BENCHMARK SERIES

MICROSOFT® OFFICE 2013

NITA RUTKOSKY
Pierce College Puyallup
Puyallup, Washington

AUDREY ROGGENKAMP
Pierce College Puyallup
Puyallup, Washington

IAN RUTKOSKY
Pierce College Puyallup
Puyallup, Washington

St. Paul

Managing Editor Christine Hurney
Director of Production Timothy W. Larson
Production Editor Sarah Kearin
Cover and Text Designers Leslie Anderson and Jaana Bykonich
Copy Editors Communicáto, Ltd.; Nan Brooks, Abshier House
Desktop Production Jaana Bykonich, Julie Johnston, Valerie King, Timothy W. Larson, Jack Ross, and Sara Schmidt Boldon
Indexer Terry Casey
VP & Director of Digital Projects Chuck Bratton
Digital Projects Manager Tom Modl

Acknowledgements: The authors, editors, and publisher thank the following instructors for their helpful suggestions during the planning and development of the books in the Benchmark Office 2013 Series: Olugbemiga Adekunle, Blue Ridge Community College, Harrisonburg, VA; Letty Barnes, Lake WA Institute of Technology, Kirkland, WA; Erika Nadas, Wilbur Wright College, Chicago, IL; Carolyn Walker, Greenville Technical College, Greenville, SC; Carla Anderson, National College, Lynchburg, VA; Judy A. McLaney, Lurleen B. Wallace Community College, Opp, AL; Sue Canter, Guilford Technical Community College, Jamestown, NC; Reuel Sample, National College, Knoxville, TN; Regina Young, Wiregrass Georgia Technical College, Valdosta, GA; William Roxbury, National College, Stow, OH; Charles Adams, II, Danville Community College, Danville, VA; Karen Spray, Northeast Community College, Norfolk, NE; Deborah Miller, Augusta Technical College, Augusta, GA; Wanda Stuparits, Lanier Technical College, Cumming, GA; Gale Wilson, Brookhaven College, Farmers Branch, TX; Jocelyn S. Pinkard, Arlington Career Institute, Grand Prairie, TX; Ann Blackman, Parkland College, Champaign, IL; Fathia Williams, Fletcher Technical Community College, Houma, LA; Leslie Martin, Gaston College, Dallas, NC; Tom Rose, Kellogg Community College, Battle Creek, MI; Casey Thompson, Wiregrass Georgia Technical College, Douglas, GA; Larry Bush, University of Cincinnati, Clermont College, Amelia, OH; Tim Ellis, Schoolcraft College, Liconia, MI; Miles Cannon, Lanier Technical College, Oakwood, GA; Irvin LaFleur, Lanier Technical College, Cumming, GA; Patricia Partyka, Schoolcraft College, Prudenville, MI.

The authors and publishing team also thanks the following individuals for their contributions to this project: checking the accuracy of the instruction and exercises—Brienna McWade, Traci Post, and Janet Blum, Fanshawe College, London, Ontario; creating annotated model answers and developing lesson plans—Ann Mills, Ivy Tech Community College, Evansville, Indiana; developing rubrics—Marjory Wooten, Laneir Techncial College, Cumming, Georgia.

ISBN 978-0-76385-342-6 (Text)
ISBN 978-0-76385-385-3 (Text + CD)
ISBN 978-0-76385-364-8 (ebook via email)
ISBN 978-0-76385-407-2 (ebook via mail)

875 Montreal Way
St. Paul, MN 55102
Email: educate@emcp.com
Website: www.emcp.com

Printed in the United States of America

23 22 21 20 19 18 17 16 15 14 3 4 5 6 7 8 9 10 11 12

Contents

Preface ix
Getting Started in Office 2013 1
Using Windows 8 13
Browsing the Internet Using Internet Explorer 10 41

Microsoft Word 2013 Level 1

Unit 1 Editing and Formatting Documents 1

Chapter 1 Preparing Documents 3
Model Answers 4
Opening Microsoft Word 5
Creating, Saving, Printing, and Closing a Document 5
Using the New Line Command 7
Saving a Document 8
Naming a Document 9
Printing a Document 9
Closing a Document 10
Creating a New Document 11
Opening a Document 12
Opening a Document from the Recent Documents List 12
Pinning a Document to the Recent Documents List 12
Saving a Document with Save As 14
Closing Word 14
Editing a Document 15
Moving the Insertion Point to a Specific Line or Page 16
Moving the Insertion Point with the Keyboard 16
Resuming Reading or Editing in a Document 17
Inserting and Deleting Text 18
Selecting Text 18
Selecting Text with the Mouse 19
Selecting Text with the Keyboard 19
Using the Undo and Redo Buttons 21
Checking the Spelling and Grammar in a Document 23
Using Help 25
Getting Help from a ScreenTip 26
Getting Help in a Dialog Box 27
**Chapter Summary, Commands Review, Concepts Check, Skills Check, Visual Benchmark, Case Study* 28

Chapter 2 Formatting Characters and Paragraphs 35
Model Answers 36
Changing Fonts 37
Choosing a Typestyle 40
Choosing a Font Effect 41
Using Keyboard Shortcuts 42
Formatting with the Mini Toolbar 42
Changing Fonts at the Font Dialog Box 45
Applying Styles from a Style Set 47
Removing Default Formatting 47
Changing the Style Set 47
Applying a Theme 48
Customizing Style Sets and Themes 49
Changing Paragraph Alignment 50
Changing Paragraph Alignment as You Type 51
Changing Paragraph Alignment of Existing Text 51
Changing Alignment at the Paragraph Dialog Box 52
Indenting Text in Paragraphs 54
Spacing Before and After Paragraphs 57
Repeating the Last Action 57
Formatting with Format Painter 58
Changing Line Spacing 60
Revealing and Comparing Formatting 61

Chapter 3 Customizing Paragraphs 71
Model Answers 72
Applying Numbering and Bullets 73
Applying Numbering to Paragraphs 73
Applying Bullets to Paragraphs 76
Inserting Paragraph Borders and Shading 77
Inserting Paragraph Borders 77
Adding Paragraph Shading 78
Customizing Borders and Shading 80
Sorting Text in Paragraphs 82
Manipulating Tabs 83
Manipulating Tabs on the Horizontal Ruler 83
Manipulating Tabs at the Tabs Dialog Box 86
Cutting, Copying, and Pasting Text 89
Deleting Selected Text 89
Cutting and Pasting Text 89
Moving Text by Dragging with the Mouse 90
Using the Paste Options Button 91
Copying and Pasting Text 92
Using the Clipboard 93

Chapter 4 Formatting Pages 103
Model Answers 104
Changing the View 107
Displaying a Document in Draft View 107
Displaying a Document in Read Mode View 107
Changing Ribbon Display Options 108
Navigating Using the Navigation Pane 108
Hiding/Showing White Space in Print Layout View 111
Changing Page Setup 111
Changing Margins 112
Changing Page Orientation 112
Changing Page Size 112
Changing Margins at the Page Setup Dialog Box 114
Changing Paper Size at the Page Setup Dialog Box 114
Inserting a Page Break 115
Inserting a Blank Page 117
Inserting a Cover Page 117
Inserting Predesigned Page Numbering 119
Inserting Predesigned Headers and Footers 120
Removing a Header or Footer 121
Editing a Predesigned Header or Footer 122
Formatting the Page Background 123
Inserting a Watermark 123
Changing Page Color 124
Inserting a Page Border 125
Changing Page Border Options 125
Finding and Replacing Text and Formatting 128
Finding and Replacing Text 130
Choosing Check Box Options 131
Finding and Replacing Formatting 133

Unit 1 Performance Assessment 143

Unit 2 Enhancing and Customizing Documents 151

Chapter 5 Applying Formatting and Inserting Objects 153
Model Answers 154
Inserting a Section Break 156
Creating Columns 157
Creating Columns with the Columns Dialog Box 158
Removing Column Formatting 159
Inserting a Column Break 159
Balancing Columns on a Page 160
Hyphenating Words 161
Automatically Hyphenating Words 161
Manually Hyphenating Words 161
Creating a Drop Cap 162
Inserting Symbols and Special Characters 163
Inserting the Date and Time 165
Using the Click and Type Feature 166
Vertically Aligning Text 167
Inserting an Image 169

**These activities appear at the end of every chapter.*

Customizing and Formatting an Image 169
Sizing an Image 169
Moving an Image 170
Inserting a Picture 170
Inserting an Image from Office.com 173
Inserting and Customizing a Pull Quote Text Box 176
Drawing Shapes 178
Copying Shapes 178
Drawing and Formatting a Text Box 180
Creating and Modifying WordArt Text 181
Creating and Inserting a Screenshot 183
Chapter 6 Maintaining Documents 197
Model Answers 198
Maintaining Documents 200
Using Print Screen 200
Creating a Folder 201
Renaming a Folder 202
Selecting Documents 202
Deleting Documents 203
Copying and Moving Documents 204
Renaming Documents 205
Deleting a Folder 205
Opening Multiple Documents 205
Saving a Document in a Different Format 206
Saving in PDF/XPS Format 209
Working with Windows 211
Arranging Windows 212
Maximizing, Restoring, and Minimizing Documents 212
Splitting a Window 212
Viewing Documents Side by Side 213
Opening a New Window 214
Inserting a File 215
Printing and Previewing a Document 216
Previewing Pages in a Document 216
Printing Pages in a Document 217
Creating and Printing Envelopes 220
Creating and Printing Labels 223
Changing Label Options 224
Creating Mailing Labels with an Image 226
Creating a Document Using a Template 226
Chapter 7 Creating Tables and SmartArt 239
Model Answers 240
Creating a Table 241
Entering Text in Cells 242
Moving the Insertion Point within a Table 242
Using the Insert Table Dialog Box 244
Changing the Table Design 245
Selecting Cells 247
Selecting in a Table with the Mouse 247
Selecting in a Table with the Keyboard 248
Changing Table Layout 249
Selecting with the Select Button 250
Viewing Gridlines 250
Inserting and Deleting Rows and Columns 250
Merging and Splitting Cells and Tables 252
Customizing Cell Size 254
Changing Cell Alignment 256
Repeating a Header Row 256
Inserting a Quick Table 257
Changing Cell Margin Measurements 258
Changing Cell Direction 260
Changing Table Alignment and Dimensions 261
Changing Table Size with the Resize Handle 262
Moving a Table 262
Converting Text to a Table and a Table to Text 264
Drawing a Table 265
Sorting Text in a Table 266
Performing Calculations in a Table 266
Creating SmartArt 269
Inserting and Formatting a SmartArt Graphic 269
Arranging and Moving a SmartArt Graphic 271
Creating an Organizational Chart with SmartArt 273
Chapter 8 Merging Documents 289
Model Answers 290
Completing a Merge 293
Creating a Data Source File 293
Creating a Main Document 295
Previewing a Merge 298
Checking for Errors 298
Merging Documents 298
Merging Envelopes 300
Merging Labels 302
Merging a Directory 304
Editing a Data Source File 306
Selecting Specific Records 306
Editing Records 308
Inputting Text during a Merge 311
Merging Using the Mail Merge Wizard 313
Unit 2 Performance Assessment 325
Word Level 1 Index 337
Microsoft Excel 2013 Level 1
Unit 1 Preparing and Formatting Worksheets 1
Chapter 1 Preparing an Excel Workbook 3
Model Answers 4
Creating a Worksheet 5
Saving a Workbook 8
Editing Data in a Cell 10
Printing a Workbook 11
Closing a Workbook 12
Closing Excel 13
Using Automatic Entering Features 13
Using AutoComplete 13
Using AutoCorrect 13
Using AutoFill 15
Opening a Workbook 16
Opening a Workbook from the Recent Workbooks List 16
Pinning a Workbook to the Recent Workbooks List 16
Inserting Formulas 18
Using the AutoSum Button to Add Numbers 18
Using the AutoSum Button to Average Numbers 19
Using the Fill Handle to Copy a Formula 19
Selecting Cells 20
Selecting Cells Using the Mouse 20
Selecting Cells Using the Keyboard 20
Selecting Data within Cells 20
Applying Basic Formatting 21
Changing Column Width 21
Merging and Centering Cells 21
Formatting Numbers 23
Using Help 25
Getting Help on a Button 26
Getting Help in a Dialog Box or Backstage Area 27
Chapter 2 Inserting Formulas in a Worksheet 35
Model Answers 36
Writing Formulas with Mathematical Operators 37
Copying a Formula with Relative Cell References 38
Checking Cell References in a Formula 39
Writing a Formula by Pointing 40
Determining the Order of Operations 40
Using the Trace Error Button 41
Identifying Common Formula/Function Errors in Excel 41
Inserting Formulas with Functions 43
Writing Formulas with Statistical Functions 45
Writing Formulas with the NOW and TODAY Functions 49
Displaying Formulas 49
Using Absolute and Mixed Cell References in Formulas 50

Using an Absolute Cell Reference in a Formula 50
Using a Mixed Cell Reference in a Formula 52

Chapter 3 Formatting an Excel Worksheet 61
Model Answers 62
Changing Column Width 63
Changing Column Width Using Column Boundaries 63
Changing Column Width at the Column Width Dialog Box 64
Changing Row Height 65
Inserting and Deleting Cells, Rows, and Columns 66
Inserting Rows 66
Inserting Columns 67
Deleting Cells, Rows, or Columns 68
Clearing Data in Cells 69
Applying Formatting 69
Applying Font Formatting 70
Formatting with the Mini Toolbar 70
Applying Alignment Formatting 70
Applying a Theme 73
Formatting Numbers 74
Formatting Numbers Using Number Group Buttons 74
Formatting Numbers Using the Format Cells Dialog Box 76
Formatting Cells Using the Format Cells Dialog Box 78
Aligning and Indenting Data 78
Changing the Font at the Format Cells Dialog Box 80
Adding Borders to Cells 82
Adding Fill and Shading to Cells 84
Repeating the Last Action 84
Formatting with Format Painter 86
Hiding and Unhiding Columns and Rows 86

Chapter 4 Enhancing a Worksheet 99
Model Answers 100
Formatting a Worksheet Page 101
Changing Margins 101
Centering a Worksheet Horizontally and/or Vertically 102
Changing Page Orientation 104
Changing the Page Size 104
Inserting and Removing Page Breaks 104
Printing Column and Row Titles on Multiple Pages 107
Scaling Data 108
Inserting a Background Picture 109
Printing Gridlines and Row and Column Headings 110
Printing a Specific Area of a Worksheet 110
Inserting Headers and Footers 112
Customizing Print Jobs 117
Completing a Spelling Check 118
Using Undo and Redo 118
Finding and Replacing Data and Cell Formatting in a Worksheet 120
Sorting Data 125
Completing a Custom Sort 125
Sorting More Than One Column 127
Filtering Data 127

Unit 1 Performance Assessment 141

Unit 2 Enhancing the Display of Workbooks 147

Chapter 5 Moving Data within and between Workbooks 149
Model Answers 150
Creating a Workbook with Multiple Worksheets 153
Inserting a New Worksheet 153
Deleting a Worksheet 153
Selecting Multiple Worksheets 153
Copying, Cutting, and Pasting Cells 154
Copying and Pasting Selected Cells 154
Using Paste Options 155
Moving Selected Cells 156
Copying and Pasting with the Clipboard Task Pane 157
Pasting Values Only 159
Managing Worksheets 160
Hiding a Worksheet in a Workbook 162
Printing a Workbook Containing Multiple Worksheets 163
Using Zoom 164
Splitting a Worksheet into Windows and Freezing and Unfreezing Panes 165
Working with Ranges 167
Working with Windows 168
Opening Multiple Workbooks 169
Arranging Workbooks 169
Hiding/Unhiding Workbooks 171
Sizing and Moving Workbooks 172
Moving, Linking, Copying, and Pasting Data 172
Moving and Copying Data 173
Linking Data 174
Copying and Pasting Data between Programs 175

Chapter 6 Maintaining Workbooks 187
Model Answers 188
Maintaining Workbooks 190
Creating a Folder 191
Renaming a Folder 192
Selecting Workbooks 192
Deleting Workbooks and Folders 193
Deleting to the Recycle Bin 193
Copying Workbooks 194
Sending Workbooks to a Different Drive or Folder 195
Cutting and Pasting a Workbook 195
Renaming Workbooks 196
Deleting a Folder and Its Contents 197
Managing the Recent Workbooks List 197
Pinning a Workbook 198
Recovering an Unsaved Workbook 199
Clearing the Recent Workbooks List and the Recent List 199
Managing Worksheets 200
Copying a Worksheet to Another Workbook 200
Moving a Worksheet to Another Workbook 201
Formatting with Cell Styles 204
Applying a Style 204
Defining a Cell Style 205
Modifying a Style 209
Copying Styles to Another Workbook 210
Removing a Style 211
Deleting a Style 211
Inserting Hyperlinks 212
Linking to an Existing Web Page or File 212
Navigating Using Hyperlinks 213
Linking to a Place in the Workbook 214
Linking to a New Workbook 214
Linking Using a Graphic 215
Linking to an Email Address 215
Modifying, Editing, and Removing a Hyperlink 216
Using Excel Templates 217

Chapter 7 Creating Charts and Inserting Formulas 229
Model Answers 230
Creating a Chart 232
Sizing and Moving a Chart 233
Editing Data and Adding a Data Series 233
Formatting with Chart Buttons 236
Printing a Chart 238
Changing the Chart Design 239
Changing the Chart Style 240
Switching Rows and Columns 240
Changing Chart Layout and Colors 241
Changing the Chart Location 242
Adding, Moving, and Deleting Chart Elements 242
Changing Chart Formatting 245
Formatting a Selection 245
Inserting Shapes 246
Applying Formatting at a Task Pane 248
Changing Chart Height and Width Measurements 248

Deleting a Chart 249
Writing Formulas with Financial Functions 252
Finding the Periodic Payments for a Loan 253
Finding the Future Value of a Series of Payments 255
Writing Formulas with the IF Logical Function 256
Writing Formulas with an IF Function Using the Function Arguments Palette 257
Writing IF Formulas Containing Text 259

Chapter 8 Adding Visual Interest to Workbooks 271
Model Answers 272
Inserting Symbols and Special Characters 273
Inserting Images 275
Customizing and Formatting an Image 276
Sizing and Moving an Image 276
Formatting an Image at the Format Picture Task Pane 278
Inserting an Image from Office.com 278
Creating and Inserting Screenshots 280
Inserting and Copying Shapes 281
Drawing and Formatting Text Boxes 284
Inserting a Picture as a Watermark 286
Inserting SmartArt Graphics 288
Entering Data in a SmartArt Graphic 288
Sizing, Moving, and Deleting a SmartArt Graphic 289
Changing the SmartArt Graphic Design 290
Changing the SmartArt Graphic Formatting 291
Creating, Sizing, and Moving WordArt 293

Unit 2 Performance Assessment 305

Excel Level 1 Index 313

Microsoft Access 2013 Level 1

Unit 1 Creating Tables and Queries 1

Chapter 1 Managing and Creating Tables 3
Model Answers 4
Exploring a Database 5
Opening a Database 6
Pinning a Database File or Folder to the Recent List 7
Closing a Database 8
Opening and Closing Objects 8
Managing Tables 11
Inserting and Deleting Records 11
Inserting, Moving, and Deleting Fields 13
Hiding, Unhiding, Freezing, and Unfreezing Column Fields 15
Changing Column Width 15
Renaming and Deleting a Table 17
Printing Tables 17
Previewing a Table 18
Changing Page Size and Margins 18
Changing Page Layout 19
Designing a Table 22
Creating a Table 23
Renaming a Field Heading 27
Inserting a Name, Caption, and Description 27
Inserting Quick Start Fields 28
Assigning a Default Value 29
Assigning a Field Size 29
Changing the AutoNumber Field 29

Chapter 2 Creating Relationships between Tables 43
Model Answers 44
Creating Related Tables 45
Determining Relationships 46
Defining the Primary Key 46
Relating Tables in a One-to-Many Relationship 50
Specifying Referential Integrity 52
Printing Relationships 53
Showing Tables 56
Editing a Relationship 56
Deleting a Relationship 56
Inserting and Deleting Records in Related Tables 60
Creating One-to-One Relationships 61
Displaying Related Records in Subdatasheets 64

Chapter 3 Performing Queries 77
Model Answers 78
Extracting Data with Queries 82
Designing Queries 82
Establishing Query Criteria 84
Sorting and Showing or Hiding Fields in a Query 92
Arranging Fields in a Query 92
Modifying a Query 95
Renaming and Deleting a Query 95
Designing Queries with *Or* and *And* Criteria 96
Performing Queries with the Simple Query Wizard 100
Creating Calculated Fields 107
Designing Queries with Aggregate Functions 109
Creating Crosstab Queries 112
Creating Find Duplicates Queries 115
Creating Find Unmatched Queries 118

Chapter 4 Creating and Modifying Tables in Design View 129
Model Answers 130
Creating Tables in Design View 132
Assigning a Default Value 136
Using the Input Mask 137
Validating Field Entries 141
Using the Lookup Wizard 141
Inserting, Moving, and Deleting Fields in Design View 142
Inserting a Total Row 143
Sorting Records 147
Printing Specific Records 147
Formatting Table Data 148
Completing a Spelling Check 152
Finding and Replacing Data 154
Using Help 157
Getting Help on a Button 157
Getting Help in a Dialog Box or Backstage Area 159

Unit 1 Performance Assessment 171

Unit 2 Creating Forms and Reports 181

Chapter 5 Creating Forms 183
Model Answers 184
Creating Forms 186
Creating a Form with the Form Button 186
Changing Views 186
Printing a Form 186
Deleting a Form 187
Navigating in a Form 187
Adding and Deleting Records 189
Sorting Records 189
Creating a Form with a Related Table 190
Customizing Forms 192
Applying Themes 193
Inserting Data in the Form Header 193
Modifying a Control Object 193
Inserting a Control 194
Moving a Form Table 197
Arranging Objects 198
Formatting a Form 201
Applying Conditional Formatting 204
Adding Existing Fields 207
Creating Split Forms 210
Creating Multiple Items Form 213
Creating Forms Using the Form Wizard 214

Chapter 6 Creating Reports and Mailing Labels 229
Model Answers 230
Creating Reports 233
Creating a Report with the Report Button 233

Modifying the Record Source 234
Modifying Control Objects 235
Sorting Records 236
Displaying and Customizing a Report in Print Preview 236
Deleting a Report 236
Finding Data in a Report 237
Customizing Reports 240
Grouping and Sorting Records 244
Creating a Report Using the Report Wizard 248
Preparing Mailing Labels 252

Chapter 7 Modifying, Filtering, and Viewing Data 263
Model Answers 264
Filtering Data 265
Filtering Using the Filter Button 265
Removing a Filter 266
Filtering on Specific Values 268
Filtering by Selection 270
Filtering by Shortcut Menu 271
Using the *Filter by Form* Option 272
Viewing Object Dependencies 274
Using Options at the Info Backstage Area 276
Compacting and Repairing a Database 276
Encrypting a Database with a Password 277
Viewing and Customizing Database Properties 278
Saving Databases and Database Objects 281
Saving an Object in PDF or XPS File Format 281
Backing Up a Database 282

Chapter 8 Importing and Exporting Data 291
Model Answers 292
Exporting Data 295
Exporting Data to Excel 295
Exporting Data to Word 298
Merging Access Data with a Word Document 300
Merging Query Data with a Word Document 301
Exporting an Access Object to a PDF or XPS File 304
Importing and Linking Data to New Tables 305
Importing Data into a New Table 305
Linking Data to an Excel Worksheet 307
Using the Office Clipboard 308

Unit 2 Performance Assessment 319
Access Level 1 Index 329

Microsoft PowerPoint 2013

Unit 1 Creating and Formatting PowerPoint Presentations 1

Chapter 1 Preparing a PowerPoint Presentation 3
Model Answers 4
Creating a PowerPoint Presentation 5
Opening a Presentation 7
Opening a Presentation from the Recent Presentations List 8
Pinning a Presentation to a Recent List 8
Running a Presentation 8
Closing a Presentation 8
Planning a Presentation 10
Creating a Presentation Using a Design Theme Template 10
Creating Slides in a Presentation 11
Choosing a Slide Layout 12
Inserting a New Slide 12
Saving a Presentation 12
Changing Views 16
Navigating in a Presentation 16
Printing and Previewing a Presentation 18
Running a Slide Show 22
Applying a Design Theme and Color Variant 27
Deleting a Presentation 28
Preparing a Presentation from a Blank Presentation 29
Preparing a Presentation in Outline View 29
Adding Transition and Sound Effects 31
Adding Transitions 32
Adding Sounds 32
Removing Transitions and Sounds 32
Advancing Slides Automatically 34

Chapter 2 Modifying a Presentation and Using Help 43
Model Answers 44
Checking Spelling 45
Using the Thesaurus 46
Managing Text in Slides 48
Inserting and Deleting Text in Slides 48
Finding and Replacing Text in Slides 49
Cutting, Copying, and Pasting Text in Slides 51
Rearranging Text in the Outline Pane 54
Sizing and Rearranging Placeholders in a Slide 55
Managing Slides 57
Inserting and Deleting Slides 57
Moving Slides 57
Copying a Slide 57
Copying a Slide between Presentations 59
Duplicating Slides 60
Reusing Slides 61
Creating Sections within a Presentation 63
Customizing the Quick Access Toolbar 65
Using Help 66
Getting Help on a Button 67
Getting Help in a Dialog Box or Backstage Area 67

Chapter 3 Formatting Slides 79
Model Answers 80
Formatting a Presentation 81
Applying Font Formatting 81
Formatting with Format Painter 85
Formatting Paragraphs 87
Fitting Contents in a Placeholder 87
Customizing Paragraphs 90
Customizing Columns 91
Rotating and Vertically Aligning Text 92
Customizing Bullets 94
Customizing Numbering 96
Customizing Placeholders 98
Customizing Placeholders at the Format Shape Task Pane 99
Changing Page Setup 103
Modifying Theme Colors and Forms 105
Customizing Slide Backgrounds 105
Creating Custom Themes 109
Creating Custom Theme Colors 109
Creating Custom Theme Fonts 111
Saving a Custom Theme 112
Editing Custom Themes 113
Deleting Custom Themes 113

Chapter 4 Inserting Elements in Slides 125
Model Answers 126
Inserting and Formatting Text Boxes 126
Formatting a Text Box 126
Selecting Multiple Objects 127
Aligning Text Boxes 127
Setting Tabs in a Text Box 133
Inserting, Formatting, and Copying Shapes 135
Displaying Rulers, Gridlines, and Guides 136
Merging Shapes 140
Grouping/Ungrouping Objects 141
Inserting an Image 142
Customizing and Formatting an Image 142
Sizing, Cropping, and Moving an Image 143
Arranging Images 143
Inserting a Picture as a Slide Background 147

Inserting an Image from Office.com 149
Sizing, Rotating, and Positioning Objects 150
Copying Objects within and between Presentations 152
Creating Screenshots 152
Creating and Formatting WordArt Text 154
Inserting Symbols 156
Inserting Headers and Footers 157
Unit 1 Performance Assessment 177

Unit 2 Customizing and Enhancing PowerPoint Presentations 185

Chapter 5 Creating Tables, Charts, and SmartArt Graphics 187
Model Answers 188
Creating a Table 189
Entering Text in Cells 189
Selecting Cells 189
Changing Table Design 191
Changing Table Layout 193
Inserting an Excel Spreadsheet 195
Drawing a Table 197
Creating SmartArt 198
Modifying SmartArt 199
Formatting SmartArt 201
Converting Text and WordArt to a SmartArt Graphic 203
Inserting Text in the Text Pane 203
Converting a SmartArt Graphic to Text or Shapes 205
Creating a Chart 206
Formatting with Chart Buttons 208
Changing Chart Design 210
Formatting a Chart and Chart Elements 212
Creating a Photo Album 217
Editing and Formatting a Photo Album 219
Formatting Pictures 222
Chapter 6 Using Slide Masters and Action Buttons 235
Model Answers 236
Customizing Slide Masters 237
Applying Themes to Slide Masters 238
Applying and Formatting Backgrounds 240
Deleting Placeholders 240
Deleting Slide Master Layouts 240
Inserting Slides in a Customized Presentation 241
Inserting Elements in a Slide Master 243
Creating and Renaming a Custom Slide Layout 244
Inserting Placeholders 244
Creating Custom Prompts 245
Inserting a New Slide Master 246
Preserving Slide Masters 247
Changing Page Setup 247
Saving a Presentation as a Template 250
Customizing the Handout Master 251
Customizing the Notes Master 253
Using VIEW Tab Options 255
Changing the Zoom 255
Managing Windows 255
Viewing in Color and Grayscale 256
Inserting Action Buttons 258
Applying an Action to an Object 260
Inserting Hyperlinks 262
Chapter 7 Applying Custom Animation and Setting Up Shows 275
Model Answers 276
Applying and Removing Animations 278
Applying Animation Effects 281
Applying Animations with Animation Painter 281
Modifying Animation Effects 283
Reordering Items 283
Customizing Animation Effects at the Animation Pane 285
Applying Sound to Animations 288
Applying a Build 288
Animating Shapes and Images 289
Animating a SmartArt Graphic 290
Animating a Chart 292
Creating a Motion Path 293
Applying a Trigger 294
Setting Up a Slide Show 296
Running a Presentation without Animation 297
Setting Up a Presentation to Loop Continuously 297
Setting Automatic Times for Slides 299
Recording Narration 300
Hiding Slides 302
Managing Monitors 303
Using Presenter View 303
Presenting a Presentation Online 304
Creating a Custom Show 306
Running a Custom Show 306
Editing a Custom Show 307
Printing a Custom Show 307
Inserting Audio and Video Files 308
Inserting an Audio File 309
Inserting a Video File 309
Optimizing and Compressing Audio and Video Files 310
Showing and Hiding Media Controls 310
Trimming a Video File 313
Playing an Audio File throughout a Presentation 314
Chapter 8 Integrating, Sharing, and Protecting Presentations 325
Model Answers 326
Importing a Word Outline 328
Copying and Pasting Data 329
Sharing Presentations 331
Exporting Presentations 334
Saving a Presentation in the PDF or XPS Formats 334
Creating a Video of a Presentation 334
Packaging a Presentation 335
Exporting a Presentation to a Word Document 336
Saving a Presentation in a Different Format 338
Embedding and Linking Objects 342
Embedding Objects 343
Linking Objects 344
Editing Linked Objects 345
Downloading Templates 346
Comparing and Combining Presentations 349
Managing Comments 351
Managing Presentation Information 353
Managing Presentation Properties 353
Protecting a Presentation 355
Encrypting a Presentation 356
Adding a Digital Signature 357
Inspecting a Presentation 358
Checking the Accessibility of a Presentation 359
Checking the Compatibility of a Presentation 361
Managing Versions 361
Customizing PowerPoint Options 362
Unit 2 Performance Assessment 379
PowerPoint Index 387

Office 2013 Integrated Project IP1

Preface

Benchmark Series Microsoft Office 2013 is designed for students who want to learn how to use the new version of Microsoft's popular suite to enhance their productivity for educational, workplace, and home use. Throughout this text, students are expected to develop and execute strategies for solving information processing and management problems using Word 2013; for solving numeric and mathematical problems using Excel 2013; for organizing, querying, and retrieving data using Access 2013; and for writing, creating, and producing presentations using PowerPoint 2013. After successfully completing a course using this textbook, students will be able to

- Analyze, synthesize, and evaluate school, work, or home information-processing needs and use application software to meet those needs efficiently and effectively
- Access the Internet and use the browse, search, and hyperlink capabilities of web browsers
- Create, design, and produce professional documents using word processing software
- Process, manipulate, and represent numeric data using spreadsheet software
- Plan, structure, and create databases for efficient data access and retrieval using database software
- Use presentation software to design and create informational and motivational slide shows that contain hyperlinks, tables, images, and animation
- Learn strategies for merging and integrating source data from different applications

In addition to mastering essentials Word, Excel, Access, and PowerPoint skills, students will learn the basic features and functions of computer hardware, the Windows 8 operating system, and Internet Explorer 10. Upon completing the text, they can expect to be proficient in using the major applications of the Office 2013 suite to organize, analyze, and present information.

Well-designed textbook pedagogy is important, but students learn technology skills through practice and problem solving. Technology provides opportunities for interactive learning as well as excellent ways to quickly and accurately assess student performance. To this end, this textbook is supported with SNAP, Paradigm Publishing's web-based training and assessment learning management system. Details about SNAP as well as additional student courseware and instructor resources can be found on page xv.

UNIT OPENERS display the unit's four chapter titles. Each program module has two units; each unit concludes with a comprehensive unit performance assessment.

Achieving Proficiency in Office 2013

Since its inception several Office versions ago, the Benchmark Series has served as a standard of excellence in software instruction. Elements of the book function individually and collectively to create an inviting, comprehensive learning environment that produces successful computer users. The following visual tour highlights the structure and features that comprise the highly popular Benchmark model.

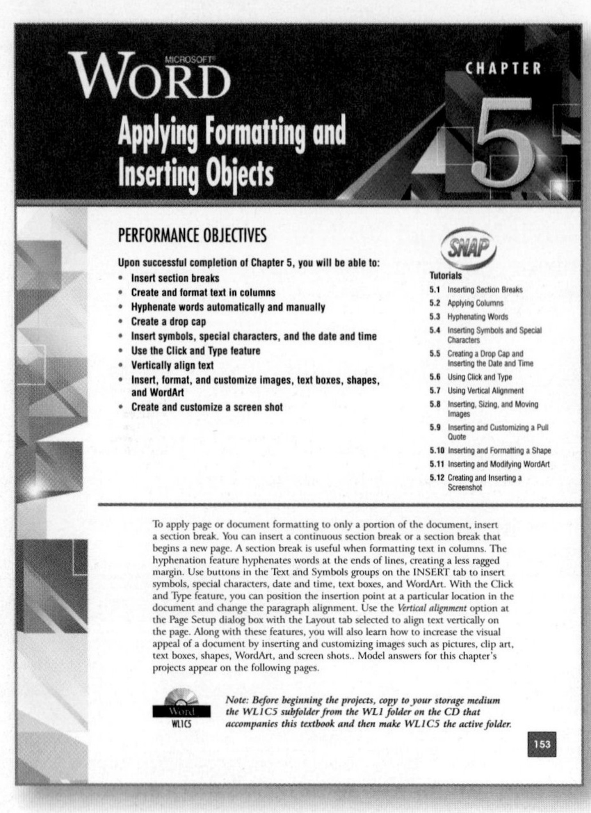
MICROSOFT® WORD

CHAPTER 5

Applying Formatting and Inserting Objects

PERFORMANCE OBJECTIVES

Upon successful completion of Chapter 5, you will be able to:

- Insert section breaks
- Create and format text in columns
- Hyphenate words automatically and manually
- Create a drop cap
- Insert symbols, special characters, and the date and time
- Use the Click and Type feature
- Vertically align text
- Insert, format, and customize images, text boxes, shapes, and WordArt
- Create and customize a screen shot

SNAP Tutorials

5.1 Inserting Section Breaks
5.2 Applying Columns
5.3 Hyphenating Words
5.4 Inserting Symbols and Special Characters
5.5 Creating a Drop Cap and Inserting the Date and Time
5.6 Using Click and Type
5.7 Using Vertical Alignment
5.8 Inserting, Sizing, and Moving Images
5.9 Inserting and Customizing a Pull Quote
5.10 Inserting and Formatting a Shape
5.11 Inserting and Modifying WordArt
5.12 Creating and Inserting a Screenshot

To apply page or document formatting to only a portion of the document, insert a section break. You can insert a continuous section break or a section break that begins a new page. A section break is useful when formatting text in columns. The hyphenation feature hyphenates words at the ends of lines, creating a less ragged margin. Use buttons in the Text and Symbols groups on the INSERT tab to insert symbols, special characters, date and time, text boxes, and WordArt. With the Click and Type feature, you can position the insertion point at a particular location in the document and change the paragraph alignment. Use the *Vertical alignment* option at the Page Setup dialog box with the Layout tab selected to align text vertically on the page. Along with these features, you will also learn how to increase the visual appeal of a document by inserting and customizing images such as pictures, clip art, text boxes, shapes, WordArt, and screen shots.. Model answers for this chapter's projects appear on the following pages.

Word WL1C5

Note: Before beginning the projects, copy to your storage medium the WL1C5 subfolder from the WL1 folder on the CD that accompanies this textbook and then make WL1C5 the active folder.

153

CHAPTER OPENERS present the performance objectives and an overview of the skills taught.

SNAP interactive tutorials are available to support chapter-specific skills at snap2013.emcp.com.

DATA FILES are provided for each chapter. A prominent note reminds students to copy the appropriate chapter data folder and make it active.

PROJECT APPROACH: Builds Skill Mastery within Realistic Context

MODEL ANSWERS provide a preview of the finished chapter projects and allow students to confirm they have completed the projects accurately.

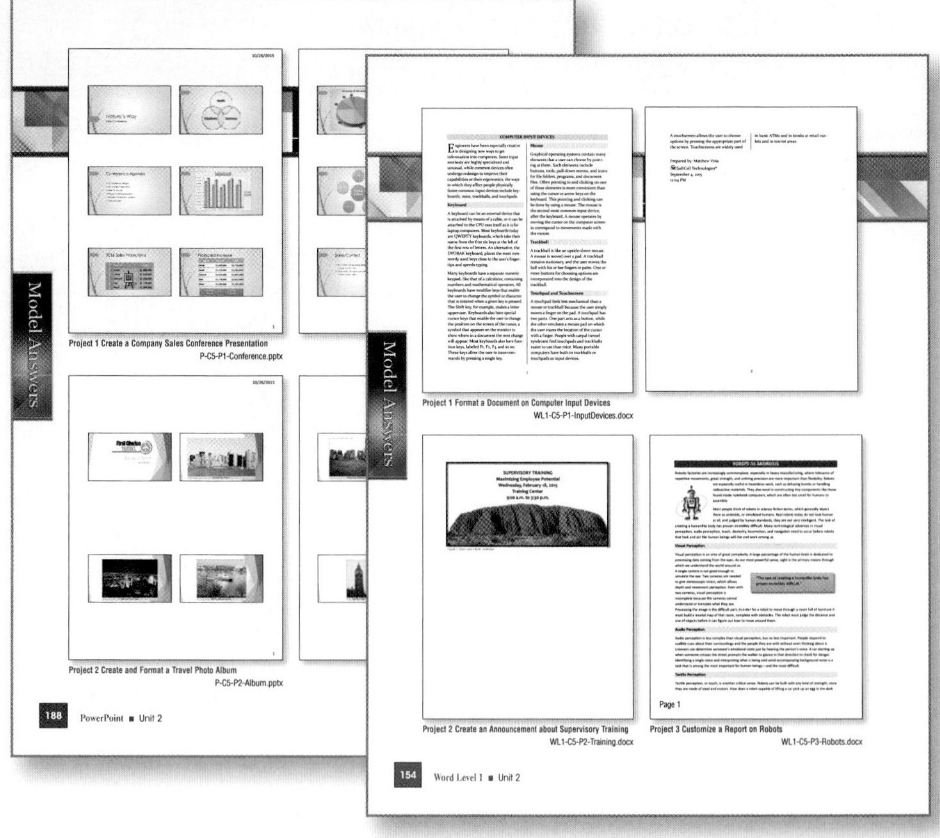
Model Answers

Project 1 Create a Company Sales Conference Presentation
P-C5-P1-Conference.pptx

Project 2 Create and Format a Travel Photo Album
P-C5-P2-Album.pptx

188 PowerPoint ■ Unit 2

Model Answers

Project 1 Format a Document on Computer Input Devices
WL1-C5-P1-InputDevices.docx

Project 2 Create an Announcement about Supervisory Training
WL1-C5-P2-Training.docx

Project 3 Customize a Report on Robots
WL1-C5-P3-Robots.docx

154 Word Level 1 ■ Unit 2

MULTIPART PROJECTS provide a framework for instruction and practice on software features. A project overview identifies tasks to accomplish and key features to use in completing the work.

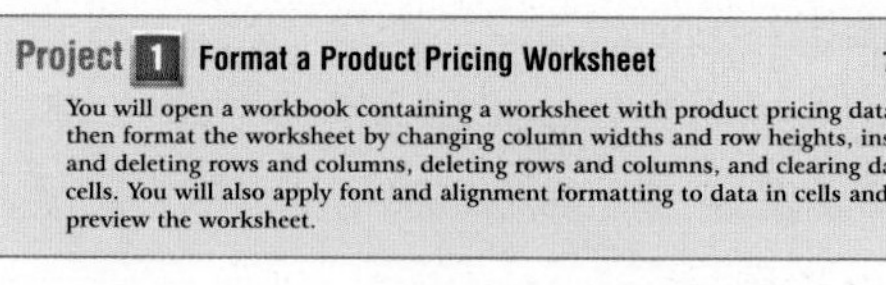

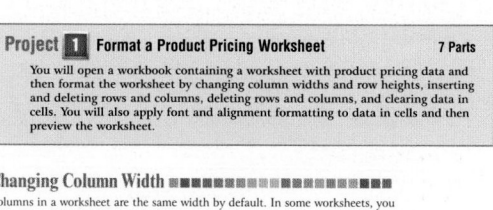

Project 1 Format a Product Pricing Worksheet **7 Parts**

You will open a workbook containing a worksheet with product pricing data and then format the worksheet by changing column widths and row heights, inserting and deleting rows and columns, deleting rows and columns, and clearing data in cells. You will also apply font and alignment formatting to data in cells and then preview the worksheet.

Changing Column Width

Columns in a worksheet are the same width by default. In some worksheets, you may want to change column widths to accommodate more or less data. You can change column width using the mouse on column boundaries or at a dialog box.

Changing Column Width Using Column Boundaries

As you learned in Chapter 1, you can adjust the width of a column by dragging the column boundary line or adjust a column width to the longest entry by double-clicking the boundary line. When you drag a column boundary, the column width displays in a box above the mouse pointer. The column width number that displays represents the average number of characters in the standard font that can fit in a cell.

You can change the width of selected adjacent columns at the same time. To do this, select the columns and then drag one of the column boundaries within the selected columns. As you drag the boundary, the column width changes for all selected columns. To select adjacent columns, position the cell pointer on the first desired column header (the mouse pointer turns into a black, down-pointing arrow), hold down the left mouse button, drag the cell pointer to the last desired column header, and then release the mouse button.

HINT To change the width of all columns in a worksheet, click the Select All button and then drag a column boundary to the desired position.

HINTS provide useful tips on how to use features efficiently and effectively.

Project 1a Changing Column Width Using a Column Boundary **Part 1 of 7**

1. Open **CMProducts.xlsx**.
2. Save the workbook with Save As and name it **EL1-C3-P1-CMProducts**.
3. Insert a formula in cell D2 that multiplies the price in cell B2 with the number in cell C2. Copy the formula in cell D2 down to cells D3 through D14.
4. Change the width of column D by completing the following steps:
   a. Position the mouse pointer on the column boundary in the column header between columns D and E until it turns into a double-headed arrow pointing left and right.
   b. Hold down the left mouse button, drag the column boundary to the right until *Width: 11.00 (106 pixels)* displays in the box, and then release the mouse button.
5. Make cell D15 active and then insert the sum of cells D2 through D14.
6. Change the width of columns A and B by completing the following steps:
   a. Select columns A and B. To do this, position the cell pointer on the column A header, hold down the left mouse button, drag the cell pointer to the column B header, and then release the mouse button.

Step 4b

Typically, a file remains open throughout all parts of the project. Students save their work incrementally. At the end of the project, students save, print, and then close the file.

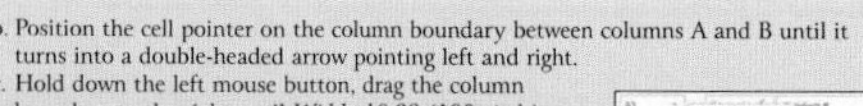

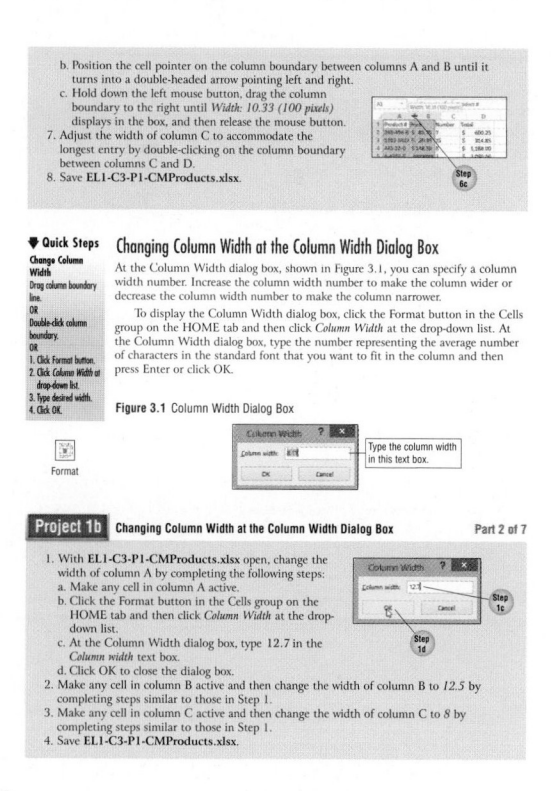

   b. Position the cell pointer on the column boundary between columns A and B until it turns into a double-headed arrow pointing left and right.
   c. Hold down the left mouse button, drag the column boundary to the right until *Width: 10.33 (100 pixels)* displays in the box, and then release the mouse button.
7. Adjust the width of column C to accommodate the longest entry by double-clicking on the column boundary between columns C and D.
8. Save **EL1-C3-P1-CMProducts.xlsx**.

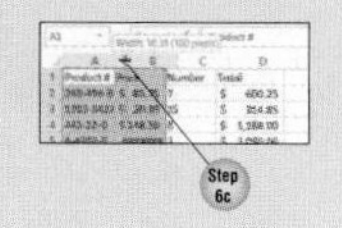

Step 6c

Quick Steps
Change Column Width
Drag column boundary line.
OR
Double-click column boundary.
OR
1. Click Format button.
2. Click *Column Width* at drop-down list.
3. Type desired width.
4. Click OK.

Format

Changing Column Width at the Column Width Dialog Box

At the Column Width dialog box, shown in Figure 3.1, you can specify a column width number. Increase the column width number to make the column wider or decrease the column width number to make the column narrower.

To display the Column Width dialog box, click the Format button in the Cells group on the HOME tab and then click *Column Width* at the drop-down list. At the Column Width dialog box, type the number representing the average number of characters in the standard font that you want to fit in the column and then press Enter or click OK.

Figure 3.1 Column Width Dialog Box

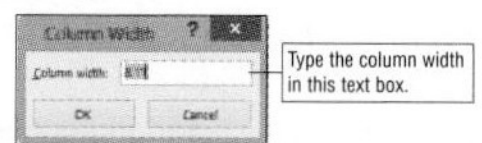

QUICK STEPS provide feature summaries for reference and review.

Project 1b Changing Column Width at the Column Width Dialog Box **Part 2 of 7**

1. With **EL1-C3-P1-CMProducts.xlsx** open, change the width of column A by completing the following steps:
   a. Make any cell in column A active.
   b. Click the Format button in the Cells group on the HOME tab and then click *Column Width* at the drop-down list.
   c. At the Column Width dialog box, type 12.7 in the *Column width* text box.
   d. Click OK to close the dialog box.
2. Make any cell in column B active and then change the width of column B to *12.5* by completing steps similar to those in Step 1.
3. Make any cell in column C active and then change the width of column C to *8* by completing steps similar to those in Step 1.
4. Save **EL1-C3-P1-CMProducts.xlsx**.

Step 1c

Step 1d

64 Excel Level 1 ■ Unit 1

Between project parts, the text presents instruction on the features and skills necessary to accomplish the next section of the project.

STEP-BY-STEP INSTRUCTIONS guide students to the desired outcome for each project part. Screen captures illustrate what the screen should look like at key points.

MAGENTA TEXT identifies material to type.

CHAPTER REVIEW ACTIVITIES: A Hierarchy of Learning Assessments

Chapter Summary

- The Page Setup group on the PAGE LAYOUT tab contains buttons for changing the margins and page orientation and size, as well as buttons for establishing the print area, inserting a page break, applying a picture background, and printing titles.
- The default left and right margins are 0.7 inch and the default top and bottom margins are 0.75 inch. Change these default margins with the Margins button in the Page Setup group on the PAGE LAYOUT tab.
- Display the Page Setup dialog box with the Margins tab selected by clicking the Margins button and then clicking *Custom Margins* at the drop-down list.
- Center a worksheet on the page with the *Horizontally* and *Vertically* options at the Page Setup dialog box with the Margins tab selected.
- Click the Orientation button in the Page Setup group on the PAGE LAYOUT tab to display the two orientation choices: *Portrait* and *Landscape*.
- Insert a page break by selecting the column or row, clicking the Breaks button in the Page Setup group on the PAGE LAYOUT tab, and then clicking *Insert Page Break* at the drop-down list.
- To insert both horizontal and vertical page breaks at the same time, make a cell active, click the Breaks button, and then click *Insert Page Break* at the drop-down list.
- Preview the page break button in the view area clicking the Page Break
- Use options at the Page printing column and/or clicking the Print Titles tab.
- Use options in the Sca to fit on a specific num
- Use the Background bu to insert a worksheet b screen but does not pri
- Use options in the She whether to view and/or
- Specify the print area b button in the Page Setu *Set Print Area* at the dr desired cells, clicking t at the drop-down list.
- Create a header and/or group on the INSERT Setup dialog box with
- Customize a print job
- To check spelling in a Spelling button.

CHAPTER SUMMARY
captures the purpose and execution of key features.

- Click the Undo button on the Quick Access toolbar to reverse the most recent action and click the Redo button to redo a previously reversed action.
- Use options at the Find and Replace dialog box with the Find tab selected to find specific data and/or formatting in a worksheet.
- Use options at the Find and Replace dialog box with the Replace tab selected to find specific data and/or formatting and replace it with other data and/or formatting.
- Sort data in a worksheet with options from the Sort & Filter button in the Editing group on the HOME tab.
- Create a custom sort with options at the Sort dialog box. Display this dialog box by clicking the Sort & Filter button and then clicking *Custom Sort* at the drop-down list.
- Use filtering to temporarily isolate specific data. Turn on the filter feature by clicking the Sort & Filter button in the Editing group on the HOME tab and then clicking *Filter* at the drop-down list. This inserts filter arrows with each column label. Click a filter arrow and then use options at the drop-down list that displays to specify the filter data.

Commands Review

FEATURE	RIBBON TAB, GROUP	BUTTON, OPTION	KEYBOARD SHORTCUT
background picture	PAGE LAYOUT, Page Setup		
filter data	HOME, Editing		
Find and Replace dialog box with Find tab selected	HOME, Editi		
Find and Replace dialog box with Replace tab selected	HOME, Editi		
header and footer	INSERT, Tex		
insert page break	PAGE LAYO		
margins	PAGE LAYO		
orientation	PAGE LAYO		
Page Layout view	VIEW, Work		
Page Setup dialog box with Margins tab selected	PAGE LAYO		
Page Setup dialog box with Sheet tab selected	PAGE LAYO		
preview page break	VIEW, Work		

COMMANDS REVIEW
summarizes visually the major features and alternative methods of access.

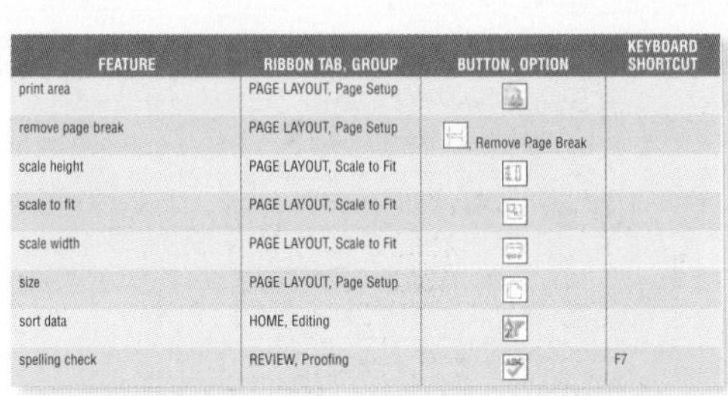

FEATURE	RIBBON TAB, GROUP	BUTTON, OPTION	KEYBOARD SHORTCUT
print area	PAGE LAYOUT, Page Setup		
remove page break	PAGE LAYOUT, Page Setup	Remove Page Break	
scale height	PAGE LAYOUT, Scale to Fit		
scale to fit	PAGE LAYOUT, Scale to Fit		
scale width	PAGE LAYOUT, Scale to Fit		
size	PAGE LAYOUT, Page Setup		
sort data	HOME, Editing		
spelling check	REVIEW, Proofing		F7

Concepts Check Test Your Knowledge SNAP

Completion: In the space provided at the right, indicate the correct term, symbol, or command.

1. This is the default left and right margin measurement. ________
2. This is the default top and bottom margin measurement. ________
3. The Margins button is located on this tab. ________
4. By default, a worksheet prints in this orientation on a page. ________
5. Click the Print Titles button in the Page Setup group on the PAGE LAYOUT tab and the Page Setup dialog box displays with this tab selected. ________
6. Use options in this group on the PAGE LAYOUT tab to adjust the printed output by a percentage to fit the number of pages specified. ________
7. Use this button in the Page Setup group on the PAGE LAYOUT tab to select and print specific areas in a worksheet. ________
8. Click the Header & Footer button in the Text group on the INSERT tab and the worksheet displays in this view. ________
9. This tab contains options for formatting and customizing a header and/or footer. ________

CONCEPTS CHECK
questions assess knowledge recall. Students enrolled in SNAP can complete the Concepts Check online. SNAP automatically scores student work.

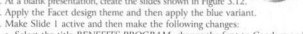

SKILLS CHECK exercises ask students to develop both standard and customized types of word processing, spreadsheet, database, or presentation documents without how-to directions.

Versions of the activities marked with a SNAP Grade It icon are available for automatic scoring in SNAP.

Skills Check Assess Your Performance

Assessment

1 CREATE, FORMAT, AND MODIFY A BENEFITS PRESENTATION (SNAP Grade It)

1. At a blank presentation, create the slides shown in Figure 3.12.
2. Apply the Facet design theme and then apply the blue variant.
3. Make Slide 1 active and then make the following changes:
   a. Select the title *BENEFITS PROGRAM*, change the font to Candara and the font size to 60 points, apply the Turquoise, Accent 1, Darker 50% font color, and apply italic formatting.
   b. Select the subtitle *Changes to Plans*, change the font to Candara and the font size to 32 points, apply the Turquoise, Accent 1 font color, and apply bold and shadow formatting.
   c. Click the title placeholder and then click the Center button in the Paragraph group.
   d. Center the subtitle in the placeholder.
4. Make Slide 2 active and then make the following changes:
   a. Select the title *INTRODUCTION*, change the font to Candara and the font size to 44 points, apply the Turquoise, Accent 1, Darker 50% font color, and apply shadow formatting.
   b. Using Format Painter, apply the title formatting to the titles in the remaining slides.
5. Center-align and middle-align the titles in Slides 2 through 5.
6. Make Slide 2 active, select the bulleted text, and then change the line spacing to double spacing (2.0).
7. Make Slide 3 active, select the bulleted text, and then change the line spacing to double spacing (2.0).
8. Make Slide 4 active, select the bulleted text, and then change the line spacing to 1.5.
9. Make Slide 5 active, select th paragraphs to *18 pt*. ***Hint: Do***
10. Make Slide 2 active and then Display the Bullets and Num selected, choose the *1. 2. 3.* o Turquoise, Accent 1, Darker 5
11. Make Slide 3 active and then Display the Bullets and Num selected, choose the *1. 2. 3.* o Turquoise, Accent 1, Darker 5 and then close the dialog box
12. Make Slide 4 active, select th change the bullets to *Hollow S*
13. Make Slide 5 active, select th change the bullets to *Hollow S*
14. Save the presentation and na
15. Print the presentation as a ha
16. Apply the Organic design the
17. Apply a transition and sound
18. Run the presentation.

118 PowerPoint ■ Unit 1

VISUAL BENCHMARK assessments test students' problem-solving skills and mastery of program features.

Visual Benchmark Demonstrate Your Proficiency

FORMAT A PRESENTATION ON HOME SAFETY

1. Open **HomeSafety.pptx** and then save the presentation with Save As and name it **P-C3-VB-HomeSafety**.
2. Format the presentation so the slides appear as shown in Figure 3.13 with the following specifications.
   a. Apply the Facet design theme and the blue variant color.
   b. Delete and rearrange slides as shown in the figure.
   c. Apply the Parchment texture slide background and change the slide background transparency to 50% for all slides in the presentation. ***Hint: Apply these options using the Format Background task pane.***
   d. Change the font size of the title in Slic formatting, apply the Blue, Accent 2, L align the title.
   e. Change the font size of the subtitle in change the font color to Turquoise, Ac the subtitle.
   f. Change the font size of the titles in Sli font color to Turquoise, Accent 1, Darl
   g. Change the line spacing, spacing after, so your slides display in a manner simi
   h. Select the bulleted text placeholder in task pane, select the *Solid fill* option, a Turquoise, Accent 1, Lighter 80%. Dis with the TEXT OPTIONS tab selected change the left margin to 1 inch and th
3. Print the presentation as a handout with page.
4. Save and then close the presentation.

Figure 3.13 Visual Benchmark

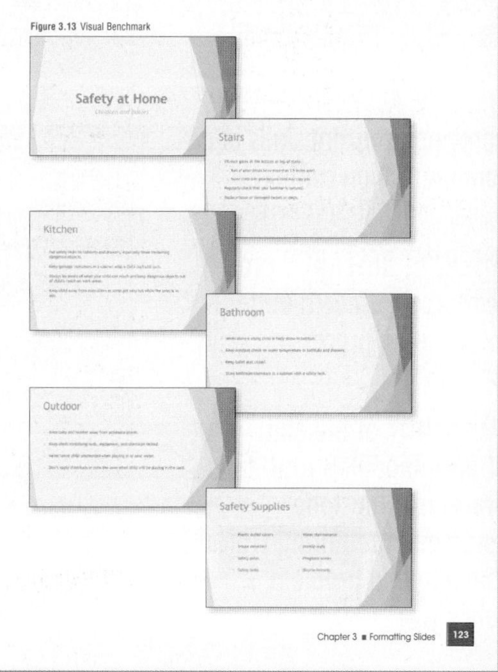

Chapter 3 ■ Formatting Slides 123

Case Study Apply Your Skills

Part 1

You are the office manager for a real estate company, Macadam Realty, and have been asked by the senior sales associate, Lucy Hendricks, to organize contract forms into a specific folder. Create a new folder named *RealEstate* and then copy into the folder documents that begin with the letters "RE." Ms. Hendricks has also asked you to prepare mailing labels for Macadam Realty. Include on the labels the name, Macadam Realty, and the address, 100 Third Street, Suite 210, Denver, CO 80803. Use a decorative font for the label and make the *M* in *Macadam* and the *R* in *Realty* larger and more pronounced than surrounding text. ***Hint: Format text in the label by selecting text, right-clicking in the selected text, and then choosing the desired option at the shortcut menu.*** Save the completed document and name it **WL1-C6-CS-RELabels**. Print and then close the document.

Part 2

One of your responsibilities is to format contract forms. Open the document named **REConAgrmnt.docx** and then save it and name it **WL1-C6-CS-REConAgrmnt**. The sales associate has asked you to insert signature information at the end of the document, and so you decide to insert at the end of the document the file named **RESig.docx**. With **WL1-C6-CS-REConAgrmnt.docx** still open, open **REBuildAgrmnt.docx**. Format the **WL1-C6-CS-REConAgrmnt.docx** document so it is formatted in a manner similar to the **REBuildAgrmnt.docx** document. Consider the following when specifying formatting: margins, fonts, and paragraph shading. Save, print, and then close **WL1-C6-CS-REConAgrmnt.docx**. Close **REBuildAgrmnt.docx**.

Part 3

Help

As part of the organization of contracts, Ms. Hendricks has asked you to insert document properties for the **REBuildAgrmnt.docx** and **WL1-C6-CS-REConAgrmnt.docx** documents. Use the Help feature to learn how to insert document properties. With the information you learn from the Help feature, open each of the two documents separately, display the Info backstage area, click the Show All Properties hyperlink, and then insert document properties in the following fields (you determine the information to type): *Title*, *Subject*, *Categories*, and *Company*. Print the document properties for each document. (Change the first gallery in the *Settings* category in the Print backstage area to *Document Properties*.) Save each document with the original name and close the documents.

Part 4

A client of the real estate company, Anna Hurley, is considering purchasing several rental properties and has asked for information on how to locate real estate rental forms. Using the Internet, locate at least three websites that offer real estate rental forms. Write a letter to Anna Hurley at 2300 South 22nd Street, Denver, CO 80205. In the letter, list the websites you found and include information on which site you thought offered the most resources. Also include in the letter that Macadam Realty is very interested in helping her locate and purchase rental properties. Save the document and name it **WL1-C6-CS-RELtr**. Create an envelope for the letter and add it to the letter document. Save, print, and then close **WL1-C6-CS-RELtr.docx**. (You may need to manually feed the envelope in the printer.)

238 Word Level 1 ■ Unit 2

CASE STUDY requires analyzing a workplace scenario and then planning and executing multipart projects.

Students search the Web and/or use the program's Help feature to locate additional information required to complete the Case Study.

UNIT PERFORMANCE ASSESSMENT: Cross-Disciplinary, Comprehensive Evaluation

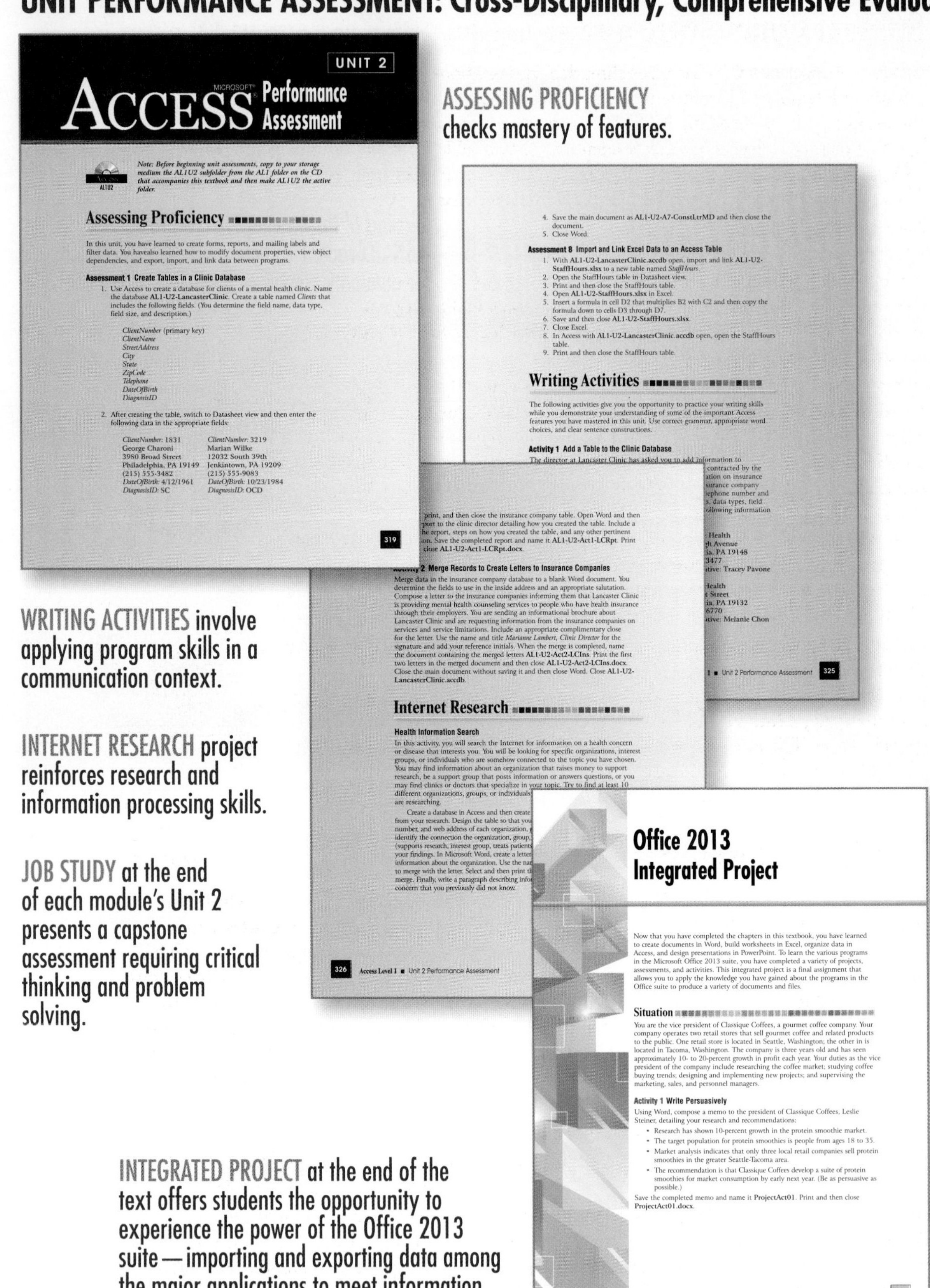

UNIT 2

MICROSOFT® ACCESS Performance Assessment

Note: Before beginning unit assessments, copy to your storage medium the AL1U2 subfolder from the AL1 folder on the CD that accompanies this textbook and then make AL1U2 the active folder.

Assessing Proficiency

In this unit, you have learned to create forms, reports, and mailing labels and filter data. You havealso learned how to modify document properties, view object dependencies, and export, import, and link data between programs.

Assessment 1 Create Tables in a Clinic Database

1. Use Access to create a database for clients of a mental health clinic. Name the database **AL1-U2-LancasterClinic**. Create a table named *Clients* that includes the following fields. (You determine the field name, data type, field size, and description.)

   ClientNumber (primary key)
   ClientName
   StreetAddress
   City
   State
   ZipCode
   Telephone
   DateOfBirth
   DiagnosisID

2. After creating the table, switch to Datasheet view and then enter the following data in the appropriate fields:

ClientNumber: 1831	*ClientNumber*: 3219
George Charoni	Marian Wilke
3980 Broad Street	12032 South 39th
Philadelphia, PA 19149	Jenkintown, PA 19209
(215) 555-3482	(215) 555-9083
DateOfBirth: 4/12/1961	*DateOfBirth*: 10/23/1984
DiagnosisID: SC	*DiagnosisID*: OCD

319

ASSESSING PROFICIENCY checks mastery of features.

4. Save the main document as **AL1-U2-A7-ConstLtrMD** and then close the document.
5. Close Word.

Assessment 8 Import and Link Excel Data to an Access Table

1. With **AL1-U2-LancasterClinic.accdb** open, import and link **AL1-U2-StaffHours.xlsx** to a new table named *StaffHours*.
2. Open the StaffHours table in Datasheet view.
3. Print and then close the StaffHours table.
4. Open **AL1-U2-StaffHours.xlsx** in Excel.
5. Insert a formula in cell D2 that multiplies B2 with C2 and then copy the formula down to cells D3 through D7.
6. Save and then close **AL1-U2-StaffHours.xlsx**.
7. Close Excel.
8. In Access with **AL1-U2-LancasterClinic.accdb** open, open the StaffHours table.
9. Print and then close the StaffHours table.

Writing Activities

The following activities give you the opportunity to practice your writing skills while you demonstrate your understanding of some of the important Access features you have mastered in this unit. Use correct grammar, appropriate word choices, and clear sentence constructions.

Activity 1 Add a Table to the Clinic Database

The director at Lancaster Clinic has asked you to add information to ... contracted by the ... ation on insurance ... surance company ... lephone number and ... s, data types, field ... ollowing information

... Health
... h Avenue
... ia, PA 19148
... 3477
... tive: Tracey Pavone

... ealth
... t Street
... ia, PA 19132
... 6770
... tive: Melanie Chon

... l ■ Unit 2 Performance Assessment 325

... print, and then close the insurance company table. Open Word and then ... port to the clinic director detailing how you created the table. Include a ... he report, steps on how you created the table, and any other pertinent ... on. Save the completed report and name it **AL1-U2-Act1-LCRpt**. Print ... close **AL1-U2-Act1-LCRpt.docx**.

Activity 2 Merge Records to Create Letters to Insurance Companies

Merge data in the insurance company database to a blank Word document. You determine the fields to use in the inside address and an appropriate salutation. Compose a letter to the insurance companies informing them that Lancaster Clinic is providing mental health counseling services to people who have health insurance through their employers. You are sending an informational brochure about Lancaster Clinic and are requesting information from the insurance companies on services and service limitations. Include an appropriate complimentary close for the letter. Use the name and title *Marianne Lambert, Clinic Director* for the signature and add your reference initials. When the merge is completed, name the document containing the merged letters **AL1-U2-Act2-LCIns**. Print the first two letters in the merged document and then close **AL1-U2-Act2-LCIns.docx**. Close the main document without saving it and then close Word. Close **AL1-U2-LancasterClinic.accdb**.

Internet Research

Health Information Search

In this activity, you will search the Internet for information on a health concern or disease that interests you. You will be looking for specific organizations, interest groups, or individuals who are somehow connected to the topic you have chosen. You may find information about an organization that raises money to support research, be a support group that posts information or answers questions, or you may find clinics or doctors that specialize in your topic. Try to find at least 10 different organizations, groups, or individuals ... are researching.

Create a database in Access and then create ... from your research. Design the table so that you ... number, and web address of each organization, ... identify the connection the organization, group, ... (supports research, interest group, treats patients ... your findings. In Microsoft Word, create a letter ... information about the organization. Use the na... to merge with the letter. Select and then print th... merge. Finally, write a paragraph describing info... concern that you previously did not know.

326 Access Level 1 ■ Unit 2 Performance Assessment

Office 2013 Integrated Project

Now that you have completed the chapters in this textbook, you have learned to create documents in Word, build worksheets in Excel, organize data in Access, and design presentations in PowerPoint. To learn the various programs in the Microsoft Office 2013 suite, you have completed a variety of projects, assessments, and activities. This integrated project is a final assignment that allows you to apply the knowledge you have gained about the programs in the Office suite to produce a variety of documents and files.

Situation

You are the vice president of Classique Coffees, a gourmet coffee company. Your company operates two retail stores that sell gourmet coffee and related products to the public. One retail store is located in Seattle, Washington; the other in is located in Tacoma, Washington. The company is three years old and has seen approximately 10- to 20-percent growth in profit each year. Your duties as the vice president of the company include researching the coffee market; studying coffee buying trends; designing and implementing new projects; and supervising the marketing, sales, and personnel managers.

Activity 1 Write Persuasively

Using Word, compose a memo to the president of Classique Coffees, Leslie Steiner, detailing your research and recommendations:

- Research has shown 10-percent growth in the protein smoothie market.
- The target population for protein smoothies is people from ages 18 to 35.
- Market analysis indicates that only three local retail companies sell protein smoothies in the greater Seattle-Tacoma area.
- The recommendation is that Classique Coffees develop a suite of protein smoothies for market consumption by early next year. (Be as persuasive as possible.)

Save the completed memo and name it **ProjectAct01**. Print and then close **ProjectAct01.docx**.

IP1

WRITING ACTIVITIES involve applying program skills in a communication context.

INTERNET RESEARCH project reinforces research and information processing skills.

JOB STUDY at the end of each module's Unit 2 presents a capstone assessment requiring critical thinking and problem solving.

INTEGRATED PROJECT at the end of the text offers students the opportunity to experience the power of the Office 2013 suite—importing and exporting data among the major applications to meet information processing needs most effectively.

Student Courseware

Student Resources CD Each Benchmark Series textbook is packaged with a Student Resources CD containing the data files required for completing the projects and assessments. A CD icon and folder name displayed on the opening page of chapters reminds students to copy a folder of files from the CD to the desired storage medium before beginning the project exercises. Directions for copying folders are printed on the inside back cover.

Internet Resource Center Additional learning tools and reference materials are available at the book-specific website at www.paradigmcollege.net/Benchmark13. Students can access the same files that are on the Student Resources CD along with study tools, study quizzes, web links, and tips for using computers effectively in academic and workplace settings.

SNAP Training and Assessment Available at snap2013.emcp.com, SNAP is a web-based program offering an interactive venue for learning Microsoft Office 2013, Windows 8, and Internet Explorer 10. Along with a web-based learning management system, SNAP provides multimedia tutorials, performance skill items, Concepts Check matching activities, Grade It Skills Check Assessment activities, comprehensive performance evaluations, a concepts test bank, an online grade book, and a set of course planning tools. A CD of tutorials teaching the basics of Office, Windows, and Internet Explorer is also available if instructors wish to assign additional SNAP tutorial work without using the web-based SNAP program.

eBook For students who prefer studying with an eBook, the texts in the Benchmark Series are available in an electronic form. The web-based, password-protected eBooks feature dynamic navigation tools, including bookmarking, a linked table of contents, and the ability to jump to a specific page. The eBook format also supports helpful study tools, such as highlighting and note taking.

Instructor Resources

Instructor's Guide and Disc Instructor support for the Benchmark Series includes an *Instructor's Guide* and Instructor Resources Disc package. This resource includes course planning resources, such as Lesson Blueprints, teaching hints, and sample course syllabi; presentation resources, such as PowerPoint slide shows with lecture notes; and assessment resources, including an overview of available assessment venues, live model answers for chapter projects, and live and annotated PDF model answers for end-of-chapter exercises. Contents of the *Instructor's Guide* and Instructor Resources Disc package are also available on the password-protected section of the Internet Resource Center for this title at www.paradigmcollege.net/Benchmark13.

Computerized Test Generator Instructors can use the ExamView® Assessment Suite and test banks of multiple-choice items to create customized web-based or print tests.

Blackboard Cartridge This set of files allows instructors to create a personalized Blackboard website for their course and provides course content, tests, and the mechanisms for establishing communication via e-discussions and online group conferences. Available content includes a syllabus, test banks, PowerPoint presentations, and supplementary course materials. Upon request, the files can be available within 24–48 hours. Hosting the site is the responsibility of the educational institution.

System Requirements

This text is designed for the student to complete projects and assessments on a computer running a standard installation of Microsoft Office Professional Plus 2013 and the Microsoft Windows 8 operating system. To effectively run this suite and operating system, your computer should be outfitted with the following:

- 1 gigahertz (GHz) processor or higher; 1 gigabyte (GB) of RAM (32 bit) or 2 GB of RAM (64 bit)
- 3 GB of available hard-disk space
- .NET version 3.5, 4.0, or 4.5
- DirectX 10 graphics card
- Minimum 1024 × 576 resolution (or 1366 × 768 to use Windows Snap feature)
- Computer mouse, multi-touch device, or other compatible pointing device

Office 2013 will also operate on computers running the Windows 7 operating system.

Screen captures in this book were created using a screen resolution display setting of 1600 × 900. Refer to the *Customizing Settings* section of *Getting Started in Office 2013* following this preface for instructions on changing your monitor's resolution. Figure G.9 on page 10 shows the Microsoft Office Word ribbon at three resolutions for comparison purposes. Choose the resolution that best matches your computer; however, be aware that using a resolution other than 1600 × 900 means that your screens may not match the illustrations in this book.

About the Authors

Nita Rutkosky began teaching business education courses at Pierce College Puyallup, Washington, in 1978. Since then she has taught a variety of software applications to students in postsecondary Information Technology certificate and degree programs. In addition to *Benchmark Office 2013,* she has co-authored *Marquee Series: Microsoft Office 2013, 2010, 2007,* and *2003; Signature Series: Microsoft Word 2013, 2010, 2007,* and *2003; Using Computers in the Medical Office: Microsoft Word, Excel, and PowerPoint 2010, 2007* and *2003*; and *Computer and Internet Essentials: Preparing for IC³*. She has also authored textbooks on keyboarding, WordPerfect, desktop publishing, and voice recognition for Paradigm Publishing, Inc.

Audrey Roggenkamp has been teaching courses in the Business Information Technology department at Pierce College Puyallup since 2005. Her courses have included keyboarding, skill building, and Microsoft Office programs. In addition to this title, she has co-authored *Marquee Series: Microsoft Office 2013, 2010,* and *2007; Signature Series: Microsoft Word 2013, 2010,* and *2007; Using Computers in the Medical Office: Microsoft Word, Excel, and PowerPoint 2010, 2007,* and *2003*; and *Computer and Internet Essentials: Preparing for IC³* for Paradigm Publishing, Inc.

Ian Rutkosky teaches Business Technology courses at Pierce College Puyallup, Washington. In addition to this title, he has coauthored *Computer and Internet Essentials: Preparing for IC³, Marquee Series: Microsoft Office 2013,* and *Using Computers in the Medical Office: Microsoft Word, Excel, and PowerPoint 2010*. He is also a co-author and consultant for Paradigm's SNAP training and assessment software.

Getting Started in Office 2013

In this textbook, you will learn to operate several computer programs that combine to make the Microsoft Office 2013 application suite. The programs you will learn are known as ***software***, and they contain instructions that tell the computer what to do. Some of the application programs in the suite include Word, a word processing program; Excel, a spreadsheet program; Access, a database program; and PowerPoint, a presentation program.

Identifying Computer Hardware

The computer equipment you will use to operate the Microsoft Office suite is referred to as ***hardware***. You will need access to a computer system that includes a CPU, monitor, keyboard, printer, drives, and mouse. If you are not sure what equipment you will be operating, check with your instructor. The computer system shown in Figure G.1 consists of six components. Each component is discussed separately in the material that follows.

Figure G.1 Computer System

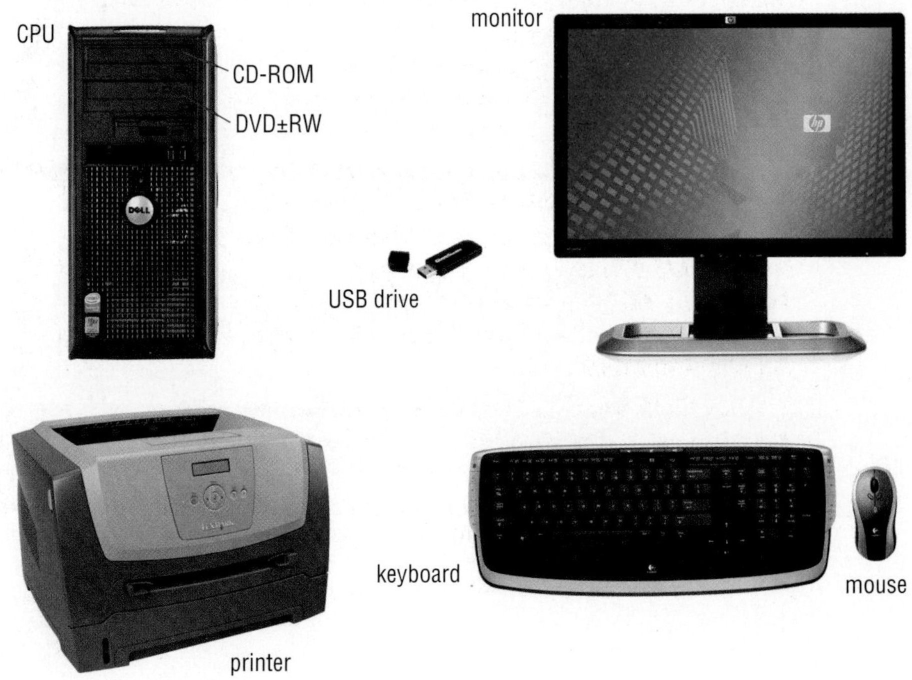

CPU

The ***central processing unit (CPU)*** is the brain of the computer and is where all processing occurs. Silicon chips, which contain miniaturized circuitry, are placed on boards that are plugged into slots within the CPU. Whenever an instruction is given to the computer, it is processed through the circuitry in the CPU.

Monitor

A computer ***monitor*** looks like a television screen. It displays the information in a program and the text you input using the keyboard. The quality of display for monitors varies depending on the type of monitor and the level of resolution. Monitors can also vary in size—generally from 13 inches to 26 inches or larger.

Keyboard

The ***keyboard*** is used to input information into the computer. The number and location of the keys on a keyboard can vary. In addition to letters, numbers, and symbols, most computer keyboards contain function keys, arrow keys, and a numeric keypad. Figure G.2 shows an enhanced keyboard.

The 12 keys at the top of the keyboard, labeled with the letter F followed by a number, are called ***function keys***. Use these keys to perform functions within each of the Office programs. To the right of the regular keys is a group of ***special*** or ***dedicated keys***. These keys are labeled with specific functions that will be performed when you press the key. Below the special keys are arrow keys. Use these keys to move the insertion point in the document screen.

Some keyboards include mode indicator lights. When you select certain modes, a light appears on the keyboard. For example, if you press the Caps Lock key, which disables the lowercase alphabet, a light appears next to Caps Lock. Similarly, pressing the Num Lock key will disable the special functions on the numeric keypad, which is located at the right side of the keyboard.

Figure G.2 Keyboard

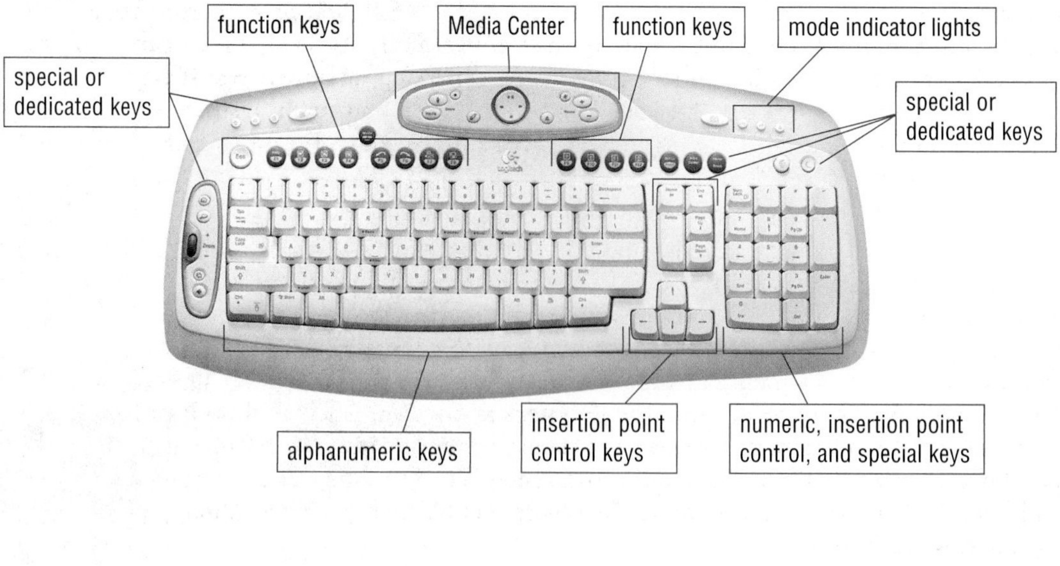

function keys
Media Center
function keys
mode indicator lights
special or dedicated keys
special or dedicated keys
alphanumeric keys
insertion point control keys
numeric, insertion point control, and special keys

Drives and Ports

Depending on the computer system you are using, Microsoft Office 2013 is installed on a hard drive or as part of a network system. Either way, you will need to have a CD or DVD drive to complete the projects and assessments in this book. If you plan to use a USB drive as your storage medium, you will also need a USB port. You will insert the CD that accompanies this textbook into the CD or DVD drive and then copy folders from the disc to your storage medium. You will also save documents you create to folders on your storage medium.

Printer

An electronic version of a file is known as a ***soft copy***. If you want to create a ***hard copy*** of a file, you need to print it. To print documents you will need to access a printer, which will probably be either a laser printer or an ink-jet printer. A ***laser printer*** uses a laser beam combined with heat and pressure to print documents, while an ***ink-jet printer*** prints a document by spraying a fine mist of ink on the page.

Mouse or Touchpad

Most functions and commands in the Microsoft Office suite are designed to be performed using a mouse or a similar pointing device. A ***mouse*** is an input device that sits on a flat surface next to the computer. You can operate a mouse with your left or right hand. Moving the mouse on the flat surface causes a corresponding pointer to move on the screen, and clicking the left or right mouse buttons allows you to select various objects and commands. Figure G.1 contains an image of a mouse.

If you are working on a laptop computer, you may use a touchpad instead of a mouse. A ***touchpad*** allows you to move the mouse pointer by moving your finger across a surface at the base of the keyboard. You click by using your thumb to press the button located at the bottom of the touchpad.

Using the Mouse

The programs in the Microsoft Office suite can be operated with the keyboard and a mouse. The mouse generally has two buttons on top, which you press to execute specific functions and commands. A mouse may also contain a wheel, which can be used to scroll in a window or as a third button. To use the mouse, rest it on a flat surface or a mouse pad. Put your hand over it with your palm resting on top of the mouse, your wrist resting on the table surface, and your index finger resting on the left mouse button. As you move your hand, and thus the mouse, a corresponding pointer moves on the screen.

When using the mouse, you should understand four terms — point, click, double-click, and drag. When operating the mouse, you may need to point to a specific command, button, or icon. To ***point*** means to position the mouse pointer on the desired item. With the mouse pointer positioned on the desired item, you may need to click a button on the mouse to select the item. To ***click*** means to quickly tap a button on the mouse once. To complete two steps at one time, such as choosing and then executing a function, double-click the mouse button. To ***double-click*** means to tap the left mouse button twice in quick succession. The term ***drag*** means to press and hold the left mouse button, move the mouse pointer to a specific location, and then release the button.

Using the Mouse Pointer

The mouse pointer will look different depending on where you have positioned it and what function you are performing. The following are some of the ways the mouse pointer can appear when you are working in the Office suite:

- The mouse pointer appears as an I-beam (called the ***I-beam pointer***) when you are inserting text in a file. The I-beam pointer can be used to move the insertion point or to select text.
- The mouse pointer appears as an arrow pointing up and to the left (called the ***arrow pointer***) when it is moved to the Title bar, Quick Access toolbar, ribbon, or an option in a dialog box, among other locations.
- The mouse pointer becomes a double-headed arrow (either pointing left and right, pointing up and down, or pointing diagonally) when you perform certain functions such as changing the size of an object.
- In certain situations, such as when you move an object or image, the mouse pointer displays with a four-headed arrow attached. The four-headed arrow means that you can move the object left, right, up, or down.
- When a request is being processed or when a program is being loaded, the mouse pointer may appear as a moving circle. The moving circle means "please wait." When the process is completed, the circle is replaced with a normal arrow pointer.
- When the mouse pointer displays as a hand with a pointing index finger, it indicates that more information is available about an item. The mouse pointer also displays as a hand with a pointing index finger when you hover the mouse over a hyperlink.

Choosing Commands

Once a program is open, you can use several methods in the program to choose commands. A ***command*** is an instruction that tells the program to do something. You can choose a command using the mouse or the keyboard. When a program such as Word or PowerPoint is open, the ribbon contains buttons and options for completing tasks, as well as tabs you can click to display additional buttons and options. To choose a button on the Quick Access toolbar or on the ribbon, position the tip of the mouse arrow pointer on the button and then click the left mouse button.

The Office suite provides ***accelerator keys*** you can press to use a command in a program. Press the Alt key on the keyboard to display KeyTips that identify the accelerator key you can press to execute a command. For example, if you press the Alt key in a Word document with the HOME tab active, KeyTips display as shown in Figure G.3. Continue pressing accelerator keys until you execute the desired command. For example, to begin spell checking a document, press the Alt key, press the R key on the keyboard to display the REVIEW tab, and then press the letter S on the keyboard.

Figure G.3 Word HOME Tab KeyTips

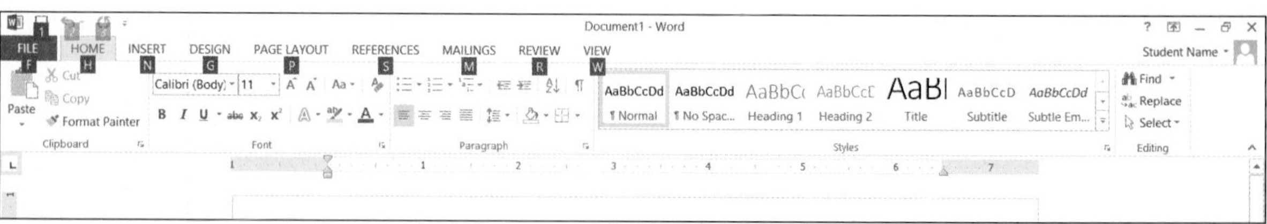

Choosing Commands from Drop-Down Lists

To choose a command from a drop-down list with the mouse, position the mouse pointer on the desired option and then click the left mouse button. To make a selection from a drop-down list with the keyboard, type the underlined letter in the desired option.

Some options at a drop-down list may appear in gray (dimmed), indicating that the option is currently unavailable. If an option at a drop-down list displays preceded by a check mark, it means the option is currently active. If an option at a drop-down list displays followed by an ellipsis (…), clicking that option will display a dialog box.

Choosing Options from a Dialog Box

A ***dialog box*** contains options for applying formatting or otherwise modifying a file or data within a file. Some dialog boxes display with tabs along the top that provide additional options. For example, the Font dialog box shown in Figure G.4 contains two tabs — the Font tab and the Advanced tab. The tab that displays in the front is the active tab. To make a tab active using the mouse, position the arrow pointer on the desired tab and then click the left mouse button. If you are using the keyboard, press Ctrl + Tab or press Alt + the underlined letter on the desired tab.

Figure G.4 Word Font Dialog Box

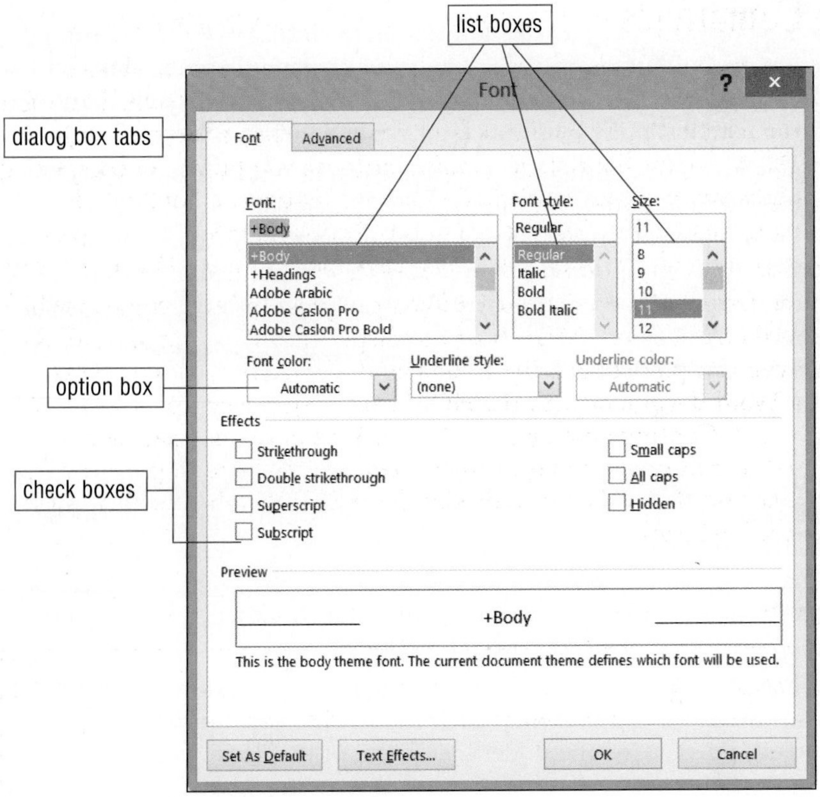

To choose options from a dialog box with the mouse, position the arrow pointer on the desired option and then click the left mouse button. If you are using the keyboard, press the Tab key to move the insertion point forward from option to option. Press Shift + Tab to move the insertion point backward from option to option. You can also hold down the Alt key and then press the underlined letter of the desired option. When an option is selected, it displays with a blue background or surrounded by a dashed box called a ***marquee***. A dialog box contains one or more of the following elements: list boxes, option boxes, check boxes, text boxes, option buttons, measurement boxes, and command buttons.

List Boxes and Option Boxes

The fonts below the *Font* option in the Font dialog box in Figure G.4 are contained in a ***list box***. To make a selection from a list box with the mouse, move the arrow pointer to the desired option and then click the left mouse button.

Some list boxes may contain a scroll bar. This scroll bar will display at the right side of the list box (a vertical scroll bar) or at the bottom of the list box (a horizontal scroll bar). Use a vertical scroll bar or a horizontal scroll bar to move through the list if the list is longer (or wider) than the box. To move down a list using a vertical scroll bar, position the arrow pointer on the down-pointing arrow and hold down the left mouse button. To scroll up through the list, position the arrow pointer on the up-pointing arrow and hold down the left mouse button. You can also move the arrow pointer above the scroll box and click the left mouse button to scroll up the list or move the arrow pointer below the scroll box and click the left mouse button to move down the list. To navigate a list with a horizontal scroll bar, click the left-pointing arrow to scroll to the left of the list or click the right-pointing arrow to scroll to the right of the list.

To use the keyboard to make a selection from a list box, move the insertion point into the box by holding down the Alt key and pressing the underlined letter of the desired option. Press the Up and/or Down Arrow keys on the keyboard to move through the list, and press Enter once the desired option is selected.

In some dialog boxes where there is not enough room for a list box, lists of options are contained in a drop-down list box called an ***option box***. Option boxes display with a down-pointing arrow. For example, in Figure G.4, the font color options are contained in an option box. To display the different color options, click the down-pointing arrow at the right of the *Font color* option box. If you are using the keyboard, press Alt + C.

Check Boxes

Some dialog boxes contain options preceded by a box. A check mark may or may not appear in the box. The Word Font dialog box shown in Figure G.4 displays a variety of check boxes within the *Effects* section. If a check mark appears in the box, the option is active (turned on). If the check box does not contain a check mark, the option is inactive (turned off). Any number of check boxes can be active. For example, in the Word Font dialog box, you can insert a check mark in several of the boxes in the *Effects* section to activate the options.

To make a check box active or inactive with the mouse, position the tip of the arrow pointer in the check box and then click the left mouse button. If you are using the keyboard, press Alt + the underlined letter of the desired option.

Text Boxes

Some options in a dialog box require you to enter text. For example, the boxes below the *Find what* and *Replace with* options at the Excel Find and Replace dialog box shown in Figure G.5 are text boxes. In a text box, you type text or edit existing text. Edit text in a text box in the same manner as normal text. Use the Left and Right Arrow keys on the keyboard to move the insertion point without deleting text and use the Delete key or Backspace key to delete text.

Option Buttons

The Word Insert Table dialog box shown in Figure G.6 contains options in the *AutoFit behavior* section preceded by ***option buttons***. Only one option button can be selected at any time. When an option button is selected, a blue or black circle displays in the button. To select an option button with the mouse, position the tip of the arrow pointer inside the option button or on the option and then click the left mouse button. To make a selection with the keyboard, hold down the Alt key and then press the underlined letter of the desired option.

Measurement Boxes

Some options in a dialog box contain measurements or amounts you can increase or decrease. These options are generally located in a ***measurement box***. For example, the Word Insert Table dialog box shown in Figure G.6 contains the *Number of columns* and *Number of rows* measurement boxes. To increase a number in a measurement box, position the tip of the arrow pointer on the up-pointing arrow at the right of the desired option and then click the left mouse button. To decrease the number, click the down-pointing arrow. If you are using the keyboard, press and hold down Alt + the underlined letter of the desired option and then press the Up Arrow key to increase the number or the Down Arrow key to decrease the number.

Command Buttons

The buttons at the bottom of the Excel Find and Replace dialog box shown in Figure G.5 are called ***command buttons***. Use a command button to execute or cancel a command. Some command buttons display with an ellipsis (...), which means another dialog box will open if you click that button. To choose a command button with the mouse, position the arrow pointer on the desired button and then click the left mouse button. To choose a command button with the keyboard, press the Tab key until the desired command button is surrounded by a marquee and then press the Enter key.

Figure G.5 Excel Find and Replace Dialog Box

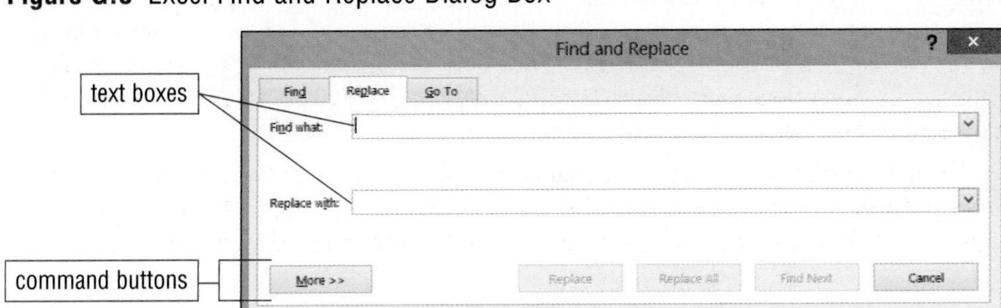

Choosing Commands with Keyboard Shortcuts

Applications in the Office suite offer a variety of keyboard shortcuts you can use to execute specific commands. Keyboard shortcuts generally require two or more keys. For example, the keyboard shortcut to display the Open dialog box in an application is Ctrl + F12. To use this keyboard shortcut, hold down the Ctrl key, press the F12 function on the keyboard, and then release the Ctrl key. For a list of keyboard shortcuts, refer to the Help files.

Choosing Commands with Shortcut Menus

The software programs in the Office suite include shortcut menus that contain commands related to different items. To display a shortcut menu, position the mouse pointer over the item for which you want to view more options, and then click the right mouse button or press Shift + F10. The shortcut menu will appear wherever the insertion point is positioned. For example, if the insertion point is positioned in a paragraph of text in a Word document, clicking the right mouse button or pressing Shift + F10 will cause the shortcut menu shown in Figure G.7 to display in the document screen (along with the Mini toolbar).

To select an option from a shortcut menu with the mouse, click the desired option. If you are using the keyboard, press the Up or Down Arrow key until the desired option is selected and then press the Enter key. To close a shortcut menu without choosing an option, click anywhere outside the shortcut menu or press the Esc key.

Figure G.6 Word Insert Table Dialog Box

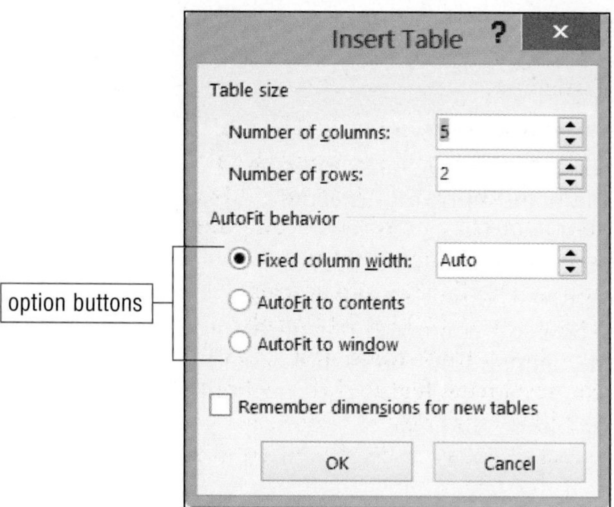

Figure G.7 Word Shortcut Menu

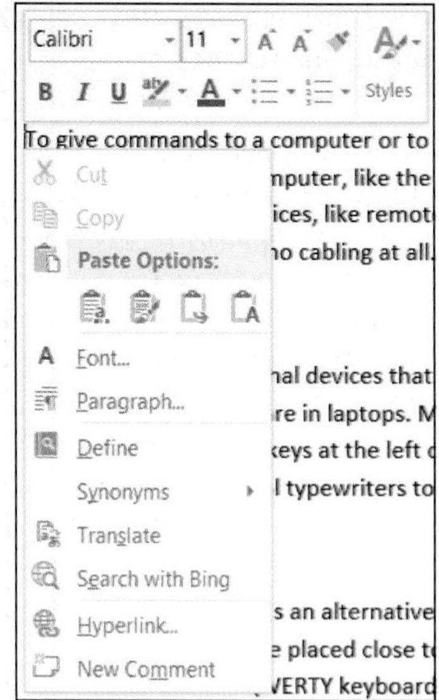

Working with Multiple Programs

As you learn the various programs in the Microsoft Office suite, you will notice many similarities between them. For example, the steps to save, close, and print are virtually the same whether you are working in Word, Excel, or PowerPoint. This consistency between programs greatly enhances a user's ability to transfer knowledge learned in one program to another within the suite. Another benefit to using Microsoft Office is the ability to have more than one program open at the same time and to integrate content from one program with another. For example, you can open Word and create a document, open Excel and create a spreadsheet, and then copy the Excel spreadsheet into Word.

When you open a program, a button containing an icon representing the program displays on the Taskbar. If you open another program, a button containing an icon representing that program displays to the right of the first program button on the Taskbar. Figure G.8 on the next page, shows the Taskbar with Word, Excel, Access, and PowerPoint open. To move from one program to another, click the Taskbar button representing the desired program.

Figure G.8 Taskbar with Word, Excel, Access, and PowerPoint Open

Customizing Settings

Before beginning computer projects in this textbook, you may need to customize your monitor's settings and turn on the display of file extensions. Projects in the chapters in this textbook assume that the monitor display is set at 1600 x 900 pixels and that the display of file extensions is turned on.

Before you begin learning the applications in the Microsoft Office 2013 suite, take a moment to check the display settings on the computer you are using. Your monitor's display settings are important because the ribbon in the Microsoft Office suite adjusts to the screen resolution setting of your computer monitor. A computer monitor set at a high resolution will have the ability to show more buttons in the ribbon than will a monitor set to a low resolution. The illustrations in this textbook were created with a screen resolution display set at 1600 × 900 pixels. In Figure G.9 on the next page, the Word ribbon is shown three ways: at a lower screen resolution (1366 × 768 pixels), at the screen resolution featured throughout this textbook, and at a higher screen resolution (1920 × 1080 pixels). Note the variances in the ribbon in all three examples. If possible, set your display to 1600 × 900 pixels to match the illustrations you will see in this textbook.

ure G.9 Monitor Resolution

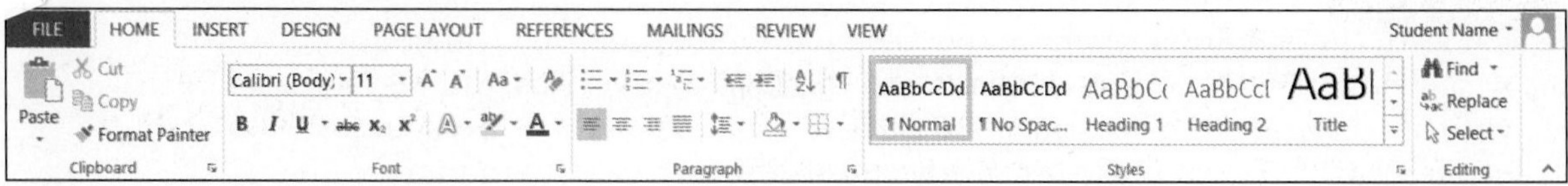

1366 × 768 screen resolution

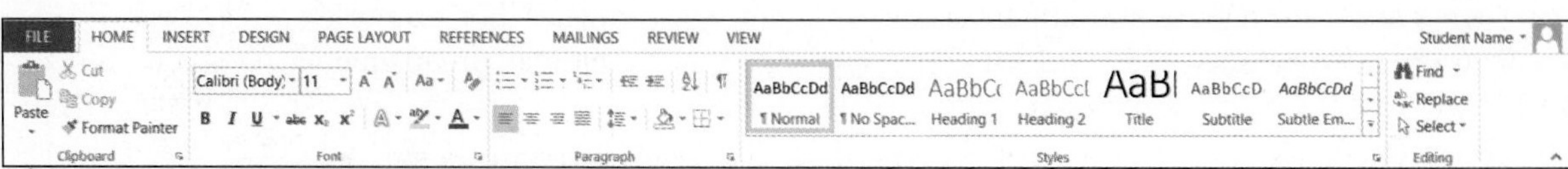

1600 × 900 screen resolution

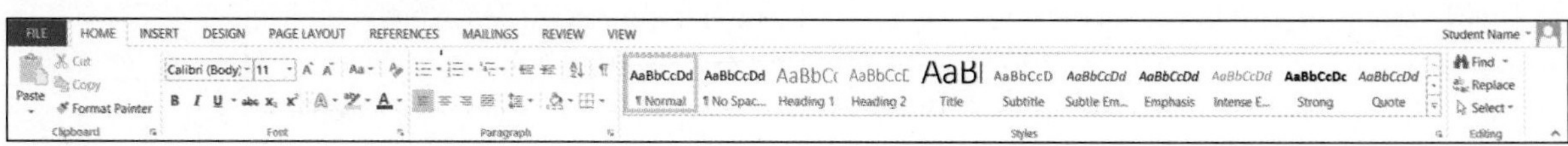

1920 × 1080 screen resolution

Project 1 Setting Monitor Display to 1600 by 900

1. At the Windows desktop, right-click a blank area of the screen.
2. At the shortcut menu, click the *Screen resolution* option.
3. At the Screen Resolution window, click the *Resolution* option box. (This displays a slider bar. Your slider bar may display differently than what you see in the image at the right.)
4. Drag the button on the slider bar until *1600 × 900* displays to the right of the slider bar.
5. Click in the Screen Resolution window to remove the slider bar.
6. Click the Apply button.
7. Click the Keep Changes button.
8. Click the OK button.

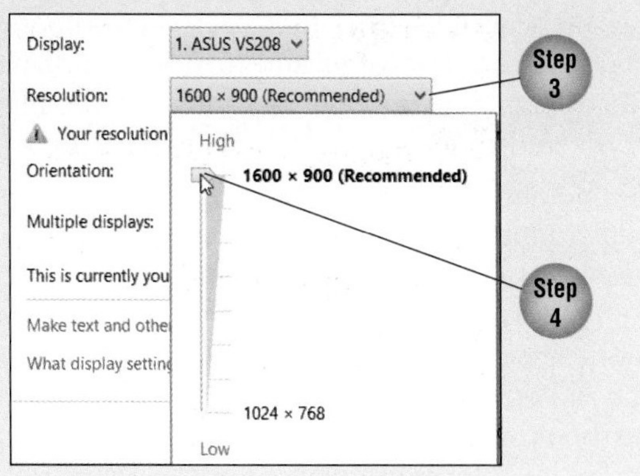

Project 2 Displaying File Extensions

1. At the Windows desktop, position the mouse pointer in the lower left corner of the Taskbar until the Start screen thumbnail displays and then click the right mouse button.
2. At the pop-up list, click the *File Explorer* option.
3. At the Computer window, click the View tab on the ribbon and then click the *File name extensions* check box in the Show/hide group to insert a check mark.
4. Close the Computer window.

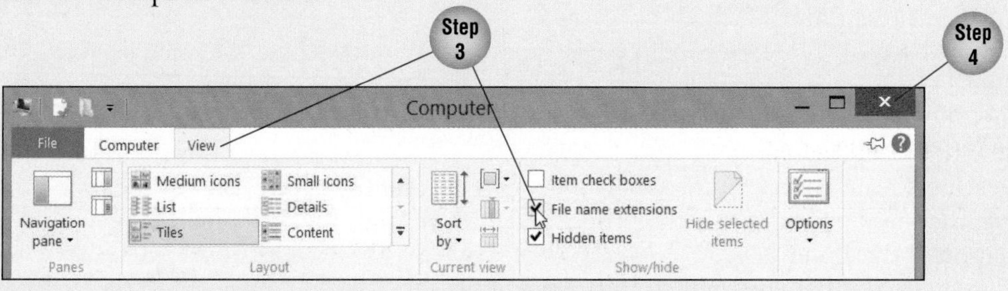

Completing Computer Projects

Some projects in this textbook require that you open an existing file. Project files are saved on the Student Resources CD in individual chapter folders. Before beginning a chapter, copy the necessary folder from the CD to your storage medium (such as a USB flash drive or your OneDrive) using the Computer window. To maximize storage capacity, delete previous chapter folders before copying a new chapter folder onto your storage medium.

Project 3 Copying a Folder from the Student Resources CD to a USB Flash Drive

1. Insert the CD that accompanies this textbook into your computer's CD/DVD drive.
2. Insert your USB flash drive into an available USB port.
3. At the Windows Start screen, click the Desktop tile.
4. Open File Explorer by clicking the File Explorer button on the Taskbar.
5. Click *Computer* in the Navigation pane at the left side of the File Explorer window.
6. Double-click the CD/DVD drive that displays with the name *BM13StudentResources* preceded by the drive letter.
7. Double-click ***StudentDataFiles*** in the Content pane.
8. Double-click the desired program folder name (and level number, if appropriate) in the Content pane.
9. Click once on the desired chapter (or unit performance assessment) folder name to select it.
10. Click the Home tab and then click the Copy button in the Clipboard group.
11. Click your USB flash drive that displays in the Navigation pane at the left side of the window.
12. Click the Home tab and then click the Paste button in the Clipboard group.
13. Close the File Explorer window by clicking the Close button located in the upper right corner of the window.

Project 4 Copying a Folder from the Student Resources CD to your OneDrive Account

Note: OneDrive is updated periodically, so the steps to create folders and upload files may vary from the steps below.

1. Insert the CD that accompanies this textbook into your computer's CD/DVD drive.
2. At the Windows Start screen, click the Desktop tile.
3. Open Internet Explorer by clicking the Internet Explorer button on the Taskbar.
4. At the Internet Explorer home page, click in the Address bar, type **www.onedrive.com**, and then press Enter.
5. At the Microsoft OneDrive login page, type your Windows Live ID (such as your email address).
6. Press the Tab key, type your password, and then press Enter.
7. Click the Documents tile in your OneDrive.
8. Click the Create option on the OneDrive menu bar and then click *Folder* at the drop-down list.
9. Type the name of the folder that you want to copy from the Student Resources CD and then press the Enter key.
10. Click the folder tile you created in the previous step.
11. Click the Upload option on the menu bar.
12. Click the CD/DVD drive that displays in the Navigation pane at the left side of the Choose File to Upload dialog box.
13. Open the chapter folder on the CD that contains the required student data files.
14. Select all of the files in the folder by pressing Ctrl + A and then click the Open button.

Project 5 Deleting a Folder

Note: Check with your instructor before deleting a folder.

1. Insert your storage medium (such as a USB flash drive) into your computer's USB port.
2. At the Windows desktop, open File Explorer by right-clicking the Start screen thumbnail and then clicking *File Explorer* at the shortcut menu.
3. Double-click the drive letter for your storage medium (the drive containing your USB flash drive, such as *Removable Disk (F:)*).
4. Click the chapter folder in the Content pane.
5. Click the Home tab and then click the Delete button in the Organize group.
6. At the message asking if you want to delete the folder, click the Yes button.
7. Close the Computer window by clicking the Close button located in the upper right corner of the window.

Using Windows 8

A computer requires an operating system to provide necessary instructions on a multitude of processes including loading programs, managing data, directing the flow of information to peripheral equipment, and displaying information. Windows 8 is an operating system that provides functions of this type (along with much more) in a graphical environment. Windows is referred to as a ***graphical user interface*** (GUI—pronounced *gooey*) that provides a visual display of information with features such as icons (pictures) and buttons. In this introduction, you will learn these basic features of Windows 8:

- Use the Start screen to launch programs
- Use desktop icons and the Taskbar to launch programs and open files or folders
- Organize and manage data, including copying, moving, creating, and deleting files and folders; and create a shortcut
- Explore the Control Panel and personalize the desktop
- Use the Windows Help and Support features
- Use search tools
- Customize monitor settings

Before using the software programs in the Microsoft Office suite, you will need to start the Windows 8 operating system. To do this, turn on the computer. Depending on your computer equipment configuration, you may also need to turn on the monitor and printer. If you are using a computer that is part of a network system or if your computer is set up for multiple users, a screen will display showing the user accounts defined for your computer system. At this screen, click your user account name; if necessary, type your password; and then press the Enter key. The Windows 8 operating system will start and, after a few moments, the Windows 8 Start screen will display as shown in Figure W.1. (Your Windows 8 Start screen may vary from what you see in Figure W.1.)

Exploring the Start Screen and Desktop

When Windows is loaded, the Windows 8 Start screen displays. This screen contains tiles that open various applications. Open an application by clicking an application's tile or display the Windows 8 desktop by clicking the Desktop tile. Click the Desktop tile and the screen displays as shown in Figure W.2. Think of the desktop in Windows as the top of a desk in an office. A businessperson places necessary tools—such as pencils, pens, paper, files, calculator—on the desktop to perform functions. Like the tools that are located on a desk, the Windows 8 desktop contains tools for operating the computer. These tools are logically grouped and placed in dialog boxes or panels that you can display using icons on the desktop. The desktop contains a variety of features for using your computer and applications installed on the computer.

Figure W.1 Windows 8 Start Screen

Figure W.2 Windows 8 Desktop

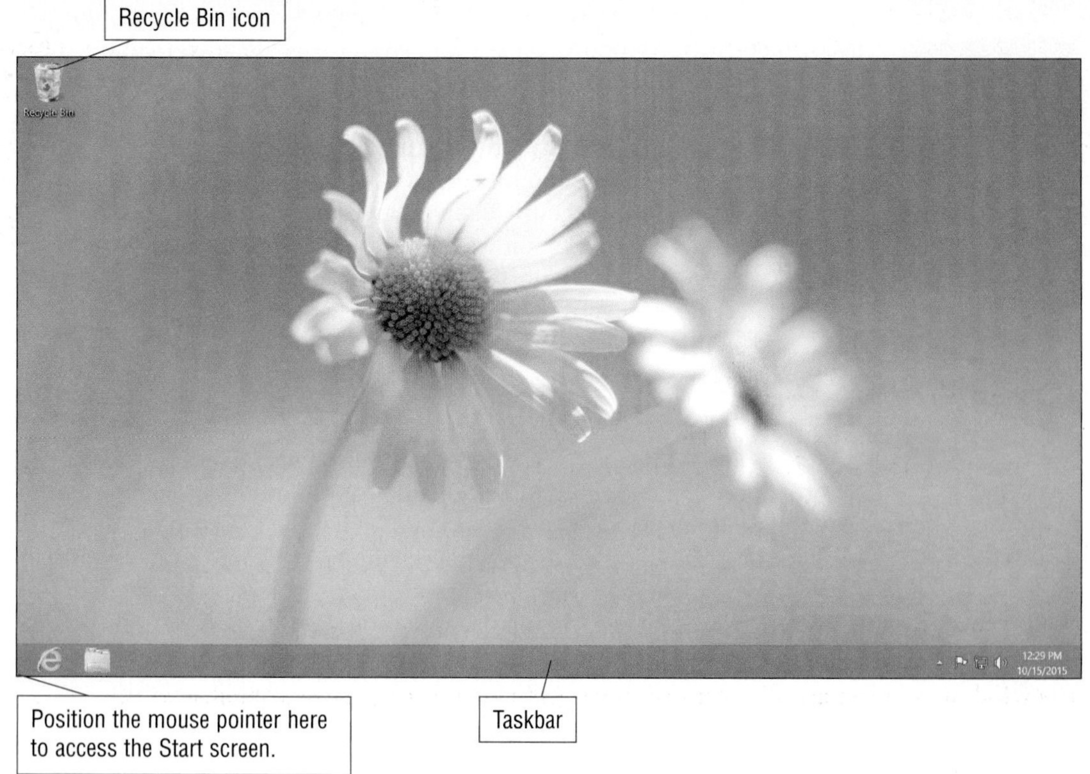

Using Icons

Icons are visual symbols that represent programs, files, or folders. Figure W.2 identifies the Recycle Bin icon on the Windows desktop. The Windows desktop on your computer may contain additional icons. Applications that have been installed on your computer may be represented by an icon on the desktop. Icons that represent files or folders may also display on your desktop. Double-click an icon and the application, file, or folder it represents opens on the desktop.

Using the Taskbar

The bar that displays at the bottom of the desktop (see Figure W.2) is called the ***Taskbar***. The Taskbar, shown in Figure W.3, contains the Start screen area (a spot where you point to access the Start screen), pinned items, a section that displays task buttons representing active tasks, the notification area, and the Show desktop button.

Position the mouse pointer in the lower left corner of the Taskbar to display the Start screen thumbnail. When the Start screen thumbnail displays, click the left mouse button to access the Windows 8 Start screen, shown in Figure W.1. (Your Start screen may look different.) You can also display the Start screen by pressing the Windows key on your keyboard or by pressing Ctrl + Esc. The left side of the Start menu contains tiles you can click to access the most frequently used applications. The name of the active user (the person who is currently logged on) displays in the upper right corner of the Start screen.

To open an application from the Start screen, drag the arrow pointer to the desired tile (referred to as ***pointing***) and then click the left mouse button. When a program is open, a task button representing the program appears on the Taskbar. If multiple programs are open, each program will appear as a task button on the Taskbar (a few specialized tools may not).

Figure W.3 Windows 8 Taskbar

Manipulating Windows

When you open a program, a defined work area known as a ***window*** displays on the screen. A Title bar displays at the top of the window and contains buttons at the right side for minimizing, maximizing, and restoring the size of the window, as well as for closing it. You can open more than one window at a time and the open windows can be cascaded or stacked. Windows 8 contains a Snap feature that causes a window to "stick" to the edge of the screen when the window is moved to the left or right side of the screen. Move a window to the top of the screen and the window is automatically maximized. If you drag down a maximized window, the window is automatically restored down (returned to its previous smaller size).

In addition to moving and sizing a window, you can change the display of all open windows. To do this, position the mouse pointer on the Taskbar and then click the right mouse button. At the pop-up menu that displays, you can choose to cascade all open windows, stack all open windows, or display all open windows side by side.

Project 1 Opening Programs, Switching between Programs, and Manipulating Windows

1. Open Windows 8. (To do this, turn on the computer and, if necessary, turn on the monitor and/or printer. If you are using a computer that is part of a network system or if your computer is set up for multiple users, you may need to click your user account name, type your password, and then press the Enter key. Check with your instructor to determine if you need to complete any additional steps.)
2. When the Windows 8 Start screen displays, open Microsoft Word by positioning the mouse pointer on the *Word 2013* tile and then clicking the left mouse button. (You may need to scroll to the right to display the Word 2013 tile.)
3. When the Microsoft Word program is open, notice that a task button representing Word displays on the Taskbar.

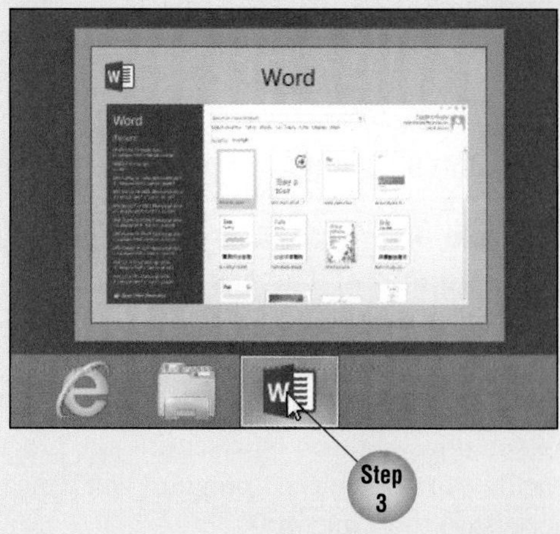

4. Open Microsoft Excel by completing the following steps:
   a. Position the arrow pointer in the lower left corner of the Taskbar until the Start screen thumbnail displays and then click the left mouse button.
   b. At the Start screen, position the mouse pointer on the *Excel 2013* tile and then click the left mouse button.
5. When the Microsoft Excel program is open, notice that a task button representing Excel displays on the Taskbar to the right of the task button representing Word.
6. Switch to the Word program by clicking the Word task button on the Taskbar.
7. Switch to the Excel program by clicking the Excel task button on the Taskbar.

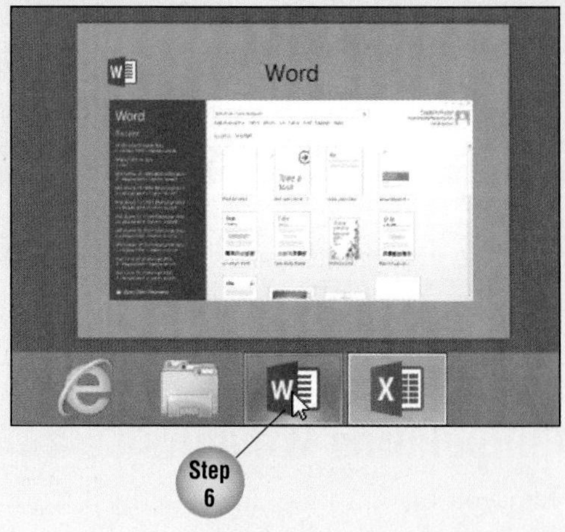

8. Restore down the Excel window by clicking the Restore Down button that displays immediately left of the Close button in the upper right corner of the screen. (This reduces the Excel window so it displays along the bottom half of the screen.)
9. Restore down the Word window by clicking the Restore Down button located immediately left of the Close button in the upper right corner of the screen.

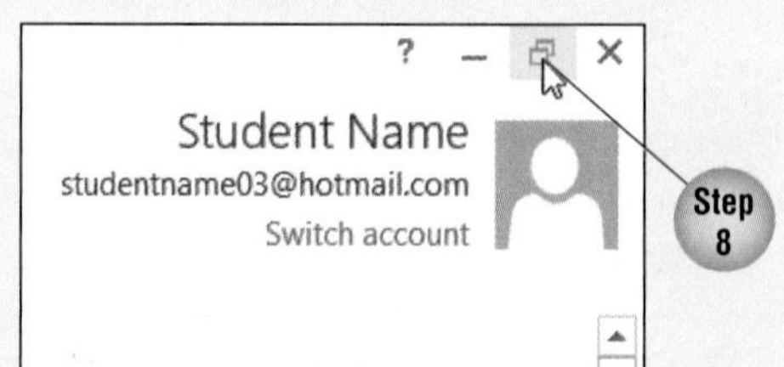

10. Position the mouse pointer at the top of the Word window screen, hold down the left mouse button, drag to the left side of the screen until an outline of the window displays in the left half of the screen, and then release the mouse button. (This "sticks" the window to the left side of the screen.)
11. Position the mouse pointer at the top of the Excel window screen, hold down the left mouse button, drag to the right until an outline of the window displays in the right half of the screen, and then release the mouse button.
12. Minimize the Excel window by clicking the Minimize button that displays in the upper right corner of the Excel window screen.

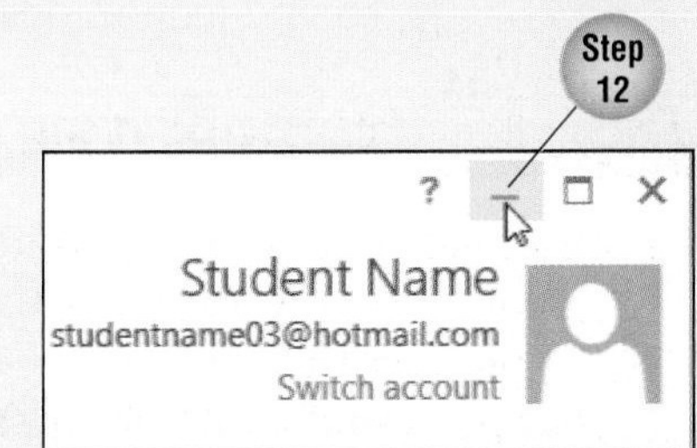

13. Hover your mouse over the Excel button on the Taskbar and then click the Excel window thumbnail that displays. (This displays the Excel window at the right side of the screen.)
14. Cascade the Word and Excel windows by positioning the arrow pointer in an empty area of the Taskbar, clicking the right mouse button, and then clicking *Cascade windows* at the shortcut menu.

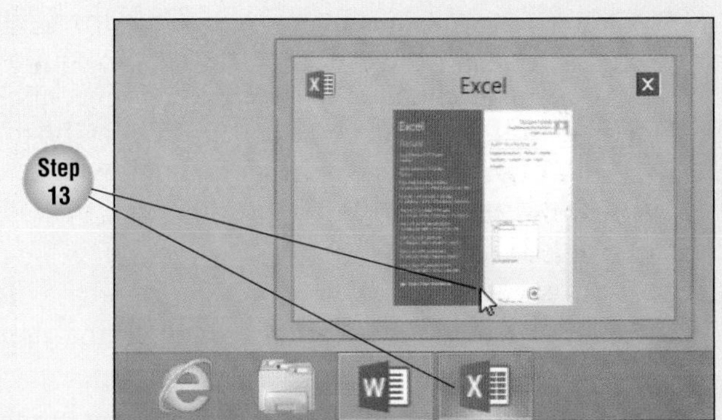

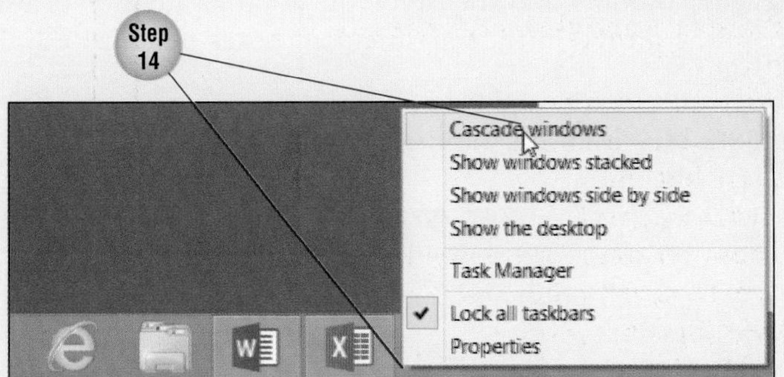

15. After viewing the windows cascaded, display them stacked by right-clicking an empty area of the Taskbar and then clicking *Show windows stacked* at the shortcut menu.
16. Display the desktop by right-clicking an empty area of the Taskbar and then clicking *Show the desktop* at the shortcut menu.
17. Display the windows stacked by right-clicking an empty area of the Taskbar and then clicking *Show open windows* at the shortcut menu.
18. Position the mouse pointer at the top of the Word window screen, hold down the left mouse button, drag the window to the top of the screen, and then release the mouse button. This maximizes the Word window so it fills the screen.
19. Close the Word window by clicking the Close button located in the upper right corner of the window.
20. At the Excel window, click the Maximize button located immediately left of the Close button in the upper right corner of the Excel window.
21. Close the Excel window by clicking the Close button located in the upper right corner of the window.

Using the Pinned Area

The icons that display immediately right of the Start screen area represent ***pinned applications***. Clicking an icon opens the application associated with the icon. Click the first icon to open the Internet Explorer web browser and click the second icon to open a File Explorer window containing Libraries.

Exploring the Notification Area

The notification area is located at the right side of the Taskbar and contains icons that show the status of certain system functions such as a network connection or battery power. The notification area contains icons for managing certain programs and Windows 8 features, as well as the system clock and date. Click the time or date in the notification area and a window displays with a clock and a calendar of the current month. Click the Change date and time settings hyperlink that displays at the bottom of the window and the Date and Time dialog box displays. To change the date and/or time, click the Change date and time button and the Date and Time Settings dialog box displays, similar to the dialog box shown in Figure W.4. (If a dialog box displays telling you that Windows needs your permission to continue, click the Continue button.)

Change the month and year by clicking the left-pointing or right-pointing arrow at the top of the calendar. Click the left-pointing arrow to display the previous month(s) and click the right-pointing arrow to display the next month(s).

To change the day, click the desired day in the monthly calendar that displays in the dialog box. To change the time, double-click either the hour, minute, or seconds number and then type the appropriate time or use the up- and down-pointing arrows in the measurement boxes to adjust the time.

Figure W.4 Date and Time Settings Dialog Box

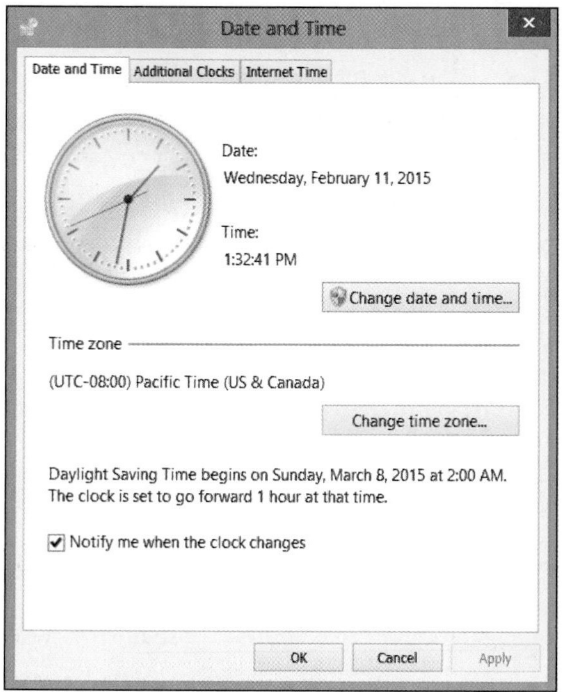

Some applications, when installed, will add an icon to the notification area of the Taskbar. To determine the name of an icon, position the mouse pointer on the icon and, after approximately one second, its label will display. If more icons have been inserted in the notification area than can be viewed at one time, an up-pointing arrow button displays at the left side of the notification area. Click this up-pointing arrow to display the remaining icons.

Setting Taskbar Properties

Customize the Taskbar with options at the Taskbar shortcut menu. Display this menu by right-clicking in an empty portion of the Taskbar. The Taskbar shortcut menu contains options for turning on or off the display of specific toolbars, specifying the display of multiple windows, displaying the Start Task Manager dialog box, locking or unlocking the Taskbar, and displaying the Taskbar Properties dialog box.

With options in the Taskbar Properties dialog box, shown in Figure W.5, you can change settings for the Taskbar. Display this dialog box by right-clicking an empty area on the Taskbar and then clicking *Properties* at the shortcut menu.

Each Taskbar property is controlled by a check box or an option box. If a property's check box contains a check mark, that property is active. Click the check box to remove the check mark and make the option inactive. If an option is inactive, clicking the check box will insert a check mark and turn on the option (make it active). A property option box displays the name of the currently active option. Click the option box to select a different option from the drop-down list.

Figure W.5 Taskbar Properties Dialog Box

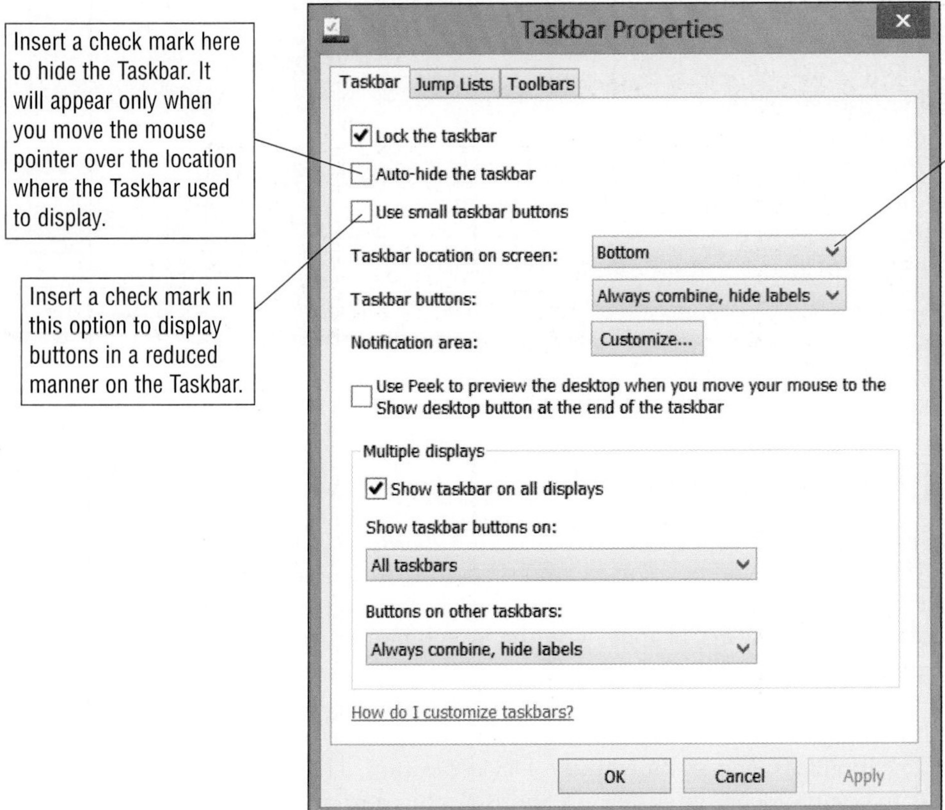

Project 2 Changing Taskbar Properties

1. Make sure the Windows 8 desktop displays.
2. Change the Taskbar properties by completing the following steps:
   a. Position the arrow pointer in an empty area of the Taskbar and then click the right mouse button.
   b. At the shortcut menu that displays, click *Properties*.
   c. At the Taskbar Properties dialog box, click the *Auto-hide the taskbar* check box to insert a check mark.
   d. Click the *Use small taskbar buttons* check box to insert a check mark.
   e. Click the option box (contains the word *Bottom*) that displays at the right side of the *Taskbar location on screen:* option and then click *Right* at the drop-down list.
   f. Click OK to close the dialog box.

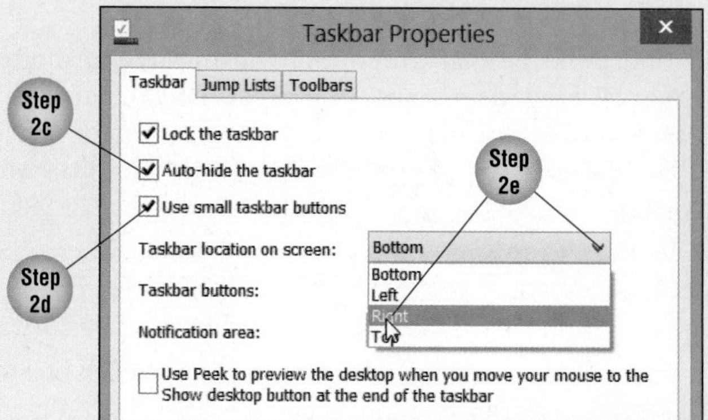

3. Since the *Auto-hide the taskbar* check box contains a check mark, the Taskbar does not display. Display the Taskbar by moving the mouse pointer to the right side of the screen. Notice that the buttons on the Taskbar are smaller than they were before.
4. Return to the default Taskbar properties by completing the following steps:
   a. Move the mouse pointer to the right side of the screen to display the Taskbar.
   b. Right-click an empty area of the Taskbar and then click *Properties* at the shortcut menu.
   c. Click the *Auto-hide the taskbar* check box to remove the check mark.
   d. Click the *Use small taskbar buttons* check box to remove the check mark.
   e. Click the *Taskbar location on screen* option box (displays with the word *Right*) and then click *Bottom* at the drop-down list.
   f. Click OK to close the dialog box.

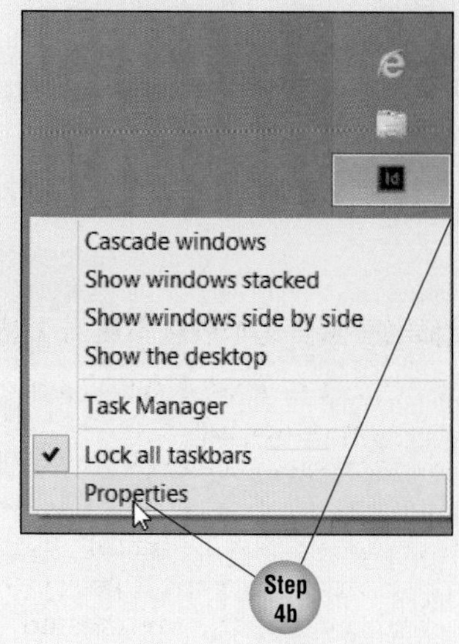

Using the Charm Bar

Windows 8 contains a new feature called the ***Charm bar***. The Charm bar is a bar that displays when you position the mouse pointer in the upper or lower right corner of the screen. Use the buttons on the Charm bar, shown in Figure W.6, to access certain features or tools. Use the Search button to search the computer for applications, files, folders and settings. With the Share button, you can share information with others via email or social networks. Clicking the Start button displays the Windows 8 Start screen. Access settings for various devices such as printers, monitors, and so on with the Devices button. The Settings button gives you access to common computer settings and is also used to power down the computer.

Figure W.6 Charm Bar

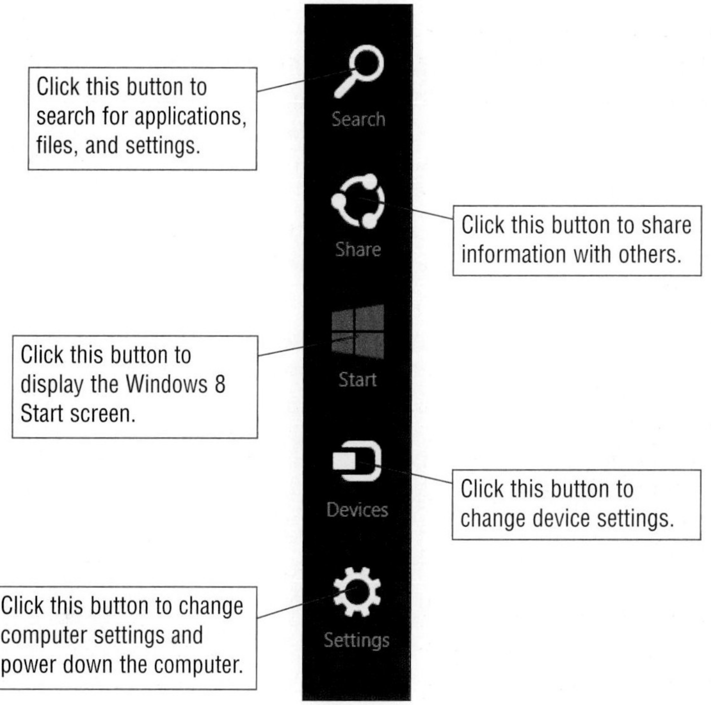
Click this button to search for applications, files, and settings.
Search
Share
Click this button to share information with others.
Click this button to display the Windows 8 Start screen.
Start
Devices
Click this button to change device settings.
Click this button to change computer settings and power down the computer.
Settings

Powering Down the Computer

If you want to shut down Windows, first close any open programs and then display the Charm bar. Click the Settings button on the Charm bar, click the Power tile, and then click the *Shut down* option. The Power tile also contains options for restarting the computer or putting the computer to sleep. Restarting the computer may be useful when installing new applications or if Windows 8 stops working properly. In sleep mode, Windows saves files and information about applications and then powers down the computer to a low-power state. To "wake up" the computer, press the computer's power button.

In a multi-user environment, you can sign out of or lock your account so that no one can tamper with your work. To access these features, display the Windows 8 Start screen and then click your user account tile in the upper right corner. This displays a shortcut menu with three options. The *Lock* option locks the computer, which means that it is still powered on but requires a user password in order to access any applications or files that were previously opened. (To unlock the computer, click the icon on the login screen representing your account, type your password, and then press Enter.) Use the *Sign out* option to sign out of your user account while still keeping the computer turned on so that others may log on to it. Click the *Change account picture* option if you want to change the picture associated with your user account.

Managing Files and Folders

As you begin working with programs in Windows 8, you will create files in which data (information) is saved. A file might be a Word document, an Excel workbook, an Access database, or a PowerPoint presentation. As you begin creating files, consider creating folders in which to store these files. Complete file management tasks such as creating a folder or moving a file at the Computer window. To display the Computer window, shown in Figure W.7, position your mouse pointer in the lower left corner of the screen to display the Start screen thumbnail, click the right mouse button, and then click *File Explorer* at the shortcut menu. The various components of the Computer window are identified in Figure W.7.

In the Content pane of the Computer window, icons display representing each hard disk drive and removable storage medium (such as a CD, DVD, or USB device) connected to your computer. Next to each storage device icon, Windows displays the amount of storage space available as well as a bar with the amount of used space shaded with color. This visual cue allows you to see at a glance the amount of space available relative to the capacity of the device. Double-click a device icon in the Content pane to change the display to show the contents stored on the device. Display contents from another device or folder using the Navigation pane or the Address bar on the Computer window.

Figure W.7 Computer Window

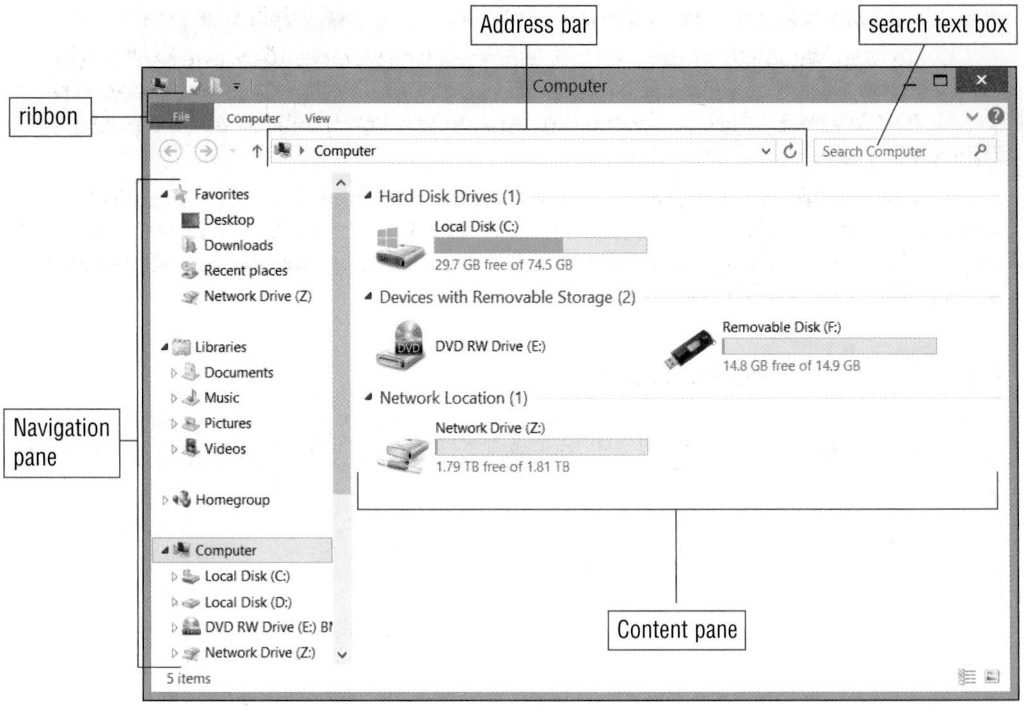

Copying, Moving, and Deleting Files and Folders

File and folder management activities include copying and moving files and folders from one folder or drive to another, as well as deleting files and folders. The Computer window offers a variety of methods for performing these actions. This section will provide you with steps for copying, moving, and deleting files and folders using options from the Home tab (shown in Figure W.8) and the shortcut menu (shown in Figure W.9).

To copy a file to another folder or drive, first display the file in the Content pane. If the file is located in the Documents folder, click the *Documents* folder in the *Libraries* section of the Navigation pane and then, in the Content pane, click the name of the file you want to copy. Click the Home tab on the ribbon and then click the Copy button in the Clipboard group. Use the Navigation pane to navigate to the location where you want to paste the file. Click the Home tab and then click the Paste button in the Clipboard group. Complete similar steps to copy and paste a folder to another location.

If the desired file is located on a storage medium such as a CD, DVD, or USB device, double-click the device in the section of the Content pane labeled *Devices with Removable Storage*. (Each removable device is assigned an alphabetic drive letter by Windows, usually starting at E or F and continuing through the alphabet depending on the number of removable devices that are currently in use.) After double-clicking the storage medium in the Content pane, navigate to the desired folder and then click the file to select it. Click the Home tab on the ribbon and then click the Copy button in the Clipboard group. Navigate to the desired folder, click the Home tab, and then click the Paste button in the Clipboard group.

To move a file, click the desired file in the Content pane, click the Home tab on the ribbon, and then click the Cut button in the Clipboard group. Navigate to the desired location, click the Home tab, and then click the Paste button in the Clipboard group.

To delete a file or folder, click the file or folder in the Content pane in the Computer window. Click the Home tab and then click the Delete button in the Organize group. At the message asking if you want to move the file or folder to the Recycle Bin, click the Yes button.

Figure W.8 File Explorer Home tab

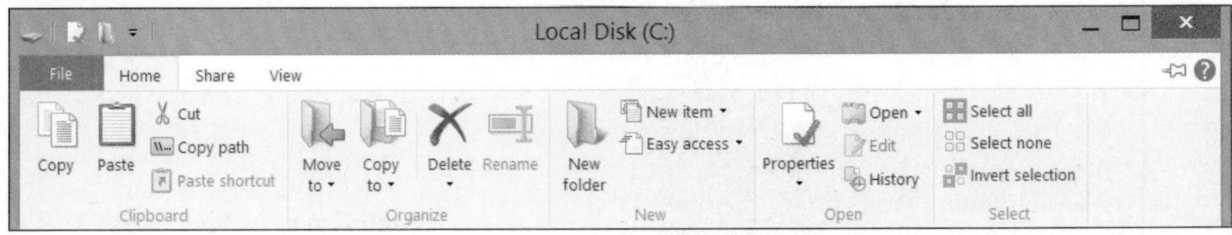

Figure W.9 Shortcut Menu

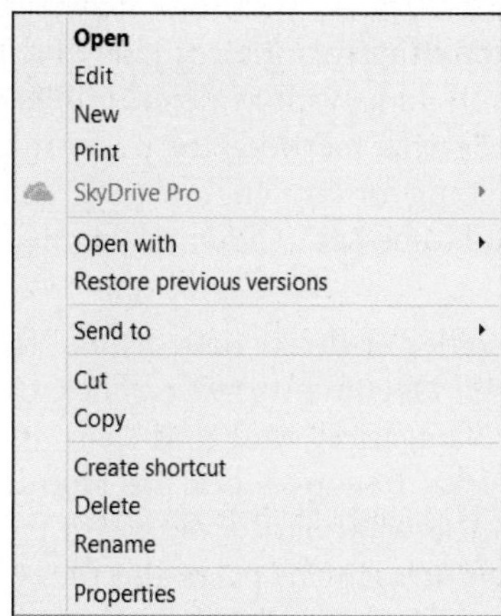

Project 3 Copying a File and Folder and Deleting a File

1. Insert the CD that accompanies this textbook into the appropriate drive.
2. Insert your storage medium (such as a USB flash drive) into the appropriate drive.
3. At the Windows 8 desktop, position the mouse pointer in the lower left corner of the Taskbar to display the Start screen thumbnail, click the right mouse button, and then click *File Explorer* at the shortcut menu.
4. Copy a file from the CD that accompanies this textbook to the drive containing your storage medium by completing the following steps:
   a. In the Content pane, double-click the drive into which you inserted the CD that accompanies this textbook.
   b. Double-click the *StudentDataFiles* folder in the Content pane.
   c. Double-click the *Windows8* folder in the Content pane.
   d. Click ***WordDocument01.docx*** in the Content pane.
   e. Click the Home tab and then click *Copy* in the Clipboard group.

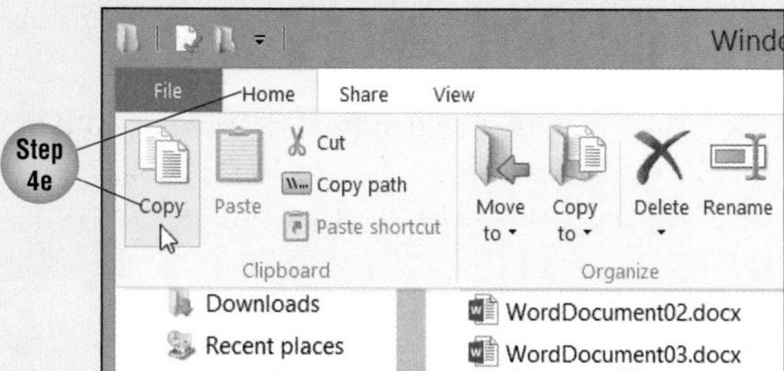

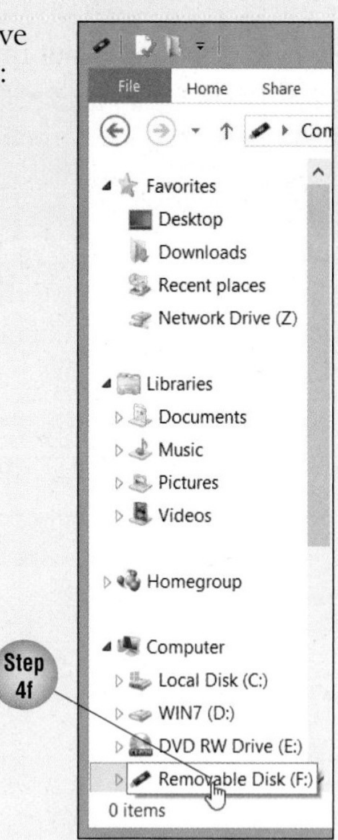

   f. In the Computer section in the Navigation pane, click the drive containing your storage medium. (You may need to scroll down the Navigation pane.)
   g. Click the Home tab and then click the Paste button in the Clipboard group.
5. Delete ***WordDocument01.docx*** from your storage medium by completing the following steps:
   a. Make sure the contents of your storage medium display in the Content pane in the Computer window.

b. Click ***WordDocument01.docx*** in the Content pane to select it.
c. Click the Home tab and then click the Delete button in the Organize group.
d. At the message asking if you want to permanently delete the file, click the Yes button.

6. Copy the Windows8 folder from the CD to your storage medium by completing the following steps:
   a. With the Computer window open, click the drive in the *Computer* section in the Navigation pane that contains the CD that accompanies this book.
   b. Double-click *StudentDataFiles* in the Content pane.
   c. Click the *Windows8* folder in the Content pane.
   d. Click the Home tab and then click the Copy button in the Clipboard group.
   e. In the *Computer* section in the Navigation pane, click the drive containing your storage medium.
   f. Click the Home tab and then click the Paste button in the Clipboard group.

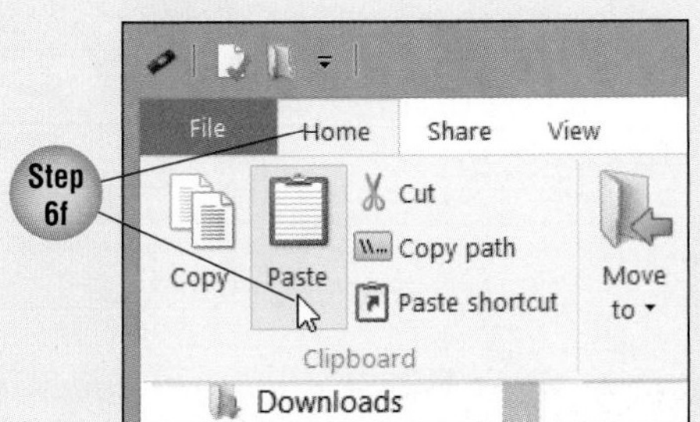

7. Close the Computer window by clicking the Close button located in the upper right corner of the window.

In addition to options on the Home tab, you can use options in a shortcut menu to copy, move, and delete files or folders. To use a shortcut menu, select the desired file(s) or folder(s), position the mouse pointer on the selected item, and then click the right mouse button. At the shortcut menu that displays, click the desired option, such as *Copy*, *Cut*, or *Delete*.

Selecting Files and Folders

You can move, copy, or delete more than one file or folder at the same time. Before moving, copying, or deleting files or folders, select the desired files or folders. To make selecting easier, consider displaying the files in the Content pane in a list or detailed list format. To change the display, click the View tab on the ribbon and then click *List* or *Details* in the Layout group.

To select adjacent files or folders, click the first file or folder, hold down the Shift key, and then click the last file or folder. To select nonadjacent files or folders, click the first file or folder, hold down the Ctrl key, and then click the other files or folders you wish to select.

Project 4 Copying and Deleting Files

1. At the Windows 8 desktop, position the mouse pointer in the lower left corner of the Taskbar to display the Start screen thumbnail, click the right mouse button, and then click *File Explorer* at the shortcut menu.
2. Copy files from the CD that accompanies this textbook to the drive containing your storage medium by completing the following steps:
   a. Make sure the CD that accompanies this textbook and your storage medium are inserted in the appropriate drives.
   b. Double-click the CD drive in the Content pane in the Computer window.

c. Double-click the *StudentDataFiles* folder in the Content pane.
d. Double-click the *Windows8* folder in the Content pane.
e. Change the display to List by clicking the View tab and then clicking *List* in the Layout group list box.

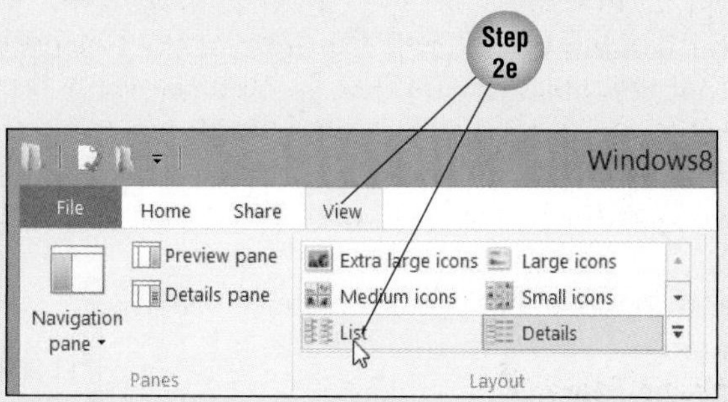

f. Click ***WordDocument01.docx*** in the Content pane.
g. Hold down the Shift key, click ***WordDocument05.docx***, and then release the Shift key. (This selects five documents.)

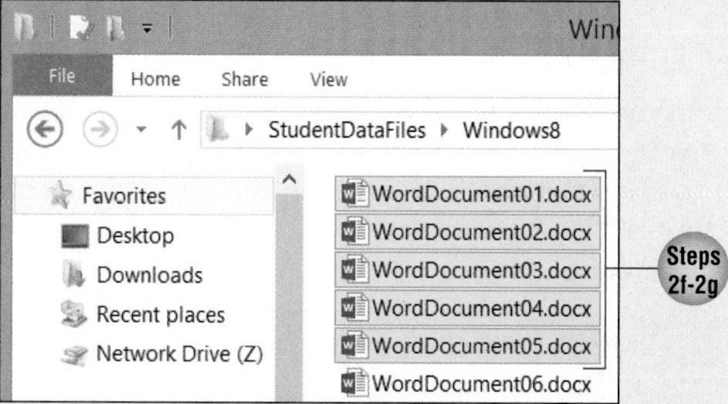

h. Click the Home tab and then click the Copy button in the Clipboard group.
i. In the *Computer* section of the Navigation pane, click the drive containing your storage medium.
j. Click the Home tab and then click the Paste button in the Clipboard group.

3. Delete the files you just copied to your storage medium by completing the following steps:
   a. Change the display by clicking the View tab and then clicking *List* in the Layout group.
   b. Click ***WordDocument01.docx*** in the Content pane.
   c. Hold down the Shift key, click ***WordDocument05.docx***, and then release the Shift key.
   d. Position the mouse pointer on any selected file, click the right mouse button, and then click *Delete* at the shortcut menu.
   e. At the message asking if you are sure you want to permanently delete the files, click Yes.
4. Close the Computer window by clicking the Close button located in the upper right corner of the window.

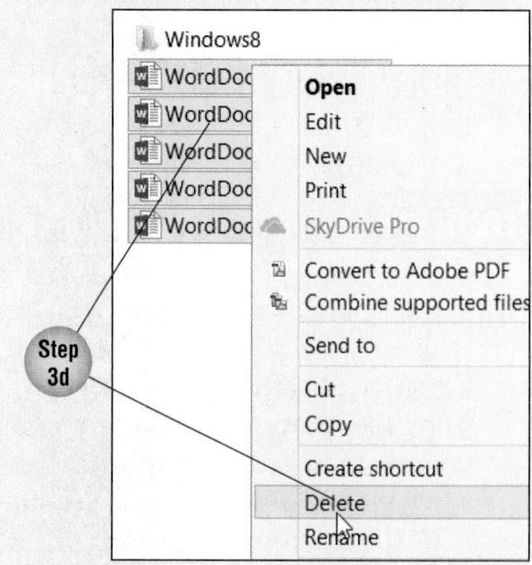

Manipulating and Creating Folders

As you begin working with and creating multiple files, consider creating folders in which you can logically group and store the files. To create a folder, display the Computer window and then display the drive or folder where you want to create the folder in the Content pane. To create the new folder, click the New folder button in the New group on the Home tab; click the New folder button on the Quick Access toolbar; or click in a blank area in the Content pane, click the right mouse button, point to *New* in the shortcut menu, and then click *Folder* at the side menu. Any of the three methods inserts a folder icon in the Content pane and names the folder *New folder*. Type the desired name for the new folder and then press Enter.

Project 5 Creating a New Folder

1. At the Windows 8 desktop, open the Computer window.
2. Create a new folder by completing the following steps:
   a. In the Content pane, double-click the drive that contains your storage medium.
   b. Double-click the *Windows8* folder in the Content pane. (This opens the folder.)
   c. Click the View tab and then click *List* in the Layout group.
   d. Click the Home tab and then click the New folder button in the New group.
   e. Type **SpellCheckFiles** and then press Enter. (This changes the name from *New folder* to *SpellCheckFiles*.)

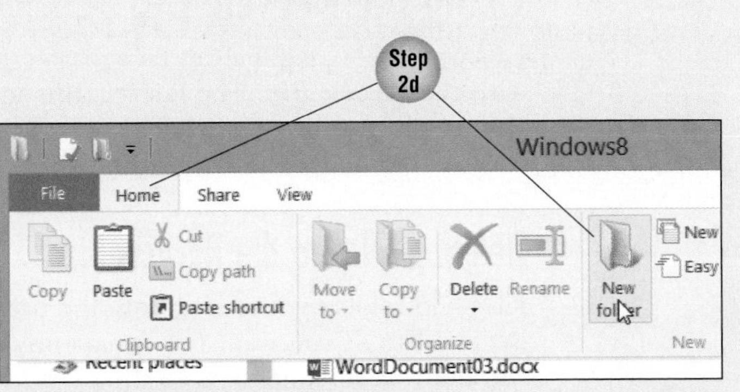

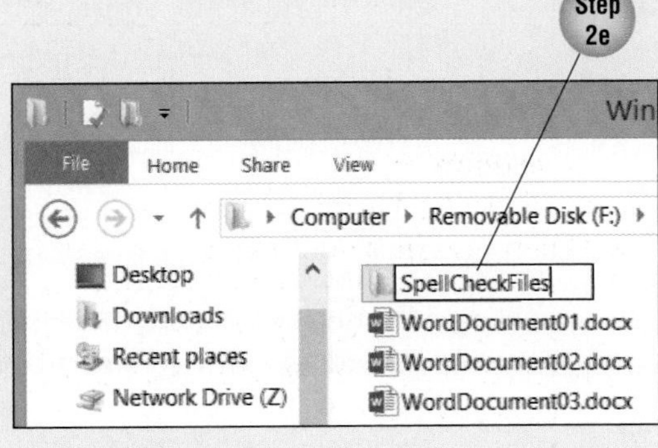

3. Copy **WordSpellCheck01.docx**, **WordSpellCheck02.docx**, and **WordSpellCheck03.docx** into the SpellCheckFiles folder you just created by completing the following steps:
   a. Click the View tab and then click *List* in the Layout group. (Skip this step if *List* is already selected.)
   b. Click ***WordSpellCheck01.docx*** in the Content pane.
   c. Hold down the Shift key, click ***WordSpellCheck03.docx***, and then release the Shift key. (This selects three documents.)
   d. Click the Home tab and then click the Copy button in the Clipboard group.
   e. Double-click the *SpellCheckFiles* folder in the Content pane.
   f. Click the Home tab and then click the Paste button in the Clipboard group.

4. Delete the SpellCheckFiles folder and its contents by completing the following steps:
   a. Click the Back button (contains a left-pointing arrow) located at the left side of the Address bar.
   b. With the SpellCheckFiles folder selected in the Content pane, click the Home tab and then click the Delete button in the Organize group.
   c. At the message asking you to confirm the deletion, click Yes.
5. Close the window by clicking the Close button located in the upper right corner of the window.

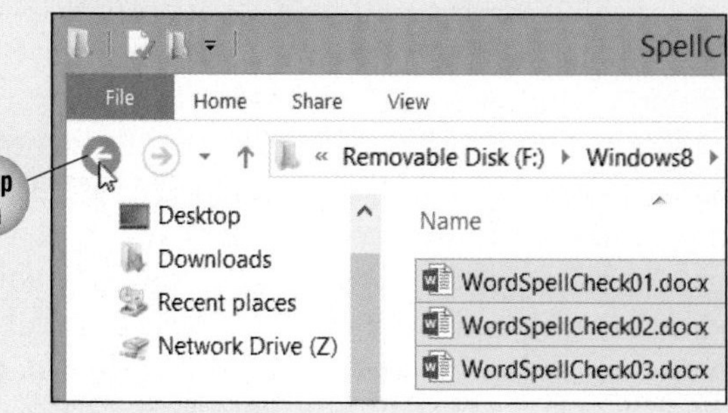

Using the Recycle Bin

Deleting the wrong file can be a disaster, but Windows 8 helps protect your work with the ***Recycle Bin***. The Recycle Bin acts just like an office wastepaper basket; you can "throw away" (delete) unwanted files, but you can also "reach in" to the Recycle Bin and take out (restore) a file if you threw it away by accident.

Deleting Files to the Recycle Bin

Files and folders you delete from the hard drive are sent automatically to the Recycle Bin. If you want to permanently delete files or folders from the hard drive without first sending them to the Recycle Bin, select the desired file(s) or folder(s), right-click one of the selected files or folders, hold down the Shift key, and then click *Delete* at the shortcut menu.

Files and folders deleted from a USB flash drive or disc are deleted permanently. (Recovery programs are available, however, that will help you recover deleted files or folders. If you accidentally delete a file or folder from a USB flash drive or disc, do not do anything more with the USB flash drive or disc until you can run a recovery program.)

You can delete files in the manner described earlier in this section and you can also delete a file by dragging the file icon to the Recycle Bin. To do this, click the desired file in the Content pane in the Computer window, drag the file icon to the Recycle Bin icon on the desktop until the text *Move to Recycle Bin* displays, and then release the mouse button.

Restoring Files from the Recycle Bin

To restore a file from the Recycle Bin, double-click the Recycle Bin icon on the desktop. This opens the Recycle Bin window, shown in Figure W.10. (The contents of the Recycle Bin will vary.) To restore a file, click the file you want restored, click the Recycle Bin Tools Manage tab and then click the Restore the selected items button in the Restore group. This removes the file from the Recycle Bin and returns it to its original location. You can also restore a file by positioning the mouse pointer on the file, clicking the right mouse button, and then clicking *Restore* at the shortcut menu.

Figure W.10 Recycle Bin Window

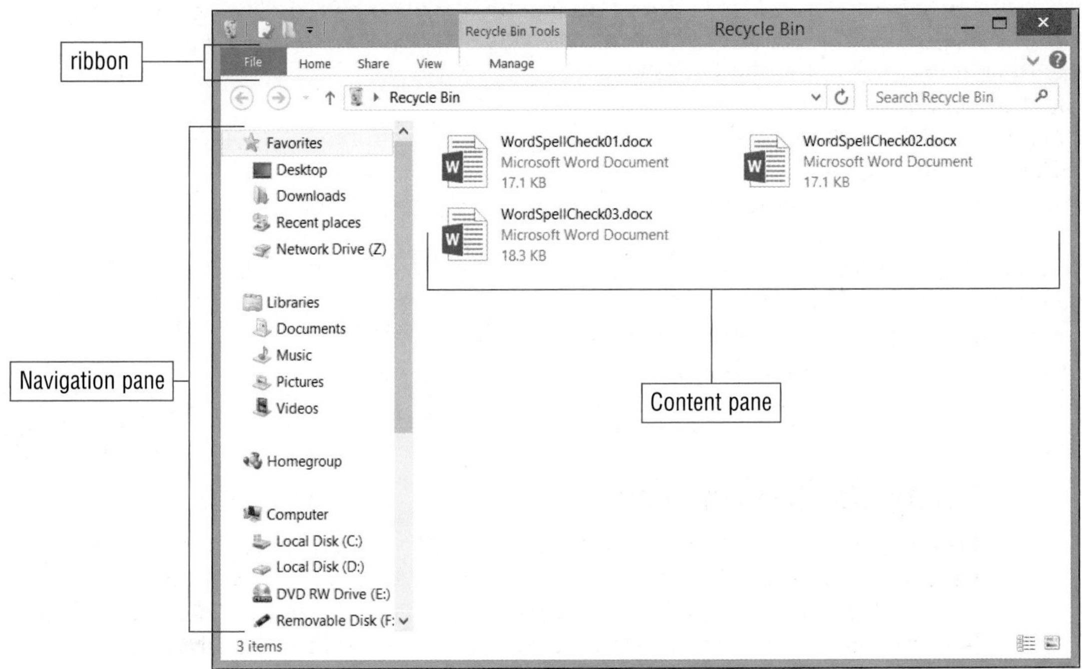

Project 6 Deleting Files to and Restoring Files from the Recycle Bin

Before beginning this project, check with your instructor to determine if you can copy files to the hard drive.

1. At the Windows 8 desktop, open the Computer window.
2. Copy files from your storage medium to the Documents folder on your hard drive by completing the following steps:
   a. In the Content pane, double-click the drive containing your storage medium.
   b. Double-click the *Windows8* folder in the Content pane.
   c. Click the View tab and then click *List* in the Layout group. (Skip this step if *List* is already selected.)
   d. Click ***WordSpellCheck01.docx*** in the Content pane.
   e. Hold down the Shift key, click ***WordSpellCheck03.docx***, and then release the Shift key.
   f. Click the Home tab and then click the Copy button in the Clipboard group.
   g. Click the *Documents* folder in the *Libraries* section of the Navigation pane.
   h. Click the Home tab and then click the Paste button in the Clipboard group.

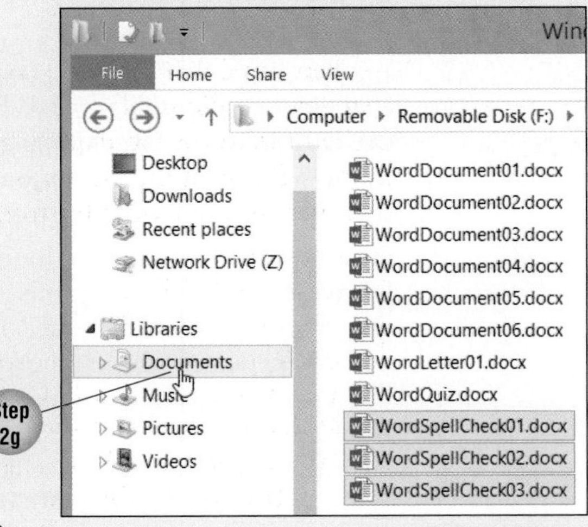

3. With **WordSpellCheck01.docx** through **WordSpellCheck03.docx** selected in the Content pane, click the Home tab and then click the Delete button in the Organize group to delete the files to the Recycle Bin.
4. Close the Computer window.
5. At the Windows 8 desktop, display the contents of the Recycle Bin by double-clicking the Recycle Bin icon.
6. Restore the files you just deleted by completing the following steps:
   a. Select **WordSpellCheck01.docx** through **WordSpellCheck03.docx** in the Recycle Bin Content pane. (If these files are not visible, you will need to scroll down the list of files in the Content pane.)
   b. Click the Recycle Bin Tools Manage tab and then click the Restore the selected items button in the Restore group.

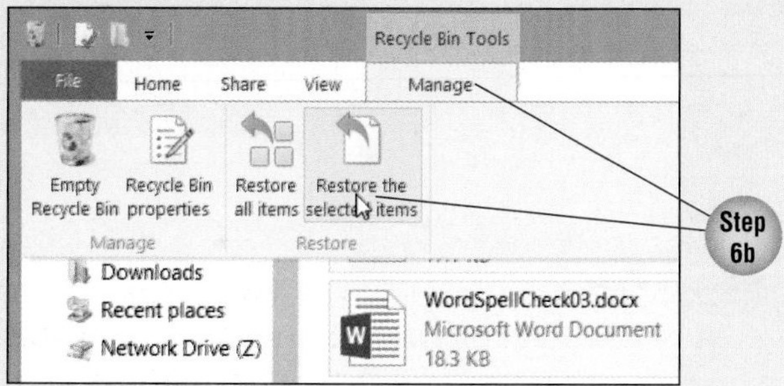

7. Close the Recycle Bin by clicking the Close button located in the upper right corner of the window.
8. Display the Computer window.
9. Click the *Documents* folder in the *Libraries* section of the Navigation pane.
10. Delete the files you restored.
11. Close the Computer window.

Emptying the Recycle Bin

Just like a wastepaper basket, the Recycle Bin can get full. To empty the Recycle Bin, position the arrow pointer on the Recycle Bin icon on the desktop and then click the right mouse button. At the shortcut menu that displays, click the *Empty Recycle Bin* option. At the message asking if you want to permanently delete the items, click Yes. You can also empty the Recycle Bin by displaying the Recycle Bin window and then clicking the Empty Recycle Bin button in the Manage group on the Recycle Bin Tools Manage tab. At the message asking if you want to permanently delete the items, click Yes. To delete a specific file from the Recycle Bin window, click the desired file in the Recycle Bin window, click the Home tab, and then click the Delete button in the Organize group. At the message asking if you want to permanently delete the file, click Yes. When you empty the Recycle Bin, the files cannot be recovered by the Recycle Bin or by Windows 8. If you have to recover a file, you will need to use a file recovery program.

Project 7 Emptying the Recycle Bin

Note: Before beginning this project, check with your instructor to determine if you can delete files/folders from the Recycle Bin.

1. At the Windows 8 desktop, double-click the Recycle Bin icon.
2. At the Recycle Bin window, empty the contents by clicking the Empty Recycle Bin button in the Manage group on the Recycle Bin Tools Manage tab.
3. At the message asking you if you want to permanently delete the items, click Yes.
4. Close the Recycle Bin by clicking the Close button located in the upper right corner of the window.

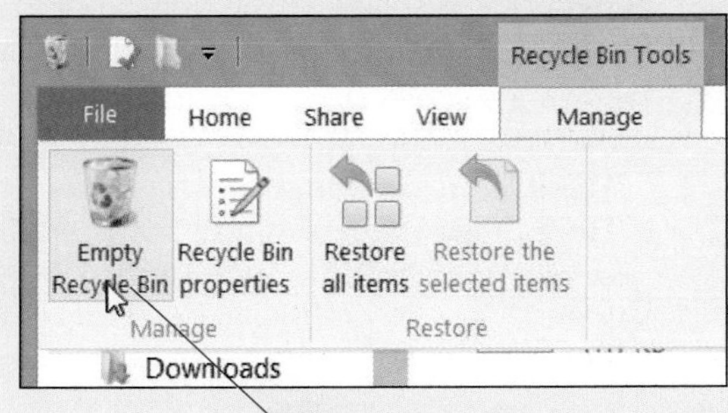

Creating a Shortcut

If you use a file or application on a consistent basis, consider creating a shortcut to the file or application. A ***shortcut*** is a specialized icon that points the operating system to an actual file, folder, or application. If you create a shortcut to a Word document, the shortcut icon is not the actual document but a very small file that contains the path to the document. Double-click the shortcut icon and Windows 8 opens the document in Word.

One method for creating a shortcut is to display the Computer window and then make active the drive or folder where the file is located. Right-click the desired file, point to *Send to*, and then click *Desktop (create shortcut)*. You can easily delete a shortcut icon from the desktop by dragging the shortcut icon to the Recycle Bin icon. This deletes the shortcut icon but does not delete the file to which the shortcut pointed.

Project 8 Creating a Shortcut

1. At the Windows 8 desktop, display the Computer window.
2. Double-click the drive containing your storage medium.
3. Double-click the *Windows8* folder in the Content pane.
4. Change the display of files to a list by clicking the View tab and then clicking *List* in the Layout group. (Skip this step if *List* is already selected.)
5. Create a shortcut to the file named **WordQuiz.docx** by right-clicking ***WordQuiz.docx***, pointing to *Send to*, and then clicking *Desktop (create shortcut)*.
6. Close the Computer window.

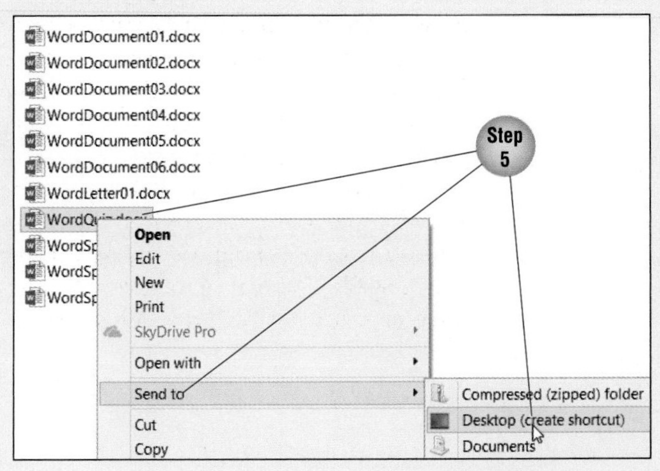

7. Open Word and **WordQuiz.docx** by double-clicking the *WordQuiz.docx* shortcut icon on the desktop.
8. After viewing the file in Word, close Word by clicking the Close button that displays in the upper right corner of the window.
9. Delete the *WordQuiz.docx* shortcut icon by completing the following steps:
   a. At the desktop, position the mouse pointer on the *WordQuiz.docx* shortcut icon.
   b. Hold down the left mouse button, drag the icon on top of the Recycle Bin icon, and then release the mouse button.

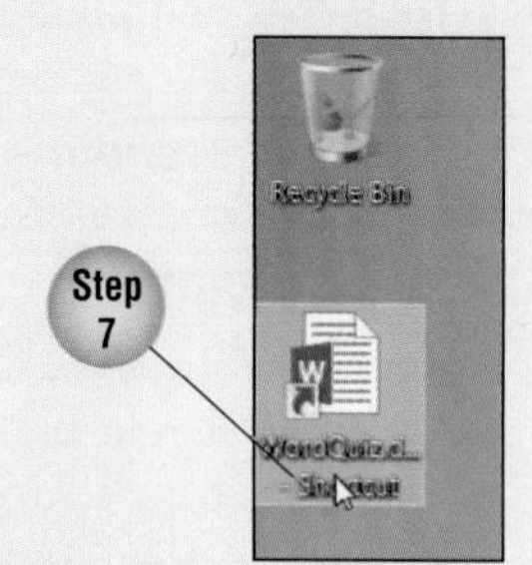

Exploring the Control Panel

The Control Panel, shown in Figure W.11, contains a variety of icons for customizing the appearance and functionality of your computer as well as accessing and changing system settings. Display the Control Panel by right-clicking the Start screen thumbnail and then clicking *Control Panel* at the shortcut menu. The Control Panel organizes settings into categories to make them easier to find. Click a category icon and the Control Panel displays lower-level categories and tasks within each of them.

Hover your mouse over a category icon in the Control Panel and a ScreenTip displays with an explanation of what options are available. For example, if you hover the mouse over the Appearance and Personalization icon, a ScreenTip displays with information about the tasks available in the category, such as changing the appearance of desktop items, applying a theme or screen saver to your computer, or customizing the Taskbar.

If you click a category icon in the Control Panel, the Control Panel displays all of the available subcategories and tasks in the category. Also, the categories display in text form at the left side of the Control Panel. For example, if you click the Appearance and Personalization icon, the Control Panel displays as shown in Figure W.12. Notice how the Control Panel categories display at the left side of the Control Panel and options for changing the appearance and personalizing your computer display in the middle of the Control Panel.

By default, the Control Panel displays categories of tasks in what is called *Category* view. You can change this view to display large or small icons. To change the view, click the down-pointing arrow that displays at the right side of the text *View by* that displays in the upper right corner of the Control Panel, and then click the desired view at the drop-down list (see Figure W.11).

Figure W.11 The Control Panel

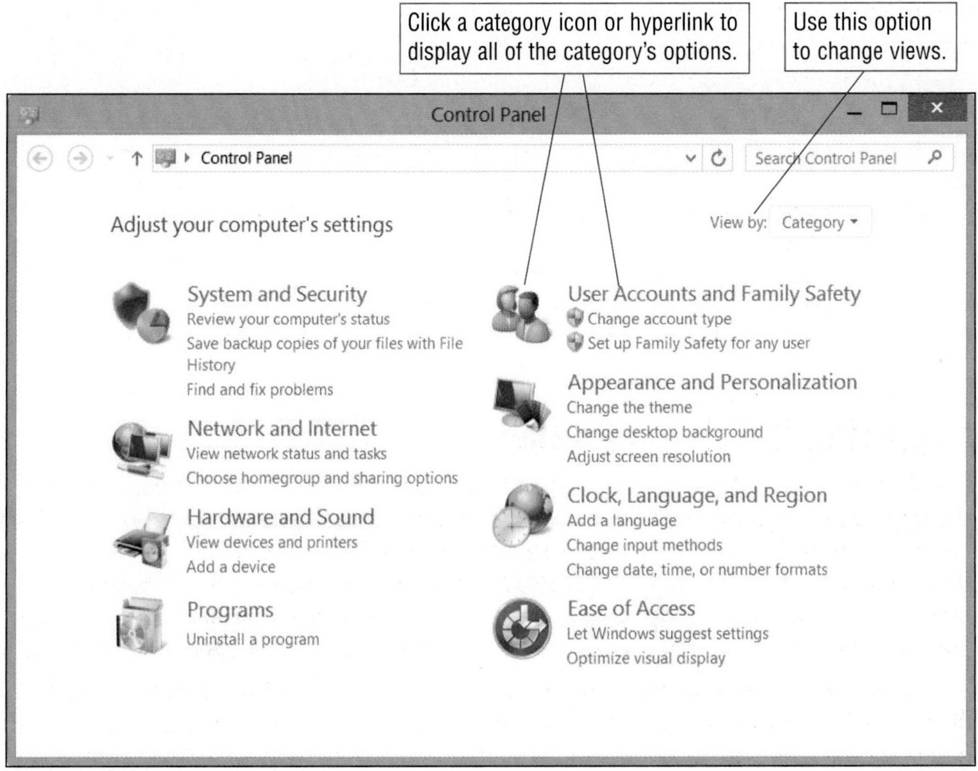

Figure W.12 Appearance and Personalization Window

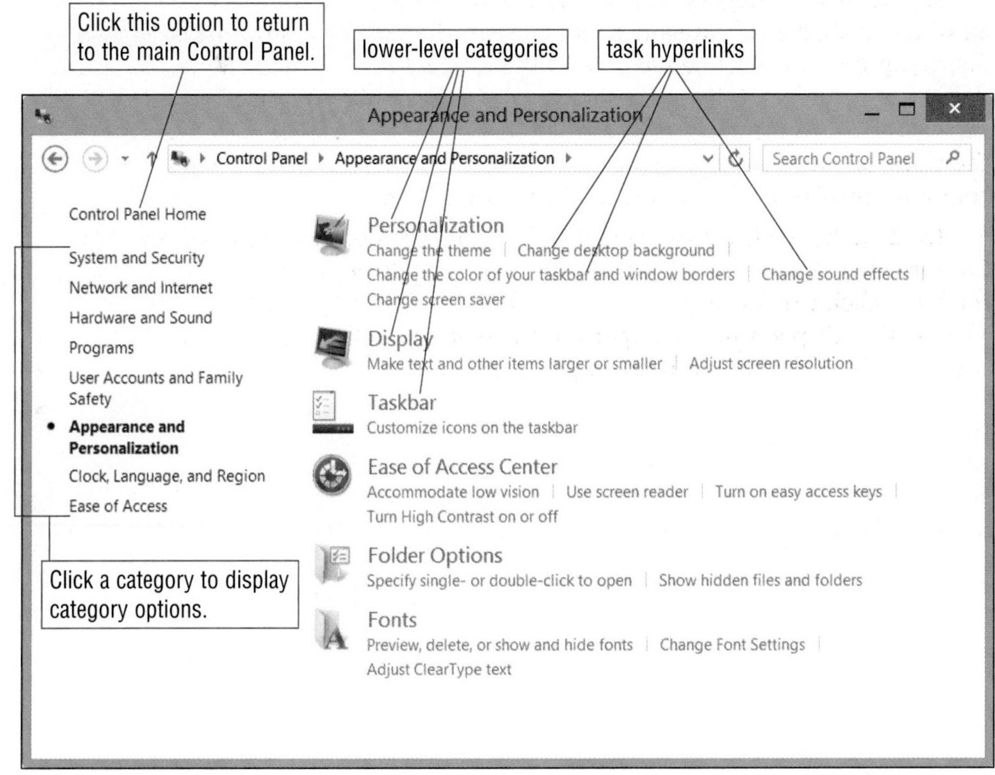

Project 9 Changing the Desktop Theme

1. At the Windows 8 desktop, right-click the Start screen thumbnail and then click *Control Panel* at the shortcut menu.
2. At the Control Panel, click the Appearance and Personalization icon.

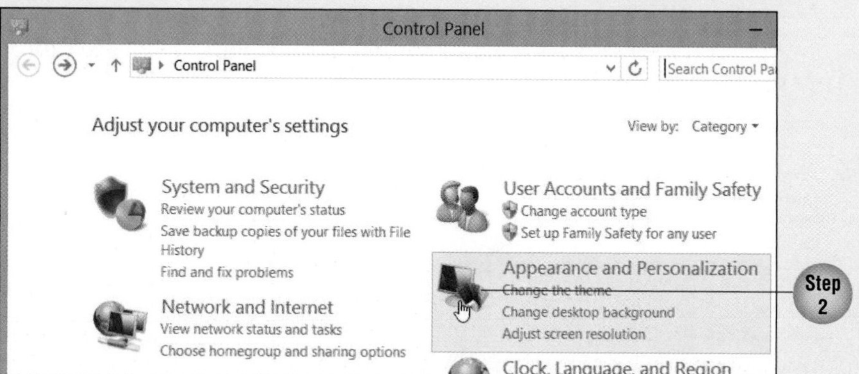

3. Click the Change the theme hyperlink that displays below *Personalization* in the panel at the right in the Control Panel.
4. At the window that displays with options for changing visuals and sounds on your computer, click *Earth* in the *Windows Default Themes* section.
5. Click the Desktop Background hyperlink that displays in the lower left corner of the panel.
6. Click the button that displays below the text *Change picture every* and then click *10 Seconds* at the drop-down list. (This tells Windows to change the picture on your desktop every 10 seconds.)
7. Click the Save changes button that displays in the lower right corner of the Control Panel.
8. Click the Close button located in the upper right corner to close the Control Panel.
9. Look at the picture that displays as the desktop background. Wait for 10 seconds and then look at the second picture that displays.
10. Right-click the Start screen thumbnail and then click *Control Panel* at the shortcut menu.
11. At the Control Panel, click the Appearance and Personalization icon.
12. Click the Change the theme hyperlink that displays below *Personalization* in the panel at the right.
13. At the window that displays with options for changing visuals and sounds on your computer, click *Windows* in the *Windows Default Themes* section. (This is the default theme.)
14. Click the Close button located in the upper right corner of the Control Panel.

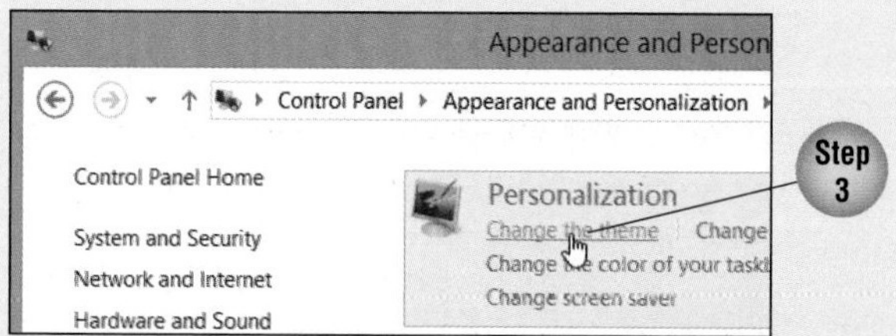

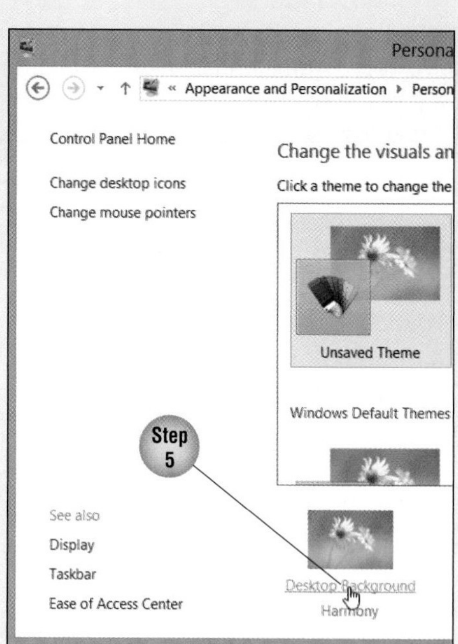

Searching in the Control Panel

The Control Panel contains a large number of options for customizing the appearance and functionality of your computer. If you want to customize a feature and are not sure where the options for the feature are located, search for the feature. To do this, display the Control Panel and then type the name of the desired feature. By default, the insertion point is positioned in the *Search Control Panel* text box. When you type the feature name in the text box, options related to the feature display in the Control Panel.

Project 10 Customizing the Mouse

1. Right-click the Start screen thumbnail and then click *Control Panel.*
2. At the Control Panel, type **mouse**. (The insertion point is automatically located in the *Search Control Panel* text box when you open the Control Panel. When you type *mouse,* features for customizing the mouse display in the Control Panel.)
3. Click the Mouse icon that displays in the Control Panel.
4. At the Mouse Properties dialog box, notice the options that display. (The *Switch primary and secondary buttons* option might be useful, for example, if you are left-handed and want to switch the buttons on the mouse.)
5. Click the Cancel button to close the dialog box.
6. At the Control Panel, click the Change the mouse pointer display or speed hyperlink.

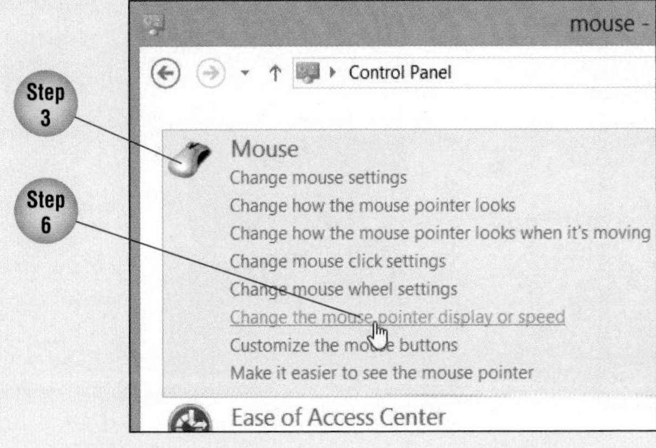

7. At the Mouse Properties dialog box with the Pointer Options tab selected, click the *Display pointer trails* check box in the *Visibility* section to insert a check mark.
8. Drag the button on the slider bar (located below the *Display pointer trails* check box) approximately to the middle of the bar.
9. Click OK to close the dialog box.
10. Close the Control Panel.
11. Move the mouse pointer around the screen to see the pointer trails.

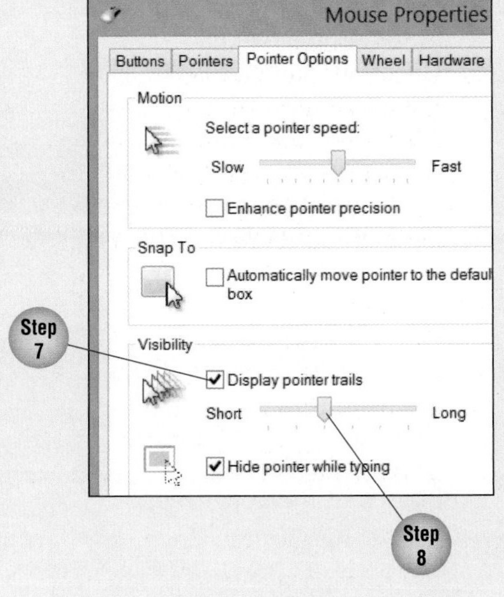

Displaying Personalize Options with a Shortcut Command

In addition to the Control Panel, display customization options with a command from a shortcut menu. Display a shortcut menu by positioning the mouse pointer in the desired position and then clicking the right mouse button. For example, display a shortcut menu with options for customizing the desktop by positioning the mouse pointer in an empty area of the desktop and then clicking the right mouse button. At the shortcut menu that displays, click the desired shortcut command.

Project 11 Customizing with a Shortcut Command

1. At the Windows 8 desktop, position the mouse pointer in an empty area on the desktop, click the right mouse button, and then click *Personalize* at the shortcut menu.
2. At the Control Panel Appearance and Personalization window that displays, click the Change mouse pointers hyperlink that displays at the left side of the window.
3. At the Mouse Properties dialog box, click the Pointer Options tab.
4. Click in the *Display pointer trails* check box to remove the check mark.
5. Click OK to close the dialog box.
6. At the Control Panel Appearance and Personalization window, click the Screen Saver hyperlink that displays in the lower right corner of the window.
7. At the Screen Saver Settings dialog box, click the option button below the *Screen saver* option and then click *Ribbons* at the drop-down list.
8. Check the number in the *Wait* measurement box. If a number other than *1* displays, click the down-pointing arrow at the right side of the measurement box until *1* displays. (This tells Windows to display the screen saver after one minute of inactivity.)
9. Click OK to close the dialog box.
10. Close the Control Panel by clicking the Close button located in the upper right corner of the window.

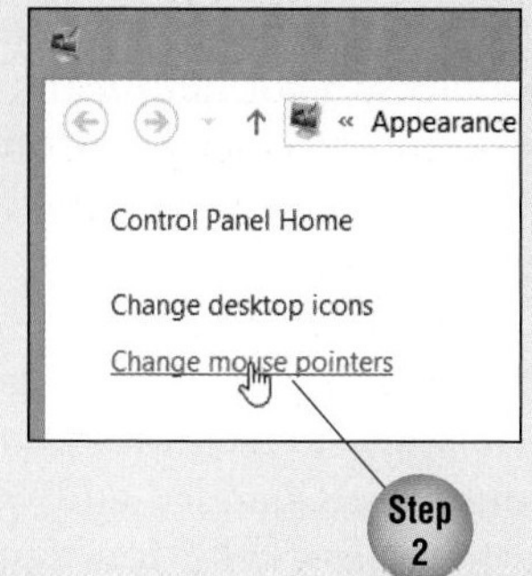

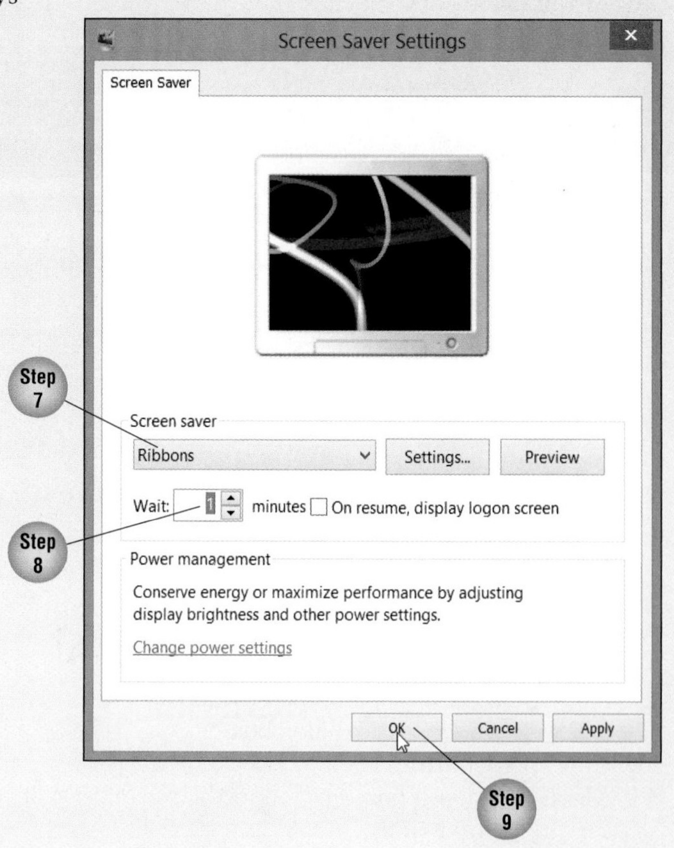

11. Do not touch the mouse or keyboard and wait over one minute for the screen saver to display. After watching the screen saver, move the mouse. (This redisplays the desktop.)
12. Right-click in an empty area of the desktop and then click *Personalize* at the shortcut menu.
13. At the Control Panel Appearance and Personalization window, click the Screen Saver hyperlink.
14. At the Screen Saver Settings dialog box, click the option button below the *Screen saver* option and then click *(None)* at the drop-down list.
15. Click OK to close the dialog box.
16. Close the Control Panel Appearance and Personalization window.

Exploring Windows Help and Support

Windows 8 includes an on-screen reference guide providing information, explanations, and interactive help on learning Windows features. Get help at the Windows Help and Support window, shown in Figure W.13. Display this window by clicking the Start screen thumbnail to display the Windows 8 Start screen. Right-click a blank area of the Start screen, click the All apps button, and then click the *Help and Support* tile in the Windows System group. Use options in the Windows Help and Support window to search for help on a specific feature; display the opening Windows Help and Support window; print the current information; and display information on getting started with Windows 8, setting up a network, and protecting your computer.

Figure W.13 Windows Help and Support Window

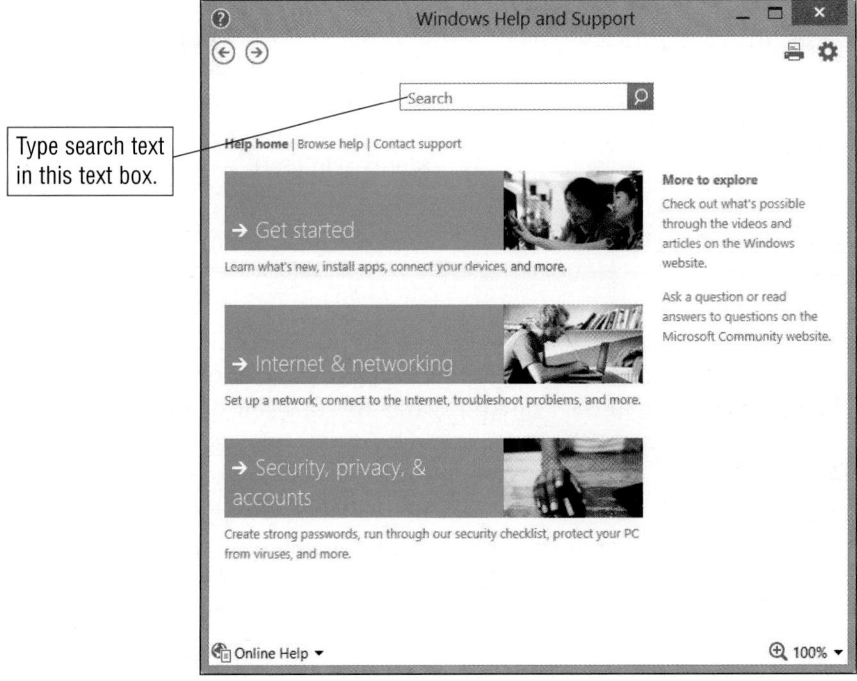

Project 12 Getting Help

1. Display the Windows 8 Help and Support window by following these steps:
   a. At the Windows 8 desktop, position the mouse pointer in the lower left corner of the screen and then click the Start screen thumbnail.
   b. Position the mouse in a blank area of the Windows 8 Start screen and then click the right mouse button.
   c. Click the All apps button that appears in the lower right corner of the Start screen and then scroll to the right of the Start screen.
   d. Click the *Help and Support* tile located in the *Windows System* category.
2. At the Windows Help and Support window, click the Get started hyperlink.
3. Click a hyperlink that interests you, read the information, and then click the Back button. (The Back button is located in the upper left corner of the window.)
4. Click another hyperlink that interests you and then read the information.
5. Click the Help home hyperlink that displays below the search text box. (This returns you to the opening Windows Help and Support window.)
6. Click in the search text box, type **delete files**, and then press Enter.
7. Click the How to work with files and folders hyperlink that displays in the window.
8. Read the information that displays about working with files or folders and then click the Print button located in the upper right corner of the Windows Help and Support window.
9. At the Print dialog box, click the Print button.
10. Click the Close button to close the Windows Help and Support window.

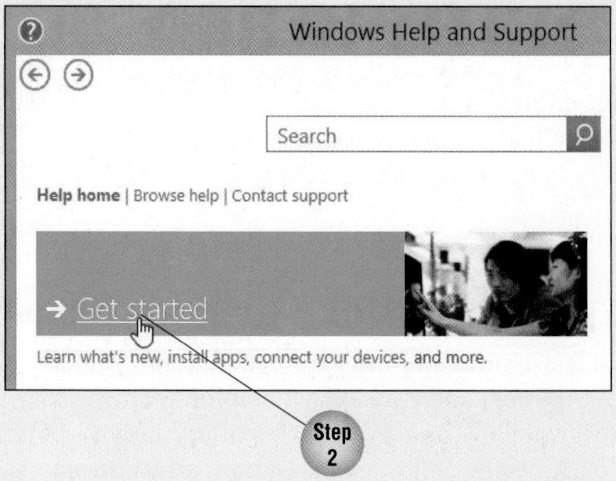

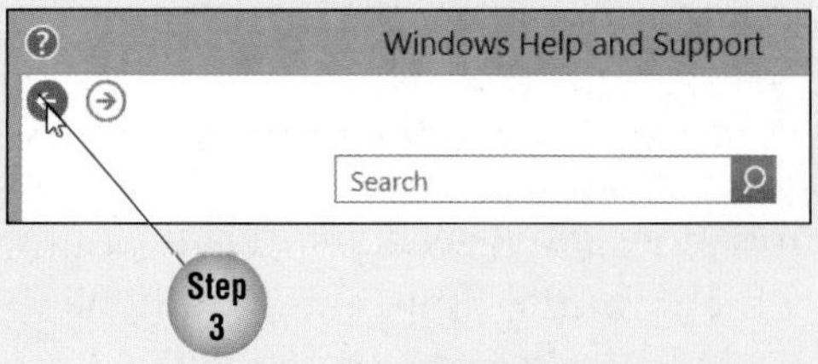

Using Search Tools

The Charm bar contains a search tool you can use to quickly find an application or file on your computer. To use the search tool, display the Charm bar, click the Search button and then type in the search text box the first few characters of the application or file for which you are searching. As you type characters in the text box, a list displays with application names or file names that begin with the characters. As you continue typing characters, the search tool refines the list.

You can also search for programs or files with the search text box in the Computer window. The search text box displays in the upper right corner of the Computer window at the right side of the Address bar. If you want to search a specific folder, make that folder active in the Content pane and then type the search text in the text box.

When conducting a search, you can use the asterisk (*) as a wildcard character in place of any letters, numbers, or symbols within a file name. For example, in the following project you will search for file names containing *check* by typing ***check** in the search text box. The asterisk indicates that the file name can start with any letter but it must contain the letters *check* somewhere in the file name.

Project 13 Searching for Programs and Files

1. At the Windows 8 desktop, display the Charm bar and then click the Search button.
2. With the insertion point positioned in the search text box, type **paint**. (Notice as you type the letters that Windows displays applications that begin with the same letters you are typing or that are associated with the same letters in a keyword. Notice that the Paint program displays below the heading *Apps* at the top of the list. Depending on the contents stored in the computer you are using, additional items may display below Paint.)

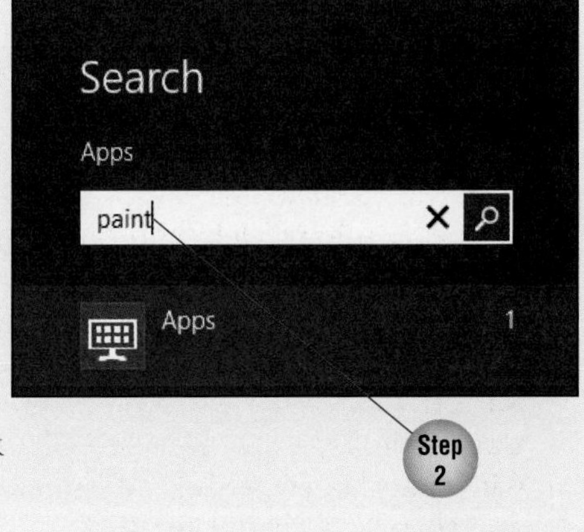

3. Click *Paint* that displays below the *Apps* heading.
4. Close the Paint window.
5. Right-click the Start screen thumbnail and then click *File Explorer*.
6. At the Computer window, double-click the icon representing your storage medium.
7. Double-click the *Windows8* folder.
8. Click in the search text box located at the right of the Address bar and then type **document**. (As you begin typing the letters, Windows filters the list of files in the Content pane to those that contain the letters you type. Notice that the Address bar displays *Search Results in Windows8* to indicate that the files that display matching your criteria are limited to the current folder.)

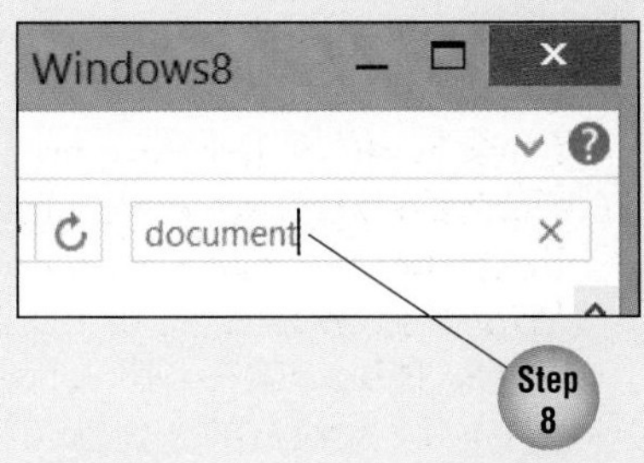

9. Select the text *document* that displays in the search text box and then type ***check**. (Notice that the Content pane displays file names containing the letters *check* no matter how the file name begins.)
10. Double-click ***WordSpellCheck02.docx*** to open the document in Word.
11. Close the document and then close Word by clicking the Close button located in the upper right corner of the window.
12. Close the Computer window.

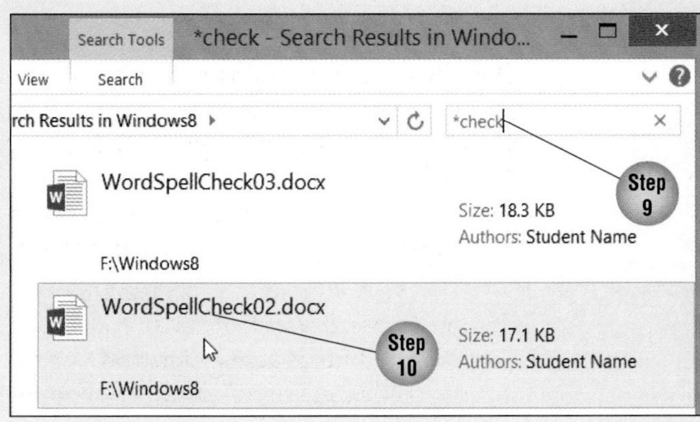

Browsing the Internet Using Internet Explorer 10

Microsoft Internet Explorer 10 is a web browser with options and features for displaying sites as well as navigating and searching for information on the Internet. The ***Internet*** is a network of computers connected around the world. Users access the Internet for several purposes: to communicate using instant messaging and/or email, to subscribe to newsgroups, to transfer files, to socialize with other users around the globe on social websites, and to access virtually any kind of information imaginable.

Using the Internet, people can find a phenomenal amount of information for private or public use. To use the Internet, three things are generally required: an ***Internet Service Provider (ISP)***, software to browse the Web (called a ***web browser***), and a ***search engine***. In this section, you will learn how to:

- Navigate the Internet using URLs and hyperlinks
- Use search engines to locate information
- Download web pages and images

You will use the Microsoft Internet Explorer web browser to locate information on the Internet. A ***Uniform Resource Locator***, referred to as a ***URL***, identifies a location on the Internet. The steps for browsing the Internet vary but generally include opening Internet Explorer, typing the URL for the desired site, navigating the various pages of the site, navigating to other sites using links, and then closing Internet Explorer.

To launch Internet Explorer 10, click the Internet Explorer icon on the Taskbar at the Windows desktop. Figure IE.1 identifies the elements of the Internet Explorer 10 window. The web page that displays in your Internet Explorer window may vary from what you see in Figure IE.1.

If you know the URL for a desired website, click in the Address bar, type the URL, and then press Enter. The website's home page displays in a tab within the Internet Explorer window. The format of a URL is *http://server-name.path*. The first part of the URL, *http*, stands for HyperText Transfer Protocol, which is the protocol or language used to transfer data within the World Wide Web. The colon and slashes separate the protocol from the server name. The server name is the second component of the URL. For example, in the URL http://www.microsoft.com, the server name is *microsoft*. The last part of the URL specifies the domain to which the server belongs. For example, *.com* refers to "commercial" and establishes that the URL is a commercial company. Examples of other domains include *.edu* for "educational," *.gov* for "government," and *.mil* for "military."

Internet Explorer 10 has been streamlined to provide users with more browsing space and reduced clutter. By default, Microsoft has turned off many features in Internet Explorer 10 such as the Menu bar, Command bar, and Status bar. You can turn these features on by right-clicking the empty space above the Address bar and to the right of the new tab button (see Figure IE.1) and then clicking the desired option at the drop-down list that displays. For example, if you want to turn on the Menu bar (the bar that contains File, Edit, and so on), right-click the empty space above the Address bar and then click *Menu bar* at the drop-down list. (This inserts a check mark next to *Menu bar*.)

Figure IE.1 Internet Explorer Window

Project 1 Browsing the Internet Using URLs

1. Make sure you are connected to the Internet through an Internet Service Provider and that the Windows 8 desktop displays. (Check with your instructor to determine if you need to complete steps for accessing the Internet such as typing a user name and password to log on.)
2. Launch Microsoft Internet Explorer by clicking the Internet Explorer icon located at the left side of the Windows Taskbar, which is located at the bottom of the Windows desktop.
3. Turn on the Command bar by right-clicking the empty space above the Address bar or to the right of the new tab button (see Figure IE.1) and then clicking *Command bar* at the drop-down list.
4. At the Internet Explorer window, explore the website for Yosemite National Park by completing the following steps:
   a. Click in the Address bar, type www.nps.gov/yose, and then press Enter.
   b. Scroll down the home page for Yosemite National Park by clicking the down-pointing arrow on the vertical scroll bar located at the right side of the Internet Explorer window.

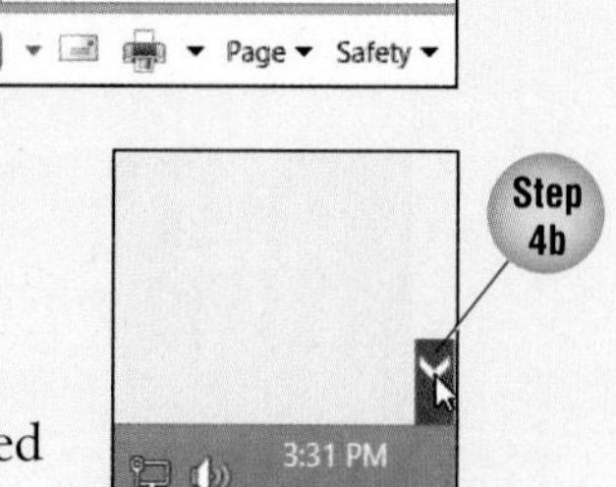

c. Print the home page by clicking the Print button located on the Command bar. (Note that some websites have a printer-friendly button you can click to print the page.)
5. Explore the website for Glacier National Park by completing the following steps:
   a. Click in the Address bar, type **www.nps.gov/glac**, and then press Enter.
   b. Print the home page by clicking the Print button located on the Command bar.
6. Close Internet Explorer by clicking the Close button (contains an X) located in the upper right corner of the Internet Explorer window.

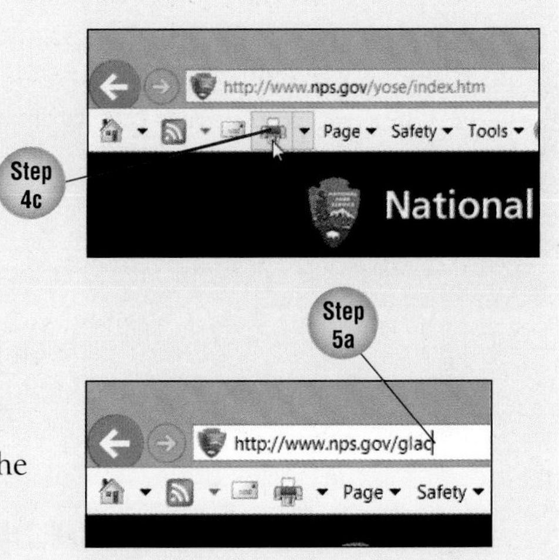

Navigating Using Hyperlinks

Most web pages contain ***hyperlinks*** that you click to connect to another page within the website or to another site on the Internet. Hyperlinks may display in a web page as underlined text in a specific color or as images or icons. To use a hyperlink, position the mouse pointer on the desired hyperlink until the mouse pointer turns into a hand and then click the left mouse button. Use hyperlinks to navigate within and between sites on the Internet. The Internet Explorer window contains a Back button (see Figure IE.1) that, when clicked, takes you to the previous web page viewed. If you click the Back button and then want to return to the previous page, click the Forward button. You can continue clicking the Back button to back your way out of several linked pages in reverse order since Internet Explorer maintains a history of the websites you visit.

Project 2 Navigating Using Hyperlinks

1. Make sure you are connected to the Internet and then click the Internet Explorer icon on the Windows Taskbar.
2. At the Internet Explorer window, display the White House web page and navigate in the page by completing the following steps:
   a. Click in the Address bar, type **whitehouse.gov**, and then press Enter.
   b. At the White House home page, position the mouse pointer on a hyperlink that interests you until the pointer turns into a hand and then click the left mouse button.
   c. At the linked web page, click the Back button. (This returns you to the White House home page.)
   d. At the White House home page, click the Forward button to return to the previous web page viewed.
   e. Print the web page by clicking the Print button on the Command bar.

3. Display the website for Amazon.com and navigate in the site by completing the following steps:
   a. Click in the Address bar, type **www.amazon.com**, and then press Enter.
   b. At the Amazon.com home page, click a hyperlink related to books.
   c. When a book web page displays, click the Print button on the Command bar.

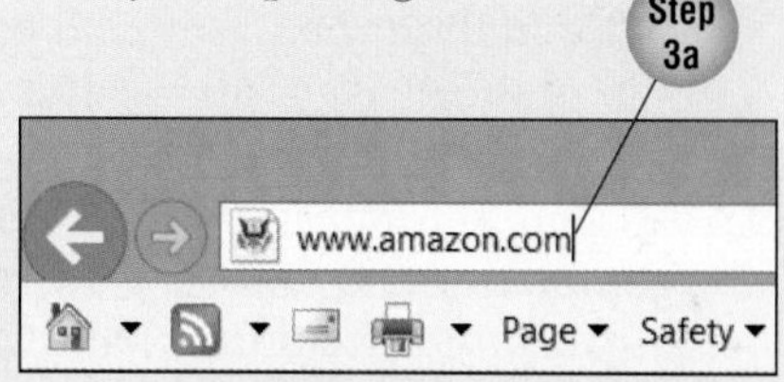

4. Close Internet Explorer by clicking the Close button (contains an X) located in the upper right corner of the Internet Explorer window.

Searching for Specific Sites

If you do not know the URL for a specific site or you want to find information on the Internet but do not know what site to visit, complete a search with a search engine. A ***search engine*** is software created to search quickly and easily for desired information. A variety of search engines are available on the Internet, each offering the opportunity to search for specific information. One method for searching for information is to click in the Address bar, type a keyword or phrase related to your search, and then press Enter. Another method for completing a search is to visit the website for a search engine and use options at the site.

Bing is Microsoft's online search portal and is the default search engine used by Internet Explorer. Bing organizes search results by topic category and provides related search suggestions.

Project 3 Searching for Information by Topic

1. Start Internet Explorer.
2. At the Internet Explorer window, search for sites on bluegrass music by completing the following steps:
   a. Click in the Address bar.
   b. Type **bluegrass music** and then press Enter.
   c. When a list of sites displays in the Bing results window, click a site that interests you.
   d. When the page displays, click the Print button.

Step
2b
bluegrass music
Page

3. Use the Yahoo! search engine to find sites on bluegrass music by completing the following steps:
   a. Click in the Address bar, type **www.yahoo.com**, and then press Enter.
   b. At the Yahoo! website, with the insertion point positioned in the search text box, type **bluegrass music** and then press Enter. (Notice that the sites displayed vary from sites displayed in the earlier search.)

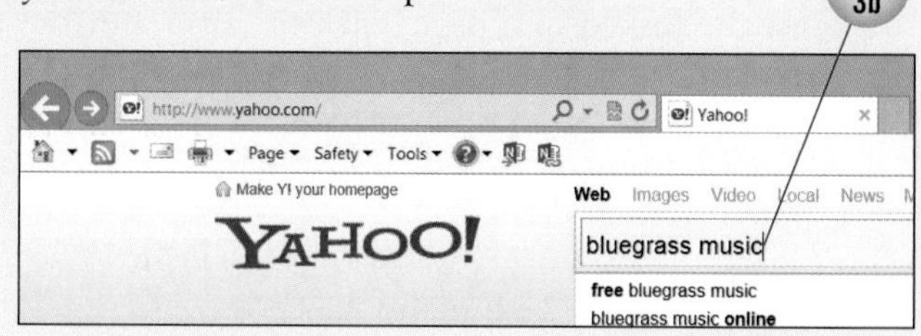

c. Click hyperlinks until a website displays that interests you.
d. Print the page.

4. Use the Google search engine to find sites on jazz music by completing the following steps:
   a. Click in the Address bar, type **www.google.com**, and then press Enter.
   b. At the Google website, with the insertion point positioned in the search text box, type **jazz music** and then press Enter.
   c. Click a site that interests you.
   d. Print the page.
5. Close Internet Explorer.

Using a Metasearch Engine

Bing, Yahoo!, and Google are search engines that search the Web for content and display search results. In addition to individual search engines, you can use a metasearch engine, such as Dogpile, that sends your search text to other search engines and then compiles the results in one list. With a metasearch engine, you type the search text once and then access results from a wider group of search engines. The Dogpile metasearch engine provides search results from Google, Yahoo!, and Yandex.

Project 4 Searching with a Metasearch Search Engine

1. Start Internet Explorer.
2. Click in the Address bar.
3. Type **www.dogpile.com** and then press Enter.
4. At the Dogpile website, type **jazz music** in the search text box and then press Enter.
5. Click a hyperlink that interests you.
6. Close the Internet Explorer window. If a message displays asking if you want to close all tabs, click the Close all tabs button.

Completing Advanced Searches for Specific Sites

The Internet contains an enormous amount of information. Depending on what you are searching for on the Internet and the search engine you use, some searches can result in several thousand "hits" (sites). Wading through a large number of sites can be very time-consuming and counterproductive. Narrowing a search to very specific criteria can greatly reduce the number of hits for a search. To narrow a search, use the advanced search options offered by the search engine.

Project 5 Narrowing a Search

1. Start Internet Explorer.
2. Search for sites on skydiving in Oregon by completing the following steps:
   a. Click in the Address bar, type **www.yahoo.com**, and then press Enter.
   b. At the Yahoo! home page, click the Search button next to the search text box.
   c. Click the More hyperlink located above the search text box and then click *Advanced Search* at the drop-down list.
   d. At the Advanced Web Search page, click in the search text box next to *all of these words*.
   e. Type **skydiving Oregon tandem static line**. (This limits the search to web pages containing all of the words typed in the search text box.)
   f. Click the Yahoo! Search button.
   g. When the list of websites displays, click a hyperlink that interests you.
   h. Click the Back button until the Yahoo! Advanced Web Search page displays.
   i. Click in the *the exact phrase* text box and then type **skydiving in Oregon**.
   j. Click the *Only .com domains* option in the *Site/Domain* section.
   k. Click the Yahoo! Search button.
   l. When the list of websites displays, click a hyperlink that interests you.
   m. Print the page.
3. Close Internet Explorer.

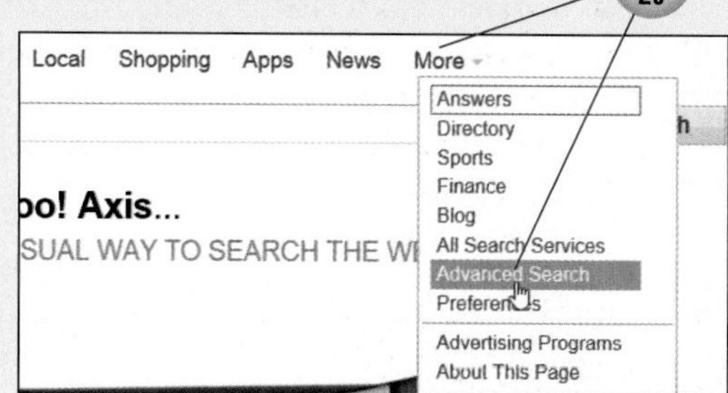

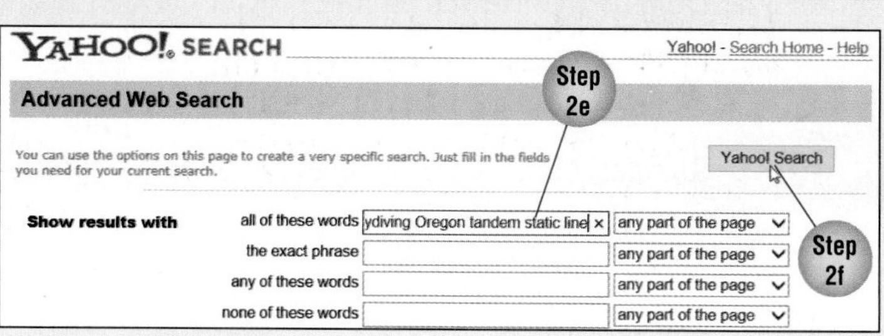

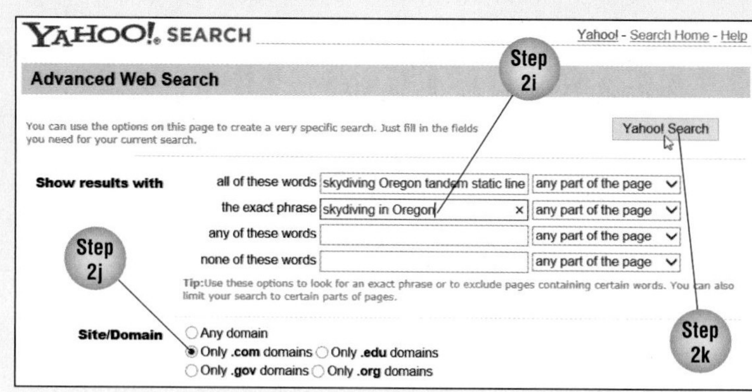

Downloading Images, Text, and Web Pages from the Internet

The image(s) and/or text that display when you open a web page, as well as the web page itself, can be saved as a separate file. This separate file can be viewed, printed, or inserted in another file. The information you want to save in a separate file is downloaded from the Internet by Internet Explorer and saved in a folder of your choosing with the name you specify. Copyright laws protect much of the information on the Internet. Before using information downloaded from the Internet, check the site for restrictions. If you do use information, make sure you properly cite the source.

Project 6 Downloading Images and Web Pages

1. Start Internet Explorer.
2. Download a web page and image from Banff National Park by completing the following steps:
   a. Search for websites related to Banff National Park.
   b. From the list of sites that displays, choose a site that contains information about Banff National Park and at least one image of the park.
   c. Make sure the Command bar is turned on. (If the Command bar is turned off, turn it on by right-clicking the empty space above the Address bar or to the right of the new tab button and then clicking *Command bar* at the drop-down list.)
   d. Save the web page as a separate file by clicking the Page button on the Command bar and then clicking *Save as* at the drop-down list.
   e. At the Save Webpage dialog box, type **BanffWebPage**.
   f. Click the down-pointing arrow for the *Save as type* option and then click *Web Archive, single file (*.mht)*.
   g. Navigate to the drive containing your storage medium and then click the Save button.

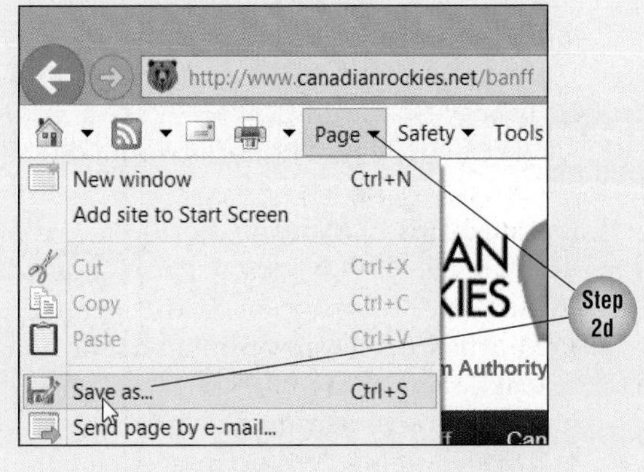

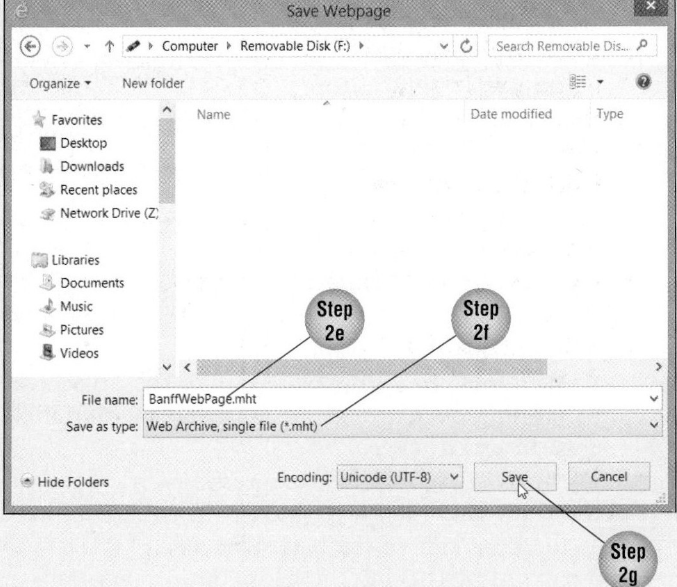

3. Save an image file by completing the following steps:
   a. Right-click an image that displays at the website.
   b. At the shortcut menu that displays, click *Save picture as*.

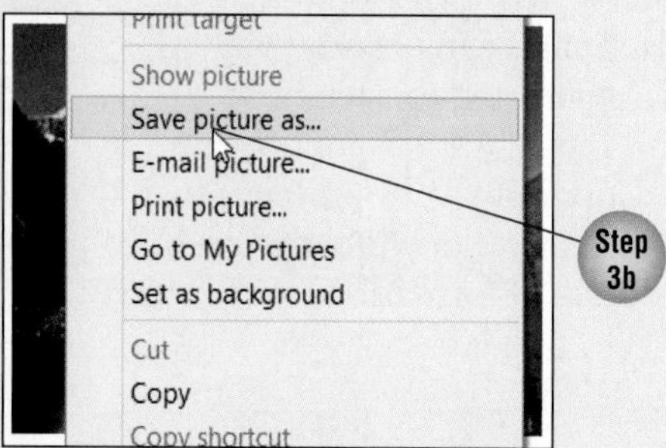

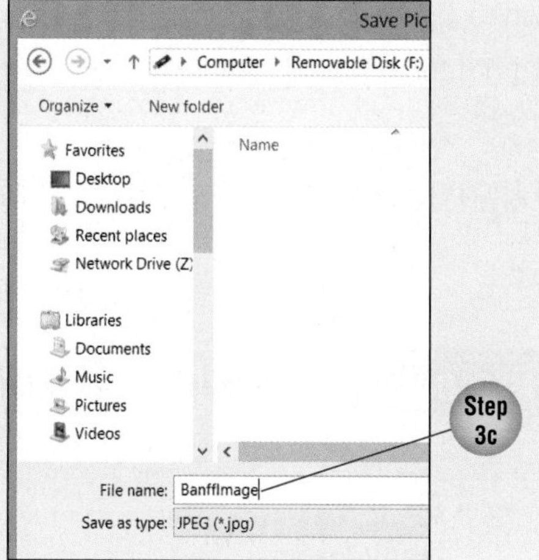

   c. At the Save Picture dialog box, type **BanffImage** in the *File name* text box.
   d. Navigate to the drive containing your storage medium and then click the Save button.
4. Close Internet Explorer.

Project 7 Opening the Saved Web Page and Image in a Word Document

1. Open Microsoft Word by positioning the mouse pointer in the lower left corner of the Taskbar, clicking the Start screen thumbnail, and then clicking the *Word 2013* tile in the Windows 8 Start screen. At the Word opening screen, click the *Blank document* template.
2. With Microsoft Word open, insert the image in a document by completing the following steps:
   a. Click the INSERT tab and then click the Pictures button in the Illustrations group.
   b. At the Insert Picture dialog box, navigate to the drive containing your storage medium and then double-click ***BanffImage.jpg***.
   c. When the image displays in the Word document, print the document by pressing Ctrl + P and then clicking the Print button.
   d. Close the document by clicking the FILE tab and then clicking the *Close* option. At the message asking if you want to save the changes, click the Don't Save button.

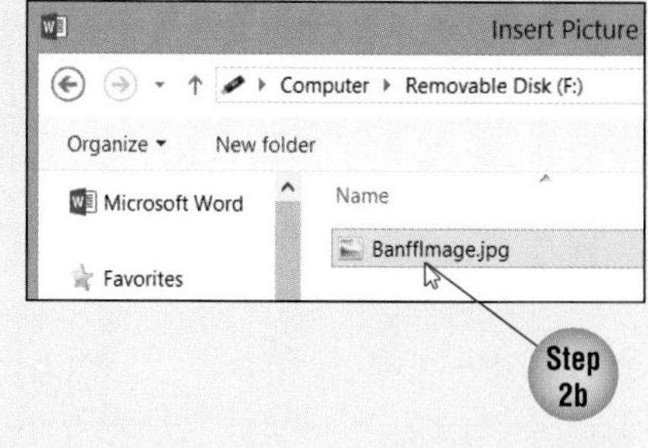

3. Open the **BanffWebPage.mht** file by completing the following steps:
   a. Click the FILE tab and then click the *Open* option.
   b. Double-click the *Computer* option.
   c. At the Open dialog box, navigate to the drive containing your storage medium and then double-click ***BanffWebPage.mht***.
   d. Preview the web page(s) by pressing Ctrl + P. At the Print backstage area, preview the page shown at the right side of the backstage area.

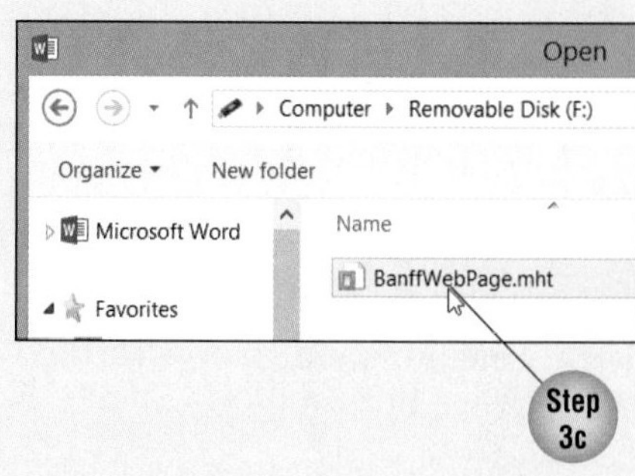

4. Close Word by clicking the Close button (contains an X) that displays in the upper right corner of the screen.

MICROSOFT® WORD Level 1

Unit 1 ■ Editing and Formatting Documents

Chapter 1 ■ Preparing Documents

Chapter 2 ■ Formatting Characters and Paragraphs

Chapter 3 ■ Customizing Paragraphs

Chapter 4 ■ Formatting Pages

MICROSOFT®
WORD

CHAPTER 1

Preparing Documents

PERFORMANCE OBJECTIVES

Upon successful completion of Chapter 1, you will be able to:

- **Open Microsoft Word**
- **Create, save, name, print, open, and close a Word document**
- **Close Word**
- **Edit a document**
- **Move the insertion point within a document**
- **Scroll within a document**
- **Select text in a document**
- **Use the Undo and Redo buttons**
- **Check spelling and grammar in a document**
- **Use the Help feature**

Tutorials

1.1 Creating, Saving, and Printing a Document

1.2 Opening a Document

1.3 Pinning Documents and Folders to the Recent Lists

1.4 Editing a Document

1.5 Checking the Spelling and Grammar in a Document

1.6 Using the Word Help Feature

In this chapter, you will learn to create, save, name, print, open, close, and edit a Word document as well as complete a spelling and grammar check. You will also learn about the Help feature, which is an on-screen reference manual providing information on features and commands for each program in the Office suite. Before continuing, make sure you read the *Getting Started* section presented at the beginning of this book. This section contains information about computer hardware and software, using the mouse, executing commands, and exploring Help files. Model answers for this chapter's projects appear on the following page.

Note: Before beginning the projects, copy to your OneDrive or storage medium (such as a USB drive) the WL1C1 subfolder from the WL1 folder on the CD that accompanies this textbook. Steps on how to copy a folder are presented on the inside of the back cover of this textbook. Do this every time you start a chapter's projects.

Model Answers

The traditional chronological resume lists your work experience in reverse-chronological order (starting with your current or most recent position). The functional style deemphasizes the "where" and "when" of your career and instead groups similar experiences, talents, and qualifications regardless of when they occurred.

Like the chronological resume, the hybrid resume includes specifics about where you worked, when you worked there, and what your job titles were. Like a functional resume, a hybrid resume emphasizes your most relevant qualifications in an expanded summary section, in several "career highlights" bullet points at the top of your resume, or in project summaries.

Created:
Thursday, December 8, 2015
Note: The two paragraphs will become the 2nd and 3rd paragraphs in the 5th section.

Project 1 Prepare a Word Document

WL1-C1-P1-Resume.docx

The majority of new jobs being created in the United States today involve daily work with computers. Computer-related careers include technical support jobs, sales and training, programming and applications development, network and database administration, and computer engineering.

A technician is an entry-level worker who installs and maintains hardware and/or software. Technical sales and technical training jobs emphasize interpersonal skills as much as they do technical skills. Programming is one of the most difficult and highly skilled jobs in the industry. Programmers create new software, such as Microsoft Windows or computer games, and often have college degrees. Software engineers are programmers trained to create software in teams with other programmers. Application developers are similar to programmers, but they use existing software such as a database to create applications for business solutions. Application development jobs include database administration, network administration, and systems analysis. Database and network administration involves overseeing and maintaining databases and networks, respectively. Systems analysts design information systems or evaluate and improve existing ones.

Project 2 Save and Edit a Word Document

WL1-C1-P2-CompCareers.docx

COMPUTER KEYBOARDS

To enter commands into a computer or to enter data into it, a user needs an input device. An input device can be built into the computer, like the keyboard in a laptop, or it can be connected to the computer by a cable. Some input devices, like remote keyboards, send directions to the computer by means of an infrared signal.

Keyboards can be external devices that are attached by a cable, or they can be attached to the CPU case itself as they are in laptops. Most keyboards today are QWERTY keyboards, which take their name from the first six keys at the left of the first row of letters. The QWERTY design was invented in the early days of mechanical typewriters to slow down typists and thus keep keys from jamming.

The DVORAK keyboard is an alternative to the QWERTY keyboard. On the DVORAK keyboard, the most commonly used keys are placed close to the user's fingertips and this increases typing speed. You can install software on a QWERTY keyboard that emulates a DVORAK keyboard. The ability to emulate other keyboards is convenient especially when working with foreign languages.

Project 4 Insert and Delete Text

WL1-C1-P4-CompKeyboards.docx

ON THE HORIZON

The march of computer technology continues to change the nature of our jobs and workplaces. Considering the global economic and technology scene, some major changes in occupations involve changes in communications media, work locations, and communications tools.

Communications Media

One key to being successful in our modern, technological world is spotting trends early and adjusting one's career direction accordingly. For example, 80 percent of daily newspaper readers are over 50 years old. Young reader are not as interested in the printed word, and each year the industry suffers from a shrinking number of subscriptions. The young are still reading, but they are reading online media sites rather than the printed page. Websites make excellent dynamic newspapers, as they can be changed at will, they require no printing or distribution costs, and they do not require the newspaper delivery person to go door to door asking for payment. This switch to the new media is causing many jobs to change. The number of printing and lithography jobs is shrinking, but web developers and graphic artists are in demand.

Industry-morphing trends are sweeping away many traditional approaches to the marketing and distribution of products. Increasingly, music and movies are being downloaded versus being bought on a disc. Fewer movies are being rented, while more people are watching them on-demand through their cable systems. Once a successful approach is discovered, every type of media that can be digitized rather than produced and distributed in physical form will come under increasing pressure to modernize in order to match the competition. Individuals managing career paths need to be aware of these trends and avoid becoming part of a downsizing effort.

Telecommuting

Telecommuting, sometimes called telework, involves working via computer from home or while traveling rather than going to the office on a daily basis. Approximately 25 million Americans telecommute at least one day per week. Telework plans have been especially successful for commissioned salespeople, who are often more productive when away from the office environment.

Project 5 Complete a Spelling and Grammar Check

WL1-C1-P5-TechOccTrends.docx

Project 1 Prepare a Word Document — 2 Parts

You will create a short document containing information on resumes and then save, print, and close the document.

Opening Microsoft Word

Microsoft Office 2013 contains a word processing program named Word that you can use to create, save, edit, and print documents. The steps to open Word may vary depending on your system setup. Generally, to open Word, you click the Word 2013 tile at the Windows Start screen. At the Word 2013 opening screen, click the *Blank document* template.

Quick Steps

Open Word and Open a Blank Document

1. Click the Word 2013 tile at the Windows Start screen.
2. Click the *Blank document* template.

Creating, Saving, Printing, and Closing a Document

When you click the Blank document template, a blank document displays on the screen, as shown in Figure 1.1. The features of the document screen are described in Table 1.1.

To avoid opening the same program twice, use the Taskbar to see which programs are open.

At a blank document, type information to create a document. A document is any information you choose — for instance, a letter, report, term paper, table, and so on. Some things to consider when typing text are:

- **Word wrap:** As you type text to create a document, you do not need to press the Enter key at the end of each line because Word wraps text to the next line. A word is wrapped to the next line if it begins before the right margin and continues past the right margin. The only times you need to press Enter are to end a paragraph, create a blank line, or end a short line.
- **AutoCorrect:** Word contains a feature that automatically corrects certain words as you type them. For example, if you type the word *adn* instead of *and*, Word automatically corrects it when you press the spacebar after the word. AutoCorrect will also superscript the letters that follow an ordinal number (a number indicating a position in a series). For example, if you type *2nd* and then press the spacebar or Enter key, Word will convert this ordinal number to *2nd*.
- **Automatic spelling checker:** By default, Word will automatically insert a red wavy line below words that are not contained in the Spelling dictionary or automatically corrected by AutoCorrect. This may include misspelled words, proper names, some terminology, and some foreign words. If you type a word not recognized by the Spelling dictionary, leave it as written if the word is correct. However, if the word is incorrect, you have two choices — you can delete the word and then type it correctly, or you can position the I-beam pointer on the word, click the *right* mouse button, and then click the correct spelling in the pop-up list.
- **Automatic grammar checker:** Word includes an automatic grammar checker. If the grammar checker detects a sentence containing a grammatical error, a blue wavy line is inserted below the error in the sentence. You can leave the sentence as written or position the mouse I-beam pointer on the error, click the *right* mouse button, and a pop-up list will display with possible corrections.
- **Spacing punctuation:** Typically, Word uses Calibri as the default typeface, which is a proportional typeface. (You will learn more about typefaces in Chapter 2.) When typing text in a proportional typeface, space once (rather than twice) after

A book icon displays in the Status bar. A check mark on the book indicates no spelling errors detected in the document by the spell checker, while an X on the book indicates errors. Double-click the book icon to move to the next error. If the book icon is not visible, right-click the Status bar and then click the *Spelling and Grammar Check* option at the pop-up list.

Figure 1.1 Blank Document

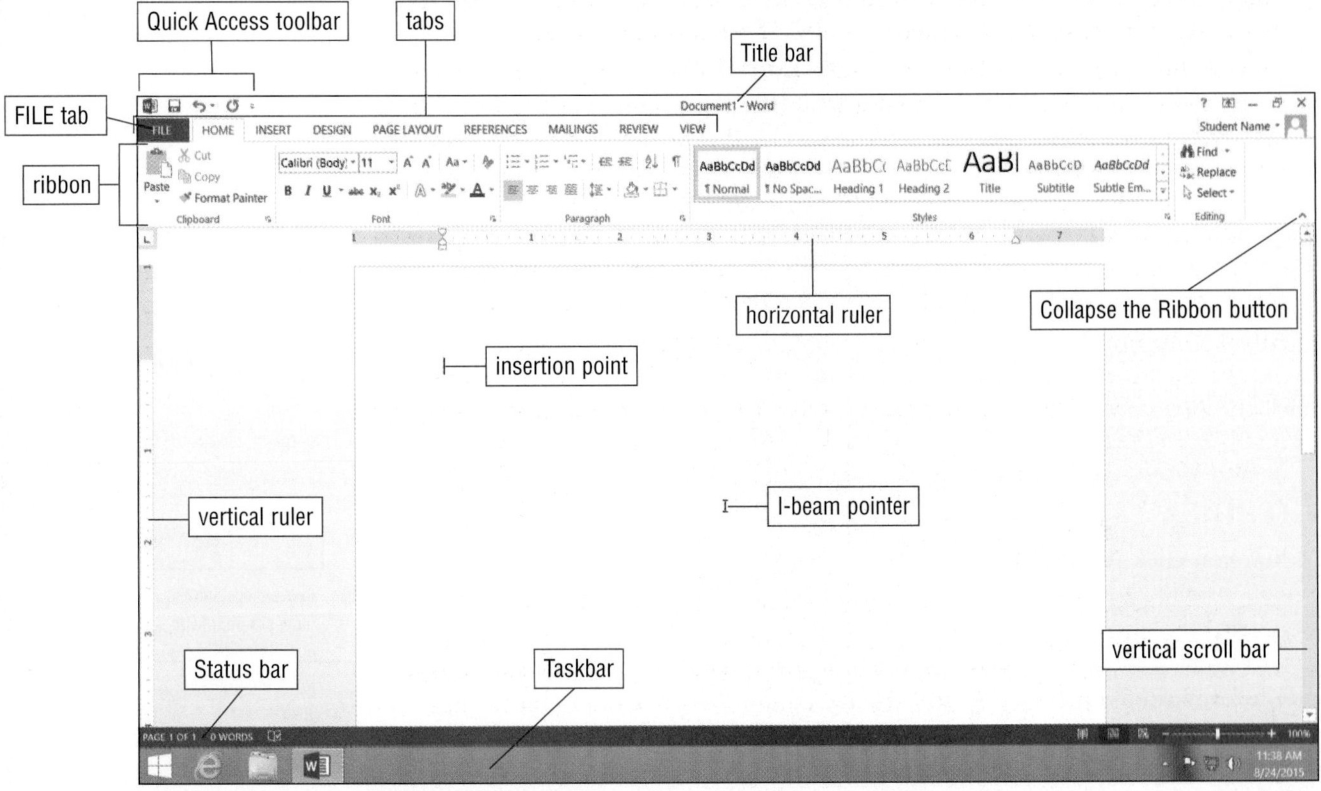

Table 1.1 Microsoft Word Screen Features

Feature	*Description*
Collapse the Ribbon button	when clicked, removes the ribbon from the screen
FILE tab	when clicked, displays backstage area that contains options for working with and managing documents
horizontal ruler	used to set margins, indents, and tabs
I-beam pointer	used to move the insertion point or to select text
insertion point	indicates location of next character entered at the keyboard
Quick Access toolbar	contains buttons for commonly used commands
ribbon	area containing the tabs with options and buttons divided into groups
Status bar	displays number of pages and words, view buttons, and Zoom slider bar
tabs	contain commands and features organized into groups
Taskbar	contains icons for launching programs, buttons for active tasks, and a notification area
Title bar	displays document name followed by program name
vertical ruler	used to set top and bottom margins
vertical scroll bar	used to view various parts of the document beyond the screen

end-of-sentence punctuation such as a period, question mark, or exclamation point, and after a colon. Proportional typeface is set closer together, and extra white space at the end of a sentence or after a colon is not needed.

- **Option buttons:** As you insert and edit text in a document, you may notice an option button popping up in your text. The name and appearance of this option button varies depending on the action. If a word you type is corrected by AutoCorrect, if you create an automatic list, or if autoformatting is applied to text, the AutoCorrect Options button appears. Click this button to undo the specific automatic action. If you paste text in a document, the Paste Options button appears near the text. Click this button to display the Paste Options gallery with buttons for controlling how the pasted text is formatted.
- **AutoComplete:** Microsoft Word and other Office applications include an AutoComplete feature that inserts an entire item when you type a few identifying characters. For example, type the letters *Mond* and *Monday* displays in a ScreenTip above the letters. Press the Enter key or press F3 and Word inserts *Monday* in the document.

Using the New Line Command

A Word document is based on a template that applies default formatting. Some basic formatting includes 1.08 line spacing and 8 points of spacing after a paragraph. Each time you press the Enter key, a new paragraph begins and 8 points of spacing is inserted after the paragraph. If you want to move the insertion point down to the next line without including the additional 8 points of spacing, use the New Line command, Shift + Enter.

Project 1a **Creating a Document** **Part 1 of 2**

1. Open Word by clicking the Word 2013 tile at the Windows Start screen. At the Word opening screen, click the *Blank document* template. (These steps may vary. Check with your instructor for specific instructions.)
2. At a blank document, type the information shown in Figure 1.2 with the following specifications:
   a. Correct any errors highlighted by the spell checker or grammar checker as they occur.
   b. Press the spacebar once after end-of-sentence punctuation.
   c. After typing *Created:* press Shift + Enter to move the insertion point to the next line without adding 8 points of additional spacing.
   d. To insert the word *Thursday* located towards the end of the document, type Thur and then press F3. (This is an example of the AutoComplete feature.)
   e. To insert the word *December*, type Dece and then press the Enter key. (This is another example of the AutoComplete feature.)
   f. Press Shift + Enter after typing *December 8, 2015*.
   g. When typing the last line (the line containing the ordinal numbers), type the ordinal number text and AutoCorrect will automatically convert the letters in the ordinal numbers to superscript.
3. When you are finished typing the text, press the Enter key once.

Figure 1.2 Project 1a

> The traditional chronological resume lists your work experience in reverse-chronological order (starting with your current or most recent position). The functional style deemphasizes the "where" and "when" of your career and instead groups similar experiences, talents, and qualifications regardless of when they occurred.
>
> Like the chronological resume, the hybrid resume includes specifics about where you worked, when you worked there, and what your job titles were. Like a functional resume, a hybrid resume emphasizes your most relevant qualifications in an expanded summary section, in several "career highlights" bullet points at the top of your resume, or in project summaries.
>
> Created:
> Thursday, December 8, 2015
> Note: The two paragraphs will become the 2nd and 3rd paragraphs in the 5th section.

Quick Steps

Save a Document

1. Click Save button on Quick Access toolbar.
2. Click desired location.
3. Click Browse button.
4. Type document name in *File name* text box.
5. Press Enter or click Save button.

Save

Save a document approximately every 15 minutes or when interrupted.

Saving a Document

Save a document if you want to use it in the future. You can use a variety of methods to save a document, such as clicking the Save button on the Quick Access toolbar, clicking the FILE tab and then clicking the *Save* option or *Save As* option, or using the keyboard shortcut Ctrl + S. When you choose one of these options, the Save As backstage area displays, as shown in Figure 1.3. At this backstage area, click the desired location. For example, click the *OneDrive* option preceded by your name if you are saving to your OneDrive or click the *Computer* option if you are saving to your computer. After specifying the place, click the Browse button and the Save As dialog box displays, as shown in Figure 1.4. If you are saving to your computer, you can double-click the *Computer* option to display the Save As dialog box. At this dialog box, type the name of the document in the *File name* text box and then press Enter or click the Save button. You can go directly to the Save As dialog box without displaying the Save As backstage area by pressing the F12 function key.

Figure 1.3 Save As Backstage Area

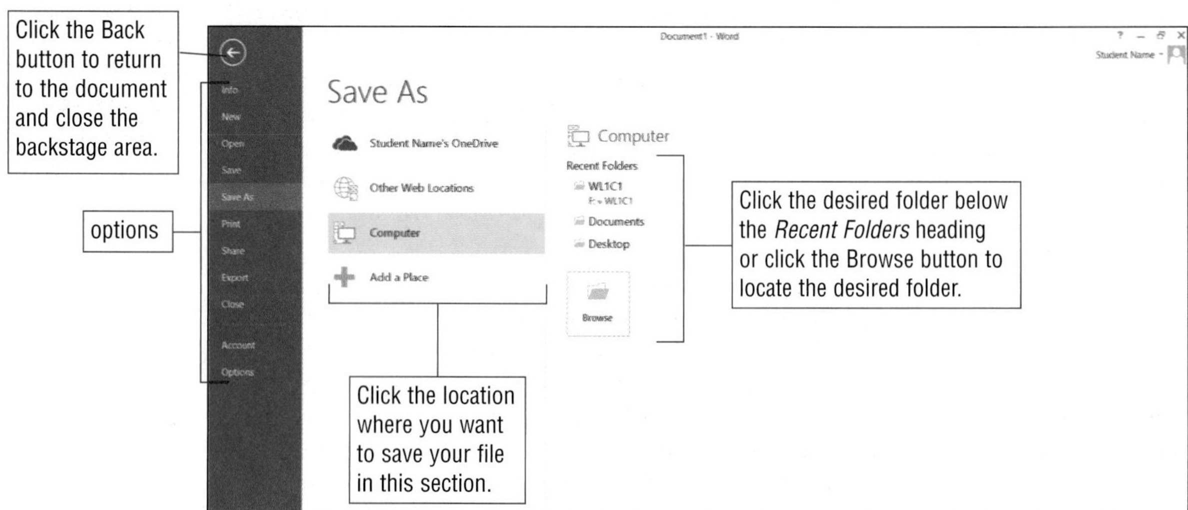

Figure 1.4 Save As Dialog Box

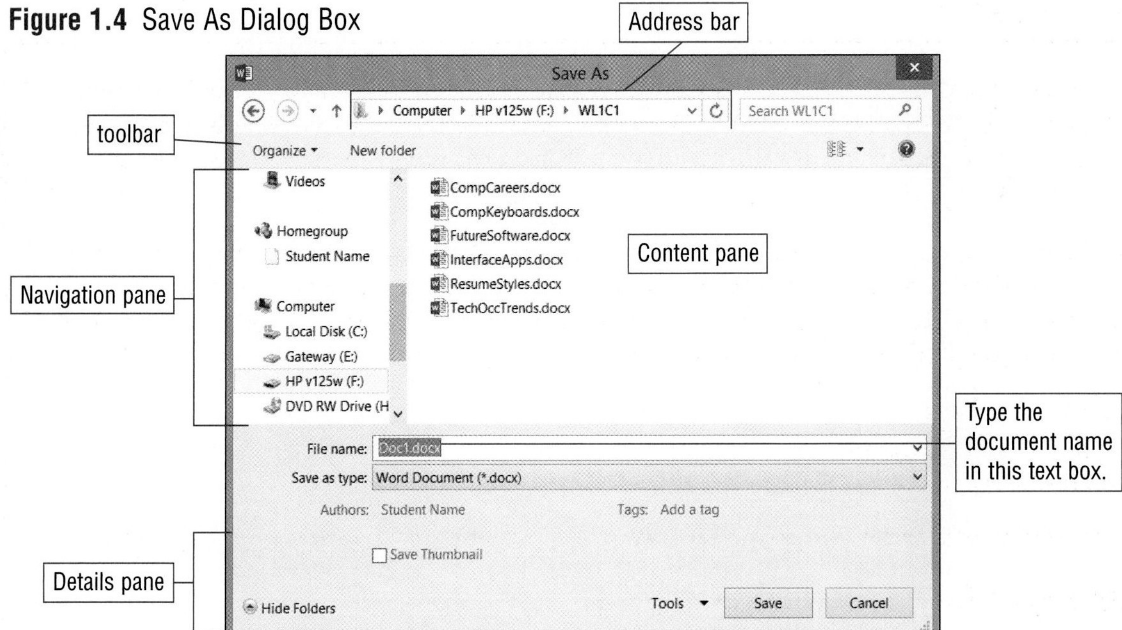

Naming a Document

Document names created in Word and other applications in the Office suite can be up to 255 characters in length, including the drive letter and any folder names, and may include spaces. File names cannot include any of the following characters:

forward slash (/)   asterisk (*)   colon (:)
backslash (\)   question mark (?)   semicolon (;)
greater than sign (>)   quotation marks (" ")   pipe symbol (|)
less than sign (<)

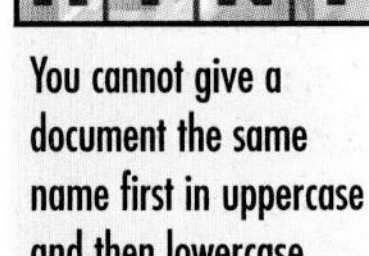

You cannot give a document the same name first in uppercase and then lowercase letters.

Printing a Document

Click the FILE tab and the backstage area displays. The buttons and options at the backstage area change depending on the option selected at the left side of the backstage area. If you want to remove the backstage area without completing an action, click the Back button located in the upper left corner of the backstage area or press the Esc key on your keyboard.

Quick Steps

Print a Document
Click Quick Print button on Quick Access toolbar.
OR
1. Click FILE tab.
2. Click *Print* option.
3. Click Print button.

Many of the files you create will need to be printed. A printing of a document on paper is referred to as ***hard copy***, and a document displayed on the screen is referred to as ***soft copy***. Print a document with options at the Print backstage area, shown in Figure 1.5. To display this backstage area, click the FILE tab and then click the *Print* option. You can also display the Print backstage area using the keyboard shortcut Ctrl + P.

Click the Print button located toward the upper left side of the backstage area to send the document to the printer and specify the number of copies you want printed with the *Copies* option. Below the Print button are two categories—*Printer* and *Settings*. Use the gallery in the *Printer* category to specify the desired printer. The *Settings* category contains a number of galleries, each with options for specifying how you want your document printed, including whether you want the pages collated when printed; the orientation, page size, and margins of your document; and how many pages of your document you want to print on a sheet of paper.

Figure 1.5 Print Backstage Area

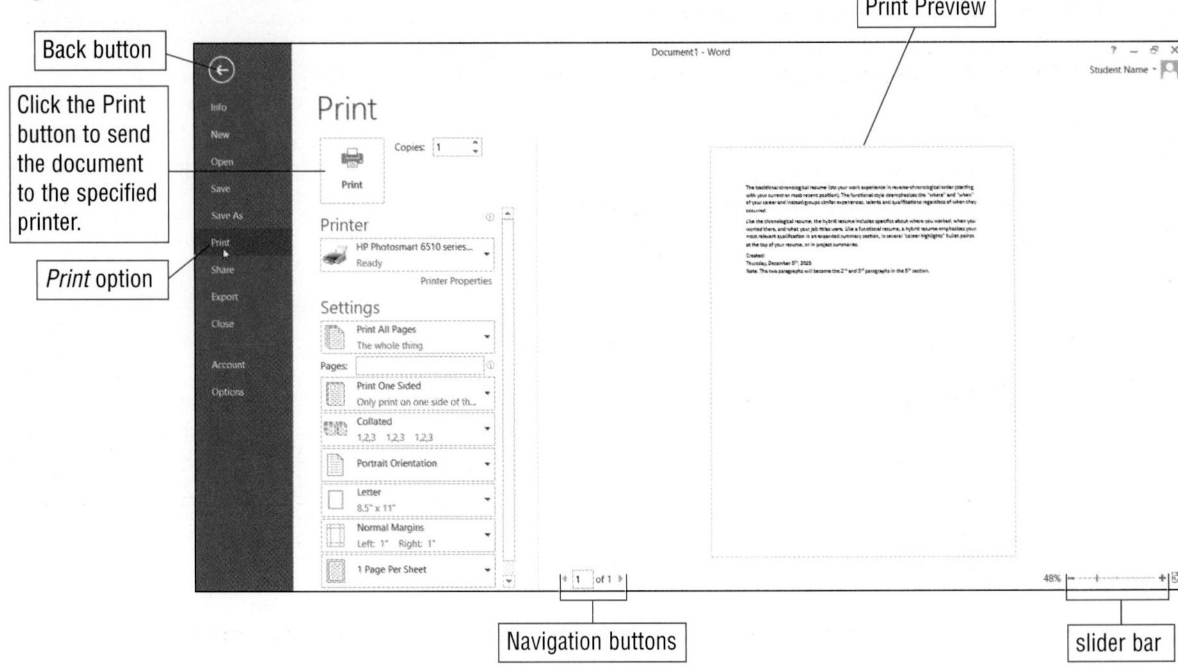

Quick Print

Another method for printing a document is to insert the Quick Print button on the Quick Access toolbar and then click the button. This sends the document directly to the printer without displaying the Print backstage area. To insert the button on the Quick Access toolbar, click the Customize Quick Access Toolbar button that displays at the right side of the toolbar and then click *Quick Print* at the drop-down list. To remove the Quick Print button from the Quick Access toolbar, right-click the button and then click the *Remove from Quick Access Toolbar* option that displays in the drop-down list.

Closing a Document

Quick Steps

Close a Document
1. Click FILE tab.
2. Click *Close* option.
OR
Press Ctrl + F4.

When you save a document, it is saved on your OneDrive or other storage medium and remains in the document screen. To remove the document from the screen, click the FILE tab and then click the *Close* option or use the keyboard shortcut Ctrl + F4. When you close a document, the document is removed and a blank screen displays. At this screen, you can open a previously saved document, create a new document, or close Word.

Project 1b **Saving, Printing, and Closing a Document** **Part 2 of 2**

1. Save the document you created for Project 1a and name it **WL1-C1-P1-Resume** (*WL1-* for Word Level 1, *C1-* for Chapter 1, *P1-* for Project 1, and *Resume* because the document is about resumes) by completing the following steps:
   a. Click the Save button on the Quick Access toolbar.
   b. At the Save As backstage area, click the *OneDrive* option preceded by your name if you are saving to your OneDrive, or click the *Computer* option if you are saving to your computer or USB flash drive.
   c. Click the Browse button.

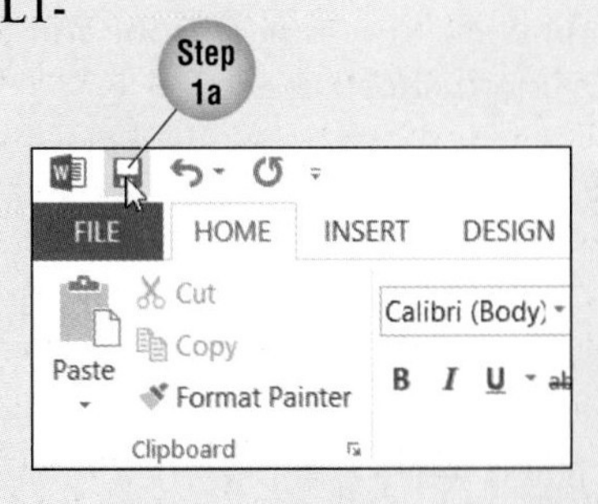

d. At the Save As dialog box, if necessary, navigate to the WL1C1 folder.

e. Click in the *File name* text box (this selects any text in the box), type **WL1-C1-P1-Resume**, and then press Enter.

2. Print the document by clicking the FILE tab, clicking the *Print* option, and then clicking the Print button at the Print backstage area.

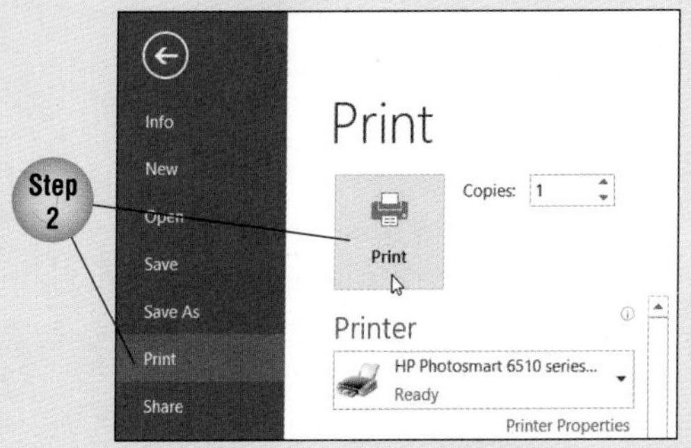

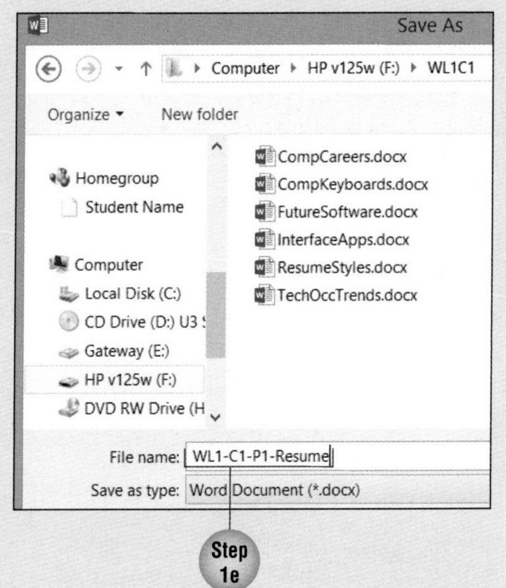

3. Close the document by clicking the FILE tab and then clicking the *Close* option.

Project 2 Save and Edit a Word Document — 2 Parts

You will open a document located in the WL1C1 folder on your storage medium, add text to the document, and then save the document with a new name.

Creating a New Document

When you close a document, a blank screen displays. If you want to create a new document, display a blank document. To do this, click the FILE tab, click the *New* option, and then click the Blank document template. You can also open a new document using the keyboard shortcut, Ctrl + N, or by inserting a New button on the Quick Access toolbar. To insert the button, click the Customize Quick Access Toolbar button that displays at the right side of the toolbar and then click *New* at the drop-down list.

Quick Steps

Create a New Document

1. Click FILE tab.
2. Click *New* option.
3. Click Blank document template.

Opening a Document

After you save and close a document, you can open it at the Open dialog box, shown in Figure 1.6. To display this dialog box, click the FILE tab and then click the *Open* option. This displays the Open backstage area. You can also display the Open backstage area with the keyboard shortcut Ctrl + O, by inserting an Open button on the Quick Access toolbar, or by clicking the Open Other Documents hyperlink that displays in the lower left corner of the Word 2013 opening screen. At the Open backstage area, click the desired location (such as your OneDrive or *Computer*) and then click the Browse button. (If you are opening a document from your computer or USB flash drive, you can double-click the *Computer* option.) When you click the Browse button (or double-click the *Computer* option) the

Quick Steps

Open a Document

1. Click FILE tab.
2. Click *Open* option.
3. Click desired location.
4. Click Browse button.
5. Double-click document name.

Open dialog box displays. You can go directly to the Open dialog box without displaying the Open backstage area by pressing Ctrl + F12. At the Open dialog box, open a document by double-clicking the document name in the Content pane.

If a document is open, Word will display the folder name where the document is located below the *Current Folder* heading in the Open backstage area with your OneDrive or the *Computer* option selected. Click this folder name to display the folder contents. In addition to the current folder, the Open backstage area also displays a list of the most recently accessed folders below the *Recent Folders* heading. Open a folder by clicking the folder name.

Opening a Document from the Recent Documents List

At the Open backstage area with Recent Documents selected, the Recent Documents list displays the names of the most recently opened documents. By default, Word displays 25 of the most recently opened documents. To open a document from the Recent Documents list, scroll down the list and then click the desired document. The Word 2013 opening screen also displays a list of the most recently opened documents. Click a document name in the Recent list at the opening screen to open the document.

Pinning a Document to the Recent Documents List

If you want a document to remain in the Recent Documents list at the Open backstage area, "pin" the document to the list. To pin a document, position the mouse pointer over the desired document name and then click the small left-pointing stick pin that displays at the right side of the document name. This changes it to a down-pointing stick pin. The next time you display the Open backstage area, the document you "pinned" displays at the top of the Recent

Figure 1.6 Open Dialog Box

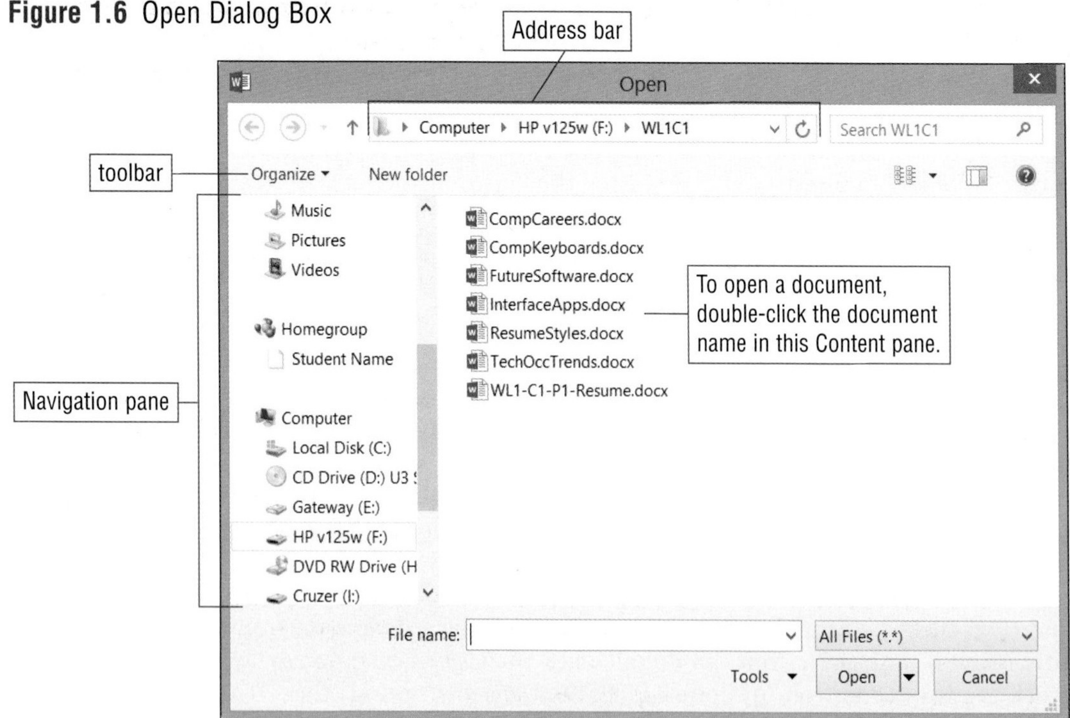

Documents list. You can also pin a document to the Recent list at the Word 2013 opening screen. When you pin a document, it displays at the top of the Recent list as well as the Recent Documents list at the Open backstage area. To “unpin” a document from the Recent or Recent Documents list, click the pin to change it from a down-pointing pin to a left-pointing pin. You can pin more than one document to a list. Another method for pinning and unpinning documents is to use the shortcut menu. Right-click a document name and then click *Pin to list* or *Unpin from list*.

In addition to pinning documents to a list, you can pin a folder to the Recent Folders list. Pin a folder in the same manner as pinning a document. If you access a particular folder on a regular basis, consider pinning it to the list.

Project 2a Opening and Pinning/Unpinning a Document — Part 1 of 2

1. Open **CompCareers.docx** by completing the following steps:
   a. Click the FILE tab and then click the *Open* option.
   b. At the Open backstage area, click the desired location. (For example, click your OneDrive if you are using your OneDrive account, or click the *Computer* option if you are opening a document from your computer’s hard drive or a USB flash drive.)
   c. Click the WL1C1 folder that displays below the *Recent Folders* heading. (If the folder name does not display, click the Browse button and then navigate to the WL1C1 folder.)
   d. At the Open dialog box, double-click ***CompCareers.docx*** in the Content pane.
2. Close **CompCareers.docx**.
3. Open **FutureSoftware.docx** by completing steps similar to those in Step 1.
4. Close **FutureSoftware.docx**.
5. Pin **CompCareers.docx** to the list of recent documents by completing the following steps:
   a. Click the FILE tab and then, if necessary, click the *Open* option.
   b. Hover the mouse over **CompCareers.docx** in the Recent Documents list and then click the left-pointing stick pin that displays at the right side of the document. (This moves the document to the top of the list and changes the left-pointing stick pin to a down-pointing stick pin.)

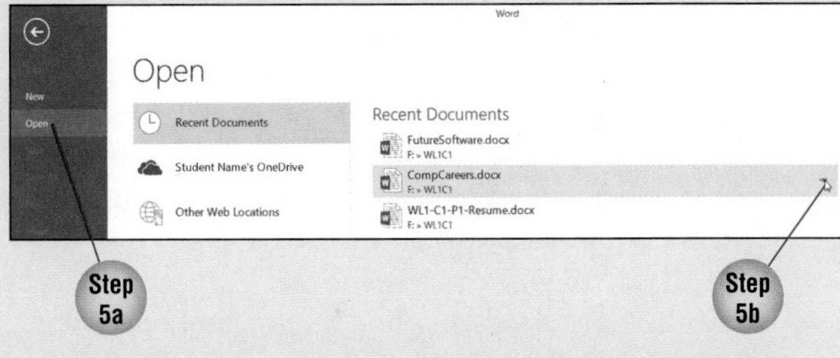

6. Click ***CompCareers.docx*** at the top of the Recent Documents list to open the document.
7. With the insertion point positioned at the beginning of the document, type the text shown in Figure 1.7.
8. Unpin **CompCareers.docx** from the Recent Documents list by completing the following steps:
   a. Click the FILE tab and then click the *Open* option.
   b. Click the down-pointing stick pin that displays at the right of **CompCareers.docx** in the Recent Documents list. (This changes the pin from a down-pointing stick pin to a left-pointing stick pin.)
   c. Click the Back button to return to the document.

Figure 1.7 Project 2a

> The majority of new jobs being created in the United States today involve daily work with computers. Computer-related careers include technical support jobs, sales and training, programming and applications development, network and database administration, and computer engineering.

Quick Steps

Save a Document with Save As
1. Click FILE tab.
2. Click *Save As* option.
3. At Save As backstage area, click desired location.
4. Click Browse button.
5. At Save As dialog box, navigate to desired folder.
6. Type document name in *File name* text box.
7. Press Enter.

Close Word
Click Close button.
OR
Press Alt + F4.

Saving a Document with Save As

If you open a previously saved document and want to give it a new name, use the *Save As* option at the backstage area rather than the *Save* option. Click the FILE tab and then click the *Save As* option. At the Save As backstage area, click the desired location and then click the Browse button or click the desired folder below the *Current Folder* or *Recent Folders* headings. At the Save As dialog box, type the new name for the document in the *File name* text box and then press Enter.

Closing Word

When you are finished working with Word and have saved all necessary information, close Word by clicking the Close button located in the upper right corner of the screen. You can also close Word with the keyboard shortcut Alt + F4.

Project 2b **Saving a Document with Save As** **Part 2 of 2**

1. With **CompCareers.docx** open, save the document with a new name by completing the following steps:
   a. Click the FILE tab and then click the *Save As* option.
   b. At the Save As backstage area, click the *WL1C1* folder below the *Current Folder* heading or the *Recent Folders* heading. (If the folder does not display, double-click your OneDrive or the *Computer* option and then navigate to the WL1C1 folder.)
   c. At the Save As dialog box, press the Home key on your keyboard to move the insertion point to the beginning of the file name and then type **WL1-C1-P2-**. (Pressing the Home key saves you from having to type the entire document name.)
   d. Press the Enter key.

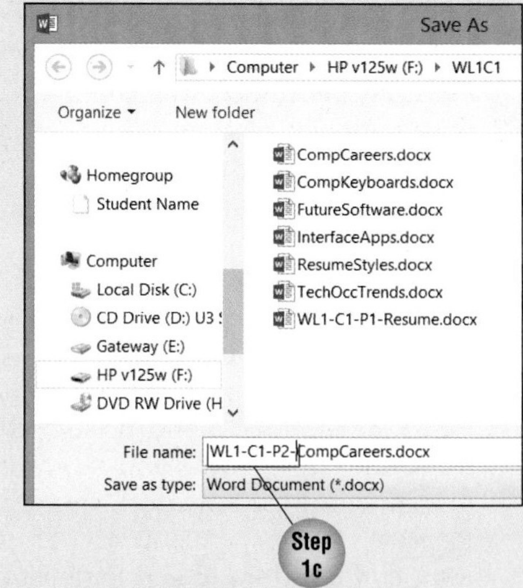

2. Print the document by clicking the FILE tab, clicking the *Print* option, and then clicking the Print button at the Print backstage area. (If your Quick Access toolbar contains the Quick Print button, you can click the button to send the document directly to the printer.)
3. Close the document by pressing Ctrl + F4.

Project 3 Scroll and Browse in a Document — 2 Parts

You will open a previously created document, save it with a new name, and then use scrolling and browsing techniques to move the insertion point to specific locations in the document.

Editing a Document

When editing a document, you may decide to insert or delete text. To edit a document, use the mouse, the keyboard, or a combination of the two to move the insertion point to a specific location in the document. To move the insertion point using the mouse, position the I-beam pointer where you want to place the insertion point and then click the left mouse button.

You can also scroll in a document, which changes the text display but does not move the insertion point. Use the mouse with the ***vertical scroll bar*** located at the right side of the screen to scroll through text in a document. Click the up scroll arrow at the top of the vertical scroll bar to scroll up through the document, and click the down scroll arrow to scroll down through the document. The scroll bar contains a scroll box that indicates the location of the text in the document screen in relation to the remainder of the document. To scroll up one screen at a time, position the arrow pointer above the scroll box (but below the up scroll arrow) and then click the left mouse button. Position the arrow pointer below the scroll box and click the left button to scroll down a screen. If you hold down the left mouse button, the action becomes continuous. You can also position the arrow pointer on the scroll box, hold down the left mouse button, and then drag the scroll box along the scroll bar to reposition text in the document screen. As you drag the scroll box along the vertical scroll bar in a longer document, page numbers display in a box at the right side of the document screen.

Project 3a Scrolling in a Document — Part 1 of 2

1. Open **InterfaceApps.docx** (from the WL1C1 folder you copied to your storage medium).
2. Save the document with Save As and name it **WL1-C1-P3-InterfaceApps**.
3. Position the I-beam pointer at the beginning of the first paragraph and then click the left mouse button.
4. Click the down scroll arrow on the vertical scroll bar several times. (This scrolls down lines of text in the document.) With the mouse pointer on the down scroll arrow, hold down the left mouse button and keep it down until the end of the document displays.
5. Position the mouse pointer on the up scroll arrow and hold down the left mouse button until the beginning of the document displays.
6. Position the mouse pointer below the scroll box and then click the left mouse button. Continue clicking the mouse button (with the mouse pointer positioned below the scroll box) until the end of the document displays.
7. Position the mouse pointer on the scroll box in the vertical scroll bar. Hold down the left mouse button, drag the scroll box to the top of the vertical scroll bar, and then release the mouse button. (Notice that the document page numbers display in a box at the right side of the document screen.)
8. Click in the title at the beginning of the document. (This moves the insertion point to the location of the mouse pointer.)

Moving the Insertion Point to a Specific Line or Page

Word includes a Go To feature you can use to move the insertion point to a specific location in a document such as a line or page. To use the feature, click the Find button arrow located in the Editing group on the HOME tab and then click *Go To* at the drop-down list. At the Find and Replace dialog box with the Go To tab selected, move the insertion point to a specific page by typing the page number in the *Enter page number* text box and then pressing Enter. Move to a specific line by clicking the *Line* option in the *Go to what* list box, typing the line number in the *Enter line number* text box and then pressing Enter. Click the Close button to close the dialog box.

Moving the Insertion Point with the Keyboard

To move the insertion point with the keyboard, use the arrow keys located to the right of the regular keyboard or use the arrow keys on the numeric keypad. If you use these keys, make sure Num Lock is off. Use the arrow keys together with other keys to move the insertion point to various locations in the document, as shown in Table 1.2.

When moving the insertion point, Word considers a word to be any series of characters between spaces. A paragraph is any text that is followed by a stroke of the Enter key. A page is text that is separated by a soft or hard page break.

Table 1.2 Insertion Point Movement Commands

To move insertion point	*Press*
one character left	Left Arrow
one character right	Right Arrow
one line up	Up Arrow
one line down	Down Arrow
one word left	Ctrl + Left Arrow
one word right	Ctrl + Right Arrow
to end of line	End
to beginning of line	Home
to beginning of current paragraph	Ctrl + Up Arrow
to beginning of next paragraph	Ctrl + Down Arrow
up one screen	Page Up
down one screen	Page Down
to top of previous page	Ctrl + Page Up
to top of next page	Ctrl + Page Down
to beginning of document	Ctrl + Home
to end of document	Ctrl + End

Resuming Reading or Editing in a Document

If you open a previously saved document, you can move the insertion point to where the insertion point was last located when the document was closed by pressing Shift + F5.

When you work in a multiple-page document and then close the document, Word remembers the page where the insertion point was last positioned. When you reopen the document, Word displays a "Welcome back!" message at the right side of the screen near the vertical scroll bar. The message tells you that you can pick up where you left off and identifies the page where your insertion point was last located. Click the message and the insertion point is positioned at the top of that page.

Project 3b Moving the Insertion Point in a Document — Part 2 of 2

1. With **WL1-C1-P3-InterfaceApps.docx** open, move the insertion point to line 15 and then to page 3 by completing the following steps:
   a. Click the Find button arrow located in the Editing group on the HOME tab and then click *Go To* at the drop-down list.
   b. At the Find and Replace dialog box with the Go To tab selected, click *Line* in the *Go to what* list box.
   c. Type 15 in the *Enter line number* text box and then press Enter.
   d. Click *Page* in the *Go to what* list box.
   e. Click in the *Enter page number* text box, type 3, and then press Enter.
   f. Click the Close button to close the Find and Replace dialog box. 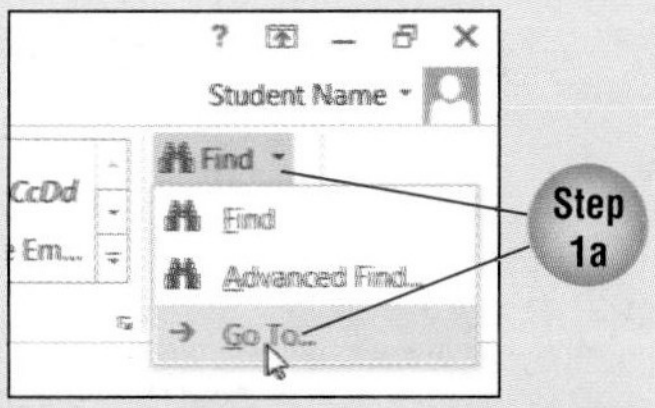 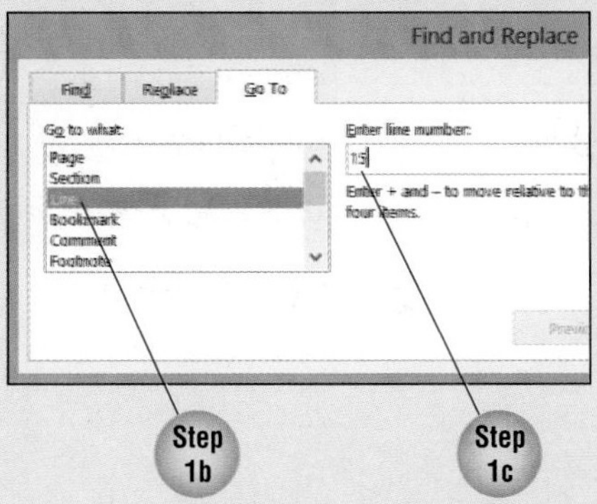
2. Close the document.
3. Open the document by clicking the FILE tab, clicking the *Open* option (if necessary), and then double-clicking the document name ***WL1-C1-P3-InterfaceApps.docx*** that displays at the top of the Recent Documents list.
4. Move the mouse pointer to the right side of the screen to display the "Welcome back!" message. Hover the mouse over the message and then click the left mouse button. (This positions the insertion point at the top of the third page—the page where the insertion point was positioned when you closed the document.) 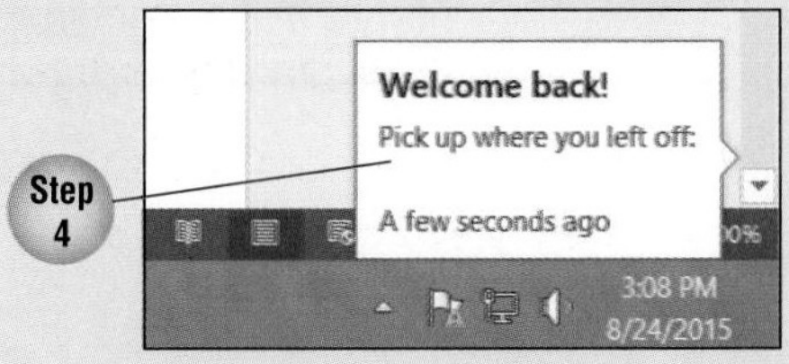
5. Press Ctrl + Home to move the insertion point to the beginning of the document.
6. Practice using the keyboard commands shown in Table 1.2 to move the insertion point within the document.
7. Close **WL1-C1-P3-InterfaceApps.docx**.

Project 4 Insert and Delete Text — 2 Parts

You will open a previously created document, save it with a new name, and then make editing changes to the document. The editing changes include selecting, inserting, and deleting text.

Inserting and Deleting Text

Editing a document may include inserting and/or deleting text. To insert text in a document, position the insertion point in the desired location and then type the text. Existing characters move to the right as you type the text. A number of options are available for deleting text. Some deletion commands are shown in Table 1.3.

Selecting Text

Use the mouse and/or keyboard to select a specific amount of text. Once you have selected the text, you can delete it or perform other Word functions on it. When text is selected, it displays with a gray background, as shown in Figure 1.8, and the Mini toolbar displays. The Mini toolbar contains buttons for common tasks. (You will learn more about the Mini toolbar in Chapter 2.)

Table 1.3 Deletion Commands

To delete	Press
character right of insertion point	Delete key
character left of insertion point	Backspace key
text from insertion point to beginning of word	Ctrl + Backspace
text from insertion point to end of word	Ctrl + Delete

Figure 1.8 Selected Text and Mini Toolbar

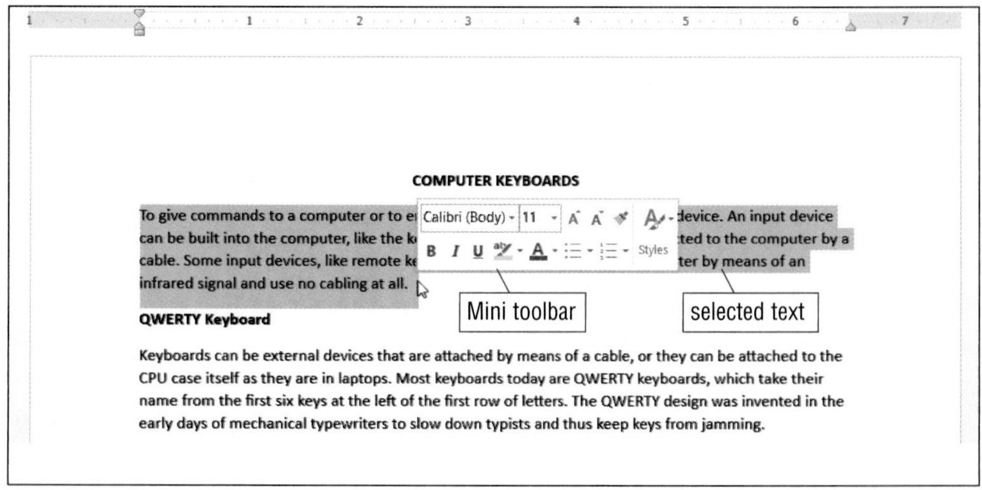

Selecting Text with the Mouse

Use the mouse to select a word, line, sentence, paragraph, or the entire document. Table 1.4 indicates the steps to follow to select various amounts of text. To select a specific amount of text, such as a line or a paragraph, click in the selection bar. The selection bar is the space located toward the left side of the document screen between the left edge of the page and the text. When the mouse pointer is positioned in the selection bar, the pointer turns into an arrow pointing up and to the right (instead of to the left).

To select an amount of text other than a word, sentence, or paragraph, position the I-beam pointer on the first character of the text to be selected, hold down the left mouse button, drag the I-beam pointer to the last character of the text to be selected, and then release the mouse button. You can also select all text between the current insertion point and the I-beam pointer. To do this, position the insertion point where you want the selection to begin, hold down the Shift key, click the I-beam pointer at the end of the selection, and then release the Shift key. To cancel a selection using the mouse, click anywhere in the document screen outside the selected text.

Select text vertically in a document by holding down the Alt key while dragging with the mouse. This is especially useful when selecting a group of text, such as text set in columns.

Selecting Text with the Keyboard

To select a specific amount of text using the keyboard, turn on the Selection mode by pressing the F8 function key. With the Selection mode activated, use the arrow keys to select the desired text. If you want to cancel the selection, press the Esc key and then press any arrow key. You can customize the Status bar to display text indicating that the Selection mode is activated. To do this, right-click any blank location on the Status bar and then click *Selection Mode* at the pop-up list. When you press F8 to turn on the Selection mode, the words *EXTEND SELECTION* display on the Status bar. You can also select text with the commands shown in Table 1.5.

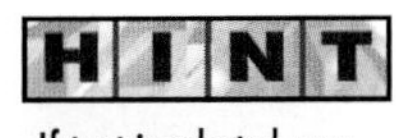

If text is selected, any character you type replaces the selected text.

Table 1.4 Selecting Text with the Mouse

To select	*Complete these steps using the mouse*
a word	Double-click the word.
a line of text	Click in the selection bar to the left of the line.
multiple lines of text	Drag in the selection bar to the left of the lines.
a sentence	Hold down the Ctrl key and then click anywhere in the sentence.
a paragraph	Double-click in the selection bar next to the paragraph, or triple-click anywhere in the paragraph.
multiple paragraphs	Drag in the selection bar.
an entire document	Triple-click in the selection bar.

Table 1.5 Selecting Text with the Keyboard

To select	*Press*
one character to right	Shift + Right Arrow
one character to left	Shift + Left Arrow
to end of word	Ctrl + Shift + Right Arrow
to beginning of word	Ctrl + Shift + Left Arrow
to end of line	Shift + End
to beginning of line	Shift + Home
one line up	Shift + Up Arrow
one line down	Shift + Down Arrow
to beginning of paragraph	Ctrl + Shift + Up Arrow
to end of paragraph	Ctrl + Shift + Down Arrow
one screen up	Shift + Page Up
one screen down	Shift + Page Down
to end of document	Ctrl + Shift + End
to beginning of document	Ctrl + Shift + Home
entire document	Ctrl + A or click Select button in Editing group and then click *Select All*

Project 4a Editing a Document

Part 1 of 2

1. Open **CompKeyboards.docx**. (This document is located in the WL1C1 folder you copied to your storage medium.)
2. Save the document with Save As and name it **WL1-C1-P4-CompKeyboards**.
3. Change the word *give* in the first sentence of the first paragraph to *enter*.
4. Change the second *to* in the first sentence to *into*.
5. Delete the words *means of* in the first sentence in the *QWERTY Keyboard* section.
6. Select the words *and use no cabling at all* and the period that follows located at the end of the last sentence in the first paragraph, and then press the Delete key.
7. Insert a period immediately following the word *signal*.

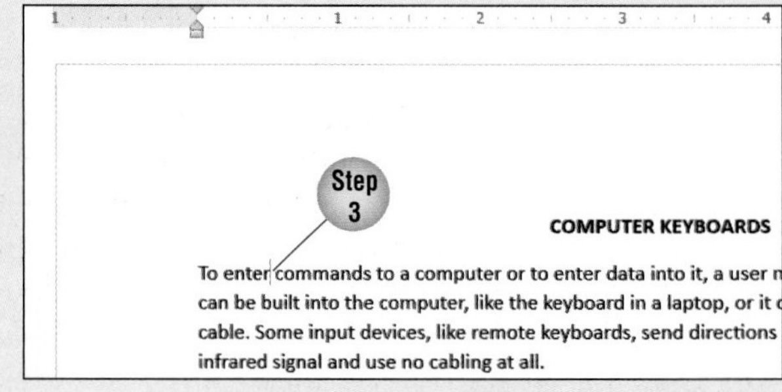

Step 3
COMPUTER KEYBOARDS
To enter commands to a computer or to enter data into it, a user
can be built into the computer, like the keyboard in a laptop, or it
cable. Some input devices, like remote keyboards, send directions
infrared signal and use no cabling at all.

8. Delete the heading line containing the text *QWERTY Keyboard* using the Selection mode by completing the following steps:
   a. Position the insertion point immediately before the *Q* in *QWERTY*.
   b. Press F8 to turn on the Selection mode.
   c. Press the Down Arrow key.
   d. Press the Delete key.
9. Complete steps similar to those in Step 8 to delete the heading line containing the text *DVORAK Keyboard*.
10. Begin a new paragraph with the sentence that reads *Keyboards have different physical appearances* by completing the following steps:
    a. Position the insertion point immediately left of the *K* in *Keyboards* (the first word of the fifth sentence in the last paragraph).
    b. Press the Enter key.
11. Save **WL1-C1-P4-CompKeyboards.docx**.

To enter commands into a c
device can be built into the
computer by a cable. Some i
means of an infrared signal.

QWERTY Keyboard

Keyboards can be external d
itself as they are in laptops.
the first six keys at the left o
of mechanical typewriters t

Steps 8a-8c

To enter commands into a computer or
device can be built into the computer, l
computer by a cable. Some input devic
means of an infrared signal.

Keyboards can be external devices that
itself as they are in laptops. Most keyb
the first six keys at the left of the first r
of mechanical typewriters to slow dow

The DVORAK keyboard is an alternative
commonly used keys are placed close t
install software on a QWERTY keyboard
keyboards is convenient especially whe

Keyboards have different physical appe
that of a calculator, containing number
"broken" into two pieces to reduce stra
change the symbol or character entere

Using the Undo and Redo Buttons

If you make a mistake and delete text that you did not intend to, or if you change your mind after deleting text and want to retrieve it, you can use the Undo or Redo buttons on the Quick Access toolbar. For example, if you type text and then click the Undo button, the text will be removed. You can undo text or commands. For example, if you add formatting such as bolding to text and then click the Undo button, the bolding is removed.

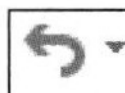
Undo

Redo

If you use the Undo button and then decide you do not want to reverse the original action, click the Redo button. For example, if you select and underline text and then decide to remove underlining, click the Undo button. If you then decide you want the underlining back on, click the Redo button. Many Word actions can be undone or redone. Some actions, however, such as printing and saving, cannot be undone or redone.

Word maintains actions in temporary memory. If you want to undo an action performed earlier, click the Undo button arrow. This causes a drop-down list to display. To make a selection from this drop-down list, click the desired action and the action, along with any actions listed above it in the drop-down list, is undone.

You cannot undo a save.

Project 4b Undoing and Redoing Deletions Part 2 of 2

1. With **WL1-C1-P4-CompKeyboards.docx** open, delete the last sentence in the last paragraph using the mouse by completing the following steps:
   a. Hover the I-beam pointer anywhere over the sentence that begins *All keyboards have modifier keys*.
   b. Hold down the Ctrl key and then click the left mouse button.

install software on a QWERTY keyboard that emulates a DVORAK keyboard. The ability to emulate other keyboards is convenient especially when working with foreign languages.

Keyboards have different physical appearances. Many keyboards have a separate numeric keypad, like that of a calculator, containing numbers and mathematical operators. Some keyboards are sloped and "broken" into two pieces to reduce strain. All keyboards have modifier keys that enable the user to change the symbol or character entered when a given key is pressed.

   c. Press the Delete key.
2. Delete the last paragraph by completing the following steps:
   a. Position the I-beam pointer anywhere in the last paragraph (the paragraph that begins *Keyboards have different physical appearances*).
   b. Triple-click the left mouse button.
   c. Press the Delete key.
3. Undo the deletion by clicking the Undo button on the Quick Access toolbar.

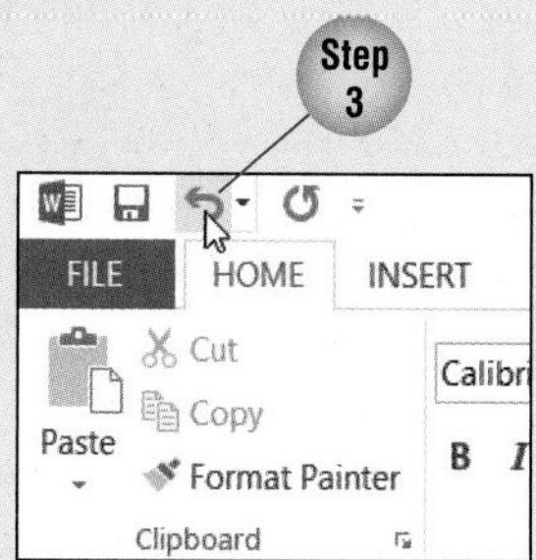

4. Redo the deletion by clicking the Redo button on the Quick Access toolbar.
5. Select the first sentence in the second paragraph and then delete it.
6. Select the first paragraph in the document and then delete it.
7. Undo the two deletions by completing the following steps:
   a. Click the Undo button arrow.
   b. Click the second *Clear* listed in the drop-down list. (This will redisplay the first sentence in the second paragraph as well as display the first paragraph. The sentence will be selected.)
8. Click outside the sentence to deselect it.
9. Save, print, and then close **WL1-C1-P4-CompKeyboards.docx**.

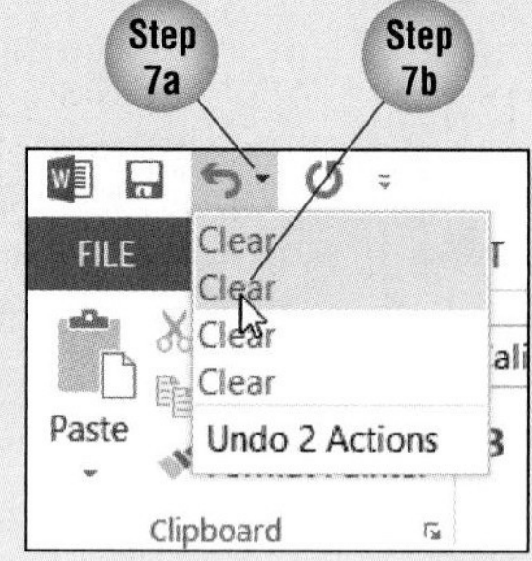

Project 5 Complete a Spelling and Grammar Check 1 Part

You will open a previously created document, save it with a new name, and then check the spelling and grammar in the document.

Checking the Spelling and Grammar in a Document

Two tools for creating thoughtful and well-written documents include a spelling checker and a grammar checker. The spelling checker finds misspelled words and offers replacement words. It also finds duplicate words and irregular capitalizations. When you spell check a document, the spelling checker compares the words in your document with the words in its dictionary. If the spelling checker finds a match, it passes over the word. If a match is not found for the word, the spelling checker will stop, select the word, and offer possible corrections.

The grammar checker will search a document for errors in grammar, punctuation, and word usage. If the grammar checker finds an error, it stops and offers possible corrections. The spelling checker and the grammar checker can help you create a well-written document but do not eliminate the need for proofreading.

Quick Steps

Check Spelling and Grammar

1. Click REVIEW tab.
2. Click Spelling & Grammar button.
3. Change or ignore errors.
4. Click OK.

Spelling & Grammar

Complete a spelling and grammar check on a portion of a document by selecting the text first and then clicking the Spelling & Grammar button.

To complete a spelling and grammar check, click the REVIEW tab and then click the Spelling & Grammar button in the Proofing group. You can also begin spelling and grammar checking by pressing the keyboard shortcut, F7. If Word detects a possible spelling error, the text containing the error is selected and the Spelling task pane displays. The Spelling task pane contains a list box with possible correction(s) along with buttons you can click to either change or ignore the spelling error, as described in Table 1.6. A definition of the selected word in the list box may display toward the bottom of the Spelling task pane if you have a dictionary installed.

If Word detects a gammar error, the word(s) or sentence is selected and possible corrections display in the Grammar task pane list box. Depending on the error selected, some or all of the buttons described in Table 1.6 may display in the Grammar task pane and a description of the grammar rule with suggestions may display toward the bottom of the task pane. With the buttons that display, you can choose to ignore or change the grammar error.

When checking the spelling and grammar in a document, you can temporarily leave the Spelling task pane or Grammar task pane by clicking in the document. To resume the spelling and grammar check, click the Resume button in the Spelling task pane or Grammar task pane.

Table 1.6 Spelling Task Pane and Grammar Task Pane Buttons

Button	Function
Ignore	During spell checking, skips that occurrence of the word; in grammar checking, leaves currently selected text as written.
Ignore All	During spell checking, skips that occurrence of the word and all other occurrences of the word in the document.
Add	Adds the selected word to the spelling check dictionary.
Delete	Deletes the currently selected word(s).
Change	Replaces the selected word with a word in the task pane list box.
Change All	Replaces the selected word and all other occurrences of it with a word in the task pane list box.

Project 5 Checking the Spelling and Grammar in a Document

Part 1 of 1

1. Open **TechOccTrends.docx**.
2. Save the document with Save As and name it **WL1-C1-P5-TechOccTrends**.
3. Click the REVIEW tab.
4. Click the Spelling & Grammar button in the Proofing group.
5. The spelling checker selects the word *tecnology* and displays the Spelling task pane. The proper spelling is selected in the Spelling task pane list box, so click the Change button (or Change All button).

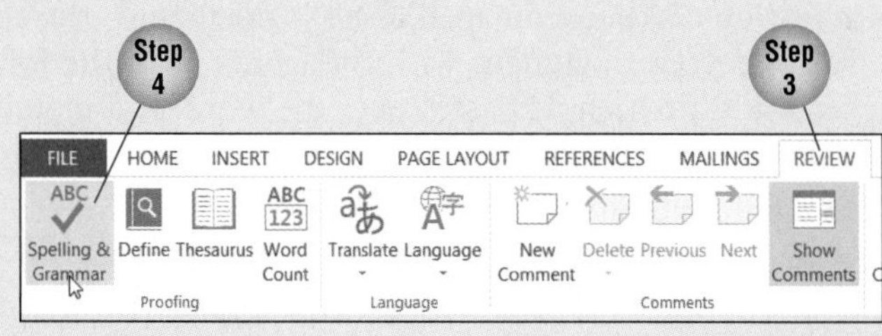

6. The grammar checker selects the sentence containing the word *job's* and displays the Grammar task pane with *jobs* selected in the list box. The grammar checker also displays toward the bottom of the Grammar task pane information about plurals or possessives. Read the information and then click the Change button.

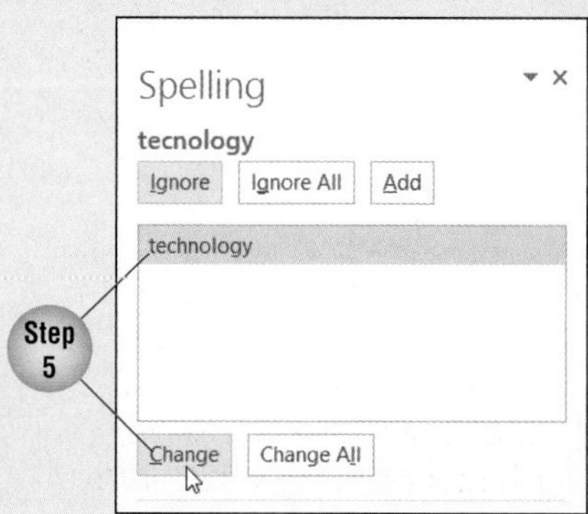

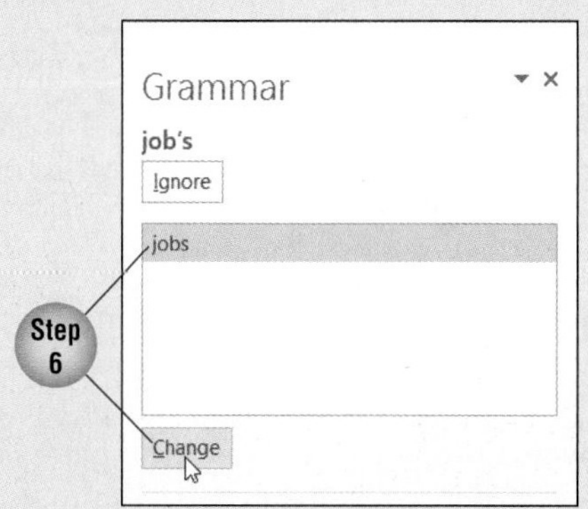

7. The grammar checker selects the word *too* in the document and displays the Grammar task pane, with *to* selected in the list box. If definitions of *to* and *too* display toward the bottom of the task pane, read the information. Click the Change button.
8. The grammar checker selects the sentence containing the words *downloaded* and *versus*, which contain two spaces between the words. The Grammar task pane displays in the list box the two words with only one space between. Read the information about spaces between words that displays toward the bottom of the Grammar task pane and then click the Change button.
9. The spelling checker selects the word *sucessful* and offers *successful* in the Spelling task pane list box. Since this word is misspelled in another location in the document, click the Change All button.
10. The spelling checker selects the word *are*, which is used twice in a row. Click the Delete button in the Spelling task pane to delete the second *are*.
11. When the message displays telling you that the spelling and grammar check is complete, click the OK button.
12. Save, print, and then close **WL1-C1-P5-TechOccTrends.docx**.

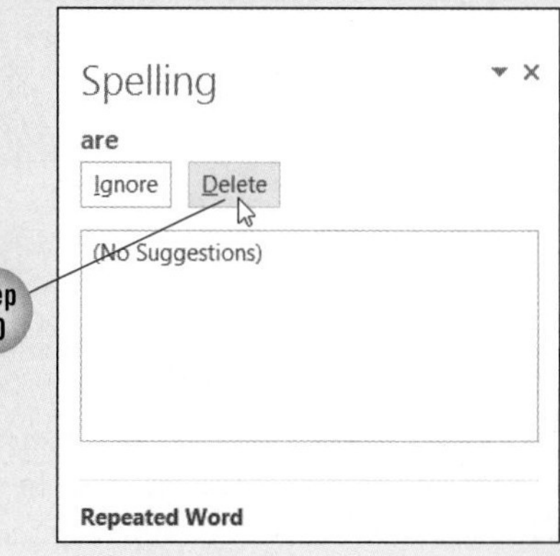

Project 6 Use the Help Feature

2 Parts

You will use the Help feature to learn more about printing and opening documents.

Using Help

Word's Help feature is an on-screen reference manual containing information about Word features and commands. Word's Help feature is similar to the Help features in Excel, PowerPoint, and Access. Get help by clicking the Microsoft Word Help button located in the upper right corner of the screen (a question mark) or by pressing the keyboard shortcut, F1. This displays the Word Help window, as shown in Figure 1.9. In this window, type a topic, feature, or question in the search text box and then press Enter. Topics related to the search text display in the Word Help window. Click a topic that interests you. If the topic window contains a Show All hyperlink in the upper right corner, click this hyperlink and the information expands to show all help information related to the topic. When you click the Show All hyperlink, it becomes the Hide All hyperlink.

Quick Steps

Use Help Feature

1. Click Microsoft Word Help button.
2. Type search text in search text box.
3. Press Enter.
4. Click desired topic.

The Word Help window contains five buttons that display to the left of the search text box. Use the Back and Forward buttons to navigate in the window. Click the Home button to return to the Word Help window opening screen. If you want to print information on a topic or feature, click the Print button and then click the Print button at the Print dialog box. You can make the text in the Word Help window larger by clicking the Use Large Text button. In addition to these five buttons, the Word Help window contains a Keep Help on Top button located near the upper right corner of the window. Click this button and the Word Help window remains on the screen even when you work in a document. Click the button again to remove the window from the screen.

Figure 1.9 Word Help Window

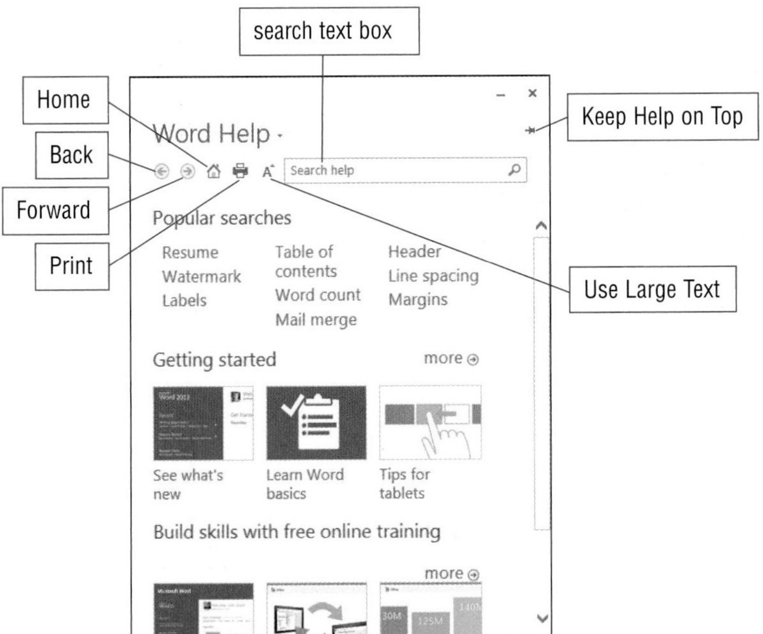

Getting Help from a ScreenTip

If you hover your mouse over some buttons, the ScreenTip that displays may include a Help icon and the Tell me more hyperlinked text. Click Tell me more, and the Word Help window opens with information about the button feature. You can also press F1 to display the Word Help window with information about the button feature.

Project 6a **Using the Help Feature** **Part 1 of 2**

1. At a blank document, click the Microsoft Word Help button located in the upper right corner of the screen.
2. At the Word Help window, click in the search text box and then type **print**.
3. Press the Enter key.
4. When the list of topics displays, click the Print and preview documents hyperlinked topic.

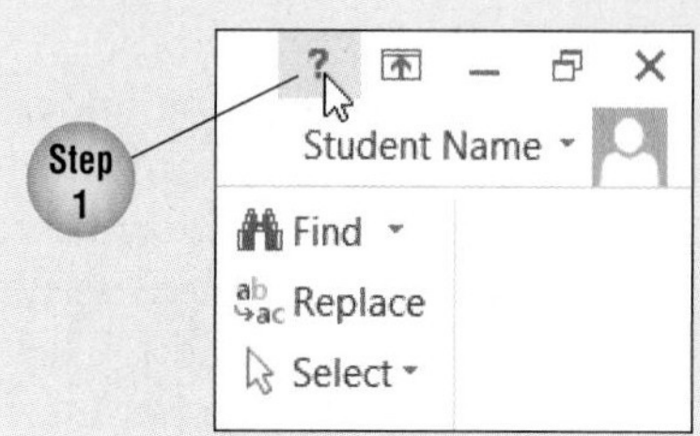

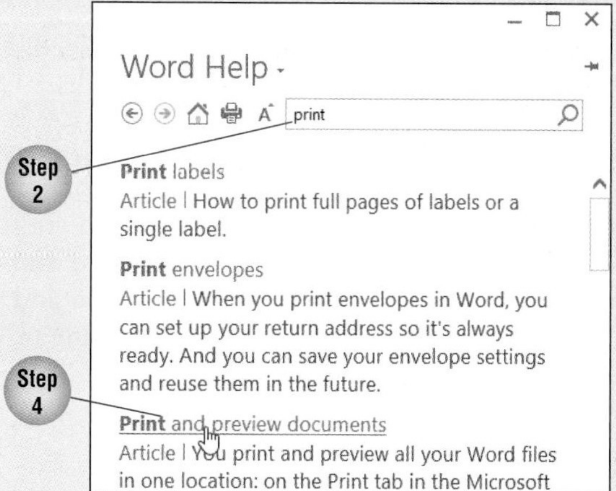

5. Scroll down the Word Help window and read the information about printing and previewing documents.
6. Click the Print button in the Word Help window. This displays the Print dialog box. If you want to print the topic, click the Print button; otherwise, click the Cancel button to close the dialog box.

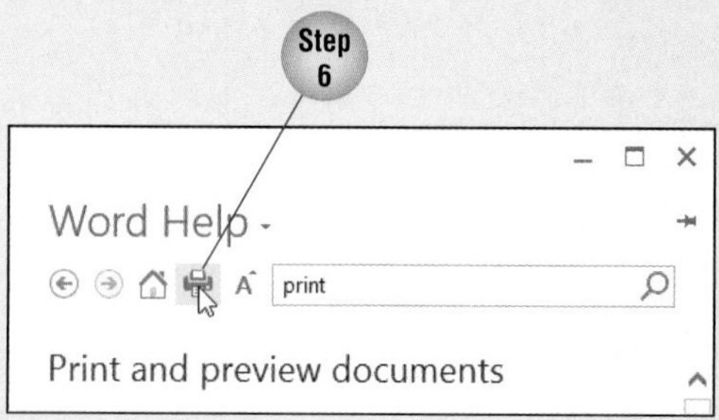

7. At the Word Help window, click the Use Large Text button to increase the size of the text in the window.
8. Click the Use Large Text button again to return the text to the normal size.
9. Click the Back button to return to the previous window.

10. Click the Forward button to redisplay the article on printing and previewing a document.
11. Click the Home button to return to the original Word Help window screen.
12. Click the Close button to close the Word Help window.
13. Hover your mouse over the Format Painter button in the Clipboard group on the HOME tab.
14. Click the Tell me more hyperlinked text, which displays at the bottom of the ScreenTip.
15. Read the information in the Word Help window about the Format Painter feature.
16. Click the Close button to close the Word Help window.

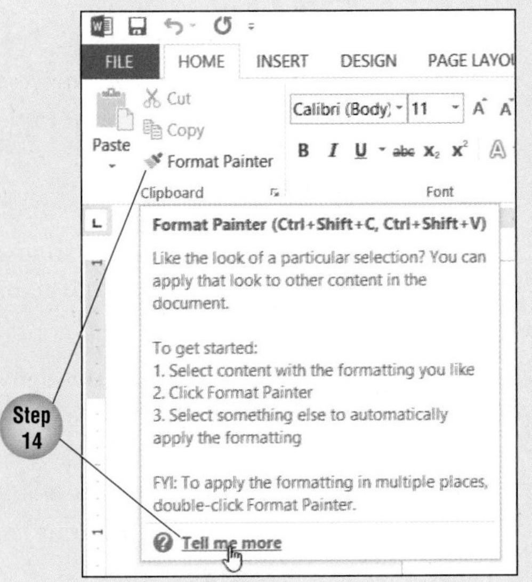

Getting Help in a Dialog Box

Some dialog boxes contain a help button you can click to display specific information about the dialog box. Open a dialog box and then click the help button and information about the dialog box displays in the Word Help window. After reading and/or printing the information, close the Word Help window and then close the dialog box by clicking the Close button located in the upper right corner.

Project 6b Getting Help in a Dialog Box — Part 2 of 2

1. At a blank document, click the Paragraph group dialog box launcher that displays in the lower right corner of the Pararaph group on the HOME tab.
2. Click the Help button that displays in the upper right corner of the Paragraph dialog box.
3. Read the information that displays in the Word Help window.
4. Close the Word Help window and then close the Paragraph dialog box.
5. Click the FILE tab and then click the *Open* option.
6. At the Open backstage area, double-click the *Computer* option.
7. At the Open dialog box, click the Get help button, which displays toward the upper right corner of the dialog box.
8. At the Windows Help and Support window, read the information that displays about opening a file or folder, and then click the Close button located in the upper right corner of the window.
9. Close the Open dialog box.
10. At the Open backstage area, press the Esc key on your keyboard.
11. Close the blank document without saving changes.

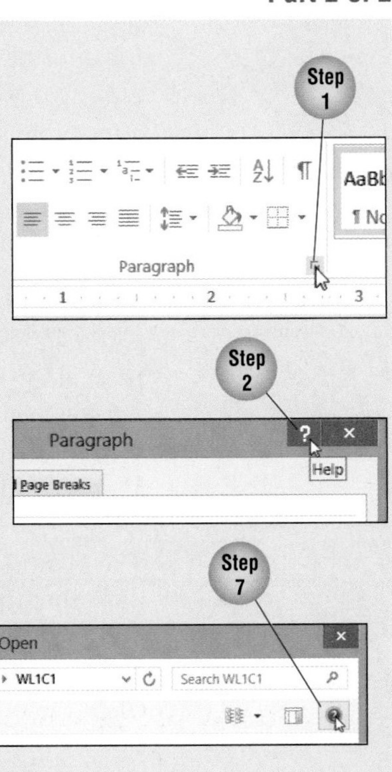

Chapter Summary

- Refer to Figure 1.1 and Table 1.1 for an example and a list of key Word screen features.
- The Quick Access toolbar contains buttons for commonly used commands.
- Click the FILE tab and the backstage area displays, containing options for working with and managing documents.
- The ribbon area contains tabs with options and buttons divided into groups.
- The insertion point displays as a blinking vertical line and indicates the position of the next character to be entered in the document.
- Document names can contain a maximum of 255 characters, including the drive letter and folder names, and may include spaces.
- The insertion point can be moved throughout the document without interfering with text by using the mouse, the keyboard, or the mouse combined with the keyboard.
- The scroll box on the vertical scroll bar indicates the location of the text in the document in relation to the remainder of the document.
- You can move the insertion point by character, word, screen, or page and from the first to the last character in a document. Refer to Table 1.2 for keyboard insertion point movement commands.
- Delete text by character, word, line, several lines, or partial page using specific keys or by selecting text using the mouse or the keyboard. Refer to Table 1.3 for deletion commands.
- You can select a specific amount of text using the mouse or the keyboard. Refer to Table 1.4 for information on selecting with the mouse, and refer to Table 1.5 for information on selecting with the keyboard.
- Use the Undo button on the Quick Access toolbar if you change your mind after typing, deleting, or formatting text and want to undo the action. Use the Redo button to redo something that had been undone with the Undo button.
- The spelling checker matches the words in your document with the words in its dictionary. If a match is not found, the word is selected and possible corrections are suggested in the Spelling task pane. The grammar checker searches a document for errors in grammar, style, punctuation, and word usage. When a grammar error is detected, possible corrections display in the Grammar task pane along with information about the grammar rule or error. Refer to Table 1.6 for Spelling task pane and Grammar task pane buttons.
- Word's Help feature is an on-screen reference manual containing information about Word features and commands. Click the Microsoft Word Help button or press F1 to display the Word Help window.
- The Word Help window contains five buttons to the left of the search text box, including the Back, Forward, Home, Print, and Use Large Text buttons.
- The Word Help window contains a Keep Help on Top button you can click to keep the Word Help window on the screen even when working in a document. Click the button again to remove the window from the screen.

- If you hover your mouse over some buttons, the ScreenTip that displays may include a Help icon and the Tell me more hyperlinked text. Click this hyperlinked text to display the Word Help window with information about the button feature.
- Some dialog boxes contain a help button you can click to display information specific to the dialog box.

Commands Review

FEATURE	RIBBON TAB, GROUP/OPTION	BUTTON, OPTION	KEYBOARD SHORTCUT
close document	FILE, *Close*		Ctrl + F4
close Word			Alt + F4
Find and Replace dialog box with Go To tab selected	HOME, Editing	, *Go To*	Ctrl + G
new blank document	FILE, *New*	*Blank document*	Ctrl + N
Open backstage area	FILE, *Open*		Ctrl + O
Print backstage area	FILE, *Print*		Ctrl + P
redo an action			Ctrl + Y
save	FILE, *Save*		Ctrl + S
Save As backstage area	FILE, *Save As*		F12
select document	HOME, Editing	, *Select All*	Ctrl + A
spelling and grammar checker	REVIEW, Proofing		F7
undo an action			Ctrl + Z
Word Help			F1

Concepts Check Test Your Knowledge

Completion: In the space provided at the right, indicate the correct term, symbol, or command.

1. This toolbar contains the Save button. ____________
2. Click this tab to display the backstage area. ____________
3. This is the area located toward the top of the screen that contains tabs with options and buttons divided into groups. ____________
4. This bar, located toward the bottom of the screen, displays the numbers of pages and words, view buttons, and the Zoom slider bar. ____________
5. This tab is active by default. ____________
6. This feature automatically corrects certain words as you type them. ____________
7. This feature inserts an entire item when you type a few identifying characters and then press Enter or F3. ____________
8. This is the keyboard shortcut to display the Print backstage area. ____________
9. This is the keyboard shortcut to close a document. ____________
10. This is the keyboard shortcut to display a new blank document. ____________
11. Use this keyboard shortcut to move the insertion point to the beginning of the previous page. ____________
12. Use this keyboard shortcut to move the insertion point to the end of the document. ____________
13. Press this key on the keyboard to delete the character left of the insertion point. ____________
14. Using the mouse, do this to select one word. ____________
15. To select various amounts of text using the mouse, click in this bar. ____________
16. Click this tab to display the Spelling & Grammar button in the Proofing group. ____________
17. This is the keyboard shortcut to display the Word Help window. ____________

Skills Check Assess Your Performance

Assessment 1

TYPE AND EDIT A DOCUMENT ON WRITING RESUMES

SNAP Grade It

1. Open Word and then type the text in Figure 1.10. Correct any errors highlighted by the spelling checker, and space once after end-of-sentence punctuation.
2. Make the following changes to the document:
   a. Delete the first occurrence of the word *currently* in the first sentence of the first paragraph.
   b. Select the word *important* in the first sentence in the first paragraph and then type **essential**.
   c. Type **and hard-hitting** between the words *concise* and *written* located in the second sentence of the second paragraph.
   d. Delete the words *over and over,* (including the comma) located in the third sentence in the second paragraph.
   e. Select and then delete the second sentence of the third paragraph (the sentence that begins *So do not take*).
   f. Join the second and third paragraphs.
   g. Delete the name *Marie Solberg* and then type your first and last names.
3. Save the document and name it **WL1-C1-A1-WriteResume**.
4. Print and then close **WL1-C1-A1-WriteResume.docx**.

Figure 1.10 Assessment 1

Writing a Resume

For every job seeker, including those currently employed and those currently not working, a powerful resume is an important component of the job search. In fact, conducting a job search without a resume is virtually impossible. A resume is your calling card that briefly communicates the skills, qualifications, experience, and value you bring to the prospective employer. It is the document that will open doors and generate interviews.

Your resume is a sales document, and you are the product. You must identify the features of that product, and then communicate them in a concise written presentation. Remind yourself over and over, as you work your way through the resume process, that you are writing marketing literature designed to market yourself.

Your resume can have tremendous power and a phenomenal impact on your job search. So do not take it lightly. You should devote the time, energy, and resources that are essential to developing a resume that is well written, visually attractive, and effective in communicating who you are and how you want to be perceived.

Created by Marie Solberg
Monday, October 5, 2015
Note: Please insert this information between the 2nd and 3rd sections.

Assessment 2

CHECK THE SPELLING AND GRAMMAR OF A RESUME STYLES DOCUMENT

1. Open **ResumeStyles.docx**.
2. Save the document with Save As and name it **WL1-C1-A2-ResumeStyles**.
3. Complete a spelling and grammar check on the document and correct the selected errors.
4. Type the sentence **Different approaches work for different people.** between the first and second sentences in the first paragraph of text below the title *RESUME STYLES*.
5. Move the insertion point to the end of the document, type your first and last names, press Shift + Enter, and then type the current date.
6. Save, print, and then close **WL1-C1-A2-ResumeStyles.docx**.

Assessment 3

CREATE A DOCUMENT DESCRIBING KEYBOARD SHORTCUTS

1. Click the Microsoft Word Help button, type **keyboard shortcuts**, and then press Enter.
2. At the Word Help window, click the Keyboard shortcuts for Microsoft Word hyperlink.
3. At the keyboard shortcut window, click the Show All hyperlink.
4. Read through the information in the Word Help window.
5. Create a document describing four keyboard shortcuts.
6. Save the document and name it **WL1-C1-A3-KeyboardShortcuts**.
7. Print and then close **WL1-C1-A3-KeyboardShortcuts.docx**.

Visual Benchmark Demonstrate Your Proficiency

CREATE A LETTER

1. At a blank document, press the Enter key three times and then type the personal business letter shown in Figure 1.11 on the next page. Follow the directions in red.
2. Save the completed letter and name it **WL1-C1-VB-CoverLtr**.
3. Print and then close the document.

Figure 1.11 Visual Benchmark

(press Enter three times)

4520 South Park Street *(press Shift + Enter)*
Newark, NJ 07122 *(press Shift + Enter)*
Current Date *(press Enter two times)*

Mrs. Sylvia Hammond *(press Shift + Enter)*
Sales Director, Eastern Division *(press Shift + Enter)*
Grand Style Products *(press Shift + Enter)*
1205 Sixth Street *(press Shift + Enter)*
Newark, NJ 07102 *(press Enter)*

Dear Mrs. Hammond: *(press Enter)*

Thank you for agreeing to meet with me next Wednesday. Based on our initial conversation, it seems that my ability to sell solutions rather than products is a good fit for your needs as you seek to expand your visibility in the region. *(press Enter)*

As noted in the enclosed resume, I have led an under-performing product division to generating 33 percent of total revenue (up from 5 percent) at our location, and delivering, from a single location, 25 percent of total sales for our 20-site company. Having completed this turnaround over the last 5 years, I'm eager for new challenges where my proven skills in sales, marketing, and program/event planning can contribute to a company's bottom line. *(press Enter)*

I have been thinking about the challenges you described in building your presence at the retail level, and I have some good ideas to share at our meeting. I am excited about the future of Grand Style Products and eager to contribute to your growth. *(press Enter)*

Sincerely, *(press Enter two times)*

Student Name *(press Enter)*

Enclosure

Case Study Apply Your Skills

Part 1

You are the assistant to Paul Brewster, the training coordinator at a medium-sized service-oriented business. You have been asked by Mr. Brewster to prepare a document for Microsoft Word users within the company explaining the steps employees need to take to save an open company contract document to a folder named *Contracts* that is located in the *Documents* main folder. Save the document and name it **WL1-C1-CS-Saving**. Print and then close the document.

Part 2

Help

Mr. Brewster would like a document containing a brief summary of some basic Word commands for use in Microsoft Word training classes. He has asked you to prepare a document containing the following information:

- A brief explanation of how to move the insertion point to a specific page
- Keyboard shortcuts to move the insertion point to the beginning and end of a text line and beginning and end of a document
- Commands to delete text from the insertion point to the beginning of a word and from the insertion point to the end of a word
- Steps to select a word and a paragraph using the mouse
- A keyboard shortcut to select the entire document

Save the document and name it **WL1-C1-CS-WordCommands**. Print and then close the document.

Part 3

WWW

According to Mr. Brewster, the company is considering updating the Resources Department computers to Microsoft Office 2013. He has asked you to use the Internet to go to the Microsoft home page at www.microsoft.com and then use the search feature to find information on the system requirements for Office Professional Plus 2013. When you find the information, type a document that contains the Office Professional Plus 2013 system requirements for the computer and processor, memory, hard disk space, and operating system. Save the document and name it **WL1-C1-CS-SystemReq**. Print and then close the document.

MICROSOFT® WORD

Formatting Characters and Paragraphs

PERFORMANCE OBJECTIVES

Upon successful completion of Chapter 2, you will be able to:

- **Change the font and font effects**
- **Format selected text with buttons on the Mini toolbar**
- **Apply styles from style sets**
- **Apply themes**
- **Change the alignment of text in paragraphs**
- **Indent text in paragraphs**
- **Increase and decrease spacing before and after paragraphs**
- **Repeat the last action**
- **Automate formatting with Format Painter**
- **Change line spacing in a document**
- **Reveal and compare formatting**

Tutorials

2.1 Modifying the Font Using the Font Group

2.2 Formatting with the Mini Toolbar

2.3 Highlighting Text

2.4 Applying Formatting Using the Font Dialog Box

2.5 Applying Styles, Style Sets, and Themes

2.6 Aligning Text in Paragraphs

2.7 Changing Text Indentation

2.8 Using the Format Painter

2.9 Setting Line and Paragraph Spacing

2.10 Revealing and Comparing Formatting

The appearance of a document in the document screen and when printed is called the ***format***. A Word document is based on a template that applies default formatting. Some of the default formats include 11-point Calibri font, line spacing of 1.08, 8 points of spacing after each paragraph, and left-aligned text. In this chapter, you will learn about changing the typeface, type size, and typestyle as well as applying font effects such as bold and italics. The Paragraph group on the HOME tab includes buttons for applying formatting to paragraphs of text. In Word, a paragraph is any amount of text followed by a press of the Enter key. In this chapter, you will learn to format paragraphs by changing text alignment, indenting text, applying formatting with Format Painter, and changing line spacing. Model answers for this chapter's projects appear on the following pages.

Note: Before beginning the projects, copy to your storage medium the WL1C2 subfolder from the WL1 folder on the CD that accompanies this textbook and then make WL1C2 the active folder.

GLOSSARY OF TERMS

A

Access time: The time a storage device spends locating a particular file.
Aggregation software: E-commerce software application that combines online activities to provide *one-stop shopping* for consumers.
Analog signals: Signals composed of continuous waves transmitted at a certain frequency range over a medium, such as a telephone line.

B

Backup: A second copy kept of valuable data.
Bandwidth: The number of *bits* that can be transferred per second over a given medium or network.
Beta-testing: One of the last steps in software development that involves allowing outside people to use the software to see if it works as designed.

C

Chinese abacus: Pebbles strung on a rod inside a frame. Pebbles in the upper part of an abacus correspond to 5×10^0, or 5, for the first column; 5×10^1, or 50, for the second column; 5×10^2, or 500, for the third column; and so on.
Chip: A thin wafer of *silicon* containing electronic circuitry that performs various functions, such as mathematical calculations, storage, or controlling computer devises.
Cluster: A group of two or more sectors on a dish, which is the smallest unit of storage space used to store data.
Coding: A term used by programmers to refer to the act of writing source code.
Crackers: A term coined by computer hackers for those who intentionally enter ~~(or hack)~~ computer systems to damage them.

CREATED BY SUSAN ASHBY
WEDNESDAY, FEBRUARY 18, 2015

Project 1 Apply Character Formatting
WL1-C2-P1-CompTerms.docx

COMMERCIAL LIFE CYCLE

The software life cycle is the term used to describe the phases involved in the process of creating, testing, and releasing new commercial software products. This cycle is similar to the process used in developing information systems, except that in this case the cycle focuses on the creation and release of a software program, not the development of a customized information system. The commercial software life cycle is repeated every time a new version of a program is needed. The phases in the software life cycle include the following: proposal and planning, design, implementation, testing, and public release.

Proposal and Planning

In the proposal and planning phase of a new software product, software developers will describe the proposed software program and what it is supposed to accomplish. In the case of existing software, the proposal and planning stage can be used to describe any new features and improvements. Older software programs are often revised to take advantage of new hardware or software developments and to add new functions or features.

Design

Developers are ready to begin the design process once the decision has been made to create or upgrade a software program. This step produces specifications documenting the details of the software to be written by programmers. Developers use problem-solving steps to determine the appropriate specifications.

Implementation

The implementation phase of the software life cycle is usually the most difficult. Development teams often spend late nights and weekends writing code and making it work. If the planning and design efforts have been successful, this phase should go well, but unanticipated problems inevitably crop up and have to be solved. The end result of the implementation phase is the production of a prototype called an alpha product, which is used by the development team for testing purposes. The alpha product can be revised to incorporate any improvements suggested by team members.

Testing

A quality assurance (QA) team usually develops a testing harness, which is a scripted set of tests that a program must undergo before being considered ready for public release. These tests might cover events such as very large input loads, maximum number of users, running on several different platforms, and simulated power outages. Once testing is finished, a beta version of the software program is created for testing outside of the development group, often by a select group of knowledgeable consumers. Any suggestions they make can be used to improve the product before it is released to the general public. Once the beta version is finalized, the user manual can be written or updated. At this point, the software developers would send the master CDs to duplicators for mass production.

Public Release and Support

When the product is deemed ready for widespread use, it is declared "gold" and released to the public. The software life cycle now goes back to the beginning phases as software developers think of new ways to improve the product.

Project 2 Apply Styles and Themes
WL1-C2-P2-SoftwareCycle.docx

PROPERTY PROTECTION ISSUES

The ability to link computers through the Internet offers many advantages. With linked computers, we can quickly and easily communicate with other users around the world, sharing files and other data with a few simple keystrokes. The convenience provided by linking computers through the Internet also has some drawbacks. Computer viruses can travel around the world in seconds, damaging programs and files. Hackers can enter into systems without authorization and steal or alter data. In addition, the wealth of information on the Web and the increased ease with which it can be copied have made plagiarizing easy. Plagiarism is using others' ideas and creations (their intellectual property) without permission.

All of these ethical issues revolve around property rights, the right of someone to protect and control the things he or she owns. A solid legal framework ensuring the protection of personal property exists, but computers have created many new issues that challenge conventional interpretations of these laws.

Intellectual Property

Intellectual property includes just about anything that can be created by the agency of the human mind. To encourage innovation and improvement and thus benefit society as a whole, our legal system grants patents to those who invent new and better ways of doing things. A patent awards ownership of an idea or invention to its creator for a fixed number of years. This allows the inventor the right to charge others for the use of the invention. To encourage and protect artistic and literary endeavors, authors and artists are awarded copyrights to the material they create, allowing them the right to control the use of their works and charge others for their use. Patent and copyright violation is punishable by law, and prosecutions and convictions are frequent. The legal framework protecting intellectual property has come under constant challenge as technology has moved forward.

With the Internet, accessing and copying written works that may be protected is easy. Today, authors are increasingly dismayed to find copies of their works appearing on the Internet without their permission. The same problem occurs with graphic and artistic images on the Internet, such as photographs and artwork. Once placed on the Web, they can be copied and reused numerous times. Unauthorized copying of items appearing on websites is difficult and sometimes even technically impossible to prevent.

Page 1

Fair Use

Situations exist in which using work written by others is permissible. Using another person's material without permission is allowed as long as the use is acknowledged, is used for noncommercial purposes, and involves only the use of limited excerpts of protected material, such as no more than 300 words of prose and one line of poetry. Such a right is called fair use and is dealt with under the U.S. Copyright Act, Section 107. Here, in part, is what the Fair Use law states:

> [A] copyrighted work, including such use by reproduction in copies of phonorecords or by any other means specified by that section, for purposes such as criticism, comment, news reporting, teaching (including multiple copies for classroom use), scholarship, or research, is not an infringement of copyright.

Even under the Fair Use provision, describing the source of the material is important. Plagiarism may be punished by law, and in many educational institutions it can result in suspension or even expulsion.

Intellectual Property Protection

The problem faced by intellectual property owners in the digital age is twofold. First, new technology has presented new difficulties in interpreting previous understandings dealing with the protection of intellectual property, such as difficulties applying the Fair Use provision to Internet material. Second, the new technical capabilities brought about by digital technologies have greatly increased the ease with which intellectual property can be appropriated and used without authorization, making policing and protecting intellectual property very difficult. Intellectual property owners have formed new organizations to ensure the protection of their property.

REFERENCES

Fuller, Floyd and Brian Larson. (2013) *Computers: Understanding Technology* (pp. 659-661). St. Paul, MN: Paradigm Publishing.

Myerson, Jean A. (2011) *Intellectual Properties* (pp. 123-126). New Orleans, LA: Robicheaux Publishing House.

Patterson, Margaret and Montgomery Littleton. (2014) *Issues of Plagiarism*. Chicago, IL: Lansing and Edelman Publishers.

Page 2

Project 3 Apply Paragraph Formatting and Use Format Painter
WL1-C2-P3-IntelProp.docx

Talbot, Lenora J. and Marcella S. Angleton. (2013) *Internet Considerations*. Portland, OR: Pacific Blue Publishing Group.

Prepared by Clarissa Markham
Edited by Joshua Streeter

Page 3

Solving Problems

In groups or individually, brainstorm possible solutions to the issues presented.

- Computers currently offer both *visual* and *audio* communications. Under development are devices and technologies that will allow users to smell various types of products while looking at them in the computer screen. What are some new applications of this technology for the food industry? Can you think of other industries that could use this capability?
- Picture yourself working in the Information Technology department of a mid-sized company. Your responsibilities include evaluating employees' computer system needs and recommending equipment purchases. Recently, the company president hired a new employee and you must evaluate her computer system needs. Considering that you have a budget of $5,500 for equipping the new employee with the computer system (or systems), research possible configurations and prepare a report outlining your recommendations, including costs. Assume that for her office she needs a complete system, including a system unit, monitor, printer, speakers, keyboard, and mouse.

Project 4 Format Computer Issues Document
WL1-C2-P4-CompIssues.docx

Project 1 Apply Character Formatting — 4 Parts

You will open a document containing a glossary of terms, add additional text, and then format the document by applying character formatting.

Changing Fonts

The Font group shown in Figure 2.1 contains a number of buttons for applying character formatting to text in a document. The top row contains buttons for changing the font and font size as well as buttons for increasing and decreasing the size of the font, changing the text case, and clearing formatting. You can remove character formatting (as well as paragraph formatting) applied to text by clicking the Clear All Formatting button in the Font group. Remove only character formatting from selected text by pressing the keyboard shortcut, Ctrl + spacebar. The bottom row contains buttons for applying typestyles such as bold, italic, and underline and for applying text effects, highlighting, and color.

A Word document is based on a template that formats text in 11-point Calibri. You may want to change this default to some other font for such reasons as changing the mood of the document, enhancing the visual appeal, and increasing the readability of the text. A font consists of three elements: typeface, type size, and typestyle.

Change the default font by selecting the desired font at the Font dialog box and then clicking the Set As Default button.

A typeface is a set of characters with a common design and shape and can be decorative or plain and either monospaced or proportional. Word refers to a typeface as a ***font***. A monospaced typeface allots the same amount of horizontal space for

Figure 2.1 Font Group Buttons

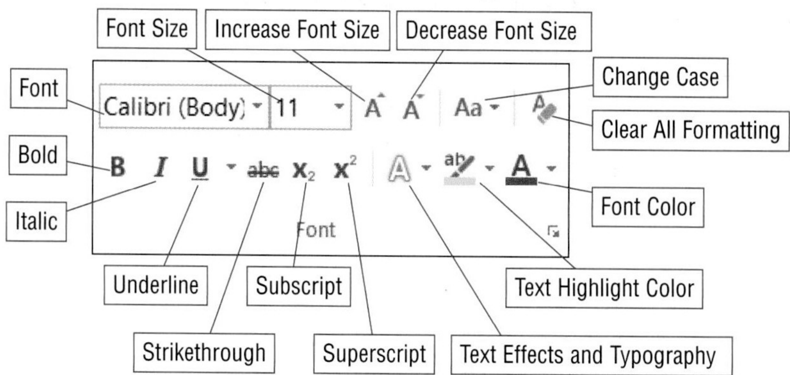

each character, while a proportional typeface allots a varying amount of space for each character. Proportional typefaces are divided into two main categories: ***serif*** and ***sans serif***. A serif is a small line at the end of a character stroke. Consider using a serif typeface for text-intensive documents because the serifs help move the reader's eyes across the page. Use a sans serif typeface for headings, headlines, and advertisements. Some of the popular typefaces are shown in Table 2.1.

Use a serif typeface for text-intensive documents.

Type is generally set in proportional size. The size of proportional type is measured vertically in units called ***points***. A point is approximately $^{1}/_{72}$ of an inch—the higher the point size, the larger the characters. Within a typeface, characters may have varying styles. Type styles are divided into four main categories: regular, bold, italic, and bold italic.

Use the Font button arrow in the Font group to change the font. When you select text and then click the Font button arrow, a drop-down gallery of font options displays. Hover your mouse pointer over a font option and the selected text in the document displays with the font applied. You can continue hovering your mouse pointer over different font options to see how the selected text displays in each specified font. The Font button arrow drop-down gallery is an example of the ***live preview*** feature, which allows you to see how the font formatting affects your text without having to return to the document. The live preview feature is also available when you click the Font Size button arrow to change the font size.

Press Ctrl +] to increase font size by one point and press Ctrl + [to decrease font size by one point.

Table 2.1 Categories of Typefaces

Serif Typefaces	***Sans Serif Typefaces***	***Monospaced Typefaces***
Cambria	Calibri	Consolas
Constantia	Candara	Courier New
Times New Roman	Corbel	Lucida Console
Bookman Old Style	Arial	MS Gothic

Project 1a Changing the Font and Font Size

Part 1 of 4

1. Open **CompTerms.docx**.
2. Save the document with Save As and name it **WL1-C2-P1-CompTerms**.
3. Change the typeface to Cambria by completing the following steps:
   a. Select the entire document by pressing Ctrl + A. (You can also select all text in the document by clicking the Select button in the Editing group and then clicking *Select All* at the drop-down list.)
   b. Click the Font button arrow, scroll down the Font drop-down gallery until *Cambria* displays, and then hover the mouse pointer over *Cambria*. This displays a live preview of the text set in Cambria.
   c. Click the mouse button on *Cambria*.

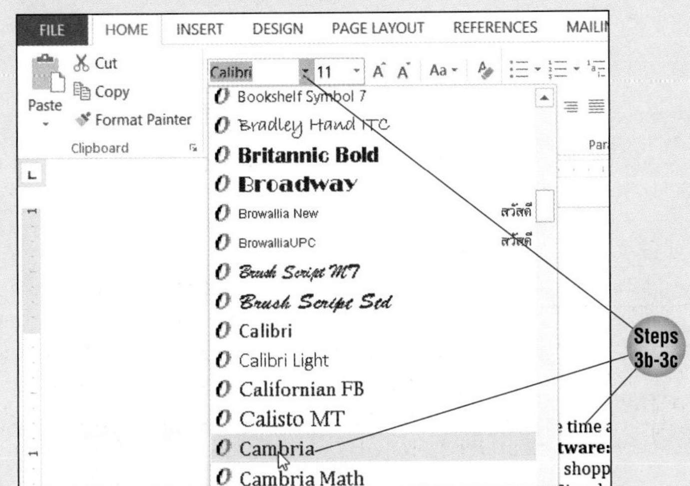

4. Change the type size to 14 points by completing the following steps:
   a. With the text in the document still selected, click the Font Size button arrow.
   b. At the drop-down gallery that displays, hover the mouse pointer on *14* and look at the live preview of the text with 14 points applied.
   c. Click the left mouse button on *14*.
5. At the document screen, deselect the text by clicking anywhere in the document.
6. Change the type size and typeface by completing the following steps:
   a. Press Ctrl + A to select the entire document.
   b. Click three times on the Decrease Font Size button in the Font group. (This decreases the size to 10 points.)
   c. Click twice on the Increase Font Size button. (This increases the size of the font to 12 points.)

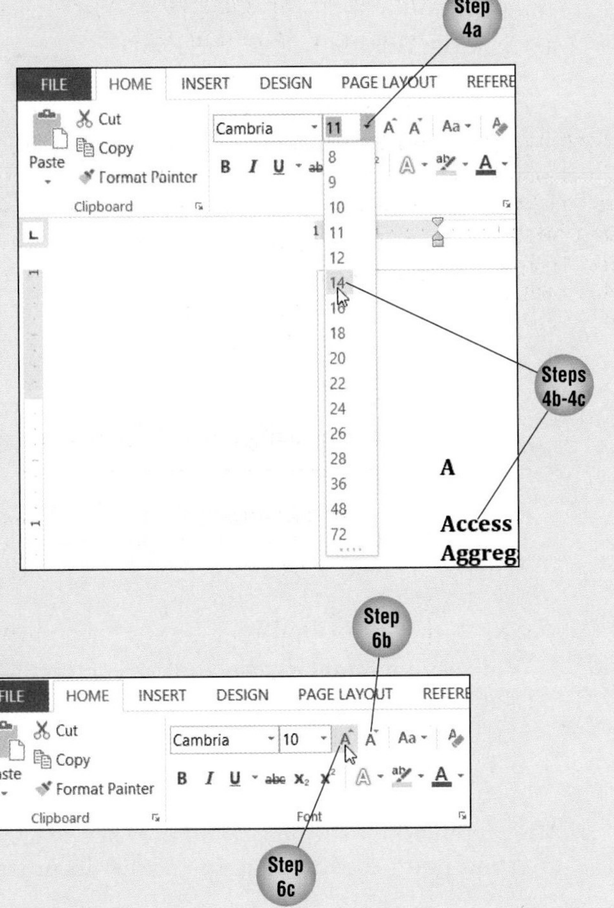

d. Click the Font button arrow, scroll down the drop-down gallery, and then click *Constantia*. (The most recently used fonts display at the beginning of the gallery, followed by a listing of all fonts.)

7. Save **WL1-C2-P1-CompTerms.docx**.

Choosing a Typestyle

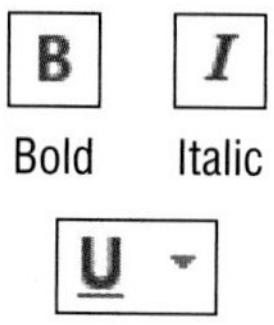

B Bold   *I* Italic   U Underline

Apply a particular typestyle to text with the Bold, Italic, or Underline buttons in the bottom row in the Font group. You can apply more than one style to text. For example, you can bold and italicize the same text or apply all three styles to the same text. Click the Underline button arrow and a drop-down gallery displays with underlining options such as a double line, dashed line, and thicker underline. Click the *Underline Color* option at the Underline button drop-down gallery and a side menu displays with color options.

Project 1b **Applying Character Formatting to Text as You Type** **Part 2 of 4**

1. With **WL1-C2-P1-CompTerms.docx** open, press Ctrl + Home to move the insertion point to the beginning of the document.
2. Type a heading for the document by completing the following steps:
   a. Click the Bold button in the Font group. (This turns on bold.)
   b. Click the Underline button in the Font group. (This turns on underline.)
   c. Type **Glossary of Terms**.
3. Press Ctrl + End to move the insertion point to the end of the document.
4. Type the text shown in Figure 2.2 with the following specifications:
   a. While typing, make the appropriate text bold as shown in the figure by completing the following steps:
      1) Click the Bold button in the Font group. (This turns on bold.)
      2) Type the text.
      3) Click the Bold button in the Font group. (This turns off bold.)
   b. Press Enter twice after typing the *C* heading.
   c. While typing, italicize the appropriate text as shown in the figure by completing the following steps:
      1) Click the Italic button in the Font group.
      2) Type the text.
      3) Click the Italic button in the Font group.
5. After typing the text, press the Enter key twice and then press Ctrl + Home to move the insertion point to the beginning of the document.

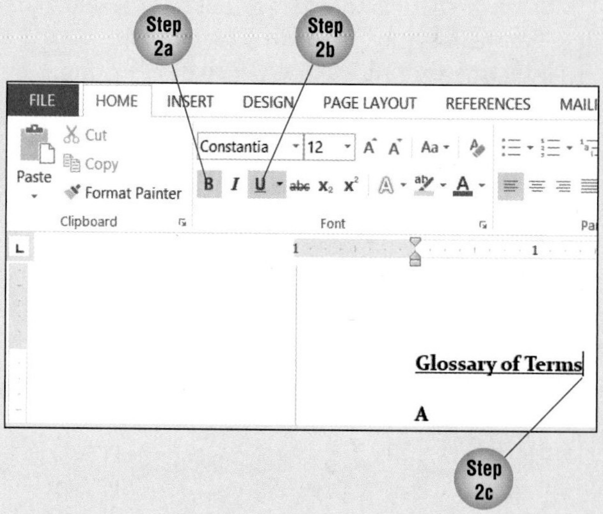

6. Change the underlining below the title by completing the following steps:
   a. Select the title *Glossary of Terms*.
   b. Click the Underline button arrow and then click the third underline option from the top of the drop-down gallery.
   c. Click the Underline button arrow, point to the *Underline Color* option, and then click the *Red* color (second color option) in the *Standard Colors* section.

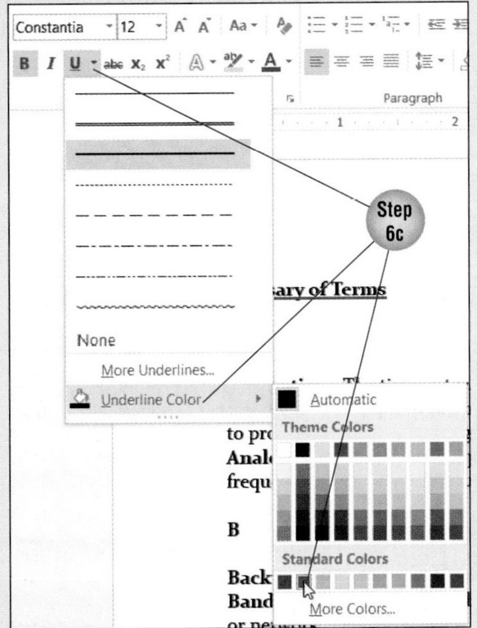

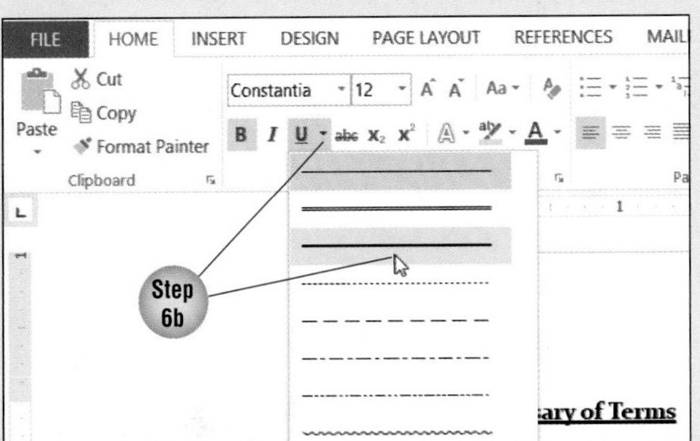

7. With the title still selected, change the font size to 14 points.
8. Save **WL1-C2-P1-CompTerms.docx**.

Figure 2.2 Project 1b

C

Chip: A thin wafer of *silicon* containing electronic circuitry that performs various functions, such as mathematical calculations, storage, or controlling computer devices.
Cluster: A group of two or more *sectors* on a disk, which is the smallest unit of storage space used to store data.
Coding: A term used by programmers to refer to the act of writing source code.
Crackers: A term coined by computer hackers for those who intentionally enter (or hack) computer systems to damage them.

Choosing a Font Effect

Apply font effects with some of the buttons in the top and bottom rows in the Font group, or clear all formatting from selected text with the Clear All Formatting button. Change the case of text with the Change Case button drop-down list. Click the Change Case button in the top row in the Font group and a drop-down list displays with the options *Sentence case*, *lowercase*, *UPPERCASE*, *Capitalize Each Word*, and *tOGGLE cASE*. You can also change the case of selected text with the keyboard shortcut Shift + F3. Each time you press Shift + F3, the selected text displays in the next case option in the list.

Clear All Formatting

Change Case

Strikethrough

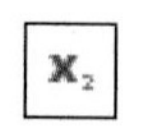
Subscript

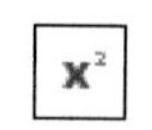
Superscript

Text Effects and Typography

Text Highlight Color

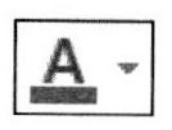
Font Color

The bottom row in the Font group contains buttons for applying font effects. Use the Strikethrough button to draw a line through selected text. This has a practical application in some legal documents in which deleted text must be retained in the document. Use the Subscript button to create text that is lowered slightly below the line, as in the chemical formula H_2O. Use the Superscript button to create text that is raised slightly above the text line, as in the mathematical equation four to the third power (written as 4^3). Click the Text Effects and Typography button in the bottom row and a drop-down gallery displays with effect options. Use the Text Highlight Color button to highlight specific text in a document and use the Font Color button to change the color of text.

Using Keyboard Shortcuts

Several of the buttons in the Font group have keyboard shortcuts. For example, you can press Ctrl + B to turn on/off bold or press Ctrl + I to turn on/off italics. Position the mouse pointer on a button and an enhanced ScreenTip displays with the name of the button; the keyboard shortcut, if any; a description of the action performed by the button; and sometimes, access to the Word Help window. Table 2.2 identifies the keyboard shortcuts available for buttons in the Font group.

Formatting with the Mini Toolbar

When you select text, the Mini toolbar displays above the selected text. Click a button on the Mini toolbar to apply formatting to the selected text. When you move the mouse pointer away from the Mini toolbar, it disappears.

Table 2.2 Font Group Button Keyboard Shortcuts

Font Group Button	*Keyboard Shortcut*
Font	Ctrl + Shift + F
Font Size	Ctrl + Shift + P
Increase Font Size	Ctrl + Shift + >
Decrease Font Size	Ctrl + Shift + <
Bold	Ctrl + B
Italic	Ctrl + I
Underline	Ctrl + U
Subscript	Ctrl + =
Superscript	Ctrl + Shift + +
Change Case	Shift + F3

Project 1c Applying Font Effects

Part 3 of 4

1. With **WL1-C2-P1-CompTerms.docx** open, move the insertion point to the beginning of the term *Chip*, press the Enter key, and then press the Up Arrow key. Type the text shown in Figure 2.3. Create each superscript number by clicking the Superscript button, typing the number, and then clicking the Superscript button.
2. Change the case of text and remove underlining from the title by completing the following steps:
   a. Select the title <u>*Glossary of Terms*</u>.
   b. Remove all formatting from the title by clicking the Clear All Formatting button in the Font group.
   c. Click the Change Case button in the Font group and then click *UPPERCASE* at the drop-down list.
   d. Click the Text Effects and Typography button in the Font group and then click the *Gradient Fill - Blue, Accent 1, Reflection* option (second column, second row) at the drop-down gallery.
   e. Change the font size to 14.
3. Strike through text by completing the following steps:
   a. Select the words and parentheses *(or hack)* in the *Crackers* definition.
   b. Click the Strikethrough button in the Font group.

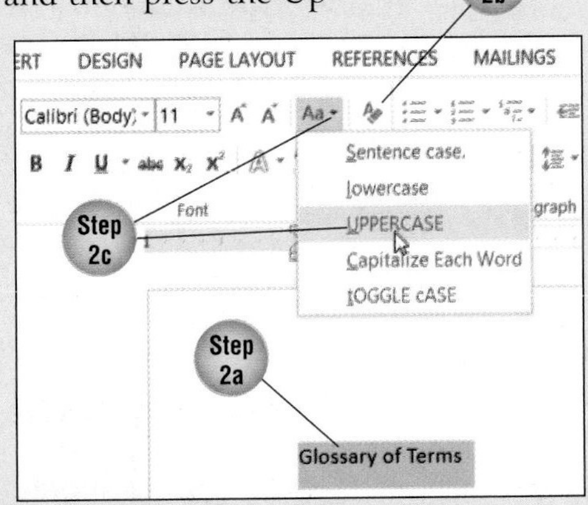

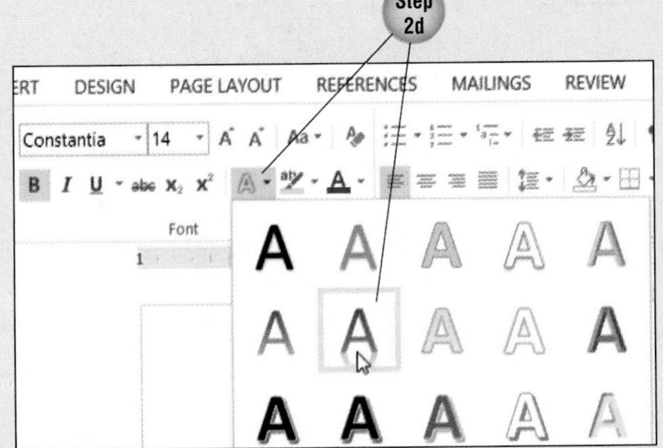

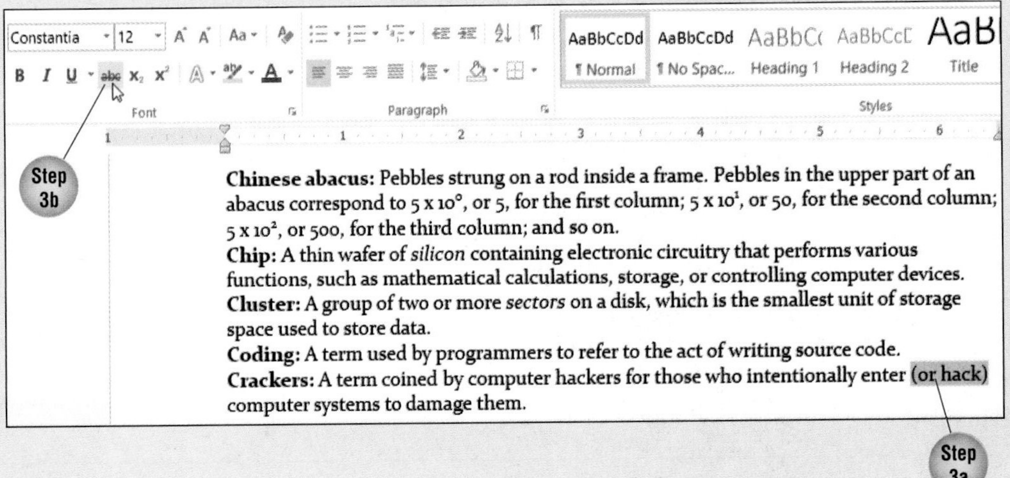

Constantia
12
AaBbCcDd
AaBbCcDd
AaBbCc
AaBbCcD
AaB
¶ Normal
¶ No Spac...
Heading 1
Heading 2
Title
Font
Paragraph
Styles
Step 3b
Chinese abacus: Pebbles strung on a rod inside a frame. Pebbles in the upper part of an abacus correspond to 5×10^0, or 5, for the first column; 5×10^1, or 50, for the second column; 5×10^2, or 500, for the third column; and so on.
Chip: A thin wafer of *silicon* containing electronic circuitry that performs various functions, such as mathematical calculations, storage, or controlling computer devices.
Cluster: A group of two or more *sectors* on a disk, which is the smallest unit of storage space used to store data.
Coding: A term used by programmers to refer to the act of writing source code.
Crackers: A term coined by computer hackers for those who intentionally enter (or hack) computer systems to damage them.
Step 3a

4. Change the font color by completing the following steps:
   a. Press Ctrl + A to select the entire document.
   b. Click the Font Color button arrow.
   c. Click the *Dark Red* color (first color option in the *Standard Colors* section) at the drop-down gallery.
   d. Click in the document to deselect text.

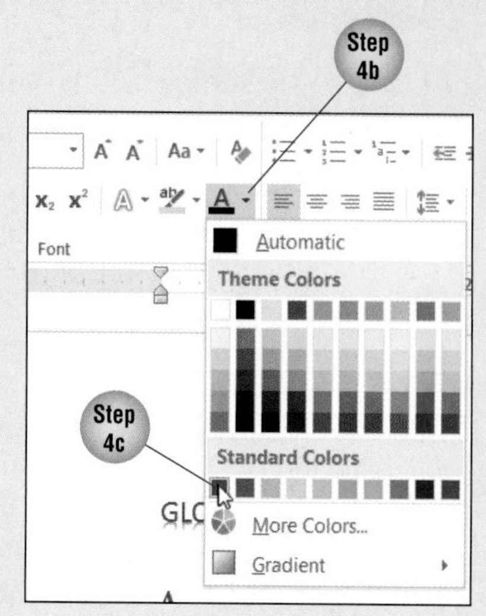

5. Highlight text in the document by completing the following steps:
   a. Click the Text Highlight Color button arrow in the Font group and then click the *Yellow* color (first column, first row) at the drop-down palette. (This causes the mouse pointer to display as an I-beam pointer with a highlighter pen attached.)
   b. Select the term *Beta-testing* and the definition that follows.
   c. Click the Text Highlight Color button arrow and then click the *Turquoise* color (third column, first row).
   d. Select the term *Cluster* and the definition that follows.
   e. Click the Text Highlight Color button arrow and then click the *Yellow* color at the drop-down gallery.
   f. Click the Text Highlight Color button to turn off highlighting.

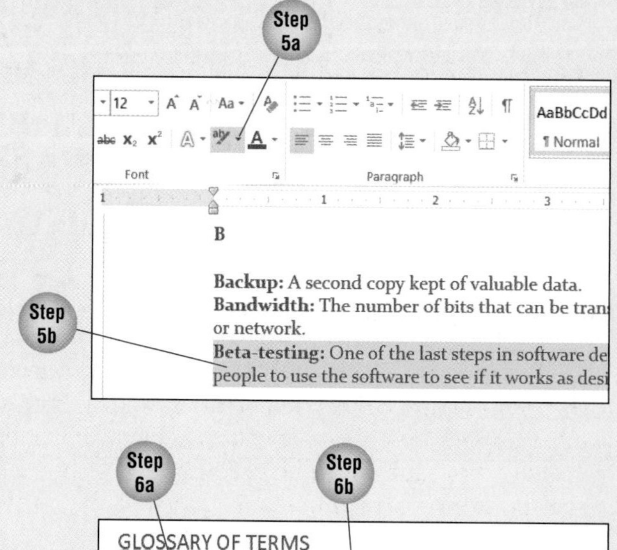

6. Apply italic formatting using the Mini toolbar by completing the following steps:
   a. Select the text *one-stop shopping* located in the definition for the term *Aggregation software*. (When you select the text, the Mini toolbar displays.)
   b. Click the Italic button on the Mini toolbar.
   c. Select the word *bits* located in the definition for the term *Bandwidth* and then click the Italic button on the Mini toolbar.

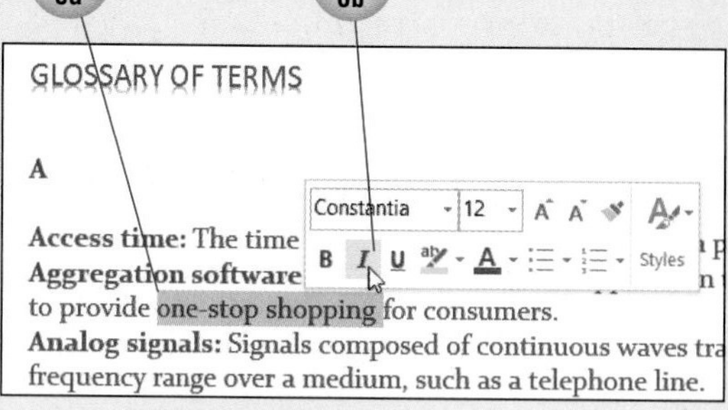

7. Save **WL1-C2-P1-CompTerms.docx**.

Figure 2.3 Project 1c

Chinese abacus: Pebbles strung on a rod inside a frame. Pebbles in the upper part of an abacus correspond to 5 x 10^0, or 5, for the first column; 5 x 10^1, or 50, for the second column; 5 x 10^2, or 500, for the third column; and so on.

Figure 2.4 Font Dialog Box

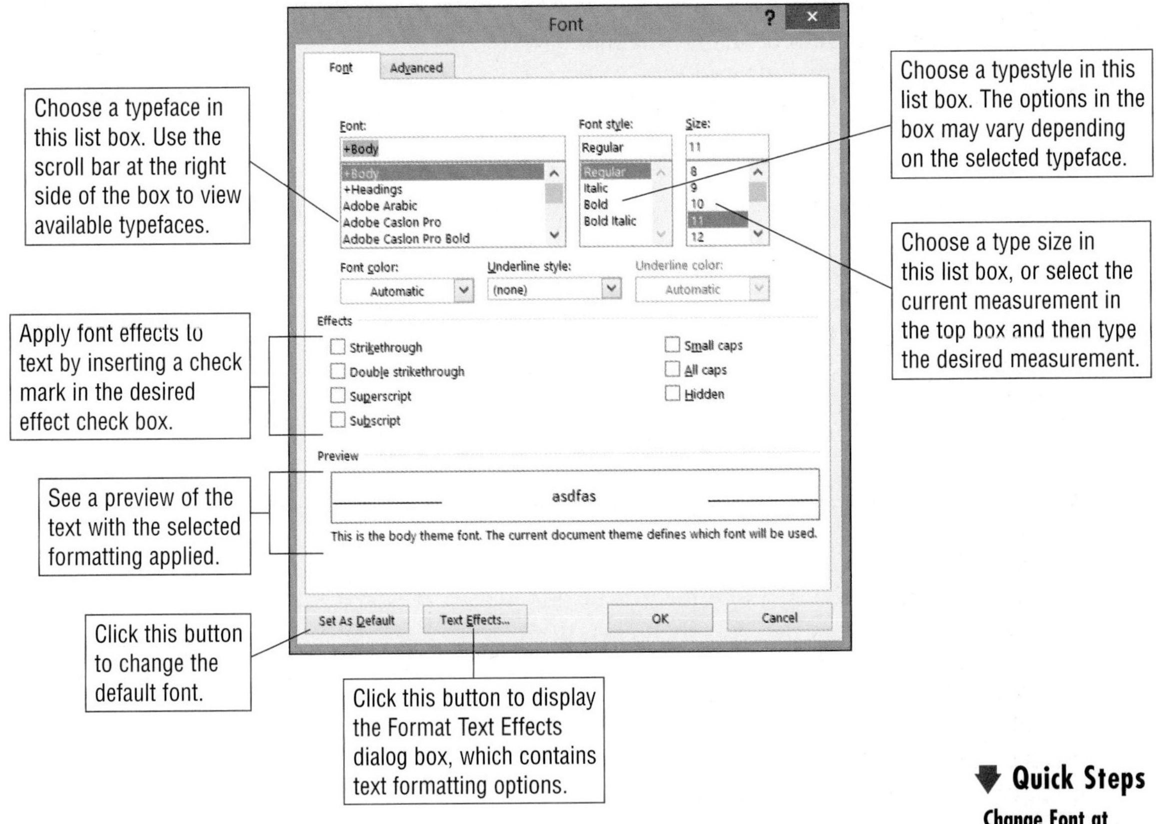

Changing Fonts at the Font Dialog Box

In addition to buttons in the Font group, you can use options at the Font dialog box shown in Figure 2.4 to change the typeface, type size, and typestyle of text as well as apply font effects. Display the Font dialog box by clicking the Font group dialog box launcher. The dialog box launcher is a small square containing a diagonal-pointing arrow that displays in the lower right corner of the Font group.

Quick Steps

Change Font at Font Dialog Box

1. Select text if necessary.
2. Click Font group dialog box launcher.
3. Choose desired options at dialog box.
4. Click OK.

Project 1d **Changing the Font at the Font Dialog Box** **Part 4 of 4**

1. With **WL1-C2-P1-CompTerms.docx** open, press Ctrl + End to move the insertion point to the end of the document. (Make sure the insertion point is positioned a double space below the last line of text.)
2. Type **Created by Susan Ashby** and then press the Enter key.
3. Type **Wednesday, February 18, 2015.**
4. Change the font to 13-point Candara and the color to dark blue for the entire document by completing the following steps:
   a. Press Ctrl + A to select the entire document.
   b. Click the Font group dialog box launcher.

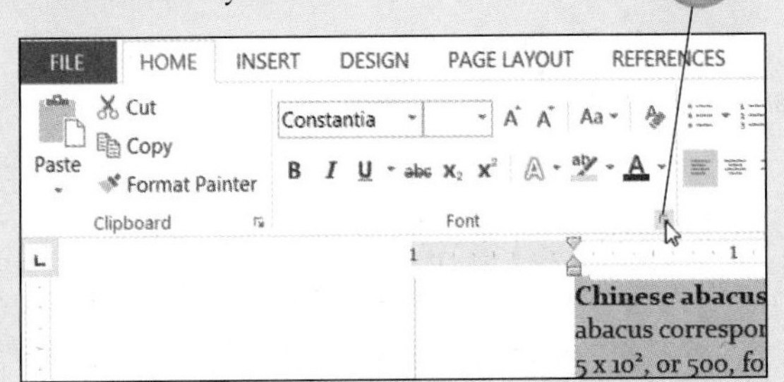

c. At the Font dialog box, click the up-pointing arrow at the right side of the *Font* list box to scroll down the list box and then click *Candara*.
d. Click in the *Size* text box, select the current number, and then type 13.
e. Click the down-pointing arrow at the right side of the *Font color* option box and then click the *Dark Blue* color in the *Standard Colors* section at the drop-down color palette.
f. Click OK to close the dialog box.

5. Double underline text by completing the following steps:
   a. Select *Wednesday, February 18, 2015*.
   b. Click the Font group dialog box launcher.
   c. At the Font dialog box, click the down-pointing arrow at the right side of the *Underline style* option box and then click the double-line option at the drop-down list.
   d. Click OK to close the dialog box.
6. Change text to small caps by completing the following steps:
   a. Select the text *Created by Susan Ashby* and *Wednesday, February 18, 2015*.
   b. Display the Font dialog box.
   c. Click the *Small caps* option in the *Effects* section. (This inserts a check mark in the check box.)
   d. Click OK to close the dialog box.

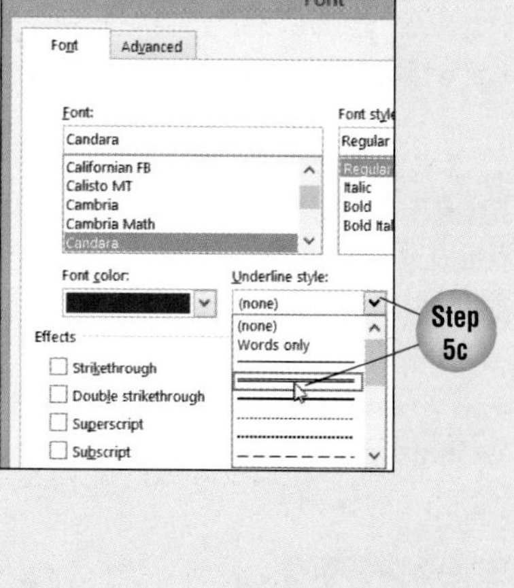

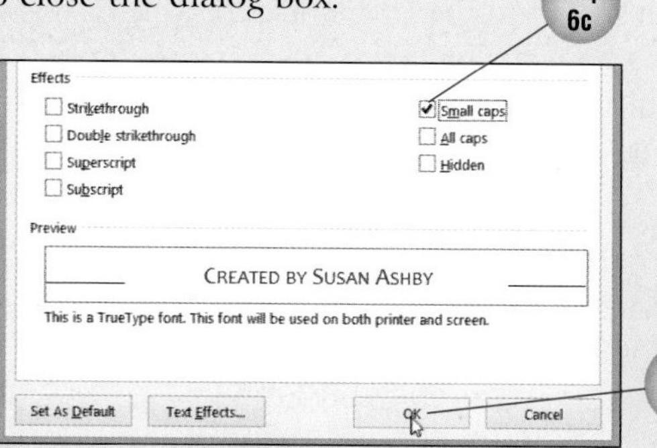

7. Save, print, and then close **WL1-C2-P1-CompTerms.docx**.

Project 2 Apply Styles and Themes — 3 Parts

You will open a document containing information on the life cycle of software, apply styles to text, and then change the style set. You will also apply a theme and then change the theme colors and fonts.

Applying Styles from a Style Set

A Word document contains a number of predesigned formats grouped into style sets. Several thumbnails of the styles in the default style set display in the Styles group on the HOME tab. Display additional styles by clicking the More button that displays at the right side of the style thumbnails. This displays a drop-down gallery of style choices. To apply a style, position the insertion point in the text or paragraph of text to which you want the style applied, click the More button at the right side of the style thumbnails in the Styles group, and then click the desired style at the drop-down gallery.

If you apply a heading style (such as Heading 1, Heading 2, and so on) to text, you can collapse and expand text below the heading(s). Hover your mouse over text with a heading style applied and a collapse triangle (solid, right- and down-pointing triangle) displays to the left of the heading. Click this collapse triangle and any text below the heading is collapsed (hidden). Redisplay the text below a heading by hovering the mouse over the heading text until an expand triangle displays (hollow, right-pointing triangle) and then click the expand triangle. This expands (redisplays) the text below the heading.

Quick Steps

Apply a Style
1. Position insertion point in desired text or paragraph of text.
2. Click More button in Styles group.
3. Click desired style.

Change Style Set
1. Click DESIGN tab.
2. Click desired style set thumbnail.

More

Removing Default Formatting

A Word document contains some default formatting, including 8 points of spacing after paragraphs and line spacing of 1.08. (You will learn more about these formatting options later in this chapter.) You can remove this default formatting, as well as any character formatting applied to text in your document by applying the No Spacing style to your text. This style is located in the Styles group.

Changing the Style Set

Word contains a number of style sets containing styles you can use to apply formatting to a document. To change to a different style set, click the DESIGN tab and then click the desired style set thumbnail in the Document Formatting group.

Project 2a **Applying Styles and Changing the Style Set** **Part 1 of 3**

1. Open **SoftwareCycle.docx**.
2. Save the document with Save As and name it **WL1-C2-P2-SoftwareCycle**.
3. Position the insertion point on any character in the title *COMMERCIAL LIFE CYCLE* and then click the *Heading 1* style thumbnail that displays in the Styles group.

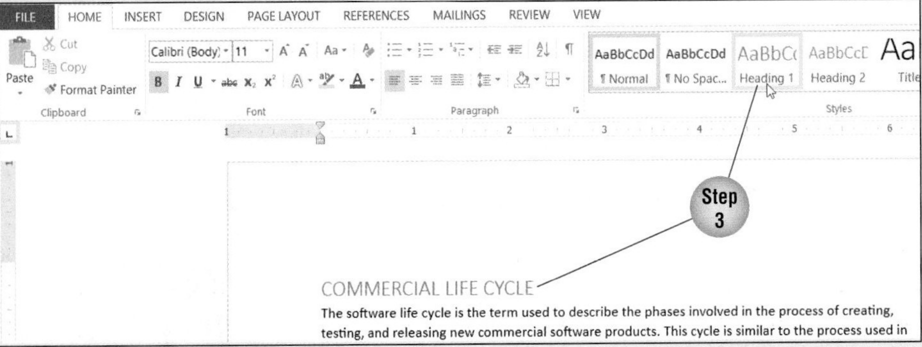

4. Position the insertion point on any character in the heading *Proposal and Planning* and then click the *Heading 2* style thumbnail that displays in the Styles group.

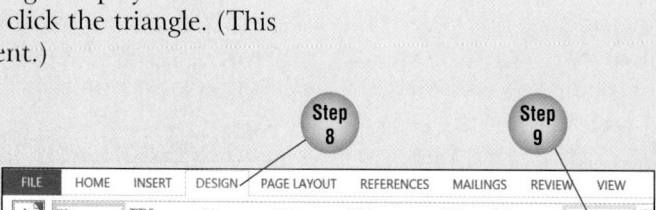

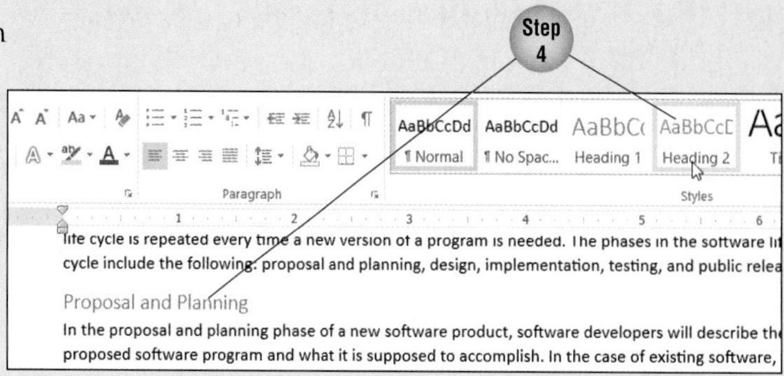

5. Position the insertion point on any character in the heading *Design* and then click the *Heading 2* style thumbnail in the Styles group.
6. Apply the Heading 2 style to the remaining headings (*Implementation*, *Testing*, and *Public Release and Support*).
7. Collapse and expand text below the heading with the Heading 1 style applied by completing the following steps:
   a. Hover the mouse over the heading *COMMERCIAL LIFE CYCLE* until a collapse triangle displays at the left side of the heading and then click the triangle. (This collapses all of the text below the heading.)
   b. Hover the mouse over the heading *COMMERCIAL LIFE CYCLE* until an expand triangle displays at the left side of the heading and then click the triangle. (This redisplays the text in the document.)
8. Click the DESIGN tab.
9. Click the *Casual* style set thumbnail in the Document Formatting group. (Notice how the Heading 1 and Heading 2 formatting changes.)
10. Save and then print **WL1-C2-P2-SoftwareCycle.docx**.

Applying a Theme

Quick Steps

Apply a Theme
1. Click DESIGN tab.
2. Click Themes button.
3. Click desired theme.

Themes

Word provides a number of themes for formatting text in your document. A theme is a set of formatting choices that include a color theme (a set of colors), a font theme (a set of heading and body text fonts), and an effects theme (a set of lines and fill effects). To apply a theme, click the DESIGN tab and then click the Themes button in the Document Formatting group. At the drop-down gallery that displays, click the desired theme. Hover the mouse pointer over a theme and the live preview feature will display your document with the theme formatting applied. With the live preview feature, you can see how the theme formatting affects your document before you make your final choice. Applying a theme is an easy way to give your document a professional look.

Project 2b Applying a Theme to Text in a Document

Part 2 of 3

1. With **WL1-C2-P2-SoftwareCycle.docx** open, click the DESIGN tab and then click the Themes button in the Document Formatting group.
2. At the drop-down gallery, hover your mouse pointer over several different themes and notice how the text formatting changes in your document.
3. Click the *Organic* theme.
4. Save and then print **WL1-C2-P2-SoftwareCycle.docx**.

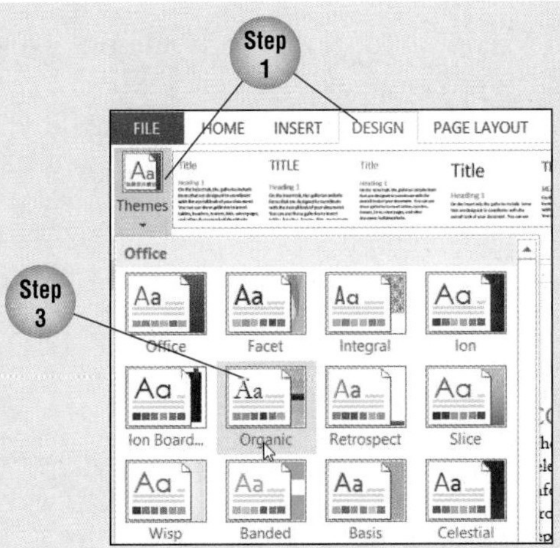

Customizing Style Sets and Themes

Customize the color applied by a style or theme with the Colors button in the Document Formatting group. Click the Colors button and a drop-down gallery displays with named color schemes. Customize the fonts applied to text in a document with the Fonts button in the Document Formatting group. Click this button and a drop-down gallery displays with font choices. Each font group in the drop-down gallery contains two choices. The first choice in the group is the font that is applied to headings, and the second choice is the font that is applied to body text in the document. If you are formatting a document containing graphics with lines and fills, you can apply a specific theme effect with options at the Effects button drop-down gallery.

The buttons in the Document Formatting group display a visual representation of the current theme. If you change the theme colors, the small color squares in the Themes button and the Colors button reflect the change. Change the theme fonts and the *As* on the Themes button as well as the uppercase *A* on the Fonts button reflect the change. If you change the theme effects, the circle in the Effects button reflects the change.

The Paragraph Spacing button in the Document Formatting group on the DESIGN tab contains predesigned paragraph spacing options. To change paragraph spacing, click the Paragraph Spacing button and then click the desired option at the drop-down gallery. You can hover your mouse over an option at the drop-down gallery and, after a moment, a ScreenTip displays with information about the formatting applied by the option. For example, if you hover the mouse over the *Compact* option at the side menu, a ScreenTip displays telling you that the Compact option will change the spacing before paragraphs to 0 points, the spacing after paragraphs to 4 points, and the line spacing to single spacing.

Quick Steps

Change Theme Color
1. Click DESIGN tab.
2. Click Colors button.
3. Click desired theme color option.

Change Theme Fonts
1. Click DESIGN tab.
2. Click Fonts button.
3. Click desired theme fonts option.

Change Paragraph Spacing
1. Click DESIGN tab.
2. Click Paragraph Spacing button.
3. Click desired paragraph spacing option.

Theme Colors

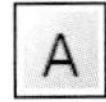
Theme Fonts

Theme Effects

Paragraph Spacing

Project 2c Customizing a Theme

Part 3 of 3

1. With **WL1-C2-P2-SoftwareCycle.docx** open, click the Colors button in the Document Formatting group and then click *Red Orange* at the drop-down gallery. (Notice how the colors in the title and headings change.)
2. Click the Fonts button arrow and then click the *Corbel* option. (Notice how the document text font changes.)
3. Click the Paragraph Spacing button and then, one at a time, hover the mouse over each of the paragraph spacing options, beginning with *Compact*. For each option, read the ScreenTip that explains the paragraph spacing applied by the option.
4. Click the *Double* option.

5. Scroll through the document and notice the paragraph spacing.
6. Change the paragraph spacing by clicking the Paragraph Spacing button and then clicking *Compact*.
7. Save, print, and then close **WL1-C2-P2-SoftwareCycle.docx**.

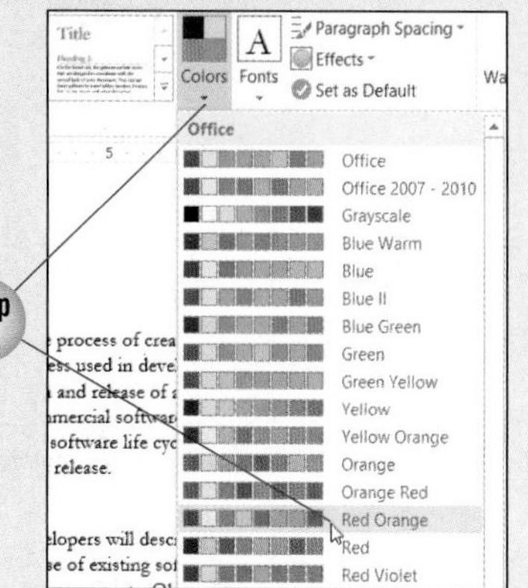

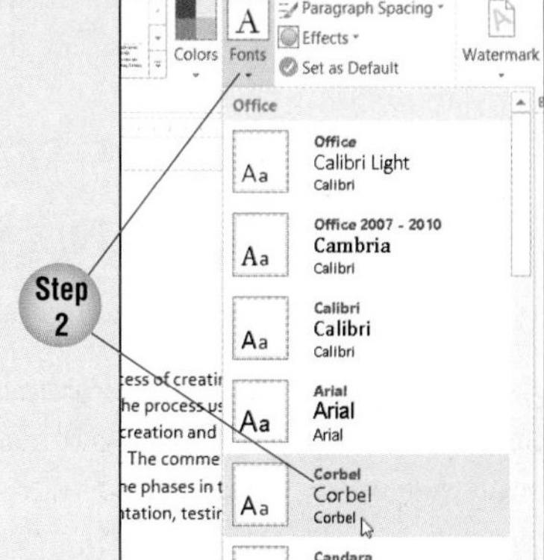

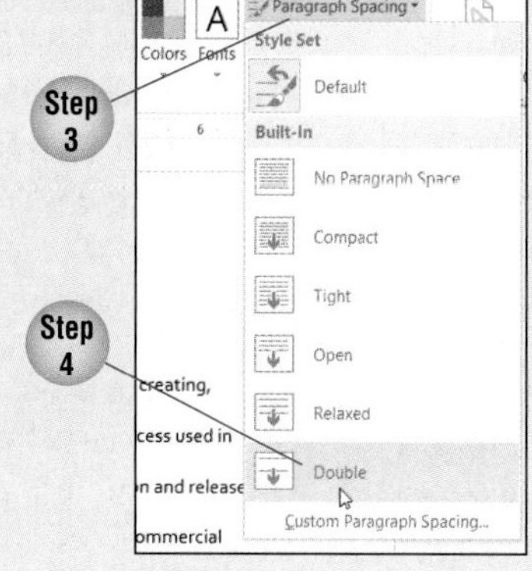

Project 3 Apply Paragraph Formatting and Use Format Painter

6 Parts

You will open a report on intellectual property and fair use issues and then format the report by changing the alignment of text in paragraphs, applying spacing before and after paragraphs of text, and repeating the last formatting action.

Changing Paragraph Alignment

By default, paragraphs in a Word document are aligned at the left margin and ragged at the right margin. Change this default alignment with buttons in the Paragraph group on the HOME tab or with keyboard shortcuts, as shown in Table 2.3. You can change the alignment of text in paragraphs before you type the text, or you can change the alignment of existing text.

Table 2.3 Paragraph Alignment Buttons and Keyboard Shortcuts

To align text	*Paragraph Group Button*	*Keyboard Shortcut*
At the left margin		Ctrl + L
Between margins		Ctrl + E
At the right margin		Ctrl + R
At the left and right margins		Ctrl + J

Changing Paragraph Alignment as You Type

If you change the alignment before typing text, the alignment formatting is inserted in the paragraph mark. As you type text and press Enter, the paragraph formatting is continued. For example, if you click the Center button in the Paragraph group, type text for the first paragraph, and then press the Enter key, the center alignment formatting is still active and the insertion point displays centered between the left and right margins. To display the paragraph symbols in a document, click the Show/Hide ¶ button in the Paragraph group. With the Show/Hide ¶ button active (displays with a light blue background), nonprinting formatting symbols display, such as the paragraph symbol ¶ indicating a press of the Enter key or a dot indicating a press of the spacebar.

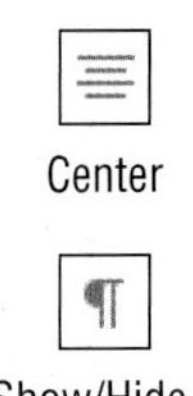

Center

Show/Hide ¶

Changing Paragraph Alignment of Existing Text

To change the alignment of existing text in a paragraph, position the insertion point anywhere within the paragraph. You do not need to select the entire paragraph. To change the alignment of several adjacent paragraphs in a document, select a portion of the first paragraph through a portion of the last paragraph. You do not need to select all of the text in the paragraphs.

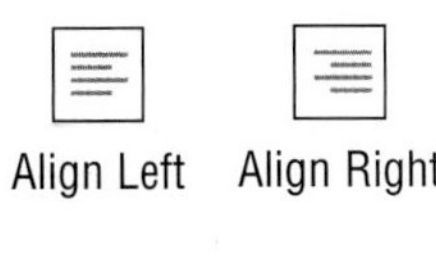

Align Left Align Right

To return paragraph alignment to the default (left-aligned), click the Align Left button in the Paragraph group. You can also return all paragraph formatting to the default with the keyboard shortcut Ctrl + Q. This keyboard shortcut removes paragraph formatting from selected text. If you want to remove all formatting from selected text, including character and paragraph formatting, click the Clear All Formatting button in the Font group.

HINT

Align text to help the reader follow the message of a document and to make the layout look appealing.

Project 3a **Changing Paragraph Alignment** **Part 1 of 6**

1. Open **IntelProp.docx**. (Some of the default formatting in this document has been changed.)
2. Save the document with Save As and name it **WL1-C2-P3-IntelProp**.
3. Click the Show/Hide ¶ button in the Paragraph group on the HOME tab to turn on the display of nonprinting characters.

Step 3

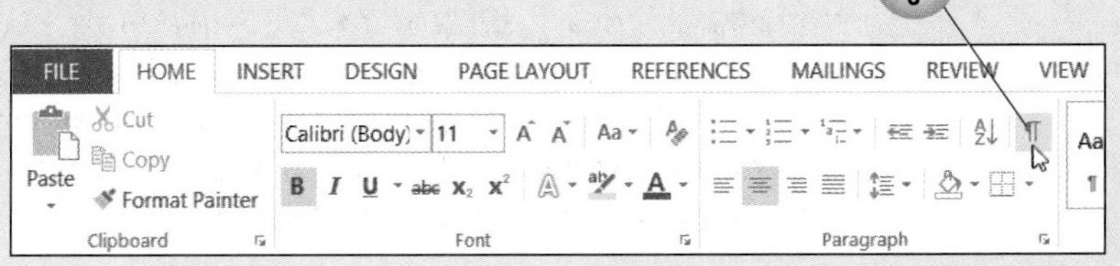

4. With the insertion point positioned immediately left of the paragraph symbol at the beginning of the document, press the Delete key to delete the blank paragraph.
5. Press Ctrl + A to select the entire document and then change the paragraph alignment to justified alignment by clicking the Justify button in the Paragraph group on the HOME tab.
6. Press Ctrl + End to move the insertion point to the end of the document.
7. Press the Enter key once.
8. Press Ctrl + E to move the insertion point to the middle of the page.
9. Type **Prepared by Clarissa Markham**.
10. Press Shift + Enter and then type **Edited by Joshua Streeter**.

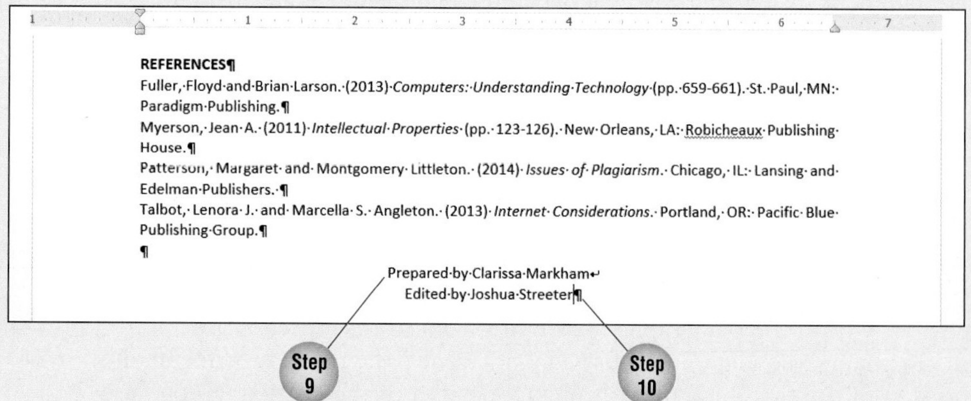

11. Click the Show/Hide ¶ button in the Paragraph group on the HOME tab to turn off the display of nonprinting characters.
12. Save **WL1-C2-P3-IntelProp.docx**.

Quick Steps

Change Paragraph Alignment

Click desired alignment button in Paragraph group on HOME tab.

OR

1. Click Paragraph group dialog box launcher.
2. Click *Alignment* option box arrow.
3. Click desired alignment.
4. Click OK.

Changing Alignment at the Paragraph Dialog Box

Along with buttons in the Paragraph group and keyboard shortcuts, you can also change paragraph alignment with the *Alignment* option box at the Paragraph dialog box shown in Figure 2.5. Display this dialog box by clicking the Paragraph group dialog box launcher. At the Paragraph dialog box, click the down-pointing arrow at the right side of the *Alignment* option box. At the drop-down list that displays, click the desired alignment option and then click OK to close the dialog box.

Figure 2.5 Paragraph Dialog Box with Alignment Options

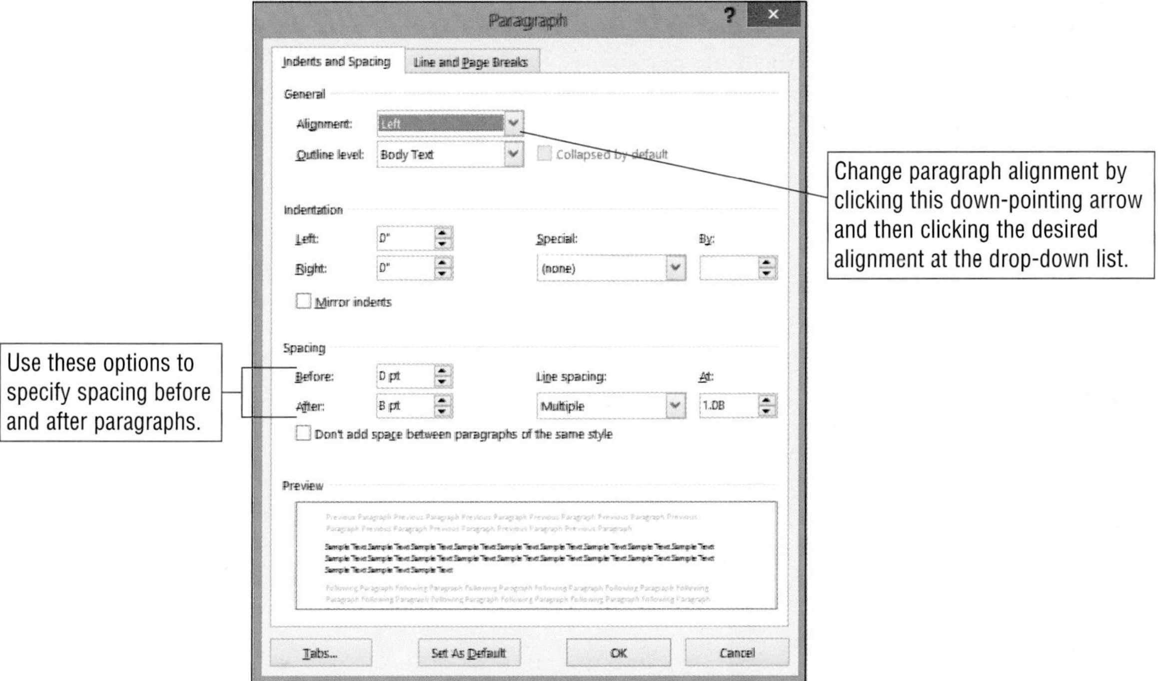

Project 3b Changing Paragraph Alignment at the Paragraph Dialog Box — Part 2 of 6

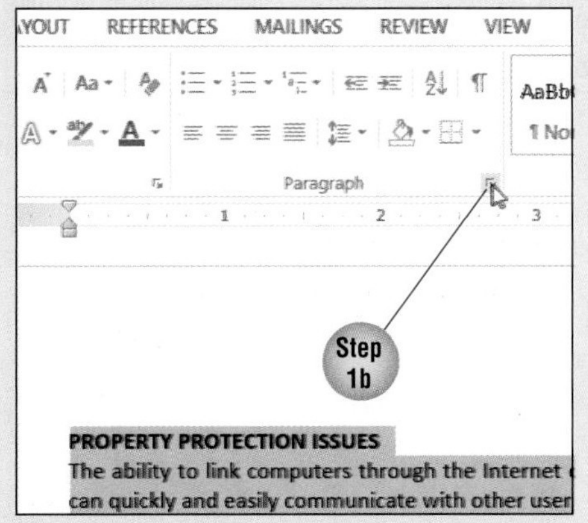

1. With **WL1-C2-P3-IntelProp.docx** open, change paragraph alignment by completing the following steps:
   a. Select the entire document.
   b. Click the Paragraph group dialog box launcher.
   c. At the Paragraph dialog box with the Indents and Spacing tab selected, click the down-pointing arrow at the right of the *Alignment* option box and then click *Left*.
   d. Click OK to close the dialog box.
   e. Deselect the text.
2. Change paragraph alignment by completing the following steps:
   a. Press Ctrl + End to move the insertion point to the end of the document.
   b. Position the insertion point on any character in the text *Prepared by Clarissa Markham*.
   c. Click the Paragraph group dialog box launcher.
   d. At the Paragraph dialog box with the Indents and Spacing tab selected, click the down-pointing arrow at the right of the *Alignment* option box and then click *Right*.

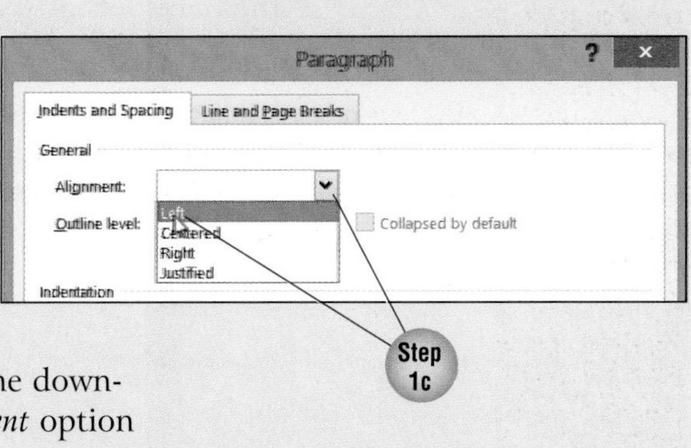

e. Click OK to close the dialog box. (The line of text containing the name *Clarissa Markham* and the line of text containing the name *Joshua Streeter* are both aligned at the right since you used the New Line command, Shift + Enter, to separate the lines of text without creating a new paragraph.)
3. Save and then print **WL1-C2-P3-IntelProp.docx**.

Quick Steps

Indent Text in Paragraph
Drag indent marker(s) on horizontal ruler.
OR
Press keyboard shortcut keys.
OR
1. Click Paragraph group dialog box launcher.
2. Insert measurement in *Left*, *Right*, and/or *By* text box.
3. Click OK.

Indenting Text in Paragraphs

By now you are familiar with the word wrap feature of Word, which ends lines and wraps the insertion point to the next line. To indent text from the left margin, the right margin, or both, use the indent buttons in the Paragraph group, on the PAGE LAYOUT tab, keyboard shortcuts, options from the Paragraph dialog box, markers on the horizontal ruler, or use the Alignment button that displays above the vertical ruler. Figure 2.6 identifies indent markers on the horizontal ruler and the Alignment button. Refer to Table 2.4 for methods for indenting text in a document. If the horizontal ruler is not visible, display the ruler by clicking the VIEW tab and then clicking the *Ruler* check box in the Show group to insert a check mark.

Figure 2.6 Horizontal Ruler and Indent Markers

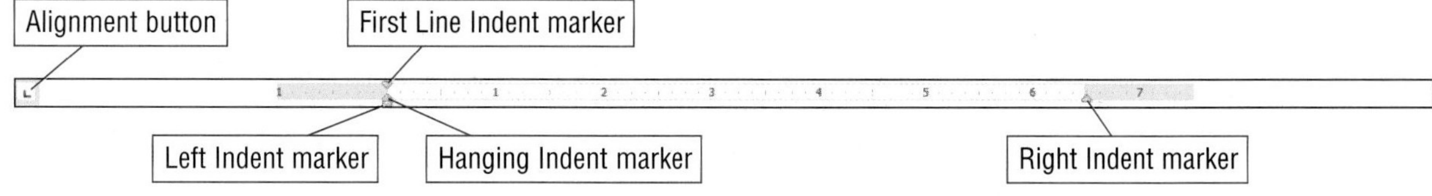

Table 2.4 Methods for Indenting Text

Indent	*Methods for Indenting*
First line of paragraph	• Press the Tab key. • Display the Paragraph dialog box, click the down-pointing arrow to the right of the *Special* list box, click *First line*, and then click OK. • Drag the First Line Indent marker on the horizontal ruler. • Click the Alignment button located left of the horizontal ruler and above the vertical ruler until the First Line Indent button displays, and then click the horizontal ruler at the desired location.

continues

Table 2.4 Methods for Indenting Text—*Continued*

Indent	*Methods for Indenting*
Text from left margin	• Click the Increase Indent button in the Paragraph group on the HOME tab to increase the indent or click the Decrease Indent button to decrease the indent. • Insert a measurement in the *Indent Left* measurement box in the Paragraph group on the PAGE LAYOUT tab. • Press Ctrl + M to increase the indent or press Ctrl + Shift + M to decrease the indent. • Display the Paragraph dialog box, type the desired indent measurement in the *Left* measurement box, and then click OK. • Drag the Left Indent marker on the horizontal ruler.
Text from right margin	• Insert a measurement in the *Indent Right* measurement box in the Paragraph group on the PAGE LAYOUT tab. • Display the Paragraph dialog box, type the desired indent measurement in the *Right* measurement box, and then click OK. • Drag the Right Indent marker on the horizontal ruler.
All lines of text except the first (called a hanging indent)	• Press Ctrl + T. (Press Ctrl + Shift + T to remove hanging indent.) • Display the Paragraph dialog box, click the down-pointing arrow to the right of the *Special* list box, click *Hanging*, and then click OK. • Click the Alignment button located left of the horizontal ruler and above the vertical ruler until the Hanging Indent button displays and then click the horizontal ruler at the desired location.
Text from both left and right margins	• Display the Paragraph dialog box, type the desired indent measurement in the *Left* measurement box, type the desired measurement in the *Right* measurement box, and then click OK. • Insert a measurement in the *Indent Right* and *Indent Left* measurement boxes in the Paragraph group on the PAGE LAYOUT tab. • Drag the Left Indent marker on the horizontal ruler; then drag the Right Indent marker on the horizontal ruler.

Project 3c Indenting Paragraphs

Part 3 of 6

1. With **WL1-C2-P3-IntelProp.docx** open, indent the first line of text in paragraphs by completing the following steps:
   a. Select the first two paragraphs of text in the document (the text after the title *PROPERTY PROTECTION ISSUES* and before the heading *Intellectual Property*.
   b. Make sure the horizontal ruler displays. (If it does not display, click the VIEW tab and then click the *Ruler* check box in the Show group to insert a check mark.)
   c. Position the mouse pointer on the First Line Indent marker on the horizontal ruler, hold down the left mouse button, drag the marker to the 0.5-inch mark, and then release the mouse button.

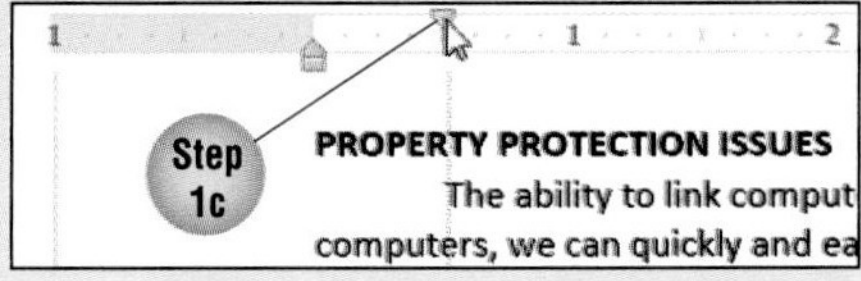

d. Select the paragraphs of text in the *Intellectual Property* section, and then drag the First Line Indent marker on the horizontal ruler to the 0.5-inch mark.

e. Select the paragraphs of text in the *Fair Use* section, click the Alignment button located at the left side of the horizontal ruler until the First Line Indent button displays, and then click the horizontal ruler at the 0.5-inch mark.

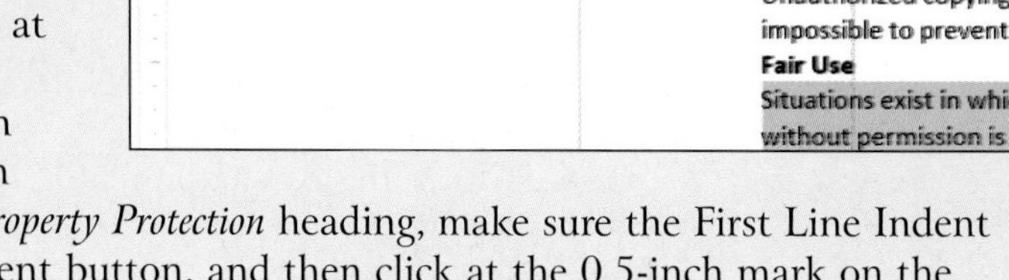

f. Position the insertion point on any character in the paragraph of text below the *Intellectual Property Protection* heading, make sure the First Line Indent button displays in the Alignment button, and then click at the 0.5-inch mark on the horizontal ruler.

2. Since the text in the second paragraph in the *Fair Use* section is a quote, indent the text from the left and right margins by completing the following steps:
   a. Position the insertion point anywhere within the second paragraph in the *Fair Use* section (the paragraph that begins *[A] copyrighted work, including such*).
   b. Click the Paragraph group dialog box launcher.
   c. At the Paragraph dialog box, with the Indents and Spacing tab selected, select the current measurement in the *Left* measurement box and then type 0.5.
   d. Select the current measurement in the *Right* measurement box and then type 0.5.
   e. Click the down-pointing arrow at the right side of the *Special* list box and then click *(none)* at the drop-down list.

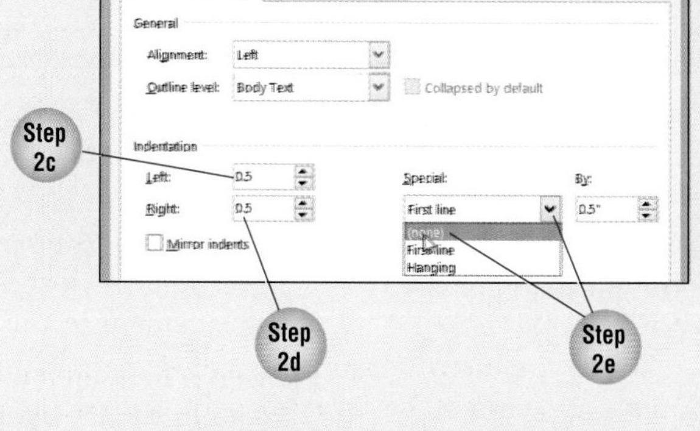

   f. Click OK or press Enter.

3. Create a hanging indent for the first paragraph in the *REFERENCES* section by positioning the insertion point anywhere in the first paragraph below *REFERENCES* and then pressing Ctrl + T.

4. Create a hanging indent for the second paragraph in the *REFERENCES* section by completing the following steps:
   a. Position the insertion point anywhere in the second paragraph in the *REFERENCES* section.
   b. Click the Alignment button located to the left of the horizontal ruler and above the vertical ruler until the Hanging Indent button displays.
   c. Click the 0.5-inch mark on the horizontal ruler.

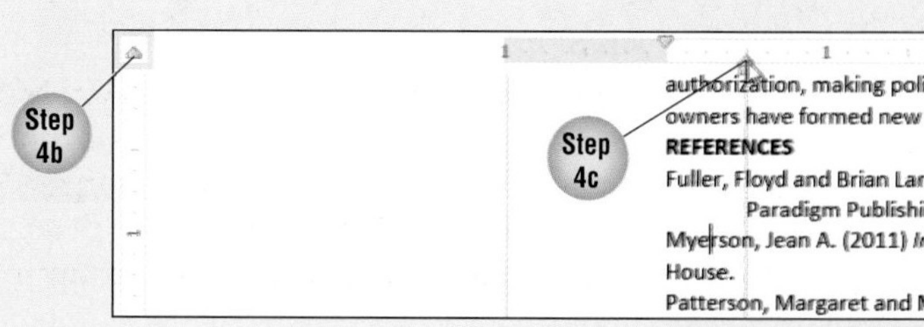

5. Create a hanging indent for the third and fourth paragraphs by completing the following steps:
   a. Select a portion of the third and fourth paragraphs.
   b. Click the Paragraph group dialog box launcher.
   c. At the Paragraph dialog box with the Indents and Spacing tab selected, click the down-pointing arrow at the right side of the *Special* list box and then click *Hanging* at the drop-down list.
   d. Click OK or press Enter.
6. Save **WL1-C2-P3-IntelProp.docx**.

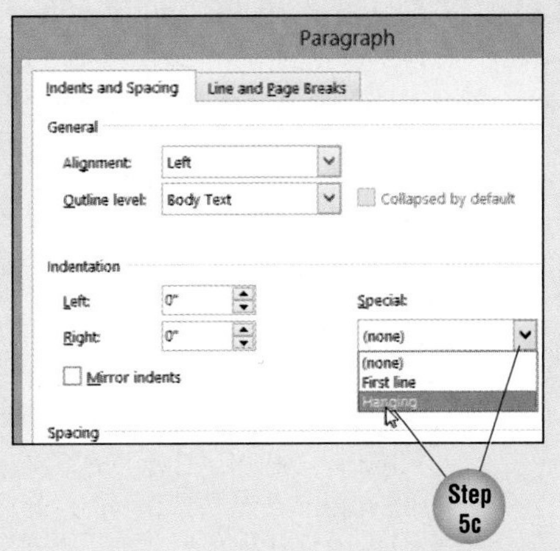

Spacing Before and After Paragraphs

By default, Word applies 8 points of additional spacing after a paragraph. You can remove this spacing, increase or decrease the spacing, and insert spacing above the paragraph. To change spacing before or after a paragraph, use the *Spacing Before* and *Spacing After* measurement boxes located in the Paragraph group on the PAGE LAYOUT tab or the *Before* and *After* options at the Paragraph dialog box with the Indents and Spacing tab selected. You can also add spacing before and after paragraphs at the Line and Paragraph Spacing button drop-down list.

HINT

Line spacing determines the amount of vertical space between lines, while paragraph spacing determines the amount of space above or below paragraphs of text.

Spacing before or after a paragraph is part of the paragraph and will be moved, copied, or deleted with the paragraph. If a paragraph, such as a heading, contains spacing before it and the paragraph falls at the top of a page, Word ignores the spacing.

Spacing before or after paragraphs is added in points, and a vertical inch contains approximately 72 points. To add spacing before or after a paragraph, click the PAGE LAYOUT tab, select the current measurement in the *Spacing Before* or the *Spacing After* measurement box, and then type the desired number of points. You can also click the up- or down-pointing arrows at the right side of the *Spacing Before* and *Spacing After* measurement boxes to increase or decrease the amount of spacing.

Repeating the Last Action

If you apply formatting to text and then want to apply the same formatting to other text in the document, consider using the Repeat command. To use this command, apply the desired formatting, move the insertion point to the next location where you want the formatting applied, and then press the F4 function key or press Ctrl + Y. The Repeat command will repeat only the last command you executed.

Quick Steps

Repeat Last Action
Press F4.
OR
Press Ctrl + Y.

Project 3d Spacing Before and After Paragraphs and Repeating Last Action Part 4 of 6

1. With **WL1-C2-P3-IntelProp.docx** open, add 6 points of spacing before and after each paragraph in the document by completing the following steps:
   a. Select the entire document.
   b. Click the PAGE LAYOUT tab.
   c. Click the up-pointing arrow at the right side of the *Spacing Before* measurement box in the Paragraph group (this inserts *6 pt* in the box).
   d. Click the up-pointing arrow at the right side of the *Spacing After* measurement box in the Paragraph group (this inserts *6 pt* in the box).
2. Add an additional 6 points of spacing above the headings by completing the following steps:
   a. Position the insertion point on any character in the heading *Intellectual Property* and then click the up-pointing arrow at the right side of the *Spacing Before* measurement box (this changes the measurement to *12 pt*).
   b. Position the insertion point on any character in the heading *Fair Use* and then press F4. (F4 is the Repeat command.)
   c. Position the insertion point on any character in the heading *Intellectual Property Protection* and then press F4.
   d. Position the insertion point on any character in the heading *REFERENCES* and then press Ctrl + Y. (Ctrl + Y is also the Repeat command.)
3. Save **WL1-C2-P3-IntelProp.docx**.

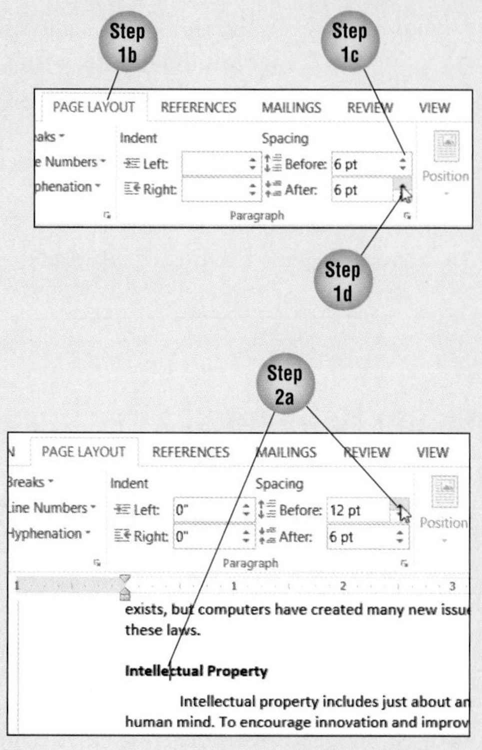

Formatting with Format Painter

Quick Steps

Format with Format Painter
1. Format text.
2. Double-click Format Painter button.
3. Select text.
4. Click Format Painter button.

Format Painter

The Clipboard group on the HOME tab contains a button for copying formatting and displays in the Clipboard group as a paintbrush. To use this button, called Format Painter, position the insertion point on a character containing the desired formatting, click the Format Painter button, and then select text to which you want the formatting applied. When you click the Format Painter button, the mouse I-beam pointer displays with a paintbrush attached. If you want to apply the formatting a single time, click the Format Painter button once. If you want to apply the formatting in more than one location in the document, double-click the Format Painter button and then select text to which you want formatting applied. When you are finished, click the Format Painter button to turn it off. You can also turn off Format Painter by pressing the Esc key.

Project 3e Formatting Headings with Format Painter Part 5 of 6

1. With **WL1-C2-P3-IntelProp.docx** open, click the HOME tab.
2. Select the entire document and then change the font to 12-point Cambria.
3. Select the title *PROPERTY PROTECTION ISSUES*, click the Center button in the Paragraph group, and then change the font to 16-point Candara bold.
4. Apply 16-point Candara bold formatting to the *REFERENCES* heading by completing the following steps:
   a. Click any character in the title *PROPERTY PROTECTION ISSUES*.
   b. Click the Format Painter button in the Clipboard group.

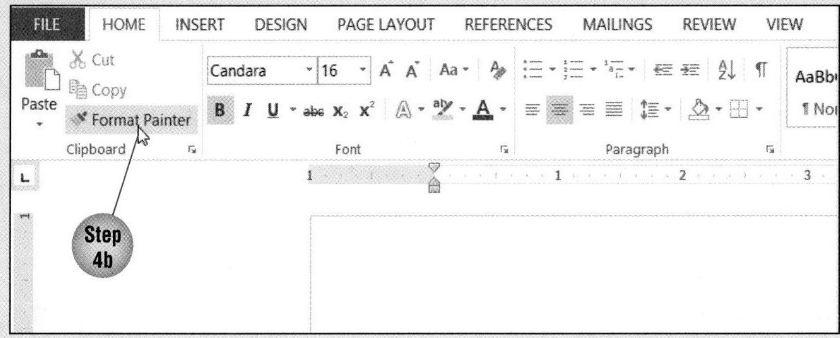

   c. Press Ctrl + End to move the insertion point to the end of the document and then click any character in the heading *REFERENCES*. (This applies the 16-point Candara bold formatting and centers the text.)
5. With the insertion point positioned on any character in the heading *REFERENCES*, add an additional 6 points of spacing before the heading (for a total of 12 points before the heading).
6. Select the heading *Intellectual Property* and then change the font to 14-point Candara bold.
7. Use the Format Painter button and apply 14-point Candara bold formatting to the other headings by completing the following steps:
   a. Position the insertion point on any character in the heading *Intellectual Property*.
   b. Double-click the Format Painter button in the Clipboard group.
   c. Using the mouse, select the heading *Fair Use*.
   d. Using the mouse, select the heading *Intellectual Property Protection*.
   e. Click the Format Painter button in the Clipboard group. (This turns off the feature.)
   f. Deselect the heading.
8. Save **WL1-C2-P3-IntelProp.docx**.

Changing Line Spacing

Quick Steps

Change Line Spacing
1. Click Line and Paragraph Spacing button in Paragraph group.
2. Click desired option at drop-down list.

OR

Press shortcut command keys.

OR

1. Click Paragraph group dialog box launcher.
2. Click *Line Spacing* option box arrow.
3. Click desired line spacing option.
4. Click OK.

OR

1. Click Paragraph group dialog box launcher.
2. Type line measurement in *At* measurement box.
3. Click OK.

Line and Paragraph Spacing

The default line spacing for a document is 1.08. (The line spacing for the **IntelProp.docx** document, which you opened at the beginning of Project 3, had been changed to single.) In certain situations, Word automatically adjusts the line spacing. For example, if you insert a large character or object, such as a graphic, Word increases the line spacing of that specific line. But you also may sometimes decide to change the line spacing for a section or for the entire document.

Change line spacing using the Line and Paragraph Spacing button in the Paragraph group on the HOME tab, with keyboard shortcuts, or with options from the Paragraph dialog box. Table 2.5 displays the keyboard shortcuts to change line spacing.

You can also change line spacing at the Paragraph dialog box with the *Line spacing* option or the *At* measurement box. If you click the down-pointing arrow at the right side of the *Line spacing* option, a drop-down list displays with a variety of spacing options. For example, to change the line spacing to double spacing, click *Double* at the drop-down list. You can type a specific line spacing measurement in the *At* measurement box. For example, to change the line spacing to 1.75, type *1.75* in the *At* measurement box.

Table 2.5 Line Spacing Keyboard Shortcuts

Press	*To change line spacing to*
Ctrl + 1	single spacing
Ctrl + 2	double spacing
Ctrl + 5	1.5 line spacing

Project 3f **Changing Line Spacing** **Part 6 of 6**

1. With **WL1-C2-P3-IntelProp.docx** open, change the line spacing for all paragraphs to double spacing by completing the following steps:
   a. Select the entire document.
   b. Click the Line and Paragraph Spacing button located in the Paragraph group on the HOME tab.
   c. Click *2.0* at the drop-down list.
2. With the entire document still selected, press Ctrl + 5. (This changes the line spacing to 1.5 line spacing.)

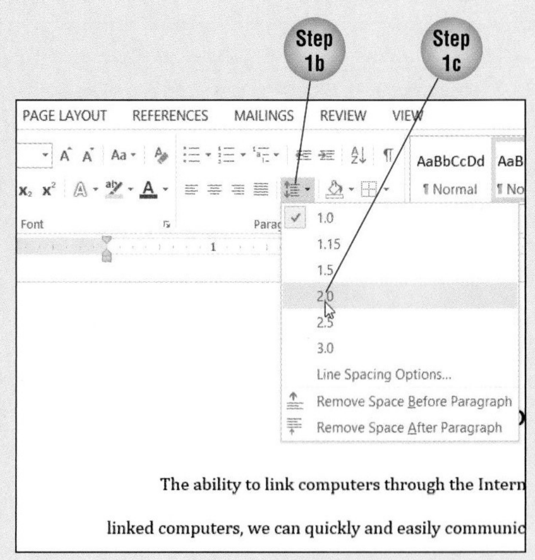

3. Change the line spacing to 1.3 using the Paragraph dialog box by completing the following steps:
   a. With the entire document still selected, click the Paragraph group dialog box launcher.
   b. At the Paragraph dialog box, make sure the Indents and Spacing tab is selected, click inside the *At* measurement box, and then type 1.3. (This measurement box is located to the right of the *Line spacing* option box.)
   c. Click OK or press Enter.
   d. Deselect the text.
4. Save, print, and then close **WL1-C2-P3-IntelProp.docx**.

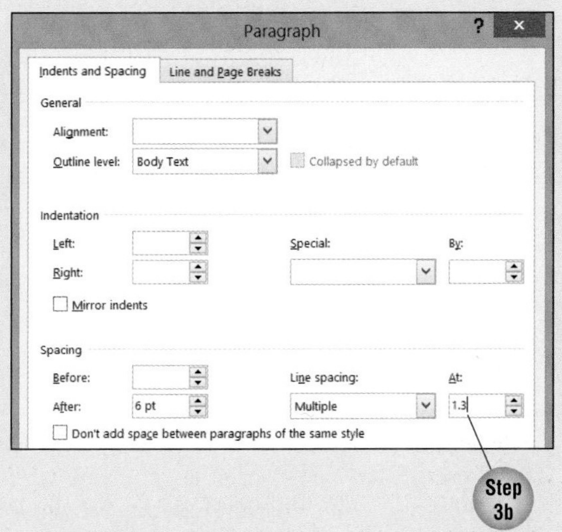

Project 4 Format Computer Issues Document — 2 Parts

You will open a document containing two computer-related problems to solve, reveal the formatting, compare the formatting, and make formatting changes.

Revealing and Comparing Formatting

Display formatting applied to specific text in a document at the Reveal Formatting task pane, as shown in Figure 2.7. The Reveal Formatting task pane displays font, paragraph, and section formatting applied to text where the insertion point is

Figure 2.7 Reveal Formatting Task Pane

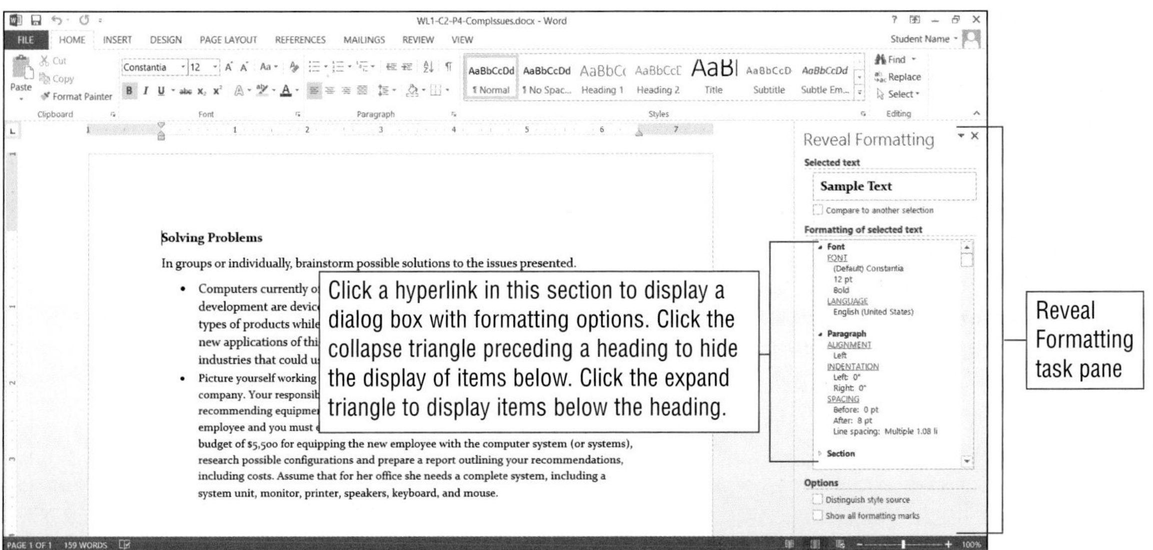

positioned or to selected text. Display the Reveal Formatting task pane with the keyboard shortcut Shift + F1. Generally, a collapse triangle (a solid, right-and-down-pointing triangle) precedes *Font* and *Paragraph*, and an expand triangle (a hollow, right-pointing triangle) precedes *Section* in the *Formatting of selected text* list box in the Reveal Formatting task pane. Click the collapse triangle to hide any items below a heading, and click the expand triangle to reveal items. Some of the items below headings in the *Formatting of selected text* list box are hyperlinks. Click a hyperlink and a dialog box displays with the specific option.

Project 4a Revealing Formatting

Part 1 of 2

1. Open **CompIssues.docx**.
2. Save the document with Save As and name it **WL1-C2-P4-CompIssues**.
3. Press Shift + F1 to display the Reveal Formatting task pane.
4. Click anywhere in the heading *Solving Problems* and then notice the formatting information that displays in the Reveal Formatting task pane.
5. Click in the bulleted paragraph and notice the formatting information that displays in the Reveal Formatting task pane.

Quick Steps

Compare Formatting
1. Press Shift + F1 to display Reveal Formatting task pane.
2. Click or select text.
3. Click *Compare to another selection* check box.
4. Click or select text.

Along with displaying formatting applied to text, you can use the Reveal Formatting task pane to compare formatting of two text selections to determine what formatting is different. To compare formatting, select the first instance of formatting to be compared, click the *Compare to another selection* check box, and then select the second instance of formatting to compare. Any differences between the two selections display in the *Formatting differences* list box.

Project 4b Comparing Formatting

Part 2 of 2

1. With **WL1-C2-P4-CompIssues.docx** open, make sure the Reveal Formatting task pane displays. If it does not, turn it on by pressing Shift + F1.
2. Select the first bulleted paragraph (the paragraph that begins *Computers currently offer both*).
3. Click the *Compare to another selection* check box to insert a check mark.
4. Select the second bulleted paragraph (the paragraph that begins *Picture yourself working in the*).
5. Determine the formatting differences by reading the information in the *Formatting differences* list box. (The list box displays *12 pt -> 11 pt* below the FONT hyperlink, indicating that the difference is point size.)
6. Format the second bulleted paragraph so it is set in 12-point size.

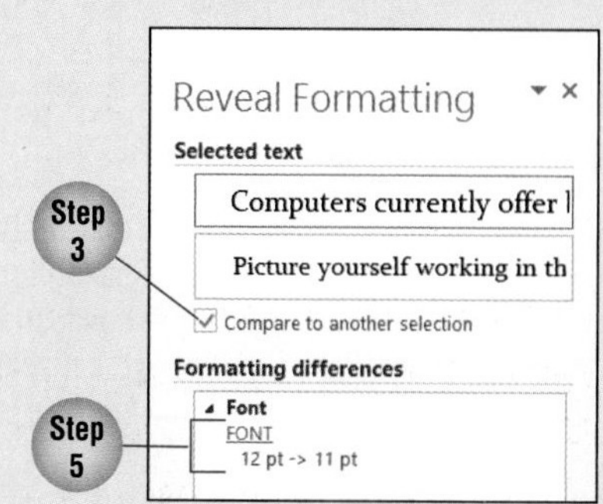

7. Click the *Compare to another selection* check box to remove the check mark.
8. Select the word *visual,* which displays in the first sentence in the first bulleted paragraph.
9. Click the *Compare to another selection* check box to insert a check mark.
10. Select the word *audio,* which displays in the first sentence of the first bulleted paragraph.
11. Determine the formatting differences by reading the information in the *Formatting differences* list box.
12. Format the word *audio* so it matches the formatting of the word *visual.*
13. Click the *Compare to another selection* check box to remove the check mark.
14. Close the Reveal Formatting task pane by clicking the Close button (contains an X), which displays in the upper right corner of the task pane.
15. Save, print, and then close **WL1-C2-P4-CompIssues.docx**.

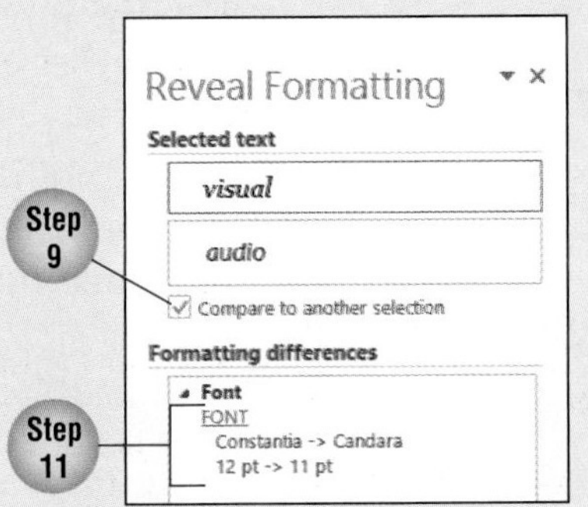

Chapter Summary

- A font consists of three parts: typeface, type size, and typestyle.
- A typeface (font) is a set of characters with a common design and shape. Typefaces are either monospaced, allotting the same amount of horizontal space for each character, or proportional, allotting a varying amount of space for each character. Proportional typefaces are divided into two main categories: serif and sans serif.
- Type size is measured in point size; the higher the point size, the larger the characters.
- A typestyle is a variation of style within a certain typeface, such as bold, italic, and underline. You can apply typestyle formatting with some of the buttons in the Font group.
- With some of the buttons in the Font group, you can apply font effects such as superscript, subscript, and strikethrough.
- The Mini toolbar automatically displays above selected text. Use buttons on this toolbar to apply formatting to selected text.
- With options at the Font dialog box, you can change the font, font size, and font style and apply specific effects. Display this dialog box by clicking the Font group dialog box launcher.
- A Word document contains a number of predesigned formats grouped into style sets. Change to a different style set by clicking the DESIGN tab and then clicking the desired style set thumbnail in the Document Formatting group.
- Apply a theme and change theme colors, fonts, and effects with buttons in the Document Formatting group on the DESIGN tab.
- Click the Paragraph Spacing button in the Document Formatting group on the DESIGN tab to apply a predesigned paragraph spacing option to text in a document.

- By default, paragraphs in a Word document are aligned at the left margin and ragged at the right margin. Change this default alignment with buttons in the Paragraph group, at the Paragraph dialog box, or with keyboard shortcuts.
- To turn on or off the display of nonprinting characters such as paragraph marks, click the Show/Hide ¶ button in the Paragraph group on the HOME tab.
- Indent text in paragraphs with indent buttons in the Paragraph group on the HOME tab, buttons in the Paragraph group on the PAGE LAYOUT tab, keyboard shortcuts, options from the Paragraph dialog box, markers on the horizontal ruler, or use the Alignment button above the vertical ruler.
- Increase and/or decrease spacing before and after paragraphs using the *Spacing Before* and *Spacing After* measurement boxes in the Paragraph group on the PAGE LAYOUT tab or using the *Before* and/or *After* options at the Paragraph dialog box.
- Use the Format Painter button in the Clipboard group on the HOME tab to copy formatting already applied to text to different locations in the document.
- Change line spacing with the Line and Paragraph Spacing button in the Paragraph group on the HOME tab, keyboard shortcuts, or options from the Paragraph dialog box.
- Display the Reveal Formatting task pane to display formatting applied to text. Use the *Compare to another selection* option in the task pane to compare formatting of two text selections to determine what formatting is different.

Commands Review

FEATURE	RIBBON TAB, GROUP	BUTTON	KEYBOARD SHORTCUT
bold text	HOME, Font	B	Ctrl + B
center-align text	HOME, Paragraph		Ctrl + E
change case of text	HOME, Font	Aa	Shift + F3
clear all formatting	HOME, Font		
clear character formatting			Ctrl + spacebar
clear paragraph formatting			Ctrl + Q
decrease font size	HOME, Font	A	Ctrl + Shift + <
display nonprinting characters	HOME, Paragraph	¶	Ctrl + Shift + *
font	HOME, Font	Calibri (Body)	
font color	HOME, Font	A	
Font dialog box	HOME, Font		Ctrl + Shift + F

FEATURE	RIBBON TAB, GROUP	BUTTON	KEYBOARD SHORTCUT
Format Painter	HOME, Clipboard		Ctrl + Shift + C Ctrl + Shift + V
highlight text	HOME, Font		
increase font size	HOME, Font		Ctrl + Shift + >
italicize text	HOME, Font		Ctrl + I
justify text	HOME, Paragraph		Ctrl + J
left-align text	HOME, Paragraph		Ctrl + L
line spacing	HOME, Paragraph		Ctrl + 1 (single) Ctrl + 2 (double) Ctrl + 5 (1.5)
Paragraph dialog box	HOME, Paragraph		
paragraph spacing	DESIGN, Document Formatting		
repeat last action			F4 or Ctrl + Y
Reveal Formatting task pane			Shift + F1
right-align text	HOME, Paragraph		Ctrl + R
spacing after paragraph	PAGE LAYOUT, Paragraph	After: 0 pt	
spacing before paragraph	PAGE LAYOUT, Paragraph	Before: 0 pt	
strikethrough text	HOME, Font		
subscript text	HOME, Font		Ctrl + =
superscript text	HOME, Font		Ctrl + Shift + +
text effects and typography	HOME, Font		
theme colors	DESIGN, Document Formatting		
theme effects	DESIGN, Document Formatting		
theme tonts	DESIGN, Document Formatting		
themes	DESIGN, Document Formatting		
underline text	HOME, Font		Ctrl + U

Concepts Check Test Your Knowledge 

Completion: In the space provided at the right, indicate the correct term, symbol, or command.

1. The Bold button is located in this group on the HOME tab. ________________
2. Click this button in the Font group to remove all formatting from selected text. ________________
3. Proportional typefaces are divided into two main categories: serif and this. ________________
4. This is the keyboard shortcut to italicize selected text. ________________
5. This term refers to text that is raised slightly above the regular text line. ________________
6. This automatically displays above selected text. ________________
7. Click this to display the Font dialog box. ________________
8. Change style sets with options in this group on the DESIGN tab. ________________
9. Apply a theme and change theme colors, fonts, and effects with buttons in the Document Formatting group on this tab. ________________
10. This is the default paragraph alignment. ________________
11. Click this button in the Paragraph group on the HOME tab to turn on the display of nonprinting characters. ________________
12. Return all paragraph formatting to normal with this keyboard shortcut. ________________
13. Click this button in the Paragraph group on the HOME tab to align text at the right margin. ________________
14. In this type of indent, the first line of text remains at the left margin and the remaining lines of text align at the first tab. ________________
15. Repeat the last action by pressing F4 or using this keyboard shortcut. ________________
16. Use this button in the Clipboard group on the HOME tab to copy formatting already applied to text to different locations in the document. ________________
17. Change line spacing to 1.5 with this keyboard shortcut. ________________
18. Press these keys to display the Reveal Formatting task pane. ________________

Skills Check Assess Your Performance

Assessment 1

APPLY CHARACTER FORMATTING TO A LEASE AGREEMENT DOCUMENT

1. Open **LeaseAgrmnt.docx**.
2. Save the document with Save As and name it **WL1-C2-A1-LeaseAgrmnt**.
3. Press Ctrl + End to move the insertion point to the end of the document and then type the text shown in Figure 2.8. Bold, italicize, and underline text as shown.
4. Select the entire document and then change the font to 12-point Candara.
5. Select and then bold *THIS LEASE AGREEMENT* located in the first paragraph.
6. Select and then italicize *12 o'clock midnight* in the *Term* section.
7. Select the title *LEASE AGREEMENT* and then change the font to 16-point Corbel and the font color to Dark Blue. (Make sure the title retains the bold formatting.)
8. Select the heading *Term*, change the font to 14-point Corbel, and apply small caps formatting. (Make sure the heading retains the bold formatting.)
9. Use Format Painter to change the formatting to small caps in 14-point Corbel for the remaining headings (*Rent*, *Damage Deposit*, *Use of Premises*, *Condition of Premises*, *Alterations and Improvements*, *Damage to Premises*, and *Inspection of Premises*).
10. Save, print, and then close **WL1-C2-A1-LeaseAgrmnt.docx**.

Figure 2.8 Assessment 1

Inspection of Premises

Lessor shall have the right at all reasonable times during the term of this Agreement to exhibit the Premises and to display the usual *for rent* or *vacancy* signs on the Premises at any time within <u>forty-five</u> days before the expiration of this Lease.

Assessment 2

APPLY STYLES, A STYLE SET, AND A THEME TO A HARDWARE TECHNOLOGY DOCUMENT

1. Open **NetworkHardware.docx**.
2. Save the document with Save As and name it **WL1-C2-A2-NetworkHardware**.
3. Apply the Heading 1 style to the title *Network Hardware*.
4. Apply the Heading 2 style to the headings in the document (*Hubs*, *Switches*, *Repeaters*, *Routers*, *Gateways*, *Bridges*, and *Network Interface Cards*).
5. Apply the Lines (Stylish) style set.
6. Apply the Savon theme.
7. Apply the Green theme colors.
8. Apply the Georgia theme fonts.
9. Apply the Open paragraph spacing.
10. Highlight in yellow the second sentence in the *Hubs* section.
11. Save, print, and then close **WL1-C2-A2-NetworkHardware.docx**.

Assessment

3 APPLY CHARACTER AND PARAGRAPH FORMATTING TO AN EMPLOYEE PRIVACY DOCUMENT

1. Open **WorkplacePrivacy.docx**.
2. Save the document with Save As and name it **WL1-C2-A3-WorkplacePrivacy**.
3. Move the insertion point to the beginning of the document and then type WORKPLACE PRIVACY.
4. Select the text from the beginning of the first paragraph to the end of the document (make sure you select the blank line at the end of the document) and then make the following changes:
   a. Change the line spacing to 1.5 lines.
   b. Change the spacing after paragraphs to 0 points.
   c. Indent the first line of each paragraph 0.5 inch.
   d. Change the paragraph alignment to justified alignment.
5. Move the insertion point to the end of the document and, if necessary, drag the First Line Indent marker on the horizontal ruler back to 0 inch. Type the text shown in Figure 2.9. (Create a hanging indent, as shown in Figure 2.9.)
6. Select the entire document and then change the font to Constantia.
7. Select the title *WORKPLACE PRIVACY*, center the title, change the font to 14-point Calibri bold, and then apply the Fill - Orange, Accent 2, Outline - Accent 2 text effect (third column, first row in the Text Effects and Typography button drop-down gallery).
8. Use the Format Painter to apply the same formatting to the title *BIBLIOGRAPHY* that you applied to the title *WORKPLACE PRIVACY*.
9. Save, print, and then close **WL1-C2-A3-WorkplacePrivacy.docx**.

Figure 2.9 Assessment 3

BIBLIOGRAPHY

Amaral, H. G. (2014). *Privacy in the workplace,* 2nd edition (pp. 103-112). Denver, CO: Goodwin Publishing Group.

Visual Benchmark Demonstrate Your Proficiency

CREATE AN ACTIVE LISTENING REPORT

1. At a blank document, press the Enter key twice and then type the document shown in Figure 2.10. Set the body text in 12-point Cambria, set the title in 16-point Candara bold, set the headings in 14-point Candara bold, change the paragraph spacing after the headings to 6 points, change the font color to dark blue for the entire document, and then apply additional formatting so the document appears as shown in the figure.
2. Save the document and name it **WL1-C2-VB-ActiveListen**.
3. Print and then close the document.

Figure 2.10 Visual Benchmark

ACTIVE LISTENING SKILLS

Speaking and listening is a two-way activity. When the audience pays attention, the speaker gains confidence, knowing that his or her message is being received and appreciated. At the same time, alert listeners obtain information, hear an amusing or interesting story, and otherwise benefit from the speaker's presentation.

Become an Active Listener

Active listeners pay attention to the speaker and to what is being said. They are respectful of the speaker and eager to be informed or entertained. In contrast, *passive listeners* "tune out" the presentation and may even display rudeness by not paying attention to the speaker, here are ways in which you can become an active listener:

Listen with a purpose: Stay focused on what the speaker is saying and you will gain useful information to hear a suspenseful story narrated well. Try to avoid letting your attention wander.

Be courteous: Consider that the speaker spent time preparing for the presentation and thus deserves your respect.

Take brief notes: If the speaker is providing information, take brief notes on the main ideas. Doing so will help you understand and remember what is being said. If you have questions or would like to hear more about a particular point, ask the speaker for clarification after the presentation.

Practice Active Listening Skills in Conversation

Most people have had the experience in being in a one-way conversation in which one person does all the talking and the others just listen. In fact, this is not a conversation, which is by definition an exchange of information and ideas. In a true conversation, everyone has a chance to be heard. Do not monopolize conversation. Give the other person or persons an opportunity to talk. Pay attention when others are speaking and show your interest in what is being said by making eye contact and asking questions. Avoid interrupting since this shows your disinterest an also suggests that what you have to say is more important.

Case Study Apply Your Skills

Part 1

You work for the local chamber of commerce and are responsible for assisting the office manager, Teresa Alexander. Ms. Alexander would like to maintain consistency in articles submitted for publication in the monthly chamber newsletter. She wants you to explore various decorative and plain fonts. She would like you to choose two handwriting fonts, two decorative fonts, and two plain fonts and then prepare a document containing an illustration of each of these fonts. Save the document and name it **WL1-C2-CS-Fonts**. Print and then close the document.

Part 2

Ms. Alexander has asked you to write a short article for the upcoming chamber newsletter. In the article, she would like you to describe an upcoming event at your school, a local college or university, or your local community. Effectively use at least two of the fonts you wrote about in the document you prepared for Case Study Part 1. Save the document and name it **WL1-C2-CS-Article**. Print and then close the document.

Part 3

Help

Ms. Alexander will be posting the Chamber of Commerce newsletter to the chamber's website and would like you to research how to save a Word document as a web page. Use the Help feature to research how to save a document as a web page—specifically, a filtered web page. With the information you find, create a Word document describing the steps for saving a document as a filtered web page. Save the document and name it **WL1-C2-CS-WebPage**. Print and then close the document. Open the **WL1-C2-CS-Article.docx** document you created in Case Study Part 2 and then save the document as a filtered web page.

MICROSOFT® WORD

CHAPTER 3

Customizing Paragraphs

PERFORMANCE OBJECTIVES

Upon successful completion of Chapter 3, you will be able to:

- **Apply numbering and bulleting formatting to text**
- **Insert paragraph borders and shading**
- **Apply custom borders and shading**
- **Sort paragraph text**
- **Set, clear, and move tabs on the horizontal ruler and at the Tabs dialog box**
- **Cut, copy, and paste text in a document**
- **Copy and paste text between documents**

Tutorials

3.1 Creating Bulleted and Numbered Lists
3.2 Adding a Border and Shading to Selected Text
3.3 Sorting Text in Paragraphs
3.4 Setting Tabs Using the Horizontal Ruler
3.5 Setting Tabs at the Tabs Dialog Box
3.6 Cutting, Copying, and Pasting Text
3.7 Using the Clipboard Task Pane

As you learned in Chapter 2, Word contains a variety of options for formatting text in paragraphs. In this chapter you will learn how to insert numbers and bullets in a document, how to apply borders and shading to paragraphs of text in a document, how to sort paragraphs of text, and how to manipulate tabs on the horizontal ruler and at the Tabs dialog box. Editing some documents might include selecting and then deleting, moving, or copying text. You can perform this type of editing with buttons in the Clipboard group on the HOME tab or with keyboard shortcuts. Model answers for this chapter's projects appear on the following pages.

Note: Before beginning the projects, copy to your storage medium the WL1C3 subfolder from the WL1 folder on the CD that accompanies this textbook and then make WL1C3 the active folder.

Model Answers

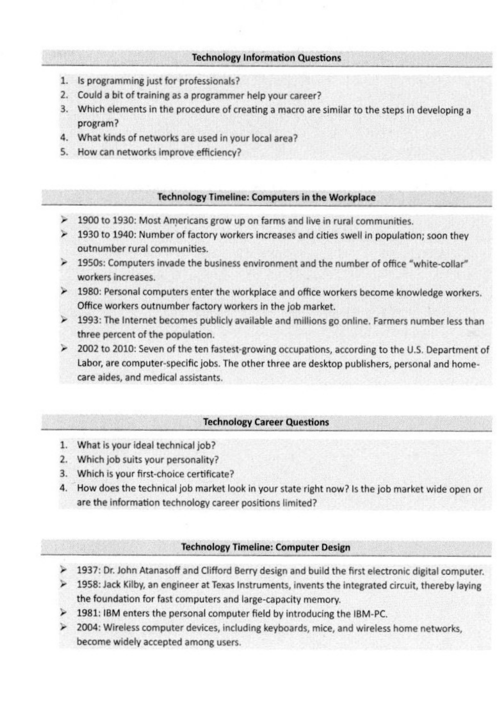

Technology Information Questions

1. Is programming just for professionals?
2. Could a bit of training as a programmer help your career?
3. Which elements in the procedure of creating a macro are similar to the steps in developing a program?
4. What kinds of networks are used in your local area?
5. How can networks improve efficiency?

Technology Timeline: Computers in the Workplace

- 1900 to 1930: Most Americans grow up on farms and live in rural communities.
- 1930 to 1940: Number of factory workers increases and cities swell in population; soon they outnumber rural communities.
- 1950s: Computers invade the business environment and the number of office "white-collar" workers increases.
- 1980: Personal computers enter the workplace and office workers become knowledge workers. Office workers outnumber factory workers in the job market.
- 1993: The Internet becomes publicly available and millions go online. Farmers number less than three percent of the population.
- 2002 to 2010: Seven of the ten fastest-growing occupations, according to the U.S. Department of Labor, are computer-specific jobs. The other three are desktop publishers, personal and home-care aides, and medical assistants.

Technology Career Questions

1. What is your ideal technical job?
2. Which job suits your personality?
3. Which is your first-choice certificate?
4. How does the technical job market look in your state right now? Is the job market wide open or are the information technology career positions limited?

Technology Timeline: Computer Design

- 1937: Dr. John Atanasoff and Clifford Berry design and build the first electronic digital computer.
- 1958: Jack Kilby, an engineer at Texas Instruments, invents the integrated circuit, thereby laying the foundation for fast computers and large-capacity memory.
- 1981: IBM enters the personal computer field by introducing the IBM-PC.
- 2004: Wireless computer devices, including keyboards, mice, and wireless home networks, become widely accepted among users.

Project 1 Format a Document on Computer Technology
WL1-C3-P1-TechInfo.docx

Online Shopping

Online shopping, also called electronic shopping or e-shopping, is defined as using a computer, modem, browser, and the Internet to locate, examine, purchase, and pay for products. Many businesses encourage consumers to shop online because it saves employee time, thus reducing staff needs and saving money for the company. For example, some major airlines offer special discounts to travelers who purchase their tickets over the Internet, and most are eliminating paper tickets altogether.

Advantages of Online Shopping

For the consumer, online shopping offers several distinct advantages over traditional shopping methods. Some of these conveniences include:

- Convenience. With e-shopping, you can browse merchandise and make purchases whenever you want from the privacy and comfort of your home or office.
- Ease of comparison shopping. E-shopping allows you to quickly find comparable items at similar stores and locate those venues with the best quality and lowest prices.
- Greater selection. Because they are not restricted by available shelf space, online stores can offer you an almost unlimited number of products.
- More product information. At many online stores, you can find detailed information about a wide variety of products, an advantage often unavailable in traditional stores.

Online Shopping Venues

Just as consumers can visit a variety of bricks-and-mortar retail outlets, such as stores and shopping malls, Internet shoppers can browse several types of online shopping venues, including online stores, superstores, and shopping malls.

Online Shopping Safety Tips

The number one concern about shopping online is security. The truth is, shopping online is safe and secure if you know what to look for. Following these guidelines can help you avoid trouble.

1. Only buy at secure sites.
2. Never provide your social security number.
3. Look for sites that follow privacy rules from a privacy watchdog such as TRUSTe.
4. Find out the privacy policy of shopping sites before you buy.
5. Keep current on the latest Internet scams.
6. Answer only the minimum questions when filling out forms.

REFERENCES

Claussen, Morgan. "Online Shopping Tips," *Technology Bytes*, October 2, 2014.
Fairmont, Gerald. "Securing Your Privacy," emcpnews.com, August 5, 2014.
Weyman, Jennifer. "Safe Online Shopping," *Computing Standards*, September 10, 2014.

Project 2 Customize a Document on Online Shopping
WL1-C3-P2-OnlineShop.docx

WORKSHOPS

Title	Price	Date
Quality Management	$240	Friday, February 6
Staff Development	229	Friday, February 20
Streamlining Production	175	Monday, March 2
Managing Records	150	Tuesday, March 17
Customer Service Training	150	Thursday, March 19
Sales Techniques	125	Tuesday, April 14

TRAINING DATES

January 6	February 3
January 15	February 12
January 20	February 17
January 22	February 24

TABLE OF CONTENTS

Computers and Creativity 1
Graphics Software 8
Page Layout Software 14
Multimedia Software 21
Educational and Reference Software 34
Programming Software 43

Project 3 Prepare a Document on Workshops and Training Dates WL1-C3-P3-Tabs.docx

Online Shopping Safety Tips

The number one concern about shopping online is security. The truth is, shopping online is safe and secure if you know what to look for. Following these guidelines should help you avoid trouble.

Find out the privacy policy of shopping sites before you buy. Ask what information they gather, how that information will be used, and whether they share that information.

Only buy at secure sites. Secure sites use encryption to scramble your credit card information so that no one except the site can read it. When you enter a secure site, you'll get a pop-up notice in your browser, and then an icon of a closed lock will appear at the bottom of the browser.

Keep current with the latest Internet scams. The U.S. Consumer Gateway reports on Internet scams and tells you what actions the Federal Trade Commission has taken against Internet scammers. The Internet Fraud Watch, run by the National Consumers League, is a great source as well.

Never provide your social security number. A legitimate site will not ask you for your social security number.

Look for sites that follow privacy rules from a privacy watchdog such as TRUSTe. TRUSTe (www.truste.org) is a nonprofit group that serves as a watchdog for Internet privacy. It allows sites to post an online seal if the site adheres to TRUSTe's Internet privacy policies.

Answer only the minimum questions when filling out forms. Many sites put an asterisk next to the questions that must be answered, so only answer those.

Project 4 Move and Copy Text in a Document on Online Shopping Tips WL1-C3-P4-ShoppingTips.docx

TECHNICAL SUPPORT TEAM
Staff Meeting
Wednesday, March 18, 2015
3:00 to 4:30 p.m., Room 20

TECHNICAL SUPPORT TEAM
Staff Meeting
Wednesday, March 18, 2015
3:00 to 4:30 p.m., Room 20

TECHNICAL SUPPORT TEAM
Staff Meeting
Wednesday, March 18, 2015
3:00 to 4:30 p.m., Room 20

TECHNICAL SUPPORT TEAM
Staff Meeting
Wednesday, March 18, 2015
3:00 to 4:30 p.m., Room 20

TECHNICAL SUPPORT TEAM
Staff Meeting
Wednesday, March 18, 2015
3:00 to 4:30 p.m., Room 20

TECHNICAL SUPPORT TEAM
Staff Meeting
Wednesday, March 18, 2015
3:00 to 4:30 p.m., Room 20

Project 5 Copy Text in a Staff Meeting Announcement
WL1-C3-P5-StaffMtg.docx

CONTRACT NEGOTIATION ITEMS

1. The Employer agrees that, during the term of this Agreement, it shall not cause or initiate any lockout of Employees.

2. During the term of this Agreement, the **LWU**, its members, and its representatives agree not to engage in, authorize, sanction, or support any strike, slowdown, or other acts of curtailment or work stoppage.

3. Employees transferring to another location at their own request due to bidding or exercise of seniority shall be provided with space-available transportation with no service charge for self and family.

4. Each employee requested by **RM** to be away from regular base on duty shall receive expenses.

5. An employee shall report to his/her **RM** supervisor that he/she is ill and unable to work at least two (2) hours prior to the start of his/her shift, if at all possible.

6. If **RM**, at any time, grants additional sick leave or assistance to any employee, the **LWU** will deem this a precedence requiring additional sick leave or assistance in any other case.

Project 6 Create a Contract Negotiations Document
WL1-C3-P6-NegotiateItems.docx

Project 1 Format a Document on Computer Technology — 5 Parts

You will open a document containing information on computer technology, type numbered text in the document, and apply numbering and bullet formatting to paragraphs in the document.

Applying Numbering and Bullets

Automatically number paragraphs or insert bullets before paragraphs using buttons in the Paragraph group on the HOME tab. Use the Bullets button to insert bullets before specific paragraphs and use the Numbering button to insert numbers.

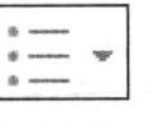
Bullets

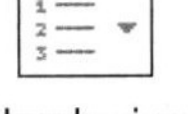
Numbering

Applying Numbering to Paragraphs

If you type *1.* and then press the spacebar, Word indents the number approximately 0.25 inch from the left margin and then hang indents the text in the paragraph approximately 0.5 inch from the left margin. Additionally, when you press Enter to end the first item, *2.* is inserted 0.25 inch from the left margin at the beginning of the next paragraph. Continue typing items, and Word inserts the next number in the list. To turn off numbering, press the Enter key twice or click the Numbering button in the Paragraph group. (You can also remove paragraph formatting from a paragraph, including automatic numbering, with the keyboard shortcut Ctrl + Q. Remove all formatting including character and paragraph formatting from selected text by clicking the Clear All Formatting button in the Font group on the HOME tab.)

Quick Steps
Type Numbered Paragraphs
1. Type **1**.
2. Press spacebar.
3. Type text.
4. Press Enter.

Define new numbering by clicking the Numbering button arrow and then clicking *Define New Number Format.*

If you press the Enter key twice between numbered paragraphs, the automatic number is removed. To turn it back on, type the next number in the list (and the period) followed by a space. Word will automatically indent the number and hang indent the text.

When the AutoFormat feature inserts numbering and indents text, the AutoCorrect Options button displays. Click this button and a drop-down list displays with options for undoing and/or stopping the automatic numbering. An AutoCorrect Options button also displays when AutoFormat inserts automatic bulleting in a document. If you want to insert a line break without inserting a bullet or number, you do not need to turn off the automatic numbering/bulleting and then turn it back on again. Instead, simply press Shift + Enter to insert the line break.

Project 1a **Typing Numbered Paragraphs** **Part 1 of 5**

1. Open **TechInfo.docx**.
2. Save the document with Save As and name it **WL1-C3-P1-TechInfo**.
3. Press Ctrl + End to move the insertion point to the end of the document and then type the text shown in Figure 3.1. Bold and center the title *Technology Career Questions*. When typing the numbered paragraphs, complete the following steps:
   a. Type 1. and then press the spacebar.
   b. Type the paragraph of text and then press the Enter key. (This moves the insertion point down to the next line, inserts *2.* indented 0.25 inch from the left margin, and also indents the first paragraph of text approximately 0.5 inch from the left margin. Also, the AutoCorrect Options button displays. Use this button if you want to undo or stop automatic numbering.)
   c. Continue typing the remaining text. (Remember, you do not need to type the paragraph number and period—these are automatically inserted. The last numbered item will wrap differently on your screen than shown in Figure 3.1.)
   d. After typing the last question, press the Enter key twice. (This turns off paragraph numbering.)
4. Save **WL1-C3-P1-TechInfo.docx**.

Figure 3.1 Project 1a

Technology Career Questions

1. What is your ideal technical job?
2. Which job suits your personality?
3. Which is your first-choice certificate?
4. How does the technical job market look in your state right now? Is the job market wide open or are the information technology career positions limited?

If you do not want automatic numbering in a document, turn off the feature at the AutoCorrect dialog box with the AutoFormat As You Type tab selected, as shown in Figure 3.2. To display this dialog box, click the FILE tab and then click *Options*. At the Word Options dialog box, click the *Proofing* option located in the left panel and then click the AutoCorrect Options button that displays in the *AutoCorrect options* section of the dialog box. At the AutoCorrect dialog box, click

Figure 3.2 AutoCorrect Dialog Box with AutoFormat As You Type Tab Selected

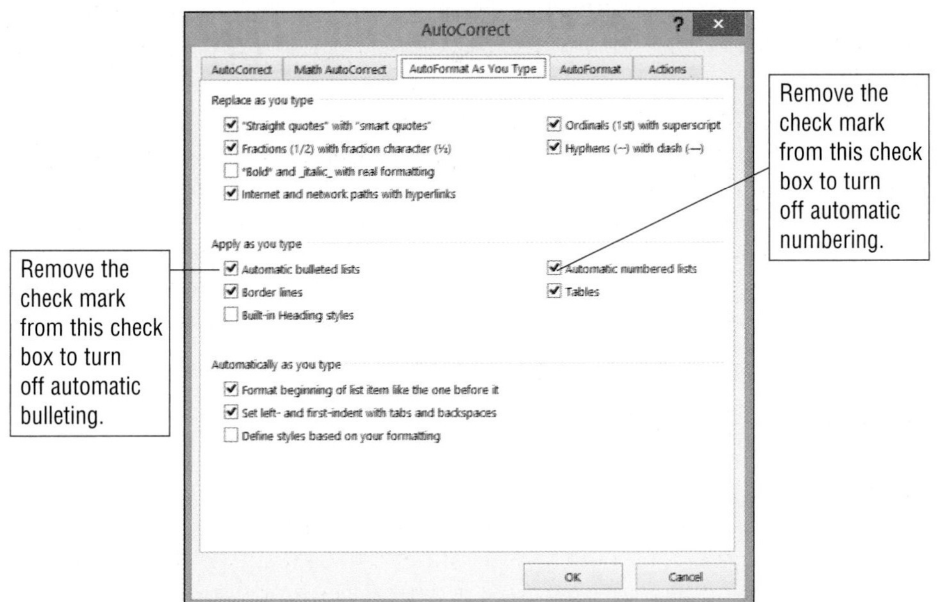

the AutoFormat As You Type tab and then click the *Automatic numbered lists* check box to remove the check mark. Click OK to close the AutoCorrect dialog box and then click OK to close the Word Options dialog box.

You can also automate the creation of numbered paragraphs with the Numbering button in the Paragraph group on the HOME tab. To use this button, type the text (do not type the number) for each paragraph to be numbered, select the paragraphs to be numbered, and then click the Numbering button in the Paragraph group. You can insert or delete numbered paragraphs in a document.

Quick Steps

Create Numbered Paragraphs
1. Select text.
2. Click Numbering button.

Project 1b Inserting Paragraph Numbering

Part 2 of 5

1. With **WL1-C3-P1-TechInfo.docx** open, apply numbers to paragraphs by completing the following steps:
   a. Select the five paragraphs of text in the *Technology Information Questions* section.
   b. Click the Numbering button in the Paragraph group on the HOME tab.

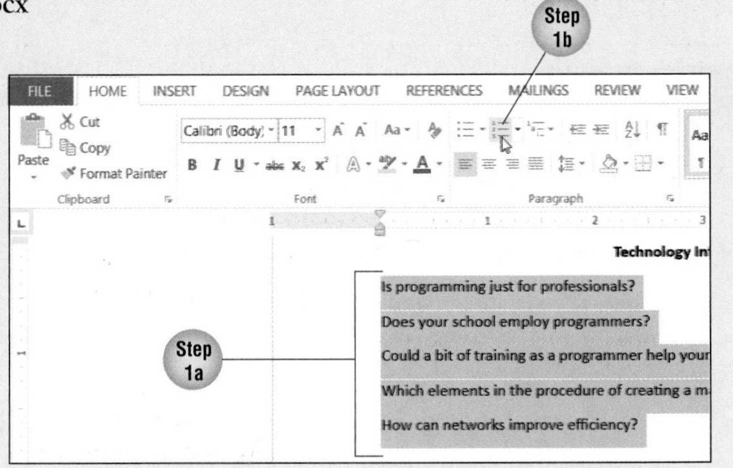

2. Add text between paragraphs 4 and 5 in the *Technology Information Questions* section by completing the following steps:
   a. Position the insertion point immediately to the right of the question mark at the end of the fourth paragraph.
   b. Press Enter.
   c. Type **What kinds of networks are used in your local area?**

Technology Information Questions
1. Is programming just for professionals?
2. Does your school employ programmers?
3. Could a bit of training as a programmer help your career?
4. Which elements in the procedure of creating a macro are similar
program?
5. What kinds of networks are used in your local area?
6. How can networks improve efficiency?
Step 2c

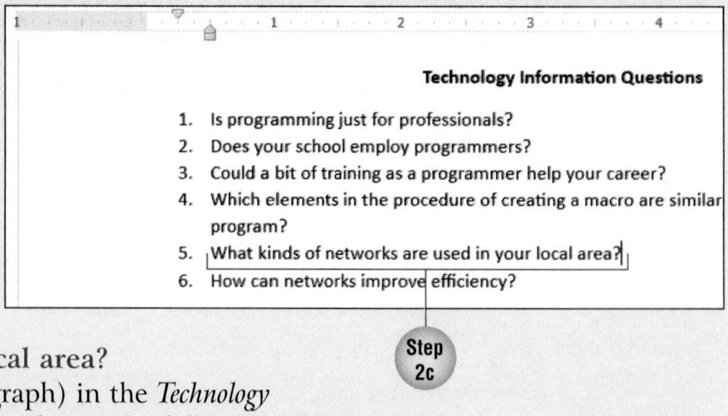

3. Delete the second question (paragraph) in the *Technology Information Questions* section by completing the following steps:
   a. Select the text of the second paragraph. (You will not be able to select the number.)
   b. Press the Delete key.
4. Save **WL1-C3-P1-TechInfo.docx**.

Applying Bullets to Paragraphs

Quick Steps

Type Bulleted Paragraphs
1. Type *, >, or - symbol.
2. Press spacebar.
3. Type text.
4. Press Enter.

Create Bulleted Paragraphs
1. Select text.
2. Click Bullets button.

In addition to automatically numbering paragraphs, Word's AutoFormat feature will create bulleted paragraphs. Bulleted lists with hanging indents are automatically created when a paragraph begins with the symbol *, >, or -. Type one of the symbols and then press the spacebar, and the AutoFormat feature inserts a bullet approximately 0.25 inch from the left margin and indents the text following the bullet another 0.25 inch. You can turn off the automatic bulleting feature at the AutoCorrect dialog box with the AutoFormat As You Type tab selected. You can demote or promote bulleted text by pressing the Tab key to demote text or pressing Shift + Tab to promote bulleted text. Word uses different bullets for demoted text.

You can also create bulleted paragraphs with the Bullets button in the Paragraph group on the HOME tab. To create bulleted paragraphs using the Bullets button, type the text of the paragraphs (do not type the bullets), select the paragraphs, and then click the Bullets button in the Paragraph group.

Project 1c Typing and Inserting Bulleted Text — Part 3 of 5

1. With **WL1-C3-P1-TechInfo.docx** open, press Ctrl + End to move the insertion point to the end of the document and then press the Enter key once.
2. Type **Technology Timeline: Computer Design** in bold and centered, as shown in Figure 3.3, and then press the Enter key.
3. Turn off bold and change to left alignment.
4. Type a greater-than symbol (>), press the spacebar, type the text of the first bulleted paragraph in Figure 3.3, and then press the Enter key.
5. Press the Tab key (this demotes the bullet to a hollow circle) and then type the bulleted text.
6. Press the Enter key (this displays another hollow circle bullet), type the bulleted text, and then press the Enter key.
7. Press Shift + Tab (this promotes the bullet to an arrow), type the bulleted text, and then press the Enter key twice (this turns off bullets).

8. Promote bulleted text by positioning the insertion point at the beginning of the text *1958: Jack Kilby, an engineer* and then pressing Shift + Tab. Promote the other hollow circle bullet to an arrow. (The four paragraphs of text should be preceded by arrow bullets.)
9. Format the paragraphs of text in the *Technology Timeline: Computers in the Workplace* section as a bulleted list by completing the following steps:
   a. Select the paragraphs of text in the *Technology Timeline: Computers in the Workplace* section.
   b. Click the Bullets button in the Paragraph group. (Word will insert the same arrow bullets that you inserted in Step 2. Word keeps the same bullet formatting until you choose a different bullet style.)

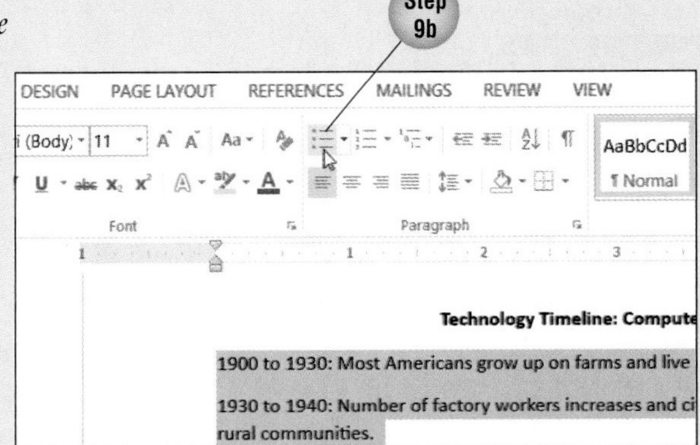

10. Save and then print **WL1-C3-P1-TechInfo.docx**.

Figure 3.3 Project 1c

Technology Timeline: Computer Design

- ➢ 1937: Dr. John Atanasoff and Clifford Berry design and build the first electronic digital computer.
  - o 1958: Jack Kilby, an engineer at Texas Instruments, invents the integrated circuit, thereby laying the foundation for fast computers and large-capacity memory.
  - o 1981: IBM enters the personal computer field by introducing the IBM-PC.
- ➢ 2004: Wireless computer devices, including keyboards, mice, and wireless home networks, become widely accepted among users.

Inserting Paragraph Borders and Shading

Every paragraph you create in Word contains an invisible frame. You can apply a border to the frame around the paragraph. You can apply a border to specific sides of the paragraph or to all sides, customize the type of border lines, and add shading and fill to the border. Add borders and shading to paragraphs in a document using the Borders and Shading buttons in the Paragraph group on the HOME tab or options from the Borders and Shading dialog box.

Inserting Paragraph Borders

Quick Steps

Apply Border
1. Select text.
2. Click Borders button.

Borders

When a border is added to a paragraph of text, the border expands and contracts as text is inserted or deleted from the paragraph. You can create a border around a single paragraph or a border around selected paragraphs. One method for creating a border is to use options from the Borders button in the Paragraph group. Click the Borders button arrow and a drop-down list displays. At the drop-down list, click the option that will insert the desired border. For example, to insert a border at the bottom of the paragraph, click the *Bottom Border* option. Clicking an option will add the border to the paragraph where the insertion point is located. To add a border to more than one paragraph, select the paragraphs first and then click the desired option.

Project 1d Adding Borders to Paragraphs of Text — Part 4 of 5

1. With **WL1-C3-P1-TechInfo.docx** open, insert an outside border to specific text by completing the following steps:
   a. Select text from the title *Technology Information Questions* through the five numbered paragraphs of text.
   b. In the Paragraph group, click the Borders button arrow.
   c. Click the *Outside Borders* option at the drop-down list.
2. Select text from the title *Technology Timeline: Computers in the Workplace* through the six bulleted paragraphs of text and then click the Borders button in the Paragraph group. (The button will apply the border option that was previously selected.)
3. Select text from the title *Technology Career Questions* through the four numbered paragraphs of text below and then click the Borders button in the Paragraph group.

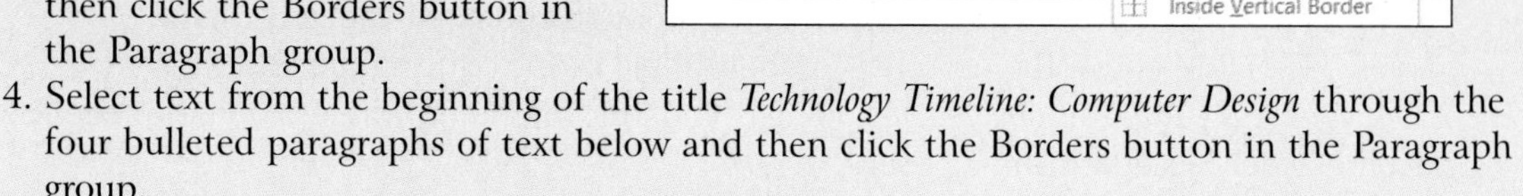

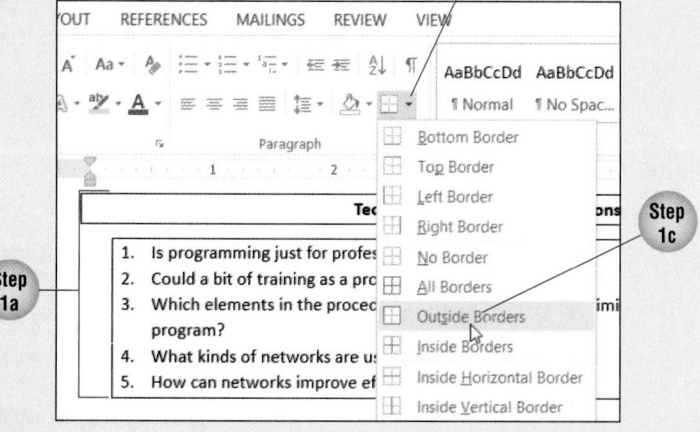

4. Select text from the beginning of the title *Technology Timeline: Computer Design* through the four bulleted paragraphs of text below and then click the Borders button in the Paragraph group.
5. Save and then print **WL1-C3-P1-TechInfo.docx**.

Adding Paragraph Shading

Quick Steps

Apply Shading
1. Select text.
2. Click Shading button.

Shading

Add shading to text in a document with the Shading button in the Paragraph group. Select text you want to shade and then click the Shading button. This applies a background color behind the text.

Click the Shading button arrow and a drop-down gallery displays. Paragraph shading colors display in themes in the drop-down gallery. Use one of the theme colors or click one of the standard colors that displays at the bottom of the gallery. Click the *More Colors* option, and the Colors dialog box displays. At the Colors dialog box with the Standard tab selected, click the desired color or click the Custom tab and then specify a custom color.

Project 1e Applying Shading to Paragraphs

Part 5 of 5

1. With **WL1-C3-P1-TechInfo.docx** open, apply paragraph shading and change border lines by completing the following steps:
   a. Position the insertion point on any character in the title *Technology Information Questions*.
   b. Click the Borders button arrow and then click *No Border* at the drop-down list.
   c. Click the Borders button arrow and then click *Bottom Border* at the drop-down list.
   d. Click the Shading button arrow and then click the *Gold, Accent 4, Lighter 60%* option (eighth column, third row).

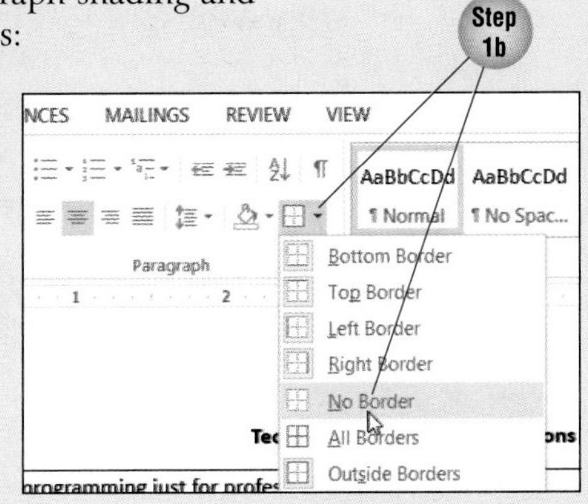

2. Apply the same formatting to the other titles by completing the following steps:
   a. With the insertion point positioned on any character in the title *Technology Information Questions*, double-click the Format Painter button in the Clipboard group.
   b. Select the title *Technology Timeline: Computers in the Workplace*.
   c. Select the title *Technology Career Questions*.
   d. Select the title *Technology Timeline: Computer Design*.
   e. Click the Format Painter button in the Clipboard group.

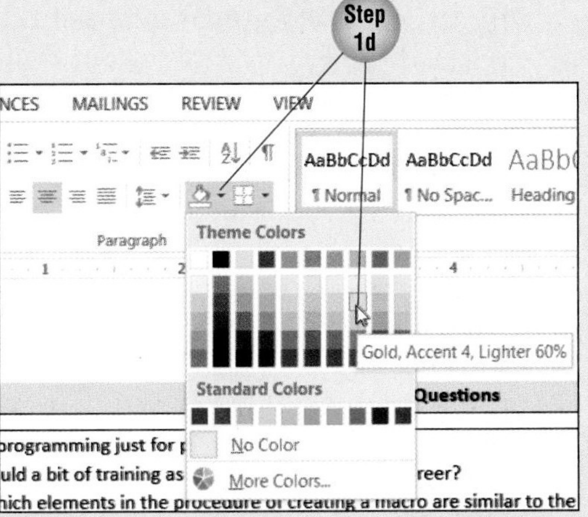

3. Remove the paragraph border and apply shading to paragraphs by completing the following steps:
   a. Select the numbered paragraphs of text below the *Technology Information Questions* title.
   b. Click the Borders button arrow and then click *No Border* at the drop-down list.
   c. Click the Shading button arrow and then click the *Gold, Accent 4, Lighter 80%* option (eighth column, second row).

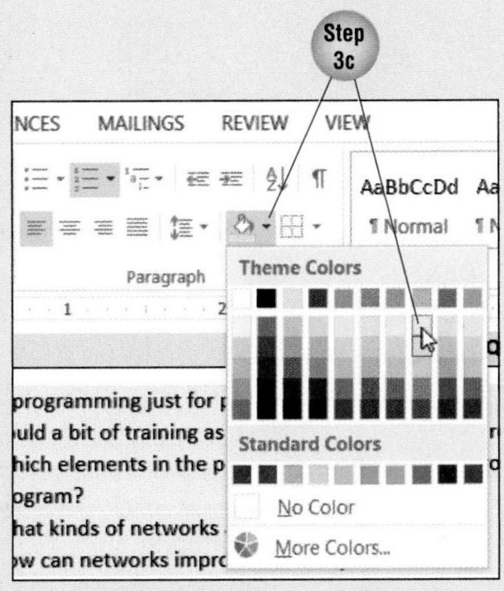

4. Select the bulleted paragraphs of text below the *Technology Timeline: Computers in the Workplace* title, click the Borders button, and then click the Shading button. (Clicking the Borders button will apply the previous border option, which was *No Border*. Clicking the Shading button will apply the previous shading option, which was *Gold, Accent 4, Lighter 80%*.)
5. Select the numbered paragraphs of text below the *Technology Career Questions* title, click the Borders button, and then click the Shading button.
6. Select the numbered paragraphs of text below the *Technology Timeline: Computer Design* title, click the Borders button, and then click the Shading button.
7. Save, print, and then close **WL1-C3-P1-TechInfo.docx**.

Project 2 Customize a Document on Online Shopping 2 Parts

You will open a document containing information on online shopping, apply and customize borders and shading, and then sort text in the document.

Customizing Borders and Shading

If you want to further customize paragraph borders and shading, use options at the Borders and Shading dialog box. Display this dialog box by clicking the Borders button arrow and then clicking *Borders and Shading* at the drop-down list. Click the Borders tab and options display for customizing the border; click the Shading tab and shading options display.

As you learned in a previous section, you can add borders to a paragraph with the Borders button in the Paragraph group. If you want to further customize borders, use options at the Borders and Shading dialog box with the Borders tab selected, as shown in Figure 3.4. At the Borders and Shading dialog box, specify the desired border setting, style, color, and width. Click the Shading tab and the dialog box displays with shading options.

Figure 3.4 Borders and Shading Dialog Box with the Borders Tab Selected

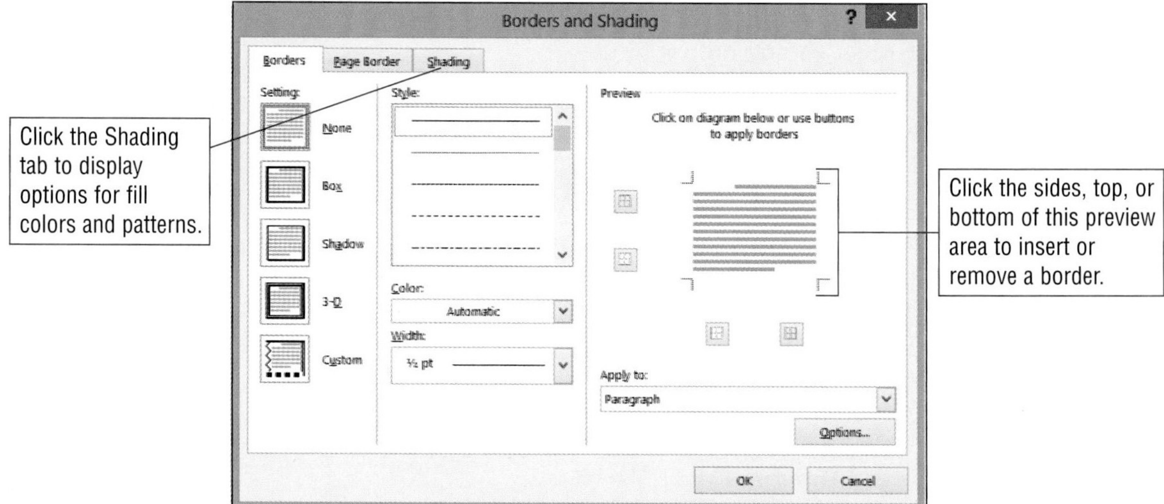

Project 2a Adding a Customized Border and Shading to a Document Part 1 of 2

1. Open **OnlineShop.docx**.
2. Save the document with Save As and name it **WL1-C3-P2-OnlineShop**.
3. Make the following changes to the document:
   a. Insert 12 points of space before and 6 points of space after the headings *Online Shopping*, *Advantages of Online Shopping*, *Online Shopping Venues*, *Online Shopping Safety Tips*, and *REFERENCES*. (Do this with the *Spacing Before* and *Spacing After* measurement boxes on the PAGE LAYOUT tab.)
   b. Center the *REFERENCES* title.

4. Insert a custom border and add shading to a heading by completing the following steps:
   a. Move the insertion point to any character in the heading *Online Shopping*.
   b. Click the Borders button arrow and then click *Borders and Shading* at the drop-down list.
   c. At the Borders and Shading dialog box with the Borders tab selected, click the down-pointing arrow at the right side of the *Color* option box and then click the *Dark Blue* color in the *Standard Colors* section.
   d. Click the down-pointing arrow at the right of the *Width* option box and then click *1 pt* at the drop-down list.

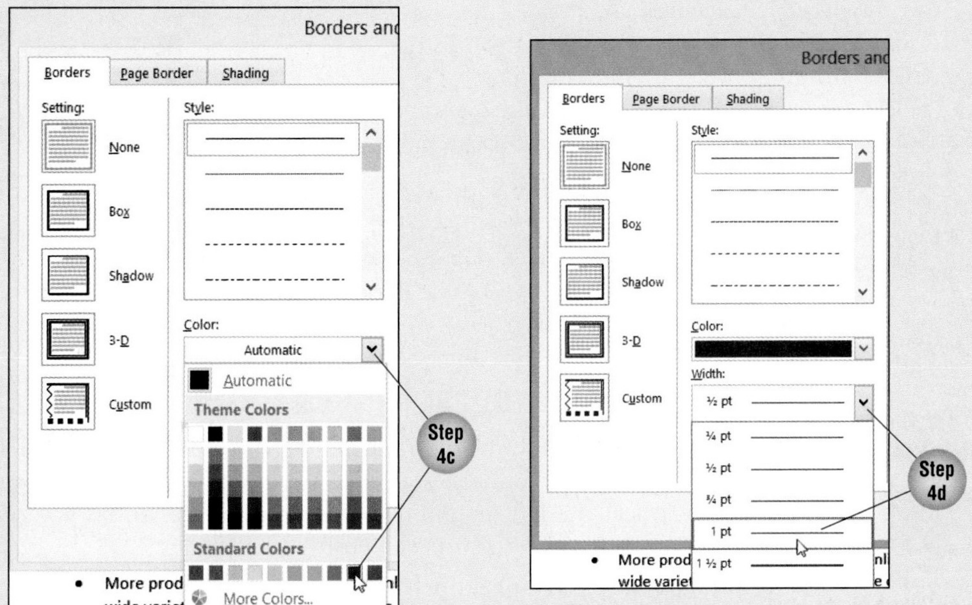

   e. Click the top border of the box in the *Preview* section of the dialog box.
   f. Scroll down the *Style* list box and then click the first thick/thin line.
   g. If necessary, click the down-pointing arrow at the right side of the *Color* option box and then click the *Dark Blue* color in the *Standard Colors* section.
   h. Click the bottom border of the box in the *Preview* section of the dialog box.

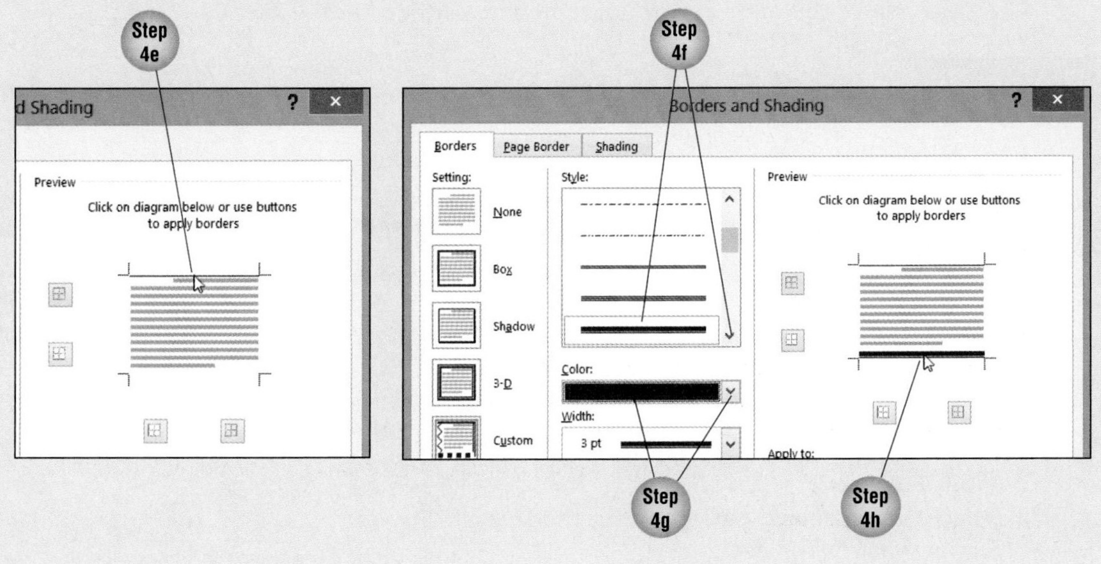

i. Click the Shading tab.
j. Click the down-pointing arrow at the right side of the *Fill* option box and then click *Green, Accent 6, Lighter 60%* (last column, third row).
k. Click OK to close the dialog box.

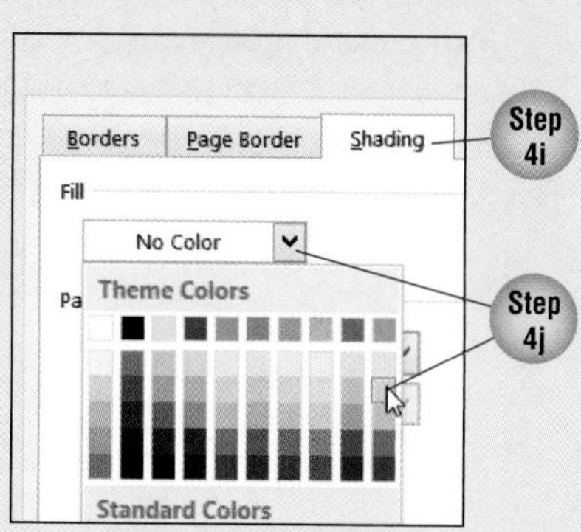

5. Use Format Painter to apply the same border and shading formatting to the remaining headings by completing the following steps:
   a. Position the insertion point on any character in the heading *Online Shopping*.
   b. Double-click the Format Painter button in the Clipboard group on the HOME tab.
   c. Select the heading *Advantages of Online Shopping*.
   d. Select the heading *Online Shopping Venues*.
   e. Select the heading *Online Shopping Safety Tips*.
   f. Click the Format Painter button once.
6. Move the insertion point to any character in the heading *Online Shopping* and then remove the 12 points of spacing above.
7. Save **WL1-C3-P2-OnlineShop.docx**.

Sorting Text in Paragraphs

Quick Steps

Sort Paragraphs of Text
1. Click Sort button.
2. Make any needed changes at Sort Text dialog box.
3. Click OK.

Sort

You can sort text arranged in paragraphs alphabetically by the first character. The first character can be a number, symbol (such as $ or #), or letter. Type paragraphs you want to sort at the left margin or indented to a tab. Unless you select specific paragraphs for sorting, Word sorts the entire document.

To sort text in paragraphs, open the document. If the document contains text you do not want sorted, select the specific paragraphs you do want sorted. Click the Sort button in the Paragraph group and the Sort Text dialog box displays. At this dialog box, click OK. The *Type* option at the Sort Text dialog box will display *Text*, *Number*, or *Date* depending on the text selected. Word will attempt to determine the data type and choose one of the three options. For example, if you select numbers with a mathematical value, Word will assign them the *Number* type. However, if you select a numbered list, Word assigns them the *Text* type since the numbers do not represent mathematical values.

Project 2b Sorting Paragraphs Alphabetically

Part 2 of 2

1. With **WL1-C3-P2-OnlineShop.docx** open, sort the bulleted text alphabetically by completing the following steps:
   a. Select the bulleted paragraphs in the *Advantages of Online Shopping* section.
   b. Click the Sort button in the Paragraph group.
   c. At the Sort Text dialog box, make sure *Paragraphs* displays in the *Sort by* option box and the *Ascending* option is selected.
   d. Click OK.

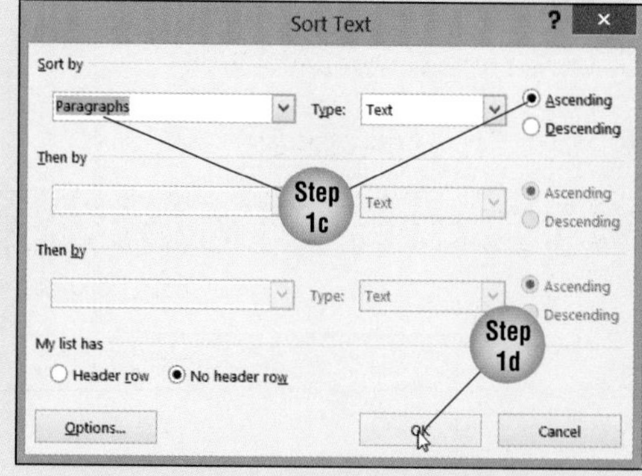

2. Sort the numbered paragraphs by completing the following steps:
   a. Select the numbered paragraphs in the *Online Shopping Safety Tips* section.

b. Click the Sort button in the Paragraph group.
c. Click OK at the Sort Text dialog box.

3. Sort alphabetically the three paragraphs of text below the *REFERENCES* title by completing the following steps:
   a. Select the paragraphs of text below the *REFERENCES* title.
   b. Click the Sort button in the Paragraph group.
   c. Click the down-pointing arrow at the right side of the *Type* option box and then click *Text* at the drop-down list.
   d. Click OK.
4. Save, print, and then close **WL1-C3-P2-OnlineShop.docx**.

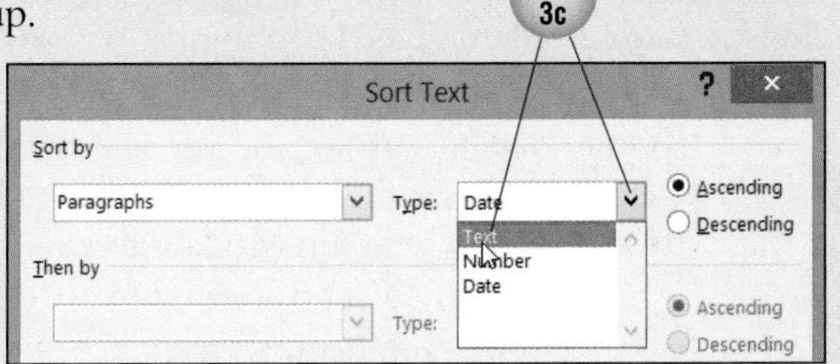

Project 3 Prepare a Document on Workshops and Training Dates — 4 Parts

You will set and move tabs on the horizontal ruler and at the Tabs dialog box and type tabbed text about workshops, training dates, and a table of contents.

Manipulating Tabs

When you work with a document, Word offers a variety of default settings, such as margins and line spacing. One of these defaults is a left tab set every 0.5 inch. In some situations, these default tabs are appropriate; in others, you may want to create your own. Two methods exist for setting tabs. Tabs can be set on the horizontal ruler or at the Tabs dialog box.

Manipulating Tabs on the Horizontal Ruler

Use the horizontal ruler to set, move, and delete tabs. If the ruler is not visible, click the VIEW tab and then click the *Ruler* check box in the Show group. By default, tabs are set every 0.5 inch on the horizontal ruler. With a left tab, text aligns at the left edge of the tab. The other types of tabs that can be set on the horizontal ruler are center, right, decimal, and bar. Use the Alignment button that displays above the vertical ruler to specify tabs. Each time you click the Alignment button, a different tab or paragraph alignment symbol displays. Table 3.1 shows the tab alignment buttons and what type of tab each will set.

Table 3.1 Tab Alignment Buttons

Tab Alignment Button	*Type of Tab*	*Tab Alignment Button*	*Type of Tab*
└	left	┴.	decimal
┴	center	I	bar
┘	right		

Setting Tabs

Quick Steps

Set Tabs on Horizontal Ruler
1. Click Alignment button above vertical ruler.
2. Click desired location on horizontal ruler.

When setting tabs on the horizontal ruler, a dotted guideline displays to help align tabs.

Position the insertion point in any paragraph of text, and tabs for the paragraph appear on the horizontal ruler.

To set a left tab on the horizontal ruler, make sure the left alignment symbol (see Table 3.1) displays in the Alignment button. Position the arrow pointer on the tick mark (the marks on the ruler) where you want the tab symbol to appear and then click the left mouse button. When you set a tab on the horizontal ruler, any default tabs to the left are automatically deleted by Word. Set a center, right, decimal, or bar tab on the horizontal ruler in a similar manner.

Before setting a tab on the horizontal ruler, click the Alignment button that displays above the vertical ruler until the appropriate tab symbol displays and then set the tab. If you change the tab symbol in the Alignment button, the symbol remains until you change it again or you close Word. If you close and then reopen Word, the Alignment button displays with the left tab symbol.

If you want to set a tab at a specific measurement on the horizontal ruler, hold down the Alt key, position the arrow pointer at the desired position, and then hold down the left mouse button. This displays two measurements in the white portion in the horizontal ruler. The first measurement displays the location of the arrow pointer on the ruler in relation to the left margin. The second measurement is the distance from the location of the arrow pointer on the ruler to the right margin. With the left mouse button held down, position the tab symbol at the desired location and then release the mouse button and the Alt key.

If you change tab settings and then create columns of text using the New Line command, Shift + Enter, the tab formatting is stored in the paragraph mark at the end of the columns. If you want to make changes to the tab settings for text in the columns, position the insertion point anywhere within the columns (all of the text in the columns does not have to be selected) and then make the changes.

Project 3a **Setting Left, Center, and Right Tabs on the Horizintal Ruler** **Part 1 of 4**

1. At a new blank document, type **WORKSHOPS** centered and bolded as shown in Figure 3.5.
2. Press the Enter key. In the new paragraph, return the paragraph alignment back to left alignment and then turn off bold formatting.
3. Set a left tab at the 0.5-inch mark, a center tab at the 3.25-inch mark, and a right tab at the 6-inch mark by completing the following steps:
   a. Click the Show/Hide ¶ button in the Paragraph group on the HOME tab to turn on the display of nonprinting characters.
   b. Make sure the horizontal ruler is displayed. (If not, click the VIEW tab and then click the *Ruler* check box in the Show group.)
   c. Make sure the left tab symbol displays in the Alignment button located above the vertical ruler.
   d. Position the arrow pointer on the 0.5-inch mark on the horizontal ruler and then click the left mouse button.

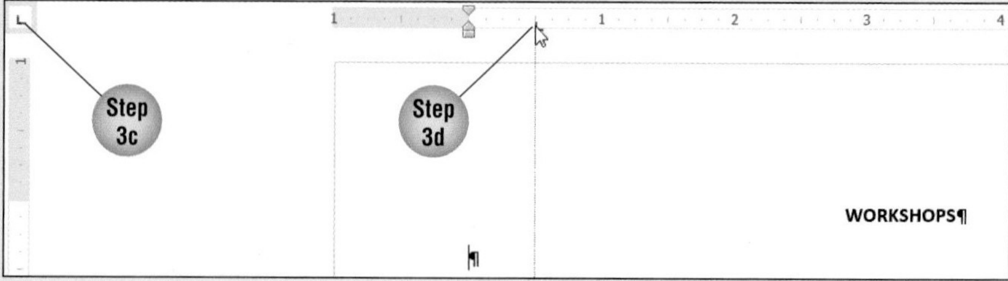

e. Position the arrow pointer on the Alignment button above the vertical ruler and then click the left mouse button until the center tab symbol displays (see Table 3.1).

f. Position the arrow pointer below the 3.25-inch mark on the horizontal ruler. Hold down the Alt key and then the left mouse button. Make sure the first measurement on the horizontal ruler displays as *3.25"* and then release the mouse button and the Alt key.

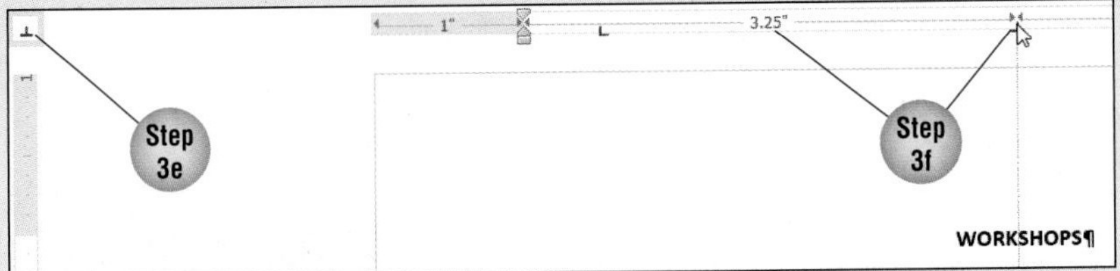

g. Position the arrow pointer on the Alignment button above the vertical ruler and then click the left mouse button until the right tab symbol displays (see Table 3.1).

h. Position the arrow pointer below the 6-inch mark on the horizontal ruler. Hold down the Alt key and then the left mouse button. Make sure the first measurement on the horizontal ruler displays as *6"* and then release the mouse button and the Alt key.

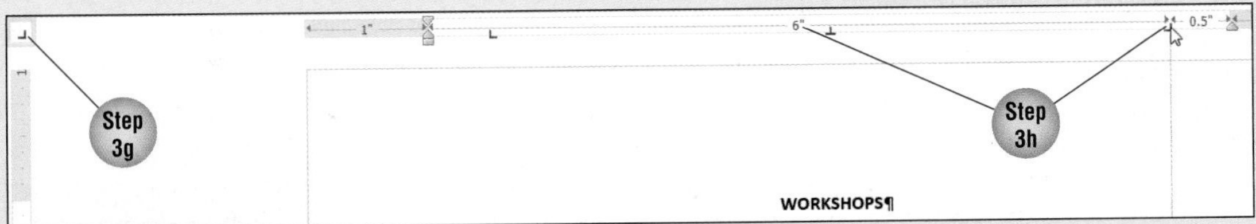

4. Type the text in columns, as shown in Figure 3.5. Press the Tab key before typing each column entry and press Shift + Enter after typing the text in the third column.
5. After typing the last column entry, press the Enter key twice.
6. Press Ctrl + Q to remove paragraph formatting (tab settings).
7. Click the Show/Hide ¶ button to turn off the display of nonprinting characters.
8. Save the document and name it **WL1-C3-P3-Tabs**.

Figure 3.5 Project 3a

WORKSHOPS

Title	**Price**	**Date**
Quality Management	$240	Friday, February 6
Staff Development	229	Friday, February 20
Streamlining Production	175	Monday, March 2
Managing Records	150	Tuesday, March 17
Customer Service Training	150	Thursday, March 19
Sales Techniques	125	Tuesday, April 14

Moving Tabs and Deleting Tabs

After a tab has been set on the horizontal ruler, it can be moved to a new location. To move a tab, position the arrow pointer on the tab symbol on the ruler, hold down the left mouse button, drag the symbol to the new location on the ruler, and then release the mouse button. To delete a tab from the ruler, position the arrow pointer on the tab symbol you want deleted, hold down the left mouse button, drag the symbol down into the document, and then release the mouse button.

Project 3b **Moving Tabs** **Part 2 of 4**

1. With **WL1-C3-P3-Tabs.docx** open, position the insertion point on any character in the first entry in the tabbed text.
2. Position the arrow pointer on the left tab symbol at the 0.5-inch mark on the horizontal ruler, hold down the left mouse button, drag the left tab symbol to the 1-inch mark on the ruler, and then release the mouse button. ***Hint: Use the Alt key to help you precisely position the tab symbol.***

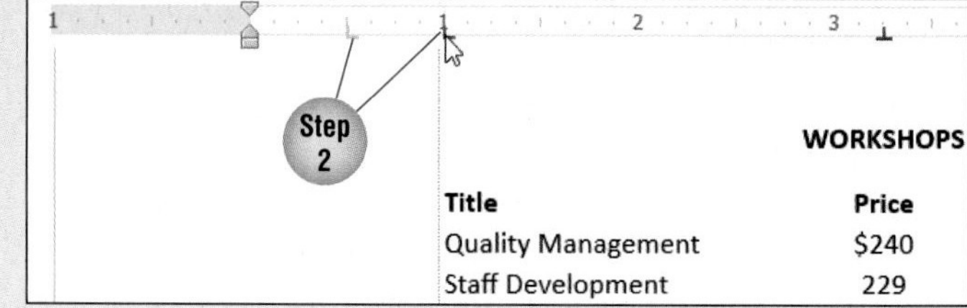

3. Position the arrow pointer on the right tab symbol at the 6-inch mark on the horizontal ruler, hold down the left mouse button, drag the right tab symbol to the 5.5-inch mark on the ruler, and then release the mouse button. ***Hint: Use the Alt key to help you precisely position the tab symbol.***
4. Save **WL1-C3-P3-Tabs.docx**.

Manipulating Tabs at the Tabs Dialog Box

Use the Tabs dialog box, shown in Figure 3.6, to set tabs at specific measurements. You can also use the Tabs dialog box to set tabs with preceding leaders and clear one tab or all tabs. To display the Tabs dialog box, click the Paragraph group dialog box launcher. At the Paragraph dialog box, click the Tabs button located in the bottom left corner of the dialog box.

Figure 3.6 Tabs Dialog Box

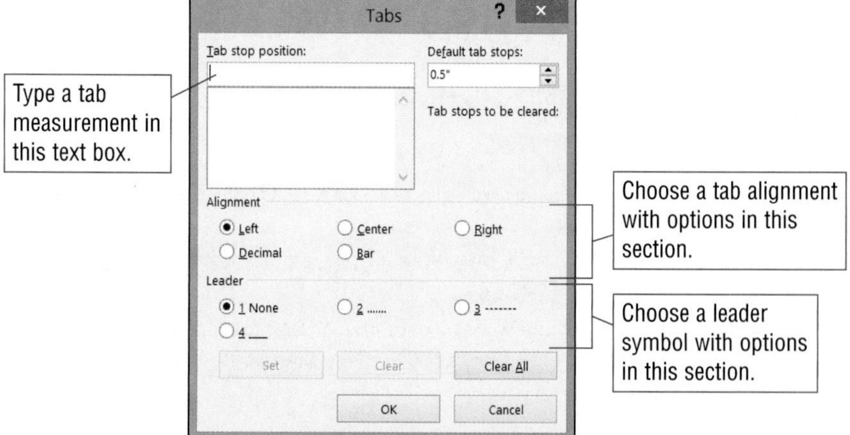

Clearing Tabs and Setting Tabs

At the Tabs dialog box, you can clear an individual tab or all tabs. To clear all tabs, click the Clear All button. To clear an individual tab, specify the tab position, and then click the Clear button.

At the Tabs dialog box, you can set a left, right, center, or decimal tab as well as a bar tab. (For an example of a bar tab, refer to Figure 3.7.) You can also set a left, right, center, or decimal tab with preceding leaders. To change the type of tab at the Tabs dialog box, display the dialog box and then click the desired tab in the *Alignment* section. Type the desired measurement for the tab in the *Tab stop position* text box.

Quick Steps

Set Tabs at Tabs Dialog Box

1. Click Paragraph group dialog box launcher.
2. Click Tabs button.
3. Specify tab positions, alignments, and leader options.
4. Click OK.

Project 3c **Setting Left Tabs and a Bar Tab at the Tabs Dialog Box** **Part 3 of 4**

1. With **WL1-C3-P3-Tabs.docx** open, press Ctrl + End to move the insertion point to the end of the document.
2. Type the title **TRAINING DATES** bolded and centered as shown in Figure 3.7, press the Enter key, return the paragraph alignment back to left, and then turn off bold formatting.
3. Display the Tabs dialog box and then set left tabs and a bar tab by completing the following steps:
   a. Click the Paragraph group dialog box launcher.
   b. At the Paragraph dialog box, click the Tabs button located in the lower left corner of the dialog box.
   c. Make sure *Left* is selected in the *Alignment* section of the dialog box.
   d. Type 1.75 in the *Tab stop position* text box.
   e. Click the Set button.
   f. Type 4 in the *Tab stop position* text box and then click the Set button.
   g. Type 3.25 in the *Tab stop position* text box, click *Bar* in the *Alignment* section, and then click the Set button.
   h. Click OK to close the Tabs dialog box.

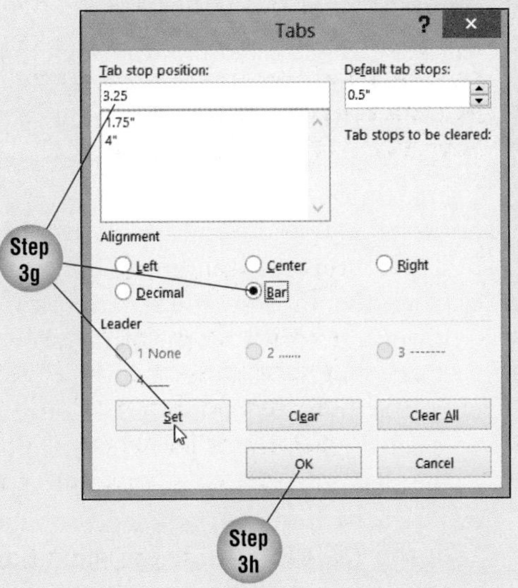

4. Type the text in columns, as shown in Figure 3.7. Press the Tab key before typing each column entry and press Shift + Enter to end each line.
5. After typing *February 24*, complete the following steps:
   a. Press the Enter key.
   b. Clear tabs by displaying the Tabs dialog box, clicking the Clear All button, and then clicking OK.
   c. Press the Enter key.
6. Remove the 8 points of spacing after the last entry in the text by completing the following steps:
   a. Position the insertion point on any character in the *January 22* entry.
   b. Click the PAGE LAYOUT tab.
   c. Click twice on the down-pointing arrow at the right side of the *Spacing After* measurement box. (This changes the measurement to *0 pt.*)
7. Save **WL1-C3-P3-Tabs.docx**.

Figure 3.7 Project 3c

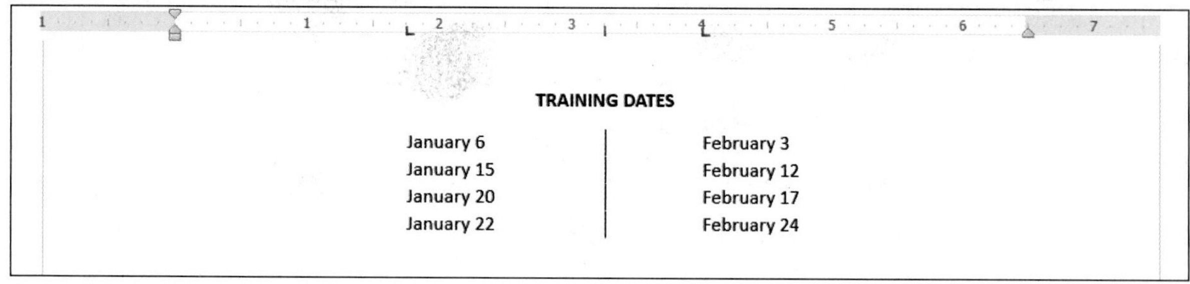

Setting Leader Tabs

Four types of tabs (left, right, center, and decimal) can be set with leaders. Leaders are useful in a table of contents or other material where you want to direct the reader's eyes across the page. Figure 3.8 shows an example of leaders. Leaders can be periods (.), hyphens (-), or underlines (_). To add leaders to a tab, click the type of leader desired in the *Leader* section of the Tabs dialog box.

Project 3d Setting a Left Tab and a Right Tab with Dot Leaders

Part 4 of 4

1. With **WL1-C3-P3-Tabs.docx** open, press Ctrl + End to move the insertion point to the end of the document.
2. Type the title TABLE OF CONTENTS bolded and centered, as shown in Figure 3.8.
3. Press the Enter key and then return the paragraph alignment back to left and turn off bold formatting.
4. Set a left tab and a right tab with dot leaders by completing the following steps:
   a. Click the Paragraph group dialog box launcher.
   b. Click the Tabs button located in the lower left corner of the Paragraph dialog box.
   c. At the Tabs dialog box, make sure *Left* is selected in the *Alignment* section of the dialog box.
   d. With the insertion point positioned in the *Tab stop position* text box, type 1 and then click the Set button.
   e. Type 5.5 in the *Tab stop position* text box.
   f. Click *Right* in the *Alignment* section of the dialog box.
   g. Click *2 ......* in the *Leader* section of the dialog box and then click the Set button.
   h. Click OK to close the dialog box.

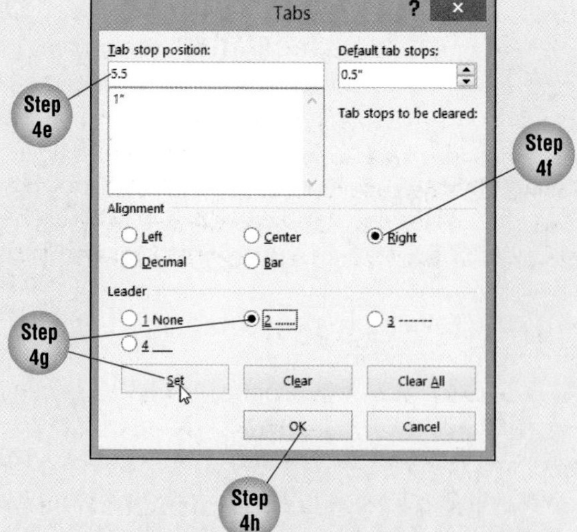

5. Type the text in columns, as shown in Figure 3.8. Press the Tab key before typing each column entry and press Shift + Enter to end each line.
6. Save, print, and then close **WL1-C3-P3-Tabs.docx**.

Figure 3.8 Project 3d

TABLE OF CONTENTS

Computers and Creativity 1
Graphics Software 8
Page Layout Software 14
Multimedia Software 21
Educational and Reference Software 34
Programming Software 43

Project 4 Move and Copy Text in a Document on Online Shopping Tips

2 Parts

You will open a document containing information on online shopping safety tips and then cut, copy, and paste text in the document.

Cutting, Copying, and Pasting Text

When editing a document, you may need to delete specific text, move text to a different location in the document, and/or copy text to various locations in the document. You can complete these activities using buttons in the Clipboard group on the HOME tab.

Deleting Selected Text

Word offers different methods for deleting text from a document. To delete a single character, you can use either the Delete key or the Backspace key. To delete more than a single character, select the text and then press the Delete key on the keyboard or click the Cut button in the Clipboard group. If you press the Delete key, the text is deleted permanently. (You can restore deleted text with the Undo button on the Quick Access toolbar.) The Cut button in the Clipboard group will remove the selected text from the document and insert it in Word's ***Clipboard***, which is a temporary area of memory. The Clipboard holds text while it is being moved or copied to a new location in the document or to a different document.

HINT

The Clipboard contents are deleted when the computer is turned off. Text you want to save permanently should be saved as a separate document.

Cutting and Pasting Text

To move text to a different location in the document, select the text, click the Cut button in the Clipboard group, position the insertion point at the location where you want the text inserted, and then click the Paste button in the Clipboard group.

You can also move selected text with a shortcut menu. To do this, select the text and then position the insertion point inside the selected text until it turns into an arrow pointer. Click the right mouse button and then click *Cut* at the shortcut menu. Position the insertion point where you want the text inserted, click the right mouse button, and then click *Paste* at the shortcut menu. Keyboard shortcuts are also available for cutting and pasting text. Use Ctrl + X to cut text and Ctrl + V to paste text.

Quick Steps

Move Selected Text

1. Select text.
2. Click Cut button.
3. Move to desired location.
4. Click Paste button.

Cut

Paste

When selected text is cut from a document and inserted in the Clipboard, it stays in the Clipboard until other text is inserted in the Clipboard. For this reason, you can paste text from the Clipboard more than just once. For example, if you cut text to the Clipboard, you can paste this text in different locations within the document or other documents as many times as desired.

Quick Steps

Move Text with the Mouse
1. Select text.
2. Position mouse pointer in selected text.
3. Hold down left mouse button and drag to desired location.
4. Release left mouse button.

Moving Text by Dragging with the Mouse

You can also use the mouse to move text. To do this, select text to be moved and then position the I-beam pointer inside the selected text until it turns into an arrow pointer. Hold down the left mouse button, drag the arrow pointer (displays with a gray box attached) to the location where you want the selected text inserted, and then release the button. If you drag and then drop selected text in the wrong location, immediately click the Undo button.

Project 4a Moving and Dragging Selected Text — Part 1 of 2

1. Open **ShoppingTips.docx**.
2. Save the document with Save As and name it **WL1-C3-P4-ShoppingTips**.
3. Move a paragraph by completing the following steps:
   a. Select the paragraph that begins with *Only buy at secure sites,* including the blank line below the paragraph.
   b. Click the Cut button in the Clipboard group on the HOME tab.
   c. Position the insertion point at the beginning of the paragraph that begins with *Look for sites that follow.*
   d. Click the Paste button in the Clipboard group. (If the first and second paragraphs are not separated by a blank line, press the Enter key once.)
4. Following steps similar to those in Step 3, move the paragraph that begins with *Never provide your social* so it is positioned before the paragraph that begins *Look for sites that follow privacy* and after the paragraph that begins *Only buy at secure.*
5. Use the mouse to select the paragraph that begins with *Keep current with the latest Internet*, including one blank line below the paragraph.
6. Move the I-beam pointer inside the selected text until it becomes an arrow pointer.
7. Hold down the left mouse button and drag the arrow pointer (displays with a small gray box attached) so that the insertion point, which displays as a black vertical bar, is positioned at the beginning of the paragraph that begins with *Never provide your social.* Release the mouse button.
8. Deselect the text.
9. Save **WL1-C3-P4-ShoppingTips.docx**.

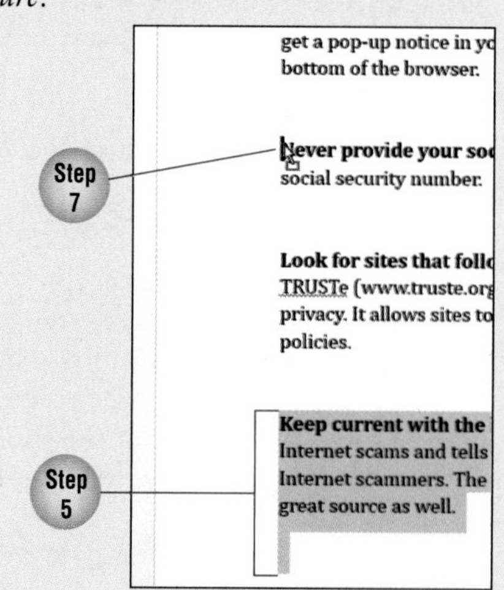

Using the Paste Options Button

When selected text is pasted, the Paste Options button displays in the lower right corner of the text. Click this button (or press the Ctrl key on the keyboard) and the *Paste Options* gallery displays, as shown in Figure 3.9. Use options from this gallery to specify how you want information pasted in the document. Hover the mouse over a button in the gallery and the live preview displays the text in the document as it will appear when pasted.

Paste Options

By default, pasted text retains the formatting of the selected text. You can choose to match the formatting of the pasted text with the formatting where the text is pasted or paste only the text without retaining formatting. To determine the function of a button in the *Paste Options* gallery, hover the mouse over a button and a ScreenTip displays with an explanation of the button function as well as the keyboard shortcut. For example, hover the mouse pointer over the first button from the left in the *Paste Options* gallery and the ScreenTip displays with the information *Keep Source Formatting (K)*. Click this button or press K on the keyboard, and the pasted text keeps its original formatting.

Figure 3.9 Paste Options Button Drop-down List

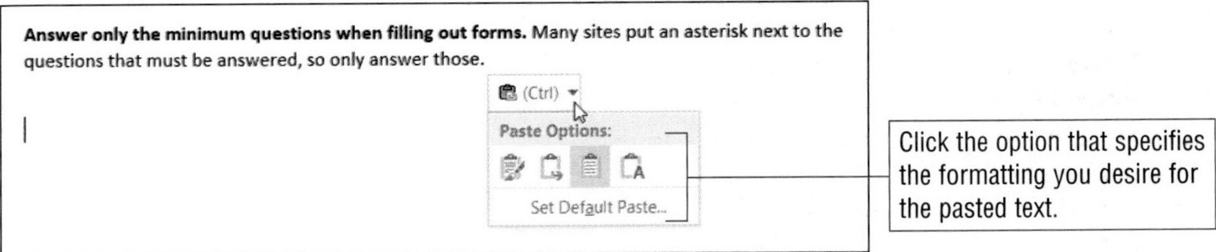

Project 4b Using the Paste Options Button

Part 2 of 2

1. With **WL1-C3-P4-ShoppingTips.docx** open, open **Tip.docx**.
2. Select the paragraph of text in the document, including the blank line below the paragraph, and then click the Copy button in the Clipboard group.
3. Close **Tip.docx**.
4. Move the insertion point to the end of **WL1-C3-P4-ShoppingTips.docx**.
5. Click the Paste button in the Clipboard group.
6. Click the Paste Options button that displays at the end of the paragraph and then click the second button in the *Paste Options* gallery (Merge Formatting (M) button). (This changes the font so it matches the formatting of the other paragraphs in the document.)

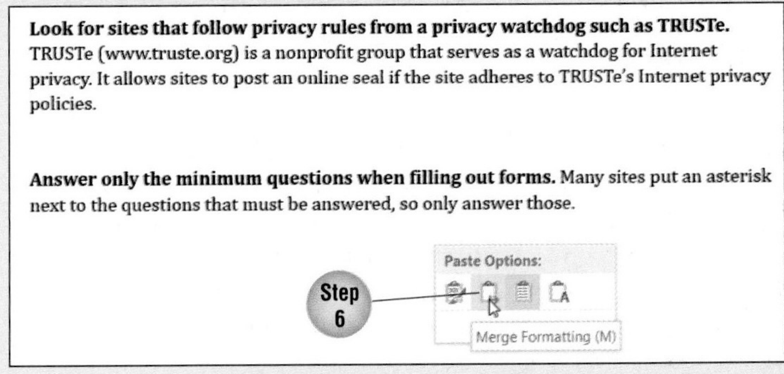

7. Save, print, and then close **WL1-C3-P4-ShoppingTips.docx**.

Project 5 Copy Text in a Staff Meeting Announcement — 1 Part

You will copy and paste text in a document announcing a staff meeting for the Technical Support Team.

Copying and Pasting Text

Quick Steps

Copy Selected Text
1. Select text.
2. Click Copy button.
3. Move to desired location.
4. Click Paste button.

Copy

Copying selected text can be useful in documents that contain repeated information. Use copy and paste to insert duplicate portions of text in a document instead of retyping them. After you have selected text, copy the text to a different location with the Copy and Paste buttons in the Clipboard group on the HOME tab or using the mouse. You can also use the keyboard shortcut Ctrl + C to copy text.

To use the mouse to copy text, select the text and then position the I-beam pointer inside the selected text until it becomes an arrow pointer. Hold down the left mouse button and hold down the Ctrl key. Drag the arrow pointer (displays with a small gray box and a box containing a plus symbol) and a black vertical bar moves with the pointer. Position the black bar in the desired location, release the mouse button, and then the Ctrl key.

Project 5 Copying Text — Part 1 of 1

1. Open **StaffMtg.docx**.
2. Save the document with Save As and name it **WL1-C3-P5-StaffMtg**.
3. Copy the text in the document to the end of the document by completing the following steps:
   a. Select all of the text in the document and include one blank line below the text. ***Hint: Click the Show/Hide ¶ button to turn on the display of nonprinting characters. When you select the text, select one of the paragraph markers below the text.***
   b. Click the Copy button in the Clipboard group.
   c. Move the insertion point to the end of the document.
   d. Click the Paste button in the Clipboard group.
4. Paste the text again at the end of the document. To do this, position the insertion point at the end of the document and then click the Paste button in the Clipboard group. (This inserts a copy of the text from the Clipboard.)
5. Select all of the text in the document using the mouse and include one blank line below the text. (Consider turning on the display of nonprinting characters.)
6. Move the I-beam pointer inside the selected text until it becomes an arrow pointer.
7. Hold down the Ctrl key and then the left mouse button. Drag the arrow pointer (displays with a box with a plus symbol inside) so the vertical black bar is positioned at the end of the document, release the mouse button, and then release the Ctrl key.
8. Deselect the text.
9. Make sure all text fits on one page. If not, consider deleting any extra blank lines.
10. Save, print, and then close **WL1-C3-P5-StaffMtg.docx**.

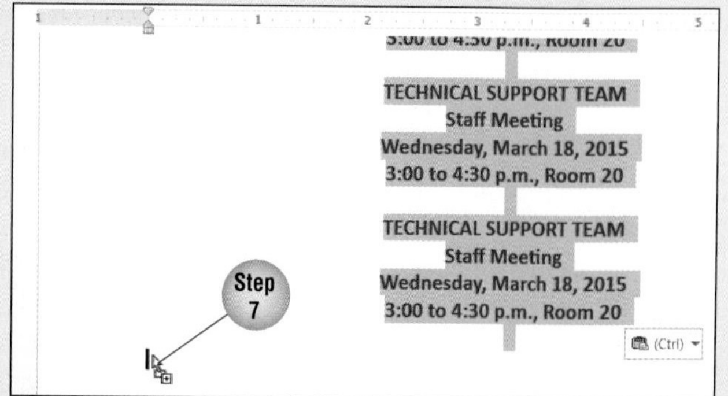

Project 6 Create a Contract Negotiations Document 1 Part

You will use the Clipboard to copy and paste paragraphs to and from separate documents to create a contract negotiations document.

Using the Clipboard

Use the Clipboard to collect and paste multiple items. You can collect up to 24 different items and then paste them in various locations. To display the Clipboard task pane, click the Clipboard task pane launcher located in the lower right corner of the Clipboard group. The Clipboard task pane displays at the left side of the screen in a manner similar to what you see in Figure 3.10.

Select text or an object you want to copy and then click the Copy button in the Clipboard group. Continue selecting text or items and clicking the Copy button. To insert an item, position the insertion point in the desired location and then click the option in the Clipboard task pane representing the item. Click the Paste All button to paste all of the items in the Clipboard into the document. If the copied item is text, the first 50 characters display in the list box on the Clipboard task pane. When all desired items are inserted, click the Clear All button to remove any remaining items.

Quick Steps

Use the Clipboard

1. Click Clipboard task pane launcher.
2. Select and copy desired text.
3. Move to desired location.
4. Click desired option in Clipboard task pane.

You can copy items to the Clipboard from various Office applications and then paste them into any Office file.

Figure 3.10 Clipboard Task Pane

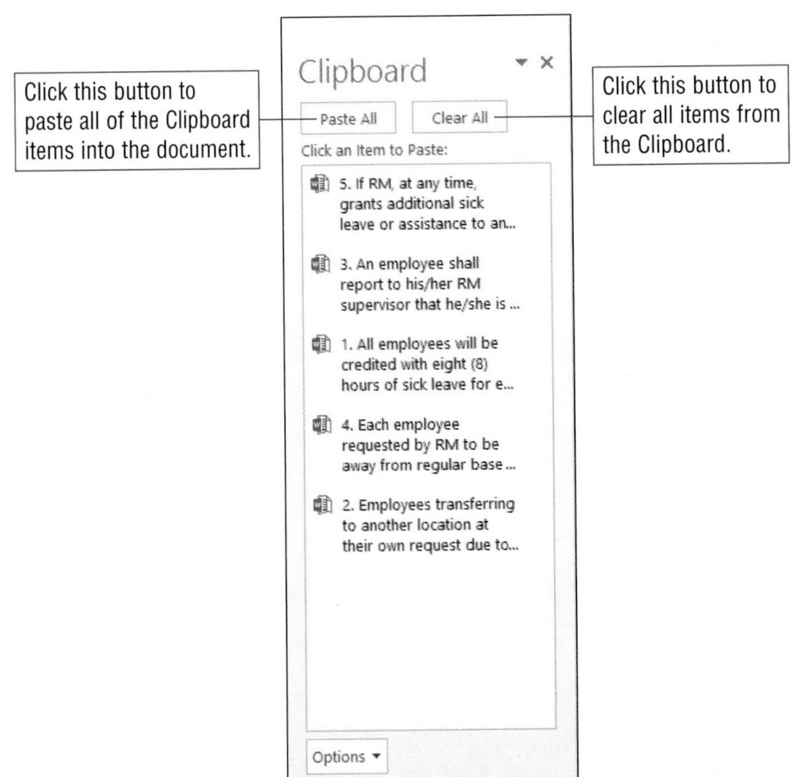

Project 6 Collecting and Pasting Paragraphs of Text

Part 1 of 1

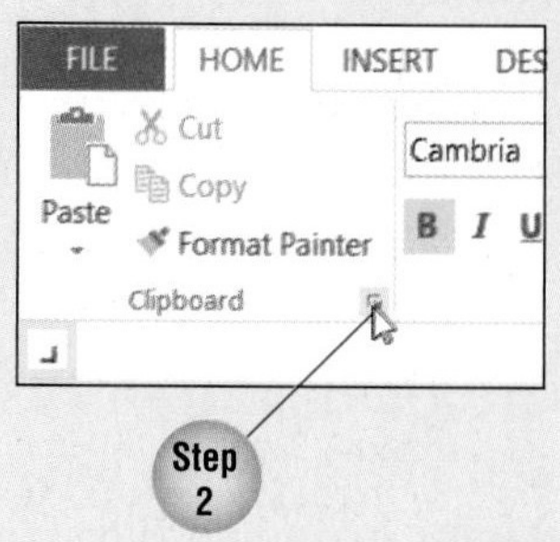

1. Open **ContractItems.docx**.
2. Turn on the display of the Clipboard task pane by clicking the Clipboard task pane launcher located in the bottom right corner of the Clipboard group. (If the Clipboard task pane list box contains any text, click the Clear All button located toward the top of the task pane.)
3. Select paragraph 1 in the document (the 1. is not selected) and then click the Copy button in the Clipboard group.
4. Select paragraph 3 in the document (the 3. is not selected) and then click the Copy button in the Clipboard group.
5. Close **ContractItems.docx**.
6. Paste the paragraphs by completing the following steps:
   a. Press Ctrl + N to display a new blank document. (If the Clipboard task pane does not display, click the Clipboard task pane launcher.)
   b. Type **CONTRACT NEGOTIATION ITEMS** centered and bolded.
   c. Press the Enter key, turn off bold formatting, and return the paragraph alignment back to left alignment.
   d. Click the Paste All button in the Clipboard task pane to paste both paragraphs in the document.
   e. Click the Clear All button in the Clipboard task pane.

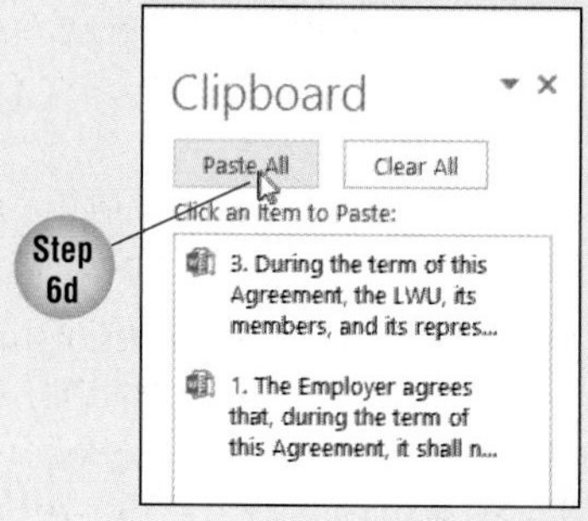

7. Open **UnionContract.docx**.
8. Select and then copy each of the following paragraphs:
   a. Paragraph 2 in the *Transfers and Moving Expenses* section.
   b. Paragraph 4 in the *Transfers and Moving Expenses* section.
   c. Paragraph 1 in the *Sick Leave* section.
   d. Paragraph 3 in the *Sick Leave* section.
   e. Paragraph 5 in the *Sick Leave* section.
9. Close **UnionContract.docx**.
10. Make sure the insertion point is positioned at the end of the document and then paste the paragraphs by completing the following steps:
    a. Click the button in the Clipboard task pane representing paragraph 2. (When the paragraph is inserted in the document, the paragraph number changes to 3.)
    b. Click the button in the Clipboard task pane representing paragraph 4.
    c. Click the button in the Clipboard task pane representing paragraph 3.
    d. Click the button in the Clipboard task pane representing paragraph 5.
11. Click the Clear All button located toward the top of the Clipboard task pane.
12. Close the Clipboard task pane.
13. Save the document and name it **WL1-C3-P6-NegotiateItems**.
14. Print and then close **WL1-C3-P6-NegotiateItems.docx**.

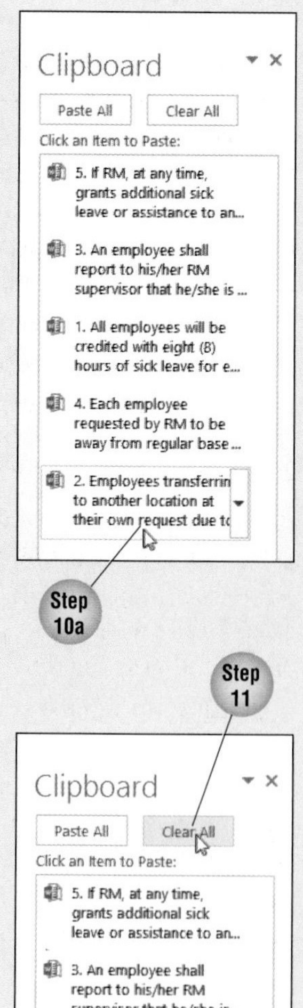

Chapter Summary

- Number paragraphs with the Numbering button in the Paragraph group on the HOME tab and insert bullets before paragraphs with the Bullets button.
- Remove all paragraph formatting from a paragraph by pressing the keyboard shortcut Ctrl + Q, and remove all character and paragraph formatting by clicking the Clear All Formatting button in the Font group.
- The AutoCorrect Options button displays when the AutoFormat feature inserts numbers. Click this button to display options for undoing and/or stopping automatic numbering.
- Bulleted lists with hanging indents are automatically created when a paragraph begins with *, >, or -. The type of bullet inserted depends on the type of character entered.
- You can turn off automatic numbering and bullets at the AutoCorrect dialog box with the AutoFormat As You Type tab selected.
- A paragraph created in Word contains an invisible frame, and you can insert a border around this frame. Click the Borders button arrow to display a drop-down list of border choices.
- Apply shading to text by clicking the Shading button arrow and then clicking the desired color at the drop-down gallery.
- Use options at the Borders and Shading dialog box with the Borders tab selected to add a customized border to a paragraph or selected paragraphs, and use options with Shading tab selected to add shading or a pattern to a paragraph or selected paragraphs.
- With the Sort button in the Paragraph group on the HOME tab, you can sort text arranged in paragraphs alphabetically by the first character, which can be a number, symbol, or letter.
- By default, tabs are set every 0.5 inch. These settings can be changed on the horizontal ruler or at the Tabs dialog box.
- Use the Alignment button that displays above the vertical ruler to select a left, right, center, decimal, or bar tab. When you set a tab on the horizontal ruler, any default tabs to the left are automatically deleted.
- After a tab has been set on the horizontal ruler, it can be moved or deleted using the mouse pointer.
- At the Tabs dialog box, you can set any of the five types of tabs at a specific measurement. You can also set tabs with preceding leaders and clear one tab or all tabs. Preceding leaders can be periods, hyphens, or underlines.
- Cut, copy, and paste text using buttons in the Clipboard group on the HOME tab or with keyboard shortcuts.
- When selected text is pasted, the Paste Options button displays in the lower right corner of the text. Click the button, and the *Paste Options* gallery displays with buttons for specifying how you want information pasted in the document.
- With the Clipboard, you can collect up to 24 items and then paste them in various locations in a document.

Commands Review

FEATURE	RIBBON TAB, GROUP	BUTTON, OPTION	KEYBOARD SHORTCUT
borders	HOME, Paragraph		
Borders and Shading dialog box	HOME, Paragraph	, *Borders and Shading*	
bullets	HOME, Paragraph		
clear all formatting	HOME, Font		
clear paragraph formatting			Ctrl + Q
Clipboard task pane	HOME, Clipboard		
copy text	HOME, Clipboard		Ctrl + C
cut text	HOME, Clipboard		Ctrl + X
New Line command			Shift + Enter
numbering	HOME, Paragraph		
Paragraph dialog box	HOME, Paragraph		
paste text	HOME, Clipboard		Ctrl + V
shading	HOME, Paragraph		
Sort Text dialog box	HOME, Paragraph		
Tabs dialog box	HOME, Paragraph	, Tabs	

Concepts Check Test Your Knowledge

Completion: In the space provided at the right, indicate the correct term, symbol, or command.

1. The Numbering button is located in this group on the HOME tab. ____________
2. Automate the creation of bulleted paragraphs with this button on the HOME tab. ____________
3. This button displays when the AutoFormat feature inserts numbers. ____________
4. You can turn off automatic numbering and bullets at the AutoCorrect dialog box with this tab selected. ____________

5. Bulleted lists with hanging indents are automatically created when you begin a paragraph with the asterisk symbol (*), the hyphen (-), or this symbol. ______________

6. The Borders button is located in this group on the HOME tab. ______________

7. Use options at this dialog box to add a customized border to a paragraph or selected paragraphs. ______________

8. Sort text arranged in paragraphs alphabetically by the first character, can be a number, symbol, or this. ______________

9. By default, tabs are set apart from one another by this measurement. ______________

10. This is the default tab type. ______________

11. When setting tabs on the horizontal ruler, choose the tab type with this button. ______________

12. Tabs can be set on the horizontal ruler or here. ______________

13. This group on the HOME tab contains the Cut, Copy, and Paste buttons. ______________

14. To copy selected text with the mouse, hold down this key while dragging selected text. ______________

15. With this task pane, you can collect up to 24 items and then paste the items in various locations in the document. ______________

Skills Check Assess Your Performance

Assessment 1

APPLY PARAGRAPH FORMATTING TO A COMPUTER ETHICS DOCUMENT

1. Open **CompEthics.docx**.
2. Save the document with Save As and name it **WL1-C3-A1-CompEthics**.
3. Move the insertion point to the end of the document and then type the text shown in Figure 3.11. Apply bullet formatting as shown in the figure.
4. Select the paragraphs of text in the *Computer Ethics* section and then apply numbering formatting.
5. Select the paragraphs of text in the *Technology Timeline* section and then apply bullet formatting.
6. Insert the following paragraph of text between paragraphs 2 and 3 in the *Computer Ethics* section: **Find sources relating to the latest federal and/or state legislation on privacy protection.**
7. Apply the Heading 1 style to the three headings in the document.
8. Apply the Shaded style set.
9. Apply the Slice theme.

10. Apply Light Turquoise, Background 2, Lighter 80% paragraph shading (third column, second row) to the numbered paragraphs in the *Computer Ethics* section and the bulleted paragraphs in the *Technology Timeline* and *ACLU Fair Electronic Monitoring Policy* sections.
11. Save, print, and then close **WL1-C3-A1-CompEthics.docx**.

Figure 3.11 Assessment 1

ACLU Fair Electronic Monitoring Policy

- Notice to employees of the company's electronic monitoring practices
- Use of a signal to let an employee know he or she is being monitored
- Employee access to all personal data collected through monitoring
- No monitoring of areas designed for the health or comfort of employees
- The right to dispute and delete inaccurate data
- A ban on the collection of data unrelated to work performance
- Restrictions on the disclosure of personal data to others without the employee's consent

Assessment 2

TYPE TABBED TEXT AND APPLY FORMATTING TO A COMPUTER SOFTWARE DOCUMENT

1. Open **ProdSoftware.docx**.
2. Save the document with Save As and name it **WL1-C3-A2-ProdSoftware**.
3. Move the insertion point to the end of the document and then set left tabs at the 0.75-inch, 2.75-inch, and 4.5-inch marks on the horizontal ruler. Type the text in Figure 3.12 and type the tabbed text at the tabs you set. Use the New Line command after typing each line of text in columns (except the last line).
4. Apply the Heading 1 style to the three headings in the document (*Productivity Software*, *Personal-Use Software*, and *Software Training Schedule*).
5. Apply the Retrospect theme.
6. Select the productivity software categories in the *Productivity Software* section (from *Word processing* through *Computer-aided design*) and then sort the text alphabetically.
7. With the text still selected, apply bullet formatting.
8. Select the personal-use software categories in the *Personal-Use Software* section (from *Personal finance software* through *Games and entertainment software*) and then sort the text alphabetically.
9. With the text still selected, apply bullet formatting.
10. Apply to the heading *Productivity Software* a single-line top border and Olive Green, Text 2, Lighter 80% paragraph shading (fourth column, second row).
11. Apply the same single-line top border and the same olive green shading to the other two headings (*Personal-Use Software* and *Software Training Schedule*).
12. With the insertion point positioned on the first line of tabbed text, move the tab symbols on the horizontal ruler as follows:
    a. Move the tab at the 0.75-inch mark to the 1-inch mark.
    b. Move the tab at the 4.5-inch mark to the 4-inch mark.
13. Save, print, and then close **WL1-C3-A2-ProdSoftware.docx**.

Figure 3.12 Assessment 2

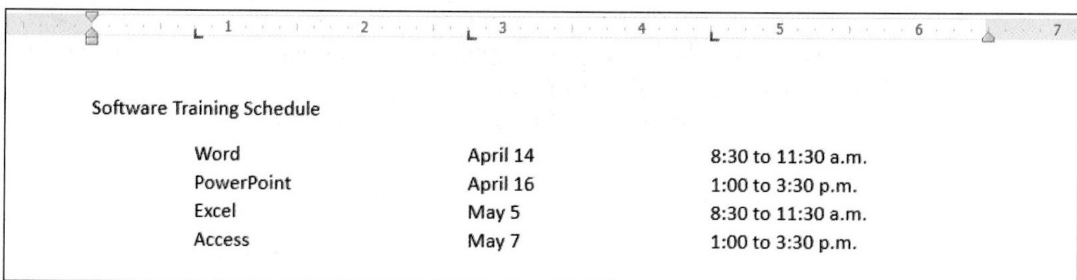

Software Training Schedule

Word	April 14	8:30 to 11:30 a.m.
PowerPoint	April 16	1:00 to 3:30 p.m.
Excel	May 5	8:30 to 11:30 a.m.
Access	May 7	1:00 to 3:30 p.m.

Assessment 3

TYPE AND FORMAT A TABLE OF CONTENTS DOCUMENT

1. At a new blank document, type the document shown in Figure 3.13 with the following specifications:
   a. Change the font to 11-point Cambria.
   b. Bold and center the title as shown.
   c. Before typing the text in columns, display the Tabs dialog box. Set two left tabs at the 1-inch mark and the 1.5-inch mark and a right tab with dot leaders at the 5.5-inch mark.
   d. Press Enter to end each line of text.
2. Save the document and name it **WL1-C3-A3-TofC**.
3. Print **WL1-C3-A3-TofC.docx**.
4. Select the text in columns and then move the tab symbols on the horizontal ruler as follows. (Because you pressed Enter instead of Shift + Enter at the end of each line of text, you need to select all the text in the columns before moving the tabs.)
   a. Delete the left tab symbol that displays at the 1.5-inch mark.
   b. Set a new left tab at the 0.5-inch mark.
   c. Move the right tab at the 5.5-inch mark to the 6-inch mark.
5. Insert single-line top and bottom borders to the title *TABLE OF CONTENTS*.
6. Apply Orange, Accent 2, Lighter 80% paragraph shading to the title *TABLE OF CONTENTS*.
7. Save, print, and then close **WL1-C3-A3-TofC.docx**.

Figure 3.13 Assessment 3

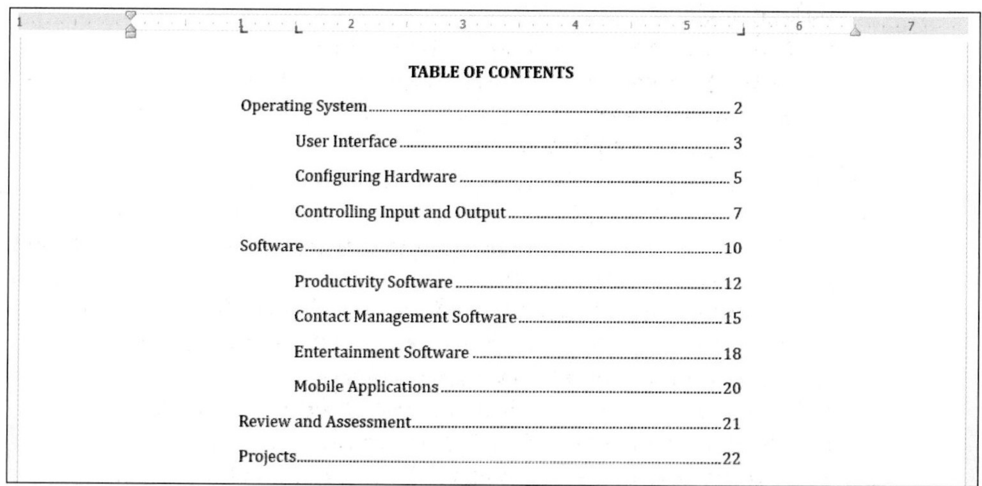

TABLE OF CONTENTS

Operating System..2
User Interface..3
Configuring Hardware..5
Controlling Input and Output..7
Software..10
Productivity Software..12
Contact Management Software..15
Entertainment Software..18
Mobile Applications..20
Review and Assessment..21
Projects..22

Assessment

4 FORMAT A BUILDING CONSTRUCTION AGREEMENT DOCUMENT

1. Open **ConstructAgrmnt.docx**.
2. Save the document with Save As and name it **WL1-C3-A4-ConstructAgrmnt**.
3. Select and then delete the paragraph (including the blank line below the paragraph) that begins *Supervision of Work*.
4. Select and then delete the paragraph (including the blank line below the paragraph) that begins *Builder's Right to Terminate Contract*.
5. Move the paragraph (including the blank line below the paragraph) that begins *Financing Arrangements* above the paragraph that begins *Start of Construction*.
6. Open **AgrmntItems.docx**.
7. Turn on the display of the Clipboard task pane and then clear all the contents, if necessary.
8. Select and then copy the first paragraph.
9. Select and then copy the second paragraph.
10. Select and then copy the third paragraph.
11. Close **AgrmntItems.docx**.
12. With **WL1-C3-A4-ConstructAgrmnt.docx** open, turn on the display of the Clipboard and then paste the *Supervision* paragraph *above* the *Changes and Alterations* paragraph and then merge the formatting. (Make sure you position the insertion point *above* the paragraph before you paste the text.)
13. Paste the *Pay Review* paragraph *above* the *Possession of Residence* paragraph and then merge the formatting.
14. Clear all items from the Clipboard and then close the Clipboard task pane.
15. Check the spacing between paragraphs. Insert or delete blank lines to maintain consistent spacing.
16. Save, print, and then close **WL1-C3-A4-ConstructAgrmnt.docx**.

Assessment

5 HYPHENATE WORDS IN A REPORT

1. In some Word documents, especially documents with left and right margins wider than 1 inch, the right margin may appear quite ragged. If the paragraph alignment is changed to justified alignment, the right margin will appear even, but there will be extra space added throughout the line. In these situations, hyphenating long words that fall at the ends of text lines provides the document with a more balanced look. Use Word's Help feature to learn how to automatically hyphenate words in a document.
2. Open **InterfaceApps.docx**.
3. Save the document with Save As and name it **WL1-C3-A5-InterfaceApps**.
4. Automatically hyphenate words in the document, limiting the number of consecutive hyphens to 2. ***Hint: Specify the number of consecutive hyphens at the Hyphenation dialog box.***

Visual Benchmark Demonstrate Your Proficiency

CREATE A RESUME

1. At a blank document, click the *No Spacing* style and then type the resume document shown in Figure 3.14 on the next page. Apply character and paragraph formatting as shown in the figure. Insert 6 points of spacing after the headings *PROFESSIONAL EXPERIENCE, EDUCATION, TECHNOLOGY SKILLS,* and *REFERENCES*. Change the font size of the name, *DEVON CHAMBERS*, to 16 points.
2. Save the document and name it **WL1-C3-VB-Resume.**
3. Print and then close the document.

Case Study Apply Your Skills

Part 1

You are the assistant to Gina Coletti, manager of La Dolce Vita, an Italian restaurant. She has been working on updating and formatting the lunch menu. She has asked you to complete the menu by opening the **Menu.docx** document (located in the WL1C3 folder), determining how the appetizer section is formatted, and then applying the same formatting to the *Soups and Salads*; *Sandwiches, Calzones and Burgers*; and *Individual Pizzas* sections. Save the document and name it **WL1-C3-CS-Menu**. Print and then close the document.

Part 2

Ms. Coletti has reviewed the completed menu and is pleased with it, but she wants to add a page border around the entire page to increase visual interest. Open **WL1-C3-CS-Menu.docx** and then save the document and name it **WL1-C3-CS-MenuPgBorder**. Display the Borders and Shading dialog box with the Page Border tab selected and then experiment with the options available. Apply an appropriate page border to the menu. (Consider applying an art page border.) Save, print, and then close **WL1-C3-CS-MenuPgBorder.docx**.

Part 3

Each week, the restaurant offers daily specials. Ms. Coletti has asked you to open and format the text in the **MenuSpecials.docx** document. She has asked you to format the specials menu in a similar manner as the main menu but to make some changes so it is unique from the main menu. Apply the same page border to the specials menu document that you applied to the main menu document. Save the document and name it **WL1-C3-CS-MenuSpecials**. Print and then close the document.

Part 4

You have been asked by the head chef to research a new recipe for an Italian dish. Using the Internet, find a recipe that interests you and then prepare a Word document containing the recipe and ingredients. Use bullets before each ingredient and use numbering for each step in the recipe preparation. Save the document and name it **WL1-C3-CS-Recipe**. Print and then close the document.

Figure 3.14 Visual Benchmark

DEVON CHAMBERS

344 North Anderson Road * Oklahoma City, OK 73177 * (404) 555-3228

PROFILE

Business manager with successful track record at entrepreneurial start-up and strong project management skills. Keen ability to motivate and supervise employees, a strong hands-on experience with customer service, marketing, and operations. Highly organized and motivated professional looking to leverage strengths in leadership and organizational skills in a project coordinator role.

PROFESSIONAL EXPERIENCE

Midwest Deli, Oklahoma City, OK .... 07/13 to present
Assistant Manager

- Coordinated the opening of a new business, which included budgeting start-up costs, establishing relationships with vendors, ordering supplies, purchasing and installing equipment, and marketing the business to the community
- Manage business personnel, which includes recruitment, interviewing, hiring, training, motivating staff, and conflict resolution
- Manage daily business operations through customer satisfaction, quality control, employee scheduling, process improvement, and maintaining product inventory

Marin Associates, Shawnee, OK.. 06/11 to 06/13
Projects Coordinator

- Developed and maintained a secure office network and installed and repaired computers
- Provided support for hardware and software issues
- Directed agency projects such as equipment purchases, office reorganization, and building maintenance and repair

Moore Insurance Agency, Shawnee, OK.. 04/09 to 04/11
Administrative Assistant

- Prepared documents and forms for staff and clients
- Organized and maintained paper and electronic files and scheduled meetings and appointments
- Disseminated information using the telephone, mail services, websites, and email

EDUCATION

Associate of Arts, Business 2013
Oklahoma City Community College

TECHNOLOGY SKILLS

- Proficient in Microsoft Word, Excel, and PowerPoint
- Knowledgeable in current and previous versions of the Windows operating system
- Experience with networking, firewalls, and security systems

REFERENCES

Professional and personal references available upon request.

MICROSOFT®
WORD

CHAPTER 4

Formatting Pages

PERFORMANCE OBJECTIVES

Upon successful completion of Chapter 4, you will be able to:

- **Change document views**
- **Navigate in a document with the Navigation pane**
- **Change margins, page orientation, and paper size in a document**
- **Format pages at the Page Setup dialog box**
- **Insert a page break, blank page, and cover page**
- **Insert page numbering**
- **Insert and edit predesigned headers and footers**
- **Insert a watermark, page color, and page border**
- **Find and replace text and formatting**

Tutorials

4.1 Changing Document Views
4.2 Navigating Using the Navigation Pane
4.3 Changing Margins, Page Orientation, and Paper Size
4.4 Inserting a Blank Page and a Cover Page
4.5 Inserting Page Numbers and Page Breaks
4.6 Creating Headers and Footers
4.7 Modifying Headers and Footers
4.8 Inserting a Watermark, Page Color, and Page Border
4.9 Finding and Replacing Text
4.10 Finding and Replacing Formatting

A document generally displays in Print Layout view. You can change this default view with buttons in the view area on the Status bar or with options on the VIEW tab. Use the Navigation pane to navigate in a document. A Word document, by default, contains 1-inch top, bottom, left, and right margins. You can change these default margins with the Margins button in the Page Setup group on the PAGE LAYOUT tab or with options at the Page Setup dialog box. You can insert a variety of features in a Word document, including a page break, blank page, and cover page as well as page numbers, headers, footers, a watermark, page color, and page border. Use options at the Find and Replace dialog box to search for specific text or formatting and replace with other text or formatting. Model answers for this chapter's projects appear on the following pages.

Note: Before beginning the projects, copy to your storage medium the WL1C4 subfolder from the WL1 folder on the CD that accompanies this textbook and then make WL1C4 thae active folder.

NETIQUETTE GUIDELINES

Distance conveys a degree of anonymity, and as a result, many people feel less inhibited in online situations than in their everyday lives. This lessening of inhibitions sometimes leads people to drop their normal standards of decorum when communicating online. In response, good cybercitizens have developed, over the years, an informal set of guidelines for online behavior called ***netiquette***. Netiquette can be summarized by three simple precepts: Remember that there is a human being on the other end of your communication, treat that human being with respect, and do not transmit any message that you wouldn't be willing to communicate face to face. Some specific guidelines include:

- Be careful what you write about others. Assume that anyone about whom you are writing will read your comments or receive them by some circuitous route.
- Be truthful. Do not pretend to be someone or something that you are not.
- Be brief. Receiving and reading messages costs time and money.
- Use titles that accurately and concisely describe the contents of email and other postings.
- Consider your audience, and use language that is appropriate. Excessive use of jargon in a nontechnical chat room, for example, can be bad manners, and remember that children sometimes join chat rooms.
- Avoid offensive language, especially comments that might be construed as racist or sexist.
- Remember that the law still applies in cyberspace. Do not commit illegal acts online, such as libeling or slandering others, and do not joke about committing illegal acts.
- Be careful with humor and sarcasm. One person's humorous comment can be another person's boorish or degrading remark.
- Do not post a message more than once.
- Generally speaking, avoid putting words into full capitals. Online, all-caps is considered SHOUTING.
- If you are following up a previous message or posting, summarize that message or posting.
- Do not post irrelevant messages, referred to in hacker's jargon as spam.
- Do not post messages whose sole purpose is to sucker others into an irrelevant or unimportant discussion. Such messages are known as trolls.
- Read existing follow-up postings and don't repeat what has already been said.
- Respect other people's intellectual property. Don't post, display, or otherwise provide access to materials belonging to others, and cite references as appropriate.
- Temper online expressions of hostility; in hacker's jargon, avoid excessive flaming of others.
- Never send online chain letters.
- Some email programs allow one to place a signature containing text and graphics at the end of a mailing. Remember that elaborate materials take up valuable transmission time, and do not overdo these signatures.
- Limit the length of typed lines to less than 78 characters, and avoid unusual formatting.
- Identify any financial interests related to an email message or posting. If you are selling something, make that fact clear.
- Do not send email to people who might have no interest in it. In particular, avoid automatically copying email to large numbers of people.
- Online messages can be quite informal, but try, nevertheless, to express yourself using proper spelling, capitalization, grammar, usage, and punctuation.
- Avoid chastising others for their online typos. To err is human. To forgive is good cybercitizenship.

Project 2 Format a Document on Online Etiquette Guidelines
WL1-C4-P2-Netiquette.docx

Cover Page

Project 3 Customize a Report on Computer Input and Output Devices
WL1-C4-P3-CompDevices.docx

COMPUTER INPUT DEVICES

Engineers have been especially creative in designing new ways to get information into computers. Some input methods are highly specialized and unusual, while common devices often undergo redesign to improve their capabilities or their ergonomics, the ways in which they affect people physically. Some common input devices include keyboards, mice, trackballs, and touchpads.

Keyboard

A keyboard can be an external device that is attached by means of a cable, or it can be attached to the CPU case itself as it is for laptop computers. Most keyboards today are QWERTY keyboards, which take their name from the first six keys at the left of the first row of letters. An alternative, the DVORAK keyboard, places the most commonly used keys close to the user's fingertips and speeds typing.

Many keyboards have a separate numeric keypad, like that of a calculator, containing numbers and mathematical operators. All keyboards have modifier keys that enable the user to change the symbol or character that is entered when a given key is pressed. The Shift key, for example, makes a letter uppercase. Keyboards also have special cursor keys that enable the user to change the position on the screen of the cursor, a symbol that appears on the monitor to show where in a document the next change will appear. Most keyboards also have function keys, labeled F1, F2, F3, and so on. These keys allow the user to issue commands by pressing a single key.

1 | Page

Page 1

Mouse

Graphical operating systems contain many elements that a user can choose by pointing at them. Such elements include buttons, tools, pull-down menus, and icons for file folders, programs, and document files. Often pointing to and clicking on one of these elements is more convenient than using the cursor or arrow keys on the keyboard. This pointing and clicking can be done by using a mouse. The mouse is the second most common input device, after the keyboard. A mouse operates by moving the cursor on the computer screen to correspond to movements made with the mouse.

Trackball

A trackball is like an upside-down mouse. A mouse is moved over a pad. A trackball remains stationary, and the user moves the ball with his or her fingers or palm. One or more buttons for choosing options are incorporated into the design of the trackball.

Touchpad and Touchscreen

A touchpad feels less mechanical than a mouse or trackball because the user simply moves a finger on the pad. A touchpad has two parts. One part acts as a button, while the other emulates a mouse pad on which the user traces the location of the cursor with a finger. People with carpal tunnel syndrome find touchpads and trackballs easier to use than mice. Many portable computers have built-in trackballs or touchpads as input devices.

A touchscreen allows the user to choose options by pressing the appropriate part of the screen. Touchscreens are widely used in bank ATMs and in kiosks at retail outlets and in tourist areas.

2 | Page

Page 2

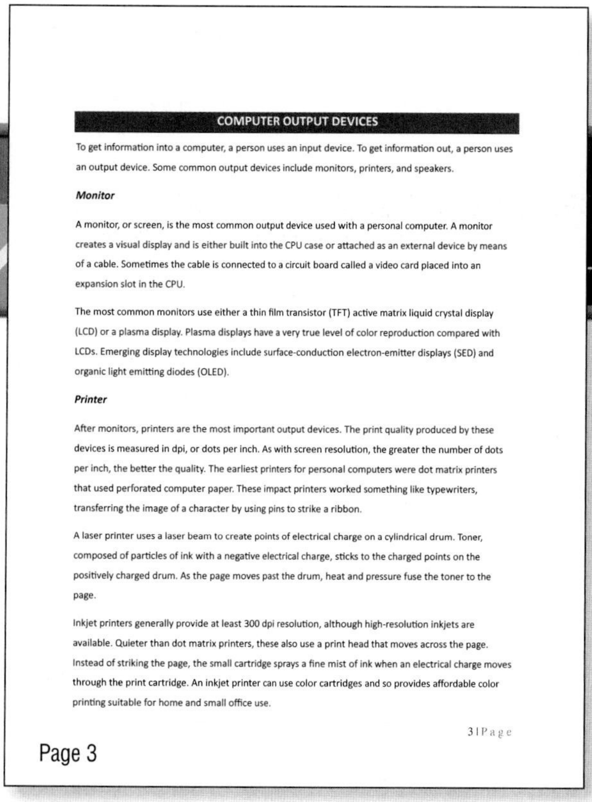

COMPUTER OUTPUT DEVICES

To get information into a computer, a person uses an input device. To get information out, a person uses an output device. Some common output devices include monitors, printers, and speakers.

Monitor

A monitor, or screen, is the most common output device used with a personal computer. A monitor creates a visual display and is either built into the CPU case or attached as an external device by means of a cable. Sometimes the cable is connected to a circuit board called a video card placed into an expansion slot in the CPU.

The most common monitors use either a thin film transistor (TFT) active matrix liquid crystal display (LCD) or a plasma display. Plasma displays have a very true level of color reproduction compared with LCDs. Emerging display technologies include surface-conduction electron-emitter displays (SED) and organic light emitting diodes (OLED).

Printer

After monitors, printers are the most important output devices. The print quality produced by these devices is measured in dpi, or dots per inch. As with screen resolution, the greater the number of dots per inch, the better the quality. The earliest printers for personal computers were dot matrix printers that used perforated computer paper. These impact printers worked something like typewriters, transferring the image of a character by using pins to strike a ribbon.

A laser printer uses a laser beam to create points of electrical charge on a cylindrical drum. Toner, composed of particles of ink with a negative electrical charge, sticks to the charged points on the positively charged drum. As the page moves past the drum, heat and pressure fuse the toner to the page.

Inkjet printers generally provide at least 300 dpi resolution, although high-resolution inkjets are available. Quieter than dot matrix printers, these also use a print head that moves across the page. Instead of striking the page, the small cartridge sprays a fine mist of ink when an electrical charge moves through the print cartridge. An inkjet printer can use color cartridges and so provides affordable color printing suitable for home and small office use.

3 | Page

Page 3

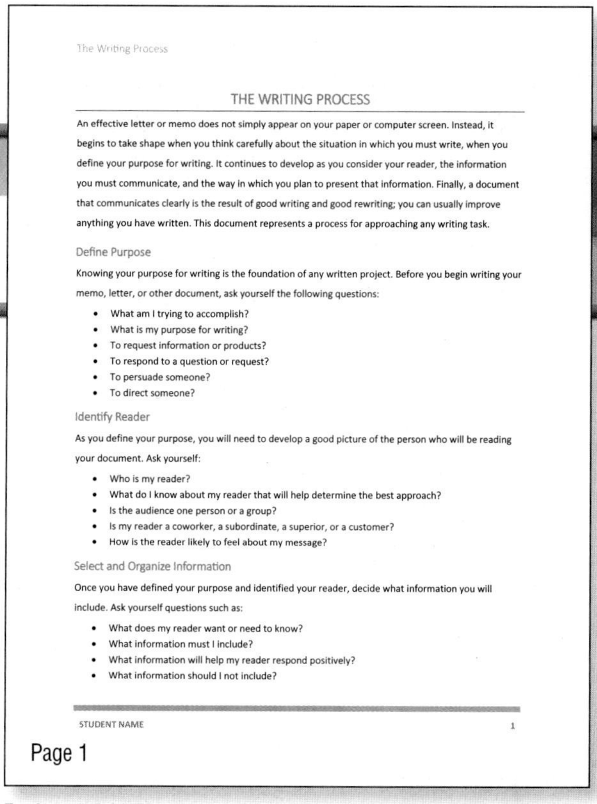

The Writing Process

THE WRITING PROCESS

An effective letter or memo does not simply appear on your paper or computer screen. Instead, it begins to take shape when you think carefully about the situation in which you must write, when you define your purpose for writing. It continues to develop as you consider your reader, the information you must communicate, and the way in which you plan to present that information. Finally, a document that communicates clearly is the result of good writing and good rewriting; you can usually improve anything you have written. This document represents a process for approaching any writing task.

Define Purpose

Knowing your purpose for writing is the foundation of any written project. Before you begin writing your memo, letter, or other document, ask yourself the following questions:

- What am I trying to accomplish?
- What is my purpose for writing?
- To request information or products?
- To respond to a question or request?
- To persuade someone?
- To direct someone?

Identify Reader

As you define your purpose, you will need to develop a good picture of the person who will be reading your document. Ask yourself:

- Who is my reader?
- What do I know about my reader that will help determine the best approach?
- Is the audience one person or a group?
- Is my reader a coworker, a subordinate, a superior, or a customer?
- How is the reader likely to feel about my message?

Select and Organize Information

Once you have defined your purpose and identified your reader, decide what information you will include. Ask yourself questions such as:

- What does my reader want or need to know?
- What information must I include?
- What information will help my reader respond positively?
- What information should I not include?

STUDENT NAME 1

Page 1

Project 4 Add Elements to a Report on the Writing Process

WL1-C4-P4-WritingProcess.docx

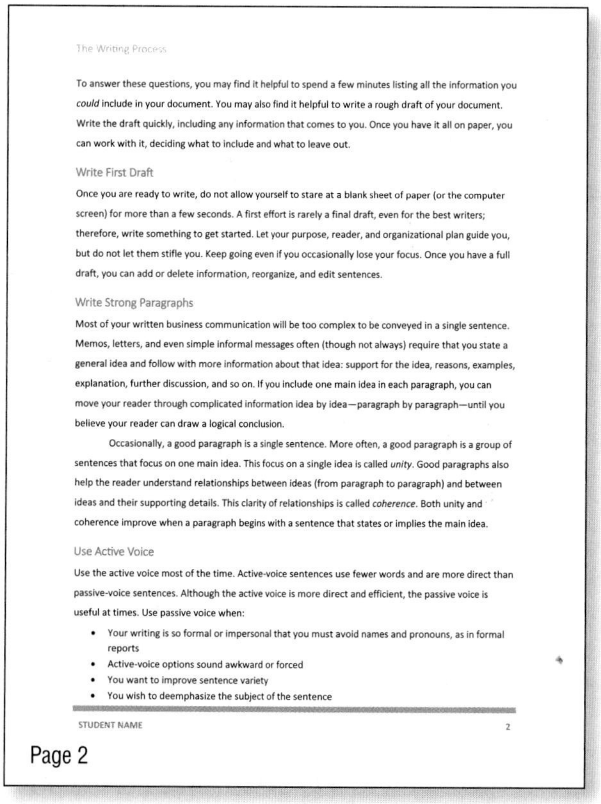

The Writing Process

To answer these questions, you may find it helpful to spend a few minutes listing all the information you *could* include in your document. You may also find it helpful to write a rough draft of your document. Write the draft quickly, including any information that comes to you. Once you have it all on paper, you can work with it, deciding what to include and what to leave out.

Write First Draft

Once you are ready to write, do not allow yourself to stare at a blank sheet of paper (or the computer screen) for more than a few seconds. A first effort is rarely a final draft, even for the best writers; therefore, write something to get started. Let your purpose, reader, and organizational plan guide you, but do not let them stifle you. Keep going even if you occasionally lose your focus. Once you have a full draft, you can add or delete information, reorganize, and edit sentences.

Write Strong Paragraphs

Most of your written business communication will be too complex to be conveyed in a single sentence. Memos, letters, and even simple informal messages often (though not always) require that you state a general idea and follow with more information about that idea: support for the idea, reasons, examples, explanation, further discussion, and so on. If you include one main idea in each paragraph, you can move your reader through complicated information idea by idea—paragraph by paragraph—until you believe your reader can draw a logical conclusion.

Occasionally, a good paragraph is a single sentence. More often, a good paragraph is a group of sentences that focus on one main idea. This focus on a single idea is called *unity*. Good paragraphs also help the reader understand relationships between ideas (from paragraph to paragraph) and between ideas and their supporting details. This clarity of relationships is called *coherence*. Both unity and coherence improve when a paragraph begins with a sentence that states or implies the main idea.

Use Active Voice

Use the active voice most of the time. Active-voice sentences use fewer words and are more direct than passive-voice sentences. Although the active voice is more direct and efficient, the passive voice is useful at times. Use passive voice when:

- Your writing is so formal or impersonal that you must avoid names and pronouns, as in formal reports
- Active-voice options sound awkward or forced
- You want to improve sentence variety
- You wish to deemphasize the subject of the sentence

STUDENT NAME 2

Page 2

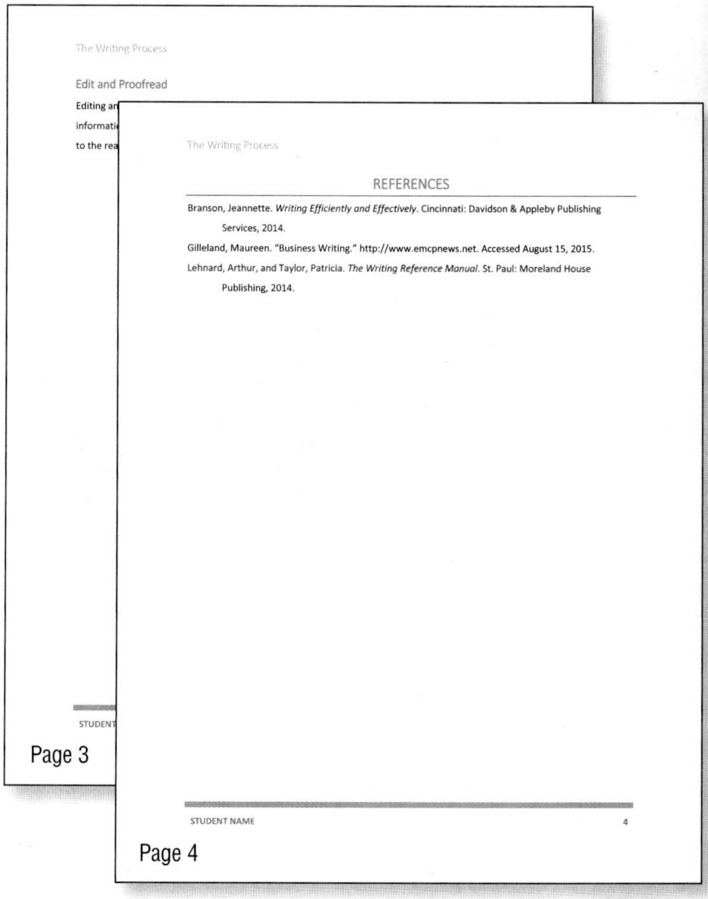

The Writing Process

Edit and Proofread

Editing ar
informati
to the rea

STUDENT

Page 3

The Writing Process

REFERENCES

Branson, Jeannette. *Writing Efficiently and Effectively*. Cincinnati: Davidson & Appleby Publishing Services, 2014.

Gilleland, Maureen. "Business Writing." http://www.emcpnews.net. Accessed August 15, 2015.

Lehnard, Arthur, and Taylor, Patricia. *The Writing Reference Manual*. St. Paul: Moreland House Publishing, 2014.

STUDENT NAME 4

Page 4

DESIREABLE EMPLOYEE QUALITIES

Communication Skills

The focus on communication skills is so common that you should assume that every job requires them—and employers say so too! Assume that communication skills are important for every job and try to demonstrate them in your resume. There is a mountain of evidence from research on employment interviews that candidates demonstrating good communication skills tend to get the highest ratings. There is no reason why you cannot demonstrate these skills in your resume.

Who Will You Communicate With?

The degree of skills you need to demonstrate will depend on the type of job you are going for. The job might involve communicating with any of the following:

- People in your team or department
- Other departments in the same organization
- Other organizations or the public
- Special groups, such as the young or elderly
- Influential or senior clients, such as corporate sponsors
- Lawyers
- Government officials
- Senior managers

What difference does it make who you communicate with? Different situations make different demands on you and you should be aware of the sorts of communication you may need. While an employer might tolerate the occasional gruff tone or mildly sarcastic remark within the confines of the office, a very dim view will be taken of such behavior in front of clients.

Look at the job ad or description and try to establish who you might be communicating with the most. The skills required may range from being able to understand and relay telephone messages clearly to writing an extensive report or proposal, or presenting a sales pitch to customers. Questions to ask yourself are the following:

- Do I speak clearly in English?
- Can I write clearly?
- Am I able to understand what people are saying to me on most occasions?
- Can I explain things to people clearly?

So How Do I Demonstrate These Skills on My Resume?

You could draw on your work history. For instance, passing a typing test might suggest you can spell accurately, as would shorthand skills. Work as a receptionist or a sales representative suggests that you can communicate verbally and effectively. Giving presentations to clients, or other public speaking experiences such as Toastmasters, look good.

Page 1

Team Skills

What this means is that you are happy and effective working in groups with other people. You are happy to work together, share information, and help out team members when they are struggling. You tend to like people, and are reasonably well liked. It sometimes seems that "team player" is added to just about every job ad without any real reason. As a general rule, it is code for saying "Do you get along with other people, or are you selfish and unpleasant?" Some people think the expression "team player" refers to membership in sporting teams. Generally, this is not the case, and it is better to use examples of your team skills drawn from work experience. Of course, if you cannot think of any convincing examples from work, then you might consider using some limited examples from your hobbies.

Attention to Detail

Many jobs request this skill. Just because this quality is not included in an advertisement, do not assume it is not important. Making silly mistakes in some jobs, such as an accounting clerk position where large sums of money may be involved, can lead to very expensive outcomes! In a study we conducted, where we deliberately included spelling mistakes on some resumes but not on others, we found that even one error reduced the chance of the candidate being interviewed by between 30 and 45 percent. Think about it—just a minor effort can reduce your chances of being interviewed by almost half!

Energy, Dynamism, Enthusiasm, Drive, and Initiative

Nobody wants to employ somebody who slumps in their seat, seems to take forever to carry out the most trivial tasks, and sighs deeply every time they are asked to do something. The organization looking for qualities such as energy and enthusiasm is looking for someone who is alert, gets on with their work quickly and without unnecessary complaint, and (within reason) will find solutions to problems rather than find problems with solutions.

Ability to Handle Pressure

Pressure varies from job to job, but the request for this ability is an indication that things might get very busy from time to time—for example, work in a fire department or with the police force, where lapses of concentration or failures of nerve have potentially fatal outcomes. What the employer wants to see is evidence that you will respond to the challenge and perhaps work faster or longer hours on occasion to meet deadlines or reduce the backlog. What they are saying is they do not expect you to lose your temper or take sick leave at the first sign of pressure. Pressure in some jobs will be immediate, such as a long line of irritated customers. Or it could be long-term stress, such as the pressure to build all the stadiums for the Olympic Games on time!

Leadership

Leadership is one of those qualities that tends to get thrown into a job ad without much justification. For a start, nobody can agree on what makes a good leader. However, if you can demonstrate that you have managed a team of people successfully—either by length of time in the position (this says that if you were not a good leader, you would have been moved on quickly) or by tasks achieved by a group under your management—this may be the sort of thing the employer is looking for. Equally, being elected to a chairperson's role or similar job would suggest that you inspire the confidence of others.

Page 2

Project 5 Format a Report on Employee Qualities

WL1-C4-P5-EmpQualities.docx

RENT AGREEMENT

THIS RENT AGREEMENT (hereinafter referred to as the "Agreement") is made and entered into this ____ day of ________________, 2015, by and between Tracy Hartford and Michael Iwami.

Term

Tracy Hartford rents to Michael Iwami and Michael Iwami rents from Tracy Hartford the described premises together with any and all appurtenances thereto, for a term of _____ year(s), such term beginning on _________________, and ending at 12 o'clock midnight on ____________________.

Rent

The total rent for the term hereof is the sum of ________________ DOLLARS ($_________) payable on the ______ day of each month of the term. All such payments shall be made to Tracy Hartford at Tracy Hartford's address on or before the due date and without demand.

Damage Deposit

Upon the due execution of this Agreement, Michael Iwami shall deposit with Tracy Hartford the sum of ____________ DOLLARS ($_________), receipt of which is hereby acknowledged by Tracy Hartford, as security for any damage caused to the Premises during the renting term hereof. Such deposit shall be returned to Michael Iwami, without interest, and minus any set off for damages to the Premises, upon the termination of this renting Agreement.

Use of Premises

The Premises shall be used and occupied by Michael Iwami and Michael Iwami's immediately family, exclusively, as a private single-family dwelling, and no part of the Premises shall be used at any time during the term of this Agreement by Michael Iwami for the purpose of carrying on any business, profession, or trade of any kind, or for any purpose other than as a private single-family dwelling. Michael Iwami shall not allow any other person, other than Michael Iwami's immediate family or transient relatives and friends who are guests of Michael Iwami, to use or occupy the Premises without first obtaining Tracy Hartford's written consent to such use.

Condition of Premises

Michael Iwami stipulates, represents, and warrants that Michael Iwami has examined the Premises, and that they are at the time of this Agreement in good order and repair and in a safe, clean, and tenantable condition.

Alterations and Improvements

Michael Iwami shall make no alterations to the buildings or improvements on the Premises without the prior written consent of Tracy Hartford. Any and all alterations, changes, and/or improvements built, constructed, or placed on the Premises by Michael Iwami shall, unminus otherwise provided by written agreement between Tracy Hartford and Michael Iwami, be and become the property of Tracy Hartford and remain on the Premises at the expiration or earlier termination of this Agreement.

Page 1

Damage to Premises

In the event the Premises are destroyed or rendered wholly unlivable, by fire, storm, earthquake, or other casualty not caused by the negligence of Michael Iwami, this Agreement shall terminate from such time except for the purpose of enforcing rights that may have then accrued hereunder.

Page 2

Project 6 Format a Lease Agreement

WL1-C4-P6-LeaseAgrmnt.docx

Project 1 Navigate in a Report on Navigating and Searching the Web — 2 Parts

You will open a document containing information on navigating and searching the web, change document views, navigate in the document using the Navigation pane, and show and hide white space at the tops and bottoms of pages.

Changing the View

By default, a Word document displays in Print Layout view. This view displays the document on the screen as it will appear when printed. Other views are available, such as Draft and Read Mode. Change views with buttons in the view area on the Status bar or with options on the VIEW tab. The buttons in the view area on the Status bar are identified in Figure 4.1. Along with the View buttons, the Status bar also contains a Zoom slider bar, as shown in Figure 4.1. Drag the button on the Zoom slider bar to increase or decrease the size of the display, or click the Zoom Out button to decrease the size and click the Zoom In button to increase the size.

Click the 100% that displays at the right side of the Zoom slider bar to display the Zoom dialog box.

Zoom Out Zoom In

Displaying a Document in Draft View

Change to Draft view and the document displays in a format for efficient editing and formatting. At this view, margins and other features such as headers and footers do not display on the screen. Change to Draft view by clicking the VIEW tab and then clicking the Draft button in the Views group.

Draft

Displaying a Document in Read Mode View

The Read Mode view displays a document in a format for easy viewing and reading. Change to Read Mode view by clicking the Read Mode button in the view area on the Status bar or by clicking the VIEW tab and then clicking the Read Mode button in the Views group. Navigate in Read Mode view using the keys on the keyboard, as shown in Table 4.1. Or, navigate with the mouse by clicking at the right side of the screen or clicking the Next button (right-pointing triangle in a circle) to display the next pages or clicking at the left side of the screen or clicking the Previous button (left-pointing triangle in a circle) to display the previous pages.

Read Mode

The FILE, TOOLS, and VIEW tabs display in the upper left corner of the screen in Read Mode view. Click the FILE tab to display the backstage area. Click the TOOLS tab and a drop-down list displays with options for finding specific text in the document and searching for information on the Internet using the Bing search engine. Click the VIEW tab and options display for customizing what you see in Read Mode view. You can display the Navigation pane to navigate to specific locations

Figure 4.1 View Buttons and Zoom Slider Bar

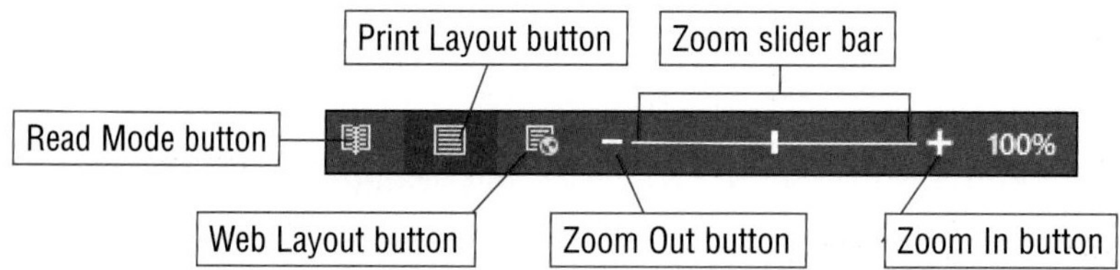

Table 4.1 Keyboard Commands in Read Mode View

Press this key	*To complete this action*
Page Down key, Right Arrow key, or spacebar	Display next two pages
Page Up key, Left Arrow key, or Backspace key	Display previous two pages
Home	Display first page in document
End	Display last page in document
Esc	Return to previous view

in the document, show comments inserted in the document, change the width of the columns or change to a page layout, and change the page colors in Read Mode view.

If your document contains an object such as a table, SmartArt graphic, image, or shape, you can zoom in on the object in Read Mode view. To do this, double-click the object. When you double-click an object, a button containing a magnifying glass with a plus symbol inside displays just outside the upper right corner of the object. Click this button to zoom in even more on the object. Click the button again and the object returns to the original zoom size. Click once outside the object to return it to its original size.

To close Read Mode view and return to the previous view, press the Esc key on your keyboard or click the VIEW tab and then click *Edit Document* at the drop-down list.

Changing Ribbon Display Options

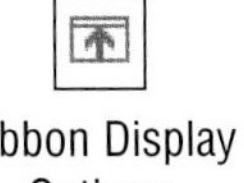
Ribbon Display Options

If you want to view more of your document, use the Ribbon Display Options button that displays in the upper right corner of the screen to the right of the Microsoft Word Help button. Click the Ribbon Display Options button and a drop-down list displays with three options—*Auto-hide Ribbon*, *Show Tabs*, and *Show Tabs and Commands*. The default is Show Tabs and Commands, which displays the Quick Access toolbar, the ribbon, and the Status bar on the screen. Click the first option, *Auto-hide Ribbon*, and the Quick Access toolbar, ribbon, and Status bar are hidden, allowing you to see more of your document. To temporarily redisplay these features, click at the top of the screen. Turn these features back on by clicking the Ribbon Display Options button and then clicking the *Show Tabs and Commands* option. Click the *Show Tabs* option at the drop-down list and the tabs display on the ribbon while the buttons and commands remain hidden.

Navigating Using the Navigation Pane

Quick Steps
Display Navigation Pane
1. Click VIEW tab.
2. Click *Navigation Pane* check box.

Word includes a number of features for navigating in a document. Along with the navigation features you have already learned, you can also navigate using the Navigation pane shown in Figure 4.2. When you click the *Navigation Pane* check box in the Show group on the VIEW tab, the Navigation pane displays at the left side of the screen and includes a search text box and a pane with three tabs. Click the HEADINGS tab to display in the pane titles and headings with styles applied. Click a title or heading in the pane to move the insertion point to that title or heading.

Figure 4.2 Navigation Pane

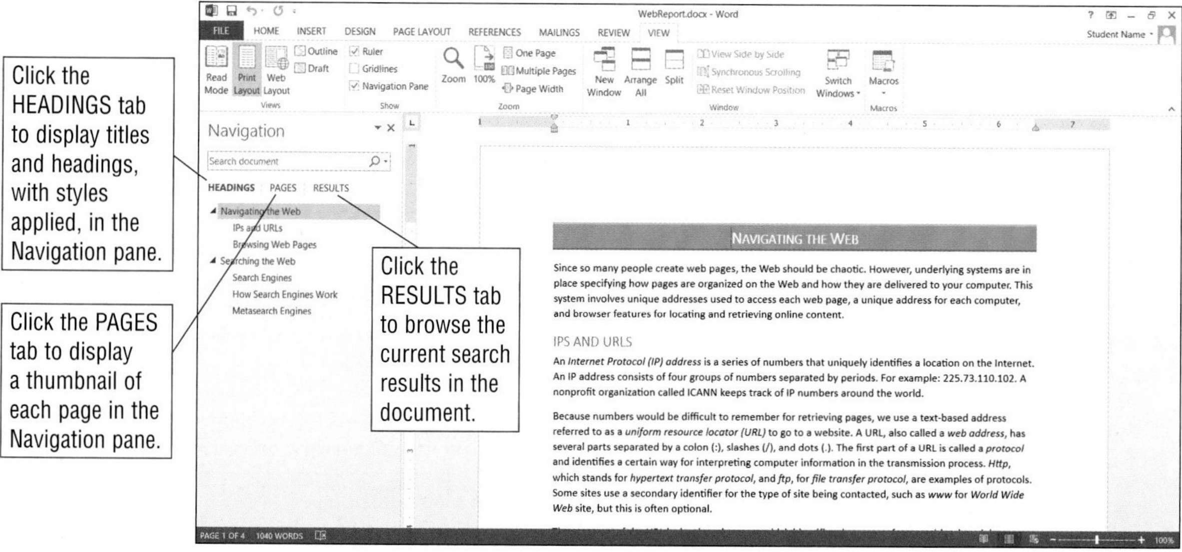

Click the PAGES tab to display a thumbnail of each page in the pane. Click a thumbnail to move the insertion point to the specific page. Click the RESULTS tab to browse the current search results in the document. Close the Navigation pane by clicking the *Navigation Pane* check box in the Show group on the VIEW tab or by clicking the Close button located in the upper right corner of the pane.

Project 1a Changing Views and Navigating in a Document — Part 1 of 2

1. Open **WebReport.docx**.
2. Click the VIEW tab and then click the Draft button in the Views group.

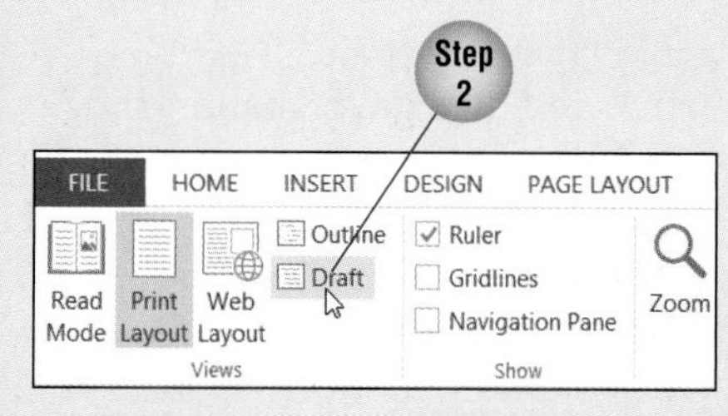

3. Click three times on the Zoom Out button that displays to the left of the Zoom slider bar. (This changes the percentage displays and *70%* displays at the right side of the Zoom In button.)
4. Using the mouse, drag the Zoom slider bar button to the middle until *100%* displays at the right side of the Zoom In button.

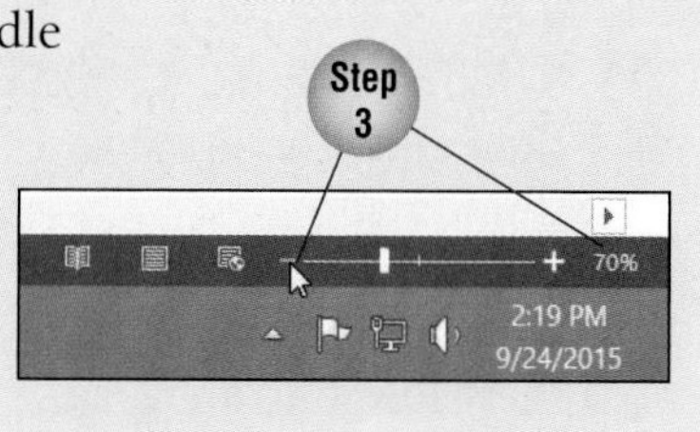

5. Click the Print Layout button located in the view area on the Status bar.
6. Click the Read Mode button located in the view area on the Status bar.
7. Increase the display of the table located at the right side of the screen by double-clicking the table. (If the table is not visible, click the right-pointing arrow located at the right side of the screen to view the next page.)
8. Click the button (contains a magnifying glass with a plus symbol) that displays outside the upper right corner of the table. (This increases the zoom.)

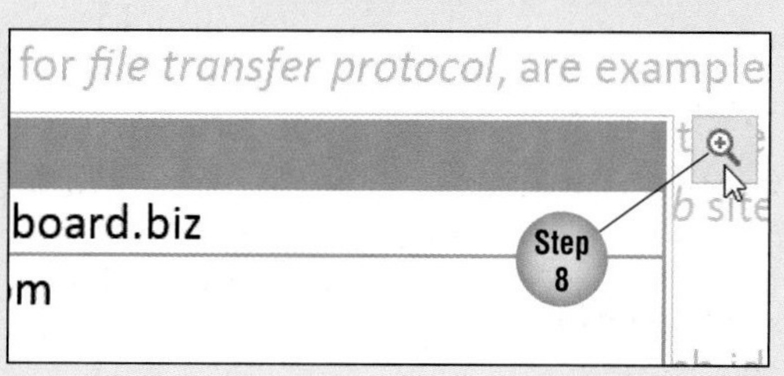

9. Click outside the table to return the table to the original size.
10. Practice navigating in Read Mode view using the actions shown in Table 4.1 (except the last option).
11. Press the Esc key to return to the Print Layout view.
12. Click the Ribbon Display Options button that displays in the upper right corner of the screen to the right of the Microsoft Word Help button and then click *Auto-hide Ribbon* at the drop-down list.
13. Press Ctrl + End to display the last page in the document and then press the Page Up key until the beginning of the document displays.
14. Click at the top of the screen to temporarily redisplay the Quick Access toolbar, ribbon, and Status bar.
15. Click the Ribbon Display Options button and then click *Show Tabs* at the drop-down list.
16. Click the Ribbon Display Options button and then click *Show Tabs and Commands* at the drop-down list.
17. Click the *Navigation Pane* check box in the Show group on the VIEW tab to insert a check mark.
18. Click the *Navigating the Web* heading that displays in the Navigation pane.
19. Click the *Searching the Web* heading that displays in the Navigation pane.
20. Click the PAGES tab in the Navigation pane to display the page thumbnails in the pane.
21. Click the number 4 thumbnail in the Navigation pane.
22. Scroll up the pane and then click the number 1 thumbnail.
23. Close the Navigation pane by clicking the Close button located in the upper right corner of the Navigation pane.

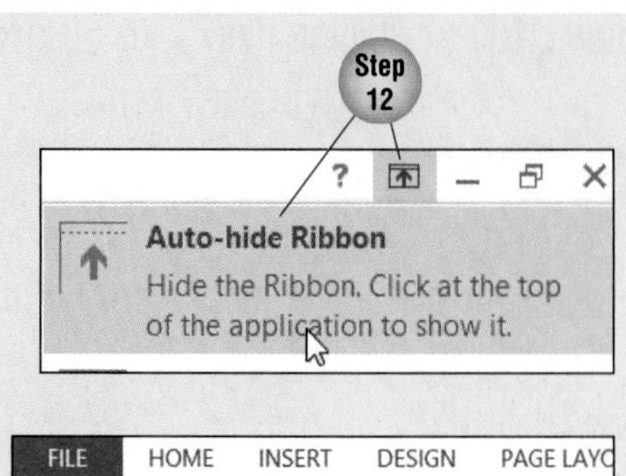

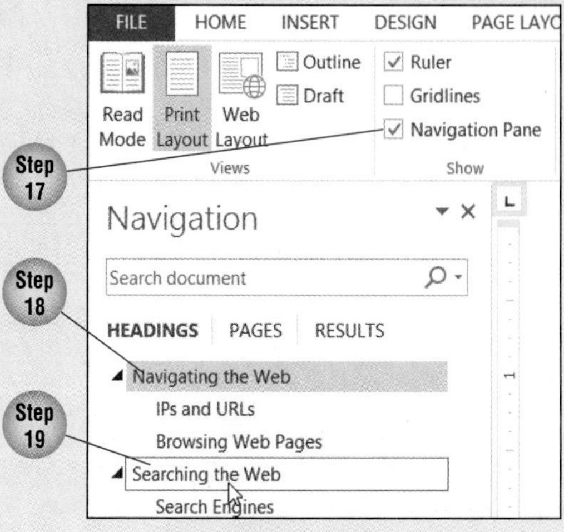

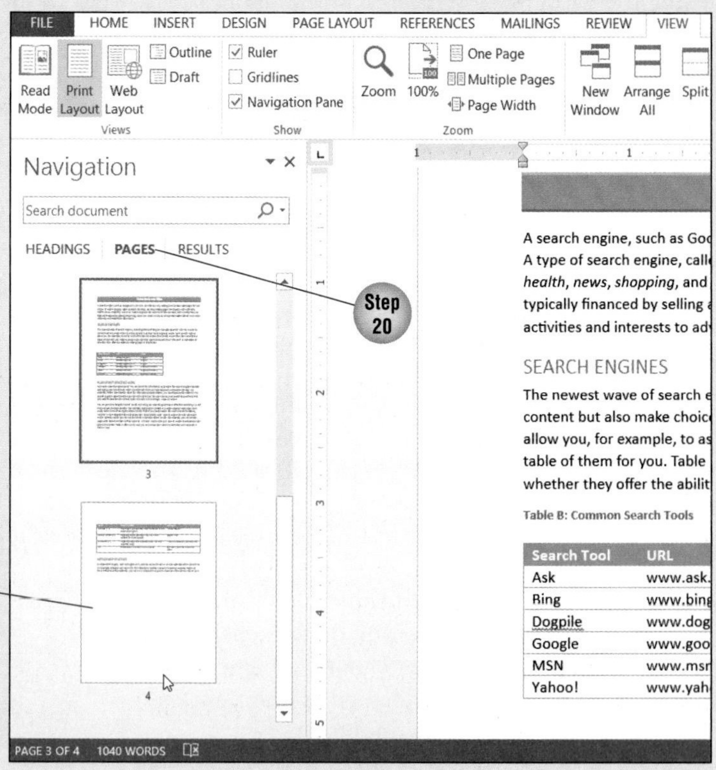

Hiding/Showing White Space in Print Layout View

In Print Layout view, a page displays as it will appear when printed including the white space at the top and bottom of the page representing the document's margins. To save space on the screen in Print Layout view, you can remove the white space by positioning the mouse pointer at the top edge or bottom edge of a page or between pages until the pointer displays as the Hide White Space icon and then double-clicking the left mouse button. To redisplay the white space, position the mouse pointer on the thin, gray line separating pages until the pointer turns into the Show White Space icon and then double-click the left mouse button.

Quick Steps

Hide/Show White Space

1. Position mouse pointer at top of page until pointer displays as Hide White Space icon or Show White Space icon.
2. Double-click left mouse button.

Hide White Space

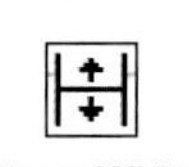

Show White Space

Project 1b Hiding/Showing White Space — Part 2 of 2

1. With **WebReport.docx** open, make sure the document displays in Print Layout view.
2. Press Ctrl + Home to move the insertion point to the beginning of the document.
3. Hide the white spaces at the tops and bottoms of pages by positioning the mouse pointer at the top edge of the page until the pointer turns into the Hide White Space icon and then double-clicking the left mouse button.

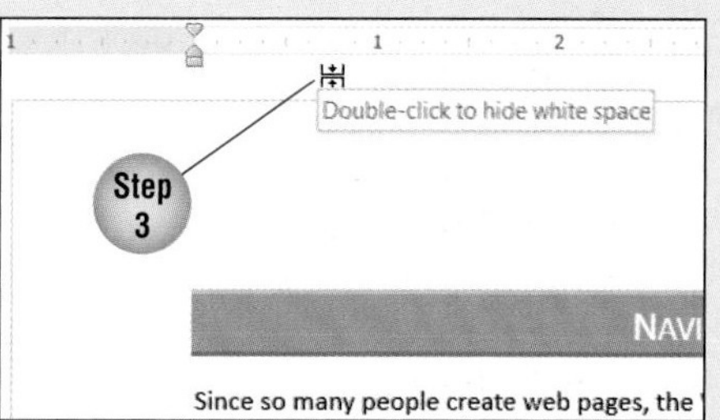

4. Scroll through the document and notice the display of pages.
5. Redisplay the white spaces at the tops and bottoms of pages by positioning the mouse pointer on any thin, gray line separating pages until the pointer turns into the Show White Space icon and then double-clicking the left mouse button.

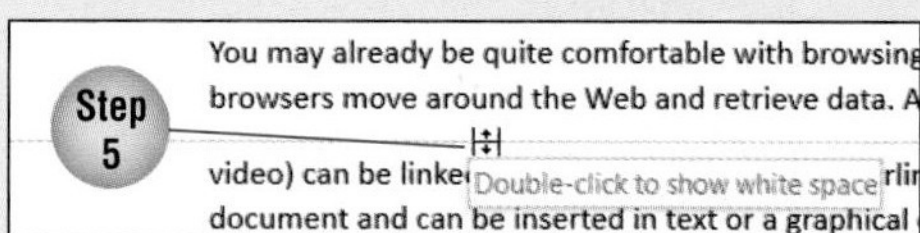

6. Close **WebReport.docx**.

Project 2 Format a Document on Online Etiquette Guidelines — 2 Parts

You will open a document containing information on guidelines for online etiquette and then change the margins, page orientation, and page size.

Changing Page Setup

The Page Setup group on the PAGE LAYOUT tab contains a number of options for affecting pages in a document. With options in the Page Setup group, you can perform such actions as changing margins, orientation, and page size and inserting page breaks. The Pages group on the INSERT tab contains three buttons for inserting a cover page, blank page, and page break.

Changing Margins

Quick Steps

Change Margins
1. Click PAGE LAYOUT tab.
2. Click Margins button.
3. Click desired margin option.

Change Page Orientation
1. Click PAGE LAYOUT tab.
2. Click Orientation button.
3. Click desired orientation.

Change Page Size
1. Click PAGE LAYOUT tab.
2. Click Size button.
3. Click desired size option.

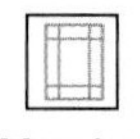
Margins

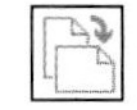
Orientation

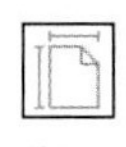
Size

Change page margins with options at the Margins button drop-down list, as shown in Figure 4.3. To display this list, click the PAGE LAYOUT tab and then click the Margins button in the Page Setup group. To change the margins, click one of the preset margins that display in the drop-down list. Be aware that most printers have a required margin (between ¼ and ⅜ inch) because printers cannot print to the edge of the page.

Changing Page Orientation

Click the Orientation button in the Page Setup group on the PAGE LAYOUT tab, and two options display—*Portrait* and *Landscape*. At the portrait orientation, which is the default, the page is 11 inches tall and 8.5 inches wide. At the landscape orientation, the page is 8.5 inches tall and 11 inches wide. Change the page orientation and the page margins automatically change.

Changing Page Size

By default, Word uses a page size of 8.5 inches wide and 11 inches tall. Change this default setting with options at the Size button drop-down list. Display this drop-down list by clicking the Size button in the Page Setup group on the PAGE LAYOUT tab.

Figure 4.3 Margins Drop-down List

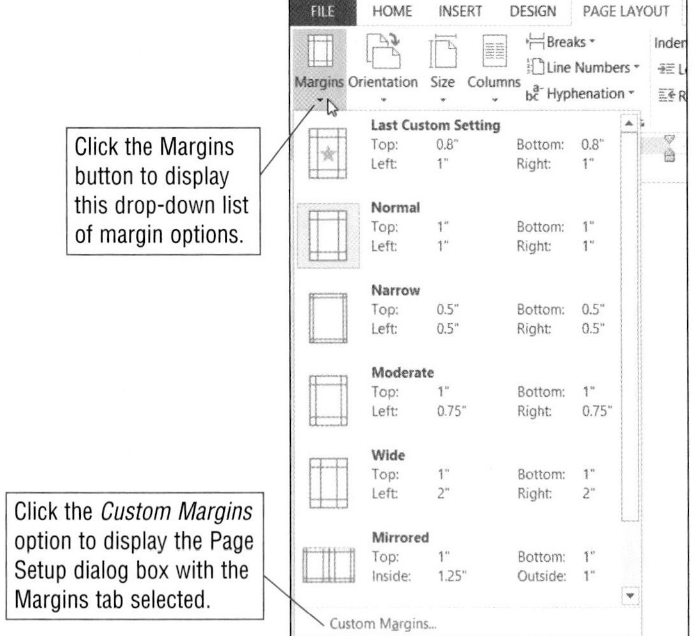

Project 2a Changing Margins, Page Orientation, and Size

Part 1 of 2

1. Open **Netiquette.docx**.
2. Save the document with Save As and name it **WL1-C4-P2-Netiquette**.
3. Click the PAGE LAYOUT tab.
4. Click the Margins button in the Page Setup group and then click the *Narrow* option.
5. Click the Orientation button in the Page Setup group.
6. Click *Landscape* at the drop-down list.

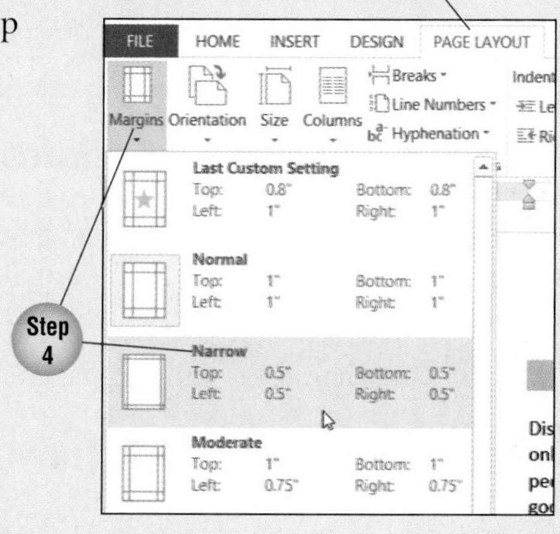

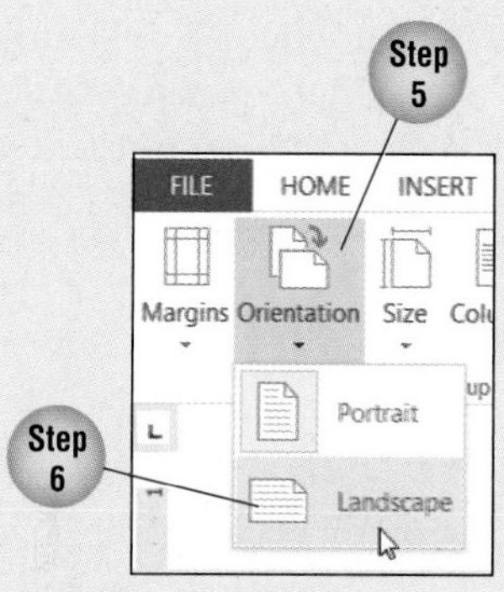

7. Scroll through the document and notice how the text displays on the page in landscape orientation.
8. Click the Orientation button in the Page Setup group and then click *Portrait* at the drop-down list. (This changes the orientation back to the default.)
9. Click the Size button in the Page Setup group.
10. Click the *Executive* option (displays with *7.25" × 10.5"* below *Executive*). If this option is not available, choose an option with a similar size.

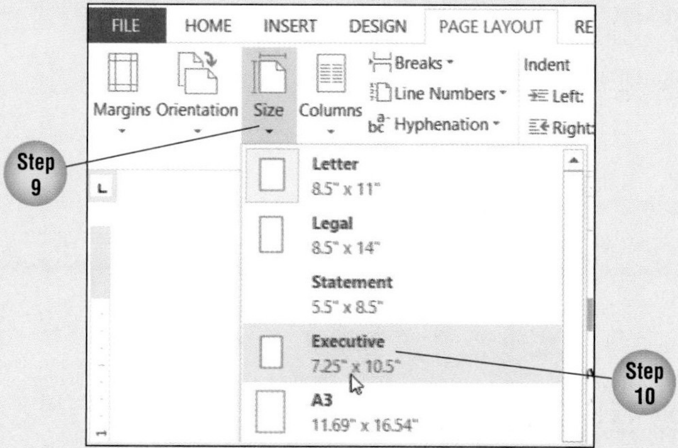

11. Scroll through the document and notice how the text displays on the page.
12. Click the Size button and then click *Legal* (displays with *8.5" × 14"* below *Legal*).
13. Scroll through the document and notice how the text displays on the page.
14. Click the Size button and then click *Letter* (displays with *8.5" × 11"* below *Letter*). (This returns the size back to the default.)
15. Save **WL1-C4-P2-Netiquette.docx**.

Changing Margins at the Page Setup Dialog Box

Quick Steps

Change Margins at the Page Setup Dialog Box

1. Click PAGE LAYOUT tab.
2. Click Page Setup group dialog box launcher.
3. Specify desired margins.
4. Click OK.

Change Page Size at the Page Setup Dialog Box

1. Click PAGE LAYOUT tab.
2. Click Size button.
3. Click *More Paper Sizes* at drop-down list.
4. Specify desired size.
5. Click OK.

The Margins button in the Page Setup group provides you with a number of preset margins. If these margins do not fit your needs, you can set specific margins at the Page Setup dialog box with the Margins tab selected, as shown in Figure 4.4. Display this dialog box by clicking the Page Setup group dialog box launcher or by clicking the Margins button and then clicking *Custom Margins* at the bottom of the drop-down list.

To change one of the margins, select the current measurement in the *Top*, *Bottom*, *Left*, or *Right* measurement box, and then type the new measurement. You can also increase a measurement by clicking the up-pointing arrow at the right side of the measurement box. Decrease a measurement by clicking the down-pointing arrow. As you make changes to the margin measurements at the Page Setup dialog box, the sample page in the *Preview* section illustrates the effects of the changes.

Changing Paper Size at the Page Setup Dialog Box

The Size button drop-down list contains a number of preset page sizes. If these sizes do not fit your needs, specify a page size at the Page Setup dialog box with the Paper tab selected. Display this dialog box by clicking the Size button in the Page Setup group and then clicking *More Paper Sizes* that displays at the bottom of the drop-down list.

Figure 4.4 Page Setup Dialog Box with Margins Tab Selected

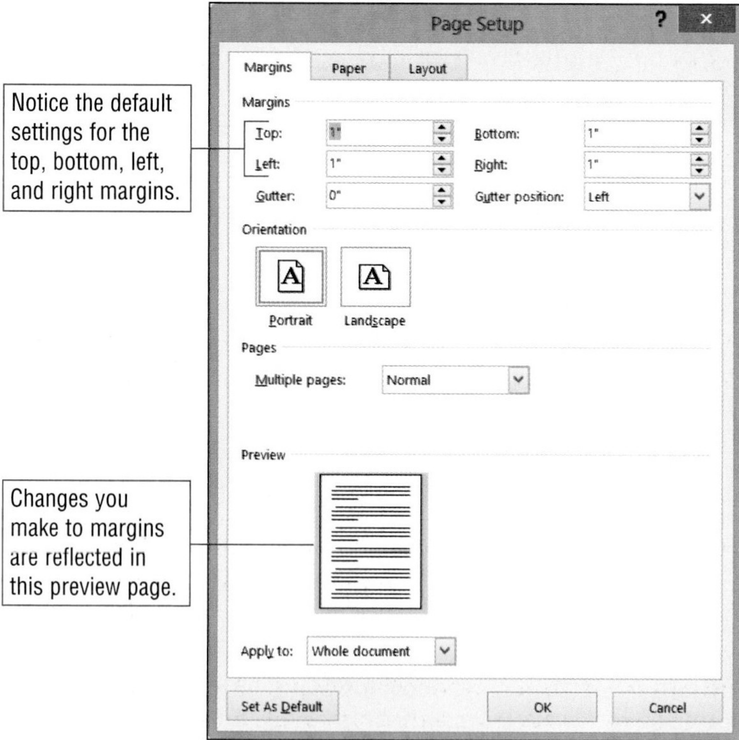

Project 2b Changing Margins at the Page Setup Dialog Box

Part 2 of 2

1. With **WL1-C4-P2-Netiquette.docx** open, make sure the PAGE LAYOUT tab is selected.
2. Click the Page Setup group dialog box launcher.
3. At the Page Setup dialog box with the Margins tab selected, click the up-pointing arrow at the right side of the *Top* measurement box until *0.7"* displays.
4. Click the up-pointing arrow at the right side of the *Bottom* measurement box until *0.7"* displays.
5. Select the current measurement in the *Left* measurement box and then type **0.75**.
6. Select the current measurement in the *Right* measurement box and then type **0.75**.

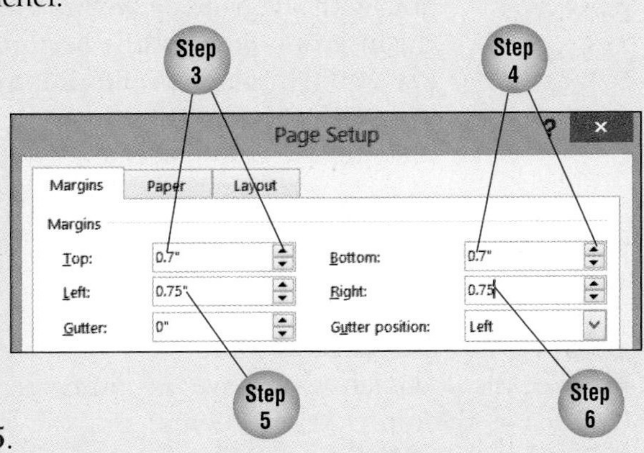

7. Click OK to close the dialog box.
8. Click the Size button in the Page Setup group and then click *More Paper Sizes* at the drop-down list.
9. At the Page Setup dialog box with the Paper tab selected, click the down-pointing arrow at the right side of the *Paper size* option box and then click *Legal* at the drop-down list.

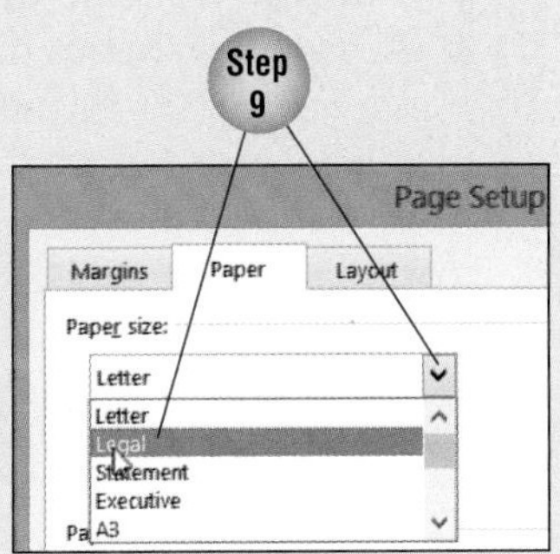

10. Click OK to close the dialog box.
11. Scroll through the document and notice how the text displays on the page.
12. Click the Size button in the Page Setup group and then click *Letter* at the drop-down list.
13. Save, print, and then close **WL1-C4-P2-Netiquette.docx**.

Project 3 Customize a Report on Computer Input and Output Devices

3 Parts

You will open a document containing information on computer input and output devices and then insert page breaks, a blank page, a cover page, and page numbering.

Inserting a Page Break

With the default top and bottom margins of 1 inch, approximately 9 inches of text print on the page. At approximately the 10-inch mark, Word automatically inserts a page break. You can insert your own page break in a document with the keyboard shortcut Ctrl + Enter or with the Page Break button in the Pages group on the INSERT tab.

Quick Steps

Insert a Page Break
1. Click INSERT tab.
2. Click Page Break button.

OR

Press Ctrl + Enter.

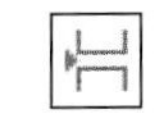

Page Break

A page break inserted by Word is considered a ***soft page break***, and a page break inserted by you is considered a ***hard page break***. Soft page breaks automatically adjust if you add or delete text from a document. Hard page breaks do not adjust and are therefore less flexible than soft page breaks.

If you add or delete text from a document with a hard page break, check the break to determine whether it is still in a desirable location. Display a hard page break along with other nonprinting characters by clicking the Show/Hide ¶ button in the Paragraph group on the HOME tab. A hard page break displays as a row of dots with the words *Page Break* in the center. To delete a hard page break, position the insertion point at the beginning of the page break and then press the Delete key. If the display of nonprinting characters is turned off, delete a hard page break by positioning the insertion point immediately below the page break and then pressing the Backspace key.

Project 3a Inserting Page Breaks — Parts 1 of 3

1. Open **CompDevices.docx**.
2. Save the document with Save As and name it **WL1-C4-P3-CompDevices**.
3. Change the top margin by completing the following steps:
   a. Click the PAGE LAYOUT tab.
   b. Click the Page Setup group dialog box launcher.
   c. At the Page Setup dialog box, click the Margins tab and then type 1.5 in the *Top* measurement box.
   d. Click OK to close the dialog box.

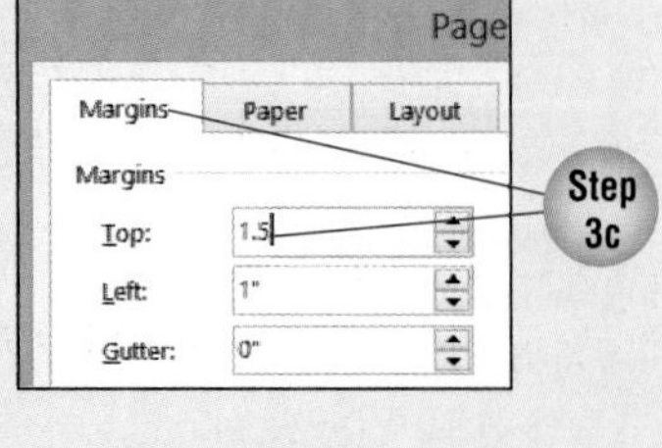

4. Insert a page break at the beginning of the heading *Mouse* by completing the following steps:
   a. Position the insertion point at the beginning of the heading *Mouse* (located toward the bottom of page 1).
   b. Click the INSERT tab and then click the Page Break button in the Pages group.

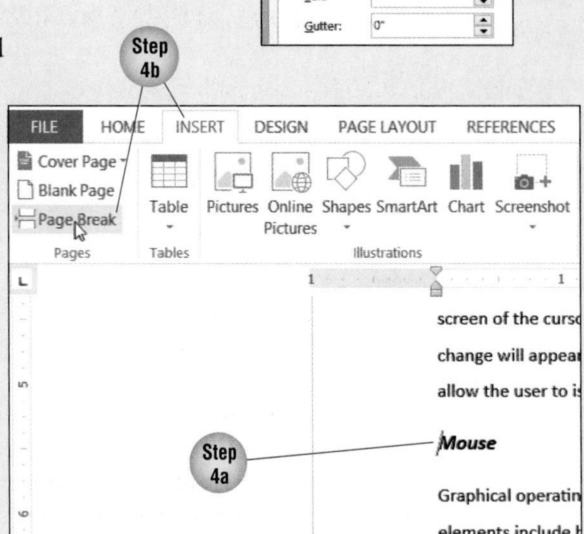

5. Move the insertion point to the beginning of the title *COMPUTER OUTPUT DEVICES* (located on the second page) and then insert a page break by pressing Ctrl + Enter.
6. Move the insertion point to the beginning of the heading *Printer* and then press Ctrl + Enter to insert a page break.
7. Delete a page break by completing the following steps:
   a. Click the HOME tab.
   b. Click the Show/Hide ¶ button in the Paragraph group.
   c. Scroll up to display the bottom of the third page, position the insertion point at the beginning of the page break (displays with the words *Page Break*), and then press the Delete key.
   d. Press the Delete key again to remove the blank line.
   e. Turn off the display of nonprinting characters by clicking the Show/Hide ¶ button in the Paragraph group on the HOME tab.
8. Save **WL1-C4-P3-CompDevices.docx**.

Inserting a Blank Page

Click the Blank Page button in the Pages group on the INSERT tab to insert a blank page at the position of the insertion point. This might be useful in a document where you want to insert a blank page for an illustration, graphic, or figure.

Inserting a Cover Page

If you are preparing a document for distribution to others or you want to simply improve the visual appeal of your document, consider inserting a cover page. With the Cover Page button in the Pages group on the INSERT tab, you can insert a predesigned and formatted cover page and then type personalized text in specific locations on the page. Click the Cover Page button and a drop-down list displays. The drop-down list provides a visual representation of the cover page. Scroll through the list and then click the desired cover page.

A predesigned cover page contains location placeholders where you enter specific information. For example, a cover page might contain the placeholder *[Document title]*. Click anywhere in the placeholder text and the placeholder text is selected. With the placeholder text selected, type the desired text. Delete a placeholder by clicking anywhere in the placeholder text, clicking the placeholder tab, and then pressing the Delete key.

Quick Steps

Insert Blank Page
1. Click INSERT tab.
2. Click Blank Page button.

Insert Cover Page
1. Click INSERT tab.
2. Click Cover Page button.
3. Click desired cover page at drop-down list.

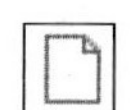

Blank Page

Cover Page

A cover page provides a polished and professional look to a document.

Project 3b **Inserting a Blank Page and a Cover Page** **Part 2 of 3**

1. With **WL1-C4-P3-CompDevices.docx** open, create a blank page by completing the following steps:
   a. Move the insertion point to the beginning of the heading *Touchpad and Touchscreen* located on the second page.
   b. Click the INSERT tab.
   c. Click the Blank Page button in the Pages group.
2. Insert a cover page by completing the following steps:
   a. Press Ctrl + Home to move the insertion point to the beginning of the document.
   b. Click the Cover Page button in the Pages group.
   c. At the drop-down list, scroll down and then click the *Motion* cover page.

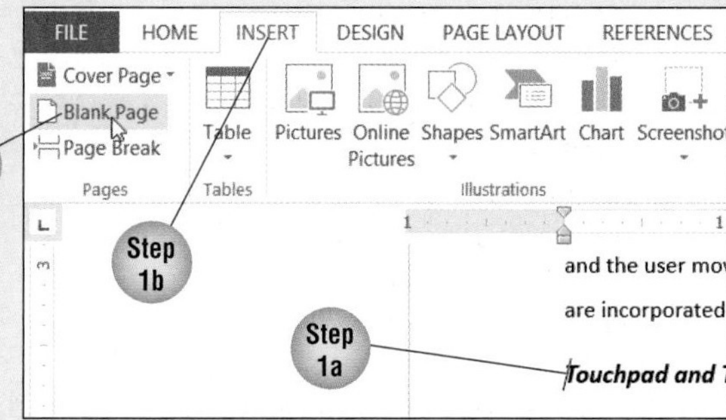

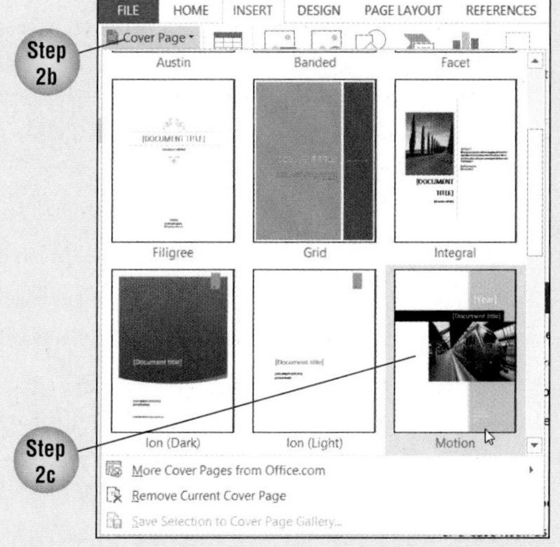

d. Click anywhere in the placeholder text *[Document title]* and then type **Computer Devices**.

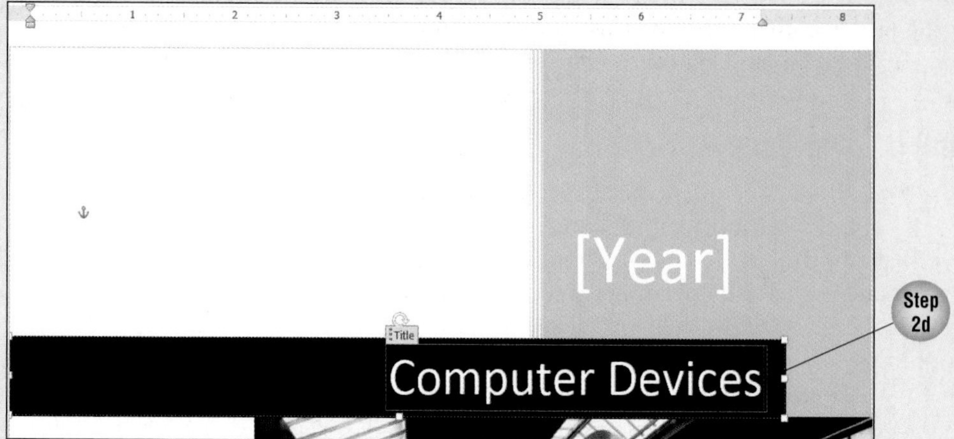

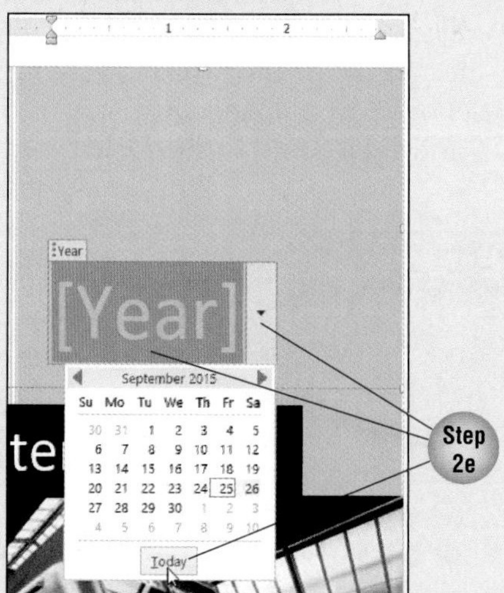

e. Click the placeholder text *[Year]*. Click the down-pointing arrow that displays at the right side of the placeholder and then click the Today button that displays at the bottom of the drop-down calendar.

f. Click anywhere in the placeholder text *[Company name]* and then type **Drake Computing**. (If a name displays in the placeholder, select the name and then type **Drake Computing**.)

g. Select the name that displays above the company name and then type your first and last names. If, instead of a name, the *[Author name]* placeholder displays above the company name, click anywhere in the placeholder text and then type your first and last names.

3. Remove the blank page you inserted in Step 1 by completing the following steps:

a. Move the insertion point immediately right of the period that ends the last sentence in the paragraph of text in the *Trackball* heading (located toward the bottom of page 3).

b. Press the Delete key on the keyboard approximately six times until the heading *Touchpad and Touchscreen* displays on page 3.

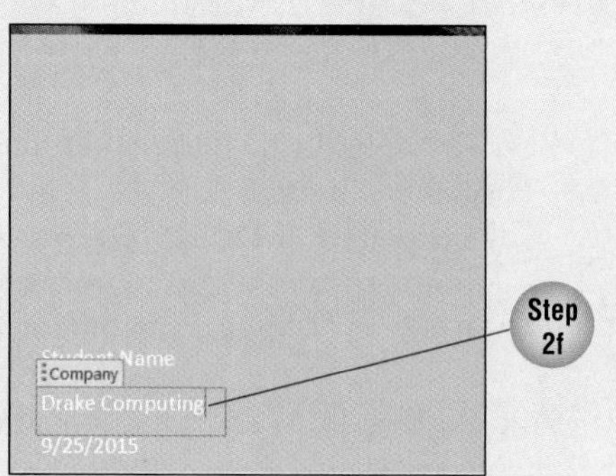

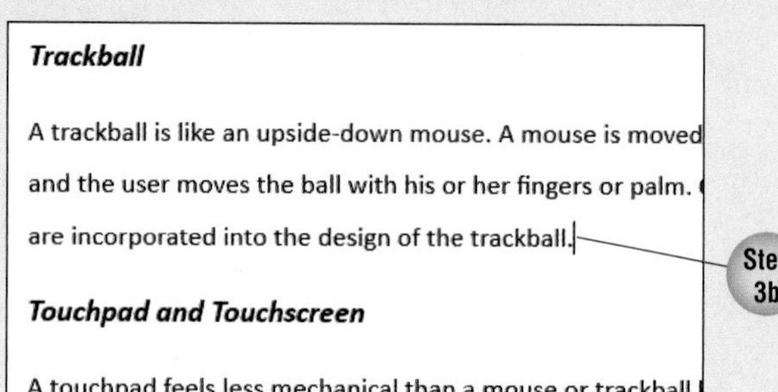

Trackball
A trackball is like an upside-down mouse. A mouse is moved
and the user moves the ball with his or her fingers or palm.
are incorporated into the design of the trackball.
Step 3b
Touchpad and Touchscreen
A touchpad feels less mechanical than a mouse or trackball

4. Save **WL1-C4-P3-CompDevices.docx**.

Inserting Predesigned Page Numbering

Word, by default, does not print page numbers on pages. If you want to insert page numbering in a document, use the Page Number button in the Header & Footer group on the INSERT tab. When you click the Page Number button, a drop-down list displays with options for specifying the page number location. Point to an option at this list and a drop-down list displays of predesigned page number formats. Scroll through the options in the drop-down list and then click the desired option.

If you want to change the format of page numbering in a document, double-click the page number, select the page number text, and then apply the desired formatting. Remove page numbering from a document by clicking the Page Number button and then clicking *Remove Page Numbers* at the drop-down list.

Quick Steps

Insert Page Numbering
1. Click INSERT tab.
2. Click Page Number button.
3. Click desired option at drop-down list.

Page Number

Project 3c **Inserting Predesigned Page Numbering** **Part 3 of 3**

1. With **WL1-C4-P3-CompDevices.docx** open, insert page numbering by completing the following steps:
   a. Move the insertion point so it is positioned on any character in the title *COMPUTER INPUT DEVICES*.
   b. Click the INSERT tab.
   c. Click the Page Number button in the Header & Footer group and then point to *Top of Page*.
   d. Scroll through the drop-down list and then click the *Brackets 2* option.

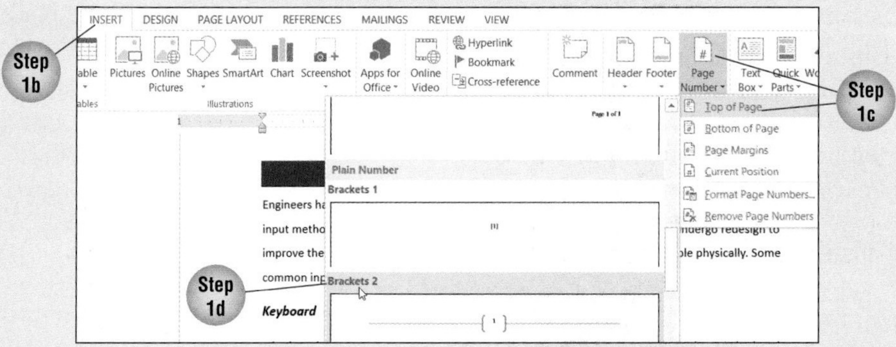

2. Double-click in the document text. (This makes the document text active and dims the page number.)
3. Scroll through the document and notice the page numbering that displays at the top of each page except the cover page. (The cover page and text are divided by a page break. Word does not include the cover page when numbering pages.)
4. Remove the page numbering by clicking the INSERT tab, clicking the Page Number button, and then clicking *Remove Page Numbers* at the drop-down list.
5. Click the Page Number button, point to *Bottom of Page*, scroll down the drop-down list, and then click the *Accent Bar 2* option.
6. Double-click in the document to make it active.
7. Save, print, and then close **WL1-C4-P3-CompDevices.docx**.

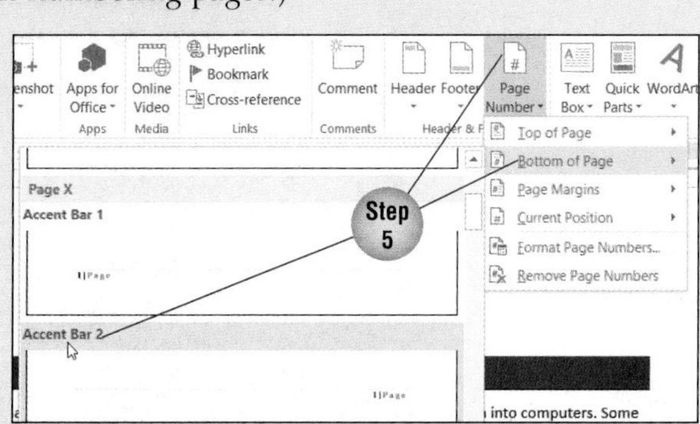

Project 4 Add Elements to a Report on the Writing Process — 3 Parts

You will open a document containing information on the process of writing effectively, insert a predesigned header and footer in the document, remove a header, and format and delete header and footer elements.

Inserting Predesigned Headers and Footers

Quick Steps

Insert Predesigned Header
1. Click INSERT tab.
2. Click Header button.
3. Click desired option at drop-down list.
4. Type text in specific placeholders in header.

Header

Text that appears in the top margin of a page is called a ***header*** and text that appears in the bottom margin of a page is referred to as a ***footer***. Headers and footers are common in manuscripts, textbooks, reports, and other publications. Insert a predesigned header in a document by clicking the INSERT tab and then clicking the Header button in the Header & Footer group. This displays the Header button drop-down list. At this list, click the desired predesigned header option and the header is inserted in the document. Headers and footers are visible in Print Layout view but not Draft view.

A predesigned header or footer may contain location placeholders for entering specific information. For example, a header might contain the placeholder *[Document title]*. Click anywhere in the placeholder text and all of the placeholder text is selected. With the placeholder text selected, type the desired text. Delete a placeholder by clicking anywhere in the placeholder text, clicking the placeholder tab, and then pressing the Delete key.

To return to your document after inserting a header or footer, double-click in the document. You can also return to the document by clicking the Close Header and Footer button on the HEADER & FOOTER TOOLS DESIGN tab.

Project 4a Inserting a Predesigned Header in a Document — Part 1 of 3

1. Open **WritingProcess.docx**.
2. Save the document with Save As and name it **WL1-C4-P4-WritingProcess**.
3. Move the insertion point to the end of the document.
4. Move the insertion point to the beginning of the *REFERENCES* heading and then insert a page break by clicking the INSERT tab and then clicking the Page Break button in the Pages group.

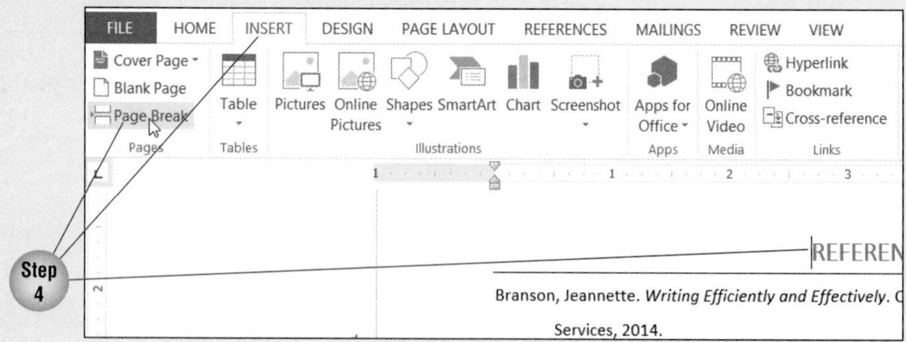

5. Press Ctrl + Home to move the insertion point to the beginning of the document and then insert a header by completing the following steps:
   a. If necessary, click the INSERT tab.
   b. Click the Header button in the Header & Footer group.
   c. Scroll to the bottom of the drop-down list that displays and then click the *Sideline* option.

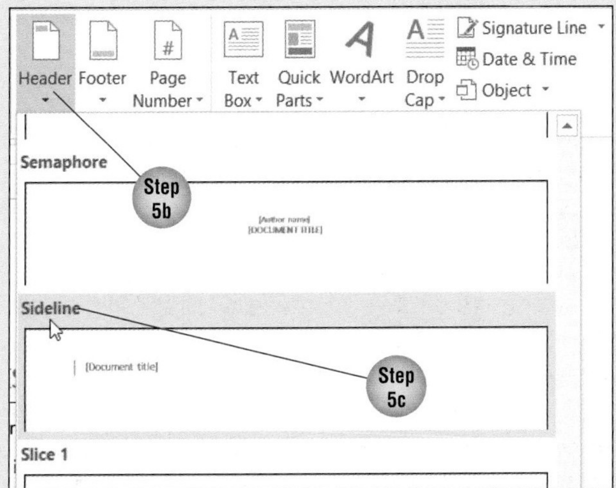

   d. Click anywhere in the placeholder text *[Document title]* and then type **The Writing Process**.
   e. Double-click in the document text. (This makes the document text active and dims the header.)

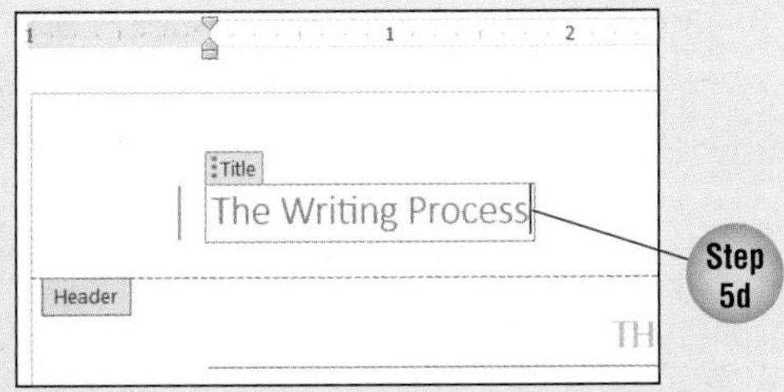

6. Scroll through the document to see how the header will print.
7. Save and then print **WL1-C4-P4-WritingProcess.docx**.

Insert a predesigned footer in the same manner as inserting a header. Click the Footer button in the Header & Footer group on the INSERT tab and a drop-down list displays similar to the Header button drop-down list. Click the desired footer and the predesigned footer formatting is applied to the document.

Quick Steps

Insert Predesigned Footer
1. Click INSERT tab.
2. Click Footer button.
3. Click desired option at drop-down list.
4. Type text in specific placeholders in footer.

Footer

Removing a Header or Footer

Remove a header from a document by clicking the INSERT tab and then clicking the Header button in the Header & Footer group. At the drop-down list that displays, click the *Remove Header* option. Complete similar steps to remove a footer.

Project 4b Removing a Header and Inserting a Predesigned Footer Part 2 of 3

1. With **WL1-C4-P4-WritingProcess.docx** open, press Ctrl + Home to move the insertion point to the beginning of the document.
2. Remove the header by clicking the INSERT tab, clicking the Header button in the Header & Footer group, and then clicking the *Remove Header* option at the drop-down menu.
3. Insert a footer in the document by completing the following steps:
   a. Click the Footer button in the Header & Footer group.
   b. Scroll down the drop-down list and then click *Ion (Light)*.

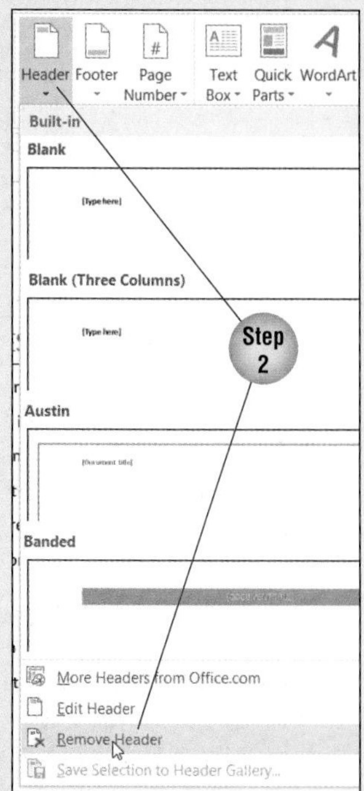

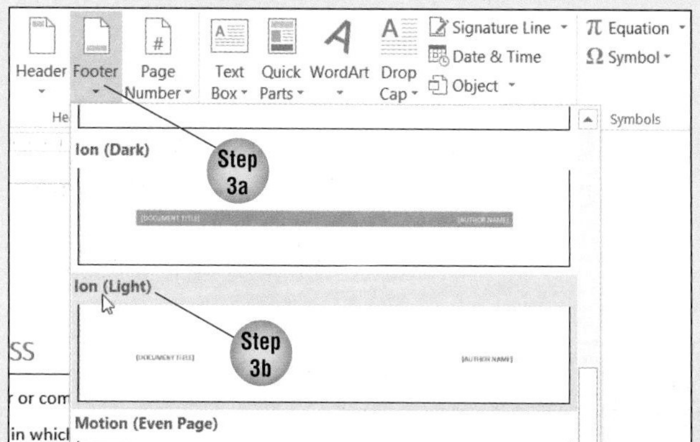

   c. Notice that Word inserted the document title at the left side of the footer (Word remembered the document title you entered in the header) and your name at the right side of the footer. If the document title does not display, click anywhere in the placeholder *[DOCUMENT TITLE]* and then type **THE WRITING PROCESS**, and if your name does not display, click anywhere in the placeholder *[AUTHOR NAME]* and then type your first and last names.
   d. Click the Close Header and Footer button on the HEADER & FOOTER TOOLS DESIGN tab to close the Footer pane and return to the document.
4. Scroll through the document to see how the footer will print.
5. Save and then print **WL1-C4-P4-WritingProcess.docx**.

Editing a Predesigned Header or Footer

Predesigned headers and footers contain elements such as page numbers and a title. You can change the formatting of the element by clicking the desired element and then applying the desired formatting. You can also select and then delete an item.

Project 4c Formatting and Deleting Header and Footer Elements Part 3 of 3

1. With **WL1-C4-P4-WritingProcess.docx** open, remove the footer by clicking the INSERT tab, clicking the Footer button, and then clicking *Remove Footer* at the drop-down list.

2. Insert and then format a header by completing the following steps:
   a. Click the Header button in the Header & Footer group on the INSERT tab, scroll down the drop-down list, and then click *Grid*. (This header inserts the document title as well as a date placeholder.)
   b. Delete the Date placeholder by clicking anywhere in the *[Date]* placeholder text, clicking the placeholder tab, and then pressing the Delete key.
   c. Double-click in the document text.
3. Insert and then format a footer by completing the following steps:
   a. Click the INSERT tab.
   b. Click the Footer button, scroll down the drop-down list, and then click *Retrospect*.
   c. Select the name that displays in the Author tab located at the left side of the footer and then type your first and last names.
   d. Select your name and the page number, turn on bold formatting, and then change the font size to 10 points.
   e. Double-click in the document text.
4. Scroll through the document to see how the header and footer will print.
5. Save, print, and then close **WL1-C4-P4-WritingProcess.docx**.

Project 5 Format a Report on Desirable Employee Qualities — 2 Parts

You will open a document containing information on desirable employee qualities and then insert a watermark, change page background color, and insert a page border.

Formatting the Page Background

The Page Background group on the DESIGN tab contains three buttons for customizing a page background. Click the Watermark button and choose a predesigned watermark from a drop-down list. If a document is going to be viewed on-screen or on the Web, consider adding a page color. In Chapter 3, you learned how to apply borders and shading to text at the Borders and Shading dialog box. This dialog box also contains options for inserting a page border.

Quick Steps

Insert a Watermark
1. Click DESIGN tab.
2. Click Watermark button.
3. Click desired option at drop-down list.

Change the Page Color
1. Click DESIGN tab.
2. Click Page Color button.
3. Click desired option at color palette.

Watermark

Inserting a Watermark

A ***watermark*** is a lightened image that displays behind text in a document. Use a watermark to add visual appeal to a document or to identify a document as a draft, sample, or confidential document. Word provides a number of predesigned watermarks you can insert in a document. Display these watermarks by clicking the Watermark button in the Page Background group on the DESIGN tab. Scroll through the list of watermarks and then click the desired option.

Changing Page Color

Page Color

Use the Page Color button in the Page Background group to apply background color to a document. This background color is intended for viewing a document on-screen or on the Web. The color is visible on the screen but does not print. Insert a page color by clicking the Page Color button and then clicking the desired color at the color palette.

Project 5a **Inserting a Watermark and Changing Page Color** **Part 1 of 2**

1. Open **EmpQualities.docx** and then save the document with Save As and name it **WL1-C4-P5-EmpQualities**.
2. Insert a watermark by completing the following steps:
   a. With the insertion point positioned at the beginning of the document, click the DESIGN tab.
   b. Click the Watermark button in the Page Background group.
   c. At the drop-down list, click the *CONFIDENTIAL 1* option.
3. Scroll through the document and notice how the watermark displays behind the text.
4. Remove the watermark and insert a different one by completing the following steps:
   a. Click the Watermark button in the Page Background group and then click *Remove Watermark* at the drop-down list.
   b. Click the Watermark button and then click the *DO NOT COPY 1* option at the drop-down list.
5. Scroll through the document and notice how the watermark displays.
6. Move the insertion point to the beginning of the document.
7. Click the Page Color button in the Page Background group and then click *Tan, Background 2* (third column, first row) at the color palette.

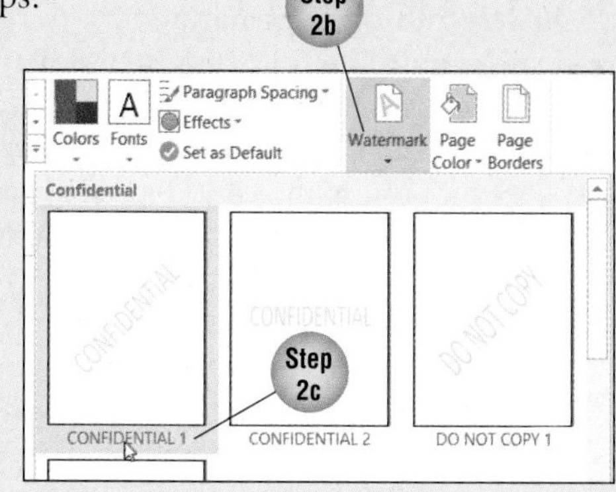

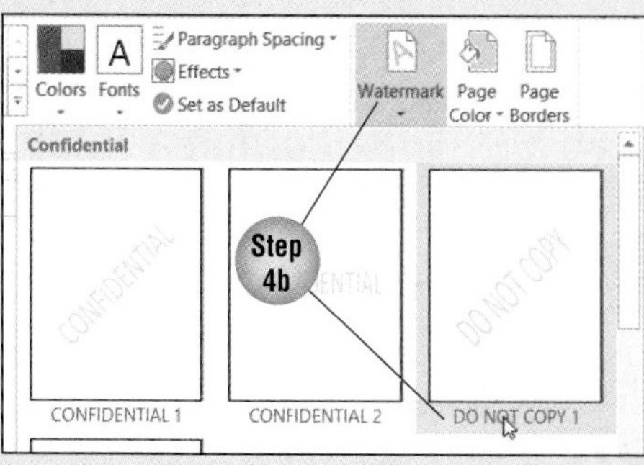

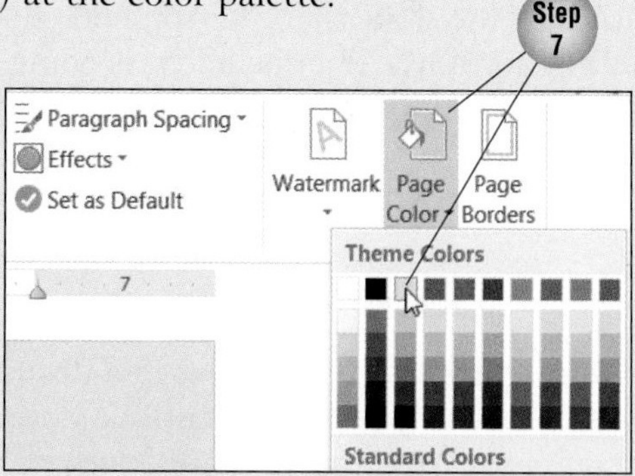

8. Save **WL1-C4-P5-EmpQualities.docx**.

Inserting a Page Border

To improve the visual appeal of a document, consider inserting a page border. When you insert a page border in a multiple-page document, the border prints on each page. To insert a page border, click the Page Borders button in the Page Background group on the DESIGN tab. This displays the Borders and Shading dialog box with the Page Border tab selected, as shown in Figure 4.5. At this dialog box, specify the border style, color, and width.

The dialog box contains an option for inserting a page border containing an image. To display the images available, click the down-pointing arrow at the right side of the *Art* option box. Scroll down the drop-down list and then click the desired image.

Quick Steps

Insert Page Border
1. Click DESIGN tab.
2. Click Page Borders button.
3. Specify desired options at dialog box.

Page Borders

Changing Page Border Options

By default, a page border displays and prints 24 points from the top, left, right, and bottom edges of the page. Some printers, particularly inkjet printers, have a nonprinting area around the outside edges of the page that can interfere with the printing of a border. Before printing a document with a page border, click the FILE tab and then click the *Print* option. Look at the preview of the page at the right side of the Print backstage area and determine whether the entire border is visible. If a portion of the border is not visible in the preview page (generally at the bottom and right sides of the page), consider changing measurements at the Border and Shading Options dialog box shown in Figure 4.6. You can also change measurements at the Border and Shading Options dialog box to control the location of the page border on the page.

Display the Border and Shading Options dialog box by clicking the DESIGN tab and then clicking the Page Borders button. At the Borders and Shading dialog box with the Page Border tab selected, click the Options button that displays in the lower right corner of the dialog box. The options at the Border and Shading Options dialog box change depending on whether you click the Options button at the Borders and Shading dialog box with the Borders tab selected or the Page Border tab selected.

Figure 4.5 Borders and Shading Dialog Box with Page Border Tab Selected

Click this down-pointing arrow to scroll through a list of page border styles.

Click this down-pointing arrow to display a list of width points.

Click this down-pointing arrow to display a list of art border images.

Preview the page border in this section.

Click this down-pointing arrow to display a palette of page border colors.

Click this button to display the Border and Shading Options dialog box.

Figure 4.6 Border and Shading Options Dialog Box

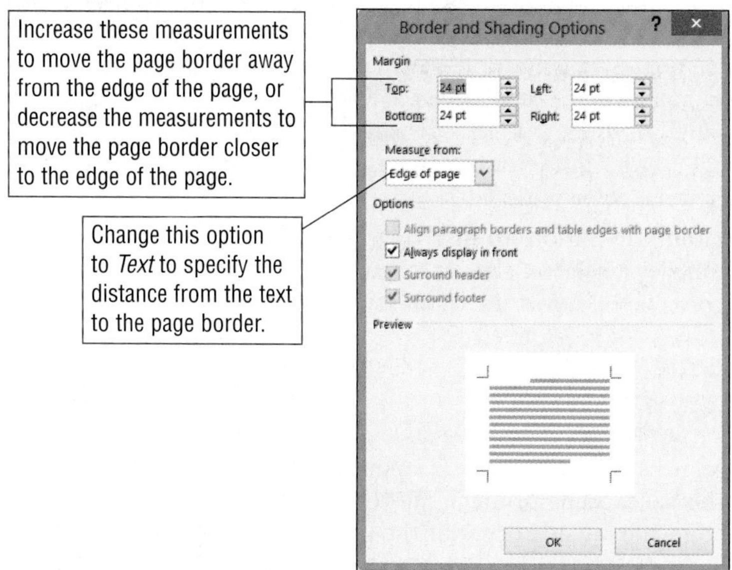

If your printer contains a nonprinting area and the entire page border will not print, consider increasing the spacing from the page border to the edge of the page. Do this with the *Top*, *Left*, *Bottom*, and/or *Right* measurement boxes. The *Measure from* option box has a default setting of *Edge of page*. You can change this option to *Text*, which changes the top and bottom measurements to *1 pt* and the left and right measurements to *4 pt* and moves the page border into the page. Use the measurement boxes to specify the distance you want the page border displayed and printed from the text in the document.

Project 5b Inserting a Page Border

Part 2 of 2

1. With **WL1-C4-P5-EmpQualities.docx** open, remove the page color by clicking the Page Color button in the Page Background group on the DESIGN tab and then clicking *No Color* at the color palette.
2. Insert a page border by completing the following steps:
   a. Click the Page Borders button in the Page Background group on the DESIGN tab.
   b. Click the *Box* option in the *Setting* section.
   c. Scroll down the list of line styles in the *Style* list box until the last line style displays and then click the third line from the end.
   d. Click the down-pointing arrow at the right of the *Color* option box and then click *Dark Red, Accent 2* (sixth column, first row) at the color palette.
   e. Click OK to close the dialog box.

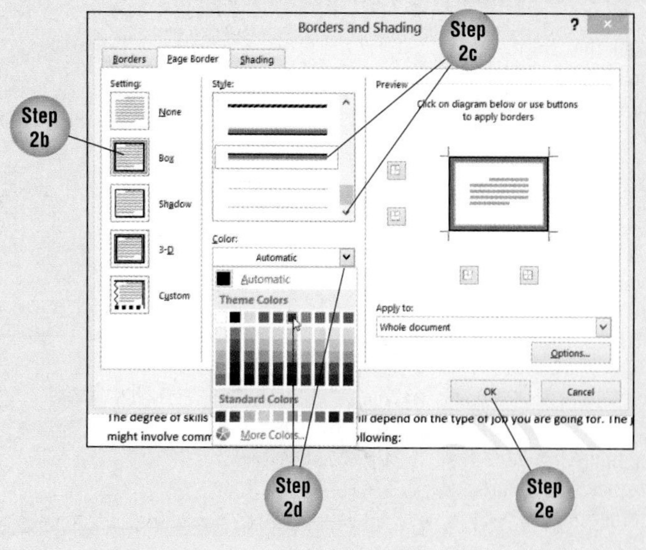

3. Increase the spacing from the page border to the edges of the page by completing the following steps:
   a. Click the Page Borders button in the Page Background group on the DESIGN tab.
   b. At the Borders and Shading dialog box with the Page Border tab selected, click the Options button located in the lower right corner.
   c. At the Border and Shading Options dialog box, click the up-pointing arrow at the right side of the *Top* measurement box until *31 pt* displays. (This is the maximum measurement allowed.)
   d. Increase the measurement for the *Left, Bottom,* and *Right* measurement boxes to *31 pt*.
   e. Click OK to close the Border and Shading Options dialog box.
   f. Click OK to close the Borders and Shading dialog box.

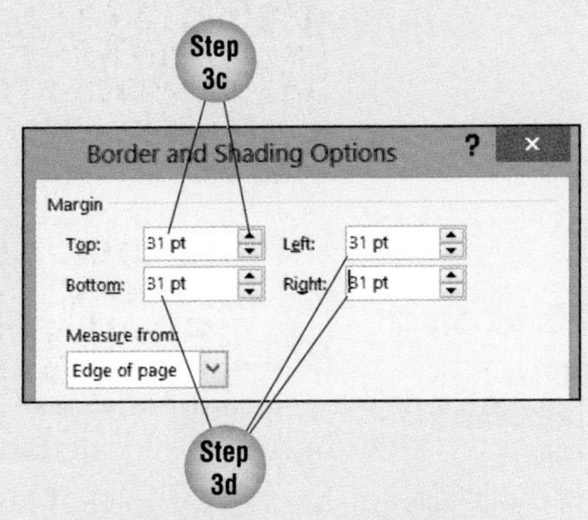

4. Save **WL1-C4-P5-EmpQualities.docx** and then print only page 1.
5. Insert an image page border and change the page border spacing options by completing the following steps:
   a. Click the Page Borders button in the Page Background group on the DESIGN tab.
   b. Click the down-pointing arrow at the right side of the *Art* option box and then click the border image shown at the right (located approximately one-third of the way down the drop-down list).

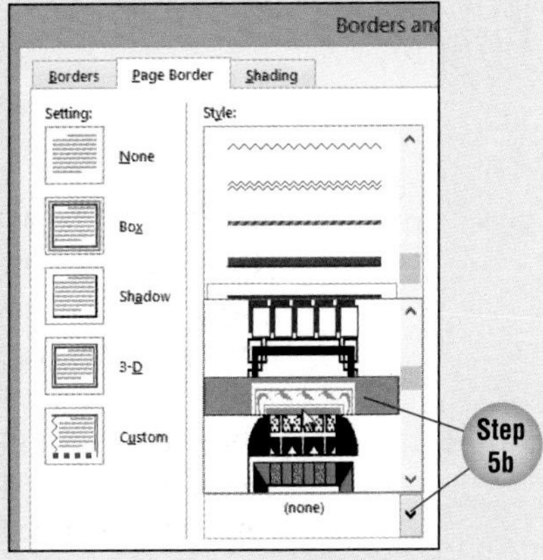

   c. Click the Options button located in the lower right corner of the Borders and Shading dialog box.
   d. At the Border and Shading Options dialog box, click the down-pointing arrow at the right of the *Measure from* option box and then click *Text* at the drop-down list.
   e. Click the up-pointing arrow at the right of the *Top* measurement box until *10 pt* displays.
   f. Increase the measurement for the *Bottom* measurement to *10 pt* and the measurements in the *Left* and *Right* measurement boxes to *14 pt*.
   g. Click the *Surround header* check box to remove the check mark.
   h. Click the *Surround footer* check box to remove the check mark.
   i. Click OK to close the Border and Shading Options dialog box.
   j. Click OK to close the Borders and Shading dialog box.

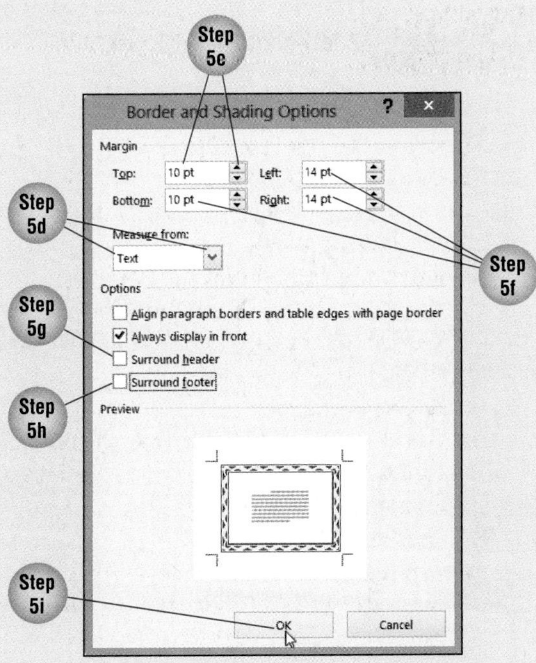

6. Save, print, and then close **WL1-C4-P5-EmpQualities.docx**.

Project 6 Format a Lease Agreement — 4 Parts

You will open a lease agreement, search for specific text and replace it with other text, and then search for specific formatting and replace it with other formatting.

Finding and Replacing Text and Formatting

Quick Steps

Find Text
1. Click Find button on HOME tab.
2. Type search text.
3. Click Next Search Result button.

Find

Replace

Use Word's Find feature to search for a specific character or format. With the Find and Replace feature, you can search for a specific character or format and replace it with another character or format. The Find button and the Replace button are located in the Editing group on the HOME tab.

Click the Find button in the Editing group on the HOME tab (or press the keyboard shortcut Ctrl + F) and the Navigation pane displays at the left side of the screen with the RESULTS tab selected. With this tab selected, type search text in the search text box, and any occurrence of the text in the document is highlighted. A fragment of the text surrounding the search text also displays in a thumbnail in the Navigation pane. For example, search for *Lessee* in the **WL1-C4-P6-LeaseAgrmnt.docx** document and the screen displays as shown in Figure 4.7. Notice that any occurrence of *Lessee* displays highlighted in yellow in the document and the Navigation pane displays thumbnails of text surrounding the occurrences of *Lessee*.

Figure 4.7 Navigation Pane Showing Search Results

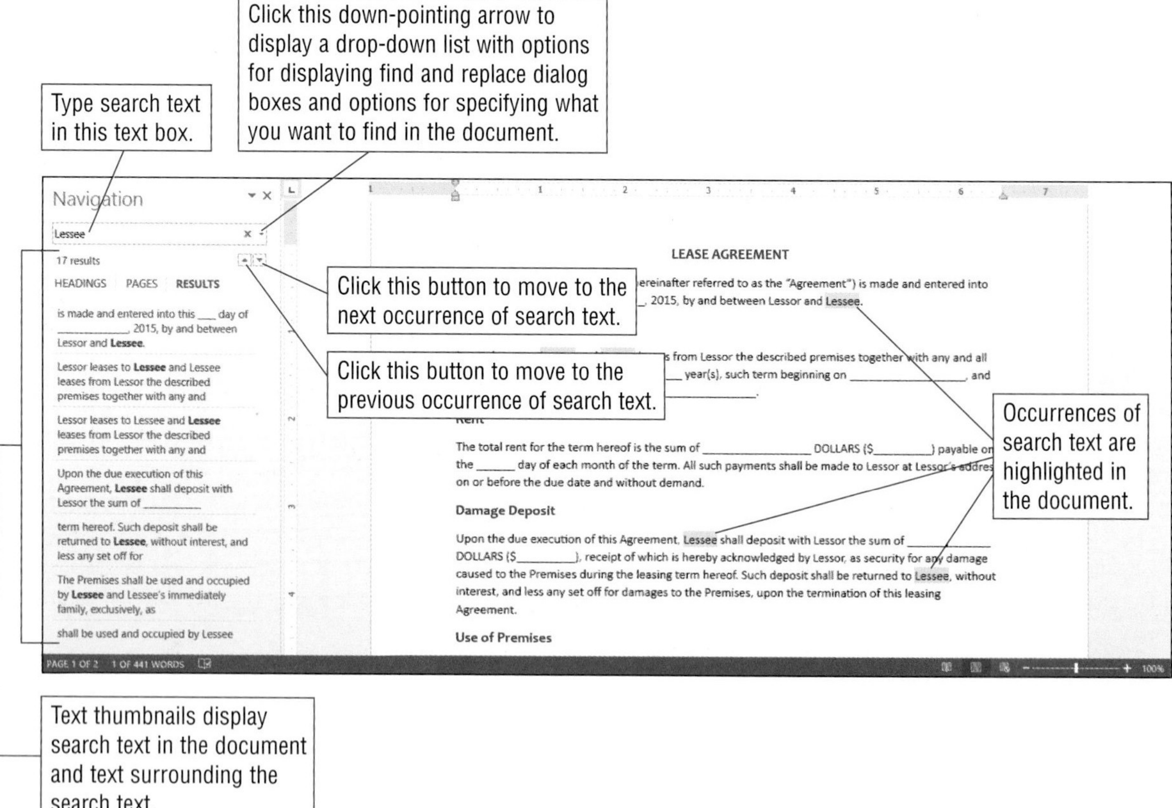

Click a text thumbnail in the Navigation pane and the occurrence of the search text is selected in the document. If you hover your mouse over a text thumbnail in the Navigation pane, the page number location displays in a small box near the mouse pointer. You can also move to the next occurrence of the search text by clicking the Next button (contains a down-pointing triangle) that displays below and to the right of the search text box. Click the Previous button (contains an up-pointing triangle) to move to the previous occurrence of the search text.

Click the down-pointing arrow at the right side of the search text box and a drop-down list displays. It shows options for displaying dialog boxes, such as the Find Options dialog box and the Find and Replace dialog box, and also options for specifying what you want to find in the document, such as figures, tables, and equations.

You can also highlight search text in a document with options at the Find and Replace dialog box with the Find tab selected. Display this dialog box by clicking the Find button arrow in the Editing group on the HOME tab and then clicking *Advanced Find* at the drop-down list. Another method for displaying the Find and Replace dialog box is to click the down-pointing arrow at the right side of the search text box in the Navigation pane and then click the *Advanced Find* option at the drop-down list. To highlight found text, type the search text in the *Find what* text box, click the Reading Highlight button, and then click *Highlight All* at the drop-down list. All occurrences of the text in the document are highlighted. To remove highlighting, click the Reading Highlight button and then click *Clear Highlighting* at the drop-down list.

Project 6a Finding and Highlighting Text — Part 1 of 4

1. Open **LeaseAgrmnt.docx** and then save the document with Save As and name it **WL1-C4-P6-LeaseAgrmnt**.
2. Find all occurrences of *lease* by completing the following steps:
   a. Click the Find button in the Editing group on the HOME tab.
   b. Click the RESULTS heading in the Navigation pane.
   c. Type lease in the search text box in the Navigation pane.
   d. After a moment, all occurrences of *lease* in the document are highlighted and text thumbnails display in the Navigation pane. Click a couple of the text thumbnails in the Navigation pane to select the text in the document.
   e. Click the Previous button (contains an up-pointing triangle) to select the previous occurrence of *lease* in the document.

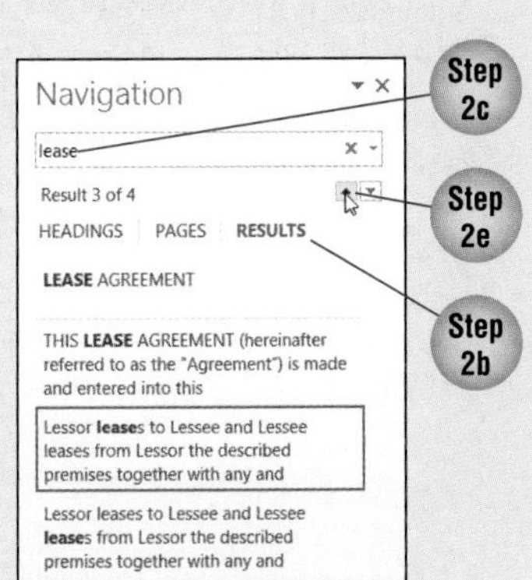

3. Use the Find and Replace dialog box with the Find tab selected to highlight all occurrences of *Premises* in the document by completing the following steps:
   a. Click in the document and press Ctrl + Home to move the insertion point to the beginning of the document.
   b. Click the down-pointing arrow at the right side of the search text box in the Navigation pane and then click *Advanced Find* at the drop-down list.

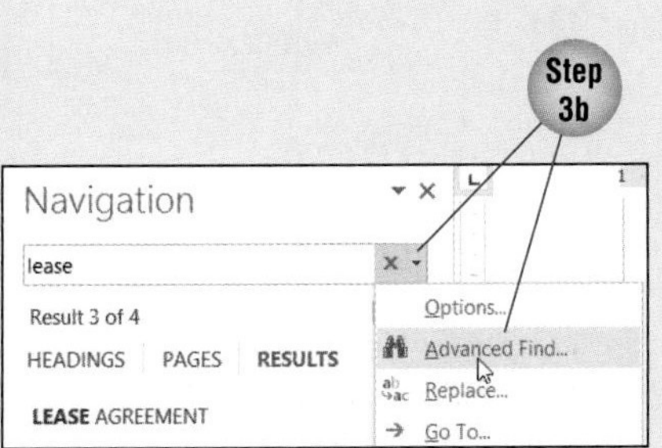

c. At the Find and Replace dialog box with the Find tab selected (and *lease* selected in the *Find what* text box), type **Premises**.
d. Click the Reading Highlight button and then click *Highlight All* at the drop-down list.
e. Click in the document to make it active and then scroll through the document and notice the occurrences of highlighted text.
f. Click in the dialog box to make it active.
g. Click the Reading Highlight button and then click *Clear Highlighting* at the drop-down list.
h. Click the Close button to close the Find and Replace dialog box.

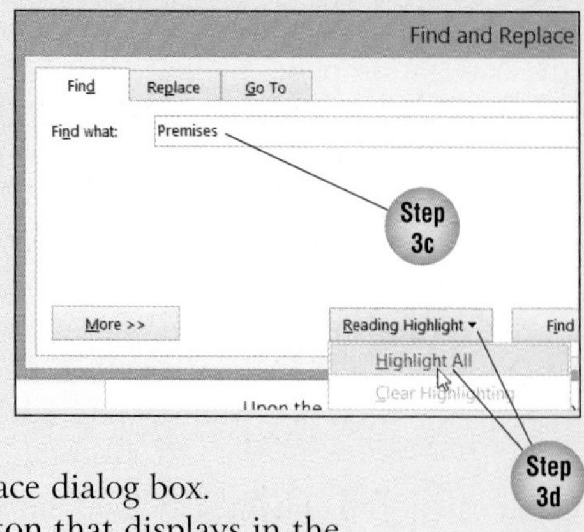

4. Close the Navigation pane by clicking the Close button that displays in the upper right corner of the pane.

Finding and Replacing Text

Quick Steps

Find and Replace Text

1. Click Replace button on HOME tab.
2. Type search text.
3. Press Tab key.
4. Type replace text.
5. Click Replace or Replace All button.

HINT

If the Find and Replace dialog box is in the way of specific text, drag the dialog box to a different location.

To find and replace text, click the Replace button in the Editing group on the HOME tab or use the keyboard shortcut Ctrl + H. This displays the Find and Replace dialog box with the Replace tab selected, as shown in Figure 4.8. Type the text you want to find in the *Find what* text box, press the Tab key, and then type the replacement text in the Replace with text box.

The Find and Replace dialog box contains several command buttons. Click the Find Next button to tell Word to find the next occurrence of the text. Click the Replace button to replace the text and find the next occurrence. If you know that you want all occurrences of the text in the *Find what* text box replaced with the text in the *Replace with* text box, click the Replace All button. This replaces every occurrence from the location of the insertion point to the beginning or end of the document (depending on the search direction).

Figure 4.8 Find and Replace Dialog Box with the Replace Tab Selected

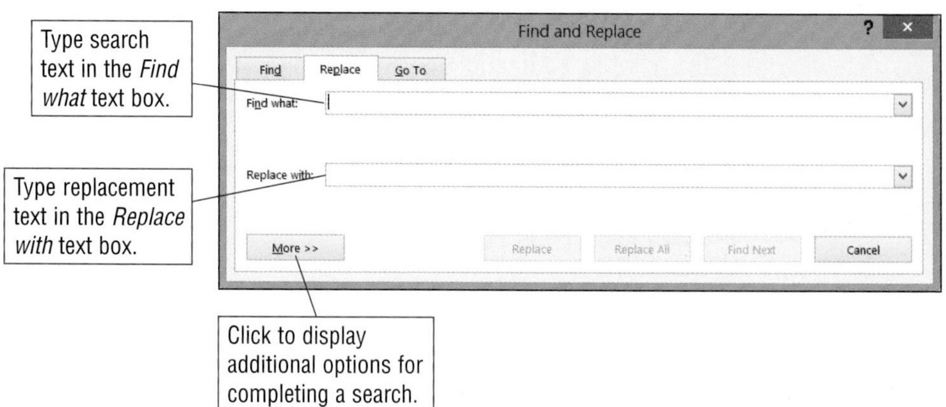

Project 6b Finding and Replacing Text

Part 2 of 4

1. With **WL1-C4-P6-LeaseAgrmnt.docx** open, make sure the insertion point is positioned at the beginning of the document.
2. Find all occurrences of *Lessor* and replace with *Tracy Hartford* by completing the following steps:
   a. Click the Replace button in the Editing group on the HOME tab.
   b. At the Find and Replace dialog box with the Replace tab selected, type **Lessor** in the *Find what* text box.
   c. Press the Tab key to move the insertion point to the *Replace with* text box.
   d. Type **Tracy Hartford**.
   e. Click the Replace All button.
   f. At the message telling you that 11 replacements were made, click OK. (Do not close the Find and Replace dialog box.)
3. With the Find and Replace dialog box still open, complete steps similar to those in Step 2 to find all occurrences of *Lessee* and replace with *Michael Iwami.*
4. Click the Close button to close the Find and Replace dialog box.
5. Save **WL1-C4-P6-LeaseAgrmnt.docx**.

Choosing Check Box Options

The Find and Replace dialog box contains a variety of check boxes with options for completing a search. To display these options, click the More button located at the bottom left side of the dialog box. This causes the Find and Replace dialog box to expand, as shown in Figure 4.9. Each option and what will occur if it is selected

Figure 4.9 Expanded Find and Replace Dialog Box

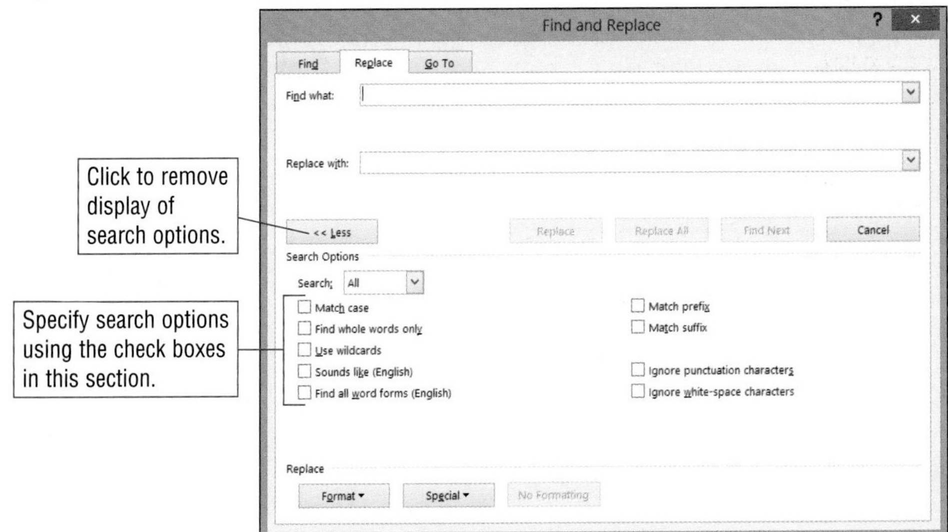

is described in Table 4.2. To remove the display of options, click the Less button. (The Less button was previously the More button.) Note that if you make a mistake when replacing text, close the Find and Replace dialog box and then click the Undo button on the Quick Access toolbar.

Table 4.2 Options at the Expanded Find and Replace Dialog Box

Choose this option	*To*
Match case	Exactly match the case of the search text. For example, if you search for *Book* and select the *Match case* option, Word will stop at *Book* but not *book* or *BOOK*.
Find whole words only	Find a whole word, not a part of a word. For example, if you search for *her* and did not select *Find whole words only*, Word will stop at *there*, *here*, *hers*, etc.
Use wildcards	Search for wildcards, special characters, or special search operators.
Sounds like	Match words that sound alike but are spelled differently, such as *know* and *no*.
Find all word forms	Find all forms of the word entered in the *Find what* text box. For example, if you enter *hold*, Word will stop at *held* and *holding*.
Match prefix	Find only those words that begin with the letters in the *Find what* text box. For example, if you enter *per*, Word will stop at words such as *perform* and *perfect* but skip words such as *super* and *hyperlink*.
Match suffix	Find only those words that end with the letters in the *Find what* text box. For example, if you enter *ly*, Word will stop at words such as *accurately* and *quietly* but skip words such as *catalyst* and *lyre*.
Ignore punctuation characters	Ignore punctuation within characters. For example, if you enter *US* in the *Find what* text box, Word will stop at *U.S.*
Ignore white-space characters	Ignore spaces between letters. For example, if you enter *F B I* in the *Find what* text box, Word will stop at *FBI*.

Project 6c Finding and Replacing Word Forms and Suffixes

Part 3 of 4

1. With **WL1-C4-P6-LeaseAgrmnt.docx** open, make sure the insertion point is positioned at the beginning of the document.
2. Find all word forms of the word *lease* and replace with *rent* by completing the following steps:
   a. Click the Replace button in the Editing group on the HOME tab.
   b. At the Find and Replace dialog box with the Replace tab selected, type **lease** in the *Find what* text box.

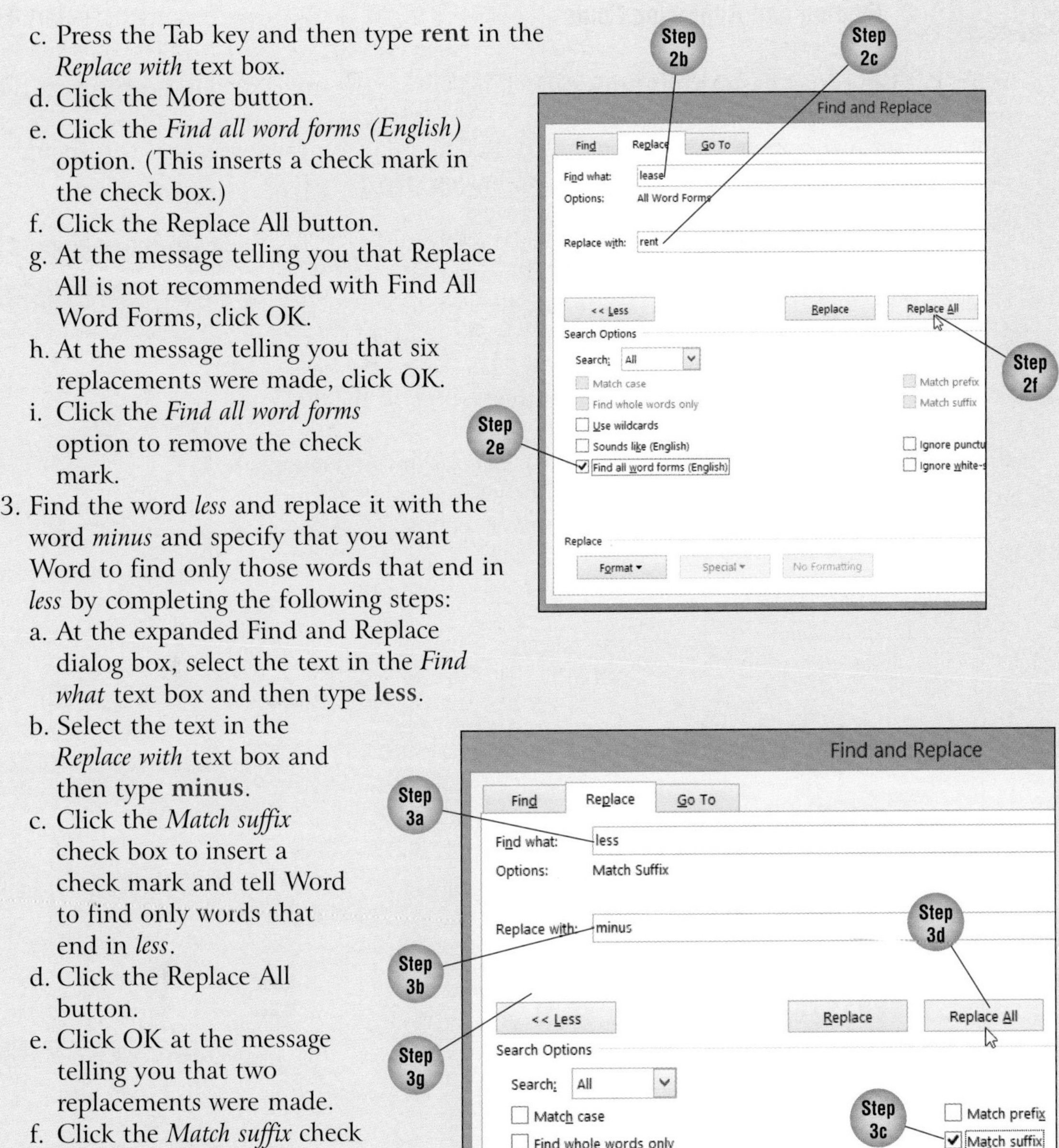

c. Press the Tab key and then type **rent** in the *Replace with* text box.
d. Click the More button.
e. Click the *Find all word forms (English)* option. (This inserts a check mark in the check box.)
f. Click the Replace All button.
g. At the message telling you that Replace All is not recommended with Find All Word Forms, click OK.
h. At the message telling you that six replacements were made, click OK.
i. Click the *Find all word forms* option to remove the check mark.

3. Find the word *less* and replace it with the word *minus* and specify that you want Word to find only those words that end in *less* by completing the following steps:
   a. At the expanded Find and Replace dialog box, select the text in the *Find what* text box and then type **less**.
   b. Select the text in the *Replace with* text box and then type **minus**.
   c. Click the *Match suffix* check box to insert a check mark and tell Word to find only words that end in *less*.
   d. Click the Replace All button.
   e. Click OK at the message telling you that two replacements were made.
   f. Click the *Match suffix* check box to remove the check mark.
   g. Click the Less button.
   h. Close the Find and Replace dialog box.
4. Save **WL1-C4-P6-LeaseAgrmnt.docx**.

Finding and Replacing Formatting

With options at the Find and Replace dialog box with the Replace tab selected, you can search for characters containing specific formatting and replace them with other characters or formatting. To specify formatting in the Find and Replace dialog box, click the More button and then click the Format button that displays toward the bottom of the dialog box. At the pop-up list that displays, identify the type of formatting you want to find.

Project 6d Finding and Replacing Fonts

Part 4 of 4

1. With **WL1-C4-P6-LeaseAgrmnt.docx** open, make sure the insertion point displays at the beginning of the document.
2. Find text set in 12-point Candara bold Dark Red and replace it with text set in 14-point Calibri bold Dark Blue by completing the following steps:
   a. Click the Replace button in the Editing group.
   b. At the Find and Replace dialog box, press the Delete key. (This deletes any text that displays in the *Find what* text box.)
   c. Click the More button. (If a check mark displays in any of the check boxes, click the option to remove the check mark.)
   d. With the insertion point positioned in the *Find what* text box, click the Format button located toward the bottom of the dialog box and then click *Font* at the pop-up list.
   e. At the Find Font dialog box, choose the *Candara* font and change the font style to *Bold*, the size to *12*, and the font color to *Dark Red* (first color option in the *Standard Colors* section).

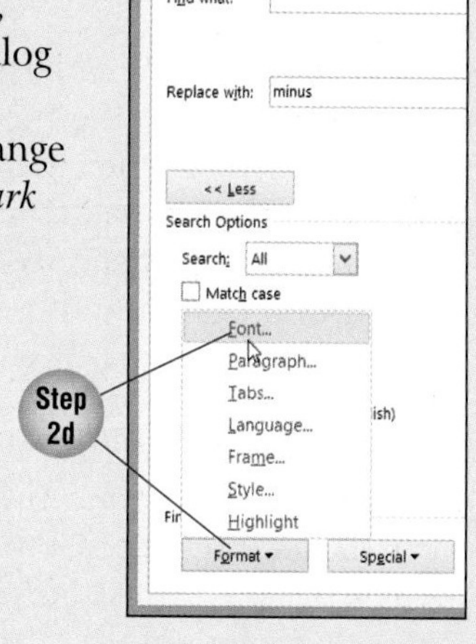

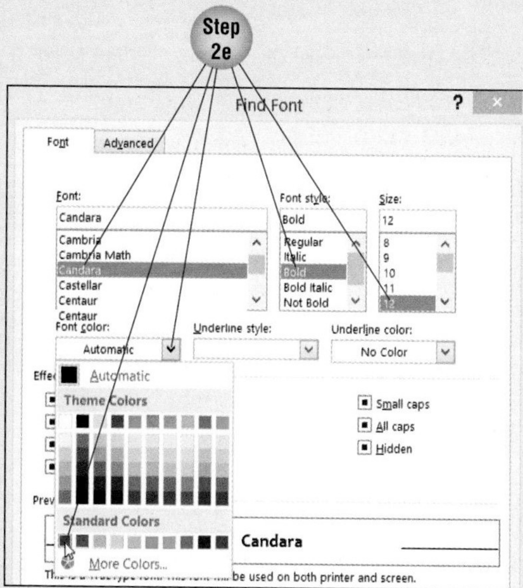

   f. Click OK to close the Find Font dialog box.
   g. At the Find and Replace dialog box, click inside the *Replace with* text box and then delete any text that displays.
   h. Click the Format button located toward the bottom of the dialog box and then click *Font* at the pop-up list.
   i. At the Replace Font dialog box, choose the *Calibri* font and change the font style to *Bold*, the size to *14*, and the font color to *Dark Blue* (second color option from the right in the *Standard Colors* section).

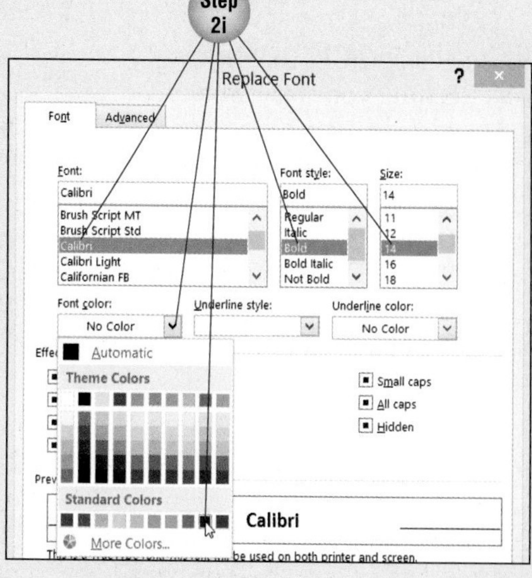

   j. Click OK to close the Replace Font dialog box.
   k. At the Find and Replace dialog box, click the Replace All button.
   l. Click OK at the message telling you that eight replacements were made.

m. Click in the *Find what* text box and then click the No Formatting button.
n. Click in the *Replace with* text box and then click the No Formatting button.
o. Click the Less button.
p. Close the Find and Replace dialog box.
3. Save, print, and then close **WL1-C4-P6-LeaseAgrmnt.docx**.

Chapter Summary

- Change the document view with buttons in the view area on the Status bar or with options in the Views group on the VIEW tab.
- Print Layout is the default view, but the view can be changed to other views, such as Draft view and Read Mode view.
- The Draft view displays the document in a format for efficient editing and formatting.
- Use the Zoom slider bar to change the percentage of the display.
- The Read Mode view displays a document in a format for easy viewing and reading.
- Use options at the Ribbon Display Options button drop-down list to specify whether you want the Quick Access toolbar, ribbon, and Status bar visible or hidden.
- Navigate in a document using the Navigation pane. Display the pane by inserting a check mark in the *Navigation Pane* check box in the Show group on the VIEW tab.
- By default, a Word document contains 1-inch top, bottom, left, and right margins. Change margins with preset margin settings at the Margins button drop-down list or with options at the Page Setup dialog box with the Margins tab selected.
- The default page orientation is portrait, which can be changed to landscape with the Orientation button in the Page Setup group on the PAGE LAYOUT tab.
- The default page size is 8.5 inches by 11 inches, which can be changed with options at the Size button drop-down list or options at the Page Setup dialog box with the Paper tab selected.
- The page break that Word inserts automatically is a soft page break. A page break that you insert is a hard page break. Insert a hard page break with the Page Break button in the Pages group on the INSERT tab or by pressing Ctrl + Enter.
- Insert a predesigned and formatted cover page by clicking the Cover Page button in the Pages group on the INSERT tab and then clicking the desired option at the drop-down list.
- Insert predesigned and formatted page numbering by clicking the Page Number button in the Header & Footer group on the INSERT tab, specifying the desired location of page numbers, and then clicking the desired page numbering option.
- Insert predesigned headers and footers in a document with the Header button and the Footer button in the Header & Footer group on the INSERT tab.
- A watermark is a lightened image that displays behind text in a document. Use the Watermark button in the Page Background group on the DESIGN tab to insert a watermark.

- Insert page color in a document with the Page Color button in the Page Background group on the DESIGN tab. Page color is designed for viewing a document on-screen and does not print.
- Click the Page Borders button in the Page Background group on the DESIGN tab and the Borders and Shading dialog box with the Page Border tab selected displays. Use options at this dialog box to insert a page border or an image page border in a document.
- Use the Find feature to search for specific characters or formatting. Use the Find and Replace feature to search for specific characters or formatting and replace with other characters or formatting.
- At the Find and Replace dialog box, click the Find Next button to find the next occurrence of the characters and/or formatting. Click the Replace button to replace the characters or formatting and find the next occurrence, or click the Replace All button to replace all occurrences of the characters or formatting.
- Click the More button at the Find and Replace dialog box to display additional options for completing a search.

Commands Review

FEATURE	RIBBON TAB, GROUP	BUTTON, OPTION	KEYBOARD SHORTCUT
blank page	INSERT, Pages		
Borders and Shading dialog box with Page Border tab selected	DESIGN, Page Background		
Border and Shading Options dialog box	DESIGN, Page Background	, *Options*	
cover page	INSERT, Pages		
Draft view	VIEW, Views		
Find and Replace dialog box with Find tab selected	HOME, Editing	, *Advanced Find*	
Find and Replace dialog box with Replace tab selected	HOME, Editing		Ctrl + H
footer	INSERT, Header & Footer		
header	INSERT, Header & Footer		
margins	PAGE LAYOUT, Page Setup		
Navigation pane	VIEW, Show	*Navigation Pane*	Ctrl + F
orientation	PAGE LAYOUT, Page Setup		
page break	INSERT, Pages		Ctrl + Enter
page color	DESIGN, Page Background		

FEATURE	RIBBON TAB, GROUP	BUTTON, OPTION	KEYBOARD SHORTCUT
page numbering	INSERT, Header & Footer		
Page Setup dialog box with Margins tab selected	PAGE LAYOUT, Page Setup	, *Custom Margins* OR	
Page Setup dialog box with Paper tab selected	PAGE LAYOUT, Page Setup	, *More Paper Sizes*	
page size	PAGE LAYOUT, Page Setup		
Print Layout view	VIEW, Views		
Read Mode view	VIEW, Views		
ribbon display options			
watermark	DESIGN, Page Background		

Concepts Check

Test Your Knowledge

Completion: In the space provided at the right, indicate the correct term, symbol, or command.

1. This is the default measurement for the top, bottom, left, and right margins. ________________
2. This view displays a document in a format for efficient editing and formatting. ________________
3. This view displays a document in a format for easy viewing and reading. ________________
4. The *Navigation Pane* check box is located in this group on the VIEW tab. ________________
5. To remove white space, double-click this icon. ________________
6. This is the default page orientation. ________________
7. Set specific margins at this dialog box with the Margins tab selected. ________________
8. Press these keys on the keyboard to insert a page break. ________________
9. The Cover Page button is located in the Pages group on this tab. ________________
10. Text that appears at the top of every page is called this. ________________
11. A lightened image that displays behind text in a document is called this. ________________
12. Change the position of the page border from the edge of the page with options at this dialog box. ________________

13. The Page Borders button displays in this group on the DESIGN tab. __________

14. If you want to replace every occurrence of what you are searching for in a document, click this button at the Find and Replace dialog box. __________

15. Click this option at the Find and Replace dialog box if you are searching for a word and all of its forms. __________

Skills Check Assess Your Performance

Assessment 1

FORMAT A COVER LETTER DOCUMENT AND CREATE A COVER PAGE

1. Open **CoverLetter.docx** and then save the document with Save As and name it **WL1-C4-A1-CoverLetter**.
2. Change the left and right margins to 1.25 inches.
3. Move the insertion point to the beginning of the heading *Writing Cover Letters to People You Know* and then insert a blank page.
4. Insert a page break at the beginning of the heading *Writing Cover Letters to People You Don't Know*.
5. Move the insertion point to the beginning of the document and then insert the Filigree cover page.
6. Insert the following text in the specified fields:
   a. Type **job search strategies** in the *[DOCUMENT TITLE]* placeholder.
   b. Type **Writing a Cover Letter** in the *[Document subtitle]* placeholder.
   c. Type **february 3, 2015** in the *[DATE]* placeholder.
   d. Type **career finders** in the *[COMPANY NAME]* placeholder.
   e. Delete the *[Company address]* placeholder.
7. Move the insertion point to any character in the title *WRITING A COVER LETTER* and then insert the Brackets 1 page numbering at the bottom of the page. (The page numbering will not appear on the cover page.)
8. Make the document active, turn on the display of nonprinting characters, move the insertion point to the blank line above the page break below the first paragraph of text in the document, and then press the Delete key six times. (This deletes the page break on the first page and the page break creating a blank page 2 as well as extra hard returns.) Turn off the display of nonprinting characters.
9. Save, print, and then close **WL1-C4-A1-CoverLetter.docx**.

Assessment 2

FORMAT AN INTELLECTUAL PROPERTY REPORT AND INSERT HEADERS AND FOOTERS

1. Open **PropProtect.docx** and then save the document with Save As and name it **WL1-C4-A2-PropProtect**.
2. Insert a page break at the beginning of the *REFERENCES* title (located on the second page).
3. Change the top margin to 1.5 inches.

4. Change the page orientation to landscape orientation.
5. Move the insertion point to the beginning of the document and then insert the Retrospect footer. Select the name that displays at the left side of the footer and then type your first and last names.
6. Save the document and then print only page 1 of the document.
7. Change the orientation back to portrait orientation.
8. Apply the Moderate page margins.
9. Remove the footer.
10. Insert the Ion (Dark) header.
11. Insert the Ion (Dark) footer. Type **property protection issues** as the title and make sure your first and last names display at the right side of the footer.
12. Select the footer text (document name and your name), turn on bold, and then change the font size to 8 points.
13. Insert the DRAFT 1 watermark in the document.
14. Apply the Green, Accent 3, Lighter 80% page color (seventh column, second row).
15. Save and then print **WL1-C4-A2-PropProtect.docx**.
16. With the document still open, change the paper size to legal (8.5 inches by 14 inches).
17. Save the document with Save As and name it **WL1-C4-A2-PropProtect-Legal**.
18. Check with your instructor to determine if you can print legal-sized documents. If so, print page 1 of the document.
19. Save and then close **WL1-C4-A2-PropProtect-Legal.docx**.

Assessment 3

FORMAT A REAL ESTATE AGREEMENT

1. Open **REAgrmnt.docx** and then save the document with Save As and name it **WL1-C4-A3-REAgrmnt**.
2. Find all occurrences of *BUYER* (matching the case) and replace with *James Berman*.
3. Find all occurrences of *SELLER* (matching the case) and replace with *Mona Trammell*.
4. Find all word forms of the word *buy* and replace with *purchase*.
5. Search for 14-point Tahoma bold formatting in Dark Red and replace with 12-point Constantia bold formatting in Black, Text 1.
6. Insert Plain Number 2 page numbers at the bottom center of the page.
7. Insert a page border with the following specifications:
   - Choose the first double-line border in the *Style* list box.
   - Change the color of the page border to *Dark Red* (located in the *Standard Colors* section).
   - Change the width of the page border to *1½ pt*.
8. Display the Border and Shading Options dialog box and then change the top, left, bottom, and right measurements to *30 pt*. ***Hint: Display the Border and Shading Options dialog box by clicking the Options button at the Borders and Shading dialog box with the Page Border tab selected.***
9. Save, print, and then close **WL1-C4-A3-REAgrmnt.docx**.

Visual Benchmark Demonstrate Your Proficiency

FORMAT A RESUME STYLES REPORT

1. Open **Resumes.docx** and then save it with Save As and name it **WL1-C4-VB-Resumes**.
2. Format the document so it appears as shown in Figure 4.10 on page 141 with the following specifications:
   - Change the top margin to 1.5 inches.
   - Apply the Heading 1 style to the title and the Heading 2 style to the headings.
   - Apply the Lines (Simple) style set.
   - Apply the Savon theme.
   - Apply the Blue Green theme colors.
   - Insert the Austin cover page and insert text in the placeholders and delete placeholders as shown in the figure. (If a name displays in the Author placeholder, delete the current name, and then type your first and last names.)
   - Insert the Ion (Dark) header and the Ion (Dark) footer.
3. Save, print, and then close **WL1-C4-VB-Resumes.docx**.

Case Study Apply Your Skills

Part 1

You work for Citizens for Consumer Safety, a nonprofit organization providing information on household safety. Your supervisor, Melinda Johansson, has asked you to attractively format a document on smoke detectors. She will be using the document as an informational handout during a presentation on smoke detectors. Open **SmokeDetectors.docx** and then save the document with Save As and name it **WL1-C4-CS1-SmokeDetectors**. Apply appropriate styles to the title and headings and apply a theme. Ms. Johansson has asked you to change the page orientation to landscape and to change the left and right margins to 1.5 inches. She wants the extra space at the left and right margins so audience members can write notes in the margins. Use the Help feature or experiment with the options in the HEADER & FOOTER TOOLS DESIGN tab and figure out how to number pages on every page but the first page. Insert page numbering in the document that prints at the top right side of every page except the first page. Save, print, and then close **WL1-C4-CS1-SmokeDetectors.docx**.

Figure 4.10 Visual Benchmark

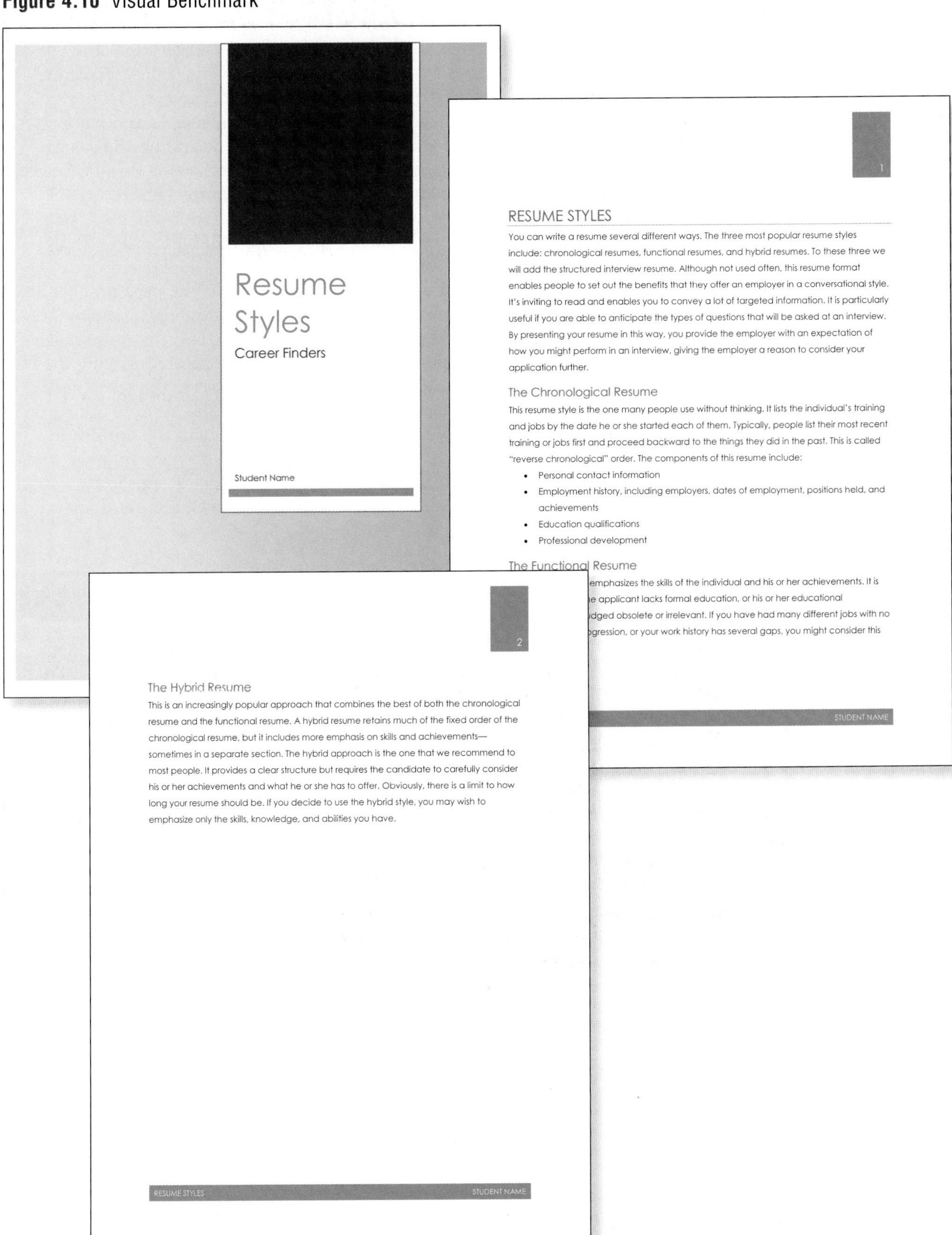

Part 2

Help

After reviewing the formatted document on smoke detectors, Ms. Johansson has decided that she wants the document to print in the default orientation (portrait) and would like to see different theme and style choices. She also noticed that the term "smoke alarm" should be replaced with "smoke detector." She has asked you to open and then format the original document. Open **SmokeDetectors.docx** and then save the document with Save As and name it **WL1-C4-CS2-SmokeDetectors**. Apply styles to the title and headings and apply a theme to the document (other than the one you chose for Part 1). Search for all occurrences of *smoke alarm* and replace with *smoke detector*. Insert a cover page of your choosing and insert the appropriate information in the page. Use the Help feature or experiment with the options in the HEADER & FOOTER TOOLS DESIGN tab and figure out how to insert odd-page and even-page footers in a document. Insert an odd-page footer that prints the page number at the right margin and insert an even-page footer that prints the page number at the left margin. You do not want the footer to print on the cover page, so make sure you position the insertion point below the cover page before inserting the footers. After inserting the footers in the document, you decide that they need to be moved down the page to create more space between the last line of text on a page and the footer. Use the Help feature or experiment with the options in the HEADER & FOOTER TOOLS DESIGN tab to figure out how to move the footers down and then edit each footer so it displays 0.3 inch from the bottom of the page. Save, print, and then close **WL1-C4-CS2-SmokeDetectors.docx**.

Part 3

Ms. Johansson has asked you to prepare a document on infant car seats and car seat safety. She wants this informational car seat safety document available for distribution at a local community center. Use the Internet to find websites that provide information on child and infant car seats and car seat safety. Write a report on the information you find that includes at least the following information:

- Description of the types of car seats (such as rear-facing, convertible, forward-facing, built-in, and booster)
- Safety rules and guidelines
- Installation information
- Specific child and infant seat models
- Sites on the Internet that sell car seats
- Price ranges
- Internet sites providing safety information

Format the report using styles and a theme and include a cover page and headers and/or footers. Save the completed document and name it **WL1-C4-CS-CarSeats**. Print and then close the document.

UNIT 1

MICROSOFT® WORD Performance Assessment

WL1U1

Note: Before beginning unit assessments, copy to your storage medium the WL1U1 subfolder from the WL1 folder on the CD that accompanies this textbook and then make WL1U1 the active folder.

Assessing Proficiency

In this unit, you have learned to create, edit, save, and print Word documents. You have also learned to format characters, paragraphs, and pages.

Assessment 1 Format a Document on Website Design

1. Open **Website.docx** and then save the document with Save As and name it **WL1-U1-A1-Website**.
2. Complete a spelling and grammar check.
3. Select from the paragraph that begins *Make your home page work for you.* through the end of the document and then apply bullet formatting.
4. Select and then bold the first sentence of each bulleted paragraph.
5. Apply a single-line bottom border to the document title and apply Gold, Accent 4, Lighter 80% paragraph shading to the title.
6. Save and then print **WL1-U1-A1-Website.docx**.
7. Change the top, left, and right margins to 1.5 inches.
8. Select the bulleted paragraphs, change the paragraph alignment to justified alignment, and then apply numbering formatting.
9. Select the entire document and then change the font to 12-point Cambria.
10. Insert the text shown in Figure U1.1 after paragraph number 2. (The number 3. should be inserted preceding the text you type.)
11. Save, print, and then close **WL1-U1-A1-Website.docx**.

Figure U1.1 Assessment 1

Avoid a cluttered look. In design, less is more. Strive for a clean look to your pages, using ample margins and white space.

Assessment 2 Format Accumulated Returns Document

1. Open **ReturnChart.docx** and then save the document with Save As and name it **WL1-U1-A2-ReturnChart**.
2. Select the entire document and then make the following changes:
   a. Apply the No Spacing style.
   b. Change the line spacing to 1.5.
   c. Change the font to 12-point Cambria.
   d. Apply 6 points of spacing after paragraphs.
3. Select the title *TOTAL RETURN CHARTS*, change the font to 14-point Corbel bold, change the alignment to centered, and apply Blue-Gray, Text 2, Lighter 80% paragraph shading.
4. Bold the following text that appears at the beginning of the second through the fifth paragraphs:
   Average annual total return: *Annual total return:*
   Accumulation units: *Accumulative rates:*
5. Select the paragraphs of text in the body of the document (all paragraphs except the title) and then change the paragraph alignment to justified alignment.
6. Select the paragraphs that begin with the bolded words, sort the paragraphs in ascending order, and then indent the text 0.5 inch from the left margin.
7. Insert a watermark that prints *DRAFT* diagonally across the page.
8. Save, print, and then close **WL1-U1-A2-ReturnChart.docx**.

Assessment 3 Format Computer Ethics Report

1. Open **FutureEthics.docx** and then save the document with Save As and name it **WL1-U1-A3-FutureEthics.docx**.
2. Apply the Heading 1 style to the titles *FUTURE OF COMPUTER ETHICS* and *REFERENCES*.
3. Apply the Heading 2 style to the headings in the document.
4. Apply the Shaded style set.
5. Apply the Open paragraph spacing.
6. Apply the Parallax theme and then change the theme fonts to Garamond.
7. Center the two titles (*FUTURE OF COMPUTER ETHICS* and *REFERENCES*).
8. Add 6 points of paragraph spacing after each heading with the Heading 1 and Heading 2 styles applied in the document.
9. Hang indent the paragraphs of text below the *REFERENCES* title.
10. Insert page numbering that prints at the bottom center of each page.
11. Save, print, and then close **WL1-U1-A3-FutureEthics.docx**.

Assessment 4 Set Tabs and Type Income by Division Text in Columns

1. At a new blank document, type the text shown in Figure U1.2 with the following specifications:
   a. Bold and center the title as shown.
   b. You determine the tab settings for the text in columns.
   c. Select the entire document and then change the font to 12-point Arial.
2. Save the document and name it **WL1-U1-A4-Income**.
3. Print and then close **WL1-U1-A4-Income.docx**.

Figure U1.2 Assessment 4

INCOME BY DIVISION

	2013	2014	2015
Public Relations	$14,375	$16,340	$16,200
Database Services	9,205	15,055	13,725
Graphic Design	18,400	21,790	19,600
Technical Support	5,780	7,325	9,600

Assessment 5 Set Tabs and Type Table of Contents Text

1. At a blank document, type the text shown in Figure U1.3 with the following specifications:
   a. Bold and center the title as shown.
   b. You determine the tab settings for the text in columns.
   c. Select the entire document, change the font to 12-point Cambria, and then change the line spacing to 1.5.
2. Save the document and name it **WL1-U1-A5-TofC**.
3. Print and then close **WL1-U1-A5-TofC.docx**.

Figure U1.3 Assessment 5

TABLE OF CONTENTS

Online Shopping. 2

Online Services. 4

Peer-to-Peer Online Transactions. 5

Transaction Payment Methods. 8

Transaction Security and Encryption 11

Establishing a Website. 14

Assessment 6 Format Union Agreement Contract

1. Open **LaborContract.docx** and then save the document with Save As and name it **WL1-U1-A6-LaborContract**.
2. Find all occurrences of *REINBERG MANUFACTURING* and replace with *MILLWOOD ENTERPRISES*.
3. Find all occurrences of *RM* and replace with *ME*.
4. Find all occurrences of *LABOR WORKERS' UNION* and replace with *SERVICE EMPLOYEES' UNION*.
5. Find all occurrences of *LWU* and replace with *SEU*.
6. Select the entire document and then change the font to 12-point Cambria and the line spacing to double spacing.

7. Select the numbered paragraphs in the *Transfers and Moving Expenses* section and change to bulleted paragraphs.
8. Select the numbered paragraphs in the *Sick Leave* section and change them to bulleted paragraphs.
9. Change the page orientation to landscape and the top margin to 1.5 inches.
10. Save and then print **WL1-U1-A6-LaborContract.docx**.
11. Change the page orientation to portrait and the left margin (previously the top margin) back to 1 inch.
12. Insert the Wisp cover page (may display as *Whisp*) and insert the current date in the Date placeholder, the title *Union Agreement* as the document title and *Millwood Enterprises* as the document subtitle. Select the Author placeholder (or the name that displays) located toward the bottom of the document and then type your first and last names. Delete the Company Name placeholder.
13. Move the insertion point to the page after the cover page, insert the Ion Dark footer, and then make sure *UNION AGREEMENT* displays in the Title placeholder and your name displays in the Author placeholder. If not, type **UNION AGREEMENT** in the Title placeholder and your first and last names in the Author placeholder.
14. Save, print, and then close **WL1-U1-A6-LaborContract.docx**.

Assessment 7 Copy and Paste Text in Health Plan Document

1. Open **KeyLifePlan.docx** and then save the document with Save As and name it **WL1-U1-A7-KeyLifePlan**.
2. Open **PlanOptions.docx** and then turn on the display of the Clipboard task pane. Make sure the Clipboard is empty.
3. Select the heading *Plan Highlights* and the six paragraphs of text below the heading and then copy the selected text to the Clipboard.
4. Select the heading *Plan Options* and the two paragraphs of text below the heading and then copy the selected text to the Clipboard.
5. Select the heading *Quality Assessment* and the six paragraphs of text below the heading and then copy the selected text to the Clipboard.
6. Close **PlanOptions.docx**.
7. With **WL1-U1-A7-KeyLifePlan.docx** open, display the Clipboard task pane.
8. Move the insertion point to the beginning of the *Provider Network* heading, paste the *Plan Options* item from the Clipboard, and merge the formatting.
9. With the insertion point positioned at the beginning of the *Provider Network* heading, paste *Plan Highlights* from the Clipboard and merge the formatting.
10. Move the insertion point to the beginning of the *Plan Options* heading, paste the *Quality Assessment* item from the Clipboard, and merge the formatting.
11. Clear the Clipboard and then close it.
12. Apply the Heading 1 style to the title, *KEY LIFE HEALTH PLAN*.
13. Apply the Heading 2 style to the four headings in the document.
14. Change the top margin to 1.5 inches.
15. Apply the Lines (Simple) style set.
16. Apply the Compact paragraph spacing.
17. Apply the Red Orange theme colors.
18. Insert a double-line, Dark Red page border.
19. Insert the Slice 1 header.
20. Insert the Slice footer and type your first and last names in the Author placeholder.
21. Insert a page break at the beginning of the heading *Plan Highlights*.
22. Save, print, and then close **WL1-U1-A7-KeyLifePlan.docx**.

Assessment 8 Create and Format a Resume

1. Apply the No spacing style to a blank document and then create the resume shown in Figure U1.4. Change the font to Candara and apply the character, paragraph, border, shading, and bullet formatting as shown in the figure.
2. Save the completed document and name it **WL1-U1-A8-Resume.**
3. Print and then close **WL1-U1-A8-Resume.docx**.

Figure U1.4 Assessment 8

KIERNAN O'MALLEY

1533 Baylor Street East, Auburn, WA 98020 (253) 555-3912

NETWORK ADMINISTRATION PROFESSIONAL
Pursuing **Cisco Certified Network Associate (CCNA)** and **Network+** credentials
Proficient in Microsoft Office applications in Windows environment

EDUCATION

Information Systems (IS), Western Washington University, Bellingham, WA...................... 2012
Medical Specialist, Seattle University, Seattle, WA .... 2010 to 2012
Medical Terminology, Green River Community College, Auburn, WA................................. 2009

APPLIED RESEARCH PROJECTS

Completed **Applied Research Projects (ARPs)**, in conjunction with IS degree requirements, covering all aspects of design and management of organizational technical resources, as follows:

- **Organizational Culture and Leadership** (2015): Evaluated the organizational culture of Bellevue Surgery Center's endoscopy unit and operating room (OR) in order to ensure that the mission and vision statements were being appropriately applied at the staff level.
- **Human Resources (HR) Management** (2015): Established a comprehensive orientation package for the Bellevue Surgery Center's clinical staff.
- **Strategic Management and Planning** (2014): Conducted internal/external environmental assessments in order to identify an approach for Bellevue Surgery Center to expand its OR facilities.
- **Financial Accounting** (2014): Created a quarterly operating budget for the Bellevue Surgery Center and implemented an expenditure tracking system.
- **Database Management Systems** (2013): Created an inventory-control system that optimizes inventory maintenance in a cost-effective manner.
- **Statistics and Research Analysis** (2013): Generated graphics to illustrate the Valley Hospital's assisted-reproduction success rate.
- **Management Support System** (2012): Identified solutions to resolve inventory-control vulnerabilities at minimal cost for Valley Hospital.

PROFESSIONAL EXPERIENCE

CERTIFIED SURGICAL TECHNOLOGIST

Bellevue Surgery Center, Bellevue, WA...2013 to present
Valley Hospital, Renton, WA ....2011 to 2013
Kenmore Ambulatory Surgery Center, Kenmore, WA ....2009 to 2011
South Sound Medical Center, Auburn, WA.. 2008 to 2009

Writing Activities

The following activities give you the opportunity to practice your writing skills along with demonstrating an understanding of some of the important Word features you have mastered in this unit. Use correct grammar, appropriate word choices, and clear sentence constructions. Follow the steps in Figure U1.5 to improve your writing skills.

Activity 1 Write Steps on Using KeyTips

Use Word's Help feature to learn about KeyTips. To do this, open the Word Help window, type **keytips**, and then press Enter. Click the Keyboard shortcuts for Microsoft Word article hyperlink. Click the Show All hyperlink and then scroll down the article to the *Navigating the ribbon* heading. Read the information about accessing any command with a few keystrokes. (Read only the information in the *Navigating the ribbon* section.)

At a blank document, write a paragraph summarizing the information you read in the Word Help article. After writing the paragraph, write steps on how to use KeyTips to accomplish the following tasks:

- Turn on bold formatting.
- Display the Font dialog box.
- Print the open document.

Save the completed document and name it **WL1-U1-Act1-KeyTips**. Print and then close **WL1-U1-Act1-KeyTips.docx**.

Activity 2 Write Information on Customizing Grammar Style Options

Use Word's Help feature to learn about grammar and style options. (You can also experiment with the *Writing Style* and *Settings* options at the Word Options dialog box with Proofing selected. Display this dialog box by clicking the FILE tab, clicking *Options*, and then clicking *Proofing* in the left panel of the Word Options dialog box.) Learn how to choose which grammar errors to detect and which style errors to detect. Also learn how to set rules for grammar and style. Once you have determined this information, create a document describing at least two grammar errors and at least two style errors you can choose for detection. Also include in this document the steps required to have Word check the grammar and style rather than just the grammar in a document. Save the completed document and name it **WL1-U1-Act2-CustomSpell**. Print and then close **WL1-U1-Act2-CustomSpell.docx**.

Figure U1.5 The Writing Process

The Writing Process

Plan Gather ideas, select which information to include, and choose the order in which to present the information.

Checkpoints
- What is the purpose?
- What information does the reader need in order to reach your intended conclusion?

Write Following the information plan and keeping the reader in mind, draft the document using clear, direct sentences that say what you mean.

Checkpoints
- What are the subpoints for each main thought?
- How can you connect paragraphs so the reader moves smoothly from one idea to the next?

Revise Improve what is written by changing, deleting, rearranging, or adding words, sentences, and paragraphs.

Checkpoints
- Is the meaning clear?
- Do the ideas follow a logical order?
- Have you included any unnecessary information?
- Have you built your sentences around strong nouns and verbs?

Edit Check spelling, sentence construction, word use, punctuation, and capitalization.

Checkpoints
- Can you spot any redundancies or clichés?
- Can you reduce any phrases to an effective word (for example, change *the fact that* to *because*)?
- Have you used commas only where there is a strong reason for doing so?
- Did you proofread the document for errors that your spelling checker cannot identify?

Publish Prepare a final copy that could be reproduced and shared with others.

Checkpoints
- Which design elements, such as boldface or different fonts, would help highlight important ideas or sections?
- Would charts or other graphics help clarify meaning?

Internet Research

Research Business Desktop Computer Systems

You hold a part-time job at the local Chamber of Commerce, where you assist the office manager, Ryan Woods. Mr. Woods will be purchasing new desktop computers for the office staff. He has asked you to research on the Internet and identify at least three PCs that can be purchased directly over the Internet, and he requests that you put your research and recommendations in writing. Mr. Woods is looking for solid, reliable, economical, and powerful desktop computers with good warranties and service plans. He has given you a budget of $800 per unit.

Search the Internet for three desktop PC computer systems from three different manufacturers. Consider price, specifications (processor speed, amount of RAM, hard drive space, and monitor type and size), performance, warranties, and service plans when making your choice of systems. Print your research findings and include them with your report. (For helpful information on shopping for a computer, read the articles "Buying and Installing a PC" and "Purchasing a Computer," posted in the Course Resources section of this book's Internet Resource Center, either at www.paradigmcollege.net/BenchmarkOffice13 or www.paradigmcollege.net/BenchmarkWord13.)

Using Word, write a brief report in which you summarize the capabilities and qualities of each of the three computer systems you recommend. Include a final paragraph detailing which system you suggest for purchase and why. If possible, incorporate user opinions and/or reviews about this system to support your decision. At the end of your report, include a table comparing the computer systems. Format your report using the concepts and techniques you learned in Unit 1. Save the report and name it **WL1-U1-InternetResearch**. Print and then close the file.

MICROSOFT®

WORD Level 1

Unit 2 ■ Enhancing and Customizing Documents

Chapter 5 ■ Applying Formatting and Inserting Objects

Chapter 6 ■ Maintaining Documents

Chapter 7 ■ Creating Tables and SmartArt

Chapter 8 ■ Merging Documents

MICROSOFT®
WORD

Applying Formatting and Inserting Objects

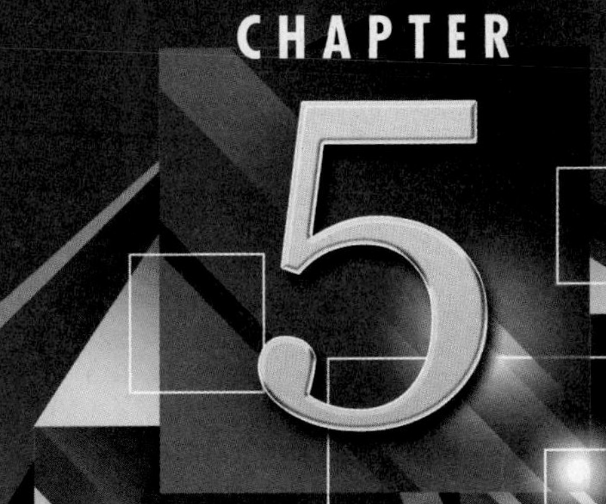

PERFORMANCE OBJECTIVES

Upon successful completion of Chapter 5, you will be able to:

- **Insert section breaks**
- **Create and format text in columns**
- **Hyphenate words automatically and manually**
- **Create a drop cap**
- **Insert symbols, special characters, and the date and time**
- **Use the Click and Type feature**
- **Vertically align text**
- **Insert, format, and customize images, text boxes, shapes, and WordArt**
- **Create and customize a screen shot**

Tutorials

5.1 Inserting Section Breaks
5.2 Creating Newspaper Columns
5.3 Hyphenating Words
5.4 Inserting a Drop Cap, Symbols, and Date and Time
5.5 Using Click and Type
5.6 Using Horizontal Alignment
5.7 Inserting and Formatting an Image
5.8 Inserting, Sizing, and Moving an Image from Office.com
5.9 Inserting and Formatting a Text Box
5.10 Inserting and Formatting a Shape
5.11 Inserting and Modifying WordArt
5.12 Creating and Inserting a Screenshot

To apply page or document formatting to only a portion of the document, insert a section break. You can insert a continuous section break or a section break that begins a new page. A section break is useful when formatting text in columns. The hyphenation feature hyphenates words at the ends of lines, creating a less ragged margin. Use buttons in the Text and Symbols groups on the INSERT tab to insert symbols, special characters, date and time, text boxes, and WordArt. With the Click and Type feature, you can position the insertion point at a particular location in the document and change the paragraph alignment. Use the *Vertical alignment* option at the Page Setup dialog box with the Layout tab selected to align text vertically on the page. Along with these features, you will also learn how to increase the visual appeal of a document by inserting and customizing images such as pictures, clip art, text boxes, shapes, WordArt, and screen shots. Model answers for this chapter's projects appear on the following pages.

Note: Before beginning the projects, copy to your storage medium the WL1C5 subfolder from the WL1 folder on the CD that accompanies this textbook and then make WL1C5 the active folder.

COMPUTER INPUT DEVICES

Engineers have been especially creative in designing new ways to get information into computers. Some input methods are highly specialized and unusual, while common devices often undergo redesign to improve their capabilities or their ergonomics, the ways in which they affect people physically. Some common input devices include keyboards, mice, trackballs, and touchpads.

Keyboard

A keyboard can be an external device that is attached by means of a cable, or it can be attached to the CPU case itself as it is for laptop computers. Most keyboards today are QWERTY keyboards, which take their name from the first six keys at the left of the first row of letters. An alternative, the DVORAK keyboard, places the most commonly used keys close to the user's fingertips and speeds typing.

Many keyboards have a separate numeric keypad, like that of a calculator, containing numbers and mathematical operators. All keyboards have modifier keys that enable the user to change the symbol or character that is entered when a given key is pressed. The Shift key, for example, makes a letter uppercase. Keyboards also have special cursor keys that enable the user to change the position on the screen of the cursor, a symbol that appears on the monitor to show where in a document the next change will appear. Most keyboards also have function keys, labeled F1, F2, F3, and so on. These keys allow the user to issue commands by pressing a single key.

Mouse

Graphical operating systems contain many elements that a user can choose by pointing at them. Such elements include buttons, tools, pull-down menus, and icons for file folders, programs, and document files. Often pointing to and clicking on one of these elements is more convenient than using the cursor or arrow keys on the keyboard. This pointing and clicking can be done by using a mouse. The mouse is the second most common input device, after the keyboard. A mouse operates by moving the cursor on the computer screen to correspond to movements made with the mouse.

Trackball

A trackball is like an upside-down mouse. A mouse is moved over a pad. A trackball remains stationary, and the user moves the ball with his or her fingers or palm. One or more buttons for choosing options are incorporated into the design of the trackball.

Touchpad and Touchscreen

A touchpad feels less mechanical than a mouse or trackball because the user simply moves a finger on the pad. A touchpad has two parts. One part acts as a button, while the other emulates a mouse pad on which the user traces the location of the cursor with a finger. People with carpal tunnel syndrome find touchpads and trackballs easier to use than mice. Many portable computers have built-in trackballs or touchpads as input devices.

1

A touchscreen allows the user to choose options by pressing the appropriate part of the screen. Touchscreens are widely used in bank ATMs and in kiosks at retail outlets and in tourist areas.

Prepared by: Matthew Viña
SoftCell Technologies®
September 4, 2015
12:04 PM

2

Project 1 Format a Document on Computer Input Devices
WL1-C5-P1-InputDevices.docx

SUPERVISORY TRAINING
Maximizing Employee Potential
Wednesday, February 18, 2015
Training Center
9:00 a.m. to 3:30 p.m.

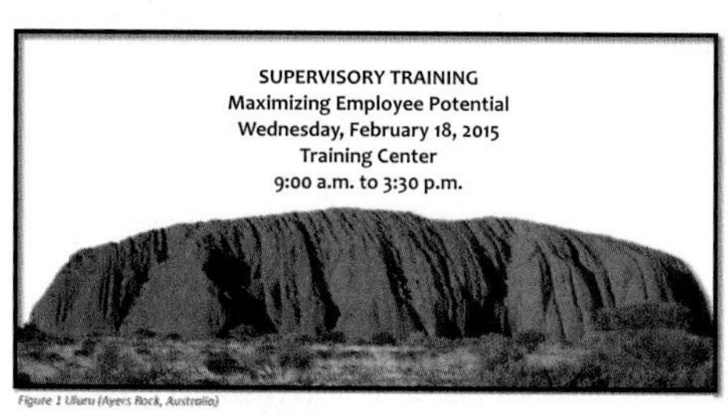

Figure 1 Uluru (Ayers Rock, Australia)

Project 2 Create an Announcement about Supervisory Training
WL1-C5-P2-Training.docx

ROBOTS AS ANDROIDS

Robotic factories are increasingly commonplace, especially in heavy manufacturing, where tolerance of repetitive movements, great strength, and untiring precision are more important than flexibility. Robots are especially useful in hazardous work, such as defusing bombs or handling radioactive materials. They also excel in constructing tiny components like those found inside notebook computers, which are often too small for humans to assemble.

Most people think of robots in science fiction terms, which generally depict them as androids, or simulated humans. Real robots today do not look human at all, and judged by human standards, they are not very intelligent. The task of creating a humanlike body has proven incredibly difficult. Many technological advances in visual perception, audio perception, touch, dexterity, locomotion, and navigation need to occur before robots that look and act like human beings will live and work among us.

Visual Perception

Visual perception is an area of great complexity. A large percentage of the human brain is dedicated to processing data coming from the eyes. As our most powerful sense, sight is the primary means through which we understand the world around us.
A single camera is not good enough to simulate the eye. Two cameras are needed to give stereoscopic vision, which allows depth and movement perception. Even with two cameras, visual perception is incomplete because the cameras cannot understand or translate what they see.

"The task of creating a humanlike body has proven incredibly difficult."

Processing the image is the difficult part. In order for a robot to move through a room full of furniture it must build a mental map of that room, complete with obstacles. The robot must judge the distance and size of objects before it can figure out how to move around them.

Audio Perception

Audio perception is less complex than visual perception, but no less important. People respond to audible cues about their surroundings and the people they are with without even thinking about it. Listeners can determine someone's emotional state just by hearing the person's voice. A car starting up when someone crosses the street prompts the walker to glance in that direction to check for danger. Identifying a single voice and interpreting what is being said amid accompanying background noise is a task that is among the most important for human beings—and the most difficult.

Tactile Perception

Tactile perception, or touch, is another critical sense. Robots can be built with any level of strength, since they are made of steel and motors. How does a robot capable of lifting a car pick up an egg in the dark

Page 1

Project 3 Customize a Report on Robots
WL1-C5-P3-Robots.docx

without dropping or crushing it? The answer is through a sense of touch. The robot must not only be able to feel an object, but also be able to sense how much pressure it is applying to that object. With this feedback it can properly judge how hard it should squeeze. This is a very difficult area, and it may prove that simulating the human hand is even more difficult than simulating the human mind.

Related to touch is the skill of dexterity, or hand-eye coordination. The challenge is to create a robot that can perform small actions, such as soldering tiny joints or placing a chip at a precise spot in a circuit board within half a millimeter.

Locomotion

Locomotion includes broad movements such as walking. Getting a robot to move around is not easy. This area of robotics is challenging, as it requires balance within an endlessly changing set of variables. How does the program adjust for walking up a hill, or down a set of stairs? What if the wind is blowing hard or a foot slips? Currently most mobile robots work with wheels or treads, which limits their mobility in some circumstances but makes them much easier to control.

Navigation

Related to perception, navigation deals with the science of moving a mobile robot through an environment. Navigation is not an isolated area of artificial intelligence, as it must work closely with a visual system or some other kind of perception system. Sonar, radar, mechanical "feelers," and other systems have been subjects of experimentation. A robot can plot a course to a location using an internal "map" built up by a navigational perception system. If the course is blocked or too difficult, the robot must be smart enough to backtrack so it can try another plan.

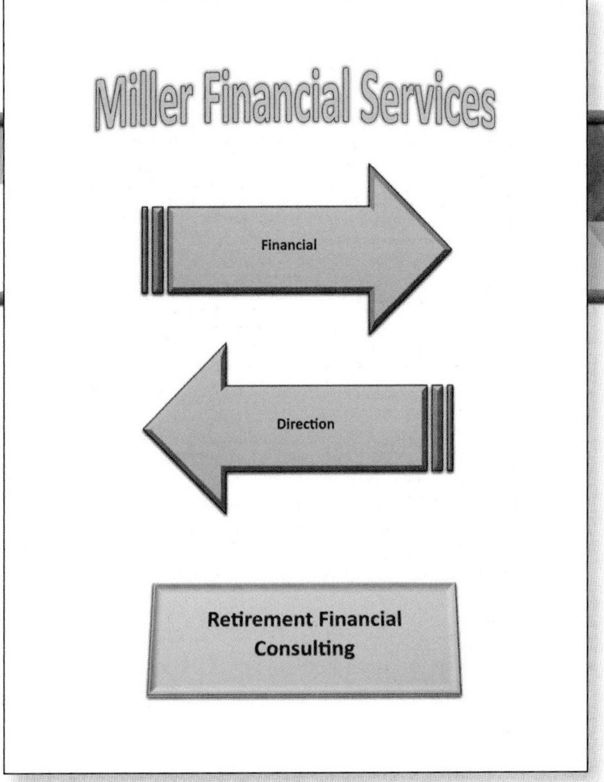

Project 4 Prepare a Company Flier

WL1-C5-P4-FinConsult.docx

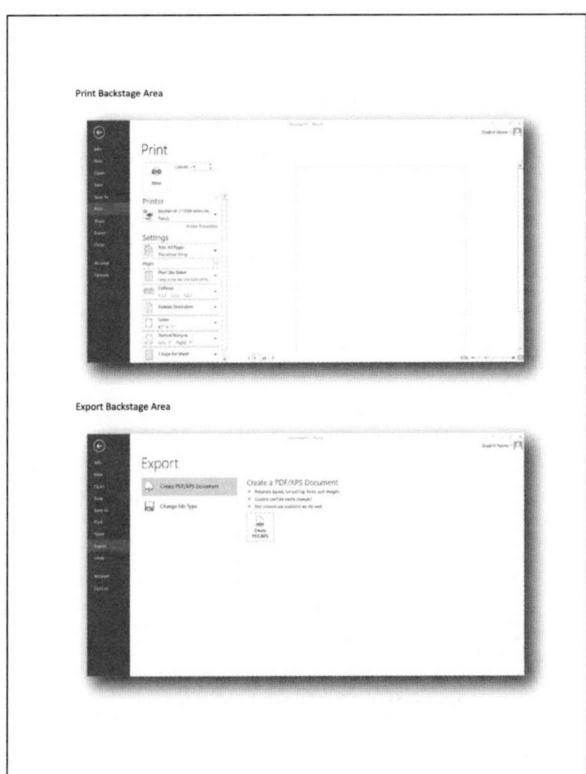

Project 5 Create and Format Screenshots

WL1-C5-P5-BackstageAreas.docx

WL1-C5-P5-NSSCoverPages.docx

Project 1 Format a Document on Computer Input Devices — 8 Parts

You will format into columns text in a document on computer input devices, improve the readability of the document by hyphenating long words, and improve the visual appeal by inserting a drop cap.

Inserting a Section Break

Quick Steps

Insert a Section Break
1. Click PAGE LAYOUT tab.
2. Click Breaks button.
3. Click section break type in drop-down list.

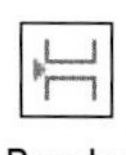

Breaks

If you delete a section break, the text that follows the section break takes on the formatting of the text preceding the break.

You can change the layout and formatting of specific portions of a document by inserting section breaks. For example, you can insert section breaks and then change margins for the text between the section breaks. If you want to format specific text in a document into columns, insert a section break.

Insert a section break in a document by clicking the PAGE LAYOUT tab, clicking the Breaks button in the Page Setup group, and then clicking the desired option in the *Section Breaks* section of the drop-down list. You can insert a section break that begins a new page or a continuous section break that does not begin a new page. A ***continuous section break*** separates the document into sections but does not insert a page break. Click one of the other three options in the *Section Breaks* section of the Breaks drop-down list if you want to insert a section break that begins a new page.

A section break inserted in a document is not visible in Print Layout view. Change to Draft view or click the Show/Hide ¶ button on the HOME tab to turn on the display of nonprinting characters and a section break displays in the document as a double row of dots with the words *Section Break* in the middle. Depending on the type of section break you insert, text follows *Section Break*. For example, if you insert a continuous section break, the words *Section Break (Continuous)* display in the middle of the row of dots. To delete a section break, change to Draft view, click on any character in the *Section Break (Continuous)* text, and then press the Delete key. (This moves the insertion point to the beginning of the section break.) Another option is to click the Show/Hide ¶ button to turn on the display of nonprinting characters, click on any character in the *Section Break (Continuous)* text, and then press the Delete key.

Project 1a Inserting a Continuous Section Break — Part 1 of 8

1. Open **InputDevices.docx** and then save it with Save As and name it **WL1-C5-P1-InputDevices**.
2. Insert a continuous section break by completing the following steps:
   a. Move the insertion point to the beginning of the *Keyboard* heading.
   b. Click the PAGE LAYOUT tab.
   c. Click the Breaks button in the Page Setup group and then click *Continuous* in the *Section Breaks* section of the drop-down list.
3. Click the HOME tab, click the Show/Hide ¶ button in the Paragraph group, and then notice the section break that displays at the end of the first paragraph of text.
4. Click the Show/Hide ¶ button to turn off the display of nonprinting characters.

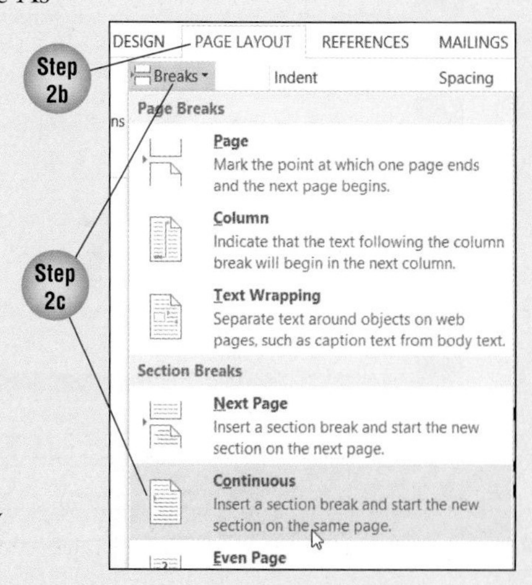

5. With the insertion point positioned at the beginning of the *Keyboard* heading, change the left and right margins to 1.5 inches. (The margin changes affect only the text after the continuous section break.)
6. Save and then print **WL1-C5-P1-InputDevices.docx**.

Creating Columns

When preparing a document containing text, an important point to consider is the readability of the document. Readability refers to the ease with which a person can read and understand groups of words. The line length of text in a document can enhance or detract from the readability of text. If the line length is too long, the reader may lose his or her place on the line and have a difficult time moving to the next line below. To improve the readability of documents such as newsletters or reports, you may want to set the text in columns. One common type of column is newspaper, which is typically used for text in newspapers, newsletters, and magazines. ***Newspaper columns*** contain text in vertical columns.

Quick Steps

Create Columns
1. Click PAGE LAYOUT tab.
2. Click Columns button.
3. Click desired number of columns.

Columns

Create newspaper columns with the Columns button in the Page Setup group on the PAGE LAYOUT tab or with options at the Columns dialog box. The Columns button creates columns of equal width. Use the Columns dialog box to create columns with varying widths. A document can include as many columns as room available on the page. Word determines how many columns can be included on the page based on the page width, the margin widths, and the size and spacing of the columns. Columns must be at least 0.5 inch in width. Changes in columns affect the entire document or the section of the document in which the insertion point is positioned.

Project 1b **Formatting Text into Columns** **Part 2 of 8**

1. With **WL1-C5-P1-InputDevices.docx** open, make sure the insertion point is positioned below the section break and then change the left and right margins back to 1 inch.
2. Delete the section break by completing the following steps:
   a. Click the Show/Hide ¶ button in the Paragraph group on the HOME tab to turn on the display of nonprinting characters.
   b. Click any character in the *Section Break (Continuous)* text located at the end of the first paragraph in the document.

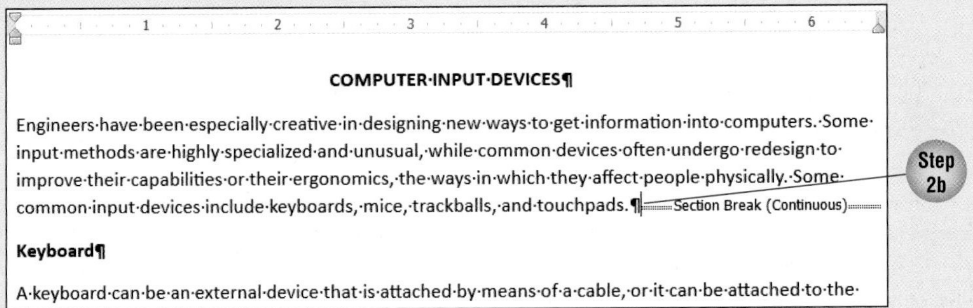

   c. Press the Delete key.
   d. Click the Show/Hide ¶ button to turn off the display of nonprinting characters.

3. Move the insertion point to the beginning of the first paragraph of text in the document and then insert a continuous section break.
4. Format the text into columns by completing the following steps:
   a. Make sure the insertion point is positioned below the section break.
   b. If necessary, click the PAGE LAYOUT tab.
   c. Click the Columns button in the Page Setup group.
   d. Click *Two* at the drop-down list.
5. Save **WL1-C5-P1-InputDevices.docx**.

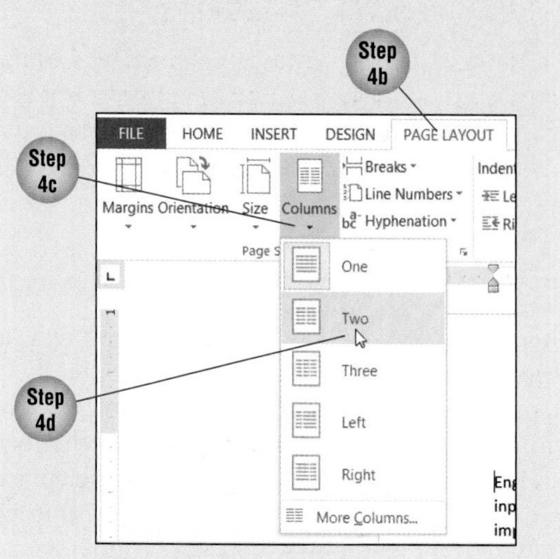

Creating Columns with the Columns Dialog Box

Quick Steps

Create Columns with the Columns Dialog Box
1. Click PAGE LAYOUT tab.
2. Click Columns button.
3. Click *More Columns* at the drop-down list.
4. Specify column options.
5. Click OK.

Use the Columns dialog box to create newspaper columns that are equal or unequal in width. To display the Columns dialog box, shown in Figure 5.1, click the Columns button in the Page Setup group on the PAGE LAYOUT tab and then click *More Columns* at the drop-down list.

With options at the Columns dialog box, specify the style and number of columns, enter your own column measurements, create unequal columns, and insert a line between columns. By default, column formatting is applied to the whole document. With the *Apply to* option box at the bottom of the Columns dialog box, you can change this from *Whole document* to *This point forward*. With the *This point forward* option, a section break is inserted and the column formatting is applied to text from the location of the insertion point to the end of the document or until other column formatting is encountered. The *Preview* section of the dialog box displays an example of how the columns will appear in the document.

Figure 5.1 Columns Dialog Box

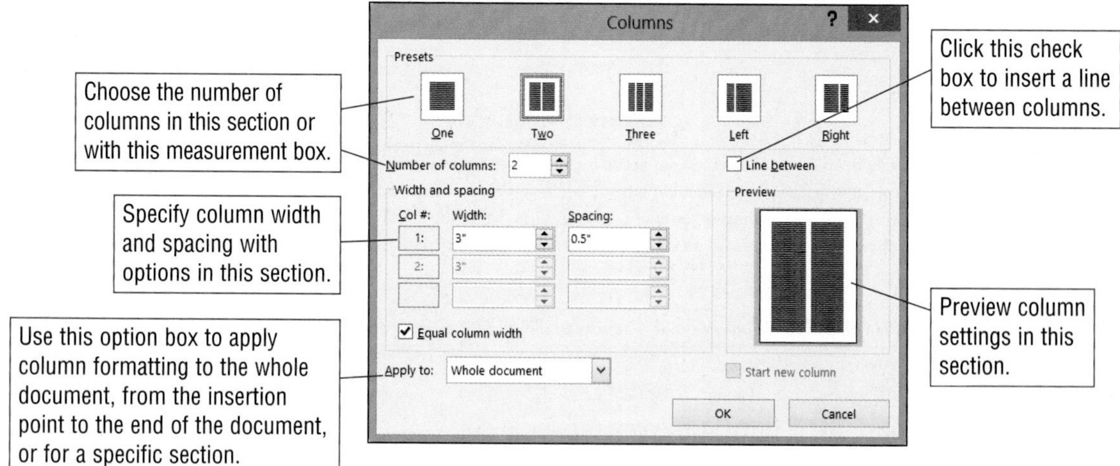

Removing Column Formatting

To remove column formatting using the Columns button, position the insertion point in the section containing columns, click the PAGE LAYOUT tab, click the Columns button, and then click *One* at the drop-down list. You can also remove column formatting at the Columns dialog box by selecting the *One* option in the *Presets* section.

Inserting a Column Break

When formatting text into columns, Word automatically breaks the columns to fit the page. At times, column breaks may appear in an undesirable location. You can insert a column break by positioning the insertion point where you want the column to end, clicking the PAGE LAYOUT tab, clicking the Breaks button, and then clicking *Column* at the drop-down list.

You can also insert a column break with the keyboard shortcut Ctrl + Shift + Enter.

Project 1c **Formatting Columns at the Columns Dialog Box** **Part 3 of 8**

1. With **WL1-C5-P1-InputDevices.docx** open, delete the section break by completing the following steps:
   a. Click the VIEW tab and then click the Draft button in the Views group.
   b. Click on any character in the *Section Break (Continuous)* text and then press the Delete key.
   c. Click the Print Layout button in the Views group on the VIEW tab.
2. Remove column formatting by clicking the PAGE LAYOUT tab, clicking the Columns button in the Page Setup group, and then clicking *One* at the drop-down list.
3. Format text in columns by completing the following steps:
   a. Position the insertion point at the beginning of the first paragraph of text in the document.
   b. Click the Columns button in the Page Setup group and then click *More Columns* at the drop-down list.
   c. At the Columns dialog box, click *Two* in the *Presets* section.
   d. Click the down-pointing arrow at the right of the *Spacing* measurement box until *0.3"* displays.
   e. Click the *Line between* check box to insert a check mark.
   f. Click the down-pointing arrow at the right side of the *Apply to* option box and then click *This point forward* at the drop-down list.
   g. Click OK to close the dialog box.

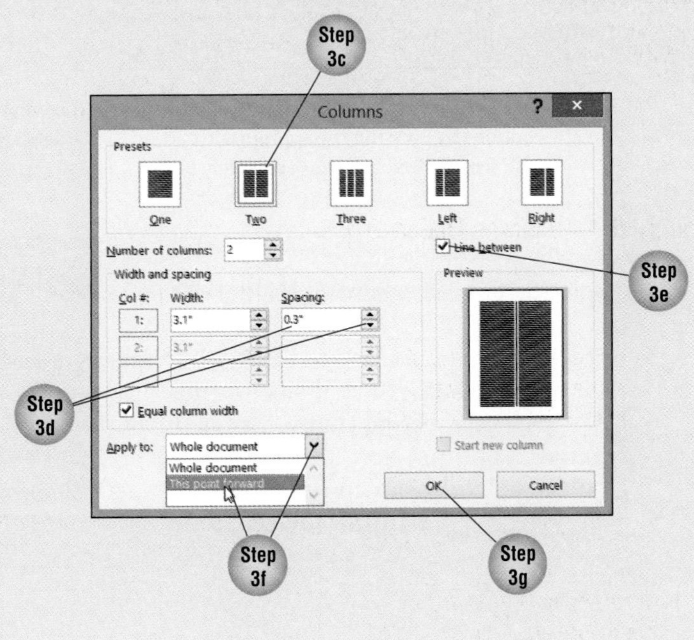

4. Insert a column break by completing the following steps:
   a. Position the insertion point at the beginning of the *Mouse* heading.
   b. Click the Breaks button in the Page Setup group and then click *Column* at the drop-down list.
5. Save and then print **WL1-C5-P1-InputDevices.docx**.

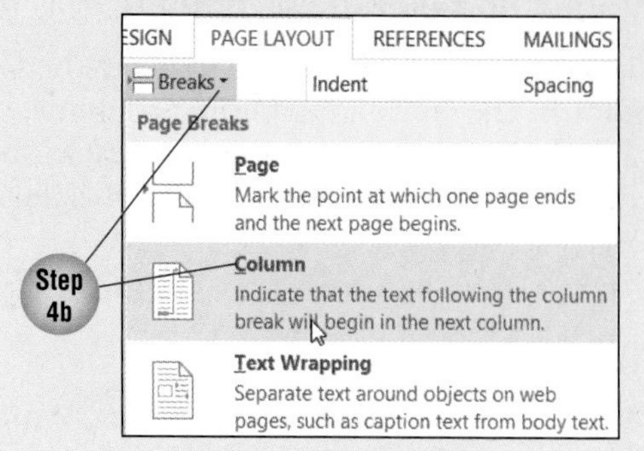

Balancing Columns on a Page

In a document containing text formatted into columns, Word automatically lines up (balances) the last line of text at the bottom of each column, except the last page. Text in the first column of the last page may flow to the end of the page, while the text in the second column may end far short of the end of the page. You can balance columns by inserting a continuous section break at the end of the text.

Project 1d **Formatting and Balancing Columns of Text** **Part 4 of 8**

1. With **WL1-C5-P1-InputDevices.docx** open, delete the column break by positioning the insertion point at the beginning of the *Mouse* heading and then pressing the Backspace key.
2. Select the entire document and then change the font to 12-point Constantia.
3. Move the insertion point to the end of the document and then balance the columns by clicking the PAGE LAYOUT tab, clicking the Breaks button, and then clicking *Continuous* at the drop-down list.

A touchscreen allows the user to choose options by pressing the appropriate part of the screen. Touchscreens are widely used in bank ATMs and in kiosks at retail outlets and in tourist areas.

Step 3

4. Apply the Green, Accent 6, Lighter 60% paragraph shading (last column, third row) to the title *COMPUTER INPUT DEVICES*.
5. Apply the Green, Accent 6, Lighter 80% paragraph shading (last column, second row) to each of the headings in the document.
6. Insert page numbering that prints at the bottom center of each page using the Plain Number 2 option.
7. Double-click in the document to make it active.
8. Save **WL1-C5-P1-InputDevices.docx**.

Hyphenating Words

In some Word documents, especially those with left and right margins wider than 1 inch or those with text set in columns, the right margin may appear quite ragged. To improve the display of text lines by making line lengths more uniform, consider hyphenating long words that fall at the ends of lines. When using the hyphenation feature, you can tell Word to hyphenate words automatically in a document or you can manually insert hyphens.

Avoid dividing words at the ends of more than two consecutive lines.

Automatically Hyphenating Words

To automatically hyphenate words in a document, click the PAGE LAYOUT tab, click the Hyphenation button in the Page Setup group, and then click *Automatic* at the drop-down list. Scroll through the document and check to see if hyphens display in appropriate locations within the words. If after hyphenating words in a document you want to remove all hyphens, immediately click the Undo button on the Quick Access toolbar.

Quick Steps

Turn on Automatic Hyphenation

1. Click PAGE LAYOUT tab.
2. Click Hyphenation button.
3. Click *Automatic* at drop-down list.

Apply Manual Hyphenation

1. Click PAGE LAYOUT tab.
2. Click Hyphenation button.
3. Click *Manual* at drop-down list.
4. Click Yes or No to hyphenate indicated words.
5. When complete, click OK.

Hyphenation

Manually Hyphenating Words

If you want to control where a hyphen appears in a word during hyphenation, choose manual hyphenation. To do this, click the PAGE LAYOUT tab, click the Hyphenation button in the Page Setup group, and then click *Manual* at the drop-down list. This displays the Manual Hyphenation dialog box, as shown in Figure 5.2. (The word in the *Hyphenate at* text box will vary.) At this dialog box, click Yes to hyphenate the word as indicated in the *Hyphenate at* text box, click No if you do not want the word hyphenated, or click Cancel to cancel hyphenation. You can also reposition the hyphen in the *Hyphenate at* text box. Word displays the word with syllable breaks indicated by hyphens. The position where the word will be hyphenated displays as a blinking black bar. If you want to hyphenate at a different location in the word, position the blinking black bar where you want the hyphen and then click Yes. Continue clicking Yes or No at the Manual Hyphenation dialog box.

Be careful with words ending in *-ed*. Several two-syllable words can be divided before that final syllable—for example, *noted*. However, one-syllable words ending in *-ed* should not be divided. An example is *served*. Watch for this type of occurrence and click No to cancel the hyphenation. At the hyphenation complete message, click OK.

Figure 5.2 Manual Hyphenation Dialog Box

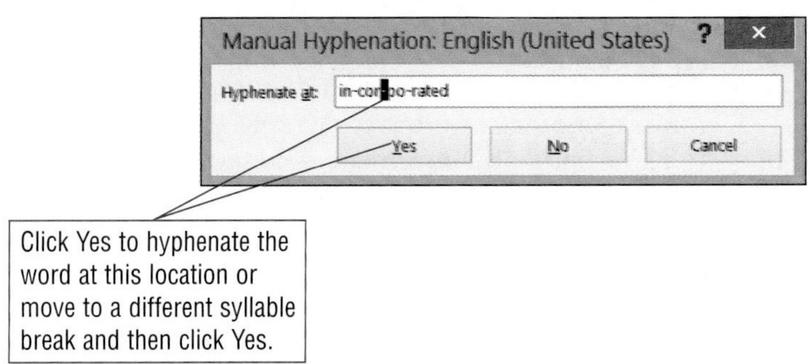
Manual Hyphenation: English (United States)
Hyphenate at:
in-cor-po-rated
Yes
No
Cancel
Click Yes to hyphenate the word at this location or move to a different syllable break and then click Yes.

If you want to remove all hyphens in a document, immediately click the Undo button on the Quick Access toolbar. To delete a few but not all of the optional hyphens inserted during hyphenation, use the Find and Replace dialog box. To do this, display the Find and Replace dialog box with the Replace tab selected, insert an optional hyphen symbol in the *Find what* text box (to do this, click the More button, click the Special button, and then click *Optional Hyphen* at the pop-up list), and make sure the *Replace with* text box is empty. Complete the find and replace, clicking the Replace button to replace the hyphen with nothing or clicking the Find Next button to leave the hyphen in the document.

Project 1e **Automatically and Manually Hyphenating Words** **Part 5 of 8**

1. With **WL1-C5-P1-InputDevices.docx** open, hyphenate words automatically by completing the following steps:
   a. Press Ctrl + Home.
   b. Click the PAGE LAYOUT tab.
   c. Click the Hyphenation button in the Page Setup group and then click *Automatic* at the drop-down list.

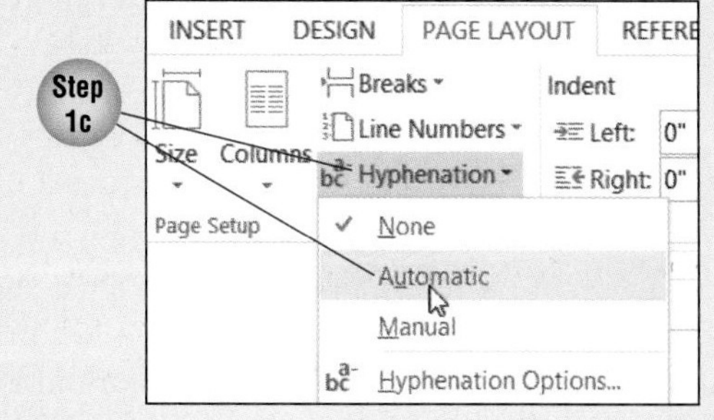

2. Scroll through the document and notice the hyphenation.
3. Click the Undo button to remove the hyphens.
4. Manually hyphenate words by completing the following steps:
   a. Click the Hyphenation button in the Page Setup group and then click *Manual* at the drop-down list.
   b. At the Manual Hyphenation dialog box, make one of the following choices:
      - Click Yes to hyphenate the word as indicated in the *Hyphenate at* text box.
      - Move the hyphen in the word to a more desirable location and then click Yes.
      - Click No if you do not want the word hyphenated.
   c. Continue clicking Yes or No at the Manual Hyphenation dialog box.
   d. At the hyphenation complete message, click OK.
5. Save **WL1-C5-P1-InputDevices.docx**.

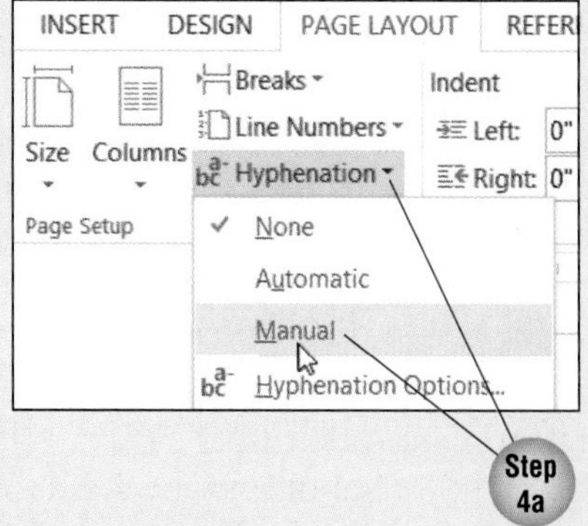

Quick Steps

Create a Drop Cap
1. Click INSERT tab.
2. Click Drop Cap button.
3. Click desired type in drop-down list.

Drop Cap

Creating a Drop Cap

Use a drop cap to enhance the appearance of text. A ***drop cap*** is the first letter of the first word of a paragraph that is set into the paragraph. Drop caps identify the beginnings of major sections or parts of a document. Create a drop cap with the Drop Cap button in the Text group on the INSERT tab. You can choose to set the drop cap in the paragraph or in the margin. At the Drop Cap dialog box, specify a font, the numbers of lines you want the letter to drop, and the distance you want the letter positioned from the text of the paragraph. Add a drop cap at the first word by selecting the word and then clicking the Drop Cap button.

Project 1f Inserting Drop Caps

Part 6 of 8

1. With **WL1-C5-P1-InputDevices.docx** open, create a drop cap by completing the following steps:
   a. Position the insertion point on the first word of the first paragraph of text (*Engineers*).
   b. Click the INSERT tab.
   c. Click the Drop Cap button in the Text group.
   d. Click *In margin* at the drop-down gallery.

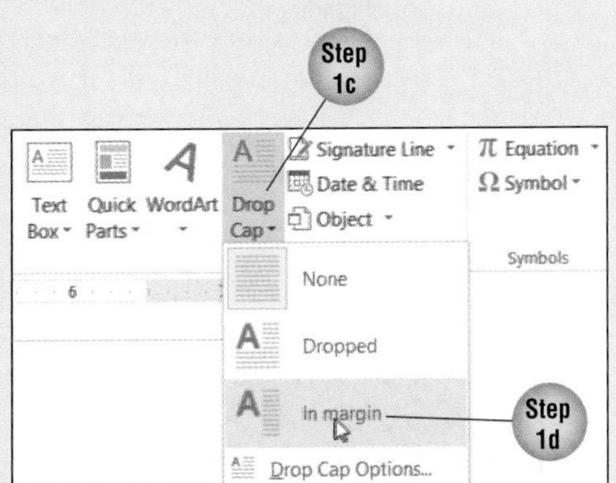

2. Looking at the drop cap, you decide that you do not like it in the margin and want it to be a little smaller. To change the drop cap, complete the following steps:
   a. With the E in the word *Engineers* selected, click the Drop Cap button in the Text group and then click *None* at the drop-down gallery.
   b. Click the Drop Cap button and then click *Drop Cap Options* at the drop-down gallery.
   c. At the Drop Cap dialog box, click *Dropped* in the *Position* section.
   d. Click the down-pointing arrow at the right side of the *Font* option box, scroll down the drop-down list, and then click *Cambria*.
   e. Click the down arrow at the right side of the *Lines to drop* measurement box to change the number to *2*.
   f. Click OK to close the dialog box.
   g. Click outside the drop cap to deselect it.
3. Save **WL1-C5-P1-InputDevices.docx**.

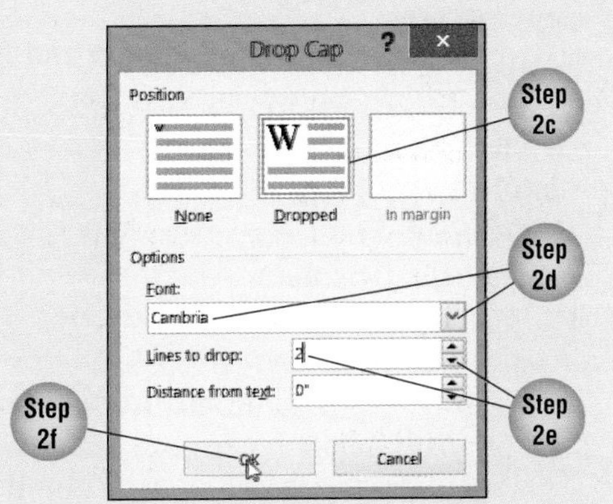

Inserting Symbols and Special Characters

Use the Symbol button on the INSERT tab to insert special symbols in a document. Click the Symbol button in the Symbols group on the INSERT tab and a drop-down list displays with the most recently inserted symbols along with a *More Symbols* option. Click one of the symbols that displays in the list to insert it in the document or click the *More Symbols* option to display the Symbol dialog box, as shown in Figure 5.3. At the Symbol dialog box, double-click the desired symbol and then click Close or click the desired symbol, click the Insert button, and then click Close.

At the Symbol dialog box with the Symbols tab selected, you can change the font with the *Font* option box. When you change the font, different symbols display in the dialog box. Click the Special Characters tab at the Symbol dialog box, and a list of special characters displays along with keyboard shortcuts to create these characters.

Quick Steps

Insert a Symbol
1. Click INSERT tab.
2. Click Symbol button.
3. Click desired symbol in drop-down list.

OR

1. Click INSERT tab.
2. Click Symbol button.
3. Click *More Symbols*.
4. Double-click desired symbol.
5. Click Close.

Symbol

Figure 5.3 Symbol Dialog Box with Symbols Tab Selected

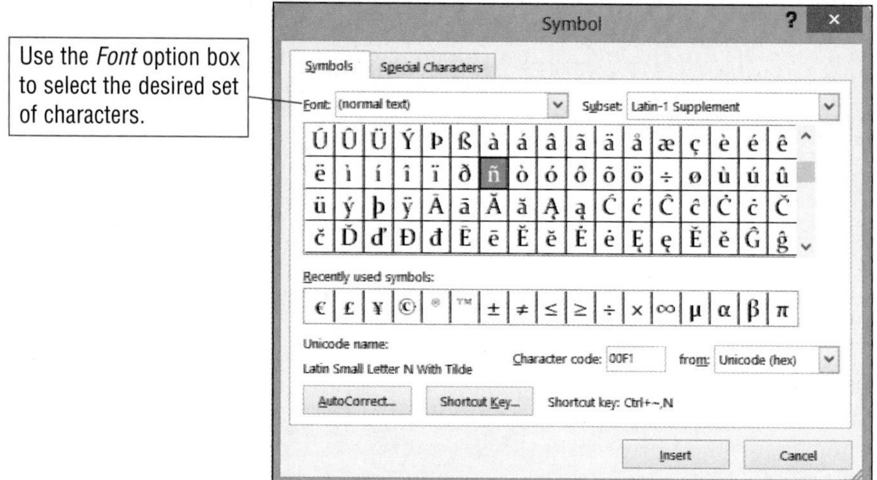

Project 1g Inserting Symbols and Special Characters

Part 7 of 8

1. With **WL1-C5-P1-InputDevices.docx** open, press Ctrl + End to move the insertion point to the end of the document.
2. Press the Enter key once, type **Prepared by:**, and then press the spacebar once.
3. Type the first name **Matthew** and then press the spacebar once.
4. Insert the last name *Viña* by completing the following steps:
   a. Type **Vi**.
   b. Click the Symbol button in the Symbols group on the INSERT tab.
   c. Click *More Symbols* at the drop-down list.
   d. At the Symbol dialog box, make sure the *Font* option box displays *(normal text)* and then double-click the ñ symbol (located in approximately the tenth through twelfth row).
   e. Click the Close button.
   f. Type **a**.

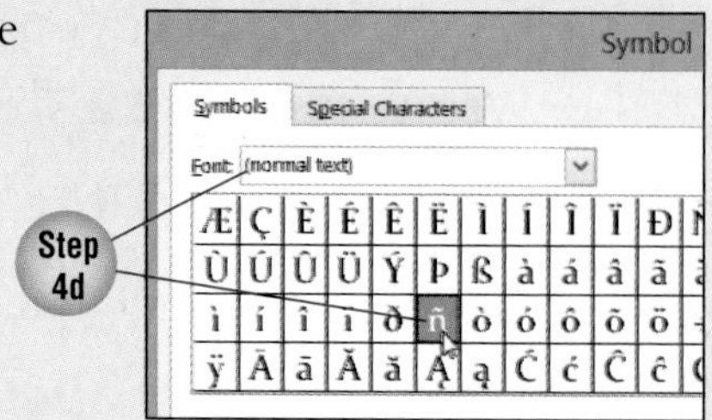

5. Press Shift + Enter.
6. Insert the keyboard symbol (⌨) by completing the following steps:
   a. Click the Symbol button and then click *More Symbols*.
   b. At the Symbol dialog box, click the down-pointing arrow at the right side of the *Font* option box and then click *Wingdings* at the drop-down list. (You will need to scroll down the list to display this option.)
   c. Double-click ⌨ (located approximately in the second row).
   d. Click the Close button.
7. Type **SoftCell Technologies**.

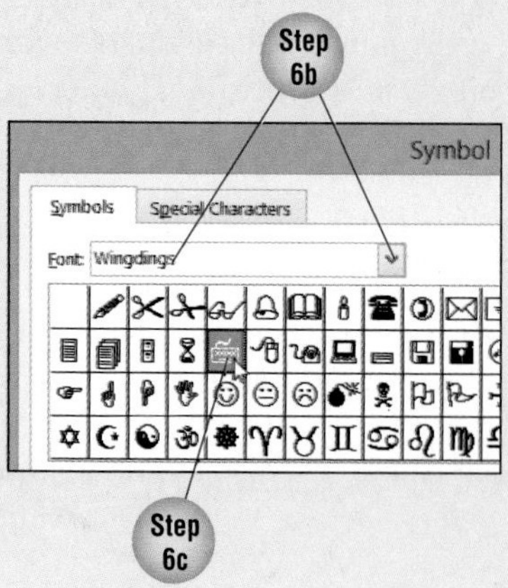

8. Insert the registered trademark symbol (®) by completing the following steps:
   a. Click the Symbol button and then click *More Symbols*.
   b. At the Symbol dialog box, click the Special Characters tab.
   c. Double-click the ® symbol (tenth option from the top).
   d. Click the Close button.
   e. Press Shift + Enter.
9. Select the keyboard symbol (⌨) and then change the font size to 18 points.
10. Save **WL1-C5-P1-InputDevices.docx**.

Step 8b

Step 8c

Symbol

Symbols | Special Characters

Character:		Shortcut key:
—	Em Dash	Alt+Ctrl+Num -
–	En Dash	Ctrl+Num -
-	Nonbreaking Hyphen	Ctrl+Shift+_
¬	Optional Hyphen	Ctrl+-
	Em Space	
	En Space	
	1/4 Em Space	
°	Nonbreaking Space	Ctrl+Shift+Space
©	Copyright	Alt+Ctrl+C
®	Registered	Alt+Ctrl+R
™	Trademark	Alt+Ctrl+T
§	Section	
¶	Paragraph	
…	Ellipsis	Alt+Ctrl+.
'	Single Opening Quote	Ctrl+``

Inserting the Date and Time

Use the Date & Time button in the Text group on the INSERT tab to insert the current date and time in a document. Click this button and the Date and Time dialog box displays, as shown in Figure 5.4. (Your date will vary from what you see in the figure.) At the Date and Time dialog box, click the desired date and/or time format in the *Available formats* list box.

If the *Update automatically* check box does not contain a check mark, the date and/or time are inserted in the document as normal text that you can edit in the normal manner. You can also insert the date and/or time as a field. The advantage to inserting the date or time as a field is that the date and time are updated when you reopen the document. You can also update the date and time in the document with the Update Field keyboard shortcut, F9. Insert a check mark in the *Update automatically* check box to insert the date and/or time as a field. You can also insert the date as a field using the keyboard shortcut Alt + Shift + D, and insert the time as a field with the keyboard shortcut Alt + Shift + T.

Quick Steps

Insert the Date and Time
1. Click INSERT tab.
2. Click Date & Time button.
3. Click desired option in list box.
4. Click OK.

Date & Time

Figure 5.4 Date and Time Dialog Box

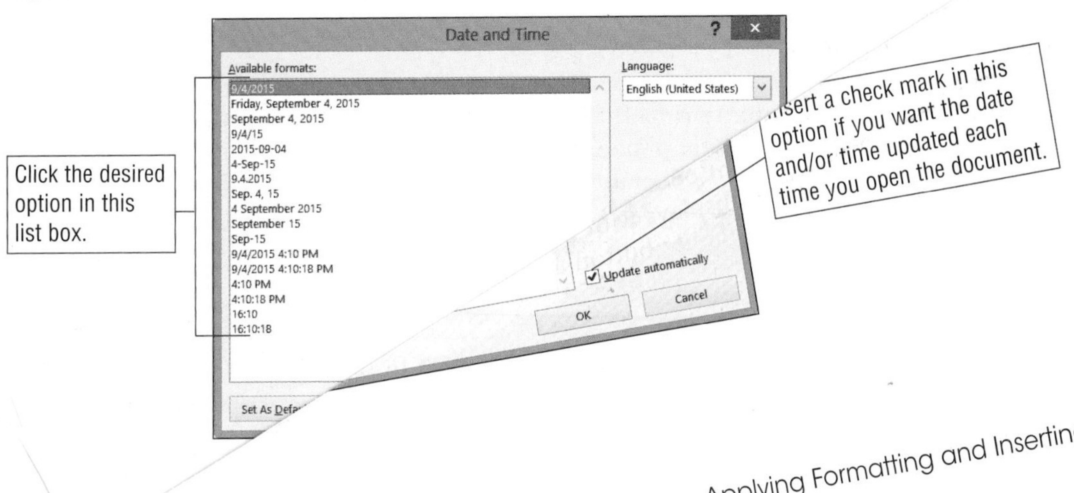

Project 1h Inserting the Date and Time

Part 8 of 8

1. With **WL1-C5-P1-InputDevices.docx** open, press Ctrl + End and make sure the insertion point is positioned below the company name.
2. Insert the current date by completing the following steps:
   a. Click the Date & Time button in the Text group on the INSERT tab.
   b. At the Date and Time dialog box, click the third option from the top in the *Available formats* list box. (Your date and times will vary from what you see in the image at the right.)
   c. Click in the *Update automatically* check box to insert a check mark.
   d. Click OK to close the dialog box.
3. Press Shift + Enter.
4. Insert the current time by pressing Alt + Shift + T.
5. Save **WL1-C5-P1-InputDevices.docx**.
6. Update the time by clicking the time and then pressing F9.
7. Save, print, and then close **WL1-C5-P1-InputDevices.docx**.

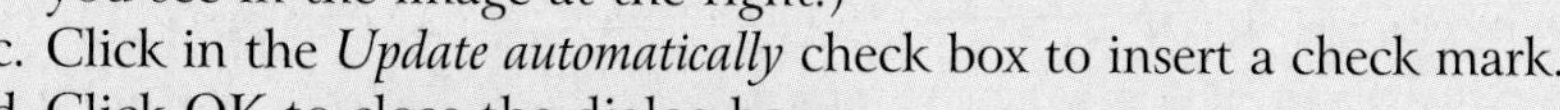

Project 2 Create an Announcement about Supervisory Training

3 Parts

You will create an announcement about upcoming supervisory training and use the Click and Type feature to center and right align text. You will vertically center the text on the page and insert and format a picture to add visual appeal to the announcement.

Using the Click and Type Feature

and ... at right margin.
2. Double-click left mouse button.

Word contains a Click and Type feature you can use to position the insertion ... at a specific location and alignment in the document. This feature allows the ... ition one or more lines of text as you type, rather than typing the text that the pointer ... ing and reformatting the text, which requires multiple steps. Double-click the mouse ... nd Type feature, make sure the document displays in Print location of the mouse pointer. ... the mouse pointer at the location where you want ... you move the mouse pointer, you will notice

If the horizontal lines do not display ... horizontal lines representing the alignment. double-click the mouse button, a left tab is set at the ... tion point is positioned at the point. If you want to change the alignment and not set a tab, ... se pointer when you ... of the insertion horizontal lines display near the mouse pointer before double-clicking ... sure the ... mouse.

Project 2a **Using Click and Type** **Part 1 of 3**

1. At a blank document, create the centered text shown in Figure 5.5 by completing the following steps:
   a. Position the I-beam pointer between the left and right margins at about the 3.25-inch mark on the horizontal ruler and the top of the vertical ruler.
   b. When the center alignment lines display below the I-beam pointer, double-click the left mouse button.

   c. Type the centered text shown in Figure 5.5. Press Shift + Enter to end each text line.
2. Change to right alignment by completing the following steps:
   a. Position the I-beam pointer near the right margin at approximately the 1-inch mark on the vertical ruler until the right alignment lines display at the left side of the I-beam pointer.
   b. Double-click the left mouse button.
   c. Type the right-aligned text shown in Figure 5.5. Press Shift + Enter to end the text line.
3. Select the centered text and then change the font to 14-point Candara bold and the line spacing to double spacing.
4. Select the right-aligned text, change the font to 10-point Candara bold, and then deselect the text.
5. Save the document and name it **WL1-C5-P2-Training**.

Figure 5.5 Project 2a

SUPERVISORY TRAINING
Maximizing Employee Potential
Wednesday, February 18, 2015
Training Center
9:00 a.m. to 3:30 p.m.

Sponsored by
Cell Systems

Vertically Aligning Text

Text in a Word document is aligned at the top of the page by default. You can change this alignment with the *Vertical alignment* option box at the Page Setup dialog box with the Layout tab selected, as shown in Figure 5.6. Display this dialog box by clicking the PAGE LAYOUT tab, clicking the Page Setup group dialog box launcher, and then clicking the Layout tab at the Page Setup dialog box.

Figure 5.6 Page Setup Dialog Box with Layout Tab Selected

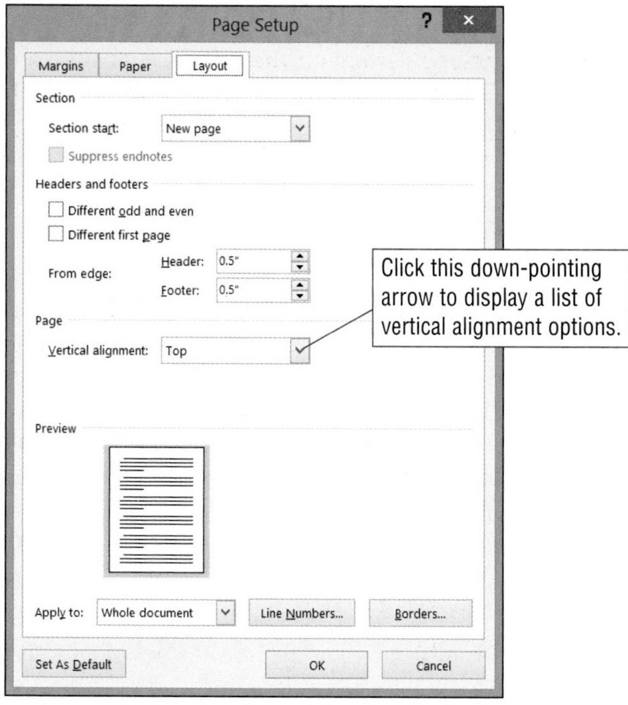

Quick Steps

Vertically Align Text

1. Click PAGE LAYOUT tab.
2. Click Page Setup group dialog box launcher.
3. Click Layout tab.
4. Click *Vertical alignment* option box.
5. Click desired alignment.
6. Click OK.

The *Vertical alignment* option box in the Page Setup dialog box contains four choices: *Top*, *Center*, *Justified*, and *Bottom*. The default setting is *Top*, which aligns text at the top of the page. Choose *Center* if you want text centered vertically on the page. The *Justified* option will align text between the top and the bottom margins. The *Center* option positions text in the middle of the page vertically, while the *Justified* option adds space between paragraphs of text (not within) to fill the page from the top to bottom margins. If you center or justify text, the text does not display centered or justified on the screen in the Draft view, but it does display centered or justified in the Print Layout view. Choose the *Bottom* option to align text in the document vertically along the bottom of the page.

Project 2b Vertically Centering Text

Part 2 of 3

1. With **WL1-C5-P2-Training.docx** open, click the PAGE LAYOUT tab and then click the Page Setup group dialog box launcher.
2. At the Page Setup dialog box, click the Layout tab.
3. Click the down-pointing arrow at the right side of the *Vertical alignment* option box and then click *Center* at the drop-down list.
4. Click OK to close the dialog box.
5. Save and then print **WL1-C5-P2-Training.docx**.

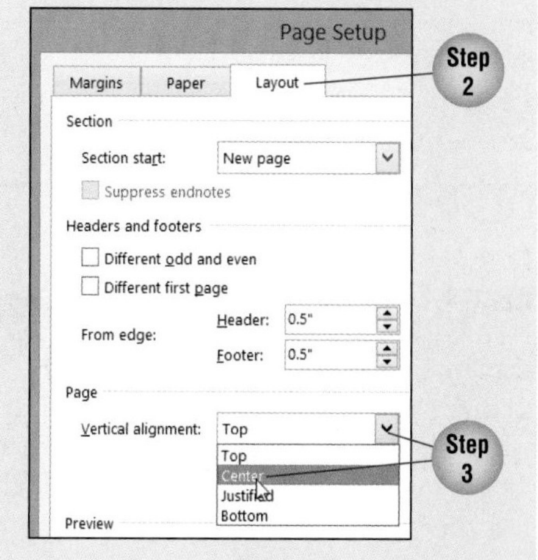

Inserting an Image

You can insert an image such as a picture or clip art in a Word document with buttons in the Illustrations group on the INSERT tab. Click the Pictures button to display the Insert Picture dialog box, where you can specify the desired picture file, or click the Online Pictures button and search online for images such as pictures and clip art. When you insert an image in a document, the PICTURE TOOLS FORMAT tab displays. Use options on this tab to customize and format the image.

Customizing and Formatting an Image

Use options in the Adjust group on the PICTURE TOOLS FORMAT tab to remove unwanted portions of the image, correct the brightness and contrast, change the image color, apply artistic effects, compress the size of the image file, change to a different image, and reset the image back to the original formatting. Use buttons in the Picture Styles group to apply a predesigned style to the image, change the image border, and apply other effects to the image. With options in the Arrange group, you can position the image on the page, specify how text will wrap around it, align the image with other elements in the document, and rotate the image. Use the Crop button in the Size group to remove any unnecessary parts of the image and specify the image size with the *Shape Height* and *Shape Width* measurement boxes.

Crop

In addition to the PICTURE TOOLS FORMAT tab, you can customize and format an image with options at the shortcut menu. Display this menu by right-clicking the image. With options at the shortcut menu, you can change the picture, insert a caption, choose text wrapping, size and position the image, and display the Format Picture task pane.

When you insert a picture or image in a document, the default text wrapping style is *Top and Bottom*. At this wrapping style, text wraps above and below the image. Change text wrapping with the Position and Wrap Text buttons on the PICTURE TOOLS FORMAT tab and with options from the Layout Options button side menu. The Layout Options button displays just outside the upper right corner of a selected image. Click this button to display a side menu with wrapping options and click the *See more* hyperlink that displays at the bottom of the side menu to display the Layout dialog box containing additional options for positioning the image on the page. Close the Layout Options button side menu by clicking the button or clicking the Close button located in the upper right corner of the side menu.

Position

Wrap Text

Layout Options

Sizing an Image

Change the size of an image with the *Shape Height* and *Shape Width* measurement boxes in the Size group on the PICTURE TOOLS FORMAT tab or with the sizing handles that display around the selected image. To change size with a sizing handle, position the mouse pointer on a sizing handle until the pointer turns into a double-headed arrow and then hold down the left mouse button. Drag the sizing handle in or out to decrease or increase the size of the image and then release the mouse button. Use the middle sizing handles at the left or right side of the image to make the image wider or thinner. Use the middle sizing handles at the top or bottom of the image to make the image taller or shorter. Use the sizing handles at the corners of the image to change both the width and height at the same time.

Resize a selected object horizontally, vertically, or diagonally from the center outward by holding down the Ctrl key and then dragging a sizing handle.

Moving an Image

Move an image to a specific location on the page with options at the Position button drop-down gallery in the Arrange group on the PICTURE TOOLS FORMAT tab. When you choose an option from this gallery, the image is moved to the specified location on the page and square text wrapping is applied to the image.

You can also move the image by dragging it to the desired location. Before dragging an image, however, you must first choose how the text will wrap around it by clicking the Wrap Text button in the Arrange group and then clicking the desired wrapping style at the drop-down list. After choosing a wrapping style, move the image by positioning the mouse pointer on the image border until the arrow pointer turns into a four-headed arrow. Hold down the left mouse button, drag the image to the desired position, and then release the mouse button. As you move an image to the top, left, right, or bottom margins or to the center of the document, green alignment guides display. Use these guides to help you position an image on the page. You can also turn on gridlines to help you precisely position an image. Do this by clicking the Align button in the Arrange group on the PICTURE TOOLS FORMAT tab and then clicking *View Gridlines*.

Rotate the image by positioning the mouse pointer on the round rotation handle (circular arrow) that displays above the image until the pointer displays with a black circular arrow attached. Hold down the left mouse button, drag in the desired direction, and then release the mouse button.

Quick Steps

Insert a Picture
1. Click INSERT tab.
2. Click Pictures button.
3. Double-click desired picture in Insert Picture dialog box.

Pictures

Inserting a Picture

To insert a picture in a document, click the INSERT tab and then click the Pictures button in the Illustrations group. At the Insert Picture dialog box, navigate to the folder containing the desired picture and then double-click the picture. Use buttons on the PICTURE TOOLS FORMAT tab to format and customize the picture.

Project 2c **Inserting and Customizing a Picture** **Part 3 of 3**

1. With **WL1-C5-P2-Training.docx** open, return the vertical alignment back to top alignment by completing the following steps:
   a. Click the PAGE LAYOUT tab.
   b. Click the Page Setup group dialog box launcher.
   c. At the Page Setup dialog box, make sure the Layout tab is selected.
   d. Click the down-pointing arrow at the right side of the *Vertical alignment* option box and then click *Top* at the drop-down list.
   e. Click OK to close the dialog box.
2. Select and then delete the text *Sponsored by* and the text *Cell Systems*.
3. Select the remaining text and change the line spacing to single spacing.
4. Move the insertion point to the beginning of the document, press the Enter key, and then move the insertion back to the beginning of the document.
5. Insert a picture by completing the following steps:
   a. Click the INSERT tab and then click the Pictures button in the Illustrations group.
   b. At the Insert Picture dialog box, navigate to your WL1C5 folder.
   c. Double-click ***Uluru.jpg*** in the Content pane.

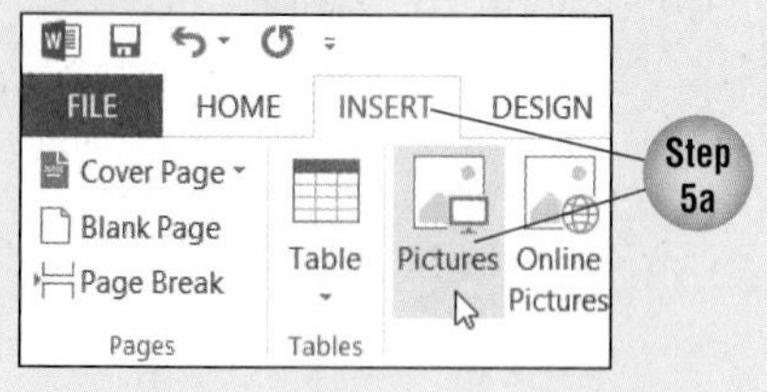

6. Crop the picture by completing the following steps:
   a. Click the Crop button in the Size group on the PICTURE TOOLS FORMAT tab.
   b. Position the mouse pointer on the bottom middle crop handle (displays as a short black line) until the pointer turns into the crop tool (displays as a small black T).
   c. Hold down the left mouse button, drag up to just below the rock as shown at the right, and then release the mouse button.
   d. Click the Crop button in the Size group to turn off the feature.

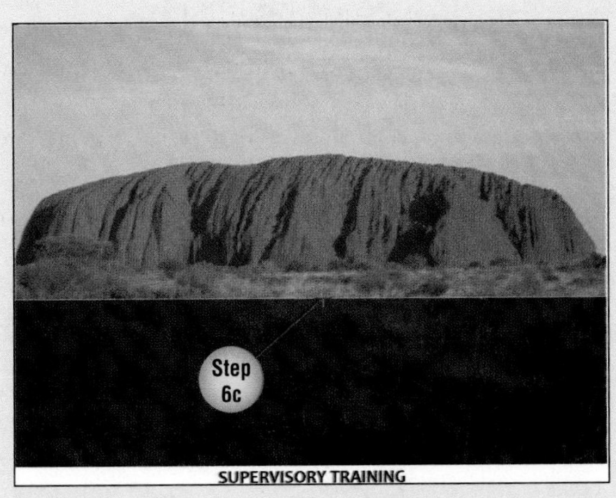

7. Change the size of the picture by clicking in the *Shape Height* measurement box in the Size group, typing 3.1, and then pressing Enter.
8. Move the picture behind the text by clicking the Layout Options button that displays outside the upper right corner of the picture and then clicking the *Behind Text* option at the side menu (second column, second row in the *With Text Wrapping* section). Close the side menu by clicking the Close button located in the upper right corner of the side menu.

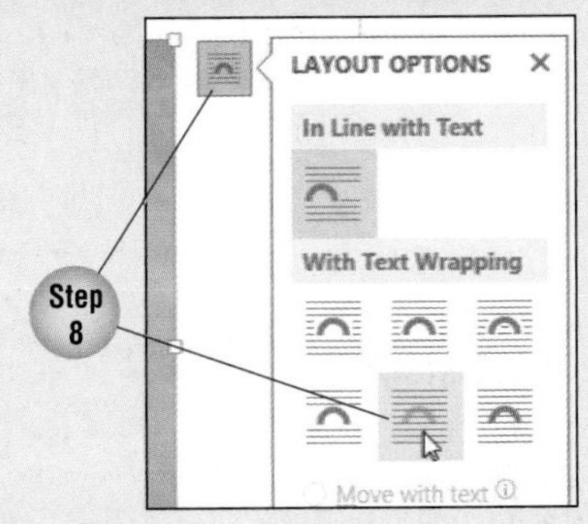

9. Rotate the image by clicking the Rotate Objects button in the Arrange group and then clicking *Flip Horizontal* at the drop-down list.

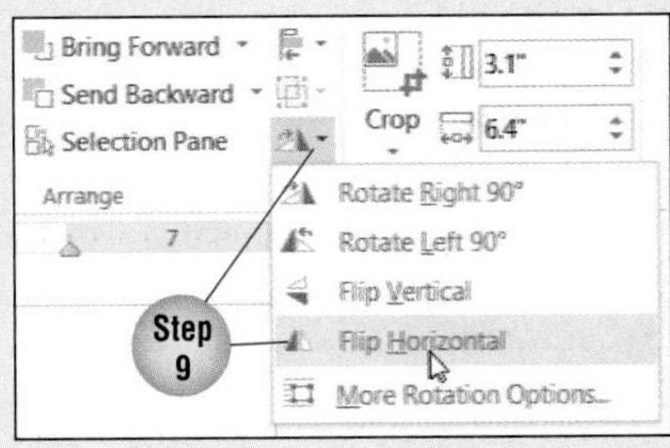

10. Change the picture color by clicking the Color button in the Adjust group and then clicking *Saturation: 300%* (sixth option in the *Color Saturation* section.)

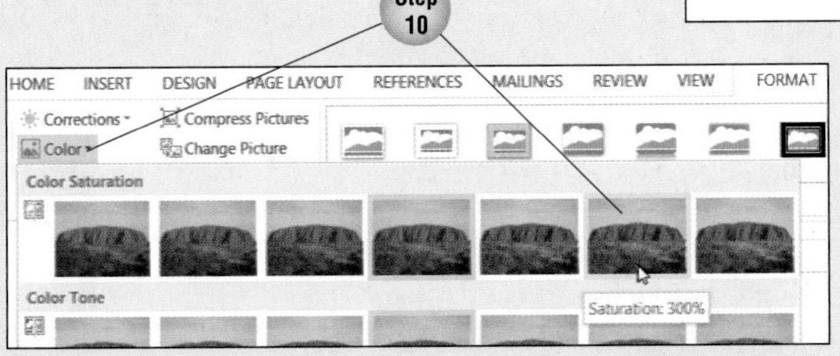

11. After looking at the coloring, you decide to return to the original color by clicking the Undo button on the Quick Access toolbar.
12. Sharpen the picture by clicking the Corrections button in the Adjust group and then clicking the *Sharpen: 25%* option (fourth option in the *Sharpen/Soften* section).

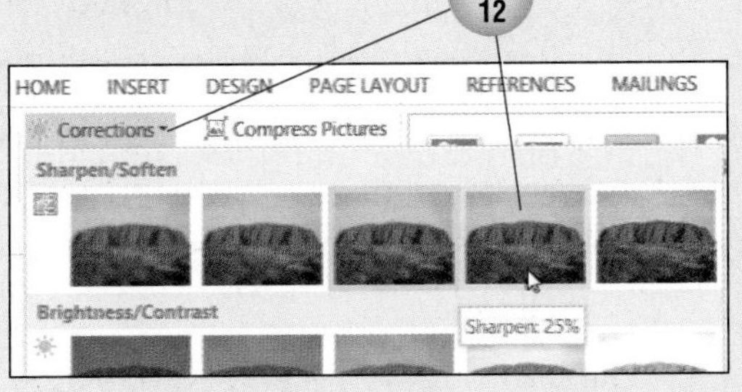

13. Change the contrast of the picture by clicking the Corrections button in the Adjust group and then clicking the *Brightness: 0% (Normal) Contrast: +40%* option (third option in the bottom row in the *Brightness/Contrast* section).
14. Apply a picture style by clicking the More button at the right side of the thumbnails in the Picture Styles group and then clicking the *Simple Frame, Black* option (second column, second row).

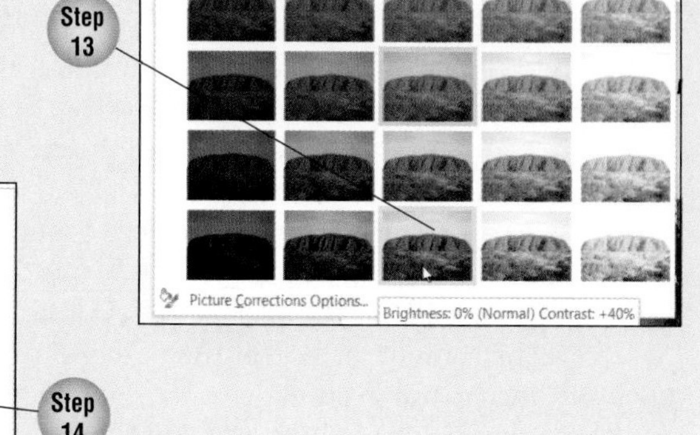

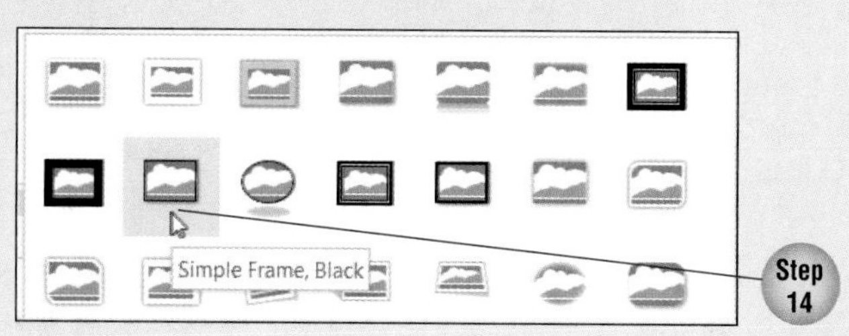

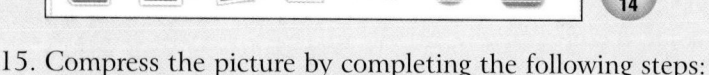

15. Compress the picture by completing the following steps:
    a. Click the Compress Pictures button in the Adjust group.
    b. At the Compress Pictures dialog box, make sure a check mark displays in both options in the *Compression options* section and then click OK.

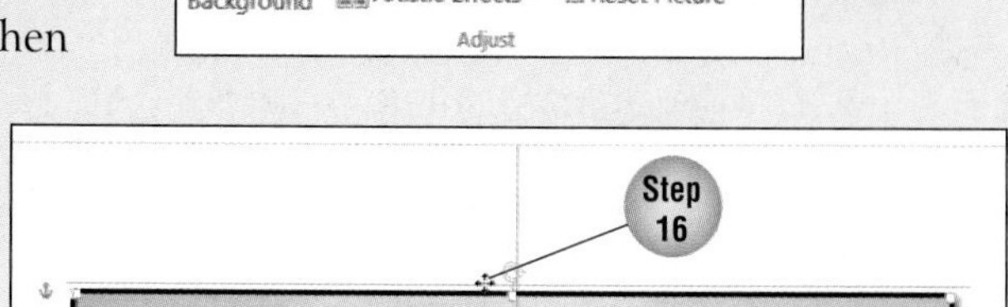

16. Position the mouse pointer on the border of the selected picture until the pointer displays with a four-headed arrow attached. Hold down the left mouse button, drag the picture up and slightly to the left until you see green alignment guides at the top margin and the center of the page, and then release the mouse button.

17. Save and then print **WL1-C5-P2-Training.docx**.
18. With the picture selected, remove the background by completing the following steps:
    a. Click the Remove Background button in the Adjust group on the PICTURE TOOLS FORMAT tab.
    b. Using the left middle sizing handle, drag the left border to the left border line of the image.
    c. Drag the right middle sizing handle to the right border line of the image.
    d. Drag the bottom middle sizing handle to the very bottom border of the image, which displays as a dashed line.
    e. Drag the top middle sizing handle down to just above the top of the rock.

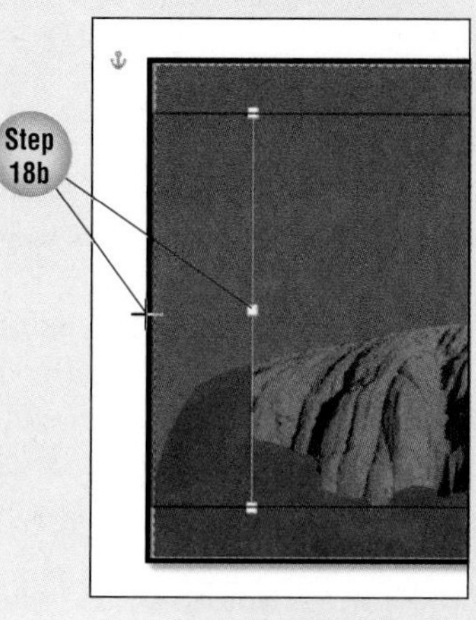

f. Click the Keep Changes button in the Close group on the BACKGROUND REMOVAL tab. (The picture should now display with the sky removed.)

19. Insert a caption by completing the following steps:
    a. Right-click the picture. (This displays the shortcut menu.)
    b. Click the *Insert Caption* option at the shortcut menu.
    c. At the Caption dialog box with the insertion point positioned in the *Caption* text box after the *Figure 1* text, press the spacebar and then type **Uluru (Ayers Rock, Australia)**.
    d. Click OK. (The caption displays below and at the left side of the picture.)
20. Save, print, and then close **WL1-C5-P2-Training.docx**.

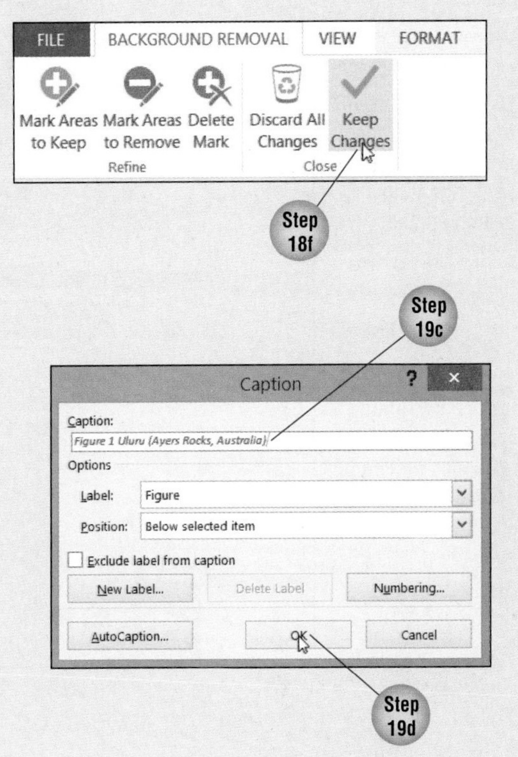

Project 3 Customize a Report on Robots — 2 Parts

You will open a report on robots and then add visual appeal to the report by inserting and formatting an image from Office.com and a built-in text box.

Inserting an Image from Office.com

Microsoft Office includes a gallery of media images you can insert in a document, such as clip art images and photographs. To insert an image in a Word document, click the INSERT tab and then click the Online Pictures button in the Illustrations group. This displays the Insert Pictures window, as shown in Figure 5.7.

At the Insert Pictures window, click in the search text box to the right of *Office.com Clip Art*, type the search term or topic, and then press Enter. Images that match your search term or topic display in the window. To insert an image, click the desired image and then click the Insert button or double-click the image. This downloads the image from the Office.com website to your document.

When you insert an image in the document, the image is selected and the PICTURE TOOLS FORMAT tab is active. Use buttons on this tab to customize an image just as you learned to customize a picture.

Quick Steps

Insert an Image from Office.com
1. Click INSERT tab.
2. Click Online Pictures button.
3. Type search word or topic.
4. Press Enter.
5. Double-click desired image.

Online Pictures

Figure 5.7 Insert Pictures Window

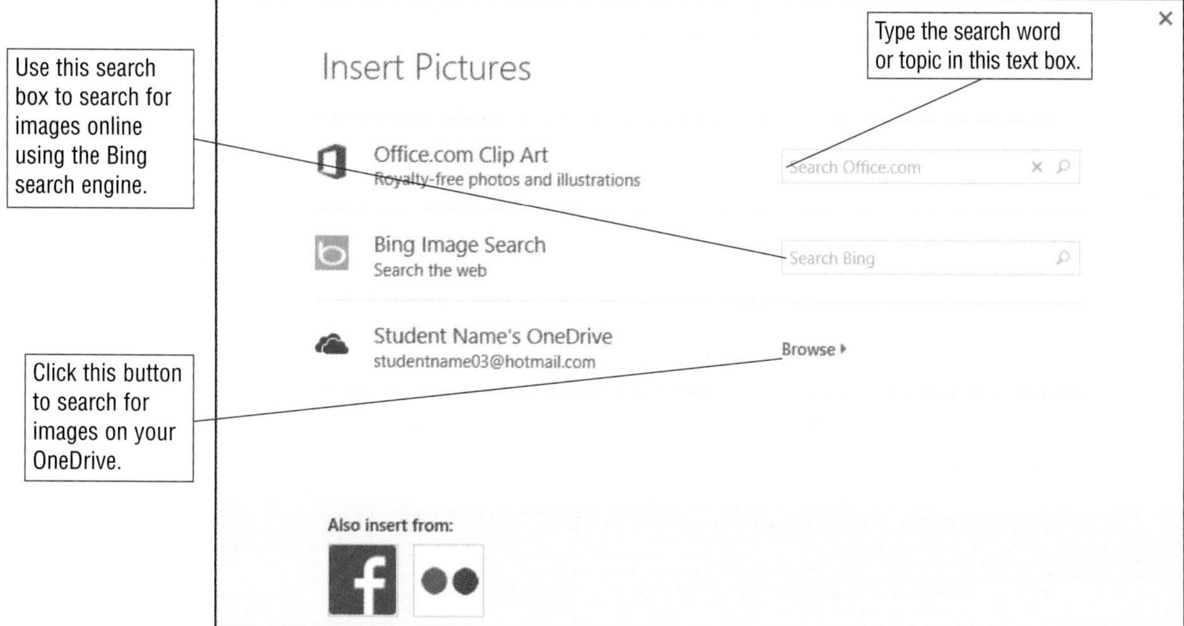

Project 3a Inserting an Image

Part 1 of 2

1. Open **Robots.docx** and then save the document with Save As and name it **WL1-C5-P3-Robots**.
2. Insert a clip art image of a robot by completing the following steps:
   a. Move the insertion point so it is positioned at the beginning of the first paragraph of text (the sentence that begins *Robotic factories are increasingly*).
   b. Click the INSERT tab.
   c. Click the Online Pictures button in the Illustrations group.
   d. At the Insert Pictures window, type **robot antenna** and then press Enter.
   e. Double-click the robot image shown at the right.

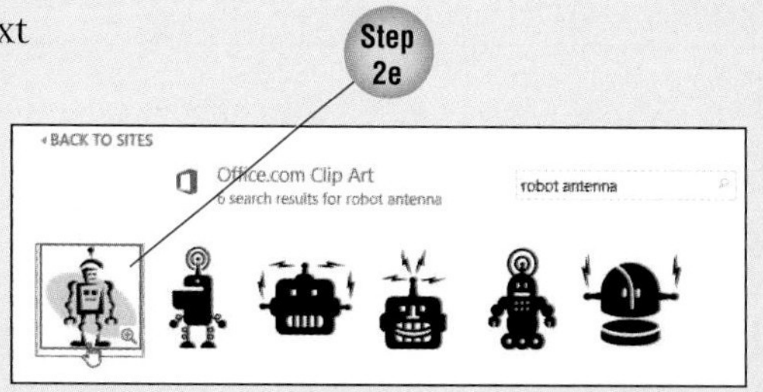

3. Format the clip art image by completing the following steps:
   a. Click the *Drop Shadow Rectangle* option in the Pictures Styles group (fourth option).
   b. Click the Color button in the Adjust group and then click the *Blue, Accent color 1 Dark* option (second column, second row).
   c. Click in the *Shape Height* measurement box in the Size group, type 3, and then press Enter.

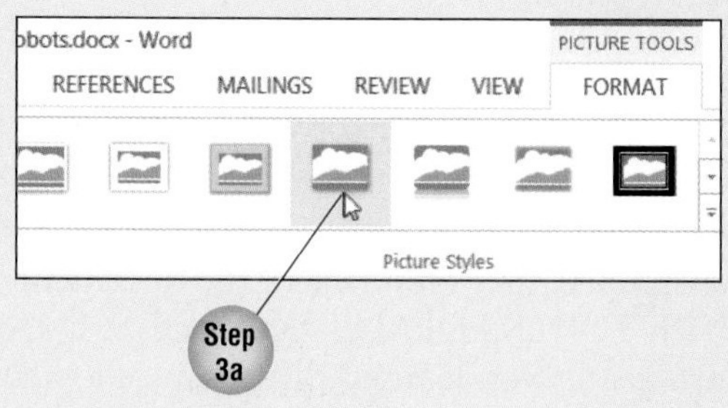

4. Reset the image and the image size by clicking the Reset Picture button arrow in the Adjust group and then clicking the *Reset Picture & Size* option at the drop-down list.

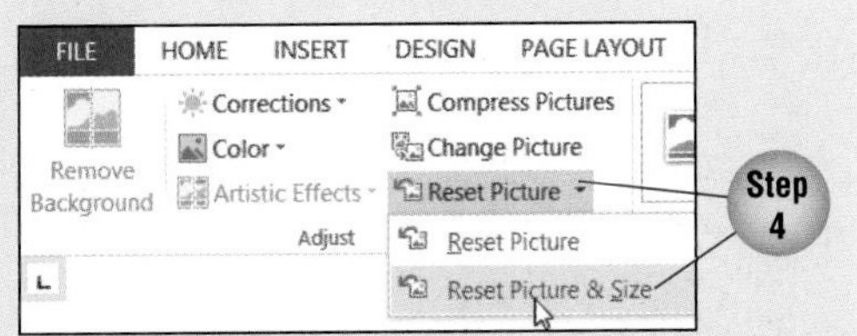

5. Make transparent the green oval behind the robot by completing the following steps:
   a. Click the Color button in the Adjust group.
   b. Click the *Set Transparent Color* option that displays toward the bottom of the drop-down list. (The mouse pointer turns into a dropper tool.)
   c. Position the dropper tool on the green color in the image and then click the left mouse button.

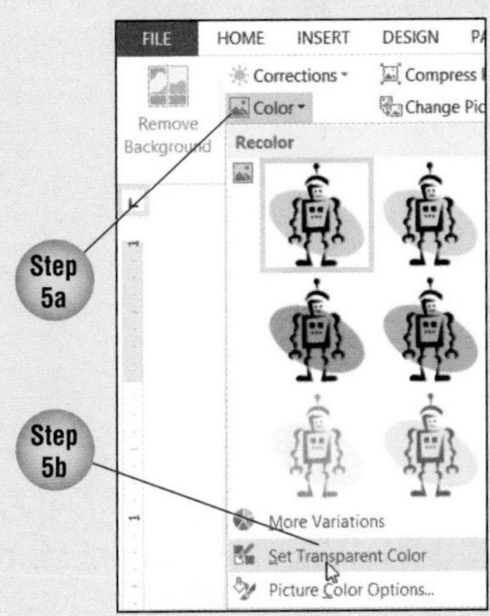

6. Decrease the size of the image by clicking in the *Shape Height* measurement box in the Size group, typing 1.3, and then pressing Enter.
7. Change the text wrapping by clicking the Wrap Text button in the Arrange group and then clicking *Square* at the drop-down list.

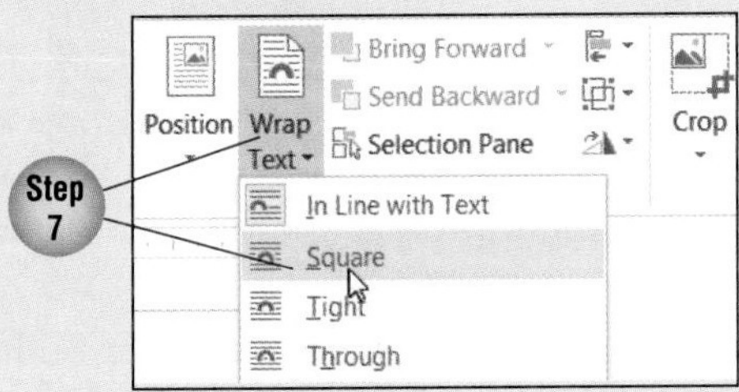

8. Rotate the image by clicking the Rotate Objects button in the Arrange group and then clicking *Flip Horizontal* at the drop-down list.
9. Click the Corrections button in the Adjust group and then click the *Brightness: -40% Contrast: 0% (Normal)* option (first column, third row).
10. Click the Picture Effects button in the Picture Styles group, point to *Shadow*, and then click the *Offset Diagonal Bottom Left* option (third column, first row in the *Outer* section).

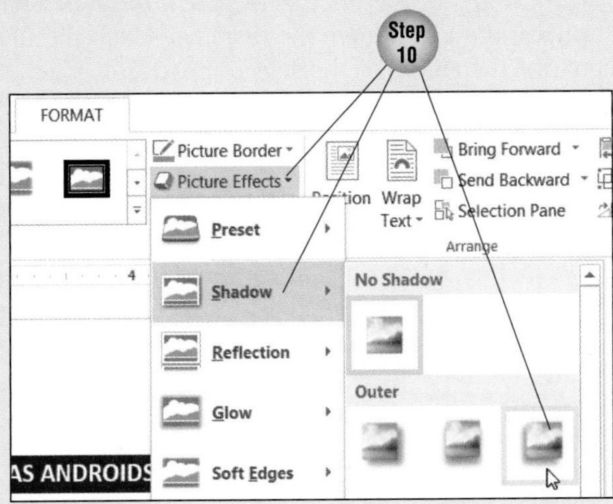

11. Position the mouse pointer on the border of the selected picture until the pointer turns into a four-headed arrow and then drag the picture so it is positioned as shown at the right. (Use the green alignment guide to position the image at the left margin.)
12. Click outside the clip art image to deselect it.
13. Save **WL1-C5-P3-Robots.docx**.

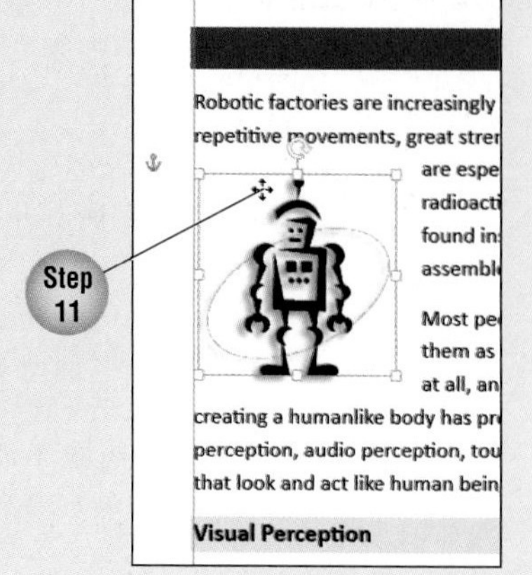

Inserting and Customizing a Pull Quote Text Box

Quick Steps

Insert a Pull Quote
1. Click INSERT tab.
2. Click Text Box button.
3. Click desired pull quote.

Text Box

Use a pull quote in a document such as an article to attract attention. A ***pull quote*** is a quote from an article that is "pulled out" and enlarged and positioned in an attractive location on the page. Some advantages of pull quotes are that they reinforce important concepts, summarize your message, and break up text blocks to make them easier to read. If you use multiple pull quotes in a document, keep them in order to ensure clear comprehension for readers.

You can insert a pull quote in a document with a predesigned built-in text box. Display the available pull quote built-in text boxes by clicking the INSERT tab and then clicking the Text Box button in the Text group. Click the desired pull quote from the drop-down list that displays and the built-in text box is inserted in the document. Type the quote inside the text box and then format the text and/or customize the text box. Use buttons on the DRAWING TOOLS FORMAT tab to format and customize the built-in text box.

Use options in the Insert Shapes group on the DRAWING TOOLS FORMAT tab to insert a shape in the document. Click the Edit Shape button in the Insert Shapes group and a drop-down list displays. Click the *Change Shape* option if you want to change the shape of the selected text box. Click the *Edit Points* option and small black squares display at points around the text box. Use the mouse on these points to increase or decrease specific points of the text box. Apply predesigned styles to a text box with options in the Shape Styles group. You can also change the shape fill, outline, and effects. Change the formatting of the text in the text box with options in the WordArt Styles group. Click the More button that displays at the right side of the WordArt style options and then click the desired style at the drop-down gallery. You can further customize text with the Text Fill, Text Outline, and Text Effects buttons in the Text group. Use options in the Arrange group to position the text box on the page, specify text wrapping in relation to the text box, align the text box with other objects in the document, and rotate the text box. Specify the text box size with the *Shape Height* and *Shape Width* measurement boxes in the Size group.

Project 3b Inserting a Built-in Text Box

Part 2 of 2

1. With **WL1-C5-P3-Robots.docx** open, click the INSERT tab.
2. Click the Text Box button in the Text group.
3. Scroll down the drop-down list and then click the *Ion Quote (Dark)* option.
4. Type the following text in the text box: **"The task of creating a humanlike body has proven incredibly difficult."**
5. Delete the line and the source placeholder in the text box by pressing the F8 function key (this turns on the Selection Mode), pressing Ctrl + End (this selects text from the location of the insertion point to the end of the text box), and then pressing the Delete key.

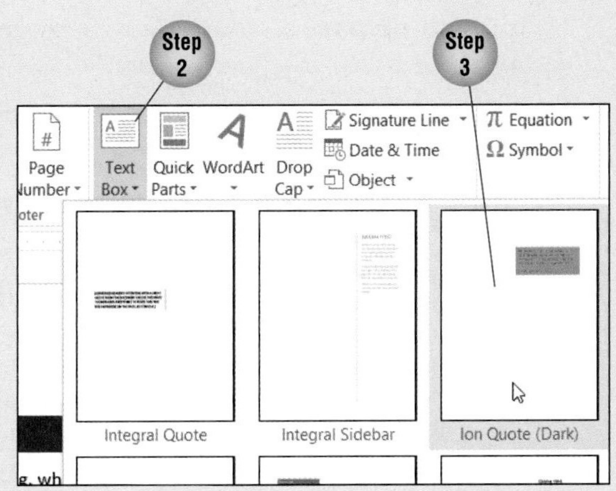

6. With the DRAWING TOOLS FORMAT tab active, click the More button at the right side of the style options in the Shape Styles group and then click the *Subtle Effect - Blue, Accent 5* option (sixth column, fourth row).
7. Click the Shape Effects button in the Shape Styles group, point to *Shadow*, and then click the *Offset Diagonal Bottom Right* option (first column, first row in the *Outer* section).

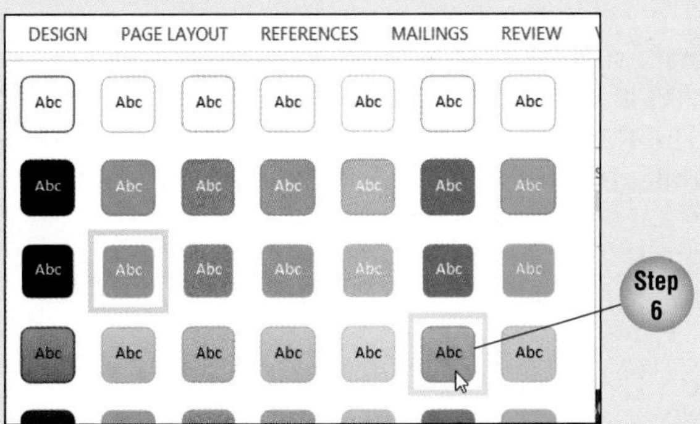

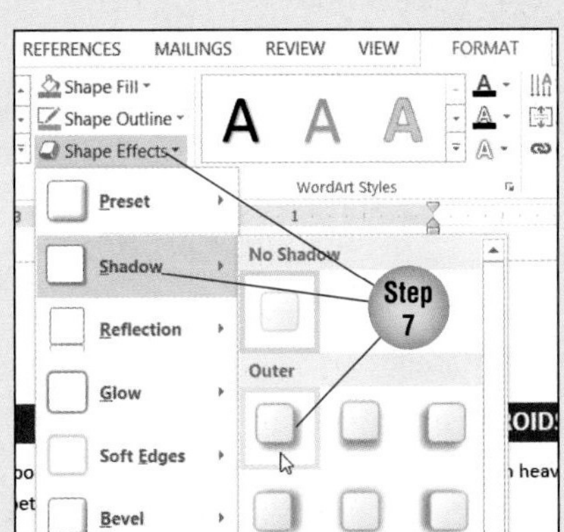

8. Position the mouse pointer on the border of the selected text box until the pointer turns into a four-headed arrow and then drag the text box so it is positioned as shown below.

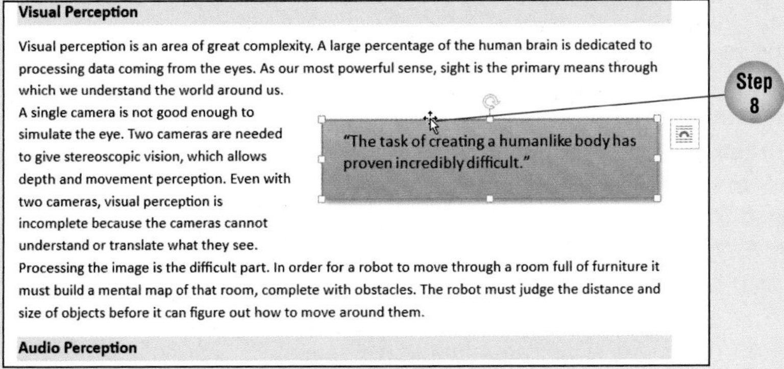
Visual Perception

Visual perception is an area of great complexity. A large percentage of the human brain is dedicated to processing data coming from the eyes. As our most powerful sense, sight is the primary means through which we understand the world around us.

A single camera is not good enough to simulate the eye. Two cameras are needed to give stereoscopic vision, which allows depth and movement perception. Even with two cameras, visual perception is incomplete because the cameras cannot understand or translate what they see.

"The task of creating a humanlike body has proven incredibly difficult."

Processing the image is the difficult part. In order for a robot to move through a room full of furniture it must build a mental map of that room, complete with obstacles. The robot must judge the distance and size of objects before it can figure out how to move around them.

Audio Perception

9. Save, print, and then close **WL1-C5-P3-Robots.docx**.

Project 4 Prepare a Company Flier

3 Parts

You will prepare a company flier by inserting and customizing shapes, text boxes, and WordArt.

Quick Steps

Draw a Shape
1. Click INSERT tab.
2. Click Shapes button.
3. Click desired shape at drop-down list.
4. Click in document or drag in document screen to create shape.

Shapes

To draw a square, choose the Rectangle shape and then hold down the Shift key while drawing the shape. To draw a circle, choose the Oval shape and then hold down the Shift key while drawing the shape.

Drawing Shapes

Use the Shapes button on the INSERT tab to draw shapes in a document, including lines, basic shapes, block arrows, flow chart shapes, stars and banners, and callouts. Click a shape and the mouse pointer displays as crosshairs (plus sign). Position the crosshairs in the document where you want the shape to display and then click the left mouse button. You can also hold down the left mouse button, drag to create the shape, and then release the mouse button. The shape is inserted in the document and the DRAWING TOOLS FORMAT tab is active.

If you choose a shape in the *Lines* section of the drop-down list, the shape you draw is considered a ***line drawing***. If you choose an option in the other sections of the drop-down list, the shape you draw is considered an ***enclosed object***. When drawing an enclosed object, you can maintain the proportions of the shape by holding down the Shift key while dragging with the mouse to create the shape.

Copying Shapes

To copy a shape, select the shape and then click the Copy button in the Clipboard group on the HOME tab. Position the insertion point at the location you want the copied shape and then click the Paste button. You can also copy a selected shape by holding down the Ctrl key while dragging a copy of the shape to the desired location.

Project 4a Drawing Arrow Shapes

Part 1 of 3

1. At a blank document, press the Enter key twice and then draw an arrow shape by completing the following steps:
   a. Click the INSERT tab.
   b. Click the Shapes button in the Illustrations group and then click the *Striped Right Arrow* shape in the *Block Arrows* section.
   c. Position the mouse pointer (displays as crosshairs) immediately right of the insertion point and then click the left mouse button. (This inserts the arrow shape in the document.)
2. Format the arrow by completing the following steps:
   a. Click in the *Shape Height* measurement box in the Size group, type 2.4, and then press Enter.
   b. Click in the *Shape Width* measurement box in the Size group, type 4.5, and then press Enter.

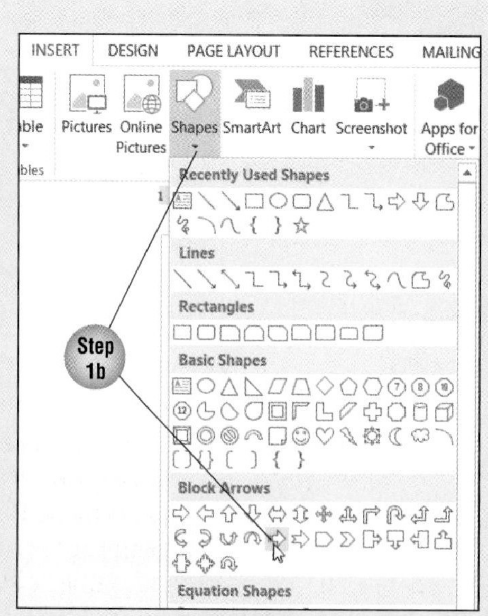

c. Horizontally align the arrow by clicking the Align button in the Arrange group and then clicking *Distribute Horizontally* at the drop-down list.

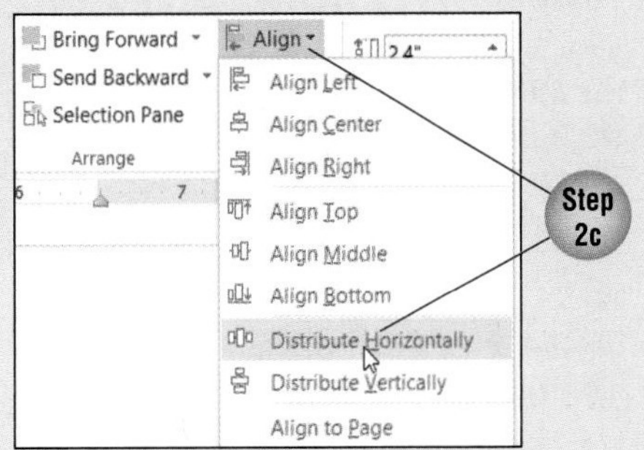

d. Click the More button at the right side of the options in the Shape Styles group and then click the *Intense Effect - Green, Accent 6* option (last option at the drop-down gallery).

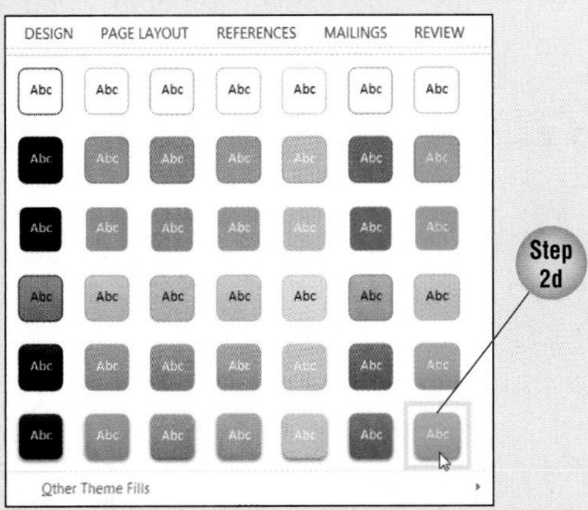

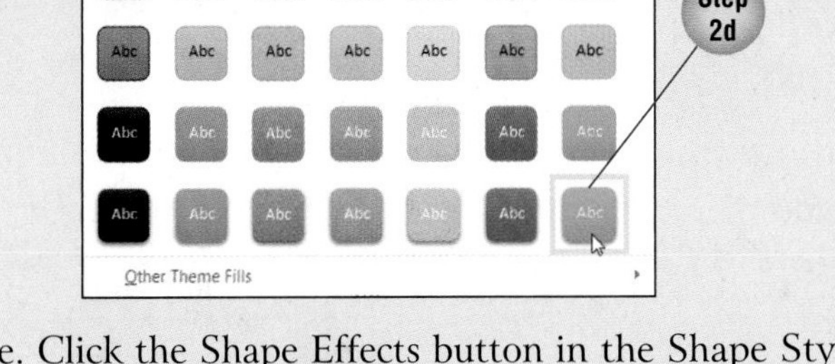

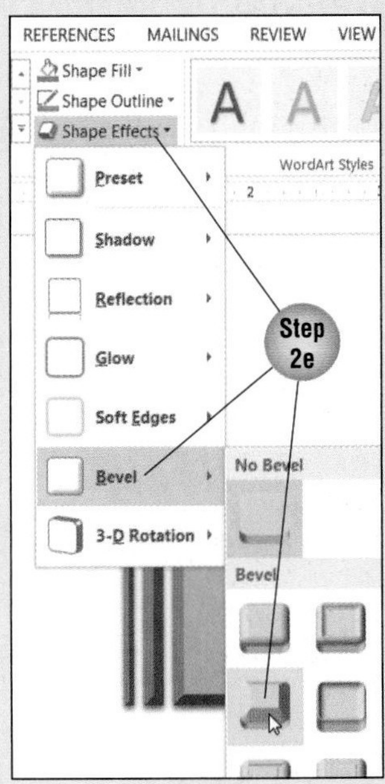

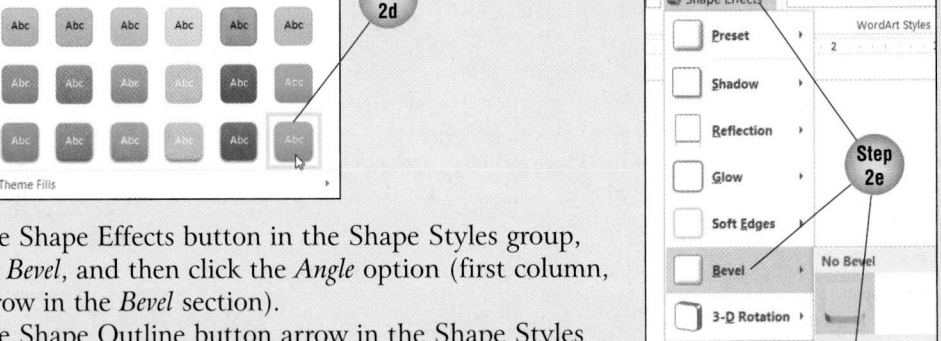

e. Click the Shape Effects button in the Shape Styles group, point to *Bevel*, and then click the *Angle* option (first column, second row in the *Bevel* section).

f. Click the Shape Outline button arrow in the Shape Styles group and then click the *Dark Blue* color (ninth option in the *Standard Colors* section).

3. Copy the arrow by completing the following steps:
   a. With the mouse pointer positioned in the arrow (mouse pointer displays with a four-headed arrow attached), hold down the Ctrl key and the left mouse button.
   b. Drag down until the copied arrow displays just below the top arrow, release the mouse button, and then release the Ctrl key.
   c. Copy the arrow again by holding down the Ctrl key and the left mouse button and then dragging the copied arrow just below the second arrow.
4. Flip the middle arrow by completing the following steps:
   a. Click the middle arrow to select it.
   b. Click the Rotate button in the Arrange group on the DRAWING TOOLS FORMAT tab and then click *Flip Horizontal* at the drop-down gallery.
5. Insert the text *Financial* in the top arrow by completing the following steps:
   a. Click the top arrow to select it.
   b. Type **Financial**.
   c. Select *Financial*.
   d. Click the HOME tab.
   e. Change the font size to 16 points, turn on bold formatting, and then apply the Dark Blue font color (ninth option in the *Standard Colors* section).
6. Complete steps similar to those in Step 5 to insert the word *Direction* in the middle arrow.
7. Complete steps similar to those in Step 5 to insert the word *Retirement* in the bottom arrow.
8. Save the document and name it **WL1-C5-P4-FinConsult**.
9. Print the document.

Quick Steps

Draw a Text Box
1. Click INSERT tab.
2. Click Text Box button in Text group.
3. Click *Draw Text Box*.
4. Click in document or drag in document to create box.

Drawing and Formatting a Text Box

You can use the built-in text boxes provided by Word, or you can draw your own text box. To draw a text box, click the INSERT tab, click the Text Box button in the Text group, and then click *Draw Text Box* at the drop-down list. The mouse pointer displays as crosshairs. Click in the document to insert the text box or position the crosshairs in the document and then drag to create the text box. When a text box is selected, the DRAWING TOOLS FORMAT tab is active. Use buttons on this tab to format text boxes in the same manner as when formatting built-in text boxes.

Project 4b Inserting and Formatting a Text Box

Part 2 of 3

1. With **WL1-C5-P4-FinConsult.docx** open, delete the bottom arrow by completing the following steps:
   a. Click the bottom arrow. (This displays a border around the arrow.)
   b. Position the mouse pointer on the border (displays with four-headed arrow attached) and then click the left mouse button. (This changes the dashed border to a solid border.)
   c. Press the Delete key.
2. Insert, size, and format a text box by completing the following steps:
   a. Click the INSERT tab.
   b. Click the Text Box button in the Text group and then click *Draw Text Box* at the drop-down list.
   c. Click in the document at about the 1-inch mark on the horizontal ruler and about 1 inch below the bottom arrow. (This inserts a text box in the document.)
   d. Click in the *Shape Height* measurement box in the Size group and then type **1.7**.
   e. Click in the *Shape Width* measurement box, type **4.5**, and then press Enter.
   f. Click the More button at the right side of the options in the Shape Styles group and then click the *Intense Effect - Green, Accent 6* option (last option at the drop-down gallery).
   g. Click the Shape Effects button in the Shape Styles group, point to *Bevel*, and then click the *Soft Round* option at the side menu (second column, second row in the *Bevel* section).

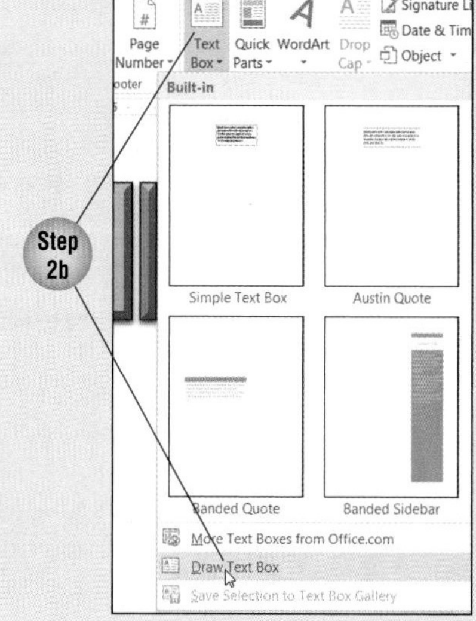

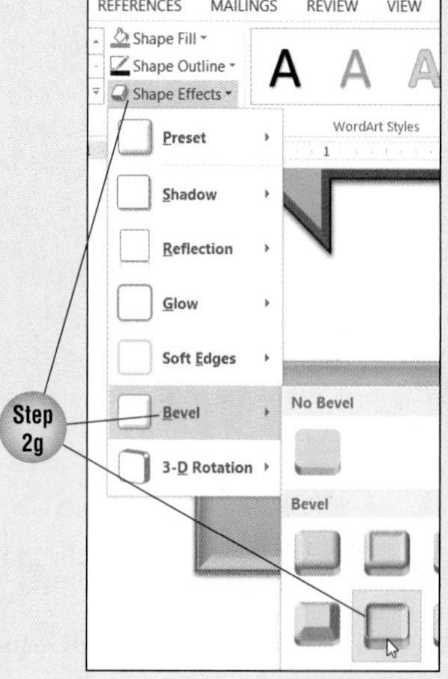

h. Click the Shape Effects button in the Shape Styles group, point to *3-D Rotation*, and then click the *Perspective Above* option (first column, second row in the *Perspective* section).

3. Insert and format text in the text box by completing the following steps:
   a. Press the Enter key twice. (The insertion point should be positioned in the text box.)
   b. Click the HOME tab.
   c. Change the font size to 24 points, turn on bold formatting, and change the font color to *Dark Blue*.
   d. Click the Center button in the Paragraph group.
   e. Type **Retirement Financial Consulting**. (Your text box should appear as shown below.)

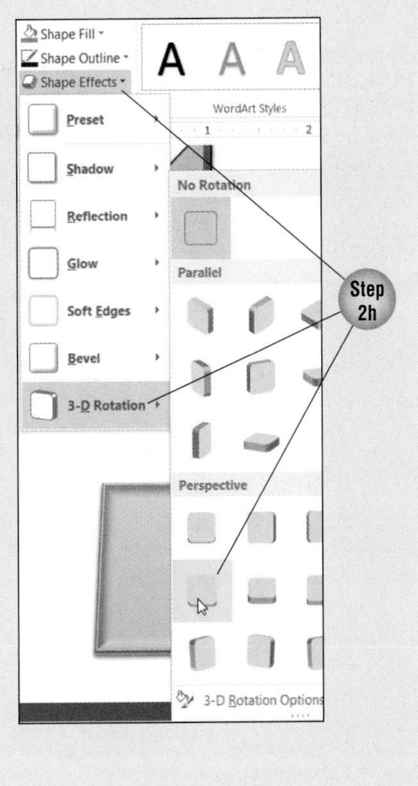

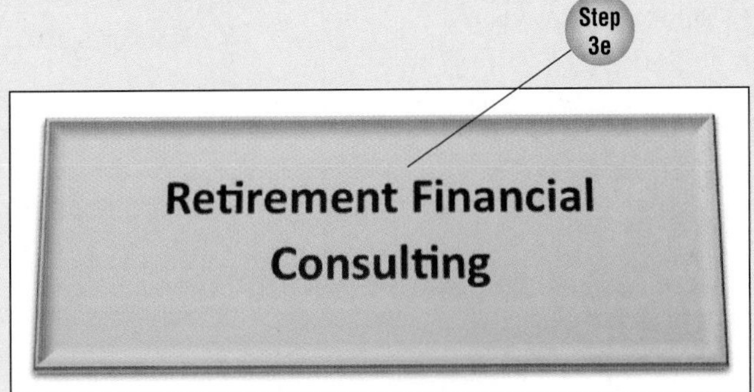

4. Save **WL1-C5-P4-FinConsult.docx**.

Creating and Modifying WordArt Text

With the WordArt feature, you can distort or modify text to conform to a variety of shapes. This is useful for creating company logos, letterheads, flier titles, or headings. To insert WordArt in a document, click the INSERT tab and then click the WordArt button in the Text group. At the drop-down list that displays, click the desired option and a WordArt text box is inserted in the document containing the words *Your text here* and the DRAWING TOOLS FORMAT tab is active. Type the desired WordArt text and then format the WordArt with options on the DRAWING TOOLS FORMAT tab. You can also type text in a document, select the text, and then choose a WordArt option at the WordArt button drop-down list.

Quick Steps

Create WordArt Text
1. Click INSERT tab.
2. Click WordArt button.
3. Click desired WordArt option at drop-down list.
4. Type WordArt text.

WordArt

Project 4c **Inserting and Modifying WordArt** **Part 3 of 3**

1. With **WL1-C5-P4-FinConsult.docx** open, press Ctrl + Home to move the insertion point to the beginning of the document.
2. Insert WordArt text by completing the following steps:
   a. Type **Miller Financial Services** and then select *Miller Financial Services*.

b. Click the INSERT tab.
c. Click the WordArt button in the Text group and then click the *Fill - Orange, Accent 2, Outline - Accent 2* option (third column, first row).

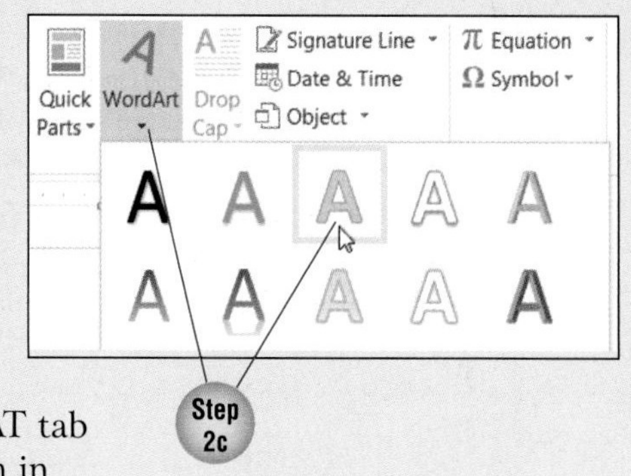

3. Format the WordArt text by completing the following steps:
   a. Make sure the WordArt text border displays as a solid line.
   b. Click the Text Fill button arrow in the WordArt Styles group on the DRAWING TOOLS FORMAT tab and then click the *Light Green* option (fifth option in the *Standard Colors* section).
   c. Click the Text Outline button arrow in the WordArt Styles group and then click the *Green, Accent 6, Darker 50%* option (last option in *Theme Colors* section).
   d. Click the Text Effects button in the WordArt Styles group, point to *Glow*, and then click the *Blue, 5 pt glow, Accent color 1* option (first option in the *Glow Variations* section).

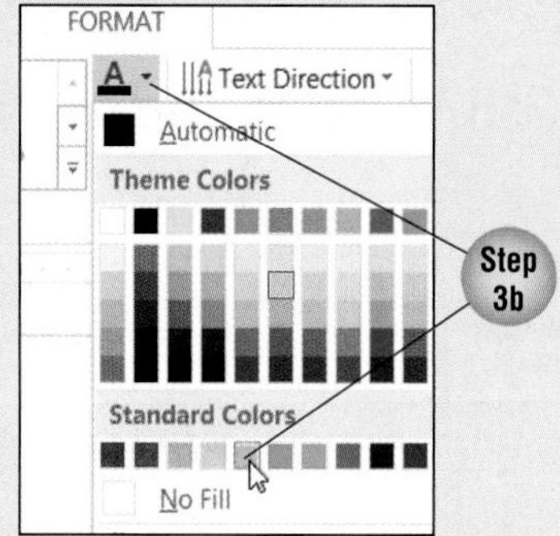

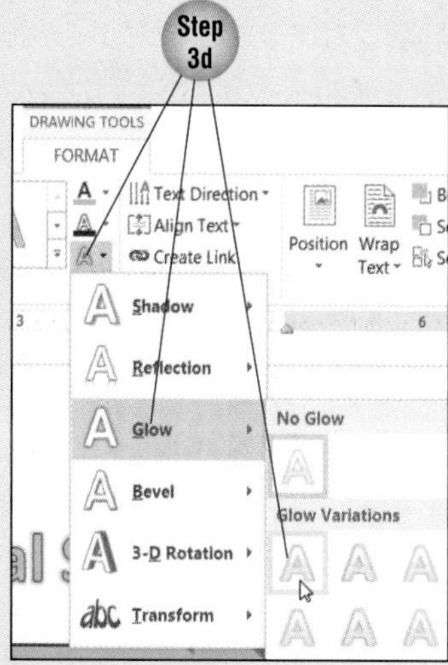

   e. Click in the *Shape Height* measurement box in the Size group and then type 1.
   f. Click in the *Shape Width* measurement box in the Size group, type 6, and then press Enter.
   g. Click the Text Effects button in the WordArt Styles group, point to *Transform*, and then click the *Can Up* option (third column, fourth row in the *Warp* section).

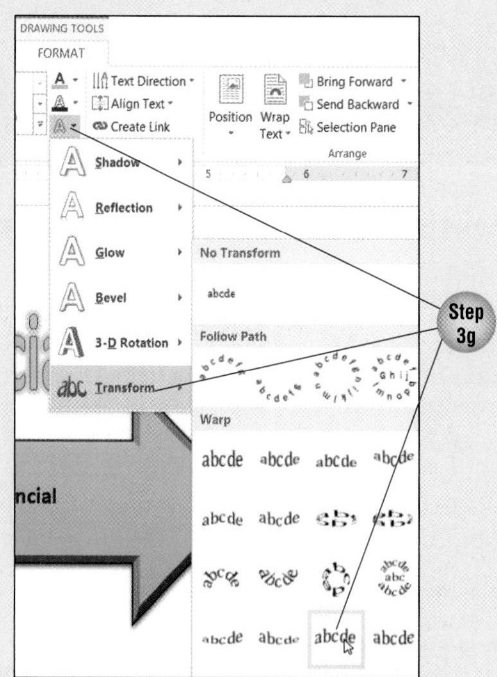

h. Click the Position button in the Arrange group and then click the *Position in Top Center with Square Text Wrapping* option (second column, first row in the *With Text Wrapping* section).
4. Check to make sure that the WordArt, the two arrows, and the text box all fit on one page. If they do not, consider moving and/or sizing the arrows or text box to ensure that they fit on one page.
5. Save, print, and then close **WL1-C5-P4-FinConsult.docx**.

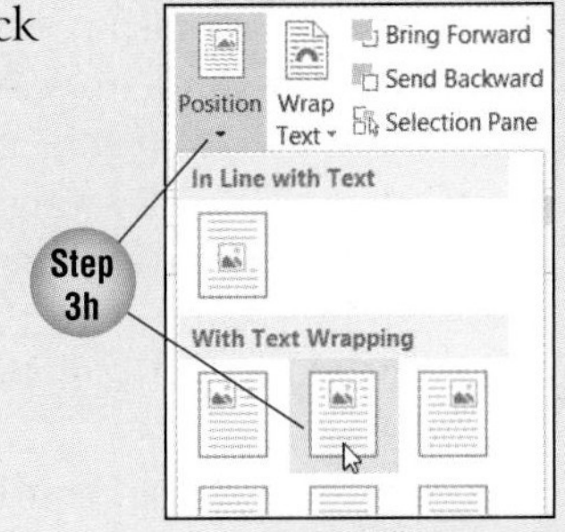

Project 5 Create and Format Screenshots — 2 Parts

You will create screenshots of the Print and Export backstage areas, screen clippings of cover pages, and a sample cover page document.

Creating and Inserting a Screenshot

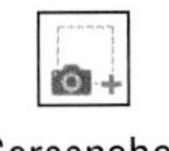

Screenshot

The Illustrations group on the INSERT tab contains a Screenshot button, which you can use to capture the contents of a screen as an image or capture a portion of a screen. If you want to capture the entire screen, open a new document, click the INSERT tab, click the Screenshot button in the Illustrations group, and then click the desired screen thumbnail at the drop-down list. The currently active document does not display as a thumbnail at the drop-down list—only any other documents or files that you have open. When you click the desired thumbnail, the screenshot is inserted as an image in the open document, the image is selected, and the PICTURE TOOLS FORMAT tab is active. Use buttons on this tab to customize the screenshot image.

Project 5a Inserting and Formatting Screenshots — Part 1 of 2

1. Press Ctrl + N to open a blank document.
2. Press Ctrl + N to open a second blank document, type **Print Backstage Area** at the left margin, and then press the Enter key.
3. Save the document and name it **WL1-C5-P5-BackstageAreas**.
4. Point to the Word button on the Taskbar and then click the thumbnail representing the blank document.
5. Display the Print backstage area by clicking the FILE tab and then clicking the *Print* option.

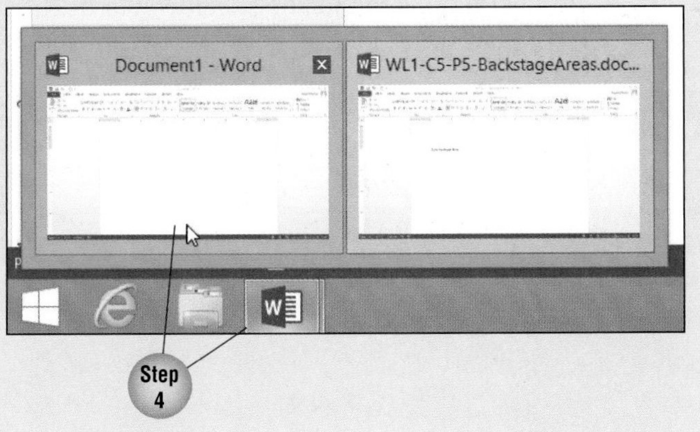

6. Point to the Word buttons on the Taskbar and then click the thumbnail representing **WL1-C5-P5-BackstageAreas.docx**.
7. Insert and format a screenshot of the Print backstage area by completing the following steps:
   a. Click the INSERT tab.
   b. Click the Screenshot button in the Illustrations group and then click the thumbnail that displays in the drop-down list. (This inserts a screenshot of the Print backstage area in the document.)
   c. With the screenshot image selected, click the *Drop Shadow Rectangle* picture style option (fourth option in the Picture Styles group).

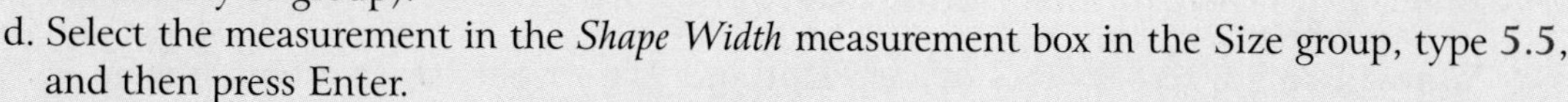

   d. Select the measurement in the *Shape Width* measurement box in the Size group, type 5.5, and then press Enter.
8. Press Ctrl + End and then press the Enter key. (The insertion point should be positioned below the screenshot image.)
9. Type **Export Backstage Area** at the left margin and then press the Enter key.
10. Point to the Word buttons on the Taskbar and then click the thumbnail representing the blank document.
11. At the backstage area, click the *Export* option. (This displays the Export backstage area.)
12. Point to the Word buttons on the Taskbar and then click the thumbnail representing **WL1-C5-P5-BackstageAreas.docx**.
13. Insert and format a screenshot of the Export backstage area by completing steps similar to those in Step 7.
14. Press Ctrl + Home to move the insertion point to the beginning of the document.
15. Save, print, and then close **WL1-C5-P5-BackstageAreas.docx**.
16. At the Export backstage area, press the Esc key to redisplay the blank document.
17. Close the blank document.

In addition to making a screenshot of an entire screen, you can make a screenshot of a specific portion of the screen by clicking the *Screen Clipping* option at the Screenshot button drop-down list. When you click this option, the other open document, file, or Windows Start screen or desktop displays in a dimmed manner and the mouse pointer displays as a crosshair. Using the mouse, draw a border around the specific area of the screen you want to capture. The specific area you identified is inserted in the other document as an image, the image is selected, and the PICTURE TOOLS FORMAT tab is active. If you have only one document or file open when you click the Screenshot button, clicking the *Screen Clipping* option will cause the Windows Start screen or desktop to display.

Project 5b Creating and Formatting a Screen Clipping

Part 2 of 2

1. Open **NSSLtrhd.docx** and save it with Save As with the new name **WL1-C5-P5-NSSCoverPages**.
2. Type the text **Sample Cover Pages** and then press the Enter key twice.
3. Select the text you just typed, change the font to 18-point Copperplate Gothic Bold, and then center the text.
4. Press Ctrl + End to move the insertion point below the text.
5. Open the document named **NSSCoverPg01.docx** and then change the zoom to 40% by clicking six times on the Zoom Out button located at the left side of the Zoom slider bar on the Status bar.
6. Point to the Word buttons on the Taskbar and then click the thumbnail representing **WL1-C5-P5-NSSCoverPages.docx**.

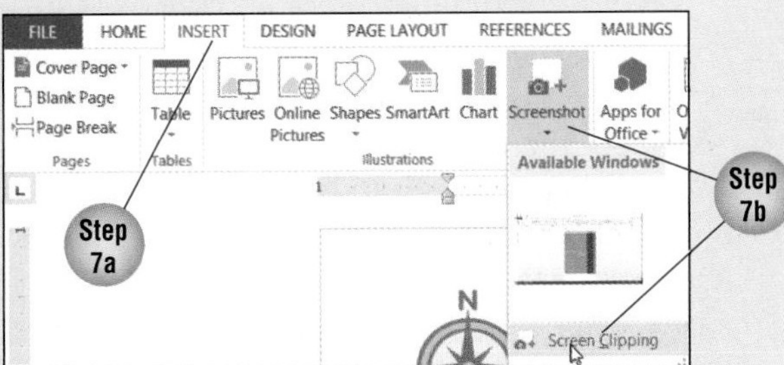

7. Create and format a screenshot screen clipping by completing the following steps:
   a. Click the INSERT tab.
   b. Click the Screenshot button in the Illustrations group and then click *Screen Clipping*.
   c. When **NSSCoverPg01.docx** displays in a dimmed manner, position the mouse crosshairs in the upper left corner of the cover page, hold down the left mouse button, drag down to the lower right corner of the cover page, and then release the mouse button. (See image at the right.)
   d. With the cover page screenshot image inserted in **WL1-C5-P5-NSSCoverPages.docx**, make sure the image is selected (sizing handles display around the cover page image).
   e. Click the Wrap Text button in the Arrange group on the PICTURE TOOLS FORMAT tab and then click *Square* at the drop-down gallery.
   f. Select the current measurement in the *Shape Width* measurement box in the Size group, type 3, and then press Enter.

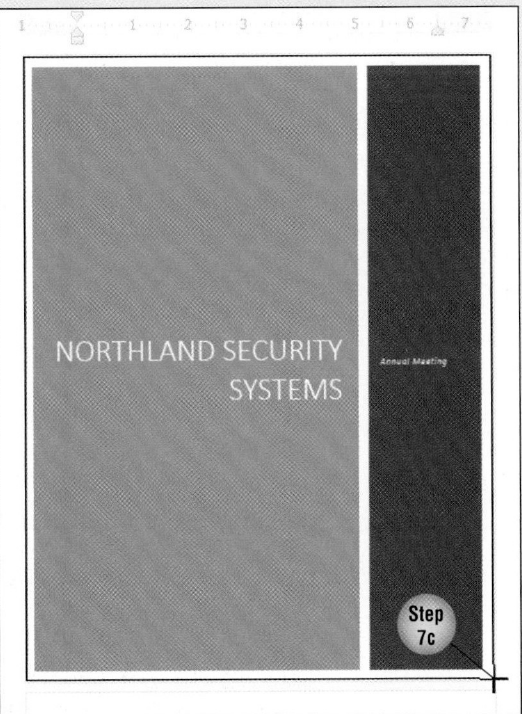

8. Point to the Word buttons on the Taskbar and then click the thumbnail representing **NSSCoverPg01.docx**.
9. Close **NSSCoverPg01.docx**.
10. Open **NSSCoverPg02.docx** and then, if neccessary, change the zoom to 40%.
11. Point to the Word buttons on the Taskbar and then click the thumbnail representing **WL1-C5-P5-NSSCoverPages.docx**.
12. Create and format a screenshot by completing steps similar to those in Step 7.
13. Position the two cover page screenshot images so they are side by side in the document.
14. Save, print, and then close **WL1-C5-P5-NSSCoverPages.docx**.
15. Close **NSSCoverPg02.docx**.

Chapter Summary

- Insert a section break in a document to apply formatting to a portion of a document. You can insert a continuous section break or a section break that begins a new page. Turn on the display of nonprinting characters or change to Draft view to see section breaks, since they are not visible in Print Layout view.
- Set text in columns to improve the readability of documents such as newsletters and reports. Format text in columns using the Columns button in the Page Setup group on the PAGE LAYOUT tab or with options at the Columns dialog box.
- Remove column formatting with the Columns button on the PAGE LAYOUT tab or at the Columns dialog box. Balance column text on the last page of a document by inserting a continuous section break at the end of the text.
- Improve the display of text lines by hyphenating long words that fall at the ends of lines. You can automatically or manually hyphenate words in a document.
- To enhance the appearance of text, use drop caps to identify the beginnings of major sections or paragraphs. Create drop caps with the Drop Cap button in the Text group on the INSERT tab.
- Insert symbols with options at the Symbol dialog box with the Symbols tab selected, and insert special characters with options at the Symbol dialog box with the Special Characters tab selected.
- Click the Date & Time button in the Text group on the INSERT tab to display the Date and Time dialog box. Insert the date or time with options at this dialog box or with keyboard shortcuts. If the date or time is inserted as a field, update the field with the Update Field key, F9.
- Use the Click and Type feature to center, right-align, and left-align text.
- Vertically align text in a document with the *Vertical alignment* option at the Page Setup dialog box with the Layout tab selected.
- Insert an image such as a picture or clip art with buttons in the Illustrations group on the INSERT tab.
- Customize and format an image with options and buttons on the PICTURE TOOLS FORMAT tab. Size an image with the *Shape Height* and *Shape Width* measurement boxes in the Size group or with the sizing handles that display around the selected image.
- Move an image with options from the Position button drop-down gallery located on the PICTURE TOOLS FORMAT tab or by choosing a text wrapping style and then moving the image by dragging it with the mouse.
- To insert a picture, click the INSERT tab, click the Pictures button, navigate to the desired folder at the Insert Picture dialog box, and then double-click the picture.
- To insert an image from Office.com, click the INSERT tab and then click the Online Pictures button. At the Insert Pictures window, type the search text or topic and then press Enter. Double-click the desired image.
- Insert a pull quote in a document with a built-in text box by clicking the INSERT tab, clicking the Text Box button, and then clicking the desired built-in text box at the drop-down list.

- Draw shapes in a document by clicking the Shapes button in the Illustrations group on the INSERT tab, clicking the desired shape at the drop-down list, and then clicking or dragging in the document to draw the shape. Customize a shape with options on the DRAWING TOOLS FORMAT tab. Copy a shape by holding down the Ctrl key while dragging the selected shape.
- Draw a text box by clicking the Text Box button in the Text group on the INSERT tab, clicking *Draw Text Box* at the drop-down list, and then clicking or dragging in the document. Customize a text box with buttons on the DRAWING TOOLS FORMAT tab.
- Use WordArt to distort or modify text to conform to a variety of shapes. Customize WordArt with options on the DRAWING TOOLS FORMAT tab.
- Use the Screenshot button in the Illustrations group on the INSERT tab to capture the contents of a screen or capture a portion of a screen. Use buttons on the PICTURE TOOLS FORMAT tab to customize a screenshot image.

Commands Review

FEATURE	RIBBON TAB, GROUP	BUTTON, OPTION	KEYBOARD SHORTCUT
columns	PAGE LAYOUT, Page Setup		
Columns dialog box	PAGE LAYOUT, Page Setup	, *More Columns*	
continuous section break	PAGE LAYOUT, Page Setup	, *Continuous*	
Date and Time dialog box	INSERT, Text		
drop cap	INSERT, Text		
hyphenate words automatically	PAGE LAYOUT, Page Setup	, *Automatic*	
insert date			Alt + Shift + D
Insert Picture dialog box	INSERT, Illustrations		
Insert Pictures window	INSERT, Illustrations		
insert time			Alt + Shift + T
Manual Hyphenation dialog box	PAGE LAYOUT, Page Setup	, *Manual*	
Page Setup dialog box	PAGE LAYOUT, Page Setup		
pull quote (built-in text box)	INSERT, Text		
screenshot	INSERT, Illustrations		
shapes	INSERT, Illustrations		

FEATURE	RIBBON TAB, GROUP	BUTTON, OPTION	KEYBOARD SHORTCUT
Symbol dialog box	INSERT, Symbols	Ω, *More Symbols*	
text box	INSERT, Text		
update field			F9
WordArt	INSERT, Text		

Concepts Check Test Your Knowledge

Completion: In the space provided at the right, indicate the correct term, symbol, or command.

1. View a section break by turning on the display of nonprinting characters or using this view. ____________
2. Format text into columns with the Columns button located in this group on the PAGE LAYOUT tab. ____________
3. Balance column text on the last page of a document by inserting this type of break at the end of the text. ____________
4. The first letter of the first word of a paragraph that is set into a paragraph is called this. ____________
5. The Symbol button is located on this tab. ____________
6. This is the keyboard shortcut to insert the current date. ____________
7. Use this feature to position the insertion point at a specific location and alignment in a document. ____________
8. Vertically align text with the *Vertical alignment* option at the Page Setup dialog box with this tab selected. ____________
9. Insert an image in a document with buttons in this group on the INSERT tab. ____________
10. Customize and format an image with options and buttons on this tab. ____________
11. Size an image with the sizing handles that display around the selected image or with these measurement boxes on the PICTURE TOOLS FORMAT tab. ____________
12. Click the Picture button on the INSERT tab and this dialog box displays. ____________
13. Click the Online Pictures button on the INSERT tab and this window displays. ____________
14. This is the term for a quote that is enlarged and positioned in an attractive location on the page. ____________

15. The Shapes button is located on this tab. ________________

16. To copy a selected shape, hold down this key while dragging the shape. ________________

17. Use this feature to distort or modify text to conform to a variety of shapes. ________________

18. To capture a portion of a screen, click the Screenshot button in the Illustrations group on the INSERT tab and then click this option at the drop-down list. ________________

Skills Check Assess Your Performance

Assessment 1

ADD VISUAL APPEAL TO A REPORT ON INTELLECTUAL PROPERTY

1. Open **ProtectIssues.docx** and then save the document with Save As and name it **WL1-C5-A1-ProtectIssues**.
2. Format the text from the first paragraph of text below the title to the end of the document into two columns with 0.4 inch between columns.
3. Move the insertion point to the end of the document and then insert a continuous section break to balance the columns on the second page.
4. Press Ctrl + Home to move the insertion point to the beginning of the document.
5. Display the Insert Pictures window (click the Online Pictures button on the INSERT tab), type **computer privacy magnifying glass** in the search text box, and then press Enter. Insert the clip art image with a man in a blue hat. (If this clip art image is not available, choose another related to *computer* and *privacy*.)
6. Make the following customizations to the clip art image:
   a. Change the height to 1 inch.
   b. Change the color of the clip art image to *Blue, Accent color 1 Light*.
   c. Correct the contrast to *Brightness: 0% (Normal) Contrast: +20%*.
   d. Change the position of the clip art image to *Position in Middle Left with Square Text Wrapping*.
   e. Use the Rotate Objects button in the Arrange group and flip the clip art image horizontally.
7. Move the insertion point to the beginning of the paragraph immediately below the *Intellectual Property Protection* heading (located on the second page). Insert the Austin Quote built-in text box and then make the following customizations:
   a. Type the following text in the text box: "**Plagiarism may be punished by law, and in many educational institutions it can result in suspension or even expulsion.**"
   b. Select the text and then change the font size to 11 points.
   c. Change the width of the text box to 2.8 inches.
   d. Change the position of the text box to *Position in Top Center with Square Text Wrapping*.

8. Press Ctrl + End to move the insertion point to the end of the document. (The insertion point will be positioned below the continuous section break you inserted on the second page to balance the columns of text.)
9. Change back to one column.
10. Press the Enter key twice and then insert a shape near the insertion point using the Plaque shape (located in the second row in the *Basic Shapes* section) and make the following customizations:
    a. Change the shape height to 1.4 inches and the shape width to 3.9 inches.
    b. Use the Align button in the Arrange group and distribute the shape horizontally.
    c. Apply the Subtle Effect - Blue Accent 1 shape style (second column, fourth row).
    d. Type the text **Felicité Compagnie** inside the shape. Insert the é symbol at the Symbol dialog box with the *(normal text)* font selected.
    e. Insert the current date below *Felicité Compagnie* and insert the current time below the date.
    f. Select the text in the shape, change the font size to 14 points, and apply bold formatting.
11. Manually hyphenate the document. (Do not hyphenate headings or proper names.)
12. Create a drop cap with the first letter of the word *The* that begins the first paragraph of text below the title.
13. Save, print, and then close **WL1-C5-A1-ProtectIssues.docx**.

Assessment 2

CREATE A SALES MEETING ANNOUNCEMENT

1. At a blank document, press the Enter key twice, and then create WordArt with the following specifications:
    a. Choose the *Fill - Black, Text 1, Outline - Background 1, Hard Shadow - Background 1* WordArt style option and then type **Inlet Corporation** in the WordArt text box.
    b. Change the width of the WordArt text box to 6.5 inches.
    c. Use the Transform option from the Text Effects button in the WordArt Styles group to apply the Chevron Up text effect.
2. Press Ctrl + End and then press the Enter key three times. Change the font to 18-point Candara, turn on bold formatting, change to center alignment, and then type the following text:

    National Sales Meeting

    Northwest Division

    Ocean View Resort

    August 19 through August 21, 2015
3. Insert the picture named **Ocean.jpg** and then make the following changes to the picture:
    a. Change the width of the picture to 6.5 inches.
    b. Apply the Brightness: +40% Contrast: -40% correction.
    c. Apply the Compound Frame, Black picture style.
    d. Change the position of the picture to *Position in Top Center with Square Text Wrapping*.
    e. Change text wrapping to *Behind Text*.
4. Save the announcement document and name it **WL1-C5-A2-SalesMtg**.
5. Print and then close **WL1-C5-A2-SalesMtg.docx**.

Assessment 3

CREATE AN ANNOUNCEMENT

1. Open **FirstAidCourse.docx** and then save the document with Save As and name it **WL1-C5-A3-FirstAidCourse**.
2. Format the announcement shown in Figure 5.8. Insert the caduceus clip art image as shown in the figure with the following specifications:
   a. Use the word *caduceus* at the Insert Pictures window to search online for the clip art image.
   b. Change the text wrapping to *Tight*.
   c. Change the clip art image color to *Blue, Accent color 1 Light*.
   d. Correct the brightness and contrast to *Brightness: -20% Contrast: +40%*.
   e. Size and move the clip art image as shown in the figure.
3. Apply paragraph shading, insert the page border, and add leaders to the tabs as shown in Figure 5.8.
4. Save, print, and then close **WL1-C5-A3-FirstAidCourse.docx**. (If some of the page border does not print, consider increasing the measurements at the Border and Shading Options dialog box.)

Figure 5.8 Assessment 3

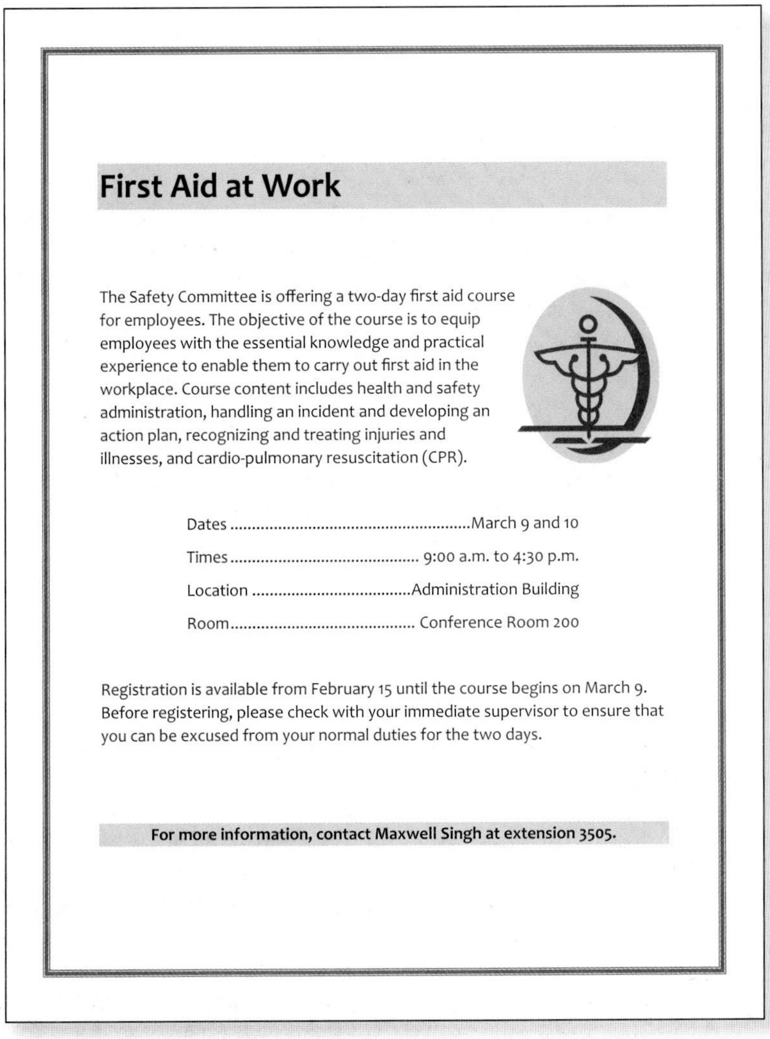

First Aid at Work

The Safety Committee is offering a two-day first aid course for employees. The objective of the course is to equip employees with the essential knowledge and practical experience to enable them to carry out first aid in the workplace. Course content includes health and safety administration, handling an incident and developing an action plan, recognizing and treating injuries and illnesses, and cardio-pulmonary resuscitation (CPR).

Dates .... March 9 and 10

Times .... 9:00 a.m. to 4:30 p.m.

Location .... Administration Building

Room .... Conference Room 200

Registration is available from February 15 until the course begins on March 9. Before registering, please check with your immediate supervisor to ensure that you can be excused from your normal duties for the two days.

For more information, contact Maxwell Singh at extension 3505.

Assessment

4 INSERT SCREENSHOTS IN A MEMO

1. Open **FirstAidMemo.docx** and then save it with Save As and name it **WL1-C5-A4-FirstAidMemo**.
2. Insert screenshots so your document appears as shown in Figure 5.9. Use the **FirstAidAnnounce.docx** document located in your WL1C5 folder to create the first screenshot, and use the document **WL1-C5-A3-FirstAidCourse.docx** you created in Assessment 3 for the second screenshot. ***Hint: Decrease the size of the document so the entire document is visible on the screen.***
3. Move the insertion point below the screenshot images and then insert the text as shown in the figure. Insert your initials in place of the *XX*.
4. Save, print, and close **WL1-C5-A4-FirstAidMemo.docx**.

Figure 5.9 Assessment 4

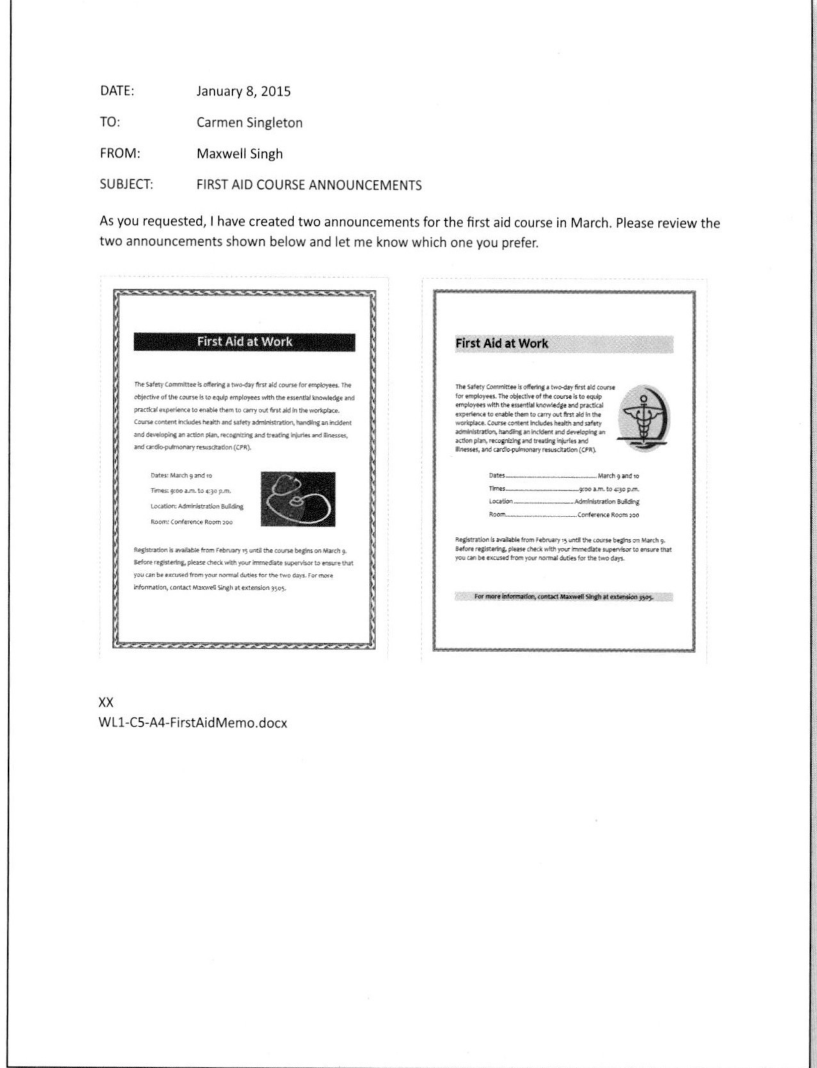

DATE: January 8, 2015

TO: Carmen Singleton

FROM: Maxwell Singh

SUBJECT: FIRST AID COURSE ANNOUNCEMENTS

As you requested, I have created two announcements for the first aid course in March. Please review the two announcements shown below and let me know which one you prefer.

XX
WL1-C5-A4-FirstAidMemo.docx

Visual Benchmark Demonstrate Your Proficiency

1 CREATE A FLIER

1. Create the flier shown in Figure 5.10 with the following specifications:
   - Create the title *Pugs on Parade!* as WordArt using the *Fill - Black, Text 1, Shadow* option. Change the width to 6.5 inches, apply the Can Up transform effect, and change the text fill color to *Dark Red*.
   - Create the shape containing the text *Admission is free!* using the Explosion 1 shape in the Stars and Banners section of the Shapes button drop-down list.
   - Insert the **Pug.jpg** picture (use the Pictures button on the INSERT tab) located in the WL1C5 folder on your storage medium. Change the text wrapping for the picture to *Behind Text* and size and position the picture as shown in the figure.
   - Create the line above the last line of text as a top border. Change the color to *Dark Red* and the width to 3 points.
   - Make any other changes so your document appears similar to Figure 5.10.
2. Save the document and name it **WL1-C5-VB1-PugFlier**.
3. Print and then close the document.

Figure 5.10 Visual Benchmark 1

2 FORMAT A REPORT

1. Open **Resume.docx** and then save it with Save As and name it **WL1-C5-VB2-Resume**.
2. Format the report so it appears as shown in Figure 5.11 with the following specifications:
   a. Insert the WordArt text *Résumé Writing* with the following specifications:
      - Use the Fill - *Black, Text 1, Outline - Background 1, Hard Shadow - Background 1* option (first column, third row).
      - Type the text **Résumé Writing** and insert the é symbol using the Insert Symbol dialog box.
      - Change the position to *Position in Top Center with Square Text Wrapping*.
      - Change the width of the WordArt to 5.5 inches.
      - Apply the Can Up transform text effect.

   b. Format the report into two columns beginning with the first paragraph of text below the title and balance the columns on the second page.
   c. Insert the pull quote with the following specifications:
      - Use the Motion Quote built in text box.
      - Type the text shown in the pull quote in Figure 5.11. (Use the Insert Symbol dialog box to insert the two é symbols in the word résumé.)
      - Select the text and then change the font size to 11 points.
      - Change the width of the text box to 2.3 inches.
      - Position the pull quote as shown in Figure 5.11.

   d. Insert the cake clip art image with the following specifications:
      - Search for the cake image using the words *cakes, desserts, dining, food* in the Insert Pictures window. Insert the cake image shown in the figure. (The original image colors are brown and black.) If this image is not available, choose a similar image of a cake.
      - Change the image color to *Black and White: 50%*.
      - Change the width to 0.9 inches.
      - Change the text wrapping to *Tight*.
      - Position the cake image as shown in Figure 5.11.

   e. Insert page numbering at the bottom center of each page with the *Thick Line* option.
3. Save, print, and then close **WL1-C5-VB2-Resume.docx**.

Figure 5.11 Visual Benchmark 2

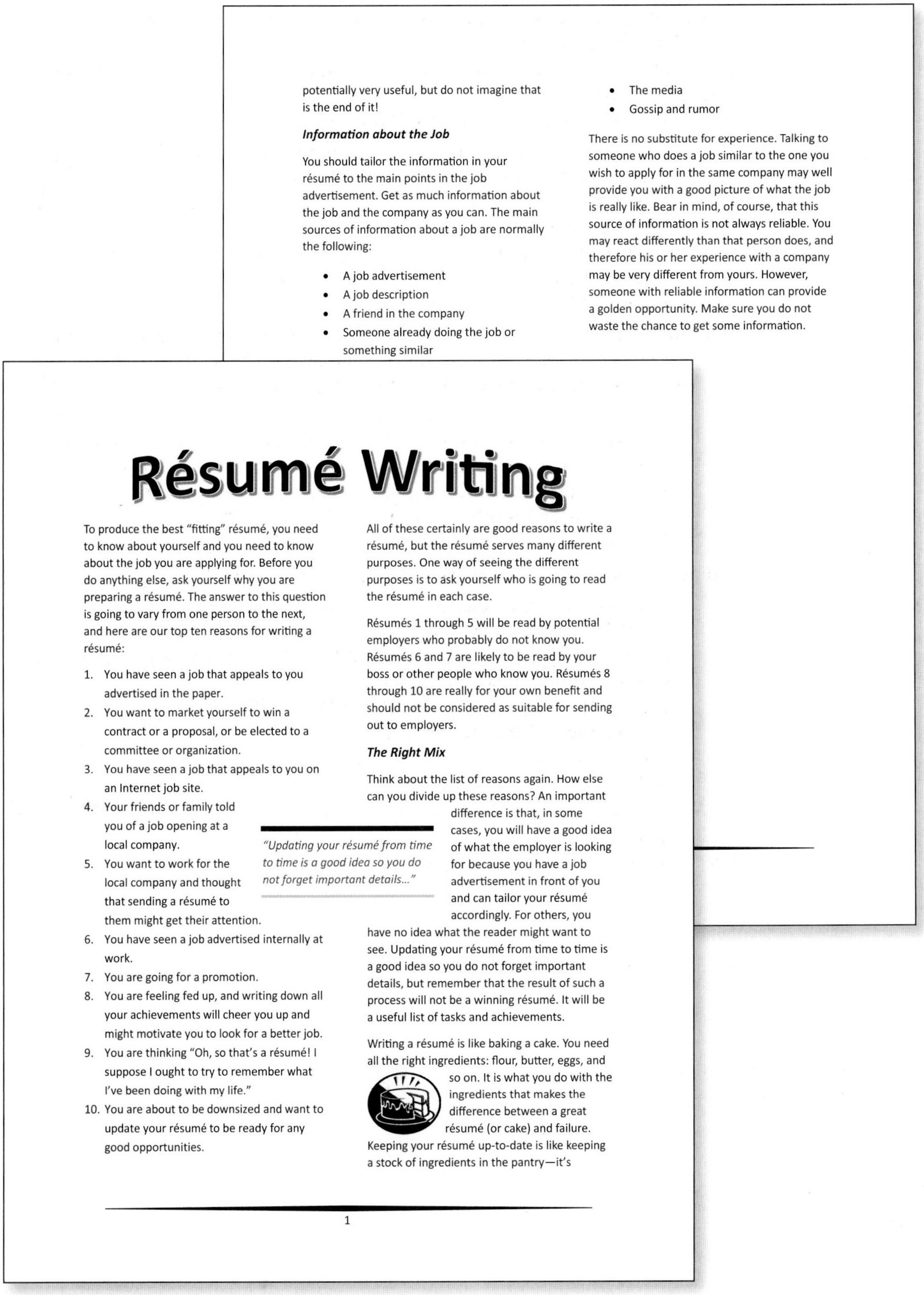

potentially very useful, but do not imagine that is the end of it!

Information about the Job

You should tailor the information in your résumé to the main points in the job advertisement. Get as much information about the job and the company as you can. The main sources of information about a job are normally the following:

- A job advertisement
- A job description
- A friend in the company
- Someone already doing the job or something similar
- The media
- Gossip and rumor

There is no substitute for experience. Talking to someone who does a job similar to the one you wish to apply for in the same company may well provide you with a good picture of what the job is really like. Bear in mind, of course, that this source of information is not always reliable. You may react differently than that person does, and therefore his or her experience with a company may be very different from yours. However, someone with reliable information can provide a golden opportunity. Make sure you do not waste the chance to get some information.

Résumé Writing

To produce the best "fitting" résumé, you need to know about yourself and you need to know about the job you are applying for. Before you do anything else, ask yourself why you are preparing a résumé. The answer to this question is going to vary from one person to the next, and here are our top ten reasons for writing a résumé:

1. You have seen a job that appeals to you advertised in the paper.
2. You want to market yourself to win a contract or a proposal, or be elected to a committee or organization.
3. You have seen a job that appeals to you on an Internet job site.
4. Your friends or family told you of a job opening at a local company.
5. You want to work for the local company and thought that sending a résumé to them might get their attention.
6. You have seen a job advertised internally at work.
7. You are going for a promotion.
8. You are feeling fed up, and writing down all your achievements will cheer you up and might motivate you to look for a better job.
9. You are thinking "Oh, so that's a résumé! I suppose I ought to try to remember what I've been doing with my life."
10. You are about to be downsized and want to update your résumé to be ready for any good opportunities.

"Updating your résumé from time to time is a good idea so you do not forget important details..."

All of these certainly are good reasons to write a résumé, but the résumé serves many different purposes. One way of seeing the different purposes is to ask yourself who is going to read the résumé in each case.

Résumés 1 through 5 will be read by potential employers who probably do not know you. Résumés 6 and 7 are likely to be read by your boss or other people who know you. Résumés 8 through 10 are really for your own benefit and should not be considered as suitable for sending out to employers.

The Right Mix

Think about the list of reasons again. How else can you divide up these reasons? An important difference is that, in some cases, you will have a good idea of what the employer is looking for because you have a job advertisement in front of you and can tailor your résumé accordingly. For others, you have no idea what the reader might want to see. Updating your résumé from time to time is a good idea so you do not forget important details, but remember that the result of such a process will not be a winning résumé. It will be a useful list of tasks and achievements.

Writing a résumé is like baking a cake. You need all the right ingredients: flour, butter, eggs, and so on. It is what you do with the ingredients that makes the difference between a great résumé (or cake) and failure. Keeping your résumé up-to-date is like keeping a stock of ingredients in the pantry—it's

1

Case Study Apply Your Skills

Part 1

You work for Honoré Financial Services and have been asked by the office manager, Jason Monroe, to prepare an information newsletter. Mr. Monroe has asked you to open the document named **Budget.docx** and then format it into columns. You are to determine the number of columns and any additional enhancements to the columns. He also wants you to proofread the document and correct any spelling and grammatical errors. Save the completed newsletter, naming it **WL1-C5-CS-Budget**, and then print the newsletter. When Mr. Monroe reviews the newsletter, he decides that it needs additional visual appeal. He wants you to insert visual elements in the newsletter, such as WordArt, clip art, a built-in text box, and/or a drop cap. Save **WL1-C5-CS-Budget.docx** and then print and close the document.

Part 2

Honoré Financial Services will be offering a free workshop titled Planning for Financial Success. Mr. Monroe has asked you to prepare an announcement containing information on the workshop. You determine what to include in the announcement such as the date, time, location, and so forth. Enhance the announcement by inserting a picture or clip art and by applying formatting such as font, paragraph alignment, and borders. Save the completed document and name it **WL1-C5-CS-Announce**. Print and then close the document.

Part 3

Honoré Financial Services has adopted a new slogan, and Mr. Monroe has asked you to create a shape with the new slogan inside. Experiment with the shadow and 3-D shape effects available on the DRAWING TOOLS FORMAT tab and then create a shape and enhance the shape with shadow and/or 3-D effects. Insert the new Honoré Financial Services slogan "Retirement Planning Made Easy" in the shape. Include any additional enhancements to improve the visual appeal of the shape and slogan. Save the completed document and name it **WL1-C5-CS-Slogan**. Print and then close the document.

Part 4

Mr. Monroe has asked you to prepare a document containing information on teaching children how to budget. Use the Internet to find websites and articles that provide information on how to teach children to budget their money. Write a synopsis of the information you find and include at least four suggestions on how to teach children to manage their money. Format the text in the document into newspaper columns. Add additional enhancements to improve the appearance of the document. Save the completed document and name it **WL1-C5-CS-ChildBudget**. Print and then close the document.

MICROSOFT®

WORD

Maintaining Documents

PERFORMANCE OBJECTIVES

Upon successful completion of Chapter 6, you will be able to:

- **Create and rename a folder**
- **Select, delete, copy, move, rename, and print documents**
- **Save documents in different file formats**
- **Open, close, arrange, split, maximize, minimize, and restore documents**
- **Insert a file into an open document**
- **Print specific pages and sections in a document**
- **Print multiple copies of a document**
- **Print envelopes and labels**
- **Create a document using a Word template**

Tutorials

6.1 Managing Folders
6.2 Managing Documents
6.3 Saving a Document in a Different Format
6.4 Working with Windows
6.5 Inserting a File
6.6 Previewing and Printing Documents
6.7 Creating and Printing Envelopes
6.8 Preparing Mailing Labels
6.9 Creating a Document Using a Word Template

Almost every company that conducts business maintains a filing system. The system may consist of documents, folders, and cabinets, or it may be a computerized filing system where information is stored on the computer's hard drive or other storage medium. Whatever type of filing system a business uses, daily maintenance of files is important to its operation. In this chapter, you will learn to maintain files (documents) in Word, performing such activities as creating additional folders and copying, moving, and renaming documents. You will also learn how to create and print documents, envelopes, and labels and create a document using a Word template. Model answers for this chapter's projects appear on the following pages.

Note: Before beginning the projects, copy to your storage medium the WL1C6 subfolder from the WL1 folder on the CD that accompanies this textbook and then make WL1C6 the active folder.

Model Answers

APARTMENT LEASE AGREEMENT
This Apartment Lease Agreement (hereinafter referred to as the "Agreement") is made and entered into this 30th day of September, 2015, by and between Monica Spellman, Lessor, and Jack Lowell, Lessee.
Term
Lessor leases to Lessee the described premises together with any and all appurtenances thereto, for a term of 1 year, such term beginning on October 1, 2015, and ending at 12 o'clock midnight on September 30, 2016.
Rent
The total rent for the term hereof is the sum of one thousand five hundred dollars ($1,500) payable on the 5th day of each month of the term. All such payments shall be made to Lessor on or before the due date and without demand.
Damage Deposit
Upon the due execution of this Agreement, Lessee shall deposit with Lessor the sum of seven hundred dollars ($700), receipt of which is hereby acknowledged by Lessor, as security for any damage caused to the Premises during the term hereof. Such deposit shall be returned to Lessee, without interest, and less any set off for damages to the Premises upon the termination of this Agreement.
Use of Premises
The Premises shall be used and occupied by Lessee and Lessee's immediate family, exclusively, as a private single family dwelling, and no part of the Premises shall be used at any time during the term of this Agreement by Lessee for the purpose of carrying on any business, profession, or trade of any kind, or for any purpose other than as a private single family dwelling. Lessee shall not allow any other person, other than Lessee's immediate family or transient relatives and friends who are guests, to use or occupy the Premises without first obtaining written consent to such use.

Project 1 Manage Documents

WL1-C6-P1-AptLease-PlainTxt.txt

APARTMENT LEASE AGREEMENT

This Apartment Lease Agreement (hereinafter referred to as the "Agreement") is made and entered into this 30th day of September, 2015, by and between Monica Spellman, Lessor, and Jack Lowell, Lessee.

Term

Lessor leases to Lessee the described premises together with any and all appurtenances thereto, for a term of 1 year, such term beginning on October 1, 2015, and ending at 12 o'clock midnight on September 30, 2016.

Rent

The total rent for the term hereof is the sum of one thousand five hundred dollars ($1,500) payable on the 5th day of each month of the term. All such payments shall be made to Lessor on or before the due date and without demand.

Damage Deposit

Upon the due execution of this Agreement, Lessee shall deposit with Lessor the sum of seven hundred dollars ($700), receipt of which is hereby acknowledged by Lessor, as security for any damage caused to the Premises during the term hereof. Such deposit shall be returned to Lessee, without interest, and less any set off for damages to the Premises upon the termination of this Agreement.

Use of Premises

The Premises shall be used and occupied by Lessee and Lessee's immediate family, exclusively, as a private single family dwelling, and no part of the Premises shall be used at any time during the term of this Agreement by Lessee for the purpose of carrying on any business, profession, or trade of any kind, or for any purpose other than as a private single family dwelling. Lessee shall not allow any other person, other than Lessee's immediate family or transient relatives and friends who are guests, to use or occupy the Premises without first obtaining written consent to such use.

WL1-C6-P1-AptLease-RichTxt.rtf

N

Northland Security Systems

NORTHLAND SECURITY SYSTEMS MISSION

Northland Security Systems is a full-service computer information security management and consulting firm offering a comprehensive range of services to help businesses protect electronic data.

SECURITY SERVICES

Northland Security Systems is dedicated to helping business, private and public, protect vital company data through on-site consultation, product installation and training, and 24-hour telephone support services. We show you how computer systems can be compromised and steps you can take to protect your company's computer system.

SECURITY SOFTWARE

We offer a range of security management software to protect your business against viruses, spyware, adware, intrusion, spam, and policy abuse.

Security Management Software

Security Software Training

On-site Consultation

24-Hour Telephone Support

WL1-C6-P1-NSS.pdf

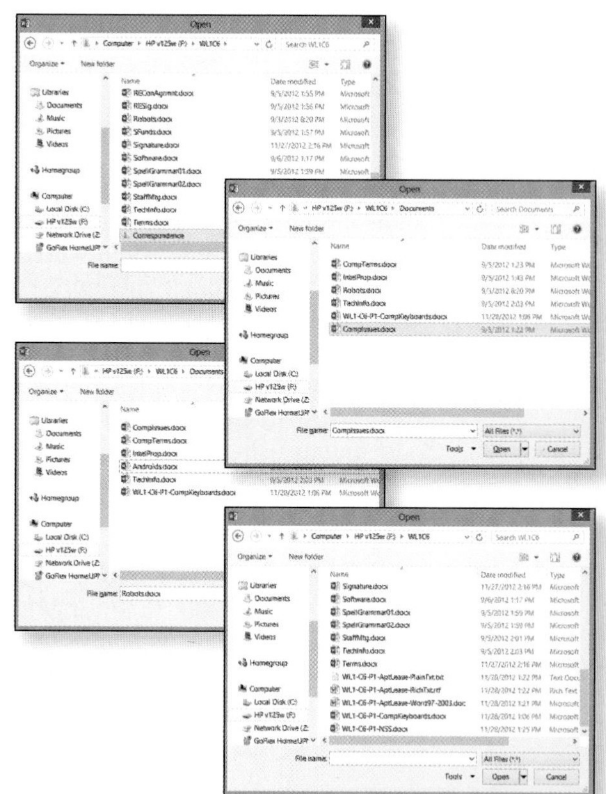

Open dialog box in Part a, Part d, Part e, and Part h

SECTION 1: GRAPHICS AND MULTIMEDIA SOFTWARE

Graphics and multimedia software allows both professional and home users to work with graphics, video, and audio. A variety of application software is focused in this area including painting and drawing software, image-editing software, video and audio editing software, and computer-aided design (CAD) software.

Painting and Drawing Software

Painting and drawing programs are available for both professional and home users. The more expensive professional versions typically include more features and greater capabilities than do the less expensive personal versions. Both painting programs and drawing programs provide an intuitive interface through which users can draw pictures, make sketches, create various shapes, and edit images. Programs typically include a variety of templates that simplify painting or drawing procedures.

Image-Editing Software

The market demand for image-editing programs has increased concurrently with the popularity of digital cameras. An image-editing program allows a user to touch up, modify, and enhance image quality. Once edited, images can be stored in a variety of forms and inserted into other files, such as letters, advertisements, and electronic scrapbooks.

Video and Audio Editing Software

As digital video cameras and other portable technologies have become more common, users have desired the ability to create and modify recorded video and audio clips using video and audio editing software. To create digital video or audio files, home users can often use basic video and audio editing software contained within their computer's operating system. Some users prefer the additional features of an application software package.

Computer-aided Design Software

Computer-aided design software is a sophisticated kind of drawing software, providing tools that enable professionals to create architectural, engineering, product, and scientific designs. Engineers can use the software to design buildings or bridges, and scientists can create graphical designs of plant, animal, and chemical structures. Some software programs display designs in three-dimensional form so they can be viewed from various angles. Once a design has been created, changes can be easily made until it is finalized.

SECTION 2: PERSONAL-USE SOFTWARE

When browsing computer stores, shoppers are likely to see numerous software applications designed for use in the household. Among the many products available are applications for writing letters, making out wills, designing a new home, landscaping a lawn, preparing and filing tax returns, and managing finances. Software suites are also available for home and personal use, although sometimes the suites available for home use do not contain all the features in business versions.

Page 1

ying bills, balancing checkbooks, keeping track of income and
other financial activities. The software also enables users to
me personal finance software provides online services available on
s to go online to learn the status of their investments and insurance
g transactions, including accessing and printing bank statements

alyzing federal and state tax status, as well as to prepare and
ide tips for preparing tax documents that can help identify
ome programs include actual state and federal tax forms for
forms provide instructions for downloading them from the
ns can be printed for mailing or filing electronically. Because federal
orms, users will probably need to obtain the software version for

and prepare a variety of legal documents, including wills and
documents, such as the forms required for real estate purchases or
ided in most packages are standard templates for various legal
g them.

ught about an increase in the availability of educational and
r learning and reference tools. Examples of educational and
naries, and tutorials.

ctionary at one time or another. An encyclopedia is a
led articles on a broad range of subjects. Before computers,
They are now available electronically and many new PCs include a

ining an alphabetical listing of words, with definitions that provide
Examples include *Webster's Dictionary* and *Webster's New World*

es, such as multi-language dictionaries, contain words
translation. Many dictionaries are available on CD.

torials. A tutorial is a form of instruction in which
cess. Tutorials are available for almost any subject,
processor, or write a letter. Once an electronic tutorial is
ayed on the screen. Many tutorials include graphics to

Project 2 Manage Multiple Documents

WL1-C6-P2-CompSoftware.docx

WENDY STEINBERG
4532 S 52 ST
BOSTON MA 21002-2334

GREGORY LINCOLN
4455 SIXTH AVE
BOSTON MA 21100-4409

Project 3 Create and Print Envelopes

WL1-C6-P3-Env.docx

DAVID LOWRY 12033 S 152 ST HOUSTON TX 77340	MARCELLA SANTOS 394 APPLE BLOSSOM FRIENDSWOOD TX 77533	KEVIN DORSEY 26302 PRAIRIE DR HOUSTON TX 77316
AL AND DONNA SASAKI 1392 PIONEER DR BAYTOWN TX 77903	JACKIE RHYNER 29039 107 AVE E HOUSTON TX 77302	MARK AND TINA ELLIS 607 FORD AVE HOUSTON TX 77307

Project 4 Create Mailing Labels

WL1-C6-P4-Labels.docx

Mr. and Mrs. Matthew Adair 12201 North 21st Street Jennings, LA 70563	Mr. and Mrs. Matthew Adair 12201 North 21st Street Jennings, LA 70563	Mr. and Mrs. Matthew Adair 12201 North 21st Street Jennings, LA 70563
Mr. and Mrs. Matthew Adair 12201 North 21st Street Jennings, LA 70563	Mr. and Mrs. Matthew Adair 12201 North 21st Street Jennings, LA 70563	Mr. and Mrs. Matthew Adair 12201 North 21st Street Jennings, LA 70563
Mr. and Mrs. Matthew Adair 12201 North 21st Street Jennings, LA 70563	Mr. and Mrs. Matthew Adair 12201 North 21st Street Jennings, LA 70563	Mr. and Mrs. Matthew Adair 12201 North 21st Street Jennings, LA 70563
Mr. and Mrs. Matthew Adair 12201 North 21st Street Jennings, LA 70563	Mr. and Mrs. Matthew Adair 12201 North 21st Street Jennings, LA 70563	Mr. and Mrs. Matthew Adair 12201 North 21st Street Jennings, LA 70563
Mr. and Mrs. Matthew Adair 12201 North 21st Street Jennings, LA 70563	Mr. and Mrs. Matthew Adair 12201 North 21st Street Jennings, LA 70563	Mr. and Mrs. Matthew Adair 12201 North 21st Street Jennings, LA 70563
Mr. and Mrs. Matthew Adair 12201 North 21st Street Jennings, LA 70563	Mr. and Mrs. Matthew Adair 12201 North 21st Street Jennings, LA 70563	Mr. and Mrs. Matthew Adair 12201 North 21st Street Jennings, LA 70563
Mr. and Mrs. Matthew Adair 12201 North 21st Street Jennings, LA 70563	Mr. and Mrs. Matthew Adair 12201 North 21st Street Jennings, LA 70563	Mr. and Mrs. Matthew Adair 12201 North 21st Street Jennings, LA 70563
Mr. and Mrs. Matthew Adair 12201 North 21st Street Jennings, LA 70563	Mr. and Mrs. Matthew Adair 12201 North 21st Street Jennings, LA 70563	Mr. and Mrs. Matthew Adair 12201 North 21st Street Jennings, LA 70563
Mr. and Mrs. Matthew Adair 12201 North 21st Street Jennings, LA 70563	Mr. and Mrs. Matthew Adair 12201 North 21st Street Jennings, LA 70563	Mr. and Mrs. Matthew Adair 12201 North 21st Street Jennings, LA 70563
Mr. and Mrs. Matthew Adair 12201 North 21st Street Jennings, LA 70563	Mr. and Mrs. Matthew Adair 12201 North 21st Street Jennings, LA 70563	Mr. and Mrs. Matthew Adair 12201 North 21st Street Jennings, LA 70563

WL1-C6-P4-LAProg.docx

WL1-C6-P4-BGCLabels.pdf

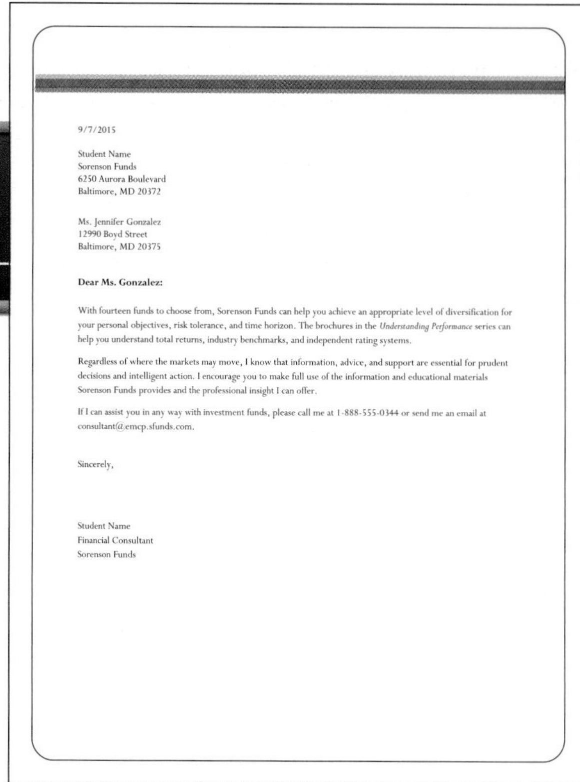

9/7/2015

Student Name
Sorenson Funds
6250 Aurora Boulevard
Baltimore, MD 20372

Ms. Jennifer Gonzalez
12990 Boyd Street
Baltimore, MD 20375

Dear Ms. Gonzalez:

With fourteen funds to choose from, Sorenson Funds can help you achieve an appropriate level of diversification for your personal objectives, risk tolerance, and time horizon. The brochures in the *Understanding Performance* series can help you understand total returns, industry benchmarks, and independent rating systems.

Regardless of where the markets may move, I know that information, advice, and support are essential for prudent decisions and intelligent action. I encourage you to make full use of the information and educational materials Sorenson Funds provides and the professional insight I can offer.

If I can assist you in any way with investment funds, please call me at 1-888-555-0344 or send me an email at consultant@emcp.sfunds.com.

Sincerely,

Student Name
Financial Consultant
Sorenson Funds

Project 5 Use a Template to Create a Business Letter

WL1-C6-P5-SFunds.docx

Project 1 Manage Documents — 8 Parts

You will perform a variety of file management tasks, including creating and renaming a folder; selecting and then deleting, copying, cutting, pasting, and renaming documents; deleting a folder; and opening, printing, and closing a document.

Maintaining Documents

Many file (document) management tasks can be completed at the Open dialog box (and some at the Save As dialog box). These tasks can include copying, moving, printing, and renaming documents; opening multiple documents; and creating a new folder and renaming a folder.

Directions and projects in this chapter assume that you are managing documents and folders on a USB flash drive or your computer's hard drive. If you are using your OneDrive, some of the document and folder management tasks may vary.

Using Print Screen

Keyboards contain a Print Screen key that will capture the contents of the screen into a file. That file can then be inserted in a Word document. Press the Print Screen key to capture the entire screen as an image or press Alt + Print Screen to capture only a dialog box or window that is open on the screen. The Print Screen feature is useful for file management in that you can print folder contents to help you keep track of documents and folders. To use the Print Screen key, display the desired information on the screen and then press the Print Screen key on your keyboard (generally located in the top row) or press Alt + Print Screen to capture a dialog box or window on the screen. When you press the Print Screen key or Alt + Print Screen, nothing seems to happen, but in fact, the screen image is captured in a file that is inserted in the Clipboard. To insert this file in a document, display a blank document and then click the Paste button in the Clipboard group on the HOME tab. You can also paste the file by right-clicking in a blank location in a document screen and then clicking the *Paste* option at the shortcut menu.

Creating a Folder

Word documents, like paper documents, should be grouped logically and placed in ***folders***. The main folder on a storage medium is called the ***root folder*** and you can create additional folders within the root folder. At the Open or Save As dialog box, documents display in the Content pane preceded by a document icon and folders display preceded by a folder icon. Create a new folder by clicking the New folder button located on the dialog box toolbar. This inserts a folder in the Content pane that contains the text *New folder*. Type a name for the folder (the name you type replaces *New folder*) and then press Enter. A folder name can contain a maximum of 255 characters. Numbers, spaces, and symbols can be used in the folder name, except those symbols explained in the *Naming a Document* section in Chapter 1.

To make the new folder active, double-click the folder name in the Open dialog box Content pane. The current folder path displays in the Address bar and includes the current folder as well as any previous folders. If the folder is located in an external storage device, the drive letter and name may display in the path. A right-pointing triangle displays to the right of each folder name in the Address bar. Click this right-pointing triangle and a drop-down list displays containing the names of any subfolders within the folder.

Quick Steps

Create a Folder
1. Display Open dialog box.
2. Click New folder button.
3. Type folder name.
4. Press Enter.

New folder

HINT

Display the Open dialog box with the keyboard shortcut Ctrl + F12.

Project 1a **Creating a Folder** **Part 1 of 8**

1. Open a blank document and then press Ctrl + F12 to display the Open dialog box.
2. In the *Computer* list in the Navigation pane, click the drive containing your storage medium. (You may need to scroll down the list to display the drive.)
3. Double-click the *WL1C6* folder in the Content pane.
4. Click the New folder button on the dialog box toolbar.
5. Type **Correspondence** and then press Enter.
6. Capture the Open dialog box as an image file and insert the file in a document by completing the following steps:
   a. With the Open dialog box displayed, hold down the Alt key and then press the Print Screen key on your keyboard (generally located in the top row of your keyboard).
   b. Close the Open dialog box.

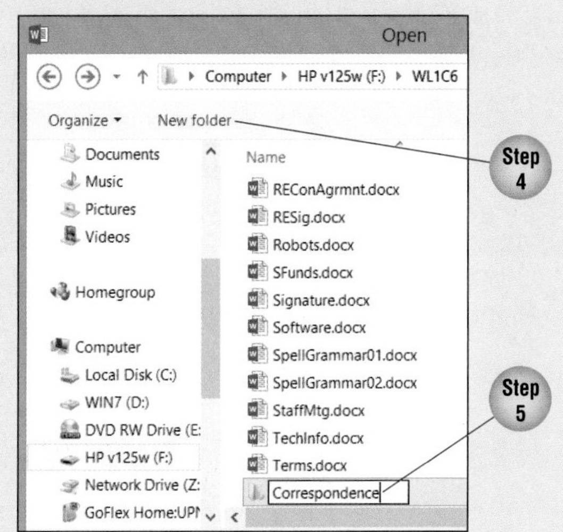

c. At the blank document, click the Paste button in the Clipboard group on the HOME tab. (If a blank document does not display on your screen, press Ctrl + N to open a blank document.)
d. With the print screen file inserted in the document, print the document by clicking the FILE tab, clicking the *Print* option, and then clicking the Print button at the Print backstage area.
7. Close the document without saving it.
8. Display the Open dialog box and make WL1C6 the active folder.

Renaming a Folder

Quick Steps

Rename a Folder
1. Display Open dialog box.
2. Right-click folder.
3. Click *Rename.*
4. Type new name.
5. Press Enter.

Organize ▾

Organize

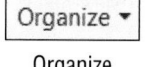

As you organize your files and folders, you may decide to rename a folder. Rename a folder using the Organize button on the toolbar in the Open or Save As dialog box or using a shortcut menu. To rename a folder using the Organize button, display the Open or Save As dialog box, click the folder you want to rename, click the Organize button located on the toolbar in the dialog box, and then click *Rename* at the drop-down list. This selects the folder name and inserts a border around the name. Type the new name for the folder and then press Enter. To rename a folder using a shortcut menu, display the Open dialog box, right-click the folder name in the Content pane, and then click *Rename* at the shortcut menu. Type a new name for the folder and then press Enter.

Project 1b **Renaming a Folder** **Part 2 of 8**

1. With the Open dialog box open, right-click the *Correspondence* folder name in the Content pane.
2. Click *Rename* at the shortcut menu.
3. Type **Documents** and then press Enter.

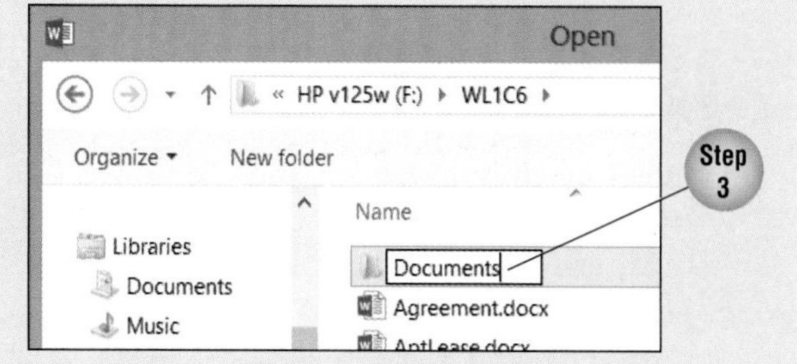

Selecting Documents

You can complete document management tasks on one document or selected documents. To select one document, display the Open dialog box and then click the desired document. To select several adjacent documents (documents that display next to each other), click the first document, hold down the Shift key, and then click the last document. To select documents that are not adjacent, click the first document, hold down the Ctrl key, click any other desired documents, and then release the Ctrl key.

Deleting Documents

At some point, you may want to delete documents from your storage medium or any other drive or folder in which you may be working. To delete a document, display the Open or Save As dialog box, select the document, click the Organize button on the toolbar, and then click *Delete* at the drop-down list. If you are deleting a document from an external drive such as a USB flash drive, click the Yes button at the message that displays asking you to confirm the deletion. This message does not display if you are deleting a document from the computer's hard drive. To delete a document using a shortcut menu, right-click the document name in the Content pane and then click *Delete* at the shortcut menu. If a confirmation message displays, click Yes.

Documents deleted from the hard drive are automatically sent to the Recycle Bin. If you accidentally send a document to the Recycle Bin, it can be easily restored. To free space on the drive, empty the Recycle Bin on a periodic basis. Restoring a document from or emptying the contents of the Recycle Bin is completed at the Windows desktop (not in Word). To display the Recycle Bin, minimize the Word window, display the Windows desktop, and then double-click the *Recycle Bin* icon located on the Windows desktop. At the Recycle Bin, you can restore a file and empty the Recycle Bin.

Quick Steps

Delete a Folder or Document

1. Display Open dialog box.
2. Click folder or document name.
3. Click Organize button.
4. Click *Delete* at drop-down list.
5. Click Yes.

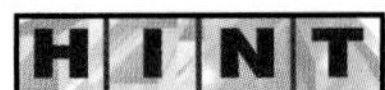

Remember to empty the Recycle Bin on a regular basis.

Project 1c **Selecting and Deleting Documents** **Part 3 of 8**

1. Open **FutureHardware.docx** and then save the document with Save As and name it **WL1-C6-P1-FutureHardware**.
2. Close **WL1-C6-P1-FutureHardware.docx**.
3. Delete **WL1-C6-P1-FutureHardware.docx** by completing the following steps:
   a. Display the Open dialog box.
   b. Click ***WL1-C6-P1-FutureHardware.docx*** to select it.
   c. Click the Organize button on the toolbar and then click *Delete* at the drop-down list.
   d. At the question asking if you want to delete **WL1-C6-P1-FutureHardware.docx**, click Yes. (This question will not display if you are deleting the file from your computer's hard drive.)
4. Delete selected documents by completing the following steps:
   a. At the Open dialog box, click ***CompCareers.docx***.
   b. Hold down the Shift key and then click ***CompEthics.docx***.
   c. Position the mouse pointer on a selected document and then click the right mouse button.
   d. At the shortcut menu that displays, click *Delete*.
   e. At the question asking if you want to delete the items, click Yes.

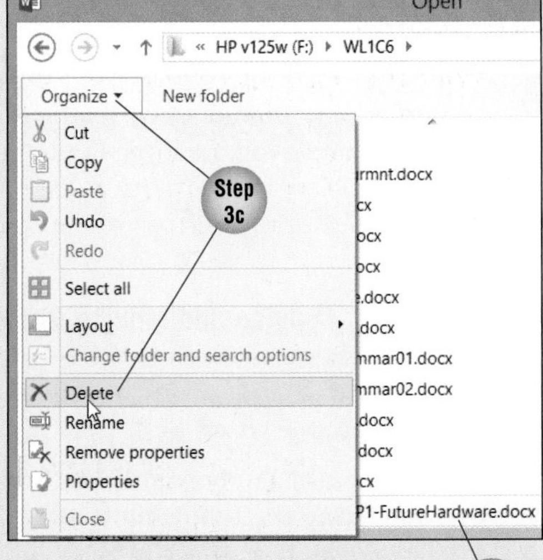

5. Open **CompKeyboards.docx** and then save the document with Save As and name it **WL1-C6-P1-CompKeyboards**.
6. Save a copy of the **WL1-C6-P1-CompKeyboards.docx** document in the Documents folder by completing the following steps.
   a. With **WL1-C6-P1-CompKeyboards.docx** open, press F12 to display the Save As dialog box.

b. At the Save As dialog box, double-click the *Documents* folder located at the beginning of the Content pane. (Folders are listed before documents.)
c. Click the Save button located in the lower right corner of the dialog box.

7. Close **WL1-C6-P1-CompKeyboards.docx**.
8. Press Ctrl + F12 to display the Open dialog box and then click *WL1C6* in the Address bar.

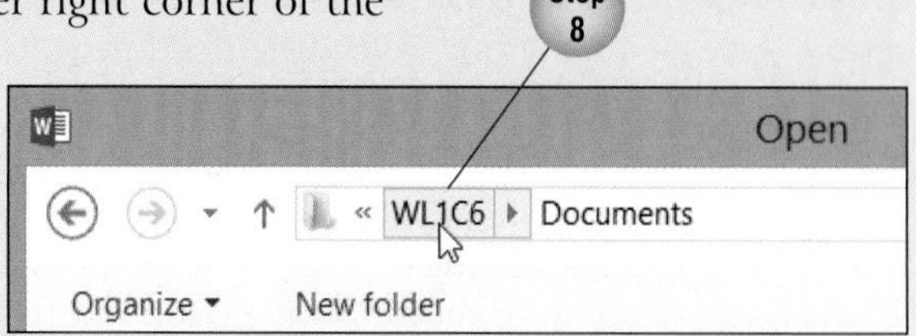

Quick Steps

Copy a Document
1. Display Open dialog box.
2. Right-click document name.
3. Click *Copy*.
4. Navigate to desired folder.
5. Right-click blank area in Content pane.
6. Click *Paste*.

Move Document
1. Display Open dialog box.
2. Right-click document name.
3. Click *Cut*.
4. Navigate to desired folder.
5. Right-click blank area in Content pane.
6. Click *Paste*.

Copying and Moving Documents

You can copy a document to another folder without opening the document first. To do this, use the *Copy* and *Paste* options from the Organize button drop-down list or the shortcut menu at the Open dialog box or the Save As dialog box. You can copy a document or selected documents into the same folder. When you do this, Word inserts a hyphen followed by the word *Copy* to the document name. You can copy one document or selected documents into the same folder.

Remove a document from one folder and insert it in another folder using the *Cut* and *Paste* options from the Organize button drop-down list or the shortcut menu at the Open dialog box. To do this with the Organize button, display the Open dialog box, select the desired document, click the Organize button, and then click *Cut* at the drop-down list. Navigate to the desired folder, click the Organize button, and then click *Paste* at the drop-down list. To do this with the shortcut menu, display the Open dialog box, position the arrow pointer on the document to be removed (cut), click the right mouse button, and then click *Cut* at the shortcut menu. Navigate to the desired folder, position the arrow pointer in a blank area in the Content pane, click the right mouse button, and then click *Paste* at the shortcut menu.

To move or copy files or folders on your OneDrive, go to onedrive.com, make sure you are logged in to your account, and then use the OneDrive.com toolbar to copy and/or move a document or folder to another location.

Project 1d **Copying and Moving Documents** **Part 4 of 8**

Note: If you are using your OneDrive, the steps for copying and moving files will vary from the steps in this project. Check with your instructor.

1. At the Open dialog box with WL1C6 the active folder, copy a document to another folder by completing the following steps:
   a. Click ***CompTerms.docx*** in the Content pane, click the Organize button, and then click *Copy* at the drop-down list.
   b. Navigate to the Documents folder by double-clicking *Documents* at the beginning of the Content pane.
   c. Click the Organize button and then click *Paste* at the drop-down list.
2. Change back to the WL1C6 folder by clicking *WL1C6* in the Address bar.
3. Copy several documents to the Documents folder by completing the following steps:
   a. Click once on ***IntelProp.docx***. (This selects the document.)

b. Hold down the Ctrl key, click ***Robots.docx***, click ***TechInfo.docx***, and then release the Ctrl key. (You may need to scroll down the Content pane to display the three documents and then select the documents.)
c. Position the arrow pointer on one of the selected documents, click the right mouse button, and then click *Copy* at the shortcut menu.
d. Double-click the *Documents* folder.
e. Position the arrow pointer in any blank area in the Content pane, click the right mouse button, and then click *Paste* at the shortcut menu.

4. Click *WL1C6* in the Address bar.
5. Move **CompIssues.docx** to the Documents folder by completing the following steps:
   a. Position the arrow pointer on ***CompIssues.docx***, click the right mouse button, and then click *Cut* at the shortcut menu.
   b. Double-click *Documents* to make it the active folder.
   c. Position the arrow pointer in any blank area in the Content pane, click the right mouse button, and then click *Paste* at the shortcut menu.
6. Capture the Open dialog box as an image file and insert the file in a document by completing the following steps:
   a. With the Open dialog box displayed, press Alt + Print Screen.
   b. Close the Open dialog box.
   c. At a blank document, click the Paste button in the Clipboard group on the HOME tab. (If a blank document does not display on your screen, press Ctrl + N to open a blank document.)
   d. With the print screen file inserted in the document, print the document by clicking the FILE tab, clicking the *Print* option, and then clicking the Print button at the Print backstage area.
7. Close the document without saving it.
8. Display the Open dialog box and make WL1C6 the active folder.

Renaming Documents

At the Open dialog box, use the *Rename* option from the Organize button drop-down list to give a document a different name. The *Rename* option changes the name of the document and keeps it in the same folder. To use Rename, display the Open dialog box, click once on the document to be renamed, click the Organize button, and then click *Rename* at the drop-down list. This causes a black border to surround the document name and the name to be selected. Type the desired name and then press Enter. You can also rename a document by right-clicking the document name at the Open dialog box and then clicking *Rename* at the shortcut menu. Type the desired name for the document and then press the Enter key.

Quick Steps

Rename a Document
1. Display Open dialog box.
2. Click document name.
3. Click Organize button and then *Rename*.
4. Type new name.
5. Press Enter.

Open a recently opened document by clicking the FILE tab, clicking the *Open* option, and then clicking the document in the Recent Documents list.

Deleting a Folder

As you learned earlier in this chapter, you can delete a document or several selected documents. Delete a folder and all its contents in the same manner as you would delete a document.

Opening Multiple Documents

To open more than one document, select the documents in the Open dialog box, and then click the Open button. You can also open multiple documents by positioning the arrow pointer on one of the selected documents, clicking the right mouse button, and then clicking *Open* at the shortcut menu.

Project 1e Renaming and Opening Documents and Deleting a Folder

1. Rename a document located in the Documents folder by completing the following steps:
   a. At the Open dialog box with the WL1C6 folder open, double-click the *Documents* folder to make it active.
   b. Click once on ***Robots.docx*** to select it.
   c. Click the Organize button.
   d. Click *Rename* at the drop-down list.
   e. Type **Androids** and then press the Enter key.

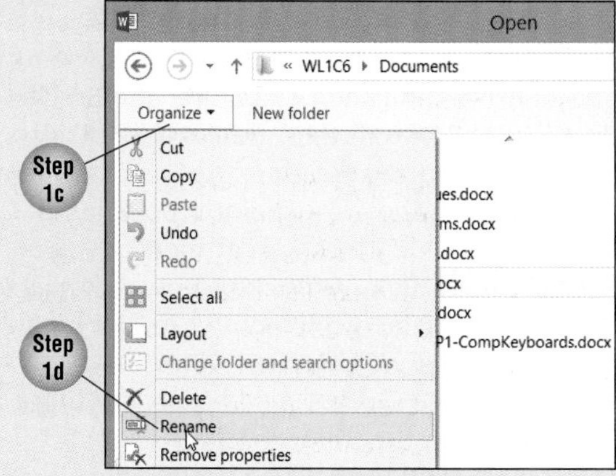

2. Capture the Open dialog box as an image file and insert the file in a document by completing the following steps:
   a. Press Alt + Print Screen.
   b. Close the Open dialog box.
   c. At a blank document, click the Paste button in the Clipboard group on the HOME tab. (If a blank document does not display on your screen, press Ctrl + N to open a blank document.)
   d. With the print screen file inserted in the document, print the document.
3. Close the document without saving it.
4. Display the Open dialog box and make WL1C6 the active folder.
5. At the Open dialog box, click the *Documents* folder to select it.
6. Click the Organize button and then click *Delete* at the drop-down list.
7. If a message displays asking if you want to remove the folder and its contents, click Yes.
8. Select ***CompKeyboards.docx***, ***CompSoftware.docx***, and ***CompTerms.docx***.
9. Click the Open button located toward the lower right corner of the dialog box.
10. Close the open documents.

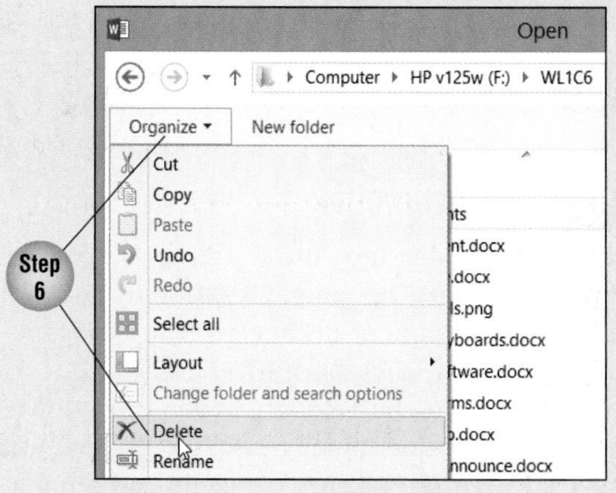

Saving a Document in a Different Format

When you save a document, the document is saved automatically as a Word document with the .docx file extension. If you need to share a document with someone who is using a different word processing program or a different version of Word, you may want to save the document in another format. At the Export backstage area, click the *Change File Type* option and the backstage area displays as shown in Figure 6.1.

With options in the *Document File Types* section below the *Change File Type* heading, you can choose to save a Word document with the default file format, save the document in a previous version of Word, save the document in the OpenDocument Text format, or save the document as a template. The OpenDocument Text format is an XML-based file format for displaying, storing, and editing files such as word processing, spreadsheet, and presentation files. OpenDocument Text format is free from any licensing, royalty payments, or other restrictions, and since technology changes at a rapid pace, saving a document in the OpenDocument Text format ensures that the information in the file can be accessed, retrieved, and used now and in the future.

Additional file types are available in the *Other File Types* section. If you need to send your document to another user who does not have access to Microsoft Word, consider saving the document in plain text or rich text file format. Use the *Plain Text (*.txt)* option to save the document with all formatting stripped, which is good for universal file exchange. Use the *Rich Text Format (*.rtf)* option to save the document with most of the character formatting applied to text in the document, such as bold, italic, underline, bullets, and fonts as well as some paragraph formatting. Before the widespread use of Adobe's portable document format (PDF), rich text format was the most portable file format used to exchange files. With the *Single File Web Page (*.mht, *.mhtml)* option, you can save your document as a single-page web document. Click the *Save as Another File Type* option and the Save As dialog box displays. Click the *Save as type* option box and a drop-down list displays with a variety of available file type options.

Quick Steps

Save a Document in a Different Format

1. Click FILE tab.
2. Click *Export* option.
3. Click *Change File Type* option.
4. Click desired format in *Document File Types* or *Other File Types* section.
5. Click Save As button.

Figure 6.1 Export Backstage Area with *Change File Type* Option Selected

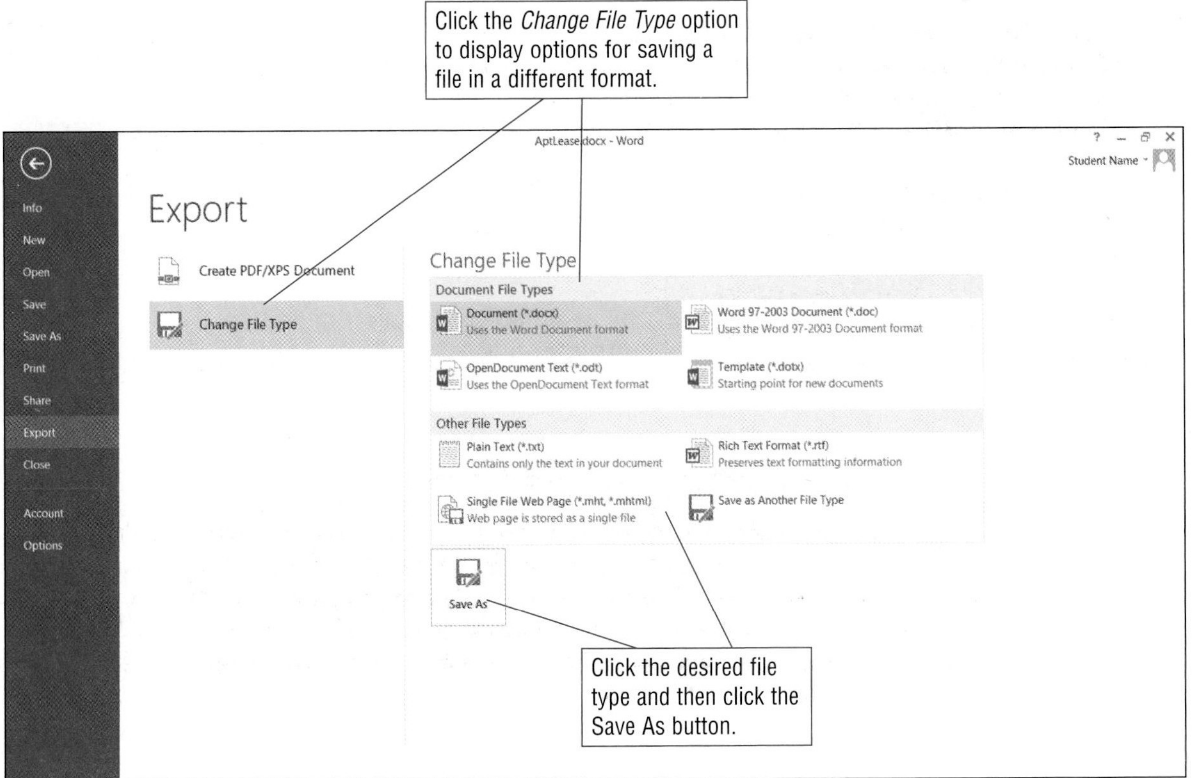

Project 1f Saving a Document in Different File Formats Part 6 of 8

1. Open **AptLease.docx** and then save the document in Word 97-2003 format by completing the following steps:
   a. Click the FILE tab and then click the *Export* option.
   b. At the Export backstage area, click the *Change File Type* option.
   c. Click the *Word 97-2003 Document (*.doc)* option in the *Document File Types* section and then click the Save As button.

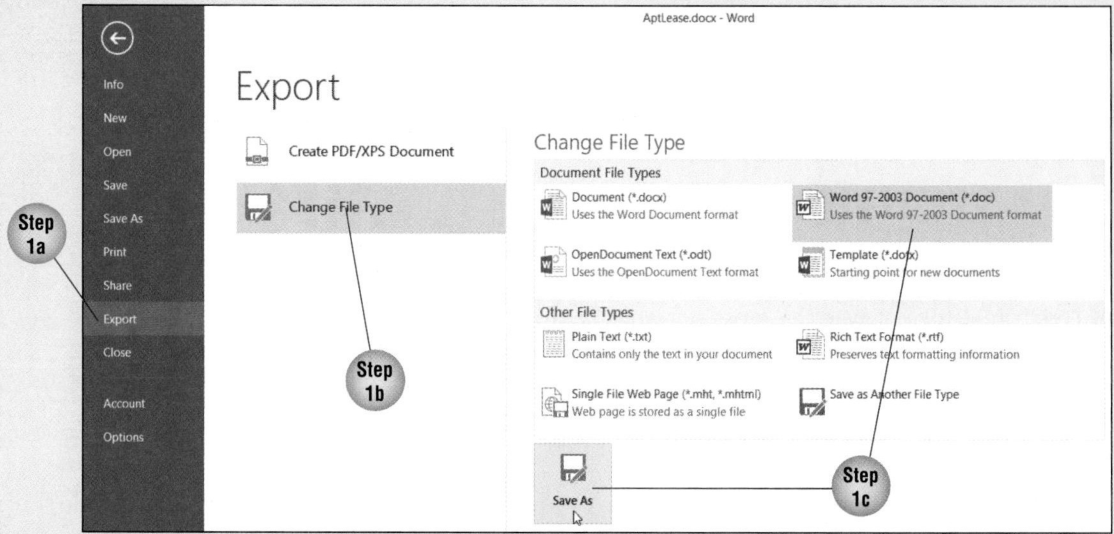

   d. At the Save As dialog box with the *Save as type* option changed to *Word 97-2003 Document (*.doc)*, type **WL1-C6-P1-AptLease-Word97-2003** in the *File name* text box and then press Enter.
2. At the document, notice the title bar displays the words *[Compatibility Mode]* after the document name.
3. Click the DESIGN tab and notice the Themes, Colors, and Fonts buttons are dimmed. (This is because the themes features were not available in Word 97 through 2003.)
4. Close **WL1-C6-P1-AptLease-Word97-2003.doc**.
5. Open **AptLease.docx**
6. Save the document in plain text format by completing the following steps:
   a. Click the FILE tab and then click the *Export* option.
   b. At the Export backstage area, click the *Change File Type* option.
   c. Click the *Plain Text (*.txt)* option in the *Other File Types* section and then click the Save As button.
   d. At the Save As dialog box, type **WL1-C6-P1-AptLease-PlainTxt** and then press Enter.
   e. At the File Conversion dialog box, click OK.
7. Close **WL1-C6-P1-AptLease-PlainTxt.txt**.
8. Display the Open dialog box and, if necessary, display all files. To do this, click the file type button at the right side of the *File name* text box and then click *All Files (*.*)* at the drop-down list.
9. Double-click ***WL1-C6-P1-AptLease-PlainTxt.txt***. (If a File Conversion dialog box displays, click OK. Notice that the character and paragraph formatting has been removed from the document.)
10. Close **WL1-C6-P1-AptLease-PlainTxt.txt**.

In addition to options in the Export backstage area with the *Change File Type* option selected, you can save a document in a different format using the *Save as type* option box at the Save As dialog box. Click the *Save as type* option box, and a drop-down list displays containing all available file formats for saving a document. Click the desired format and then click the Save button.

Quick Steps

Save a Document in a Different Format at the Save As Dialog Box

1. Display Save As dialog box.
2. Type document name.
3. Click *Save as type* option box.
4. Click desired format.
5. Click Save button.

Project 1g **Saving a Document in a Different Format at the Save As Dialog Box** **Part 7 of 8**

1. Open **AptLease.docx**.
2. Save the document in rich text format by completing the following steps:
   a. Press F12 to display the Save As dialog box.
   b. At the Save As dialog box, type **WL1-C6-P1-AptLease-RichTxt** in the *File name* text box.
   c. Click in the *Save as type* option box.
   d. Click *Rich Text Format (*.rtf)* at the drop-down list.
   e. Click the Save button.
3. Close the document.
4. Display the Open dialog box and, if necessary, display all files.
5. Double-click ***WL1-C6-P1-AptLease-RichTxt.rtf***. (Notice that the formatting was retained in the document.)
6. Close the document.

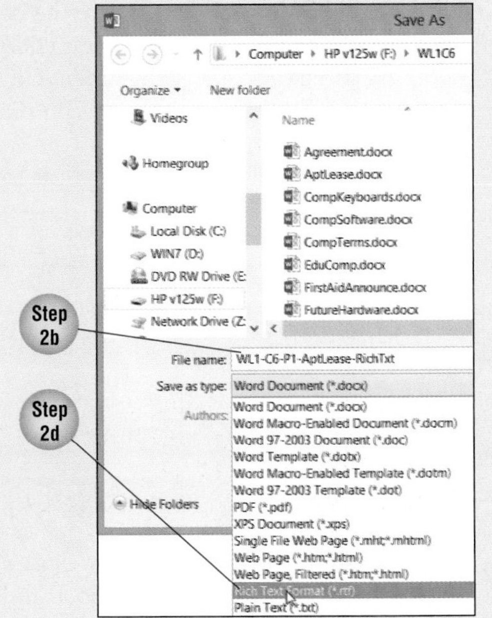

Saving in PDF/XPS Format

A Word document can be saved in the PDF or XPS file format. PDF stands for *portable document format* and is a file format that preserves fonts, formatting, and images in a printer-friendly version that looks the same on most computers. A person who receives a Word file saved in PDF format does not need to have the Word application on his or her computer to open, read, and print the file. Exchanging PDF files is a popular method for collaborating with others, since this file type has cross-platform compatibility, allowing users to open PDF files on a Windows-based personal computer, Macintosh computer, tablet, and smartphone. The XML paper specification (XPS) format is a fixed-layout format with all formatting preserved (similar to PDF) that was developed by Microsoft.

To save a document in PDF or XPS format, click the FILE tab, click the *Export* option, and then click the Create PDF/XPS button. This displays the Publish as PDF or XPS dialog box with the *PDF (*.pdf)* option selected in the *Save as type* option box.

Quick Steps

Save a Document in PDF/XPS Format

1. Click FILE tab.
2. Click *Export* option.
3. Click Create PDF/XPS button.
4. At Publish as PDF or XPS dialog box, specify PDF or XPS format.
5. Click Publish button.

If you want to save the document in XPS format, click the *Save as type* option box and then click *XPS Document (*.xps)* at the drop-down list. At the Save As dialog box, type a name in the *File name* text box and then click the Publish button.

A PDF file will open in Adobe Reader, Internet Explorer, Microsoft Word, and Windows Reader. An XPS file will open in Internet Explorer, Windows Reader, and XPS Viewer. One method for opening a PDF or XPS file is to open File Explorer, navigate to the folder containing the file, right-click on the file, and then point to *Open with*. This displays a side menu with the programs you can choose from to open the file. You can open a PDF file in Word and make edits to the file, but you cannot open an XPS file in Word.

Project 1h Saving a Document in PDF Format and Editing a PDF File in Word — Part 8 of 8

1. Open **NSS.docx** and then save the document in PDF format by completing the following steps:
   a. Click the FILE tab and then click the *Export* option.
   b. At the Export backstage area, click the Create PDF/XPS button.
   c. At the Publish as PDF or XPS dialog box, make sure *PDF (*.pdf)* is selected in the *Save as type* option box and that the *Open file after publishing* check box contains a check mark and then click the Publish button.

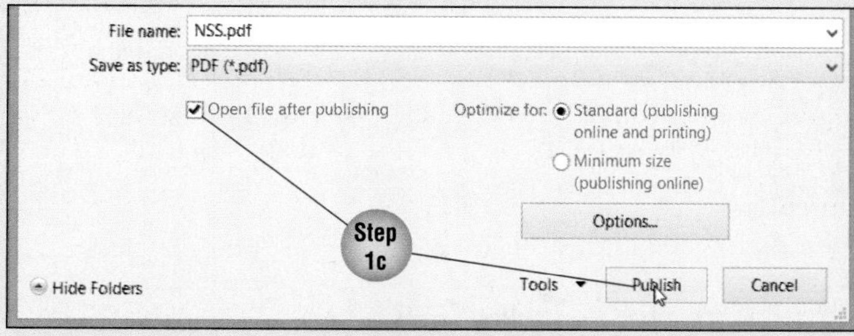

2. Scroll through the document in Adobe Reader and then click the Close button in the upper right corner of the window to close Adobe Reader. (If Adobe Reader is not installed on your computer, the file will open in Windows Reader. Close the Windows Reader window by positioning the mouse pointer at the top of the window [mouse turns into a hand], holding down the left mouse button, dragging down to the bottom of the screen, and then releasing the mouse button. At the Windows Start screen, click the Desktop icon.)
3. Close **NSS.docx**.
4. Open the **NSS.pdf** file in Windows Reader by completing the following steps:
   a. Click the File Explorer button on the Taskbar.
   b. At the Libraries dialog box, navigate to the WL1C6 folder on your storage medium.
   c. Right-click the **NSS.pdf** file in the Content pane, point to *Open with* at the shortcut menu, and then click *Reader* at the side menu.

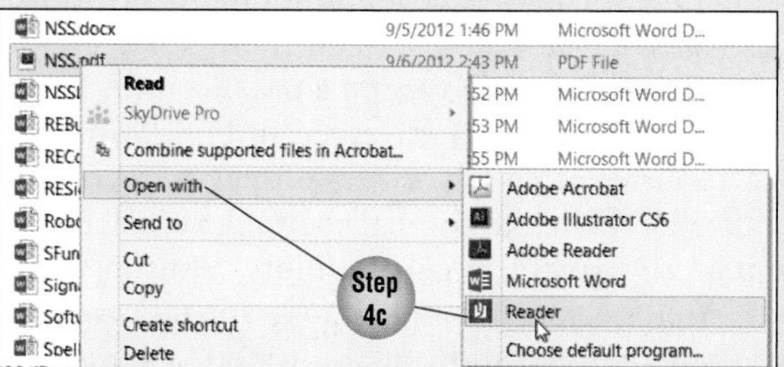

   d. After looking at the file in Windows Reader, close the window by positioning the mouse pointer at the top of the window (mouse turns into a hand), holding down the left mouse button, dragging down to the bottom of the screen, and then releasing the mouse button.

e. At the Windows Start screen, click the Desktop icon. (This step may vary.)
f. Close the WL1C6 window.
5. In Word, open the **NSS.pdf** file you saved to your WL1C6 folder. At the message that displays telling you that Word will convert the file to an editable Word document, click the OK button.
6. Notice that the formatting of the text is slightly different than the original formatting and that the graphic was moved to the second page. Edit the file by completing the following steps:
a. Click the DESIGN tab and then click the *Lines (Distinctive)* style set.
b. Delete the text "We are" in the text below the first heading and replace it with **Northland Security Systems is**.
7. Save the file with Save As and name it **WL1-C6-P1-NSS**. (The file will save in the *.docx* file format.)
8. Print and then close **WL1-C6-P1-NSS.docx**.
9. Display the Open dialog box, capture the Open dialog box as an image file, and then close the Open dialog box. Press Ctrl + N to open a blank document, paste the image file in the document, print the document, and then close the document without saving it.

Project 2 Manage Multiple Documents — 7 Parts

You will work with windows by arranging, maximizing, restoring, and minimizing windows; move selected text between split windows; compare formatting of documents side by side; print specific text, pages, and multiple copies; and create and modify document properties.

Working with Windows

In Word, you can open multiple documents and move the insertion point between the documents. You can also move and copy information between documents or compare the contents of documents. The maximum number of documents that you can have open at one time depends on the memory of your computer system and the amount of data in each document. When you open a new window, it displays on top of any previously opened window(s). Once you have multiple windows open, you can resize the windows to see all or a portion of each on the screen.

When a document is open, a Word button displays on the Taskbar. Hover the mouse over this button and a thumbnail of the document displays above the button. If you have more than one document open, another Word button displays behind the first button in a cascaded manner with only a portion of the button displaying at the right side of the first button. If you have multiple documents open, hovering the mouse over the Word buttons on the Taskbar will cause thumbnails of all of the documents to display above the buttons. To change to the desired document, click the thumbnail that represents the document.

Press Ctrl + F6 to switch between open documents.

Press Ctrl + W or Ctrl + F4 to close the active document window.

Another method for determining what documents are open is to click the VIEW tab and then click the Switch Windows button in the Window group. The document name that displays in the list with the check mark in front of it is the ***active document***. The active document contains the insertion point. To make one of the other documents active, click the document name. If you are using the keyboard, type the number shown in front of the desired document.

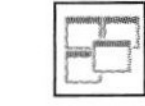

Switch Windows

Arranging Windows

Quick Steps

Arrange Windows
1. Open documents.
2. Click VIEW tab.
3. Click Arrange All button.

Arrange All

If you have several documents open, you can arrange them so a portion of each document displays. The portions that display are the title (if present) and the opening paragraph of each document. To arrange a group of open documents, click the VIEW tab and then click the Arrange All button in the Window group.

Maximizing, Restoring, and Minimizing Documents

Maximize Minimize

Restore

Use the Maximize and Minimize buttons located in the upper right corner of the active document to change the size of the window. The two buttons are located to the left of the Close button. (The Close button is located in the upper right corner of the screen and contains an X.)

If you arrange all open documents and then click the Maximize button in the active document, the active document expands to fill the document screen. In addition, the Maximize button changes to the Restore button. To return the active document back to its size before it was maximized, click the Restore button. If you click the Minimize button in the active document, the document is reduced and a button displays on the Taskbar representing the document. To maximize a document that has been minimized, click the button on the Taskbar representing the document.

Project 2a **Arranging, Maximizing, Restoring, and Minimizing Windows** **Part 1 of 7**

Note: If you are using Word on a network system that contains a virus checker, you may not be able to open multiple documents at once. Continue by opening each document individually.

1. Open the following documents: **AptLease.docx**, **CompSoftware.docx**, **IntelProp.docx**, and **NSS.docx**.
2. Arrange the windows by clicking the VIEW tab and then clicking the Arrange All button in the Window group.
3. Make **AptLease.docx** the active document by clicking the Switch Windows button in the Window group on the VIEW tab of the document at the top of your screen, and then clicking ***AptLease.docx*** at the drop-down list.
4. Close **AptLease.docx**.
5. Make **IntelProp.docx** active and then close it.
6. Make **CompSoftware.docx** active and minimize it by clicking the Minimize button in the upper right corner of the active window.
7. Maximize **NSS.docx** by clicking the Maximize button (located immediately left of the Close button).
8. Close **NSS.docx**.
9. Restore **CompSoftware.docx** by clicking the button on the Taskbar representing the document.
10. Maximize **CompSoftware.docx**.

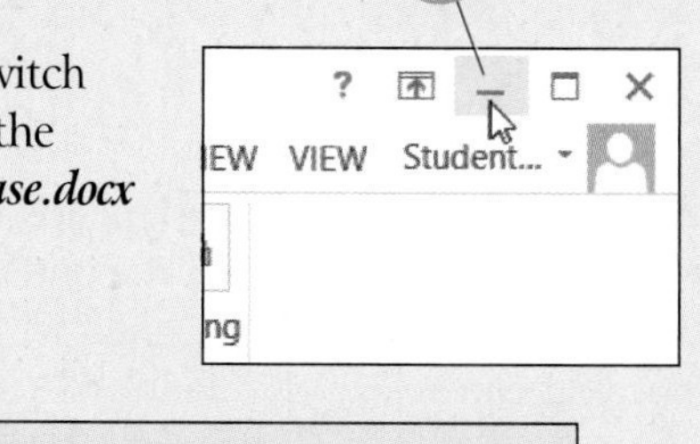

Splitting a Window

You can divide a window into two ***panes***, which is helpful if you want to view different parts of the same document at one time. You may want to display an outline for a report in one pane, for example, and the portion of the report that you are editing in the other. The original window is split into two panes that extend horizontally across the screen.

Split a window by clicking the VIEW tab and then clicking the Split button in the Window group. This splits the window in two with a split bar and another horizontal ruler. You can change the location of the split bar by positioning the mouse pointer on the split bar until it displays as an up-and-down-pointing arrow with two small lines in the middle, holding down the left mouse button, dragging to the desired position, and then releasing the mouse button.

Quick Steps

Split a Window
1. Open document.
2. Click VIEW tab.
3. Click Split button.

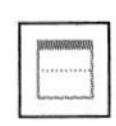

Split

When a window is split, the insertion point is positioned in the bottom pane. To move the insertion point to the other pane with the mouse, position the I-beam pointer in the other pane, and then click the left mouse button. To remove the split bar from the document, click the VIEW tab and then click the Remove Split button in the Window group. You can also double-click the split bar or drag the split bar to the top or bottom of the screen.

Project 2b **Moving Selected Text between Split Windows** **Part 2 of 7**

1. With **CompSoftware.docx** open, save the document with Save As and name it **WL1-C6-P2-CompSoftware**.
2. Click the VIEW tab and then click the Split button in the Window group.
3. Move the first section below the second section by completing the following steps:
   a. Click in the top pane and then click the HOME tab.
   b. Select the *SECTION 1: PERSONAL-USE SOFTWARE* section from the title to right above *SECTION 2: GRAPHICS AND MULTIMEDIA SOFTWARE*.
   c. Click the Cut button in the Clipboard group in the HOME tab.
   d. Click in the bottom pane and then move the insertion point to the end of the document.
   e. Click the Paste button in the Clipboard group on the HOME tab.
   f. Change the number in the two titles to *SECTION 1: GRAPHICS AND MULTIMEDIA SOFTWARE* and *SECTION 2: PERSONAL-USE SOFTWARE*.
4. Remove the split from the window by clicking the VIEW tab and then clicking the Remove Split button in the Window group.
5. Press Ctrl + Home to move the insertion point to the beginning of the document.

Viewing Documents Side by Side

If you want to compare the contents of two documents, open both documents, click the VIEW tab, and then click the View Side by Side button in the Window group. Both documents are arranged in the screen side by side, as shown in Figure 6.2. By default, synchronous scrolling is active. With this feature active, scrolling in one document causes the same scrolling to occur in the other document. This feature is useful in situations where you want to compare text, formatting, or other features between documents. If you want to scroll in one document and not the other, click the Synchronous Scrolling button in the Window group to turn it off.

Quick Steps

View Side by Side
1. Open two documents.
2. Click VIEW tab.
3. Click View Side by Side button.

View Side by Side

Synchronous Scrolling

Figure 6.2 Viewing Documents Side by Side

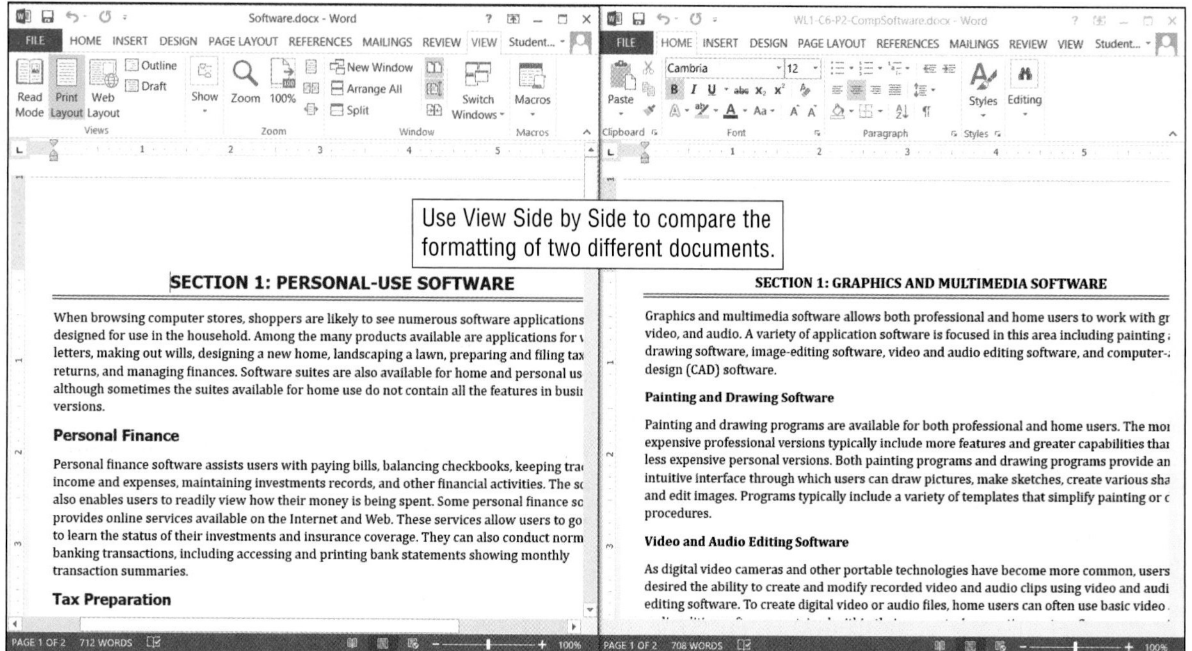

Project 2c Viewing Documents Side by Side

Part 3 of 7

1. With **WL1-C6-P2-CompSoftware.docx** open, open **Software.docx**.
2. Click the VIEW tab and then click the View Side by Side button in the Window group.
3. Scroll through both documents simultaneously. Notice the difference between the two documents. (The titles and headings are set in different fonts and colors.) Select and then format the title and headings in **WL1-C6-P2-CompSoftware.docx** so they match the formatting in **Software.docx**. ***Hint: Use the Format Painter to copy the formats.***
4. Save **WL1-C6-P2-CompSoftware.docx**.
5. Turn off synchronous scrolling by clicking the Synchronous Scrolling button in the Window group on the VIEW tab.
6. Scroll through the document and notice that the other document does not scroll.
7. Make **Software.docx** the active document and then close it.

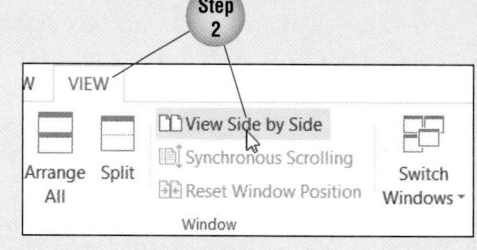

Step 2

VIEW
Arrange All
Split
View Side by Side
Synchronous Scrolling
Reset Window Position
Switch Windows
Window

Quick Steps

Open a New Window
1. Open document.
2. Click VIEW tab.
3. Click New Window button.

New Window

Opening a New Window

In addition to splitting a document to view two locations of the same document, you can open a new window containing the same document. When you open a new window, the document name in the Title bar displays followed by *:2*. The document name in the original window displays followed by *:1*. Any change you make to the document in one window is reflected in the document in the other window. If you want to view both documents on the screen, click the Arrange All button to arrange them horizontally or click the View Side by Side button to arrange them vertically.

Project 2d Opening a New Window

Part 4 of 7

1. With **WL1-C6-P2-CompSoftware.docx** open, open a new window by clicking the New Window button in the Window group on the VIEW tab. (Notice the document name in the Title bar displays followed by *:2*.)
2. Click the VIEW tab and then click the View Side by Side button in the Window group.
3. Click the Synchronous Scrolling button to turn off synchronous scrolling.
4. With the **WL1-C6-P2-CompSoftware.docx:2** window active, look at the first paragraph of text and notice the order in which the software is listed in the last sentence (painting and drawing software, image-editing software, video and audio editing software, and computer-aided design [CAD] software).
5. Click in the **WL1-C6-P2-CompSoftware.docx:1** window and then cut and paste the headings and text so the software displays in the order listed in the paragraph.
6. Click the Save button on the Quick Access toolbar.
7. Close the second version of the document by hovering the mouse pointer over the Word buttons on the Taskbar and then clicking the Close button in the upper right corner of the **WL1-C6-P2-CompSoftware.docx:2** thumbnail (the thumbnail that displays above the Word button on the Taskbar).

Inserting a File

If you want to insert the contents of one document into another, use the Object button in the Text group on the INSERT tab. Click the Object button arrow and then click *Text from File* and the Insert File dialog box displays. This dialog box contains similar features as the Open dialog box. Navigate to the desired folder and then double-click the document you want to insert in the open document.

Quick Steps

Insert a File
1. Click INSERT tab.
2. Click Object button arrow.
3. Click *Text from File.*
4. Navigate to folder.
5. Double-click document.

Object

Project 2e Inserting a File

Part 5 of 7

1. With **WL1-C6-P2-CompSoftware.docx** open, move the insertion point to the end of the document.
2. Insert a file into the open document by completing the following steps:
   a. Click the INSERT tab.
   b. Click the Object button arrow in the Text group.
   c. Click *Text from File* at the drop-down list.
   d. At the Insert File dialog box, navigate to the WL1C6 folder and then double-click *EduComp.docx*.
3. Save **WL1-C6-P2-CompSoftware.docx**.

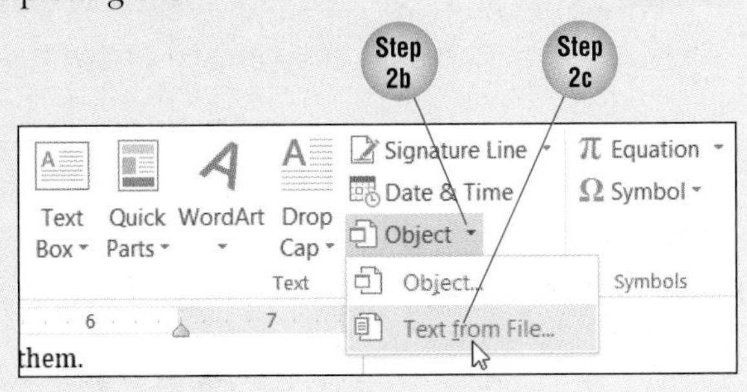

Printing and Previewing a Document

Display the Print backstage area with the keyboard shortcut Ctrl + P.

Use options at the Print backstage area, shown in Figure 6.3, to specify what you want to print and also preview the pages before printing. To display the Print backstage area, click the FILE tab and then click the *Print* option.

Previewing Pages in a Document

Zoom to Page

When you display the Print backstage area, a preview of the page where the insertion point is positioned displays at the right side (see Figure 6.3). Click the Next Page button (right-pointing triangle), located below and to the left of the page, to view the next page in the document, and click the Previous Page button (left-pointing triangle) to display the previous page in the document. Use the Zoom slider bar to increase/decrease the size of the page, and click the Zoom to Page button to fit the page in the viewing area in the Print backstage area.

Figure 6.3 Print Backstage Area

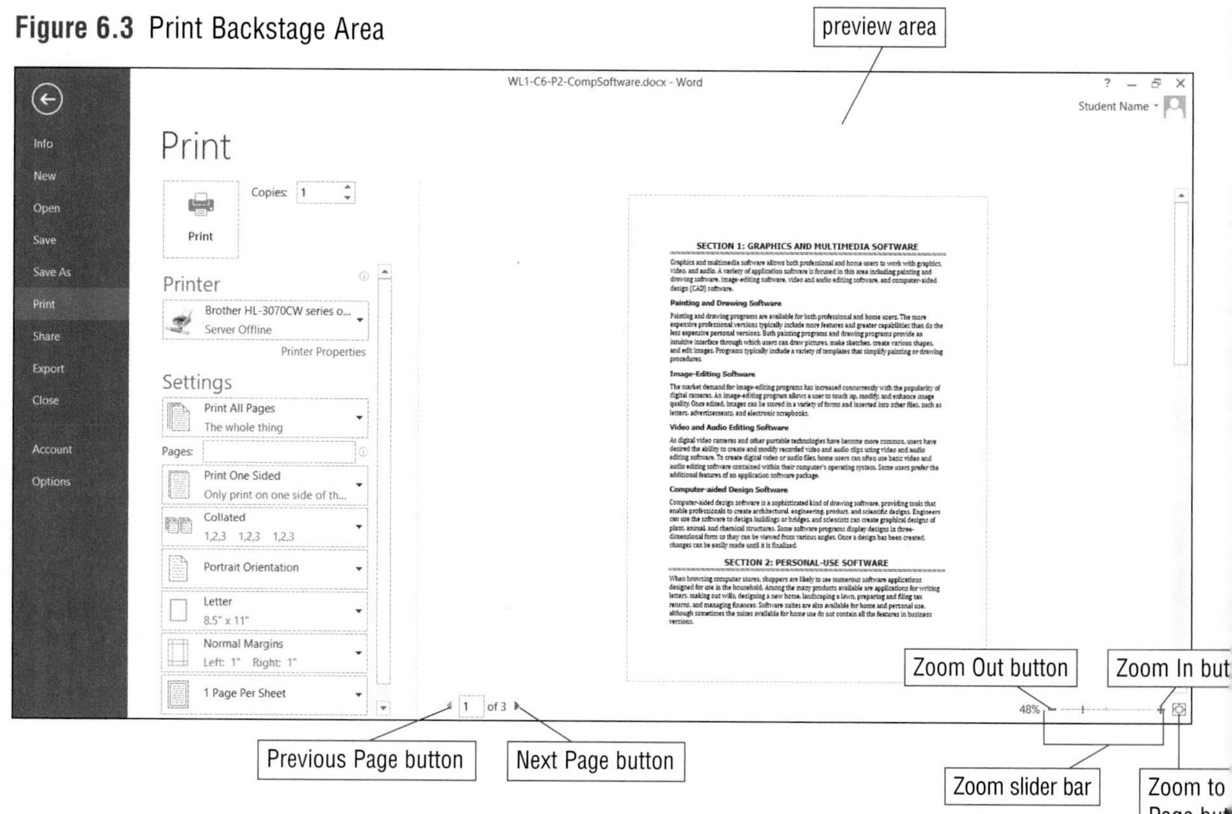

Project 2f Previewing the Document

Part 6 of 7

1. With **WL1-C6-P2-CompSoftware.docx** open, press Ctrl + Home to move the insertion point to the beginning of the document.
2. Preview the document by clicking the FILE tab and then clicking the *Print* option.
3. At the Print backstage area, click the Next Page button located below and to the left of the preview page. (This displays page 2 in the preview area.)
4. Click twice on the Zoom In button (plus symbol) that displays at the right side of the Zoom slider bar. (This increases the size of the preview page.)
5. Click the Zoom Out button (minus symbol) that displays at the left side of the Zoom slider bar until two pages of the document display in the preview area.
6. Change the zoom at the Zoom dialog box by completing the following steps:
   a. Click the percentage number that displays at the left side of the Zoom slider bar.
   b. At the Zoom dialog box, click the *Many pages* option in the *Zoom to* section.
   c. Click OK to close the dialog box. (Notice that all pages in the document display as thumbnails in the preview area.)
7. Click the Zoom to Page button that displays at the right side of the Zoom slider bar. (This returns the page to the default size.)
8. Click the Back button to return to the document.

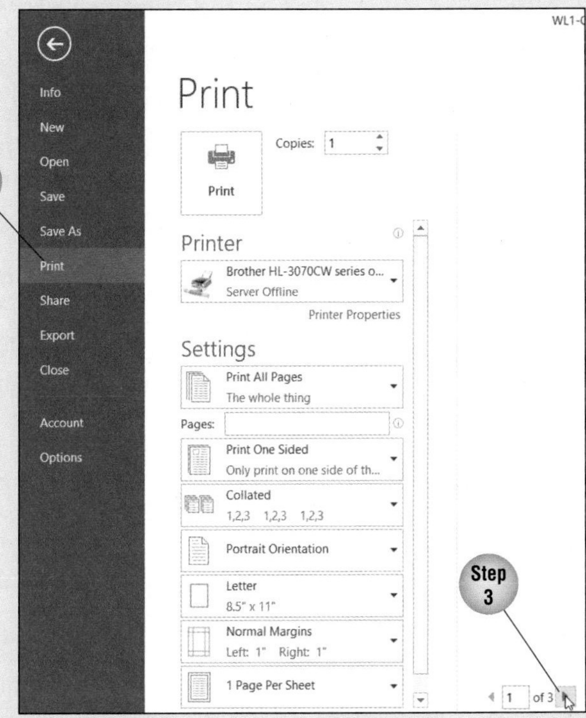

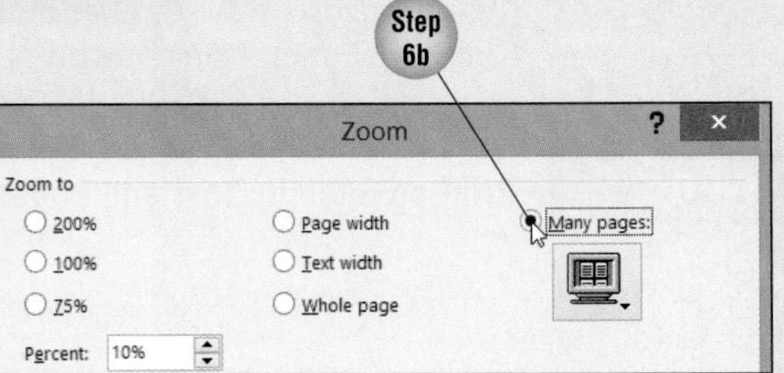

Printing Pages in a Document

If you want control over what prints in a document, use options at the Print backstage area. Click the first gallery in the *Settings* category and a drop-down list displays with options for printing all pages in the document, selected text, the current page, or a custom range of pages in the document. If you want to select and then print a portion of the document, choose the *Print Selection* option. With this option, only the text that you have selected in the current document prints. (This option is dimmed unless text is selected in the document.) Click the *Print Current Page* option to print only the page on which the insertion point is located.

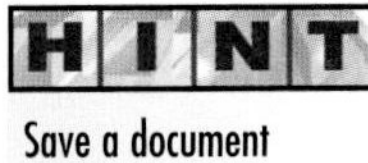

Save a document before printing it.

With the *Custom Print* option, you can identify a specific page, multiple pages, or a range of pages to print. If you want specific pages printed, use a comma (,) to indicate *and* and use a hyphen (-) to indicate *through*. For example, to print pages 2 and 5, you would type **2,5** in the *Pages* text box. To print pages 6 through 10, you would type **6-10**.

With the other galleries available in the *Settings* category of the Print backstage area, you can specify whether you want to print on one or both sides of the page, change the page orientation (portrait or landscape), specify how you want the pages collated, choose a paper size, and specify margins of a document. The last gallery contains options for printing 1, 2, 4, 6, 8, or 16 pages of a multiple-page document on one sheet of paper. This gallery also contains the *Scale to Paper Size* option. Click this option and then use the side menu to choose the paper size to which you want to scale the document.

If you want to print more than one copy of a document, use the *Copies* text box located to the right of the Print button. If you print several copies of a document that has multiple pages, Word collates the pages as they print. For example, if you print two copies of a three-page document, pages 1, 2, and 3 print, and then the pages print a second time. Printing collated pages is helpful for assembly but takes more printing time. To reduce printing time, you can tell Word *not* to print collated pages. To do this, click the *Collated* gallery in the *Settings* category and then click *Uncollated*.

If you want to send a document directly to the printer without displaying the Print backstage area, consider adding the Quick Print button to the Quick Access toolbar. To do this, click the Customize Quick Access Toolbar button located at the right side of the toolbar and then click *Quick Print* at the drop-down gallery. Click the Quick Print button and all pages of the active document print.

Project 2g Printing Specific Text and Pages — Part 7 of 7

1. With **WL1-C6-P2-CompSoftware.docx** open, print selected text by completing the following steps:
   a. Select the heading *Painting and Drawing Software* and the paragraph of text that follows it.
   b. Click the FILE tab and then click the *Print* option.
   c. At the Print backstage area, click the first gallery in the *Settings* category and then click *Print Selection* at the drop-down list.
   d. Click the Print button.
2. Change the margins and page orientation and then print only the first page by completing the following steps:
   a. Press Ctrl + Home to move the insertion point to the beginning of the document.

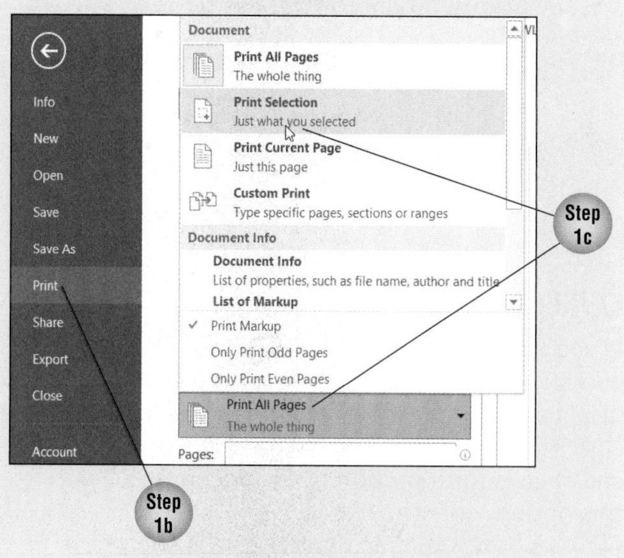

b. Click the FILE tab and then click the *Print* option.
c. At the Print backstage area, click the fourth gallery (displays with *Portrait Orientation)* in the *Settings* category and then click *Landscape Orientation* at the drop-down list.
d. Click the sixth gallery (displays with *Normal Margins*) in the *Settings* category and then click *Narrow* at the drop-down list.
e. Click the first gallery (displays with *Print All Pages*) in the *Settings* category and then click *Print Current Page* at the drop-down list.
f. Click the Print button. (The first page of the document prints in landscape orientation with 0.5-inch margins.)

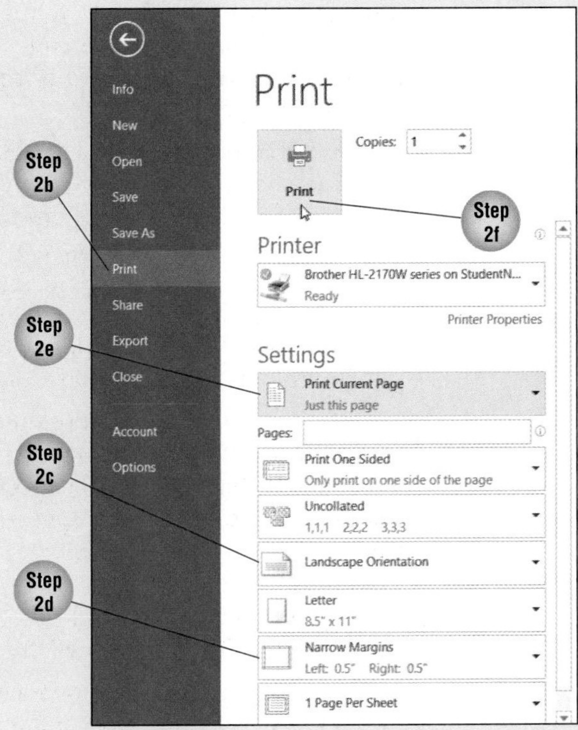

3. Print all of the pages as thumbnails on one page by completing the following steps:
   a. Click the FILE tab and then click the *Print* option.
   b. At the Print backstage area, click the bottom gallery (displays with *1 Page Per Sheet*) in the *Settings* category and then click *4 Pages Per Sheet* at the drop-down list.
   c. Click the first gallery (displays with *Print Current Page*) in the *Settings* category and then click *Print All Pages* at the drop-down list.
   d. Click the Print button.
4. Select the entire document, change the line spacing to 1.5, and then deselect the text.
5. Print two copies of specific pages by completing the following steps:
   a. Click the FILE tab and then click the *Print* option.

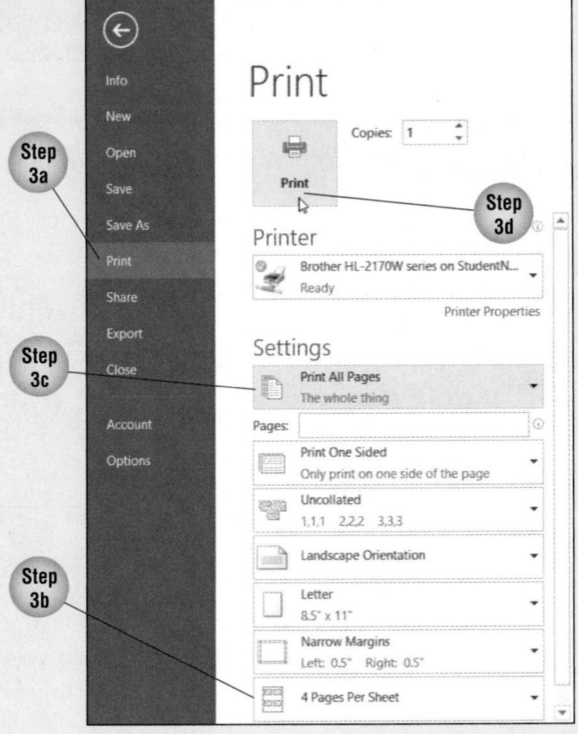

b. Click the fourth gallery (displays with (*Landscape Orientation*) in the *Settings* category and then click *Portrait Orientation* in the drop-down list.
c. Click in the *Pages* text box located below the first gallery in the *Settings* category and then type 1,3.
d. Click the up-pointing arrow at the right side of the *Copies* text box (located to the right of the Print button) to display *2*.
e. Click the third gallery (displays with *Collated*) in the *Settings* category and then click *Uncollated* at the drop-down list.
f. Click the bottom gallery (displays with *4 Pages Per Sheet*) in the *Settings* category and then click *1 Page Per Sheet* at the drop-down list.
g. Click the Print button. (The first page of the document will print twice and then the third page will print twice.)

6. Save and then close **WL1-C6-P2-CompSoftware.docx**.

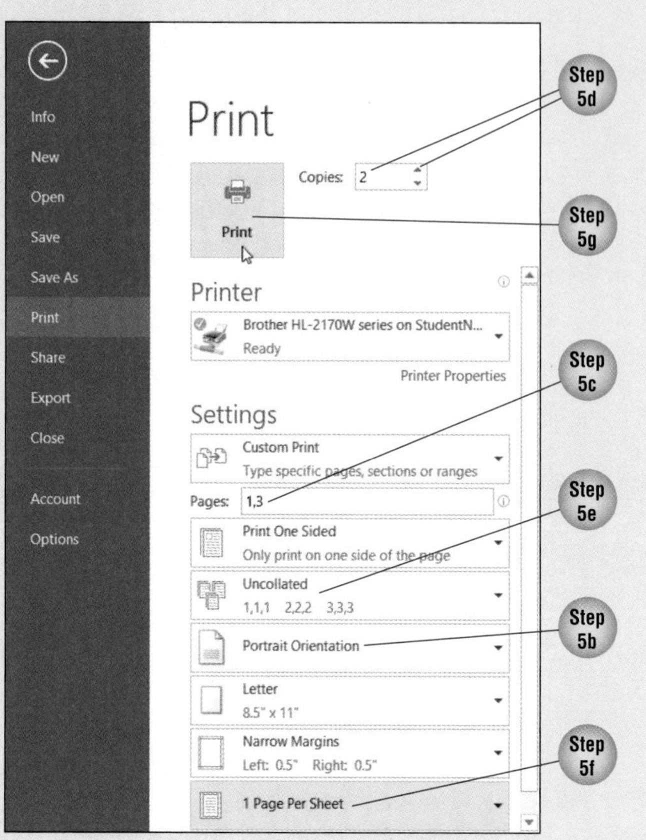

Project 3 Create and Print Envelopes — 2 Parts

You will create an envelope document and type the return address and delivery address using envelope addressing guidelines issued by the United States Postal Service. You will also open a letter document and then create an envelope using the inside address.

Creating and Printing Envelopes

Envelopes

Word automates the creation of envelopes with options at the Envelopes and Labels dialog box with the Envelopes tab selected, as shown in Figure 6.4. Display this dialog box by clicking the MAILINGS tab and then clicking the Envelopes button in the Create group. At the dialog box, type the delivery address in the *Delivery address* text box and the return address in the *Return address* text box. Send the envelope directly to the printer by clicking the Print button or insert the envelope in the current document by clicking the Add to Document button.

Figure 6.4 Envelopes and Labels Dialog Box with Envelopes Tab Selected

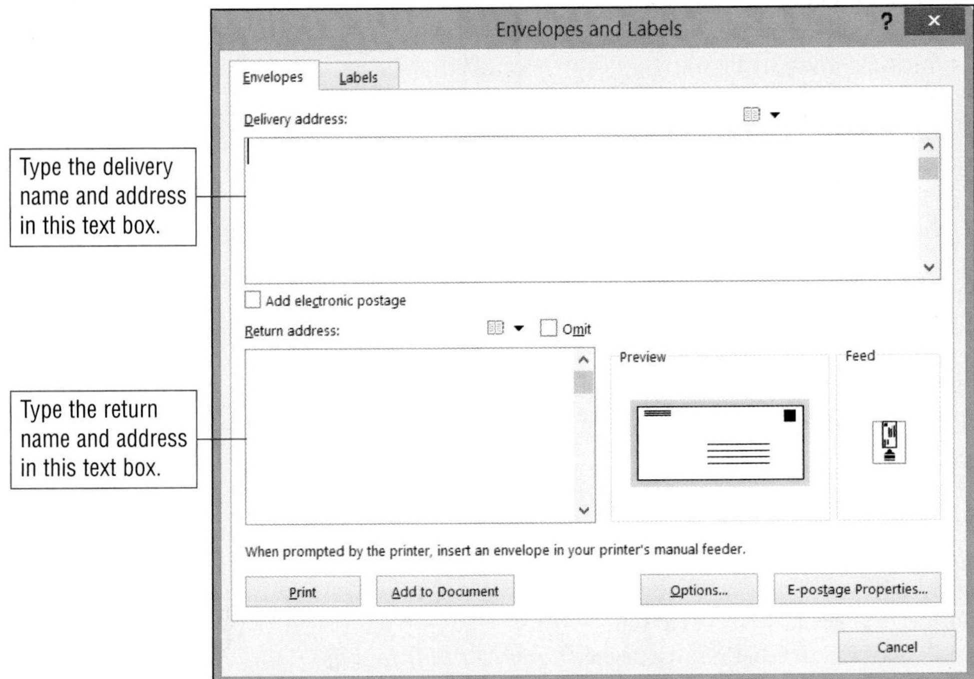

If you enter a return address before printing the envelope, Word will display the question *Do you want to save the new return address as the default return address?* At this question, click Yes if you want the current return address available for future envelopes or click No if you do not want the current return address used as the default. If a default return address displays in the *Return address* section of the dialog box, you can tell Word to omit the return address when printing the envelope. To do this, click the *Omit* check box to insert a check mark.

The Envelopes and Labels dialog box contains a *Preview* sample box and a *Feed* sample box. The *Preview* sample box shows how the envelope will appear when printed and the *Feed* sample box shows how the envelope should be inserted into the printer.

When addressing envelopes, consider following general guidelines issued by the United States Postal Service (USPS). The USPS guidelines suggest using all capital letters with no commas or periods for return and delivery addresses. Figure 6.5 shows envelope addresses that follow the USPS guidelines. Use abbreviations for street suffixes (such as *ST* for *Street* and *AVE* for *Avenue*). For a complete list of address abbreviations, visit the www.emcp.net/usps site and then search for *Official USPS Abbreviations*.

Quick Steps

Create an Envelope
1. Click MAILINGS tab.
2. Click Envelopes button.
3. Type delivery address.
4. Click in *Return address* text box.
5. Type return address.
6. Click Add to Document button or Print button.

Project 3a Printing an Envelope

Part 1 of 2

1. At a blank document, create an envelope that prints the delivery address and return address shown in Figure 6.5. Begin by clicking the MAILINGS tab.
2. Click the Envelopes button in the Create group.

3. At the Envelopes and Labels dialog box with the Envelopes tab selected, type the delivery address shown in Figure 6.5 (the one containing the name *GREGORY LINCOLN*). (Press the Enter key to end each line in the name and address.)
4. Click in the *Return address* text box. (If any text displays in the *Return address* text box, select and then delete it.)
5. Type the return address shown in Figure 6.5 (the one containing the name *WENDY STEINBERG*). (Press the Enter key to end each line in the name and address.)
6. Click the Add to Document button.
7. At the message *Do you want to save the new return address as the default return address?*, click No.
8. Save the document and name it **WL1-C6-P3-Env**.
9. Print and then close **WL1-C6-P3-Env.docx**. ***Note: Manual feed of the envelope may be required. Please check with your instructor.***

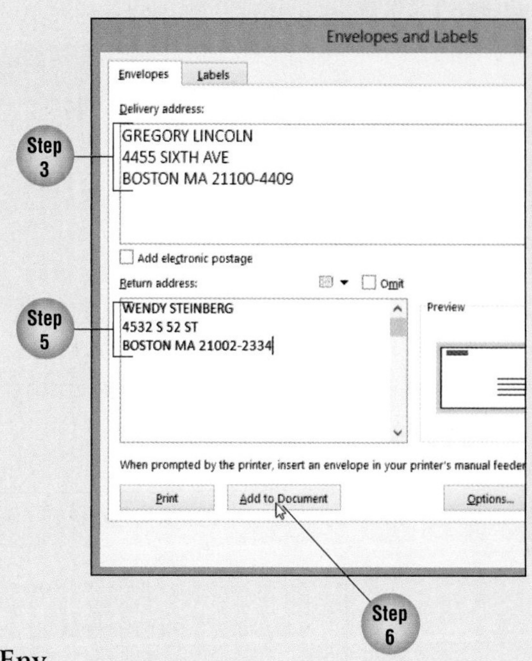

Figure 6.5 Project 3a

WENDY STEINBERG
4532 S 52 ST
BOSTON MA 21002-2334

GREGORY LINCOLN
4455 SIXTH AVE
BOSTON MA 21100-4409

If you open the Envelopes and Labels dialog box in a document containing a name and address (the name and address lines must end with a press of the Enter key and not Shift + Enter), the name and address are automatically inserted in the *Delivery address* text box in the dialog box. To do this, open a document containing a name and address and then click the Envelopes button to display the Envelopes and Labels dialog box. The name and address are inserted in the *Delivery address* text box as they appear in the letter and may not conform to the USPS guidelines. The USPS guidelines for addressing envelopes are only suggestions, not requirements.

Project 3b Creating an Envelope in an Existing Document

Part 2 of 2

1. Open **LAProg.docx**.
2. Click the MAILINGS tab.
3. Click the Envelopes button in the Create group.
4. At the Envelopes and Labels dialog box (with the Envelopes tab selected), make sure the delivery address displays properly in the *Delivery address* text box.
5. If any text displays in the *Return address* text box, insert a check mark in the *Omit* check box (located to the right of the *Return address* option). (This tells Word not to print the return address on the envelope.)
6. Click the Print button.
7. Close **LAProg.docx** without saving changes.

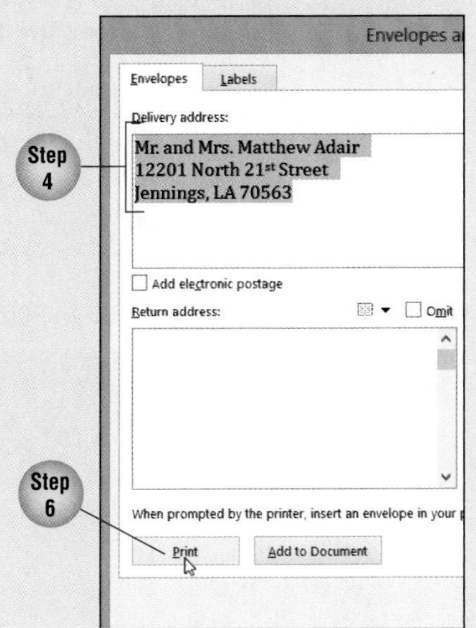

Project 4 Create Mailing Labels

2 Parts

You will create mailing labels containing names and addresses and then create mailing labels containing the inside address of a letter.

Creating and Printing Labels

Use Word's labels feature to print text on mailing labels, file labels, disc labels, or other types of labels. Word includes a variety of predefined formats for labels that can be purchased at any office supply store. With the Labels feature, you can create a sheet of mailing labels with the same name and address or image or enter a different name and address on each label.

To create a sheet of mailing labels, click the Labels button in the Create group on the MAILINGS tab. At the Envelopes and Labels dialog box with the Labels tab selected, as shown in Figure 6.6, type the desired address in the *Address* text box if you want to create a sheet of labels with the same name and address. If you want to create a sheet of labels with different names and addresses in each label, leave the *Address* text box empty. Click the New Document button to insert the mailing label in a new document or click the Print button to send the mailing label directly to the printer.

Quick Steps

Create Labels

1. Click MAILINGS tab.
2. Click Labels button.
3. Type desired address(es).
4. Click New Document button or Print button.

If you are creating labels with different names and addresses, the insertion point is positioned in the first label form when you click the New Document button. Type the name and address in the label and then press the Tab key once or twice (depending on the label) to move the insertion point to the next label. Pressing Shift + Tab will move the insertion point to the preceding label.

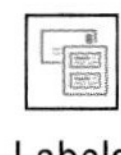
Labels

Changing Label Options

Click the Options button at the Envelopes and Labels dialog box with the Labels tab selected and the Label Options dialog box displays as shown in Figure 6.7. At the Label Options dialog box, choose the type of printer, the desired label product, and the product number. This dialog box also displays information about the selected label, such as type, height, width, and paper size. When you select a label, Word automatically determines label margins. If you want to customize these default settings, click the Details button at the Label Options dialog box.

Figure 6.6 Envelopes and Labels Dialog Box with Labels Tab Selected

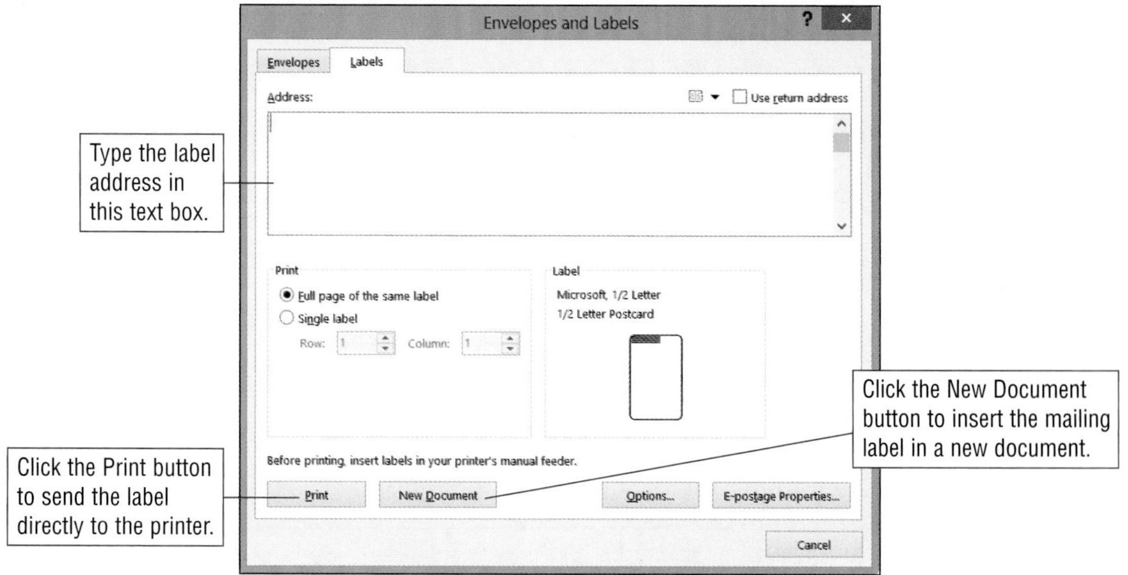

Figure 6.7 Label Options Dialog Box

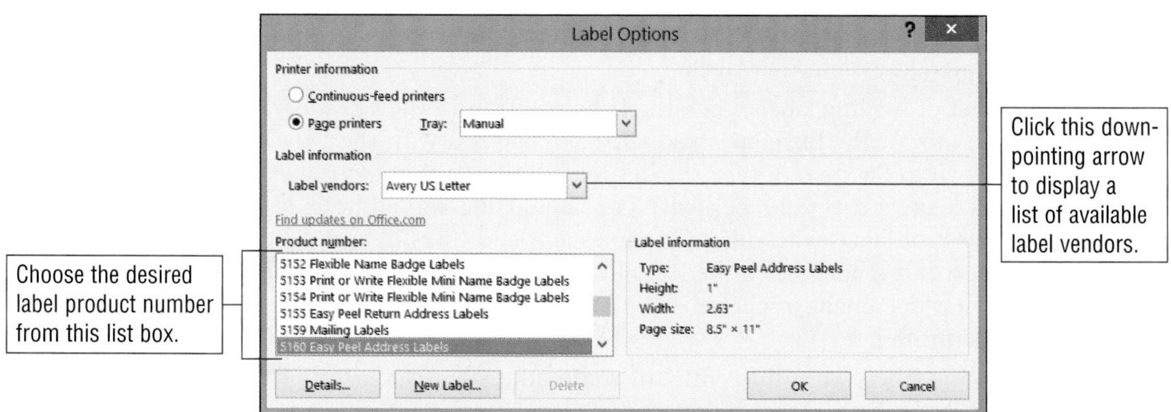

Project 4a Creating Mailing Labels

Part 1 of 2

1. At a blank document, click the MAILINGS tab.
2. Click the Labels button in the Create group.
3. At the Envelopes and Labels dialog box with the Labels tab selected, click the Options button.
4. At the Label Options dialog box, click the down-pointing arrow at the right side of the *Label vendors* option box and then click *Avery US Letter* at the drop-down list.
5. Scroll down the *Product number* list box and then click *5160 Easy Peel Address Labels*.
6. Click OK or press Enter.
7. At the Envelopes and Labels dialog box, click the New Document button.
8. At the document screen, type the first name and address shown in Figure 6.8 in the first label.
9. Press the Tab key twice to move the insertion point to the next label and then type the second name and address shown in Figure 6.8.
10. Continue in this manner until all names and addresses in Figure 6.8 have been typed.
11. Save the document and name it **WL1-C6-P4-Labels**.
12. Print and then close **WL1-C6-P4-Labels.docx**.
13. Open **LAProg.docx** and create mailing labels with the delivery address. Begin by clicking the MAILINGS tab.
14. Click the Labels button in the Create group.
15. At the Envelopes and Labels dialog box with the Labels tab selected, make sure the delivery address displays properly in the *Address* text box.
16. Make sure *Avery US Letter, 5160 Easy Peel Address Labels* displays in the *Label* section; if not, refer to Steps 3 through 6 to select the label type.
17. Click the New Document button.
18. Save the mailing label document and name it **WL1-C6-P4-LAProg.docx**.
19. Print and then close **WL1-C6-P4-LAProg.docx**.
20. Close **LAProg.docx**.

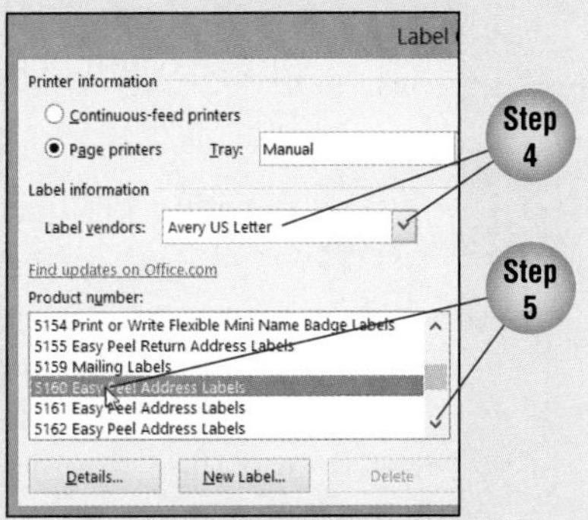

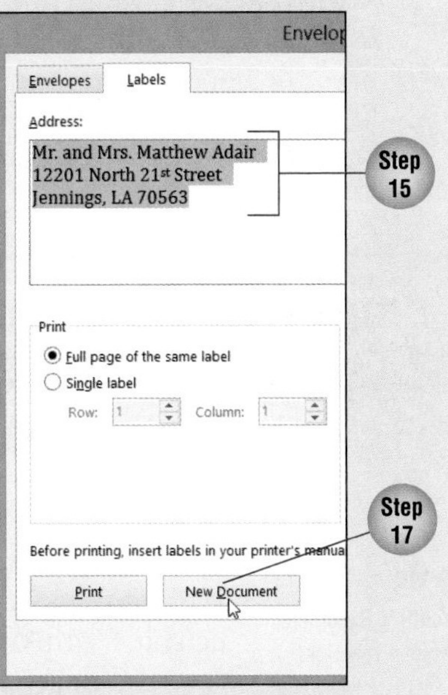

Figure 6.8 Project 4a

DAVID LOWRY 12033 S 152 ST HOUSTON TX 77340	MARCELLA SANTOS 394 APPLE BLOSSOM FRIENDSWOOD TX 77533	KEVIN DORSEY 26302 PRAIRIE DR HOUSTON TX 77316
AL AND DONNA SASAKI 1392 PIONEER DR BAYTOWN TX 77903	JACKIE RHYNER 29039 107 AVE E HOUSTON TX 77302	MARK AND TINA ELLIS 607 FORD AVE HOUSTON TX 77307

Creating Mailings Labels with an Image

Labels can be created with a graphic image. For example, you may want to create mailing labels with a company's logo and address or create labels with a company's slogan. Create labels with a graphic image by inserting the image in a blank document, clicking the MAILINGS tab and then clicking the Labels button. At the Envelopes and Labels dialog box, make sure the desired label vendor and product number are selected, and then click the New Document button.

Project 4b **Creating Mailing Labels with an Image** **Part 2 of 2**

1. At a blank document, insert a graphic image by completing the following steps:
   a. Click the INSERT tab and then click the Pictures button.
   b. At the Insert Picture dialog box, make sure the WL1C6 folder on your storage medium is active and then double-click ***BGCLabels.png***.
2. With the image selected in the document, click the MAILINGS tab and then click the Labels button.
3. At the Envelopes and Labels dialog box, make sure *Avery US Letter, 5160 Easy Peel Address Labels* displays in the *Label* section and then click the New Document button.
4. Save the document and name it **WL1-C6-P4-BGCLabels**.
5. Print and then close **WL1-C6-P4-BGCLabels.docx**.
6. Close the document containing the image without saving changes.

Project 5 **Use a Template to Create a Business Letter** **1 Part**

You will use a letter template provided by Word to create a business letter.

Creating a Document Using a Template

Quick Steps

Create a Document Using a Template
1. Click FILE tab.
2. Click *New* option.
3. Click desired template.

OR
1. Click FILE tab.
2. Click *New* option.
3. Click in search text box.
4. Type search text.
5. Press Enter.
6. Double-click desired template.

Word includes a number of template documents formatted for specific uses. Each Word document is based on a template document with the Normal template the default. With Word templates, you can easily create a variety of documents with special formatting, such as letters, calendars, and awards. Display templates by clicking the FILE tab and then clicking the *New* option. This displays the New backstage area, as shown in Figure 6.9. Open one of the templates that displays in the New backstage area by clicking the desired template. This opens a document based on the template, not the template file.

In addition to the templates that display at the New backstage area, you can download templates from the Office.com website. To do this, click in the search text box, type the search text or category, and then press Enter. Templates that match the search text or category display in the New backstage area. Click the desired template once and then click the Create button, or double-click the desired template. This downloads the template from the Office.com website and opens a document based on the template. Locations for personalized text may display in placeholders in the document. Click in the placeholder or select placeholder text and then type the personalized text.

Figure 6.9 New Backstage Area

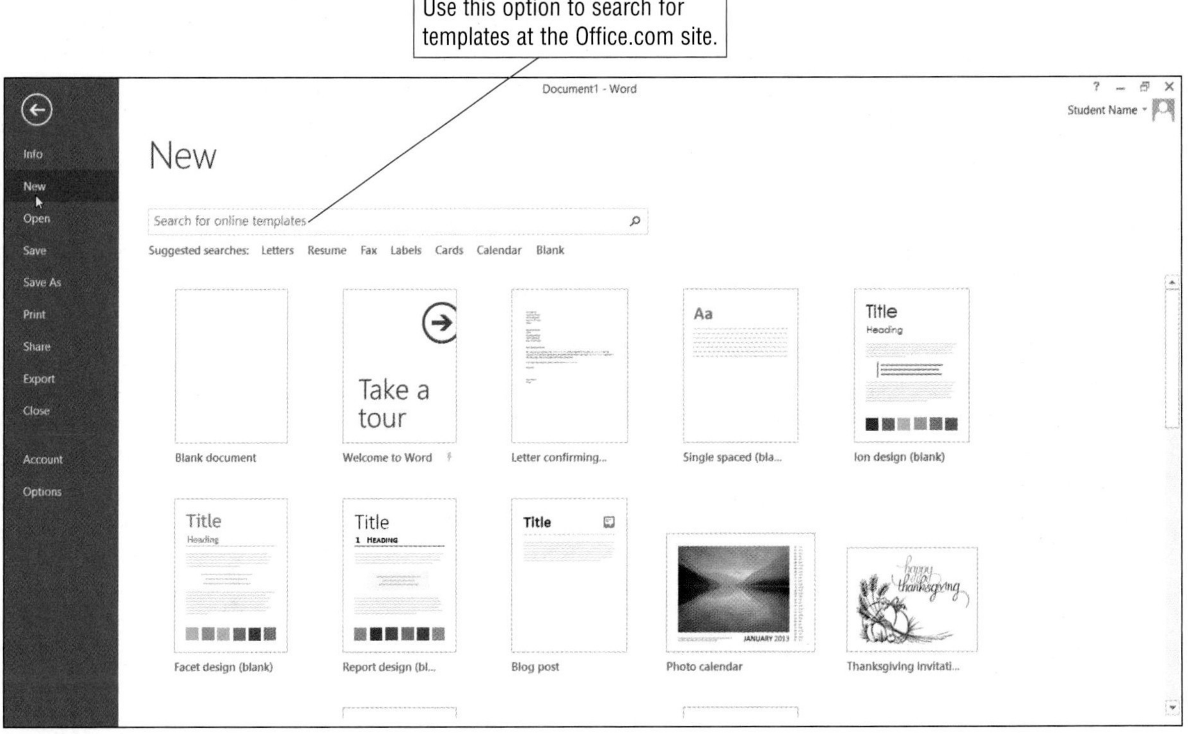

If you use a template on a regular basis, consider pinning the template to the New backstage area. To do this, search for the desired template, hover your mouse over the template, and then click the gray, left-pointing stick pin (Pin to list) that displays to the right of the template name. To unpin a template, click the down-pointing stick pin (Unpin from list).

Project 5 Creating a Letter Using a Template

Part 1 of 1

1. Click the FILE tab and then click the *New* option.
2. At the New backstage area, click in the search text box, type **letter**, and then press Enter.
3. When templates display that match *letter*, notice the Category list box that displays at the right side of the New backstage area.
4. Click the *Business* option in the Category list box. (This displays only business letter templates.)

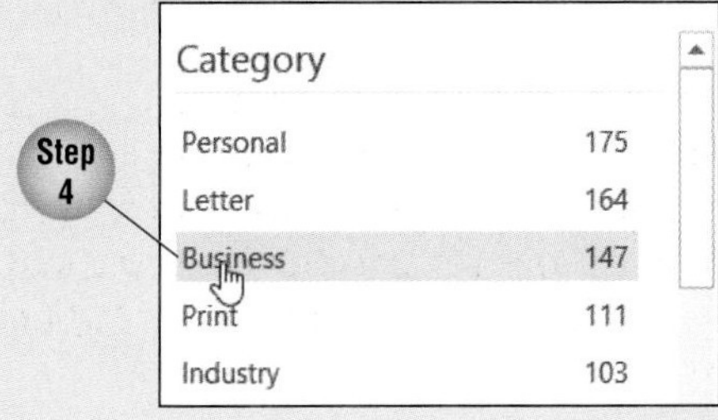

5. Scroll down the template list and then double-click the *Letter (Equity theme)* template.

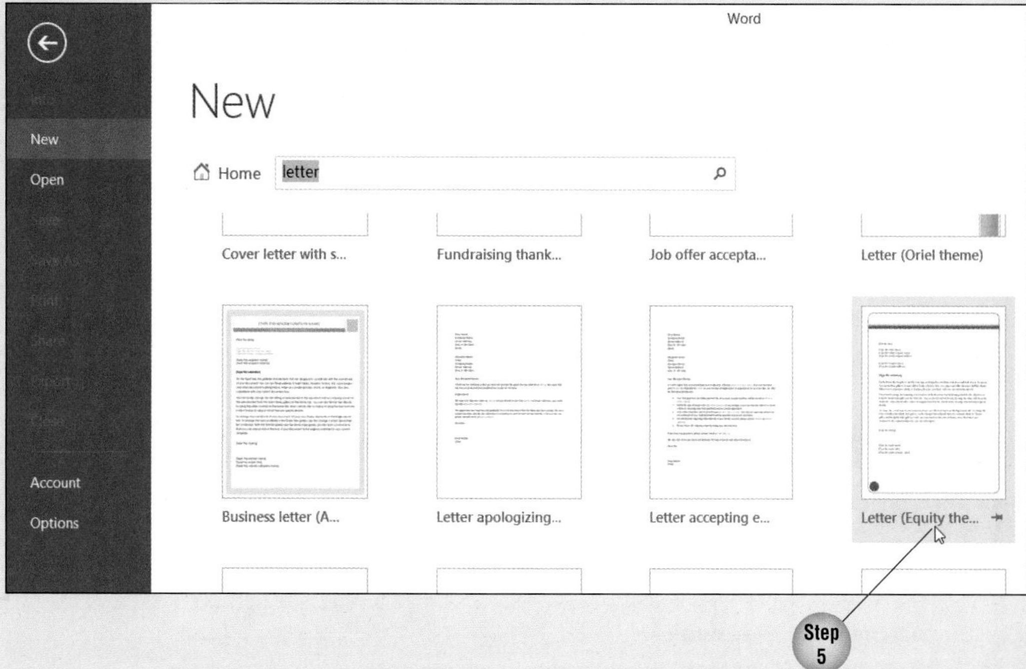

6. When the letter document displays on the screen, click the placeholder text *[Pick the date]*, click the down-pointing arrow at the right side of the placeholder, and then click the Today button located at the bottom of the calendar.
7. Click in the name that displays below the date, select the name, and then type your first and last names.
8. Click the placeholder text *[Type the sender company name]* and then type **Sorenson Funds**.
9. Click the placeholder text *[Type the sender company address]*, type **6250 Aurora Boulevard**, press the Enter key, and then type **Baltimore, MD 20372**.
10. Click the placeholder text *[Type the recipient name]* and then type **Ms. Jennifer Gonzalez**.
11. Click the placeholder text *[Type the recipient address]*, type **12990 Boyd Street**, press the Enter key, and then type **Baltimore, MD 20375**.
12. Click the placeholder text *[Type the salutation]* and then type **Dear Ms. Gonzalez:**.
13. Insert a file in the document by completing the following steps:
    a. Click anywhere in the three paragraphs of text in the body of the letter and then click the Delete key.
    b. Click the INSERT tab.
    c. Click the Object button arrow in the Text group and then click *Text from File* at the drop-down list.
    d. At the Insert File dialog box, navigate to the WL1C6 folder on your storage medium and then double-click ***SFunds.docx***.
    e. Press the Backspace key once to delete a blank line.
14. Click the placeholder text *[Type the closing]* and then type **Sincerely,**.
15. If your name does not display above the placeholder text *[Type the sender title]*, select the name and then type your first and last names.
16. Click the placeholder text *[Type the sender title]* and then type **Financial Consultant**.
17. Save the document and name it **WL1-C6-P5-SFunds**.
18. Print and then close **WL1-C6-P5-SFunds.docx**.

Chapter Summary

- Group Word documents logically into folders. Create a new folder at the Open or Save As dialog box.
- You can select one or several documents at the Open dialog box. Copy, move, rename, delete, or open a document or selected documents.
- Use the *Cut*, *Copy*, and *Paste* options from the Organize button drop-down list or the Open dialog box shortcut menu to move or copy a document from one folder to another. (If you are using your OneDrive, go to www.onedrive.com, log in to your account, and then use the onedrive.com toolbar to move or copy a document or folder to another location.)
- Delete documents and/or folders with the *Delete* option from the Organize button drop-down list or shortcut menu.
- Click the *Change File Type* option at the Export backstage area and options display for saving the document in a different file format. You can also save documents in a different file format with the *Save as type* option box at the Save As dialog box.
- Move among the open documents by clicking the buttons on the Taskbar representing the various documents, or by clicking the VIEW tab, clicking the Switch Windows button in the Window group, and then clicking the desired document name.
- View a portion of all open documents by clicking the VIEW tab and then clicking the Arrange All button in the Window group.
- Use the Minimize, Restore, and Maximize buttons located in the upper right corner of the window to reduce or increase the size of the active window.
- Divide a window into two panes by clicking the VIEW tab and then clicking the Split button in the Window group. This enables you to view different parts of the same document at one time.
- View the contents of two open documents side by side by clicking the VIEW tab and then clicking the View Side by Side button in the Window group.
- Open a new window containing the same document by clicking the VIEW tab and then clicking the New Window button in the Window group.
- Insert a document into the open document by clicking the INSERT tab, clicking the Object button arrow, and then clicking *Text from File* at the drop-down list. At the Insert File dialog box, double-click the desired document.
- Preview a document at the Print backstage area. Scroll through the pages in the document with the Next Page and the Previous Page buttons that display below the preview page. Use the Zoom slider bar to increase/decrease the display size of the preview page.
- Use options at the Print backstage area to customize the print job by changing the page orientation, size, and margins; specify how many pages you want to print on one page; indicate the number of copies and whether or not to collate the pages; and specify the printer.
- With Word's envelope feature, you can create and print an envelope at the Envelopes and Labels dialog box with the Envelopes tab selected.

- If you open the Envelopes and Labels dialog box in a document containing a name and address (with each line ending with a press of the Enter key), that information is automatically inserted in the *Delivery address* text box in the dialog box.
- Use Word's labels feature to print text on mailing labels, file labels, disc labels, or other types of labels.
- Available templates display in the New backstage area. Double-click a template to open a document based on the template. Search for templates online by typing in the search text or category in the search text box and then pressing Enter.

Commands Review

FEATURE	RIBBON TAB, GROUP/OPTION	BUTTON, OPTION	KEYBOARD SHORTCUT
arrange documents	VIEW, Window		
Envelopes and Labels dialog box with Envelopes tab selected	MAILINGS, Create		
Envelopes and Labels dialog box with Labels tab selected	MAILINGS, Create		
Export backstage area	FILE, *Export*		
Insert File dialog box	INSERT, Text	, *Text from File*	
maximize document			Ctrl + F10
minimize document			
New backstage area	FILE, *New*		
new window	VIEW, Window		
Open dialog box	FILE, *Open*	Double-click *Computer*	Ctrl + F12
Print backstage area	FILE, *Print*		Ctrl + P
restore document			
Save As dialog box	FILE, *Save As*	Double-click *Computer*	F12
split window	VIEW, Window		Alt + Ctrl + S
switch windows	VIEW, Window		
synchronous scrolling	VIEW, Window		
view documents side by side	VIEW, Window		

Concepts Check Test Your Knowledge

Completion: In the space provided at the right, indicate the correct term, command, or number.

1. Create a new folder with this button at the Open dialog box or the Save As dialog box. ________________
2. At the Open dialog box, the current folder path displays in this. ________________
3. Using the mouse, select nonadjacent documents at the Open dialog box by holding down this key while clicking the desired documents. ________________
4. Documents deleted from the computer's hard drive are automatically sent here. ________________
5. The letters *PDF* stand for this. ________________
6. Saving a document in this format strips out all formatting. ________________
7. Click this button in the Window group on the VIEW tab to arrange all open documents so a portion of each document displays. ________________
8. Click this button and the active document fills the editing window. ________________
9. Click this button to reduce the active document to a button on the Taskbar. ________________
10. To display documents side by side, click this button in the Window group on the VIEW tab. ________________
11. Display the Insert File dialog box by clicking the Object button arrow on the INSERT tab and then clicking this option. ________________
12. Type this in the *Pages* text box at the Print backstage area to print pages 3 through 6 of the open document. ________________
13. Type this in the *Pages* text box at the Print backstage area to print pages 4 and 9 of the open document. ________________
14. The Envelopes button is located in the Create group on this tab. ________________
15. Download a template at this backstage area. ________________

Skills Check Assess Your Performance

Assessment 1

MANAGE DOCUMENTS

Note: If you are using your OneDrive, please check with your instructor before completing this assessment.

1. Display the Open dialog box with WL1C6 on your storage medium the active folder and then create a new folder named *CheckingTools*.
2. Copy (be sure to copy and not cut) all documents that begin with *SpellGrammar* into the CheckingTools folder.
3. With the CheckingTools folder as the active folder, rename **SpellGrammar01.docx** to ***Technology.docx***.
4. Rename **SpellGrammar02.docx** to ***Software.docx***.
5. Capture the Open dialog box as an image file by completing the following steps:
   a. With the Open dialog box displayed, press Alt + Print Screen.
   b. Close the Open dialog box.
   c. If necessary, press Ctrl + N to display a blank document and then click the Paste button.
   d. Print the document.
   e. Close the document without saving it.
6. Display the Open dialog box and make WL1C6 on your storage medium the active folder.
7. Delete the CheckingTools folder and all documents contained within it.
8. Open **StaffMtg.docx**, **Agreement.docx**, and **Robots.docx**.
9. Make **Agreement.docx** the active document.
10. Make **StaffMtg.docx** the active document.
11. Arrange all of the windows.
12. Make **Robots.docx** the active document and then minimize it.
13. Minimize the remaining documents.
14. Restore **StaffMtg.docx**.
15. Restore **Agreement.docx**.
16. Restore **Robots.docx**.
17. Maximize and then close **StaffMtg.docx** and then maximize and close **Robots.docx**.
18. Maximize **Agreement.docx** and then save the document and name it **WL1-C6-A1-Agreement**.
19. Open **AptLease.docx**.
20. View the **WL1-C6-A1-Agreement.docx** document and **AptLease.docx** document side by side.
21. Scroll through both documents simultaneously and notice the formatting differences between the title, headings, and font in the two documents. Change the font and apply shading to only the title and headings in **WL1-C6-A1-Agreement.docx** to match the font and shading of the title and headings in **AptLease.docx**.
22. Make **AptLease.docx** active and then close it.
23. Save **WL1-C6-A1-Agreement.docx**.
24. Move the insertion point to the end of the document and then insert the document named **Terms.docx**.

25. Apply formatting to the inserted text so it matches the formatting of the text in the **WL1-C6-A1-Agreement.docx** document.
26. Move the insertion point to the end of the document and then insert the document named **Signature.docx**.
27. Save, print, and then close **WL1-C6-A1-Agreement.docx**.

Assessment 2

CREATE AN ENVELOPE

1. At a blank document, create an envelope with the text shown in Figure 6.10.
2. Save the envelope document and name it **WL1-C6-A2-Env**.
3. Print and then close **WL1-C6-A2-Env.docx**.

Figure 6.10 Assessment 2

DR ROSEANNE HOLT
21330 CEDAR DR
LOGAN UT 84598

GENE MIETZNER
4559 CORRIN AVE
SMITHFIELD UT 84521

Assessment 3

CREATE MAILING LABELS

SNAP Grade It

1. Create mailing labels with the names and addresses shown in Figure 6.11. Use a label option of your choosing. (You may need to check with your instructor before choosing an option.) When entering street numbers such as 147TH, Word will convert the th to superscript letters when you press the spacebar after typing *147TH*. To remove the superscript formatting, immediately click the Undo button on the Quick Access toolbar.

Figure 6.11 Assessment 3

SUSAN LUTOVSKY 1402 MELLINGER DR FAIRHOPE OH 43209	JIM AND PAT KEIL 413 JACKSON ST AVONDALE OH 43887	IRENE HAGEN 12930 147TH AVE E CANTON OH 43296
VINCE KILEY 14005 288TH S CANTON OH 43287	LEONARD KRUEGER 13290 N 120TH CANTON OH 43291	HELGA GUNDSTROM PO BOX 3112 AVONDALE OH 43887

2. Save the document and name it **WL1-C6-A3-Labels**.
3. Print and then close **WL1-C6-A3-Labels.docx**.
4. At the blank document screen, close the document without saving changes.

Assessment 4

PREPARE A FAX

1. At the New backstage area, search for *fax*, download the Fax (Equity theme) template and then insert the following information in the specified fields:
   To: **Frank Gallagher**
   From: (your first and last names)
   Fax: **(206) 555-9010**
   Pages: **3**
   Phone: **(206) 555-9005**
   Date: (insert current date)
   Re: **Consultation Agreement**
   CC: **Jolene Yin**
   Insert an X in the *For Review* check box.
   Comments: **Please review the Consultation Agreement and advise me of any legal issues.**
2. Save the fax document and name it **WL1-C6-A4-Fax**.
3. Print and then close the document.

Assessment 5

SAVE A DOCUMENT AS A WEB PAGE

1. Experiment with the *Save as type* option box at the Save As dialog box and figure out how to save a document as a single-file web page.
2. Open **NSS.docx**, display the Save As dialog box, and then change the *Save as type* option to a single-file web page. Click the Change Title button that displays in the Save As dialog box. At the Enter Text dialog box, type **Northland Security Systems** in the *Page title* text box and then close the dialog box by clicking the OK button. Click the Save button in the Save As dialog box.
3. Close the **NSS.mht** file.
4. Open your web browser and then open the **NSS.mht** file.
5. Close your web browser.

Assessment

CREATE PERSONAL MAILING LABELS

1. At a blank document, type your name and address and then apply formatting to enhance the appearance of the text. (You determine the font, font size, and font color.)
2. Create labels with your name and address. (You determine the label vendor and product number.)
3. Save the label document and name it **WL1-C6-A6-PersonalLabels**.
4. Print and then close the document.

Assessment

7 DOWNLOAD AND COMPLETE A STUDENT AWARD CERTIFICATE

1. Display the New backstage area and then search for and download a student of the month award certificate template. (Type **certificate for student of the month** in the search text box and then download the Basic certificate for student of the month template. If this template is not available, choose another student of the month award template.)
2. Insert the appropriate information in the award template placeholders, identifying yourself as the recipient of the student of the month award.
3. Save the completed award and name the document **WL1-C6-A7-Award**.
4. Print and then close the document.

Visual Benchmark Demonstrate Your Proficiency

1 CREATE CUSTOM LABELS

1. You can create a sheet of labels with the same information in each label by typing the information in the *Address* text box at the Envelopes and Labels dialog box, or you can type the desired information, select it, and then create the label. Using this technique, create the sheet of labels shown in Figure 6.12 with the following specifications:
   - Open **NSSLabels.docx**.
   - Set the text in 12-point Magneto.
   - Select the entire document and then create the labels by displaying the Envelopes and Labels dialog box with the Labels tab selected. Use the Avery US Letter label vendor and the 5161 product number, and then click the New Document button.
2. Save the label document and name it **WL1-C6-VB-NSSLabels**.
3. Print and then close the document.
4. Close **NSSLabels.docx** without saving it.

2 CREATE AN INVITATION

1. At the New backstage area, search for *movie awards party invitation* and then download the template document shown in Figure 6.13. (The template does not include the background image of the movie reel.)
2. Bold the text below the *hooray for hollywood!* heading.
3. Insert the movie reel clip art image (using the Online Pictures button) with the following specifications:
   - Size the image so it appears as shown in the figure and change the position of the image so it is positioned at the bottom center of the page.
   - Move the image behind the text.
4. Make any other changes so your document is similar to what you see in Figure 6.13.
5. Save the invitation and name it **WL1-C6-VB-MovieInvite**.
6. Save the invitation document in PDF format with the same name.
7. Open the **WL1-C6-VB-MovieInvite.pdf** file in Adobe Reader, print the file, and then close Adobe Reader. If Adobe Reader is not available, open the file in Internet Explorer, print the file, and then close Internet Explorer.

Figure 6.12 Visual Benchmark 1

Northland Security Systems
3200 North 22nd Street
Springfield, IL 62102

Northland Security Systems
3200 North 22nd Street
Springfield, IL 62102

Northland Security Systems
3200 North 22nd Street
Springfield, IL 62102

Northland Security Systems
3200 North 22nd Street
Springfield, IL 62102

Northland Security Systems
3200 North 22nd Street
Springfield, IL 62102

Northland Security Systems
3200 North 22nd Street
Springfield, IL 62102

Northland Security Systems
3200 North 22nd Street
Springfield, IL 62102

Northland Security Systems
3200 North 22nd Street
Springfield, IL 62102

Northland Security Systems
3200 North 22nd Street
Springfield, IL 62102

Northland Security Systems
3200 North 22nd Street
Springfield, IL 62102

Northland Security Systems
3200 North 22nd Street
Springfield, IL 62102

Northland Security Systems
3200 North 22nd Street
Springfield, IL 62102

Northland Security Systems
3200 North 22nd Street
Springfield, IL 62102

Northland Security Systems
3200 North 22nd Street
Springfield, IL 62102

Northland Security Systems
3200 North 22nd Street
Springfield, IL 62102

Northland Security Systems
3200 North 22nd Street
Springfield, IL 62102

Northland Security Systems
3200 North 22nd Street
Springfield, IL 62102

Northland Security Systems
3200 North 22nd Street
Springfield, IL 62102

Northland Security Systems
3200 North 22nd Street
Springfield, IL 62102

Northland Security Systems
3200 North 22nd Street
Springfield, IL 62102

Figure 6.13 Visual Benchmark 2

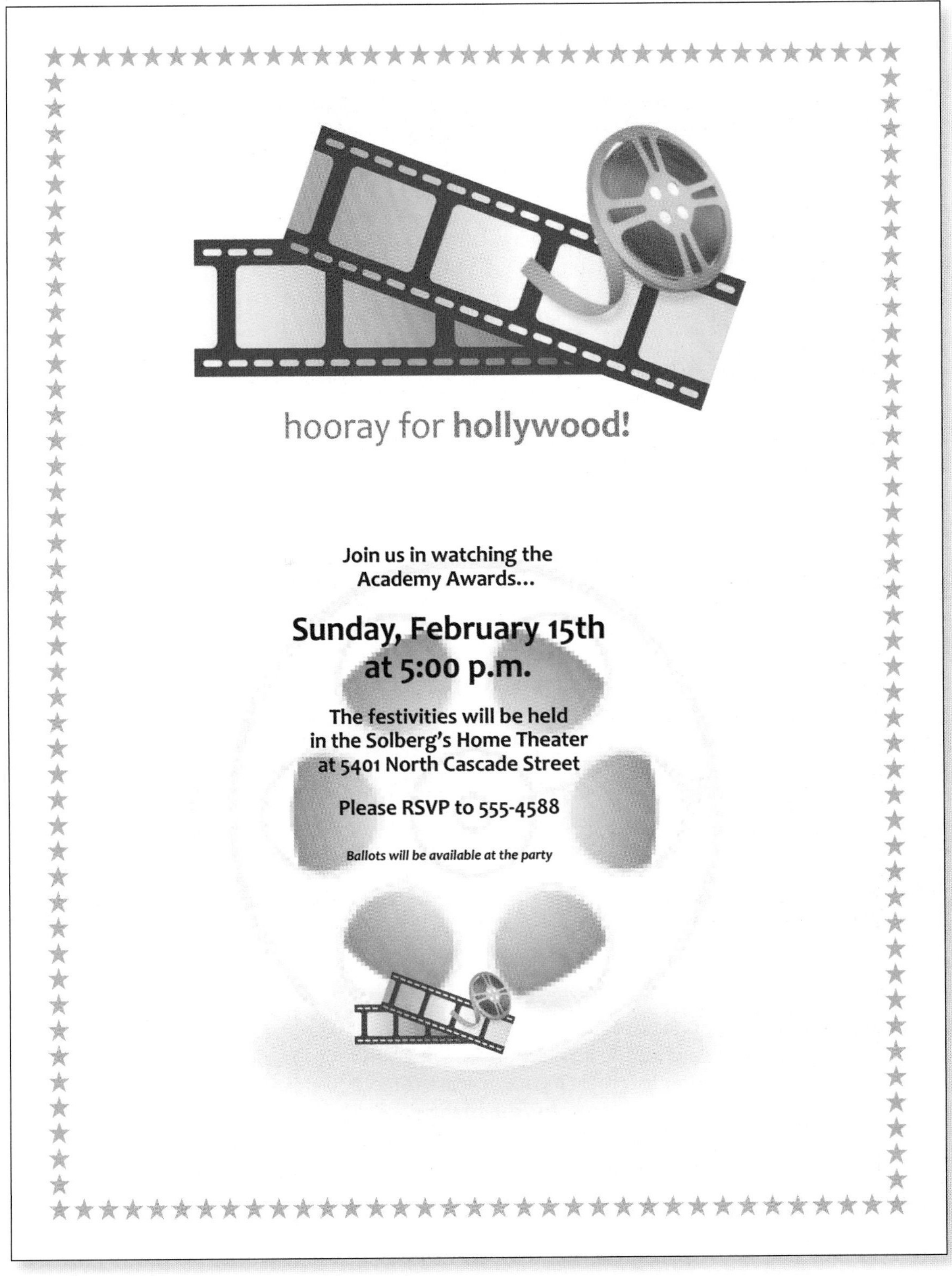

hooray for **hollywood!**
Join us in watching the
Academy Awards...
Sunday, February 15th
at 5:00 p.m.
The festivities will be held
in the Solberg's Home Theater
at 5401 North Cascade Street
Please RSVP to 555-4588
Ballots will be available at the party

Case Study Apply Your Skills

Part 1

You are the office manager for a real estate company, Macadam Realty, and have been asked by the senior sales associate, Lucy Hendricks, to organize contract forms into a specific folder. Create a new folder named *RealEstate* and then copy into the folder documents that begin with the letters "RE." Ms. Hendricks has also asked you to prepare mailing labels for Macadam Realty. Include on the labels the name, Macadam Realty, and the address, 100 Third Street, Suite 210, Denver, CO 80803. Use a decorative font for the name and address and make the *M* in *Macadam* and the *R* in *Realty* larger and more pronounced than surrounding text. Save the completed document and name it **WL1-C6-CS-RELabels**. Print and then close the document.

Part 2

One of your responsibilities is to format contract forms. Open the document named **REConAgrmnt.docx** and then save it and name it **WL1-C6-CS-REConAgrmnt**. The sales associate has asked you to insert signature information at the end of the document, and so you decide to insert at the end of the document the file named **RESig.docx**. With **WL1-C6-CS-REConAgrmnt.docx** still open, open **REBuildAgrmnt.docx**. Format the **WL1-C6-CS-REConAgrmnt.docx** document so it is formatted in a manner similar to the **REBuildAgrmnt.docx** document. Consider the following when specifying formatting: fonts, font sizes, and paragraph shading. Save, print, and then close **WL1-C6-CS-REConAgrmnt.docx**. Close **REBuildAgrmnt.docx**.

Part 3

Help

As part of the organization of contracts, Ms. Hendricks has asked you to insert document properties for the **REBuildAgrmnt.docx** and **WL1-C6-CS-REConAgrmnt.docx** documents. Use the Help feature to learn how to insert document properties. With the information you learn from the Help feature, open each of the two documents separately, display the Info backstage area, click the Show All Properties hyperlink (you may need to scroll down the backstage area to display this hyperlink), and then insert document properties in the following fields (you determine the information to type): *Title*, *Subject*, *Categories*, and *Company*. Print the document properties for each document. (Change the first gallery in the *Settings* category in the Print backstage area to *Document Info*.) Save each document with the original name and close the documents.

Part 4

A client of the real estate company, Anna Hurley, is considering purchasing several rental properties and has asked for information on how to locate real estate rental forms. Using the Internet, locate at least three websites that offer real estate rental forms. Write a letter to Anna Hurley at 2300 South 22nd Street, Denver, CO 80205. In the letter, list the websites you found and include information on which site you thought offered the most resources. Also include in the letter that Macadam Realty is very interested in helping her locate and purchase rental properties. Save the document and name it **WL1-C6-CS-RELtr**. Create an envelope for the letter and add it to the letter document. Save, print, and then close **WL1-C6-CS-RELtr.docx**. (You may need to manually feed the envelope in the printer.)

MICROSOFT® WORD

CHAPTER 7

Creating Tables and SmartArt

PERFORMANCE OBJECTIVES

Upon successful completion of Chapter 7, you will be able to:

- **Create, format, and modify a table**
- **Sort text in a table**
- **Perform calculations on data in a table**
- **Create, format, and modify a SmartArt graphic**

Tutorials

7.1 Creating Tables
7.2 Changing the Table Design
7.3 Changing the Table Layout
7.4 Merging and Splitting Cells and Tables
7.5 Changing Column Width and Height and Cell Margins
7.6 Inserting a Quick Table
7.7 Converting Text to a Table and a Table to Text
7.8 Drawing a Table
7.9 Sorting Text in a Table and Performing Calculations
7.10 Creating SmartArt
7.11 Arranging and Moving SmartArt

Some Word data can be organized in a table, which is a combination of columns and rows. Use the Tables feature to insert data in columns and rows. This data can consist of text, values, and formulas. In this chapter, you will learn how to create and format a table and insert and format data in the table. Word also includes a SmartArt feature that provides a number of predesigned graphics. In this chapter, you will learn how to use these graphics to create diagrams and organizational charts. Model answers for this chapter's projects appear on the following pages.

Note: Before beginning the projects, copy to your storage medium the WL1C7 subfolder from the WL1 folder on the CD that accompanies this textbook and then make WL1C7 the active folder.

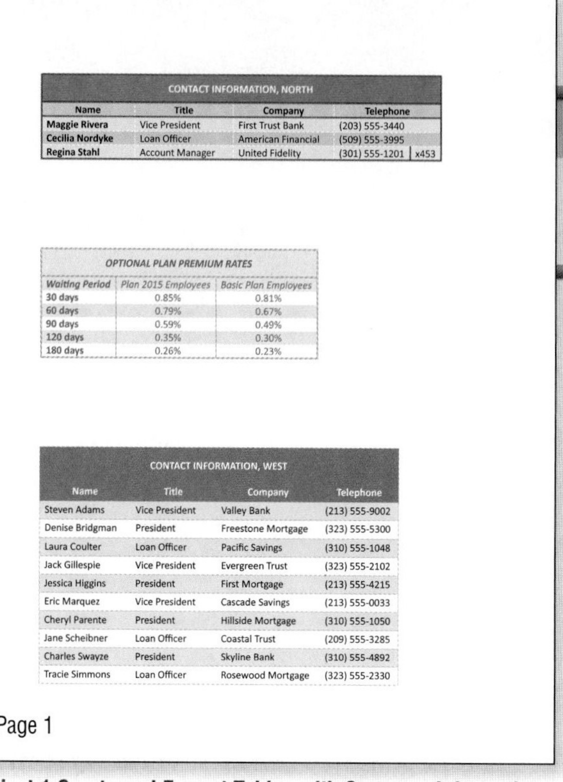

CONTACT INFORMATION, NORTH			
Name	Title	Company	Telephone
Maggie Rivera	Vice President	First Trust Bank	(203) 555-3440
Cecilia Nordyke	Loan Officer	American Financial	(509) 555-3995
Regina Stahl	Account Manager	United Fidelity	(301) 555-1201 x453

OPTIONAL PLAN PREMIUM RATES		
Waiting Period	*Plan 2015 Employees*	*Basic Plan Employees*
30 days	0.85%	0.81%
60 days	0.79%	0.67%
90 days	0.59%	0.49%
120 days	0.35%	0.30%
180 days	0.26%	0.23%

CONTACT INFORMATION, WEST			
Name	Title	Company	Telephone
Steven Adams	Vice President	Valley Bank	(213) 555-9002
Denise Bridgman	President	Freestone Mortgage	(323) 555-5300
Laura Coulter	Loan Officer	Pacific Savings	(310) 555-1048
Jack Gillespie	Vice President	Evergreen Trust	(323) 555-2102
Jessica Higgins	President	First Mortgage	(213) 555-4215
Eric Marquez	Vice President	Cascade Savings	(213) 555-0033
Cheryl Parente	President	Hillside Mortgage	(310) 555-1050
Jane Scheibner	Loan Officer	Coastal Trust	(209) 555-3285
Charles Swayze	President	Skyline Bank	(310) 555-4892
Tracie Simmons	Loan Officer	Rosewood Mortgage	(323) 555-2330

Page 1

CONTACT INFORMATION, WEST			
Name	Title	Company	Telephone
Carole Wagner	President	Main Street Bank	(310) 555-5394
Dawn Wingstrand	Vice President	Lakeland Savings	(323) 555-2348
Cora Yates	Loan Officer	Douglas Mortgage	(213) 555-6588
Robert Ziebell	President	Central Trust	(310) 555-3444

SEPTEMBER

SUN	MON	TUE	WED	THU	FRI	SAT
		1	2	3	4	5
6	7	8	9	10	11	12
13	14	15	16	17	18	19
20	21	22	23	24	25	26
27	28	29	30			

Page 2

Project 1 Create and Format Tables with Company Information

WL1-C7-P1-Tables.docx

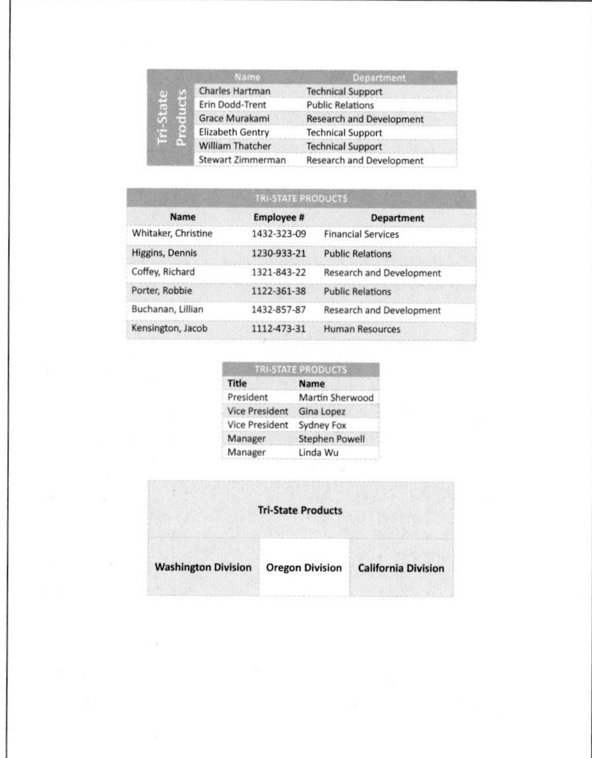

Tri-State Products	Name	Department
	Charles Hartman	Technical Support
	Erin Dodd-Trent	Public Relations
	Grace Murakami	Research and Development
	Elizabeth Gentry	Technical Support
	William Thatcher	Technical Support
	Stewart Zimmerman	Research and Development

TRI-STATE PRODUCTS		
Name	Employee #	Department
Whitaker, Christine	1432-323-09	Financial Services
Higgins, Dennis	1230-933-21	Public Relations
Coffey, Richard	1321-843-22	Research and Development
Porter, Robbie	1122-361-38	Public Relations
Buchanan, Lillian	1432-857-87	Research and Development
Kensington, Jacob	1112-473-31	Human Resources

TRI-STATE PRODUCTS	
Title	Name
President	Martin Sherwood
Vice President	Gina Lopez
Vice President	Sydney Fox
Manager	Stephen Powell
Manager	Linda Wu

Tri-State Products		
Washington Division	Oregon Division	California Division

Project 2 Create and Format Tables with Employee Information

WL1-C7-P2-TSPTables.docx

TRI-STATE PRODUCTS
Sales Division

Salesperson	Sales, 2014	Sales, 2015
Guthrie, Jonathon	$623,214	$635,099
Novak, Diana	$543,241	$651,438
Byers, Darren	$490,655	$500,210
Kurkova, Martina	$490,310	$476,005
Whittier, Michelle	$395,630	$376,522
Sogura, Jeffrey	$375,630	$399,120
Lagasa, Brianna	$294,653	$300,211
Total	$3,213,333	$3,338,605
Average	$459,048	$476,944
Top Sales	$623,214	$651,438

Region	First Qtr.	Second Qtr.	Third Qtr.	Fourth Qtr.	Total
Northwest	$125,430	$157,090	$139,239	$120,340	$542,099
Southwest	$133,450	$143,103	$153,780	$142,498	$572,831
Northeast	$275,340	$299,342	$278,098	$266,593	$1,119,373
Southeast	$211,349	$222,330	$201,849	$239,432	$874,960
Total	$745,569	$821,865	$772,966	$768,863	$3,109,263
Average	$186,392	$205,466	$193,242	$192,216	$777,316

Project 3 Sort and Calculate Sales Data

WL1-C7-P3-TSPSalesTables.docx

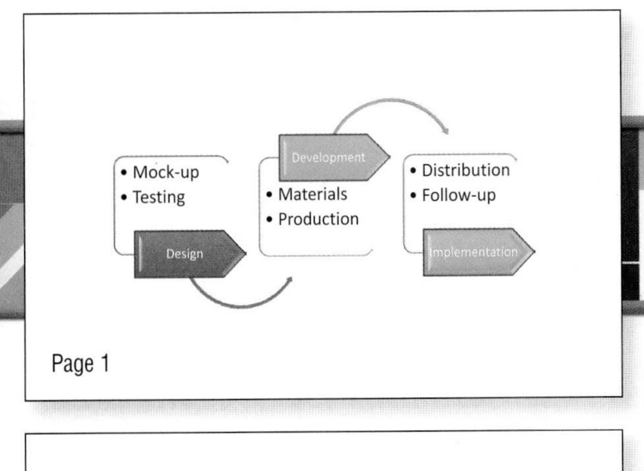

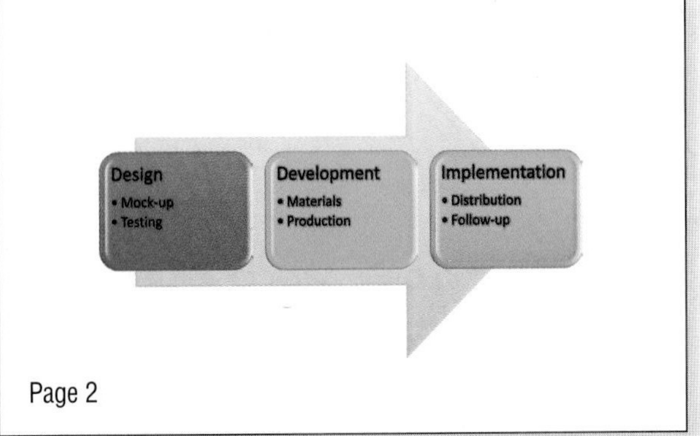

Project 4 Prepare and Format a SmartArt Graphic
WL1-C7-P4-SAGraphics.docx

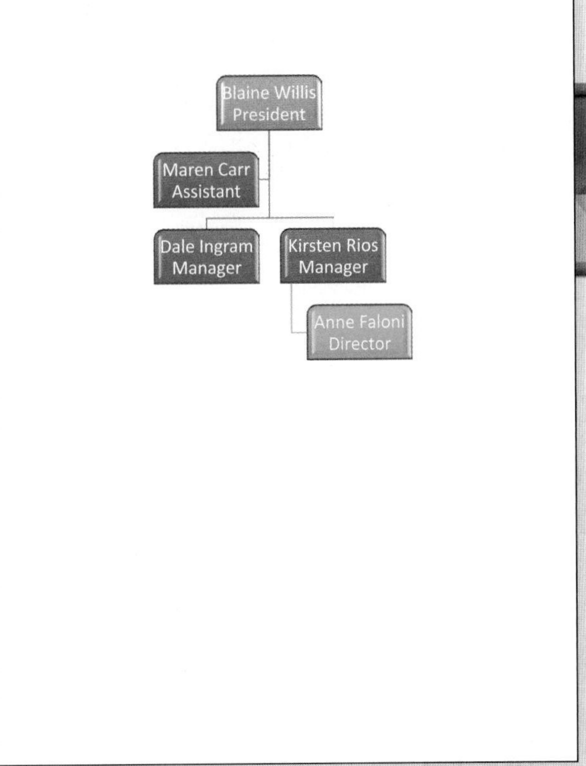

Project 5 Prepare and Format a Company Organizational Chart
WL1-C7-P5-OrgChart.docx

Project 1 Create and Format Tables with Company Information

9 Parts

You will create one table containing contact information and another containing information on plans offered by the company. You will then change the design and layout of each table.

Creating a Table

Use the Tables feature to create boxes of information called ***cells***. A cell is the intersection between a row and a column. A cell can contain text, characters, numbers, data, graphics, or formulas. Create a table by clicking the INSERT tab, clicking the Table button, dragging down and to the right in the drop-down grid until the correct number of rows and columns displays, and then clicking the mouse button. You can also create a table with options at the Insert Table dialog box. Display this dialog box by clicking the Table button in the Tables group on the INSERT tab and then clicking *Insert Table* at the drop-down list.

Figure 7.1 shows an example of a table with three columns and four rows. Various parts of the table are identified in Figure 7.1, such as the gridlines, move table column marker, end-of-cell marker, end-of-row marker, table move handle, and resize handle. In a table, nonprinting characters identify the ends of cells and the ends of rows. To view these characters, click the Show/Hide ¶ button in the

Quick Steps

Create a Table
1. Click INSERT tab.
2. Click Table button.
3. Drag to create desired number of columns and rows.
4. Click mouse button.
OR
1. Click INSERT tab.
2. Click Table button.
3. Click *Insert Table*.
4. Specify number of columns and rows.
5. Click OK.

Figure 7.1 Table with Nonprinting Characters Displayed

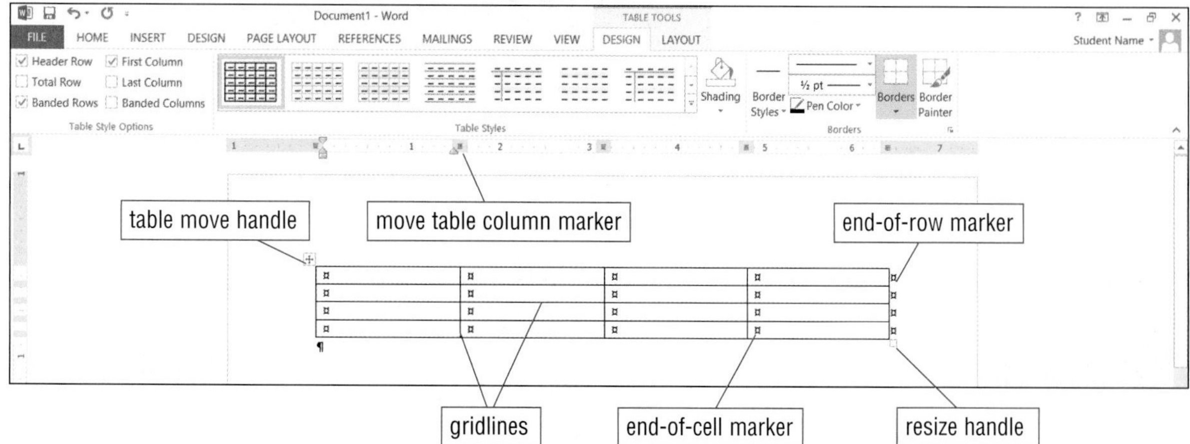

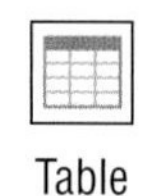

Table

You can create a table within a table, creating a *nested* table.

Paragraph group on the HOME tab. The end-of-cell marker displays inside each cell and the end-of-row marker displays at the end of a row of cells. These markers are identified in Figure 7.1.

When you create a table, the insertion point is located in the cell in the upper left corner of the table. Cells in a table contain a cell designation. Columns in a table are lettered from left to right, beginning with *A*. Rows in a table are numbered from top to bottom beginning with *1*. The cell in the upper left corner of the table is cell A1. The cell to the right of A1 is B1, the cell to the right of B1 is C1, and so on.

When the insertion point is positioned in a cell in the table, move table column markers display on the horizontal ruler. These markers represent the end of a column and are useful in changing the widths of columns. Figure 7.1 identifies a move table column marker.

Entering Text in Cells

Pressing the Tab key in a table moves the insertion point to the next cell. Pressing Ctrl + Tab moves the insertion point to the next tab within a cell.

With the insertion point positioned in a cell, type or edit text. Move the insertion point to another cell with the mouse by clicking in the desired cell. If you are using the keyboard, press the Tab key to move the insertion point to the next cell or press Shift + Tab to move the insertion point to the previous cell.

If the text you type does not fit on one line, it wraps to the next line within the same cell, or if you press Enter within a cell, the insertion point is moved to the next line within the same cell. The cell vertically lengthens to accommodate the text, and all cells in that row also lengthen. Pressing the Tab key in a table causes the insertion point to move to the next cell in the table. If you want to move the insertion point to a tab within a cell, press Ctrl + Tab. If the insertion point is located in the last cell of the table and you press the Tab key, Word adds another row to the table. Insert a page break within a table by pressing Ctrl + Enter. The page break is inserted between rows, not within a row.

Moving the Insertion Point within a Table

To use the mouse to move the insertion point to a different cell within the table, click in the desired cell. To use the keyboard to move the insertion point to a different cell within the table, refer to the information shown in Table 7.1.

Table 7.1 Insertion Point Movement within a Table Using the Keyboard

To move the insertion point	*Press these keys*
to next cell	Tab
to preceding cell	Shift + Tab
forward one character	Right Arrow key
backward one character	Left Arrow key
to previous row	Up Arrow key
to next row	Down Arrow key
to first cell in row	Alt + Home
to last cell in row	Alt + End
to top cell in column	Alt + Page Up
to bottom cell in column	Alt + Page Down

Project 1a Creating a Table

Part 1 of 9

1. At a blank document, turn on bold and then type the title CONTACT INFORMATION, as shown in Figure 7.2.
2. Turn off bold and then press the Enter key.
3. Create the table shown in Figure 7.2. To do this, click the INSERT tab, click the Table button in the Tables group, drag down and to the right in the drop-down grid until the number above the grid displays as *3x5*, and then click the mouse button.
4. Type the text in the cells as indicated in Figure 7.2. Press the Tab key to move to the next cell or press Shift + Tab to move to the preceding cell. (If you accidentally press the Enter key within a cell, immediately press the Backspace key. Do not press Tab after typing the text in the last cell. If you do, another row is inserted in the table. If this happens, immediately click the Undo button on the Quick Access toolbar.)
5. Save the table and name it **WL1-C7-P1-Tables**.

Figure 7.2 Project 1a

CONTACT INFORMATION

Maggie Rivera	First Trust Bank	(203) 555-3440
Les Cromwell	Madison Trust	(602) 555-4900
Cecilia Nordyke	American Financial	(509) 555-3995
Regina Stahl	United Fidelity	(301) 555-1201
Justin White	Key One Savings	(360) 555-8963

Using the Insert Table Dialog Box

You can also create a table with options at the Insert Table dialog box shown in Figure 7.3. To display this dialog box, click the INSERT tab, click the Table button in the Tables group, and then click *Insert Table*. At the Insert Table dialog box, enter the desired number of columns and rows and then click OK.

Figure 7.3 Insert Table Dialog Box

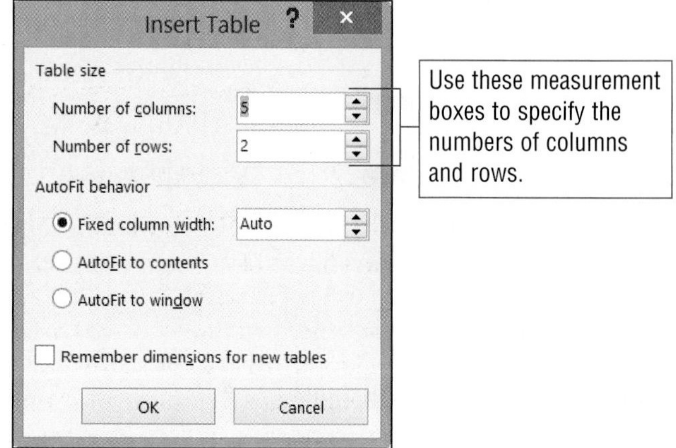

Project 1b **Creating a Table with the Insert Table Dialog Box** **Part 2 of 9**

1. With **WL1-C7-P1-Tables.docx** open, press Ctrl + End to move the insertion point below the table.
2. Press the Enter key twice.
3. Turn on bold and then type the title **OPTIONAL PLAN PREMIUM RATES**, as shown in Figure 7.4.
4. Turn off bold and then press the Enter key.
5. Click the INSERT tab, click the Table button in the Tables group, and then click *Insert Table* at the drop-down list.
6. At the Insert Table dialog box, type 3 in the *Number of columns* measurement box. (The insertion point is automatically positioned in this text box.)
7. Press the Tab key (this moves the insertion point to the *Number of rows* measurement box) and then type 5.
8. Click OK.
9. Type the text in the cells as indicated in Figure 7.4. Press the Tab key to move to the next cell or press Shift + Tab to move to the preceding cell. To indent the text in cells B2 through B5 and cells C2 through C5, press Ctrl + Tab to move the insertion point to a tab within a cell and then type the text.
10. Save **WL1-C7-P1-Tables.docx**.

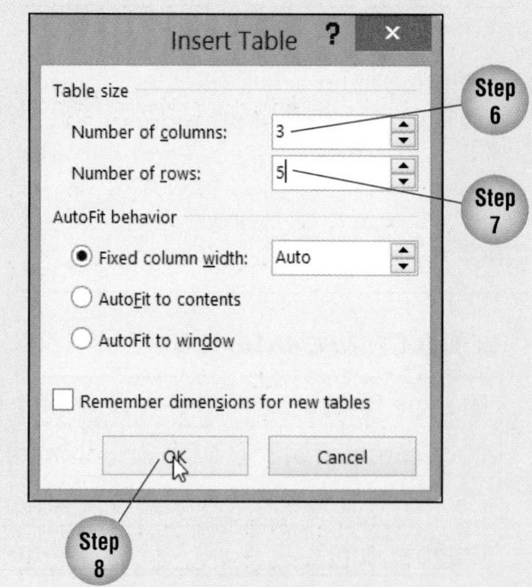

Figure 7.4 Project 1b

OPTIONAL PLAN PREMIUM RATES

Waiting Period	Basic Plan Employees	Plan 2015 Employees
60 days	0.67%	0.79%
90 days	0.49%	0.59%
120 days	0.30%	0.35%
180 days	0.23%	0.26%

Changing the Table Design

When you create a table, the TABLE TOOLS DESIGN tab is active. This tab contains a number of options for enhancing the appearance of the table, as shown in Figure 7.5. With options in the Table Styles group, apply a predesigned style that applies color and border lines to a table as well as shading to cells. Maintain further control over the predesigned style formatting applied to columns and rows with options in the Table Style Options group. For example, if your table contains a total row, you would insert a check mark in the *Total Row* option.

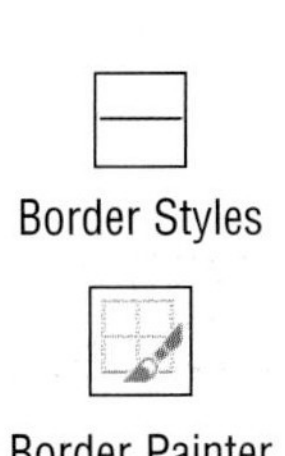

With options in the Borders group, you can customize the borders of cells in a table. Click the Border Styles button to display a drop-down list of predesigned border lines. Use other buttons in the Borders group to change the line style, width, and color; add or remove borders; and apply the same border style formatting to other cells with the Border Painter button.

Figure 7.5 TABLE TOOLS DESIGN Tab

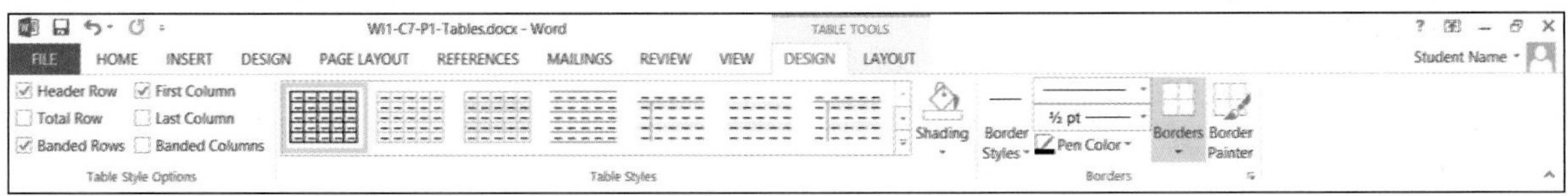

Project 1c Applying Table Styles — Part 3 of 9

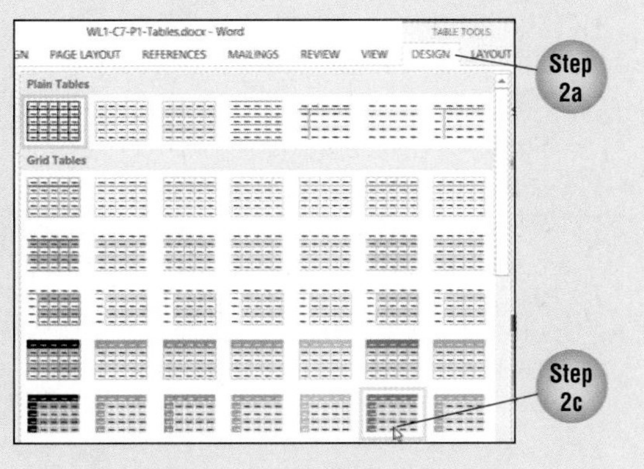

1. With **WL1-C7-P1-Tables.docx** open, click in any cell in the top table.
2. Apply a table style by completing the following steps:
   a. Make sure the TABLE TOOLS DESIGN tab is active.
   b. Click the More button at the right side of the table style thumbnails in the Table Styles group.
   c. Click the *Grid Table 5 Dark - Accent 5* style thumbnail (sixth column, fifth row in the *Grid Tables* section).

3. After looking at the table, you realize that the first row is not a header row and the first column should not be formatted differently than the other columns. To format the first row and first column in the same manner as the other rows and columns, click the *Header Row* check box and the *First Column* check box in the Table Style Options group to remove the check marks.
4. Click in any cell in the bottom table, apply the List Table 6 Colorful - Accent 5 table style (sixth column, sixth row in the *List Tables* section).
5. Add color borders to the top table by completing the following steps:
   a. Click in any cell in the top table.
   b. Click the Pen Color button arrow in the Borders group and then click the *Orange, Accent 2, Darker 50%* color (sixth column, bottom row in the *Theme Colors* section).
   c. Click the Line Weight button arrow in the Borders group and then click *1 ½ pt* at the drop-down list. (When you choose a line weight, the Border Painter button is automatically activated.)

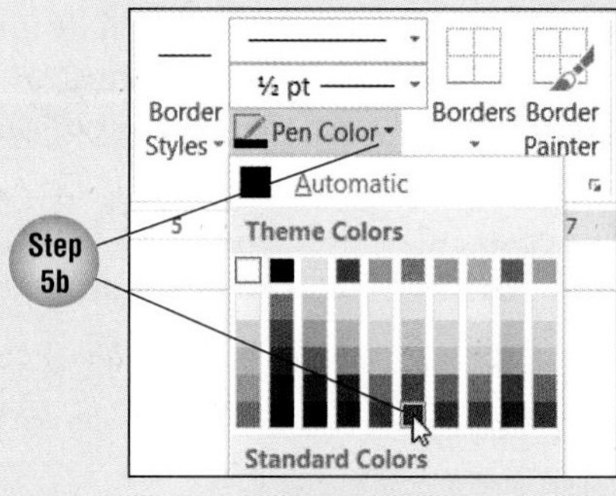

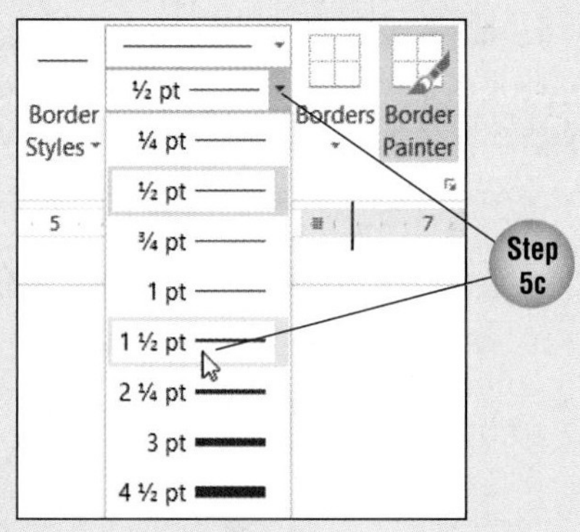

   d. Using the mouse (mouse pointer displays as a pen), drag along all four sides of the table. (As you drag with the mouse, a thick, brown border line is inserted. If you make a mistake or the line does not display as you intended, click the Undo button and then continue drawing along each side of the table.)
6. Click the Border Styles button arrow and then click the *Double solid lines, 1/2 pt, Accent 2* option (third column, third row in the *Theme Borders* section).
7. Drag along all four sides of the bottom table.

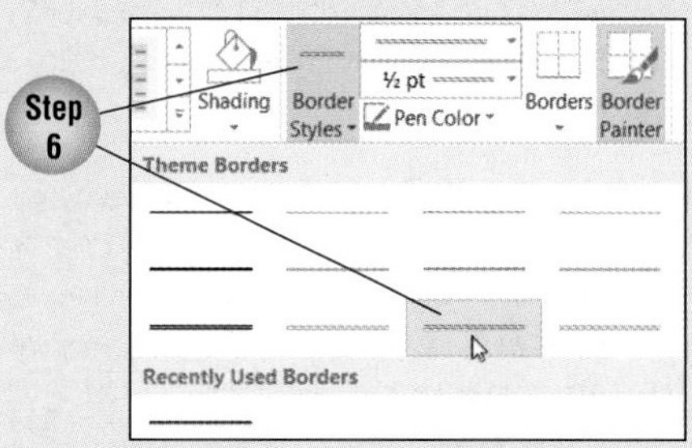

8. Click the Border Painter button to turn off the feature.
9. Save **WL1-C7-P1-Tables.docx**.

Selecting Cells

You can format data within a table in several ways. For example, you can change the alignment of text within cells or rows, select and then move or copy rows or columns, or add character formatting such as bold, italic, or underlining. To format specific cells, rows, or columns, you must first select them.

Selecting in a Table with the Mouse

Use the mouse pointer to select a cell, row, or column, or to select an entire table. Table 7.2 describes methods for selecting in a table with the mouse. The left edge of each cell, between the left column border and the end-of-cell marker or first character in the cell, is called the ***cell selection bar***. When you position the mouse pointer in the cell selection bar, it turns into a small, black arrow pointing up and to the right. Each row in a table contains a ***row selection bar***, which is the space just to the left of the left edge of the table. When you position the mouse pointer in the row selection bar, the mouse pointer turns into a white arrow pointing up and to the right.

Table 7.2 Selecting in a Table with the Mouse

To select this	*Do this*
cell	Position the mouse pointer in the cell selection bar at the left edge of the cell until it turns into a small, black arrow pointing up and to the right and then click the left mouse button.
row	Position the mouse pointer in the row selection bar at the left edge of the table until it turns into an arrow pointing up and to the right and then click the left mouse button.
column	Position the mouse pointer on the uppermost horizontal gridline of the table in the appropriate column until it turns into a small, black, down-pointing arrow and then click the left mouse button.
adjacent cells	Position the mouse pointer in the first cell to be selected, hold down the left mouse button, drag the mouse pointer to the last cell to be selected, and then release the mouse button.
all cells in a table	Click the table move handle or position the mouse pointer in the row selection bar for the first row at the left edge of the table until it turns into an arrow pointing up and to the right, hold down the left mouse button, drag down to select all rows in the table, and then release the left mouse button.
text within a cell	Position the mouse pointer at the beginning of the text and then hold down the left mouse button as you drag the mouse across the text. (When a cell is selected, the cell background color changes to gray. When text within cells is selected, only those lines containing text are selected.)

Selecting in a Table with the Keyboard

In addition to the mouse, you can also use the keyboard to select specific cells within a table. Table 7.3 displays the commands for selecting specific amounts of a table.

If you want to select only the text within a cell, rather than the entire cell, press F8 to turn on the Extend mode and then move the insertion point with an arrow key. When a cell is selected, the cell background color changes to gray. When text within a cell is selected, only those lines containing text are selected.

Table 7.3 Selecting in a Table with the Keyboard

To select	*Press*
next cell's contents	Tab
preceding cell's contents	Shift + Tab
entire table	Alt + 5 (on numeric keypad with Num Lock off)
adjacent cells	Hold down the Shift key and then press an arrow key repeatedly.
column	Position the insertion point in the top cell of the column, hold down the Shift key, and then press the down-pointing arrow key until the column is selected.

Project 1d Selecting, Moving and Formatting Cells in a Table — Part 4 of 9

1. With **WL1-C7-P1-Tables.docx** open, move two rows in the top table by completing the following steps:
   a. Position the mouse pointer in the row selection bar at the left side of the row containing the name *Cecilia Nordyke*, hold down the left mouse button, and then drag down to select two rows (the *Cecilia Nordyke* row and the *Regina Stahl* row).
   b. Click the HOME tab and then click the Cut button in the Clipboard group.
   c. Move the insertion point so it is positioned at the beginning of the name *Les Cromwell* and then click the Paste button in the Clipboard group.
2. Move the third column in the bottom table by completing the following steps:
   a. Position the mouse pointer on the top border of the third column in the bottom table until the pointer turns into a short, black, down-pointing arrow and then click the left mouse button. (This selects the entire column.)
   b. Click the Cut button in the Clipboard group on the HOME tab.
   c. With the insertion point positioned at the beginning of the text *Basic Plan Employees*, click the Paste button in the Clipboard group. (Moving the column removed the right border.)
   d. Insert the right border by clicking the TABLE TOOLS DESIGN tab, clicking the Border Styles button arrow, and then clicking the *Double solid lines, 1/2 pt, Accent 2* option at the drop-down list (third column, third row in the *Theme Borders* section).

e. Drag along the right border of the bottom table.
f. Click the Border Painter button to turn off the feature.

3. Apply shading to a row by completing the following steps:
   a. Position the mouse pointer in the row selection bar at the left edge of the first row in the bottom table until the pointer turns into an arrow pointing up and to the right and then click the left mouse button. (This selects the entire first row of the bottom table.)
   b. Click the Shading button arrow in the Table Styles group and then click the *Orange, Accent 2, Lighter 80%* color option (sixth column, second row in the *Theme Colors* section).
4. Apply a border line to the right side of two columns by completing the following steps:
   a. Position the mouse pointer on the top border of the first column in the bottom table until the pointer turns into a short, black, down-pointing arrow and then click the left mouse button.
   b. Click the Line Style button arrow and then click the top line option (a single line).
   c. Click the Borders button arrow and then click *Right Border* at the drop-down list.

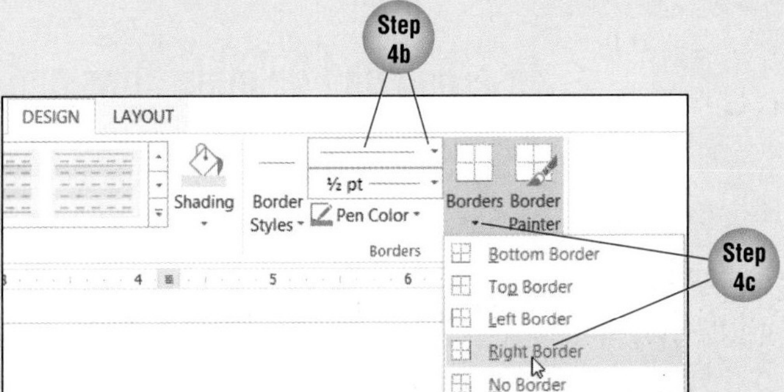

   d. Select the second column in the bottom table.
   e. Click the Borders button arrow and then click *Right Border* at the drop-down list.
5. Apply italic formatting to a column by completing the following steps:
   a. Click in the first cell of the first row in the top table.
   b. Hold down the Shift key and then press the Down Arrow key four times. (This should select all cells in the first column.)
   c. Press Ctrl + I.
6. Save **WL1-C7-P1-Tables.docx**.

Changing Table Layout

To further customize a table, consider changing the table layout by inserting or deleting columns and rows and specifying cell alignments. Change table layout with options at the TABLE TOOLS LAYOUT tab shown in Figure 7.6. Use options and buttons on the tab to select specific cells, delete and insert rows and columns, merge and split cells, specify cell height and width, sort data in cells, and insert formulas.

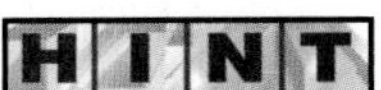

Some table layout options are available at a shortcut menu that can be viewed by right-clicking a table.

Figure 7.6 TABLE TOOLS LAYOUT Tab

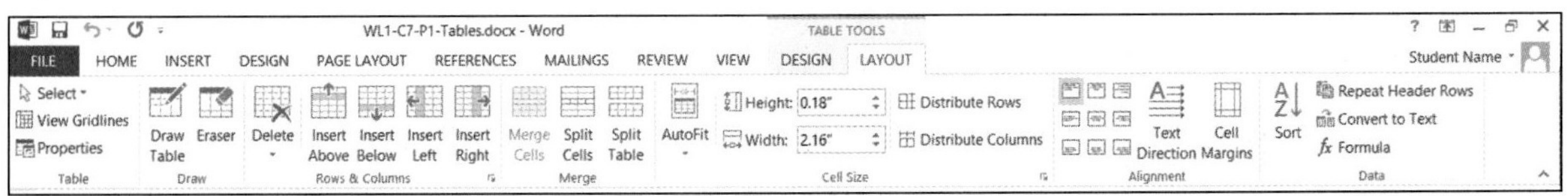

Selecting with the Select Button

Select

Along with selecting cells with the keyboard and mouse, you can also select specific cells with the Select button in the Table group on the TABLE TOOLS LAYOUT tab. To select with this button, position the insertion point in the desired cell, column, or row and then click the Select button. At the drop-down list that displays, specify what you want to select: the entire table or a column, row, or cell.

Viewing Gridlines

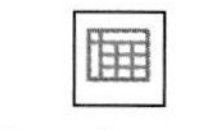
View Gridlines

When you create a table, cell borders are identified by horizontal and vertical thin, black gridlines. You can remove a cell border gridline but maintain the cell border. If you remove cell border gridlines or apply a table style that removes gridlines, nonprinting gridlines display as dashed lines. This helps you visually determine cell borders. You can turn on or off the display of these nonprinting, dashed gridlines with the View Gridlines button in the Table group on the TABLE TOOLS LAYOUT tab.

Inserting and Deleting Rows and Columns

Insert Above

Insert Below

Insert Left

Insert Right

Delete

Insert a row or column and delete a row or column with buttons in the Rows & Columns group on the TABLE TOOLS LAYOUT tab. Click the button in the group that inserts the row or column in the desired location, such as above, below, to the left, or to the right. Add a row to the bottom of a table by positioning the insertion point in the last cell and then pressing the Tab key. To delete a table, row, or column, click the Delete button and then click the option identifying what you want to delete. If you make a mistake while formatting a table, immediately click the Undo button on the Quick Access toolbar.

You can also insert a row or column with insert icons. Display the insert row icon by positioning the mouse pointer just outside the left border of the table at the left of the desired row border. When the insert row icon displays (a plus symbol in a circle and a border line), click the icon and a row is inserted below the insert icon border line. To insert a column, position the mouse pointer above the column border line until the column icon displays and then click the icon. This inserts a new column immediately left of the insert column icon border line.

Project 1e **Selecting, Inserting, and Deleting Columns and Rows** **Part 5 of 9**

1. Make sure **WL1-C7-P1-Tables.docx** is open.
2. The table style applied to the bottom table removed row border gridlines. If you do not see dashed row border gridlines in the bottom table, turn on the display of these nonprinting gridlines by positioning your insertion point in the table, clicking the TABLE TOOLS LAYOUT tab, and then clicking the View Gridlines button in the Table group. (The button should display with a light blue background indicating it is active.)
3. Select a column and apply formatting by completing the following steps:
   a. Click in any cell in the first column in the top table.
   b. Click the Select button in the Table group and then click *Select Column* at the drop-down list.
   c. With the first column selected, press Ctrl + I to remove italics and then press Ctrl + B to apply bold formatting.

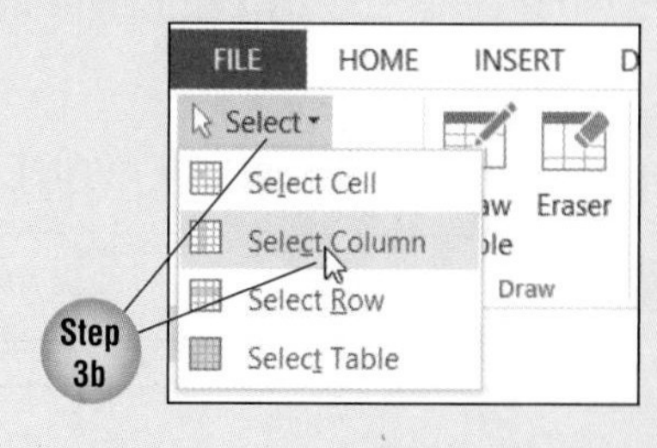

4. Select a row and apply formatting by completing the following steps:
   a. Click in any cell in the first row in the bottom table.
   b. Click the Select button in the Table group and then click *Select Row* at the drop-down list.
   c. With the first row selected in the bottom table, press Ctrl + I to apply italic formatting.
5. Insert a new row in the bottom table and type text in the new cells by completing the following steps:
   a. Click in the cell containing the text *60 days*.
   b. Click the Insert Above button in the Rows & Columns group.
   c. Type **30 days** in the first cell of the new row. Press the Tab key, press Ctrl + Tab, and then type **0.85%** in the second cell of the new row. Press the Tab key, press Ctrl + Tab, and then type **0.81%** in the third cell of the new row:

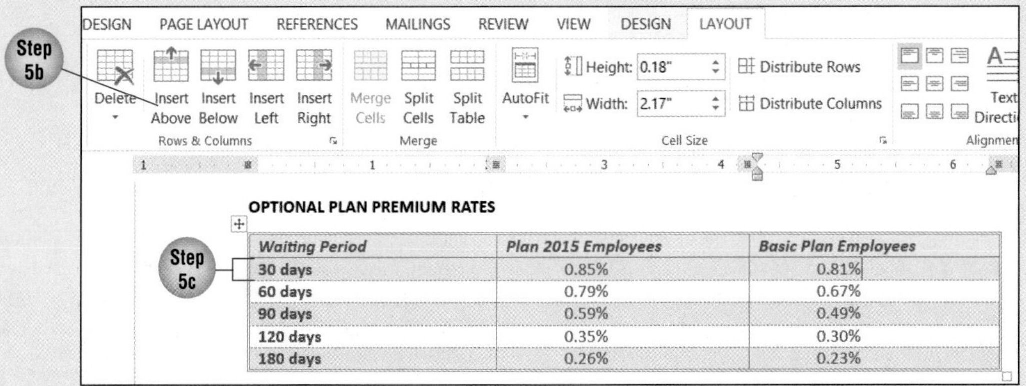

6. Insert two new rows in the top table by completing the following steps:
   a. Select the two rows of cells that begin with the names *Cecilia Nordyke* and *Regina Stahl*.
   b. Click the Insert Below button in the Rows & Columns group.
   c. Click in any cell of the top table to deselect the new rows.
7. Insert a new row in the top table by positioning the mouse pointer at the left side of the table next to the border line below *Regina Stahl* until the insert row icon displays and then click the icon.

CONTACT INFORMATION

Maggie Rivera
Cecilia Nordyke
Regina Stahl
Les Cromwell
Justin White

Step 7

8. Type the following text in the new cells:

Teresa Getty	Meridian Bank	(503) 555-9800
Michael Vazquez	New Horizon Bank	(702) 555-2435
Samantha Roth	Cascade Mutual	(206) 555-6788

CONTACT INFORMATION

Maggie Rivera	First Trust Bank	(203) 555-3440
Cecilia Nordyke	American Financial	(509) 555-3995
Regina Stahl	United Fidelity	(301) 555-1201
Teresa Getty	Meridian Bank	(503) 555-9800
Michael Vazquez	New Horizon Bank	(702) 555-2435
Samantha Roth	Cascade Mutual	(206) 555-6788
Les Cromwell	Madison Trust	(602) 555-4900
Justin White	Key One Savings	(360) 555-8963

Step 8

9. Delete a row by completing the following steps:
   a. Click in the cell containing the name *Les Cromwell*.
   b. Click the Delete button in the Rows & Columns group and then click *Delete Rows* at the drop-down list.
10. Insert a new column in the top table by completing the following steps:
    a. Position the mouse pointer immediately above the border line between the first and second columns in the top table until the insert column icon displays.
    b. Click the insert column icon.

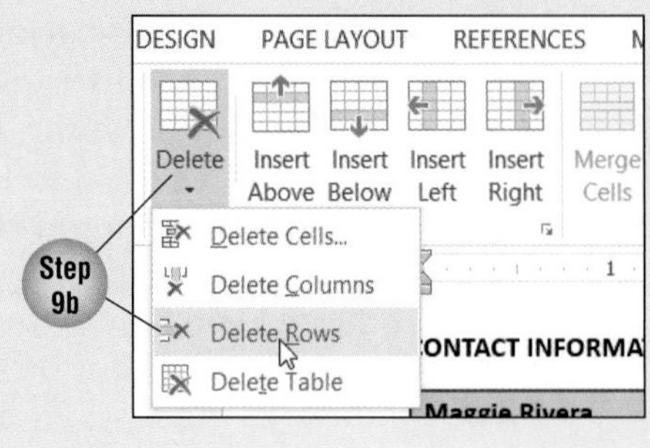

Step 10b

CONTACT INFORMATION

Maggie Rivera	First Trust Bank
Cecilia Nordyke	American Financial

11. Type the following text in the new cells:
    B1 = Vice President
    B2 = Loan Officer
    B3 = Account Manager
    B4 = Branch Manager
    B5 = President
    B6 = Vice President
    B7 = Regional Manager
12. Save **WL1-C7-P1-Tables.docx**.

Step 11

CONTACT INFORMATION

Maggie Rivera	Vice President	First Tru
Cecilia Nordyke	Loan Officer	America
Regina Stahl	Account Manager	United F
Teresa Getty	Branch Manager	Meridiar
Michael Vazquez	President	New Ho
Samantha Roth	Vice President	Cascade
Justin White	Regional Manager	Key One

Merging and Splitting Cells and Tables

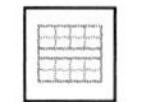
Merge Cells

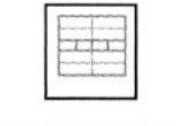
Split Cells

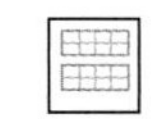
Split Table

Click the Merge Cells button in the Merge group on the TABLE TOOLS LAYOUT tab to merge selected cells and click the Split Cells button to split the currently active cell. When you click the Split Cells button, the Split Cells dialog box displays where you specify the number of columns or rows into which you want to split the active cell. If you want to split one table into two tables, position the insertion point in a cell in the row that you want to be the first row in the new table and then click the Split Table button.

Project 1f Merging and Splitting Cells and Splitting a Table — Part 6 of 9

1. With **WL1-C7-P1-Tables.docx** open, insert a new row and merge cells in the row by completing the following steps:
   a. Click in the cell containing the text *Waiting Period* (located in the bottom table).
   b. Click the Insert Above button in the Rows & Columns group on the TABLE TOOLS LAYOUT tab.

c. With all of the cells in the new row selected, click the Merge Cells button in the Merge group.

d. Type **OPTIONAL PLAN PREMIUM RATES** and then press Ctrl + E to center-align the text in the cell. (The text you type will be italicized.)

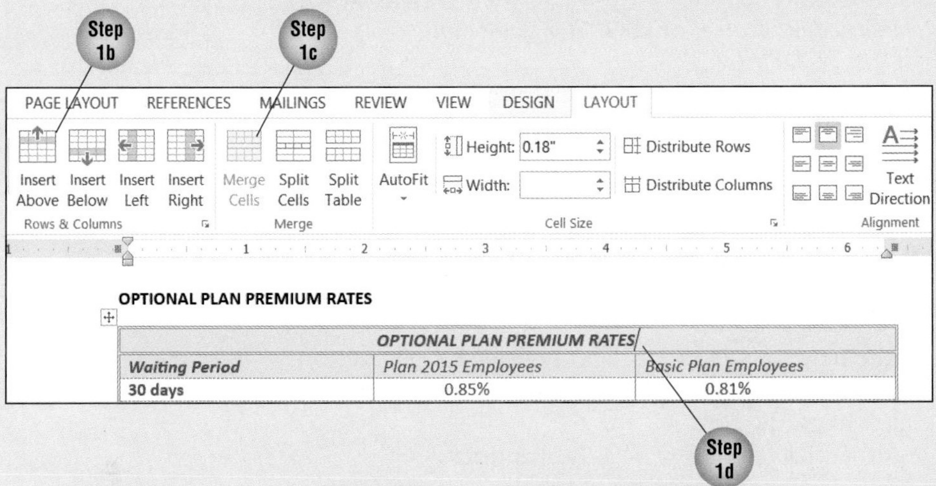

2. Select and then delete the text *OPTIONAL PLAN PREMIUM RATES* that displays above the bottom table.
3. Insert rows and text in the top table and merge cells by completing the following steps:
   a. Click in the cell containing the text *Maggie Rivera*.
   b. Click the TABLE TOOLS LAYOUT tab.
   c. Click the Insert Above button twice. (This inserts two rows at the top of the table.)
   d. With the cells in the top row selected, click the Merge Cells button in the Merge group.
   e. Type **CONTACT INFORMATION, NORTH** and then press Ctrl + E to change the paragraph alignment to center.
   f. Type the following text in the four cells in the new second row.

      Name **Title** **Company** **Telephone**

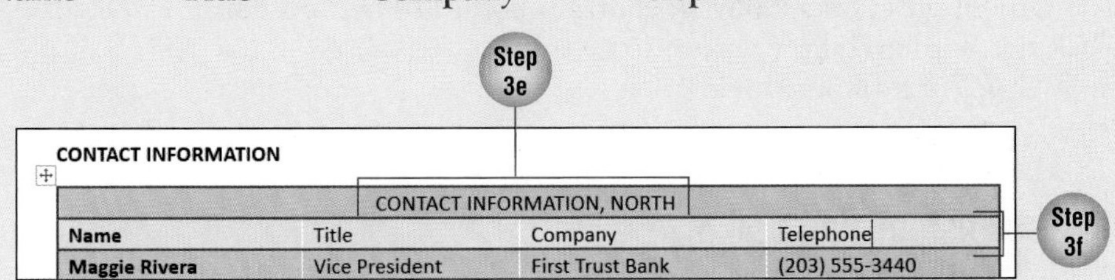

4. Apply heading formatting to the new top row by completing the following steps:
   a. Click the TABLE TOOLS DESIGN tab.
   b. Click the *Header Row* check box in the Table Style Options group.
5. Select and then delete the text *CONTACT INFORMATION* that displays above the top table.
6. Split a cell by completing the following steps:
   a. Click in the cell containing the telephone number *(301) 555-1201*.
   b. Click the TABLE TOOLS LAYOUT tab.
   c. Click the Split Cells button in the Merge group.
   d. At the Split Cells dialog box, click OK. (The telephone number will wrap to a new line. You will change this in the next project.)

e. Click in the new cell.

f. Type x453 in the new cell. If AutoCorrect automatically capitalizes the *x*, hover the mouse pointer over the *X* until the AutoCorrect Options button displays. Click the AutoCorrect Options button and then click *Undo Automatic Capitalization* or click *Stop Auto-capitalizing First Letter of Table Cells*.

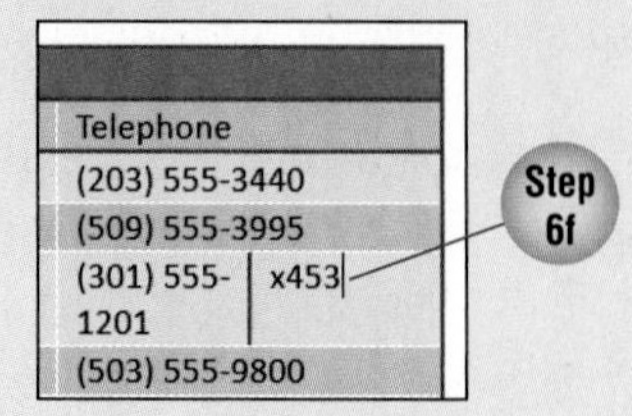

Telephone
(203) 555-3440
(509) 555-3995
(301) 555-1201
x453
(503) 555-9800
Step 6f

7. Split the cell containing the telephone number *(206) 555-6788* and then type **x2310** in the new cell. (If necessary, make the *x* lowercase.)
8. Split the top table into two tables by completing the following steps:
   a. Click in the cell containing the name *Teresa Getty*.
   b. Click the Split Table button in the Merge group.
   c. Click in the cell containing the name *Teresa Getty* (in the first row of the new table).
   d. Click the Insert Above button in the Rows and Columns group on the TABLE TOOLS LAYOUT tab.
   e. With the new row selected, click the Merge Cells button.
   f. Type **CONTACT INFORMATION, SOUTH** in the new row and then press Ctrl + E to center-align the text.
9. Save and then print **WL1-C7-P1-Tables.docx**.
10. Delete the middle table by completing the following steps:
    a. Click in any cell in the middle table.
    b. Click the TABLE TOOLS LAYOUT tab.
    c. Click the Delete button in the Rows & Columns group and then click *Delete Table* at the drop-down list.
11. Draw a dark orange border at the bottom of the top table by completing the following steps:
    a. Click in any cell in the top table and then click the TABLE TOOLS DESIGN tab.
    b. Click the Line Weight button arrow in the Borders group and then click *1 ½ pt* at the drop-down list. (This activates the Border Painter button.)
    c. Click the Pen Color button and then click the *Orange, Accent 2, Darker, 50%* option (sixth column, bottom row in the *Theme Colors* section).
    d. Using the mouse, drag along the bottom border of the top table.
    e. Click the Border Painter button to turn it off.
12. Save **WL1-C7-P1-Tables.docx**.

Customizing Cell Size

When you create a table, column width and row height are equal. You can customize the width of columns or height of rows with buttons in the Cell Size group on the TABLE TOOLS LAYOUT tab. Use the *Table Row Height* measurement box to increase or decrease the height of rows and use the *Table Column Width* measurement box to increase or decrease the width of columns. The Distribute Rows button will distribute equally the height of selected rows, and the Distribute Columns button will distribute equally the width of selected columns.

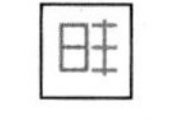
Distribute Rows

Distribute Columns

You can also change column width using the move table column markers on the horizontal ruler or by using the table gridlines. To change column width using the horizontal ruler, position the mouse pointer on a move table column marker until it turns into a left-and-right-pointing arrow, and then drag the marker to the desired position. Hold down the Shift key while dragging a table column marker and the horizontal ruler remains stationary while the table column marker moves.

Hold down the Alt key while dragging a table column marker and measurements display on the horizontal ruler. To change column width using gridlines, position the arrow pointer on the gridline separating columns until the insertion point turns into a left-and-right-pointing arrow with a vertical line in the middle and then drag the gridline to the desired position. If you want to see the column measurements on the horizontal ruler as you drag a gridline, hold down the Alt key.

Adjust row height in a manner similar to adjusting column width. You can drag the adjust table row marker on the vertical ruler or drag the gridline separating rows. Hold down the Alt key while dragging the adjust table row marker or the row gridline, and measurements display on the vertical ruler.

Use the AutoFit button in the Cell Size group to make the column widths in a table automatically fit the contents. To do this, position the insertion point in any cell in the table, click the AutoFit button in the Cell Size group, and then click *AutoFit Contents* at the drop-down list.

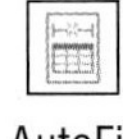
AutoFit

Project 1g Changing Column Width and Row Height

Part 7 of 9

1. With **WL1-C7-P1-Tables.docx** open, change the width of the first column in the top table by completing the following steps:
   a. Click in the cell containing the name *Maggie Rivera*.
   b. Position the mouse pointer on the move table column marker that displays just right of the 1.5-inch mark on the horizontal ruler until the pointer turns into a left-and-right-pointing arrow.
   c. Hold down the Shift key and then the left mouse button.
   d. Drag the marker to the 1.25-inch mark, release the mouse button, and then release the Shift key.

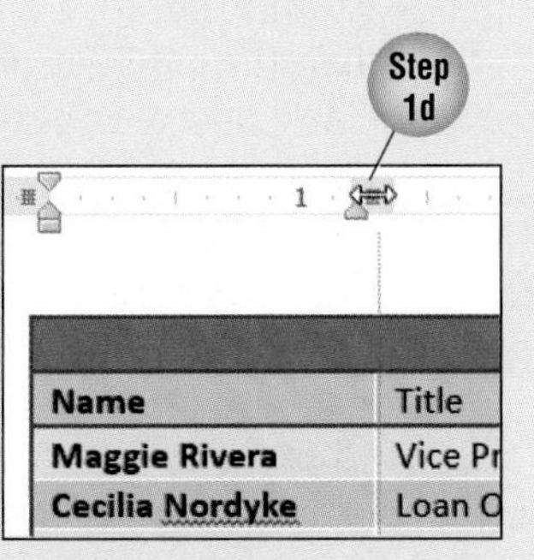

2. Complete steps similar to those in Step 1 to drag the move table column marker that displays just right of the 3-inch mark on the horizontal ruler to the 2.75-inch mark. (Make sure the text *Account Manager* in the second column does not wrap to the next line. If it does, slightly increase the width of the column.)
3. Change the width of the third column in the top table by completing the following steps:
   a. Position the mouse pointer on the gridline separating the third and fourth columns until the pointer turns into a left-and-right-pointing arrow with a vertical double line in the middle.
   b. Hold down the Alt key and then the left mouse button, drag the gridline to the left until the measurement for the third column on the horizontal ruler displays as *1.31"*, and then release the Alt key and then the mouse button.

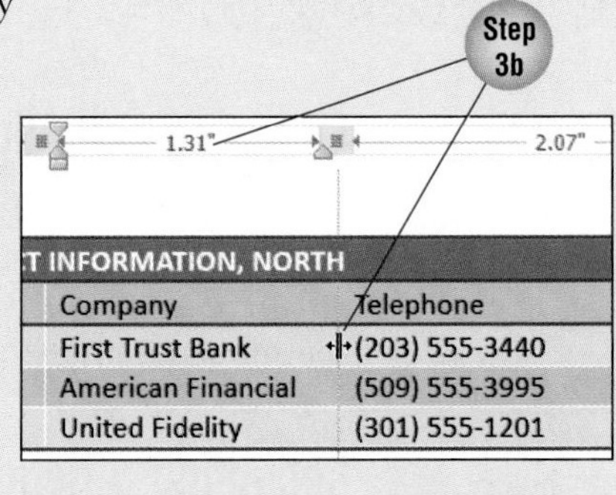

4. Position the mouse pointer on the gridline that separates the telephone number *(301) 555-1201* from the extension *x453* and then drag the gridline to the 5.25-inch mark on the horizontal ruler. (Make sure the phone number does not wrap down to the next line.)
5. Drag the right border of the top table to the 5.75-inch mark on the horizontal ruler.

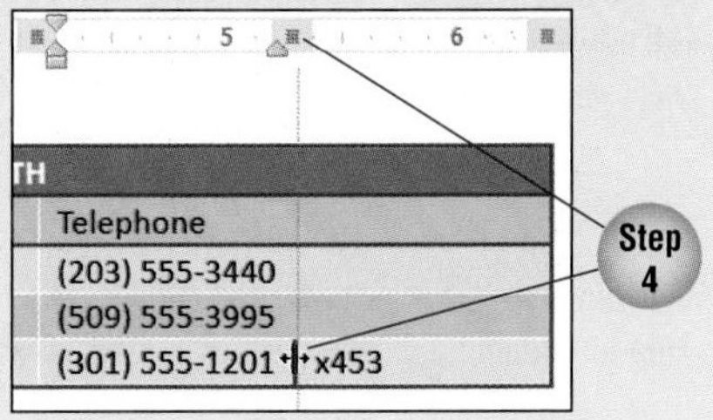

6. Automatically fit the columns in the bottom table by completing the following steps:
   a. Click in any cell in the bottom table.
   b. Click the AutoFit button in the Cell Size group on the TABLE TOOLS LAYOUT tab and then click *AutoFit Contents* at the drop-down list.

7. Increase the height of the first row in the bottom table by completing the following steps:
   a. Make sure the insertion point is located in one of the cells in the bottom table.
   b. Position the mouse pointer on the top adjust table row marker on the vertical ruler.
   c. Hold down the left mouse button and hold down the Alt key.
   d. Drag the adjust table row marker down until the first row measurement on the vertical ruler displays as *0.39"*, release the mouse button, and then release the Alt key.

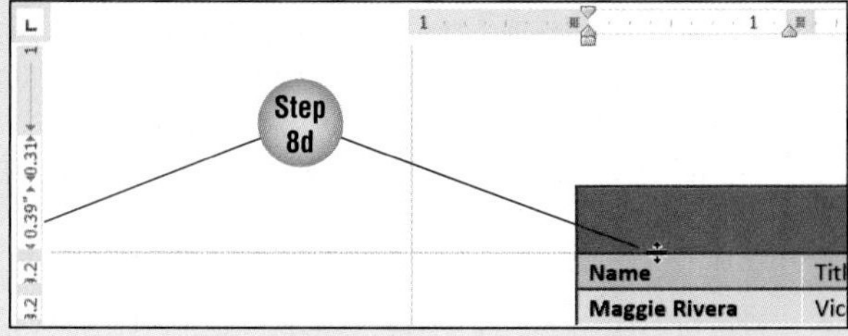

8. Increase the height of the first row in the top table by completing the following steps:
   a. Click in any cell in the top table.
   b. Position the arrow pointer on the gridline that displays at the bottom of the top row until the arrow pointer turns into an up-and-down-pointing arrow with a vertical double line in the middle.
   c. Hold down the left mouse button and then hold down the Alt key.
   d. Drag the gridline down until the first row measurement on the vertical ruler displays as *0.39"*, release the mouse button, and then release the Alt key.
9. Save **WL1-C7-P1-Tables.docx**.

Changing Cell Alignment

The Alignment group on the TABLE TOOLS LAYOUT tab contains a number of buttons for specifying the horizontal and vertical alignment of text in cells. Each button contains a visual representation of the alignment, and you can also hover the mouse pointer over a button to determine the alignment.

Quick Steps

Repeat a Header Row
1. Click in header row or select rows.
2. Click TABLE TOOLS LAYOUT tab.
3. Click Repeat Header Rows button.

Repeat Header Rows

Repeating a Header Row

If a table is divided between pages, consider adding the header row at the beginning of the table that continues on the next page. This helps the reader understand the data that displays in each column. To repeat a header row, click in the header row and then click the Repeat Header Rows button in the Data group on the TABLE TOOLS LAYOUT tab. If you want to repeat more than one header row, select the rows and then click the Repeat Header Rows button.

Project 1h Aligning Text in Cells and Repeating Header Rows Part 8 of 9

1. With **WL1-C7-P1-Tables.docx** open, click in the top cell in the top table (the cell containing the title *CONTACT INFORMATION, NORTH*).
2. Click the Align Center button in the Alignment group on the TABLE TOOLS LAYOUT tab.
3. Format and align text in the second row in the top table by completing the following steps:
   a. Select the second row.
   b. Press Ctrl + B to turn off bold formatting for the entry in the first cell and then press Ctrl + B again to turn on bold formatting for all entries in the second row.
   c. Click the Align Top Center button in the Alignment group.
4. Click in the top cell in the bottom table and then click the Align Center button in the Alignment group.
5. Press Ctrl + End to move the insertion point to the end of the document, press the Enter key four times, and then insert a table into the current document by completing the following steps:
   a. Click the INSERT tab.
   b. Click the Object button arrow in the Text group and then click *Text from File* at the drop-down list.
   c. At the Insert File dialog box, navigate to the WL1C7 folder on your storage medium and then double-click ***ContactsWest.docx***.
6. Repeat the header row by completing the following steps:
   a. Select the first two rows in the table you just inserted.
   b. Click the TABLE TOOLS LAYOUT tab.
   c. Click the Repeat Header Rows button in the Data group.

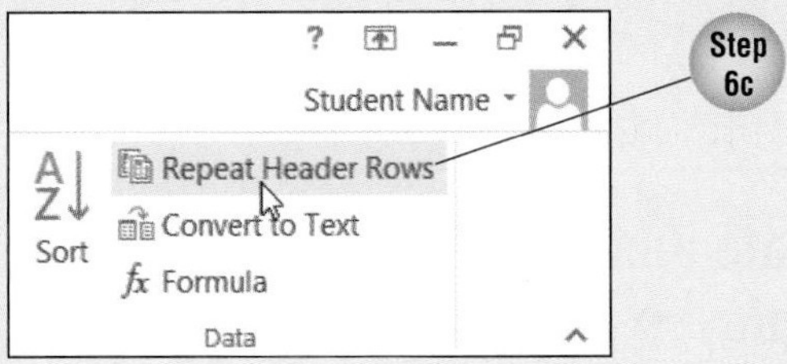

7. Save **WL1-C7-P1-Tables.docx**.

Inserting a Quick Table

Word includes a Quick Tables feature you can use to insert predesigned tables in a document. To insert a quick table, click the INSERT tab, click the Table button, point to *Quick Tables*, and then click the desired table at the side menu. A quick table has formatting applied, but you can further format the table with options at the TABLE TOOLS DESIGN tab and the TABLE TOOLS LAYOUT tab.

Quick Steps

Insert a Quick Table
1. Click INSERT tab.
2. Click Table button.
3. Point to *Quick Tables*.
4. Click desired table.

Project 1i Inserting a Quick Table

Part 9 of 9

1. With **WL1-C7-P1-Tables.docx** open, press Ctrl + End to move the insertion point to the end of the document and then press the Enter key.
2. Insert a quick table by clicking the INSERT tab, clicking the Table button, pointing to *Quick Tables*, and then clicking the *Calendar 3* option at the side menu.

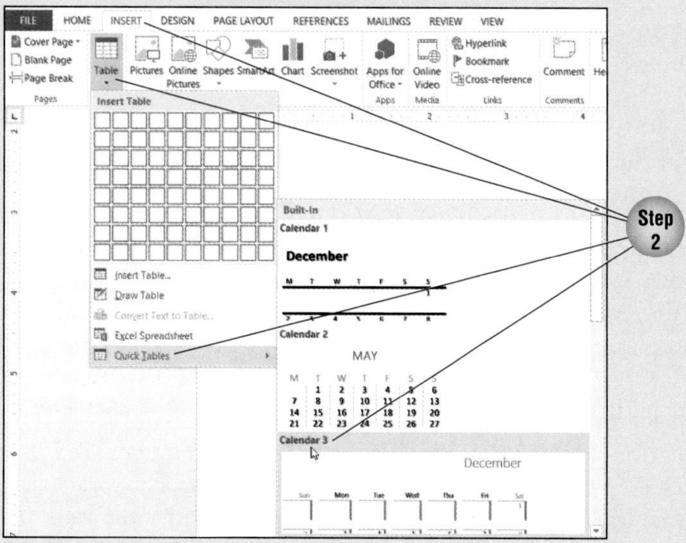

3. Edit text in each cell so the calendar reflects the current month. (If the bottom row is empty, select and then delete the row.)
4. Select the entire table by clicking the table move handle that displays outside the upper left corner of the table and then change the font to Copperplate Gothic Light.
5. Save, print, and then close **WL1-C7-P1-Tables.docx**.

Project 2 Create and Format Tables with Employee Information

5 Parts

You will create and format a table containing information on the names and departments of employees of Tri-State Products and also insert a table containing additional information on employees and then format the table.

Changing Cell Margin Measurements

Cell Margins

By default, cells in a table contain specific margin settings. Top and bottom margins in a cell have a default measurement of 0 inch and left and right margins have a default setting of 0.08 inch. Change these default settings with options at the Table Options dialog box shown in Figure 7.7. Display this dialog box by clicking the Cell Margins button in the Alignment group on the TABLE TOOLS LAYOUT tab. Use the measurement boxes in the *Default cell margins* section to change the top, bottom, left, and/or right cell margin measurements.

Figure 7.7 Table Options Dialog Box

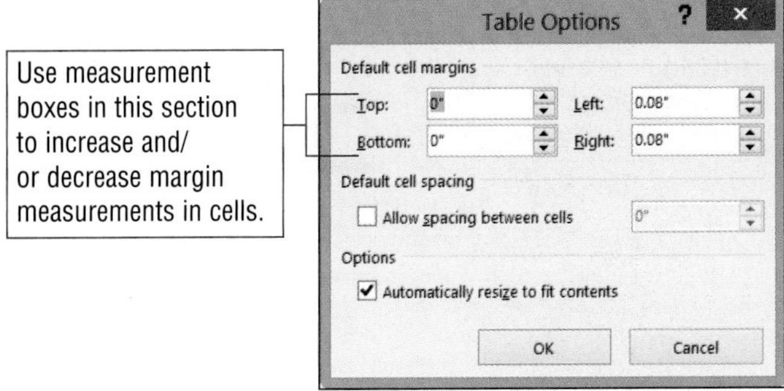

Changes to cell margins will affect all cells in a table. If you want to change the cell margin measurements for one cell or for selected cells, position the insertion point in the cell or select the desired cells and then click the Properties button in the Table group on the TABLE TOOLS LAYOUT tab. (You can also click the Cell Size group dialog box launcher.) At the Table Properties dialog box that displays, click the Cell tab and then the Options button that displays in the lower right corner of the dialog box. This displays the Cell Options dialog box shown in Figure 7.8.

Properties

Before setting the new cell margin measurements, remove the check mark from the *Same as the whole table* option. With the check mark removed from this option, the cell margin options become available. Specify the new cell margin measurements and then click OK to close the dialog box.

Figure 7.8 Cell Options Dialog Box

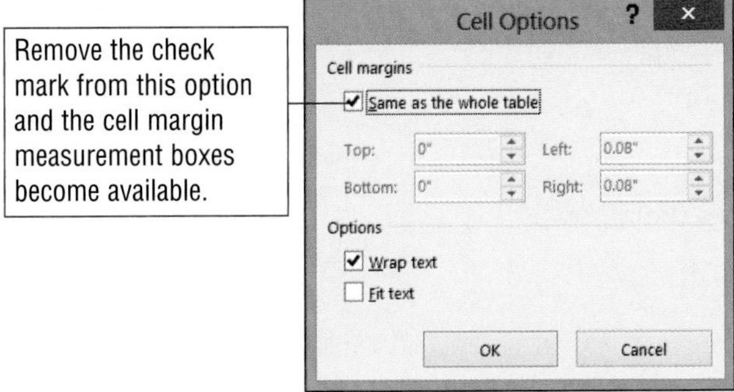

Project 2a **Changing Cell Margin Measurements** **Part 1 of 5**

1. Open **TSPTables.docx** and then save the document with Save As and name it **WL1-C7-P2-TSPTables**.
2. Change the top and bottom margins for all cells in the table by completing the following steps:
   a. Position the insertion point in any cell in the table and then click the TABLE TOOLS LAYOUT tab.
   b. Click the Cell Margins button in the Alignment group.

c. At the Table Options dialog box, change the *Top* and *Bottom* measurements to 0.05 inch.
d. Click OK to close the Table Options dialog box.

3. Change the top and bottom cell margin measurements for the first row of cells by completing the following steps:
   a. Select the first row of cells (the cells containing *Name* and *Department*).
   b. Click the Properties button in the Table group.
   c. At the Table Properties dialog box, click the Cell tab.
   d. Click the Options button located in the lower right corner of the dialog box.
   e. At the Cell Options dialog box, remove the check mark from the *Same as the whole table* option.
   f. Change the *Top* and *Bottom* measurements to 0.1 inch.
   g. Click OK to close the Cell Options dialog box.
   h. Click OK to close the Table Properties dialog box.
4. Change the left cell margin measurement for specific cells by completing the following steps:
   a. Select all rows in the table *except* the top row.
   b. Click the Cell Size group dialog box launcher.
   c. At the Table Properties dialog box, make sure the Cell tab is active.
   d. Click the Options button.
   e. At the Cell Options dialog box, remove the check mark from the *Same as the whole table* option.
   f. Change the *Left* measurement to 0.3 inch.
   g. Click OK to close the Cell Options dialog box.
   h. Click OK to close the Table Properties dialog box.
5. Save **WL1-C7-P2-TSPTables.docx**.

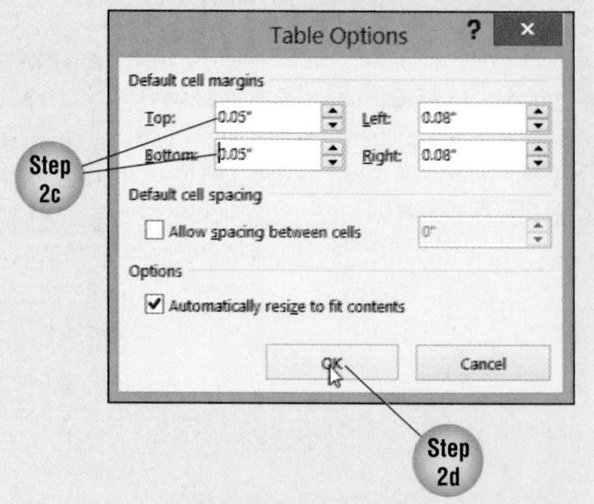

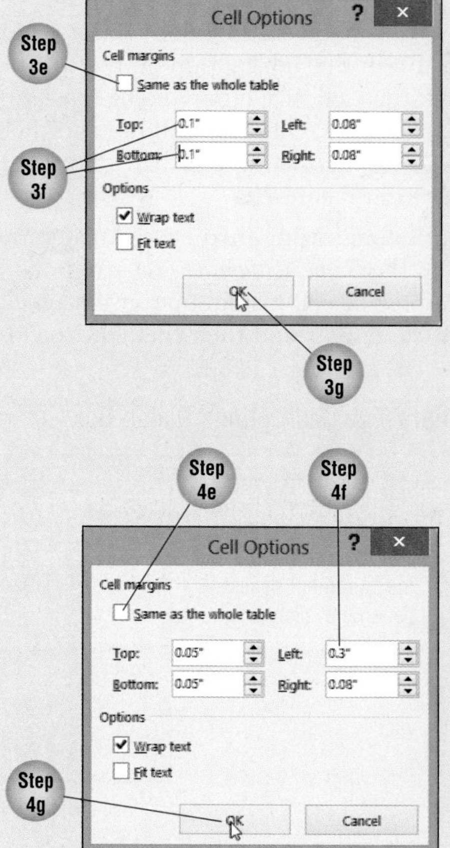

Changing Cell Direction

Text Direction

Change the direction of text in a cell using the Text Direction button in the Alignment group on the TABLE TOOLS LAYOUT tab. Each time you click the Text Direction button, the text rotates in the cell 90 degrees.

Changing Table Alignment and Dimensions

By default, a table aligns at the left margin. Change this alignment with options at the Table Properties dialog box with the Table tab selected, as shown in Figure 7.9. To change the alignment, click the desired alignment option in the *Alignment* section of the dialog box. Change table dimensions by clicking the *Preferred width* check box to insert a check mark. This makes the width measurement box active as well as the *Measure in* option box. Type a width measurement in the measurement box and specify whether the measurement type is inches or a percentage with the *Measurement in* option box.

Figure 7.9 Table Properties Dialog Box with Table Tab Selected

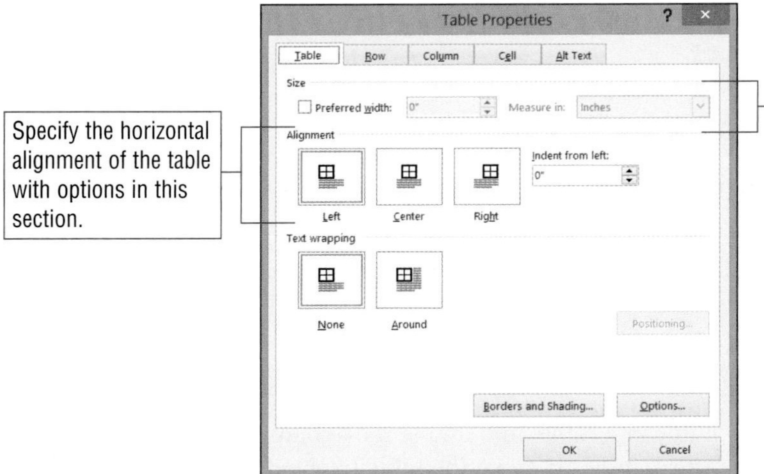

Change table dimensions by inserting a check mark in the *Preferred width* check box and then specifying the table width and measurement type.

Project 2b **Changing Table Alignment and Dimensions** **Part 2 of 5**

1. With **WL1-C7-P2-TSPTables.docx** open, insert a new column and change text direction by completing the following steps:
   a. Click in any cell in the first column.
   b. Click the Insert Left button in the Rows & Columns group.
   c. With the cells in the new column selected, click the Merge Cells button in the Merge group.
   d. Type **Tri-State Products**.
   e. Click the Align Center button in the Alignment group.
   f. Click twice on the Text Direction button in the Alignment group.
   g. With *Tri-State Products* selected, click the HOME tab and then increase the font size to 16 points.

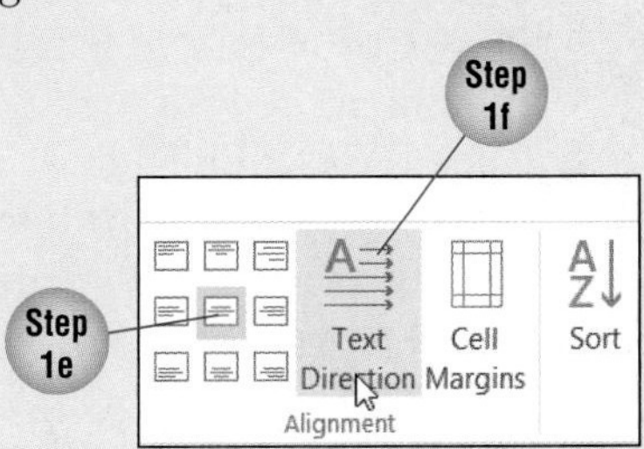

2. Automatically fit the contents by completing the following steps:
   a. Click in any cell in the table.
   b. Click the TABLE TOOLS LAYOUT tab.
   c. Click the AutoFit button in the Cell Size group and then click *AutoFit Contents* at the drop-down list.

3. Change the table dimension and alignment by completing the following steps:
   a. Click the Properties button in the Table group on the TABLE TOOLS LAYOUT tab.
   b. At the Table Properties dialog box, click the Table tab.
   c. Click the *Preferred width* check box.
   d. Select the measurement in the measurement box and then type 4.5.
   e. Click the *Center* option in the *Alignment* section.
   f. Click OK.
4. Select the two cells containing the text *Name* and *Department* and then click the Align Center button in the Alignment group.
5. Save **WL1-C7-P2-TSPTables.docx**.

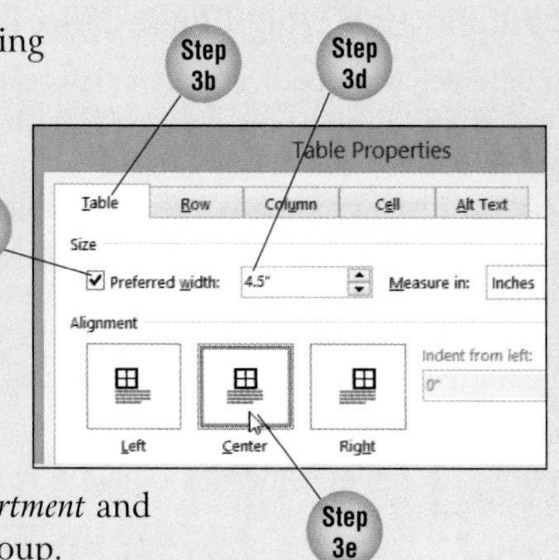

Changing Table Size with the Resize Handle

When you hover the mouse pointer over a table, a resize handle displays in the lower right corner of the table. The resize handle displays as a small, white square. Drag this resize handle to increase and/or decrease the size and proportion of the table.

Quick Steps

Move a Table

1. Position mouse pointer on table move handle until pointer displays with four-headed arrow attached.
2. Hold down left mouse button.
3. Drag table to desired position.
4. Release mouse button.

Moving a Table

Position the mouse pointer in a table and a table move handle displays in the upper left corner. Use this handle to move the table in the document. To move a table, position the mouse pointer on the table move handle until the pointer displays with a four-headed arrow attached, hold down the left mouse button, drag the table to the desired position, and then release the mouse button.

Project 2c **Resizing and Moving Tables** Part 3 of 5

1. With **WL1-C7-P2-TSPTables.docx** open, insert a table into the current document by completing the following steps:
   a. Press Ctrl + End to move the insertion point to the end of the document and then press the Enter key.
   b. Click the INSERT tab.
   c. Click the Object button arrow in the Text group and then click *Text from File* at the drop-down list.
   d. At the Insert File dialog box, navigate to the WL1C7 folder and then double-click ***TSPEmps.docx***.
2. Automatically fit the bottom table by completing the following steps:
   a. Click in any cell in the bottom table.
   b. Click the TABLE TOOLS LAYOUT tab.
   c. Click the AutoFit button in the Cell Size group and then click *AutoFit Contents* at the drop-down list.
3. Format the bottom table by completing the following steps:
   a. Click the TABLE TOOLS DESIGN tab.

b. Click the More button that displays at the right side of the styles thumbnails in the Table Styles group and then click the *List Table 4 - Accent 6* table style thumbnail (last column, fourth row in the *List Tables* section).

c. Click the *First Column* check box in the Table Style Options group to remove the check mark.

d. Select the first and second rows, click the TABLE TOOLS LAYOUT tab, and then click the Align Center button in the Alignment group.

e. Select the second row and then press Ctrl + B to turn on bold formatting.

Step 3b

4. Resize the bottom table by completing the following steps:

a. Position the mouse pointer on the resize handle located in the lower right corner of the bottom table.

b. Hold down the left mouse button, drag down and to the right until the width and height of the table increase approximately 1 inch, and then release the mouse button.

TRI-STATE PRODUCTS		
Name	**Employee #**	**Department**
Whitaker, Christine	1432-323-09	Financial Services
Higgins, Dennis	1230-933-21	Public Relations
Coffey, Richard	1321-843-22	Research and Development
Lee, Yong	1411-322-76	Human Resources
Fleishmann, Jim	1246-432-90	Public Relations
Schaffer, Mitchell	1388-340-44	Purchasing
Porter, Robbie	1122-361-38	Public Relations
Buchanan, Lillian	1432-857-87	Research and Development
Kensington, Jacob	1112-473-31	Human Resources

Steps 4a-4b

5. Move the bottom table by completing the following steps:

a. Move the mouse pointer over the bottom table and then position the mouse pointer on the table move handle until the pointer displays with a four-headed arrow attached.

b. Hold down the left mouse button, drag the table so it is positioned equally between the left and right margins, and then release the mouse button.

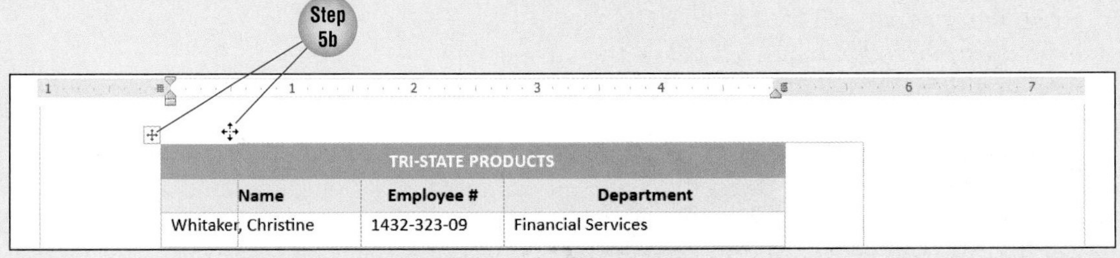

6. Select the cells in the column below the heading *Employee #* and then click the Align Top Center button in the Alignment group.

7. Save **WL1-C7-P2-TSPTables.docx**.

Quick Steps

Convert Text to a Table
1. Select text.
2. Click INSERT tab.
3. Click Table button.
4. Click *Convert Text to Table.*
5. Click OK.

Convert a Table to Text
1. Click TABLE TOOLS LAYOUT tab.
2. Click Convert to Text button.
3. Specify separator.
4. Click OK.

Convert to Text

Converting Text to a Table and a Table to Text

You can create a table and then enter text in the cells, or you can create the text and then convert it to a table. When typing the text, separate it with a separator character, such as a comma or tab. The separator character identifies where you want text divided into columns. To convert text, select the text, click the INSERT tab, click the Table button in the Tables group, and then click *Convert Text to Table* at the drop-down list.

You can convert a table to text by positioning the insertion point in any cell of the table, clicking the TABLE TOOLS LAYOUT tab, and then clicking the Convert to Text button in the Data group. At the Convert Table to Text dialog box, specify the desired separator and then click OK.

Project 2d Converting Text to a Table — Part 4 of 5

1. With **WL1-C7-P2-TSPTables.docx** open, press Ctrl + End to move the insertion point to the end of the document. (If the insertion point does not display below the second table, press the Enter key until the insertion point is below the second table.)
2. Insert the document named **TSPExecs.docx** into the current document.
3. Convert the text to a table by completing the following steps:
   a. Select the text you just inserted.
   b. Make sure the INSERT tab is active.
   c. Click the Table button in the Tables group and then click *Convert Text to Table* at the drop-down list.
   d. At the Convert Text to Table dialog box, type 2 in the *Number of columns* measurement box.
   e. Click the *AutoFit to contents* option in the *AutoFit behavior* section.
   f. Click the *Commas* option in the *Separate text at* section.
   g. Click OK.

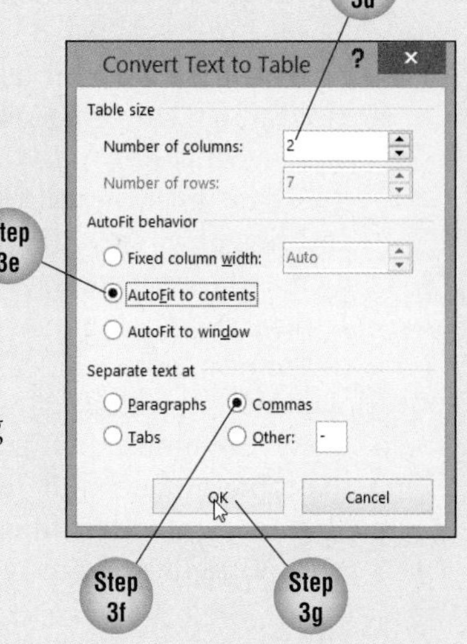

4. Select and merge the cells in the top row (the row containing the title *TRI-STATE PRODUCTS*) and then center-align the text in the merged cell.
5. Apply the List Table 4 - Accent 6 style (last column, fourth row in the *List Tables* section) and remove the check mark from the *First Column* check box in the Table Style Options group on the TABLE TOOLS DESIGN tab.
6. Drag the table so it is centered below the table above.
7. Apply the List Table 4 - Accent 6 style to the top table. Increase the width of the columns so the text *TRI-STATE PRODUCTS* is visible and the text in the second and third columns displays on one line.
8. Drag the table so it is centered above the middle table. Make sure the three tables fit on one page.
9. Click in the middle table and then convert the table to text by completing the following steps:
   a. Click the TABLE TOOLS LAYOUT tab and then click the Convert to Text button in the Data group.
   b. At the Convert Table to Text dialog box, click *Tabs* and then click OK.
10. Print **WL1-C7-P2-TSPTables.docx**.
11. Click the Undo button to return the text to a table.
12. Save **WL1-C7-P2-TSPTables.docx**.

Drawing a Table

In Project 1, you used options in the Borders group in the TABLE TOOLS DESIGN tab to draw borders around an existing table. You can also use these options to draw an entire table. To draw a table, click the INSERT tab, click the Table button in the Tables group, and then click *Draw Table* at the drop-down list; or, click the Draw Table button in the Draw group on the TABLE TOOLS LAYOUT tab. This turns the mouse pointer into a pen. Drag the pen pointer in the document to create the table. If you make a mistake while drawing a table, click the Eraser button in the Draw group on the TABLE TOOLS LAYOUT tab (which changes the mouse pointer to an eraser) and then drag over any border lines you want to erase. You can also click the Undo button to undo your most recent action.

Eraser

Project 2e **Drawing and Formatting a Table** **Part 5 of 5**

1. With **WL1-C7-P2-TSPTables.docx** open, select and then delete three rows in the middle table from the row that begins with the name *Lee, Yong* through the row that begins with the name *Schaffer, Mitchell*.
2. Move the insertion point to the end of the document (outside of any table) and then press the Enter key.
3. Click the INSERT tab, click the Table button, and then click the *Draw Table* option at the drop-down list. (This turns the insertion point into a pen.)
4. Using the mouse, drag in the document (below the bottom table) to create the table shown at the right. If you make a mistake, click the Undo button. You can also click the Eraser button in the Draw group on the TABLE TOOLS LAYOUT tab and drag over a border line to erase it. Click the Draw Table button in the Draw group to turn the pen off.

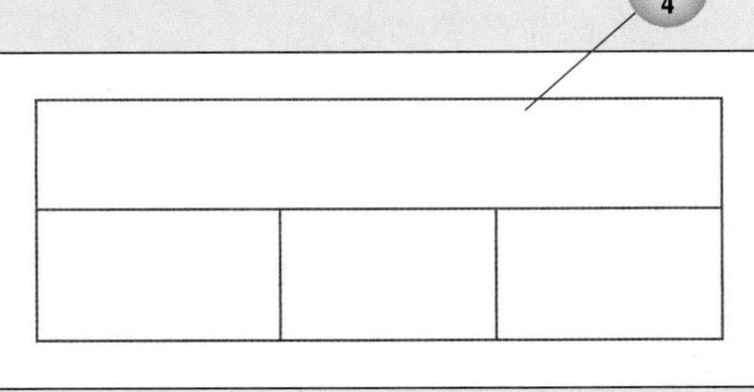

5. After drawing the table, type **Tri-State Products** in the top cell, **Washington Division** in the cell at the left, **Oregon Division** in the middle bottom cell, and **California Division** in the cell at the right.
6. Apply the Grid Table 4 - Accent 6 table style.
7. Select the table, change the font size to 12 points, turn on bold formatting, and then center-align the text in the cells.
8. Make any adjustments needed to border lines so text displays on one line in each cell.
9. Drag the table so it is centered and positioned below the bottom table.
10. Save, print, and then close **WL1-C7-P2-TSPTables.docx**.

Project 3 **Sort and Calculate Sales Data** **2 Parts**

You will sort data in tables on Tri-State Products sales and then insert formulas to calculate total sales, average sales, and top sales.

Sort

Quick Steps

Sort Text in a Table
1. Select desired rows.
2. Click Sort button on TABLE TOOLS LAYOUT tab.
3. Specify column containing text to sort.
4. Click OK.

Sorting Text in a Table

Use the Sort button in the Data group on the TABLE TOOLS LAYOUT tab to sort text in selected cells in a table in ascending or descending alphabetic or numeric order. To sort text, select the desired rows in the table and then click the Sort button in the Data group. At the Sort dialog box, specify the column containing the text on which you want to sort, and then click OK.

Project 3a **Sorting Text in a Table** **Part 1 of 2**

1. Open **TSPSalesTables.docx** and then save the document with Save As and name it **WL1-C7-P3-TSPSalesTables**.
2. Sort text in the top table by completing the following steps:
   a. Select all of the rows containing names (from *Novak, Diana* through *Sogura, Jeffrey*).
   b. Click the TABLE TOOLS LAYOUT tab.
   c. Click the Sort button in the Data group.
   d. At the Sort dialog box, click OK. (This sorts the last names in the first column in alphabetical order.)

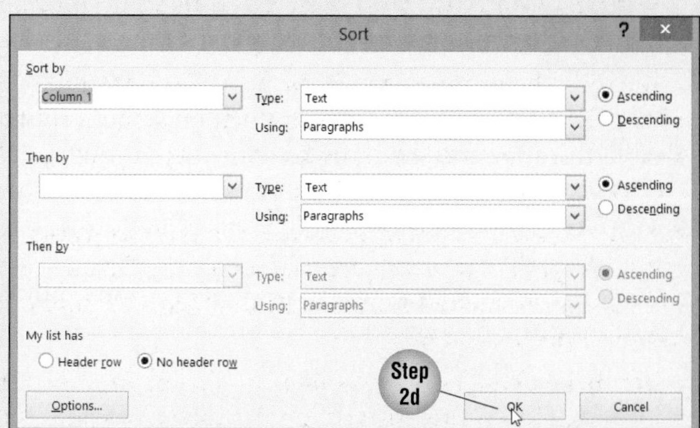

3. After looking at the table, you decide to sort by sales in 2014. To do this, complete the following steps:
   a. With the rows still selected, click the Sort button in the Data group.
   b. At the Sort dialog box, click the down-pointing arrow at the right side of the *Sort by* option box and then click *Column 2* at the drop-down list.
   c. Click the Descending option in the *Sort by* section.
   d. Click OK.
   e. Deselect the rows.
4. Save **WL1-C7-P3-TSPSalesTables.docx**.

Performing Calculations in a Table

Quick Steps

Insert a Formula in a Table
1. Click in cell.
2. Click TABLE TOOLS LAYOUT tab.
3. Click Formula button.
4. Type formula in Formula dialog box.
5. Click OK.

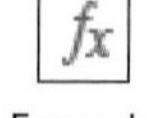
Formula

Use the Formula button in the Data group on the TABLE TOOLS LAYOUT tab to insert formulas that calculate data in a table. Numbers in cells in a table can be added, subtracted, multiplied, and divided. In addition, you can perform other calculations, such as determine averages, count items, and identify minimum and maximum values. You can calculate data in a Word table, but for complex calculations you should use an Excel worksheet.

To perform a calculation on data in a table, position the insertion point in the cell where you want the result of the calculation inserted and then click the Formula button in the Data group on the TABLE TOOLS LAYOUT tab. This displays the Formula dialog box, as shown in Figure 7.10. At this dialog box, accept the default formula that displays in the *Formula* text box or type the desired calculation, and then click OK.

Figure 7.10 Formula Dialog Box

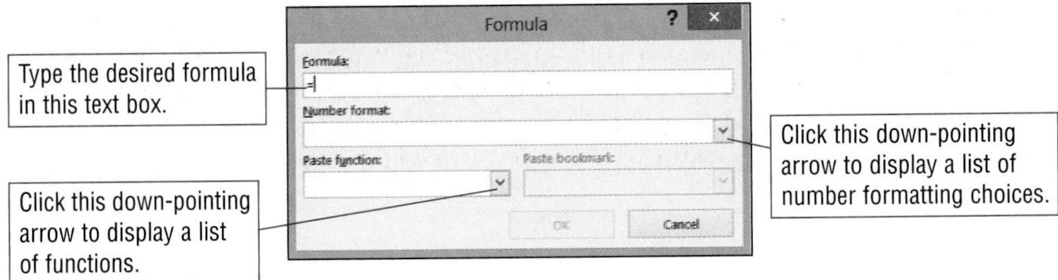

You can use four basic operators when writing a formula, including the plus sign (+) for addition, the minus sign (–) for subtraction, the asterisk (*) for multiplication, and the forward slash (/) for division. If a calculation contains two or more operators, Word calculates from left to right. If you want to change the order of calculation, use parentheses around the part of the calculation to be performed first.

In the default formula, the **SUM** part of the formula is called a ***function***. Word provides other functions you can use to write a formula. These functions are available in the *Paste function* option box in the Formula dialog box. For example, you can use the AVERAGE function to average numbers in cells.

Specify the numbering format with the *Number format* option box in the Formula dialog box. For example, if you are calculating money amounts, you can specify that the calculated numbers display with no numbers or two numbers following the decimal point.

If you make changes to the values in a formula, you need to update the result of the formula. To do this, right-click the formula result and then click *Update Field* at the shortcut menu. You can also select the formula result and then press the F9 function key, which is the Update Field keyboard shortcut. To update the results of all formulas in a table, select the entire table and then press the F9 function key.

Project 3b **Inserting Formulas** **Part 2 of 2**

1. With **WL1-C7-P3-TSPSalesTables.docx** open, insert a formula by completing the following steps:
   a. Click in cell B9. (Cell B9 is the empty cell located immediately below the cell containing the amount *$294,653.*)
   b. Click the TABLE TOOLS LAYOUT tab.
   c. Click the Formula button in the Data group.
   d. At the Formula dialog box, make sure *=SUM(ABOVE)* displays in the *Formula* text box.
   e. Click the down-pointing arrow at the right side of the *Number format* option box and then click *#,##0* at the drop-down list (top option in the list).
   f. Click OK to close the Formula dialog box.
   g. At the table, type a dollar sign ($) before the number just inserted in cell B9.

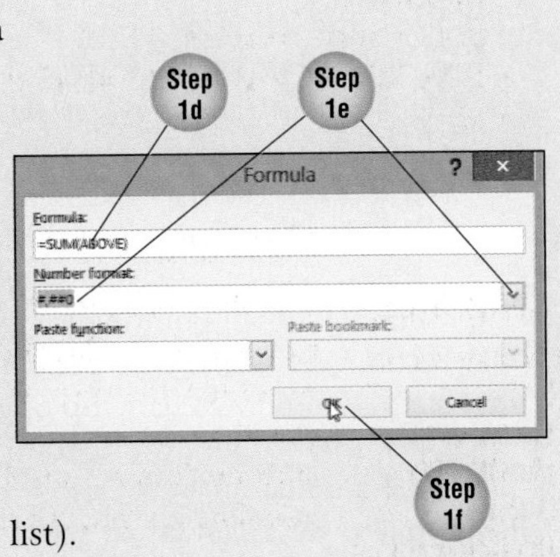

2. Complete steps similar to those in Steps 1c through 1g to insert a formula in cell C9. (Cell C9 is the empty cell located immediately below the cell containing the amount *$300,211.*)

3. Complete steps similar to those in Steps 1c through 1g to insert in the bottom table formulas that calculate totals. Insert formulas in the cells in the *Total* row and *Total* column. When inserting formulas in cells F2 through F6, make sure the formula at the Formula dialog box displays as *=SUM(LEFT)*.
4. Insert a formula that calculates the average of amounts by completing the following steps:
   a. Click in cell B10 in the top table. (Cell B10 is the empty cell immediately right of the cell containing the word *Average*.)
   b. Click the Formula button in the Data group.
   c. At the Formula dialog box, delete the formula in the *Formula* text box *except* the equals sign.
   d. With the insertion point positioned immediately right of the equals sign, click the down-pointing arrow at the right side of the *Paste function* option box and then click *AVERAGE* at the drop-down list.
   e. With the insertion point positioned between the left and right parentheses, type B2:B8. (When typing cell designations in a formula, you can type either uppercase or lowercase letters.)
   f. Click the down-pointing arrow at the right side of the *Number format* option box and then click *#,##0* at the drop-down list (top option in the list).
   g. Click OK to close the Formula dialog box.
   h. Type a dollar sign ($) before the number just inserted in cell B10.

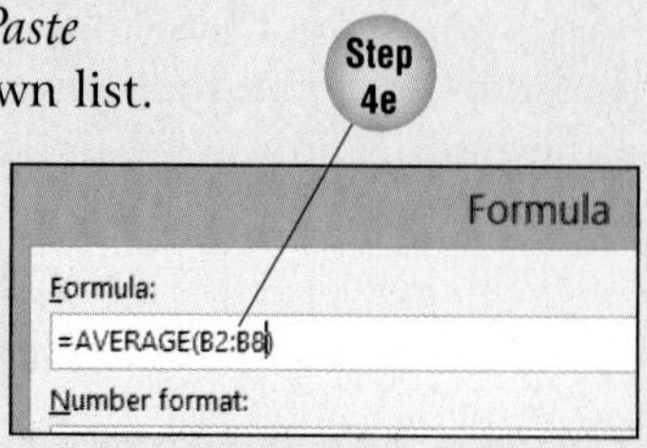

5. Complete steps similar to those in Steps 4b through 4h to insert a formula in cell C10 in the top table that calculates the average of cells C2 through C8.
6. Complete steps similar to those in Steps 4b through 4h to insert a formula in cell B7 in the bottom table that calculates the average of cells B2 through B5. Complete similar steps to insert in cell C7 the average of cells C2 through C5; insert in cell D7 the average of cells D2 through D5; insert in cell E7 the average of cells E2 through E5; and insert in cell F7 the average of cells F2 through F5.
7. Insert a formula that calculates the maximum number by completing the following steps:
   a. Click in cell B11 in the top table. (Cell B11 is the empty cell immediately right of the cell containing the words *Top Sales*.)
   b. Click the Formula button in the Data group.
   c. At the Formula dialog box, delete the formula in the *Formula* text box *except* the equals sign.
   d. With the insertion point positioned immediately right of the equals sign, click the down-pointing arrow at the right side of the *Paste function* option box and then click *MAX* at the drop-down list. (You will need to scroll down the list to display the *MAX* option.)
   e. With the insertion point positioned between the left and right parentheses, type B2:B8.
   f. Click the down-pointing arrow at the right side of the *Number format* option box and then click *#,##0* at the drop-down list (top option in the list).
   g. Click OK to close the Formula dialog box.
   h. Type a dollar sign ($) before the number just inserted in cell B11.

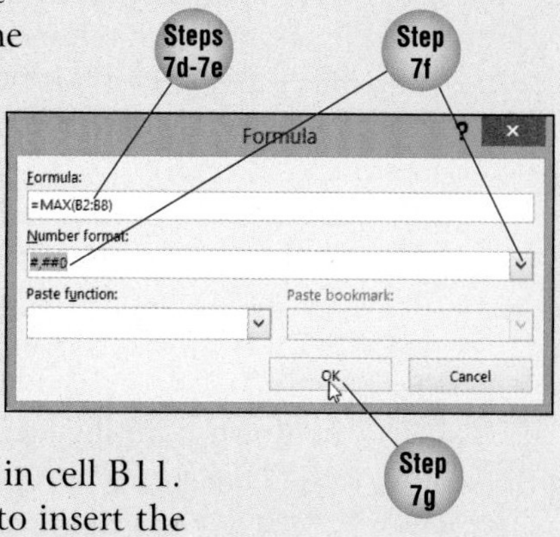

8. Complete steps similar to those in Steps 7b through 7h to insert the maximum number in cell C11.
9. Apply to each table the Grid Table 2 - Accent 6 table style and remove the check mark from the *First Column* option.
10. Drag the tables so they are centered and positioned below the title and subtitle.
11. Save, print, and then close **WL1-C7-P3-TSPSalesTables.docx**.

Project 4 Prepare and Format a SmartArt Graphic — 2 Parts

You will prepare a SmartArt process graphic identifying steps in the production process and then apply formatting to enhance the graphic.

Creating SmartArt

Use SmartArt to communicate your message and ideas in a visual manner.

With Word's SmartArt feature you can insert graphics such as diagrams and organizational charts in a document. SmartArt offers a variety of predesigned graphics that are available at the Choose a SmartArt Graphic dialog box, as shown in Figure 7.11. At this dialog box, by default, *All* is selected in the left panel and all available predesigned SmartArt graphics display in the middle panel.

Inserting and Formatting a SmartArt Graphic

Quick Steps

Insert a SmartArt Graphic

1. Click INSERT tab.
2. Click SmartArt button.
3. Double-click desired graphic.

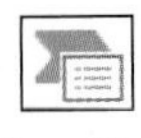

SmartArt

HINT

Limit the number of shapes and the amount of text in your SmartArt graphic.

To insert a SmartArt graphic, click the INSERT tab and then click the SmartArt button in the Illustrations group to open the Choose a SmartArt Graphic dialog box. Predesigned SmartArt graphics display in the middle panel of the dialog box. Use the scroll bar at the right side of the middle panel to scroll down the list of choices. Click a graphic in the middle panel and its name displays in the right panel along with a description. SmartArt includes graphics for presenting a list of data; showing data processes, cycles, and relationships; and presenting data in a matrix or pyramid. Double-click a graphic in the middle panel of the dialog box and the graphic is inserted in the document.

When you double-click a graphic at the dialog box, the graphic is inserted in the document and a text pane displays at the left side of the graphic. Type text in the text pane or directly in the graphic. Apply formatting to a graphic with options at the SMARTART TOOLS DESIGN tab. This tab becomes active when the graphic is inserted in the document. With options and buttons on this tab, you add objects, change the graphic layout, apply a style to the graphic, and reset the graphic back to the original formatting.

Figure 7.11 Choose a SmartArt Graphic Dialog Box

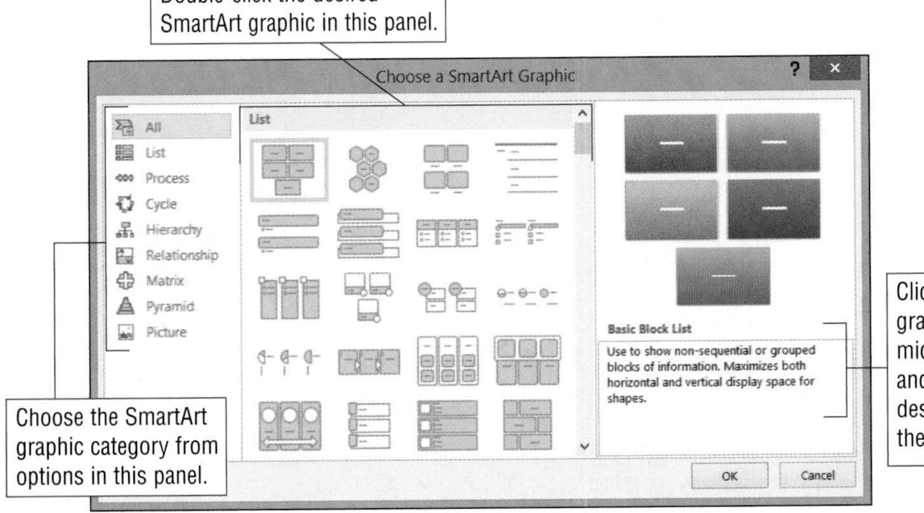

Apply formatting to a graphic with options on the SMARTART TOOLS FORMAT tab. Use options and buttons on this tab to change the size and shape of objects in the graphic; apply shape styles and WordArt styles; change the shape fill, outline, and effects; and arrange and size the graphic.

Project 4a Inserting and Formatting a SmartArt Graphic — Part 1 of 2

1. At a blank document, insert the SmartArt graphic shown in Figure 7.12 by completing the following steps:
   a. Click the INSERT tab.
   b. Click the SmartArt button in the Illustrations group.
   c. At the Choose a SmartArt Graphic dialog box, click *Process* in the left panel and then double-click the *Alternating Flow* graphic.
   d. If a *Type your text here* text pane does not display at the left side of the graphic, click the Text Pane button in the Create Graphic group to display the pane.
   e. With the insertion point positioned after the top bullet in the *Type your text here* text pane, type **Design**.
   f. Click *[Text]* that displays below *Design* and then type **Mock-up**.
   g. Continue clicking occurrences of *[Text]* and typing text so the text pane displays as shown at the right.
   h. Close the text pane by clicking the Close button (a gray X) that displays in the upper right corner of the pane. (You can also click the Text Pane button in the Create Graphic group.)

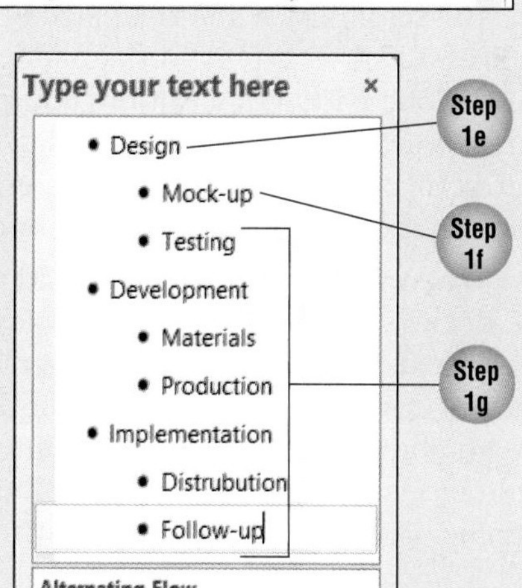

2. Change the graphic colors by clicking the Change Colors button in the SmartArt Styles group and then clicking the *Colorful Range - Accent Colors 5 to 6* option (last option in the *Colorful* section).

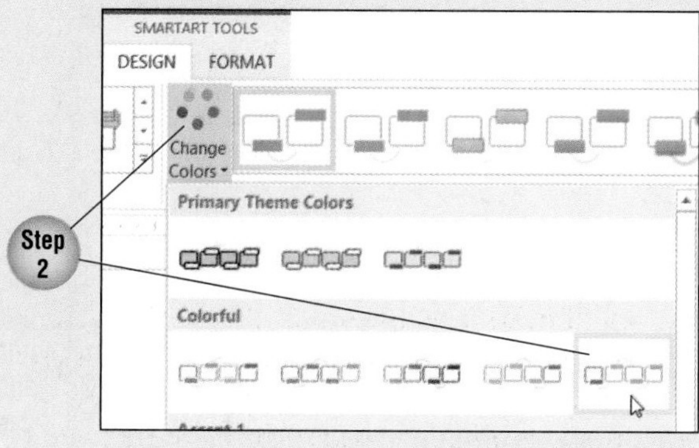

3. Apply a style by clicking the More button that displays at the right side of the option in the SmartArt Styles group and then clicking the *Inset* option (second column, first row in the *3-D* section).
4. Copy the graphic and then change the layout by completing the following steps:
   a. Click inside the SmartArt graphic border but outside any shapes.
   b. Click the HOME tab and then click the Copy button in the Clipboard group.
   c. Press Ctrl + End, press the Enter key once, and then press Ctrl + Enter to insert a page break.
   d. Click the Paste button in the Clipboard group.
   e. With the SmartArt graphic on the second page selected (the one you just pasted), click the SMARTART TOOLS DESIGN tab.
   f. Click the More button that displays at the right side of the options in the Layouts group and then click the *Continuous Block Process* layout.
   g. Click outside the graphic to deselect it.
5. Save the document and name it **WL1-C7-P4-SAGraphics**.

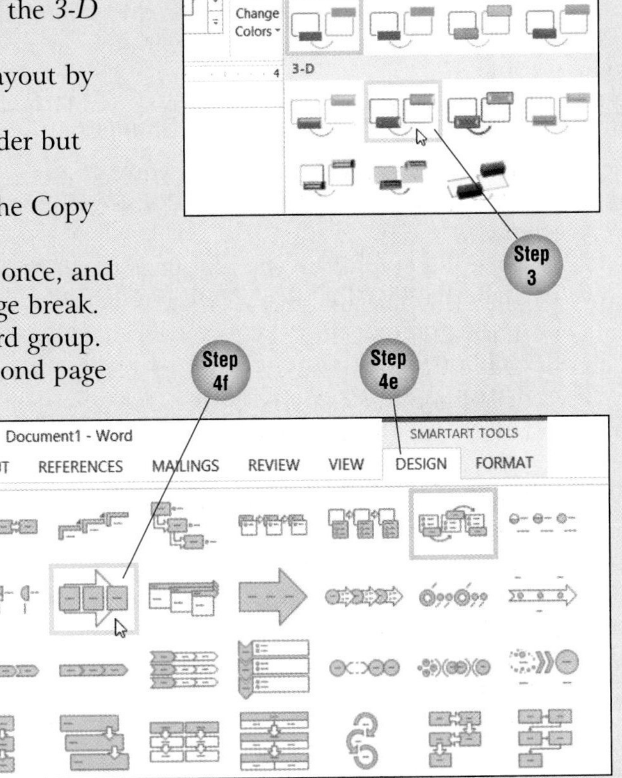

Figure 7.12 Project 4a

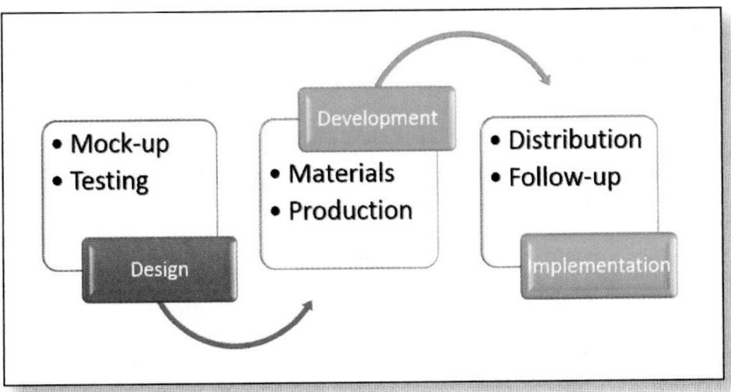

Arranging and Moving a SmartArt Graphic

Position a SmartArt graphic by clicking the Arrange button on the SMARTART TOOLS FORMAT tab, clicking the Position button, and then clicking the desired position option at the drop-down gallery. Along with positioning the SmartArt graphic, the options at the Position button drop-down gallery apply the Square text wrapping. You can also apply text wrapping by clicking the Arrange button, clicking the Wrap Text button, and then clicking the desired wrapping style at the drop-down

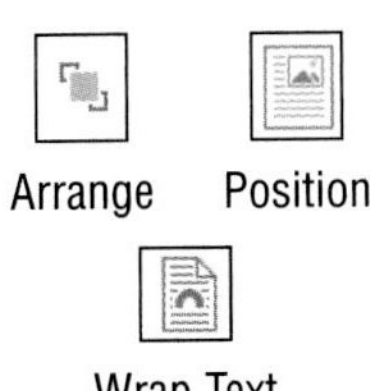

gallery or with options from the Layout Options button that displays outside the upper right corner of the selected SmartArt graphic. Move a SmartArt graphic by positioning the arrow pointer on the graphic border until the pointer displays with a four-headed arrow attached, holding down the left mouse button, and then dragging the graphic to the desired location. Nudge the SmartArt graphic or a shape or selected shapes in the graphic with the up, down, left, or right arrow keys on the keyboard.

Project 4b Formatting SmartArt Graphics — Part 2 of 2

1. With **WL1-C7-P4-SAGraphics.docx** open, format shapes by completing the following steps:
   a. Click the graphic on the first page to select it (a border surrounds the graphic).
   b. Click the SMARTART TOOLS FORMAT tab.
   c. In the graphic, click the rectangle shape containing the word *Design*.
   d. Hold down the Shift key and then click the shape containing the word *Development*.
   e. With the Shift key still down, click the shape containing the word *Implementation*. (All three shapes should now be selected.)
   f. Click the Change Shape button in the Shapes group.
   g. Click the *Pentagon* shape (seventh column, second row in the *Block Arrows* section).
   h. With the shapes still selected, click the Larger button in the Shapes group.
   i. With the shapes still selected, click the Shape Outline button arrow in the Shape Styles group and then click the *Dark Blue* option (ninth option in the *Standard Colors* section).
   j. Click inside the graphic border but outside any shape. (This deselects the shapes but keeps the graphic selected.)

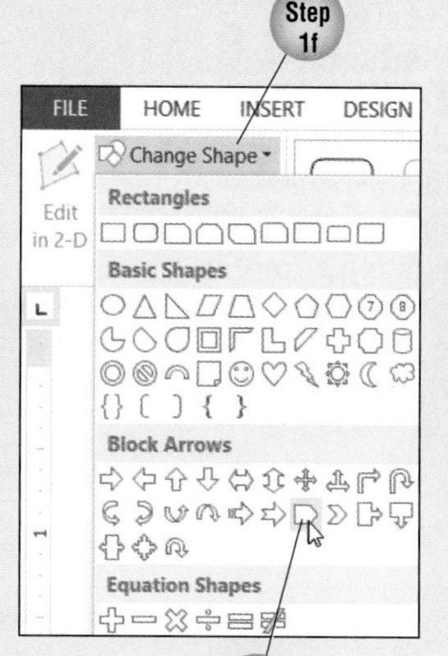

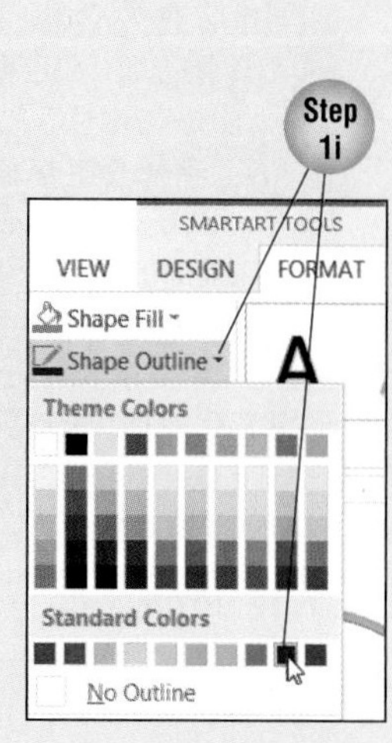

2. Change the size of the graphic by completing the following steps:
   a. Click the Size button located at the right side of the SMARTART TOOLS FORMAT tab.
   b. Click in the *Shape Height* measurement box, type 4, and then press Enter.
3. Position the graphic by completing the following steps:
   a. Click the Arrange button on the SMARTART TOOLS FORMAT tab and then click the Position button at the drop-down list.
   b. Click the *Position in Middle Center with Square Text Wrapping* option (second column, second row in the *With Text Wrapping* section).
   c. Click outside the graphic to deselect it.

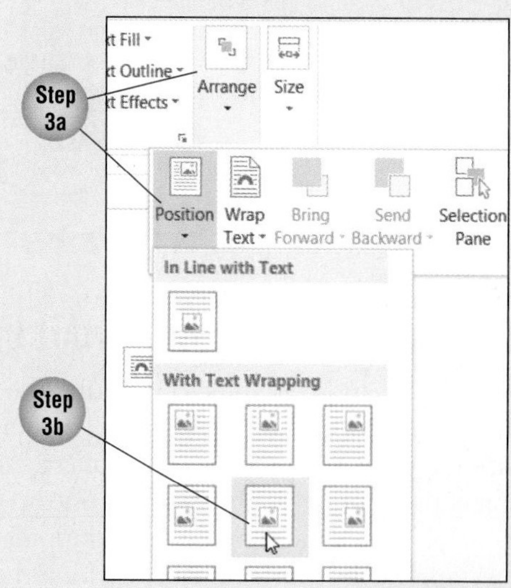

4. Format the bottom SmartArt graphic by completing the following steps:
   a. Press Ctrl + End to move to the end of the document and then click in the bottom SmartArt graphic to select it.
   b. Hold down the Shift key and then click each of the three shapes.
   c. Click the More button at the right side of the style options in the WordArt Styles group on the SMARTART TOOLS FORMAT tab.
   d. Click the *Fill - Black, Text 1, Shadow* option (first column, first row).
   e. Click the Text Outline button arrow in the WordArt Styles group and then click the *Dark Blue* option (ninth color in the *Standard Colors* section).
   f. Click the Text Effects button in the WordArt Styles group, point to *Glow* at the drop-down list, and then click the *Orange, 5 pt glow, Accent color 2* option (second column, first row in the *Glow Variations* section).
   g. Click inside the SmartArt graphic border but outside any shape.
5. Arrange the graphic by clicking the Arrange button, clicking the Position button, and then clicking the *Position in Middle Center with Square Text Wrapping* option (second column, second row in the *With Text Wrapping* section).
6. Click outside the graphic to deselect it.
7. Save, print, and then close **WL1-C7-P4-SAGraphics.docx**.

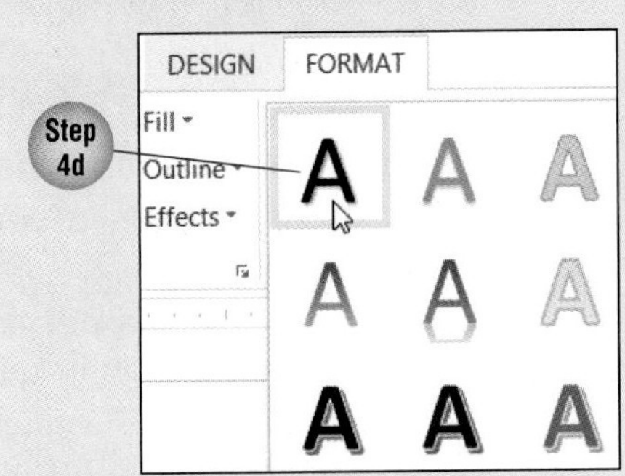

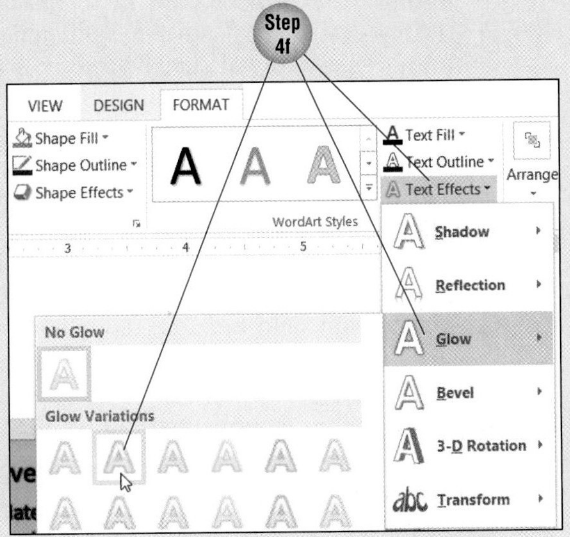

Project 5 Prepare and Format a Company Organizational Chart 1 Part

You will prepare an organizational chart for a company and then apply formatting to enhance the visual appeal of the chart.

Creating an Organizational Chart with SmartArt

If you need to visually illustrate hierarchical data, consider creating an organizational chart with a SmartArt option. To display organizational chart SmartArt options, click the INSERT tab and then click the SmartArt button in the Illustrations group. At the Choose a SmartArt Graphic dialog box, click *Hierarchy* in the left panel. Organizational chart options display in the middle panel of the dialog box. Double-click the desired organizational chart, and the chart is inserted in the document. Type text in a SmartArt graphic by selecting

Quick Steps

Insert an Organizational Chart
1. Click INSERT tab.
2. Click SmartArt button.
3. Click *Hierarchy*.
4. Double-click desired organizational chart.

the shape and then typing text in the shape, or type text in the *Type your text here* window that displays at the left side of the graphic. Format a SmartArt organizational chart with options and buttons on the SMARTART TOOLS DESIGN tab, the SMARTART TOOLS FORMAT tab, and the Layout Options button.

Project 5 Creating and Formatting a SmartArt Organizational Chart Part 1 of 1

1. At a blank document, create the organizational chart shown in Figure 7.13. To begin, click the INSERT tab.
2. Click the SmartArt button in the Illustrations group.
3. At the Choose a SmartArt Graphic dialog box, click *Hierarchy* in the left panel of the dialog box and then double-click the *Organization Chart* option (first option in the middle panel).
4. If a *Type your text here* pane displays at the left side of the organizational chart, close the pane by clicking the Text Pane button in the Create Graphic group.
5. Delete one of the boxes in the organizational chart by clicking the border of the box in the lower right corner to select it and then pressing the Delete key. (Make sure that the selection border that surrounds the box is a solid line and not a dashed line. If a dashed line displays, click the box border again. This should change it to a solid line.)
6. With the bottom right box selected, click the Add Shape button arrow in the Create Graphic group and then click the *Add Shape Below* option.
7. Click *[Text]* in the top box, type **Blaine Willis**, press Shift + Enter, and then type **President**. Click in each of the remaining boxes and type the text as shown in Figure 7.13. (Press Shift + Enter after typing the name.)
8. Click the More button located at the right side of the style options in the SmartArt Styles group and then click the *Inset* style (second column, first row in the *3-D* section).
9. Click the Change Colors button in the SmartArt Styles group and then click the *Colorful Range - Accent Colors 4 to 5* option (fourth column, first row in the *Colorful* section).
10. Click the SMARTART TOOLS FORMAT tab.
11. Click the text pane control (displays with a left-pointing arrow) that displays at the left side of the graphic border. (This displays the *Type your text here* window.)
12. Using the mouse, select all of the text that displays in the *Type your text here* window.

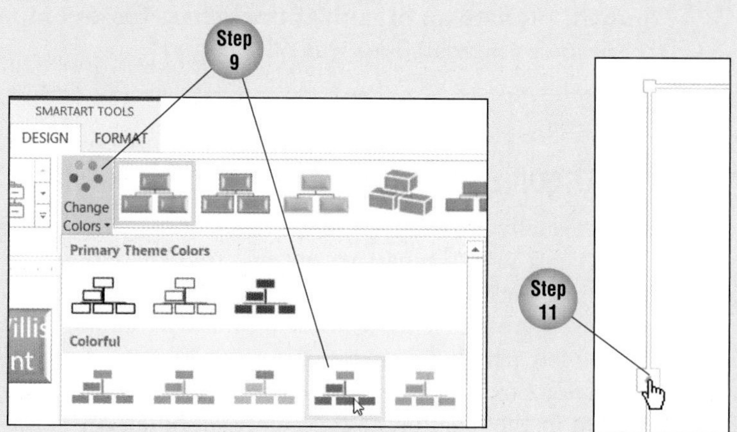

13. Click the Change Shape button in the Shapes group and then click the *Round Same Side Corner Rectangle* option (eighth option in the *Rectangles* section).
14. Click the Shape Outline button arrow in the Shape Styles group and then click the *Dark Blue* color (ninth option in the *Standard Colors* section).
15. Close the *Type your text here* window by clicking the Close button (gray X) located in the upper right corner of the window.
16. Click inside the organizational chart border but outside any shape.
17. Click the Size button located at the right side of the SMARTART TOOLS FORMAT tab, click in the *Shape Height* measurement box, and then type 4. Click in the *Shape Width* measurement box, type 6.5, and then press Enter.
18. Click outside the chart to deselect it.
19. Save the document and name it **WL1-C7-P5-OrgChart**.
20. Print and then close the document.

Figure 7.13 Project 5

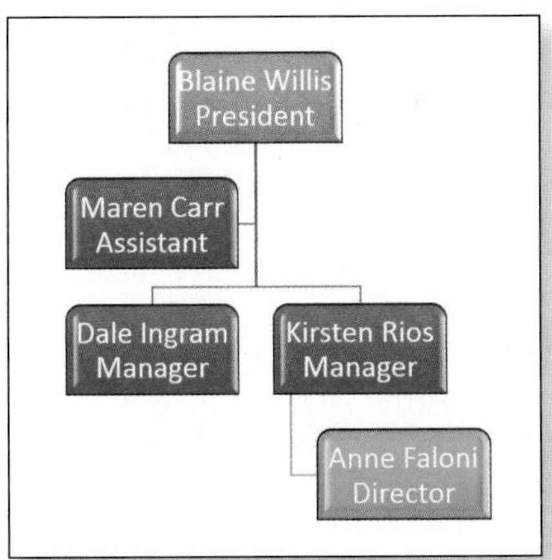

Chapter Summary

- Use the Tables feature to create columns and rows of information. Create a table with the Table button in the Tables group on the INSERT tab or with options at the Insert Table dialog box.
- A cell is the intersection between a row and a column. The lines that form the cells of the table are called gridlines.
- Move the insertion point to cells in a document using the mouse by clicking in the desired cell, or use the keyboard commands shown in Table 7.1.
- Change the table design with options and buttons on the TABLE TOOLS DESIGN tab.
- Refer to Table 7.2 for a list of mouse commands for selecting specific cells in a table and Table 7.3 for a list of keyboard commands for selecting specific cells in a table.
- Change the layout of a table with options and buttons on the TABLE TOOLS LAYOUT tab.

- Select a table, column, row, or cell using the Select button in the Table group on the TABLE TOOLS LAYOUT tab.
- Turn on and off the display of gridlines by clicking the TABLE TOOLS LAYOUT tab and then clicking the View Gridlines button in the Table group.
- Insert and delete columns and rows with buttons in the Rows & Columns group on the TABLE TOOLS LAYOUT tab.
- Merge selected cells with the Merge Cells button and split cells with the Split Cells button, both located in the Merge group on the TABLE TOOLS LAYOUT tab.
- Change column width and row height using the height and width measurement boxes in the Cell Size group on the TABLE TOOLS LAYOUT tab; by dragging move table column markers on the horizontal ruler, adjust table row markers on the vertical ruler, or gridlines in the table; or with the AutoFit button in the Cell Size group.
- Change alignment of text in cells with buttons in the Alignment group on the TABLE TOOLS LAYOUT tab.
- If a table spans two pages, you can insert a header row at the beginning of the rows that extend to the next page. To do this, click in the header row or select the desired header rows, and then click the Repeat Header Rows button in the Data group on the TABLE TOOLS LAYOUT tab.
- Quick Tables are predesigned tables you can insert in a document by clicking the INSERT tab, clicking the Table button, pointing to *Quick Tables*, and then clicking the desired table at the side menu.
- Change cell margins with options in the Table Options dialog box.
- Change text direction in a cell with the Text Direction button in the Alignment group.
- Change the table dimensions and alignment with options at the Table Properties dialog box with the Table tab selected.
- Use the resize handle to change the size of the table and the table move handle to move the table.
- Convert text to a table with the *Convert Text to Table* option at the Table button drop-down list. Convert a table to text with the Convert to Text button in the Data group on the TABLE TOOLS LAYOUT tab.
- Draw a table in a document by clicking the INSERT tab, clicking the Table button, and then clicking *Draw Table*. Using the mouse, drag in the document to create the table.
- Sort selected rows in a table with the Sort button in the Data group.
- Perform calculations on data in a table by clicking the Formula button in the Data group on the TABLE TOOLS LAYOUT tab and then specifying the formula and number format at the Formula dialog box.
- Use the SmartArt feature to insert predesigned graphics and organizational charts in a document. Click the SmartArt button on the INSERT tab to display the Choose a SmartArt Graphic dialog box.
- Format a SmartArt graphic with options and buttons on the SMARTART TOOLS DESIGN tab and the SMARTART TOOLS FORMAT tab.
- Choose a position or a text wrapping style for a SmartArt graphic with the Arrange button in the SMARTART TOOLS FORMAT tab or the Layout Options button that displays outside the upper right corner of the selected SmartArt graphic.

Commands Review

FEATURE	RIBBON TAB, GROUP	BUTTON	OPTION
AutoFit table contents	TABLE TOOLS LAYOUT, Cell Size		
cell alignment	TABLE TOOLS LAYOUT, Alignment		
Choose a SmartArt Graphic dialog box	INSERT, Illustrations		
convert table to text	TABLE TOOLS LAYOUT, Data		
convert text to table	INSERT, Tables		*Convert Text to Table*
delete column	TABLE TOOLS LAYOUT, Rows & Columns		*Delete Columns*
delete row	TABLE TOOLS LAYOUT, Rows & Columns		*Delete Rows*
delete table	TABLE TOOLS LAYOUT, Rows & Columns		*Delete Table*
draw table	INSERT, Tables		*Draw Table*
Formula dialog box	TABLE TOOLS LAYOUT, Data	fx	
insert column left	TABLE TOOLS LAYOUT, Rows & Columns		
insert column right	TABLE TOOLS LAYOUT, Rows & Columns		
insert row above	TABLE TOOLS LAYOUT, Rows & Columns		
insert row below	TABLE TOOLS LAYOUT, Rows & Columns		
Insert Table dialog box	INSERT, Tables		*Insert Table*
merge cells	TABLE TOOLS LAYOUT, Merge		
Quick Table	INSERT, Tables		*Quick Tables*
repeat header row	TABLE TOOLS LAYOUT, Data		
sort text in table	TABLE TOOLS LAYOUT, Data	A Z ↓	
Split Cells dialog box	TABLE TOOLS LAYOUT, Merge		
table	INSERT, Tables		
Table Options dialog box	TABLE TOOLS LAYOUT, Alignment		
text direction	TABLE TOOLS LAYOUT, Alignment		
view gridlines	TABLE TOOLS LAYOUT, Table		

Concepts Check Test Your Knowledge 

Completion: In the space provided at the right, indicate the correct term, command, or number.

1. The Table button is located on this tab. ____________________
2. This is another name for the lines that form the cells of the table. ____________________
3. Use this keyboard shortcut to move the insertion point to the preceding cell in a table. ____________________
4. Use this keyboard shortcut to move the insertion point to a tab within a cell in a table. ____________________
5. This tab contains table styles you can apply to a table. ____________________
6. Click this button on the TABLE TOOLS LAYOUT tab to insert a column at the left side of the column containing the insertion point. ____________________
7. Insert and delete columns and rows with buttons in this group on the TABLE TOOLS LAYOUT tab. ____________________
8. One method for changing column width in a table is dragging this on the horizontal ruler. ____________________
9. Use this button in the Cell Size group to make the column widths in a table automatically fit the contents. ____________________
10. Change the table alignment at this dialog box with the Table tab selected. ____________________
11. Position the mouse pointer in a table and this displays in the lower right corner of the table. ____________________
12. Position the mouse pointer in a table and this displays in the upper left corner. ____________________
13. Display the Formula dialog box by clicking the Formula button in this group on the TABLE TOOLS LAYOUT tab. ____________________
14. A variety of predesigned graphics and organizational charts are available at this dialog box. ____________________
15. The SmartArt button is located on this tab. ____________________
16. If you need to visually illustrate hierarchical data, consider creating this with the SmartArt feature. ____________________

Skills Check Assess Your Performance

Assessment 1

CREATE, FORMAT, AND MODIFY A TRAINING SCHEDULE TABLE

1. At a blank document, create a table with four columns and five rows.
2. Type text in cells as shown in Figure 7.14.
3. Insert a new column at the right side of the table and then type the following text in the new cells:
   Trainer
   Marsden
   Trujillo
   Yong
   Stein
4. Change the width of each column to the following measurements:
   First column = 0.8 inch
   Second column = 1.2 inches
   Third column = 0.7 inch
   Fourth column = 1.3 inches
   Fifth column = 0.9 inch
5. Insert a new row above the first row and then with the new row selected, merge the cells. Type **APPLICATION TRAINING SCHEDULE** in the cell and then center the text.
6. Select the second row (contains the text *Section*, *Training*, *Days*, and so on) and then bold and center the text.
7. Display the TABLE TOOLS DESIGN tab, apply the Grid Table 4 table style (first column, fourth row in the *Grid Tables* section), and then remove the check mark from the *First Column* check box.
8. Horizontally center the table on the page. ***Hint: Do this at the Table Properties dialog box with the Table tab selected.***
9. Save the document and name it **WL1-C7-A1-SchTable**.
10. Print and then close **WL1-C7-A1-SchTable.docx**.

Figure 7.14 Assessment 1

Section	Training	Days	Time
WD100	Word Level 1	MWF	9:00-10:00 a.m.
WD110	Word Level 2	TTh	1:30-3:00 p.m.
EX100	Excel Level 1	MTW	3:00-4:00 p.m.
EX110	Excel Level 2	TTh	2:00-3:30 p.m.

Assessment

2 CREATE, FORMAT, AND MODIFY A PROPERTY REPLACEMENT COSTS TABLE

1. At a blank document, create a table with two columns and six rows.
2. Type the text in the cells in the table as shown in Figure 7.15. (Press the Enter key after typing the word *PROPERTY* in the first cell.)
3. Merge the cells in the top row and then center the text in the merged cell.
4. Right-align the cells containing the money amounts as well as the blank cell below the last amount (cells B2 through B6).
5. Click in the *Accounts receivable* cell and then insert a row below. Type **Equipment** in the new cell at the left, and type **$83,560** in the new cell at the right.
6. Select rows 2 through 6 and then sort the amounts in column 2 in descending order.
7. Insert a formula in cell B7 that sums the amounts in cells B2 through B6 and change the number format to *#,##0*. Insert a dollar sign before the amount in cell B7.
8. Automatically fit the contents of the cells.
9. Apply the Grid Table 4 - Accent 1 table style (second column, fourth row in the *Grid Tables* section) and remove the check mark from the *First Column* check box.
10. Click the Border Styles button arrow, click the *Double solid lines, 1/2 pt* option (first column, third row in the *Theme Borders* section), and then draw a border around all four sides of the table.
11. Save the document and name it **WL1-C7-A2-CostsTable.**
12. Print and then close **WL1-C7-A2-CostsTable.docx.**

Figure 7.15 Assessment 2

PROPERTY REPLACEMENT COSTS	
Accounts receivable	$95,460
Business personal property	$1,367,340
Legal liability	$75,415
Earnings and expenses	$945,235
Total	

Assessment 3

FORMAT A TABLE ON TRANSPORTATION SERVICES

1. Open **ServicesTable.docx** and then save the document with Save As and name it **WL1-C7-A3-ServicesTable**.
2. Insert a new column at the left and then merge the cells. Type Metro Area in the merged cell, press the Enter key, and then type Transportation Services.
3. Select the text in the first column, change the font size to 16 points, and then click the Text Direction button twice to rotate the text. ***Hint: The Text Direction button is located in the Alignment group on the TABLE TOOLS LAYOUT tab.***
4. Center-align (use the Align Center button) the text in the first column.
5. Change the width of the first column to 0.9 inch and the width of the third column to 1.1 inches.
6. Apply the Grid Table 5 Dark - Accent 5 table style (sixth column, fifth row in the *Grid Tables* section).
7. Horizontally center the table on the page.
8. Indent the text in the three cells below the cell containing the text *Valley Railroad,* as shown in Figure 7.16.
9. Apply italic and bold formatting to the four headings in the second column (*Langley City Transit*, *Valley Railroad*, *Mainline Bus*, and *Village Travel Card*).
10. Save, print, and then close **WL1-C7-A3-ServicesTable.docx**.

Figure 7.16 Assessment 3

Metro Area Transportation Services	Service	Telephone
	Langley City Transit	
	Subway and bus information	(507) 555-3049
	Service status hotline	(507) 555-4123
	Travel information	(507) 555-4993
	Valley Railroad	
	Railway information	(202) 555-2300
	Status hotline	(202) 555-2343
	Travel information	(202) 555-2132
	Mainline Bus	
	Bus routes	(507) 555-6530
	Emergency hotline	(507) 555-6798
	Travel information	(507) 555-7542
	Village Travel Card	
	Village office	(507) 555-1232
	Card inquiries	(507) 555-1930

Assessment

4 CREATE AND FORMAT A COMPANY SMARTART GRAPHIC

1. At a blank document, create the SmartArt graphic shown in Figure 7.17 with the following specifications:
   a. Use the Titled Matrix SmartArt graphic.
   b. Apply the Colorful - Accent Colors SmartArt style.
   c. Apply the Polished SmartArt style.
   d. With the middle shape selected, apply the Intense Effect - Green, Accent 6 shape style (located on the SMARTART TOOLS FORMAT tab).
   e. Type all of the text shown in Figure 7.17.
   f. Select only the SmartArt graphic (not a specific shape) and then apply the Fill - Black, Text 1, Outline - Background 1, Hard Shadow - Background 1 WordArt style (first column, third row) to the text.
   g. Change the height of the SmartArt graphic to 3.2 inches and the width to 5.3 inches.
   h. Change the position of the SmartArt graphic to *Position in Top Center with Square Text Wrapping*.
2. Save the document and name it **WL1-C7-A4-OCGraphic**.
3. Print and then close **WL1-C7-A4-OCGraphic.docx**.

Figure 7.17 Assessment 4

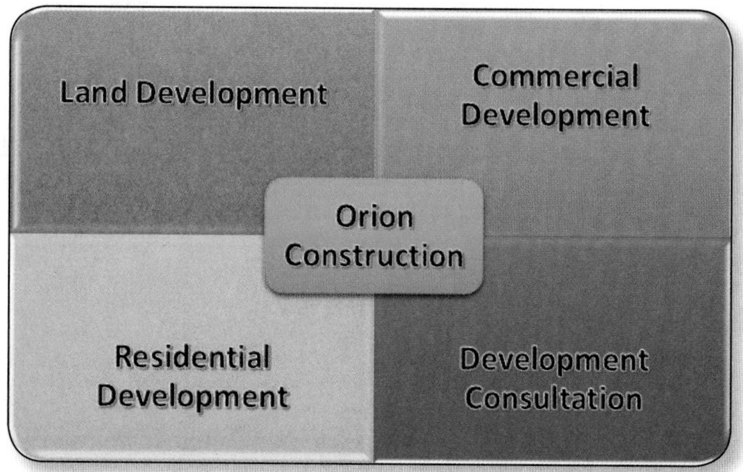

Assessment

5 CREATE AND FORMAT A COMPANY ORGANIZATIONAL CHART

1. At a blank document, create the organizational chart shown in Figure 7.18 with the following specifications:
   a. Use the Hierarchy SmartArt graphic.
   b. With the top text box selected, insert a shape above.
   c. Select the text box at the right in the third row and then add a shape below.
   d. Type the text shown in the organizational chart in Figure 7.18.
   e. Apply the Colorful Range - Accent Colors 3 to 4 SmartArt style.
   f. Increase the height to 4.5 inches and the width to 6.5 inches.
   g. Position the organizational chart in the middle of the page with square text wrapping.
2. Save the document and name it **WL1-C7-A5-OrgChart**.
3. Print and then close **WL1-C7-A5-OrgChart.docx**.

Figure 7.18 Assessment 5

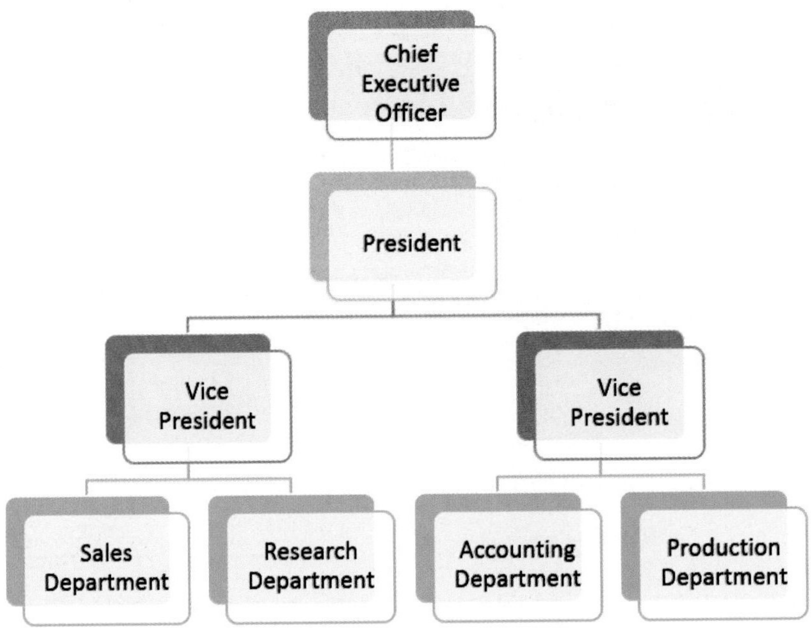

Assessment 6

INSERT FORMULAS IN A TABLE

1. In this chapter, you learned how to insert formulas in a table. Experiment with writing formulas (consider using the Help feature or other reference) and then open **FinAnalysis.docx**. Save the document with Save As and name it **WL1-C7-A6-FinAnalysis**.
2. Apply the Grid Table 4 - Accent 6 table style to the table and then apply other formatting so your table appears similar to the table in Figure 7.19.
3. Insert a formula in cell B13 that sums the amounts in cells B6 through B12. Type a dollar sign before the amount. Complete similar steps to insert formulas and dollar signs in cells C13, D13, and E13.
4. Insert a formula in cell B14 that subtracts the amount in B13 from the amount in B4. ***Hint: The formula should look like this:*** **=(B4-B13)**. Type a dollar sign before the amount. Complete similar steps to insert formulas and dollar signs in cells C14, D14, and E14.
5. Save, print, and then close **WL1-C7-A6-FinAnalysis.docx**.

Figure 7.19 Assessment 6

TRI-STATE PRODUCTS				
Financial Analysis				
	2012	**2013**	**2014**	**2015**
Revenue	$1,450,348	$1,538,239	$1,634,235	$1,523,455
Expenses				
Facilities	$250,220	$323,780	$312,485	$322,655
Materials	$93,235	$102,390	$87,340	$115,320
Payroll	$354,390	$374,280	$380,120	$365,120
Benefits	$32,340	$35,039	$37,345	$36,545
Marketing	$29,575	$28,350	$30,310	$31,800
Transportation	$4,492	$5,489	$5,129	$6,349
Miscellaneous	$4,075	$3,976	$4,788	$5,120
Total				
Net Revenue				

Visual Benchmark Demonstrate Your Proficiency

1 CREATE A COVER LETTER CONTAINING A TABLE

1. Click the FILE tab, click the *New* option, and then double-click the *Single spaced (blank)* template.
2. At the single-spaced blank document, type the letter shown in Figure 7.20. Create and format the table in the letter as shown in the figure. ***Hint: Apply the Grid Table 4 - Accent 1 table style.***
3. Save the completed document and name it **WL1-C7-VB1-CoverLtr**.
4. Print and then close **WL1-C7-VB1-CoverLtr.docx**.

Figure 7.20 Visual Benchmark 1

10234 Larkspur Drive
Cheyenne, WY 82002
July 15, 2015

Dr. Theresa Sullivan
Rocky Mountain News
100 Second Avenue
Cheyenne, WY 82001

Dear Dr. Sullivan:

Your advertised opening for a corporate communications staff writer describes interesting challenges. As you can see from the table below, my skills and experience are excellent matches for the position.

QUALIFICATIONS AND SKILLS	
Your Requirement	**My Experience, Skills, and Value Offered**
Two years of business writing experience	Four years of experience creating diverse business messages, from corporate communications to feature articles and radio broadcast material.
Ability to complete projects by deadline	Proven project coordination skills and tight deadline focus. My current role as producer of a daily three-hour talk-radio program requires planning, coordination, and execution of many detailed tasks, always in the face of inflexible deadlines.
Oral presentation skills	Unusually broad experience, including high-profile roles as an on-air radio presence and "the voice" for an on-hold telephone message company.
Relevant education (BA or BS)	BA in Mass Communications; one year post-graduate study in Multimedia Communications.

As you will note from the enclosed résumé, my experience encompasses corporate, print media, and multimedia environments. I offer a diverse and proven skill set that can help your company create and deliver its message to various audiences to build image, market presence, and revenue. I look forward to meeting with you to discuss the value I can offer your company.

Sincerely,

Marcus Tolliver

Enclosure: Résumé

2 CREATE AND FORMAT A SMARTART GRAPHIC

1. At a blank document, create the document shown in Figure 7.21. Create and format the SmartArt graphic as shown in the figure. ***Hint: Use the Step Up Process graphic***. Change the width of the SmartArt graphic to 6.5 inches.
2. Save the completed document and name it **WL1-C7-VB2-SalesGraphic**.
3. Print and then close **WL1-C7-VB2-SalesGraphic.docx**.

Figure 7.21 Visual Benchmark 2

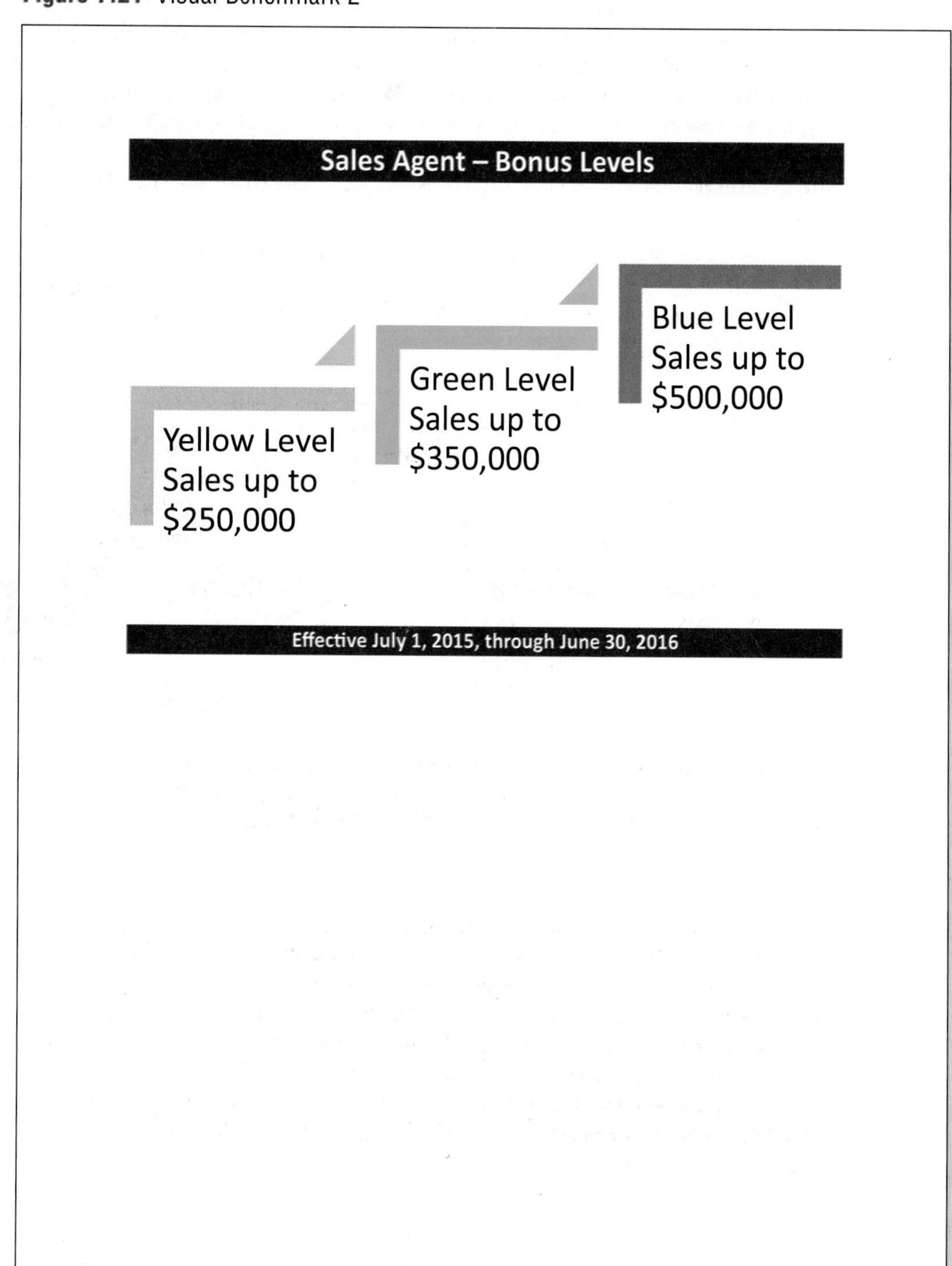

Case Study — Apply Your Skills

Part 1

You have recently been hired as an accounting clerk for a landscaping business, Landmark Landscaping, which has two small offices in your city. The accounting clerk prior to you kept track of monthly sales using Word, and the manager would prefer that you continue using that application. Open the file named **LLMoSales.docx** and then save the document with Save As and name it **WL1-C7-CS-LLMoSales**. After reviewing the information, you decide that a table would be a better format for maintaining and displaying the data. Convert the data to a table and modify its appearance so that it is easy to read and understand. Insert a total row at the bottom of the table and then insert formulas to sum the totals in the columns containing amounts. Apply formatting to the table to enhance the appearance of the table. Determine a color theme for the table and then continue that same color theme when preparing other documents for Landmark Landscaping. Save, print, and then close the document.

Part 2

The president of Landmark Landscaping has asked you to prepare an organizational chart for the company that will become part of the company profile. Create a SmartArt organizational chart with the following company titles (in the order shown below):

President

Westside Manager

Landscape Architect | Landscape Director

Assistant

Eastside Manager

Landscape Architect | Landscape Director

Assistant

Format the organizational chart to enhance the appearance of the chart and apply colors that match the color scheme you chose for the company in Part 1. Save the document and name it **WL1-C7-CS-LLOrgChart**. Print and then close the document.

Part 3

As part of the company profile, the president of the company would like to include a graphic that represents the services offered by the company and use the graphic as a company marketing tool. Use SmartArt to create a graphic that contains the following services: Maintenance Contracts, Planting Services, Landscape Design, and Landscape Consultation. Format the SmartArt graphic to enhance the appearance of the graphic and apply colors that match the color scheme you chose for the company in Part 1. Save the document and name it **WL1-C7-CS-LLServices**. Print and then close the document.

Part 4

The office manager has started a training document with information on using SmartArt. He has asked you to add information on keyboard shortcuts for working with shapes in a SmartArt graphic. Use the Help feature to learn about the keyboard shortcuts available for working with shapes and then create a table and insert the information in the table. Format the table to enhance the appearance of the table and apply colors that match the color scheme you chose for the company in Part 1. Save the document and name it **WL1-C7-CS-SAShortcuts**. Print and then close the document.

Part 5

One of the landscape architects has asked you to prepare a table containing information on trees that need to be ordered next month. She would also like to have you include the Latin names for the trees, since this information is important when ordering. Create a table that contains the common name of each tree, the Latin name, the number required, and the price per tree, as shown in Figure 7.22. Use the Internet (or any other resource available to you) to find the Latin name of each tree listed in Figure 7.22. Create a column in the table that multiplies the number of trees required by the price and include this formula for each tree. Format and enhance the table so it is attractive and easy to read. Save the document and name it **WL1-C7-CS-LLTrees**. Print and then close the document.

Figure 7.22 Case Study, Part 5

Douglas-fir, 15 required, $1.99 per tree
White Elm, 10 required, $2.49 per tree
Western Hemlock, 10 required, $1.89 per tree
Red Maple, 8 required, $6.99 per tree
Ponderosa Pine, 5 required, $2.69 per tree

MICROSOFT®
WORD

Merging Documents

PERFORMANCE OBJECTIVES

Upon successful completion of Chapter 8, you will be able to:

- **Create a data source file**
- **Create a main document and merge with a data source file**
- **Create an envelope, labels, or directory main document and then merge with a data source file**
- **Create custom fields for a merge**
- **Edit main documents and data source files**
- **Input text during a merge**

Tutorials

8.1 Merging Documents

8.2 Creating a Data Source File

8.3 Creating a Main Document

8.4 Merging Envelopes and Labels

8.5 Merging a Directory

8.6 Editing a Data Source File

8.7 Inputting Text During a Merge

8.8 Using the Mail Merge Wizard

Word includes a Mail Merge feature you can use to create customized letters, envelopes, labels, directories, email messages, and faxes. The Mail Merge feature is useful for situations when you need to send the same letter to a number of people and create an envelope for each letter. Use Mail Merge to create a main document that contains a letter, envelope, or other data and then merge the main document with a data source. In this chapter, you will use Mail Merge to create letters, envelopes, labels, and directories. Model answers for this chapter's projects appear on the following pages.

Note: Before beginning the projects, copy to your storage medium the WL1C8 subfolder from the WL1 folder on the CD that accompanies this textbook and then make WL1C8 the active folder.

February 23, 2015

«AddressBlock»

«GreetingLine»

McCormack Funds is lowering its expense charges beginning May 1, 2015. The reduction in expense charges mean that more of your account investment performance in the «Fund» is returned to you, «Title» «Last_Name». The reductions are worth your attention because most of our competitors' fees have gone up.

Lowering expense charges is noteworthy because before the reduction, McCormack expense deductions were already among the lowest, far below most mutual funds and variable annuity accounts with similar objectives. At the same time, services for you, our client, will continue to expand. If you would like to discuss this change, please call us at (212) 555-2277. Your financial future is our main concern at McCormack.

Sincerely,

Jodie Langstrom
Director, Financial Services

XX
WL1-C8-P1-MFMD.docx

February 23, 2015

Mr. Kenneth Porter
7645 Tenth Street
Apt. 314
New York, NY 10192

Dear Mr. Porter:

McCormack Funds is lowering its expense charges beginning May 1, 2015. The reduction in expense charges mean that more of your account investment performance in the Mutual Investment Fund is returned to you, Mr. Porter. The reductions are worth your attention because most of our competitors' fees have gone up.

Lowering expense charges is noteworthy because before the reduction, McCormack expense deductions were already among the lowest, far below most mutual funds and variable annuity accounts with similar objectives. At the same time, services for you, our client, will continue to expand. If you would like to discuss this change, please call us at (212) 555-2277. Your financial future is our main concern at McCormack.

Sincerely,

Jodie Langstrom
Director, Financial Services

XX
WL1-C8-P1-MFMD.docx

Page 1

Project 1 Merge Letters to Customers

WL1-C8-P1-MFMD.docx

WL1-C8-P1-MFLtrs.docx

February 23, 2015

Ms. Carolyn Renquist
13255 Meridian Street
New York, NY 10435

Dear Ms. Renquist:

McCormack Funds is lowering its expense charges beginni
charges mean that more of your account investment perf
you, Ms. Renquist. The reductions are worth your attentio
gone up.

Lowering expense charges is noteworthy because before t
were already among the lowest, far below most mutual fu
objectives. At the same time, services for you, our client,
discuss this change, please call us at (212) 555-2277. Your
McCormack.

Sincerely,

Jodie Langstrom
Director, Financial Services

XX
WL1-C8-P1-MFMD.docx

Page 2

February 23, 2015

Dr. Amil Ranna
433 South 17th
Apt. 17-D
New York, NY 10322

Dear Dr. Ranna:

McCormack Funds is lowering its expense charges beginni
charges mean that more of your account investment perf
you, Dr. Ranna. The reductions are worth your attention b
gone up.

Lowering expense charges is noteworthy because before t
were already among the lowest, far below most mutual fu
objectives. At the same time, services for you, our client, v
discuss this change, please call us at (212) 555-2277. Your
McCormack.

Sincerely,

Jodie Langstrom
Director, Financial Services

XX
WL1-C8-P1-MFMD.docx

Page 3

February 23, 2015

Mrs. Wanda Houston
566 North 22nd Avenue
New York, NY 10634

Dear Mrs. Houston:

McCormack Funds is lowering its expense charges beginning May 1, 2015. The reduction in expense charges mean that more of your account investment performance in the Quality Care Fund is returned to you, Mrs. Houston. The reductions are worth your attention because most of our competitors' fees have gone up.

Lowering expense charges is noteworthy because before the reduction, McCormack expense deductions were already among the lowest, far below most mutual funds and variable annuity accounts with similar objectives. At the same time, services for you, our client, will continue to expand. If you would like to discuss this change, please call us at (212) 555-2277. Your financial future is our main concern at McCormack.

Sincerely,

Jodie Langstrom
Director, Financial Services

XX
WL1-C8-P1-MFMD.docx

Page 4

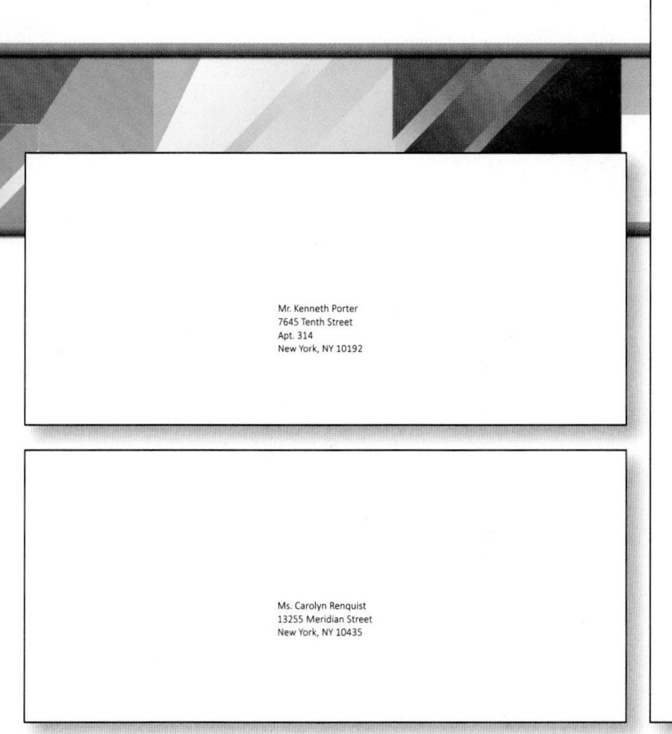

Mr. Kenneth Porter
7645 Tenth Street
Apt. 314
New York, NY 10192

Ms. Carolyn Renquist
13255 Meridian Street
New York, NY 10435

Project 2 Merge Envelopes

WL1-C8-P2-MFEnvs.docx

Mr. Kenneth Porter
7645 Tenth Street
Apt. 314
New York, NY 10192

Ms. Carolyn Renquist
13255 Meridian Street
New York, NY 10435

Dr. Amil Ranna
433 South 17th
Apt. 17-D
New York, NY 10322

Mrs. Wanda Houston
566 North 22nd Avenue
New York, NY 10634

Project 3 Merge Mailing Labels

WL1-C8-P3-MFLabels.docx

Last Name	First Name	Fund
Porter	Kenneth	Mutual Investment Fund
Renquist	Carolyn	Quality Care Fund
Ranna	Amil	Priority One Fund
Houston	Wanda	Quality Care Fund

Project 4 Merge a Directory

WL1-C8-P4-Directory.docx

Mr. Martin Saunders
231 South 41st Street
P.O. Box 3321
Baltimore, MD 20156

Ms. Amanda Perkins
9033 North Ridge Drive
Apt. #401
Baltimore, MD 20487

Ms. Anita Grenwald
580 Capital Lane
#1002-B
Baltimore, MD 20384

Mr. Steve Dutton
3490 East 145th
Apt. B
Baltimore, MD 20468

Mrs. Darlene Fernandez
12115 South 42nd
#20-G
Baltimore, MD 20376

Mrs. Kaycee Stahl
450 Washington Ave.
Baltimore, MD 20376

Project 5 Select Records and Merge Mailing Labels

WL1-C8-P5-SFLabels.docx

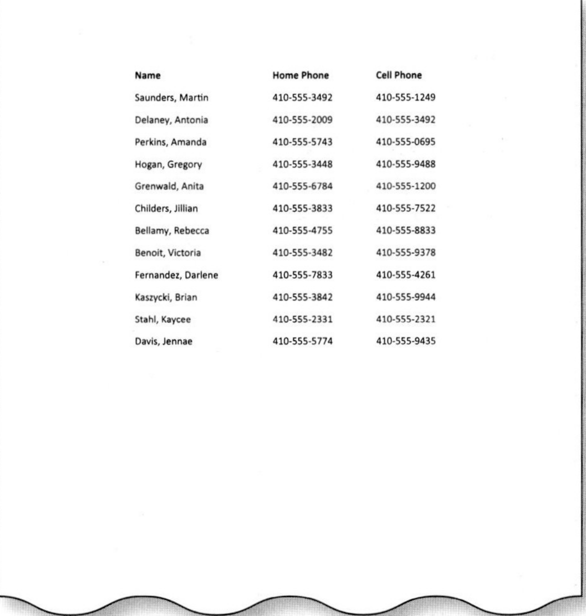

Name	Home Phone	Cell Phone
Saunders, Martin	410-555-3492	410-555-1249
Delaney, Antonia	410-555-2009	410-555-3492
Perkins, Amanda	410-555-5743	410-555-0695
Hogan, Gregory	410-555-3448	410-555-9488
Grenwald, Anita	410-555-6784	410-555-1200
Childers, Jillian	410-555-3833	410-555-7522
Bellamy, Rebecca	410-555-4755	410-555-8833
Benoit, Victoria	410-555-3482	410-555-9378
Fernandez, Darlene	410-555-7833	410-555-4261
Kaszycki, Brian	410-555-3842	410-555-9944
Stahl, Kaycee	410-555-2331	410-555-2321
Davis, Jennae	410-555-5774	410-555-9435

Project 6 Edit Records in a Data Source File

WL1-C8-P6-Directory.docx

February 23, 2015

Mr. Kenneth Porter
7645 Tenth Street
Apt. 314
New York, NY 10192

Dear Mr. Porter:

McCormack Funds is lowering its expense charges beginning May 1, 2015. The reduction in exp
charges mean that more of your account investment performance in the Mutual Investment Fu
returned to you, Mr. Porter. The reductions are worth your attention because most of our com
fees have gone up.

Lowering expense charges is noteworthy because before the reduction, McCormack expense d
were already among the lowest, far below most mutual funds and variable annuity accounts w
objectives. At the same time, services for you, our client, will continue to expand. If you would
discuss this change, please call our service representative, Marilyn Smythe, at (646) 555-8944.

Sincerely,

Jodie Langstrom
Director, Financial Services

XX
WL1-C8-P1-MFMD.docx

Page 1

February 23, 2015

Ms. Carolyn Renquist
13255 Meridian Street
New York, NY 10435

Dear Ms. Renquist:

McCormack Funds is lowering its exp
charges mean that more of your acco
you, Ms. Renquist. The reductions ar
gone up.

Lowering expense charges is notewo
were already among the lowest, far b
objectives. At the same time, service
discuss this change, please call our se

Sincerely,

Jodie Langstrom
Director, Financial Services

XX
WL1-C8-P1-MFMD.docx

Page 2

February 23, 2015

Dr. Amil Ranna
433 South 17th
Apt. 17-D
New York, NY 10322

Dear Dr. Ranna:

McCormack Funds is lowering its exp
charges mean that more of your acco
you, Dr. Ranna. The reductions are w
gone up.

Lowering expense charges is notewo
were already among the lowest, far b
objectives. At the same time, service
discuss this change, please call our se

Sincerely,

Jodie Langstrom
Director, Financial Services

XX
WL1-C8-P1-MFMD.docx

Page 3

February 23, 2015

Mrs. Wanda Houston
566 North 22nd Avenue
New York, NY 10634

Dear Mrs. Houston:

McCormack Funds is lowering its expense charges beginning May 1, 2015. The reduction in expense charges mean that more of your account investment performance in the Quality Care Fund is returned to you, Mrs. Houston. The reductions are worth your attention because most of our competitors' fees have gone up.

Lowering expense charges is noteworthy because before the reduction, McCormack expense deductions were already among the lowest, far below most mutual funds and variable annuity accounts with similar objectives. At the same time, services for you, our client, will continue to expand. If you would like to discuss this change, please call our service representative, Thomas Rivers, at (646) 555-0793.

Sincerely,

Jodie Langstrom
Director, Financial Services

XX
WL1-C8-P1-MFMD.docx

Page 4

Project 7 Add Fill-in Fields to a Main Document
WL1-C8-P7-MFLtrs.docx

January 22, 2015

Mr. Martin Saunders
231 South 41st Street
P.O. Box 3321
Baltimore, MD 20156

Dear Mr. Saunders:

Last year, a law went into effect that changes the maximum amounts that may be contributed to defined contribution pension and tax-deferred annuity plans, such as those using Sorenson Funds annuities. Generally, the changes slow down the rate at which the maximums will increase in the future. A likely result is that more people will reach the maximum and, if they wish to save more for their retirement, they will have to use after-tax savings instruments.

The amount of money you can voluntarily contribute to your fund was expected to rise above the current maximum. The amendments will delay any cost-of-living adjustments, and the limit will probably not go up for several years. The changes in the law will have an effect on your next annuity statement. If you want to increase or decrease the amount you contribute to your fund, please let us know.

Sincerely,

Jennifer Tann
Director of Financial Services

XX
SFLtrMD.docx

6250 Aurora Boulevard + Baltimore, MD 20372 + 1-888-555-0344

Page 1

Sorenson Funds

January 22, 2015

Mrs. Antonia Delaney
11220 East Madison
Rosedale, MD 21237

Dear Mrs. Delaney:

Last year, a law went into effect that changes the maximum amounts that may be contributed to defined contribution pension and tax-deferred annuity plans, such as those using Sorenson Funds annuities. Generally, the changes slow down the rate at which the maximums will increase in the future. A likely result is that more people will reach the maximum and, if they wish to save more for their retirement, they will have to use after-tax savings instruments.

The amount of money you can voluntarily contribute to your fund was expected to rise above the current maximum. The amendments will delay any cost-of-living adjustments, and the limit will probably not go up for several years. The changes in the law will have an effect on your next annuity statement. If you want to increase or decrease the amount you contribute to your fund, please let us know.

Sincerely,

Jennifer Tann
Director of Financial Services

XX
SFLtrMD.docx

6250 Aurora Boulevard + Baltimore, MD 20372 + 1-888-555-0344

Page 2

Project 8 Use Mail Merge Wizard
WL1-C8-P8-SFLtrs.docx

Project 1 Merge Letters to Customers — 3 Parts

You will create a data source file and a letter main document and then merge the main document with the records in the data source file.

Completing a Merge

Use buttons and options on the MAILINGS tab to complete a merge. A merge generally takes two files: the ***data source*** file and the ***main document***. The main document contains the standard text along with fields identifying where variable information is inserted during the merge. The data source file contains the variable information that will be inserted in the main document.

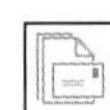

Start Mail Merge

Select Recipients

Use the Start Mail Merge button on the MAILINGS tab to identify the type of main document you want to create and use the Select Recipients button to create a data source file or specify an existing data source file. You can also use the Mail Merge Wizard to guide you through the merge process.

Creating a Data Source File

Before creating a data source file, determine what type of correspondence you will be creating and the type of information you will need to insert in the correspondence. Word provides predetermined field names you can use when creating the data source file. Use these field names if they represent the data you are creating. Variable information in a data source file is saved as a ***record***. A record contains all of the information for one unit (for example, a person, family, customer, client, or business). A series of fields makes one record, and a series of records makes a data source file.

Quick Steps

Create a Data Source File

1. Click MAILINGS tab.
2. Click Select Recipients button.
3. Click *Type a New List* at drop-down list.
4. Type data in predesigned or custom fields.
5. Click OK.

Create a data source file by clicking the Select Recipients button in the Start Mail Merge group on the MAILINGS tab and then clicking *Type a New List* at the drop-down list. At the New Address List dialog box, shown in Figure 8.1, use the predesigned fields offered by Word or edit the fields by clicking the Customize Columns button. At the Customize Address List dialog box that displays, insert new fields or delete existing fields and then click OK. With the desired fields established,

Figure 8.1 New Address List Dialog Box

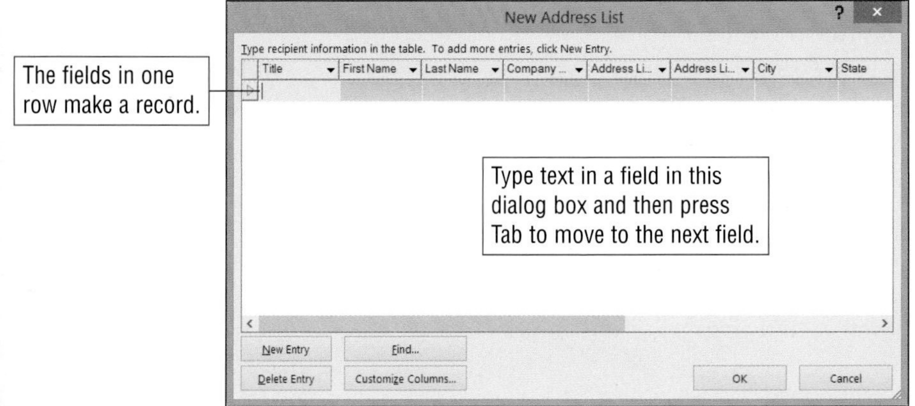

type the required data. Note that fields in the main document correspond to the column headings in the data source file. When all records have been entered, click OK. At the Save Address List dialog box, navigate to the desired folder, type a name for the data source file, and then click OK. Word saves a data source file as an Access database. You do not need Access on your computer to complete a merge with a data source file.

Project 1a Creating a Data Source File Part 1 of 3

1. At a blank document, click the MAILINGS tab.
2. Click the Start Mail Merge button in the Start Mail Merge group and then click *Letters* at the drop-down list.
3. Click the Select Recipients button in the Start Mail Merge group and then click *Type a New List* at the drop-down list.

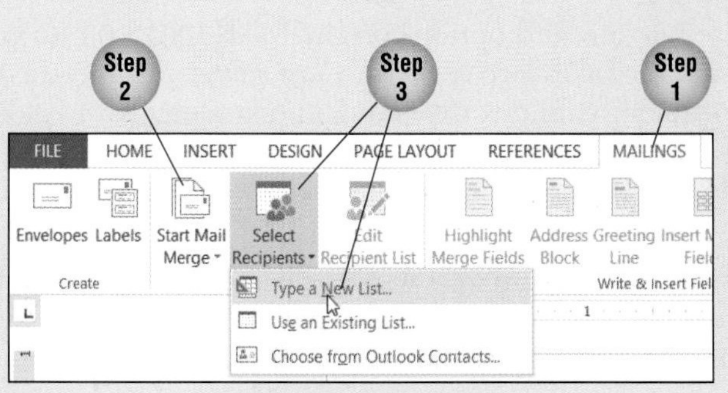

4. At the New Address List dialog box, Word provides a number of predesigned fields. Delete the fields you do not need by completing the following steps:
   a. Click the Customize Columns button.
   b. At the Customize Address List dialog box, click *Company Name* to select it and then click the Delete button.
   c. At the message that displays, click the Yes button.
   d. Complete steps similar to those in 4b and 4c to delete the following fields:
      Country or Region
      Home Phone
      Work Phone
      E-mail Address

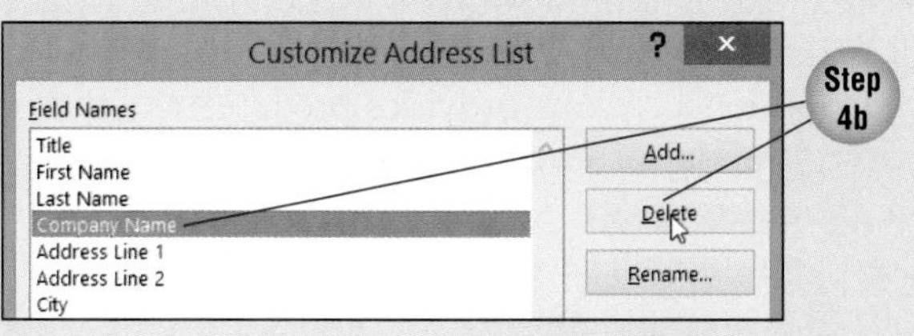

5. Insert a custom field by completing the following steps:
   a. At the Customize Address List dialog box, click the Add button.
   b. At the Add Field dialog box, type **Fund** and then click OK.
   c. Click the OK button to close the Customize Address List dialog box.

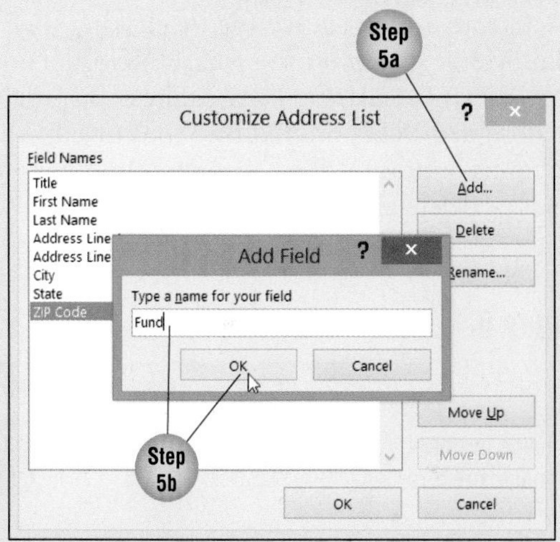

6. At the New Address List dialog box, enter the information for the first client shown in Figure 8.2 by completing the following steps:
   a. Type **Mr.** in the Title field and then press the Tab key. (This moves the insertion point to the *First Name* field. You can also press Shift + Tab to move to the previous field.)
   b. Type **Kenneth** and then press the Tab key.
   c. Type **Porter** and then press the Tab key.
   d. Type **7645 Tenth Street** and then press the Tab key.

e. Type **Apt. 314** and then press the Tab key.
f. Type **New York** and then press the Tab key.
g. Type **NY** and then press the Tab key.
h. Type **10192** and then press the Tab key.
i. Type **Mutual Investment Fund** and then press the Tab key. (This makes the Title field active in the next row.)
j. With the insertion point positioned in the Title field, complete steps similar to those in 6a through 6i to enter the information for the three other clients shown in Figure 8.2 (reading the records from left to right).

7. After entering all of the information for the last client in Figure 8.2 (Mrs. Wanda Houston), click the OK button located in the bottom right corner of the New Address List dialog box.
8. At the Save Address List dialog box, navigate to the WL1C8 folder on your storage medium, type **WL1-C8-P1-MFDS** in the *File name* text box, and then click the Save button.

Figure 8.2 Project 1a

Title	= Mr.	Title	= Ms.
First Name	= Kenneth	First Name	= Carolyn
Last Name	= Porter	Last Name	= Renquist
Address Line 1	= 7645 Tenth Street	Address Line 1	= 13255 Meridian Street
Address Line 2	= Apt. 314	Address Line 2	= (leave this blank)
City	= New York	City	= New York
State	= NY	State	= NY
Zip Code	= 10192	Zip Code	= 10435
Fund	= Mutual Investment Fund	Fund	= Quality Care Fund
Title	= Dr.	Title	= Mrs.
First Name	= Amil	First Name	= Wanda
Last Name	= Ranna	Last Name	= Houston
Address Line 1	= 433 South 17th	Address Line 1	= 566 North 22nd Avenue
Address Line 2	= Apt. 17-D	Address Line 2	= (leave this blank)
City	= New York	City	= New York
State	= NY	State	= NY
Zip Code	= 10322	Zip Code	= 10634
Fund	= Priority One Fund	Fund	= Quality Care Fund

Creating a Main Document

When you begin a mail merge, you specify the type of main document you are creating. After creating and typing the records in the data source file, type the main document. Insert in the main document fields identifying where you want the variable information inserted when the document is merged with the data source file. Use buttons in the Write & Insert Fields group to insert fields and field blocks in the main document.

Quick Steps

Create a Main Document
1. Click MAILINGS tab.
2. Click Start Mail Merge button.
3. Click desired document type at drop-down list.
4. Type main document text and insert fields as needed.

Address Block

Greeting Line

Insert Merge Field

Insert all of the fields required for the inside address of a letter with the Address Block button in the Write & Insert Fields group. Click this button and the Insert Address Block dialog box displays with a preview of how the fields will be inserted in the document to create the inside address; the dialog box also contains buttons and options for customizing the fields. Click OK and the «AddressBlock» field is inserted in the document. The «AddressBlock» field is an example of a composite field that groups a number of fields together (such as *Title*, *First Name*, *Last Name*, *Address Line 1*, and so on).

Click the Greeting Line button and the Insert Greeting Line dialog box displays with options for customizing how the fields are inserted in the document to create the greeting line. When you click OK at the dialog box, the «GreetingLine» composite field is inserted in the document.

If you want to insert an individual field from the data source file, click the Insert Merge Field button. This displays the Insert Merge Field dialog box with a list of fields from the data source file. Click the Insert Merge Field button arrow and a drop-down list displays containing the fields in the data source file.

A field or composite field is inserted in the main document surrounded by chevrons (« and »). The chevrons distinguish fields in the main document and do not display in the merged document. If you want merged data formatted, you can format the merge fields at the main document.

Project 1b Creating a Main Document

Part 2 of 3

1. At the blank document, create the letter shown in Figure 8.3. Begin by clicking the *No Spacing* style thumbnail in the Styles group on the HOME tab.
2. Press the Enter key six times and then type **February 23, 2015**.
3. Press the Enter key four times and then insert the address composite field by completing the following steps:
   a. Click the MAILINGS tab and then click the Address Block button in the Write & Insert Fields group.
   b. At the Insert Address Block dialog box, click the OK button.
   c. Press the Enter key twice.
4. Insert the greeting line composite field by completing the following steps:
   a. Click the Greeting Line button in the Write & Insert Fields group.
   b. At the Insert Greeting Line dialog box, click the down-pointing arrow at the right of the option box containing the comma (the box to the right of the box containing *Mr. Randall*).
   c. At the drop-down list that displays, click the colon.
   d. Click OK to close the Insert Greeting Line dialog box.
   e. Press the Enter key twice.

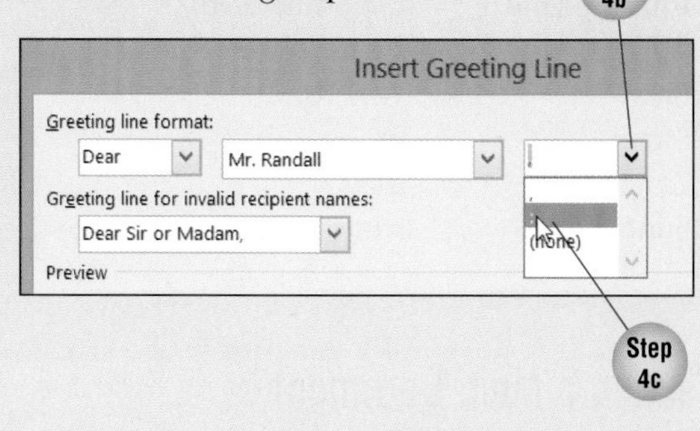

5. Type the letter shown in Figure 8.3 to the point where «Fund» displays and then insert the «Fund» field by clicking the Insert Merge Field button arrow and then clicking *Fund* at the drop-down list.
6. Type the letter to the point where the «Title» field displays and then insert the «Title» field by clicking the Insert Merge Field button arrow and then clicking *Title* at the drop-down list.
7. Press the spacebar and then insert the «Last_Name» field by clicking the Insert Merge Field button arrow and then clicking *Last_Name* at the drop-down list.
8. Type the remainder of the letter shown in Figure 8.3. (Insert your initials instead of *XX* at the end of the letter.)
9. Save the document and name it **WL1-C8-P1-MFMD**.

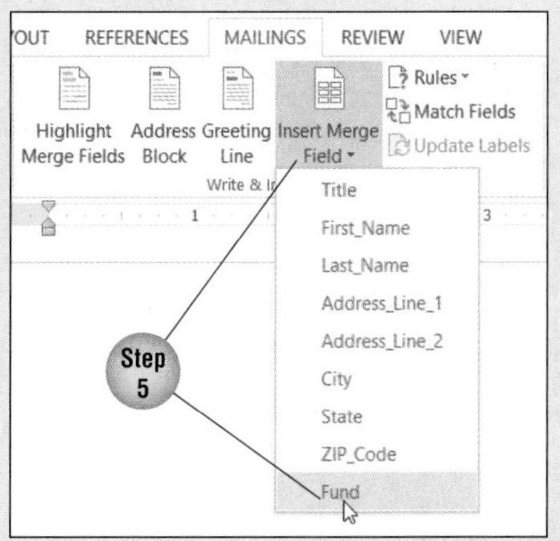

Figure 8.3 Project 1b

February 23, 2015

«AddressBlock»

«GreetingLine»

McCormack Funds is lowering its expense charges beginning May 1, 2015. The reductions in expense charges mean that more of your account investment performance in the «Fund» is returned to you, «Title» «Last_Name». The reductions are worth your attention because most of our competitors' fees have gone up.

Lowering expense charges is noteworthy because before the reduction, McCormack expense deductions were already among the lowest, far below most mutual funds and variable annuity accounts with similar objectives. At the same time, services for you, our client, will continue to expand. If you would like to discuss this change, please call us at (212) 555-2277. Your financial future is our main concern at McCormack.

Sincerely,

Jodie Langstrom
Director, Financial Services

XX
WL1-C8-P1-MFMD.docx

Previewing a Merge

Preview Results

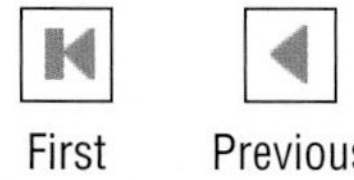

First Record Previous Record

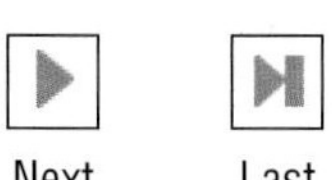

Next Record Last Record

Find Recipient

To view how the main document will appear when merged with the first record in the data source file, click the Preview Results button on the MAILINGS tab. You can view the main document merged with other records by using the navigation buttons in the Preview Results group. This group contains the First Record, Previous Record, Next Record, and Last Record buttons and the Go to Record text box. Click the button that will display the main document merged with the desired record. Viewing the merged document before printing is helpful to ensure that the merged data is correct. To use the Go to Record text box, click in the text box, type the number of the desired record, and then press Enter. Turn off the preview feature by clicking the Preview Results button.

The Preview Results group on the MAILINGS tab also includes a Find Recipient button. If you want to search for and preview merged documents with specific entries, click the Preview Results button and then click the Find Recipient button. At the Find Entry dialog box that displays, type the specific field entry for which you are searching in the *Find* text box and then click the Find Next button. Continue clicking the Find Next button until Word displays a message telling you that there are no more entries that contain the text you typed.

Checking for Errors

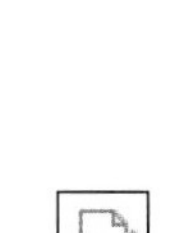

Check for Errors

Before merging documents, you can check for errors using the Check for Errors button in the Preview Results group on the MAILINGS tab. Click this button and the Checking and Reporting Errors dialog box, shown in Figure 8.4, displays containing three options. Click the first option, *Simulate the merge and report errors in a new document,* to tell Word to test the merge, not make any changes, and report errors in a new document. Choose the second option, *Complete the merge, pausing to report each error as it occurs,* and Word will merge the documents and display errors as they occur during the merge. Choose the third option, *Complete the merge without pausing. Report errors in a new document,* and Word will complete the merge without pausing and insert any errors in a new document.

Merging Documents

Finish & Merge

To complete the merge, click the Finish & Merge button in the Finish group on the MAILINGS tab. At the drop-down list that displays, you can choose to merge the records and create a new document, send the merged documents directly to the printer, or send the merged documents by email.

Figure 8.4 Checking and Reporting Errors Dialog Box

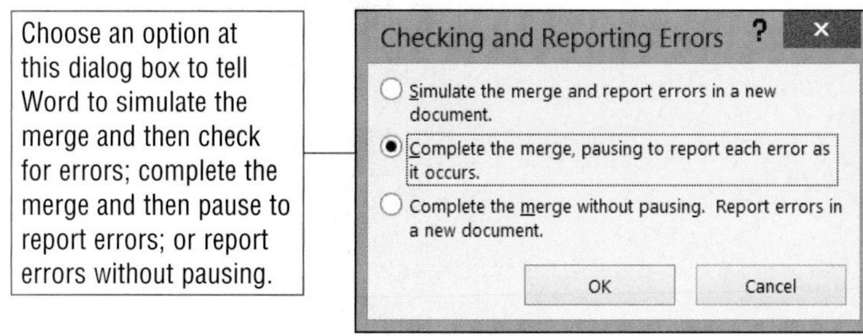
Choose an option at this dialog box to tell Word to simulate the merge and then check for errors; complete the merge and then pause to report errors; or report errors without pausing.
Checking and Reporting Errors
Simulate the merge and report errors in a new document.
Complete the merge, pausing to report each error as it occurs.
Complete the merge without pausing. Report errors in a new document.
OK
Cancel

To merge the documents and create a new document with the merged records, click the Finish & Merge button and then click *Edit Individual Documents* at the drop-down list. At the Merge to New Document dialog box, make sure *All* is selected in the *Merge records* section and then click OK. This merges the records in the data source file with the main document and inserts the merged documents in a new document. You can also display the Merge to New Document dialog box by pressing Alt + Shift + N. Press Alt + Shift + M to display the Merge to Printer dialog box.

Identify specific records you want merged with options at the Merge to New Document dialog box. Display this dialog box by clicking the Finish & Merge button on the MAILINGS tab and then clicking the *Edit Individual Documents* option at the drop-down list. Click the *All* option in the Merge to New Document dialog box to merge all records in the data source and click the *Current record* option if you want to merge only the current record. If you want to merge specific adjacent records, click in the *From* text box, type the beginning record number, press the Tab key, and then type the ending record number in the *To* text box.

Quick Steps

Merge Documents

1. Click Finish & Merge button.
2. Click *Edit Individual Documents* at drop-down list.
3. Make sure *All* is selected in Merge to New Document dialog box.
4. Click OK.

Project 1c Merging the Main Document with the Data Source File

Part 3 of 3

1. With **WL1-C8-P1-MFMD.docx** open, preview the main document merged with the first record in the data source file by clicking the Preview Results button on the MAILINGS tab.
2. Click the Next Record button to view the main document merged with the second record in the data source file.
3. Click the Preview Results button to turn off the preview feature.

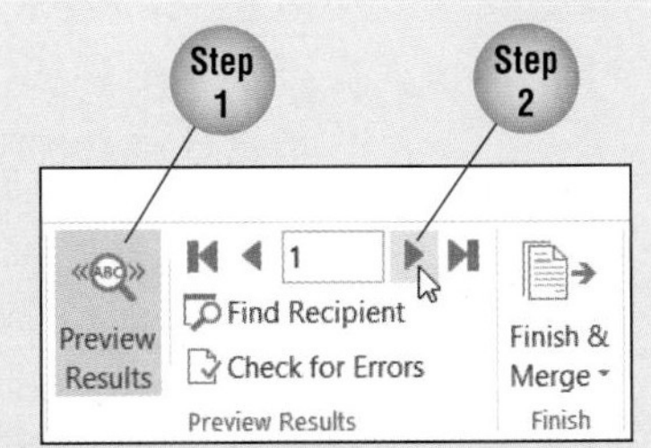

4. Automatically check for errors by completing the following steps:
   a. Click the Check for Errors button in the Preview Results group on the MAILINGS tab.
   b. At the Checking and Reporting Errors dialog box, click the first option, *Simulate the merge and report errors in a new document*.
   c. Click OK.
   d. If a new document displays with any errors, print the document and then close it without saving it. If a message displays telling you that no errors were found, click OK.

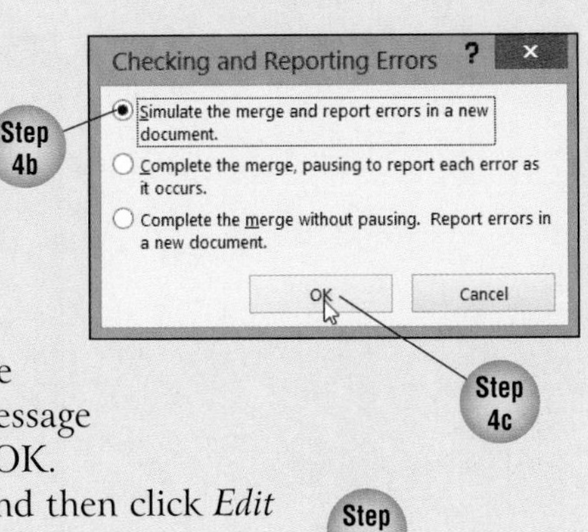

5. Click the Finish & Merge button in the Finish group and then click *Edit Individual Documents* at the drop-down list.
6. At the Merge to New Document dialog box, make sure *All* is selected and then click OK.
7. Save the merged letters and name the document **WL1-C8-P1-MFLtrs**.
8. Print **WL1-C8-P1-MFLtrs.docx**. (This document will print four letters.)
9. Close **WL1-C8-P1-MFLtrs.docx**.
10. Save and then close **WL1-C8-P1-MFMD.docx**.

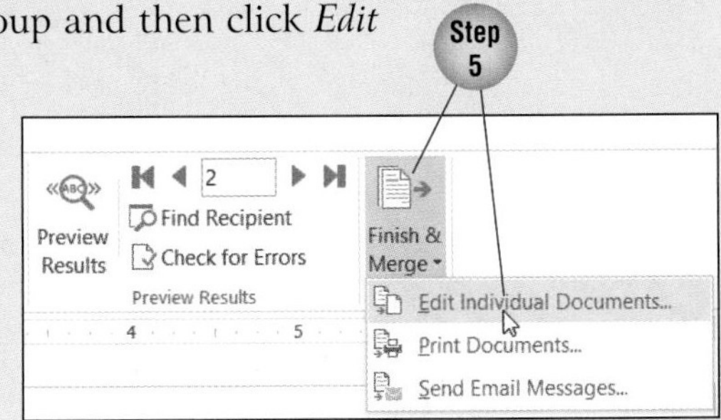

Project 2 Merge Envelopes

1 Part

You will use Mail Merge to prepare envelopes with customer names and addresses.

Merging Envelopes

If you create a letter as a main document and then merge it with a data source file, more than likely you will need properly addressed envelopes in which to send the letters. To prepare an envelope main document that is merged with a data source file, click the MAILINGS tab, click the Start Mail Merge button, and then click *Envelopes* at the drop-down list. This displays the Envelope Options dialog box, as shown in Figure 8.5. At this dialog box, specify the desired envelope size, make any other changes, and then click OK.

The next step in the envelope merge process is to create the data source file or identify an existing data source file. To identify an existing data source file, click the Select Recipients button in the Start Mail Merge group and then click *Use an Existing List* at the drop-down list. At the Select Data Source dialog box, navigate to the folder containing the desired data source file and then double-click the file.

With the data source file attached to the envelope main document, the next step is to insert the appropriate fields. Click in the envelope in the approximate location the recipient's address will appear, and a box with a dashed gray border displays. Click the Address Block button in the Write & Insert Fields group and then click OK at the Insert Address Block dialog box.

Figure 8.5 Envelope Options Dialog Box

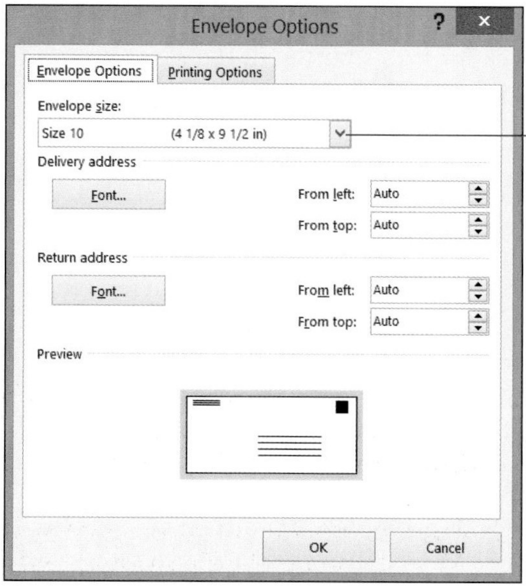

Click this down-pointing arrow to display a list of available envelope sizes.

Project 2 Merging Envelopes

Part 1 of 1

1. At a blank document, click the MAILINGS tab.
2. Click the Start Mail Merge button in the Start Mail Merge group and then click *Envelopes* at the drop-down list.
3. At the Envelope Options dialog box, make sure the envelope size is Size 10 and then click OK.
4. Click the Select Recipients button in the Start Mail Merge group and then click *Use an Existing List* at the drop-down list.
5. At the Select Data Source dialog box, navigate to the WL1C8 folder on your storage medium and then double-click the data source file named ***WL1-C8-P1-MFDS.mdb***.
6. Click in the approximate location in the envelope document where the recipient's address will appear. (This causes a box with a dashed gray border to display. If you do not see this box, try clicking in a different location on the envelope.)

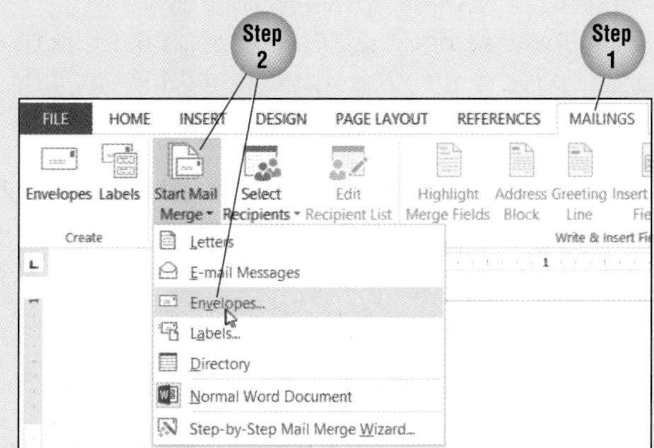

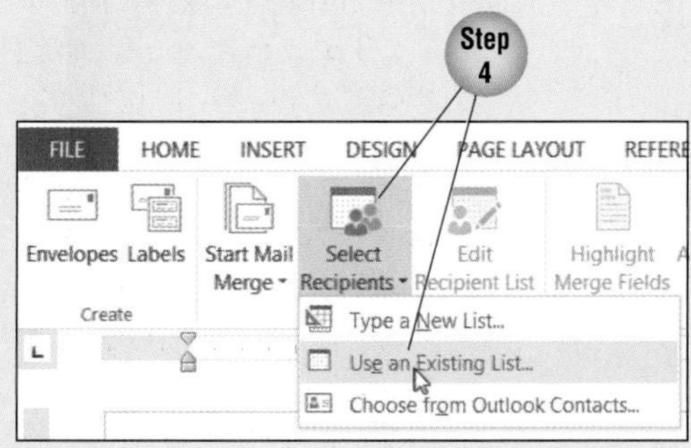

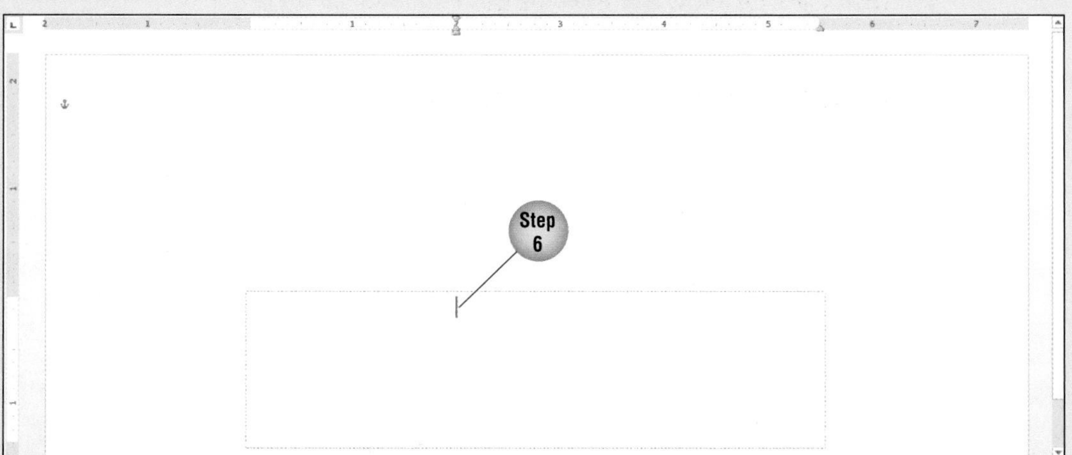

7. Click the Address Block button in the Write & Insert Fields group.
8. At the Insert Address Block dialog box, click the OK button.
9. Click the Preview Results button to see how the envelope appears merged with the first record in the data source file.
10. Click the Preview Results button to turn off the preview feature.
11. Click the Finish & Merge button in the Finish group and then click *Edit Individual Documents* at the drop-down list.

12. At the Merge to New Document dialog box, specify that you want only the first two records to merge by completing the following steps:
    a. Click in the *From* text box and then type **1**.
    b. Click in the *To* text box and then type **2**.
    c. Click OK. (This merges only the first two records and opens a document with two merged envelopes.)
13. Save the merged envelopes and name the document **WL1-C8-P2-MFEnvs**.
14. Print **WL1-C8-P2-MFEnvs.docx**. (This document will print two envelopes. Manual feeding of the envelopes may be required. Please check with your instructor.)
15. Close **WL1-C8-P2-MFEnvs.docx**.
16. Save the envelope main document and name it **WL1-C8-P2-EnvMD**.
17. Close **WL1-C8-P2-EnvMD.docx**.

Project 3 Merge Mailing Labels — 1 Part

You will use Mail Merge to prepare mailing labels with customer names and addresses.

Merging Labels

Create mailing labels for records in a data source file in much the same way that you create envelopes. Click the Start Mail Merge button and then click *Labels* at the drop-down list. This displays the Label Options dialog box, as shown in Figure 8.6. Make sure the desired label is selected and then click OK to close the dialog box. The next step is to create the data source file or identify an existing data source file. With the data source file attached to the label main document, insert the appropriate fields and then complete the merge.

Figure 8.6 Label Options Dialog Box

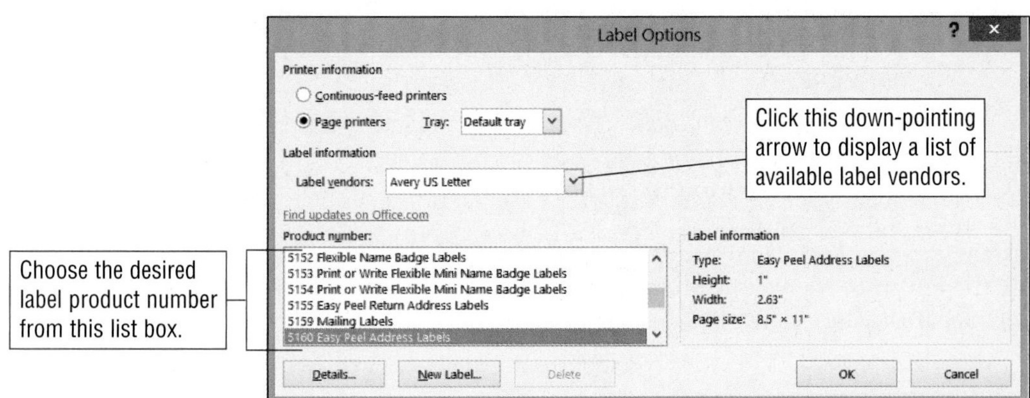

Project 3 Merging Mailing Labels

Part 1 of 1

1. At a blank document, change the document zoom to 100% and then click the MAILINGS tab
2. Click the Start Mail Merge button in the Start Mail Merge group and then click *Labels* at the drop-down list.
3. At the Label Options dialog box, complete the following steps:
   a. If necessary, click the down-pointing arrow at the right side of the *Label vendors* option box and then click *Avery US Letter* at the drop-down list. (If this product vendor is not available, choose a vendor name that offers labels that print on a full page.)
   b. Scroll in the *Product number* list box and then click *5160 Easy Peel Address Labels*. (If this option is not available, choose a label number that prints labels in two or three columns down a full page.)
   c. Click OK to close the dialog box.

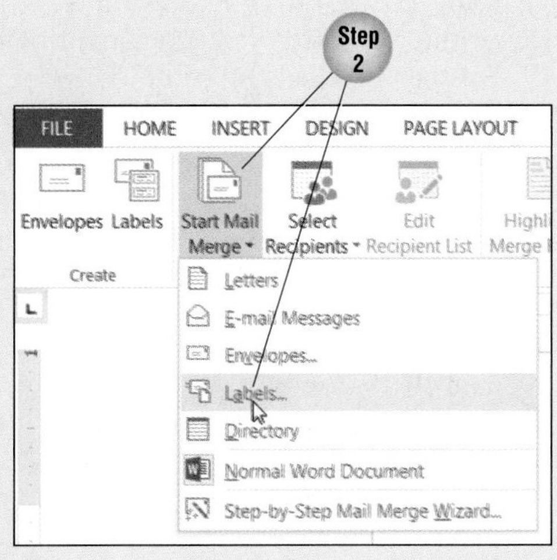

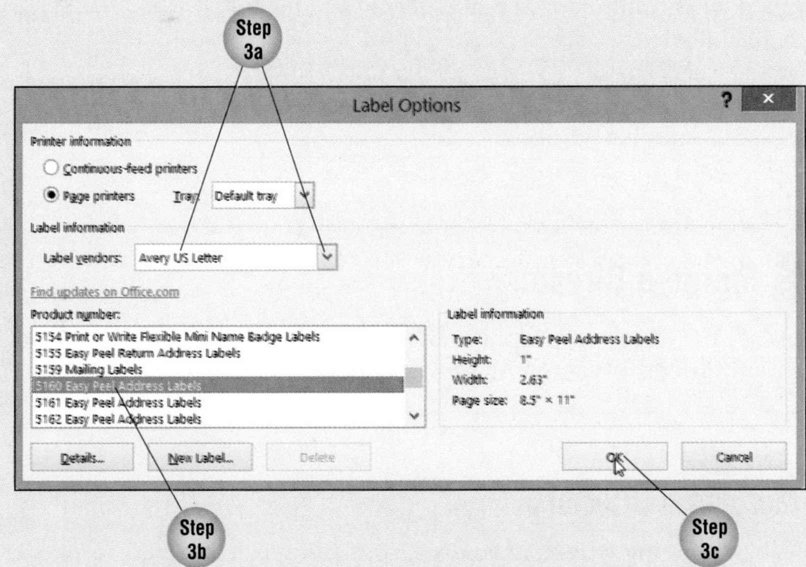

4. Click the Select Recipients button in the Start Mail Merge group and then click *Use an Existing List* at the drop-down list.
5. At the Select Data Source dialog box, navigate to the WL1C8 folder on your storage medium and then double-click the data source file named ***WL1-C8-P1-MFDS.mdb***.
6. At the labels document, click the Address Block button in the Write & Insert Fields group.
7. At the Insert Address Block dialog box, click the OK button. (This inserts «AddressBlock» in the first label. The other labels contain the «Next Record» field.)
8. Click the Update Labels button in the Write & Insert Fields group. (This adds the «AddressBlock» field after each «Next Record» field in the second and subsequent labels.)
9. Click the Preview Results button to see how the labels appear merged with the records in the data source file.
10. Click the Preview Results button to turn off the preview feature.

11. Click the Finish & Merge button in the Finish group and then click *Edit Individual Documents* at the drop-down list.
12. At the Merge to New Document dialog box, make sure *All* is selected, and then click OK.
13. Format the labels by completing the following steps:
    a. Click the TABLE TOOLS LAYOUT tab.
    b. Click the Select button in the Table group and then click *Select Table*.
    c. Click the Align Center Left button in the Alignment group.
    d. Click the HOME tab and then click the Paragraph group dialog box launcher.
    e. At the Paragraph dialog box, click the up-pointing arrow at the right of the *Before* measurement box to change the measurement to 0 points.
    f. Click the up-pointing arrow at the right of the *After* measurement box to change the measurement to 0 points.
    g. Click the up-pointing arrow at the right of the *Inside* measurement box to change the measurement to 0.3 inch.
    h. Click OK.

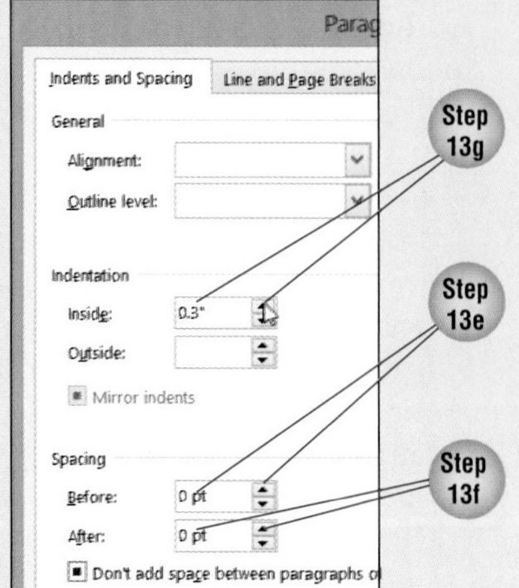

14. Save the merged labels and name the document **WL1-C8-P3-MFLabels**.
15. Print and then close **WL1-C8-P3-MFLabels.docx**.
16. Save the label main document and name it **WL1-C8-P3-LabelsMD**.
17. Close **WL1-C8-P3-LabelsMD.docx**.

Project 4 Merge a Directory — 1 Part

You will use Mail Merge to prepare a directory list containing customer names and types of financial investment funds.

Merging a Directory

When merging letters, envelopes, or mailing labels, a new form is created for each record. For example, if the data source file merged with the letter contains eight records, eight letters are created. If the data source file merged with a mailing label contains twenty records, twenty labels are created. In some situations, you may want merged information to remain on the same page. This is useful, for example, when creating a list such as a directory or address list.

Begin creating a merged directory by clicking the Start Mail Merge button and then clicking *Directory* at the drop-down list. Create or identify an existing data source file and then insert the desired fields in the directory document. You may want to set tabs to insert text in columns.

Project 4 Merging a Directory

Part 1 of 1

1. At a blank document, click the MAILINGS tab.
2. Click the Start Mail Merge button in the Start Mail Merge group and then click *Directory* at the drop-down list.
3. Click the Select Recipients button in the Start Mail Merge group and then click *Use an Existing List* at the drop-down list.
4. At the Select Data Source dialog box, navigate to the WL1C8 folder on your storage medium and then double-click the data source file named ***WL1-C8-P1-MFDS.mdb***.
5. At the document screen, set left tabs at the 1-inch mark, the 2.5-inch mark, and the 4-inch mark on the horizontal ruler and then press the Tab key. (This moves the insertion point to the tab set at the 1-inch mark.)

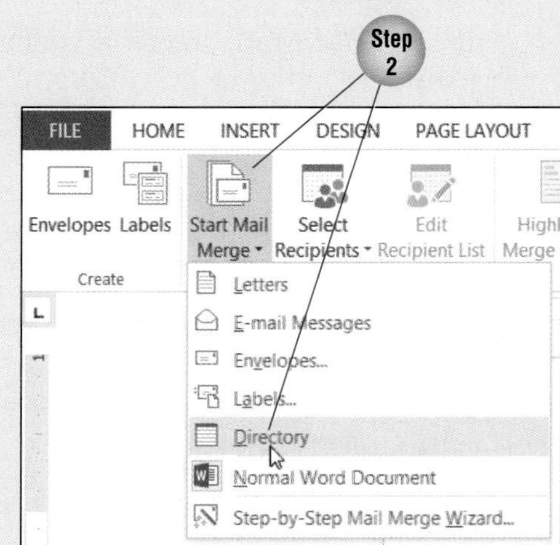

6. Click the Insert Merge Field button arrow and then click *Last_Name* at the drop-down list.
7. Press the Tab key to move the insertion point to the 2.5-inch mark.
8. Click the Insert Merge Field button arrow and then click *First_Name* at the drop-down list.
9. Press the Tab key to move the insertion point to the 4-inch mark.
10. Click the Insert Merge Field button arrow and then click *Fund* at the drop-down list.
11. Press the Enter key once.
12. Click the Finish & Merge button in the Finish group and then click *Edit Individual Documents* at the drop-down list.
13. At the Merge to New Document dialog box, make sure *All* is selected and then click OK. (This merges the fields in the document.)
14. Press Ctrl + Home, press the Enter key once, and then press the Up Arrow key once.
15. Press the Tab key, turn on bold, and then type **Last Name**.
16. Press the Tab key and then type **First Name**.
17. Press the Tab key and then type **Fund**.

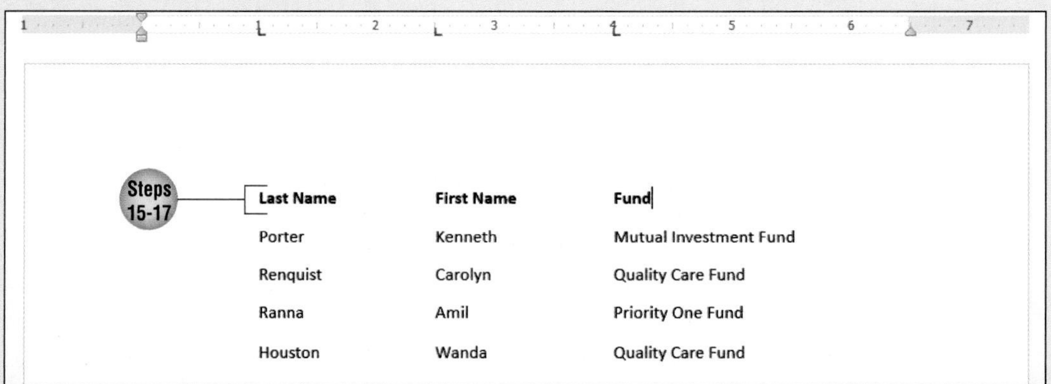

18. Save the directory document and name it **WL1-C8-P4-Directory**.
19. Print and then close the document.
20. Close the directory main document without saving it.

Project 5 Select Records and Merge Mailing Labels — 1 Part

You will use Mail Merge to prepare mailing labels with names and addresses of customers living in Baltimore.

Editing a Data Source File

Quick Steps

Edit a Data Source File

1. Open main document.
2. Click MAILINGS tab.
3. Click Edit Recipient List button.
4. Make desired changes at Mail Merge Recipients dialog box.
5. Click OK.

Edit Recipient List

Edit a main document in the normal manner. Open the document, make the required changes, and then save the document. Since a data source is actually an Access database file, you cannot open it in the normal manner. Open a data source file for editing using the Edit Recipient List button in the Start Mail Merge group on the MAILINGS tab. When you click the Edit Recipient List button, the Mail Merge Recipients dialog box displays, as shown in Figure 8.7. Select or edit records at this dialog box.

Selecting Specific Records

Each record in the Mail Merge Recipients dialog box contains a check mark before the first field. If you want to select specific records, remove the check marks from those records you do not want included in a merge. This way, you can select and then merge only certain records in the data source file with the main document.

Figure 8.7 Mail Merge Recipients Dialog Box

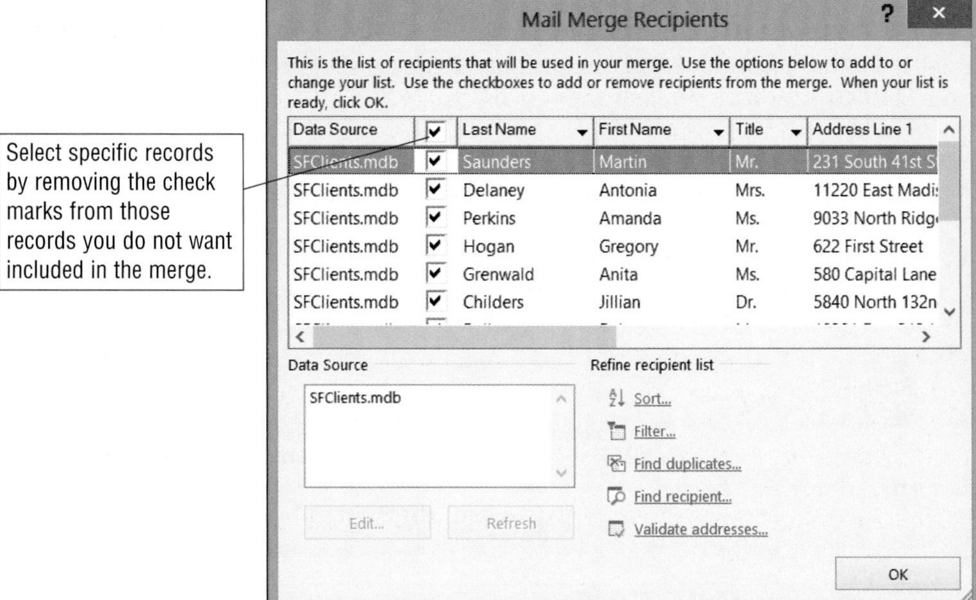

Project 5 Selecting Records and Merging Mailing Labels Part 1 of 1

1. At a blank document, create mailing labels for customers living in Baltimore. Begin by clicking the MAILINGS tab.
2. Click the Start Mail Merge button in the Start Mail Merge group and then click *Labels* at the drop-down list.
3. At the Label Options dialog box, make sure *Avery US Letter* displays in the *Label vendors* option box and *5160 Easy Peel Address Labels* displays in the *Product number* list box. Click OK.
4. Click the Select Recipients button in the Start Mail Merge group and then click *Use an Existing List* at the drop-down list.
5. At the Select Data Source dialog box, navigate to the WL1C8 folder on your storage medium and then double-click the data source file named ***SFClients.mdb***.
6. Click the Edit Recipient List button in the Start Mail Merge group.
7. At the Mail Merge Recipients dialog box, complete the following steps:
   a. Click the check box located immediately left of the *Last Name* field column heading to remove the check mark. (This removes all of the check marks from the check boxes.)
   b. Click the check box immediately left of each of the following last names: *Saunders*, *Perkins*, *Grenwald*, *Dutton*, *Fernandez*, and *Stahl*. (These are the customers who live in Baltimore.)
   c. Click OK to close the dialog box.

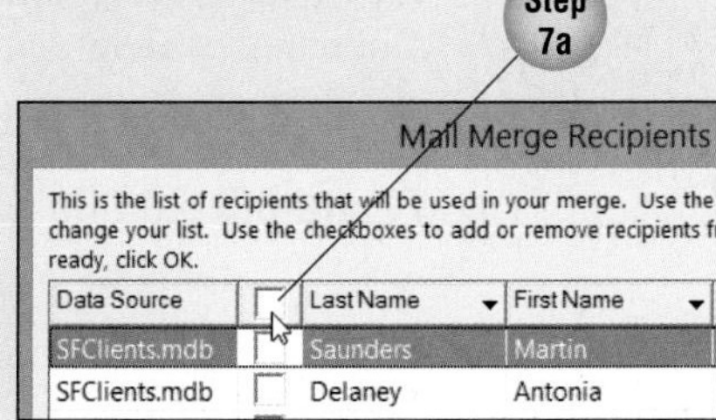

8. At the labels document, click the Address Block button in the Write & Insert Fields group.
9. At the Insert Address Block dialog box, click the OK button.
10. Click the Update Labels button in Write & Insert Fields group.
11. Click the Preview Results button and then click the Previous Record button to display each label. Make sure only labels for those customers living in Baltimore display.
12. Click the Preview Results button to turn off the preview feature.
13. Click the Finish & Merge button in the Finish group and then click *Edit Individual Documents* at the drop-down list.
14. At the Merge to New Document dialog box, make sure *All* is selected and then click OK.
15. Format the labels by completing the following steps:
    a. Click the TABLE TOOLS LAYOUT tab.
    b. Click the Select button in the Table group and then click *Select Table*.
    c. Click the Align Center Left button in the Alignment group.
    d. Click the HOME tab and then click the Paragraph group dialog box launcher.
    e. At the Paragraph dialog box, click the up-pointing arrow at the right of the *Before* measurement box to change the measurement to 0 points.
    f. Click the up-pointing arrow at the right of the *After* measurement box to change the measurement to 0 points.
    g. Click the up-pointing arrow at the right of the *Inside* measurement box to change the measurement to 0.3 inch.
    h. Click OK.
16. Save the merged labels and name the document **WL1-C8-P5-SFLabels**.
17. Print and then close **WL1-C8-P5-SFLabels.docx**.
18. Close the main labels document without saving it.

Project 6 Edit Records in a Data Source File 1 Part

You will edit records in a data source file and then use Mail Merge to prepare a directory with the edited records that contains customer names, telephone numbers, and cell phone numbers.

Editing Records

A data source file may need editing on a periodic basis to add or delete customer names, update fields, insert new fields, or delete existing fields. To edit a data source file, click the Edit Recipient List button in the Start Mail Merge group. At the Mail Merge Recipients dialog box, click the data source file name in the *Data Source* list box and then click the Edit button that displays below the list box. This displays the Edit Data Source dialog box, as shown in Figure 8.8. At this dialog box, you can add a new entry, delete an entry, find a particular entry, and customize columns.

Figure 8.8 Edit Data Source Dialog Box

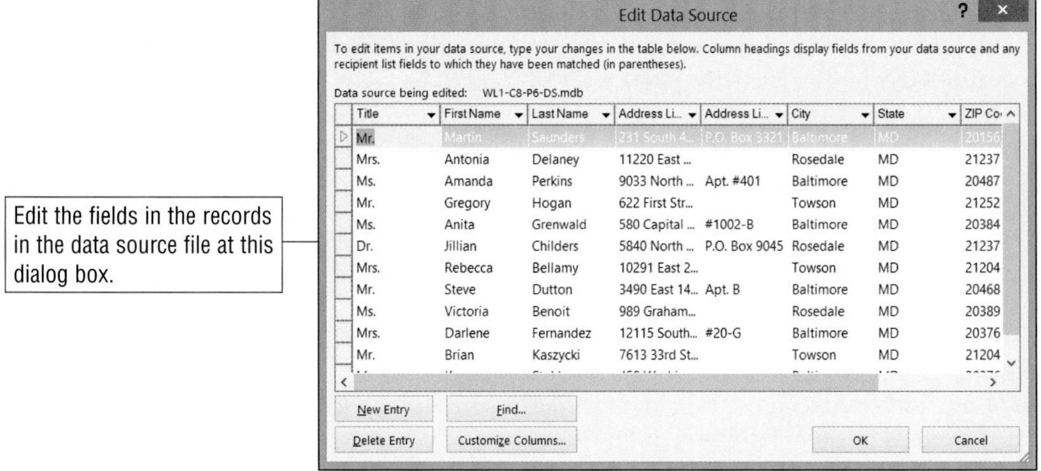

Project 6 Editing Records in a Data Source File Part 1 of 1

1. Make a copy of the **SFClients.mdb** file by completing the following steps:
   a. Display the Open dialog box and make WL1C8 the active folder.
   b. If necessary, change the file type option to *All Files (*.*)*.
   c. Right-click on the ***SFClients.mdb*** file and then click *Copy* at the shortcut menu.
   d. Position the mouse pointer in a white portion of the Open dialog box Content pane (outside any file name), click the right mouse button, and then click *Paste* at the shortcut menu. (This inserts a copy of the file in the dialog box Content pane and names the file **SFClients - Copy.mdb**.)
   e. Right-click on the file name ***SFClients - Copy.mdb*** and then click *Rename* at the shortcut menu.

f. Type **WL1-C8-P6-DS** and then press Enter.
g. Close the Open dialog box.

2. At a blank document, click the MAILINGS tab.
3. Click the Select Recipients button and then click *Use an Existing List* from the drop-down list.
4. At the Select Data Source dialog box, navigate to the WL1C8 folder on your storage medium and then double-click the data source file named ***WL1-C8-P6-DS.mdb***.
5. Click the Edit Recipient List button in the Start Mail Merge group.
6. At the Mail Merge Recipients dialog box, click ***WL1-C8-P6-DS.mdb*** that displays in the *Data Source* list box and then click the Edit button.
7. Delete the record for Steve Dutton by completing the following steps:
   a. Click the square that displays at the beginning of the row for *Mr. Steve Dutton*.
   b. Click the Delete Entry button.
   c. At the message asking if you want to delete the entry, click the Yes button.
8. Insert a new record by completing the following steps:
   a. Click the New Entry button in the dialog box.
   b. Type the following text in the new record in the specified fields:
      Title: **Ms.**
      First Name: **Jennae**
      Last Name: **Davis**
      Address Line 1: **3120 South 21st**
      Address Line 2: (none)
      City: **Rosedale**
      State: **MD**
      ZIP Code: **20389**
      Home Phone: **410-555-5774**
9. Insert a new field and type text in the field by completing the following steps:
   a. At the Edit Data Source dialog box, click the Customize Columns button.
   b. At the message asking if you want to save the changes made to the data source file, click Yes.
   c. At the Customize Address List dialog box, click *ZIP Code* in the *Field Names* list box. (A new field is inserted below the selected field.)
   d. Click the Add button.
   e. At the Add Field dialog box, type **Cell Phone** and then click OK.
   f. You decide that you want the *Cell Phone* field to display after the *Home Phone* field. To move the *Cell Phone* field, make sure it is selected and then click the Move Down button.
   g. Click OK to close the Customize Address List dialog box.

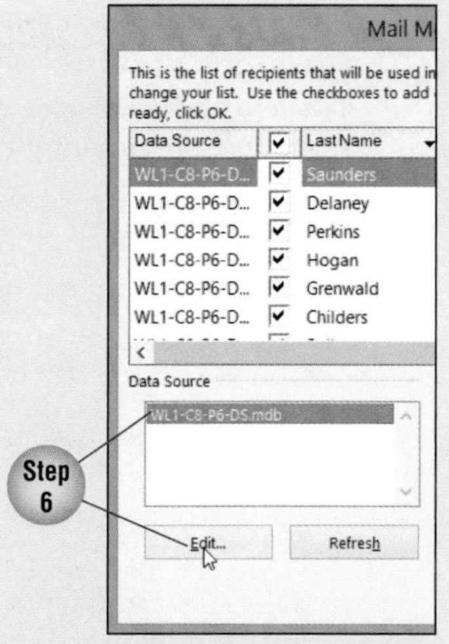

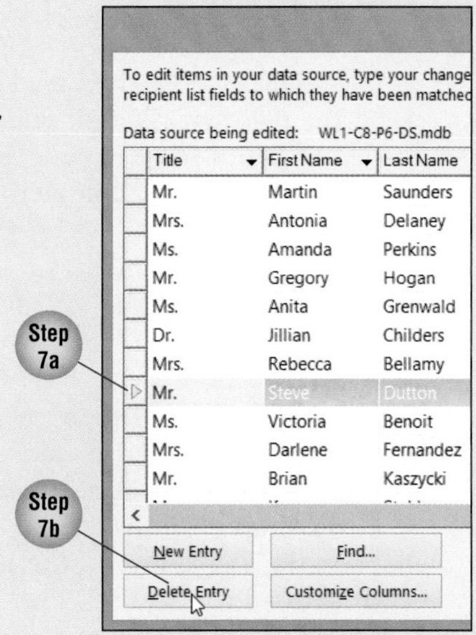

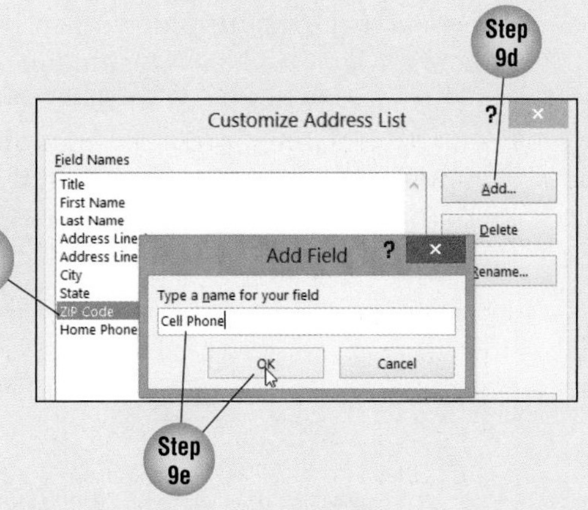

h. At the Edit Data Source dialog box, scroll to the right to display the *Cell Phone* field (last field in the file) and then type the following cell phone numbers (after typing each cell phone number except the last number, press the Down Arrow key to make the next cell below active):

Record 1: 410-555-1249
Record 2: 410-555-3492
Record 3: 410-555-0695
Record 4: 410-555-9488
Record 5: 410-555-1200
Record 6: 410-555-7522
Record 7: 410-555-8833
Record 8: 410-555-9378
Record 9: 410-555-4261
Record 10: 410-555-9944
Record 11: 410-555-2321
Record 12: 410-555-9435

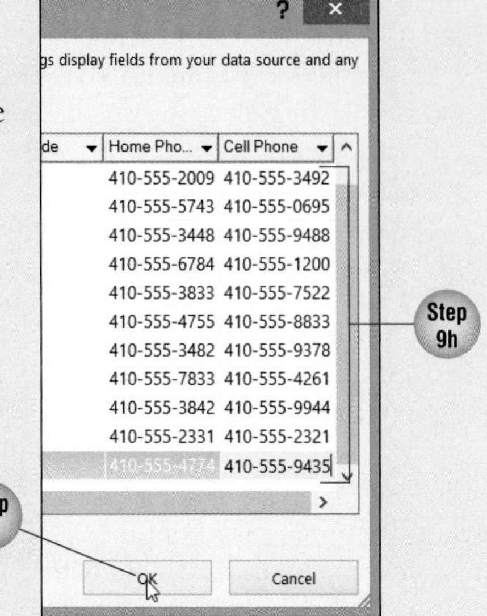

i. Click OK to close the Edit Data Source dialog box.
j. At the message asking if you want to update the recipient list and save changes, click Yes.
k. At the Mail Merge Recipients dialog box, click OK.

10. Create a directory by completing the following steps:
    a. Click the Start Mail Merge button and then click *Directory* at the drop-down list.
    b. At the blank document, set left tabs on the horizontal ruler at the 1-inch mark, the 3-inch mark, and the 4.5-inch mark.
    c. Press the Tab key. (This moves the insertion point to the first tab set at the 1-inch mark.)
    d. Click the Insert Merge Field button arrow and then click *Last_Name* at the drop-down list.
    e. Type a comma and then press the spacebar.
    f. Click the Insert Merge Field button arrow and then click *First_Name* at the drop-down list.
    g. Press the Tab key, click the Insert Merge Field button arrow, and then click *Home_Phone* at the drop-down list.
    h. Press the Tab key, click the Insert Merge Field button arrow, and then click *Cell_Phone* at the drop-down list.
    i. Press the Enter key once.
    j. Click the Finish & Merge button in the Finish group and then click *Edit Individual Documents* at the drop-down list.
    k. At the Merge to New Document dialog box, make sure *All* is selected and then click OK. (This merges the fields in the document.)
11. Press Ctrl + Home, press the Enter key once, and then press the Up Arrow key once.
12. Press the Tab key, turn on bold, and then type **Name**.
13. Press the Tab key and then type **Home Phone**.
14. Press the Tab key and then type **Cell Phone**.

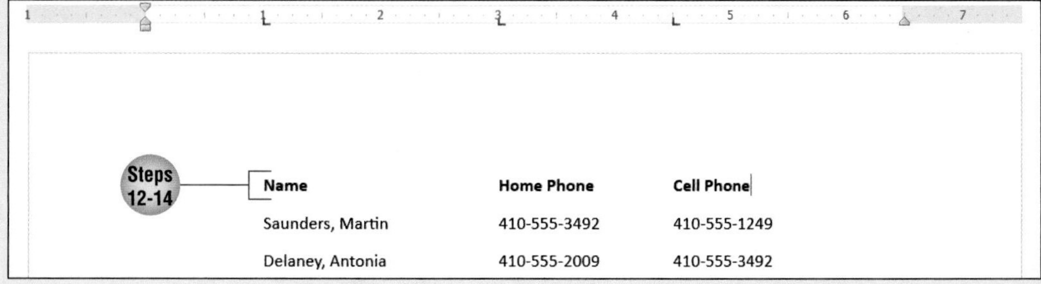

15. Save the directory document and name it **WL1-C8-P6-Directory**.
16. Print and then close the document.
17. Close the directory main document without saving it.

Project 7 Add Fill-in Fields to a Main Document — 1 Part

You will edit a form letter and insert sales representative contact information during a merge.

Inputting Text during a Merge

Word's Merge feature contains a large number of merge fields you can insert in a main document. In this section, you will learn about the Fill-in field that is used for information input at the keyboard during a merge. For more information on the other merge fields, please refer to the on-screen help.

In some situations, you may not need to keep all variable information in a data source file. For example, variable information that changes on a regular basis might include a customer's monthly balance, a product price, and so on. Word lets you input variable information into a document during the merge using the keyboard. A Fill-in field is inserted in a main document by clicking the Rules button in the Write & Insert Fields group on the MAILINGS tab and then clicking *Fill-in* at the drop-down list. This displays the Insert Word Field: Fill-in dialog box, shown in Figure 8.9. At this dialog box, type a short message indicating what should be entered at the keyboard and then click OK. At the Microsoft Word dialog box with the message you entered displayed in the upper left corner, type the text you want to display in the document and then click OK. When the Fill-in field or fields are added, save the main document in the normal manner. A document can contain any number of Fill-in fields.

When you merge the main document with the data source file, the first record is merged with the main document and the Microsoft Word dialog box displays with the message you entered displayed in the upper left corner. Type the required information for the first record in the data source file and then click

Quick Steps

Insert a Fill-in Field in a Main Document
1. Click MAILINGS tab.
2. Click Rules button.
3. Click *Fill-in* at drop-down list.
4. Type prompt text.
5. Click OK.
6. Type text to be inserted in document.
7. Click OK.

Rules

Figure 8.9 Insert Word Field: Fill-in Dialog Box

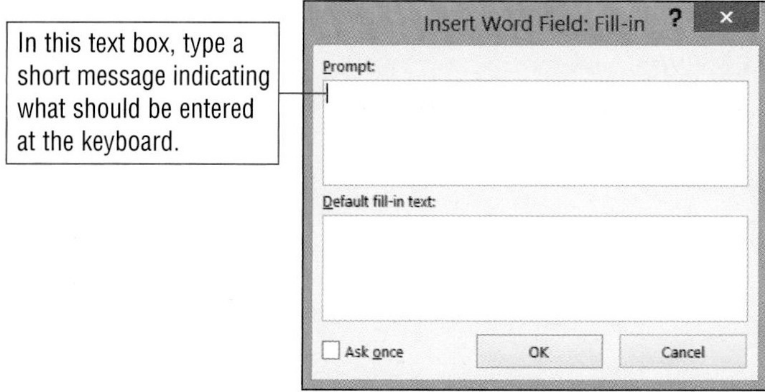
In this text box, type a short message indicating what should be entered at the keyboard.
Insert Word Field: Fill-in
Prompt:
Default fill-in text:
Ask once
OK
Cancel

the OK button. Word displays the dialog box again. Type the required information for the second record in the data source file and then click OK. Continue in this manner until the required information has been entered for each record in the data source file. Word then completes the merge.

Project 7 Adding Fill-in Fields to a Main Document — Part 1 of 1

1. Open the document named **WL1-C8-P1-MFMD.docx**. (At the message asking if you want to continue, click Yes.) Save the document with Save As and name it **WL1-C8-P7-MFMD**.
2. Change the second paragraph in the body of the letter to the paragraph shown in Figure 8.10. Insert the first Fill-in field (representative's name) by completing the following steps:
   a. Click the MAILINGS tab.
   b. Click the Rules button in the Write & Insert Fields group and then click *Fill-in* at the drop-down list.
   c. At the Insert Word Field: Fill-in dialog box, type **Insert rep name** in the *Prompt* text box and then click OK.
   d. At the Microsoft Word dialog box with *Insert rep name* displayed in the upper left corner, type **(representative's name)** and then click OK.

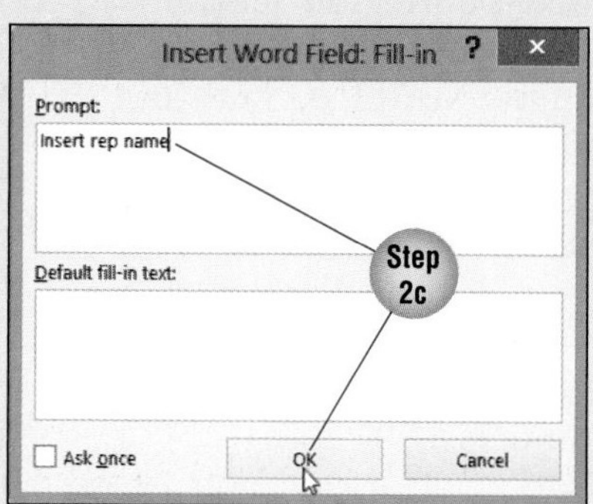

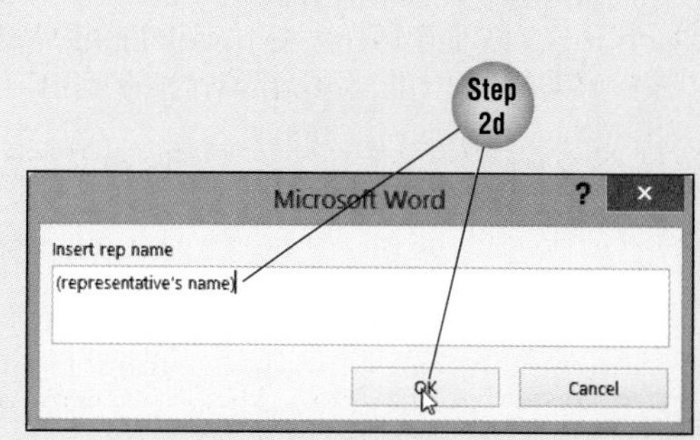

3. Complete steps similar to those in Step 2 to insert the second Fill-in field (phone number), except type **Insert phone number** in the *Prompt* text box at the Insert Word Field: Fill-in dialog box and type **(phone number)** at the Microsoft Word dialog box.
4. Save **WL1-C8-P7-MFMD.docx**.
5. Merge the main document with the data source file by completing the following steps:
   a. Click the Finish & Merge button and then click *Edit Individual Documents* at the drop-down list.
   b. At the Merge to New Document dialog box, make sure *All* is selected and then click OK.
   c. When Word merges the main document with the first record, a dialog box displays with the message *Insert rep name* and the text *(representative's name)* selected. At this dialog box, type **Marilyn Smythe** and then click OK.
   d. At the dialog box with the message *Insert phone number* and *(phone number)* selected, type **(646) 555-8944** and then click OK.

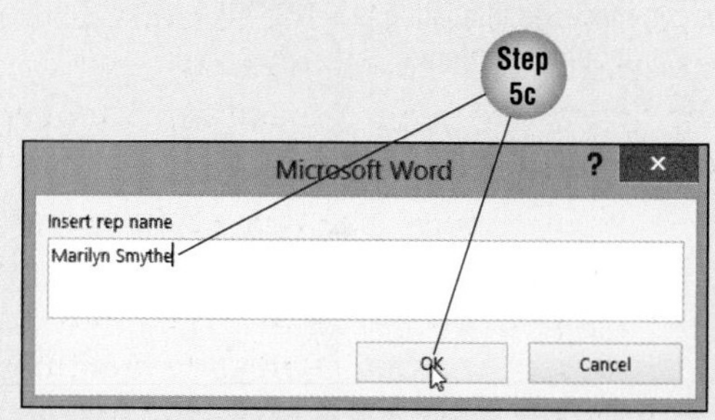

e. At the dialog box with the message *Insert rep name*, type **Anthony Mason** (over *Marilyn Smythe*) and then click OK.
f. At the dialog box with the message *Insert phone number*, type **(646) 555-8901** (over the previous number) and then click OK.
g. At the dialog box with the message *Insert rep name*, type **Faith Ostrom** (over *Anthony Mason*) and then click OK.
h. At the dialog box with the message *Insert phone number*, type **(646) 555-8967** (over the previous number) and then click OK.
i. At the dialog box with the message *Insert rep name*, type **Thomas Rivers** (over *Faith Ostrom*) and then click OK.
j. At the dialog box with the message *Insert phone number*, type **(646) 555-0793** (over the previous number) and then click OK.

6. Save the merged document and name it **WL1-C8-P7-MFLtrs**.
7. Print and then close **WL1-C8-P7-MFLtrs.docx**.
8. Save and then close **WL1-C8-P7-MFMD.docx**.

Figure 8.10 Project 7

Lowering expense charges is noteworthy because before the reduction, McCormack expense deductions were already among the lowest, far below most mutual funds and variable annuity accounts with similar objectives. At the same time, services for you, our client, will continue to expand. If you would like to discuss this change, please call our service representative, **(representative's name)**, at **(phone number)**.

Project 8 Use Mail Merge Wizard — 1 Part

You will use the Mail Merge wizard to merge a main document with a data source file and create letters to clients of Sorenson Funds.

Merging Using the Mail Merge Wizard

The Mail Merge feature includes a Mail Merge wizard that guides you through the merge process. To access the Wizard, click the MAILINGS tab, click the Start Mail Merge button, and then click the *Step-by-Step Mail Merge Wizard* option at the drop-down list. The first of six Mail Merge task panes displays at the right side of the screen. Completing the tasks at one task pane displays the next task pane. The options in each task pane may vary depending on the type of merge you are performing. Generally, you complete one of the following steps at each task pane:

- Step 1: Select the type of document you want to create such as a letter, email message, envelope, label, or directory.
- Step 2: Specify whether you want to use the current document to create the main document, start from a template, or start from an existing document.
- Step 3: Specify whether you are typing a new list, using an existing list, or selecting from an Outlook contacts list.

- Step 4: Use the items in this task pane to help you prepare the main document by performing tasks such as inserting fields.
- Step 5: Preview the merged documents.
- Step 6: Complete the merge.

Project 8 Preparing Form Letters Using the Mail Merge Wizard

Part 1 of 1

1. At a blank document, click the MAILINGS tab, click the Start Mail Merge button in the Start Mail Merge group, and then click *Step-by-Step Mail Merge Wizard* at the drop-down list.
2. At the first Mail Merge task pane, make sure *Letters* is selected in the *Select document type* section and then click the Next: Starting document hyperlink located toward the bottom of the task pane.
3. At the second Mail Merge task pane, click the *Start from existing document* option in the *Select starting document* section.
4. Click the Open button in the *Start from existing* section of the task pane.
5. At the Open dialog box, navigate to the WL1C8 folder on your storage medium and then double-click ***SFLtrMD.docx***.
6. Click the Next: Select recipients hyperlink located toward the bottom of the task pane.
7. At the third Mail Merge task pane, click the Browse hyperlink that displays in the *Use an existing list* section of the task pane.
8. At the Select Data Source dialog box, navigate to the WL1C8 folder on your storage medium and then double-click ***SFClients.mdb***.
9. At the Mail Merge Recipients dialog box, click OK.
10. Click the Next: Write your letter hyperlink that displays toward the bottom of the task pane.
11. At the fourth Mail Merge task pane, enter fields in the form letter by completing the following steps:
    a. Position the insertion point a double space above the first paragraph of text in the letter.
    b. Click the Address block hyperlink located in the *Write your letter* section of the task pane.
    c. At the Insert Address Block dialog box, click the OK button.
    d. Press the Enter key twice and then click the Greeting line hyperlink located in the *Write your letter* section of the task pane.
    e. At the Insert Greeting Line dialog box, click the down-pointing arrow at the right of the option box containing the comma (the box to the right of the box containing *Mr. Randall*).
    f. At the drop-down list that displays, click the colon.
    g. Click OK to close the Insert Greeting Line dialog box.

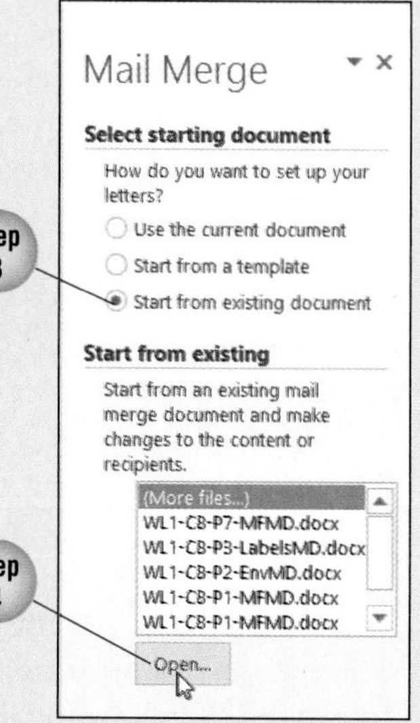

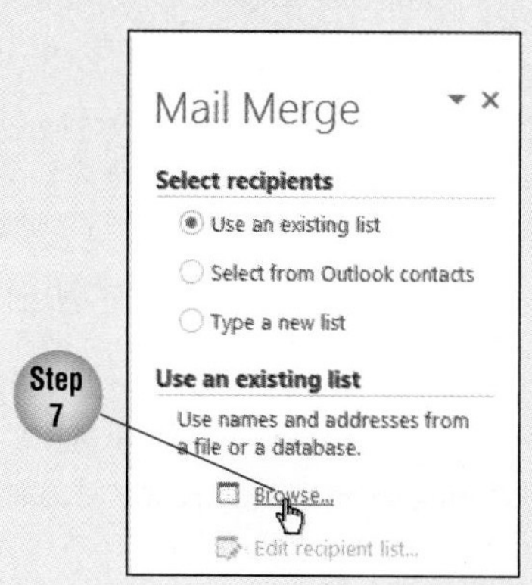

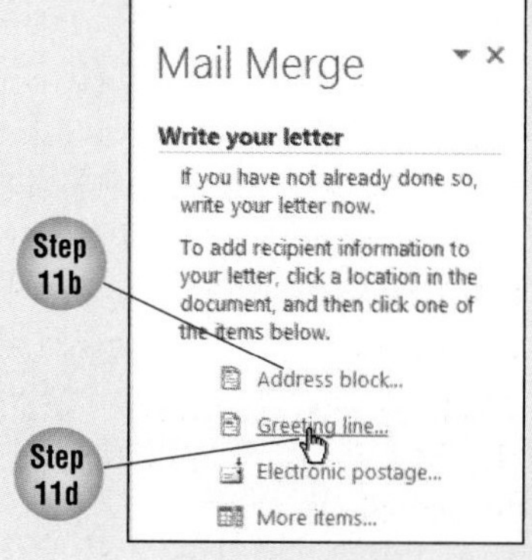

12. Click the Next: Preview your letters hyperlink located toward the bottom of the task pane.
13. At the fifth Mail Merge task pane, look over the letter that displays in the document window and make sure the information merged properly. If you want to see the letters for the other recipients, click the button in the Mail Merge task pane containing the right-pointing arrow.
14. Click the Preview Results button in the Preview Results group to turn off the preview feature.
15. Click the Next: Complete the merge hyperlink that displays toward the bottom of the task pane.
16. At the sixth Mail Merge task pane, click the Edit individual letters hyperlink that displays in the *Merge* section of the task pane.
17. At the Merge to New Document dialog box, make sure *All* is selected and then click the OK button.
18. Save the merged letters document with the name **WL1-C8-P8-SFLtrs**.
19. Print only the first two pages of **WL1-C8-P8-SFLtrs.docx**.
20. Close the document.
21. At the sixth Mail Merge task pane, close the letter main document without saving it.

Chapter Summary

- Use the Mail Merge feature to create documents such as letters, envelopes, labels, and directories with personalized information.
- Generally, a merge takes two documents—the data source file containing the variable information and the main document containing standard text—along with fields identifying where variable information is inserted during the merge process.
- Variable information in a data source file is saved as a record. A record contains all of the information for one unit. A series of fields makes a record, and a series of records makes a data source file.
- A data source file is saved as an Access database, but you do not need Access on your computer to complete a merge with a data source.
- Use predesigned fields when creating a data source file, or create your own custom field at the Customize Address List dialog box.
- Use the Address Block button in the Write & Insert Fields group on the MAILINGS tab to insert all of the fields required for the inside address of a letter. This inserts the «AddressBlock» field, which is considered a composite field because it groups a number of fields.
- Click the Greeting Line button in the Write & Insert Fields group on the MAILINGS tab to insert the «GreetingLine» composite field in the document.
- Click the Insert Merge Field button arrow in the Write & Insert Fields group on the MAILINGS tab to display a drop-down list of fields contained in the data source file.
- Click the Preview Results button on the MAILINGS tab to view the main document merged with the first record in the data source. Use the navigation buttons in the Preview Results group on the MAILINGS tab to display the main document merged with the desired record.

- Before merging documents, check for errors by clicking the Check for Errors button in the Preview Results group on the MAILINGS tab. This displays the Checking and Reporting Errors dialog box with three options for checking errors.
- Click the Finish & Merge button on the MAILINGS tab to complete the merge.
- Select specific records for merging by inserting or removing check marks from the desired records in the Mail Merge Recipients dialog box. Display this dialog box by clicking the Edit Recipient List button on the MAILINGS tab.
- Edit specific records in a data source file at the Edit Data Source dialog box. Display this dialog box by clicking the Edit Recipient List button on the MAILINGS tab, clicking the desired data source file name in the *Data Source* list box, and then clicking the Edit button.
- Use the Fill-in field in a main document to insert variable information at the keyboard during a merge.
- Word includes a Mail Merge wizard to guide you through the process of creating letters, envelopes, labels, directories, and email messages with personalized information.

Commands Review

FEATURE	RIBBON TAB, GROUP	BUTTON	OPTION
Address Block field	MAILINGS, Write & Insert Fields		
Checking and Reporting Errors dialog box	MAILINGS, Preview Results		
directory main document	MAILINGS, Start Mail Merge		*Directory*
envelopes main document	MAILINGS, Start Mail Merge		*Envelopes*
Fill-in merge field	MAILINGS, Write & Insert Fields		*Fill-in*
Greeting Line field	MAILINGS, Write & Insert Fields		
insert merge fields	MAILINGS, Write & Insert Fields		
labels main document	MAILINGS, Start Mail Merge		*Labels*
letter main document	MAILINGS, Start Mail Merge		*Letters*
Mail Merge Recipients dialog box	MAILINGS, Start Mail Merge		
Mail Merge wizard	MAILINGS, Start Mail Merge		*Step-by-Step Mail Merge Wizard*
New Address List dialog box	MAILINGS, Start Mail Merge		*Type a New List*
preview merge results	MAILINGS, Preview Results		

Concepts Check Test Your Knowledge

Completion: In the space provided at the right, indicate the correct term, command, o

1. A merge generally takes two files: a data source file and this. ________________
2. This term refers to all of the information for one unit in a data source file. ________________
3. Create a data source file by clicking this button on the MAILINGS tab and then clicking *Type a New List* at the drop-down list. ________________
4. A data source file is saved as this type of file. ________________
5. Create your own custom fields in a data source file with options at this dialog box. ________________
6. Use this button on the MAILINGS tab to insert all of the required fields for the inside address in a letter. ________________
7. The «GreetingLine» field is considered this type of field because it includes all of the fields required for the greeting line. ________________
8. Click this button on the MAILINGS tab to display the first record merged with the main document. ________________
9. Before merging a document, check for errors using this button in the Preview Results group on the MAILINGS tab. ________________
10. To complete a merge, click this button in the Finish group on the MAILINGS tab. ________________
11. When creating the envelope main document, click in the approximate location the recipient's address will appear and then click this button in the Write & Insert Fields group. ________________
12. Select specific records in a data source file by inserting or removing check marks from the records in this dialog box. ________________
13. Use this field to insert variable information at the keyboard during a merge. ________________
14. Click this option at the Start Mail Merge button drop-down list to begin the Mail Merge wizard. ________________

...eck Assess Your Performance

...ILE

..., display the New Address List dialog
...ay the Customize Address List dialog box.
...e Address List dialog box, delete the following fields: *Company* ...*or Region*, *Work Phone*, and *E-mail Address* and then add a custom ...*Cell Phone*.
...Customize Address List box and then type the following information ...New Address List dialog box as the first record:

...tle: Mr.
First Name: Tony
Last Name: Benedetti
Address Line 1: 1315 Cordova Road
Address Line 2: Apt. 402
City: Santa Fe
State: NM
ZIP Code: 87505
Home Phone: (505) 555-0489
Cell Phone: (505) 555-0551

4. Type the following information as the second record:
   Title: Ms.
   First Name: Theresa
   Last Name: Dusek
   Address Line 1: 12044 Ridgeway Drive
   Address Line 2: (leave blank)
   City: Santa Fe
   State: NM
   ZIP Code: 87504
   Home Phone: (505) 555-1120
   Cell Phone: (505) 555-6890
5. Type the following information as the third record:
   Title: Mrs.
   First Name: Mary
   Last Name: Arguello
   Address Line 1: 2554 Country Drive
   Address Line 2: #105
   City: Santa Fe
   State: NM
   ZIP Code: 87504
   Home Phone: (505) 555-7663
   Cell Phone: (505) 555-5472
6. Type the following information as the fourth record:
   Title: Mr.
   First Name: Preston
   Last Name: Miller
   Address Line 1: 120 Second Street
   Address Line 2: (leave blank)

City: **Santa Fe**
State: **NM**
ZIP Code: **87505**
Home Phone: **(505) 555-3551**
Cell Phone: **(505) 555-9630**

7. Save the data source file and name it **WL1-C8-A1-CCDS**.
8. Close the blank document without saving changes.

Assessment 2

CREATE A MAIN DOCUMENT AND MERGE WITH A DATA SOURCE FILE

1. Open **CCVolunteerLtr.docx** and then save the document with Save As and name it **WL1-C8-A2-CCMD**.
2. Select **WL1-C8-A1-CCDS.mdb** you created in Assessment 1 as the data source file.
3. Move the insertion point to the beginning of the first paragraph of text in the body of the letter, insert the «AddressBlock» field, and then press Enter twice.
4. Insert the «GreetingLine» field specifying a colon rather than a comma as the greeting line format and then press Enter twice.
5. Move the insertion point one space to the right of the period that ends the second paragraph of text in the body of the letter and then type the following text inserting the «Title», «Last_Name», «Home_Phone», «Cell_Phone» fields where indicated:

   Currently, *«Title» «Last_Name»*, **our records indicate your home telephone number is** *«Home_Phone»* **and your cell phone number is** *«Cell_Phone»*. **If this information is not accurate, please contact our office with the correct numbers.**
6. Merge the main document with all records in the data source file.
7. Save the merged letters document as **WL1-C8-A2-CCLetters**.
8. Print and then close **WL1-C8-A2-CCLetters.docx**.
9. Save and then close **WL1-C8-A2-CCMD.docx**.

Assessment 3

CREATE AN ENVELOPE MAIN DOCUMENT AND MERGE WITH A DATA SOURCE FILE

1. Create an envelope main document using the Size 10 envelope size.
2. Select **WL1-C8-A1-CCDS.mdb** as the data source file.
3. Insert the «AddressBlock» field in the appropriate location in the envelope document.
4. Merge the envelope main document with all records in the data source file.
5. Save the merged envelopes document and name it **WL1-C8-A3-CCEnvs**.
6. Print and then close the envelopes document. (Check with your instructor before printing the envelopes.)
7. Close the envelope main document without saving it.

Assessment

4 CREATE A LABELS MAIN DOCUMENT AND MERGE WITH A DATA SOURCE FILE

1. Create a labels main document using the *Avery US Letter 5160 Easy Peel Address Labels* option.
2. Select **WL1-C8-A1-CCDS.mdb** as the data source file.
3. Insert the «AddressBlock» field.
4. Update the labels.
5. Merge the labels main document with all records in the data source file.
6. Select the entire document and then apply the No Spacing style.
7. Save the merged labels document and name it **WL1-C8-A4-CCLabels**.
8. Print and then close the labels document.
9. Close the labels main document without saving it.

Assessment

5 EDIT A DATA SOURCE FILE

1. Open **WL1-C8-A2-CCMD.docx**. (At the message asking if you want to continue, click Yes.) Save the main document with Save As and name it **WL1-C8-A5-CCMD**.
2. Edit the **WL1-C8-A1-CCDS.mdb** data source file by making the following changes:
   a. Change the address for Ms. Theresa Dusek from *12044 Ridgeway Drive* to *1390 Fourth Avenue*.
   b. Delete the record for Mrs. Mary Arguello.
   c. Insert a new record with the following information:

      Mr. Cesar Rivera
      3201 East Third Street
      Santa Fe, NM 87505
      Home Phone: (505) 555-6675
      Cell Phone: (505) 555-3528
3. At the main document, edit the third sentence of the second paragraph so it reads as follows (insert a Fill-in field for the *(number of hours)* shown in the sentence below):

   According to our volunteer roster, you have signed up to volunteer for *(number of hours)* during the summer session.
4. Merge the main document with the data source file and type the following text for each record:

   Record 1: **four hours a week**
   Record 2: **six hours a week**
   Record 3: **twelve hours a week**
   Record 4: **four hours a week**
5. Save the merged document and name it **WL1-C8-A5-CCLtrs**.
6. Print and then close **WL1-C8-A5-CCLtrs.docx**.
7. Save and then close **WL1-C8-A5-CCMD.docx**.

Visual Benchmark Demonstrate Your Proficiency

PREPARE AND MERGE LETTERS

1. Open **FPLtrhd.docx** and then save the document with Save As and name it **WL1-C8-VB-FPMD**.
2. Look at the information in Figure 8.13 and Figure 8.14 and then use Mail Merge to prepare four letters. (When creating the main document, as shown in Figure 8.14, insert the appropriate fields where you see the text *Title*; *First Name*; *Last Name*; *Street Address*; and *City*, *State ZIP*. Insert the appropriate fields where you see the text *Title* and *Last Name* in the first paragraph of text.) Create the data source file with the information in Figure 8.13 and then save the file and name it **WL1-C8-VB-FPDS**.
3. Merge the **WL1-C8-VB-FPMD.docx** main document with the **WL1-C8-VB-FPDS.mdb** data source file and then save the merged letters document and name it **WL1-C8-VB-FPLtrs**.
4. Print and then close **WL1-C8-VB-FPLtrs.docx**.
5. Save and then close **WL1-C8-VB-FPMD.docx**.

Figure 8.13 Visual Benchmark Data Source Records

Mr. and Mrs. Chris Gallagher
17034 234th Avenue
Newport, VT 05855

Ms. Heather Segarra
4103 Thompson Drive
Newport, VT 05855

Mr. Gene Goodrich
831 Cromwell Lane
Newport, VT 05855

Mrs. Sonya Kraus
15933 Ninth Street
Newport, VT 05855

Figure 8.14 Visual Benchmark Main Document

Frontline Photography Equipment and Supplies

Current Date

Title First Name Last Name
Street Address
City, State ZIP

Dear Title Last Name:

We have enjoyed being a part of the Newport community for the past two years. Our success in the community is directly related to you, Title Last Name, and all of our other loyal customers. Thank you for shopping at our store for all of your photography equipment and supply needs.

To show our appreciation for your loyalty and your business, we are enclosing a coupon for 20 percent off any item in our store, even our incredibly low-priced clearance items. Through the end of the month, all of our camera accessories are on sale. So, use your coupon and take advantage of additional savings on items such as camera lenses, tripods, cleaning supplies, and camera bags.

To accommodate our customers' schedules, we have increased our weekend hours. Our store will be open Saturdays until 7:00 p.m. and Sundays until 5:00 p.m. Come by and let our sales associates find just the right camera and camera accessories for you.

Sincerely,

Student Name

XX
WL1-C8-VB-FPMD.docx

Enclosure

559 Tenth Street, Suite A ◈ Newport, VT 05855 ◈ (802) 555-4411

Case Study Apply Your Skills

Part 1

You are the office manager for Freestyle Extreme, a sporting goods store that specializes in snowboarding and snow skiing equipment and supplies. The store has two branches: one on the east side of town and the other on the west side. One of your job responsibilities is to send letters to customers letting them know about sales, new equipment, and upcoming events. Next month, both stores are having a sale and all snowboard and snow skiing supplies will be 15 percent off the regular price. Create a data source file that contains the following customer information: first name, last name, address, city, state, ZIP code, and branch. Add six customers to the data source file. Indicate that three usually shop at the East branch and three usually shop at the West branch. Create a letter as a main document that includes information about the upcoming sale. The letter should contain at least two paragraphs, and in addition to the information on the sale, it might include information about the store, snowboarding, and/or snow skiing. Save the data source file with the name **WL1-C8-CS-FEDS**, save the main document with the name **WL1-C8-CS-FEMD**, and save the merged document with the name **WL1-C8-CS-FELtrs**. Create envelopes for the six merged letters, and name the merged envelope document **WL1-C8-CS-FEEnvs**. Do not save the envelope main document. Print the merged letters document and the merged envelopes document.

Part 2

A well-known extreme snowboarder will be visiting both branches of the store to meet with customers and sign autographs. Use the Help feature to learn how to insert an If...Then...Else... merge field in a document, and then create a letter that includes the name of the extreme snowboarder (you determine the name), the time (1:00 p.m. to 4:30 p.m.), and any additional information that might interest customers. Also include in the letter an If...Then...Else... merge field that will insert *Wednesday, September 23* if the customer's Branch is *East* and will insert *Thursday, September 24* if the Branch is *West*. Add visual appeal to the letter by inserting a picture, clip art image, WordArt, or any other feature that will attract readers' attention. Save the letter main document and name it **WL1-C8-CS-MD**. Merge the letter main document with the **WL1-C8-CS-FEDS.mdb** data source. Save the merged letters document and name it **WL1-C8-CS-AnnLtrs**. Print the merged letters document.

Part 3

The store owner wants to try selling short skis known as "snow blades" or "skiboards." He has asked you to research these skis and identify one type and model to sell only at the West branch of the store. If the model sells well, he will consider selling it at the East branch at a future time. Prepare a main document letter that describes the new snow blade or skiboard that the West branch is selling. Include information about pricing and tell customers that the new item is being offered at a 40 percent discount if purchased within the next week. Merge the letter main document with the **WL1-C8-CS-FEDS.mdb** data source file and include only those customers that shop at the West branch. Save the merged letters document and name it **WL1-C8-CS-SBLtrs**. Print the merged letters document. Save the letter main document and name it **WL1-C8-CS-SBMD**. Print and then close the main document.

UNIT 2

MICROSOFT® WORD Performance Assessment

Word
WL1U2

Note: Before beginning unit assessments, copy to your storage medium the WL1U2 subfolder from the WL1 folder on the CD that accompanies this textbook and then make WL1U2 the active folder.

Assessing Proficiency

In this unit, you have learned to format text into columns; insert, format, and customize objects to enhance the appearance of a document; manage files, print envelopes and labels, and create documents using templates; create and edit tables; visually represent data in SmartArt graphics and organizational charts; and use Mail Merge to create letters, envelopes, labels, and directories.

Assessment 1 Format a Bioinformatics Document

1. Open **Bioinformatics.docx** and then save the document with Save As and name it **WL1-U2-A01-Bioinformatics**.
2. Move the insertion point to the end of the document and then insert the file named **GenomeMapping.docx**.
3. Change the line spacing for the entire document to 1.5 spacing.
4. Insert a continuous section break at the beginning of the first paragraph of text (the paragraph that begins *Bioinformatics is the mixed application*).
5. Format the text below the section break into two columns.
6. Balance the columns on the second page.
7. Press Ctrl + Home to move the insertion point to the beginning of the document, insert the Motion Quote text box, and then type **"Understanding our DNA is similar to understanding a number that is billions of digits long."** in the text box. Select the text in the text box, change the font size to 12 points, change the width of the text box to 2.6 inches, and then position the text box in the middle of the page with square text wrapping.
8. Create a drop cap with the first letter of the first word *Bioinformatics* that begins the first paragraph of text. Make the drop cap two lines in height.
9. Manually hyphenate words in the document.
10. Insert page numbering at the bottom of the page using the Thin Line page numbering option.
11. Save, print, and then close **WL1-U2-A01-Bioinformatics.docx**.

Assessment 2 Create a Workshop Flier

1. Create the flier shown in Figure U2.1 with the following specifications:
   a. Create the WordArt with the following specifications:
      - Use the *Fill - White, Outline - Accent 1, Shadow* option (first row, fourth column) at the WordArt button drop-down gallery.
      - Increase the width to 6.5 inches and the height to 1 inch.
      - Apply the Deflate text effect transform shape.
      - Change the text fill color to *Green, Accent 6, Lighter 40%*.

   b. Type the text shown in the figure. Change the font to 22-point Calibri bold and center-align the text.
   c. Insert the clip art image shown in the figure (use the keyword *Paris* to find the clip art) and then change the wrapping style to *Square*. Position and size the image as shown in the figure.
2. Save the document and name it **WL1-U2-A02-TravelFlier**.
3. Print and then close **WL1-U2-A02-TravelFlier.docx**.

Figure U2.1 Assessment 2

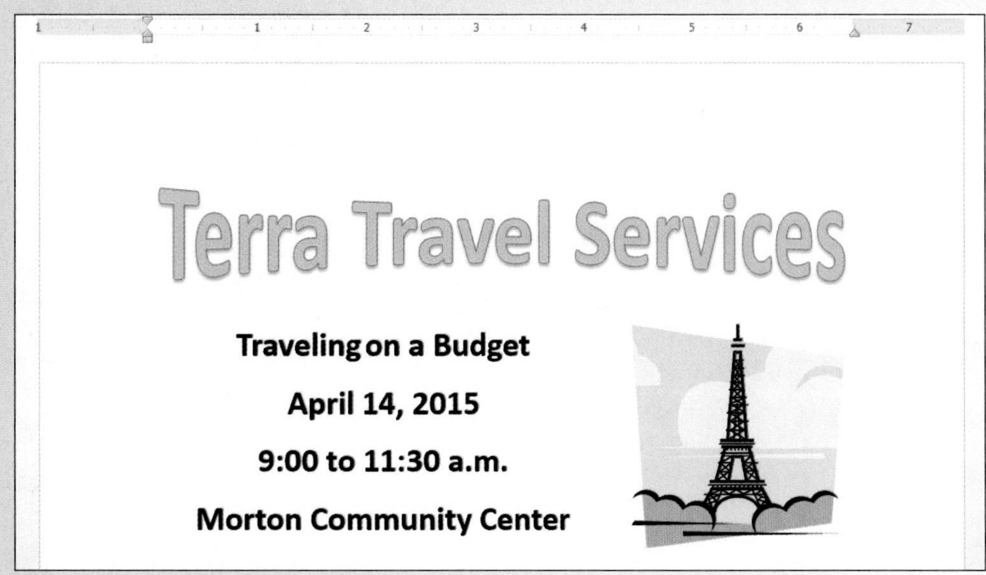

Assessment 3 Create a Staff Meeting Announcement

1. Create the announcement shown in Figure U2.2 with the following specifications:
   a. Use the Hexagon shape in the *Basic Shapes* section of the Shapes drop-down list to create the shape.
   b. Apply the Subtle Effect - Blue, Accent 1 shape style.
   c. Apply the Art Deco bevel shape effect.
   d. Type the letter A (this makes active many of the tab options), click the HOME tab, and then click the *No Spacing* style thumbnail in the Styles group.
   e. Type the remaining text in the shape as shown in the figure. Insert the ñ as a symbol (in the normal text font), and insert the clock as a symbol (in the Wingdings font). Set the text and clock symbol in larger font sizes.
2. Save the completed document and name it **WL1-U2-A03-MeetNotice**.
3. Print and then close **WL1-U2-A03-MeetNotice.docx**.

Figure U2.2 Assessment 3

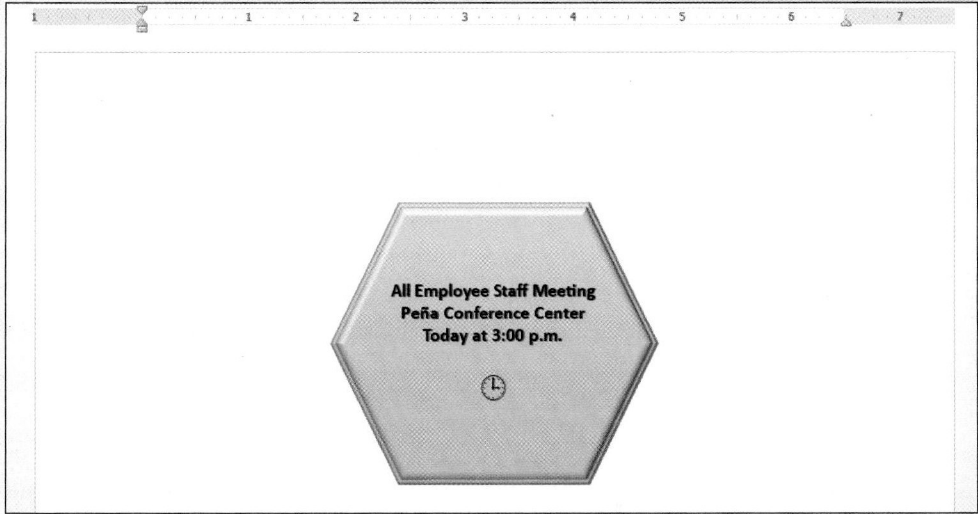

Assessment 4 Create a River Rafting Flier

1. At a blank document, insert the picture named **River.jpg**. (Insert the picture using the Picture button.)
2. Crop out a portion of the trees at the left and right and a portion of the hill at the top.
3. Correct the brightness and contrast to *Brightness: +20% Contrast: +40%*.
4. Specify that the picture should wrap behind text.
5. Type the text **River Rafting Adventures** on one line, **Salmon River, Idaho** on the next line, and **1-888-555-3322** on the third line.
6. Increase the size of the picture so it is easier to see and the size of the text so it is easier to read. Center the text and position it on the picture on top of the river so the text is readable.
7. Save the document and name it **WL1-U2-A04-RaftingFlier**.
8. Print and then close **WL1-U2-A04-RaftingFlier.docx**.

Assessment 5 Create an Envelope

1. At a blank document, create an envelope with the text shown in Figure U2.3.
2. Save the envelope document and name it **WL1-U2-A05-Env**.
3. Print and then close **WL1-U2-A05-Env.docx**.

Figure U2.3 Assessment 5

Mrs. Eileen Hebert
15205 East 42nd Street
Lake Charles, LA 71098

Mr. Earl Robicheaux
1436 North Sheldon Street
Jennings, LA 70542

Assessment 6 Create Mailing Labels

1. Create mailing labels with the name and address for Mrs. Eileen Hebert shown in Figure U2.3 using a label vendor and product of your choosing.
2. Save the document and name it **WL1-U2-A06-Labels**.
3. Print and then close **WL1-U2-A06-Labels.docx**.

Assessment 7 Create and Format a Table with Software Training Information

1. At a blank document, create the table shown in Figure U2.4. Format the table and the text (do not apply a table style) in a manner similar to what is shown in Figure U2.4.
2. Insert a formula in cell B8 that totals the numbers in cells B4 through B7.
3. Insert a formula in cell C8 that totals the numbers in cells C4 through C7.
4. Save the document and name it **WL1-U2-A07-TechTraining**.
5. Print and then close **WL1-U2-A07-TechTraining.docx**.

Figure U2.4 Assessment 7

TRI-STATE PRODUCTS		
Computer Technology Department Microsoft® Office 2013 Training		
Application	**# Enrolled**	**# Completed**
Access 2013	20	15
Excel 2013	62	56
PowerPoint 2013	40	33
Word 2013	80	72
Total		

Assessment 8 Create and Format a Table Containing Training Scores

1. Open **TrainingScores.docx** and then save the document with Save As and name it **WL1-U2-A08-TrainingScores**.
2. Insert formulas that calculate the averages in the appropriate row and column. (When writing the formulas, change the *Number format* option to *0*.)
3. Autofit the contents of the table.
4. Apply a table style of your choosing to the table.
5. Apply any other formatting to improve the appearance of the table.
6. Save, print, and then close **WL1-U2-A08-TrainingScores.docx**.

Assessment 9 Create an Organizational Chart

1. Use SmartArt to create an organizational chart for the text shown in Figure U2.5 (in the order displayed). Change the colors to *Colorful Range - Accent Colors 4 to 5* and apply the Metallic Scene SmartArt style.
2. Save the completed document and name it **WL1-U2-A09-OrgChart**.
3. Print and then close **WL1-U2-A09-OrgChart.docx**.

Figure U2.5 Assessment 9

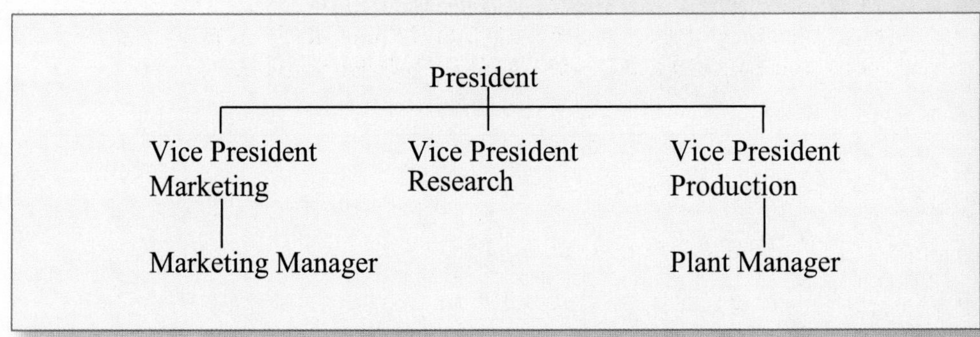

Assessment 10 Create a SmartArt Graphic

1. At a blank document, create the WordArt and SmartArt graphic shown in Figure U2.6 with the following specifications:
   a. Create the WordArt text using the *Fill - Blue, Accent 1, Outline - Background 1, Hard Shadow - Accent 1* option. Change the shape height to 1 inch and the shape width to 6 inches and then apply the Square transform text effect. Position the WordArt at the top center of the page with square text wrapping.
   b. Create the SmartArt graphic using the Vertical Picture Accent List graphic. Click the picture icon that displays in the top circle and then insert the picture named **Seagull.jpg** located in the WL1U2 folder. Insert the same picture in the other two circles. Type the text in each rectangle shape as shown in Figure U2.6. Change the colors to *Colorful Range - Accent Colors 5 to 6* and apply the Cartoon SmartArt style.
2. Save the document and name it **WL1-U2-A10-SPGraphic**.
3. Print and then close **WL1-U2-A10-SPGraphic.docx**.

Figure U2.6 Assessment 10

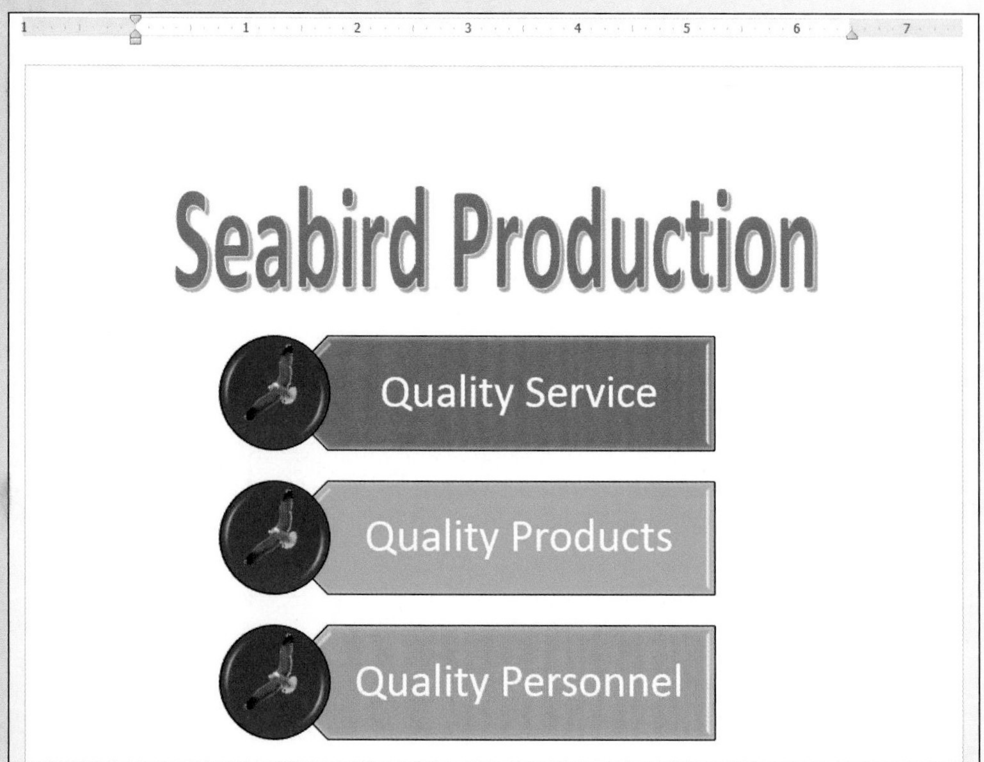

Assessment 11 Merge and Print Letters

1. Look at the information shown in Figure U2.7 and Figure U2.8. Use the Mail Merge feature to prepare six letters using the information shown in the figures. When creating the letter main document, open **SMLtrhd.docx** and then save the document with Save As and name it **WL1-U2-A11-MD**. Insert Fill-in fields in the main document in place of the *(coordinator name)* and *(telephone number)* text. Create the data source file with the text shown in Figure U2.7 and name the file **WL1-U2-A11-DS**.
2. Type the text in the main document as shown in Figure U2.8 and then merge the document with the **WL1-U2-A11-DS.mdb** data source file. When merging, enter the first name and telephone number shown below for the first three records and enter the second name and telephone number shown below for the last three records:

    Jeff Greenswald (813) 555-9886
    Grace Ramirez (813) 555-9807

3. Save the merged letters document and name it **WL1-U2-A11-Ltrs**. Print and then close the document.
4. Save and then close the main document.

Figure U2.7 Assessment 11

Mr. Antonio Mercado
3241 Court G
Tampa, FL 33623

Ms. Kristina Vukovich
1120 South Monroe
Tampa, FL 33655

Ms. Alexandria Remick
909 Wheeler South
Tampa, FL 33620

Mr. Minh Vu
9302 Lawndale Southwest
Tampa, FL 33623

Mr. Curtis Iverson
10139 93rd Court South
Tampa, FL 33654

Mrs. Holly Bernard
8904 Emerson Road
Tampa, FL 33620

Figure U2.8 Assessment 11

December 14, 2015

«AddressBlock»

«GreetingLine»

Sound Medical is switching hospital care in Tampa to St. Jude's Hospital beginning January 1, 2016. As mentioned in last month's letter, St. Jude's Hospital was selected because it meets our requirements for high-quality, customer-pleasing care that is also affordable and accessible. Our physicians look forward to caring for you in this new environment.

Over the past month, staff members at Sound Medical have been working to make this transition as smooth as possible. Surgeries planned after January 1 are being scheduled at St. Jude's Hospital. Mothers delivering babies any time after January 1 are receiving information about delivery room tours and prenatal classes available at St. Jude's. Your Sound Medical doctor will have privileges at St. Jude's and will continue to care for you if you need to be hospitalized.

You are a very important part of our patient family, «Title» «Last_Name», and we hope this information is helpful. If you have any additional questions or concerns, please call your Sound Medical health coordinator, (coordinator name), at (telephone number), between 8:00 a.m. and 4:30 p.m.

Sincerely,

Jody Tiemann
District Administrator

XX
WL1-U2-A11-MD.docx

Assessment 12 Merge and Print Envelopes

1. Use the Mail Merge feature to prepare envelopes for the letters created in Assessment 11.
2. Specify **WL1-U2-A11-DS.mdb** as the data source document.
3. Save the merged envelopes document and name the document **WL1-U2-A12-Envs**.
4. Print and then close **WL1-U2-A12-Envs.docx**.
5. Do not save the envelope main document.

Writing Activities

The following activities give you the opportunity to practice your writing skills along with demonstrating an understanding of some of the important Word features you have mastered in this unit. Use correct grammar, appropriate word choices, and clear sentence construction.

Activity 1 Compose a Letter to Volunteers

You are an employee of the city of Greenwater and are responsible for coordinating volunteers for the city's Safe Night program. Compose a letter to the volunteers listed in Figure U2.9 and include the following information in the letter:

- Safe Night event scheduled for Saturday, June 13, 2015.
- Volunteer orientation scheduled for Thursday, May 14, 2015, at 7:30 p.m. At the orientation, participants will learn about the types of volunteer positions available and the work schedule.

Include additional information in the letter, including a thank you to the volunteers. Use the Mail Merge feature to create a data source with the names and addresses shown in Figure U2.9 that is attached to the main document, which is the letter to the volunteers. Save the merged letters as **WL1-U2-Act01-Ltrs** and then print them.

Figure U2.9 Activity 1

Mrs. Laura Reston
376 Thompson Avenue
Greenwater, OR 99034

Ms. Cecilia Sykes
1430 Canyon Road
Greenwater, OR 99034

Mr. Ralph Emerson
1103 Highlands Avenue
Greenwater, OR 99034

Mr. Matthew Klein
7408 Ryan Road
Greenwater, OR 99034

Mr. Brian McDonald
8980 Union Street
Greenwater, OR 99034

Mrs. Nola Alverez
598 McBride Street
Greenwater, OR 99034

Activity 2 Create a Business Letterhead

You have just opened a new mailing and shipping business and need letterhead stationery. Click the INSERT tab, click the Header button, and then click *Edit Header* at the drop-down list. Look at the options in the Options group on the HEADER & FOOTER TOOLS DESIGN tab and then figure out how to create a header that displays and prints only on the first page. Create a letterhead for your company in a header that displays and prints only on the first page and include *at least* one of the following: a clip art image, a picture, a shape, a text box, and/or WordArt. Include the following information in the header:

Global Mailing
4300 Jackson Avenue
Toronto, ON M4C 3X4
(416) 555-0095
www.emcp.net/globalmailing

Save the completed letterhead and name it **WL1-U2-Act02-Ltrhd**. Print and then close the document.

Internet Research

Create a Flier on an Incentive Program

The owner of Terra Travel Services is offering an incentive to motivate travel consultants to increase travel bookings. The incentive is a sales contest with a grand prize of a one-week paid vacation to Cancun, Mexico. The owner has asked you to create a flier that will be posted on the office bulletin board that includes information about the incentive program, as well as some information about Cancun. Create this flier using information about Cancun that you find on the Internet. Include a photo you find on a website (make sure it is not copyrighted), or include a clip art image representing travel. Include any other information or object to add visual interest to the flier. Save the completed flier and name it **WL1-U2-InternetResearch**. Print and then close the document.

Job Study

Develop Recycling Program Communications

The Chief Operating Officer of Harrington Engineering has just approved your draft of the company's new recycling policy. (Open the file named **RecyclingPolicy.docx** located in the WL1U2 folder.) Edit the draft and prepare a final copy of the policy, along with a memo to all employees describing the new guidelines. To support the company's energy resources conservation effort, you will send hard copies of the new policy to the Somerset Recycling Program president and to directors of the Somerset Chamber of Commerce.

Using the concepts and techniques you learned in this unit, prepare the following documents:

- Format the recycling policy manual, including a cover page, appropriate headers and footers, and page numbers. Add at least one graphic where appropriate. Format the document using styles and a style set. Save the manual and name it **WL1-U2-JobStudyManual**. Print the manual.
- Download a memo template at the New backstage area and then create a memo from Susan Gerhardt, Chief Operating Officer of Harrington Engineering, to all employees that introduces the new recycling program. Copy the *Procedure* section of the recycling policy manual into the memo where appropriate. Include a table listing five employees who will act as Recycling Coordinators at Harrington Engineering (make up the names). Add columns for the employees' department names and telephone extensions. Save the memo and name it **WL1-U2-JobStudyMemo**. Print the memo.
- Write a letter to the president of the Somerset Recycling Program, William Elizondo, enclosing a copy of the recycling policy manual. Add a notation indicating that copies with enclosures were sent to all members of the Somerset Chamber of Commerce. Save the letter and name it **WL1-U2-JobStudyLetter**. Print the letter.
- Create mailing labels (see Figure U2.10). Save the labels and name the file **WL1-U2-JobStudyLabels**. Print the file.

Figure U2.10 Mailing Labels

William Elizondo, President
Somerset Recycling Program
700 West Brighton Road
Somerset, NJ 55123

Paul Schwartz
Somerset Chamber of Commerce
45 Wallace Road
Somerset, NJ 55123

Ashley Crighton
Somerset Chamber of Commerce
45 Wallace Road
Somerset, NJ 55123

Carol Davis
Somerset Chamber of Commerce
45 Wallace Road
Somerset, NJ 55123

Robert Knight
Somerset Chamber of Commerce
45 Wallace Road
Somerset, NJ 55123

Index

A

active document, 211
addition formula, 267
Address Block button, 296
Align Left button, 51, 83
alignment
  changing cell alignment, 256–257
  changing table alignment, 261–262
  vertical, of text, 167–168
Alignment button, 54, 83
Align Right button, 51, 83
Arrange All button, 212
arrow shape, drawing, 178–179
asterisk, 267
AutoComplete, 7
AutoCorrect, 5
AutoCorrect dialog box, 75
AutoFit button, 255
AVERAGE function, 267

B

background
  inserting page border, 125–127
  inserting watermark, 123–124
Backstage area
  Open document, 11–12
  Print button, 9–10
  Save As, 8
blank document, 5, 6
blank page, inserting, 117–118
Blank Page button, 117
Bold button, 40
bold typeface, 38, 40
Border and Shading Options dialog box, 125–127
Border Painter button, 245
borders
  customizing, 80–82
  inserting and changing page borders, 125–127
  inserting paragraph, 77–78, 80–82
Borders and Shading dialog box, 80–82
Borders button, 77–78
Border Styles button, 245
Breaks button, 156
built-in text box, 176–177
bulleting, paragraphs, 76–77

C

calculations, performing in table, 266–268
Calibri, 5
Cell Margins button, 258
Cell Options dialog box, 259
cells
  changing cell alignment, 256–257
  changing cell margin measurements, 258–260
  changing column width and row height, 255–256
  changing text direction, 260
  customizing size of, 254–256
  defined, 241
  entering text in, 242
  merging and splitting, 252–254
  selecting
    with keyboard, 248–249
    with mouse, 247
cell selection bar, 247
Center button, 51, 83
centering, vertical, of text, 168
Change Case button, 41
charts, creating organizational chart with SmartArt, 273–275
Check for Error button, 298
Checking and Reporting Errors dialog box, 298
Clear All Formatting button, 37, 41
Click and Type feature, 166–167
Clipboard
  in cutting and pasting text, 89–90
  defined, 89
  in deleting selected text, 89
  using, 93–94
Clipboard task pane, 93–94
closing
  documents, 10
  Word, 14
Collapse the Ribbon button, 6
color
  changing page color, 124
  customizing, 49–50
columns
  balancing on page, 160
  changing width in table, 255–256
  creating with Columns dialog box, 158–160
  formatting text into, 157–158
  inserting and deleting in tables, 250–252
  inserting column break, 159
  newspaper, 157
  removing formatting, 159
Columns button, 157
Columns dialog box, 158–160
Compact option, 49
continuous section break, 156–157
Convert to Text button, 264
Copy button, 92
copying
  documents, 204–205
  shapes, 178
copying and pasting text, 92
cover page, inserting, 117–118
Cover Page button, 117
Crop button, 169
customizing
  borders, 80–82
  cell size, 254–256
  images, 169–173
  picture, 170–173
  shading, 80–82
Cut button, 89
cutting and pasting text, 89–90

D

data source file
  creating, 293–295

defined, 293
editing, 306–311
date, inserting, 165–166
Date and Time dialog box, 165–166
deleting
documents, 203–204
folder, 205
rows and columns, 250–252
tabs, 86
text, 18, 89
undo and redo, 21–22
DESIGN tab, 48
directory, merging, 304–305
Distribute Columns button, 254
Distribute Rows button, 254
division formula, 267
Document Formatting group, 49
documents
active, 211
blank, 5, 6
closing, 10
copying, 204–205
creating new, 7, 11–12
deleting, 203–204
editing, 15–18
indenting text in, 54–55
inserting file into, 215
maintaining, 200–211
moving, 204–205
moving insertion point in, 16–17
naming, 9
navigating, 108–110
opening, 11–12
multiple, 205, 211
pinning and unpinning, 12–13
previewing pages in, 216–217
printing, 9–10, 217–220
renaming, 205
saving, 8–9, 14
in different formats, 206–211
scrolling in, 15
selecting, 202–204
template to create, 226–228
view, changing, 107–108
viewing side by side, 213–214
Draft view, 107
drawing
arrow shape, 178–179
enclosed object, 178
line drawing, 178
shapes, 178–179
table, 265
text box, 180–181
drop cap, 162–163

E

Edit Data Source dialog box, 308
editing
data source file, 306–311
documents, 15–18
predesigned header and footer, 122–123
Edit Recipient List button, 306
enclosed object, 178
Envelope Options dialog box, 300
envelopes
creating and printing, 220–223
general guidelines for addressing, 221
mailing labels, 223–226
merging, 300–305
Envelopes and Labels dialog box, 221, 222, 224
Eraser button, 265
Export backstage area, 206–208

F

file, inserting, 215
FILE tab, 6
Fill-in dialog box, 311–312
Find and Replace dialog box, 130–133
options in expanded, 131–132
Find button, 128
finding and replacing
formatting, 133–135
text, 130–133
Find option, find and highlight text, 129–130
Find Recipient button, 298
Finish & Merge button, 298–299
First Record button, 298
folder
copying and moving documents from, 204–205
creating, 201–202
deleting, 205
pinning, 13
renaming, 202
root folder, 201
Font Color button, 42
Font dialog box, 45
fonts
changing with Font dialog box, 45
choosing font effects, 41–42
default, 35, 37
defined, 37
finding and replacing, 134–135
Font group buttons, 37–38
typefaces, 37–38
type styles, 38, 40
footers
editing, 122–123
inserting predesigned, 120–123
removing, 121–122
format, defined, 35
Format Painter button, 58–59
formatting
Click and Type feature, 166–167
columns, 157–160
date and time, 165–166
drop cap, 162–163
finding and replacing, 133–135
fonts, 37–46
with Format Painter, 58–59
image, 173
indenting text in paragraphs, 54–57
line spacing changes, 60–61
page background, 123–127

paragraph alignment, 50–54
paragraph spacing, 57
pull quote text box, 176–177
removing default, 47
repeating last action, 57–58
revealing and comparing, 61–62
screen clipping, 185
screenshots, 183–184
section breaks, 156–157
SmartArt graphic, 269–271
style sets, 47–48, 49–50
symbols and special characters, 163–165
text box, 180–181
themes, 48–50
vertically aligning text, 168
WordArt Text, 181–183
Formula button, 266
Formula dialog box, 267
formulas, inserting, 266–268
forward slash, 267
function, 267

G

Go To option, 16
grammar
automatic grammar checker, 5
Grammar task pane, 23
spelling and grammar checker, 23–24
Greeting Line button, 296
gridlines, viewing, 250

H

hard copy, 9
hard page break, 115–116
headers
editing, 122–123
inserting predesigned, 120–123
removing, 121–122
repeat header row, 256–257
headings, collapse/expand text below, 47
HEADINGS tab, 108–109
Help feature
in dialog box, 27
Help window, 25
ScreenTip, 26
horizontal ruler, 6
indenting text, 54–57
manipulating tabs on, 83–85
show/hide, 83
hyphenation
automatic, 161
manual, 161–162
Hyphenation button, 161

I

I-beam pointer, 6
images
customizing, 169–173
formatting, 173
inserting, 174–176
mailing labels with, 226
moving, 170
from Office.com, 173
sizing, 169
indenting, text in paragraphs, 54–57
inserting
blank page, 117–118
bulleted text, 76–77
cover page, 117–118
date and time, 165–166
drop cap, 162–163
file, 215
formulas, 267–268
image, 169–176, 173–176
page border, 125–127
page breaks, 115–116
paragraph numbering, 75–76
picture, 170–173
predesigned headers and footers, 120–123
predesigned page numbering, 119
pull quote text box, 176–177
Quick Table, 257–258
rows and columns, 250–252
screenshots, 183–184
section break, 156–157
SmartArt graphic, 269–271
symbols and special characters, 163–165
text, 18
text box, 180–181
watermark, 123–124
WordArt Text, 181–183
insertion point, moving, 6
keyboard commands for, 16
to last location in document, 17
with mouse, 15
moving between windows, 211
moving within table using keyboard, 242–243
to specific line or page, 16
in split window, 213
in table, when created, 242
Insert Merge Field button, 296
Insert Picture window, 173, 174
Insert Table dialog box, 244
Italic button, 40
italic typeface, 38, 40

K

keyboard shortcuts
case of text, 41
closing Word, 14
deleting text, 18
font group buttons, 42
Help, 25
line spacing, 60
moving insertion point, 16
in tables, 242–243
new document, 11
Open backstage area, 11
Open dialog box, 12
paragraph alignment, 51
repeat last action, 57
selecting cells in table with, 248–249
selecting text, 19–20

L

Label Options dialog box, 302

labels
  creating and printing, 223–226
  merging, 302–304
landscape orientation, 112, 113
Last Record button, 298
Layout Options button, 169
leader tab, setting, 88
letter, template to create, 227–228
Line and Paragraph Spacing button, 60
line drawing, 178
line spacing
  automatic adjustments, 60
  default setting, 60
  keyboard shortcut for changing, 60
  Paragraph dialog box, 60
live preview feature, 38

M

mailing labels
  with an image, 226
  creating and printing, 223–226
MAILINGS tab, 293–295
Mail Merge
  adding Fill-in fields to main document, 311–313
  check for errors, 298
  create data source file, 293–295
  create main document, 295–297
  editing data source file, 306–311
  inputting text during merge, 311–313
  merge directory, 304–305
  merge documents, 298–299
  merge envelopes, 300–305
  merge labels, 302–304
  previewing merge, 298
  selecting specific records, 306–307
  using Mail Merge Wizard, 313–315
Mail Merge Wizard, 313–315
main document
  adding Fill-in fields to, 311–313
  creating, 295–297
  defined, 293
  editing, 306
Manual Hyphenation dialog box, 161–162
margins
  changing cell margin measurements, 258–260
  changing page margins, 112–115
Margins drop-down list, 112, 113
Maximize button, 212
Merge Cell button, 252
merging
  cells, 252–254
  directory, 304–305
  documents, 298–299
  envelopes, 300–305
  labels, 302–304
  previewing, 298
Minimize button, 212
Mini toolbar, 18
  formatting text, 42
minus sign, 267
monospaced typeface, 37–38
mouse
  dragging text with, 90
  selecting cells in table with, 247
  selecting text with, 19
moving
  cells in table, 248–249
  documents, 204–205
  SmartArt graphic, 271–272
  table, 262–263
multiplication formula, 267

N

naming, document, 9
navigating documents, 108–110
Navigation pane, 108–110
New Address List dialog box, 293
New backstage area, 226–227
New Folder button, 201
New Line command, 7
newspaper columns, 157
Next Record button, 298
No Spacing style, 47
numbering
  automatic, 73–74
  inserting predesigned page numbering, 119
  paragraphs, 73–76
  turning off, 74–75
Numbering button, 73–76

O

Object button, 215
objects, enclosed object, 178
Office.com, inserting image from, 173
Online Pictures button, 173
Open dialog box, 11–12
  copying and moving documents, 204–205
  create folder, 201–202
  delete document, 203–204
  opening multiple documents, 205
  rename folder, 202
  renaming documents, 205
  select document, 202
opening
  documents, 11–12
  multiple documents, 211
  from recent document list, 12
  Word, 5
option buttons, 7
organizational chart with SmartArt, 273–275
Organize button, 202

P

page border, inserting and changing, 125–127
Page Break button, 115
page breaks, 115–116
Page Number button, 119

page numbers, inserting
predesigned, 119
page orientation, 112, 113
pages
formatting background
changing page color, 124
inserting and changing page border, 125–127
inserting watermark, 123–124
hiding/showing white space, 111
inserting
blank page, 117–118
cover page, 117–118
page breaks, 115–116
predesigned headers and footers, 120–123
predesigned page numbering, 119
navigating, 108–110
setup changes
margins, 112–115
page orientation, 112
size, 112–113, 114
view, changing, 107–108
Page Setup dialog box
margin changes, 114–115
paper size changes, 114–115
vertical alignment option box, 167–168
page size, 112–113, 114
PAGES tab, 109
panes, dividing window into, 212–213
Paragraph dialog box, 52–54
change line spacing on, 60
paragraphs
alignment
changing as you type, 51
changing at Dialog Box, 52–54
changing existing text, 51
borders, 77–78, 80–82
bulleting, 76–77
collecting and pasting with Clipboard, 94
customizing theme, 61–62
cutting, copying and pasting text, 89–92
display paragraph symbol, 51
indenting text in, 54–57
manipulating tabs, 83–88
numbering, 73–76
shading, 78–82
sorting text in, 82–83
spacing
before and after, 57
changing with Paragraph Spacing button, 49–50
Paste button, 89
Paste Options button, 91
PDF file, saving document as, 209–211
pictures. *See also* images
inserting and customizing, 170–173
PICTURE TOOLS FORMAT tab, 169
pinning
document, 12–13
folder, 13
plain text, saving document as, 207–208
plus sign, 267
points, 38
portrait orientation, 112, 113
Position button, 169, 170
previewing
merge, 298
pages in document, 216–217
Preview Results button, 298
Previous Record button, 298
printing
document, 9–10
envelopes, 220–223
labels, 223–226
pages in document, 217–220
previewing pages, 216–217
Print backstage area, 9–10
Quick Print button, 10
Print Layout view
as default view, 107
hiding/showing white space in, 111
Print Screen feature, 200–201
Properties button, 259
proportional typeface, 5, 7, 38
pull quote text box, 176–177

Q

Quick Access toolbar, 6
Open button, 11
Quick Print button on, 10
Save As button on, 10
Undo and Redo button, 21–22
Quick Print button, 10
Quick Table, inserting, 257–258

R

readability, 157
Read Mode view, 107–108
Recent Documents list
opening document from, 12
pinning and unpinning document to, 12–13
record, in data source file, 293
Recycle bin
displaying, 203
restoring document from, 203
Redo button, 21–22
renaming, documents, 205
Repeat command, 57
Repeat Header Rows button, 256–257
Replace button, 128
resize handle, 262
resizing table, 262–263
Restore button, 212
restoring, windows, 212
Reveal Formatting task pane, 61–62
ribbon, 6
Ribbon Display Options button, 108
Rich Text Format (RTF), saving document as, 207–208
root folder, 201
rows
changing height in table, 255–256
inserting and deleting in table, 250–252

row selection bar, 247
ruler
horizontal, 6
vertical, 6
Rules button, 311

S

san serif typeface, 38
Save As dialog box, 8–9, 14
copying and moving documents, 204–205
deleting documents, 203–204
documents in different format, 209
Save button, 8
saving documents, 8–9
in different formats, 206–211
in PDF/XPS format, 209–211
with Save As, 14
screen clipping, creating and formatting, 185
Screenshot button, 183
screenshots, inserting and formatting, 183–184
ScreenTip, 26
scrolling
in documents, 15
synchronous, 213
section break
continuous, 156
inserting, 156–157
Select button, 250
Selection Mode, 19, 20
Select Recipients button, 293
serif typeface, 38
shading
customizing, 80–82
paragraphs, 78–82
Shading button, 78
shapes
copying, 178
drawing, 178–179
Shapes button, 178
shortcuts. *See* keyboard shortcuts
Show/Hide ¶ button, 156
sizing
image, 169
resizing table, 262–263
SmartArt graphic
arranging and moving, 271–272
creating organizational chart with, 273–275
inserting and formatting, 269–271
soft copy, 9
soft page break, 115
Sort button, 266
sorting
text in paragraphs, 82–83
text in table, 266
Sort Text dialog box, 82–83
spacing
changing before/after paragraphs, 57
changing with Paragraph Spacing button, 49–50
line spacing changes, 60–61
special characters, inserting, 163–164
spelling
automatic spelling checker, 5
spelling and grammar check, 23–24
Spelling task pane, 23
Split Cell button, 252
Split Table button, 252
split window, 212–213
Start Mail Merge button, 293
Status bar, 6
Strikethrough button, 42
styles
applying, 47–48
No Spacing style, 47
style set
changing, 47
customizing, 49–50
Subscript button, 42
subtraction formula, 267
suffixes, finding and replacing, 132–133
SUM part of formula, 267
Superscript button, 42
Symbol button, 163
Symbol dialog box, 164
Synchronous Scrolling button, 213

T

table
converting text to table, 264
creating
entering text in cells, 242
Insert Table dialog box, 244
moving cells in, 248–249
moving insertion point within, 242–243
parts of, 242
with Quick Table, 257–258
with Table button, 241, 243
design changes, 245–246
drawing, 265
inserting formulas, 266–268
layout changes
alignment and dimensions, 261–262
cell alignment, 256–257
cell direction, 260
cell margin measurements, 258–260
customizing cells size, 254–256
inserting and deleting rows and columns, 250–252
merging and splitting cells and tables, 252–254
repeating header rows, 256–257
resizing and moving, 262–263
TABLE TOOLS LAYOUT tab, 249
performing calculations in, 266–268
selecting cells
with keyboard, 248–249
with mouse, 247
with Select button, 250
sorting text in, 266
Table button, 241, 243
Table Options dialog box, 259

Tables Properties dialog box, 261
TABLE TOOLS DESIGN tab, 245, 250
TABLE TOOLS LAYOUT tab, 249
tabs, 6
  alignment buttons, 83–84
  clearing, 87
  default setting, 83
  deleting, 86
  manipulating
    on horizontal ruler, 83–85
    at Tabs dialog box, 86–87
  moving, 86
  setting, 84
  setting leader tab, 88
Tabs dialog box, 86
Taskbar, 6
  Word button on, 211
template, creating letter with, 227–228
text
  built-in text box, 176–177
  changing direction of, in cells, 260
  Click and Type feature, 166–167
  collecting and pasting with Clipboard, 94
  converting to table, 264
  copying and pasting, 92
  cutting and pasting, 89–90
  deleting, 18, 89
  dragging with mouse, 90
  drop cap, 162–163
  entering text in cells, 242
  finding and highlighting, 129–130
  finding and replacing, 130–133
  formatting into columns, 157–158
  hyphenating words, 161–162
  indenting in paragraphs, 54–55
  inserting, 18
  Paste Options button, 91
  pull quote text box, 176–177
  readability, 157
  selecting, 18–20
  sorting in paragraphs, 82–83
  sorting in table, 266
  symbols and special characters, 163–165
  undo and redo deletions, 21–22
  vertically aligning, 167–168
  vertically centering, 168
  WordArt Text, 181–183
text box
  built-in text box, 176–177
  drawing, 180–181
Text Box button, 176
Text Direction button, 260
Text Effects and Typography button, 42
Text Highlight Color button, 42
Theme button, 48
themes
  applying, 48–49
  customizing, 49–50
time, inserting, 165–166
Title bar, 6
typeface. *See also* fonts
  examples of, 38
  monospaced, 37–38
  proportional, 5, 7, 38
  san serif, 38
  serif, 38
type styles, 38, 40

U

Underline button, 40
underline typeface, 40
Undo button, 21–22
unpinning document, 13

V

Vertical alignment option box, 167–168
vertically aligning text, 167–168
vertically centering text, 168
vertical ruler, 6
vertical scroll bar, 6, 15
view
  changing, 107–108
  Draft view, 107
  Read Mode view, 107–108
  Ribbon Display Options button, 108
View Side by Side button, 213

W

watermark, inserting, 123–124
white space, hiding/showing, 111
windows
  arranging, 212
  maximizing and minimizing, 212
  opening new, 214–215
  restoring, 212
  splitting, 212–213
  viewing documents side by side, 213–214
Word
  closing, 14
  opening, 5
WordArt Text, inserting and modifying, 181–183
word forms, finding and replacing, 132–133
word wrap, 5
Wrap Text button, 169

X

XPS file, saving document as, 209–211

Z

Zoom In button, 107
Zoom Out button, 107
Zoom slider bar, 107

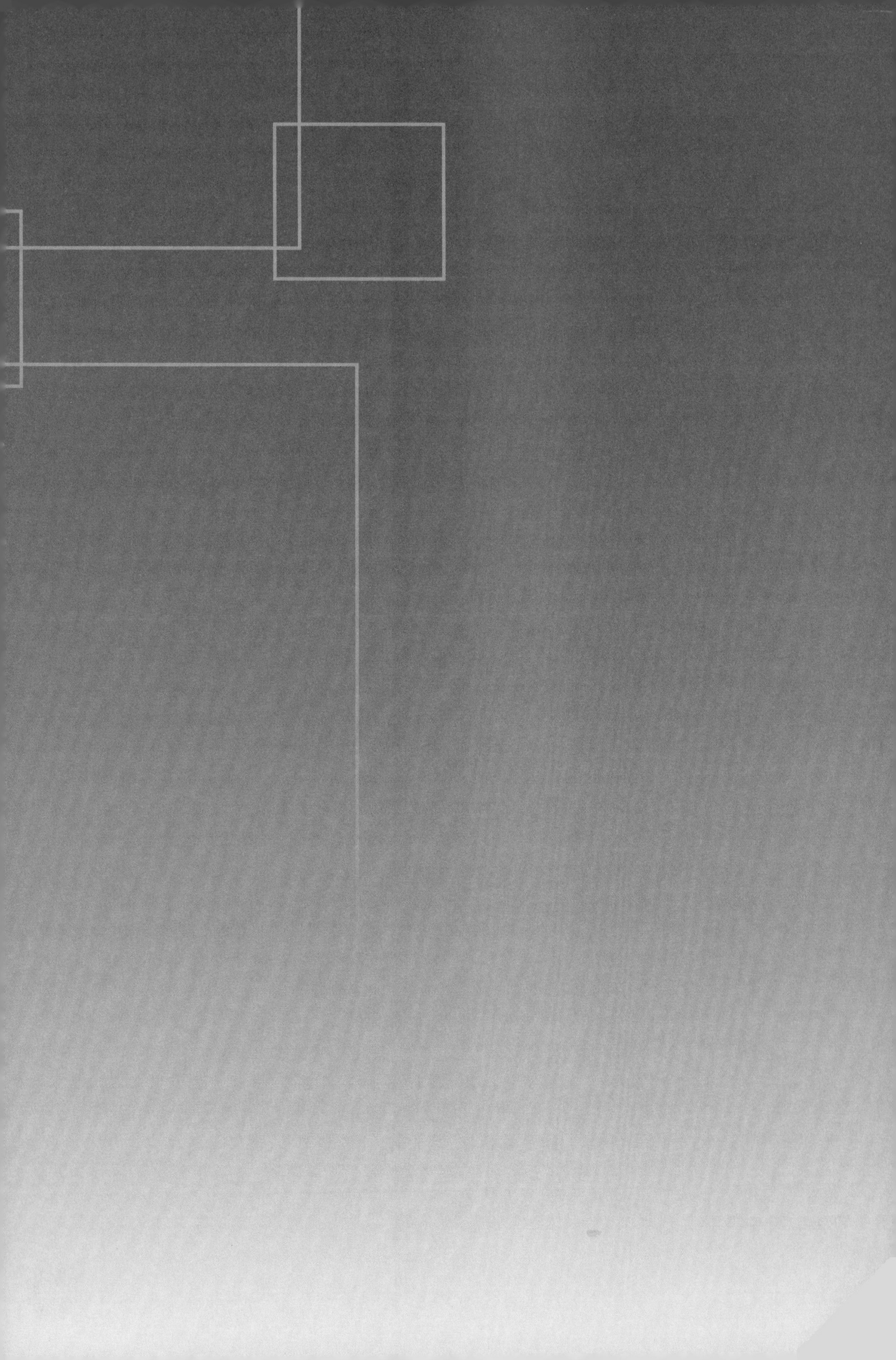

MICROSOFT® EXCEL® Level 1

Unit 1 ■ Preparing and Formatting Worksheets

Chapter 1 ■ Preparing an Excel Workbook

Chapter 2 ■ Inserting Formulas in a Worksheet

Chapter 3 ■ Formatting an Excel Worksheet

Chapter 4 ■ Enhancing a Worksheet

MICROSOFT® EXCEL®

Preparing an Excel Workbook

PERFORMANCE OBJECTIVES

Upon successful completion of Chapter 1, you will be able to:

- **Identify the various elements of an Excel workbook**
- **Create, save, and print a workbook**
- **Enter data in a workbook**
- **Edit data in a workbook**
- **Insert a formula using the AutoSum button**
- **Apply basic formatting to cells in a workbook**
- **Use the Help feature**

Tutorials

1.1 Opening, Saving, and Closing an Excel Workbook

1.2 Entering Data in Cells and Saving a Workbook with a New Name

1.3 Editing Cells and Using Proofing Tools

1.4 Printing a Worksheet

1.5 Performing Calculations Using the AutoSum Button

1.6 Navigating and Scrolling in a Worksheet

1.7 Applying Basic Formatting

1.8 Applying Number Formatting

1.9 Getting Help at the Excel Help Window

Many companies use spreadsheets to organize numerical and financial data and to analyze and evaluate information. An Excel spreadsheet can be used for such activities as creating financial statements, preparing budgets, managing inventory, and analyzing cash flow. In addition, numbers and values can be easily manipulated to create "What if?" situations. For example, using a spreadsheet, a person in a company can ask questions such as "What if the value in this category is decreased? How would that change affect the department budget?" Questions like these can be easily answered using the information in an Excel spreadsheet. Change the value in a category and Excel will recalculate formulas for the other values. In this way, a spreadsheet can be used not only for creating financial statements or budgets, but also as a planning tool. Model answers for this chapter's projects appear on the following page.

EL1C1

Note: Before beginning the projects, copy to your storage medium the EL1C1 subfolder from the EL1 folder on the CD that accompanies this textbook. Steps on how to copy a folder are presented on the inside of the back cover of this textbook. Do this every time you start a chapter's projects.

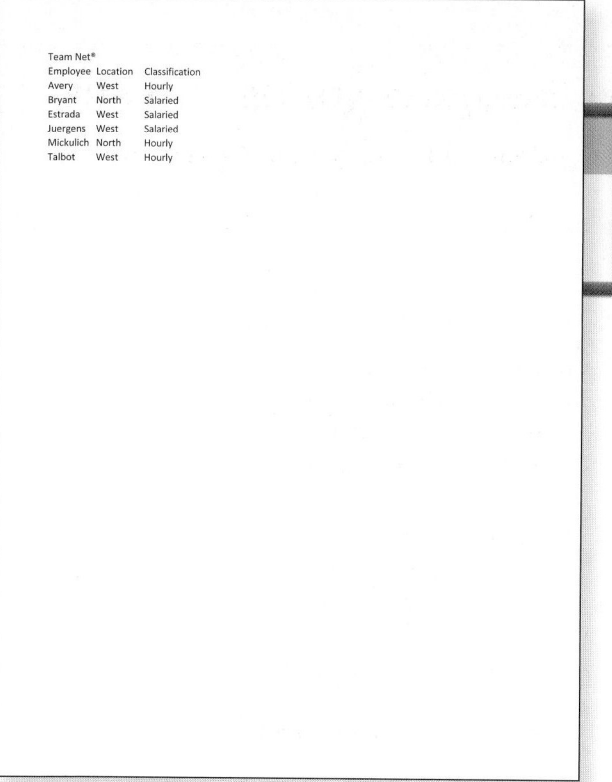

Team Net®		
Employee	Location	Classification
Avery	West	Hourly
Bryant	North	Salaried
Estrada	West	Salaried
Juergens	West	Salaried
Mickulich	North	Hourly
Talbot	West	Hourly

Project 1 Prepare a Worksheet with Employee Information

EL1-C1-P1-EmpBene.xlsx

	January	February	March	April	May	June
Year 1	**100**	100	100	100	125	125
Year 3	**150**	150	150	150	175	175
Year 5	**200**	200	200	150	150	150
Year 7	**250**	250	250	250	250	250
Total	700	700	700	650	700	700

Qtr 1	$5,500	$6,250	$7,000	$8,500	$5,500	$4,500
Qtr 2	$6,000	$7,250	$6,500	$9,000	$4,000	$5,000
Qtr 3	$4,500	$8,000	$6,000	$7,500	$6,000	$5,000
Qtr 4	$6,500	$8,500	$7,000	$8,000	$5,500	$6,000
Average	$5,625	$7,500	$6,625	$8,250	$5,250	$5,125

Project 2 Open and Format a Workbook and Insert Formulas

EL1-C1-P2-FillCells.xlsx

Monthly Expenses
January, 2015

Expense	Budget	Actual
Accounting Services	$ 500	$ 423
Advertising	3,200	3,475
Utilities	2,700	3,045
Estimated Taxes	25,000	25,000
Health Insurance	9,420	9,595
Inventory Purchases	4,200	2,155
Equipment Repair	500	214
Loan Payment	5,586	5,586
Office Supplies	225	415
Total	$ 51,331	$ 49,908

Budget Percentages

Department	Percentage
Personnel	26%
Development	22%
Sales	18%
Production	13%
Maintenance	8%
Accounting	7%
Administration	6%

Project 3 Format a Worksheet

EL1-C1-P3-MoExps.xlsx

Project 1 Prepare a Worksheet with Employee Information 3 Parts

You will create a worksheet containing employee information, edit the contents, and then save and close the workbook.

Creating a Worksheet

Open Excel by clicking the Excel 2013 tile at the Windows Start screen. (Depending on your operating system, these steps may vary.) At the Excel 2013 opening screen that displays, click the *Blank workbook* template. This displays a workbook with a blank worksheet, as shown in Figure 1.1. The elements of a blank Excel worksheet are described in Table 1.1.

A file created in Excel is referred to as a ***workbook***. An Excel workbook consists of an individual worksheet (or *sheet*) by default, but it can contain multiple worksheets, like the sheets of paper in a notebook. Notice the tab named *Sheet1*, located toward the bottom of the Excel window. The area containing the gridlines in the Excel window is called the ***worksheet area***. Figure 1.2 identifies the elements of the worksheet area. Create a worksheet in the worksheet area that will be saved as part of a workbook. Columns in a worksheet are labeled with letters of the alphabet and rows are numbered.

Figure 1.1 Blank Excel Worksheet

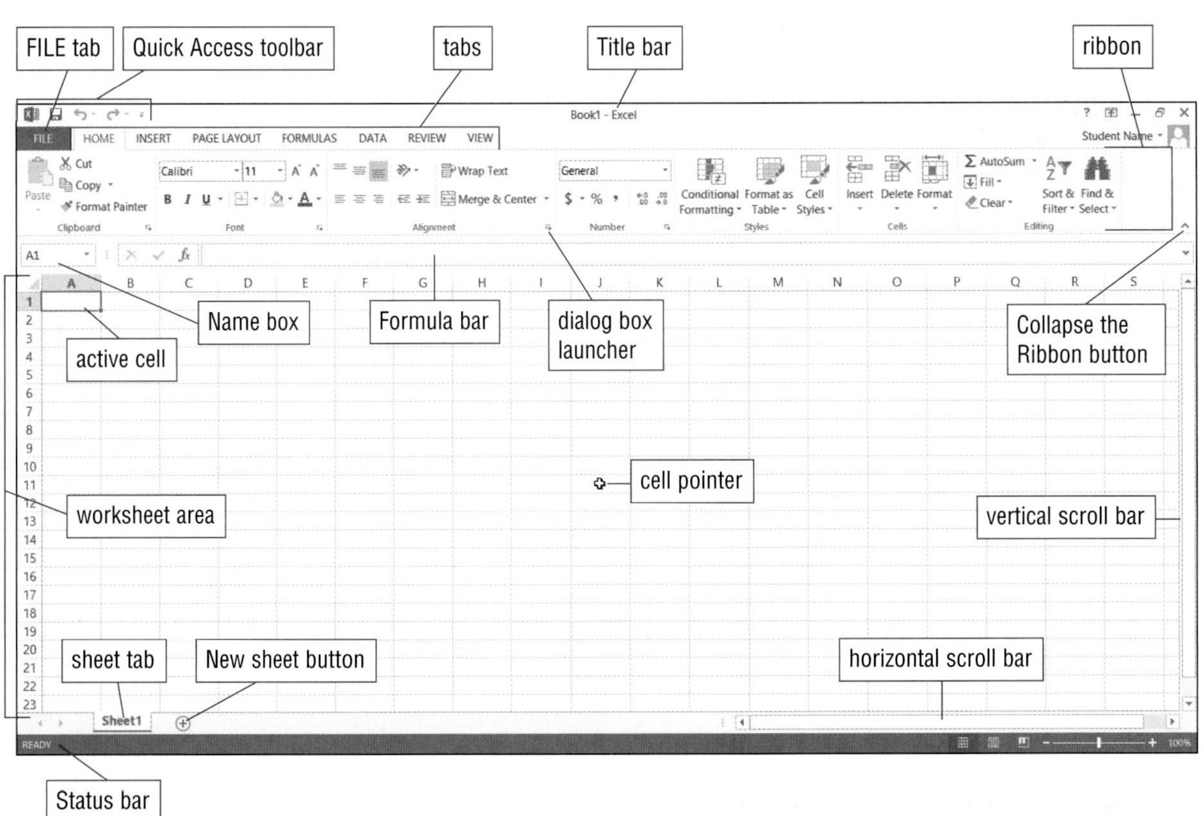

Table 1.1 Elements of an Excel Worksheet

Feature	*Description*
active cell	location in the worksheet that will display typed data or that will be affected by a command
cell pointer	when this icon appears, select cells by clicking or dragging the mouse
dialog box launcher	click to open a dialog box with more options for that group
FILE tab	displays the backstage area that contains options for working with and managing files
Formula bar	displays the contents stored in the active cell
horizontal and vertical scroll bars	used to view various parts of the worksheet beyond the current screen
Name box	displays the active cell address or name assigned to the active cell
New sheet button	click to insert a new worksheet in the workbook
Quick Access toolbar	contains buttons for commonly used commands that can be executed with a single mouse click
ribbon	area containing the tabs with commands and buttons
sheet tab	identifies the current worksheet in the workbook
Status bar	displays the current mode, action messages, view buttons, and Zoom slider bar
tab	contains commands and buttons organized into groups
Title bar	displays the workbook name followed by the application name
Collapse the Ribbon button	when clicked, removes the ribbon from the screen
worksheet area	contains the cells used to create a worksheet

Figure 1.2 Elements of a Worksheet Area

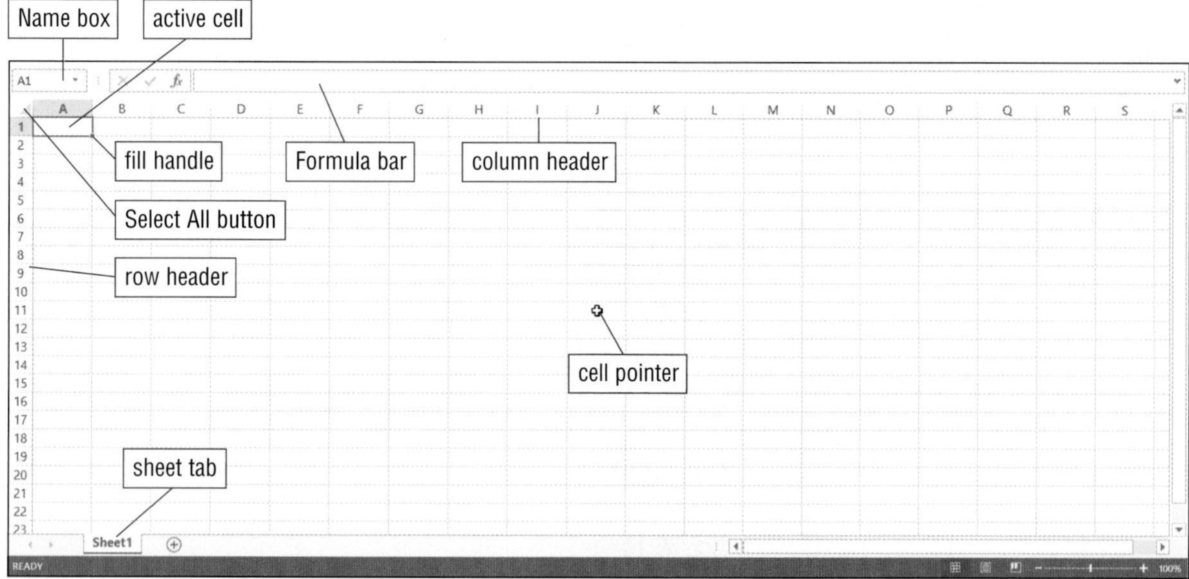

The horizontal and vertical lines that define the cells in the worksheet area are called ***gridlines***. When a cell is active (displays with a green border), the ***cell address***, also called the ***cell reference***, displays in the ***Name box***. The cell reference includes the column letter and row number. For example, if the first cell of the worksheet is active, the cell reference *A1* displays in the Name box. A green border surrounds the active cell.

HINT

To make a cell active, position the cell pointer in the cell and then click the left mouse button.

Enter data such as text, a number, or a value in a cell. To enter data in a cell, make the desired cell active and then type the data. To make the next cell active, press the Tab key. Table 1.2 displays additional commands for making a specific cell active.

Another method for making a specific cell active is to use the Go To feature. To use this feature, click the Find & Select button in the Editing group on the HOME tab and then click *Go To*. At the Go To dialog box, type the cell reference in the *Reference* text box and then click OK.

Find & Select

Ctrl + G is the keyboard shortcut to display the Go To dialog box.

When you are ready to type data into the active cell, check the Status bar. The word *READY* should display at the left side. As you type data, the word *Ready* changes to *ENTER*. Data you type in a cell displays in the cell as well as in the Formula bar. If the data you type is longer than the cell can accommodate, the data overlaps the next cell to the right. (It does not become a part of the next cell—it simply overlaps it.) You will learn how to change column widths to accommodate data later in this chapter.

Table 1.2 Commands for Making a Specific Cell Active

To make this cell active	*Press*
cell below current cell	Enter
cell above current cell	Shift + Enter
next cell	Tab
previous cell	Shift + Tab
cell at beginning of row	Home
next cell in direction of arrow	Up, Down, Left, or Right Arrow keys
last cell in worksheet	Ctrl + End
first cell in worksheet	Ctrl + Home
cell in next window	Page Down
cell in previous window	Page Up
cell in window to right	Alt + Page Down
cell in window to left	Alt + Page Up

If the data you enter in a cell consists of text and the text does not fit into the cell, it overlaps the next cell. If, however, you enter a number in a cell, specify it as a number (rather than text), and the number is too long to fit in the cell, Excel changes the display of the number to number symbols *(###)*. This change is made because Excel does not want you to be misled by a number when you see only a portion of it in the cell.

Along with the keyboard, the mouse can be used to make a specific cell active. To make a specific cell active with the mouse, position the mouse pointer, which displays as a white plus sign (called the ***cell pointer***), on the desired cell and then click the left mouse button. The cell pointer displays as a white plus sign when positioned in a cell in the worksheet and displays as an arrow pointer when positioned on other elements of the Excel window, such as options on tabs or scroll bars.

Scroll through a worksheet using the horizontal and/or vertical scroll bars. Scrolling shifts the display of cells in the worksheet area but does not change the active cell. Scroll through a worksheet until the desired cell is visible and then click the desired cell.

Saving a Workbook

Quick Steps

Save a Workbook

1. Click Save button on Quick Access toolbar.
2. At Save As backstage area, click desired location.
3. Click Browse button.
4. At Save As dialog box, navigate to desired folder.
5. Type workbook name.
6. Press Enter.

Save

Ctrl + S is the keyboard shortcut to save a workbook.

Save an Excel workbook, which consists of one or more worksheets, by clicking the Save button on the Quick Access toolbar or by clicking the FILE tab and then clicking the *Save As* option at the backstage area. At the Save As backstage area, click the location where you want to save the workbook. For example, click the OneDrive option preceded by your name if you are saving to your OneDrive or click the *Computer* option if you are saving to a USB flash drive (or other location on your computer). After specifying the place, click the Browse button and the Save As dialog box displays. If you are saving the workbook to your computer or a flash drive, you can double-click the *Computer* option at the Save As backstage area to display the Save As dialog box. At the Save As dialog box, type a name for the workbook in the *File name* text box and then press Enter or click the Save button. You can bypass the Save As backstage area and go directly to the Save As dialog box by using the keyboard shortcut F12.

When you click your OneDrive or the *Computer* option at the Save As backstage area, the names of the most recently accessed folders display below the Recent Folders heading in the *Computer* section. Open a folder by clicking the folder name.

A workbook file name can contain up to 255 characters, including the drive letter and any folder names, and can include spaces. You cannot give a workbook the same name in first uppercase and then lowercase letters. Also, some symbols cannot be used in a file name, such as:

forward slash (/)	question mark (?)
backslash (\)	quotation mark (“)
greater-than symbol (>)	colon (:)
less-than symbol (<)	semicolon (;)
asterisk (*)	pipe symbol (|)

To save an Excel workbook in the EL1C1 folder on your storage medium, display the Save As dialog box, click the drive representing your storage medium in the Navigation pane, and then double-click *EL1C1* in the Content pane.

Project 1a Creating and Saving a Document — Part 1 of 3

1. Open Excel by clicking the Excel 2013 tile at the Windows Start screen. (Depending on your operating system, these steps may vary.)
2. At the Excel 2013 opening screen, click the *Blank workbook* template. (This opens a workbook with a blank worksheet.)
3. At the blank Excel worksheet that displays, create the worksheet shown in Figure 1.3 by completing the following steps:
   a. Press the Enter key once to make cell A2 the active cell.
   b. Type **Employee** in cell A2 .
   c. Press the Tab key. (This makes cell B2 active.)
   d. Type **Location** and then press the Tab key. (This makes cell C2 active.)
   e. Type **Benefits** and then press the Enter key to move the insertion point to cell A3.
   f. Type **Avery** (a name) in cell A3.
   g. Continue typing the data shown in Figure 1.3. (For commands that make specific cells active, refer to Table 1.2.)
4. After typing the data shown in the cells in Figure 1.3, save the workbook by completing the following steps:
   a. Click the Save button on the Quick Access toolbar.
   b. At the Save As backstage area, click the desired location, such as your OneDrive or *Computer,* and then click the Browse button.
   c. At the Save As dialog box, navigate to the EL1C1 folder in the Navigation pane and then double-click the *EL1C1* folder that displays in the Content pane.
   d. Select the text in the *File name* text box and then type **EL1-C1-P1-EmpBene** (for Excel Level 1, Chapter 1, Project 1, and the workbook that contains information about employee benefits).
   e. Press the Enter key or click the Save button.

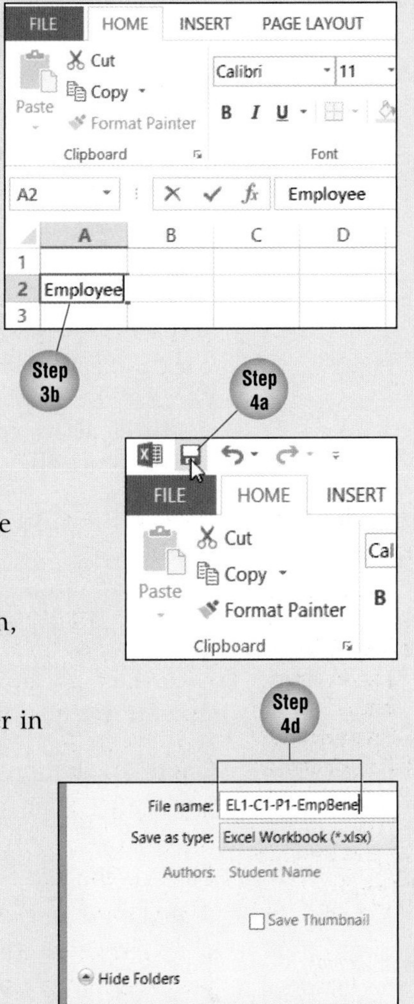

Figure 1.3 Project 1a

	A	B	C	D
1				
2	Employee	Location	Benefits	
3	Avery			
4	Connors			
5	Estrada			
6	Juergens			
7	Mikulich			
8	Talbot			
9				

Editing Data in a Cell

Edit data being typed in a cell by pressing the Backspace key to delete the character to the left of the insertion point or pressing the Delete key to delete the character to the right of the insertion point. To change the data in a cell, click the cell once to make it active and then type the new data. When a cell containing data is active, anything typed will take the place of the existing data.

If you want to edit only a portion of the data in a cell, double-click in the cell. This makes the cell active, moves the insertion point inside the cell, and displays the word *Edit* at the left side of the Status bar. Move the insertion point using the arrow keys or the mouse and then make the needed corrections. If you are using the keyboard, press the Home key to move the insertion point to the first character in the cell or Formula bar or press the End key to move the insertion point to the last character.

When you are finished editing the data in the cell, be sure to change out of the Edit mode. To do this, make another cell active by pressing Enter, Tab, or Shift + Tab. You can also change out of the Edit mode and return to the Ready mode by clicking another cell or clicking the Enter button on the Formula bar.

Cancel

Enter

If the active cell does not contain data, the Formula bar displays only the cell reference (by column letter and row number). As you type data, two buttons display on the Formula bar to the right of the Name box, as shown in Figure 1.4. Click the Cancel button to delete the current cell entry. You can also delete the cell entry by pressing the Delete key. Click the Enter button to indicate that you are finished typing or editing the cell entry. When you click the Enter button on the Formula bar, the word *Enter* (or *Edit*) located at the left side of the Status bar changes to *Ready*.

Figure 1.4 Buttons on the Formula Bar

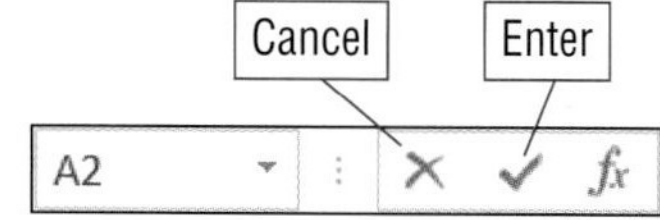

Project 1b **Editing Data in a Cell** **Part 2 of 3**

1. With **EL1-C1-P1-EmpBene.xlsx** open, double-click in cell A7 (contains *Mikulich*).
2. Move the insertion point immediately left of the *k* and then type c. (This changes the spelling to *Mickulich*.)
3. Click once in cell A4 (contains *Connors*), type **Bryant**, and then press the Tab key. (Clicking only once allows you to type over the existing data.)
4. Edit cell C2 by completing the following steps:
   a. Click the Find & Select button in the Editing group on the HOME tab and then click *Go To* at the drop-down list.

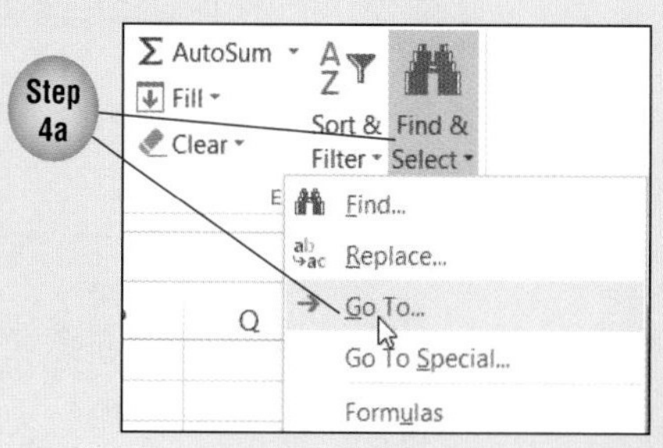

b. At the Go To dialog box, type C2 in the *Reference* text box and then click OK.
c. Type Classification (over *Benefits*).
5. Click once in any other cell.
6. Click the Save button on the Quick Access toolbar to save the workbook again.

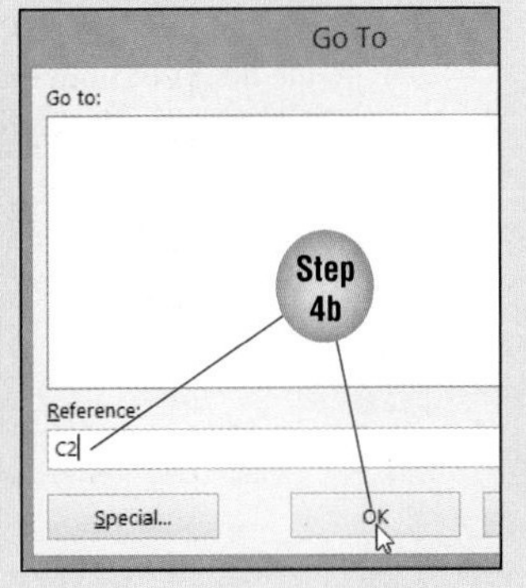

Printing a Workbook

With a workbook open, click the FILE tab and the Info backstage area displays, as shown in Figure 1.5. Use buttons and options at the backstage area to perform functions such as opening, closing, saving, and printing a workbook. If you want to exit the backstage area without completing an action, click the Back button (located in the upper left corner of the backstage area) or press the Esc key on your keyboard.

Many of the computer projects you create will need to be printed. Print a workbook from the Print backstage area, as shown in Figure 1.6. To display this backstage area, click the FILE tab and then click the *Print* option. You can also display the Print backstage area with the keyboard shortcut Ctrl + P.

Ctrl + P is the keyboard shortcut to display the Print backstage area.

Figure 1.5 Info Backstage Area

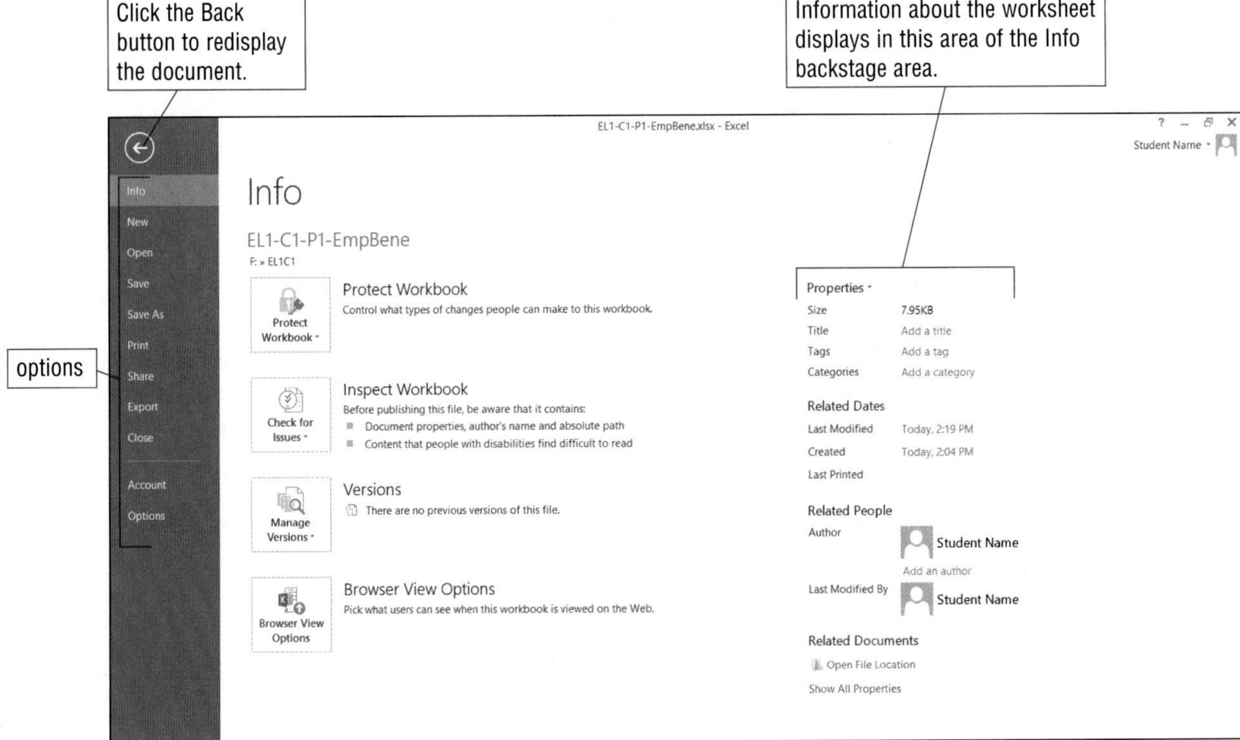

Figure 1.6 Print Backstage Area

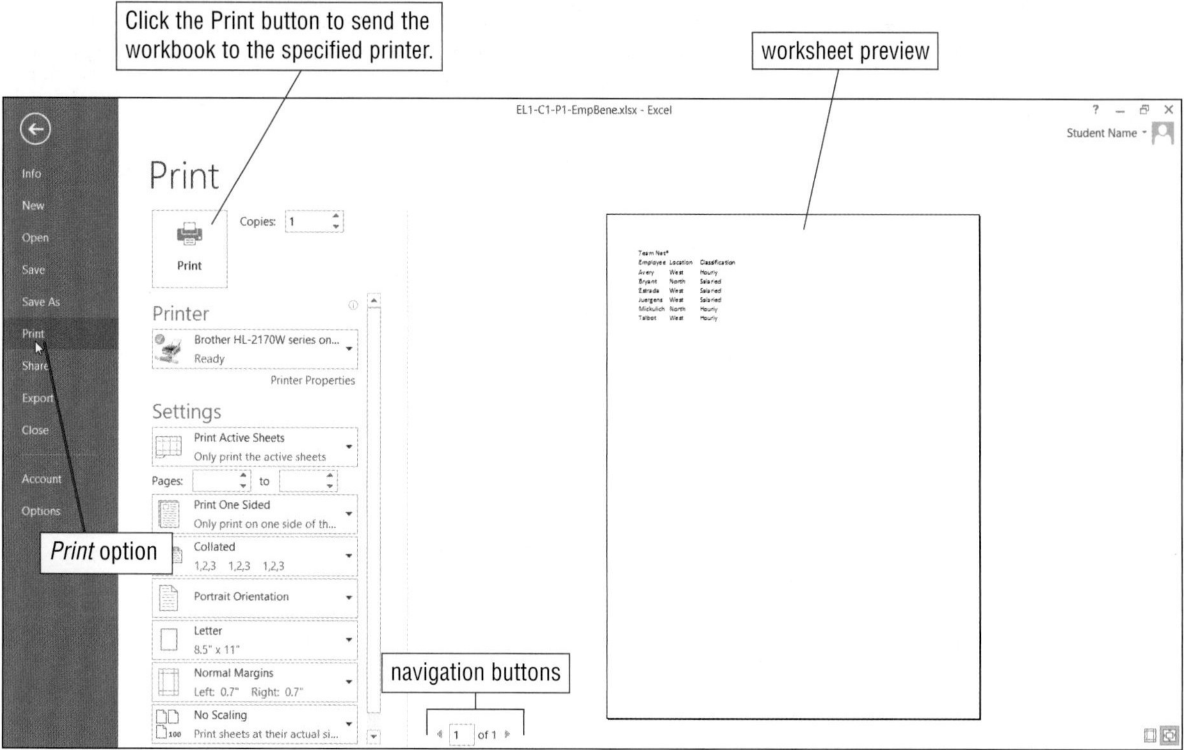

Quick Steps

Print a Workbook
1. Click FILE tab.
2. Click *Print* option.
3. Click Print button.
OR
Click Quick Print button on Quick Access toolbar.

The left side of the Print backstage area displays three categories: *Print, Printer*, and *Settings*. Click the Print button in the Print backstage area to send the workbook to the printer and use the *Copies* measurement box to specify the number of copies you want printed. Use the gallery in the *Printer* category to specify the desired printer. The *Settings* category contains a number of galleries, each with options for specifying how you want your workbook printed. Use the galleries to specify whether you want the pages collated when printed; what orientation, page size, and margins your workbook should have; and whether you want the worksheet scaled to print all rows and columns of data on one page.

Another method for printing a workbook is to insert the Quick Print button on the Quick Access toolbar and then click the button. This sends the workbook directly to the printer without displaying the Print backstage area. To insert this button on the Quick Access toolbar, click the Customize Quick Access Toolbar button that displays at the right side of the toolbar and then click *Quick Print* at the drop-down list. To remove the Quick Print button from the Quick Access toolbar, right-click the button and then click *Remove from Quick Access Toolbar* at the drop-down list.

Quick Steps

Close a Workbook
1. Click FILE tab.
2. Click *Close* option.

Closing a Workbook

To close an Excel workbook without closing Excel, click the FILE tab and then click the *Close* option. You can also close a workbook with the keyboard shortcut Ctrl + F4.

Closing Excel

To close Excel, click the Close button that displays in the upper right corner of the screen. The Close button contains an X, and if you position the mouse pointer on the button, a ScreenTip displays with the name *Close*. You can also close Excel with the keyboard shortcut Alt + F4.

Quick Steps

Close Excel
Click Close button.

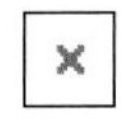

Close

Using Automatic Entering Features

Excel contains several features that help you enter data into cells quickly and efficiently. These features include ***AutoComplete***, which automatically inserts data in a cell that begins the same as a previous entry; ***AutoCorrect***, which automatically corrects many common typographical errors; and ***AutoFill***, which automatically inserts words, numbers, or formulas in a series.

Using AutoComplete

The AutoComplete feature automatically inserts data in a cell that begins the same as a previous entry. If the data inserted by AutoComplete is the data you want in the cell, press the Tab key or the Enter key. If it is not the desired data, simply continue typing the correct data. This feature can be very useful in a worksheet that contains repetitive data entries. For example, consider a worksheet that repeats the word *Payroll*. The second and subsequent times this word is to be inserted in a cell, simply typing the letter *P* will cause AutoComplete to insert the entire word.

Using AutoCorrect

The AutoCorrect feature automatically corrects many common typing errors. To see what symbols and words are in the AutoCorrect feature, click the FILE tab and then click *Options*. At the Excel Options dialog box, click *Proofing* in the left panel and then click the AutoCorrect Options button located in the right panel. This displays the AutoCorrect dialog box with the AutoCorrect tab selected, as shown in Figure 1.7, with a list box containing the replacement data.

Figure 1.7 AutoCorrect Dialog Box with AutoCorrect Tab Selected

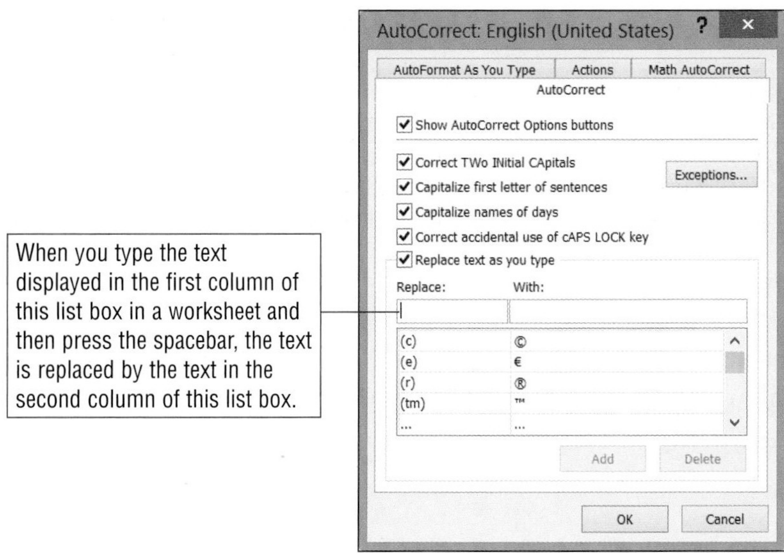

At the AutoCorrect dialog box, type the text shown in the first column in the list box and the text in the second column is inserted in the cell. Along with symbols, the AutoCorrect dialog box contains commonly misspelled words and common typographical errors.

Project 1c Inserting Data in Cells with AutoComplete — Part 3 of 3

1. With **EL1-C1-P1-EmpBene.xlsx** open, make cell A1 active.
2. Type the text in cell A1, as shown in Figure 1.8. Insert the ® symbol by typing (r) and then pressing Enter. (AutoCorrect will change (r) to ®.)
3. Type the remaining text in the cells. When you type the W in *West* in cell B5, the AutoComplete feature will insert *West*. Accept this by pressing the Tab key. (Pressing the Tab key accepts *West* and also makes the cell to the right active.) Use the AutoComplete feature to enter *West* in cells B6 and B8 and *North* in cell B7. Use AutoComplete to enter the second and subsequent occurrences of *Salaried* and *Hourly*.
4. Click the Save button on the Quick Access toolbar.
5. Print **EL1-C1-P1-EmpBene.xlsx** by clicking the FILE tab, clicking the *Print* option, and then clicking the Print button at the Print backstage area. (The gridlines will not print.)

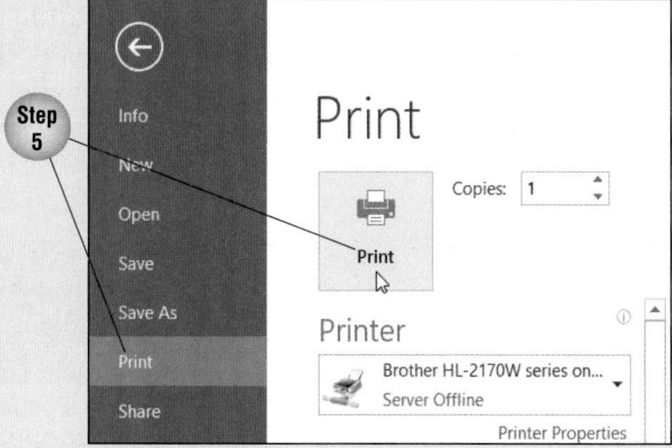

6. Close the workbook by clicking the FILE tab and then clicking the *Close* option at the backstage area.

Figure 1.8 Project 1c

	A	B	C	D
1	Team Net®			
2	Employee	Location	Classification	
3	Avery	West	Hourly	
4	Bryant	North	Salaried	
5	Estrada	West	Salaried	
6	Juergens	West	Salaried	
7	Mickulich	North	Hourly	
8	Talbot	West	Hourly	
9				

Project 2 Open and Format a Workbook and Insert Formulas 3 Parts

You will open an existing workbook and insert formulas to find the sums and averages of numbers.

Using AutoFill

When a cell is active, a thick, green border surrounds it and a small, green square displays in the bottom right corner of the border. This green square is called the AutoFill ***fill handle*** (see Figure 1.2 on page 6). With the fill handle, you can quickly fill a range of cells with the same data or with consecutive data. For example, suppose you need to insert the year 2015 in a row or column of cells. To do this quickly, type *2015* in the first cell, position the mouse pointer on the fill handle, hold down the left mouse button, drag across the cells in which you want the year inserted, and then release the mouse button.

You can also use the fill handle to insert a series in a row or column of cells. For example, suppose you are creating a worksheet with data for all of the months in the year. Type *January* in the first cell, position the mouse pointer on the fill handle, hold down the left mouse button, drag down or across to 11 more cells, and then release the mouse button. Excel automatically inserts the other 11 months in the year in the proper order. When using the fill handle, the cells must be adjacent. Table 1.3 identifies the sequences inserted in cells by Excel when specific types of data are entered.

When filling cells with the fill handle, hold down the Ctrl key if you want to copy the same data instead of displaying the next instance in the series.

Certain sequences, such as *2, 4* and *Jan 12, Jan 13,* require that both cells be selected before using the fill handle. If only the cell containing *2* is active, the fill handle will insert *2*s in the selected cells. The list in Table 1.3 is only a sampling of what the fill handle can do. You may find a variety of other sequences that can be inserted in a worksheet using the fill handle.

An Auto Fill Options button displays when you fill cells with the fill handle. Click this button and a list of options displays for filling the cells. By default, data and formatting are filled in each cell. You can choose to fill only the formatting in the cells or fill only the data without the formatting. You can also choose to copy data into the selected cells or fill the data as a series.

Auto Fill Options

Table 1.3 AutoFill Fill Handle Series

Enter this data *(commas represent data in separate cells)*	***And the fill handle will insert this sequence in adjacent cells***
January	February, March, April, and so on
Jan	Feb, Mar, Apr, and so on
Jan 12, Jan 13	14-Jan, 15-Jan, 16-Jan, and so on
Monday	Tuesday, Wednesday, Thursday, and so on
Product 1	Product 2, Product 3, Product 4, and so on
Qtr 1	Qtr 2, Qtr 3, Qtr 4
2, 4	6, 8, 10, and so on

Opening a Workbook

Quick Steps

Open a Workbook
1. Click FILE tab.
2. Click *Open* option.
3. Click the desired location (your OneDrive or *Computer*).
4. Click the Browse button.
5. Display desired folder.
6. Double-click workbook name.

Open an Excel workbook at the Open dialog box. To display this dialog box, click the FILE tab and then click the *Open* option. This displays the Open backstage area. You can also display the Open backstage area with the keyboard shortcut Ctrl + O or by inserting an Open button on the Quick Access toolbar. At the Open backstage area, click the desired location, such as your OneDrive or *Computer*, and then click the Browse button. (If you are opening a workbook from your computer or USB flash drive, you can double-click the *Computer* option.) At the Open dialog box, navigate to the desired folder and then double-click the desired workbook name in the Content pane. You can bypass the Open backstage area and go directly to the Open dialog box by using the keyboard shortcut Ctrl + F12.

When you click your OneDrive or the *Computer* option at the Open backstage area, a list of the most recently accessed folders displays below the *Recent Folders* heading in the *Computer* section. Open a folder by clicking the folder name.

Opening a Workbook from the Recent Workbooks List

Click the *Recent Workbooks* option in the middle panel at the Open backstage area and a list of the most recently opened workbooks displays below the Recent Workbooks heading at the right side of the backstage area. Up to twenty-five workbook names display in the list by default. Open a workbook from this list by clicking the workbook name.

Pinning a Workbook to the Recent Workbooks List

If you want a workbook to remain in the Recent Workbooks list at the Open backstage area, "pin" the workbook to the list. To do this, position the mouse pointer over the desired workbook name and then click the small, left-pointing stick pin that displays at the right side of the workbook name. This changes it to a down-pointing stick pin. The next time you display the Open backstage area, the workbook you pinned displays at the top of the Recent Workbooks list. You can also pin a workbook to the Recent list at the Excel 2013 opening screen. When you pin a workbook here, it will display in the Recent Workbooks list at the Open backstage area as well. To "unpin" the workbook, click the stick pin to change it from a down-pointing pin to a left-pointing pin. You can pin more than one workbook to the list.

Project 2a **Inserting Data in Cells with the Fill Handle** **Part 1 of 3**

1. Open **FillCells.xlsx**. (This workbook is located in the EL1C1 folder on your storage medium.)
2. Save the workbook with Save As and name it **EL1-C1-P2-FillCells**.
3. Add data to cells as shown in Figure 1.9. Begin by making cell B1 active and then typing January.
4. Position the mouse pointer on the fill handle for cell B1, hold down the left mouse button, drag across to cell G1, and then release the mouse button.

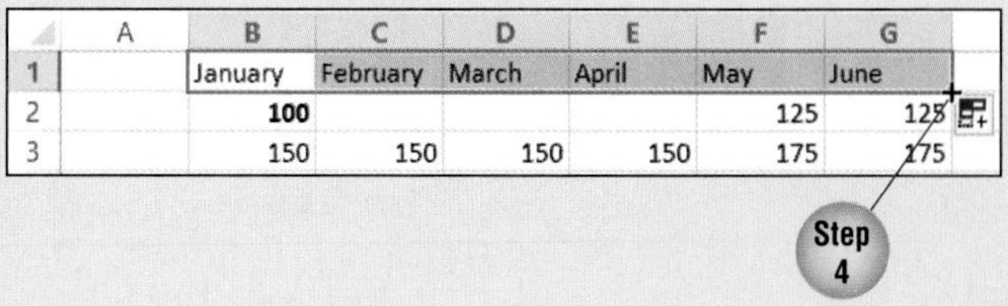

	A	B	C	D	E	F	G
1		January	February	March	April	May	June
2		100				125	125
3		150	150	150	150	175	175

Step 4

5. Type a sequence and then use the fill handle to fill the remaining cells by completing the following steps:
   a. Make cell A2 active and then type **Year 1**.
   b. Make cell A3 active and then type **Year 3**.
   c. Select cells A2 and A3 by positioning the mouse pointer in cell A2, holding down the left mouse button, dragging down to cell A3, and then releasing the mouse button.
   d. Drag the fill handle for cell A3 to cell A5. (This inserts *Year 5* in cell A4 and *Year 7* in cell A5.)
6. Use the fill handle to fill adjacent cells with a number but not the formatting by completing the following steps:
   a. Make cell B2 active. (This cell contains *100* with bold formatting.)
   b. Drag the fill handle for cell B2 to cell E2. (This inserts ***100*** in cells C2, D2, and E2.)
   c. Click the Auto Fill Options button that displays at the bottom right of the selected cells.
   d. Click the *Fill Without Formatting* option at the drop-down list.

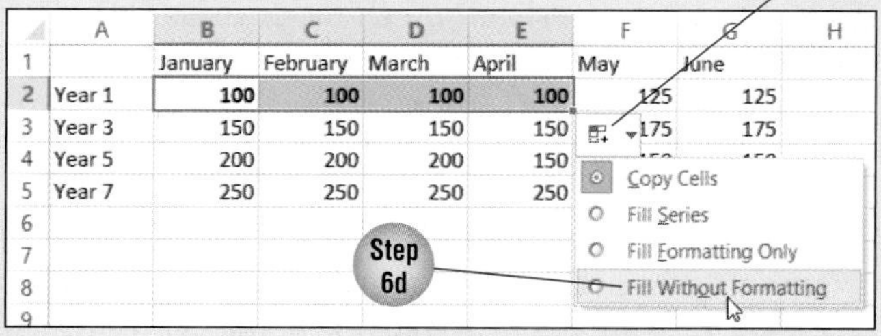

	A	B	C	D	E	F	G	H
1		January	February	March	April	May	June	
2	Year 1	100	100	100	100	125	125	
3	Year 3	150	150	150	150	175	175	
4	Year 5	200	200	200	150			
5	Year 7	250	250	250	250			

Copy Cells
Fill Series
Fill Formatting Only
Fill Without Formatting

Step 6c

Step 6d

7. Use the fill handle to apply formatting only by completing the following steps:
   a. Make cell B2 active.
   b. Drag the fill handle to cell B5.
   c. Click the Auto Fill Options button and then click *Fill Formatting Only* at the drop-down list.
8. Make cell A10 active and then type **Qtr 1**.
9. Drag the fill handle for cell A10 to cell A13.
10. Save **EL1-C1-P2-FillCells.xlsx**.

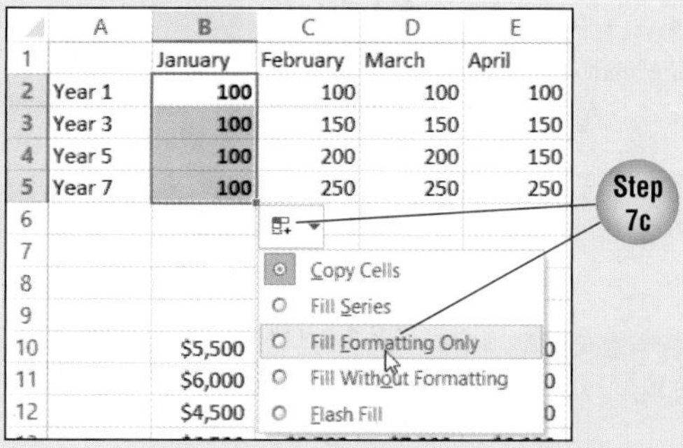

	A	B	C	D	E
1		January	February	March	April
2	Year 1	100	100	100	100
3	Year 3	100	150	150	150
4	Year 5	100	200	200	150
5	Year 7	100	250	250	250
10		$5,500			
11		$6,000			
12		$4,500			

Copy Cells
Fill Series
Fill Formatting Only
Fill Without Formatting
Flash Fill

Step 7c

Figure 1.9 Project 2a

	A	B	C	D	E	F	G	H
1		January	February	March	April	May	June	
2	Year 1	**100**	100	100	100	125	125	
3	Year 3	**150**	150	150	150	175	175	
4	Year 5	**200**	200	200	150	150	150	
5	Year 7	**250**	250	250	250	250	250	
6								
7								
8								
9								
10	Qtr 1	$5,500	$6,250	$7,000	$8,500	$5,500	$4,500	
11	Qtr 2	$6,000	$7,250	$6,500	$9,000	$4,000	$5,000	
12	Qtr 3	$4,500	$8,000	$6,000	$7,500	$6,000	$5,000	
13	Qtr 4	$6,500	$8,500	$7,000	$8,000	$5,500	$6,000	
14								

Inserting Formulas

Quick Steps

Insert a Formula Using the AutoSum button

1. Click in desired cell.
2. Click AutoSum button.
3. Check range identified and make changes if necessary.
4. Press Enter.

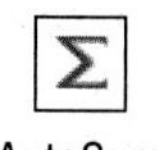

AutoSum

HINT You can use the keyboard shortcut Alt + = to insert the SUM function in a cell.

Excel is a powerful decision-making tool you can use to manipulate data to answer questions in "What if?" situations. Insert a formula in a worksheet and then manipulate the data to make projections, answer specific questions, and plan for the future. For example, the manager of a department might use an Excel worksheet to prepare a department budget and then determine the impact on the budget of hiring a new employee or increasing the volume of production.

Insert a ***formula*** in a worksheet to perform calculations on values. A formula contains a mathematical operator, value, cell reference, cell range, and function. Formulas can be written that add, subtract, multiply, and/or divide values. Formulas can also be written that calculate averages, percentages, minimum and maximum values, and much more. Excel includes an AutoSum button in the Editing group on the HOME tab that inserts a formula to calculate the total of a range of cells.

Using the AutoSum Button to Add Numbers

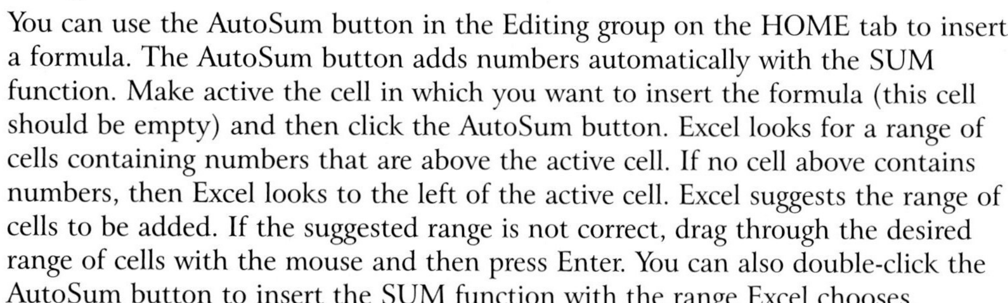

You can use the AutoSum button in the Editing group on the HOME tab to insert a formula. The AutoSum button adds numbers automatically with the SUM function. Make active the cell in which you want to insert the formula (this cell should be empty) and then click the AutoSum button. Excel looks for a range of cells containing numbers that are above the active cell. If no cell above contains numbers, then Excel looks to the left of the active cell. Excel suggests the range of cells to be added. If the suggested range is not correct, drag through the desired range of cells with the mouse and then press Enter. You can also double-click the AutoSum button to insert the SUM function with the range Excel chooses.

Project 2b **Adding Values with the AutoSum Button** **Part 2 of 3**

1. With **EL1-C1-P2-FillCells.xlsx** open, make cell A6 active and then type Total.
2. Make cell B6 active and then calculate the sum of the cells by clicking the AutoSum button in the Editing group on the HOME tab.
3. Excel inserts the formula *=SUM(B2:B5)* in cell B6. This is the correct range of cells, so press Enter.

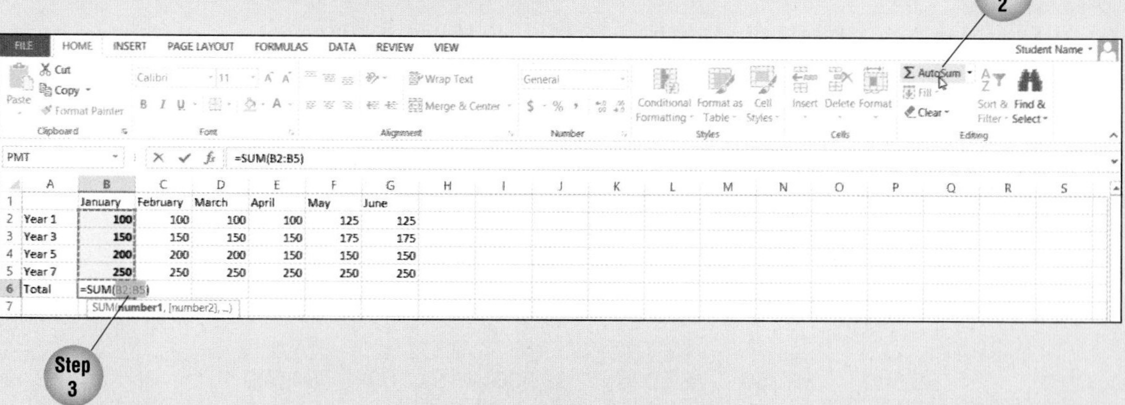

4. Make cell C6 active and then click the AutoSum button in the Editing group.
5. Excel inserts the formula *=SUM(C2:C5)* in cell C6. This is the correct range of cells, so press Enter.

6. Make cell D6 active.
7. Double-click the AutoSum button. This inserts the formula *=SUM(D2:D5)* in cell D6 and inserts the sum *700*.
8. Insert the sum in cells E6, F6, and G6.
9. Save **EL1-C1-P2-FillCells.xlsx**.

Using the AutoSum Button to Average Numbers

A common function in a formula is the AVERAGE function. With this function, a range of cells is added together and then divided by the number of cell entries. The AVERAGE function is available on the AutoSum button. Click the AutoSum button arrow and a drop-down list displays with a number of common functions.

Using the Fill Handle to Copy a Formula

In a worksheet, you may want to insert the same basic formula in other cells. In a situation where a formula is copied to other locations in a worksheet, use a ***relative cell reference***. Copy a formula containing relative cell references and the cell references change. For example, if you enter the formula *=SUM(A2:C2)* in cell D2 and then copy it relatively to cell D3, the formula in cell D3 displays as *=SUM(A3:C3)*. You can use the fill handle to copy a formula relatively in a worksheet. To do this, position the mouse pointer on the fill handle until the mouse pointer turns into a thin, black cross; hold down the left mouse button; drag and select the desired cells; and then release the mouse button.

Quick Steps

Insert an Average Formula Using the AutoSum Button
1. Click in desired cell.
2. Click AutoSum button arrow.
3. Click *Average*.
4. Specify range.
5. Press Enter.

Copy a Formula Using the Fill Handle
1. Insert formula in cell.
2. Make active cell containing formula.
3. Using fill handle, drag through cells you want to contain formula.

Project 2c **Inserting the AVERAGE Function and Copying a Formula Relatively** **Part 3 of 3**

1. With **EL1-C1-P2-FillCells.xlsx** open, make cell A14 active and then type Average.
2. Insert the average of cells B10 through B13 by completing the following steps:
   a. Make cell B14 active.
   b. Click the AutoSum button arrow in the Editing group and then click *Average* at the drop-down list.
   c. Excel inserts the formula *=AVERAGE(B10:B13)* in cell B14. This is the correct range of cells, so press Enter.

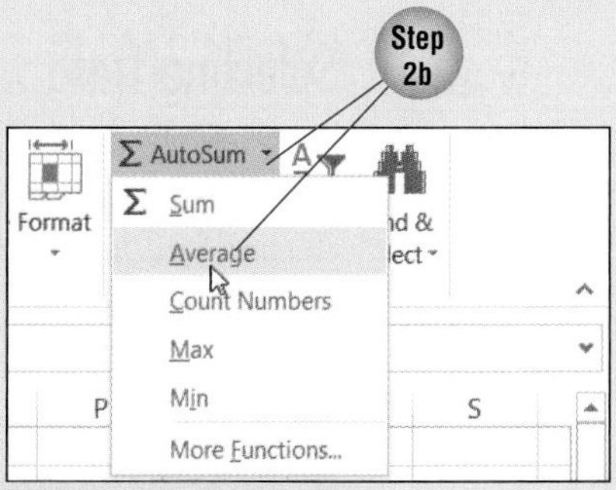

Step 2b

Σ AutoSum
Format
Σ Sum
Average
Count Numbers
Max
Min
More Functions...

3. Copy the formula relatively to cells C14 through G14 by completing the following steps:
   a. Make cell B14 active.
   b. Position the mouse pointer on the fill handle, hold down the left mouse button, drag across to cell G14, and then release the mouse button.

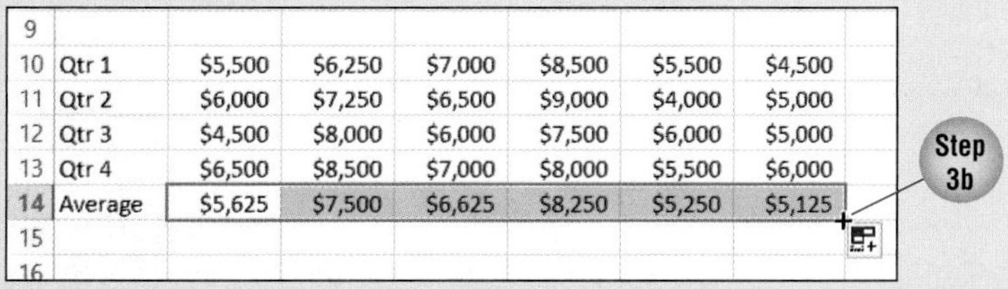

9							
10	Qtr 1	$5,500	$6,250	$7,000	$8,500	$5,500	$4,500
11	Qtr 2	$6,000	$7,250	$6,500	$9,000	$4,000	$5,000
12	Qtr 3	$4,500	$8,000	$6,000	$7,500	$6,000	$5,000
13	Qtr 4	$6,500	$8,500	$7,000	$8,000	$5,500	$6,000
14	Average	$5,625	$7,500	$6,625	$8,250	$5,250	$5,125
15							
16							

Step 3b

4. Save, print, and then close **EL1-C1-P2-FillCells.xlsx**.

Project 3 Format a Worksheet — 2 Parts

You will open a monthly expenses workbook and then change column width, merge and center cells, and apply number formatting to numbers in cells.

Selecting Cells

You can use a variety of methods for formatting cells in a worksheet. For example, you can change the alignment of data in cells or rows or add character formatting. To identify the cells that are to be affected by the formatting, select the specific cells.

Selecting Cells Using the Mouse

Select specific cells in a worksheet using the mouse or select columns or rows. Table 1.4 displays the methods for selecting cells using the mouse.

HINT

The first cell in a range displays with a white background and is the active cell.

Selected cells, except the active cell, display with a gray background (this may vary) rather than a white background. The active cell is the first cell in the selection block and displays in the normal manner (white background with black data). Selected cells remain selected until you click a cell with the mouse or press an arrow key on the keyboard.

Selecting Cells Using the Keyboard

You can use the keyboard to select specific cells within a worksheet. Table 1.5 displays the commands for selecting specific cells. If a worksheet contains data, Ctrl + A selects the cells containing data. If the worksheet contains groups of data separated by empty cells, Ctrl + A or Ctrl + Shift + spacebar will select a group of cells rather than all of the cells.

Selecting Data within Cells

The selection commands presented select the entire cell. You can also select specific characters within a cell. To do this with the mouse, position the cell pointer in the desired cell and then double-click the left mouse button. Drag with the I-beam pointer through the data you want selected. Data selected within a cell displays in

Table 1.4 Selecting with the Mouse

To select this	*Do this*
column	Position the cell pointer on the column header (a letter) and then click the left mouse button.
row	Position the cell pointer on the row header (a number) and then click the left mouse button.
adjacent cells	Drag with the mouse to select specific cells.
nonadjacent cells	Hold down the Ctrl key while clicking the column header, row header, or specific cells.
all cells in worksheet	Click Select All button. (Refer to Figure 1.2 on page 6.)

Table 1.5 Selecting Cells Using the Keyboard

To select	*Press*
cells in direction of arrow key	Shift + arrow key
from active cell to beginning of row	Shift + Home
from active cell to beginning of worksheet	Shift + Ctrl + Home
from active cell to last cell in worksheet containing data	Shift + Ctrl + End
entire column	Ctrl + spacebar
entire row	Shift + spacebar
cells containing data	Ctrl + A
groups of data separated by empty cells	Ctrl + Shift + spacebar

black with a gray background. If you are using the keyboard to select data in a cell, hold down the Shift key and then press the arrow key that moves the insertion point in the desired direction. All data the insertion point passes through will be selected. You can also press F8 to turn on the Extend Selection mode, move the insertion point in the desired direction to select the data, and then press F8 to turn off the Extend Selection mode. When the Extend Selection mode is on, the words *EXTEND SELECTION* display toward the left side of the Status bar.

Select nonadjacent columns or rows by holding down the Ctrl key while selecting cells.

Applying Basic Formatting

Excel provides a wide range of formatting options you can apply to cells in a worksheet. Some basic formatting options that are helpful when creating a worksheet include changing column width, merging and centering cells, and formatting numbers.

Changing Column Width

If data such as text or numbers overlaps in a cell, you can increase the width of the column to accommodate the data. To do this, position the mouse pointer on the gray boundary line between columns in the column header (Figure 1.2 identifies the column header) until the pointer turns into a left-and-right-pointing arrow and then drag the boundary to the desired location. If the column contains data, double-click the column boundary at the right side of the column to automatically adjust the width of the column to accommodate the longest entry.

Quick Steps

Change the Column Width
Drag column boundary line.
OR
Double-click column boundary.

Merge and Center Cells
1. Select cells.
2. Click Merge & Center button on HOME tab.

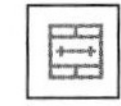
Merge & Center

Merging and Centering Cells

As you learned earlier in this chapter, if the text you type is longer than the cell can accommodate, the text overlaps the next cell to the right (unless you are typing numbers). You can merge cells to accommodate the text and also center the text within the merged cells. To merge cells and center the text, select the desired cells and then click the Merge & Center button located in the Alignment group on the HOME tab.

Project 3a Changing Column Width and Merging and Centering Cells

1. Open **MoExps.xlsx** from the EL1C1 folder on your storage medium.
2. Save the workbook with Save As and name it **EL1-C1-P3-MoExps**.
3. Change the column width by completing the following steps:
   a. Position the mouse pointer in the column header on the boundary line between columns A and B until the pointer turns into a double-headed arrow pointing left and right.

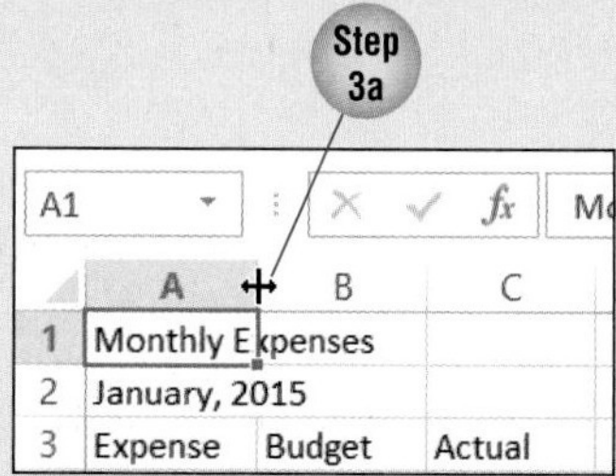

   b. Double-click the left mouse button.
   c. Position the mouse pointer in the column header on the boundary line between columns E and F and then double-click the left mouse button.
   d. Position the mouse pointer in the column header on the boundary line between columns F and G and then double-click the left mouse button.
4. Merge and center cells by completing the following steps:
   a. Select cells A1 through C1.
   b. Click the Merge & Center button in the Alignment group on the HOME tab.

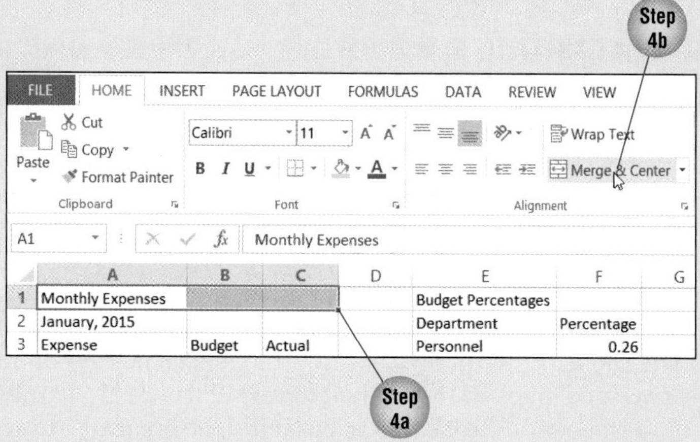

   c. Select cells A2 through C2.
   d. Click the Merge & Center button.
   e. Select cells E1 and F1 and then click the Merge & Center button.
5. Save **EL1-C1-P3-MoExps.xlsx**.

Formatting Numbers

Numbers in a cell, by default, are aligned at the right and decimals and commas do not display unless they are typed in the cell. Change the format of numbers with buttons in the Number group on the HOME tab. Symbols you can use to format numbers include a percent sign (%), a comma (,), and a dollar sign ($). For example, if you type the number *$45.50* in a cell, Excel automatically applies the Currency format to the number. If you type *45%*, Excel automatically applies the Percent format to the number. The Number group on the HOME tab contains five buttons you can use to format numbers in cells. The five buttons are shown and described in Table 1.6.

Specify the formatting for numbers in cells in a worksheet before typing the numbers or format existing numbers in a worksheet. The Increase Decimal and Decrease Decimal buttons in the Number group on the HOME tab will change decimal places for existing numbers only. The Number group on the HOME tab also contains the Number Format button. Click the Number Format button arrow and a drop-down list displays of common number formats. Click the desired format at the drop-down list to apply the number formatting to the cell or selected cells.

A general guideline in accounting is to insert a dollar sign before the first number amount in a column and before the total number amount but not before the number amounts in between. You can format a worksheet following this guideline by applying accounting formatting to the first amount and total amount (using the Accounting Number Format button) and applying comma formatting to the number amounts in between (using the Comma Style button).

Table 1.6 Number Formatting Buttons

Click this button		*To do this*
$ ▾	Accounting Number Format	Add a dollar sign, any necessary commas, and a decimal point followed by two decimal digits, if none are typed; right-align the number in the cell.
%	Percent Style	Multiply the cell value by 100 and display the result with a percent symbol; right-align the number in the cell.
,	Comma Style	Add any necessary commas and a decimal point followed by two decimal digits, if none are typed; right-align the number in the cell.
←.0 .00	Increase Decimal	Increase the number of decimal places displayed after the decimal point in the selected cell.
.00 →.0	Decrease Decimal	Decrease the number of decimal places displayed after the decimal point in the selected cell.

Project 3b Formatting Numbers

Part 2 of 2

1. With **EL1-C1-P3-MoExps.xlsx** open, make cell B13 active and then double-click the AutoSum button. (This inserts the total of the numbers in cells B4 through B12.)
2. Make cell C13 active and then double-click the AutoSum button.
3. Apply accounting formatting to cells by completing the following steps:
   a. Select cells B4 and C4.
   b. Click the Accounting Number Format button in the Number group on the HOME tab.
   c. Decrease the decimals by clicking twice on the Decrease Decimal button in the Number group.

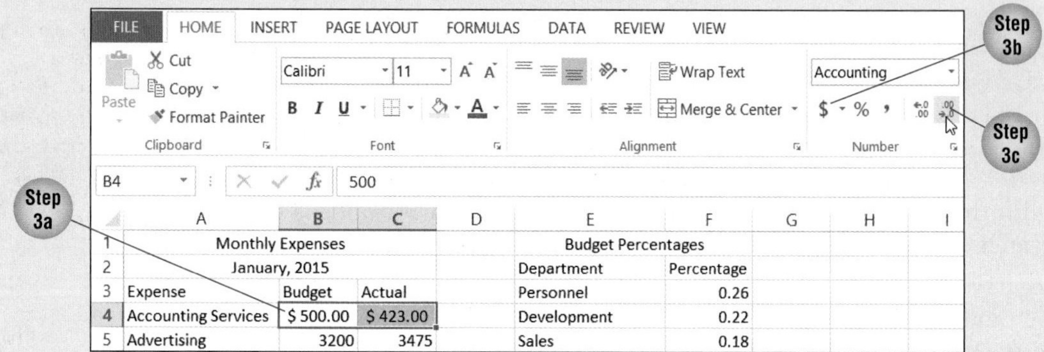

   d. Select cells B13 and C13.
   e. Click the Accounting Number Format button.
   f. Click twice on the Decrease Decimal button.
4. Apply comma formatting to numbers by completing the following steps:
   a. Select cells B5 through C12.
   b. Click the Comma Style button in the Number group.
   c. Click twice on the Decrease Decimal button.

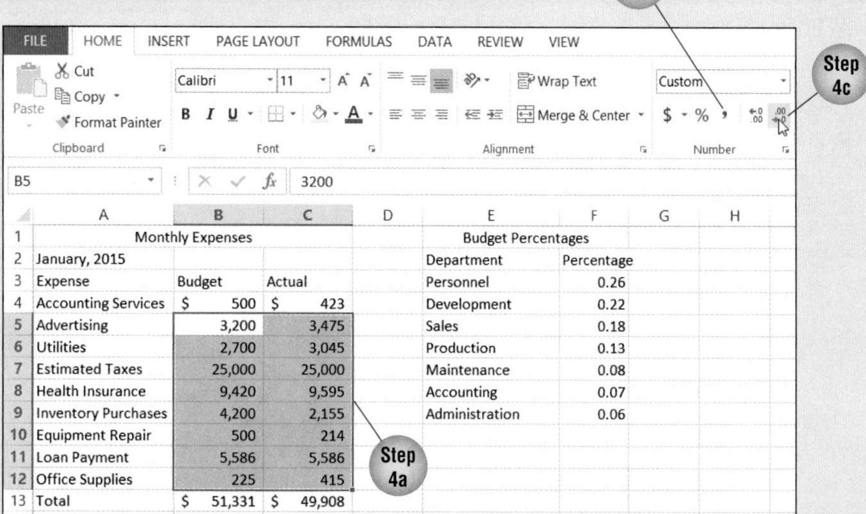

5. Apply percent formatting to numbers by completing the following steps:
   a. Select cells F3 through F9.
   b. Click the Percent Style button in the Number group on the HOME tab.
6. Click in cell A1.
7. Save, print, and then close **EL1-C1-P3-MoExps.xlsx**.

Project 4 Use the Help Feature **2 Parts**

You will use the Help feature to learn more about entering data in cells, printing a workbook, and number formats, as well as use the ScreenTip to display information about a specific button.

Using Help

Microsoft Excel includes a Help feature that contains information about Excel features and commands. This on-screen reference manual is similar to Windows Help and the Help features in Word, PowerPoint, and Access. Click the Microsoft Excel Help button (the question mark) located in the upper right corner of the screen or press the keyboard shortcut F1 to display the Excel Help window, as shown in Figure 1.10. In this window, type a topic, feature, or question in the search text box and then press the Enter key or click the Search help button. Topics related to the search text display in the Excel Help window. Click a topic that interests you. If the topic window contains a Show All hyperlink in the upper right corner, click this hyperlink and the topic options expand to show additional information related to the topic. When you click the Show All hyperlink, it becomes the Hide All hyperlink.

Quick Steps

Use the Help Feature
1. Click Microsoft Excel Help button.
2. Type topic or feature.
3. Press Enter.
4. Click desired topic.

Help

The Excel Help window contains five buttons that display to the left of the search text box as identified in Figure 1.10. Use the Back and Forward buttons to navigate in the window. Click the Home button to return to the Excel Help window opening screen. If you want to print information on a topic or feature,

Figure 1.10 Excel Help Window

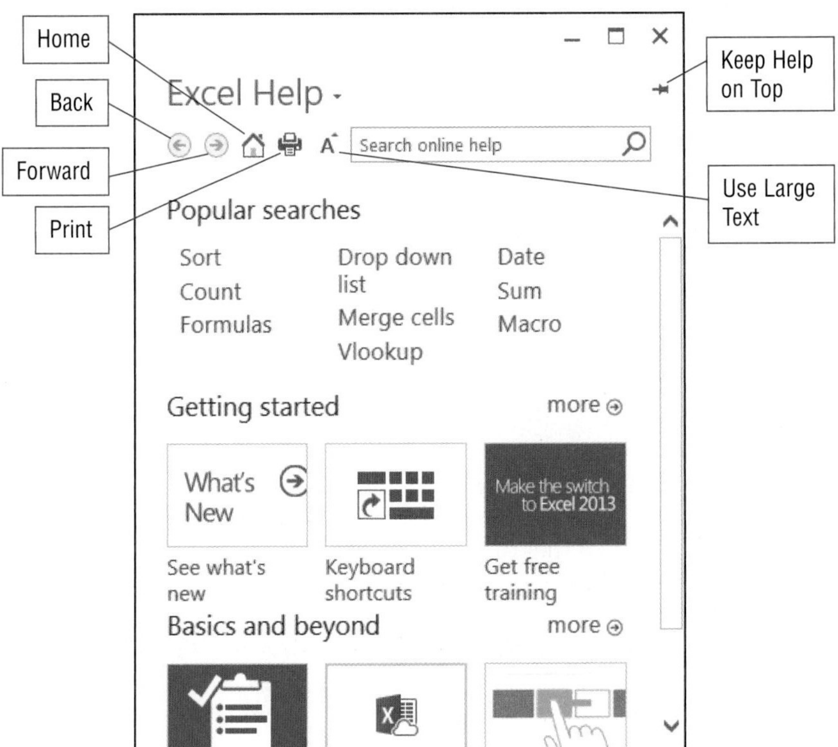

click the Print button and then click the Print button at the Print dialog box. Make the text in the Excel Help window larger by clicking the Use Large Text button. In addition to these five buttons, the Excel Help window contains a Keep Help on Top button located near the upper right corner of the window. Click this button and the Excel Help window remains on the screen (pinned to the screen) even when you work in a worksheet. Click the button again to remove the window from the screen.

Getting Help on a Button

When you position the mouse pointer on a button, a ScreenTip displays with information about the button. Some button ScreenTips display with a Help icon and the hyperlinked text Tell me more. Click this hyperlinked text or press F1 and the Excel Help window opens with information about the button feature.

Project 4a **Using the Help Feature** **Part 1 of 2**

1. At the blank screen, press Ctrl + N to display a blank workbook. (Ctrl + N is the keyboard shortcut to open a blank workbook.)
2. Click the Microsoft Excel Help button located in the upper right corner of the screen.
3. At the Excel Help window, type **enter data** in the search text box and then press the Enter key.
4. When the list of topics displays, click the Enter data manually in worksheet cells hyperlink.
5. Read the information about entering data in cells.
6. Click the Print button in the Excel Help window. This displays the Print dialog box. If you want to print the topic, click the Print button; otherwise, click the Cancel button to remove the dialog box.
7. Click the Use Large Text button in the Excel Help window to increase the size of the text.
8. Click the Use Large Text button again to return the text to the normal size.
9. Click the Back button to return to the previous window.
10. Click the Forward button to return to the article on entering data manually in worksheet cells.
11. Click the Home button to return to the original Excel Help window screen.
12. Click the Close button to close the Excel Help window.

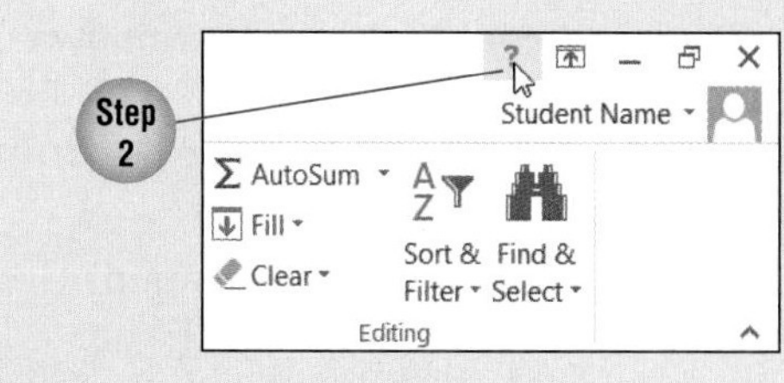

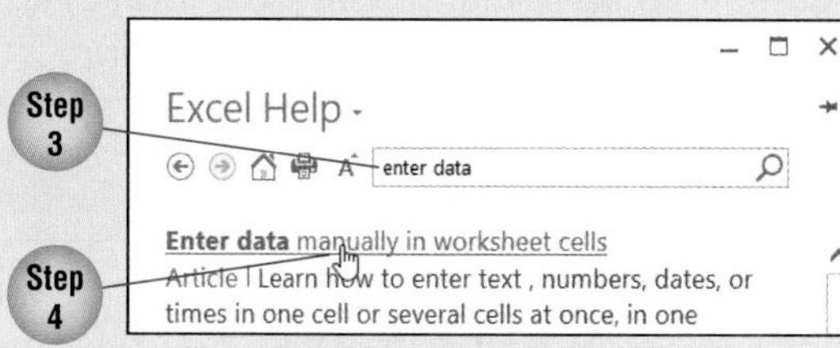

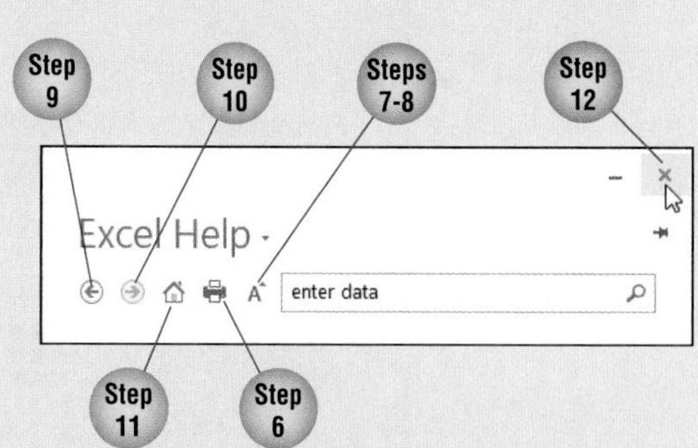

13. Hover the mouse pointer over the Wrap Text button in the Alignment group on the HOME tab until the ScreenTip displays and then click the hyperlinked text Tell me more that displays at the bottom of the ScreenTip.
14. At the Excel Help window, read the information that displays and then close the window.

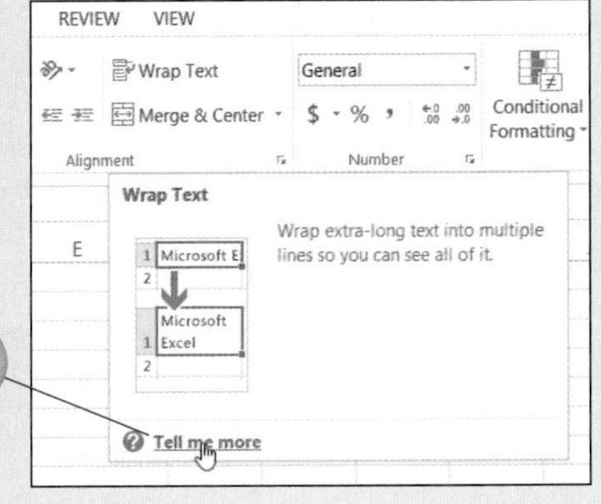

Getting Help in a Dialog Box or Backstage Area

Some dialog boxes and backstage areas contain a help button you can click to display the Excel Help window with specific information about the dialog box or backstage area. After reading and/or printing the information, close the dialog box by clicking the Close button located in the upper right corner of the dialog box or close the backstage area by clicking the Back button or pressing the Esc key.

Project 4b **Getting Help in a Dialog Box or Backstage Area** **Part 2 of 2**

1. At the blank workbook, click the FILE tab and then click the *Print* option.
2. At the Print backstage area, click the Microsoft Excel Help button that displays in the upper right corner.
3. At the Excel Help window that displays, click the hyperlink to an article on printing that interests you. Read the article and then close the Excel Help window.
4. Click the Back button to return to the blank workbook.
5. At the blank workbook, click the Number group dialog box launcher.
6. At the Format Cells dialog box with the Number tab selected, click the Help button that displays in the upper right corner of the dialog box.

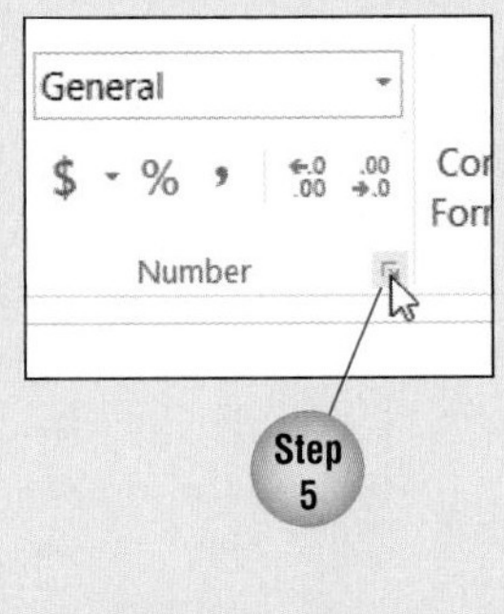

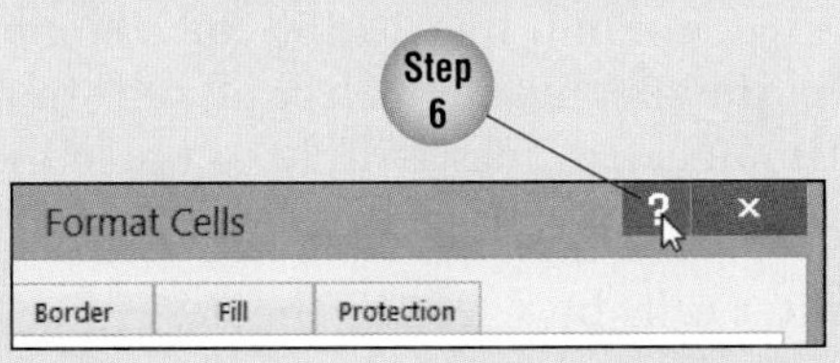

7. Click the hyperlink to the article on available number formats.
8. Read the article, close the Excel Help window and then close the Format Cells dialog box.

Chapter Summary

- A file created in Excel is called a workbook and it consists of individual worksheets.
- The intersection of columns and rows in a worksheet is referred to as a cell. Gridlines are the horizontal and vertical lines that define cells.
- When the insertion point is positioned in a cell, the cell name (also called the cell reference) displays in the Name box located at the left side of the Formula bar. The cell name includes the column letter and row number.
- If data entered in a cell consists of text (letters) and does not fit into the cell, it overlaps the cell to the right. If the data consists of numbers and does not fit into the cell, the numbers are changed to number symbols (###).
- Save a workbook by clicking the Save button on the Quick Access toolbar or by clicking the FILE tab and then clicking the *Save As* option. At the Save As backstage area, click the desired location and then click the Browse button. At the Save As dialog box, navigate to the desired folder, type the workbook name in the *File name* text box, and then press Enter.
- To replace data in a cell, click the cell once and then type the new data. To edit data within a cell, double-click the cell and then make necessary changes.
- Print a workbook by clicking the FILE tab, clicking the *Print* option, and then clicking the Print button.
- Close a workbook by clicking the FILE tab and then clicking the *Close* option or by using the keyboard shortcut Ctrl + F4.
- Close Excel by clicking the Close button located in the upper right corner of the screen or with the keyboard shortcut Alt + F4.
- The AutoComplete feature automatically inserts a previous entry if the character or characters being typed in a cell match a previous entry. The AutoCorrect feature corrects many common typographical errors. The AutoFill fill handle fills a range of cells with the same or consecutive data.
- Open a workbook by clicking the FILE tab and then clicking the *Open* option. At the Open backstage area, click the desired location and then click the Browse button. At the Open dialog box, double-click the desired workbook.
- Use the AutoSum button in the Editing group on the HOME tab to find the total or average of data in columns or rows.
- Select all cells in a column by clicking the column header. Select all cells in a row by clicking the row header. Select all cells in a worksheet by clicking the Select All button located immediately to the left of the column headers.
- Change column width by dragging or double-clicking the column boundary.
- Merge and center cells by selecting the desired cells and then clicking the Merge & Center button in the Alignment group on the HOME tab.
- Format numbers in cells with buttons in the Number group on the HOME tab.
- Click the Microsoft Excel Help button or press F1 to display the Excel Help window. At this window, type a topic in the search text box and then press Enter.
- The ScreenTip for some buttons displays with the hyperlinked text Tell me more. Click this hyperlink (or press F1) and the Excel Help window opens with information about the button feature.
- Some dialog boxes and backstage areas contain a help button you can click to display information specific to the dialog box or backstage area.

Commands Review

FEATURE	RIBBON TAB, GROUP/OPTION	BUTTON	KEYBOARD SHORTCUT
Accounting format	HOME, Number	$	
AutoSum	HOME, Editing	Σ	Alt + =
close Excel		×	Alt + F4
close workbook	FILE, *Close*		Ctrl + F4
Comma format	HOME, Number	,	
decrease decimal places	HOME, Number	.00 →.0	
Excel Help window		?	F1
Go To dialog box	HOME, Editing		Ctrl + G
increase decimal places	HOME, Number	←.0 .00	
merge and center cells	HOME, Alignment		
Open backstage area	FILE, *Open*		Ctrl + O
Percent format	HOME, Number	%	Ctrl + Shift + %
Print backstage area	FILE, *Print*		Ctrl + P
Save As backstage area	FILE, *Save As*		Ctrl + S

Concepts Check

Test Your Knowledge

Completion: In the space provided at the right, indicate the correct term, symbol, or command.

1. The horizontal and vertical lines that define the cells in a worksheet area are referred to as this. ____________________
2. Columns in a worksheet are labeled with these. ____________________
3. Rows in a worksheet are labeled with these. ____________________
4. Press this key on the keyboard to move the insertion point to the next cell. ____________________

5. Press these keys on the keyboard to move the insertion point to the previous cell. ____________

6. Data being typed in a cell displays in the cell as well as here. ____________

7. If a number entered in a cell is too long to fit inside the cell, the number is changed to this. ____________

8. This feature automatically inserts words, numbers, or formulas in a series. ____________

9. This is the name of the small black square that displays in the bottom right corner of the active cell. ____________

10. Use this button in the Editing group on the HOME tab to insert a formula in a cell. ____________

11. With this function, a range of cells are added together and then divided by the number of cell entries. ____________

12. To select nonadjacent columns using the mouse, hold down this key on the keyboard while clicking the column headers. ____________

13. Click this button to merge selected cells and center data within the merged cells. ____________

14. The Accounting Number Format button is located in this group on the HOME tab. ____________

15. Press this function key to display the Excel Help window. ____________

Skills Check Assess Your Performance

Assessment

1 CREATE A WORKSHEET USING AUTOCOMPLETE

1. Create the worksheet shown in Figure 1.12 with the following specifications:
   a. To create the © symbol in cell A1, type (c).
   b. Type the misspelled words as shown and let the AutoCorrect feature correct them. Use the AutoComplete feature to insert the second occurrence of *Category, Available,* and *Balance*.
   c. Merge and center cells A1 and B1.
2. Save the workbook and name it **EL1-C1-A1-Plan**.
3. Print and then close **EL1-C1-A1-Plan.xlsx**.

Figure 1.12 Assessment 1

	A	B	C
1	Premiere Plan©		
2	Plan A	Catagory	
3		Availalbe	
4		Balence	
5	Plan B	Category	
6		Available	
7		Balance	
8			

Assessment 2

CREATE AND FORMAT A WORKSHEET

SNAP Grade It

1. Create the worksheet shown in Figure 1.13 with the following specifications:
   a. Merge and center cells A1 through C1.
   b. After typing the data, automatically adjust the width of column A.
   c. Insert in cell B8 the sum of cells B3 through B7 and insert in cell C8 the sum of cells C3 through C7.
   d. Apply accounting formatting and decrease the decimal point by two positions to cells B3, C3, B8, and C8.
   e. Apply comma formatting and decrease the decimal point by two positions to cells B4 through C7.
   f. If any of the number amounts display as number symbols (###), automatically adjust the width of the appropriate columns.
2. Save the workbook and name it **EL1-C1-A2-Exp**.
3. Print and then close **EL1-C1-A2-Exp.xlsx**.

Figure 1.13 Assessment 2

	A	B	C	D
1	Construction Project			
2	Expense	Original	Current	
3	Material	129000	153000	
4	Labor	97000	98500	
5	Equipment rental	14500	11750	
6	Permits	1200	1350	
7	Tax	1950	2145	
8	Total			
9				

Assessment 3

CREATE A WORKSHEET USING THE FILL HANDLE

1. Type the worksheet data shown in Figure 1.14 with the following specifications:
   a. Type **Monday** in cell B2 and then use the fill handle to fill in the remaining days of the week.
   b. Type **350** in cell B3 and then use the fill handle to fill in the remaining numbers in the row.
   c. Merge and center cells A1 through G1.
2. Insert in cell G3 the sum of cells B3 through F3 and insert in cell G4 the sum of cells B4 through F4.
3. After typing the data, select cells B3 through G4 and then apply accounting formatting with two places past the decimal point.
4. If necessary, adjust column widths.
5. Save the workbook and name it **EL1-C1-A3-Invest**.
6. Print and then close **EL1-C1-A3-Invest.xlsx**.

Figure 1.14 Assessment 3

	A	B	C	D	E	F	G	H
1	CAPITAL INVESTMENTS							
2		Monday	Tuesday	Wednesday	Thursday	Friday	Total	
3	Budget	350	350	350	350	350		
4	Actual	310	425	290	375	400		
5								

Assessment 4

INSERT FORMULAS IN A WORKSHEET

1. Open **DIAnalysis.xlsx** and then save the workbook with Save As and name it **EL1-C1-A4-DIAnalysis**.
2. Insert a formula in cell B15 that totals the amounts in cells B4 through B14.
3. Use the fill handle to copy relatively the formula in cell B15 to cell C15.
4. Insert a formula in cell D4 that finds the average of the amounts in cells B4 and C4.
5. Use the fill handle to copy relatively the formula in cell D4 down to cells D5 through D14.
6. Select cells D5 through D14 and then apply comma formatting with no places past the decimal point.
7. Save, print, and then close **EL1-C1-A4-DIAnalysis.xlsx**.

Visual Benchmark Demonstrate Your Proficiency

CREATE, FORMAT, AND INSERT FORMULAS IN A WORKSHEET

1. At a blank workbook, create the worksheet shown in Figure 1.15 with the following specifications:
   a. Type the data in cells, as shown in the figure. Use the fill handle when appropriate, merge and center the text *Personal Expenses - July through December*, and automatically adjust column widths.

b. Insert formulas to determine averages and totals.
c. Apply accounting formatting with no places past the decimal point to the amounts in cells B4 through H4 and cells B12 through H12.
d. Apply comma formatting with no places past the decimal point to the amounts in cells B5 through H11.
2. Save the workbook and name it **EL1-C1-VB-PersExps**.
3. Print and then close **EL1-C1-VB-PersExps.xlsx**.

Figure 1.15 Visual Benchmark

	A	B	C	D	E	F	G	H	I
1									
2			Personal Expenses - July through December						
3	Expense	July	August	September	October	November	December	Average	
4	Rent	850	850	850	850	850	850		
5	Rental insurance	55	55	55	55	55	55		
6	Health insurance	120	120	120	120	120	120		
7	Electricity	129	135	110	151	168	173		
8	Utilities	53	62	49	32	55	61		
9	Telephone	73	81	67	80	82	75		
10	Groceries	143	137	126	150	147	173		
11	Gasoline	89	101	86	99	76	116		
12	Total								
13									

Case Study Apply Your Skills

Part 1

You are the office manager for Deering Industries. One of your responsibilities is to create a monthly calendar containing information on staff meetings, training, and due dates for time cards. Open **DICalendar.xlsx** and then insert the following information:

- Type the text November, 2015 in cell A2.
- Insert the days of the week (*Sunday*, *Monday*, *Tuesday*, *Wednesday*, *Thursday*, *Friday*, and *Saturday*) in cells A3 through G3. (Use the fill handle to fill in the days of the week and fill without formatting.)
- Insert the numbers *1* through *7* in cells A4 through G4.
- Insert in the calendar the remaining numbers of the days (numbers *8* through *14* in cells A6 through G6, numbers *15* through *21* in cells A8 through G8, numbers *22* through *28* in cells A10 through G10, and numbers *29* and *30* in cells A12 and B12. If you use the fill handle, fill without formatting.
- Excel training will be held Thursday, November 5, from 9:00 to 11:00 a.m. Insert this information in cell E5. (Insert the text on two lines by typing Excel Training, pressing Alt + Enter to move the insertion point to the next line, and then typing 9-11 a.m.)
- A staff meeting is held the second and fourth Monday of each month from 9:00 to 10:00 a.m. Insert this information in cell B7 and cell B11.

- Time cards are due the first and third Fridays of the month. Insert in cells F5 and F9 information indicating that time cards are due.
- A production team meeting is scheduled for Tuesday, November 24, from 1:00 to 3:00 p.m. Insert this information in cell C11.

Save the workbook and name it **EL1-C1-CS-DICalendar**. Print and then close the workbook.

Part 2

The manager of the purchasing department has asked you to prepare a worksheet containing information on quarterly purchases. Open **DIExpenditures.xlsx** and then insert the data as shown in Figure 1.16. After typing the data, insert in the appropriate cells formulas to calculate averages and totals. Apply comma formatting to cells F5 through F8. Save the workbook and name it **EL1-C1-CS-DIExpenditures**. Print and then close the workbook.

Figure 1.16 Case Study, Part 2

	A	B	C	D	E	F	G
1	DEERING INDUSTRIES						
2	PURCHASING DEPARTMENT - EXPENDITURES						
3	*Category*					*Average*	
4	**Supplies**	$ 645.75	$ 756.25	$ 534.78	$ 78,950.00		
5	**Equipment**	4,520.55	10,789.35	3,825.00	12,890.72		
6	**Furniture**	458.94	2,490.72	851.75	743.20		
7	**Training**	1,000.00	250.00	1,200.00	800.00		
8	**Software**	249.00	1,574.30	155.45	3,458.70		
9	**Total**						
10							

Part 3

The manager of the purchasing department has asked you to prepare a note to the finances coordinator, Jennifer Strauss. In Word, type a note to Jennifer Strauss explaining that you have prepared an Excel worksheet with the purchasing department expenditures. You are including the cells from the worksheet containing the expenditure information. In Excel, open **EL1-C1-CS-DIExpenditures.xlsx**, copy cells A3 through F9, and then paste them in the Word document. Make any corrections to the table so the information is readable. Save the document and name it **EL1-C1-CS-DINotetoJS**. Print and then close the document. Close **EL1-C1-CS-DIExpenditures.xlsx**.

Part 4

You will be ordering copy machines for several departments in the company and have decided to research prices. Using the Internet, find three companies that sell copiers and write down information on different copier models. Open **DICopiers.xlsx** and then type the company, model number, and price in the designated cells. Save the completed workbook and name it **EL1-C1-CS-DICopiers**. Print and then close **EL1-C1-CS-DICopiers.xlsx**.

WWW

MICROSOFT® EXCEL®

Inserting Formulas in a Worksheet

PERFORMANCE OBJECTIVES

Upon successful completion of Chapter 2, you will be able to:

- **Write formulas with mathematical operators**
- **Type a formula in the Formula bar**
- **Copy a formula**
- **Use the Insert Function feature to insert a formula in a cell**
- **Write formulas with the AVERAGE, MAX, MIN, COUNT, NOW, and TODAY functions**
- **Create absolute and mixed cell references**

Tutorials

2.1 Performing Calculations Using Formulas

2.2 Copying and Testing Formulas

2.3 Using Statistical Functions

2.4 Writing Formulas with Date Functions and Dates

2.5 Displaying Formulas in a Worksheet

2.6 Creating Formulas and Absolute Addressing

Excel is a powerful decision-making tool containing data that can be manipulated to answer "What if?" situations. Insert a formula in a worksheet and then manipulate the data to make projections, answer specific questions, and plan for the future. For example, the owner of a company might prepare a worksheet on production costs and then determine the impact on company revenues if production is increased or decreased. Insert a formula in a worksheet to perform calculations on values. A formula contains a mathematical operator, value, cell reference, cell range, and function. Formulas can be written that add, subtract, multiply, and/or divide values. Formulas can also be written that calculate averages, percentages, minimum and maximum values, and much more. As you learned in Chapter 1, Excel includes an AutoSum button in the Editing group on the HOME tab that inserts a formula to calculate the total of a range of cells and also includes some commonly used formulas. Along with the AutoSum button, Excel includes a FORMULAS tab that offers a variety of functions to create formulas. Model answers for this chapter's projects appear on the following pages.

Note: Before beginning the projects, copy to your storage medium the EL1C2 subfolder from the EL1 folder on the CD that accompanies this textbook and make EL1C2 the active folder.

Highland Construction

Customer	Actual	Planned	Difference
Sellar Corporation	$ 30,349	$ 34,109	$ 3,760
Main Street Photos	46,425	48,100	1,675
Sunset Automotive	34,192	32,885	(1,307)
Linstrom Enterprises	63,293	60,000	(3,293)
Morcos Media	29,400	30,500	1,100
Green Valley Optics	57,415	58,394	979
Detailed Designs	14,115	13,100	(1,015)
Arrowstar Company	87,534	86,905	(629)

Name	Hours	Rate	Salary
Carolyn Bentley	35	$ 23.15	$ 810.25
Lindon Cassini	28	19.00	532.00
Michelle DeFord	40	19.10	764.00
Javier Farias	24	16.45	394.80
Deborah Gould	24	11.50	276.00
William Jarman	15	11.50	172.50

Expense	Actual	Budget	% of Actual
Salaries	$ 126,000	$ 124,000	98%
Commissions	58,000	54,500	94%
Media space	8,250	10,100	122%
Travel expenses	6,350	6,000	94%
Dealer display	4,140	4,500	109%
Payroll taxes	2,430	2,200	91%
Telephone	1,450	1,500	103%

EQUIPMENT USAGE REPORT						
Hours	January	February	March	April	May	June
Total hours available	2,300	2,430	2,530	2,400	2,440	2,240
Avoidable delays	19	12	16	20	14	15
Unavoidable delays	9	8	6	12	9	10
Repairs	5	7	12	9	10	6
Servicing	6	13	7	6	4	5
Unassigned	128	95	85	135	95	75
In use	2,040	2,105	2,320	2,180	2,050	1,995
% of down time	11%	13%	8%	9%	16%	11%
Jan - March hours	7,260					
April - June hours	7,080					

Project 1 Insert Formulas in a Worksheet

EL1-C2-P1-HCReports.xlsx

Dollar Wise
Financial Services

Technical Support Department

Employee	Test 1	Test 2	Test 3	Average
Arnson, Patrick	91%	87%	82%	87%
Barclay, Jeanine	76%	74%	72%	74%
Calahan, Jack	67%	71%	65%	68%
Cumpston, Kurt	86%	91%	90%	89%
Donovan, Nancy	85%	89%	78%	84%
Fisher-Edwards, Teri	70%	70%	70%	70%
Flanery, Stephanie	70%	70%	72%	71%
Herbertson, Wynn	91%	80%	85%	85%
Jewett, Troy	97%	94%	92%	94%
Leibrand, Maxine	72%	63%	65%	67%
Markovits, Claude	68%	93%	70%	77%
Nyegaard, Curtis	90%	89%	88%	89%
Pherson, Douglas	72%	82%	55%	70%

Highest Test Average	94%
Lowest Test Average	67%
Average of All Tests	79%
Test 2 Completed	13
Test 3 Completed	13

Prepared by:
Student Name
9/18/2015 14:05

Project 2 Insert Formulas with Statistical Functions

EL1-C2-P2-DWTests.xlsx

Dollar Wise
Financial Services

Technical Support Department

Employee	Test 1	Test 2
Arnson, Patrick	0.91	0.87
Barclay, Jeanine	0.76	0.74
Calahan, Jack	0.67	0.71
Cumpston, Kurt	0.86	0.91
Donovan, Nancy	0.85	0.89
Fisher-Edwards, Teri	0.7	0.7
Flanery, Stephanie	0.7	0.7
Herbertson, Wynn	0.91	0.8
Jewett, Troy	0.97	0.94
Leibrand, Maxine	0.72	0.63
Markovits, Claude	0.68	0.93
Nyegaard, Curtis	0.9	0.89
Pherson, Douglas	0.72	0.82

Highest Test Average	=MAX(E4:E16)
Lowest Test Average	=MIN(E4:E16)
Average of All Tests	=AVERAGE(E4:E16)
Test 2 Completed	=COUNT(C4:C16)
Test 3 Completed	=COUNT(D4:D16)

Prepared by:
Student Name
=NOW()

Page 1

Test 3	Average
0.82	=AVERAGE(B4:D4)
0.72	=AVERAGE(B5:D5)
0.65	=AVERAGE(B6:D6)
0.9	=AVERAGE(B7:D7)
0.78	=AVERAGE(B8:D8)
0.7	=AVERAGE(B9:D9)
0.72	=AVERAGE(B10:D10)
0.85	=AVERAGE(B11:D11)
0.92	=AVERAGE(B12:D12)
0.65	=AVERAGE(B13:D13)
0.7	=AVERAGE(B14:D14)
0.88	=AVERAGE(B15:D15)
0.55	=AVERAGE(B16:D16)

Page 2

EL1-C2-P2-DWTests.xlsx, Formulas

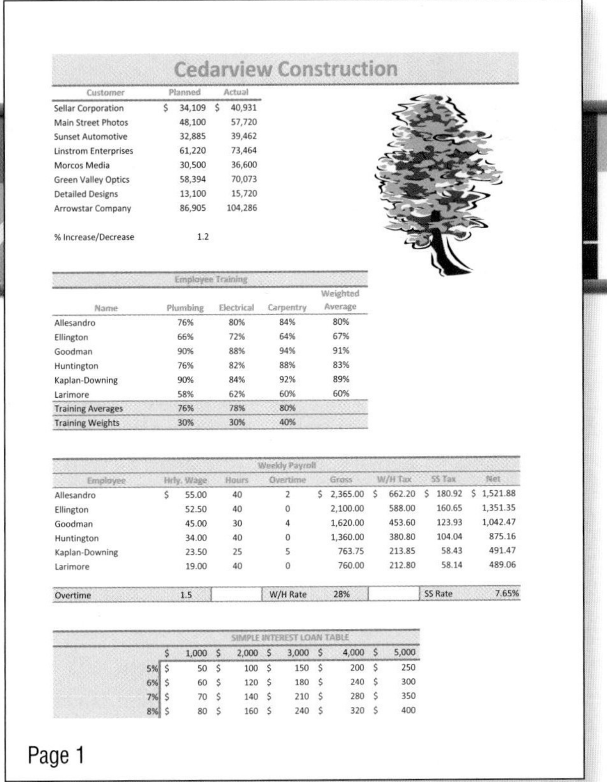

Cedarview Construction

Customer	Planned	Actual
Sellar Corporation	$ 34,109	$ 40,931
Main Street Photos	48,100	57,720
Sunset Automotive	32,885	39,462
Linstrom Enterprises	61,220	73,464
Morcos Media	30,500	36,600
Green Valley Optics	58,394	70,073
Detailed Designs	13,100	15,720
Arrowstar Company	86,905	104,286
% Increase/Decrease	1.2	

Employee Training

Name	Plumbing	Electrical	Carpentry	Weighted Average
Allesandro	76%	80%	84%	80%
Ellington	66%	72%	64%	67%
Goodman	90%	88%	94%	91%
Huntington	76%	82%	88%	83%
Kaplan-Downing	90%	84%	92%	89%
Larimore	58%	62%	60%	60%
Training Averages	76%	78%	80%	
Training Weights	30%	30%	40%	

Weekly Payroll

Employee	Hrly. Wage	Hours	Overtime	Gross	W/H Tax	SS Tax	Net
Allesandro	$ 55.00	40	2	$ 2,365.00	$ 662.20	$ 180.92	$ 1,521.88
Ellington	52.50	40	0	2,100.00	588.00	160.65	1,351.35
Goodman	45.00	30	4	1,620.00	453.60	123.93	1,042.47
Huntington	34.00	40	0	1,360.00	380.80	104.04	875.16
Kaplan-Downing	23.50	25	5	763.75	213.85	58.43	491.47
Larimore	19.00	40	0	760.00	212.80	58.14	489.06
Overtime	1.5		W/H Rate	28%		SS Rate	7.65%

SIMPLE INTEREST LOAN TABLE

	$ 1,000	$ 2,000	$ 3,000	$ 4,000	$ 5,000
5%	$ 50	$ 100	$ 150	$ 200	$ 250
6%	$ 60	$ 120	$ 180	$ 240	$ 300
7%	$ 70	$ 140	$ 210	$ 280	$ 350
8%	$ 80	$ 160	$ 240	$ 320	$ 400

Page 1

9%	$ 90	$ 180	$ 270	$ 360	$ 450
10%	$ 100	$ 200	$ 300	$ 400	$ 500
11%	$ 110	$ 220	$ 330	$ 440	$ 550
12%	$ 120	$ 240	$ 360	$ 480	$ 600
13%	$ 130	$ 260	$ 390	$ 520	$ 650
14%	$ 140	$ 280	$ 420	$ 560	$ 700
15%	$ 150	$ 300	$ 450	$ 600	$ 750

Page 2

Project 3 Insert Formulas Using Absolute and Mixed Cell References EL1-C2-P3-CCReports.xlsx

Project 1 Insert Formulas in a Worksheet — 4 Parts

You will open a worksheet containing data and then insert formulas to calculate differences, salaries, and percentages of budgets.

Writing Formulas with Mathematical Operators

As you learned in Chapter 1, the AutoSum button in the Editing group on the HOME tab creates the formula for you. You can also write your own formulas using ***mathematical operators***. Commonly used mathematical operators and their functions are displayed in Table 2.1. When writing your own formula, begin the formula with the equals sign (=). For example, to create a formula that divides the contents of cell B2 by the contents of cell C2 and inserts the result in cell D2, you would make D2 the active cell and then type *=B2/C2*.

After typing a formula in a cell, press the Enter key, the Tab key, Shift + Tab, or click Formula bar.

Table 2.1 Mathematical Operators

Operator	Function	Operator	Function
+	addition	/	division
-	subtraction	%	percentage
*	multiplication	^	exponentiation

Copying a Formula with Relative Cell References

Quick Steps

Copy a Formula Relatively
1. Insert formula in cell.
2. Select cell containing formula and all cells you want to contain formula.
3. Click Fill button.
4. Click desired direction.

Fill

In many worksheets, the same basic formula is used repetitively. In a situation where a formula is copied to other locations in a worksheet, use a ***relative cell reference***. Copy a formula containing relative cell references and the cell references change. For example, if you enter the formula *=SUM(A2:C2)* in cell D2 and then copy it relatively to cell D3, the formula in cell D3 displays as *=SUM(A3:C3)*. (Additional information on cell references is discussed later in this chapter in the "Using an Absolute Cell Reference in a Formula" section.)

To copy a formula relatively in a worksheet, use the Fill button or the fill handle. (You used the fill handle to copy a formula in Chapter 1.) To use the Fill button, select the cell containing the formula as well as the cells to which you want the formula copied and then click the Fill button in the Editing group on the HOME tab. At the Fill button drop-down list, click the desired direction. For example, if you are copying the formula down cells, click the *Down* option.

Project 1a **Finding Differences by Inserting and Copying a Formula** **Part 1 of 4**

1. Open **HCReports.xlsx**.
2. Save the workbook with Save As and name it **EL1-C2-P1-HCReports**.
3. Insert a formula by completing the following steps:
   a. Make cell D3 active.
   b. Type the formula =C3-B3.
   c. Press Enter.
4. Copy the formula to cells D4 through D10 by completing the following steps:
   a. Select cells D3 through D10.
   b. Click the Fill button in the Editing group on the HOME tab and then click *Down* at the drop-down list.
5. Save **EL1-C2-P1-HCReports.xlsx**.
6. With the worksheet open, make the following changes to cell contents:
   B4: Change *48,290* to *46425*
   C6: Change *61,220* to *60000*
   B8: Change *55,309* to *57415*
   B9: Change *12,398* to *14115*
7. Make cell D3 active, apply Accounting formatting, and then decrease the places past the decimal point to none.
8. Save **EL1-C2-P1-HCReports.xlsx**.

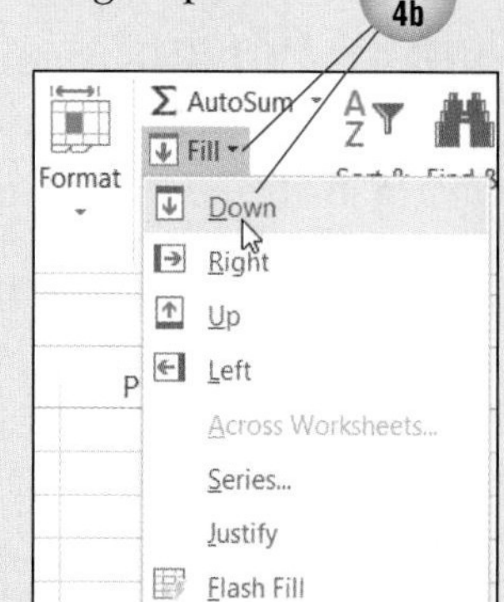

As you learned in Chapter 1, you can use the fill handle to copy a formula up, down, left, or right within a worksheet. To use the fill handle, insert the desired data in the cell (text, value, formula, etc.). With the cell active, position the mouse pointer on the fill handle until the mouse pointer turns into a thin, black cross. Hold down the left mouse button, drag and select the desired cells, and then release the mouse button. If you are dragging a cell containing a formula, a relative version of the formula is copied to the selected cells.

Use the fill handle to copy a relative version of a formula.

Checking Cell References in a Formula

To verify if a formula is using the correct cell references, double-click in a cell containing a formula and the cells referenced in the formula display with a colored border and shading in the worksheet. This feature makes identifying which cells are being referenced in a formula easy and is helpful when trying to identify errors that may occur in a formula.

Project 1b Calculating Salary by Inserting and Copying a Formula with the Fill Handle

Part 2 of 4

1. With **EL1-C2-P1-HCReports.xlsx** open, insert a formula by completing the following steps:
   a. Make cell D15 active.
   b. Click in the Formula bar text box and then type =C15*B15.
   c. Click the Enter button on the Formula bar.
2. Copy the formula to cells D16 through D20 by completing the following steps:
   a. Make sure cell D15 is still the active cell.
   b. Position the mouse pointer on the fill handle that displays at the lower right corner of cell D15 until the pointer turns into a thin, black cross.
   c. Hold down the left mouse button, drag down to cell D20, and then release the mouse button.
3. Save **EL1-C2-P1-HCReports.xlsx**.
4. Double-click in cell D20 to display the formula with cell references color coded to ensure the formula was copied relatively.
5. Make the following changes to cell contents in the worksheet:
   B16: Change *20* to *28*
   C17: Change *18.75* to *19.10*
   B19: Change *15* to *24*
6. Select cells D16 through D20 and then apply Comma formatting.
7. Save **EL1-C2-P1-HCReports.xlsx**.

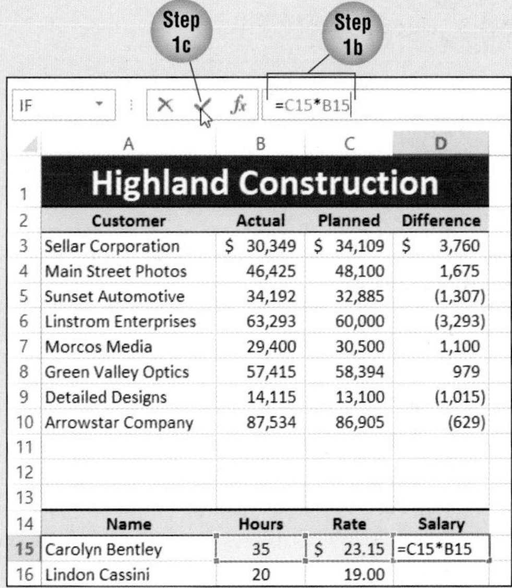

	A	B	C	D
1	Highland Construction			
2	Customer	Actual	Planned	Difference
3	Sellar Corporation	$ 30,349	$ 34,109	$ 3,760
4	Main Street Photos	46,425	48,100	1,675
5	Sunset Automotive	34,192	32,885	(1,307)
6	Linstrom Enterprises	63,293	60,000	(3,293)
7	Morcos Media	29,400	30,500	1,100
8	Green Valley Optics	57,415	58,394	979
9	Detailed Designs	14,115	13,100	(1,015)
10	Arrowstar Company	87,534	86,905	(629)
11				
12				
13				
14	Name	Hours	Rate	Salary
15	Carolyn Bentley	35	$ 23.15	=C15*B15
16	Lindon Cassini	20	19.00	

	A	B	C	D
13				
14	Name	Hours	Rate	Salary
15	Carolyn Bentley	35	$ 23.15	$ 810.25
16	Lindon Cassini	20	19.00	$ 380.00
17	Michelle DeFord	40	18.75	$ 750.00
18	Javier Farias	24	16.45	$ 394.80
19	Deborah Gould	15	11.50	$ 172.50
20	William Jarman	15	11.50	$ 172.50
21				

Writing a Formula by Pointing

Quick Steps

Write a Formula by Pointing

1. Click cell that will contain formula.
2. Type equals sign.
3. Click cell you want to reference in formula.
4. Type desired mathematical operator.
5. Click next cell reference.
6. Press Enter.

In Project 1a and Project 1b, you wrote formulas using cell references such as *=C3-B3*. Another method for writing a formula is to "point" to the specific cells that are to be part of the formula. Creating a formula by pointing is more accurate than typing the cell reference since a mistake can happen when typing the cell reference.

To write a formula by pointing, click in the cell that will contain the formula, type the equals sign to begin the formula, and then click in the cell you want to reference in the formula. This inserts a moving border around the cell and also changes the mode from Enter to Point. (The word *POINT* displays at the left side of the Status bar.) Type the desired mathematical operator and then click the next cell reference. Continue in this manner until all cell references are specified and then press the Enter key. This ends the formula and inserts the result of the calculation of the formula in the active cell. When writing a formula by pointing, you can also select a range of cells you want included in the formula.

Project 1c **Writing a Formula by Pointing that Calculates Percentage of Actual Budget** **Part 3 of 4**

1. With **EL1-C2-P1-HCReports.xlsx** open, enter a formula by pointing that calculates the percentage of actual budget by completing the following steps:
   a. Make cell D25 active.
   b. Type the equals sign (=).
   c. Click in cell C25. (This inserts a moving border around the cell and changes the mode from Enter to Point.)
   d. Type the forward slash symbol (/).
   e. Click in cell B25.
   f. Make sure the formula in D25 is *=C25/B25* and then press Enter.
2. Make cell D25 active, position the mouse pointer on the fill handle, drag down to cell D31, and then release the mouse button.
3. Save **EL1-C2-P1-HCReports.xlsx**.

	A	B	C	D
23				
24	Expense	Actual	Budget	% of Actual
25	Salaries	$ 126,000	$ 124,000	=C25/B25
26	Commissions	58,000	54,500	
27	Media space	8,250	10,100	
28	Travel expenses	6,350	6,000	
29	Dealer display	4,140	4,500	
30	Payroll taxes	2,430	2,200	
31	Telephone	1,450	1,500	

Steps 1a-1e

C	D
Budget	% of Actual
$ 124,000	98%
54,500	94%
10,100	122%
6,000	94%
4,500	109%
2,200	91%
1,500	103%

Step 2

Determining the Order of Operations

If a formula contains two or more operators, Excel uses the same ***order of operations*** used in algebra. From left to right in a formula, this order is negations (negative number—a number preceded by -) first, then percentages (%), then exponentiations (^), followed by multiplications (*), divisions (/), additions (+), and subtractions (-). If you want to change the order of operations, use parentheses around the part of the formula you want calculated first. For example, suppose you want to create a formula using cells A1, B1, and C1, and each cell contains the value *5*. If the formula is written as *=A1+B1*C1*, the result would be 30 (because 5*5=25 and 5+25=30). However, if you place parentheses around the first two cell references so the formula displays as *=(A1+B1)*C1*, the result would be 50 (because 5+5=10 and 10*5=50).

Excel requires each left parenthesis to be paired with a right parenthesis. If a formula is missing a left or right parenthesis, a message box will display explaining that an error exists in the formula and providing a possible correction, which you can accept or decline. This feature is useful when creating a formula that contains multiple layers of parentheses (called ***nested parentheses***) because it will identify any missing left or right parentheses in the formula. Parentheses can also be used in various functions to further determine the order of operations in the function.

Using the Trace Error Button

As you are working in a worksheet, you may occasionally notice a button pop up near the active cell. The general term for this button is ***smart tag***. The display of the smart tag button varies depending on the action performed. In Project 1d, you will insert a formula that will cause a smart tag button, named the Trace Error button, to appear. When the Trace Error button appears, a small, dark green triangle also displays in the upper left corner of the cell. Click the Trace Error button and a drop-down list displays with options for updating the formula to include specific cells, getting help with the error, ignoring the error, editing the error in the Formula bar, and completing an error check. In Project 1d, two of the formulas you insert return the desired results. You will click the Trace Error button, read information on what Excel perceives as the error, and then tell Excel to ignore the error.

Trace Error

Identifying Common Formula/Function Errors in Excel

Excel is a sophisticated program that requires data input and formula creation to follow strict guidelines in order to function properly. When guidelines that specify how data or formulas are entered are not followed, Excel will display one of many ***error codes***. When an error is identified with a code, determining and then fixing the problem is easier than if no information is provided. Table 2.2 lists some common error codes.

Most errors in Excel are the result of the user incorrectly inputting data into a worksheet. However, most error messages will not display until the data is used in a formula or function. Common mistakes made while inputting data include placing text in a cell that requires a number, entering data in the wrong location, and entering numbers in an incorrect format. Other errors are the result of entering a formula or function improperly. A formula will often display an error message if it is trying to divide a number by zero or it contains a circular reference (that is, when a formula within a cell uses the results of that formula in the same cell). Functions tend to display error messages if the arguments of a particular function are not correctly defined or if a function name is typed incorrectly.

Table 2.2 Common Error Codes

Error Code	*Meaning*
#DIV/O	A formula is attempting to divide a number by zero.
#N/A	An argument parameter has been left out of a function.
#NAME?	A function name is not entered correctly.
#NUM!	An argument parameter does not meet a function's requirements.
#REF!	A referenced cell no longer exists within a worksheet.
#VALUE	The data entered is the wrong type (for example, text instead of numbers).

Project 1d Writing a Formula by Pointing That Calculates Percentage of Down Time

1. With **EL1-C2-P1-HCReports.xlsx** open, enter a formula by pointing that computes the percentage of equipment down time by completing the following steps:
   a. Make cell B45 active.
   b. Type the equals sign followed by the left parenthesis (=().
   c. Click in cell B37. (This inserts a moving border around the cell and changes the mode from Enter to Point.)
   d. Type the minus symbol (-).
   e. Click in cell B43.
   f. Type the right parenthesis followed by the forward slash ()/).
   g. Click in cell B37.
   h. Make sure the formula in cell B45 is *=(B37-B43)/B37* and then press Enter.

34				
35	EQUIPMENT USAGE REPORT			
36	Hours	January	February	March
37	Total hours available	2,300	2,430	2,530
38	Avoidable delays	19	12	16
39	Unavoidable delays	9	8	6
40	Repairs	5	7	12
41	Servicing	6	13	7
42	Unassigned	128	95	85
43	In use	2,040	2,105	2,320
44				
45	% of down time	=(B37-B43)/B37		
46	Jan - March hours			
47	April - June hours			
48				

Steps 1a-1h

2. Make cell B45 active, position the mouse pointer on the fill handle, drag across to cell G45, and then release the mouse button.
3. Enter a formula by dragging through a range of cells by completing the following steps:
   a. Click in cell B46 and then click the AutoSum button in the Editing group on the HOME tab.
   b. Select cells B37 through D37.
   c. Click the Enter button on the Formula bar. (This inserts *7,260* in cell B46.)

Step 3c Step 3b

B37 =SUM(B37:D37)

	A	B	C	D	E
34					
35	EQUIPMENT USAGE REPORT				
36	Hours	January	February	March	April
37	Total hours available	2,300	2,430	2,530	2,400
38	Avoidable delays	19	12	16	20
39	Unavoidable delays	9	8	6	12
40	Repairs	5	7	12	9
41	Servicing	6	13	7	6
42	Unassigned	128	95	85	135
43	In use	2,040	2,105	2,320	2,180
44					
45	% of down time	11%	13%	8%	9%
46	Jan - March hours	=SUM(B37:D37)			
47	April - June hours	SUM(**number1**, [number2], ...)			

4. Click in cell B47 and then complete steps similar to those in Step 3 to create a formula that totals hours available from April through June (cells E37 through G37). (This inserts *7,080* in cell B47.)
5. Click in cell B46 and notice the Trace Error button that displays. Complete the following steps to read about the error and then tell Excel to ignore the error:
   a. Click the Trace Error button.
   b. At the drop-down list that displays, click the *Help on this error* option.
   c. Read the information that displays in the Excel Help window and then close the window.
   d. Click the Trace Error button again and then click *Ignore Error* at the drop-down list.

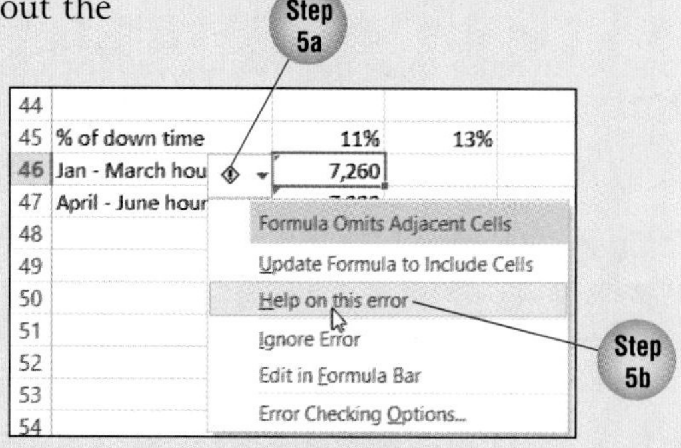

6. Remove the dark green triangle from cell B47 by completing the following steps:
   a. Click in cell B47.
   b. Click the Trace Error button and then click *Ignore Error* at the drop-down list.
7. Save, print, and then close **EL1-C2-P1-HCReports.xlsx**.

Project 2 Insert Formulas with Statistical Functions 4 Parts

You will use the AVERAGE function to determine average test scores, use the MINIMUM and MAXIMUM functions to determine lowest and highest averages, use the COUNT function to count the number of students taking a test, and display a formula in a cell rather than the result of the formula.

Inserting Formulas with Functions

In Project 2b in Chapter 1, you used the AutoSum button to insert the formula *=SUM(B2:B5)* in a cell. The beginning section of the formula, *=SUM*, is called a ***function***, and it is a built-in formula. Using a function takes fewer keystrokes when creating a formula. For example, using the *=SUM* function saved you from having to type each cell to be included in the formula with the plus (+) symbol between cell entries.

Excel provides other functions for writing formulas. A function operates on what is referred to as an ***argument***. An argument may consist of a constant, a cell reference, or another function. In the formula *=SUM(B2:B5)*, the cell range *(B2:B5)* is an example of a cell reference argument. An argument may also contain a ***constant***. A constant is a value entered directly into the formula. For example, if you enter the formula *=SUM(B3:B9,100)*, the cell range *B3:B9* is a cell reference argument and *100* is a constant. In this formula, 100 is always added to the sum of the cells.

When a value calculated by the formula is inserted in a cell, this process is referred to as ***returning the result***. The term *returning* refers to the process of calculating the formula and the term *result* refers to inserting the value in the cell.

fx

Insert Function

You can type a function in a cell in a worksheet or you can use the Insert Function button on the Formula bar or on the FORMULAS tab to help you write the formula. Figure 2.1 displays the FORMULAS tab, which provides the Insert Function button as well as other buttons for inserting functions in a worksheet. The Function Library group on the FORMULAS tab contains a number of buttons for inserting functions from a variety of categories, such as *Financial*, *Logical*, *Text*, and *Date & Time*.

Click the Insert Function button on the Formula bar or on the FORMULAS tab and the Insert Function dialog box displays, as shown in Figure 2.2. At the Insert Function dialog box, the most recently used functions display in the *Select a function* list box. Choose a function category by clicking the down-pointing arrow

Figure 2.1 FORMULAS Tab

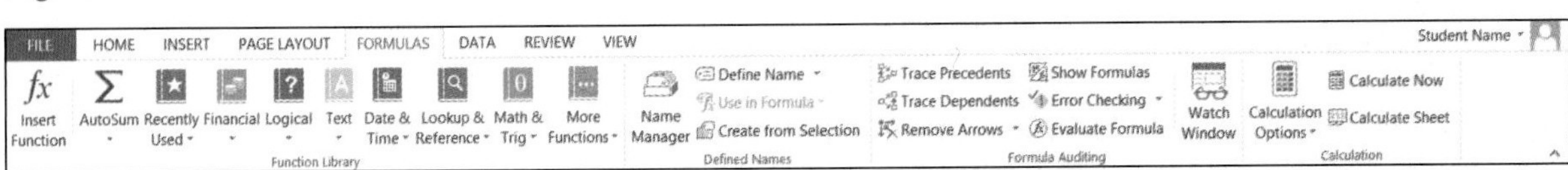

Figure 2.2 Insert Function Dialog Box

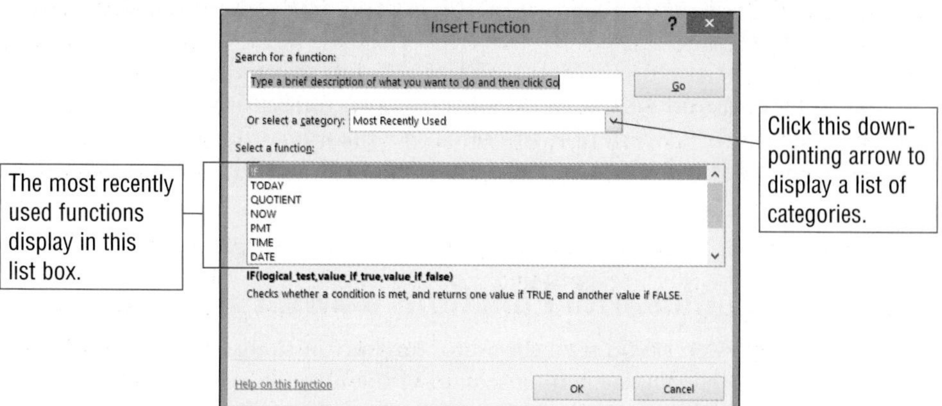

You can also display the Insert Function dialog box by clicking the down-pointing arrow at the right side of the AutoSum button and then clicking *More Functions.*

Click the AutoSum button arrow on the FORMULAS tab and common functions display in a drop-down list.

at the right side of the *Or select a category* option box and then clicking the desired category at the drop-down list. Use the *Search for a function* search box to locate a specific function.

With the desired function category selected, choose a function in the *Select a function* list box and then click OK. This displays a Function Arguments palette like the one shown in Figure 2.3. At this palette, enter in the *Number1* text box the range of cells you want included in the formula, any constants that are to be included as part of the formula, or another function. You can either type a cell reference or a range of cells in an argument text box or you can point to a cell or select a range of cells with the mouse pointer. Pointing to cells or selecting a range of cells using the mouse pointer is the preferred method of entering data into an argument text box because there is less chance of making errors. After entering a range of cells, a constant, or another function, click the OK button. You can include more than one argument in a function. If the function you are creating contains more than one argument, press the Tab key to move the insertion point to the *Number2* text box and then enter the second argument. If you need to display a specific cell or cells behind the function palette, move the palette by clicking and dragging it.

Figure 2.3 Example of a Function Arguments Palette

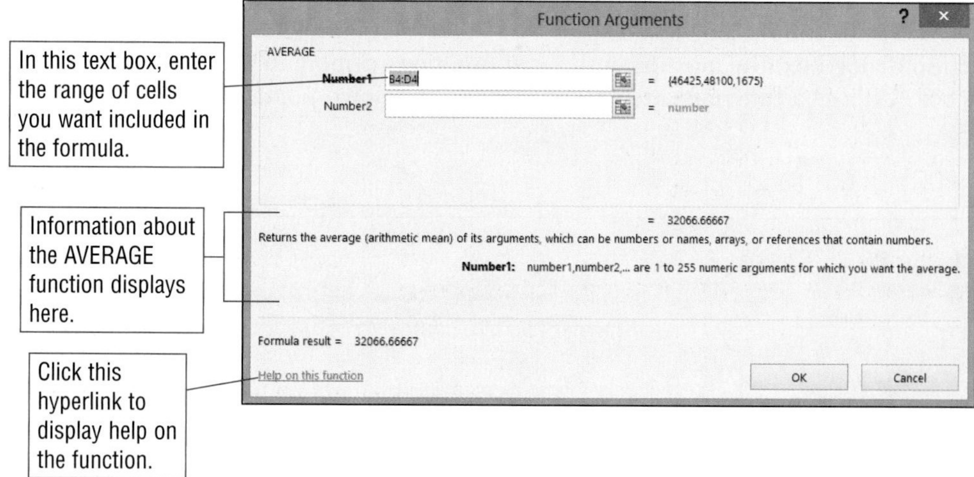

Excel performs over 300 functions that are divided into these 13 categories: *Financial*, *Date & Time*, *Math & Trig*, *Statistical*, *Lookup & Reference*, *Database*, *Text*, *Logical*, *Information*, *Engineering*, *Cube*, *Compatibility*, and *Web*. Clicking the AutoSum button in the Function Library group on the FORMULAS tab or the Editing group on the HOME tab automatically adds numbers with the SUM function. The SUM function is included in the *Math & Trig* category. In some projects in this chapter, you will write formulas with functions in other categories, including *Statistical* and *Date & Time*.

Excel includes the Formula AutoComplete feature that displays a drop-down list of functions. To use this feature, click in the desired cell or click in the Formula bar text box, type the equals sign (=), and then type the first letter of the desired function. This displays a drop-down list with functions that begin with the letter. Double-click the desired function, enter the cell references, and then press Enter.

Writing Formulas with Statistical Functions

In this section, you will learn to write formulas with the statistical functions AVERAGE, MAX, MIN, and COUNT. The AVERAGE function returns the average (arithmetic mean) of the arguments. The MAX function returns the largest value in a set of values, and the MIN function returns the smallest value in a set of values. Use the COUNT function to count the number of cells that contain numbers within the list of arguments.

Finding Averages

A common function in a formula is the ***AVERAGE function***. With this function, a range of cells is added together and then divided by the number of cell entries. In Project 2a, you will use the AVERAGE function, which will add all of the test scores for a student and then divide that number by the total number of tests. You will use the Insert Function button to simplify the creation of the formula containing an AVERAGE function.

One of the advantages to using formulas in a worksheet is that you can easily manipulate data to answer certain questions. In Project 2a, you will learn the impact of retaking certain tests on the final average score.

Project 2a **Averaging Test Scores in a Worksheet** **Part 1 of 4**

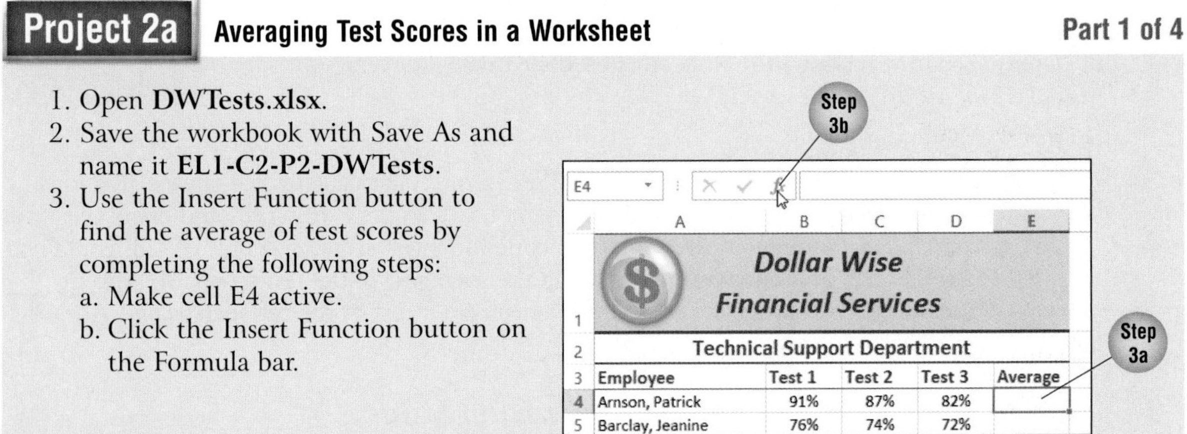

1. Open **DWTests.xlsx**.
2. Save the workbook with Save As and name it **EL1-C2-P2-DWTests**.
3. Use the Insert Function button to find the average of test scores by completing the following steps:
   a. Make cell E4 active.
   b. Click the Insert Function button on the Formula bar.

c. At the Insert Function dialog box, click the down-pointing arrow at the right side of the *Or select a category* option box and then click *Statistical* at the drop-down list.
d. Click *AVERAGE* in the *Select a function* list box.
e. Click OK.
f. At the Function Arguments palette, make sure *B4:D4* displays in the *Number1* text box. (If not, type B4:D4 in the *Number1* text box.)
g. Click OK.

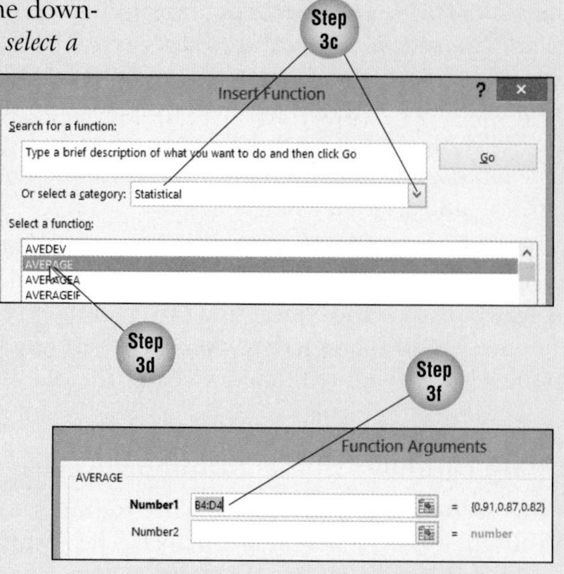

4. Copy the formula by completing the following steps:
   a. Make sure cell E4 is still active.
   b. Position the mouse pointer on the fill handle until the pointer turns into a thin black cross.
   c. Hold down the left mouse button, drag down to cell E16, and then release the mouse button.
5. Save and then print **EL1-C2-P2-DWTests.xlsx**.
6. After viewing the averages of test scores, you notice that a couple of students have low averages. You decide to see what happens to these average scores if students make up the tests on which they scored the lowest. You decide that a student can score a maximum of 70% on a retake of the test. Make the following changes to test scores to see how the changes will affect the test averages:
   B9: Change *50* to *70*
   C9: Change *52* to *70*
   D9: Change *60* to *70*
   B10: Change *62* to *70*
   B14: Change *0* to *70*
   D14: Change *0* to *70*
   D16: Change *0* to *70*
7. Save and then print **EL1-C2-P2-DWTests.xlsx**. (Compare the test averages of Teri Fisher-Edwards, Stephanie Flanery, Claude Markovits, and Douglas Pherson to see how retaking the tests affected their final test averages.)

tment

Test 3	Average
82%	87%
72%	74%
65%	68%
90%	89%
78%	84%
60%	54%
72%	68%
85%	85%
92%	94%
65%	67%
0%	31%
88%	89%
0%	51%

Step 4c

When a formula such as the AVERAGE formula calculates cell entries, it ignores certain cell entries. The AVERAGE function will ignore text in cells and blank cells (not zeros). For example, in the worksheet containing test scores, a couple of cells contained a *0%* entry. This entry was included in the averaging of the test scores. To prevent including that particular test in the average, enter text in the cell such as *N/A* (for *not applicable*) or leave the cell blank.

Finding Maximum and Minimum Values

The ***MAX function*** in a formula returns the maximum value in a cell range and the ***MIN function*** returns the minimum value in a cell range. As an example, you could use the MAX and MIN functions in a worksheet containing employee hours to determine which employee worked the most number of hours and which worked the least. In a worksheet containing sales commissions, you could use the MAX and MIN functions to determine the salesperson who earned the most commission dollars and the one who earned the least.

Insert a MAX or a MIN function into a formula in the same manner as an AVERAGE function. In Project 2b, you will use the Formula AutoComplete feature to insert the MAX function in cells to determine the highest test score average and the Insert Function button to insert the MIN function to determine the lowest test score average.

Project 2b Finding Maximum and Minimum Values in a Worksheet — Part 2 of 4

1. With **EL1-C2-P2-DWTests.xlsx** open, type the following in the specified cells:
   A19: Highest Test Average
   A20: Lowest Test Average
   A21: Average of All Tests
2. Insert a formula to identify the highest test score average by completing the following steps:
   a. Make cell B19 active.
   b. Type =M. (This displays the Formula AutoComplete list.)
   c. Double-click *MAX* in the Formula AutoComplete list.
   d. Type E4:E16) and then press Enter.

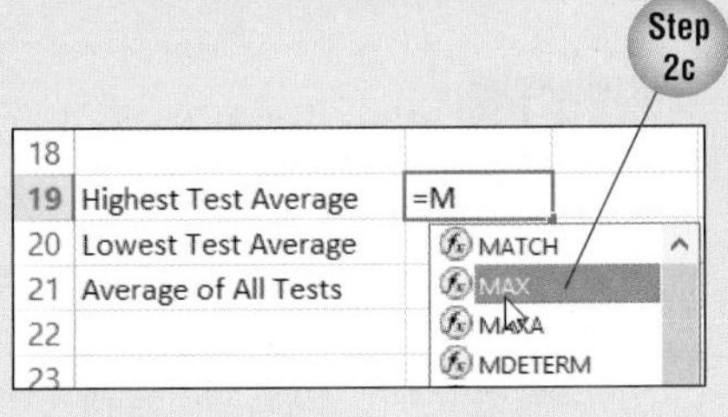

3. Insert a formula to identify the lowest test score average by completing the following steps:
   a. Make sure cell B20 is active.
   b. Click the Insert Function button on the Formula bar.
   c. At the Insert Function dialog box, make sure *Statistical* is selected in the *Or select a category* option box, and then click *MIN* in the *Select a function* list box. (You will need to scroll down the list to display *MIN*.)
   d. Click OK.
   e. At the Function Arguments palette, type E4:E16 in the *Number1* text box.
   f. Click OK.

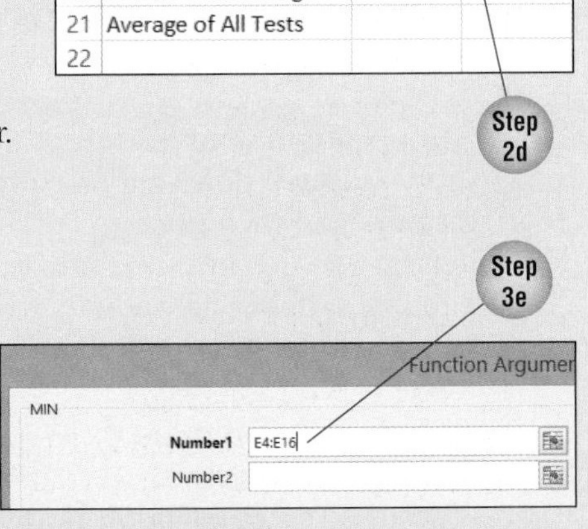

4. Insert a formula to determine the average of all test scores by completing the following steps:
   a. Make cell B21 active.
   b. Click the FORMULAS tab.
   c. Click the Insert Function button in the Function Library group.
   d. At the Insert Function dialog box, make sure *Statistical* is selected in the *Or select a category* option box and then click *AVERAGE* in the *Select a function* list box.
   e. Click OK.
   f. At the Function Arguments palette, make sure the insertion point is positioned in the *Number1* text box with existing text selected, use the mouse pointer to select the range E4:E16 in the worksheet, (you may need to move the palette to display the cells) and then click OK.

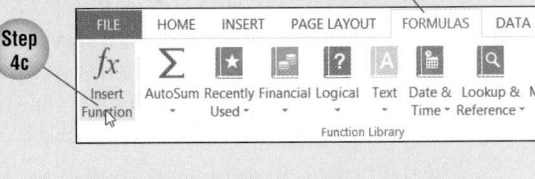

5. Save and then print **EL1-C2-P2-DWTests.xlsx**.
6. Change the *70%* values (which were previously *0%*) in cells B14, D14, and D16 to *N/A*. (This will cause the average test scores for Claude Markovits and Douglas Pherson to increase and will change the minimum number and average of all test scores.)
7. Save and then print **EL1-C2-P2-DWTests.xlsx**.

Counting Numbers in a Range

Use the ***COUNT function*** to count the numeric values in a range. For example, in a range of cells containing cells with text and cells with numbers, you can count how many cells in the range contain numbers. In Project 2c, you will use the COUNT function to specify the number of students taking Test 2 and Test 3. In the worksheet, the cells containing the text N/A are not counted by the COUNT function.

Project 2c **Counting the Number of Students Taking Tests** **Part 3 of 4**

1. With **EL1-C2-P2-DWTests.xlsx** open, make cell A22 active.
2. Type **Test 2 Completed**.
3. Make cell B22 active.
4. Insert a formula counting the number of students who have taken Test 2 by completing the following steps:
   a. With cell B22 active, click in the Formula bar text box.
   b. Type **=C**.
   c. At the Formula AutoComplete list that displays, scroll down the list until *COUNT* displays and then double-click *COUNT*.
   d. Type **C4:C16)** and then press Enter.

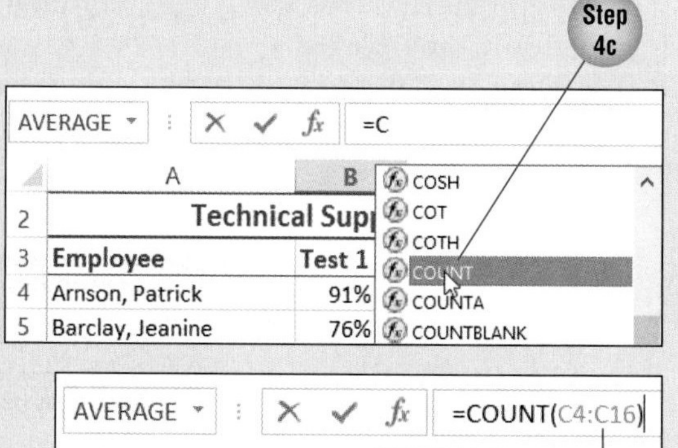

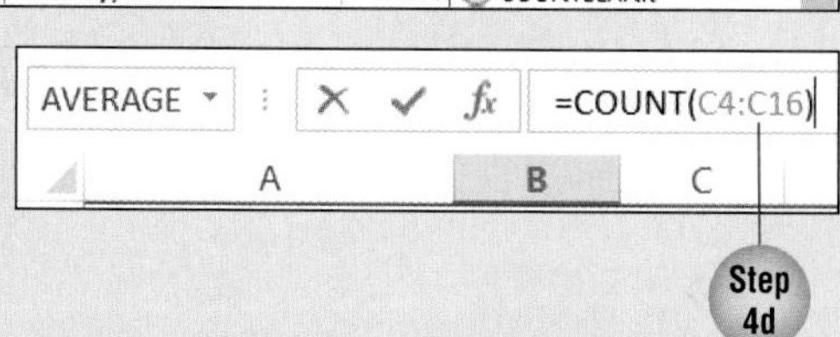

5. Count the number of students who have taken Test 3 by completing the following steps:
   a. Make cell A23 active.
   b. Type **Test 3 Completed**.
   c. Make cell B23 active.
   d. Click the Insert Function button on the Formula bar.
   e. At the Insert Function dialog box, make sure *Statistical* is selected in the *Or select a category* option box.
   f. Scroll down the list of functions in the *Select a function* list box until *COUNT* is visible and then double-click *COUNT*.
   g. At the formula palette, type **D4:D16** in the *Value1* text box and then click OK.
6. Save and then print **EL1-C2-P2-DWTests.xlsx**.
7. Add the test scores by completing the following steps:
   a. Make cell B14 active and then type **68**.
   b. Make cell D14 active and then type **70**.
   c. Make cell D16 active and then type **55**.
   d. Press Enter.
8. Save and then print **EL1-C2-P2-DWTests.xlsx**.

Writing Formulas with the NOW and TODAY Functions

The NOW and TODAY functions are part of the *Date & Time* category of functions. The ***NOW function*** returns the current date and time in a date and time format. The ***TODAY function*** returns the current date in a date format. Both the NOW and TODAY functions automatically update when a workbook is opened. To access the NOW and TODAY functions, click the Date & Time button in the Function Library group on the FORMULAS tab. You can also access these functions at the Insert Function dialog box.

Date & Time

The NOW and TODAY functions can also be updated without closing and then reopening the workbook. To update a workbook that contains a NOW or TODAY function, click the Calculate Now button in the Calculation group on the FORMULAS tab or press the F9 function key.

Calculate Now

Displaying Formulas

In some situations, you may need to display the formulas in a worksheet rather than the results of the formula. For instance, you may want to turn on formulas for auditing purposes or to check formulas for accuracy. Display all formulas in a worksheet, rather than the results, by clicking the FORMULAS tab and then clicking the Show Formulas button in the Formula Auditing group. You can also turn on the display of formulas with the keyboard shortcut Ctrl + `. (This is the grave accent, generally located to the left of the 1 key on the keyboard.) Press Ctrl + ` to turn off the display of formulas or click the Show Formulas button on the FORMULAS tab.

Press Ctrl + ` to display formulas in a worksheet rather than the results.

Show Formulas

Project 2d **Using a NOW Function and Displaying Formulas** **Part 4 of 4**

1. With **EL1-C2-P2-DWTests.xlsx** open, make cell A26 active and then type **Prepared by:**.
2. Make cell A27 active and then type your first and last names.
3. Insert the current date and time by completing the following steps:
   a. Make cell A28 active.
   b. Click the Date & Time button in the Function Library group on the FORMULAS tab and then click *NOW* at the drop-down list.
   c. At the Function Arguments palette telling you that the function takes no argument, click OK.
4. Update the time in cell A28 by completing the following steps:
   a. Wait for 1 minute.
   b. Click the Calculate Now button in the Calculations group on the FORMULAS tab.
5. Click the Show Formulas button in the Formula Auditing group to turn on the display of formulas.
6. Print the worksheet with the formulas. (The worksheet will print on two pages.)
7. Press Ctrl + ` to turn off the display of formulas.
8. Save, print, and then close **EL1-C2-P2-DWTests.xlsx**.

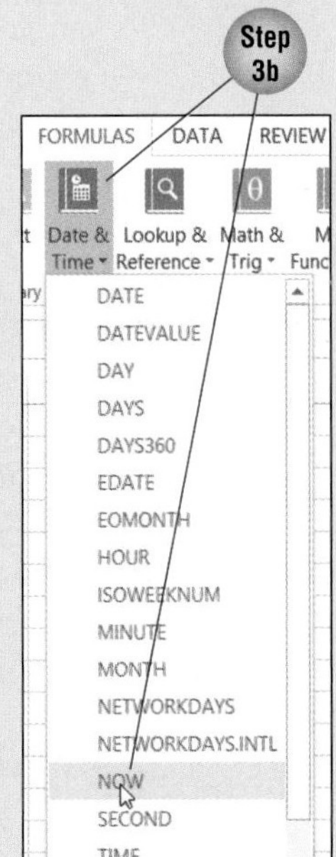

Project 3 Insert Formulas Using Absolute and Mixed Cell References

4 Parts

You will insert a formula containing an absolute cell reference that determines the effect on earnings with specific increases, insert a formula with multiple absolute cell references that determine the weighted average of scores, and use mixed cell references to determine simple interest.

Using Absolute and Mixed Cell References in Formulas

A reference identifies a cell or a range of cells in a worksheet and can be relative, absolute, or mixed. A ***relative cell reference*** refers to a cell relative to a position in a formula. An ***absolute cell reference*** refers to a cell in a specific location. When a formula is copied, a relative cell reference adjusts while an absolute cell reference remains constant. A ***mixed cell reference*** does both: either the column remains absolute and the row is relative or the column is relative and the row remains absolute. Distinguish among relative, absolute, and mixed cell references using the dollar sign ($). Type a dollar sign before the column and/or row cell reference in a formula to specify that the column or row is an absolute cell reference.

Using an Absolute Cell Reference in a Formula

In this chapter, you have learned to copy a relative formula. For example, if the formula *=SUM(A2:C2)* in cell D2 is copied relatively to cell D3, the formula changes to *=SUM(A3:C3)*. In some situations, you may want a formula to contain an absolute cell reference, which always refers to a cell in a specific location. In Project 3a, you will add a column for projected job earnings and then perform "What if?" situations using a formula with an absolute cell reference. To identify an absolute cell reference, insert a $ sign before the row and the column. For example, the absolute cell reference C12 would be typed as *$C$12* in a formula.

Project 3a Inserting and Copying a Formula with an Absolute Cell Reference

Part 1 of 4

1. Open **CCReports.xlsx**.
2. Save the workbook with Save As and name it **EL1-C2-P3-CCReports**.
3. Determine the effect on actual job earnings with a 10% increase by completing the following steps:
   a. Make cell C3 active, type the formula **=B3*$B$12**, and then press Enter.
   b. Make cell C3 active and then use the fill handle to copy the formula to cells C4 through C10.
   c. Make cell C3 active, click the Accounting Number Format button on the HOME tab, and then click the Decrease Decimal button twice.

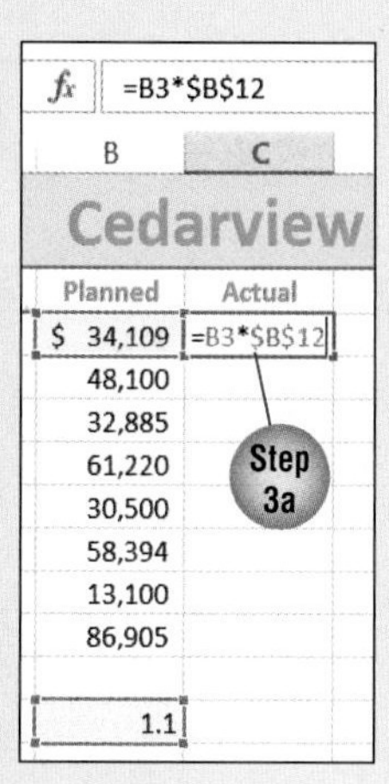

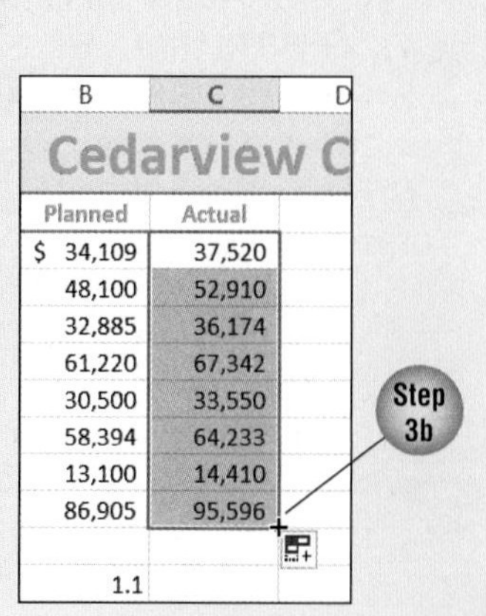

4. Save and then print **EL1-C2-P3-CCReports.xlsx**.
5. With the worksheet still open, determine the effect on actual job earnings with a 10% decrease by completing the following steps:
   a. Make cell B12 active.
   b. Type 0.9 and then press Enter.
6. Save and then print the **EL1-C2-P3-CCReports.xlsx**.
7. Determine the effects on actual job earnings with a 20% increase. (To do this, type 1.2 in cell B12 and then press Enter.)
8. Save and then print **EL1-C2-P3-CCReports.xlsx**.

B	C
Cedarview	
Planned	Actual
$ 34,109	$ 30,698
48,100	43,290
32,885	29,597
61,220	55,098
30,500	27,450
58,394	52,555
13,100	11,790
86,905	78,215
0.9	

Step 5b

In Project 3a, you created a formula with one absolute cell reference. You can also create a formula with multiple absolute cell references. For example, in Project 3b. you will create a formula that contains both relative and absolute cell references to determine the average of training scores based on specific weight percentages. In a weighted average, some scores have more value (weight) than others. For example, in project 3b, you will create a formula that determines the weighted average of training scores that gives more weight to the Carpentry percentages then the Plumbing or Electrical percentages.

Project 3b Inserting and Copying a Formula with Multiple Absolute Cell References

Part 2 of 4

1. With **EL1-C2-P3-CCReports.xlsx** open, insert the following formulas:
   a. Insert a formula in cell B23 that averages the percentages in cells B17 through B22.
   b. Copy the formula in cell B23 to the right to cells C23 and D23.
2. Insert a formula that determines the weighted average of training scores by completing the following steps:
   a. Make cell E17 active.
   b. Type the following formula:
      =$B$24*B17+$C$24*C17+$D$24*D17
   c. Press the Enter key.
   d. Copy the formula in cell E17 down to cells E18 through E22.
   e. With cells E17 through E22 selected, click the Decrease Decimal button three times.
3. Save and then print **EL1-C2-P3-CCReports.xlsx**.
4. With the worksheet still open, determine the effect on weighted training scores if the weighted values change by completing the following steps:
   a. Make cell B24 active, type 30, and then press Enter.
   b. Make cell D24 active, type 40, and then press Enter.
5. Save and then print **EL1-C2-P3-CCReports.xlsx**.

Employee Training				
Name	Plumbing	Electrical	Carpentry	Weighted Average
Allesandro	76%	80%	84%	80%
Ellington	66%	72%	64%	67%
Goodman	90%	88%	94%	91%
Huntington	76%	82%	88%	83%
Kaplan-Downing	90%	84%	92%	89%
Larimore	58%	62%	60%	60%
Training Averages	76%	78%	80%	
Training Weights	30%	30%	40%	

Step 4a

Step 4b

Using a Mixed Cell Reference in a Formula

The formula you created in Step 3a in Project 3a contained a relative cell reference (B3) and an absolute cell reference ($B$12). A formula can also contain a mixed cell reference. As stated earlier, in a mixed cell reference, either the column remains absolute and the row is relative or the column is relative and the row remains absolute. In Project 3c, you will insert a number of formulas—two of which will contain mixed cell references. You will insert the formula *=E29*E$26* to calculate withholding tax and *=E29*H$36* to calculate social security tax. The dollar sign before each row indicates that the row is an absolute cell reference.

Project 3c **Determining Payroll Using Formulas with Absolute and Mixed Cell References** **Part 3 of 4**

1. With **EL1-C2-P3-CCReports.xlsx** open, make cell E29 active and then type the following formula that calculates the gross pay, including overtime (press Enter after typing each of the formulas):
   =(B29*C29+(B29*$B$36*D29))
2. Copy the formula in cell E29 down to cells E30 through E34.
3. Make cell F29 active and then type the following formula that calculates the amount of withholding tax:
   =E29*E$36
4. Copy the formula in cell F29 down to cells F30 through F34.
5. Make cell G29 active and then type the following formula that calculates the amount of social security tax:
   =E29*H$36
6. Copy the formula in cell G29 down to cells G30 through G34.
7. Make cell H29 active and then type the following formula that calculates net pay:
   =E29-(F29+G29)
8. Copy the formula in cell H29 down to cells H30 through H34.
9. Select cells E29 through H29 and then click the Accounting Number Format button.
10. Save **EL1-C2-P3-CCReports.xlsx**.

As you learned in Project 3c, a formula can contain a mixed cell reference. In Project 3d, you will create the formula *=$A41*B$40*. In the first cell reference in the formula, *$A41*, the column is absolute and the row is relative. In the second cell reference, *B$40*, the column is relative and the row is absolute. The formula containing the mixed cell reference allows you to fill in the column and row data using only one formula.

Identify an absolute or mixed cell reference by typing a dollar sign before the column and/or row reference or press the F4 function key to cycle through the various cell references. For example, type *=A41* in a cell, press F4, and the cell reference changes to *=$A$41*. Press F4 again and the cell reference changes to *=A$41*. The next time you press F4, the cell reference changes to *=$A41* and if you press it again, the cell reference changes back to *=A41*.

Project 3d Determining Simple Interest Using a Formula with Mixed Cell References

Part 4 of 4

1. With **EL1-C2-P3-CCReports.xlsx** open, make cell B41 the active cell and then insert a formula containing mixed cell references by completing the following steps:
   a. Type =A41 and then press the F4 function key three times. (This changes the cell reference to *$A41*.)
   b. Type *B40 and then press the F4 function key twice. (This changes the cell reference to *B$40*.)
   c. Make sure the formula displays as *=$A41*B$40* and then press Enter.

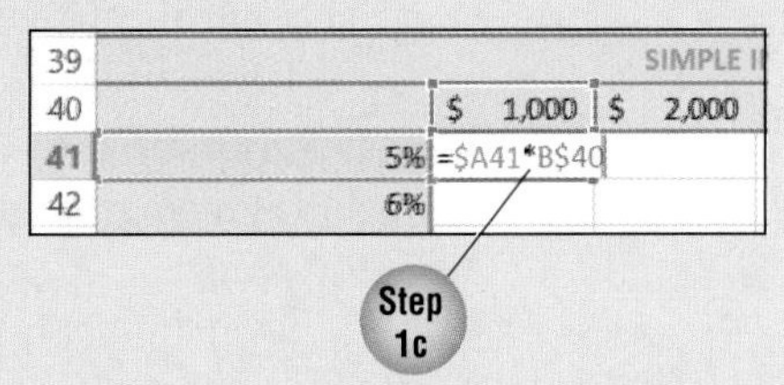

2. Copy the formula to the right by completing the following steps:
   a. Make cell B41 active and then use the fill handle to copy the formula right to cell F41.
   b. With cells B41 through F41 selected, use the fill handle to copy the formula down to cell F51.

	B	C	D	E	F
	SIMPLE INTEREST LOAN TABLE				
	$ 1,000	$ 2,000	$ 3,000	$ 4,000	$ 5,000
5%	$ 50	$ 100	$ 150	$ 200	$ 250
6%					

Step 2a

	B	C	D	E	F
	SIMPLE INTEREST LOAN TABLE				
	$ 1,000	$ 2,000	$ 3,000	$ 4,000	$ 5,000
5%	$ 50	$ 100	$ 150	$ 200	$ 250
6%	$ 60	$ 120	$ 180	$ 240	$ 300
7%	$ 70	$ 140	$ 210	$ 280	$ 350
8%	$ 80	$ 160	$ 240	$ 320	$ 400
9%	$ 90	$ 180	$ 270	$ 360	$ 450
10%	$ 100	$ 200	$ 300	$ 400	$ 500
11%	$ 110	$ 220	$ 330	$ 440	$ 550
12%	$ 120	$ 240	$ 360	$ 480	$ 600
13%	$ 130	$ 260	$ 390	$ 520	$ 650
14%	$ 140	$ 280	$ 420	$ 560	$ 700
15%	$ 150	$ 300	$ 450	$ 600	$ 750

Step 2b

3. Save, print, and then close **EL1-C2-P3-CCReports.xlsx**.

Chapter Summary

- Type a formula in a cell and the formula displays in the cell as well as in the Formula bar. If cell entries are changed, a formula automatically recalculates the values and inserts the result in the cell.
- Create your own formula with commonly used operators, such as addition (+), subtraction (-), multiplication (*), division (/), percentage (%), and exponentiation (^). When writing a formula, begin with the equals sign (=).
- Excel uses the same order of operations as algebra and that order can be modified by adding parentheses around certain parts of a formula.

- Copy a formula to other cells in a row or column with the Fill button in the Editing group on the HOME tab or with the fill handle that displays in the bottom right corner of the active cell.
- Double-click in a cell containing a formula and the cell references will display with a colored border and cell shading.
- Another method for writing a formula is to point to specific cells that are part of the formula as the formula is being built.
- If Excel detects an error in a formula, a Trace Error button appears and a dark green triangle displays in the upper left corner of the cell containing the formula.
- Excel displays different error codes for different formula errors. An error code helps identify an error in a formula by providing information on the specific issue.
- Excel performs over 300 functions that are divided into 13 categories.
- A function operates on an argument, which may consist of a cell reference, a constant, or another function. When a value calculated by a formula is inserted in a cell, this is referred to as returning the result.
- The AVERAGE function returns the average (arithmetic mean) of the arguments. The MAX function returns the largest value in a set of values and the MIN function returns the smallest value in a set of values. The COUNT function counts the number of cells containing numbers within the list of arguments.
- The NOW function returns the current date and time and the TODAY function returns the current date.
- Turn on the display of formulas in a worksheet with the Show Formulas button on the FORMULAS tab or with the keyboard shortcut Ctrl + ` (grave accent).
- A reference identifies a cell or a range of cells in a worksheet and can be relative, absolute, or mixed. Identify an absolute cell reference by inserting a dollar sign ($) before the column and row. Cycle through the various cell reference options by typing the cell reference and then pressing F4.

Commands Review

FEATURE	RIBBON TAB, GROUP	BUTTON	KEYBOARD SHORTCUT
display formulas	FORMULAS, Formula Auditing		Ctrl + `
cycle through cell references			F4
Insert Function dialog box	FORMULAS, Function Library	*fx*	Shift + F3
SUM function	HOME, Editing OR FORMULAS, Function Library	Σ	Alt + =
update formulas	FORMULAS, Calculation		F9

Concepts Check Test Your Knowledge 

Completion: In the space provided at the right, indicate the correct term, symbol, or command.

1. When typing a formula, begin the formula with this sign. ________________
2. This is the operator for division that is used when writing a formula. ________________
3. This is the operator for multiplication that is used when writing a formula. ________________
4. As an alternative to the fill handle, use this button to copy a formula relatively in a worksheet. ________________
5. To display cell references for a formula, perform this action on a cell containing a formula. ________________
6. A formula's order of operations can be modified with these. ________________
7. Excel inserts this symbol in a cell that may contain a possible error. ________________
8. A function operates on this, which may consist of a constant, a cell reference, or another function. ________________
9. This function returns the largest value in a set of values. ________________
10. This is the keyboard shortcut to display formulas in a worksheet. ________________
11. This function returns the current date and time. ________________
12. To identify an absolute cell reference, type this symbol before the column and row. ________________

Skills Check Assess Your Performance

Assessment 1

INSERT AVERAGE, MAX, AND MIN FUNCTIONS

1. Open **DISalesAnalysis.xlsx**.
2. Save the workbook with Save As and name it **EL1-C2-A1-DISalesAnalysis**.
3. Use the AVERAGE function to determine the monthly sales (cells H4 through H9).
4. Apply accounting formatting with no places past the decimal point to cell H4.
5. Total each monthly column, including the *Average* column (cells B10 through H10).
6. Use the MAX function to determine the highest monthly total (for cells B10 through G10) and insert the amount in cell B11.
7. Use the MIN function to determine the lowest monthly total (for cells B10 through G10) and insert the amount in cell B12.
8. Save, print, and then close **EL1-C2-A1-DISalesAnalysis.xlsx**.

Assessment 2

INSERT THE SUM FUNCTION AND ENTER FORMULAS WITH MATHEMATICAL OPERATORS

1. Open **CMQrtlyIncome.xlsx**.
2. Save the workbook with Save As and name it **EL1-C2-A2-CMQrtlyIncome**.
3. The manager of Capstan Marine needs a condensed quarterly statement of income for the third quarter. Insert each of the following formulas by typing the formula, using the pointing method, or using the AutoSum button.
   a. In cell B7, subtract cost of goods sold from sales by entering **=B5-B6**.
   b. In cell B12, add the three expenses by entering **=SUM(B9:B11)**.
   c. In cell B14, subtract total expenses from gross margin by entering **=B7-B12**.
   d. In cell B15, multiply net income before taxes by 22% and then subtract that value from net income before taxes by entering **=B14-(B14*22%)**.
4. Relatively copy the formulas in column B to columns C and D using the fill handle as follows.
   a. Fill the formula in cell B7 to cells C7 and D7 .
   b. Fill the formula in cell B12 to cells C12 and D12.
   c. Fill the formula in cell B14 to C14 and D14.
   d. Fill the formula in cell B15 to C15 and D15.
5. Insert the total in cell E5 by using the AutoSum button to add the range B5:D5.
6. Fill the SUM function in cell E5 to the range E6:E15. (Cells E8 and E13 will contain hyphens.)
7. Apply accounting formatting with a dollar sign and one place past the decimal point to cells B5 through E5.
8. Insert a TODAY function in cell A18.
9. Save, print, and then close **EL1-C2-A2-CMQrtlyIncome.xlsx**.

Assessment 3

WRITE FORMULAS WITH ABSOLUTE CELL REFERENCES

1. Open **CCQuotas.xlsx**.
2. Save the workbook with Save As and name it **EL1-C2-A3-CCQuotas**.
3. Make the following changes to the worksheet:
   a. Insert a formula using an absolute reference to determine the projected quotas with a 10% increase from the current quota.
   b. Save and then print **EL1-C2-A3-CCQuotas.xlsx**.
   c. Determine the projected quotas with a 15% increase from the current quota by changing cell A15 to *15% Increase* and cell B15 to *1.15*.
   d. Save and then print **EL1-C2-A3-CCQuotas.xlsx**.
   e. Determine the projected quotas with a 20% increase from the current quota.
4. Apply accounting formatting with no places after the decimal point to cell C4.
5. Save, print, and then close **EL1-C2-A3-CCQuotas.xlsx**.

Assessment 4

WRITE FORMULAS WITH MIXED CELL REFERENCES

1. Open **AASMileageChart.xlsx**.
2. Save the workbook with Save As and name it **EL1-C2-A4-AASMileageChart**.
3. Determine the mileage range of vehicles that have differing miles per gallon and fuel tank capacities by following these steps:
   a. In cell C5, multiply vehicle fuel tank capacity by vehicle miles per gallon rating by entering =B5*C4.
   b. Change the cell references in the formula so when it is copied, it will multiply the correct values in the chart. Either type dollar signs in the formula or press the F4 function key until the correct mixed cell references display. ***Hint: Refer to Project 3d for assistance.***
   c. Use the fill handle to complete the chart (fill without formatting).
4. Save, print, and then close **EL1-C2-A4-AASMileageChart.xlsx**.

Assessment 5

USE HELP TO LEARN ABOUT EXCEL OPTIONS

1. Learn more about using parentheses within formulas by completing the following steps:
   a. At a blank workbook, display the Excel Help window, click in the search text box, type overview of formulas, and then press Enter.

   b. Click the Overview of formulas article hyperlink and then scroll down approximately one-third of the article to the heading *Use of parentheses*.
   c. Read the information about using parentheses in formulas.
   d. Close the Excel Help window.
2. Open **ParenFormulas.xlsx**.
3. Save the workbook with Save As and name it **EL1-C2-A5-ParenFormulas**.
4. Change the results of the formulas individually (do not use the fill handle) in the range B6:B10 by editing the formulas to include parentheses. Consider writing the formulas on paper before inserting them in the cells. ***Note: The last formula will require nested parentheses.***

5. Once the formulas have been edited, compare the new results to the values in column C.
6. Make sure that YES displays in column D for each formula.
7. Turn on the display of formulas.
8. Save, print, and then close **EL1-C2-A5-ParenFormulas.xlsx**.

Visual Benchmark Demonstrate Your Proficiency

CREATE A WORKSHEET AND INSERT FORMULAS

1. At a blank workbook, type the data in the cells indicated in Figure 2.4 but **do not** type the data in the following cells. Instead, insert the formulas as indicated:
   - Cells D3 through D9: Insert a formula that calculates the salary.
   - Cells D14 through D19: Insert a formula that calculates the differences.
   - Cells B29 through D29: Insert a formula that calculates the averages.
   - Cells E24 through E28: Insert a formula that calculates the weighted average of test scores. ***Hint: Refer to Project 3b, Step 2, for assistance on writing a formula with weighted averages.***

   The results of your formulas should match the results you see in the figure.
2. Apply any other formatting so your worksheet looks similar to the worksheet shown in Figure 2.4.
3. Save the workbook and name it **EL1-C2-VB-Formulas**.
4. Print **EL1-C2-VB-Formulas.xlsx**.
5. Press Ctrl + ` to turn on the display of formulas and then print the worksheet again.
6. Turn off the display of formulas and then close the workbook.

Figure 2.4 Visual Benchmark

	A	B	C	D	E	F
1	Weekly Payroll					
2	Employee	Hours	Rate	Salary		
3	Alvarez, Rita	40	$ 22.50	$ 900.00		
4	Campbell, Owen	15	22.50	337.50		
5	Heitmann, Luanne	25	19.00	475.00		
6	Malina, Susan	40	18.75	750.00		
7	Parker, Kenneth	40	18.75	750.00		
8	Reitz, Collette	20	15.00	300.00		
9	Shepard, Gregory	15	12.00	180.00		
10						
11						
12	Construction Projects					
13	Project	Projected	Actual	Difference		
14	South Cascade	$145,000	$ 141,597	$ (3,403)		
15	Rogue River Park	120,000	124,670	4,670		
16	Meridian	120,500	99,450	(21,050)		
17	Lowell Ridge	95,250	98,455	3,205		
18	Walker Canyon	70,000	68,420	(1,580)		
19	Nettleson Creek	52,000	49,517	(2,483)		
20						
21						
22	Test Scores					
23	Employee	Test No. 1	Test No. 2	Test No. 3	Wgt. Avg.	
24	Coffey, Annette	62%	64%	76%	70%	
25	Halverson, Ted	88%	96%	90%	91%	
26	Kohler, Jeremy	80%	76%	82%	80%	
27	McKnight, Carol	68%	72%	78%	74%	
28	Parkhurst, Jody	98%	96%	98%	98%	
29	Test Averages	79%	81%	85%		
30	Test Weights	25%	25%	50%		
31						

Case Study Apply Your Skills

Part 1

You are the office manager for Allenmore Auto Sales and are responsible for preparing the monthly sales worksheet. Open **AASFebSales.xlsx** and then save the workbook with Save As and name it **EL1-C2-CS-AASFebSales**. Complete the workbook by inserting the following formulas:

- In column F, insert a formula that displays the gross profit, which is the price minus the dealer cost.
- In column H, insert a formula that multiplies the gross profit by the commission percentage.
- In column I, insert a formula that displays the net profit, which is the gross profit minus the total commission.
- Apply accounting formatting with a dollar sign to the amounts in cells D4, E4, F4, H4, and I4.

Save the workbook, print the workbook (it will print on two pages), and then close the workbook.

Part 2

The sales manager at Allenmore Auto Sales has asked you to determine the percentage of total commissions each salesperson has earned for the month of February. Open **AASFebCommissions.xlsx** and then save the workbook with Save As and name it **EL1-C2-CS-AASFebCommissions**. Insert a formula in cell C5 that divides B5 by the amount in cell C3. Use an absolute cell reference for cell C3 when writing the formula. Copy the formula down to cells C6 through C12. Save, print, and then close the workbook.

Part 3

You have created a workbook for automobile trade-ins for the month of February. The sales manager wants used automobiles to be wholesaled if they are not sold within a specific period of time. She wants you to determine the date each February trade-in is to be wholesaled. She wants any used automobile older than 2010 to be wholesaled after 45 days and any automobile newer than 2009 to be wholesaled after 60 days. Open **AASFebTradeIns.xlsx** and then save the workbook with Save As and name it **EL1-C2-CS-AASFebTradeIns**. Insert a formula in column G that adds 45 days to the date in column B for trade-ins 2009 and older and adds 60 days to trade-ins 2010 and newer. Save, print, and then close the workbook.

Part 4

The sales manager has asked you to locate at least two websites that provide estimates on the value of used automobiles (such as Kelley Blue Book (kbb.com) and Edmunds.com). She wants you to add at least two hyperlinks to the February trade-ins workbook. Sales people can use the hyperlinks in the worksheet to quickly determine the value of a used automobile. Use the Help feature to learn how to create hyperlinks in Excel. Open the **EL1-C2-CS-AASFebTradeIns.xlsx** workbook and save it with Save As and name it **EL1-C2-CS-AASFebTradeIns-2**. Add at least two hyperlinks to the workbook that link to websites that provide estimates on the value of used automobiles. Save, print, and then close the workbook.

MICROSOFT®

EXCEL®

Formatting an Excel Worksheet

PERFORMANCE OBJECTIVES

Upon successful completion of Chapter 3, you will be able to:

- **Change column widths**
- **Change row heights**
- **Insert rows and columns in a worksheet**
- **Delete cells, rows, and columns in a worksheet**
- **Clear data in cells**
- **Apply formatting to data in cells**
- **Apply formatting to selected data using the Mini toolbar**
- **Apply a theme and customize the theme font and color**
- **Format numbers**
- **Repeat the last action**
- **Automate formatting with Format Painter**
- **Hide and unhide rows and columns**

Tutorials

3.1 Adjusting Column Width and Row Height
3.2 Inserting and Deleting Columns and Rows
3.3 Applying Font Formatting
3.4 Applying Alignment Formatting
3.5 Applying Cell Styles and Themes
3.6 Formatting Numbers
3.7 Adding Borders and Shading to Cells
3.8 Using Format Painter
3.9 Hiding and Unhiding Columns and/or Rows

The appearance of a worksheet on the screen and how it looks when printed is called the ***format***. In Chapter 1, you learned how to apply basic formatting to cells in a worksheet. Additional types of formatting you may want to apply to a worksheet include changing column width and row height; applying character formatting such as bold, italic, and underlining; specifying number formatting; inserting and deleting rows and columns; and applying borders, shading, and patterns to cells. You can also apply formatting to a worksheet with a theme. A theme is a set of formatting choices that include colors and fonts. Model answers for this chapter's projects appear on the following page.

Note: Before beginning the projects, copy to your storage medium the EL1C3 subfolder from the EL1 folder on the CD that accompanies this textbook and then make EL1C3 the active folder.

Capstan Marine Products

Purchasing Department

Company	***Product #***	***Price***	***Number***	***Total***
RD Manufacturing	240-490-B	$ 85.75	7	$ 600.25
	443-22-0	148.50	8	1,188.00
	855-495	42.75	5	213.75
Ray Enterprises	S894-T	4.99	30	149.70
	B-3448	25.50	12	306.00
	43-GB-39	45.00	20	900.00
Sunrise Corporation	341-453	19.99	8	159.92
	CT-342	304.75	5	1,523.75
	83-492	9.75	35	341.25
	L-756-M	95.40	4	381.60
Geneva Systems	340-19	15.99	20	319.80
	T-3491-S	450.50	5	2,252.50
	900-599	35.95	15	539.25
	43-49CE	120.00	5	600.00
	Total			$9,475.77

Project 1 Format a Product Pricing Worksheet

EL1-C3-P1-CMProducts.xlsx

Stanton & Barnett Associates

Weekly Payroll

Employee	Hrly. Rate	Hours	Overtime	Gross	W/H Tax	SS Tax	Net
Lowell	$ 40.00	40	1	$ 1,660.00	$ 464.80	$ 126.99	$ 1,068.21
McIntyre	$ 40.00	40	3	$ 1,780.00	$ 498.40	$ 136.17	$ 1,145.43
Rawlings	$ 37.50	30	0	$ 1,125.00	$ 315.00	$ 86.06	$ 723.94
Fratzke	$ 32.00	40	2	$ 1,376.00	$ 385.28	$ 105.26	$ 885.46
Singleton	$ 25.00	25	0	$ 625.00	$ 175.00	$ 47.81	$ 402.19
Gleason	$ 22.00	40	1	$ 913.00	$ 255.64	$ 69.84	$ 587.52
Overtime	1.5		W/H Rate	28%		SS Rate	7.65%

Project 2 Apply a Theme to a Payroll Worksheet

EL1-C3-P2-SBAPayroll.xlsx

REAL PHOTOGRAPHY

Invoices

Invoice #	Client #	Service	Amount	Tax	Amount Due
2930	03-392	Family Portraits	$ 450.00	8.5%	$ 488.25
2942	02-498	Wedding Portraits	$ 1,075.00	8.8%	$ 1,169.60
2002	11-279	Development	$ 225.00	0.0%	$ 225.00
2007	04-325	Sports Portraits	$ 750.00	8.5%	$ 813.75
2376	03-392	Senior Portraits	$ 850.00	8.5%	$ 922.25
2129	11-279	Development	$ 350.00	0.0%	$ 350.00
2048	11-325	Wedding Portraits	$ 875.00	8.5%	$ 949.38
2054	04-325	Sports Portraits	$ 750.00	8.5%	$ 813.75
2064	05-665	Family Portraits	$ 560.00	8.8%	$ 609.28
2077	11-279	Development	$ 400.00	0.0%	$ 400.00
2079	04-325	Sports Portraits	$ 600.00	8.5%	$ 651.00
2908	55-340	Senior Portraits	$ 725.00	8.8%	$ 788.80
3001	11-279	Development	$ 310.00	8.8%	$ 337.28

Project 3 Format an Invoices Worksheet

EL1-C3-P3-RPInvoices.xlsx

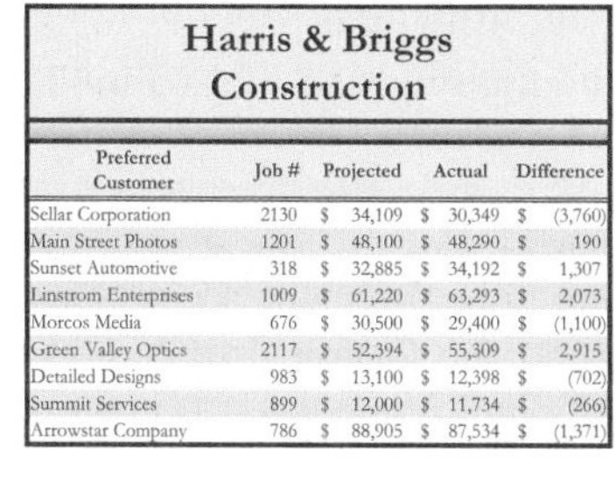

Harris & Briggs Construction

Preferred Customer	Job #	Projected	Actual	Difference
Sellar Corporation	2130	$ 34,109	$ 30,349	$ (3,760)
Main Street Photos	1201	$ 48,100	$ 48,290	$ 190
Sunset Automotive	318	$ 32,885	$ 34,192	$ 1,307
Linstrom Enterprises	1009	$ 61,220	$ 63,293	$ 2,073
Morcos Media	676	$ 30,500	$ 29,400	$ (1,100)
Green Valley Optics	2117	$ 52,394	$ 55,309	$ 2,915
Detailed Designs	983	$ 13,100	$ 12,398	$ (702)
Summit Services	899	$ 12,000	$ 11,734	$ (266)
Arrowstar Company	786	$ 88,905	$ 87,534	$ (1,371)

Project 4 Format a Company Budget Worksheet

EL1-C3-P4-HBCJobs.xlsx

Project 1 Format a Product Pricing Worksheet — 7 Parts

You will open a workbook containing a worksheet with product pricing data and then format the worksheet by changing column widths and row heights, inserting and deleting rows and columns, and clearing data in cells. You will also apply font and alignment formatting to data in cells.

Changing Column Width

Columns in a worksheet are the same width by default. In some worksheets, you may want to change column widths to accommodate more or less data. Change column width using the mouse on column boundaries or at a dialog box.

Changing Column Width Using Column Boundaries

As you learned in Chapter 1, you can adjust the width of a column by dragging the column boundary line or adjust a column width to the longest entry by double-clicking the boundary line. When you drag a column boundary, the column width displays in a box above the mouse pointer. The column width number that displays represents the average number of characters in the standard font that can fit in a cell.

You can change the width of selected adjacent columns at the same time. To do this, select the columns and then drag one of the column boundaries within the selected columns. As you drag the boundary, the column width changes for all selected columns. To select adjacent columns, position the cell pointer on the first desired column header (the mouse pointer turns into a black, down-pointing arrow), hold down the left mouse button, drag the cell pointer to the last desired column header, and then release the mouse button.

To change the width of all columns in a worksheet, click the Select All button and then drag a column boundary to the desired position.

Project 1a **Changing Column Width Using a Column Boundary** — **Part 1 of 7**

1. Open **CMProducts.xlsx**.
2. Save the workbook with Save As and name it **EL1-C3-P1-CMProducts**.
3. Insert a formula in cell D2 that multiplies the price in cell B2 with the number in cell C2. Copy the formula in cell D2 down to cells D3 through D14.
4. Change the width of column D by completing the following steps:
   a. Position the mouse pointer on the column boundary in the column header between columns D and E until it turns into a double-headed arrow pointing left and right.
   b. Hold down the left mouse button, drag the column boundary to the right until *Width: 11.00 (106 pixels)* displays in the box, and then release the mouse button.
5. Make cell D15 active and then insert the sum of cells D2 through D14.
6. Change the width of columns A and B by completing the following steps:
   a. Select columns A and B. To do this, position the cell pointer on the column A header, hold down the left mouse button, drag the cell pointer to the column B header, and then release the mouse button.

b. Position the cell pointer on the column boundary between columns A and B until it turns into a double-headed arrow pointing left and right.

c. Hold down the left mouse button, drag the column boundary to the right until *Width: 10.33 (100 pixels)* displays in the box, and then release the mouse button.

7. Adjust the width of column C to accommodate the longest entry by double-clicking on the column boundary between columns C and D.
8. Save **EL1-C3-P1-CMProducts.xlsx**.

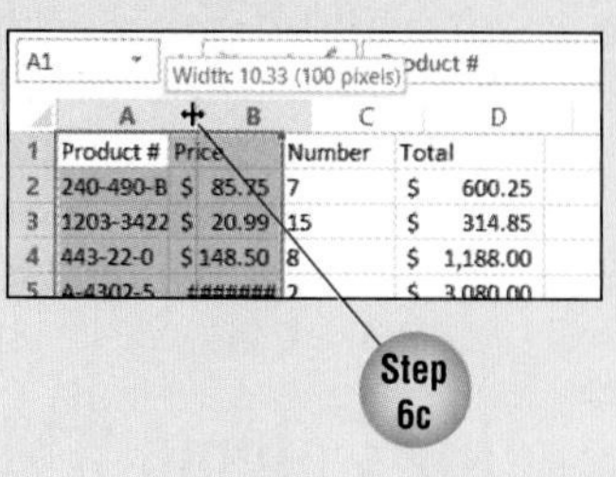

Changing Column Width at the Column Width Dialog Box

Quick Steps

Change Column Width

Drag column boundary line.

OR

Double-click column boundary.

OR

1. Click Format button.
2. Click *Column Width* at drop-down list.
3. Type desired width.
4. Click OK.

Format

At the Column Width dialog box, shown in Figure 3.1, you can specify a column width number. Increase the column width number to make the column wider or decrease the column width number to make the column narrower.

To display the Column Width dialog box, click the Format button in the Cells group on the HOME tab and then click *Column Width* at the drop-down list. At the Column Width dialog box, type the number representing the average number of characters in the standard font that you want to fit in the column and then press Enter or click OK.

Figure 3.1 Column Width Dialog Box

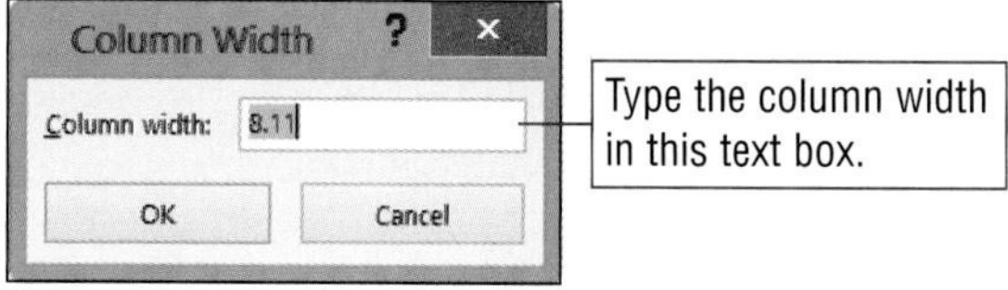

Project 1b **Changing Column Width at the Column Width Dialog Box** **Part 2 of 7**

1. With **EL1-C3-P1-CMProducts.xlsx** open, change the width of column A by completing the following steps:
   a. Make any cell in column A active.
   b. Click the Format button in the Cells group on the HOME tab and then click *Column Width* at the drop-down list.
   c. At the Column Width dialog box, type 12.7 in the *Column width* text box.
   d. Click OK to close the dialog box.
2. Make any cell in column B active and then change the width of column B to *12.5* by completing steps similar to those in Step 1.
3. Make any cell in column C active and then change the width of column C to *8* by completing steps similar to those in Step 1.
4. Save **EL1-C3-P1-CMProducts.xlsx**.

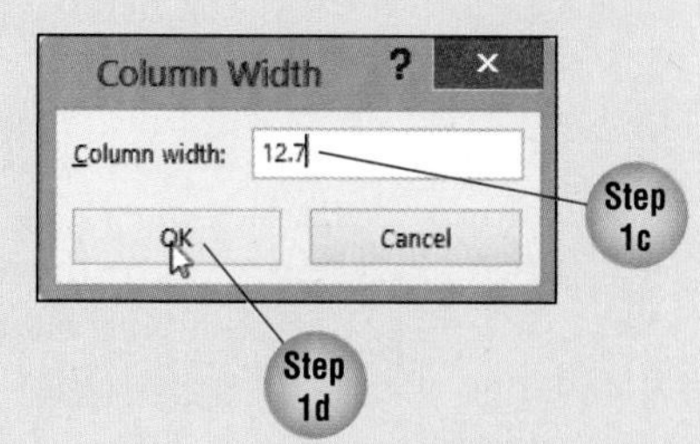

Changing Row Height

Row height can be changed in much the same manner as column width. For example, you can change the row height using the mouse on a row boundary or at the Row Height dialog box. Change row height using a row boundary in the same manner as you learned to change column width. To do this, position the cell pointer on the boundary between rows in the row header until it turns into a double-headed arrow pointing up and down, hold down the left mouse button, drag up or down until the row is the desired height, and then release the mouse button.

The height of selected rows that are adjacent can be changed at the same time. (The height of nonadjacent rows will not all change at the same time.) To do this, select the rows and then drag one of the row boundaries within the selected rows. As the boundary is being dragged, the row height changes for all selected rows.

As a row boundary is being dragged, the row height displays in a box above the mouse pointer. The row height number that displays represents a point measurement. A vertical inch contains approximately 72 points. Increase the point size to increase the row height; decrease the point size to decrease the row height.

At the Row Height dialog box, shown in Figure 3.2, you can specify a row height number. To display the Row Height dialog box, click the Format button in the Cells group on the HOME tab and then click *Row Height* at the drop-down list.

Quick Steps

Change Row Height
Drag row boundary line.
OR
1. Click Format button.
2. Click *Row Height* at drop-down list.
3. Type desired height.
4. Click OK.

To change the height of all rows in a worksheet, click the Select All button and then drag a row boundary to the desired position.

Excel measures row height in points and column width in characters.

Figure 3.2 Row Height Dialog Box

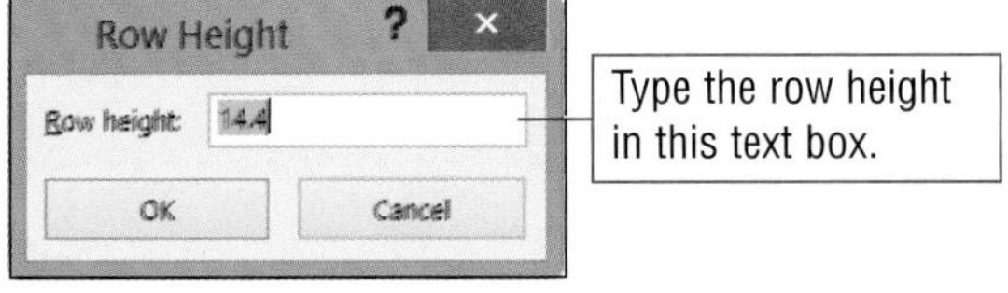

Project 1c **Changing Row Height** **Part 3 of 7**

1. With **EL1-C3-P1-CMProducts.xlsx** open, change the height of row 1 by completing the following steps:
   a. Position the cell pointer in the row header on the row boundary between rows 1 and 2 until it turns into a double-headed arrow pointing up and down.
   b. Hold down the left mouse button, drag the row boundary down until *Height: 19.80 (33 pixels)* displays in the box, and then release the mouse button.
2. Change the height of rows 2 through 14 by completing the following steps:
   a. Select rows 2 through 14. To do this, position the cell pointer on the number 2 in the row header, hold down the left mouse button, drag the cell pointer to the number 14 in the row header, and then release the mouse button.
   b. Position the cell pointer on the row boundary between rows 2 and 3 until it turns into a double-headed arrow pointing up and down.

c. Hold down the left mouse button, drag the row boundary down until *Height: 16.80 (28 pixels)* displays in the box, and then release the mouse button.

3. Change the height of row 15 by completing the following steps:
   a. Make cell A15 active.
   b. Click the Format button in the Cells group on the HOME tab and then click *Row Height* at the drop-down list.
   c. At the Row Height dialog box, type 20 in the *Row height* text box and then click OK.

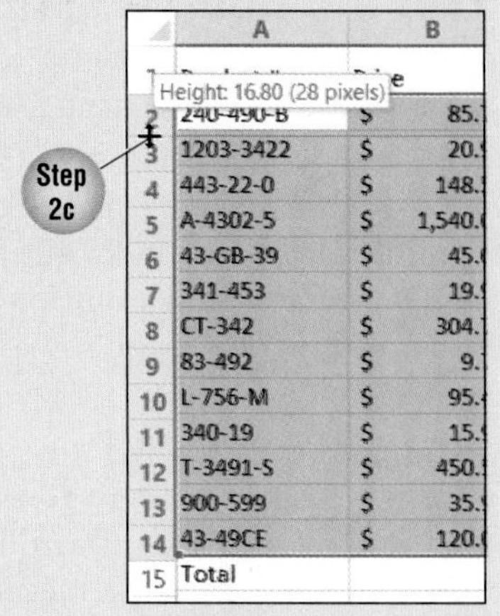

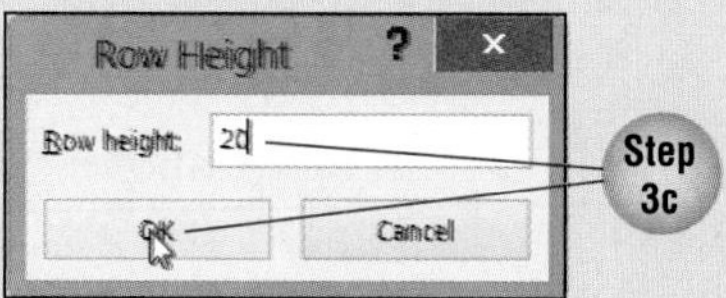

4. Save **EL1-C3-P1-CMProducts.xlsx**.

HINT When you insert cells, rows, or columns in a worksheet, all references affected by the insertion are automatically adjusted.

Inserting and Deleting Cells, Rows, and Columns

New data may need to be included in an existing worksheet. For example, a row or several rows of new data may need to be inserted into a worksheet or data may need to be removed from a worksheet.

Quick Steps

Insert a Row
Click Insert button.
OR
1. Click Insert button arrow.
2. Click *Insert Sheet Rows* at drop-down list.

OR
1. Click Insert button arrow.
2. Click *Insert Cells*.
3. Click *Entire row* in dialog box.
4. Click OK.

Insert

Inserting Rows

After you create a worksheet, you can add (insert) rows to the worksheet. Insert a row with the Insert button in the Cells group on the HOME tab or with options at the Insert dialog box. By default, a row is inserted above the row containing the active cell. To insert a row in a worksheet, select the row below where the row is to be inserted and then click the Insert button. If you want to insert more than one row, select the number of rows in the worksheet that you want inserted and then click the Insert button.

You can also insert a row by making a cell active in the row below where the row is to be inserted, clicking the Insert button arrow, and then clicking *Insert Sheet Rows*. Another method for inserting a row is to click the Insert button arrow and then click *Insert Cells*. This displays the Insert dialog box, as shown in Figure 3.3. At the Insert dialog box, click *Entire row*. This inserts a row above the active cell.

Figure 3.3 Insert Dialog Box

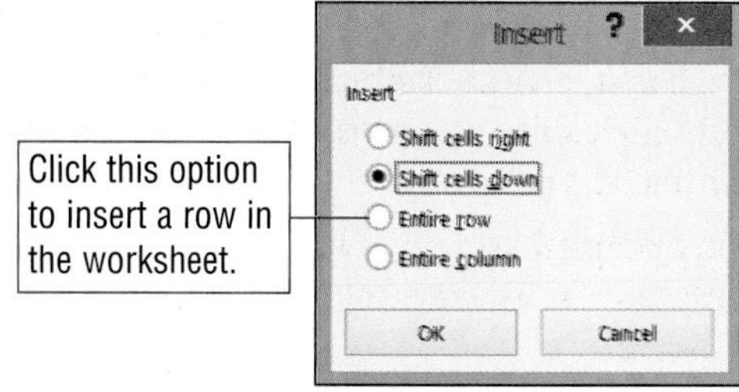

Project 1d Inserting Rows

Part 4 of 7

1. With **EL1-C3-P1-CMProducts.xlsx** open, insert two rows at the beginning of the worksheet by completing the following steps:
   a. Make cell A1 active.
   b. Click the Insert button arrow in the Cells group on the HOME tab.
   c. At the drop-down list that displays, click *Insert Sheet Rows*.
   d. With cell A1 active, click the Insert button arrow and then click *Insert Sheet Rows* at the drop-down list.

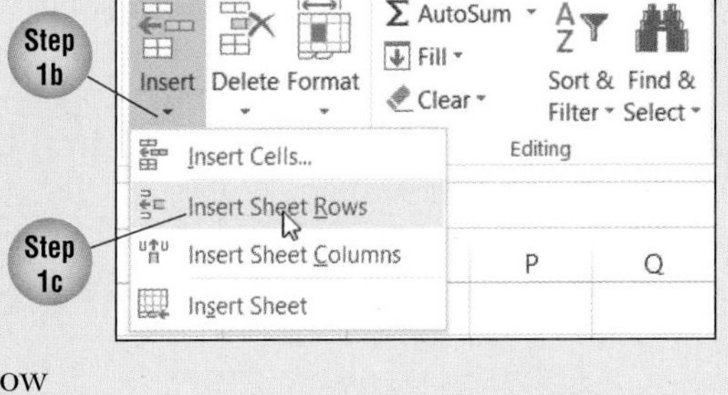

2. Type the text **Capstan Marine Products** in cell A1.
3. Make cell A2 active and then type **Purchasing Department**.
4. Change the height of row 1 to *42.00 (70 pixels)*.
5. Change the height of row 2 to *21.00 (35 pixels)*.
6. Insert two rows by completing the following steps:
   a. Select rows 7 and 8 in the worksheet.
   b. Click the Insert button in the Cells group on the HOME tab.

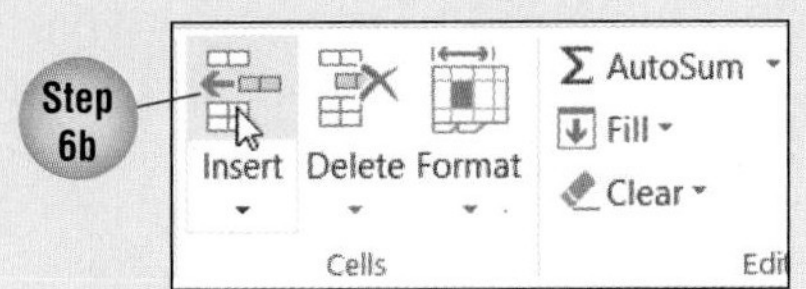

7. Type the following data in the specified cells. For the cells that contain money amounts, you do not need to type the dollar sign:
   A7: 855-495
   B7: 42.75
   C7: 5
   A8: ST039
   B8: 12.99
   C8: 25
8. Make cell D6 active and then use the fill handle to copy the formula down to cells D7 and D8.
9. Save **EL1-C3-P1-CMProducts.xlsx**.

Inserting Columns

Insert columns in a worksheet in much the same way as rows. Insert a column with options from the Insert button drop-down list or with options at the Insert dialog box. By default, a column is inserted immediately to the left of the column containing the active cell. To insert a column in a worksheet, make a cell active in the column immediately to the right of where the new column is to be inserted, click the Insert button arrow, and then click *Insert Sheet Columns* at the drop-down list. If you want to insert more than one column, select the number of columns in the worksheet that you want inserted, click the Insert button arrow, and then click *Insert Sheet Columns*.

You also can insert a column by making a cell active in the column immediately to the right of where the new column is to be inserted, clicking the Insert button arrow, and then clicking *Insert Cells* at the drop-down list. At the Insert dialog box that displays, click *Entire column*. This inserts an entire column immediately to the left of the active cell.

Excel includes an especially helpful and time-saving feature related to inserting columns. When you insert columns in a worksheet, all references affected by the insertion are automatically adjusted.

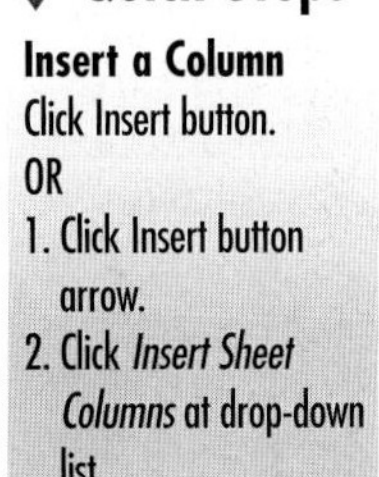

Quick Steps

Insert a Column
Click Insert button.
OR
1. Click Insert button arrow.
2. Click *Insert Sheet Columns* at drop-down list.
OR
1. Click Insert button arrow.
2. Click *Insert Cells*.
3. Click *Entire column*.
4. Click OK.

Project 1e Inserting a Column Part 5 of 7

1. With **EL1-C3-P1-CMProducts.xlsx** open, insert a column by completing the following steps:
   a. Click in any cell in column A.
   b. Click the Insert button arrow in the Cells group on the HOME tab and then click *Insert Sheet Columns* at the drop-down list.
2. Type the following data in the specified cell:
   A3: **Company**
   A4: **RD Manufacturing**
   A8: **Smithco, Inc.**
   A11: **Sunrise Corporation**
   A15: **Geneva Systems**
3. Make cell A1 active and then adjust the width of column A to accommodate the longest entry.
4. Insert another column by completing the following steps:
   a. Make cell B1 active.
   b. Click the Insert button arrow and then click *Insert Cells* at the drop-down list.
   c. At the Insert dialog box, click *Entire column*.
   d. Click OK.
5. Type Date in cell B3 and then press Enter.
6. Save **EL1-C3-P1-CMProducts.xlsx**.

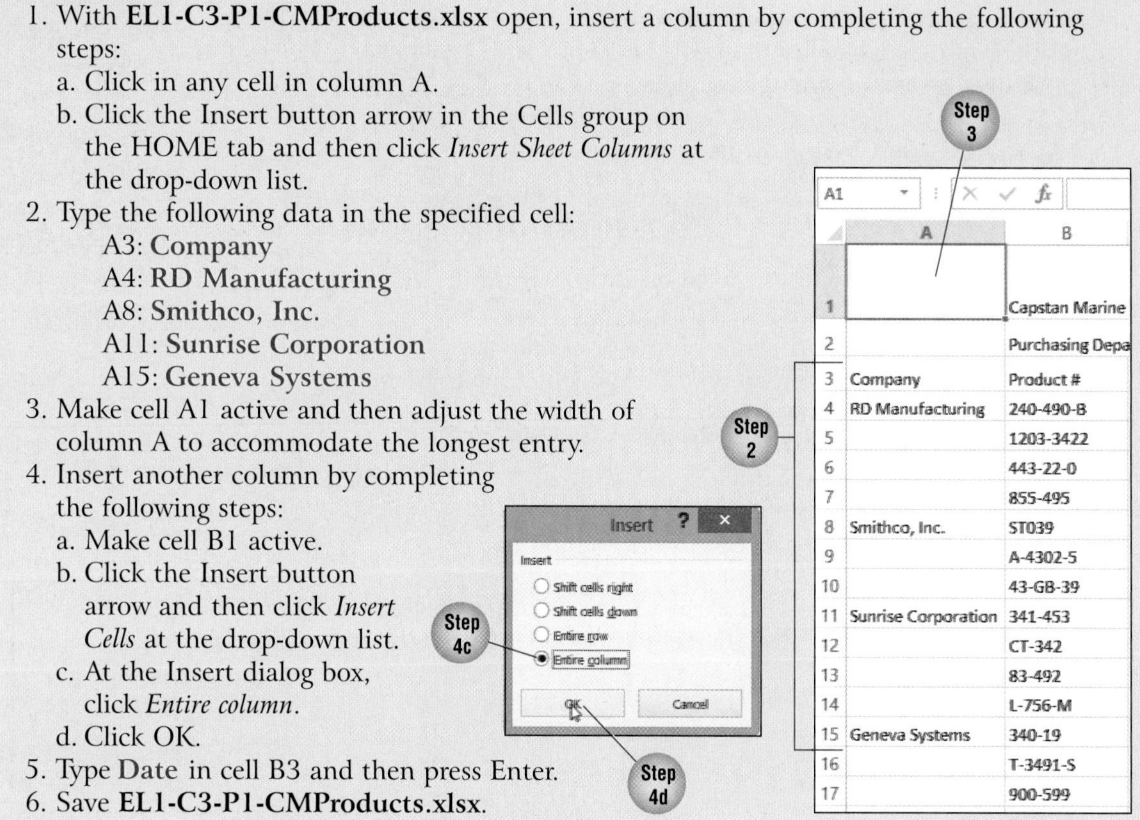

Deleting Cells, Rows, or Columns

Delete

You can delete specific cells in a worksheet or rows or columns in a worksheet. To delete a row, select the row and then click the Delete button in the Cells group on the HOME tab. To delete a column, select the column and then click the Delete button. Delete a specific cell by making the cell active, clicking the Delete button arrow, and then clicking *Delete Cells* at the drop-down list. This displays the Delete dialog box, shown in Figure 3.4. At the Delete dialog box, specify what you want deleted and then click OK. You can also delete adjacent cells by selecting the cells and then displaying the Delete dialog box.

HINT Display the Delete dialog box by positioning the cell pointer in the worksheet, clicking the right mouse button, and then clicking *Delete* at the shortcut menu.

Figure 3.4 Delete Dialog Box

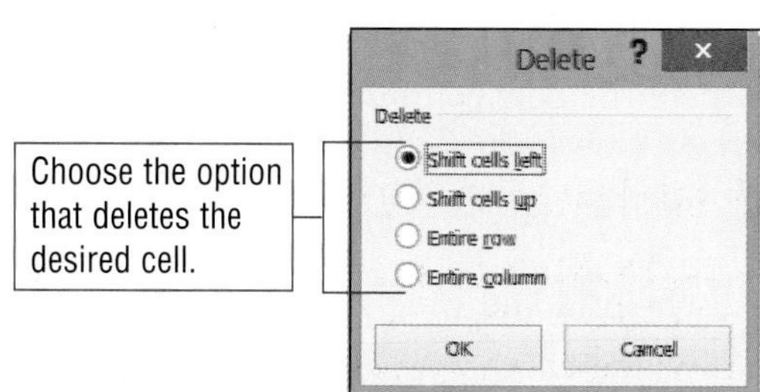

Clearing Data in Cells

If you want to delete the cell contents but not the cell, make the cell active or select desired cells and then press the Delete key. A quick method for clearing the contents of a cell is to right-click in the cell and then click *Clear Contents* at the shortcut menu. Another method for deleting cell content is to make the cell active or select desired cells, click the Clear button in the Editing group on the HOME tab, and then click *Clear Contents* at the drop-down list.

With the options at the Clear button drop-down list, you can clear the contents of the cell or selected cells as well as the formatting and comments. Click the *Clear Formats* option to remove formatting from cells or selected cells while leaving the data. You can also click the *Clear All* option to clear the contents of the cell or selected cells as well as the formatting.

Quick Steps

Clear Data in Cells
1. Select desired cells.
2. Press Delete key.

OR
1. Select desired cells.
2. Click Clear button.
3. Click *Clear Contents* at drop-down list.

Clear

Project 1f **Deleting and Clearing Rows in a Worksheet** **Part 6 of 7**

1. With **EL1-C3-P1-CMProducts.xlsx** open, delete column B in the worksheet by completing the following steps:
   a. Click in any cell in column B.
   b. Click the Delete button arrow in the Cells group on the HOME tab and then click *Delete Sheet Columns* at the drop-down list.
2. Delete row 5 by completing the following steps:
   a. Select row 5.
   b. Click the Delete button in the Cells group.
3. Clear row contents by completing the following steps:
   a. Select rows 7 and 8.
   b. Click the Clear button in the Editing group on the HOME tab and then click *Clear Contents* at the drop-down list.
4. Type the following data in the specified cell:
   A7: **Ray Enterprises**
   B7: **S894-T**
   C7: **4.99**
   D7: **30**
   B8: **B-3448**
   C8: **25.50**
   D8: **12**
5. Make cell E6 active and then copy the formula down to cells E7 and E8.
6. Save **EL1-C3-P1-CMProducts.xlsx**.

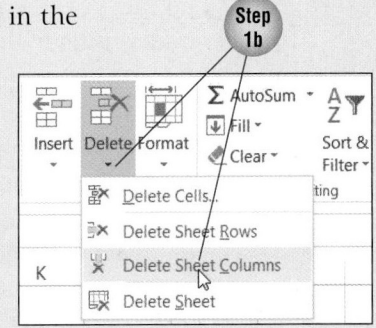

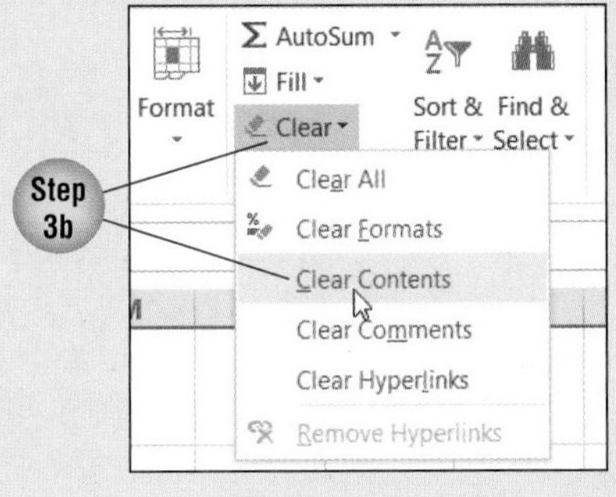

Applying Formatting

With many of the groups on the HOME tab, you can apply formatting to text in the active cell or selected cells. Use buttons in the Font group to apply font formatting to text and use buttons in the Alignment group to apply alignment formatting to text.

Figure 3.5 Font Group

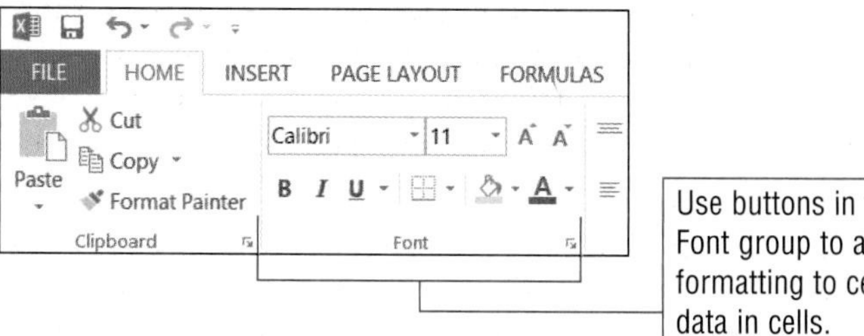

Applying Font Formatting

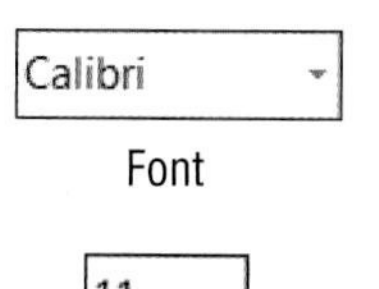

Font

Font Size

Bold

Italic

Underline

Apply a variety of formatting to cells in a worksheet with buttons in the Font group on the HOME tab. With buttons in the Font group, shown in Figure 3.5, you can change the font, font size, and font color; bold, italicize, and underline data in cells; change the text color; and apply a border or add fill to cells.

Use the Font button in the Font group to change the font of text in a cell and use the Font Size button to specify the size for the text. Apply bold formatting to text in a cell with the Bold button, italic formatting with the Italic button, and underlining with the Underline button.

Click the Increase Font Size button and the text in the active cell or selected cells increases to the next font size in the Font Size button arrow drop-down gallery. Click the Decrease Font Size button and text in the active cell or selected cells decreases in point size.

With the Borders button in the Font group, you can insert a border on any or all sides of the active cell or any or all sides of selected cells. The name of the button changes depending on the most recent border applied to a cell or selected cells. Use the Fill Color button to insert color in the active cell or in selected cells. With the Font Color button, you can change the color of text within a cell.

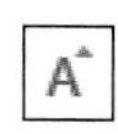

Increase Font Size

Formatting with the Mini Toolbar

Double-click in a cell and then select data within the cell and the Mini toolbar displays above the selected data. The Mini toolbar also displays when you right-click in any cell. The Mini toolbar contains buttons for applying font formatting such as font, font size, and font color, as well as bold and italic formatting. Click a button on the Mini toolbar to apply formatting to selected text.

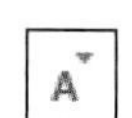

Decrease Font Size

Applying Alignment Formatting

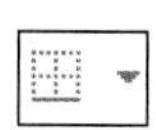

Borders

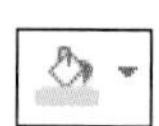

Fill Color

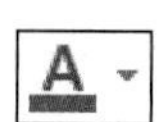

Font Color

Merge & Center

The alignment of data in cells depends on the type of data entered. Enter words or text combined with numbers in a cell and the text is aligned at the left edge of the cell. Enter numbers in a cell and the numbers are aligned at the right side of the cell. Use options in the Alignment group to align text at the left, center, or right side of the cell; align text at the top, center, or bottom of the cell; increase and/or decrease the indent of text; and change the orientation of text in a cell.

As you learned in Chapter 1, you can merge selected cells by clicking the Merge & Center button. If you merged cells, you can split the merged cell into the original cells by selecting the cell and then clicking the Merge & Center button. If you click the Merge & Center button arrow, a drop-down list of options displays. Click the *Merge & Center* option to merge all of the selected cells and change to center cell alignment. Click the *Merge Across* option to merge each row of the selected cells. For example, if you select three cells and two rows, clicking the *Merge Across* option will merge the three cells in the first row and merge the three cells in the second row so you end up with two cells. Click the *Merge Cells* option to merge all selected cells but not change to center cell alignment. Use the last option, *Unmerge Cells* to split cells that were previously merged. If you select and merge cells containing data, only the data in the upper left cell will remain. Data in any other cells in the merged cells is deleted.

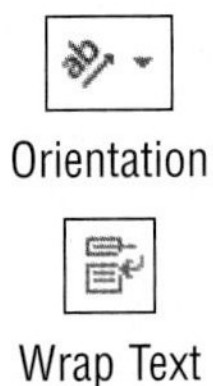

Click the Orientation button to rotate data in a cell. Click the Orientation button and a drop-down list displays with options for rotating text in a cell. If data typed in a cell is longer than the cell, it overlaps the next cell to the right. If you want data to remain in a cell and wrap to the next line within the same cell, click the Wrap Text button in the Alignment group.

Project 1g Applying Font and Alignment Formatting — Part 7 of 7

1. With **EL1-C3-P1-CMProducts.xlsx** open, make cell B1 active and then click the Wrap Text button in the Alignment group on the HOME tab. (This wraps the company name within the cell.)
2. Select cells B1 through C2, click the Merge & Center button arrow in the Alignment group on the HOME tab, and then click *Merge Across* at the drop-down list.
3. After looking at the merged cells, you decide to merge additional cells and horizontally and vertically center text in the cells by completing the following steps:
   a. With cells B1 through C2 selected, click the Merge & Center button arrow and then click *Unmerge Cells* at the drop-down list.
   b. Select cells A1 through E2.
   c. Click the Merge & Center button arrow and then click the *Merge Across* option at the drop-down list.
   d. Click the Middle Align button in the Alignment group and then click the Center button.

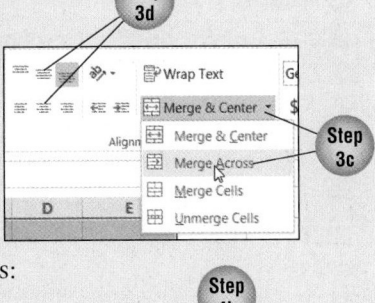

Step 3d

Wrap Text
Merge & Center
Merge & Center
Merge Across
Merge Cells
Unmerge Cells

Step 3c

4. Rotate text in the third row by completing the following steps:
   a. Select cells A3 through E3.
   b. Click the Orientation button in the Alignment group and then click *Angle Counterclockwise* at the drop-down list.
   c. After looking at the rotated text, you decide to return the orientation back to horizontal by clicking the Undo button on the Quick Access toolbar.

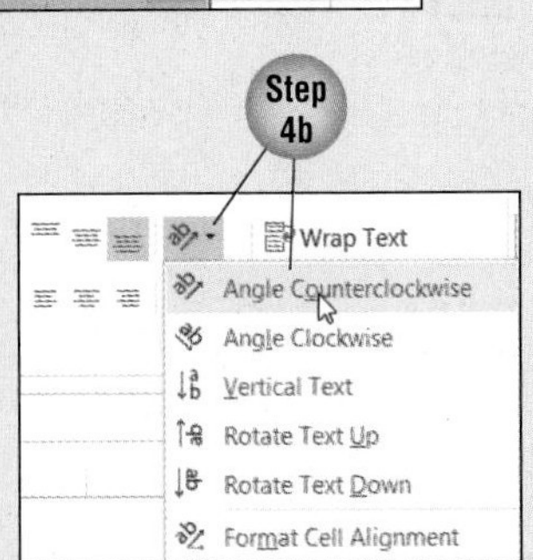

5. Change the font, font size, and font color for text in specific cells by completing the following steps:
   a. Make cell A1 active.
   b. Click the Font button arrow in the Font group, scroll down the drop-down gallery, and then click *Bookman Old Style*.
   c. Click the Font Size button arrow in the Font group and then click *22* at the drop-down gallery.

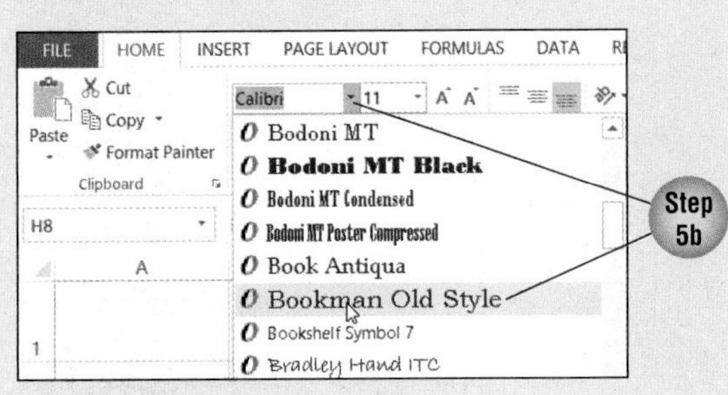

d. Click the Font Color button arrow and then click the *Dark Blue* option (ninth option in the *Standard Colors* section).

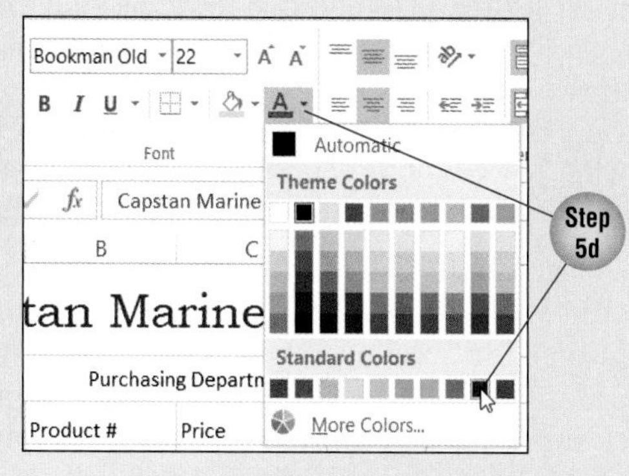

6. Make cell A2 active and then complete steps similar to those in Step 5 to change the font to Bookman Old Style, the font size to 16 points, and the font color to Dark Blue.
7. Select cells A3 through E3 and then click the Center button in the Alignment group.
8. With cells A3 through E3 still selected, click the Bold button in the Font group and then click the Italic button.
9. Select cells A3 through E18 and then change the font to Bookman Old Style.
10. Use the Mini toolbar to apply formatting to selected data by completing the following steps:
    a. Double-click in cell A4.
    b. Select the letters *RD*. (This displays the Mini toolbar above the selected word.)
    c. Click the Increase Font Size button on the Mini toolbar.
    d. Double-click in cell A14.
    e. Select the word *Geneva* and then click the Italic button on the Mini toolbar.

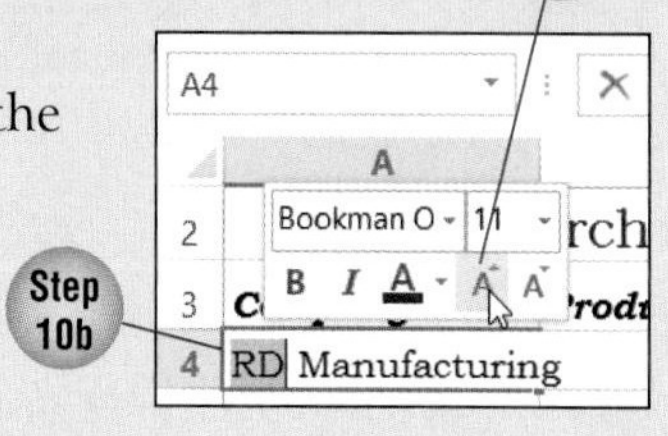

11. Adjust columns A through E to accommodate the longest entry in each column. To do this, select columns A through E and then double-click any selected column boundary.
12. Select cells D4 through D17 and then click the Center button in the Alignment group.
13. Add a double-line bottom border to cell A2 by completing the following steps:
    a. Make cell A2 active.
    b. Click the Borders button arrow in the Font group. (The name of this button varies depending on the last option selected.)
    c. Click the *Bottom Double Border* option at the drop-down list.

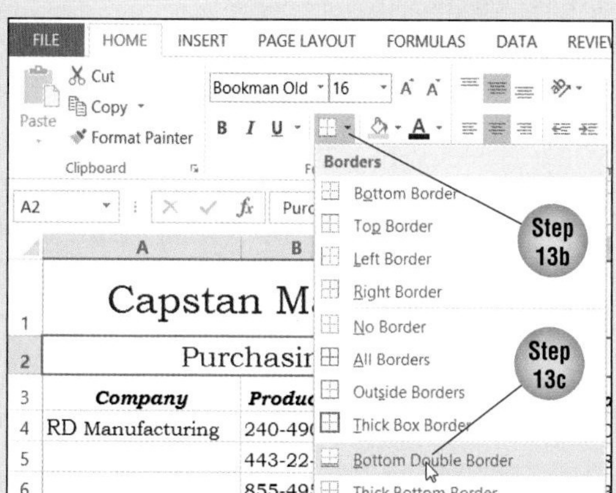

14. Add a single-line bottom border to cells A3 through E3 by completing the following steps:
    a. Select cells A3 through E3.
    b. Click the Borders button arrow and then click the *Bottom Border* option.
15. Apply fill color to specific cells by completing the following steps:
    a. Select cells A1 through E3.
    b. Click the Fill Color button arrow in the Font group.
    c. Click the *Blue, Accent 5, Lighter 80%* color option (ninth column, second row in the *Theme Colors* section).

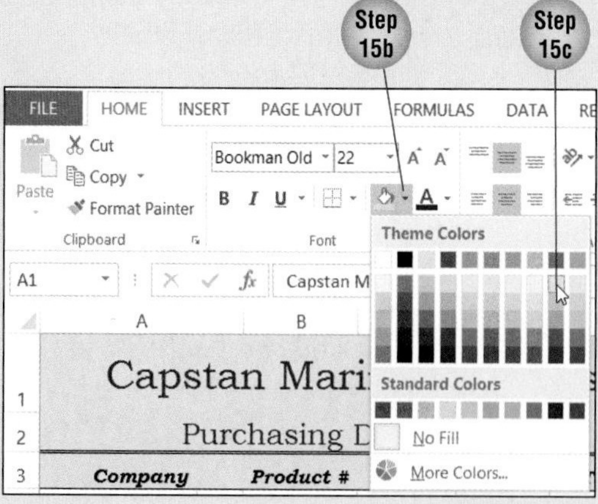

16. Select cells C5 through C17 and then click the Comma Style button.
17. Select cells E5 through E17 and then click the Comma Style button.
18. Save, print, and then close **EL1-C3-P1-CMProducts.xlsx**.

Project 2 Apply a Theme to a Payroll Worksheet 1 Part

You will open a workbook containing a worksheet with payroll information and then insert text, apply formatting to cells and cell contents, apply a theme, and then change the theme font and colors.

Applying a Theme

Excel provides a number of themes you can use to format text and cells in a worksheet. A ***theme*** is a set of formatting choices that includes a color theme (a set of colors), a font theme (a set of heading and body text fonts), and an effects theme (a set of lines and fill effects). To apply a theme, click the PAGE LAYOUT tab and then click the Themes button in the Themes group. At the drop-down gallery that displays, click the desired theme. Position the mouse pointer over a theme and the ***live preview*** feature will display the worksheet with the theme formatting applied. With the live preview feature, you can see how the theme formatting affects your worksheet before you make your final choice.

Apply a theme to give your worksheet a professional look.

Themes

Project 2 Applying a Theme Part 1 of 1

1. Open **SBAPayroll.xlsx** and then save it with Save As and name it **EL1-C3-P2-SBAPayroll**.
2. Make cell G4 active and then insert a formula that calculates the amount of social security tax. (Multiply the gross pay amount in cell E4 with the social security rate in cell H11; you will need to use the mixed cell reference H$11 when writing the formula.)
3. Copy the formula in cell G4 down to cells G5 through G9.
4. Make H4 the active cell and then insert a formula that calculates the net pay (gross pay minus withholding and social security tax).
5. Copy the formula in cell H4 down to cells H5 through H9.
6. Increase the height of row 1 to 36.00 points.
7. Make cell A1 active, click the Middle Align button in the Alignment group, click the Font Size button arrow, click *18* at the drop-down list, and then click the Bold button.
8. Type **Stanton & Barnett Associates** in cell A1.
9. Select cells A2 through H3 and then click the Bold button in the Font group.
10. Apply a theme and customize the font and colors by completing the following steps:
    a. Make cell A1 active.
    b. Click the PAGE LAYOUT tab.
    c. Click the Themes button in the Themes group and then click *Wisp* at the drop-down gallery. (You might want to point the mouse to individual themes to see how each theme's formatting affects the worksheet.)

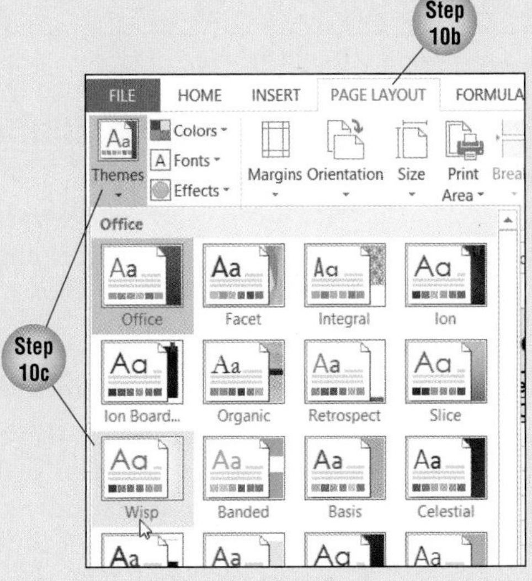

d. Click the Colors button in the Themes group and then click *Red Orange* at the drop-down gallery.
e. Click the Fonts button in the Themes group, scroll down the drop-down gallery, and then click *TrebuchetMS*.

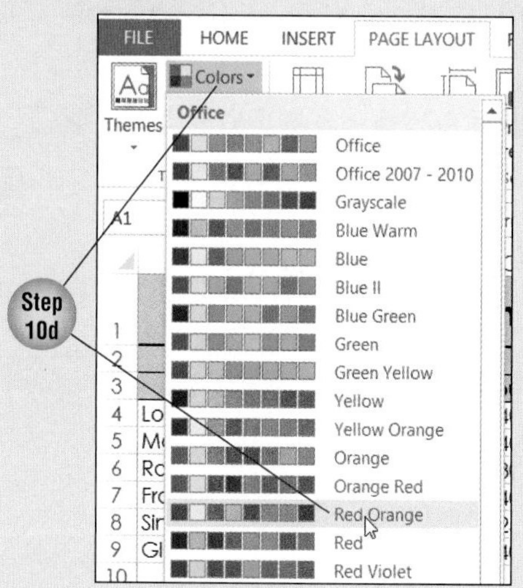

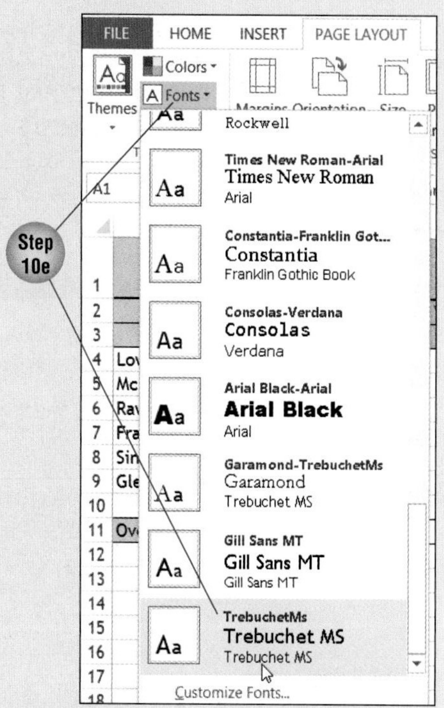

11. Select columns A through H and adjust the width of the columns to accommodate the longest entries.
12. Save, print, and then close **EL1-C3-P2-SBAPayroll.xlsx**.

Project 3 Format an Invoices Worksheet — 2 Parts

You will open a workbook containing an invoice worksheet and apply number formatting to numbers in cells.

Formatting Numbers

Numbers in a cell, by default, are aligned at the right and decimals and commas do not display unless they are typed in the cell. Change the format of numbers with buttons in the Number group on the HOME tab or with options at the Format Cells dialog box with the Number tab selected.

Formatting Numbers Using Number Group Buttons

The format symbols you can use to format numbers include a percent sign (%), comma (,), and dollar sign ($). For example, if you type the number *$45.50* in a cell, Excel automatically applies currency formatting to the number. If you type *45%*, Excel automatically applies percent formatting to the number. The Number group on the HOME tab contains five buttons you can use to format numbers in cells. You learned about these buttons in Chapter 1.

Specify the formatting for numbers in cells in a worksheet before typing the numbers or format existing numbers in a worksheet. The Increase Decimal and Decrease Decimal buttons in the Number group on the HOME tab will change the number of places after the decimal point for existing numbers only.

The Number group on the HOME tab also contains the Number Format button. Click the Number Format button arrow and a drop-down list displays of common number formats. Click the desired format at the drop-down list to apply the number formatting to the cell or selected cells.

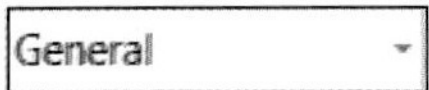

Number Format

Project 3a Formatting Numbers with Buttons in the Number Group

Part 1 of 2

1. Open **RPInvoices.xlsx**.
2. Save the workbook with Save As and name it **EL1-C3-P3-RPInvoices**.
3. Make the following changes to column widths:
   a. Change the width of column C to 17.00 characters.
   b. Change the width of column D to 10.00 characters.
   c. Change the width of column E to 7.00 characters.
   d. Change the width of column F to 12.00 characters.
4. Select row 1 and then click the Insert button in the Cells group on the HOME tab.
5. Change the height of row 1 to 42.00 points.
6. Select cells A1 through F1 and then make the following changes:
   a. Click the Merge & Center button in the Alignment group on the HOME tab.
   b. With cell A1 active, change the font size to 24 points.
   c. Click the Fill Color button arrow in the Font group and then click *Green, Accent 6, Lighter 80%* (last column, second row in the *Theme Colors* section).
   d. Click the Borders button arrow in the Font group and then click the *Top and Thick Bottom Border* option.
   e. With cell A1 active, type **REAL PHOTOGRAPHY** and then press Enter.
7. Change the height of row 2 to 24.00 points.
8. Select cells A2 through F2 and then make the following changes:
   a. Click the Merge & Center button in the Alignment group.
   b. With cell A2 active, change the font size to 18 points.
   c. Click the Fill Color button in the Font group. (This will fill the cell with green color.)
   d. Click the Borders button arrow in the Font group and then click the *Bottom Border* option.
9. Make the following changes to row 3:
   a. Change the height of row 3 to 18.00 points.
   b. Select cells A3 through F3, click the Bold button in the Font group, and then click the Center button in the Alignment group.
   c. With the cells still selected, click the Borders button arrow and then click the *Bottom Border* option.

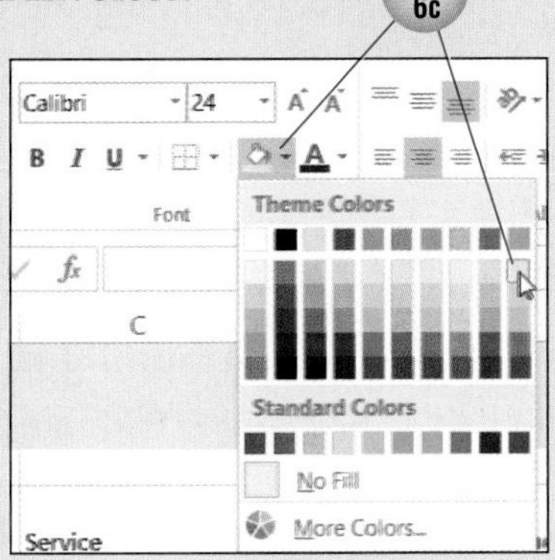

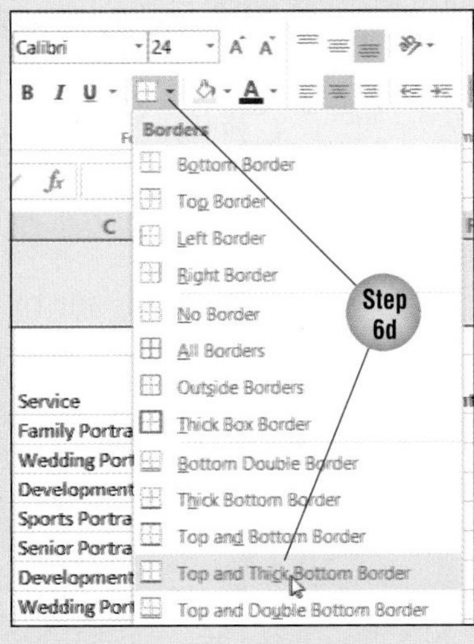

10. Make the following number formatting changes:
    a. Select cells E4 through E16 and then click the Percent Style button in the Number group on the HOME tab.
    b. With the cells still selected, click once on the Increase Decimal button in the Number group. (The percentages should include one place after the decimal point.)

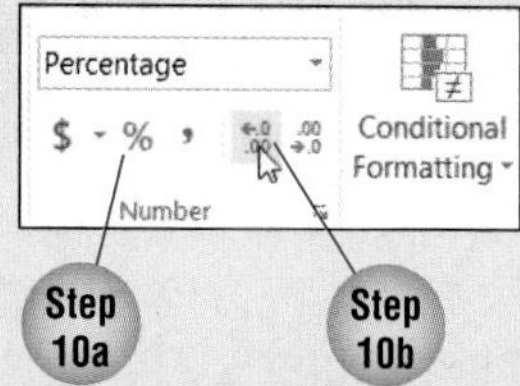

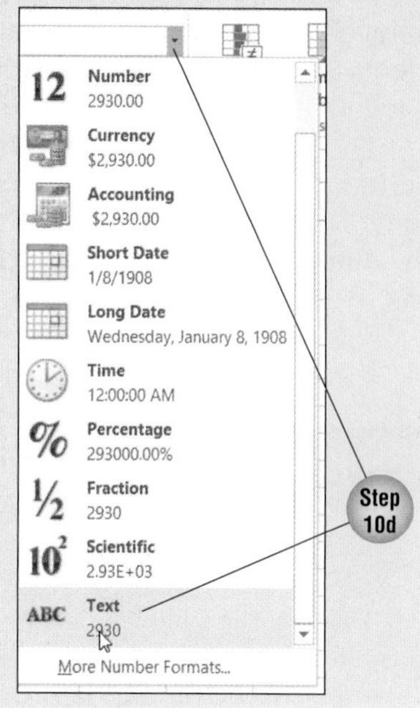

    c. Select cells A4 through B16.
    d. Click the Number Format button arrow, scroll down the drop-down list, and then click *Text*.
    e. With cells A4 through B16 still selected, click the Center button in the Alignment group.
11. Save **EL1-C3-P3-RPInvoices.xlsx**.

Formatting Numbers Using the Format Cells Dialog Box

Along with buttons in the Number group, you can format numbers with options at the Format Cells dialog box with the Number tab selected, as shown in Figure 3.6. Display this dialog box by clicking the Number group dialog box launcher or by clicking the Number Format button arrow and then clicking *More Number Formats* at the drop-down list. The left side of the dialog box displays

Figure 3.6 Format Cells Dialog Box with Number Tab Selected

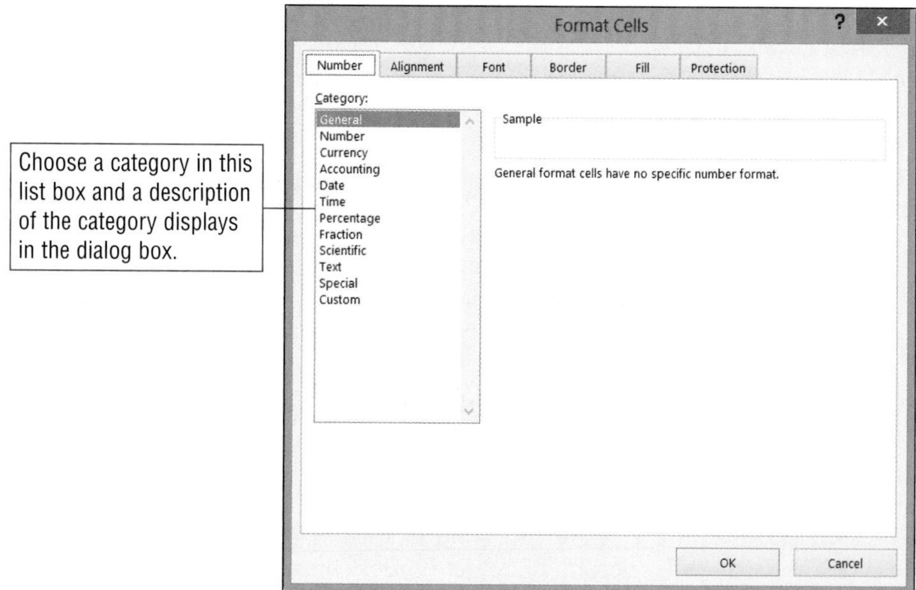

number categories with a default category of *General*. At this setting, no specific formatting is applied to numbers except right alignment in the cells. The other number categories are described in Table 3.1.

Table 3.1 Number Categories at the Format Cells Dialog Box

Click this category	*To apply this number formatting*
Number	Specify the number of places after the decimal point and whether a thousand separator should be used; choose the display of negative numbers; right-align numbers in the cell.
Currency	Apply general monetary values; add a dollar sign as well as commas and decimal points, if needed; right-align numbers in the cell.
Accounting	Line up the currency symbols and decimal points in a column; add a dollar sign and two places after the decimal point; right-align numbers in the cell.
Date	Display the date as a date value; specify the type of formatting desired by clicking an option in the *Type* list box; right-align the date in the cell.
Time	Display the time as a time value; specify the type of formatting desired by clicking an option in the *Type* list box; right-align the time in the cell.
Percentage	Multiply the cell value by 100 and display the result with a percent symbol; add a decimal point followed by two places by default; change the number of digits with the *Decimal places* option; right-align numbers in the cell.
Fraction	Specify how a fraction displays in the cell by clicking an option in the *Type* list box; right-align a fraction in the cell.
Scientific	Use for very large or very small numbers; use the letter *E* to tell Excel to move the decimal point a specified number of places.
Text	Treat a number in the cell as text; the number is displayed in the cell exactly as typed.
Special	Choose a number type, such as *Zip Code, Phone Number,* or *Social Security Number,* in the *Type* option list box; useful for tracking list and database values.
Custom	Specify a numbering type by choosing an option in the *Type* list box.

Project 3b Formatting Numbers at the Format Cells Dialog Box — Part 2 of 2

1. With **EL1-C3-P3-PRInvoices.xlsx** open, make cell F4 active, insert the formula =(D4*E4)+D4, and then press Enter.
2. Make cell F4 active and then copy the formula down to cells F5 through F16.
3. Apply accounting formatting by completing the following steps:
   a. Select cells D4 through D16.
   b. Click the Number group dialog box launcher.

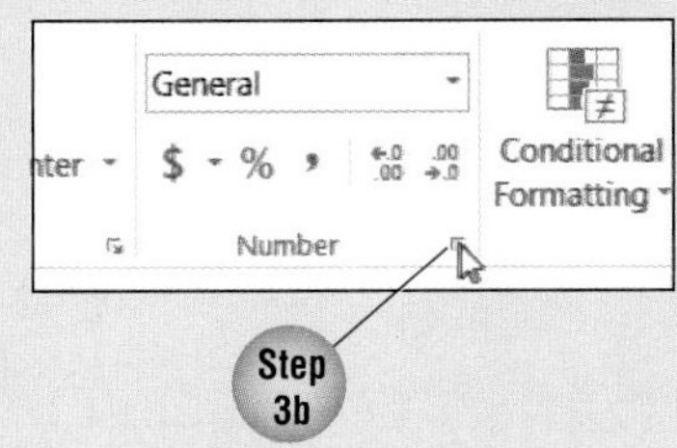

c. At the Format Cells dialog box with the Number tab selected, click *Accounting* in the *Category* list box.
d. Make sure a *2* displays in the *Decimal places* option box and a *$* (dollar sign) displays in the *Symbol* option box.
e. Click OK.

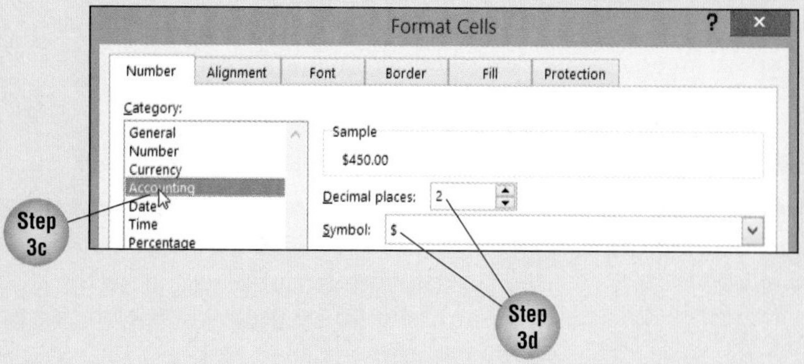

4. Apply accounting formatting to cells F4 through F16 by completing actions similar to those in Step 3.
5. Save, print, and then close **EL1-C3-P3-RPInvoices.xlsx**.

Project 4 Format a Company Budget Worksheet — 6 Parts

You will open a workbook containing a company budget worksheet and then apply formatting to cells with options at the Format Cells dialog box, use the Format Painter to apply formatting, and hide and unhide rows and columns in the worksheet.

Formatting Cells Using the Format Cells Dialog Box

In the previous section, you learned how to format numbers with options at the Format Cells dialog box with the Number tab selected. This dialog box also contains a number of other tabs you can select to format cells.

Aligning and Indenting Data

Align and indent data in cells using buttons in the Alignment group on the HOME tab or with options at the Format Cells dialog box with the Alignment tab selected, as shown in Figure 3.7. Display this dialog box by clicking the Alignment group dialog box launcher.

In the *Orientation* section, you can choose to rotate data. A portion of the *Orientation* section shows points on an arc. Click a point on the arc to rotate the text along that point. You can also type a rotation degree in the *Degrees* measurement box. Type a positive number to rotate selected text from the lower left to the upper right of the cell. Type a negative number to rotate selected text from the upper left to the lower right of the cell.

If data typed in a cell is longer than the cell, it overlaps the next cell to the right. If you want data to remain in a cell and wrap to the next line within the same cell, insert a check mark in the *Wrap text* check box in the *Text control* section of the dialog box. Insert a check mark in the *Shrink to fit* check box if you want to reduce the size of the text font so all selected data fits within the column. Insert a check mark in the *Merge cells* check box to combine two or more selected cells into a single cell.

If you want to enter data on more than one line within a cell, enter the data on the first line and then press Alt + Enter. Pressing Alt + Enter moves the insertion point to the next line within the same cell.

Figure 3.7 Format Cells Dialog Box with Alignment Tab Selected

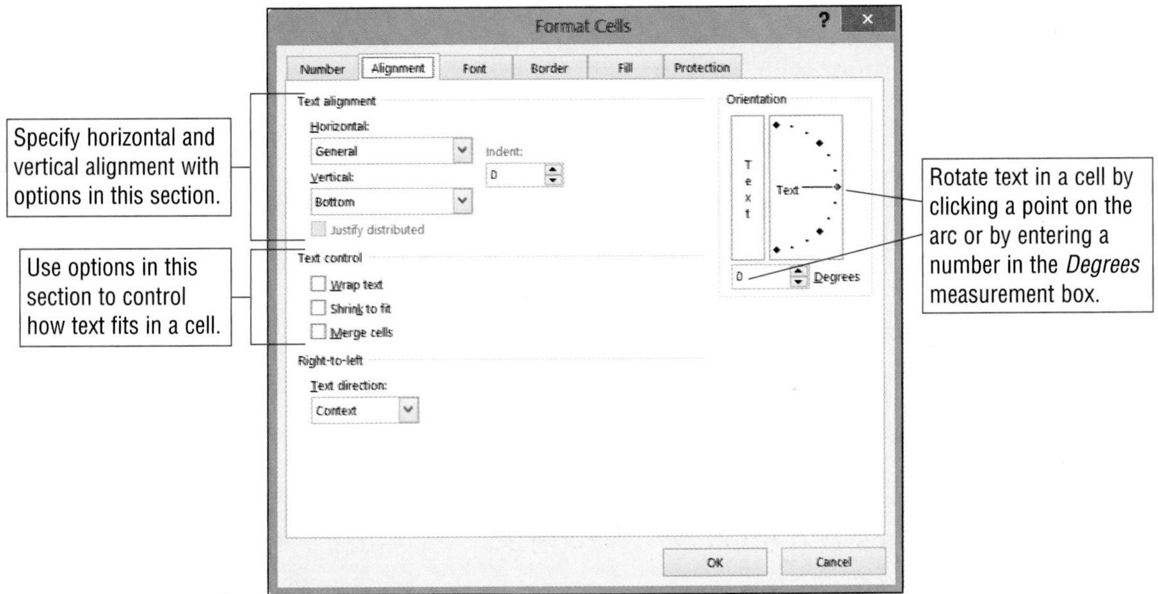

Project 4a Aligning and Rotating Data in Cells — Part 1 of 6

1. Open **HBCJobs.xlsx**.
2. Save the workbook with Save As and name it **EL1-C3-P4-HBCJobs**.
3. Make the following changes to the worksheet:
   a. Insert a new row at the beginning of the worksheet.
   b. Change the height of row 1 to 66.00 points.
   c. Merge and center cells A1 through E1.
   d. Type Harris & Briggs in cell A1 and then press Alt + Enter. (This moves the insertion point down to the next line in the same cell.)
   e. Type Construction and then press Enter.
   f. With cell A2 active, type Preferred, press Alt + Enter, type Customer, and then press Enter.
   g. Change the width of column A to 22.00 characters.
   h. Change the width of column B to 7.00 characters.
   i. Change the widths of columns C, D, and E to 10.00 characters.
4. Change number formatting for specific cells by completing the following steps:
   a. Select cells C3 through E11.
   b. Click the Number group dialog box launcher.
   c. At the Format Cells dialog box with the Number tab selected, click *Accounting* in the *Category* list box.
   d. Click the down-pointing arrow at the right side of the *Decimal places* measurement box until *0* displays.
   e. Make sure a *$* (dollar sign) displays in the *Symbol* option box.
   f. Click OK.

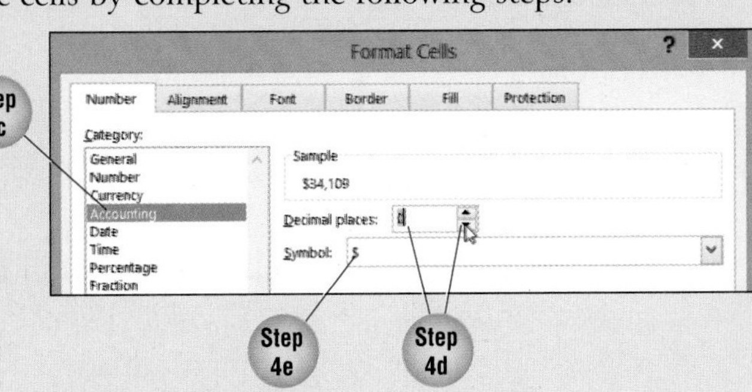

5. Make cell E3 active and then insert the formula =D3-C3. Copy this formula down to cells E4 through E11.

6. Change the orientation of data in cells by completing the following steps:
   a. Select cells B2 through E2.
   b. Click the Alignment group dialog box launcher.
   c. At the Format Cells dialog box with the Alignment tab selected, select *0* in the *Degrees* measurement box and then type 45.
   d. Click OK.

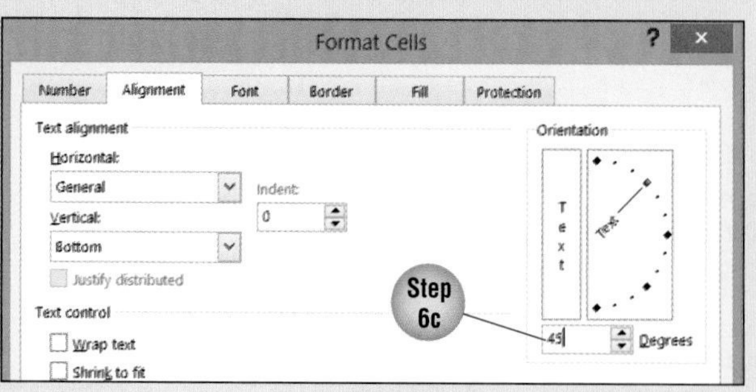

7. Change the vertical alignment of text in cells by completing the following steps:
   a. Select cells A1 through E2.
   b. Click the Alignment group dialog box launcher.
   c. At the Format Cells dialog box with the Alignment tab selected, click the down-pointing arrow at the right side of the *Vertical* option box.
   d. Click *Center* at the drop-down list.
   e. Click OK.

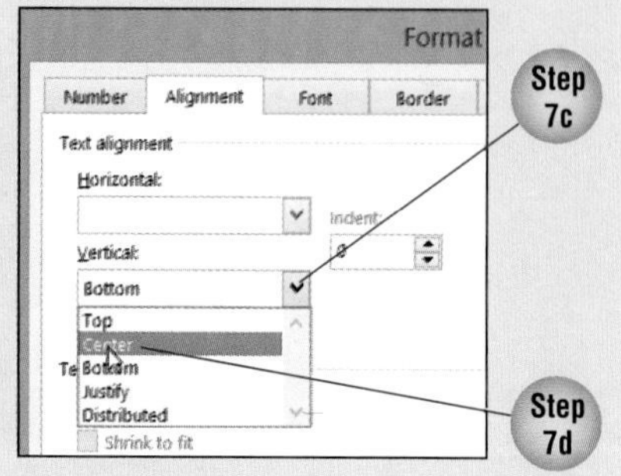

8. Change the horizontal alignment of text in cells by completing the following steps:
   a. Select cells A2 through E2.
   b. Click the Alignment group dialog box launcher.
   c. At the Format Cells dialog box with the Alignment tab selected, click the down-pointing arrow at the right side of the *Horizontal* option box.
   d. Click *Center* at the drop-down list.
   e. Click OK.

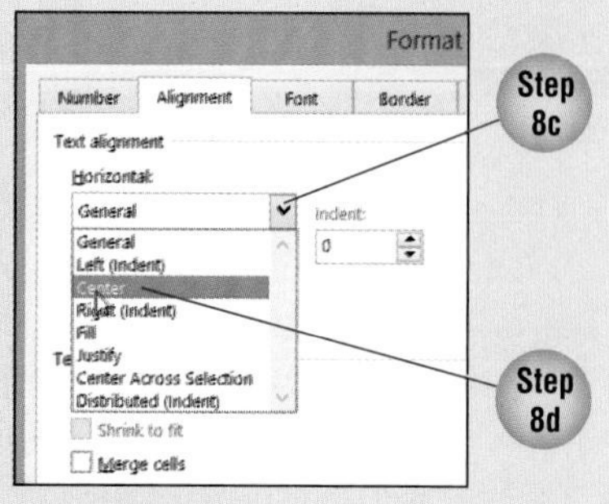

9. Change the horizontal alignment and indent of text in cells by completing the following steps:
   a. Select cells B3 through B11.
   b. Click the Alignment group dialog box launcher.
   c. At the Format Cells dialog box with the Alignment tab selected, click the down-pointing arrow at the right side of the *Horizontal* option box and then click *Right (Indent)* at the drop-down list.
   d. Click once on the up-pointing arrow at the right side of the *Indent* measurement box. (This displays *1*.)
   e. Click OK.

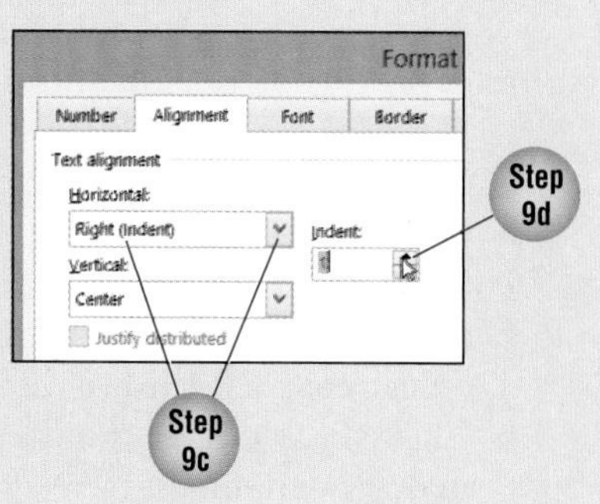

10. Save **EL1-C3-P4-HBCJobs.xlsx**.

Changing the Font at the Format Cells Dialog Box

As you learned earlier in this chapter, the Font group on the HOME tab contains buttons for applying font formatting to data in cells. You can also change the font for data in cells with options at the Format Cells dialog box with the Font tab selected, as shown in Figure 3.8. At the Format Cells dialog box with the Font tab selected, you can change the font, font style, font size, and font color. You can also change the underlining method and add effects such as superscript and subscript. Click the Font group dialog box launcher to display this dialog box.

Figure 3.8 Format Cells Dialog Box with Font Tab Selected

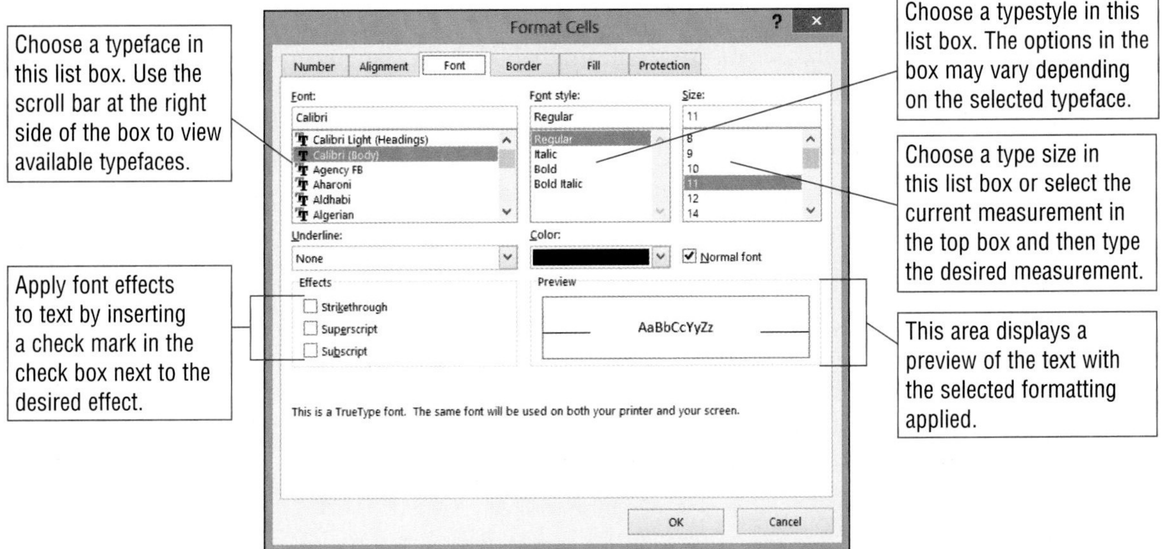
Choose a typeface in this list box. Use the scroll bar at the right side of the box to view available typefaces.
Apply font effects to text by inserting a check mark in the check box next to the desired effect.
Choose a typestyle in this list box. The options in the box may vary depending on the selected typeface.
Choose a type size in this list box or select the current measurement in the top box and then type the desired measurement.
This area displays a preview of the text with the selected formatting applied.
Format Cells
Number
Alignment
Font
Border
Fill
Protection
Font:
Calibri
Font style:
Regular
Size:
11
Underline:
None
Color:
Normal font
Effects
Strikethrough
Superscript
Subscript
Preview
AaBbCcYyZz
This is a TrueType font. The same font will be used on both your printer and your screen.
OK
Cancel

Project 4b Applying Font Formatting at the Format Cells Dialog Box

Part 2 of 6

1. With **EL1-C3-P4-HBCJobs.xlsx** open, change the font and font color by completing the following steps:
   a. Select cells A1 through E11.
   b. Click the Font group dialog box launcher.
   c. At the Format Cells dialog box with the Font tab selected, click *Garamond* in the *Font* list box. (You will need to scroll down the list to make this font visible.)
   d. Click *12* in the *Size* list box.
   e. Click the down-pointing arrow at the right of the *Color* option box.
   f. At the palette of color choices that displays, click the *Dark Red* color (first option in the *Standard Colors* section).
   g. Click OK to close the dialog box.
2. Make cell A1 active and then change the font to 24-point Garamond and apply bold formatting.
3. Select cells A2 through E2 and then apply bold formatting.
4. Save and then print **EL1-C3-P4-HBCJobs.xlsx**.

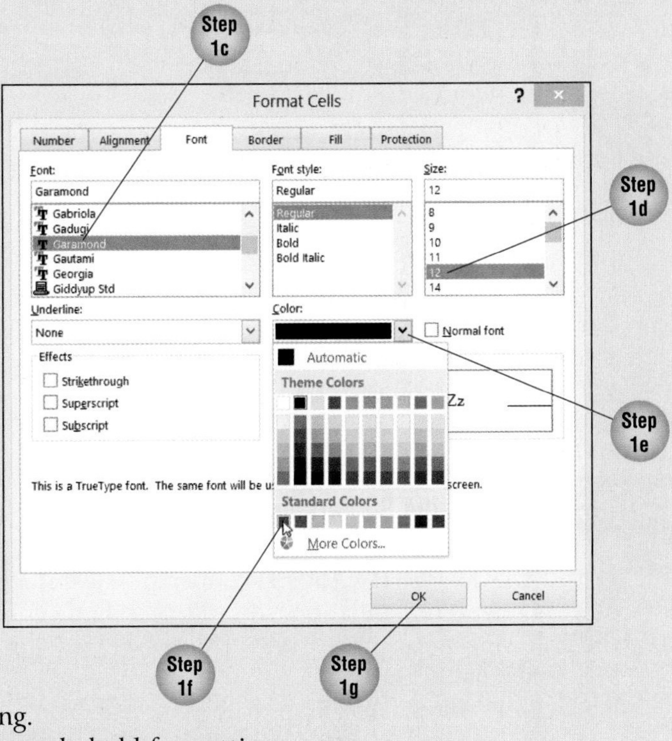
Step 1c
Step 1d
Step 1e
Step 1f
Step 1g
Format Cells
Number
Alignment
Font
Border
Fill
Protection
Font:
Garamond
Font style:
Regular
Size:
12
Underline:
None
Color:
Normal font
Automatic
Theme Colors
Standard Colors
More Colors...
OK
Cancel

Adding Borders to Cells

Quick Steps

Add Borders to Cells
1. Select cells.
2. Click Borders button arrow.
3. Click desired border.

OR

1. Select cells.
2. Click Borders button arrow.
3. Click *More Borders*.
4. Use options in dialog box to apply desired border.
5. Click OK.

The gridlines that display in a worksheet do not print. As you learned earlier in this chapter, you can use the Borders button in the Font group to add borders to cells that will print. You can also add borders to cells with options at the Format Cells dialog box with the Border tab selected, as shown in Figure 3.9. Display this dialog box by clicking the Borders button arrow in the Font group and then clicking *More Borders* at the drop-down list.

With options in the *Presets* section, you can remove borders with the *None* option, add only outside borders with the *Outline* option, or click the *Inside* option to add borders to the inside of selected cells. In the *Border* section of the dialog box, specify the side of the cell or selected cells to which you want to apply a border. Choose the style of line desired for the border with the options that display in the *Style* list box. Add color to border lines with choices from the color palette that displays when you click the down-pointing arrow at the right side of the *Color* option box.

Figure 3.9 Format Cells Dialog Box with Border Tab Selected

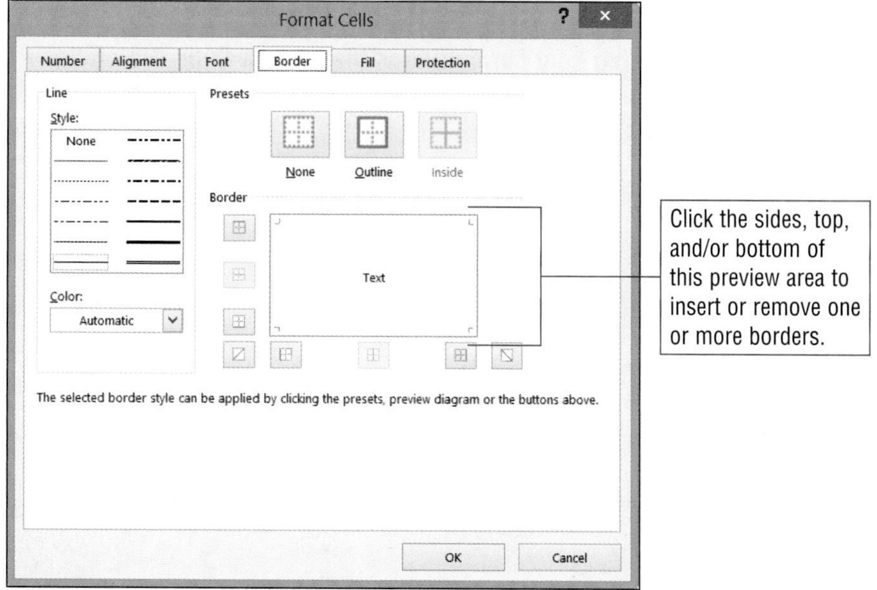

Project 4c **Adding Borders to Cells** **Part 3 of 6**

1. With **EL1-C3-P4-HBCJobs.xlsx** open, remove the 45 degrees orientation you applied in Project 4a by completing the following steps:
   a. Select cells B2 through E2.
   b. Click the Alignment group dialog box launcher.
   c. At the Format Cells dialog box with the Alignment tab selected, select *45* in the *Degrees* measurement box and then type 0.
   d. Click OK.
2. Change the height of row 2 to 33.00 points.

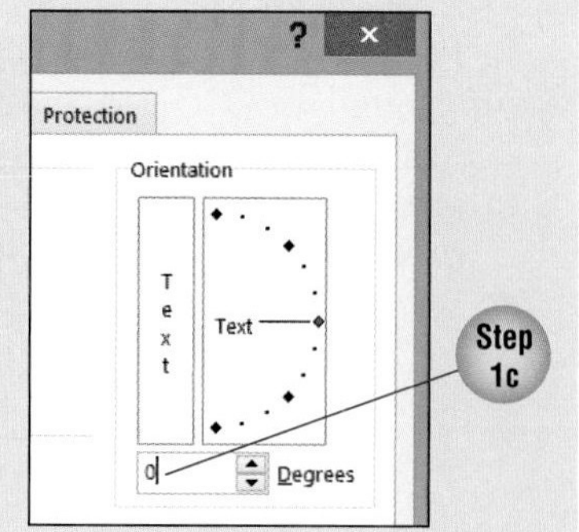

3. Add a thick, Dark Red border line to cells by completing the following steps:
   a. Select cells A1 through E11 (cells containing data).
   b. Click the Borders button arrow in the Font group and then click the *More Borders* option at the drop-down list.
   c. At the Format Cells dialog box with the Border tab selected, click the down-pointing arrow at the right side of the *Color* option box and then click the *Dark Red* color (first option in the *Standard Colors* section).
   d. Click the thick, single-line option in the *Style* list box in the *Line* section (sixth option in the second column).
   e. Click the *Outline* option in the *Presets* section.
   f. Click OK.
4. Add borders above and below cells by completing the following steps:
   a. Select cells A2 through E2.
   b. Click the Borders button arrow in the Font group and then click *More Borders* at the drop-down list.
   c. At the Format Cells dialog box with the Border tab selected, make sure the color is still Dark Red.

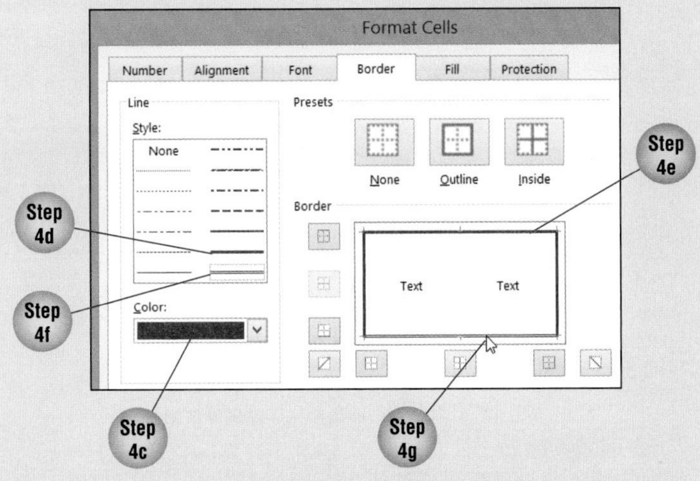

   d. Make sure the thick, single-line option is still selected in the *Style* list box in the *Line* section.
   e. Click the top border of the sample cell in the *Border* section of the dialog box.
   f. Click the double-line option in the *Style* list box (last option in the second column).
   g. Click the bottom border of the sample cell in the *Border* section of the dialog box.
   h. Click OK.
5. Save **EL1-C3-P4-HBCJobs.xlsx**.

Adding Fill and Shading to Cells

Quick Steps

Add Fill and Shading to Cells
1. Select cells.
2. Click Fill Color button arrow.
3. Click desired color.

OR

1. Select cells.
2. Click Format button.
3. Click *Format Cells* at drop-down list.
4. Click Fill tab.
5. Use options in dialog box to apply desired shading.
6. Click OK.

Repeat Last Action
1. Apply formatting.
2. Move to desired location.
3. Press F4 or Ctrl + Y.

To enhance the visual display of cells and data within cells, consider adding fill and/or shading to cells. As you learned earlier in this chapter, you can add fill color to cells with the Fill Color button in the Font group. You can also add fill color and/or shading to cells in a worksheet with options at the Format Cells dialog box with the Fill tab selected, as shown in Figure 3.10. Display the Format Cells dialog box by clicking the Format button in the Cells group and then clicking *Format Cells* at the drop-down list. You can also display the dialog box by clicking the Font group, Alignment group, or Number group dialog box launcher. At the Format Cells dialog box, click the Fill tab or right-click in a cell and then click *Format Cells* at the shortcut menu.

Choose a fill color for a cell or selected cells by clicking a color choice in the *Background Color* section. To add shading to a cell or selected cells, click the Fill Effects button and then click the desired shading style at the Fill Effects dialog box.

Repeating the Last Action

If you want to apply other types of formatting, such as number, border, or shading formatting to other cells in a worksheet, use the Repeat command by pressing F4 or Ctrl + Y. The Repeat command repeats the last action performed.

Figure 3.10 Format Cells Dialog Box with Fill Tab Selected

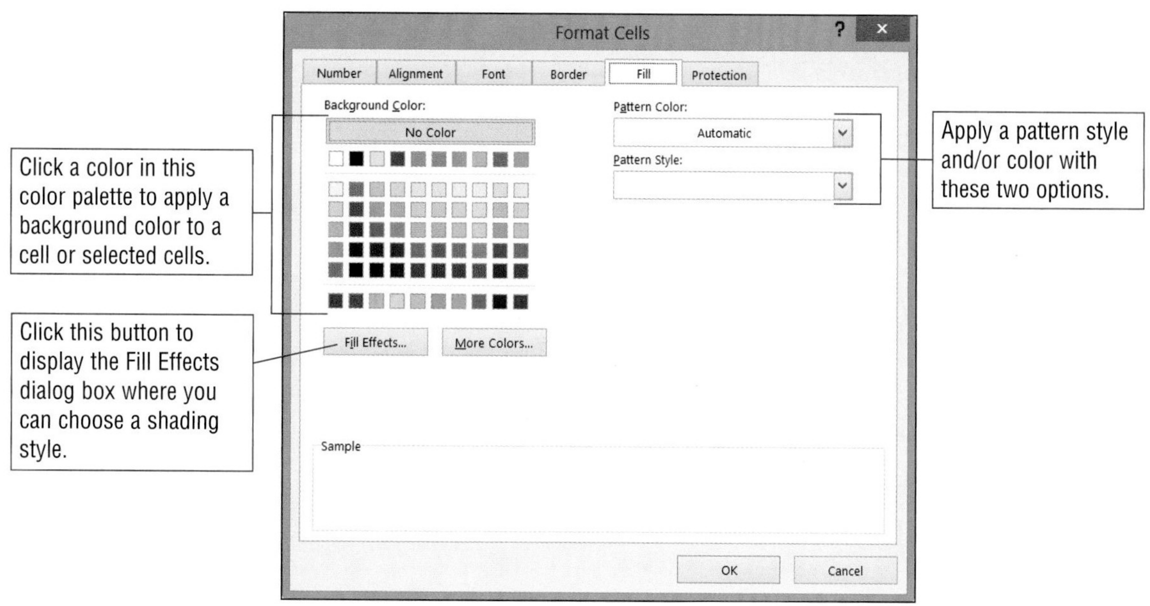
Format Cells
Number
Alignment
Font
Border
Fill
Protection
Background Color:
No Color
Fill Effects...
More Colors...
Pattern Color:
Automatic
Pattern Style:
Sample
OK
Cancel
Click a color in this color palette to apply a background color to a cell or selected cells.
Click this button to display the Fill Effects dialog box where you can choose a shading style.
Apply a pattern style and/or color with these two options.

Project 4d Adding Fill Color and Shading to Cells

Part 4 of 6

1. With **EL1-C3-P4-HBCJobs.xlsx** open, add fill color to cell A1 and repeat the formatting by completing the following steps:
   a. Make cell A1 active.
   b. Click the Format button in the Cells group and then click *Format Cells* at the drop-down list.
   c. At the Format Cells dialog box, click the Fill tab.
   d. Click the light gold color in the *Background Color* section (eighth column, second row—see image below).

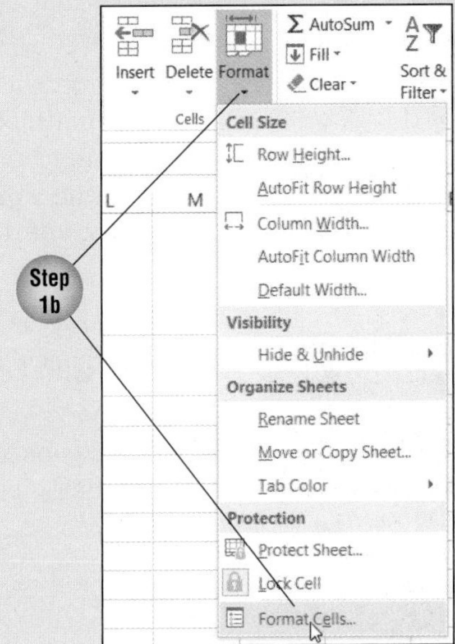

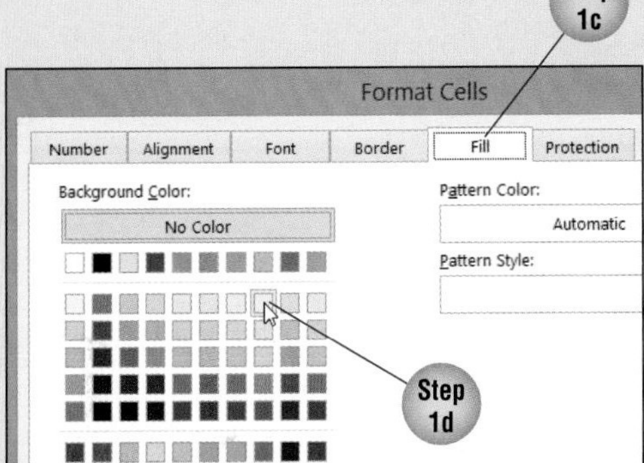

   e. Click OK.
   f. Select cells A2 through E2 and then press the F4 function key. (This repeats the light gold fill.)
2. Select row 2, insert a new row, and then change the height of the new row to 12.00 points.
3. Add shading to cells by completing the following steps:
   a. Select cells A2 through E2.
   b. Click the Format button in the Cells group and then click *Format Cells* at the drop-down list.
   c. At the Format Cells dialog box, if necessary, click the Fill tab.
   d. Click the Fill Effects button.
   e. At the Fill Effects dialog box, click the down-pointing arrow at the right side of the *Color 2* option box and then click *Gold, Accent 4* in the *Theme Colors* section (eighth column, top row).
   f. Click OK to close the Fill Effects dialog box.
   g. Click OK to close the Format Cells dialog box.
4. Save **EL1-C3-P4-HBCJobs.xlsx**.

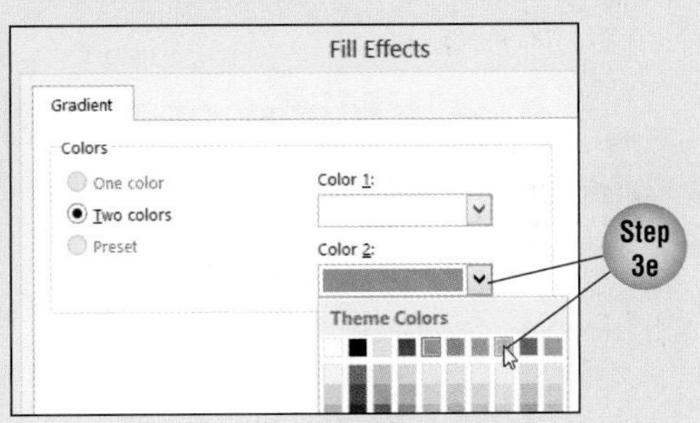

Formatting with Format Painter

Quick Steps

Format with Format Painter

1. Select cells with desired formatting.
2. Double-click Format Painter button.
3. Select desired cells.
4. Click Format Painter button.

Format Painter

Use the Format Painter button in the Clipboard group on the HOME tab to copy formatting to different locations in the worksheet. To use the Format Painter button, make active a cell or selected cells that contain the desired formatting, click the Format Painter button, and then click in the cell or selected cells to which you want the formatting applied.

When you click the Format Painter button, the mouse pointer displays with a paintbrush attached. If you want to apply formatting a single time, click the Format Painter button once. If you want to apply the formatting in more than one location in the worksheet, double-click the Format Painter button, selected the desired cells, and then click the Format Painter button to turn off the feature.

Project 4e **Formatting with Format Painter** **Part 5 of 6**

1. With **EL1-C3-P4-HBCJobs.xlsx** open, select cells A5 through E5.
2. Click the Font group dialog box launcher.
3. At the Format Cells dialog box, click the Fill tab.
4. Click the light green color in the *Background Color* section (last column, second row).
5. Click OK to close the dialog box.
6. Use Format Painter to "paint" formatting to rows by completing the following steps:
   a. With cells A5 through E5 selected, double-click the Format Painter button in the Clipboard group.
   b. Select cells A7 through E7.
   c. Select cells A9 through E9.
   d. Select cells A11 through E11.
   e. Turn off Format Painter by clicking the Format Painter button.
7. Save and then print **EL1-C3-P4-HBCJobs.xlsx**.

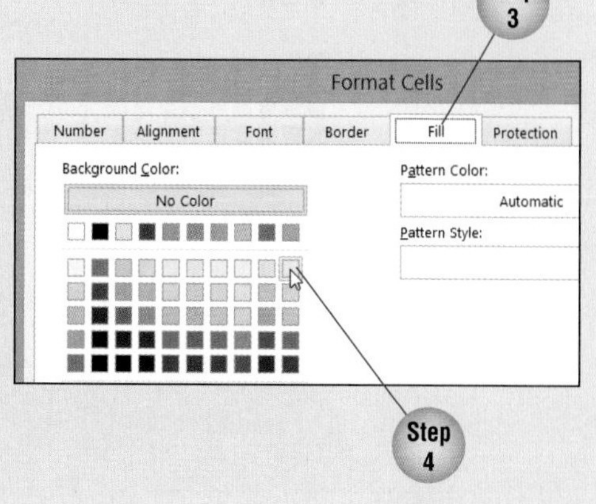

Hiding and Unhiding Columns and Rows

Quick Steps

Hide Columns

1. Select columns.
2. Click Format button.
3. Point to *Hide & Unhide*.
4. Click *Hide Columns*.

Hide Rows

1. Select rows.
2. Click Format button.
3. Point to *Hide & Unhide*.
4. Click *Hide Rows*.

If a worksheet contains columns and/or rows of sensitive data or data that you are not using or do not want to view, consider hiding the columns and/or rows. To hide columns in a worksheet, select the columns to be hidden, click the Format button in the Cells group on the HOME tab, point to *Hide & Unhide*, and then click *Hide Columns*. To hide selected rows, click the Format button in the Cells group, point to *Hide & Unhide*, and then click *Hide Rows*. To make a hidden column visible, select the column to the left and the column to the right of the hidden column, click the Format button in the Cells group, point to *Hide & Unhide*, and then click *Unhide Columns*. To make a hidden row visible, select the row above and the row below the hidden row, click the Format button in the Cells group, point to *Hide & Unhide*, and then click *Unhide Rows*.

If the first row or column is hidden, use the Go To feature to make the row or column visible. To do this, click the Find & Select button in the Editing group on the HOME tab and then click *Go To* at the drop-down list. At the Go To dialog box, type *A1* in the *Reference* text box and then click OK. At the worksheet, click the Format button in the Cells group, point to *Hide & Unhide*, and then click *Unhide Columns* or click *Unhide Rows*.

You can also unhide columns or rows using the mouse. If a column or row is hidden, the light gray boundary line in the column or row header displays as a slightly thicker gray line. To unhide a column, position the mouse pointer on the slightly thicker gray line that displays in the column header until the mouse pointer changes into a left-and-right-pointing arrow with a double line in the middle. (Make sure the mouse pointer displays with two lines between the arrows. If a single line displays, you will simply change the size of the visible column.) Hold down the left mouse button, drag to the right until the column displays at the desired width, and then release the mouse button. Unhide a row in a similar manner. Position the mouse pointer on the slightly thicker gray line in the row header until the mouse pointer changes into an up-and-down-pointing arrow with a double line in the middle. Drag down to display the row and then release the mouse button. If two or more adjacent columns or rows are hidden, you will need to unhide each column or row separately.

Set the column width to zero and the column is hidden. Set the row height to zero and the row is hidden.

Project 4f Hiding and Unhiding Columns and Rows

Part 6 of 6

1. With **EL1-C3-P4-HBCJobs.xlsx** open, hide the row for Linstrom Enterprises and the row for Summit Services by completing the following steps:
   a. Click the row 7 header to select the entire row.
   b. Hold down the Ctrl key and then click the row 11 header to select the entire row.
   c. Click the Format button in the Cells group on the HOME tab, point to *Hide & Unhide*, and then click *Hide Rows*.

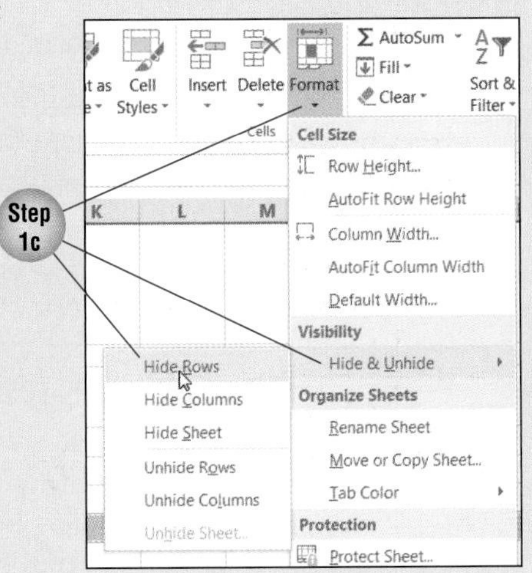

2. Hide the column containing the actual amounts by completing the following steps:
   a. Click in cell D3 to make it the active cell.
   b. Click the Format button in the Cells group, point to *Hide & Unhide*, and then click *Hide Columns*.
3. Save and then print **EL1-C3-P4-HBCJobs.xlsx**.
4. Unhide the rows by completing the following steps:
   a. Select rows 6 through 12.
   b. Click the Format button in the Cells group, point to *Hide & Unhide*, and then click *Unhide Rows*.
   c. Click in cell A4.
5. Unhide column D by completing the following steps:
   a. Position the mouse pointer on the thicker gray line that displays between columns C and E in the column header until the pointer turns into a left-and-right-pointing arrow with a double line in the middle.
   b. Hold down the left mouse button, drag to the right until *Width: 9.56 (93 pixels)* displays in a box above the mouse pointer, and then release the mouse button.

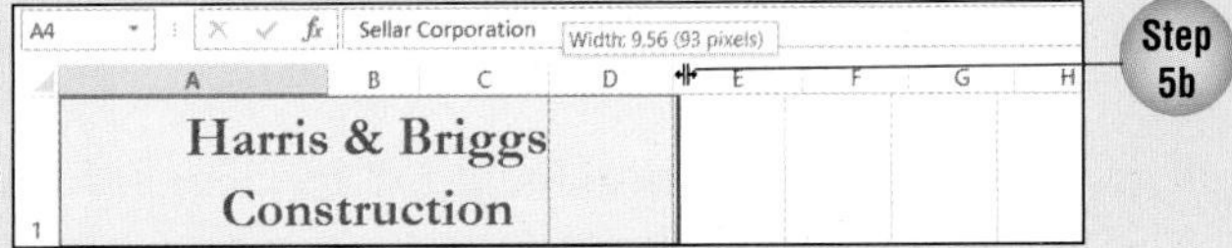

6. Save, print, and then close **EL1-C3-P4-HBCJobs.xlsx**.

Chapter Summary

- Change column width using the mouse on column boundaries or with options at the Column Width dialog box.
- Change row height using the mouse on row boundaries or with options at the Row Height dialog box.
- Insert a row in a worksheet with the Insert button in the Cells group on the HOME tab or with options at the Insert dialog box.
- Insert a column in a worksheet with the Insert button in the Cells group or with options at the Insert dialog box.
- Delete a specific cell by clicking the Delete button arrow and then clicking *Delete Cells* at the drop-down list. At the Delete dialog box, specify if you want to delete just the cell or an entire row or column.
- Delete a selected row(s) or column(s) by clicking the Delete button in the Cells group.
- Delete cell contents by pressing the Delete key or clicking the Clear button in the Editing group on the HOME tab and then clicking *Clear Contents* at the drop-down list.
- Apply font formatting with buttons in the Font group on the HOME tab.
- Use the Mini toolbar to apply font formatting to selected data in a cell.
- Apply alignment formatting with buttons in the Alignment group on the HOME tab.
- Use the Themes button in the Themes group on the PAGE LAYOUT tab to apply a theme to cells in a worksheet that applies formatting such as color, font, and effects. Use the other buttons in the Themes group to customize the theme.
- Format numbers in cells with buttons in the Number group on the HOME tab or with options at the Format Cells dialog box with the Number tab selected.
- Apply formatting to cells in a worksheet with options at the Format Cells dialog box. This dialog box includes the following tabs for formatting cells: Number, Alignment, Font, Border, and Fill.
- Press F4 or Ctrl + Y to repeat the last action performed.
- Use the Format Painter button in the Clipboard group on the HOME tab to apply formatting to different locations in a worksheet.
- Hide selected columns or rows in a worksheet by clicking the Format button in the Cells group on the HOME tab, pointing to *Hide & Unhide*, and then clicking *Hide Columns* or *Hide Rows*.
- To make a hidden column visible, select the columns to the left and right, click the Format button in the Cells group, point to *Hide & Unhide*, and then click *Unhide Columns*.
- To make a hidden row visible, select the rows above and below, click the Format button in the Cells group, point to *Hide & Unhide*, and then click *Unhide Rows*.

Commands Review

FEATURE	RIBBON TAB, GROUP	BUTTON	KEYBOARD SHORTCUT
bold text	HOME, Font	B	Ctrl + B
borders	HOME, Font		
bottom-align (in row)	HOME, Alignment		
center-align (in column)	HOME, Alignment		
clear cell or cell contents	HOME, Editing		
decrease font size	HOME, Font	A	
decrease indent	HOME, Alignment		Ctrl + Alt + Shift + Tab
delete cells, rows, or columns	HOME, Cells		
fill color	Home, Font		
font	HOME, Font	Calibri	
font color	Home, Font	A	
font size	HOME, Font	11	
format	HOME, Cells		
Format Painter	HOME, Clipboard		
increase font size	HOME, Font	A	
increase indent	HOME, Alignment		Ctrl + Alt + Tab
insert cells, rows, or columns	HOME, Cells		
italicize text	HOME, Font	I	Ctrl + I
left-align (in column)	HOME, Alignment		
merge and center cells	HOME, Alignment		
middle-align (in row)	HOME, Alignment		
number format	HOME, Number	General	
orientation	HOME, Alignment		
repeat last action			F4 or Ctrl + Y
right-align (in column)	HOME, Alignment		
themes	PAGE LAYOUT, Themes	Aa	

FEATURE	RIBBON TAB, GROUP	BUTTON	KEYBOARD SHORTCUT
top-align (in row)	HOME, Alignment		
underline text	HOME, Font		Ctrl + U
wrap text	HOME, Alignment		

Concepts Check Test Your Knowledge

Completion: In the space provided at the right, indicate the correct term, symbol, or command.

1. By default, a column is inserted on this side of the column containing the active cell. __________
2. To delete a row, select the row and then click the Delete button in this group on the HOME tab. __________
3. Use the options at this button's drop-down list to clear the contents of the cell or selected cells. __________
4. Use this button to insert color in the active cell or selected cells. __________
5. Select data in a cell and this displays above the selected text. __________
6. By default, numbers are aligned at this side of a cell. __________
7. Click this button in the Alignment group on the HOME tab to rotate data in a cell. __________
8. The Themes button is located on this tab. __________
9. If you type a number with a dollar sign, such as *$50.25*, Excel automatically applies this formatting to the number. __________
10. If you type a number with a percent sign, such as *25%*, Excel automatically applies this formatting to the number. __________
11. Align and indent data in cells using buttons in the Alignment group on the HOME tab or with options at this dialog box with the Alignment tab selected. __________
12. You can repeat the last action performed by pressing Ctrl + Y or this function key. __________
13. The Format Painter button is located in this group on the HOME tab. __________
14. To hide a column, select the column, click this button in the Cells group on the HOME tab, point to *Hide & Unhide*, and then click *Hide Columns*. __________

Skills Check Assess Your Performance

Assessment 1

FORMAT A SALES WORKSHEET

1. Open **NSPSales.xlsx**.
2. Save the workbook with Save As and name it **EL1-C3-A1-NSPSales**.
3. Change the width of columns as follows:
   Column A: 14.00
   Columns B–E: 10.00
4. Select row 2 and then insert a new row.
5. Merge and center cells A2 through E2.
6. Type **Sales Department** in cell A2 and then press Enter.
7. Increase the height of row 1 to 33.00 points.
8. Increase the height of row 2 to 21.00 points.
9. Increase the height of row 3 to 18.00 points.
10. Make the following formatting changes to the worksheet:
    a. Make cell A1 active, change the font size to 18 points, and turn on bold formatting.
    b. Make cell A2 active, change the font size to 14 points, and turn on bold formatting.
    c. Select cells A3 through E3, click the Bold button in the Font group, and then click the Center button in the Alignment group.
    d. Select cells A1 through E3 and change the vertical alignment to *Middle Align*.
11. Insert the following formulas in the worksheet:
    a. Insert a formula in cell D4 that adds the amounts in cells B4 and C4. Copy the formula down to cells D5 through D11.
    b. Insert a formula in cell E4 that averages the amounts in cells B4 and C4. Copy the formula down to cells E5 through E11.
12. Make the following changes to the worksheet:
    a. Select cells B4 through E4 and then apply accounting formatting with a dollar sign and no places past the decimal point.
    b. Select cells B5 through E11 and then apply comma formatting and change the number of places past the decimal point to zero.
    c. Apply the Facet theme to the worksheet.
    d. Add a double-line border outline around cells A1 through E11.
    e. Select cells A1 and A2 and then apply Blue-Gray, Text 2, Lighter 80% fill color (fourth column, second row in the *Theme Colors* section).
    f. Select cells A3 through E3 and then apply Blue-Gray, Text 2, Lighter 60% fill color (fourth column, third row in the *Theme Colors* section).
13. Save, print, and then close **EL1-C3-A1-NSPSales.xlsx**.

Assessment 2

FORMAT AN OVERDUE ACCOUNTS WORKSHEET

1. Open **CCorpAccts.xlsx**.
2. Save the workbook with Save As and name it **EL1-C3-A2-CCorpAccts**.
3. Change the width of columns as follows:
   Column A: 21.00 characters
   Column B: 10.00 characters
   Column C: 12.00 characters
   Column D: 13.00 characters
   Column E: 7.00 characters
   Column F: 12.00 characters
4. Make cell A1 active and then insert a new row.
5. Merge and center cells A1 through F1.
6. Type **Compass Corporation** in cell A1 and then press Enter.
7. Increase the height of row 1 to 42.00 points.
8. Increase the height of row 2 to 24.00 points.
9. Make the following formatting changes to the worksheet:
   a. Select cells A1 through F11 and then change the font to 10-point Cambria.
   b. Make cell A1 active, change the font size to 24 points, and turn on bold formatting.
   c. Make cell A2 active, change the font size to 18 points, and turn on bold formatting.
   d. Select cells A3 through F3, click the Bold button in the Font group, and then click the Center button in the Alignment group.
   e. Select cell A1 and then click the Middle Align button in the Alignment group.
   f. Select cells B4 through B11 and then click the Center button in the Alignment group.
   g. Select cells E4 through E11 and then click the Center button in the Alignment group.
10. Enter a formula in cell F4 that inserts the due date (the purchase date plus the number of days in the *Terms* column). Copy the formula down to cells F5 through F11.
11. Apply the following borders and fill color:
    a. Add a thick line outline border around cells A1 through F11.
    b. Make cell A2 active and then add a double-line border at the top and the bottom of the cell.
    c. Select cells A3 through F3 and then add a single line border to the bottom of the cells.
    d. Select cells A1 and A2 and then apply Blue, Accent 1, Lighter 80% fill color (fifth column, second row in the *Theme Colors* section).
12. Save, print, and then close **EL1-C3-A2-CCorpAccts.xlsx**.

Assessment 3

FORMAT A SUPPLIES AND EQUIPMENT WORKSHEET

1. Open **OEBudget.xlsx**.
2. Save the workbook with Save As and name it **EL1-C3-A3-OEBudget**.
3. Select and then merge across cells A1 through D2. ***Hint: Use the*** **Merge Across** ***option at the Merge & Center button drop-down list.***

4. With cells A1 and A2 selected, click the Middle Align button in the Alignment group and then click the Center button.
5. Make cell A1 active and then change the font size to 22 points and turn on bold formatting.
6. Make cell A2 active and then change the font size to 12 points and turn on bold formatting.
7. Change the height of row 1 to 36.00 points.
8. Change the height of row 2 to 21.00 points.
9. Change the width of column A to 15.00 characters.
10. Select cells A3 through A17, turn on bold, and then click the Wrap Text button in the Alignment group.
11. Make cell B3 active and then apply currency formatting with no places past the decimal point.
12. Select cells C6 through C19 and then apply percentage formatting with one place past the decimal point.
13. Make cell D6 active and then type a formula that multiplies the absolute cell reference $B$3 with the percentage in cell C6. Copy the formula down to cells D7 through D19.
14. With cells D6 through D19 selected, apply currency formatting with no places past the decimal point.
15. Make cell D8 active and then clear the cell contents. Use the Repeat command, F4, to clear the contents from cells D11, D14, and D17.
16. Select cells A1 through D19, change the font to Constantia, and then change the font color to Dark Blue (in the *Standard Colors* section).
17. Add Green, Accent 6, Lighter 80% green fill color (last column, second row in the *Theme Colors* section) to the following cells: A1, A2, A5–D5, A8–D8, A11–D11, A14–D14, and A17–D17.
18. Automatically adjust the width of column B.
19. Save, print, and then close **EL1-C3-A3-OEBudget.xlsx**.

Assessment 4

FORMAT A FINANCIAL ANALYSIS WORKSHEET

1. At a blank workbook, display the Format Cells dialog box with the Alignment tab selected and then experiment with the options in the *Text control* section.
2. Open **FinAnalysis.xlsx**.
3. Save the workbook with Save As and name it **EL1-C3-A4-FinAnalysis**.
4. Make cell B9 active and then insert a formula that averages the percentages in cells B3 through B8. Copy the formula to the right to cells C9 and D9.
5. Select cells B3 through D9, display the Format Cells dialog box with the Alignment tab selected, change the horizontal alignment to *Right (Indent)* and the indent to *2*, and then close the dialog box.
6. Select cells A1 through D9 and then change the font size to 14 points.
7. Select cells B2 through D2 and then change the orientation to 45 degrees.
8. Save, print, and then close **EL1-C3-A4-FinAnalysis.xlsx**.

Visual Benchmark Demonstrate Your Proficiency

CREATE A WORKSHEET AND INSERT FORMULAS

1. At a blank workbook, type the data in the cells indicated in Figure 3.11 but **do not** type the data in the following cells: B8:D8, B14:D14, B20:D20, B22:D22, and B25:D25. For these cells, enter the appropriate formulas so your results match what you see in the figure.
2. Apply formatting so your worksheet looks similar to the worksheet shown in Figure 3.11.
3. Save the workbook and name it **EL1-C3-VB-BTBookings**.
4. Print **EL1-C3-VB-BTBookings.xlsx**.
5. Press Ctrl + ` to turn on the display of formulas and then print the worksheet again.
6. Turn off the display of formulas and then close the workbook.

Figure 3.11 Visual Benchmark

	A	B	C	D	E
1	**Bayside Travel**				
2	**First Quarter Booking Totals**				
3		**January**	**February**	**March**	
4	**Los Angeles**				
5	Tours	$ 65,395	$ 62,103	$ 58,450	
6	Cruises	48,525	43,218	54,055	
7	Other	29,329	26,398	30,391	
8	**Total**	143,249	131,719	142,896	
9					
10	**San Francisco**				
11	Tours	41,438	39,493	56,461	
12	Cruises	23,147	18,530	40,530	
13	Other	18,642	14,320	17,305	
14	**Total**	83,227	72,343	114,296	
15					
16	**Toronto**				
17	Tours	50,229	42,519	52,403	
18	Cruises	49,260	41,490	39,230	
19	Other	31,322	21,579	27,430	
20	**Total**	130,811	105,588	119,063	
21					
22	TOTAL	$357,287	$309,650	$376,255	
23					
24	**Gross Profit Factor**	26%			
25	**Estimated Gross Profit**	$ 92,895	$ 80,509	$ 97,826	

Case Study Apply Your Skills

Part 1

You are the office manager for HealthWise Fitness Center and decide to prepare an Excel worksheet that displays the various plans offered by the health club. In this worksheet, you want to include yearly dues for each plan as well as quarterly and monthly payments. Open the **HFCDues.xlsx** workbook and then save it with Save As and name it **EL1-C3-CS-HFCDues-1**. Make the following changes to the worksheet:

- Select cells B3 through D8 and then apply accounting formatting with two places past the decimal point and without dollar signs.
- Make cell B3 active and then insert *500.00*.
- Make cell B4 active and then insert a formula that adds the amount in cell B3 with the product (multiplication) of cell B3 multiplied by 10%. (The formula should look like this: **=B3+(B3*10%)**. The Economy plan is the base plan and each additional plan costs 10% more than the previous plan.)
- Copy the formula in cell B4 down to cells B5 through B8.
- Insert a formula in cell C3 that divides the amount in cell B3 by 4 and then copy the formula down to cells C4 through C8.
- Insert a formula in cell D3 that divides the amount in cell B3 by 12 and then copy the formula down to cells D4 through D8.
- Apply formatting to enhance the visual display of the worksheet.

Save and print the completed worksheet.

With **EL1-C3-CS-HFCDues-1.xlsx** open, save the workbook with Save As and name it **EL1-C3-CS-HFCDues-2** and then make the following changes:

- You have been informed that the base rate for yearly dues has increased from $500.00 to $600.00. Change this amount in cell B3 of the worksheet.
- If clients are late with their quarterly or monthly dues payments, a late fee is charged. You decide to add the late fee information to the worksheet. Insert a new column to the right of column C. Type **Late Fees** in cell D2 and also in cell F2.
- Insert a formula in cell D3 that multiplies the amount in C3 by 5%. Copy this formula down to cells D4 through D8.
- Insert a formula in cell F3 that multiplies the amount in cell E3 by 7%. Copy this formula down to cells F4 through F8. If necessary, apply accounting formatting to cells F3 through F8 with two places after the decimal point and without dollar signs.
- Select cells B3 through F3 and change the accounting formatting to include dollar signs.
- Select cells B8 through F8 and change the accounting formatting to include dollar signs.
- Apply formatting to enhance the visual display of the worksheet.

Save, print, and then close **EL1-C3-CS-HFCDues-2.xlsx**.

Part 2

Prepare a payroll sheet for the employees of the fitness center using the information in Figure 3.12, and include the following information:

Insert a formula in the *Overtime Pay* column that multiples the hourly wage by the overtime rate, which is 1.5, and then multiple that amount by the number of overtime hours. (Make sure you include parentheses around the first part of the formula.)

Insert a formula in the *Weekly Salary* column that multiplies the hourly wage by the number of hours plus the overtime pay. (Make sure you include parentheses in the first part of the formula.)

Apply formatting to enhance the visual display of the worksheet. Save the workbook and name it **EL1-C3-CS-HFCPayroll**. Press Ctrl + ` to turn on the display of formulas, print the worksheet, and then turn off the display of formulas.

Make the following changes to the worksheet:

- Change the hourly wage for Amanda Turney to *$22.00*.
- Increase the hours for Daniel Joyner to *20*.
- Remove the row for Grant Baker.
- Insert a row between Jean Overmeyer and Bonnie Haddon and then type the following information in the cells in the new row: *Employee:* **McGuire, Tonya**; *Hourly Wage:* **$17.50**; *Hours:* **15**; *Overtime Hours:* **0**.

Save and then print **EL1-C3-CS-HFCPayroll.xlsx**. Press Ctrl + ` to turn on the display of formulas, print the worksheet again, and then turn off the display of formulas. Save and close **EL1-C3-CS-HFCPayroll.xlsx**.

Figure 3.12 Case Study Part 2

HealthWise Fitness Center
Weekly Payroll

Employee	Hourly Wage	Hours	Overtime Hours	Overtime Pay	Weekly Salary
Heaton, Kelly	$26.50	40	2		
Severson, Joel	$25.00	40	0		
Turney, Amanda	$20.00	15	0		
Walters, Leslie	$19.65	30	0		
Overmeyer, Jean	$18.00	20	0		
Haddon, Bonnie	$16.00	40	3		
Baker, Grant	$15.00	40	0		
Calveri, Shannon	$12.00	15	0		
Dugan, Emily	$10.50	40	4		
Joyner, Daniel	$10.50	10	0		
Lee, Alexander	$10.50	10	0		

Part 3

Your boss is interested in ordering new equipment for the health club. She is interested in ordering three elliptical machines, three recumbent bikes, and three upright bikes. She has asked you to use the Internet to research models and prices for this new equipment. She then wants you to prepare a worksheet with the information. Using the Internet, search for information about the following equipment:

- Search for elliptical machines for sale. Locate two different models and, if possible, find at least two companies that sell each model. Make a note of the company names, model numbers, and prices.
- Search for recumbent bikes for sale. Locate two different models and, if possible, find at least two companies that sell each model. Make a note of the company names, model numbers, and prices.
- Search for upright bikes for sale. Locate two different models and, if possible, find at least two companies that sell each model. Make a note of the company names, model numbers, and prices.

Using the information you found on the Internet, prepare an Excel worksheet with the following information:

- Company name
- Equipment name
- Equipment model
- Price
- A column that multiplies the price by the number required (which is 3)

Include the fitness center name, HealthWise Fitness Center, and any other information you think is necessary to the worksheet. Apply formatting to enhance the visual display of the worksheet. Save the workbook and name it **EL1-C3-CS-HFCEquip**. Print and then close **EL1-C3-CS-HFCEquip.xlsx**.

Part 4

When a prospective client contacts HealthWise about joining, you send a letter containing information about the fitness center, the plans offered, and the dues amounts. Use a letter template in Word to create a letter to send to a prospective client. (You determine the client's name and address). Copy the cells in **EL1-C3-CS-HFCDues-02.xlsx** containing data and paste them into the body of the letter. Make formatting changes to make the data readable. Save the document and name it **HFCLetter**. Print and then close **HFCLetter.docx**.

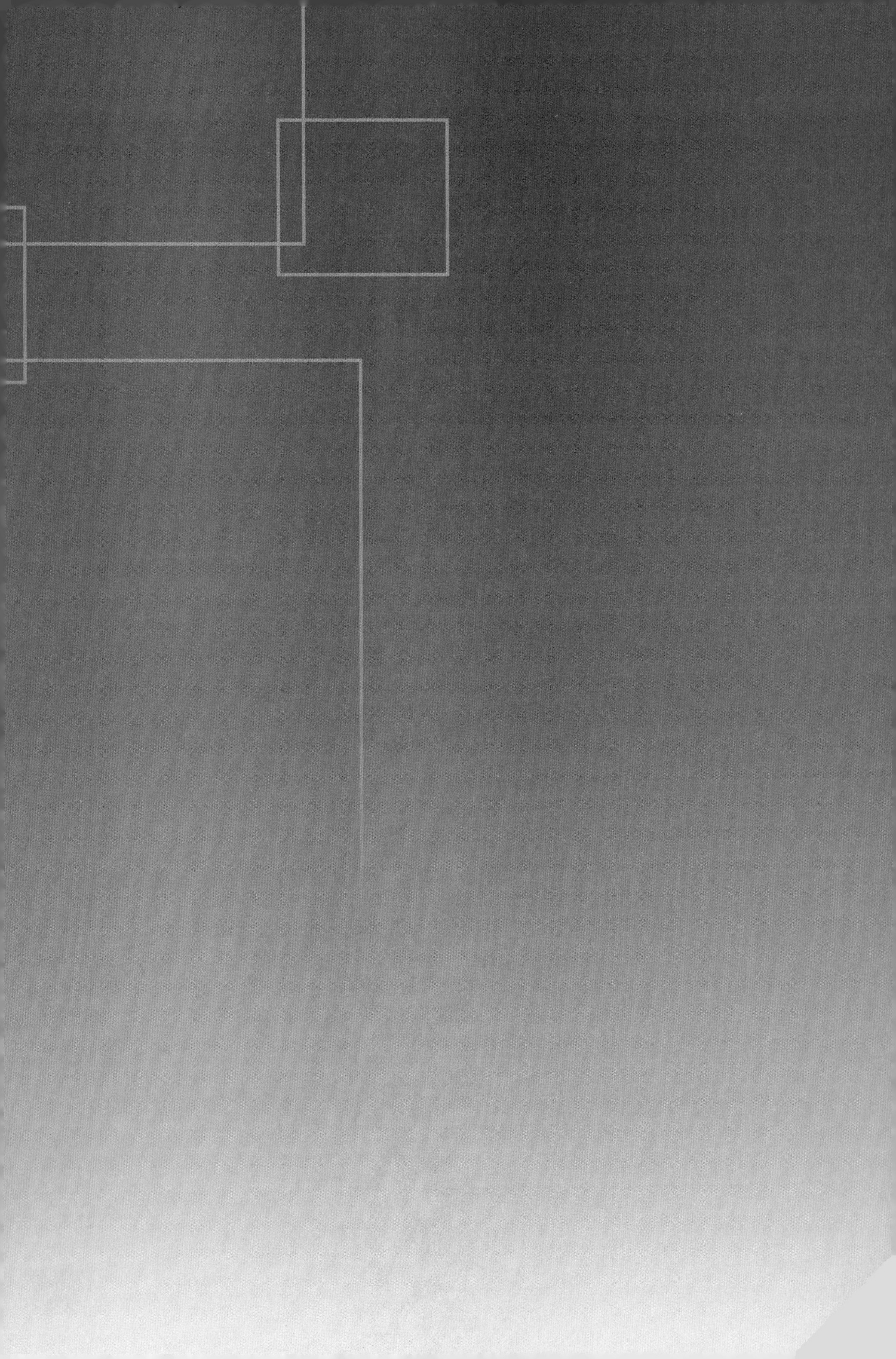

MICROSOFT® EXCEL®

Enhancing a Worksheet

PERFORMANCE OBJECTIVES

Upon successful completion of Chapter 4, you will be able to:

- **Change worksheet margins**
- **Center a worksheet horizontally and vertically on the page**
- **Insert a page break in a worksheet**
- **Print gridlines and row and column headings**
- **Set and clear a print area**
- **Insert headers and footers**
- **Customize print jobs**
- **Complete a spelling check on a worksheet**
- **Find and replace data and cell formatting in a worksheet**
- **Sort data in cells in ascending and descending order**
- **Filter a list using AutoFilter**

Tutorials

4.1 Changing Page Layout Options
4.2 Formatting a Worksheet Page for Printing
4.3 Using Page Break Preview
4.4 Inserting Headers and Footers
4.5 Formatting and Printing Multiple Worksheets
4.6 Completing a Spelling Check
4.7 Using Undo and Redo
4.8 Using Find and Replace
4.9 Finding and Replacing Text and Formatting
4.10 Sorting Data
4.11 Filtering Data Using a Custom AutoFilter

Excel contains features you can use to enhance and control the formatting of a worksheet. In this chapter, you will learn how to change worksheet margins, orientation, size, and scale; print column and row titles; print gridlines; and center a worksheet horizontally and vertically on the page. You will also learn how to complete a spelling check on text in a worksheet, find and replace specific data and formatting in a worksheet, sort and filter data, and plan and create a worksheet. Model answers for this chapter's projects appear on the following pages.

EL1C4

Note: Before beginning the projects, copy to your storage medium the EL1C4 subfolder from the EL1 folder on the CD that accompanies this textbook and make EL1C4 the active folder.

1

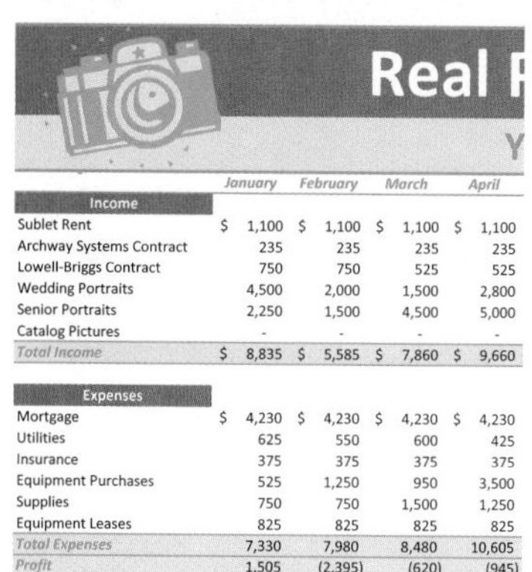

Real P

Y

	January	February	March	April
Income				
Sublet Rent	$ 1,100	$ 1,100	$ 1,100	$ 1,100
Archway Systems Contract	235	235	235	235
Lowell-Briggs Contract	750	750	525	525
Wedding Portraits	4,500	2,000	1,500	2,800
Senior Portraits	2,250	1,500	4,500	5,000
Catalog Pictures	-	-	-	-
Total Income	$ 8,835	$ 5,585	$ 7,860	$ 9,660
Expenses				
Mortgage	$ 4,230	$ 4,230	$ 4,230	$ 4,230
Utilities	625	550	600	425
Insurance	375	375	375	375
Equipment Purchases	525	1,250	950	3,500
Supplies	750	750	1,500	1,250
Equipment Leases	825	825	825	825
Total Expenses	7,330	7,980	8,480	10,605
Profit	1,505	(2,395)	(620)	(945)

Yearly Budget 2

hotography

early Budget

May	June	July	August	September	October
$ 1,100	$ 1,100	$ 1,100	$ 1,100	$ 1,100	$ 1,100
235	235	235	235	235	235
-	-	450	450	450	575
4,000	8,250	7,500	6,850	4,500	3,500
3,250	1,000	300	500	650	650
500	500	500	500	500	-
$ 9,085	$ 11,085	$ 10,085	$ 9,635	$ 7,435	$ 6,060
$ 4,230	$ 4,230	$ 4,230	$ 4,230	$ 4,230	$ 4,230
400	500	650	700	700	500
375	375	375	375	375	375
-	-	-	-	-	-
1,500	2,500	2,250	1,750	950	850
825	825	825	825	825	825
7,330	8,430	8,330	7,880	7,080	6,780
1,755	2,655	1,755	1,755	355	(720)

Student Name

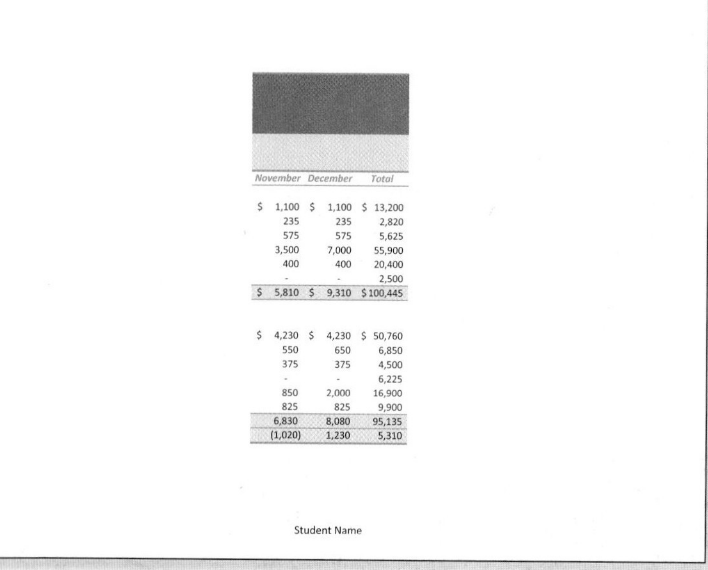

Yearly Budget 3

November	December	Total
$ 1,100	$ 1,100	$ 13,200
235	235	2,820
575	575	5,625
3,500	7,000	55,900
400	400	20,400
-	-	2,500
$ 5,810	$ 9,310	$ 100,445
$ 4,230	$ 4,230	$ 50,760
550	650	6,850
375	375	4,500
-	-	6,225
850	2,000	16,900
825	825	9,900
6,830	8,080	95,135
(1,020)	1,230	5,310

Student Name

Project 1 Format a Yearly Budget Worksheet

EL1-C4-P1-RPBudget.xlsx

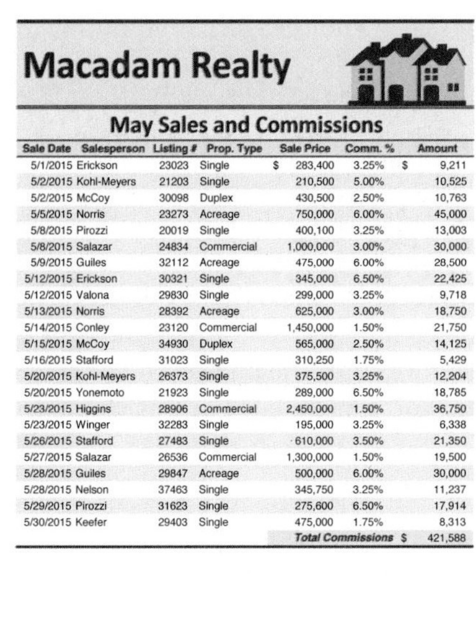

Macadam Realty

May Sales and Commissions

Sale Date	Salesperson	Listing #	Prop. Type	Sale Price	Comm. %	Amount
5/1/2015	Erickson	23023	Single	$ 283,400	3.25%	$ 9,211
5/2/2015	Kohl-Meyers	21203	Single	210,500	5.00%	10,525
5/2/2015	McCoy	30098	Duplex	430,500	2.50%	10,763
5/5/2015	Norris	23273	Acreage	750,000	6.00%	45,000
5/8/2015	Pirozzi	20019	Single	400,100	3.25%	13,003
5/8/2015	Salazar	24834	Commercial	1,000,000	3.00%	30,000
5/9/2015	Guiles	32112	Acreage	475,000	6.00%	28,500
5/12/2015	Erickson	30321	Single	345,000	6.50%	22,425
5/12/2015	Valona	29830	Single	299,000	3.25%	9,718
5/13/2015	Norris	28392	Acreage	625,000	3.00%	18,750
5/14/2015	Conley	23120	Commercial	1,450,000	1.50%	21,750
5/15/2015	McCoy	34930	Duplex	565,000	2.50%	14,125
5/16/2015	Stafford	31023	Single	310,250	1.75%	5,429
5/20/2015	Kohl-Meyers	26373	Single	375,500	3.25%	12,204
5/20/2015	Yonemoto	21923	Single	289,000	6.50%	18,785
5/23/2015	Higgins	28906	Commercial	2,450,000	1.50%	36,750
5/23/2015	Winger	32283	Single	195,000	3.25%	6,338
5/26/2015	Stafford	27483	Single	610,000	3.50%	21,350
5/27/2015	Salazar	26536	Commercial	1,300,000	1.50%	19,500
5/28/2015	Guiles	29847	Acreage	500,000	6.00%	30,000
5/28/2015	Nelson	37463	Single	345,750	3.25%	11,237
5/29/2015	Pirozzi	31623	Single	275,600	6.50%	17,914
5/30/2015	Keefer	29403	Single	475,000	1.75%	8,313
					Total Commissions	$ 421,588

Project 2 Format a May Sales and Commissions Worksheet

EL1-C4-P2-MRSales.xlsx

Ace Physical Therapy

Billing - Week of August 10, 2015

Client #	Treatment	Date	Hours	Rate	Total
2085	Test Consultation	8/10/2015	0.25	$ 75.00	$ 18.75
3102	Therapeutic Massage	8/10/2015	1.00	$ 65.00	$ 65.00
3102	Consultation	8/10/2015	0.75	$ 50.00	$ 37.50
1403	Physical Therapy	8/11/2015	1.00	$ 60.00	$ 60.00
1502	Physical Therapy	8/11/2015	1.25	$ 60.00	$ 75.00
1884	Physical Therapy	8/11/2015	1.00	$ 60.00	$ 60.00
2188	Pool Therapy	8/11/2015	0.50	$ 45.00	$ 22.50
1215	Physical Therapy	8/12/2015	1.00	$ 60.00	$ 60.00
3102	Therapeutic Massage	8/12/2015	1.00	$ 65.00	$ 65.00
3402	Physical Examination	8/12/2015	0.50	$ 50.00	$ 25.00
3675	Therapeutic Massage	8/12/2015	1.00	$ 65.00	$ 65.00
3675	Physical Therapy	8/12/2015	0.50	$ 60.00	$ 30.00
1008	Physical Therapy	8/13/2015	1.00	$ 60.00	$ 60.00
1403	Physical Therapy	8/13/2015	1.00	$ 60.00	$ 60.00
1502	Physical Therapy	8/13/2015	1.00	$ 60.00	$ 60.00
2188	Pool Therapy	8/13/2015	0.50	$ 45.00	$ 22.50
3211	Consultation	8/13/2015	0.75	$ 50.00	$ 37.50
3322	Physical Examination	8/13/2015	0.50	$ 50.00	$ 25.00
1434	Pool Therapy	8/14/2015	0.50	$ 45.00	$ 22.50
1566	Therapeutic Massage	8/14/2015	1.00	$ 65.00	$ 65.00
3211	Physical Therapy	8/14/2015	1.00	$ 60.00	$ 60.00
1403	Physical Therapy	8/15/2015	1.00	$ 60.00	$ 60.00
1722	Physical Therapy	8/15/2015	1.00	$ 65.00	$ 65.00
2188	Pool Therapy	8/15/2015	0.50	$ 45.00	$ 22.50
3211	Test Consultation	8/15/2015	0.50	$ 50.00	$ 25.00
2085	Physical Examination	8/20/2015	0.50	$ 50.00	$ 25.00

Project 3 Format a Billing Worksheet

EL1-C4-P3-APTBilling.xlsx

Project 1 Format a Yearly Budget Worksheet — 12 Parts

You will format a yearly budget worksheet by inserting formulas; changing margins, page orientation, and page size; inserting a page break; printing column headings on multiple pages; scaling data to print on one page; inserting a background picture; inserting headers and footers; and identifying a print area and customizing a print job.

Formatting a Worksheet Page

An Excel worksheet contains default page formatting. For example, a worksheet contains left and right margins of 0.7 inch and top and bottom margins of 0.75 inch. In addition, a worksheet prints in portrait orientation and the worksheet page size is 8.5 inches by 11 inches. These defaults, along with additional settings, can be changed and/or controlled with options on the PAGE LAYOUT tab.

Changing Margins

The Page Setup group on the PAGE LAYOUT tab contains buttons for changing the margins and the page orientation and size, as well as buttons for establishing a print area, inserting a page break, applying a picture background, and printing titles.

Change the worksheet margins by clicking the Margins button in the Page Setup group on the PAGE LAYOUT tab. This displays a drop-down list of

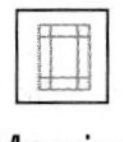
Margins

Quick Steps

Change Worksheet Margins
1. Click PAGE LAYOUT tab.
2. Click Margins button.
3. Click desired predesigned margin.
OR
1. Click PAGE LAYOUT tab.
2. Click Margins button.
3. Click *Custom Margins* at drop-down list.
4. Change the top, left, right, and/or bottom measurements.
5. Click OK.

predesigned margin choices. If one of the predesigned choices is what you want to apply to the worksheet, click the option. If you want to customize the margins, click the *Custom Margins* option at the bottom of the Margins button drop-down list. This displays the Page Setup dialog box with the Margins tab selected, as shown in Figure 4.1.

A worksheet page showing the cells and margins displays in the dialog box. As you increase or decrease the top, bottom, left, or right margin measurements, the sample worksheet page reflects the change. You can also increase or decrease the measurement from the top of the page to the header with the *Header* measurement box or the measurement from the footer to the bottom of the page with the *Footer* measurement box. (You will learn about headers and footers later in this chapter.)

Figure 4.1 Page Setup Dialog Box with Margins Tab Selected

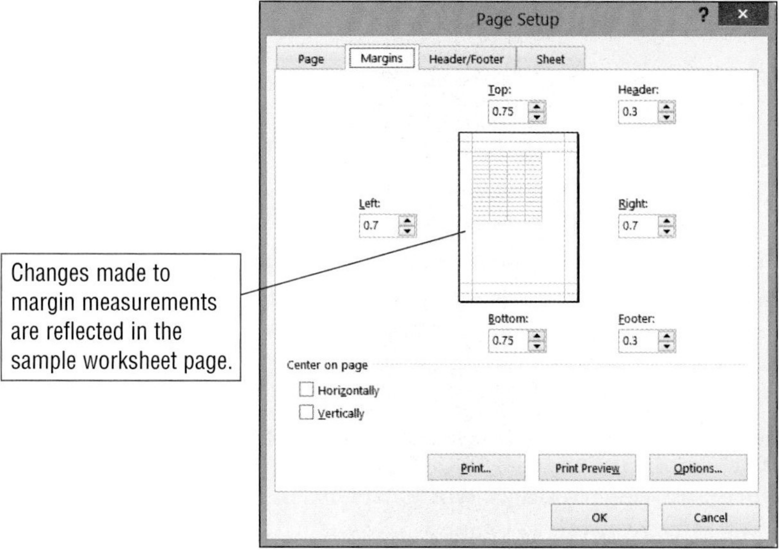

Quick Steps

Center a Worksheet Horizontally and/or Vertically
1. Click PAGE LAYOUT tab.
2. Click Margins button.
3. Click *Custom Margins* at drop-down list.
4. Click *Horizontally* option and/or click *Vertically* option.
5. Click OK.

Centering a Worksheet Horizontally and/or Vertically

By default, a worksheet prints in the upper left corner of the page. You can center a worksheet on the page by changing the margins. However, an easier method for centering a worksheet is to use the *Horizontally* and/or *Vertically* options that display in the Page Setup dialog box with the Margins tab selected. If you choose one or both of these options, the worksheet page in the preview section displays how the worksheet will print on the page.

Project 1a **Changing Margins and Horizontally and Vertically Centering a Worksheet** **Part 1 of 12**

1. Open **RPBudget.xlsx**.
2. Save the workbook with Save As and name it **EL1-C4-P1-RPBudget**.
3. Insert the following formulas in the worksheet:
   a. Insert formulas in column N, rows 5 through 10 that sum the totals for each income item.
   b. Insert formulas in row 11, columns B through N that sum the income as well as the total for all income items.

c. Insert formulas in column N, rows 14 through 19 that sum the totals for each expense item.
d. Insert formulas in row 20, columns B through N that sum the expenses as well as the total of expenses.
e. Insert formulas in row 21, columns B through N that subtract the total expenses from the income. (To begin the formula, make cell B21 active and then type the formula =B11-B20. Copy this formula to columns C through N.)
f. Apply the Accounting format with no places past the decimal point to cells N5 and N14.

4. Click the PAGE LAYOUT tab.
5. Click the Margins button in the Page Setup group and then click *Custom Margins* at the drop-down list.
6. At the Page Setup dialog box with the Margins tab selected, click the up-pointing arrow at the right side of the *Top* measurement box until *3.5* displays.
7. Click the up-pointing arrow at the right side of the *Bottom* measurement box until *1.5* displays.
8. Preview the worksheet by clicking the Print Preview button located toward the bottom of the Page Setup dialog box. The worksheet appears to be a little low on the page so you decide to horizontally and vertically center it by completing the following steps:
   a. Click the Page Setup hyperlink that displays below the galleries in the *Settings* category in the Print backstage area.
   b. Click the Margins tab at the Page Setup dialog box.
   c. Change the *Top* and *Bottom* measurements to *1*.
   d. Click the *Horizontally* check box.
   e. Click the *Vertically* check box.
   f. Click OK to close the dialog box.
   g. Look at the preview of the worksheet and then click the Back button to return to the worksheet.
9. Save **EL1-C4-P1-RPBudget.xlsx**.

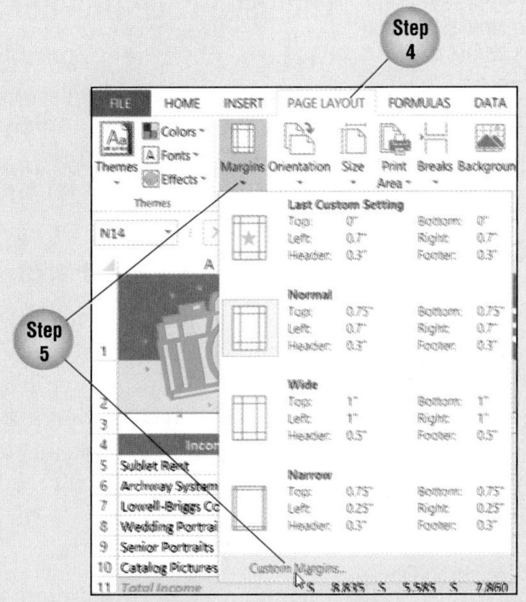

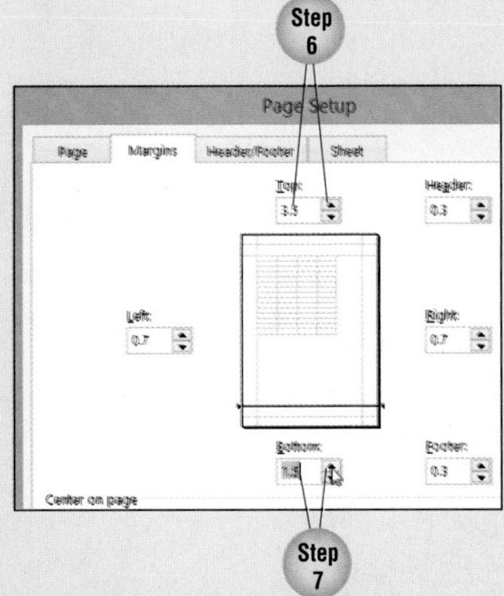

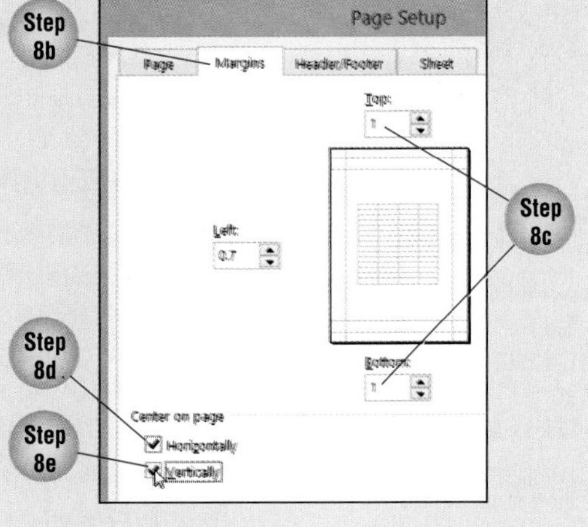

Quick Steps

Change Page Orientation
1. Click PAGE LAYOUT tab.
2. Click Orientation button.
3. Click desired orientation at drop-down list.

Change Page Size
1. Click PAGE LAYOUT tab.
2. Click Size button.
3. Click desired size at drop-down list.

Orientation

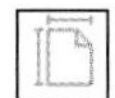
Size

Changing Page Orientation

Click the Orientation button in the Page Setup group and a drop-down list displays with two choices: *Portrait* and *Landscape*. The two choices are represented by sample pages. A sample page that is taller than it is wide shows how the default orientation (*Portrait*) prints data on the page. The other choice, *Landscape*, rotates the data and prints it on a page that is wider than it is tall.

Changing the Page Size

An Excel worksheet page size, by default, is set at 8.5 inches × 11 inches. You can change this default page size by clicking the Size button in the Page Setup group. At the drop-down list that displays, notice that the default setting is *Letter* and that the measurement *8.5" × 11"* displays below *Letter*. This drop-down list also contains a number of page sizes, such as *Executive* and *Legal*, and a number of envelope sizes.

Project 1b **Changing Page Orientation and Size** **Part 2 of 12**

1. With **EL1-C4-P1-RPBudget.xlsx** open, click the Orientation button in the Page Setup group on the PAGE LAYOUT tab and then click *Landscape* at the drop-down list.
2. Click the Size button in the Page Setup group and then click *Legal* at the drop-down list.
3. Preview the worksheet by clicking the FILE tab and then clicking the *Print* option. After viewing the worksheet in the Print backstage area, press the Esc key to return to the worksheet.
4. Save **EL1-C4-P1-RPBudget.xlsx**.

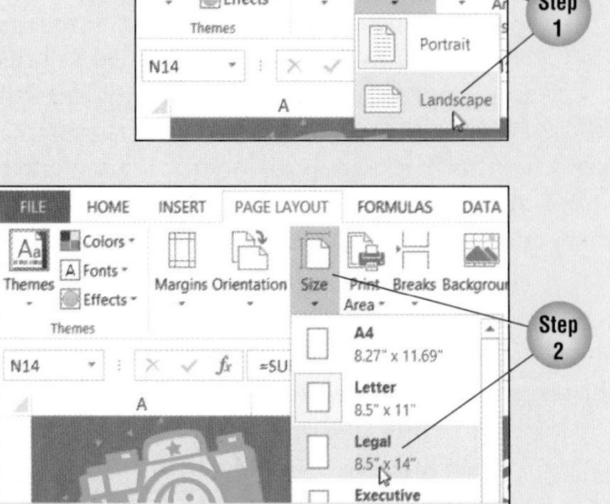

Inserting and Removing Page Breaks

Quick Steps

Insert a Page Break
1. Select column or row.
2. Click PAGE LAYOUT tab.
3. Click Breaks button.
4. Click *Insert Page Break* at drop-down list.

The default left and right margins of 0.7 inch allow approximately 7 inches of cells across the page (8.5 inches minus 1.4 inches equals 7.1 inches). If a worksheet contains more than 7 inches of cells across the page, a page break is inserted and the remaining columns are moved to the next page. A page break displays as a broken line along cell borders. Figure 4.2 shows the page break in **EL1-C4-P1-RPBudget.xlsx** when the paper size is set to *Letter*.

A page break also displays horizontally in a worksheet. By default, a worksheet can contain approximately 9.5 inches of cells vertically down the page. This is because the paper size is set by default at 11 inches. With the default top and bottom margins of 0.75 inch, this allows 9.5 inches of cells to print on one page.

Figure 4.2 Page Break

Real Photography

Yearly Budget

	January	February	March	April	May	June	July	August	September	October	November	December	Total
Income													
Sublet Rent	$ 1,100	$ 1,100	$ 1,100	$ 1,100	$ 1,100	$ 1,100	$ 1,100	$ 1,100	$ 1,100	$ 1,100	$ 1,100	$ 1,100	$ 13,200
Archway Systems Contract	235	235	235	235	235	235	235	235	235	235	235	235	2,820
Lowell-Briggs Contract	750	750	525	525	-	-	450	450	450	575	575	575	5,625
Wedding Portraits	4,500	2,000	1,500	2,800	4,000	8,250	7,500	6,850	4,500	3,500	3,500	7,000	55,900
Senior Portraits	2,250	1,500	4,500	5,000	3,250	1,000	300	500	650	650	400	400	20,400
Catalog Pictures	-	-	-	-	500	500	500	500	500	-	-	-	2,500
Total Income	$ 8,835	$ 5,585	$ 7,860	$ 9,660	$ 9,085	$ 11,085	$ 10,085	$ 9,635	$ 7,435	$ 6,060	$ 5,810	$ 9,310	$ 100,445
Expenses													
Mortgage	$ 4,230	$ 4,230	$ 4,230	$ 4,230	$ 4,230	$ 4,230	$ 4,230	$ 4,230	$ 4,230	$ 4,230	$ 4,230	$ 4,230	$ 50,760
Utilities	625	550	600	425	400	500	650	700	700	500	550	650	6,850
Insurance	375	375	375	375	375	375	375	375	375	375	375	375	4,500
Equipment Purchases	525	1,250	950	3,500	-	-	-	-	-	-	-	-	6,225
Supplies	750	750	1,500	1,250	1,500	2,500	2,250	1,750	950	850	850	2,000	16,900

Sheet1

page break

Excel automatically inserts page breaks in a worksheet. Insert your own page break if you would like more control over what cells print on a page. To insert your own page break, select the column or row, click the Breaks button in the Page Setup group on the PAGE LAYOUT tab, and then click *Insert Page Break* at the drop-down list. A page break is inserted immediately left of the selected column or immediately above the selected row.

Breaks

If you want to insert both horizontal and vertical page breaks at the same time, make a cell active, click the Breaks button in the Page Setup group, and then click *Insert Page Break*. This causes a horizontal page break to be inserted immediately above the active cell and a vertical page break to be inserted at the left side of the active cell. To remove a page break, select the column or row or make the desired cell active, click the Breaks button in the Page Setup group, and then click *Remove Page Break* at the drop-down list.

A page break automatically inserted by Excel may not be visible initially in a worksheet. One way to display the page break is to display the worksheet in the Print backstage area. When you return to the worksheet, the page break will display in the worksheet.

Excel provides a page break view that displays worksheet pages and page breaks. To display this view, click the Page Break Preview button located in the view area at the right side of the Status bar or click the VIEW tab and then click the Page Break Preview button in the Workbook Views group. This causes the worksheet to display similar to the worksheet shown in Figure 4.3. The word *Page* along with the page number displays in gray behind the cells in the worksheet. A dashed blue line indicates a page break inserted by Excel and a solid blue line indicates a page break inserted manually.

Page Break Preview

You can edit a worksheet in Page Break Preview.

Move a page break by positioning the arrow pointer on the blue line, holding down the left mouse button, dragging the line to the desired location, and then releasing the mouse button. To return to the Normal view, click the Normal button in the view area on the Status bar or click the VIEW tab and then click the Normal button in the Workbook Views group.

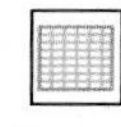

Normal

Figure 4.3 Worksheet in Page Break Preview

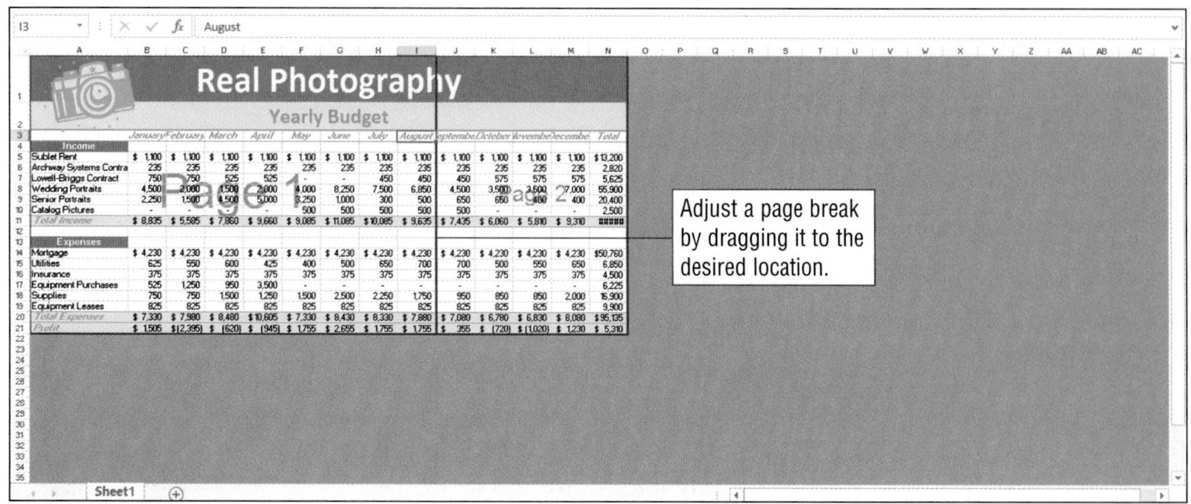

Project 1c Inserting a Page Break in a Worksheet

Part 3 of 12

1. With **EL1-C4-P1-RPBudget.xlsx** open, click the Size button in the Page Setup group on the PAGE LAYOUT tab and then click *Letter* at the drop-down list.
2. Click the Margins button and then click *Custom Margins* at the drop-down list.
3. At the Page Setup dialog box with the Margins tab selected, click in the *Horizontally* check box to remove the check mark, click in the *Vertically* check box to remove the check mark, and then click OK to close the dialog box.
4. Insert a page break between columns I and J by completing the following steps:
   a. Select column J.
   b. Click the Breaks button in the Page Setup group and then click *Insert Page Break* at the drop-down list. Click in any cell in column I.
5. View the worksheet in Page Break Preview by completing the following steps:
   a. Click the Page Break Preview button located in the view area on the Status bar.
   b. View the pages and page breaks in the worksheet.
   c. You decide to include the first six months of the year on one page. To do this, position the arrow pointer on the vertical blue line until the arrow pointer displays as a left-and-right-pointing arrow, hold down the left mouse button, drag the line to the left so it is between columns G and H, and then release the mouse button.

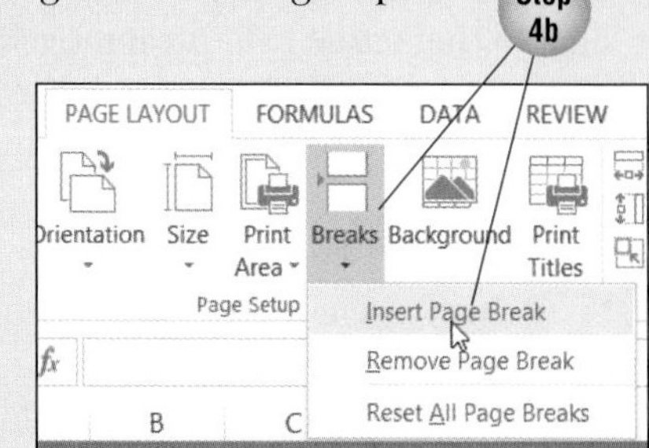

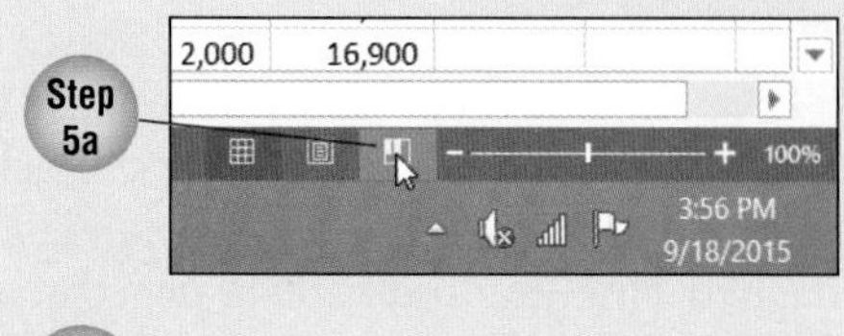

Step 5c

d. Click the Normal button located in the view area on the Status bar.

6. Save **EL1-C4-P1-RPBudget.xlsx**.

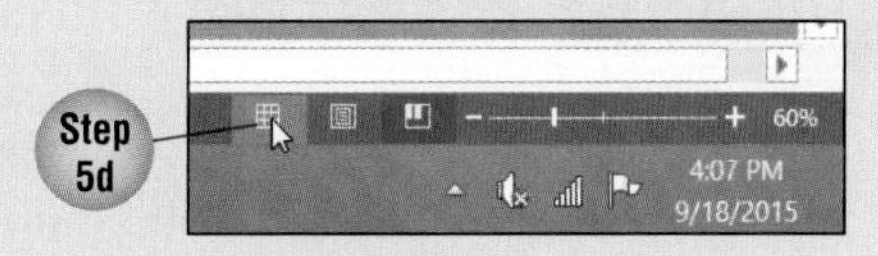

Printing Column and Row Titles on Multiple Pages

The columns and rows in a worksheet are usually titled. For example, in **EL1-C4-P1-RPBudget.xlsx**, the column titles include *Income*, *Expenses*, *January*, *February*, *March*, and so on. The row titles include the income and expenses categories. If a worksheet prints on more than one page, having column and/or row titles printing on each page can be useful. To do this, click the Print Titles button in the Page Setup group on the PAGE LAYOUT tab. This displays the Page Setup dialog box with the Sheet tab selected, as shown in Figure 4.4.

At the Page Setup dialog box with the Sheet tab selected, specify the range of row cells you want to print on every page in the *Rows to repeat at top* text box. Type a cell range using a colon. For example, if you want cells A1 through J1 to print on every page, type *A1:J1* in the *Rows to repeat at top* text box. Type the range of column cells you want to print on every page in the *Columns to repeat at left* text box. To make rows and columns easier to identify on the printed page, specify that row and/or column headings print on each page.

Quick Steps

Print Column and Row Titles

1. Click PAGE LAYOUT tab.
2. Click Print Titles button.
3. Type row range in *Rows to repeat at top* option.
4. Type column range in *Columns to repeat at left* option.
5. Click OK.

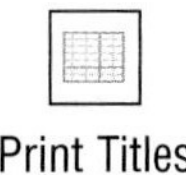

Print Titles

Figure 4.4 Page Setup Dialog Box with Sheet Tab Selected

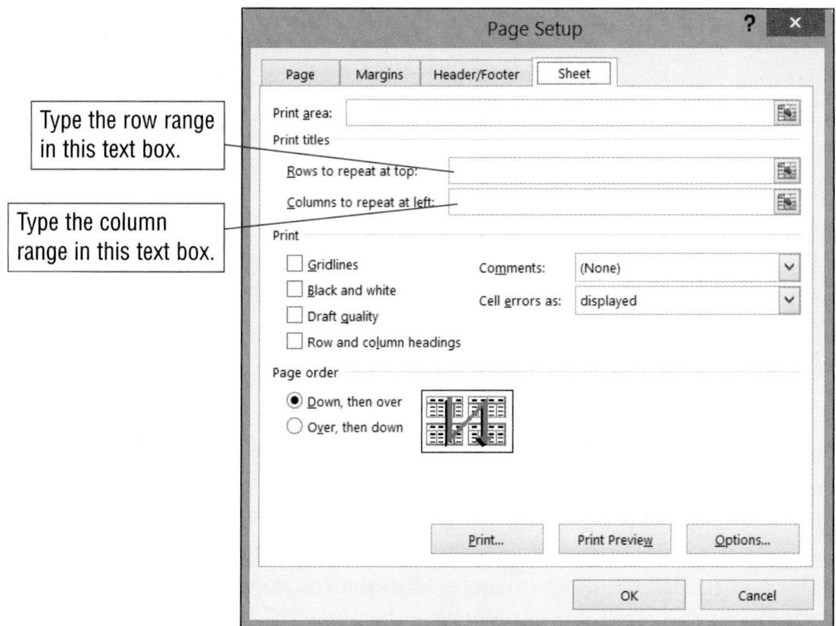

Project 1d Printing Column Titles on Each Page of a Worksheet Part 4 of 12

1. With **EL1-C4-P1-RPBudget.xlsx** open, click the PAGE LAYOUT tab and then click the Print Titles button in the Page Setup group.
2. At the Page Setup dialog box with the Sheet tab selected, click in the *Columns to repeat at left* text box.
3. Type A1:A21.
4. Click OK to close the dialog box.
5. Save and then print **EL1-C4-P1-RPBudget.xlsx**.

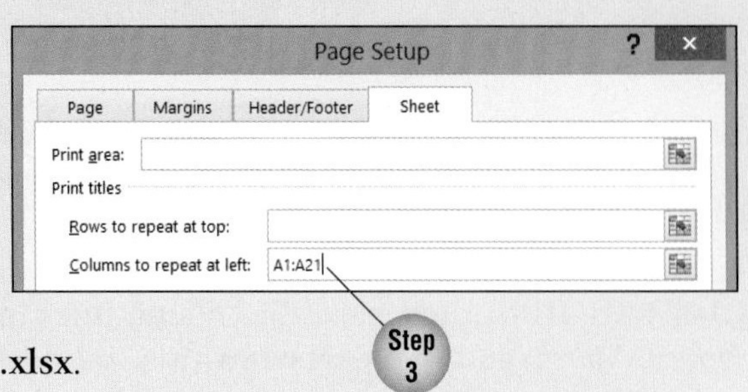

Scaling Data

Width

Using buttons in the Scale to Fit group on the PAGE LAYOUT tab, you can adjust the printed output by a percentage to fit the number of pages specified. For example, if a worksheet contains too many columns to print on one page, click the down-pointing arrow at the right side of the *Width* option box in the Scale to Fit group on the PAGE LAYOUT tab and then click *1 page*. This causes the data to shrink so all columns display and print on one page.

Project 1e Scaling Data to Fit on One Page and Printing Row Titles on Each Page Part 5 of 12

1. With **EL1-C4-P1-RPBudget.xlsx** open, click the down-pointing arrow at the right side of the *Width* option box in the Scale to Fit group on the PAGE LAYOUT tab.
2. At the drop-down list that displays, click the *1 page* option.
3. Display the Print backstage area, notice that all cells containing data display on one page in the worksheet, and then return to the worksheet.
4. Change margins by completing the following steps:
   a. Click the Margins button in the Page Setup group and then click *Custom Margins* at the drop-down list.
   b. At the Page Setup dialog box with the Margins tab selected, select the current number in the *Top* measurement box and then type 3.5.
   c. Select the current number in the *Left* measurement box and then type 0.3.
   d. Select the current number in the *Right* measurement box and then type 0.3.
   e. Click OK to close the Page Setup dialog box.
5. Specify that you want row titles to print on each page by completing the following steps:
   a. Click the Print Titles button in the Page Setup group on the PAGE LAYOUT tab.
   b. At the Page Setup dialog box with the Sheet tab selected, select and then delete the text that displays in the *Columns to repeat at left* text box.

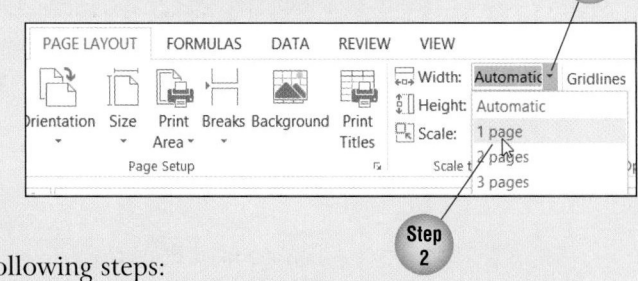

c. Click in the *Rows to repeat at top* text box and then type A3:N3.

d. Click OK to close the dialog box.

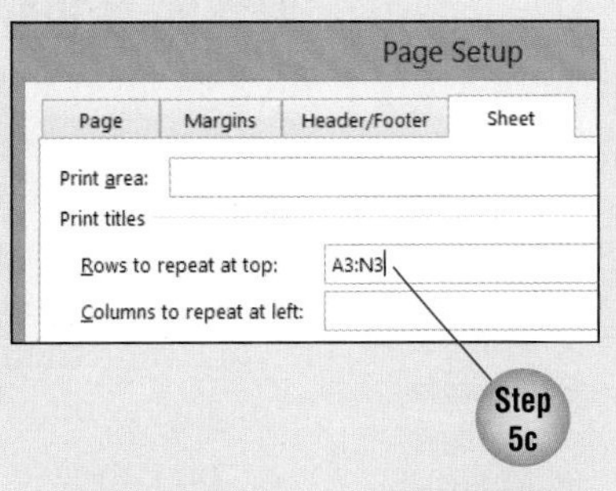

6. Save and then print **EL1-C4-P1-RPBudget.xlsx**. (The worksheet will print on two pages with the row titles repeated on the second page.)
7. At the worksheet, return to the default margins by clicking the PAGE LAYOUT tab, clicking the Margins button, and then clicking the *Normal* option at the drop-down list.
8. Prevent titles from printing on second and subsequent pages by completing the following steps:
   a. Click the Print Titles button in the Page Setup group.
   b. At the Page Setup dialog box with the Sheet tab selected, select and then delete the text that displays in the *Rows to repeat at top* text box.
   c. Click OK to close the dialog box.
9. Change the scaling back to the default by completing the following steps:
   a. Click the down-pointing arrow at the right side of the *Width* option box in the Scale to Fit group and then click *Automatic* at the drop-down list.
   b. Click the up-pointing arrow at the right side of the *Scale* measurement box until *100%* displays in the box.

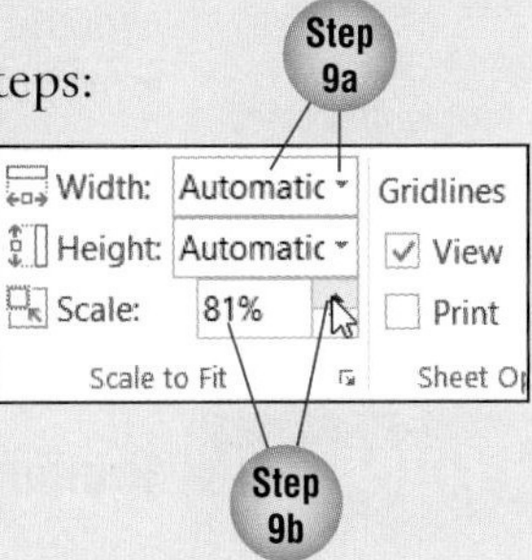

10. Save **EL1-C4-P1-RPBudget.xlsx**.

Inserting a Background Picture

Using the Background button in the Page Setup group on the PAGE LAYOUT tab, you can insert a picture as a background to the worksheet. The picture displays only on the screen and does not print. To insert a picture, click the Background button in the Page Setup group and then click the Browse button at the Insert Pictures window. At the Sheet Background dialog box, navigate to the folder containing the desired picture and then double-click the picture. To remove the picture from the worksheet, click the Delete Background button.

Quick Steps

Insert a Background Picture
1. Click PAGE LAYOUT tab.
2. Click Background button.
3. Navigate to desired picture and double-click picture.

Background

Project 1f Inserting a Background Picture

Part 6 of 12

1. With **EL1-C4-P1-RPBudget.xlsx** open, insert a background picture by completing the following steps:
   a. Click the Background button in the Page Setup group on the PAGE LAYOUT tab.
   b. At the Insert Pictures window, click the Browse button.
   c. At the Sheet Background dialog box, navigate to the EL1C4 folder and then double-click ***Ship.jpg***.
   d. Scroll down the worksheet to display the ship.

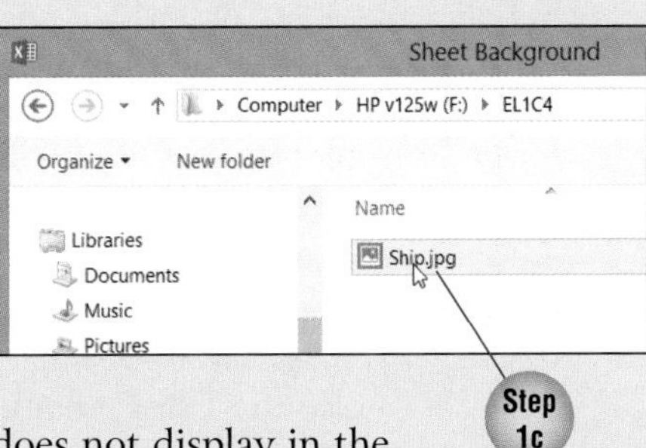

2. Display the Print backstage area, notice that the picture does not display in the preview worksheet, and then return to the worksheet.
3. Remove the picture by clicking the Delete Background button in the Page Setup group on the PAGE LAYOUT tab.
4. Save **EL1-C4-P1-RPBudget.xlsx**.

Printing Gridlines and Row and Column Headings

Quick Steps

Print Gridlines and/or Row and Column Headings
1. Click PAGE LAYOUT tab.
2. Click *Print* check boxes in *Gridlines* and/or *Headings* section in Sheet Options group.

OR

1. Click PAGE LAYOUT tab.
2. Click Sheet Options dialog box launcher.
3. Click *Gridlines* and/or *Row and column headings* check boxes.
4. Click OK.

By default, the gridlines that create the cells in a worksheet and the row numbers and column letters that label the cells do not print. The Sheet Options group on the PAGE LAYOUT tab contain check boxes for gridlines and headings. The *View* check boxes for gridlines and headings contain check marks. At these settings, gridlines and row and column headings display on the screen but do not print. If you want them to print, insert check marks in the *Print* check boxes. Complex worksheets may be easier to read with the gridlines printed.

You can also control the display and printing of gridlines and headings with options at the Page Setup dialog box with the Sheet tab selected. Display this dialog box by clicking the Sheet Options dialog box launcher. To print gridlines and headings, insert check marks in the check boxes located in the *Print* section of the dialog box. The *Print* section contains two additional options: *Black and white* and *Draft quality*. If you are printing with a color printer, you can print the worksheet in black and white by inserting a check mark in the *Black and white* check box. Insert a check mark in the *Draft quality* option if you want to print a draft of the worksheet. With this option checked, some formatting, such as shading and fill, does not print.

Project 1g **Printing Gridlines and Row and Column Headings** **Part 7 of 12**

Width: Automatic | Gridlines | Headings
Height: Automatic | View | View
Scale: 100% | Print | Print
Scale to Fit | Sheet Options
Step 1 | Step 2

1. With **EL1-C4-P1-RPBudget.xlsx** open, click in the *Print* check box below *Gridlines* in the Sheet Options group on the PAGE LAYOUT tab to insert a check mark.
2. Click in the *Print* check box below *Headings* in the Sheet Options group to insert a check mark.
3. Click the Margins button in the Page Setup group and then click *Custom Margins* at the drop-down list.
4. At the Page Setup dialog box with the Margins tab selected, click in the *Horizontally* check box to insert a check mark.
5. Click in the *Vertically* check box to insert a check mark.
6. Click OK to close the dialog box.
7. Save and then print **EL1-C4-P1-RPBudget.xlsx**.
8. Click in the *Print* check box below *Headings* in the Sheet Options group to remove the check mark.
9. Click in the *Print* check box below *Gridlines* in the Sheet Options group to remove the check mark.
10. Save **EL1-C4-P1-RPBudget.xlsx**.

Printing a Specific Area of a Worksheet

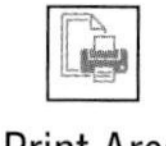

Print Area

Use the Print Area button in the Page Setup group on the PAGE LAYOUT tab to select and print specific areas in a worksheet. To do this, select the cells you want to print, click the Print Area button in the Page Setup group, and then click *Set Print Area* at the drop-down list. This inserts a border around the selected cells. Display the Print backstage area and click the Print button and the cells within the border are printed.

You can specify more than one print area in a worksheet. To do this, select the first group of cells, click the Print Area button in the Page Setup group, and then click *Set Print Area*. Select the next group of cells, click the Print Area button, and then click *Add to Print Area*. Clear a print area by clicking the Print Area button in the Page Setup group and then clicking *Clear Print Area* at the drop-down list.

Each area specified as a print area will print on a separate page. If you want nonadjacent print areas to print on the same page, consider hiding columns and/or rows in the worksheet to bring the areas together.

Project 1h Printing Specific Areas

Part 8 of 12

1. With **EL1-C4-P1-RPBudget.xlsx** open, print the first half of the year's income and expenses by completing the following steps:
   a. Select cells A3 through G21.
   b. Click the Print Area button in the Page Setup group on the PAGE LAYOUT tab and then click *Set Print Area* at the drop-down list.
   c. With the border surrounding the cells A3 through G21, click the FILE tab, click the *Print* option, and then click the Print button at the Print backstage area.
   d. Clear the print area by clicking the Print Area button in the Page Setup group and then clicking *Clear Print Area* at the drop-down list.

Step 1b

PAGE LAYOUT FORMULAS DATA
Orientation Size Print Area Breaks Background
Set Print Area
Clear Print Area

2. Suppose you want to print the income and expenses information as well as the totals for the month of April. To do this, hide columns and select a print area by completing the following steps:
   a. Select columns B through D.
   b. Click the HOME tab.
   c. Click the Format button in the Cells group, point to *Hide & Unhide*, and then click *Hide Columns*.
   d. Click the PAGE LAYOUT tab.
   e. Select cells A3 through E21. (Columns A and E are now adjacent.)
   f. Click the Print Area button in the Page Setup group and then click *Set Print Area* at the drop-down list.
3. Click the FILE tab, click the *Print* option, and then click the Print button.
4. Clear the print area by ensuring cells A3 through E21 are selected, clicking the Print Area button in the Page Setup group, and then clicking *Clear Print Area* at the drop-down list.
5. Unhide the columns by completing the following steps:
   a. Click the HOME tab.
   b. Select columns A and E. (These columns are adjacent.)
   c. Click the Format button in the Cells group, point to *Hide & Unhide*, and then click *Unhide Columns*.
   d. Deselect the text by clicking in any cell containing data in the worksheet.
6. Save **EL1-C4-P1-RPBudget.xlsx**.

Inserting Headers and Footers

> **Quick Steps**
> **Insert a Header or Footer**
> 1. Click INSERT tab.
> 2. Click Header & Footer button.
> 3. Click Header button and then click predesigned header or click Footer button and then click predesigned footer.
>
> OR
> 1. Click INSERT tab.
> 2. Click Header & Footer button.
> 3. Click desired header or footer elements.

Header & Footer

Text that prints at the top of each worksheet page is called a ***header*** and text that prints at the bottom of each worksheet page is called a ***footer***. Create a header and/or footer with the Header & Footer button in the Text group on the INSERT tab, in Page Layout View, or with options at the Page Setup dialog box with the Header/Footer tab selected.

To create a header with the Header & Footer button, click the INSERT tab and then click the Header & Footer button in the Text group. This displays the worksheet in Page Layout view and displays the HEADER & FOOTER TOOLS DESIGN tab. Use buttons on this tab, shown in Figure 4.5, to insert predesigned headers and/or footers or insert header and footer elements such as page numbers, date, time, path name, and file name. You can also create a different header or footer on the first page of the worksheet or create a header or footer for even pages and another for odd pages.

At the Print backstage area, you can preview your headers and footers before printing. Click the FILE tab and then the *Print* option to display the Print backstage area. A preview of the worksheet displays at the right side of the backstage area. If your worksheet will print on more than one page, you can view the different pages by clicking the Next Page button or the Previous Page button. These buttons are located below and to the left of the preview worksheet at the Print backstage area. Two buttons display in the bottom right corner of the Print backstage area. Click the Zoom to Page button to zoom in or out of the preview of the worksheet. Click the Show Margins button in the Print backstage area and margin guidelines and handles display on the preview page. The handles display as black squares that you can use to increase or decrease the page margins and column widths. To do this, position the mouse pointer on the desired handle, hold down the left mouse button, and then drag to the desired position.

Figure 4.5 HEADER & FOOTER TOOLS DESIGN Tab

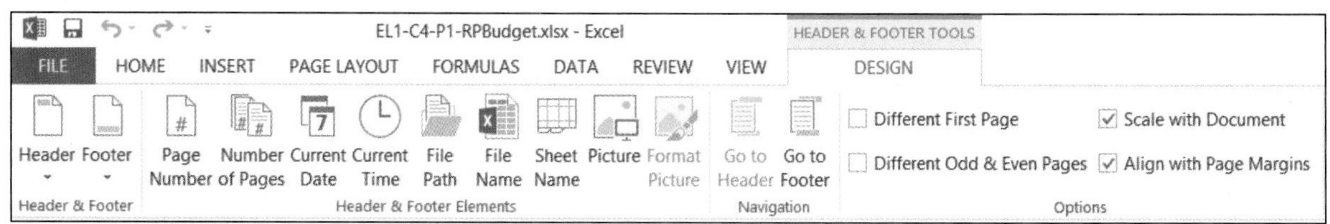

Project 1i Inserting a Header in a Worksheet

Part 9 of 12

1. With **EL1-C4-P1-RPBudget.xlsx** open, create a header by completing the following steps:
   a. Click the INSERT tab.
   b. Click the Header & Footer button in the Text group.

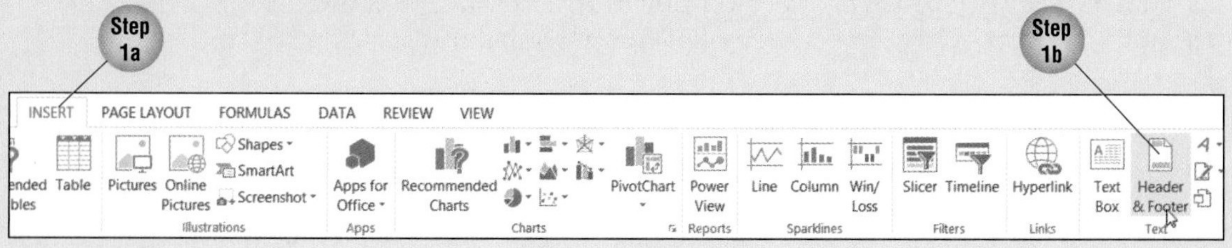

c. Click the Header button located at the left side of the HEADER & FOOTER TOOLS DESIGN tab and then click *Page 1, EL1-C4-P1-RPBudget.xlsx* at the drop-down list. (This inserts the page number in the middle header box and the workbook name in the right header box.)

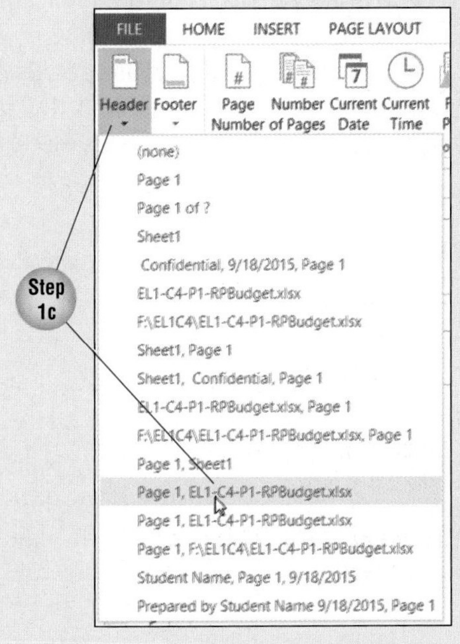

2. Preview the worksheet by completing the following steps:
   a. Click the FILE tab and then click the *Print* option.
   b. At the Print backstage area, look at the preview worksheet that displays at the right side of the backstage area.
   c. View the next page of the worksheet by clicking the Next Page button that displays below and to the left of the preview worksheet.

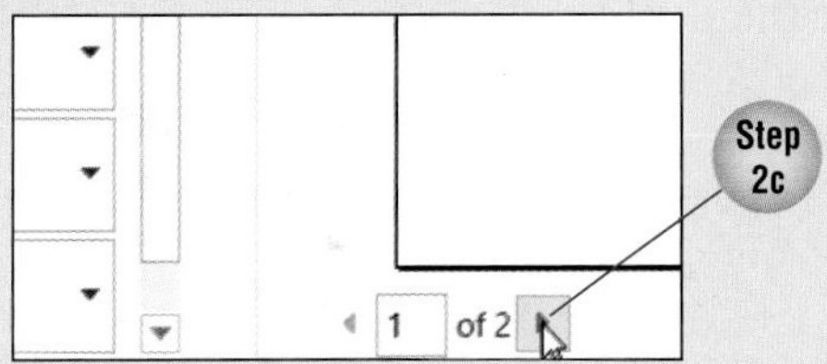

   d. View the first page by clicking the Previous Page button that displays left of the Next Page button.
   e. Click the Zoom to Page button in the lower right corner of the backstage area. (Notice that the preview page has zoomed in on the worksheet.)
   f. Click the Zoom to Page button.
   g. Click the Page Margins button in the lower right corner of the backstage area. (Notice the guidelines and handles that display on the preview page.)

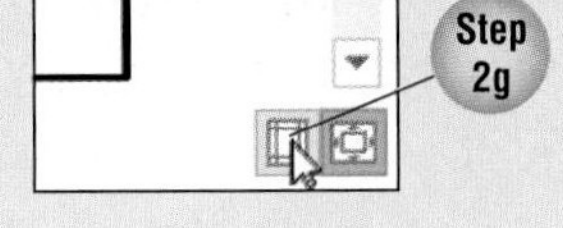

   h. Click the Page Margins button to remove the guidelines and handles.
   i. Click the Back button to return to the workbook.
3. Save **EL1-C4-P1-RPBudget.xlsx**.

You also can insert a header and/or footer by switching to Page Layout view. In Page Layout view, the top of the worksheet page displays with the text *Click to add header*. Click this text and the insertion point is positioned in the middle header box. Type the desired header in this box or click in the left box or the right box and then type the header. Create a footer in a similar manner. Scroll down the worksheet until the bottom of the page displays and then click the text *Click to add footer*. Type the footer in the center footer box or click the left or right box and then type the footer.

Project 1j Inserting a Footer and Modifying a Header in a Worksheet Part 10 of 12

1. With **EL1-C4-P1-RPBudget.xlsx** open, make sure the workbook displays in Page Layout view.
2. Scroll down the worksheet until the text *Click to add footer* displays and then click the text.

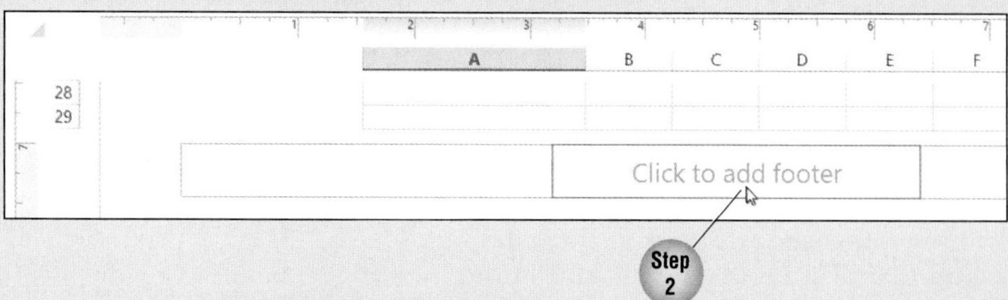

3. Type your first and last names.
4. Click in the left footer box, click the HEADER & FOOTER TOOLS DESIGN tab, and then click the Current Date button in the Header & Footer Elements group. (This inserts a date code. The date will display when you click outside the footer box.)
5. Click in the right footer box and then click the Current Time button in the Header & Footer Elements group. (This inserts the time as a code. The time will display when you click outside the footer box.)
6. View the header and footer at the Print backstage area and then return to the worksheet.
7. Modify the header by completing the following steps:
   a. Scroll to the beginning of the worksheet and display the header text.
   b. Click the page number in the middle header box. (This displays the HEADER & FOOTER TOOLS DESIGN tab, changes the header to a field, and selects the field.)
   c. Press the Delete key to delete the header.
   d. Click the header text that displays in the right header box and then press the Delete key.
   e. With the insertion point positioned in the right header box, insert the page number by clicking the HEADER & FOOTER TOOLS DESIGN tab and then clicking the Page Number button in the Header & Footer Elements group.
   f. Click in the left header box and then click the File Name button in the Header & Footer Elements group.

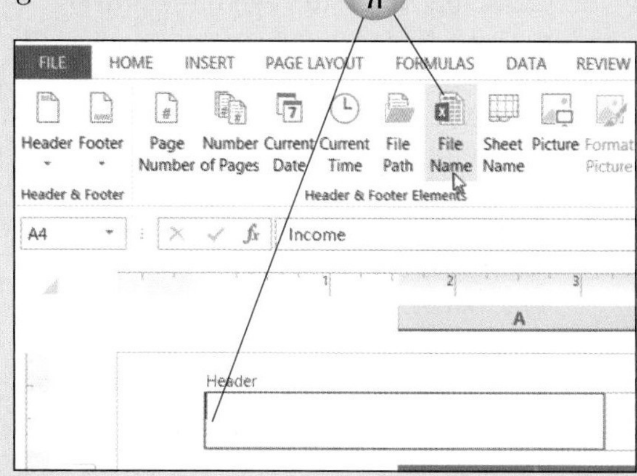

8. Click in any cell in the worksheet that contains data.
9. View the header and footer at the Print backstage area and then return to the worksheet.
10. Save **EL1-C4-P1-RPBudget.xlsx**.

In addition to selecting options on the HEADER & FOOTER TOOLS DESIGN tab, you can insert and customize headers and footers with options at the Page Setup dialog box with the Header/Footer tab selected, as shown in Figure 4.6. Display this dialog box by clicking the PAGE LAYOUT tab and then clicking the Page Setup group dialog box launcher. At the Page Setup dialog box, click the Header/Footer tab. If your worksheet contains headers or footers, they will display in the dialog box. With the check box options that display in

Figure 4.6 Page Setup Dialog Box with Header/Footer Tab Selected

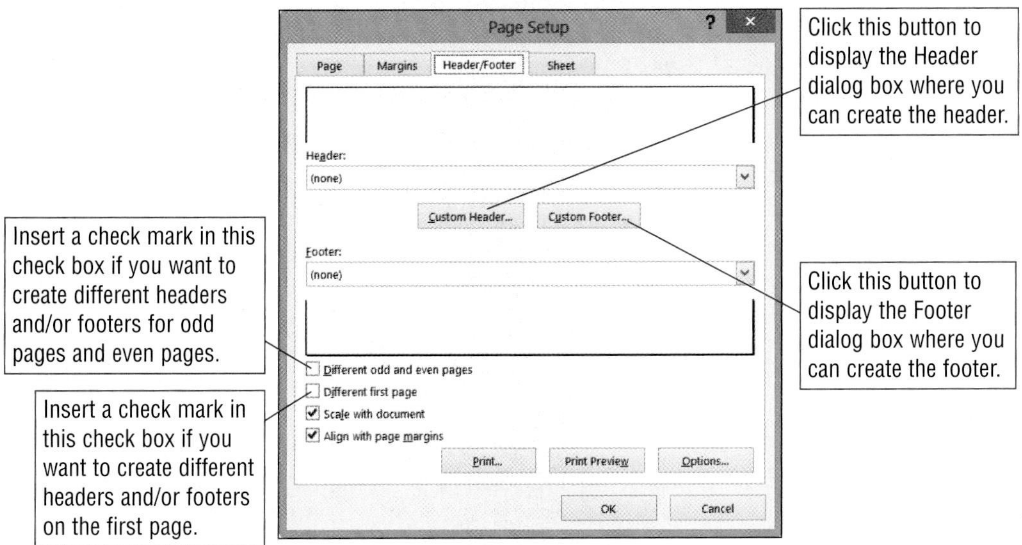
Page Setup
Page
Margins
Header/Footer
Sheet
Header:
(none)
Custom Header...
Custom Footer...
Footer:
(none)
Different odd and even pages
Different first page
Scale with document
Align with page margins
Print...
Print Preview
Options...
OK
Cancel
Click this button to display the Header dialog box where you can create the header.
Click this button to display the Footer dialog box where you can create the footer.
Insert a check mark in this check box if you want to create different headers and/or footers for odd pages and even pages.
Insert a check mark in this check box if you want to create different headers and/or footers on the first page.

the lower left corner of the dialog box, you can specify that you want to insert different odd and even page headers and/or footers or insert a different first page header and/or footer. The bottom two check box options are active by default. These defaults scale the header and footer text with the worksheet text and align the header and footer with the page margins.

To create different odd and even page headers, click the *Different odd and even pages* check box to insert a check mark and then click the Custom Header button. This displays the Header dialog box with the Odd Page Header tab selected. Type or insert the desired odd page header data in the *Left section*, *Center section*, or *Right section* text box and then click the Even Page Header tab. Type or insert the desired even page header data in the desired section text box and then click OK. Use the buttons that display above the section boxes to format the header text and insert information such as the page number, current date, current time, file name, worksheet name, and so on. Complete similar steps to create different odd and even page footers and a different first page header or footer.

Project 1k Creating Different Odd and Even Page Headers and Footers and a Different First Page Header and Footer — Part 11 of 12

1. With **EL1-C4-P1-RPBudget.xlsx** open, remove the page break by clicking the PAGE LAYOUT tab, clicking the Breaks button in the Page Setup group, and then clicking *Reset All Page Breaks* at the drop-down list.
2. Change the margins by completing the following steps:
   a. Click the Margins button in the Page Setup group on the PAGE LAYOUT tab and then click *Custom Margins* at the drop-down list.
   b. At the Page Setup dialog box with the Margins tab selected, select the current number in the *Left* measurement box and then type 3.
   c. Select the current number in the *Right* measurement box and then type 3.
   d. Click OK to close the dialog box.
3. Click the Page Setup group dialog box launcher on the PAGE LAYOUT tab.

4. At the Page Setup dialog box, click the Header/Footer tab.
5. At the Page Setup dialog box with the Header/Footer tab selected, click the *Different odd and even pages* check box to insert a check mark and then click the Custom Header button.
6. At the Header dialog box with the Odd Page Header tab selected, click the Format Text button (located above the *Left section* text box). At the Font dialog box, click *12* in the *Size* list box box and then click OK.
7. At the Header dialog box, type **Yearly Budget** in the *Left section* text box.

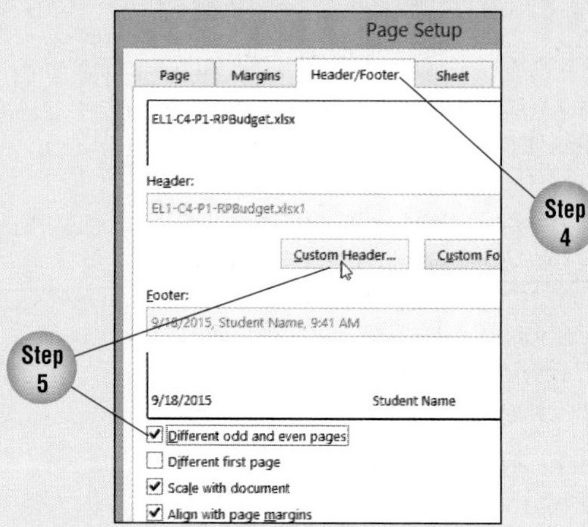

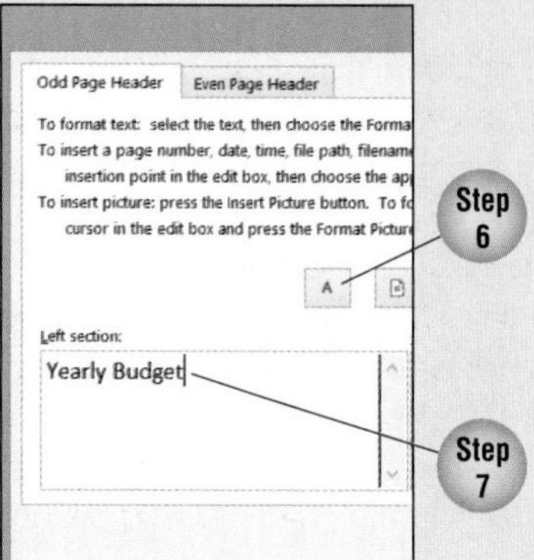

8. Click the Even Page Header tab, click in the *Left section* text box, and then click the Insert Page Number button.
9. Click in the *Right section* text box and then type **Yearly Budget**.
10. Select the text *Yearly Budget*, click the Format Text button, click *12* in the *Size* list box box, and then click OK.
11. Click OK to close the Header dialog box.
12. Click the Custom Footer button and at the Footer dialog box with the Odd Page Footer tab selected, delete the data in the *Left section* text box and select and delete the data in the *Right section* text box. (The footer should contain only your name.)
13. Select your name, click the Format Text button, click *12* in the *Size* list box box, and then click OK.
14. Click the Even Page Footer tab, type your name in the *Center section* text box, select your name, and then change the font size to 12 points.
15. Click OK to close the Footer dialog box and then click OK to close the Page Setup dialog box. (View the header and footer in the Print backstage area and then return to the worksheet.)
16. Click the Page Setup group dialog box launcher on the PAGE LAYOUT tab.
17. At the Page Setup dialog box, click the Header/Footer tab.
18. At the Page Setup dialog box with the Header/Footer tab selected, click the *Different odd and even pages* check box to remove the check mark.
19. Click the *Different first page* check box to insert a check mark and then click the Custom Header button.
20. At the Header dialog box with the Header tab selected, click the First Page Header tab.
21. Click in the *Right section* text box and then click the Insert Page Number button located above the section boxes.

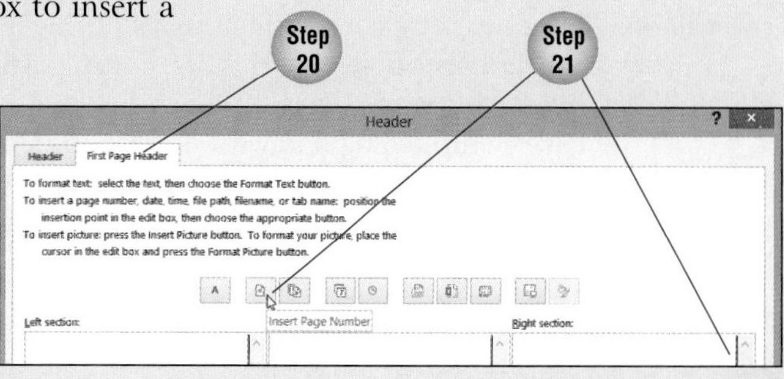

22. Click OK to close the Header dialog box and then click OK to close the Page Setup dialog box.
23. View the header and footer in the Print backstage area and then return to the worksheet.
24. Save **EL1-C4-P1-RPBudget.xlsx**.

Customizing Print Jobs

As you learned earlier in this chapter, you can preview worksheets in the Print backstage area. Use options in the *Settings* category at the Print backstage area, to specify what you want printed. By default, the active worksheet prints. You can change this by clicking the first gallery that displays in the *Settings* category. At the drop-down list that displays, you can specify to print the entire workbook (which is useful when a workbook contains more than one worksheet) or only selected cells. With the other galleries in the *Settings* category, you can specify if you want pages printed on one side or both sides (this is dependent on your printer) and collated. You can also specify the worksheet orientation, size, and margins and whether you want the worksheet scaled to fit all columns or rows on one page.

With the *Pages* text boxes in the *Settings* category, specify the pages of your worksheet you want printed. For example, if you want to print pages 2 and 3 of your active worksheet, type *2* in the measurement box immediately right of the word *Pages* in the *Settings* category and then type *3* in the measurement box immediately right of the word *to*. You can also use the up- and down-pointing arrows to insert page numbers.

Project 1l **Printing Specific Pages of a Worksheet** **Part 12 of 12**

1. With **EL1-C4-P1-RPBudget.xlsx** open, print the first two pages of the worksheet by completing the following steps:
   a. Click the FILE tab and then click the *Print* option.
   b. At the Print backstage area, click in the measurement box immediately right of *Pages* and below the first gallery in the *Settings* category and then type 1.
   c. Click in the measurement box immediately right of *to* in the *Settings* category and then type 2.
   d. Click the Print button.

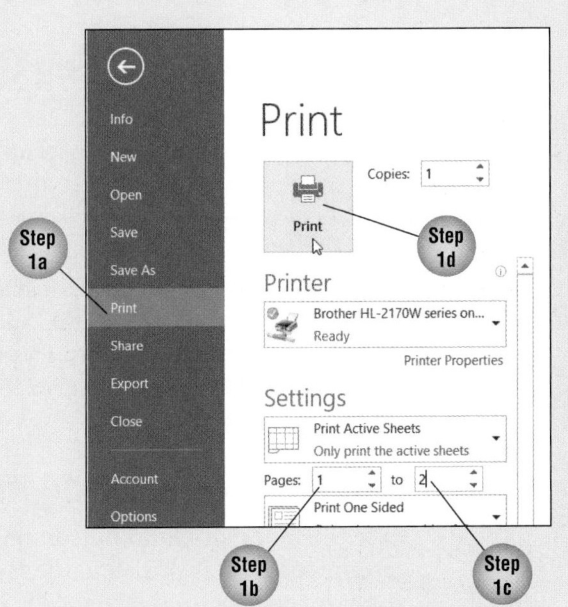

2. Print selected cells by completing the following steps:
   a. Display the worksheet in Normal view.
   b. Select cells A3 through D11.
   c. Click the FILE tab and then the *Print* option.
   d. At the Print backstage area, select and then delete the numbers in the *Pages* measurement boxes. (These are the numbers you inserted in Steps 1b and 1c.)
   e. Click the first gallery in the *Settings* category (displays with *Print Active Sheets*) and then click *Print Selection* at the drop-down list.
   f. Click the Print button.
3. Save and then close **EL1-C4-P1-RPBudget.xlsx**.

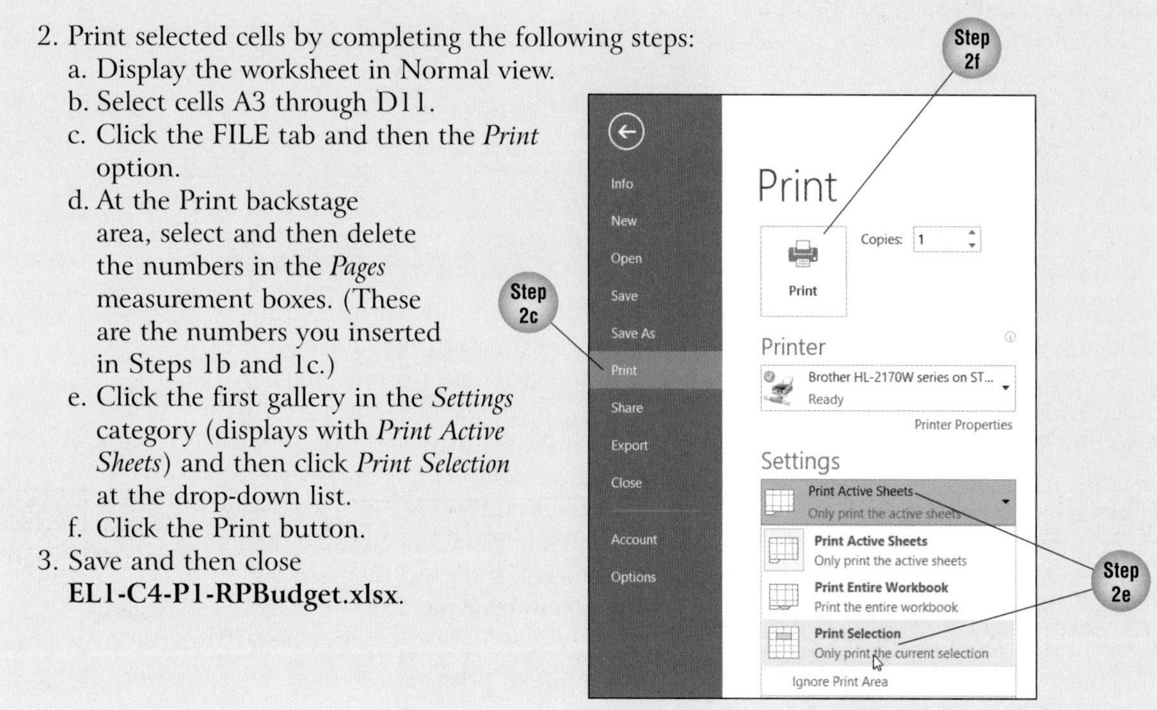

Project 2 Format a May Sales and Commissions Worksheet 3 Parts

You will format a sales commission worksheet by inserting a formula, completing a spelling check, and finding and replacing data and cell formatting.

Completing a Spelling Check

Quick Steps

Complete a Spelling Check
1. Click REVIEW tab.
2. Click Spelling button.
3. Replace or ignore selected words.

Spelling

HINT

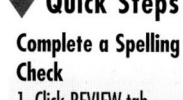

Customize spell checking options at the Excel Options dialog box with *Proofing* selected.

Excel includes a spelling checker you can use to verify the spelling of text in a worksheet. The spelling checker uses an electronic dictionary to identity misspelled words and suggest alternatives. Before checking the spelling in a worksheet, make the first cell active. The spelling checker reviews the worksheet from the active cell to the last cell in the worksheet that contains data.

To use the spelling checker, click the REVIEW tab and then click the Spelling button. Figure 4.7 displays the Spelling dialog box. At this dialog box, you can click a button to tell Excel to ignore a word or you can replace a misspelled word with a word from the *Suggestions* list box.

Using Undo and Redo

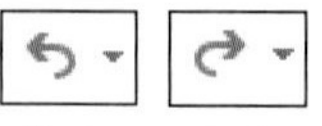

Undo Redo

Excel includes an Undo button on the Quick Access toolbar that will reverse certain commands or delete the last data typed in a cell. For example, if you apply formatting to selected cells in a worksheet and then decide you want the formatting removed, click the Undo button on the Quick Access toolbar. If you decide you want the formatting back again, click the Redo button on the Quick Access toolbar.

Figure 4.7 Excel Spelling Dialog Box

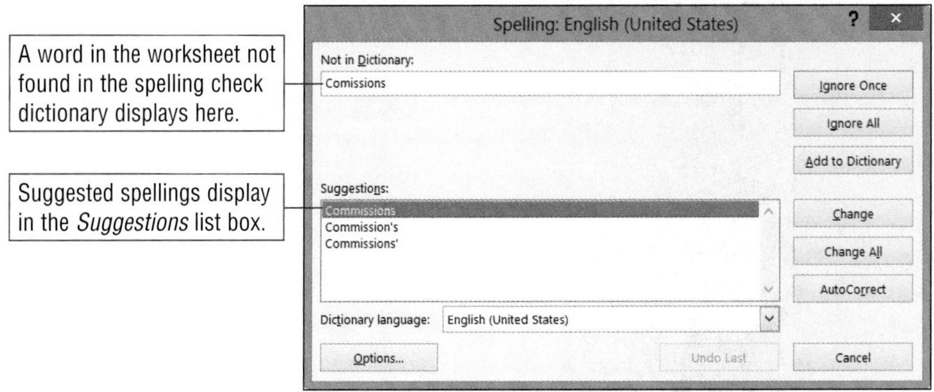

Excel maintains actions in temporary memory. If you want to undo an action, click the down-pointing arrow at the right side of the Undo button and a drop-down list displays containing the actions performed on the worksheet. Click the desired action at the drop-down list. Any actions preceding a chosen action are also undone. You can do the same with the Redo drop-down list. Multiple actions must be undone or redone in sequence.

Ctrl + Z is the keyboard shortcut to undo a command.

Project 2a Spell Checking and Formatting a Worksheet — Part 1 of 3

1. Open **MRSales.xlsx**.
2. Save the workbook with Save As and name it **EL1-C4-P2-MRSales**.
3. Complete a spelling check on the worksheet by completing the following steps:
   a. Make cell A1 active.
   b. Click the REVIEW tab.
   c. Click the Spelling button in the Proofing group.
   d. Click the Change button as needed to correct misspelled words in the worksheet. (When the spelling check stops at the proper names *Pirozzi* and *Yonemoto*, click the Ignore All button.)
   e. At the message telling you the spelling check is complete, click OK.

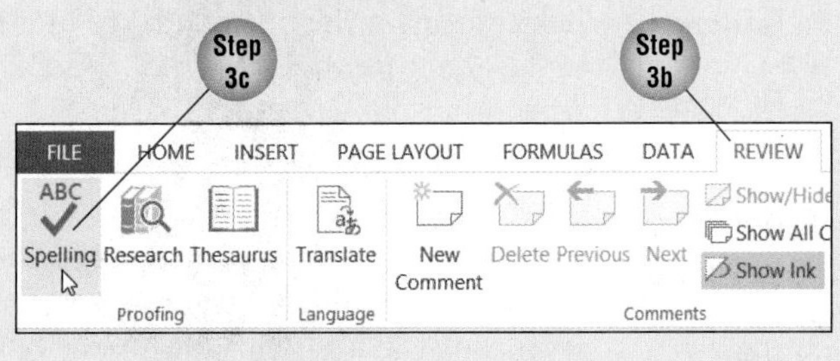

4. Insert a formula and then copy the formula without the formatting by completing the following steps:
   a. Make cell G4 active and then insert a formula that multiplies the sale price by the commission percentage.
   b. Copy the formula down to cells G5 through G26.
   c. Some of the cells contain shading that you do not want removed, so click the Auto Fill Options button that displays at the bottom right of the selected cells and then click the *Fill Without Formatting* option at the drop-down list.

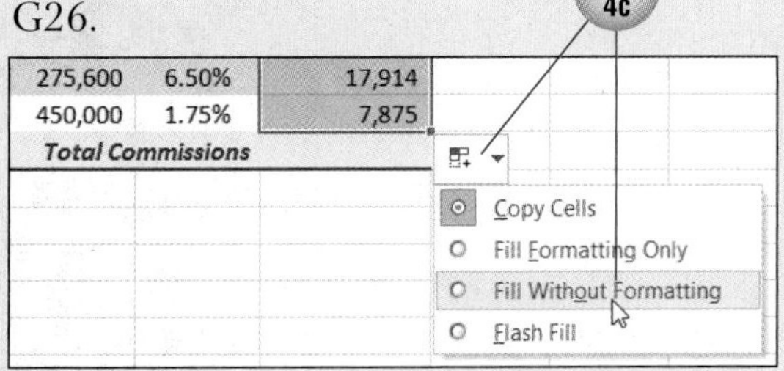

5. Make cell G27 active and then insert the sum of cells G4 through G26.
6. Apply accounting formatting with no places past the decimal point and add a dollar sign to cells G4 and G27.
7. Apply a theme by clicking the PAGE LAYOUT tab, clicking the Themes button, and then clicking *Ion* at the drop-down gallery.
8. After looking at the worksheet with the Ion theme applied, you decide you want to return to the original formatting. To do this, click the Undo button on the Quick Access toolbar.

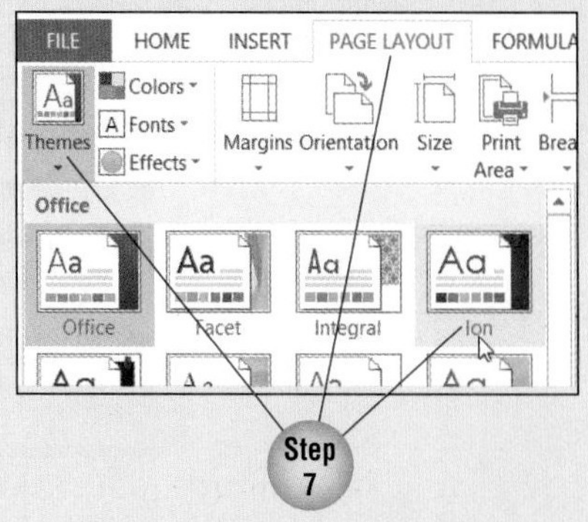

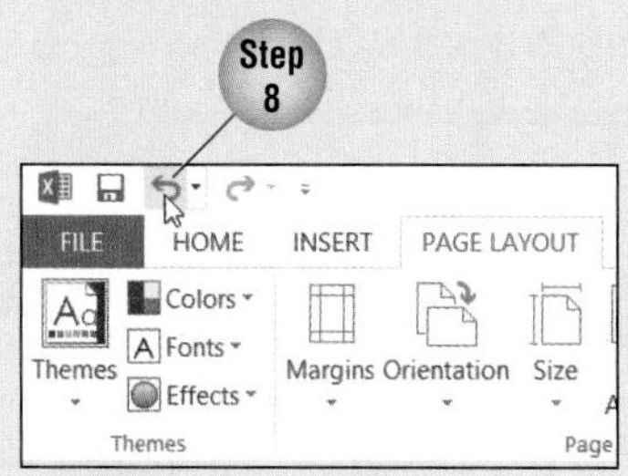

9. Save **EL1-C4-P2-MRSales.xlsx**.

Finding and Replacing Data and Cell Formatting in a Worksheet

Quick Steps

Find Data
1. Click Find & Select button.
2. Click *Find* at drop-down list.
3. Type data in *Find what* text box.
4. Click Find Next button.

Find & Select

Excel provides a Find feature you can use to look for specific data and either replace it with nothing or replace it with other data. This feature is particularly helpful for finding data quickly in a large worksheet. Excel also includes a find and replace feature. Use this tool to look for specific data in a worksheet and replace it with other data.

To find specific data in a worksheet, click the Find & Select button located in the Editing group on the HOME tab and then click *Find* at the drop-down list. This displays the Find and Replace dialog box with the Find tab selected, as shown in Figure 4.8. Type the data you want to find in the *Find what* text box and then click the Find Next button. Continue clicking the Find Next button to move to the next occurrence of the data. If the Find and Replace dialog box obstructs your view of the worksheet, use the mouse pointer on the title bar to drag the dialog box to a different location.

Figure 4.8 Find and Replace Dialog Box with Find Tab Selected

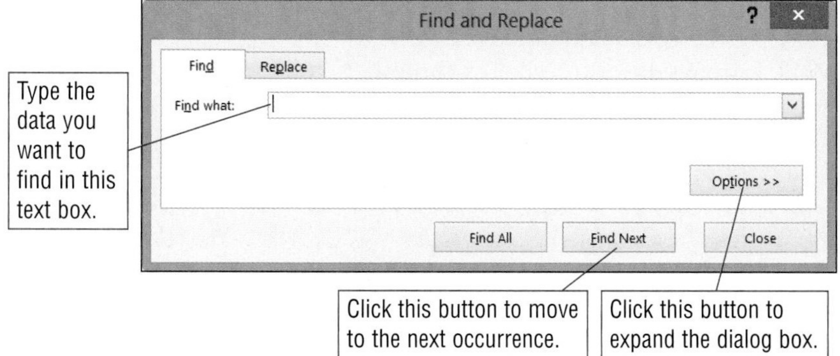

To find specific data in a worksheet and replace it with other data, click the Find & Select button in the Editing group on the HOME tab and then click *Replace* at the drop-down list. This displays the Find and Replace dialog box with the Replace tab selected, as shown in Figure 4.9. Enter the data you want to find in the *Find what* text box. Press the Tab key or click in the *Replace with* text box and then enter the data that is to replace the data in the *Find what* text box.

Click the Find Next button to tell Excel to find the next occurrence of the data. Click the Replace button to replace the data and find the next occurrence. If you know that you want to replace all occurrences of the data in the *Find what* text box with the data in the *Replace with* text box, click the Replace All button. Click the Close button to close the Replace dialog box.

Display additional find and replace options by clicking the Options button. This expands the dialog box, as shown in Figure 4.10. By default, Excel will look for any data that contains the same characters as the data in the *Find what* text box, without concern for the characters before or after the entered data. For example, in Project 2b, you will look for sale prices of $450,000 and replace them with sale prices of $475,000. If you do not specify to Excel that you want to find cells that contain only *450000,* Excel will stop at any cell containing *450000.* In this example, Excel will stop at a cell containing *$1,450,000* and a cell containing *$2,450,000.* To specify that the only data that should be contained in the cell is what is entered in the *Find what* text box, click the Options button to expand the dialog box and then insert a check mark in the *Match entire cell contents* check box.

Quick Steps

Find and Replace Data

1. Click Find & Select button.
2. Click *Replace* at drop-down list.
3. Type data in *Find what* text box.
4. Type data in *Replace with* text box.
5. Click Replace button or Replace All button.

Figure 4.9 Find and Replace Dialog Box with Replace Tab Selected

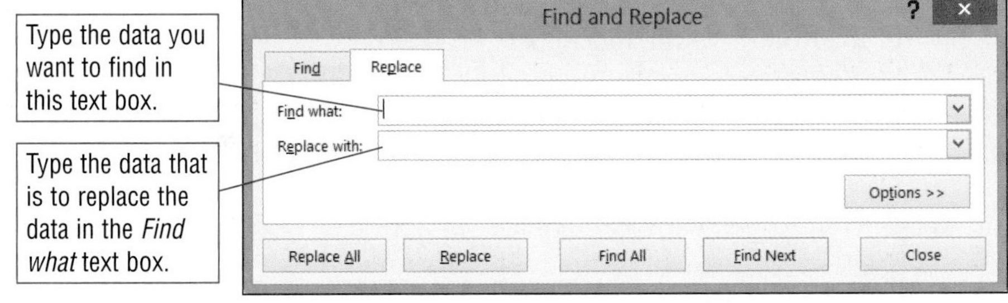

Figure 4.10 Expanded Find and Replace Dialog Box

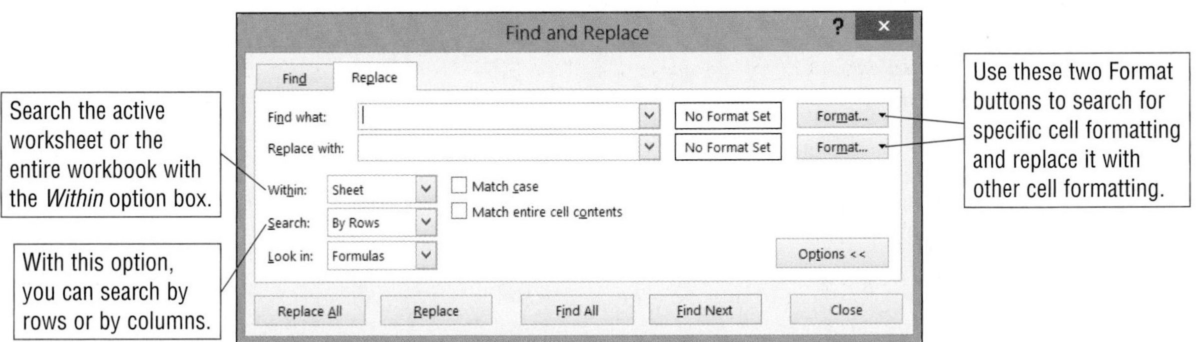

If the *Match case* option is active (contains a check mark), Excel will look for only that data that matches the case of the data entered in the *Find what* text box. Remove the check mark from this check box if you do not want Excel to find exact case matches. Excel will search in the current worksheet. If you want Excel to search an entire workbook, change the *Within* option to *Workbook*. Excel, by default, searches by rows in a worksheet. You can change this to *By Columns* with the *Search* option.

Project 2b Finding and Replacing Data — Part 2 of 3

1. With **EL1-C4-P2-MRSales.xlsx** open, find all occurrences of *Land* in the worksheet and replace with *Acreage* by completing the following steps:
   a. Click the Find & Select button in the Editing group on the HOME tab and then click *Replace* at the drop-down list.
   b. At the Find and Replace dialog box with the Replace tab selected, type **Land** in the *Find what* text box.
   c. Press the Tab key. (This moves the insertion point to the *Replace with* text box.)
   d. Type **Acreage**.
   e. Click the Replace All button.
   f. At the message telling you that four replacements were made, click OK.
   g. Click the Close button to close the Find and Replace dialog box.

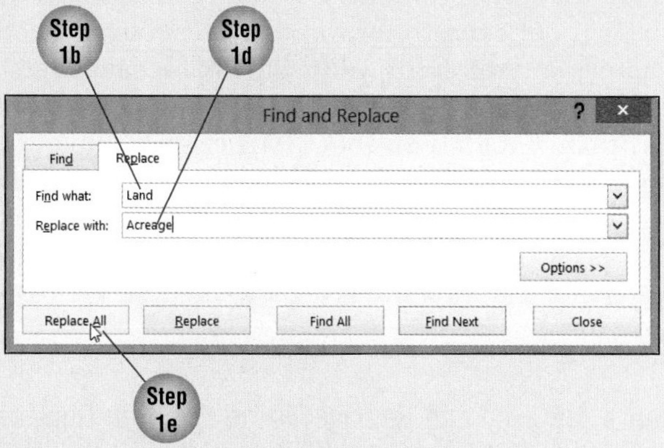

2. Find all occurrences of *$450,000* and replace them with *$475,000* by completing the following steps:
   a. Click the Find & Select button in the Editing group and then click *Replace* at the drop-down list.
   b. At the Find and Replace dialog box with the Replace tab selected, type **450000** in the *Find what* text box.
   c. Press the Tab key.
   d. Type **475000**.
   e. Click the Options button to display additional options. (If additional options already display, skip this step.)
   f. Click the *Match entire cell contents* check box to insert a check mark.
   g. Click the Replace All button.
   h. At the message telling you that two replacements were made, click OK.
   i. At the Find and Replace dialog box, click the *Match entire cell contents* check box to remove the check mark.
   j. Click the Close button to close the Find and Replace dialog box.

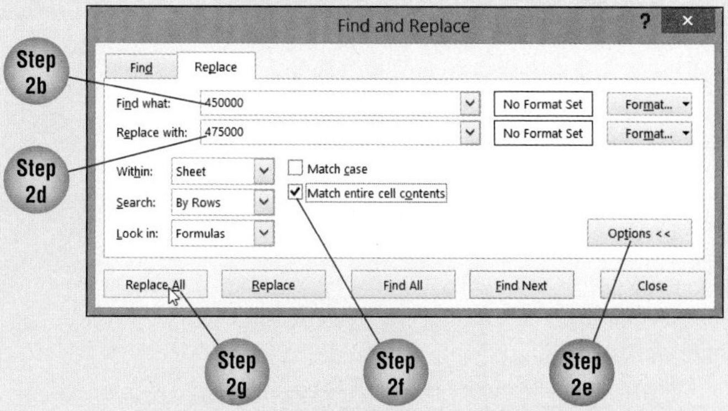

3. Save **EL1-C4-P2-MRSales.xlsx**.

Use the Format buttons at the expanded Find and Replace dialog box (see Figure 4.10) to search for specific cell formatting and replace it with other formatting. Click the down-pointing arrow at the right side of the Format button and a drop-down list displays. Click the *Format* option and the Find Format dialog box displays with the Number, Alignment, Font, Border, Fill, and Protection tabs. Specify formatting at this dialog box. Click the *Choose Format From Cell* option from the Format button drop-down list or click the Choose Format From Cell button in the Find Format dialog box and the mouse pointer displays with a pointer tool attached. Click in the cell containing the desired formatting and the formatting displays in the *Preview* box to the left of the Format button. Click the *Clear Find Format* option at the Find button drop-down list and any formatting in the *Preview* box is removed.

Project 2c Finding and Replacing Cell Formatting

Part 3 of 3

1. With **EL1-C4-P2-MRSales.xlsx** open, search for a light turquoise fill color and replace it with a light green fill color by completing the following steps:
   a. Click the Find & Select button in the Editing group on the HOME tab and then click *Replace* at the drop-down list.
   b. At the Find and Replace dialog box with the Replace tab selected, make sure the dialog box is expanded. (If not, click the Options button.)
   c. Select and then delete any text that displays in the *Find what* text box.
   d. Select and then delete any text that displays in the *Replace with* text box.
   e. Make sure the boxes immediately preceding the two Format buttons display with the text *No Format Set*. (If not, click the down-pointing arrow at the right of the Format button, and then click the *Clear Find Format* option at the drop-down list. Do this for each Format button.)
   f. Click the top Format button.
   g. At the Find Format dialog box, click the Fill tab.
   h. Click the More Colors button.
   i. At the Colors dialog box with the Standard tab selected, click the light turquoise color shown at the right.
   j. Click OK to close the Colors dialog box.
   k. Click OK to close the Find Format dialog box.
   l. Click the bottom Format button.
   m. At the Replace Format dialog box with the Fill tab selected, click the light green color (last column, second row), as shown at the right.
   n. Click OK to close the dialog box.
   o. At the Find and Replace dialog box, click the Replace All button.
   p. At the message telling you that 10 replacements were made, click OK.

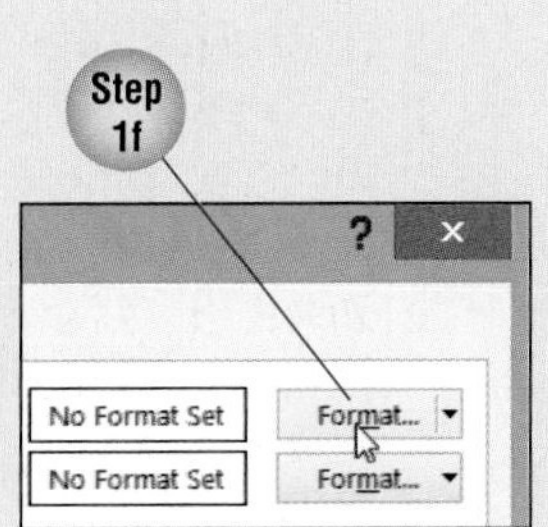

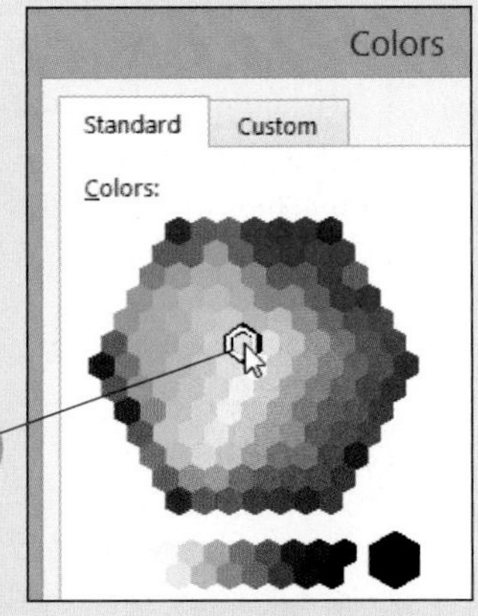

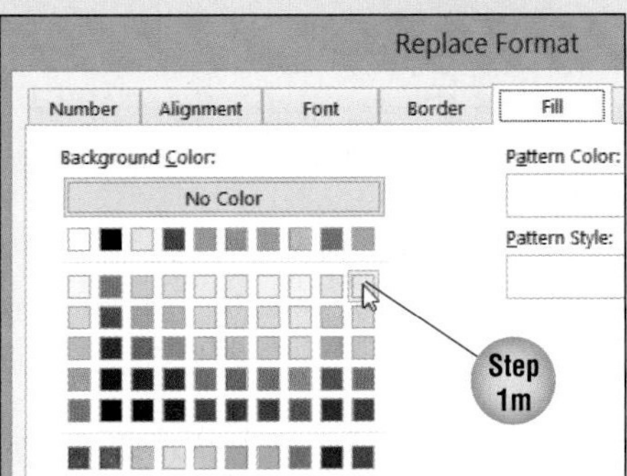

2. Search for a light gray fill color and replace it with a light yellow fill color by completing the following steps:
   a. At the Find and Replace dialog box, click the top Format button.
   b. At the Find Format dialog box with the Fill tab selected, click the light gray color (fourth column, second row), as shown at the right.
   c. Click OK to close the Find Format dialog box.
   d. Click the bottom Format button.
   e. At the Replace Format dialog box with the Fill tab selected, click the yellow color (eighth column, second row), as shown below and to the right.
   f. Click OK to close the dialog box.
   g. At the Find and Replace dialog box, click the Replace All button.
   h. At the message telling you that 78 replacements were made, click OK.

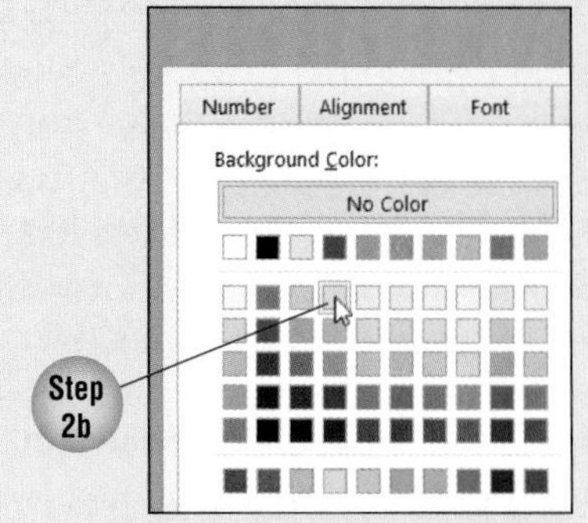

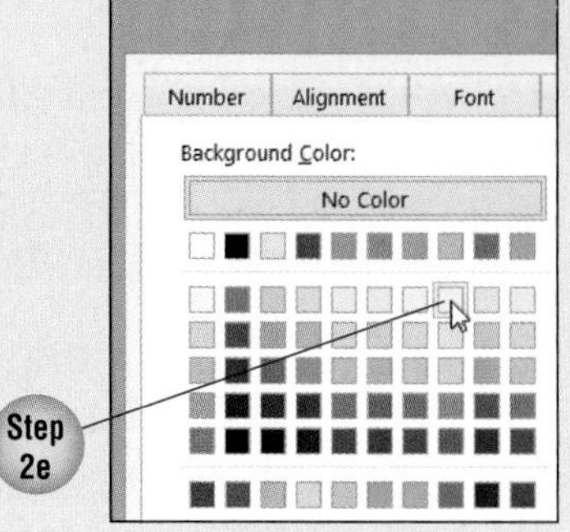

3. Search for 11-point Calibri formatting and replace it with 10-point Arial formatting by completing the following steps:
   a. With the Find and Replace dialog box open, clear formatting from the top Format button by clicking the down-pointing arrow at the right side of the top Format button and then clicking the *Clear Find Format* option at the drop-down list.
   b. Clear formatting from the bottom Format button by clicking the down-pointing arrow at the right side of the bottom Format button and then clicking *Clear Replace Format.*
   c. Click the top Format button.
   d. At the Find Format dialog box, click the Font tab.
   e. Scroll down the *Font* list box and then click *Calibri.*
   f. Click *11* in the *Size* list box.
   g. Click OK to close the dialog box.
   h. Click the bottom Format button.
   i. At the Replace Format dialog box with the Font tab selected, scroll down the *Font* list box and then click *Arial.*
   j. Click *10* in the *Size* list box.
   k. Click OK to close the dialog box.
   l. At the Find and Replace dialog box, click the Replace All button.
   m. At the message telling you that 174 replacements were made, click OK.
   n. At the Find and Replace dialog box, remove formatting from both Format buttons.
   o. Click the Close button to close the Find and Replace dialog box.

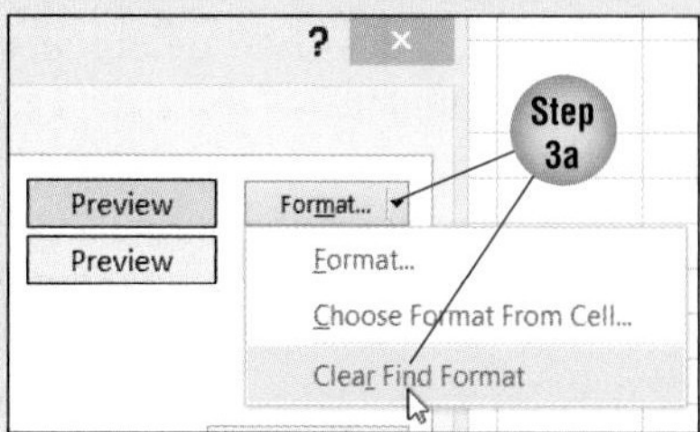

4. Save, print, and then close **EL1-C4-P2-MRSales.xlsx**.

Project 3 Format a Billing Worksheet — 4 Parts

You will insert a formula in a weekly billing worksheet and then sort and filter specific data in the worksheet.

Sorting Data

Excel is primarily a spreadsheet program, but it also includes some basic database functions. With a database program, you can alphabetize information or arrange numbers numerically. Data can even be sorted by columns in a worksheet. To sort data in a worksheet, use the Sort & Filter button in the Editing group on the HOME tab.

To sort data in a worksheet, select the cells containing the data you want to sort, click the Sort & Filter button in the Editing group, and then click the option representing the desired sort. The sort option names vary depending on the data in selected cells. For example, if the first column of selected cells contains text, the sort options in the drop-down list display as *Sort A to Z* and *Sort Z to A*. If the selected cells contain dates, the sort options in the drop-down list display as *Sort Oldest to Newest* and *Sort Newest to Oldest*, and if the cells contain numbers or values, the sort options display as *Sort Smallest to Largest* and *Sort Largest to Smallest*. If you select more than one column in a worksheet, Excel will sort the data in the first selected column.

Quick Steps

Sort Data

1. Select cells.
2. Click Sort & Filter button.
3. Click desired sort option at drop-down list.

Sort & Filter

If you are not satisfied with the results of the sort, immediately click the Undo button.

Project 3a **Sorting Data** **Part 1 of 4**

1. Open **APTBilling.xlsx** and save it with Save As and name it **EL1-C4-P3-APTBilling**.
2. Insert a formula in cell F4 that multiplies the rate by the hours. Copy the formula down to cells F5 through F29.
3. Sort the data in the first column in descending order by completing the following steps:
   a. Make cell A4 active.
   b. Click the Sort & Filter button in the Editing group on the HOME tab.
   c. Click the *Sort Largest to Smallest* option at the drop-down list.
4. Sort in ascending order by clicking the Sort & Filter button and then clicking *Sort Smallest to Largest* at the drop-down list.
5. Save **EL1-C4-P3-APTBilling.xlsx**.

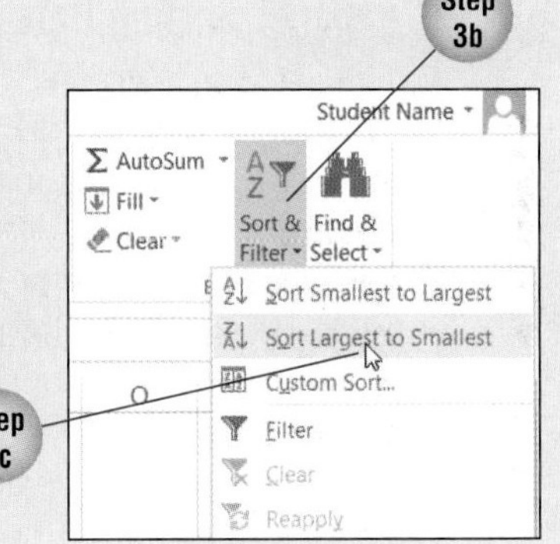

Completing a Custom Sort

If you want to sort data in a column other than the first column, use the Sort dialog box. If you select just one column in a worksheet, click the Sort & Filter button, and then click the desired sort option, only the data in that column is sorted. If this data is related to data to the left or right of the data in the sorted column, that relationship is broken. For example, if you sort cells C4 through C29 in EL1-C4-P3-APTBilling.xlsx, the client number, treatment, hours, and total no longer match the date.

Use the Sort dialog box to sort data and maintain the relationship among all cells. To sort using the Sort dialog box, select the cells you want sorted, click the Sort & Filter button, and then click *Custom Sort*. This displays the Sort dialog box, shown in Figure 4.11.

Quick Steps

Complete a Custom Sort

1. Select cells.
2. Click Sort & Filter button.
3. Click *Custom Sort* at drop-down list.
4. Specify options at Sort dialog box.
5. Click OK.

Figure 4.11 Sort Dialog Box

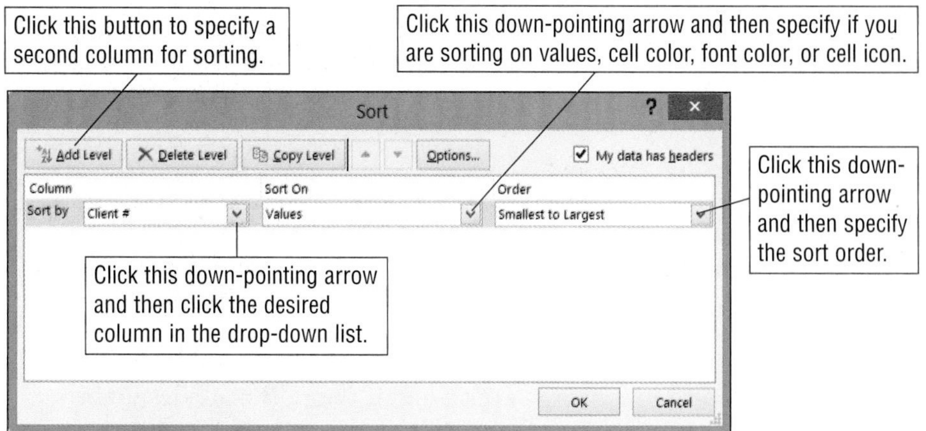

The data displayed in the *Sort by* option box will vary depending on what you have selected. Generally, the data that displays is the title of the first column of selected cells. If the selected cells do not have a title, the data may display as *Column A*. Use this option to specify what column you want sorted. Using the Sort dialog box to sort data in a column maintains the relationship among the data.

Project 3b Sorting Data Using the Sort Dialog Box — Part 2 of 4

1. With **EL1-C4-P3-APTBilling.xlsx** open, sort the rates in cells E4 through E29 in descending order and maintain the relationship to the other data by completing the following steps:
   a. Select cells A3 through F29.
   b. Click the Sort & Filter button and then click *Custom Sort*.
   c. At the Sort dialog box, click the down-pointing arrow at the right of the *Sort by* option box and then click *Rate* at the drop-down list.
   d. Click the down-pointing arrow at the right of the *Order* option box and then click *Largest to Smallest* at the drop-down list.

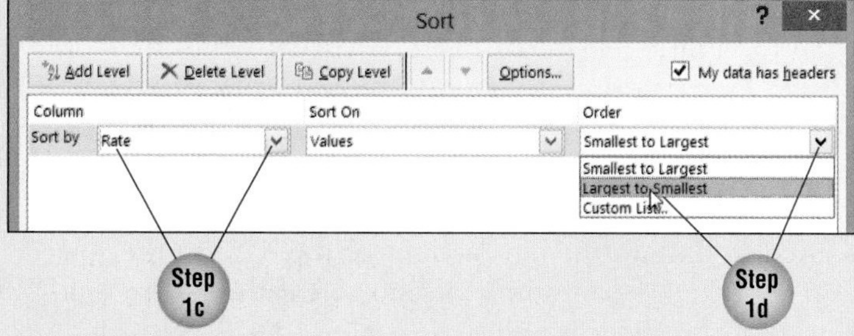

   e. Click OK to close the Sort dialog box.
   f. Deselect the cells.
2. Sort the dates in ascending order (oldest to newest) by completing steps similar to those in Step 1.
3. Save and then print **EL1-C4-P3-APTBilling.xlsx**.

Sorting More Than One Column

When sorting data in cells, you can sort in more than one column. For example, in Project 3c, you will sort the dates from oldest to newest and the client numbers from lowest to highest. In this sort, the dates are sorted first and then the client numbers are sorted in ascending order within the same date.

To sort in more than one column, select all columns in the worksheet that need to remain relative and then display the Sort dialog box. At the Sort dialog box, specify the first column you want sorted in the *Sort by* option box, click the *Add Level* button, and then specify the second column in the first *Then by* option box. In Excel, you can sort on multiple columns. Add additional *Then by* option boxes by clicking the *Add Level* button.

Project 3c Sorting Data in Two Columns

Part 3 of 4

1. With **EL1-C4-P3-APTBilling.xlsx** open, select cells A3 through F29.
2. Click the Sort & Filter button and then click *Custom Sort*.
3. At the Sort dialog box, click the down-pointing arrow at the right side of the *Sort by* option box and then click *Date* in the drop-down list. (Skip this step if *Date* already displays in the *Sort by* option box.)
4. Make sure *Oldest to Newest* displays in the *Order* option box.
5. Click the Add Level button.
6. Click the down-pointing arrow at the right of the *Then by* option box and then click *Client #* in the drop-down list.
7. Click OK to close the dialog box.
8. Deselect the cells.
9. Save and then print **EL1-C4-P3-APTBilling.xlsx**.

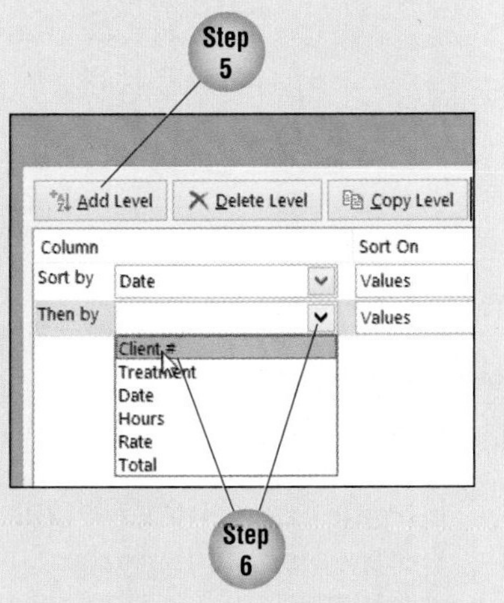

Filtering Data

You can place a restriction, called a ***filter***, on data in a worksheet to temporarily isolate specific data. To turn on filtering, make a cell containing data active, click the Sort & Filter button in the Editing group on the HOME tab, and then click *Filter* at the drop-down list. This turns on filtering and causes a filter arrow to appear with each column label in the worksheet, as shown in Figure 4.12. You do not need to select data before turning on filtering because Excel automatically searches for column labels in a worksheet.

To filter data in a worksheet, click the filter arrow in the heading you want to filter. This causes a drop-down list to display with options to filter all records, create a custom filter, or select an entry that appears in one or more of the cells in the column. When you filter data, the filter arrow changes to a funnel icon. The funnel icon indicates that rows in the worksheet have been filtered. To turn off filtering, click the Sort & Filter button and then click *Filter*.

If a column contains numbers, click the filter arrow and point to *Number Filters* and a side menu displays with options for filtering numbers. For example, you can filter numbers that are equal to, greater than, or less than a number you specify; filter the top ten numbers; and filter numbers that are above or below a specified number.

Quick Steps

Filter a List

1. Select cells.
2. Click Sort & Filter button.
3. Click *Filter* at drop-down list.
4. Click down-pointing arrow of heading to filter.
5. Click desired option at drop-down list.

Figure 4.12 Filtering Data

Turn on filtering and filter arrows display with column headings.

	A	B	C	D	E	F
1	Ace Physical Therapy					
2	Billing - Week of August 10, 2015					
3	Client	Treatment	Date	Hours	Rate	Total
4	2085	Test Consultation	8/10/2015	0.25	$ 75.00	$ 18.75
5	3102	Therapeutic Massage	8/10/2015	1.00	$ 65.00	$ 65.00
6	3102	Consultation	8/10/2015	0.75	$ 50.00	$ 37.50
		l Therapy	8/11/2015	1.00	$ 60.00	$ 60.00
		l Therapy	8/11/2015	1.25	$ 60.00	$ 75.00

Click the filter in the *Client #* heading, click the *(Select All)* check box to remove the check mark, and then click the *3102* check box to display only those rows containing client number 3102.

	A	B	C	D	E	F
1	Ace Physical Therapy					
2	Billing - Week of August 10, 2015					
3	Client	Treatment	Date	Hours	Rate	Total
5	3102	Therapeutic Massage	8/10/2015	1.00	$ 65.00	$ 65.00
6	3102	Consultation	8/10/2015	0.75	$ 50.00	$ 37.50
12	3102	Therapeutic Massage	8/12/2015	1.00	$ 65.00	$ 65.00
30						

Project 3d Filtering Data

Part 4 of 4

1. With **EL1-C4-P3-APTBilling.xlsx** open, click in cell A4.
2. Turn on filtering by clicking the Sort & Filter button in the Editing group on the HOME tab and then clicking *Filter* at the drop-down list.
3. Filter rows for client number 3102 by completing the following steps:
   a. Click the filter arrow in the *Client #* heading.
   b. Click the *(Select All)* check box to remove the check mark.
   c. Scroll down the list box and then click *3102* to insert a check mark in the check box.
   d. Click OK.
4. Redisplay all rows containing data by completing the following steps:
   a. Click the funnel icon in the *Client #* heading.
   b. Click the *(Select All)* check box to insert a check mark. (This also inserts check marks for all items in the list.)
   c. Click OK.

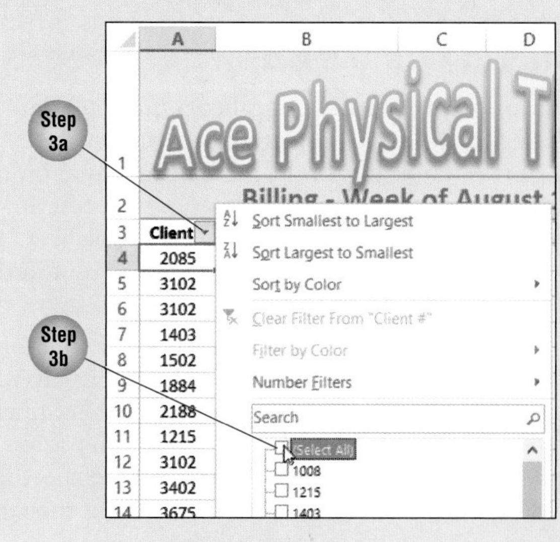

5. Filter a list of clients receiving physical therapy by completing the following steps:
   a. Click the filter arrow in the *Treatment* heading.
   b. Click the *(Select All)* check box.
   c. Click the *Physical Therapy* check box.
   d. Click OK.
6. Redisplay all rows containing data by completing the following steps:
   a. Click the funnel icon in the *Treatment* heading.
   b. Click the *Clear Filter From "Treatment"* option.
7. Display the top two highest rates by completing the following steps:
   a. Click the filter arrow in the *Rate* heading.
   b. Point to *Number Filters* and then click *Top 10* at the side menu.
   c. At the Top 10 AutoFilter dialog box, select the *10* that displays in the middle measurement box and then type 2.
   d. Click OK to close the dialog box.

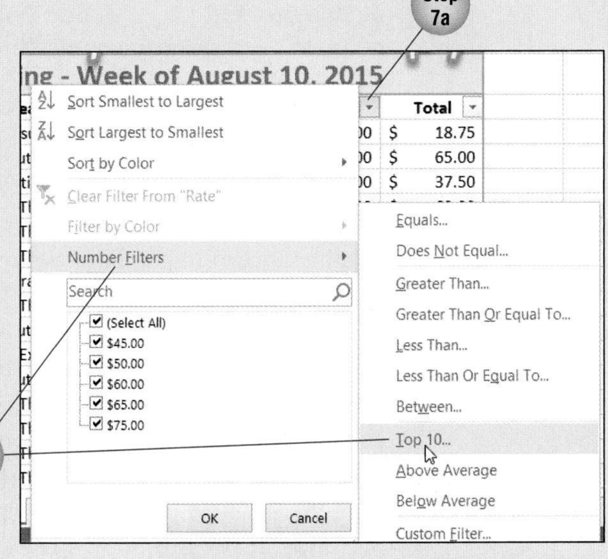

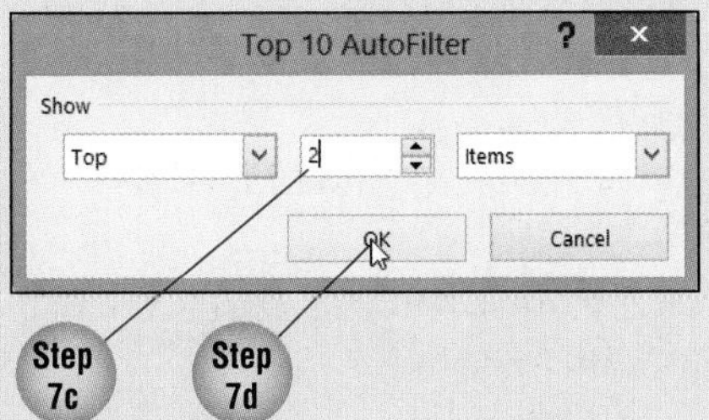

8. Redisplay all rows that contain data by completing the following steps:
   a. Click the funnel icon in the *Rate* heading.
   b. Click the *Clear Filter From "Rate"* option.
9. Display totals greater than $60 by completing the following steps:
   a. Click the filter arrow in the *Total* heading.
   b. Point to *Number Filters* and then click *Greater Than*.
   c. At the Custom AutoFilter dialog box, type 60 and then click OK.
10. Print the worksheet by clicking the FILE tab, clicking the *Print* option, and then clicking the Print button.
11. Turn off the filtering feature by clicking the Sort & Filter button and then clicking *Filter* at the drop-down list.
12. Save, print, and then close **EL1-C4-P3-APTBilling.xlsx**.

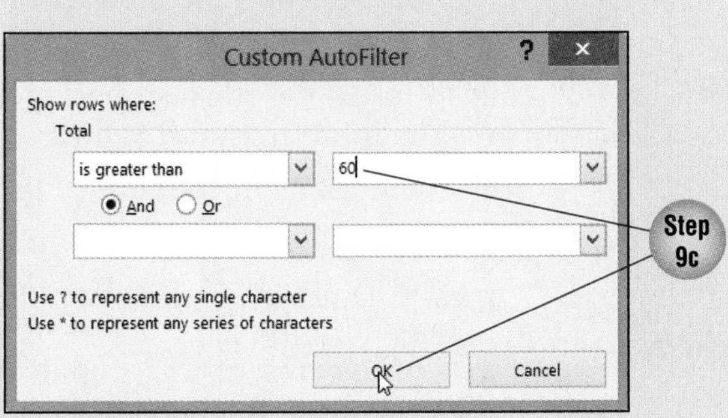

Chapter Summary

- The Page Setup group on the PAGE LAYOUT tab contains buttons for changing the margins and page orientation and size, as well as buttons for establishing the print area, inserting a page break, applying a picture background, and printing titles.
- The default left and right margins are 0.7 inch and the default top and bottom margins are 0.75 inch. Change these default margins with the Margins button in the Page Setup group on the PAGE LAYOUT tab.
- Display the Page Setup dialog box with the Margins tab selected by clicking the Margins button in the Page Setup group on the PAGE LAYOUT tab and then clicking *Custom Margins* at the drop-down list.
- Center a worksheet on the page with the *Horizontally* and *Vertically* options at the Page Setup dialog box with the Margins tab selected.
- Click the Orientation button in the Page Setup group on the PAGE LAYOUT tab to display the two orientation choices: *Portrait* and *Landscape*.
- Insert a page break by selecting the column or row, clicking the Breaks button in the Page Setup group on the PAGE LAYOUT tab, and then clicking *Insert Page Break* at the drop-down list.
- To insert both horizontal and vertical page breaks at the same time, make a cell active, click the Breaks button, and then click *Insert Page Break* at the drop-down list.
- Preview the page breaks in a worksheet by clicking the Page Break Preview button in the view area on the Status bar or clicking the VIEW tab and then clicking the Page Break Preview button in the Workbook Views group.
- Use options at the Page Setup dialog box with the Sheet tab selected to specify printing column and/or row titles on each page. Display this dialog box by clicking the Print Titles button in the Page Setup group on the PAGE LAYOUT tab.
- Use options in the Scale to Fit group on the PAGE LAYOUT tab to scale data to fit on a specific number of pages.
- Use the Background button in the Page Setup group on the PAGE LAYOUT tab to insert a worksheet background picture. A background picture displays on the screen but does not print.
- Use options in the Sheet Options group on the PAGE LAYOUT tab to specify whether to view and/or print gridlines and headings.
- Specify the print area by selecting the desired cells, clicking the Print Area button in the Page Setup group on the PAGE LAYOUT tab, and then clicking *Set Print Area* at the drop-down list. Add another print area by selecting the desired cells, clicking the Print Area button, and then clicking *Add to Print Area* at the drop-down list.
- Create a header and/or footer with the Header & Footer button in the Text group on the INSERT tab, in Page Layout view, or with options at the Page Setup dialog box with the Header/Footer tab selected.
- Customize a print job with options at the Print backstage area.
- To check spelling in a worksheet, click the REVIEW tab and then click the Spelling button.

- Click the Undo button on the Quick Access toolbar to reverse the most recent action and click the Redo button to redo a previously reversed action.
- Use options at the Find and Replace dialog box with the Find tab selected to find specific data and/or formatting in a worksheet.
- Use options at the Find and Replace dialog box with the Replace tab selected to find specific data and/or formatting and replace it with other data and/or formatting.
- Sort data in a worksheet with options from the Sort & Filter button in the Editing group on the HOME tab.
- Create a custom sort with options at the Sort dialog box. Display this dialog box by clicking the Sort & Filter button and then clicking *Custom Sort* at the drop-down list.
- Use filtering to temporarily isolate specific data. Turn on the filter feature by clicking the Sort & Filter button in the Editing group on the HOME tab and then clicking *Filter* at the drop-down list. This inserts filter arrows with each column label. Click a filter arrow and then use options at the drop-down list that displays to specify the filter data.

Commands Review

FEATURE	RIBBON TAB, GROUP	BUTTON, OPTION	KEYBOARD SHORTCUT
background picture	PAGE LAYOUT, Page Setup		
filter data	HOME, Editing		
Find and Replace dialog box with Find tab selected	HOME, Editing	, *Find*	Ctrl + F
Find and Replace dialog box with Replace tab selected	HOME, Editing	, *Replace*	Ctrl + H
header and footer	INSERT, Text		
insert page break	PAGE LAYOUT, Page Setup	, *Insert Page Break*	
margins	PAGE LAYOUT, Page Setup		
orientation	PAGE LAYOUT, Page Setup		
Page Layout view	VIEW, Workbook Views		
Page Setup dialog box with Margins tab selected	PAGE LAYOUT, Page Setup	, *Custom Margins*	
Page Setup dialog box with Sheet tab selected	PAGE LAYOUT, Page Setup		
preview page break	VIEW, Workbook Views		

FEATURE	RIBBON TAB, GROUP	BUTTON, OPTION	KEYBOARD SHORTCUT
print area	PAGE LAYOUT, Page Setup		
remove page break	PAGE LAYOUT, Page Setup	, *Remove Page Break*	
scale height	PAGE LAYOUT, Scale to Fit		
scale to fit	PAGE LAYOUT, Scale to Fit		
scale width	PAGE LAYOUT, Scale to Fit		
size	PAGE LAYOUT, Page Setup		
sort data	HOME, Editing		
spelling checker	REVIEW, Proofing		F7

Concepts Check Test Your Knowledge

Completion: In the space provided at the right, indicate the correct term, symbol, or command.

1. This is the default left and right margin measurement. __________
2. This is the default top and bottom margin measurement. __________
3. The Margins button is located on this tab. __________
4. By default, a worksheet prints in this orientation on a page. __________
5. Click the Print Titles button in the Page Setup group on the PAGE LAYOUT tab and the Page Setup dialog box displays with this tab selected. __________
6. Use options in this group on the PAGE LAYOUT tab to adjust the printed output by a percentage to fit the number of pages specified. __________
7. Use this button in the Page Setup group on the PAGE LAYOUT tab to select and print specific areas in a worksheet. __________
8. Click the Header & Footer button in the Text group on the INSERT tab and the worksheet displays in this view. __________
9. This tab contains options for formatting and customizing a header and/or footer. __________

10. Click this tab to display the Spelling button. ____________

11. The Undo and Redo buttons are located on this toolbar. ____________

12. Click this button in the Find and Replace dialog box to expand the dialog box. ____________

13. Use these two buttons at the expanded Find and Replace dialog box to search for specific cell formatting and replace it with other formatting. ____________

14. Use this button in the Editing group on the HOME tab to sort data in a worksheet. ____________

15. Use this feature to temporarily isolate specific data in a worksheet. ____________

Skills Check Assess Your Performance

Assessment 1

FORMAT A DATA ANALYSIS WORKSHEET

1. Open **DISemiSales.xlsx**.
2. Save the workbook with Save As and name it **EL1-C4-A1-DISemiSales**.
3. Make the following changes to the worksheet:
   a. Insert a formula in cell H4 that averages the amounts in cells B4 through G4.
   b. Copy the formula in cell H4 down to cells H5 through H9.
   c. Insert a formula in cell B10 that adds the amounts in cells B4 through B9.
   d. Copy the formula in cell B10 over to cells C10 through H10. (Click the Auto Fill Options button and then click *Fill Without Formatting* at the drop-down list.)
   e. Apply accounting formatting to cell H4.
   f. Change the orientation of the worksheet to landscape.
   g. Change the top margin to 3 inches and the left margin to 1.5 inches.
4. Save and then print **EL1-C4-A1-DISemiSales.xlsx**.
5. Make the following changes to the worksheet:
   a. Change the orientation back to portrait.
   b. Change the top margin to 1 inch and the left margin to 0.7 inch.
   c. Horizontally and vertically center the worksheet on the page.
   d. Scale the worksheet so it fits on one page.
6. Save, print, and then close **EL1-C4-A1-DISemiSales.xlsx**.

Assessment 2

FORMAT A TEST RESULTS WORKSHEET

1. Open **CMTests.xlsx**.
2. Save the workbook with Save As and name it **EL1-C4-A2-CMTests**.
3. Make the following changes to the worksheet:
   a. Insert a formula in cell N4 that averages the test scores in cells B4 through M4.
   b. Copy the formula in cell N4 down to cells N5 through N21.
   c. Type Average in cell A22.
   d. Insert a formula in cell B22 that averages the test scores in cells B4 through B21.
   e. Copy the formula in cell B22 across to cells C22 through N22.
   f. Insert a page break between columns G and H.
4. View the worksheet using Page Break Preview.
5. Change back to the Normal view.
6. Specify that the column titles (A3 through A22) are to print on each page.
7. Create a header that prints the page number at the right side of the page.
8. Create a footer that prints your name at the left side of the page and the workbook file name at the right side of the page.
9. Display the worksheet in Normal view.
10. Save and then print the worksheet.
11. Set a print area for cells N3 through N22 and then print the cells.
12. Clear the print area.
13. Save and then close **EL1-C4-A2-CMTests.xlsx**.

Assessment 3

FORMAT AN EQUIPMENT RENTAL WORKSHEET

1. Open **HERInvoices.xlsx**.
2. Save the workbook with Save As and name it **EL1-C4-A3-HERInvoices**.
3. Insert a formula in cell H3 that multiplies the rate in cell G3 by the hours in cell F3. Copy the formula in cell H3 down to cells H4 through H16.
4. Insert a formula in cell H17 that sums the amounts in cells H3 through H16.
5. Complete the following find and replaces:
   a. Find all occurrences of cells containing *75* and replace them with *90*.
   b. Find all occurrences of cells containing *55* and replace them with *60*.
   c. Find all occurrences of *Barrier Concrete* and replace them with *Lee Sand and Gravel*.
   d. Find all occurrences of 11-point Calibri and replace them with 10-point Cambria.
   e. After completing the find and replaces, clear all formatting from the Format buttons.
6. Insert a header that prints the date at the left side of the page and the time at the right side of the page.
7. Insert a footer that prints your name at the left side of the page and the workbook file name at the right side of the page.
8. Print the worksheet horizontally and vertically centered on the page.
9. Save and then close **EL1-C4-A3-HERInvoices.xlsx**.

Assessment

4 FORMAT AN INVOICES WORKSHEET

1. Open **RPInvoices.xlsx**.
2. Save the workbook with Save As and name it **EL1-C4-A4-RPInvoices**.
3. Insert a formula in G4 that multiplies the amount in E4 with the percentage in F4 and then adds the product to cell E4. (If you write the formula correctly, the result in G4 will display as *$488.25*.)
4. Copy the formula in cell G4 down to cells G5 through G17, click the Auto Fill Options button, and then click the *Fill Without Formatting* option.
5. Complete a spelling check on the worksheet.
6. Find all occurrences of *Picture* and replace them with *Portrait*. (Do not type a space after *Picture* or *Portrait* because you want to find occurrences that end with an *s*. Make sure the *Match entire cell contents* check box does not contain a check mark.)
7. Sort the records by invoice number in ascending order (smallest to largest).
8. Complete a new sort that sorts the records by client number in ascending order (A to Z).
9. Complete a new sort that sorts by date in ascending order (oldest to newest).
10. Insert a footer in the worksheet that prints your name at the left side of the page and the current date at the right side of the page.
11. Display the worksheet in Normal view.
12. Center the worksheet horizontally and vertically on the page.
13. Save and then print **EL1-C4-A4-RPInvoices.xlsx**.
14. Select cells A3 through G3 and then turn on the filter feature and complete the following filters:
    a. Filter and then print a list of rows containing client number 11-279 and then clear the filter.
    b. Filter and then print a list of rows containing the top three highest amounts due and then clear the filter.
    c. Filter and then print a list of rows containing amounts due that are less than $500 and then clear the filter.
15. Save and then close **EL1-C4-A4-RPInvoices.xlsx**.

Assessment

5 CREATE A WORKSHEET CONTAINING KEYBOARD SHORTCUTS

1. Use Excel's Help feature to learn about keyboard shortcuts in Excel. After reading the information presented, create a worksheet with the following features:
    - Create a title for the worksheet.
    - Include at least 10 keyboard shortcuts along with an explanation of each shortcut.
    - Set the data in cells in a typeface other than Calibri and change the data color.
    - Add borders to the cells. (You determine the border style.)
    - Add a color of shading to cells. (You determine the color; make it complement the data color.)
    - Create a header that prints the date at the right margin and create a footer that prints your name at the left margin and the file name at the right margin.
2. Save the workbook and name it **EL1-C4-A5-KeyboardShortcuts**.
3. Print and then close **EL1-C4-A5-KeyboardShortcuts.xlsx**.

Visual Benchmark Demonstrate Your Proficiency

CREATE AND FORMAT AN EXPENSE WORKSHEET

1. At a blank workbook, type the data in the cells as indicated in Figure 4.13 on the next page, but **do not** type the data in the cells noted below. Instead, insert the formulas as indicated:
   - Cells N3 through N8: Insert a formula that sums the monthly expenses for the year.
   - Cells B9 through N9: Insert a formula that sums the monthly expenses for each month and the entire year.

   (The results of your formulas should match the results you see in the figure.)
2. Change the left and right margins to 0.45 inch and change the top margin to 1.5 inches.
3. Apply formatting so your worksheet looks similar to the worksheet shown in Figure 4.13. (Set the heading in 26-point Cambria and set the remaining data in 10-point Cambria. Apply bold formatting as shown in the figure.)
4. Save the workbook and name it **EL1-C4-VB-HERExpenses**.
5. Look at the printing of the worksheet shown in Figure 4.14 and then make the following changes:
   - Insert a page break between columns G and H.
   - Insert the headers and footer as shown.
   - Specify that the column titles print on the second page, as shown in Figure 4.14.
6. Save and then print **EL1-C4-VB-HERExpenses.xlsx**. (Your worksheet should print on two pages and appear as shown in Figure 4.14 on the next page.)
7. Close **EL1-C4-VB-HERExpenses.xlsx**.

Figure 4.13 Visual Benchmark Data

	A	B	C	D	E	F	G	H	I	J	K	L	M	N
1	**Hilltop Equipment Rental**													
2	**Expenses**	**January**	**February**	**March**	**April**	**May**	**June**	**July**	**August**	**September**	**October**	**November**	**December**	***Total***
3	Lease	$ 3,250	$ 3,250	$ 3,250	$ 3,250	$ 3,250	$ 3,250	$ 3,250	$ 3,250	$ 3,250	$ 3,250	$ 3,250	$ 3,250	$ 39,000
4	Utilities	3,209	2,994	2,987	2,500	2,057	1,988	1,845	1,555	1,890	2,451	2,899	3,005	29,380
5	Payroll	10,545	9,533	11,542	10,548	11,499	12,675	13,503	13,258	12,475	10,548	10,122	9,359	135,607
6	Insurance	895	895	895	895	895	895	895	895	895	895	895	895	10,740
7	Maintenance	2,439	1,856	2,455	5,410	3,498	3,110	2,479	3,100	1,870	6,105	4,220	3,544	40,086
8	Supplies	341	580	457	330	675	319	451	550	211	580	433	601	5,528
9	***Total Expenses***	$ 20,679	$ 19,108	$ 21,586	$ 22,933	$ 21,874	$ 22,237	$ 22,423	$ 22,608	$ 20,591	$ 23,829	$ 21,819	$ 20,654	$ 260,341
10														

Figure 4.14 Visual Benchmark Printed Pages

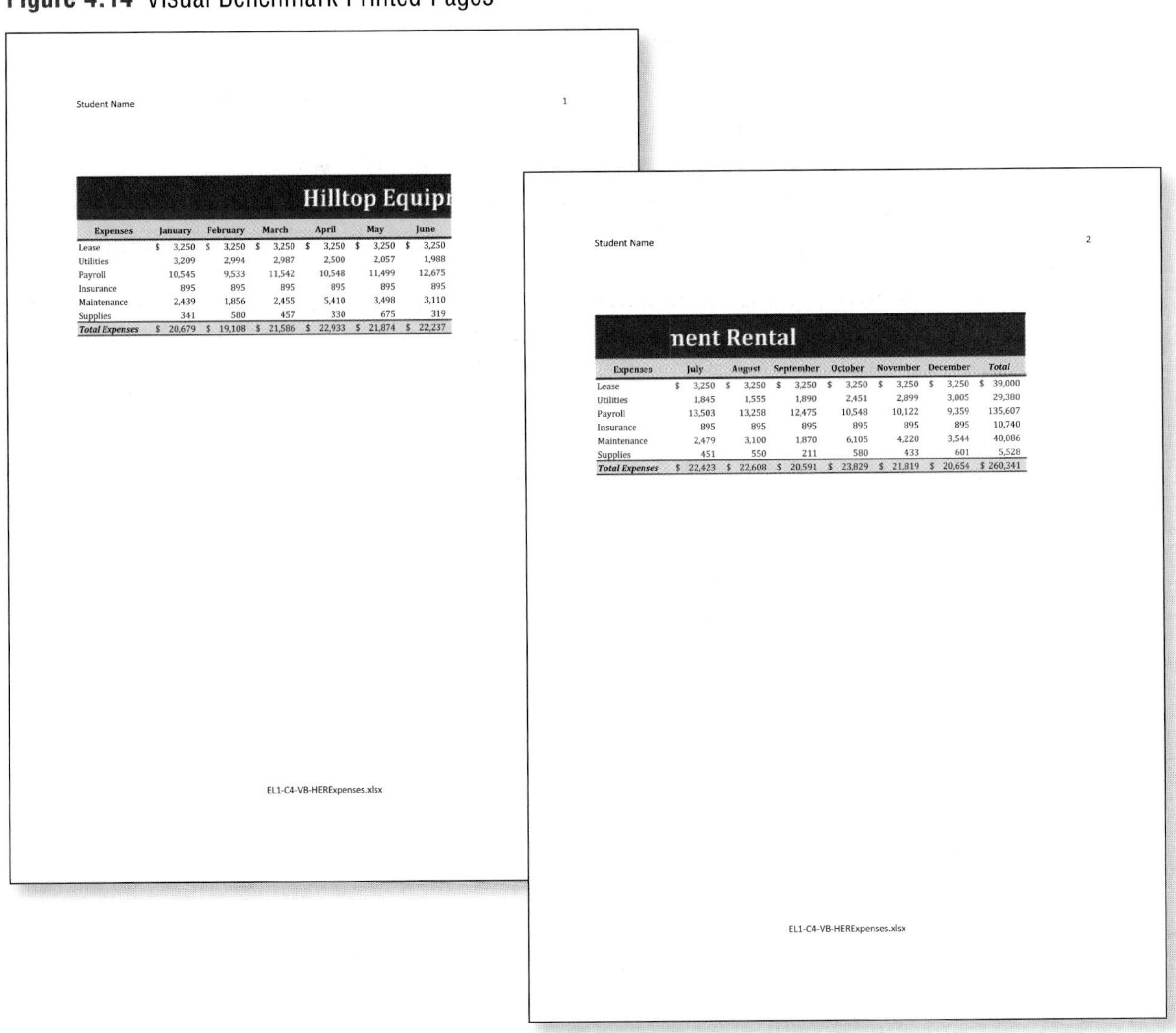

Student Name 1

Hilltop Equipr						
Expenses	January	February	March	April	May	June
Lease	$ 3,250	$ 3,250	$ 3,250	$ 3,250	$ 3,250	$ 3,250
Utilities	3,209	2,994	2,987	2,500	2,057	1,988
Payroll	10,545	9,533	11,542	10,548	11,499	12,675
Insurance	895	895	895	895	895	895
Maintenance	2,439	1,856	2,455	5,410	3,498	3,110
Supplies	341	580	457	330	675	319
Total Expenses	$ 20,679	$ 19,108	$ 21,586	$ 22,933	$ 21,874	$ 22,237

EL1-C4-VB-HERExpenses.xlsx

Student Name 2

nent Rental							
Expenses	July	August	September	October	November	December	*Total*
Lease	$ 3,250	$ 3,250	$ 3,250	$ 3,250	$ 3,250	$ 3,250	$ 39,000
Utilities	1,845	1,555	1,890	2,451	2,899	3,005	29,380
Payroll	13,503	13,258	12,475	10,548	10,122	9,359	135,607
Insurance	895	895	895	895	895	895	10,740
Maintenance	2,479	3,100	1,870	6,105	4,220	3,544	40,086
Supplies	451	550	211	580	433	601	5,528
Total Expenses	$ 22,423	$ 22,608	$ 20,591	$ 23,829	$ 21,819	$ 20,654	$ 260,341

EL1-C4-VB-HERExpenses.xlsx

Case Study Apply Your Skills

Part 1

You are a sales associate for Macadam Realty. Your supervisor has asked you to complete a form that she started containing information on sample mortgages. She wants to display the form in the reception area display rack. She has already inserted a formula (in cell G4) that calculates monthly payments using the PMT function. (You will learn more about this function in Chapter 5.) Open **MRMortgages.xlsx** and then save it with Save As and name it **EL1-C4-CS-MRMortgages-01**. Add the following information and make the following changes:

- In column C, insert a formula that determines the down payment amount.
- In column D, insert a formula that determines the loan amount.
- In column G, drag the formula in cell G4 down to cells G5 through G47.
- Insert the date and time as a header and your name and the workbook name (**EL1-C4-CS-MRMortgages-01.xlsx**) as a footer.
- Find 11-point Calibri formatting and replace it with 11-point Candara formatting.
- Scale the worksheet so it prints on one page.

Save and then print **EL1-C4-CS-MRMortgages-01.xlsx**. After looking at the printed worksheet, you decide that you need to make the following changes:

- Sort the values in the *Price of Home* column from smallest to largest.
- Change the percentage amount in column E from 6% to 7%.
- Shade the cells in row 4 that contain data in the light gold color that matches the fill in cell A2. Copy this shading to every other row of cells in the worksheet (stopping at row 46). *Apply accounting formatting with a dollar sign and no places past the decimal point to cells A4, C4, D4, and G4.

Save the edited worksheet with Save As and name it **EL1-C4-CS-MRMortgages-02**. Make sure the worksheet prints on one page. Save, print, and then close **EL1-C4-CS-MRMortgages-02.xlsx**.

Part 2

You are responsible for preparing a worksheet containing sales and commissions for the year. You will print the worksheet for distribution to staff members who attend an upcoming meeting. You have created the worksheet and included the sales and commission totals and now need to insert formulas and format the worksheet. Open **MRSalesComms.xlsx** and then save the workbook with Save As and name it **EL1-C4-CS-MRSalesComms**. Make the following changes to the worksheet:

- Calculate the sales and commissions and insert the totals in the appropriate locations in the worksheet.
- Calculate the total sales and total commissions and insert the totals in the appropriate locations in the worksheet.
- Apply appropriate number formatting.
- Apply formatting so the worksheet is formatted similar to the worksheet you prepared in Part 1.
- Change the left margin to 1.2 inches and the top margin to 1.5 inches.
- Include a header that prints the page number and a footer that prints your name.

Save the worksheet and then print it so that the row titles (A4:A14) print on both pages. After looking at the worksheet, you decide to make the following changes:

- Remove the header containing the page number.
- Edit the footer so the date prints at the left margin and your name prints at the right margin.
- Change the orientation to landscape.
- Scale the worksheet so it prints on one page.

Print, save, and then close **EL1-C4-CS-MRSalesComms.xlsx**.

Part 3

You have clients living in Canada that are interested in purchasing real estate in the United States. For those clients, you like to keep a dollar conversion worksheet available. Using the Internet, search for a site that converts the US dollar to the Canadian dollar. Determine the current currency exchange rate for the Canadian dollar and then create a worksheet with the following specifications:

- Apply formatting that is similar to the formatting in the worksheets you worked with in the first two parts of the case study.
- Create a column for home prices in US dollars with home amounts that begin with $100,000, increment every $50,000, and end with $1,000,000.
- Create a column for home prices converted to Canadian dollars.
- Apply any other formatting you feel is necessary to improve the worksheet.

Save the completed workbook and name it **EL1-C4-CS-CanadaPrices**. Display formulas and then print the worksheet. Turn off the display of formulas and then save and close the workbook.

MICROSOFT® EXCEL® Performance Assessment

Excel L1U1

Note: Before beginning unit assessments, copy to your storage medium the EL1U1 subfolder from the EL1U1 folder on the CD that accompanies this textbook and then make EL1U1 the active folder.

Assessing Proficiency

In this unit, you have learned to create, save, print, edit, and format Excel worksheets; create and insert formulas; and enhance worksheets with features such as headers and footers, page numbering, sorting, and filtering.

Assessment 1 Calculate Total, Maximum, Minimum, and Average Yearly Sales

1. Open **DI2015Sales.xlsx** and then save the workbook with Save As and name it **EL1-U1-A1-DI2015Sales**.
2. Insert in cells D4 through D14 the appropriate sales totals.
3. Insert in cells B15, C15, and D15 the appropriate first half, second half, and total sales, respectively. (If you use the fill handle to copy the formula in cell B15 to cells C15 and D15, you will need to fill without formatting so the right border remains in cell D15.)
4. Insert in cell B17 a formula that inserts the maximum total sales amount from cells D4 through D14.
5. Insert in cell B18 a formula that inserts the minimum total sales amount from cells D4 through D14.
6. Insert in cell B19 a formula that inserts the average of total sales in cells D4 through D14.
7. Apply accounting formatting to cell D4 with a dollar sign. (Make sure the places after the decimal point remain set at zero.)
8. Save, print, and then close **EL1-U1-A1-DI2015Sales.xlsx**.

Assessment 2 Create Worksheet with AutoFill and Calculate Hours and Gross Pay

1. Create the Excel worksheet shown in Figure U1.1. Use AutoFill to fill in the days of the week and some of the hours.
2. Insert a formula in cells H4 through H10 that calculates the total hours.
3. Insert a formula in cells J4 through J10 that calculates the gross pay (total hours multiplied by pay rate).
4. Insert a formula in cells B11 through J11 that totals the hours, total hours, pay rate, and gross pay.

5. Apply formatting to the cells as shown in the figure.
6. Change the page orientation to landscape.
7. Save the worksheet and name it **EL1-U1-A2-CPPayroll**.
8. Turn on the display of formulas, print the worksheet (prints on two pages), and then turn off the display of formulas.
9. Save and then close **EL1-U1-A2-CPPayroll.xlsx**.

Figure U1.1 Assessment 2

	A	B	C	D	E	F	G	H	I	J
1	**Capstan Products**									
2	**Payroll - Week Ended: March 14, 2015**									
3	**Employee**	**Monday**	**Tuesday**	**Wednesday**	**Thursday**	**Friday**	**Saturday**	**Total Hours**	**Pay Rate**	**Gross Pay**
4	Loftus, Maureen	8	8	8	8	8	0	40	$ 28.50	$1,140.00
5	Banyai, Robert	3	3	3	3	0	8	20	15.35	307.00
6	Martinez, Michelle	0	8	8	8	8	8	40	19.00	760.00
7	Wilhelm, Marshall	0	5	5	5	5	8	28	13.50	378.00
8	Ziegler, Cathleen	0	0	0	0	4	4	8	22.45	179.60
9	Hope, Trevor	0	0	0	0	4	4	8	13.50	108.00
10	Anthony, Charles	0	4	4	4	4	4	20	13.50	270.00
11	**Total**	11	28	28	28	33	36	164	$ 125.80	$3,142.60

Assessment 3 Sales Bonuses Workbook

1. Create the Excel worksheet shown in Figure U1.2. Format the cells as you see them in the figure.
2. Insert a formula in cells D4 through D11 that calculates the bonus amount (sales times bonus).
3. Insert a formula in cells E4 through E11 that calculates the net sales (sales minus bonus amount).
4. Insert the sum of cells B4 through B11 in cell B12, the sum of cells D4 through D11 in cell D12, and the sum of cells E4 through E11 in cell E12.
5. Apply accounting formatting with no places after the decimal point and no dollar sign to cells B5 through B11 and cells D5 through E11.
6. Apply accounting formatting with a dollar sign and no places after the decimal point to cells B4, D4, E4, B12, D12, and E12.
7. Insert a footer that contains your first and last names and the current date.
8. Print the worksheet horizontally and vertically centered on the page.
9. Save the workbook and name it **EL1-U1-A3-SBASales**.
10. Close **EL1-U1-A3-SBASales.xlsx**.

Figure U1.2 Assessment 3

	A	B	C	D	E	F
1	**Stanton & Barnet Associates**					
2	**Sales Department**					
3	**Associate**	**Sales**	**Bonus**	**Bonus Amount**	**Net Sales**	
4	Conway, Amanda	$ 101,450	5%			
5	Eckhart, Geneva	94,375	2%			
6	Farris, Edward	73,270	0%			
7	Greenwood, Wayne	110,459	5%			
8	Hagen, Chandra	120,485	5%			
9	Logan, Courtney	97,520	2%			
10	Pena, Geraldo	115,850	5%			
11	Rubin, Alex	76,422	0%			
12	**Total**					
13						

Assessment 4 Format a Department Budget

1. Open **CMDeptBudgets.xlsx** and then save the workbook with Save As and name it **EL1-U1-A4-CMDeptBudgets**.
2. Insert a formula using an absolute cell reference to determine the projected budget with an increase of 10% over the current budget. (Use the number *1.1* in cell B3 when writing the formula.)
3. Insert formulas to total the budget amounts and the projected budget amounts.
4. Make cell A15 active and then use the NOW function to insert the current date and time.
5. Save and then print the worksheet.
6. Determine the projected budget with an increase of 5% over the current budget by changing the text in cell A3 to *5% Increase* and the number in cell B3 to *1.05*.
7. Save, print, and then close **EL1-U1-A4-CMDeptBudgets.xlsx**.

Assessment 5 Format Weekly Payroll Workbook

1. Open **CCPayroll.xlsx** and then save the workbook with Save As and name it **EL1-U1-A5-CCPayroll**.
2. Insert a formula in cell E3 that multiplies the hourly rate by the hours and then adds that to the multiplication of the hourly rate by the overtime pay rate (1.5) and then overtime hours. (Use parentheses in the formula and use an absolute cell reference for the overtime pay rate. Refer to Chapter 2, Project 3c.) Copy the formula down to cells E4 through E16.
3. Insert a formula in cell F3 that multiplies the gross pay by the withholding tax rate (W/H Rate). (Use an absolute cell reference for the cell containing the withholding rate. Refer to Chapter 2, Project 3c.) Copy the formula down to cells F4 through F16.

4. Insert a formula in cell G3 that multiplies the gross pay by the social security rate (SS Rate). Use an absolute cell reference for the cell containing the social security rate. (Refer to Chapter 2, Project 3c.) Copy the formula down to cells G4 through G16.
5. Insert a formula in cell H4 that adds together the social security tax and the withholding tax and subtracts that sum from the gross pay. (Refer to Chapter 2, Project 3c.) Copy the formula down to cells H4 through H16.
6. Sort the employee last names alphabetically in ascending order (A to Z).
7. Center the worksheet horizontally and vertically on the page.
8. Insert a footer that prints your name at the left side of the page and the file name at the right side of the page.
9. Save, print, and then close **EL1-U1-A5-CCPayroll.xlsx**.

Assessment 6 Format Customer Sales Analysis Workbook

1. Open **DIAnnualSales.xlsx** and then save the workbook with Save As and name it **EL1-U1-A6-DIAnnualSales**.
2. Insert formulas and drag formulas to complete the worksheet. After dragging the total formula in row 10, specify that you want to fill without formatting. (This retains the right border in cell N10.) Do this with the Auto Fill Options button.
3. Insert in cell B11 the highest total from cells B10 through M10. Insert in cell B12 the lowest total from cells B10 through M10.
4. Change the orientation to landscape.
5. Insert a header that prints the page number at the right side of the page.
6. Insert a footer that prints your name at the right side of the page.
7. Horizontally and vertically center the worksheet on the page.
8. Specify that the column headings in cells A3 through A12 print on both pages.
9. Save, print, and then close **EL1-U1-A6-DIAnnualSales.xlsx**.

Assessment 7 Format Invoices Workbook

1. Open **RPInvoices.xlsx** and then save the workbook with Save As and name it **EL1-U1-A7-RPInvoices**.
2. Insert a formula in cell G4 that multiplies the amount in cell E4 by the percentage in cell F4 and then adds that total to the amount in cell E4. (Use parentheses in this formula.)
3. Copy the formula in cell G4 down to cells G5 through G18.
4. Apply accounting formatting with two places after the decimal point and a dollar sign to cell G4, and then apply comma formatting with two places after the decimal point to cells G5 through G18.
5. Find all occurrences of cells containing *11-279* and replace them with *10-005*.
6. Find all occurrences of cells containing *8.5* and replace them with *9.0*.
7. Search for all occurrences of the Calibri font and replace them with the Candara font. (Do not specify a type size so that Excel replaces all sizes of Calibri with Candara.)
8. Print **EL1-U1-A7-RPInvoices.xlsx**.
9. Filter and then print a list of rows containing only the client number *04-325*. (After printing, return the list to *(Select All)*.)
10. Filter and then print a list of rows containing only the service *Development*. (After printing, return the list to *(Select All)*.)
11. Filter and then print a list of rows containing the three highest totals in the *Amount Due* column. (After printing, turn off the filter feature.)
12. Save and then close **EL1-U1-A7-RPInvoices.xlsx**.

Writing Activities

The following activities give you the opportunity to practice your writing skills along with demonstrating an understanding of some of the important Excel features you have mastered in this unit. Use correct grammar, appropriate word choices, and clear sentence construction.

Activity 1 Plan and Prepare Orders Summary Workbook

Plan and prepare a worksheet with the information shown in Figure U1.3. Apply formatting of your choosing to the worksheet. Save the completed worksheet and name it **EL1-U1-Act1-OrdersSumm**. Print and then close **EL1-U1-Act1-OrdersSumm.xlsx**.

Figure U1.3 Activity 1

Prepare a weekly summary of orders taken that itemizes the products coming into the company and the average order size. The products and average order size include:

Black and gold wall clock: $2,450 worth of orders, average order size of $125
Traveling alarm clock: $1,358 worth of orders, average order size of $195
Waterproof watch: $890 worth of orders, average order size of $90
Dashboard clock: $2,135 worth of orders, average order size of $230
Pyramid clock: $3,050 worth of orders, average order size of $375
Gold chain watch: $755 worth of orders, average order size of $80

In the worksheet, total the amount ordered and also calculate the average weekly order size. Sort the data in the worksheet by the order amount in descending order.

Activity 2 Prepare Depreciation Workbook

Assets within a company, such as equipment, can be depreciated over time. Several methods are available for determining the amount of depreciation, such as the straight-line depreciation method, the fixed-declining balance method, and the double-declining method. Use Excel's Help feature to learn about two depreciation methods: straight-line and double-declining depreciation. (The straight-line depreciation function, SLN, and the double-declining depreciation function, DDB, are located in the *Financial* category.) After reading about the two methods, create an Excel worksheet describing the methods with the following information:

- An appropriate title
- A heading for straight-line depreciation
- The straight-line depreciation function
- The name of and a description for each straight-line depreciation function argument category
- A heading for double-declining depreciation

- The double-declining depreciation function
- The name of and a description for each double-declining depreciation function argument category

Apply formatting of your choosing to the worksheet. Save the completed workbook and name it **EL1-U1-Act2-DepMethods**. Print the worksheet horizontally and vertically centered on the page. Close **EL1-U1-Act2-DepMethods.xlsx**.

Activity 3 Insert Straight-Line Depreciation Formula

Open **RPDepreciation.xlsx** and then save the workbook and name it **EL1-U1-Act3-RPDepreciation**. Insert the function to determine straight-line depreciation in cell E4. Copy the formula down to cells E5 through E9. Print the worksheet horizontally and vertically centered on the page. Save and then close **EL1-U1-Act3-RPDepreciation.xlsx**.

Optional: Briefly research straight-line and double-declining depreciation to find out why businesses depreciate their assets. What purpose does it serve? Locate information about the topics on the Internet or in your school library. Then use Word 2013 to write a half-page, single-spaced report explaining the financial reasons for using depreciation methods. Save the document and name it **EL1-U1-Act3-DepReport**. Print and then close the document.

Internet Research

Create a Travel Planning Worksheet

Search for information on the Internet on traveling to a specific country that interests you. Find sites that provide cost information for airlines, hotels, meals, entertainment, and car rentals. Using the first week of the next month as the travel dates, create a travel planning worksheet for the country that includes the following:

- An appropriate title
- Appropriate headings
- Airline costs
- Hotel costs (off-season and in-season rates if available)
- Estimated meal costs
- Entertainment costs
- Car rental costs

Save the completed workbook and name it **EL1-U1-Act4-TrvlWksht**. Print and then close the workbook.

MICROSOFT®

EXCEL®

Level 1

Unit 2 ■ Enhancing the Display of Workbooks

Chapter 5 ■ Moving Data within and between Workbooks

Chapter 6 ■ Maintaining Workbooks

Chapter 7 ■ Creating Charts and Inserting Formulas

Chapter 8 ■ Adding Visual Interest to Workbooks

MICROSOFT® EXCEL®

Moving Data within and between Workbooks

PERFORMANCE OBJECTIVES

Upon successful completion of Chapter 5, you will be able to:

- **Create a workbook with multiple worksheets**
- **Move, copy, and paste cells within and between worksheets**
- **Split a worksheet into windows and freeze panes**
- **Name a range of cells and use a range in a formula**
- **Open multiple workbooks**
- **Arrange, size, and move workbooks**
- **Copy and paste data between workbooks**
- **Link data between worksheets**

Tutorials

5.1 Moving and Copying Cells
5.2 Inserting, Moving, Renaming, and Deleting a Worksheet
5.3 Formatting Multiple Worksheets
5.4 Using Paste Options
5.5 Printing a Workbook Containing Multiple Worksheets
5.6 Freezing Panes and Changing the Zoom
5.7 Splitting a Worksheet into Windows
5.8 Naming and Using a Range
5.9 Working with Windows
5.10 Linking Data between Worksheets
5.11 Copying and Pasting Data between Programs

Up to this point, the workbooks you have been working in have consisted of only single worksheets. In this chapter, you will learn to create a workbook with several worksheets and complete tasks such as copying and pasting data within and between worksheets. Moving and pasting or copying and pasting selected cells in and between worksheets is useful for rearranging data and saving time. You will also work with multiple workbooks and complete tasks such as arranging, sizing, and moving workbooks and opening and closing multiple workbooks. Model answers for this chapter's projects appear on the following pages.

Note: Before beginning the projects, copy to your storage medium the EL1C5 subfolder from the EL1 folder on the CD that accompanies this textbook and then make EL1C5 the active folder.

Model Answers

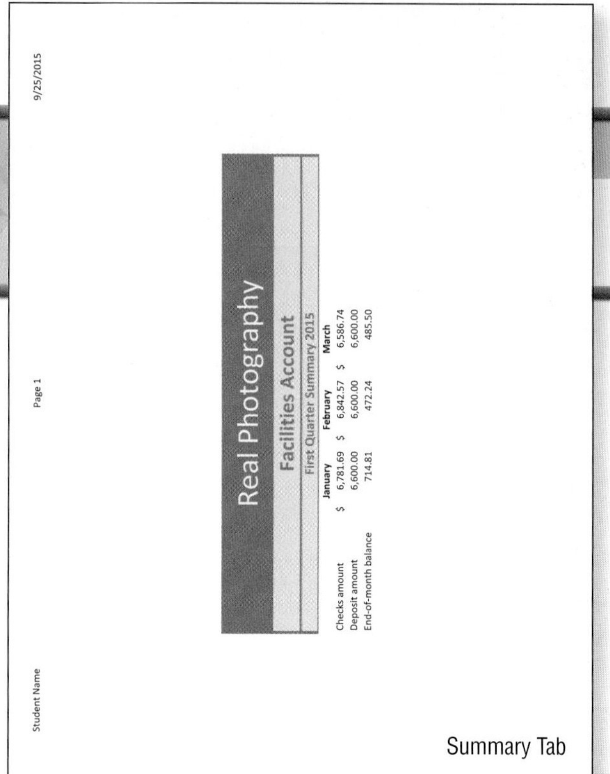

Student Name | Page 1 | 9/25/2015

Real Photography
Facilities Account
First Quarter Summary 2015

	January	February	March
Checks amount	$ 6,781.69	$ 6,842.57	$ 6,586.74
Deposit amount	6,600.00	6,600.00	6,600.00
End-of-month balance	714.81	472.24	485.50

Summary Tab

Student Name | Page 2 | 9/25/2015

Real Photography
Facilities Account
January 2015

Date	Check No.	Payee	Description	Amount	Deposit	Balance
1-Jan			Balance from previous month			$ 896.50
1-Jan			Deposit - General Account		$ 5,500.00	6,396.50
2-Jan	501	Cascade Insurance	Facilities insurance	$ 225.00		6,171.50
2-Jan	502	Quality Insurance	Equipment insurance	150.00		6,021.50
5-Jan	503	Stationery Plus	Paper supplies	205.55		5,815.95
6-Jan	504	Firstline Mortgage	Mortgage payment	4,230.00		1,585.95
8-Jan	505	Clear Source	Developer supplies	123.74		1,462.21
9-Jan			Deposit - sublet rent		1,100.00	2,562.21
12-Jan	506	Rainier Suppliers	Camera supplies	119.62		2,442.59
13-Jan	507	A1 Wedding Supplies	Photo albums	323.58		2,119.01
12-Jan	508	General Systems	Developer payment	525.00		1,594.01
14-Jan	509	Randall Machines	Copier lease payment	250.00		1,344.01
16-Jan	510	Hometown Energy	Electric bill payment	413.74		930.27
19-Jan	511	Steward-Holmes Energy	Natural gas bill payment	86.51		843.76
23-Jan	512	Parkland City Services	Water/sewer payment	45.70		798.06
28-Jan	513	New Century Telephones	Telephone bill payment	83.25		714.81
			Total	$ 6,781.69	$ 6,600.00	

January Tab

Project 1 Manage Data in a Multiple-Worksheet Account Workbook EL1-C5-P1-RPFacAccts.xlsx

Student Name | Page 3 | 9/25/2015

Real Photography
Facilities Account
February 2015

Date	Check No.	Payee	Description	Amount	Deposit	Balance
1-Feb			Balance from previous month			$ 714.81
2-Feb			Deposit - General Account		$ 5,500.00	6,214.81
3-Feb	514	Firstline Mortgage	Mortgage payment	$ 4,230.00		1,984.81
5-Feb	515	Cascade Insurance	Facilities insurance	225.00		1,759.81
10-Feb	516	Quality Insurance	Equipment insurance	150.00		1,609.81
11-Feb	517	Stationery Plus	Paper supplies	266.43		1,343.38
12-Feb	518	Clear Source	Developer supplies	123.74		1,219.64
13-Feb			Deposit - sublet rent		1,100.00	2,319.64
16-Feb	519	Rainier Suppliers	Camera supplies	119.62		2,200.02
17-Feb	520	A1 Wedding Supplies	Photo albums	323.58		1,876.44
17-Feb	521	General Systems	Developer payment	525.00		1,351.44
20-Feb	522	Randall Machines	Copier lease payment	250.00		1,101.44
20-Feb	523	Hometown Energy	Electric bill payment	413.74		687.70
23-Feb	524	Steward-Holmes Energy	Natural gas bill payment	86.51		601.19
24-Feb	525	Parkland City Services	Water/sewer payment	45.70		555.49
26-Feb	526	New Century Telephones	Telephone bill payment	83.25		472.24
			Total	$ 6,842.57	$ 6,600.00	

February Tab

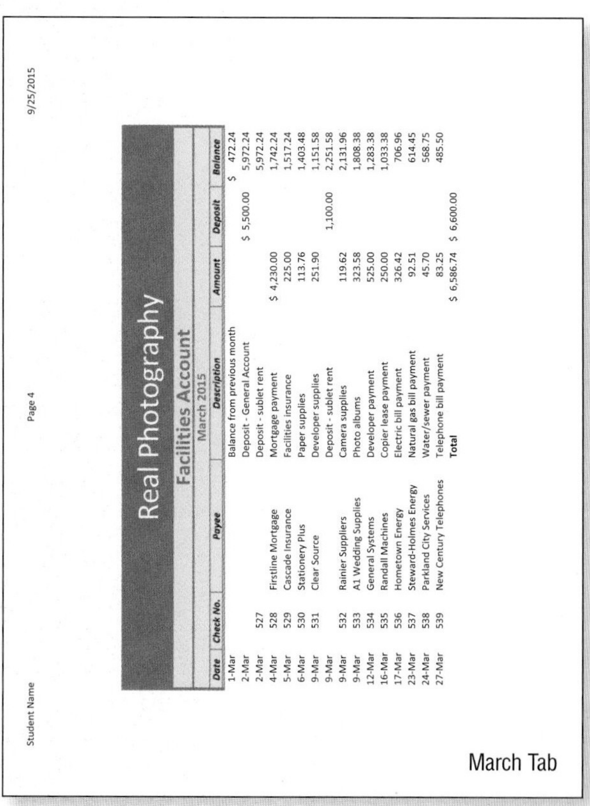

Student Name | Page 4 | 9/25/2015

Real Photography
Facilities Account
March 2015

Date	Check No.	Payee	Description	Amount	Deposit	Balance
1-Mar			Balance from previous month			$ 472.24
2-Mar			Deposit - General Account		$ 5,500.00	5,972.24
2-Mar	527		Deposit - sublet rent			5,972.24
4-Mar	528	Firstline Mortgage	Mortgage payment	$ 4,230.00		1,742.24
5-Mar	529	Cascade Insurance	Facilities insurance	225.00		1,517.24
6-Mar	530	Stationery Plus	Paper supplies	113.76		1,403.48
9-Mar	531	Clear Source	Developer supplies	251.90		1,151.58
9-Mar			Deposit - sublet rent		1,100.00	2,251.58
9-Mar	532	Rainier Suppliers	Camera supplies	119.62		2,131.96
9-Mar	533	A1 Wedding Supplies	Photo albums	323.58		1,808.38
12-Mar	534	General Systems	Developer payment	525.00		1,283.38
16-Mar	535	Randall Machines	Copier lease payment	250.00		1,033.38
17-Mar	536	Hometown Energy	Electric bill payment	326.42		706.96
23-Mar	537	Steward-Holmes Energy	Natural gas bill payment	92.51		614.45
24-Mar	538	Parkland City Services	Water/sewer payment	45.70		568.75
27-Mar	539	New Century Telephones	Telephone bill payment	83.25		485.50
			Total	$ 6,586.74	$ 6,600.00	

March Tab

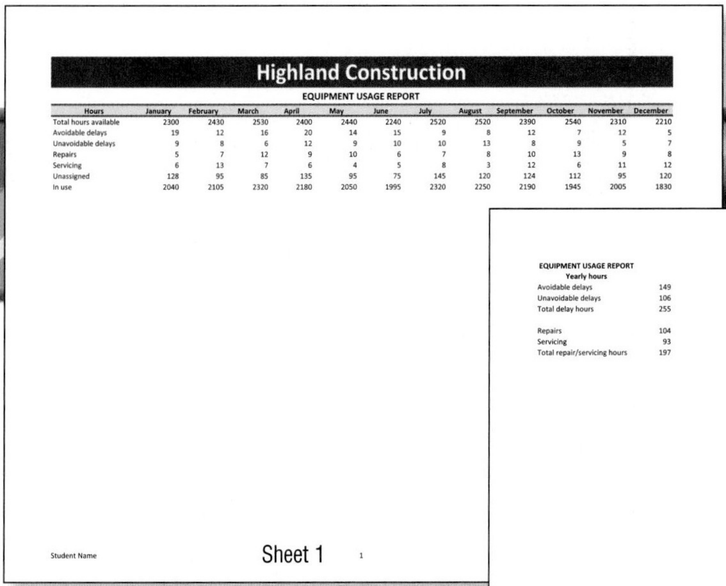

Highland Construction

EQUIPMENT USAGE REPORT

Hours	January	February	March	April	May	June	July	August	September	October	November	December
Total hours available	2300	2430	2530	2400	2440	2240	2520	2520	2390	2540	2310	2210
Avoidable delays	19	12	16	20	14	15	9	8	12	7	12	5
Unavoidable delays	9	8	6	12	9	10	10	13	8	9	5	7
Repairs	5	7	12	9	10	6	7	8	10	13	9	8
Servicing	6	13	7	6	4	5	8	3	12	6	11	12
Unassigned	128	95	85	135	95	75	145	120	124	112	95	120
In use	2040	2105	2320	2180	2050	1995	2320	2250	2190	1945	2005	1830

Student Name 1

Sheet 1

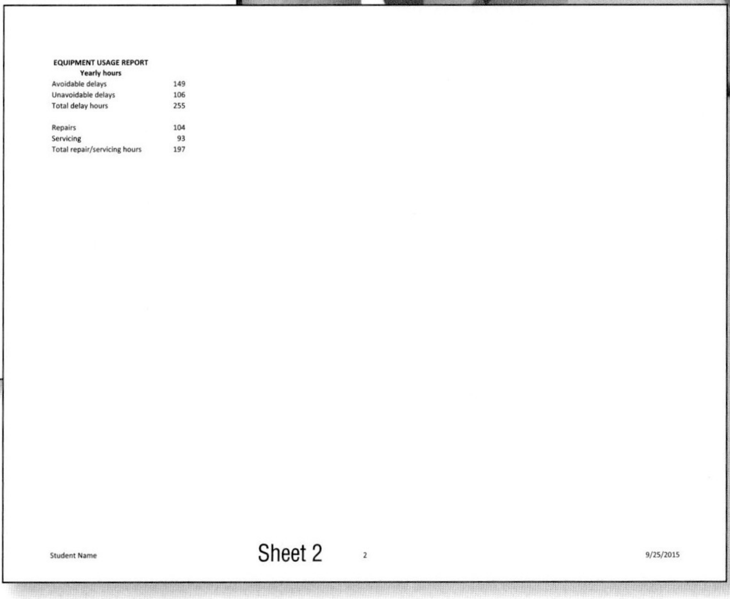

EQUIPMENT USAGE REPORT

Yearly hours

Avoidable delays	149
Unavoidable delays	106
Total delay hours	255
Repairs	104
Servicing	93
Total repair/servicing hours	197

Student Name 2 9/25/2015

Sheet 2

Project 2 Write Formulas Using Ranges in an Equipment Usage Workbook

EL1-C5-P2-HCEqpRpt.xlsx

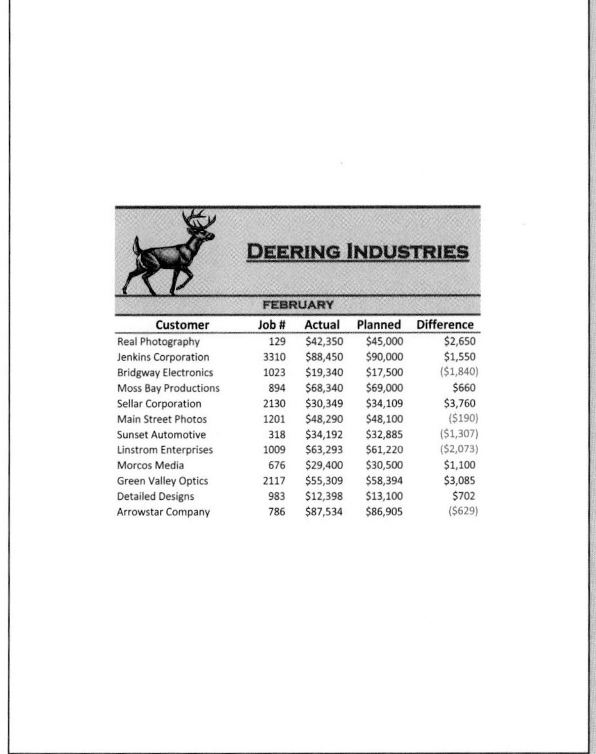
DEERING INDUSTRIES

FEBRUARY

Customer	Job #	Actual	Planned	Difference
Real Photography	129	$42,350	$45,000	$2,650
Jenkins Corporation	3310	$88,450	$90,000	$1,550
Bridgway Electronics	1023	$19,340	$17,500	($1,840)
Moss Bay Productions	894	$68,340	$69,000	$660
Sellar Corporation	2130	$30,349	$34,109	$3,760
Main Street Photos	1201	$48,290	$48,100	($190)
Sunset Automotive	318	$34,192	$32,885	($1,307)
Linstrom Enterprises	1009	$63,293	$61,220	($2,073)
Morcos Media	676	$29,400	$30,500	$1,100
Green Valley Optics	2117	$55,309	$58,394	$3,085
Detailed Designs	983	$12,398	$13,100	$702
Arrowstar Company	786	$87,534	$86,905	($629)

Project 3 Arrange, Size, and Copy Data between Workbooks

EL1-C5-P3-DIFebJobs.xlsx

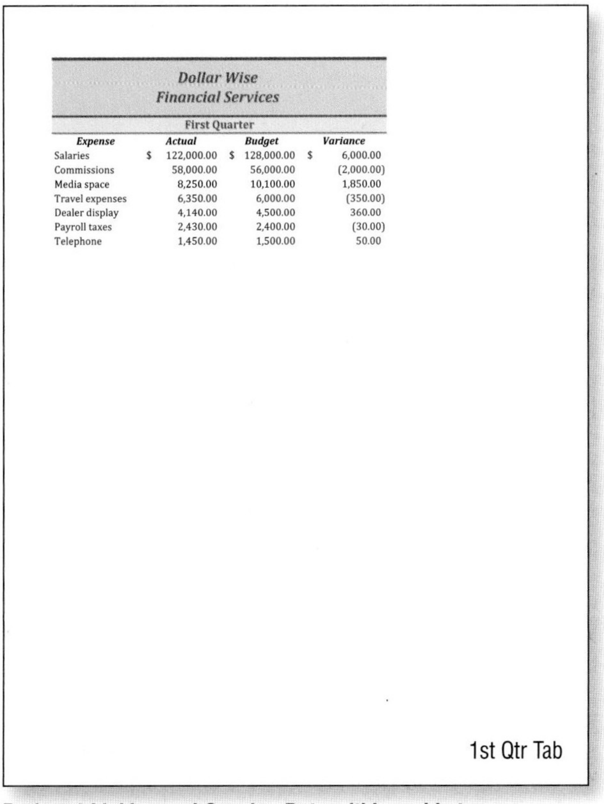

Dollar Wise
Financial Services

First Quarter

Expense	*Actual*	*Budget*	*Variance*
Salaries	$ 122,000.00	$ 128,000.00	$ 6,000.00
Commissions	58,000.00	56,000.00	(2,000.00)
Media space	8,250.00	10,100.00	1,850.00
Travel expenses	6,350.00	6,000.00	(350.00)
Dealer display	4,140.00	4,500.00	360.00
Payroll taxes	2,430.00	2,400.00	(30.00)
Telephone	1,450.00	1,500.00	50.00

1st Qtr Tab

Project 4 Linking and Copying Data within and between Worksheets and Word

EL1-C5-P4-DWQtrlyExp.xlsx

Dollar Wise
Financial Services

Second Quarter			
Expense	*Actual*	*Budget*	*Variance*
Salaries	$ 98,200.00	$ 128,000.00	$ 29,800.00
Commissions	42,300.00	56,000.00	13,700.00
Media space	9,150.00	10,100.00	950.00
Travel expenses	6,350.00	6,000.00	(350.00)
Dealer display	3,140.00	4,500.00	1,360.00
Payroll taxes	1,675.00	2,400.00	725.00
Telephone	1,255.00	1,500.00	245.00

2nd Qtr Tab

Dollar Wise
Financial Services

Third Quarter			
Expense	*Actual*	*Budget*	*Variance*
Salaries	$ 129,000.00	$ 128,000.00	$ (1,000.00)
Commissions	48,000.00	56,000.00	8,000.00
Media space	9,000.00	10,100.00	1,100.00
Travel expenses	5,250.00	6,000.00	750.00
Dealer display	5,140.00	4,500.00	(640.00)
Payroll taxes	2,150.00	2,400.00	250.00
Telephone	1,250.00	1,500.00	250.00

3rd Qtr Tab

Dollar Wise
Financial Services

Fourth Quarter			
Expense	*Actual*	*Budget*	*Variance*
Salaries	$ 125,200.00	$ 128,000.00	$ 2,800.00
Commissions	49,300.00	56,000.00	6,700.00
Media space	9,150.00	10,100.00	950.00
Travel expenses	5,850.00	6,000.00	150.00
Dealer display	3,240.00	4,500.00	1,260.00
Payroll taxes	1,975.00	2,400.00	425.00
Telephone	1,355.00	1,500.00	145.00

4th Qtr Tab

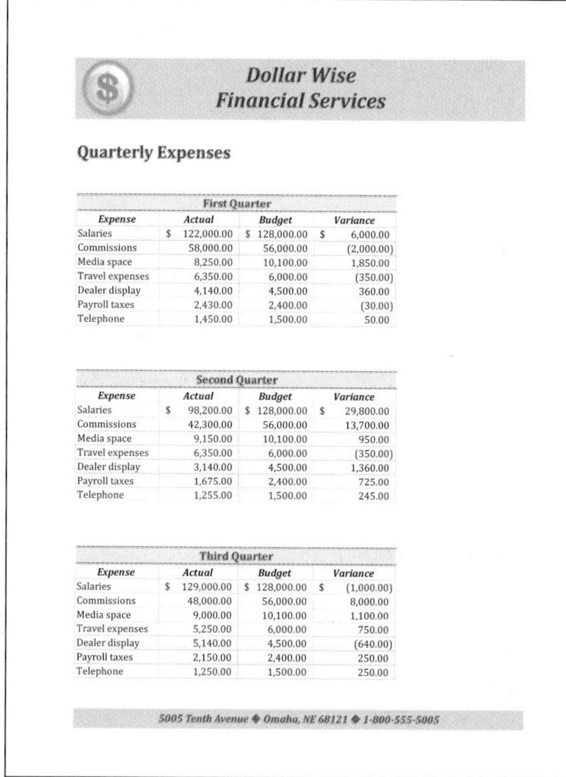

Dollar Wise
Financial Services

Quarterly Expenses

First Quarter			
Expense	*Actual*	*Budget*	*Variance*
Salaries	$ 122,000.00	$ 128,000.00	$ 6,000.00
Commissions	58,000.00	56,000.00	(2,000.00)
Media space	8,250.00	10,100.00	1,850.00
Travel expenses	6,350.00	6,000.00	(350.00)
Dealer display	4,140.00	4,500.00	360.00
Payroll taxes	2,430.00	2,400.00	(30.00)
Telephone	1,450.00	1,500.00	50.00

Second Quarter			
Expense	*Actual*	*Budget*	*Variance*
Salaries	$ 98,200.00	$ 128,000.00	$ 29,800.00
Commissions	42,300.00	56,000.00	13,700.00
Media space	9,150.00	10,100.00	950.00
Travel expenses	6,350.00	6,000.00	(350.00)
Dealer display	3,140.00	4,500.00	1,360.00
Payroll taxes	1,675.00	2,400.00	725.00
Telephone	1,255.00	1,500.00	245.00

Third Quarter			
Expense	*Actual*	*Budget*	*Variance*
Salaries	$ 129,000.00	$ 128,000.00	$ (1,000.00)
Commissions	48,000.00	56,000.00	8,000.00
Media space	9,000.00	10,100.00	1,100.00
Travel expenses	5,250.00	6,000.00	750.00
Dealer display	5,140.00	4,500.00	(640.00)
Payroll taxes	2,150.00	2,400.00	250.00
Telephone	1,250.00	1,500.00	250.00

5005 Tenth Avenue ◆ Omaha, NE 68121 ◆ 1-800-555-5005

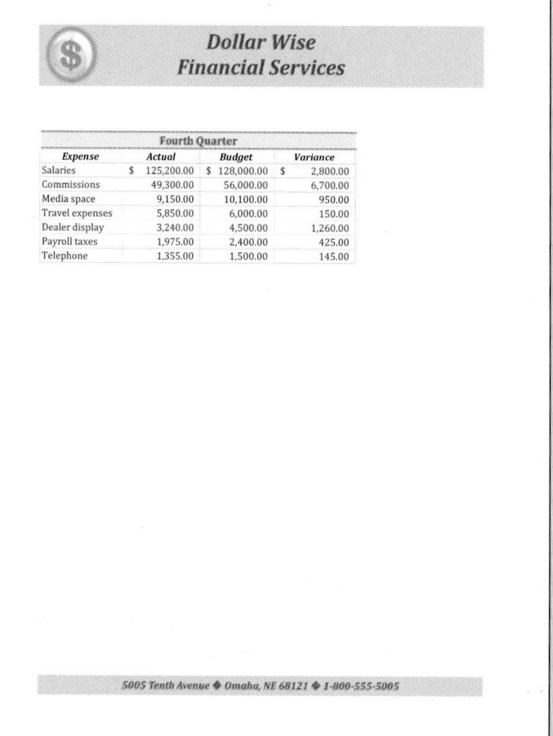

Dollar Wise
Financial Services

Fourth Quarter			
Expense	*Actual*	*Budget*	*Variance*
Salaries	$ 125,200.00	$ 128,000.00	$ 2,800.00
Commissions	49,300.00	56,000.00	6,700.00
Media space	9,150.00	10,100.00	950.00
Travel expenses	5,850.00	6,000.00	150.00
Dealer display	3,240.00	4,500.00	1,260.00
Payroll taxes	1,975.00	2,400.00	425.00
Telephone	1,355.00	1,500.00	145.00

5005 Tenth Avenue ◆ Omaha, NE 68121 ◆ 1-800-555-5005

EL1-C5-P4-DWQtrlyRpt.docx

Project 1 Manage Data in a Multiple-Worksheet Account Workbook

7 Parts

You will open an account workbook containing multiple worksheets and then insert and delete worksheets and move, copy, and paste data between the worksheets. You will also hide and unhide worksheets and format and print multiple worksheets in the workbook.

Creating a Workbook with Multiple Worksheets

An Excel workbook, by default, contains one worksheet, but you can add additional worksheets to it. Add additional worksheets to a workbook to store related data. For example, you might want to create a workbook with a worksheet for the expenses for each salesperson in the company and another worksheet for the monthly payroll for each department within the company. Another example is recording sales statistics for each quarter in individual worksheets within a workbook.

Creating multiple worksheets within a workbook is helpful for saving related data.

Inserting a New Worksheet

Insert a new worksheet in a workbook by clicking the New sheet button that displays to the right of the Sheet1 tab at the bottom of the worksheet area. You can also insert a new worksheet with the keyboard shortcut Shift + F11. A new worksheet tab is inserted to the right of the active tab. To move between worksheets, click the desired tab. The active worksheet tab displays with a white background and the worksheet name displays in green. Any inactive tabs display with a light gray background and gray text.

Quick Steps

Insert a Worksheet
Click New sheet button.
OR
Press Shift + F11.

New sheet

Deleting a Worksheet

If you no longer need a worksheet in a workbook, delete the worksheet by clicking the desired worksheet tab, clicking the Delete button arrow in the Cells group on the HOME tab, and then clicking *Delete Sheet* at the drop-down list. You can also delete a worksheet by right-clicking the worksheet tab and then clicking *Delete* at the shortcut menu. When you click the Delete button or option, Excel displays a message telling you that you cannot undo deleting sheets. At this message, click the Delete button.

Quick Steps

Delete a Worksheet
1. Click worksheet tab.
2. Click Delete button arrow.
3. Click *Delete Sheet*.
4. Click Delete button.

Selecting Multiple Worksheets

To work with more than one worksheet at a time, select the desired worksheets. You might want to select multiple worksheets to apply the same formatting to cells or to delete multiple worksheets. To select adjacent worksheet tabs, click the first tab, hold down the Shift key, and then click the last tab. To select nonadjacent worksheet tabs, click the first tab, hold down the Ctrl key, and then click any other tabs you want selected.

Copy

Cut

Paste

Copying, Cutting, and Pasting Cells

At times, you may need to copy cells or move cells to a different location within a worksheet or to another worksheet or workbook. You can move or copy cells in a worksheet or between worksheets or workbooks. Perform these actions by selecting cells and then using the Cut, Copy, and/or Paste buttons in the Clipboard group on the HOME tab.

Quick Steps

Copy and Paste Cells
1. Select cells.
2. Click Copy button.
3. Click desired cell.
4. Click Paste button.

Ctrl + C is the keyboard shortcut to copy selected data.

Copying and Pasting Selected Cells

Copying selected cells can be useful in worksheets that contain repetitive data. To copy cells, select the cells and then click the Copy button in the Clipboard group on the HOME tab. This causes a moving dashed line border (called a ***marquee***) to display around the selected cells. If you are copying cells to another worksheet, click the worksheet tab. Click the cell where you want the first selected cell copied and then click the Paste button in the Clipboard group. Remove the moving marquee from selected cells by pressing the Esc key or double-clicking in any cell.

You can also copy selected cells in the same worksheet using the mouse and the Ctrl key. To do this, select the cells you want to copy and then position the mouse pointer on any border around the selected cells until the pointer turns into an arrow pointer. Hold down the Ctrl key and the left mouse button, drag the outline of the selected cells to the desired location, release the left mouse button, and then release the Ctrl key.

Project 1a **Inserting, Deleting, Selecting, Copying, Pasting, and Formatting Worksheets** **Part 1 of 7**

1. Open **RPFacAccts.xlsx** and then save the workbook with Save As and name it **EL1-C5-P1-RPFacAccts**.
2. Insert a new worksheet in the workbook by completing the following steps:
   a. Click the 2ndHalfSales worksheet tab to make it active.
   b. Click the New sheet button that displays to the right of the 2ndHalfSales worksheet tab. (This inserts a new worksheet to the right of the 2ndHalfSales worksheet with the name Sheet4.)

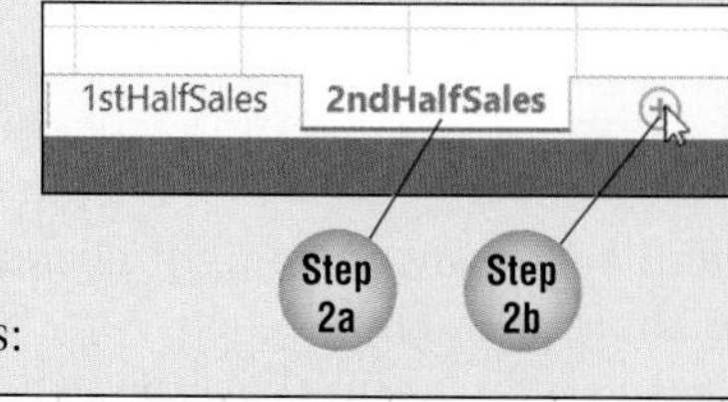

3. Delete two worksheet tabs by completing the following steps:
   a. Click the 1stHalfSales worksheet tab.
   b. Hold down the Shift key and then click the 2ndHalfSales worksheet tab. (These tabs must be adjacent. If they are not, hold down the Ctrl key when clicking the 2ndHalfSales worksheet tab.)
   c. With the two worksheet tabs selected, click the Delete button arrow in the Cells group on the HOME tab and then click *Delete Sheet* at the drop-down list.
   d. At the message that displays telling you that you cannot undo deleting sheets, click the Delete button.

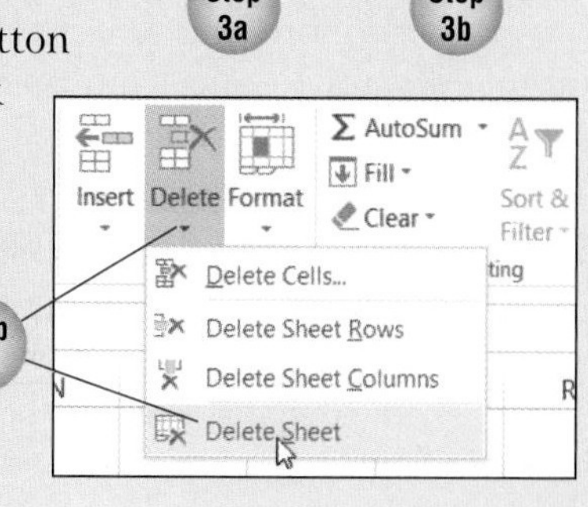

4. Copy cells from Sheet1 to Sheet4 by completing the following steps:
   a. Click the Sheet1 tab to make it the active worksheet.
   b. Select cells A1 through A3 (the first three rows of data).
   c. Click the Copy button in the Clipboard group on the HOME tab.
   d. Click the Sheet4 tab to make it the active tab.
   e. With A1 the active cell, click the Paste button in the Clipboard group on the HOME tab.

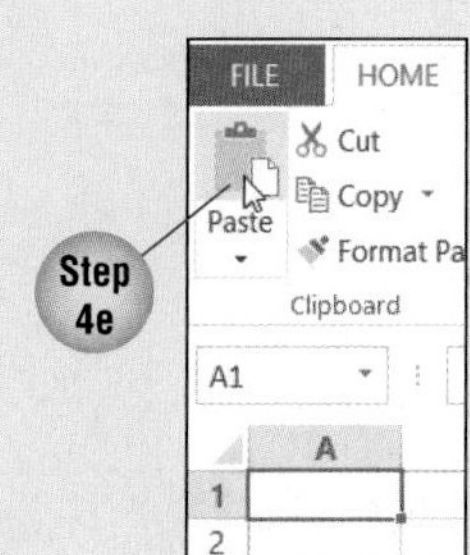

5. Make the following changes to the new worksheet:
   a. Make cell A3 active and then type **First Quarter Summary 2015**.
   b. Change the width of column A to 20.00 characters.
   c. Change the widths of columns B, C, and D to 12.00 characters.
   d. Type the following text in the specified cells:
      B4: **January**
      C4: **February**
      D4: **March**
      A5: **Checks amount**
      A6: **Deposit amount**
      A7: **End-of-month balance**
   e. Select cells B4 through D4, click the Bold button in the Font group on the HOME tab, and then click the Center button in the Alignment group.
   f. Select cells B5 through D7 and then apply accounting formatting without dollar signs and with two places after the decimal point.
6. Apply formatting to cells in all four worksheets by completing the following steps:
   a. Click Sheet1 to make it active and then click in cell A1 to make it the active cell.
   b. Hold down the Shift key and then click Sheet4. (This selects all four worksheets.)
   c. With cell A1 active, change the row height to 51.00 points.
   d. Make cell A3 active.
   e. Change the font size to 14 points.
   f. Click each remaining worksheet tab (Sheet2, Sheet3, and Sheet4) and notice the formatting changes applied to all of the cells.
7. Change column widths for the three worksheets by completing the following steps:
   a. Click Sheet1 to make it active.
   b. Hold down the Shift key and then click Sheet3.
   c. Select columns E, F, and G and then change the column width to 10.00 characters.
   d. Click Sheet2 and then click Sheet 3. Notice that the widths of columns E, F, and G have changed to 10.00 characters. Click Sheet4 and notice that the column widths did not change.
8. Save **EL1-C5-P1-RPFacAccts.xlsx**.

Using Paste Options

When you paste cells in a worksheet, you can specify how you want the cells pasted by clicking the Paste button arrow and then clicking the desired paste option button at the drop-down list. You can also click the Paste button (not the button arrow) and a Paste Options button displays in the lower right corner of the pasted cell(s). Display a list of paste options by clicking the button or pressing

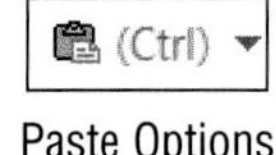

Paste Options

Figure 5.1 Paste Option Buttons

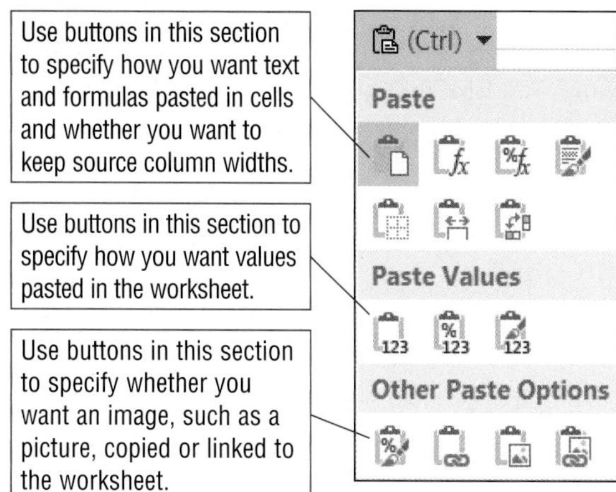
Use buttons in this section to specify how you want text and formulas pasted in cells and whether you want to keep source column widths.
Use buttons in this section to specify how you want values pasted in the worksheet.
Use buttons in this section to specify whether you want an image, such as a picture, copied or linked to the worksheet.
(Ctrl)
Paste
Paste Values
Other Paste Options

the Ctrl key. This causes a drop-down list to display, as shown in Figure 5.1. The same option buttons display when you click the Paste button arrow. Hover your mouse over a button in the drop-down list and the descriptive name of the button displays along with the keyboard shortcut. Use buttons in this drop-down list to specify what you want pasted.

Moving Selected Cells

Quick Steps

Move and Paste Cells
1. Select cells.
2. Click Cut button.
3. Click desired cell.
4. Click Paste button.

Ctrl + X is the keyboard shortcut to cut selected data. Ctrl + V is the keyboard shortcut to paste data.

You can move selected cells and cell contents within and between worksheets. Move selected cells with the Cut and Paste buttons in the Clipboard group on the HOME tab or by dragging with the mouse.

To move selected cells with buttons on the HOME tab, select the cells and then click the Cut button in the Clipboard group. Click the cell where you want the first selected cell inserted and then click the Paste button in the Clipboard group.

To move selected cells with the mouse, select the cells and then position the mouse pointer on any border of the selected cells until the pointer turns into an arrow pointer with a four-headed arrow attached. Hold down the left mouse button, drag the outline of the selected cells to the desired location, and then release the mouse button.

Project 1b **Copying and Moving Cells and Pasting Cells Using Paste Options** **Part 2 of 7**

1. With **EL1-C5-P1-RPFacAccts.xlsx** open, copy cells from Sheet2 to Sheet3 using the Paste Options button by completing the following steps:
   a. Click the Sheet2 tab to make it active.
   b. Select cells C7 through E9.
   c. Click the Copy button in the Clipboard group.
   d. Click the Sheet3 tab.
   e. Make cell C7 active.
   f. Click the Paste button in the Clipboard group.

g. Click the Paste Options button that displays in the lower right corner of the pasted cells and then click the Keep Source Column Widths button at the drop-down list.
h. Make Sheet2 active and then press the Esc key to remove the moving marquee.

2. Make Sheet1 active.
3. You realize that the sublet rent deposit was recorded on the wrong day. The correct day is January 9. To move the cells containing information on the deposit, complete the following steps:
    a. Make cell A13 active and then insert a row. (The new row should display above the row containing information on *Rainier Suppliers*.)
    b. Select cells A7 through F7.
    c. Click the Cut button in the Clipboard group on the HOME tab.
    d. Click in cell A13 to make it active.
    e. Click the Paste button in the Clipboard group.
    f. Change the date of the deposit from January 1 to January 9.
    g. Select row 7 and then delete it.

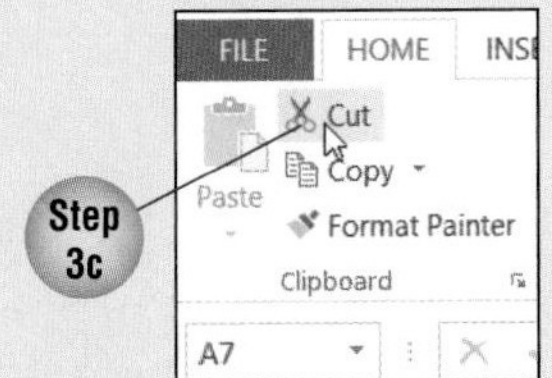

4. Move cells using the mouse by completing the following steps:
    a. Click the Sheet2 tab.
    b. Make cell A13 active and then insert a new row.
    c. Using the mouse, select cells A7 through F7.
    d. Position the mouse pointer on any boundary of the selected cells until it turns into an arrow pointer with a four-headed arrow attached. Hold down the left mouse button, drag the outline of the selected cells to row 13, and then release the mouse button.

12	12-Feb	518	Clear Source	Developer supplies	123.74
13					
14	16-Feb	519	Rainier Su A13:F13	Camera supplies	119.62
15	17-Feb	520	A1 Wedding Supplies	Photo albums	323.58

Step 4d

    e. Change the date of the deposit to February 13.
    f. Delete row 7.
5. Save **EL1-C5-P1-RPFacAccts.xlsx**.

Copying and Pasting with the Clipboard Task Pane

Use the Clipboard task pane to copy and paste multiple items. To use the task pane, click the Clipboard task pane launcher. This button is located in the lower right corner of the Clipboard group on the HOME tab. The Clipboard task pane displays at the left side of the screen in a manner similar to what you see in Figure 5.2.

Select data or an object you want to copy and then click the Copy button in the Clipboard group. Continue selecting cells, text, or other items and clicking the Copy button. To paste an item into a worksheet, make the desired cell active and then click the item in the Clipboard task pane. If the copied item is text, the first 50 characters display in the task pane. If you want to paste all of the selected items into a single location, make the desired cell active and then click the Paste All button in the task pane. When all desired items have been pasted into the worksheet, click the Clear All button to remove any remaining items from the task pane.

Quick Steps

Copy and Paste Multiple Items

1. Click Clipboard task pane launcher.
2. Select desired cells.
3. Click Copy button.
4. Repeat Steps 2 and 3 as desired.
5. Make desired cell active.
6. Click item in Clipboard task pane to be inserted in worksheet.
7. Repeat Step 6 as desired.

Figure 5.2 Clipboard Task Pane

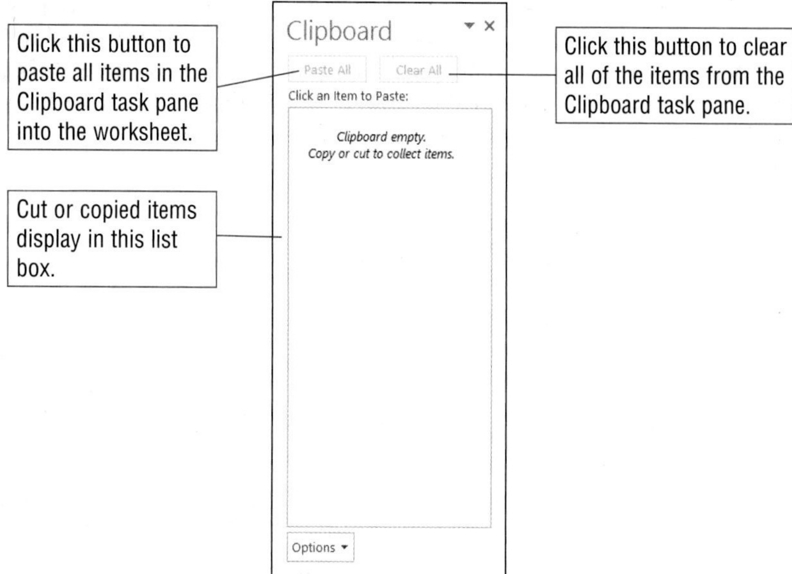

Project 1c Copying and Pasting Cells Using the Clipboard Task Pane

Part 3 of 7

1. With **EL1-C5-P1-RPFacAccts.xlsx** open, select cells for copying by completing the following steps:
   a. Display the Clipboard task pane by clicking the Clipboard task pane launcher. (If the Clipboard task pane contains any copied data, click the Clear All button.)
   b. Click the Sheet1 tab.
   c. Select cells C15 through E16.
   d. Click the Copy button in the Clipboard group.
   e. Select cells C19 through E19.
   f. Click the Copy button in the Clipboard group.

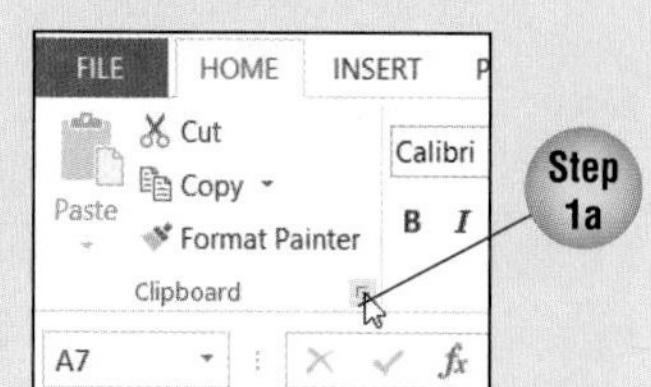

2. Paste the copied cells by completing the following steps:
   a. Click the Sheet2 tab.
   b. Make cell C15 active.
   c. Click the item in the Clipboard task pane representing *General Systems Developer*.
   d. Click the Sheet3 tab.
   e. Make cell C15 active.
   f. Click the item in the Clipboard task pane representing *General Systems Developer*.
   g. Make cell C19 active.
   h. Click the item in the Clipboard task pane representing *Parkland City Services*.

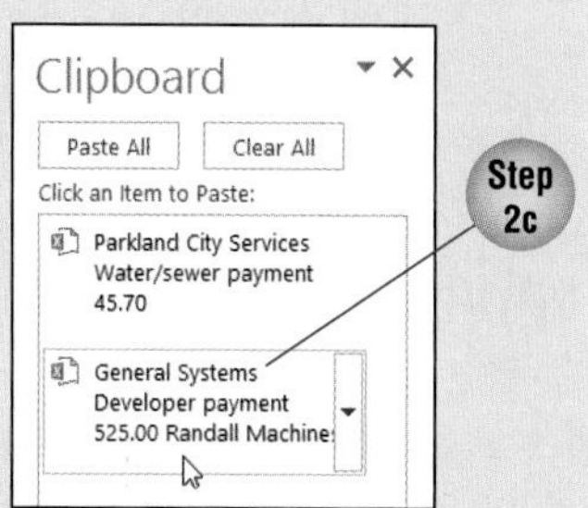

3. Click the Clear All button located toward the top of the Clipboard task pane.
4. Close the Clipboard task pane by clicking the Close button (contains an X) located in the upper right corner of the task pane.
5. Save **EL1-C5-P1-RPFacAccts.xlsx**.

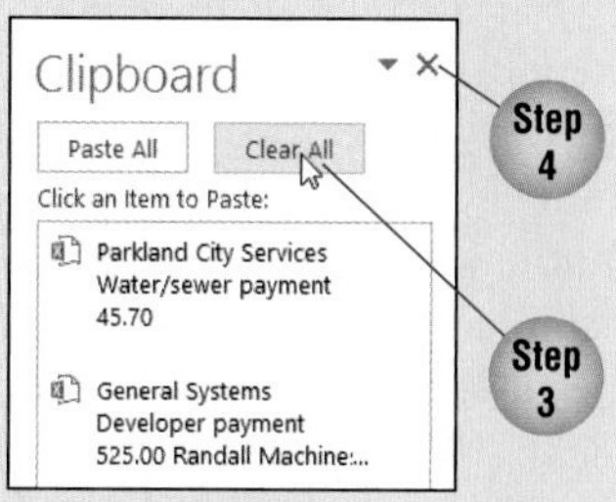

Pasting Values Only

When you paste cells containing a value as well as a formula, use button options from the Paste button or Paste Options button drop-down list to specify what you want pasted. With the buttons in the *Paste Values* section of the drop-down list, you can choose to insert the value only, the value with numbering formatting, or the value with the source formatting.

Project 1d Copying and Pasting Values — Part 4 of 7

1. With **EL1-C5-P1-RPFacAccts.xlsx** open, make Sheet1 the active tab.
2. Make cell G6 active, type the formula **=(F6-E6)+G5**, and then press Enter.
3. Copy the formula in cell G6 down to cells G7 through G20.
4. Copy as a value (and not a formula) the final balance amount from Sheet1 to Sheet2 by completing the following steps:
   a. Make cell G20 active.
   b. Click the Copy button in the Clipboard group.
   c. Click the Sheet2 tab.
   d. Make cell G5 active and then click the Paste button arrow.
   e. At the drop-down list that displays, click the Values button in the *Paste Values* section of the drop-down list. (This inserts the value and not the formula.)

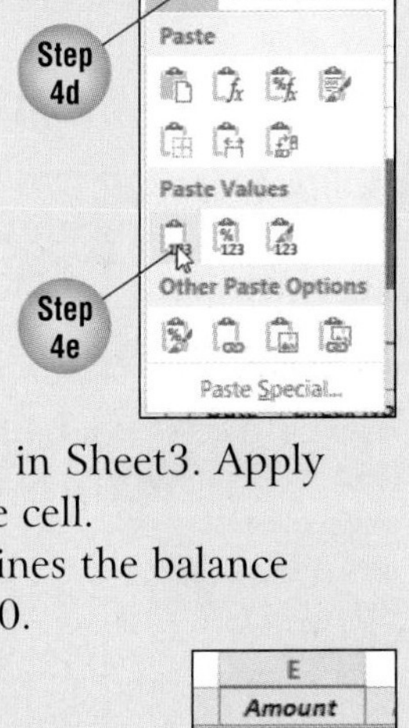

5. Make cell G6 active, insert a formula that determines the balance (see Step 2), and then copy the formula down to cells G7 through G20.
6. Copy the amount in cell G20 and then paste the value only in cell G5 in Sheet3. Apply accounting formatting with a dollar sign and two decimal places to the cell.
7. With Sheet3 active, make cell G6 active, insert a formula that determines the balance (see Step 2), and then copy the formula down to cells G7 through G20.
8. Insert formulas and apply formatting to cells in three worksheets by completing the following steps:
   a. Click Sheet1 to make it active.
   b. Hold down the Shift key and then click Sheet3.
   c. Make cell D21 active, click the Bold button in the Font group on the HOME tab, and then type **Total**.
   d. Make cell E21 active and then click once on the AutoSum button in the Editing group on the HOME tab. (This inserts the formula *=SUM(E13:E20)*.)
   e. Change the formula to *=SUM(E7:E20)* and then press Enter.
   f. Make cell F21 active and then click once on the AutoSum button. (This inserts the formula *=SUM(F12:F20)*.)
   g. Change the formula to *=SUM(F6:F20)* and then press Enter.
   h. Select cells E21 and F21 and then click the Accounting Number Format button. Make cell G5 active and then click the Accounting Number Format button. (Cell G5 in Sheet1 already contains accounting formatting but cells G5 in Sheet2 and Sheet3 do not.)
   i. Click the Sheet2 tab and notice the text and formulas inserted in the worksheet, click Sheet3 and notice the text and formulas, and then click Sheet4 (to deselect the tabs).
9. Copy values from Sheet1 to Sheet4 by completing the following steps:
   a. Make Sheet1 active.
   b. Make cell E21 active and then click the Copy button in the Clipboard group.
   c. Make Sheet4 active.
   d. Make cell B5 active and then click the Paste button in the Clipboard group.

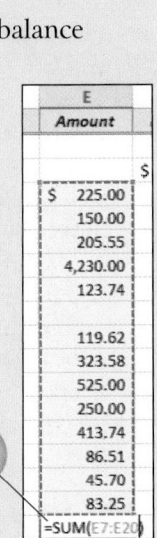

e. Click the Paste Options button and then click the Values button in the *Paste Values* section of the drop-down list.
f. Make Sheet1 active.
g. Make cell F21 active and then click the Copy button.
h. Make Sheet4 active.
i. Make cell B6 active, click the Paste button arrow, and then click the Values button at the drop-down list.
j. Make Sheet1 active.
k. Make cell G20 active and then click the Copy button.
l. Make Sheet4 active.
m. Make cell B7 active, click the Paste button arrow, and then click the Values button at the drop-down list.

10. Complete steps similar to those in Step 9 to insert amounts and balances for February and March.
11. Select cells B5 through D5 and then click the Accounting Number Format button.
12. Save **EL1-C5-P1-RPFacAccts.xlsx**.

Managing Worksheets

Quick Steps

Move or Copy a Worksheet
1. Right-click sheet tab.
2. Click *Move or Copy*.
3. At Move or Copy dialog box, click desired worksheet name in *Before sheet* list box.
4. Click OK.

OR

Drag worksheet tab to desired position. (To copy, hold down Ctrl key while dragging.)

Use the tab scroll button to bring into view any worksheet tabs not currently visible.

Quick Steps

Apply Color to a Sheet Tab
1. Right-click sheet tab.
2. Point to *Tab Color*.
3. Click desired color at color palette.

Right-click a sheet tab and a shortcut menu displays, as shown in Figure 5.3, with the options for managing worksheets. For example, remove a worksheet by clicking the *Delete* option. Move or copy a worksheet by clicking the *Move or Copy* option. Clicking this option causes a Move or Copy dialog box to display, in which you specify where you want to move or copy the selected sheet. By default, Excel names worksheets in a workbook *Sheet1, Sheet2, Sheet3,* and so on. To rename a worksheet, click the *Rename* option (which selects the default sheet name) and then type the desired name.

In addition to the shortcut menu options, you can use the mouse to move or copy worksheets. To move a worksheet, position the mouse pointer on the worksheet tab, hold down the left mouse button (a page icon displays next to the mouse pointer), drag the page icon to the desired position, and then release the mouse button. For example, to move the Sheet2 tab after the Sheet3 tab, position the mouse pointer on the Sheet2 tab, hold down the left mouse button, drag the page icon so it is positioned after the Sheet3 tab, and then release the mouse button. To copy a worksheet, hold down the Ctrl key while dragging the sheet tab.

Use the *Tab Color* option at the shortcut menu to apply a color to a worksheet tab. Right-click a worksheet tab, point to *Tab Color* at the shortcut menu, and then click the desired color at the color palette.

Figure 5.3 Sheet Tab Shortcut Menu

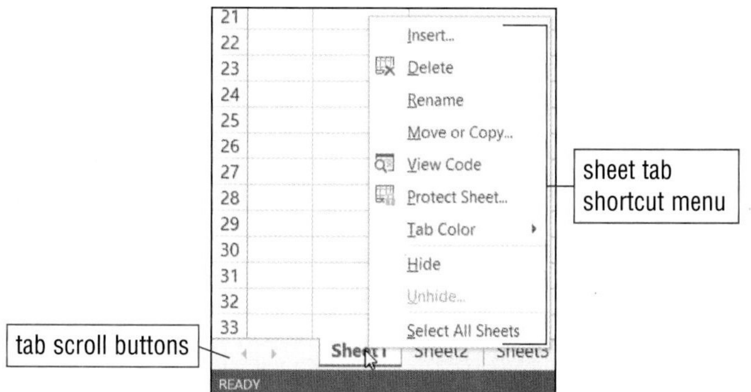

Project 1e Selecting, Moving, Renaming, and Changing the Color of Worksheet Tabs Part 5 of 7

1. With **EL1-C5-P1-RPFacAccts.xlsx** open, move Sheet4 by completing the following steps:
   a. Right-click Sheet4 and then click *Move or Copy* at the shortcut menu.
   b. At the Move or Copy dialog box, make sure *Sheet1* is selected in the *Before sheet* list box, and then click OK.

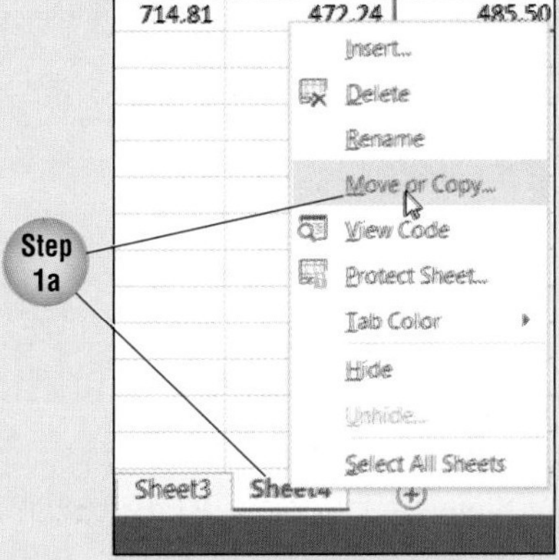

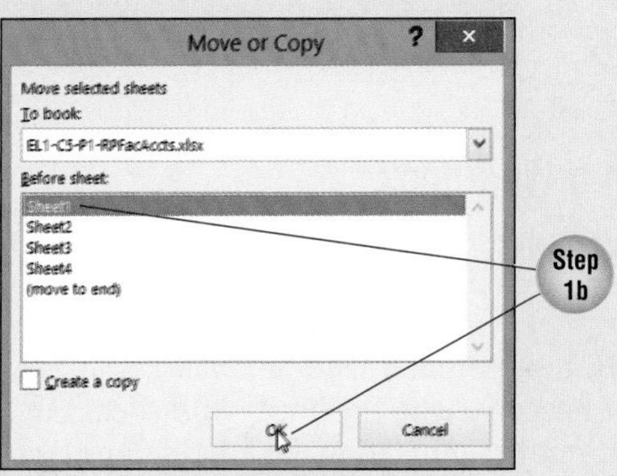

2. Rename Sheet4 by completing the following steps:
   a. Right-click the Sheet4 tab and then click *Rename*.
   b. Type Summary and then press Enter.
3. Complete steps similar to those in Step 2 to rename Sheet1 to *January*, Sheet2 to *February*, and Sheet3 to *March*.

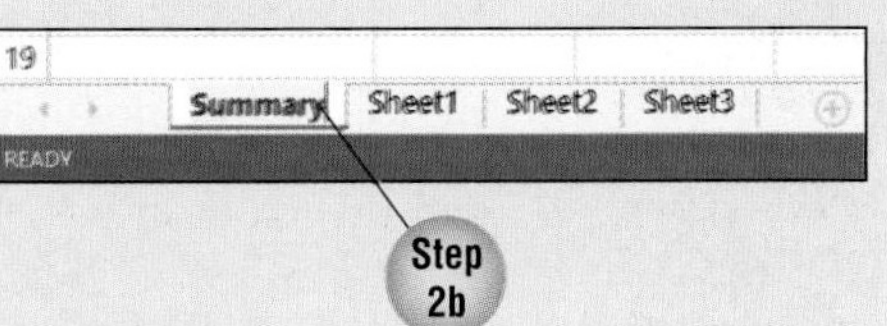

4. Change the color of the Summary sheet tab by completing the following steps:
   a. Right-click the Summary sheet tab.
   b. Point to *Tab Color* at the shortcut menu.
   c. Click the *Red* color option in the *Standard Colors* section (second color option).

5. Follow steps similar to those in Step 4 to change the January sheet tab to Blue (eighth color option in the *Standard Colors* section), the February sheet tab to Purple (last color option in the *Standard Colors* section), and the March sheet tab to Green (sixth color option in the *Standard Colors* section).
6. Save **EL1-C5-P1-RPFacAccts.xlsx**.

Quick Steps

Hide a Worksheet
1. Click Format button.
2. Point to *Hide & Unhide*.
3. Click *Hide Sheet*.

OR
1. Right-click worksheet tab.
2. Click *Hide* at shortcut menu.

Unhide a Worksheet
1. Click Format button.
2. Point to *Hide & Unhide*.
3. Click *Unhide Sheet*.
4. Double-click desired hidden worksheet in Unhide dialog box.

OR
1. Right-click worksheet tab.
2. Click *Unhide* at shortcut menu.
3. Double-click desired hidden worksheet in Unhide dialog box.

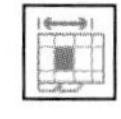

Format

Figure 5.4 Unhide Dialog Box

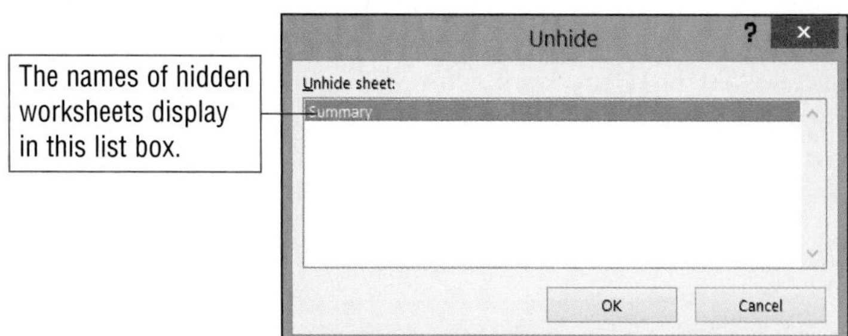

Hiding a Worksheet in a Workbook

In a workbook containing multiple worksheets, you can hide a worksheet that may contain sensitive data or data you do not want to display or print with the workbook. To hide a worksheet in a workbook, click the Format button in the Cells group on the HOME tab, point to *Hide & Unhide*, and then click *Hide Sheet*. You can also hide a worksheet by right-clicking a worksheet tab and then clicking the *Hide* option at the shortcut menu. To make a hidden worksheet visible, click the Format button in the Cells group, point to *Hide & Unhide*, and then click *Unhide Sheet*, or right-click a worksheet tab and then click *Unhide* at the shortcut menu. At the Unhide dialog box, as shown in Figure 5.4, double-click the name of the hidden worksheet you want to display.

Project 1f **Hiding a Worksheet and Formatting Multiple Worksheets** **Part 6 of 7**

1. With **EL1-C5-P1-RPFacAccts.xlsx** open, hide the Summary worksheet by completing the following steps:
   a. Click the Summary tab.
   b. Click the Format button in the Cells group on the HOME tab, point to *Hide & Unhide*, and then click *Hide Sheet*.

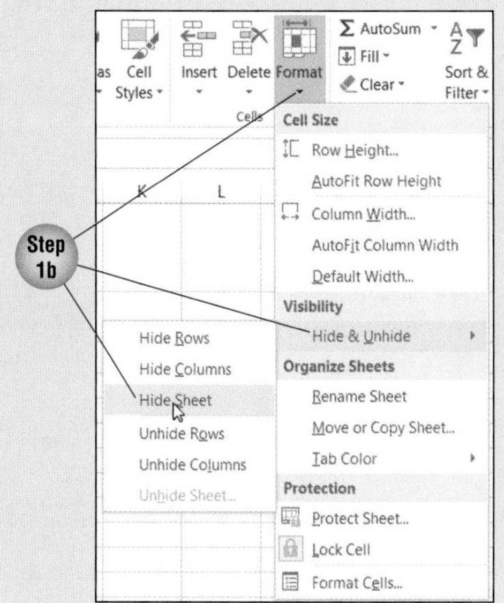

2. Unhide the worksheet by completing the following steps:
   a. Click the Format button in the Cells group, point to *Hide & Unhide*, and then click *Unhide Sheet*.
   b. At the Unhide dialog box, make sure *Summary* is selected and then click OK.

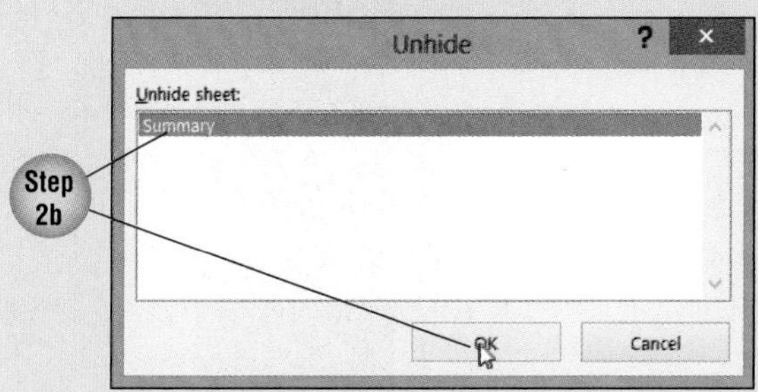

3. Insert a header for each worksheet by completing the following steps:
   a. With the Summary tab active, hold down the Shift key and then click the March tab. (This selects all four tabs.)
   b. Click the INSERT tab.
   c. Click the Header & Footer button in the Text group.
   d. Click the Header button in the Header & Footer group on the HEADER & FOOTER TOOLS DESIGN tab and then click the option at the drop-down list that prints your name at the left side of the page (if a name displays at the left side of the page, select the name and then type your first and last names), the page number in the middle, and the date at the right side.
4. With all the sheet tabs selected, horizontally and vertically center each worksheet on the page. ***Hint: Do this at the Page Setup dialog box with the Margins tab selected.***
5. With all of the sheet tabs still selected, change the page orientation to landscape. ***Hint: Do this with the Orientation button on the PAGE LAYOUT tab.***
6. Save **EL1-C5-P1-RPFacAccts.xlsx**.

Printing a Workbook Containing Multiple Worksheets

By default, Excel prints the currently displayed worksheet. If you want to print all of the worksheets in a workbook, display the Print backstage area, click the first gallery in the *Settings* category, click *Print Entire Workbook* at the drop-down list, and then click the Print button. You can also print specific worksheets in a workbook by selecting the tabs of the worksheets you want printed. With the desired worksheet tabs selected, display the Print backstage area and then click the Print button.

Quick Steps

Print All Worksheets in a Workbook

1. Click FILE tab.
2. Click *Print* option.
3. Click first gallery in *Settings* category.
4. Click *Print Entire Workbook*.
5. Click Print button.

Project 1g Printing All Worksheets in a Workbook Part 7 of 7

1. With **EL1-C5-P1-RPFacAccts.xlsx** open, click the FILE tab and then click the *Print* option.
2. At the Print backstage area, click the first gallery in the *Settings* category and then click *Print Entire Workbook* at the drop-down list.
3. Click the Print button.
4. Save and then close **EL1-C5-P1-RPFacAccts.xlsx**.

Project 2 Write Formulas Using Ranges in an Equipment Usage Workbook 2 Parts

You will open an equipment usage workbook, view the document at different zoom percentages, and then split the window and edit cells. You will also name ranges and then use the range names to write formulas in the workbook.

Using Zoom

Zoom

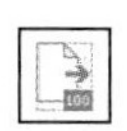

100%

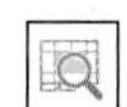

Zoom to Selection

The VIEW tab contains a Zoom group with three buttons to change zoom settings. Click the Zoom button in the Zoom group to open the Zoom dialog box, which contains options for changing the zoom percentage. Click the 100% button in the Zoom group to return the view to 100%, which is the default. Select a range of cells and then click the Zoom to Selection button to cause Excel to scale the zoom setting so that the selected range fills the worksheet area.

Use the zoom slider bar that displays at the right side of the Status bar to change the zoom percentage. Click the Zoom Out button (displays with a minus symbol) to decrease the zoom percentage or click the Zoom In button (displays with a plus symbol) to increase the zoom percentage. Another method for increasing or decreasing zoom percentage is to click and drag the zoom slider bar button on the slider bar.

Splitting a Worksheet into Windows and Freezing and Unfreezing Panes

Split

In some worksheets, not all cells display at one time in the worksheet area (for example, in **EL1-C5-P2-HCEqpRpt.xlsx**). When working in a worksheet with more cells than can display at one time, you may find splitting the worksheet window into panes helpful. Split the worksheet window into panes with the Split button in the Window group on the VIEW tab. When you click the Split button, the worksheet splits into four window panes, as shown in Figure 5.5. The windows are split by thick, light gray lines called ***split lines***. To remove split lines from a worksheet, click the Split button to deactivate it.

Remove a split line by double-clicking anywhere on the split line that divides the panes.

Freeze Panes

A window pane will display the active cell. As the insertion point is moved through the pane, another active cell may display. This additional active cell displays when the insertion point passes over one of the split lines that creates the pane. As you move through a worksheet, you may see both active cells. If you make a change to one active cell, the change is made in the other as well. If you want only one active cell to display, freeze the window panes by clicking the Freeze Panes button in the Window group on the VIEW tab and then clicking *Freeze Panes* at the drop-down list. You can maintain the display of column headings while editing or typing text in cells by clicking the Freeze Panes button and then clicking *Freeze Top Row*. Maintain the display of row headings by clicking the Freeze Panes button and then clicking *Freeze First Column*. Unfreeze window panes by clicking the Freeze Panes button and then clicking *Unfreeze Panes* at the drop-down list.

Using the mouse, you can move the split lines that divide the window. To do this, position the mouse pointer on a split line until the pointer turns into a left-and-right-pointing arrow with a double line in the middle. Hold down the left mouse button, drag the outline of the split line to the desired location, and then release the mouse button. If you want to move both the horizontal and vertical split lines at the same time, position the mouse pointer on the intersection of the split lines until the pointer turns into a four-headed arrow. Hold down the left mouse button, drag the split lines to the desired direction, and then release the mouse button.

Figure 5.5 Split Window

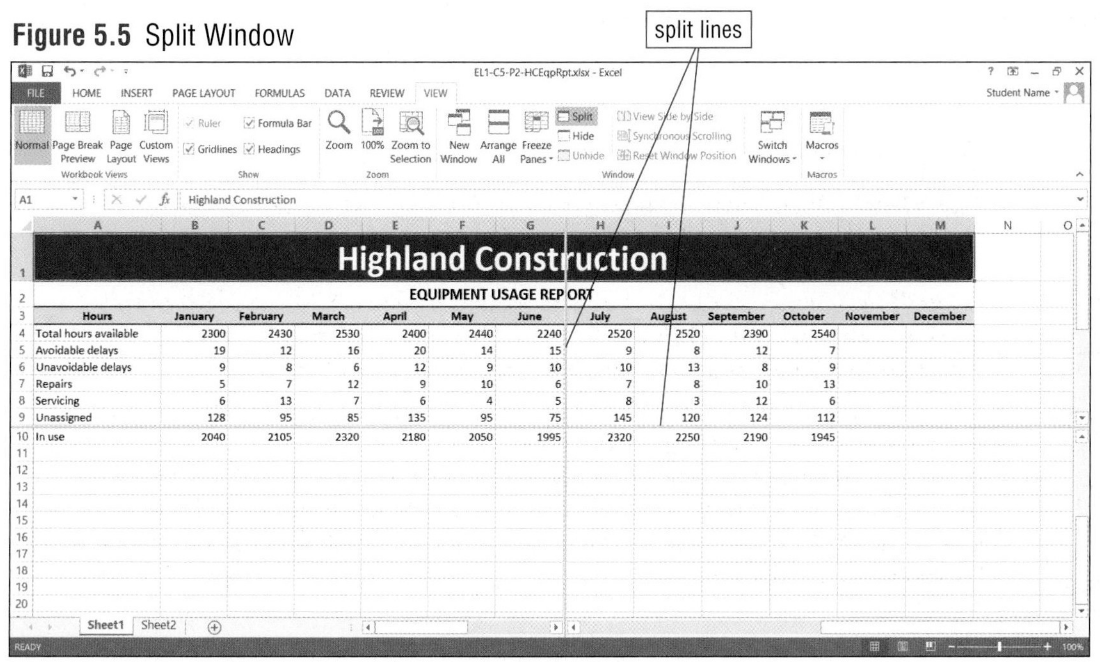

Project 2a Using Zoom, Splitting Windows, and Editing Cells **Part 1 of 2**

1. Open **HCEqpRpt.xlsx** and then save the workbook with Save As and name it **EL1-C5-P2-HCEqpRpt**.
2. Increase the Zoom percentage by clicking twice on the Zoom In button at the right side of the zoom slider bar.
3. Select cells G3 through I10, click the VIEW tab, and then click the Zoom to Selection button in the Zoom group.
4. Click the Zoom button in the Zoom group, click the *75%* option at the Zoom dialog box, and then click OK.
5. Click the 100% button in the Zoom group.
6. Make cell A1 active and then split the window by clicking the Split button in the Window group on the VIEW tab. (This splits the window into four panes.)
7. Drag the vertical split line by completing the following steps:
   a. Position the mouse pointer on the vertical split line until the pointer turns into a left-and-right-pointing arrow with a double line in the middle.
   b. Hold down the left mouse button, drag to the left until the vertical split line is immediately to the right of the first column, and then release the mouse button.

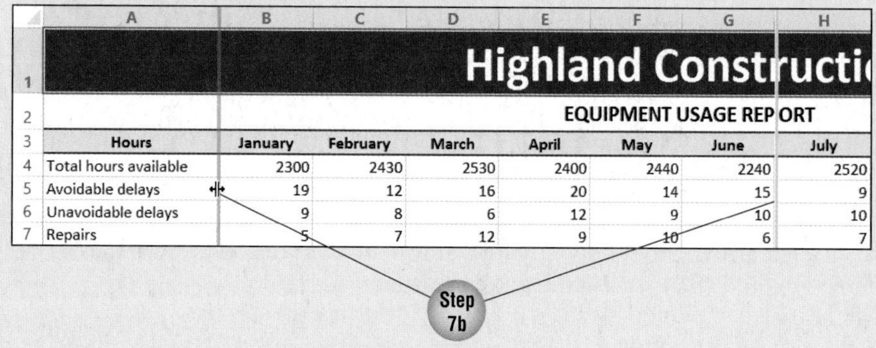

	A	B	C	D	E	F	G	H
1	Highland Constructi							
2	EQUIPMENT USAGE REPORT							
3	Hours	January	February	March	April	May	June	July
4	Total hours available	2300	2430	2530	2400	2440	2240	2520
5	Avoidable delays	19	12	16	20	14	15	9
6	Unavoidable delays	9	8	6	12	9	10	10
7	Repairs	5	7	12	9	10	6	7

8. Freeze the window panes by clicking the Freeze Panes button in the Window group on the VIEW tab and then clicking *Freeze Panes* at the drop-down list.
9. Make cell L4 active and then type the following data in the specified cells:

   L4: 2310 M4: 2210
   L5: 12 M5: 5
   L6: 5 M6: 7
   L7: 9 M7: 8
   L8: 11 M8: 12
   L9: 95 M9: 120
   L10: 2005 M10: 1830

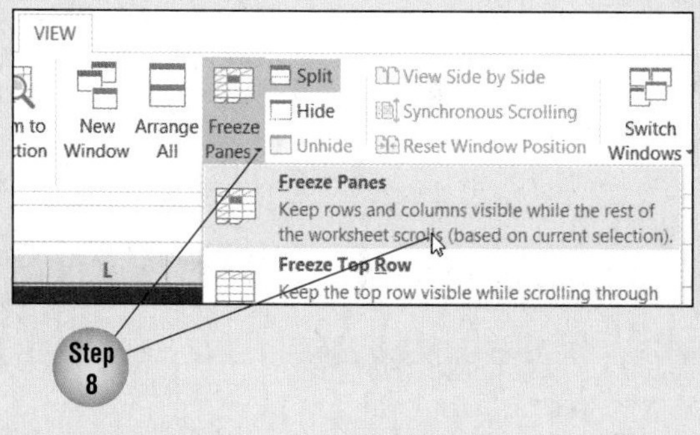

10. Unfreeze the window panes by clicking the Freeze Panes button and then clicking *Unfreeze Panes* at the drop-down list.
11. Remove the panes by clicking the Split button in the Window group to deactivate it.
12. Save **EL1-C5-P2-HCEqpRpt.xlsx**.

Working with Ranges

A selected group of cells is referred to as a ***range***. A range of cells can be formatted, moved, copied, or deleted. You can also name a range of cells and then move the insertion point to the range or use a named range as part of a formula.

To name a range, select the cells and then click in the Name box located at the left of the Formula bar. Type a name for the range (do not use a space) and then press Enter. To move the insertion point to a specific range and select the range, click the down-pointing arrow at the right side of the Name box and then click the range name.

You can also name a range using the Define Name button on the FORMULAS tab. To do this, click the FORMULAS tab and then click the Define Name button in the Defined Names group. At the New Name dialog box, type a name for the range and then click OK.

A range name can be used in a formula. For example, if a range is named *Profit* and you want to insert the average of all cells in the Profit range, make the desired cell active and then type *=AVERAGE(Profit)*. Use a named range in the current worksheet or in another worksheet within the workbook.

Quick Steps

Name a Range
1. Select cells.
2. Click in Name box.
3. Type range name.
4. Press Enter.

HINT

Another method for moving to a range is to click the Find & Select button in the Editing group on the HOME tab and then click *Go To*. At the Go To dialog box, double-click the range name.

Project 2b Naming a Range and Using a Range in a Formula — Part 2 of 2

1. With **EL1-C5-P2-HCEqpRpt.xlsx** open, click the Sheet2 tab and then type the following text in the specified cells:
   A1: **EQUIPMENT USAGE REPORT**
   A2: **Yearly hours**
   A3: **Avoidable delays**
   A4: **Unavoidable delays**
   A5: **Total delay hours**
   A6: (leave blank)
   A7: **Repairs**
   A8: **Servicing**
   A9: **Total repair/servicing hours**

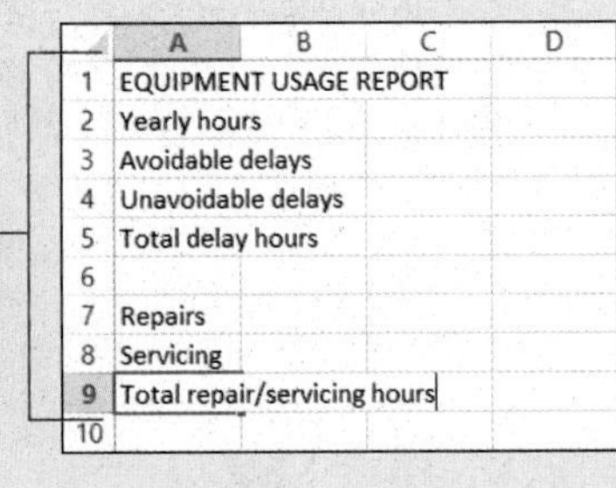

2. Make the following formatting changes to the worksheet:
   a. Automatically adjust the width of column A.
   b. Center and bold the text in cells A1 and A2.
3. Select a range of cells in Sheet1, name the range, and use it in a formula in Sheet2 by completing the following steps:
   a. Click the Sheet1 tab.
   b. Select cells B5 through M5.
   c. Click in the Name box located to the left of the Formula bar.
   d. Type **adhours** (for Avoidable Delays Hours) and then press Enter.
   e. Click the Sheet2 tab.
   f. Make cell B3 active.
   g. Type the equation **=SUM(adhours)** and then press Enter.

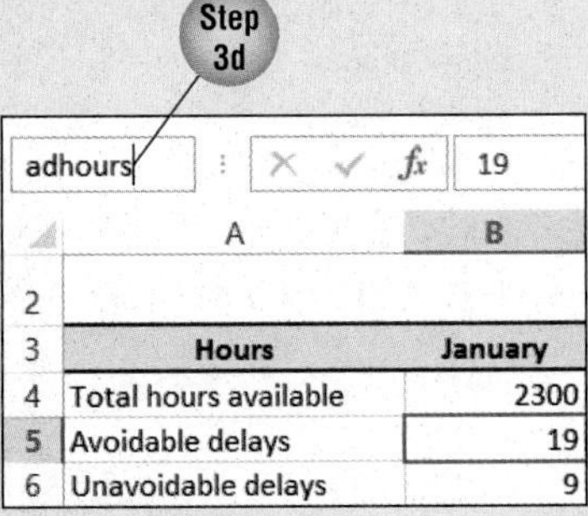

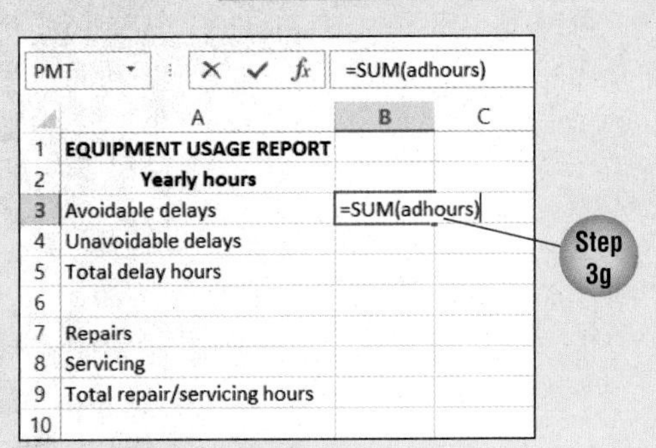

4. Click the Sheet1 tab and then complete the following steps:
   a. Select cells B6 through M6.
   b. Click the FORMULAS tab.
   c. Click the Define Name button in the Defined Names group.
   d. At the New Name dialog box, type **udhours** and then click OK.
   e. Click the Sheet2 tab, make sure cell B4 is active, type the equation **=SUM(udhours)**, and then press Enter.

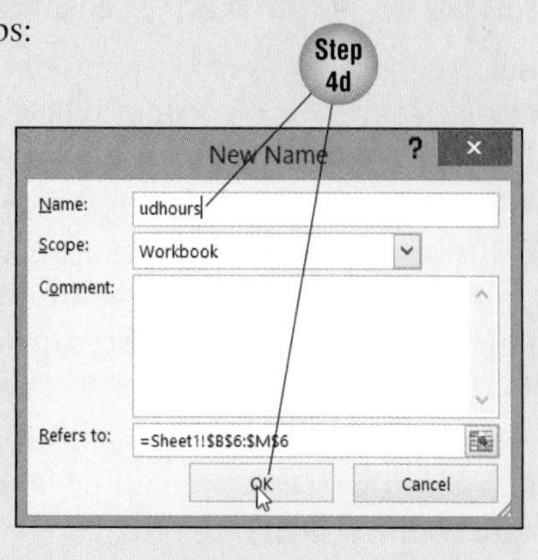

5. Click the Sheet1 tab and then complete the following steps:
   a. Select cells B7 through M7 and then name the range *rhours*.
   b. Click the Sheet2 tab, make cell B7 active, type the equation **=SUM(rhours)**, and then press Enter.
   c. Click the Sheet1 tab.
   d. Select cells B8 through M8 and then name the range *shours*.
   e. Click the Sheet2 tab, make sure cell B8 is active, type the equation **=SUM(shours)**, and then press Enter.
6. With Sheet2 still active, make the following changes:
   a. Make cell B5 active.
   b. Double-click the AutoSum button in the Editing group on the HOME tab.
   c. Make cell B9 active.
   d. Double-click the AutoSum button in the Editing group.
7. Click the Sheet1 tab and then move to the adhours range by clicking the down-pointing arrow at the right side of the Name box and then clicking *adhours* at the drop-down list.
8. Select both sheet tabs, change the orientation to landscape, scale the contents to fit on one page (by changing the width to *1 page* on the PAGE LAYOUT tab), and then insert a custom footer with your name, the page number, and the date.
9. With both worksheet tabs selected, print both worksheets in the workbook.
10. Save and then close **EL1-C5-P2-HCEqpRpt.xlsx**.

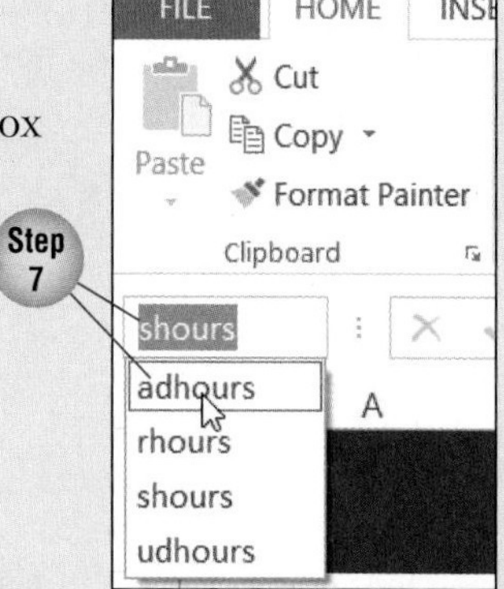

Project 3 Arrange, Size, and Copy Data between Workbooks 3 Parts

You will open, arrange, hide, unhide, size, and move multiple workbooks. You will also copy cells from one workbook and paste them in another workbook.

Working with Windows

You can open multiple workbooks in Excel, open a new window with the current workbook, and arrange the open workbooks in the Excel window. With multiple workbooks open, you can cut and paste or copy and paste cell entries from one workbook to another using the same techniques discussed earlier in this chapter with the exception that you make the destination workbook active before using the Paste command.

Opening Multiple Workbooks

With multiple workbooks open, or more than one version of the current workbook open, you can move or copy information between workbooks and compare the contents of several workbooks. When you open a new workbook or a new window of the current workbook, it is placed on top of the original workbook.

Open a new window of the current workbook by clicking the VIEW tab and then clicking the New Window button in the Window group. Excel adds a colon followed by the number *2* to the end of the workbook title and adds a colon followed by the number *1* to the end of the originating workbook name.

New Window

Open multiple workbooks at one time at the Open dialog box. Select adjacent workbooks by clicking the name of the first workbook to be opened, holding down the Shift key, clicking the name of the last workbook to be opened, and then clicking the Open button. If workbooks are nonadjacent, click the name of the first workbook to be opened, hold down the Ctrl key, and then click the names of any other workbooks you want to open.

To see what workbooks are currently open, click the VIEW tab and then click the Switch Windows button in the Window group. The names of the open workbooks display in a drop-down list and the workbook name preceded by a check mark is the active workbook. To make one of the other workbooks active, click the desired workbook name at the drop-down list.

Switch Windows

Another method for determining which workbooks are open is to hover your mouse over the Excel icon button that displays on the Taskbar. This causes a thumbnail to display of each open workbook. If you have more than one workbook open, the Excel button on the Taskbar displays additional layers in a cascaded manner. The layer behind the Excel button displays only a portion of the edge at the right side of the button. If you have multiple workbooks open, hovering the mouse over the Excel button on the Taskbar will cause thumbnails of all of the workbooks to display above the button. (This depends on your monitor size.) To change to the desired workbook, click the thumbnail that represents the workbook.

Arranging Workbooks

If you have more than one workbook open, you can arrange the workbooks at the Arrange Windows dialog box, shown in Figure 5.6. To display this dialog box, open several workbooks and then click the Arrange All button in the Window group on the VIEW tab. At the Arrange Windows dialog box, click *Tiled* to display a portion of each open workbook. Figure 5.7 displays four tiled workbooks.

Quick Steps

Arrange Workbooks

1. Click VIEW tab.
2. Click Arrange All button.
3. At Arrange Windows dialog box, click desired arrangement.
4. Click OK.

Arrange All

Figure 5.6 Arrange Windows Dialog Box

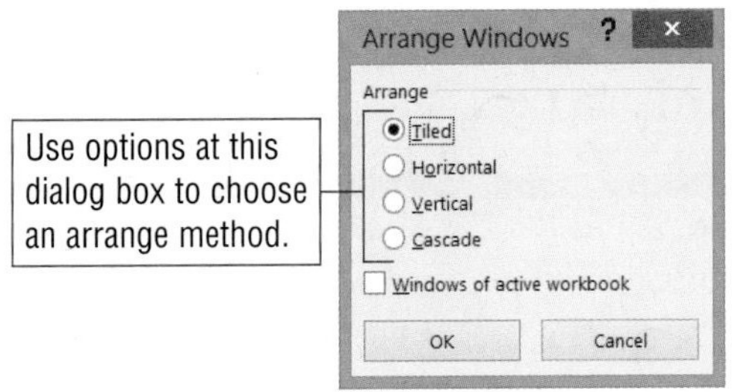

Figure 5.7 Tiled Workbooks

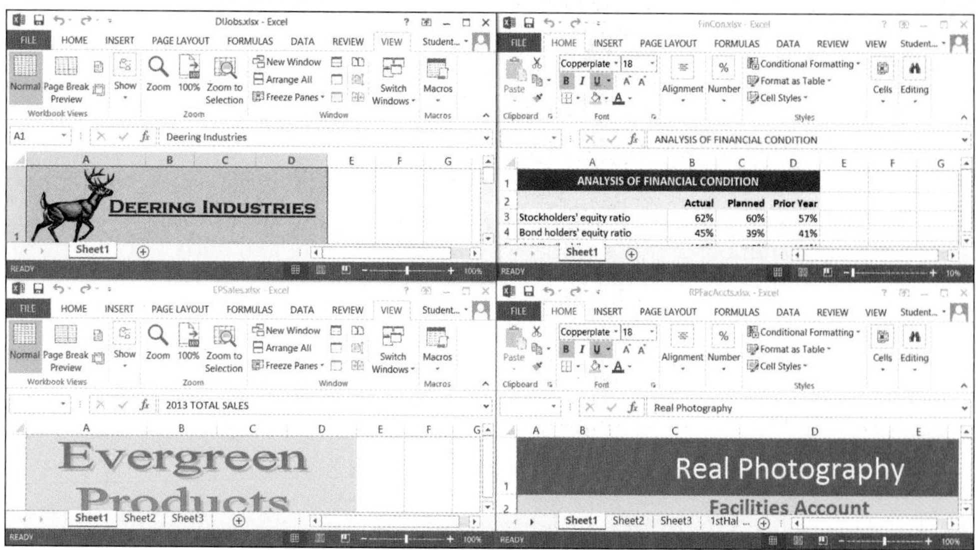

Choose the *Horizontal* option at the Arrange Windows dialog box and the open workbooks display across the screen. The *Vertical* option displays the open workbooks up and down the screen. The last option, *Cascade*, displays the Title bar of each open workbook. Figure 5.8 shows four cascaded workbooks.

The option you select for displaying multiple workbooks depends on which part of the workbooks is most important to view simultaneously. For example, the tiled workbooks in Figure 5.7 allow you to view the company names and the first few rows and columns of each workbook.

Figure 5.8 Cascaded Workbooks

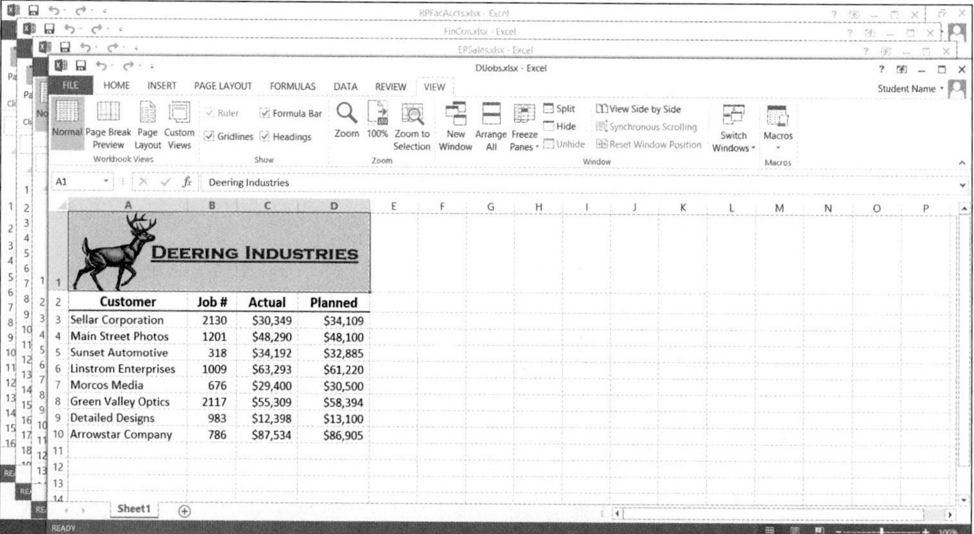

Hiding/Unhiding Workbooks

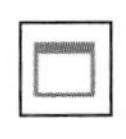

With the Hide button in the Window group on the VIEW tab, you can hide the active workbook. If a workbook has been hidden, redisplay it by clicking the Unhide button in the Window group. At the Unhide dialog box, make sure the desired workbook is selected in the list box and then click OK.

Project 3a **Opening, Arranging, and Hiding/Unhiding Workbooks** **Part 1 of 3**

1. Open several workbooks at the same time by completing the following steps:
   a. Display the Open dialog box with EL1C5 the active folder.
   b. Click the workbook named ***DIJobs.xlsx***.
   c. Hold down the Ctrl key, click ***EPSales.xlsx***, click ***FinCon.xlsx***, and then click ***RPFacAccts.xlsx***.
   d. Release the Ctrl key and then click the Open button in the dialog box.
2. Make **DIJobs.xlsx** the active workbook by clicking the VIEW tab, clicking the Switch Windows button, and then clicking ***DIJobs.xlsx*** at the drop-down list.

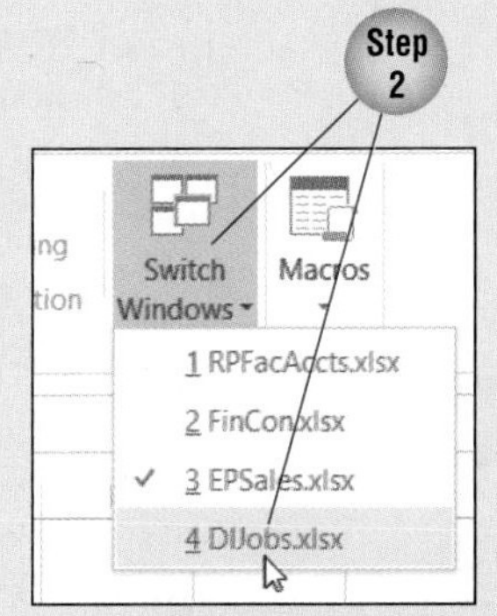

3. Tile the workbooks by completing the following steps:
   a. Click the VIEW tab and then click the Arrange All button in the Window group.
   b. At the Arrange Windows dialog box, make sure *Tiled* is selected and then click OK.

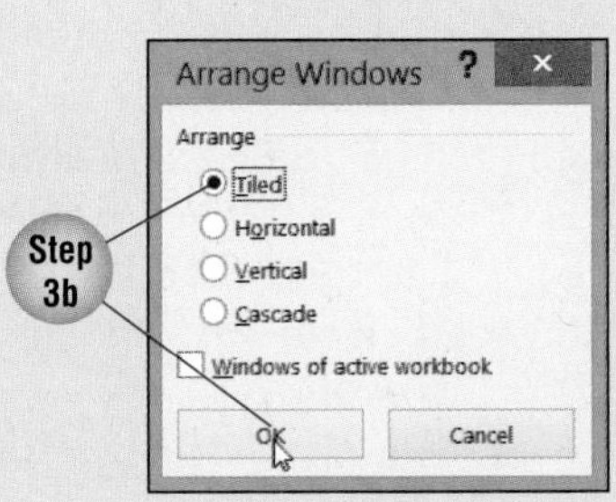

4. Cascade the workbooks by completing the following steps:
   a. Click the Arrange All button in the **DIJobs.xlsx** workbook.
   b. At the Arrange Windows dialog box, click *Cascade* and then click OK.
5. Hide and unhide workbooks by completing the following steps:
   a. Make sure **DIJobs.xlsx** is the active workbook. (The file name displays on top of each workbook file.)
   b. Click the Hide button in the Window group on the VIEW tab.
   c. Make sure **RPFacAccts.xlsx** is the active workbook. (The file name displays at the top of each workbook file.)
   d. Click the VIEW tab and then click the Hide button.
   e. At the active workbook, click the Unhide button.
   f. At the Unhide dialog box, click ***RPFacAccts.xlsx*** in the list box and then click OK.
   g. Click the Unhide button.
   h. At the Unhide dialog box, make sure **DIJobs.xlsx** is selected in the list box and then click OK. (If the workbook is not selected, click the **RPFacAccts.xlsx** title bar to make it active.)

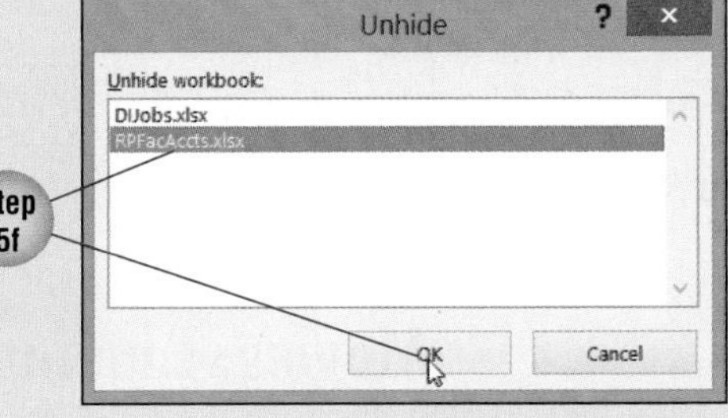

6. Close all of the open workbooks (without saving changes) except **DIJobs.xlsx**.
7. Open a new window with the current workbook by clicking the New Window button in the Window group on the VIEW tab. (Notice that the new window contains the workbook name followed by a colon and the number *2*.)
8. Switch back and forth between the two versions of the workbook.
9. Make **DIJobs.xlsx:2** the active window and then close the workbook.

Sizing and Moving Workbooks

Maximize

Minimize

Close

Restore Down

Use the Maximize and Minimize buttons located in the upper right corner of the active workbook to change the size of the window. The Maximize button is the button in the upper right corner of the active workbook immediately to the left of the Close button. (The Close button is the button containing the *X*.) The Minimize button is located immediately to the left of the Maximize button.

If you arrange all open workbooks and then click the Maximize button in the active workbook, the active workbook expands to fill the screen. In addition, the Maximize button changes to the Restore Down button. To return the active workbook back to its original size, click the Restore Down button.

If you click the Minimize button in the active workbook, the workbook is reduced and displays as a layer behind the Excel button on the Taskbar. To maximize a workbook that has been minimized, click the Excel button on the Taskbar and then click the thumbnail representing the workbook.

Project 3b **Minimizing, Maximizing, and Restoring Workbooks** **Part 2 of 3**

1. Make sure **DIJobs.xlsx** is open.
2. Maximize **DIJobs.xlsx** by clicking the Maximize button located in the upper right corner of the screen immediately left of the Close button.
3. Open **EPSales.xlsx** and **FinCon.xlsx**.
4. Make the following changes to the open workbooks:
   a. Tile the workbooks.
   b. Click the **DIJobs.xlsx** Title bar to make it the active workbook.
   c. Minimize **DIJobs.xlsx** by clicking the Minimize button that displays at the right side of the Title bar.
   d. Make **EPSales.xlsx** the active workbook and then minimize it.
   e. Minimize **FinCon.xlsx**.
5. Click the Excel button on the Taskbar, click the **DIJobs.xlsx** thumbnail, and then close the workbook without saving changes.
6. Complete steps similar to Step 5 to close the other two workbooks.

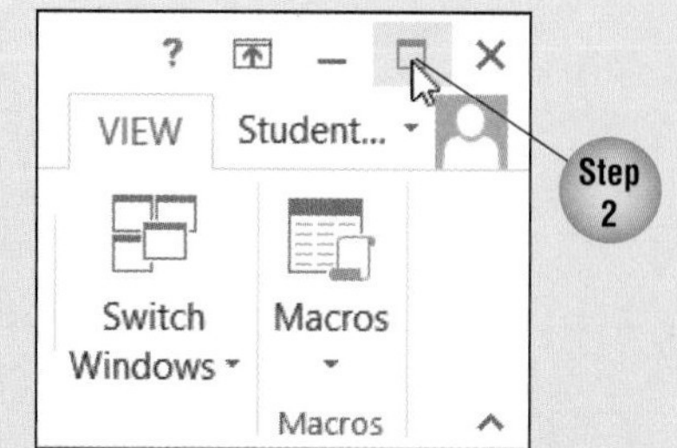

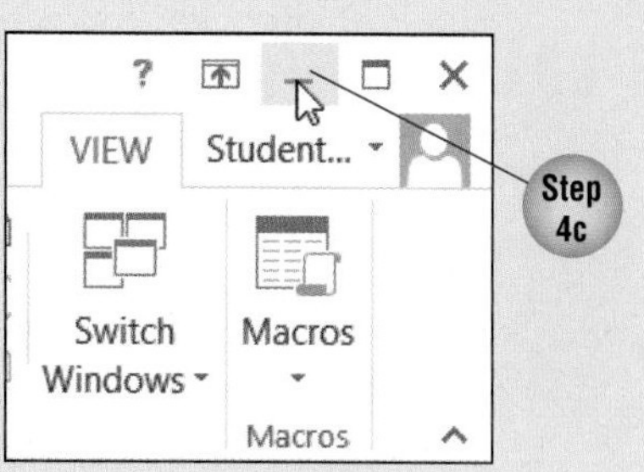

Moving, Linking, Copying, and Pasting Data

With more than one workbook open, you can move, link, copy, and/or paste data from one workbook to another. To move, link, copy, and/or paste data between workbooks, use the cutting and pasting options you learned earlier in this chapter together with the information about windows.

Moving and Copying Data

You can move or copy data within a worksheet, between worksheets, and between workbooks and other programs, such as Word, PowerPoint, and Access. The Paste Options button provides a variety of options for pasting data in a worksheet, another workbook, or another program. In addition to pasting data, you can also link data and paste data as an object or a picture object.

Project 3c Copying Selected Cells from One Open Worksheet to Another — Part 3 of 3

1. Open **DIFebJobs.xlsx**.
2. If you just completed Project 3b, click the Maximize button so the worksheet fills the entire worksheet window.
3. Save the workbook with Save As and name it **EL1-C5-P3-DIFebJobs**.
4. With **EL1-C5-P3-DIFebJobs.xlsx** open, open **DIJobs.xlsx**.
5. Select and then copy text from **DIJobs.xlsx** to **EL1-C5-P3-DIFebJobs.xlsx** by completing the following steps:
   a. With **DIJobs.xlsx** the active workbook, select cells A3 through D10.
   b. Click the Copy button in the Clipboard group on the HOME tab.
   c. Click the Excel button on the Taskbar and then click the **EL1-C5-P3-DIFebJobs.xlsx** thumbnail.

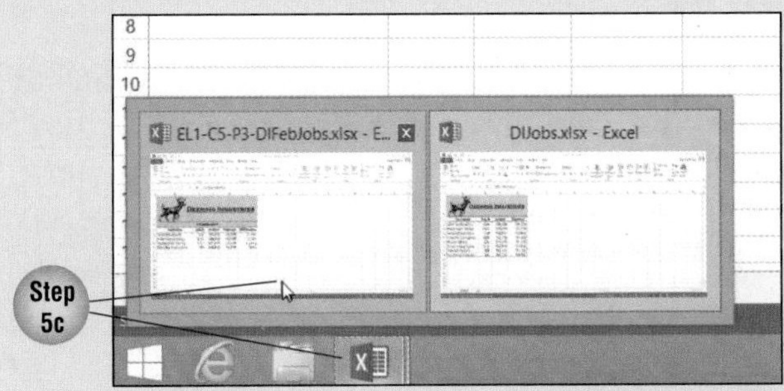

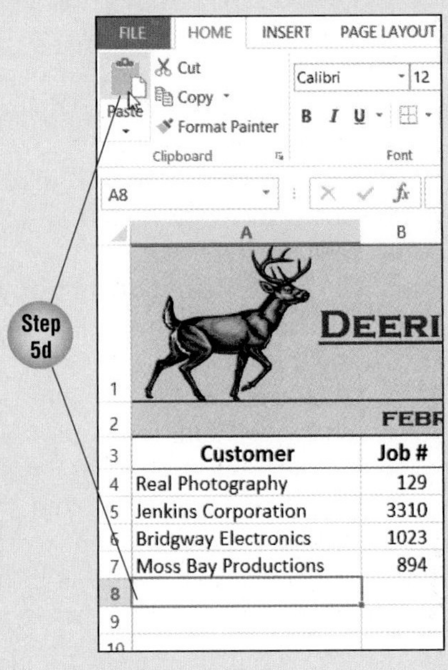

   d. Make cell A8 active and then click the Paste button in the Clipboard group.
   e. Make cell E7 active and then drag the fill handle down to cell E15.
6. Print **EL1-C5-P3-DIFebJobs.xlsx** horizontally and vertically centered on the page.
7. Save and then close **EL1-C5-P3-DIFebJobs.xlsx**.
8. Close **DIJobs.xlsx**.

Project  4 Linking and Copying Data within and between Worksheets and Word — 2 Parts

You will open a workbook containing four worksheets with quarterly expenses data, copy and link cells between the worksheets, and then copy and paste the worksheets into Word as picture objects.

Linking Data

Quick Steps

Link Data between Worksheets
1. Select cells.
2. Click Copy button.
3. Click desired worksheet tab.
4. Click in desired cell.
5. Click Paste button arrow.
6. Click *Paste Link* at drop-down list.

In some situations, you may want to copy and link data within or between worksheets or workbooks rather than copy and paste data. Linking data is useful when you need to maintain consistency and control over critical data in worksheets or workbooks. When data is linked, a change made in a linked cell is automatically made to the other cells in the link. You can make links with individual cells or with a range of cells. When linking data, the worksheet that contains the original data is called the ***source worksheet*** and the worksheet relying on the source worksheet for the data in the link is called the ***dependent worksheet***.

To create a link, make active the cell containing the data to be linked (or select the cells) and then click the Copy button in the Clipboard group on the HOME tab. Make active the worksheet where you want to paste the cells, click the Paste button arrow, and then click the Paste Link button located in the *Other Paste Options* section in the drop-down list. You can also create a link by clicking the Paste button, clicking the Paste Options button, and then clicking the Paste Link button in the *Other Paste Options* section in the drop-down list.

Project 4a **Linking Cells between Worksheets** **Part 1 of 2**

1. Open **DWQtrlyExp.xlsx** and then save the workbook with Save As and name it **EL1-C5-P4-DWQtrlyExp**.
2. Link cells in the first quarter worksheet to the other three worksheets by completing the following steps:
   a. With the 1st Qtr tab active, select cells C4 through C10.
   b. Click the Copy button in the Clipboard group on the HOME tab.
   c. Click the 2nd Qtr tab.
   d. Make cell C4 active.
   e. Click the Paste button arrow and then click the Paste Link button located in the *Other Paste Options* section in the drop-down list.
   f. Click the 3rd Qtr tab and then make cell C4 active.
   g. Click the Paste button arrow and then click the Paste Link button.
   h. Click the 4th Qtr tab and then make cell C4 active.
   i. Click the Paste button.
   j. Click the Paste Options button and then click the Paste Link button in the *Other Paste Options* section in the drop-down list.

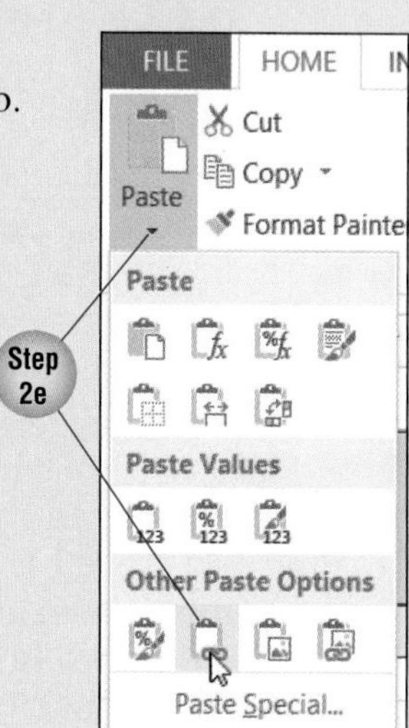

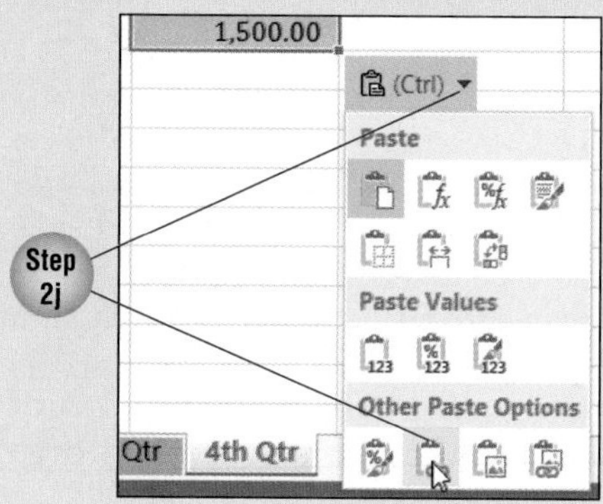

3. Click the 1st Qtr tab and then press the Esc key to remove the moving marquee.
4. Insert a formula in each worksheet that subtracts the budget amount from the variance amount by completing the following steps:
   a. Make sure the first quarter worksheet displays.
   b. Hold down the Shift key and then click the 4th Qtr tab. (This selects all four tabs.)
   c. Make cell D4 active and then type the formula =C4-B4 and press Enter.
   d. Copy the formula in cell D4 down to cells D5 through D10.
   e. Make cell D4 active and then apply accounting formatting with two places after the decimal point and a dollar sign.
   f. Click the 2nd Qtr tab and notice that the formula was inserted and copied in this worksheet.
   g. Click the other worksheet tabs and notice the amounts in column D.
   h. Click the 1st Qtr tab.

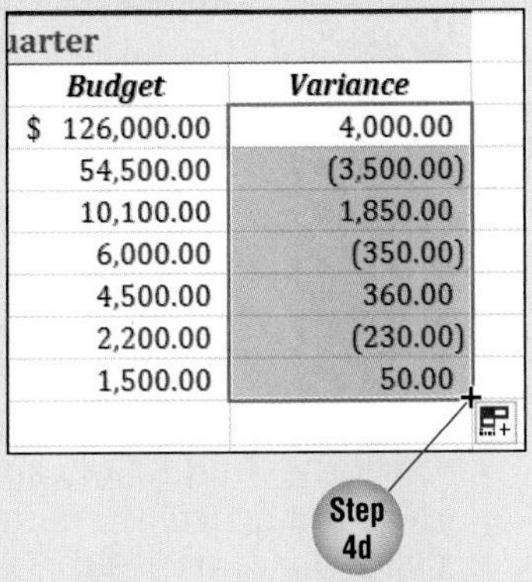

uarter

Budget	*Variance*
$ 126,000.00	4,000.00
54,500.00	(3,500.00)
10,100.00	1,850.00
6,000.00	(350.00)
4,500.00	360.00
2,200.00	(230.00)
1,500.00	50.00

Step 4d

5. With the first quarter worksheet active, make the following changes to some of the linked cells:

   C4: Change *$126,000* to *$128,000*

   C5: Change *54,500* to *56,000*

   C9: Change *2,200* to *2,400*
6. Click the 2nd Qtr tab and notice that the values in cells C4, C5, and C9 automatically changed (because they were linked to the first quarter worksheet).
7. Click the other tabs and notice that the values changed.
8. Save **EL1-C5-P4-DWQtrlyExp.xlsx** and then print all four worksheets in the workbook.

Copying and Pasting Data between Programs

Microsoft Office is a suite that allows ***integration***, which is the combining of data from two or more programs into one file. Integration can occur by copying and pasting data between programs. For example, you can create a worksheet in Excel, select specific data in the worksheet, and then copy it to a Word document. When pasting Excel data in a Word document, you can choose to keep the source formatting, use destination styles, link the data, insert the data as a picture, or keep the text only.

Project 4b Copying and Pasting Excel Data into a Word Document — Part 2 of 2

1. With **EL1-C5-P4-DWQtrlyExp.xlsx** open, open the Word program.
2. In Word, open the document named **DWQtrlyRpt.docx** located in the EL1C5 folder on your storage medium.
3. Save the Word document with Save As and name it **EL1-C5-P4-DWQtrlyRpt**.
4. Click the Excel button on the Taskbar.
5. Copy the first quarter data into the Word document by completing the following steps:
   a. Click the 1st Qtr tab.
   b. Select cells A2 through D10.
   c. Click the Copy button in the Clipboard group on the HOME tab.
   d. Click the Word button on the Taskbar.

e. In the **EL1-C5-P4-DWQtrlyRpt.docx** document, press Ctrl + End to move the insertion point below the heading.
f. Click the Paste button arrow. (This displays a drop-down list of paste option buttons.)
g. Move your mouse over the various buttons in the drop-down list to see how each option will insert the data in the document.
h. Click the Picture button. (This inserts the data as a picture object.)
i. Press Ctrl + End and then press the Enter key twice. (This moves the insertion point below the data.)
j. Click the Excel button on the Taskbar.

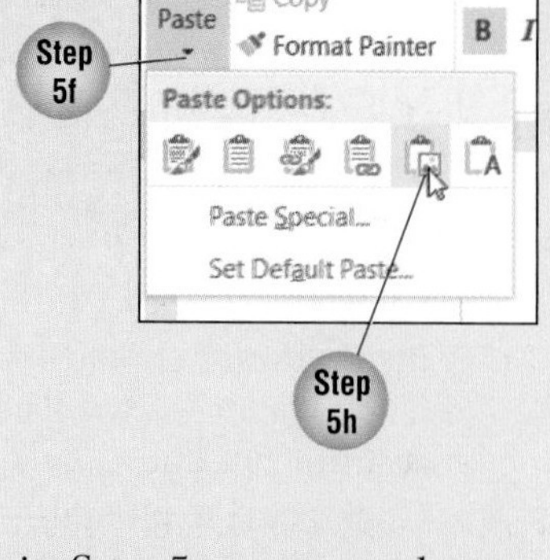

6. Click the 2nd Qtr tab and then complete steps similar to those in Step 5 to copy and paste the second quarter data to the Word document.
7. Click the 3rd Qtr tab and then complete steps similar to those in Step 5 to copy and paste the third quarter data to the Word document.
8. Click the 4th Qtr tab and then complete steps similar to those in Step 5 to copy and paste the fourth quarter data to the Word document. (The data will display on two pages.)
9. Print the document by clicking the FILE tab, clicking the *Print* option, and then clicking the Print button at the Print backstage area.
10. Save and close **EL1-C5-P4-DWQtrlyRpt.docx** and then close Word.
11. In Excel, press the Esc key to remove the moving marquee and then make cell A1 active.
12. Save and then close **EL1-C5-P4-DWQtrlyExp.xlsx**.

Chapter Summary

- An Excel workbook, by default, contains one worksheet. Add a new worksheet to a workbook by clicking the New sheet button or with the keyboard shortcut Shift + F11.
- Delete a worksheet with the Delete button in the Cells group on the HOME tab or by right-clicking a worksheet tab and then clicking *Delete* at the shortcut menu.
- Manage more than one worksheet at a time by first selecting the worksheets. Use the mouse together with the Shift key to select adjacent worksheet tabs and use the mouse together with the Ctrl key to select nonadjacent worksheet tabs.
- Copy or move selected cells and cell contents in and between worksheets using the Cut, Copy, and Paste buttons in the Clipboard group on the HOME tab or by dragging with the mouse.
- Move selected cells with the mouse by dragging the outline of the selected cells to the desired position.
- Copy selected cells with the mouse by holding down the Ctrl key while dragging the cells to the desired position.
- When pasting data, specify how you want cells pasted by clicking the Paste button arrow or pasting the cells and then clicking the Paste Options button. Clicking either button causes a drop-down list of paste option buttons to display. Click the desired button in the drop-down list.

- Use the Clipboard task pane to copy and paste data within and between worksheets and workbooks. Display the Clipboard task pane by clicking the Clipboard task pane launcher.
- Perform maintenance activities, such as deleting and renaming, on worksheets within a workbook by clicking the right mouse button on a worksheet tab and then clicking the desired option at the shortcut menu.
- You can use the mouse to move or copy worksheets. To move a worksheet, drag the worksheet tab with the mouse. To copy a worksheet, hold down the Ctrl key and then drag the worksheet tab with the mouse.
- Use the *Tab Color* option at the worksheet tab shortcut menu to apply a color to a worksheet tab.
- Hide and unhide a worksheet by clicking the Format button in the Cells group and then clicking the desired option at the drop-down list or by right-clicking the worksheet tab and then clicking the desired option at the shortcut menu.
- To print all worksheets in a workbook, display the Print backstage area, click the first gallery in the *Settings* category, and then click *Print Entire Workbook* at the drop-down list. You can also print specific worksheets by selecting the tabs of the worksheets you want to print.
- Use buttons in the Zoom group on the VIEW tab or the zoom slider bar located at the right side of the Status bar to change the display zoom percentage.
- Split the worksheet window into panes with the Split button in the Window group on the VIEW tab. To remove a split from a worksheet, click the Split button to deactivate it.
- Freeze window panes by clicking the Freeze Panes button in the Window group on the VIEW tab and then clicking *Freeze Panes* at the drop-down list. Unfreeze window panes by clicking the Freeze Panes button and then clicking *Unfreeze Panes* at the drop-down list.
- A selected group of cells is referred to as a range. A range can be named and used in a formula. Name a range by typing the name in the Name box located to the left of the Formula bar or at the New Name dialog box.
- To open multiple workbooks that are adjacent, display the Open dialog box, click the first workbook, hold down the Shift key, click the last workbook, and then click the Open button. To open workbooks that are nonadjacent, click the first workbook, hold down the Ctrl key, click the desired workbooks, and then click the Open button.
- To see a list of open workbooks, click the VIEW tab and then click the Switch Windows button in the Window group.
- Arrange multiple workbooks in a window with options at the Arrange Windows dialog box.
- Hide the active workbook by clicking the Hide button and unhide a workbook by clicking the Unhide button in the Window group on the VIEW tab.
- Click the Maximize button located in the upper right corner of the active workbook to make the workbook fill the entire window area. Click the Minimize button to shrink the active workbook to a button on the Taskbar. Click the Restore Down button to return the workbook to its previous size.
- You can move, link, copy, and/or paste data between workbooks.

Commands Review

FEATURE	RIBBON TAB, GROUP	BUTTON, OPTION	KEYBOARD SHORTCUT
Arrange Windows dialog box	VIEW, Window		
Clipboard task pane	HOME, Clipboard		
copy selected cells	HOME, Clipboard		Ctrl + C
cut selected cells	HOME, Clipboard		Ctrl + X
freeze window panes	VIEW, Window	, *Freeze Panes*	
hide worksheet	HOME, Cells	, *Hide & Unhide, Hide Sheet*	
insert new worksheet			Shift + F11
maximize window			
minimize window			
New Name dialog box	FORMULAS, Defined Names		
paste selected cells	HOME, Clipboard		Ctrl + V
restore down			
split window into panes	VIEW, Window		
unfreeze window panes	VIEW, Window	, *Unfreeze Panes*	
unhide worksheet	HOME, Cells	, *Hide & Unhide, Unhide Sheet*	

Concepts Check

Test Your Knowledge

Completion: In the space provided at the right, indicate the correct term, symbol, or command.

1. By default, a workbook contains this number of worksheets. ____________
2. Click this button to insert a new worksheet in a workbook. ____________
3. To select nonadjacent worksheet tabs, click the first tab, hold down this key, and then click any other tabs you want selected. ____________
4. To select adjacent worksheet tabs, click the first tab, hold down this key, and then click the last tab. ____________

5. The Cut, Copy, and Paste buttons are located in this group on the HOME tab. ____________________

6. This button displays in the lower right corner of pasted cells. ____________________

7. Use this task pane to copy and paste multiple items. ____________________

8. Click this option at the worksheet tab shortcut menu to apply a color to a worksheet tab. ____________________

9. To print all of the worksheets in a workbook, display the Print backstage area, click the first gallery in the *Settings* category, and then click this option at the drop-down list. ____________________

10. The Split button is located on this tab. ____________________

11. Display the Arrange Windows dialog box by clicking this button in the Window group on the VIEW tab. ____________________

12. Click this button to make the active workbook expand to fill the screen. ____________________

13. Click this button to reduce the active workbook to a layer behind the Excel button on the Taskbar. ____________________

14. When linking data between worksheets, the worksheet containing the original data is called this. ____________________

Skills Check Assess Your Performance

Assessment 1

COPY AND PASTE DATA BETWEEN WORKSHEETS IN A SALES WORKBOOK

1. Open **EPSales.xlsx** and then save the workbook with Save As and name it **EL1-C5-A1-EPSales**.
2. Turn on the display of the Clipboard task pane, click the Clear All button to clear any content, and then complete the following steps:
   a. Select and copy cells A7 through C7.
   b. Select and copy cells A10 through C10.
   c. Select and copy cells A13 through C13.
   d. Display the second worksheet, make cell A7 active, and then paste the *Avalon Clinic* cells.
   e. Make cell A10 active and then paste the *Stealth Media* cells.
   f. Make A13 active and then paste the *Danmark Contracting* cells.
   g. Make the third worksheet active and then complete similar steps to paste the cells in the same location as in the second worksheet.
   h. Clear the contents of the Clipboard task pane and then close the task pane.

3. Change the name of the Sheet1 tab to *2013 Sales*, the name of the Sheet2 tab to *2014 Sales*, and the name of the Sheet3 tab to *2015 Sales*.
4. Change the color of the 2013 Sales tab to Blue, the color of the 2014 Sales tab to Green, and the color of the 2015 Sales tab to Yellow.
5. Make 2013 Sales the active worksheet, select all three tabs, and then insert a formula in cell D4 that sums the amounts in cells B4 and C4. Copy the formula in cell D4 down to cells D5 through D14.
6. Make cell D15 active and then insert a formula that sums the amounts in cells D4 through D14.
7. Apply accounting formatting with a dollar sign and no places after the decimal point to cell D4 (on all three worksheets).
8. Insert a footer on all three worksheets that prints your name at the left side and the current date at the right.
9. Save **EL1-C5-A1-EPSales.xlsx**.
10. Print all three worksheets and then close **EL1-C5-A1-EPSales.xlsx**.

Assessment 2 COPY, PASTE, AND FORMAT WORKSHEETS IN AN INCOME STATEMENT WORKBOOK

1. Open **CMJanIncome.xlsx** and then save the workbook with Save As and name it **EL1-C5-A2-CMJanIncome**.
2. Copy cells A1 through B17 in Sheet1 and paste them into Sheet2. (Click the Paste Options button and then click the Keep Source Column Widths button at the drop-down list.)
3. Make the following changes to the Sheet2 worksheet:
   a. Adjust the row heights so they match the heights in the Sheet1 worksheet.
   b. Change the month from *January* to *February*.
   c. Change the amount in cell B4 to *97,655*.
   d. Change the amount in cell B5 to *39,558*.
   e. Change the amount in cell B11 to *1,105*.
4. Select both sheet tabs and then insert the following formulas:
   a. Insert a formula in cell B6 that subtracts the cost of sales from the sales revenue (*=B4-B5*).
   b. Insert a formula in cell B16 that sums the amounts in cells B8 through B15.
   c. Insert a formula in cell B17 that subtracts the total expenses from the gross profit (*=B6-B16*).
5. Change the name of the Sheet1 tab to *January* and the name of the Sheet2 tab to *February*.
6. Change the color of the January tab to Blue and the color of the February tab to Red.
7. Insert a custom header on both worksheets that prints your name at the left side, the date in the middle, and the file name at the right side.
8. Save, print, and then close **EL1-C5-A2-CMJanIncome.xlsx**.

Assessment

3 FREEZE AND UNFREEZE WINDOW PANES IN A TEST SCORES WORKBOOK

1. Open **CMCertTests.xlsx** and then save the workbook with Save As and name it **EL1-C5-A3-CMCertTests**.
2. Make sure cell A1 is active and then split the window by clicking the VIEW tab and then clicking the Split button in the Window group. (This causes the window to split into four panes.)
3. Drag both the horizontal and vertical split lines up and to the left until the horizontal split line is immediately below the second row and the vertical split line is immediately to the right of the first column.
4. Freeze the window panes.
5. Add two rows immediately above row 18 and then type the following text in the specified cells:

A18: **Nauer, Sheryl**	A19: **Nunez, James**
B18: **75**	B19: **98**
C18: **83**	C19: **96**
D18: **85**	D19: **100**
E18: **78**	E19: **90**
F18: **82**	F19: **95**
G18: **80**	G19: **93**
H18: **79**	H19: **88**
I18: **82**	I19: **91**
J18: **92**	J19: **89**
K18: **90**	K19: **100**
L18: **86**	L19: **96**
M18: **84**	M19: **98**

6. Insert a formula in cell N3 that averages the percentages in cells B3 through M3 and then copy the formula down to cells N4 through N22.
7. Unfreeze the window panes.
8. Remove the split.
9. Change the orientation to landscape and then scale the worksheet to print on one page. ***Hint: Do this with the* Width *option in the Scale to Fit group on the PAGE LAYOUT tab.***
10. Save, print, and then close **EL1-C5-A3-CMCertTests.xlsx**.

Assessment

4 CREATE, COPY, PASTE, AND FORMAT CELLS IN AN EQUIPMENT USAGE WORKBOOK

1. Create the worksheet shown in Figure 5.9. (Change the width of column A to 21.00 characters.)
2. Save the workbook and name it **EL1-C5-A4-HCMachRpt**.
3. With **EL1-C5-A4-HCMachRpt.xlsx** open, open **HCEqpRpt.xlsx**.

4. Select and copy the following cells from **HCEqpRpt.xlsx** to **EL1-C5-A4-HCMachRpt.xlsx**:
   a. Copy cells A4 through G4 in **HCEqpRpt.xlsx** and paste them into **EL1-C5-A4-HCMachRpt.xlsx** beginning with cell A12.
   b. Copy cells A10 through G10 in **HCEqpRpt.xlsx** and paste them into **EL1-C5-A4-HCMachRpt.xlsx** beginning with cell A13.
5. With **EL1-C5-A4-HCMachRpt.xlsx** the active workbook, make cell A1 active and then apply the following formatting:
   a. Change the height of row 1 to 25.20 points.
   b. Change the font size of the text in cell A1 to 14 points.
   c. Apply the Blue, Accent 5, Lighter 80% fill color (ninth column, second row in the *Theme Colors* section) to cell A1.
6. Select cells A2 through G2 and apply the Blue, Accent 5, Darker 50% fill color (ninth column, last row in the *Theme Colors* section).
7. Select cells B2 through G2 and apply the White, Background 1 text color (first column, first row in the *Theme Colors* section). (Make sure the text in the cells is right-aligned.)
8. Select and then apply the Blue, Accent 5, Lighter 80% fill color (ninth column, second row in the *Theme Colors* section) to the following cells: A3 through G3, A7 through G7, and A11 through G11.
9. Print the worksheet centered horizontally and vertically on the page.
10. Save and then close **EL1-C5-A4-HCMachRpt.xlsx**.
11. Close **HCEqpRpt.xlsx** without saving the changes.

Figure 5.9 Assessment 4

	A	B	C	D	E	F	G	H
1			**EQUIPMENT USAGE REPORT**					
2		**January**	**February**	**March**	**April**	**May**	**June**	
3	**Machine #12**							
4	Total hours available	2200	2330	2430	2300	2340	2140	
5	In use	1940	2005	2220	2080	1950	1895	
6								
7	**Machine #25**							
8	Total hours available	2100	2240	2450	2105	2390	1950	
9	In use	1800	1935	2110	1750	2215	1645	
10								
11	**Machine #30**							
12								

Assessment 5 COPYING AND LINKING DATA IN A WORD DOCUMENT

1. In this chapter you learned how to link data in cells between worksheets. You can also copy data in an Excel worksheet and then paste and link the data in a file in another program such as Word. Use buttons in the Paste Options button drop-down list to link data or use options at the Paste Special dialog box. Open Word and then open the document named **DWLtr.docx** located in the EL1C5 folder. Save the document with Save As and name it **EL1-C5-A5-DWLtr**.

2. Click the Excel button on the Taskbar, open **DWMortgages.xlsx**, and then save the workbook with Save As and name it **EL1-C5-A5-DWMortgages**.
3. Select cells A2 through G10 and then click the Copy button.
4. Click the Word button on the Taskbar. (This displays **EL1-C5-A5-DWLtr.docx**.)
5. Move the insertion point between the two paragraphs of text.
6. Click the Paste button arrow and then click *Paste Special* at the drop-down list.
7. At the Paste Special dialog box, look at the options available and click the *Paste link* option, click *Microsoft Excel Worksheet Object* in the *As* list box, and then click OK.
8. Save, print, and then close **EL1-C5-A5-DWLtr.docx**.
9. Click the Excel button on the Taskbar.
10. Make cell A3 active and then change the number from *$300,000* to *$400,000*. Copy the number in cell A3 down to cells A4 through A10. (Cells A3 through A10 should now contain the amount *$400,000*.) Select cells A4 through A10 and then apply accounting formatting with no dollars signs and no places after the decimal point.
11. Save, print, and then close **EL1-C5-A5-DWMortgages.xlsx**.
12. Click the Word button on the Taskbar.
13. Open **EL1-C5-A5-DWLtr.docx**. At the message that displays asking if you want to update the data from the linked files, click Yes.
14. Save, print, and then close **EL1-C5-A5-DWLtr.docx**.
15. Close Word.

Visual Benchmark Demonstrate Your Proficiency

CREATE AND FORMAT A SALES WORKSHEET USING FORMULAS

1. At a blank workbook, create the worksheet shown in Figure 5.10 with the following specifications:
   - Do not type the data in cells D4 through D9. Instead, enter a formula that totals the first-half and second-half yearly sales.
   - Apply the formatting shown in the figure, including changing font sizes, column widths, and row heights and inserting shading and border lines.
   - Rename the sheet tab and change the tab color as shown in the figure.
2. Copy cells A1 through D9 and then paste the cells in Sheet2.
3. Edit the cells and apply formatting so your worksheet matches the worksheet shown in Figure 5.11. Rename the sheet tab and change the tab color as shown in the figure.
4. Save the completed workbook and name it **EL1-C5-VB-CMSemiSales**.
5. Print both worksheets.
6. Close **EL1-C5-VB-CMSemiSales.xlsx**.

Figure 5.10 Sales 2014 Worksheet

	A	B	C	D
1	Clearline Manufacturing			
2	SEMIANNUAL SALES - 2014			
3	Customer	1st Half	2nd Half	Total
4	Lakeside Trucking	$ 84,300	$ 73,500	$ 157,800
5	Gresham Machines	33,000	40,500	73,500
6	Real Photography	30,890	35,465	66,355
7	Genesis Productions	72,190	75,390	147,580
8	Landower Company	22,000	15,000	37,000
9	Jewell Enterprises	19,764	50,801	70,565

Sales 2014 | Sales 2015

Figure 5.11 Sales 2015 Worksheet

	A	B	C	D
1	Clearline Manufacturing			
2	SEMIANNUAL SALES - 2015			
3	Customer	1st Half	2nd Half	Total
4	Lakeside Trucking	$ 84,300	$ 73,500	$ 157,800
5	Gresham Machines	33,000	40,500	73,500
6	Real Photography	20,750	15,790	36,540
7	Genesis Productions	51,270	68,195	119,465
8	Landower Company	22,000	15,000	37,000
9	Jewell Enterprises	14,470	33,770	48,240

Sales 2014 | Sales 2015

Case Study Apply Your Skills

Part 1

You are an administrator for Gateway Global, an electronics manufacturing corporation. You are gathering information on money spent on supplies and equipment purchases. You have gathered information for the first quarter of the year and decide to create a workbook containing worksheets for monthly information. To do this, create a worksheet that contains the following information:

- Company name is Gateway Global.
- Create the title *January Expenditures*.
- Create the columns shown in Figure 5.12.

Figure 5.12 Case Study Part 1

Department	**Supplies**	**Equipment**	**Total**
Production	$25,425	$135,500	
Technical Support	$14,500	$65,000	
Finance	$5,790	$22,000	
Sales and Marketing	$35,425	$8,525	
Facilities	$6,000	$1,200	
Total			

- Insert a formula in the *Total* column that sums the amounts in the *Supplies* and *Equipment* columns and insert a formula in the *Total* row that sums the supplies amounts, equipment amounts, and total amounts.
- Apply formatting such as fill color, borders, font color, and shading to enhance the appearance of the worksheet.

After creating and formatting the worksheet, complete the following:

- Insert a new worksheet and then copy the data in Sheet1 to Sheet2.
- Insert a new worksheet and then copy the data in Sheet1 to Sheet3.
- Make the following changes to data in Sheet2:
    - Change *January Expenditures* to *February Expenditures*.
    - Change the Production department supplies amount to *$38,550* and the equipment amount to *$88,500*.
    - Change the Technical Support department equipment amount to *$44,250*.
    - Change the Finance department supplies amount to *$7,500*.
- Make the following changes to data in Sheet3:
    - Change *January Expenditures* to *March Expenditures*.
    - Change the Production department supplies amount to *$65,000* and the equipment amount to *$150,000*.
    - Change the Technical Support department supplies amount to *$21,750* and the equipment amount to *$43,525*.
    - Change the Facilities department equipment amount to *$18,450*.

Create a new worksheet that summarizes the supplies and equipment totals for January, February, and March. Apply the same formatting to the worksheet as you applied to the other three. Change the tab name for Sheet1 to *Jan. Expenditures*, the tab name for Sheet2 to *Feb. Expenditures*, the tab name for Sheet3 to *Mar. Expenditures*, and the tab name for Sheet4 to *Qtr. Summary*. Change the color of each tab. (You determine the colors.)

Insert a header that prints your name at the left side of each worksheet and the current date at the right side of each worksheet. Save the workbook and name it **EL1-C5-CS-GGExp**. Print all the worksheets in the workbook and then close the workbook.

Part 2

Employees of Gateway Global have formed two intramural co-ed softball teams and you have volunteered to keep statistics for the players. Open **GGStats.xlsx** and then make the following changes to both worksheets in the workbook:

- Insert a formula that calculates a player's batting average (Hits / At Bats).
- Insert a formula that calculates a player's on-base percentage: (Walks + Hits) / (At Bats + Walks). Select cells E5 through F15 and then specify that you want to display three places after the decimal point.
- Insert the company name.
- Apply formatting to enhance the appearance of the worksheets.
- Horizontally and vertically center the worksheets.
- Insert a footer that prints on both worksheets and prints your name at the left side of the worksheet and the date at the right of the worksheet.

Use the Help feature to learn about applying cell styles or click the Cells Styles button in the Styles group on the HOME tab and then experiment with applying different styles. Apply the Good cell style to any cell in the *Batting Average* column with an average over .400. Apply this style to cells in both worksheets. Save the workbook and name it **EL1-C5-CS-GGStats**. Print both worksheets and then close **EL1-C5-CS-GGStats.xlsx**.

Part 3

Many of the suppliers for Gateway Global are international and use metric measurements. The purchasing manager has asked you to prepare a worksheet in Excel that converts length measurements..

Use the Internet to locate information on converting the following length measurements:

- 1 inch to centimeters
- 1 foot to centimeters
- 1 yard to meters
- 1 mile to kilometers

Locate a site on the Internet that provides the formula for converting Fahrenheit temperatures to Celsius temperatures and then create another worksheet in the workbook with the following information:

- Insert Fahrenheit temperatures beginning with 0 and continuing to 100 in increments of 5 (for example, 0, 5, 10, 15, and so on).
- Insert a formula that converts the Fahrenheit temperature to a Celsius temperature.

Include the company name, Gateway Global, in both worksheets. Apply additional formatting to improve the appearance of both worksheets. Rename both sheet names and apply a color to each tab. (You determine the names and colors.) Save the workbook and name it **EL1-C5-CS-GGConv**. Print both worksheets centered horizontally and vertically on the page and then close **EL1-C5-CS-GGConv.xlsx**.

Part 4

Open Microsoft Word and then create a letterhead document that contains the company name, *Gateway Global*; the address (you decide the street address, city, state, and ZIP code or street address, city, province, and postal code); and the telephone number (you decide). Apply formatting to improve the appearance of the letterhead. Save the document and name it **EL1-C5-CS-GGLtrhd**. Save the document again and name it **EL1-C5-CS-GGConvLtr**.

In Excel, open **EL1-C5-CS-GGConv.xlsx** (the workbook you created in Part 3). In the Fahrenheit conversion worksheet, copy the cells containing data and then paste the cells in **EL1-C5-CS-GGConvLtr.docx** as a picture object. Center the cells (picture object) between the left and right margins. Save, print, and then close **EL1-C5-CS-GGConvLtr.docx**. Close Microsoft Word and then in Excel close **EL1-C5-CS-GGConv.xlsx**.

MICROSOFT® EXCEL®

Maintaining Workbooks

PERFORMANCE OBJECTIVES

Upon successful completion of Chapter 6, you will be able to:

- **Create and rename a folder**
- **Delete workbooks and folders**
- **Copy and move workbooks within and between folders**
- **Copy and move worksheets between workbooks**
- **Maintain consistent formatting with styles**
- **Insert, modify, and remove hyperlinks**
- **Create financial forms using templates**

Tutorials

6.1 Maintaining Workbooks
6.2 Managing Folders
6.3 Managing the Recent Workbooks List
6.4 Managing Worksheets
6.5 Formatting with Cell Styles
6.6 Inserting Hyperlinks
6.7 Using Excel Templates

Once you have been working with Excel for a period of time, you will have accumulated several workbook files. You should organize your workbooks into folders to facilitate fast retrieval of information. Occasionally, you should perform file maintenance activities, such as copying, moving, renaming, and deleting workbooks, to ensure the workbook lists in your various folders are manageable. You will learn these file management tasks in this chapter, along with creating and applying styles to a workbook, inserting hyperlinks in a workbook, and using an Excel template to create a workbook. Model answers for this chapter's projects appear on the following pages.

Note: Before beginning the projects, copy to your storage medium the EL1C6 subfolder from the EL1 folder on the CD that accompanies this textbook and then make EL1C6 the active folder.

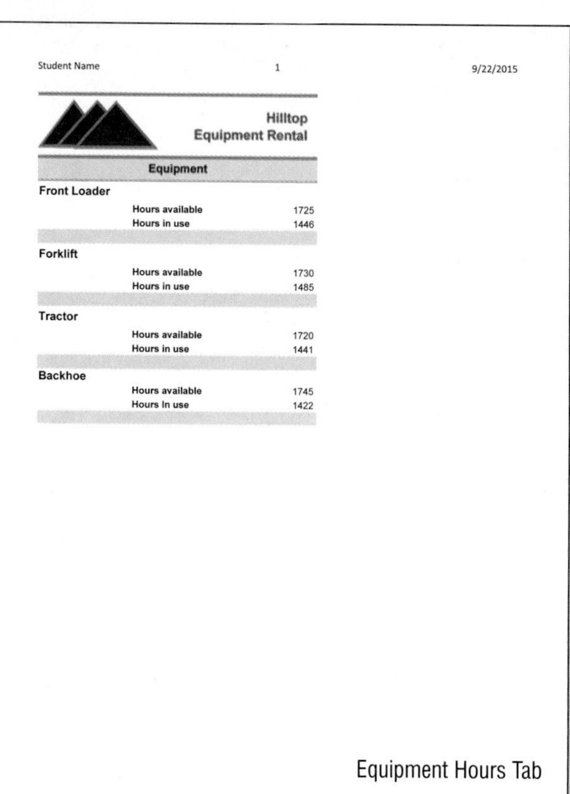

Student Name 1 9/22/2015

Hilltop
Equipment Rental

Equipment		
Front Loader		
	Hours available	1725
	Hours in use	1446
Forklift		
	Hours available	1730
	Hours in use	1485
Tractor		
	Hours available	1720
	Hours in use	1441
Backhoe		
	Hours available	1745
	Hours in use	1422

Equipment Hours Tab

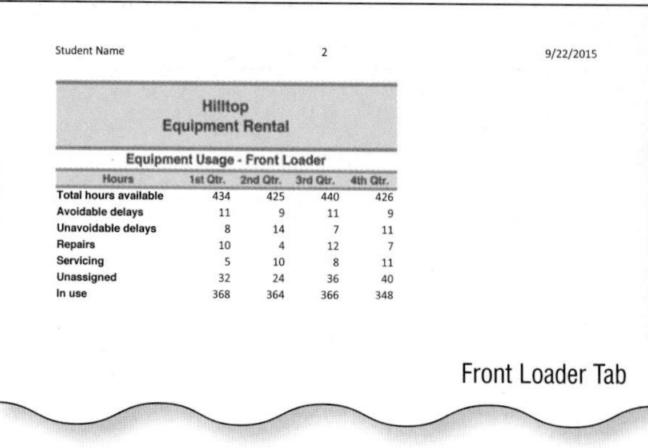

Student Name 2 9/22/2015

Hilltop
Equipment Rental

Equipment Usage - Front Loader

Hours	1st Qtr.	2nd Qtr.	3rd Qtr.	4th Qtr.
Total hours available	434	425	440	426
Avoidable delays	11	9	11	9
Unavoidable delays	8	14	7	11
Repairs	10	4	12	7
Servicing	5	10	8	11
Unassigned	32	24	36	40
In use	368	364	366	348

Front Loader Tab

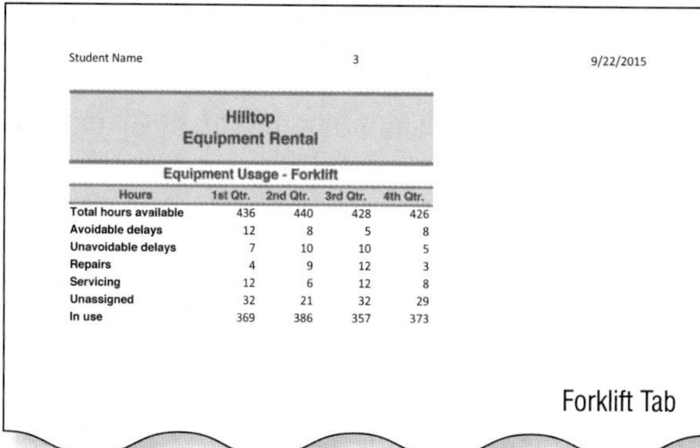

Student Name 3 9/22/2015

Hilltop
Equipment Rental

Equipment Usage - Forklift

Hours	1st Qtr.	2nd Qtr.	3rd Qtr.	4th Qtr.
Total hours available	436	440	428	426
Avoidable delays	12	8	5	8
Unavoidable delays	7	10	10	5
Repairs	4	9	12	3
Servicing	12	6	12	8
Unassigned	32	21	32	29
In use	369	386	357	373

Forklift Tab

Project 2 Copy and Move Worksheets into an Equipment Rental Workbook EL1-C6-P2-HEREquip.xlsx

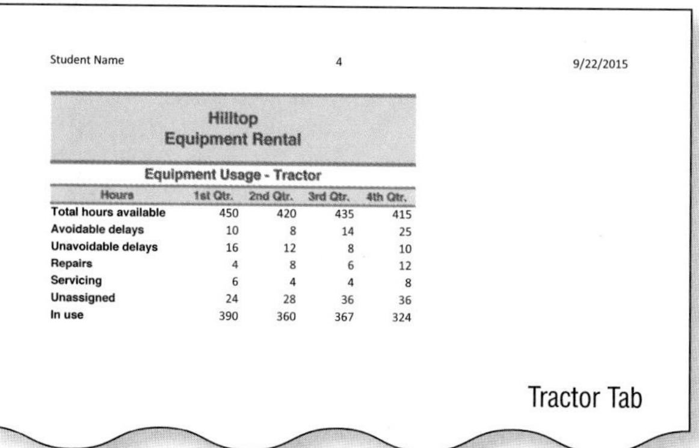

Student Name 4 9/22/2015

Hilltop
Equipment Rental

Equipment Usage - Tractor

Hours	1st Qtr.	2nd Qtr.	3rd Qtr.	4th Qtr.
Total hours available	450	420	435	415
Avoidable delays	10	8	14	25
Unavoidable delays	16	12	8	10
Repairs	4	8	6	12
Servicing	6	4	4	8
Unassigned	24	28	36	36
In use	390	360	367	324

Tractor Tab

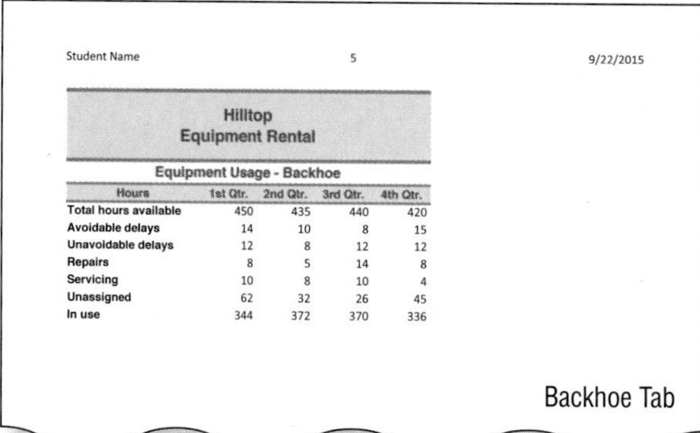

Student Name 5 9/22/2015

Hilltop
Equipment Rental

Equipment Usage - Backhoe

Hours	1st Qtr.	2nd Qtr.	3rd Qtr.	4th Qtr.
Total hours available	450	435	440	420
Avoidable delays	14	10	8	15
Unavoidable delays	12	8	12	12
Repairs	8	5	14	8
Servicing	10	8	10	4
Unassigned	62	32	26	45
In use	344	372	370	336

Backhoe Tab

O'Rourke Enterprises

Maintenance Department - Weekly Payroll

Employee	Hrly. Rate	Hours	Gross	W/H Tax	SS Tax	Net
Williams, Pamela	$ 43.00	40	$ 1,720.00	$ 481.60	$ 131.58	$ 1,106.82
Ternes, Reynaldo	41.50	40	1,660.00	464.80	126.99	1,068.21
Sinclair, Jason	38.00	30	1,140.00	319.20	87.21	733.59
Pierson, Rhea	38.00	40	1,520.00	425.60	116.28	978.12
Nyegaard, James	25.00	25	625.00	175.00	47.81	402.19
Lunde, Beverly	21.00	40	840.00	235.20	64.26	540.54

Withholding rate	28%
Social Security rate	7.65%

Weekly Payroll Tab

O'Rourke Enterprises

Invoices

Invoice #	Customer #	Date	Amount	Tax	Amount Due
1001	34002	4/2/2012	$ 450.00	8.50%	$ 488.25
1002	12034	4/4/2012	1,075.00	8.80%	1,169.60
1003	40059	4/6/2012	225.00	0.00%	225.00
1004	23002	4/10/2012	750.00	8.50%	813.75
1005	59403	4/10/2012	350.00	0.00%	350.00
1006	80958	4/11/2012	875.00	8.50%	949.38
1007	23494	4/13/2012	750.00	8.50%	813.75
1008	45232	4/17/2012	560.00	8.80%	609.28
1009	76490	4/18/2012	400.00	0.00%	400.00
1010	45466	4/19/2012	600.00	8.50%	651.00
1011	34094	4/23/2012	95.00	0.00%	95.00
1012	45450	4/25/2012	2,250.00	8.50%	2,441.25
1013	23044	4/26/2012	225.00	8.80%	244.80
1014	48933	4/30/2012	140.00	0.00%	140.00

Invoices Tab

Project 3 Create and Apply Styles to a Payroll Workbook EL1-C6-P3-OEPayroll.xlsx

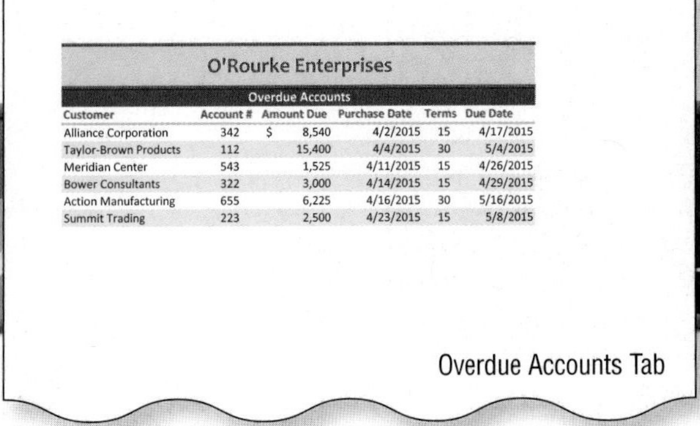

O'Rourke Enterprises

Overdue Accounts

Customer	Account #	Amount Due	Purchase Date	Terms	Due Date
Alliance Corporation	342	$ 8,540	4/2/2015	15	4/17/2015
Taylor-Brown Products	112	15,400	4/4/2015	30	5/4/2015
Meridian Center	543	1,525	4/11/2015	15	4/26/2015
Bower Consultants	322	3,000	4/14/2015	15	4/29/2015
Action Manufacturing	655	6,225	4/16/2015	30	5/16/2015
Summit Trading	223	2,500	4/23/2015	15	5/8/2015

Overdue Accounts Tab

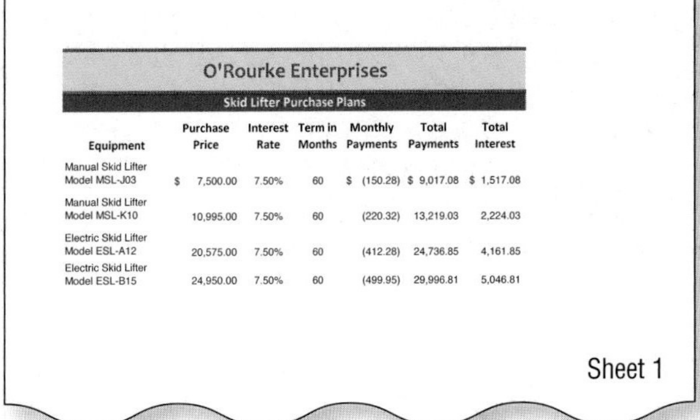

O'Rourke Enterprises

Skid Lifter Purchase Plans

Equipment	Purchase Price	Interest Rate	Term in Months	Monthly Payments	Total Payments	Total Interest
Manual Skid Lifter Model MSL-J03	$ 7,500.00	7.50%	60	$ (150.28)	$ 9,017.08	$ 1,517.08
Manual Skid Lifter Model MSL-K10	10,995.00	7.50%	60	(220.32)	13,219.03	2,224.03
Electric Skid Lifter Model ESL-A12	20,575.00	7.50%	60	(412.28)	24,736.85	4,161.85
Electric Skid Lifter Model ESL-B15	24,950.00	7.50%	60	(499.95)	29,996.81	5,046.81

Sheet 1

EL1-C6-P3-OEPlans.xlsx

Pyramid Sales

Facilities Account

First Quarter Summary

	January	February	March
Checks amount	$ 15,102.00	$ 14,613.79	$ 12,195.96
Deposits amount	$ 12,600.00	$ 12,600.00	$ 12,600.00
End-of-month balance	$ 2,394.50	$ 380.71	$ 380.71

Customer sales analysis

Summary Tab

Project 4 Insert, Modify, and Remove Hyperlinks

EL1-C6-P4-PSAccts.xlsx

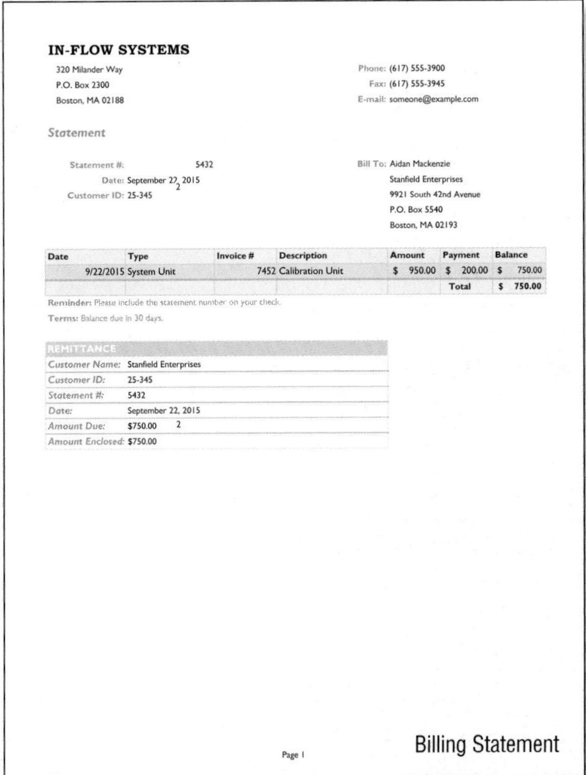

IN-FLOW SYSTEMS

320 Milander Way
P.O. Box 2300
Boston, MA 02188

Phone: (617) 555-3900
Fax: (617) 555-3945
E-mail: someone@example.com

Statement

Statement #: 5432
Date: September 22, 2015
Customer ID: 25-345

Bill To: Aidan Mackenzie
Stanfield Enterprises
9921 South 42nd Avenue
P.O. Box 5540
Boston, MA 02193

Date	Type	Invoice #	Description	Amount	Payment	Balance
9/22/2015	System Unit	7452	Calibration Unit	$ 950.00	$ 200.00	$ 750.00
					Total	$ 750.00

Reminder: Please include the statement number on your check.

Terms: Balance due in 30 days.

REMITTANCE	
Customer Name:	Stanfield Enterprises
Customer ID:	25-345
Statement #:	5432
Date:	September 22, 2015
Amount Due:	$750.00
Amount Enclosed:	$750.00

Page 1

Billing Statement

Project 5 Create a Billing Statement Workbook Using a Template

EL1-C6-P5-Billing.xlsx

Project 1 Manage Workbooks — 8 Parts

You will perform a variety of file management tasks, including creating and renaming a folder; selecting and then deleting, copying, cutting, pasting, and renaming workbooks; deleting a folder; and opening, printing, and closing a workbook.

Maintaining Workbooks

You can complete many workbook management tasks at the Open and Save As dialog boxes. These tasks include copying, moving, printing, and renaming workbooks; opening multiple workbooks; and creating and renaming new folders. Perform some file maintenance tasks, such as creating a folder and deleting files, with options from the Organize button drop-down list or a shortcut menu and navigate to folders using the Address bar. The elements of the Open dialog box are identified in Figure 6.1.

Figure 6.1 Open Dialog Box

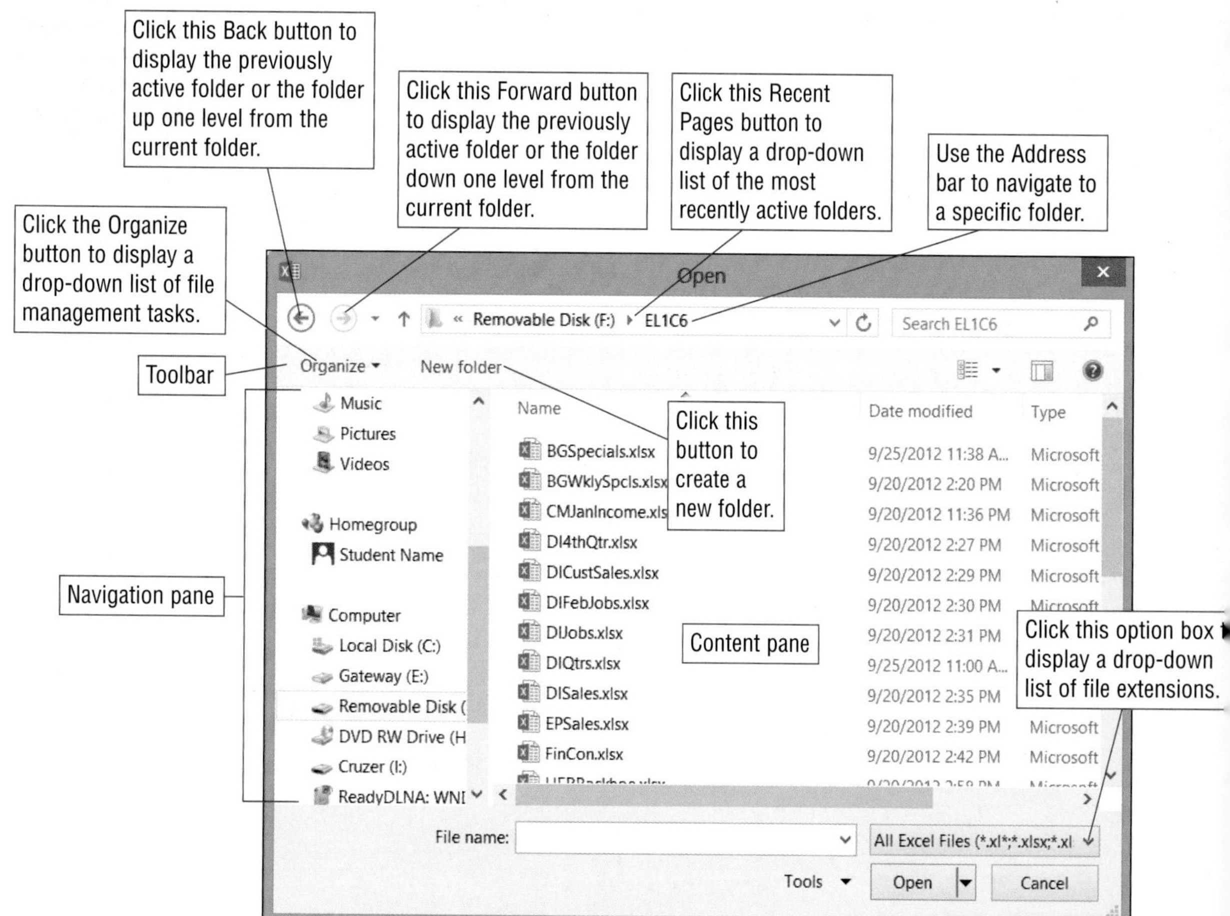

Directions and projects in this chapter assume that you are managing workbooks and folders on a USB flash drive or your computer's hard drive. If you are using your OneDrive, some of the workbook and folder management tasks may vary.

Creating a Folder

In Excel, you should logically group and store workbooks in ***folders***. For example, you could store all of the workbooks related to one department in one folder with the department name being the folder name. You can also create a folder within a folder (called a ***subfolder***). If you create workbooks for a department by individuals, each individual name could have a subfolder within the department folder. The main folder on a disk or drive is called the root folder. You create additional folders as branches of this root folder.

At the Open dialog box and Save As dialog box, workbook file names display in the Content pane preceded by workbook icons and folder names display preceded by folder icons. Create a new folder by clicking the New folder button located in the toolbar at the Open dialog box or Save As dialog box. This inserts a new folder in the Content pane. Type the name for the folder and then press Enter.

A folder name can contain a maximum of 255 characters. Numbers, spaces, and symbols can be used in the folder name, except those symbols identified in the Saving a Workbook section in Chapter 1.

Quick Steps

Create a Folder

1. Press Ctrl + F12 to display the Open dialog box.
2. Click New folder button.
3. Type folder name.
4. Press Enter.

New folder

HINT

Change the default folder with the *Default local file location* option at the Excel Options dialog box with *Save* selected in the left panel.

Project 1a **Creating a Folder** **Part 1 of 8**

1. With Excel open, create a folder named *Payroll* on your storage medium by completing the following steps:
   a. Press Ctrl + F12 to display the Open dialog box.
   b. At the Open dialog box, navigate to your storage medium.
2. Double-click the *EL1C6* folder name to make it the active folder.
3. Click the New folder button on the toolbar.
4. Type **Payroll** and then press Enter.
5. Close the Open dialog box.

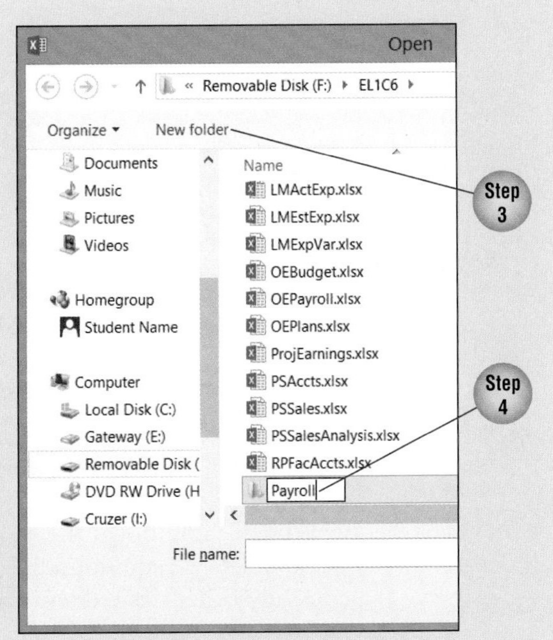

Renaming a Folder

Quick Steps

Rename a Folder

1. Display Open dialog box.
2. Click desired folder.
3. Click Organize button.
4. Click *Rename* at drop-down list.
5. Type new name.
6. Press Enter.

OR

1. Display Open dialog box.
2. Right-click folder name.
3. Click *Rename*.
4. Type new name.
5. Press Enter.

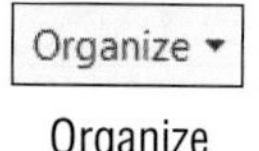

Organize

As you organize your files and folders, you may decide to rename a folder. Rename a folder using the Organize button in the Open dialog box or using a shortcut menu. To rename a folder using the Organize button, display the Open dialog box, click in the Content pane the folder you want to rename, click the Organize button located on the toolbar, and then click *Rename* at the drop-down list. This selects the folder name and inserts a border around the name. Type the new name for the folder and then press Enter. To rename a folder using a shortcut menu, display the Open dialog box, right-click the folder name in the Content pane, and then click *Rename* at the shortcut menu. Type a new name for the folder and then press Enter.

A tip to remember when you are organizing files and folders is to make sure your system is set up to display all of the files in a particular folder and not just the Excel files, for example. You can display all files in a folder in the Open dialog box by clicking the button to the right of the *File name* text box and then clicking *All Files (*.*)* at the drop-down list.

Project 1b **Renaming a Folder** **Part 2 of 8**

1. Press Ctrl + F12 to display the Open dialog box and make sure the EL1C6 folder is the active folder.
2. Right-click the *Payroll* folder name in the Content pane.
3. Click *Rename* at the shortcut menu.
4. Type **Finances** and then press Enter.

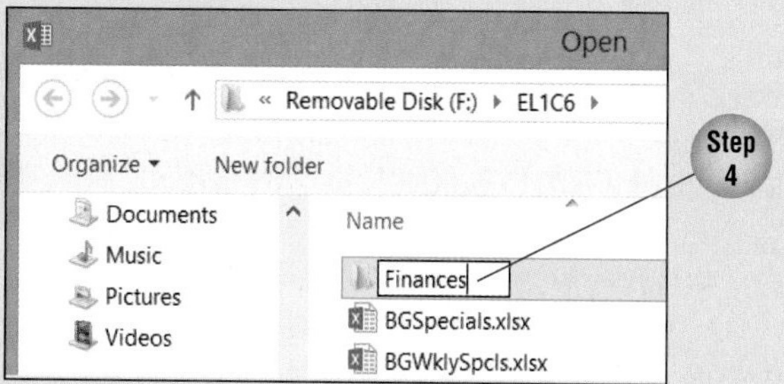

Selecting Workbooks

You can complete workbook management tasks on one workbook or selected workbooks. To select one workbook, display the Open dialog box and then click the desired workbook. To select several adjacent workbooks, click the first workbook, hold down the Shift key, and then click the last workbook. To select workbooks that are not adjacent, click the first workbook, hold down the Ctrl key, click any other desired workbooks, and then release the Ctrl key.

Deleting Workbooks and Folders

At some point, you may want to delete certain workbooks from your storage medium or any other drive or folder in which you may be working. To delete a workbook, display the Open or Save As dialog box, click the workbook in the Content pane, click the Organize button, and then click *Delete* at the drop-down list. If you are deleting a file from a removable storage medium such as a USB drive, a message will display asking you to confirm the deletion. At this message, click the Yes button. To delete a workbook using a shortcut menu, display the Open dialog box, right-click the workbook name in the Content pane, and then click *Delete* at the shortcut menu. If you are deleting a file from a removable storage medium such as a USB flash drive, click Yes at the confirmation dialog box.

Quick Steps

Delete a Workbook or Folder

1. Display Open dialog box.
2. Right-click workbook or folder name.
3. Click *Delete*.
4. If deleting from a removable drive, click Yes.

Deleting to the Recycle Bin

Workbooks deleted from a removable drive are deleted permanently while workbooks deleted from the hard drive are automatically sent to the Windows Recycle Bin. You can easily restore a deleted workbook from the Recycle Bin. To free space on the drive, empty the Recycle Bin on a periodic basis. Restoring a workbook from or emptying the contents of the Recycle Bin is completed at the Windows desktop (not in Excel). To display the Recycle Bin, minimize the Excel window and then double-click the Recycle Bin icon located on the Windows desktop. At the Recycle Bin, you can restore file(s) and empty the Recycle Bin.

Project 1c Selecting and Deleting Workbooks

Part 3 of 8

1. At the Open dialog box, open **RPFacAccts.xlsx** (located in the EL1C6 folder).
2. Save the workbook with Save As and name it **EL1-C6-P1-RPFacAccts**.
3. Close **EL1-C6-P1-RPFacAccts.xlsx**.
4. Delete **EL1-C6-P1-RPFacAccts.xlsx** by completing the following steps:
   a. Display the Open dialog box with the EL1C6 folder the active folder.
   b. Click ***EL1-C6-P1-RPFacAccts.xlsx*** to select it.
   c. Click the Organize button and then click *Delete* at the drop-down list.
   d. If a message displays asking if you are sure you want to delete the worksheet, click Yes.

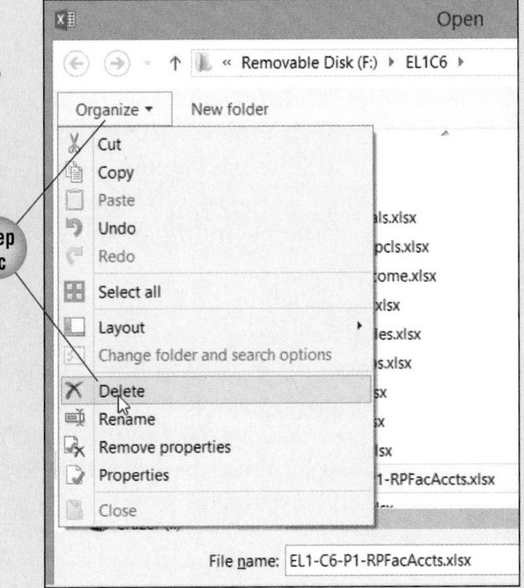

5. Delete selected workbooks by completing the following steps:
   a. Click ***DICustSales.xlsx*** in the Content pane.
   b. Hold down the Shift key and then click ***DIJobs.xlsx***.
   c. Position the mouse pointer on one of the selected workbooks and then click the right mouse button.
   d. At the shortcut menu that displays, click *Delete*.
   e. If a message displays asking if you are sure you want to delete the items, click Yes.
6. Close the Open dialog box.

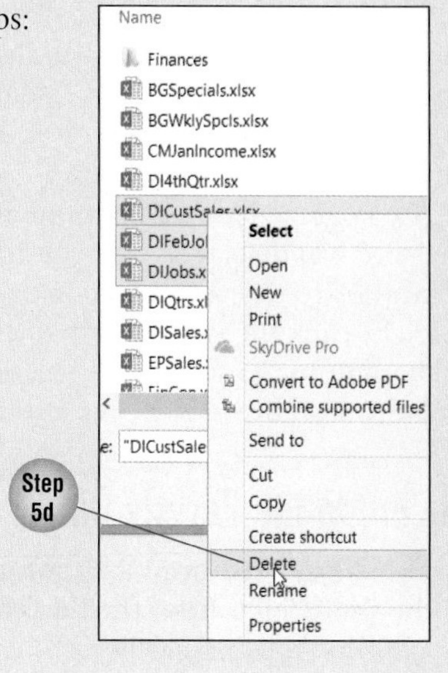

Copying Workbooks

In previous chapters, you have been opening a workbook from your storage medium and saving it with a new name in the same location. This process makes an exact copy of the workbook, preserving the original file on your storage medium. You can also copy a workbook into another folder.

Project 1d Saving a Copy of an Open Workbook to Another Folder — Part 4 of 8

1. Open **EPSales.xlsx**.
2. Save the workbook with Save As and name it **TotalSales**. (Make sure the EL1C6 folder is the active folder.)
3. Save a copy of **TotalSales.xlsx** in the Finances folder you created in Project 1a (and renamed in Project 1b) by completing the following steps:
   a. With **TotalSales.xlsx** open, press F12 to display the Save As dialog box.
   b. At the Save As dialog box, change to the Finances folder. To do this, double-click *Finances* at the beginning of the Content pane. (Folders are listed before workbooks.)
   c. Click the Save button located in the lower right corner of the dialog box.
4. Close **TotalSales.xlsx**.
5. Change back to the EL1C6 folder by completing the following steps:
   a. Press Ctrl + F12 to display the Open dialog box.
   b. Click *EL1C6* that displays in the Address bar.
6. Close the Open dialog box.

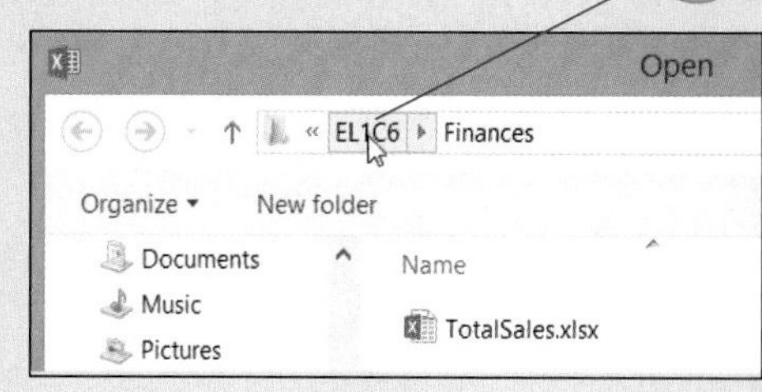

You can copy a workbook to another folder without opening the workbook first. To do this, use the *Copy* and *Paste* options from the shortcut menu at the Open dialog box or the Save As dialog box. You can also copy a workbook or selected workbooks into the same folder. When you do this, Excel adds a hyphen followed by the word *Copy* to the end of the document name.

To move or copy files or folders on your OneDrive, go to onedrive.com, make sure you are logged in to your account, and then use the onedrive.com toolbar to move a workbook or folder to another location or copy and then move a workbook or folder to another location.

Quick Steps

Copy a Workbook

1. Display Open or Save As dialog box.
2. Right-click workbook name.
3. Click *Copy*.
4. Navigate to desired folder.
5. Right-click blank area in Content pane.
6. Click *Paste*.

Project 1e **Copying a Workbook at the Open Dialog Box** **Part 5 of 8**

Note: If you are using your OneDrive, the steps for copying, cutting, and pasting workbooks will vary from the steps in Project 1e and 1f. Please check with your instructor.

1. Copy **CMJanIncome.xlsx** to the Finances folder. To begin, display the Open dialog box with the EL1C6 folder active.
2. Position the arrow pointer on **CMJanIncome.xlsx**, click the right mouse button, and then click *Copy* at the shortcut menu.
3. Change to the Finances folder by double-clicking *Finances* at the beginning of the Content pane.
4. Position the arrow pointer in any blank area in the Content pane, click the right mouse button, and then click *Paste* at the shortcut menu.
5. Change back to the EL1C6 folder by clicking *EL1C6* that displays in the Address bar.
6. Close the Open dialog box.

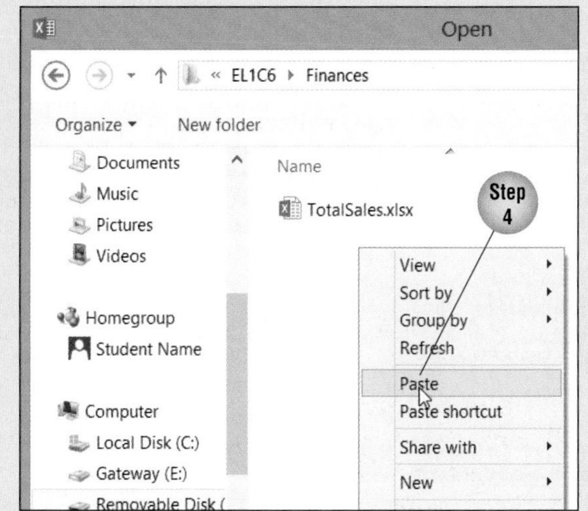

Sending Workbooks to a Different Drive or Folder

You can copy a workbook to another folder or drive without having to navigate to the new location. With the *Send to* option, you can send a copy of a workbook to another drive or folder. To use this option, position the arrow pointer on the workbook you want to copy, click the right mouse button, point to *Send to* (which causes a side menu to display), and then click the desired drive or folder.

Cutting and Pasting a Workbook

You can remove a workbook from one folder and insert it in another folder using the *Cut* and *Paste* options from the shortcut menu at the Open dialog box. To do this, display the Open dialog box, position the arrow pointer on the workbook to be removed (cut), click the right mouse button, and then click *Cut* at the shortcut menu. Change to the desired folder or drive, position the arrow pointer in any blank area in the Content pane, click the right mouse button, and then click *Paste* at the shortcut menu.

Quick Steps

Move a Workbook

1. Display Open dialog box.
2. Right-click workbook name.
3. Click *Cut*.
4. Navigate to desired folder.
5. Right-click blank area in Content pane.
6. Click *Paste*.

Project 1f Cutting and Pasting a Workbook — Part 6 of 8

1. Display the Open dialog box with the EL1C6 folder active.
2. Position the arrow pointer on **FinCon.xlsx**, click the right mouse button, and then click *Cut* at the shortcut menu.
3. Double-click *Finances* to make it the active folder.
4. Position the arrow pointer in any blank area in the Content pane, click the right mouse button, and then click *Paste* at the shortcut menu.
5. Click *EL1C6* that displays in the Address bar.

Quick Steps

Rename a Workbook

1. Display Open dialog box.
2. Click desired workbook.
3. Click Organize button.
4. Click *Rename*.
5. Type new name.
6. Press Enter.

OR

1. Display Open dialog box.
2. Right-click workbook name.
3. Click *Rename*.
4. Type new name.
5. Press Enter.

Renaming Workbooks

At the Open dialog box, use the *Rename* option from the Organize button drop-down list or the shortcut menu to give a workbook a different name. The *Rename* option changes the name of the workbook and keeps it in the same folder. To use *Rename*, display the Open dialog box, click once on the workbook to be renamed, click the Organize button, and then click *Rename* at the drop-down list. This causes a thin black border to surround the workbook name and the name to be selected. Type the new name and then press Enter.

You can also rename a workbook by right-clicking the workbook name at the Open dialog box and then clicking *Rename* at the shortcut menu. Type the new name for the workbook and then press the Enter key.

Project 1g Renaming a Workbook — Part 7 of 8

1. Make sure the Open dialog box displays with the EL1C6 folder the active folder.
2. Double-click *Finances* to make it the active folder.
3. Click once on ***FinCon.xlsx*** to select it.
4. Click the Organize button on the toolbar.
5. Click *Rename* at the drop-down list.
6. Type **Analysis** and then press the Enter key.

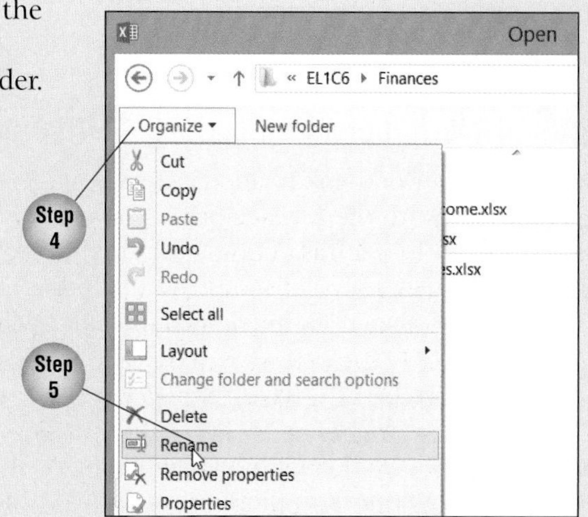

7. Complete steps similar to those in Steps 3 through 6 to rename **CMJanIncome.xlsx** to **CMJanProfits**.
8. Click the Back button (displays as *Back to EL1C6*) at the left side of the Address bar.

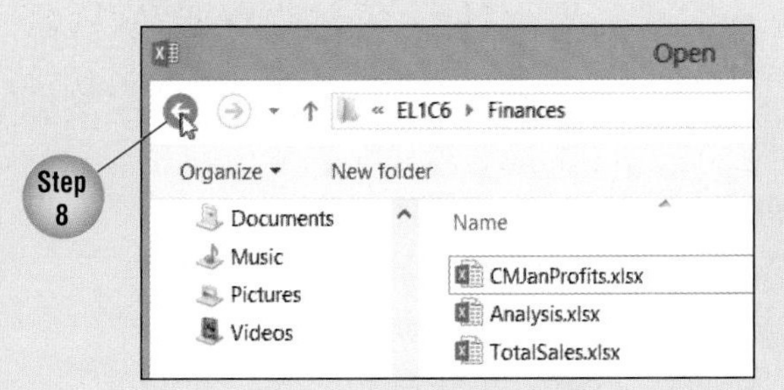

Deleting a Folder and Its Contents

As you learned earlier in this chapter, you can delete a workbook or selected workbooks. In addition to workbooks, you can delete a folder and all of its contents. Delete a folder in the same manner as you delete a workbook.

Project 1h **Deleting a Folder and Its Contents** **Part 8 of 8**

1. Make sure the Open dialog box displays with the EL1C6 folder active.
2. Right-click the *Finances* folder name in the Content pane.
3. Click *Delete* at the shortcut menu.
4. If you are deleting the folder from a removable drive, click Yes at the message that displays asking if you want to delete the folder.
5. Close the Open dialog box.

Project 2 Copy and Move Worksheets into an Equipment Rental Workbook

3 Parts

You will manage workbooks at the Open backstage area and then open multiple workbooks and copy and move worksheets between the workbooks.

Managing the Recent Workbooks List

When you open and close workbooks, Excel keeps a list of the most recently opened workbooks. To view this list, click the FILE tab and then click the *Open* option. This displays the Open backstage area, similar to what you see in Figure 6.2. (Your workbook names may vary from what you see in the figure.) The most recently opened workbook names display in the Recent Workbooks list, which displays when the *Recent Workbooks* option is selected. The most recently accessed folder names display in the Recent Folders list, which displays when the *Computer* option is selected. Generally, the 25 most recently opened workbook names display in the Recent Workbooks list. To open a workbook, scroll down the list and then click the desired workbook name.

The Excel opening screen contains a Recent list that displays the most recently opened workbooks. The workbook names in the Recent list are the same that display in the Recent Workbooks list at the Open backstage area.

Figure 6.2 Open Backstage Area

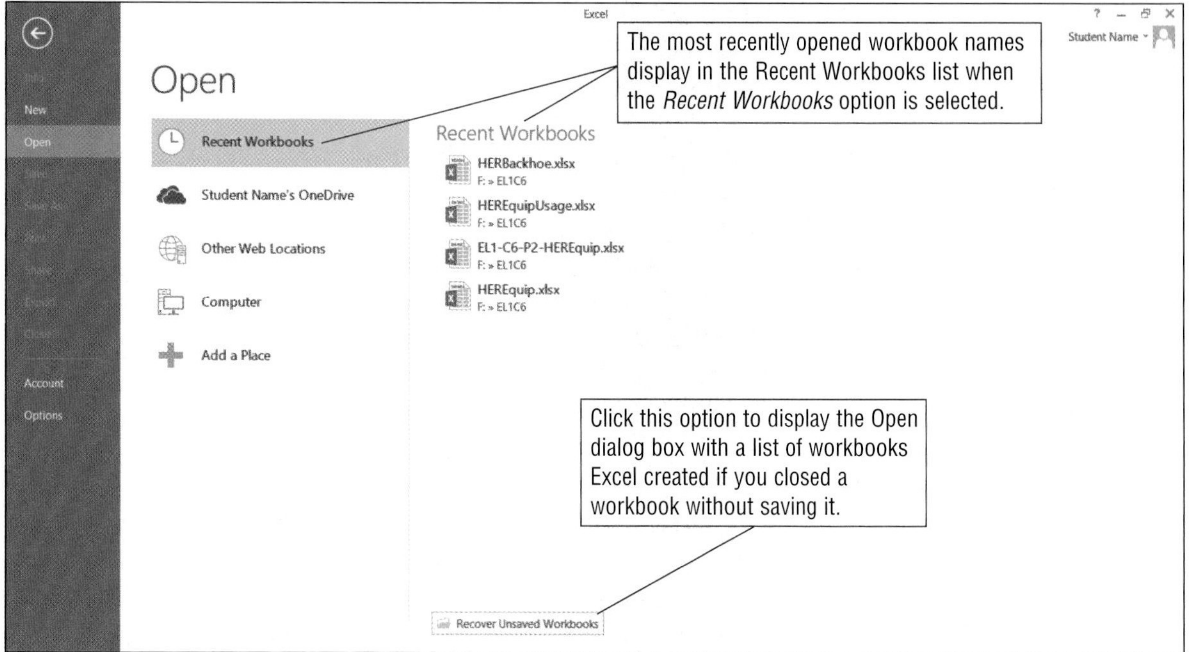

Pinning a Workbook

If you want a workbook name to remain at the top of the Recent Workbooks list, at the Open backstage area or the Recent list at the Excel opening screen "pin" the workbook name. To do this, click the gray pin that displays at the right side of the workbook name. This changes the left-pointing pin to a down-pointing pin. The next time you display the Open backstage area or the Excel opening screen, the workbook name you pinned displays at the top of the list. To "unpin" a workbook name, click the down-pointing pin to change it to a left-pointing pin. You can also pin a workbook name to the Recent Workbooks list or Recent list by right-clicking the workbook name and then clicking *Pin to list* at the shortcut menu. To unpin the workbook name, right-click the workbook name and then click *Unpin from list* at the shortcut menu.

Recovering an Unsaved Workbook

If you close a workbook without saving it, you can recover it with the *Recover Unsaved Workbooks* option located below the Recent Workbooks list. Click this option and the Open dialog box displays with workbook names that Excel automatically saved. At this dialog box, double-click the desired workbook name to open the workbook.

Clearing the Recent Workbooks List and the Recent List

Clear the contents (except pinned workbooks) of the Recent Workbooks list or Recent list by right-clicking a workbook name in the list and then clicking *Clear unpinned Workbooks* at the shortcut menu. At the message asking if you are sure you want to remove the items, click the Yes button. To clear a folder in the Recent Folders list, right-click a folder in the list and then click *Remove from list* at the shortcut menu.

Project 2a **Managing Workbooks at the Open Backstage Area** **Part 1 of 3**

1. Close any open workbooks.
2. Click the FILE tab and then click the *Open* option.
3. Make sure the *Recent Workbooks* option is selected. Notice the workbook names that display in the Recent Workbooks list.
4. Navigate to the EL1C6 folder on your storage medium, open **HEREquip.xlsx**, and then save the workbook with Save As and name it **EL1-C6-P2-HEREquip**.
5. Close **EL1-C6-P2-HEREquip.xlsx**.
6. Open **HEREquipUsage.xlsx** and then close it.
7. Open **HERBackhoe.xlsx** and then close it.
8. Pin the three workbooks to the Recent Workbooks list (you will use them in Project 2b) by completing the following steps:
   a. Click the FILE tab and then make sure the *Open* option is selected. (This displays the Open backstage area with the *Recent Workbooks* option selected.)
   b. Click the left-pointing pin that displays at the right side of **EL1-C6-P2-HEREquip.xlsx**. (This rotates the pin from left pointing to down pointing.)

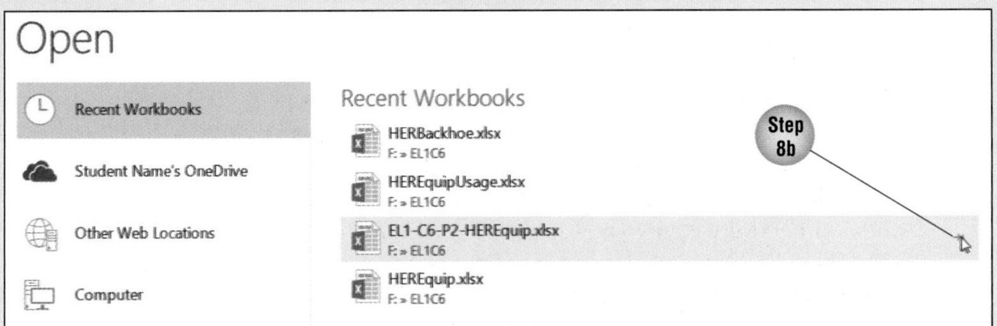

   c. Click the left-pointing pin that displays at the right side of **HEREquipUsage.xlsx**.

d. Right-click **HERBackhoe.xlsx** and then click *Pin to list* at the shortcut menu.
e. Click the Back button to exit the Open backstage area.

9. Open **EL1-C6-P2-HEREquip.xlsx** by clicking the FILE tab and then clicking ***EL1-C6-P2-HEREquip.xlsx*** in the Recent Workbooks list. (After clicking the FILE tab, make sure the *Open* option is selected. This displays the Open backstage area with *Recent Workbooks* selected.)

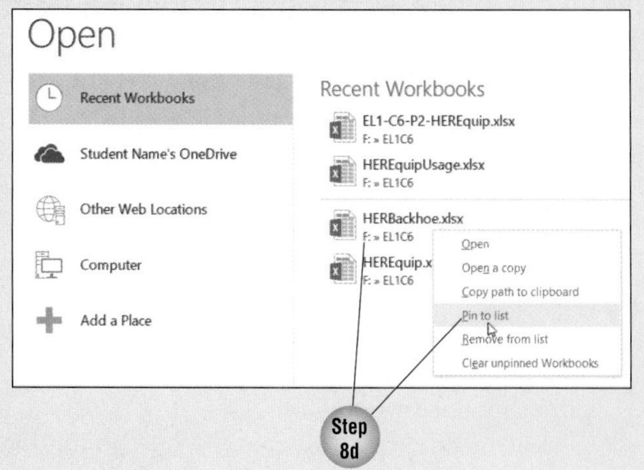

Managing Worksheets

Quick Steps

Copy a Worksheet to Another Workbook

1. Right-click desired sheet tab.
2. Click *Move or Copy*.
3. Select desired destination workbook.
4. Select desired worksheet location.
5. Click *Create a copy* check box.
6. Click OK.

You can move or copy individual worksheets within the same workbook or to another existing workbook. Exercise caution when moving sheets, since calculations or charts based on data in a worksheet might become inaccurate if you move the worksheet. To make a duplicate of a worksheet in the same workbook, hold down the Ctrl key and then drag the worksheet tab to the desired position.

Copying a Worksheet to Another Workbook

To copy a worksheet to another existing workbook, open both the source and the destination workbooks. Right-click the worksheet tab and then click *Move or Copy* at the shortcut menu. At the Move or Copy dialog box, shown in Figure 6.3, select the destination workbook name from the *To book* drop-down list, select the worksheet that you want the copied worksheet placed before in the *Before sheet* list box, click the *Create a copy* check box, and then click OK.

Figure 6.3 Move or Copy Dialog Box

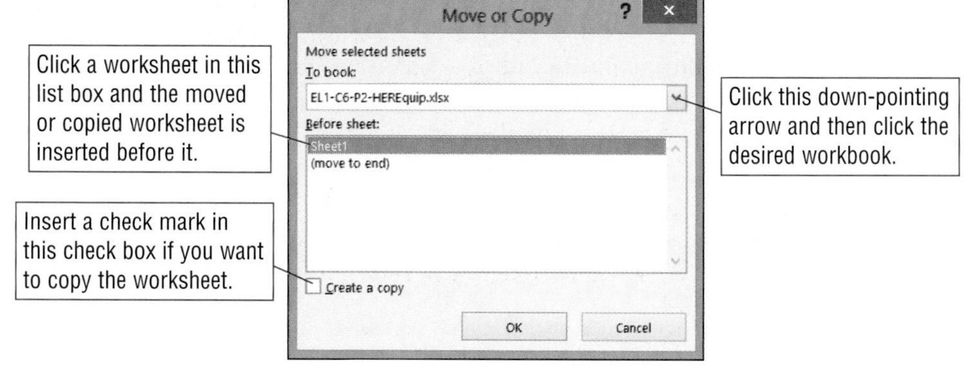

Project 2b **Copying a Worksheet to Another Workbook** **Part 2 of 3**

1. With **EL1-C6-P2-HEREquip.xlsx** open, open **HEREquipUsage.xlsx**.
2. Copy the Front Loader worksheet by completing the following steps:
   a. With **HEREquipUsage.xlsx** the active workbook, right-click the Front Loader tab and then click *Move or Copy* at the shortcut menu.
   b. Click the down-pointing arrow next to the *To book* option box and then click ***EL1-C6-P2-HEREquip.xlsx*** at the drop-down list.
   c. Click *(move to end)* in the *Before sheet* list box.
   d. Click the *Create a copy* check box to insert a check mark.
   e. Click OK. (Excel switches to the **EL1-C6-P2-HEREquip.xlsx** workbook and inserts the copied Front Loader worksheet after Sheet1.)
3. Complete steps similar to those in Step 2 to copy the Tractor worksheet to the **EL1-C6-P2-HEREquip.xlsx** workbook.
4. Complete steps similar to those in Step 2 to copy the Forklift worksheet to the **EL1-C6-P2-HEREquip.xlsx** workbook and insert the Forklift worksheet before the Tractor worksheet.
5. Save **EL1-C6-P2-HEREquip.xlsx**.
6. Make **HEREquipUsage.xlsx** the active workbook and then close it.

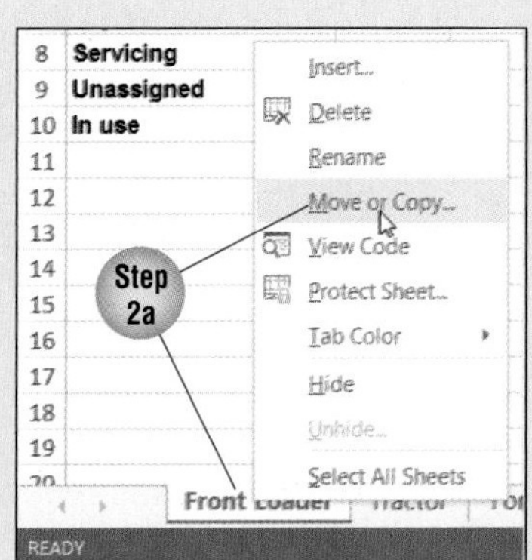

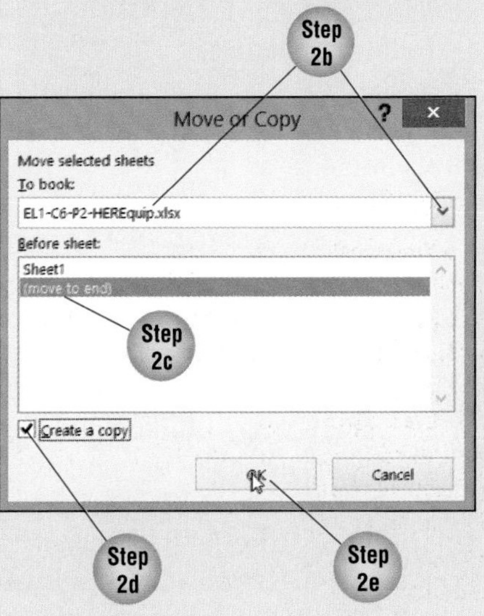

Moving a Worksheet to Another Workbook

To move a worksheet to another existing workbook, open both the source and the destination workbooks. Make active the worksheet you want to move in the source workbook, right-click the worksheet tab, and then click *Move or Copy* at the shortcut menu. At the Move or Copy dialog box, shown in Figure 6.3, select the destination workbook name from the *To book* drop-down list, select the worksheet before which you want the worksheet placed in the *Before sheet* list box, and then click OK. If you need to reposition a worksheet tab, drag the tab to the desired position.

Be careful when moving a worksheet to another workbook file. If formulas exist in the source workbook that depend on the contents of the cells in the worksheet that is moved, they will no longer calculate properly.

Quick Steps

Move a Worksheet to Another Workbook

1. Right-click desired worklsheet tab.
2. Click *Move or Copy*.
3. Select desired destination workbook.
4. Select desired worksheet location.
5. Click OK.

Project 2c Moving a Worksheet to Another Workbook Part 3 of 3

1. With **EL1-C6-P2-HEREquip.xlsx** open, open **HERBackhoe.xlsx**.
2. Move Sheet1 from **HERBackhoe.xlsx** to **EL1-C6-P2-HEREquip.xlsx** by completing the following steps:
   a. With **HERBackhoe.xlsx** the active workbook, right-click the Sheet1 tab and then click *Move or Copy* at the shortcut menu.
   b. Click the down-pointing arrow next to the *To book* option box and then click ***EL1-C6-P2-HEREquip.xlsx*** at the drop-down list.
   c. Click *(move to end)* in the *Before sheet* list box.
   d. Click OK.

3. With **EL1-C6-P2-HEREquip.xlsx** open, make the following changes:
   a. Rename Sheet1 as *Equipment Hours*.
   b. Rename Sheet1 (2) as *Backhoe*.
4. Create a range for the front loader total hours available by completing the following steps:
   a. Click the Front Loader tab.
   b. Select cells B4 through E4.
   c. Click in the Name box.
   d. Type **FrontLoaderHours**.
   e. Press Enter.

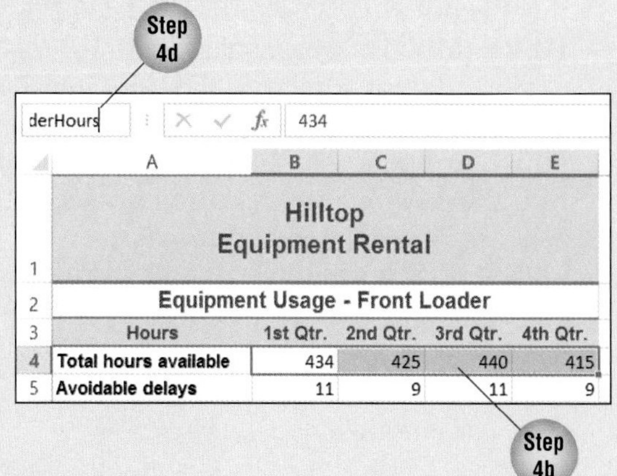

	A	B	C	D	E
1	Hilltop Equipment Rental				
2	Equipment Usage - Front Loader				
3	Hours	1st Qtr.	2nd Qtr.	3rd Qtr.	4th Qtr.
4	Total hours available	434	425	440	415
5	Avoidable delays	11	9	11	9

5. Complete steps similar to those in Step 4 to create the following ranges:
   a. In the Front Loader worksheet, create a range with cells B10 through E10 and name it *FrontLoaderHoursInUse*.
   b. Click the Forklift tab and then create a range with cells B4 through E4 and name it *ForkliftHours* and create a range with cells B10 through E10 and name it *ForkliftHoursInUse*.
   c. Click the Tractor tab and then create a range with cells B4 through E4 and name it *TractorHours* and create a range with cells B10 through E10 and name it *TractorHoursInUse*.
   d. Click the Backhoe tab and then create a range with cells B4 through E4 and name it *BackhoeHours* and create a range with cells B10 through E10 and name it *BackhoeHoursInUse*.
6. Click the Equipment Hours tab to make it the active worksheet and then insert a formula that calculates the total hours for the front loader by completing the following steps:
   a. Make cell C4 active.
   b. Type =SUM(Fr.
   c. When you type *Fr*, a drop-down list displays with the front loader ranges. Double-click *FrontLoaderHours*.

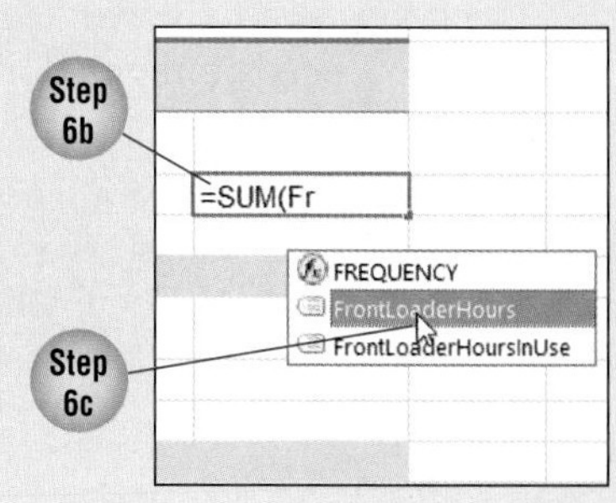

d. Type) (the closing parenthesis).
e. Press Enter.

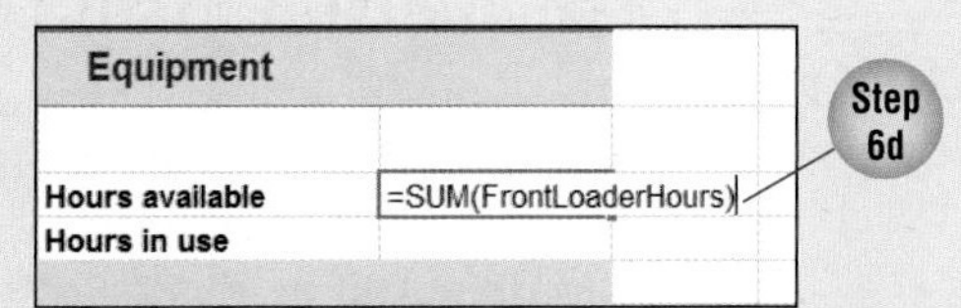

7. Complete steps similar to those in Step 6 to insert ranges in the following cells:
   a. Make cell C5 active and then insert a formula that calculates the total in-use hours for the front loader.
   b. Make cell C8 active and then insert a formula that calculates the total hours available for the forklift.
   c. Make cell C9 active and then insert a formula that calculates the total in-use hours for the forklift.
   d. Make cell C12 active and then insert a formula that calculates the total hours available for the tractor.
   e. Make cell C13 active and then insert a formula that calculates the total in-use hours for the tractor.
   f. Make cell C16 active and then insert a formula that calculates the total hours available for the backhoe.
   g. Make cell C17 active and then insert a formula that calculates the total in-use hours for the backhoe.
8. Make the following changes to specific worksheets:
   a. Click the Front Loader tab and then change the number in cell E4 from *415* to *426* and change the number in cell C6 from *6* to *14*.
   b. Click the Forklift tab and then change the number in cell E4 from *415* to *426* and change the number in cell D8 from *4* to *12*.
9. Select all of the worksheet tabs and then create a header that prints your name at the left side of each worksheet, the page number in the middle, and the current date at the right side.
10. Save and then print all of the worksheets in **EL1-C6-P2-HEREquip.xlsx**.
11. Close the workbook. (Make sure all workbooks are closed.)
12. Make the following changes to the Open backstage area.
    a. Click the FILE tab.
    b. Make sure the *Open* option is selected and *Recent Workbooks* is selected.
    c. Unpin **EL1-C6-P2-HEREquip.xlsx** from the Recent Workbooks list by clicking the down-pointing pin that displays at the right side of **EL1-C6-P2-HEREquip.xlsx**. (This changes the down-pointing pin to a left-pointing pin and moves the file down the list.)
    d. Unpin **HERBackhoe.xlsx** and **HEREquipUsage.xlsx**.
    e. Click the Back button to exit the Open backstage area.

Project 3 Create and Apply Styles to a Payroll Workbook — 5 Parts

You will open a payroll workbook, define and apply styles, and then modify the styles. You will also copy the styles to another workbook and then apply the styles in the new workbook.

Formatting with Cell Styles

In some worksheets, you may want to apply formatting to highlight or accentuate certain cells. You can apply formatting to a cell or selected cells with a cell style. A ***style*** is a predefined set of formatting attributes, such as font, font size, alignment, borders, shading, and so forth. You can use one of the predesigned styles from the Cell Styles drop-down gallery or create your own style.

Quick Steps

Apply a Cell Style
1. Select desired cell(s).
2. Click Cell Styles button.
3. Click desired style.

Cell Styles

Applying a Style

To apply a style, select the desired cell(s), click the Cell Styles button in the Styles group on the HOME tab, and then click the desired option at the drop-down gallery shown in Figure 6.4. If you hover your mouse pointer over a style in the drop-down gallery, the cell or selected cells display with the formatting applied.

Figure 6.4 Cell Styles Drop-Down Gallery

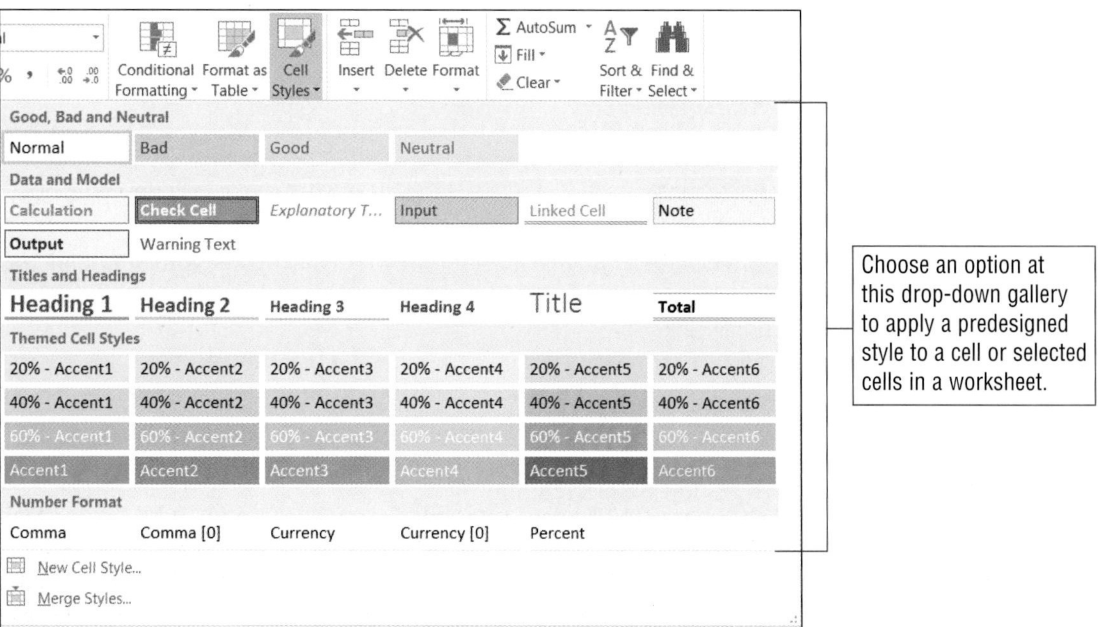

Project 3a **Formatting with Cell Styles** **Part 1 of 5**

1. Open **OEPayroll.xlsx** and then save the workbook with Save As and name it **EL1-C6-P3-OEPayroll**.
2. With Sheet1 the active worksheet, insert the necessary formulas to calculate gross pay, withholding tax amount, social security tax amount, and net pay. ***Hint: Refer to Project 3c in Chapter 2 for assistance***. Select cells D4 through G4 and then click the Accounting Number Format button to insert dollar signs.
3. Make Sheet2 active and then insert a formula that calculates the amount due. Make cell F4 active and then click the Accounting Number Format button to insert a dollar sign.

4. Make Sheet3 active and then insert a formula in the *Due Date* column that calculates the purchase date plus the number of days in the *Terms* column. ***Hint: The formula in cell F4 will be =D4+E4.***
5. Apply cell styles to cells by completing the following steps:
   a. Make Sheet1 active and then select cells A11 and A12.
   b. Click the Cell Styles button in the Styles group on the HOME tab.
   c. At the drop-down gallery, hover your mouse over styles to see how the style formatting affects the selected cells.
   d. Click the *Check Cell* option in the *Data and Model* section.
6. Select cells B11 and B12, click the Cell Styles button, and then click the *Output* option in the *Data and Model* section (first column, second row in the *Data and Model* section).

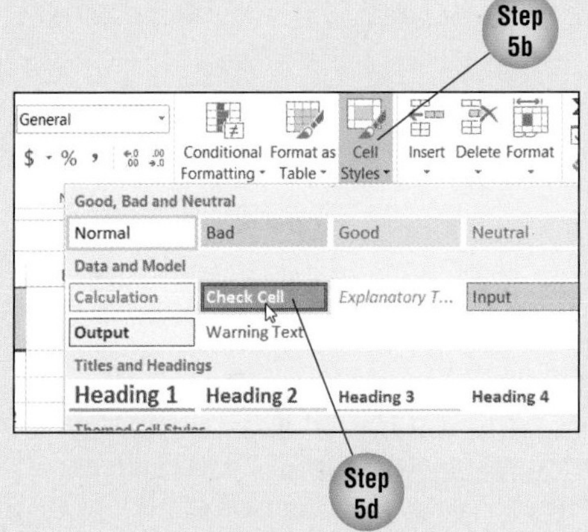

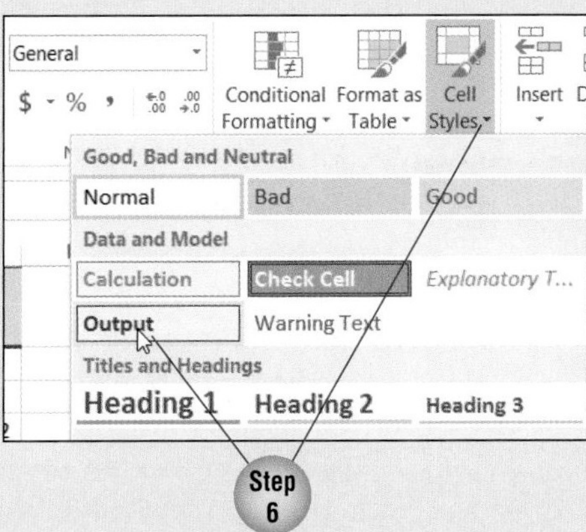

7. Save **EL1-C6-P3-OEPayroll.xlsx.**

Defining a Cell Style

You can apply a style from the Cell Styles drop-down gallery or you can create your own style. Using a style to apply formatting has several advantages. A style helps to ensure consistent formatting from one worksheet to another. Once you define all attributes for a particular style, you do not have to redefine them again. If you need to change the formatting, change the style and all cells formatted with that style automatically reflect the change.

Two basic methods are available for defining your own cell style. You can define a style with formats already applied to a cell or you can display the Style dialog box, click the Format button, and then choose formatting options at the Format Cells dialog box. Styles you create are available only in the workbook in which they are created.

To define a style with existing formatting, select the cell or cells containing the desired formatting, click the Cell Styles button in the Styles group on the HOME tab, and then click the *New Cell Style* option located toward the bottom of the drop-down gallery. At the Style dialog box, shown in Figure 6.5, type a name for the new style in the *Style name* text box and then click OK to close the dialog box. The styles you create display at the top of the drop-down gallery in the *Custom* section when you click the Cell Styles button.

Quick Steps

Define a Cell Style with Existing Formatting
1. Select cell containing formatting.
2. Click Cell Styles button.
3. Click *New Cell Style.*
4. Type name for new style.
5. Click OK.

Cell styles are based on the workbook theme.

Figure 6.5 Style Dialog Box

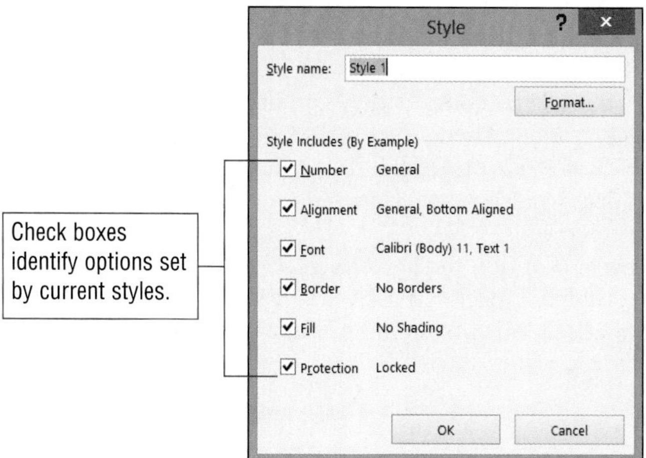

Project 3b Defining and Applying a Style

Part 2 of 5

1. With **EL1-C6-P3-OEPayroll.xlsx** open, define a style named *C06Title* with the formatting in cell A1 by completing the following steps:
   a. Make sure Sheet1 is active and then make cell A1 active.
   b. Click the Cell Styles button in the Styles group on the HOME tab and then click the *New Cell Style* option located toward the bottom of the drop-down gallery.
   c. At the Style dialog box, type **C06Title** in the *Style name* text box.
   d. Click OK.

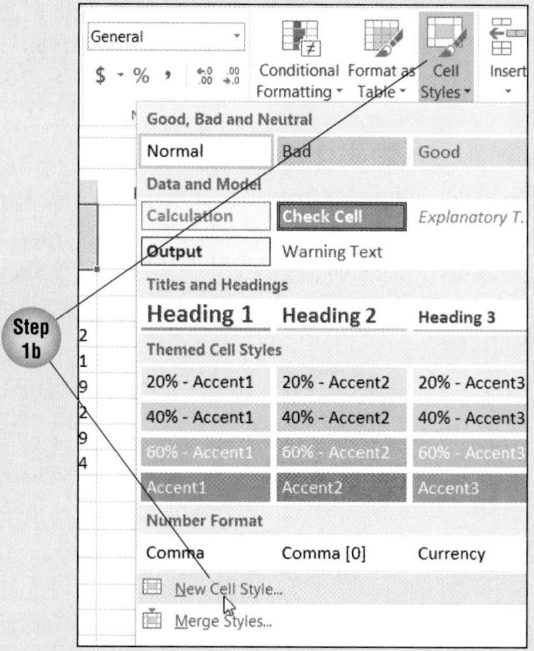

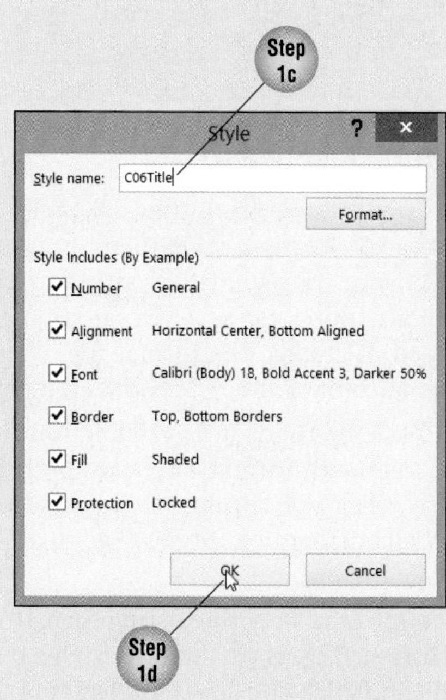

2. Even though cell A1 is already formatted, the style has not been applied to it. (Later, you will modify the style and the style must be applied to the cell for the change to affect it.) Apply the C06Title style to cell A1 by completing the following steps:
   a. Make sure cell A1 is the active cell.

b. Click the Cell Styles button in the Styles group on the HOME tab.
c. Click the *C06Title* style in the *Custom* section located toward the top of the drop-down gallery.

3. Apply the C06Title style to other cells by completing the following steps:
   a. Click the Sheet2 tab.
   b. Make cell A1 active.
   c. Click the Cell Styles button in the Styles group and then click the *C06Title* style at the drop-down gallery. (Notice that the style did not apply the row height formatting. The style applies only cell formatting.)
   d. Click the Sheet3 tab.
   e. Make cell A1 active.
   f. Click the Cell Styles button and then click the *C06Title* style at the drop-down gallery.
   g. Click the Sheet1 tab.
4. Save **EL1-C6-P3-OEPayroll.xlsx**.

In addition to defining a style based on cell formatting, you can also define a new style without first applying the formatting. To do this, you would display the Style dialog box, type a name for the new style, and then click the Format button. At the Format Cells dialog box, apply any desired formatting and then click OK to close the dialog box. At the Style dialog box, remove the check mark from any formatting that you do not want included in the style and then click OK to close the Style dialog box.

Quick Steps

Define a Style
1. Click in blank cell.
2. Click Cell Styles button.
3. Click *New Cell Style.*
4. Type name for style.
5. Click Format button.
6. Choose formatting options.
7. Click OK.
8. Click OK.

Project 3c Defining a Style without First Applying Formatting — Part 3 of 5

1. With **EL1-C6-P3-OEPayroll.xlsx** open, define a new style named *C06Subtitle* without first applying the formatting by completing the following steps:
   a. With Sheet1 active, click in any empty cell.
   b. Click the Cell Styles button in the Styles group and then click *New Cell Style* at the drop-down gallery.
   c. At the Style dialog box, type **C06Subtitle** in the *Style name* text box.
   d. Click the Format button in the Style dialog box.
   e. At the Format Cells dialog box, click the Font tab.
   f. At the Format Cells dialog box with the Font tab selected, change the font to Candara, the font style to bold, the size to 12 points, and the color to White, Background 1.

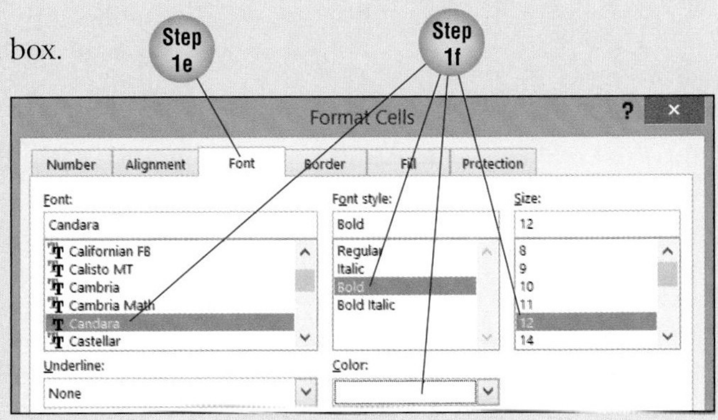

g. Click the Fill tab.
h. Click the green option shown at the right (last column, fifth row in the palette).
i. Click the Alignment tab.
j. Change the horizontal alignment to center alignment.
k. Click OK to close the Format Cells dialog box.
l. Click OK to close the Style dialog box.

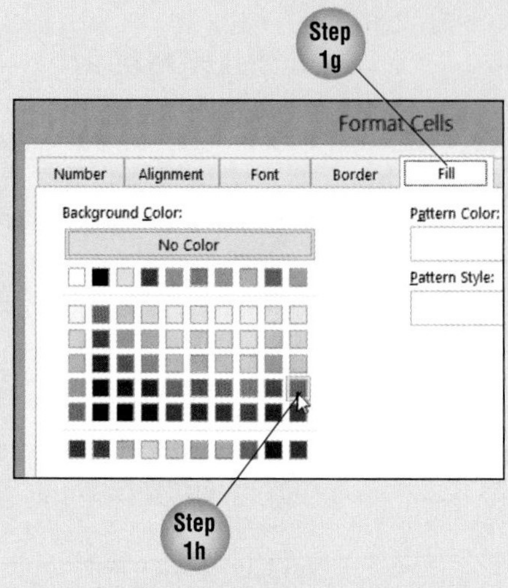

2. Apply the C06Subtitle style by completing the following steps:
   a. Make cell A2 active.
   b. Click the Cell Styles button and then click the *C06Subtitle* style located toward the top of the drop-down gallery in the *Custom* section.
   c. Click the Sheet2 tab.
   d. Make cell A2 active.
   e. Click the Cell Styles button and then click the *C06Subtitle* style.
   f. Click the Sheet3 tab.
   g. Make cell A2 active.
   h. Click the Cell Styles button and then click the *C06Subtitle* style.
   i. Click the Sheet1 tab.
3. Apply the following predesigned cell styles:
   a. Select cells A3 through G3.
   b. Click the Cell Styles button and then click the *Heading 3* style at the drop-down gallery.
   c. Select cells A5 through G5.
   d. Click the Cell Styles button and then click the *20% - Accent3* style.
   e. Apply the 20% - Accent3 style to cells A7 through G7 and cells A9 through G9.
   f. Click the Sheet2 tab.
   g. Select cells A3 through F3 and then apply the Heading 3 style.
   h. Select cells A5 through F5 and then apply the 20% - Accent3 style.
   i. Apply the 20% - Accent3 style to every other row of cells (cells A7 through F7, A9 through F9, and so on, finishing with cells A17 through F17).
   j. Click the Sheet3 tab.
   k. Select cells A3 through F3 and then apply the Heading 3 style.
   l. Apply the 20% - Accent3 style to cells A5 through F5, A7 through F7, and A9 through F9.
4. With Sheet3 active, change the height of row 1 to 36.00 points.
5. Make Sheet2 active and then change the height of row 1 to 36.00 points.
6. Make Sheet1 active.
7. Save **EL1-C6-P3-OEPayroll.xlsx** and then print only the first worksheet.

Modifying a Style

One of the advantages to formatting with a style is that you can modify the formatting of the style and all cells formatted with that style automatically reflect the change. You can modify a style you create or one of the predesigned styles provided by Excel. When you modify a predesigned style, only the style in the current workbook is affected. If you open a blank workbook, the cell styles available are the default styles.

To modify a style, click the Cell Styles button in the Styles group on the HOME tab and then right-click the desired style at the drop-down gallery. At the shortcut menu that displays, click *Modify*. At the Style dialog box, click the Format button. Make the desired formatting changes at the Format Cells dialog box and then click OK. Click OK to close the Style dialog box and any cells formatted with the specific style are automatically updated.

Quick Steps

Modify a Style

1. Click Cell Styles button.
2. Right-click desired style at drop-down gallery.
3. Click *Modify*.
4. Click Format button.
5. Make desired formatting changes.
6. Click OK to close Format Cells dialog box.
7. Click OK to close Style dialog box.

Project 3d **Modifying Styles** **Part 4 of 5**

1. With **EL1-C6-P3-OEPayroll.xlsx** open, modify the C06Title style by completing the following steps:
   a. Click in any empty cell.
   b. Click the Cell Styles button in the Styles group.
   c. At the drop-down gallery, right-click the *C06Title* style located toward the top of the gallery in the *Custom* section and then click *Modify*.
   d. At the Style dialog box, click the Format button.
   e. At the Format Cells dialog box, click the Font tab and then change the font to Candara.
   f. Click the Alignment tab.
   g. Click the down-pointing arrow to the right of the *Vertical* option box and then click *Center* at the drop-down list.
   h. Click the Fill tab.
   i. Click the light blue fill color as shown at the right (fifth column, third row in the palette).
   j. Click OK to close the Format Cells dialog box.
   k. Click OK to close the Style dialog box.

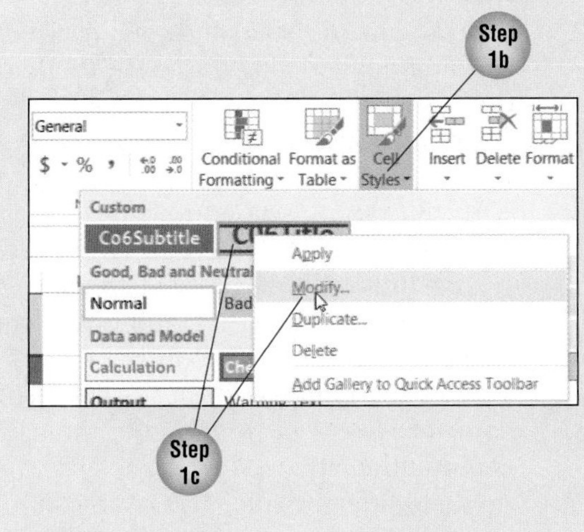

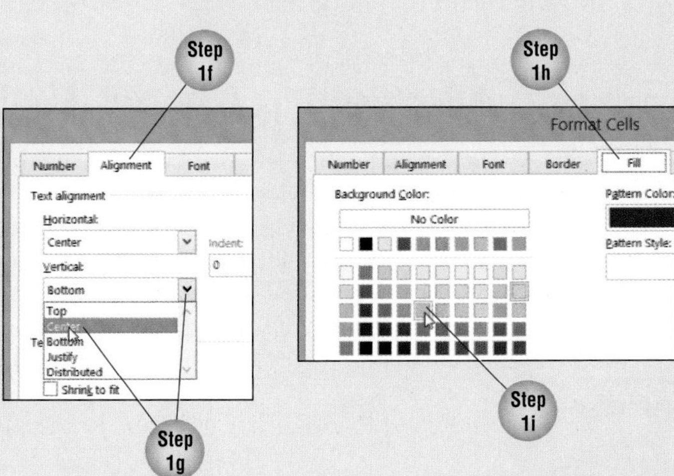

2. Modify the C06Subtitle style by completing the following steps:
   a. Click in any empty cell.
   b. Click the Cell Styles button in the Styles group.
   c. At the drop-down gallery, right-click on the *C06Subtitle* style located toward the top of the gallery in the *Custom* section and then click *Modify*.
   d. At the Style dialog box, click the Format button.
   e. At the Format Cells dialog box, click the Font tab and then change the font to Calibri.
   f. Click the Fill tab.
   g. Click the dark blue fill color as shown at the right (fifth column, sixth row in the palette).
   h. Click OK to close the Format Cells dialog box.
   i. Click OK to close the Style dialog box.

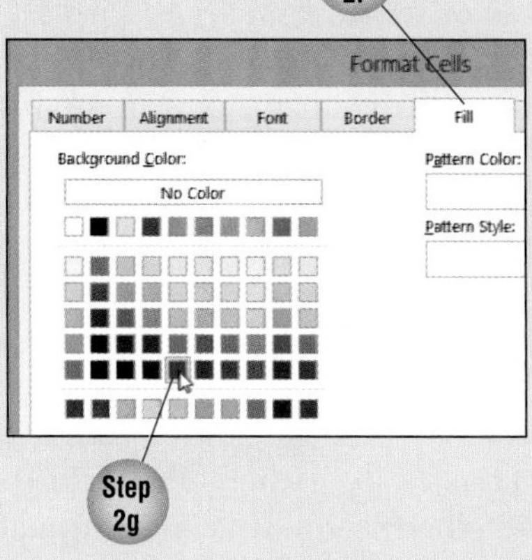

3. Modify the predefined 20% - Accent3 style by completing the following steps:
   a. Click the Cell Styles button in the Styles group.
   b. At the drop-down gallery, right-click on the *20% - Accent3* style and then click *Modify*.
   c. At the Style dialog box, click the Format button.
   d. At the Format Cells dialog box, make sure the Fill tab is active.
   e. Click the light blue fill color as shown at the right (fifth column, second row in the palette).
   f. Click OK to close the Format Cells dialog box.
   g. Click OK to close the Style dialog box.

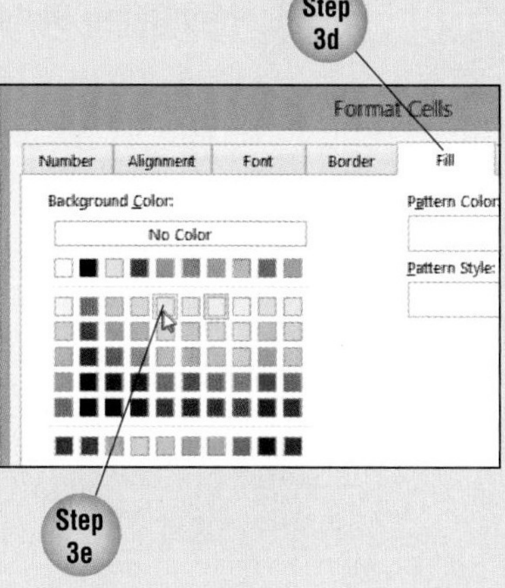

4. Click each worksheet tab and notice the formatting changes made by the modified styles.
5. Change the name of Sheet1 to *Weekly Payroll*, the name of Sheet2 to *Invoices*, and the name of Sheet3 to *Overdue Accounts*.
6. Apply a different color to each of the three worksheet tabs.
7. Save and then print all the worksheets in **EL1-C6-P3-OEPayroll.xlsx**.

Quick Steps

Copy Styles to Another Workbook
1. Open workbook containing desired styles.
2. Open workbook to be modified.
3. Click Cell Styles button.
4. Click *Merge Styles* option.
5. Double-click name of workbook that contains styles.

Copying Styles to Another Workbook

Styles you define are saved with the workbook in which they are created. You can, however, copy styles from one workbook to another. To do this, open the workbook containing the styles you want to copy and open the workbook into which you want to copy the styles. Click the Cell Styles button in the Styles group on the HOME tab and then click the *Merge Styles* option located at the bottom of the drop-down gallery. At the Merge Styles dialog box, shown in Figure 6.6, double-click the name of the workbook that contains the styles you want to copy.

Figure 6.6 Merge Styles Dialog Box

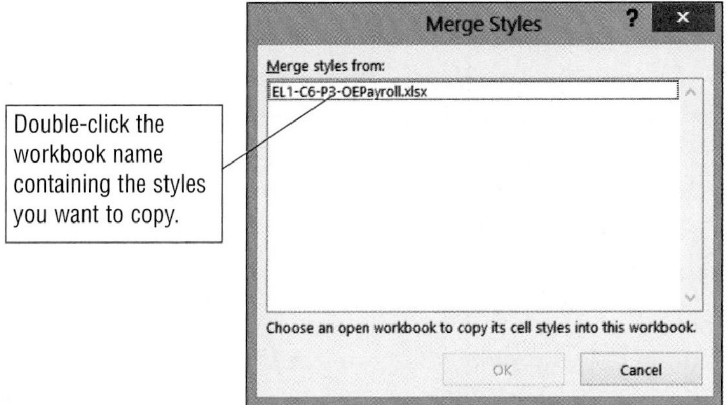

The Undo command will not reverse the effects of the Merge Styles dialog box.

Quick Steps

Remove a Style
1. Select cells formatted with style to be removed.
2. Click Cell Styles button.
3. Click *Normal* at drop-down gallery.

Delete a Style
1. Click Cell Styles button.
2. Right-click style to be deleted.
3. Click *Delete* at shortcut menu.

Removing a Style

If you apply a style to text and then decide you do not want it applied, return the formatting to Normal, which is the default. To do this, select the cells formatted with the style you want to remove, click the Cell Styles button, and then click *Normal* at the drop-down gallery.

Deleting a Style

To delete a style, click the Cell Styles button in the Styles group on the HOME tab. At the drop-down gallery that displays, right-click the style you want to delete and then click *Delete* at the shortcut menu. Formatting applied by the deleted style is removed from cells in the workbook.

You cannot delete the Normal style.

Project 3e **Copying Styles** **Part 5 of 5**

1. With **EL1-C6-P3-OEPayroll.xlsx** open, open **OEPlans.xlsx**.
2. Save the workbook with Save As and name it **EL1-C6-P3-OEPlans**.
3. Copy the styles in **EL1-C6-P3-OEPayroll.xlsx** into **EL1-C6-P3-OEPlans.xlsx** by completing the following steps:
   a. Click the Cell Styles button in the Styles group on the HOME tab.
   b. Click the *Merge Styles* option located toward the bottom of the drop-down gallery.
   c. At the Merge Styles dialog box, double-click ***EL1-C6-P3-OEPayroll.xlsx*** in the *Merge styles from* list box.
   d. At the message that displays asking if you want to merge styles that have the same names, click Yes.

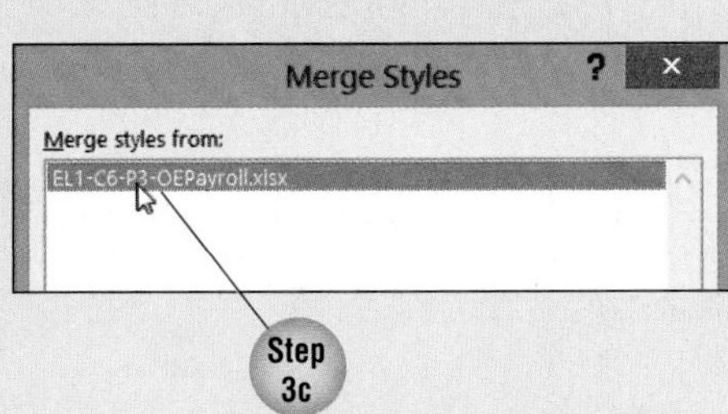

4. Apply the C06Title style to cell A1 and the C06Subtitle style to cell A2.
5. Increase the height of row 1 to 36.00 points.
6. Save, print, and then close **EL1-C6-P3-OEPlans.xlsx**.
7. Close **EL1-C6-P3-OEPayroll.xlsx**.

Project 4 Insert, Modify, and Remove Hyperlinks — 3 Parts

You will open a facilities account workbook and then insert hyperlinks to a website, to cells in other worksheets in the workbook, and to another workbook. You will modify and edit hyperlinks and then remove a hyperlink from the workbook.

Inserting Hyperlinks

Quick Steps

Insert Hyperlink
1. Click INSERT tab.
2. Click Hyperlink button.
3. Make desired changes at Insert Hyperlink dialog box.
4. Click OK.

Hyperlink

A hyperlink in a workbook can serve a number of purposes: Click it to navigate to a web page on the Internet or a specific location in the workbook, to display a different workbook, to open a file in a different program, to create a new document, or to link to an email address. Create a customized hyperlink by clicking the desired cell in a workbook, clicking the INSERT tab, and then clicking the Hyperlink button in the Links group. This displays the Insert Hyperlink dialog box, shown in Figure 6.7. At this dialog box, identify what you want to link to and the location of the link. Click the ScreenTip button to customize the hyperlink ScreenTip.

Linking to an Existing Web Page or File

Link to a web page on the Internet by typing a web address or with the Existing File or Web Page button in the *Link to* section. To link to an existing web page, type the address of the web page, such as *www.emcp.com*. By default, the automatic formatting of hyperlinks is turned on and the web address is formatted as a hyperlink. (The text is underlined and the color is changed to blue.)

You can turn off the automatic formatting of hyperlinks at the AutoCorrect dialog box. Display this dialog box by clicking the FILE tab, clicking *Options*, and then clicking *Proofing* in the left panel of the Excel Options dialog box. Click the AutoCorrect Options button to display the AutoCorrect dialog box. At this dialog

Figure 6.7 Insert Hyperlink Dialog Box

Type the text to display in the hyperlink.

Click this button to edit the hyperlink ScreenTip.

Click a button in this section to indicate the hyperlink location.

Type a web address in this text box.

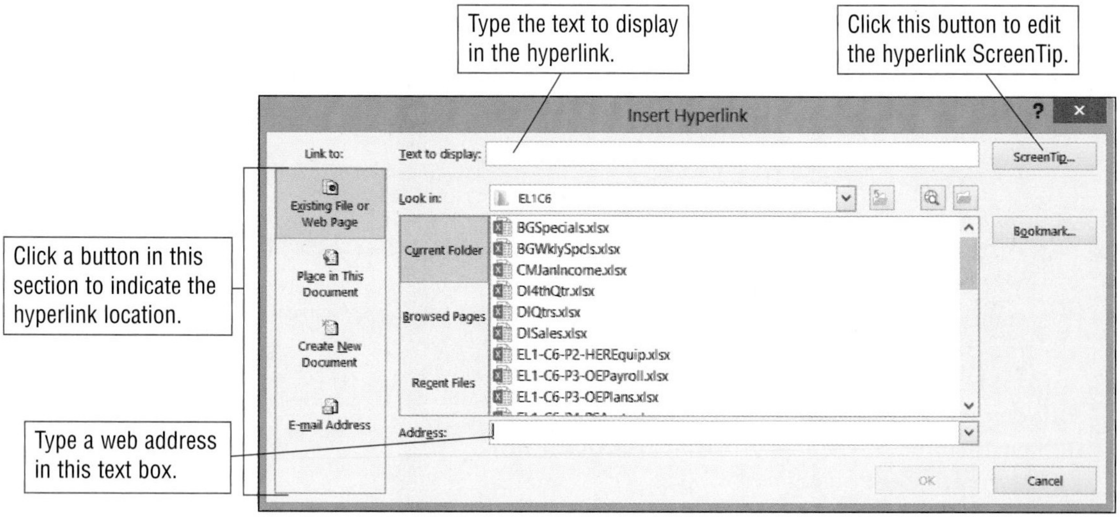

box, click the AutoFormat As You Type tab and then remove the check mark from the *Internet and network paths with hyperlinks* check box. To link to a web page at the Insert Hyperlink dialog box, display the dialog box, click the Existing File or Web Page button in the *Link to* section and then type the web address in the *Address* text box.

In some situations, you may want to provide information to your readers from a variety of sources. For example, you may want to provide additional information in an Excel workbook, a Word document, or a PowerPoint presentation. To link an Excel workbook to a workbook or file in another application, display the Insert Hyperlink dialog box and then click the Existing File or Web Page button in the *Link to* section. Use buttons in the *Look in* section to navigate to the folder containing the desired file and then click the file. Make other changes in the Insert Hyperlink dialog box as needed and then click OK.

Navigating Using Hyperlinks

Navigate to a hyperlinked location by clicking the hyperlink in the worksheet. Hover the mouse over the hyperlink and a ScreenTip displays with the address of the hyperlinked location. If you want specific information to display in the ScreenTip, click the ScreenTip button in the Insert Hyperlink dialog box, type the desired text in the Set Hyperlink ScreenTip dialog box, and then click OK.

Project 4a Linking to a Website and Another Workbook — Part 1 of 3

1. Open **PSAccts.xlsx** and then save the workbook with Save As and name it **EL1-C6-P4-PSAccts**.
2. Insert a hyperlink to information about Pyramid Sales, a fictitious company (the hyperlink will connect to the publishing company website), by completing the following steps:
   a. Make cell A13 active.
   b. Click the INSERT tab and then click the Hyperlink button in the Links group.
   c. At the Insert Hyperlink dialog box, if necessary, click the Existing File or Web Page button in the *Link to* section.
   d. Type **www.emcp.com** in the *Address* text box.
   e. Select the text that displays in the *Text to display* text box and then type **Company information**.
   f. Click the ScreenTip button located in the upper right corner of the dialog box.

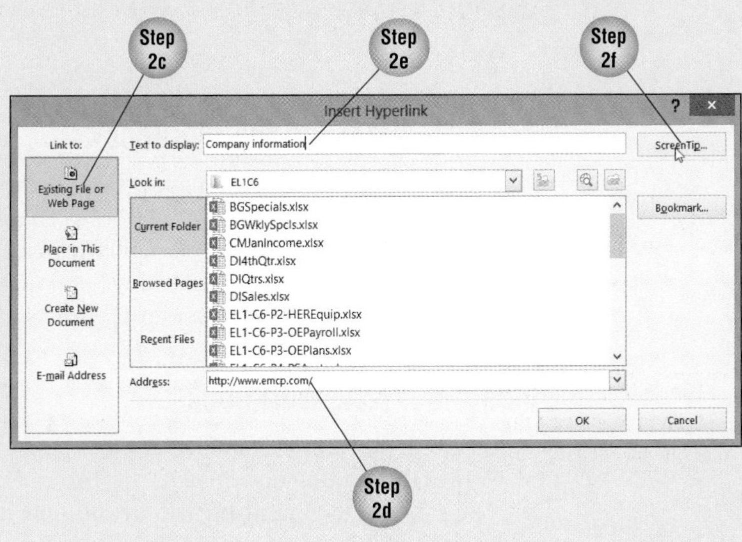

g. At the Set Hyperlink ScreenTip dialog box, type **View the company website.** and then click OK.
h. Click OK to close the Insert Hyperlink dialog box.

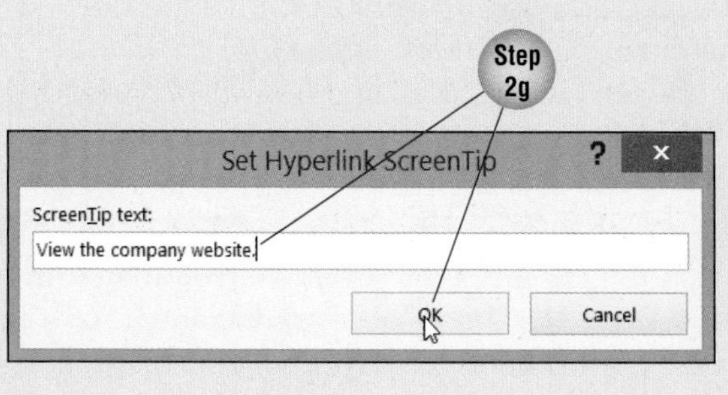

3. Navigate to the company website (in this case, the publishing company website) by clicking the Company information hyperlink in cell A13.
4. Close the Web browser.

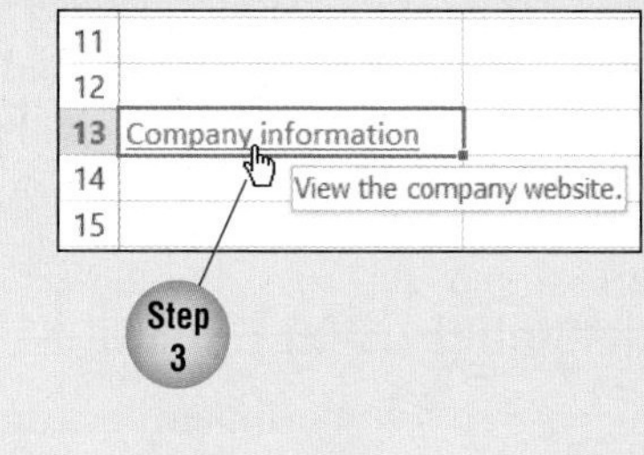

5. Create a link to another workbook by completing the following steps:
   a. Make cell A11 active, type **Semiannual sales**, and then press the Enter key.
   b. Make cell A11 active and then click the Hyperlink button in the Links group on the INSERT tab.
   c. At the Insert Hyperlink dialog box, make sure the Existing File or Web Page button is selected.
   d. If necessary, click the down-pointing arrow at the right side of the *Look in* option box and then navigate to the EL1C6 folder on your storage medium.
   e. Double-click ***PSSalesAnalysis.xlsx***.
6. Click the Semiannual sales hyperlink to open **PSSalesAnalysis.xlsx**.
7. Look at the information in the workbook and then close it.
8. Save **EL1-C6-P4-PSAccts.xlsx**.

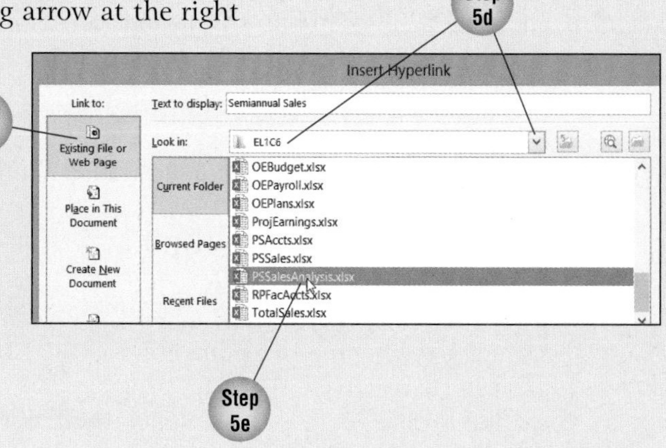

Linking to a Place in the Workbook

To create a hyperlink to another location in the workbook, click the Place in This Document button in the *Link to* section in the Edit Hyperlink dialog box. If you are linking to a cell within the same worksheet, type the cell name in the *Type the cell reference* text box. If you are linking to another worksheet in the workbook, click the desired worksheet name in the *Or select a place in this document* list box.

Linking to a New Workbook

In addition to linking to an existing workbook, you can create a hyperlink to a new workbook. To do this, display the Insert Hyperlink dialog box and then click the Create New Document button in the *Link to* section. Type a name for the new workbook in the *Name of new document* text box and then specify if you want to edit the workbook now or later.

Linking Using a Graphic

You can use a graphic, such as a clip art image, picture, or text box, to hyperlink to a file or website. To hyperlink with a graphic, select the graphic, click the INSERT tab, and then click the Hyperlink button. You can also right-click the graphic and then click *Hyperlink* at the shortcut menu. At the Insert Hyperlink dialog box, specify the location you want to link to and the text you want to display in the hyperlink.

Linking to an Email Address

You can insert a hyperlink to an email address at the Insert Hyperlink dialog box. To do this, click the E-mail Address button in the *Link to* section, type the desired address in the *E-mail address* text box, and then type a subject for the email in the *Subject* text box. Click in the *Text to display* text box and then type the text you want to display in the worksheet.

Project 4b **Linking to a Place in a Workbook, to Another Workbook, and Using a Graphic** **Part 2 of 3**

1. With **EL1-C6-P4-PSAccts.xlsx** open, create a link from the checks amount in cell B6 to the checks amount in cell G20 in the January worksheet by completing the following steps:
   a. Make cell B6 active.
   b. Click the Hyperlink button in the Links group on the INSERT tab.
   c. At the Insert Hyperlink dialog box, click the Place in This Document button in the *Link to* section.
   d. Select the text in the *Type the cell reference* text box and then type G20.
   e. Click *January* in the *Or select a place in this document* list box.
   f. Click OK to close the Insert Hyperlink dialog box.

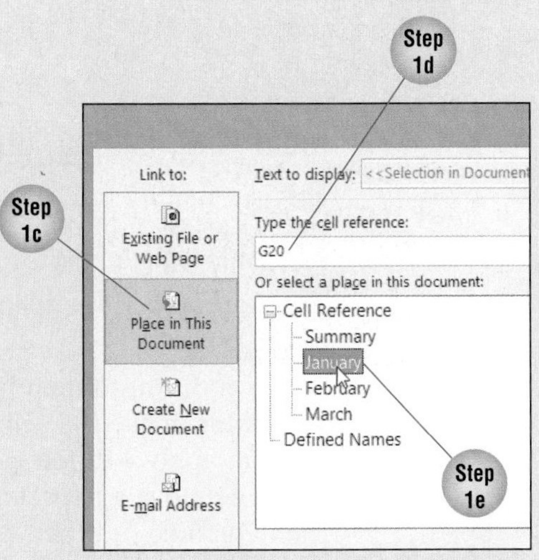

2. Make cell C6 active and then complete steps similar to those in Steps 1b through 1f except click *February* in the *Or select a place in this document* list box.
3. Make cell D6 active and then complete steps similar to those in Steps 1b through 1f except click *March* in the *Or select a place in this document* list box.
4. Click the hyperlinked amount in cell B6. (This makes cell G20 active in the January worksheet.)
5. Click the Summary worksheet tab.
6. Click the hyperlinked amount in cell C6. (This makes cell G20 active in the February worksheet.)
7. Click the Summary worksheet tab.
8. Click the hyperlinked amount in cell D6. (This makes cell G20 active in the March worksheet.)
9. Click the Summary worksheet tab.

10. Use the first pyramid graphic image in cell A1 to create a link to the company web page by completing the following steps:
    a. Right-click the first pyramid graphic image in cell A1 and then click *Hyperlink* at the shortcut menu.
    b. At the Insert Hyperlink dialog box, if necessary, click the Existing File or Web Page button in the *Link to* section.
    c. Type **www.emcp.com** in the *Address* text box.
    d. Click the ScreenTip button located in the upper right corner of the dialog box.
    e. At the Set Hyperlink ScreenTip dialog box, type **View the company website.** and then click OK.
    f. Click OK to close the Insert Hyperlink dialog box.
11. Make cell A5 active.
12. Navigate to the company website (the publishing company website) by clicking the first pyramid graphic image.
13. Close the Web browser.
14. Save **EL1-C6-P4-PSAccts.xlsx**.

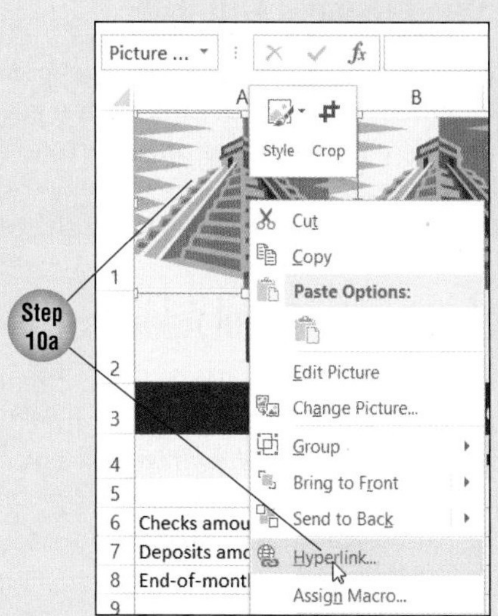

Modifying, Editing, and Removing a Hyperlink

You can modify or change the hyperlink text or destination. To do this, right-click the hyperlink and then click *Edit Hyperlink* at the shortcut menu. At the Edit Hyperlink dialog box, make any desired changes and then close the dialog box. The Edit Hyperlink dialog box contains the same options as the Insert Hyperlink dialog box.

In addition to modifying the hyperlink, you can edit hyperlink text in a cell. To do this, make the cell active and then make the desired changes. For example, you can apply a different font or font size, change the text color, and apply a text effect. Remove a hyperlink from a workbook by right-clicking the cell containing the hyperlink and then clicking *Remove Hyperlink* at the shortcut menu.

Project 4c Modifying, Editing, and Removing a Hyperlink — Part 3 of 3

1. With **EL1-C6-P4-PSAccts.xlsx** open, modify the Semiannual sales hyperlink by completing the following steps:
    a. Position the mouse pointer on the Semiannual sales hyperlink in cell A11, click the right mouse button, and then click *Edit Hyperlink* at the shortcut menu.
    b. At the Edit Hyperlink dialog box, select the text *Semiannual sales* in the *Text to display* text box and then type **Customer sales analysis**.

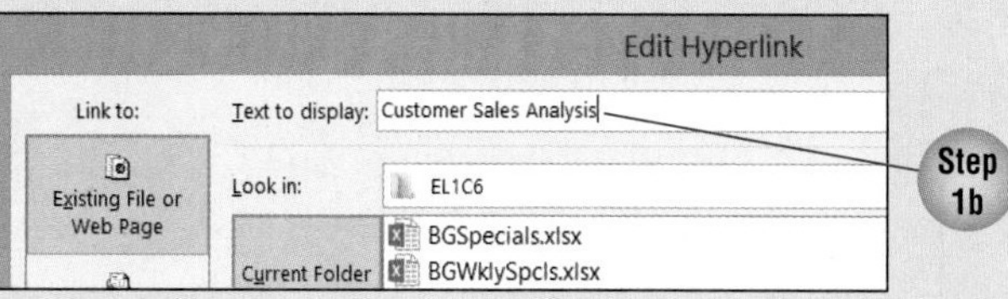

c. Click the ScreenTip button located in the upper right corner of the dialog box.
d. At the Set Hyperlink ScreenTip dialog box, type **Click this hyperlink to display the workbook containing customer sales analysis.**
e. Click OK to close the Set Hyperlink ScreenTip dialog box.
f. Click OK to close the Edit Hyperlink dialog box.

2. Click the Customer sales analysis hyperlink.
3. After looking at the **PSSalesAnalysis.xlsx** workbook, close it.
4. With cell A11 active, edit the Customer sales analysis hyperlink text by completing the following steps:
   a. Click the HOME tab.
   b. Click the Font Color button arrow in the Font group and then click the *Dark Red* color option (first option in the *Standard Colors* section).
   c. Click the Bold button.
   d. Click the Underline button. (This removes underlining from the text.)
5. Remove the Company information hyperlink by right-clicking in cell A13 and then clicking *Remove Hyperlink* at the shortcut menu.
6. Press the Delete key to remove the contents of cell A13.
7. Save, print only the first worksheet (the Summary worksheet), and then close **EL1-C6-P4-PSAccts.xlsx**.

Project 5 Create a Billing Statement Workbook Using a Template — 1 Part

You will open a Billing Statement template provided by Excel, add data, save it as an Excel workbook, and then print the workbook.

Using Excel Templates

Excel provides a number of template worksheet forms formatted for specific uses. With Excel templates, you can create a variety of worksheets with specialized formatting, such as balance sheets, billing statements, loan amortizations, sales invoices, and time cards. Display installed templates by clicking the FILE tab and then clicking the *New* option. This displays the New backstage area, as shown in Figure 6.8.

Quick Steps

Use an Excel Template
1. Click FILE tab.
2. Click *New* option.
3. Double-click desired template.

Click the desired template in the New backstage area and a preview of the template displays in a window. Click the Create button that displays below the template preview and a workbook based on the template opens and displays on the screen. Locations for personalized text display in placeholders in the worksheet. To enter information in the worksheet, position the mouse pointer (white plus sign) in the location you want to type data and then click the left mouse button. After typing the data, click the next location. You can also move the insertion point to another cell using the commands learned in Chapter 1. For example, press the Tab key to make the next cell active or press Shift + Tab to make the previous cell active. If you are connected to the Internet, you can download a number of predesigned templates offered by Microsoft.

Figure 6.8 New Backstage Area

Use this option to search for templates at Office.com.

The templates that display in this section of your New backstage area will vary from what you see in this figure.

Project 5 Preparing a Billing Statement Using a Template

Part 1 of 1

1. Click the FILE tab and then click the *New* option.
2. At the New backstage area, type **billing statement** in the search text box and then press Enter.
3. Double-click the *Billing statement* template (first row, first column).

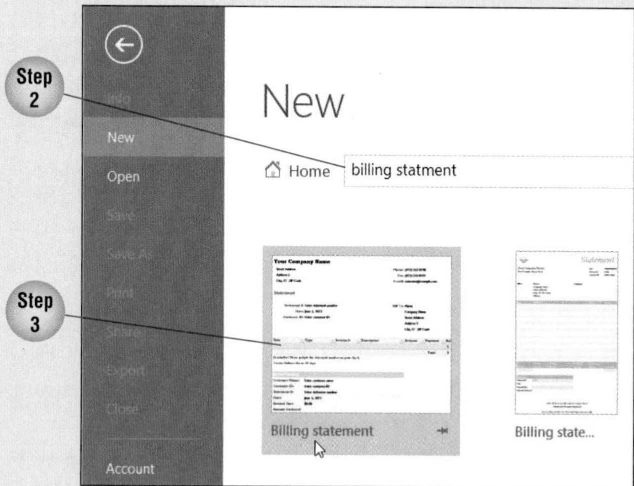

4. Click the Normal button in the view area on the Status bar.

5. With cell B1 active, type **IN-FLOW SYSTEMS**.
6. Click the text *Street Address* (cell B2) and then type **320 Milander Way**.
7. Click in each specified location (cell) and then type the text indicated:
   Address 2 (cell B3): **P.O. Box 2300**
   City, ST ZIP Code (cell B4): **Boston, MA 02188**
   Phone (cell F2): **(617) 555-3900**
   Fax (cell F3): **(617) 555-3945**
   Statement # (cell C8): **5432**
   Customer ID (cell C10): **25-345**
   Name (cell F8): **Aidan Mackenzie**
   Company Name (cell F9): **Stanfield Enterprises**
   Street Address (cell F10): **9921 South 42nd Avenue**
   Address 2 (cell F11): **P.O. Box 5540**
   City, ST ZIP Code (cell F12): **Boston, MA 02193**
   Date (cell B15): (insert current date in numbers as ##/##/#### and if necessary, adjust the width of the column)
   Type (cell C15): **System Unit**
   Invoice # (cell D15): **7452**
   Description (cell E15): **Calibration Unit**
   Amount (cell F15): **950**
   Payment (cell G15): **200**
   Customer Name (cell C21): **Stanfield Enterprises**
   Amount Enclosed (cell C26): **750**

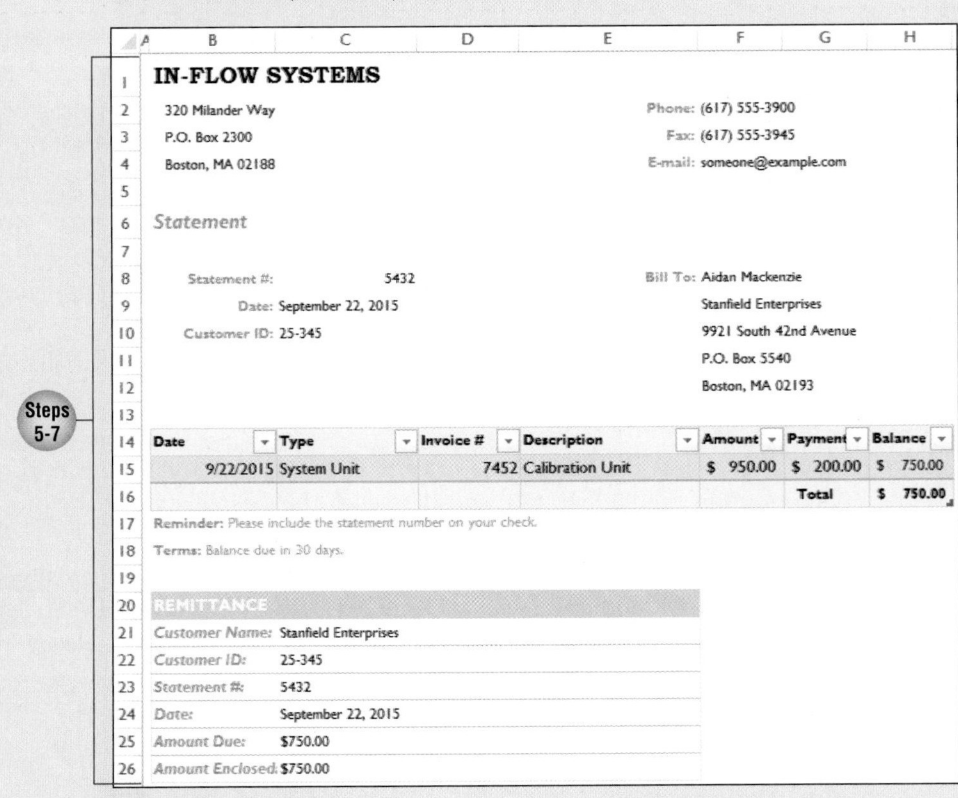

8. Save the completed invoice and name it **EL1-C6-P5-Billing**.
9. Print and then close **EL1-C6-P5-Billing.xlsx**.

Chapter Summary

- Perform file management tasks, such as copying, moving, printing, and renaming workbooks and creating and renaming folders, at the Open dialog box or Save As dialog box.
- Create a new folder by clicking the New folder button located on the toolbar at the Open dialog box or Save As dialog box.
- Rename a folder with the *Rename* option from the Organize button drop-down list or with a shortcut menu.
- Use the Shift key to select adjacent workbooks in the Open dialog box and use the Ctrl key to select nonadjacent workbooks.
- To delete a workbook, use the *Delete* option from the Organize button drop-down list or use a shortcut menu option. Workbooks deleted from the hard drive are automatically sent to the Windows Recycle Bin, where they can be restored or permanently deleted.
- Use the *Copy* and *Paste* options from the shortcut menu at the Open dialog box or Save As dialog box to copy a workbook from one folder to another folder or drive.
- Use the *Send to* option from the shortcut menu to send a copy of a workbook to another drive or folder.
- Remove a workbook from a folder or drive and insert it in another folder or drive using the *Cut* and *Paste* options from the shortcut menu.
- Use the *Rename* option from the Organize button drop-down list or the shortcut menu to give a workbook a different name.
- To move or copy a worksheet to another existing workbook, open both the source workbook and the destination workbook and then open the Move or Copy dialog box.
- Use options from the Cell Styles button drop-down gallery to apply predesigned styles to a cell or selected cells.
- Automate the formatting of cells in a workbook by defining and then applying styles. A style is a predefined set of formatting attributes.
- Define a style with formats already applied to a cell or display the Style dialog box, click the Format button, and then choose formatting options at the Format Cells dialog box.
- To apply a style, select the desired cell or cells, click the Cell Styles button in the Styles group in the HOME tab, and then click the desired style at the drop-down gallery.
- Modify a style and all of the cells to which the style is applied automatically reflect the change. To modify a style, click the Cell Styles button in the Styles group on the HOME tab, right-click the desired style, and then click *Modify* at the shortcut menu.
- Styles are saved in the workbook in which they are created. Styles can be copied, however, to another workbook. Do this with options at the Merge Styles dialog box.
- With options at the Insert Hyperlink dialog box, you can create a hyperlink to a web page, another workbook, a location within a workbook, a new workbook, or an email. You can also create a hyperlink using a graphic.
- You can modify, edit, and remove hyperlinks.

- Excel provides preformatted templates for creating forms. Search for and download templates at the New backstage area.
- Templates contain unique areas where information is entered at the keyboard.

Commands Review

FEATURE	RIBBON TAB, GROUP/OPTION	BUTTON, OPTION	KEYBOARD SHORTCUT
cell styles	HOME, Styles		
Insert Hyperlink dialog box	INSERT, Links		
Merge Styles dialog box	HOME, Styles	, *Merge Styles*	
New backstage area	FILE, *New*		
new folder	FILE, *Open*	New folder	
Open backstage area	FILE, *Open*		Ctrl + O
Open dialog box			Ctrl + F12
Save As backstage area	FILE, *Save As*		Ctrl + S
Save As dialog box			F12
Style dialog box	HOME, Styles	, *New Cell Style*	

Concepts Check Test Your Knowledge

Completion: In the space provided at the right, indicate the correct term, symbol, or command.

1. Perform file management tasks, such as copying, moving, and deleting workbooks, with options at the Open dialog box or this dialog box. ____________________
2. At the Open dialog box, a list of folders and files displays in this pane. ____________________
3. Rename a folder or file at the Open dialog box using a shortcut menu or this button. ____________________
4. At the Open dialog box, hold down this key while selecting nonadjacent workbooks. ____________________

5. Workbooks deleted from the hard drive are automatically sent to this location. ________________

6. The most recently opened workbook names display in this list, which displays when the *Recent Workbooks* option is selected at the Open backstage area. ________________

7. Do this to a workbook name you want to remain at the top of the Recent Workbooks list at the Open backstage area. ________________

8. If you close a workbook without saving it, you can recover it with this option at the Open backstage area. ________________

9. The Cell Styles button is located in this group on the HOME tab. ________________

10. Click the *New Cell Style* option at the Cell Styles button drop-down gallery and this dialog box displays. ________________

11. A style you create displays in this section of the Cell Styles button drop-down gallery. ________________

12. Copy styles from one workbook to another with options at this dialog box. ________________

13. To link a workbook to another workbook, click this button in the *Link to* section of the Insert Hyperlink dialog box. ________________

14. Templates display at this backstage area. ________________

Skills Check Assess Your Performance

Assessment 1

MANAGE WORKBOOKS

1. Display the Open dialog box with the EL1C6 folder the active folder.
2. Create a new folder named *O'Rourke* in the EL1C6 folder.
3. Copy **OEBudget.xlsx**, **OEPayroll.xlsx**, and **OEPlans.xlsx** to the O'Rourke folder.
4. Display the contents of the O'Rourke folder and then rename **OEBudget.xlsx** as **OEEquipBudget.xlsx**.
5. Rename **OEPlans.xlsx** as **OEPurchasePlans.xlsx** in the O'Rourke folder.
6. Change the active folder back to EL1C6.
7. Close the Open dialog box.

Assessment 2

MOVE AND COPY WORKSHEETS BETWEEN SALES ANALYSIS WORKBOOKS

1. Open **DISales.xlsx** and then save the workbook with Save As and name it **EL1-C6-A2-DISales**.
2. Rename Sheet1 as *1st Qtr*.
3. Open **DIQtrs.xlsx**.
4. Rename Sheet1 as *2nd Qtr* and then copy it to **EL1-C6-A2-DISales.xlsx** following the 1st Qtr worksheet. (When copying the worksheet, make sure you insert a check mark in the *Create a copy* check box in the Move or Copy dialog box.)
5. Make **DIQtrs.xlsx** active, rename Sheet2 as *3rd Qtr,* and then copy it to **EL1-C6-A2-DISales.xlsx** following the 2nd Qtr tab. (Make sure you insert a check mark in the *Create a copy* check box.)
6. Make **DIQtrs.xlsx** active and then close it without saving the changes.
7. Open **DI4thQtr.xlsx**.
8. Rename Sheet1 as *4th Qtr* and then move it to **EL1-C6-A2-DISales.xlsx** following the 3rd Qtr worksheet.
9. With **EL1-C6-A2-DISales.xlsx** open, make the following changes to all four quarterly worksheets at the same time:
   a. Make 1st Qtr the active worksheet.
   b. Hold down the Shift key and then click the 4th Qtr tab. (This selects the four quarterly worksheet tabs.)
   c. Insert in cell E4 a formula to calculate the average of cells B4 through D4 and then copy the formula down to cells E5 through E9.
   d. Insert in cell B10 a formula to calculate the sum of cells B4 through B9 and then copy the formula across to cells C10 through E10.
   e. Make cell E4 active and apply accounting formatting with a dollar sign and no places after the decimal point.
10. Insert a footer on all worksheets that prints your name at the left, the page number in the middle, and the current date at the right.
11. Horizontally and vertically center all of the worksheets.
12. Save and then print all four worksheets.
13. Close **EL1-C6-A2-DISales.xlsx**.

Assessment 3

DEFINE AND APPLY STYLES TO A PROJECTED EARNINGS WORKBOOK

1. At a blank worksheet, define a style named *C06Heading* that contains the following formatting:
   a. Font:14-point Cambria bold in dark blue
   b. Horizontal alignment: Center alignment
   c. Borders: Top and bottom in dark blue
   d. Fill: Light yellow (eighth column, second row)
2. Define a style named *C06Subheading* that contains the following formatting:
   a. Font: 12-point Cambria bold in dark blue
   b. Horizontal alignment: Center alignment
   c. Borders: Top and bottom in dark blue
   d. Fill: Light green (last column, second row)

3. Define a style named *C06Column* that contains the following formatting:
   a. Number: At the Style dialog box, click the *Number* check box to remove the check mark.
   b. Font: 12-point Cambria in dark blue
   c. Fill: Light green (last column, second row)
4. Save the workbook and name it **EL1-C6-A3-Styles**.
5. With **EL1-C6-A3-Styles.xlsx** open, open **ProjEarnings.xlsx**.
6. Save the workbook with Save As and name it **EL1-C6-A3-ProjEarnings**.
7. Make cell C6 active and then insert a formula that multiplies the content of cell B6 by the amount in cell B3. (When writing the formula, identify cell B3 as an absolute reference.) Copy the formula down to cells C7 through C17.
8. Make cell C6 active and then click the Accounting Number Format button.
9. Copy the styles from **EL1-C6-A3-Styles.xlsx** into **EL1-C6-A3-ProjEarnings.xlsx**. ***Hint: Do this at the Merge Styles dialog box.***
10. Apply the following styles:
    a. Select cells A1 and A2 and then apply the C06Heading style.
    b. Select cells A5 through C5 and then apply the C06Subheading style.
    c. Select cells A6 through A17 and then apply the C06Column style.
11. Save the workbook again and then print **EL1-C6-A3-ProjEarnings.xlsx**.
12. With **EL1-C6-A3-ProjEarnings.xlsx** open, modify the following styles:
    a. Modify the C06Heading style so it changes the font color to dark green (last column, sixth row) instead of dark blue, changes the vertical alignment to center alignment, and inserts top and bottom borders in dark green (last column, sixth row) instead of dark blue.
    b. Modify the C06Subheading style so it changes the font color to dark green (last column, sixth row) instead of dark blue and inserts top and bottom borders in dark green (instead of dark blue).
    c. Modify the C06Column style so it changes the font color to dark green (last column, sixth row) instead of dark blue. Do not change any of the other formatting attributes.
13. Save and then print the workbook.
14. Close **EL1-C6-A3-ProjEarnings.xlsx** and then close **EL1-C6-A3-Styles.xlsx** without saving the changes.

Assessment 4

INSERT HYPERLINKS IN A BOOKSTORE WORKBOOK

1. Open **BGSpecials.xlsx** and then save the workbook with Save As and name it **EL1-C6-A4-BGSpecials.xlsx**.
2. Make cell E3 active and then create a hyperlink to www.microsoft.com.
3. Make cell E4 active and then create a hyperlink to www.symantec.com
4. Make cell E5 active and then create a hyperlink to www.nasa.gov.
5. Make cell E6 active and then create a hyperlink to www.cnn.com.
6. Make cell A8 active, type **Weekly specials!**, and then create a hyperlink to the workbook named **BGWklySpcls.xlsx**.
7. Click the hyperlink to the Microsoft website, explore the site, and then close the web browser.
8. Click the hyperlink to the NASA website, explore the site, and then close the web browser.
9. Click the Weekly specials! hyperlink, view the workbook, and then close the workbook.
10. Save, print, and then close **EL1-C6-A4-BGSpecials.xlsx**.

Assessment

5 APPLY CONDITIONAL FORMATTING TO A SALES WORKBOOK

1. Use Excel Help files or experiment with the options at the Conditional Formatting button drop-down gallery to learn about conditional formatting.
2. Open **PSSales.xlsx** and then save the workbook with Save As and name it **EL1-C6-A5-PSSales**.
3. Select cells D5 through D19 and then use conditional formatting to display the amounts as data bars. (You choose the type of data bars.)
4. Insert a header that prints your name, a page number, and the current date.
5. Save, print, and then close **EL1-C6-A5-PSSales.xlsx**.

Visual Benchmark Demonstrate Your Proficiency

FILL IN AN EXPENSE REPORT FORM

1. Display the New backstage area, search for an expense report template, and then double-click the *Expense report* template shown in Figure 6.9.
2. With the expense report open, apply the Retrospect theme.
3. Select cells J1 through L1 and then apply the Note cell style.
4. Type the information in the cells as indicated in Figure 6.9.
5. Make cell L18 active and apply the Bad cell style.
6. Save the completed workbook and name it **EL1-C6-VB-OEExpRpt**.
7. Print and then close **EL1-C6-VB-OEExpRpt.xlsx**.

Figure 6.9 Visual Benchmark

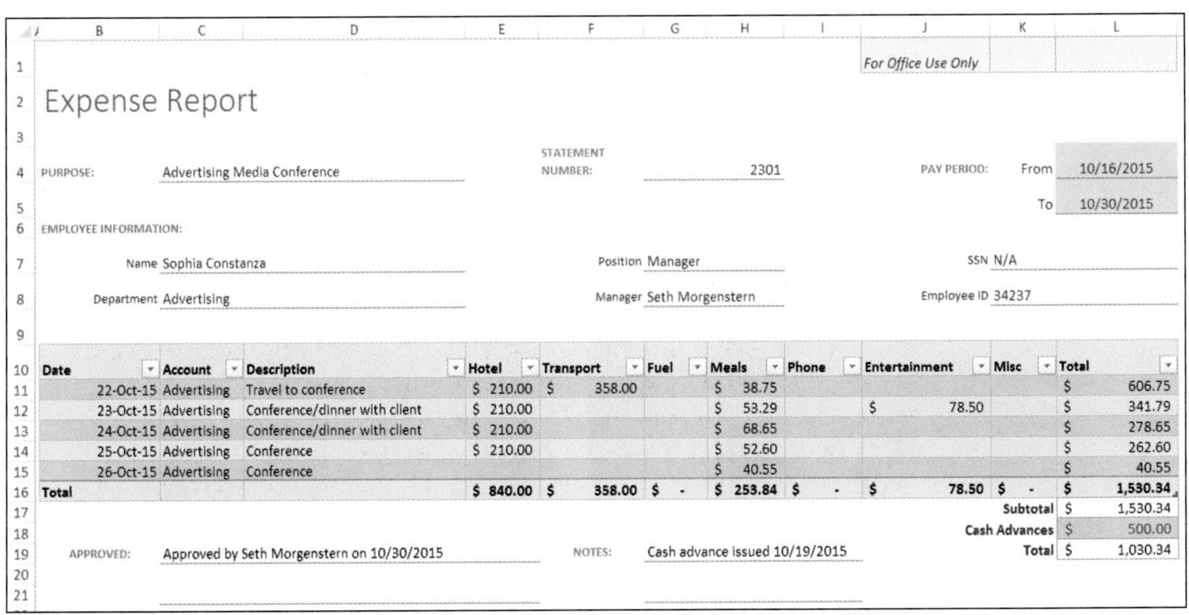

For Office Use Only

Expense Report

PURPOSE: Advertising Media Conference | STATEMENT NUMBER: 2301 | PAY PERIOD: From 10/16/2015 To 10/30/2015

EMPLOYEE INFORMATION:

Name Sophia Constanza | Position Manager | SSN N/A

Department Advertising | Manager Seth Morgenstern | Employee ID 34237

Date	Account	Description	Hotel	Transport	Fuel	Meals	Phone	Entertainment	Misc	Total
22-Oct-15	Advertising	Travel to conference	$ 210.00	$ 358.00		$ 38.75				$ 606.75
23-Oct-15	Advertising	Conference/dinner with client	$ 210.00			$ 53.29		$ 78.50		$ 341.79
24-Oct-15	Advertising	Conference/dinner with client	$ 210.00			$ 68.65				$ 278.65
25-Oct-15	Advertising	Conference	$ 210.00			$ 52.60				$ 262.60
26-Oct-15	Advertising	Conference				$ 40.55				$ 40.55
Total			**$ 840.00**	**$ 358.00**	**$ -**	**$ 253.84**	**$ -**	**$ 78.50**	**$ -**	**$ 1,530.34**
									Subtotal	$ 1,530.34
									Cash Advances	$ 500.00
									Total	$ 1,030.34

APPROVED: Approved by Seth Morgenstern on 10/30/2015 | NOTES: Cash advance issued 10/19/2015

Case Study Apply Your Skills

Part 1

You are the office manager for Leeward Marine and you decide to consolidate into one workbook several worksheets containing information on expenses. Open **LMEstExp.xlsx** and then save the workbook and name it **EL1-C6-CS-LMExpSummary**. Open **LMActExp.xlsx**, copy the worksheet into **EL1-C6-CS-LMExpSummary.xlsx**, make **LMActExp.xlsx** the active workbook, and then close it. Apply appropriate formatting to numbers and insert necessary formulas in each worksheet. (Use the Clear button in the HOME tab to clear the contents of cells N8, N9, N13, and N14 in both worksheets.) Include the company name, Leeward Marine, in both worksheets. Create styles and apply the styles to cells in both worksheets to maintain consistent formatting. Automatically adjust the widths of the columns to accommodate the longest entries. Save **EL1-C6-CS-LMExpSummary.xlsx**.

Part 2

You decide that you want to include another worksheet that displays the yearly estimated expenses, actual expenses, and variances (differences) between the two. With **EL1-C6-CS-LMExpSummary.xlsx** open, open **LMExpVar.xlsx**. Copy the worksheet into **EL1-C6-CS-LMExpSummary.xlsx**, make **LMExpVar.xlsx** the active workbook, and then close it. Rename the sheet tab containing the estimated expenses as *Estimated Exp*, rename the sheet tab containing the actual expenses as *Actual Exp*, and rename the sheet tab containing the variances as *Summary*. Recolor the three sheet tabs you just renamed.

Select the yearly estimated expense amounts (column N) in the Estimated Exp worksheet and then paste the amounts in the appropriate cells in the Summary worksheet. Click the Paste Options button and then click the Values & Number Formatting button in the *Paste Values* section of the drop-down list. (This pastes the value and the cell formatting, rather than the formula.) Select the yearly actual expense amounts (column N) in the Actual Exp worksheet and then paste the amounts in the appropriate cells in the Summary worksheet. Click the Paste Options button and then click the Values & Number Formatting button in the *Paste Values* section of the drop-down list. Apply appropriate formatting to the numbers and insert a formula to calculate the variances (differences) between estimated and actual expenses. Clear the contents of cells D8, D9, D13, and D14. Apply styles to the Summary worksheet so it is formatted similar to the Estimated Exp and Actual Exp worksheets.

Insert an appropriate header or footer in each worksheet. Scale the worksheets so each prints on one page. Save, print all of the worksheets, and then close **EL1-C6-CS-LMExpSummary.xlsx**.

Part 3

Based on the summary of the yearly expense variances, your supervisor has created projected expenses for next year and has asked you to format the worksheet. Open **LMProjectedExp.xlsx** and then save it and name it **EL1-C6-CS-LMProjectedExp**. Format the worksheet in a similar manner to the formatting you applied to **EL1-C6-CS-LMExpSummary.xlsx** (use the styles you created). Save and then close **EL1-C6-CS-LMProjectedExp.xlsx**. Open **EL1-C6-CS-LMExpSummary.xlsx**, make the Summary worksheet active and then insert a hyperlink to the **EL1-C6-CS-LMProjectedExp.xlsx** workbook. You determine the cell location and hyperlink text for the hyperlink. Save **EL1-C6-CS-LMExpSummary.xlsx** and then print only the Summary worksheet.

Part 4

You need to print a number of copies of the summary worksheet in the **EL1-C6-CS-LMExpSummary.xlsx** workbook and you want the company letterhead to print at the top of the page. You decide to use the letterhead in a Word document and copy the summary data from Excel into the Word letterhead document. To do this, open Word and then open the document named **LMLtrd.docx** (located in the EL1C6 folder on your storage medium). Press the Enter key two times. Make Excel the active program and with **EL1-C6-CS-LMExpSummary.xlsx** open, make the Summary worksheet active, select and then copy cells containing information on the yearly expense variances, and then paste them into the **LMLtrhd.docx** Word document as a picture object. (Click the Paste Options button and then click the Picture button.) Save the document with Save As and name it **EL1-C6-CS-LMExpSummary**. Print and then close **EL1-C6-CS-LMExpSummary.docx** and then close Word. In Excel, close **EL1-C6-CS-LMExpSummary.xlsx**.

MICROSOFT® EXCEL®

Creating Charts and Inserting Formulas

PERFORMANCE OBJECTIVES

Upon successful completion of Chapter 7, you will be able to:

- **Create a chart with data in an Excel worksheet**
- **Size, move, edit, format, and delete charts**
- **Print a selected chart and print a worksheet containing a chart**
- **Change a chart location**
- **Insert, move, size, and delete chart elements and shapes**
- **Write formulas with the PMT and FV financial functions**
- **Write formulas with the IF logical function**

Tutorials

7.1 Creating Charts in Excel
7.2 Editing Chart Data
7.3 Formatting with Chart Buttons
7.4 Printing Charts
7.5 Changing Chart Design
7.6 Changing Chart Formatting
7.7 Inserting and Formatting a Shape
7.8 Moving, Sizing, and Deleting a Chart
7.9 Using Financial Functions
7.10 Using the Logical IF Function

In the previous Excel chapters, you learned to create data in worksheets. While a worksheet does an adequate job of representing data, some data are better represented visually with a chart. A ***chart***, which is sometimes referred to as a ***graph***, is a picture of numeric data. In this chapter, you will learn to create and customize charts in Excel. You will also learn how to write formulas using financial and logical functions. Model answers for this chapter's projects appear on the following pages.

Note: Before beginning the projects, copy to your storage medium the EL1C7 subfolder from the EL1 folder on the CD that accompanies this textbook and then make EL1C7 the active folder.

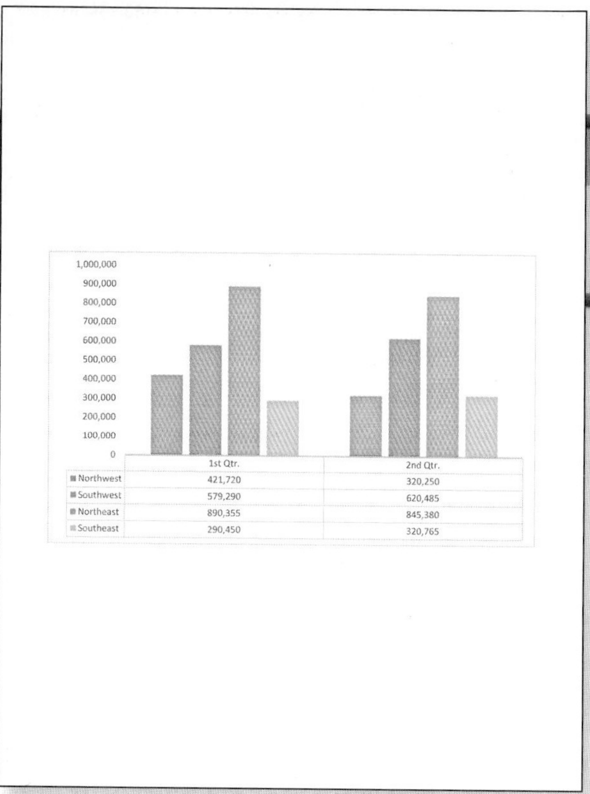

Project 1 Create a Quarterly Sales Column Chart
EL1-C7-P1-SalesChart.xlsx

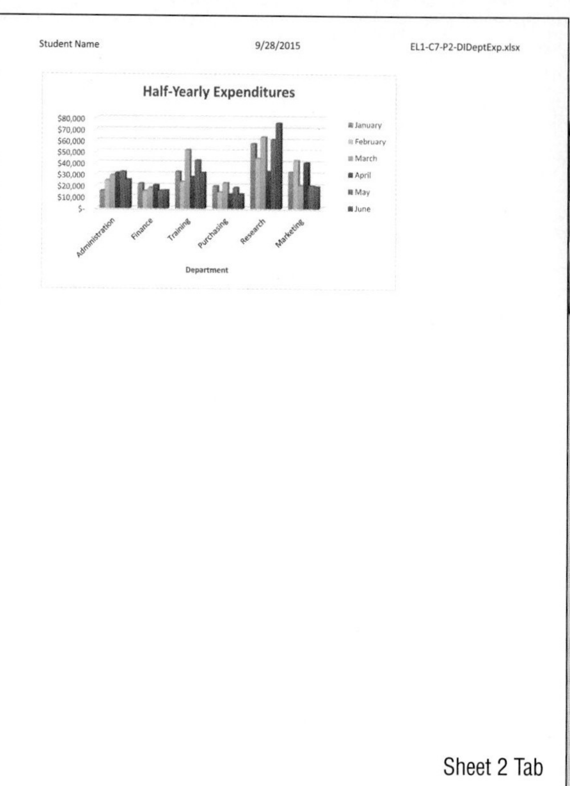

Project 2 Create a Technology Purchases Bar Chart and Column Chart
EL1-C7-P2-DIDeptExp.xlsx

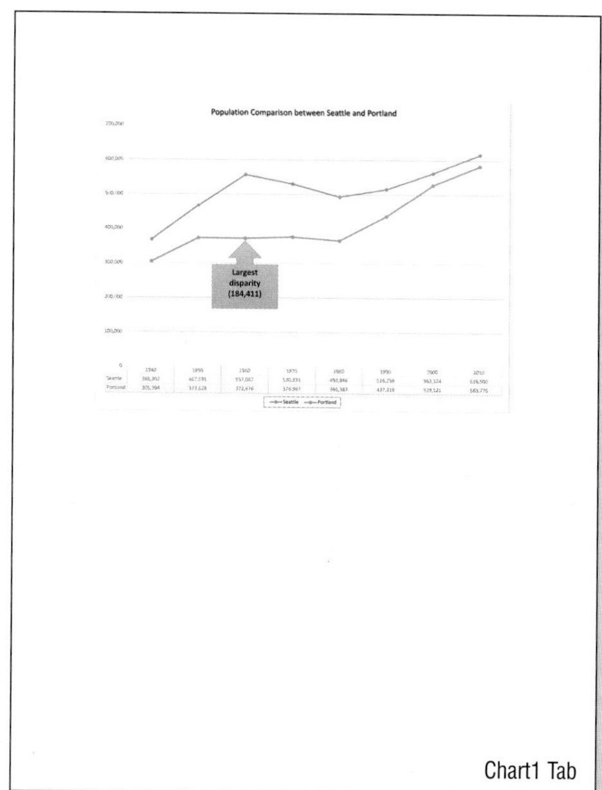

Project 3 Create a Population Comparison Line Chart
EL1-C7-P3-PopComp.xlsx

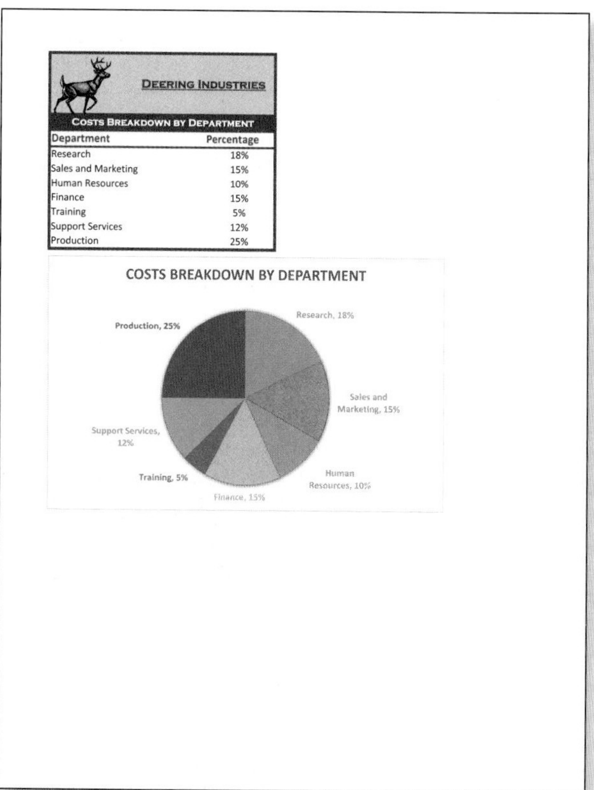

DEERING INDUSTRIES

COSTS BREAKDOWN BY DEPARTMENT

Department	Percentage
Research	18%
Sales and Marketing	15%
Human Resources	10%
Finance	15%
Training	5%
Support Services	12%
Production	25%

Project 4 Create a Costs Percentage Pie Chart
EL1-C7-P4-DIDeptCosts.xlsx

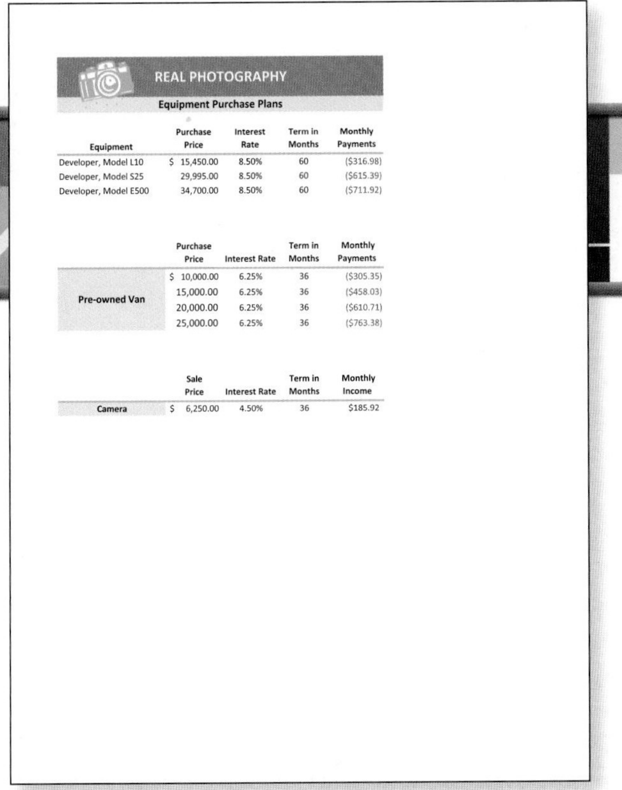

REAL PHOTOGRAPHY

Equipment Purchase Plans

Equipment	Purchase Price	Interest Rate	Term in Months	Monthly Payments
Developer, Model L10	$ 15,450.00	8.50%	60	($316.98)
Developer, Model S25	29,995.00	8.50%	60	($615.39)
Developer, Model E500	34,700.00	8.50%	60	($711.92)

	Purchase Price	Interest Rate	Term in Months	Monthly Payments
Pre-owned Van	$ 10,000.00	6.25%	36	($305.35)
	15,000.00	6.25%	36	($458.03)
	20,000.00	6.25%	36	($610.71)
	25,000.00	6.25%	36	($763.38)

	Sale Price	Interest Rate	Term in Months	Monthly Income
Camera	$ 6,250.00	4.50%	36	$185.92

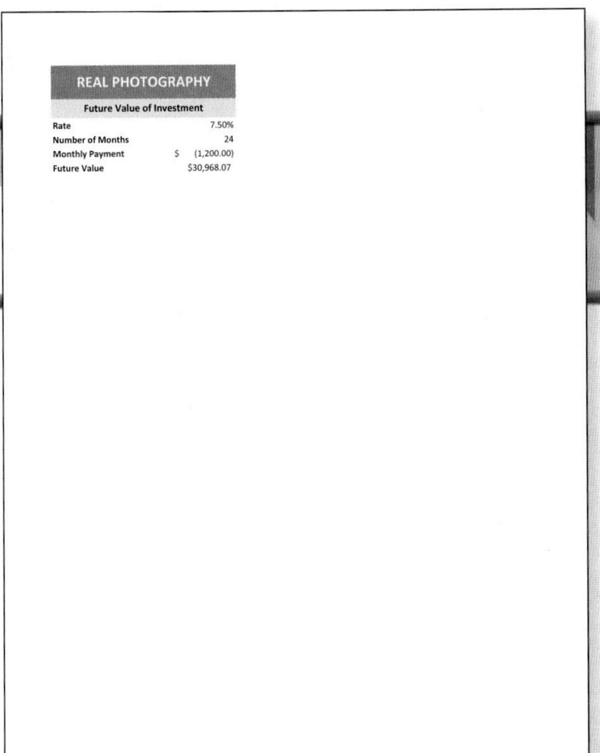

REAL PHOTOGRAPHY

Future Value of Investment

Rate	7.50%
Number of Months	24
Monthly Payment	$ (1,200.00)
Future Value	$30,968.07

Project 5 Calculate Payments and the Future Value of an Investment

EL1-C7-P5-RPReports.xlsx

EL1-C7-P5-RPInvest.xlsx

Capstan Marine Products

Sales Department

Salesperson	Quota	Actual Sales	Bonus
Allejandro	$ 95,500.00	$ 103,295.00	$ 20,659.00
Crispin	137,000.00	129,890.00	-
Frankel	124,000.00	133,255.00	26,651.00
Hiesmann	85,500.00	94,350.00	18,870.00
Jarvis	159,000.00	167,410.00	33,482.00
Littleman	110,500.00	109,980.00	-

Sales Department

Product #	Price	Discount Price	Discount
C-2340	$ 1,250.00	$ 1,187.50	YES
C-3215	695.00	660.25	YES
C-4390	475.00	475.00	NO
E-2306	225.00	225.00	NO
E-3420	520.00	520.00	NO
G-2312	2,150.00	2,042.50	YES
G-4393	2,450.00	2,327.50	YES
J-1203	755.00	717.25	YES
J-3288	455.00	455.00	NO
J-4594	1,050.00	997.50	YES
M-2355	890.00	845.50	YES
M-3129	645.00	612.75	YES
M-4392	475.00	475.00	NO

New Employee Orientation

Name	Quiz 1	Quiz 2	Quiz 3	Average	Grade
Angelo	78	69	88	78	FAIL
Cunningham	90	95	86	90	PASS
Elliot	82	88	94	88	PASS
Kennedy	100	98	96	98	PASS
Lipscomb	64	76	62	67	FAIL

Project 6 Insert Formulas with the IF Logical Function

EL1-C7-P6-CMPReports.xlsx

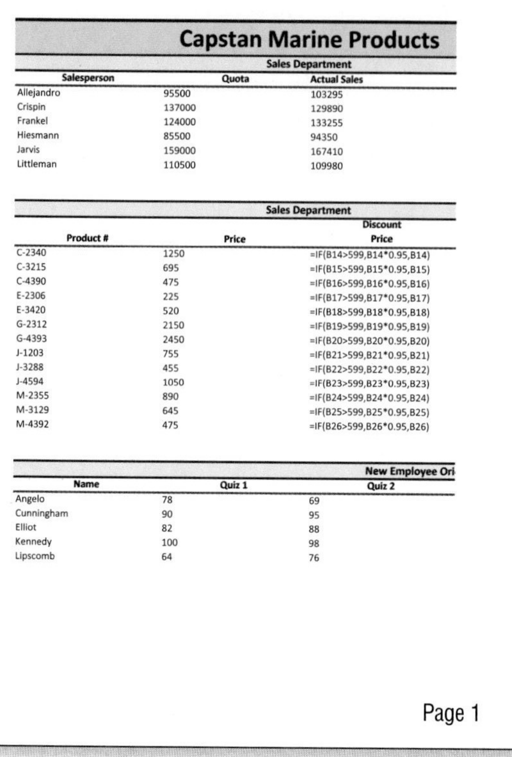

Capstan Marine Products

Salesperson	Quota	Actual Sales
		Sales Department
Allejandro	95500	103295
Crispin	137000	129890
Frankel	124000	133255
Hiesmann	85500	94350
Jarvis	159000	167410
Littleman	110500	109980

Product #	Price	Discount Price
		Sales Department
C-2340	1250	=IF(B14>599,B14*0.95,B14)
C-3215	695	=IF(B15>599,B15*0.95,B15)
C-4390	475	=IF(B16>599,B16*0.95,B16)
E-2306	225	=IF(B17>599,B17*0.95,B17)
E-3420	520	=IF(B18>599,B18*0.95,B18)
G-2312	2150	=IF(B19>599,B19*0.95,B19)
G-4393	2450	=IF(B20>599,B20*0.95,B20)
J-1203	755	=IF(B21>599,B21*0.95,B21)
J-3288	455	=IF(B22>599,B22*0.95,B22)
J-4594	1050	=IF(B23>599,B23*0.95,B23)
M-2355	890	=IF(B24>599,B24*0.95,B24)
M-3129	645	=IF(B25>599,B25*0.95,B25)
M-4392	475	=IF(B26>599,B26*0.95,B26)

Name	Quiz 1	Quiz 2
		New Employee Ori
Angelo	78	69
Cunningham	90	95
Elliot	82	88
Kennedy	100	98
Lipscomb	64	76

Page 1

Bonus
=IF(C4>B4,C4*0.2,0)
=IF(C5>B5,C5*0.2,0)
=IF(C6>B6,C6*0.2,0)
=IF(C7>B7,C7*0.2,0)
=IF(C8>B8,C8*0.2,0)
=IF(C9>B9,C9*0.2,0)

Discount
=IF(B14>599,"YES","NO")
=IF(B15>599,"YES","NO")
=IF(B16>599,"YES","NO")
=IF(B17>599,"YES","NO")
=IF(B18>599,"YES","NO")
=IF(B19>599,"YES","NO")
=IF(B20>599,"YES","NO")
=IF(B21>599,"YES","NO")
=IF(B22>599,"YES","NO")
=IF(B23>599,"YES","NO")
=IF(B24>599,"YES","NO")
=IF(B25>599,"YES","NO")
=IF(B26>599,"YES","NO")

Quiz 3	Average	Grade
entation		
88	=AVERAGE(B31:D31)	=IF(E31>79,"PASS","FAIL")
86	=AVERAGE(B32:D32)	=IF(E32>79,"PASS","FAIL")
94	=AVERAGE(B33:D33)	=IF(E33>79,"PASS","FAIL")
96	=AVERAGE(B34:D34)	=IF(E34>79,"PASS","FAIL")
62	=AVERAGE(B35:D35)	=IF(E35>79,"PASS","FAIL")

Page 2

EL1-C7-P6-CMReports(Formulas).xlsx

Project 1 Create a Quarterly Sales Column Chart — 3 Parts

You will open a workbook containing quarterly sales data and then use the data to create a column chart. You will decrease the size of the chart, move it to a different location in the worksheet, and then make changes to sales numbers. You will also use buttons to customize and filter chart elements.

Creating a Chart

Quick Steps

Create a Chart
1. Select cells.
2. Click INSERT tab.
3. Click desired chart button.
4. Click desired chart style at drop-down gallery.

Recommended Charts

To provide a visual representation of your data, consider inserting data in a chart. With buttons in the Charts group on the INSERT tab, you can create a variety of charts, such as a column chart, line chart, pie chart, and much more. Excel provides ten basic chart types, as described in Table 7.1.

To create a chart, select the cells in the worksheet that you want to chart, click the INSERT tab, and then click the desired chart button in the Charts group. At the drop-down gallery that displays, click the desired chart style. If you are not sure what type of chart will best illustrate your data, consider letting Excel recommend a chart. To do this, select the data, click the INSERT tab, and then click the Recommended Charts button. This displays the data in a chart in the Insert Chart dialog box. Customize the recommended chart with options in the left panel of the dialog box. Click the OK button to insert the recommended chart in the worksheet. You can also insert a recommended chart in the worksheet with the keyboard shortcut Alt+ F1.

Table 7.1 Types of Charts

Chart	*Description*
area	Emphasizes the magnitude of change rather than time and the rate of change. Also shows the relationship of the parts to the whole by displaying the sum of the plotted values.
bar	Shows individual figures at a specific time or shows variations between components but not in relationship to the whole.
column	Compares separate (noncontinuous) items as they vary over time.
combo	Combines two or more chart types to make data easy to understand.
line	Shows trends and overall change across time at even intervals. Emphasizes the rate of change across time rather than the magnitude of change.
pie	Shows proportions and the relationship of the parts to the whole.
radar	Emphasizes differences and amounts of change over time and variations and trends. Each category has a value axis radiating from the center point. Lines connect all values in the same series.
stock	Shows four values for a stock: open, high, low, and close.
surface	Shows trends in values across two dimensions in a continuous curve.
xy (scatter)	Shows the relationships among numeric values in several data series or plots the interception points between *x* and *y* values. Shows uneven intervals of data and is commonly used in scientific data.

Sizing and Moving a Chart

When you create a chart, it is inserted in the same worksheet as the selected cells. Figure 7.1 displays the worksheet and chart you will create in Project 1a. The chart is inserted in a box, which you can size and/or move in the worksheet.

Change the size of the chart using the sizing handles (white squares) that display on the chart borders. Drag the top and bottom middle sizing handles to increase or decrease the height of the chart; use the left and right middle sizing handles to increase or decrease the width; and use the corner sizing handles to increase or decrease the height and width at the same time. To increase or decrease the size of the chart but maintain its proportions, hold down the Shift key while dragging one of the chart's corner borders.

To move the chart, make sure the chart is selected (border with sizing handles displays around the chart), position the mouse pointer on a border until the pointer displays with a four-headed arrow attached, hold down the left mouse button, and then drag to the desired position.

Quick Steps

Create a Recommended Chart

1. Select cells.
2. Click INSERT tab.
3. Click Recommended Charts button.
4. Click OK at Insert Chart dialog box.

OR

1. Select cells.
2. Press Alt + F1.

Hide rows or columns that you do not want to chart.

Editing Data and Adding a Data Series

The cells you select to create the chart are linked to it. If you need to change the data for a chart, edit the data in the desired cell and the corresponding section of the chart will be automatically updated. If you add data to cells within the range of cells used for the chart, called the source data, the new data will be included in the chart. If you add a data series in cells next to or below the source data, you will need to click in the chart to display the source data with sizing handles and then drag with a sizing handle to include the new data.

Figure 7.1 Project 1a Chart

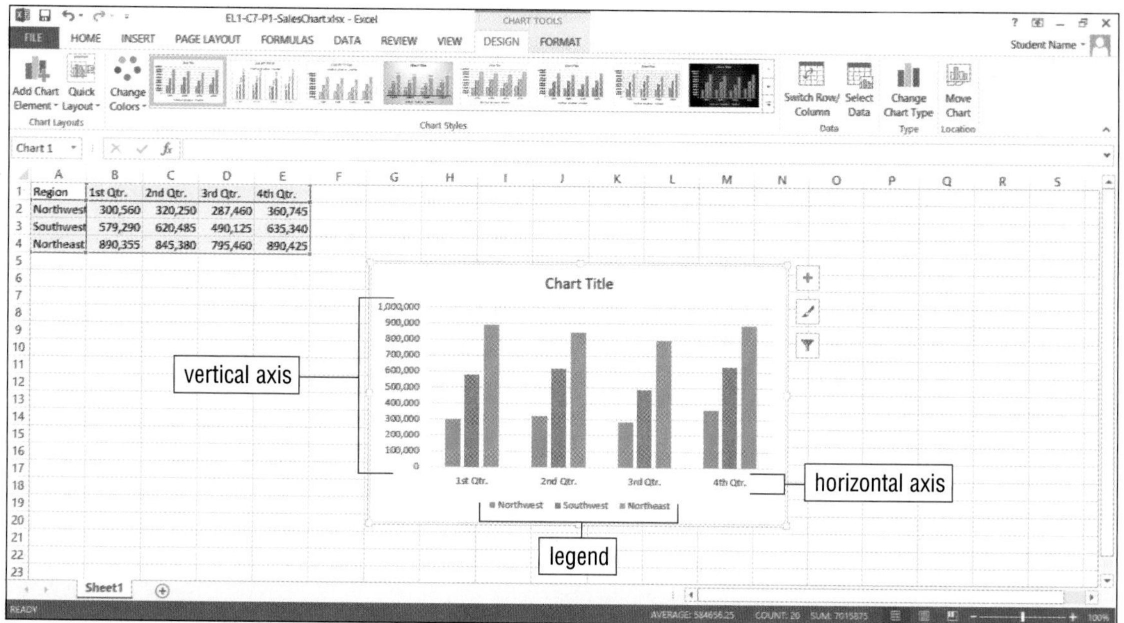

Project 1a Creating a Chart

Part 1 of 3

1. Open **SalesChart.xlsx** and then save the workbook with Save As and name it **EL1-C7-P1-SalesChart**.
2. Select cells A1 through E4.
3. Let Excel recommend a chart type by completing the following steps:
   a. Click the INSERT tab.
   b. Click the Recommended Charts button in the Charts group.

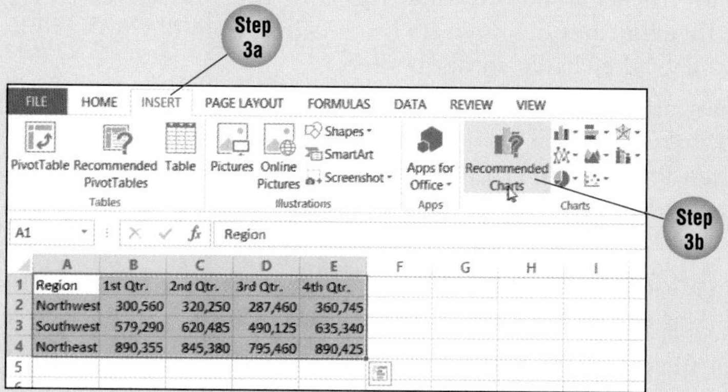

   c. At the Insert Chart dialog box, look at the options that display in the left panel and then click OK.

4. Slightly increase the size of the chart and maintain its proportions by completing the following steps:
   a. Position the mouse pointer on the sizing handle in the lower right corner of the chart border until the pointer turns into a two-headed arrow pointing diagonally.
   b. Hold down the Shift key and then hold down the left mouse button.
   c. Drag out approximately 0.5 inch. Release the mouse button and then release the Shift key.

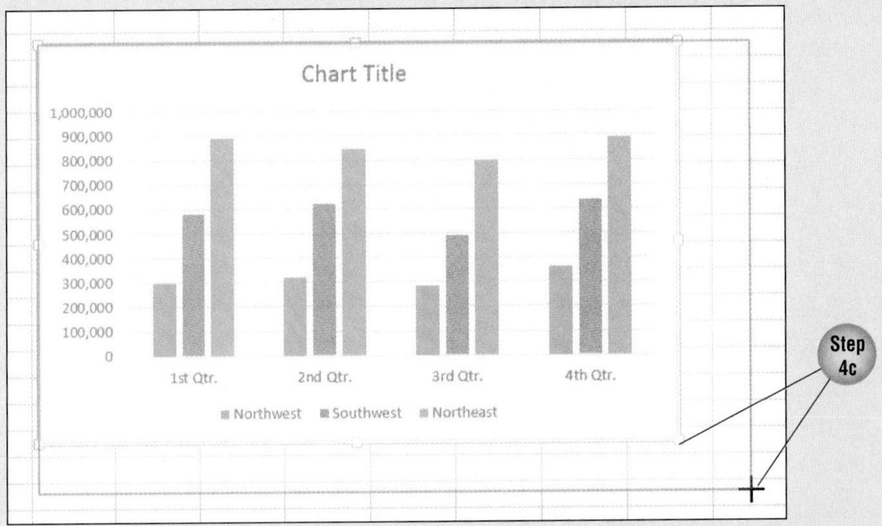

5. Move the chart below the cells containing data by completing the following steps:
   a. Make sure the chart is selected. (When the chart is selected, the border surrounding it displays with sizing handles.)
   b. Position the mouse pointer on the chart border until the pointer displays with a four-headed arrow attached.
   c. Hold down the left mouse button, drag the chart so it is positioned in row 6 below the cells containing data, and then release the mouse button.
6. Make the following changes to the specified cells:
   a. Make cell B2 active and then change *300,560* to *421,720*.
   b. Make cell D2 active and then change *287,460* to *397,460*.

	A	B	C	D	E	F
1	Region	1st Qtr.	2nd Qtr.	3rd Qtr.	4th Qtr.	
2	Northwest	300,560	320,250	287,460	360,745	
3	Southwest	579,290	620,485	490,125	635,340	
4	Northeast	890,355	845,380	795,460	890,425	
5						
6						
7			Step 5c		Chart Title	
8	1,000,000					

7. Add a new data series by typing data in the following cells:
   A5: Southeast
   B5: 290,450
   C5: 320,765
   D5: 270,450
   E5: 300,455

8. Add the new data series to the chart by completing the following steps:
   a. Click in the chart. (This selects the data source A1 through E4.)
   b. Position the mouse pointer on the sizing handle in the lower right corner of cell E4 until the pointer displays as a two-headed diagonally pointing arrow.
   c. Hold down the left mouse button, drag down to cell E5, and then release the mouse button. (This incorporates the data row E in the chart.)
9. Save **EL1-C7-P1-SalesChart.xlsx**.

Formatting with Chart Buttons

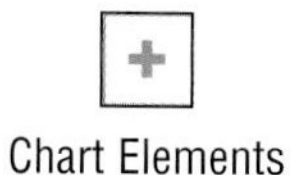

Chart Elements

When you insert a chart in a worksheet, three buttons display at the right side of the chart border. Click the top button, Chart Elements, and a side menu displays with chart elements, as shown in Figure 7.2. The check boxes containing check marks indicate the elements that are currently part of the chart. Add a new element to your chart by inserting a check mark in the check box for the desired element and remove an element by removing the check mark.

Chart Styles

Excel offers a variety of chart styles you can apply to your chart. Click the Chart Styles button that displays at the right side of the chart and a side menu gallery of styles displays, as shown in Figure 7.3 on the next page. Scroll down the gallery, hover your mouse over an option, and the style formatting is applied to your chart. In this way, you can scroll down the gallery and then choose the desired chart style.

In addition to applying a chart style, you can use the Chart Styles button side menu gallery to change the chart colors. Click the Chart Styles button and then click the COLOR tab that displays to the right of the STYLE tab. Click the desired color option at the color palette that displays. Hover your mouse over a color option to view how the color change affects the elements in your chart.

Chart Filters

Use the bottom button, Chart Filters, to isolate specific data in your chart. When you click the button, a side menu displays, as shown in Figure 7.4. Specify the series or categories you want to display in your chart. To do this, remove check marks from those elements that you do not want to appear in your chart. After removing the desired check marks, click the Apply button that displays toward the bottom of the side menu. Click the NAMES tab at the Chart Filters button side menu and options display for turning on/off the display of column and row names.

Figure 7.2 Chart Elements Button Side Menu Gallery

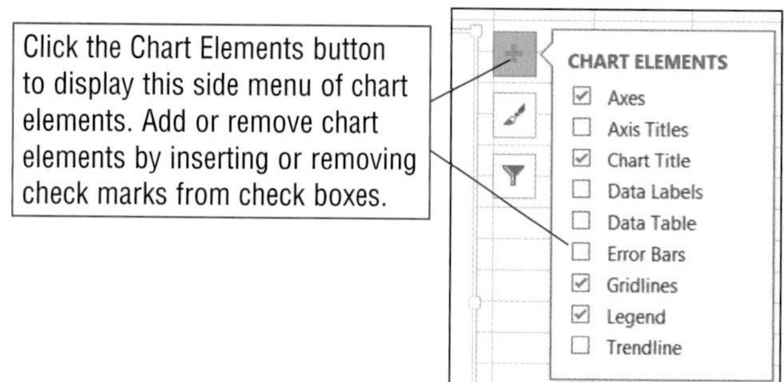

Figure 7.3 Chart Styles Button Side Menu Gallery

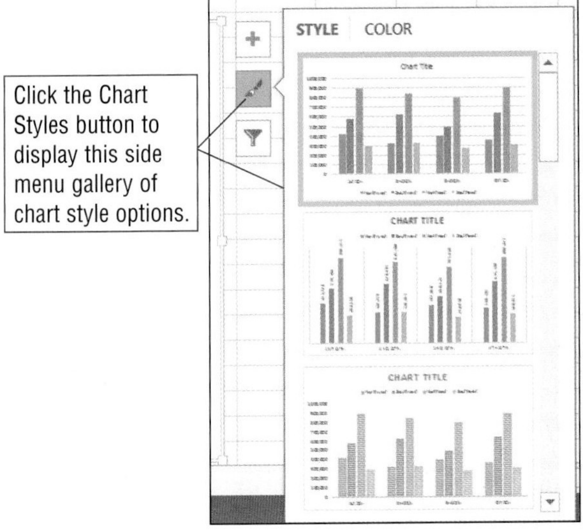

Figure 7.4 Chart Filters Button Side Menu

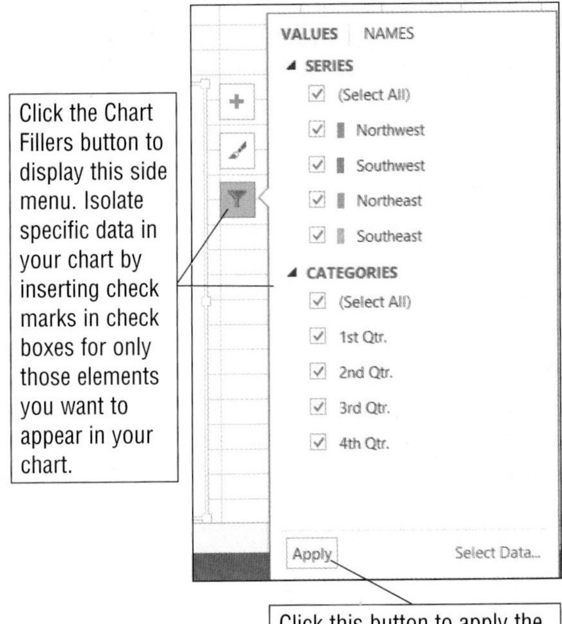

Project 1b Formatting with Chart Buttons

Part 2 of 3

1. With **EL1-C7-P1-SalesChart.xlsx** open, make the chart active by clicking inside the chart but outside any elements.
2. Insert and remove chart elements by completing the following steps:
   a. Click the Chart Elements button that displays outside the upper right side of the chart.
   b. At the side menu that displays, click the *Chart Title* check box to remove the check mark.
   c. Click the *Data Table* check box to insert a check mark.
   d. Hover your mouse over *Gridlines* in the Chart Elements button side menu and then click the right-pointing triangle that displays.
   e. At the side menu that displays, click the *Primary Major Vertical* check box to insert a check mark.
   f. Click the *Legend* check box to remove the check mark.

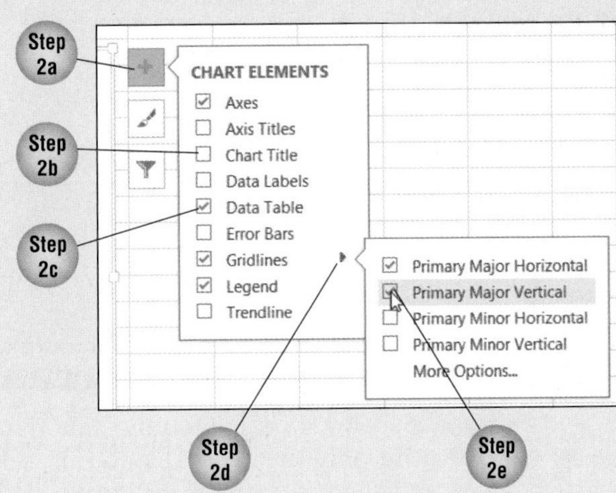

3. Apply a different chart style by completing the following steps:
   a. Click the Chart Styles button that displays outside the upper right side of the chart (below the Chart Elements button).
   b. At the side menu gallery, click the *Style 3* option (third option in the gallery).
4. Display only the first quarter and second quarter sales by completing the following steps:
   a. Click the Chart Filters button that displays outside the upper right corner of the chart (below the Chart Styles button).
   b. Click the *3rd Qtr.* check box in the *CATEGORIES* section to remove the check mark.
   c. Click the *4th Qtr.* check box in the *CATEGORIES* section to remove the check mark.
   d. Click the Apply button that displays toward the bottom of the side menu.
   e. Click the Chart Filters button to remove the side menu.

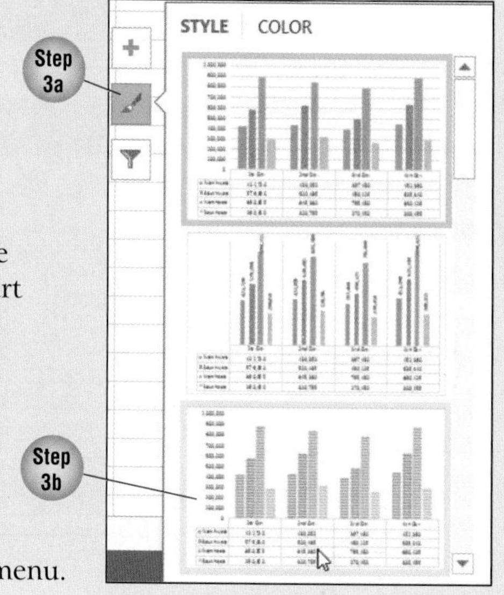

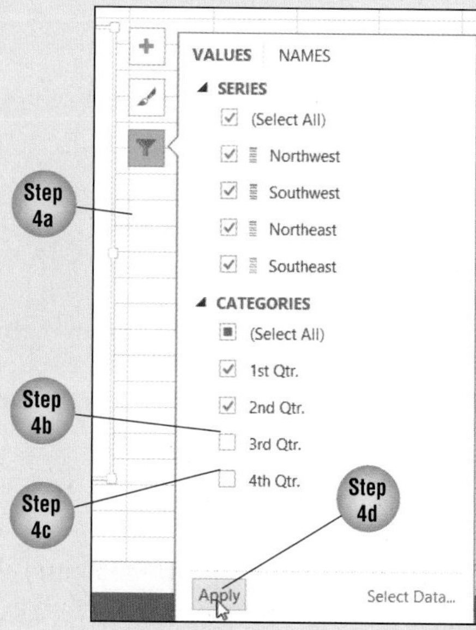

5. Save **EL1-C7-P1-SalesChart.xlsx**.

Printing a Chart

In a worksheet containing data in cells as well as a chart, you have the option to print only the chart. To do this, select the chart, display the Print backstage area, and then click the Print button. With a chart selected, the first gallery in the *Settings* category is automatically changed to *Print Selected Chart*. A preview of the chart displays at the right side of the Print backstage area.

Project 1c Printing a Chart

Part 3 of 3

1. With **EL1-C7-P1-SalesChart.xlsx** open, make sure the chart is selected.
2. Click the FILE tab and then click the *Print* option.
3. At the Print backstage area, look at the preview of the chart that displays at the right side and notice that the first gallery in the *Settings* category is set to *Print Selected Chart*.
4. Click the Print button.
5. Save and then close **EL1-C7-P1-SalesChart.xlsx**.

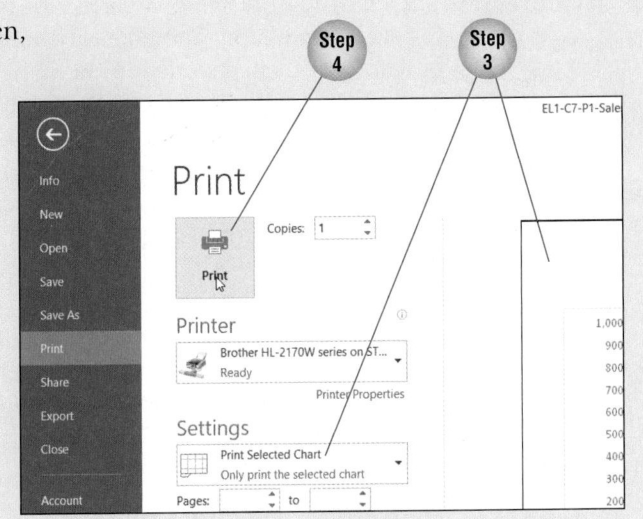

Project 2 Create a Department Expenditures Bar Chart and Column Chart

2 Parts

You will open a workbook containing expenditure data by department and then create a bar chart with the data. You will then change the chart type, layout, and style; add chart elements; and move the chart to a new worksheet.

Changing the Chart Design

Along with the buttons that display outside the upper right side of the chart, you can apply formatting to change the chart design with options on the CHART TOOLS DESIGN tab. This tab, shown in Figure 7.5, displays when you insert a chart in a worksheet. Use options on this tab to add chart elements, change the chart type, specify a different layout or style for the chart, and change the location of the chart so it displays in a separate worksheet.

Figure 7.5 CHART TOOLS DESIGN Tab

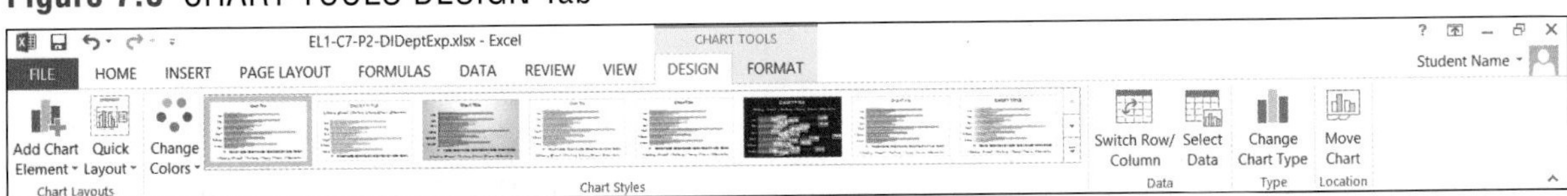

Changing the Chart Style

Quick Steps

Change the Chart Type and Style
1. Make chart active.
2. Click CHART TOOLS DESIGN tab.
3. Click Change Chart Type button.
4. Click desired chart type.
5. Click desired chart style.
6. Click OK.

Change Chart Type

The chart feature offers a variety of preformatted custom charts and varying styles for each chart type. You chose a chart style in Project 1b using the Chart Styles button that displays outside the right border of the chart. You can also choose a chart style with options in the Chart Styles group on the CHART TOOLS DESIGN tab. To do this, click the desired chart style thumbnail that displays in the Chart Styles group or click the More button that displays to the right of the thumbnails and then click the desired chart style thumbnail.

You can also choose a chart style with the Change Chart Type button in the Type group. Click this button and the Change Chart Type dialog box with the All Charts tab active displays, as shown in Figure 7.6. Click the desired chart type in the panel at the left side of the dialog box, click the desired chart style in the row of options at the top at the right, and then click a specific style that displays below the row of styles. Click the Recommended Chart tab to display chart styles recommended for the data by Excel.

Switching Rows and Columns

Quick Steps

Switch Rows and Columns
1. Make chart active.
2. Click CHART TOOLS DESIGN tab.
3. Click Switch Row/Column button.

Switch Row/Column

When creating a chart, Excel uses row headings for grouping data along the bottom of the chart (the horizontal axis) and uses column headings for the legend. You can change this order by clicking the Switch Row/Column button in the Data group on the CHART TOOLS DESIGN tab. When you click this button, Excel uses the column headings for grouping data along the horizontal axis and uses row headings for the legend.

Figure 7.6 Change Chart Type Dialog Box

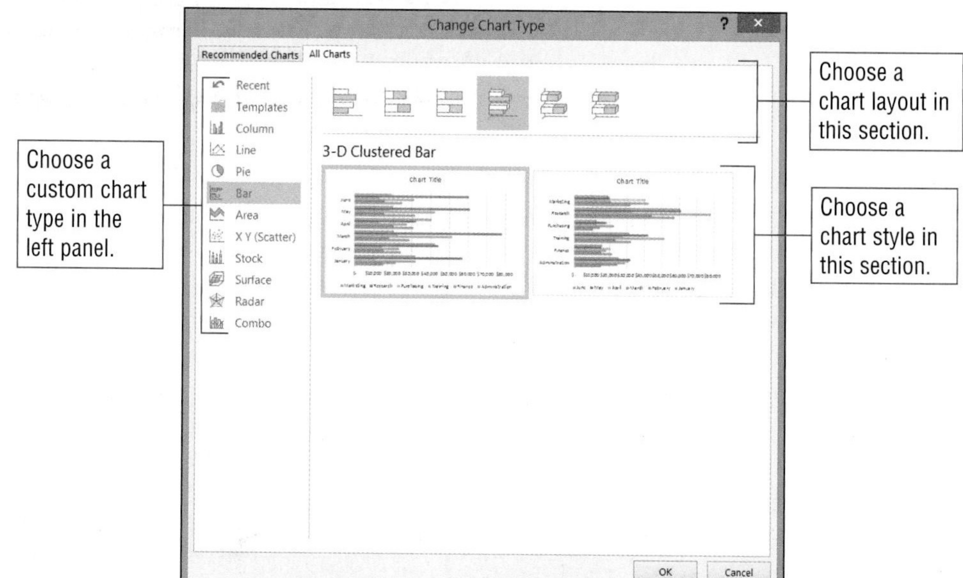

Project 2a **Creating a Chart and Changing the Design** **Part 1 of 2**

1. Open **DIDeptExp.xlsx** and then save the workbook with Save As and name it **EL1-C7-P2-DIDeptExp**.
2. Create a bar chart by completing the following steps:
   a. Select cells A3 through G9.
   b. Click the INSERT tab.
   c. Click the Insert Bar Chart button in the Charts group.
   d. Click the *3-D Clustered Bar* option (first option in the *3-D Bar* section).

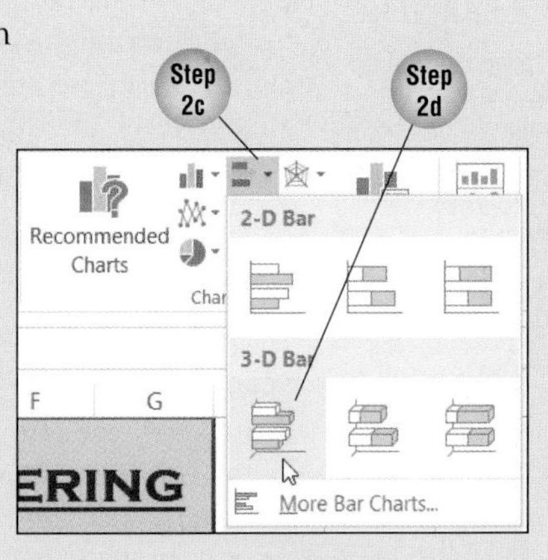

3. With the CHART TOOLS DESIGN tab active, change the chart type by completing the following steps:
   a. Click the Change Chart Type button located in the Type group.
   b. At the Change Chart Type dialog box, click the *Column* option in the left panel.
   c. Click the *3-D Clustered Column* option in the top row (fourth option from left).
   d. Click OK to close the Change Chart Type dialog box.
4. With the chart selected and the CHART TOOLS DESIGN tab active, click the Switch Row/Column button located in the Data group.

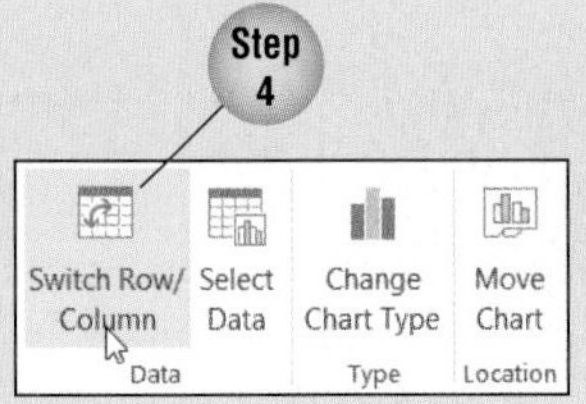

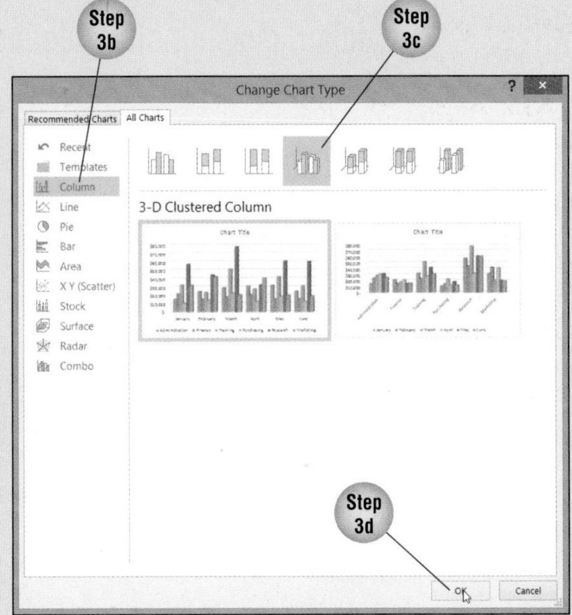

5. Save **EL1-C7-P2-DIDeptExp.xlsx**.

Changing Chart Layout and Colors

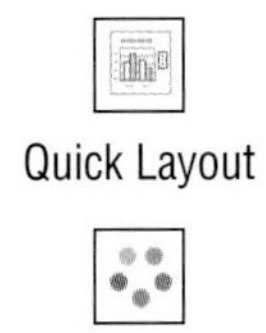

The CHART TOOLS DESIGN tab contains options for changing the chart layout and chart colors. Click the Quick Layout button in the Chart Layouts group and a drop-down gallery of layout options displays. Hover the mouse over a layout option at the drop-down gallery and the chart will reflect the layout. Change the colors used in the chart by clicking the Change Colors button in the Chart Styles group and then clicking the desired color at the drop-down gallery.

Changing the Chart Location

Quick Steps
Change the Chart Location
1. Make chart active.
2. Click CHART TOOLS DESIGN tab.
3. Click Move Chart button.
4. Click *New Sheet* option.
5. Click OK.

Move Chart

Create a chart and the chart is inserted in the currently open worksheet as an embedded object. Change the location of a chart with the Move Chart button in the Location group on the CHART TOOLS DESIGN tab. Click this button and the Move Chart dialog box displays, as shown in Figure 7.7. To move the chart to a new sheet in the workbook, click the *New sheet* option; Excel automatically names the new sheet *Chart1*. Earlier in this chapter you learned that pressing Alt + F1 will insert a recommended chart in the currently open worksheet. If you want the recommended chart inserted into a separate worksheet, press F11.

If you move a chart to a separate sheet, you can move it back to the original sheet or move it to a different sheet within the workbook. To move a chart to a sheet, click the Move Chart button in the Location group. At the Move Chart dialog box, click the down-pointing arrow at the right side of the *Object in* option and then click the desired sheet at the drop-down list. Click OK and the chart is inserted in the specified sheet as an object that you can move, size, and format.

Adding, Moving, and Deleting Chart Elements

Add Chart Element

As you learned earlier in this chapter, you can add chart elements to a chart with the Chart Elements button that displays at the right side of a selected chart. You can also add chart elements with the Add Chart Element button on the CHART TOOLS DESIGN tab. Click this button to display a drop-down list of elements, point to a category of elements, and then click the element you want to apply at the side menu that displays.

Quick Steps
Delete a Chart Element
1. Click chart element.
2. Press Delete key.
OR
1. Right-click chart element.
2. Click *Delete*.

You can also move and/or size a chart element. To move a chart element, click the element to select it and then move the mouse pointer over the border line until the pointer turns into a four-headed arrow. Hold down the left mouse button, drag the element to the desired location, and then release the mouse button. To size a chart element, click to select the element and then use the sizing handles that display around it to increase or decrease the size. To delete a chart element, click the element to select it and then press the Delete key. You can also delete an element by right-clicking the element and then clicking *Delete* at the shortcut menu.

Figure 7.7 Move Chart Dialog Box

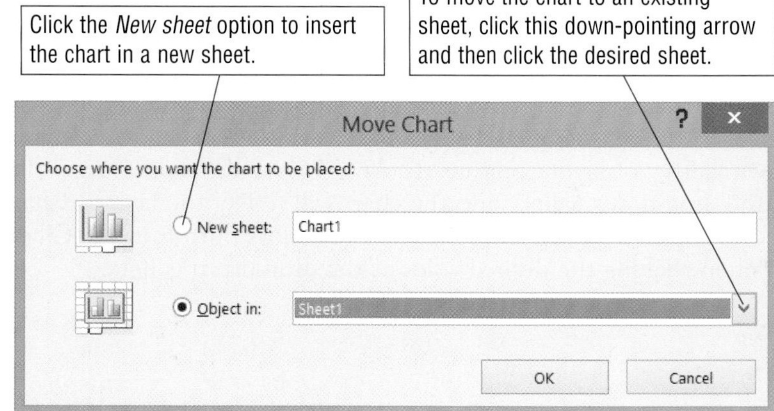
Click the *New sheet* option to insert the chart in a new sheet.
To move the chart to an existing sheet, click this down-pointing arrow and then click the desired sheet.
Move Chart
Choose where you want the chart to be placed:
New sheet:
Chart1
Object in:
Sheet1
OK
Cancel

Project 2b Changing Chart Layout and Location and Adding Chart Elements Part 2 of 2

1. With **EL1-C7-P2-DIDeptExp.xlsx** open, make sure the CHART TOOLS DESIGN tab is active. (If it is not, make sure the chart is selected and then click the CHART TOOLS DESIGN tab.)
2. Change the chart style by clicking the *Style 5* thumbnail in the Chart Styles group (fifth option from the left).

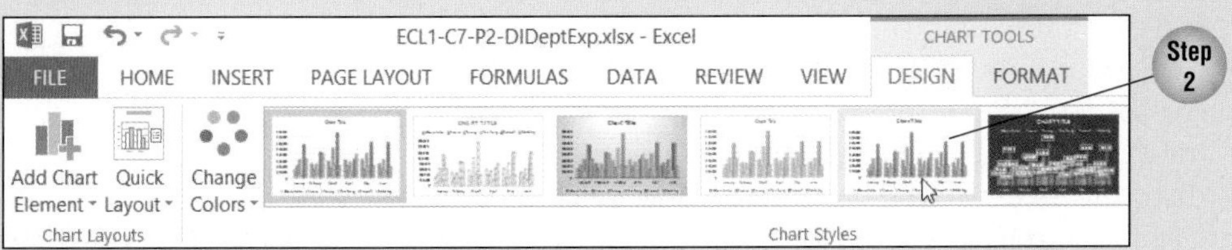

3. Change the chart colors by clicking the Change Colors button in the Chart Styles group and then clicking the *Color 3* option (third row in the *Colorful* group).
4. Change the chart layout by clicking the Quick Layout button in the Chart Layouts group and then clicking the *Layout 1* option (first option in the drop-down gallery).

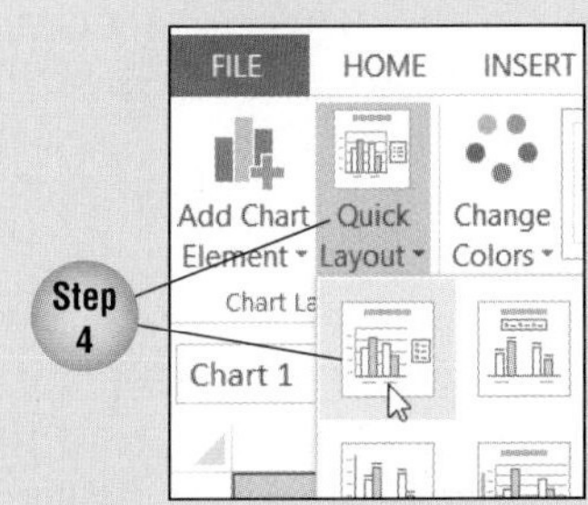

5. Add axis titles by completing the following steps:
   a. Click the Add Chart Element button in the Chart Layouts group on the CHART TOOLS DESIGN tab.
   b. Point to *Axis Titles* and then click *Primary Horizontal* at the side menu.
   c. Type **Department** and then press Enter. (The word *Department* will display in the Formula bar.)
   d. Click the Add Chart Element button, point to *Axis Titles*, and then click *Primary Vertical* at the side menu.
   e. Type **Expenditure Amounts** and then press Enter.

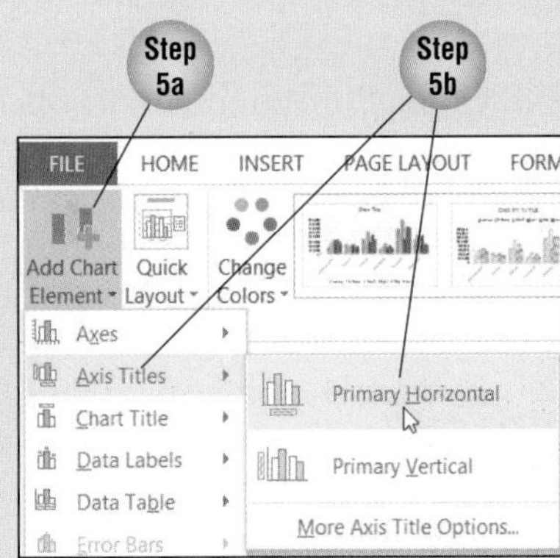

6. Click in the text *Chart Title* that displays toward the top of the chart, type **Half-Yearly Expenditures**, and then press Enter.
7. Delete the *Expenditure Amounts* axis title by clicking on any character in the axis title and then pressing the Delete key.
8. Move the legend by completing the following steps:
   a. Click on any character in the legend to select it.
   b. Move the mouse pointer over the border line until the pointer turns into a four-headed arrow.
   c. Hold down the left mouse button, drag up until the top border of the legend aligns with the top gridline in the chart, and then release the mouse button.

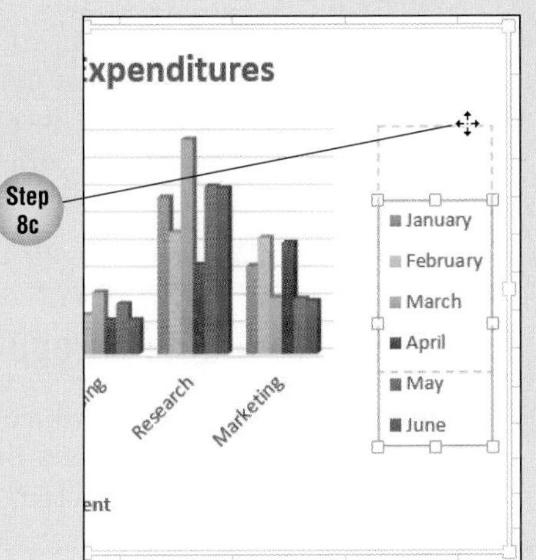

9. Move the chart to a new location by completing the following steps:
   a. Click the Move Chart button in the Location group.
   b. At the Move Chart dialog box, click the *New sheet* option and then click OK. (The chart is inserted in a worksheet named *Chart1*.) 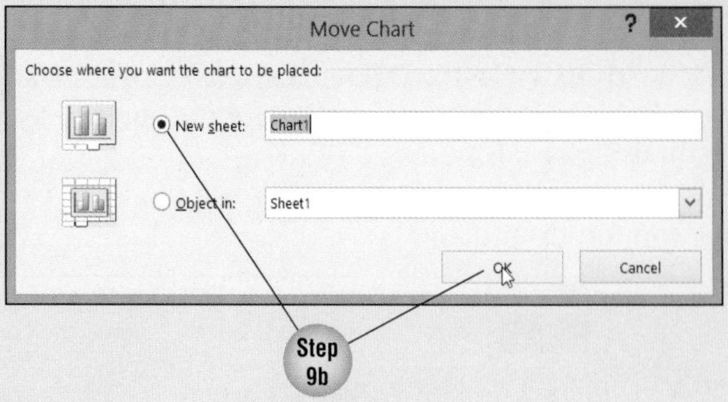
10. Save **EL1-C7-P2-DIDeptExp.xlsx**.
11. Print the Chart1 worksheet.
12. Move the chart from Chart1 to Sheet2 by completing the following steps:
   a. Make sure Chart1 is the active worksheet and that the chart is selected (not just an element in the chart).
   b. Make sure the CHART TOOLS DESIGN tab is active.
   c. Click the Move Chart button in the Location group.
   d. At the Move Chart dialog box, click the down-pointing arrow at the right side of the *Object in* option box and then click *Sheet2* at the drop-down list.
   e. Click OK. 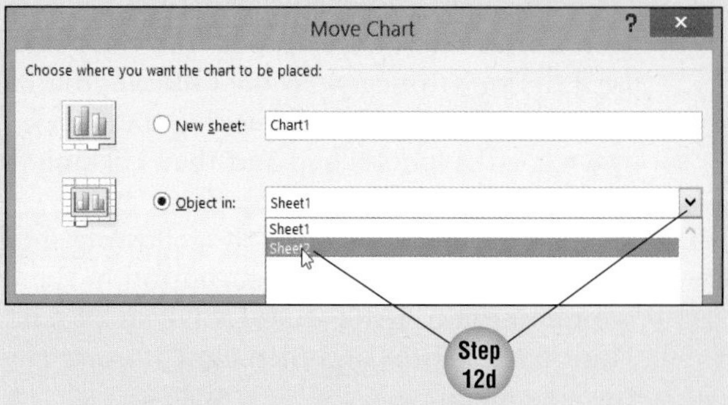
13. Change the amounts in Sheet1 by completing the following steps:
   a. Click Sheet1.
   b. Make cell B7 active and then change the amount from *10,540* to *19,750*.
   c. Make cell D8 active and then change the amount from *78,320* to *63,320*.
   d. Make cell G8 active and then change the amount from *60,570* to *75,570*.
   e. Make cell A2 active.
   f. Click the Sheet2 tab and notice that the chart displays the updated amounts.
14. Click outside the chart to deselect it.
15. Insert a header in the Sheet2 worksheet that prints your name at the left side, the current date in the middle, and the workbook file name at the right side.
16. Display the worksheet at the Print backstage area and make sure it will print on one page. If the chart does not fit on the page, return to the worksheet and then move and/or decrease the size of the chart until it fits on one page.
17. Print the active worksheet (Sheet2).
18. Save and then close **EL1-C7-P2-DIDeptExp.xlsx**.

Move Chart
Choose where you want the chart to be placed:
New sheet: Chart1
Object in: Sheet1
OK Cancel
Step 9b

Move Chart
Choose where you want the chart to be placed:
New sheet: Chart1
Object in: Sheet1
Sheet1
Sheet2
Step 12d

Project 3 Create a Population Comparison Line Chart — 2 Parts

You will open a workbook containing population comparison data for Seattle and Portland and then create a line chart with the data. You will move the chart to a new worksheet, format chart elements, and insert a shape in the chart.

Changing Chart Formatting

Customize the formatting of a chart and chart elements with options on the CHART TOOLS FORMAT tab, as shown in Figure 7.8. With buttons in the Current Selection group, you can identify specific elements in the chart and then apply formatting. Insert a shape in a chart with options in the Insert Shapes group and format shapes with options in the Shape Styles group. Apply WordArt formatting to data in a chart with options in the WordArt Styles group. Arrange, align, and size a chart with options in the Arrange and Size groups.

Formatting a Selection

Identify a specific element in a chart for formatting by clicking the Chart Elements button arrow in the Current Selection group on the CHART TOOLS FORMAT tab and then clicking the desired element at the drop-down list. This selects the specific element in the chart. Click the Reset to Match Style button to return the formatting of the element back to the original style. Use buttons in the Shapes Styles group to apply formatting to a selected object and use buttons in the WordArt Styles group to apply formatting to selected data.

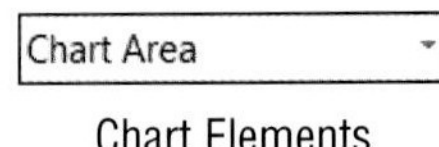

Chart Elements

Figure 7.8 CHART TOOLS FORMAT Tab

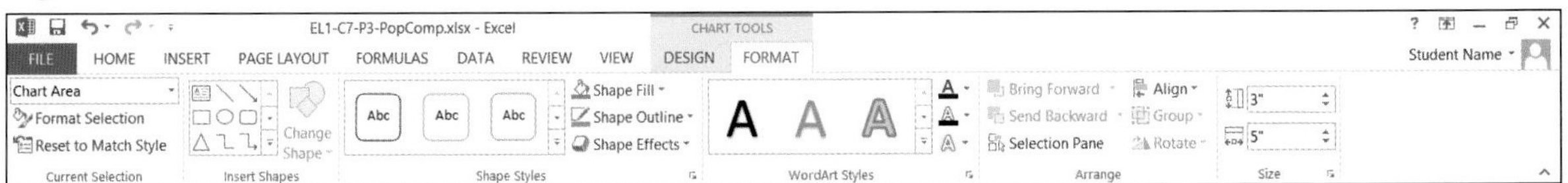

Project 3a **Creating and Formatting a Line Chart** **Part 1 of 2**

1. Open **PopComp.xlsx** and then save the workbook with Save As and name it **EL1-C7-P3-PopComp**.
2. Create a line chart and add a chart element by completing the following steps:
   a. Select cells A2 through I4.
   b. Click the INSERT tab.
   c. Click the Insert Line Chart button in the Charts group.
   d. Click the *Line with Markers* option at the drop-down list (first column, second row in the *2-D Line* section).
   e. Click the Chart Elements button that displays outside the upper right side of the chart.
   f. Hover your mouse over the *Data Table* option at the side menu, click the right-pointing triangle that displays, and then click *No Legend Keys* at the side menu that appears.
   g. Click the Chart Elements button to remove the side menu.
3. Move the chart to a new sheet by completing the following steps:
   a. Click the Move Chart button in the Location group on the CHART TOOLS DESIGN tab.
   b. At the Move Chart dialog box, click the *New sheet* option.
   c. Click OK.

4. Format the *Portland* line by completing the following steps:
   a. Click the CHART TOOLS FORMAT tab.
   b. Click the Chart Elements button arrow in the Current Selection group and then click *Series "Portland"* at the drop-down list.
   c. Click the Shape Fill button arrow in the Shape Styles group and then click the *Green* color at the drop-down color palette (sixth color in the *Standard Colors* section).

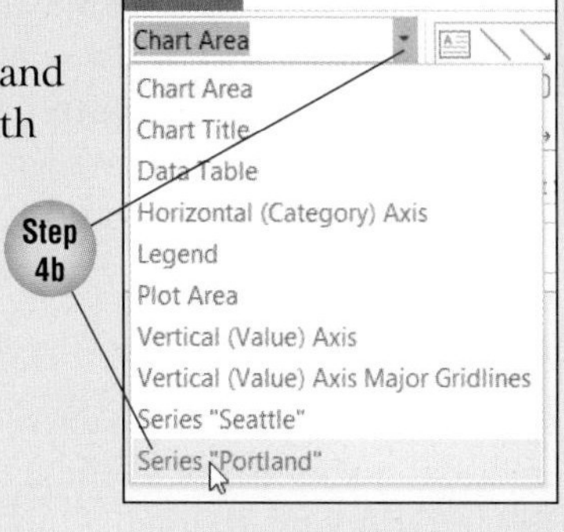

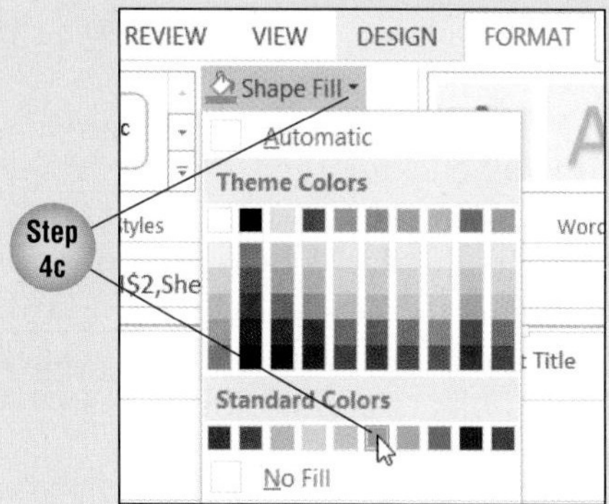

   d. Click the Shape Outline button arrow in the Shape Styles group and then click the *Green* color.
5. Type a title for the chart and format the title by completing the following steps:
   a. Click Chart Elements button arrow in the Current Selection group and then click *Chart Title* at the drop-down list.
   b. Type **Population Comparison between Seattle and Portland** and then press Enter.
   c. Click the *Fill - Black, Text 1, Shadow* WordArt style thumbnail in the WordArt Styles group (first WordArt style thumbnail).
6. Format the legend by completing the following steps:
   a. Click the Chart Elements button arrow in the Current Selection group and then click *Legend* at the drop-down list.
   b. Click the *Colored Outline - Blue, Accent 1* shape style thumbnail in the Shape Styles group (second shape style thumbnail).
7. Save **EL1-C7-P3-PopComp.xlsx**.

Inserting Shapes

Quick Steps

Insert a Shape
1. Make chart active.
2. Click CHART TOOLS FORMAT tab.
3. Click More button at right side of shapes.
4. Click desired shape at drop-down list.
5. Click or drag to create shape in chart.

The Insert Shapes group on the CHART TOOLS FORMAT tab contains options for inserting shapes in a chart. Click a shape option and the mouse pointer turns into a thin, black plus symbol. Click in the chart or drag with the mouse to create the shape in the chart. The shape is inserted in the chart and the DRAWING TOOLS FORMAT tab is active. This tab contains many of the same options as the CHART TOOLS FORMAT tab. For example, you can insert a shape, apply a shape or WordArt style, and arrange and size the shape. Size a shape by clicking the up- or down-pointing arrows that display at the right side of the *Shape Height* or *Shape Width* measurement boxes in the Size group on the DRAWING TOOLS FORMAT tab. You can also select the current measurement and then type a specific measurement.

Project 3b Inserting and Customizing a Shape

1. With **EL1-C7-P3-PopComp.xlsx** open, create a shape similar to the one shown in Figure 7.9 on the next page by completing the following steps:
   a. Click the More button at the right side of the shapes in the Insert Shapes group on the CHART TOOLS FORMAT tab.
   b. Click the *Up Arrow Callout* shape in the *Block Arrows* section.
   c. Click in the chart to insert the shape.
   d. Click in the *Shape Height* measurement box in the Size group on the DRAWING TOOLS FORMAT tab, type 1.5, and then press Enter.
   e. Click in the *Shape Width* measurement box, type 1.5, and then press Enter.
   f. Apply a shape style by clicking the More button at the right side of the shape style thumbnails in the Shape Style group and then clicking the *Subtle Effect - Blue, Accent 1* option (second column, fourth row).

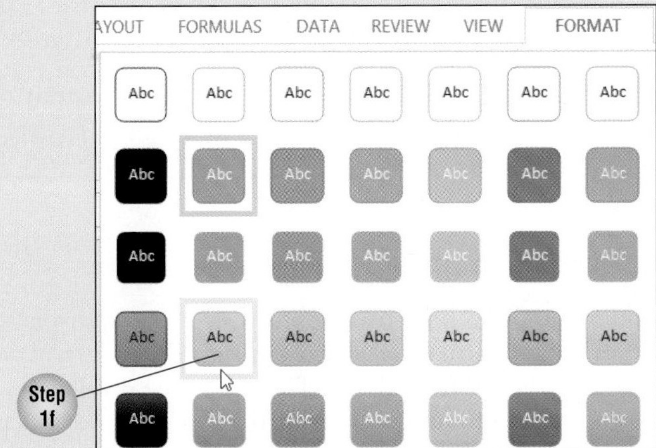

   g. Type **Largest disparity** in the shape, press Enter, and then type **(184,411)**.
   h. Select the text you just typed.
   i. Click the HOME tab.
   j. Click the Bold button in the Font group.
   k. Click the Font Size button arrow and then click *14*.
   l. Click the Center button in the Alignment group.
2. With the shape selected, drag the shape so it is positioned as shown in Figure 7.9.
3. Save **EL1-C7-P3-PopComp.xlsx**, print the Chart1 worksheet, and then close the workbook.

Figure 7.9 Project 3 Chart

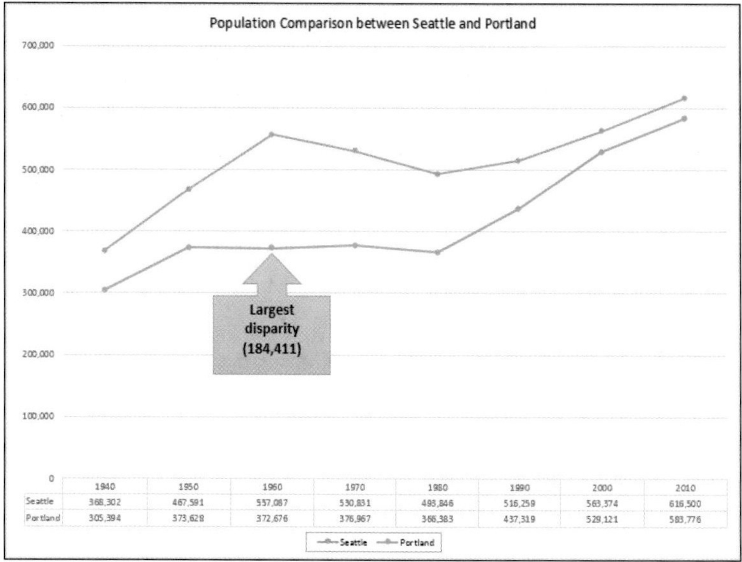

Project 4 Create a Costs Percentage Pie Chart — 1 Part

You will create a pie chart, add data labels, apply a style, format chart elements, and then size and move the pie chart.

Quick Steps

Display a Task Pane
1. Select chart or specific element.
2. Click CHART TOOLS FORMAT tab.
3. Click Format Selection button.

Format Selection

Applying Formatting at a Task Pane

To view and apply more formatting options for charts, display the formatting task pane by clicking the Format Selection button in the Current Selection group on the CHART TOOLS FORMAT tab. The task pane displays at the right side of the screen and the name of and contents in the task pane vary depending on what is selected. If the entire chart is selected, the Format Chart Area task pane displays, as shown in Figure 7.10. Format the chart by clicking the desired formatting options in the task pane. Display additional formatting options by clicking the icons that display toward the top of the task pane. For example, click the Effects icon in the Format Chart Area task pane and options for applying shadow, glow, soft edges, and 3-D formatting display.

Click a chart element and then click the Format Selection button and the task pane name and options change. You can also right-click a chart or chart element and then click the format option at the shortcut menu. The name of the format option varies depending on the selected element.

Quick Steps

Change Chart Height and/or Width
1. Make chart active.
2. Click CHART TOOLS FORMAT tab.
3. Insert desired height and/or width with *Shape Height* and/or *Shape Width* measurement boxes.

Changing Chart Height and Width Measurements

As you learned earlier in this chapter, if you insert a chart into the current worksheet (not into a separate, new worksheet), you can size the chart by selecting it and then dragging a sizing handle. You can also size a chart to specific measurements. To do this, display the CHART TOOLS FORMAT tab and then click the up- or down-pointing arrow that displays at the right side of the *Shape*

Figure 7.10 Format Chart Area Task Pane

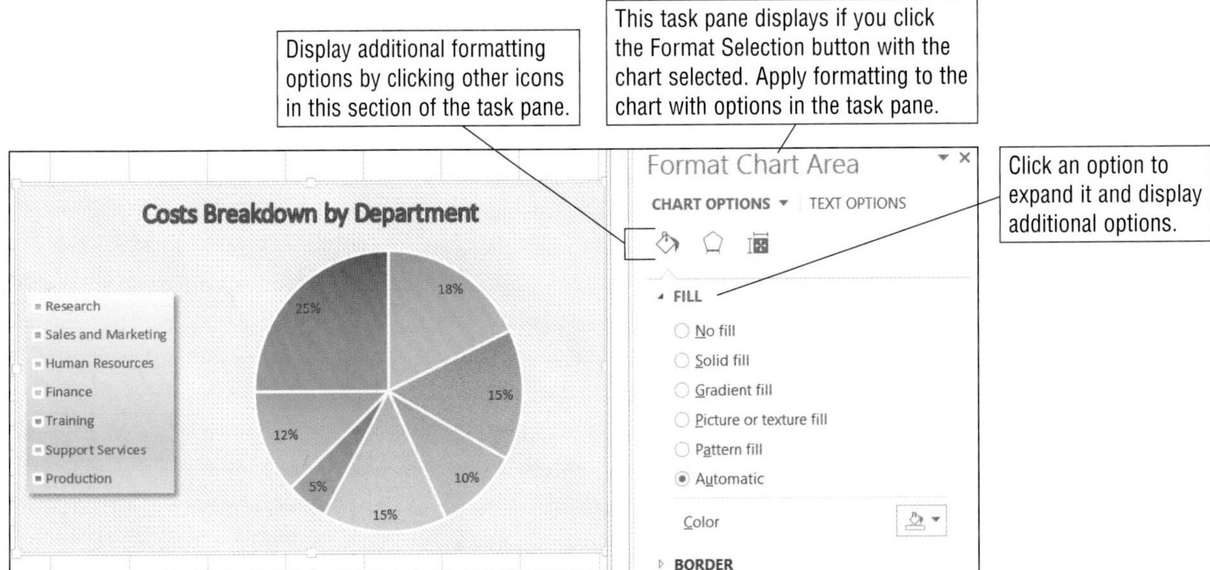

Height or *Shape Width* measurement box or select the current measurement and then type a specific measurement. In addition to using the *Shape Height* and *Shape Width* measurement boxes on the CHART TOOLS FORMAT tab, you can change the chart size with options at the Format Chart Area task pane.

Deleting a Chart

Delete a chart created in Excel by clicking once in the chart to select it and then pressing the Delete key. If you move a chart to a different worksheet in the workbook and then delete the chart, the chart will be deleted but the worksheet will not. To delete the worksheet as well as the chart, position the mouse pointer on the Chart1 tab, click the right mouse button, and then click *Delete* at the shortcut menu. At the message box telling you that selected sheets will be permanently deleted, click Delete.

Quick Steps

Delete a Chart
1. Click once in chart.
2. Press Delete key.
OR
1. Right-click chart tab.
2. Click *Delete*.

Project 4 **Deleting a Chart and Creating and Formatting a Pie Chart** **Part 1 of 1**

1. Open **DIDeptCosts.xlsx** and then save the workbook with Save As and name it **EL1-C7-P4-DIDeptCosts**.
2. Delete the column chart by completing the following steps:
   a. Click the column chart to select the chart. (Make sure the chart is selected and not a specific element in the chart.)
   b. Press the Delete key.
3. Create the pie chart shown in Figure 7.10 by completing the following steps:
   a. Select cells A3 through B10.
   b. Click the INSERT tab.

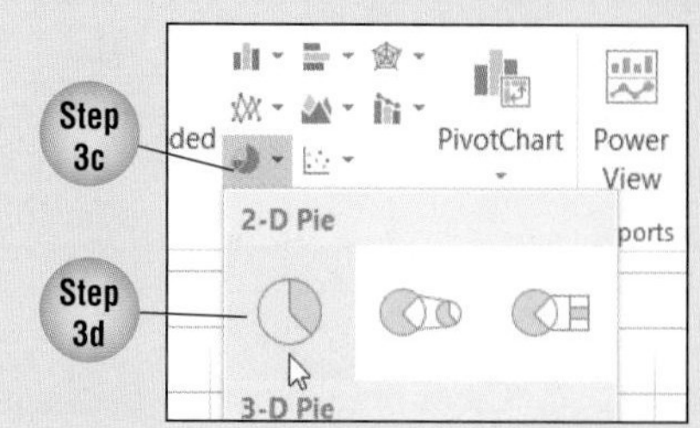

c. Click the Insert Pie or Doughnut Chart button.
d. Click the *Pie* option (first option in the *2-D Pie* section).
4. Insert data labels in the chart by completing the following steps:
a. Click the Chart Elements button that displays outside the upper right border of the chart.
b. Hover the mouse over the *Data Labels* option and click the right-pointing triangle that displays.
c. Click *Inside End* at the side menu.
d. Click the Chart Elements button to hide the side menu.

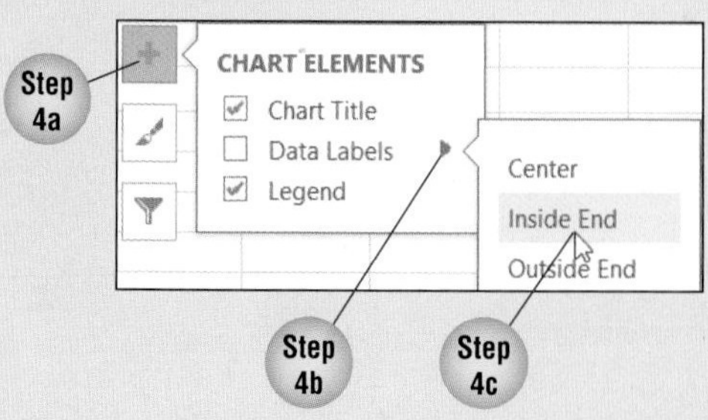

5. Click the *Style 6* thumbnail in the Chart Styles group.
6. Type a title and then apply a WordArt style to the title by completing the following steps:
a. Click the CHART TOOLS FORMAT tab.
b. Click the Chart Elements button arrow in the Current Selection group.
c. Click *Chart Title* at the drop-down list.
d. Type **C** and Excel's AutoComplete feature inserts the entire title *Costs Breakdown by Department* in the Formula bar. Accept this name by pressing the Enter key.
e. Click the More button at the right side of the WordArt style thumbnails in the WordArt Styles group.
f. Click the *Pattern Fill - Gray-50%, Accent 3, Narrow Horizontal, Inner Shadow* style thumbnail at the drop-down gallery (second column, fourth row).
7. Use the Format Legend task pane to apply formatting to the legend by completing the following steps:
a. Click the Chart Elements button arrow and then click *Legend* at the drop-down list.
b. Click the Format Selection button in the Current Selection group.

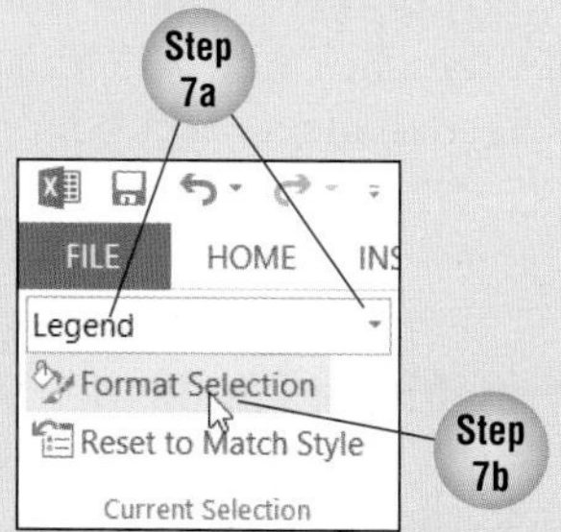

c. At the Format Legend task pane, click the *Left* option in the *LEGEND OPTIONS* section.
d. Click the Effects icon in the task pane. (This changes the options in the task pane.)

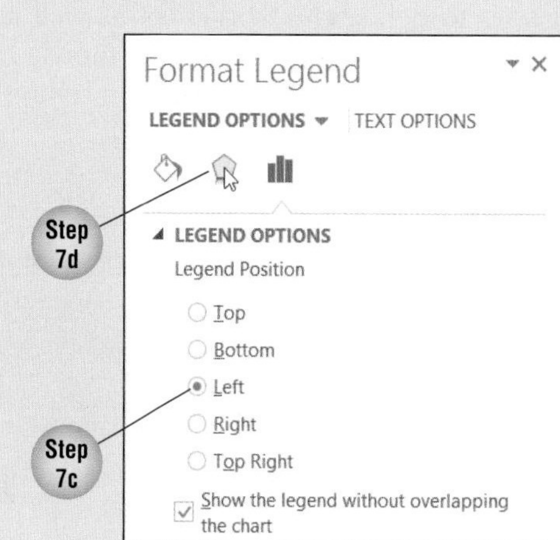

e. Click the *SHADOW* option. (This displays shadow options in the task pane.)
f. Click the Shadow button that displays to the right of *Presets* and then click the *Offset Diagonal Bottom Right* option (first option in the *Outer* section).
g. Click the Fill & Line icon in the task pane.
h. Click the *FILL* option.
i. Click the *Gradient fill* option.
j. Close the task pane by clicking the Close button located in the upper right corner of the task pane.

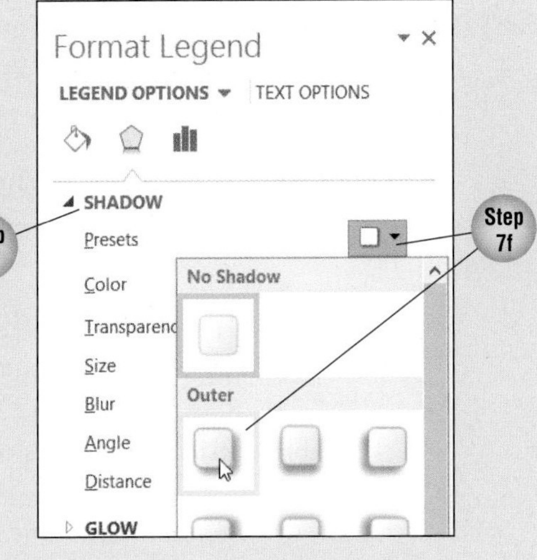

8. Use the Format Chart Area task pane to apply formatting to the chart by completing the following steps:
   a. Click inside the chart but outside any chart elements.
   b. Click the Format Selection button in the Current Selection group.
   c. Make sure the Fill & Line icon in the Format Chart Area task pane is selected. (If not, click the icon.)
   d. Make sure the *FILL* option is expanded. (If not, click the *FILL* option.)
   e. Click the *Gradient fill* option.
   f. Click the Size & Properties icon in the task pane.
   g. Click the *SIZE* option to display size options.
   h. Select the current measurement in the *Height* measurement box, type 4, and then press Enter.
   i. Close the task pane.

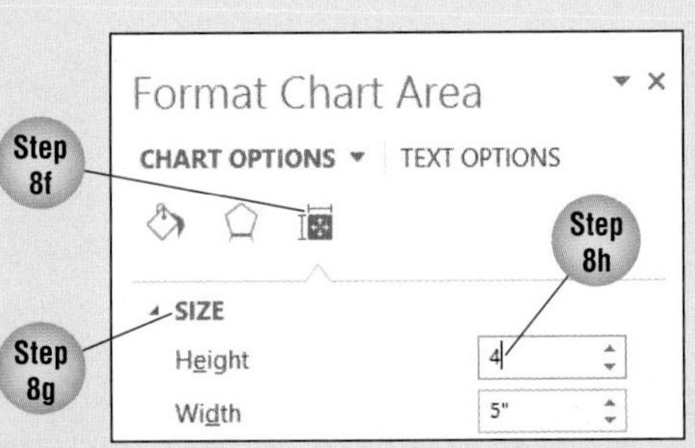

9. Save **EL1-C7-P4-DIDeptCosts.xlsx** and then print only the chart.
10. Change the chart style by completing the following steps:
    a. Click the CHART TOOLS DESIGN tab.
    b. Click the More button at the right side of the chart style thumbnails.
    c. Click the *Style 9* thumbnail at the drop-down gallery.
11. Change the size of the chart by completing the following steps:
    a. Click the CHART TOOLS FORMAT tab.
    b. Click in the *Shape Height* measurement box, type 3.5, and then press Enter.
    c. Click in the *Shape Width* measurement box, type 5.5, and then press Enter.
12. Drag the chart so it is positioned below the cells containing data.
13. Click outside the chart to deselect it.
14. Display the Print backstage area, make sure the chart fits on the page with the data, and then click the Print button.
15. Save **EL1-C7-P4-DIDeptCosts.xlsx** and then close the workbook.

Project 5 Calculate Payments and the Future Value of an Investment

2 Parts

You will use the PMT financial function to calculate payments and the FV financial function to find the future value of an investment.

Writing Formulas with Financial Functions

In Chapter 2, you learned how to insert formulas in a worksheet using mathematical operators and functions. In this section, you will continue learning about writing formulas with functions.

Excel provides a number of financial functions you can use in a formula. With financial functions, you can determine different aspects of a financial loan or investment, such as the payment amount, present value, future value, interest rate, and number of payment periods. Each financial function requires some of the variables listed below in order to return a result. Two such financial functions are the PMT function and FV function. The ***PMT function*** calculates the payment for a loan based on constant payments and a constant interest rate. The ***FV function*** calculates the future value of an investment.

Financial functions use some of the following arguments:

- **Rate:** The rate is the interest rate for a payment period. The rate may need to be modified for the function to display the desired results. For example, most rate values are given as an APR (annual percentage rate), which is the percentage rate for one year, not a payment period. So a percentage rate may be given as 12% APR but if the payment period is a month, then the percentage rate for the function is 1%, not 12%. If your worksheet contains the annual percentage rate, you can enter the cell reference in the function argument and specify that you want it divided by 12 months. For example, if cell B6 contains the annual interest rate, enter *B6/12* as the Rate argument.
- **Nper:** The Nper is the number of payment periods in an investment. The Nper may also need to be modified depending on what information is provided. For example, if a loan duration is expressed in years but the payments are paid each month, the Nper value needs to be adjusted accordingly. A five-year loan has an Nper of 60 (five years times 12 months in each year).
- **Pmt:** The Pmt is the payment amount for each period. This variable describes the payment amount for a period and is commonly expressed as a negative value because it is an outflow of cash. However, the Pmt value can be entered as a positive value if the present value (Pv) or future value (Fv) is entered as a negative value. Whether the Pmt value is positive or negative depends on who created the workbook. For example, a home owner lists the variable as outflow, while the lending institution lists it as inflow.
- **Pv:** The Pv is the present value of an investment, expressed in a lump sum. The Pv variable is generally the initial loan amount. For example, if a person is purchasing a new home, the Pv is the amount of money the buyer borrowed to buy the home. Pv can be expressed as a negative value, which denotes it as an investment instead of a loan. For example, if a bank issues a loan to a home buyer, it enters the Pv value as a negative because it is an outflow of cash for the bank.

- **Fv:** The Fv is the future value of an investment, expressed in a lump sum amount. The Fv variable is generally the loan amount plus the amount of interest paid during the loan. In the example of a home buyer, the Fv is the sum of payments, which includes both the principle and interest paid on the loan. In the example of a bank, the Fv is the total amount received after a loan has been paid off. Fv can also be expressed as either a positive or negative value depending on which side of the transaction you review.

Finding the Periodic Payments for a Loan

The PMT function finds the payment for a loan based on constant payments and a constant interest rate. In Project 5a, you will use the PMT function to determine monthly payments for equipment and a used van as well as monthly income from selling equipment. The formulas you will create with the PMT function in Project 5a will include Rate, Nper, and Pv arguments. The Nper argument is the number of payments that will be made on the loan or investment, Pv is the current value of amounts to be received or paid in the future, and Fv is the value of the loan or investment at the end of all periods.

Financial

To write the PMT function, click the FORMULAS tab, click the Financial button in the Function Library group, and then click the PMT function at the drop-down list. This displays the Function Arguments palette with options for inserting cell designations for Rate, Nper, and Pv. (These are the arguments in bold. The palette also contains the Fv and Type functions, which are dimmed.)

Project 5a **Calculating Payments** **Part 1 of 2**

1. Open **RPReports.xlsx** and then save the workbook with Save As and name it **EL1-C7-P5-RPReports**.
2. The owner of Real Photography is interested in purchasing a new developer and needs to determine monthly payments on three different models. Insert a formula that calculates monthly payments and then copy that formula by completing the following steps:
   a. Make cell E5 active.
   b. Click the FORMULAS tab.
   c. Click the Financial button in the Function Library group, scroll down the drop-down list, and then click *PMT*.

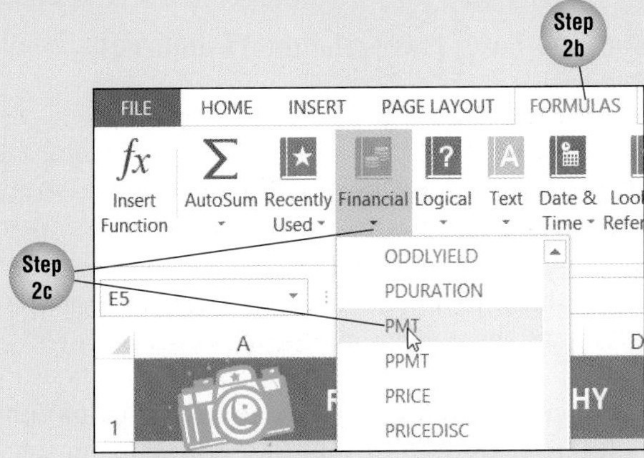

d. At the Function Arguments palette, type **C5/12** in the *Rate* text box. (This tells Excel to divide the interest rate by 12 months.)
e. Press the Tab key. (This moves the insertion point to the *Nper* text box).
f. Type **D5**. (This is the total number of months for the investment.)
g. Press the Tab key. (This moves the insertion point to the *Pv* text box.)
h. Type **B5**. (This is the purchase price of the developer.)
i. Click OK. (This closes the palette and inserts the monthly payment of *($316.98)* in cell E5. Excel displays the result of the PMT function as a negative number since the loan represents money going out of the company—a negative cash flow.)
j. Copy the formula in cell E5 down to cells E6 and E7.

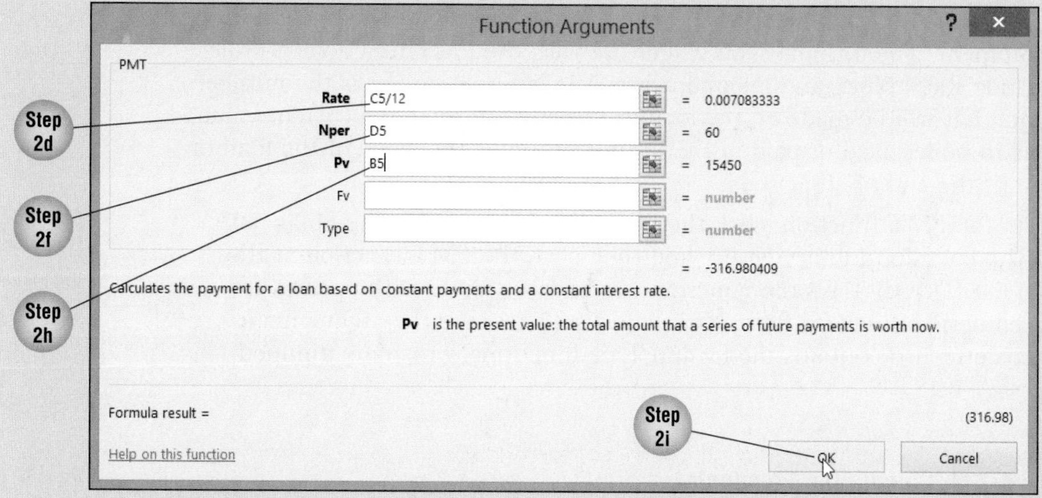

3. The owner is interested in purchasing a used van for the company and wants an idea of what monthly payments would be at various terms and rates. Insert a formula that calculates monthly payments for a three-year loan at 5% interest by completing the following steps:
   a. Make cell E12 active.
   b. Make sure the FORMULAS tab is active
   c. Click the Financial button in the Function Library group, scroll down the drop-down list, and then click *PMT*.
   d. At the Function Arguments palette, type **C12/12** in the *Rate* text box. (This tells Excel to divide the interest rate by 12 months.)
   e. Press the Tab key.
   f. Type **D12** in the *Nper* text box. (This is the total number of months for the investment.)
   g. Press the Tab key.
   h. Type **B12** in the *Pv* text box.
   i. Click OK. (This closes the palette and inserts the monthly payment of *($299.71)* in cell E12.)
   j. Copy the formula in cell E12 down to cells E13 through E15.

Term in Months	Monthly Payments
36	($299.71)
36	($449.56)
36	($599.42)
36	($749.27)

Step 3j

4. The owner has discovered that the interest rate for a used van will be 6.25% instead of 5%. Change the percentages in cells C12 through C15 to 6.25%.
5. The owner is selling a camera and wants you to determine the monthly payments for a two-year loan at 4.5% interest. Determine monthly payments on the camera (income to Real Photography) by completing the following steps:

a. Make cell E20 active.
b. Make sure the FORMULAS tab is active.
c. Click the Financial button in the Function Library group, scroll down the drop-down list, and then click *PMT*.
d. At the Function Arguments palette, type **C20/12** in the *Rate* text box.
e. Press the Tab key.
f. Type **D20** in the *Nper* text box.
g. Press the Tab key.
h. Type **-B20**. In the *Pv* text box. (Excel displays the result of the PMT function as a negative number since the loan represents a negative cash flow. The sale of the camera represents a cash outflow because the business is selling the camera in order to receive payments—cash in flow).
i. Click OK. (This closes the palette and inserts the monthly income of *$185.92* in cell E20.)

6. Save, print, and then close **EL1-C7-P5-RPReports.xlsx**.

Finding the Future Value of a Series of Payments

The FV function calculates the future value of a series of equal payments or an annuity. Use this function to determine information such as how much money can be earned in an investment account with a specific interest rate and over a specific period of time.

Project 5b Finding the Future Value of an Investment — Part 2 of 2

1. Open **RPInvest.xlsx** and then save the workbook with Save As and name it **EL1-C7-P5-RPInvest**.
2. The owner of Real Photography has decided to save money to purchase a new developer and wants to compute how much money can be earned by investing the money in an investment account that returns 7.5% annual interest. The owner determines that $1,200 per month can be invested in the account for three years. Complete the following steps to determine the future value of the investment account:
   a. Make cell B6 active.
   b. Make sure the FORMULAS tab is active.
   c. Click the Financial button in the Function Library group.
   d. At the drop-down list that displays, scroll down the list and then click *FV*.
   e. At the Function Arguments palette, type **B3/12** in the *Rate* text box.
   f. Press the Tab key.
   g. Type **B4** in the *Nper* text box.
   h. Press the Tab key.
   i. Type **B5** in the *Pmt* text box.
   j. Click OK. (This closes the palette and also inserts the future value of *$48,277.66* in cell B6.)
3. Save and then print **EL1-C7-P5-RPInvest.xlsx**.
4. The owner decides to determine the future return after two years. To do this, change the amount in cell B4 from *36* to *24* and then press Enter. (This recalculates the future investment amount in cell B6.)
5. Save, print, and then close **EL1-C7-P5-RPInvest.xlsx**.

Project 6 Insert Formulas with the IF Logical Function

3 Parts

You will use the IF logical function to calculate sales bonuses, determine pass/fail grades based on averages, and identify discounts and discount amounts.

Writing Formulas with the IF Logical Function

A question that can be answered with true or false is considered a ***logical test***. You can use the ***IF function*** to create a logical test that performs a particular action if the answer is true (condition met) and another action if the answer is false (condition not met).

For example, an IF function can be used to write a formula that calculates a salesperson's bonus as 10% if the salesperson sells more than $99,999 worth of product and 0% if he or she does not sell more than $99,999 worth of product. When writing a formula with an IF function, think about the words *if* and *then*. For example, the formula written out for the bonus example would look like this:

> ***If*** the salesperson sells more than $99,999 of product, ***then*** he or she receives a bonus of 10%.
>
> ***If*** the salesperson does not sell more than $99,999 of product, ***then*** he or she receives a bonus of 0%.

When writing a formula with an IF function, commas separate the condition and the action. The formula for the bonus example would look like this: ***=IF(sales>99999,sales*0.1,0)***. The formula contains three parts:

- the condition or logical test: ***IF(sales>99999***
- the action taken if the condition or logical test is true: ***sales*0.1***
- the action taken if the condition or logical test is false: ***0***

In Project 6a, you will write a formula with cell references rather than cell data. In the project, you will write a formula with an IF function that determines the following:

> ***If*** the sales amount is greater than the quota amount, ***then*** the salesperson will receive a 15% bonus.
>
> ***If*** the sales amount is not greater than the quota amount, ***then*** the salesperson will not receive a bonus.

Written with cell references in the project, the formula looks like this: ***=IF(C4>B4,C4*0.15,0)***. In this formula the condition or logical test is whether or not the number in cell C4 is greater than the number in cell B4. If the condition is true and the number is greater, then the number in cell C4 is multiplied by 0.15 (providing a 15% bonus). If the condition is false and the number in cell C4 is less than the number in cell B4, then nothing happens (no bonus). Notice how commas are used to separate the logical test from the action.

Project 6a Writing a Formula with an IF Function

Part 1 of 3

1. Open **CMPReports.xlsx** and then save it with Save As and name it **EL1-C7-P6-CMPReports**.
2. Write a formula with the IF function that determines if a sales quota has been met and, if it has, inserts the bonus: 15% of actual sales. (If the quota has not been met, the formula will insert a 0.) Write the formula by completing the following steps:
   a. Make cell D4 active.
   b. Type =IF(C4>B4,C4*0.15,0) and then press Enter.

D4 | =IF(C4>B4,C4*0.15,0)

	A	B	C	D
1	Capstan Marine Products			
2	Sales Department			
3	Salesperson	Quota	Actual Sales	Bonus
4	Allejandro	$ 95,500.00	$	=IF(C4>B4,C4*0.15,0)
5	Crispin	137,000.00	129,890.00	

Step 2b

   c. Make cell D4 active and then use the fill handle to copy the formula to cells D5 through D9.
3. Print the worksheet.
4. Revise the formula so it inserts a 20% bonus if the quota has been met by completing the following steps:
   a. Make cell D4 active.
   b. Click in the Formula bar, edit the formula so it displays as *=IF(C4>B4,C4*0.2,0)*, and then click the Enter button on the Formula bar.
   c. Copy the formula in cell D4 down to cells D5 through D9.
   d. Apply accounting formatting with a dollar sign and two places beyond the decimal point.
5. Save **EL1-C7-P6-CMPReports.xlsx**.

Writing Formulas with an IF Function Using the Function Arguments Palette

You can type a formula containing an IF function directly into a cell or you can use the Function Arguments palette to help you write the formula. To use the Function Arguments palette to write a formula with the IF function, click the FORMULAS tab, click the Logical button in the Function Library group, and then click *IF* at the drop-down list. This displays the Function Arguments palette, shown in Figure 7.11. The Function Arguments palette displays the information you will type in the three argument text boxes for Project 6b.

Logical

At the Function Arguments palette, click in the *Logical_test* text box and information about the Logical_test argument displays in the palette. In this text box, type the cell designation followed by what is evaluated. In the figure, the *Logical_test* text box contains *B14>599*, indicating that what is being evaluated is whether or not the amount in cell B14 is greater than $599. The *Value_if_true* text box contains *B14*0.95*, indicating that if the logical test is true, then multiply the amount in cell B14 by 0.95. (The discount for any product price greater than $599

Figure 7.11 Function Arguments Palette

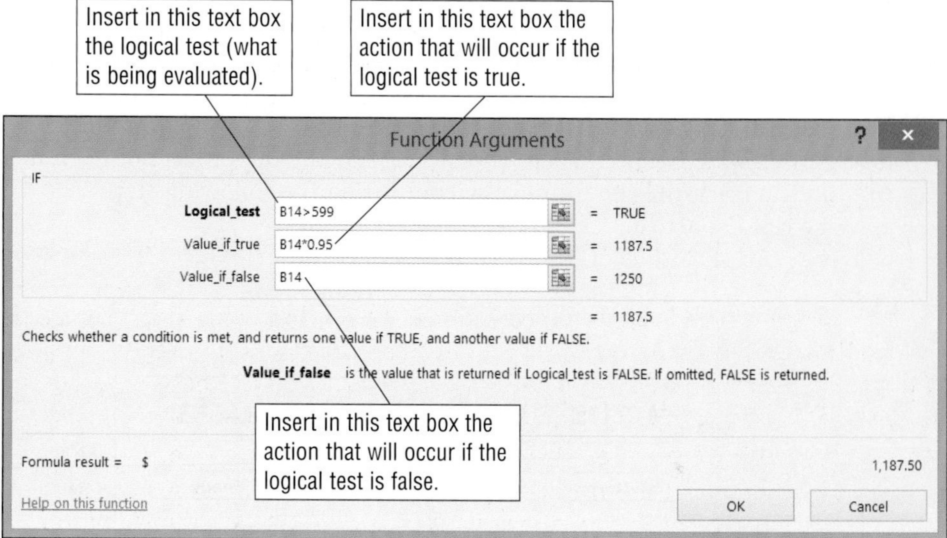

is 5% and multiplying the product price by 0.95 determines the price after the 5% discount is applied.) The *Value_if_false* text box contains *B14*, indicating that if the logical test is false (the product price is not greater than $599), then simply insert the amount from cell B14.

Project 6b Writing a Formula with an IF Function Using the Function Arguments Palette

Part 2 of 3

1. With **EL1-C7-P6-CMPReports.xlsx** open, insert a formula with an IF function using the Function Arguments palette by completing the following steps:
   a. Make cell C14 active.
   b. Click the FORMULAS tab.
   c. Click the Logical button in the Function Library group.
   d. Click *IF* at the drop-down list.
   e. At the Function Arguments palette, type **B14>599** in the *Logical_test* text box.
   f. Press the Tab key and then type **B14*0.95** in the *Value_if_true* text box.
   g. Press the Tab key and then type **B14** in the *Value_if_false* text box.
   h. Click OK to close the Function Arguments palette.

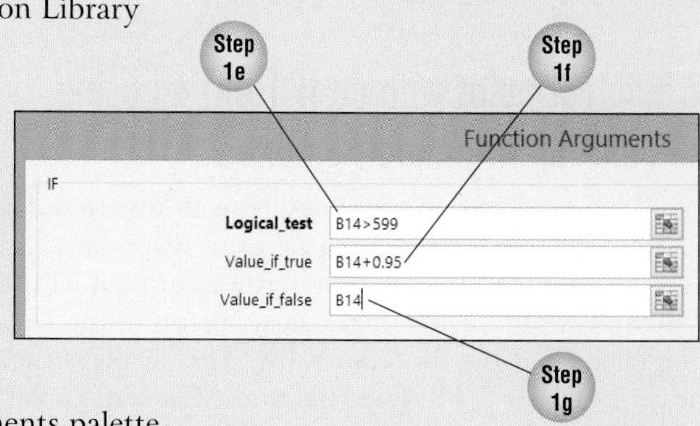

2. Copy the formula in cell C14 down to cells C15 through C26.
3. Apply accounting formatting with a dollar sign and two places after the decimal point to cell C14.
4. Save **EL1-C7-P6-CMPReports.xlsx**.

Writing IF Formulas Containing Text

If you write a formula with an IF function and want text inserted in a cell rather than a value, you must insert quotation marks around the text. For example, in Step 2 of Project 6c, you will write a formula with an IF function that, when written out, looks like this:

> ***If*** the employee averages more than 79 on the quizzes, ***then*** he or she passes.
>
> ***If*** the employee does not average more than 79 on the quizzes, ***then*** he or she fails.

When writing the formula in the project, the word *PASS* is inserted in a cell if the average of the new employee quizzes is greater than 79 and inserts the word *FAIL* if the condition is not met. To write this formula in Project 6c, you will type ***=IF(E31>79, "PASS", "FAIL")***. The quotation marks before and after *PASS* and *FAIL* identify the data as text rather than a value.

You can use the Function Arguments palette to write a formula with an IF function that contains text. For example, in Step 3 of Project 6c, you will write a formula with an IF function using the Function Arguments palette that, when written out, looks like this:

> ***If*** the product price is greater than $599, ***then*** insert *YES*.
>
> ***If*** the product price is not greater than $599, ***then*** insert *NO*.

To create the formula in Step 3 in the Function Arguments palette, display the palette and then type **B14>599** in the *Logical_test* text box, **YES** in the *Value_if_true* text box, and **NO** in the *Value_if_false* text box. When you press Enter after typing YES in the *Value_if_true* text box, Excel automatically inserts quotations marks around the text. Excel will do the same thing for NO in the *Value_if_false* text box.

Project 6c **Writing IF Statements Containing Text** **Part 3 of 3**

1. With **EL1-C7-P6-CMPReports.xlsx** open, insert quiz averages by completing the following steps:
   a. Make cell E31 active and then insert a formula that calculates the average of the test scores in cells B31 through D31.
   b. Copy the formula in cell E31 down to cells E32 through E35.
2. Write a formula with an IF function that inserts the word *PASS* if the quiz average is greater than 79 and inserts the word *FAIL* if the quiz average is not greater than 79. Write the formula by completing the following steps:
   a. Make cell F31 active.
   b. Type =IF(E31>79,"PASS","FAIL") and then press Enter.

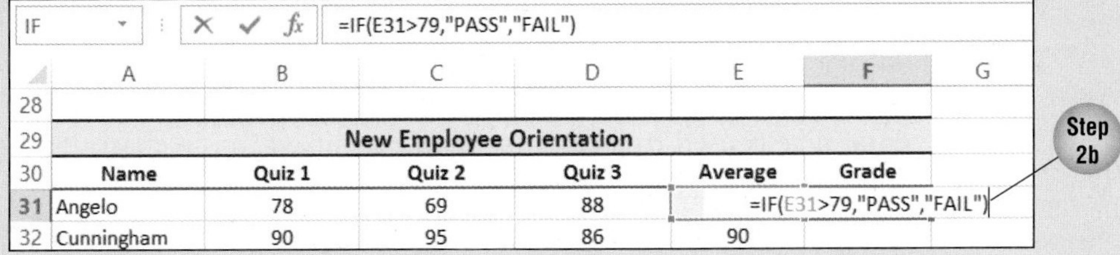

   c. Copy the formula in cell F31 down to cells F32 through F35.

3. Write a formula with an IF function using the Function Arguments palette that inserts the word *YES* in the cell if the product price is greater than $599 and inserts the word *NO* if the price is not greater than $599. Write the formula by completing the following steps:
   a. Make cell D14 active.
   b. Click the FORMULAS tab.
   c. Click the Logical button in the Function Library group.
   d. Click *IF* at the drop-down list.
   e. Type **B14>599** in the *Logical_test* text box.
   f. Press the Tab key and then type **YES** in the *Value_if_true* text box.
   g. Press the Tab key and then type **NO** in the *Value_if_false* text box.
   h. Click OK to close the Function Arguments palette.
   i. Copy the formula in cell D14 down to cells D15 through D26. 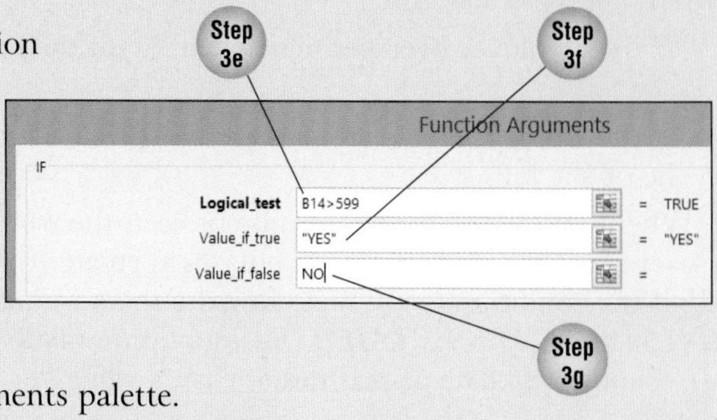
4. Save and then print **EL1-C7-P6-CMPReports.xlsx**.
5. Press Ctrl + ` to turn on the display of formulas.
6. Print the worksheet again. (The worksheet will print on two pages.)
7. Press Ctrl + ` to turn off the display of formulas.
8. Save and then close **EL1-C7-P6-CMPReports.xlsx**.

Chapter Summary

- A chart is a visual presentation of data. Excel provides 11 basic chart types: area, bar, bubble, column, doughnut, line, pyramid, radar, stock, surface, and xy (scatter).
- To create a chart, select the cells containing data you want to chart, click the INSERT tab, and then click the desired chart button in the Charts group. Click the Recommended Charts button in the Charts group and Excel will recommend a type of chart for the data.
- A chart you create is inserted in the same worksheet as the selected cells.
- Change the size of a chart using the mouse by dragging one of the sizing handles that display around the border of the chart. When changing the chart size, maintain the proportion of the chart by holding down the Shift key while dragging a sizing handle.
- Move a chart by positioning the mouse pointer on the chart border until the pointer displays with a four-headed arrow attached and then dragging with the mouse.
- The data in cells used to create the chart are linked to the chart. If you change the data in cells, the chart reflects the changes.
- Three buttons appear outside the right border of a selected chart. Use the Chart Elements button to insert or remove chart elements, use the Chart Styles button to apply a chart style, and use the Chart Filters button to isolate specific data in the chart.

- Print a chart by selecting the chart, displaying the Print backstage area, and then clicking the Print button.
- When you insert a chart in a worksheet, the CHART TOOLS DESIGN tab is active. Use options on this tab to add chart elements, change the chart type, specify a different layout or style, and change the location of the chart.
- Choose a chart style with options in the Chart Styles group on the CHART TOOLS DESIGN tab or at the Change Chart Type dialog box.
- Click the Switch Row/Column button in the Data group to change what Excel uses to determine the grouping of data along the horizontal axis and legend.
- Use the Quick Layout button in the Chart Layouts group to change the chart layout.
- Use the Change Colors button to apply different colors to a chart.
- By default, a chart is inserted in the active worksheet. You can move the chart to a new worksheet within the workbook with the *New sheet* option at the Move Chart dialog box.
- Add chart elements with the Add Chart Element button arrow in the Chart Layouts group on the CHART TOOLS DESIGN tab.
- Move a chart element by selecting the element and then dragging it with the mouse. Use the sizing handles that display around a chart element to change the size of the element. Delete a chart element by selecting it and then pressing the Delete key or right-clicking the selected element and then clicking Delete at the shortcut menu.
- Customize the formatting of a chart and chart elements with options on the CHART TOOLS FORMAT tab. With options on the tab, you can identify specific elements in the chart for formatting, insert a shape, apply formatting to a shape, apply WordArt formatting to data in a chart, and arrange, align, and size a chart.
- Insert a shape by clicking the desired shape in the Insert Shapes group on the CHART TOOLS FORMAT tab and then clicking or dragging in the chart.
- Excel provides additional formatting options at a formatting task pane. A formatting task pane displays at the right side of the screen and the name and the contents in the task pane vary depending on whether the entire chart or an element in the chart is selected. Display a task pane by clicking the chart or element in the chart and then clicking the Format Selection button in the Current Selection group on the CHART TOOLS FORMAT tab.
- Change the size of a chart with shape height and width measurement boxes on the CHART TOOLS FORMAT tab or at the Format Chart Area task pane.
- To delete a chart in a worksheet, click the chart to select it and then press the Delete key. To delete a chart created in a separate sheet, position the mouse pointer on the chart tab, click the right mouse button, and then click *Delete*.
- Write a formula with the PMT function to calculate the payment for a loan based on constant payments and a constant interest rate. Write a formula with the FV function to calculate the future value of an investment based on periodic, constant payments and a constant interest rate.
- A logical test is a question that can be answered with true or false. Use the IF function to create a logical test that performs a particular action if the answer is true (condition met) or another action if the answer is false (condition not met).

Commands Review

FEATURE	RIBBON TAB, GROUP	BUTTON, OPTION	KEYBOARD SHORTCUT
Change Chart Type dialog box	CHART TOOLS DESIGN, Type		
chart in separate sheet			F11
chart or chart element task pane	CHART TOOLS FORMAT, Current Selection		
financial functions	FORMULAS, Function Library		
logical functions	FORMULAS, Function Library		
Move Chart dialog box	CHART TOOLS DESIGN, Location		
recommended chart	INSERT, Charts		Alt + F1

Concepts Check Test Your Knowledge

Completion: In the space provided at the right, indicate the correct term, symbol, or command.

1. Let Excel determine a chart type for selected data in a worksheet by clicking this button in the Charts group on the INSERT tab. ____________________

2. This type of chart shows proportions and relationships of the parts to the whole. ____________________

3. When you create a chart, the chart is inserted in this location by default. ____________________

4. Size a chart by dragging one of these on the selected chart border. ____________________

5. When a chart is selected, three buttons display at the right side of the chart border: the Chart Elements button, the Chart Styles button, and this button. ____________________

6. Select a chart in a worksheet, display the Print backstage area, and the first gallery in the *Settings* category is automatically changed to this option. ____________________

7. The Switch Row/Column button is located in this group on the CHART TOOLS DESIGN tab. ________________

8. Click this option at the Move Chart dialog box to move the chart to a separate sheet. ________________

9. Insert a shape in a chart and this tab is active. ________________

10. Select a chart (not a chart element), click the Format Selection button in the Current Selection group on the CHART TOOLS FORMAT tab, and this task pane displays at the right side of the screen. ________________

11. This function finds the payment for a loan based on constant payments and a constant interest rate. ________________

12. Suppose cell B2 contains the total sales amount. Write a formula that inserts the word *BONUS* in cell C2 if the sales amount is greater than $49,999 and inserts the words *NO BONUS* if the sales amount is not greater than $49,999. ________________

Skills Check Assess Your Performance

Assessment 1

CREATE A NET PROFIT CHART

1. Open **NetProfit.xlsx** and then save the workbook with Save As and name it **EL1-C7-A1-NetProfit**.
2. Select cells A2 through E7 and then create a chart using the Recommended Charts button. (Accept the chart recommended by Excel.)
3. Use the Chart Elements button that displays outside the right border of the chart to insert a data table and remove the legend.
4. Use the Chart Styles button that displays outside the right border of the chart to apply the Style 7 chart style.
5. Use the Chart Filters button that displays outside the right border of the chart to display only New York and Philadelphia net profits in the chart. (Make sure you click the Apply button.)
6. Click the text *Chart Title*, type **Net Profit by Office**, and then press Enter.
7. Move the chart below the cells containing data, deselect the chart, make sure the data and chart fit on one page, and then print the worksheet (data and chart).
8. Save and then close **EL1-C7-A1-NetProfit.xlsx**.

Assessment 2

CREATE A COMPANY SALES COLUMN CHART

1. Open **CMSales.xlsx** and then save the workbook with Save As and name it **EL1-C7-A2-CMSales**.
2. Select cells A3 through C15 and then create a column chart with the following specifications:
   a. Click the *3-D Clustered Column* option at the Insert Column Chart button drop-down list.
   b. At the CHART TOOLS DESIGN tab, click the Quick Layout button and then click the *Layout 3* option at the drop-down gallery.
   c. Apply the Style 11 chart style.
   d. Click the text *Chart Title*, type **2015 Company Sales**, and then press Enter.
   e. Move the location of the chart to a new sheet.
3. Print only the worksheet containing the chart.
4. Save and then close **EL1-C7-A2-CMSales.xlsx**.

Assessment 3

CREATE QUARTERLY DOMESTIC AND FOREIGN SALES BAR CHART

1. Open **CMPQtrlySales.xlsx** and then save the workbook with Save As and name it **EL1-C7-A3-CMPQtrlySales**.
2. Select cells A3 through E5 and then create a bar chart with the following specifications:
   a. Click the *3-D Clustered Bar* option at the Insert Bar Chart button drop-down list.
   b. Apply the Layout 2 quick layout. (Use the Quick Layout button.)
   c. Apply the Style 6 chart style.
   d. Type **Quarterly Sales** as the chart title. (Excel will convert the text to uppercase letters.)
   e. Click in the chart but outside any chart element.
   f. Click the CHART TOOLS FORMAT tab and then apply the Subtle Effect - Gold, Accent 4 shape style (fifth column, fourth row).
   g. Click the Chart Elements button arrow, click *Series "Foreign"* at the drop-down list, and then apply Dark Red shape fill. (Use the Shape Fill button arrow in the Shape Styles group and choose Dark Red in the *Standard Colors* section.)
   h. Select the chart title and then apply the Fill - Black, Text 1, Shadow WordArt style (first column, first row).
   i. Increase the height of the chart to 4 inches and the width to 6 inches.
3. Move the chart below the cells containing data, deselect the chart, make sure the data and chart fit on one page, and then print the worksheet (data and chart).
4. Save and then close **EL1-C7-A3-CMPQtrlySales.xlsx**.

Assessment 4

CREATE A FUND ALLOCATIONS PIE CHART

1. Open **SMFFunds.xlsx** and then save the workbook with Save As and name it **EL1-C7-A4-SMFFunds**.
2. Select cells A3 through B7 and then create a pie chart with the following specifications:
   a. Click the *3-D Pie* option at the Insert Pie or Doughnut Chart button drop-down gallery.
   b. Apply the Layout 1 quick layout.
   c. Apply the Style 2 chart style.
   d. Change the color to Color 3.
   e Move the pie chart to a new worksheet.
   f. Change the title to *Fund Allocations*.
   g. Click the CHART TOOLS FORMAT tab, make sure the chart is selected and not a chart element, and then click the Format Selection button.
   h. At the Format Chart Area task pane, make sure the Fill & Line icon is active, click the *FILL* option to display additional options, click the *Gradient fill* option, and then close the task pane.
   i. Use the Chart Elements button arrow to select *Series "Allocation" Data Labels*.
   j. With the data labels selected, click the Text Fill button arrow (located in the WordArt Styles group) and then click the *Orange, Accent 2, Darker 50%* option (sixth column, bottom row in the *Theme Colors* section).
   k. With the data labels still selected, click the HOME tab and then change the font size to 18 points.
3. Print only the worksheet containing the chart.
4. Save and then close **EL1-C7-A4-SMFFunds.xlsx**.

Assessment 5

WRITE A FORMULA WITH THE PMT FUNCTION

1. Open **CMRefiPlan.xlsx** and then save the workbook with Save As and name it **EL1-C7-A5-CMRefiPlan**.
2. The manager of Clearline Manufacturing is interested in refinancing a loan for either $125,000 or $300,000 and wants to determine the monthly payments. Make cell E4 active and then insert a formula using the PMT function. (For assistance, refer to Project 5a. The monthly payment amounts will display as negative numbers representing outflows of cash.)
3. Copy the formula in cell E4 down to cells E5 through E7.
4. Save, print, and then close **EL1-C7-A5-CMRefiPlan.xlsx**.

Assessment 6

WRITE A FORMULA WITH THE FV FUNCTION

1. Open **CMInvest.xlsx** and then save the workbook with Save As and name it **EL1-C7-A6-CMInvest**.
2. Make cell B6 active and then use the FV function to insert a formula that calculates the future value of the investment.
3. Save and then print the worksheet.

4. Make the following changes to the worksheet:
   a. Change the percentage in cell B3 from *6.5%* to *8.0%*.
   b. Change the number in cell B4 from *48* to *60*.
   c. Change the amount in cell B5 from *(-1000)* to *-500*.
5. Save, print, and then close **EL1-C7-A6-CMInvest.xlsx**.

Assessment

WRITE A FORMULA WITH THE IF FUNCTION

1. Open **DISalesBonuses.xlsx** and then save the workbook with Save As and name it **EL1-C7-A7-DISalesBonuses**.
2. Insert a formula in cell C4 that inserts the word *YES* if the amount in B4 is greater than 99999 and inserts *NO* if the amount is not greater than 99999. Copy the formula in cell C4 down to cells C5 through C14.
3. Make cell D4 active and then insert the formula =IF(C4="YES",B4*0.05,0). If sales are over $99,999, this formula will multiply the sales amount by 5% and then insert the product (result) of the formula in the cell. Copy the formula in cell D4 down to cells D5 through D14.
4. Apply accounting formatting with a dollar sign and no places past the decimal point to cell D4.
5. Save and then print **EL1-C7-A7-DISalesBonuses.xlsx**.
6. Display the formulas in the worksheet and then print the worksheet.
7. Turn off the display of formulas.
8. Save and then close **EL1-C7-A7-DISalesBonuses.xlsx**

Assessment

CREATE A STACKED COLUMN CHART

1. Use Excel's Help feature to learn more about chart types and specifically about 3-D stacked column charts.
2. Open **CMPerSales.xlsx** and then save the workbook with Save As and name it **EL1-C7-A8-CMPerSales**.
3. With the data in the worksheet, create a 3-D 100% stacked column chart in a separate sheet. Create an appropriate title for the chart and apply any other formatting to enhance the appearance of the chart.
4. Print only the worksheet containing the chart.
5. Close **EL1-C7-A8-CMPerSales.xlsx**.

Assessment

9 LEARN ABOUT EXCEL OPTIONS

1. Learn about specific options in the Excel Options dialog box by completing the following steps:
   a. At a blank workbook, display the Excel Options dialog box by clicking the FILE tab and then clicking *Options*.
   b. At the Excel Options dialog box, click the *Advanced* option in the left panel.
   c. Scroll down the dialog box and look for the section *Display options for this workbook* and then read the information in the section. Also read the information in the *Display options for this worksheet* section.
   d. Write down the check box options available in the *Display options for this workbook* section and the *Display options for this worksheet* section and identify whether or not the check box contains a check mark. (Record only check box options and ignore buttons and options preceded by circles.)
2. With the information you wrote down about the options, create an Excel worksheet with the following information:
   a. In column C, type each option you wrote down. (Include an appropriate heading.)
   b. In column B, insert an X in the cell that precedes any option that contains a check mark in the check box. (Include an appropriate heading.)
   c. In column A, write a formula with the IF function that inserts the word *ON* in the cell if the cell in column B contains an X and inserts the word *OFF* if it does not (the cell is blank). (Include an appropriate heading.)
   d. Apply formatting to improve the appearance of the worksheet.
3. Save the workbook and name it **EL1-C7-A9-DisplayOptions**.
4. Turn on the display of formulas.
5. Print the worksheet.
6. Turn off the display of formulas.
7. Save, print, and then close **EL1-C7-A9-DisplayOptions.xlsx**.

Visual Benchmark Demonstrate Your Proficiency

CREATE AND FORMAT A PIE CHART

1. At a blank workbook, enter data and then create a pie chart in a separate sheet, as shown in Figure 7.12. Use the information shown in the pie chart to create the data. Format the pie chart so it appears similar to what you see in Figure 7.12. (Apply the Layout 4 quick style and the Style 8 chart style. Create and format the title as shown in the figure and change the size of the data labels to 12 points.)
2. Save the completed workbook and name it **EL1-C7-VB-CMFebExp**.
3. Print both worksheets in the workbook.
4. Close **EL1-C7-VB-CMFebExp.xlsx.**

Figure 7.12 Visual Benchmark

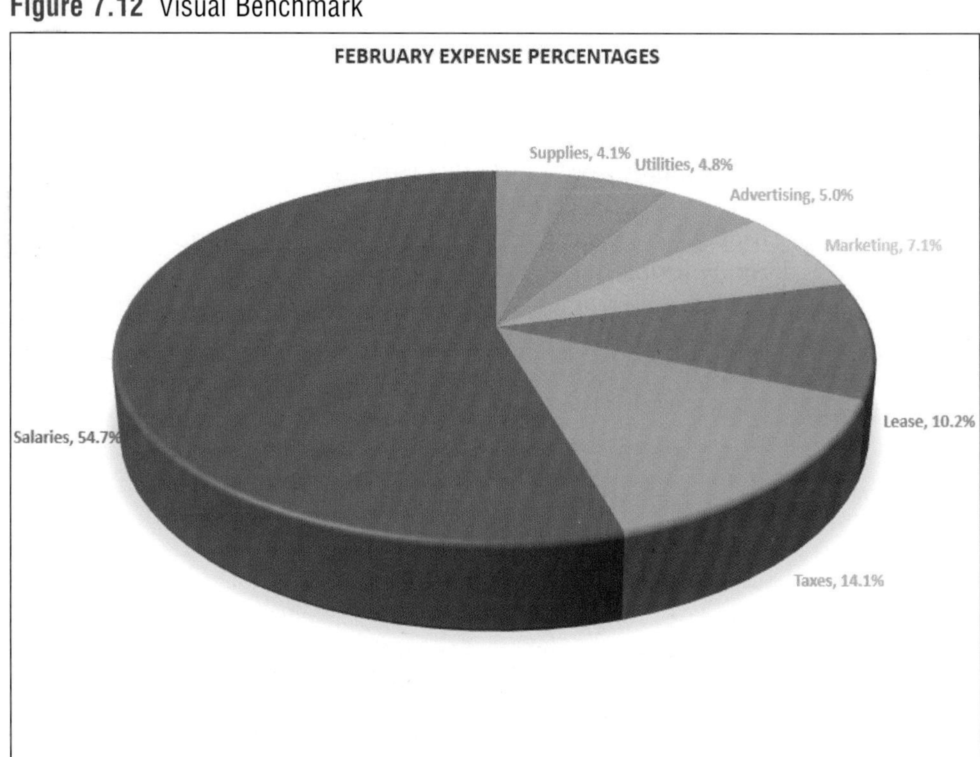

Case Study Apply Your Skills

Part 1

You are an administrator for Dollar Wise Financial Services and need to prepare charts indicating home loan and commercial loan amounts for the past year. Use the information below to prepare a chart in Excel. You determine the type and style of the chart and the layout and formatting of the chart. Insert a shape in the Commercial Loans chart that contains the text *All-time High* and points to the second quarter amount (*$6,785,250*).

Home Loans
- 1st Qtr. = $2,675,025
- 2nd Qtr. = $3,125,750
- 3rd Qtr. = $1,975,425
- 4th Qtr. = $875,650

Commercial Loans
- 1st Qtr. = $5,750,980
- 2nd Qtr. = $6,785,250
- 3rd Qtr. = $4,890,625
- 4th Qtr. = $2,975,900

Save the workbook and name it **EL1-C7-CS-DWQtrSales**. Print only the chart and then close **EL1-C7-CS-DWQtrSales.xlsx**.

Part 2

You need to present information on the budget for the company. You have the dollar amounts and need to convert each amount to a percentage of the entire budget. Use the information below to calculate the percentage of the budget for each item and then create a pie chart with the information. You determine the chart style, layout, and formatting.

Total Budget: $6,000,000
- Building Costs = $720,000
- Salaries = $2,340,000
- Benefits = $480,000
- Advertising = $840,000
- Marketing = $600,000
- Client Expenses = $480,000
- Equipment = $420,000
- Supplies = $120,000

Save the workbook containing the pie chart and name it **EL1-C7-CS-DWBudget**. Print only the chart and then close **EL1-C7-CS-DWBudget.xlsx**.

Part 3

The loan officer for Dollar Wise Financial Services has asked you to prepare a sample home mortgage worksheet to show prospective clients. This mortgage worksheet will show the monthly payments on variously priced homes with varying interest rates. Open the **DWMortgageWksht.xlsx** worksheet and then complete the home mortgage worksheet by inserting the following formulas:

- Since many homes in your area sell for at least $400,000, you decide to use that amount in the worksheet with down payments of 5%, 10%, 15%, and 20%. (Insert the amount $400,000 in cells A11 through A14.)
- In column C, insert a formula that determines the down payment amount.
- In column D, insert a formula that determines the loan amount.
- In column G, insert a formula using the PMT function. (The monthly payment will display as a negative number.)

Save the worksheet and name it **EL1-C7-CS-DWMortgageWksht**.

Part 4

If home buyers put down less than 20% of the home's purchase price, mortgage insurance is required. With **EL1-C7-CS-DWMortgageWksht.xlsx** open, insert an IF statement in the cells in column H that inserts the word *NO* if the percentage in column B is equal to or greater than 20% and inserts the word *YES* if the percentage in column B is less than 20%. Save and then print **EL1-C7-CS-DWMortgageWksht.xlsx**.

Part 5

You need to prepare information on mortgage interest rates for a community presentation. You decide to provide the information on mortgage rates in a chart for easy viewing. Use the Internet to search for historical data on the national average for mortgage interest rates. Determine the average mortgage rate for a 30-year FRM (fixed-rate mortgage) for each January and July beginning with the year 2011 and continuing to the current year. Also include the current average interest rate. Use this information to create the chart. Save the workbook and name it **EL1-C7-CS-DWRates**. Print only the chart and then close **EL1-C7-CS-DWRates.xlsx**.

MICROSOFT® EXCEL®

Adding Visual Interest to Workbooks

PERFORMANCE OBJECTIVES

Upon successful completion of Chapter 8, you will be able to:

- **Insert symbols and special characters**
- **Insert, size, move, and format images**
- **Insert a screenshot**
- **Draw, format, and copy shapes**
- **Insert, format, and type text in a text box**
- **Insert a picture image as a watermark**
- **Insert and format SmartArt graphics**
- **Insert and format WordArt**

Tutorials

8.1 Inserting Symbols and Special Characters
8.2 Inserting and Modifying Images from the Insert Picture dialog box
8.3 Inserting and Modifying Images from Office.com
8.4 Creating and Inserting Screenshots
8.5 Inserting and Formatting a Shape
8.6 Drawing and Formatting Text Boxes
8.7 Inserting a Picture as a Watermark
8.8 Inserting and Formatting a SmartArt Graphic
8.9 Creating WordArt

Microsoft Excel includes a variety of features that you can use to enhance the appearance of a workbook. Some methods for adding visual appeal that you will learn in this chapter include inserting and modifying pictures and clip art images, screenshots, shapes, text boxes, SmartArt, and WordArt. Model answers for this chapter's projects appear on the following pages.

Note: Before beginning the projects, copy to your storage medium the EL1C8 subfolder from the EL1 folder on the CD that accompanies this textbook and make EL1C8 the active folder.

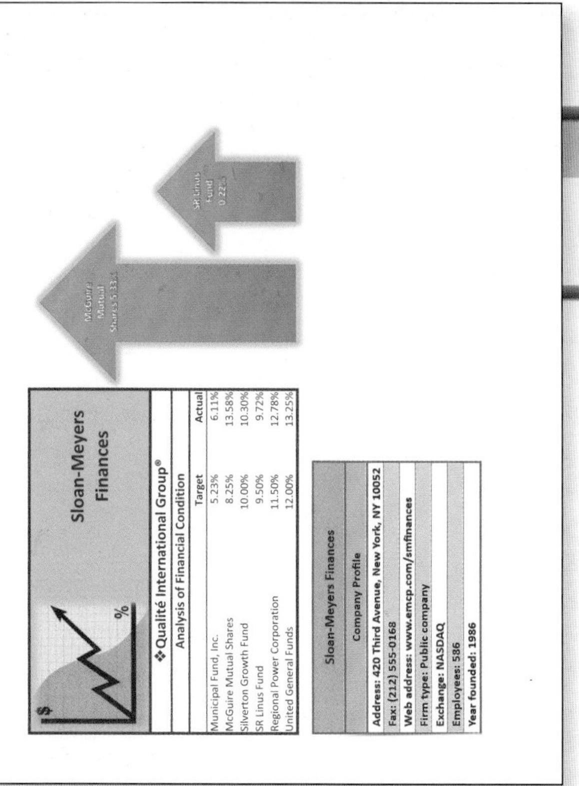

Sloan-Meyers Finances

❖Qualité International Group®

Analysis of Financial Condition

	Target	Actual
Municipal Fund, Inc.	5.23%	6.11%
McGuire Mutual Shares	8.25%	13.58%
Silverton Growth Fund	10.00%	10.30%
SR Linus Fund	9.50%	9.72%
Regional Power Corporation	11.50%	12.78%
United General Funds	12.00%	13.25%

Sloan-Meyers Finances

Company Profile

Address: 420 Third Avenue, New York, NY 10052
Fax: (212) 555-0168
Web address: www.emcp.com/smfinances
Firm type: Public company
Exchange: NASDAQ
Employees: 586
Year founded: 1986

Project 1 Insert a Clip Art Image and Shapes in a Financial Analysis Workbook EL1-C8-P1-SMFFinCon.xlsx

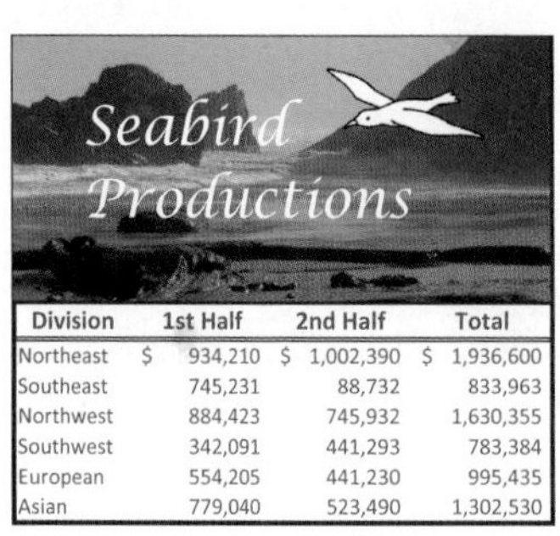

Division	1st Half	2nd Half	Total
Northeast	$ 934,210	$ 1,002,390	$ 1,936,600
Southeast	745,231	88,732	833,963
Northwest	884,423	745,932	1,630,355
Southwest	342,091	441,293	783,384
European	554,205	441,230	995,435
Asian	779,040	523,490	1,302,530

Project 2 Insert a Picture and Text Box in a Division Sales Workbook EL1-C8-P2-SPDivSales.xlsx

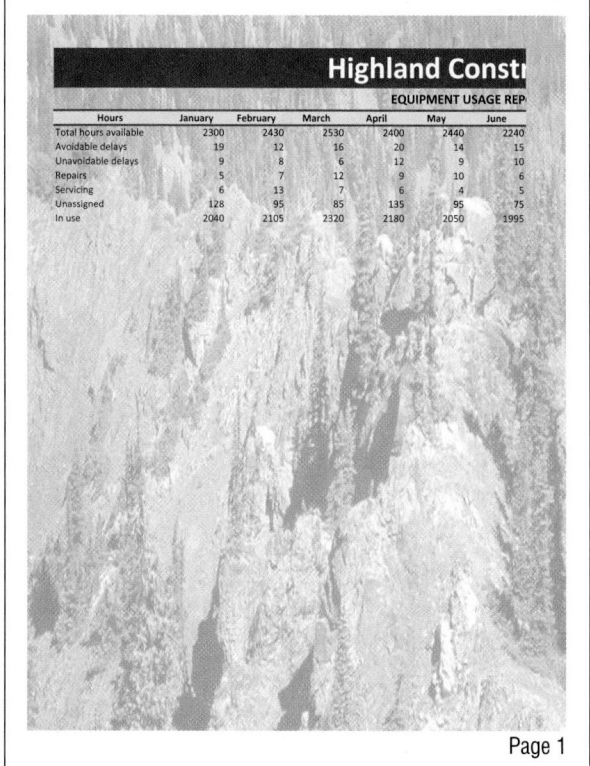

Highland Constr

EQUIPMENT USAGE REP

Hours	January	February	March	April	May	June
Total hours available	2300	2430	2530	2400	2440	2240
Avoidable delays	19	12	16	20	14	15
Unavoidable delays	9	8	6	12	9	10
Repairs	5	7	12	9	10	6
Servicing	6	13	7	6	4	5
Unassigned	128	95	85	135	95	75
In use	2040	2105	2320	2180	2050	1995

Page 1

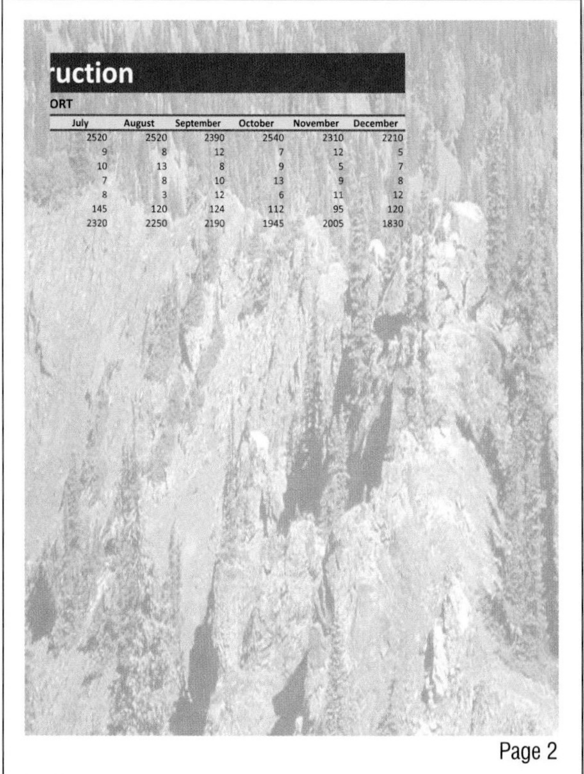

ruction

ORT

July	August	September	October	November	December
2520	2520	2390	2540	2310	2210
9	8	12	7	12	5
10	13	8	9	5	7
7	8	10	13	9	8
8	3	12	6	11	12
145	120	124	112	95	120
2320	2250	2190	1945	2005	1830

Page 2

Project 3 Insert a Watermark in an Equipment Usage Workbook EL1-C8-P3-HCEqpRpt.xlsx

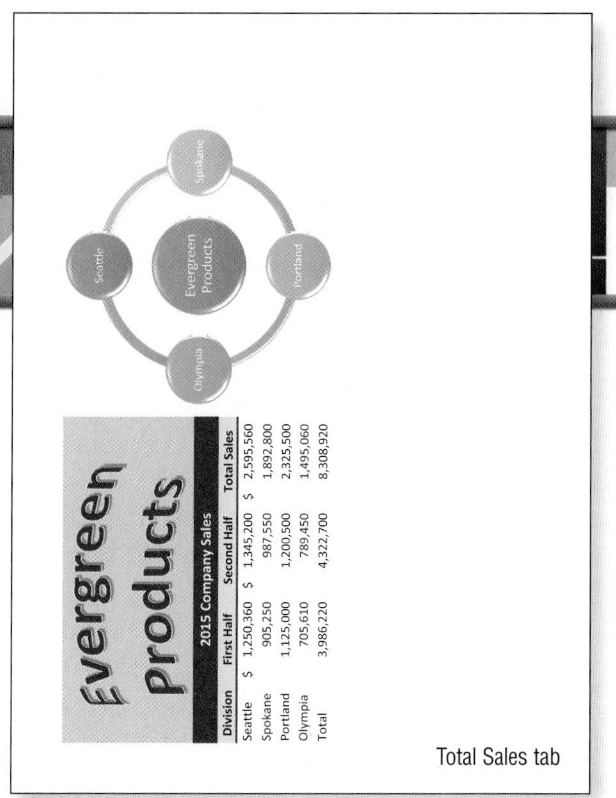

Evergreen Products

2015 Company Sales			
Division	First Half	Second Half	Total Sales
Seattle	$ 1,250,360	$ 1,345,200	$ 2,595,560
Spokane	905,250	987,550	1,892,800
Portland	1,125,000	1,200,500	2,325,500
Olympia	705,610	789,450	1,495,060
Total	3,986,220	4,322,700	8,308,920

Total Sales tab

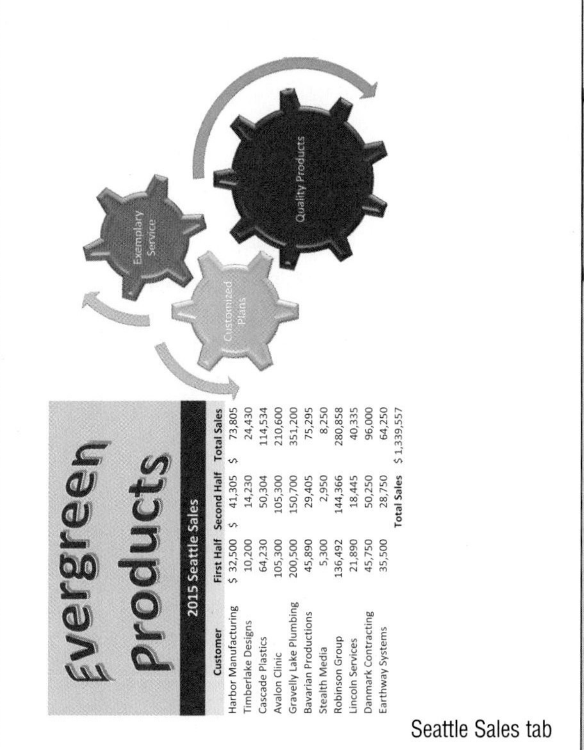

Evergreen Products

2015 Seattle Sales			
Customer	First Half	Second Half	Total Sales
Harbor Manufacturing	$ 32,500	$ 41,305	$ 73,805
Timberlake Designs	10,200	14,230	24,430
Cascade Plastics	64,230	50,304	114,534
Avalon Clinic	105,300	105,300	210,600
Gravelly Lake Plumbing	200,500	150,700	351,200
Bavarian Productions	45,890	29,405	75,295
Stealth Media	5,300	2,950	8,250
Robinson Group	136,492	144,366	280,858
Lincoln Services	21,890	18,445	40,335
Danmark Contracting	45,750	50,250	96,000
Earthway Systems	35,500	28,750	64,250
		Total Sales	$ 1,339,557

Seattle Sales tab

Project 4 Insert and Format SmartArt Graphics in a Company Sales Workbook EL1-C8-P4-EPSales.xlsx

Project 1 Insert a Clip Art Image and Shapes in a Financial Analysis Workbook — 5 Parts

You will open a financial analysis workbook and then insert symbols and move, size, and format an image in the workbook. You will also insert an arrow shape, type and format text in the shape, and then copy the shape.

Inserting Symbols and Special Characters

Use the Symbol button on the INSERT tab to insert special symbols in a worksheet. Click the Symbol button in the Symbols group on the INSERT tab and the Symbol dialog box displays, as shown in Figure 8.1. At the Symbol dialog box, double-click the desired symbol and then click Close or click the desired symbol, click the Insert button, and then click Close. At the Symbol dialog box with the Symbols tab selected, you can change the font at the *Font* option box. When you change the font, different symbols display in the dialog box. Click the Special Characters tab at the Symbol dialog box and a list of special characters displays. Click the desired character, click the Insert button, and then click the Close button.

Quick Steps

Insert a Symbol

1. Click in desired cell.
2. Click INSERT tab.
3. Click Symbol button.
4. Double-click desired symbol.
5. Click Close.

Symbol

Quick Steps

Insert a Special Character

1. Click in desired cell.
2. Click INSERT tab.
3. Click Symbol button.
4. Click Special Characters tab.
5. Double-click desired special character.
6. Click Close.

You can increase or decrease the size of the Symbol dialog box by positioning the mouse pointer on the lower right corner until the pointer displays as a two-headed arrow and then dragging with the mouse.

Figure 8.1 Symbol Dialog Box with Symbols Tab Selected

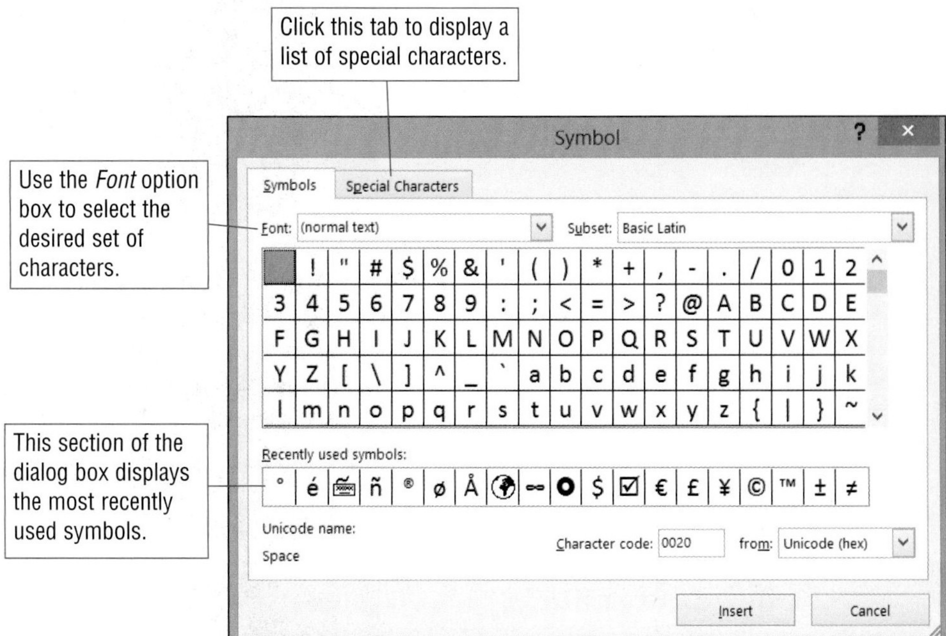

Project 1a Inserting Symbols and Special Characters

Part 1 of 5

1. Open **SMFFinCon.xlsx** and then save the workbook with Save As and name it **EL1-C8-P1-SMFFinCon**.
2. Insert a symbol by completing the following steps:
   a. Double-click in cell A2.
   b. Delete the *e* that displays at the end of *Qualite*.
   c. With the insertion point positioned immediately right of the *t* in *Qualit*, click the INSERT tab.
   d. Click the Symbol button in the Symbols group.
   e. At the Symbol dialog box, scroll down the list box and then click the *é* symbol (located in approximately the ninth through eleventh row).
   f. Click the Insert button and then click the Close button.

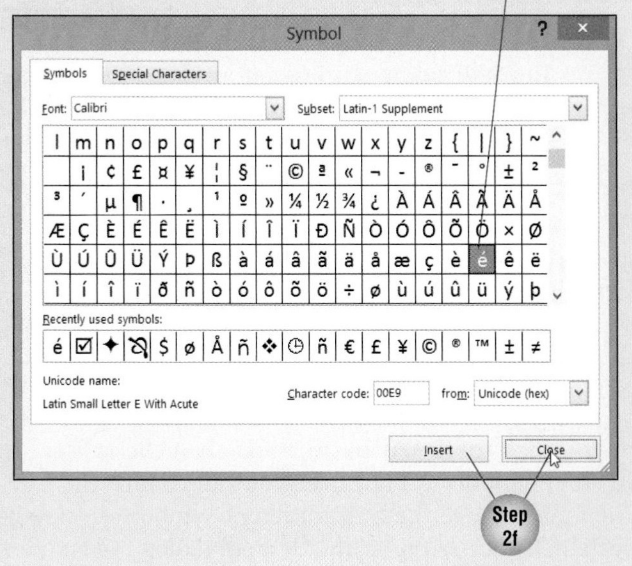

3. Insert a special character by completing the following steps:
   a. With cell A2 selected and in EDIT mode, move the insertion point so it is positioned immediately right of *Group*.
   b. Click the Symbol button in the Symbols group.
   c. At the Symbol dialog box, click the Special Characters tab.
   d. Double-click the ® symbol (tenth option from the top).
   e. Click the Close button.

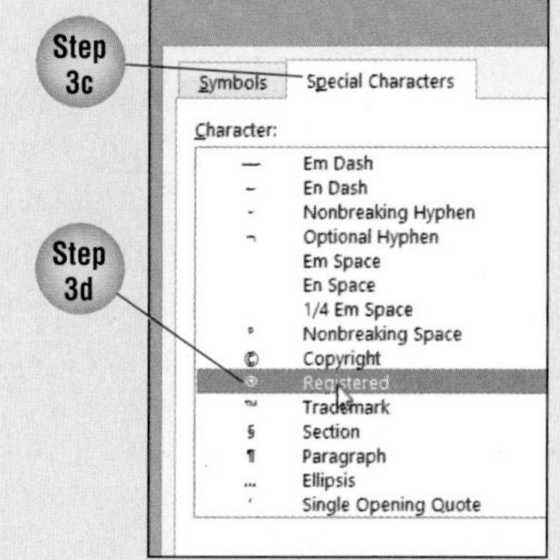

4. Insert a symbol by completing the following steps:
   a. With cell A2 selected and in EDIT mode, move the insertion point so it is positioned immediately left of the *Q* in *Qualité*.
   b. Click the Symbol button in the Symbols group.
   c. At the Symbol dialog box, click the down-pointing arrow at the right side of the *Font* option box and then click *Wingdings* at the drop-down list. (You will need to scroll down the list to display this option.)
   d. Click the ❖ symbol (located in approximately the fifth or sixth row).
   e. Click the Insert button and then click the Close button.
5. Click in cell A3.
6. Save **EL1-C8-P1-SMFFinCon.xlsx**.

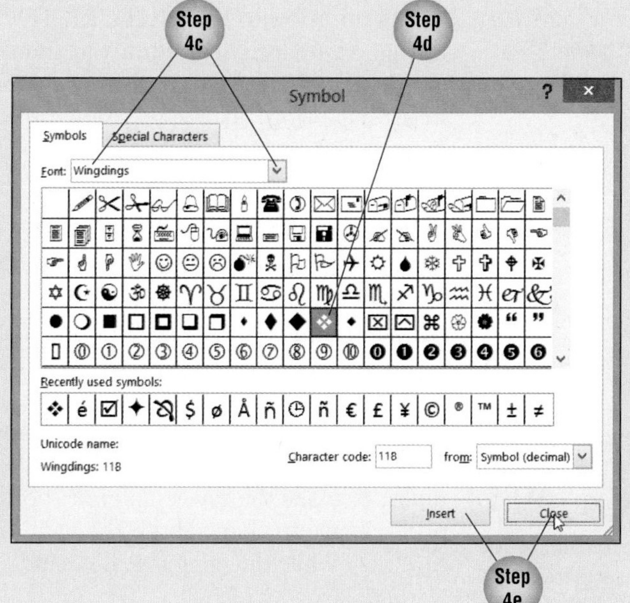

Inserting Images

Insert an image, such as a picture or clip art, in an Excel workbook with buttons in the Illustrations group on the INSERT tab. Click the Pictures button to display the Insert Picture dialog box, where you can specify the desired picture file, or click the Online Pictures button and search for images online. When you insert an image in a worksheet, the PICTURE TOOLS FORMAT tab displays, as shown in Figure 8.2.

Quick Steps

Insert a Picture
1. Click INSERT tab.
2. Click Pictures button.
3. Navigate to desired folder.
4. Double-click desired picture.

Pictures

Figure 8.2 PICTURE TOOLS FORMAT Tab

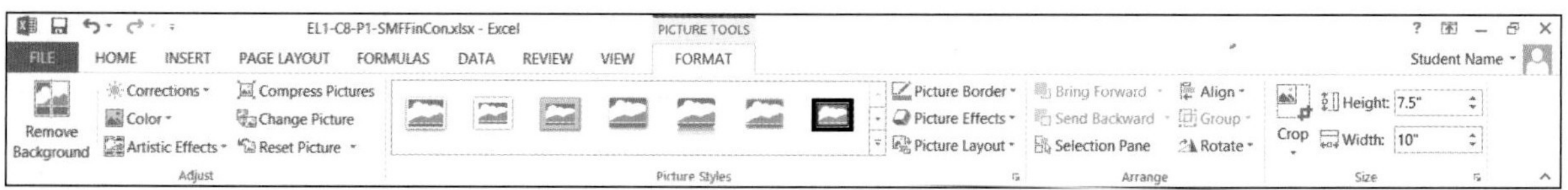

Customizing and Formatting an Image

Use buttons in the Adjust group on the PICTURE TOOLS FORMAT tab to remove unwanted portions of an image, correct the brightness and contrast, change the image color, apply artistic effects, change to a different image, and reset the image back to the original formatting. Use the Compress Pictures button in the Adjust group to compress the size of an image file and reduce the amount of space the image requires on your storage medium. Use buttons in the Picture Styles group to apply a predesigned style to the image, change the image border, or apply other effects to the image. With options in the Arrange group, you can position the image on the page, specify how text will wrap around it, align the image with other elements in the worksheet, and rotate the image. Use the Crop button in the Size group to remove any unnecessary parts of the image and use the *Shape Height* and *Shape Width* measurement boxes to specify the image size.

Compress Pictures

Crop

In addition to the PICTURE TOOLS FORMAT tab, you can customize and format an image with options at the shortcut menu. Display this menu by right-clicking the image. With options at the shortcut menu, you can change the image, insert a caption, choose text wrapping, size and position the image, and display the Format Picture task pane.

Sizing and Moving an Image

Change the size of an image with the *Shape Height* and *Shape Width* measurement boxes in the Size group on the PICTURE TOOLS FORMAT tab or with the sizing handles that display around the selected image. To change size with a sizing handle, position the mouse pointer on a sizing handle until the pointer turns into a double-headed arrow and then drag in or out to decrease or increase the size of the image. Use the middle sizing handles at the left and right sides of the image to make the image wider or thinner. Use the middle sizing handles at the top and bottom of the image to make the image taller or shorter. Use the sizing handles at the corners of the image to change both the width and height at the same time. Hold down the Shift key while dragging a sizing handle to maintain the proportions of the image.

You can use arrow keys on the keyboard to move a selected image. To move the image in small increments, hold down the Ctrl key while pressing one of the arrow keys.

Move an image by positioning the mouse pointer on the image border until the pointer displays with a four-headed arrow attached and then dragging the image to the desired location. Rotate the image by positioning the mouse pointer on the white, round rotation handle until the pointer displays as a circular arrow. Hold down the left mouse button, drag in the desired direction, and then release the mouse button.

Project 1b **Formatting an Image** **Part 2 of 5**

1. With **EL1-C8-P1-SMFFinCon.xlsx** open, insert a picture by completing the following steps:
   a. Click the INSERT tab and then click the Pictures button in the Illustrations group.
   b. At the Insert Picture dialog box, navigate to the EL1C8 folder on your storage medium and then double-click ***WallStreet.jpg***.
2. Change the size of the image by clicking in the *Shape Height* measurement box in the Size group on the PICTURE TOOLS FORMAT tab, typing 2, and then pressing Enter.
3. Remove the yellow background from the image by completing the following steps:
   a. Click the Remove Background button in the Adjust group.
   b. Position the mouse pointer on the middle sizing handle at the top of the image until the pointer displays as an up-and-down-pointing arrow.

c. Hold down the left mouse button, drag the border up to the top of the image, and then release the mouse.
d. Position the mouse pointer on the middle sizing handle at the bottom of the image until the pointer displays as an up-and-down-pointing arrow.
e. Hold down the left mouse button, drag the border up approximately 0.25 inch, and then release the mouse button.
f. Click the Keep Changes button in the Close group on the BACKGROUND REMOVAL tab.

4. Change the color by clicking the Color button in the Adjust group and then clicking the *Blue, Accent color 1 Light* option (second column, third row in the *Recolor* section).
5. Apply a correction by clicking the Corrections button and then clicking the *Brightness: +20% Contrast: +20%* option (fourth column, fourth row in the *Brightness and Contrast* section).

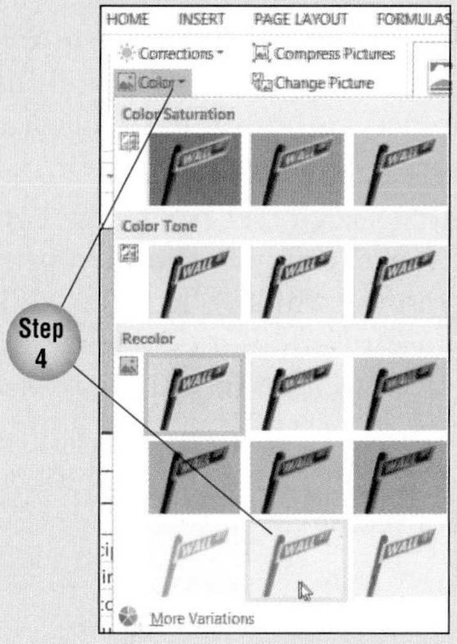

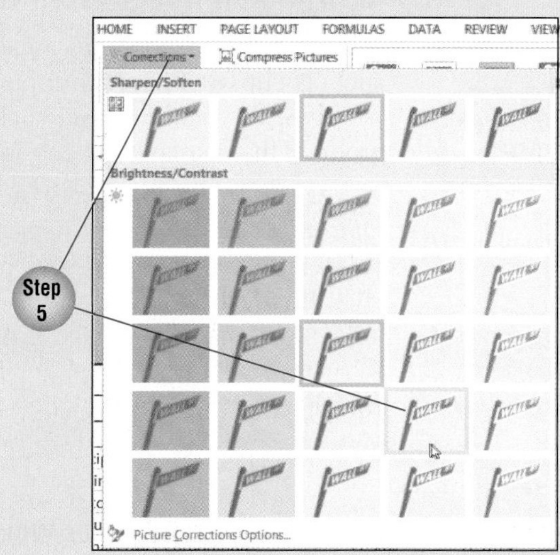

6. Apply an artistic effect by clicking the Artistic Effects button and then clicking the *Glow Edges* option (last option in the drop-down gallery).
7. Move the image by completing the following steps:
   a. Position the mouse pointer on the image (displays with a four-headed arrow attached).
   b. Hold down the left mouse button, drag the image to the upper left corner of the worksheet, and then release the mouse button.

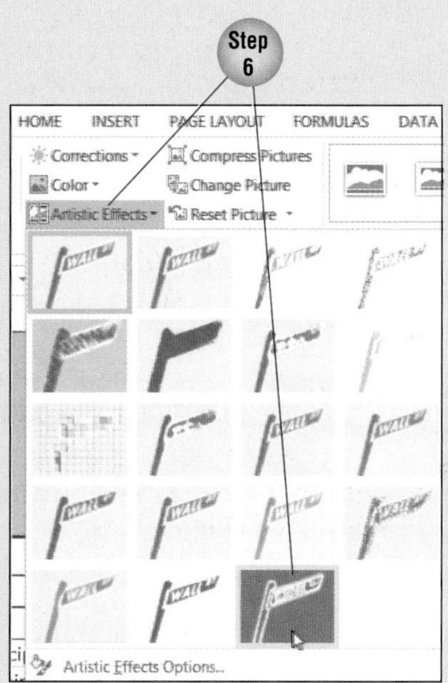

8. Save and then print **EL1-C8-P1-SMFFinCon.xlsx**.

Formatting an Image at the Format Picture Task Pane

In addition to the PICTURES TOOLS FORMAT tab, the Format Picture task pane is available for formatting an image. Click the Picture Styles group task pane launcher or the Size group task pane launcher and the Format Picture task pane displays at the right side of the screen. If you click the Picture Styles group task pane launcher, the task pane displays with the Effects icon selected, and if you click the Size group task pane launcher, the Size & Properties icon is selected. Two other icons are also available in this task pane: the Fill & Line icon and the Picture icon. You may need to display (expand) the formatting options within the icons. For example, click SIZE with the Size & Properties icon selected and options for changing the size of the image display. Close the task pane by clicking the Close button located in the upper right corner of the task pane.

Inserting an Image from Office.com

Quick Steps

Insert an Image from Office.com

1. Click INSERT tab.
2. Click Online Pictures button.
3. Type search word or topic.
4. Press Enter.
5. Double-click desired image.
6. Click desired image.

Online Pictures

Microsoft Office includes a gallery of media images you can insert in a worksheet, such as clip art images and photographs. To insert an image in a worksheet, click the INSERT tab and then click the Online Pictures button in the Illustrations group. This displays the Insert Pictures window, as shown in Figure 8.3.

At the Insert Pictures window, click in the search text box to the right of *Office.com Clip Art*; type the search word(s), term, or topic; and then press Enter. Images that match your search text display in the window. To insert an image, click the desired image and then click the Insert button or double-click the image. This downloads the image from the Office.com website to your worksheet.

When you insert an image in the worksheet, the image is selected and the PICTURE TOOLS FORMAT tab is active. Use buttons on this tab to customize an image, just as you learned to customize a picture.

Figure 8.3 Insert Pictures Window

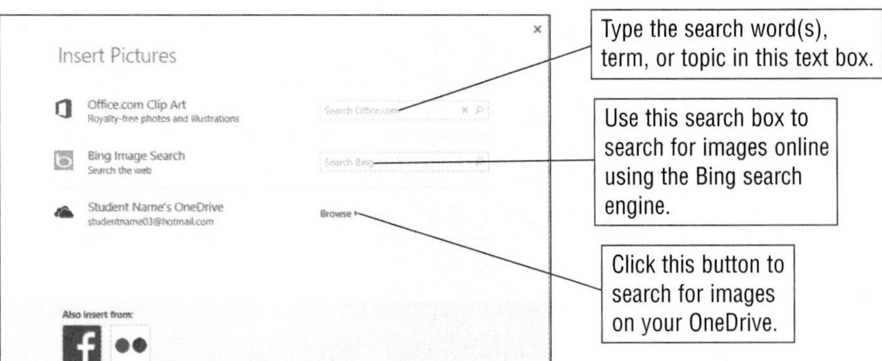

Project 1c **Inserting and Formatting a Clip Art Image** **Part 3 of 5**

1. With **EL1-C8-P1-SMFFinCon.xlsx** open, delete the Wall Street sign image by clicking the image and then pressing the Delete key.
2. Insert a clip art image by completing the following steps:
   a. Make cell A1 active.
   b. Click the INSERT tab and then click the Online Pictures button in the Illustrations group.

c. At the Insert Pictures window, type **charts, graphs, stock market** in the search box and then press Enter.
d. Double-click the image shown below and to the right.

3. Apply a border to the image by clicking the Picture Border button arrow, pointing to *Weight* at the drop-down list, and then clicking *1 pt* at the side menu.
4. Change the image border to a picture style by clicking the *Soft Edge Rectangle* thumbnail in the Picture Styles group (sixth thumbnail).

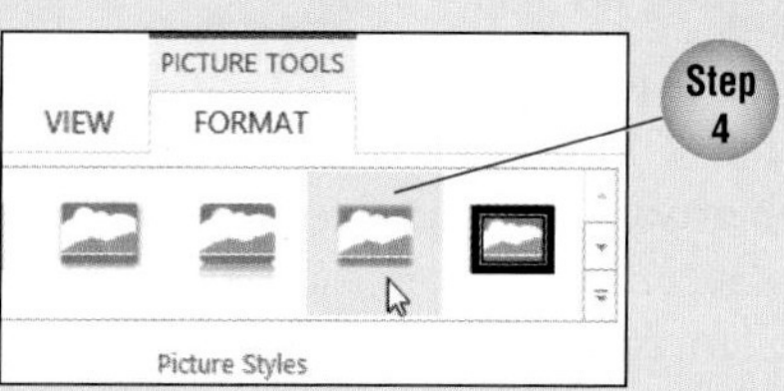

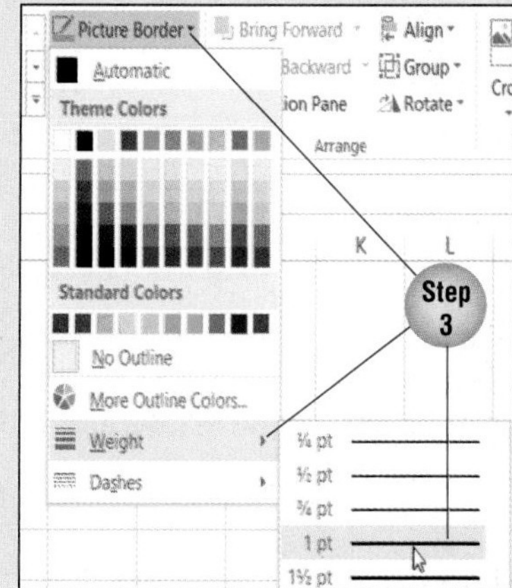

5. Display the Format Picture task pane with the Size & Properties icon selected by clicking the Size group task pane launcher on the PICTURE TOOLS FORMAT tab.
6. If necessary, click *SIZE* in the task pane to display the sizing options.
7. Change the height of the image by selecting the current measurement in the *Height* measurement box, typing 1.7, and then pressing Enter. (The width automatically changes to maintain the proportions of the image.)
8. Change the properties of the image by clicking PROPERTIES to expand the options and then clicking the *Move and size with cells* option. (With this option selected, if you change the size of the row, the size of the image will also change.)
9. Apply a correction to the image by completing the following steps:
   a. Click the Picture icon located toward the top of the task pane.
   b. Click PICTURE CORRECTIONS to expand the options.
   c. Select the current percentage in the *Brightness* text box and then type -23.
   d. Select the current percentage in the *Contract* text box, type 45, and then press Enter.
10. Close the Format Picture task pane by clicking the Close button in the upper right corner of the task pane.
11. Click outside the clip art image to deselect it.
12. Increase the height of row 1 to 126.00 pixels and notice that the image size increases with the row height.
13. Save **EL1-C8-P1-SMFFinCon.xlsx**.

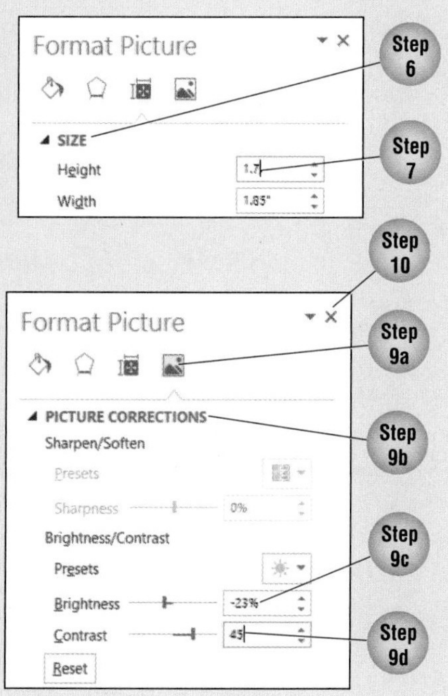

Creating and Inserting Screenshots

Quick Steps

Insert a Screenshot
1. Open workbook.
2. Open another file.
3. Display desired information.
4. Make workbook active.
5. Click INSERT tab.
6. Click Screenshot button.
7. Click desired window at drop-down list.

OR

6. Click Screenshot button and then *Screen Clipping*.
7. Drag to specify capture area.

Screenshot

The Illustrations group on the INSERT tab contains a Screenshot button you can use to capture all or part of the contents of a screen as an image. This is useful for capturing information from a web page or a file in another program. If you want to capture the entire screen, display the desired web page or open the desired file from a program, make Excel active, and then open a workbook or blank workbook. Click the INSERT tab, click the Screenshot button, and then click the desired screen thumbnail at the drop-down list. The currently active worksheet does not display as a thumbnail at the drop-down list—only any other file or program you have open. If you do not have another file or program open, the Windows desktop displays. When you click the desired thumbnail, the screenshot is inserted as an image in the open workbook, the image is selected, and the PICTURE TOOLS FORMAT tab is active. Use buttons on this tab to customize the screenshot image.

In addition to making a screenshot of an entire screen, you can make a screenshot of a specific portion of the screen by clicking the *Screen Clipping* option at the Screenshot button drop-down list. When you click this option, the open web page, file, or Windows desktop displays in a dimmed manner and the mouse pointer displays as crosshairs (a plus sign). Using the mouse, draw a border around the specific area of the screen you want to capture. The specific area you identify is inserted in the workbook as an image, the image is selected, and the PICTURE TOOLS FORMAT tab is active. If you have only one workbook or file open when you click the Screenshot button, clicking the *Screen Clipping* option will cause the Windows desktop to display.

Project 1d **Inserting and Formatting a Screenshot** **Part 4 of 5**

1. With **EL1-C8-P1-SMFFinCon.xlsx** open, make sure that no other programs are open.
2. Open Word and then open the document named **SMFCoProfile.docx** from the EL1C8 folder on your storage medium.
3. Click the Excel button on the Taskbar.
4. Insert a screenshot of the table in the Word document by completing the following steps:
   a. Click the INSERT tab.
   b. Click the Screenshot button in the Illustrations group and then click *Screen Clipping* at the drop-down list.
   c. When the **SMFCoProfile.docx** document displays in a dimmed manner, position the mouse crosshairs in the upper left corner of the table, hold down the left mouse button, drag down to the lower right corner of the table, and then release the mouse button. (This creates a screenshot of the entire table.)

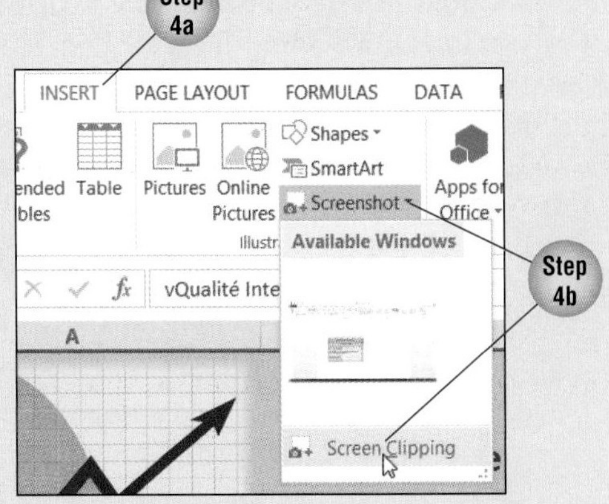

5. With the screenshot image inserted in the **EL1-C8-P1-SMFFinCon.xlsx** workbook, make the following changes:
   a. Click in the *Shape Width* measurement box in the Size group on the PICTURE TOOLS FORMAT tab, type 3.7, and then press Enter.

b. Click the Corrections button and then click the *Sharpen: 25%* option (fourth option in the *Sharpen/Soften* section).
c. Click the Corrections button and then click the *Brightness: 0% (Normal) Contrast: -40%* (third column, first row in the *Brightness/Contrast* section).
d. Using the mouse, drag the screenshot image one row below the data in row 10.

6. Make cell A4 active.
7. Save **EL1-C8-P1-SMFFinCon.xlsx**.
8. Click the Word button on the Taskbar, close **SMFCoProfile.docx**, and then close Word.

Inserting and Copying Shapes

In Chapter 7, you learned how to insert shapes in a chart. With the Shapes button in the Illustrations group on the INSERT tab, you can also insert shapes in a worksheet. Use the Shapes button to draw shapes in a worksheet, including lines, basic shapes, block arrows, flow chart shapes, callouts, stars, and banners. Click a shape and the mouse pointer displays as crosshairs. Click in the worksheet or position the crosshairs where you want the shape to begin, hold down the left mouse button, drag to create the shape, and then release the mouse button. If you click or drag in the worksheet, the shape is inserted in the worksheet and the DRAWING TOOLS FORMAT tab, shown in Figure 8.4, becomes active. Use the buttons on this tab to change the shape, apply a style to the shape, arrange the shape, and change the size of the shape.

If you choose a shape in the *Lines* section of the Shapes button drop-down list, the shape you draw is considered a line drawing. If you choose an option in the other sections of the drop-down list, the shape you draw is considered an enclosed object. When drawing an enclosed object, you can maintain the proportions of the shape by holding down the Shift key while dragging with the mouse to create the shape. You can type text in an enclosed object and then use buttons in the WordArt Styles group (or options on the HOME tab) to format the text.

Copy a shape in a worksheet by selecting the shape and then clicking the Copy button in the Clipboard group on the HOME tab. Make active the cell where you want to copy the shape and then click the Paste button. You can also copy a selected shape by holding down the Ctrl key while dragging the shape to the desired location.

Quick Steps

Insert a Shape
1. Click INSERT tab.
2. Click Shapes button.
3. Click desired shape at drop-down list.
4. Click or drag in worksheet.

Copy a Shape
1. Select shape.
2. Click Copy button.
3. Position insertion point in desired location.
4. Click Paste button.

OR

1. Select shape.
2. Hold down Ctrl key.
3. Drag shape to desired location.

Shapes

Figure 8.4 DRAWING TOOLS FORMAT Tab

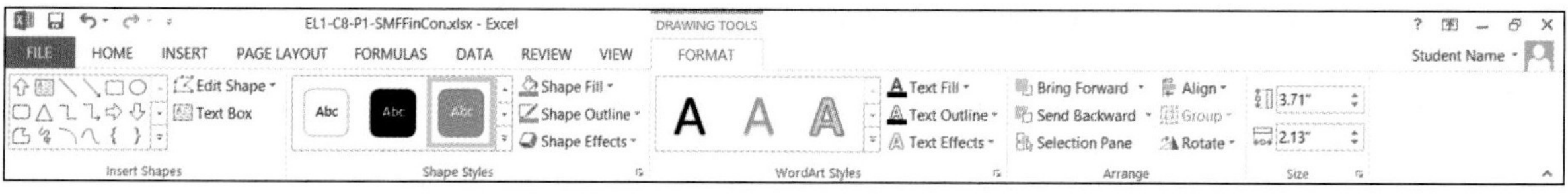

Project 1e Drawing Arrow Shapes

Part 5 of 5

1. With **EL1-C8-P1-SMFFinCon.xlsx** open, create the larger arrow shown in Figure 8.5 on page 284 by completing the following steps:
   a. Click the INSERT tab.
   b. Click the Shapes button in the Illustrations group and then click the *Up Arrow* shape (third column, top row in the *Block Arrows* section).
   c. Position the mouse pointer (displays as crosshairs) near the upper left corner of cell D1 and then click the left mouse button. (This inserts the arrow shape in the worksheet.)

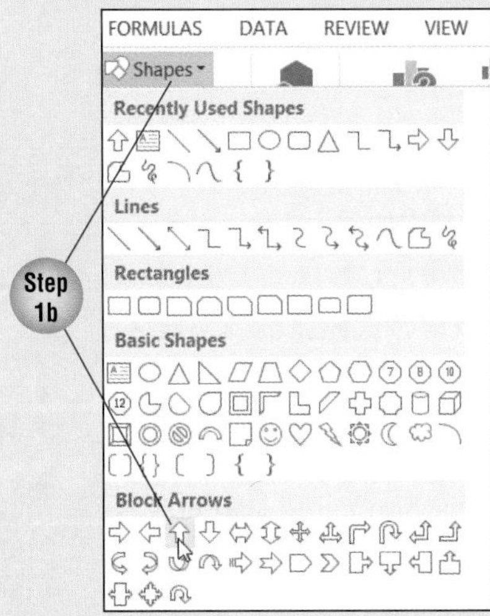

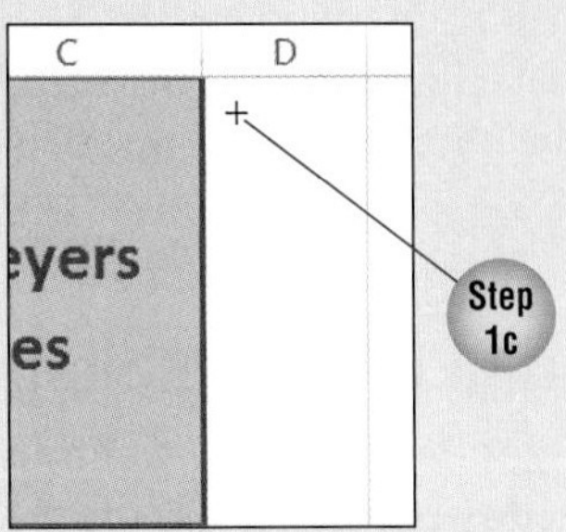

   d. Click in the *Shape Height* measurement box and then type 3.7.
   e. Click in the *Shape Width* measurement box, type 2.1, and then press Enter.
   f. If necessary, drag the arrow so it is positioned as shown in Figure 8.5 on page 284. (To drag the arrow, position the mouse pointer on the border of the selected arrow until the pointer displays with a four-headed arrow attached, hold down the left mouse button, drag the arrow to the desired position, and then release the mouse button.)
   g. Click the More button at the right side of the thumbnails in the Shape Styles group on the DRAWING TOOLS FORMAT tab and then click the *Intense Effect - Blue, Accent 1* option (second column, bottom row).

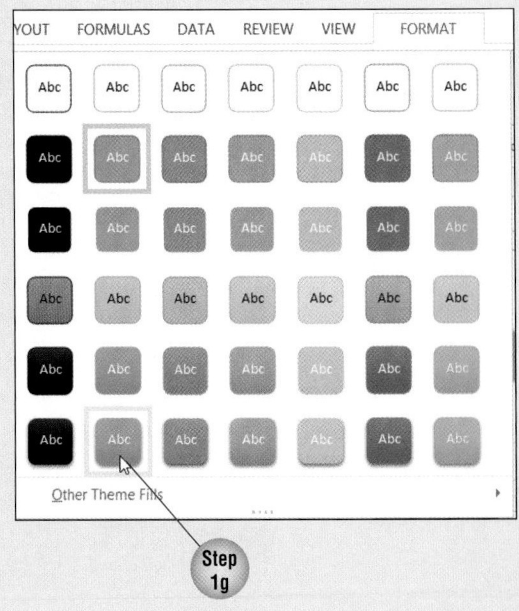

h. Click the Shape Effects button in the Shape Styles group, point to *Glow*, and then click the *Orange, 11 pt glow, Accent color 2* option (second column, third row in the *Glow Variations* section).

2. Insert text in the arrow shape by completing the following steps:
   a. With the arrow shape selected, type **McGuire Mutual Shares 5.33%**.
   b. Select the text you just typed (*McGuire Mutual Shares 5.33%*).
   c. Click the More button at the right side of the thumbnails in the WordArt Styles group and then click the *Fill - White, Outline - Accent 2, Hard Shadow - Accent 2* option (fourth column, third row).
   d. Press Ctrl + E to center the text.
3. With the arrow selected, copy the arrow by completing the following steps:
   a. Hold down the Ctrl key.
   b. Position the mouse pointer on the arrow border until the pointer displays with a square box and plus symbol attached.
   c. Hold down the left mouse button and drag to the right so the outline of the arrow is positioned at the right side of the existing arrow.
   d. Release the mouse button and then release the Ctrl key.
4. Format the second arrow by completing the following steps:
   a. With the second arrow selected, click in the *Shape Height* measurement box on the DRAWING TOOLS FORMAT tab and then type 2.
   b. Click in the *Shape Width* measurement box, type 1.6, and then press Enter
   c. Select the text *McGuire Mutual Shares 5.33%* and then type **SR Linus Fund 0.22%**.
   d. Drag the arrow so it is positioned as shown in Figure 8.5.
5. Change the orientation to landscape. (Make sure the cells containing data, the screenshot image, and the arrows will print on the same page.)
6. Save, print, and then close **EL1-C8-P1-SMFFinCon.xlsx**.

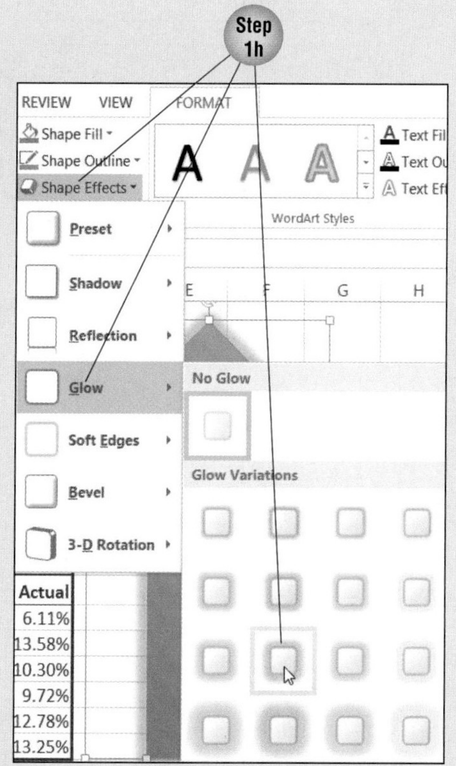

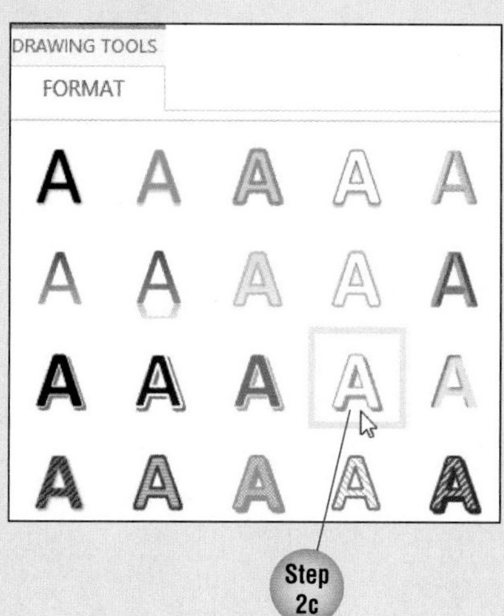

Figure 8.5 Project 1e

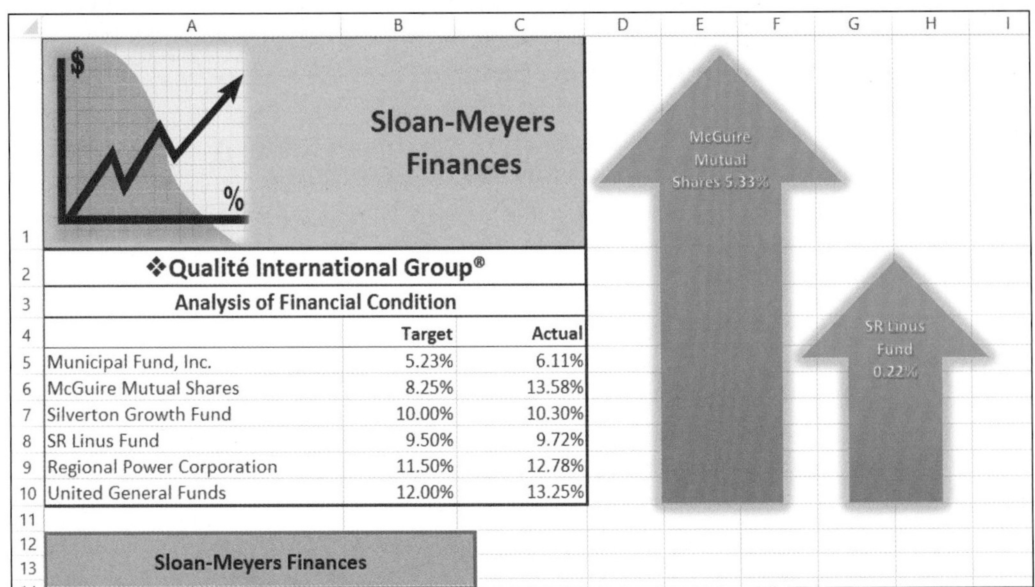

	A	B	C
1	Sloan-Meyers Finances		
2	❖Qualité International Group®		
3	Analysis of Financial Condition		
4		Target	Actual
5	Municipal Fund, Inc.	5.23%	6.11%
6	McGuire Mutual Shares	8.25%	13.58%
7	Silverton Growth Fund	10.00%	10.30%
8	SR Linus Fund	9.50%	9.72%
9	Regional Power Corporation	11.50%	12.78%
10	United General Funds	12.00%	13.25%
11			
12			
13	Sloan-Meyers Finances		

Project 2 Insert a Picture and Text Box in a Division Sales Workbook — 1 Part

You will open a division sales workbook and then insert, move, and size a picture. You will also insert a text box and then format the text.

Drawing and Formatting Text Boxes

Quick Steps

Draw a Text Box
1. Click INSERT tab.
2. Click Text Box button.
3. Click or drag in worksheet to create text box.

Text Box

Use the Text Box button on the INSERT tab to draw a text box in a worksheet. To draw a text box, click the INSERT tab and then click the Text Box button in the Text group. This causes the mouse pointer to display as a long, thin, crosslike pointer. Position the pointer in the worksheet and then drag to create the text box. When a text box is selected, the DRAWING TOOLS FORMAT tab displays with options for customizing the text box.

Click a text box to select it and a dashed border and sizing handles display around the text box. If you want to delete the text box, click the text box border again to change the dashed border lines to solid border lines and then press the Delete key.

Project 2 **Inserting and Customizing a Picture and Text Box** — **Part 1 of 1**

1. Open **SPDivSales.xlsx** and then save the workbook with Save As and name it **EL1-C8-P2-SPDivSales**.
2. Make the following changes to the bird clip art image:
   a. Click the bird clip art image to select it.
   b. Click the PICTURE TOOLS FORMAT tab.

c. Click the Rotate button in the Arrange group and then click *Flip Horizontal* at the drop-down list.

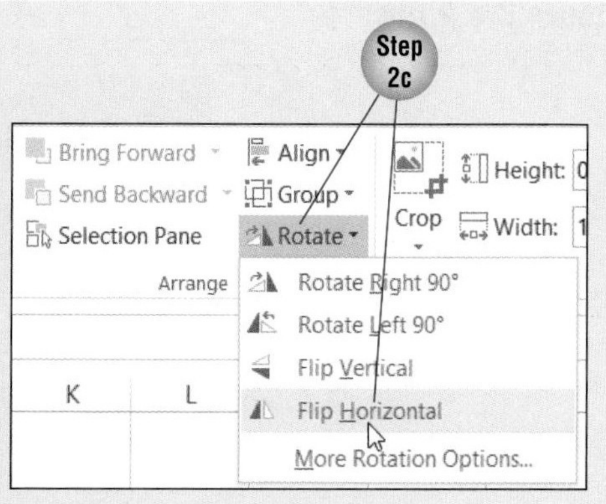

3. Insert and format a picture by completing the following steps:
   a. Click in cell A1 outside the bird image.
   b. Click the INSERT tab.
   c. Click the Pictures button in the Illustrations group.
   d. At the Insert Picture dialog box, navigate to the EL1C8 folder on your storage medium and then double-click ***Ocean.jpg***.
   e. With the picture selected, click the Send Backward button in the Arrange group on the PICTURE TOOLS FORMAT tab.

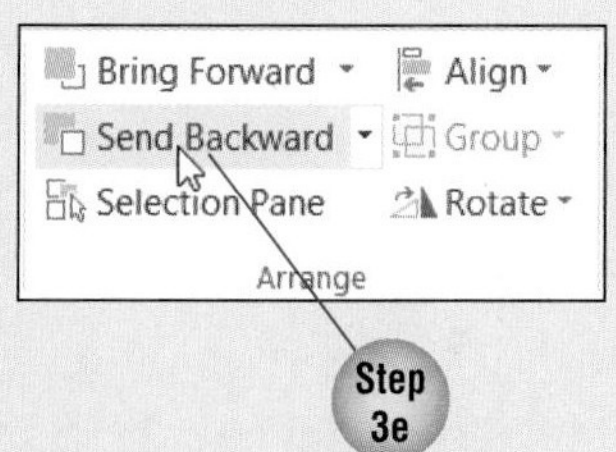

   f. Use the sizing handles that display around the picture image to move and size it so it fills cell A1, as shown in Figure 8.6.
   g. If necessary, click the bird clip art image and then drag the image so it is positioned as shown in Figure 8.6 on the next page.

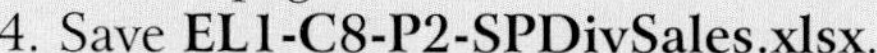

4. Save **EL1-C8-P2-SPDivSales.xlsx**.
5. Draw a text box by completing the following steps:
   a. Click the INSERT tab.
   b. Click the Text Box button in the Text group.
   c. Drag in cell A1 to draw a text box the approximate size and shape shown at the right.

6. Format the text box by completing the following steps:
   a. Click the DRAWING TOOLS FORMAT tab.
   b. Click the Shape Fill button arrow in the Shape Styles group and then click *No Fill* at the drop-down gallery.
   c. Click the Shape Outline button arrow in the Shape Styles group and then click *No Outline* at the drop-down gallery.

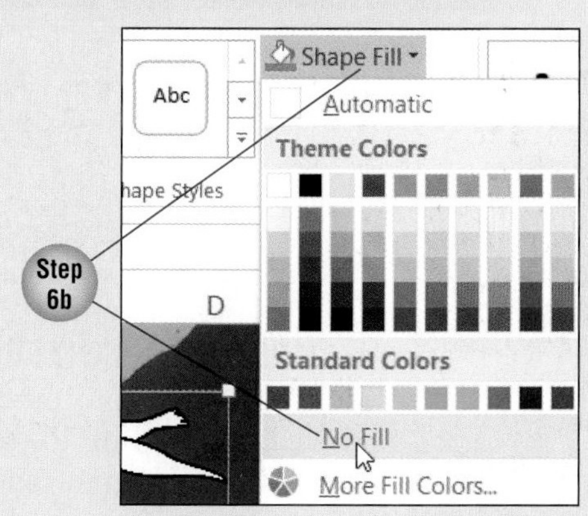

7. Insert text in the text box by completing the following steps:
   a. With the text box selected, click the HOME tab.
   b. Click the Font button arrow and then click *Lucida Calligraphy* at the drop-down gallery. (You will need to scroll down the gallery to display this font.)
   c. Click the Font Size button arrow and then click *32* at the drop-down gallery.
   d. Click the Font Color button arrow and then click *White, Background 1* (first column, first row in the *Theme Colors* section).
   e. Type **Seabird Productions**.
8. Move the text box so the text is positioned in cell A1 as shown in Figure 8.6.
9. Save, print, and then close **EL1-C8-P2-SPDivSales.xlsx**.

Figure 8.6 Project 2

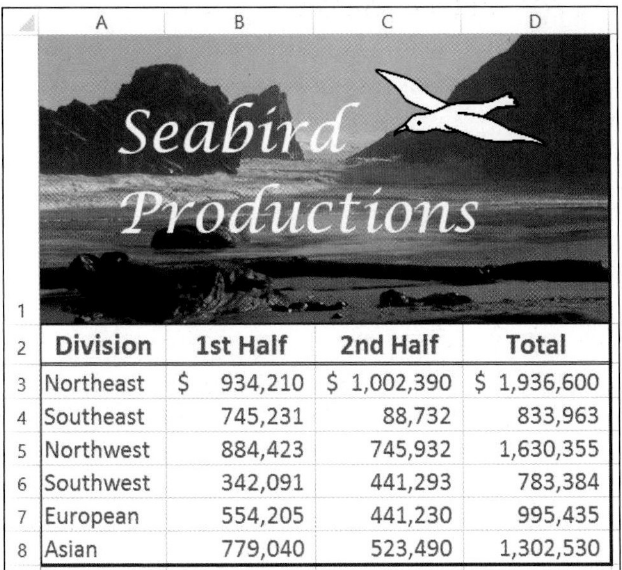

	A	B	C	D
2	Division	1st Half	2nd Half	Total
3	Northeast	$ 934,210	$ 1,002,390	$ 1,936,600
4	Southeast	745,231	88,732	833,963
5	Northwest	884,423	745,932	1,630,355
6	Southwest	342,091	441,293	783,384
7	European	554,205	441,230	995,435
8	Asian	779,040	523,490	1,302,530

Project 3 Insert a Watermark in an Equipment Usage Workbook — 1 Part

You will open an equipment usage report workbook and then insert a picture as a watermark that prints on both pages of the worksheet.

Inserting a Picture as a Watermark

Quick Steps

Insert a Picture as a Watermark

1. Click INSERT tab.
2. Click Header & Footer button.
3. Click Picture button.
4. Click Browse button.
5. Navigate to desired folder.
6. Double-click desired picture.
7. Click Format Picture button.
8. Change size, brightness, and contrast of image.
9. Click OK.

Format Picture

A ***watermark*** is a lightened image that displays behind data in a file. You can create a watermark in a Word document but the watermark functionality is not available in Excel. You can, however, insert a picture in a header or footer and then resize and format the picture to display behind each page of the worksheet.

To create a picture watermark in a worksheet, click the INSERT tab and then click the Header & Footer button in the Text group. With the worksheet in Print Layout view, click the Picture button in the Header & Footer Elements group on the HEADER & FOOTER TOOLS DESIGN tab. At the Insert Pictures window, click the Browse button to the right of the *From a file* option. At the Insert Picture dialog box, navigate to the desired folder and then double-click the desired picture. This inserts *&[Picture]* in the header. Resize and format the picture by clicking the Format Picture button in the Header & Footer Elements group. Use options at the Format Picture dialog box with the Size tab selected to specify the size of the picture and use options in the dialog box with the Picture tab selected to specify brightness and contrast.

Project 3 Inserting a Picture as a Watermark

Part 1 of 1

1. Open **HCEqpRpt.xlsx** and then save it and name it **EL1-C8-P3-HCEqpRpt**.
2. Insert a picture as a watermark by completing the following steps:
   a. Click the INSERT tab.
   b. Click the Header & Footer button in the Text group.
   c. Click the Picture button in the Header & Footer Elements group on the HEADER & FOOTER TOOLS DESIGN tab.
   d. At the Insert Pictures window, click the Browse button that displays to the right of the *From a file* option.
   e. At the Insert Picture dialog box, navigate to the EL1C8 folder on your storage medium and then double-click ***Olympics.jpg***.
   f. Click the Format Picture button in the Header & Footer Elements group.
   g. At the Format Picture dialog box with the Size tab selected, click the *Lock aspect ratio* check box in the *Scale* section to remove the check mark.
   h. Select the current measurement in the *Height* measurement box in the *Size and rotate* section and then type 10.
   i. Select the current measurement in the *Width* measurement box in the *Size and rotate* section and then type 7.5.
   j. Click the Picture tab.
   k. Select the current percentage in the *Brightness* measurement box in the *Image control* section and then type 75.
   l. Select the current percentage in the *Contrast* measurement box and then type 25.
   m. Click OK to close the Format Picture dialog box.
3. Click in the worksheet.
4. Display the worksheet in the Print backstage area to view how the image will print on page 1 and page 2 and then print the worksheet.
5. Save and then close **EL1-C8-P3-HCEqpRpt.xlsx**.

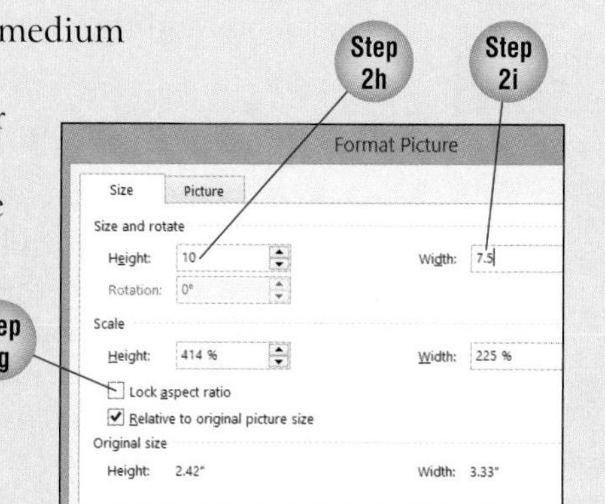

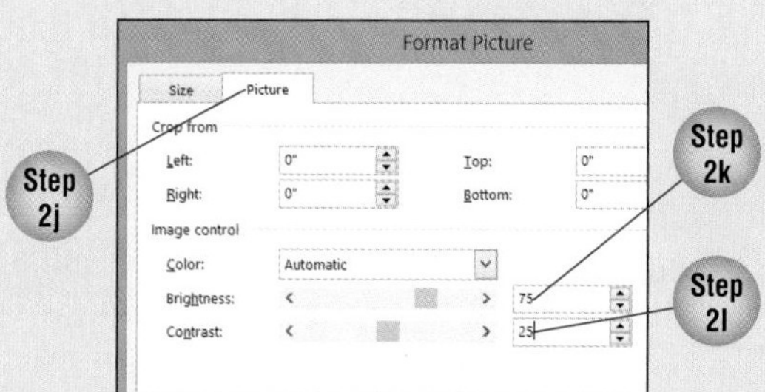

Project 4 Insert and Format SmartArt Graphics in a Company Sales Workbook

4 Parts

You will open a workbook that contains two company sales worksheets. You will insert and format a SmartArt cycle graphic in one worksheet and insert and format a SmartArt relationship graphic in the other. You will also create and format WordArt text.

Inserting SmartArt Graphics

Quick Steps

Insert a SmartArt Graphic
1. Click INSERT tab.
2. Click SmartArt button.
3. Double-click desired graphic.

SmartArt

Use the SmartArt feature included in Excel to insert graphics, such as diagrams and organizational charts, in a worksheet. SmartArt offers a variety of predesigned graphics that are available at the Choose a SmartArt Graphic dialog box, shown in Figure 8.7. Display this dialog box by clicking the INSERT tab and then clicking the SmartArt button in the Illustrations group. At the dialog box, *All* is selected in the left panel and all available predesigned graphics display in the middle panel. Use the scroll bar at the right side of the middle panel to scroll down the list of graphic choices. Click a graphic in the middle panel and the name of the graphic displays in the right panel along with a description of the graphic type. SmartArt includes graphics for presenting a list of data; showing data processes, cycles, and relationships; and presenting data in a matrix or pyramid. Double-click a graphic in the middle panel of the dialog box and the graphic is inserted in the worksheet.

Generally, you would use a SmartArt graphic to represent text and a chart to represent numbers.

Entering Data in a SmartArt Graphic

Text Pane

Some SmartArt graphics are designed to include text. Type text in a graphic by selecting a shape in the graphic and then typing text in the shape or you can display a text pane and then type text in the pane. Display the text pane by clicking the Text Pane button in the Create Graphic group on the SMARTART TOOLS DESIGN tab. Turn off the display of the pane by clicking the Text Pane button or clicking the Close button that displays in the upper right corner of the text pane.

Figure 8.7 Choose a SmartArt Graphic Dialog Box

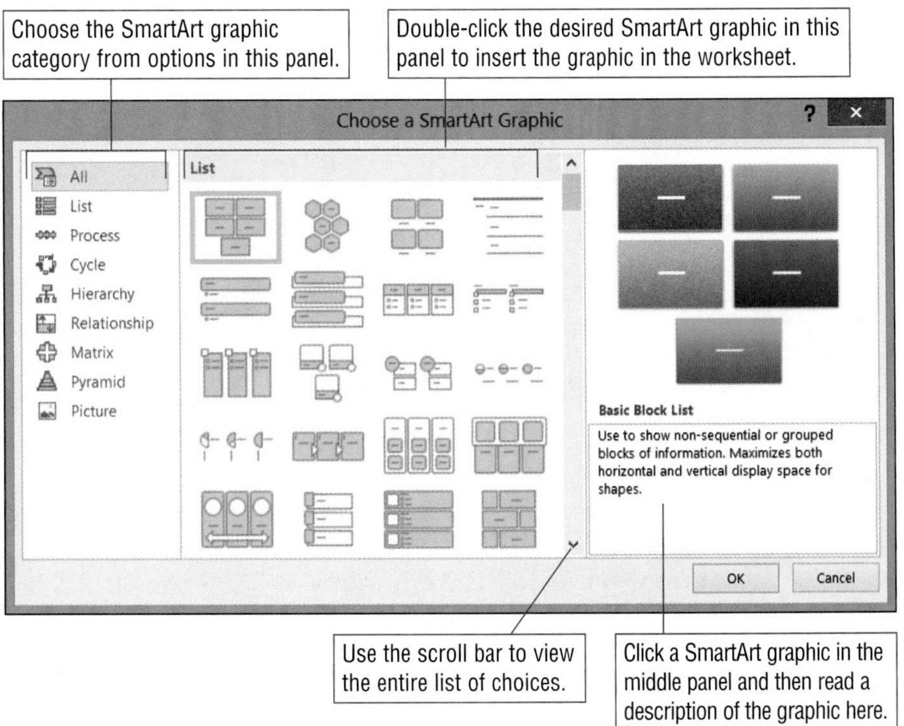

Sizing, Moving, and Deleting a SmartArt Graphic

Increase or decrease the size of a SmartArt graphic by dragging one of the sizing handles that display around the selected graphic. Use the corner sizing handles to increase or decrease the height and width at the same time. Use the middle sizing handles to increase or decrease the height or width of the SmartArt graphic.

To move a SmartArt graphic, select the graphic and then position the mouse pointer on the graphic border until the pointer displays with a four-headed arrow attached. Hold down the left mouse button, drag the graphic to the desired position, and then release the mouse button. Delete a graphic by selecting the graphic and then pressing the Delete key.

Project 4a Inserting, Moving, and Sizing a SmartArt Graphic in a Worksheet — Part 1 of 4

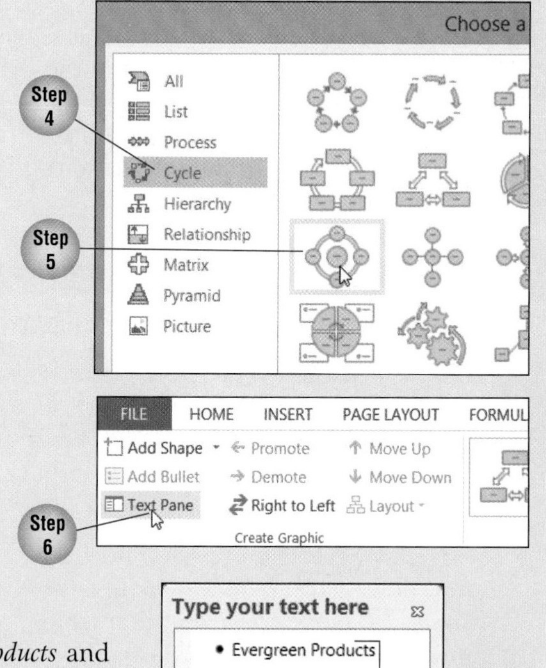

1. Open **EPSales.xlsx** and then save the workbook with Save As and name it **EL1-C8-P4-EPSales**.
2. Create the SmartArt graphic shown in Figure 8.8 on page 291. To begin, click the INSERT tab.
3. Click the SmartArt button in the Illustrations group.
4. At the Choose a SmartArt Graphic dialog box, click *Cycle* in the left panel.
5. Double-click *Radial Cycle* in the middle panel.
6. If the text pane is not open, click the Text Pane button in the Create Graphic group. (The text pane will display at the left side of the SmartArt graphic.)
7. With the insertion point positioned after the top bullet in the text pane, type **Evergreen Products**.
8. Click the *[Text]* placeholder below *Evergreen Products* and then type **Seattle**.
9. Click the next *[Text]* placeholder and then type **Olympia**.
10. Click the next *[Text]* placeholder and then type **Portland**.
11. Click the next *[Text]* placeholder and then type **Spokane**.
12. Click the Text Pane button to turn off the display of the text pane.
13. Drag the SmartArt graphic so it is positioned as shown in Figure 8.8. To drag the graphic, position the mouse pointer on the graphic border until the pointer displays with a four-headed arrow attached. Hold down the left mouse button, drag the graphic to the desired position, and then release the mouse button.
14. Use the sizing handles that display around the SmartArt graphic to increase or decrease the size of the graphic so it displays as shown in Figure 8.8.
15. Save **EL1-C8-P4-EPSales.xlsx**.

Changing the SmartArt Graphic Design

To restore the SmartArt default layout and color, click the Reset Graphic button in the Reset group on the SMARTART TOOLS DESIGN tab.

When you double-click a SmartArt graphic at the Choose a SmartArt Graphic dialog box, the graphic is inserted in the worksheet and the SMARTART TOOLS DESIGN tab is active. Use options and buttons on this tab to add objects, change the graphic layout, apply a style to the graphic, and reset the graphic back to the original formatting.

Project 4b **Changing the SmartArt Graphic Design** **Part 2 of 4**

1. With **EL1-C8-P4-EPSales.xlsx** open, make sure the SMARTART TOOLS DESIGN tab is active and then click the *Spokane* circle shape in the graphic to select it.
2. Click the Right to Left button in the Create Graphic group. (This switches *Olympia* and *Spokane*.) 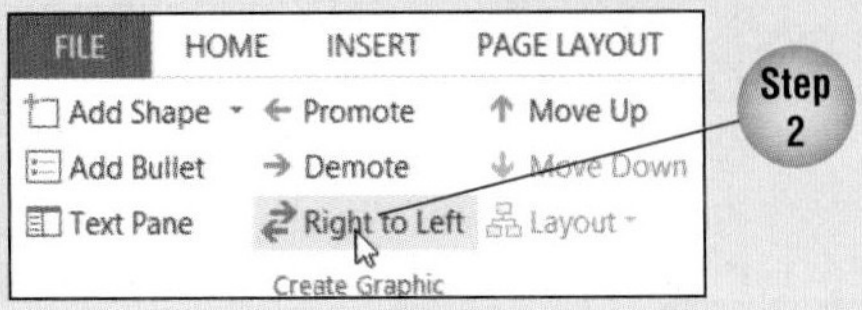
3. Click the More button located at the right side of the SmartArt Styles group and then click the *Polished* option at the drop-down list (first column, first row in the *3-D* section).

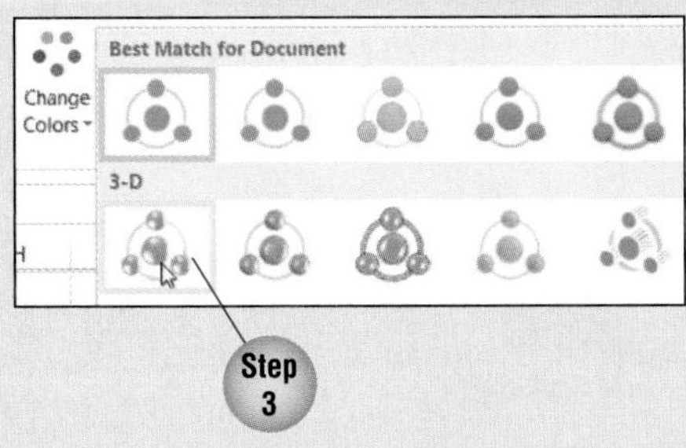

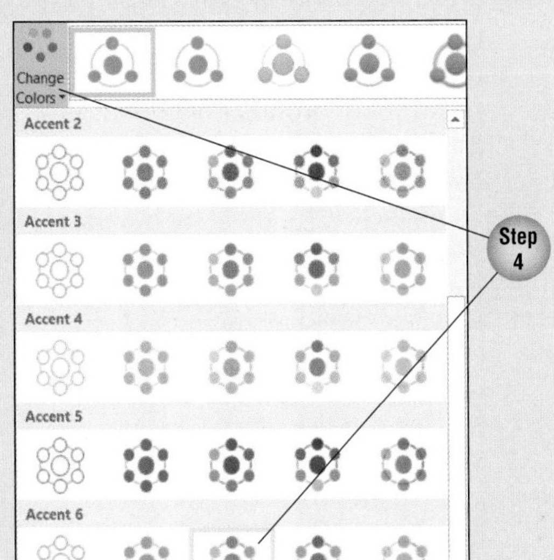

4. Click the Change Colors button in the SmartArt Styles group, scroll down the drop-down gallery, and then click the *Gradient Range - Accent 6* option (third option in the *Accent 6* section).
5. Click outside the SmartArt graphic to deselect it.
6. Change the orientation to landscape. (Make sure the graphic fits on the first page.)
7. Save **EL1-C8-P4-EPSales.xlsx** and then print the Total Sales worksheet.

Figure 8.8 Projects 4a and 4b

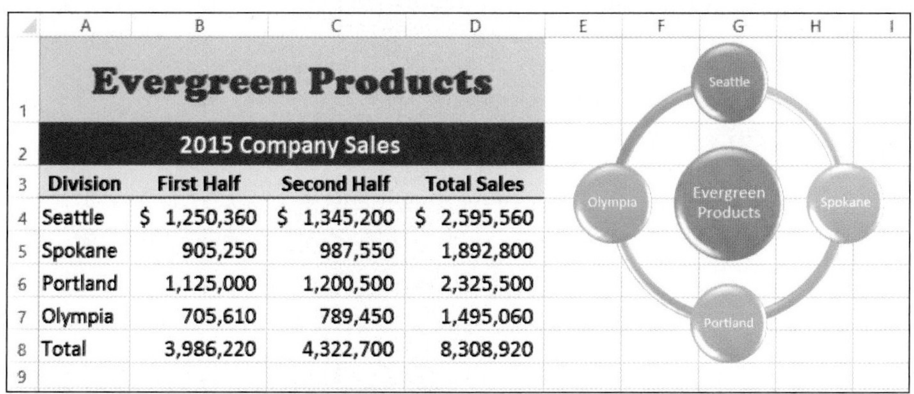

	A	B	C	D
1	**Evergreen Products**			
2	2015 Company Sales			
3	Division	First Half	Second Half	Total Sales
4	Seattle	$ 1,250,360	$ 1,345,200	$ 2,595,560
5	Spokane	905,250	987,550	1,892,800
6	Portland	1,125,000	1,200,500	2,325,500
7	Olympia	705,610	789,450	1,495,060
8	Total	3,986,220	4,322,700	8,308,920
9				

Changing the SmartArt Graphic Formatting

Click the SMARTART TOOLS FORMAT tab and options display for formatting a SmartArt graphic. Use buttons on this tab to insert and customize shapes; apply a shape style; apply WordArt styles; and specify the position, alignment, rotation, wrapping style, height, and width of the graphic.

Project 4c Changing the SmartArt Graphic Formatting — Part 3 of 4

1. With **EL1-C8-P4-EPSales.xlsx** open, click the Seattle Sales worksheet tab.
2. Create the SmartArt graphic shown in Figure 8.9 on the next page. To begin, click the INSERT tab and then click the SmartArt button in the Illustrations group.
3. At the Choose a SmartArt Graphic dialog box, click *Relationship* in the left panel and then double-click *Gear* in the middle panel.
4. Click *[Text]* in the bottom gear and then type **Quality Products**.
5. Click *[Text]* in the left gear and then type **Customized Plans**.
6. Click *[Text]* in the top gear and then type **Exemplary Service**.
7. Click inside the SmartArt graphic border but outside any graphic element.
8. Click the More button that displays at the right side of the SmartArt Styles group and then click the *Inset* option (second column, first row in the *3-D* section).

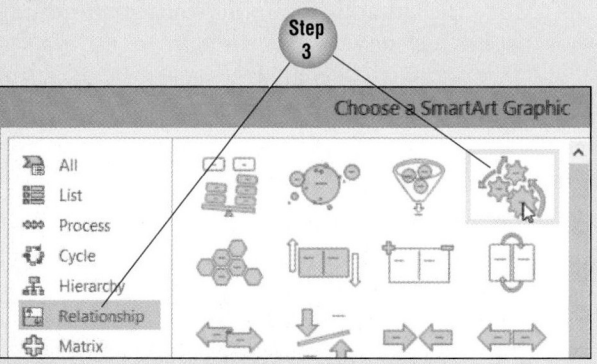

Step 3

Choose a SmartArt Graphic

All
List
Process
Cycle
Hierarchy
Relationship
Matrix

9. Click the Change Colors button in the SmartArt Styles group and then click the *Gradient Loop - Accent 6* option (fourth option in the *Accent 6* section).
10. Click the SMARTART TOOLS FORMAT tab.
11. Click in the *Shape Height* measurement box in the Size group and then type 4.
12. Click in the *Shape Width* measurement box, type 4.5, and then press Enter.

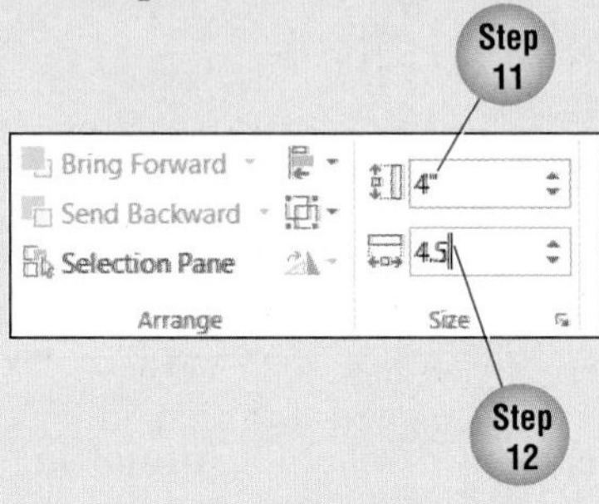

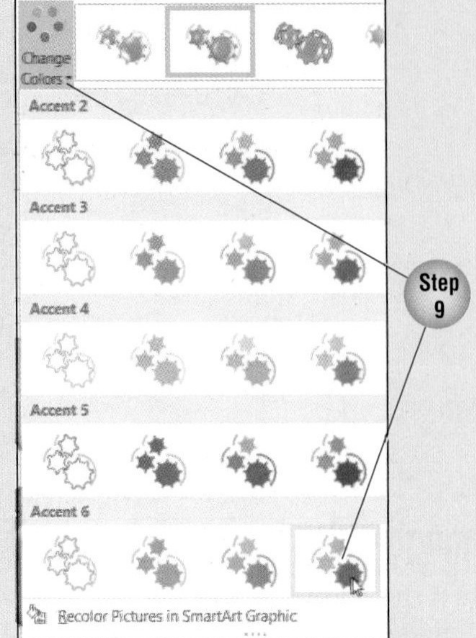

13. Click the bottom gear to select it.
14. Click the Shape Fill button arrow in the Shape Styles group and then click the *Green, Accent 6, Darker 50%* option (last column, last row in the *Theme Colors* section).
15. Click the top gear to select it.
16. Click the Shape Fill button arrow and then click the *Green, Accent 6, Darker 25%* option (last column, fifth row in the *Theme Colors* section).
17. Change the orientation to landscape.
18. Move the SmartArt graphic so it fits on the first page and displays as shown in Figure 8.9.
19. Click outside the chart to deselect it.
20. Save **EL1-C8-P4-EPSales.xlsx** and then print the Seattle Sales worksheet.

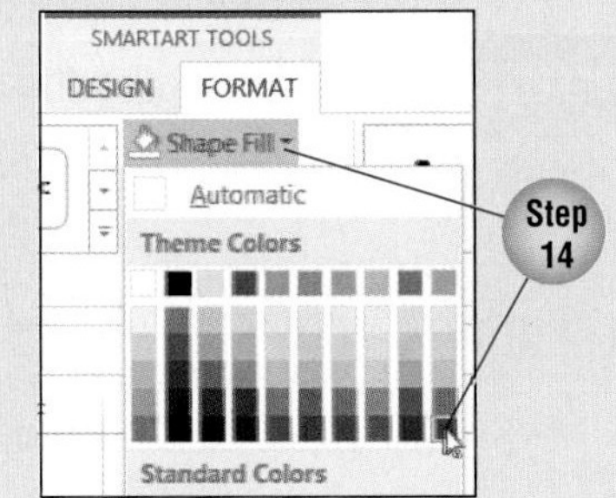

Figure 8.9 Project 4c

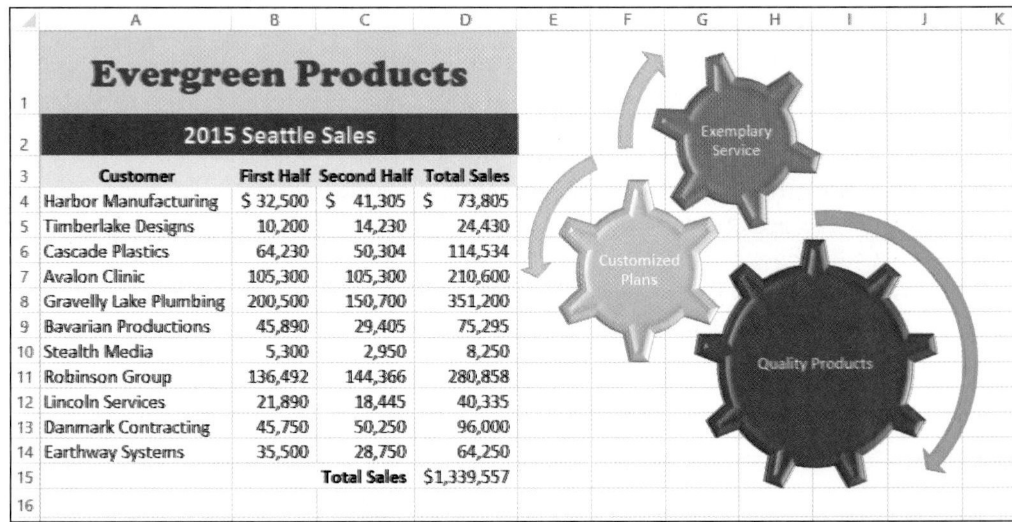

Evergreen Products			
2015 Seattle Sales			
Customer	First Half	Second Half	Total Sales
Harbor Manufacturing	$ 32,500	$ 41,305	$ 73,805
Timberlake Designs	10,200	14,230	24,430
Cascade Plastics	64,230	50,304	114,534
Avalon Clinic	105,300	105,300	210,600
Gravelly Lake Plumbing	200,500	150,700	351,200
Bavarian Productions	45,890	29,405	75,295
Stealth Media	5,300	2,950	8,250
Robinson Group	136,492	144,366	280,858
Lincoln Services	21,890	18,445	40,335
Danmark Contracting	45,750	50,250	96,000
Earthway Systems	35,500	28,750	64,250
		Total Sales	$1,339,557

Creating, Sizing, and Moving WordArt

With the WordArt feature, you can distort or modify text to conform to a variety of shapes. This is useful for creating company logos and headings. With WordArt, you can change the font, style, and alignment of text. You can also use different fill patterns and colors, customize border lines, and add shadow and three-dimensional effects.

To insert WordArt in an Excel worksheet, click the INSERT tab, click the Insert WordArt button in the Text group, and then click the desired option at the drop-down list. This inserts the text *Your text here* in the worksheet, formatted in the WordArt option you selected at the drop-down list. Type the desired text and then use the buttons on the DRAWING TOOLS FORMAT tab to format the WordArt.

WordArt text inserted in a worksheet is surrounded by white sizing handles. Use these sizing handles to change the height and width of the WordArt text. To move WordArt text, position the arrow pointer on the border of the WordArt text box until the pointer displays with a four-headed arrow attached and then drag the outline of the WordArt text box to the desired location.

Conform WordArt text to a variety of shapes using the *Transform* option from Text Effects button drop-down list. When you apply a transform shape, the WordArt border displays with a small, purple, square shape. Use this shape to change the slant of the WordArt text.

Quick Steps

Create WordArt

1. Click INSERT tab.
2. Click Insert WordArt button.
3. Click desired WordArt style at drop-down list.
4. Type desired text.

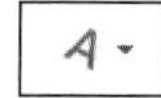

Insert WordArt

To remove a WordArt style from text and still retain the text, click the More button in the WordArt Styles group on the DRAWING TOOLS FORMAT tab and then click *Clear WordArt*.

Project 4d **Inserting and Formatting WordArt** **Part 4 of 4**

1. With **EL1-C8-P4-EPSales.xlsx** open, click the Total Sales worksheet tab.
2. Make cell A1 active and then press the Delete key. (This removes the text from the cell.)
3. Increase the height of row 1 to 137 points.
4. Click the INSERT tab.
5. Click the Insert WordArt button in the Text group and then click the *Fill - Black, Text 1, Outline - Background 1, Hard Shadow - Background 1* option (first column, third row).
6. Type **Evergreen**, press the Enter key, and then type **Products**.
7. Click the WordArt border to change the border to a solid line (not a dashed line).
8. Click the Text Fill button arrow in the WordArt Styles group and then click the *Green, Accent 6, Darker 50%* option (last column, last row in the *Theme Colors* section).

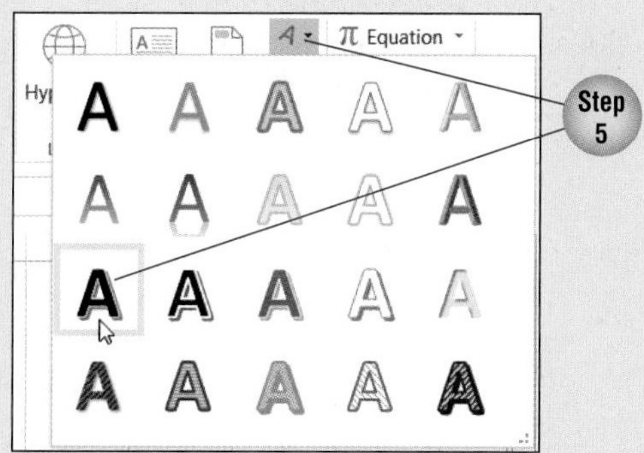

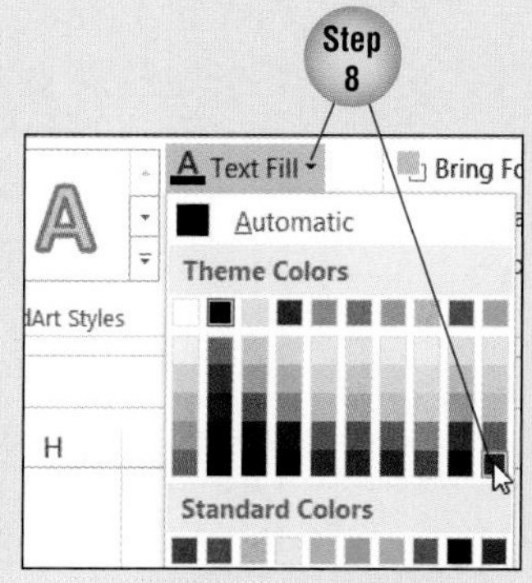

9. Click the Text Effects button in the WordArt Styles group, point to *Transform*, and then click the *Can Up* option (third column, fourth row in the *Warp* section).
10. Position the mouse pointer (turns into a white arrow) on the small, purple square that displays right below the *d* in *Products*, hold down the left mouse button, drag up approximately 0.25 inch, and then release the mouse button. (This changes the slant of the text.)
11. Drag the WordArt text so it is positioned in cell A1.
12. If necessary, resize the SmartArt graphic and position it so it prints on one page with the data.
13. Click the Seattle Sales worksheet tab and then complete steps similar to those in Steps 2 through 11 to insert *Evergreen Products* as WordArt in cell A1.
14. Make sure the SmartArt graphic fits on the page with the data. If necessary, decrease the size of the graphic.
15. Save **EL1-C8-P4-EPSales.xlsx** and then print both worksheets.
16. Close **EL1-C8-P4-EPSales.xlsx**.

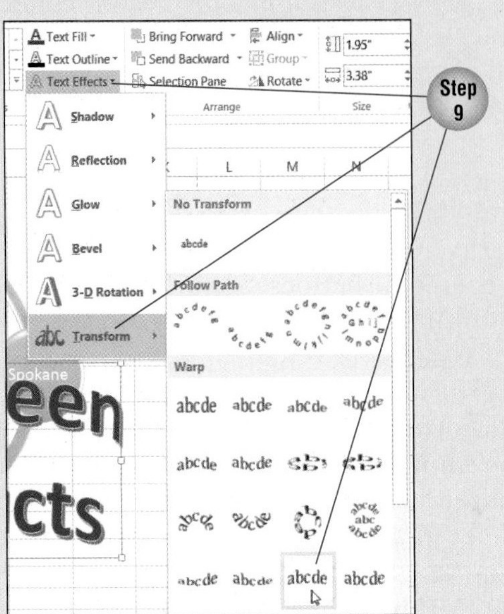

Chapter Summary

- Insert symbols with options at the Symbol dialog box with the Symbols tab or the Special Characters tab selected.
- With buttons in the Illustrations group on the INSERT tab, you can insert a picture, clip art image, screenshot, shape, or SmartArt graphic.
- Insert a picture by clicking the INSERT tab, clicking the Pictures button in the Illustrations group, and then double-clicking the desired picture at the Insert Picture dialog box.
- When you insert an image, such as a picture or clip art image, in a worksheet, the PICTURE TOOLS FORMAT tab is active and includes options for adjusting the image, applying preformatted styles, and arranging and sizing the image.
- Change the size of an image with the *Shape Height* and *Shape Width* measurement boxes in the Size group on the PICTURE TOOLS FORMAT tab or with the sizing handles that display around the selected image.
- Move an image by positioning the mouse pointer on the image border until the pointer displays with a four-headed arrow attached and then drag the image to the desired location.
- Insert an image from Office.com with options at the Insert Pictures window. Display this window by clicking the INSERT tab and then clicking the Online Pictures button in the Illustrations group.

- Use the Screenshot button in the Illustrations group on the INSERT tab to capture all or part of the contents of a screen.
- To draw shapes in a workbook, click the INSERT tab, click the Shapes button in the Illustrations group, and then click the desired shape at the drop-down list. Click or drag in the worksheet to insert the shape. To maintain the proportions of the shape, hold down the Shift key while dragging in the worksheet.
- Copy a shape with the Copy and Paste buttons in the Clipboard group on the HOME tab or by holding down the Ctrl key while dragging the shape.
- Draw a text box in a worksheet by clicking the INSERT tab, clicking the Text Box button in the Text group, and then clicking or dragging in the worksheet. Use options on the DRAWING TOOLS FORMAT tab to format and customize the text box.
- A watermark is a lightened image that displays behind data in a file. Create a picture watermark in a worksheet by inserting a picture in a header or footer and then changing the size and formatting of the picture.
- Insert a SmartArt graphic in a worksheet by clicking the INSERT tab, clicking the SmartArt button in the Illustrations group, and then double-clicking the desired graphic at the Choose a SmartArt Graphic dialog box. Customize a SmartArt graphic with options on the SMARTART TOOLS DESIGN tab and the SMARTART TOOLS FORMAT tab.
- Use WordArt to create, distort, modify, and/or conform text to a variety of shapes. Insert WordArt in a worksheet with the WordArt button in the Text group on the INSERT tab. Customize WordArt text with options on the DRAWING TOOLS FORMAT tab.

Commands Review

FEATURE	RIBBON TAB, GROUP	BUTTON
Choose a SmartArt Graphic dialog box	INSERT, Illustrations	
Insert Picture dialog box	INSERT, Illustrations	
Insert Pictures window	INSERT, Illustrations	
Insert WordArt button drop-down list	INSERT, Text	A ▾
screenshot	INSERT, Illustrations	
Shapes button drop-down list	INSERT, Illustrations	
Symbol dialog box	INSERT, Symbols	Ω
text box	INSERT, Text	

Concepts Check Test Your Knowledge

Completion: In the space provided at the right, indicate the correct term, symbol, or command.

1. The Symbol button is located on this tab. ____________
2. The *Font* option is available at the Symbol dialog box with this tab selected. ____________
3. Insert a picture, clip art image, screenshot, shape, or SmartArt graphic with buttons in this group on the INSERT tab. ____________
4. Display the Insert Pictures window by clicking this button on the INSERT tab. ____________
5. When you insert an image, such as a picture or clip art, in a worksheet, this tab is active. ____________
6. Maintain the proportions of an image by holding down this key while dragging a sizing handle. ____________
7. To move an image, position the mouse pointer on the image border until the mouse pointer displays with this attached and then drag the image to the desired location. ____________
8. To capture a portion of a screen, click the Screenshot button and then click this option at the drop-down list. ____________
9. To copy a shape, hold down this key while dragging the shape. ____________
10. When you draw a text box in a worksheet and then release the mouse button, this tab is active. ____________
11. This term refers to a lightened image that displays behind data in a file. ____________
12. Click the SmartArt button in the Illustrations group on the INSERT tab and this dialog box displays. ____________

Skills Check Assess Your Performance

Assessment

1 INSERT A CLIP ART IMAGE AND WORDART IN AN EQUIPMENT SALES WORKBOOK

1. Open **MSSalesPlans.xlsx** and then save the workbook with Save As and name it **EL1-C8-A1-MSSalesPlans**.
2. Insert a formula in cell E4 using the PMT function that calculates monthly payments. (Type a minus sign before the cell designation in the *Pv* text box at the Function Arguments palette.) ***Hint: For assistance, refer to Chapter 7, Project 5a.***

3. Copy the formula in cell E4 down to cells E5 and E6.
4. Insert a formula in cell F4 that calculates the total amount of the payments.
5. Copy the formula in cell F4 down to cells F5 and F6.
6. Insert a formula in cell G4 that calculates the total amount of interest paid.
7. Copy the formula in cell G4 down to cells G5 and G6.
8. Insert the clip art image shown in Figure 8.10 with the following specifications:
   a. Click the INSERT tab and then click the Online Pictures button. At the Insert Pictures window, search for images related to maple leaves. (The colors of the original clip art image are green and white.)
   b. Apply the Orange, Accent color 2 Dark clip art image color (third column, second row).
   c. Apply the Brightness: -20% Contrast: +20% correction (second column, fourth row).
   d. Apply the Drop Shadow Rectangle picture style (fourth thumbnail).
   e. Size and move the image so it is positioned as shown in Figure 8.10.
9. Insert the company name *Maplewood Suppliers* in cell A1 as WordArt with the following specifications:
   a. Click the WordArt button on the INSERT tab and then click the *Fill - White, Outline - Accent 2, Hard Shadow - Accent 2* option (fourth column, third row).
   b. Apply the Orange, Accent 2, Darker 50% text fill (sixth column, bottom row in the *Theme Colors* section).
   c. Apply the Orange, Accent 2, Lighter 60% text outline (sixth column, third row in the *Theme Colors* section).
   d. Using the Text Effects button, apply the Square transform text effect.
   e. Change the width of the WordArt to 5 inches.
   f. Move the WordArt so it is positioned in cell A1 as shown in Figure 8.10.
10. Change the worksheet orientation to landscape.
11. Save, print, and then close **EL1-C8-A1-MSSalesPlans.xlsx**.

Figure 8.10 Assessment 1

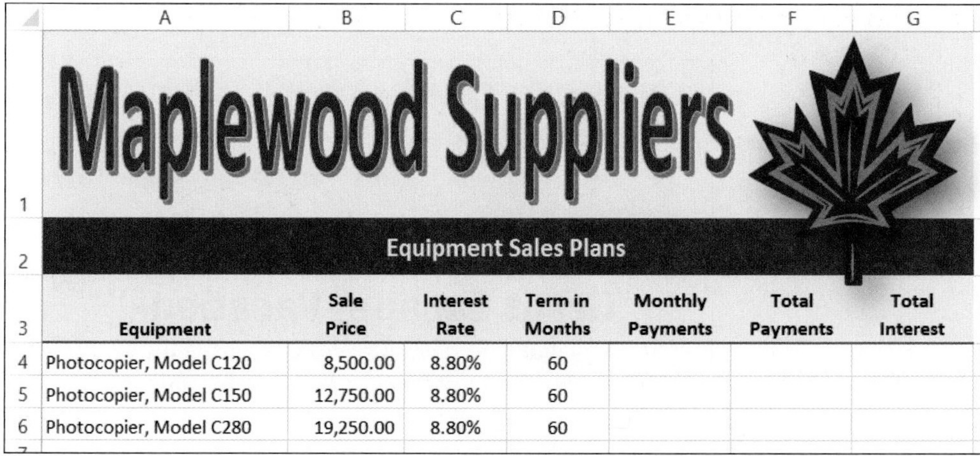

	A	B	C	D	E	F	G
1	Maplewood Suppliers						
2	Equipment Sales Plans						
3	Equipment	Sale Price	Interest Rate	Term in Months	Monthly Payments	Total Payments	Total Interest
4	Photocopier, Model C120	8,500.00	8.80%	60			
5	Photocopier, Model C150	12,750.00	8.80%	60			
6	Photocopier, Model C280	19,250.00	8.80%	60			

Assessment 2

INSERT FORMULAS AND FORMAT A TRAVEL COMPANY WORKBOOK

Grade It

1. Open **TSGEVacs.xlsx** and then save the workbook with Save As and name it **EL1-C8-A2-TSGEVacs**.
2. Insert appropriate formulas to calculate the prices based on 10% and 20% discounts and apply the appropriate number formatting. ***Hint: For the 10% discount column, multiply the price per person by 0.90 (which determines 90% of the price) and for the 20% discount column, multiply the price per person by 0.80 (which determines 80% of the price).***
3. Format the image of the airplane and position it as shown in Figure 8.11 with the following specifications:
   a. Use the Remove Background button in the Adjust group on the PICTURE TOOLS FORMAT tab to remove a portion of the yellow background so the image displays similar to what you see in the figure.
   b. Rotate the image to flip it horizontally.
   c. Apply the Brightness: +20% Contrast: +20% correction.
   d. Change the height of the image to 1.4 inches and then position the image as shown in the figure.
4. Open Word and then open the document named **TSAirfare.docx** located in the EL1C8 folder on your storage medium. Click the Excel button on the Taskbar and then use the Screenshot button (with the *Screen Clipping* option) to select and then insert the airfare information in **EL1-C8-A2-TSGEVacs.xlsx**. Position the information at the right side of the data in the worksheet.
5. Change the orientation to landscape.
6. Make sure the data and the airfare information display on one page and then print the worksheet.
7. Save and then close **EL1-C8-A2-TSGEVacs.xslx**.
8. Click the Word button on the Taskbar, close **TSAirfare.docx**, and then close Word.

Figure 8.11 Assessment 2

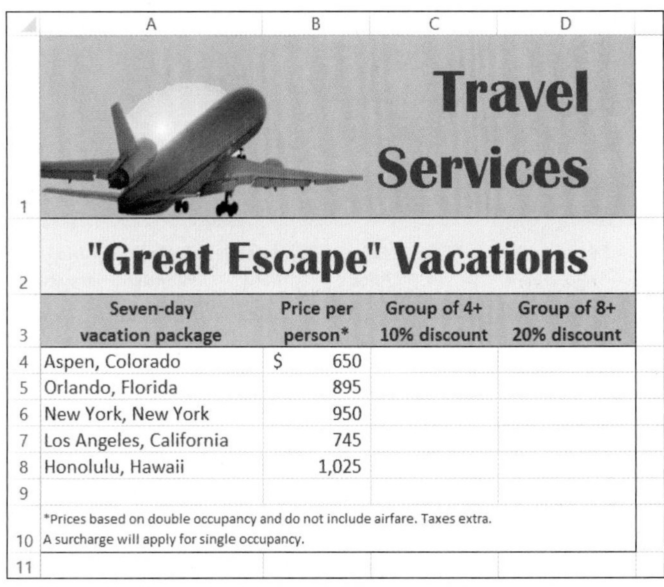

	A	B	C	D
1	Travel Services			
2	"Great Escape" Vacations			
3	Seven-day vacation package	Price per person*	Group of 4+ 10% discount	Group of 8+ 20% discount
4	Aspen, Colorado	$ 650		
5	Orlando, Florida	895		
6	New York, New York	950		
7	Los Angeles, California	745		
8	Honolulu, Hawaii	1,025		
9				
10	*Prices based on double occupancy and do not include airfare. Taxes extra. A surcharge will apply for single occupancy.			
11				

Assessment

3 INSERT AND FORMAT SHAPES IN A COMPANY SALES WORKBOOK

1. Open **MGSales.xlsx** and then save the workbook with Save As and name it **EL1-C8-A3-MGSales**.
2. Use the Isosceles Triangle shape located in the *Basic Shapes* section of the Shapes drop-down palette to draw a triangle as shown in Figure 8.12.
3. Apply Green, Accent 6, Darker 50% shape outline color (last column, last row in the *Theme Colors* section) to the triangle.
4. Apply Green, Accent 6, Darker 25% shape fill (last column, fifth row in the *Theme Colors* section) to the triangle.
5. Copy the triangle three times.
6. Position the triangles as shown in Figure 8.12.
7. Select the second and fourth triangles and then apply the Green, Accent 6, Lighter 80% shape fill (last column, second row in the *Theme Colors* section).
8. Insert the total amounts in cells B10 through D10. (If you use the fill handle to copy the formula from B10 to cells C10 and D10, use the Auto Fill options button to fill without formatting.)
9. Insert an arrow pointing to *$97,549* with the following specifications:
   a. Use the Left Arrow shape to draw the arrow.
   b. Change the height of the arrow to 0.6 inch and the width to 1.2 inches.
   c. Apply Green, Accent 6, Darker 25% shape fill (last column, fifth row in the *Theme Colors* section) to the arrow.
   d. Type the text **Largest Order** in the arrow and then select the text and change the font to 10-point Calibri bold.
   e. Position the arrow as shown in Figure 8.12.
10. Save, print, and then close **EL1-C8-A3-MGSales.xlsx**.

Figure 8.12 Assessment 3

	A	B	C	D	E	F
1	**Mountain Group**					
2	**FIRST QUARTER SALES - 2015**					
3	**Customer**	**January**	**February**	**March**		
4	Lakeside Trucking	$ 84,231	$ 73,455	$ 97,549	Largest Order	
5	Gresham Machines	33,199	40,390	50,112		
6	Real Photography	30,891	35,489	36,400		
7	Genesis Productions	72,190	75,390	83,219		
8	Landower Company	22,188	14,228	38,766		
9	Jewell Enterprises	19,764	50,801	32,188		
10	***Total***					
11						

Assessment 4

INSERT AND FORMAT A SMARTART GRAPHIC IN A SALES WORKBOOK

1. Open **PS2ndQtrSales.xlsx** and then save the workbook with Save As and name it **EL1-C8-A4-PS2ndQtrSales**.
2. Change the orientation to landscape.
3. Insert the Pyramid List SmartArt graphic at the right side of the worksheet data with the following specifications:
   a. Apply the Gradient Loop - Accent 2 color (fourth option in the *Accent 2* section).
   b. Apply the Cartoon SmartArt style (third column, first row in the *3-D* section).
   c. In the bottom text box, type **Red Level**, press Enter, and then type **$25,000 to $49,999**.
   d. In the middle text box, type **Blue Level**, press Enter, and then type **$50,000 to $99,999**.
   e. In the top text box, type **Gold Level**, press Enter, and then type **$100,000+**.
   f. Apply fill color to each text box to match the level color. (Use the Orange fill color for the Gold Level text box.)
4. Size and/or move the SmartArt graphic so it displays attractively at the right side of the worksheet data. (Make sure the entire graphic will print on the same page as the worksheet data.)
5. Save, print, and then close **EL1-C8-A4-PS2ndQtrSales.xlsx**.

Assessment 5

CREATE AND INSERT A SCREENSHOT

1. Open **RPRefiPlan.xlsx**, save it with Save As and name it **EL1-C8-A5-RPRefiPlan**, and then display the formulas by pressing Ctrl + `.
2. Insert the arrow shape shown in Figure 8.13 on the next page. Add fill to the shape, remove the shape outline, bold the text in the shape, and then determine how to rotate the shape using the rotation handle (white circle). Rotate, size, and position the arrow as shown in the figure.
3. Open Word.
4. At a blank document, press Ctrl + E to center the insertion point, press Ctrl + B to turn on bold, type **Excel Worksheet with PMT Formula**, and then press the Enter key twice.
5. Click the INSERT tab, click the Screenshot button, and then click the thumbnail of the Excel worksheet.
6. Save the Word document and name it **EL1-C8-A5-PMTFormula**.
7. Print and then close the document and then close Word.
8. In Excel, save and then close **EL1-C8-A5-RPRefiPlan.xlsx**.

Figure 8.13 Assessment 5

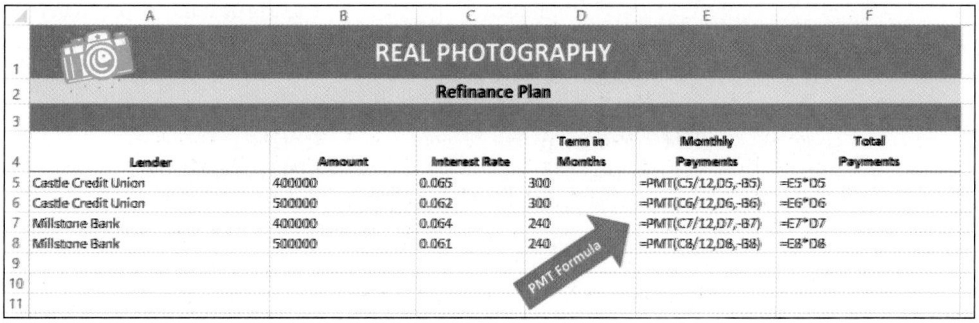

	A	B	C	D	E	F
1	REAL PHOTOGRAPHY					
2	Refinance Plan					
3						
4	**Lender**	**Amount**	**Interest Rate**	**Term in Months**	**Monthly Payments**	**Total Payments**
5	Castle Credit Union	400000	0.065	300	=PMT(C5/12,D5,-B5)	=E5*D5
6	Castle Credit Union	500000	0.062	300	=PMT(C6/12,D6,-B6)	=E6*D6
7	Millstone Bank	400000	0.064	240	=PMT(C7/12,D7,-B7)	=E7*D7
8	Millstone Bank	500000	0.061	240	=PMT(C8/12,D8,-B8)	=E8*D8
9						
10						
11						

PMT Formula

Visual Benchmark Demonstrate Your Proficiency

INSERT FORMULAS, WORDART, AND CLIP ART IN A WORKSHEET

1. Open **TSYrlySales.xlsx** and then save the workbook with Save As and name it **EL1-C8-VB-TSYrlySales**.
2. Insert formulas that will calculate the results shown in the worksheet in Figure 8.14 on the next page. (***Do not*** type the data in the cells. Instead, insert the following formulas. The results of your formulas should match the results you see in the figure.)
   - Cells C4 through C14: Insert a formula with an IF function that inserts *5%* if the amount in the cell in column B is greater than $249,999 and inserts *2%* if the amount is not greater than $249,999.
   - Cells D4 through D14: Insert a formula that multiplies the amount in column B with the amount in column C.
   - Apply accounting formatting with a dollar sign and no places past the decimal point to cell D4.
3. Insert the company name *Target Supplies* as WordArt with the following specifications:
   - Choose the *Fill - Black, Text 1, Outline - Background 1, Hard Shadow - Accent 1* option (second column, third row).
   - To type the WordArt text, press Ctrl + L (which changes to left text alignment), type **Target**, press Enter, and then type **Supplies**.
   - Apply Orange, Accent 2, Darker 50% text fill color (sixth column, bottom row in the *Theme Colors* section).
   - Apply the Orange, Accent 2, Lighter 40% text outline color (sixth column, fourth row in the *Theme Colors* section).
   - Move the WordArt so it is positioned as shown in Figure 8.14.
4. Insert the target clip art image (use the Insert Pictures window and search with the words *archery, arrows, target* to find this clip art image) with the following specifications:
   - Apply the Orange, Accent color 2 light color (third column, third row).
   - Apply the Brightness: -20% Contrast: -20% correction (second column, second row).
   - Size and position the clip art image as shown in the figure.

5. Draw the shape that displays below the data with the following specifications:
    - Use the Bevel shape (located in the *Basic Shapes* section).
    - Type the text in the shape, apply bold formatting, and change to center and middle alignment.
    - Apply the Orange, Accent 2, Darker 50% shape fill color (sixth column, bottom row in the *Theme Colors* section).
    - Apply the Orange, Accent 2 shape outline color (sixth column, top row in the *Theme Colors* section).
6. Save and then print the worksheet.
7. Press Ctrl + ` to turn on the display of formulas and then print the worksheet again.
8. Turn off the display of formulas and then close the workbook.

Figure 8.14 Visual Benchmark

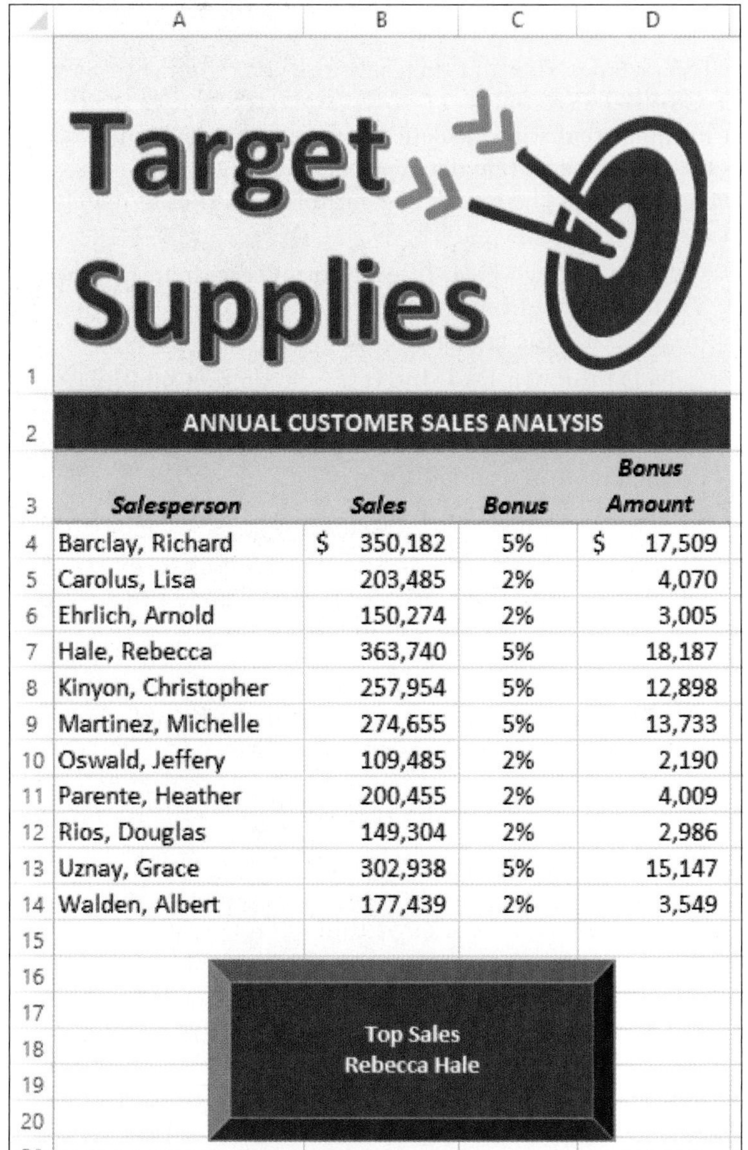

Target Supplies

ANNUAL CUSTOMER SALES ANALYSIS

Salesperson	Sales	Bonus	Bonus Amount
Barclay, Richard	$ 350,182	5%	$ 17,509
Carolus, Lisa	203,485	2%	4,070
Ehrlich, Arnold	150,274	2%	3,005
Hale, Rebecca	363,740	5%	18,187
Kinyon, Christopher	257,954	5%	12,898
Martinez, Michelle	274,655	5%	13,733
Oswald, Jeffery	109,485	2%	2,190
Parente, Heather	200,455	2%	4,009
Rios, Douglas	149,304	2%	2,986
Uznay, Grace	302,938	5%	15,147
Walden, Albert	177,439	2%	3,549

Top Sales
Rebecca Hale

Case Study Apply Your Skills

Part 1

You are the office manager for Ocean Truck Sales and are responsible for maintaining a spreadsheet of the truck and SUV inventory. Open **OTSales.xlsx** and then save the workbook and name it **EL1-C8-CS-OTSales**. Apply formatting to improve the appearance of the worksheet and insert at least one clip art image (related to a truck or ocean). Save **EL1-C8-CS-OTSales.xlsx** and then print the worksheet.

Part 2

With **EL1-C8-CS-OTSales.xlsx** open, save the workbook with Save As and name it **EL1-C8-CS-OTSalesF&C**. You make the inventory workbook available to each salesperson at the beginning of the week. For easier viewing, you decide to divide the workbook into two worksheets, with one worksheet containing all Ford vehicles and the other worksheet containing all Chevrolet vehicles. Rename the worksheet tabs to reflect the contents. Sort the data in each worksheet by price from most expensive to least expensive.

The owner offers incentives each week to help motivate the sales force. Insert in the first worksheet a SmartArt graphic of your choosing that contains the following information:

Small-sized truck: $200

2WD regular cab: $150

SUV 4x4: $100

Copy the SmartArt graphic in the first worksheet and then paste it into the second worksheet. Change the orientation to landscape and then save, print, and close both worksheets in **EL1-C8-CS-OTSalesF&C.xlsx**.

Part 3

You have been asked to save the inventory worksheet as a web page for viewing online. Open **EL1-C8-CS-OTSales.xlsx**, display the Save As dialog box, click the *Save as type* option, and then determine how to save the workbook as a single-file web page (*.mht, *.mhtml). Save the workbook as a single-file web page with the name **EL1-C8-CS-OTSales-WebPage**. Open your Internet browser and then open the web page. Look at the information in the file and then close the Internet browser.

Part 4

As part of your weekly duties, you post the incentive SmartArt graphic in various locations throughout the company. You decide to insert the graphic in PowerPoint for easy printing. Open **EL1-C8-CS-OTSalesF&C.xlsx** and then open PowerPoint. Change the slide layout in PowerPoint to Blank. Copy the SmartArt graphic in the first worksheet and paste it into the PowerPoint blank slide. Increase and/or move the graphic so it better fills the slide. Print the slide and then close PowerPoint without saving the presentation. Close **EL1-C8-CS-OTSalesF&C.xlsx**.

UNIT 2

MICROSOFT® EXCEL® Performance Assessment

Note: Before beginning unit assessments, copy to your storage medium the EL1U2 subfolder from the EL1 folder on the CD that accompanies this textbook and then make EL1U2 the active folder.

Assessing Proficiency

In this unit, you have learned how to work with multiple windows; move, copy, link, and paste data within and between workbooks and applications; create and customize charts with data in a worksheet; write formulas with PMT, FV, and IF functions; save a workbook as a web page; insert hyperlinks; and insert and customize images, shapes, SmartArt graphics, and WordArt.

Assessment 1 Copy and Paste Data and Insert WordArt in a Training Scores Workbook

1. Open **RLTraining.xlsx** and then save the workbook with Save As and name it **EL1-U2-A01-RLTraining**.
2. Delete row 15 (the row for *Kwieciak, Kathleen*).
3. Insert a formula in cell D4 that averages the percentages in cells B4 and C4.
4. Copy the formula in cell D4 down to cells D5 through D20.
5. Make cell A22 active, turn on bold formatting, and then type Highest Averages.
6. Display the Clipboard task pane and make sure it is empty.
7. Select and then copy each of the following rows (individually): 7, 10, 14, 16, and 18.
8. Make cell A23 active and then paste row 14 (the row for *Jewett, Troy*).
9. Make cell A24 active and then paste row 7 (the row for *Cumpston, Kurt*).
10. Make cell A25 active and then paste row 10 (the row for *Fisher-Edwards, Theresa*).
11. Make cell A26 active and then paste row 16 (the row for *Mathias, Caleb*).
12. Make cell A27 active and then paste row 18 (the row for *Nyegaard, Curtis*).
13. Click the Clear All button in the Clipboard task pane and then close the task pane.
14. Insert in cell A1 the text *Roseland* as WordArt. Format the WordArt text to add visual appeal to the worksheet.
15. Save, print, and then close **EL1-U2-A01-RLTraining.xlsx**.

Assessment 2 Manage Multiple Worksheets in a Projected Earnings Workbook

1. Open **RLProjEarnings.xlsx** and then save the workbook with Save As and name it **EL1-U2-A02-RLProjEarnings**.
2. Delete *Roseland* in cell A1. Open **EL1-U2-A01-RLTraining.xlsx**, copy the *Roseland* WordArt text, and then paste it into cell A1 in **EL1-U2-A02-RLProjEarnings.xlsx**. If necessary, increase the height of row 1 to accommodate the WordArt text.
3. Close **EL1-U2-A01-RLTraining.xlsx**.
4. Insert a new worksheet in the **EL1-U2-A02-RLProjEarnings.xlsx** workbook.
5. Select cells A1 through C11 in Sheet1 and then copy and paste the cells to Sheet2, keeping the source column widths.
6. With Sheet2 displayed, make the following changes:
   a. Increase the height of row 1 to accommodate the WordArt text.
   b. Delete the contents of cell B2.
   c. Change the contents of the following cells:
      A6: Change *January* to *July*
      A7: Change *February* to *August*
      A8: Change *March* to *September*
      A9: Change *April* to *October*
      A10: Change *May* to *November*
      A11: Change *June* to *December*
      B6: Change *8.30%* to *8.10%*
      B8: Change *9.30%* to *8.70%*
7. Make Sheet1 active, copy cell B2, and then paste link it to cell B2 in Sheet2.
8. Rename Sheet1 *First Half* and rename Sheet2 *Second Half*.
9. Make the First Half worksheet active and then determine the effect on projected monthly earnings if the projected yearly income is increased by 10% by changing the number in cell B2 to *$1,480,380*.
10. Horizontally and vertically center both worksheets in the workbook and insert a custom header that prints your name at the left, the current date in the center, and the sheet name (click the Sheet Name button in the Header & Footer Elements group on the Header & Footer Tools Design tab) at the right.
11. Print both worksheets.
12. Determine the effect on projected monthly earnings if the projected yearly income is increased by 20% by changing the number in cell B2 to *$1,614,960*.
13. Save the workbook again and then print both worksheets.
14. Close **EL1-U2-A02-RLProjEarnings.xlsx**.

Assessment 3 Create Charts in Worksheets in a Sales Totals Workbook

1. Open **EPYrlySales.xlsx** and then save the workbook with Save As and name it **EL1-U2-A03-EPYrlySales**.
2. Rename Sheet1 as *2013 Sales*, rename Sheet2 as *2014 Sales*, and rename Sheet3 as *2015 Sales*.
3. Select all three sheet tabs, make cell A12 active, turn on bold formatting, and then type **Total**. Make cell B12 active and then insert a formula to total the amounts in cells B4 through B11. Make cell C12 active and then insert a formula to total the amounts in cells C4 through C11.
4. Make the 2013 Sales worksheet active, select cells A3 through C11 (being careful not to select the totals in row 12), and then create a column chart. Click the Switch Row/Column button on the Chart Tools Design tab. Apply formatting to increase the visual appearance of the chart. Drag the chart below the worksheet data. (Make sure the chart fits on one page.)
5. Make the 2014 Sales worksheet active and then create the same type of chart you created in Step 4.
6. Make the 2015 Sales worksheet active and then create the same type of chart you created in Step 4. Filter the records in this chart so that only the following companies display: *Harbor Manufacturing*, *Avalon Clinic*, and *Stealth Media*.
7. Save the workbook and then print the entire workbook.
8. Close **EL1-U2-A03-EPYrlySales.xlsx**.

Assessment 4 Create and Format a Line Chart

1. Open **ProfitCompare.xlsx** and then save the workbook with Save As and name it **EL1-U2-A04-ProfitCompare**.
2. Use the data in the workbook to create a line chart with the following specifications:
   a. Apply the Style 11 chart style.
   b. Include the chart title *NET PROFIT COMPARISON*.
   c. Apply the Green shape fill and shape outline color of the Asia series (in the *Standard Colors* section).
   d. Move the chart to a new worksheet.
3. Save the workbook and then print only the worksheet containing the chart.
4. Close **EL1-U2-A04-ProfitCompare.xlsx**.

Assessment 5 Create and Format a Pie Chart

1. Open **EPProdDept.xlsx** and then save the workbook with Save As and name it **EL1-U2-A05-EPProdDept**.
2. Create a pie chart as a separate worksheet with the data in cells A3 through B10. You determine the type of pie chart. Include an appropriate title for the chart, as well as percentage labels.
3. Print only the worksheet containing the chart.
4. Save and then close **EL1-U2-A05-EPProdDept.xlsx**.

Assessment 6 Use the PMT Function and Apply Formatting to a Workbook

1. Open **HERSalesInfo.xlsx** and then save the workbook with Save As and name it **EL1-U2-A06-HERSalesInfo**.
2. The owner of Hilltop Equipment Rental is interested in selling three tractors owned by the business and needs to determine the possible monthly income from the sales. Using the PMT function, insert a formula in cell E4 that calculates monthly payments. (Type a minus sign before the cell designation in the *Pv* text box at the Function Arguments palette.)
3. Copy the formula in cell E4 down to cells E5 and E6.
4. Insert a formula in cell F4 that multiplies the amount in cell E4 by the amount in cell D4.
5. Copy the formula in cell F4 down to cells F5 and F6.
6. Insert a formula in cell G4 that subtracts the amount in cell B4 from the amount in cell F4. ***Hint: The formula should return a positive number.***
7. Copy the formula in cell G4 down to cells G5 and G6.
8. Save, print, and then close **EL1-U2-A06-HERSalesInfo.xlsx**.

Assessment 7 Use the IF Function and Apply Formatting to a Workbook

1. Open **PSQtrlySales.xlsx** and then save the workbook with Save As and name it **EL1-U2-A07-PSQtrlySales**.
2. Insert an IF statement in cell F4 that inserts *Yes* if cell E4 contains a number greater than 74999 and inserts *No* if the number in cell E4 is not greater than 74999. Copy the formula in cell F4 down to cells F5 through F18. Center align the text in cells F4 through F18.
3. Insert a footer that prints your name at the left, the current date in the middle, and the current time at the right.
4. Turn on the display of formulas, print the worksheet in landscape orientation, and then turn off the display of formulas. (The worksheet will print on two pages.)
5. Save and then close **EL1-U2-A07-PSQtrlySales.xlsx**.

Assessment 8 Insert a Text Box and Hyperlinks in a Travel Workbook

1. Open **TravDest.xlsx** and then save the workbook with Save As and name it **EL1-U2-A08-TravDest**.
2. Insert a text box in the workbook with the following specifications:
   a. Draw the text box at the right side of the clip art image.
   b. Type **Call 1-888-555-1288 for last-minute vacation specials!**
   c. Select the text and then change the font to 24-point Forte and apply the Blue color in the *Standard Colors* section.
   d. Size and position the text box so it appears visually balanced with the travel clip art image.
3. Make sure you are connected to the Internet and then, for each city in the worksheet, search for sites that might be of interest to tourists. Write down the web address of the best web page you find for each city.
4. Create a hyperlink with each city name to the web address you wrote down in Step 3. (Select the hyperlink text in each cell and change the font size to 18 points.)
5. Test each hyperlink to make sure you entered the web address correctly. Click the hyperlink and then close the web browser after the page has loaded.
6. Save, print, and then close **EL1-U2-A08-TravDest.xlsx**.

Assessment 9 Insert an Image and a SmartArt Graphic in a Workbook

1. Open **SalesQuotas.xlsx** and then save the workbook with Save As and name it **EL1-U2-A09-SalesQuotas**.
2. Insert a formula in cell C3 using an absolute reference to determine the projected quotas at a 10% increase of the current quotas.
3. Copy the formula in cell C3 down to cells C4 through C12. Apply the Accounting format with two places past the decimal point and a dollar sign to cell C3.
4. In row 1, insert a clip art image related to money. You determine the size and position of the clip art image. If necessary, increase the height of the row.
5. Insert a SmartArt graphic at the right side of the data that contains three shapes. Insert the following quota ranges in the shapes and apply the specified fill colors:
   $50,000 to $99,999 (apply a green color)
   $100,000 to $149,999 (apply a blue color)
   $150,000 to $200,000 (apply a red color)
6. Apply formatting to the SmartArt graphic to improve the visual appearance.
7. Insert a custom header that prints your name at the left, the current date in the middle, and the file name at the right.
8. Change the orientation to landscape and make sure the graphic fits on the page.
9. Save, print, and then close **EL1-U2-A09-SalesQuotas.xlsx**.

Assessment 10 Insert a Symbol, WordArt, and Screenshot in a Sales Workbook

1. Open **CISales.xlsx** and then save the workbook with Save As and name it **EL1-U2-A10-CISales**.
2. Delete the text *Landower Company* in cell A7 and then type **Económico** in the cell. (Use the Symbol dialog box to insert *ó*.)
3. Insert a new row at the beginning of the worksheet.
4. Select and then merge cells A1 through D1.
5. Increase the height of row 1 to approximately 141.00 points.
6. Insert the text *Custom Interiors* as WordArt in cell A1. You determine the formatting of the WordArt. Move and size the WordArt so it fits in cell A1.
7. Open Word and then open **CICustomers.docx** located in the EL1U2 folder on your storage medium. Click the Excel button and with **EL1-U2-A10-CISales.xlsx** open, make a screenshot (using the *Screen Clipping* option) of the customer information in the Word document. Position the screenshot image below the data in the cells.
8. Insert a custom footer that prints your name at the left and the file name at the right.
9. Make sure the data in the cells and the screenshot display on the same page and then print the worksheet.
10. Save and then close **EL1-U2-A10-CISales.xlsx**.
11. Make Word the active program, close **CICustomers.docx**, and then close Word.

Assessment 11 Insert and Format a Shape in a Budget Workbook

1. Open **SEExpenses.xlsx** and then save the workbook with Save As and name it **EL1-U2-A11-SEExpenses**.
2. Make the following changes to the worksheet so it displays as shown in Figure U2.1:
   a. Select and then merge cells A1 through D1.
   b. Add fill to the cells as shown in Figure U2.1. (Use the Green, Accent 6, Lighter 40% fill color.)
   c. Increase the height of row 1 to the approximate size shown in Figure U2.1.
   d. Make cell A1 active, type **SOLAR**, press Alt + Enter, and then type **ENTERPRISES**. Set the text you just typed in 20-point Calibri bold, center and middle aligned, and change the font color to *Green, Accent 6, Darker 25%*.
   e. Insert the sun shape (located in the *Basic Shapes* section of the Shapes button drop-down list). Apply orange shape fill (using the Orange option in the *Standard Colors* section) and change the shape outline to *Green, Accent 6, Darker 25%*. Copy the shape in the cell and then size and position the shapes as shown in the figure.
3. Save, print, and then close **EL1-U2-A11-SEExpenses.xlsx**.

Figure U2.1 Assessment 11

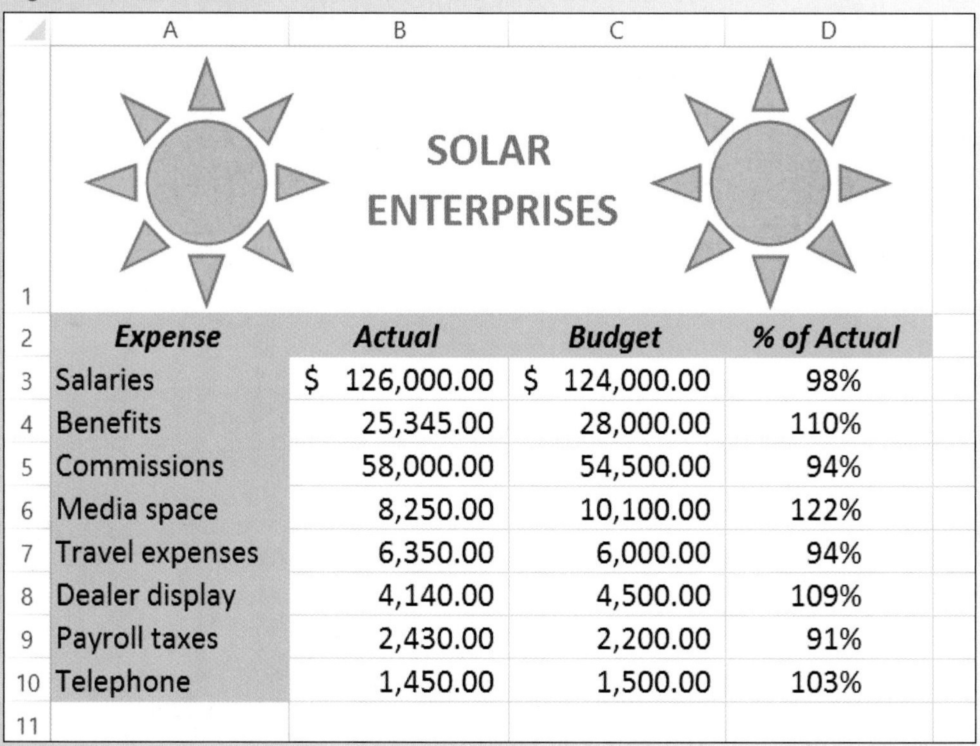

	A	B	C	D
1	SOLAR ENTERPRISES			
2	***Expense***	***Actual***	***Budget***	***% of Actual***
3	Salaries	$ 126,000.00	$ 124,000.00	98%
4	Benefits	25,345.00	28,000.00	110%
5	Commissions	58,000.00	54,500.00	94%
6	Media space	8,250.00	10,100.00	122%
7	Travel expenses	6,350.00	6,000.00	94%
8	Dealer display	4,140.00	4,500.00	109%
9	Payroll taxes	2,430.00	2,200.00	91%
10	Telephone	1,450.00	1,500.00	103%
11				

Writing Activities

The following activities give you the opportunity to practice your writing skills along with demonstrating an understanding of some of the important Excel features you have mastered in this unit. Use correct grammar, appropriate word choices, and clear sentence constructions.

Activity 1 Prepare a Projected Budget

You are the accounting assistant in the financial department of McCormack Funds and you have been asked to prepare a proposed annual department budget. The total amount available to the department is $1,450,000. You are given these percentages for the proposed budget items: salaries, 45%; benefits, 12%; training, 14%; administrative costs, 10%; equipment, 11%; and supplies, 8%. Create a worksheet with this information that shows the projected yearly budget, the budget items in the department, the percentage for each item, and the amount for each item. After the worksheet is completed, save the workbook and name it **EL1-U2-Act1-MFBudget**. Print and then close the workbook.

Optional: Using Word 2013, write a memo to members of the McCormack Funds Finance Department explaining that the proposed annual department budget is attached for their review. Comments and suggestions are to be sent to you within one week. Save the file and name it **EL1-U2-Act1-MFMemo**. Print and then close the file.

Activity 2 Create a Travel Tours Bar Chart

Prepare a worksheet in Excel for Carefree Travels that includes the following information:

Scandinavian Tours

Country	**Tours Booked**
Norway	52
Sweden	62
Finland	29
Denmark	38

Use the information in the worksheet to create and format a bar chart as a separate sheet. Save the workbook and name it **EL1-U2-Act2-CTTours**. Print only the sheet containing the chart and then close **EL1-U2-Act2-CTTours.xlsx**.

Activity 3 Prepare a Ski Vacation Worksheet

Prepare a worksheet for Carefree Travels that advertises a snow skiing trip. Include the following information in the announcement:

- At the beginning of the worksheet, create a company logo that includes the company name *Carefree Travels* and a clip art image related to travel.
- Include the heading *Whistler Ski Vacation Package* in the worksheet.
- Include the following details below the heading:
    - Round-trip air transportation: $395
    - Seven nights' hotel accommodations: $1,550
    - Four all-day ski passes: $425
    - Compact rental car with unlimited mileage: $250
    - Total price of the ski package: (calculate the total price)

- Include the following information somewhere in the worksheet:
    - Book your vacation today at special discount prices.
    - Two-for-one discount at many of the local ski resorts.

Save the workbook and name it **EL1-U2-Act3-CTSkiTrips**. Print and then close **EL1-U2-Act3-CTSkiTrips.xlsx**.

Internet Research

Find Information on Excel Books and Present the Data in a Worksheet

Locate two companies on the Internet that sell new books. At the first new book company site, locate three books on Microsoft Excel. Record the title, author, and price for each book. At the second new book company site, locate the same three books and record the prices. Create an Excel worksheet that includes the following information:

- Name of each new book company
- Title and author of each book
- Prices for each book from the two book company sites

Create a hyperlink to the website of each book company. Then save the completed workbook and name it **EL1-U2-IR-Books**. Print and then close the workbook.

Job Study

Create a Customized Time Card for a Landscaping Company

You are the manager of Landmark Landscaping Company and are responsible for employee time cards. At the New backstage area, search for and download a time card using the words *weekly time sheet portrait* to narrow the search. Use the template to create a customized time card workbook for your company. With the workbook based on the template open, insert additional blank rows to increase the spacing above the Employee row. Insert a clip art image related to landscaping or gardening and position and size it attractively in the form. Include a text box with the text *Lawn and Landscaping Specialists* inside the box. Format, size, and position the text attractively in the form. Fill in the form for the current week with the following employee information:

Employee: Jonathan Holder
Manager: (Your name)
Employee phone: (225) 555-3092
Employee email: None
Regular hours: 8 hours for Monday, Tuesday, Wednesday, and Thursday
Overtime: 2 hours on Wednesday
Sick hours: None
Vacation: 8 hours on Friday
Rate per hour: $20.00
Overtime pay: $30.00

Save the completed form and name it **EL1-U2-JS-TimeCard**. Print and then close **EL1-U2-JS-TimeCard.xlsx**.

Index

A

absolute cell reference
  defined, 50
  using in formula, 50–51
Accounting, as category in Format Cells dialog box, 77
accounting formatting, 23
Accounting Number Format button, 23
active cell, 5, 6
Add Chart Elements button, 242
addition, AutoSum to add numbers, 19
alignment
  aligning data, 78–80
  applying formatting, 70–72
area chart, 233
argument, defined, 43
Arrange All button, 169
Arrange Windows dialog box, 169
arrow shapes, drawing, 282–284
AutoComplete, 13, 14
AutoCorrect, 13–14
AutoCorrect dialog box, 13–14, 212–213
AutoFill, 15
automatic entering features, 13–15
AutoSum button, 45
  to add numbers, 18–19
  to average numbers, 19
average
  AutoSum to average numbers, 19
  finding, 45–46
AVERAGE function, 19, 45
  writing formulas with, 45–46

B

background picture, inserting, 109
bar chart, 233
billing statement, preparing, using template, 218–219
Bold button, 70
borders, adding, to cells, 82–83
Borders button, 70
Breaks button, 105
bubble chart, 233
budget, calculating percentage of actual, 40

C

Calculate Now button, 49
Cancel button, 10
cascaded workbook, 170
cell address, 7
cell pointer, 5, 6, 8
cell reference, 7
  absolute, 50–51
  checking in formula, 39
  mixed, 50, 52–53
  relative, 50
cells
  active
    keyboard commands for, 7
    mouse for, 8
  clearing data in, 69
  copying and pasting
    cells from one worksheet to another, 173
    with Clipboard task pane, 157–158
    pasting values only, 159–160
    selected cells, 154–155
    using Paste Options button, 155–157
  deleting, 68–69
  editing data in, 10–11
  entering data in
    with fill handle, 15, 16–17
    typing in, 7–8
  formatting
    adding borders to, 82–83
    adding fill and shading to, 84–85
    centering, 21–22
    finding and replacing, 123–124
    with Format Cells dialog box, 78–85
    merging, 21–22
  linking between worksheets, 174–175
  range
    naming, 167
    using in formula, 167–168
  selecting, 20–21
    with keyboard, 20–21
    with mouse, 20
cell styles
  applying, 204, 206–207
  copying to another workbook, 210–211
  defining, 205–208
  deleting, 211
  formatting with, 204–211
  modifying, 209–210
  removing, 211
    Cell Styles button, 204
centering
  cells, 21–22
  worksheet horizontally/vertically, 102–103
Change Chart Type button, 240
Change Chart Type dialog box, 240
Change Colors button, 241
Chart Elements button, 236, 245
Chart Filters button, 236–237
charts
  adding data series, 233–234
  creating, 232–235
  deleting, 249–251
  design changes
    adding, moving and deleting chart elements, 242–244
    chart layout and colors, 241
    chart location, 242
    chart style, 240
    switching rows and columns, 240
  editing data in, 233–234
  formatting
    changing chart height and width measurements, 248–249
    with chart buttons, 236–238
    with CHART TOOLS FORMAT tab, 245–246

Format Chart Area task pane, 248, 249
line chart, 245–246
pie chart, 249–251
inserting and customizing shapes, 246–248
moving, 233
printing, 238–239
sizing, 233
types of, 232–233
Chart Styles button, 236–237
CHART TOOLS DESIGN tab, 239, 240
CHART TOOLS FORMAT tab, 245
Clear button, 69
clip art, inserting and formatting, 278–279
Clipboard task pane, 157–158
Close button, 172
closing
Excel, 13
workbook, 12
Collapse the Ribbon button, 5, 6
color
change colors in charts, 241
change worksheet color, 160–161
font formatting and, 70
column boundary line, changing width with, 63–64
column chart, 233
columns
deleting, 68–69
formatting
row height, 65–66
width, 21–22, 63–64
hiding and unhiding, 86–87
inserting, 67–68
printing column headings, 110
printing titles on multiple pages, 107–108
sorting in more than one, 127
switching in charts, 240
Column Width dialog box, changing column width at, 64–65
comma formatting, 23
Comma Style button, 23
Compress Pictures button, 276
constant, defined, 43
Copy button, 154
copying
cell styles, 210–211
data, 173
between programs, 175–176
formulas
with fill handle, 19
with relative cell references, 38–39
shapes, 281–284
workbook, 194–195
worksheet, 160
to another workbook, 200–201
copying and pasting, cells
with Clipboard task pane, 157–158
pasting values only, 159–160
selected cells, 154–155
using Paste Options button, 155–157
COUNT function, 45
writing formulas with, 48
Crop button, 276
Currency, as category in Format Cells dialog box, 77
Custom, as category in Format Cells dialog box, 77
customizing
images, 276–277
print jobs, 117–118
shapes in charts, 246–248
Cut button, 154
cutting
cells, 154–155
workbooks, 195–196

D

data
aligning, 78–80
clearing, in cells, 69
copying, 173
editing
in cell, 10–11
in chart, 233–234
entering into cells
with fill handle, 15, 16–17
typing in, 7–8
filtering, 127–128
finding and replacing, 120–122
indenting, 78–80
linking, 174–175
moving, 173
rotating, 79–80
scaling, 108–109
selecting within cell
with keyboard, 21
with mouse, 20–21
sorting, 125–127
data series, adding to chart, 233–234
Date, as category in Format Cells dialog box, 77
Date & Time button, 49
Decrease Decimal button, 23, 75
Decrease Font Size button, 70
Define Name button, 167
Delete button, 68
Delete dialog box, 68
Delete key, 69
deleting
cells, 68–69
cell styles, 211
chart element, 242
charts, 249–251
columns, 68–69
data in cell, 10
folder, 193, 197
hyperlink, 216–217
to Recycle Bin, 193
rows, 68–69
SmartArt graphic, 289
workbook, 193
worksheet, 153–155, 160
dependent worksheet, 174
dialog box launder, 5, 6
DIV/O error code, 41
doughnut chart, 233
down time, writing formula to calculate percentage of, 42
drawing
arrow shapes, 282–284
text boxes, 284–286
DRAWING TOOLS FORMAT tab, 281, 284–286

E

editing
  data in cell, 10–11
  data in chart, 233–234
  hyperlinks, 216–217
email address, linking using, 215
Enter button, 10
error codes, common formula and function, 41
Esc key, to escape backstage area, 11
Excel
  closing, 13
  copying and pasting data into Word document, 175–176
  opening, 5

F

FILE tab, 5, 6
fill, adding to cells, 84–85
fill button, copying formula relatively in worksheet, 38
Fill Color button, 70
fill handle
  to copy formula, 19
  copying formula relatively in worksheet, 39
  inserting data in cells with, 15, 16–17
filter, 127
filtering data, 127–128
financial functions, writing formulas with, 252–255
Find and Replace dialog box, 120–121
find and replace feature
  cell formatting, 123–124
  data, 120–122
Find and Select button, 120
folders
  copying workbook into another, 194
  creating, 191
  deleting, 193, 197
  naming, 191
  renaming, 192
  root folder, 191
  sending workbook to different, 195
  subfolder, 191
font
  changing, at Format Cells dialog box, 80–81
  formatting, 70–72
Font button, 70
Font Color button, 70
Font Size button, 70
footers
  inserting, 112–117
  insert picture watermark, 286–287
Format button, 162
Format Cells dialog box
  adding fill and shading, 84–85
  aligning and indenting data, 78–80
  changing fonts, 80–81
  formatting cells with, 78–85
  formatting numbers with, 76–78
Format Chart Area task pane, 248, 249
Format Painter, formatting with, 86
Format Picture button, 286–287
Format Picture task pane, 278
Format Selection button, 248
formatting
  alignment, 70–72, 78–80
  applying theme, 73–74
  cells
    adding borders to, 82–83
    adding fill and shading, 84–85
    centering, 21–22
    finding and replacing, 123–124
    Format Cells dialog box, 79–80
    merging, 21–22
  with cell styles, 204–211
  charts
    changing chart height and width measurements, 248–249
    with chart buttons, 236–238
    with CHART TOOLS FORMAT tab, 245–246
    Format Chart Area task pane, 248, 249
    line chart, 245–246
    pie chart, 249–251
  clearing data in cells, 69
  clip art, 278–279
  column row height, 65–66
  column width, 21–22, 63–64
  deleting cells, rows or columns, 68–69
  font, 70–72, 80–81
  with Format Painter, 86
  images, 276–278
  inserting columns, 67–68
  inserting rows, 66–67
  with Mini toolbar, 70
  numbers, 23–24, 74–78
  repeating last action, 84
  screenshots, 280–281
  text boxes, 284–286
  WordArt, 293–294
  worksheet
    background picture, inserting, 109
    centering horizontally vertically, 102–103
    headers and footers, inserting, 112–117
    margin changes, 101–102
    page breaks, inserting and removing, 104–107
    page orientation changes, 104
    page size changes, 104
    scaling data, 108–109
    undo and redo, 118–119
Formula AutoComplete, 45
Formula bar, 5, 6, 10
formulas
  absolute cell references in, 50–51
  checking cell references in, 39
  copying, with relative cell references, 38–39
  defined, 18
  determining order of operations, 40–41
  displaying, 49
  finding future value of investment, 255
  finding periodic payments for loan, 253–255

identifying common errors, 41
inserting
AutoSum, 18–19
fill handle to copy formula, 19
with functions, 43–49
mixed cell references in, 52–53
ranges in, 167–168
Trace Error button, 41
writing
with AVERAGE, MIN, MAX, COUNT functions, 45–48
with financial functions, 252–255
with IF logical function, 256–260
with mathematical operators, 37–42
with NOW and TODAY function, 49
by pointing, 40, 41
with statistical functions, 45–48
FORMULA tab, 43
Fraction, as category in Format Cells dialog box, 77
Freeze Panes button, 165–166
Function Arguments palette, 44, 257–258
Function Library group, 43
functions
argument, 43
AVERAGE, 45–46
constants, 43
COUNT function, 48
defined, 43
finding future value of investment, 255
finding periodic payments for loan, 253–255
FV function, 252
identifying common errors, 41
inserting formulas with, 43–48
MAX function, 46–48
MIN function, 46–48
NOW function, 49
PMT function, 252
TODAY function, 49
writing formulas
with financial functions, 252–255
with IF logical function, 256–260
writing formulas with statistical functions, 45–48
future value, 253
finding, 255
Fv, in financial functions, 253
FV function, 252

G

Go To feature, 7
graphic, linking using, 215–216
gridlines, 7
printing, 110

H

Header & Footer button, 112
HEADER & FOOTER TOOLS DESIGN tab, 112–113, 286–287
headers
inserting, 112–117
insert picture watermark, 286–287
headings, printing row and column headings, 110
Help feature
in dialog box or backstage area, 27
Help window, 25–26
ScreenTips, 26
Hide button, 171
hiding
columns and rows, 86–87
worksheet, 162–163
horizontal scroll bar, 5, 6, 8
Hyperlink button, 212
hyperlinks
automatic formatting of, 212–213
editing, 216–217
inserting, 212–217
linking
to existing web page or file, 212–213
to new workbook, 214–216
to place in workbook, 214–216
using email address, 215
using graphic, 215–216
modifying, 216–217
navigating using, 213–214
purposes of, 212
removing, 216–217

I

IF function, writing formulas with, 257–260
images
compress and crop, 276
customizing and formatting, 276–277
formatting with Format Picture task pane, 278
inserting, 275–279
inserting and formatting clip art images, 278–279
sizing and moving, 276
Increase Decimal button, 23, 75
Increase Font Size button, 70
indenting, data, 78–80
Info backstage area, 11
Insert button, 66
Insert dialog box, 66
Insert Function button, 43
Insert Function dialog box, 43–44
Insert Hyperlink dialog box, 212
inserting
background picture, 109
clip art, 278–279
columns, 67–68
data in cells with fill handle, 15, 16–17
footers, 112–117
formulas
AutoSum, 18–19
fill handle to copy, 19
with functions, 43–49
headers, 112–117
hyperlinks, 212–217
images, 275–279
new worksheet, 153–155
page breaks, 104–107
picture as watermark, 286–287

rows, 66–67
screenshots, 280–281
shapes, 246–248, 281–284
SmartArt graphic, 288–292
symbols and special characters, 273–275
WordArt, 293–294
Insert WordArt button, 293
integration, 175–176
interest, simple, formula with mixed cell references, 53
Italic button, 70

K

keyboard shortcuts
to activate cells, 7
repeat last action, 84
selecting cell with, 20–21
selecting data within cell, 21

L

landscape orientation, 104
line chart, 233
creating and formatting, 245–246
linking
cells between worksheets, 174–175
data, 174–175
live preview feature, 73
loan, finding periodic payments for, 253–255
logical test, 256

M

margins
changing in worksheet, 101–103
default settings, 101
Margins button, 101
marquee, 154
mathematical operations, writing formulas with, 37–42
MAX function, 45
writing formulas with, 46–48
Maximize button, 172
Merge & Center button, 21, 70–71
Merge Styles dialog box, 210–211
merging, cells, 21–22
MIN function, 45
writing formulas with, 46–48
Minimize button, 172
Mini toolbar, formatting with, 70
mixed cell reference, 50
mouse
to activate cells, 8
moving split lines, 165
selecting cell with, 20
selecting data within cell, 20–21
Move Chart button, 242
Move Chart dialog box, 242
Move or Copy dialog box, 200
moving
chart, 233
chart element, 242
chart location, 242
data, 173
images, 276
SmartArt graphic, 289
split lines, 165
WordArt, 293
workbook, 172
worksheet, 160–161
worksheet to another workbook, 201–203
multiple cell reference, using in formula, 52–53

N

N/A error code, 41
Name box, 5, 6, 7
NAME? error code, 41
navigating, using hyperlinks, 213–214
nested parentheses, 41
New folder button, 191
New sheet button, 5, 6, 153
New Window button, 169
Normal button, 105
NOW function, writing formulas with, 49
Nper, in financial functions, 252
Number, as category in Format Cells dialog box, 77
Number Format button, 23, 75
numbers
AutoSum
to add, 18–19
to average numbers, 19
formatting, 23–24
with Format Cells dialog box, 76–78
with Number group buttons, 74–76
number symbol (###) for exceeding space in cell, 8
NUM! error code, 41

O

Office.com, inserting images from, 278–279
100% button, 164
Online Pictures button, 278
Open dialog box, 16
copying workbook to another folder, 195
creating folder, 191
cutting and pasting workbook, 195–196
deleting workbooks and folders, 193
elements of, 190–191
renaming folder, 192
renaming workbook, 196–197
selecting workbook, 192
opening, workbook
multiple, 169
from Open dialog box, 16
from Recent Workbook list, 16
order of operations, 40–41
Orientation button, 71, 104

P

page break, inserting and removing, 104–107
Page Break Preview button, 105–106
page orientation
changing, 104
default, 101
Page Setup dialog box
centering horizontally/vertically, 102–103
changing margins, 102

inserting headers and footers, 114–117
printing column and row titles on multiple pages, 107–108
printing gridlines and column and row headings, 110
printing specific area of worksheet, 110–111
page size
changing, 104
default, 101
pane, freezing and unfreezing, 165–166
Paste button, 154
Paste Options button, 155–157
pasting
cells, 154–156
data, between programs, 175–176
workbooks, 195–196
payroll, formulas with absolute and mixed cell references, 52–53
Percentage, as category in Format Cells dialog box, 77
Percent Style button, 23
pictures
compress and crop, 276
customizing and formatting, 276
formatting with Format Picture task pane, 278
inserting and customizing picture and text box, 284–286
inserting background picture, 109
sizing and moving, 276
as watermark, 286–287
Pictures button, 275
PICTURE TOOLS FORMAT tab, 275
pie chart, 233
formatting, 249–251
pinning, workbook to Recent Workbooks list, 16, 198
Pmt, in financial functions, 252
PMT function, 252
pointing, writing formula by, 40, 42
portrait orientation, 104
Print Area button, 110–111
Print backstage area, 11–12
printing
charts, 238–239
column and row titles on multiple pages, 107–108
gridlines, 110
row and column headings, 110
specific area of worksheet, 110–111
specific pages of worksheet, 117–118
workbook, 11–12
with multiple worksheets, 163–164
Print Titles button, 107
Pv, in financial functions, 252

Q

Quick Access toolbar, 5, 6
Print button on, 12
Quick Layout button, 241

R

radar chart, 233
range
defined, 167
naming, 167
using in formula, 167–168
rate, in financial functions, 252
Recent Workbooks list
clearing, 199
opening workbook from, 16
pinning workbook to, 16, 198
recovering unsaved workbook, 198
Recommended Charts button, 232
Recycle Bin
deleting workbook to, 193
display contents of, 193
restoring workbooks from, 193
Redo button, 118–119
REF! error code, 41
relative cell reference, 19
copying formulas with, 38–39
defined, 50
removing
cell styles, 211
hyperlink, 216–217
page breaks, 104–107
worksheet, 160
renaming
folder, 192
workbook, 196–197
worksheet, 160–161
Repeat command, 84
Reset to Match Style button, 245
Restore Down button, 172
returning the result, 43
ribbon, 5, 6
root folder, 191
rotating, text, 79–80
Row Height dialog box, 65–66
rows
deleting, 68–69
hiding and unhiding, 86–87
inserting, 66–67
printing row headings, 110
printing titles on multiple pages, 107–108
switching in charts, 240

S

salary, calculating by inserting and copying formula, 39
Save As backstage area, 8
Save As dialog box, creating folder, 191
Save button, 8
saving, workbook, 8–9
scaling data, 108–109
scatter chart, 233
Scientific, as category in Format Cells dialog box, 77
Screenshot button, 280
screenshots, inserting and formatting, 280–281
ScreenTips, 26
scroll bar, 8
horizontal, 5, 6
vertical, 5, 6
selecting
cells, 20–21

multiple worksheets, 153–155
workbook, 192
shading, adding to cells, 84–85
shapes
drawing arrow shapes, 282–284
inserting and copying, 281–284
Shapes button, 281
sheet tab, 5, 6
Sheet Tab shortcut menu, 160–162
Show Formulas button, 49
simple interest, formula with mixed cell references, 53
Size button, 104
sizing
chart, 233
image, 276
SmartArt graphic, 289
WordArt, 293
workbook, 172
SmartArt button, 288
SmartArt graphic
changing design of, 290–291
changing formatting of, 291–293
entering data in, 288
sizing, moving and deleting, 289
SmartArt Graphic dialog box, 288
SMARTART TOOLS DESIGN tab, 288
smart tag, 41
Sort dialog box, 125–127
Sort & Filter button, 125, 127
sorting data, 125–127
custom sort, 125–126
more than one column, 127
source worksheet, 174
Special, as category in Format Cells dialog box, 77
special characters, inserting, 273–275
Spelling button, 118
spelling checker, 118, 119–120
Spelling dialog box, 119
Split button, 165
split lines, 165
statistical functions, writing formulas with, 45–48
Status bar, 5, 6, 7
stock chart, 233
style, 204
Style dialog box, 205–208
subfolder, 191
subtraction, inserting and copying formula, 38
SUM function, 18, 45
surface chart, 233
Switch Row/Column button, 240
Switch Windows button, 169
Symbol button, 273
Symbol dialog box, 274
symbols, inserting, 273–275

T

tab, 5, 6
templates, for worksheets, 217–219
Text, as category in Format Cells dialog box, 77
text, rotating, 79–80
Text Box button, 284
text boxes, drawing and formatting, 284–286
Text Pane button, 288
theme
applying, 73–74
defined, 73
Themes button, 73
tiled workbook, 170
Time, as category in Format Cells dialog box, 77
Title bar, 5, 6
TODAY function, writing formulas with, 49
Trace Error button, 41

U

Underline button, 70
Undo button, 118–119
Unfreeze Panes, 165–166
Unhide button, 171
Unhide dialog box, 162–163
unhiding, columns and rows, 86–87

V

VALUE error code, 41
vertical scroll bar, 5, 6, 8

W

watermark, inserting picture as, 286–287
web page, linking to existing, 212–213
Width option box, 108
windows
arranging workbooks in, 169–170
cascaded workbooks, 170
hiding/unhiding workbooks, 171
opening multiple workbooks, 169
opening new window, 169
sizing and moving workbooks, 172
splitting worksheet into, 165–166
tiled workbooks, 170
WordArt, inserting and formatting, 293–294
Word document, copying and pasting Excel data into, 175–176
workbook
arranging, 169–170
automatic entering features, 13–15
cascaded, 170
closing, 12
copying, 194–195
worksheet to another, 200–201
creating, 5–8
with multiple worksheets, 153–155
cutting and pasting, 195–196
defined, 5
deleting, 193
worksheet in, 153–155
folders to organize, 191–192
hide/unhiding, 171
hide worksheet in, 162–163
inserting new worksheet, 153–155
linking
to new workbook, 214–216
to place in, 214–216
maintaining, 190–197

maximizing, 172
minimizing, 172
moving, 172
moving and copying data between, 173
moving worksheet to another, 201–203
naming, 8
opening, 16
multiple, 169
pinning to Recent Workbook list, 16, 199
printing, 11–12
with multiple worksheets, 163–164
Recent List of, 197–200
recovering unsaved workbook, 198
renaming, 196–197
restoring, 172
saving, 8–9
selecting, 192
sending to different drive or folder, 195
sizing, 172
tiled, 170
worksheet
change color, 160–161
column width changes, 63–66
copying, 160
to another workbook, 200–201
defined, 5
deleting, 153–155, 160
dependent, 174
elements of, 5–8
filtering data, 127–128
finding and replacing data, 120–124
finding averages in, 45–46
finding maximum and minimum values in, 47–48
formatting
background picture, inserting, 109
centering horizontally/vertically, 102–103
headers and footers, inserting, 112–117
margin changes, 101–102
page breaks, inserting and removing, 104–107
page orientation changes, 104
page size changes, 104
scaling data, 108–109
undo and redo, 118–119
freezing and unfreezing panes, 165–166
hiding, 162–163
inserting
columns, 67–68
formulas, 18–19
headers and footers, 112–117
new, 153–155
rows, 66–67
linking cells between, 174–175
managing, 160–166, 200–203
moving, 160–161
to another workbook, 201–203
moving and copying data between, 173
printing
column and row titles on multiple pages, 107–108
gridlines and row and column headings, 110
specific area of, 110–111
specific pages of, 117–118
workbook containing multiple, 163–164
removing, 160
renaming, 160–161
selecting multiple, 153–155
sorting data
custom sort, 125–126
sorting more than one column, 127
source, 174
spelling check, 118, 119–120
splitting into windows, 165–166
templates for, 217–219
worksheet area, 5, 6
Wrap Text button, 71
writing, formulas
with financial functions, 252–255
with IF logical function, 256–260
with mathematical operations, 37–42
by pointing, 40, 41

X

xy (scatter) chart, 233

Z

zoom, using, 164, 166
Zoom button, 164
Zoom to Selection button, 164

MICROSOFT®

ACCESS®

Level 1

Unit 1 ■ Creating Tables and Queries

Chapter 1 ■ Managing and Creating Tables

Chapter 2 ■ Creating Relationships between Tables

Chapter 3 ■ Performing Queries

Chapter 4 ■ Creating and Modifying Tables in Design View

MICROSOFT®
ACCESS®

Managing and Creating Tables

PERFORMANCE OBJECTIVES

Upon successful completion of Chapter 1, you will be able to:

- **Open and close objects in a database**
- **Insert, delete, and move rows and columns in a table**
- **Hide, unhide, freeze, and unfreeze columns**
- **Adjust table column width**
- **Preview and print a table**
- **Design and create a table**
- **Rename column headings**
- **Insert a column name, caption, and description**
- **Insert Quick Start fields**
- **Assign a default value and field size**

Tutorials

1.1 Opening and Closing an Access Database and Table
1.2 Using the Recent List
1.3 Navigating in Objects
1.4 Adding Records in a Table
1.5 Deleting Records in a Table
1.6 Adjusting Column Width
1.7 Previewing and Printing a Table
1.8 Creating a New Database; Creating a Table in Datasheet View
1.9 Creating a Table Using Quick Start Fields
1.10 Modifying Field Size, Caption, and Default Value Properties

Managing information is an integral part of operating a business. Information can come in a variety of forms, such as data about customers, including names, addresses, and telephone numbers; product data; and purchasing and buying data. Most companies today manage data using a system software program. Microsoft Office Professional Plus includes a database management system software program named *Access*. With Access, you can organize, store, maintain, retrieve, sort, and print all types of business data.

This chapter contains just a few ideas on how to manage data with Access. With a properly designed and maintained database management system, a company can operate smoothly with logical, organized, and useful information. Model answers for this chapter's projects appear on the following pages.

AL1C1

Note: Before beginning the projects, copy to your storage medium the AL1C1 subfolder from the AL1 folder on the CD that accompanies this textbook. Make sure you have copied the files from the CD to your storage medium. Open all database files from your removable storage device and not directly from the CD since Access database files on the CD are read-only. Steps on how to copy a folder are presented on the inside of the back cover of this textbook. Do this every time you start a chapter's projects.

Project 1 Establish Relationships between Tables

Suppliers 10/2/2015

SupplierID	SupplierName	StreetAddress	City	Prov/State	PostalCode	Field1	EmailAddress
10	Hopewell, Inc.	5600 Carver Road	Port Moody	BC	V3H 1A4	(604) 555-3843	hopewell@emcp.net
25	Langley Corporation	805 First Avenue	Burnaby	BC	V3J 1C9	(604) 555-1200	langley@emcp.net
31	Sound Supplies	2104 Union Street	Seattle	WA	98105	(206) 555-4855	ssupplies@emcp.net
35	Emerald City Products	1059 Pike Street	Seattle	WA	98102	(206) 555-7728	ecproducts@emcp.net
38	Hadley Company	5845 Jefferson Street	Seattle	WA	98107	(206) 555-8003	hcompany@emcp.net
42	Fraser Valley Products	3894 Old Yale Road	Abbotsford	BC	V2S 1A9	(604) 555-1455	fvproducts@emcp.net
54	Manning, Inc.	1039 South 22nd	Vancouver	BC	V5K 1R1	(604) 555-0087	manning@emcp.net
68	Freedom Corporation	14 Fourth Avenue	Vancouver	BC	V5K 2C7	(604) 555-2155	freedom@emcp.net
70	Rosewood, Inc.	998 North 42nd Street	Vancouver	BC	V5K 2N8	(778) 555-6643	rosewood@emcp.net
84	Macadam, Inc.	675 Third Street	Vancouver	BC	V5K 2R9	(604) 555-5522	macadam@emcp.net
99	KL Distributions	402 Yukon Drive	Bellingham	WA	98435	(360) 555-3711	kldist@emcp.net

Page 1

Suppliers Table

Products 10/2/2015

ProductID	Product	SupplierID	UnitsInStock	UnitsOnOrder	ReorderLevel
101-S1B	SL 0-degrees down sleeping bag, black	54	16	0	15
101-S1R	SL 0-degrees down sleeping bag, red	54	17	0	15
101-S2B	SL 15-degrees synthetic sleeping bag, blac	54	21	0	15
101-S2R	SL 15-degrees synthetic sleeping bag, red	54	12	15	15
101-S3B	SL 20-degrees synthetic sleeping bag, blac	54	8	15	15
101-S3R	SL 20-degrees synthetic sleeping bag, red	54	4	10	10
209-L	Gordon wool ski hat, L	68	21	25	25
209-XL	Gordon wool ski hat, XL	68	14	25	25
209-XXL	Gordon wool ski hat, XXL	68	10	20	20
210-L	Tech-lite ski hat, L	68	17	25	25
210-M	Tech-lite ski hat, M	68	6	15	15
210-XL	Tech-lite ski hat, XL	68	22	0	20
299-M1	HT waterproof hiking boots, MS13	31	8	0	10
299-M2	HT waterproof hiking boots, MS12	31	2	10	10
299-M3	HT waterproof hiking boots, MS11	31	6	10	10
299-M4	HT waterproof hiking boots, MS10	31	7	0	10
299-M5	HT waterproof hiking boots, MS9	31	9	10	10
299-W1	HT waterproof hiking boots, WS11	31	5	8	8
299-W2	HT waterproof hiking boots, WS10	31	9	0	8
299-W3	HT waterproof hiking boots, WS9	31	3	10	10
299-W4	HT waterproof hiking boots, WS8	31	2	10	10
299-W5	HT waterproof hiking boots, WS7	31	3	10	10
299-W6	HT waterproof hiking boots, WS6	31	11	0	10
371-L	Lite-tech ski gloves, ML	68	3	10	10
371-M	Lite-tech ski gloves, MM	68	5	0	15
371-XL	Lite-tech ski gloves, MXL	68	3	10	10
371-XXL	Lite-tech ski gloves, MXXL	68	12	0	10
375-L	Lite-tech ski gloves, WL	68	22	0	20
375-M	Lite-tech ski gloves, WM	68	3	20	20
375-S	Lite-tech ski gloves, WS	68	6	20	20
442-1A	Polar backpack, 150BR	42	12	0	10
442-1B	Polar backpack, 150RW	42	9	10	10
443-1A	Polar backpack, 250BR	42	14	0	15
443-1B	Polar backpack, 250RW	42	6	15	15
558-C	ICE snow goggles, clear	68	18	0	15
559-B	ICE snow goggles, bronze	68	22	0	20

Page 1

Products Table, Page 1

Products 10/2/2015

ProductID	Product	SupplierID	UnitsInStock	UnitsOnOrder	ReorderLevel
602-XR	Binoculars, 8 x 42	35	3	5	5
602-XT	Binoculars, 10.5 x 45	35	5	0	4
602-XX	Binoculars, 10 x 50	35	7	0	5
647-1	Two-person dome tent	99	10	15	15
648-2	Three-person dome tent	99	5	0	10
651-1	K-2 one-person tent	99	8	0	10
652-2	K-2 two-person tent	99	12	0	10
804-50	AG freestyle snowboard, X50	70	7	0	10
804-60	AG freestyle snowboard, X60	70	8	0	5
897-L	Lang blunt snowboard	70	8	0	7
897-W	Lang blunt snowboard, wide	70	4	0	3
901-S	Solar battery pack	38	16	0	15
917-S	Silo portable power pack	38	8	0	10

Page 2

Products Table, Page 2

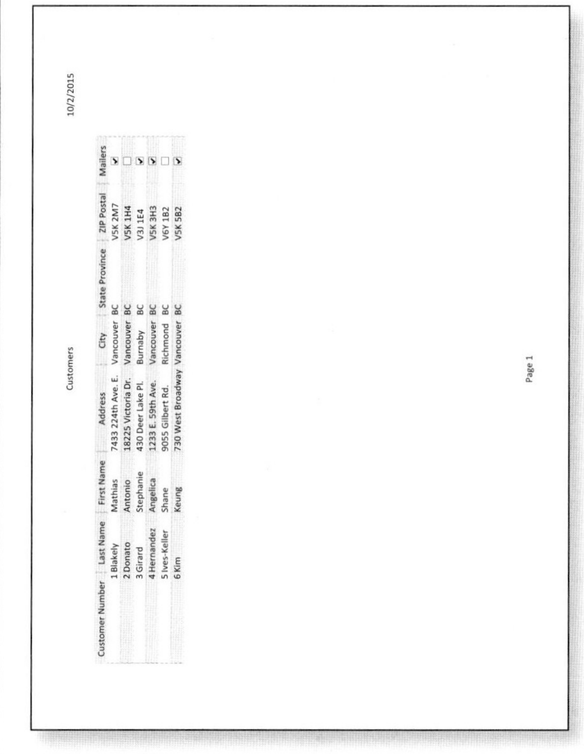

10/2/2015

Customers

Customer Number	Last Name	First Name	Address	City	State Province	ZIP Postal	Mailers
1	Blakely	Mathias	7433 224th Ave. E.	Vancouver	BC	V5K 2M7	☑
2	Donato	Antonio	18225 Victoria Dr.	Vancouver	BC	V5K 1H4	☐
3	Girard	Stephanie	430 Deer Lake Pl.	Burnaby	BC	V3J 1E4	☑
4	Hernandez	Angelica	1233 E. 59th Ave.	Vancouver	BC	V5K 3H3	☑
5	Ives-Keller	Shane	9055 Gilbert Rd.	Richmond	BC	V6Y 1B2	☐
6	Kim	Keung	730 West Broadway	Vancouver	BC	V5K 5B2	☑

Page 1

Customers Table

10/2/2015

Orders

OrderID	Supplier Number	Product Number	UnitsOrdered	Order Amount	OrderDate
1	54	101-S3	10	$1,137.50	1/5/2015
2	68	209-L	25	$173.75	1/5/2015
3	68	209-XL	25	$180.00	1/5/2015
4	68	209-XXL	20	$145.80	1/5/2015
5	68	210-M	15	$97.35	1/5/2015
6	68	210-L	25	$162.25	1/5/2015
7	31	299-M2	10	$887.90	1/19/2015
8	31	299-M3	10	$887.90	1/19/2015
9	31	299-M5	10	$887.90	1/19/2015
10	31	299-W1	8	$602.32	1/19/2015
11	31	299-W3	10	$752.90	1/19/2015
12	31	299-W4	10	$752.90	1/19/2015
13	31	299-W5	10	$752.90	1/19/2015
14	35	602-XR	5	$2,145.00	1/19/2015

Page 1

Orders Table

Project 1 Explore an Access Database — 1 Part

You will open a database and open and close objects in the database, including tables, queries, forms, and reports.

Exploring a Database

A ***database*** is comprised of a series of objects (such as tables, queries, forms, and reports) that you use to enter, manage, view, and print data. Data in a database is organized into tables, which contain information for related items (such as customers, employees, orders, and products). To view the various objects in a database, you will open a previously created database and then navigate in the database and open objects.

To create a new database or open a previously created database, click the Access 2013 tile at the Windows Start screen. (This step may vary depending on your system configuration.) This displays the Access 2013 opening screen, as shown in Figure 1.1. At this opening screen, you can open a recently opened database, a blank database, a database from the Open backstage area, or a database based on a template.

Quick Steps

Create a New Database

1. Open Access.
2. Click Blank desktop database template.
3. Type database name.
4. Click Create button.

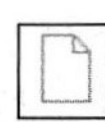

Create

To create a new blank database, click the Blank desktop database template. At the Blank desktop database window that displays, type a name for the database in the *File Name* text box, and then click the Create button. If you want to save the database in a particular location, click the Browse button at the right side of the *File Name* text box. At the File New Database dialog box that displays, navigate to the desired location or folder, type the database name in the *File name* text box, and then click OK.

Figure 1.1 Access 2013 Opening Screen

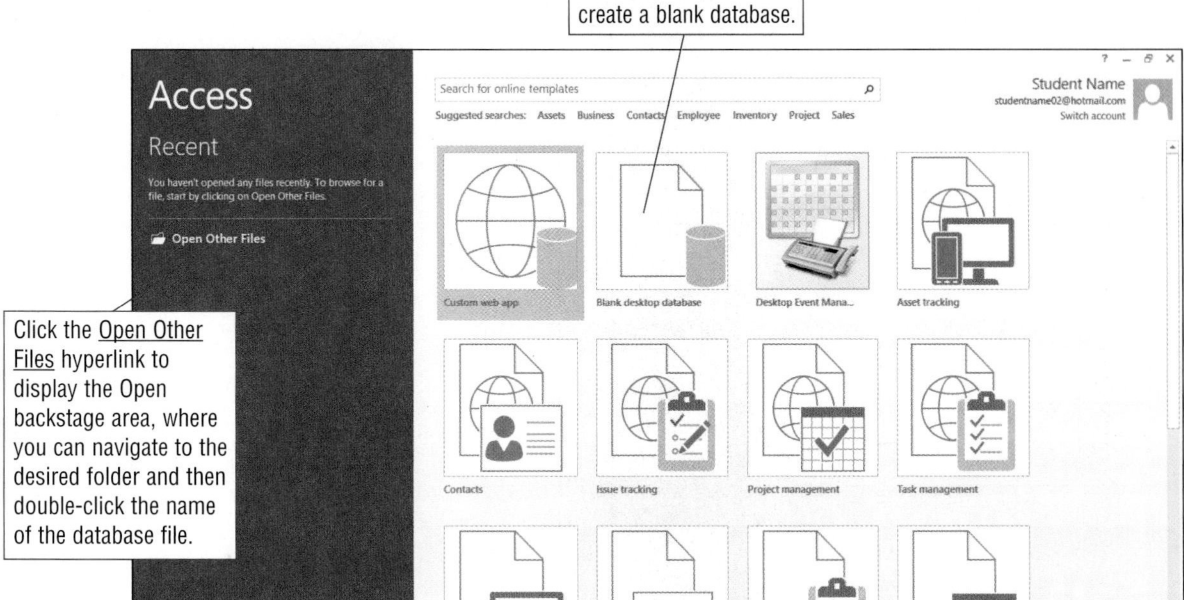

Opening a Database

Quick Steps

Open a Database

1. Open Access.
2. Click Open Other Files hyperlink.
3. Double-click OneDrive or *Computer* option.
4. Navigate to desired location.
5. Double-click database.

To open an existing Access database, click the Open Other Files hyperlink that displays in the left panel at the Access 2013 opening screen. This displays the Open backstage area. You can also display the Open backstage area with the keyboard shortcut Ctrl + O or by inserting an Open button on the Quick Access toolbar and clicking that button. At the Open backstage area, click the desired location, such as your OneDrive or the *Computer* option, and then click the Browse button. (If you are opening a database from your computer or USB flash drive, double-click the *Computer* option.) At the Open dialog box that displays, navigate to the desired folder and then double-click the desired database name in the Content pane.

If you are opening a database from your OneDrive, Access requires you to save a copy of the database to a location such as your computer's hard drive or a USB flash drive. Any changes you make to the database will be saved to the local copy of the database but not the database on your OneDrive. If you want to save the database back to your OneDrive, you will need to upload the database by opening a web browser, going to onedrive.com, logging in to your OneDrive account, and then clicking the Upload link. Microsoft constantly updates the Onedrive.com website, so these steps may vary.

When you click your OneDrive or the *Computer* option at the Open backstage area, a list of the most recently accessed folders displays in the Recent Folders list in the *Computer* section. Open a folder from this list by clicking the folder name.

At the Open backstage area with *Recent* selected in the middle panel, a list of the most recently opened databases displays in the Recent list. Open a database from this list by clicking the database name. When you open a database, the Access screen displays, as shown in Figure 1.2. Refer to Table 1.1 for descriptions of the Access screen elements.

Figure 1.2 Access Screen

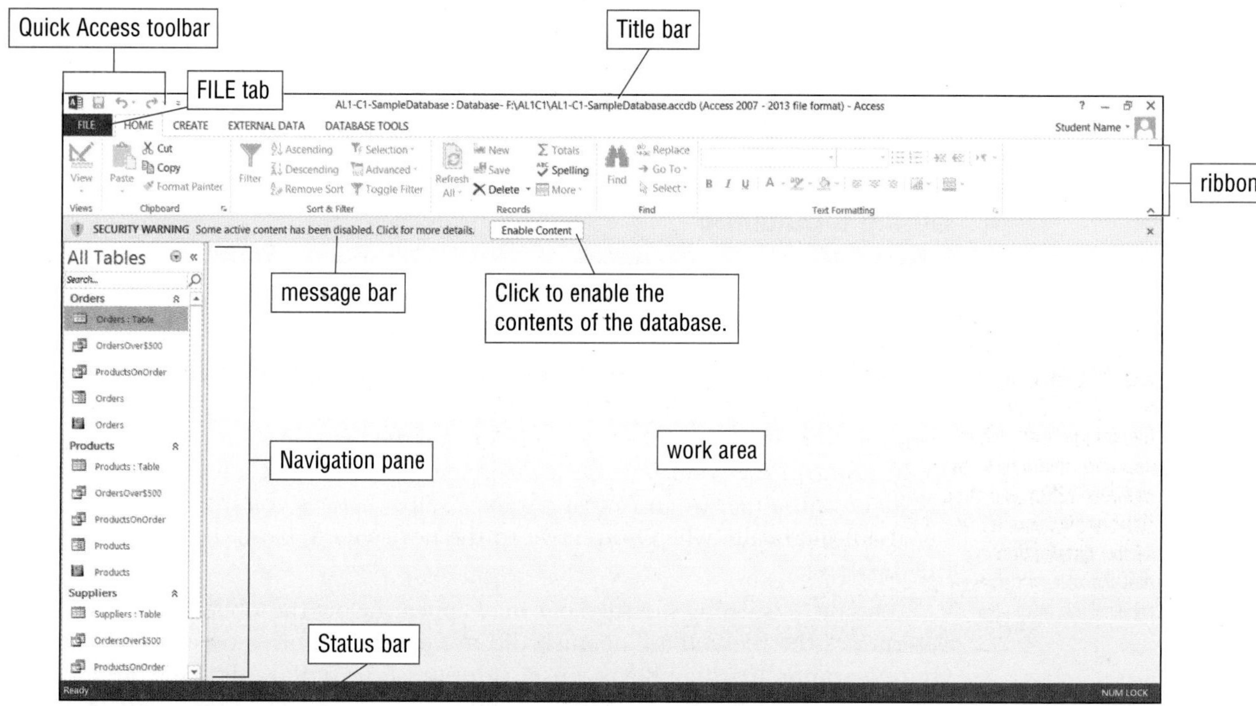

Table 1.1 Access Screen Elements

Feature	*Description*
FILE tab	When clicked, displays the backstage area that contains options for working with and managing databases.
message bar	Displays security alerts if the database being opened contains potentially unsafe content.
Navigation pane	Displays the names of objects within the database grouped by categories.
Quick Access toolbar	Contains buttons for commonly used commands.
ribbon	Contains the tabs with commands and buttons divided into groups.
Status bar	Displays messages, the current view, and view buttons.
tabs	Contain commands and features organized into groups.
Title bar	Displays the database name followed by the program name.
work area	Displays opened objects.

Pinning a Database File or Folder to the Recent List

If you want a database to remain in the Recent list at the Open backstage area, "pin" the database to the list. To do this, position the mouse pointer over the desired database file name and then click the small, left-pointing stick pin that displays at the right side of the list. When you click the stick pin, it changes to a down-pointing stick pin. The next time you display the Open backstage area, the database file name you pinned displays at the top of the Recent list.

You can also pin a folder name to the Recent Folders list in the same manner as you pin a database file name. The Recent Folders list displays at the Open backstage area when you click the OneDrive or *Computer* option. You can pin more than one database file name to the Recent list or more than one folder name to the Recent Folders list. To "unpin" a database or folder name, click the stick pin to change it from a down-pointing pin to a left-pointing pin.

Closing a Database

Close

HINT

The active database is saved automatically on a periodic basis and when you make another record active, close the table, or close the database.

To close a database, click the FILE tab and then click the *Close* option. Close Access by clicking the Close button that displays in the upper right corner of the screen or with the keyboard shortcut Alt + F4.

Only one Access database can be open at a time. If you open a new database in the current Access window, the existing database closes. You can, however, open multiple instances of Access and open a database in each instance. In other applications in the Microsoft Office suite, you have to save a revised file after you edit data in the file. In an Access database, any changes you make to data are saved automatically when you move to the next record, close the table, or close the database.

A security warning message bar may appear below the ribbon if Access determines the file you are opening did not originate from a trusted location on your computer and may have viruses or other security hazards. This often occurs when you copy a file from another medium (such as a CD or the Web). Active content in the file is disabled until you click the Enable Content button. The message bar closes when you identify the database as a trusted source. Before making any changes to the database, you must click the Enable Content button.

The Navigation pane at the left side of the Access screen displays the objects contained in the database. Some common objects found in a database include tables, queries, forms, and reports. Refer to Table 1.2 for descriptions of these four types of objects.

Opening and Closing Objects

Database objects display in the Navigation pane. Control what displays in the pane by clicking the menu bar at the top of the Navigation pane and then clicking the desired option at the drop-down list or by clicking the button on the menu bar containing the down-pointing triangle. (The name of this button changes

Table 1.2 Database Objects

Object Type	*Description*
table	Organizes data in fields (columns) and records (rows). A database must contain at least one table. The table is the base upon which other objects are created.
query	Displays data from a table or related tables that meets a conditional statement and/or performs calculations. For example, all records from a specific month can be displayed or only those records containing a specific city.
form	Allows fields and records to be presented in a layout different from the datasheet. Used to facilitate data entry and maintenance.
report	Prints data from tables or queries.

depending on what is selected.) For example, to display a list of all saved objects in the database, click the *Object Type* option at the drop-down list. This view displays the objects grouped by type: *Tables*, *Queries*, *Forms*, and *Reports*. To open an object, double-click the object in the Navigation pane. The object opens in the work area and a tab displays with the object name at the left side of the object.

Hide the Navigation pane by clicking the Shutter Bar Open/Close Button or by pressing F11.

To view more of an object, consider closing the Navigation pane by clicking the Shutter Bar Open/Close Button located in the upper right corner of the Navigation pane or by using the keyboard shortcut F11. Click the button or press F11 again to reopen the Navigation pane. You can open more than one object in the work area. Each object opens with a visible tab. Navigate to objects by clicking the object tab. To close an object, click the Close button that displays in the upper right corner of the work area or use the keyboard shortcut Ctrl + F4.

Shutter Bar Open/Close Button

Project 1 Opening and Closing a Database and Objects in a Database — Part 1 of 1

1. Open Access by clicking the Access 2013 tile at the Windows Start screen.
2. At the Access 2013 opening screen, click the Open Other Files hyperlink that displays in the left panel.
3. At the Open backstage area, click the desired location in the middle panel of the backstage area. (For example, click your OneDrive if you are using your OneDrive account or click the *Computer* option if you are opening a database from your computer's hard drive or a USB flash drive.)
4. Click the Browse button (or click *AL1C1* if it displays in the Recent Folders list).
5. At the Open dialog box, navigate to the AL1C1 folder on your storage medium and then double-click ***AL1-C1-SampleDatabase.accdb***. (This database contains data on orders, products, and suppliers for a specialty hiking and backpacking outfitters store named Pacific Trek.)
6. Click the Enable Content button in the message bar if a security warning message appears. (The message bar will display immediately below the ribbon.)
7. With the database open, click the Navigation pane menu bar and then click *Object Type* at the drop-down list. (This option displays the objects grouped by type: *Tables*, *Queries*, *Forms*, and *Reports*.)
8. Double-click *Suppliers* in the Tables group in the Navigation pane. This opens the Suppliers table in the work area, as shown in Figure 1.3.
9. Close the Suppliers table by clicking the Close button in the upper right corner of the work area.
10. Double-click *OrdersOver$500* in the Queries group in the Navigation pane. A query displays data that meets a conditional statement. This query displays orders that meet the criterion of being more than $500.
11. Close the query by clicking the Close button in the upper right corner of the work area.
12. Double-click *SuppliersNotVancouver* in the Queries group in the Navigation pane and notice that the query displays information about suppliers but excludes those located in Vancouver.

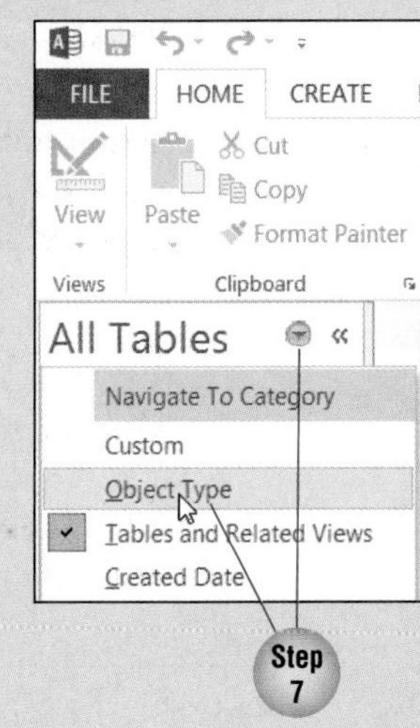

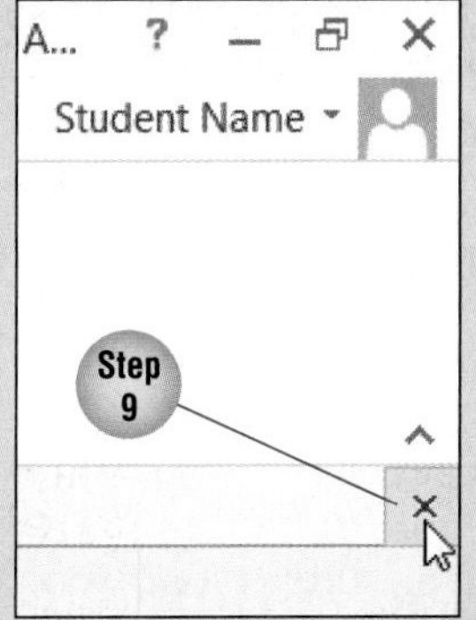

13. Click the Close button in the work area.
14. Double-click *Orders* in the Forms group in the Navigation pane. This displays an order form. A form is used to view and edit data in a table one record at a time.
15. Click the Close button in the work area.
16. Double-click *Orders* in the Reports group in the Navigation pane. This displays a report with information about orders and order amounts.
17. Close the Navigation pane by clicking the Shutter Bar Open/Close Button located in the upper right corner of the pane.
18. After viewing the report, click the Shutter Bar Open/Close Button again to open the Navigation pane.
19. Click the Close button in the work area to close the report.
20. Close the database by clicking the FILE tab and then clicking the *Close* option.
21. Close Access by clicking the Close button (contains an X) that displays in the upper right corner of the screen.

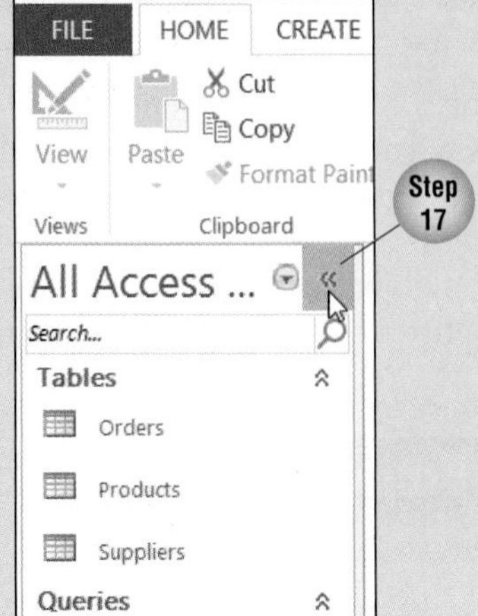

Figure 1.3 Open Suppliers Table

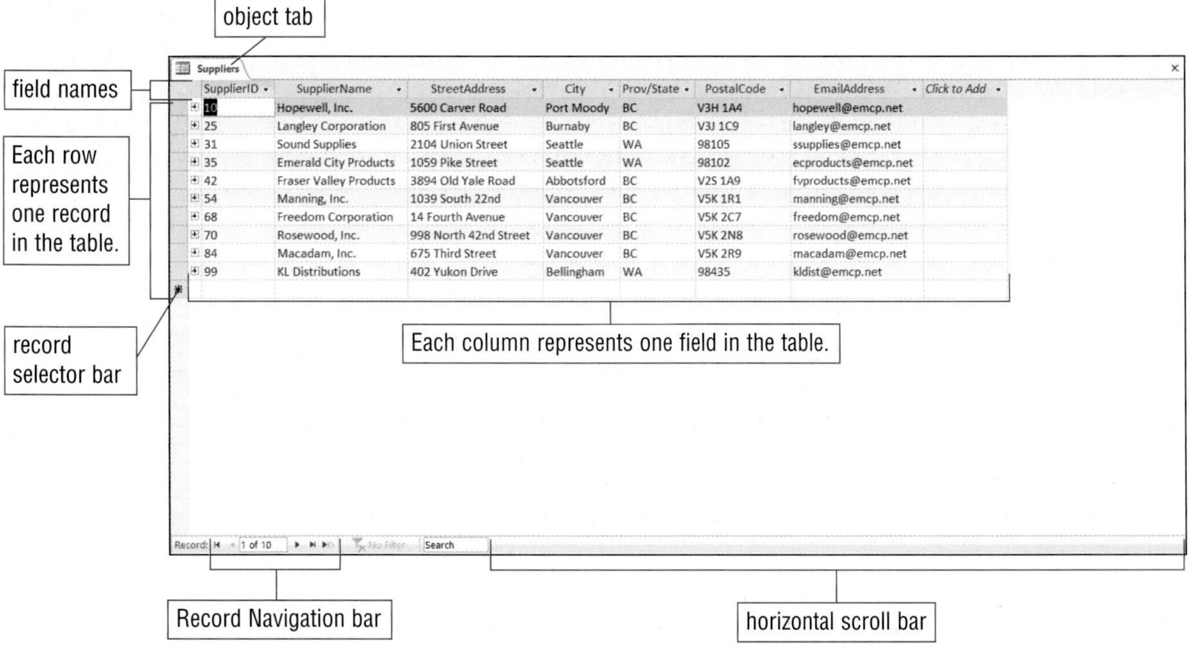

SupplierID	SupplierName	StreetAddress	City	Prov/State	PostalCode	EmailAddress	Click to Add
10	Hopewell, Inc.	5600 Carver Road	Port Moody	BC	V3H 1A4	hopewell@emcp.net	
25	Langley Corporation	805 First Avenue	Burnaby	BC	V3J 1C9	langley@emcp.net	
31	Sound Supplies	2104 Union Street	Seattle	WA	98105	ssupplies@emcp.net	
35	Emerald City Products	1059 Pike Street	Seattle	WA	98102	ecproducts@emcp.net	
42	Fraser Valley Products	3894 Old Yale Road	Abbotsford	BC	V2S 1A9	fvproducts@emcp.net	
54	Manning, Inc.	1039 South 22nd	Vancouver	BC	V5K 1R1	manning@emcp.net	
68	Freedom Corporation	14 Fourth Avenue	Vancouver	BC	V5K 2C7	freedom@emcp.net	
70	Rosewood, Inc.	998 North 42nd Street	Vancouver	BC	V5K 2N8	rosewood@emcp.net	
84	Macadam, Inc.	675 Third Street	Vancouver	BC	V5K 2R9	macadam@emcp.net	
99	KL Distributions	402 Yukon Drive	Bellingham	WA	98435	kldist@emcp.net	

Project 2 Manage Tables in a Database — 7 Parts

Pacific Trek is an outfitting store specializing in hiking and backpacking gear. Information about the store, including suppliers and products, is contained in a database. You will open the database and then insert and delete records; insert, move, and delete fields; preview and print tables; rename and delete a table; and create two new tables for the database.

Managing Tables

In a new database, tables are the first objects created, since all other database objects rely on a table as the source for their data. Managing the tables in the database is important for keeping the database up to date and may include inserting or deleting records, inserting or deleting fields, renaming fields, creating a hard copy of the table by printing the table, and renaming and deleting tables.

Inserting and Deleting Records

When you open a table, it displays in Datasheet view in the work area. The Datasheet view displays the contents of a table in a column and row format similar to an Excel worksheet. Columns contain the field data, with the field names in the header row at the top of the table, and rows contain the records. A Record Navigation bar displays at the bottom of the screen just above the Status bar and contains buttons to navigate in the table. Figure 1.4 identifies the buttons and other elements on the Record Navigation bar.

To add a new record to the open table, make sure the HOME tab is active and then click the New button in the Records group. This moves the insertion point to the first field in the blank row at the bottom of the table and the *Current Record* box on the Record Navigation bar indicates what record you are creating (or editing). You can also create a new record by clicking the New (blank) record button on the Record Navigation bar.

When working in a table, press the Tab key to make the next field active or press Shift + Tab to make the previous field active. You can also click in the desired field using the mouse. When you begin typing data for the first field in the record, another row of cells is automatically inserted below the current row and a pencil icon displays in the record selector bar at the beginning of the current record. The pencil icon indicates that the record is being edited and that the changes to the data have not been saved. When you enter the data in the last field in the record and then move the insertion point out of the field, the pencil icon is removed, indicating that the data is saved.

When managing a table, you may need to delete a record when you no longer want the data in the record. One method for deleting a record is to click in one of the fields in the record, make sure the HOME tab is active, click the Delete button arrow, and then click *Delete Record* at the drop-down list. At the message that displays asking if you want to delete the record, click the Yes button. When you click in a field in a record, the Delete button displays in a dimmed manner unless specific data is selected.

When you are finished entering data in a record in a table, the data is automatically saved. Changes to the layout of a table, however, are not automatically saved. For example, if you delete a column in a table, when you close the table you will be asked if you are sure you want to delete the selected field.

Quick Steps

Add a New Record
1. Open table.
2. Click New button on HOME tab.
3. Type data.

OR
1. Open table.
2. Click New (blank) record button on Record Navigation bar.
3. Type data.

Delete a Record
1. Open table.
2. Click Delete button arrow on HOME tab.
3. Click *Delete Record.*
4. Click Yes button.

New

Delete

Figure 1.4 Record Navigation Bar

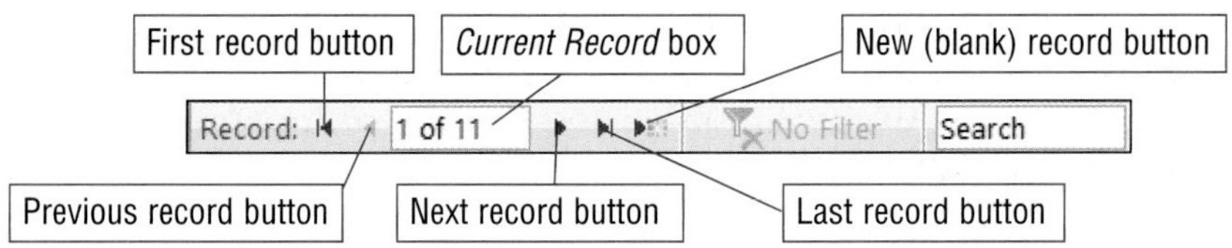

Project 2a Inserting and Deleting Records in a Table

1. Open Access.
2. At the Access 2013 opening screen, click the Open Other Files hyperlink.
3. At the Open backstage area, double-click the *Computer* option or your OneDrive (depending on where your AL1C1 folder is located).
4. At the Open dialog box, navigate to the AL1C1 folder on your storage medium or OneDrive and then double-click ***AL1-C1-PacTrek.accdb***.
5. Click the Enable Content button in the message bar if a security warning message appears. (The message bar will display immediately below the ribbon.)
6. With the database open, make sure the Navigation pane displays object types. (If it does not, click the Navigation pane menu bar and then click *Object Type* at the drop-down list.)
7. Double-click *Suppliers* in the Tables group in the Navigation pane. (This opens the table in Datasheet view.)
8. With the Suppliers table open and the HOME tab active, create a new record by completing the following steps:
   a. Click the New button in the Records group on the HOME tab. (This moves the insertion point to the first field in the blank record at the bottom of the table and the *Current Record* box in the Record Navigation bar indicates what record you are creating or editing.)
   b. Type 38. (This inserts *38* in the field immediately below *99*.)
   c. Press the Tab key (to make the next field active) and then type Hadley Company.
   d. Press the Tab key and then type 5845 Jefferson Street.
   e. Press the Tab key and then type Seattle.
   f. Press the Tab key and then type WA.
   g. Press the Tab key and then type 98107.
   h. Press the Tab key and then type hcompany@emcp.net.
   i. Press the Tab key and then type Jurene Miller.

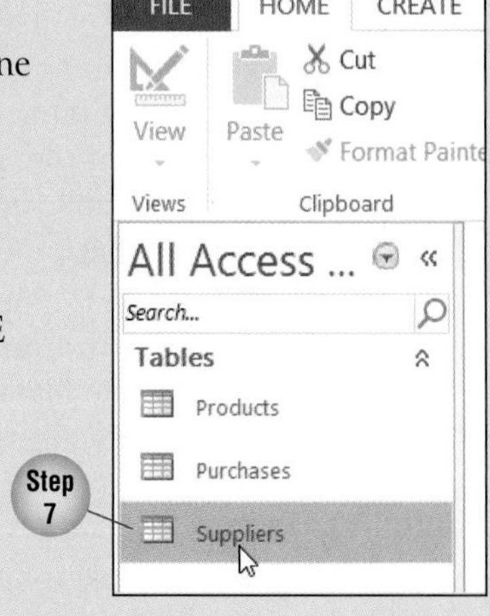

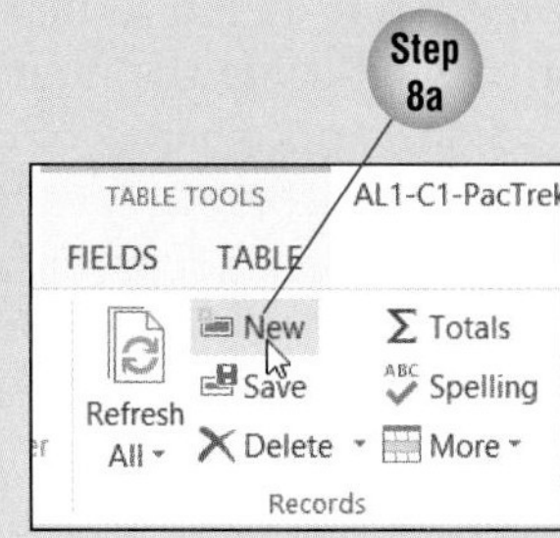

Suppliers

SupplierID	SupplierName	StreetAddres	City	Prov/State	PostalCode	EmailAddres	Contact	Click to Add
10	Hopewell, Inc.	5600 Carver Ro	Port Moody	BC	V3H 1A4	hopewell@emc	Jacob Hopewel	
25	Langley Corporation	805 First Avenu	Burnaby	BC	V3J 1C9	langley@emcp.	Mandy Shin	
31	Sound Supplies	2104 Union Str	Seattle	WA	98105	ssupplies@emc	Regan Levine	
35	Emerald City Products	1059 Pike Stree	Seattle	WA	98102	ecproducts@er	Howard Greer	
42	Fraser Valley Products	3894 Old Yale F	Abbotsford	BC	V2S 1A9	fvproducts@en	Layla Adams	
54	Manning, Inc.	1039 South 22n	Vancouver	BC	V5K 1R1	manning@emc	Jack Silverstein	
68	Freedom Corporation	14 Fourth Aven	Vancouver	BC	V5K 2C7	freedom@emc	Opal Northwoc	
70	Rosewood, Inc.	998 North 42nc	Vancouver	BC	V5K 2N8	rosewood@em	Clint Rivas	
84	Macadam, Inc.	675 Third Stree	Vancouver	BC	V5K 2R9	macadam@em	Hans Reiner	
99	KL Distributions	402 Yukon Driv	Bellingham	WA	98435	kldist@emcp.n	Noland Dannis	
38	Hadley Company	5845 Jefferson	Seattle	WA	98107	hcompany@en	Jurene Miller	

Steps 8b-8i

9. Close the Suppliers table by clicking the Close button in the work area.
10. Open the Products table by double-clicking *Products* in the Tables group in the Navigation pane. (This opens the table in Datasheet view.)
11. Insert two new records by completing the following steps:
    a. Click the New button in the Records group and then enter the data for a new record as shown in Figure 1.5. (See the record that begins with *901-S*.)

b. After you type the last field entry in the record for product number 901-S, press the Tab key. This moves the insertion point to the blank field below *901-S*.

c. Type the new record as shown in Figure 1.5. (See the record that begins with *917-S*.)

12. With the Products table open, delete a record by completing the following steps:

    a. Click in the field containing the data *780-2*.

    b. Click the Delete button arrow in the Records group (notice that the button displays in a dimmed manner) and then click *Delete Record* at the drop-down list.

    c. At the message asking if you want to delete the record, click the Yes button.

13. Close the Products table by clicking the Close button in the work area.

Figure 1.5 Project 2a, Step 11

Products

ProductID	Product	SupplierID	UnitsInStock	UnitsOnOrder	ReorderLevel	Click to Add
559-B	ICE snow goggles, bronze	68	22	0	20	
602-XR	Binoculars, 8 x 42	35	3	5	5	
602-XT	Binoculars, 10.5 x 45	35	5	0	4	
602-XX	Binoculars, 10 x 50	35	7	0	5	
647-1	Two-person dome tent	99	10	15	15	
648-2	Three-person dome tent	99	5	0	10	
651-1	K-2 one-person tent	99	8	0	10	
652-2	K-2 two-person tent	99	12	0	10	
780-2	Two-person tent	99	17	10	20	
804-50	AG freestyle snowboard, X50	70	7	0	10	
804-60	AG freestyle snowboard, X60	70	8	0	5	
897-L	Lang blunt snowboard	70	8	0	7	
897-W	Lang blunt snowboard, wide	70	4	0	3	
901-S	Solar battery pack	38	16	0	15	
917-S	Silo portable power pack	38	8	0	10	

Step 11

Inserting, Moving, and Deleting Fields

When managing a database, you may determine that you need to add additional information to a table. For example, you might decide that you want to insert a field for contact information, a field for cell phone numbers, or a field for the number of items in stock. To insert a new field in a table, open the table in Datasheet view and then click in the first field below the *Click to Add* heading. Type the desired data in the field for the first record, press the Down Arrow key to make the field below active, and then type the desired data for the second record. Continue in this manner until you have entered data in the new field for all records in the table. Instead of pressing the Down Arrow key to move the

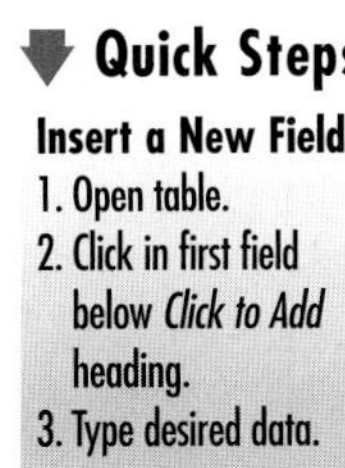

Quick Steps

Insert a New Field

1. Open table.
2. Click in first field below *Click to Add* heading.
3. Type desired data.

insertion point down to the next field, you can click in the desired field using the mouse or you can press the Tab key until the desired field is active.

Quick Steps

Move a Field Column
1. Select column.
2. Position mouse pointer on heading.
3. Hold down left mouse button.
4. Drag to desired location.
5. Release mouse button.

Delete a Field Column
1. Click in field.
2. Click Delete button arrow on HOME tab.
3. Click *Delete Column.*
4. Click Yes button.

A new field is added to the right of existing fields. Move a field by positioning the mouse pointer on the field heading until the pointer displays as a down-pointing black arrow and then clicking the left mouse button. This selects the entire column. With the field column selected, position the mouse pointer on the heading; hold down the left mouse button; drag to the left or right until a thick, black vertical line displays in the desired location; and then release the mouse button. The thick, black vertical line indicates where the field column will be positioned when you release the mouse button. In addition, the pointer displays with the outline of a gray box attached to it, indicating that you are performing a move operation.

Delete a field column in a manner similar to deleting a row. Click in one of the fields in the column, make sure the HOME tab is active, click the Delete button arrow, and then click *Delete Column* at the drop-down list. At the message that displays asking if you want to delete the column, click the Yes button.

Project 2b Inserting, Moving, and Deleting Fields

Part 2 of 7

1. With **AL1-C1-PacTrek.accdb** open, you decide to add a new field to the Suppliers table. Do this by completing the following steps:
   a. Double-click *Suppliers* in the Tables group in the Navigation pane.
   b. Click in the field immediately below the heading *Click to Add*.
   c. Type (604) 555-3843 and then press the Down Arrow key on your keyboard.
   d. Type the remaining telephone numbers as shown at the right.

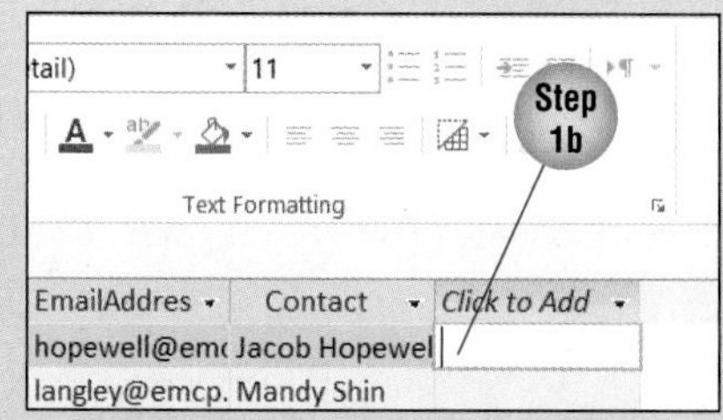

Contact	Field1
Jacob Hopewel	(604) 555-3843
Mandy Shin	(604) 555-1200
Regan Levine	(206) 555-4855
Howard Greer	(206) 555-7728
Jurene Miller	(206) 555-8003
Layla Adams	(604) 555-1455
Jack Silverstein	(604) 555-0087
Opal Northwoc	(604) 555-2155
Clint Rivas	(778) 555-6643
Hans Reiner	(604) 555-5522
Noland Dannis	(360) 555-3711

Step 1d

2. Move the field column so it is positioned immediately left of the *EmailAddress* field by completing the following steps:
   a. Position the mouse pointer on the heading *Field1* until the pointer displays as a down-pointing black arrow and then click the left mouse button. (This selects the column.)
   b. Position the mouse pointer on the heading. (The pointer displays as the normal, white arrow pointer.) Hold down the left mouse button; drag to the left until the thick, black vertical line displays immediately left of the *EmailAddress* field; and then release the mouse button.

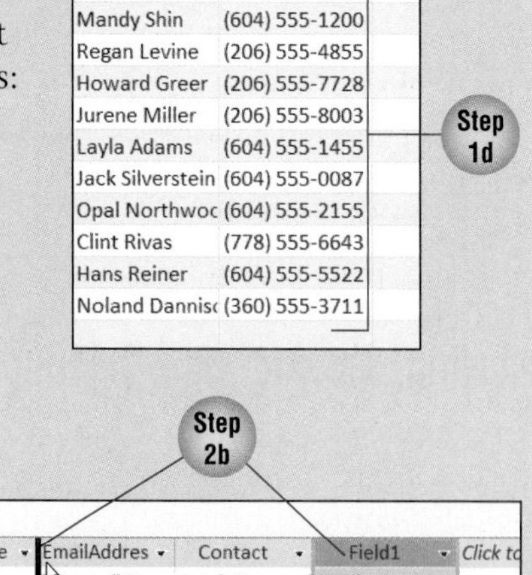

PostalCode	EmailAddres	Contact	Field1	Click to
V3H 1A4	hopewell@emc	Jacob Hopewel	(604) 555-3843	
V3J 1C9	langley@emcp.	Mandy Shin	(604) 555-1200	
98105	ssupplies@emc	Regan Levine	(206) 555-4855	
98102	ecproducts@er	Howard Greer	(206) 555-7728	

3. You realize that you no longer need the supplier contact information so you decide to delete the field. Do this by completing the following steps:
   a. Position the mouse pointer on the heading *Contact* until the pointer displays as a down-pointing black arrow and then click the left mouse button. (This selects the column.)

b. Click the Delete button arrow in the Records group and then click *Delete Column* at the drop-down list.
c. At the message asking if you want to permanently delete the selected fields, click the Yes button.
4. Close the Suppliers table. At the message that displays asking if you want to save the changes to the layout of the table, click the Yes button.

Hiding, Unhiding, Freezing, and Unfreezing Column Fields

You can hide columns of data in a table if you do not want the data visible or you want to make it easier to view two nonadjacent columns containing data you want to compare. To hide a column, click in any field in the column you want to hide, click the More button in the Records group on the HOME tab, and then click *Hide Fields* at the drop-down list. Hide adjacent columns by selecting the columns, clicking the More button in the Records group, and then clicking *Hide Fields* at the drop-down list. To unhide columns, click the More button and then click *Unhide Fields*. At the Unhide Columns dialog box that displays, insert a check mark in the check boxes for those columns you want to be visible.

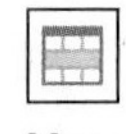
More

Another method for comparing column fields side by side is to freeze a column. Freezing a column is also helpful when not all of the columns of data are visible at one time. To freeze a column, click in any field in the column you want to freeze, click the More button, and then click *Freeze Fields* at the drop-down list. To freeze adjacent columns, select the columns first, click the More button, and then click *Freeze Fields* at the drop-down list. To unfreeze all columns in a table, click the More button and then click *Unfreeze All Fields* at the drop-down list.

Changing Column Width

When entering data in the Suppliers and Products table, did you notice that not all of the data was visible? To remedy this, you can adjust the widths of columns so that all data is visible. You can adjust the width of one column in a table to accommodate the longest entry in the column by positioning the arrow pointer on the column boundary at the right side of the column until the pointer turns into a left-and-right-pointing arrow with a vertical line in the middle and then double-clicking the left mouse button.

Adjust the widths of adjacent columns by selecting the columns first and then double-clicking on one of the selected column boundaries. To select adjacent columns, position the arrow pointer on the first column heading until the pointer turns into a down-pointing black arrow, hold down the left mouse button, drag to the last column you want to adjust, and then release the mouse button. With the columns selected, double-click one of the column boundaries.

You can also adjust the width of a column by dragging the boundary to the desired position. To do this, position the arrow pointer on the column boundary until it turns into a left-and-right-pointing arrow with a vertical line in the middle, hold down the left mouse button, drag until the column is the desired width, and then release the mouse button.

Quick Steps

Change a Table Column Width
Double-click column boundary.
OR
Select columns and then double-click column boundary.
OR
Drag column boundary to desired position.

Automatically adjust column widths in an Access table in the same manner as adjusting column widths in an Excel worksheet.

Project 2c Hiding, Unhiding, Freezing, and Unfreezing Columns and Changing Column Widths

Part 3 of 7

1. With **AL1-C1-PacTrek.accdb** open, open the Suppliers table.
2. Hide the *PostalCode* column by clicking in any field in the *PostalCode* column, clicking the More button in the Records group on the HOME tab, and then clicking *Hide Fields* at the drop-down list.
3. Unhide the column by clicking the More button and then clicking *Unhide Fields* at the drop-down list. At the Unhide Columns dialog box, click in the *PostalCode* check box to insert a check mark, and then click the Close button.

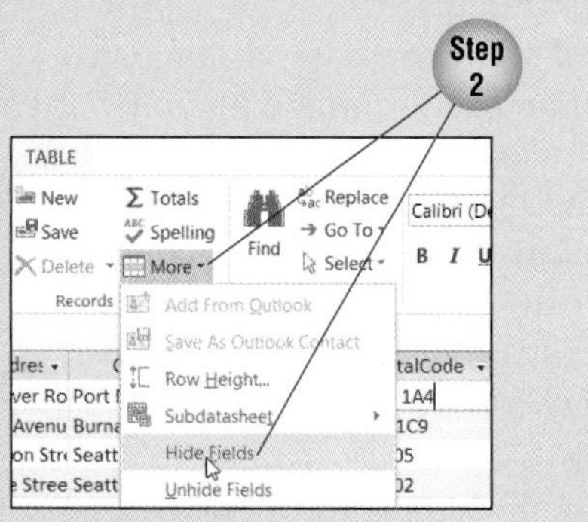

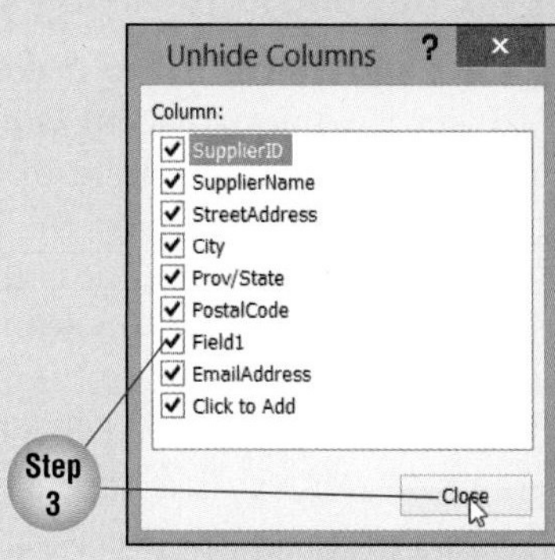

4. Adjust the width of the *SupplierID* column by positioning the arrow pointer on the column boundary at the right side of the *SupplierID* column until it turns into a left-and-right-pointing arrow with a vertical line in the middle and then double-clicking the left mouse button.

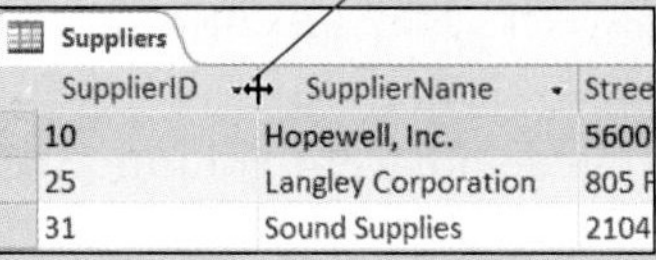

5. Adjust the width of the remaining columns by completing the following steps:
   a. Position the arrow pointer on the *SupplierName* heading until the pointer turns into a down-pointing black arrow, hold down the left mouse button, drag to the *EmailAddress* heading, and then release the mouse button.
   b. With the columns selected, double-click one of the column boundaries.
   c. Click in any field in the table to deselect the columns.
6. Increase the width of the *EmailAddress* column by positioning the arrow pointer on the column boundary at the right side of the *EmailAddress* column until it turns into a left-and-right-pointing arrow with a vertical line in the middle, holding down the left mouse button while dragging all of the way to the right side of the screen, and then releasing the mouse button. (Check the horizontal scroll bar located toward the bottom of the table and notice that the scroll bar contains a scroll box.)
7. Position the mouse pointer on the scroll box on the horizontal scroll bar and then drag to the left until the *SupplierID* field is visible.
8. Freeze the *SupplierID* column by clicking in any field in the *SupplierID* column, clicking the More button in the Records group, and then clicking *Freeze Fields* at the drop-down list.

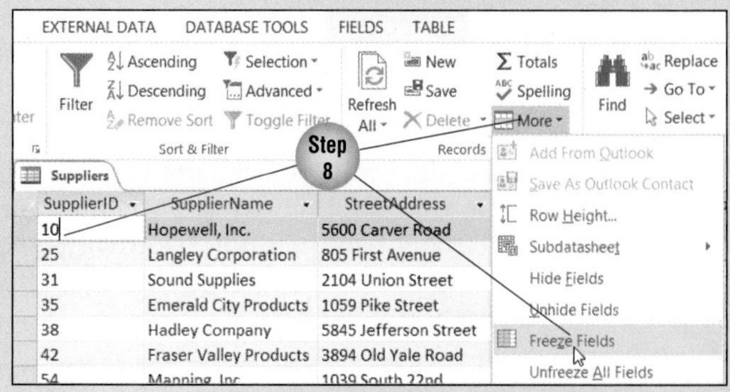

9. Using the mouse, drag the scroll box along the horizontal scroll to the right and then to the left and notice that the *SupplierID* column remains visible on the screen.
10. Unfreeze the column by clicking the More button in the Records group and then clicking *Unfreeze All Fields* at the drop-down list.
11. Double-click on the column boundary at the right side of the *EmailAddress* column.
12. Close the Suppliers table and click the Yes button at the message that asks if you want to save the changes to the layout.
13. Open the Products table and then complete steps similar to those in Step 5 to select and then adjust the column widths.
14. Close the Products table and click the Yes button at the message that asks if you want to save the changes to the layout.

Renaming and Deleting a Table

Managing tables might include actions such as renaming and deleting a table. Rename a table by right-clicking the table name in the Navigation pane, clicking *Rename* at the shortcut menu, typing the new name, and then pressing Enter. Delete a table from a database by right-clicking the table name in the Navigation pane, clicking the Delete button in the Records group on the HOME tab, and then clicking the Yes button at the message asking if you want to permanently delete the table. Another method is to right-click the table in the Navigation pane, click *Delete* at the shortcut menu, and then click the Yes at the message. If you are deleting a table from your computer's hard drive, the message asking if you want to permanently delete the table will not display. This is because Access automatically sends the deleted table to the Recycle Bin, where it can be retrieved if necessary.

Quick Steps

Rename a Table
1. Right-click table name in Navigation pane.
2. Click *Rename*.
3. Type new name.
4. Press Enter

Delete a Table
1. Right-click table name in Navigation pane.
2. Click *Delete*.
3. Click Yes, if necessary.

Printing Tables

In some situations, you may want to print a table. To do this, open the table, click the FILE tab, and then click the *Print* option. This displays the Print backstage area, as shown in Figure 1.6. Click the Quick Print button to send the table directly to the printer without making any changes to the printer setup or the table formatting. Click the Print button to display the Print dialog box, where you can specify the printer, page range, and specific records to print. Click OK to close the dialog box and send the table to the printer. By default, Access prints a table on letter-size paper in portrait orientation.

Quick Steps

Print a Table
1. Click FILE tab.
2. Click *Print* option.
3. Click Quick Print button.

OR
1. Click FILE tab.
2. Click *Print* option.
3. Click Print button.
4. Click OK.

Figure 1.6 Print Backstage Area

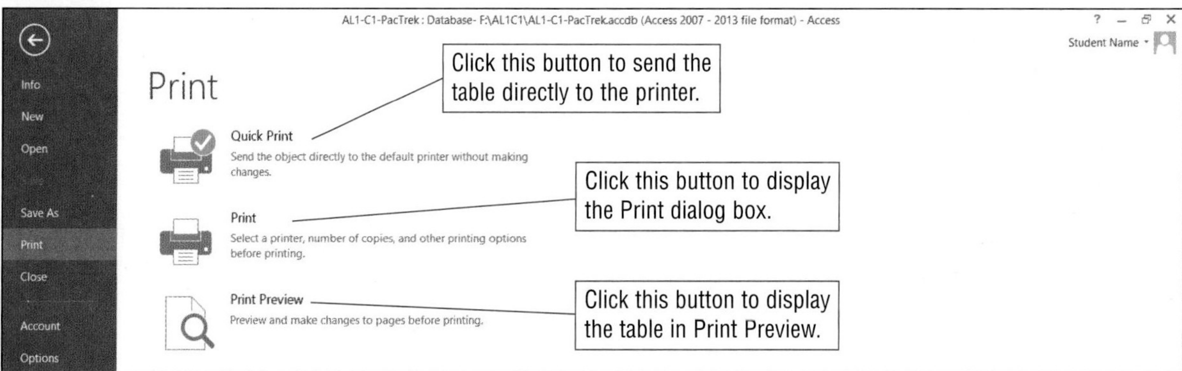

Previewing a Table

Quick Steps

Preview a Table

1. Click FILE tab.
2. Click *Print* option.
3. Click Print Preview button.

Print Preview

Print

Close Print Preview

Size

Margins

Before printing a table, you may want to display the table in Print Preview to see how the table will print on the page. To display a table in Print Preview, as shown in Figure 1.7, click the Print Preview button at the Print backstage area.

Use options in the Zoom group on the PRINT PREVIEW tab to increase or decrease the size of the page display. You can also change the size of the page display using the Zoom slider bar located at the right side of the Status bar. If your table spans more than one page, use buttons on the Navigation bar to display the next or previous page.

Print a table from Print Preview by clicking the Print button located at the left side of the PRINT PREVIEW tab. Click the Close Print Preview button if you want to close Print Preview and continue working in the table without printing it.

Changing Page Size and Margins

By default, Access prints a table in standard letter size (8.5 inches wide and 11 inches tall). Click the Size button in the Page Size group on the PRINT PREVIEW tab and a drop-down list displays with options for changing the page size to legal, executive, envelope, and so on. Access uses default top, bottom, left, and right margins of 1 inch. Change these default margins by clicking the Margins button in the Page Size group and then clicking one of the predesigned margin options.

Figure 1.7 Print Preview

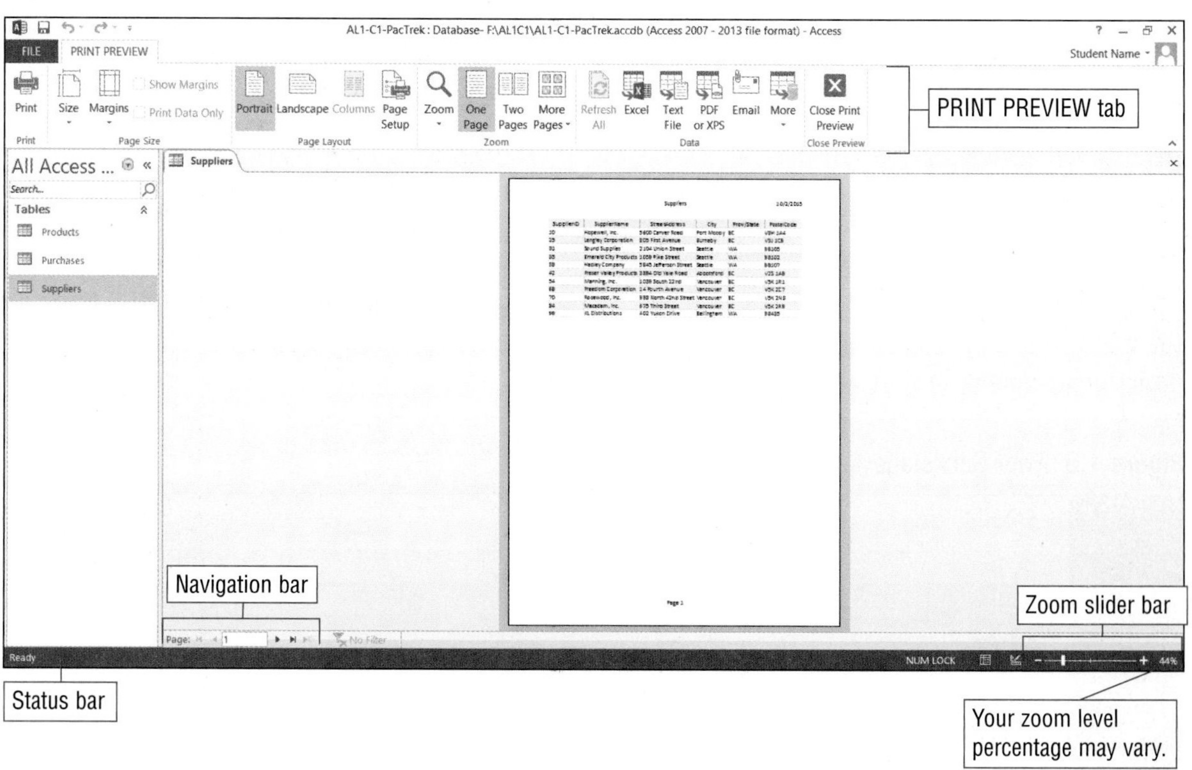

Changing Page Layout

The PRINT PREVIEW tab contains the Page Layout group with buttons for controlling how data is printed on the page. By default, Access prints a table in portrait orientation, which prints the text on the page so that it is taller than it is wide (like a page in this textbook). If a table contains a number of columns, changing to landscape orientation allows more columns to fit on a page. Landscape orientation rotates the printout to be wider than it is tall. To change from the default portrait orientation to landscape orientation, click the Landscape button in the Page Layout group on the PRINT PREVIEW tab.

Landscape

Click the Page Setup button in the Page Layout group and the Page Setup dialog box displays as shown in Figure 1.8. At the Page Setup dialog box with the Print Options tab selected, notice that the default margins are 1 inch. Change these defaults by typing a different number in the desired margin text box. By default, the table name prints at the top center of the page and the current date prints in the upper right corner of the page. In addition, the word *Page* followed by the page number prints at the bottom of the page. If you do not want the name of the table, date, and page number to print, remove the check mark from the *Print Headings* option at the Page Setup dialog box with the Print Options tab selected.

Quick Steps

Display Page Setup Dialog Box

1. Click FILE tab.
2. Click *Print* option.
3. Click Print Preview button.
4. Click Page Setup button.

Click the Page tab at the Page Setup dialog box and the dialog box displays as shown in Figure 1.9. Change the orientation with options in the *Orientation* section and change the paper size with options in the *Paper* section. Click the *Size* option box arrow and a drop-down list displays with paper sizes similar to the options available at the *Size* button drop-down list in the Page Size group on the PRINT PREVIEW tab. Specify the printer with options in the *Printer for (table name)* section of the dialog box.

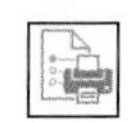

Page Setup

Figure 1.8 Page Setup Dialog Box with Print Options Tab Selected

Enter measurements in these boxes to change the page margins.

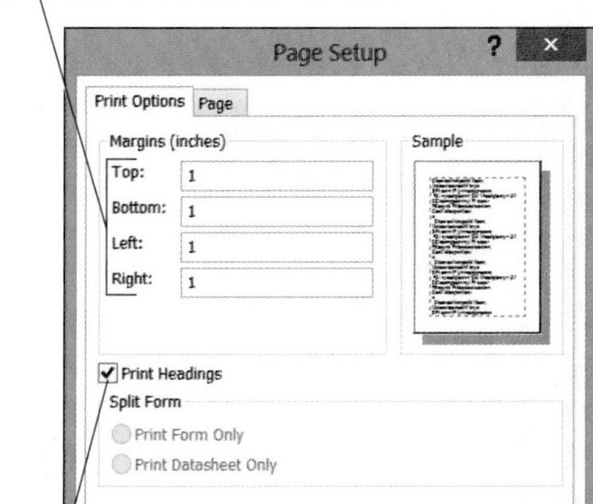

Remove the check mark from this check box if you do not want the table name, date, and page number printed.

Figure 1.9 Page Setup Dialog Box with Page Tab Selected

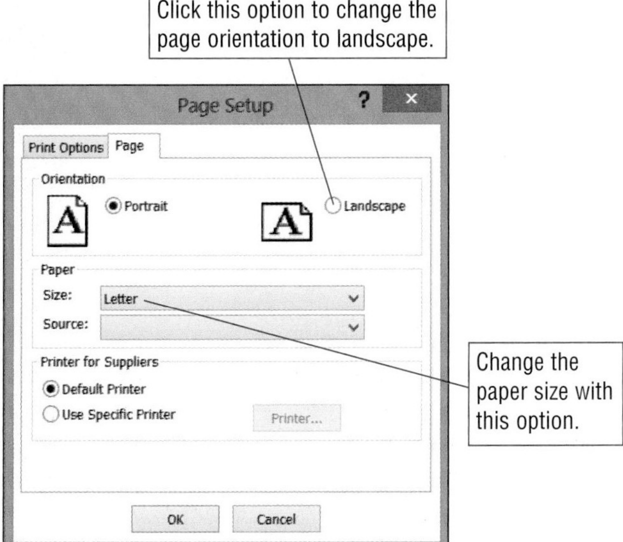

Project 2d Previewing, Changing Page Layout, Renaming, Deleting, and Printing Tables Part 4 of 7

1. With **AL1-C1-PacTrek.accdb** open, open the Suppliers table.
2. Preview and then print the Suppliers table in landscape orientation by completing the following steps:
   a. Click the FILE tab and then click the *Print* option.
   b. At the Print backstage area, click the Print Preview button.
   c. Click the Two Pages button in the Zoom group on the PRINT PREVIEW tab. (This displays two pages of the table.)
   d. Click the Zoom button arrow in the Zoom group on the PRINT PREVIEW tab and then click *75%* at the drop-down list.

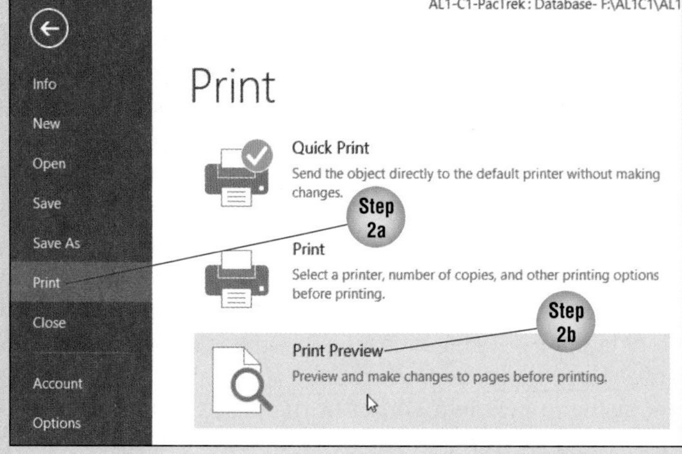

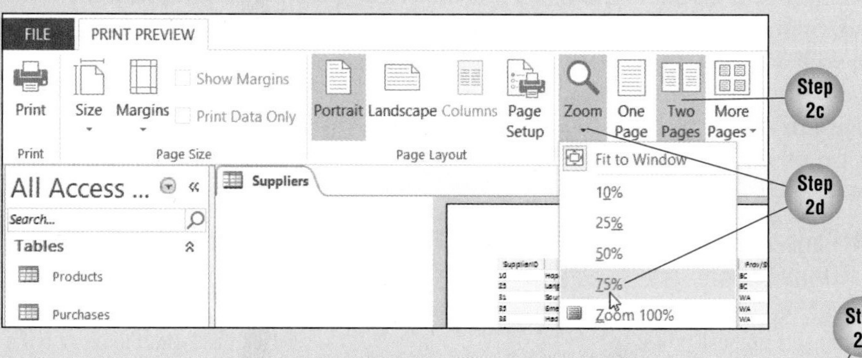

   e. Position the arrow pointer on the Zoom slider bar button that displays at the right side of the Status bar, hold down the left mouse button, drag to the right until *100%* displays at the right of the Zoom slider bar, and then release the mouse button.
   f. Return the display to a full page by clicking the One Page button in the Zoom group on the PRINT PREVIEW tab.
   g. Click the Margins button in the Page Size group on the PRINT PREVIEW tab and then click the *Narrow* option at the drop-down list. (Notice how the data will print on the page with the narrow margins.)
   h. Change the margins back to the default by clicking the Margins button in the Page Size group and then clicking the *Normal* option at the drop-down list.
   i. Change to landscape orientation by clicking the Landscape button in the Page Layout group. (Check the Next Page button on the Record Navigation bar and notice that it is dimmed. This indicates that the table will print on only one page.)

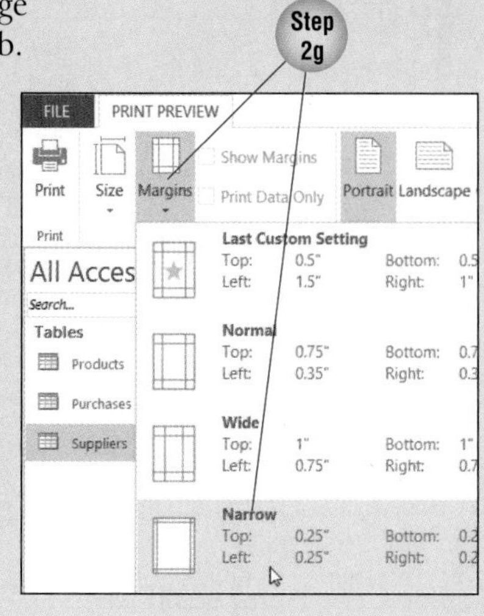

j. Print the table by clicking the Print button located at the left side of the PRINT PREVIEW tab and then clicking the OK button at the Print dialog box.

3. Close the Suppliers table.
4. Open the Products table and then print the table by completing the following steps:
   a. Click the FILE tab and then click the *Print* option.
   b. At the Print backstage area, click the Print Preview button.
   c. Click the Page Setup button in the Page Layout group on the PRINT PREVIEW tab. (This displays the Page Setup dialog box with the Print Options tab selected.)
   d. At the Page Setup dialog box, click the Page tab.
   e. Click the *Landscape* option.

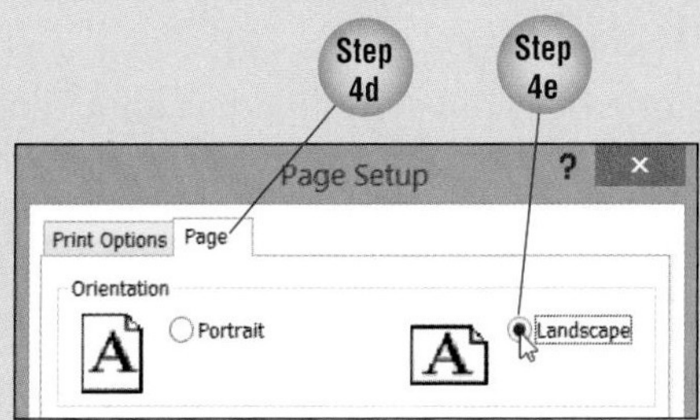

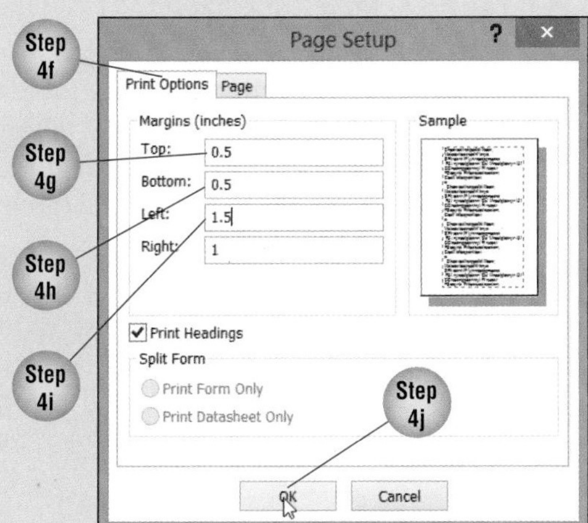

   f. Click the Print Options tab.
   g. Select the current measurement in the *Top* text box and then type **0.5**.
   h. Select the current measurement in the *Bottom* text box and then type **0.5**.
   i. Select the current measurement in the *Left* text box and then type **1.5**.
   j. Click OK to close the dialog box.
   k. Click the Print button on the PRINT PREVIEW tab and then click the OK button at the Print dialog box. (This table will print on two pages.)
5. Close the Products table.
6. Rename the Purchases table by right-clicking *Purchases* in the Navigation pane, clicking *Rename* at the shortcut menu, typing **Orders**, and then pressing Enter.
7. Delete the Orders table by right-clicking *Orders* in the Navigation pane and then clicking *Delete* at the shortcut menu. If a message displays asking if you want to permanently delete the table, click Yes.

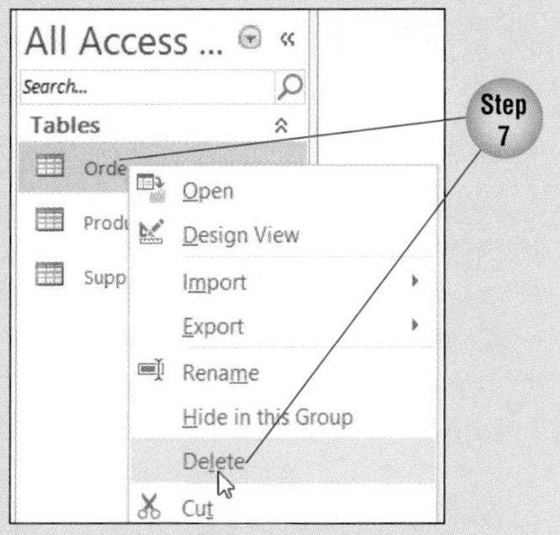

Designing a Table

Tables are the first objects created in a new database and all other objects in a database rely on tables for data. Designing a database involves planning the number of tables needed and the fields that will be included in each table. Each table in a database should contain information about only one subject. For example, the Suppliers table in the AL1-C1-PacTrek.accdb database contains data only about suppliers and the Products table contains data only about products.

Database designers often create a visual representation of the database's structure in a diagram similar to the one shown in Figure 1.10. Each table is represented by a box with the table name at the top. Within each box, the fields that will be stored in the table are listed with the field names that will be used when the table is created.

Notice that one field in each table has an asterisk next to its name. The field with the asterisk is called the ***primary key***. A primary key holds data that uniquely identifies each record in a table and is usually an identification number. The lines drawn between each table in Figure 1.10 are called ***join lines,*** and they represent links established between tables (called ***relationships***) so that data can be extracted from one or more tables. Notice the join lines point to a common field name included in each table that is to be linked. (You will learn how to join, or relate, tables in Chapter 2.) A database with related tables is called a ***relational database***.

Notice the join line in the database diagram that connects the *SupplierID* field in the Suppliers table with the *SupplierID* field in the Products table and another join line that connects the *SupplierID* field in the Suppliers table with the *SupplierID* field in the Orders table. In the database diagram, a join line connects the *ProductID* field in the Products table with the *ProductID* field in the Orders table.

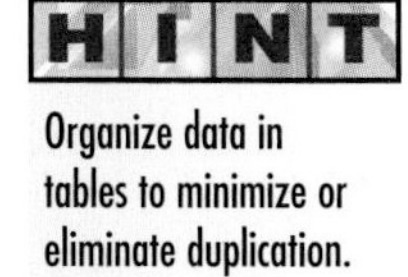

Organize data in tables to minimize or eliminate duplication.

When designing a database, you need to consider certain design principles. The first principle is to reduce redundant (duplicate) data, for several reasons. Redundant data increases the amount of data entry required, increases the chances for errors and inconsistencies, and takes up additional storage space. The Products table contains a *SupplierID* field and that field reduces the redundant

Figure 1.10 Database Diagram

Suppliers
*SupplierID
SupplierName
StreetAddress
City
Prov/State
PostalCode
EmailAddress
Contact

Products
*ProductID
Product
SupplierID
UnitsInStock
UnitsOnOrder
ReorderLevel

Orders
*OrderID
SupplierID
ProductID
UnitsOrdered
Amount
OrderDate

data needed in the table. For example, rather than typing the supplier information in the Suppliers table *and* the Products table, you type the information once in the Suppliers table and then "join" the tables with the connecting field *SupplierID*. If you need information on suppliers as well as specific information about products, you can draw the information into one object, such as a query or report using data from both tables. When you create the Orders table, you will use the *SupplierID* field and the *ProductID* field rather than typing all of the information for the suppliers and the product description. Typing a two-letter unique identifier number for a supplier greatly reduces the amount of typing required to create the Orders table. Inserting the *ProductID* field in the Orders table eliminates the need to type the product description for each order; instead, you type a unique five-, six-, or seven-digit identifier number.

Creating a Table

Creating a new table generally involves determining fields, assigning a data type to each field, modifying properties, designating the primary key, and naming the table. This process is referred to as ***defining the table structure***.

The first step in creating a table is to determine the fields. A ***field***, commonly called a column, is one piece of information about a person, place, or item. Each field contains data about one aspect of the table subject, such as a company name or product number. All fields for one unit, such as a customer or product, are considered a ***record***. For example, in the Suppliers table in the AL1-C1-PacTrek.accdb database, a record is all of the information pertaining to one supplier. A collection of records becomes a ***table***.

A database table contains fields that describe a person, customer, client, object, place, idea, or event.

When designing a table, determine fields for information to be included on the basis of how you plan to use the data. When organizing fields, be sure to consider not only current needs for the data but also any future needs. For example, a company may need to keep track of customer names, addresses, and telephone numbers for current mailing lists. In the future, the company may want to promote a new product to customers who purchase a specific type of product. For this information to be available at a later date, a field that identifies product type must be included in the database. When organizing fields, consider all potential needs for the data but also try to keep the fields logical and manageable.

You can create a table in Access in Datasheet view or in Design view. To create a table in Datasheet view, open the desired database (or create a new database), click the CREATE tab, and then click the Table button in the Tables group. This inserts a blank table in the work area with the tab labeled *Table1*, as shown in Figure 1.11. Notice the column with the field name *ID* has been created automatically. Access creates *ID* as an AutoNumber field in which the field value is assigned automatically by Access as you enter each record. In many tables, you can use this AutoNumber field to create the unique identifier for the table. For example, in Project 2e, you will create an Orders table and use the ID AutoNumber field to assign automatically a number to each order, since each order must contain a unique number.

Table

Assign a data type to each field that determines the type of information that can be entered into the field.

When creating a new field (column), determine the type of data you will insert in the field. For example, one field might contain text such as a name or product description, another field might contain an amount of money, and another might contain a date. The data type defines the type of information Access will allow to be entered into the field. For example, Access will not allow alphabetic

Figure 1.11 Blank Table

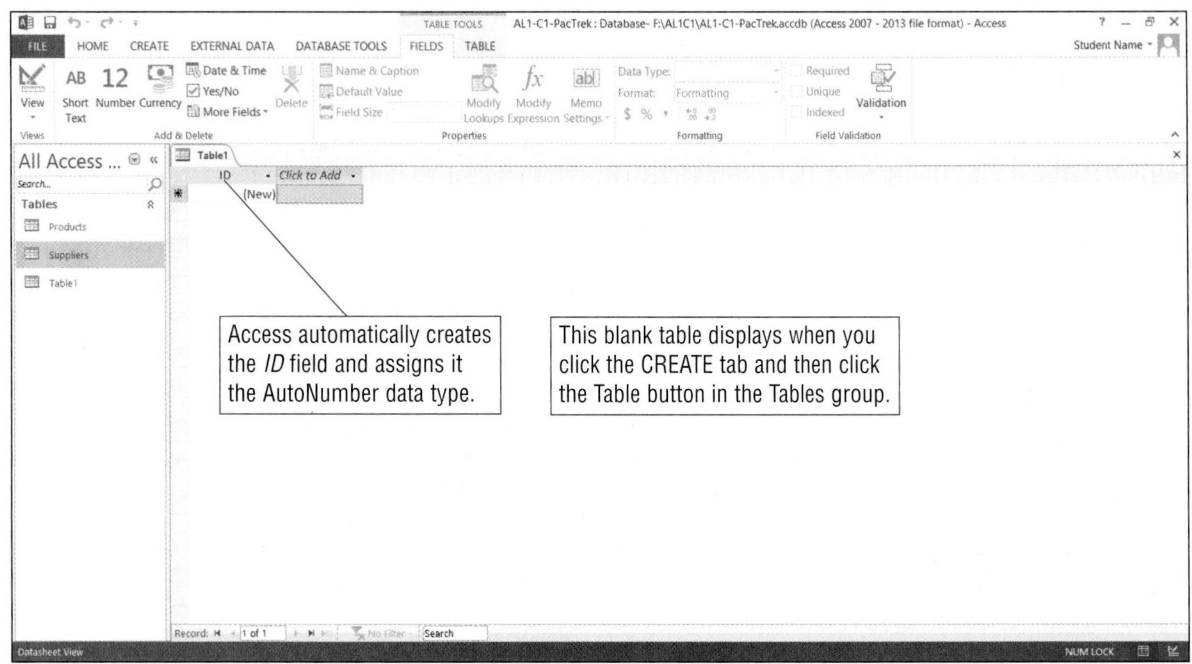

Access automatically creates the *ID* field and assigns it the AutoNumber data type.
This blank table displays when you click the CREATE tab and then click the Table button in the Tables group.

More Fields

characters to be entered into a field with a data type set to Date & Time. The Add & Delete group on the TABLE TOOLS FIELDS tab contains five buttons for assigning data types plus a More Fields button. Descriptions of the five data types assigned by the buttons are provided in Table 1.3.

Table 1.3 Data Types

Data Type Button	*Description*
Short Text	Alphanumeric data up to 255 characters in length—for example, a name, an address, or a value such as a telephone number or social security number that is used as an identifier and not for calculating.
Number	Positive or negative values that can be used in calculations; not to be used for values that will calculate monetary amounts (see Currency).
Currency	Values that involve money; Access will not round off during calculations.
Date & Time	Used to ensure dates and times are entered and sorted properly.
Yes/No	Data in the field will be either *Yes* or *No*; *True* or *False*, *On* or *Off*.

In Project 2e, you will create the Orders table, as shown in Figure 1.12. Looking at the diagram in Figure 1.10, you will assign the following data types to the columns:

OrderID:	AutoNumber (Access automatically assigns this data type to the first column)
SupplierID:	Short Text (the supplier numbers are identifiers, not numbers for calculating)
ProductID:	Short Text (the product numbers are identifiers, not numbers for calculating)
UnitsOrdered:	Number (the unit numbers are values for calculating)
Amount:	Currency
OrderDate:	Date & Time

When you click a data type button, Access inserts a field to the right of the *ID* field and selects the field heading *Field1*. Type a name for the field; press the Enter key; and Access selects the next field column, named *Click to Add,* and displays a drop-down list of data types. This drop-down list contains the same five data types as the buttons in the Add & Delete group as well as additional data types. Click the desired data type at the drop-down list, type the desired field name, and then press Enter. Continue in this manner until you have entered all field names for the table. When naming a field, consider the following guidelines:

- Each field must have a unique name.
- The name should describe the contents of the field.
- A field name can contain up to 64 characters.
- A field name can contain letters and numbers. Some symbols are permitted but others are excluded, so avoid using symbols other than the underscore (to separate words) and the number symbol (to indicate an identifier number).
- Do not use spaces in field names. Although a space is an accepted character, most database designers avoid using spaces in field names and object names. Use field compound words for field names or the underscore character as a word separator. For example, a field name for a person's last name could be named *LastName*, *Last_Name*, or *LName*.
- Abbreviate field names so that they are as short as possible but still easily understood. For example, a field such as *CompanyName* could be shortened to *CoName* and a field such as *EmailAddress* could be shortened to *Email*.

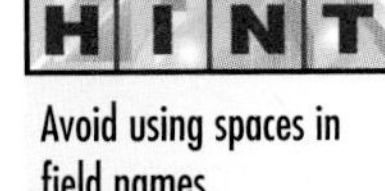

Avoid using spaces in field names.

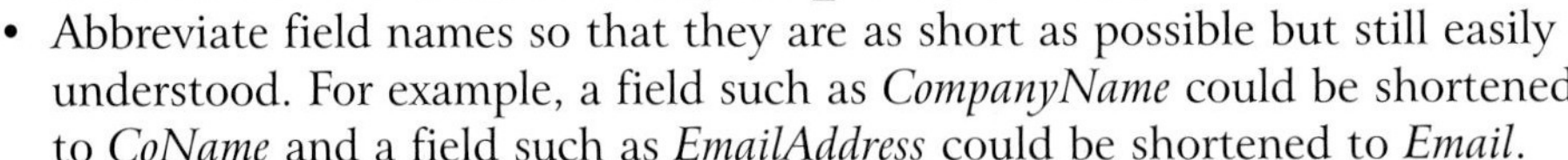

Project 2e Creating a Table and Entering Data — Part 5 of 7

1. With **AL1-C1-PacTrek.accdb** open, create a new table and specify data types and column headings by completing the following steps:
   a. Click the CREATE tab.
   b. Click the Table button in the Tables group.
   c. Click the Short Text button in the Add & Delete group.

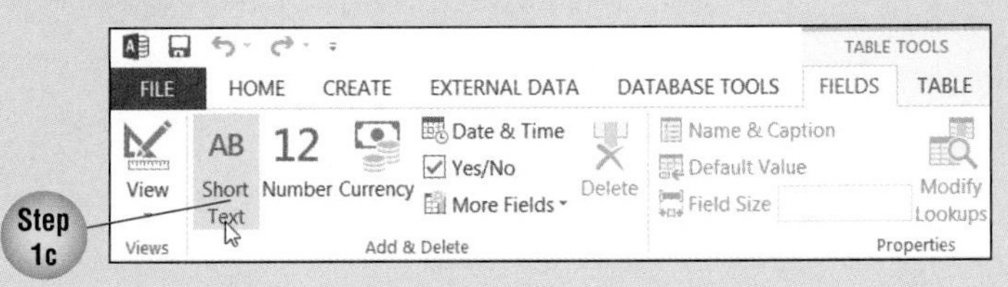

d. With the *Field1* column heading selected, type **SupplierID** and then press the Enter key. (This displays a drop-down list of data types below the *Click to Add* heading.)

e. Click the *Short Text* option at the drop-down list.

f. Type **ProductID** and then press Enter.

g. Click *Number* at the drop-down list, type **UnitsOrdered**, and then press Enter.

h. Click *Currency* at the drop-down list, type **Amount**, and then press Enter.

i. Click *Date & Time* at the drop-down list and then type **OrderDate**. (Do not press the Enter key since this is the last column in the table.)

2. Enter the first record in the table, as shown in Figure 1.12, by completing the following steps:
   a. Click twice in the first field below the *SupplierID* column heading. (The first time you click the mouse button, the row is selected. Clicking the second time makes active only the field below *SupplierID*.)
   b. Type the data in the fields as shown in Figure 1.12. Press the Tab key to move to the next field or press Shift + Tab to move to the previous field. Access will automatically insert the next number in the sequence in the first column (the *ID* column). When typing the money amounts in the *Amount* column, you do not need to type the dollar sign or the comma. Access will automatically insert them when you make the next field active.
3. When the 14 records have been entered, click the Save button on the Quick Access toolbar.
4. At the Save As dialog box, type **Orders** and then press the Enter key. (This saves the table with the name *Orders*.)
5. Close the Orders table by clicking the Close button located in the upper right corner of the work area.

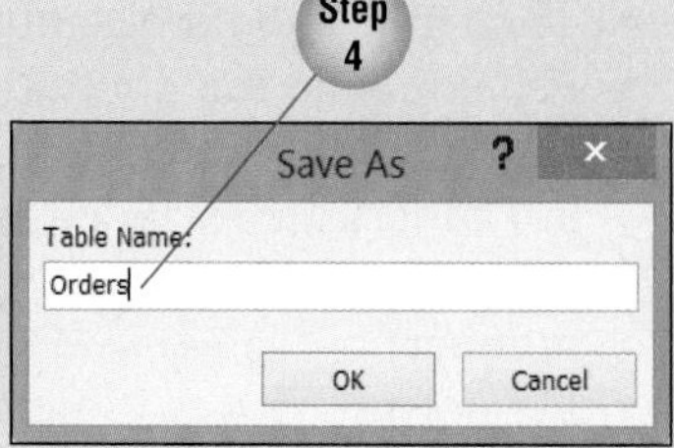

Figure 1.12 Project 2e

Orders

	ID	SupplierID	ProductID	UnitsOrderec	Amount	OrderDate	Click to Add
	1	54	101-S3	10	$1,137.50	1/5/2015	
	2	68	209-L	25	$173.75	1/5/2015	
	3	68	209-XL	25	$180.00	1/5/2015	
	4	68	209-XXL	20	$145.80	1/5/2015	
	5	68	210-M	15	$97.35	1/5/2015	
	6	68	210-L	25	$162.25	1/5/2015	
	7	31	299-M2	10	$887.90	1/19/2015	
	8	31	299-M3	10	$887.90	1/19/2015	
	9	31	299-M5	10	$887.90	1/19/2015	
	10	31	299-W1	8	$602.32	1/19/2015	
	11	31	299-W3	10	$752.90	1/19/2015	
	12	31	299-W4	10	$752.90	1/19/2015	
	13	31	299-W5	10	$752.90	1/19/2015	
	14	35	602-XR	5	$2,145.00	1/19/2015	
*	(New)			0	$0.00		

Renaming a Field Heading

When you click a data type button or click a data type at the data type drop-down list, the default heading (such as *Field1*) is automatically selected. You can type a name for the field heading that takes the place of the selected text. If you create a field heading and then decide to change the name, right-click the heading, click *Rename Field* at the shortcut menu (which selects the current column heading), and then type the new name.

Inserting a Name, Caption, and Description

When you create a table that others will use, consider providing additional information so users understand the fields in the table and what should be entered in each one. Along with the field heading name, you can provide a caption and description for each field with options at the Enter Field Properties dialog box, shown in Figure 1.13. Display this dialog by clicking the Name & Caption button in the Properties group on the TABLE TOOLS FIELDS tab.

Name & Caption

At the Enter Field Properties dialog box, type the desired name for the field heading in the *Name* text box. If you want a more descriptive name for the field heading, type the heading in the *Caption* text box. The text you type will display as the field heading but the actual field name will still be part of the table structure. Creating a caption is useful if you abbreviate a field name or want to show spaces between words in a field name. A caption also provides more information for others using the database. The name is what Access uses for the table and the caption is what displays to users.

The *Description* text box is another source for providing information about the field to others using the database. Type information in the text box that specifies what should be entered in the field. The text you type in the *Description* text box displays at the left side of the Status bar when a field in the column is active. For example, if you type *Enter the total amount of the order* in the *Description* text box for the *Amount* field column, that text will display at the left side of the Status bar when a field in the column is active.

Figure 1.13 Enter Field Properties Dialog Box

Type in the *Caption* text box a more descriptive name for the field heading.
Type information in the *Description* text box that specifies what should be entered in the field.
Enter Field Properties
?
Name
SupplierID
Caption
Description
OK
Cancel

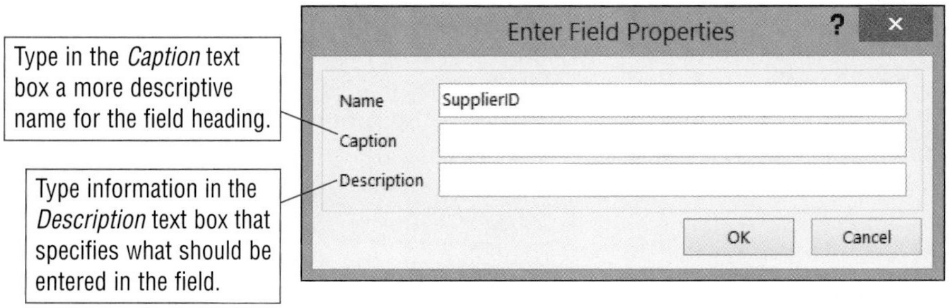

Project 2f Inserting a Name, Caption, and Description

Part 6 of 7

1. With **AL1-C1-PacTrek.accdb** open, open the Orders table.
2. Access automatically named the first field *ID*. You want to make the heading more descriptive so you decide to rename the heading. To do this, right-click the *ID* heading and then click *Rename Field* at the drop-down list.
3. Type **OrderID** and then press the Enter key.
4. To provide more information for others using the table, you decide to add information for the *SupplierID* field by creating a caption and description. To do this, complete the following steps:
   a. Click the *SupplierID* field heading. (This selects the entire column.)
   b. Click the TABLE TOOLS FIELDS tab.
   c. Click the Name & Caption button in the Properties group. (At the Enter Field Properties dialog box, notice that *SupplierID* is already inserted in the *Name* text box.)
   d. At the Enter Field Properties dialog box, click in the *Caption* text box and then type **Supplier Number**.
   e. Click in the *Description* text box and then type **Supplier identification number**.
   f. Click OK to close the dialog box. (Notice that the field name now displays as *Supplier Number*. The field name is still *SupplierID* but what displays is *Supplier Number*.)
5. Click the *ProductID* field heading and then complete steps similar to those in Steps 4c through 4f to create the caption *Product Number* and the description *Product identification number*.
6. Click the *Amount* field heading and then complete steps similar to those in Steps 4c through 4f to create the caption *Order Amount* and the description *Total amount of order*.
7. Click the Save button on the Quick Access toolbar to save the changes to the Orders table.
8. Close the Orders table.

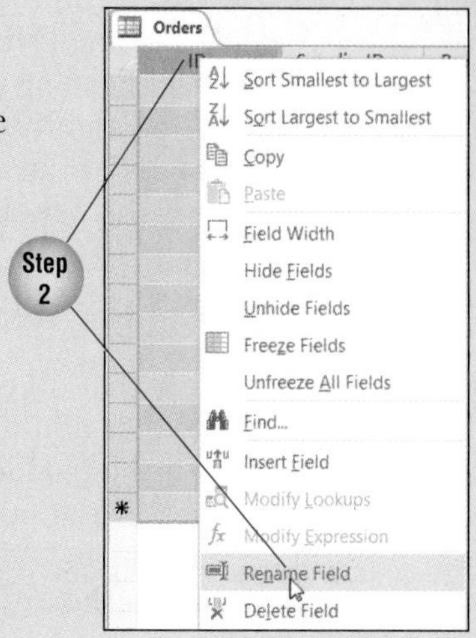

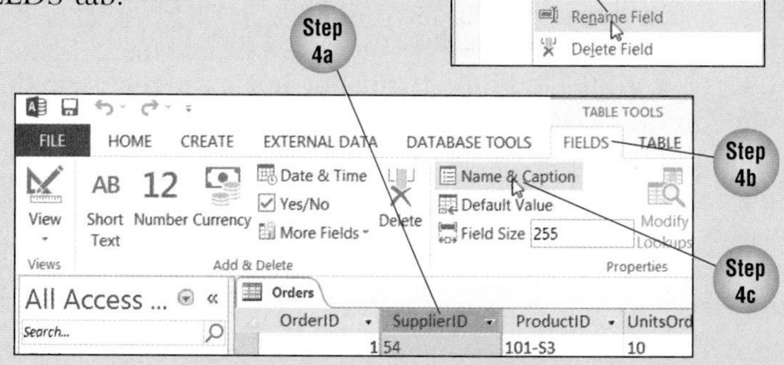

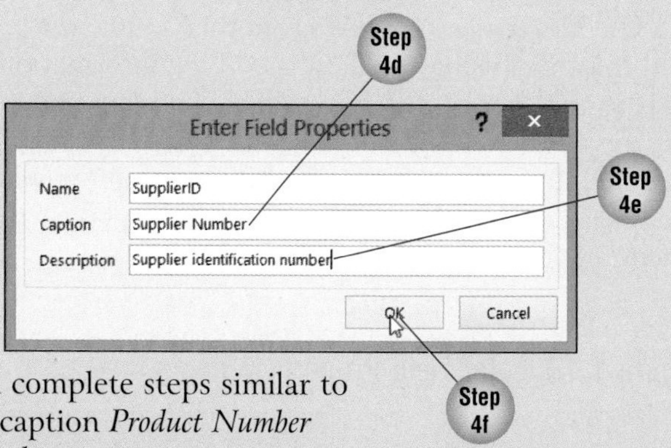

Inserting Quick Start Fields

Short Text

The Add & Delete group on the TABLE TOOLS FIELDS tab contains buttons for specifying data types. You used the Short Text button to specify the data type for the *SupplierID* field when you created the Orders table. You also used the field heading drop-down list to choose a data type. In addition to these two methods, you can specify a data type by clicking the More Fields button in the Add & Delete group on the TABLE TOOLS FIELDS tab. When you click this button, a drop-down list displays with data types grouped into categories such as *Basic Types*, *Number*, *Date and Time*, *Yes/No*, and *Quick Start*.

The options in the *Quick Start* category not only define a data type but also assign a field name. Additionally, with options in the *Quick Start* category, you can add a group of related fields in one step. For example, if you click the *Name* option in the *Quick Start* category, Access inserts the *LastName* field in one column and the *FirstName* field in the next column. Both fields are automatically assigned a short text data type. If you click the *Address* option in the *Quick Start* category, Access inserts five fields, including *Address*, *City*, *StateProvince*, *ZIPPostal*, and *CountryRegion*—all with the short text data type assigned.

Assigning a Default Value

The Properties group on the TABLE TOOLS FIELDS tab contains additional buttons for defining field properties in a table. If most records in a table are likely to contain the same field value in a column, consider inserting that value by default. Do this by clicking the Default Value button in the Properties group. At the Expression Builder dialog box, type the desired default value and then click OK.

Default Value

For example, in Project 2g, you will create a new table in the AL1-C1-PacTrek database containing information on customers, most of whom live in Vancouver, British Columbia. You will create a default value of *Vancouver* for the *City* field and a default value of *BC* for the *Prov/State* field. You can replace the default value with different text, so if a customer lives in Abbotsford instead of Vancouver, simply type *Abbotsford* in the *City* field instead.

Assigning a Field Size

The default field size property varies depending on the data type. For example, if you assign a short text data type to a field, the maximum length of the data you can enter in the field is 255 characters. You can decrease this number depending on what data will be entered in the field. You can also change the field size number to control how much data is entered and help reduce errors. For example, if you have a field for states and you want a two-letter state abbreviation inserted in each field in the column, you can assign a field size of 2 characters. If someone entering data into the table tries to type more than two letters, Access will not accept the additional text. To change field size, click in the *Field Size* text box in the Properties group on the TABLE TOOLS FIELDS tab and then type the desired number.

Changing the AutoNumber Field

Access automatically applies the AutoNumber data type to the first field in a table and assigns a unique number to each record in the table. In many cases, letting Access automatically assign a number to a record is a good idea. Some situations may arise, however, when you want the unique value in the first field to be something other than a number.

If you try to change the AutoNumber data type in the first column by clicking one of the data type buttons in the Add & Delete group on the TABLE TOOLS FIELDS tab, Access creates another field. To change the AutoNumber data type for the first field, click the down-pointing arrow at the right side of the *Data Type* option box in the Formatting group on the TABLE TOOLS FIELDS tab and then click the desired data type at the drop-down list.

Project 2g Creating a Customers Table

1. The owners of Pacific Trek have decided to publish a semiannual product catalog and have asked customers who want to receive the catalog to fill out a form and include on the form whether or not they want to receive notices of upcoming sales in addition to the catalog. Create a table to store the data for customers by completing the following steps:
   a. With **AL1-C1-PacTrek.accdb** open, click the CREATE tab.
   b. Click the Table button in the Tables group.
   c. With the *Click to Add* field heading active, click the More Fields button in the Add & Delete group on the TABLE TOOLS FIELDS tab.
   d. Scroll down the drop-down list and then click *Name* located in the *Quick Start* category. (This inserts the *Last Name* and *First Name* field headings in the table.)

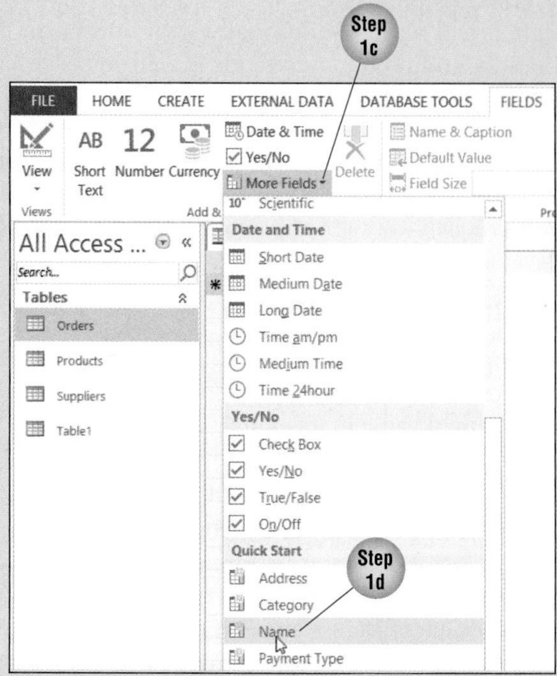

   e. Click the *Click to Add* field heading that displays immediately right of the *First Name* field heading. (The data type drop-down list displays. You are going to use the More Fields button rather than the drop-down list to create the next fields.)
   f. Click the More Fields button, scroll down the drop-down list, and then click *Address* in the *Quick Start* category. (This inserts five more fields in the table.)
   g. Scroll to the right in the table to display the *Click to Add* field heading that follows the *Country Region* column heading. (You can scroll in the table using the horizontal scroll bar that displays to the right of the Record Navigation bar.)
   h. Click the *Click to Add* field heading and then click *Yes/No* at the drop-down list.
   i. With the name *Field1* selected, type Mailers. (When entering records in the table, you will insert a check mark in the field check box if a customer wants to receive sales promotion mailers. If a customer does not want to receive the mailers, you will leave the check box blank.)

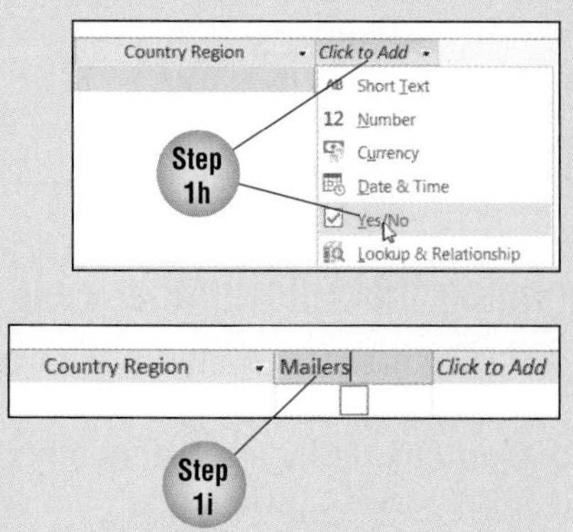

2. Rename and create a caption and description for the *ID* column heading by completing the following steps:
   a. Scroll to the beginning of the table and then click the *ID* column heading. (You can scroll in the table using the horizontal scroll bar that displays to the right of the Record Navigation bar.)
   b. Click the Name & Caption button in the Properties group on the TABLE TOOLS FIELDS tab.

c. At the Enter Field Properties dialog box, select the text *ID* that displays in the *Name* text box and then type **CustomerID**.
d. Press the Tab key and then type **Customer Number** in the *Caption* text box.
e. Press the Tab key and then type **Access will automatically assign the record the next number in the sequence.**
f. Click OK to close the Enter Field Properties dialog box. (Notice the description that displays at the left side of the Status bar.)

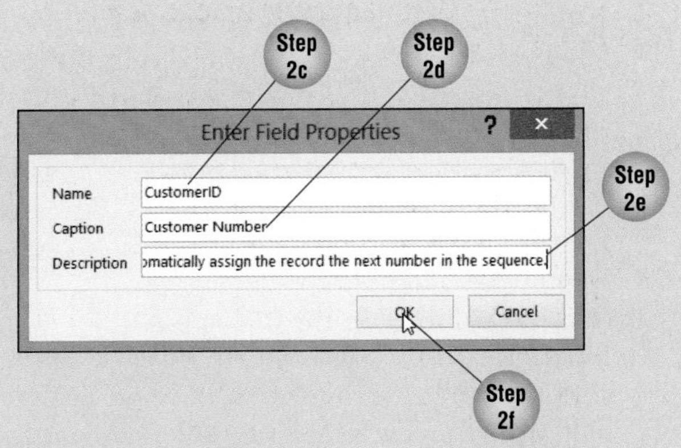

3. Add a description to the *Last Name* column by completing the following steps:
   a. Click the *Last Name* column heading.
   b. Click the Name & Caption button in the Properties group.
   c. At the Enter Field Properties dialog box notice that Access named the field *LastName* but provided the caption *Last Name*. You do not want to change the name and caption so press the Tab key twice to make the *Description* text box active and then type **Customer last name.**
   d. Click OK to close the dialog box.
4. You know that a customer's last name will not likely exceed 30 characters, so you decide to limit the field size. To do this, click in the *Field Size* text box in the Properties group (this selects *255*), type **30**, and then press the Enter key.
5. Click the *First Name* column heading and then complete steps similar to those in Steps 3 and 4 to create the description *Customer first name* and change the field size to 30 characters.
6. Since most of Pacific Trek's customers live in the city of Vancouver, you decide to make it the default field value. To do this, complete the following steps:
   a. Click the *City* column heading.
   b. Click the Default Value button in the Properties group.
   c. At the Expression Builder dialog box, type **Vancouver**.
   d. Click the OK button to close the dialog box.

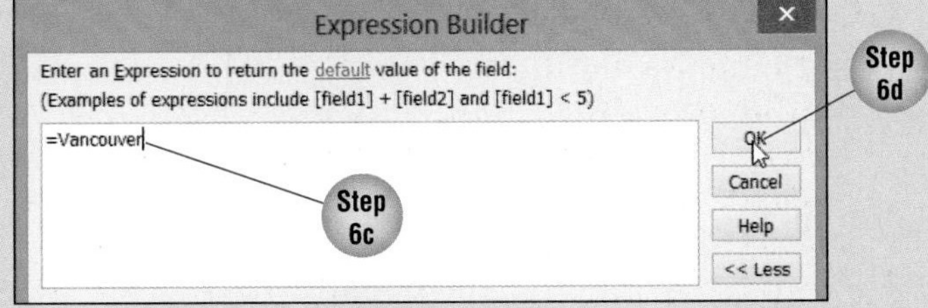

7. Change the name of the *State Province* field name and insert a default value by completing the following steps:
   a. Right-click the *State Province* column heading and then click *Rename Field* at the shortcut menu.
   b. Type **Province**.
   c. Click the Default Value button in the Properties group.
   d. Type **BC** in the Expression Builder dialog box and then click the OK button.
8. Click the *ZIP Postal* column heading and then limit the field size to 7 characters by clicking

in the *Field Size* text box (which selects *255*), typing 7, and then pressing the Enter key.

9. Since most customers want to be sent the sales promotional mailers, you decide to insert a check mark as the default value in the check boxes in the *Yes/No* column. To do this, complete the following steps:
   a. Click the *Mailers* field heading.
   b. Click the Default Value button in the Properties group.
   c. At the Expression Builder dialog box, press the Backspace key two times to delete *No* and then type **Yes**.
   d. Click OK to close the dialog box.
10. Delete the *Country Region* field by clicking the *Country Region* field heading and then clicking the Delete button in the Add & Delete group.
11. Save the table by completing the following steps:
    a. Click the Save button on the Quick Access toolbar.
    b. At the Save As dialog box, type **Customers** and then press Enter.
12. Enter the six records in the table shown in Figure 1.14. To remove a check mark in the *Mailers* column, press the spacebar.
13. Adjust the column widths to accommodate the longest entry in each column by completing the following steps:
    a. Position the arrow pointer on the *Customer Number* field heading until the pointer turns into a down-pointing black arrow, hold down the left mouse button, drag to the *Mailers* field heading, and then release the mouse button.
    b. With the columns selected, double-click one of the column boundaries.
14. Click the Save button to save the Customers table.
15. Print the Customers table by completing the following steps:
    a. Click the FILE tab and then click the *Print* option.
    b. At the Print backstage area, click the Print Preview button.
    c. Click the Landscape button in the Page Layout group on the PRINT PREVIEW tab.
    d. Click the Print button that displays at the left side of the PRINT PREVIEW tab.
    e. At the Print dialog box, click OK.
16. Close the Customers table.
17. Open the Orders table.
18. Automatically adjust the column widths to accommodate the longest entry in each column.
19. Click the Save button to save the Orders table.
20. Print the table in landscape orientation (refer to Step 15) and then close the table.
21. Close **AL1-C1-PacTrek.accdb**.

Figure 1.14 Project 2g

Customers

	Customer Number	Last Name	First Name	Address	City	State Province	ZIP Postal	Mailers
	1	Blakely	Mathias	7433 224th Ave. E.	Vancouver	BC	V5K 2M7	✔
	2	Donato	Antonio	18225 Victoria Dr.	Vancouver	BC	V5K 1H4	☐
	3	Girard	Stephanie	430 Deer Lake Pl.	Burnaby	BC	V3J 1E4	✔
	4	Hernandez	Angelica	1233 E. 59th Ave.	Vancouver	BC	V5K 3H3	✔
	5	Ives-Keller	Shane	9055 Gilbert Rd.	Richmond	BC	V6Y 1B2	☐
	6	Kim	Keung	730 West Broadway	Vancouver	BC	V5K 5B2	✔
*	(New)				Vancouver	BC		✔

Chapter Summary

- Microsoft Access is a database management system software program that can organize, store, maintain, retrieve, sort, and print all types of business data.
- In Access, open an existing database by clicking the Open Other Files hyperlink at the Access 2013 opening screen. At the Open backstage area, double-click your OneDrive or the *Computer* option. At the Open dialog box, navigate to the location of the database and then double-click the desired database.
- Some common objects found in a database include tables, queries, forms, and reports.
- The Navigation pane displays at the left side of the Access screen and displays the objects that are contained in the database.
- Open a database object by double-clicking the object in the Navigation pane. Close an object by clicking the Close button that displays in the upper right corner of the work area.
- When a table is open, the Record Navigation bar displays at the bottom of the screen and contains buttons for displaying records in the table.
- Insert a new record in a table by clicking the New button in the Records group on the HOME tab or by clicking the New (blank) record button in the Record Navigation bar. Delete a record by clicking in a field in the record you want to delete, clicking the Delete button arrow on the HOME tab, and then clicking *Delete Record* at the drop-down list.
- To add a column to a table, click the first field below the *Click to Add* column heading and then type the desired data. To move a column, select the column and then use the mouse to drag a thick, black, vertical line (representing the column) to the desired location. To delete a column, click the column heading, click the Delete button arrow, and then click *Delete Column* at the drop-down list.
- Data you enter in a table is automatically saved while changes to the layout of a table are not automatically saved.
- Hide, unhide, freeze, and unfreeze columns with options at the More button drop-down list. Display this list by clicking the More button in the Records group on the HOME tab.
- Adjust the width of a column (or selected columns) to accommodate the longest entry by double-clicking the column boundary. You can also adjust the width of a column by dragging the column boundary.
- Rename a table by right-clicking the table name in the Navigation pane, clicking *Rename*, and then typing the new name. Delete a table by right-clicking the table name in the Navigation pane and then clicking *Delete*.
- Print a table by clicking the FILE tab, clicking the *Print* option, and then clicking the Quick Print button. You can also preview a table before printing by clicking the Print Preview button at the Print backstage area.
- With buttons and option on the PRINT PREVIEW tab, you can change the page size, orientation, and margins.
- The first principle in database design is to reduce redundant data, because redundant data increases the amount of data entry required, increases the chances for errors, and takes up additional storage space.
- A data type defines the type of data Access will allow in the field. Assign a data type to a field with buttons in the Add & Delete group on the TABLE TOOLS

FIELDS tab, by clicking an option from the column heading drop-down list, or with options at the More button drop-down list.

- Rename a column heading by right-clicking the heading, clicking *Rename Field* at the shortcut menu, and then typing the new name.
- Type a name, caption, and description for a column with options at the Enter Field Properties dialog box.
- Use options in the *Quick Start* category in the More Fields button drop-down list to define a data type and assign a field name to a group of related fields.
- Insert a default value in a column with the Default Value button and assign a field size with the *Field Size* text box in the Properties group on the TABLE TOOLS FIELDS tab.
- Use the *Data Type* option box in the Formatting group on the TABLE TOOLS FIELDS tab to change the AutoNumber data type for the first column in a table.

Commands Review

FEATURE	RIBBON TAB, GROUP/OPTION	BUTTON, OPTION	KEYBOARD SHORTCUT
close Access			Alt + F4
close database	FILE, *Close*		
create table	CREATE, Tables		
Currency data type	TABLE TOOLS FIELDS, Add & Delete		
Date & Time data type	TABLE TOOLS FIELDS, Add & Delete		
delete column	HOME, Records	, *Delete Column*	
delete record	HOME, Records	, *Delete Record*	
Enter Field Properties dialog box	TABLE TOOLS FIELDS, Properties		
Expression Builder dialog box	TABLE TOOLS FIELDS, Properties		
freeze column	HOME, Records	, *Freeze Fields*	
hide column	HOME, Records	, *Hide Fields*	
landscape orientation	FILE, *Print*	Print Preview,	
new record	HOME, Records		Ctrl + +
next field			Tab
Number data type	TABLE TOOLS FIELDS, Add & Delete	12	
Page Setup dialog box	FILE, *Print*	Print Preview,	

FEATURE	RIBBON TAB, GROUP/OPTION	BUTTON, OPTION	KEYBOARD SHORTCUT
page size	FILE, *Print*	Print Preview,	
page margins	FILE, *Print*	Print Preview,	
portrait orientation	FILE, *Print*	Print Preview,	
previous field			Shift + Tab
Print backstage area	FILE, *Print*		
Print dialog box	FILE, *Print*	Print	Ctrl + P
Print Preview	FILE, *Print*	Print Preview	
Short Text data type	TABLE TOOLS FIELDS, Add & Delete	AB	
unfreeze column	HOME, Records	, *Unfreeze Fields*	
unhide column	HOME, Records	, *Unhide Fields*	
Yes/No data type	TABLE TOOLS FIELDS, Add & Delete		

Concepts Check Test Your Knowledge

Completion: In the space provided at the right, indicate the correct term, symbol, or command.

1. Click this template at the Access 2013 opening screen to create a new database. ________________
2. This toolbar contains buttons for commonly used commands. ________________
3. This displays the names of objects within a database grouped by categories. ________________
4. When you open a table, it displays in this view. ________________
5. Use buttons on this bar to navigate in a table. ________________
6. To add a new record, click the New button in this group on the HOME tab. ________________
7. At the Print backstage area, click this button to send the table directly to the printer. ________________
8. The Landscape button is located in this group on the PRINT PREVIEW tab. ________________

9. All fields for one unit, such as an employee or customer, are considered to be this. ________________

10. Assign this data type to values that involve money. ________________

11. Click this button in the Properties group on the TABLE TOOLS FIELDS tab to display the Enter Field Properties dialog box. ________________

12. With options in this category in the More Fields button drop-down list, you can define a data type and also assign a field name. ________________

13. If you want to assign the same field value to a column, click this button to display the Expression Builder dialog box and then type the desired value. ________________

Skills Check Assess Your Performance

The database designer for Griffin Technologies has created the database diagram shown in Figure 1.15 to manage data about company employees. You will open the Griffin database and maintain and create tables that follow the diagram.

Figure 1.15 Griffin Technologies Database Diagram

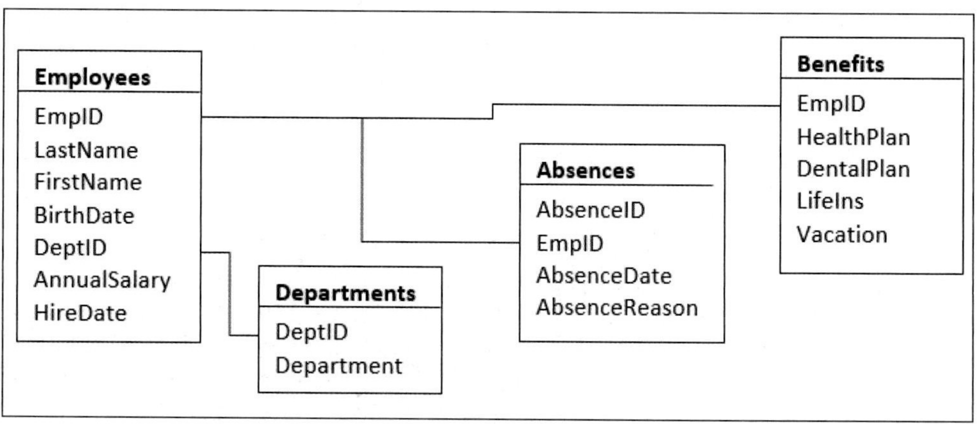

Assessment 1

INSERTING AND DELETING ROWS AND COLUMNS

1. In Access, open **AL1-C1-Griffin.accdb** from the AL1C1 folder on your storage medium and enable the contents.
2. Double-click *Employees* in the Tables group in the Navigation pane.
3. Delete the record for Scott Jorgensen (employee number 1025).
4. Delete the record for Leanne Taylor (employee number 1060).

5. Insert the following records:

EmpID: **1010**	EmpID: **1052**
LastName: **Harrington**	LastName: **Reeves**
FirstName: **Tyler**	FirstName: **Carrie**
Birthdate: **9/7/1976**	Birthdate: **12/4/1978**
AnnualSalary: **$53,350**	AnnualSalary: **$38,550**
HireDate: **10/1/2010**	HireDate: **10/1/2012**

6. Close the Employees table.
7. Looking at the database diagram in Figure 1.15, you realize that the Employees table includes a *DeptID* field. Open the Employees table, insert the new field in the Employees table, and name it *DeptID*. Change the field size to 2 characters (since department abbreviations are only one or two letters in length). At the message telling you that some data may be lost, click the Yes button. Type the department identification for each record as shown below (the records are listed from left to right):

1001: HR	1002: RD	1003: IT	1005: DP	1010: DP
1013: RD	1015: HR	1020: A	1023: IT	1030: PR
1033: A	1040: DP	1043: HR	1045: RD	1050: IT
1052: PR	1053: HR	1063: DP	1065: DP	1080: IT
1083: HR	1085: PR	1090: RD	1093: A	1095: RD

8. Move the *DeptID* column so it is positioned between the *BirthDate* column and the *AnnualSalary* column.
9. Automatically adjust the widths of the columns.
10. Save the table.
11. Display the table in Print Preview, change the top margin to 1.5 inches, change the left margin to 1.25 inches, and then print the table.
12. Close the Employees table.

Assessment 2

CREATE A DEPARTMENTS TABLE

SNAP Grade It

1. You entered a one- or two-letter abbreviation representing each department within the company. Creating the abbreviations saved you from having to type the entire department name for each record. You need to create the Departments table that will provide the department name for each abbreviation. Create a new table in the **AL1-C1-Griffin.accdb** database with the column headings and data shown in Figure 1.16 by completing the following steps:
   a. Click the CREATE tab and then click the Table button.
   b. Click the *ID* column heading, click the down-pointing arrow at the right side of the *Data Type* option box in the Formatting group, and then click *Short Text* at the drop-down list.
   c. Limit the field size to 2 characters and rename the heading as *DeptID*.
   d. Click the *Click to Add* column heading, click *Short Text* at the drop-down list, and then type **Department**.
   e. Type the data in the fields as shown in Figure 1.16 on the next page.
   f. Automatically adjust the widths of the columns.
2. Save the table and name it *Departments*.
3. Print and then close the table.

Figure 1.16 Departments Table

DeptID	Department	Click to Add
A	Accounting	
DP	Design and Production	
HR	Human Resources	
IT	Information Technology Services	
PR	Public Relations	
RD	Research and Development	
*		

Assessment 3

CREATE A BENEFITS TABLE

SNAP Grade It

1. Create a new table in **AL1-C1-Griffin.accdb** with the data shown in Figure 1.17 and with the following specifications:
   a. Name the fields as shown in the Benefits table in the diagram in Figure 1.15 and create the caption names for the fields as shown in Figure 1.17. (For example, name the life insurance field *LifeIns* and create the caption *Life Insurance*.)
   b. For the first column (EmpID), click the *ID* column heading, click the down-pointing arrow at the right side of the *Data Type* option box in the Formatting group, and then click *Short Text* at the drop-down list. Limit the field size to 4 characters and rename the field as *EmpID*.
   c. Apply the Yes/No data type to the second column, make the default value a check mark (by typing Yes at the Expression Builder dialog box), and provide the description *A check mark indicates the employee has signed up for the health plan.*

Figure 1.17 Benefits Table

EmployeeID	Health Plan	Dental Plan	Life Insurance	Vacation	Click to Add
103	✔	✔	$100,000.00	4 weeks	
105	✔	✔	$200,000.00	3 weeks	
106	☐	✔	$150,000.00	3 weeks	
109	✔	✔	$200,000.00	3 weeks	
110	✔	✔	$185,000.00	4 weeks	
112	☐	✔	$200,000.00	3 weeks	
117	☐	☐	$100,000.00	3 weeks	
120	✔	✔	$200,000.00	4 weeks	
122	☐	☐	$75,000.00	2 weeks	
125	✔	✔	$125,000.00	3 weeks	
128	✔	✔	$200,000.00	3 weeks	
130	✔	✔	$200,000.00	3 weeks	
132	☐	☐	$50,000.00	2 weeks	
138	✔	☐	$125,000.00	2 weeks	
141	✔	✔	$85,000.00	3 weeks	
143	✔	✔	$175,000.00	3 weeks	
149	✔	☐	$100,000.00	2 weeks	
152	✔	✔	$150,000.00	2 weeks	
153	✔	✔	$200,000.00	2 weeks	
155	☐	✔	$150,000.00	1 week	
159	✔	☐	$75,000.00	1 week	
163	✔	✔	$125,000.00	1 week	
165	✔	☐	$150,000.00	1 week	
170	☐	✔	$185,000.00	1 week	
173	✔	✔	$125,000.00	1 week	
*	✔	✔			

d. Apply the Yes/No data type to the third column, make the default value a check mark (by typing **Yes** at the Expression Builder dialog box), and provide the description *A check mark indicates the employee has signed up for the dental plan.*
e. Apply the Currency data type to the fourth column.
f. Apply the Short Text data type to the fifth column and limit the field size to 8 characters.
g. Type the data in each record as shown in Figure 1.17.
h. Automatically adjust the column widths.
i. Save the table and name it *Benefits*.
2. Display the table in Print Preview, change the top and left margins to 1.5 inches, and then print the table.
3. Close the Benefits table.

Assessment 4

SORT DATA

1. With **AL1-C1-Griffin.accdb** open, open the Employees table.
2. Experiment with the buttons in the Sort & Filter group on the HOME tab and determine how to sort columns of data in ascending and descending order.
3. Sort the records in the Employees table in ascending order by last name.
4. Save, print, and then close the Employees table.
5. Open the Benefits table and then sort the records in descending order by life insurance amounts.
6. Save, print, and then close the Benefits table.

Visual Benchmark Demonstrate Your Proficiency

CREATE AN ABSENCES TABLE

1. With **AL1-C1-Griffin.accdb** open, create the Absences table shown in Figure 1.18 (using the field names as shown in Figure 1.15 on page 36) with the following specifications:
   a. Use the default AutoNumber data type for column 1. Apply the appropriate data type to the other columns.
   b. Create an appropriate caption and description for the *EmpID*, *AbsenceDate*, and *AbsenceReason* columns.
   c. Apply the default value of Sick Day to the *AbsenceReason* column. (You will need to type "**Sick Day**" in the Expression Builder dialog box.)
2. Save the table and name it *Absences*.
3. Print the table in landscape orientation with top and left margins of 1.5 inches.
4. Close the Absences table and then close **AL1-C1-Griffin.accdb**.

Figure 1.18 Visual Benchmark

Absences

AbsenceID	EmpID	Absent Date	Absent Reason	Click to Add
1	141	1/2/2015	Sick Day	
2	141	1/5/2015	Sick Day	
3	105	1/6/2015	Sick Day	
4	163	1/9/2015	Sick Day	
5	125	1/9/2015	Bereavement	
6	125	1/12/2015	Bereavement	
7	125	1/12/2015	Bereavement	
8	117	1/13/2015	Sick Day	
9	170	1/14/2015	Personal Day	
10	153	1/16/2015	Sick Day	
11	153	1/19/2015	Sick Day	
12	103	1/19/2015	Personal Day	
13	109	1/20/2015	Sick Day	
14	109	1/22/2015	Sick Day	
15	167	1/23/2015	Personal Day	
16	138	1/29/2015	Sick Day	
17	159	1/30/2015	Sick Day	
* (New)			Sick Day	

Case Study Apply Your Skills

You are the office manager for Elite Limousines, and your company is switching over to Access for managing company data. The database designer has provided you with the database diagram in Figure 1.19. She wants you to follow the diagram when creating the database.

Figure 1.19 Elite Limousines Database Diagram

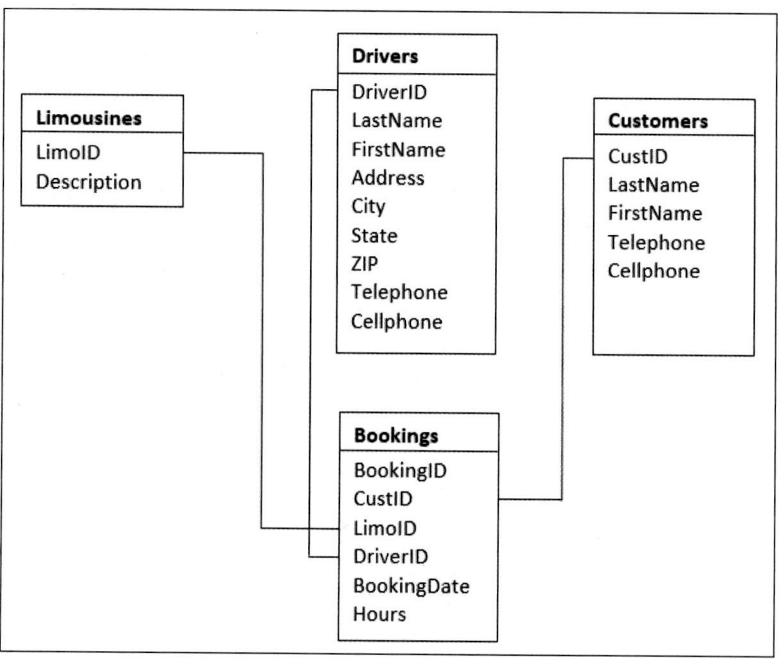

Part 1

Create a new database named **AL1-C1-Elite.accdb** and then create the Limousines table shown in the database diagram in Figure 1.19. The database designer has asked you to include an appropriate caption and description for each field and to change the field size for the *LimoID* field. Type the following records in the table:

LimoID: **01**
Description: **2011 White stretch**

LimoID: **02**
Description: **2011 Black stretch**

LimoID: **04**
Description: **2012 Black minibus**

LimoID: **06**
Description: **2012 Black standard**

LimoID: **08**
Description: **2014 Black SUV stretch**

LimoID: **10**
Description: **2015 Black stretch**

Part 2

With **AL1-C1-Elite.accdb** open, create the Drivers table shown in the database diagram shown in Figure 1.19. Include appropriate captions and descriptions for each field and change the field sizes where appropriate. Type the following records in the table:

DriverID#: **101**
LastName: **Brennan**
FirstName: **Andrea**
Address: **4438 Gowan Rd.**
City: **Las Vegas**
State: **NV**
ZIP: **89115**
Telephone: **(702) 555-3481**
Cellphone: **(702) 555-1322**

DriverID: **114**
LastName: **Gould**
FirstName: **Randall**
Address: **330 Aura Ave.**
City: **Las Vegas**
State: **NV**
ZIP: **89052**
Telephone: **(702) 555-1239**
Cellphone: **(702) 555-7474**

DriverID: **120**
LastName: **Martinelli**
FirstName: **Albert**
Address: **107 Cameo Dr.**
City: **Las Vegas**
State: **NV**
ZIP: **89138**
Telephone: **(702) 555-0349**
Cellphone: **(702) 555-6649**

DriverID: **125**
LastName: **Nunez**
FirstName: **Frank**
Address: **4832 Helena St.**
City: **Las Vegas**
State: **NV**
ZIP: **89129**
Telephone: **(702) 555-3748**
Cellphone: **(702) 555-2210**

Part 3

With **AL1-C1-Elite.accdb** open, create the Customers table shown in the database diagram in Figure 1.19. Include appropriate captions and descriptions for the fields and change the field sizes where appropriate. Type the following records in the table:

CustID: 1001
LastName: Spencer
FirstName: Maureen
Telephone: (513) 555-3943
Cellphone: (513) 555-4884

CustID: 1002
LastName: Tsang
FirstName: Lee
Telephone: (702) 555-4775
Cellphone: (702) 555-4211

CustID: 1028
LastName: Gabriel
FirstName: Nicholas
Telephone: (612) 555-7885
Cellphone: (612) 555-7230

CustID: 1031
LastName: Marshall
FirstName: Patricia
Telephone: (702) 555-6410
Cellphone: (702) 555-0137

CustID: 1010
LastName: Chavez
FirstName: Blake
Telephone: (206) 555-3774
Cellphone: (206) 555-3006

CustID: 1044
LastName: Vanderhage
FirstName: Vernon
Telephone: (213) 555-8846
Cellphone: (213) 555-4635

Part 4

With **AL1-C1-Elite.accdb** open, create the Bookings table shown in the database diagram in Figure 1.19. Include appropriate captions and descriptions for the fields and change the field sizes where appropriate. Type the following records in the table:

BookingID: (AutoNumber)
CustID: 1044
LimoID: 02
DriverID: 114
BookingDate: 7/1/2015
Hours: 6

BookingID: (AutoNumber)
CustID: 1001
LimoID: 10
DriverID: 120
BookingDate: 7/1/2015
Hours: 8

BookingID: (AutoNumber)
CustID: 1002
LimoID: 04
DriverID: 101
BookingDate: 7/6/2015
Hours: 8

BookingID: (AutoNumber)
CustID: 1028
LimoID: 02
DriverID: 125
BookingDate: 7/6/2015
Hours: 4

BookingID: (AutoNumber)
CustID: 1010
LimoID: 06
DriverID: 125
BookingDate: 7/3/2015
Hours: 3

BookingID: (AutoNumber)
CustID: 1031
LimoID: 08
DriverID: 120
BookingDate: 7/7/2015
Hours: 5

Automatically adjust the column widths of each table to accommodate the longest entry in each column. Print each table so all records fit on one page.

MICROSOFT®

ACCESS®

Creating Relationships between Tables

PERFORMANCE OBJECTIVES

Upon successful completion of Chapter 2, you will be able to:

- **Define a primary key in a table**
- **Create a one-to-many relationship**
- **Specify referential integrity**
- **Print, edit, and delete relationships**
- **Create a one-to-one relationship**
- **View and edit a subdatasheet**

Tutorials

2.1 Defining a Primary Key

2.2 Deleting a Relationship; Printing a Relationships Report

2.3 Creating a Relationship between Two Tables in a Database

2.4 Creating a One-to-One Relationship between Tables

2.5 Editing a Relationship; Enforcing Referential Integrity; Viewing a Subdatasheet

Access is a relational database program you can use to create tables that are related or connected within the same database. When a relationship is established between tables, you can view and edit records in related tables with a subdatasheet. In this chapter, you will learn how to identify a primary key in a table that is unique to that table, how to join tables by creating a relationship between them, and how to view and edit subdatasheets. Model answers for this chapter's projects appear on the following pages.

AL1C2

Note: Before beginning the projects, copy the AL1C2 subfolder from the AL1 folder on the CD that accompanies this textbook to your storage medium and make AL1C2 the active folder.

Project 1 Establish Relationships between Tables

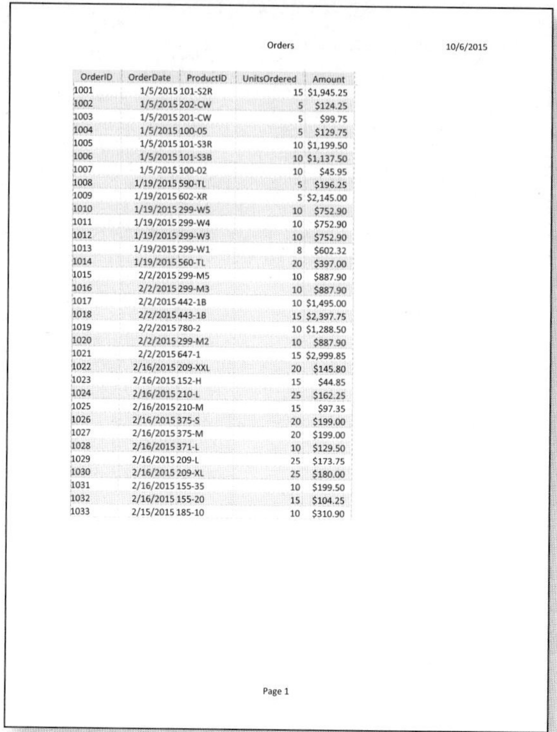

Orders 10/6/2015

OrderID	OrderDate	ProductID	UnitsOrdered	Amount
1001	1/5/2015	101-S2R	15	$1,945.25
1002	1/5/2015	202-CW	5	$124.25
1003	1/5/2015	201-CW	5	$99.75
1004	1/5/2015	100-05	5	$129.75
1005	1/5/2015	101-S3R	10	$1,199.50
1006	1/5/2015	101-S3B	10	$1,137.50
1007	1/5/2015	100-02	10	$45.95
1008	1/19/2015	590-TL	5	$196.25
1009	1/19/2015	602-XR	5	$2,145.00
1010	1/19/2015	299-W5	10	$752.90
1011	1/19/2015	299-W4	10	$752.90
1012	1/19/2015	299-W3	10	$752.90
1013	1/19/2015	299-W1	8	$602.32
1014	1/19/2015	560-TL	20	$397.00
1015	2/2/2015	299-M5	10	$887.90
1016	2/2/2015	299-M3	10	$887.90
1017	2/2/2015	442-1B	10	$1,495.00
1018	2/2/2015	443-1B	15	$2,397.75
1019	2/2/2015	780-2	10	$1,288.50
1020	2/2/2015	299-M2	10	$887.90
1021	2/2/2015	647-1	15	$2,999.85
1022	2/16/2015	209-XXL	20	$145.80
1023	2/16/2015	152-H	15	$44.85
1024	2/16/2015	210-L	25	$162.25
1025	2/16/2015	210-M	15	$97.35
1026	2/16/2015	375-S	20	$199.00
1027	2/16/2015	375-M	20	$199.00
1028	2/16/2015	371-L	10	$129.50
1029	2/16/2015	209-L	25	$173.75
1030	2/16/2015	209-XL	25	$180.00
1031	2/16/2015	155-35	10	$199.50
1032	2/16/2015	155-20	15	$104.25
1033	2/15/2015	185-10	10	$310.90

Page 1

Orders Table

Products 10/6/2015

ProductID	Product	SupplierID	UnitsInStock	UnitsOnOrder	ReorderLevel
100-01	Wrist compass	84	12	0	10
100-02	Multi-function compass	84	8	10	5
100-03	Lenspro plastic compass	84	6	0	5
100-04	Lenspro metal compass	84	8	0	5
100-05	Deluxe map compass	84	2	5	5
101-S1B	SL 0-degrees down sleeping bag, black	54	16	0	15
101-S1R	SL 0-degrees down sleeping bag, red	54	17	0	15
101-S2B	SL 15-degrees synthetic sleeping bag, blac	54	21	0	15
101-S2R	SL 15-degrees synthetic sleeping bag, red	54	12	15	15
101-S3B	SL 20-degrees synthetic sleeping bag, blac	54	8	15	15
101-S3R	SL 20-degrees synthetic sleeping bag, red	54	4	10	10
152-H	Lantern hanger	10	12	15	15
155-20	Shursite angle-head flashlight	10	14	20	20
155-30	Shursite aluminum flashlight	10	8	0	5
155-35	Shursite portable camp light	10	7	10	10
155-45	Shursite propane lantern	10	12	0	10
155-55	Shursite waterproof headlamp	10	7	0	5
200-CW	Four-piece titanium cookware	33	6	0	5
201-CW	Eight-piece stainless steel cookware	33	3	5	5
202-CW	Ten-piece hiker cookware	33	2	5	5
209-L	Gordon wool ski hat, L	68	21	25	25
209-XL	Gordon wool ski hat, XL	68	14	25	25
209-XXL	Gordon wool ski hat, XXL	68	10	20	20
210-L	Tech-lite ski hat, L	68	17	25	25
210-M	Tech-lite ski hat, M	68	6	15	15
210-XL	Tech-lite ski hat, XL	68	22	0	20
299-M1	HT waterproof hiking boots, MS13	31	8	0	10
299-M2	HT waterproof hiking boots, MS12	31	2	10	10
299-M3	HT waterproof hiking boots, MS11	31	6	10	10
299-M4	HT waterproof hiking boots, MS10	31	7	0	10
299-M5	HT waterproof hiking boots, MS9	31	9	10	10
299-W1	HT waterproof hiking boots, WS11	31	5	8	8
299-W2	HT waterproof hiking boots, WS10	31	9	0	8
299-W3	HT waterproof hiking boots, WS9	31	3	10	10
299-W4	HT waterproof hiking boots, WS8	31	2	10	10
299-W5	HT waterproof hiking boots, WS7	31	3	10	10
299-W6	HT waterproof hiking boots, WS6	31	11	0	10

Page 1

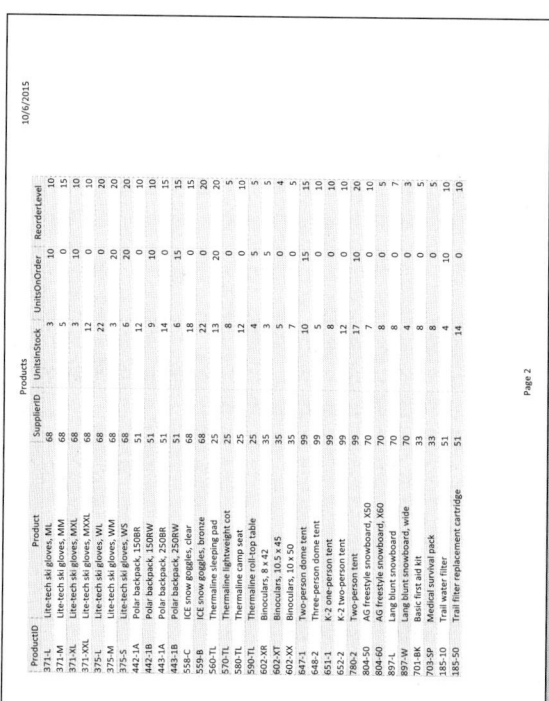

Products Table, Page 1

Products 10/6/2015

ProductID	Product	SupplierID	UnitsInStock	UnitsOnOrder	ReorderLevel
371-L	Lite-tech ski gloves, ML	68	3	10	10
371-M	Lite-tech ski gloves, MM	68	5	0	15
371-XL	Lite-tech ski gloves, MXL	68	3	10	10
371-XXL	Lite-tech ski gloves, MXXL	68	12	0	10
375-L	Lite-tech ski gloves, WL	68	22	0	20
375-M	Lite-tech ski gloves, WM	68	3	20	20
375-S	Lite-tech ski gloves, WS	68	6	20	20
442-1A	Polar backpack, 150BR	51	12	0	10
442-1B	Polar backpack, 150RW	51	9	10	10
443-1A	Polar backpack, 250BR	51	14	0	15
443-1B	Polar backpack, 250RW	51	6	15	15
558-C	ICE snow goggles, clear	68	18	0	15
559-B	ICE snow goggles, bronze	68	22	0	20
560-TL	Thermaline sleeping pad	25	13	20	20
570-TL	Thermaline lightweight cot	25	8	0	5
580-TL	Thermaline camp seat	25	12	0	10
590-TL	Thermaline roll-top table	25	4	5	5
602-XR	Binoculars, 8 x 42	35	3	5	5
602-XT	Binoculars, 10.5 x 45	35	5	0	4
602-XX	Binoculars, 10 x 50	35	7	0	5
647-1	Two-person dome tent	99	10	15	15
648-2	Three-person dome tent	99	5	0	10
651-1	K-2 one-person tent	99	8	0	10
652-2	K-2 two-person tent	99	12	0	10
780-2	Two-person tent	99	17	10	20
804-50	AG freestyle snowboard, X50	70	7	0	10
804-60	AG freestyle snowboard, X60	70	8	0	5
897-L	Lang blunt snowboard	70	8	0	7
897-W	Lang blunt snowboard, wide	70	4	0	3
701-BK	Basic first aid kit	33	8	0	5
703-SP	Medical survival pack	33	8	0	5
185-10	Trail water filter	51	4	10	10
185-50	Trail filter replacement cartridge	51	14	0	10

Page 2

Products Table, Page 2

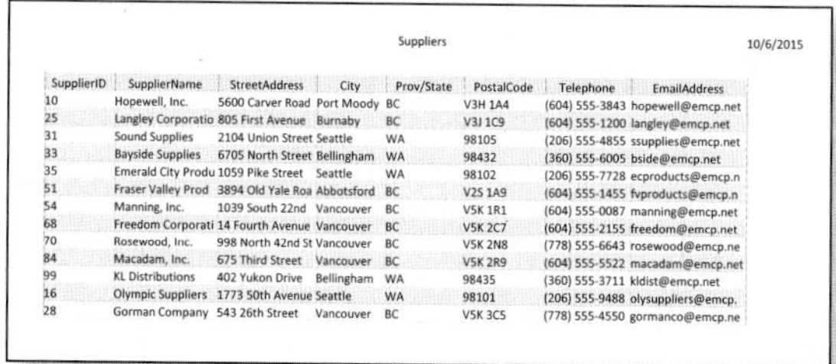

Suppliers 10/6/2015

SupplierID	SupplierName	StreetAddress	City	Prov/State	PostalCode	Telephone	EmailAddress
10	Hopewell, Inc.	5600 Carver Road	Port Moody	BC	V3H 1A4	(604) 555-3843	hopewell@emcp.net
25	Langley Corporatio	805 First Avenue	Burnaby	BC	V3J 1C9	(604) 555-1200	langley@emcp.net
31	Sound Supplies	2104 Union Street	Seattle	WA	98105	(206) 555-4855	ssupplies@emcp.net
33	Bayside Supplies	6705 North Street	Bellingham	WA	98432	(360) 555-6005	bside@emcp.net
35	Emerald City Produ	1059 Pike Street	Seattle	WA	98102	(206) 555-7728	ecproducts@emcp.n
51	Fraser Valley Prod	3894 Old Yale Roa	Abbotsford	BC	V2S 1A9	(604) 555-1455	fvproducts@emcp.n
54	Manning, Inc.	1039 South 22nd	Vancouver	BC	V5K 1R1	(604) 555-0087	manning@emcp.net
68	Freedom Corporati	14 Fourth Avenue	Vancouver	BC	V5K 2C7	(604) 555-2155	freedom@emcp.net
70	Rosewood, Inc.	998 North 42nd St	Vancouver	BC	V5K 2N8	(778) 555-6643	rosewood@emcp.ne
84	Macadam, Inc.	675 Third Street	Vancouver	BC	V5K 2R9	(604) 555-5522	macadam@emcp.net
99	KL Distributions	402 Yukon Drive	Bellingham	WA	98435	(360) 555-3711	kldist@emcp.net
16	Olympic Suppliers	1773 50th Avenue	Seattle	WA	98101	(206) 555-9488	olysuppliers@emcp.
28	Gorman Company	543 26th Street	Vancouver	BC	V5K 3C5	(778) 555-4550	gormanco@emcp.ne

Suppliers Table

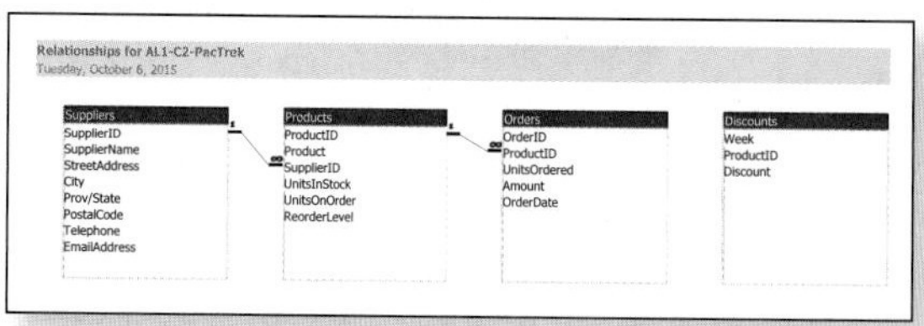

Relationships Report

Project 2 Create Relationships and Display Subdatasheets in a Database

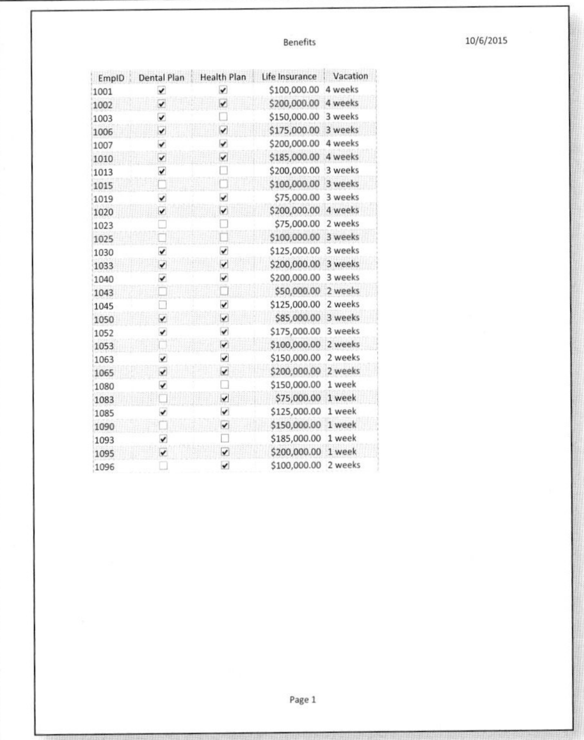

Benefits 10/6/2015

EmpID	Dental Plan	Health Plan	Life Insurance	Vacation
1001	☑	☑	$100,000.00	4 weeks
1002	☑	☑	$200,000.00	4 weeks
1003	☑	☐	$150,000.00	3 weeks
1006	☑	☑	$175,000.00	3 weeks
1007	☑	☑	$200,000.00	4 weeks
1010	☑	☑	$185,000.00	4 weeks
1013	☑	☐	$200,000.00	3 weeks
1015	☐	☐	$100,000.00	3 weeks
1019	☑	☑	$75,000.00	3 weeks
1020	☑	☑	$200,000.00	4 weeks
1023	☐	☐	$75,000.00	2 weeks
1025	☐	☐	$100,000.00	3 weeks
1030	☑	☑	$125,000.00	3 weeks
1033	☑	☑	$200,000.00	3 weeks
1040	☑	☑	$200,000.00	3 weeks
1043	☐	☐	$50,000.00	2 weeks
1045	☐	☑	$125,000.00	2 weeks
1050	☑	☑	$85,000.00	3 weeks
1052	☑	☑	$175,000.00	3 weeks
1053	☐	☑	$100,000.00	2 weeks
1063	☑	☑	$150,000.00	2 weeks
1065	☑	☑	$200,000.00	2 weeks
1080	☑	☐	$150,000.00	1 week
1083	☐	☑	$75,000.00	1 week
1085	☑	☑	$125,000.00	1 week
1090	☐	☑	$150,000.00	1 week
1093	☑	☐	$185,000.00	1 week
1095	☑	☑	$200,000.00	1 week
1096	☐	☑	$100,000.00	2 weeks

Page 1

Benefits Table

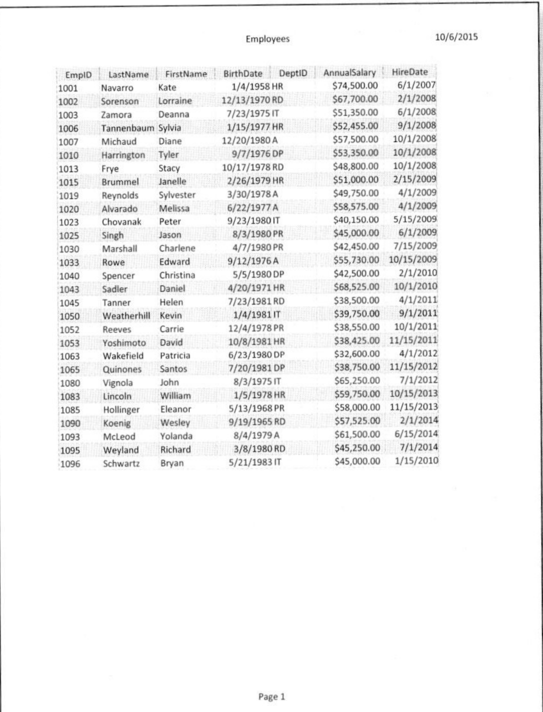

Employees 10/6/2015

EmpID	LastName	FirstName	BirthDate	DeptID	AnnualSalary	HireDate
1001	Navarro	Kate	1/4/1958	HR	$74,500.00	6/1/2007
1002	Sorenson	Lorraine	12/13/1970	RD	$67,700.00	2/1/2008
1003	Zamora	Deanna	7/23/1975	IT	$51,350.00	6/1/2008
1006	Tannenbaum	Sylvia	1/15/1977	HR	$52,455.00	9/1/2008
1007	Michaud	Diane	12/20/1980	A	$57,500.00	10/1/2008
1010	Harrington	Tyler	9/7/1976	DP	$53,350.00	10/1/2008
1013	Frye	Stacy	10/17/1978	RD	$48,800.00	10/1/2008
1015	Brummel	Janelle	2/26/1979	HR	$51,000.00	2/15/2009
1019	Reynolds	Sylvester	3/30/1978	A	$49,750.00	4/1/2009
1020	Alvarado	Melissa	6/22/1977	A	$58,575.00	4/1/2009
1023	Chovanak	Peter	9/23/1980	IT	$40,150.00	5/15/2009
1025	Singh	Jason	8/3/1980	PR	$45,000.00	6/1/2009
1030	Marshall	Charlene	4/7/1980	PR	$42,450.00	7/15/2009
1033	Rowe	Edward	9/12/1976	A	$55,730.00	10/15/2009
1040	Spencer	Christina	5/5/1980	DP	$42,500.00	2/1/2010
1043	Sadler	Daniel	4/20/1971	HR	$68,525.00	10/1/2010
1045	Tanner	Helen	7/23/1981	RD	$38,500.00	4/1/2011
1050	Weatherhill	Kevin	1/4/1981	IT	$39,750.00	9/1/2011
1052	Reeves	Carrie	12/4/1978	PR	$38,550.00	10/1/2011
1053	Yoshimoto	David	10/8/1981	HR	$38,425.00	11/15/2011
1063	Wakefield	Patricia	6/23/1980	DP	$32,600.00	4/1/2012
1065	Quinones	Santos	7/20/1981	DP	$38,750.00	11/15/2012
1080	Vignola	John	8/3/1975	IT	$65,250.00	7/1/2012
1083	Lincoln	William	1/5/1978	HR	$59,750.00	10/15/2013
1085	Hollinger	Eleanor	5/13/1968	PR	$58,000.00	11/15/2013
1090	Koenig	Wesley	9/19/1965	RD	$57,525.00	2/1/2014
1093	McLeod	Yolanda	8/4/1979	A	$61,500.00	6/15/2014
1095	Weyland	Richard	3/8/1980	RD	$45,250.00	7/1/2014
1096	Schwartz	Bryan	5/21/1983	IT	$45,000.00	1/15/2010

Page 1

Employees Table

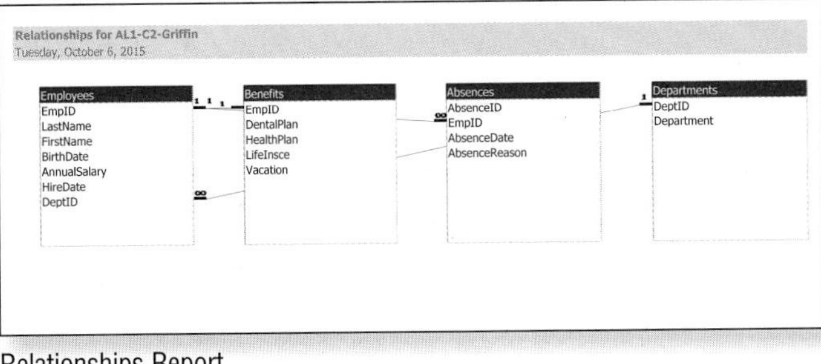

Relationships Report

Project 1 Establish Relationships between Tables **4 Parts**

You will specify primary keys in tables, establish one-to-many relationships between tables, specify referential integrity, and print the relationships. You will also edit and delete a relationship.

Creating Related Tables

Generally, a database management system fits into one of two categories: a file management system (also sometimes referred to as a ***flat file database***) or a relational database management system. A flat file management system stores all data in a single directory and cannot contain multiple tables. This type of management system is a simple way to store data but becomes more inefficient as more data is added. In a

Defining a relationship between tables is one of the most powerful features of a relational database management system.

relational database management system, like Access, relationships are defined between sets of data, allowing greater flexibility in manipulating data and eliminating data redundancy (entering the same data in more than one place).

In Project 1, you will define relationships between tables in the AL1-C2-PacTrek.accdb database. Because the tables in the database will be related, information on the same product does not need to be repeated in a table on orders. If you used a flat file management system to maintain product information, you would need to repeat the product description for each order.

Determining Relationships

Taking time to plan a database is extremely important. Creating a database with related tables takes even more consideration. You need to determine how to break down the required data and what tables to create to eliminate redundancies. One idea to help you determine what tables are necessary in a database is to think of the word *about*. For example, the Pacific Trek store needs a table *about* products, another *about* suppliers, and another *about* orders. A table should be about only one subject, such as products, suppliers, or orders.

Along with determining the necessary tables for a database, you need to determine the relationship between tables. The ability to relate, or "join," tables is what makes Access a relational database system. As you learned in Chapter 1, database designers often create a visual representation of the database's structure in a diagram. Figure 2.1 displays the database diagram for the AL1-C2-PacTrek.accdb database. (Some of the fields in the tables have been slightly modified from the database you used in Chapter 1.)

Defining the Primary Key

A database table can contain two different types of keys: a primary key and a foreign key. In the database diagram in Figure 2.1, notice that one field in each table contains an asterisk. The asterisk indicates a ***primary key field***, which is a field that holds data that uniquely identifies each record in a table. For example,

Figure 2.1 AL1-C2-PacTrek.accdb Database Diagram

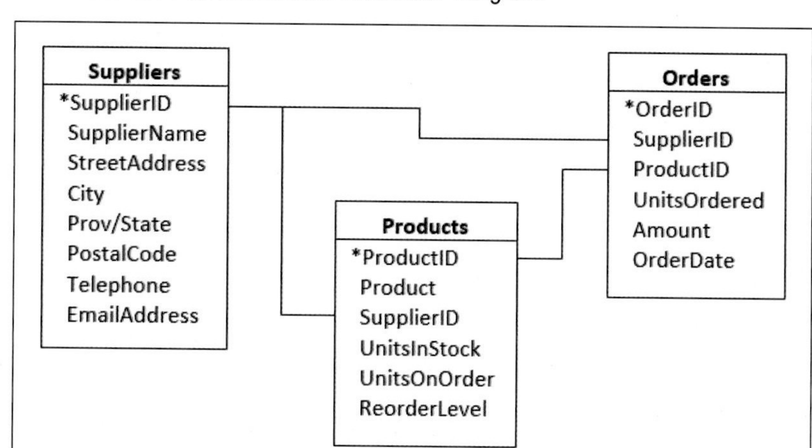

the *SupplierID* field in the Suppliers table contains a unique supplier number for each record in the table and the *ProductID* field in the Products table contains a unique product number for each product. A table can have only one primary key field and it is the field by which the table is sorted whenever the table is opened.

When a new record is added to a table, Access checks to ensure that there is no existing record with the same data in the primary key. If there is, Access displays an error message indicating there are duplicate values and does not allow the record to be saved. When adding a new record to a table, the primary key field cannot be left blank. Access expects a value in each record in the table and this is referred to as ***entity integrity***. If a value is not entered in a field, Access actually enters a null value. A null value cannot be given to a primary key field. Access will not let you close a database containing a primary key field with a null value.

By default, Access includes the *ID* field as the first field in a table, assigns the AutoNumber data type, and identifies the field as the primary key. The AutoNumber data type assigns the first record a field value of *1* and each new record is assigned the next sequential number. You can use this default field as the primary key or define your own. To determine what field is the primary key or to define a primary key field, you must display the table in Design view. To do this, open the table and then click the View button located at the left side of the HOME tab. You can also display the table in Design view by clicking the View button arrow and then clicking *Design View* at the drop-down list. To add or remove a primary key from a field, click the desired field in the *Field Name* column and then click the Primary Key button in the Tools group on the TABLE TOOLS DESIGN tab. A key icon is inserted in the field selector bar (the blank column to the left of the field names) for the desired field. Figure 2.2 displays the Products table in Design view with the *ProductID* field identified as the primary key.

Quick Steps

Define a Primary Key
1. Open table.
2. Click View button.
3. Click desired field.
4. Click Primary Key button.
5. Click Save button.

Primary Key

Figure 2.2 Products Table in Design View

A key icon in the field selector bar specifies the primary key field.

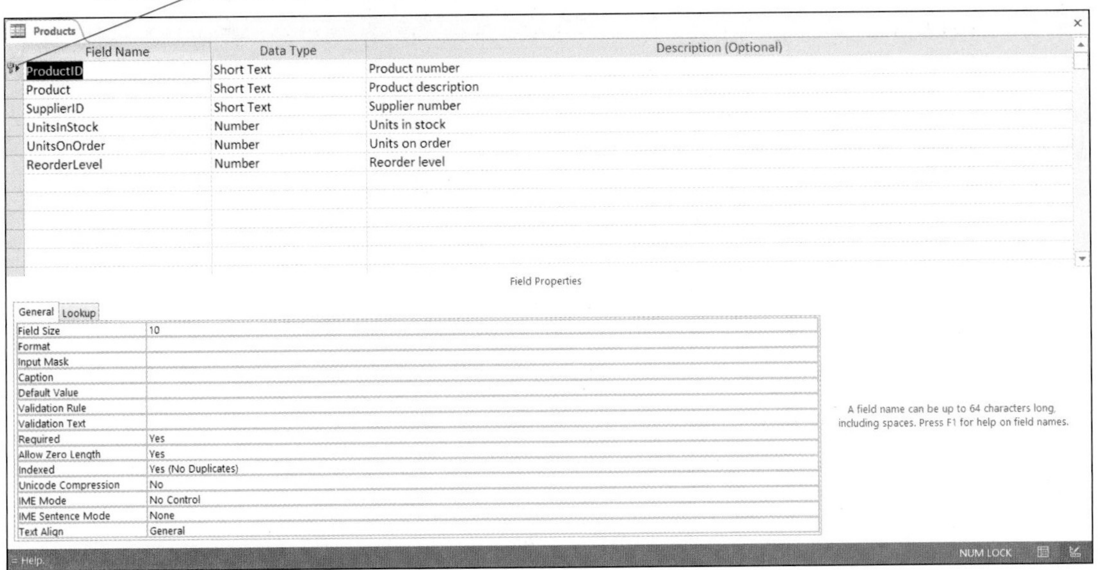

Typically, a primary key field in one table becomes the ***foreign key field*** in a related table. For example, the primary key field *SupplierID* in the Suppliers table is considered the foreign key field in the Orders table. In the Suppliers table, each entry in the *SupplierID* field must be unique since it is the primary key field but the same supplier number may appear more than once in the *SupplierID* field in the Orders table (for instance, in a situation when more than one product is ordered from the same supplier).

HINT

Access uses a primary key to associate data from multiple tables.

Data in the foreign key field must match data in the primary key field of the related table. For example, any supplier number you enter in the *SupplierID* field in the Orders table must be contained in the Suppliers table. In other words, you would not make an order to a supplier that does not exist in the Suppliers table. Figure 2.3 identifies the primary and foreign keys in the tables in the AL1-C2-PacTrek.accdb database. Primary keys are identified with *(PK)* and foreign keys are identified with *(FK)* in the figure.

You must enter a value in the primary key in every record.

Figure 2.3 AL1-C2-PacTrek.accdb Database Diagram with Primary and Foreign Keys Identified

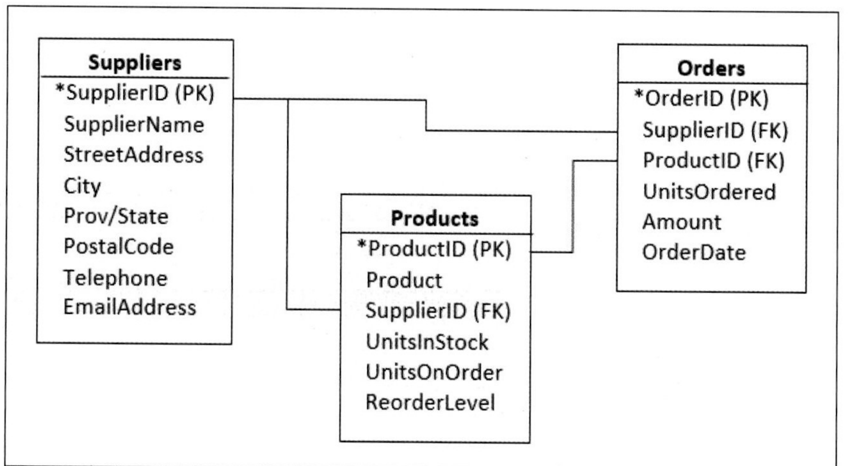

Project 1a Defining a Primary Key Field **Part 1 of 4**

1. Open Access.
2. At the Access 2013 opening screen, click the Open Other Files hyperlink that displays at the left side of the screen.
3. At the Open backstage area, double-click the *Computer* option or your OneDrive (depending on where your student data files are located).
4. At the Open dialog box, navigate to the AL1C2 folder on your storage medium and then double-click the database ***AL1-C2-PacTrek.accdb***.
5. Click the Enable Content button in the message bar if the security warning message appears. (The message bar will display immediately below the ribbon.)
6. Open the Products table.
7. View the primary key field by completing the following steps:
   a. Click the View button located at the left side of the HOME tab. (This displays the table in Design view.)

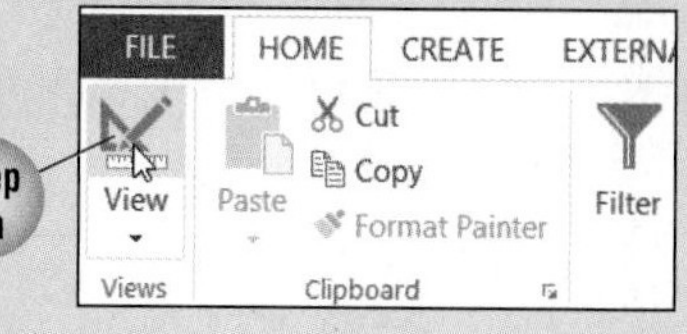

b. In Design view, notice the *Field Name*, *Data Type*, and *Description* columns and notice the information that displays for each field. The first field, *ProductID* is the primary key field and is identified by the key icon that displays in the field selector bar.
c. Click the View button to return to the Datasheet view.
d. Close the Products table.

8. Open the Suppliers table, click the View button to display the table in Design view, and then notice the *SupplierID* field is defined as the primary key field.
9. Click the View button to return to Datasheet view and then close the table.
10. Open the Orders table. (The first field in the Orders table has been changed from the AutoNumber field automatically assigned by Access in the AL1-C2-PacTrek.accdb database to a Short Text data type field.)
11. Define the *OrderID* field as the primary key field by completing the following steps:
   a. Click the View button located at the left side of the HOME tab.
   b. With the table in Design view and the *OrderID* field selected in the *Field Name* column, click the Primary Key button located in the Tools group on the TABLE TOOLS DESIGN tab.

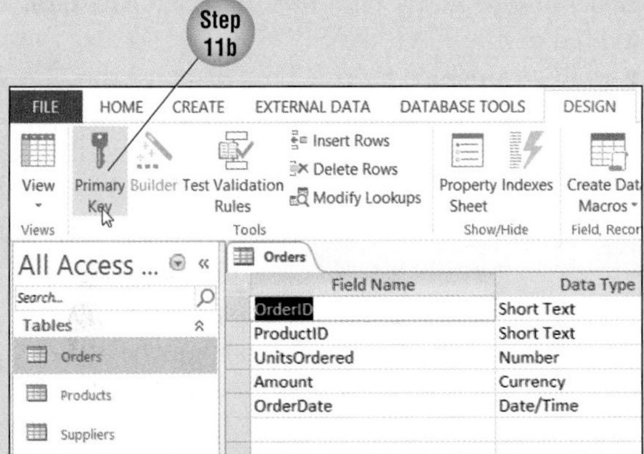

   c. Click the Save button on the Quick Access toolbar.
   d. Click the View button to return the table to Datasheet view.

12. Move the *OrderDate* field by completing the following steps:
   a. Click the *OrderDate* field heading. (This selects the column.)
   b. Position the mouse pointer on the heading; hold down the left mouse button; drag to the left until the thick, black vertical line displays immediately left of the *ProductID* field; and then release the mouse button.

Step 12b

Orders

OrderID	ProductID	UnitsOrderec	Amount	OrderDate	Click to Add
1001	101-S2R	15	$1,945.25	1/5/2015	
1002	202-CW	5	$124.25	1/5/2015	
1003	201-CW	5	$99.75	1/5/2015	
1004	100-05	5	$129.75	1/5/2015	

13. Automatically adjust the column widths.
14. Save and then close the Orders table.

Relating Tables in a One-to-Many Relationship

In Access, one table can be related to another, which is generally referred to as performing a ***join***. When tables with a common field are joined, data can be extracted from both tables as if they were one large table. Relate tables to ensure the integrity of the data. For example, in Project 1b, you will create a relationship between the Suppliers table and the Products table. The relationship you establish will ensure that a supplier number cannot be entered in the Products table without first being entered in the Suppliers table. This type of relationship is called a ***one-to-many relationship***, which means that one record in the Suppliers table will match zero, one, or many records in the Products table.

In a one-to-many relationship, the table containing the "one" is referred to as the ***primary table*** and the table containing the "many" is referred to as the ***related table***. Access follows a set of rules that provide ***referential integrity***, which enforces consistency between related tables. These rules are enforced when data is updated in related tables. The referential integrity rules ensure that a record added to a related table has a matching record in the primary table.

Quick Steps

Create a One-to-Many Relationship

1. Click DATABASE TOOLS tab.
2. Click Relationships button.
3. At Show Table dialog box, add tables.
4. In Relationships window, drag "one" field from primary table to "many" field in related table.
5. At Edit Relationships dialog box, enforce referential integrity.
6. Click Create button.
7. Click Save button.

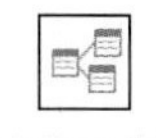

Relationships

To create a one-to-many relationship, open the database containing the tables to be related. Click the DATABASE TOOLS tab and then click the Relationships button in the Relationships group. This displays the Show Table dialog box, as shown in Figure 2.4. At the Show Table dialog box, each table that will be related must be added to the Relationships window. To do this, click the first table name to be included and then click Add (or double-click the desired table). Continue in this manner until all necessary table names have been added to the Relationships window and then click the Close button.

At the Relationships window, such as the one shown in Figure 2.5, use the mouse to drag the common field from the primary table's field list box (the "one") to the related table's field list box (the "many"). This causes the Edit Relationships dialog box to display, as shown in Figure 2.6. At the Edit Relationships dialog box, check to make sure the correct field name displays in the *Table/Query* and *Related Table/Query* list boxes and the relationship type at the bottom of the dialog box displays as *One-To-Many*.

Specify the relationship options by choosing *Enforce Referential Integrity*, as well as *Cascade Update Related Fields* and/or *Cascade Delete Related Records*, and then click the Create button. This causes the Edit Relationships dialog box to close and the Relationships window to display showing the relationship between the tables.

Figure 2.4 Show Table Dialog Box

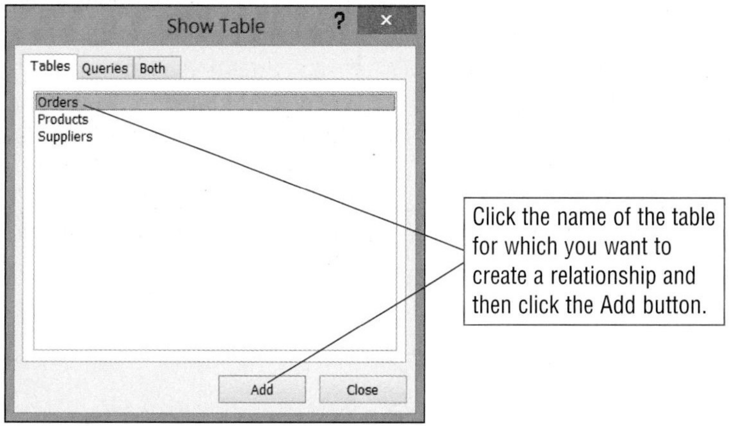
Show Table
Tables
Queries
Both
Orders
Products
Suppliers
Add
Close
Click the name of the table for which you want to create a relationship and then click the Add button.

Figure 2.5 Relationships Window

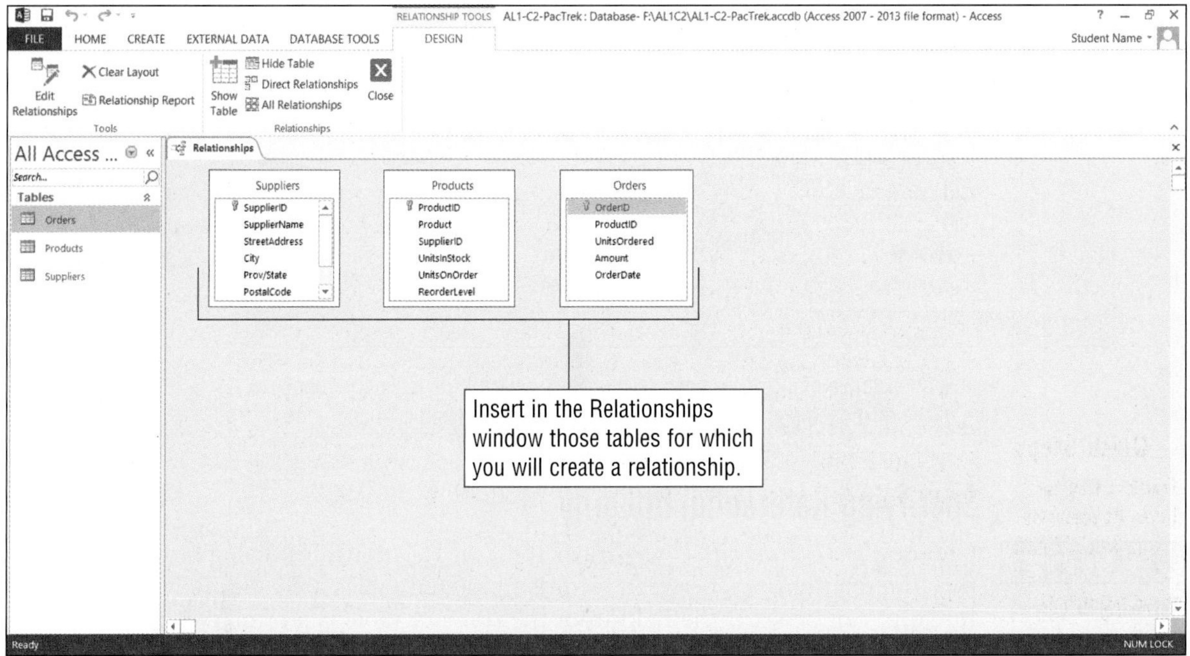
Insert in the Relationships window those tables for which you will create a relationship.

Figure 2.6 Edit Relationships Dialog Box

Make sure the correct field names display here.
Make sure the relationship type is One-To-Many.

In Figure 2.7, the *Suppliers* field list box displays with a black line attached along with the number *1* (signifying the "one" side of the relationship). The black line is connected to the *Products* field list box along with the infinity symbol, ∞ (signifying the "many" side of the relationship). The black line, called the ***join line***, is thick at both ends if the *Enforce Referential Integrity* option is chosen. If this option is not chosen, the line is thin at both ends. Click the Save button on the Quick Access toolbar to save the relationship. Close the Relationships window by clicking the Close button located in the upper right corner of the window.

Figure 2.7 One-to-Many Relationship

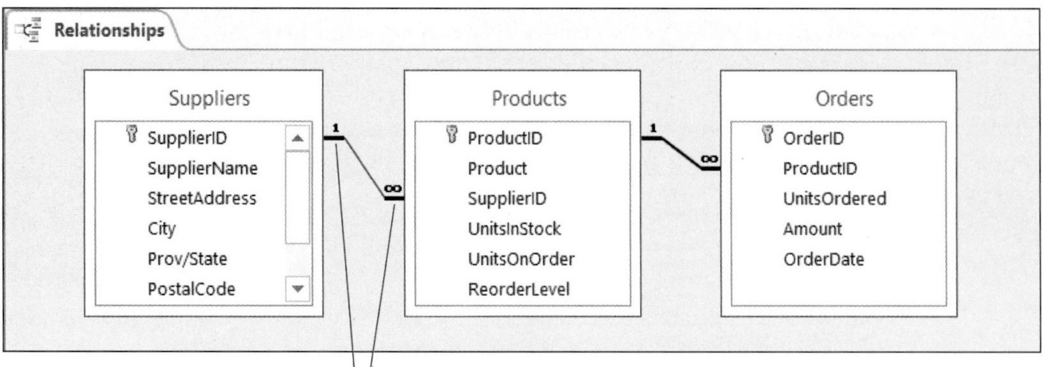

This is an example of a one-to-many relationship, where 1 identifies the "one" side of the relationship and the infinity symbol (∞) identifies the "many" side.

Specifying Referential Integrity

Referential integrity ensures that a record exists in the "one" table before the record can be entered in the "many" table.

Choose *Enforce Referential Integrity* at the Edit Relationships dialog box to ensure that the relationships between records in related tables are valid. Referential integrity can be set if the field from the primary table is a primary key and the related fields have the same data type. When referential integrity is established, a value for the primary key must first be entered in the primary table before it can be entered in the related table.

If you select only *Enforce Referential Integrity* and the related table contains a record, you will not be able to change a primary key field value in the primary table. You will not be able to delete a record in the primary table if its key value equals a foreign key in the related table. If you choose *Cascade Update Related Fields*, you will be able to change a primary key field value in the primary table and Access will automatically update the matching value in the related table. Choose *Cascade Delete Related Records* and you will be able to delete a record in the primary table and Access will delete any related records in the related table.

In Project 1b, you will create a one-to-many relationship between tables in the AL1-C2-PacTrek.accdb database. Figure 2.8 displays the Relationships window with the relationships identified that you will create in the project.

Figure 2.8 Relationships in the AL1-C2-PacTrek Database

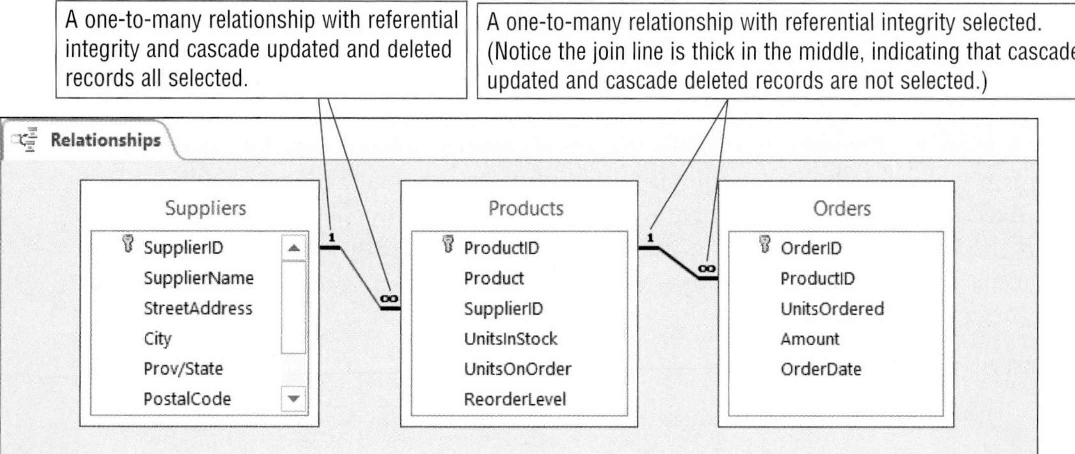

Printing Relationships

You can print a report displaying the relationships between tables. To do this, display the Relationships window and then click the Relationship Report button in the Tools group. This displays the relationships report in Print Preview. Click the Print button in the Print group on the PRINT PREVIEW tab and then click OK at the Print dialog box. After printing the relationships report, click the Close button to close the relationships report.

Quick Steps

Print a Relationship

1. Click DATABASE TOOLS tab.
2. Click Relationships button.
3. Click Relationships Report button.
4. Click Print button.
5. Click OK.
6. Click Close button.

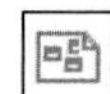

Relationship Report

Project 1b **Creating Relationships between Tables** **Part 2 of 4**

1. With **AL1-C2-PacTrek.accdb** open, click the DATABASE TOOLS tab and then click the Relationships button in the Relationships group. (The Show Table dialog box should display in the Relationships window. If it does not display, click the Show Table button in the Relationships group on the RELATIONSHIP TOOLS DESIGN tab.)

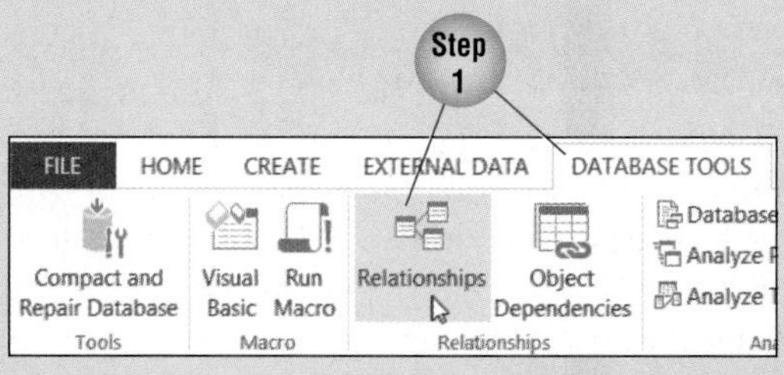

2. At the Show Table dialog box with the Tables tab selected, add the Suppliers, Products, and Orders tables to the Relationships window by completing the following steps:
   a. Click *Suppliers* in the list box and then click the Add button.
   b. Click *Products* in the list box and then click the Add button.
   c. Click *Orders* in the list box and then click the Add button.
3. Click the Close button to close the Show Table dialog box.

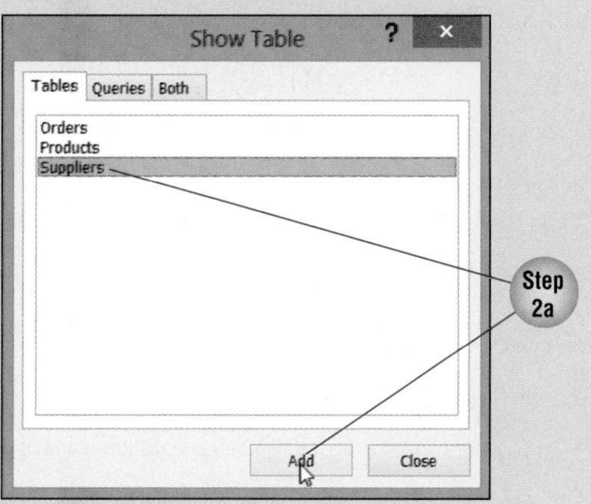

4. At the Relationships window, drag the *SupplierID* field from the *Suppliers* field list box to the *Products* field list box by completing the following steps:
   a. Position the arrow pointer on the *SupplierID* field that displays in the *Suppliers* field list box.
   b. Hold down the left mouse button, drag the arrow pointer (with a field icon attached) to the *SupplierID* field in the *Products* field list box, and then release the mouse button. (This causes the Edit Relationships dialog box to display.)

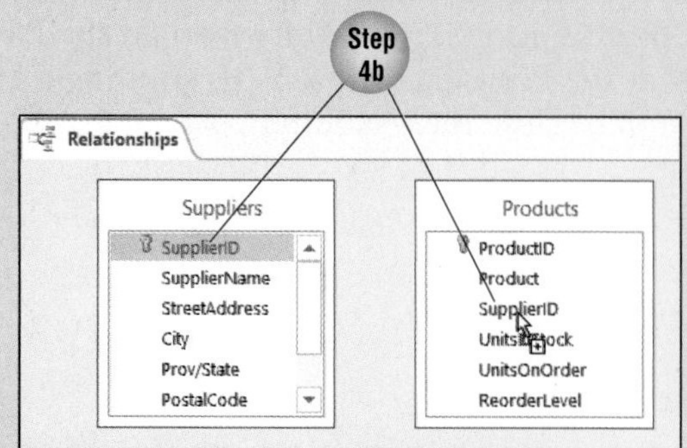

5. At the Edit Relationships dialog box, make sure *SupplierID* displays in the *Table/Query* and *Related Table/Query* list boxes and the relationship type at the bottom of the dialog box displays as *One-To-Many*.
6. Enforce the referential integrity of the relationship by completing the following steps:
   a. Click the *Enforce Referential Integrity* check box to insert a check mark. (This makes the other two options available.)
   b. Click the *Cascade Update Related Fields* check box to insert a check mark.
   c. Click the *Cascade Delete Related Records* check box to insert a check mark.

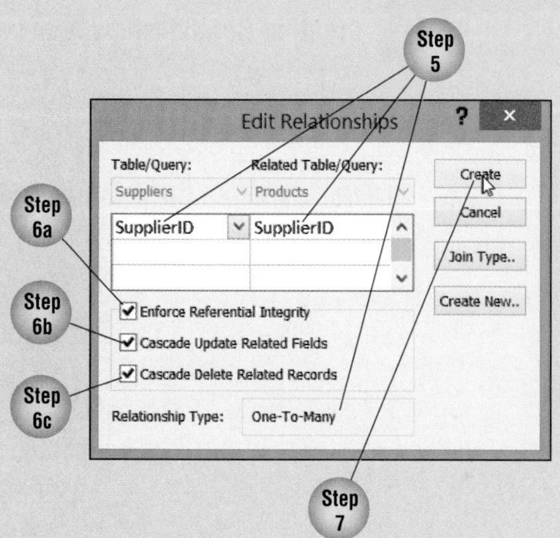

7. Click the Create button. (This causes the Edit Relationships dialog box to close and the Relationships window to display, showing a black line (thick on the ends and thin in the middle) connecting the *SupplierID* field in the *Suppliers* field list box to the *SupplierID* field in the *Products* field list box. A *1* appears at the Suppliers table side and an infinity symbol (∞) appears at the Products table side of the black line.)
8. Click the Save button on the Quick Access toolbar to save the relationship.
9. Create a one-to-many relationship between the Products table and the Orders table with the *ProductID* field by completing the following steps:
   a. Position the arrow pointer on the *ProductID* field that displays in the *Products* field list box.
   b. Hold down the left mouse button, drag the arrow pointer (with a field icon attached) to the *ProductID* field in the *Orders* field list box, and then release the mouse button.

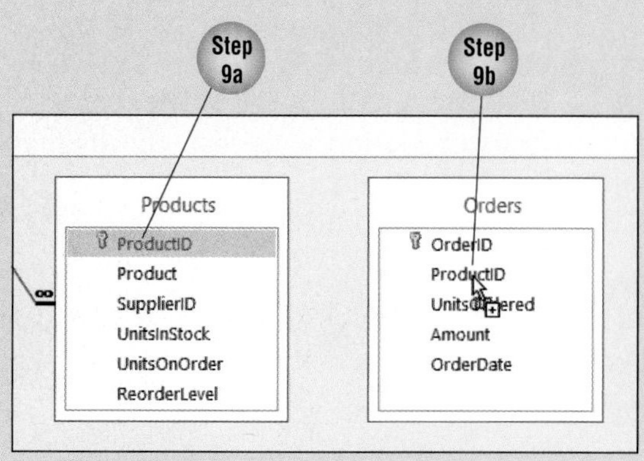

c. At the Edit Relationships dialog box, make sure *ProductID* displays in the *Table/Query* and *Related Table/Query* list boxes and the relationship type displays as *One-To-Many*.

d. Click the *Enforce Referential Integrity* check box. (Do not insert check marks in the other two check boxes.)

e. Click the Create button.

10. Click the Save button on the Quick Access toolbar to save the relationships.

11. Print the relationships by completing the following steps:

a. At the Relationships window, click the Relationship Report button in the Tools group. This displays the relationships report in Print Preview. (If a security notice displays, click the Open button.)

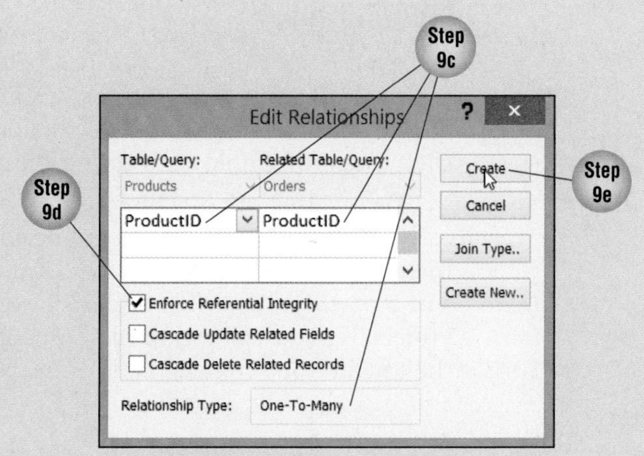

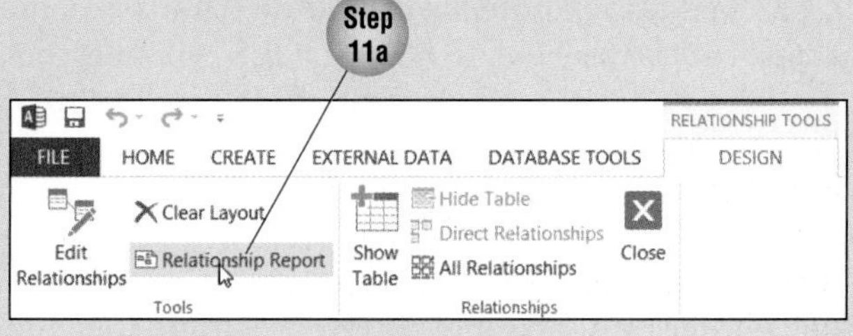

b. Click the Print button in the Print group at the left side of the PRINT PREVIEW tab.

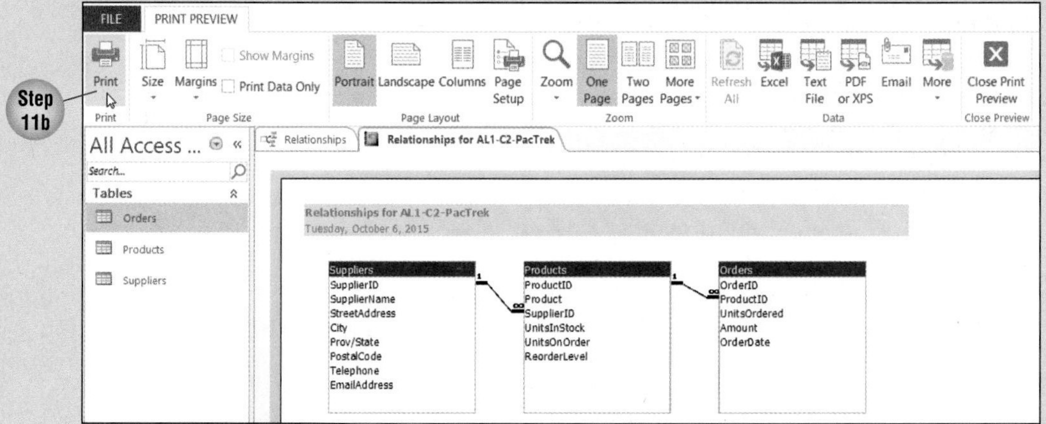

c. Click OK at the Print dialog box.

d. Close the report by clicking the Close button that displays in the upper right corner of the work area.

e. At the message asking if you want to save changes to the design of the report, click No.

12. Close the Relationships window by clicking the Close button that displays in the upper right corner of the work area.

Showing Tables

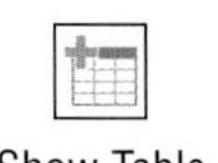

Show Table

Once a relationship is established between tables and the Relationships window is closed, clicking the Relationships button causes the Relationships window to display without the Show Table dialog box. To display the Show Table dialog box, click the Show Table button in the Relationships group.

Pacific Trek offers a discount on one product each week. You want to keep track of this information so you decide to create a Discounts table that includes the discount item for each week of the first three months of the year. (You will add a new record to this field each week when the discount item is chosen.) In Project 1c, you will create the Discounts table shown in Figure 2.9 on page 59 and then relate the Products table with the Discounts table using the *ProductID* field.

Editing a Relationship

Quick Steps

Edit a Relationship

1. Click DATABASE TOOLS tab.
2. Click Relationships button.
3. Click Edit Relationships button.
4. Make desired changes at Edit Relationships dialog box.
5. Click OK.

You can edit a relationship between tables or delete the relationship altogether. To edit a relationship, open the database containing the tables with the relationship, click the DATABASE TOOLS tab, and then click the Relationships button in the Relationships group. This displays the Relationships window with the related tables. Click the Edit Relationships button located in the Tools group to display the Edit Relationships dialog box. The dialog box will be similar to the one shown in Figure 2.6 on page 51. Identify the relationship you want to edit by clicking the down-pointing arrow at the right side of the *Table/Query* option box and then clicking the table name containing the "one" field. Click the down-pointing arrow at the right side of the *Related Table/Query* option box and then click the table name containing the "many" field.

Edit Relationships

To edit a specific relationship, position the arrow pointer on the middle portion of the black line that connects the related tables and then click the right mouse button. At the shortcut menu that displays, click the *Edit Relationship* option. This displays the Edit Relationships dialog box with the specific related field in both list boxes.

Deleting a Relationship

Quick Steps

Delete a Relationship

1. Click DATABASE TOOLS tab.
2. Click Relationships button.
3. Right-click black line connecting related tables.
4. Click *Delete*.
5. Click Yes.

To delete a relationship between tables, display the related tables in the Relationships window. Position the arrow pointer on the middle portion of the black line connecting the related tables and then click the right mouse button. At the shortcut menu that displays, click *Delete*. At the message asking if you are sure you want to permanently delete the selected relationship from your database, click Yes.

Project 1c Creating a Table and Creating and Editing Relationships Part 3 of 4

1. With **AL1-C2-PacTrek.accdb** open, create the Discounts table shown in Figure 2.9 on page 59 by completing the following steps:
   a. Click the CREATE tab.
   b. Click the Table button in the Tables group.
   c. Click the Short Text button in the Add & Delete group. (This creates and then selects the *Field1* heading that displays to the right of the *ID* column.)

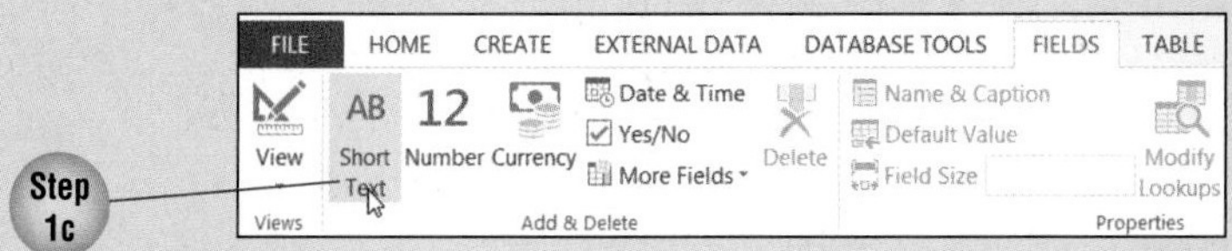

   d. Type **ProductID** and then press Enter.
   e. Click the *Short Text* option at the drop-down list and then type **Discount**.
   f. Click the *ID* heading (the first column), click the down-pointing arrow at the right side of the *Data Type* option box in the Formatting group, and then click *Date/Time* at the drop-down list.

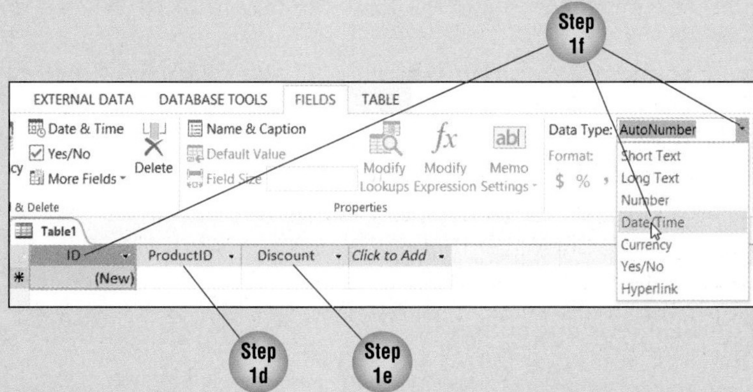

   g. Right-click the *ID* heading, click *Rename Field* at the shortcut menu, type **Week**, and then press Enter.
   h. Type the 13 records in the Discounts table shown in Figure 2.9 on page 59.
2. After typing the records, save the table by completing the following steps:
   a. Click the Save button on the Quick Access toolbar.
   b. At the Save As dialog box, type **Discounts** and then press Enter.
3. Close the Discounts table.
4. Create a relationship from the Products table to the Discounts table by completing the following steps:
   a. Click the DATABASE TOOLS tab and then click the Relationships button in the Relationships group.
   b. Display the Show Table dialog box by clicking the Show Table button in the Relationships group.
   c. At the Show Table dialog box, double-click the Discounts table.
   d. Click the Close button to close the Show Table dialog box.

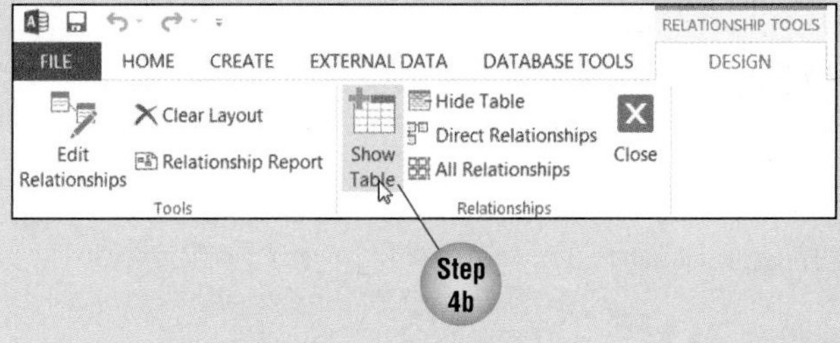

5. At the Relationships window, create a one-to-many relationship between the Products table and the Discounts table with the *ProductID* field by completing the following steps:
   a. Drag the *ProductID* field from the *Products* field list box to the *ProductID* field in the *Discounts* field list box.

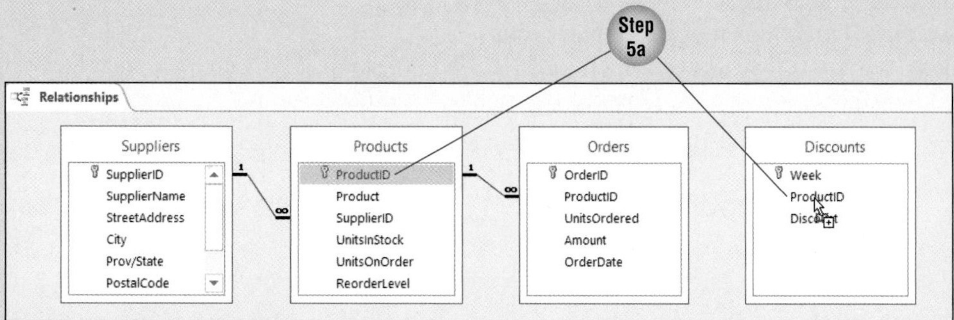

   b. At the Edit Relationships dialog box, make sure *ProductID* displays in the *Table/Query* and *Related Table/Query* list boxes and the relationship type at the bottom of the dialog box displays as *One-To-Many*.
   c. Click the *Enforce Referential Integrity* check box.
   d. Click the *Cascade Update Related Fields* check box.
   e. Click the *Cascade Delete Related Records* check box.
   f. Click the Create button. (At the Relationships window, notice the join line that displays between the Products table and the Discounts table. If a message occurs telling you that the relationship cannot be created, click the Cancel button. Open the Discounts table, check to make sure the product numbers are entered correctly in the *ProductID* field, and then close the Discounts table. Try again to create the relationship.)
6. Edit the one-to-many relationship between the *ProductID* field in the Products table and the Orders table and specify that you want to cascade updated and related fields and cascade and delete related records by completing the following steps:
   a. Click the Edit Relationships button located in the Tools group on the RELATIONSHIP TOOLS DESIGN tab.
   b. At the Edit Relationships dialog box, click the down-pointing arrow at the right side of the *Table/Query* option box and then click *Products* at the drop-down list.
   c. Click the down-pointing arrow at the right side of the *Related Table/Query* option box and then click *Orders* at the drop-down list.
   d. Click the *Cascade Update Related Fields* check box.
   e. Click the *Cascade Delete Related Records* check box.
   f. Click the OK button.

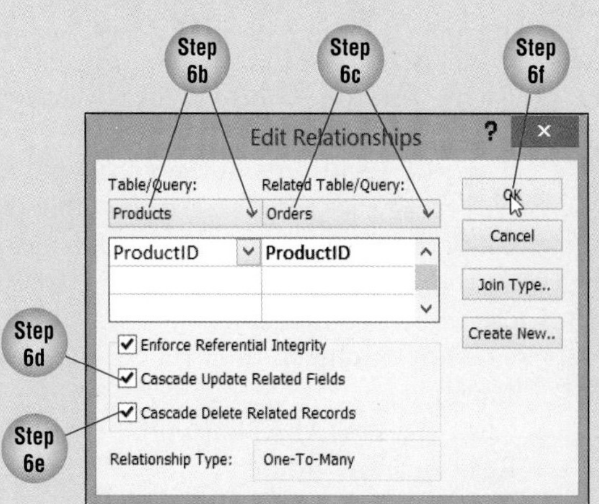

7. Click the Save button on the Quick Access toolbar to save the relationship.
8. Print the relationships by completing the following steps:
   a. Click the Relationship Report button in the Tools group.
   b. Click the Print button in the Print group.
   c. Click OK at the Print dialog box.

d. Close the report by clicking the Close button that displays in the upper right corner of the work area.
e. At the message asking if you want to save changes to the design of the report, click No.

9. Delete the relationship between the Products table and the Discounts table by completing the following steps:
   a. Position the arrow pointer on the thin portion of the black line connecting the *ProductID* field in the *Products* field list box with the *ProductID* field in the *Discounts* field list box and then click the right mouse button.
   b. Click the *Delete* option at the shortcut menu.

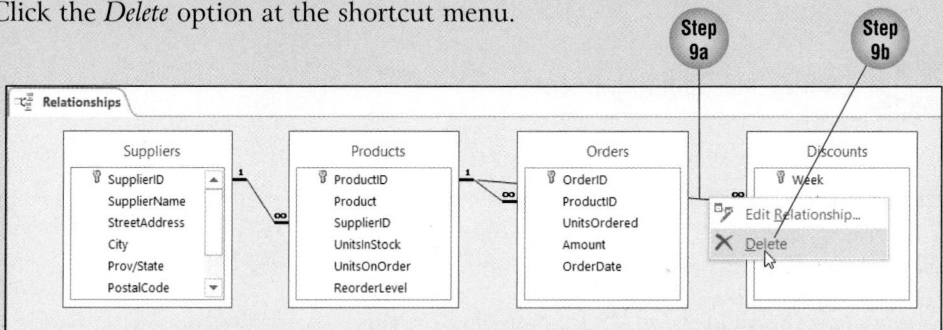

   c. At the message asking if you are sure you want to permanently delete the selected relationship from your database, click Yes.
10. Click the Save button on the Quick Access toolbar to save the relationship.
11. Print the relationships by completing the following steps:
   a. Click the RELATIONSHIP TOOLS DESIGN tab and then click the Relationship Report button in the Tools group.
   b. Click the Print button in the Print group.
   c. Click OK at the Print dialog box.
   d. Close the report by clicking the Close button that displays in the upper right corner of the work area.
   e. At the message asking if you want to save changes to the design of the report, click No.
12. Close the Relationships window by clicking the Close button that displays in the upper right corner of the work area.

Figure 2.9 Discounts Table

Discounts

Week	ProductID	Discount	Click to Add
1/5/2015	155-45	20%	
1/12/2015	652-2	15%	
1/19/2015	443-1A	20%	
1/26/2015	202-CW	15%	
2/2/2015	804-60	10%	
2/9/2015	652-2	15%	
2/16/2015	101-S1B	5%	
2/23/2015	560-TL	20%	
3/2/2015	652-2	20%	
3/9/2015	602-XX	15%	
3/16/2015	100-05	10%	
3/23/2015	652-2	15%	
3/30/2015	202-CW	15%	

Inserting and Deleting Records in Related Tables

In the relationship established in Project 1b, a record must first be added to the Suppliers table before a related record can be added to the Products table. This is because you chose the *Enforce Referential Integrity* option at the Edit Relationships dialog box. Because you chose the two options *Cascade Update Related Fields* and *Cascade Delete Related Records*, records in the Suppliers table (the primary table) can be updated or deleted and related records in the Products table (the related table) are automatically updated or deleted.

Project 1d Editing and Updating Records — Part 4 of 4

1. With **AL1-C2-PacTrek.accdb** open, open the Suppliers table.
2. Change two supplier numbers in the Suppliers table (Access will automatically change them in the Products table and the Orders table) by completing the following steps:
   a. Double-click the field value *15* that displays in the *SupplierID* field.
   b. Type 33.
   c. Double-click the field value *42* that displays in the *SupplierID* field.
   d. Type 51.
   e. Click the Save button on the Quick Access toolbar.
   f. Close the Suppliers table.
   g. Open the Products table and notice that supplier number *15* changed to *33* and supplier number *42* changed to *51*.
   h. Close the Products table.

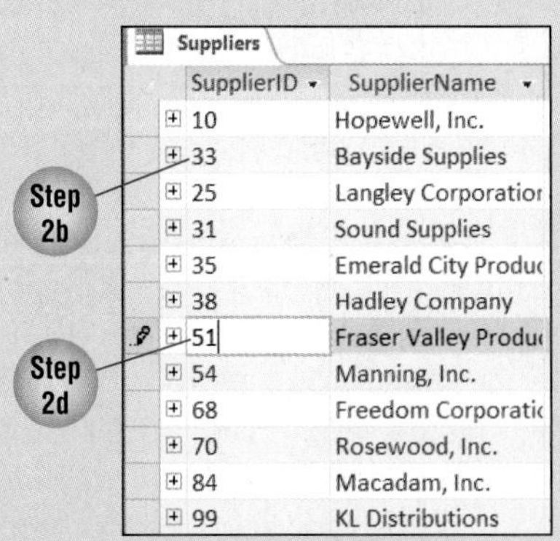

Suppliers

SupplierID	SupplierName
10	Hopewell, Inc.
33	Bayside Supplies
25	Langley Corporatior
31	Sound Supplies
35	Emerald City Produc
38	Hadley Company
51	Fraser Valley Produ
54	Manning, Inc.
68	Freedom Corporatic
70	Rosewood, Inc.
84	Macadam, Inc.
99	KL Distributions

Step 2b

Step 2d

3. Open the Suppliers table and then add the following records:

SupplierID: 16
SupplierName: Olympic Suppliers
StreetAddress: 1773 50th Avenue
City: Seattle
Prov/State: WA
PostalCode: 98101
Telephone: (206) 555-9488
EmailAddress: olysuppliers@emcp.net

SupplierID: 28
SupplierName: Gorman Company
StreetAddress: 543 26th Street
City: Vancouver
Prov/State: BC
PostalCode: V5K 3C5
Telephone: (778) 555-4550
EmailAddress: gormanco@emcp.net

Suppliers

SupplierID	SupplierName	StreetAddress	City	Prov/State	PostalCode	Telephone	EmailAddress	Click to Add
10	Hopewell, Inc.	5600 Carver Road	Port Moody	BC	V3H 1A4	(604) 555-3843	hopewell@emcp.net	
25	Langley Corporatior	805 First Avenue	Burnaby	BC	V3J 1C9	(604) 555-1200	langley@emcp.net	
31	Sound Supplies	2104 Union Street	Seattle	WA	98105	(206) 555-4855	ssupplies@emcp.net	
33	Bayside Supplies	6705 North Street	Bellingham	WA	98432	(360) 555-6005	bside@emcp.net	
35	Emerald City Produc	1059 Pike Street	Seattle	WA	98102	(206) 555-7728	ecproducts@emcp.ne	
38	Hadley Company	5845 Jefferson Stre	Seattle	WA	98107	(206) 555-8003	hcompany@emcp.net	
51	Fraser Valley Produ	3894 Old Yale Roac	Abbotsford	BC	V2S 1A9	(604) 555-1455	fvproducts@emcp.ne	
54	Manning, Inc.	1039 South 22nd	Vancouver	BC	V5K 1R1	(604) 555-0087	manning@emcp.net	
68	Freedom Corporatic	14 Fourth Avenue	Vancouver	BC	V5K 2C7	(604) 555-2155	freedom@emcp.net	
70	Rosewood, Inc.	998 North 42nd Str	Vancouver	BC	V5K 2N8	(778) 555-6643	rosewood@emcp.net	
84	Macadam, Inc.	675 Third Street	Vancouver	BC	V5K 2R9	(604) 555-5522	macadam@emcp.net	
99	KL Distributions	402 Yukon Drive	Bellingham	WA	98435	(360) 555-3711	kldist@emcp.net	
16	Olympic Suppliers	1773 50th Avenue	Seattle	WA	98101	(206) 555-9488	olysuppliers@emcp.n	
28	Gorman Company	543 26th Street	Vancouver	BC	V5K 3C5	(778) 555-4550	gormanco@emcp.net	

Step 3

4. Delete the record for supplier number 38 (Hadley Company). At the message telling you that relationships that specify cascading deletes are about to cause records in this table and related tables to be deleted, click Yes.
5. Display the table in Print Preview, change to landscape orientation, and then print the table.
6. Close the Suppliers table.
7. Open the Products table and then add the following records to the table:

   ProductID: 701-BK
   Product: Basic first aid kit
   SupplierID: 33
   UnitsInStock: 8
   UnitsOnOrder: 0
   ReorderLevel: 5

   ProductID: 703-SP
   Product: Medical survival pack
   SupplierID: 33
   UnitsInStock: 8
   UnitsOnOrder: 0
   ReorderLevel: 5

   ProductID: 185-10
   Product: Trail water filter
   SupplierID: 51
   UnitsInStock: 4
   UnitsOnOrder: 10
   ReorderLevel: 10

   ProductID: 185-50
   Product: Trail filter replacement cartridge
   SupplierID: 51
   UnitsInStock: 14
   UnitsOnOrder: 0
   ReorderLevel: 10
8. Display the Products table in Print Preview, change to landscape orientation, change the top and bottom margins to 0.4 inch and then print the table. (The table will print on two pages.)
9. Close the Products table.
10. Open the Orders table and then add the following record:

    OrderID: 1033
    OrderDate: 2/15/2015
    ProductID: 185-10
    UnitsOrdered: 10
    Amount: $310.90
11. Print and then close the Orders table.
12. Close **AL1-C2-PacTrek.accdb**.

Project 2 Create Relationships and Display Subdatasheets in a Database

2 Parts

You will open a company database and then create one-to-many relationships between tables, as well as a one-to-one relationship. You will also display and edit subdatasheets.

Creating One-to-One Relationships

You can create a ***one-to-one relationship*** between tables in which each record in the first table matches only one record in the second table and one record in the second table matches only one record in the first table. A one-to-one relationship is not as common as a one-to-many relationship, since the type of information used to create the relationship can be stored in one table. A one-to-one relationship is generally used when you want to break a large table with many fields into two smaller tables.

The Relationships window displays any relationship you have defined between tables.

In Project 2a, you will create a one-to-one relationship between the Employees table and the Benefits table. Each record in the Employees table and each record in the Benefits table pertains to one employee. These two tables could be merged into one but the data in each table is easier to manage when separated. Figure 2.10 shows the relationships you will define between the tables in AL1-C2-Griffin.accdb. The Benefits table and the Departments table have been moved down so you can more easily see the relationships.

Figure 2.10 AL1-C2-Griffin.accdb Table Relationships

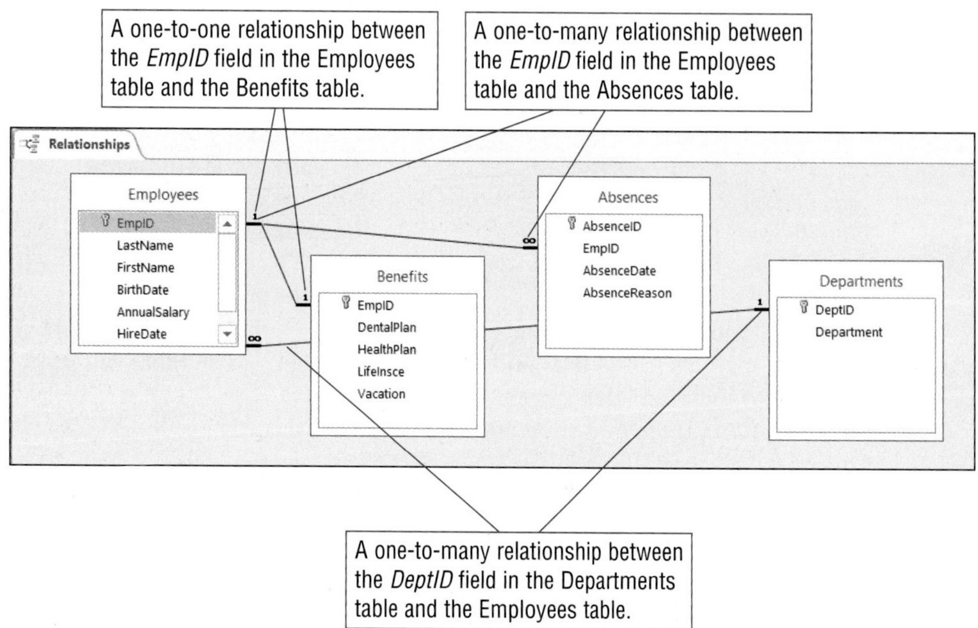

Project 2a Creating One-to-Many and One-to-One Relationships — Part 1 of 2

1. Open **AL1-C2-Griffin.accdb** and enable the contents.
2. Click the DATABASE TOOLS tab.
3. Click the Relationships button in the Relationships group.
4. At the Show Table dialog box with the Tables tab selected, add all of the tables to the Relationships window by completing the following steps:
   a. Double-click *Employees* in the list box. (This inserts the table in the Relationships window.)
   b. Double-click *Benefits* in the list box.
   c. Double-click *Absences* in the list box.
   d. Double-click *Departments* in the list box.
   e. Click the Close button to close the Show Table dialog box.
5. At the Relationships window, create a one-to-many relationship with the *EmpID* field in the Employees table as the "one" and the *EmpID* field in the Absences table the "many" by completing the following steps:
   a. Position the arrow pointer on the *EmpID* field that displays in the *Employees* field list box.

b. Hold down the left mouse button, drag the arrow pointer (with a field icon attached) to the *EmpID* field in the *Absences* field list box, and then release the mouse button. (This causes the Edit Relationships dialog box to display.)

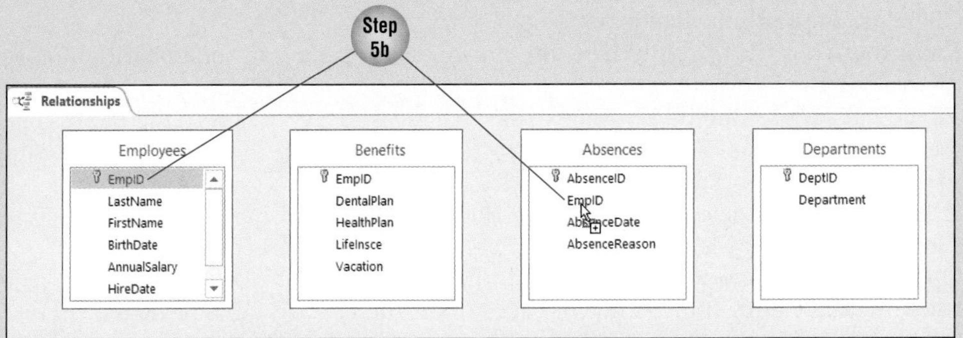

c. At the Edit Relationships dialog box, make sure *EmpID* displays in the *Table/Query* and *Related Table/Query* list boxes and the relationship type at the bottom of the dialog box displays as *One-To-Many*.
d. Click the *Enforce Referential Integrity* check box to insert a check mark.
e. Click the *Cascade Update Related Fields* check box to insert a check mark.
f. Click the *Cascade Delete Related Records* check box to insert a check mark.
g. Click the Create button. (A *1* appears at the *Employees* field list box side and an infinity symbol (∞) appears at the *Absences* field list box side of the black line.)

6. Complete steps similar to those in Step 5 to create a one-to-many relationship with the *DeptID* field in the Departments table the "one" and the *DeptID* field in the Employees table the "many." (You may need to scroll down the Employees field list box to display the *DeptID* field.)
7. Create a one-to-one relationship with the *EmpID* field in the Employees table and the *EmpID* field in the Benefits table by completing the following steps:
   a. Position the arrow pointer on the *EmpID* field in the *Employees* field list box.
   b. Hold down the left mouse button, drag the arrow pointer to the *EmpID* field in the *Benefits* field list box, and then release the mouse button. (This displays the Edit Relationships dialog box; notice at the bottom of the dialog box that the relationship type displays as *One-To-One*.)
   c. Click the *Enforce Referential Integrity* check box to insert a check mark.
   d. Click the *Cascade Update Related Fields* check box.
   e. Click the *Cascade Delete Related Records* check box.
   f. Click the Create button. (Notice that a *1* appears at the side of the *Employees* field list box and at the side of the *Benefits* field list box, indicating a one-to-one relationship.)

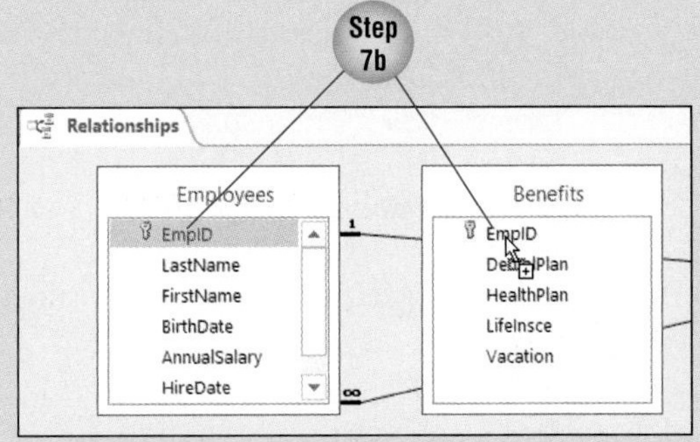

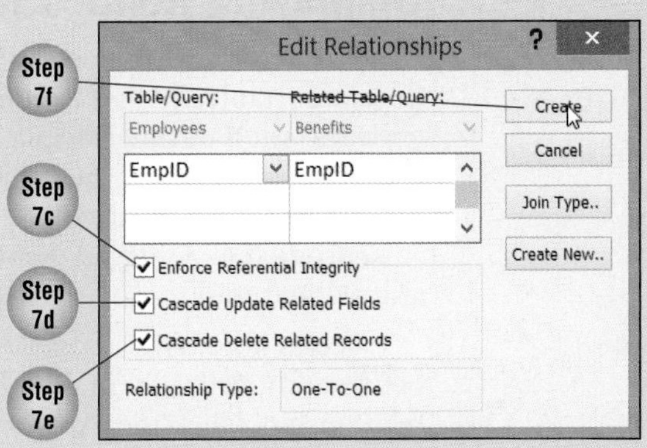

8. Click the Save button on the Quick Access toolbar to save the relationships.
9. Print the relationships by completing the following steps:
   a. Click the Relationship Report button in the Tools group.
   b. Click the Print button in the Print group.
   c. Click OK at the Print dialog box.
   d. Close the report by clicking the Close button that displays in the upper right corner of the work area.
   e. At the message asking if you want to save changes to the design of the report, click No.
10. Close the Relationships window by clicking the Close button that displays in the upper right corner of the work area.
11. Add a record to and delete a record from the Employees and Benefits tables by completing the following steps:
    a. Open the Employees table.
    b. Click the New button in the Records group on the HOME tab and then type the following data in the specified field:
       EmpID: 1096
       LastName: Schwartz
       FirstName: Bryan
       BirthDate: 5/21/1983
       DeptID: IT
       AnnualSalary: $45,000.00
       HireDate: 1/15/2010
    c. Delete the record for Trevor Sargent (employee number 1005). At the message telling you that relationships that specify cascading deletes are about to cause records in this table and related tables to be deleted, click Yes.
    d. Print and then close the Employees table.
12. Open the Benefits table and notice that the record for Trevor Sargent is deleted but the new employee record you entered in the Employees table is not reflected in the Benefits table. Add a new record for Bryan Schwartz with the following information:
    EmpID: 1096
    Dental Plan: (Press spacebar to remove check mark.)
    Health Plan: (Leave check mark.)
    Life Insurance: $100,000.00
    Vacation: 2 weeks
13. Print and then close the Benefits table.

Displaying Related Records in Subdatasheets

When a relationship is established between tables, you can view and edit records in related tables with a ***subdatasheet***. Figure 2.11 displays the Employees table with the subdatasheet displayed for employee Kate Navarro. The subdatasheet displays the fields in the Benefits table related to Kate Navarro. Use this subdatasheet to view and edit information in both the Employees table and Absences table. Changes made to fields in a subdatasheet affect the table and any related table.

Access automatically inserts a plus symbol (referred to as an ***expand indicator***) before each record in a table that is joined to another table by a one-to-many relationship. Click the expand indicator and if the table is related to only one other table, a subdatasheet containing fields from the related table displays below the record, as shown in Figure 2.11. To remove the subdatasheet, click the minus sign (referred to as a ***collapse indicator***) preceding the record. (The plus symbol turns into the minus symbol when a subdatasheet displays.)

If a table has more than one relationship defined, clicking the expand indicator will display the Insert Subdatasheet dialog box, as shown in Figure 2.12. At this dialog box, click the desired table in the Tables list box and then click OK. You can also display the Insert Subdatasheet dialog box by clicking the More button in the Records group on the HOME tab, pointing to *Subdatasheet*, and then clicking *Subdatasheet*. Display subdatasheets for all records by clicking the More button, pointing to *Subdatasheet*, and then clicking *Expand All*. Remove all subdatasheets by clicking the More button, pointing to *Subdatasheet*, and then clicking *Collapse All*.

If a table is related to two or more tables, specify the desired subdatasheet at the Insert Subdatasheet dialog box. If you decide to display a different subdatasheet, remove the subdatasheet first, before selecting the next subdatasheet. Do this by clicking the More button, pointing to *Subdatasheet*, and then clicking *Remove*.

Quick Steps

Display a Subdatasheet

1. Open table.
2. Click expand indicator at left side of desired record.
3. Click desired table at Insert Subdatasheet dialog box.
4. Click OK.

Figure 2.11 Table with Subdatasheet Displayed

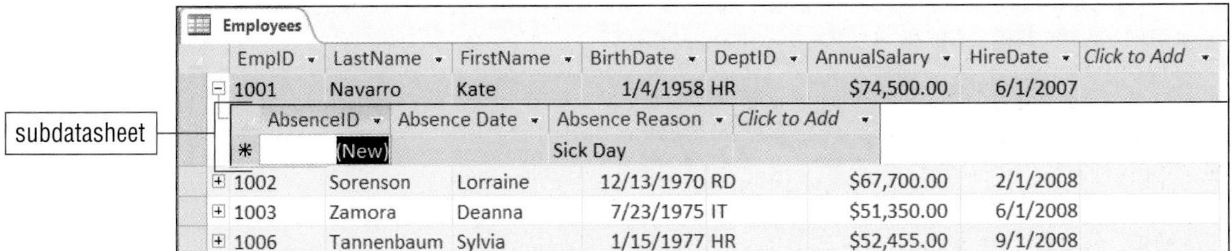

Figure 2.12 Insert Subdatasheet Dialog Box

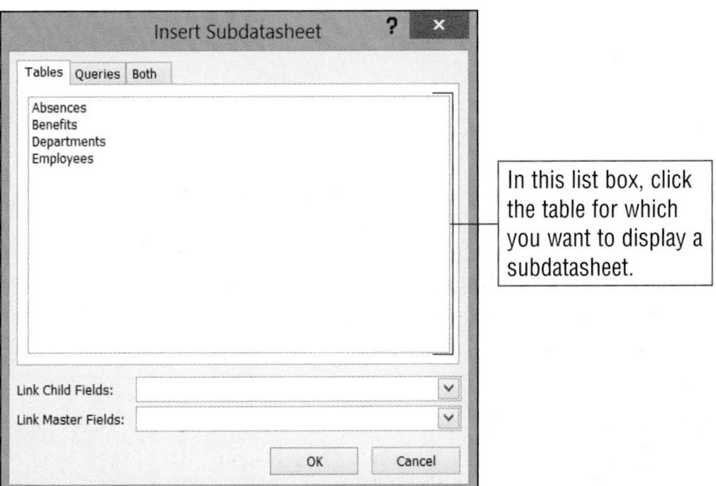

Project 2b Viewing and Editing a Subdatasheet

1. With the **AL1-C2-Griffin.accdb** database open, open the Employees table.
2. Display a subdatasheet by clicking the expand indicator (plus symbol) that displays at the left side of the first row (the row for Kate Navarro).

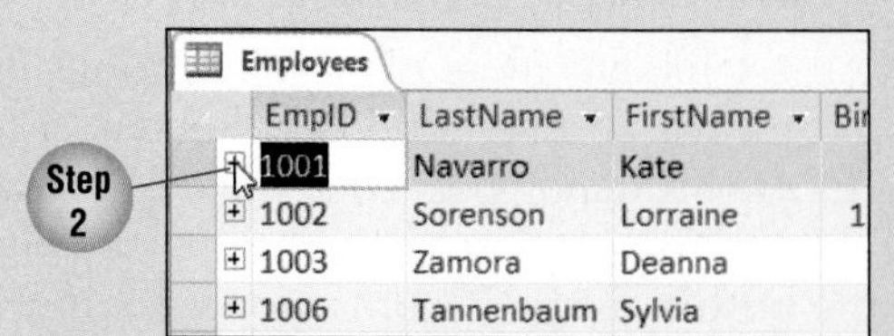

3. Remove the subdatasheet by clicking the collapse indicator (minus sign) that displays at the left side of the record for Kate Navarro.
4. Display subdatasheets for all of the records by clicking the More button in the Records group, pointing to *Subdatasheet*, and then clicking *Expand All*.

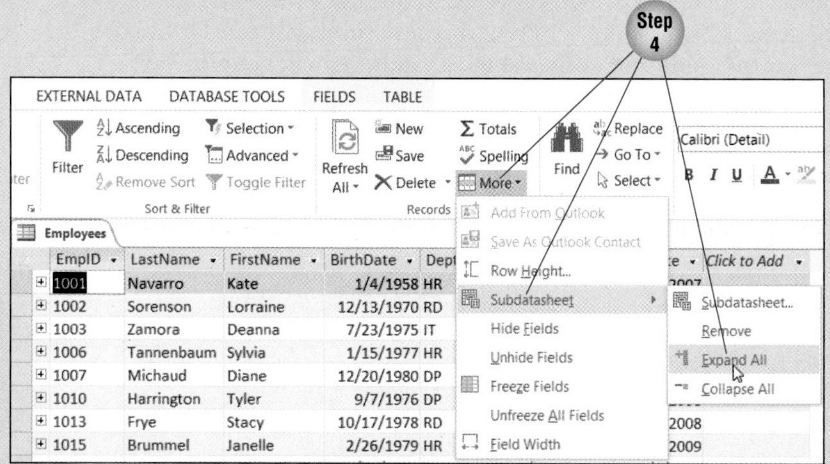

5. Remove the display of all subdatasheets by clicking the More button, pointing to *Subdatasheet*, and then clicking *Collapse All*.
6. Remove the connection between the Employees table and Absences table by clicking the More button, pointing to *Subdatasheet*, and then clicking *Remove*. (Notice that the expand indicators [plus symbols] no longer display before each record.)

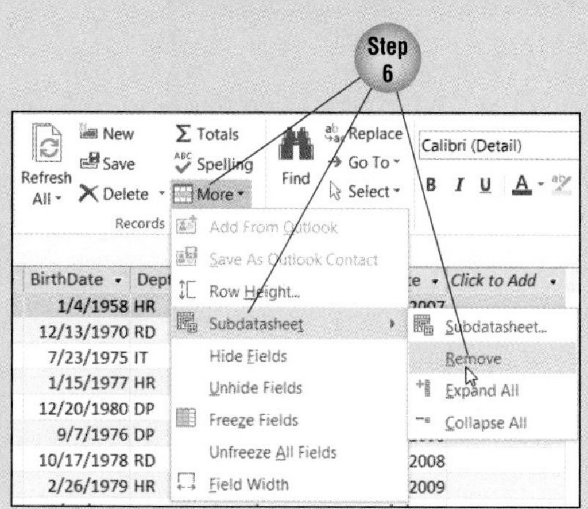

7. Suppose that the employee, Diane Michaud, has moved to a different department and has had an increase in salary. Display the Benefits subdatasheet and make changes to fields in the Employees table and Benefits table by completing the following steps:
   a. Click the More button in the Records group, point to *Subdatasheet*, and then click *Subdatasheet* at the side menu.
   b. At the Insert Subdatasheet dialog box, click *Benefits* in the list box and then click OK.
   c. Change the department ID for the record for *Diane Michaud* from *DP* to *A*.
   d. Change the salary from *$56,250.00* to *$57,500.00*.
   e. Click the expand indicator (plus symbol) that displays at the left side of the record for Diane Michaud.
   f. Insert a check mark in the *Dental Plan* check box and change the vacation from 3 weeks to 4 weeks.
   g. Click the collapse indicator (minus symbol) that displays at the left side of the record for Diane Michaud.

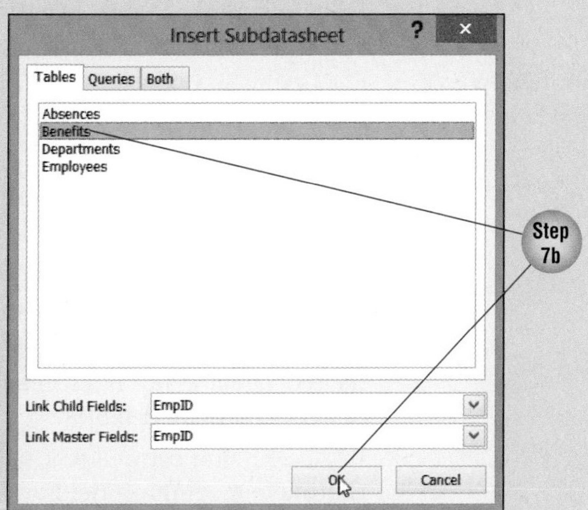

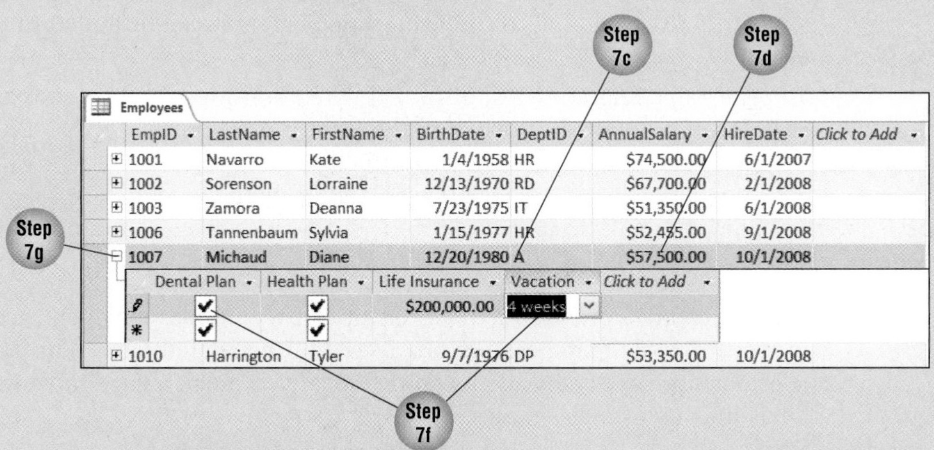

8. Click the Save button on the Quick Access toolbar.
9. Print and then close the Employees table.
10. Open, print, and then close the Benefits table.
11. Close the **AL1-C2-Griffin.accdb** database.

Chapter Summary

- Access is a relational database software program in which you can create tables that are related or connected.
- When planning a table, take time to determine how to break down the required data and what relationships need to be defined to eliminate data redundancies.
- Generally, one field in a table must be unique so that one record can be distinguished from another. A field with a unique value is considered a primary key field.
- A table can have only one primary key field and it is the field by which the table is sorted whenever it is opened.
- In a field defined as a primary key field, duplicate values are not allowed. Access also expects a value in each record in the primary key field.
- Typically, a primary key field in one table becomes the foreign key field in a related table. Data in a foreign key field must match data in the primary key field of the related tables.
- In Access, you can relate a table to another by performing a join. When tables that have a common field are joined, you can extract data from both tables as if they were one large table.
- You can create a one-to-many relationship between tables. In this relationship, a record must be added to the "one" table before it can be added to the "many" table.
- To print table relationships, display the Relationships window, click the Relationship Report button, click the Print button on the PRINT PREVIEW tab, and then click OK at the Print dialog box.
- At the Relationships window, click the Show Table button to display the Show Table dialog box.
- You can edit or delete a relationship between tables.
- You can create a one-to-one relationship between tables in which each record in the first table matches only one record in the related table. This type of relationship is generally used when you want to break a large table with many fields into two smaller tables.
- When a relationship is established between tables, you can view and edit fields in related tables with a subdatasheet.
- To display a subdatasheet for a record, click the expand indicator (plus symbol) that displays to the left of the record. To display subdatasheets for all records, click the More button in the Records group on the HOME tab, point to *Subdatasheet*, and then click *Expand All*.
- Display the Insert Subdatasheet dialog box by clicking the More button in the Reports group on the HOME tab, pointing to *Subdatasheet*, and then clicking *Subdatasheet*.
- Turn off the display of a subdatasheet by clicking the collapse indicator (minus symbol) at the beginning of the record. To turn off the display of subdatasheets for all records, click the More button, point to *Subdatasheet*, and then click *Collapse All*.

Commands Review

FEATURE	RIBBON, GROUP	BUTTON	OPTION
Edit Relationships dialog box	RELATIONSHIP TOOLS DESIGN, Tools		
Insert Subdatasheet dialog box	HOME, Records		*Subdatasheet, Subdatasheet*
primary key	TABLE TOOLS DESIGN, Tools		
print relationships report	RELATIONSHIP TOOLS DESIGN, Tools		
Relationships window	DATABASE TOOLS, Relationships		
Show Table dialog box	RELATIONSHIP TOOLS DESIGN, Relationships		

Concepts Check

Test Your Knowledge

Completion: In the space provided at the right, indicate the correct term, symbol, or command.

1. In Access, one table can be related to another, which is generally referred to as performing this. ____________
2. A database table can contain a foreign key field and this type of key field. ____________
3. Open a table, click the View button on the HOME tab, and the table displays in this view. ____________
4. In a one-to-many relationship, the table containing the "one" is referred to as this. ____________
5. In a one-to-many relationship, the table containing the "many" is referred to as this. ____________
6. In a one-to-many relationship, Access follows a set of rules that enforces consistency between related tables and is referred to as this. ____________
7. In related tables, this symbol displays near the black line next to the field list box of the related table. ____________
8. The black line that connects the field list boxes of related tables is referred to as this. ____________

9. Establish this type of relationship between tables in which each record in the first table matches only one record in the second table and only one record in the second table matches each record in the first table. ________________

10. The plus symbol that displays at the beginning of a record in a related table is referred to as this. ________________

11. The minus symbol that displays at the beginning of a record in a related table with a subdatasheet displayed is referred to as this. ________________

12. Display subdatasheets for all records by clicking the More button, pointing to *Subdatasheet*, and then clicking this option. ________________

Skills Check Assess Your Performance

The database designer for Copper State Insurance has created the database diagram shown in Figure 2.13 to manage company data. You will open the Copper State Insurance database and maintain and create tables that follow the diagram.

Figure 2.13 Copper State Insurance Database Design

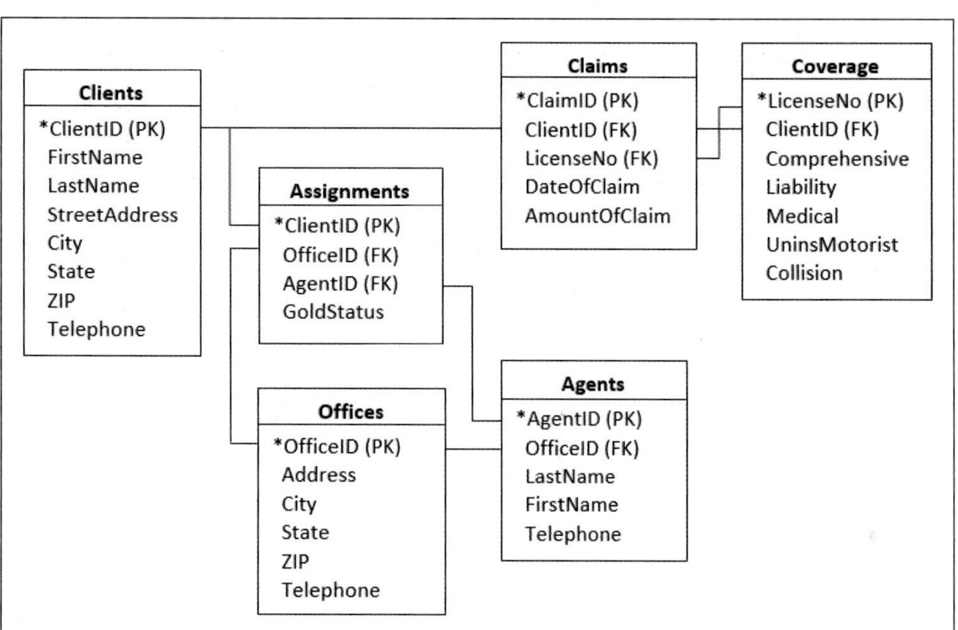

Assessment 1

CREATE RELATIONSHIPS IN AN INSURANCE COMPANY DATABASE

1. Open **AL1-C2-CopperState.accdb** and enable the contents.
2. Open the Claims table.
3. Display the table in Design view, define the *ClaimID* field as the primary key field, click the Save button on the Quick Access toolbar, and then close the Claims table.
4. Display the Relationships window and then insert the Clients, Claims, and Coverage tables.
5. Create a one-to-many relationship with the *ClientID* field in the Clients table the "one" and the *ClientID* field in the Claims table the "many." Enforce referential integrity and cascade fields and records.
6. Create a one-to-many relationship with the *ClientID* field in the Clients table the "one" and the *ClientID* field in the Coverage table the "many." Enforce referential integrity and cascade fields and records.
7. Create a one-to-many relationship with the *LicenseNo* field in the Coverage table the "one" and the *LicenseNo* field in the Claims table the "many." Enforce referential integrity and cascade fields and records.
8. Save and then print the relationships.
9. Close the relationships report without saving it and close the Relationships window.

Assessment 2

CREATE A NEW TABLE AND RELATE THE TABLE

SNAP Grade It

1. With **AL1-C2-CopperState.accdb** open, create the Offices table shown in Figure 2.14. Change the data type of the first column to *Short Text*. (Do this with the *Data Type* option box in the Formatting group on the TABLE TOOLS FIELDS tab.) Change the field size to 2 characters. Change the default value for the *State* field to *AZ*.
2. After typing the records, adjust the column widths to accommodate the longest entry in each column and then save the Offices table.
3. Print and then close the Offices table.
4. Display the Relationships window and then add the Offices table and the Assignments table to the window.
5. Create a one-to-many relationship with the *OfficeID* field in the Offices table the "one" and the *OfficeID* field in the Assignments table the "many." Enforce referential integrity and cascade fields and records.
6. Create a one-to-one relationship with the *ClientID* field in the Clients table and the *ClientID* field in the Assignments table. Enforce referential integrity and cascade fields and records.
7. Save and then print the relationships in landscape orientation. To do this, click the Landscape button in the Page Layout group in Print Preview.
8. Close the relationships report without saving it and then close the Relationships window.

Figure 2.14 Assessment 2 Offices Table

Offices

	OfficeID	Address	City	State	ZIP	Telephone	Click to Add
	GN	North 51st Avenue	Glendale	AZ	85305	(653) 555-8800	
	GW	West Bell Road	Glendale	AZ	85312	(623) 555-4300	
	PG	Grant Street West	Phoenix	AZ	85003	(602) 555-6200	
	PM	McDowell Road	Phoenix	AZ	85012	(602) 555-3800	
	SE	East Thomas Road	Scottsdale	AZ	85251	(480) 555-5500	
	SN	North 68th Street	Scottsdale	AZ	85257	(480) 555-9000	
*				AZ			

Assessment 3

DELETE AND EDIT RECORDS IN TABLES

1. With **AL1-C2-CopperState.accdb** open, open the Clients table.
2. Delete the record for Harold McDougal (client number 9879). (At the message telling you that relationships that specify cascading deletes are about to cause records in this table and related tables to be deleted, click Yes.)
3. Delete the record for Vernon Cook (client number 7335). (At the message telling you that relationships that specify cascading deletes are about to cause records in this table and related tables to be deleted, click Yes.)
4. Change the client number for Paul Vuong from *4300* to *2560*.
5. Print the Clients table in landscape orientation and then close the table.
6. Open the Claims table, print the table, and then close the table. (The Claims table initially contained two entries for client number 9879 and one entry for 7335. These entries were deleted automatically when you deleted the records in the Clients table.)

Assessment 4

DISPLAY AND EDIT RECORDS IN A SUBDATASHEET

1. With **AL1-C2-CopperState.accdb** open, open the Clients table.
2. Click the expand indicator (plus symbol) that displays at the left side of the record for Erin Hagedorn. At the Insert Subdatasheet dialog box, click *Claims* in the list box and then click OK.
3. Change the amount of the claim from *$1,450.00* to *$1,797.00*, change Erin's street address from *4818 Oakes Boulevard* to *763 51st Avenue*, and change her zip code from *85018* to *85014*.
4. Click the collapse indicator (minus symbol) that displays at the left side of the record for Erin Hagedorn.
5. Remove the connection between the Clients and Claims tables by clicking the More button in the Records group on the HOME tab, pointing to *Subdatasheet*, and then clicking *Remove*.
6. Click the More button in the Records group, point to *Subdatasheet*, and then click *Subdatasheet*.
7. At the Insert Subdatasheet dialog box, click *Coverage* in the list box and then click OK.
8. Expand all records by clicking the More button, pointing to *Subdatasheet*, and then clicking *Expand All*.
9. Change the telephone number for Claire Azevedo (client number 1379) from *480-555-2154* to *480-555-2143* and insert check marks in the *Medical* field and the *UninsMotorist* field.
10. Change the last name of Joanne Donnelly (client number 1574) to *Marquez* and remove the check mark from the *Collision* field.
11. At the record for Brenda Lazzuri (client number 3156), insert check marks in the *UninsMotorist* field and *Collision* field for both vehicles.
12. Click in any field heading and then collapse all records.
13. Remove the connection between the Clients and Coverage tables.
14. Save, print, and then close the Clients table. (Make sure the table displays in landscape orientation.)
15. Open the Coverage table, print the table, and then close the table.
16. Close **AL1-C2-CopperState.accdb**.

Visual Benchmark Demonstrate Your Proficiency

CREATE A BOOKINGS TABLE

1. Open **AL1-C2-CarefreeTravel.accdb** and then create the Bookings table shown in Figure 2.15. You determine the data types and field sizes. Create a more descriptive caption for each field name and create a description for each field.
2. Save, print, and then close the Bookings table.
3. Create a relationship between the Agents table and Bookings table. You determine what table contains the "one" and what table contains the "many." Enforce referential integrity and cascade fields and records.
4. Create a relationship between the Tours table and Bookings table. You determine what table contains the "one" and what table contains the "many." Enforce referential integrity and cascade fields and records.
5. Save and then print the relationships and then close the Relationships window.
6. Open the Agents table.
7. Change the AgentID for Wayne Postovic from *137* to *115*.
8. Change Jenna Williamson's last name from *Williamson* to *Parr*.
9. Print and then close the Agents table.
10. Open the Bookings table, print the table, and then close the table. (Notice that the *137* AgentID in the Bookings table is changed to *115*. This is because the tables are related and the changes you make in the primary table are made automatically in the related table.)
11. Close **AL1-C2-CarefreeTravel.accdb**.

Figure 2.15 Visual Benchmark Bookings Table

Bookings

	BookingID	BookingDate	TourID	AgentID	NumberPersons	*Click to Add*
	1	6/1/2015	AF02	114	8	
	2	6/1/2015	HC01	109	2	
	3	6/3/2015	CR02	103	2	
	4	6/4/2015	AK01	137	4	
	5	6/5/2015	HC01	109	2	
	6	6/6/2015	AT02	109	4	
	7	6/8/2015	HS02	104	2	
	8	6/10/2015	HC01	125	2	
	9	6/11/2015	AK01	142	4	
	10	6/13/2015	AT01	112	2	
	11	6/15/2015	HC03	129	2	
*	(New)				0	

Case Study Apply Your Skills

You are the manager for Gold Star Cleaning Services and your company is switching over to Access for managing company data. The database designer has provided you with the database diagram in Figure 2.17. He wants you to follow the diagram when creating the database.

Figure 2.17 Gold Star Cleaning Services Database Diagram

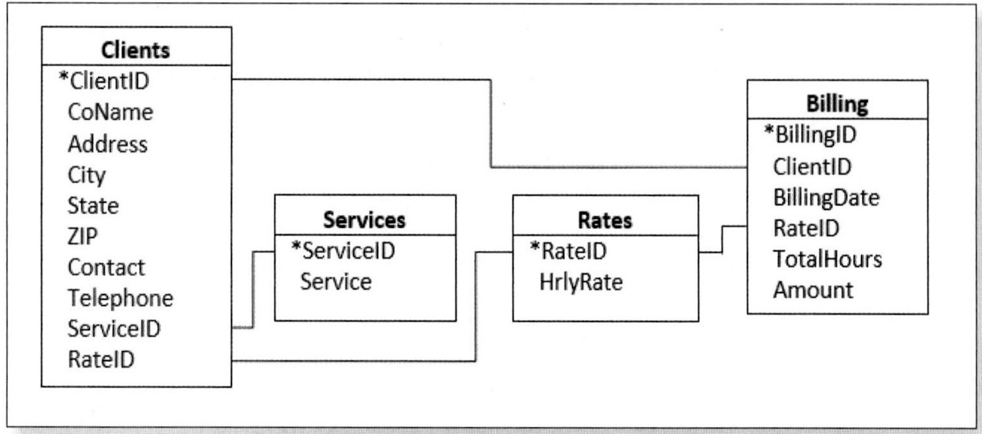

Part 1

Create a new database named **AL1-C2-GoldStar.accdb** and then create the Clients table shown in the database diagram. The database designer has asked you to include an appropriate caption and description for each field. Specify a field size of 3 characters for the *ClientID* field, 4 characters for the *ServiceID* field, and 1 character for the *RateID* field. You determine the field sizes for the *State*, *ZIP*, and *Telephone* fields. The designer also wants you to set the default value for the *City* field to *St. Louis* and the *State* field to *MO*. Type the following records in the table:

ClientID: 101
CoName: Smithson Realty
Address: 492 Papin Street
City: (default value)
State: (default value)
ZIP: 63108
Contact: Danielle Snowden
Telephone: (314) 555-3588
ServiceID: GS-1
RateID: B

*ClientID:*102
CoName: Air-Flow Systems
Address: 1058 Pine Street
City: (default value)
State: (default value)
ZIP: 63186
Contact: Nick Cline
Telephone: (314) 555-9452
ServiceID: GS-3
RateID: A

ClientID: 107
CoName: Mainstreet Mortgage
Address: North 22nd Street
City: (default value)
State: (default value)
ZIP: 63134
Contact: Ted Farrell
Telephone: (314) 555-7744
ServiceID: GS-1
RateID: D

ClientID: 110
CoName: Firstline Finances
Address: 104 Scott Avenue
City: (default value)
State: (default value
ZIP: 63126
Contact: Robert Styer
Telephone: (314) 555-8343
ServiceID: GS-2
RateID: A

ClientID: 112
CoName: GB Construction
Address: 988 Lucas Avenue
City: (default value)
State: (default value)
ZIP: 63175
Contact: Joy Ewing
Telephone: (314) 555-0036
ServiceID: GS-1
RateID: C

ClientID: 115
CoName: Simko Equipment
Address: 1200 Market Street
City: (default value)
State: (default value)
ZIP: 63140
Contact: Dale Aldrich
Telephone: (314) 555-3315
ServiceID: GS-3
RateID: C

Create the Services table shown in the database diagram. Change the *ServiceID* field size to 4 characters. Type the following records in the table:

ServiceID: GS-1
Service: Deep cleaning all rooms and surfaces, garbage removal, recycling, carpet cleaning, disinfecting

ServiceID: GS-2
Service: Deep cleaning all rooms and surfaces, garbage removal, disinfecting

ServiceID: GS-3
Service: Deep cleaning all rooms and surfaces, disinfecting

Create the Rates table shown in the database diagram. Change the *RateID* field size to 1 character. Type the following records in the table:

RateID: A
HrlyRate: $75.50

RateID: B
HrlyRate: $65.00

RateID: C
HrlyRate: $59.75

RateID: D
HrlyRate: $50.50

Create the Billing table shown in the database diagram. Change the *BillingID* field size to 2 characters, the *ClientID* field size to 3 characters, and the *RateID* field size to 1 character. Apply the appropriate data types to the fields. Type the following records in the table:

BillingID: 40
ClientID: 101
BillingDate: 4/1/2015
RateID: B
TotalHours: 26
Amount: $1,690.00

BillingID: 41
ClientID: 102
BillingDate: 4/1/2015
RateID: A
TotalHours: 32
Amount: $2,416.00

BillingID: 42
ClientID: 107
BillingDate: 4/1/2015
RateID: D
TotalHours: 15
Amount: $747.50

BillingID: 43
ClientID: 110
BillingDate: 4/1/2015
RateID: A
TotalHours: 30
Amount: $2,265.00

BillingID: 44
ClientID: 112
BillingDate: 4/1/2015
RateID: C
TotalHours: 20
Amount: $1,195.00

BillingID: 45
ClientID: 115
BillingDate: 4/1/2015
RateID: C
TotalHours: 22
Amount: $1,314.50

Automatically adjust the column widths of each table to accommodate the longest entry in each column and then print each table on one page. ***Hint: Check the table in Print Preview and, if necessary, change to landscape orientation and change the margins.***

Part 2

With **AL1-C2-GoldStar.accdb** open, create the one-to-many relationships required to connect the tables. (Refer to Figure 2.17 as a guide.) You will need to increase the size of the Clients field list box to view all of the fields. To do this, position the mouse pointer on the bottom border of the Clients field list box in the Relationships window until the pointer turns into a white arrow pointing up and down. Hold down the left mouse button, drag down to the desired position, and then release the mouse button. Print the relationships report.

Part 3

Open the Services table and then make the following changes to the field values in the *ServiceID* field:

Change *GS-1* to *GS-A*
Change *GS-2* to *GS-B*
Change *GS-3* to *GS-C*

Print and then close the Services table. Open the Clients table, delete the record for client number 112, and then insert the following record:

ClientID: **108**
Name: **Cedar Ridge Products**
Address: **6400 Olive Street**
City: (default value)
State: (default value)
ZIP: **63114**
Contact: **Penny Childers**
Telephone: **(314) 555-7660**
ServiceID: **GS-B**
RateID: **B**

Print and then close the Clients table. Open the Billing table, print the table, and then close the table. Close **AL1-C2-GoldStar.accdb**.

MICROSOFT®

ACCESS®

Performing Queries

PERFORMANCE OBJECTIVES

Upon successful completion of Chapter 3, you will be able to:

- **Design queries to extract specific data from tables**
- **Modify queries**
- **Design queries with *Or* and *And* criteria**
- **Use the Simple Query Wizard to create queries**
- **Create a calculated field**
- **Use aggregate functions in queries**
- **Create crosstab, duplicate, and unmatched queries**

Tutorials

3.1 Creating a Query in Design View
3.2 Extracting Records Using Criteria Statements
3.3 Creating a Query in Design View Using Multiple Tables
3.4 Extracting Records Using AND Criteria; Sorting Query Results
3.5 Renaming and Deleting Objects
3.6 Extracting Records Using OR Criteria
3.7 Creating Queries Using the Simple Query Wizard
3.8 Performing Calculations in a Query
3.9 Using Aggregate Functions
3.10 Creating a Crosstab Query
3.11 Creating a Find Duplicates Query
3.12 Creating a Find Unmatched Query

One of the primary uses of a database is to extract the specific information needed to answer questions and make decisions. A company might need to know information such as how much inventory is currently on hand, which products have been ordered, which accounts are past due, or which customers live in a particular city. You can extract specific information from a table or multiple tables by completing a query. You will learn how to perform a variety of queries on information in tables in this chapter. Model answers for this chapter's projects appear on the following pages.

AL1C3

Note: Before beginning the projects, copy the AL1C3 subfolder from the AL1 folder on the CD that accompanies this textbook to your storage medium and make AL1C3 the active folder.

Project 1 Design Queries

Project 1a

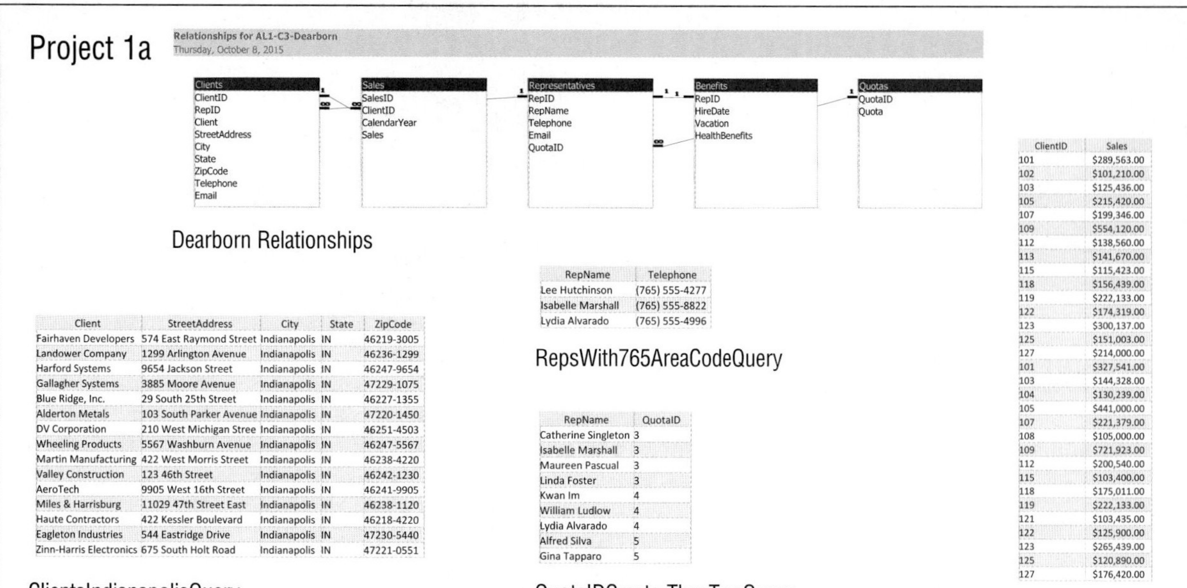

Dearborn Relationships

Client	StreetAddress	City	State	ZipCode
Fairhaven Developers	574 East Raymond Street	Indianapolis	IN	46219-3005
Landower Company	1299 Arlington Avenue	Indianapolis	IN	46236-1299
Harford Systems	9654 Jackson Street	Indianapolis	IN	46247-9654
Gallagher Systems	3885 Moore Avenue	Indianapolis	IN	47229-1075
Blue Ridge, Inc.	29 South 25th Street	Indianapolis	IN	46227-1355
Alderton Metals	103 South Parker Avenue	Indianapolis	IN	47220-1450
DV Corporation	210 West Michigan Stree	Indianapolis	IN	46251-4503
Wheeling Products	5567 Washburn Avenue	Indianapolis	IN	46247-5567
Martin Manufacturing	422 West Morris Street	Indianapolis	IN	46238-4220
Valley Construction	123 46th Street	Indianapolis	IN	46242-1230
AeroTech	9905 West 16th Street	Indianapolis	IN	46241-9905
Miles & Harrisburg	11029 47th Street East	Indianapolis	IN	46238-1120
Haute Contractors	422 Kessler Boulevard	Indianapolis	IN	46218-4220
Eagleton Industries	544 Eastridge Drive	Indianapolis	IN	47230-5440
Zinn-Harris Electronics	675 South Holt Road	Indianapolis	IN	47221-0551

ClientsIndianapolisQuery

RepName	Telephone
Lee Hutchinson	(765) 555-4277
Isabelle Marshall	(765) 555-8822
Lydia Alvarado	(765) 555-4996

RepsWith765AreaCodeQuery

RepName	QuotaID
Catherine Singleton	3
Isabelle Marshall	3
Maureen Pascual	3
Linda Foster	3
Kwan Im	4
William Ludlow	4
Lydia Alvarado	4
Alfred Silva	5
Gina Tapparo	5

QuotaIDGreaterThanTwoQuery

ClientID	Sales
101	$289,563.00
102	$101,210.00
103	$125,436.00
105	$215,420.00
107	$199,346.00
109	$554,120.00
112	$138,560.00
113	$141,670.00
115	$115,423.00
118	$156,439.00
119	$222,133.00
122	$174,319.00
123	$300,137.00
125	$151,003.00
127	$214,000.00
101	$327,541.00
103	$144,328.00
104	$130,239.00
105	$441,000.00
107	$221,379.00
108	$105,000.00
109	$721,923.00
112	$200,540.00
115	$103,400.00
118	$175,011.00
119	$222,133.00
121	$103,435.00
122	$125,900.00
123	$265,439.00
125	$120,890.00
127	$176,420.00

SalesOver$99999Query

Project 1b

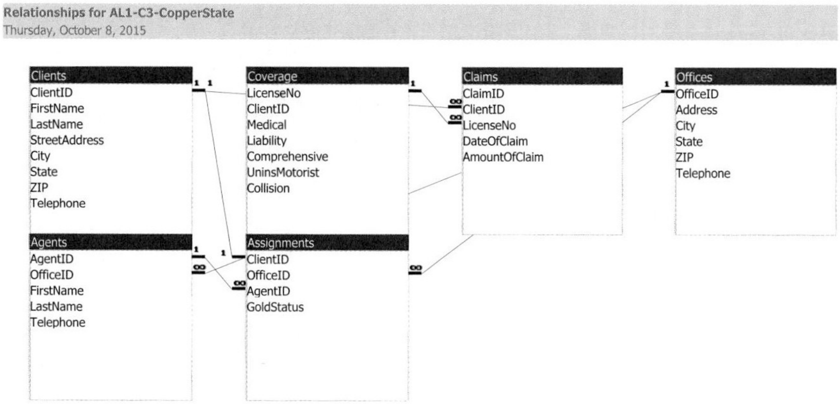

Relationships for AL1-C3-CopperState
Thursday, October 8, 2015

Clients	Coverage	Claims	Offices	Agents	Assignments
ClientID	LicenseNo	ClaimID	OfficeID	AgentID	ClientID
FirstName	ClientID	ClientID	Address	OfficeID	OfficeID
LastName	Medical	LicenseNo	City	FirstName	AgentID
StreetAddress	Liability	DateOfClaim	State	LastName	GoldStatus
City	Comprehensive	AmountOfClaim	ZIP	Telephone	
State	UninsMotorist		Telephone		
ZIP	Collision				
Telephone					

CopperState Relationships

RepName	HireDate
Alfred Silva	3/15/2011
Cecilia Ortega	4/12/2011
Isabelle Marshall	3/7/2011

MarToNov2011HiresQuery

ProductID	Product	OrderDate
250-XL	Cascade R4 jacket, MXL	2/2/2015
100-02	Multi-function compass	2/2/2015
202-CW	Ten-piece hiker cookware	2/2/2015
201-CW	Eight-piece stainless steel cookware	2/2/2015
100-05	Deluxe map compass	2/2/2015
101-S3R	SL 20-degrees synthetic sleeping bag, red	2/2/2015
101-S3B	SL 20-degrees synthetic sleeping bag, blac	2/2/2015
255-M	Cascade R4 jacket, WM	2/2/2015
250-L	Cascade R4 jacket, ML	2/2/2015
255-XL	Cascade R4 jacket, WXL	2/2/2015
299-W4	HT waterproof hiking boots, WS8	2/16/2015
299-W5	HT waterproof hiking boots, WS7	2/16/2015
602-XR	Binoculars, 8 x 42	2/16/2015
590-TL	Thermaline roll-top table	2/16/2015
299-W3	HT waterproof hiking boots, WS9	2/16/2015
299-W1	HT waterproof hiking boots, WS11	2/16/2015
560-TL	Thermaline sleeping pad	2/16/2015

Feb1-28OrdersQuery

ClientID	FirstName	LastName	UninsMotorist
3120	Spenser	Winters	✓
7335	Vernon	Cook	✓
4300	Paul	Vuong	✓
3120	Spenser	Winters	✓
4852	Phillip	Cole	✓
5645	Eileen	Hanley	✓
7521	Fredrick	Guthrie	✓
0214	Alice	Ryckman	✓
8223	Cecilia	Ortiz	✓
5665	Suzanne	Lundberg	✓
9879	Harold	McDougal	✓
4852	Phillip	Cole	✓
6478	Parma	Moreno	✓
9775	Carla	Waterman	✓
5645	Eileen	Hanley	✓
9897	Rachel	Kaelin	✓
2768	Marcus	LeVigne	✓
7139	Donald	Rutledge	✓
9872	Sun	Cheong	✓
5982	Alan	Couturier	✓
4875	Michael	Nicolo	✓
1574	Joanne	Donnelly	✓
4786	Lenora	Chisham	✓
5231	Helena	Myerson	✓
4567	Bonnie	Metzger	✓
4868	Eric	Zadinski	✓

UninsMotoristCoverageQuery

RepID	RepName	HireDate
15	Lee Hutchinson	2/1/2012
22	Gina Tapparo	10/1/2012
25	Lydia Alvarado	4/1/2012

RepsHiredIn2012Query

ClientID	Client	Sales
110	Blue Ridge, Inc.	$17,542.00
110	Blue Ridge, Inc.	$83,210.00

BlueRidgeSalesQuery

ClientID	FirstName	LastName	ClaimID	DateOfClaim	AmountOfClaim
9383	Elaine	Hueneka	102394	1/2/2015	$1,235.00
7335	Vernon	Cook	104366	1/5/2015	$834.95
4300	Paul	Vuong	121039	1/8/2015	$5,230.00
9383	Elaine	Hueneka	153001	1/17/2015	$535.00
1574	Joanne	Donnelly	158954	1/19/2015	$1,050.75
4875	Michael	Nicolo	147858	1/16/2015	$875.00
8223	Cecilia	Ortiz	158962	1/21/2015	$2,830.50
4300	Paul	Vuong	178545	1/30/2015	$4,858.30
8854	Edward	Bakalarski	174223	1/23/2015	$950.50
9879	Harold	McDougal	174589	1/26/2015	$752.45
4567	Bonnie	Metzger	136695	1/10/2015	$1,840.00
5982	Alan	Couturier	147851	1/12/2015	$3,250.50

JanClaimsOver$500Query

Project 1c

ProductID	SupplierID	UnitsOrdered	Amount
442-1B	42	10	$1,495.00
780-2	99	10	$1,288.50
250-XL	60	10	$1,285.00
250-L	60	10	$1,285.00
101-S3R	54	10	$1,199.50
101-S3B	54	10	$1,137.50
299-M3	31	10	$887.90
299-M2	31	10	$887.90
299-M5	31	10	$887.90
299-W4	31	10	$752.90
299-W5	31	10	$752.90
299-W3	31	10	$752.90
299-W1	31	8	$602.32
255-XL	60	5	$599.50
255-M	60	5	$599.50
560-TL	25	20	$397.00
155-35	10	10	$199.50
375-S	68	20	$199.00
375-M	68	20	$199.00
590-TL	25	5	$196.25
209-XL	68	25	$180.00
209-L	68	25	$173.75
210-L	68	25	$162.25
209-XXL	68	20	$145.80
100-05	84	5	$129.75
371-L	68	10	$129.50
202-CW	15	5	$124.25
155-20	10	15	$104.25
201-CW	15	5	$99.75
210-M	68	15	$97.35
100-02	84	10	$45.95
152-H	10	15	$44.85

OrdersLessThan$1500Query

OfficeID	FirstName	LastName
GW	Carlos	Alvarez
GW	Joanne	Donnelly
GW	Cecilia	Ortiz
GW	Donald	Rutledge
GW	Paul	Vuong

GWClientsQuery

RepName	Client	Sales
Andre Kulisek	HE Systems	$721,923.00
Andre Kulisek	HE Systems	$554,120.00
Lee Hutchinson	Harford Systems	$441,000.00
Linda Foster	Bering Company	$327,541.00
Kwan Im	Eagleton Industries	$300,137.00
Linda Foster	Bering Company	$289,563.00
Kwan Im	Eagleton Industries	$265,439.00
Craig Johnson	Miles & Harrisburg	$222,133.00
Craig Johnson	Miles & Harrisburg	$222,133.00
Catherine Singleton	Gallagher Systems	$221,379.00
Lee Hutchinson	Harford Systems	$215,420.00
Catherine Singleton	Zinn-Harris Electronics	$214,000.00
Gina Tapparo	DV Corporation	$200,540.00
Catherine Singleton	Gallagher Systems	$199,346.00
Catherine Singleton	Zinn-Harris Electronics	$176,420.00
David DeBruler	AeroTech	$175,011.00
Jaren Newman	Haute Contractors	$174,319.00
David DeBruler	AeroTech	$156,439.00
Cecilia Ortega	Dover Industries	$151,003.00
Alfred Silva	Clearwater Service	$144,328.00
Catherine Singleton	Franklin Services	$141,670.00
Gina Tapparo	DV Corporation	$138,560.00
Robin Rehberg	Landower Company	$130,239.00
Jaren Newman	Haute Contractors	$125,900.00
Alfred Silva	Clearwater Service	$125,436.00
Cecilia Ortega	Dover Industries	$120,890.00
Craig Johnson	Wheeling Products	$115,423.00
Edward Harris	Karris Supplies	$105,000.00
William Ludlow	Madison Electrics	$103,435.00
Craig Johnson	Wheeling Products	$103,400.00
Kwan Im	Fairhaven Developers	$101,210.00

SalesMoreThan$100000Query

Project 1d

RepName	Client	Sales
William Ludlow	Madison Electrics	$99,450.00
Robin Rehberg	Landower Company	$97,653.00
Kwan Im	Fairhaven Developers	$95,630.00
Isabelle Marshall	Providence, Inc.	$85,628.00
Maureen Pascual	Blue Ridge, Inc.	$83,210.00
Isabelle Marshall	Providence, Inc.	$75,462.00
Catherine Singleton	Franklin Services	$65,411.00
Lydia Alvarado	Martin Manufacturing	$61,539.00
Edward Harris	Karris Supplies	$61,349.00
Jaren Newman	Paragon Corporation	$51,237.00
Alfred Silva	Alderton Metals	$45,230.00
Lydia Alvarado	Martin Manufacturing	$35,679.00
Craig Johnson	Hoosier Corporation	$31,935.00
Kwan Im	Milltown Contractors	$31,230.00
Craig Johnson	Hoosier Corporation	$24,880.00
Lee Hutchinson	Valley Construction	$22,478.00
Jaren Newman	Paragon Corporation	$20,137.00
Maureen Pascual	Blue Ridge, Inc.	$17,542.00
Lee Hutchinson	Valley Construction	$15,248.00
Alfred Silva	Northstar Services	$15,094.00
Alfred Silva	Alderton Metals	$9,547.00
Alfred Silva	Northstar Services	$9,457.00
Kwan Im	Milltown Contractors	$2,356.00

SalesLessThan$100000Query

RepName	Vacation
Alfred Silva	3 weeks
Cecilia Ortega	3 weeks
Isabelle Marshall	3 weeks
Craig Johnson	3 weeks
Gina Tapparo	3 weeks
Edward Harris	3 weeks

RepsWith3WeekVacationsQuery

Project 1e

RepName	Vacation
William Ludlow	4 weeks
Alfred Silva	3 weeks
Cecilia Ortega	3 weeks
Robin Rehberg	4 weeks
Isabelle Marshall	3 weeks
Craig Johnson	3 weeks
Gina Tapparo	3 weeks
Edward Harris	3 weeks

RepsWith3Or4WeekVacationsQuery

Client	City	Sales
Fairhaven Developers	Indianapolis	$101,210.00
Landower Company	Indianapolis	$130,239.00
Harford Systems	Indianapolis	$215,420.00
Harford Systems	Indianapolis	$441,000.00
Gallagher Systems	Indianapolis	$199,346.00
Gallagher Systems	Indianapolis	$221,379.00
DV Corporation	Indianapolis	$138,560.00
DV Corporation	Indianapolis	$200,540.00
Wheeling Products	Indianapolis	$115,423.00
Wheeling Products	Indianapolis	$103,400.00
AeroTech	Indianapolis	$156,439.00
AeroTech	Indianapolis	$175,011.00
Miles & Harrisburg	Indianapolis	$222,133.00
Miles & Harrisburg	Indianapolis	$222,133.00
Haute Contractors	Indianapolis	$174,319.00
Haute Contractors	Indianapolis	$125,900.00
Eagleton Industries	Indianapolis	$300,137.00
Eagleton Industries	Indianapolis	$265,439.00
Zinn-Harris Electronics	Indianapolis	$214,000.00
Zinn-Harris Electronics	Indianapolis	$176,420.00

SalesOver$100000IndianapolisQuery

SupplierID	SupplierName	Product
25	Langley Corporation	Thermaline sleeping pad
25	Langley Corporation	Thermaline light-weight cot
25	Langley Corporation	Thermaline camp seat
25	Langley Corporation	Thermaline roll-top table
31	Sound Supplies	HT waterproof hiking boots, MS13
31	Sound Supplies	HT waterproof hiking boots, MS12
31	Sound Supplies	HT waterproof hiking boots, MS11
31	Sound Supplies	HT waterproof hiking boots, MS10
31	Sound Supplies	HT waterproof hiking boots, MS9
31	Sound Supplies	HT waterproof hiking boots, WS11
31	Sound Supplies	HT waterproof hiking boots, WS10
31	Sound Supplies	HT waterproof hiking boots, WS9
31	Sound Supplies	HT waterproof hiking boots, WS8
31	Sound Supplies	HT waterproof hiking boots, WS7
31	Sound Supplies	HT waterproof hiking boots, WS6
42	Fraser Valley Products	Polar backpack, 150BR
42	Fraser Valley Products	Polar backpack, 150RW
42	Fraser Valley Products	Polar backpack, 250BR
42	Fraser Valley Products	Polar backpack, 250RW

Suppliers25-31-42Query

OrderID	SupplierName	Product	UnitsOrdered
1017	Freedom Corporation	Gordon wool ski hat, L	25
1009	Freedom Corporation	Gordon wool ski hat, XL	25
1008	Freedom Corporation	Gordon wool ski hat, XXL	20
1012	Freedom Corporation	Tech-lite ski hat, L	25
1013	Freedom Corporation	Tech-lite ski hat, M	15
1016	Freedom Corporation	Lite-tech ski gloves, ML	10
1015	Freedom Corporation	Lite-tech ski gloves, WM	20
1014	Freedom Corporation	Lite-tech ski gloves, WS	20

SkiHatsGlovesOnOrderQuery

ProductID	Product	SupplierName
443-1B	Polar backpack, 250RW	Fraser Valley Products
101-S1B	SL 0-degrees down sleeping bag, black	Manning, Inc.
101-S1R	SL 0-degrees down sleeping bag, red	Manning, Inc.
101-S2B	SL 15-degrees synthetic sleeping bag, blac	Manning, Inc.
101-S2R	SL 15-degrees synthetic sleeping bag, red	Manning, Inc.
101-S3B	SL 20-degrees synthetic sleeping bag, blac	Manning, Inc.
101-S3R	SL 20-degrees synthetic sleeping bag, red	Manning, Inc.
299-M1	HT waterproof hiking boots, MS13	Sound Supplies
299-M2	HT waterproof hiking boots, MS12	Sound Supplies
299-M3	HT waterproof hiking boots, MS11	Sound Supplies
299-M4	HT waterproof hiking boots, MS10	Sound Supplies
299-M5	HT waterproof hiking boots, MS9	Sound Supplies
299-W1	HT waterproof hiking boots, WS11	Sound Supplies
299-W2	HT waterproof hiking boots, WS10	Sound Supplies
299-W3	HT waterproof hiking boots, WS9	Sound Supplies
299-W4	HT waterproof hiking boots, WS8	Sound Supplies
299-W5	HT waterproof hiking boots, WS7	Sound Supplies

BootsSleepingBagsBackpacksQuery

FirstName	LastName	Medical	Liability	Comprehensive	UninsMotorist	Collision
Brenda	Lazzuri	☐	☑	☐	☐	☐
Edward	Bakalarski	☐	☑	☐	☐	☐
Brenda	Lazzuri	☐	☑	☐	☐	☐
Bret	Mardock	☐	☑	☐	☐	☐
Carlos	Alvarez	☐	☑	☐	☐	☐

ClientsWithOnlyLiabilityQuery

Project 1f

ClientID	Client	Sales
101	Bering Company	$289,563.00
101	Bering Company	$327,541.00
102	Fairhaven Developers	$101,210.00
102	Fairhaven Developers	$95,630.00
103	Clearwater Service	$125,436.00
103	Clearwater Service	$144,328.00
104	Landower Company	$97,653.00
104	Landower Company	$130,239.00
105	Harford Systems	$215,420.00
105	Harford Systems	$441,000.00
106	Providence, Inc.	$85,628.00
106	Providence, Inc.	$75,462.00
107	Gallagher Systems	$199,346.00
107	Gallagher Systems	$221,379.00
108	Karris Supplies	$61,349.00
108	Karris Supplies	$105,000.00
109	HE Systems	$554,120.00
109	HE Systems	$721,923.00
110	Blue Ridge, Inc.	$17,542.00
110	Blue Ridge, Inc.	$83,210.00
111	Alderton Metals	$9,547.00
111	Alderton Metals	$45,230.00
112	DV Corporation	$138,560.00
112	DV Corporation	$200,540.00
113	Franklin Services	$141,670.00
113	Franklin Services	$65,411.00
114	Milltown Contractors	$2,356.00
114	Milltown Contractors	$31,230.00
115	Wheeling Products	$115,423.00
115	Wheeling Products	$103,400.00
116	Martin Manufacturing	$35,679.00
116	Martin Manufacturing	$61,539.00
117	Valley Construction	$15,248.00
117	Valley Construction	$22,478.00
118	AeroTech	$156,439.00
118	AeroTech	$175,011.00
119	Miles & Harrisburg	$222,133.00
119	Miles & Harrisburg	$222,133.00
120	Paragon Corporation	$51,237.00
120	Paragon Corporation	$20,137.00
121	Madison Electrics	$99,450.00
121	Madison Electrics	$103,435.00
122	Haute Contractors	$174,319.00

ClientSalesQuery, Page 1

ClientID	Client	Sales
122	Haute Contractors	$125,900.00
123	Eagleton Industries	$300,137.00
123	Eagleton Industries	$265,439.00
124	Hoosier Corporation	$24,880.00
124	Hoosier Corporation	$31,935.00
125	Dover Industries	$151,003.00
125	Dover Industries	$120,890.00
126	Northstar Services	$9,457.00
126	Northstar Services	$15,094.00
127	Zinn-Harris Electronics	$214,000.00
127	Zinn-Harris Electronics	$176,420.00

ClientSalesQuery, Page 2

SupplierID	SupplierName	ProductID	Amount
42	Fraser Valley Products	443-1B	$2,397.75
25	Langley Corporation	560-TL	$397.00
25	Langley Corporation	590-TL	$196.25
35	Emerald City Products	602-XR	$2,145.00
99	KL Distributions	647-1	$2,999.85
99	KL Distributions	780-2	$1,288.50
84	Macadam, Inc.	100-02	$45.95
84	Macadam, Inc.	100-05	$129.75
54	Manning, Inc.	101-S2R	$1,945.25
54	Manning, Inc.	101-S3B	$1,137.50
54	Manning, Inc.	101-S3R	$1,199.50
10	Hopewell, Inc.	152-H	$44.85
10	Hopewell, Inc.	155-20	$104.25
10	Hopewell, Inc.	155-35	$199.50
15	Bayside Supplies	201-CW	$99.75
15	Bayside Supplies	202-CW	$124.25
68	Freedom Corporation	209-L	$173.75
68	Freedom Corporation	209-XL	$180.00
68	Freedom Corporation	209-XXL	$145.80
68	Freedom Corporation	210-L	$162.25
68	Freedom Corporation	210-M	$97.35
60	Cascade Gear	250-L	$1,285.00
60	Cascade Gear	250-XL	$1,285.00
60	Cascade Gear	255-M	$599.50
60	Cascade Gear	255-XL	$599.50
31	Sound Supplies	299-M2	$887.90
31	Sound Supplies	299-M3	$887.90
31	Sound Supplies	299-M5	$887.90
31	Sound Supplies	299-W1	$602.32
31	Sound Supplies	299-W3	$752.90
31	Sound Supplies	299-W4	$752.90
31	Sound Supplies	299-W5	$752.90
68	Freedom Corporation	371-L	$129.50
68	Freedom Corporation	375-M	$199.00
68	Freedom Corporation	375-S	$199.00
42	Fraser Valley Products	442-1B	$1,495.00

ProductOrderAmountsQuery

Project 1g

SupplierName	StreetAddress	City	Prov/State	PostalCode
Bayside Supplies	6705 North Street	Bellingham	WA	98432
Hadley Company	5845 Jefferson Street	Seattle	WA	98107
Cascade Gear	540 Broadway	Seattle	WA	98106
Sound Supplies	2104 Union Street	Seattle	WA	98105
Emerald City Products	1059 Pike Street	Seattle	WA	98102
KL Distributions	402 Yukon Drive	Bellingham	WA	96435

SuppliersNotBCQuery

Client	StreetAddress	City	State	ZipCode
Bering Company	4521 East Sixth Street	Muncie	IN	47310-5500
Clearwater Service	10385 North Gavin Street	Muncie	IN	47308-1236
Providence, Inc.	12490 141st Street	Muncie	IN	47306-3410
Paragon Corporation	4500 Meridian Street	Muncie	IN	47302-4338
Dover Industries	4839 Huchins Road	Muncie	IN	47306-4839
Northstar Services	5135 West Second Street	Muncie	IN	47301-7774

ClientsMuncieQuery

ClientID	FirstName	LastName	StreetAddress	City	State	ZIP	ClaimID	AmountOfClaim
7335	Vernon	Cook	1230 South Mesa	Phoenix	AZ	85018	104366	$834.95
1331	Erin	Hagedorn	4818 Oakes Boulevard	Phoenix	AZ	85018	198745	$1,797.00
9879	Harold	McDougal	7115 Elizabeth Lane	Phoenix	AZ	85009	174589	$752.45
9775	Carla	Waterman	3979 19th Avenue	Phoenix	AZ	85031	241485	$4,500.00
6478	Parma	Moreno	610 Sheridan Avenue	Phoenix	AZ	85031	200147	$925.75
4868	Eric	Zadinski	1301 North Meridian	Phoenix	AZ	85031	210369	$2,675.00
9879	Harold	McDougal	7115 Elizabeth Lane	Phoenix	AZ	85009	247823	$775.75

PhoenixClientClaimsOver$500Query

Project 1h

EmpID	FirstName	LastName	AnnualSalary	PensionContrib
101	Joseph	Ammons	$52,350.00	1570.5
102	Walter	Irving	$50,750.00	1522.5
103	Francine	Prescott	$52,500.00	1575
104	Mary	Vanderhoff	$59,750.00	1792.5
105	Corey	Gadeau	$60,150.00	1804.5
106	Stephanie	Wendt	$42,000.00	1260
108	Nathan	Holmes	$53,350.00	1600.5
110	Thomas	Byrnes	$42,500.00	1275
111	Ray	Bannerman	$32,600.00	978
112	Noreen	Blanca	$38,750.00	1162.5
114	Blaine	Kaiser	$64,500.00	1935
115	Sean	O'Callaghan	$52,455.00	1573.65
116	Silas	Workman	$51,000.00	1530
118	Glenn	Ishimoto	$68,525.00	2055.75
119	Lucinda	Larsen	$38,425.00	1152.75
121	Patricia	Ochoa	$59,750.00	1792.5
124	Antonio	Silvestri	$51,350.00	1540.5
125	Debra	Tapparo	$40,150.00	1204.5
126	Michelle	Vincent	$39,750.00	1192.5
127	Kurt	Ziegler	$65,250.00	1957.5
129	Shilo	Alvarado	$45,000.00	1350
130	Norman	Curis	$42,450.00	1273.5
133	Brett	Dupree	$58,550.00	1756.5
134	Sally	Farrell	$58,000.00	1740
135	Dorothy	Griswold	$67,700.00	2031
137	Leslie	Jacobsen	$48,800.00	1464
138	Susan	Masui	$38,500.00	1155
139	Jerry	Prentiss	$57,525.00	1725.75
140	Kathleen	Schreiber	$45,250.00	1357.5

PensionContributionsQuery

EmpID	FirstName	LastName	AnnualSalary	Salary&Pension
101	Joseph	Ammons	$52,350.00	53920.5
102	Walter	Irving	$50,750.00	52272.5
103	Francine	Prescott	$52,500.00	54075
104	Mary	Vanderhoff	$59,750.00	61542.5
105	Corey	Gadeau	$60,150.00	61954.5
106	Stephanie	Wendt	$42,000.00	43260
108	Nathan	Holmes	$53,350.00	54950.5
110	Thomas	Byrnes	$42,500.00	43775
111	Ray	Bannerman	$32,600.00	33578
112	Noreen	Blanca	$38,750.00	39912.5
114	Blaine	Kaiser	$64,500.00	66435
115	Sean	O'Callaghan	$52,455.00	54028.65
116	Silas	Workman	$51,000.00	52530
118	Glenn	Ishimoto	$68,525.00	70580.75
119	Lucinda	Larsen	$38,425.00	39577.75
121	Patricia	Ochoa	$59,750.00	61542.5
124	Antonio	Silvestri	$51,350.00	52890.5
125	Debra	Tapparo	$40,150.00	41354.5
126	Michelle	Vincent	$39,750.00	40942.5
127	Kurt	Ziegler	$65,250.00	67207.5
129	Shilo	Alvarado	$45,000.00	46350
130	Norman	Curis	$42,450.00	43723.5
133	Brett	Dupree	$58,550.00	60306.5
134	Sally	Farrell	$58,000.00	59740
135	Dorothy	Griswold	$67,700.00	69731
137	Leslie	Jacobsen	$48,800.00	50264
138	Susan	Masui	$38,500.00	39655
139	Jerry	Prentiss	$57,525.00	59250.75
140	Kathleen	Schreiber	$45,250.00	46607.5

Salary&PensionQuery

Product	OrderID	UnitsOrdered	Amount	Total
Two-person tent	1001	10	$1,288.50	$12,885.00
HT waterproof hiking boots, MS9	1002	10	$887.90	$8,879.00
HT waterproof hiking boots, MS11	1003	10	$887.90	$8,879.00
Polar backpack, 250RW	1004	15	$2,397.75	$35,966.25
HT waterproof hiking boots, MS12	1005	10	$887.90	$8,879.00
Two-person dome tent	1006	15	$2,999.85	$44,997.75
Polar backpack, 150RW	1007	10	$1,495.00	$14,950.00
Gordon wool ski hat, XXL	1008	20	$145.80	$2,916.00
Gordon wool ski hat, XL	1009	25	$180.00	$4,500.00
Shursite portable camp light	1010	10	$199.50	$1,995.00
Lantern hanger	1011	15	$44.85	$672.75
Tech-lite ski hat, L	1012	25	$162.25	$4,056.25
Tech-lite ski hat, M	1013	15	$97.35	$1,460.25
Lite-tech ski gloves, WS	1014	20	$199.00	$3,980.00
Lite-tech ski gloves, WM	1015	20	$199.00	$3,980.00
Lite-tech ski gloves, ML	1016	10	$129.50	$1,295.00
Gordon wool ski hat, L	1017	25	$173.75	$4,343.75
Shursite angle-head flashlight	1018	15	$104.25	$1,563.75
Cascade R4 jacket, MXL	1019	10	$1,285.00	$12,850.00
Multi-function compass	1020	10	$45.95	$459.50
Ten-piece hiker cookware	1021	5	$124.25	$621.25
Eight-piece stainless steel cookware	1022	5	$99.75	$498.75
Deluxe map compass	1023	5	$129.75	$648.75
SL 20-degrees synthetic sleeping bag, re	1024	10	$1,199.50	$11,995.00
SL 20-degrees synthetic sleeping bag, bla	1025	10	$1,137.50	$11,375.00
Cascade R4 jacket, WM	1026	5	$599.50	$2,997.50
SL 15-degrees synthetic sleeping bag, re	1027	15	$1,945.25	$29,178.75
Cascade R4 jacket, ML	1028	10	$1,285.00	$12,850.00
Cascade R4 jacket, WXL	1029	5	$599.50	$2,997.50
HT waterproof hiking boots, WS8	1030	10	$752.90	$7,529.00
HT waterproof hiking boots, WS7	1031	10	$752.90	$7,529.00
Binoculars, 8 x 42	1032	5	$2,145.00	$10,725.00
Thermaline roll-top table	1033	5	$196.25	$981.25
HT waterproof hiking boots, WS9	1034	10	$752.90	$7,529.00
HT waterproof hiking boots, WS11	1035	8	$602.32	$4,818.56
Thermaline sleeping pad	1036	20	$397.00	$7,940.00

UnitsOrderedTotalQuery

Project 2 Create Aggregate Functions, Crosstab, Find Duplicates, and Find Unmatched Queries

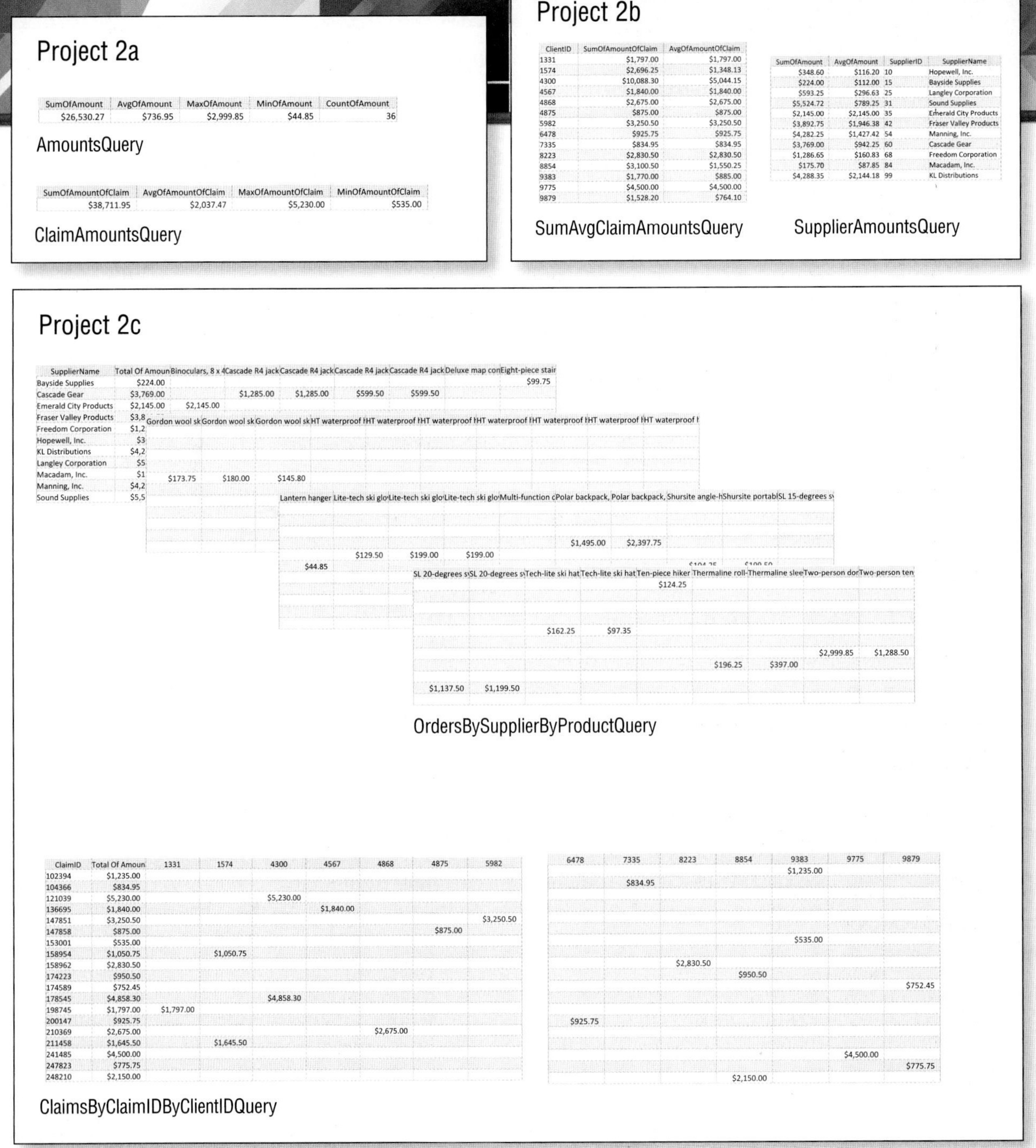

Project 2a

SumOfAmount	AvgOfAmount	MaxOfAmount	MinOfAmount	CountOfAmount
$26,530.27	$736.95	$2,999.85	$44.85	36

AmountsQuery

SumOfAmountOfClaim	AvgOfAmountOfClaim	MaxOfAmountOfClaim	MinOfAmountOfClaim
$38,711.95	$2,037.47	$5,230.00	$535.00

ClaimAmountsQuery

Project 2b

ClientID	SumOfAmountOfClaim	AvgOfAmountOfClaim
1331	$1,797.00	$1,797.00
1574	$2,696.25	$1,348.13
4300	$10,088.30	$5,044.15
4567	$1,840.00	$1,840.00
4868	$2,675.00	$2,675.00
4875	$875.00	$875.00
5982	$3,250.50	$3,250.50
6478	$925.75	$925.75
7335	$834.95	$834.95
8223	$2,830.50	$2,830.50
8854	$3,100.50	$1,550.25
9383	$1,770.00	$885.00
9775	$4,500.00	$4,500.00
9879	$1,528.20	$764.10

SumAvgClaimAmountsQuery

SumOfAmount	AvgOfAmount	SupplierID	SupplierName
$348.60	$116.20	10	Hopewell, Inc.
$224.00	$112.00	15	Bayside Supplies
$593.25	$296.63	25	Langley Corporation
$5,524.72	$789.25	31	Sound Supplies
$2,145.00	$2,145.00	35	Emerald City Products
$3,892.75	$1,946.38	42	Fraser Valley Products
$4,282.25	$1,427.42	54	Manning, Inc.
$3,769.00	$942.25	60	Cascade Gear
$1,286.65	$160.83	68	Freedom Corporation
$175.70	$87.85	84	Macadam, Inc.
$4,288.35	$2,144.18	99	KL Distributions

SupplierAmountsQuery

Project 2c

SupplierName	Total Of Amoun	Binoculars, 8 x 4	Cascade R4 jack	Cascade R4 jack	Cascade R4 jack	Cascade R4 jack	Deluxe map con	Eight-piece stair
Bayside Supplies	$224.00							$99.75
Cascade Gear	$3,769.00		$1,285.00	$1,285.00	$599.50	$599.50		
Emerald City Products	$2,145.00	$2,145.00						
Fraser Valley Products	$3,8							
Freedom Corporation	$1,2							
Hopewell, Inc.	$3							
KL Distributions	$4,2							
Langley Corporation	$5							
Macadam, Inc.	$1							
Manning, Inc.	$4,2							
Sound Supplies	$5,5							

Gordon wool sk	Gordon wool sk	Gordon wool sk	HT waterproof I	HT waterproof I	HT waterproof I	HT waterproof I	HT waterproof I	HT waterproof I	HT waterproof I
$173.75	$180.00	$145.80							

Lantern hanger	Lite-tech ski glo	Lite-tech ski glo	Lite-tech ski glo	Multi-function c	Polar backpack,	Polar backpack,	Shursite angle-h	Shursite portabl	SL 15-degrees s
					$1,495.00	$2,397.75			
	$129.50	$199.00	$199.00						
$44.85									

SL 20-degrees s	SL 20-degrees s	Tech-lite ski hat	Tech-lite ski hat	Ten-piece hiker	Thermaline roll-	Thermaline slee	Two-person dor	Two-person ten
				$124.25				
		$162.25	$97.35					
							$2,999.85	$1,288.50
					$196.25	$397.00		
$1,137.50	$1,199.50							

OrdersBySupplierByProductQuery

ClaimID	Total Of Amoun	1331	1574	4300	4567	4868	4875	5982	6478	7335	8223	8854	9383	9775	9879
102394	$1,235.00												$1,235.00		
104366	$834.95									$834.95					
121039	$5,230.00			$5,230.00											
136695	$1,840.00				$1,840.00										
147851	$3,250.50							$3,250.50							
147858	$875.00						$875.00								
153001	$535.00												$535.00		
158954	$1,050.75		$1,050.75												
158962	$2,830.50										$2,830.50				
174223	$950.50											$950.50			
174589	$752.45														$752.45
178545	$4,858.30			$4,858.30											
198745	$1,797.00	$1,797.00													
200147	$925.75								$925.75						
210369	$2,675.00					$2,675.00									
211458	$1,645.50		$1,645.50												
241485	$4,500.00													$4,500.00	
247823	$775.75														$775.75
248210	$2,150.00											$2,150.00			

ClaimsByClaimIDByClientIDQuery

Project 2d

SupplierName	SupplierID	StreetAddress	City	Prov/State	PostalCode	EmailAddress	Telephone
Langley Corporation	25	805 First Avenue	Burnaby	BC	V3J 1C9	langley@emcp.net	(604) 555-1200
Langley Corporation	29	1248 Larson Avenue	Burnaby	BC	V5V 9K2	lc@emcp.net	(604) 555-1200

DuplicateSuppliersQuery

Project 2e

SupplierName Field	NumberOfDups
Bayside Supplies	2
Cascade Gear	4
Fraser Valley Products	2
Freedom Corporation	8
Hopewell, Inc.	3
KL Distributions	2
Langley Corporation	2
Macadam, Inc.	2
Manning, Inc.	3
Sound Supplies	7

SupplierOrdersCountQuery

Project 2f

ProductID	Product	SupplierID	UnitsInStock	UnitsOnOrder	ReorderLevel
558-C	ICE snow goggles, clear	68	18	0	15
559-B	ICE snow goggles, bronze	68	22	0	20
570-TL	Thermaline light-weight cot	25	8	0	5
580-TL	Thermaline camp seat	25	12	0	10
602-XT	Binoculars, 10.5 x 45	35	5	0	4
602-XX	Binoculars, 10 x 50	35	7	0	5
648-2	Three-person dome tent	99	5	0	10
651-1	K-2 one-person tent	99	8	0	10
652-2	K-2 two-person tent	99	12	0	10
804-50	AG freestyle snowboard, X50	70	7	0	10
804-60	AG freestyle snowboard, X60	70	8	0	5
897-L	Lang blunt snowboard	70	8	0	7
897-W	Lang blunt snowboard, wide	70	4	0	3
901-S	Solar battery pack	38	16	0	15
917-S	Silo portable power pack	38	8	0	10
100-01	Wrist compass	84	12	0	10
100-03	Lenspro plastic compass	84	6	0	5
100-04	Lenspro metal compass	84	8	0	5
101-S1B	SL 0-degrees down sleeping bag, black	54	16	0	15
101-S1R	SL 0-degrees down sleeping bag, red	54	17	0	15
101-S2B	SL 15-degrees synthetic sleeping bag, blac	54	21	0	15
155-30	Shursite aluminum flashlight	10	8	0	5
155-45	Shursite propane lantern	10	12	0	10
155-55	Shursite waterproof headlamp	10	7	0	5
200-CW	Four-piece titanium cookware	15	6	0	5
210-XL	Tech-lite ski hat, XL	68	22	0	20
250-M	Cascade R4 jacket, MM	60	6	0	5
250-XXL	Cascade R4 jacket, MXXL	60	5	0	0
255-L	Cascade R4 jacket, WL	60	6	0	5
299-M1	HT waterproof hiking boots, MS13	31	8	0	10
299-M4	HT waterproof hiking boots, MS10	31	7	0	10

Products Without Matching Orders

Model Answers

Project 1 Design Queries — 8 Parts

You will design and run a number of queries including queries with fields from one table and queries with fields from more than one table. You will also use the Simple Query Wizard to design queries.

Extracting Data with Queries

Being able to extract (pull out) specific data from a table is one of the most important functions of a database. Extracting data in Access is referred to as performing a query. The word ***query*** means "question" and to perform a query means to ask a question. Access provides several methods for performing a query. You can design your own query, use a simple query wizard, or use complex query wizards. In this chapter, you will learn to design your own query; use the Simple Query Wizard; create a calculated field; use aggregate functions in a query; and use the Crosstab, Find Duplicates, and Unmatched Query wizards.

The first step in designing a query is to choose the fields that you want to display in the query results datasheet.

Query Design

Designing Queries

Designing a query consists of identifying the table from which you are gathering data, the field or fields from which the data will be drawn, and the criteria for selecting the data. To design a query and perform the query, open a database, click the CREATE tab, and then click the Query Design button in the Queries group. This displays a query window in the work area and also displays the Show Table dialog box, as shown in Figure 3.1.

Figure 3.1 Query Window with Show Table Dialog Box

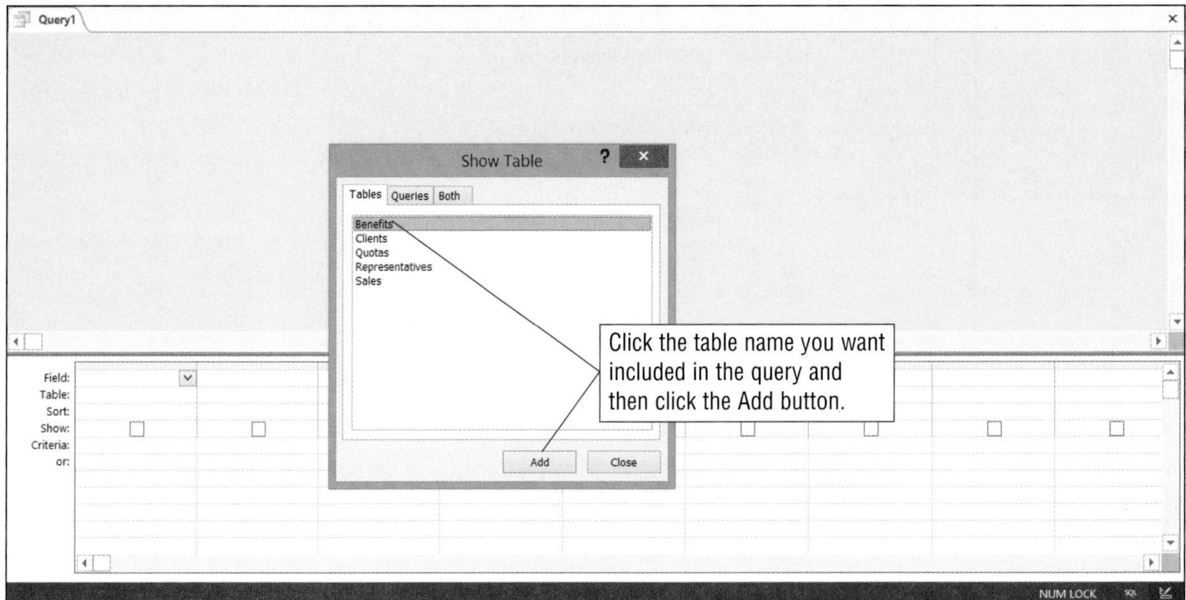

Click the table name in the Show Table dialog box that you want included in the query and then click the Add button or double-click the desired table. This inserts a field list box for the table. Add any other tables required for the query. When all tables have been added, click the Close button. In the query window, click the down-pointing arrow at the right of the first *Field* row field in the query design grid and then click the desired field from the drop-down list. Figure 3.2 displays a sample query window.

To establish a criterion, click inside the *Criteria* row field in the column containing the desired field name in the query design grid and then type the criterion. With the fields and criteria established, click the Run button in the Results group on the QUERY TOOLS DESIGN tab. Access searches the specified tables for records that match the criteria and then displays those records in the query results datasheet. If you plan to use the query in the future, save the query and name it. If you will not need the query again, close the query results datasheet without saving it.

To insert a field in the query design grid, click the down-pointing arrow at the right side of a *Field* row field and then click the desired field at the drop-down list. You can also double-click a field in a table field list box to insert the field in the first available *Field* row field in the query design grid. For example, suppose you want to find out how many purchase orders were issued on a specific date. To do this, double-click *PurchaseOrderID* in the table field list box (which inserts *PurchaseOrderID* in the first *Field* row field in the query design grid) and then double-click *OrderDate* in the table field list box (which inserts *OrderDate* in the second *Field* row field in the query design grid). In this example, both fields are needed, so the purchase order ID is displayed along with the specific order date. After inserting the fields, you insert the criterion. The criterion for this example is something like *#1/15/2015#*. After you insert the criterion, click the Run button in the Results group and the results of the query display in the query results datasheet.

Quick Steps

Design a Query
1. Click CREATE tab.
2. Click Query Design button.
3. At Show Table dialog box, click desired table, and then click Add button.
4. Add any additional tables.
5. In query design grid, click down-pointing arrow in *Field* row field and click desired field from drop-down list.
6. Insert criterion.
7. Click Run button.
8. Save query.

Run

Figure 3.2 Query Window

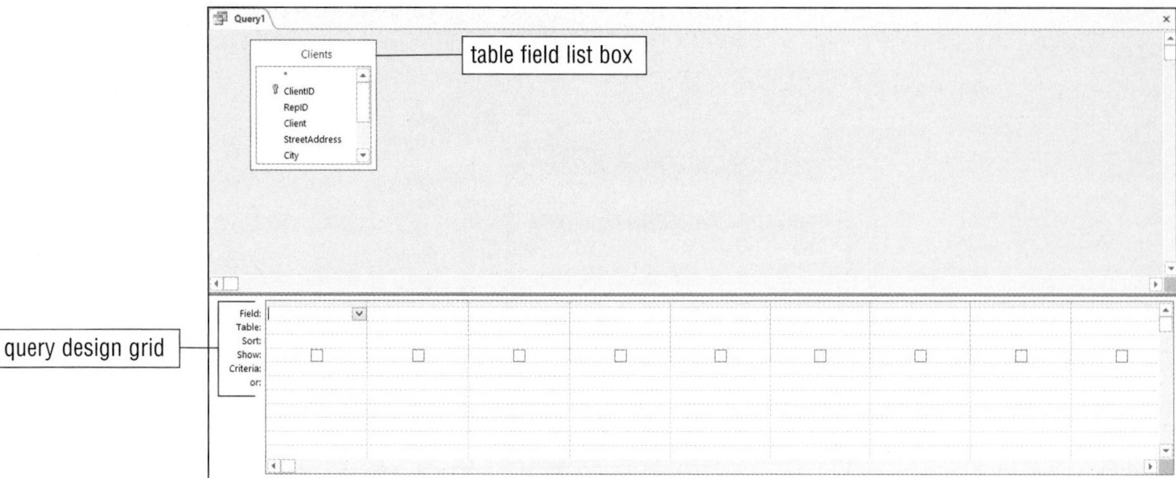

A third method for inserting a field in the query design grid is to drag a field from the table field list box to the desired field in the query design grid. To do this, position the mouse pointer on the desired field in the table field list box, hold down the left mouse button, drag to the desired *Field* row field in the query design grid, and then release the mouse button.

Establishing Query Criteria

Quick Steps

Establish a Query Criterion

1. At query window, click in desired *Criteria* row field in query design grid.
2. Type criterion and then press Enter.
3. Click Run button.

Performing a query does not require specific criteria to be established. In the example described on the previous page, if the criterion for the date was not included, the query would return all purchase order numbers with the dates. (*Return* is the term used for the results of the query.) While this information may be helpful, you could easily find this information in the table. The value of performing a query is to extract specific information from a table. To do this, you must insert a criterion like the one described in the example.

Insert fields in the *Field* row fields in the query design grid in the order in which you want the fields to display in the query results datasheet.

Access makes writing a criterion fairly simple by inserting the necessary symbols in the criterion. If you type a city name, such as *Indianapolis*, in the *Criteria* row field and then press Enter, Access changes the criterion to "*Indianapolis*". The quotation marks are inserted by Access and are necessary for the query to run properly. You can either let Access put the proper symbols in the *Criteria* row field, or you can type the criterion with the symbols. Table 3.1 shows some examples of criteria, including what is typed and what is returned.

Access inserts quotation marks around text criteria and pound symbols around date criteria.

In the criteria examples, the asterisk is used as a so-called ***wildcard character***, or a symbol that can be used to indicate any character. This is consistent with many other software applications. Two of the criteria examples in Table 3.1 use less-than and greater-than symbols. You can use these symbols for fields containing numbers, values, dates, amounts, and so forth. In the next several projects, you will design queries to extract specific information from different tables in databases.

Table 3.1 Criteria Examples

Typing This Criterion	Returns This Result
"Smith"	Field value that matches *Smith*
"Smith" Or "Larson"	Field value that matches either *Smith* or *Larson*
Not "Smith"	Field value that is not *Smith* (the opposite of "Smith")
"s*"	Field value that begins with *S* or *s* and ends in anything
"*s"	Field value that begins with anything and ends in *S* or *s*
"[A-D]*"	Field value that begins with *A*, *B*, *C*, or *D* and ends in anything
#01/01/2015#	Field value that matches the date 01/01/2015
<#04/01/2015#	Field value that is less than (before) 04/01/2015
>#04/01/2015#	Field value that is greater than (after) 04/01/2015
Between #01/01/2015# And #03/31/2015#	Field value that is between 01/01/2015 and 03/31/2015

Project 1a Performing Queries on Tables

Part 1 of 8

1. Open **AL1-C3-Dearborn.accdb** from the AL1C3 folder on your storage medium and enable the contents.
2. Create the following relationships and enforce referential integrity (and cascade fields and records) for each relationship:
   a. Create a one-to-many relationship with the *ClientID* field in the *Clients* field list box the "one" and the *ClientID* field in the *Sales* field list box the "many."
   b. Create a one-to-one relationship with the *RepID* field in the *Representatives* field list box the "one" and the *RepID* field in the *Benefits* field list box the "one."
   c. Create a one-to-many relationship with the *RepID* field in the *Representatives* field list box the "one" and the *RepID* field in the *Clients* field list box the "many."
   d. Create a one-to-many relationship with the *QuotaID* field in the *Quotas* field list box the "one" and the *QuotaID* field in the *Representatives* field list box the "many."
3. Click the Save button on the Quick Access toolbar.
4. Print the relationships by completing the following steps:
   a. Click the Relationship Report button in the Tools group on the RELATIONSHIP TOOLS DESIGN tab.
   b. At the relationship report window, click the Landscape button in the Page Layout group on the PRINT PREVIEW tab.
   c. Click the Print button that displays at the left side of the PRINT PREVIEW tab.
   d. At the Print dialog box, click OK.
5. Close the relationship report window without saving the report.
6. Close the Relationships window.

7. Extract records of those clients located in Indianapolis by completing the following steps:
   a. Click the CREATE tab.
   b. Click the Query Design button in the Queries group.

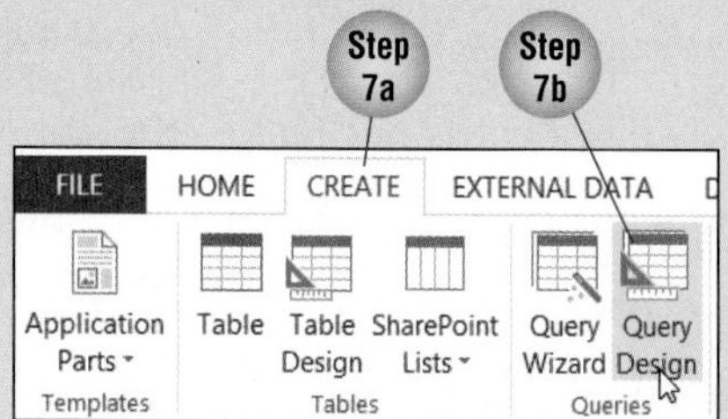

   c. At the Show Table dialog box with the Tables tab selected (see Figure 3.1), click *Clients* in the list box, click the Add button, and then click the Close button.
   d. Insert fields from the *Clients* field list box to the *Field* row fields in the query design grid by completing the following steps:
      1) Click the down-pointing arrow located at the right of the first *Field* row field in the query design grid and then click *Client* in the drop-down list.
      2) Click inside the next *Field* row field (to the right of *Client*) in the query design grid, click the down-pointing arrow, and then click *StreetAddress* in the drop-down list.
      3) Click inside the next *Field* row field (to the right of *StreetAddress*), click the down-pointing arrow, and then click *City* in the drop-down list.
      4) Click inside the next *Field* row field (to the right of *City*), click the down-pointing arrow, and then click *State* in the drop-down list.
      5) Click inside the next *Field* row field (to the right of *State*), click the down-pointing arrow, and then select *ZipCode* in the drop-down list.

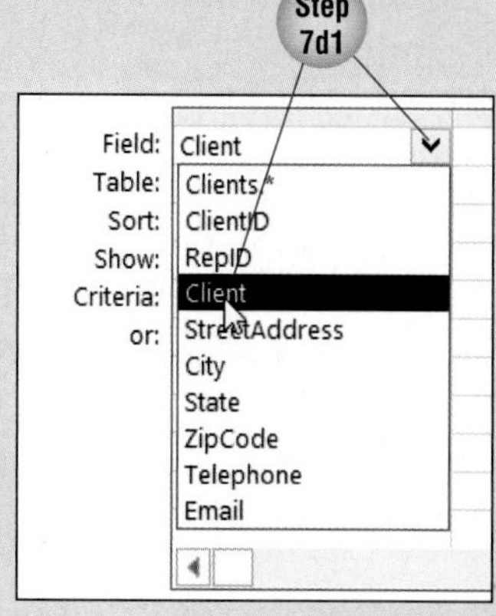

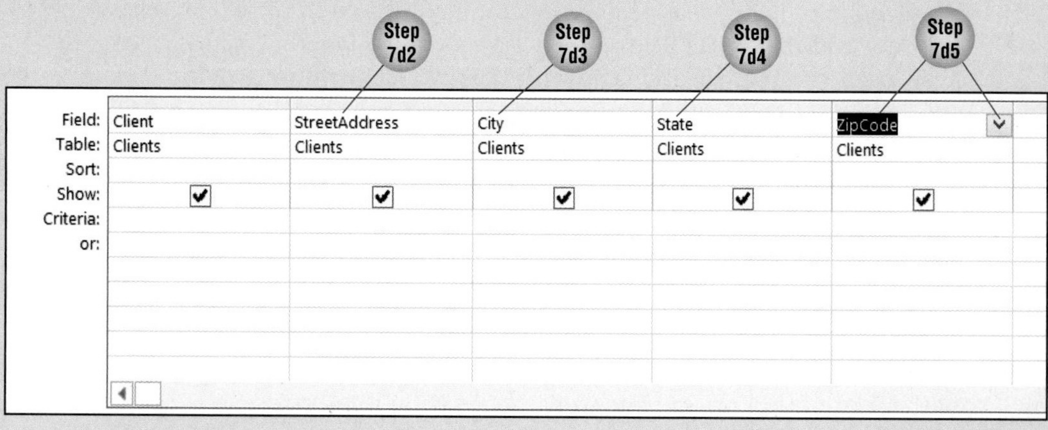

e. Insert the criterion text telling Access to display only those suppliers located in Indianapolis by completing the following steps:
   1) Click in the *Criteria* row field in the *City* column in the query design grid. (This positions the insertion point in the field.)
   2) Type **Indianapolis** and then press Enter. (This changes the criterion to "Indianapolis".)

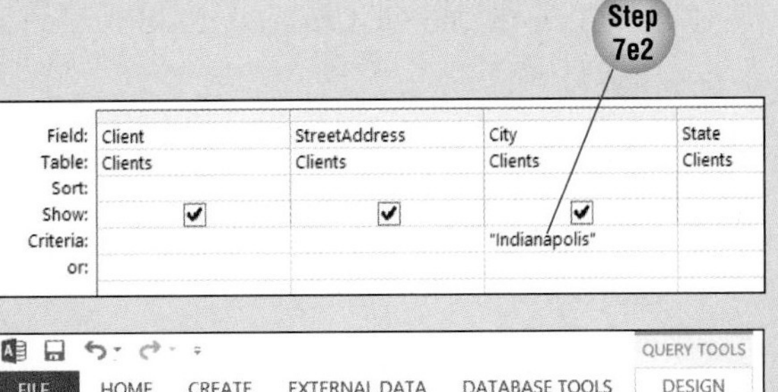

f. Return the results of the query by clicking the Run button in the Results group on the QUERY TOOLS DESIGN tab. (This displays the results in the query results datasheet.)

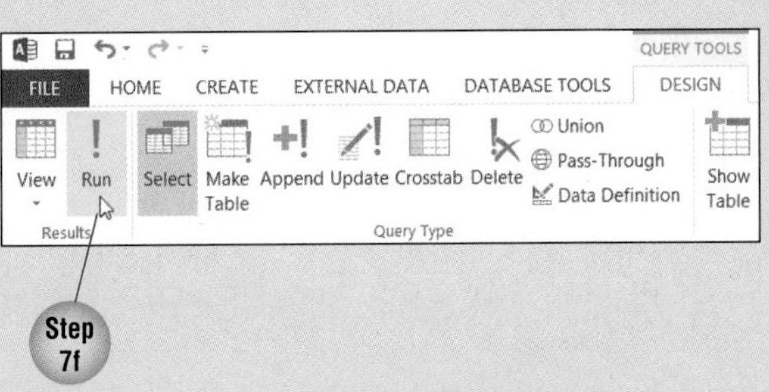

g. Save the results of the query by completing the following steps:
   1) Click the Save button on the Quick Access toolbar.
   2) At the Save As dialog box, type **ClientsIndianapolisQuery** and then press Enter or click OK. (See Project 1a query results on page 78.)
h. Print the query results datasheet by clicking the FILE tab, clicking the *Print* option, and then clicking the Quick Print button.
i. Close ClientsIndianapolisQuery.

8. Extract those records with quota identification numbers greater than 2 by completing the following steps:
   a. Click the CREATE tab and then click the Query Design button in the Queries group.
   b. Double-click *Representatives* in the Show Table dialog box and then click the Close button.
   c. In the query window, double-click *RepName*. (This inserts the field in the first *Field* row field in the query design grid.)
   d. Double-click *QuotaID*. (This inserts the field in the second *Field* row field in the query design grid.)
   e. Insert the query criterion by completing the following steps:
      1) Click in the *Criteria* row field in the *QuotaID* column in the query design grid.
      2) Type >2 and then press Enter. (Access will automatically insert quotation marks around *2* since the data type for the field is identified as *Short Text* [rather than *Number*].)

Field:	RepName	QuotaID
Table:	Representatives	Representatives
Sort:		
Show:	✔	✔
Criteria:		>"2"
or:		

Step 8e2

   f. Return the results of the query by clicking the Run button in the Results group.
   g. Save the query and name it *QuotaIDGreaterThanTwoQuery*. (See Project 1a query results on page 78.)
   h. Print and then close the query.

9. Extract those sales greater than $99,999 by completing the following steps:
   a. Click the CREATE tab and then click the Query Design button.
   b. Double-click *Sales* in the Show Table dialog box and then click the Close button.
   c. At the query window, double-click *ClientID*. (This inserts the field in the first *Field* row field in the query design grid.)
   d. Insert the *Sales* field in the second *Field* row field.

e. Insert the query criterion by completing the following steps:
   1) Click in the *Criteria* row field in the *Sales* column in the query design grid.
   2) Type >99999 and then press Enter. (Access will not insert quotation marks around *99999* since the field is identified as *Currency*.)

Field:	ClientID	Sales
Table:	Sales	Sales
Sort:		
Show:	✔	✔
Criteria:		>99999
or:		

Step 9e2

f. Return the results of the query by clicking the Run button in the Results group.
g. Save the query and name it *SalesOver$99999Query*. (See Project 1a query results on page 78.)
h. Print and then close the query.

10. Extract records of those representatives with a telephone number that begins with the 765 area code by completing the following steps:
   a. Click the CREATE tab and then click the Query Design button.
   b. Double-click *Representatives* in the Show Table dialog box and then click the Close button.
   c. Insert the *RepName* field in the first *Field* row field.
   d. Insert the *Telephone* field in the second *Field* row field.
   e. Insert the query criterion by completing the following steps:
      1) Click in the *Criteria* row field in the *Telephone* column.
      2) Type "(765*" and then press Enter. (You need to type the quotation marks in this criterion because the criterion contains a left parenthesis.)

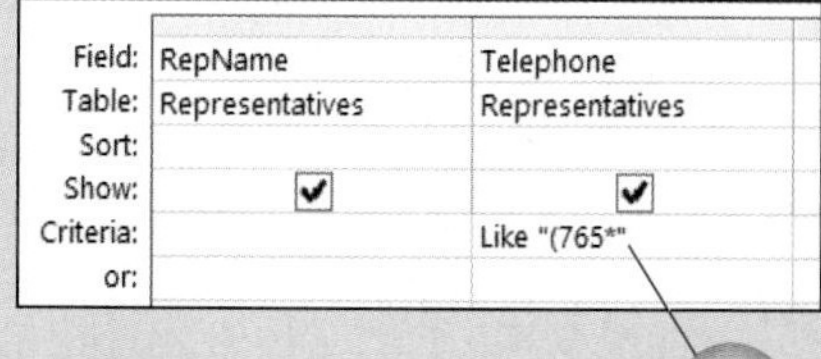

   f. Return the results of the query by clicking the Run button in the Results group.
   g. Save the query and name it *RepsWith765AreaCodeQuery*. (See Project 1a query results on page 78.)
   h. Print and then close the query.

In Project 1a, you performed several queries on specific tables. You can also perform queries on fields from more than one table. In Project 1b, you will perform queries on related tables.

When completing steps in Project 1b, you will be instructed to open AL1-C3-CopperState.accdb. Two of the tables in the database contain yes/no check boxes. When designing a query, you can extract records that contain a check mark or records that do not contain a check mark. If you want to extract records that contain a check mark, click in the *Criteria* row field in the desired column in the query design grid, type a *1*, and then press Enter. When you press the Enter key, Access changes the *1* to *True*. If you want to extract records that do not contain a check mark, type *0* in the *Criteria* row field and then press Enter. Access changes the 0 to *False*.

You can use the Zoom box when entering a criterion in a query to provide a larger area for typing. To display the Zoom box, press Shift + F2 or right-click in the desired *Criteria* row field and then click *Zoom* at the shortcut menu. Type the desired criterion in the Zoom box and then click OK.

Project 1b Performing Queries on Related Tables

Part 2 of 8

1. With **AL1-C3-Dearborn.accdb** open, extract information on representatives hired between March 2011 and November 2011 and include the representatives' names by completing the following steps:
   a. Click the CREATE tab and then click the Query Design button.
   b. Double-click *Representatives* in the Show Table dialog box.
   c. Double-click *Benefits* in the Show Table dialog box and then click the Close button.
   d. At the query window, double-click *RepName* in the *Representatives* field list box.
   e. Double-click *HireDate* in the *Benefits* field list box.

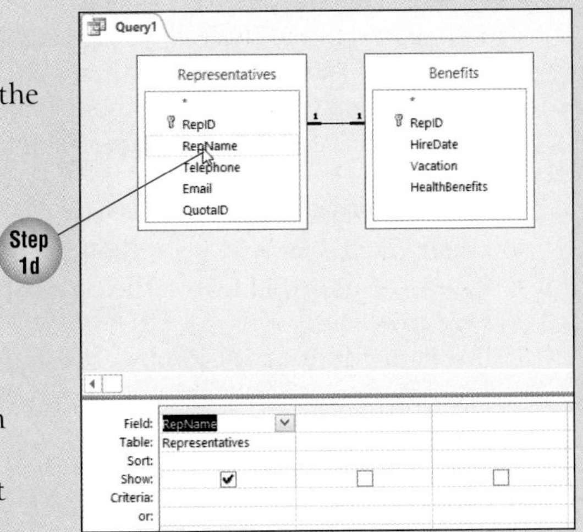

   f. Insert the query criterion in the Zoom box by completing the following steps:
      1) Click in the *Criteria* row field in the *HireDate* column.
      2) Press Shift + F2 to display the Zoom box.
      3) Type **Between 3/1/2011 And 11/30/2011**. (Make sure you type zeros and not capital *O*s.)
      4) Click OK.
   g. Return the results of the query by clicking the Run button in the Results group.
   h. Save the query and name it *MarToNov2011HiresQuery*. (See Project 1b query results on page 78.)
   i. Print and then close the query.

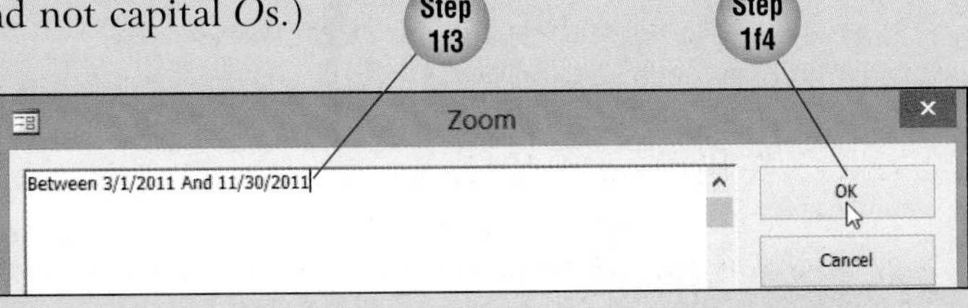

2. Extract records of those representatives who were hired in 2012 by completing the following steps:
   a. Click the CREATE tab and then click the Query Design button.
   b. Double-click *Representatives* in the Show Table dialog box.
   c. Double-click *Benefits* in the Show Table dialog box and then click the Close button.
   d. At the query window, double-click the *RepID* field in the *Representatives* field list box.
   e. Double-click *RepName* in the *Representatives* field list box.
   f. Double-click *HireDate* in the *Benefits* field list box.
   g. Insert the query criterion by completing the following steps:
      1) Click in the *Criteria* row field in the *HireDate* column.
      2) Type ***2012** and then press Enter.
   h. Return the results of the query by clicking the Run button in the Results group.
   i. Save the query and name it *RepsHiredIn2012Query*. (See Project 1b query results on page 78.)
   j. Print and then close the query.

Field:	RepID	RepName	HireDate
Table:	Representatives	Representatives	Benefits
Sort:			
Show:	☑	☑	☑
Criteria:			Like "*2012"
or:			

Step 2g2

3. Suppose you need to determine sales for a company but you can only remember that the company name begins with *Blue*. Create a query that finds the company and identifies the sales by completing the following steps:
   a. Click the CREATE tab and then click the Query Design button.
   b. Double-click *Clients* in the Show Table dialog box.
   c. Double-click *Sales* in the Show Table dialog box and then click the Close button.
   d. At the query window, insert the *ClientID* field from the *Clients* field list box in the first *Field* row field in the query design grid.
   e. Insert the *Client* field from the *Clients* field list box in the second *Field* row field.
   f. Insert the *Sales* field from the *Sales* field list box in the third *Field* row field.
   g. Insert the query criterion by completing the following steps:
      1) Click in the *Criteria* row field in the *Client* column.
      2) Type **Blue*** and then press Enter.
   h. Return the results of the query by clicking the Run button in the Results group.
   i. Save the query and name it *BlueRidgeSalesQuery*. (See Project 1b query results on page 78.)
   j. Print and then close the query.

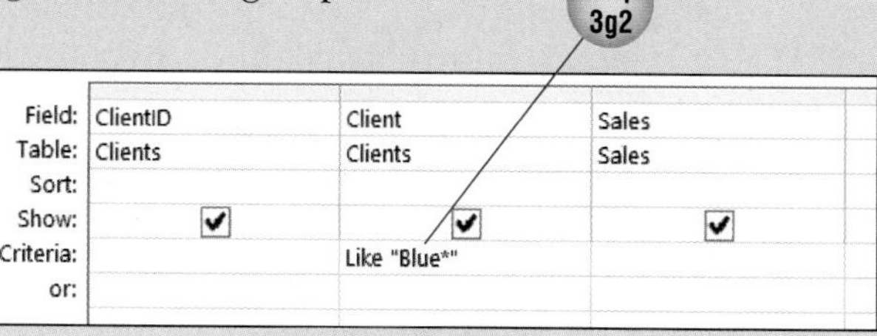

4. Close **AL1-C3-Dearborn.accdb.**
5. Display the Open dialog box with the AL1C3 folder on your storage medium active.
6. Open **AL1-C3-PacTrek.accdb** and enable the contents.
7. Extract information on products ordered between February 1, 2015, and February 28, 2015, by completing the following steps:
   a. Click the CREATE tab and then click the Query Design button.
   b. Double-click *Products* in the Show Table dialog box.
   c. Double-click *Orders* in the Show Table dialog box and then click the Close button.
   d. At the query window, insert the *ProductID* field from the *Products* field list box in the first *Field* row field.
   e. Insert the *Product* field from the *Products* field list box in the second *Field* row field.
   f. Insert the *OrderDate* field from the *Orders* field list box in the third *Field* row field.
   g. Insert the query criterion by completing the following steps:
      1) Click in the *Criteria* row field in the *OrderDate* column.
      2) Type **Between 2/1/2015 And 2/28/2015** and then press Enter. (Make sure you type zeros and not capital *O*s.)
   h. Return the results of the query by clicking the Run button in the Results group.
   i. Save the query and name it *Feb1-28OrdersQuery*. (See Project 1b query results on page 78.)
   j. Print and then close the query.

Field:	ProductID	Product	OrderDate
Table:	Products	Products	Orders
Sort:			
Show:	✔	✔	✔
Criteria:			Between #2/1/2015# An
or:			

Step 7g2

8. Close **AL1-C3-PacTrek.accdb**.
9. Open **AL1-C3-CopperState.accdb** and enable the contents.
10. Display the Relationships window and create the following additional relationships (enforce referential integrity and cascade fields and records):
    a. Create a one-to-many relationship with the *AgentID* field in the Agents field list box the "one" and the *AgentID* field in the Assignments field list box the "many."

b. Create a one-to-many relationship with the *OfficeID* field in the Offices field list box the "one" and the *OfficeID* field in the Assignments field list box the "many."
c. Create a one-to-many relationship with the *OfficeID* field in the Offices field list box the "one" and the *OfficeID* field in the Agents field list box the "many."

11. Save and then print the relationships.
12. Close the relationship report without saving it and then close the Relationships window.
13. Extract records of clients that have uninsured motorist coverage by completing the following steps:
    a. Click the CREATE tab and then click the Query Design button.
    b. Double-click *Clients* in the Show Table dialog box.
    c. Double-click *Coverage* in the Show Table dialog box and then click the Close button.
    d. At the query window, insert the *ClientID* field from the *Clients* field list box in the first *Field* row field.
    e. Insert the *FirstName* field from the *Clients* field list box in the second *Field* row field.
    f. Insert the *LastName* field from the *Clients* field list box in the third *Field* row field.
    g. Insert the *UninsMotorist* field from the *Coverage* field list box in the fourth *Field* row field. (You may need to scroll down the Coverage field list box to display the *UninsMotorist* field.)
    h. Insert the query criterion by clicking in the *Criteria* row field in the *UninsMotorist* column, typing 1, and then pressing the Enter key. (Access changes the *1* to *True*.)

Field:	ClientID	FirstName	LastName	UninsMotorist
Table:	Clients	Clients	Clients	Coverage
Sort:				
Show:	✔	✔		✔
Criteria:				True
or:				

Step 13h

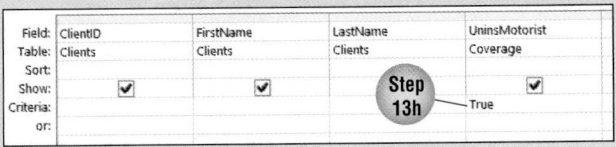

    i. Click the Run button in the Results group.
    j. Save the query and name it *UninsMotoristCoverageQuery*. (See Project 1b query results on page 78.)
    k. Print and then close the query.
14. Extract records of claims in January over $500 by completing the following steps:
    a. Click the CREATE tab and then click the Query Design button.
    b. Double-click *Clients* in the Show Table dialog box.
    c. Double-click *Claims* in the Show Table dialog box and then click the Close button.
    d. At the query window, insert the *ClientID* field from the *Clients* field list box in the first *Field* row field.
    e. Insert the *FirstName* field from the *Clients* field list box in the second *Field* row field.
    f. Insert the *LastName* field from the *Clients* field list box in the third *Field* row field.
    g. Insert the *ClaimID* field from the *Claims* field list box in the fourth *Field* row field.
    h. Insert the *DateOfClaim* field from the *Claims* field list box in the fifth *Field* row field.
    i. Insert the *AmountOfClaim* field from the *Claims* field list box in the sixth *Field* row field.
    j. Click in the *Criteria* row field in the *DateOfClaim* column, type **Between 1/1/2015 And 1/31/2015**, and then press Enter.
    k. With the insertion point positioned in the *Criteria* row field in the *AmountOfClaim* column, type **>500** and then press Enter.

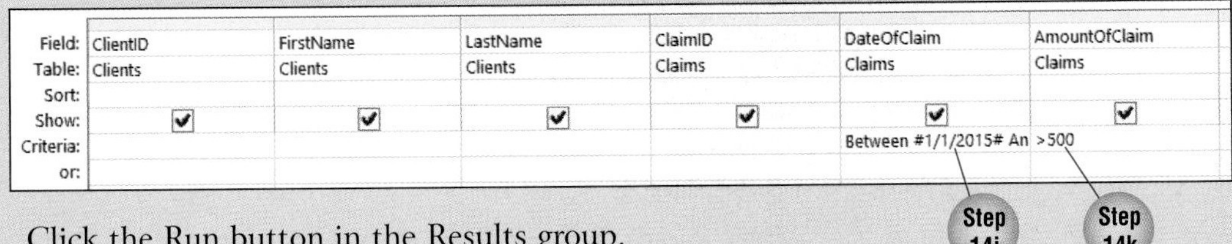

    l. Click the Run button in the Results group.
    m. Save the query and name it *JanClaimsOver$500Query*. (See Project 1b query results on page 78.)
    n. Print and then close the query.

Quick Steps

Sort Fields in a Query

1. At query window, click in *Sort* row field in query design grid.
2. Click down arrow in *Sort* row field.
3. Click *Ascending* or *Descending*.

Sorting and Showing or Hiding Fields in a Query

When designing a query, you can specify the sort order of a field or fields. Click inside one of the columns in the *Sort* row field and a down-pointing arrow displays at the right of the field. Click this down-pointing arrow and a drop-down list displays with the choices *Ascending*, *Descending*, and *(not sorted)*. Click *Ascending* to sort from lowest to highest or click *Descending* to sort from highest to lowest. You can hide specific fields in the query result by removing the check mark from the check box in the *Show* row in the design grid for the field you do not want to show.

Arranging Fields in a Query

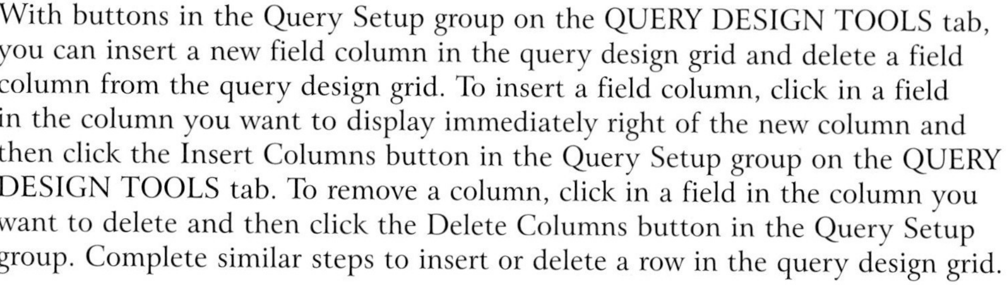

With buttons in the Query Setup group on the QUERY DESIGN TOOLS tab, you can insert a new field column in the query design grid and delete a field column from the query design grid. To insert a field column, click in a field in the column you want to display immediately right of the new column and then click the Insert Columns button in the Query Setup group on the QUERY DESIGN TOOLS tab. To remove a column, click in a field in the column you want to delete and then click the Delete Columns button in the Query Setup group. Complete similar steps to insert or delete a row in the query design grid.

Insert Columns

Delete Columns

You can also rearrange columns in the query design grid by selecting the desired field column and then dragging the column to the desired position. To select a column in the query design grid, position the mouse pointer at the top of the column until the pointer turns into a small, black, down-pointing arrow and then click the left mouse button. Position the mouse pointer toward the top of the selected column until the mouse displays as a pointer, hold down the left mouse button, drag to the desired position in the design grid, and then release the mouse button. As you drag the column, a thick, black, vertical line displays identifying the location where the column will be inserted.

Project 1c **Performing Queries on Related Tables and Sorting in Field Values** **Part 3 of 8**

1. With **AL1-C3-CopperState.accdb** open, extract information on clients with agents from the West Bell Road Glendale office and sort the information alphabetically by client last name by completing the following steps:
   a. Click the CREATE tab and then click the Query Design button.
   b. Double-click *Assignments* in the Show Table dialog box.
   c. Double-click *Clients* in the Show Table dialog box and then click the Close button.
   d. At the query window, insert the *OfficeID* field from the *Assignments* field list box in the first *Field* row field.
   e. Insert the *AgentID* field from the *Assignments* field list box in the second *Field* row field.
   f. Insert the *FirstName* field from the *Clients* field list box in the third *Field* row field.
   g. Insert the *LastName* field from the *Clients* field list box in the fourth *Field* row field.

h. Click in the *Criteria* row field in the *OfficeID* column, type **GW**, and then press Enter.

i. Sort the *LastName* field in ascending alphabetical order (A–Z) by completing the following steps:
   1) Click in the *Sort* row field in the *LastName* column. (This causes a down-pointing arrow to display at the right side of the field.)
   2) Click the down-pointing arrow at the right side of the *Sort* row field and then click *Ascending*.

j. Specify that you do not want the *AgentID* field to show in the query results by clicking in the check box in the *Show* row field in the *AgentID* column to remove the check mark.

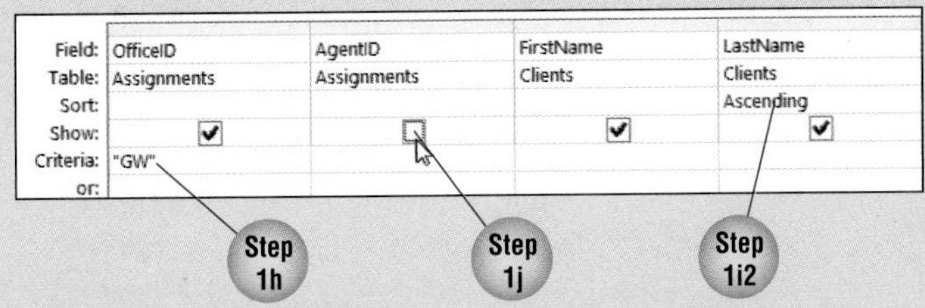

k. Click the Run button in the Results group.

l. Save the query and name it *GWClientsQuery*. (See Project 1c query results on page 79.)

m. Print and then close the query.

2. Close **AL1-C3-CopperState.accdb**.
3. Open **AL1-C3-PacTrek.accdb**.
4. Extract information on orders less than $1,500 by completing the following steps:
   a. Click the CREATE tab and then click the Query Design button.
   b. Double-click *Products* in the Show Table dialog box.
   c. Double-click *Orders* in the Show Table dialog box and then click the Close button.
   d. At the query window, insert the *ProductID* field from the *Products* field list box in the first *Field* row field.
   e. Insert the *SupplierID* field from the *Products* field list box in the second *Field* row field.
   f. Insert the *UnitsOrdered* field from the Orders field list box in the third *Field* row field.
   g. Insert the *Amount* field from the Orders field list box in the fourth *Field* row field.
   h. Insert the query criterion by completing the following steps:
      1) Click in the *Criteria* row field in the *Amount* column.
      2) Type **<1500** and then press Enter. (Make sure you type zeros and not capital Os.)

Field:	ProductID	SupplierID	UnitsOrdered	Amount
Table:	Products	Products	Orders	Orders
Sort:				
Show:	✔	✔	✔	✔
Criteria:				<1500
or:				

Step 4h2

   i. Sort the *Amount* field values from highest to lowest by completing the following steps:
      1) Click in the *Sort* row field in the *Amount* column. (This causes a down-pointing arrow to display at the right side of the field.)
      2) Click the down-pointing arrow at the right side of the *Sort* field and then click *Descending*.

Ordered | Amount
s | Orders
Descending
Ascending
Descending
(not sorted)

Step 4i2

   j. Return the results of the query by clicking the Run button in the Results group.
   k. Save the query and name it *OrdersLessThan$1500Query*. (See Project 1c query results on page 79.)
   l. Print and then close the query.

5. Close **AL1-C3-PacTrek.accdb**.
6. Open **AL1-C3-Dearborn.accdb**.
7. Design a query by completing the following steps:
   a. Click the CREATE tab and then click the Query Design button.
   b. Double-click *Representatives* in the Show Table dialog box.

c. Double-click *Clients* in the Show Table dialog box.
d. Double-click *Sales* in the Show Table dialog box and then click the Close button.
e. At the query window, insert the *RepID* field from the *Representatives* field list box in the first *Field* row field.
f. Insert the *RepName* field from the *Representatives* field list box in the second *Field* row field.
g. Insert the *ClientID* field from the *Clients* field list box in the third *Field* row field.
h. Insert the *Sales* field from the *Sales* field list box in the fourth *Field* row field.

8. Move the *RepName* field by completing the following steps:
   a. Position the mouse pointer at the top of the *RepName* column until the pointer turns into a small, black, down-pointing arrow and then click the left mouse button. (This selects the entire column.)

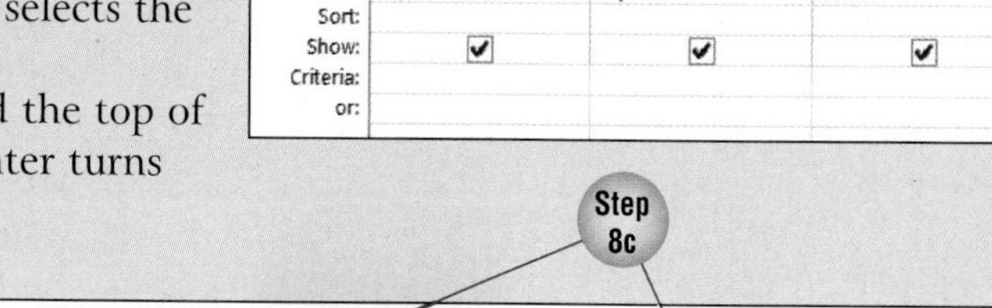

   b. Position the mouse pointer toward the top of the selected column until the pointer turns into a white arrow.
   c. Hold down the left mouse button; drag to the right until a thick, black horizontal line displays between the *ClientID* column and the *Sales* column; and then release the mouse button.

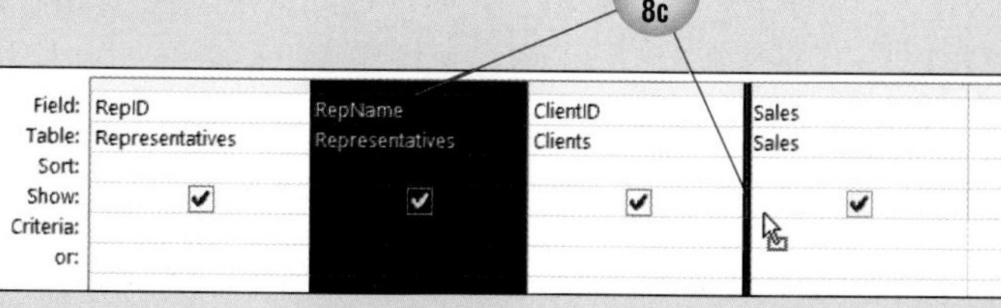

9. Delete the *RepID* field by clicking in a field in the column and then clicking the Delete Columns button in the Query Setup group.
10. Insert a new field column and insert a new field in the column by completing the following steps:
    a. Click in the *Sales* field and then click the Insert Columns button in the Query Setup group.
    b. Click the down-pointing arrow at the right side of the new field and then click *Clients.Client* at the drop-down list.

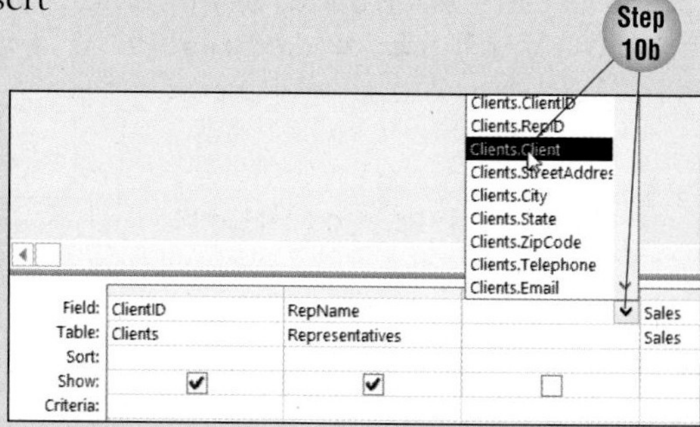

11. Hide the *ClientID* field so it does not display in the query results by clicking the *Show* check box in the *ClientID* column to remove the check mark.
12. Insert the query criterion that extracts information on sales over $100,000 by completing the following steps:
    a. Click in the *Criteria* row field in the *Sales* column.
    b. Type **>100000** and then press Enter. (Make sure you type zeros and not capital *O*s.)
13. Sort the *Sales* field values from highest to lowest by completing the following steps:
    a. Click in the *Sort* row field in the *Sales* column.
    b. Click the down-pointing arrow at the right side of the *Sort* row field and then click *Descending*.
14. Return the results of the query by clicking the Run button in the Results group.
15. Save the query and name it *SalesMoreThan$100000Query*. (See Project 1c query results on page 79.)
16. Print and then close the query.

Modifying a Query

You can modify a saved query and use it for a new purpose. For example, suppose that after designing the query that displays sales of more than $100,000, you decide that you want to find sales that are less than $100,000. Rather than design a new query, open the existing query, make any needed changes, and then run the query.

To modify an existing query, double-click the query in the Navigation pane. (This displays the query in Datasheet view.) Click the View button to display the query in Design view. You can also open a query in Design view by right-clicking the query in the Navigation pane and then clicking *Design View* at the shortcut menu. Make the desired changes and then click the Run button in the Results group. Click the Save button on the Quick Access toolbar to save the query with the same name. If you want to save the query with a new name, click the FILE tab, click the *Save As* option, click the *Save Object As* option, and then click the Save As button. At the Save As dialog box, type a name for the query and then press Enter.

If your database contains a number of queries, you can group and display them in the Navigation pane. To do this, click the down-pointing arrow in the Navigation pane menu bar and then click *Object Type* at the drop-down list. This displays objects grouped in categories, such as *Tables* and *Queries*.

Quick Steps

Modify a Query
1. Double-click query in Navigation pane.
2. Click View button.
3. Make desired changes to query.
4. Click Run button.
5. Click Save button.

Save time designing a new query by modifying an existing query.

Renaming and Deleting a Query

If you modify a query, you may want to rename it. To do this, right-click the query name in the Navigation pane, click *Rename* at the shortcut menu, type the new name, and then press Enter. If you no longer need the query in the database, delete it by clicking the query name in the Navigation pane, clicking the Delete button in the Records group on the HOME tab, and then clicking the Yes button at the message asking if you want to permanently delete the query. Another method is to right-click the query in the Navigation pane, click *Delete* at the shortcut menu, and then click the Yes at the message. If you are deleting a query from your computer's hard drive, the message asking if you want to permanently delete the query will not display. This is because Access automatically sends the deleted query to the Recycle Bin, where it can be retrieved if necessary.

Project 1d **Modifying Queries** **Part 4 of 8**

1. With **AL1-C3-Dearborn.accdb** open, find sales less than $100,000 by completing the following steps:
   a. Double-click *SalesMoreThan$100000Query* in the Queries group in the Navigation pane.
   b. Click the View button in the Views group to switch to Design view.
   c. Click in the *Criteria* row field containing the text *>100000* and then edit the text so it displays as *<100000*.

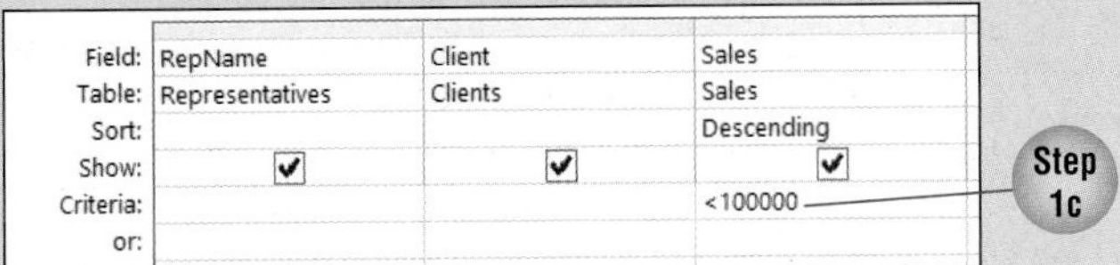

   d. Click the Run button in the Results group.

2. Save the query with a new name by completing the following steps:
   a. Click the FILE tab, click the *Save As* option, click the *Save Object As* option, and then click the Save As button.
   b. At the Save As dialog box, type **SalesLessThan$100000Query** and then press Enter. (See Project 1d query results on page 79.)
   c. Print and then close the query.
3. Modify an existing query and find employees with three weeks of vacation by completing the following steps:
   a. Right-click *MarToNov2011HiresQuery* in the Queries group in the Navigation pane and then click *Design View* at the shortcut menu.
   b. Click in the *Field* row field containing the text *HireDate*.
   c. Click the down-pointing arrow that displays at the right side of the field and then click *Vacation* at the drop-down list.
   d. Select the current text in the *Criteria* row field in the *Vacation* column, type **3 weeks**, and then press Enter.
   e. Click the Run button in the Results group.
   f. Save and then close the query.

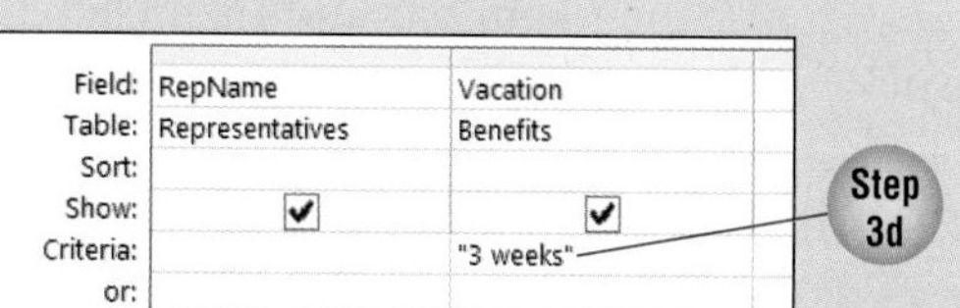

4. Rename the query by completing the following steps:
   a. Right-click *MarToNov2011HiresQuery* in the Navigation pane and then click *Rename* at the shortcut menu.
   b. Type **RepsWith3WeekVacationsQuery** and then press Enter. (See Project 1d query results on page 79.)
   c. Open, print and then close the query.
5. Delete the *SalesOver$99999Query* by right-clicking the query name in the Navigation pane and then clicking *Delete* at the shortcut menu. If a message displays asking if you want to permanently delete the query, click Yes.

Designing Queries with *Or* and *And* Criteria

The query design grid contains an *or* row that you can use to design a query that instructs Access to display records matching any of the criteria. Multiple criterion statements on different rows in a query become an Or statement, which means that any of the criterion can be met for a record to be displayed in the query results datasheet. For example, to display a list of employees with three weeks of vacation *or* four weeks of vacation, type *3 weeks* in the *Criteria* row field for the *Vacation* column and then type *4 weeks* in the field immediately below *3 weeks* in the *or* row. Other examples include finding clients that live in *Muncie* or *Lafayette* and finding representatives with quotas of *1* or *2*.

HINT
You can design a query that combines *And* and *Or* statements.

You can also select records by entering criteria statements into more than one *Criteria* field. Multiple criteria all entered in the same row become an *And* statement, for which each criterion must be met for Access to select the record. For example, you can search for clients in the Indianapolis area with sales greater than $100,000.

Project 1e Designing Queries with *Or* and *And* Criteria Part 5 of 8

1. With **AL1-C3-Dearborn.accdb** open, modify an existing query and find employees with three weeks or four weeks of vacation by completing the following steps:
   a. Double-click the *RepsWith3WeekVacationsQuery*.
   b. Click the View button in the Views group to switch to Design view.
   c. Click in the empty field below "*3 weeks*" in the *or* row, type **4 weeks**, and then press Enter.
   d. Click the Run button in the Results group.

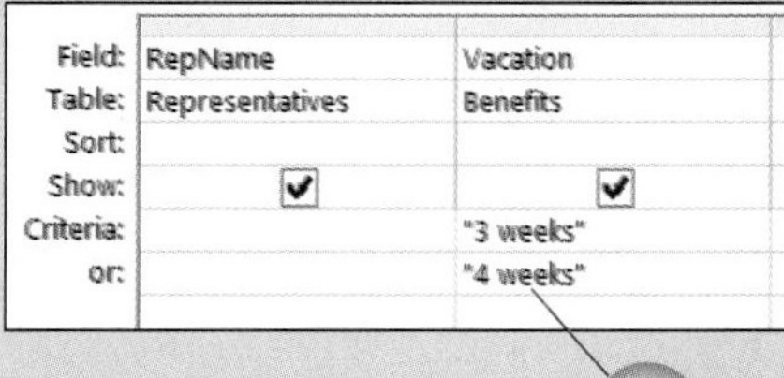

Field:	RepName	Vacation
Table:	Representatives	Benefits
Sort:		
Show:	✔	✔
Criteria:		"3 weeks"
or:		"4 weeks"

2. Save the query with a new name by completing the following steps:
   a. Click the FILE tab, click the *Save As* option, click the *Save Object As* option, and then click the Save As button.
   b. At the Save As dialog box, type **RepsWith3Or4WeekVacationsQuery** and then press Enter. (See Project 1e query results on page 79.)
   c. Print and then close the query.
3. Design a query that finds records of clients in the Indianapolis area with sales over $100,000 by completing the following steps:
   a. Click the CREATE tab and then click the Query Design button.
   b. Double-click *Clients* in the Show Table dialog box.
   c. Double-click *Sales* in the Show Table dialog box and then click the Close button.
   d. At the query window, insert the *Client* field from the *Clients* field list box in the first *Field* row field.
   e. Insert the *City* field from the *Clients* field list box in the second *Field* row field.
   f. Insert the *Sales* field from the *Sales* field list box in the third *Field* row field.
   g. Insert the query criteria by completing the following steps:
      1) Click in the *Criteria* row field in the *City* column.
      2) Type **Indianapolis** and then press Enter.
      3) With the insertion point positioned in the *Criteria* row field in the *Sales* column, type **>100000** and then press Enter.

Field:	Client	City	Sales
Table:	Clients	Clients	Sales
Sort:			
Show:	✔	✔	✔
Criteria:		"Indianapolis"	>100000
or:			

Step 3g2 Step 3g3

   h. Click the Run button in the Results group.
   i. Save the query and name it *SalesOver$100000IndianapolisQuery*. (See Project 1e query results on page 79.)
   j. Print and then close the query.
4. Close **AL1-C3-Dearborn.accdb**.
5. Open **AL1-C3-PacTrek.accdb**.
6. Design a query that finds products available from supplier numbers 25, 31, and 42 by completing the following steps:
   a. Click the CREATE tab and then click the Query Design button.
   b. Double-click *Suppliers* in the Show Table dialog box.
   c. Double-click *Products* in the Show Table dialog box and then click the Close button.
   d. At the query window, insert the *SupplierID* field from the *Suppliers* field list box in the first *Field* row field.

e. Insert the *SupplierName* field from the *Suppliers* field list box in the second *Field* row field.
f. Insert the *Product* field from the *Products* field list box in the third *Field* row field.
g. Insert the query criteria by completing the following steps:
   1) Click in the *Criteria* row field in the *SupplierID* column.
   2) Type **25** and then press the Down Arrow key on your keyboard. (This makes active the field below *25*.)
   3) Type **31** and then press the Down Arrow key on your keyboard. (This makes active the field below *31*.)
   4) Type **42** and then press Enter.

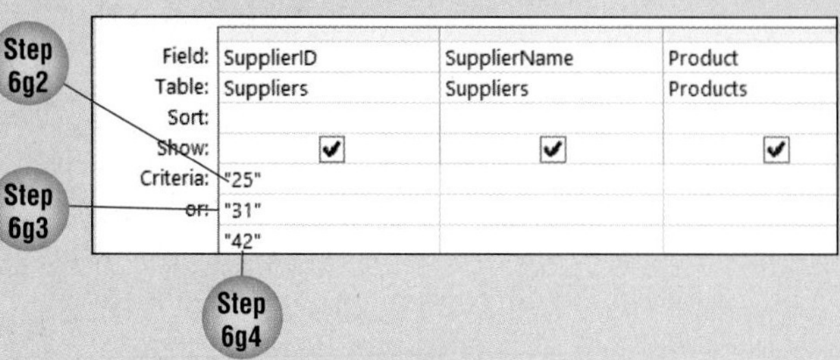

h. Click the Run button in the Results group.
i. Save the query and name it *Suppliers25-31-42Query*. (See Project 1e query results on page 79.)
j. Print and then close the query.

7. Design a query that finds ski hats or gloves on order and the numbers ordered by completing the following steps:
   a. Click the CREATE tab and then click the Query Design button.
   b. Double-click *Orders* in the Show Table dialog box.
   c. Double-click *Suppliers* in the Show Table dialog box.
   d. Double-click *Products* in the Show Table dialog box and then click the Close button.
   e. At the query window, insert the *OrderID* field from the *Orders* field list box in the first *Field* row field.
   f. Insert the *SupplierName* field from the *Suppliers* field list box in the second *Field* row field.
   g. Insert the *Product* field from the *Products* field list box in the third *Field* row field.
   h. Insert the *UnitsOrdered* field from the *Orders* field list box in the fourth *Field* row field.
   i. Insert the query criteria by completing the following steps:
      1) Click in the *Criteria* row field in the *Product* column.
      2) Type ***ski hat*** and then press the Down Arrow key on your keyboard. (You need to type the asterisk before and after *ski hat* so the query will find any product that includes the words *ski hat* in the description, no matter what text comes before or after the words.)
      3) Type ***gloves*** and then press Enter.

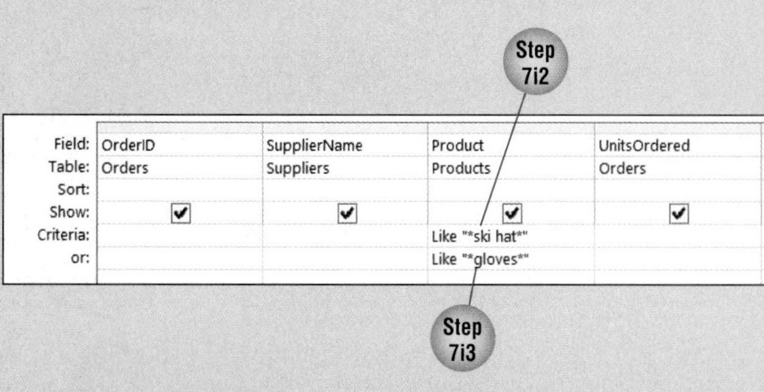

   j. Click the Run button in the Results group.
   k. Save the query and name it *SkiHatsGlovesOnOrderQuery*. (See Project 1e query results on page 79.)
   l. Print and then close the query.

8. Design a query that finds boots, sleeping bags, or backpacks and the suppliers that produce them by completing the following steps:
   a. Click the CREATE tab and then click the Query Design button.
   b. Double-click *Products* in the Show Table dialog box.
   c. Double-click *Suppliers* in the Show Table dialog box and then click the Close button.
   d. At the query window, insert the *ProductID* field from the *Products* field list box in the first *Field* row field.
   e. Insert the *Product* field from the *Products* field list box in the second *Field* row field.
   f. Insert the *SupplierName* field from the *Suppliers* field list box in the third *Field* row field.
   g. Insert the query criteria by completing the following steps:
      1) Click in the *Criteria* row field in the *Product* column.
      2) Type ***boots*** and then press the Down Arrow key on your keyboard.
      3) Type ***sleeping bag*** and then press the Down Arrow key on your keyboard.
      4) Type ***backpack*** and then press Enter.

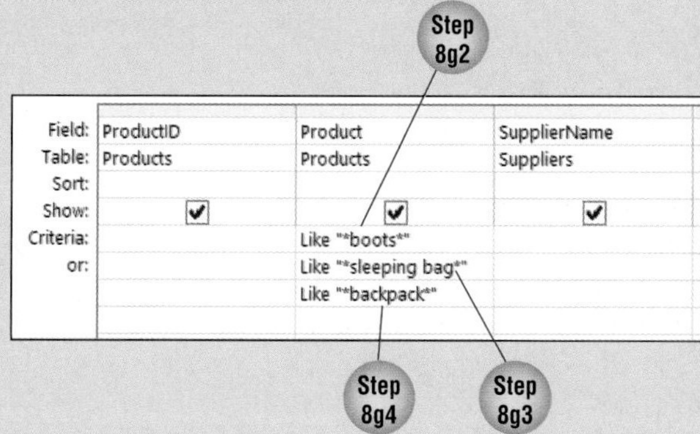

   h. Click the Run button in the Results group.
   i. Save the query and name it *BootsSleepingBagsBackpacksQuery*. (See Project 1e query results on page 79.)
   j. Print and then close the query.
9. Close **AL1-C3-PacTrek.accdb**.
10. Open **AL1-C3-CopperState.accdb**.
11. Design a query that finds clients that have only liability auto coverage by completing the following steps:
   a. Click the CREATE tab and then click the Query Design button.
   b. Double-click *Clients* in the Show Table dialog box.
   c. Double-click *Coverage* in the Show Table dialog box and then click the Close button.
   d. At the query window, insert the *ClientID* field from the *Clients* field list box in the first *Field* row field.
   e. Insert the *FirstName* field from the *Clients* field list box in the second *Field* row field.
   f. Insert the *LastName* field from the *Clients* field list box in the third *Field* row field.
   g. Insert the *Medical* field from the *Coverage* field list box in the fourth *Field* row field.
   h. Insert the *Liability* field from the *Coverage* field list box in the fifth *Field* row field.
   i. Insert the *Comprehensive* field from the *Coverage* field list box in the sixth *Field* row field.
   j. Insert the *UninsMotorist* field from the *Coverage* field list box in the seventh *Field* row field. (You may need to scroll down the *Coverage* field list box to display the *UninsMotorist* field.)
   k. Insert the *Collision* field from the *Coverage* field list box in the eighth *Field* row field. (You may need to scroll down the *Coverage* field list box to display the *Collision* field.)

l. Insert the query criteria by completing the following steps:
   1) Click in the *Criteria* row field in the *Medical* column, type **0**, and then press Enter. (Access changes the *0* to *False*.)
   2) With the insertion point in the *Liability* column, type **1** and then press Enter. (Access changes the *1* to *True*.)
   3) With the insertion point in the *Comprehensive* column, type **0** and then press Enter.
   4) With the insertion point in the *UninsMotorist* column, type **0** and then press Enter.
   5) With the insertion point in the *Collision* column, type **0** and then press Enter.

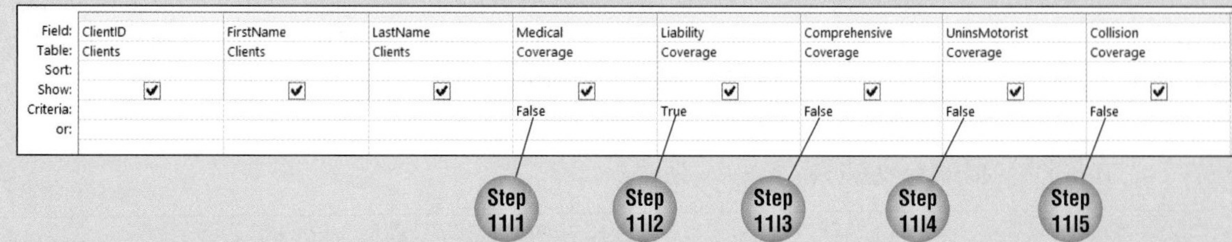

Field: ClientID FirstName LastName Medical Liability Comprehensive UninsMotorist Collision
Table: Clients Clients Clients Coverage Coverage Coverage Coverage Coverage
Sort:
Show:
Criteria: False True False False False
or:
Step 11l1
Step 11l2
Step 11l3
Step 11l4
Step 11l5

m. Click the Run button in the Results group.
n. Save the query and name it *ClientsWithOnlyLiabilityQuery*. (See Project 1e query results on page 79.)
o. Print the query in landscape orientation.
p. Close the query.

12. Close **AL1-C3-CopperState.accdb**.

Performing Queries with the Simple Query Wizard

Query Wizard

The Simple Query Wizard provided by Access guides you through the steps for preparing a query. To use this wizard, open the database, click the CREATE tab, and then click the Query Wizard button in the Queries group. At the New Query dialog box, make sure *Simple Query Wizard* is selected in the list box and then click the OK button. At the first Simple Query Wizard dialog box, shown in Figure 3.3, specify the table(s) in the *Tables/Queries* option box. After specifying the table(s), insert the fields you want included in the query in the *Selected Fields* list box and then click the Next button.

Figure 3.3 First Simple Query Wizard Dialog Box

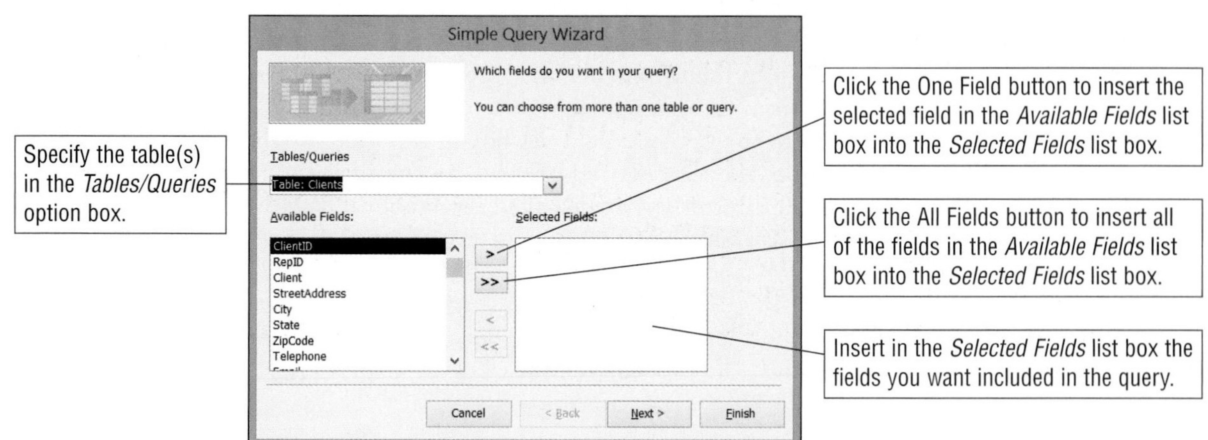

At the second Simple Query Wizard dialog box, specify whether you want a detail or summary query and then click the Next button. At the third (and last) Simple Query Wizard dialog box, shown in Figure 3.4, type a name for the completed query or accept the name provided by the wizard. At this dialog box, you can also specify that you want to open the query to view the information or modify the query design. If you want to extract specific information, be sure to choose the *Modify the query design* option. After making any necessary changes, click the Finish button.

If you do not modify the query design in the last Simple Query Wizard dialog box, the query displays all records for the fields identified in the first Simple Query Wizard dialog box. In Project 1f, you will perform a query without modifying the design, and in Project 1g, you will modify the query design.

Quick Steps

Create a Query with the Simple Query Wizard

1. Click CREATE tab.
2. Click Query Wizard button.
3. Make sure *Simple Query Wizard* is selected in list box and then click OK.
4. Follow query steps.

Figure 3.4 Last Simple Query Wizard Dialog Box

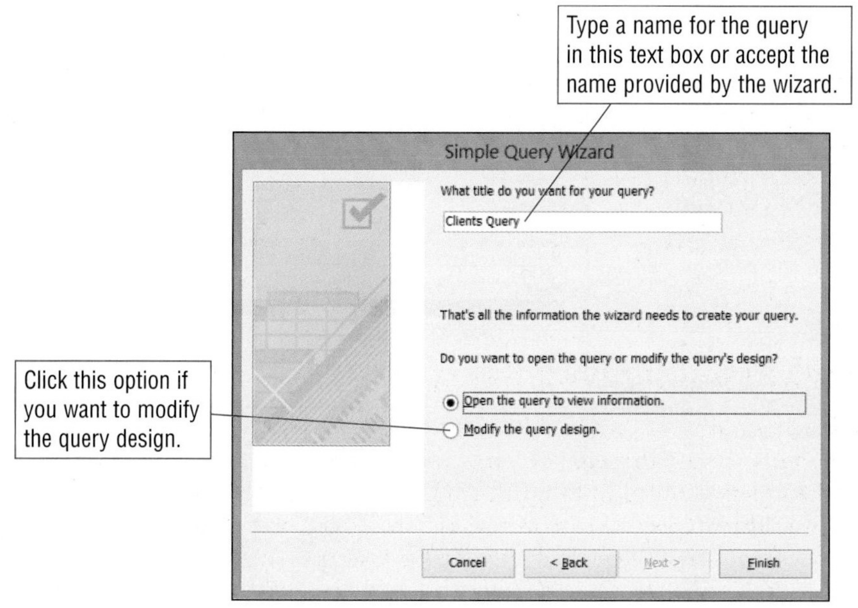

Project 1f Performing Queries with the Simple Query Wizard — Part 6 of 8

1. Open **AL1-C3-Dearborn.accdb** and then use the Simple Query Wizard to create a query that displays client names along with sales by completing the following steps:
   a. Click the CREATE tab and then click the Query Wizard button in the Queries group.
   b. At the New Query dialog box, make sure *Simple Query Wizard* is selected in the list box and then click OK.
   c. At the first Simple Query Wizard dialog box, click the down-pointing arrow at the right of the *Tables/Queries* option box and then click *Table: Clients*.

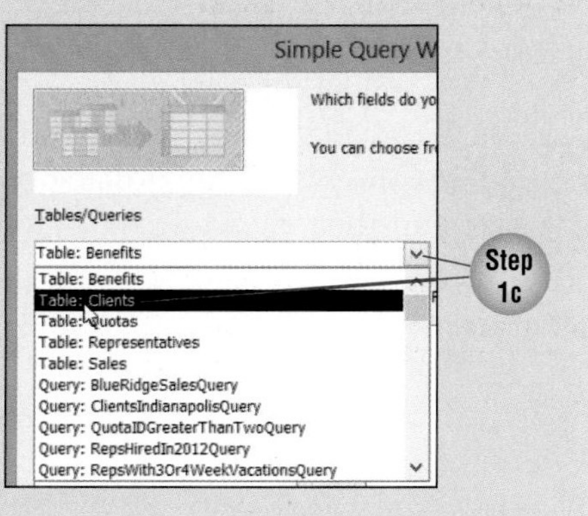

d. With *ClientID* selected in the *Available Fields* list box, click the One Field button (the button containing the greater-than symbol, >). This inserts the *ClientID* field in the *Selected Fields* list box.

e. Click *Client* in the *Available Fields* list box and then click the One Field button.

f. Click the down-pointing arrow at the right of the *Tables/Queries* option box and then click *Table: Sales*.

g. Click *Sales* in the *Available Fields* list box and then click the One Field button.

h. Click the Next button.

i. At the second Simple Query Wizard dialog box, click the Next button.

j. At the last Simple Query Wizard dialog box, select the name in the *What title do you want for your query?* text box, type **ClientSalesQuery**, and then press Enter.

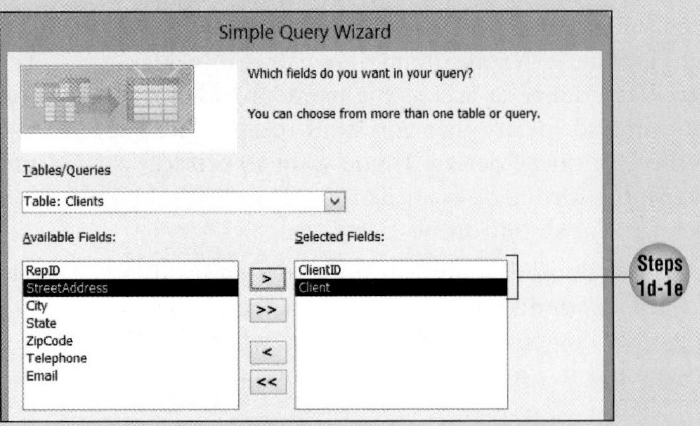

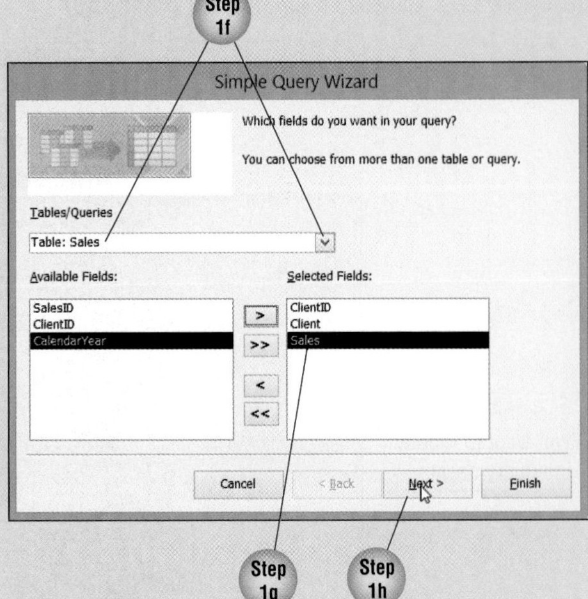

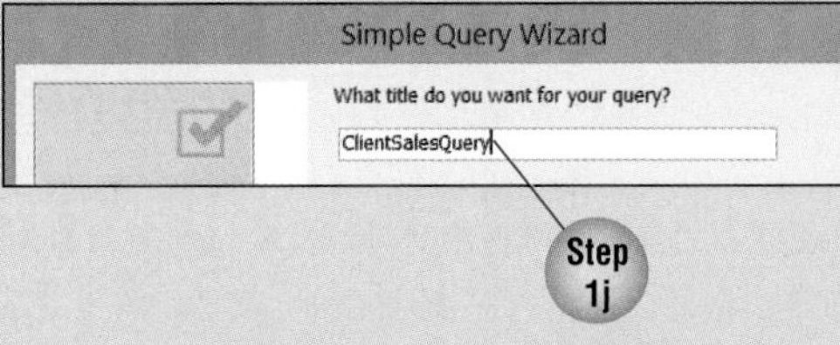

k. When the results of the query display, print the results. (See Project 1f query results on page 80.)

2. Close the query.
3. Close **AL1-C3-Dearborn.accdb**.
4. Open **AL1-C3-PacTrek.accdb**.
5. Create a query that displays the products on order, order amounts, and supplier names by completing the following steps:
   a. Click the CREATE tab and then click the Query Wizard button.
   b. At the New Query dialog box, make sure *Simple Query Wizard* is selected in the list box and then click OK.

c. At the first Simple Query Wizard dialog box, click the down-pointing arrow at the right side of the *Tables/Queries* option box and then click *Table: Suppliers*.
d. With *SupplierID* selected in the *Available Fields* list box, click the One Field button. (This inserts the *SupplierID* field in the *Selected Fields* list box.)
e. With *SupplierName* selected in the *Available Fields* list box, click the One Field button.
f. Click the down-pointing arrow at the right of the *Tables/Queries* option box and then click *Table: Orders*.
g. Click *ProductID* in the *Available Fields* list box and then click the One Field button.
h. Click *Amount* in the *Available Fields* list box and then click the One Field button.
i. Click the Next button.
j. At the second Simple Query Wizard dialog box, click the Next button.

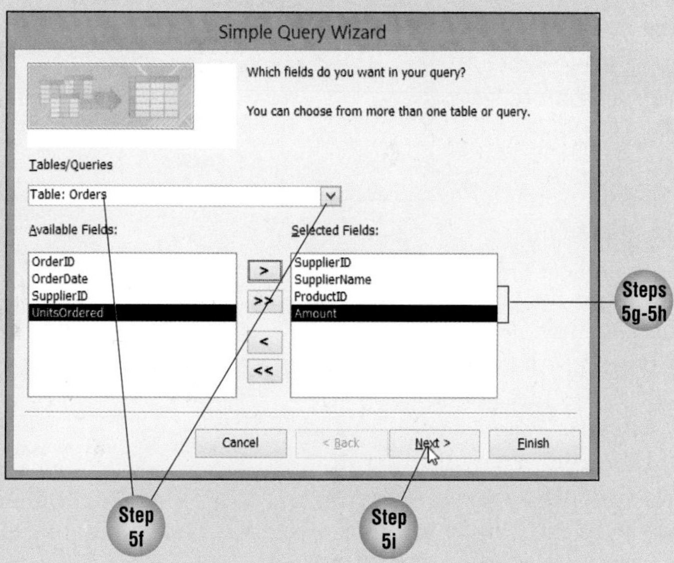

k. At the last Simple Query Wizard dialog box, select the text in the *What title do you want for your query?* text box, type **ProductOrderAmountsQuery**, and then press Enter.
l. When the results of the query display, print the results. (See Project 1f query results on page 80.)
m. Close the query.

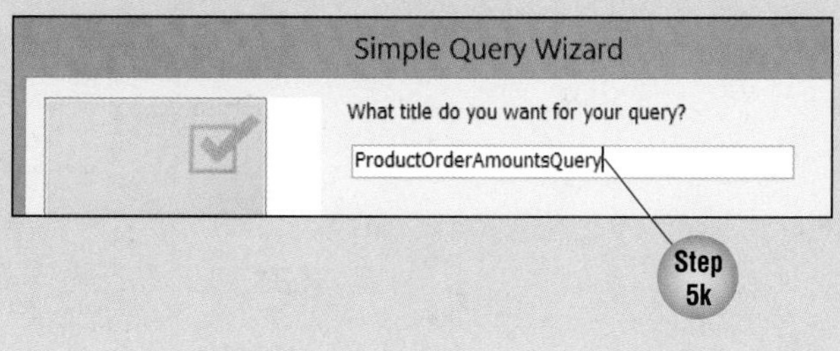

To extract specific information when using the Simple Query Wizard, tell the wizard that you want to modify the query design. This displays the query window with the query design grid, where you can insert query criteria.

Project 1g **Performing and Modifying Queries with the Simple Query Wizard** **Part 7 of 8**

1. With **AL1-C3-PacTrek.accdb** open, use the Simple Query Wizard to create a query that displays suppliers outside British Columbia by completing the following steps:
   a. Click the CREATE tab and then click the Query Wizard button.
   b. At the New Query dialog box, make sure *Simple Query Wizard* is selected and then click OK.
   c. At the first Simple Query Wizard dialog box, click the down-pointing arrow at the right side of the *Tables/Queries* option box and then click *Table: Suppliers*.
   d. Insert the following fields in the *Selected Fields* list box:
      SupplierName
      StreetAddress
      City
      Prov/State
      PostalCode
   e. Click the Next button.
   f. At the last Simple Query Wizard dialog box, select the current text in the *What title do you want for your query?* text box and then type **SuppliersNotBCQuery**.
   g. Click the *Modify the query design* option and then click the Finish button.
   h. At the query window, complete the following steps:
      1) Click in the *Criteria* row field in the *Prov/State* column in the query design grid.
      2) Type **Not BC** and then press Enter.

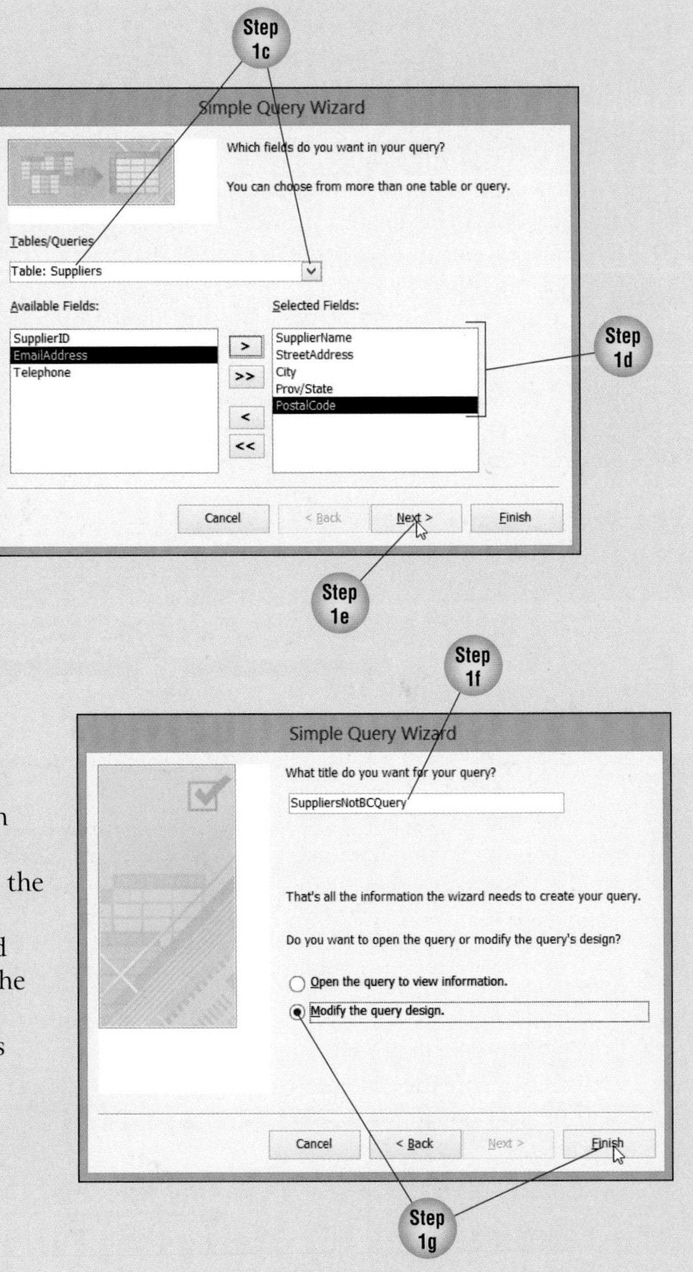

i. Specify that the fields are to be sorted in descending order by postal code by completing the following steps:
   1) Click in the *Sort* row field in the *PostalCode* column.
   2) Click the down-pointing arrow that displays at the right side of the field and then click *Descending*.

Field:	[SupplierName]	[StreetAddress]	[City]	[Prov/State]	[PostalCode]
Table:	Suppliers	Suppliers	Suppliers	Suppliers	Suppliers
Sort:					Descending (Ascending / Descending / (not sorted))
Show:	✔	✔	✔	✔	
Criteria:				Not "BC"	
or:					

Step 1i2

j. Click the Run button in the Results group. (This displays suppliers that are not located in British Columbia and displays the records sorted by postal code in descending order. See Project 1g query results on page 80.)
k. Save, print, and then close the query.

2. Close **AL1-C3-PacTrek.accdb**.
3. Open **AL1-C3-Dearborn.accdb**.
4. Use the Simple Query Wizard to create a query that displays clients in Muncie by completing the following steps:
   a. Click the CREATE tab and then click the Query Wizard button.
   b. At the New Query dialog box, make sure *Simple Query Wizard* is selected and then click OK.
   c. At the first Simple Query Wizard dialog box, click the down-pointing arrow at the right of the *Tables/Queries* option box and then click *Table: Clients*. (You may need to scroll up the list to display this table.)
   d. Insert the following fields in the *Selected Fields* list box:
      Client
      StreetAddress
      City
      State
      ZipCode
   e. Click the Next button.
   f. At the last Simple Query Wizard dialog box, select the current text in the *What title do you want for your query?* text box and then type **ClientsMuncieQuery**.
   g. Click the *Modify the query design* option and then click the Finish button.
   h. At the query window, complete the following steps:
      1) Click in the *Criteria* row field in the *City* column in the query design grid.
      2) Type **Muncie** and then press Enter.

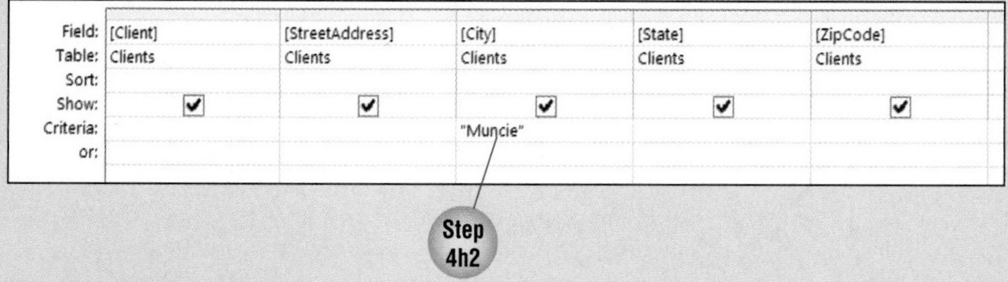

   i. Click the Run button in the Results group. (This displays clients located in Muncie. See Project 1g query results on page 80.)
   j. Save, print, and then close the query.

5. Close **AL1-C3-Dearborn.accdb**.
6. Open **AL1-C3-CopperState.accdb**.
7. Use the Simple Query Wizard to display clients that live in Phoenix with claims over $500 by completing the following steps:
   a. Click the CREATE tab and then click the Query Wizard button in the Queries group.
   b. At the New Query dialog box, make sure *Simple Query Wizard* is selected in the list box and then click OK.
   c. At the first Simple Query Wizard dialog box, click the down-pointing arrow at the right of the *Tables/Queries* option box and then click *Table: Clients*.
   d. Insert the following fields in the *Selected Fields* list box:
      ClientID
      FirstName
      LastName
      StreetAddress
      City
      State
      ZIP
   e. Click the down-pointing arrow at the right of the *Tables/Queries* option box and then click *Table: Claims*.
   f. With *ClaimID* selected in the *Available Fields* list box, click the One Field button.
   g. Click *AmountOfClaim* in the *Available Fields* list box and then click the One Field button.
   h. Click the Next button.
   i. At the second Simple Query Wizard dialog box, click the Next button.
   j. At the last Simple Query Wizard dialog box, select the current text in the *What title do you want for your query?* text box and then type **PhoenixClientClaimsOver$500Query**.
   k. Click the *Modify the query design* option and then click the Finish button.
   l. At the query window, complete the following steps:
      1) Click in the *Criteria* row field in the *City* column in the query design grid.
      2) Type **"Phoenix"** and then press Enter. (Type the quotation marks to tell Access that this is a criterion, otherwise Access will insert the query name *PhoenixClientClaimsOver$500Query* in the *Criteria* field.)
      3) Click in the *Criteria* row field in the *AmountOfClaim* column. (You may need to scroll to the right to display this field.)
      4) Type **>500** and then press Enter.

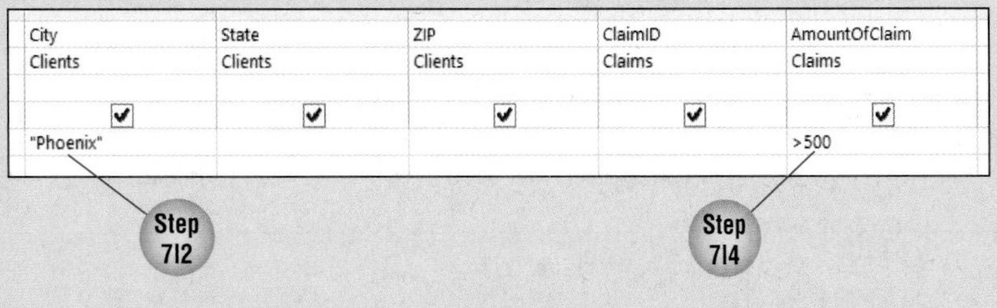

City	State	ZIP	ClaimID	AmountOfClaim
Clients	Clients	Clients	Claims	Claims
✔	✔	✔	✔	✔
"Phoenix"				>500

Step 7l2 Step 7l4

   m. Click the Run button in the Results group. (This displays clients located in Phoenix with claims greater than $500. See Project 1g query results on page 80.)
   n. Save the query, print the query in landscape orientation, and then close the query.
8. Close **AL1-C3-CopperState.accdb**.

Creating Calculated Fields

In a query, you can calculate values from a field by inserting a ***calculated field*** in a *Field* row field in the query design grid. To insert a calculated field, click in the *Field* row field, type the desired field name followed by a colon, and then type the equation. For example, to determine pension contributions as 3% of an employee's annual salary, type *PensionContribution:[AnnualSalary]*0.03* in the *Field* row field. Use brackets to specify field names and use mathematical operators to perform the equation. Some basic operators include the plus (+) for addition, the hyphen (-) for subtraction, the asterisk (*) for multiplication, and the forward slash (/) for division.

Type a calculated field in the field or in the Expression Builder dialog box. To display the Expression Builder dialog box, display the query in Design view, click in the field where you want the calculated field expression inserted, and then click the Builder button in the Query Setup group on the QUERY TOOLS DESIGN tab. You can type field names in the Expression Builder and when you click OK, the equation is inserted in the field with the correct symbols. For example, you can type *AnnualSalary*0.03* in the Expression Builder and when you click OK, *Expr1: [AnnualSalary]*0.03* is inserted in the *Criteria* row field. If you do not type a name for the field, Access creates the alias *Expr1* for the field name. If you want a specific name for the field, such as *PensionContribution*, first type that in the Expression Builder, followed by a colon, and then type the expression.

Builder

Project 1h **Creating a Calculated Field in a Query** **Part 8 of 8**

1. Open **AL1-C3-MRInvestments.accdb** and enable the contents.
2. Create a query that displays employer pension contributions at 3% of employees' annual salary by completing the following steps:
   a. Click the CREATE tab and then click the Query Design button.
   b. Double-click *Employees* in the Show Table dialog box and then click the Close button.
   c. At the query window, insert the *EmpID* field from the *Employees* field list box in the first *Field* row field.
   d. Insert the *FirstName* field in the second *Field* row field.
   e. Insert the *LastName* field in the third *Field* row field.
   f. Insert the *AnnualSalary* field in the fourth *Field* row field.
   g. Click in the fifth *Field* row field.
   h. Type **PensionContribution:[AnnualSalary]*0.03** and then press Enter.
   i. Click the Run button in the Results group.
   j. Save the query and name it *PensionContributionsQuery*. (See Project 1h query results on page 80.)
   k. Print and then close the query.

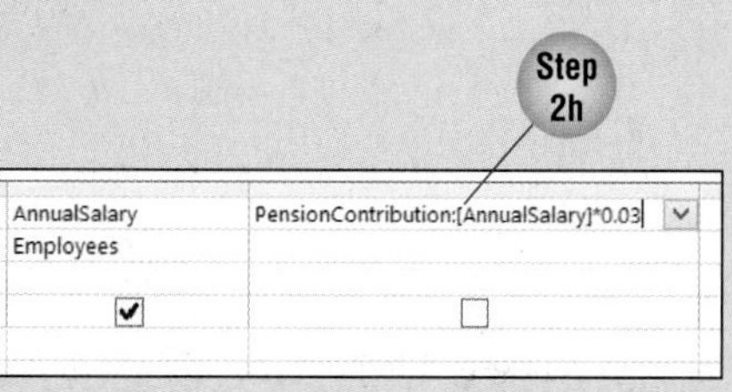

3. Modify *PensionContributionsQuery* and use the Expression Builder to write an equation finding the total amount of annual salary plus a 3% employer pension contribution by completing the following steps:
   a. Right-click *PensionContributionsQuery* in the Queries group in the Navigation pane and then click *Design View* at the shortcut menu.
   b. Click in the field containing *PensionContribution:[AnnualSalary]*0.03*.
   c. Click the Builder button in the Query Setup group on the QUERY TOOLS DESIGN tab.

d. In the Expression Builder, select the existing expression *PensionContribution: [AnnualSalary]*0.03*.
e. Type **Salary&Pension: [AnnualSalary]*1.03** and then click OK.
4. Click the Run button in the Results group.
5. Save the query by completing the following steps:
a. Click the FILE tab, click the *Save As* option, click the *Save Object As* option, and then click the Save As button.
b. At the Save As dialog box, type **Salary&PensionQuery** and then click OK. (See Project 1h query results on page 80.)

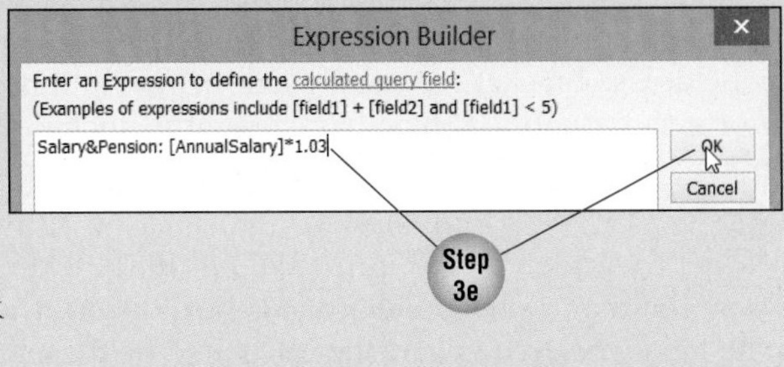

6. Print and then close the query.
7. Close **AL1-C3-MRInvestments.accdb**.
8. Open **AL1-C3-PacTrek.accdb**.
9. Create a query that displays orders and total order amounts by completing the following steps:
a. Click the CREATE tab and then click the Query Design button.
b. Double-click *Products* in the Show Table dialog box.
c. Double-click *Orders* in the Show Table dialog box and then click the Close button.
d. At the query window, insert the *Product* field from the *Products* field list box in the first *Field* row field.
e. Insert the *OrderID* field from the *Orders* field list box in the second *Field* row field.
f. Insert the *UnitsOrdered* field from the *Orders* field list box in the third *Field* row field.
g. Insert the *Amount* field from the *Orders* field list box in the fourth *Field* row field.
h. Click in the fifth *Field* row field.
i. Click the Builder button in the Query Setup group on the QUERY TOOLS DESIGN tab.
j. Type **Total:Amount*UnitsOrdered** in the Expression Builder and then click OK.
k. Click the Run button in the Results group.
l. Adjust the width of the columns to fit the longest entries.
m. Save the query and name it *UnitsOrderedTotalQuery*. (See Project 1h query results on page 80.)
n. Print and then close the query.

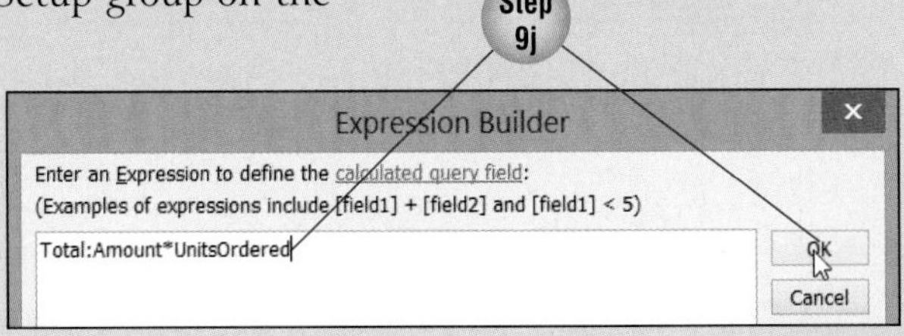

Project 2 Create Aggregate Functions, Crosstab, Find Duplicates, and Find Unmatched Queries — 6 Parts

You will create an aggregate functions query that determines the total, average, minimum, and maximum order amounts and then calculate total and average order amounts grouped by supplier. You will also use the Crosstab, Find Duplicates, and Find Unmatched query wizards to design queries.

Designing Queries with Aggregate Functions

You can include an ***aggregate function***—such as Sum, Avg, Min, Max, or Count—in a query to calculate statistics from numeric field values of all the records in the table. When an aggregate function is used, Access displays one row in the query results datasheet with the formula result for the function used. For example, in a table with a numeric field containing annual salary amounts, you can use the Sum function to calculate the total of all salary amount values.

To display the aggregate function list, click the Totals button in the Show/Hide group on the QUERY TOOLS DESIGN tab. Access adds a *Total* row to the design grid with a drop-down list from which you select the desired function. Access also inserts the words *Group By* in the *Total* row field. Click the down-pointing arrow and then click the desired aggregate function from the drop-down list. In Project 2a, Step 1, you will create a query in Design view and use aggregate functions to find the total of all sales, average sales amount, maximum and minimum sales, and total number of sales. The completed query will display as shown in Figure 3.5. Access automatically determines the column heading names.

Quick Steps

Design a Query with an Aggregate Function

1. At query window, click Totals button.
2. Click down-pointing arrow in *Total* row field.
3. Click desired aggregate function.

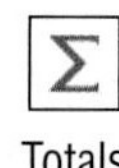
Totals

Figure 3.5 Query Results for Project 2a, Step 1

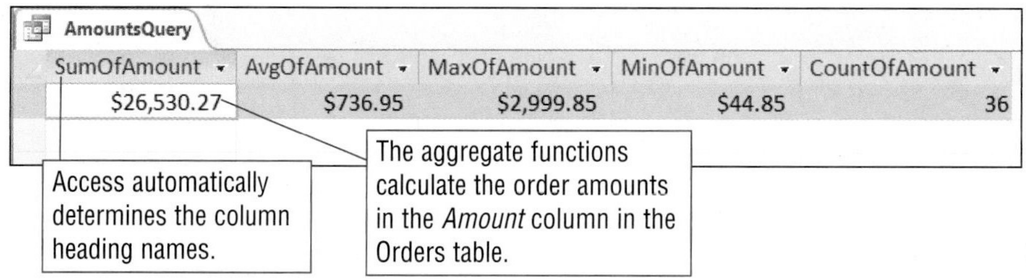

Project 2a **Using Aggregate Functions in Queries** **Part 1 of 6**

1. With **AL1-C3-PacTrek.accdb** open, create a query with aggregate functions that determines total, average, maximum, and minimum order amounts, as well as the total number of orders, by completing the following steps:
   a. Click the CREATE tab and then click the Query Design button.
   b. At the Show Table dialog box, make sure *Orders* is selected in the list box, click the Add button, and then click the Close button.
   c. Insert the *Amount* field in the first, second, third, fourth, and fifth *Field* row fields. (You may need to scroll down the *Orders* field list box to display the *Amount* field.)
   d. Click the Totals button in the Show/Hide group on the QUERY TOOLS DESIGN tab. (This adds a *Total* row to the design grid between *Table* and *Sort* with the default option of *Group By*.)

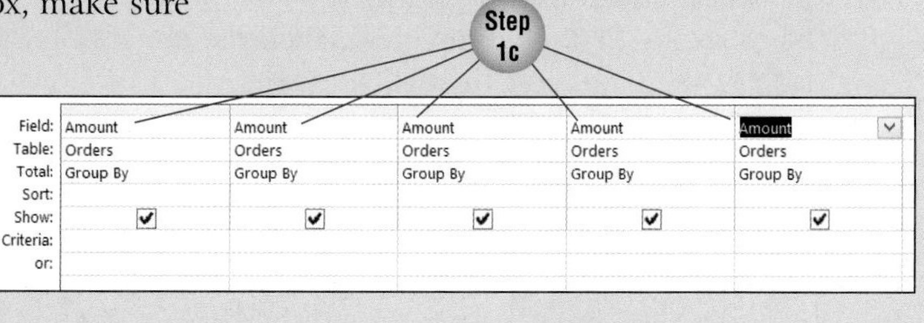

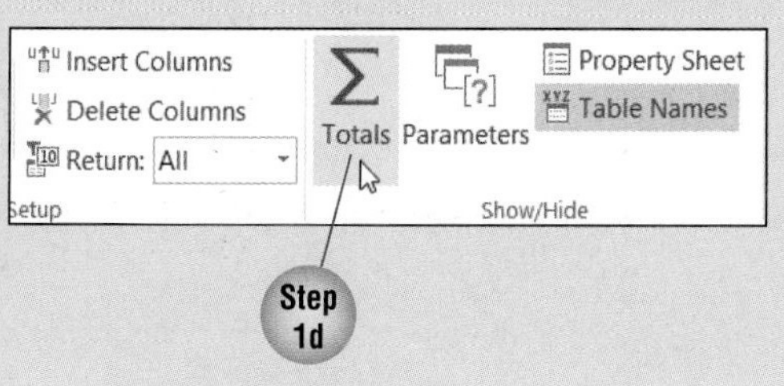

e. Specify a Sum function for the first *Total* row field by completing the following steps:
   1) Click in the first *Total* row field.
   2) Click the down-pointing arrow that displays at the right side of the field.
   3) Click *Sum* at the drop-down list.

f. Complete steps similar to those in Step 1e to insert *Avg* in the second *Total* row field.

g. Complete steps similar to those in Step 1e to insert *Max* in the third *Total* row field.

h. Complete steps similar to those in Step 1e to insert *Min* in the fourth *Total* row field.

i. Complete steps similar to those in Step 1e to insert *Count* in the fifth *Total* row field.

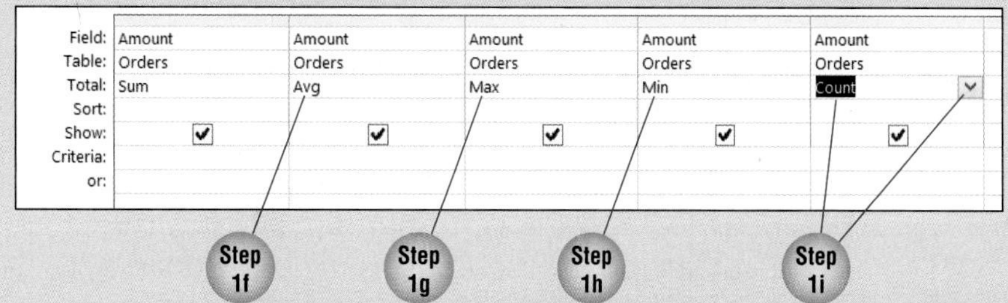

j. Click the Run button in the Results group. (Notice the headings that Access assigns to the columns.)

k. Automatically adjust the widths of the columns.

l. Save the query and name it *AmountsQuery*. (See Project 2a query results on page 81.)

m. Print and then close the query.

2. Close **AL1-C3-PacTrek.accdb**.
3. Open **AL1-C3-CopperState.accdb**.
4. Create a query with aggregate functions that determines total, average, maximum, and minimum claim amounts by completing the following steps:
   a. Click the CREATE tab and then click the Query Design button.
   b. At the Show Table dialog box, double-click *Claims*.
   c. Click the Close button to close the Show Table dialog box.
   d. Insert the *AmountOfClaim* field in the first, second, third, and fourth *Field* row fields.
   e. Click the Totals button in the Show/Hide group.
   f. Click in the first *Total* row field, click the down-pointing arrow that displays at the right side of the field, and then click *Sum* at the drop-down list.

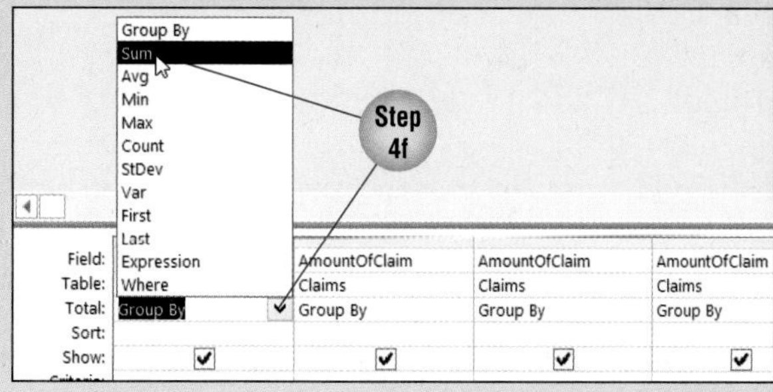

g. Click in the second *Total* row field, click the down-pointing arrow, and then click *Avg* at the drop-down list.
h. Click in the third *Total* row field, click the down-pointing arrow, and then click *Max* at the drop-down list.
i. Click in the fourth *Total* row field, click the down-pointing arrow, and then click *Min* at the drop-down list.
j. Click the Run button in the Results group. (Notice the headings that Access chooses for the columns.)
k. Automatically adjust the widths of the columns.
l. Save the query and name it *ClaimAmountsQuery*. (See Project 2a query results on page 81.)
m. Print the query in landscape orientation and then close the query.

Using the *Group By* option in the *Total* field, you can add a field to the query on which you want Access to group records for statistical calculations. For example, to calculate the total of all orders for a specific supplier, add the *SupplierID* field to the design grid with the *Total* field set to *Group By*. In Project 2b, Step 1, you will create a query in Design view and use aggregate functions to find the total of all order amounts and the average order amounts grouped by supplier number.

Project 2b Using Aggregate Functions and Grouping Records — Part 2 of 6

1. With **AL1-C3-CopperState.accdb** open, determine the sum and average of client claims by completing the following steps:
   a. Click the CREATE tab and then click the Query Design button.
   b. At the Show Table dialog box, double-click *Clients* in the list box.
   c. Double-click *Claims* in the list box and then click the Close button.
   d. Insert the *ClientID* field from the *Clients* field list box to the first *Field* row field.
   e. Insert the *AmountOfClaim* field from the *Claims* field list box to the second *Field* row field.
   f. Insert the *AmountOfClaim* field from the *Claims* field list box to the third *Field* row field.
   g. Click the Totals button in the Show/Hide group.
   h. Click in the second *Total* row field, click the down-pointing arrow, and then click *Sum* at the drop-down list.
   i. Click in the third *Total* row field, click the down-pointing arrow, and then click *Avg* at the drop-down list.
   j. Make sure *Group By* displays in the first *Total* row field.

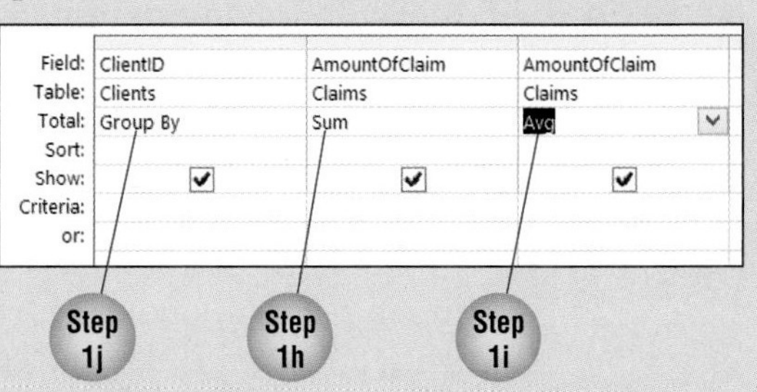

   k. Click the Run button in the Results group.
   l. Automatically adjust column widths.
   m. Save the query and name it *SumAvgClaimAmountsQuery*. (See Project 2b query results on page 81.)
   n. Print and then close the query.
2. Close **AL1-C3-CopperState.accdb**.

3. Open **AL1-C3-PacTrek.accdb**.
4. Determine the total and average order amounts for each supplier by completing the following steps:
   a. Click the CREATE tab and then click the Query Design button.
   b. At the Show Table dialog box, make sure *Orders* is selected in the list box and then click the Add button.
   c. Click *Suppliers* in the list box, click the Add button, and then click the Close button.
   d. Insert the *Amount* field from the *Orders* field list box to the first *Field* row field. (You may need to scroll down the *Orders* field list box to display the *Amount* field.)
   e. Insert the *Amount* field from the *Orders* field list box to the second *Field* row field.
   f. Insert the *SupplierID* field from the *Suppliers* field list box to the third *Field* row field.
   g. Insert the *SupplierName* field from the *Suppliers* field list box to the fourth *Field* row field.
   h. Click the Totals button in the Show/Hide group.
   i. Click in the first *Total* row field, click the down-pointing arrow, and then click *Sum* at the drop-down list.
   j. Click in the second *Total* row field, click the down-pointing arrow, and then click *Avg* at the drop-down list.
   k. Make sure *Group By* displays in the third and fourth *Total* row fields.
   l. Click the Run button in the Results group.
   m. Automatically adjust column widths.
   n. Save the query and name it *SupplierAmountsQuery*. (See Project 2b query results on page 81.)
   o. Print and then close the query.

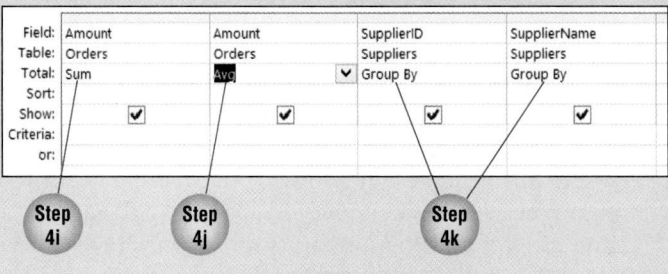

Creating Crosstab Queries

> **Quick Steps**
> **Create a Crosstab Query**
> 1. Click CREATE tab.
> 2. Click Query Wizard button.
> 3. Double-click *Crosstab Query Wizard*.
> 4. Complete wizard steps.

A ***crosstab query*** calculates aggregate functions, such as Sum and Avg, in which field values are grouped by two fields. A wizard is included that guides you through the steps to create the query. The first field selected causes one row to display in the query results datasheet for each group. The second field selected displays one column in the query results datasheet for each group. A third field is specified that is the numeric field to be summarized. The intersection of each row and column holds a value that is the result of the specified aggregate function for the designated row and column group.

Create a crosstab query from fields in one table. If you want to include fields from more than one table, you must first create a query containing the desired fields, and then create the crosstab query. For example, in Project 2c, Step 2, you will create a new query that contains fields from each of the three tables in AL1-C3-PacTrek.accdb. Using this query, you will use the Crosstab Query Wizard to create a query that summarizes the order amounts by supplier name and product ordered. Figure 3.6 displays the results of that crosstab query. The first column displays the supplier names, the second column displays the total amount for each supplier, and the remaining columns display the amounts by suppliers for specific items.

Figure 3.6 Crosstab Query Results for Project 2c, Step 2

Order amounts are grouped by supplier name and individual product.

OrdersBySupplierByProductQuery

SupplierName	Total Of Amc	Binoculars, 8	Cascade R4 ja	Cascade R4 ja	Cascade R4 ja	Cascade R4 ja	Deluxe map c	Eight-piece st
Bayside Supplies	$224.00							$99.75
Cascade Gear	$3,769.00		$1,285.00	$1,285.00	$599.50	$599.50		
Emerald City Products	$2,145.00	$2,145.00						
Fraser Valley Products	$3,892.75							
Freedom Corporation	$1,286.65							
Hopewell, Inc.	$348.60							
KL Distributions	$4,288.35							
Langley Corporation	$593.25							
Macadam, Inc.	$175.70						$129.75	
Manning, Inc.	$4,282.25							
Sound Supplies	$5,524.72							

Project 2c Creating Crosstab Queries

Part 3 of 6

1. With **AL1-C3-PacTrek.accdb** open, create a query containing fields from the three tables by completing the following steps:
   a. Click the CREATE tab and then click the Query Design button.
   b. At the Show Table dialog box with *Orders* selected in the list box, click the Add button.
   c. Double-click *Products* in the list box.
   d. Double-click *Suppliers* in the list box and then click the Close button.
   e. Insert the following fields to the specified *Field* row fields:
      1) From the *Orders* field list box, insert the *ProductID* field in the first *Field* row field.
      2) From the *Products* field list box, insert the *Product* field in the second *Field* row field.
      3) From the *Orders* field list box, insert the *UnitsOrdered* field in the third *Field* row field.
      4) From the *Orders* field list box, insert the *Amount* field in the fourth *Field* row field.
      5) From the *Suppliers* field list box, insert the *SupplierName* field in the fifth *Field* row field.
      6) From the *Orders* field list box, insert the *OrderDate* field in the sixth *Field* row field.

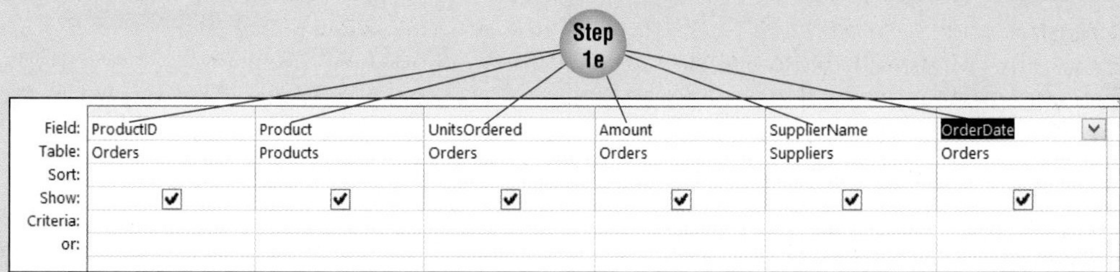

   f. Click the Run button to run the query.
   g. Save the query and name it *ItemsOrderedQuery*.
   h. Close the query.

2. Create a crosstab query that summarizes the orders by supplier name and by product ordered by completing the following steps:
   a. Click the CREATE tab and then click the Query Wizard button.
   b. At the New Query dialog box, double-click *Crosstab Query Wizard* in the list box.
   c. At the first Crosstab Query Wizard dialog box, click the *Queries* option in the *View* section and then click *Query: ItemsOrderedQuery* in the list box.
   d. Click the Next button.
   e. At the second Crosstab Query Wizard dialog box, click *SupplierName* in the *Available Fields* list box and then click the One Field button. (This inserts *SupplierName* in the *Selected Fields* list box and specifies that you want *SupplierName* for the row headings.)
   f. Click the Next button.
   g. At the third Crosstab Query Wizard dialog box, click *Product* in the list box. (This specifies that you want *Product* for the column headings.)
   h. Click the Next button.
   i. At the fourth Crosstab Query Wizard dialog box, click *Amount* in the *Fields* list box and then click *Sum* in the *Functions* list box.
   j. Click the Next button.
   k. At the fifth Crosstab Query Wizard dialog box, select the current text in the *What do you want to name your query?* text box and then type **OrdersBySupplierByProductQuery**.
   l. Click the Finish button. (See Project 2c query results on page 81.)

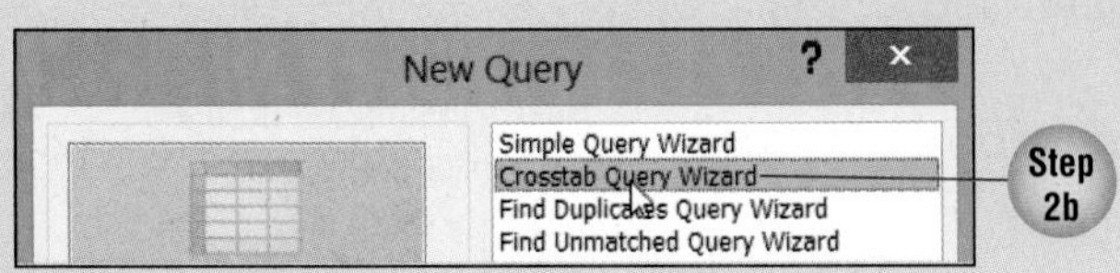

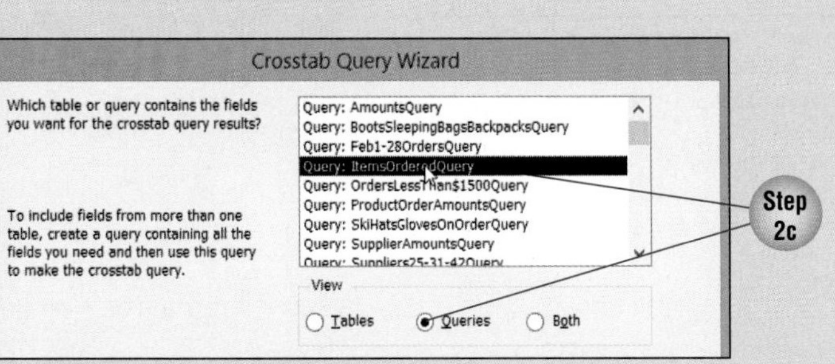

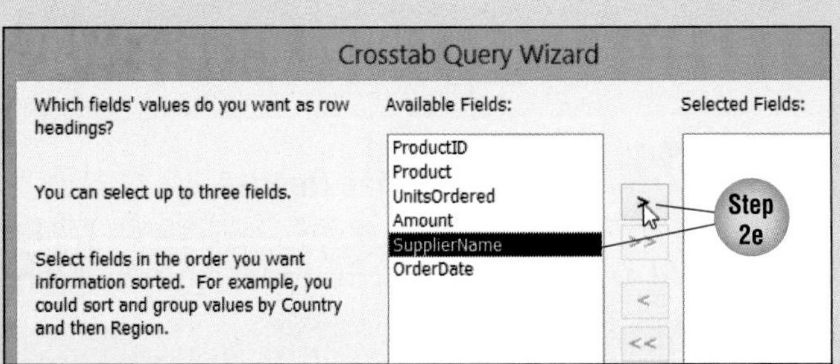

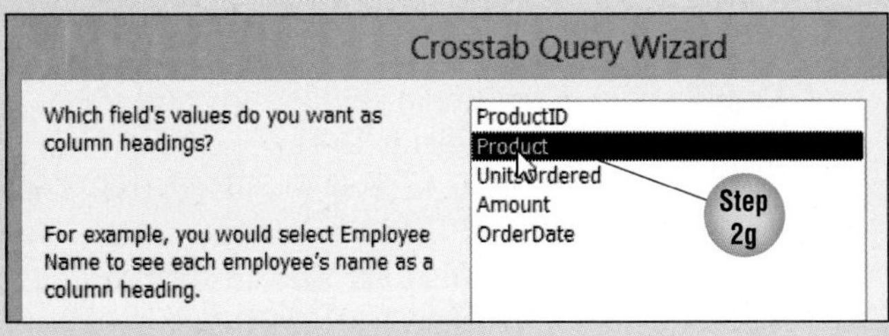

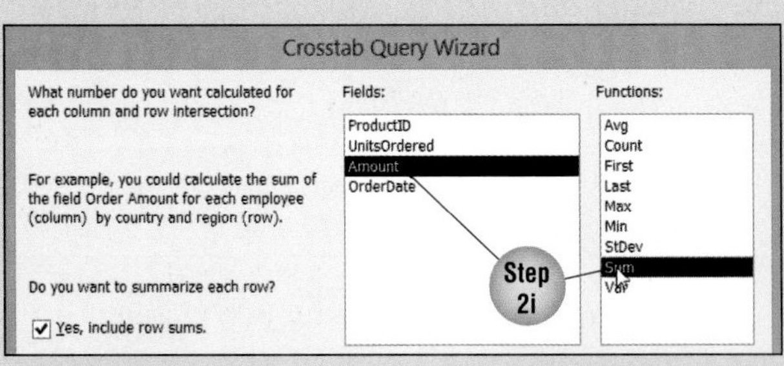

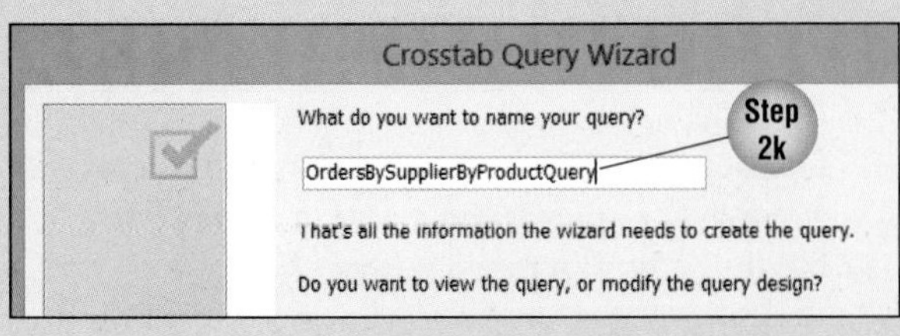

3. Display the query in Print Preview, change the orientation to landscape, change the left and right margins to 0.5 inch, and then print the query. (The query will print on four pages.)

4. Close the query.
5. Close **AL1-C3-PacTrek.accdb**.
6. Open **AL1-C3-CopperState.accdb**.
7. Create a crosstab query from fields in one table that summarizes clients' claims by completing the following steps:
   a. Click the CREATE tab and then click the Query Wizard button.
   b. At the New Query dialog box, double-click *Crosstab Query Wizard* in the list box.
   c. At the first Crosstab Query Wizard dialog box, click *Table: Claims* in the list box.
   d. Click the Next button.
   e. At the second Crosstab Query Wizard dialog box, click the One Field button. (This inserts the *ClaimID* field in the *Selected Fields* list box.)
   f. Click the Next button.
   g. At the third Crosstab Query Wizard dialog, make sure *ClientID* is selected in the list box and then click the Next button.
   h. At the fourth Crosstab Query Wizard dialog box, click *AmountOfClaim* in the *Fields* list box and click *Sum* in the *Functions* list box.
   i. Click the Next button.
   j. At the fifth Crosstab Query Wizard dialog box, select the current text in the *What do you want to name your query?* text box and then type **ClaimsByClaimIDByClientIDQuery**.
   k. Click the Finish button. (See Project 2c query results on page 81.)
8. Change the orientation to landscape and then print the query. The query will print on two pages.
9. Close the query.
10. Close **AL1-C3-CopperState.accdb**.

Creating Find Duplicates Queries

Use a ***find duplicates query*** to search a specified table or query for duplicate field values within a designated field or fields. Create this type of query, for example, if you suspect a record (such as a product record) has inadvertently been entered twice (perhaps under two different product numbers). A find duplicates query has many applications. Here are a few other examples of how you can use a find duplicates query:

- In an orders table, find records with the same customer number so you can identify loyal customers.
- In a customers table, find records with the same last name and mailing address so you can send only one mailing to a household and save on printing and postage costs.
- In an employee expenses table, find records with the same employee number so you can see which employee is submitting the most claims.

Access provides the Find Duplicates Query Wizard to build the query based on the selections made in a series of dialog boxes. To use this wizard, open the desired database, click the CREATE tab, and then click the Query Wizard button. At the New Query dialog box, double-click *Find Duplicates Query Wizard* in the list box and then complete the steps provided by the wizard.

In Project 2d, you will assume that you have been asked to update the address for a supplier in AL1-C3-PacTrek.accdb. Instead of updating the address, you create a new record. You will then use the Find Duplicates Query Wizard to find duplicate field values in the Suppliers table.

Quick Steps

Create a Find Duplicates Query
1. Click CREATE tab.
2. Click Query Wizard button.
3. Double-click *Find Duplicates Query Wizard*.
4. Complete wizard steps.

Project 2d Creating a Find Duplicates Query

1. Open **AL1-C3-PacTrek.accdb** and then open the Suppliers table.
2. Add the following record to the table:

   SupplierID# **29**
   SupplierName **Langley Corporation**
   StreetAddress **1248 Larson Avenue**
   City **Burnaby**
   Prov/State **BC**
   PostalCode **V5V 9K2**
   EmailAddress **lc@emcp.net**
   Telephone **(604) 555-1200**
3. Close the Suppliers table.
4. Use the Find Duplicates Query Wizard to find any duplicate supplier names by completing the following steps:
   a. Click the CREATE tab and then click the Query Wizard button.
   b. At the New Query dialog box, double-click *Find Duplicates Query Wizard*.
   c. At the first wizard dialog box, click *Table: Suppliers* in the list box.

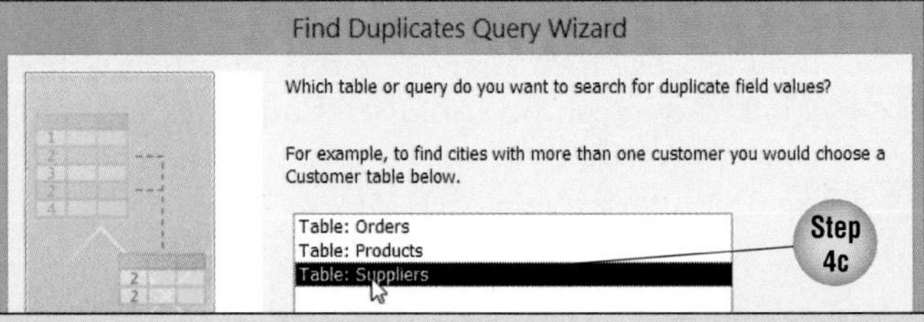

   d. Click the Next button.
   e. At the second wizard dialog box, click *SupplierName* in the *Available fields* list box and then click the One Field button. (This moves the *SupplierName* field to the *Duplicate-value fields* list box.)

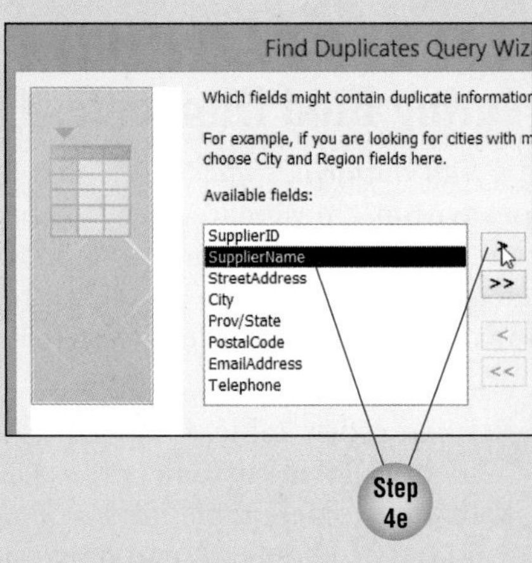

   f. Click the Next button.
   g. At the third wizard dialog box, click the All Fields button (the button containing the two greater-than symbols, >>). This moves all the fields to the *Additional query fields* list box. You are doing this because if you find a duplicate supplier name, you want to view all the fields to determine which record is accurate.
   h. Click the Next button.
   i. At the fourth (and last) wizard dialog box, type **DuplicateSuppliersQuery** in the *What do you want to name your query?* text box.
   j. Click the Finish button. (See Project 2d query results on page 81.)
   k. Change the orientation to landscape and then print the query.

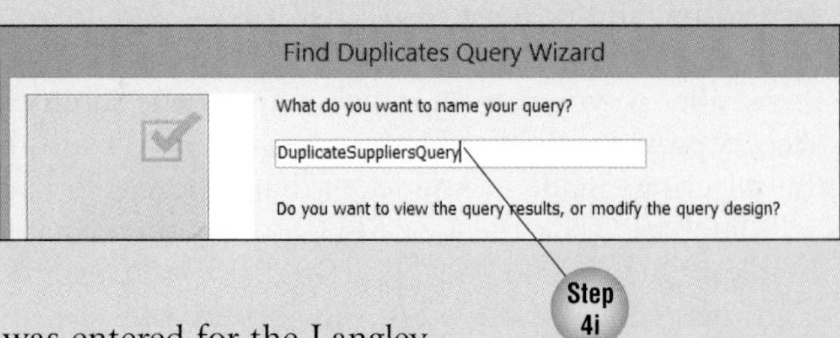

5. As you look at the query results, you realize that an inaccurate record was entered for the Langley Corporation, so you decide to delete one of the records. To do this, complete the following steps:

a. With the query open, click in the record selector bar next to the record with a supplier ID of *29*. (This selects the entire row.)
b. Click the HOME tab and then click the Delete button in the Records group.
c. At the message asking you to confirm, click the Yes button.
d. Close the query.

6. Change the street address for Langley Corporation by completing the following steps:
   a. Open the Suppliers table in Datasheet view.
   b. Change the address for Langley Corporation from *805 First Avenue* to *1248 Larson Avenue*. Leave the other fields as displayed.
   c. Close the Suppliers table.

In Project 2d, you used the Find Duplicates Query Wizard to find records containing the same field.In Project 2e, you will use the Find Duplicates Query Wizard to find information on the suppliers you order from the most. You could use this information to negotiate for better prices or to ask for discounts.

Project 2e Finding Duplicate Orders — Part 5 of 6

1. With **AL1-C3-PacTrek.accdb** open, create a query with the following fields (in the order shown) from the specified tables:

SupplierID	Suppliers table
SupplierName	Suppliers table
ProductID	Orders table
Product	Products table

2. Run the query.
3. Save the query with the name *SupplierOrdersQuery* and then close the query.
4. Use the Find Duplicates Query Wizard to find the suppliers you order from the most by completing the following steps:
   a. Click the CREATE tab and then click the Query Wizard button.
   b. At the New Query dialog box, double-click *Find Duplicates Query Wizard*.
   c. At the first wizard dialog box, click the *Queries* option in the *View* section and then click *Query: SupplierOrdersQuery*. (You may need to scroll down the list to display this query.)

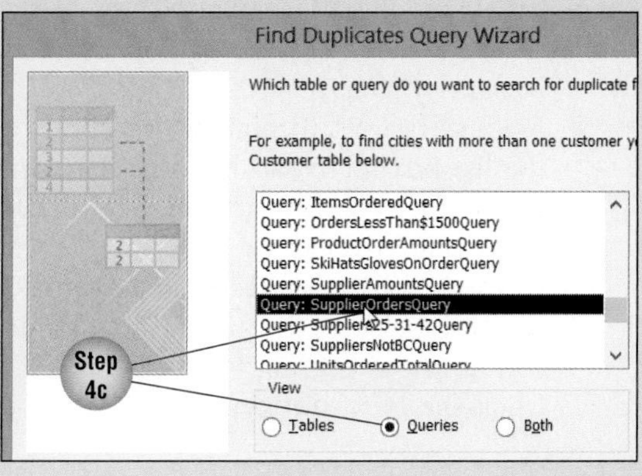

d. Click the Next button.
e. At the second wizard dialog box, click *SupplierName* in the *Available fields* list box and then click the One Field button.
f. Click the Next button.
g. At the third wizard dialog box, click the Next button.
h. At the fourth (and last) wizard dialog box, type **SupplierOrdersCountQuery** in the *What do you want to name your query?* text box.
i. Click the Finish button.
j. Adjust the widths of the columns to fit the longest entries.
k. Print the query. (See Project 2e query results on page 82.)

5. Close the query.

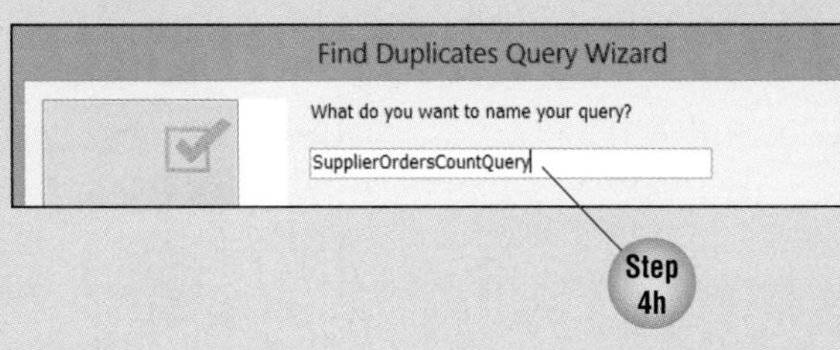

Creating Find Unmatched Queries

Create a ***find unmatched query*** to compare two tables and produce a list of the records in one table that have no matching record in the other table. This type of query is useful to produce lists such as customers who have never placed orders and invoices that have no records of payment. Access provides the Find Unmatched Query Wizard to build the select query by guiding you through a series of dialog boxes.

In Project 2f, you will use the Find Unmatched Query Wizard to find all of the products that have no units on order. This information is helpful in identifying which products are not selling and might need to be discontinued or returned. To use the Find Unmatched Query Wizard, click the CREATE tab and then click the Query Wizard button in the Queries group. At the New Query dialog box, double-click *Find Unmatched Query Wizard* in the list box and then follow the wizard steps.

Quick Steps

Create a Find Unmatched Query
1. Click CREATE tab.
2. Click Query Wizard button.
3. Double-click *Find Unmatched Query Wizard.*
4. Complete wizard steps.

Project 2f **Creating a Find Unmatched Query** **Part 6 of 6**

1. With **AL1-C3-PacTrek.accdb** open, use the Find Unmatched Query Wizard to find all products that do not have units on order by completing the following steps:
   a. Click the CREATE tab and then click the Query Wizard button.
   b. At the New Query dialog box, double-click *Find Unmatched Query Wizard.*
   c. At the first wizard dialog box, click *Table: Products* in the list box. (This is the table containing the fields you want to see in the query results.)
   d. Click the Next button.
   e. At the second wizard dialog box, make sure *Table: Orders* is selected in the list box. (This is the table containing the related records.)
   f. Click the Next button.

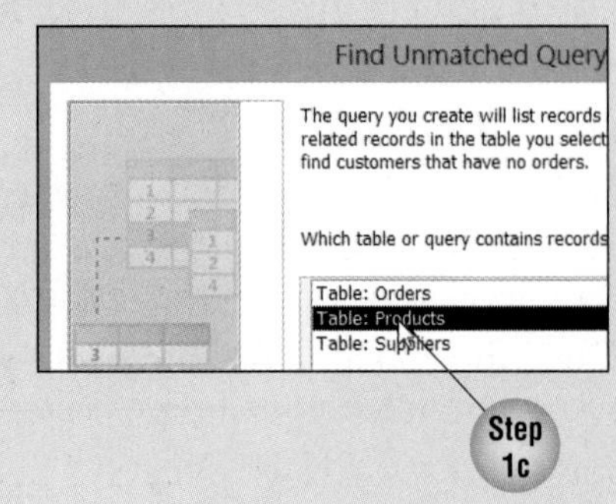

g. At the third wizard dialog box, make sure *ProductID* is selected in both the *Fields in 'Products'* list box and in the *Fields in 'Orders'* list box.
h. Click the Next button.
i. At the fourth wizard dialog box, click the All Fields button to move all of the fields from the *Available fields* list box to the *Selected fields* list box.
j. Click the Next button.
k. At the fifth wizard dialog box, click the Finish button. (Let the wizard determine the query name: *Products Without Matching Orders*. See Project 2f query results on page 82.)

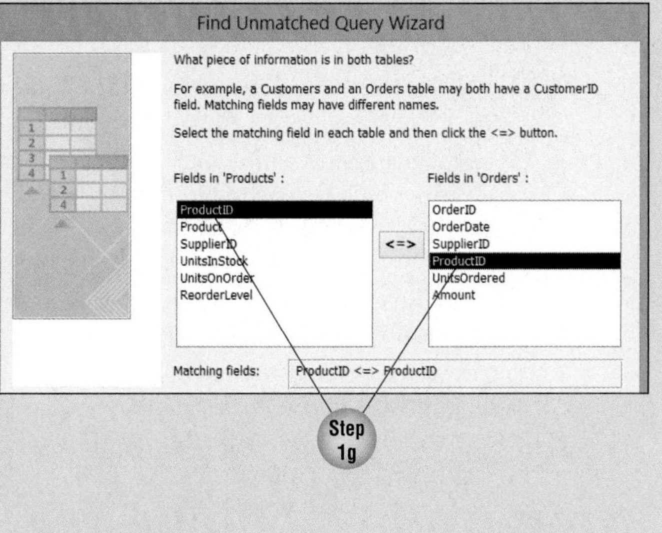

2. Print the query in landscape orientation and then close the query.
3. Close **AL1-C3-PacTrek.accdb**.

Chapter Summary

- One of the most important uses of a database is to select the information needed to answer questions and make decisions. Data can be extracted from an Access database by performing a query, which can be accomplished by designing a query or using a query wizard.
- Designing a query consists of identifying the table, the field or fields from which the data will be drawn, and the criteria for selecting the data.
- In designing a query, type the criterion (or criteria) for extracting the specific data. Access inserts any necessary symbols in the criterion when the Enter key is pressed.
- In a criterion, quotation marks surround field values and pound symbols (#) surround dates. Use the asterisk (*) as a wildcard character.
- You can perform a query on fields within one table or on fields from related tables.
- When designing a query, you can specify the sort order of a field or fields.
- You can modify an existing query and use it for a new purpose.
- Enter a criterion in the *or* row in the query design grid to instruct Access to display records that match any of the criteria.
- Multiple criteria entered in the *Criteria* row in the query design grid become an *And* statement, where each criterion must be met for Access to select the record.
- The Simple Query Wizard guides you through the steps for preparing a query. You can modify a query you create with the wizard.
- You can insert a calculated field in a *Field* row field when designing a query.

- Include an aggregate function (such as Sum, Avg, Min, Max, or Count) to calculate statistics from numeric field values. Click the Totals button in the Show/Hide group on the QUERY TOOLS DESIGN tab to display the aggregate function list.
- Use the *Group By* option in the *Total* row field to add a field to a query on which you want Access to group records for statistical calculations.
- Create a crosstab query to calculate aggregate functions (such as Sum and Avg), in which fields are grouped by two. Create a crosstab query from fields in one table. If you want to include fields from more than one table, create a query first and then create the crosstab query.
- Use a find duplicates query to search a specified table for duplicate field values within a designated field or fields.
- Create a find unmatched query to compare two tables and produce a list of the records in one table that have no matching records in the other related table.

Commands Review

FEATURE	RIBBON TAB, GROUP	BUTTON, OPTION
add *Total* row to query design	QUERY TOOLS DESIGN, Show/Hide	Σ
Crosstab Query Wizard	CREATE, Queries	, *Crosstab Query Wizard*
Find Duplicates Query Wizard	CREATE, Queries	, *Find Duplicates Query Wizard*
Find Unmatched Query Wizard	CREATE, Queries	, *Find Unmatched Query Wizard*
New Query dialog box	CREATE, Queries	
query results	QUERY TOOLS DESIGN, Results	!
query window	CREATE, Queries	
Simple Query Wizard	CREATE, Queries	, *Simple Query Wizard*

records in one table that have no matching records in the other related table.

Completion: In the space provided at the right, indicate the correct term, symbol, or command.

1. The Query Design button is located in the Queries group on this tab. ____________
2. Click the Query Design button and the query window displays with this dialog box open. ____________
3. To establish a criterion for a query, click in this row in the column containing the desired field name and then type the criterion. ____________
4. This is the term used for the results of the query. ____________
5. This is the symbol Access automatically inserts before and after a date when writing a criterion for the query. ____________
6. Use this symbol to indicate a wildcard character when writing a query criterion. ____________
7. This is the criterion you would type to return field values greater than $500. ____________
8. This is the criterion you would type to return field values that begin with the letter *L*. ____________
9. This is the criterion you would type to return field values that are not in Oregon. ____________
10. You can sort a field in a query in ascending order or in this order. ____________
11. Multiple criteria entered in the *Criteria* row in the query design grid become this type of statement. ____________
12. This wizard guides you through the steps for preparing a query. ____________
13. This type of query calculates aggregate functions, in which field values are grouped by two fields. ____________
14. Use this type of query to compare two tables and produce a list of the records in one table that have no matching records in the other table. ____________

Skills Check Assess Your Performance

Assessment 1

DESIGN QUERIES IN A LEGAL SERVICES DATABASE

1. Display the Open dialog box with the AL1C3 folder on your storage medium the active folder.
2. Open **AL1-C3-WarrenLegal.accdb** and enable the contents.
3. Design a query that extracts information from the Billing table with the following specifications:
   a. Include the fields *BillingID*, *ClientID*, and *CategoryID* in the query.
   b. Extract those records with the *SE* category. (Type "SE" in the *Criteria* row field in the *CategoryID* column. You need to type the quotation marks to tell Access that SE is a criterion and not a built-in Access function.)
   c. Save the query and name it *SECategoryBillingQuery*.
   d. Print and then close the query.
4. Design a query that extracts information from the Billing table with the following specifications:
   a. Include the fields *BillingID*, *ClientID*, and *Date*.
   b. Extract those records in the *Date* field with dates between 6/8/2015 and 6/15/2015.
   c. Save the query and name it *June8-15BillingQuery*.
   d. Print and then close the query.
5. Design a query that extracts information from the Clients table with the following specifications:
   a. Include the fields *FirstName*, *LastName*, and *City*.
   b. Extract those records with cities other than Kent in the *City* field.
   c. Save the query and name it *ClientsNotInKentQuery*.
   d. Print and then close the query.
6. Design a query that extracts information from two tables with the following specifications:
   a. Include the fields *BillingID*, *ClientID*, *Date*, and *RateID* from the Billing table.
   b. Include the field *Rate* from the Rates table.
   c. Extract those records with rate IDs greater than *2*.
   d. Save the query and name it *RateIDGreaterThan2Query*.
   e. Print and then close the query.
7. Design a query that extracts information from three tables with the following specifications:
   a. Include the fields *AttorneyID, FName,* and *LName* from the Attorneys table.
   b. Include the fields *FirstName* and *LastName* from the Clients table.
   c. Include the fields *Date* and *Hours* from the Billing table.
   d. Extract those records with an attorney ID of *12*.
   e. Save the query and name it *Attorney12Query*.
   f. Print and then close the query.
8. Design a query that extracts information from four tables with the following specifications:
   a. Include the fields *AttorneyID*, *FName*, and *LName* from the Attorneys table.
   b. Include the field *Category* from the Categories table.
   c. Include the fields *RateID* and *Rate* from the Rates table.

d. Include the fields *Date* and *Hours* from the Billing table.
e. Extract those records with an attorney ID of *17* and a rate ID of *4*.
f. Save the query and name it *Attorney17RateID4Query*.
g. Print the query in landscape orientation and then close the query.

9. Open the Attorney17RateID4Query query, click the View button on the HOME tab to display the query in Design view, and then modify the query so it displays records with a rate ID of *4* and attorney IDs of *17* and *19* by making the following changes:
   a. Click below the field value "*17*" in the *AttorneyID* column and then type 19.
   b. Click below the field value "*4*" in the *RateID* column, type 4, and then press Enter.
   c. Run the query.
   d. Save the query with the new name *Attorney17&19RateID4Query*. ***Hint: Do this at the Save As dialog box. Display this dialog box by clicking the FILE tab,* clicking *the* Save As *option, clicking the* Save Object As *option, and then clicking the Save As button.***
   e. Print the query in landscape orientation and then close the query.

Assessment 2

USE THE SIMPLE QUERY WIZARD AND DESIGN QUERIES

1. With **AL1-C3-WarrenLegal.accdb** open, use the Simple Query Wizard to extract specific information from three tables with the following specifications:
   a. At the first Simple Query Wizard dialog box, include the following fields:
      From Attorneys table: *AttorneyID*, *FName,* and *LName*
      From Categories table: *Category*
      From Billing table: *Hours*
   b. At the second Simple Query Wizard dialog box, click Next.
   c. At the third Simple Query Wizard dialog box, click the *Modify the query design* option and then click the Finish button.
   d. At the query window, insert *14* in the *Criteria* row field in the *AttorneyID* column.
   e. Run the query.
   f. Save the query with the default name.
   g. Print and then close the query.
2. Create a query in Design view with the Billing table with the following specifications:
   a. Insert the *Hours* field from the *Billing* field list box to the first, second, third, and fourth *Field* row fields.
   b. Click the Totals button in the Show/Hide group.
   c. Insert *Sum* in the first *Total* row field.
   d. Insert *Min* in the second *Total* row field.
   e. Insert *Max* in the third *Total* row field.
   f. Insert *Count* in the fourth *Total* row field.
   g. Run the query.
   h. Automatically adjust the widths of the columns.
   i. Save the query and name it *HoursAmountQuery*.
   j. Print and then close the query.
3. Create a query in Design view with the following specifications:
   a. Add the Attorneys table and Billing table to the query window.
   b. Insert the *FName* field from the *Attorneys* field list box to the first *Field* row field.
   c. Insert the *LName* field from the *Attorneys* field list box to the second *Field* row field.

d. Insert the *AttorneyID* field from the *Billing* field list box to the third *Field* row field. (You will need to scroll down the *Billing* field list box to display the *AttorneyID* field.)
e. Insert the *Hours* field from the *Billing* field list box to the fourth *Field* row field.
f. Click the Totals button in the Show/Hide group.
g. Insert *Sum* in the fourth *Total* row field in the *Hours* column.
h. Run the query.
i. Save the query and name it *AttorneyHoursQuery*.
j. Print and then close the query.

4. Create a query in Design view with the following specifications:
a. Add the Attorneys, Clients, Categories, and Billing tables to the query window.
b. Insert the *AttorneyID* field from the *Attorneys* field list box to the first *Field* row field.
c. Insert the *ClientID* field from the *Clients* field list box to the second *Field* row field.
d. Insert the *Category* field from the *Categories* field list box to the third *Field* row field.
e. Insert the *Hours* field from the *Billing* field list box to the fourth *Field* row field.
f. Run the query.
g. Save the query and name it *AttorneyClientHours*.
h. Print and then close the query.

Assessment

3 CREATE A CROSSTAB QUERY AND USE THE FIND DUPLICATES AND FIND UNMATCHED QUERY WIZARDS

1. With **AL1-C3-WarrenLegal.accdb** open, create a crosstab query that summarizes the hours by attorney by category with the following specifications:
a. At the first Crosstab Query Wizard dialog box, click the *Queries* option in the *View* section and then click *Query: AttorneyClientHours* in the list box.
b. At the second Crosstab Query Wizard dialog box with *AttorneyID* selected in the *Available Fields* list box, click the One Field button.
c. At the third Crosstab Query Wizard dialog box, click *Category* in the list box.
d. At the fourth Crosstab Query Wizard dialog box, click *Hours* in the *Fields* list box and click *Sum* in the *Functions* list box.
e. At the fifth Crosstab Query Wizard dialog box, select the current name in the *What do you want to name your query?* text box and then type **HoursByAttorneyByCategory**.
f. Display the query in Print Preview, change to landscape orientation, change the left and right margins to 0.5 inch, and then print the query.
g. Close the query.

2. Use the Find Duplicates Query Wizard to find those clients with the same last name with the following specifications:
a. At the first wizard dialog box, click *Table: Clients* in the list box.
b. At the second wizard dialog box, click *LastName* in the *Available fields* list box and then click the One Field button.
c. At the third wizard dialog box, click the All Fields button.

d. At the fourth wizard dialog box, name the query *DuplicateLastNamesQuery*.
e. Print the query in landscape orientation and then close the query.
3. Use the Find Unmatched Query Wizard to find all clients who do not have any billing hours with the following specifications:
a. At the first wizard dialog box, click *Table: Clients* in the list box.
b. At the second wizard dialog box, click *Table: Billing* in the list box.
c. At the third wizard dialog box, make sure *ClientID* is selected in both the *Fields in 'Clients'* list box and in the *Fields in 'Billing'* list box.
d. At the fourth wizard dialog box, click the All Fields button to move all fields from the *Available fields* list box to the *Selected fields* list box.
e. At the fifth wizard dialog box, click the Finish button. (Let the wizard determine the query name: *Clients Without Matching Billing*.)
4. Print the query in landscape orientation and then close the query.

Assessment 4

DESIGN AND HIDE FIELDS IN A QUERY

1. You can use the check boxes in the query design grid *Show* row to show or hide fields in the query. Experiment with these check boxes and then with **AL1-C3-WarrenLegal.accdb** open design the following query:
a. At the Show Table dialog box, add the Clients table, the Billing table, and the Rates table.
b. At the query window, insert the following fields in *Field* row fields:
Clients table: *FirstName*
LastName
Billing table: *Hours*
Rates table: *Rate*
c. Insert in the fifth *Field* row field the calculated field *Total:[Hours]*[Rate]*.
d. Hide the *Hours* and *Rate* fields.
e. Run the query.
f. Save the query and name it *ClientBillingQuery*.
g. Print and then close the query. (The query will print on two pages.)
2. Close **AL1-C3-WarrenLegal.accdb**.

Visual Benchmark Demonstrate Your Proficiency

CREATING RELATIONSHIPS AND DESIGNING A QUERY

1. Open **AL1-C3-MRInvestments.accdb** from the AL1C3 folder on your storage medium and, if necessary, enable the contents.
2. Display the Relationships window and then create the relationships shown in Figure 3.7. Enforce referential integrity and cascade fields and records. (The tables in Figure 3.7 have been rearranged in the Relationships window so you have a better view of the relationships.)
3. Save and then print the relationships.
4. Close the relationship report without saving it and then close the Relationships window.
5. Design the query shown in Figure 3.8.

6. Run the query.
7. Save the query with an appropriate name and then print the query.
8. Close **AL1-C3-MRInvestments.accdb**.

Figure 3.7 Visual Benchmark Relationships Window

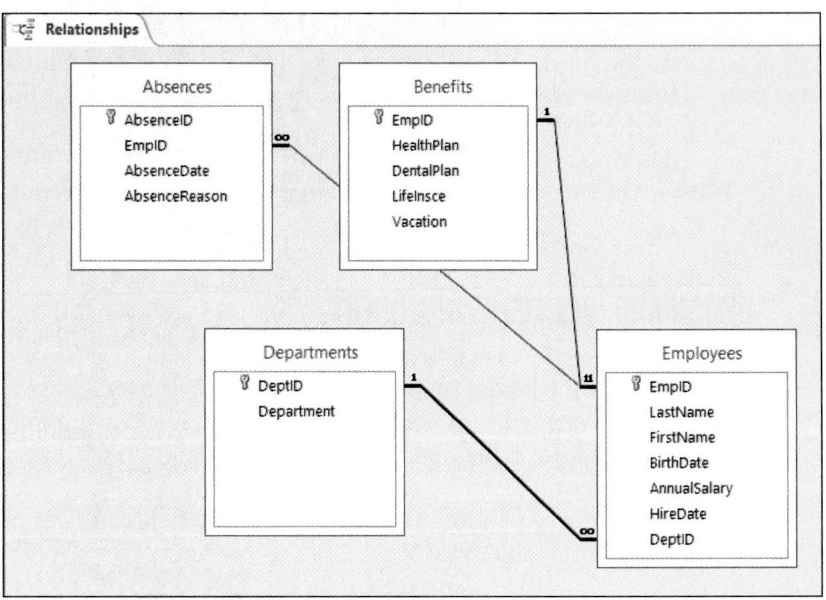

Figure 3.8 Visual Benchmark Query

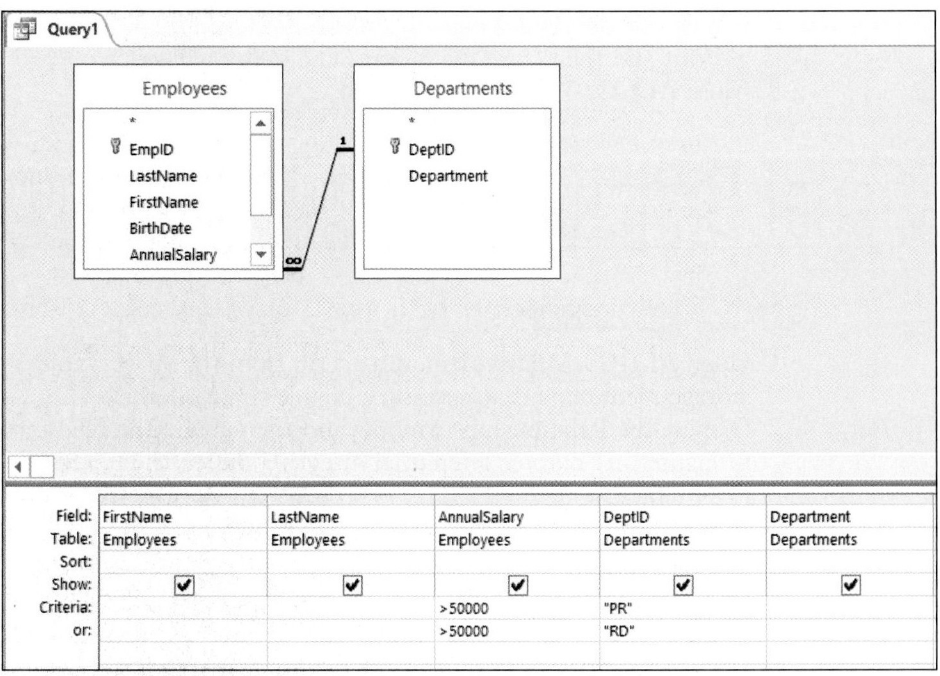

Case Study Apply Your Skills

Part 1

You work for the Skyline Restaurant in Fort Myers, Florida. Your supervisor is reviewing the restaurant's operations and has asked for a number of query reports. Before running the queries, you realize that the tables in the restaurant database, **AL1-C3-Skyline.accdb**, are not related. Open **AL1-C3-Skyline.accdb**, enable the contents, and then create the following relationships (enforce referential integrity and cascade fields and records):

Field Name	"One" Table	"Many" Table
EmployeeID	Employees	Banquets
ItemID	Inventory	Orders
SupplierID	Suppliers	Orders
SupplierID	Suppliers	Inventory
EventID	Events	Banquets

Save and then print the relationships. Close the relationship report without saving it and then close the Relationships window.

Part 2

As part of the review of the restaurant's records, your supervisor has asked you for the following information. Create a separate query for each bulleted item listed below and save, name, and print the queries. (You determine the query names.)

- Suppliers in Fort Myers: From the Suppliers table, include the supplier identification number, supplier name, city, and telephone number.
- Suppliers not located in Fort Myers: From the Suppliers table, include the supplier identification number and supplier name, city, and telephone number.
- Employees hired in 2012: From the Employees table, include the employee identification number, first and last names, and hire date.
- Employees signed up for health insurance: From the Employees table, include employee first and last names and the health insurance field.
- Wedding receptions (event identification "WR") booked in the banquet room: From the Banquets table, include the reservation identification number; reservation date; event identification; and first name, last name, and telephone number of the person making the reservation.
- Banquet reservations between 6/14/2015 and 6/30/2015 and the employees making the reservations: From the Banquets table, include the reservation identification number; reservation date; and first name, last name, and telephone number of the person making the reservation; from the Employees table include the employee first and last names.
- Banquet reservations that have not been confirmed and the employees making the reservations: From the Banquets table, include the reservation identification number; reservation date; confirmed field; and first and last names of person making the reservation; from the Employees table, include employee first and last names.
- Banquet room reserved by someone whose last name begins with the letters *Wie:* From the Employees table, include the first and last names of the employee who booked the reservation; from the Banquets table, include the first and last names and telephone number of the person making the reservation.

- A query that inserts a calculated field that multiplies the number of units ordered by the unit price for all orders for supplier number *2:* From the Orders table, include the order identification number, the supplier identification number, the units ordered, and the unit price; from the Inventory table, include the item field.

Part 3

Use the Find Duplicates Query Wizard to find duplicate items in the Orders table with the following specifications:

- At the first wizard dialog box, specify the Orders table.
- At the second wizard dialog box, specify *ItemID* as the duplicate value field.
- At the third wizard dialog, specify that you want all of the fields in the query.
- At the fourth wizard dialog box, determine the query name.
- Print and then close the query.

Use the Find Unmatched Query Wizard to find all of the employees who have not made banquet reservations with the following specifications:

- At the first wizard dialog box, specify the Employees table.
- At the second wizard dialog box, specify the Banquets table.
- At the third wizard dialog box, specify the *EmployeeID* field in both list boxes.
- At the fourth wizard dialog box, specify that you want all of the fields in the query.
- At the fifth wizard dialog box, determine the query name.
- Print the query in landscape orientation with 0.5-inch left and right margins and then close the query.

Use the Crosstab Query Wizard to create a query that summarizes order amounts by supplier with the following specifications:

- At the first wizard dialog box, specify the Orders table.
- At the second wizard dialog box, specify the *SupplierID* field for row headings.
- At the third wizard dialog box, specify the *ItemID* field for column headings.
- At the fourth wizard dialog box, click *UnitPrice* in the *Fields* list box and click *Sum* in the *Functions* list box.
- At the fifth wizard dialog box, determine the query name.
- Automatically adjust the columns in the query. (You will need to scroll to the right to view and adjust all of the columns containing data.)
- Print the query in landscape orientation and then close the query.

Part 4

Design three additional queries that require fields from at least two tables. Run the queries and then save and print the queries. In Microsoft Word, write the query information (including specific information about each query) and format the document to enhance the visual appearance. Save the document and name it **AL1-C3-CS-Queries**. Print and then close **AL1-C3-CS-Queries.docx**. Close **AL1-C3-Skyline.accdb**.

MICROSOFT®

ACCESS®

Creating and Modifying Tables in Design View

PERFORMANCE OBJECTIVES

Upon successful completion of Chapter 4, you will be able to:

- **Create a table in Design view**
- **Assign a default value**
- **Use the Input Mask Wizard and the Lookup Wizard**
- **Validate field entries**
- **Insert, move, and delete fields in Design view**
- **Insert a *Total* row**
- **Sort records in a table**
- **Print selected records in a table**
- **Complete a spelling check**
- **Find and replace data in records in a table**
- **Apply text formatting**
- **Use the Help feature**

Tutorials

4.1 Creating a Table in Design View
4.2 Creating an Input Mask and Formatting a Field
4.3 Validating Field Entries
4.4 Creating a Lookup Field
4.5 Modifying Table Structure in Design View; Inserting a *Total* Row
4.6 Sorting Records in a Table
4.7 Formatting Table Data and Printing Specific Records
4.8 Completing a Spelling Check
4.9 Finding and Replacing Data in Records
4.10 Using Help

In Chapter 1, you learned how to create a table in Datasheet view. You can also create a table in Design view, where you can establish the table's structure and properties before entering data. In this chapter, you will learn how to create a table in Design view and use the Input Mask Wizard and Lookup Wizards; insert, move, and delete fields in Design view; sort records; check spelling in a table; find and replace data; apply text formatting to a table; and use the Access Help feature. Model answers for this chapter's projects appear on the following pages.

Note: Before beginning the projects, copy the AL1C4 subfolder from the AL1 folder on the CD that accompanies this textbook to your storage medium and make AL1C4 the active folder.

Project 1 Create and Modify Tables in a Property Management Database

Project 1c

EmpID	EmpCategory	FName	LName	Address	City	State	ZIP	Telephone	HealthIns	DentalIns	LifeIns
02-59	Hourly	Christina	Solomon	12241 East 51st	Citrus Heights	CA	95611	(916) 555-8844	☑	☑	$100,000.00
03-23	Salaried	Douglas	Ricci	903 Mission Road	Roseville	CA	95678	(916) 555-4125	☑	☐	$25,000.00
03-55	Hourly	Tatiana	Kasadev	6558 Orchard Drive	Citrus Heights	CA	95610	(916) 555-8534	☑	☐	$0.00
04-14	Salaried	Brian	West	12232 142nd Avenue East	Citrus Heights	CA	95611	(916) 555-0967	☑	☑	$50,000.00
04-32	Temporary	Kathleen	Addison	21229 19th Street	Citrus Heights	CA	95621	(916) 555-3408	☑	☑	$50,000.00
05-20	Hourly	Teresa	Villanueva	19453 North 42nd Street	Citrus Heights	CA	95611	(916) 555-2302	☑	☑	$0.00
05-31	Salaried	Marcia	Griswold	211 Haven Road	North Highlands	CA	95660	(916) 555-1449	☐	☐	$100,000.00
06-24	Temporary	Tiffany	Gentry	12312 North 20th	Roseville	CA	95661	(916) 555-0043	☑	☑	$50,000.00
06-33	Hourly	Joanna	Gallegos	6850 York Street	Roseville	CA	95747	(956) 555-7446	☐	☐	$25,000.00
07-20	Salaried	Jesse	Scholtz	3412 South 21st Street	Fair Oaks	CA	95628	(916) 555-4204	☑	☐	$0.00
07-23	Salaried	Eugene	Bond	530 Laurel Road	Orangevale	CA	95662	(916) 555-9412	☑	☐	$100,000.00

Step 11, Employees Table

EmpID	FName	LName	Address	City	State	ZIP	Telephone	EmpCategory	HealthIns	LifeIns
02-59	Christina	Solomon	12241 East 51st	Citrus Heights	CA	95611	(916) 555-8844	Hourly	☑	$100,000.00
03-23	Douglas	Ricci	903 Mission Road	Roseville	CA	95678	(916) 555-4125	Salaried	☑	$25,000.00
03-55	Tatiana	Kasadev	6558 Orchard Drive	Citrus Heights	CA	95610	(916) 555-8534	Hourly	☑	$0.00
04-14	Brian	West	12232 142nd Avenue East	Citrus Heights	CA	95611	(916) 555-0967	Salaried	☑	$50,000.00
04-32	Kathleen	Addison	21229 19th Street	Citrus Heights	CA	95621	(916) 555-3408	Temporary	☑	$50,000.00
05-20	Teresa	Villanueva	19453 North 42nd Street	Citrus Heights	CA	95611	(916) 555-2302	Hourly	☑	$0.00
05-31	Marcia	Griswold	211 Haven Road	North Highlands	CA	95660	(916) 555-1449	Salaried	☐	$100,000.00
06-24	Tiffany	Gentry	12312 North 20th	Roseville	CA	95661	(916) 555-0043	Temporary	☑	$50,000.00
06-33	Joanna	Gallegos	6850 York Street	Roseville	CA	95747	(956) 555-7446	Hourly	☐	$25,000.00
07-20	Jesse	Scholtz	3412 South 21st Street	Fair Oaks	CA	95628	(916) 555-4204	Salaried	☑	$0.00
07-23	Eugene	Bond	530 Laurel Road	Orangevale	CA	95662	(916) 555-9412	Salaried	☑	$100,000.00

Step 16, Employees Table

PymntID	RenterID	PymntDate	PymntAmount	LateFee
1	130	3/1/2015	$1,800.00	
2	111	3/1/2015	$1,900.00	
3	136	3/1/2015	$1,250.00	
4	110	3/1/2015	$1,300.00	
5	135	3/2/2015	$1,900.00	
6	123	3/2/2015	$1,000.00	
7	117	3/2/2015	$1,100.00	
8	134	3/3/2015	$1,400.00	
9	131	3/3/2015	$1,200.00	
10	118	3/3/2015	$900.00	
11	125	3/5/2015	$1,650.00	
12	119	3/5/2015	$1,500.00	
13	133	3/8/2015	$1,650.00	
14	129	3/9/2015	$1,650.00	
15	115	3/12/2015	$1,375.00	$25.00
16	121	3/12/2015	$950.00	$25.00
17	127	3/19/2015	$1,300.00	$50.00
Total			**$23,825.00**	**$100.00**

Payments Table

Project 1d

RenterID	FirstName	LastName	PropID	EmpID	CreditScore	LeaseBegDate	LeaseEndDate
118	Mason	Ahn	1004	07-23	538	3/1/2015	2/28/2016
119	Michelle	Bertram	1001	03-23	621	3/1/2015	2/28/2016
110	Greg	Hamilton	1029	04-14	624	1/1/2015	12/31/2015
121	Travis	Jorgenson	1010	04-14	590	3/1/2015	2/28/2016
135	Marty	Lobdell	1006	04-14	510	6/1/2015	5/31/2016
129	Susan	Lowrey	1002	04-14	634	4/1/2015	3/31/2016
130	Ross	Molaski	1027	03-23	688	5/1/2015	4/30/2016
136	Nadine	Paschal	1022	05-31	702	6/1/2015	5/31/2016
111	Julia	Perez	1013	07-20	711	1/1/2015	12/31/2015
115	Dana	Rozinski	1026	02-59	538	2/1/2015	1/31/2016
131	Danielle	Rubio	1020	07-20	722	5/1/2015	4/30/2016
133	Katie	Smith	1018	07-23	596	5/1/2015	4/30/2016
123	Richard	Terrell	1014	07-20	687	3/1/2015	2/28/2016
117	Miguel	Villegas	1007	07-20	695	2/1/2015	1/31/2016
125	Rose	Wagoner	1015	07-23	734	4/1/2015	3/31/2016
134	Carl	Weston	1009	03-23	655	6/1/2015	5/31/2016
127	William	Young	1023	05-31	478	4/1/2015	3/31/2016

Step 2c, Renters Table

RenterID	FirstName	LastName	PropID	EmpID	CreditScore	LeaseBegDate	LeaseEndDate
125	Rose	Wagoner	1015	07-23	734	4/1/2015	3/31/2016
131	Danielle	Rubio	1020	07-20	722	5/1/2015	4/30/2016
111	Julia	Perez	1013	07-20	711	1/1/2015	12/31/2015
136	Nadine	Paschal	1022	05-31	702	6/1/2015	5/31/2016
117	Miguel	Villegas	1007	07-20	695	2/1/2015	1/31/2016
130	Ross	Molaski	1027	03-23	688	5/1/2015	4/30/2016
123	Richard	Terrell	1014	07-20	687	3/1/2015	2/28/2016
134	Carl	Weston	1009	03-23	655	6/1/2015	5/31/2016
129	Susan	Lowrey	1002	04-14	634	4/1/2015	3/31/2016
110	Greg	Hamilton	1029	04-14	624	1/1/2015	12/31/2015
119	Michelle	Bertram	1001	03-23	621	3/1/2015	2/28/2016
133	Katie	Smith	1018	07-23	596	5/1/2015	4/30/2016
121	Travis	Jorgenson	1010	04-14	590	3/1/2015	2/28/2016
118	Mason	Ahn	1004	07-23	538	3/1/2015	2/28/2016
115	Dana	Rozinski	1026	02-59	538	2/1/2015	1/31/2016
135	Marty	Lobdell	1006	04-14	510	6/1/2015	5/31/2016
127	William	Young	1023	05-31	478	4/1/2015	3/31/2016

Step 3c, Renters Table

PropID	CatID	MoRent	Address	City	State	ZIP
1007	A	$1,100.00	904 Everson Road	Fair Oaks	CA	95628
1004	A	$900.00	1932 Oakville Drive	North Highlands	CA	95660
1010	A	$950.00	19334 140th East	Citrus Heights	CA	95621
1014	A	$1,000.00	9045 Valley Avenue	Citrus Heights	CA	95611

Step 6f, Properties Table

PropID	CatID	MoRent	Address	City	State	ZIP
1007	A	$1,100.00	904 Everson Road	Fair Oaks	CA	95628
1004	A	$900.00	1932 Oakville Drive	North Highlands	CA	95660
1010	A	$950.00	19334 140th East	Citrus Heights	CA	95621
1014	A	$1,000.00	9045 Valley Avenue	Citrus Heights	CA	95611
1029	C	$1,300.00	155 Aldrich Road	Roseville	CA	95678
1002	C	$1,650.00	2650 Crestline Drive	Citrus Heights	CA	95611
1001	C	$1,500.00	4102 Tenth Street	Citrus Heights	CA	95611
1026	C	$1,375.00	10057 128th Avenue	Citrus Heights	CA	95611
1023	C	$1,300.00	750 Birch Drive	Orangevale	CA	95662
1009	C	$1,400.00	159 Meridian Street	Orangevale	CA	95662
1019	C	$1,700.00	765 Chellis Street	Fair Oaks	CA	95628
1018	C	$1,650.00	9945 North 20th Road	North Highlands	CA	95660
1017	D	$1,300.00	4500 Maple Lane	Orangevale	CA	95662
1011	D	$1,350.00	348 Hampton Avenue	Citrus Heights	CA	95611
1008	D	$1,575.00	5009 North Garden	Roseville	CA	95661
1020	D	$1,200.00	23390 South 22nd Street	Citrus Heights	CA	95610
1006	S	$1,900.00	3412 Mango Street	Orangevale	CA	95662
1003	S	$1,800.00	10234 122nd Avenue	North Highlands	CA	95660
1012	S	$1,775.00	1212 Fairhaven Road	North Highlands	CA	95660
1013	S	$1,900.00	2606 30th Street	Citrus Heights	CA	95610
1016	S	$1,825.00	21388 South 42nd Street	Citrus Heights	CA	95621
1030	S	$1,950.00	5430 112th Southeast	Citrus Heights	CA	95611
1021	S	$1,875.00	652 Seventh Street	Fair Oaks	CA	95628
1024	S	$1,650.00	1195 24th Street	North Highlands	CA	95660
1027	S	$1,800.00	2203 Center Road	Orangevale	CA	95662
1028	S	$1,750.00	488 Franklin Drive	Fair Oaks	CA	95628
1022	T	$1,250.00	4572 152nd Avenue	Citrus Heights	CA	95621
1005	T	$1,350.00	12110 55th Southeast	Citrus Heights	CA	95611
1025	T	$1,200.00	3354 North 62nd Street	Citrus Heights	CA	95610
1015	T	$1,650.00	560 Tenth Street East	North Highlands	CA	95660

Step 7f, Properties Table

Model Answers

Project 1d–*continued*

PymntID	RenterID	PymntDate	PymntAmount	LateFee
1	130	3/1/2015	$1,800.00	
2	111	3/1/2015	$1,900.00	
3	136	3/1/2015	$1,250.00	
4	110	3/1/2015	$1,300.00	
5	135	3/2/2015	$1,900.00	
6	123	3/2/2015	$1,000.00	
7	117	3/2/2015	$1,100.00	
8	134	3/3/2015	$1,400.00	
9	131	3/3/2015	$1,200.00	
10	118	3/3/2015	$900.00	
11	125	3/5/2015	$1,650.00	
12	119	3/5/2015	$1,500.00	
13	133	3/8/2015	$1,650.00	
14	129	3/9/2015	$1,650.00	
15	115	3/12/2015	$1,375.00	$25.00
16	121	3/12/2015	$950.00	$25.00
17	127	3/19/2015	$1,300.00	$50.00
Total			**$23,825.00**	**$100.00**

Step 8g, Payments Table

RenterID	FirstName	LastName	PropID	EmpID	CreditScore	LeaseBegDate	LeaseEndDate
110	Greg	Hamilton	1029	04-14	624	1/1/2015	12/31/2015
111	Julia	Perez	1013	07-20	711	1/1/2015	12/31/2015
115	Dana	Rozinski	1026	02-59	538	2/1/2015	1/31/2016
117	Miguel	Villegas	1007	07-20	695	2/1/2015	1/31/2016
118	Mason	Ahn	1004	07-23	538	3/1/2015	2/28/2016
119	Michelle	Bertram	1001	03-23	621	3/1/2015	2/28/2016
121	Travis	Jorgenson	1010	04-14	590	3/1/2015	2/28/2016
123	Richard	Terrell	1014	07-20	687	3/1/2015	2/28/2016
125	Rose	Wagoner	1015	07-23	734	4/1/2015	3/31/2016
127	William	Young	1023	05-31	478	4/1/2015	3/31/2016
129	Susan	Lowrey	1002	04-14	634	4/1/2015	3/31/2016
130	Ross	Molaski	1027	03-23	688	5/1/2015	4/30/2016
131	Danielle	Rubio	1020	07-20	722	5/1/2015	4/30/2016
133	Katie	Smith	1018	07-23	596	5/1/2015	4/30/2016
134	Carl	Weston	1009	03-23	655	6/1/2015	5/31/2016
135	Marty	Lobdell	1006	04-14	510	6/1/2015	5/31/2016
136	Nadine	Paschal	1022	05-31	702	6/1/2015	5/31/2016

Step 10j, Renters Table

Project 1e

EmpID	FName	LName	Address	City	State	ZIP	Telephone	EmpCategory	HealthIns
02-59	Christina	Solomon	12241 East 51st	Citrus Heights	CA	95611	(916) 555-8844	Hourly	☑
03-23	Douglas	Ricci	903 Mission Road	Roseville	CA	95678	(916) 555-4125	Salaried	☑
03-55	Tatiana	Kasadev	6558 Orchard Drive	Citrus Heights	CA	95610	(916) 555-8534	Hourly	☑
04-14	Brian	West	12232 142nd Avenue East	Citrus Heights	CA	95611	(916) 555-0967	Salaried	☑
04-32	Kathleen	Addison	21229 19th Street	Citrus Heights	CA	95621	(916) 555-3408	Temporary	☑
05-20	Teresa	Villanueva	19453 North 42nd Street	Citrus Heights	CA	95611	(916) 555-2302	Hourly	☑
05-31	Marcia	Griswold	211 Haven Road	North Highlands	CA	95660	(916) 555-1449	Salaried	☐
06-24	Tiffany	Gentry	12312 North 20th	Roseville	CA	95661	(916) 555-0043	Temporary	☑
06-33	Joanna	Gallegos	6850 York Street	Roseville	CA	95747	(956) 555-7446	Hourly	☐
07-20	Jesse	Scholtz	3412 South 21st Street	Fair Oaks	CA	95628	(916) 555-4204	Salaried	☑
07-23	Eugene	Bond	530 Laurel Road	Orangevale	CA	95662	(916) 555-9412	Salaried	☑
02-72	Robin	Wilder	9945 Valley Avenue	Citrus Heights	CA	95610	(916) 555-6522	Salaried	☐

Employees Table

Project 1f

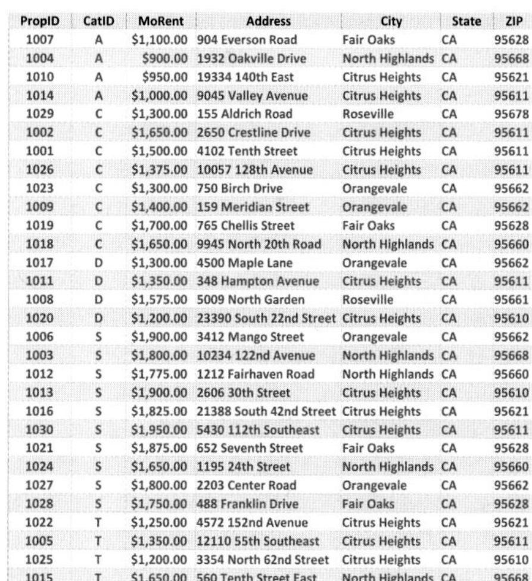

PropID	CatID	MoRent	Address	City	State	ZIP
1007	A	$1,100.00	904 Everson Road	Fair Oaks	CA	95628
1004	A	$900.00	1932 Oakville Drive	North Highlands	CA	95668
1010	A	$950.00	19334 140th East	Citrus Heights	CA	95621
1014	A	$1,000.00	9045 Valley Avenue	Citrus Heights	CA	95611
1029	C	$1,300.00	155 Aldrich Road	Roseville	CA	95678
1002	C	$1,650.00	2650 Crestline Drive	Citrus Heights	CA	95611
1001	C	$1,500.00	4102 Tenth Street	Citrus Heights	CA	95611
1026	C	$1,375.00	10057 128th Avenue	Citrus Heights	CA	95611
1023	C	$1,300.00	750 Birch Drive	Orangevale	CA	95662
1009	C	$1,400.00	159 Meridian Street	Orangevale	CA	95662
1019	C	$1,700.00	765 Chellis Street	Fair Oaks	CA	95628
1018	C	$1,650.00	9945 North 20th Road	North Highlands	CA	95660
1017	D	$1,300.00	4500 Maple Lane	Orangevale	CA	95662
1011	D	$1,350.00	348 Hampton Avenue	Citrus Heights	CA	95611
1008	D	$1,575.00	5009 North Garden	Roseville	CA	95661
1020	D	$1,200.00	23390 South 22nd Street	Citrus Heights	CA	95610
1006	S	$1,900.00	3412 Mango Street	Orangevale	CA	95662
1003	S	$1,800.00	10234 122nd Avenue	North Highlands	CA	95668
1012	S	$1,775.00	1212 Fairhaven Road	North Highlands	CA	95660
1013	S	$1,900.00	2606 30th Street	Citrus Heights	CA	95610
1016	S	$1,825.00	21388 South 42nd Street	Citrus Heights	CA	95621
1030	S	$1,950.00	5430 112th Southeast	Citrus Heights	CA	95611
1021	S	$1,875.00	652 Seventh Street	Fair Oaks	CA	95628
1024	S	$1,650.00	1195 24th Street	North Highlands	CA	95660
1027	S	$1,800.00	2203 Center Road	Orangevale	CA	95662
1028	S	$1,750.00	488 Franklin Drive	Fair Oaks	CA	95628
1022	T	$1,250.00	4572 152nd Avenue	Citrus Heights	CA	95621
1005	T	$1,350.00	12110 55th Southeast	Citrus Heights	CA	95611
1025	T	$1,200.00	3354 North 62nd Street	Citrus Heights	CA	95610
1015	T	$1,650.00	560 Tenth Street East	North Highlands	CA	95668

PropertiesTable

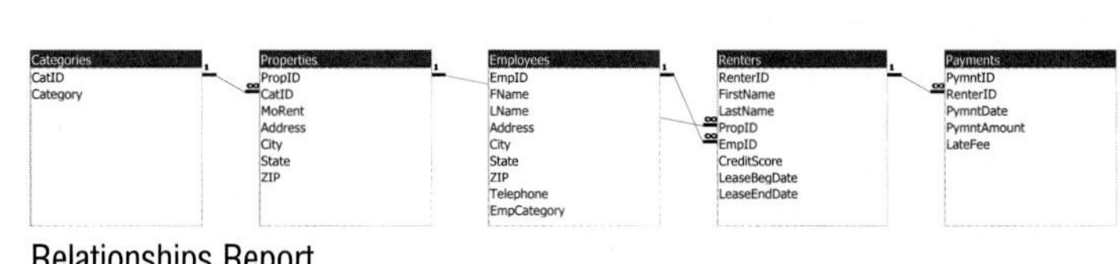

Relationships Report

FName	LName	HealthIns
Christina	Solomon	☑
Douglas	Ricci	☑
Tatiana	Kasadev	☑
Brian	West	☑
Kathleen	Addison	☑
Teresa	Villanueva	☑
Tiffany	Gentry	☑
Jesse	Scholtz	☑
Eugene	Bond	☑

EmpsWithHealthInsQuery

PropID	Category	Address	City	State	ZIP
1010	Apartment	19334 140th East	Citrus Heights	CA	95621
1014	Apartment	9045 Valley Avenue	Citrus Heights	CA	95611
1001	Condominium	4102 Tenth Street	Citrus Heights	CA	95611
1002	Condominium	2650 Crestline Drive	Citrus Heights	CA	95611
1026	Condominium	10057 128th Avenue	Citrus Heights	CA	95611
1013	Single-family house	2606 30th Street	Citrus Heights	CA	95610
1016	Single-family house	21388 South 42nd Street	Citrus Heights	CA	95621
1030	Single-family house	5430 112th Southeast	Citrus Heights	CA	95611
1011	Duplex	348 Hampton Avenue	Citrus Heights	CA	95611
1020	Duplex	23390 South 22nd Street	Citrus Heights	CA	95610
1005	Townhouse	12110 55th Southeast	Citrus Heights	CA	95611
1022	Townhouse	4572 152nd Avenue	Citrus Heights	CA	95621
1025	Townhouse	3354 North 62nd Street	Citrus Heights	CA	95610

CitrusHeightsPropsQuery

Project 1f–*continued*

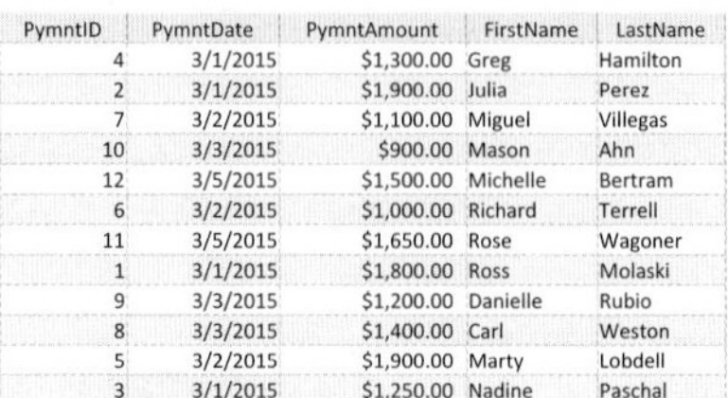

PymntID	PymntDate	PymntAmount	FirstName	LastName
4	3/1/2015	$1,300.00	Greg	Hamilton
2	3/1/2015	$1,900.00	Julia	Perez
7	3/2/2015	$1,100.00	Miguel	Villegas
10	3/3/2015	$900.00	Mason	Ahn
12	3/5/2015	$1,500.00	Michelle	Bertram
6	3/2/2015	$1,000.00	Richard	Terrell
11	3/5/2015	$1,650.00	Rose	Wagoner
1	3/1/2015	$1,800.00	Ross	Molaski
9	3/3/2015	$1,200.00	Danielle	Rubio
8	3/3/2015	$1,400.00	Carl	Weston
5	3/2/2015	$1,900.00	Marty	Lobdell
3	3/1/2015	$1,250.00	Nadine	Paschal

Pymnts3/1To3/5Query

Category	PropID	MoRent	Address	City	State	ZIP
Apartment	1010	$950.00	19334 140th East	Citrus Heights	CA	95621
Apartment	1014	$1,000.00	9045 Valley Avenue	Citrus Heights	CA	95611
Condominium	1001	$1,500.00	4102 Tenth Street	Citrus Heights	CA	95611
Condominium	1009	$1,400.00	159 Meridian Street	Orangevale	CA	95662
Condominium	1023	$1,300.00	750 Birch Drive	Orangevale	CA	95662
Condominium	1026	$1,375.00	10057 128th Avenue	Citrus Heights	CA	95611
Duplex	1011	$1,350.00	348 Hampton Avenue	Citrus Heights	CA	95611
Duplex	1017	$1,300.00	4500 Maple Lane	Orangevale	CA	95662
Duplex	1020	$1,200.00	23390 South 22nd Street	Citrus Heights	CA	95610
Townhouse	1005	$1,350.00	12110 55th Southeast	Citrus Heights	CA	95611
Townhouse	1022	$1,250.00	4572 152nd Avenue	Citrus Heights	CA	95621
Townhouse	1025	$1,200.00	3354 North 62nd Street	Citrus Heights	CA	95610

RentLessThan$1501InCHAndOVQuery

EmpID	FName	LName	Address	City	State	ZIP
07-20	Jesse	Scholtz	4102 Tenth Street	Citrus Heights	CA	95611
07-20	Jesse	Scholtz	2650 Crestline Drive	Citrus Heights	CA	95611
07-20	Jesse	Scholtz	12110 55th Southeast	Citrus Heights	CA	95611
07-20	Jesse	Scholtz	19334 140th East	Citrus Heights	CA	95621
07-20	Jesse	Scholtz	348 Hampton Avenue	Citrus Heights	CA	95611
07-20	Jesse	Scholtz	2606 30th Street	Citrus Heights	CA	95610
07-20	Jesse	Scholtz	9045 Valley Avenue	Citrus Heights	CA	95611
07-20	Jesse	Scholtz	21388 South 42nd Street	Citrus Heights	CA	95621
07-20	Jesse	Scholtz	23390 South 22nd Street	Citrus Heights	CA	95610
07-20	Jesse	Scholtz	4572 152nd Avenue	Citrus Heights	CA	95621
07-20	Jesse	Scholtz	3354 North 62nd Street	Citrus Heights	CA	95610
07-20	Jesse	Scholtz	10057 128th Avenue	Citrus Heights	CA	95611
07-20	Jesse	Scholtz	5430 112th Southeast	Citrus Heights	CA	95611

Emp07-20CHPropsQuery

Model Answers

Project 1 Create and Modify Tables in a Property Management Database — 8 Parts

You will open the Sun Properties database, create two new tables in Design view, modify existing tables, and sort data in tables. You will also complete a spelling check on data in tables, find data in a table and replace it with other data, create relationships and perform queries, and get help using the Access Help feature.

Creating Tables in Design View

Quick Steps

Create a Table in Design View

1. Open database.
2. Click CREATE tab.
3. Click Table button.
4. Click View button.
5. Type name for table.
6. Press Enter or click OK.
7. Type field names, specify data types, and include descriptions.
8. Click Save button.

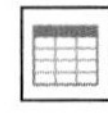

Table

View

In Datasheet view, you can create a table by assigning each column a data type and typing the field name. Once the columns are defined, you enter the data into records. You can also create a table in Design view, where you can set field properties before you begin entering data. To display a table in Design view, open the desired database, click the CREATE tab, and then click the Table button. This opens a new blank table in Datasheet view. Display the table in Design view by clicking the View button that displays at the left side of the TABLE TOOLS FIELDS tab in the Views group. When you click the View button in a new table, Access displays the Save As dialog box, where you type the table name and then press Enter or click OK. Figure 4.1 displays the Properties table in Design view in AL1-C4-SunProperties.accdb.

In Design view, each row in the top section of the work area represents one field in the table and is used to define the field name, the field data type, and a description. The *Field Properties* section in the lower half of the work area displays the properties for the active field. The properties vary depending on the active field. In the lower right corner of Design view, Help information displays about an option as you make an option active in the Design window. In Figure 4.1, the *PropID* field name is active in Design view, so Access displays information on field names in the Help area.

Figure 4.1 Properties Table in Design View

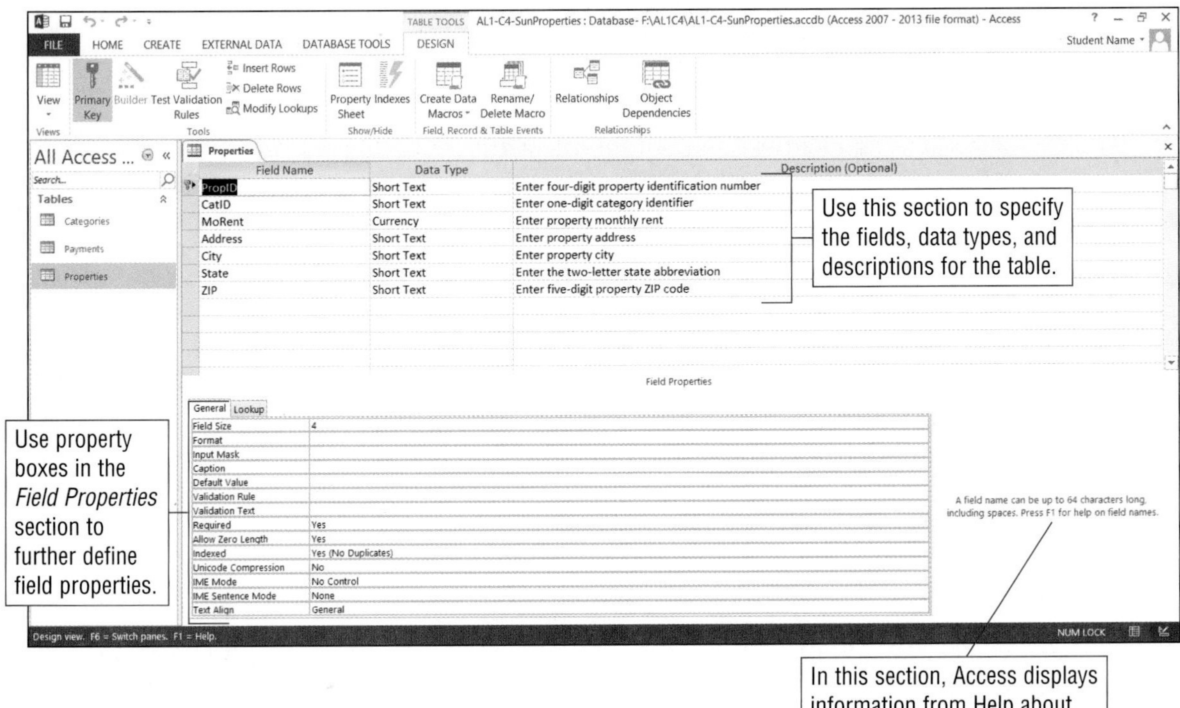
Use this section to specify the fields, data types, and descriptions for the table.
Use property boxes in the *Field Properties* section to further define field properties.
In this section, Access displays information from Help about the active field.

Define each field in the table in the rows in the top section of Design view. When you create a new table in Design view, Access automatically assigns the first field the name *ID* and assigns the AutoNumber data type. You can leave this field name or type a new name and you can also change the data type. To create a new field in the table, click in the field in the *Field Name* column, type the field name, and then press the Tab key or Enter key. This makes active the *Data Type* field. Click the down-pointing arrow in the *Data Type* field and then click the desired data type at the drop-down list. In Chapter 1, you created tables in Datasheet view and assigned data types of Short Text, Date/Time, Currency, and Yes/No. The *Data Type* field drop-down list includes these data types plus additional types, as described in Table 4.1.

When you click the desired data type at the drop-down list and then press the Tab key, the *Description* field becomes active. Type a description in the field that provides useful information to someone entering data in the table. When typing a description, consider identifying the field's purpose or contents or providing instructional information for data entry. The description you type displays in the Status bar when the field is active in the table in Datasheet view.

When creating the table, continue typing field names, assigning data types to fields, and typing field descriptions. When you have completed the table design, save the table by clicking the Save button on the Quick Access toolbar. Return to Datasheet view by clicking the View button in the Views group on the TABLE TOOLS DESIGN tab. In Datasheet view, type the records for the table.

Save

Table 4.1 Data Types

Data Type	*Description*
Short Text	Used for alphanumeric data up to 255 characters in length—for example, a name, address, or value (such as a telephone number or social security number) that is used as an identifier and not for calculating.
Long Text	Used for alphanumeric data up to 64,000 characters in length.
Number	Used for positive and negative values that can be used in calculations. Do not use for values that will calculate monetary amounts (see Currency).
Date/Time	Used to ensure dates and times are entered and sorted properly.
Currency	Used for values that involve money. Access will not round off during calculations.
AutoNumber	Used to automatically number records sequentially (incrementing by 1); each new record is numbered as it is typed.
Yes/No	Used for values of *Yes* or *No*, *True* or *False*, or *On* or *Off*.
OLE Object	Used to embed or link objects created in other Office applications.
Hyperlink	Used to store a hyperlink, such as a URL.
Attachment	Used to add file attachments to a record such as a Word document or Excel workbook.
Calculated	Used to display the Expression Builder dialog box, where an expression is entered to calculate the value of the calculated column.
Lookup Wizard	Used to enter data in the field from another existing table or to display a list of values in a drop-down list from which the user chooses.

Project 1a Creating a Table in Design View

Part 1 of 8

1. Open Access and then open **AL1-C4-SunProperties.accdb** located in the AL1C4 folder on your storage medium.
2. Click the Enable Content button in the message bar. (The message bar will display immediately below the ribbon.)
3. View the Properties table in Design view by completing the following steps:
   a. Open the Properties table.
   b. Click the View button in the Views group on the HOME tab.
   c. Click each field name and then look at the information that displays in the *Field Properties* section.
   d. Click in various options in the work area and then read the information that displays in the Help area located in the lower right corner of Design view.
   e. Click the View button to return the table to Datasheet view.
   f. Close the Properties table.

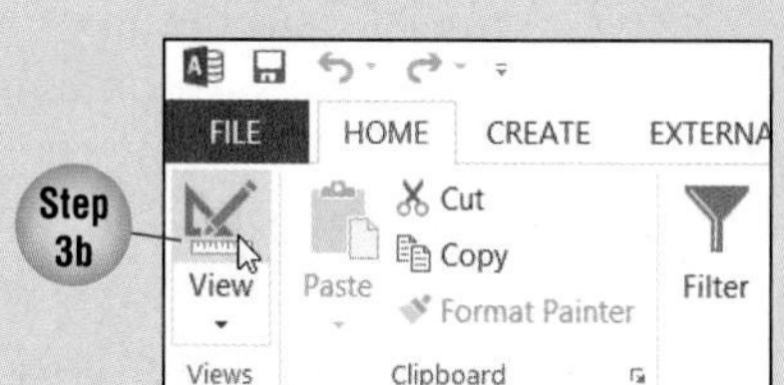

4. Create a new table in Design view, as shown in Figure 4.2, by completing the following steps:
   a. Click the CREATE tab and then click the Table button in the Tables group.
   b. Click the View button in the Views group on the TABLE TOOLS FIELDS tab.
   c. At the Save As dialog box, type **Renters** and then press Enter.
   d. Type **RenterID** in the *Field Name* column in the first row and then press the Tab key.
   e. Change the data type to Short Text by clicking the down-pointing arrow located in the *Data Type* column and then clicking *Short Text* at the drop-down list.
   f. Change the field size from the default of 255 characters to 3 characters by selecting *255* in the *Field Size* property box in the *Field Properties* section and then typing 3.
   g. Click in the *Description* column for the *RenterID* row, type **Enter three-digit renter identification number**, and then press the Tab key.

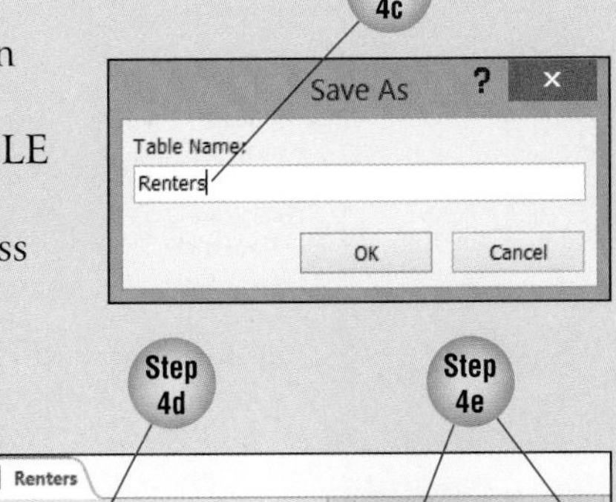

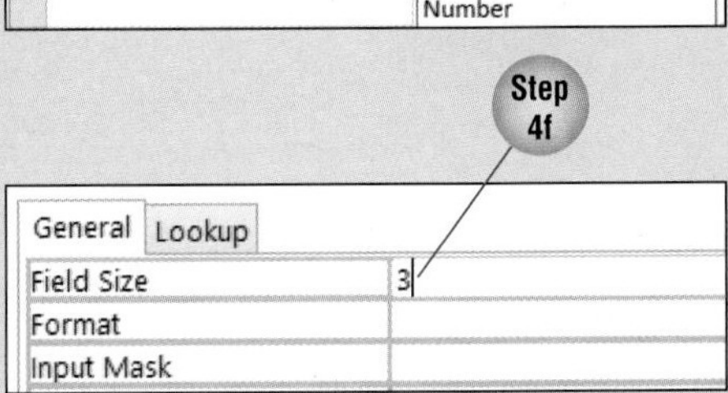

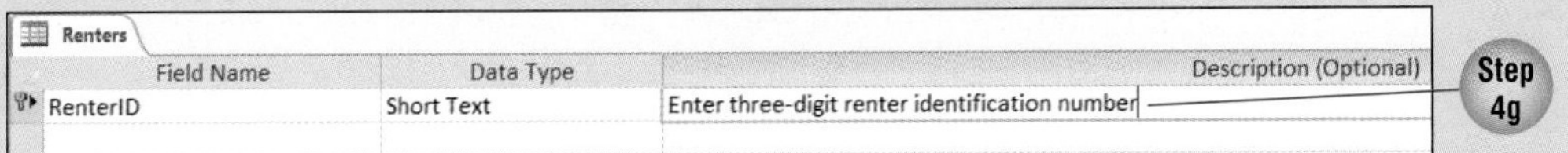

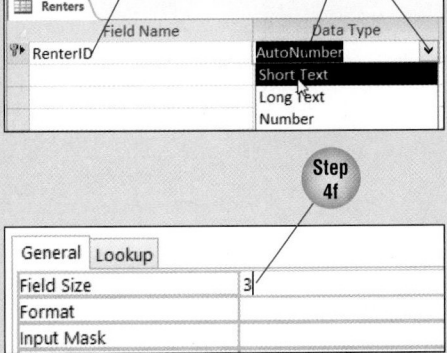

   h. Type **FirstName** in the *Field Name* column and then press the Tab key.
   i. Select *255* in the *Field Size* property box in the *Field Properties* section and then type **20**.
   j. Click in the *Description* column for the *FirstName* row, type **Enter renter's first name**, and then press the Tab key.
   k. Type **LastName** in the *Field Name* column and then press the Tab key.
   l. Change the field size to 30 characters (at the *Field Size* property box).
   m. Click in the *Description* column for the *LastName* row, type **Enter renter's last name**, and then press the Tab key.
   n. Enter the remaining field names, data types, and descriptions as shown in Figure 4.2. (Change the field sizes to 4 characters for the *PropID* field, 5 characters for the *EmpID* field, and 3 characters for the *CreditScore* field.)
   o. After all of the fields are entered, click the Save button on the Quick Access toolbar.
   p. Make sure the *RenterID* field is identified as the primary key. (A key icon displays in the *RenterID* field selector bar.)
   q. Click the View button to return the table to Datasheet view.
5. Enter the records in the Renters table as shown in Figure 4.3.
6. After all of the records are entered, automatically adjust the column widths.
7. Save and then close the Renters table.

Figure 4.2 Project 1a Renters Table in Design View

Renters

Field Name	Data Type	Description (Optional)
RenterID	Short Text	Enter three-digit renter identification number
FirstName	Short Text	Enter renter's first name
LastName	Short Text	Enter renter's last name
PropID	Short Text	Enter four-digit property identification number
EmpID	Short Text	Enter five-digit employee identification number
CreditScore	Short Text	Enter renter's current credit score
LeaseBegDate	Date/Time	Enter beginning date of lease
LeaseEndDate	Date/Time	Enter ending date of lease

Field Properties

General | Lookup

Field Size	3
Format	
Input Mask	
Caption	
Default Value	
Validation Rule	
Validation Text	
Required	Yes
Allow Zero Length	Yes
Indexed	Yes (No Duplicates)
Unicode Compression	No
IME Mode	No Control
IME Sentence Mode	None
Text Align	General

Figure 4.3 Project 1a Renters Table in Datasheet View

Renters

RenterID	FirstName	LastName	PropID	EmpID	CreditScore	LeaseBegDate	LeaseEndDate	Click to Add
110	Greg	Hamilton	1029	04-14	624	1/1/2015	12/31/2015	
111	Julia	Perez	1013	07-20	711	1/1/2015	12/31/2015	
115	Dana	Rozinski	1026	02-59	538	2/1/2015	1/31/2016	
117	Miguel	Villegas	1007	07-20	695	2/1/2015	1/31/2016	
118	Mason	Ahn	1004	07-23	538	3/1/2015	2/28/2016	
119	Michelle	Bertram	1001	03-23	621	3/1/2015	2/28/2016	
121	Travis	Jorgenson	1010	04-14	590	3/1/2015	2/28/2016	
123	Richard	Terrell	1014	07-20	687	3/1/2015	2/28/2016	
125	Rose	Wagoner	1015	07-23	734	4/1/2015	3/31/2016	
127	William	Young	1023	05-31	478	4/1/2015	3/31/2016	
129	Susan	Lowrey	1002	04-14	634	4/1/2015	3/31/2016	
130	Ross	Molaski	1027	03-23	688	5/1/2015	4/30/2016	
131	Danielle	Rubio	1020	07-20	722	5/1/2015	4/30/2016	
133	Katie	Smith	1018	07-23	596	5/1/2015	4/30/2016	
134	Carl	Weston	1009	03-23	655	6/1/2015	5/31/2016	
135	Marty	Lobdell	1006	04-14	510	6/1/2015	5/31/2016	
136	Nadine	Paschal	1022	05-31	702	6/1/2015	5/31/2016	
*								

Assigning a Default Value

In Chapter 1, you learned how to specify a default value for a field in a table in Datasheet view using the Default Value button in the Properties group on the TABLE TOOLS FIELDS tab. In addition to this method, you can create a default value for a field in Design view with the *Default Value* property box in the *Field Properties* section. Click in the *Default Value* property box and then type the desired field value.

In Project 1b, you will create a health insurance field with a Yes/No data type. Since most of the agents of Sun Properties have signed up for health insurance benefits, you set the default value for the field to *Yes*. If you add a new field that contains a default value to an existing table, the existing records do not reflect the default value. Only new records entered in the table reflect the default value.

Using the Input Mask

For some fields, you may want to control the data entered in the field. For example, in a zip code field, you may want the nine-digit zip code entered (rather than the five-digit zip code) or you may want the three-digit area code included in a telephone number. Use the *Input Mask* field property to set a pattern for how data is entered in a field. An input mask ensures that data in records conforms to a standard format. Access includes an Input Mask Wizard that guides you through creating an input mask. The Input Mask is available for fields with a data type of Short Text or Date/Time.

Use the Input Mask Wizard when assigning a data type to a field. In Design view, click in the Input Mask property box in the *Field Properties* section and then run the Input Mask Wizard by clicking the Build button (contains three black dots) that appears at the right side of the Input Mask property box. This displays the first Input Mask Wizard dialog box, as shown in Figure 4.4. In the *Input Mask* list box, choose which input mask you want your data to look like and then click the Next button. At the second Input Mask Wizard dialog box, as shown in Figure 4.5, specify the appearance of the input mask and the desired placeholder character and then click the Next button. At the third Input Mask Wizard dialog box, specify whether you want the data stored with or without the symbol in the mask and then click the Next button. At the fourth dialog box, click the Finish button.

Quick Steps

Use the Input Mask Wizard

1. Open table in Design view.
2. Type text in *Field Name* column.
3. Press Tab key.
4. Change data type to *Short Text* or *Date/Time*.
5. Click Save button.
6. Click in *Input Mask* property box.
7. Click Build button.
8. Complete wizard steps.

Build

HINT

An input mask is a set of characters that control what you can and cannot enter in a field.

Figure 4.4 First Input Mask Wizard Dialog Box

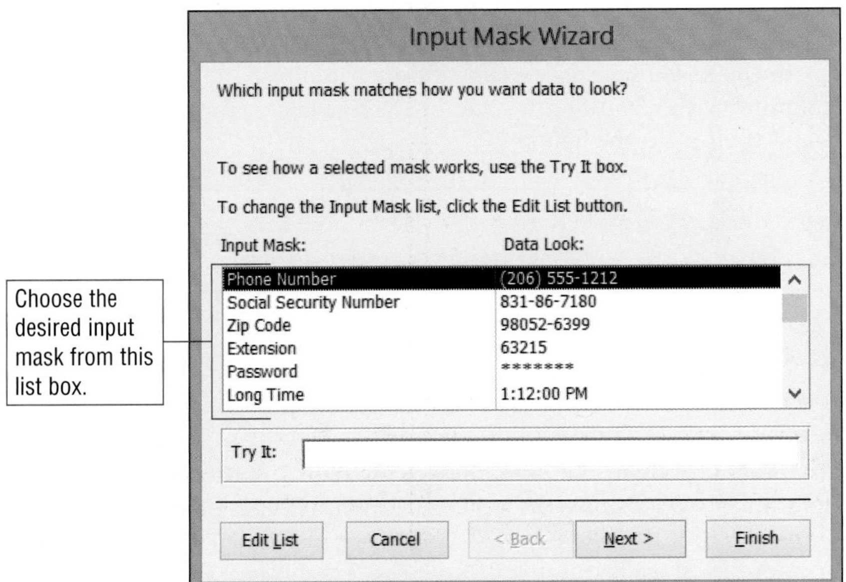

Figure 4.5 Second Input Mask Wizard Dialog Box

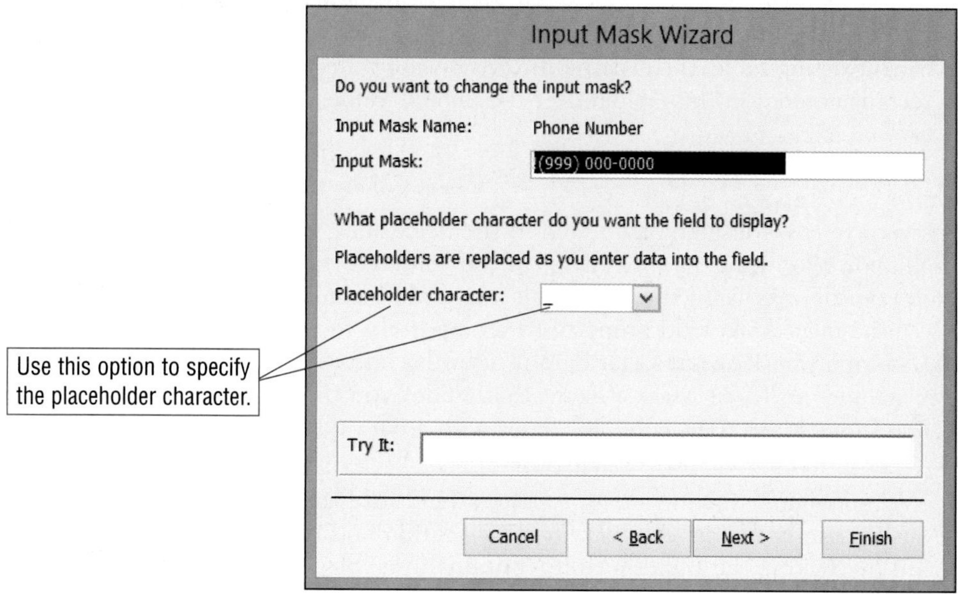

Project 1b Creating an Employees Table

Part 2 of 8

1. With **AL1-C4-SunProperties.accdb** open, create the Employees table in Design view as shown in Figure 4.6 on page 140. Begin by clicking the CREATE tab and then clicking the Table button.
2. Click the View button to switch to Design view.
3. At the Save As dialog box, type **Employees** and then press Enter.
4. Type **EmpID** in the *Field Name* column in the first row and then press the Tab key.
5. Change the data type to Short Text by clicking the down-pointing arrow located in the *Data Type* column and then clicking *Short Text* at the drop-down list.
6. Change the field size from the default of 255 characters to 5 characters by selecting *255* in the *Field Size* property box in the *Field Properties* section and then typing **5**.
7. Click in the *Description* column for the *EmpID* row, type **Enter five-digit employee identification number**, and then press the Tab key.

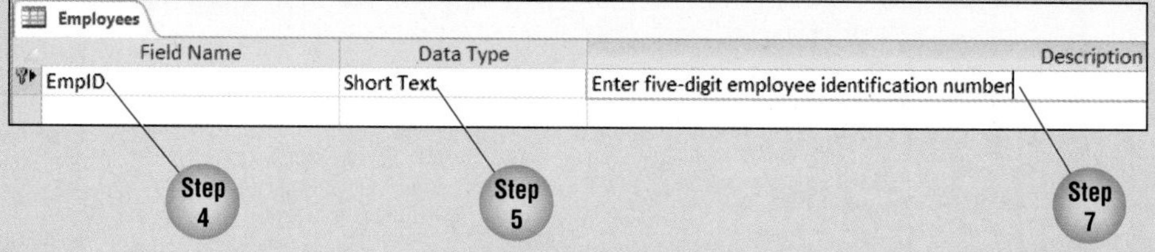

8. Type **FName** in the *Field Name* column and then press the Tab key.
9. Select *255* in the *Field Size* property box in the *Field Properties* section and then type **20**.
10. Click in the *Description* column for the *FName* row, type **Enter employee's first name**, and then press the Tab key.
11. Complete steps similar to those in Steps 8 through 10 to create the *LName*, *Address*, and *City* fields as shown in Figure 4.6. Change the field size for the *LName* field and *Address* field to 30 characters and change the *City* field to 20 characters.

12. Create the *State* field with a default value of *CA,* since all employees live in California, by completing the following steps:
    a. Type **State** in the *Field Name* column in the row below the *City* row and then press the Tab key.
    b. Click in the *Default Value* property box in the *Field Properties* section and then type **CA**.
    c. Click in the *Description* column for the *State* row, type **CA automatically entered as state**, and then press the Tab key.
13. Type **ZIP** and then press the Tab key.
14. Select *255* that displays in the *Field Size* property box in the *Field Properties* section and then type **5**.
15. Click in the *Description* column for the *ZIP* row, type **Enter five-digit ZIP code**, and then press the Tab key.
16. Type **Telephone** and then press the Tab key.
17. Create an input mask for the telephone number by completing the following steps:
    a. Click the Save button on the Quick Access toolbar to save the table. (You must save the table before using the Input Mask Wizard.)
    b. Click in the *Input Mask* property box in the *Field Properties* section.
    c. Click the Build button (contains three black dots) that displays at the right side of the *Input Mask* property box.

General	Lookup
Field Size	255
Format	
Input Mask	
Caption	
Default Value	CA
Validation Rule	
Validation Text	
Required	No

Step 12b

    d. At the first Input Mask Wizard dialog box, make sure *Phone Number* is selected in the *Input Mask* list box and then click the Next button.
    e. At the second Input Mask Wizard dialog box, click the down-pointing arrow at the right side of the *Placeholder character* option box and then click # at the drop-down list.

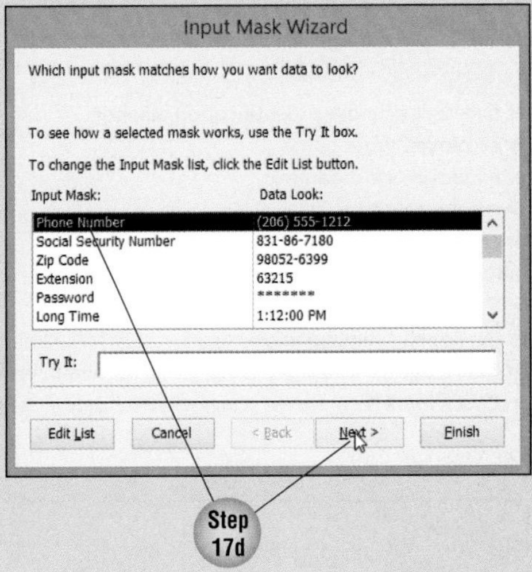

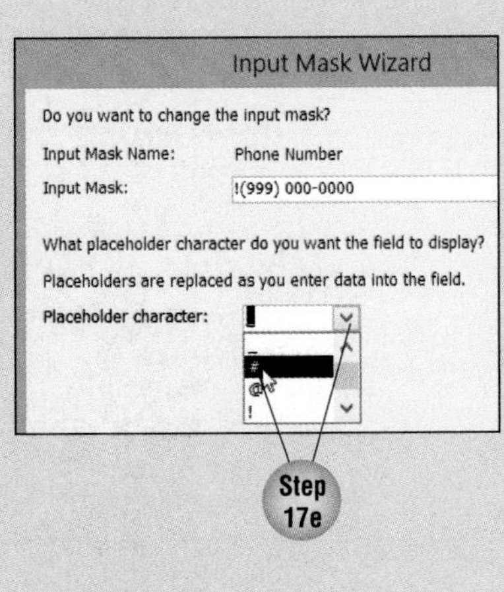

f. Click the Next button.
g. At the third Input Mask Wizard dialog box, click the *With the symbols in the mask, like this* option.
h. Click the Next button.
i. At the fourth Input Mask Wizard dialog box, click the Finish button.

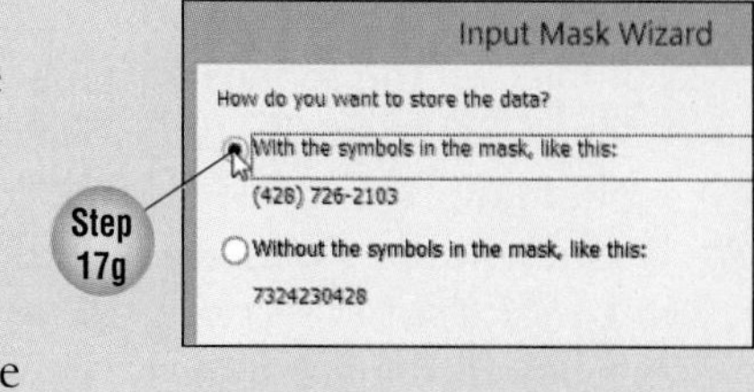

18. Click in the *Description* column in the *Telephone* row, type **Enter employee's telephone number**, and then press the Tab key.
19. Type **HealthIns** and then press the Tab key.
20. Click the down-pointing arrow in the *Data Type* column and then click *Yes/No* at the drop-down list.
21. Click in the *Default Value* property box in the *Field Properties* section, delete the text *No*, and then type **Yes**.
22. Click in the *Description* column for the *HealthIns* row, type **Leave check mark if employee is signed up for health insurance**, and then press the Tab key.

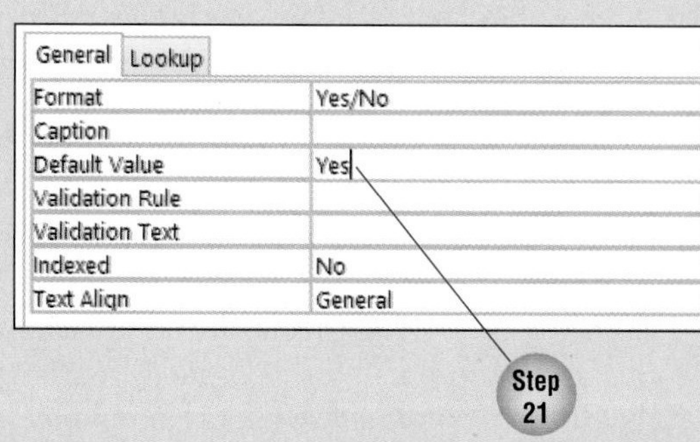

23. Type **DentalIns** and then press the Tab key.
24. Click the down-pointing arrow in the *Data Type* column and then click *Yes/No* at the drop-down list. (The text in the *Default Value* property box will remain as *No*.)
25. Click in the *Description* column for the *DentalIns* row, type **Insert check mark if employee is signed up for dental insurance**, and then press the Tab key.
26. After all of the fields are entered, click the Save button on the Quick Access toolbar.
27. Click the View button to return the table to Datasheet view.
28. Enter the records in the Employees table as shown in Figure 4.7.
29. After all of the records are entered, automatically adjust the widths of the columns in the table.
30. Save and then close the Employees table.

Figure 4.6 Project 1b Employees Table in Design View

Employees

Field Name	Data Type	Description (Optional)
EmpID	Short Text	Enter five-digit employee identification number
FName	Short Text	Enter employee's first name
LName	Short Text	Enter employee's last name
Address	Short Text	Enter employee's address
City	Short Text	Enter employee's city
State	Short Text	CA automatically entered as state
ZIP	Short Text	Enter five-digit ZIP code
Telephone	Short Text	Enter employee's telephone number
HealthIns	Yes/No	Leave check mark if employee is signed up for health insurance
DentalIns	Yes/No	Insert check mark if employee is signed up for dental insurance

Field Properties

Figure 4.7 Project 1b Employees Table in Datasheet View

Employees

	EmpID	FName	LName	Address	City	State	ZIP	Telephone	HealthIns	DentalIns
	02-59	Christina	Solomon	12241 East 51st	Citrus Heights	CA	95611	(916) 555-8844	☑	☑
	03-23	Douglas	Ricci	903 Mission Road	Roseville	CA	95678	(916) 555-4125	☑	☐
	03-55	Tatiana	Kasadev	6558 Orchard Drive	Citrus Heights	CA	95610	(916) 555-8534	☑	☐
	04-14	Brian	West	12232 142nd Avenue East	Citrus Heights	CA	95611	(916) 555-0967	☑	☑
	04-32	Kathleen	Addison	21229 19th Street	Citrus Heights	CA	95621	(916) 555-3408	☑	☑
	05-20	Teresa	Villanueva	19453 North 42nd Street	Citrus Heights	CA	95611	(916) 555-2302	☑	☑
	05-31	Marcia	Griswold	211 Haven Road	North Highlands	CA	95660	(916) 555-1449	☐	☐
	06-24	Tiffany	Gentry	12312 North 20th	Roseville	CA	95661	(916) 555-0043	☑	☑
	06-33	Joanna	Gallegos	6850 York Street	Roseville	CA	95747	(956) 555-7446	☐	☐
	07-20	Jesse	Scholtz	3412 South 21st Street	Fair Oaks	CA	95628	(916) 555-4204	☑	☐
	07-23	Eugene	Bond	530 Laurel Road	Orangevale	CA	95662	(916) 555-9412	☑	☐
*						CA			☑	☐

Validating Field Entries

Use the *Validation Rule* property box in the *Field Properties* section in Design view to enter a statement containing a conditional test that is checked each time data is entered into a field. If data is entered that fails to satisfy the conditional test, Access does not accept the entry and displays an error message. By entering a conditional statement in the *Validation Rule* property box that checks each entry against the acceptable range, you can reduce errors. Enter in the *Validation Text* property box the content of the error message that you want to display.

Enter a validation rule in a field to control what is entered in the field and to reduce errors. Create validation text that displays when someone enters invalid data in the field.

Using the Lookup Wizard

Like the Input Mask Wizard, the Lookup Wizard can be used to control the data entered in a field. Use the Lookup Wizard to confine the data entered into a field to a specific list of items. For example, in Project 1c, you will use the Lookup Wizard to restrict the new *EmpCategory* field to one of three choices: *Salaried*, *Hourly*, and *Temporary*. When the user clicks in the field in the datasheet, a down-pointing arrow displays. The user clicks this down-pointing arrow to display a drop-down list of available entries and then clicks the desired item.

Use the Lookup Wizard when assigning a data type to a field. Click in the desired field in the *Data Type* column and then click the down-pointing arrow that displays at the right side of the field. At the drop-down list that displays, click *Lookup Wizard*. This displays the first Lookup Wizard dialog box, as shown in Figure 4.8. At this dialog box, indicate that you want to enter the field choices by clicking the *I will type in the values that I want* option and then click the Next button. At the second Lookup Wizard dialog box, shown in Figure 4.9, click in the blank text box below *Col1* and then type the first choice. Press the Tab key and then type the second choice. Continue in this manner until you have entered all the desired choices and then click the Next button. At the third Lookup Wizard dialog box, make sure the proper name displays in the *What label would you like for your lookup column?* text box and then click the Finish button.

Quick Steps

Use the Lookup Wizard

1. Open table in Design view.
2. Type text in *Field Name* column.
3. Press Tab key.
4. Click down-pointing arrow.
5. Click *Lookup Wizard*.
6. Complete wizard steps.

Figure 4.8 First Lookup Wizard Dialog Box

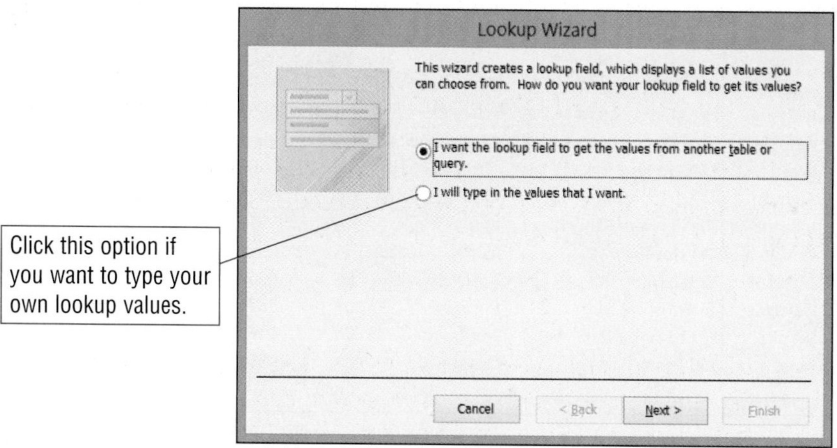

Figure 4.9 Second Lookup Wizard Dialog Box

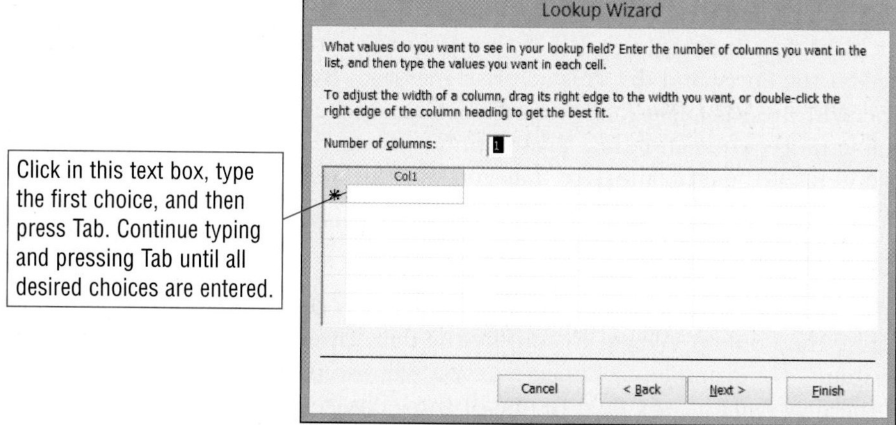

Inserting, Moving, and Deleting Fields in Design View

Quick Steps

Insert a Field in Design View

1. Open table in Design view.
2. Click in row that will follow new field.
3. Click Insert Rows button.

Insert Rows

In Chapter 1, you learned how to insert, move, and delete fields in a table in Datasheet view. You can also perform these tasks in Design view. To insert a new field in a table in Design view, position the insertion point in a field in the row that will be located immediately *below* the new field and then click the Insert Rows button in the Tools group on the TABLE TOOLS DESIGN tab. Another option is to position the insertion point on any text in the row that will display immediately *below* the new field, click the right mouse button, and then click *Insert Rows* at the shortcut menu. If you insert a row for a new field and then change your mind, immediately click the Undo button on the Quick Access toolbar. Remember that a *row* in the Design view creates a *field* in the table.

You can move a field in a table to a different location in Datasheet view or Design view. To move a field in Design view, click in the field selector bar at the left side of the row you want to move. With the row selected, position the arrow pointer in the field selector bar at the left side of the selected row, hold down the left mouse button, drag the arrow pointer with a gray square attached until a thick black line displays in the desired position, and then release the mouse button.

Delete a field in a table and all data entered in that field is also deleted. When you delete a field, it cannot be undone with the Undo button. Delete a field only if you are sure you really want it and the data associated with it completely removed from the table. To delete a field in Design view, click in the field selector bar at the left side of the row you want to delete and then click the Delete Rows button in the Tools group. At the message asking if you want to permanently delete the field and all of the data in the field, click Yes. You can also delete a row by positioning the mouse pointer in the row you want to delete, clicking the right mouse button, and then clicking *Delete Rows* at the shortcut menu.

Quick Steps

Delete a Field in Design View

1. Open table in Design view.
2. Click in row to be deleted.
3. Click Delete Rows button.
4. Click Yes.

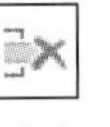

Delete Rows

Inserting a Total Row

You can add a *Total* row in a table in Datasheet view and then choose from a list of functions to find the sum, average, maximum, minimum, count, standard deviation, or variance result in a numeric column. To insert a *Total* row, click the Totals button in the Records group on the HOME tab. Access adds a row to the bottom of the table with the label *Total* at the left. Click in the *Total* row, click the down-pointing arrow that appears, and then click the desired function at the drop-down list.

Quick Steps

Insert a Total Row

1. Open table in Datasheet view.
2. Click Totals button.
3. Click in *Total* row.
4. Click down-pointing arrow.
5. Click desired function.

Totals

Project 1c **Validating Field Entries; Using the Lookup Wizard; and Inserting, Moving, and Deleting a Field** **Part 3 of 8**

1. With **AL1-C4-SunProperties.accdb** open, open the Employees table.
2. Insert in the Employees table a new field and apply a validation rule by completing the following steps:
   a. Click the View button to switch to Design view.
   b. Click in the empty field immediately below the *DentalIns* field in the *Field Name* column and then type **LifeIns**.
   c. Press the Tab key.
   d. Click the down-pointing arrow at the right side of the *Data Type* field and then click *Currency* at the drop-down list.
   e. Click in the *Validation Rule* property box, type **<=100000**, and then press Enter.
   f. With the insertion point positioned in the *Validation Text* property box, type **Enter a value that is equal to or less than $100,000**.
   g. Click in the field in the *Description* column for the *LifeIns* row and then type **Enter optional life insurance amount**.
   h. Click the Save button on the Quick Access toolbar. Since the validation rule was created *after* data was entered into the table, Access displays a warning message indicating that some data may not be valid. At this message, click No.
   i. Click the View button to switch to Datasheet view.
3. Click in the first empty field in the *LifeIns* column, type **200000**, and then press the Down Arrow key.

Step 2e

General | Lookup

Format	Currency
Decimal Places	Auto
Input Mask	
Caption	
Default Value	0
Validation Rule	<=100000
Validation Text	Enter a value that is equal to or less than $100,000
Required	No

Step 2f

4. Access displays the error message telling you to enter an amount that is equal to or less than $100,000. At this error message, click OK.
5. Edit the amount in the field so it displays as *100000* and then press the Down Arrow key.
6. Type the following entries in the remaining fields in the *LifeIns* column:
   Record 2: 25000
   Record 3: 0
   Record 4: 50000
   Record 5: 50000
   Record 6: 0
   Record 7: 100000
   Record 8: 50000
   Record 9: 25000
   Record 10: 0
   Record 11: 100000
7. Insert the field *EmpCategory* in the Employees table and use the Lookup Wizard to specify field choices by completing the following steps:
   a. Click the View button to change to Design view.
   b. Click on any character in the *FName* field entry in the *Field Name* column.
   c. Click the Insert Rows button in the Tools group.
   d. With the insertion point positioned in the new blank field in the *Field Name* column, type **EmpCategory**.
   e. Press the Tab key. (This moves the insertion point to the *Data Type* column.)
   f. Click the down-pointing arrow at the right side of the *Data Type* field and then click *Lookup Wizard* at the drop-down list.
   g. At the first Lookup Wizard dialog box, click the *I will type in the values that I want* option and then click the Next button.

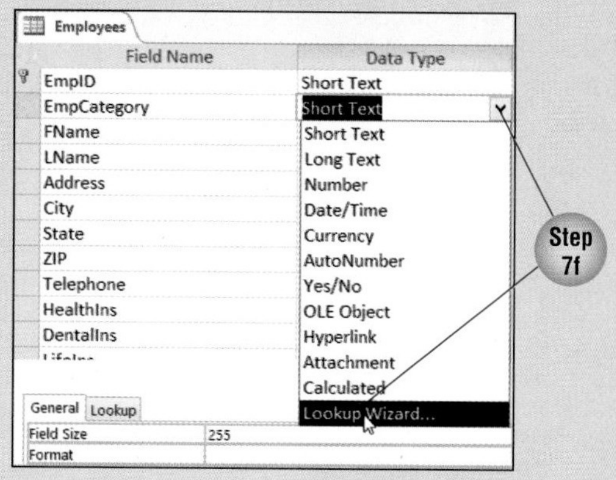

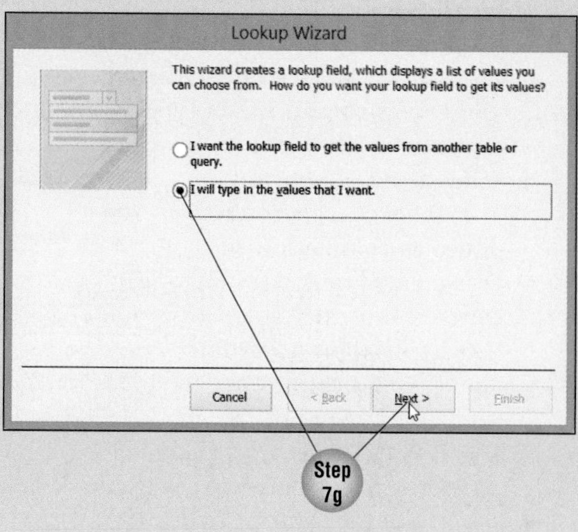

h. At the second Lookup Wizard dialog box, click in the blank text box below *Col1*, type **Salaried**, and then press the Tab key.
i. Type **Hourly** and then press the Tab key.
j. Type **Temporary**.
k. Click the Next button.
l. At the third Lookup Wizard dialog box, click the Finish button.
m. Press the Tab key and then type **Click down-pointing arrow and then click employee category** in the *Description* column.

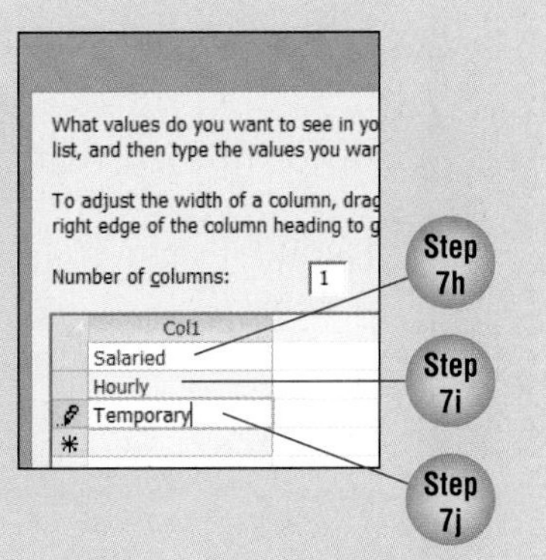

8. Click the Save button on the Quick Access toolbar.
9. Click the View button to switch to Datasheet view.
10. Insert information in the *EmpCategory* column by completing the following steps:
    a. Click in the first blank field in the new *EmpCategory* field.
    b. Click the down-pointing arrow at the right side of the field and then click *Hourly* at the drop-down list.
    c. Click in the next blank field in the *EmpCategory* column, click the down-pointing arrow, and then click *Salaried* at the drop-down list.
    d. Continue entering information in the *EmpCategory* column by completing similar steps. Choose the following in the specified record:

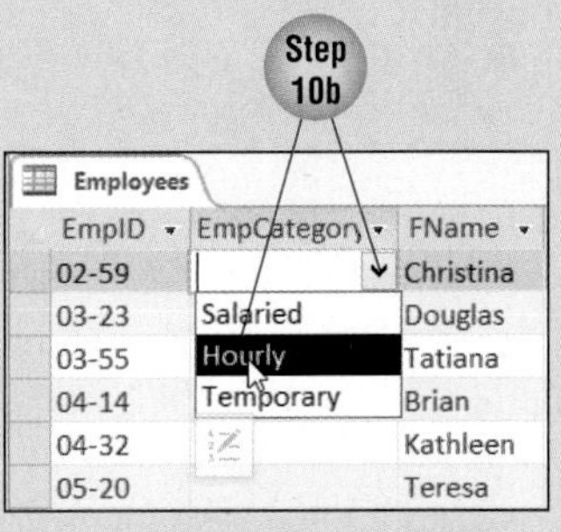

Third record: *Hourly*
Fourth record: *Salaried*
Fifth record: *Temporary*
Sixth record: *Hourly*
Seventh record: *Salaried*
Eighth record: *Temporary*
Ninth record: *Hourly*
Tenth record: *Salaried*
Eleventh record: *Salaried*

11. Print the Employees table. (The table will print on two pages.)
12. After looking at the printed table, you decide to move the *EmpCategory* field. You also need to delete the *DentalIns* field, since Sun Properties no longer offers dental insurance benefits to employees. Move the *EmpCatgory* field and delete the *DentalIns* field in Design view by completing the following steps:
    a. With the Employees table open, click the View button to switch to Design view.
    b. Click in the field selector bar at the left side of the *EmpCategory* field to select the row.
    c. Position the arrow pointer in the *EmpCategory* field selector bar, hold down the left mouse button, drag down until a thick black line displays below the *Telephone* field, and then release the mouse button.

Employees

Field Name	Data Type
EmpID	Short Text
EmpCategory	Short Text
FName	Short Text
LName	Short Text
Address	Short Text
City	Short Text
State	Short Text
ZIP	Short Text
Telephone	Short Text
HealthIns	Yes/No
DentalIns	Yes/No

Step 12c

13. Delete the *DentalIns* field by completing the following steps:
    a. Click in the field selector bar at the left side of the *DentalIns* row. (This selects the row.)
    b. Click the Delete Rows button in the Tools group.
    c. At the message asking if you want to permanently delete the field and all of the data in the field, click Yes.

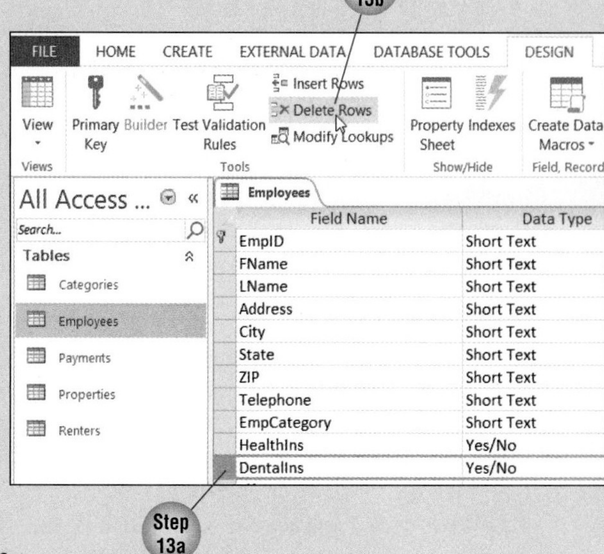

14. Click the Save button on the Quick Access toolbar.
15. Click the View button to switch to Datasheet view.
16. Print the Employees table. (The table will print on two pages.)
17. Close the Employees table.
18. Open the Payments table and then insert a new field and apply a validation rule by completing the following steps:
    a. Click the View button to switch to Design view.
    b. Click in the empty field immediately below the *PymntAmount* field in the *Field Name* column and then type **LateFee**.
    c. Press the Tab key.
    d. Click the down-pointing arrow at the right side of the *Data Type* field and then click *Currency* at the drop-down list.
    e. Click in the *Validation Rule* property box, type **<=50**, and then press Enter.
    f. With the insertion point positioned in the *Validation Text* property box, type **Late fee must be $50 or less.**
    g. Click in the box in the *Description* column for the *LateFee* field and then type **Enter a late fee amount if applicable.**

General	Lookup
Format	Currency
Decimal Places	Auto
Input Mask	
Caption	
Default Value	0
Validation Rule	<=50
Validation Text	Late fee must be $50 or less
Required	No

Step 18e

Step 18f

    h. Click the Save button on the Quick Access toolbar. Since the validation rule was created *after* data was entered into the table, Access displays a warning message indicating that some data may not be valid. At this message, click No.
    i. Click the View button to switch to Datasheet view.
19. Insert late fees for the last three records by completing the following steps:
    a. Click in the *LateFee* field for record 15, type **25**, and then press the Down Arrow key.
    b. With the *LateFee* field for record 16 active, type **25** and then press the Down Arrow key.
    c. With the *LateFee* field for record 17 active, type **50** and then press the Up Arrow key.

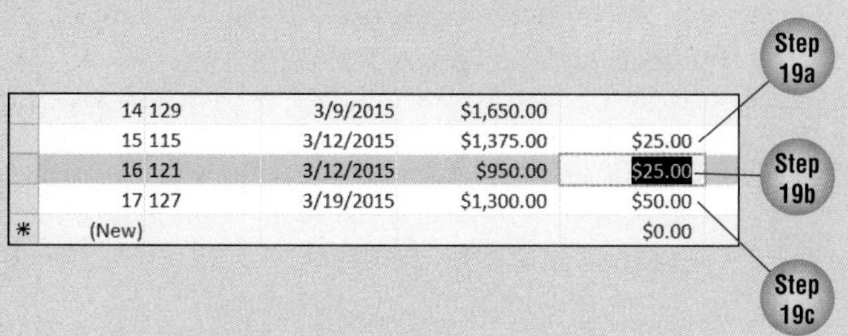

14	129	3/9/2015	$1,650.00	
15	115	3/12/2015	$1,375.00	$25.00
16	121	3/12/2015	$950.00	$25.00
17	127	3/19/2015	$1,300.00	$50.00
*	(New)			$0.00

20. Insert a *Total* row by completing the following steps:
   a. In Datasheet view, click the Totals button in the Records group on the HOME tab.
   b. Click in the blank field in the *PymntAmount* column in the *Total* row.
   c. Click the down-pointing arrow at the left side of the field and then click *Sum* at the drop-down list.
   d. Click in the blank field in the *LateFee* column in the *Total* row.
   e. Click the down-pointing arrow at the left side of the field and then click *Sum* at the drop-down list.
   f. Click in any other field.
21. Save, print, and then close the Payments table.

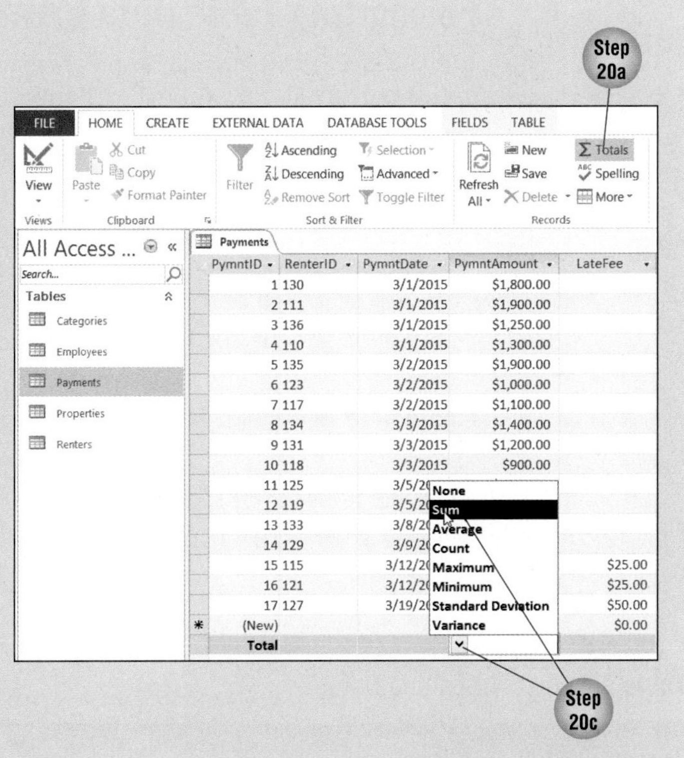

Sorting Records

The Sort & Filter group on the HOME tab contains two buttons for sorting data in records. When you click the Ascending button to sort data in the active field, text is sorted in alphabetical order from A to Z and numbers are sorted from lowest to highest. When you click the Descending button to sort data in the active field, text is sorted in alphabetical order from Z to A and numbers are sorted from highest to lowest.

Quick Steps

Sort Records
1. Open table in Datasheet view.
2. Click in field in desired column.
3. Click Ascending button or Descending button.

Ascending

Descending

Printing Specific Records

If you want to print specific records in a table, select the records and then display the Print dialog box by clicking the FILE tab, clicking the *Print* option, and then clicking the Print button. At the Print dialog box, click the *Selected Record(s)* option in the *Print Range* section and then click OK. To select specific records, display the table in Datasheet view, click the record selector of the first record, and then drag to select the desired records. The record selector is the light gray square that displays at the left side of the record. When you position the mouse pointer on the record selector, the pointer turns into a right-pointing black arrow.

Quick Steps

Print Selected Records
1. Open table and select records.
2. Click FILE tab.
3. Click *Print* option.
4. Click Print button.
5. Click *Selected Record(s)*.
6. Click OK.

Formatting Table Data

In Datasheet view, you can apply formatting to data in a table. Formatting options are available in the Text Formatting group on the HOME tab, as shown in Figure 4.10. To apply formatting, open a table in Datasheet view and then click the desired button in the Text Formatting group. The button formatting is applied to all of the data in the table. (Some of the buttons in the Text Formatting group are dimmed and unavailable. These buttons are available for fields formatted as rich text.) The buttons available for formatting a table are shown in Table 4.2.

Click the Align Left, Center, or Align Right button and formatting is applied to text in the currently active column. Click one of the other buttons shown in

Figure 4.10 HOME Tab Text Formatting Group

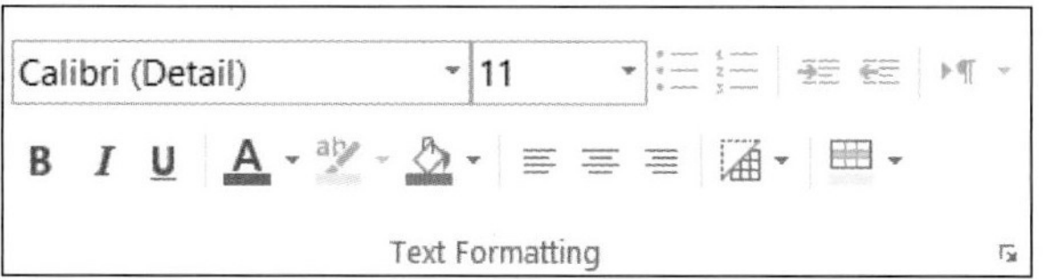

Table 4.2 Text Formatting Buttons

Button	Name	Description
Calibri (Detail)	Font	Change the text font.
11	Font Size	Change the text size.
B	Bold	Bold the text.
I	Italic	Italicize the text.
U	Underline	Underline the text.
A	Font Color	Change the text color.
	Background Color	Apply a background color to all fields.
	Align Left	Align all text in the currently active column at the left side of the fields.
	Center	Center all text in the currently active column in the center of the fields.
	Align Right	Align all text in the currently active column at the right side of the fields.
	Gridlines	Specify whether to display vertical and/or horizontal gridlines.
	Alternate Row Color	Apply a specified color to alternating rows in the table.

Table 4.2 and formatting is applied to all columns and rows of data in the table. The exception is the Background Color button, which applies formatting to all fields in the table.

When creating a table, you specify a data type for a field, such as the Short Text, Date/Time, or Currency data type. If you want to format text in a field rather than all of the fields in a column or the entire table, choose the Long Text data type and then specify rich text formatting. For example, in Project 1d, you will format specific credit scores in the *CreditScore* field column. To be able to format specific scores, you change the data type to Long Text and then specify rich text formatting. Use the Long Text data type only for fields containing text—not for fields containing currency amounts, numbers, and dates.

By default, the Long Text data type uses plain text formatting. To change to rich text, click in the *Text Format* property box in the *Field Properties* section (displays with the text *Plain Text*), click the down-pointing arrow that displays at the right side of the property box, and then click *Rich Text* at the drop-down list.

Project 1d Sorting, Printing, and Formatting Records and Fields in Tables — Part 4 of 8

1. With **AL1-C4-SunProperties.accdb** open, open the Renters table.
2. With the table in Datasheet view, sort records in ascending alphabetical order by last name by completing the following steps:
   a. Click any last name in the *LastName* field in the table.
   b. Click the Ascending button in the Sort & Filter group on the HOME tab.
   c. Print the Renters table in landscape orientation. 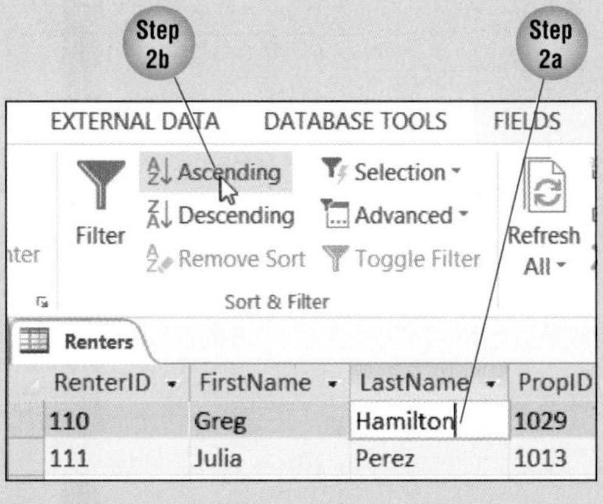
3. Sort records in descending order (highest to lowest) by credit score number by completing the following steps:
   a. Click any number in the *CreditScore* field.
   b. Click the Descending button in the Sort & Filter group.
   c. Print the Renters table in landscape orientation.
4. Close the Renters table without saving the changes.
5. Open the Properties table.
6. Sort and then print selected records with the apartment property type by completing the following steps:
   a. Click any entry in the *CatID* field.
   b. Click the Ascending button in the Sort & Filter group.
   c. Position the mouse pointer on the record selector of the first record with *A* for a category ID, hold down the mouse button, and then drag to select the four records with a category ID of *A*.

d. Click the FILE tab and then click the *Print* option.
e. Click the Print button.
f. At the Print dialog box, click the *Selected Record(s)* option in the *Print Range* section.
g. Click OK.

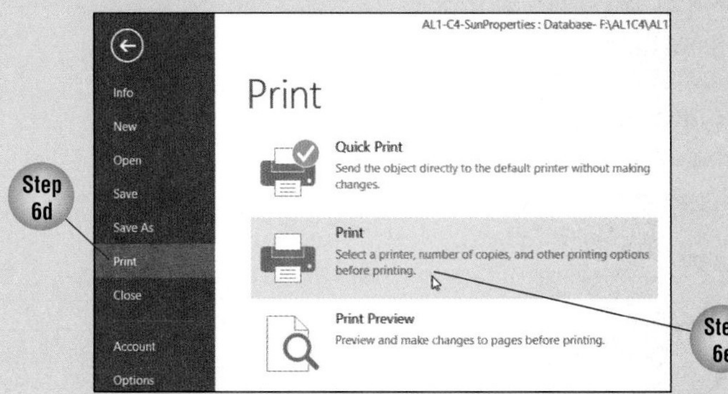

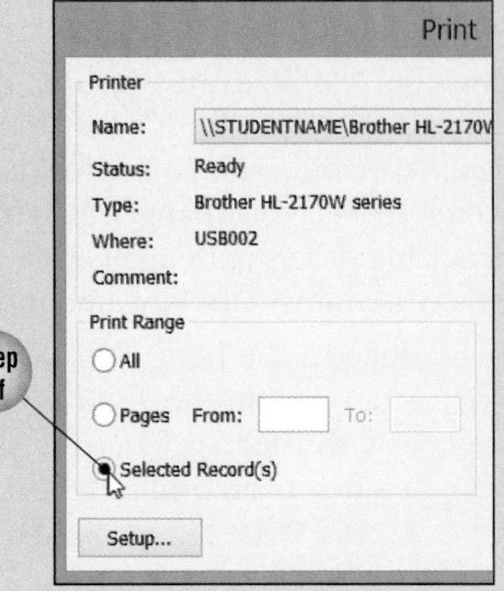

7. With the Properties table open, apply the following text formatting:
   a. Click in any field in the *CatID* column and then click the Center button in the Text Formatting group on the HOME tab.

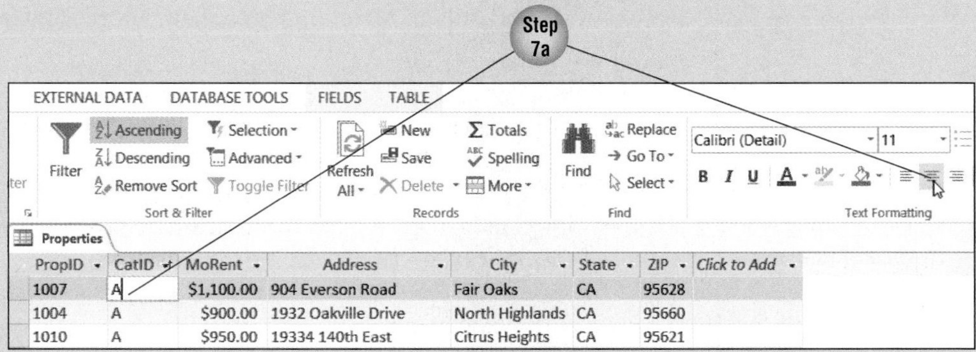

   b. Click in any field in the *PropID* column and then click the Center button in the Text Formatting group.
   c. Click the Bold button in the Text Formatting group. (This applies bold to all text in the table.)
   d. Click the Font Color button arrow and then click *Dark Blue* (fourth column, first row in the *Standard Colors* section).
   e. Adjust the column widths.
   f. Save, print, and then close the Properties table.
8. Open the Payments table and apply the following text formatting:
   a. With the first field active in the *PymntID* column, click the Center button in the Text Formatting group on the HOME tab.

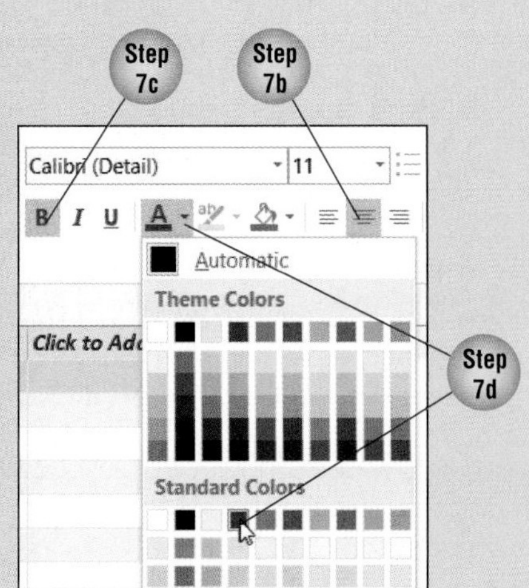

b. Click in any field in the *RenterID* column and then click the Center button in the Text Formatting group.
c. Click the Font button arrow, scroll down the drop-down list that displays, and then click *Candara*. (Fonts are listed in alphabetical order in the drop-down list.)
d. Click the Font Size button arrow and then click *12* at the drop-down list.
e. Click the Alternate Row Color button arrow and then click *Green 2* (seventh column, third row in the *Standard Colors* section).

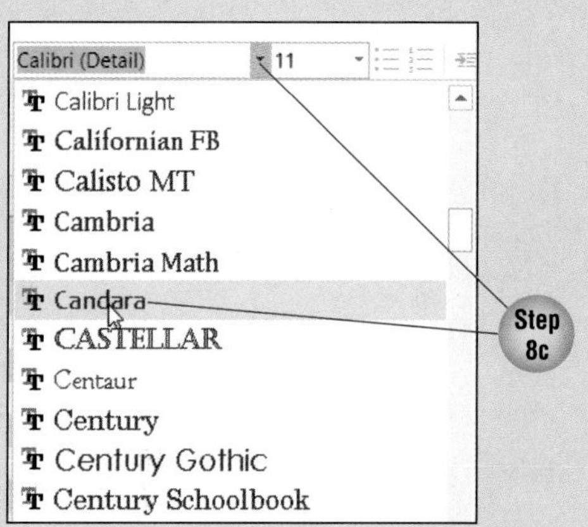

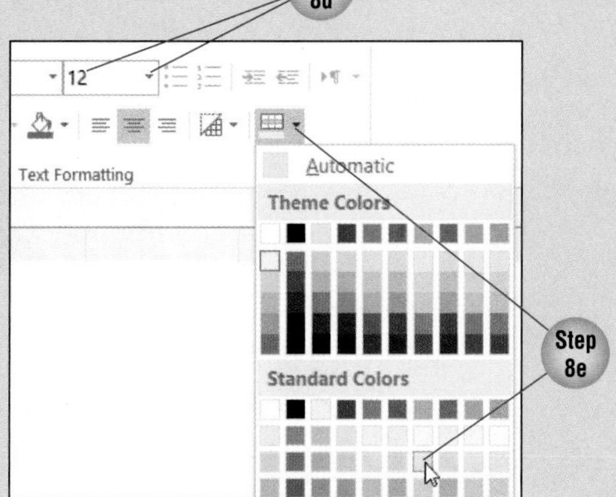

f. Adjust the column widths.
g. Save, print, and then close the Payments table.

9. Open the Renters table and then apply the following formatting to columns in the table:
   a. With the first field active in the *RenterID* column, click the Center button in the Text Formatting group on the HOME tab.
   b. Click in any field in the *PropID* column and then click the Center button.
   c. Click in any field in the *EmpID* column and then click the Center button
   d. Click in any field in the *CreditScore* column and then click the Center button.
10. Change the data type for the *CreditScore* field to Long Text with rich text formatting and apply formatting by completing the following steps:
    a. Click the View button to switch to Design view.
    b. Click in the *Data Type* column in the *CreditScore* row, click the down-pointing arrow that displays in the field, and then click *Long Text* at the drop-down list.
    c. Click in the *Text Format* property box in the *Field Properties* section (displays with the words *Plain Text*), click the down-pointing arrow that displays at the right side of the property box, and then click *Rich Text* at the drop-down list.

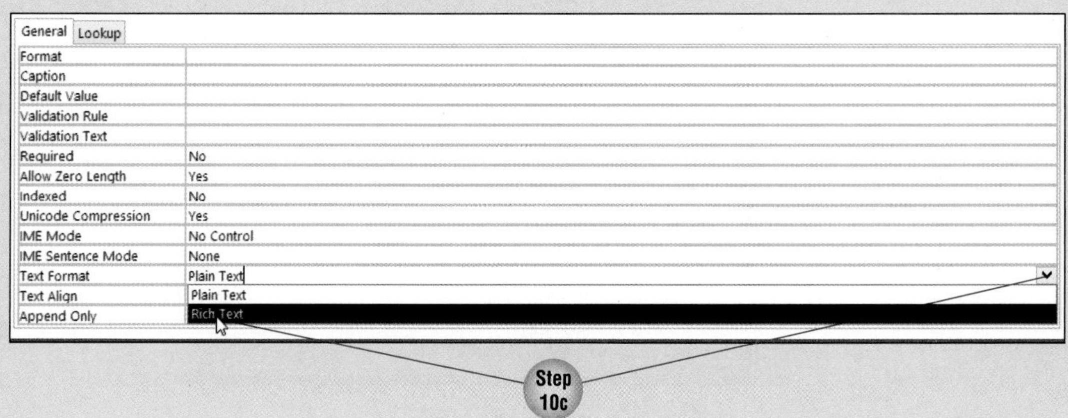

d. At the message that displays telling you that the field will be converted to rich text, click the Yes button.
e. Click the Save button on the Quick Access toolbar.
f. Click the View button to switch to Datasheet view.
g. Double-click the field value *538* that displays in the *CreditScore* column in the row for Dana Rozinski. (Double-clicking in the field selects the field value *538*.)
h. With *538* selected, click the Font Color button in the Text Formatting group. (This changes the number to red. If the font color does not change to red, click the Font Color button arrow and then click *Red* in the second column, bottom row of the *Standard Colors* section.)
i. Change the font to red for any credit scores below 600.
j. Print the Renters table in landscape orientation and then close the table.

Step 10h

Step 10g

CreditScore	LeaseBegDate	LeaseEndDate	Click to Add
624	1/1/2015	12/31/2015	
711	1/1/2015	12/31/2015	
538	2/1/2015	1/31/2016	
695	2/1/2015	1/31/2016	

Quick Steps

Complete a Spelling Check
1. Open table in Datasheet view.
2. Click Spelling button.
3. Change or ignore spelling as needed.
4. Click OK.

Spelling

You can also begin a spelling check with the keyboard shortcut F7.

Completing a Spelling Check

The spelling check feature in Access finds misspelled words and suggests replacement words. It also finds duplicate words and irregular capitalizations. When you spell check an object in a database, such as a table, the spelling check compares the words in your table with the words in its dictionary. If a match is found, the word is passed over. If no match is found, the spelling check selects the word and suggests possible replacements.

To complete a spelling check, open the desired table in Datasheet view and then click the Spelling button in the Records group on the HOME tab. If the spelling check does not find a match for a word in your table, the Spelling dialog box displays with replacement options. Figure 4.11 displays the Spelling dialog box with the word *Citruis* selected and possible replacements displayed in the *Suggestions* list box. At the Spelling dialog box, you can choose to ignore the word (for example, if the spelling check has selected a proper name), change to one of the replacement options, or add the word to the dictionary or AutoCorrect feature. You can also complete a spelling check on other objects in a database, such as a query, form, and report. (You will learn about forms and reports in future chapters.)

Figure 4.11 Spelling Dialog Box

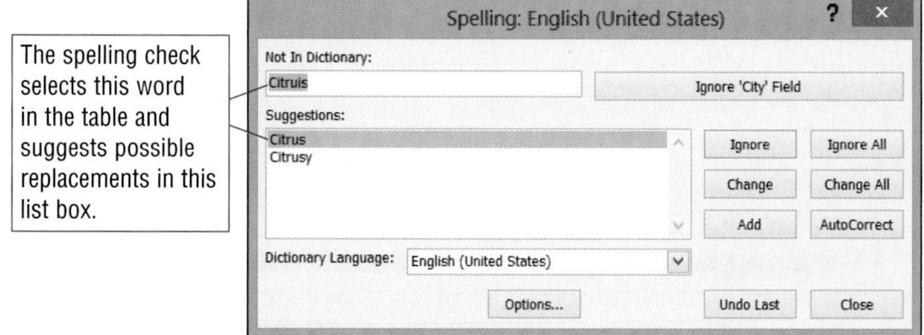

Project 1e Checking Spelling in a Table

Part 5 of 8

1. With **AL1-C4-SunProperties.accdb** open, open the Employees table.
2. Delete the *LifeIns* field by completing the following steps:
   a. Click the View button to switch to the Design view.
   b. Click in the field selector bar at the left side of the *LifeIns* row. (This selects the row.)
   c. Click the Delete Rows button in the Tools group.
   d. At the message asking if you want to permanently delete the field and all of the data in the field, click Yes.
   e. Click the Save button on the Quick Access toolbar.
   f. Click the View button to switch to Datasheet view.
3. Add the following record to the Employees table. (Type the misspelled words as shown below. You will correct the spelling in a later step.)

EmpID	02-72
FName	Roben
LName	Wildre
Address	9945 Valley Avenue
City	Citruis Heights
State	(CA automatically inserted)
ZIP	95610
Telephone	9165556522
EmpCategory	(choose *Salaried*)
HealthIns	No (Remove check mark)

4. Save the Employees table.
5. Click in the first entry in the *EmpID* column.
6. Click the Spelling button in the Records group on the HOME tab.
7. The spelling check selects the name *Kasadev*. This is a proper name, so click the Ignore button to tell the spelling check to leave the name as written.

8. The spelling check selects the name *Scholtz*. This is a proper name, so click the Ignore button to tell the spelling check to leave the name as written.
9. The spelling check selects *Roben*. The proper spelling *(Robin)* is selected in the *Suggestions* list box, so click the Change button.

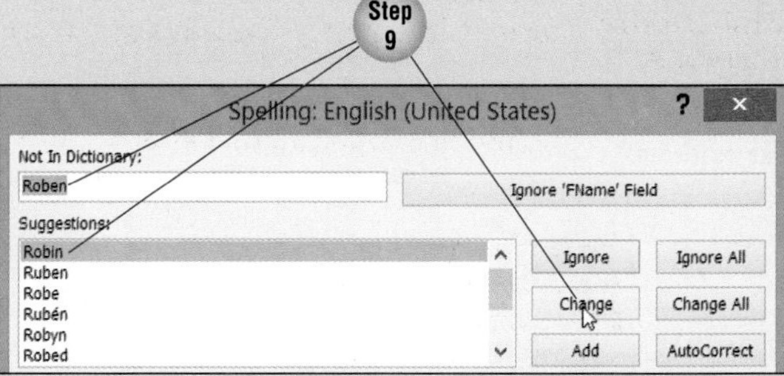

10. The spelling check selects *Wildre*. The proper spelling *(Wilder)* is selected in the *Suggestions* list box, so click the Change button.
11. The spelling check selects *Citruis*. The proper spelling *(Citrus)* is selected in the *Suggestions* list box, so click the Change button.
12. At the message telling you that the spelling check is complete, click the OK button.
13. Print the Employees table in landscape orientation and then close the table.

Finding and Replacing Data

Quick Steps

Find Data
1. Open table in Datasheet view.
2. Click Find button.
3. Type data in *Find What* text box.
4. Click Find Next button.

Find and Replace Data
1. Open table in Datasheet view.
2. Click Replace button.
3. Type find data in *Find What* text box.
4. Type replace data in *Replace With* text box.
5. Click Find Next button.
6. Click Replace button or Find Next button.

Find

Replace

Press Ctrl + F to display the Find and Replace dialog box with the Find tab selected.

Press Ctrl + H to display the Find and Replace dialog box with the Replace tab selected.

If you need to find a specific entry in a field in a table, consider using options at the Find and Replace dialog box with the Find tab selected, as shown in Figure 4.12. Display this dialog box by clicking the Find button in the Find group on the HOME tab. At the Find and Replace dialog box, enter the data you want to locate in the *Find What* text box. By default, Access looks only in the specific column where the insertion point is positioned. Click the Find Next button to find the next occurrence of the data or click the Cancel button to close the Find and Replace dialog box.

The *Look In* option defaults to the column where the insertion point is positioned. You can choose to look in the entire table by clicking the down-pointing arrow at the right side of the *Look In* option and then clicking the table name at the drop-down list. The *Match* option has a default setting of *Whole Field*. You can change this to *Any Part of Field* or *Start of Field*. The *Search* option has a default setting of *All*, which means that Access will search all of the data in a specific column. This can be changed to *Up* or *Down*. If you want to find data that contains specific uppercase and lowercase letters, insert a check mark in the *Match Case* check box and Access will return results that match the case formatting of the search text you entered.

Use the Find and Replace dialog box with the Replace tab selected to search for specific data and replace it with other data. Display this dialog box by clicking the Replace button in the Find group on the HOME tab.

Figure 4.12 Find and Replace Dialog Box with Find Tab Selected

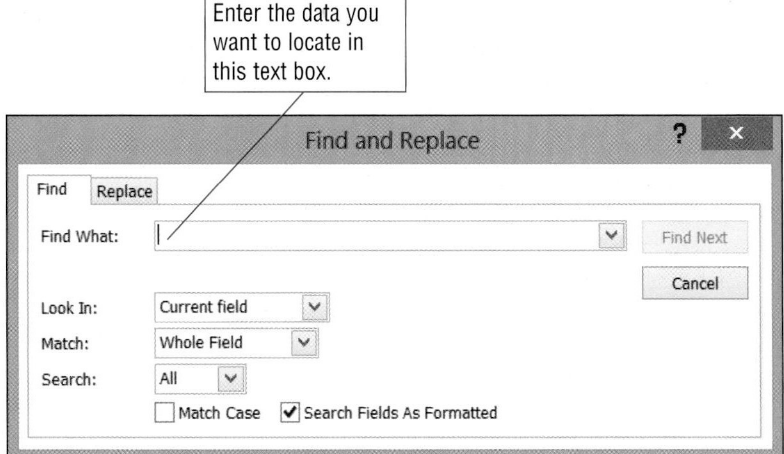

Project 1f Finding and Replacing Data, Creating Relationships, and Performing Queries

Part 6 of 8

1. With **AL1-C4-SunProperties.accdb** open, open the Properties table.
2. Find records containing the zip code *95610* by completing the following steps:
   a. Click in the first field in the *ZIP* column.
   b. Click the Find button in the Find group on the HOME tab.
   c. At the Find and Replace dialog box with the Find tab selected, type 95610 in the *Find What* text box.
   d. Click the Find Next button. (Access finds and selects the first occurrence of *95610*. If the Find and Replace dialog box covers the data, drag the dialog box to a different location on the screen.)

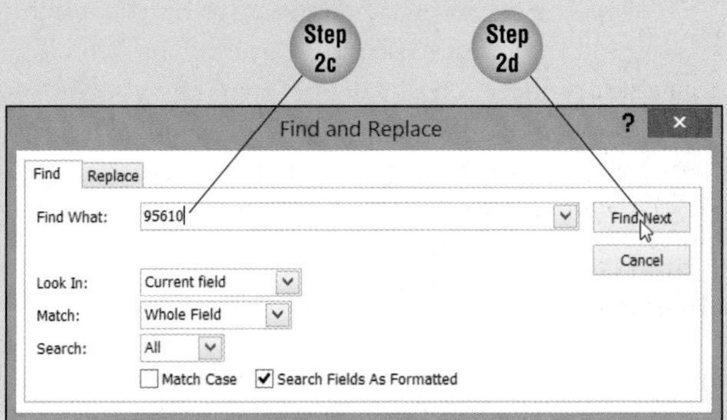

   e. Continue clicking the Find Next button until a message displays telling you that Access has finished searching the records. At this message, click OK.
   f. Click the Cancel button to close the Find and Replace dialog box.
3. Suppose a new zip code has been added to the city of North Highlands and you need to change to this new zip for some of the North Highlands properties. Complete the following steps to find *95660* and replace it with *95668*:
   a. Click in the first field in the *ZIP* column.
   b. Click the Replace button in the Find group.
   c. At the Find and Replace dialog box with the Replace tab selected, type 95660 in the *Find What* text box.
   d. Press the Tab key. (This moves the insertion point to the *Replace With* text box.)
   e. Type 95668 in the *Replace With* text box.
   f. Click the Find Next button.
   g. When Access selects the first occurrence of *95660*, click the Replace button.
   h. When Access selects the second occurrence of *95660*, click the Find Next button.

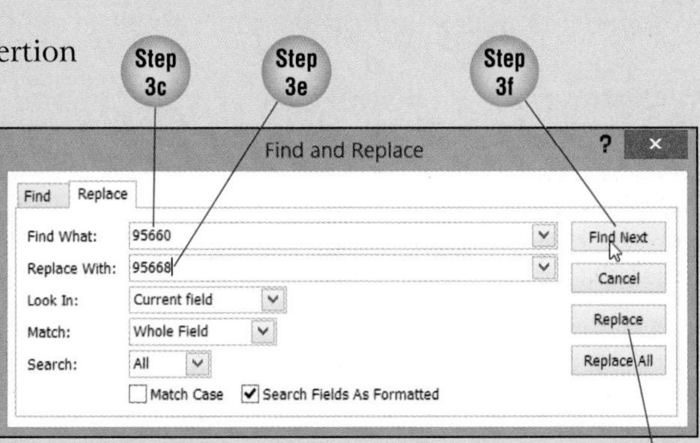

   i. When Access selects the third occurrence of *95660*, click the Replace button.
   j. When Access selects the fourth occurrence of *95660*, click the Find Next button.
   k. When Access selects the fifth occurrence of *95660*, click the Find Next button.
   l. When Access selects the sixth occurrence of *95660*, click the Replace button.
   m. Access selects the first occurrence of *95660* (record 1018) in the table. Click the Cancel button to close the Find and Replace dialog box.
4. Print and then close the Properties table.

5. Display the Relationships window and then create the following relationships (enforce referential integrity and cascade fields and records):
   a. Create a one-to-many relationship with the *CatID* field in the Categories table the "one" and the *CatID* field in the Properties table the "many."
   b. Create a one-to-many relationship with the *EmpID* field in the Employees table the "one" and the *EmpID* field in the Renters table the "many."
   c. Create a one-to-many relationship with the *PropID* field in the Properties table the "one" and the *PropID* field in the Renters table the "many."
   d. Create a one-to-many relationship with the *RenterID* field in the Renters table the "one" and the *RenterID* field in the Payments table the "many."
   e. Save the relationships and then print the relationships in landscape orientation.
   f. Close the relationships report without saving it and then close the Relationships window.
6. Design a query that displays employees with health insurance benefits with the following specifications:
   a. Insert the Employees table in the query window.
   b. Insert the *EmpID* field in the first *Field* row field.
   c. Insert the *FName* field in the second *Field* row field.
   d. Insert the *LName* field in the third *Field* row field.
   e. Insert the *HealthIns* field in the fourth *Field* row field.
   f. Click in the check box in the *Show* row field in the *EmpID* column to remove the check mark. (This hides the EmpID numbers in the query results.)

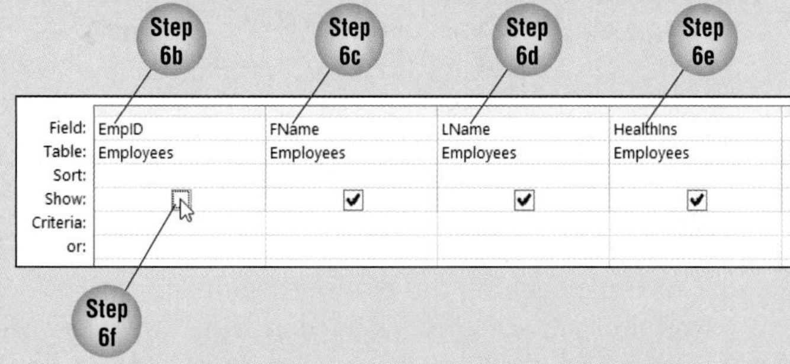

   g. Extract those employees with health benefits. (Type a *1* for the criteria.)
   h. Run the query.
   i. Save the query and name it *EmpsWithHealthInsQuery*.
   j. Print and then close the query.
7. Design a query that displays all properties in the city of Citrus Heights with the following specifications:
   a. Insert the Properties table and the Categories table in the query window.
   b. Insert the *PropID* field from the Properties table in the first *Field* row field.
   c. Insert the *Category* field from the Categories table in the second *Field* row field.
   d. Insert the *Address*, *City*, *State*, and *ZIP* fields from the Properties table to the third, fourth, fifth, and sixth *Field* row fields, respectively.
   e. Extract those properties in the city of Citrus Heights.
   f. Run the query.
   g. Save the query and name it *CitrusHeightsPropsQuery*.
   h. Print and then close the query.
8. Design a query that displays rent payments made between 3/1/2015 and 3/5/2015 with the following specifications:
   a. Insert the Payments table and the Renters table in the query window.
   b. Insert the *PymntID*, *PymntDate*, and *PymntAmount* fields from the Payments table in the first, second, and third *Field* row fields, respectively.
   c. Insert the *FirstName* and *LastName* fields from the Renters table in the fourth and fifth *Field* row fields, respectively.

d. Extract those payments made between 3/1/2015 and 3/5/2015.
e. Run the query.
f. Save the query and name it *Pymnts3/1To3/5Query*.
g. Print and then close the query.

9. Design a query that displays properties in Citrus Heights or Orangevale that rent for less than $1,501 a month as well as the type of property with the following specifications:
   a. Insert the Categories table and the Properties table in the query window.
   b. Insert the *Category* field from the Categories table.
   c. Insert the *PropID*, *MoRent*, *Address*, *City*, *State*, and *ZIP* fields from the Properties table.
   d. Extract those properties in Citrus Heights and Orangevale that rent for less than $1,501.
   e. Run the query.
   f. Save the query and name it *RentLessThan$1501InCHAndOVQuery*.
   g. Print the query in landscape orientation and then close the query.
10. Design a query that displays properties in Citrus Heights assigned to employee identification number *07-20* with the following specifications:
   a. Insert the Employees table and Properties table in the query window.
   b. Insert the *EmpID*, *FName*, and *LName* fields from the Employees table.
   c. Insert the *Address*, *City*, *State*, and *ZIP* fields from the Properties table.
   d. Extract those properties in Citrus Heights assigned to EmpID 07-20.
   e. Run the query.
   f. Save the query and name it *Emp07-20CHPropsQuery*.
   g. Print and then close the query.

Using Help

Microsoft Access includes a Help feature that contains information about Access features and commands. This on-screen reference manual is similar to Windows Help and the Help features in Word, PowerPoint, and Excel. Click the Microsoft Access Help button (the question mark) located in the upper right corner of the screen or press the keyboard shortcut F1 to display the Access Help window, as shown in Figure 4.13. In this window, type a topic, feature, or question in the search text box and then press the Enter key. Topics related to the search text display in the Access Help window. Click a topic that interests you. If the topic window contains a Show All hyperlink in the upper right corner, click this hyperlink to expand the topic options to show additional help information related to the topic. When you click the Show All hyperlink, it becomes the Hide All hyperlink.

Quick Steps

Use the Help Feature
1. Click Microsoft Access Help button.
2. Type topic or feature.
3. Press Enter.
4. Click desired topic.

?

Help

Press F1 to display the Access Help window.

Getting Help on a Button

When you position the mouse pointer on a button, a ScreenTip displays with information about the button. Some button ScreenTips display with a Help icon and the text *Tell me more*. Click this hyperlinked text or press F1 and the Access Help window opens with information about the button feature.

Figure 4.13 Access Help Window

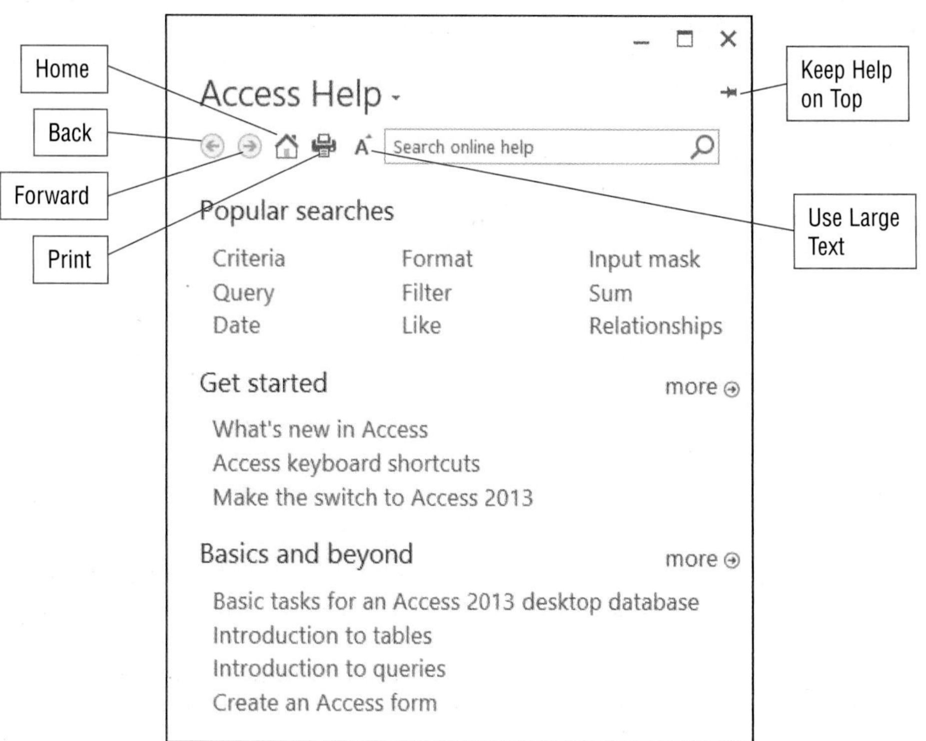

Project 1g Using the Help Feature

Part 7 of 8

1. With **AL1-C4-SunProperties.accdb** open, click the Microsoft Access Help button located in the upper right corner of the screen.
2. At the Access Help window, type **input mask** in the search text box and then press Enter.
3. When the list of topics displays, click the Guide data entry by using input masks hyperlink. (If this article is not available, choose a similar article.)
4. Read the information on creating an input mask. (If you want a printout of the information, click the Print button located toward the top of the Access Help window and then click the Print button at the Print dialog box.)
5. Close the Access Help window by clicking the Close button located in the upper right corner of the window.

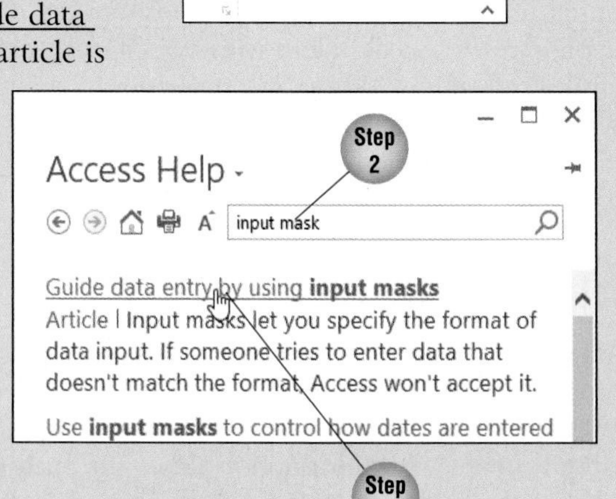

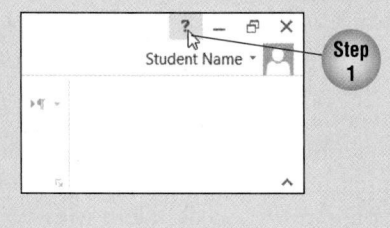

6. Click the CREATE tab.
7. Hover the mouse over the Table button and then click the Tell me more hyperlink that displays toward the bottom of the ScreenTip.
8. At the Access Help window, read the information on tables and then click the Close button located in the upper right corner of the Access Help window.

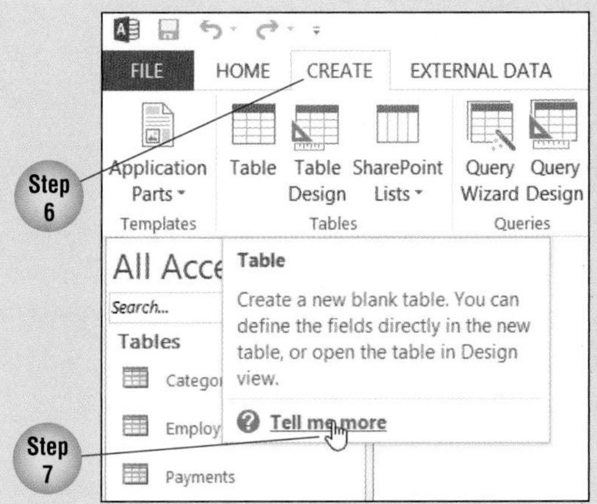

Getting Help in a Dialog Box or Backstage Area

Some dialog boxes and backstage areas provide a Help button you can click to display the Access Help window with specific information about the dialog box or backstage area. After reading and/or printing the information, close the dialog box by clicking the Close button located in the upper right corner of the dialog box or close the backstage area by clicking the Back button or pressing the Esc key.

Project 1h Getting Help in a Dialog Box and Backstage View — Part 8 of 8

1. With **AL1-C4-SunProperties.accdb** open, click the DATABASE TOOLS tab.
2. Click the Relationships button. (Make sure the Show Table dialog box displays. If it does not, click the Show Table button in the Relationships group.)
3. Click the Help button that displays in the upper right corner of the Show Table dialog box.

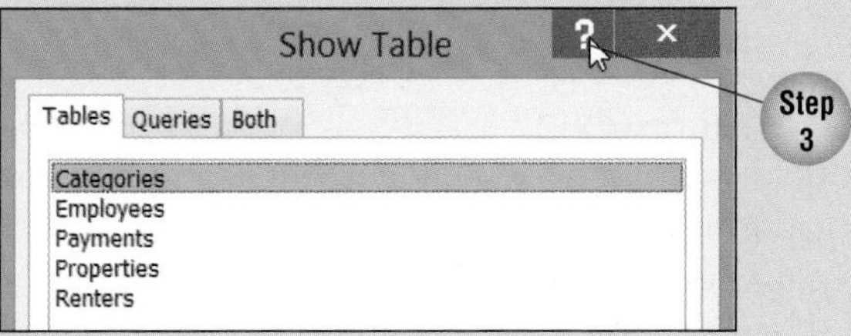

4. Click the Guide to table relationships hyperlink. (If this article is not available, choose a similar article.)
5. Read the information that displays about table relationships and then close the Access Help window.
6. Close the Show Table dialog box and then close the Relationships window.
7. Click the FILE tab and then click the *Open* option.

8. At the Open backstage area, click the Microsoft Access Help button that displays in the upper right corner.
9. Read the information that displays in the Access Help window.
10. Close the Access Help window and then press the Esc key to return to the database.
11. Close **AL1-C4-SunProperties.accdb**.

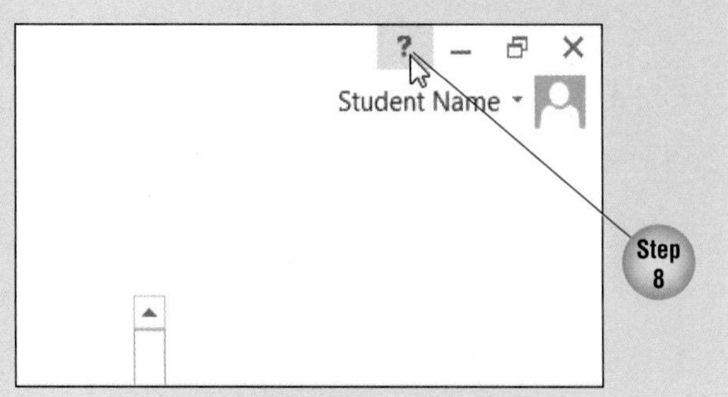

Chapter Summary

- You can create a table in Datasheet view or Design view. Click the View button on the TABLE TOOLS FIELDS tab or the HOME tab to switch between Datasheet view and Design view.
- Define each field in a table in the rows in the top section of Design view. Access automatically assigns the first field the name *ID* and assigns the AutoNumber data type.
- In Design view, specify a field name, data type, and description for each field.
- Assign a data type in Design view by clicking in the *Data Type* field in the desired row, clicking the down-pointing arrow at the right side of the field, and then clicking the desired data type at the drop-down list.
- Create a default value for a field in Design view with the *Default Value* property box in the *Field Properties* section.
- Use the Input Mask Wizard to set a pattern for how data is entered in a field.
- Use the *Validation Rule* property box in the *Field Properties* section in Design view to enter a statement containing a conditional test. Enter in the *Validation Text* property box the error message you want to display if the data entered violates the validation rule.
- Use the Lookup Wizard to confine data entered in a field to a specific list of items.
- Insert a field in Design view by clicking in the row immediately below where you want the new field inserted and then clicking the Insert Rows button.
- Move a field in Design view by clicking in the field selector bar of the field you want to move and then dragging with the mouse to the desired position.
- Delete a field in Design view by clicking in the field selector bar at the left side of the row you want deleted and then clicking the Delete Rows button.
- Insert a *Total* row in a table in Datasheet view by clicking the Totals button in the Records group on the HOME tab, clicking the down-pointing arrow in the *Total* row field, and then clicking the desired function at the drop-down list.
- Click the Ascending button in the Sort & Filter group on the HOME tab to sort records in ascending order and click the Descending button to sort records

in descending order.

- To print specific records in a table, select the records, display the Print dialog box, make sure *Selected Record(s)* is selected, and then click OK.
- Apply formatting to a table in Datasheet view with buttons in the Text Formatting group on the HOME tab. Depending on the button you click in the Text Formatting group, formatting is applied to all of the data in a table or data in a specific column in the table.
- If you want to format text in a specific field, change the data type to Long Text and then specify rich text formatting. Do this in Design view with the *Text Format* property box in the *Field Properties* section.
- Use the spelling check to find misspelled words in a table and consider possible replacement words.
- Use options at the Find and Replace dialog box with the Find tab selected to search for specific field entries in a table. Use options at the Find and Replace dialog box with the Replace tab selected to search for specific data and replace it with other data.
- Click the Microsoft Access Help button or press F1 to display the Access Help window. At this window, type a topic in the search text box and then press Enter.
- The ScreenTip for some buttons displays with a Help icon and the text *Tell me more*. Click this hyperlinked text or press F1 and the Access Help window opens with information about the button.
- Some dialog boxes and backstage areas contain a Help button you can click to display information specific to the dialog box or backstage area.

Commands Review

FEATURE	RIBBON TAB, GROUP	BUTTON, OPTION	KEYBOARD SHORTCUT
Access Help window			F1
align text left	HOME, Text Formatting		
align text right	HOME, Text Formatting		
alternate row color	HOME, Text Formatting		
background color	HOME, Text Formatting		
bold formatting	HOME, Text Formatting		
center text	HOME, Text Formatting		
delete field	TABLE TOOLS DESIGN, Tools		
Design view	HOME, Views OR TABLE TOOLS FIELDS, Views		

FEATURE	RIBBON TAB, GROUP	BUTTON, OPTION	KEYBOARD SHORTCUT
Find and Replace dialog box with Find tab selected	HOME, Find		Ctrl + F
Find and Replace dialog box with Replace tab selected	HOME, Find		Ctrl + H
font	HOME, Text Formatting	Calibri (Detail)	
font color	HOME, Text Formatting		
font size	HOME, Text Formatting	11	
gridlines	HOME, Text Formatting		
insert field	TABLE TOOLS DESIGN, Tools		
italic formatting	HOME, Text Formatting		
sort records ascending	HOME, Sort & Filter		
sort records descending	HOME, Sort & Filter		
spelling check	HOME, Records		F7
Total row	HOME, Records		
underline formatting	HOME, Text Formatting		

Concepts Check Test Your Knowledge

Completion: In the space provided at the right, indicate the correct term, symbol, or command.

1. The lower half of the work area in Design view that displays the properties for the active field is referred to as this. ____________________
2. When you create a new table in Design view, Access automatically assigns the first field the name *ID* and assigns this data type. ____________________
3. The description you type in the *Description* field displays in this location when the field is active in the table in Datasheet view. ____________________
4. Use this field property to set a pattern for how data is entered in a field. ____________________
5. Use this property box in Design view to enter a statement containing a conditional test that is checked each time data is entered into a field. ____________________

6. Use this wizard to confine the data entered in a field to a specific list of items. __________

7. To insert a new field in a table in Design view, click this button. __________

8. To insert a *Total* row in a table, click the Totals button in this group on the HOME tab. __________

9. The Ascending and Descending sort buttons are located in this group on the HOME tab. __________

10. Click this button to change the text size of data in a table. __________

11. Click this button to align all text in the active column in the center of the fields. __________

12. Click this button to specify a color for alternating rows in a table. __________

13. Use options at the Find and Replace dialog box with this tab selected to search for specific data and replace it with other data. __________

14. This is the keyboard shortcut to display the Access Help window. __________

Skills Check Assess Your Performance

Assessment 1

CREATE AN EMPLOYEES TABLE WITH THE INPUT MASK AND LOOKUP WIZARDS

1. Open Access and then create a new database by completing the following steps:
   a. At the Access 2013 opening screen, click the Blank desktop database template.
   b. Type **AL1-C4-Hudson** in the *File Name* text box.
   c. Click the Browse button.
   d. At the File New Database dialog box, navigate to the AL1C4 folder on your storage medium and then click OK.
   e. Click the Create button.
2. Create the Employees table in Design view as shown in Figure 4.14 with the following specifications:
   a. Limit the *EmpID* field size to 4 characters, the *FirstName* and *LastName* fields to 20 characters, and the *Address* field to 30 characters.
   b. Create a default value of *Pueblo* for the *City* field since most of the employees live in Pueblo.

Figure 4.14 Employees Table in Design View

Field Name	Data Type	Description
EmpID	Short Text	Enter four-digit employee identification number
FirstName	Short Text	Enter employee first name
LastName	Short Text	Enter employee last name
Address	Short Text	Enter employee street address
City	Short Text	Pueblo automatically inserted
State	Short Text	CO automatically inserted
ZIP	Short Text	Enter employee ZIP code
Telephone	Short Text	Enter employee telephone number
Status	Short Text	Click down-pointing arrow and then click employee status
HireDate	Date/Time	Enter employee hire date

c. Create a default value of *CO* for the *State* field, since all of the employees live in Colorado.

d. Create an input mask for the telephone number.

e. Use the Lookup Wizard to specify field choices for the *Status* field and include the following choices: *Full-time*, *Part-time*, *Temporary*, and *Contract*.

3. Save the table, switch to Datasheet view, and then enter the records as shown in Figure 4.15.
4. Adjust the column widths.
5. Save the table and then print it in landscape orientation.
6. Switch to Design view and then add a row immediately above the *FirstName* row. Type **Title** in the *Field Name* field, limit the field size to 20 characters, and type the description **Enter employee job title**.
7. Delete the *HireDate* field.
8. Move the *Status* field so it is positioned between the *EmpID* row and the *Title* row.
9. Save the table and then switch to Datasheet view.
10. Enter the following information in the *Title* field:

EmpID	Title	EmpID	Title
1466	**Design Director**	2301	**Assistant**
1790	**Assistant**	2440	**Assistant**
1947	**Resources Director**	3035	**Clerk**
1955	**Accountant**	3129	**Clerk**
1994	**Assistant**	3239	**Assistant**
2019	**Production Director**	4002	**Contractor**
2120	**Assistant**	4884	**Contractor**

11. Apply the following text formatting to the table:
    a. Change the font to Arial and the font size to 10 points.
    b. Center the data in the *EmpID* field column and the *State* field column.
    c. Apply the Aqua Blue 2 alternating row color (ninth column, third row in the *Standard Colors* section) to the table.
12. Adjust the column widths.
13. Save the table and then print it in landscape orientation with left and right margins of 0.5 inch.

Figure 4.15 Employees Table in Datasheet View

Employees

	EmpID	FirstName	LastName	Address	City	State	ZIP	Telephone	Status	HireDate	Click
	1466	Samantha	O'Connell	9105 Pike Avenue	Pueblo	CO	81011	(719) 555-7658	Full-time	8/15/2013	
	1790	Edward	Sorrell	9958 Franklin Avenue	Pueblo	CO	81006	(719) 555-3724	Full-time	11/15/2009	
	1947	Brandon	Byrne	102 Hudson Avenue	Pueblo	CO	81012	(719) 555-1202	Full-time	8/1/2011	
	1955	Leland	Hughes	4883 Caledonia Road	Pueblo	CO	81005	(719) 555-1211	Full-time	3/1/2013	
	1994	Rosa	Martinez	310 Graham Avenue	Pueblo	CO	81004	(719) 555-8394	Part-time	8/15/2010	
	2019	Jean	Perrault	123 Chinook Lake	Pueblo	CO	81012	(719) 555-4027	Full-time	11/15/2009	
	2120	Michael	Turek	5503 East 27th Street	Boone	CO	81025	(719) 555-5423	Full-time	3/15/2011	
	2301	Gregory	Nitsche	12055 East 18th Street	Pueblo	CO	81007	(719) 555-6657	Part-time	3/15/2010	
	2440	Bethany	Rosario	858 West 27th Street	Pueblo	CO	81012	(719) 555-9481	Part-time	2/15/2014	
	3035	Alia	Shandra	7740 West Second Street	Avondale	CO	81022	(719) 555-0059	Temporary	2/1/2013	
	3129	Gloria	Cushman	6590 East 14th Street	Pueblo	CO	81006	(719) 555-0332	Temporary	5/1/2015	
	3239	Rudolph	Powell	8874 Hood Avenue	Pueblo	CO	81008	(719) 555-2223	Temporary	4/1/2015	
	4002	Alice	Murray	4300 East 14th Street	Pueblo	CO	81003	(719) 555-4230	Contract	9/12/2009	
	4884	Simon	Banister	1022 Division Avenue	Boone	CO	81025	(719) 555-2378	Contract	5/15/2015	
*					Pueblo	CO					

14. Find all occurrences of *Director* and replace them with *Manager*. ***Hint: Position the insertion point in the first entry in the* Title *column and then display the Find and Replace dialog box. At the dialog box, change the* Match *option to* Any Part of Field.**
15. Find all occurrences of *Assistant* and replace them with *Associate*.
16. Save the table, print it in landscape orientation with left and right margins of 0.5 inch, and then close it.

Assessment 2

CREATE A PROJECTS TABLE

1. With **AL1-C4-Hudson.accdb** open, create a Projects table in Design view. Include the following fields (making sure the *ProjID* field is identified as the primary key) and create an appropriate description for each field:

Field Name	**Data Type**
ProjID	Short Text (field size = 4 characters)
EmpID	Short Text (field size = 4 characters)
BegDate	Date/Time
EndDate	Date/Time
EstCosts	Currency

2. Save the table, switch to Datasheet view, and then type the following data in the specified field:

ProjID	08-A	*ProjID*	08-B
EmpID	2019	*EmpID*	1466
BegDate	8/1/2015	*BegDate*	8/15/2015
EndDate	10/31/2015	*EndDate*	12/15/2015
EstCosts	$5,250.00	EstCosts	$2,000.00
ProjID	10-A	*ProjID*	10-B
EmpID	1947	*EmpID*	2019
BegDate	10/1/2015	*BegDate*	10/1/2015
EndDate	1/15/2016	*EndDate*	12/15/2015
EstCosts	$10,000.00	*EstCosts*	$3,500.00

ProjID	11-A	*ProjID*	11-B
EmpID	1466	*EmpID*	1947
BegDate	11/1/2015	*BegDate*	11/1/2015
EndDate	2/1/2016	*EndDate*	3/31/2016
EstCosts	$8,000.00	*EstCosts*	$12,000.00

3. Adjust the column widths.
4. Save, print, and then close the Projects table.

Assessment 3

CREATE AN EXPENSES TABLE WITH A VALIDATION RULE AND INPUT MASK

1. With **AL1-C4-Hudson.accdb** open, create an Expenses table in Design view. Include the following fields (making sure the *ItemID* field is identified as the primary key) and include an appropriate description for each field:

Field Name	Data Type
ItemID	AutoNumber
EmpID	Short Text (field size = 4 characters)
ProjID	Short Text (field size = 4 characters)
Amount	Currency (Type a condition in the *Validation Rule* property box that states the entry must be $500 or less. Type an appropriate error message in the *Validation Text* property box.)
DateSubmitted	Date/Time (Use the Input Mask to control the date so it is entered as a short date.)

2. Save the table, switch to Datasheet view, and then type the following data in the fields (recall that Access automatically fills in the *ItemID* field):

EmpID	1466	*EmpID*	2019
ProjID	08-B	*ProjID*	08-A
Amount	$245.79	*Amount*	$500.00
DateSubmitted	09/04/2015	*DateSubmitted*	09/10/2015
EmpID	4002	*EmpID*	1947
ProjID	08-B	*ProjID*	10-A
Amount	$150.00	*Amount*	$500.00
DateSubmitted	09/18/2015	*DateSubmitted*	10/03/2015
EmpID	2019	*EmpID*	1947
ProjID	10-B	*ProjID*	10-A
Amount	$487.25	*Amount*	$85.75
DateSubmitted	10/22/2015	*DateSubmitted*	10/24/2015
EmpID	1466	*EmpID*	1790
ProjID	08-B	*ProjID*	08-A
Amount	$175.00	*Amount*	$110.50
DateSubmitted	10/29/2015	*DateSubmitted*	10/30/2015
EmpID	2120	*EmpID*	1466
ProjID	10-A	*ProjID*	08-B
Amount	$75.00	*Amount*	$300.00
DateSubmitted	11/05/2015	*DateSubmitted*	11/07/2015
EmpID	1466	*EmpID*	2019
ProjID	11-A	*ProjID*	10-B
Amount	$75.00	*Amount*	$300.00
DateSubmitted	11/14/2015	*DateSubmitted*	11/19/2015

3. Adjust the column widths.
4. Insert a *Total* row with the following specifications:
   a. Click the Totals button in the Records group on the HOME tab.
   b. Click in the blank field in the *Amount* column in the *Total* row.
   c. Click the down-pointing arrow at the left side of the field and then click *Sum* at the drop-down list.
   d. Click in any other field.
5. Save, print, and then close the Expenses table.
6. Create a one-to-many relationship where *EmpID* in the Employees table is the "one" and *EmpID* in the Expenses table is the "many." (Enforce referential integrity and cascade fields and records.)
7. Create a one-to-many relationship where *EmpID* in the Employees table is the "one" and *EmpID* in the Projects table is the "many." (Enforce referential integrity and cascade fields and records.)
8. Create a one-to-many relationship where *ProjID* in the Projects table is the "one" and *ProjID* in the Expenses table is the "many." (Enforce referential integrity and cascade fields and records.)
9. Save the relationships, print the relationships, and then close the relationship report and the Relationships window.
10. Design and run a query that displays all full-time employees with the following specifications:
    a. Insert the Employees table in the query window.
    b. Insert the *EmpID*, *FirstName*, *LastName*, and *Status* fields.
    c. Click in the check box in the *Show* row field in the *EmpID* column to remove the check mark. (This hides the EmpID numbers in the query results.)
    d. Extract full-time employees.
    e. Save the query and name it *FTEmpsQuery*.
    f. Print and then close the query.
11. Design and run a query that displays projects managed by employee number 1947 with the following specifications:
    a. Insert the Employees table and Projects table in the query window.
    b. Insert the *EmpID*, *FirstName*, and *LastName* fields from the Employees table.
    c. Insert the *ProjID* field from the Projects table.
    d. Extract those projects managed by employee number 1947.
    e. Save the query and name it *ProjsManagedByEmp1947Query*.
    f. Print and then close the query.
12. Design and run a query that displays expense amounts over $250 and the employees submitting the expenses with the following specifications:
    a. Insert the Expenses table and Employees table in the query window.
    b. Insert the *ItemID*, *Amount*, and *DateSubmitted* fields from the Expenses table.
    c. Insert the *FirstName* and *LastName* fields from the Employees table.
    d. Hide the *ItemID* field in the query results by clicking in the check box in the *Show* row field in the *ItemID* column to remove the check mark.
    e. Extract those expense amounts over $250.
    f. Save the query and name it *ExpensesOver$250Query*.
    g. Print and then close the query.
13. Design and run a query that displays expenses submitted by employee number 1947 with the following specifications:
    a. Insert the Employees table and Expenses table in the query window.
    b. Insert the *EmpID*, *FirstName*, and *LastName* fields from the Employees table.
    c. Insert the *ProjID*, *Amount*, and *DateSubmitted* from the Expenses table.

d. Click in the check box in the *Show* row field in the *EmpID* column to remove the check mark. (This hides the EmpID numbers in the query results.)
e. Extract those expenses submitted by employee number 1947.
f. Save the query and name it *ExpSubmittedBy1947Query*.
g. Print and then close the query.

Assessment 4

EDIT THE EMPLOYEES TABLE

1. With **AL1-C4-Hudson.accdb** open, open the Employees table.
2. Display the table in Design view, click in the *ZIP* field row in the *Data Type* column, and then click in the *Input Mask* property box in the *Field Properties* section.
3. Use the Input Mask Wizard to create a nine-digit zip code input mask.
4. Save the table and then switch to Datasheet view.
5. Delete the records for employee number 3035 (Alia Shandra), employee number 3129 (Gloria Cushman), and employee number 4884 (Simon Banister).
6. Insert the following new records:

EmpID	**2286**	EmpID	**2970**
Status	**Full-time**	Status	**Full-time**
Title	**Associate**	Title	**Associate**
FirstName	**Erica**	FirstName	**Daniel**
LastName	**Bonari**	LastName	**Ortiz**
Address	**4850 55th Street**	Address	**12021 Cedar Lane**
City	(Pueblo automatically inserted)	City	(Pueblo automatically inserted)
State	(CO automatically inserted)	State	(CO automatically inserted)
ZIP	**81005-5002**	ZIP	**81011-1255**
Telephone	**(719) 555-1293**	Telephone	**(719) 555-0790**

7. Adjust the width of the *ZIP* column. (Only the two new records will contain the nine-digit zip code.)
8. Save the Employees table.
9. Display the table in Print Preview, change to landscape orientation, and then change the left and right margins to 0.5 inch. Print and then close the table.
10. Close **AL1-C4-Hudson.accdb**.

Visual Benchmark Demonstrate Your Proficiency

DESIGN AND FORMAT A QUERY

1. Open **AL1-C4-AlpineServices.accdb** from the AL1C4 folder on your storage medium and enable the contents.
2. Design and run the query that displays in Figure 4.16. (Make sure you include the calculated field to determine the order totals and the *Total* row.)
3. Change the font for the data in the query to 12-point Candara, add an alternating row color, and adjust column widths so your query displays in a manner similar to the query in Figure 4.16.
4. Save, print the query in landscape orientation, and then close the query.
5. Close **AL1-C4-AlpineServices.accdb**.

Figure 4.16 Visual Benchmark

OrderTotal

OrderDate	SupplierName	ProductID	UnitsOrdered	UnitPrice	Total
5/4/2015	Manning, Inc.	101-S2R	15	$129.95	1949.25
5/4/2015	Manning, Inc.	101-S3B	15	$119.95	1799.25
5/4/2015	Freedom Corporation	209-L	25	$6.95	173.75
5/4/2015	Freedom Corporation	209-XL	25	$7.20	180
5/4/2015	Freedom Corporation	209-XXL	20	$7.29	145.8
5/4/2015	Freedom Corporation	210-M	15	$6.49	97.35
5/4/2015	Freedom Corporation	210-L	25	$6.49	162.25
5/18/2015	Sound Supplies	299-M2	10	$88.79	887.9
5/18/2015	Sound Supplies	299-M3	10	$88.79	887.9
5/18/2015	Sound Supplies	299-M5	10	$88.79	887.9
5/18/2015	Sound Supplies	299-W1	8	$75.29	602.32
5/18/2015	Sound Supplies	299-W3	10	$75.29	752.9
5/18/2015	Sound Supplies	299-W4	10	$75.29	752.9
5/18/2015	Sound Supplies	299-W5	10	$75.29	752.9
5/18/2015	Emerald City Products	602-XR	5	$429.00	2145
Total				**$1,280.85**	**12177.37**

Case Study Apply Your Skills

Part 1

You work for Blue Ridge Enterprises and your supervisor has asked you to create a database with information about representatives and clients. Create a new database named **AL1-C4-BlueRidge.accdb** and then create a Representatives table with the following fields:

- Create a field for the representative identification number, change the data type to Short Text, and limit the field size to 3 characters. (This is the primary key field.)
- Create a field for the representative's first name and limit the field size to 20 characters.
- Create a field for the representative's last name and limit the field size to 20 characters.
- Create a field for the representative's telephone number and use the Input Mask Wizard.
- Create a field for the insurance plan and use the Lookup Wizard and include four options: *Platinum*, *Premium*, *Standard*, and *None*.
- Create a field for the yearly bonus amount, type a validation rule that states the bonus must be less than $10,001, and include an error message. (You determine the message.)

In Datasheet view, enter six records in the table. (You determine the data to enter.) When entering the data, make sure that at least two representatives will receive a yearly bonus over $5,000 and that at least two representatives are signed up for the *Platinum* insurance plan. Insert a *Total* row that sums the yearly bonus amounts. Change the font for the data in the table to Cambria, change the font size to 10 points, and apply a light green alternating row color. Center the data in the representative identification column. Adjust the column widths and then save the Representatives table. Print the table in landscape orientation and then close the table.

Part 2

With **AL1-C4-BlueRidge.accdb** open, create a second table named Clients (containing information on companies doing business with Blue Ridge Enterprises) with the following fields:

- Create a field for the client identification number and limit the field size to 2 characters. (This is the primary key field.)
- Create a field for the representative identification number (using the same field name you used in Part 1 in the Representatives table) and limit the field size to 3 characters.
- Create fields for the company name, address, city, state (or province), and zip (or postal code). Insert the city you live in as the default value for the city field and insert the two-letter state or province abbreviation where you live as the default value for the state or province field.
- Create a field for the client's telephone number and use the Input Mask.
- Create a field for the client's type of business and insert the word *Wholesaler* as the default value.

In Datasheet view, enter at least eight companies. (You determine the data to enter.) Make sure you use the representative identification numbers in the Clients table that match numbers in the Representatives table. Identify at least one company as a *Retailer*, rather than a *Wholesaler*, and make at least one representative represent two or more companies. Change the font for the data in the table to Cambria, change the font size to 10 points, and apply a light green alternating row color (the same color you chose in Part 1). Center the data in the client identification column, the representative identification column, and the state (or province) column. Adjust the column widths and then save the Clients table. Print the table in landscape orientation and then close the table.

Part 3

Create a one-to-many relationship with the representative identification number in the Representatives table as the "one" and the representative identification number in the Clients table as the "many." Save the relationship, print the relationships report, and then close the report without saving it.

Part 4

Your supervisor has asked you for specific information about representatives and clients. To provide answers to your supervisor, create and print the following queries:

- Create a query that extracts records of representatives earning a yearly bonus over $5,000. (You determine the fields to insert in the query window.) Save, print, and then close the query.
- Create a query that extracts records of representatives signed up for the Platinum insurance plan. (You determine the fields to insert in the query window.) Save, print, and then close the query.
- Create a query that extracts records of wholesale clients. (You determine the fields to insert in the query window.) Save, print, and then close the query.
- Create a query that extracts records of companies represented by a specific representative. (Use a representative identification number you entered in Part 2 that represents two or more companies.) Save, print, and then close the query.

UNIT 1

MICROSOFT® ACCESS® Performance Assessment

Note: The Student Resources CD does not include an Access Level 1, Unit 1 subfolder of files because no data files are required for the Unit 1 assessments. You will create all of the files yourself. Before beginning the assessments, create a folder for the new files and name it AL1U1.

Assessing Proficiency

In this unit, you have learned to design, create, and modify tables and to create one-to-many relationships and one-to-one relationships between tables. You have also learned how to perform queries on data in tables.

Assessment 1 Create Tables in a Cornerstone Catering Database

1. Use Access to create tables for Cornerstone Catering. Name the database **AL1-U1-Cornerstone**. Create a table named *Employees* that includes the following fields. If no data type is specified for a field, use the Short Text data type. You determine the field size and specify the same field size for a field that is contained in different tables. For example, if you specify a field size of 2 characters for the *EmployeeID* field in the Employees table, specify a field size of 2 characters for the *EmployeeID* field in the Events table. Provide a description for each field.

   EmployeeID (primary key)
   FirstName
   LastName
   CellPhone (Use the Input Mask Wizard for this field.)

2. After creating the table, switch to Datasheet view and then enter the following data in the appropriate fields:

EmployeeID	10	*EmployeeID*	14
FirstName	Erin	*FirstName*	Mikio
LastName	Jergens	*LastName*	Ogami
CellPhone	(505) 555-3193	*CellPhone*	(505) 555-1087
EmployeeID	19	*EmployeeID*	21
FirstName	Martin	*FirstName*	Isabelle
LastName	Vaughn	*LastName*	Baptista
CellPhone	(505) 555-4461	*CellPhone*	(505) 555-4425

EmployeeID 24
FirstName Shawn
LastName Kettering
CellPhone (505) 555-3885

EmployeeID 26
FirstName Madison
LastName Harris
CellPhone (505) 555-2256

EmployeeID 28
FirstName Victoria
LastName Lamesa
CellPhone (505) 555-6650

EmployeeID 30
FirstName Isaac
LastName Hobart
CellPhone (505) 555-7430

EmployeeID 32
FirstName Lester
LastName Franklin
CellPhone (505) 555-0440

EmployeeID 35
FirstName Manuela
LastName Harte
CellPhone (505) 555-1221

3. Change the font for data in the table to Cambria, change the font size to 10 points, and apply a light blue alternating row color. Center-align the data in the *EmployeeID* column.
4. Adjust the column widths.
5. Save, print, and then close the Employees table.
6. Create a table named *Plans* that includes the following fields:

   PlanCode (primary key)
   Plan

7. After creating the table, switch to Datasheet view and then enter the following data in the appropriate fields:

   PlanCode A
   Plan Sandwich Buffet

   PlanCode B
   Plan Cold Luncheon Buffet

   PlanCode C
   Plan: Hot Luncheon Buffet

   PlanCode D
   Plan Combination Dinner

   PlanCode E
   Plan: Vegetarian Luncheon Buffet

   PlanCode F
   Plan: Vegetarian Dinner Buffet

   PlanCode G
   Plan: Seafood Luncheon Buffet

   PlanCode H
   Plan Seafood Dinner Buffet

8. Change the font for data in the table to Cambria, change the font size to 10 points, and apply a light blue alternating row color. Center-align the data in the *PlanCode* column.
9. Adjust the column widths.
10. Save, print, and then close the Plans table.
11. Create a table named *Prices* that includes the following fields:

   PriceCode (primary key)
   PricePerPerson (Identify as the Currency data type.)

12. After creating the table, switch to Datasheet view and then enter the following data in the appropriate fields:

PriceCode	1	*PriceCode*	2
PricePerPerson	$11.50	*PricePerPerson*	$12.75
PriceCode	3	*PriceCode*	4
PricePerPerson	$14.50	*PricePerPerson*	$16.00
PriceCode	5	*PriceCode*	6
PricePerPerson	$18.50	*PricePerPerson*	$21.95

13. Change the font for data in the table to Cambria, change the font size to 10 points, and apply a light blue alternating row color. Center-align the data in both columns.
14. Adjust the column widths.
15. Save, print, and then close the Prices table.
16. Create a table named *Clients* that includes the following fields:

    ClientID (primary key)
    ClientName
    StreetAddress
    City
    State (Insert *NM* as the default value.)
    ZIP
    Telephone (Use the Input Mask Wizard for this field.)

17. After creating the table, switch to Datasheet view and then enter the following data in the appropriate fields:

ClientID	104	*ClientID*	155
ClientName	Sarco Corporation	*ClientName*	Creative Concepts
StreetAddress	340 Cordova Road	*StreetAddress*	1026 Market Street
City	Santa Fe	*City*	Los Alamos
State	NM	*State*	NM
ZIP	87510	*ZIP*	87547
Telephone	(505) 555-3880	*Telephone*	(505) 555-1200
ClientID	218	*ClientID*	286
ClientName	Allenmore Systems	*ClientName*	Sol Enterprises
StreetAddress	7866 Second Street	*StreetAddress*	120 Cerrillos Road
City	Espanola	*City*	Santa Fe
State	NM	*State*	NM
ZIP	87535	*ZIP*	87560
Telephone	(505) 555-3455	*Telephone*	(505) 555-7700
ClientID	295	*ClientID*	300
ClientName	Benson Productions	*ClientName*	Old Town Corporation
StreetAddress	555 Junction Road	*StreetAddress*	1035 East Adams Way
City	Santa Fe	*City*	Santa Fe
State	NM	*State*	NM
ZIP	87558	*ZIP*	87561
Telephone	(505) 555-8866	*Telephone*	(505) 555-2125

ClientID	305	*ClientID*	350
ClientName	Cromwell Company	*ClientName*	GH Manufacturing
StreetAddress	752 Rialto Way	*StreetAddress*	9550 Stone Road
City	Santa Fe	*City*	Los Alamos
State	NM	*State*	NM
ZIP	87512	*ZIP*	87547
Telephone	(505) 555-7500	*Telephone*	(505) 555-3388

18. Change the font for data in the table to Cambria, change the font size to 10 points, and apply a light blue alternating row color. Center-align the data in the *ClientID* column.
19. Adjust the column widths.
20. Save the table and then print it in landscape orientation.
21. Close the Clients table.
22. Create a table named *Events* that includes the following fields:

    EventID (primary key) (Identify as the AutoNumber data type.)
    ClientID
    EmployeeID
    DateOfEvent (Identify as the Date/Time data type.)
    PlanCode
    PriceCode
    NumberOfPeople (Identify as the Number data type.)

23. After creating the table, switch to Datasheet view and then enter the following data in the appropriate fields:

EventID	(AutoNumber)	*EventID*	(AutoNumber)
ClientID	218	*ClientID*	104
EmployeeID	14	*EmployeeID*	19
DateOfEvent	7/11/2015	*DateOfEvent*	7/12/2015
PlanCode	B	*PlanCode*	D
PriceCode	3	*PriceCode*	5
NumberOfPeople	250	*NumberOfPeople*	120

EventID	(AutoNumber)	*EventID*	(AutoNumber)
ClientID	155	*ClientID*	286
EmployeeID	24	*EmployeeID*	10
DateOfEvent	7/17/2015	*DateOfEvent*	7/18/2015
PlanCode	A	*PlanCode*	C
PriceCode	1	*PriceCode*	4
NumberOfPeople	300	*NumberOfPeople*	75

EventID	(AutoNumber)	*EventID*	(AutoNumber)
ClientID	218	*ClientID*	104
EmployeeID	14	*EmployeeID*	10
DateOfEvent	7/19/2015	*DateOfEvent*	7/22/2015
PlanCode	C	*PlanCode*	B
PriceCode	4	*PriceCode*	3
NumberOfPeople	50	*NumberOfPeople*	30

EventID	(AutoNumber)	*EventID*	(AutoNumber)
ClientID	305	*ClientID*	295
EmployeeID	30	*EmployeeID*	35
DateOfEvent	7/24/2015	*DateOfEvent*	7/25/2015
PlanCode	H	*PlanCode*	E
PriceCode	6	*PriceCode*	4
NumberOfPeople	150	*NumberOfPeople*	75

EventID	(AutoNumber)	*EventID*	(AutoNumber)
ClientID	300	*ClientID*	350
EmployeeID	32	*EmployeeID*	28
DateOfEvent	7/26/2015	*DateOfEvent*	7/30/2015
PlanCode	B	*PlanCode*	D
PriceCode	3	*PriceCode*	6
NumberOfPeople	200	*NumberOfPeople*	100

24. Change the font for data in the table to Cambria, change the font size to 10 points, and apply a light blue alternating row color. Center-align the data in all of the columns except the *DateOfEvent* column.
25. Adjust the column widths.
26. Save the table and then print it in landscape orientation.
27. Close the Events table.

Assessment 2 Create Relationships between Tables

1. With **AL1-U1-Cornerstone.accdb** open, create the following one-to-many relationships and enforce referential integrity:
   a. *ClientID* in the Clients table is the "one" and *ClientID* in the Events table is the "many."
   b. *EmployeeID* in the Employees table is the "one" and *EmployeeID* in the Events table is the "many."
   c. *PlanCode* in the Plans table is the "one" and *PlanCode* in the Events table is the "many."
   d. *PriceCode* in the Prices table is the "one" and *PriceCode* in the Events table is the "many."
2. Save and then print the relationships in landscape orientation.
3. Close the relationship report without saving it and then close the Relationships window.

Assessment 3 Modify Tables

1. With **AL1-U1-Cornerstone.accdb** open, open the Plans table in Datasheet view and then add the following record at the end of the table:

   PlanCode I
   Plan Hawaiian Luau Dinner Buffet

2. Adjust the column widths.
3. Save, print, and then close the Plans table.
4. Open the Events table in Datasheet view and then add the following record at the end of the table:

EventID	(AutoNumber)	*PlanCode*	I
ClientID	104	*PriceCode*	5
EmployeeID	21	*NumberOfPeople*	125
Date	7/31/2015		

5. Save, print (in landscape orientation), and then close the Events table.

Assessment 4 Design Queries

1. With **AL1-U1-Cornerstone.accdb** open, create a query to extract records from the Events table with the following specifications:
   a. Include the fields *ClientID*, *DateOfEvent*, and *PlanCode*.
   b. Extract those records with a PlanCode of C. (You will need to type "C" in the *Criteria* row.)
   c. Run the query.
   d. Save the query and name it *PlanCodeCQuery*.
   e. Print and then close the query.
2. Extract records from the Clients table with the following specifications:
   a. Include the fields *ClientName*, *City*, and *Telephone*.
   b. Extract those records with a city of Santa Fe.
   c. Run the query.
   d. Save the query and name it *SantaFeClientsQuery*.
   e. Print and then close the query.
3. Extract information from two tables with the following specifications:
   a. From the Clients table, include the fields *ClientName* and *Telephone*.
   b. From the Events table, include the fields *DateOfEvent*, *PlanCode*, and *NumberOfPeople*.
   c. Extract those records with dates between July 1, 2015, and July 15, 2015.
   d. Run the query.
   e. Save the query and name it *July1-15EventsQuery*.
   f. Print and then close the query.

Assessment 5 Design a Query with a Calculated Field Entry

1. With **AL1-U1-Cornerstone.accdb** open, create a query in Design view with the Events table and Prices table and insert the following fields in the specified locations:
   a. Insert *EventID* from the Events table to the first *Field* row field.
   b. Insert *DateOfEvent* from the Events table to the second *Field* row field.
   c. Insert *NumberOfPeople* from the Events table to the third *Field* row field.
   d. Insert *PricePerPerson* from the Prices table to the fourth *Field* row field.
2. Insert the following calculated field entry in the fifth *Field* row field: *Amount: [NumberOfPeople]*[PricePerPerson]*.

3. Run the query.
4. Save the query and name it *EventAmountsQuery*.
5. Print and then close the query.

Assessment 6 Design a Query with Aggregate Functions

1. With **AL1-U1-Cornerstone.accdb** open, create a query in Design view using EventAmountsQuery with the following specifications:
   a. Click the CREATE tab and then click the Query Design button.
   b. At the Show Tables dialog box, click the Queries tab.
   c. Double-click *EventAmountsQuery* in the list box and then click the Close button.
   d. Insert the *Amount* field in the first, second, third, and fourth *Field* row field.
   e. Click the Totals button in the Show/Hide group.
   f. Insert *Sum* in the first *Total* row field.
   g. Insert *Avg* in the second *Total* row field.
   h. Insert *Min* in the third *Total* row field.
   i. Insert *Max* in the fourth *Total* row field.
2. Run the query.
3. Automatically adjust the column widths.
4. Save the query and name it *AmountTotalsQuery*.
5. Print and then close the query.

Assessment 7 Design a Query Using Fields from Tables and a Query

1. With **AL1-U1-Cornerstone.accdb** open, create a query in Design view using the Employees table, Clients table, Events table, and EventAmountsQuery with the following specifications:
   a. Click the CREATE tab and then click the Query Design button.
   b. At the Show Tables dialog box, double-click *Employees*.
   c. Double-click *Clients*.
   d. Double-click *Events*.
   e. Click the Queries tab, double-click *EventAmountsQuery* in the list box, and then click the Close button.
   f. Insert the *LastName* field from the *Employees* field list box to the first *Field* row field.
   g. Insert the *ClientName* field from the *Clients* field list box to the second *Field* row field.
   h. Insert the *Amount* field from *EventAmountsQuery* field list box to the third *Field* row field.
   i. Insert the *DateOfEvent* field from the *Events* field list box to the fourth *Field* row field.
2. Run the query.
3. Save the query and name it *EmployeeEventsQuery*.
4. Close the query.
5. Using the Crosstab Query Wizard, create a query that summarizes the total event amounts by employee by client using the following specifications:
   a. At the first Crosstab Query Wizard dialog box, click the *Queries* option in the *View* section and then click *Query: EmployeeEventsQuery* in the list box.
   b. At the second Crosstab Query Wizard dialog box, click *LastName* in the *Available Fields* list box and then click the One Field button.

c. At the third Crosstab Query Wizard dialog box, make sure *ClientName* is selected in the list box.
d. At the fourth Crosstab Query Wizard dialog box, make sure *Amount* is selected in the *Fields* list box and then click *Sum* in the *Functions* list box.
e. At the fifth Crosstab Query Wizard dialog box, type AmountsByEmployeeByClientQuery in the *What do you want to name your query?* text box.

6. Automatically adjust the column widths.
7. Print the query in landscape orientation and then close the query.

Assessment 8 Use the Find Duplicates Query Wizard

1. With **AL1-U1-Cornerstone.accdb** open, use the Find Duplicates Query Wizard to find employees who are responsible for at least two events with the following specifications:
   a. At the first wizard dialog box, double-click *Table: Events* in the list box.
   b. At the second wizard dialog box, click *EmployeeID* in the *Available fields* list box and then click the One Field button.
   c. At the third wizard dialog box, move the *DateOfEvent* field and the *NumberOfPeople* field from the *Available fields* list box to the *Additional query fields* list box.
   d. At the fourth wizard dialog box, name the query *DuplicateEventsQuery*.
2. Print and then close the query.

Assessment 9 Use the Find Unmatched Query Wizard

1. With **AL1-U1-Cornerstone.accdb** open, use the Find Unmatched Query Wizard to find employees who do not have upcoming events scheduled with the following specifications:
   a. At the first wizard dialog box, click *Table: Employees* in the list box.
   b. At the second wizard dialog box, click *Table: Events* in the list box.
   c. At the third wizard dialog box, make sure *EmployeeID* is selected in the *Fields in 'Employees'* list box and in the *Fields in 'Events'* list box.
   d. At the fourth wizard dialog box, click the All Fields button to move all fields from the *Available fields* list box to the *Selected fields* list box.
   e. At the fifth wizard dialog box, click the Finish button. (Let the wizard determine the query name: *Employees Without Matching Events*.)
2. Print and then close the *Employees Without Matching Events* query.

Writing Activities

The following activity gives you the opportunity to practice your writing skills along with demonstrating an understanding of some of the important Access features you have mastered in this unit. Use correct grammar, appropriate word choices, and clear sentence constructions.

Create a Payroll Table and Word Report

The manager of Cornerstone Catering has asked you to add information to the **AL1-U1-Cornerstone.accdb** database on employee payroll. You need to create another table that will contain information on payroll. The manager wants the table to include the following information (you determine the appropriate field name, data type, field size, and description):

Employee Number	10	*Employee Number*	14
Status	Full-time	*Status*	Part-time
Monthly Salary	$2,850	*Monthly Salary*	$1,500
Employee Number	19	*Employee Number*	21
Status	Part-time	*Status*	Full-time
Monthly Salary	$1,400	*Monthly Salary*	$2,500
Employee Number	24	*Employee Number*	26
Status	Part-time	*Status*	Part-time
Monthly Salary	$1,250	*Monthly Salary*	$1,000
Employee number	28	*Employee number*	30
Status	Full-time	*Status*	Part-time
Monthly salary	$2,500	*Monthly salary*	$3,000
Employee number	32	*Employee number*	35
Status	Full-time	*Status*	Full-time
Monthly salary	$2,300	*Monthly salary*	$2,750

Print and then close the payroll table. Open Word and then write a report to the manager detailing how you created the table. Include a title for the report, steps on how the table was created, and any other pertinent information. Save the completed report and name it **AL1-U1-Act01-TableRpt**. Print and then close **AL1-U1-Act01-TableRpt.docx** and then close Word.

Internet Research

Vehicle Search

In this activity, you will search the Internet for information on different vehicles before doing actual test drives. Learning about a major product, such as a vehicle, can increase your chances of finding a good buy, potentially guide you away from making a poor purchase, and help speed up the process of narrowing the search to the type of vehicle that will meet your needs. Before you begin, list the top five criteria you would look for in a vehicle. For example, it must be a four-door vehicle, needs to be four-wheel drive, and so on.

Using key search words, find at least two websites that provide vehicle reviews. Use the search engines provided within the different review sites to find vehicles that fulfill the criteria you listed. Create a database in Access and create a table in that database that will contain the results from your vehicle search. Design the table to accommodate the types of data you need to record for each vehicle that meets your requirements. Include at least the make, model, year, price, description, and special problems in the table. Also include the ability to rate the vehicle as poor, fair, good, or excellent. You will decide on the rating of each vehicle depending on your findings. Print the table you created and then close the database.

MICROSOFT®

ACCESS®

Level 1

Unit 2 ■ Creating Forms and Reports

Chapter 5 ■ Creating Forms

Chapter 6 ■ Creating Reports and Mailing Labels

Chapter 7 ■ Modifying, Filtering, and Viewing Data

Chapter 8 ■ Exporting and Importing Data

MICROSOFT®

ACCESS®

Creating Forms

PERFORMANCE OBJECTIVES

Upon successful completion of Chapter 5, you will be able to:

- **Create a form using the Form button**
- **Change views in a form**
- **Print and navigate in a form**
- **Add records to and delete records from a form**
- **Create a form with a related table**
- **Customize a form**
- **Create a split form and multiple items form**
- **Create a form using the Form Wizard**

Tutorials

5.1 Creating a Form Using the Form Button

5.2 Navigating in a Form

5.3 Adding Records in a Form

5.4 Creating a Form with a Related Table

5.5 Managing Control Objects

5.6 Adding Control Objects

5.7 Formatting a Form

5.8 Applying Conditional Formatting to a Form

5.9 Adding Fields to a Form from Another Table

5.10 Creating a Split Form and Multiple Items Form

In this chapter, you will learn how to create forms from database tables, improving the data display and making data entry easier. Access offers several methods for presenting data on the screen for easier data entry. You will create a form using the Form button, create a split form and multiple items form, and use the Form Wizard to create a form. You will also learn how to customize control objects in a form and insert control objects and fields in a form. Model answers for this chapter's projects appear on the following pages.

Note: Before beginning the projects, copy to your storage medium the AL1C5 subfolder from the AL1 folder on the CD that accompanies this textbook and make AL1C5 the active folder.

Project 1 Create Forms with the Form Button

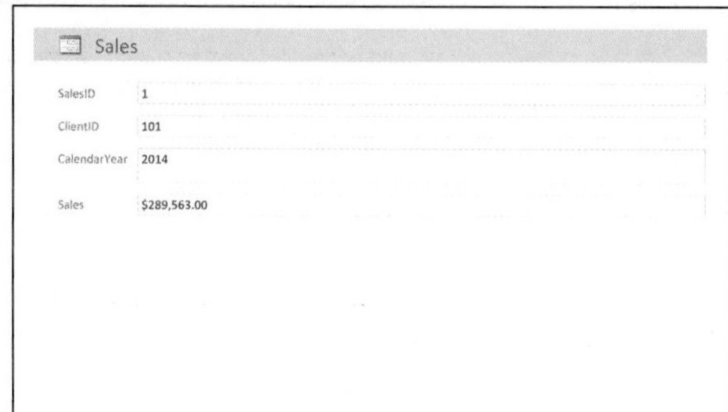

Sales

SalesID 1
ClientID 101
CalendarYear 2014
Sales $289,563.00

Project 1a, Dearborn Clients Form

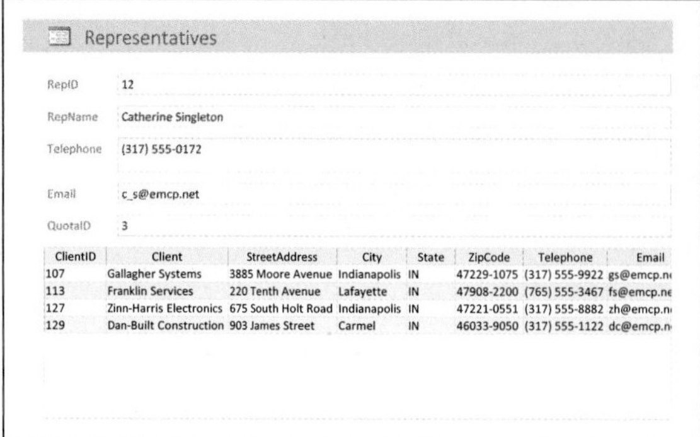

Representatives

RepID 12
RepName Catherine Singleton
Telephone (317) 555-0172
Email c_s@emcp.net
QuotaID 3

ClientID	Client	StreetAddress	City	State	ZipCode	Telephone	Email
107	Gallagher Systems	3885 Moore Avenue	Indianapolis	IN	47229-1075	(317) 555-9922	gs@emcp.n
113	Franklin Services	220 Tenth Avenue	Lafayette	IN	47908-2200	(765) 555-3467	fs@emcp.ne
127	Zinn-Harris Electronics	675 South Holt Road	Indianapolis	IN	47221-0551	(317) 555-8882	zh@emcp.n
129	Dan-Built Construction	903 James Street	Carmel	IN	46033-9050	(317) 555-1122	dc@emcp.n

Project 1c, Dearborn Representatives Form

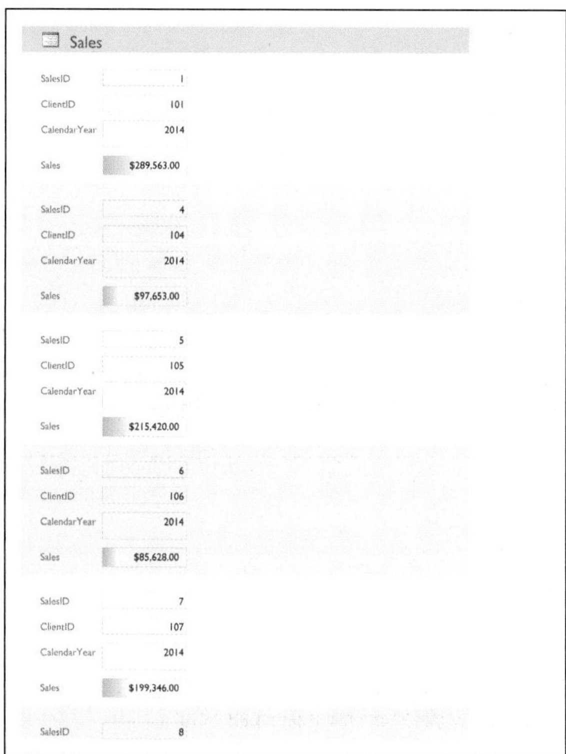

Sales

SalesID 1
ClientID 101
CalendarYear 2014
Sales $289,563.00

SalesID 4
ClientID 104
CalendarYear 2014
Sales $97,653.00

SalesID 5
ClientID 105
CalendarYear 2014
Sales $215,420.00

SalesID 6
ClientID 106
CalendarYear 2014
Sales $85,628.00

SalesID 7
ClientID 107
CalendarYear 2014
Sales $199,346.00

SalesID 8

Project 1g, Dearborn Sales Form

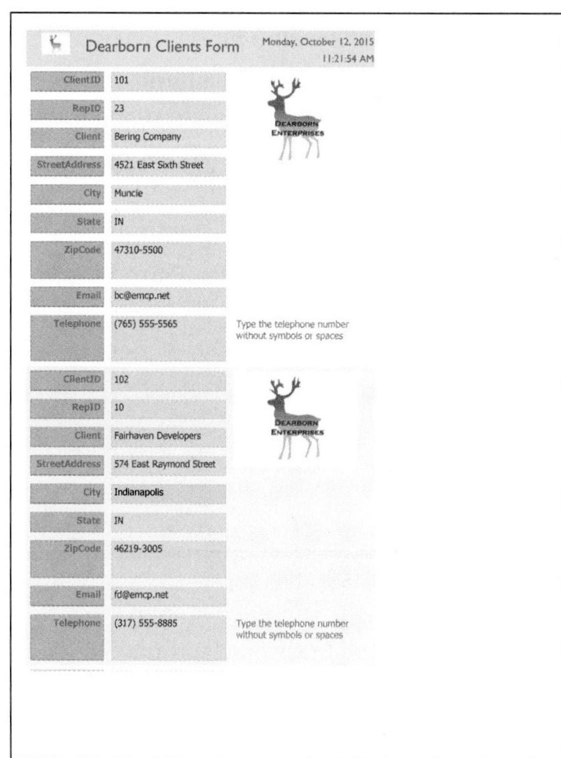

Dearborn Clients Form

Monday, October 12, 2015
11:21:54 AM

ClientID 101
RepID 23
Client Bering Company
StreetAddress 4521 East Sixth Street
City Muncie
State IN
ZipCode 47310-5500
Email bc@emcp.net
Telephone (765) 555-5565 Type the telephone number without symbols or spaces

ClientID 102
RepID 10
Client Fairhaven Developers
StreetAddress 574 East Raymond Street
City Indianapolis
State IN
ZipCode 46219-3005
Email fd@emcp.net
Telephone (317) 555-8885 Type the telephone number without symbols or spaces

Project 1g, Dearborn Clients Form

Project 2 Add Fields, Create a Split Form and Multiple Items Form, and Use the Form Wizard

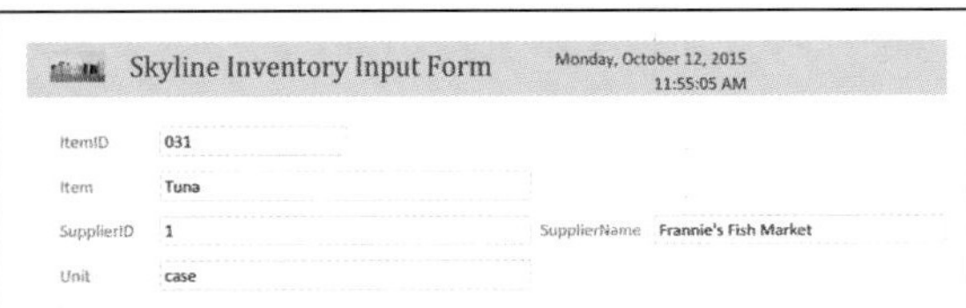

Project 2a, Skyline Inventory Form

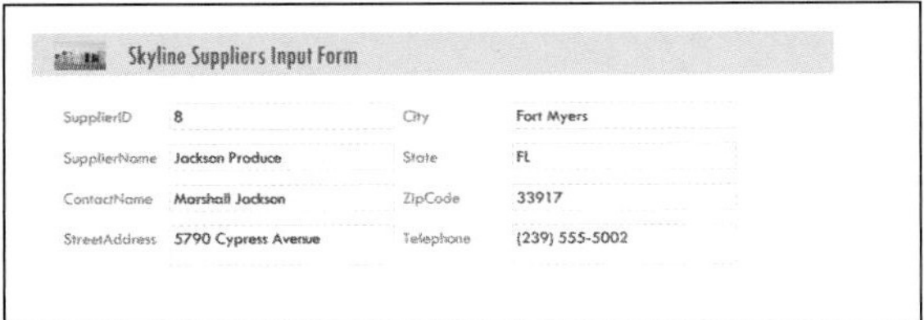

Project 2b, Skyline Suppliers Form

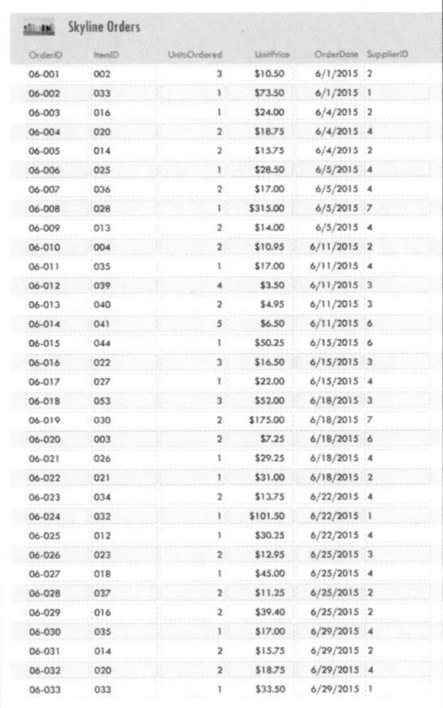

Skyline Orders

OrderID	ItemID	UnitsOrdered	UnitPrice	OrderDate	SupplierID
06-001	002	3	$10.50	6/1/2015	2
06-002	033	1	$73.50	6/1/2015	1
06-003	016	1	$24.00	6/4/2015	2
06-004	020	2	$18.75	6/4/2015	4
06-005	014	2	$15.75	6/4/2015	2
06-006	025	1	$28.50	6/5/2015	4
06-007	036	2	$17.00	6/5/2015	4
06-008	028	1	$315.00	6/5/2015	7
06-009	013	2	$14.00	6/5/2015	4
06-010	004	2	$10.95	6/11/2015	2
06-011	035	1	$17.00	6/11/2015	4
06-012	039	4	$3.50	6/11/2015	3
06-013	040	2	$4.95	6/11/2015	3
06-014	041	5	$6.50	6/11/2015	6
06-015	044	1	$50.25	6/15/2015	6
06-016	022	3	$16.50	6/15/2015	3
06-017	027	1	$22.00	6/15/2015	4
06-018	053	3	$52.00	6/18/2015	3
06-019	030	2	$175.00	6/18/2015	7
06-020	003	2	$7.25	6/18/2015	6
06-021	026	1	$29.25	6/18/2015	4
06-022	021	1	$31.00	6/18/2015	2
06-023	034	2	$13.75	6/22/2015	4
06-024	032	1	$101.50	6/22/2015	1
06-025	012	1	$30.25	6/22/2015	4
06-026	023	2	$12.95	6/25/2015	3
06-027	018	1	$45.00	6/25/2015	4
06-028	037	2	$11.25	6/25/2015	2
06-029	016	2	$39.40	6/25/2015	2
06-030	035	1	$17.00	6/29/2015	4
06-031	014	2	$15.75	6/29/2015	2
06-032	020	2	$18.75	6/29/2015	4
06-033	033	1	$33.50	6/29/2015	1

Project 2c, Skyline Orders Form

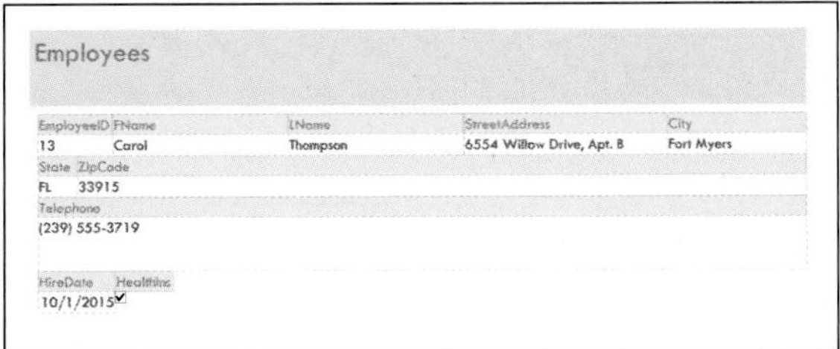

Project 2d, Skyline Employees Form, Carol Thompson

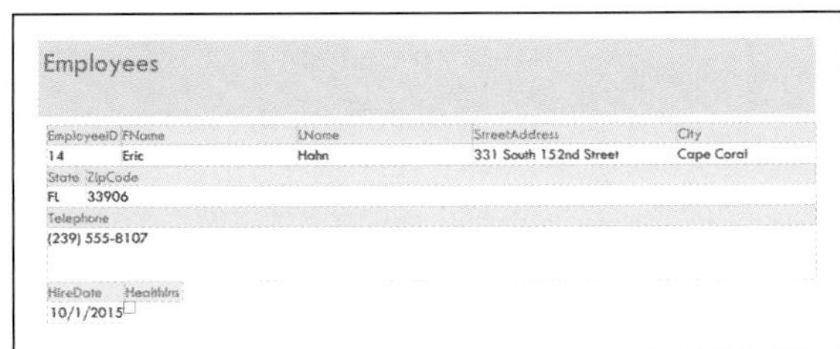

Project 2d, Skyline Employees Form, Eric Hahn

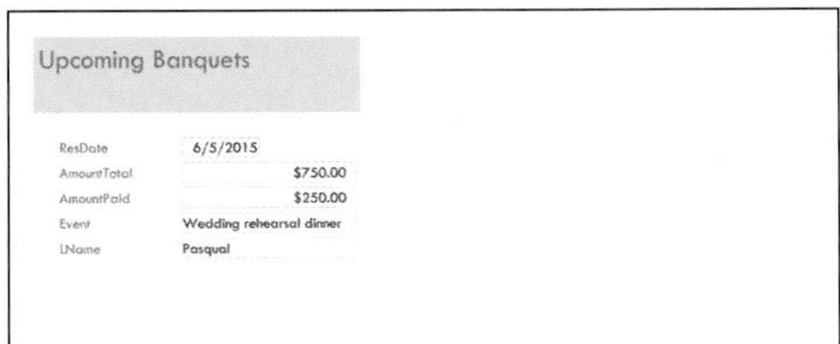

Project 2e, Skyline Upcoming Banquets Form

Project 1 Create Forms with the Form Button — 7 Parts

You will use the Form button to create forms with fields in the Clients, Representatives, and Sales tables. You will also add, delete, and print records and use buttons in the FORM LAYOUT TOOLS FORMAT tab to apply formatting to control objects in the forms.

Creating Forms

HINT

A form allows you to focus on a single record at a time.

Save a form before making changes or applying formatting to it.

Access offers a variety of options for presenting data in a clear and attractive format. For instance, you can view, add, or edit data in a table in Datasheet view. When you enter data in a table in Datasheet view, you will see multiple records at the same time. If a record contains several fields, you may not be able to view all of the fields within the record at the same time. If you create a form, however, all of the fields for a record are generally visible on the screen.

A *form* is an object you can use to enter and edit data in a table or query. It is a user-friendly interface for viewing, adding, editing, and deleting records. A form is also useful in helping to prevent incorrect data from being entered and it can be used to control access to specific data.

Several methods are available for creating forms. In this chapter, you will learn how to create forms using the Form, Split Form, and Multiple Items buttons as well as the Form Wizard.

Creating a Form with the Form Button

Quick Steps

Create a Form with the Form Button
1. Click desired table.
2. Click CREATE tab.
3. Click Form button.

The simplest method for creating a form is to click a table in the Navigation pane, click the CREATE tab, and then click the Form button in the Forms groups. Figure 5.1 shows the form you will create in Project 1a with the Sales table in AL1-C5-Dearborn.accdb. Access creates the form using all fields in the table in a vertical layout and displays the form in Layout view with the FORM LAYOUT TOOLS DESIGN tab active.

Changing Views

Form

Form View

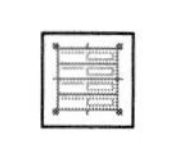

Layout View

When you click the Form button to create a form, the form displays in Layout view. This is one of three views for working with forms. Use the Form view to enter and manage records. Use the Layout view to view the data and modify the appearance and contents of the form. Use the Design view to view the structure of the form and modify the form. Change views with the View button in the Views group on the FORM LAYOUT TOOLS DESIGN tab or with buttons in the view area located at the right side of the Status bar.

You can open an existing form in Layout view. To do this, right-click the form name in the Navigation pane and then click *Layout View* at the shortcut menu.

Printing a Form

Print all of the records in a form by clicking the FILE tab, clicking the *Print* option, and then clicking the Quick Print button. If you want to print a specific record in a form, click the FILE tab, click the *Print* option, and then click the Print button.

Figure 5.1 Form Created from Data in the Sales Table

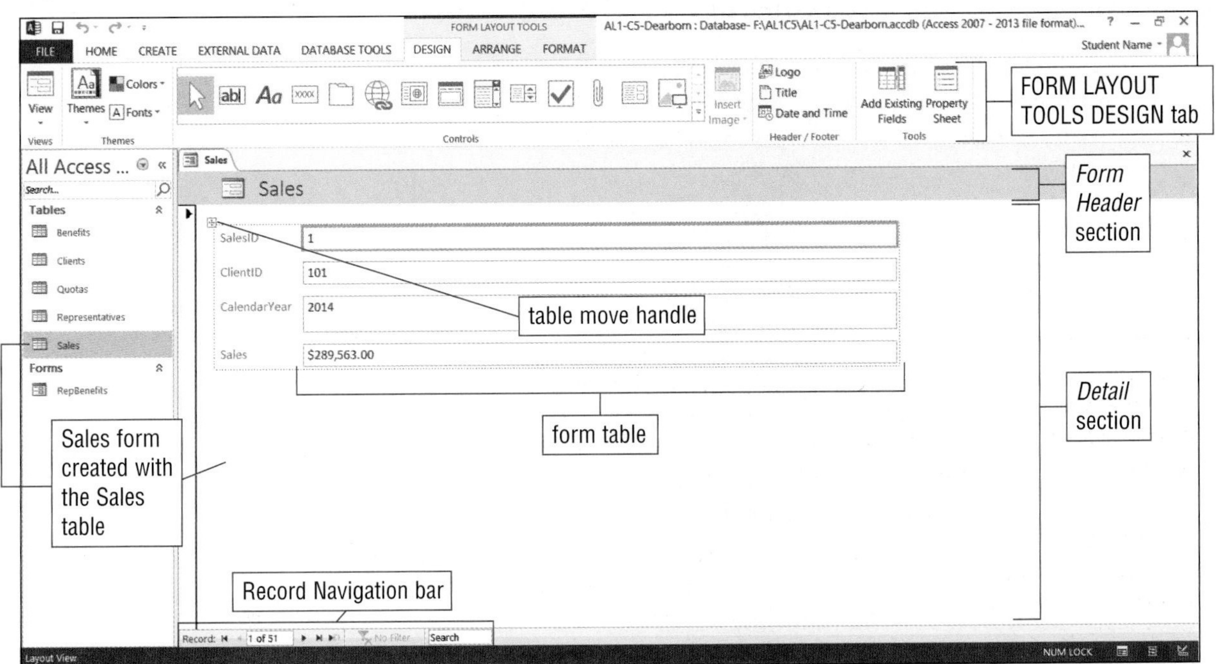

At the Print dialog box that displays, click the *Selected Record(s)* option and then click OK. You can also print a range of records by clicking the *Pages* option in the *Print Range* section of the Print dialog box and then entering the beginning record number in the *From* text box and the ending record number in the *To* text box.

Quick Steps

Print a Specific Record

1. Display form.
2. Click FILE tab.
3. Click *Print* option.
4. Click Print button.
5. Click *Selected Record(s).*
6. Click OK.

Deleting a Form

If you no longer need a form in a database, delete the form. Delete a form by clicking the form name in the Navigation pane, clicking the Delete button in the Records group on the HOME tab, and then clicking the Yes button at the message asking if you want to permanently delete the form. Another method is to right-click the form name in the Navigation pane, click *Delete* at the shortcut menu, and then click Yes at the message. If you are deleting a form from your computer's hard drive, the message asking if you want to permanently delete the form will not display. This is because Access automatically sends the deleted form to the Recycle Bin, where it can be retrieved if necessary.

Navigating in a Form

When a form displays in Form view or Layout view, navigation buttons display along the bottom of the form in the Record Navigation bar, as identified in Figure 5.1. Use these navigation buttons to display the first, previous, next, or last record in the form or add a new record. Navigate to a specific record by clicking in the *Current Record* box, selecting the current number, typing the number of the record you want to view, and then pressing Enter. You can also navigate using the keyboard. Press the Page Down key to move forward or press the Page Up key to move back a single record. Press Ctrl + Home to display the first record or Press Ctrl + End to display the last record.

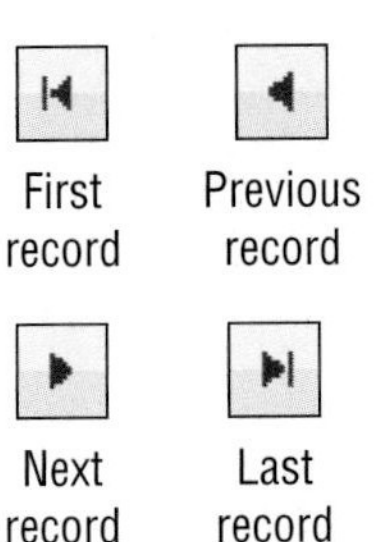

Project 1a Creating a Form with the Sales Table and Deleting a Form Part 1 of 7

1. Display the Open dialog box with the AL1C5 folder on your storage medium the active folder.
2. Open **AL1-C5-Dearborn.accdb** and enable the contents.
3. Create a form with the Sales table by completing the following steps:
   a. Click the Sales table in the Tables group in the Navigation pane.
   b. Click the CREATE tab.
   c. Click the Form button in the Forms group.
4. Switch to Form view by clicking the View button in the Views group on the FORM LAYOUT TOOLS DESIGN tab.
5. Navigate in the form by completing the following steps:
   a. Click the Next record button in the Record Navigation bar to display the next record.
   b. Click in the *Current Record* box, select any numbers that display, type 15, and then press Enter.
   c. Click the First record button in the Record Navigation bar to display the first record.
6. Save the form by completing the following steps:
   a. Click the Save button on the Quick Access toolbar.
   b. At the Save As dialog box, with *Sales* inserted in the *Form Name* text box, click OK.
7. Print the current record in the form by completing the following steps:
   a. Click the FILE tab and then click the *Print* option.
   b. Click the Print button.
   c. At the Print dialog box, click the *Selected Record(s)* option in the *Print Range* section and then click OK.
8. Close the Sales form.
9. Delete the RepBenefits form by right-clicking *RepBenefits* in the Navigation pane, clicking *Delete* at the shortcut menu, and then clicking Yes at the message asking if you want to permanently delete the form.

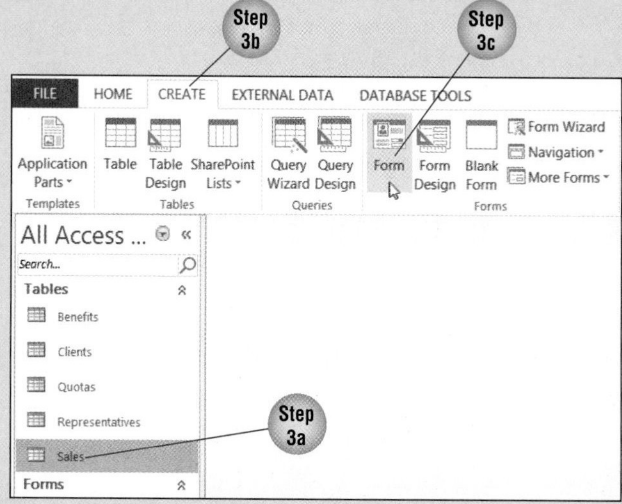

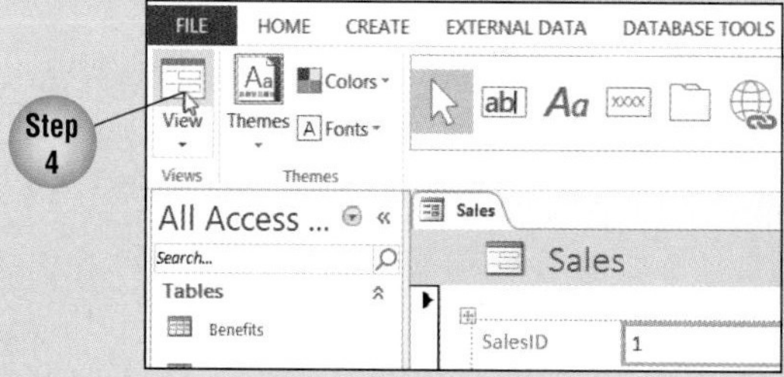

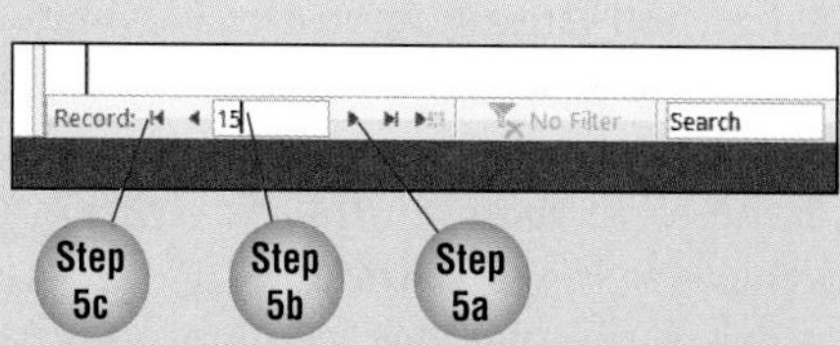

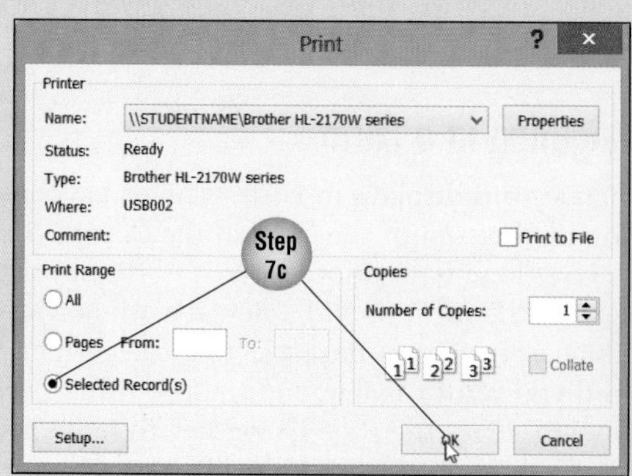

Adding and Deleting Records

Add a new record to the form by clicking the New (blank) record button (contains a right-pointing arrow and a yellow asterisk) that displays on the Record Navigation bar along the bottom of the form. You can also add a new record to a form by clicking the HOME tab and then clicking the New button in the Records group. To delete a record, display the record, click the HOME tab, click the Delete button arrow in the Records group, and then click *Delete Record* at the drop-down list. At the message telling you that the record will be deleted permanently, click Yes. Add records to or delete records from the table from which the form was created and the form will reflect the additions or deletions. Also, if you make additions or deletions to the form, the changes are reflected in the table on which the form was created.

Quick Steps

Add a Record
Click New (blank) record button on Record Navigation bar.
OR
1. Click HOME tab.
2. Click New button.

Delete a Record
1. Click HOME tab.
2. Click Delete button arrow.
3. Click *Delete Record.*
4. Click Yes.

New (blank) record

Delete

Sorting Records

Sort data in a form by clicking in the field containing data on which you want to sort and then clicking the Ascending button or Descending button in the Sort & Filter group on the HOME tab. Click the Ascending button to sort text in alphabetic order from A to Z or numbers from lowest to highest or click the Descending button to sort text in alphabetic order from Z to A or numbers from highest to lowest.

Project 1b **Adding and Deleting Records in a Form** **Part 2 of 7**

1. Open the Sales table (not the form) and add a new record by completing the following steps:
   a. Click the New (blank) record button located in the Record Navigation bar.

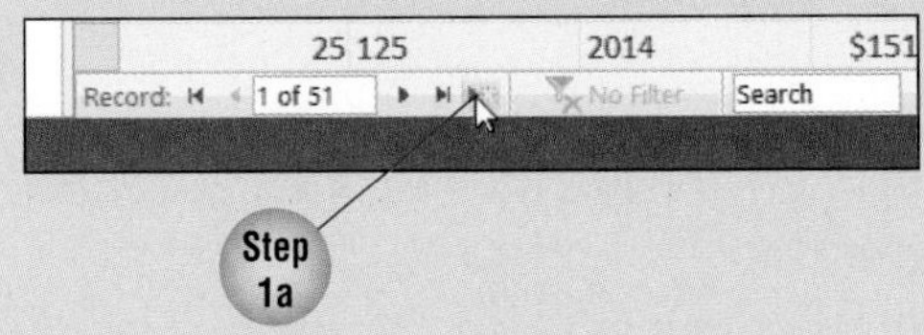

Step 1a

   b. At the new blank record, type the following information in the specified fields. (Move to the next field by pressing Tab or Enter; move to the previous field by pressing Shift + Tab.)

SalesID	(This is an AutoNumber field, so press Tab.)
ClientID	127
CalendarYear	2015
Sales	176420

2. Close the Sales table.
3. Open the Sales form.
4. Click the Last record button on the Record Navigation bar and notice that the new record you added to the table has been added to the form.

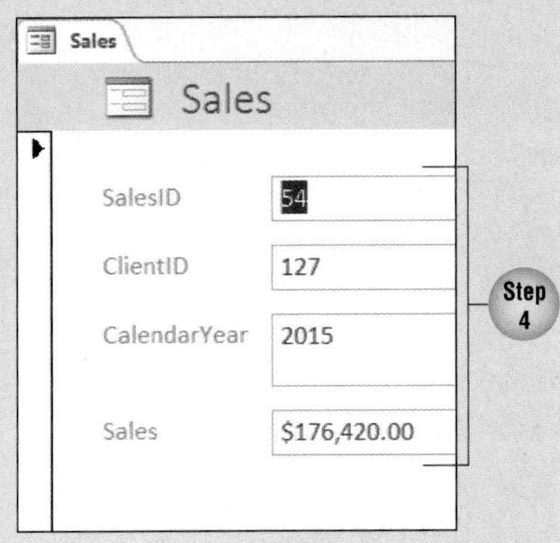

Step 4

5. Delete the second record (sales ID 3) in the form by completing the following steps:
   a. Click the First record button in the Record Navigation bar.
   b. Click the Next record button in the Record Navigation bar.
   c. With Record 2 active, click the Delete button arrow in the Records group on the HOME tab and then click *Delete Record* at the drop-down list.

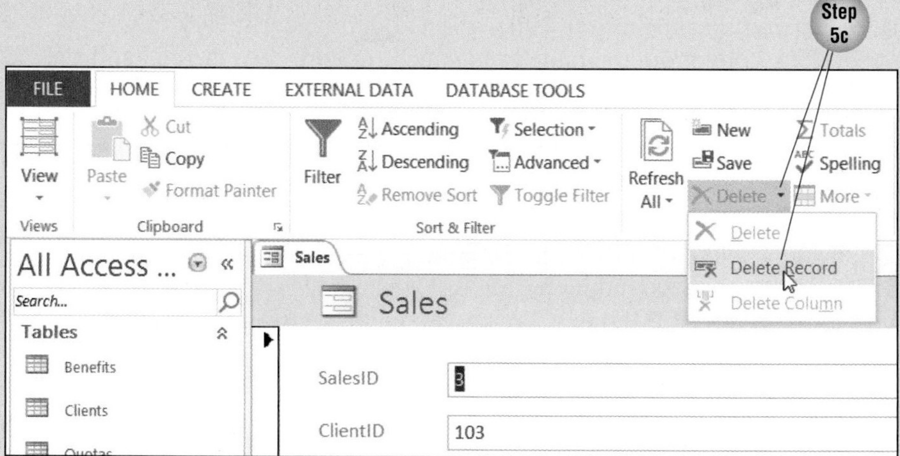

   d. At the message that displays telling you that you will not be able to undo the deletion, click the Yes button.
6. Click the New (blank) record button in the Record Navigation bar and then type the following information in the specified fields:

SalesID	(Press Tab.)
ClientID	103
CalendarYear	2014
Sales	110775

7. Sort the records in the form by completing the following steps:
   a. Click in the field containing the data *103* and then click the Ascending button in the Sort & Filter group on the HOME tab.
   b. Click in the field containing the data *$289,563.00* and then click the Descending button in the Sort & Filter group.
   c. Click in the field containing the data *36* and then click the Ascending button in the Sort & Filter group.
8. Close the Sales form.

Creating a Form with a Related Table

When you created the form with the Sales table, only the Sales table fields displayed in the form. If you create a form with a table that has a one-to-many relationship established, Access adds a datasheet to the form that is based on the related table.

For example, in Project 1c, you will create a form with the Representatives table, and since it is related to the Clients table by a one-to-many relationship, Access inserts a datasheet at the bottom of the form containing all of the records in the Clients table. Figure 5.2 displays the form you will create in Project 1c. Notice the datasheet that displays at the bottom of the form.

If you have created only a single one-to-many relationship, the datasheet for the related table displays in the form. If you have created multiple one-to-many relationships in a table, Access will not display any datasheets when you create a form with the table.

Figure 5.2 Representatives Form with Clients Datasheet

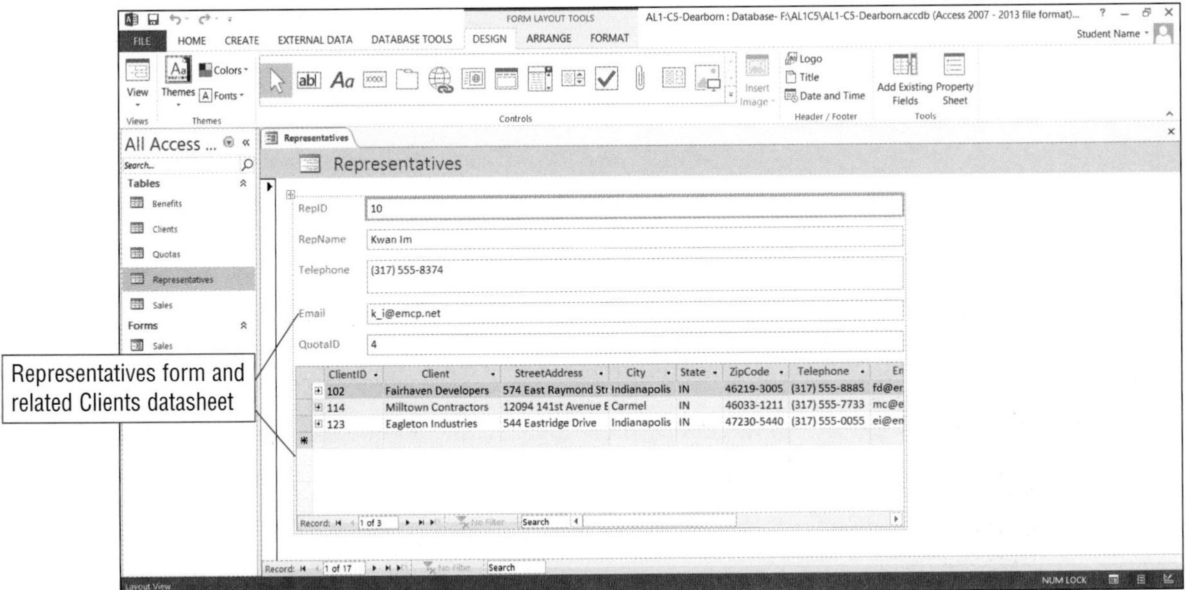

Project 1c Creating a Form with a Related Table

Part 3 of 7

1. With **AL1-C5-Dearborn.accdb** open, create a form with the Representatives table by completing the following steps:
   a. Click the Representatives table in the Navigation pane.
   b. Click the CREATE tab.
   c. Click the Form button in the Forms group.
2. Insert a new record in the Clients table for representative 12 (Catherine Singleton) by completing the following steps:
   a. Click twice on the Next record button in the Record Navigation bar at the bottom of the form window (not the Record Navigation bar in the Clients datasheet) to display the record for Catherine Singleton.
   b. Click in the cell immediately below *127* in the *ClientID* field in the Clients datasheet.

c. Type the following information in the specified fields:

ClientID	**129**
Client	**Dan-Built Construction**
StreetAddress	**903 James Street**
City	**Carmel**
State	**IN**
ZipCode	**460339050**
Telephone	**3175551122**
Email	**dc@emcp.net**

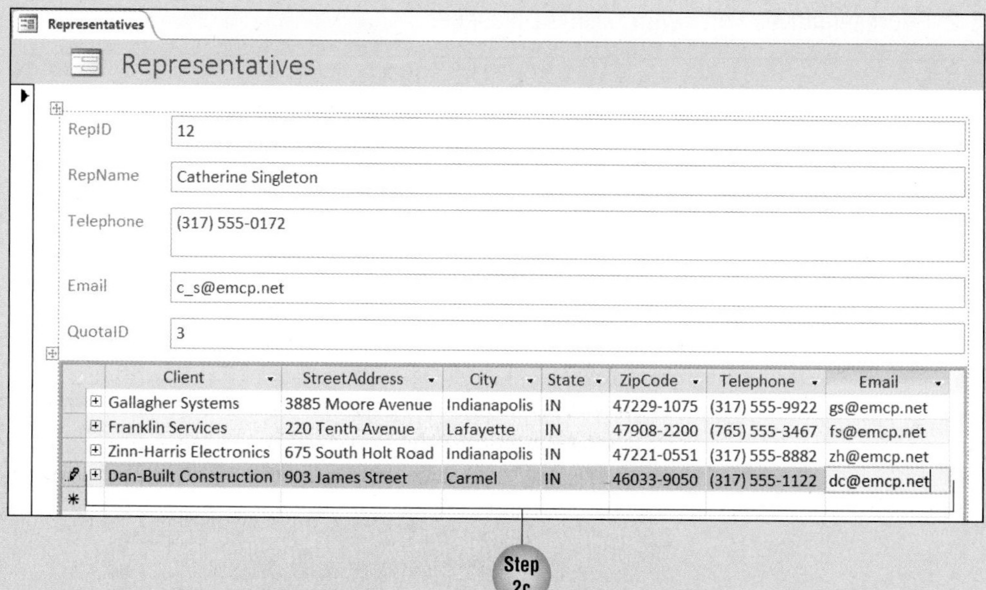

3. Click the Save button on the Quick Access toolbar and at the Save As dialog box with *Representatives* in the *Form Name* text box, click OK.
4. Print the current record in the form by completing the following steps:
   a. Click the FILE tab and then click the *Print* option.
   b. Click the Print button.
   c. At the Print dialog box, click the *Select Record(s)* option in the *Print Range* section and then click OK.
5. Close the Representatives form.

Customizing Forms

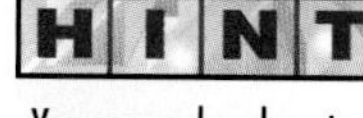

You can make almost all changes to a form in Layout view.

A form is comprised of a series of ***control objects***, which are objects that display titles or descriptions, accept data, or perform actions. Control objects are contained in the *Form Header* section and *Detail* section of the form. (Refer to Figure 5.1 on page 187.) The control objects in the *Detail* section are contained within a form table.

You can customize control objects in the *Detail* section and data in the *Form Header* section with buttons on the FORM LAYOUT TOOLS ribbon with the DESIGN tab, ARRANGE tab, or FORMAT tab selected. When you open a form in Layout view, the FORM LAYOUT TOOLS DESIGN tab is active. This tab contains options for applying a theme, inserting controls, inserting header or footer data, and adding existing fields.

Applying Themes

Themes

Access provides a number of themes for formatting objects in a database. A ***theme*** is a set of formatting choices that include a color theme (a set of colors) and a font theme (a set of heading and body text fonts). To apply a theme, click the Themes button in the Themes group on the FORM LAYOUT TOOLS DESIGN tab. At the drop-down gallery that displays, click the desired theme. Position the mouse pointer over a theme and the ***live preview feature*** will display the form with the theme formatting applied. With the live preview feature, you can see how the theme formatting affects your form before you make your final choice. When you apply a theme, any new objects you create in the database will be formatted with the theme.

Themes available in Access are the same as the themes available in Word, Excel, and PowerPoint.

You can further customize the formatting of a form with the Colors button and the Fonts button in the Themes group on the FORM LAYOUT TOOLS DESIGN tab. If you want to customize the theme colors, click the Colors button in the Themes group and then click the desired option at the drop-down list. Change the theme fonts by clicking the Themes button and then clicking the desired option at the drop-down list.

Colors

Font

Inserting Data in the Form Header

Use buttons in the Header/Footer group on the FORM LAYOUT TOOLS DESIGN tab to insert a logo, form title, or date and time. Click the Logo button and the Insert Picture dialog box displays. Browse to the folder containing the desired image and then double-click the image file. Click the Title button and the current title is selected. Type the new title and then press the Enter key. Click the Date and Time button in the Header/Footer group and the Date and Time dialog box displays. At this dialog box, choose the desired date and time format and then click OK. The date and time are inserted at the right side of the *Form Header* section.

Logo

Title

Date and Time

You can resize and move control objects in the *Form Header* section. To resize an object, click the object to select it and then drag a left or right border to increase or decrease the width. To increase or decrease the height of the object, as well as the *Form Header* section, drag a top or bottom border. To move a selected object in the *Form Header* section, position the mouse pointer over the selected object until the pointer displays with a four-headed arrow attached. Hold down the left mouse button, drag the object to the desired position, and then release the mouse button.

Modifying a Control Object

When Access creates a form from a table, the first column in the form contains the label control objects and displays the field names from the table. The second column contains the text box control objects that display the field values you entered in the table. The width of either column can be resized. To do this, click in any control object in the desired column, position the mouse pointer on the right or left border of the selected control object until the pointer displays as a black left-and-right-pointing arrow. Hold down the left mouse button, drag left or right to change the width of the column, and then release the mouse button. Complete similar steps to change the height of the row containing the selected control object. As you drag a border, a line and character count displays at the left side of the Status bar. Use the line and character count numbers to move the border to a precise location.

To delete a control object from the form, click the desired object and then press the Delete key. You can also right-click the object and then click *Delete* at the shortcut menu. If you want to delete a form row, right-click an object in the row you want to delete and then click *Delete Row* at the shortcut menu. To delete a column, right-click in one of the objects in the column you want to delete and then click *Delete Column* at the shortcut menu. In addition to the label and text box control objects, the sizes and positions of objects in the *Form Header* section, such as the logo and title, can be modified.

Inserting a Control

Select

Text Box

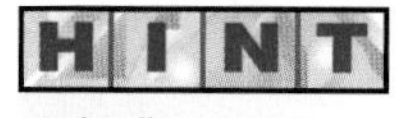

Each cell can contain only one control object.

The Controls group on the FORM LAYOUT TOOLS DESIGN tab contains a number of control objects you can insert in a form. By default, the Select button is active. With this button active, use the mouse pointer to select control objects. You can insert a new label control and text box control object in your form by clicking the Text Box button in the Controls group and then clicking in the desired position in the form. Click in the label control object, select the default text, and then type the label text. You can enter text in a label control object in Layout view but you cannot enter data in a text box control object. In Form view, you can enter data in a text box control object but you cannot edit text in a label control object. The Controls group contains a number of additional buttons for inserting control objects in a form, such as a hyperlink, combo box, or image.

Project 1d **Creating a Form and Customizing the Design of a Form** **Part 4 of 7**

1. With **AL1-C5-Dearborn.accdb** open, create a form with the Clients table and delete the datasheet by completing the following steps:
   a. Click the Clients table in the Navigation pane.
   b. Click the CREATE tab.
   c. Click the Form button in the Forms group.
   d. Click in the SalesID field in the datasheet that displays below the form.
   e. Click the table move handle that displays in the upper left corner of the datasheet (see image at right).
   f. Press the Delete key.
2. Apply a theme to the form by clicking the Themes button in the Themes group on the FORM LAYOUT TOOLS DESIGN tab and then clicking *Facet* at the drop-down gallery (first row, second column).

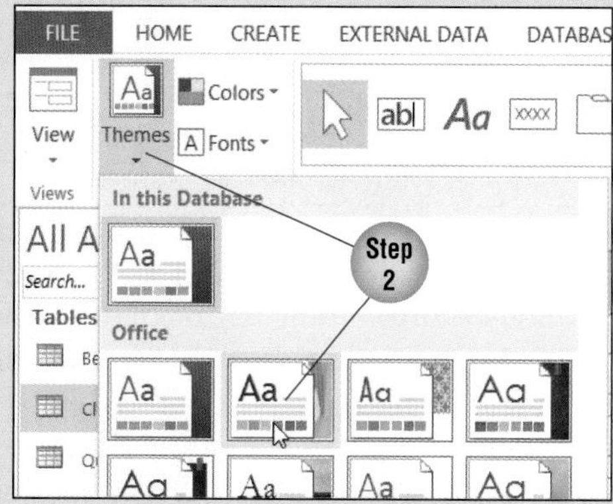

3. Change the theme fonts by clicking the Fonts button in the Themes group and then clicking *Gill Sans MT* at the drop-down gallery. (You will need to scroll down the list to display *Gill Sans MT*.)
4. Change the theme colors by clicking the Colors button in the Themes group and then clicking *Orange* at the drop-down gallery.
5. Insert a logo image in the *Form Header* section by completing the following steps:
   a. Right-click the logo object that displays in the *Form Header* section (located to the left of the title *Clients*) and then click *Delete* at the shortcut menu.
   b. Click the Logo button in the Header/Footer group.
   c. At the Insert Picture dialog box, navigate to the AL1C5 folder on your storage medium and then double-click the file named ***DearbornLogo.jpg***.
6. Change the title by completing the following steps:
   a. Click the Title button in the Header/Footer group. (This selects *Clients* in the *Form Header* section.)
   b. Type **Dearborn Clients Form** and then press Enter.
7. Insert the date and time in the *Form Header* section by completing the following steps:
   a. Click the Date and Time button in the Header/Footer group.
   b. At the Date and Time dialog box, click OK.
8. Size the control object containing the title by completing the following steps:
   a. Click in any field outside the title and then click the title to select the header control object.
   b. Position the mouse pointer on the right border of the selected object until the pointer displays as a black left-and-right-pointing arrow.
   c. Hold down the left mouse button, drag to the left until the right border is immediately right of the title, and then release the mouse button.

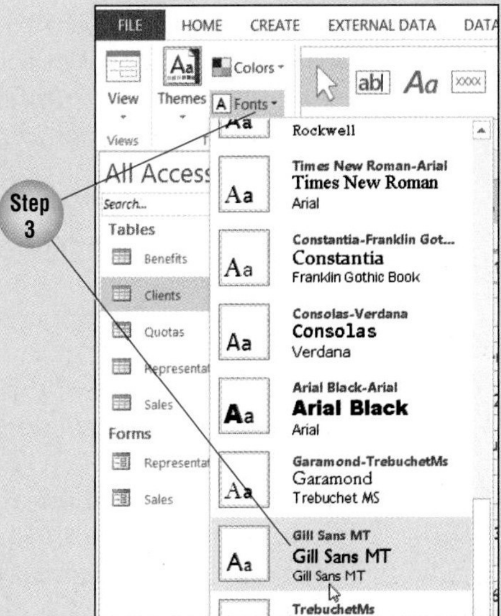

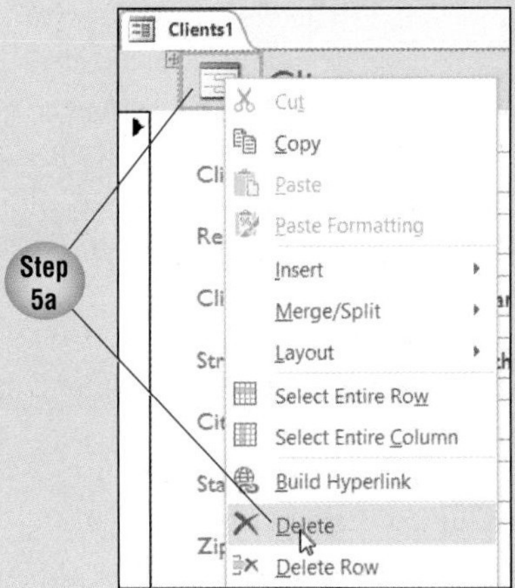

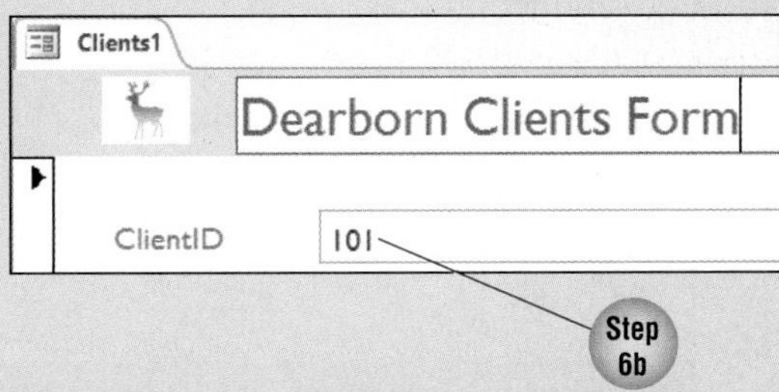

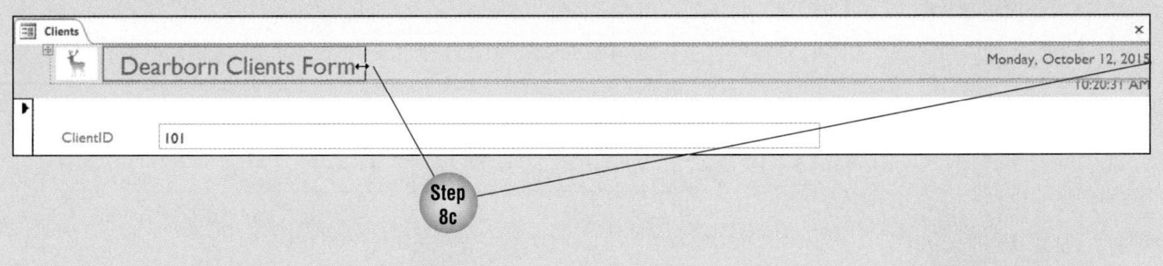

9. Size and move the control objects containing the date and time by completing the following steps:
   a. Click the date to select the control object.
   b. Hold down the Shift key, click the time, and then release the Shift key. (Both control objects should be selected.)
   c. Position the mouse pointer on the left border of the selected objects until the pointer displays as a black left-and-right-pointing arrow.
   d. Hold down the left mouse button, drag to the right until the border displays immediately left of the date, and then release the mouse button.
   e. Position the mouse pointer in the selected objects until the pointer displays with a four-headed arrow attached.
   f. Hold down the left mouse button and then drag the outline of the date and time objects to the left until the outline displays near the title.

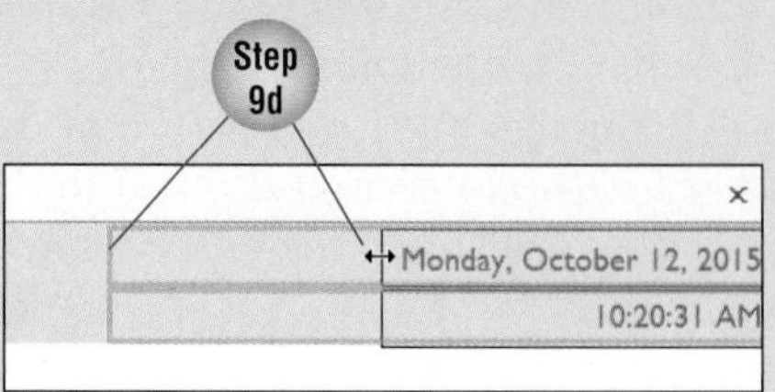

10. Decrease the size of the second column of control objects in the *Detail* section by completing the following steps:
    a. Click in the text box control object containing the client number *101*. (This selects and inserts an orange border around the object.)
    b. Position the mouse pointer on the right border of the selected object until the pointer displays as a black left-and-right-pointing arrow.
    c. Hold down the left mouse button, drag to the left until *Lines: 1 Characters: 30* displays at the left side of the Status bar, and then release the mouse button.

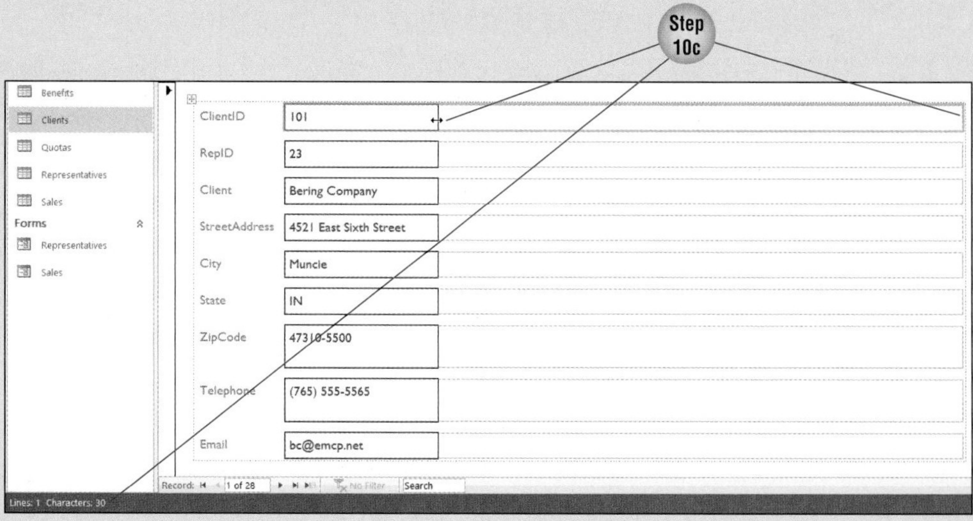

11. Insert a label control object by completing the following steps:
    a. Click the Label button in the Controls group.

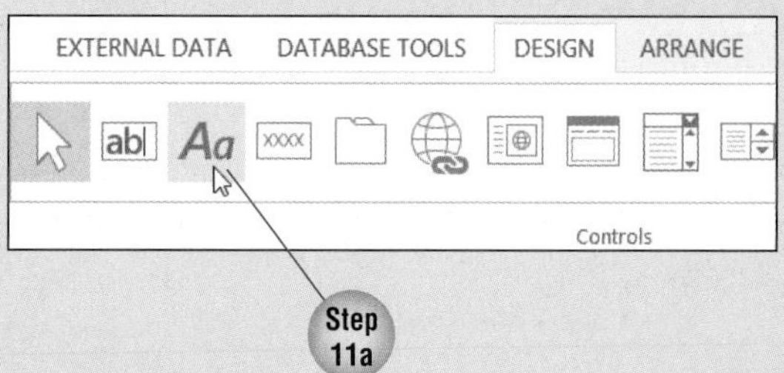

b. Click immediately right of the text box containing the telephone number *(765) 555-5565*. (This inserts the label to the right of the *Telephone* text box.)

c. With the insertion point positioned inside the label, type **Type the telephone number without symbols or spaces** and then press the Enter key.

12. Change the size of the new label control object by completing the following steps:
    a. Position the arrow pointer on the right border of the new label control object until the pointer displays as a black left-and-right-pointing arrow.
    b. Hold down the left mouse button, drag the border to the right until *Lines: 6 Characters: 32* displays at the left side of the Status bar, and then release the mouse button. The text line in the label should break after the word *number*.
    c. Decrease the height of the new label control object by dragging the bottom border up so it is positioned just below the second line of text.

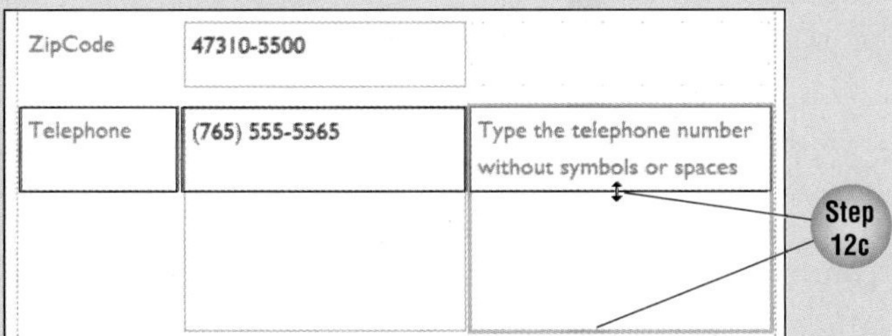

13. Click the Save button on the Quick Access toolbar. At the Save As dialog box with *Clients* in the *Form Name* text box, click OK.

Moving a Form Table

The control objects in the *Detail* section in a form in Layout view are contained within the form table. Click in a control object and the table is selected and the table move handle is visible. The table move handle is a small square with a four-headed arrow inside that displays in the upper left corner of the table. (Refer to Figure 5.1 on page 187.) Move the table and all of the control objects within the table by dragging the table move handle using the mouse. When you position the mouse pointer on the table move handle and then hold down the left mouse button, all of the control objects are selected. You can also click the table move handle to select the control objects.

You can move a control object by dragging it to the desired location.

Arranging Objects

With options on the FORM LAYOUT TOOLS ARRANGE tab, you can select, insert, delete, arrange, merge, and split cells. When you inserted a label control object to the right of the *Telephone* text box control in Project 1d, empty cells were inserted in the form above and below the new label control object. Select a control object or cell by clicking in the desired object or cell. Select adjacent objects or cells by holding down the Shift key while clicking in the desired objects or cells. To select nonadjacent objects or cells, hold down the Ctrl key while clicking in the desired objects or cells.

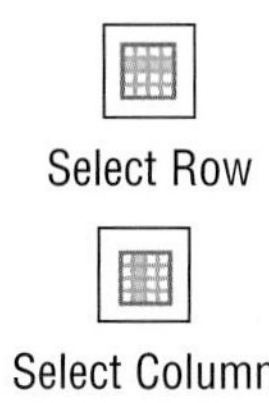

Select Row

Select Column

Select a row of control objects and cells by clicking the Select Row button in the Rows & Columns group or by right-clicking in an object or cell and then clicking *Select Entire Row* at the shortcut menu. To select a column of control objects and cells, click the Select Column button in the Rows & Columns group or right-click an object or cell and then click *Select Entire Column* at the shortcut menu. You can also select a column by positioning the mouse pointer at the top of the column until the pointer displays as a small, black, down-pointing arrow and then clicking the left mouse button.

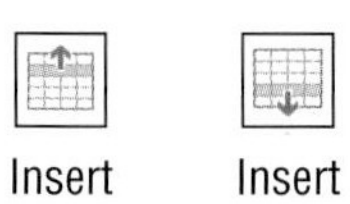

Insert Above Insert Below

The Rows & Columns group contains buttons for inserting a row or column of blank cells. To insert a new row, select a cell or object in a row and then click the Insert Above button to insert a row of blank cells above the current row or click the Insert Below button to insert a row of blank cells below the current row. Complete similar steps to insert a new column of blank cells to the left or right of the current column.

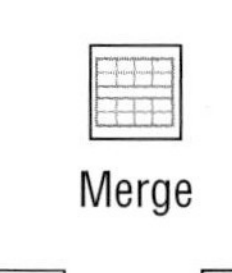

Merge

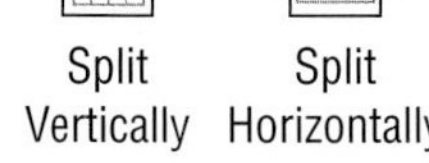

Split Vertically Split Horizontally

Merge adjacent selected cells by clicking the Merge button in the Merge/Split group on the FORM LAYOUT TOOLS ARRANGE tab. Split a control object or cell by clicking the object or cell to make it active and then clicking the Split Vertically button or Split Horizontally button in the Merge/Split group. When you split a control object, an empty cell is created to the right of the control object or below the control object.

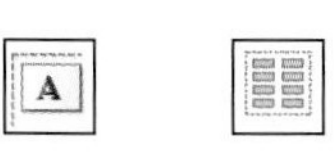

Control Margins Control Padding

You can also move up or down a row of control objects. To do this, select the desired row and then click the Move Up button in the Move group to move the row above the current row or click the Move Down button to move the row below the current row. Use the Control Margins button in the Position group to increase or decrease margins within control objects. The Position group also contains a Control Padding button you can use to increase or decrease spacing between control objects.

The Table group is located at the left side of the FORM LAYOUT TOOLS ARRANGE tab. It contains buttons for applying gridlines to control objects and changing the layout of the objects to a stacked layout or columnar layout.

Project 1e Arranging Objects in a Form

Part 5 of 7

1. With the Clients form in **AL1-C5-Dearborn.accdb** open in Design view, select and merge cells by completing the following steps:
   a. Click to the right of the text box control object containing the text *101*. (This selects the empty cell.)
   b. Hold down the Shift key and then click to the right of the text box control containing the text *Muncie*. (This selects five adjacent cells.)
   c. Click the FORM LAYOUT TOOLS ARRANGE tab.
   d. Click the Merge button in the Merge/Split group.

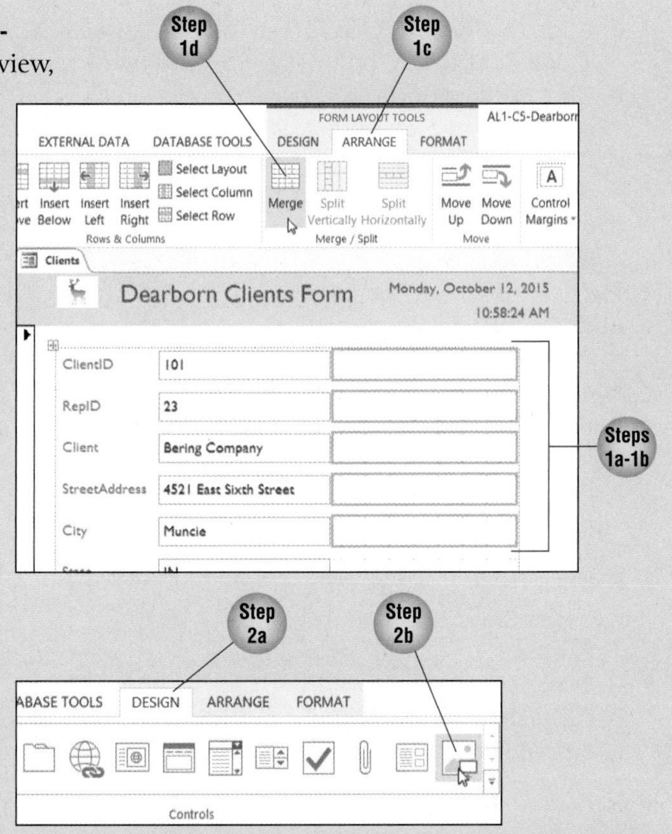

2. With the cells merged, insert an image control object and then insert an image by completing the following steps:
   a. Click the FORM LAYOUT TOOLS DESIGN tab.
   b. Click the Image button in the Controls group.
   c. Move the mouse pointer (which displays as a plus symbol next to an image icon) to the location of the merged cell until the cell displays with pink fill color and then click the left mouse button.

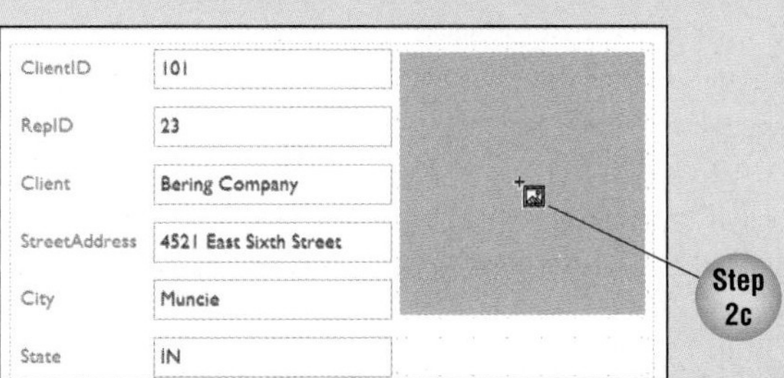

   d. At the Insert Picture dialog box, navigate to the AL1C5 folder on your storage medium and then double-click ***Dearborn.jpg***.

3. Move down the telephone row by completing the following steps:
   a. Click the FORM LAYOUT TOOLS ARRANGE tab.
   b. Click in the control object containing the text *Telephone*.
   c. Click the Select Row button in the Rows & Columns group.
   d. Click the Move Down button in the Move group.

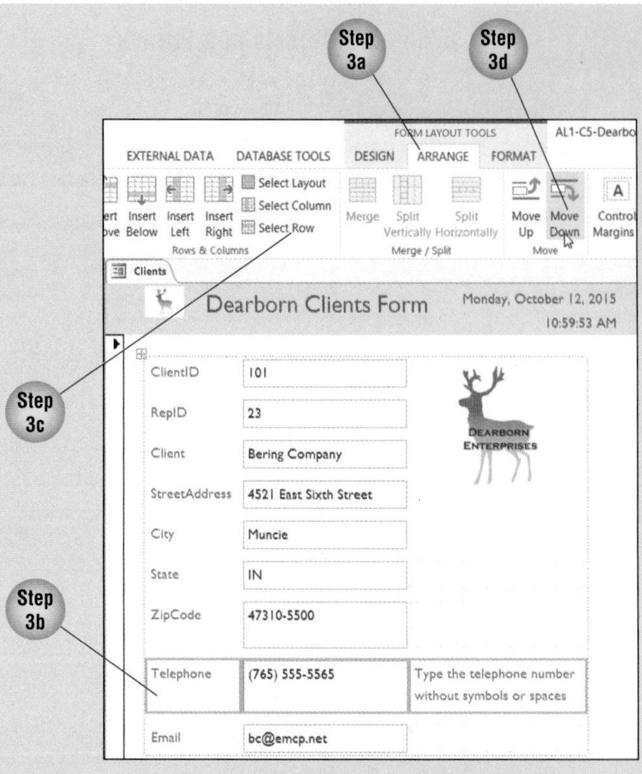

4. Decrease the margins within objects and cells, increase the spacing (padding) between objects and cells in the form, and apply gridlines by completing the following steps:
   a. If necessary, click the FORM LAYOUT TOOLS ARRANGE tab.
   b. Click the Select Layout button in the Rows & Columns group. (This selects all objects and cells in the form.)
   c. Click the Control Margins button in the Position group and then click *Narrow* at the drop-down list.

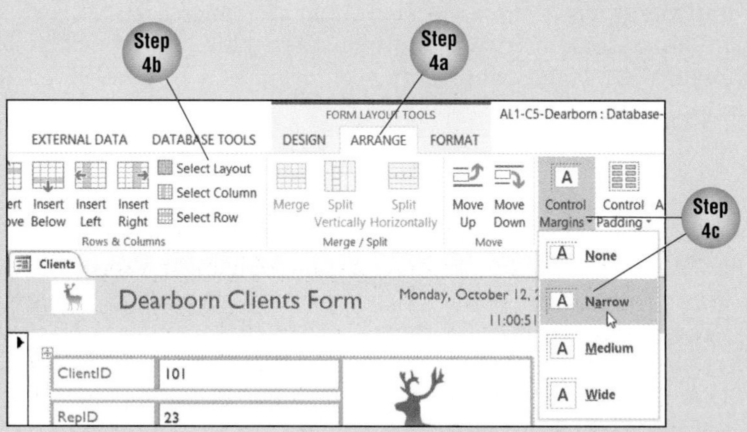

   d. Click the Control Padding button in the Position group and then click *Medium* at the drop-down list.

e. Click the Gridlines button in the Table group and then click *Top* at the drop-down list.
f. Click the Gridlines button in the Table group, point to *Color*, and then click the *Orange, Accent 2, Darker 50%* option (sixth column, bottom row in the *Theme Colors* section).

5. Move the form table by completing the following steps:
   a. Position the mouse pointer on the table move handle (which displays as a small square with a four-headed arrow inside and is located in the upper left corner of the table).
   b. Hold down the left mouse button, drag the form table up and to the left so it is positioned close to the top left border of the *Detail* section, and then release the mouse button.

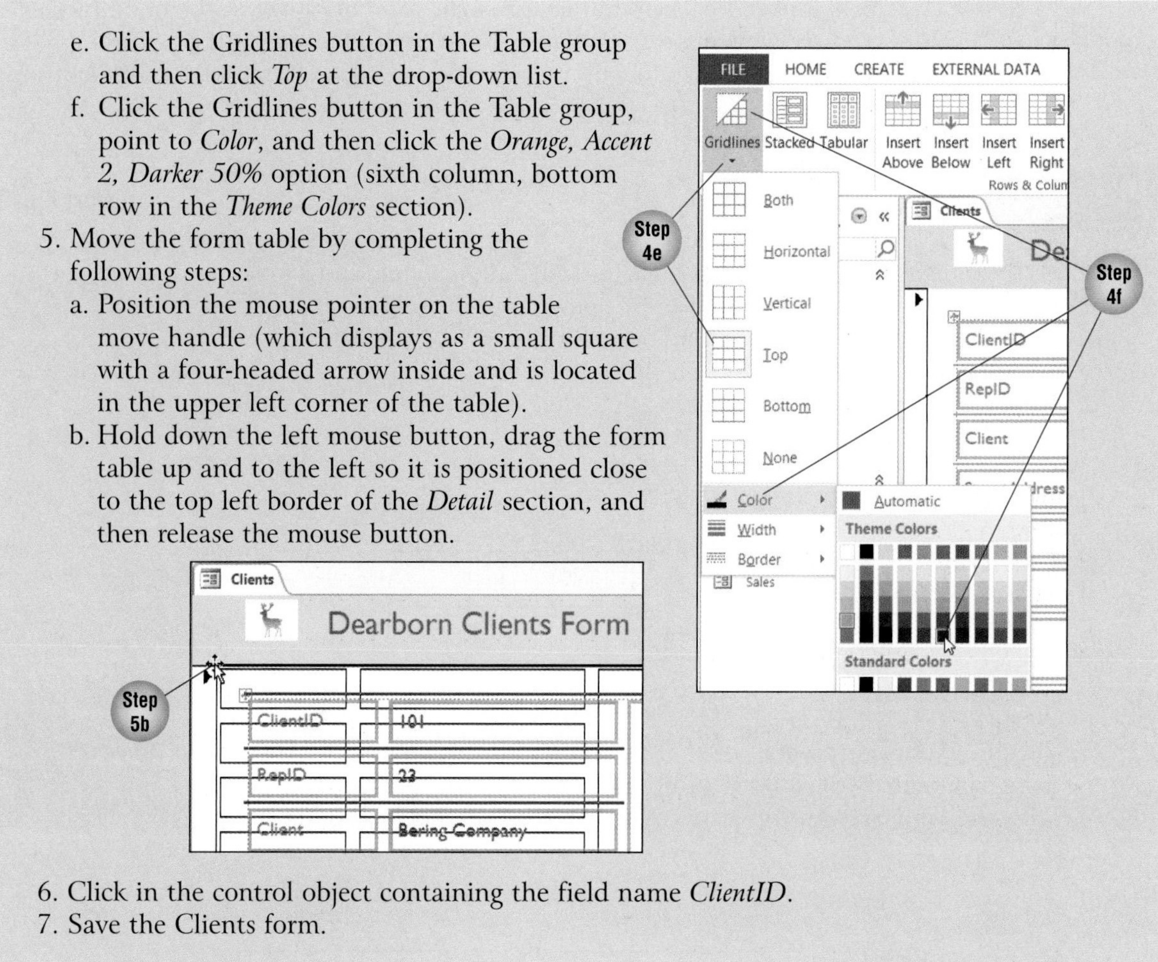

6. Click in the control object containing the field name *ClientID*.
7. Save the Clients form.

Formatting a Form

Click the FORM LAYOUT TOOLS FORMAT tab and buttons and options display for applying formatting to a form or specific objects in a form. If you want to apply formatting to a specific object, click the object in the form or click the Object button arrow in the Selection group and then click the desired object at the drop-down list. To format all objects in the form, click the Select All button in the Selection group. This selects all objects in the form, including objects in the *Form Header* section. If you want to select all of the objects in the *Detail* section (and not the *Form Header* section), click an object in the *Detail* section and then click the table move handle.

Object

Select All

With buttons in the Font, Number, Background, and Control Formatting groups, you can apply formatting to a control object or cell and to selected objects and cells in a form. Use buttons in the Font group to change the font, apply a different font size, apply text effects (such as bold and underline), and change the alignment of data in objects. If the form contains data with a Number or Currency data type, use buttons in the Number group to apply specific formatting

to numbers. Insert a background image in the form using the Background Image button and apply formatting to objects or cells with buttons in the Control Formatting group. Depending on what is selected in the form, some of the buttons may not be active.

Project 1f Formatting a Form

Part 6 of 7

1. With the Clients form in **AL1-C5-Dearborn.accdb** open and in Layout view, change the font and font size of text in the form by completing the following steps:
   a. Click in any control object in the form.
   b. Select all control objects and cells in the form by clicking the table move handle that displays in the upper left corner of the *Detail* section.

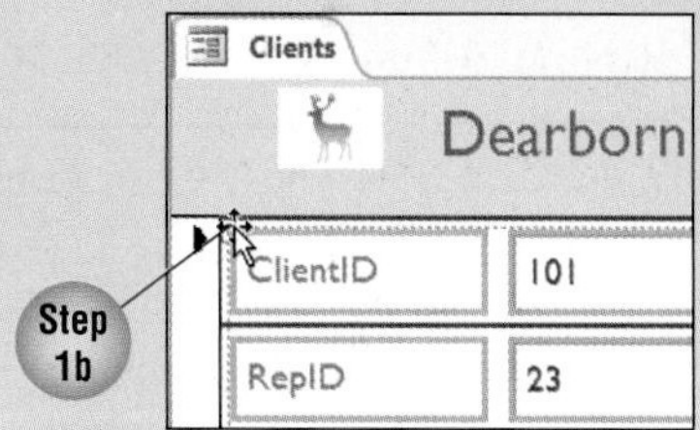

   c. Click the FORM LAYOUT TOOLS FORMAT tab.
   d. Click the Font button arrow, scroll down the drop-down list, and then click *Tahoma*. (Fonts are alphabetized in the drop-down list.)
   e. Click the Font Size button arrow and then click *10* at the drop-down list.

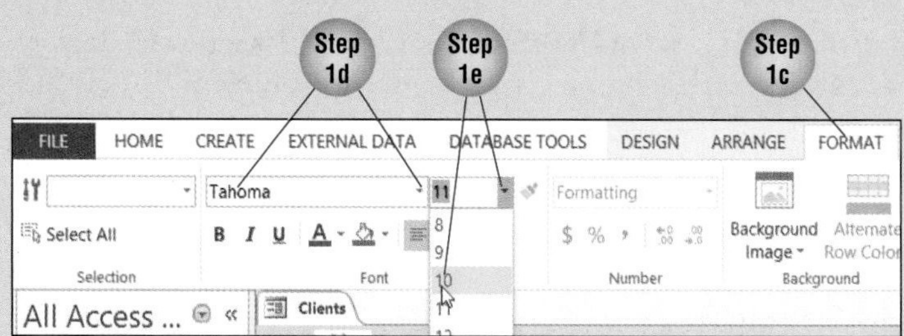

2. Apply formatting and change the alignment of the first column by completing the following steps:
   a. Click the control object containing the field name *ClientID*, hold down the Shift key, click the bottom control object containing the field name *Telephone*, and then release the Shift key.
   b. Click the Bold button in the Font group.
   c. Click the Shape Fill button in the Control Formatting group and then click the *Brown, Accent 3, Lighter 60%* color option (seventh column, third row in the *Theme Colors* section).
   d. Click the Shape Outline button in the Control Formatting group and then click the *Brown, Accent 3, Darker 50%* option (seventh column, bottom row in the *Theme Colors* section).
   e. Click the Align Right button in the Font group.

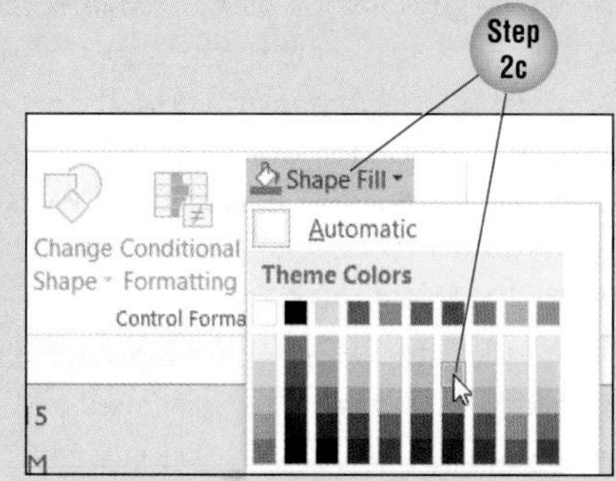

3. Apply shape fill to the second column by completing the following steps:
   a. Click the text box control object containing the text *101*.
   b. Position the mouse pointer at the top border of the selected object until the pointer displays as a small, black, down-pointing arrow and then click the left mouse button. (Make sure all of the objects in the second column are selected.)

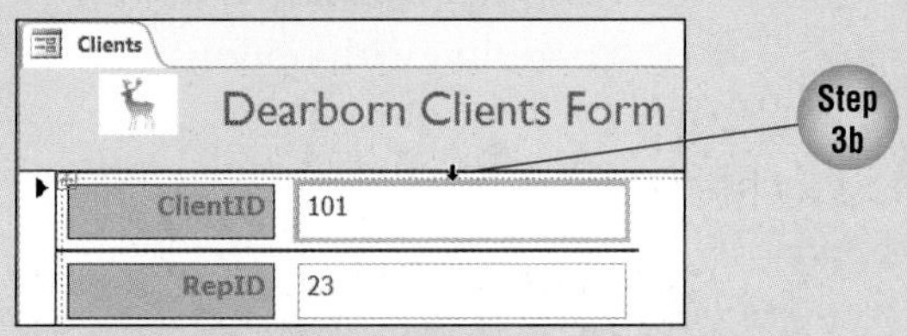

   c. Click the Shape Fill button in the Control Formatting group and then click the *Brown, Accent 3, Lighter 80%* color option (seventh column, second row in the *Theme Colors* section).
4. Remove the gridlines by completing the following steps:
   a. Click the FORM LAYOUT TOOLS ARRANGE tab.
   b. Click the Select Layout button in the Rows & Columns group.
   c. Click the Gridlines button in the Table group and then click *None* at the drop-down list.
5. Click the Save button on the Quick Access toolbar to save the Clients form.
6. Insert a background image by completing the following steps:
   a. Click the FORM LAYOUT TOOLS FORMAT tab.
   b. Click the Background Image button in the Background group and then click *Browse* at the drop-down list.
   c. Navigate to the AL1C5 folder on your storage medium and then double-click ***Mountain.jpg***.
   d. View the form and background image in Print Preview. (To display Print Preview, click the FILE tab, click the *Print* option, and then click the Print Preview button.)
   e. After viewing the form in Print Preview, return to the form by clicking the Close Print Preview button.
7. Click the Undo button on the Quick Access toolbar to remove the background image. (If this does not remove the image, close the form without saving it and then reopen the form.)
8. Save the Clients form.

Applying Conditional Formatting

With the Conditional Formatting button in the Control Formatting group on the FORM LAYOUT TOOLS FORMAT tab, you can apply formatting to data that meets a specific criterion or apply conditional formatting to data in all records in a form. For example, you can apply conditional formatting to sales amounts in a form that displays amounts higher than a specified number in a different color or you can apply conditional formatting to states' names and specify a color for companies in a particular state. You can also include conditional formatting that inserts data bars that visually compare data among records. The data bars provide a visual representation of the comparison of data in records. For example, in Project 1g, you will insert data bars in the *Sales* field that provide a visual representation of how the sales amount in one record compares to the sales amounts in other records.

To apply conditional formatting, click the Conditional Formatting button in the Control Formatting group and the Conditional Formatting Rules Manager dialog box displays. At this dialog box, click the New Rule button and the New Formatting Rule dialog box displays, as shown in Figure 5.3. In the *Select a rule type* list box, choose the *Check values in the current record or use an expression* option if the conditional formatting is applied to a field in the record that matches a specific condition. Click the *Compare to other records* option if you want to insert data bars in a field in all records that compare the data among the records.

If you want to apply conditional formatting to a field, specify the field and field condition with options in the *Edit the rule description* section of the dialog box. Specify the type of formatting you want applied to data in a field that meets the specific criterion. For example, in Project 1g, you will specify that you want to change the shape fill to a light green for all *City* fields containing *Indianapolis*. When you have made all the desired changes to the dialog box, click OK to close the dialog box and then click OK to close the Conditional Formatting Rules Manager dialog box.

To insert data bars in a field, click the Conditional Formatting button, click the New Rule button at the Conditional Formatting Rules Manager dialog box, and then click the *Compare to other records* option in the *Select a rule type* list box. This changes the options in the dialog box, as shown in Figure 5.4. Make the desired changes in the *Edit the rule description* section.

Figure 5.3 New Formatting Rule Dialog Box with the *Check values in the current record or use an expression* Option Selected

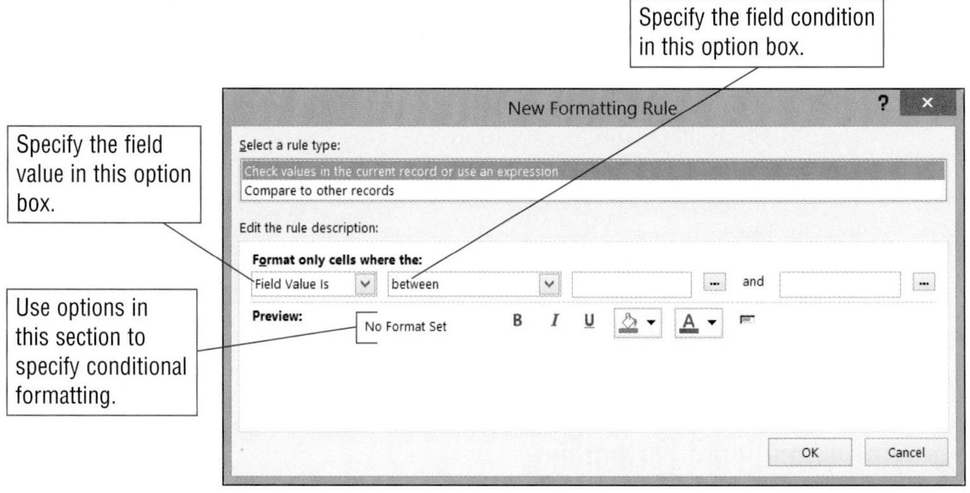

Figure 5.4 New Formatting Rule Dialog Box with the *Compare to other records* Option Selected

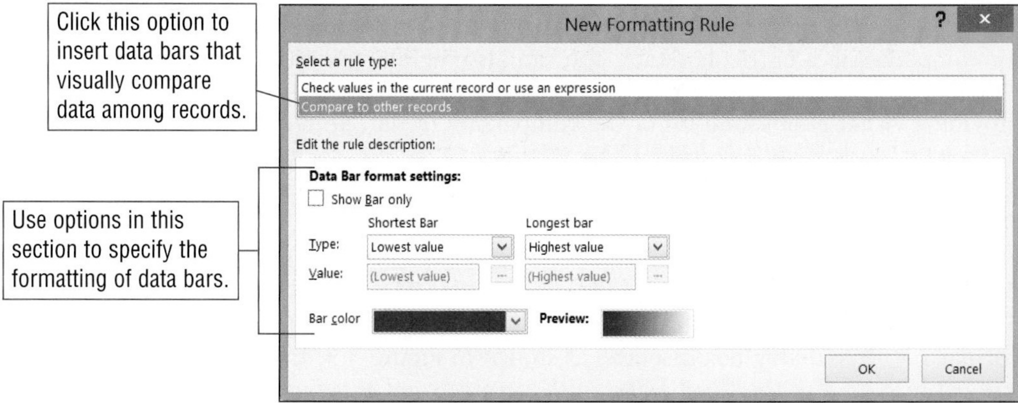

Project 1g Applying Conditional Formatting to Fields in Forms Part 7 of 7

1. With the Clients form in **AL1-C5-Dearborn.accdb** open and in Layout view, apply conditional formatting so that the *City* field displays all Indianapolis entries with a light green shape fill by completing the following steps:
   a. Click in the text box control object containing the text *Muncie*.
   b. Click the FORM LAYOUT TOOLS FORMAT tab.
   c. Click the Conditional Formatting button in the Control Formatting group.
   d. At the Conditional Formatting Rules Manager dialog box, click the New Rule button.

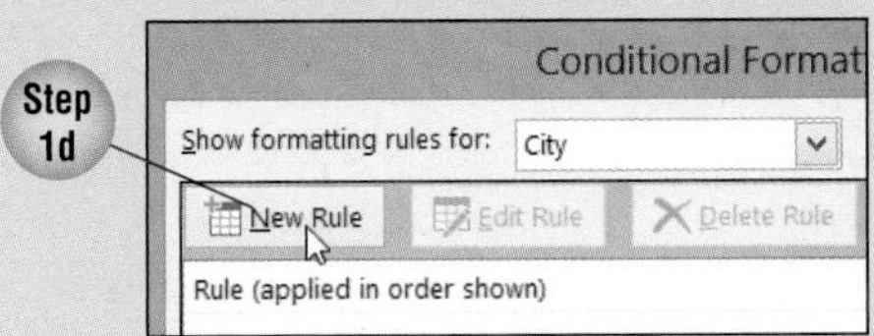

   e. At the New Formatting Rule dialog box, click the down-pointing arrow at the right side of the option box containing the word *between* and then click *equal to* at the drop-down list.
   f. Click in the text box to the right of the *equal to* option box and then type **Indianapolis**.
   g. Click the Background color button arrow and then click the *Green 3* color option (seventh column, fourth row).
   h. Click OK to close the New Formatting Rule dialog box.
   i. Click OK to close the Conditional Formatting Rules Manager dialog box.

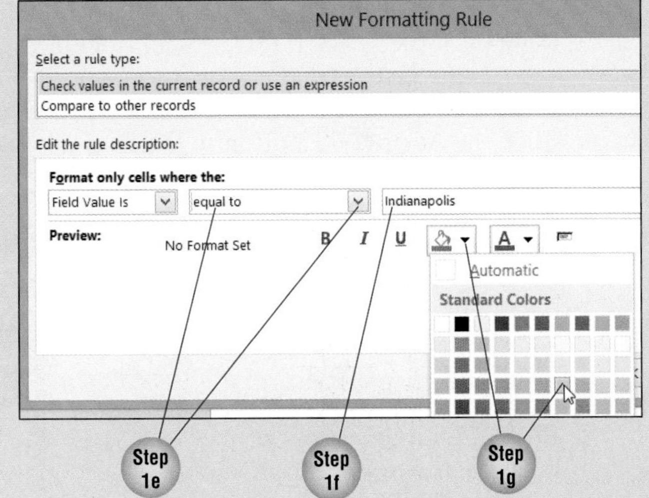

2. Click the HOME tab and then click the View button to switch to Form view.
3. Click the Next record button to display the next record in the form. Continue clicking the Next record button to view records and notice that *Indianapolis* entries display with a light green shape fill.
4. Click the First record button in the Record Navigation bar.
5. Click the Save button on the Quick Access toolbar.
6. Print page 1 of the form by completing the following steps:
   a. Click the FILE tab and then click the *Print* option.
   b. Click the Print button.
   c. At the Print dialog box, click the *Pages* option in the *Print Range* section, type 1 in the *From* text box, press the Tab key, and then type 1 in the *To* text box.
   d. Click OK.
7. Close the Clients form.
8. Open the Sales form and switch to Layout View by clicking the View button in the Views group on the HOME tab.

9. With the text box control object containing the sales ID number *1* selected, drag the right border to the left until *Lines: 1 Characters: 21* displays at the left side of the Status bar.

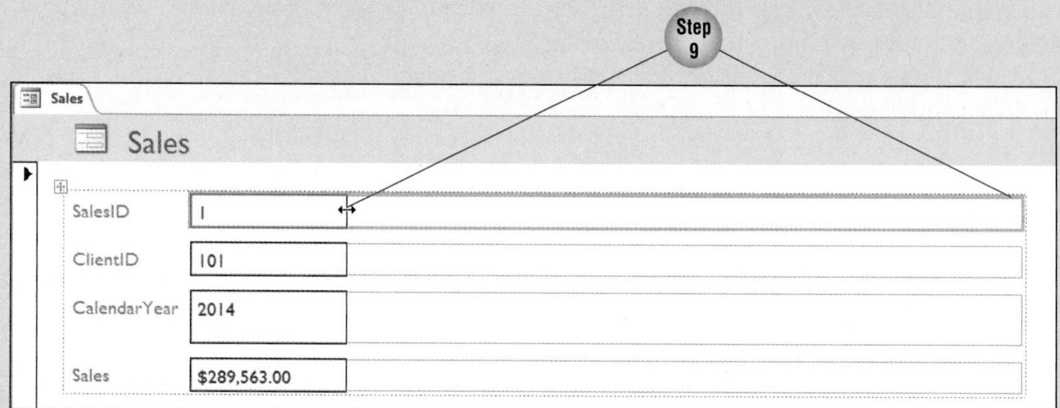

10. Change the alignment of text by completing the following steps:
    a. Right-click the selected text box control object (the object containing *1*) and then click *Select Entire Column* at the shortcut menu.
    b. Click the FORM LAYOUT TOOLS FORMAT tab.
    c. Click the Align Right button in the Font group.
11. Apply data bars to the *Sales* field by completing the following steps:
    a. Click in the text box control object containing the text *$289,563.00*.
    b. Make sure the FORM LAYOUT TOOLS FORMAT tab is active.
    c. Click the Conditional Formatting button.
    d. At the Conditional Formatting Rules Manager dialog box, click the New Rule button.
    e. At the New Formatting Rule dialog box, click the *Compare to other records* option in the *Select a rule type* list box.
    f. Click the down-pointing arrow at the right side of the *Bar color* option box and then click the *Green 4* color option (seventh column, fifth row).

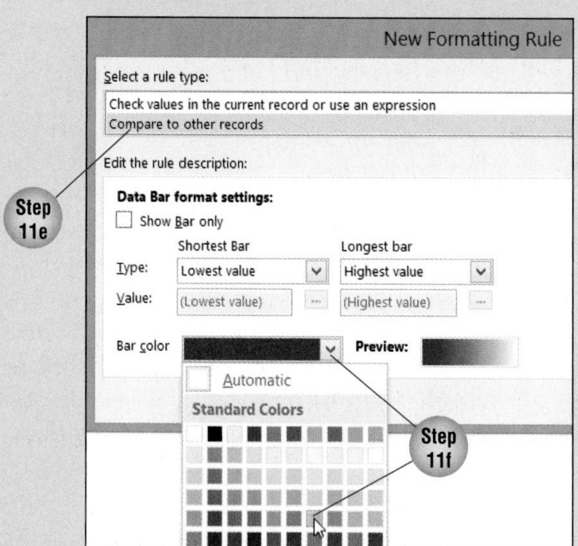

    g. Click OK to close the New Formatting Rule dialog box and then click OK to close the Conditional Formatting Rules Manager dialog box.
12. Click the Next record button in the Record Navigation bar to display the next record. Continue clicking the Next record button and notice the data bars that display in the *Sales* field.
13. Click the First record button in the Record Navigation bar.
14. Click the Save button on the Quick Access toolbar.

15. Print page 1 of the form by completing the following steps:
    a. Click the FILE tab and then click the *Print* option.
    b. Click the Print button.
    c. At the Print dialog box, click the *Pages* option in the *Print Range* section, type 1 in the *From* text box, press the Tab key, type 1 in the *To* text box, and then click OK.
16. Close the Sales form.
17. Close **AL1-C5-Dearborn.accdb**.

Project 2 Add Fields, Create a Split Form and Multiple Items Form, and Use the Form Wizard — 5 Parts

You will open the Skyline database, create a form and add related fields to the form, create a split and multiple items form, and create a form using the Form Wizard.

Adding Existing Fields

If you create a form and then realize that you forgot a field or want to insert an existing field in the form, display the form in Layout view and then click the Add Existing Fields button located in the Tools group on the FORM LAYOUT TOOLS DESIGN tab. When you click the Add Existing Fields button, the Field List task pane opens and displays at the right side of the screen. This task pane displays the fields available in the current view, fields available in related tables, and fields available in other tables. Figure 5.5 displays the Field List task pane that you will open in Project 2a.

Add Existing Fields

In the *Fields available for this view* section, Access displays all fields in any tables used to create the form. So far, you have been creating a form with all fields in one table. In the *Fields available in related tables* section, Access displays tables that are related to the table(s) used to create the form. To display the fields in the related table, click the plus symbol that displays before the table name in the Field List task pane and the list expands to display all of the field names.

Alt + F8 is the keyboard shortcut to display the Field List task pane.

To add a field to the form, double-click the desired field in the Field List task pane. This inserts the field below the existing fields in the form. You can also drag a field from the Field List task pane into the form. To do this, position the mouse pointer on the desired field in the Field List task pane, hold down the left mouse button, drag into the form window, and then release the mouse button. A pink insert indicator bar displays as you drag the field in the existing fields in the form. When you drag over a cell, the cell displays with pink fill. When the insert indicator bar is in the desired position or the desired cell is selected, release the mouse button.

HINT

Use the Field List task pane to add fields from a table or query to your form.

You can insert multiple fields in a form from the Field List task pane. To do this, hold down the Ctrl key while clicking the desired fields and then drag the fields into the form. If you try to drag a field from a table in the *Fields available in other tables* section, the Specify Relationship dialog box will display. To move a field from the Field List task pane to the form, the field must be located in a table that is related to the table(s) used to create the form.

Figure 5.5 Field List Task Pane

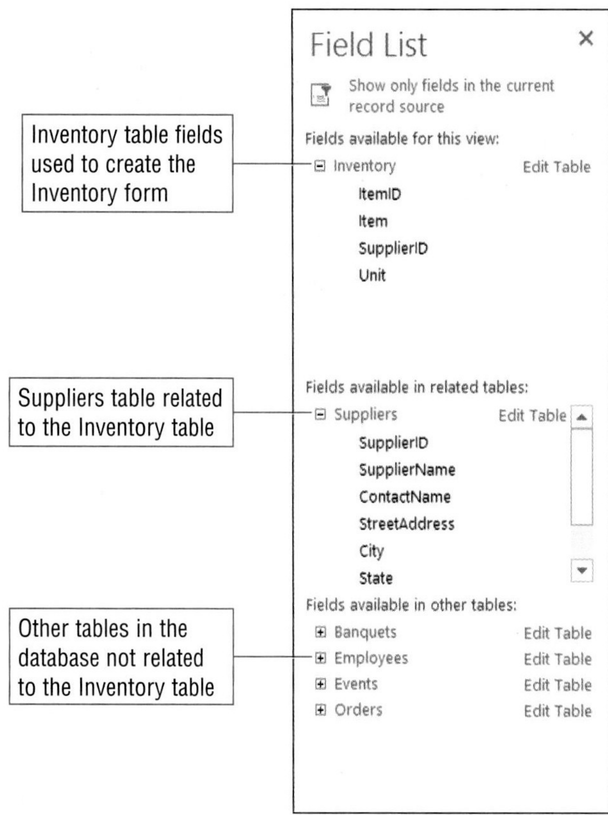

Project 2a Adding Existing Fields to a Form — Part 1 of 5

1. Display the Open dialog box with the AL1C5 folder on your storage medium the active folder, open **AL1-C5-Skyline.accdb**, and enable the contents.
2. Create a form with the Inventory table by clicking the Inventory table in the Navigation pane, clicking the CREATE tab, and then clicking the Form button in the Forms group.
3. With the text box control object containing the text *001* selected, drag the right border to the left until the selected object is approximately one-half the original width.

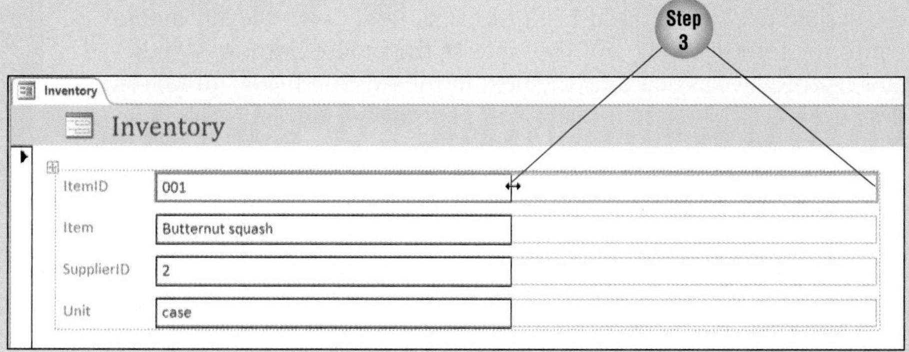

4. With the text box control object still selected, click the FORM LAYOUT TOOLS ARRANGE tab and then click the Split Horizontally button in the Merge/Split group. (This splits the text box control object into one object and one empty cell.)
5. You decide that you want to add the supplier name to the form so the name displays when the form is entered. Add the supplier name field by completing the following steps:
   a. Click the FORM LAYOUT TOOLS DESIGN tab.
   b. Click the Add Existing Fields button in the Tools group.
   c. Click the Show all tables hyperlink that displays toward the top of the Field List task pane.
   d. Click the plus symbol that displays immediately left of the Suppliers table name located in the *Fields available in related tables* section of the Field List task pane.

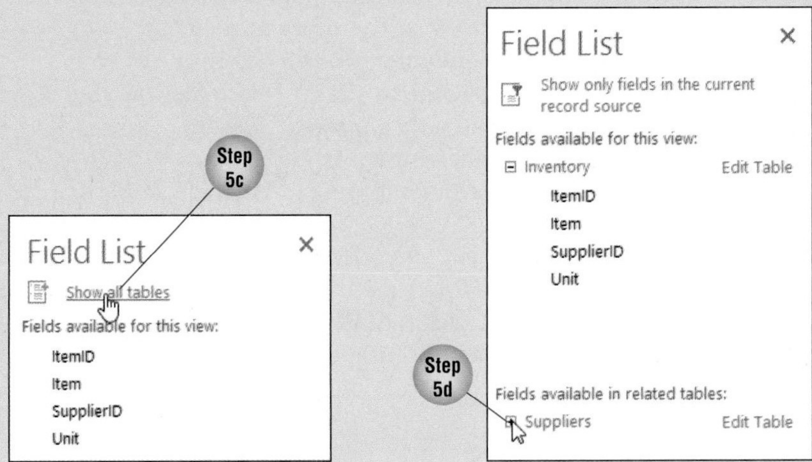

   e. Position the mouse pointer on the *SupplierName* field, hold down the left mouse button, drag into the form until the pink insert indicator bar displays immediately right of the text box control containing *2* (the text box control that displays at the right side of the *SupplierID* label control), and then release the mouse button. Access inserts the field as a Lookup field (a down-pointing arrow displays at the right side of the field).

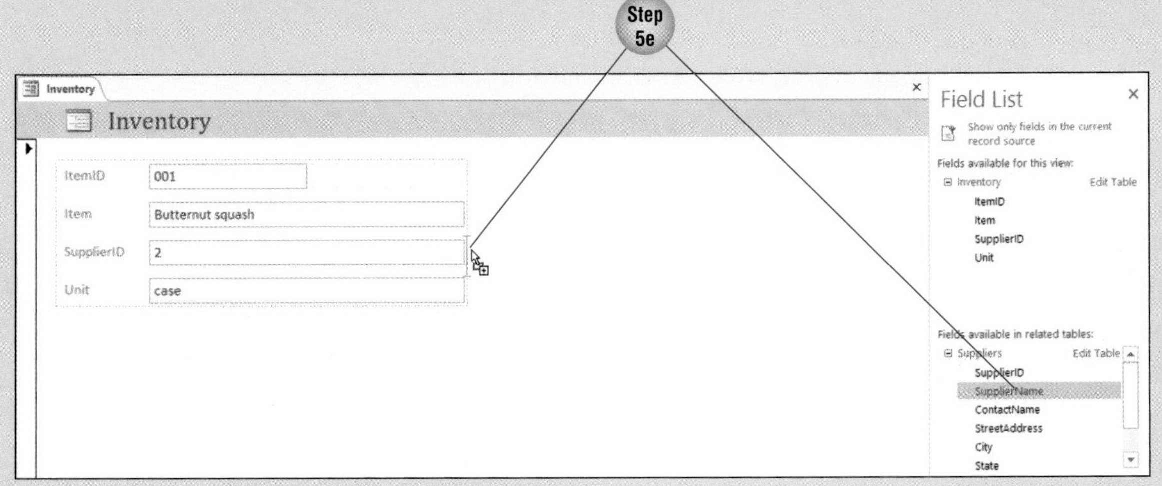

f. Change the *SupplierName* field from a Lookup field to a text box by clicking the Options button that displays below the field and then clicking *Change to Text Box* at the drop-down list. (This removes the down-pointing arrow at the right side of the field.)

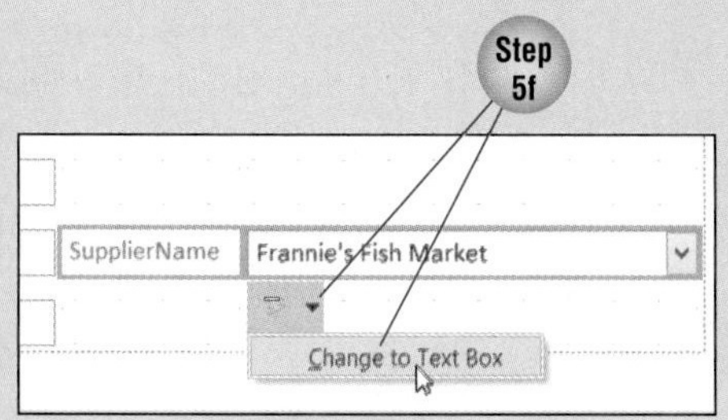

g. Close the Field List task pane by clicking the Close button located in the upper right corner of the task pane.

6. Insert a logo image in the *Form Header* section by completing the following steps:
   a. Right-click the logo object that displays in the *Form Header* section (located to the left of the title *Inventory*) and then click *Delete* at the shortcut menu.
   b. Click the Logo button in the Header/Footer group.
   c. At the Insert Picture dialog box, navigate to the AL1C5 folder on your storage medium and then double-click the file named ***Cityscape.jpg***.
7. Change the title by completing the following steps:
   a. Click the Title button in the Header/Footer group. (This selects *Inventory* in the *Form Header* section.)
   b. Type Skyline Inventory Input Form and then press Enter.
8. Insert the date and time in the *Form Header* section by clicking the Date and Time button in the Header/Footer group and then clicking OK at the Date and Time dialog box.
9. Click in any field outside the title, click the title to select the header control object, and then drag the right border of the title control object to the left until the border displays near the title.
10. Select the date and time control objects, drag in the left border until the border displays near the date and time, and then drag the objects so they are positioned near the title.
11. Scroll through the records in the form.
12. Click the First record button in the Record Navigation bar.
13. Click the Save button on the Quick Access toolbar and save the form with the name *Inventory*.
14. Print the current record.
15. Close the Inventory form.

Creating Split Forms

Quick Steps

Create a Split Form
1. Click desired table.
2. Click CREATE tab.
3. Click More Forms button.
4. Click *Split Form*.

More Forms

Another method for creating a form is to use the *Split Form* option at the More Forms button drop-down list in the Forms group on the CREATE tab. When you use this option to create a form, Access splits the screen in the work area and provides two views of the form. The top half of the work area displays the form in Layout view and the bottom half of the work area displays the form in Datasheet view. The two views are connected and are ***synchronous***, which means that displaying or modifying a specific field in the Form view portion will cause the same action to occur in the field in the Datasheet view portion. Figure 5.6 displays the split form you will create for Project 2b.

Figure 5.6 Split Form

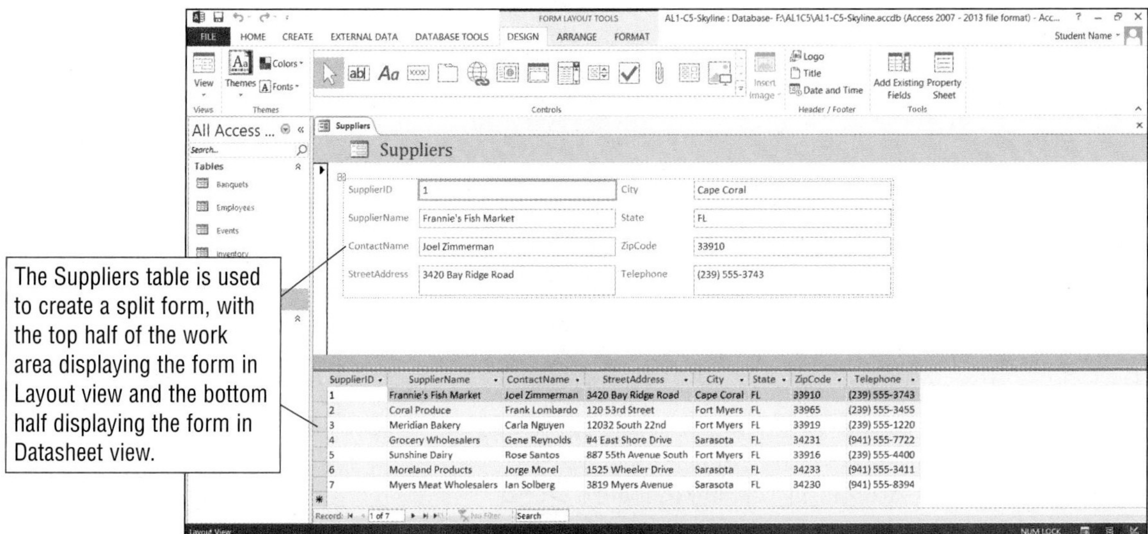
The Suppliers table is used to create a split form, with the top half of the work area displaying the form in Layout view and the bottom half displaying the form in Datasheet view.

Project 2b Creating a Split Form

Part 2 of 5

1. With **AL1-C5-Skyline.accdb** open, create a split form with the Suppliers table by completing the following steps:
   a. Click the Suppliers table in the Navigation pane.
   b. Click the CREATE tab.
   c. Click the More Forms button in the Forms group and then click *Split Form* at the drop-down list.

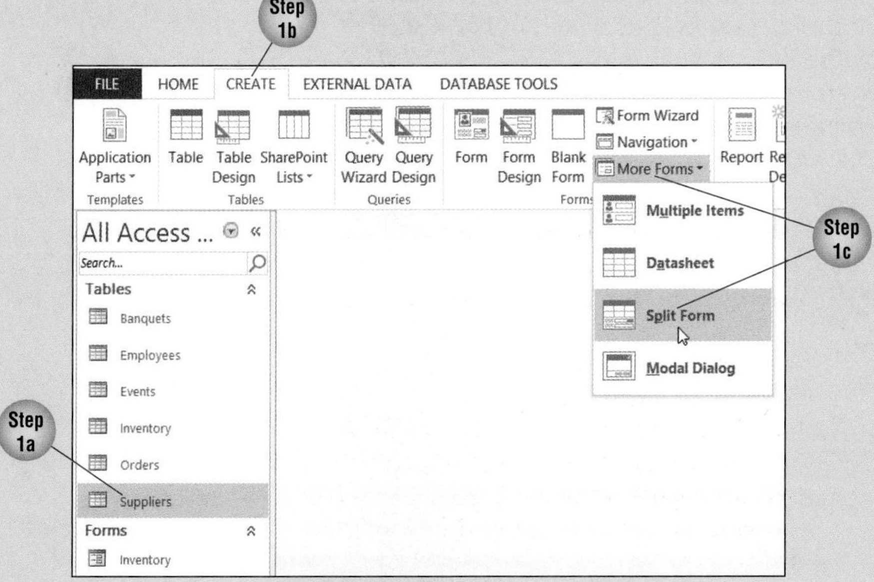
Step 1b
Step 1c
Step 1a

   d. Click several times on the Next record button in the Record Navigation bar. (As you display records, notice that the current record in the Form view in the top portion of the window is the same record selected in Datasheet view in the lower portion of the window.)
   e. Click the First record button.

2. Apply a theme by clicking the Themes button in the Themes group on the FORM LAYOUT TOOLS DESIGN tab and then clicking *Integral* at the drop-down gallery (third column, first row).
3. Insert a logo image in the *Form Header* section by completing the following steps:
   a. Right-click the logo object that displays in the *Form Header* section (located to the left of the title *Suppliers*) and then click *Delete* at the shortcut menu.
   b. Click the Logo button in the Header/Footer group.
   c. At the Insert Picture dialog box, navigate to the AL1C5 folder on your storage medium and then double-click ***Cityscape.jpg***.
4. Change the title by completing the following steps:
   a. Click the Title button in the Header/Footer group. (This selects *Suppliers* in the *Form Header* section.)
   b. Type **Skyline Suppliers Input Form** and then press Enter.
   c. Click in any field outside the title, click the title again to select the header control object, and then drag the right border to the left until the border displays near the title.
5. Click the text box control object containing the supplier identification number *1*, and then drag the right border of the text box control object to the left until *Lines: 1 Characters: 35* displays at the left side of the Status bar.
6. Click the text box control object containing the city *Cape Coral* and drag the right border of the text box control object to the left until *Lines: 1 Characters: 35* displays at the left side of the Status bar.
7. Insert a new record in the Suppliers form by completing the following steps:
   a. Click the View button to switch to Form view.
   b. Click the New (blank) record button in the Record Navigation bar.
   c. Click in the *SupplierID* field in the Form view portion of the window and then type the following information in the specified fields:

SupplierID	**8**
SupplierName	**Jackson Produce**
ContactName	**Marshall Jackson**
StreetAddress	**5790 Cypress Avenue**
City	**Fort Myers**
State	**FL**
ZipCode	**33917**
Telephone	**2395555002**

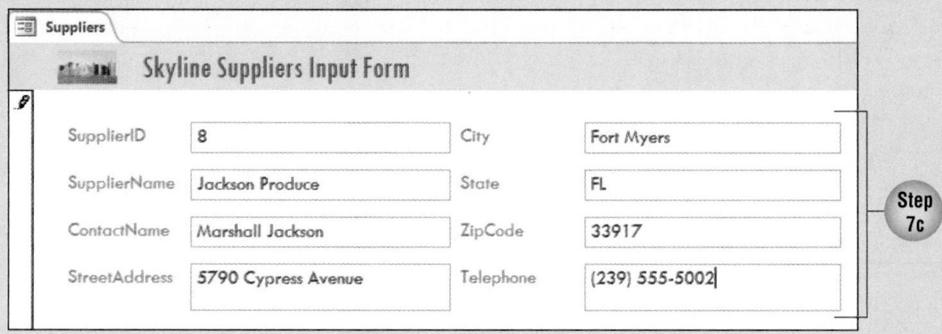

8. Click the Save button on the Quick Access toolbar and save the form with the name *Suppliers*.
9. Print the current form by completing the following steps:
   a. Click the FILE tab and then click the *Print* option.
   b. Click the Print button.
   c. At the Print dialog box, click the Setup button.
   d. At the Page Setup dialog box, click the *Print Form Only* option in the *Split Form* section of the dialog box and then click OK.
   e. At the Print dialog box, click the *Selected Record(s)* option and then click OK.
10. Close the Suppliers form.

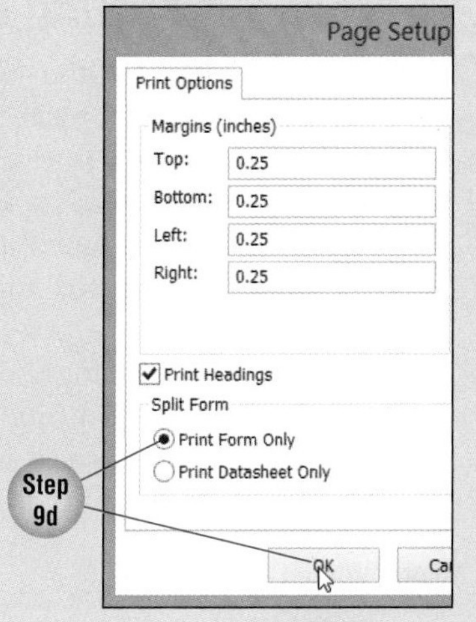

Creating Multiple Items Forms

When you create a form with the Form button, a single record displays. You can use the *Multiple Items* option at the More Forms button drop-down list to create a form that displays multiple records. The advantage to creating a multiple items form over displaying the table in Datasheet view is that you can customize the form using buttons in the FORM LAYOUT TOOLS ribbon with the DESIGN, ARRANGE, or FORMAT tab selected.

Quick Steps

Create a Multiple Items Form

1. Click desired table.
2. Click CREATE tab.
3. Click More Forms button.
4. Click *Multiple Items.*

Project 2c Creating a Multiple Items Form Part 3 of 5

1. With **AL1-C5-Skyline.accdb** open, create a multiple items form by completing the following steps:
   a. Click the Orders table in the Navigation pane.
   b. Click the CREATE tab.
   c. Click the More Forms button in the Forms group and then click *Multiple Items* at the drop-down list.
2. Insert the **Cityscape.jpg** image as the logo.
3. Insert the title *Skyline Orders*.
4. Click in any field outside the title, click the title again to select the header control object, and then drag the right border to the left until the border displays near the title.
5. Save the form with the name *Orders*.
6. Print the first page of the form by completing the following steps:
   a. Click the FILE tab and then click the *Print* option.
   b. Click the Print button.
   c. At the Print dialog box, click the *Pages* option in the *Print Range* section.
   d. Type 1 in the *From* text box, press the Tab key, and then type 1 in the *To* text box.
   e. Click OK.
7. Close the Orders form.

Creating Forms Using the Form Wizard

Quick Steps

Create a Form Using the Form Wizard
1. Click CREATE tab.
2. Click Form Wizard button.
3. Choose desired options at each Form Wizard dialog box.

Form Wizard

With the Form Wizard, you can be more selective about what fields you insert in a form.

Access offers a Form Wizard that guides you through the creation of a form. To create a form using the Form Wizard, click the CREATE tab and then click the Form Wizard button in the Forms group. At the first Form Wizard dialog box, shown in Figure 5.7, specify the table and then the fields you want included in the form. To select the table, click the down-pointing arrow at the right side of the *Table/Queries* option box and then click the desired table. Select the desired field in the *Available Fields* list box and then click the button containing the One Field button (the button containing the greater-than [>] symbol). This inserts the field in the *Selected Fields* list box. Continue in this manner until you have inserted all of the desired fields in the *Selected Fields* list box. If you want to insert all of the fields into the *Selected Fields* list box at one time, click the All Fields button (the button containing two greater-than symbols). After specifying the fields, click the Next button.

At the second Form Wizard dialog box, specify the layout for the records. You can choose from these layout type options: *Columnar*, *Tabular*, *Datasheet*, and *Justified*. Click the Next button and the third and final Form Wizard dialog box displays. It offers a title for the form and also provides the option *Open the form to view or enter information*. Make any necessary changes in this dialog box and then click the Finish button.

Figure 5.7 First Form Wizard Dialog Box

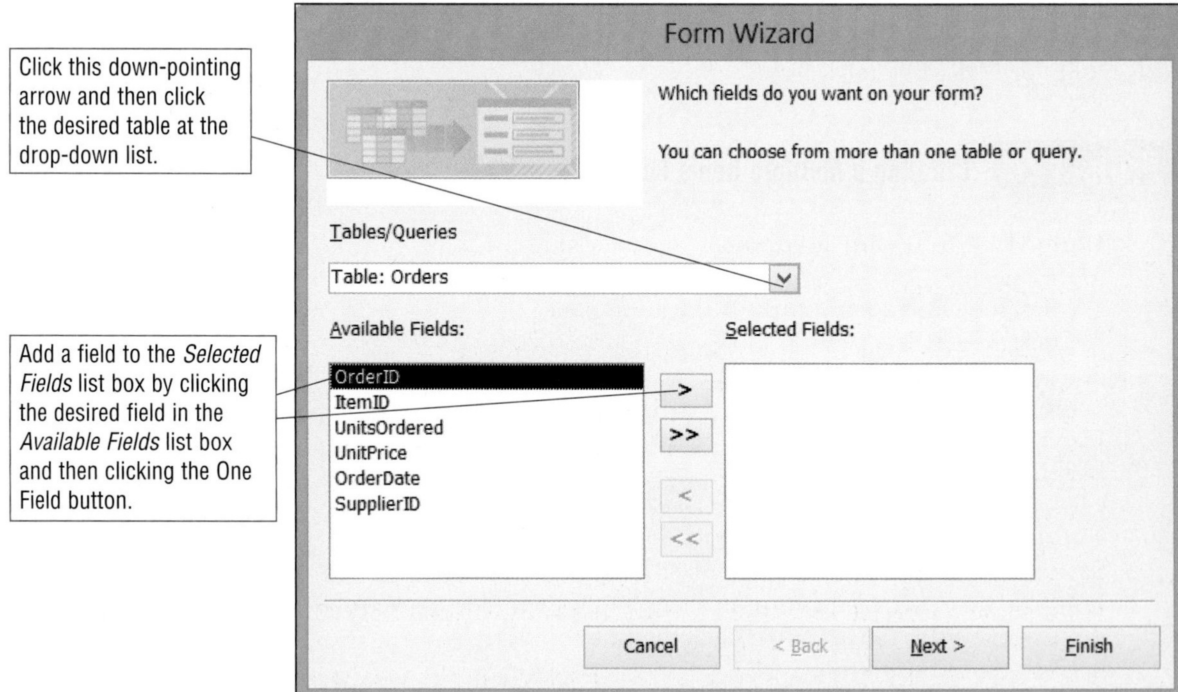
Click this down-pointing arrow and then click the desired table at the drop-down list.
Add a field to the Selected Fields list box by clicking the desired field in the Available Fields list box and then clicking the One Field button.
Form Wizard
Which fields do you want on your form?
You can choose from more than one table or query.
Tables/Queries
Table: Orders
Available Fields:
Selected Fields:
OrderID
ItemID
UnitsOrdered
UnitPrice
OrderDate
SupplierID
>
>>
<
<<
Cancel
< Back
Next >
Finish

Project 2d Creating a Form Using the Form Wizard

Part 4 of 5

1. With **AL1-C5-Skyline.accdb** open, create a form with the Form Wizard by completing the following steps:
   a. Click the CREATE tab.
   b. Click the Form Wizard button in the Forms group.
   c. At the first Form Wizard dialog box, click the down-pointing arrow at the right side of the *Tables/Queries* option box and then click *Table: Employees* at the drop-down list.
   d. Specify that you want all of the fields included in the form by clicking the All Fields button (the button containing the two greater-than symbols).
   e. Click the Next button.
   f. At the second Form Wizard dialog box, click the *Justified* option and then click the Next button.

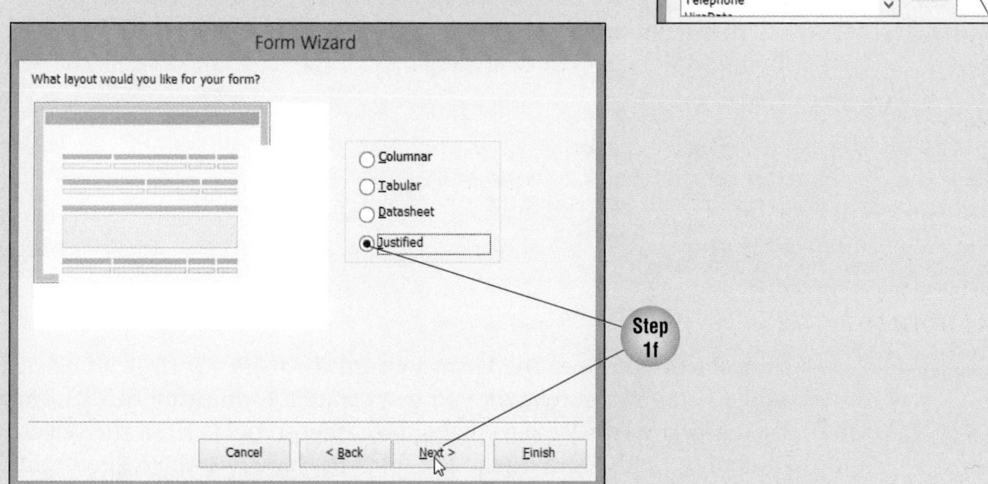

   g. At the third and final Form Wizard dialog box, click the Finish button.
2. Format the field headings by completing the following steps:
   a. Click the View button to switch to Layout view.
   b. Click the *EmployeeID* label control object. (This selects the object.)
   c. Hold down the Ctrl key and then click on each of the following label control objects: *FName*, *LName*, *StreetAddress*, *City*, *State*, *ZipCode*, *Telephone*, *HireDate*, and *HealthIns*.
   d. With all of the label control objects selected, release the Ctrl key.
   e. Click the FORM LAYOUT TOOLS FORMAT tab.
   f. Click the Shape Fill button and then click the *Aqua Blue 2* color option (ninth column, third row in the *Standard Colors* section).
   g. Click the FORM LAYOUT TOOLS DESIGN tab and then click the View button to switch to Form view.

3. In Form view, click the New (blank) record button and then add the following records:

EmployeeID	13
FName	Carol
LName	Thompson
StreetAddress	6554 Willow Drive, Apt. B
City	Fort Myers
State	FL
ZipCode	33915
Telephone	2395553719
HireDate	10/1/2015
HealthIns	(Click in the check box to insert a check mark.)
EmployeeID	14
FName	Eric
LName	Hahn
StreetAddress	331 South 152nd Street
City	Cape Coral
State	FL
ZipCode	33906
Telephone	2395558107
HireDate	10/1/2015
HealthIns	(Leave blank.)

4. Click the Save button on the Quick Access toolbar.
5. Print the record for Eric Hahn and then print the record for Carol Thompson.
6. Close the Employees form.

In Project 2d, you used the Form Wizard to create a form with all of the fields in one table. If tables are related, you can create a form using fields from related tables. At the first Form Wizard dialog box, choose fields from the selected table and then choose fields from a related table. To change to the related table, click the down-pointing arrow at the right of the *Tables/Queries* option box and then click the name of the desired table.

Project 2e Creating a Form with Related Tables

1. With **AL1-C5-Skyline.accdb** open, create a form with related tables by completing the following steps:
   a. Click the CREATE tab.
   b. Click the Form Wizard button in the Forms group.
   c. At the first Form Wizard dialog box, click the down-pointing arrow at the right of the *Tables/Queries* option box and then click *Table: Banquets*.
   d. Click *ResDate* in the *Available Fields* list box and then click the One Field button. (This inserts *ResDate* in the *Selected Fields* list box.)
   e. Click *AmountTotal* in the *Available Fields* list box, click the One Field button.
   f. With *AmountPaid* selected in the *Available Fields* list box, click the One Field button.
   g. Click the down-pointing arrow at the right side of the *Tables/Queries* option box and then click *Table: Events* at the drop-down list.
   h. Click *Event* in the *Available Fields* list box and then click the One Field button.
   i. Click the down-pointing arrow at the right side of the *Tables/Queries* option box and then click *Table: Employees* at the drop-down list.
   j. Click *LName* in the *Available Fields* list box and then click the One Field button.
   k. Click the Next button.
   l. At the second Form Wizard dialog box, click the Next button.
   m. At the third Form Wizard dialog box, click the Next button.
   n. At the fourth Form Wizard dialog box, select the text in the *What title do you want for your form?* text box, type **Upcoming Banquets**, and then click the Finish button.
2. When the first record displays, print the record.
3. Save and then close the form.
4. Close **AL1-C5-Skyline.accdb**.

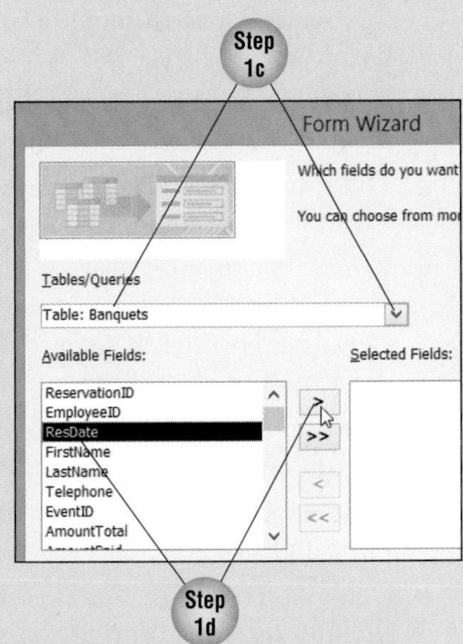

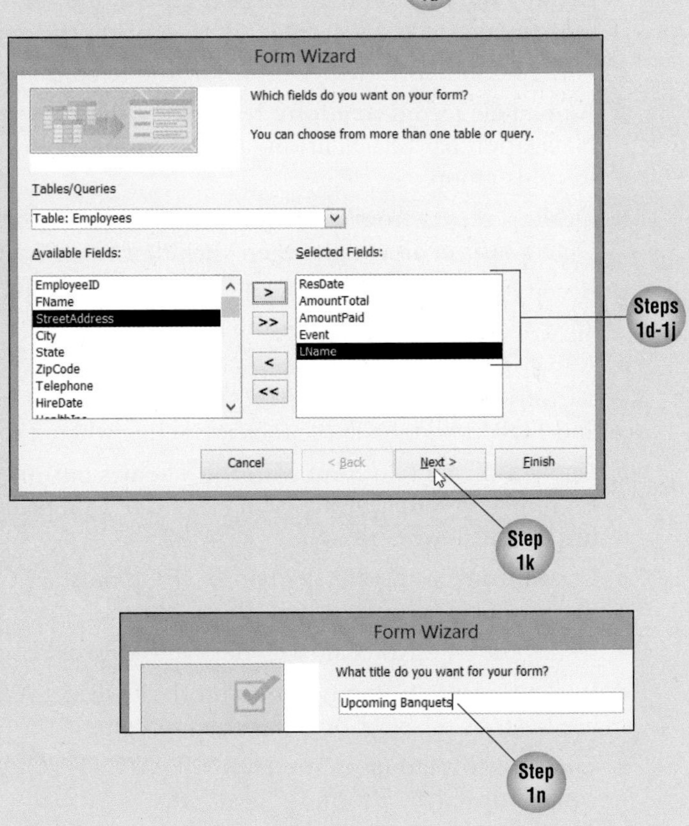

Chapter Summary

- Creating a form generally improves the ease of entering data into a table. Some methods for creating a form include using the Form, Split Form, and Multiple Items buttons or the Form Wizard.
- A form is an object you can use to enter and edit data in a table or query and to help prevent incorrect data from being entered in a database.
- The simplest method for creating a form is to click a table in the Navigation pane, click the CREATE button, and then click the Form button in the Forms group.
- When you create a form, it displays in Layout view. Use this view to display data and modify the appearance and contents of the form. Other form views include Form view and Design view. Use Form view to enter and manage records and use Design view to view and modify the structure of the form.
- Open an existing form in Layout view by right-clicking the form in the Navigation pane and then clicking *Layout View* at the shortcut menu.
- Print a form with options at the Print dialog box. To print an individual record, display the Print dialog box, click the *Selected Record(s)* option, and then click OK.
- Delete a form with the Delete button in the Records group on the HOME tab or by right-clicking the form in the Navigation pane and then clicking *Delete* at the shortcut menu. A message may display asking you to confirm the deletion.
- Navigate in a form with buttons in the Record Navigation bar.
- Add a new record to a form by clicking the New (blank) record button in the Record Navigation bar or by clicking the HOME tab and then clicking the New button in the Records group.
- Delete a record from a form by displaying the record, clicking the HOME tab, clicking the Delete button arrow, and then clicking *Delete Record* at the drop-down list.
- If you create a form with a table that has a one-to-many relationship established, Access adds a datasheet at the bottom of the form.
- A form is comprised of a series of control objects. Customize these control objects with buttons on the FORM LAYOUT TOOLS ribbon under the DESIGN tab, ARRANGE tab, and FORMAT tab. These tabs are active when a form displays in Layout view.
- Apply a theme to a form with the Themes button in the Themes group on the FORM LAYOUT TOOLS DESIGN tab. Use the Colors and Fonts buttons in the Themes group to further customize a theme.
- Use buttons in the Header/Footer group on the FORM LAYOUT TOOLS DESIGN tab to insert a logo, form title, and date and time.
- In Layout view, you can size, delete, and insert control objects.
- In the Rows & Columns group on the FORM LAYOUT TOOLS ARRANGE tab, you can use buttons to select or insert rows or columns.
- The Controls group on the FORM LAYOUT TOOLS DESIGN tab contains control objects you can insert in a form.
- Merge cells in a form by selecting cells and then clicking the Merge button in the Merge/Split group on the FORM LAYOUT TOOLS ARRANGE tab. Split selected cells by clicking the Split Vertically or Split Horizontally button.

- Format control objects and cells in a form with buttons on the FORM LAYOUT TOOLS FORMAT tab.
- Use the Conditional Formatting button in the Control Formatting group on the FORM LAYOUT TOOLS FORMAT tab to apply specific formatting to data that matches a specific criterion.
- Click the Add Existing Fields button in the Tools group on the FORM LAYOUT TOOLS DESIGN tab to display the Field List task pane. Add fields to the form by double-clicking a field or dragging the field from the task pane.
- Create a split form by clicking the More Forms button on the CREATE tab and then clicking *Split Form* in the drop-down list. Access displays the form in Form view in the top portion of the work area and in Datasheet view in the bottom portion of the work area. The two views are connected and synchronous.
- Create a Multiple Items form by clicking the More Forms button on the CREATE tab and then clicking *Multiple Items* in the drop-down list.
- The Form Wizard walks you through the steps for creating a form and lets you specify the fields you want included in the form, a layout for the records, and a name for the form.
- You can create a form with the Form Wizard that contains fields from tables connected by a one-to-many relationship.

Commands Review

FEATURE	RIBBON TAB, GROUP	BUTTON, OPTION
Conditional Formatting Rules Manager dialog box	FORM LAYOUT TOOLS FORMAT, Control Formatting	
Field List task pane	FORM LAYOUT TOOLS DESIGN, Tools	
form	CREATE, Forms	
Form Wizard	CREATE, Forms	
multiple items form	CREATE, Forms	, *Multiple Items*
split form	CREATE, Forms	, *Split Form*

Concepts Check Test Your Knowledge

Completion: In the space provided at the right, indicate the correct term, symbol, or command.

1. The simplest method for creating a form is to click this tab and then click the Form button. ________________
2. When you click the Form button to create a form, the form displays in this view. ________________
3. To print the current record in a form, click this option at the Print dialog box and then click OK. ________________
4. Navigate in a form using buttons in this bar. ________________
5. Click this button to add a new record to a form. ________________
6. The FORM LAYOUT TOOLS DESIGN tab is active when a form displays in this view. ________________
7. The Themes group on the FORM LAYOUT TOOLS DESIGN tab contains three buttons: the Themes button, the Colors button, and this button. ________________
8. Click the Logo button on the FORM LAYOUT TOOLS DESIGN tab and this dialog box displays. ________________
9. To select nonadjacent objects or cells, hold down this key on the keyboard while clicking the desired objects or cells. ________________
10. This group on the FORM LAYOUT TOOLS ARRANGE tab contains buttons for selecting and inserting rows and columns in a form. ________________
11. With this button in the Control Formatting group on the FORM LAYOUT TOOLS FORMAT tab, you can apply formatting to data that meets a specific criterion. ________________
12. Click the Add Existing Fields button in the Tools group on the FORM LAYOUT TOOLS DESIGN tab and this task pane displays. ________________
13. Create a split form or multiple items form with options at this button's drop-down list. ________________
14. When you create a form with the *Split Form* option, the form displays in this view in the top half of the work area. ________________

Skills Check Assess Your Performance

Assessment 1

CREATE AND CUSTOMIZE A SUPPLIERS FORM

1. Display the Open dialog box with the AL1C5 folder on your storage medium the active folder.
2. Open **AL1-C5-PacTrek.accdb** and enable the contents.
3. Use the Form button in the Forms group on the CREATE tab to create a form with the Suppliers table.
4. Switch to Form view and then add the following records to the Suppliers form:

SupplierID	**12**
SupplierName	**Seaside Suppliers**
StreetAddress	**4120 Shoreline Drive**
City	**Vancouver**
Prov/State	**BC**
PostalCode	**V2V 8K4**
EmailAddress	**seaside@emcp.net**
Telephone	**6045557945**

SupplierID	**34**
SupplierName	**Carson Company**
StreetAddress	**120 Plaza Center**
City	**Vancouver**
Prov/State	**BC**
PostalCode	**V2V 1K6**
EmailAddress	**carson@emcp.net**
Telephone	**6045551955**

5. Delete the record containing information on Manning, Inc.
6. Switch to Layout view and then apply the Organic theme to the form.
7. Select and delete the logo object in the *Form Header* section and then click the Logo button in the Header/Footer group. At the Insert Picture dialog box, navigate to the AL1C5 folder on your storage medium and then double-click ***River.jpg***.
8. Create the title *Pacific Trek Suppliers* for the form. Click in any field outside the title and then click in the title (which selects the header control object). Drag the right border of the title control object to the left until the border displays near the title.
9. Insert the date and time in the *Form Header* section.
10. Select the date and time control objects, drag in the left border until the border displays near the date and time, and then drag the objects so they are positioned near the title.
11. Click the text box control object containing the supplier number and then drag the right border to the left until *Lines: 1 Characters: 30* displays at the left side of the Status bar.

12. Select the fields in the first column (*SupplierID* through *Telephone*) and then apply the following formatting:
    a. Apply bold formatting.
    b. Apply the Dark Blue font color (ninth column, bottom row in the *Standard Colors* section).
    c. Apply the Align Right alignment.
    d. Apply the Light Blue 2 shape fill (fifth column, third row in the *Standard Colors* section).
    e. Apply the Dark Blue shape outline color (ninth column, bottom row in the *Standard Colors* section).
13. Select the second column and then apply the following formatting:
    a. Apply the Light Blue 1 shape fill (fifth column, second row in the *Standard Colors* section).
    b. Apply the Dark Blue shape outline color (ninth column, bottom row in the *Standard Colors* section).
14. Switch to Form view.
15. Save the form with the name *Suppliers*.
16. Make active the record for supplier number 12 (one of the new records you entered) and then print the record. (Make sure you print only the record for supplier number 12.)
17. Make active the record for supplier number 34 and then print the record.
18. Close the Suppliers table.

Assessment 2

CREATE AND CUSTOMIZE AN ORDERS FORM

1. With **AL1-C5-PacTrek.accdb** open, create a form with the Orders table using the Form button on the CREATE tab.
2. Insert a field from a related table by completing the following steps:
    a. Display the Field List task pane and then, if necessary, click the Show all tables hyperlink.
    b. Expand the Suppliers table in the *Fields available in related tables* section.
    c. Drag the field named *SupplierName* into the form and position it between *SupplierID* and *ProductID*.
    d. Change the *SupplierName* field from a Lookup field to a text box by clicking the Options button that displays below the field and then clicking *Change to Text Box* at the drop-down list.
    e. Close the Field List task pane.
3. Click the text box control object containing the text *1010* and then drag the right border to the left until *Lines: 1 Characters: 30* displays at the left side of the Status bar.
4. Select all of the objects in the *Detail* section by clicking an object in the *Detail* section and then clicking the table move handle (the small, square button with a four-headed arrow inside). With the objects selected, apply the following formatting:
    a. Change the font to Cambria and the font size to 12 points.
    b. Apply the Align Right alignment.

5. Select the first column and then apply the following formatting:
   a. Apply the Green 2 shape fill (seventh column, third row in the *Standard Colors* section).
   b. Apply bold formatting.
6. Apply conditional formatting that changes the font color to blue for any *Amount* field entry that contains an amount greater than $999. ***Hint: Click the text box control object containing the amount $199.50, click the Conditional Formatting button, click the New Rule button, change the second option in the* Edit the rule description *section to* greater than, *and then enter 999 in the third option box (without the dollar sign).***
7. Save the form with the name *Orders*.
8. Print the fifteenth record in the form and then close the form.

Assessment 3

CREATE A SPLIT FORM WITH THE PRODUCTS TABLE

1. With **AL1-C5-PacTrek.accdb** open, create a form with the Products table using the *Split Form* option from the More Forms button drop-down list.
2. Decrease the width of the second column until *Lines: 1 Characters: 35* displays at the left side of the Status bar
3. Select the first column and then apply the following formatting:
   a. Apply bold formatting.
   b. Apply the Aqua Blue 1 shape fill (ninth column, second row in the *Standard Colors* section).
   c. Apply the Blue shape outline color (eighth column, bottom row in the *Standard Colors* section).
4. Click in the text box control object containing the number *0* (the *UnitsOnOrder* number) and then apply conditional formatting that displays the number in red in any field value equal to zero.
5. Change to Form view, create a new record, and then enter the following information in the specified fields:

ProductID	**205-CS**
Product	**Timberline solo cook set**
SupplierID	**15**
UnitsInStock	**8**
UnitsOnOrder	**0**
ReorderLevel	**5**

6. Save the form with the name *Products*.
7. Print the current record (the record you just typed). ***Hint: At the Print dialog box, click the Setup button. At the Page Setup dialog box, click the* Print Form Only *option.***
8. Close the Products form.
9. Close **AL1-C5-PacTrek.accdb**.

Assessment

4 CREATE AND CUSTOMIZE AN EMPLOYEES FORM

1. Open **AL1-C5-Griffin.accdb** from the AL1C5 folder on your storage medium and enable the contents.
2. Suppose you want to create a form for entering employee information but you do not want to include the employees' salaries, since that is confidential information and accessible only to the account manager. Use the Form Wizard to create an Employees form that includes all fields *except* the *AnnualSalary* field and name the form *Employees*.
3. Type a new record with the following information in the specified fields:

EmpID	**1099**
LastName	**Williamson**
FirstName	**Carrie**
BirthDate	**6/24/1986**
HireDate	**8/1/2014**
DeptID	**RD**

4. Switch to layout view, apply the Slice theme, change the theme colors to *Blue Warm*, and change the theme fonts to *Franklin Gothic*.
5. Print the new record you typed.
6. Close the Employees form.

Visual Benchmark — Demonstrate Your Proficiency

CREATE AND FORMAT A PROPERTIES FORM

1. Open **AL1-C5-SunProperties.accdb** located in the AL1C5 folder on your storage medium and enable the contents.
2. Create a form with the Properties table and format the form so it appears similar to the form in Figure 5.8 using the following specifications:
   a. Apply the Facet theme and apply the Paper theme colors.
   b. Insert the logo, title, date, and time in the *Form Header* section, as shown in the figure. (Insert the file **SunPropLogo.jpg** for the logo. Adjust the size of the title control object and then move the date and time, as shown in the figure.)
   c. Select all of the objects in the *Detail* section and then change the font color to Maroon 5 (sixth column, sixth row in the *Standard Colors* section).
   d. Select the first column; apply bold formatting; apply Light Yellow, Background 2, Darker 10% shape fill (third column, second row in the *Theme Colors* section); apply the Maroon 5 shape outline color (sixth column, sixth row in the *Standard Colors* section); and then change the alignment to Align Right.

e. Decrease the size of the second column as shown in the figure.
f. Insert a new column to the right of the second column, merge cells in the new column to accommodate the sun image, and then insert the image **SunProp.jpg** (as a control object). Adjust the width of the third column so the image displays as shown in Figure 5.8.
g. Apply conditional formatting to the *MoRent* field that displays in green any rent amount greater than $999.
h. Adjust the position of the control objects so that the form displays similar to what is shown in Figure 5.8.

3. Save the form with the name *Properties* and then print the current record.
4. Close the form and then close **AL1-C5-SunProperties.accdb**.

Figure 5.8 Visual Benchmark

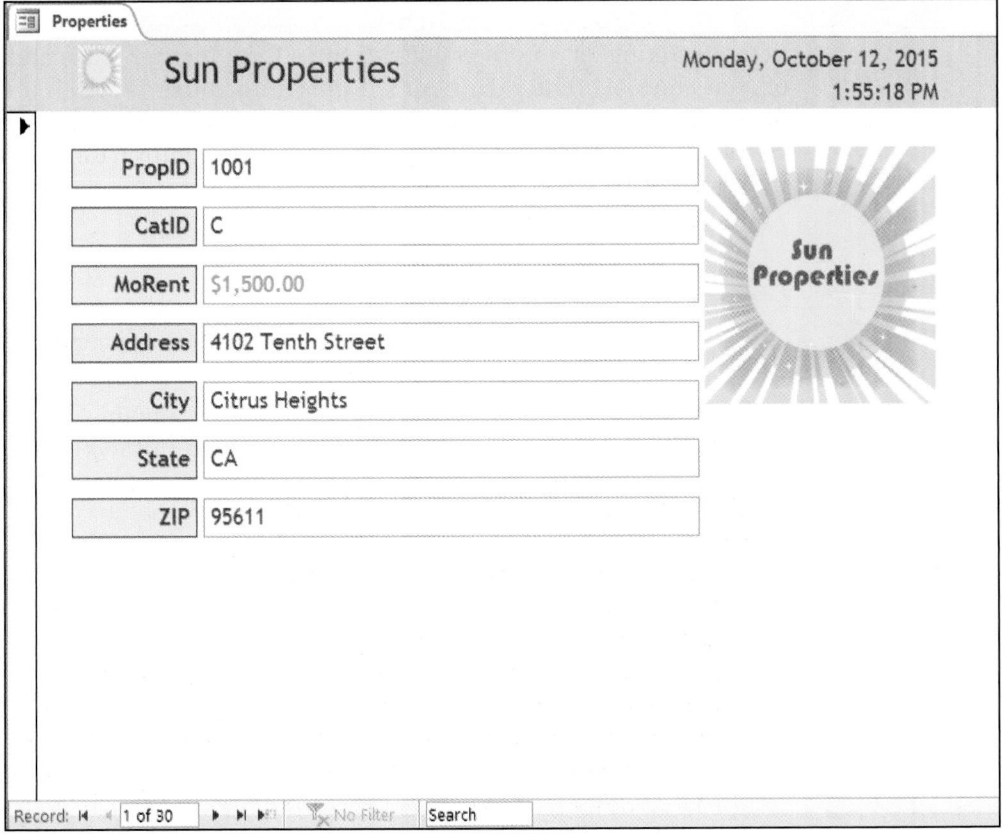

Case Study Apply Your Skills

Part 1

You are the office manager at the Lewis Vision Care Center and your center is switching over to Access to manage files. You have already created four basic tables and now need to create relationships and enter data. Open **AL1-C5-LewisCenter.accdb** and then create the following relationships between tables (enforce referential integrity and cascade fields and records):

Field Name	"One" Table	"Many" Table
PatientID	Patients	Billing
ServiceID	Services	Billing
DoctorID	Doctors	Billing

Save and then print the relationships.

Part 2

Before entering data in the tables, create a form for each table and apply a theme of your choosing. Enter data in the forms in the order in which it appears in Figure 5.10 on the next page. Apply any additional formatting to enhance the visual appearance of each form. After entering the information in the forms, print the first record of each form.

Part 3

Apply the following conditions to fields in forms:

- In the Patients form, apply the condition that the city *Tulsa* displays in red and the city *Broken Arrow* displays in blue in the *City* field. Print the first record of the Patients form and then close the form.
- In the Billing form, apply the condition that amounts in the *Fee* field over $99 display in green. Print the second record of the Billing form and then close the form.

Close **AL1-C5-LewisCenter.accdb**.

Part 4

Your center has a procedures manual that describes workplace processes and procedures. Open Word and then create a document for the procedures manual that describes the formatting and conditions you applied to the forms in **AL1-C5-LewisCenter.accdb**. Save the completed document and name it **AL1-C5-CS-Manual**. Print and then close **AL1-C5-CS-Manual.docx**.

Figure 5.10 Case Study Part 2

Patients form

Patient number 030 Rhonda J. Mahler 130 East 41st Street Tulsa, OK 74155 (918) 555-3107	Patient number 076 Patrick S. Robbins 3281 Aspen Avenue Tulsa, OK 74108 (918) 555-9672	Patient number 092 Oren L. Vargas 21320 Tenth Street Broken Arrow, OK 74012 (918) 555-1188
Patient number 085 Michael A. Dempsey 506 Houston Street Tulsa, OK 74142 (918) 555-5541	Patient number 074 Wendy L. Holloway 23849 22nd Street Broken Arrow, OK 74009 (918) 555-8842	Patient number 023 Maggie M. Winters 4422 South 121st Tulsa, OK 74142 (918) 555-8833

Doctors form

Doctor number 1 Carolyn Joswick (918) 555-4772	Doctor number 2 Gerald Ingram (918) 555-9890	Doctor number 3 Kay Feather (918) 555-7762
Doctor number 4 Sean Granger (918) 555-1039	Doctor number 5 Jerome Deltoro (918) 555-8021	

Services form

Co = Consultation	V = Vision Screening	G = Glaucoma Testing
C = Cataract Testing	S = Surgery	E = Emergency

Billing form

Patient number 076 Doctor number 2 Date of visit = 4/1/2015 Service ID = C Fee = $85	Patient number 076 Doctor number 3 Date of visit = 4/1/2015 Service ID = V Fee = $150	Patient number 085 Doctor number 1 Date of visit = 4/1/2015 Service ID = Co Fee = $0
Patient number 074 Doctor number 3 Date of visit = 4/1/2015 Service ID = V Fee = $150	Patient number 023 Doctor number 5 Date of visit = 4/1/2015 Service ID = S Fee = $750	Patient number 092 Doctor number 1 Date of visit = 4/1/2015 Service ID = G Fee = $85

MICROSOFT®

ACCESS®

Creating Reports and Mailing Labels

PERFORMANCE OBJECTIVES

Upon successful completion of Chapter 6, you will be able to:

- **Create a report using the Report button**
- **Display a report in Print Preview**
- **Create a report with a query**
- **Format and customize a report**
- **Group and sort records in a report**
- **Create a report using the Report Wizard**
- **Create mailing labels using the Label Wizard**

Tutorials

6.1 Creating and Editing a Report

6.2 Modifying a Report

6.3 Adding a Calculation to a Report

6.4 Applying Conditional Formatting to a Report

6.5 Grouping, Sorting, and Adding Totals to a Report

6.6 Creating a Report Using the Report Wizard

6.7 Creating Mailing Labels

In this chapter, you will learn how to prepare reports from data in a table using the Report button in the Reports group on the CREATE tab and using the Report Wizard. You will also learn how to format and customize a report and create mailing labels using the Label Wizard. Model answers for this chapter's projects appear on the following pages.

AL1C6

Note: Before beginning the projects, copy to your storage medium the AL1C6 subfolder from the AL1 folder on the CD that accompanies this textbook and make AL1C6 the active folder.

Project 1 Create and Customize Reports Using Tables and Queries

Sales2014Query

Thursday, October 15, 2015
1:55:23 PM

Representative	Client	Sales 2014
Andre Kulisek	HE Systems	$554,120.00
Kwan Im	Eagleton Industries	$300,137.00
Linda Foster	Bering Company	$289,563.00
Craig Johnson	Miles & Harrisburg	$222,133.00
Lee Hutchinson	Harford Systems	$215,420.00
Catherine Singleton	Zinn-Harris Electronics	$214,000.00
Catherine Singleton	Gallagher Systems	$199,346.00
Jaren Newman	Haute Contractors	$174,319.00
David DeBruler	AeroTech	$156,439.00
Cecilia Ortega	Dover Industries	$151,003.00
Catherine Singleton	Franklin Services	$141,670.00
Gina Tapparo	DV Corporation	$138,560.00
Alfred Silva	Clearwater Service	$125,436.00
Craig Johnson	Wheeling Products	$115,423.00
William Ludlow	Madison Electrics	$99,450.00
Robin Rehberg	Landower Company	$97,653.00
Isabelle Marshall	Providence, Inc.	$85,628.00
Edward Harris	Karris Supplies	$61,349.00
Jaren Newman	Paragon Corporation	$51,237.00
Lydia Alvarado	Martin Manufacturing	$35,679.00
Craig Johnson	Hoosier Corporation	$24,880.00
Maureen Pascual	Blue Ridge, Inc.	$17,542.00
Lee Hutchinson	Valley Construction	$15,248.00
Alfred Silva	Alderton Metals	$9,547.00
Alfred Silva	Northstar Services	$9,457.00
Kwan Im	Milltown Contractors	$2,356.00

Page 1 of 1

Project 1b, Dearborn 2014Sales Report

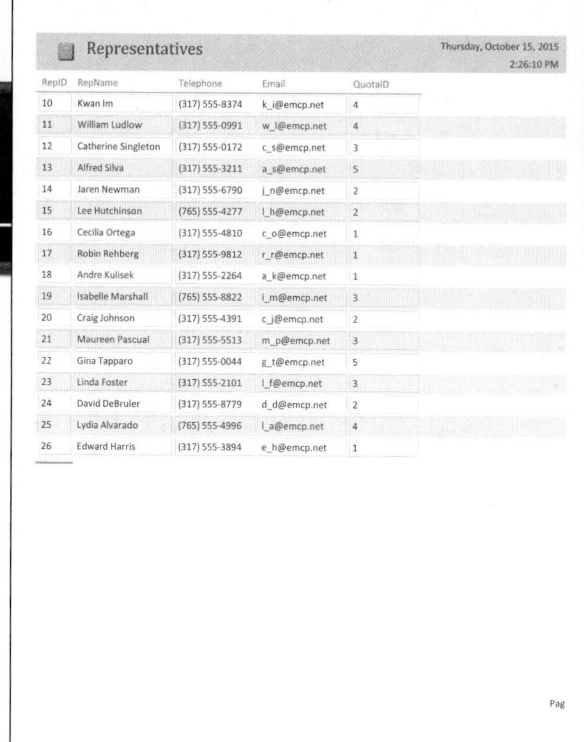

Representatives

Thursday, October 15, 2015
2:26:10 PM

RepID	RepName	Telephone	Email	QuotaID
10	Kwan Im	(317) 555-8374	k_i@emcp.net	4
11	William Ludlow	(317) 555-0991	w_l@emcp.net	4
12	Catherine Singleton	(317) 555-0172	c_s@emcp.net	3
13	Alfred Silva	(317) 555-3211	a_s@emcp.net	5
14	Jaren Newman	(317) 555-6790	j_n@emcp.net	2
15	Lee Hutchinson	(765) 555-4277	l_h@emcp.net	2
16	Cecilia Ortega	(317) 555-4810	c_o@emcp.net	1
17	Robin Rehberg	(317) 555-9812	r_r@emcp.net	1
18	Andre Kulisek	(317) 555-2264	a_k@emcp.net	1
19	Isabelle Marshall	(765) 555-8822	i_m@emcp.net	3
20	Craig Johnson	(317) 555-4391	c_j@emcp.net	2
21	Maureen Pascual	(317) 555-5513	m_p@emcp.net	3
22	Gina Tapparo	(317) 555-0044	g_t@emcp.net	5
23	Linda Foster	(317) 555-2101	l_f@emcp.net	3
24	David DeBruler	(317) 555-8779	d_d@emcp.net	2
25	Lydia Alvarado	(765) 555-4996	l_a@emcp.net	4
26	Edward Harris	(317) 555-3894	e_h@emcp.net	1

Pag

Project 1b, Dearborn Representatives Report

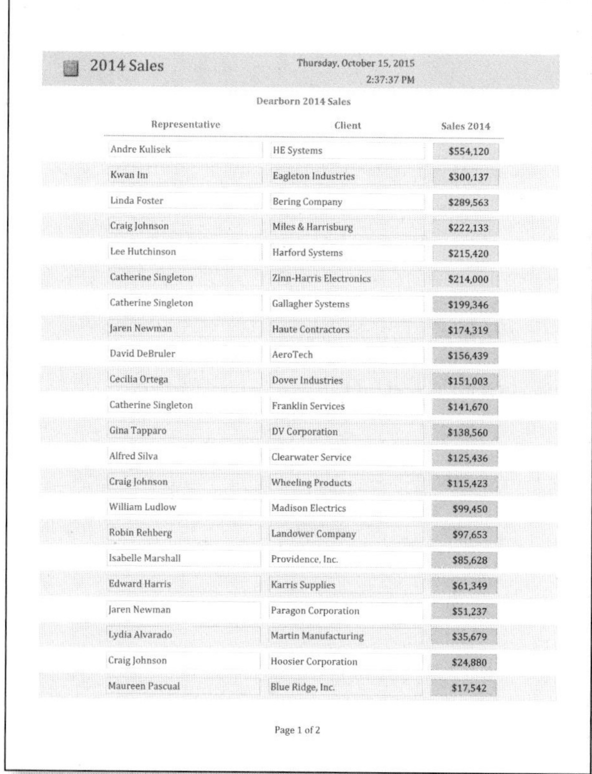

2014 Sales

Thursday, October 15, 2015
2:37:37 PM

Dearborn 2014 Sales

Representative	Client	Sales 2014
Andre Kulisek	HE Systems	$554,120
Kwan Im	Eagleton Industries	$300,137
Linda Foster	Bering Company	$289,563
Craig Johnson	Miles & Harrisburg	$222,133
Lee Hutchinson	Harford Systems	$215,420
Catherine Singleton	Zinn-Harris Electronics	$214,000
Catherine Singleton	Gallagher Systems	$199,346
Jaren Newman	Haute Contractors	$174,319
David DeBruler	AeroTech	$156,439
Cecilia Ortega	Dover Industries	$151,003
Catherine Singleton	Franklin Services	$141,670
Gina Tapparo	DV Corporation	$138,560
Alfred Silva	Clearwater Service	$125,436
Craig Johnson	Wheeling Products	$115,423
William Ludlow	Madison Electrics	$99,450
Robin Rehberg	Landower Company	$97,653
Isabelle Marshall	Providence, Inc.	$85,628
Edward Harris	Karris Supplies	$61,349
Jaren Newman	Paragon Corporation	$51,237
Lydia Alvarado	Martin Manufacturing	$35,679
Craig Johnson	Hoosier Corporation	$24,880
Maureen Pascual	Blue Ridge, Inc.	$17,542

Page 1 of 2

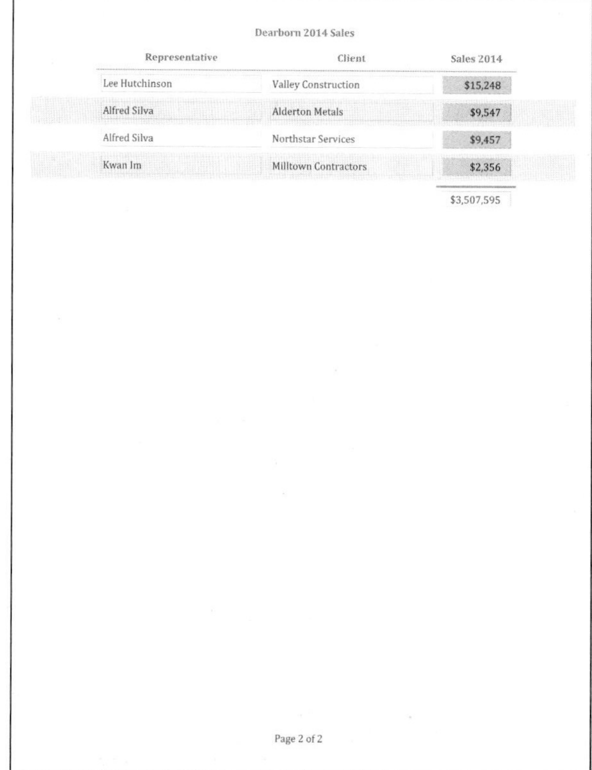

Dearborn 2014 Sales

Representative	Client	Sales 2014
Lee Hutchinson	Valley Construction	$15,248
Alfred Silva	Alderton Metals	$9,547
Alfred Silva	Northstar Services	$9,457
Kwan Im	Milltown Contractors	$2,356
		$3,507,595

Page 2 of 2

Project 1c, Dearborn 2014Sales Report

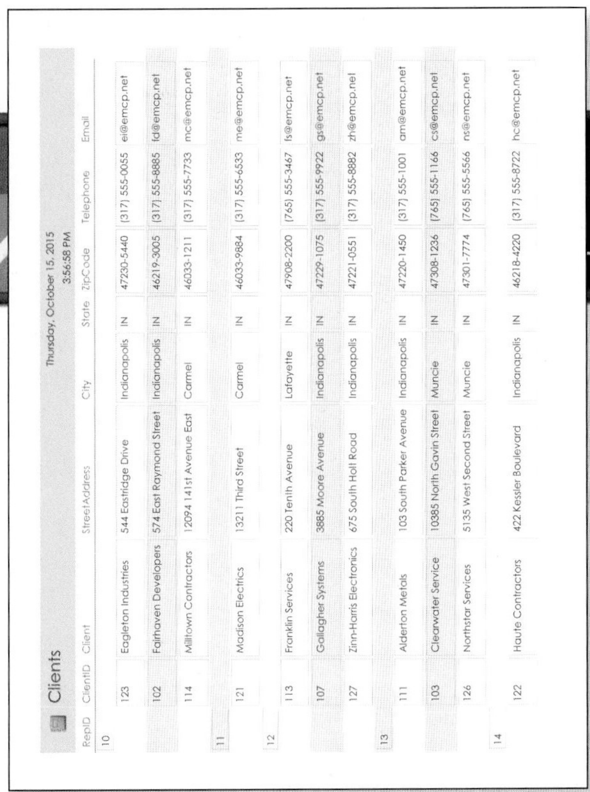

Clients

Thursday, October 15, 2015
3:56:58 PM

RepID	ClientID	Client	StreetAddress	City	State	ZipCode	Telephone	Email
10								
	123	Eagleton Industries	544 Eastridge Drive	Indianapolis	IN	47230-5440	(317) 555-0055	ei@emcp.net
	102	Fairhaven Developers	574 East Raymond Street	Indianapolis	IN	46219-3005	(317) 555-8885	fd@emcp.net
	114	Milltown Contractors	12094 141st Avenue East	Carmel	IN	46033-1211	(317) 555-7733	mc@emcp.net
11								
	121	Madison Electrics	13211 Third Street	Carmel	IN	46033-9884	(317) 555-6533	me@emcp.net
12								
	113	Franklin Services	220 Tenth Avenue	Lafayette	IN	47908-2200	(765) 555-3467	fs@emcp.net
	107	Gallagher Systems	3885 Moore Avenue	Indianapolis	IN	47229-1075	(317) 555-9922	gs@emcp.net
	127	Zinn-Harris Electronics	675 South Holt Road	Indianapolis	IN	47221-0551	(317) 555-8882	zh@emcp.net
13								
	111	Alderton Metals	103 South Parker Avenue	Indianapolis	IN	47220-1450	(317) 555-1001	am@emcp.net
	103	Clearwater Service	10385 North Gavin Street	Muncie	IN	47308-1236	(765) 555-1166	cs@emcp.net
	126	Northstar Services	5135 West Second Street	Muncie	IN	47301-7774	(765) 555-5566	ns@emcp.net
14								
	122	Haute Contractors	422 Kessler Boulevard	Indianapolis	IN	46218-4220	(317) 555-8722	hc@emcp.net

Project 1d, Dearborn ClientsGroupedRpt Report

InOrMunSalesOver$99999Query

Thursday, October 15, 2015
3:45:38 PM

City	Client	StreetAddress	Sta
Indianapolis			
	AeroTech	9905 West 16th Street	IN
	AeroTech	9905 West 16th Street	IN
	DV Corporation	210 West Michigan Street	IN
	DV Corporation	210 West Michigan Street	IN
	Eagleton Industries	544 Eastridge Drive	IN
	Eagleton Industries	544 Eastridge Drive	IN
	Gallagher Systems	3885 Moore Avenue	IN
	Gallagher Systems	3885 Moore Avenue	IN
	Harford Systems	9654 Jackson Street	IN
	Harford Systems	9654 Jackson Street	IN
	Haute Contractors	422 Kessler Boulevard	IN
	Haute Contractors	422 Kessler Boulevard	IN
	Landower Company	1299 Arlington Avenue	IN
	Miles & Harrisburg	11029 47th Street East	IN
	Miles & Harrisburg	11029 47th Street East	IN
	Wheeling Products	5567 Washburn Avenue	IN
	Wheeling Products	5567 Washburn Avenue	IN
	Zinn-Harris Electronics	675 South Holt Road	IN
	Zinn-Harris Electronics	675 South Holt Road	IN
Muncie			
	Bering Company	4521 East Sixth Street	IN
	Bering Company	4521 East Sixth Street	IN
	Clearwater Service	10385 North Gavin Street	IN
	Clearwater Service	10385 North Gavin Street	IN
	Dover Industries	4839 Huchins Road	IN
	Dover Industries	4839 Huchins Road	IN

Page

Project 1d, Dearborn InOrMunOver$99999 Report

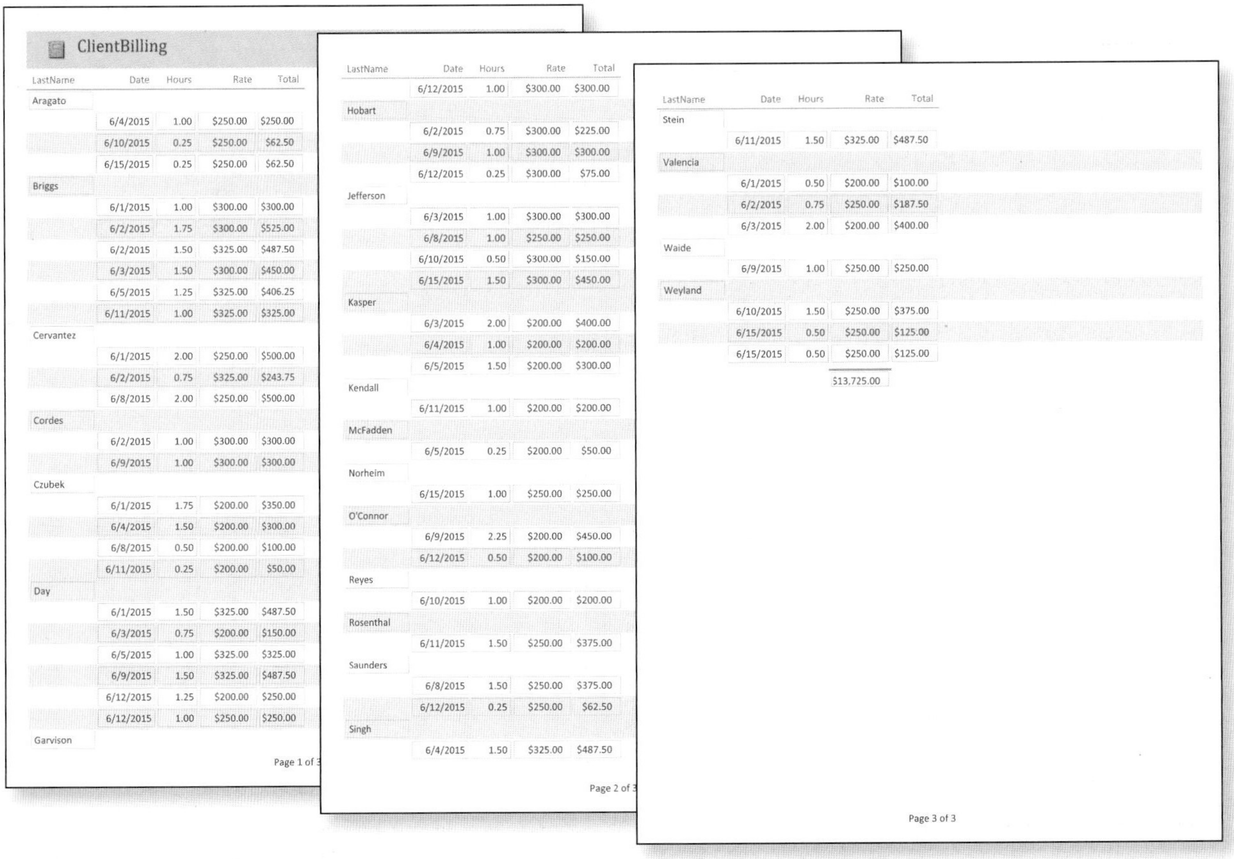

ClientBilling

LastName	Date	Hours	Rate	Total
Aragato				
	6/4/2015	1.00	$250.00	$250.00
	6/10/2015	0.25	$250.00	$62.50
	6/15/2015	0.25	$250.00	$62.50
Briggs				
	6/1/2015	1.00	$300.00	$300.00
	6/2/2015	1.75	$300.00	$525.00
	6/2/2015	1.50	$325.00	$487.50
	6/3/2015	1.50	$300.00	$450.00
	6/5/2015	1.25	$325.00	$406.25
	6/11/2015	1.00	$325.00	$325.00
Cervantez				
	6/1/2015	2.00	$250.00	$500.00
	6/2/2015	0.75	$325.00	$243.75
	6/8/2015	2.00	$250.00	$500.00
Cordes				
	6/2/2015	1.00	$300.00	$300.00
	6/9/2015	1.00	$300.00	$300.00
Czubek				
	6/1/2015	1.75	$200.00	$350.00
	6/4/2015	1.50	$200.00	$300.00
	6/8/2015	0.50	$200.00	$100.00
	6/11/2015	0.25	$200.00	$50.00
Day				
	6/1/2015	1.50	$325.00	$487.50
	6/3/2015	0.75	$200.00	$150.00
	6/5/2015	1.00	$325.00	$325.00
	6/9/2015	1.50	$325.00	$487.50
	6/12/2015	1.25	$200.00	$250.00
	6/12/2015	1.00	$250.00	$250.00
Garvison				

Page 1 of 3

LastName	Date	Hours	Rate	Total
	6/12/2015	1.00	$300.00	$300.00
Hobart				
	6/2/2015	0.75	$300.00	$225.00
	6/9/2015	1.00	$300.00	$300.00
	6/12/2015	0.25	$300.00	$75.00
Jefferson				
	6/3/2015	1.00	$300.00	$300.00
	6/8/2015	1.00	$250.00	$250.00
	6/10/2015	0.50	$300.00	$150.00
	6/15/2015	1.50	$300.00	$450.00
Kasper				
	6/3/2015	2.00	$200.00	$400.00
	6/4/2015	1.00	$200.00	$200.00
	6/5/2015	1.50	$200.00	$300.00
Kendall				
	6/11/2015	1.00	$200.00	$200.00
McFadden				
	6/5/2015	0.25	$200.00	$50.00
Norheim				
	6/15/2015	1.00	$250.00	$250.00
O'Connor				
	6/9/2015	2.25	$200.00	$450.00
	6/12/2015	0.50	$200.00	$100.00
Reyes				
	6/10/2015	1.00	$200.00	$200.00
Rosenthal				
	6/11/2015	1.50	$250.00	$375.00
Saunders				
	6/8/2015	1.50	$250.00	$375.00
	6/12/2015	0.25	$250.00	$62.50
Singh				
	6/4/2015	1.50	$325.00	$487.50

Page 2 of 3

LastName	Date	Hours	Rate	Total
Stein				
	6/11/2015	1.50	$325.00	$487.50
Valencia				
	6/1/2015	0.50	$200.00	$100.00
	6/2/2015	0.75	$250.00	$187.50
	6/3/2015	2.00	$200.00	$400.00
Waide				
	6/9/2015	1.00	$250.00	$250.00
Weyland				
	6/10/2015	1.50	$250.00	$375.00
	6/15/2015	0.50	$250.00	$125.00
	6/15/2015	0.50	$250.00	$125.00
			$13,725.00	

Page 3 of 3

Project 1d, Warren Legal ClientBillingRpt Report

Project 2 Use Wizards to Create Reports and Labels

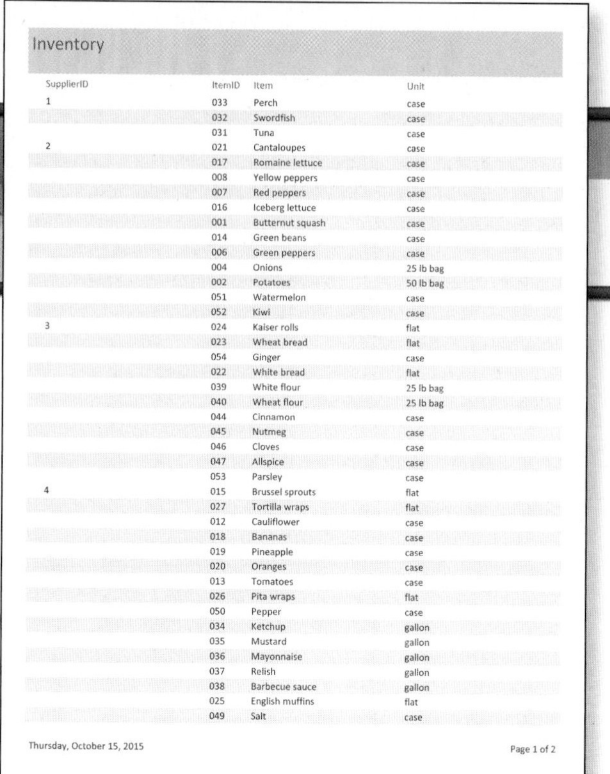

Inventory

SupplierID	ItemID	Item	Unit
1	033	Perch	case
	032	Swordfish	case
	031	Tuna	case
2	021	Cantaloupes	case
	017	Romaine lettuce	case
	008	Yellow peppers	case
	007	Red peppers	case
	016	Iceberg lettuce	case
	001	Butternut squash	case
	014	Green beans	case
	006	Green peppers	case
	004	Onions	25 lb bag
	002	Potatoes	50 lb bag
	051	Watermelon	case
	052	Kiwi	case
3	024	Kaiser rolls	flat
	023	Wheat bread	flat
	054	Ginger	case
	022	White bread	flat
	039	White flour	25 lb bag
	040	Wheat flour	25 lb bag
	044	Cinnamon	case
	045	Nutmeg	case
	046	Cloves	case
	047	Allspice	case
	053	Parsley	case
4	015	Brussel sprouts	flat
	027	Tortilla wraps	flat
	012	Cauliflower	case
	018	Bananas	case
	019	Pineapple	case
	020	Oranges	case
	013	Tomatoes	case
	026	Pita wraps	flat
	050	Pepper	case
	034	Ketchup	gallon
	035	Mustard	gallon
	036	Mayonnaise	gallon
	037	Relish	gallon
	038	Barbecue sauce	gallon
	025	English muffins	flat
	049	Salt	case

Thursday, October 15, 2015 Page 1 of 2

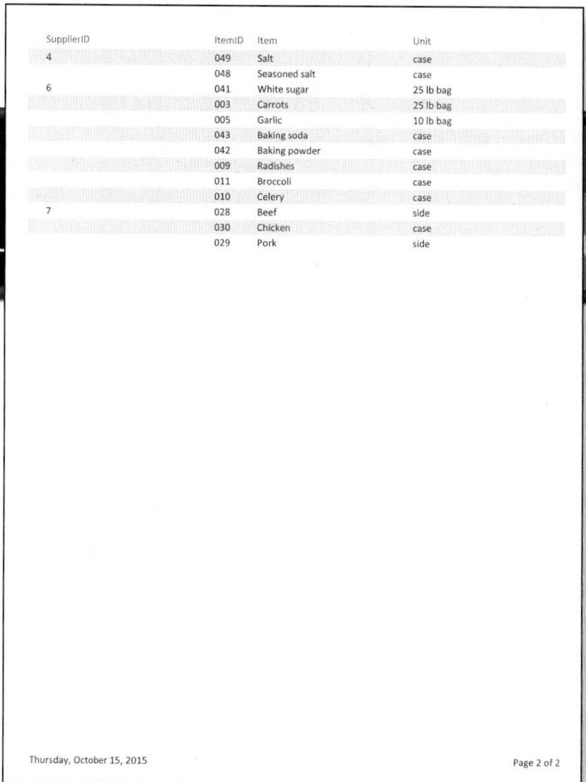

SupplierID	ItemID	Item	Unit
4	049	Salt	case
	048	Seasoned salt	case
6	041	White sugar	25 lb bag
	003	Carrots	25 lb bag
	005	Garlic	10 lb bag
	043	Baking soda	case
	042	Baking powder	case
	009	Radishes	case
	011	Broccoli	case
	010	Celery	case
7	028	Beef	side
	030	Chicken	case
	029	Pork	side

Thursday, October 15, 2015 Page 2 of 2

Project 2a, Skyline Inventory Report

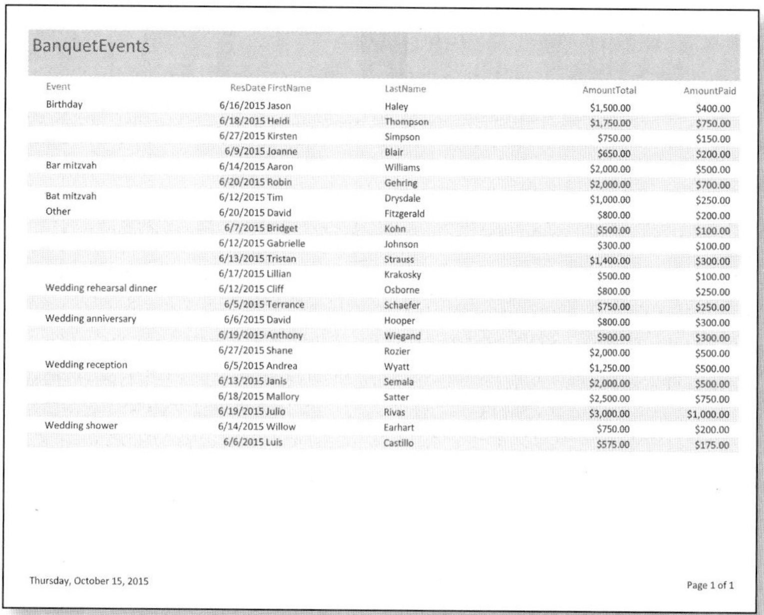

BanquetEvents

Event	ResDate	FirstName	LastName	AmountTotal	AmountPaid
Birthday	6/16/2015	Jason	Haley	$1,500.00	$400.00
	6/18/2015	Heidi	Thompson	$1,750.00	$750.00
	6/27/2015	Kirsten	Simpson	$750.00	$150.00
	6/9/2015	Joanne	Blair	$650.00	$200.00
Bar mitzvah	6/14/2015	Aaron	Williams	$2,000.00	$500.00
	6/20/2015	Robin	Gehring	$2,000.00	$700.00
Bat mitzvah	6/12/2015	Tim	Drysdale	$1,000.00	$250.00
Other	6/20/2015	David	Fitzgerald	$800.00	$200.00
	6/7/2015	Bridget	Kohn	$500.00	$100.00
	6/12/2015	Gabrielle	Johnson	$300.00	$100.00
	6/13/2015	Tristan	Strauss	$1,400.00	$300.00
	6/17/2015	Lillian	Krakosky	$500.00	$100.00
Wedding rehearsal dinner	6/12/2015	Cliff	Osborne	$800.00	$250.00
	6/5/2015	Terrance	Schaefer	$750.00	$250.00
Wedding anniversary	6/6/2015	David	Hooper	$800.00	$300.00
	6/19/2015	Anthony	Wiegand	$900.00	$300.00
	6/27/2015	Shane	Rozier	$2,000.00	$500.00
Wedding reception	6/5/2015	Andrea	Wyatt	$1,250.00	$500.00
	6/13/2015	Janis	Semala	$2,000.00	$500.00
	6/18/2015	Mallory	Satter	$2,500.00	$750.00
	6/19/2015	Julio	Rivas	$3,000.00	$1,000.00
Wedding shower	6/14/2015	Willow	Earhart	$750.00	$200.00
	6/6/2015	Luis	Castillo	$575.00	$175.00

Thursday, October 15, 2015 Page 1 of 1

Project 2b, Skyline BanquetEvents Report

Haley Brown 3219 North 33rd Street Auburn, WA 98001	Margaret Kasper 40210 42nd Avenue Auburn, WA 98001	Abigail Jefferson 1204 Meridian Road Auburn, WA 98001
Doris Sturtevant 3713 Nelton Road Auburn, WA 98001	Carlina McFadden 7809 52nd Street East Auburn, WA 98001	Ewan Aragato 904 Marine View Drive Auburn, WA 98002
Tricia O'Connor 3824 Sanders Court Auburn, WA 98002	Carol Kendall 24 Ferris Parkway Kent, WA 98003	James Weyland 2533 145th Street East Kent, WA 98031
Janice Saunders 2757 179th Avenue East Kent, WA 98032	Jeffrey Day 317 Meridian Street Kent, WA 98033	Mindy Garvison 68 Queens Avenue Kent, WA 98033
Kevin Stein 12034 South 22nd Avenue Kent, WA 98035	Jean Briggs 2110 West Valley Avenue Kent, WA 98036	Arthur Norheim 10533 Ashton Boulevard Kent, WA 98036
Consuelo Day 13321 North Lake Drive Kent, WA 98036	Christina Miles 13043 South 25th Avenue Kent, WA 98036	Matthew Waide 18391 North 45th Street Renton, WA 98055

Karl Cordes 240 Mill Avenue Renton, WA 98055	Mira Valencia 114 Springfield Avenue Renton, WA 98056	Charles Hobart 11038 132nd Street Renton, WA 98056
Taylor Reyes 201 Northwest Boulevard Renton, WA 98056	Eric Rosenthal 1230 Maplewood Road Auburn, WA 98071	Jennifer Czubek 8790 34th Avenue Renton, WA 98228
Maddie Singh 450 Mill Avenue Renton, WA 98228	Chris Cervantez 8722 Riverside Road Renton, WA 98228	Arthur Jefferson 23110 North 33rd Street Renton, WA 98230

Project 2c, WarrenLegal Mailing Labels

Project 1 Create and Customize Reports Using Tables and Queries — 4 Parts

You will create reports with the Report button using tables and queries. You will change the report views; select, move, and resize control objects; sort records; customize reports; apply conditional formatting; and group and sort fields in a report.

Creating Reports

The primary purposes for inserting data in a form are to improve the display of the data and to make data entry easier. You can also insert data in a report. The purpose for doing this is to control what data appears on the page when printed. Reports generally answer specific questions (queries). For example, a report could answer the question *What customers have submitted claims?* or *What products do we currently have on order?* The record source for a report can be a table or query. Create a report with the Report button in the Reports group or use the Report Wizard, which walks you through the process of creating a report.

Quick Steps

Create a Report

1. Click desired table or query in Navigation pane.
2. Click CREATE tab.
3. Click Report button.

Report

Creating a Report with the Report Button

To create a report with the Report button, click the desired table or query in the Navigation pane, click the CREATE tab, and then click the Report button in the Reports group. This displays the report in columnar style in Layout view with the REPORT LAYOUT TOOLS DESIGN tab active, as shown in Figure 6.1. Access creates the report using all of the fields in the table or query.

Create a report to control what data appears on the page when printed.

Figure 6.1 Report Created with Sales Table

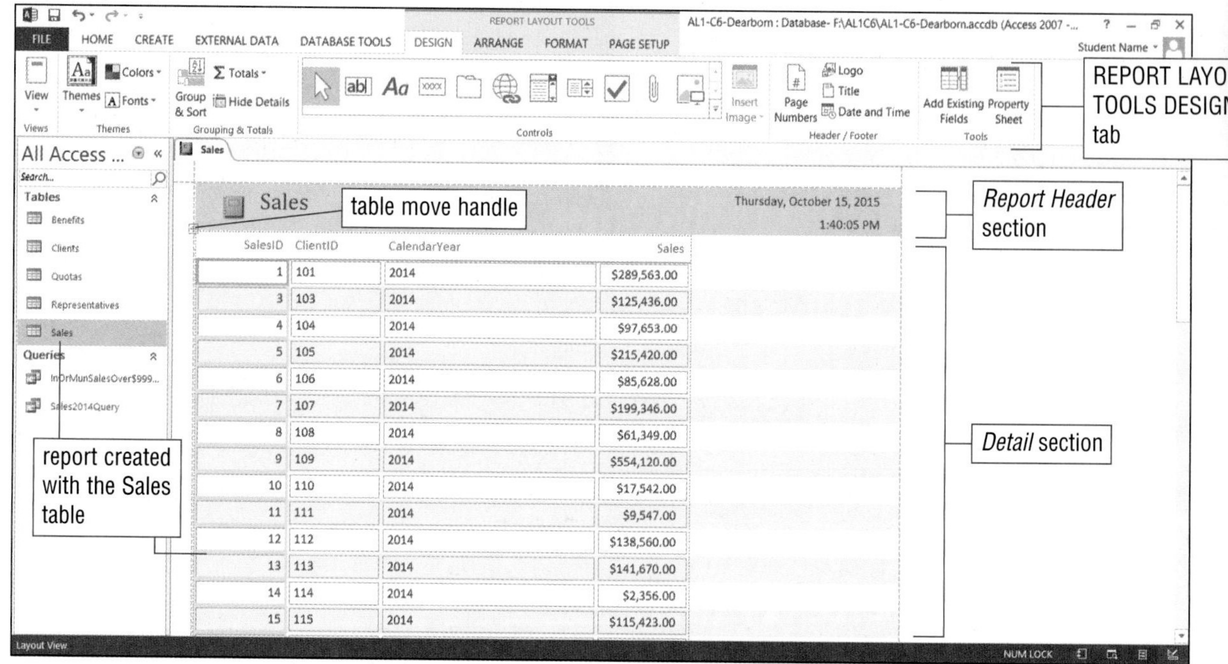

Modifying the Record Source

The record source for a report is the table or query used to create the report. If changes are made to the record source, such as adding or deleting records, those changes are reflected in the report. For example, in Project 1a, you will create a report based on the Sales table. You will then add a record to the Sales table (the record source for the report) and the added record will display in the Sales report.

Project 1a Creating a Report with the Report Button — Part 1 of 4

1. Display the Open dialog box with the AL1C6 folder on your storage medium the active folder.
2. Open **AL1-C6-Dearborn.accdb** and enable the contents.
3. Create a report based on the Sales table by completing the following steps:
   a. Click the Sales table in the Navigation pane.
   b. Click the CREATE tab.
   c. Click the Report button in the Reports group.

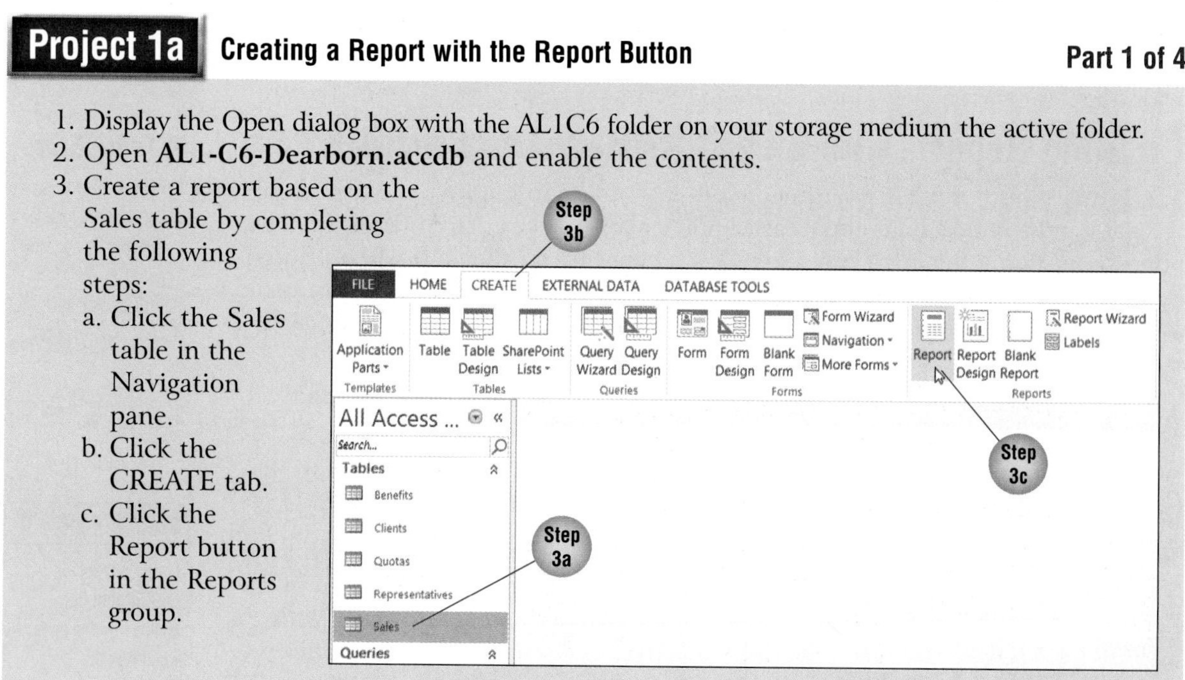

d. Save the report by clicking the Save button on the Quick Access toolbar and then clicking OK at the Save As dialog box. (This saves the report with the default name, *Sales*.)
e. Close the Sales report.

4. Add a record to the Sales table by completing the following steps:
   a. Double-click the Sales table in the Navigation pane. (Make sure you open the Sales table and not the Sales report.)
   b. Click the New button in the Records group on the HOME tab.
   c. Press the Tab key to accept the default number in the *SalesID* field.
   d. Type 127 in the *ClientID* field and then press the Tab key.
   e. Type 2015 in the *CalendarYear* field and then press the Tab key.
   f. Type 176420 in the *Sales* field.
   g. Close the Sales table.
5. Open the Sales report and then scroll down to the bottom. Notice that the new record you added to the Sales table displays in the report.
6. Close the Sales report.
7. Use the query named *Sales2014Query* to create a report by completing the following steps:
   a. Click *Sales2014Query* in the Queries group in the Navigation pane.
   b. Click the CREATE tab.
   c. Click the Report button in the Reports group.
8. Access automatically inserted a total amount for the *Sales* column of the report. Delete this amount by scrolling down to the bottom of the report, clicking the total amount at the bottom of the *Sales* column, and then pressing the Delete key. (This deletes the total amount but not the underline above the amount.)
9. Save the report by clicking the Save button on the Quick Access toolbar, typing **2014Sales** in the *Report Name* text box in the Save As dialog box, and then clicking OK.

Modifying Control Objects

A report, like a form, is comprised of control objects, such as logos, titles, labels, and text boxes. You can select an object in a report by clicking the object. A selected object displays with an orange border. If you click a data field in the report, Access selects all of the objects in the column except the column heading.

Like a form, a report contains a *Header* section and a *Detail* section. Select all of the control objects in the report in both the *Header* and *Detail* sections by pressing Ctrl + A. Control objects in the *Detail* section are contained in a report table. To select the control objects in the report table, click in any cell in the report and then click the table move handle. The table move handle is a small square with a four-headed arrow inside that displays in the upper left corner of the table (see Figure 6.1). Move the table and all of the control objects within the table by dragging the table move handle using the mouse.

Adjust column widths in a report by dragging the column border left or right. In addition to adjusting column width, you can change the position of a selected column. To do this, select the desired column, position the mouse pointer in the column heading until the pointer displays with a four-headed arrow attached, and then drag the column left or right to the desired position. As you drag the column, a vertical pink bar displays indicating where the column will be placed when you release the mouse button.

Some control objects in a report, such as a column heading or title, are label control objects. Edit a label control by double-clicking in the object and then making the desired change. For example, if you want to rename a label control, double-click in the label control and then edit or type the desired text.

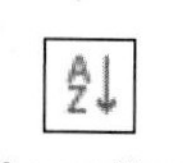
Ascending

Descending

Quick Steps

Sort Records
1. Click in field containing data.
2. Click Ascending button or click Descending button.

Sorting Records

Sort data in a report by clicking in the field containing the data you want to sort and then clicking the Ascending button or Descending button in the Sort & Filter group on the HOME tab. Click the Ascending button to sort text in alphabetical order from A to Z or sort numbers from lowest to highest or click the Descending button to sort text in alphabetical order from Z to A or sort numbers from highest to lowest.

Displaying and Customizing a Report in Print Preview

Print Preview

View

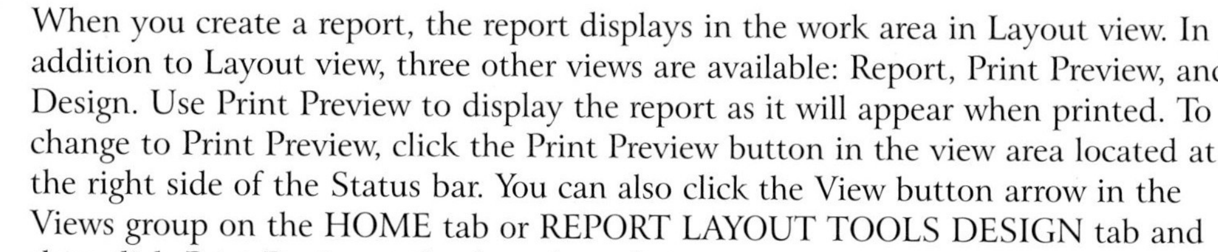

When you create a report, the report displays in the work area in Layout view. In addition to Layout view, three other views are available: Report, Print Preview, and Design. Use Print Preview to display the report as it will appear when printed. To change to Print Preview, click the Print Preview button in the view area located at the right side of the Status bar. You can also click the View button arrow in the Views group on the HOME tab or REPORT LAYOUT TOOLS DESIGN tab and then click *Print Preview* at the drop-down list.

In Print Preview, send the report to the printer by clicking the Print button on the PRINT PREVIEW tab. Use options in the Page Size group to change the page size and margins. If you want to print only the report data and not the column headings, report title, shading, and gridlines, insert a check mark in the *Print Data Only* check box. Use options in the Page Layout group to specify the page orientation, specify columns, and display the Page Setup dialog box. Click the Page Setup button and the Page Setup dialog box displays with options for customizing margins, orientation, size, and columns.

Deleting a Report

If you no longer need a report in a database, delete the report. Delete a report by clicking the report name in the Navigation pane, clicking the Delete button in the Records group on the HOME tab, and then clicking the Yes button at the message asking if you want to permanently delete the report. Another method is to right-click the report in the Navigation pane, click *Delete* at the shortcut menu, and then click the Yes at the message. If you are deleting a report from your computer's hard drive, the message asking if you want to permanently delete the report will not display. This is because Access automatically sends the deleted report to the Recycle Bin, where it can be retrieved if necessary.

Finding Data in a Report

You can find specific data in a report with options at the Find dialog box. Display this dialog box by clicking the Find button in the Find group on the HOME tab. At the Find dialog box, enter the data you want to search for in the *Find What* text box. The *Match* option at the Find dialog box is set at *Whole Field* by default. At this setting, the data you enter must match the entire entry in a field. If you want to search for partial data in a field, change the *Match* option to *Any Part of Field* or *Start of Field*. If you want the text you enter in the *Find What* text box to match the case in a field entry, click the *Match Case* option check box to insert a check mark. Access will search the entire report by default. You can change this to *Up* if you want to search from the currently active field to the beginning of the report or *Down* if you want to search from the currently active field to the end of the report. Click the Find Next button to find data that matches the data in the *Find What* text box.

Project 1b **Adjusting Control Objects, Renaming Labels, Finding and Sorting Data, Displaying a Report in Print Preview, and Deleting a Report** **Part 2 of 4**

1. With the 2014Sales report open, reverse the order of the *RepName* and *Client* columns by completing the following steps:
   a. Make sure the report displays in Layout view.
   b. Click the *RepName* column heading.
   c. Hold down the Shift key and then click in the last control object in the *RepName* column (the control object containing *Catherine Singleton*).
   d. Position the mouse pointer inside the *RepName* column heading until the pointer displays with a four-headed arrow attached.
   e. Hold down the left mouse button, drag to the left until the vertical pink bar displays to the left of the *Client* column, and then release the mouse button.

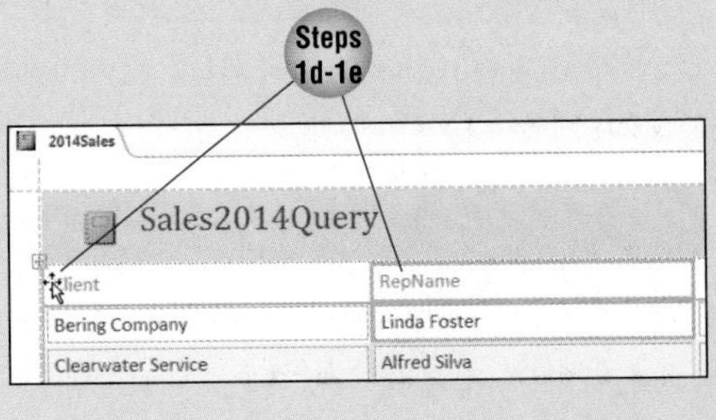

2. Sort the data in the *Sales* column in descending order by completing the following steps:
   a. Click the HOME tab.
   b. Click in any field in the *Sales* column.
   c. Click the Descending button in the Sort & Filter group.
3. Rename the *RepName* label control as *Representative* by double-clicking in the label control object containing the text *RepName*, selecting *RepName*, and then typing **Representative**.
4. Double-click in the *Sales* label control and then rename it *Sales 2014*.

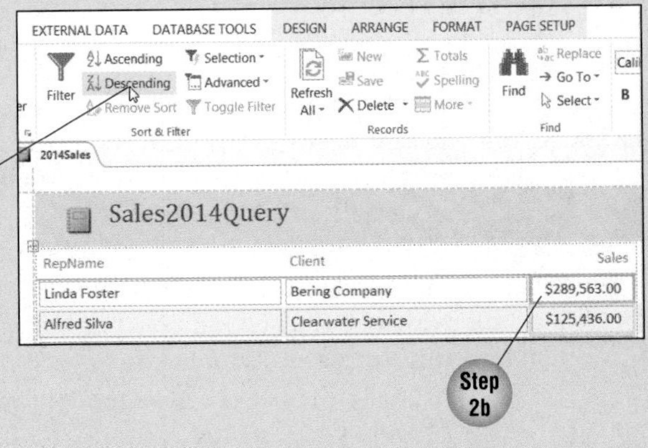

5. Move the report table by completing the following steps:
   a. Click in a cell in the report.
   b. Position the mouse pointer on the table move handle (which displays as a small square with a four-headed arrow inside and is located in the upper left corner of the table).
   c. Hold down the left mouse button, drag the report table to the right until it is centered between the left and right sides of the *Detail* section, and then release the mouse button. (When you drag with the mouse, you will see only outlines of some of the control objects.)

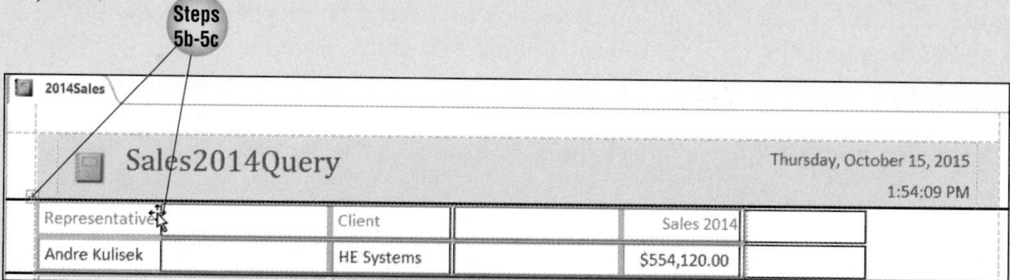

6. Display the report in Print Preview by clicking the Print Preview button in the view area at the right side of the Status bar.

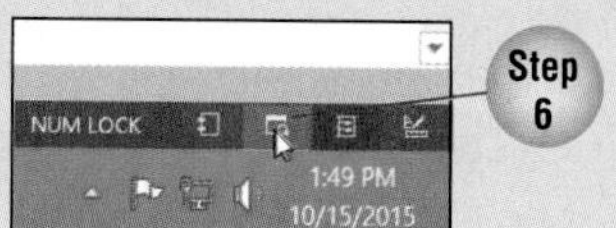

7. Click the One Page button (already active) in the Zoom group to display the entire page.
8. Click the Zoom button arrow in the Zoom group and then click *50%* at the drop-down list.
9. Click the One Page button in the Zoom group.
10. Print the report by clicking the Print button on the PRINT PREVIEW tab and then clicking OK at the Print dialog box.
11. Close Print Preview by clicking the Close Print Preview button located at the right side of the PRINT PREVIEW tab.

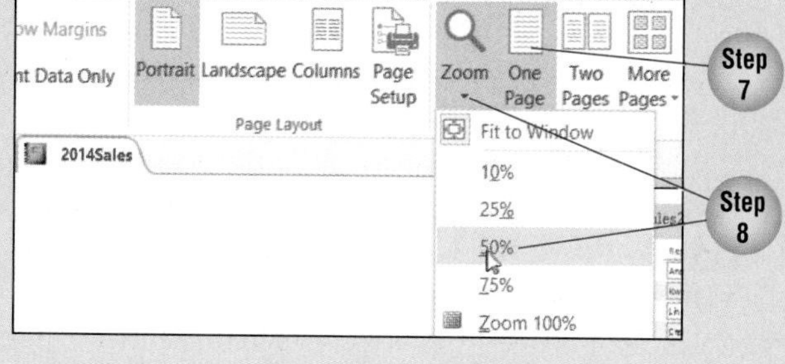

12. Save and then close the 2014Sales report.
13. Create a report with the Representatives table by completing the following steps:
   a. Click *Representatives* in the Tables group in the Navigation pane.
   b. Click the CREATE tab.
   c. Click the Report button in the Reports group.
14. Adjust the width of the second column by completing the following steps:
   a. Click in the *RepName* column heading.
   b. Drag the right border of the selected column heading to the left until the border displays near the longest entry in the column.
15. Complete steps similar to those in Step 14 to decrease the width of the third column (*Telephone*) and the fourth column (*Email*).
16. Search for fields containing a quote of *2* by completing the following steps:
   a. Click in the *RepID* column heading.
   b. Click the HOME tab and then click the Find button in the Find group.

c. At the Find dialog box, type 2 in the *Find What* text box.
d. Make sure the *Match* option is set to *Whole Field*. (If not, click the down-pointing arrow at the right side of the *Match* option and then click *Whole Field* at the drop-down list.)
e. Click the Find Next button.
f. Continue clicking the Find Next button until a message displays telling you that Access has finished searching the records. At this message, click OK.
g. Click the Cancel button to close the Find dialog box.

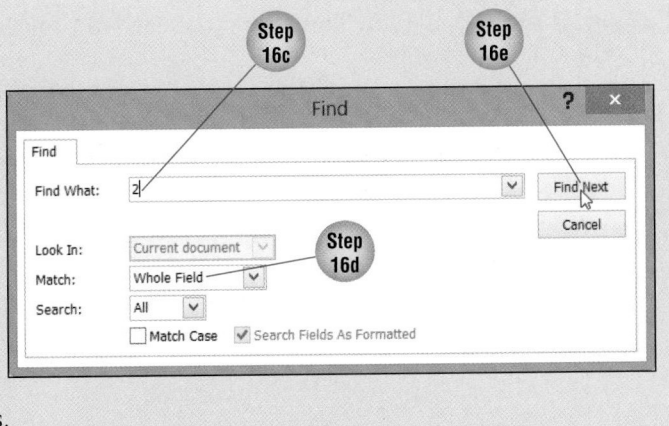

17. Suppose you want to find information on a representative and you remember the first name but not the last name. Search for a field containing the first name *Lydia* by completing the following steps:
    a. Click in the *RepID* column heading.
    b. Click the Find button in the Find group.
    c. At the Find dialog box, type Lydia in the *Find What* text box.
    d. Click the down-pointing arrow at the right side of the *Match* option and then click *Any Part of Field* at the drop-down list.
    e. Click the Find Next button. (Access will find and select the representative name *Lydia Alvarado*.)
    f. Click the Cancel button to close the Find dialog box.

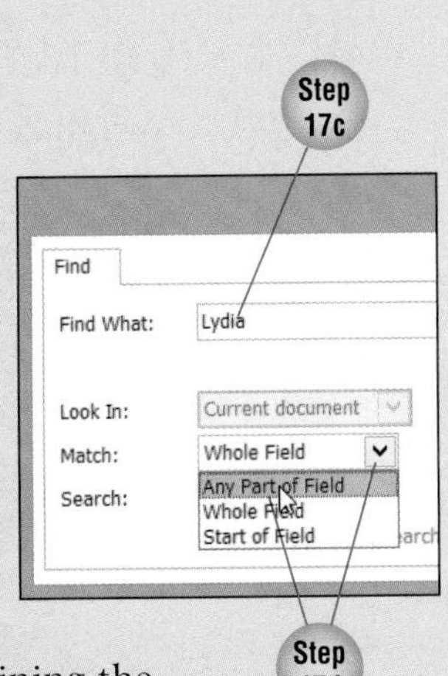

18. Click the control object at the bottom of the *RepID* column containing the number *17* and then press the Delete key. (This does not delete the underline above the amount.)
19. Switch to Print Preview by clicking the View button arrow in the Views group on the REPORT LAYOUT TOOLS DESIGN tab and then clicking *Print Preview* at the drop-down list.
20. Click the Margins button in the Page Size group and then click *Normal* at the drop-down list.

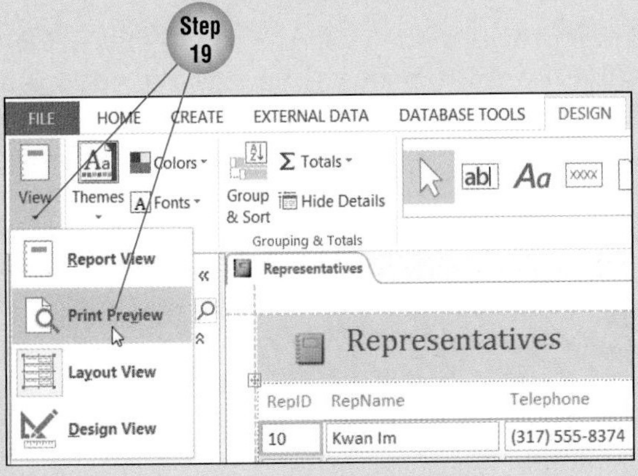

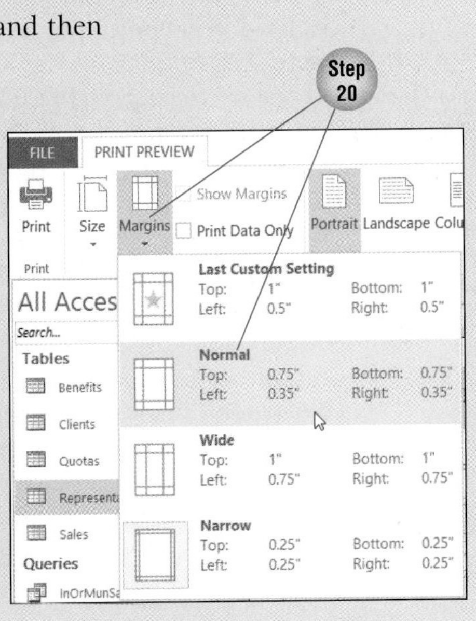

21. Print the first page of the report (the second page contains only shading) by completing the following steps:
    a. Click the Print button that displays at the left side of the PRINT PREVIEW tab.
    b. At the Print dialog box, click the *Pages* option in the *Print Range* section.
    c. Type 1 in the *From* text box, press the Tab key, and then type 1 in the *To* text box.
    d. Click OK.
22. Close Print Preview by clicking the Close Print Preview button.
23. Save the report with the name *Representatives*.
24. Close the Representatives report.
25. Delete the Sales report by right-clicking the Sales report in the Navigation pane, clicking *Delete* at the shortcut menu, and then clicking Yes at the message that displays.

Customizing Reports

Customize a report in much the same manner as you customize a form. When you first create a report, the report displays in Layout view and the REPORT LAYOUT TOOLS DESIGN tab is active. Customize control objects in the *Detail* section and the *Header* section with buttons on the REPORT LAYOUT TOOLS ribbon using the DESIGN tab, ARRANGE tab, FORMAT tab, or PAGE SETUP tab selected.

The themes available in Access are the same as the themes available in Word, Excel, and PowerPoint.

Totals

The REPORT LAYOUT TOOLS DESIGN tab contains many of the same options at the FORM LAYOUT TOOLS DESIGN tab. Use options on this tab to apply a theme, insert controls, insert header or footer data, and add existing fields. The tab also contains the Grouping & Totals group, which you will learn about in the next section. Use the Totals button in the Grouping & Totals group to perform functions such as finding the sum, average, maximum, or minimum of the numbers in a column. To use the Totals button, click the column heading of the column containing the data you want to total, click the Totals button, and then click the desired function at the drop-down list. Use the Page Number button on the REPORT LAYOUT TOOLS DESIGN tab to insert and format page numbers.

Click the REPORT LAYOUT TOOLS ARRANGE tab and options display for inserting and selecting rows, splitting cells horizontally and vertically, moving data up or down, controlling margins, and changing the padding between objects and cells. The options on the REPORT LAYOUT TOOLS ARRANGE tab are the same as the options on the FORM LAYOUT TOOLS ARRANGE tab.

Customize the formatting of control objects with options at the REPORT LAYOUT TOOLS FORMAT tab.

Select and format data in a report with options on the REPORT LAYOUT TOOLS FORMAT tab. The options on this tab are the same as the options on the FORM LAYOUT TOOLS FORMAT tab. You can apply formatting to a report or specific objects in a report. If you want to apply formatting to a specific object, click the object in the report or click the Object button arrow in the Selection group on the REPORT LAYOUT TOOLS FORMAT tab and then click the desired object at the drop-down list. To format all objects in the report, click the Select All button in the Selection group. This selects all objects in the report, including objects in the *Header* section. If you want to select all of the objects in the report, click the table move handle. You can also click the table move handle and then drag with the mouse to move the objects in the form.

With buttons in the Font, Number, Background, and Control Formatting groups, you can apply formatting to a control object or cell and to selected objects or cells in a report. Use buttons in the Font group to change the font, apply a different font size, apply text effects (such as bold and underline), and change the alignment of data in objects. Insert a background image in the report using the Background button and apply formatting to objects or cells with buttons in the Control Formatting group. Depending on what is selected in the report, some of the buttons may not be active.

Background

Click the REPORT LAYOUT TOOLS PAGE SETUP tab and the buttons that display are buttons that are also available in Print Preview. For example, you can change the page size and page layout of the report and display the Page Setup dialog box.

Project 1c Applying Formatting to a Report — Part 3 of 4

1. With **AL1-C6-Dearborn.accdb** open, open the 2014Sales report.
2. Display the report in Layout view.
3. Click the Themes button in the Themes group on the REPORT LAYOUT TOOLS DESIGN tab and then click *Ion* at the drop-down gallery (fourth column, first row).

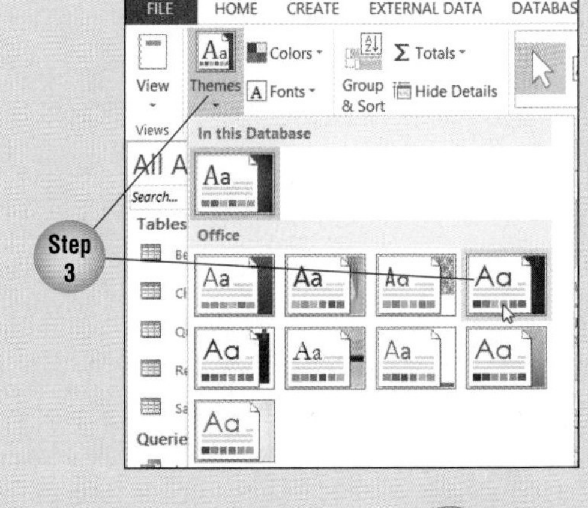

4. Click the Title button in the Header/Footer group (which selects the current title), type **2014 Sales**, and then press Enter.
5. Insert new control objects by completing the following steps:
   a. Click in the *Representative* cell.
   b. Click the REPORT LAYOUT TOOLS ARRANGE tab.
   c. Click the Insert Above button in the Rows & Columns group.
6. Merge the cells in the new row by completing the following steps:
   a. Click in the blank cell immediately above the *Representative* cell.
   b. Hold down the Shift key and then click immediately above the *Sales 2014* cell. (This selects three cells.)
   c. Click the Merge button in the Merge/Split group.
   d. Type **Dearborn 2014 Sales** in the new cell.

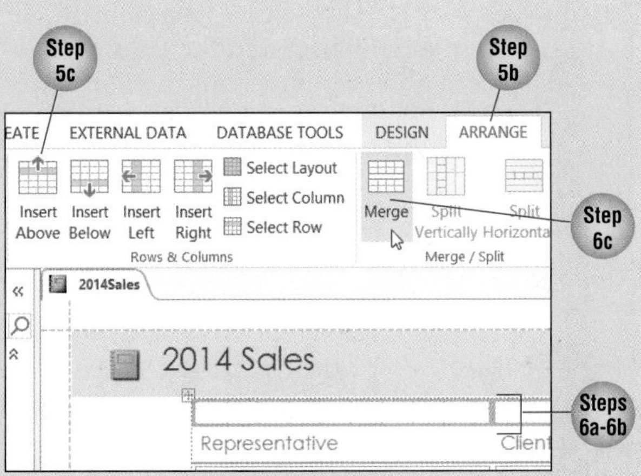

7. Split a cell by completing the following steps:
   a. Click in the *2014 Sales* title in the *Header* section.
   b. Split the cell containing the title by clicking the Split Horizontally button in the Merge/Split group.
   c. Click in the empty cell immediately right of the cell containing the title *Sales 2014* and then press the Delete key. (Deleting the empty cell causes the date and time to move to the left in the *Header* section.)
8. Change the report table margins and padding by completing the following steps:
   a. Click in any cell in the *Detail* section and then click the table move handle that displays in the upper left corner of the *Dearborn 2014 Sales* cell. (This selects the control objects in the report table in the *Detail* section.)

b. Click the Control Margins button in the Position group and then click *Narrow* at the drop-down list.
c. Click the Control Padding button in the Position group and then click *Medium* at the drop-down list.

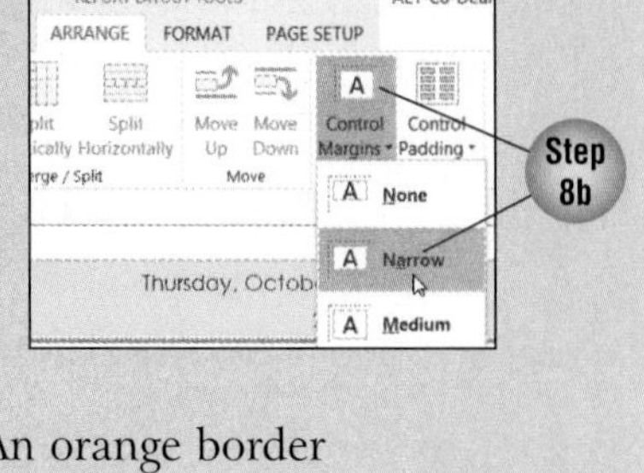

9. Click in the *Dearborn 2014 Sales* cell and then drag down the bottom border so all of the text in the cell is visible.
10. Change the font for all control objects in the report by completing the following steps:
    a. Press Ctrl + A to select all control objects in the report. (An orange border displays around selected objects.)
    b. Click the REPORT LAYOUT TOOLS FORMAT tab.
    c. Click the Font button arrow in the Font group and then click *Cambria* at the drop-down list. (You may need to scroll down the list to display *Cambria*.)

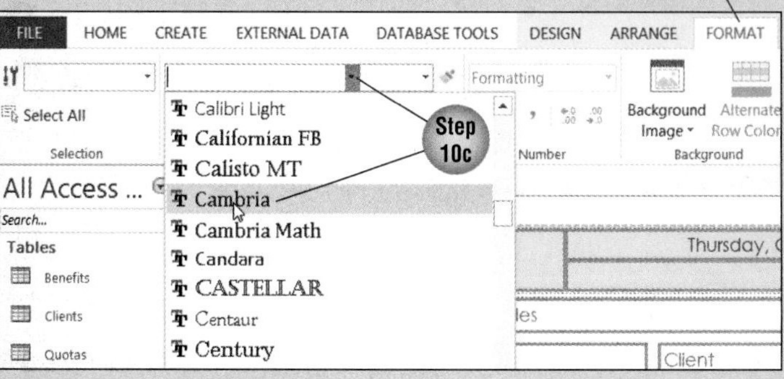

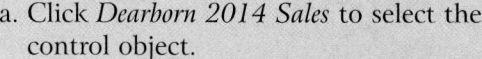

11. Apply bold formatting and change the alignment of the column headings by completing the following steps:
    a. Click *Dearborn 2014 Sales* to select the control object.
    b. Hold down the Shift key and then click *Sales 2014*. (This selects four cells.)
    c. Click the Bold button in the Font group.
    d. Click the Center button in the Font group.

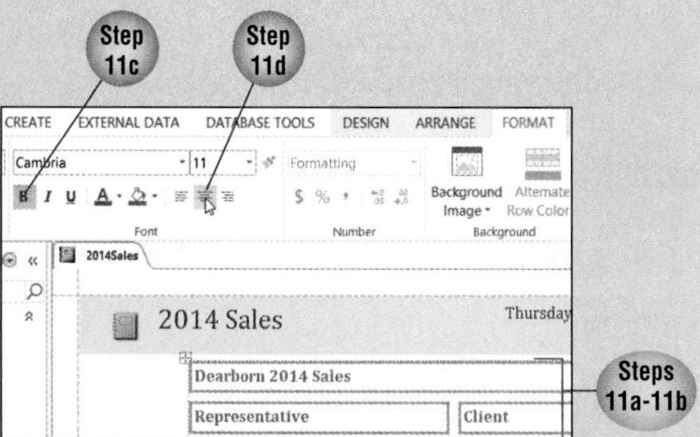

12. Format amounts and apply conditional formatting to the amounts by completing the following steps:
    a. Click the first field value below the *Sales 2014* column heading. (This selects all of the amounts in the column.)
    b. Click twice on the Decrease Decimals button in the Number group.

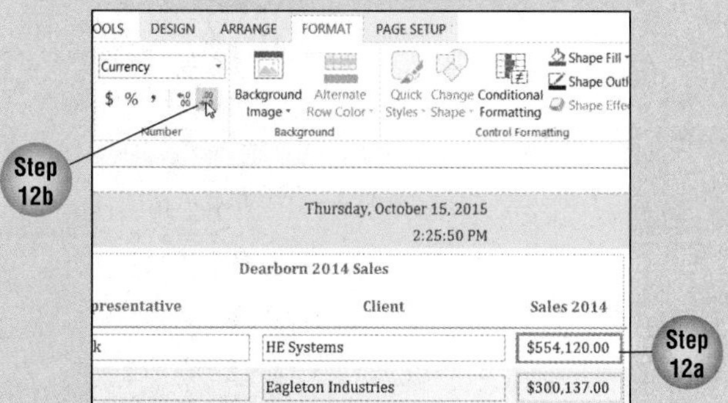

    c. Click the Conditional Formatting button in the Control Formatting group.

d. At the Conditional Formatting Rules Manager dialog box, click the New Rule button.
e. At the New Formatting Rule dialog box, click the down-pointing arrow at the right side of the second option box in the *Edit the rule description* section and then click *greater than* at the drop-down list.
f. Click in the text box immediately right of the option box containing *greater than* and then type 199999.
g. Click the Background color button arrow and then click the *Green 2* color option (seventh column, third row).
h. Click the OK button.
i. At the Conditional Formatting Rules Manager dialog box, click the New Rule button.
j. At the New Formatting Rule dialog box, click the down-pointing arrow at the right side of the second option box in the *Edit the rule description* section and then click *less than* at the drop-down list.
k. Click in the text box immediately right of the option containing *less than* and then type 200000.
l. Click the Background color button arrow and then click the *Maroon 2* color option (sixth column, third row).
m. Click OK to close the New Formatting Rule dialog box.
n. Click OK to close the Conditional Formatting Rules Manager dialog box.

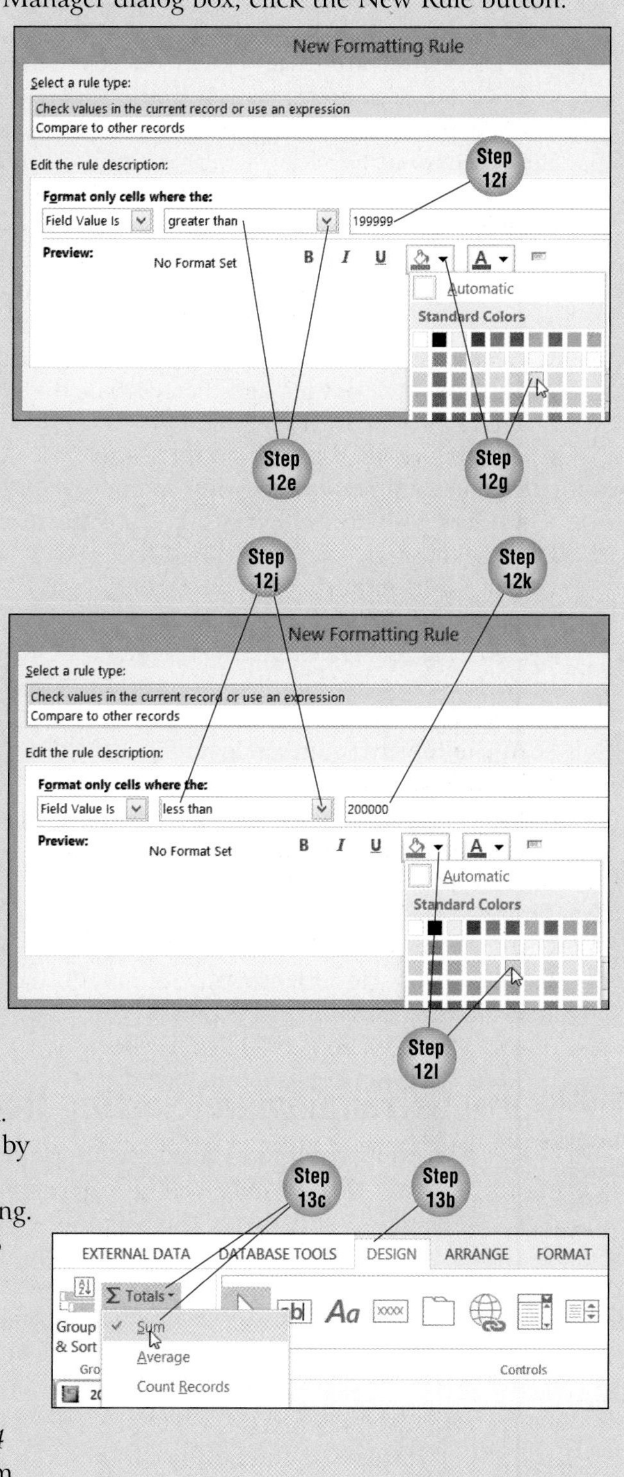

13. Sum the totals in the *Sales 2014* column by completing the following steps:
    a. Click in the *Sales 2014* column heading.
    b. Click the REPORT LAYOUT TOOLS DESIGN tab.
    c. Click the Totals button in the Grouping & Totals group and then click *Sum* at the drop-down list.
14. Click in the *Sales 2014* sum amount (located at the bottom of the *Sales 2014* column) and then drag down the bottom border so the entire amount is visible in the cell.

15. Change the top margin by completing the following steps:
    a. Click in the *Representative* column heading and then click the REPORT LAYOUT TOOLS PAGE SETUP tab.
    b. Click the Page Setup button in the Page Layout group.
    c. At the Page Setup dialog box with the Print Options tab selected, select the current measurement in the *Top* measurement box and then type **0.5**.
    d. Click OK to close the Page Setup dialog box.
16. Change the page size by clicking the Size button in the Page Size group and and then clicking *Legal* at the drop-down list.

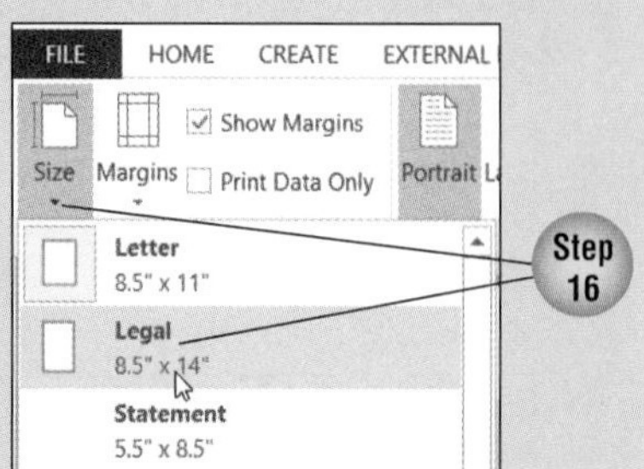

17. Display the report in Print Preview by clicking the FILE tab, clicking the *Print* option, and then clicking the Print Preview button.
18. Click the One Page button in the Zoom group and notice that the entire report will print on one legal-sized page.
19. Click the Close Print Preview button to return to the report.
20. Change the page size by clicking the PAGE LAYOUT TOOLS PAGE SETUP tab, clicking the Size button in the Page Size group, and then clicking *Letter* at the drop-down list.
21. Insert and then remove a background image by completing the following steps:
    a. Click the REPORT LAYOUT TOOLS FORMAT tab.
    b. Click the Background Image button in the Background group and then click *Browse* at the drop-down list.
    c. At the Insert Picture dialog box, navigate to the AL1C6 folder on your storage medium and then double-click ***Mountain.jpg***.
    d. Scroll through the report and notice how the image displays in the report.
    e. Click the Undo button on the Quick Access toolbar to remove the background image. (You may need to click the Undo button more than once.)
22. Print the report by clicking the FILE tab, clicking the *Print* option, and then clicking the Quick Print button.
23. Save and then close the report.

Quick Steps

Group and Sort Records

1. Open desired report in Layout view.
2. Click Group & Sort button.
3. Click Add a group button.
4. Click desired group field.

Group & Sort

Add a group

Grouping and Sorting Records

A report presents database information in a printed form and generally displays data that answers a specific question. To make the data in a report easy to understand, divide the data into groups. For example, you can divide data in a report by regions, sales, dates, or any other division that helps clarify the data for the reader. Access contains a powerful group and sort feature that you can use in a report. In this section, you will complete basic group and sort functions. For more detailed information on grouping and sorting, refer to the Access help files.

Click the Group & Sort button in the Grouping & Totals group on the REPORT LAYOUT TOOLS DESIGN tab and the Group, Sort, and Total pane displays at the bottom of the work area, as shown in Figure 6.2. Click the Add a group button in the Group, Sort, and Total pane and Access adds a new grouping level row to the pane, along with a list of available fields. Click the field on which you want to group data in the report and Access adds the grouping level in the report. With options in the grouping level row, change the group, specify the sort order, and expand the row to display additional options.

Figure 6.2 Group, Sort, and Total Pane

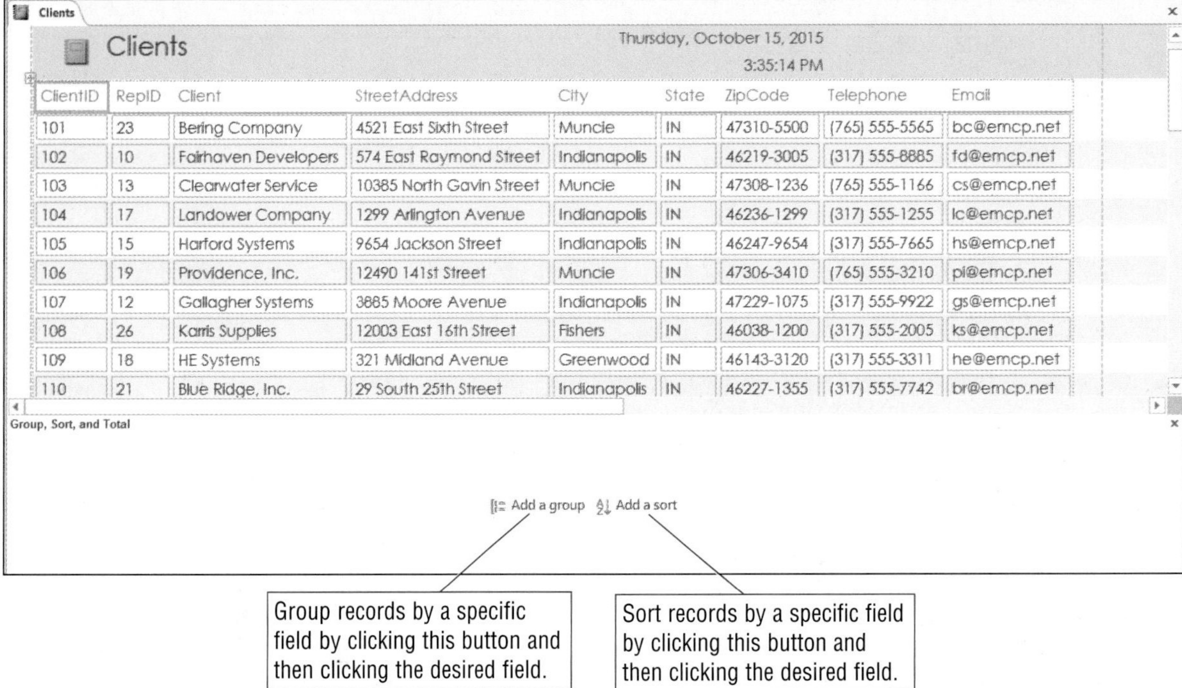
Clients
Clients
Thursday, October 15, 2015
3:35:14 PM

ClientID	RepID	Client	StreetAddress	City	State	ZipCode	Telephone	Email
101	23	Bering Company	4521 East Sixth Street	Muncie	IN	47310-5500	(765) 555-5565	bc@emcp.net
102	10	Fairhaven Developers	574 East Raymond Street	Indianapolis	IN	46219-3005	(317) 555-8885	fd@emcp.net
103	13	Clearwater Service	10385 North Gavin Street	Muncie	IN	47308-1236	(765) 555-1166	cs@emcp.net
104	17	Landower Company	1299 Arlington Avenue	Indianapolis	IN	46236-1299	(317) 555-1255	lc@emcp.net
105	15	Harford Systems	9654 Jackson Street	Indianapolis	IN	46247-9654	(317) 555-7665	hs@emcp.net
106	19	Providence, Inc.	12490 141st Street	Muncie	IN	47306-3410	(765) 555-3210	pi@emcp.net
107	12	Gallagher Systems	3885 Moore Avenue	Indianapolis	IN	47229-1075	(317) 555-9922	gs@emcp.net
108	26	Karris Supplies	12003 East 16th Street	Fishers	IN	46038-1200	(317) 555-2005	ks@emcp.net
109	18	HE Systems	321 Midland Avenue	Greenwood	IN	46143-3120	(317) 555-3311	he@emcp.net
110	21	Blue Ridge, Inc.	29 South 25th Street	Indianapolis	IN	46227-1355	(317) 555-7742	br@emcp.net

Group, Sort, and Total
Add a group
Add a sort
Group records by a specific field by clicking this button and then clicking the desired field.
Sort records by a specific field by clicking this button and then clicking the desired field.

When you specify a grouping level, Access automatically sorts that level in ascending order (from A to Z or lowest to highest). You can then sort additional data within the report by clicking the Add a sort button in the Group, Sort, and Total pane. This inserts a sorting row in the pane below the grouping level row, along with a list of available fields. At this list, click the field on which you want to sort. For example, in Project 1d, you will specify that a report is grouped by city (which will display in ascending order) and then specify that the client names display in alphabetical order within the city.

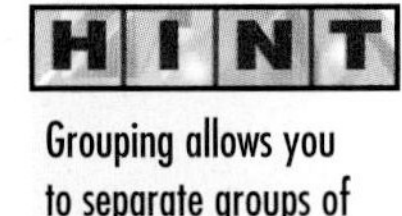
HINT

Grouping allows you to separate groups of records visually.

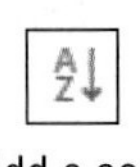

Add a sort

To delete a grouping or sorting level in the Group, Sort, and Total pane, click the Delete button that displays at the right side of the level row. After specifying the grouping and sorting levels, close the Group, Sort, and Total pane by clicking the Close button located in the upper right corner of the pane.

Project 1d Grouping and Sorting Data — Part 4 of 4

1. With **AL1-C6-Dearborn.accdb** open, create a report with the Clients table using the Report button on the CREATE tab.
2. Click each column heading individually and then decrease the size of each column so the right border is just right of the longest entry.
3. Change the orientation to landscape by completing the following steps:
   a. Click the REPORT LAYOUT TOOLS PAGE SETUP tab.
   b. Click the Landscape button in the Page Layout group.
4. Group the report by representative ID and then sort by clients by completing the following steps:
   a. Click the REPORT LAYOUT TOOLS DESIGN tab.
   b. Click the Group & Sort button in the Grouping & Totals group.

c. Click the Add a group button in the Group, Sort, and Total pane.

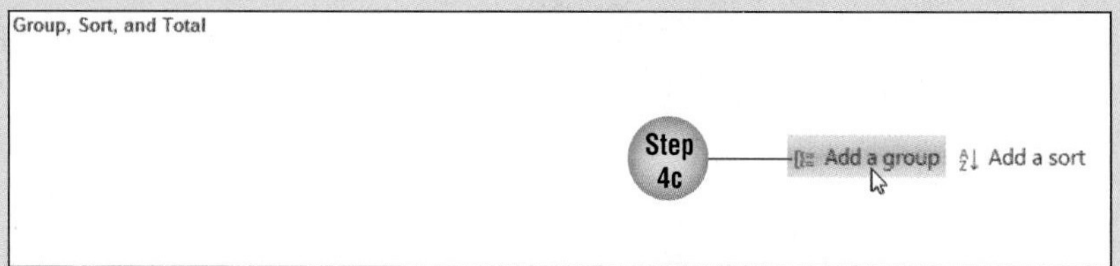

d. Click the *RepID* field in the list box.
e. Scroll through the report and notice that the records are grouped by the *RepID* field. Also, notice that the client names within each RepID field group are not in alphabetic order.
f. Click the Add a sort button in the Group, Sort, and Total pane.
g. Click the *Client* field in the list box.
h. Scroll through the report and notice that client names are now alphabetized within *RepID* field groups.
i. Close the Group, Sort, and Total pane by clicking the Close button located in the upper right corner of the pane.

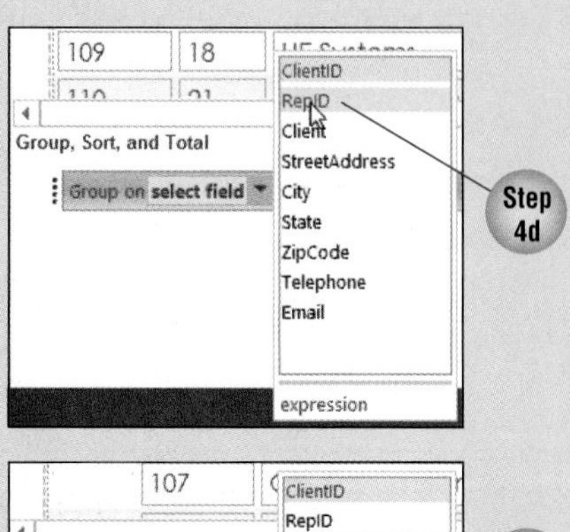

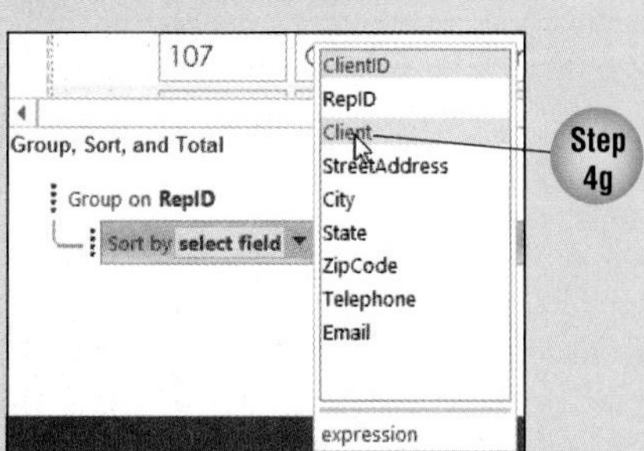

5. Save the report and name it *ClientsGroupedRpt*.
6. Print the first page of the report by completing the following steps:
   a. Click the FILE tab, click the *Print* option, and then click the Print button.
   b. At the Print dialog box, click the *Pages* option in the *Print Range* section.
   c. Type 1 in the *From* text box, press the Tab key, and then type 1 in the *To* text box.
   d. Click OK.
7. Close the ClientsGroupedRpt report.
8. Create a report with the InOrMunSalesOver$99999Query query using the Report button on the CREATE tab.
9. Make sure the report displays in Layout view.
10. Group the report by city and then sort by clients by completing the following steps:
    a. Click the Group & Sort button in the Grouping & Totals group on the REPORT LAYOUT TOOLS DESIGN tab.
    b. Click the Add a group button in the Group, Sort, and Total pane.
    c. Click the *City* field in the list box.
    d. Click the Add a sort button in the Group, Sort, and Total pane and then click the *Client* field in the list box.
    e. Close the Group, Sort, and Total pane by clicking the Close button located in the upper right corner of the pane.
11. Print the first page of the report. (Refer to Step 6.)
12. Save the report and name it *InMunSalesOver$99999*.
13. Close the report.
14. Close **AL1-C6-Dearborn.accdb**.
15. Display the Open dialog box with the AL1C6 folder on your storage medium the active folder, open **AL1-C6-WarrenLegal.accdb**, and enable the contents.

16. Design a query that extracts records from three tables with the following specifications:
   a. Add the Billing, Clients, and Rates tables to the query window.
   b. Insert the *LastName* field from the *Clients* field list box to the first *Field* row field.
   c. Insert the *Date* field from the *Billing* field list box to the second *Field* row field.
   d. Insert the *Hours* field from the *Billing* field list box to the third *Field* row field.
   e. Insert the *Rate* field from the *Rates* field list box to the fourth *Field* row field.
   f. Click in the fifth *Field* row field, type **Total: [Hours]*[Rate]**, and then press Enter.

Step 16b Step 16c Step 16d Step 16e Step 16f

Field:	LastName	Date	Hours	Rate	Total: [Hours]*[Rate]
Table:	Clients	Billing	Billing	Rates	
Sort:					
Show:	✔	✔	✔	✔	✔
Criteria:					
or:					

   g. Run the query.
   h. Save the query and name it *ClientBilling*.
   i. Close the query.
17. Create a report with the ClientBilling query using the Report button on the CREATE tab.
18. Click each column heading individually and then decrease the size of each column so the right border is near the longest entry.
19. Apply Currency formatting to the numbers in the *Total* column by completing the following steps:
   a. Click the REPORT LAYOUT TOOLS FORMAT tab.
   b. Click in the first field below the *Total* column (the field containing the number *350*).
   c. Click the Apply Currency Format button in the Number group.
   d. If necessary, increase the size of the *Total* column so the entire amounts (including the dollar signs) are visible.

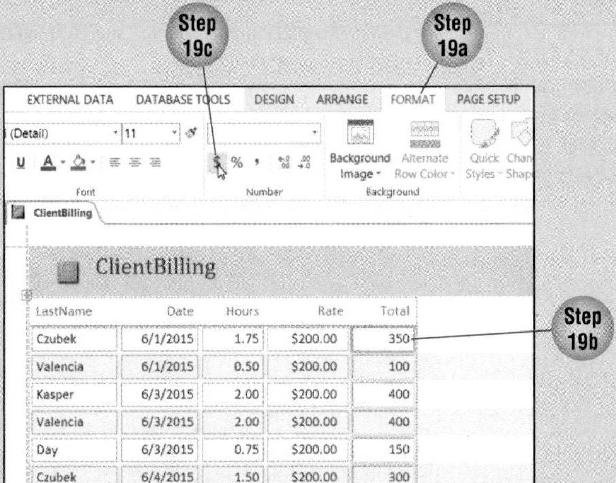

20. Group the report by last name by completing the following steps:
   a. Click the REPORT LAYOUT TOOLS DESIGN tab.
   b. Click the Group & Sort button in the Grouping & Totals group.
   c. Click the Add a group button in the Group, Sort, and Total pane.
   d. Click the *LastName* field in the list box.
   e. Click the Add a sort button in the Group, Sort, and Total pane.
   f. Click the *Date* field in the list box.
   g. Close the Group, Sort, and Total pane by clicking the Close button located in the upper right corner of the pane.
21. Scroll to the bottom of the report and, if necessary, increase the size of the column and row so the total amount in the *Rate* column is visible.
22. Save the report and name it *ClientBillingRpt*.
23. Print and then close the report. (The report will print on three pages.)
24. Close **AL1-C6-WarrenLegal.accdb**.

Project 2 Use Wizards to Create Reports and Labels **3 Parts**

You will create reports using the Report Wizard and prepare mailing labels using the Label Wizard.

Creating Reports Using the Report Wizard

Quick Steps

Create a Report Using the Report Wizard
1. Click CREATE tab.
2. Click Report Wizard button.
3. Choose desired options at each Report Wizard dialog box.

Report Wizard

Use the Report Wizard to select specific fields and specify how data is grouped and sorted.

Access offers a Report Wizard that will guide you through the steps for creating a report. To create a report using the wizard, click the CREATE tab and then click the Report Wizard button in the Reports group. At the first wizard dialog box, shown in Figure 6.3, choose the desired table or query with options from the *Tables/Queries* option box. Specify the fields you want included in the report by inserting them in the *Selected Fields* list box and then clicking the Next button.

At the second Report Wizard dialog box, shown in Figure 6.4, specify the grouping level of data in the report. To group data by a specific field, click the field in the list box at the left side of the dialog box and then click the One Field button. Use the button containing the left-pointing arrow to remove an option as a grouping level. Use the up-pointing and down-pointing arrows to change the priority of the field.

Specify a sort order with options at the third Report Wizard dialog box, shown in Figure 6.5. To specify a sort order, click the down-pointing arrow at the right of the option box preceded by the number *1* and then click the field name. The default sort order is ascending. You can change this to descending by clicking the button that displays at the right side of the text box. After identifying the sort order, click the Next button.

Figure 6.3 First Report Wizard Dialog Box

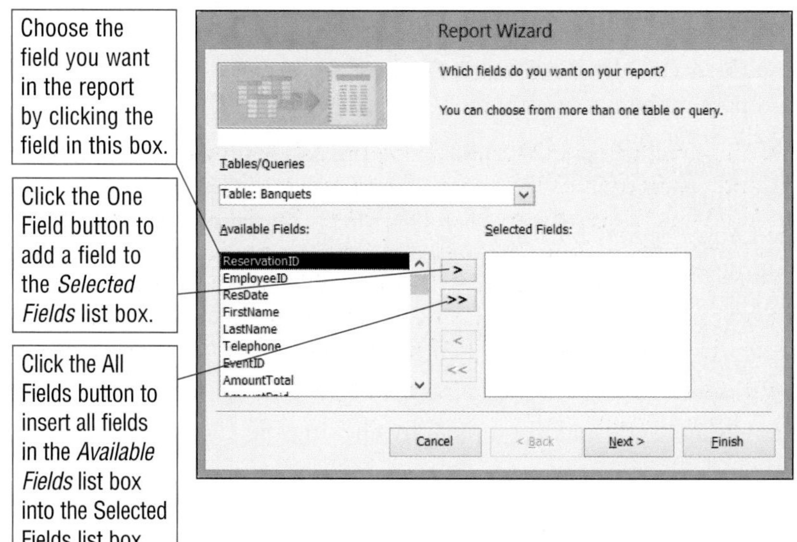
Choose the field you want in the report by clicking the field in this box.
Click the One Field button to add a field to the *Selected Fields* list box.
Click the All Fields button to insert all fields in the *Available Fields* list box into the Selected Fields list box.
Report Wizard
Which fields do you want on your report?
You can choose from more than one table or query.
Tables/Queries
Table: Banquets
Available Fields:
Selected Fields:
ReservationID
EmployeeID
ResDate
FirstName
LastName
Telephone
EventID
AmountTotal
>
>>
<
<<
Cancel
< Back
Next >
Finish

Figure 6.4 Second Report Wizard Dialog Box

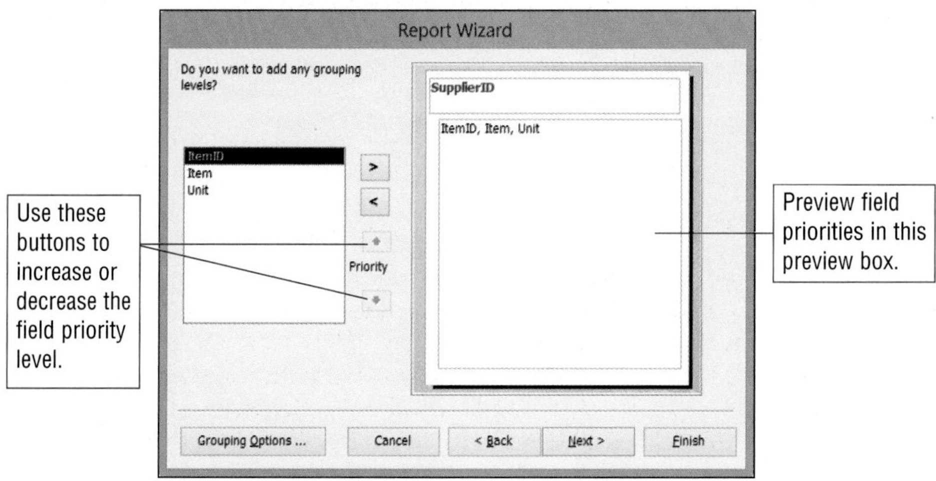

Figure 6.5 Third Report Wizard Dialog Box

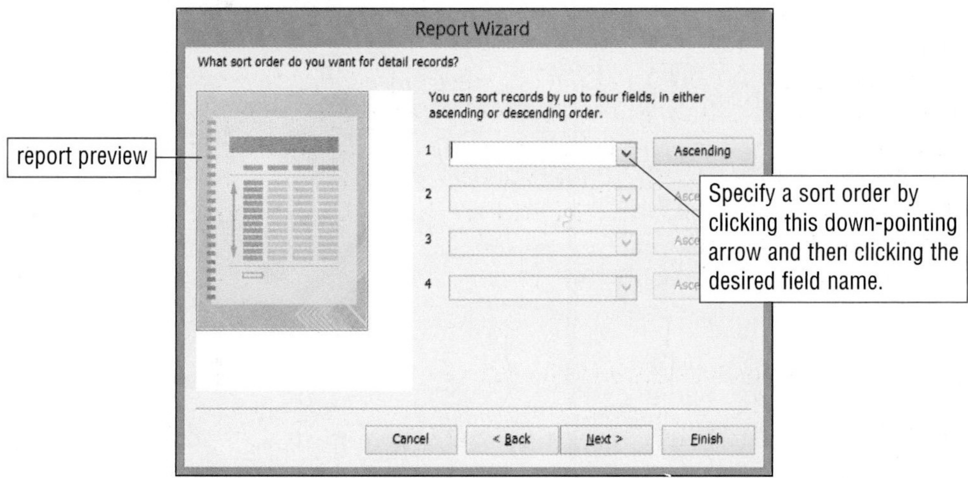

Use options at the fourth Report Wizard dialog box, shown in Figure 6.6, to specify the layout and orientation of the report. The *Layout* section has the default setting of *Stepped*. You can change this to *Block* or *Outline*. By default, the report will print in portrait orientation. You can change to landscape orientation in the *Orientation* section of the dialog box. Access will adjust field widths in the report so all of the fields fit on one page. If you do not want Access to make this adjustment, remove the check mark from the *Adjust the field width so all fields fit on a page* option.

At the fifth and final Report Wizard dialog box, type a name for the report and then click the Finish button.

Figure 6.6 Fourth Report Wizard Dialog Box

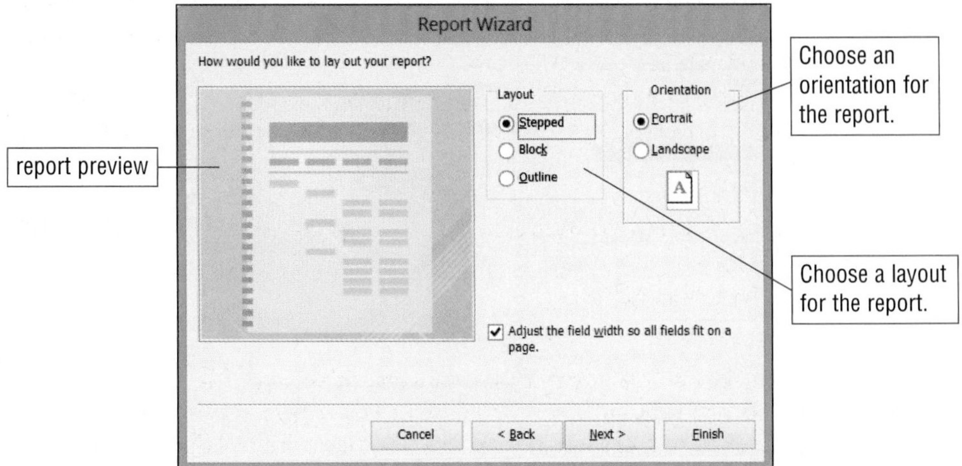

Project 2a Using the Report Wizard to Prepare a Report

Part 1 of 3

1. Display the Open dialog box with the AL1C6 folder on your storage medium the active folder.
2. Open **AL1-C6-Skyline.accdb** and enable the contents.
3. Create a report using the Report Wizard by completing the following steps:
   a. Click the CREATE tab.
   b. Click the Report Wizard button in the Reports group.
   c. At the first Report Wizard dialog box, click the down-pointing arrow at the right side of the *Tables/Queries* option box and then click *Table: Inventory* at the drop-down list.
   d. Click the All Fields button to insert all of the Inventory fields in the *Selected Fields* list box.
   e. Click the Next button.
   f. At the second Report Wizard dialog box, make sure *SupplierID* displays in blue at the top of the preview page at the right side of the dialog box and then click the Next button.
   g. At the third Report Wizard dialog box, click the Next button. (You want to use the sorting defaults.)
   h. At the fourth Report Wizard dialog box, click the *Block* option in the *Layout* section and then click the Next button.

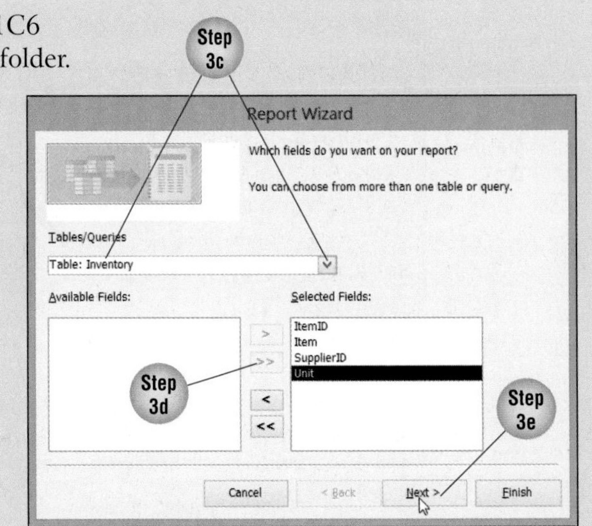

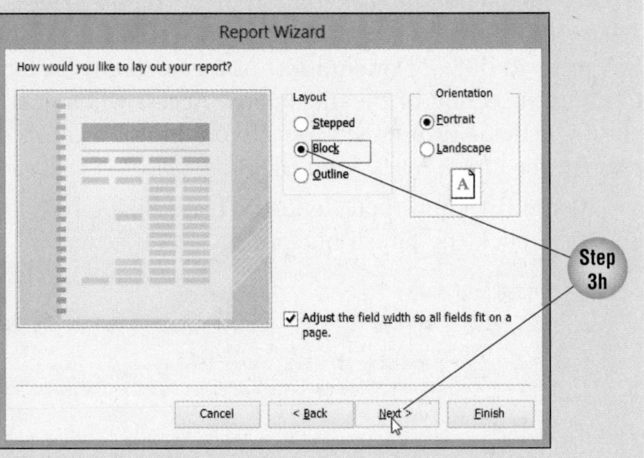

i. At the fifth Report Wizard dialog box, make sure *Inventory* displays in the *What title do you want for your report?* text box and then click the Finish button. (The report displays in Print Preview.)
4. With the report in Print Preview, click the Print button at the left side of the PRINT PREVIEW tab and then click OK at the Print dialog box. (The report will print on two pages.)
5. Close Print Preview.
6. Switch to Report view by clicking the View button on the REPORT DESIGN TOOLS DESIGN tab.
7. Close the Inventory report.

If you create a report with fields from only one table, you will choose options from five Report Wizard dialog boxes. If you create a report with fields from more than one table, you will choose options from six Report Wizard dialog boxes. After choosing the tables and fields at the first dialog box, the second dialog box that displays asks how you want to view the data. For example, if you specify fields from a Suppliers table and fields from an Orders table, the second Report Wizard dialog box will ask you if you want to view data "by Suppliers" or "by Orders."

Project 2b Creating a Report with Fields from Multiple Tables Part 2 of 3

1. With **AL1-C6-Skyline.accdb** open, create a report with the Report Wizard by completing the following steps:
   a. Click the CREATE tab.
   b. Click the Report Wizard button in the Reports group.
   c. At the first Report Wizard dialog box, click the down-pointing arrow at the right side of the *Tables/Queries* option box and then click *Table: Events* at the drop-down list.
   d. Click the *Event* field in the *Available Fields* list box and then click the One Field button.
   e. Click the down-pointing arrow at the right side of the *Tables/Queries* option box and then click *Table: Banquets* at the drop-down list.
   f. Insert the following fields in the *Selected Fields* list box:
      ResDate
      FirstName
      LastName
      AmountTotal
      AmountPaid
   g. After inserting the fields, click the Next button.
   h. At the second Report Wizard dialog box, make sure *by Events* is selected and then click the Next button.

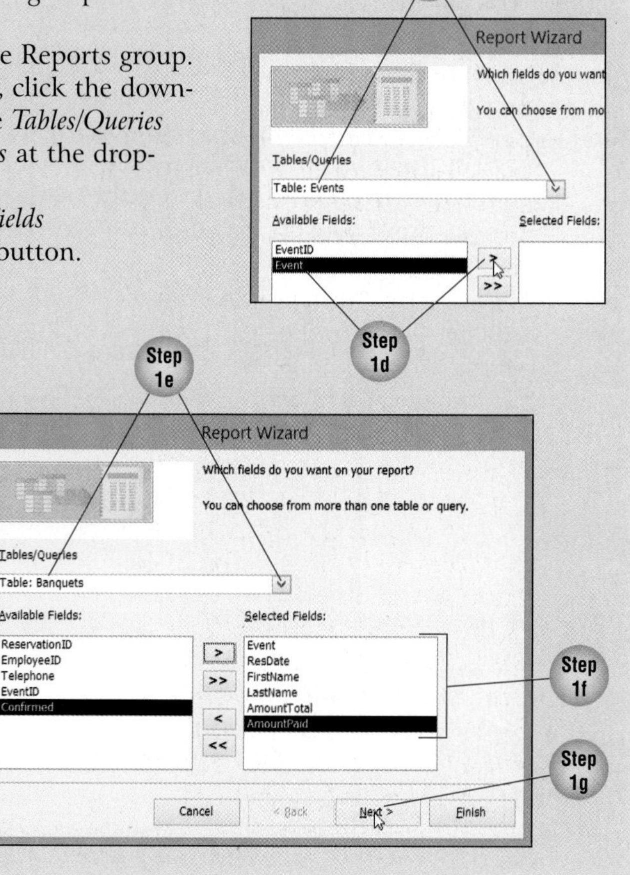

i. At the third Report Wizard dialog box, click the Next button. (The report preview shows that the report will be grouped by event.)
j. At the fourth Report Wizard dialog box, click the Next button. (You want to use the sorting defaults.)
k. At the fifth Report Wizard dialog box, click the *Block* option in the *Layout* section, click *Landscape* in the *Orientation* section, and then click the Next button.
l. At the sixth Report Wizard dialog box, select the current name in the *What title do you want for your report?* text box, type **BanquetEvents**, and then click the Finish button.

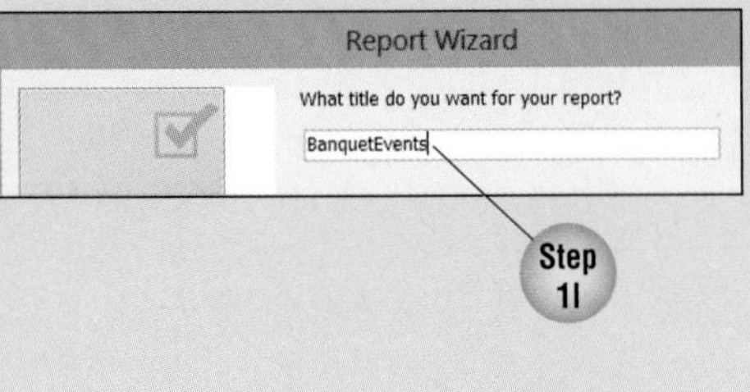

2. Close Print Preview and then change to Layout view.
3. Print and then close the BanquetEvents report.
4. Close **AL1-C6-Skyline.accdb**.

Preparing Mailing Labels

Quick Steps
Create Mailing Labels Using the Label Wizard
1. Click desired table.
2. Click CREATE tab.
3. Click Labels button.
4. Choose desired options at each Label Wizard dialog box.

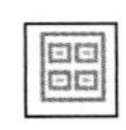
Labels

Access includes a mailing label wizard that walks you through the steps for creating mailing labels with fields in a table. To create mailing labels, click the desired table, click the CREATE tab, and then click the Labels button in the Reports group. At the first Label Wizard dialog box, shown in Figure 6.7, specify the label size, units of measure, and label type and then click the Next button. At the second Label Wizard dialog box, shown in Figure 6.8, specify the font name, size, weight, and color and then click the Next button.

Specify the fields you want included in the mailing labels at the third Label Wizard dialog box, shown in Figure 6.9. To do this, click the field in the *Available fields* list box and then click the One Field button. This moves the field to the *Prototype label* box. Insert the fields in the *Prototype label* box as you want the text to display on the label. After inserting the fields in the *Prototype label* box, click the Next button.

Figure 6.7 First Label Wizard Dialog Box

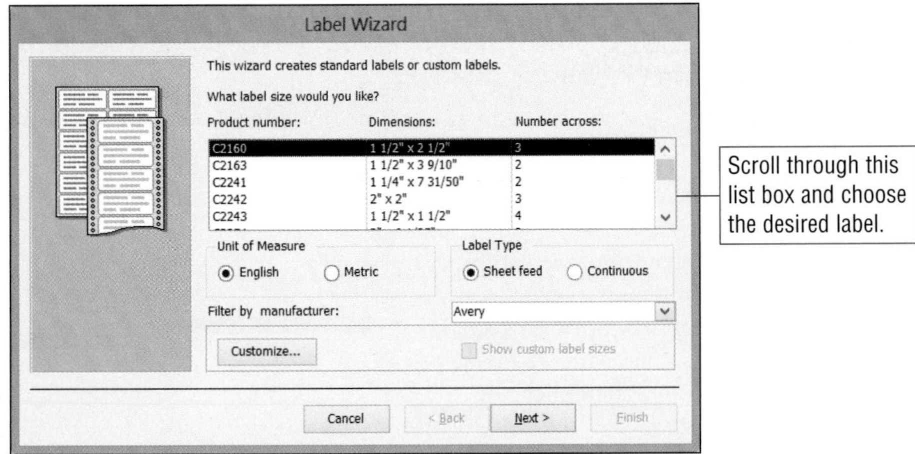

Figure 6.8 Second Label Wizard Dialog Box

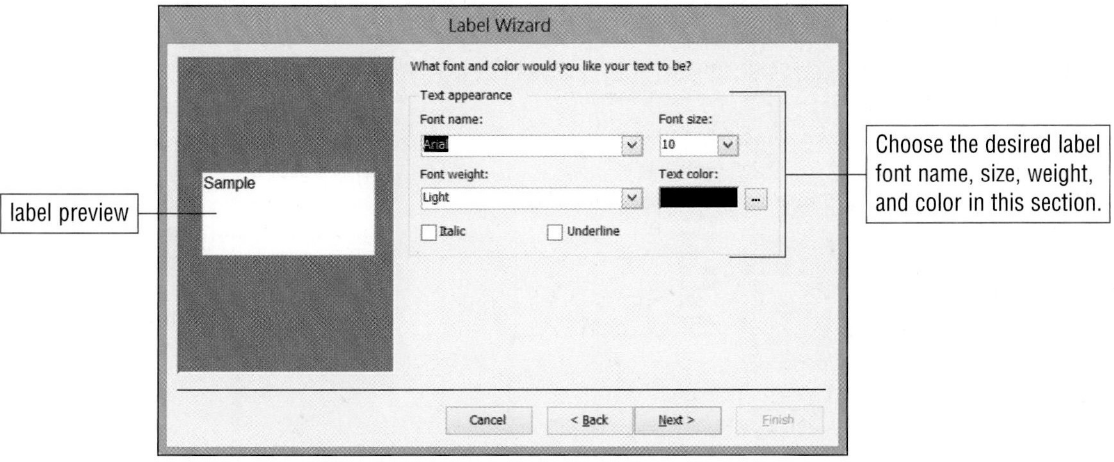

Figure 6.9 Third Label Wizard Dialog Box

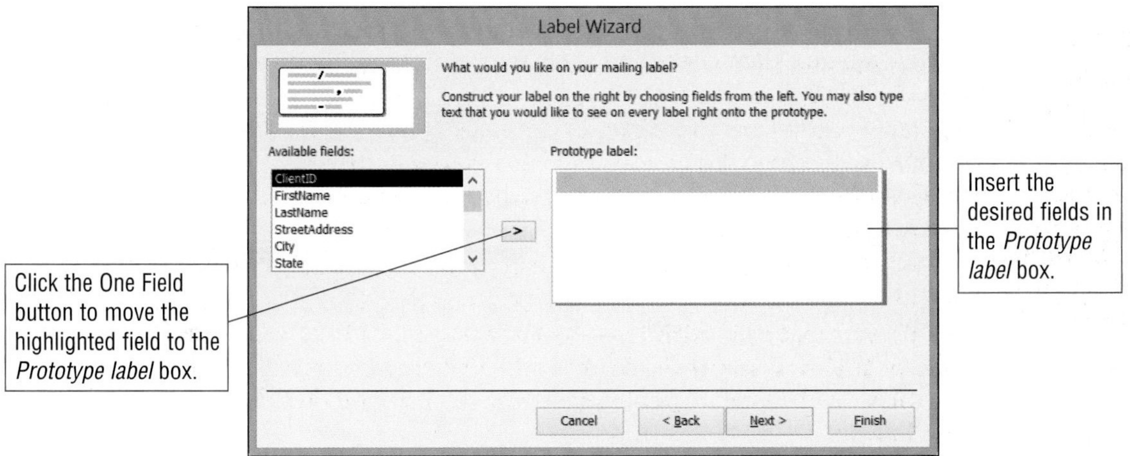

At the fourth Label Wizard dialog box, shown in Figure 6.10, specify a field from the database by which the labels will be sorted. If you want the labels sorted (for example, by last name, postal code, etc.), insert the field in the *Sort by* list box and then click the Next button.

At the last Label Wizard dialog box, type a name for the label file and then click the Finish button. After a few moments, the labels display on the screen in Print Preview. Print the labels and/or close Print Preview.

Figure 6.10 Fourth Label Wizard Dialog Box

Project 2c Preparing Mailing Labels

Part 3 of 3

1. Open **AL1-C6-WarrenLegal.accdb**.
2. Click *Clients* in the Tables group in the Navigation pane.
3. Click the CREATE tab and then click the Labels button in the Reports group.
4. At the first Label Wizard dialog box, make sure *English* is selected in the *Unit of Measure* section, *Avery* is selected in the *Filter by manufacturer* list box, *Sheet feed* is selected in the *Label Type* section, and *C2160* is selected in the *Product number* list box and then click the Next button.

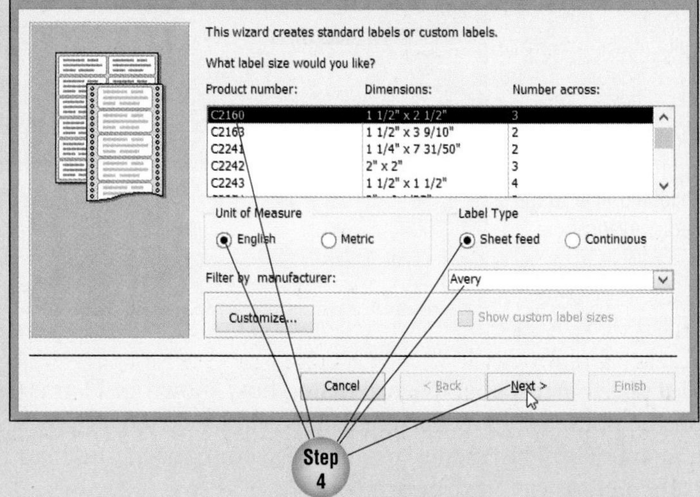

5. At the second Label Wizard dialog box, if necessary, change the font size to 10 points and then click the Next button.
6. At the third Label Wizard dialog box, complete the following steps to insert the fields in the *Prototype label* box:
   a. Click *FirstName* in the *Available fields* list box and then click the One Field button.
   b. Press the spacebar, make sure *LastName* is selected in the *Available fields* list box, and then click the One Field button.
   c. Press the Enter key. (This moves the insertion point down to the next line in the *Prototype label* box.)
   d. With *StreetAddress* selected in the *Available fields* list box, click the One Field button.
   e. Press the Enter key.
   f. With *City* selected in the *Available fields* list box, click the One Field button.
   g. Type a comma (,) and then press the spacebar.

h. With *State* selected in the *Available fields* list box, click the One Field button.
i. Press the spacebar.
j. With *ZipCode* selected in the *Available fields* list box, click the One Field button.
k. Click the Next button.

7. At the fourth Label Wizard dialog box, sort by zip code. To do this, click *ZipCode* in the *Available fields* list box and then click the One Field button.

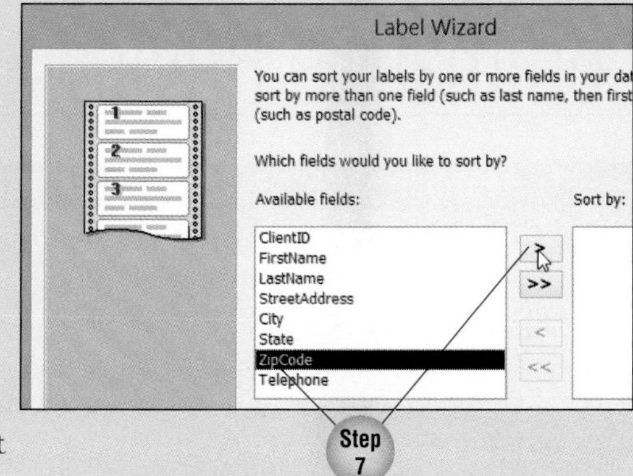

8. Click the Next button.
9. At the last Label Wizard dialog box, click the Finish button. (The Label Wizard automatically names the label report *Labels Clients*.)
10. Print the labels by clicking the Print button that displays at the left side of the PRINT PREVIEW tab and then click OK at the Print dialog box.
11. Close Print Preview.
12. Switch to Report view by clicking the View button on the REPORT DESIGN TOOLS DESIGN tab.
13. Close the labels report and then close **AL1-C6-WarrenLegal.accdb**.

Chapter Summary

- Create a report with data in a table or query to control how data appears on the page when printed.
- Create a report with the Report button in the Reports group on the CREATE tab.
- Four views are available for viewing a report: Report view, Print Preview, Layout view, and Design view.
- Use options on the PRINT PREVIEW tab to specify how a report prints.
- In Layout view, you can select a report control object and then size or move the object. You can also change the column width by clicking a column heading and then dragging the border to the desired width.
- Sort data in a record using the Ascending button or Descending button in the Sort & Filter group on the HOME tab.
- Customize a report with options on the REPORT LAYOUT TOOLS ribbon with the DESIGN tab, ARRANGE tab, FORMAT tab, or PAGE SETUP tab selected.

- To make data in a report easier to understand, divide the data into groups using the Group, Sort, and Total pane. Display this pane by clicking the Group & Sort button in the Grouping & Totals group on the REPORT LAYOUT TOOLS DESIGN tab.
- Use the Report Wizard to guide you through the steps for creating a report. Begin the wizard by clicking the CREATE tab and then clicking the Report Wizard button in the Reports group.
- Create mailing labels with data in a table using the Label Wizard. Begin the wizard by clicking the desired table, clicking the CREATE tab, and then clicking the Labels button in the Reports group.

Commands Review

FEATURE	RIBBON TAB, GROUP	BUTTON
Group, Sort, and Total pane	REPORT LAYOUT TOOLS DESIGN, Grouping & Totals	
Labels Wizard	CREATE, Reports	
report	CREATE, Reports	
Report Wizard	CREATE, Reports	

Concepts Check

Test Your Knowledge

Completion: In the space provided at the right, indicate the correct term, symbol, or command.

1. The Report button is located in the Reports group on this tab. ____________
2. Press these keys on the keyboard to select all control objects in a report in Layout view. ____________
3. The Ascending button is located in this group on the HOME tab. ____________
4. Four views are available in a report, including Layout view, Report view, Design view, and this view. ____________
5. With options on this tab, you can insert controls, insert header or footer data, and add existing fields. ____________

6. Click this button in the Grouping & Totals group on the REPORT LAYOUT TOOLS DESIGN tab to perform functions such as finding the sum, average, maximum, and minimum of the numbers in a column. ________________

7. The Group & Sort button is located in this group on the REPORT LAYOUT TOOLS DESIGN tab. ________________

8. Click the Group & Sort button and this pane displays. ________________

9. Use this to guide you through the steps for creating a report. ________________

10. To create mailing labels, click the desired table, click the CREATE tab, and then click the Labels button in this group. ________________

Skills Check Assess Your Performance

Assessment 1

CREATE AND FORMAT REPORTS IN THE HILLTOP DATABASE

1. Open **AL1-C6-Hilltop.accdb** and enable the contents.
2. Create a report with the Inventory table using the Report button.
3. With the report in Layout view, apply the following formatting:
   a. Center the data below each of the following column headings: *EquipmentID*, *AvailableHours*, *ServiceHours*, and *RepairHours*.
   b. Select all of the control objects and then change the font to Constantia.
   c. Select the money amounts below the *PurchasePrice* column heading and then click the Decrease Decimals button (in the Number group) until the amounts display without any places past the decimal point.
   d. Click in the *$473,260.00* amount and then click the Decrease Decimals button until the amount displays with no places past the decimal point.
   e. If necessary, increase the height of the total amount row so the entire amount is visible.
   f. Change the title of the report to *Inventory Report*.
4. Save the report and name it *InventoryReport*.
5. Print and then close InventoryReport.
6. Create a query in Design view with the following specifications:
   a. Add the Customers, Equipment, Invoices, and Rates tables to the query window.
   b. Insert the *Customer* field from the *Customers* field list box in the first *Field* row field.
   c. Insert the *Equipment* field from the *Equipment* field list box in the second *Field* row field.
   d. Insert the *Hours* field from the *Invoices* field list box in the third *Field* row field.
   e. Insert the *Rate* field from the *Rates* field list box in the fourth *Field* row field.
   f. Click in the fifth *Field* row field, type **Total: [Hours]*[Rate]**, and then press Enter.

g. Run the query.
h. Save the query and name it *CustomerRentals* and then close the query.
7. Create a report with the CustomerRentals query using the Report button.
8. With the report in Layout view, apply the following formatting:
a. Decrease the widths of the columns so the right border of each column displays near the right side of the longest entry.
b. Select the money amounts and then click the Decrease Decimals button until the amounts display with no places past the decimal point.
c. Click in the *Total* column and then total the amounts by clicking the REPORT LAYOUT TOOLS DESIGN tab, clicking the Totals button in the Grouping & Totals group, and then clicking *Sum* at the drop-down list.
d. Click the total amount (located at the bottom of the *Total* column), click the REPORT LAYOUT TOOLS FORMAT tab, and then click the Apply Currency Format button in the Number group.
e. Increase the height of the total amount row so the entire amount is visible.
f. Select and then delete the amount that displays at the bottom of the *Rate* column.
g. Display the Group, Sort, and Total pane; group the records by *Customer*; sort by *Equipment*; and then close the pane.
h. Apply the Integral theme. (Do this with the Themes button in the Themes group on the REPORT LAYOUT TOOLS DESIGN tab.)
i. Select the five column headings and change the font color to black.
j. Change the title of the report to *Rentals*.
9. Save the report and name it *RentalReport*.
10. Print and then close RentalReport.

Assessment 2

CREATE REPORTS USING THE REPORT WIZARD

1. With **AL1-C6-Hilltop.accdb** open, create a report using the Report Wizard with the following specifications:
a. At the first Report Wizard dialog box, insert the following fields in the *Selected Fields* list box:

From the Equipment table:	*Equipment*
From the Inventory table:	*PurchaseDate* *PurchasePrice* *AvailableHours*

b. Do not make any changes at the second Report Wizard dialog box.
c. Do not make any changes at the third Report Wizard dialog box.
d. At the fourth Report Wizard dialog box, choose the *Columnar* option.
e. At the fifth and last Report Wizard dialog box, click the Finish button. (This accepts the default report name *Equipment*.)
2. Print and then close the report.

3. Create a report using the Report Wizard with the following specifications:
   a. At the first Report Wizard dialog box, insert the following fields in the *Selected Fields* list box:

From the Customers table:	*Customer*
From the Invoices table:	*BillingDate* *Hours*
From the Equipment table:	*Equipment*
From the Rates table:	*Rate*

   b. Do not make any changes at the second Report Wizard dialog box.
   c. Do not make any changes at the third Report Wizard dialog box.
   d. Do not make any changes at the fourth Report Wizard dialog box.
   e. At the fifth Report Wizard dialog box, choose the *Block* option.
   f. At the sixth and last Report Wizard dialog box, name the report *Rentals*.
4. Print and then close the report.

Assessment 3 CREATE MAILING LABELS

1. With **AL1-C6-Hilltop.accdb** open, click *Customers* in the Tables group in the Navigation pane.
2. Use the Label Wizard to create mailing labels (you determine the label type) with customer names and addresses and sort the labels by customer names. Name the mailing label report *CustomerMailingLabels*.
3. Print the mailing labels.
4. Close the mailing labels report.

Assessment 4 ADD A FIELD TO A REPORT

1. In Chapter 5, you added a field list to an existing form using the Field List task pane. Experiment with adding a field to an existing report and then complete the following:
   a. Open the RentalReport report (created in Assessment 1) in Layout view.
   b. Display the Field List task pane and display all of the tables.
   c. Drag the *BillingDate* field from the Invoices table so the field is positioned between the *Equipment* column and *Hours* column.
   d. At the message indicating that Access will modify the RecordSource property and asking if you want to continue, click Yes.
   e. Close the Field List task pane.
2. Save, print, and then close the report.
3. Close **AL1-C6-Hilltop.accdb**.

Visual Benchmark Demonstrate Your Proficiency

DESIGN A QUERY AND CREATE A REPORT WITH THE QUERY

1. Open **AL1-C6-Skyline.accdb** and then create and run the query shown in Figure 6.11.
2. Save the query and name it *Suppliers2&4Orders* and then close the query.
3. Use the Report button to create the report shown in Figure 6.12 using the *Suppliers2&4Orders* query with the following specifications:
   a. Apply the Facet theme.
   b. Adjust the column widths and change the alignment of data as shown in Figure 6.12.
   c. Change the title as shown in Figure 6.12.
   d. Select the column headings and then apply the Black font color.
   e. Insert the total of the amounts in the *Total* column. Format the total amount as shown in Figure 6.12.
   f. Delete the sum amount at the bottom of the *UnitPrice* column.
4. Save the report and name it *Suppliers2&4OrdersRpt*.
5. Print the report, close the report, and then close **AL1-C6-Skyline.accdb**.

Figure 6.11 Visual Benchmark Query

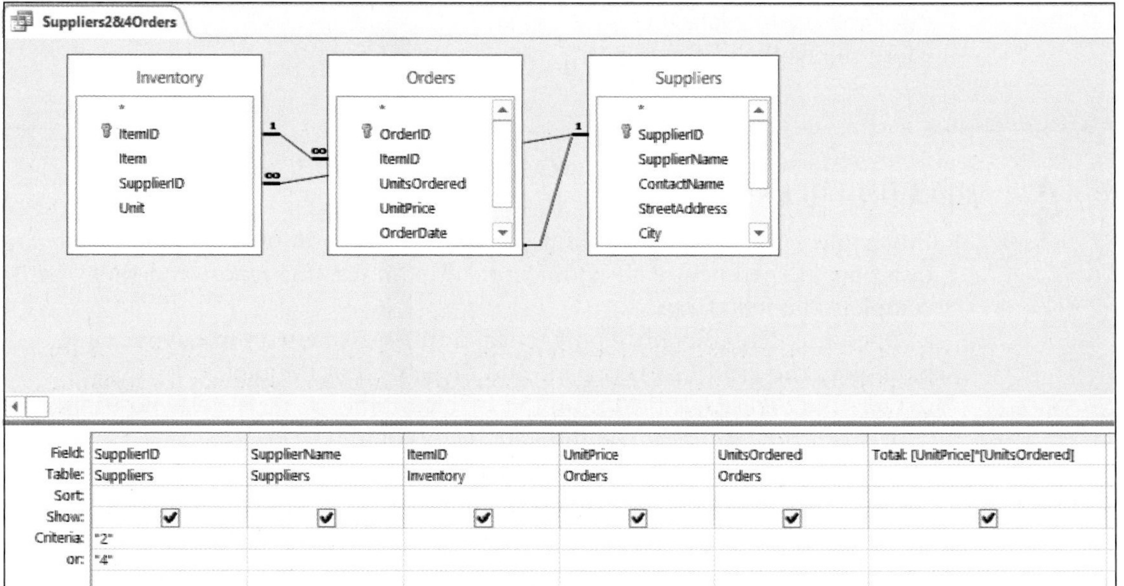

Figure 6.12 Visual Benchmark Report

Suppliers 2 and 4 Orders

Thursday, October 15, 2015
4:45:53 PM

SupplierID	SupplierName	ItemID	UnitPrice	UnitsOrdered	Total
2	Coral Produce	002	$10.50	3	$31.50
2	Coral Produce	016	$24.00	1	$24.00
4	Grocery Wholesalers	020	$18.75	2	$37.50
2	Coral Produce	014	$15.75	2	$31.50
4	Grocery Wholesalers	025	$28.50	1	$28.50
4	Grocery Wholesalers	036	$17.00	2	$34.00
4	Grocery Wholesalers	013	$14.00	2	$28.00
2	Coral Produce	004	$10.95	2	$21.90
4	Grocery Wholesalers	035	$17.00	1	$17.00
4	Grocery Wholesalers	027	$22.00	1	$22.00
4	Grocery Wholesalers	026	$29.25	1	$29.25
2	Coral Produce	021	$31.00	1	$31.00
4	Grocery Wholesalers	034	$13.75	2	$27.50
4	Grocery Wholesalers	012	$30.25	1	$30.25
4	Grocery Wholesalers	018	$45.00	1	$45.00
2	Coral Produce	016	$39.40	2	$78.80
4	Grocery Wholesalers	035	$17.00	1	$17.00
2	Coral Produce	014	$15.75	2	$31.50
4	Grocery Wholesalers	020	$18.75	2	$37.50
					$603.70

Case Study Apply Your Skills

Part 1

As the office manager at Millstone Legal Services, you need to enter records for three new clients in **AL1-C6-Millstone.accdb**. Using the following information, enter the data in the appropriate tables:

Client number 42
Martin Costanzo
1002 Thomas Drive
Casper, WY 82602
(307) 555-5001
Mr. Costanzo saw Douglas Sheehan regarding divorce proceedings with a billing date of 3/15/2015 and a fee of $150.

Client number 43
Susan Nordyke
23193 Ridge Circle East
Mills, WY 82644
(307) 555-2719
Ms. Nordyke saw Loretta Ryder regarding support enforcement with a billing date of 3/15/2015 and a fee of $175.

Client number 44
Monica Sommers
1105 Riddell Avenue
Casper, WY 82609
(307) 555-1188
Ms. Sommers saw Anita Leland regarding a guardianship with a billing date of 3/15/2015 and a fee of $250.

Part 2

Create and print the following queries, reports, and labels:

- Create a report with the Clients table. Apply formatting to enhance the appearance of the report.
- Create a query that displays the client ID, first name, and last name; attorney last name; billing date; and fee. Name the query *ClientBilling*.
- Create a report with the ClientBilling query. Group the records in the report by attorney last name (the *LName* field in the drop-down list) and sort alphabetically in ascending order by client last name (the *LastName* field in the drop-down list). Apply formatting to enhance the appearance of the report.
- Produce a telephone directory by creating a report that includes client last names, first names, and telephone numbers. Sort the records in the report alphabetically by last name in ascending order.
- Edit the ClientBilling query so it includes a criterion that displays only billing dates between 3/10/2015 and 3/13/2015. Save the query with Save Object As and name it *ClientBilling10-13*.
- Create a report with the ClientBilling10-13 query. Apply formatting to enhance the appearance of the report.
- Create mailing labels for the clients.

Part 3

Apply the following conditions to fields in reports and then print the reports:

- In the Clients report, apply the condition that the city *Casper* displays in the Red font color and the city *Mills* displays the Blue font color in the *City* field.
- In the ClientBilling report, apply the condition that fees over $199 display in the Green font color and fees less than $200 display in the Blue font color.

Part 4

Your center has a manual that describes processes and procedures in the workplace. Open Word and create a document for the manual that describes how to create a report using the Report button and Report Wizard and how to create mailing labels using the Label Wizard. Save the completed document and name it **AL1-C6-CS-Manual**. Print and then close **AL1-C6-CS-Manual.docx**.

MICROSOFT®

ACCESS®

Modifying, Filtering, and Viewing Data

PERFORMANCE OBJECTIVES

Upon successful completion of Chapter 7, you will be able to:

- **Filter data by selection and form**
- **Remove a filter**
- **View object dependencies**
- **Compact and repair a database**
- **Encrypt a database with a password**
- **View and customize document properties**
- **Save a database in an earlier version of Access**
- **Save a database object in PDF file format**

Tutorials

7.1 Filtering Records

7.2 Viewing Object Dependencies

7.3 Compacting, Repairing, and Backing Up a Database

7.4 Encrypting a Database with a Password and Modifying Document Properties

7.5 Saving Databases and Database Objects in Different Formats

You can filter data in a database object to view specific records without having to change the design of the object. In this chapter, you will learn how to filter data by selection and form. You will also learn how to view object dependencies, manage a database with options at the Info backstage area, save a database in an earlier version of Access, and save a database object in PDF file format. Model answers for this chapter's projects appear on the following pages.

Note: Before beginning the projects, copy to your storage medium the AL1C7 subfolder from the AL1 folder on the CD that accompanies this textbook and make AL1C7 the active folder.

Project 1 Filter Records

Project 1a

EmployeeID	FName	LName	StreetAddress	City	State	ZipCode
02	Wayne	Weber	17362 North Tenth	Fort Myers	FL	33994
03	Owen	Pasqual	4010 Shannon Drive	Fort Myers	FL	33910
04	Vadim	Sayenko	1328 St. Paul Avenue	Fort Myers	FL	33907
07	Donald	Sellars	23103 Summer Highway	Fort Myers	FL	33919
09	Elizabeth	Mohr	1818 Brookdale Road	Fort Myers	FL	33902
11	Nicole	Bateman	5001 150th Street	Fort Myers	FL	33908

Skyline Employees Filtered Records, Page 1

Telephone	HireDate	HealthIns
(239) 555-6041	4/1/2010	☐
(239) 555-3492	4/15/2009	☐
(239) 555-9487	6/15/2009	☑
(239) 555-4348	6/6/2012	☑
(239) 555-0430	5/1/2011	☑
(239) 555-2631	2/1/2013	☐

Skyline Employees Filtered Records, Page 2

Project 1b

ResDate	FirstName	LastName	Telephone	Event	EmployeeID
6/5/2015	Terrance	Schaefer	(239) 555-6239	Wedding rehearsal dinner	03
6/5/2015	Andrea	Wyatt	(239) 555-4282	Wedding reception	01
6/6/2015	Luis	Castillo	(239) 555-4001	Wedding shower	11
6/6/2015	David	Hooper	(941) 555-2338	Wedding anniversary	04
6/7/2015	Bridget	Kohn	(239) 555-1299	Other	02
6/9/2015	Joanne	Blair	(239) 555-7783	Birthday	03
6/12/2015	Tim	Drysdale	(941) 555-0098	Bat mitzvah	02
6/12/2015	Gabrielle	Johnson	(239) 555-1882	Other	05
6/12/2015	Cliff	Osborne	(239) 555-7823	Wedding rehearsal dinner	12
6/13/2015	Janis	Semala	(239) 555-0476	Wedding reception	06
6/13/2015	Tristan	Strauss	(941) 555-7746	Other	03
6/14/2015	Aaron	Williams	(239) 555-3821	Bar mitzvah	04
6/14/2015	Willow	Earhart	(239) 555-0034	Wedding shower	04

Skyline Banquet Reservations Query

BanquetReservations

Friday, October 16, 2015
1:41:29 PM

ResDate	FirstName	LastName	Telephone	Event	EmployeeID
6/9/2015	Joanne	Blair	(239) 555-7783	Birthday	03
6/5/2015	Terrance	Schaefer	(239) 555-6239	Wedding rehearsal dinner	03

Skyline Banquet Report

Project 1c

ItemID	Item	SupplierID	Unit
003	Carrots	6	25 lb bag
005	Garlic	6	10 lb bag
009	Radishes	6	case
010	Celery	6	case
011	Broccoli	6	case
041	White sugar	6	25 lb bag
042	Baking powder	6	case
043	Baking soda	6	case

Skyline Filtered Inventory Records, Step 2c

ItemID	Item	SupplierID	Unit
006	Green peppers	2	case
007	Red peppers	2	case
008	Yellow peppers	2	case

Skyline Filtered Inventory Records, Step 3d

ResDate	FirstName	LastName	Telephone	Event	EmployeeID
6/6/2015	Luis	Castillo	(239) 555-4001	Wedding shower	11
6/14/2015	Willow	Earhart	(239) 555-0034	Wedding shower	04
6/9/2015	Joanne	Blair	(239) 555-7783	Birthday	03
6/16/2015	Jason	Haley	(239) 555-6641	Birthday	06
6/18/2015	Heidi	Thompson	(941) 555-3215	Birthday	01
6/27/2015	Kirsten	Simpson	(941) 555-4425	Birthday	02
6/14/2015	Aaron	Williams	(239) 555-3821	Bar mitzvah	04
6/20/2015	Robin	Gehring	(239) 555-0126	Bar mitzvah	06
6/12/2015	Tim	Drysdale	(941) 555-0098	Bat mitzvah	02
6/7/2015	Bridget	Kohn	(239) 555-1299	Other	02
6/12/2015	Gabrielle	Johnson	(239) 555-1882	Other	05
6/13/2015	Tristan	Strauss	(941) 555-7746	Other	03
6/17/2015	Lillian	Krakosky	(239) 555-8890	Other	03
6/20/2015	David	Fitzgerald	(941) 555-3792	Other	01
6/5/2015	Terrance	Schaefer	(239) 555-6239	Wedding rehearsal dinner	03
6/12/2015	Cliff	Osborne	(239) 555-7823	Wedding rehearsal dinner	12
6/6/2015	David	Hooper	(941) 555-2338	Wedding anniversary	04
6/19/2015	Anthony	Wiegand	(239) 555-7853	Wedding anniversary	11
6/27/2015	Shane	Rozier	(239) 555-1033	Wedding anniversary	12

Skyline Filtered Banquet Reservations Records, Step 6c

ResDate	FirstName	LastName	Telephone	Event	EmployeeID
6/14/2015	Aaron	Williams	(239) 555-3821	Bar mitzvah	04
6/20/2015	Robin	Gehring	(239) 555-0126	Bar mitzvah	06
6/12/2015	Tim	Drysdale	(941) 555-0098	Bat mitzvah	02

Skyline Filtered Banquet Reservations Records, Step 7d

Project 1d

ReservationID	EmployeeID	ResDate	FirstName	LastName	Telephone	EventID	AmountTotal	AmountPaid	Confirmed
1	03	6/5/2015	Terrance	Schaefer	(239) 555-6239	RD	$750.00	$250.00	☑
6	03	6/9/2015	Joanne	Blair	(239) 555-7783	BD	$650.00	$200.00	☑
11	03	6/13/2015	Tristan	Strauss	(941) 555-7746	OT	$1,400.00	$300.00	☐
15	03	6/17/2015	Lillian	Krakosky	(239) 555-8890	OT	$500.00	$100.00	☐

Skyline Filtered Banquets Records, Step 3c

ItemID	Item	SupplierID	Unit
001	Butternut squash	2	case
002	Potatoes	2	50 lb bag
004	Onions	2	25 lb bag
006	Green peppers	2	case
007	Red peppers	2	case
008	Yellow peppers	2	case
014	Green beans	2	case
016	Iceberg lettuce	2	case
017	Romaine lettuce	2	case
021	Cantaloupes	2	case
028	Beef	7	side
029	Pork	7	side
030	Chicken	7	case
051	Watermelon	2	case
052	Kiwi	2	case

Skyline Filtered Inventory Records, Step 6h

Project 2 View Object Dependencies, Manage a Database, and Save a Database in a Different File Format

Project 2d

Orders 10/16/2015

OrderID	ItemID	UnitsOrdered	UnitPrice	OrderDate	SupplierID
06-001	002	3	$10.50	6/1/2015	2
06-002	033	1	$73.50	6/1/2015	1
06-003	016	1	$24.00	6/4/2015	2
06-004	020	2	$18.75	6/4/2015	4
06-005	014	2	$15.75	6/4/2015	2
06-006	025	1	$28.50	6/5/2015	4
06-007	036	2	$17.00	6/5/2015	4
06-008	028	1	$315.00	6/5/2015	7
06-009	013	2	$14.00	6/5/2012	4
06-010	004	2	$10.95	6/11/2015	2
06-011	035	1	$17.00	6/11/2015	4
06-012	039	4	$3.50	6/11/2015	3
06-013	040	2	$4.95	6/11/2015	3
06-014	041	5	$6.50	6/11/2015	6
06-015	044	1	$50.25	6/15/2015	6
06-016	022	3	$16.50	6/15/2015	3
06-017	027	1	$22.00	6/15/2015	4
06-018	053	3	$52.00	6/18/2015	3
06-019	030	2	$175.00	6/18/2015	7
06-020	003	2	$7.25	6/18/2015	6
06-021	026	1	$29.25	6/18/2015	4
06-022	021	1	$31.00	6/18/2015	2
06-023	034	2	$13.75	6/22/2015	4
06-024	032	1	$101.50	6/22/2015	1
06-025	012	1	$30.25	6/22/2015	4
06-026	023	2	$12.95	6/25/2015	3
06-027	018	1	$45.00	6/25/2015	4
06-028	037	2	$11.25	6/25/2015	2
06-029	016	2	$39.40	6/25/2015	2
06-030	035	1	$17.00	6/29/2015	4
06-031	014	2	$15.75	6/29/2015	2
06-032	020	2	$18.75	6/29/2015	4
06-033	033	1	$33.50	6/29/2015	1

Skyline Orders Table

Project 1 Filter Records — 4 Parts

You will filter records in a table, query, and report in the Skyline database using the Filter button, Selection button, Toggle Filter button, and shortcut menu. You will also remove filters and filter by form.

Filtering Data

You can place a set of restrictions, called a ***filter***, on records in a table, query, form, or report to isolate temporarily specific records. A filter, like a query, lets you view specific records without having to change the design of the table, query, form, or report. Access provides a number of buttons and options for filtering data. You can filter data using the Filter button in the Sort & Filter group on the HOME tab, right-click specific data in a record and then specify a filter, and use the Selection and Advanced buttons in the Sort & Filter group.

Quick Steps

Filter Records

1. Open desired object.
2. Click in entry of desired field column to filter.
3. Click Filter button.
4. Select desired sorting option at drop-down list.

Filtering Using the Filter Button

Filter

Use the Filter button in the Sort & Filter group on the HOME tab to filter records in an object (a table, query, form, or report). To use this button, open the desired object, click in any entry in the field column on which you want to filter, and then click the Filter button. This displays a drop-down list with sorting options and a list of all of the field entries. In a table, display this drop-down list by clicking the

Figure 7.1 *City* Field Drop-down List

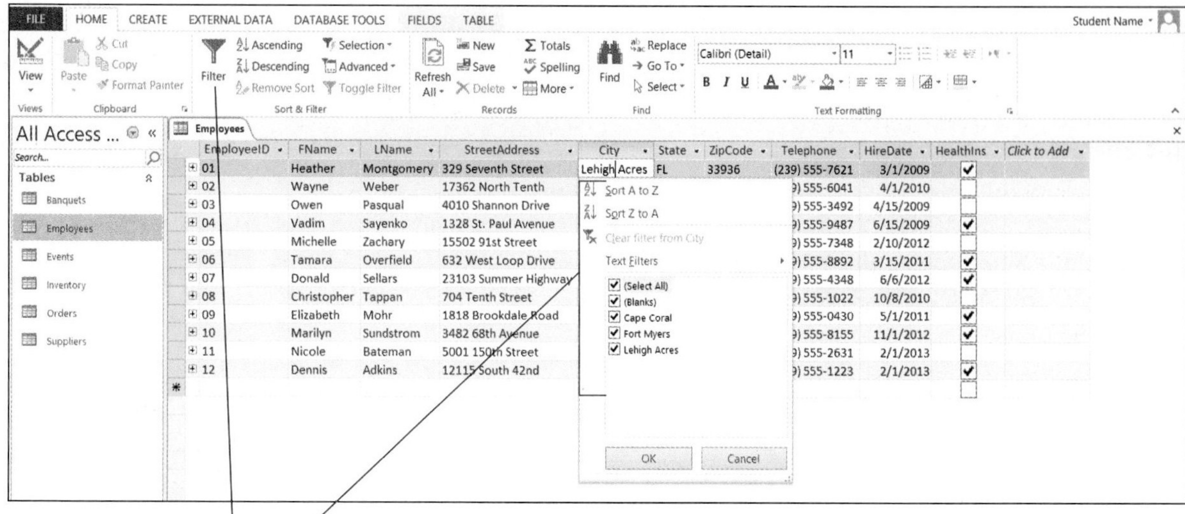

To filter on the *City* field, click in any entry in the field column and then click the Filter button. This displays a drop-down list with sorting options and a list of all field entries.

Filters available depend on the type of data selected in a column.

filter arrow that displays at the right side of a column heading. Figure 7.1 displays the drop-down list that displays when you click in the *City* field and then click the Filter button. To sort on a specific criterion, click the *(Select All)* check box to remove all check marks from the list of field entries. Click the item in the list box on which you want to sort and then click OK.

When you open a table, query, or form, the Record Navigation bar contains the dimmed words *No Filter* preceded by a filter icon with a delete symbol (X). If you filter records in one of these objects, *Filtered* displays in place of *No Filter*, the delete symbol is removed, and the text and filter icon display with an orange background. In a report, if you apply a filter to records, the word *Filtered* displays at the right side of the Status bar.

Removing a Filter

Quick Steps

Remove a Filter

1. Click in field column containing filter.
2. Click Filter button.
3. Click *Clear filter from xxx.*

OR

1. Click Advanced button.
2. Click *Clear All Filters* at drop-down list.

Toggle Filter

When you filter data, the underlying data in the object is not deleted. You can switch back and forth between the data and filtered data by clicking the Toggle Filter button in the Sort & Filter group on the HOME tab. If you click the Toggle Filter button and turn off the filter, all of the data in the table, query, or form displays and the message *Filtered* in the Record Navigation bar changes to *Unfiltered*.

Clicking the Toggle Filter button may redisplay all of the data in an object, but it does not remove the filter. To remove the filter, click in the field column containing the filter and then click the Filter button in the Sort & Filter group on the HOME tab. At the drop-down list that displays, click *Clear filter from xxx* (where *xxx* is the name of the field). You can remove all of the filters from an object by clicking the Advanced button in the Sort & Filter group and then clicking the *Clear All Filters* option.

Project 1a Filtering Records in a Table, Form, and Report

Part 1 of 4

1. Display the Open dialog box with the AL1C7 folder on your storage medium the active folder.
2. Open **AL1-C7-Skyline.accdb** and enable the contents.
3. Filter records in the Employees table by completing the following steps:
   a. Open the Employees table.
   b. Click in any entry in the *City* field.
   c. Click the Filter button in the Sort & Filter group on the HOME tab. (This displays a drop-down list of options for the *City* field.)

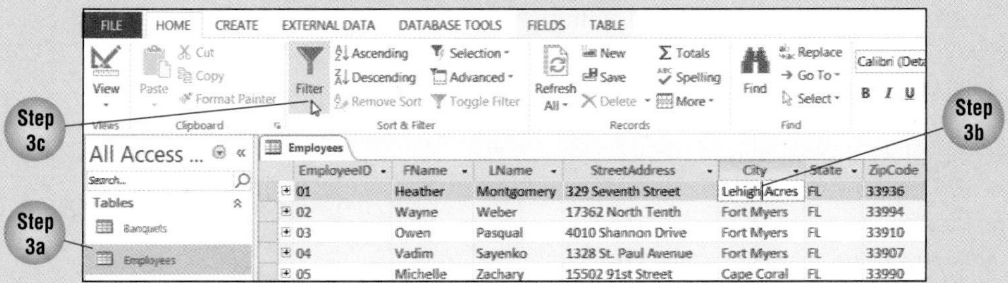

   d. Click the *(Select All)* check box in the filter drop-down list box. (This removes all check marks from the list options.)
   e. Click the *Fort Myers* check box in the list box. (This inserts a check mark in the check box.)
   f. Click OK. (Access displays only those records with a city field of *Fort Myers* and also displays *Filtered* and the filter icon with an orange background in the Record Navigation bar.)
   g. Print the filtered records by pressing Ctrl + P (the keyboard shortcut to display the print dialog box) and then clicking OK at the Print dialog box.
4. Toggle the display of filtered data by clicking the Toggle Filter button in the Sort & Filter group on the HOME tab. (This redisplays all of the data in the table.)
5. Remove the filter by completing the following steps:
   a. Click in any entry in the *City* field.
   b. Click the Filter button in the Sort & Filter group.
   c. Click the *Clear filter from City* option at the drop-down list. (Notice that the message on the Record Navigation bar changes to *No Filter* and dims the words.)

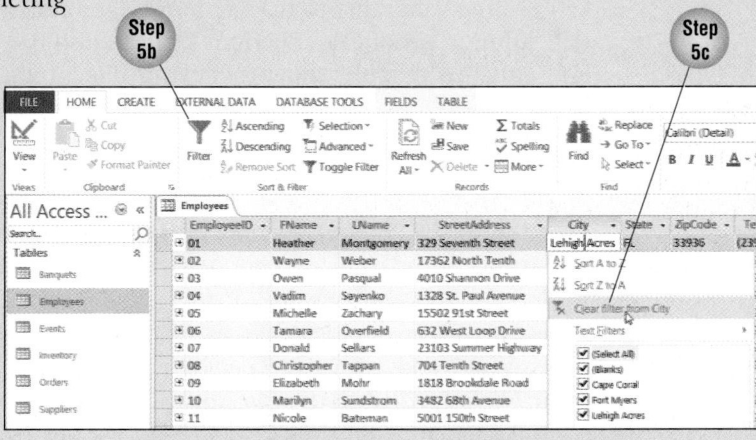

6. Save and then close the Employees table.
7. Create a form by completing the following steps:
   a. Click *Orders* in the Tables group in the Navigation pane.
   b. Click the CREATE tab and then click the Form button in the Forms group.
   c. Click the Form View button in the view area at the right side of the Status bar.
   d. Save the form with the name *Orders*.
8. Filter the records and display only those records with a supplier identification number of 2 by completing the following steps:
   a. Click in the *SupplierID* field containing the text *2*.
   b. Click the Filter button in the Sort & Filter group.
   c. At the filter drop-down list, click *(Select All)* to remove all of the check marks from the list options.
   d. Click the *2* option to insert a check mark.
   e. Click OK.
   f. Navigate through the records and notice that only the records with a supplier identification number of 2 display.
9. Close the Orders form.

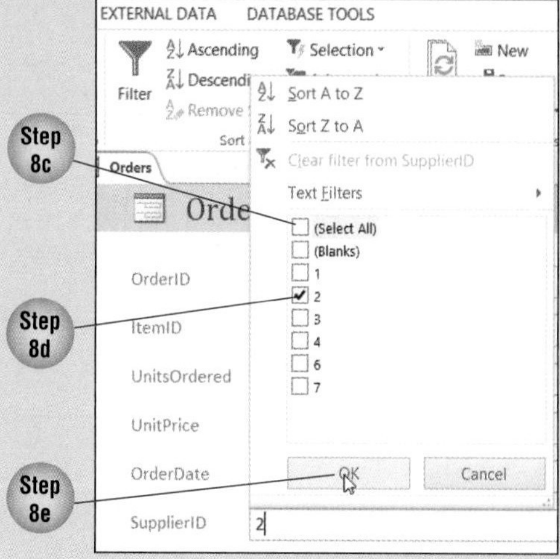

Filtering on Specific Values

When you filter on a specific field, you can display a list of unique values for that field. If you click the Filter button for a field containing text, the drop-down list for the specific field will contain a *Text Filters* option. Click this option and a values list displays next to the drop-down list. The options in the values list vary depending on the type of data in the field. If you click the Filter button for a field containing number values, the option in the drop-down list displays as *Number Filters* and if you are filtering dates, the option in the drop-down list displays as *Date Filters*. Use the options in the values list to refine a filter for a specific field. For example, you can use the values list to display money amounts within a specific range or order dates from a certain time period. You can also use the values list to find fields that are "equal to" or "not equal to" text in the current field.

Project 1b Filtering Records in a Query and Report — Part 2 of 4

1. With **AL1-C7-Skyline.accdb** open, create a query in Design view with the following specifications:
   a. Add the Banquets and Events tables to the query window.
   b. Insert the *ResDate* field from the *Banquets* field list box to the first *Field* row field.
   c. Insert the *FirstName* field from the *Banquets* field list box to the second *Field* row field.
   d. Insert the *LastName* field from the *Banquets* field list box to the third *Field* row field.
   e. Insert the *Telephone* field from the *Banquets* field list box to the fourth *Field* row field.
   f. Insert the *Event* field from the *Events* field list box to the fifth *Field* row field.
   g. Insert the *EmployeeID* field from the *Banquets* field list box to the sixth *Field* row field.
   h. Run the query.
   i. Save the query and name it *BanquetReservations*.

2. Filter records of reservations on or before June 15, 2015, in the query by completing the following steps:
   a. With the BanquetReservations query open, make sure the first entry is selected in the *ResDate* field.
   b. Click the Filter button in the Sort & Filter group on the HOME tab.
   c. Point to the *Date Filters* option in the drop-down list box.
   d. Click *Before* in the values list.
   e. At the Custom Filter dialog box, type 6/15/2015 and then click OK.

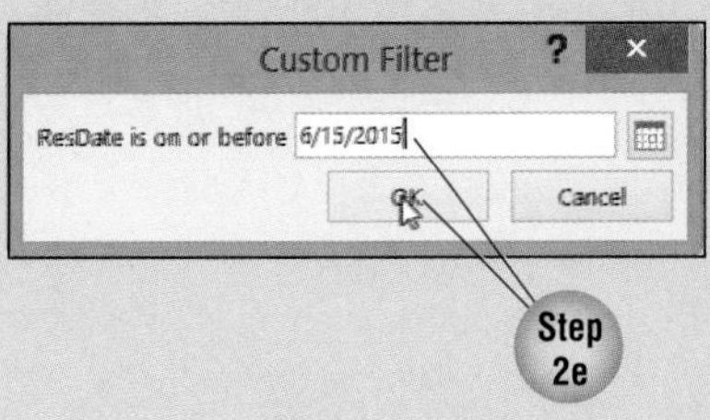

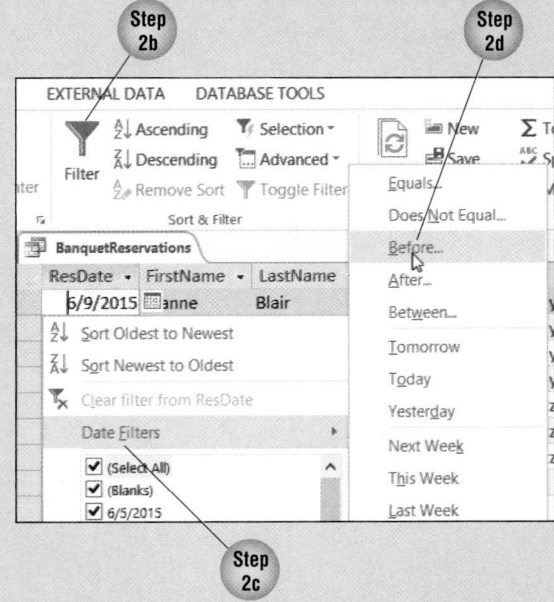

   f. Print the filtered query by pressing Ctrl + P and then clicking OK at the Print dialog box.
3. Remove the filter by clicking the filter icon that displays at the right side of the *ResDate* column heading and then clicking *Clear filter from ResDate* at the drop-down list.

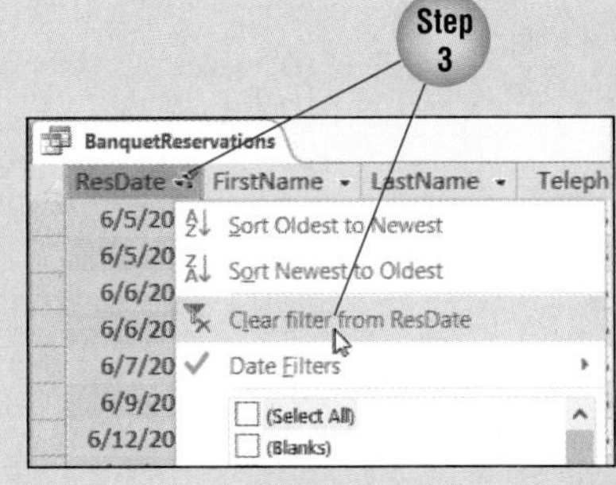

4. Save and then close the BanquetReservations query.
5. Create a report by completing the following steps:
   a. Click *BanquetReservations* in the Queries group in the Navigation pane.
   b. Click the CREATE tab and then click the Report button in the Reports group.
   c. Delete the total amount at the bottom of the *ResDate* column.
   d. With the report in Layout view, decrease the column widths so the right column border displays near the longest entry in each column.
   e. Click the Report View button in the view area at the right side of the Status bar.
   f. Save the report and name it *BanquetReport*.
6. Filter the records and display all records of events except *Other* events by completing the following steps:
   a. Click in the first entry in the *Event* field.
   b. Click the Filter button in the Sort & Filter group.
   c. Point to the *Text Filters* option in the drop-down list box and then click *Does Not Equal* at the values list.
   d. At the Custom Filter dialog box, type Other and then click OK.

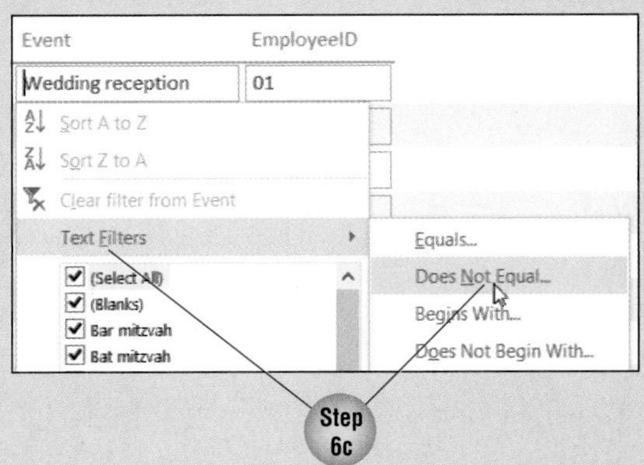

7. Further refine the filter by completing the following steps:
   a. Click in the first entry in the *EmployeeID* field.
   b. Click the Filter button.
   c. At the filter drop-down list, click the *(Select All)* check box to remove all of the check marks from the list options.
   d. Click the *03* check box to insert a check mark.
   e. Click OK.
8. Print only the first page of the report (the second page contains only shading) by completing the following steps:
   a. Press Ctrl + P to display the Print dialog box.
   b. Click the *Pages* option in the *Print Range* section.
   c. Type 1 in the *From* text box, press the Tab key, and then type 1 in the *To* text box.
   d. Click OK.
9. Save and then close the BanquetReport report.

Filtering by Selection

Selection

If you click in a field in an object and then click the Selection button in the Sort & Filter group on the HOME tab, a drop-down list displays below the button with options for filtering on the data in the field. For example, if you click in a field containing the city name *Fort Myers*, clicking the Selection button will cause a drop-down list to display as shown in Figure 7.2. Click one of the options at the drop-down list to filter records. You can select specific text in a field entry and then filter based on the specific text. For example, in Project 1c you will select the word *peppers* in the entry *Green peppers* and then filter records containing the word *peppers*.

Figure 7.2 Selection Button Drop-down List

To filter by selection, click in a field containing the text on which to filter and then click the Selection button. This displays a drop-down list of filtering options.

EXTERNAL DATA DATABASE TOOLS FIELDS TABLE

Ascending, Descending, Remove Sort, Filter, Sort & Filter; Selection: Equals "Fort Myers", Does Not Equal "Fort Myers", Contains "Fort Myers", Does Not Contain "Fort Myers"; New, Totals, Spelling, More; Find, Replace, Go To, Select

Employees

EmployeeID	FName	LName	StreetAddress	City	State	ZipCode
01	Heather	Montgomery	329 Seventh Street	Lehigh Acres	FL	33936
02	Wayne	Weber	17362 North Tenth	Fort Myers	FL	33994
03	Owen	Pasqual	4010 Shannon Drive	Fort Myers	FL	33910
04	Vadim	Sayenko	1328 St. Paul Avenue	Fort Myers	FL	33907
05	Michelle	Zachary	15502 91st Street	Cape Coral	FL	33990
06	Tamara	Overfield	632 West Loop Drive	Cape Coral	FL	33905
07	Donald	Sellars	23103 Summer Highway	Fort Myers	FL	33919
08	Christopher	Tappan	704 Tenth Street	Lehigh Acres	FL	33970
09	Elizabeth	Mohr	1818 Brookdale Road	Fort Myers	FL	33902
10	Marilyn	Sundstrom	3482 68th Avenue	Cape Coral	FL	33914
11	Nicole	Bateman	5001 150th Street	Fort Myers	FL	33908
12	Dennis	Adkins	12115 South 42nd	Cape Coral	FL	33915

Filtering by Shortcut Menu

If you right-click a field entry, a shortcut menu displays with options to sort the text, display a values list, or filter on a specific value. For example, if you right-click the field entry *Birthday* in the *Event* field, a shortcut menu displays, as shown in Figure 7.3. Click a sort option to sort text in the field in ascending or descending order, point to the *Text Filters* option to display a values list, or click one of the values filters located toward the bottom of the menu. You can also select specific text within a field entry and then right-click the selection to display the shortcut menu.

Figure 7.3 Filtering Shortcut Menu

Right-click a field entry to display a shortcut menu with sorting and filtering options.

Project 1c **Filtering Records by Selection** **Part 3 of 4**

1. With **AL1-C7-Skyline.accdb** open, open the Inventory table.
2. Filter only those records with a supplier number of 6 by completing the following steps:
   a. Click in the first entry containing *6* in the *SupplierID* field.
   b. Click the Selection button in the Sort & Filter group on the HOME tab and then click *Equals "6"* at the drop-down list.
   c. Print the filtered table by pressing Ctrl + P and then clicking OK at the Print dialog box.
   d. Click the Toggle Filter button in the Sort & Filter group.

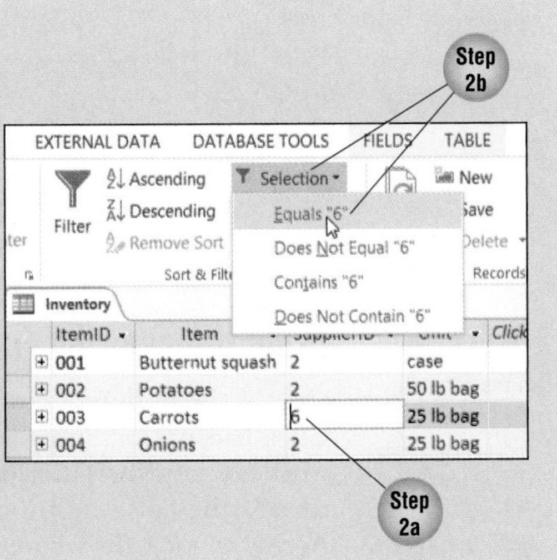

3. Filter any records in the *Item* field containing the word *peppers* by completing the following steps:
    a. Click in an entry in the *Item* field containing the text *Green peppers*.
    b. Using the mouse, select the word *peppers*.
    c. Click the Selection button and then click *Contains "peppers"* at the drop-down list.
    d. Print the filtered table by pressing Ctrl + P and then clicking OK at the Print dialog box.
4. Close the Inventory table without saving the changes.
5. Open the BanquetReservations query.
6. Filter records in the *Event* field except *Wedding reception* by completing the following steps:
    a. Right-click in the first *Wedding reception* entry in the *Event* field.
    b. Click *Does Not Equal "Wedding reception"* at the shortcut menu.
    c. Print the filtered query.
    d. Click the Toggle Filter button in the Sort & Filter group.
7. Filter any records in the *Event* field containing the word *mitzvah* by completing the following steps:
    a. Click in an entry in the *Event* field containing the entry *Bar mitzvah*.
    b. Using the mouse, select the word *mitzvah*.
    c. Right-click on the selected word and then click *Contains "mitzvah"* at the shortcut menu.
    d. Print the filtered query.
8. Close the BanquetReservations query without saving the changes.

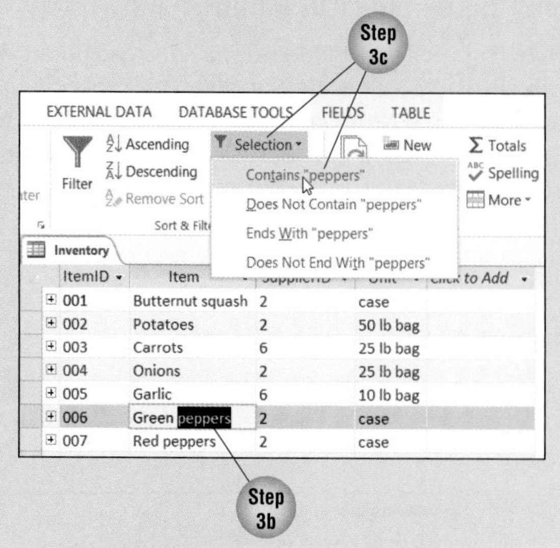

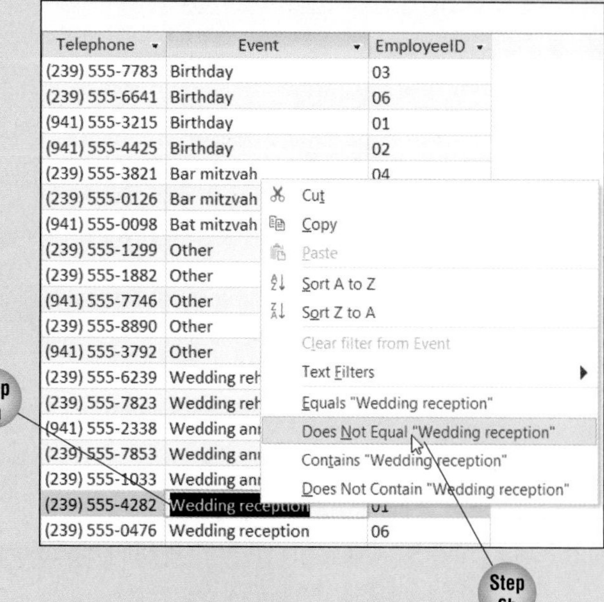

Quick Steps

Use the *Filter By Form* Option

1. Click Advanced button.
2. Click *Filter By Form*.
3. Click in empty field below desired column to filter.
4. Click down-pointing arrow.
5. Click item to filter.

Advanced

Using the *Filter By Form* Option

One of the options from the Advanced button drop-down list is *Filter By Form*. Click this option and a blank record displays in a Filter by Form window in the work area. In the Filter by Form window, the Look for tab and the Or tab display toward the bottom of the form. The Look for tab is active by default and tells Access to look for whatever data you insert in a field. Click in the empty field below the desired column and a down-pointing arrow displays at the right side of the field. Click the down-pointing arrow and then click the item on which you want to filter. Click the Toggle Filter button to display the desired records. Add an additional value to a filter by clicking the Or tab at the bottom of the form.

Project 1d Using the *Filter By Form* Option to Display Specific Records — Part 4 of 4

1. With **AL1-C7-Skyline.accdb** open, open the Banquets table.
2. Filter records for a specific employee identification number by completing the following steps:
   a. Click the Advanced button in the Sort & Filter group on the HOME tab and then click *Filter By Form* at the drop-down list.

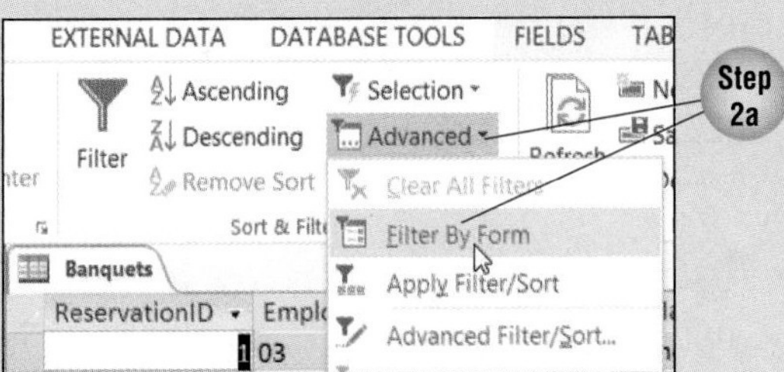

   b. At the Filter by Form window, click in the blank record below the *EmployeeID* field.
   c. Click the down-pointing arrow at the right side of the field and then click *03* at the drop-down list.
   d. Click the Toggle Filter button in the Sort & Filter group.

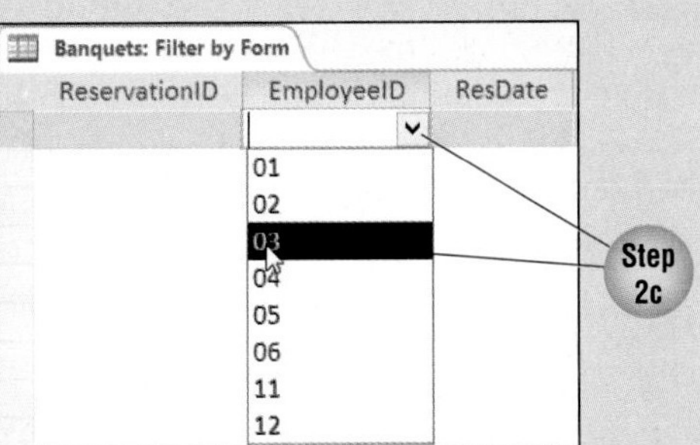

3. Print the filtered table by completing the following steps:
   a. Click the FILE tab, click the *Print* option, and then click the Print Preview button.
   b. Change the orientation to landscape and the left and right margins to 0.5 inch.
   c. Click the Print button and then click OK at the Print dialog box.
   d. Click the Close Print Preview button.
4. Close the Banquets table without saving the changes.
5. Open the Inventory table.
6. Filter records for the supplier number 2 or 7 by completing the following steps:
   a. Click the Advanced button in the Sort & Filter group on the HOME tab and then click *Filter By Form* at the drop-down list.
   b. At the Filter by Form window, click in the blank record below the *SupplierID* field.
   c. Click the down-pointing arrow at the right side of the field and then click *2* at the drop-down list.
   d. Click the Or tab located toward the bottom of the form.
   e. If necessary, click in the blank record below the *SupplierID* field.
   f. Click the down-pointing arrow at the right side of the field and then click *7* at the drop-down list.
   g. Click the Toggle Filter button in the Sort & Filter group.
   h. Print the filtered table.
   i. Click the Toggle Filter button to redisplay all records in the table.
   j. Click the Advanced button and then click *Clear All Filters* from the drop-down list.
7. Close the Inventory table without saving the changes.

Look for Or

Step 6d

Project 2 View Object Dependencies, Manage a Database, and Save a Database in a Different File Format

4 Parts

You will display object dependencies in the Skyline database, compact and repair the database, encrypt it with a password, view and customize document properties, save an object in the database in PDF file format, and save the database in a previous version of Access.

Viewing Object Dependencies

Quick Steps

View Object Dependencies
1. Open desired database.
2. Click object in Navigation pane.
3. Click DATABASE TOOLS tab.
4. Click Object Dependencies button.

Object Dependencies

The structure of a database is comprised of table, query, form, and report objects. Tables are related to other tables by the relationships that have been created. Queries, forms, and reports draw the source data from the records in the tables to which they have been associated, and forms and reports can include subforms and subreports, which further expand the associations between objects. A database with a large number of interdependent objects is more complex to work with than a simpler database. Viewing a list of the objects within a database and viewing the dependencies between objects can be beneficial to ensure an object is not deleted or otherwise modified, causing an unforeseen effect on another object.

Display the structure of a database—including tables, queries, forms, and reports, as well as relationships—at the Object Dependencies task pane. Display this task pane by opening the database, clicking the desired object in the Navigation pane, clicking the DATABASE TOOLS tab, and then clicking the Object Dependencies button in the Relationships group. The Object Dependencies task pane, shown in Figure 7.4, displays the objects in AL1-C7-Skyline.accdb that depend on the Banquets table.

Figure 7.4 Object Dependencies Task Pane

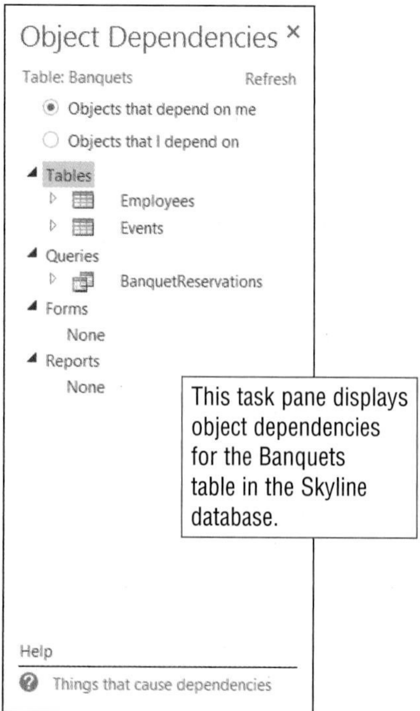

By default, *Objects that depend on me* is selected in the Object Dependencies task pane and the list box displays the names of the objects for which the selected object is the source. Next to each object in the task pane list is an expand button (a right-pointing, white triangle). Clicking the expand button next to an object shows the other objects that depend on it. For example, if a query is based on the Banquets and Events tables and the query is used to generate a report, clicking the expand button next to the query name will show the report name. Clicking an object name in the Object Dependencies task pane opens the object in Design view.

Project 2a Viewing Object Dependencies — Part 1 of 4

1. With **AL1-C7-Skyline.accdb** open, display the structure of the database by completing the following steps:
   a. Click *Banquets* in the Tables group in the Navigation pane.
   b. Click the DATABASE TOOLS tab and then click the Object Dependencies button in the Relationships group. (This displays the Object Dependencies task pane. By default, *Objects that depend on me* is selected and the task pane lists the names of the objects for which the Banquets table is the source.)

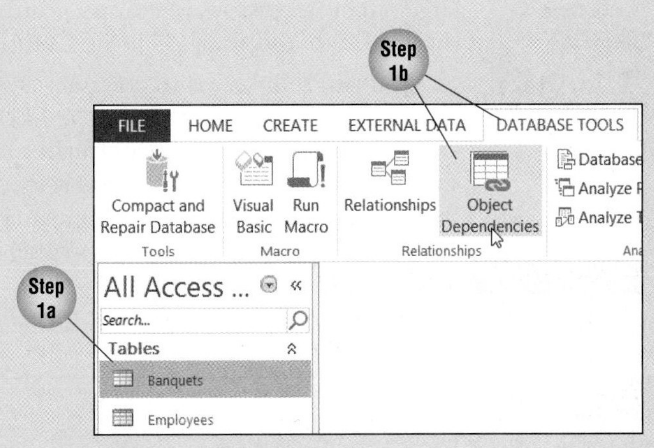

   c. Click the expand button (the right-pointing, white triangle that turns pink when you hover your mouse pointer over it) to the left of *Employees* in the *Tables* section. (This displays all of the objects that depend on the Employees table.)
   d. Click the *Objects that I depend on* option located toward the top of the Object Dependencies task pane.

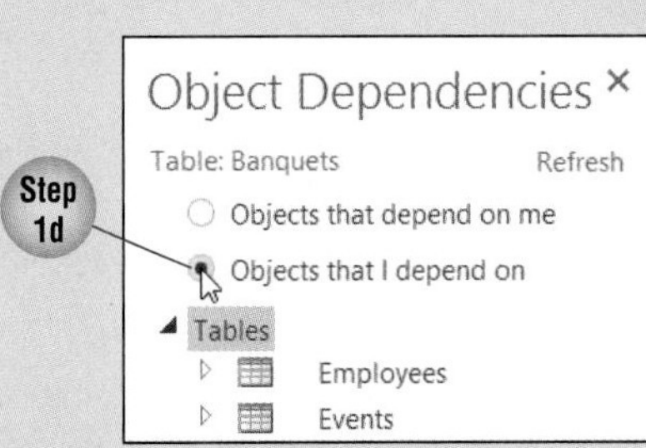

   e. Click *Events* in the Tables group in the Navigation pane. (Make sure to click *Events* in the Navigation pane and not the Object Dependencies task pane.)
   f. Click the Refresh hyperlink in the upper right corner of the Object Dependencies task pane.
   g. Click the *Objects that depend on me* option located toward the top of the Object Dependencies task pane.

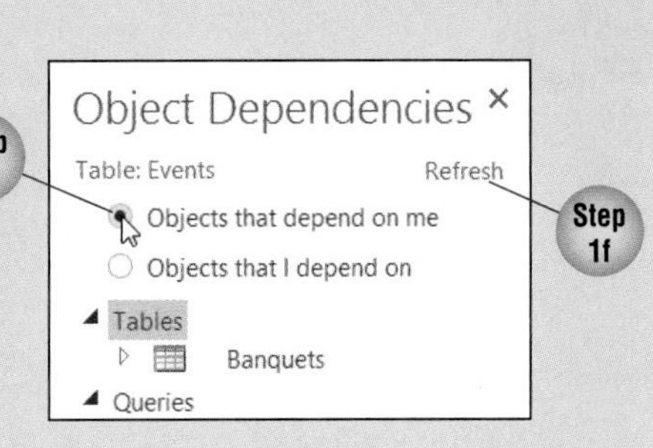

2. Close the Object Dependencies task pane.

Using Options at the Info Backstage Area

The Info backstage area contains options for compacting and repairing a database, encrypting a database with a password, and displaying and customizing database properties. Display the Info backstage area, shown in Figure 7.5, by opening a database and then clicking the FILE tab.

Compacting and Repairing a Database

Quick Steps

Compact and Repair a Database

1. Open database.
2. Click FILE tab.
3. Click Compact & Repair Database button.

Compact & Repair Database

To optimize the performance of your database, compact and repair it on a regular basis. As you work with a database, data in it can become fragmented, causing the amount of space the database takes on the storage medium or in the folder to be larger than necessary. To compact and repair a database, open the database, click the FILE tab and then click the Compact & Repair Database button.

You can tell Access to compact and repair a database each time you close the database. To do this, click the FILE tab and then click *Options*. At the Access Options dialog box, click the *Current Database* option in the left panel. Click the *Compact on Close* option to insert a check mark and then click OK to close the dialog box. Before compacting and repairing a database in a multi-user environment, make sure that no other user has the database open.

Figure 7.5 Info Backstage Area

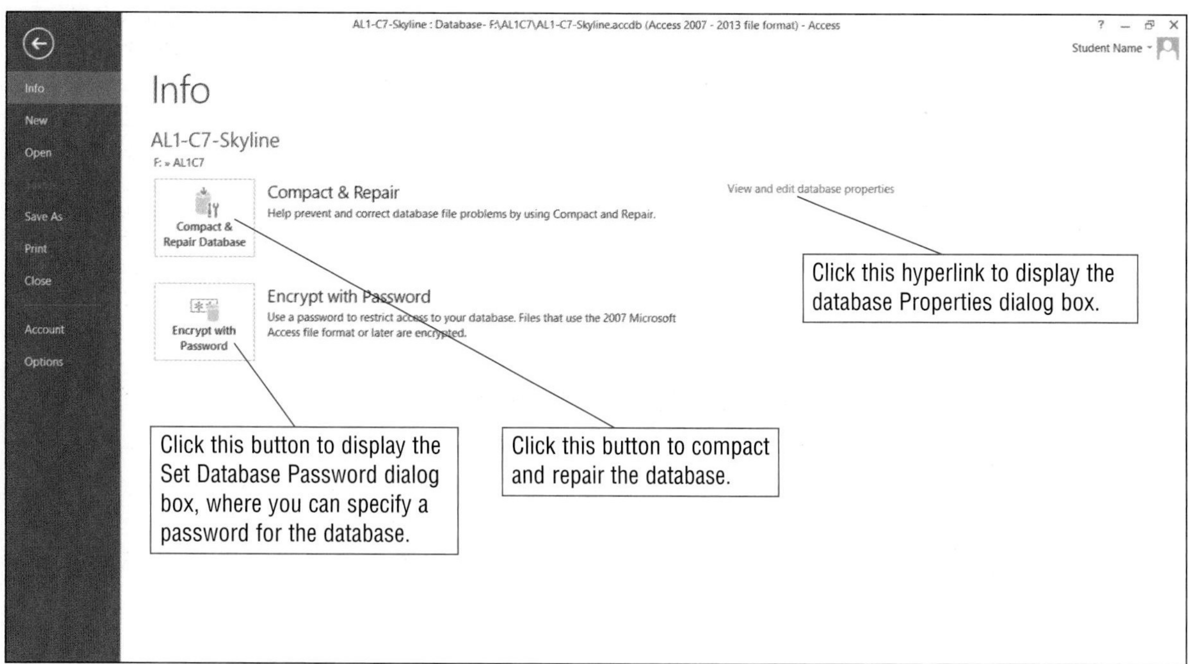

Encrypting a Database with a Password

If you want to prevent unauthorized access to a database, encrypt the database with a password to ensure that it can be opened only by someone who knows the password. Be careful when encrypting a database with a password because if you lose the password, you will be unable to use the database. You will not be able to remove the password from a database if you do not remember the password.

To encrypt a database with a password, you must open the database in Exclusive mode. To do this, display the Open dialog box, navigate to the desired folder, and then click the database to select it. Click the down-pointing arrow at the right side of the Open button located in the lower right corner of the dialog box and then click *Open Exclusive* at the drop-down list. When the database opens, click the FILE tab and then click the Encrypt with Password button in the Info backstage area. This displays the Set Database Password dialog box, as shown in Figure 7.6. At this dialog box, type a password in the *Password* text box, press the Tab key, and then type the password again. The text you type will display as asterisks. Click OK to close the Set Database Password dialog box. To remove a password from a database, open the database in Exclusive mode, click the FILE tab, and then click the Decrypt Database button. At the Unset Database Password dialog box, type the password and then click OK.

Quick Steps

Open a Database in Exclusive Mode
1. Display Open dialog box.
2. Click desired database.
3. Click down-pointing arrow at right of Open button.
4. Click *Open Exclusive*.

Encrypt a Database with a Password
1. Open database in Exclusive mode.
2. Click FILE tab.
3. Click Encrypt with Password button.
4. Type password, press Tab, and type password again.
5. Click OK.

Encrypt with Password

Decrypt Database

When encrypting a database with a password, use a password that combines uppercase and lowercase letters, numbers, and symbols.

Figure 7.6 Set Database Password Dialog Box

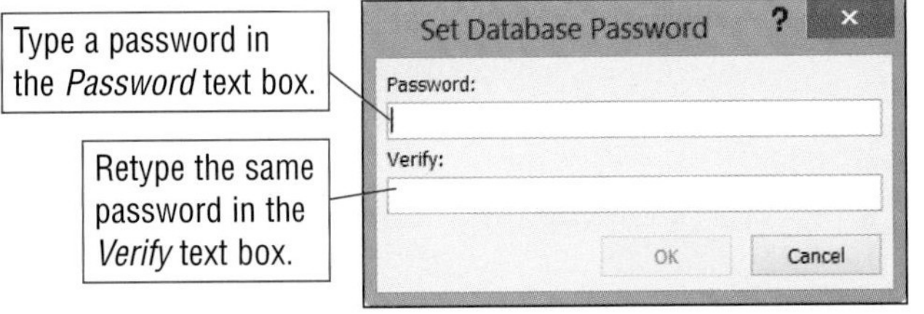

Project 2b **Compact and Repair and Encrypt a Database** **Part 2 of 4**

1. With **AL1-C7-Skyline.accdb** open, compact and repair the database by completing the following steps:
   a. Click the FILE tab. (This displays the Info backstage area.)
   b. Click the Compact & Repair Database button.
2. Close **AL1-C7-Skyline.accdb**.
3. Open the database in Exclusive mode by completing the following steps:
   a. Display the Open dialog box and make AL1C7 the active folder.
   b. Click **AL1-C7-Skyline.accdb** in the Content pane to select it.

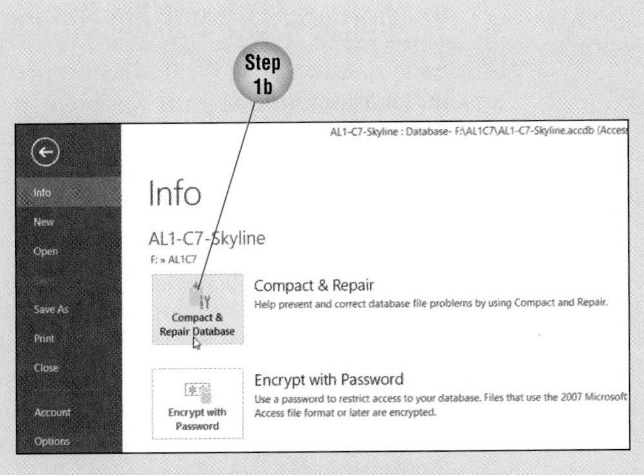

c. Click the down-pointing arrow at the right side of the Open button that displays in the lower right corner of the dialog box and then click *Open Exclusive* at the drop-down list.

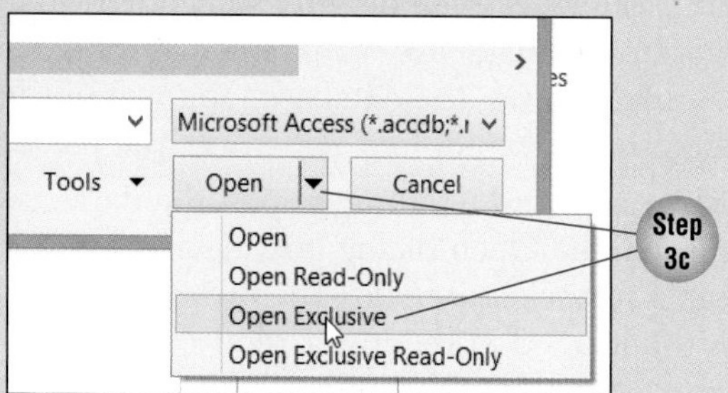

4. Encrypt the database with a password by completing the following steps:
   a. Click the FILE tab.
   b. At the Info backstage area, click the Encrypt with Password button.
   c. At the Set Database Password dialog box, type your first and last names in all lowercase letters with no space, press the Tab key, and then type your first and last names again in lowercase letters.
   d. Click OK to close the dialog box.
   e. If a message displays with information about encrypting with a block cipher, click OK.

5. Close **AL1-C7-Skyline.accdb**.
6. Display the Open dialog box with AL1C7 the active folder and then open **AL1-C7-Skyline.accdb** in Exclusive mode.
7. At the Password Required dialog box, type your password and then click OK.
8. Remove the password by completing the following steps:
   a. Click the FILE tab.
   b. Click the Decrypt Database button.
   c. At the Unset Database Password dialog box, type your first and last names in lowercase letters and then press the Enter key.

Viewing and Customizing Database Properties

Each database you create has properties associated with it, such as the type of file, its location, and when it was created, accessed, and modified. You can view and modify database properties at the Properties dialog box. To view properties for the currently open database, click the FILE tab to display the Info backstage area and then click the View and edit database properties hyperlink that displays at the right side of the backstage area. This displays the Properties dialog box, similar to what is shown in Figure 7.7.

The Properties dialog box for an open database contains tabs with information about the database. With the General tab selected, the dialog box displays information about the database type, size, and location. Click the Summary tab to display fields such as *Title*, *Subject*, *Author*, *Category*, *Keywords*, and *Comments*. Some fields contain data and others are blank. You can insert, edit, or delete text in the fields. Move the insertion point to a field by clicking in the field or by pressing the Tab key until the insertion point is positioned in the desired field.

Figure 7.7 Properties Dialog Box

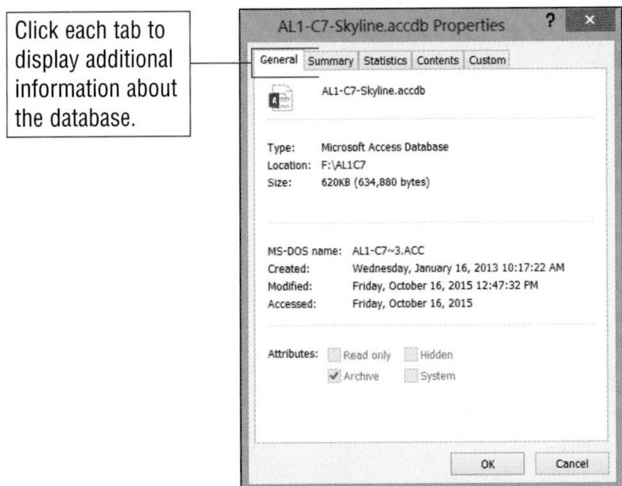

Click the Statistics tab to display information such as the dates the database was created, modified, accessed, and printed. Click the Contents tab and look in the *Document contents* section to see the objects in the database, including tables, queries, forms, reports, macros, and modules.

Use options at the Properties dialog box with the Custom tab selected to add custom properties to the database. For example, you can add a property that displays the date the database was completed, information on the department in which the database was created, and much more. The list box below the *Name* option box displays the predesigned properties provided by Access. You can choose a predesigned property or create your own.

To choose a predesigned property, select the desired property in the list box, specify what type of property it is (such as value, date, number, yes/no), and then type a value. For example, to specify the department in which the database was created, you would click *Department* in the list box, make sure the *Type* displays as *Text*, click in the *Value* text box, and then type the name of the department.

Project 2c Viewing and Customizing Database Properties **Part 3 of 4**

1. With **AL1-C7-Skyline.accdb** open, click the FILE tab and then click the View and edit database properties hyperlink that displays at the right side of the backstage area.

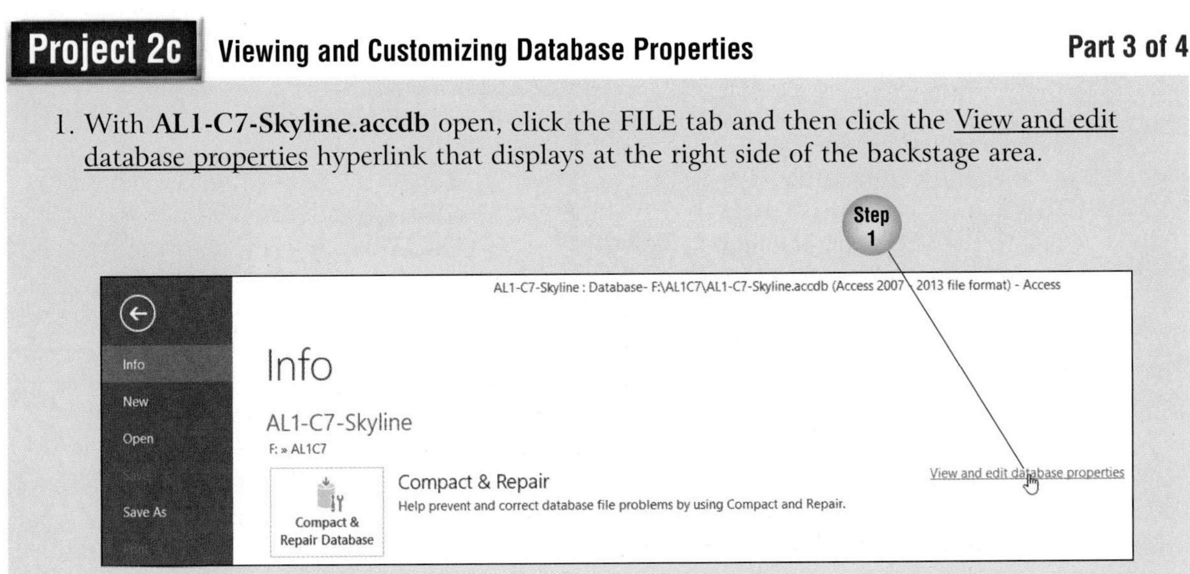

2. At the AL1-C7-Skyline.accdb Properties dialog box, click the General tab and then read the information that displays in the dialog box.
3. Click the Summary tab and then type the following text in the specified text boxes:

Title	**AL1-C7-Skyline database**
Subject	**Restaurant and banquet facilities**
Author	*(type your first and last names)*
Category	**restaurant**
Keywords	**restaurant, banquet, event, Fort Myers**
Comments	**This database contains information on Skyline Restaurant employees, banquets, inventory, and orders.**

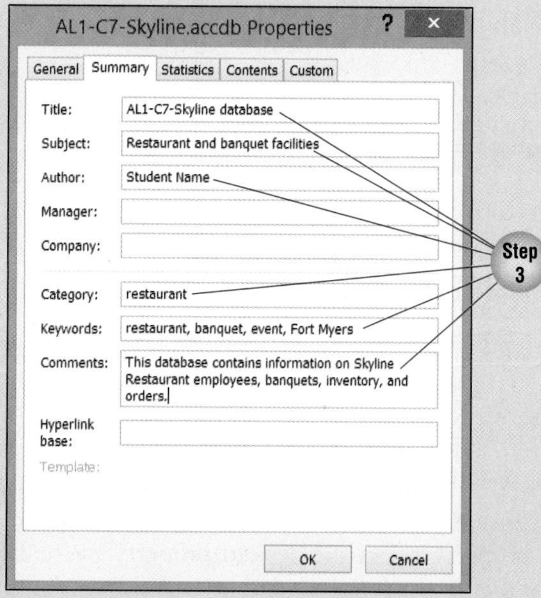

4. Click the Statistics tab and read the information that displays in the dialog box.
5. Click the Contents tab and notice that the *Document contents* section of the dialog box displays the objects in the database.
6. Click the Custom tab and then create custom properties by completing the following steps:
   a. Click the *Date completed* option in the *Name* list box.
   b. Click the down-pointing arrow at the right of the *Type* option box and then click *Date* at the drop-down list.
   c. Click in the *Value* text box and then type the current date in this format: *dd/mm/yyyy*.
   d. Click the Add button.
   e. With the insertion point positioned in the *Name* text box, type **Course**.
   f. Click the down-pointing arrow at the right of the *Type* option box and then click *Text* at the drop-down list.
   g. Click in the *Value* text box, type your current course number, and then press Enter.
   h. Click OK to close the dialog box.

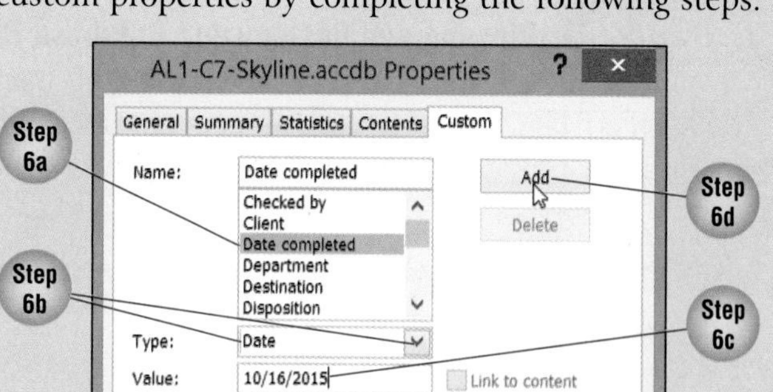

7. Click the Back button to return to the database.

Saving Databases and Database Objects

An Access 2013, Access 2010, or Access 2007 database is saved with the file extension *.accdb*. Earlier versions of Access (such as 2003, 2002, and 2000) use the file extension *.mdb*. To open an Access 2013, 2010, or 2007 database in an earlier version, you need to save the database in the .mdb file format.

To save an Access database in the 2002 to 2003 file format, open the database, click the FILE tab, and then click the *Save As* option. This displays the Save As backstage area, as shown in Figure 7.9. Click the *Access 2002-2003 Database (*.mdb)* option in the *Save Database As* section and then click the Save As button that displays at the bottom of the *Save Database As* section. This displays the Save As dialog box with the *Save as type* option set to *Microsoft Access Database (2002-2003) (*.mdb)* and the current database file name with the file extension *.mdb* inserted in the *File name* text box. At this dialog box, click the Save button.

Quick Steps

Save a Database in an Earlier Version
1. Open database.
2. Click FILE tab.
3. Click *Save As* option.
4. Click desired version in Save Database As category.
5. Click Save As button.

An Access 2007, 2010, or 2013 database cannot be opened with an earlier version of Access.

With an object open in a database, clicking the *Save Object As* option in the *File Types* section of the Save As backstage area displays options for saving the object. Click the *Save Object As* option to save the selected object in the database or click the *PDF or XPS* option if you want to save the object in PDF or XPS file format. The letters *PDF* stand for *portable document format*, a file format developed by Adobe Systems that captures all of the elements of a file as an electronic image. An XPS file is a Microsoft file format for publishing content in an easily viewable format. The letters *XPS* stand for *XML paper specification* and the letters *XML* stand for *extensible markup language*, which is a set of rules for encoding files electronically.

Saving an Object in PDF or XPS File Format

To save an object in PDF or XPS file format, open the desired object, click the FILE tab, and then click the *Save As* option. At the Save As backstage area, click the *Save Object As* option in the *File Types* section, click the *PDF or XPS* option in the *Save the current database object* section, and then click the Save As button. This displays the Publish as PDF or XPS dialog box with the name of the object inserted in the *File name* text box followed by the file extension *.pdf*, and the *Save as type* option set at *PDF (*.pdf)*. Click the Publish button and the object is saved

Quick Steps

Save an Object in PDF File Format
1. Click desired object in Navigation pane.
2. Click FILE tab.
3. Click *Save As* option.
4. Click *Save Object As* option.
5. Click *PDF or XPS* option.
6. Click Save As button.

Figure 7.9 Save As Backstage Area with *Save Database As* Option Selected

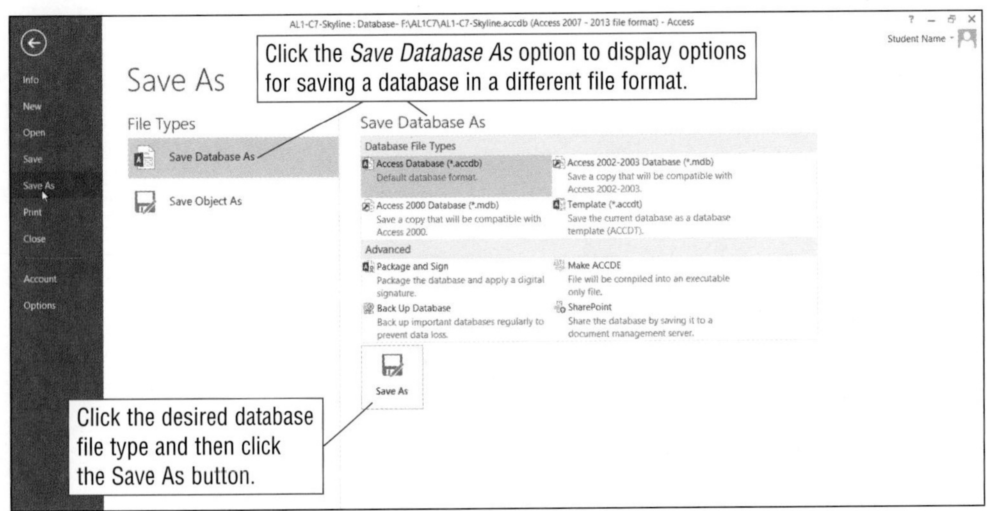

in PDF file format. If you want the object to open in Adobe Reader, click the *Open file after publishing* check box to insert a check box. With this check box active, the object will open in Adobe Reader when you click the Publish button.

You can open a PDF file in Adobe Reader, Internet Explorer, Microsoft Word, or Windows Reader. You can open an XPS file in Internet Explorer, Windows Reader, or XPS Viewer. One method for opening a PDF or XPS file is to open File Explorer, navigate to the folder containing the file, right-click on the file, and then point to *Open with*. This displays a side menu with the programs you can choose to open the file.

Backing Up a Database

Databases often contain important company information, and loss of this information can cause major problems. Backing up a database is important to minimize the chances of losing critical company data and is especially important when several people update and manage a database.

To back up a database, open the database, click the FILE tab, and then click the *Save As* option. At the Save As backstage area, click the *Back Up Database* option in the *Advanced* section and then click the Save As button. This displays the Save As dialog box with a default database file name, which is the original database name followed by the current date, in the *File name* text box. Click the Save button to save the backup database while keeping the original database open.

Project 2d **Saving a Database in a Previous Version, Saving an Object in PDF Format, and Backing Up a Database** **Part 4 of 4**

1. With **AL1-C7-Skyline.accdb** open, save the Orders table in PDF file format by completing the following steps:
   a. Open the Orders table.
   b. Click the FILE tab and then click the *Save As* option.
   c. At the Save As backstage area, click the *Save Object As* option in the *File Types* section.
   d. Click the *PDF or XPS* option in the *Save the current database object* section.
   e. Click the Save As button.

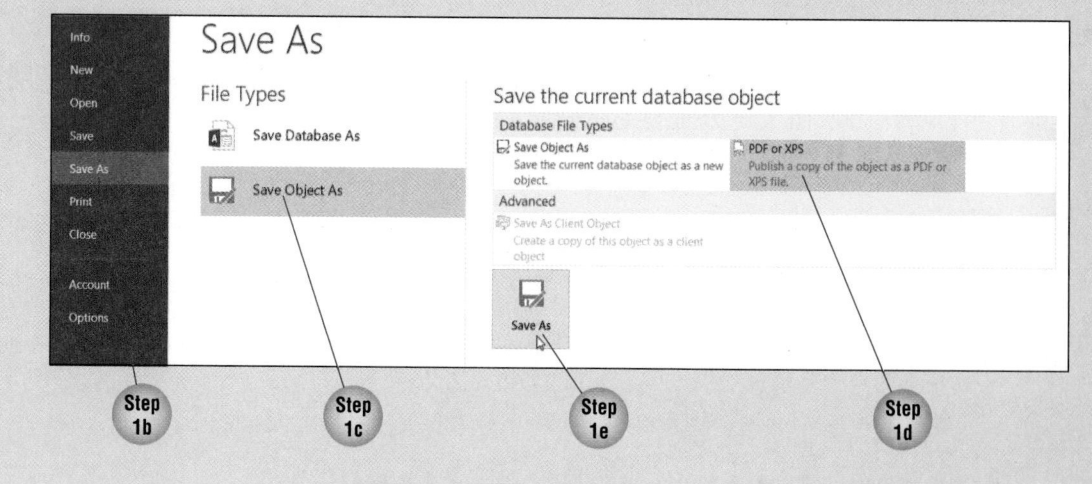

f. At the Publish as PDF or XPS dialog box, make sure the AL1C7 folder on your storage medium is the active folder and then click the *Open file after publishing* check box to insert a check mark. (Skip this step if the check box already contains a check mark.)
g. Click the Publish button.
h. When the Orders table opens in Adobe Reader, scroll through the file and then close the file by clicking the Close button located in the upper right corner of the screen.

2. Close the Orders table.
3. Save the database in a previous version of Access by completing the following steps:
   a. Click the FILE tab and then click the *Save As* option.
   b. At the Save As backstage area, click the *Access 2002-2003 Database (*.mdb)* option in the *Save Database As* section.
   c. Click the Save As button.

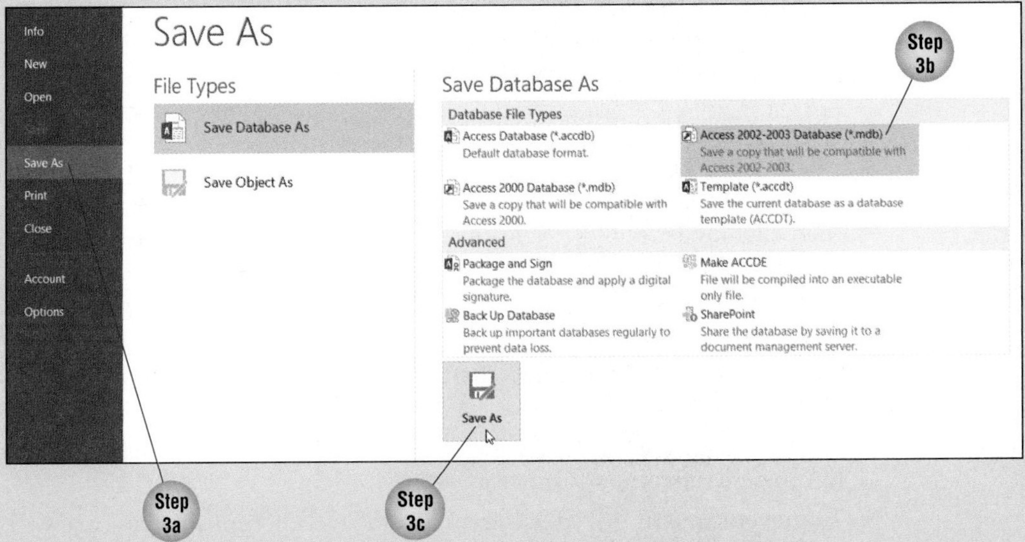

   d. At the Save As dialog box, make sure the AL1C7 folder on your storage medium is the active folder and then click the Save button. This saves the database with the same name (**AL1-C7-Skyline**) but with the file extension *.mdb*.
   e. Notice that the Title bar displays the database file name *AL1-C7-Skyline : Database (Access 2002 - 2003 file format)*.
4. Close the database.
5. Open AL1-C7-Skyline.accdb. (Make sure you open the AL1-C7-Skyline database with the .accdb file extension.)
6. Create a backup of the database by completing the following steps:
   a. Click the FILE tab and then click the *Save As* option.
   b. At the Save As backstage area, click the *Back Up Database* option in the *Advanced* section and then click the Save As button.
   c. At the Save As dialog box, notice that the database name in the *File name* text box displays the original file name followed by the current date (year, month, day).
   d. Make sure the AL1C7 folder on your storage medium is the active folder and then click the Save button. (This saves the backup copy of the database to your folder and the original database remains open.)
7. Close **AL1-C7-Skyline.accdb**.

Chapter Summary

- A set of restrictions called a filter can be set on records in a table or form. A filter lets you select specific field values.
- Filter records with the Filter button in the Sort & Filter group on the HOME tab.
- Click the Toggle Filter button in the Sort & Filter group to switch back and forth between data and filtered data.
- Remove a filter by clicking the Filter button in the Sort & Filter group and then clicking the *Clear filter from xxx* (where *xxx* is the name of the field).
- Another method for removing a filter is to click the Advanced button in the Sort & Filter group and then click *Clear All Filters*.
- Display a list of filter values by clicking the Filter button and then pointing to *Text Filters* (if the data is text), *Number Filters* (if the data is numbers), or *Date Filters* (if the data is dates).
- Filter by selection by clicking the Selection button in the Sort & Filter group.
- Right-click a field entry to display a shortcut menu with filtering options.
- Filter by form by clicking the Advanced button in the Sort & Filter group and then clicking *Filter By Form* at the drop-down list. This displays a blank record with two tabs: Look for and Or.
- Display the structure of a database and relationships between objects at the Object Dependencies task pane. Display this task pane by clicking the DATABASE TOOLS tab and then clicking the Object Dependencies button in the Relationships group.
- Click the Compact & Repair Database button in the Info backstage area to optimize database performance.
- To prevent unauthorized access to a database, encrypt the database with a password. To encrypt a database, you must first open it in Exclusive mode using the Open button drop-down list in the Open dialog box. While in Exclusive mode, encrypt a database with a password using the Encrypt with Password button in the Info backstage area.
- To view properties for the current database, click the View and edit database properties hyperlink in the Info backstage area. The Properties dialog box contains a number of tabs containing information about the database.
- Save a database in a previous version of Access using options in the *Save Database As* section of the Save As backstage area.
- To save a database object in PDF or XPS file format, display the Save As backstage area, click the *Save Object As* option, click the *PDF or XPS* option, and then click the Save As button.
- Backup a database to maintain critical data. Backup a database with the *Back Up Database* option at the Save As backstage area.

Commands Review

FEATURE	RIBBON TAB, GROUP/OPTION	BUTTON, OPTION
filter	HOME, Sort & Filter	
filter by form	HOME, Sort & Filter	, *Filter By Form*
filter by selection	HOME, Sort & Filter	
Info backstage area	FILE, *Info*	
Object Dependencies task pane	DATABASE TOOLS, Relationships	
remove filter	HOME, Sort & Filter	, *Clear filter from xxx* OR , *Clear All Filters*
toggle filter	HOME, Sort & Filter	

Concepts Check Test Your Knowledge

Completion: In the space provided at the right, indicate the correct term, symbol, or command.

1. The Filter button is located in this group on the HOME tab. ________________
2. When you filter data, you can switch between the filtered and unfiltered data by clicking this button. ________________
3. Remove all filtering from an object by pressing the Filter button or clicking this button and then clicking *Clear All Filters*. ________________
4. In the Filter by Form window, these two tabs display toward the bottom of the form. ________________
5. Display the structure of a database at this task pane. ________________
6. Optimize database performance by doing this to the database. ________________
7. Before encrypting a database with a password, you must open the database in this mode. ________________
8. Display the Set Database Password dialog box by clicking this button in the Info backstage area. ________________
9. Data in this dialog box provides details about a database, such as its title, author name, and subject. ________________
10. Save a database object in PDF file format with the *PDF or XPS* option in this backstage area. ________________

Skills Check Assess Your Performance

Assessment 1

FILTER RECORDS IN TABLES

1. Display the Open dialog box with the AL1C7 folder on your storage medium the active folder.
2. Open **AL1-C7-WarrenLegal.accdb** and enable the contents.
3. Open the Clients table and then filter the records to display the following records:
   a. Display only those records of clients who live in Renton. When the records of clients in Renton display, print the results in landscape orientation and then remove the filter. ***Hint: Change to landscape orientation in Print Preview.***
   b. Display only those records of clients with the zip code of 98033. When the records of clients with the zip code 98033 display, print the results in landscape orientation and then remove the filter.
4. Close the Clients table without saving the changes.
5. Open the Billing table and then filter the records by selection to display the following records:
   a. Display only those records with a category of CC. Print the records and then remove the filter.
   b. Display only those records with an attorney ID of 12. Print the records and then remove the filter.
   c. Display only those records with dates between 6/1/2015 and 6/10/2015. Print the records and then remove the filter.
6. Close the Billing table without saving the changes.
7. Open the Clients table and then use the *Filter By Form* option to display clients in Auburn or Renton. (Be sure to use the Or tab at the bottom of the table.) Print the table in landscape orientation and then remove the filter.
8. Close the Clients table without saving the changes.
9. Open the Billing table and then use the *Filter By Form* option to display category G or P. Print the table and then remove the filter.
10. Close the Billing table without saving the changes.
11. Close **AL1-C7-WarrenLegal.accdb**.

Assessment 2

SAVE A TABLE AND DATABASE IN DIFFERENT FILE FORMATS

1. Open **AL1-C7-Hilltop.accdb** in Exclusive mode and enable the contents.
2. Create a password for the database (you determine the password), and with the Set Database Password dialog box open, create a screen capture of the screen with the dialog box by completing the following steps:
   a. Press the Print Screen button on your keyboard.
   b. Open a blank document in Microsoft Word.
   c. Click the Paste button located in the Clipboard group on the HOME tab. (This pastes the screen capture image in the Word document.)
   d. Click the FILE tab, click the *Print* option, and then click the Print button at the Print backstage area.
   e. Close Word by clicking the Close button located in the upper right corner of the screen. At the message asking if you want to save the document, click the Don't Save button.

3. Click OK to close the Set Database Password dialog box.
4. At the message telling you that block cipher is incompatible with row level locking, click OK.
5. Close the database.
6. Open **AL1-C7-Hilltop.accdb** in Exclusive mode and enter the password when prompted.
7. Remove the password. ***Hint: Do this with the Decrypt Database button in the Info backstage area.***
8. Open the Invoices table and then save the table in PDF file format with the default file name. Specify that you want the object to open when published.
9. When the table opens in Adobe Reader, print the table by clicking the Print button located toward the upper left side of the screen and then clicking OK at the Print dialog box. (If the Print button is not visible, click the FILE option, click *Print* at the drop-down list, and then click OK at the Print dialog box.)
10. Close Adobe Reader and then close the Invoices table.
11. Save **AL1-C7-Hilltop.accdb** in the *Access 2002-2003 Database (*.mdb)* file format.
12. With the database open, make a screen capture using the Print Screen key on the keyboard. Open Word, paste the screen capture image in the Word document, print the document, and then close Word without saving the changes.
13. Close the database.

Assessment 3

DELETE AND RENAME OBJECTS

1. Open **AL1-C7-Hilltop.accdb**. (Make sure you open the AL1-C7-Hilltop database with the .accdb file extension.)
2. Right-click an object in the Navigation pane, experiment with options in the shortcut menu, and then complete these steps using the shortcut menu:
   a. Delete the Inventory form.
   b. Rename the form Equipment as *EquipForm*.
   c. Rename the report InvReport as *InventoryReport*.
   d. Export (using the shortcut menu) the *EquipmentQuery* to a Word RTF file. ***Hint: Click the Browse button at the Export - RTF File dialog box and make the folder AL1C7 the active folder.***
   e. Open the *EquipmentQuery.rtf* file in Word, print the file, and then close Word.
3. Close **AL1-C7-Hilltop.accdb**.

Visual Benchmark Demonstrate Your Proficiency

DESIGN A QUERY AND FILTER THE QUERY

1. Open **AL1-C7-PacTrek.accdb** and enable the contents.
2. Create and run the query shown in Figure 7.10.
3. Save the query and name it *ProductsOnOrderQuery.*
4. Print the query.
5. Filter the query so the records display as shown in Figure 7.11. ***Hint: Filter the supplier names as shown in Figure 7.11 and then filter the*** **UnitsOnOrder** ***field to show records that do not equal 0.***
6. Print the filtered query.
7. Remove the filters and then close the query without saving the changes.
8. Close **AL1-C7-PacTrek.accdb**.

Figure 7.10 Visual Benchmark Query

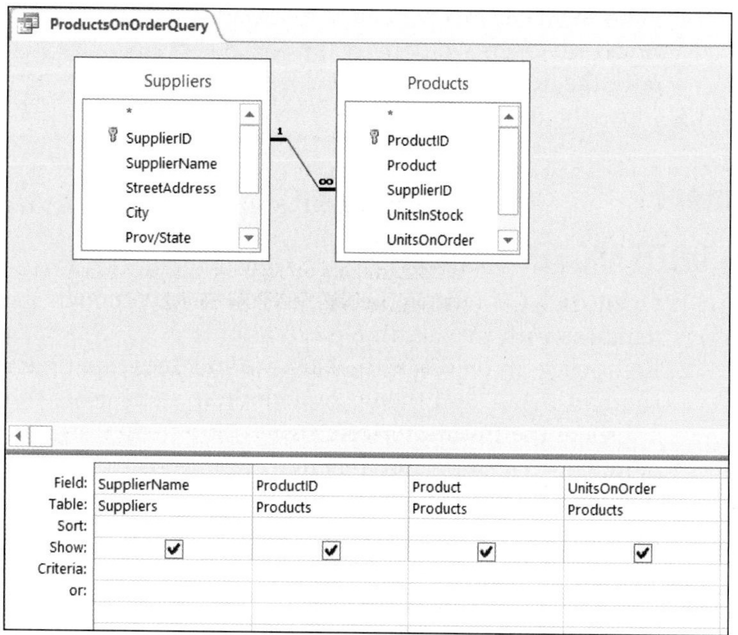

Figure 7.11 Visual Benchmark Filtered Query

ProductsOnOrderQuery

SupplierName	ProductID	Product	UnitsOnOrder
Hopewell, Inc.	152-H	Lantern hanger	15
Hopewell, Inc.	155-20	Shursite angle-head flashlight	20
Hopewell, Inc.	155-35	Shursite portable camp light	10
Cascade Gear	250-L	Cascade R4 jacket, ML	10
Cascade Gear	250-XL	Cascade R4 jacket, MXL	10
Cascade Gear	255-M	Cascade R4 jacket, WM	5
Cascade Gear	255-XL	Cascade R4 jacket, WXL	5
*			

Case Study Apply Your Skills

Part 1

As the office manager at Summit View Medical Services, you are responsible for maintaining clinic records. Open **AL1-C7-SummitView.accdb**, enable the contents, and then insert the following additional services into the appropriate table:

- Edit the *Doctor visit* entry in the Services table so it displays as *Clinic visit*.
- Add the entry *X-ray* with a service identification of *X*.
- Add the entry *Cholesterol screening* with a service identification of *CS*.

Add the following new patient information in the database in the appropriate tables:

Patient number 121
Brian M. Gould
2887 Nelson Street
Helena, MT 59604
(406) 555-3121
Mr. Gould saw Dr. Wallace for a clinic visit on 4/6/2015,
which has a fee of $75.

Patient number 122
Ellen L. Augustine
12990 148th Street
East Helena, MT 59635
(406) 555-0722
Ms. Augustine saw Dr. Kennedy for cholesterol screening
on 4/6/2015, which has a fee of $90.

Patient number 123
Jeff J. Masura
3218 Eldridge Avenue
Helena, MT 59624
(406) 555-6212
Mr. Masura saw Dr. Rowe for an x-ray on 4/6/2015,
which has a fee of $75.

Add the following information to the Billing table:

- Patient 109 came for cholesterol screening with Dr. Kennedy on 4/6/2015 with a $90 fee.
- Patient 106 came for immunizations with Dr. Pena on 4/6/2015 with a $100 fee.
- Patient 114 came for an x-ray with Dr. Kennedy on 4/6/2015 with a $75 fee.

Part 2

Create the following filters and queries:

- Open the Billing table and then filter and print the records for the date 4/2/2015. Clear the filter and then filter and print the records with a doctor number of 18. Save and then close the table.
- Create a report that displays the patient's first name, last name, street address, city, state, and zip code. Apply formatting to enhance the appearance of the report. Filter and print the records of those patients living in Helena, remove the filter, and then filter and print the records of those patients living in East Helena. Close the report.
- Design a query that includes the doctor number, doctor last name, patient number, date of visit, and fee. Save the query with the name *DoctorBillingFees* and then print the query. Filter and print the records for Dr. Kennedy and Dr. Pena, remove the filter, and then filter and print the records for the dates 4/5/2015 and 4/6/2015. Save and then close the query.

Part 3

You want to make the Billing table available for viewing on computers without Access, so you decide to save the table in PDF file format. Save the Billing table in PDF file format, print the table in Adobe Reader, and then close Adobe Reader. Close **AL1-C7-SummitView.accdb**.

Part 4

Your clinic has a manual that describes processes and procedures in the workplace. Open Word and then create a document for the manual that describes the steps you followed to create the *DoctorBillingFees* query and to create and print the two filters. Save the completed document and name it **AL1-C7-CS-Manual**. Print and then close **AL1-C7-CS-Manual.docx**.

MICROSOFT® ACCESS®

Exporting and Importing Data

PERFORMANCE OBJECTIVES

Upon successful completion of Chapter 8, you will be able to:

- **Export Access data to Excel**
- **Export Access data to Word**
- **Merge Access data with a Word document**
- **Export an Access object to a PDF or XPS file**
- **Import data to a new table**
- **Link data to a new table**
- **Use the Office Clipboard**

Tutorials

8.1 Exporting Access Data to Excel
8.2 Exporting Access Data to Word
8.3 Merging Access Data with a Word Document
8.4 Importing and Linking Data to a New Table
8.5 Using the Office Clipboard

Microsoft Office 2013 is a suite of programs that allows easy data exchange between programs. In this chapter, you will learn how to export data from Access to Excel and Word, merge Access data with a Word document, export an Access object to a PDF or XPS file, import and link data to a new table, and copy and paste data between programs. You will also learn how to copy and paste data between applications. Model answers for this chapter's projects appear on the following pages.

Note: Before beginning the projects, copy to your storage medium the AL1C8 subfolder from the AL1 folder on the CD that accompanies this textbook and make AL1C8 the active folder.

Project 1 Export Data to Excel and Export and Merge Data to Word

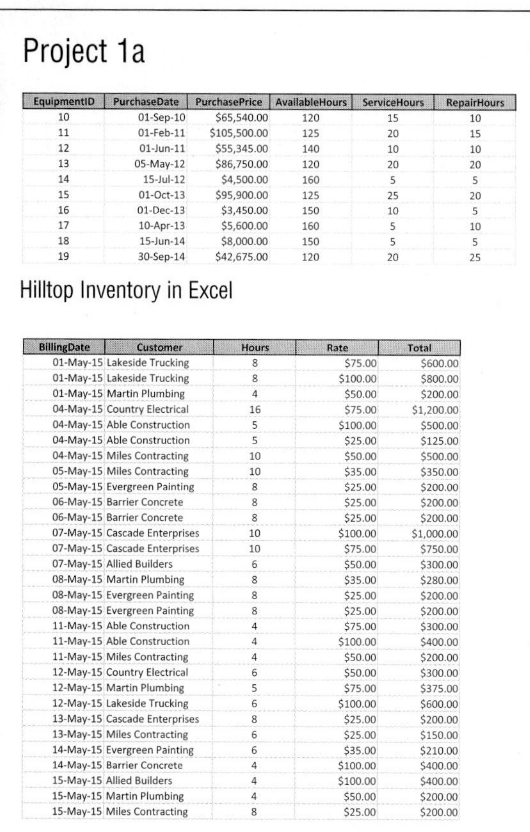

Project 1a

EquipmentID	PurchaseDate	PurchasePrice	AvailableHours	ServiceHours	RepairHours
10	01-Sep-10	$65,540.00	120	15	10
11	01-Feb-11	$105,500.00	125	20	15
12	01-Jun-11	$55,345.00	140	10	10
13	05-May-12	$86,750.00	120	20	20
14	15-Jul-12	$4,500.00	160	5	5
15	01-Oct-13	$95,900.00	125	25	20
16	01-Dec-13	$3,450.00	150	10	5
17	10-Apr-13	$5,600.00	160	5	10
18	15-Jun-14	$8,000.00	150	5	5
19	30-Sep-14	$42,675.00	120	20	25

Hilltop Inventory in Excel

BillingDate	Customer	Hours	Rate	Total
01-May-15	Lakeside Trucking	8	$75.00	$600.00
01-May-15	Lakeside Trucking	8	$100.00	$800.00
01-May-15	Martin Plumbing	4	$50.00	$200.00
04-May-15	Country Electrical	16	$75.00	$1,200.00
04-May-15	Able Construction	5	$100.00	$500.00
04-May-15	Able Construction	5	$25.00	$125.00
04-May-15	Miles Contracting	10	$50.00	$500.00
05-May-15	Miles Contracting	10	$35.00	$350.00
05-May-15	Evergreen Painting	8	$25.00	$200.00
06-May-15	Barrier Concrete	8	$25.00	$200.00
06-May-15	Barrier Concrete	8	$25.00	$200.00
07-May-15	Cascade Enterprises	10	$100.00	$1,000.00
07-May-15	Cascade Enterprises	10	$75.00	$750.00
07-May-15	Allied Builders	6	$50.00	$300.00
08-May-15	Martin Plumbing	8	$35.00	$280.00
08-May-15	Evergreen Painting	8	$25.00	$200.00
08-May-15	Evergreen Painting	8	$25.00	$200.00
11-May-15	Able Construction	4	$75.00	$300.00
11-May-15	Able Construction	4	$100.00	$400.00
11-May-15	Miles Contracting	4	$50.00	$200.00
12-May-15	Country Electrical	6	$50.00	$300.00
12-May-15	Martin Plumbing	5	$75.00	$375.00
12-May-15	Lakeside Trucking	6	$100.00	$600.00
13-May-15	Cascade Enterprises	8	$25.00	$200.00
13-May-15	Miles Contracting	6	$25.00	$150.00
14-May-15	Evergreen Painting	6	$35.00	$210.00
14-May-15	Barrier Concrete	4	$100.00	$400.00
15-May-15	Allied Builders	4	$100.00	$400.00
15-May-15	Martin Plumbing	4	$50.00	$200.00
15-May-15	Miles Contracting	8	$25.00	$200.00

Hilltop Customer Invoices Query in Excel

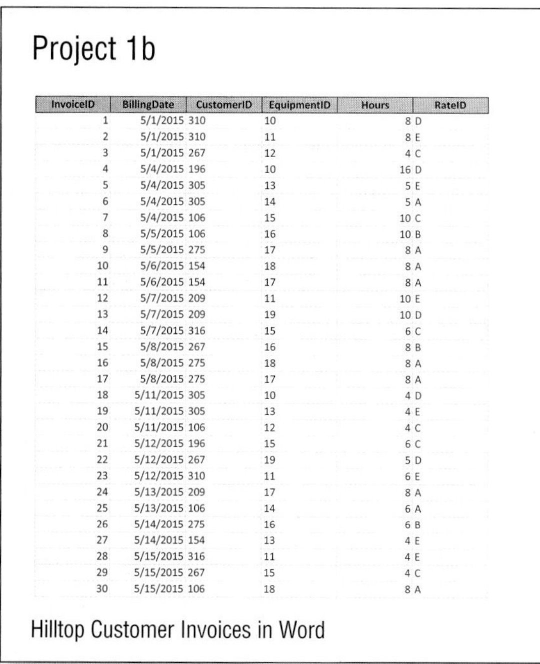

Project 1b

InvoiceID	BillingDate	CustomerID	EquipmentID	Hours	RateID
1	5/1/2015	310	10	8	D
2	5/1/2015	310	11	8	E
3	5/1/2015	267	12	4	C
4	5/4/2015	196	10	16	D
5	5/4/2015	305	13	5	E
6	5/4/2015	305	14	5	A
7	5/4/2015	106	15	10	C
8	5/5/2015	106	16	10	B
9	5/5/2015	275	17	8	A
10	5/6/2015	154	18	8	A
11	5/6/2015	154	17	8	A
12	5/7/2015	209	11	10	E
13	5/7/2015	209	19	10	D
14	5/7/2015	316	15	6	C
15	5/8/2015	267	16	8	B
16	5/8/2015	275	18	8	A
17	5/8/2015	275	17	8	A
18	5/11/2015	305	10	4	D
19	5/11/2015	305	13	4	E
20	5/11/2015	106	12	4	C
21	5/12/2015	196	15	6	C
22	5/12/2015	267	19	5	D
23	5/12/2015	310	11	6	E
24	5/13/2015	209	17	8	A
25	5/13/2015	106	14	6	A
26	5/14/2015	275	16	6	B
27	5/14/2015	154	13	4	E
28	5/15/2015	316	11	4	E
29	5/15/2015	267	15	4	C
30	5/15/2015	106	18	8	A

Hilltop Customer Invoices in Word

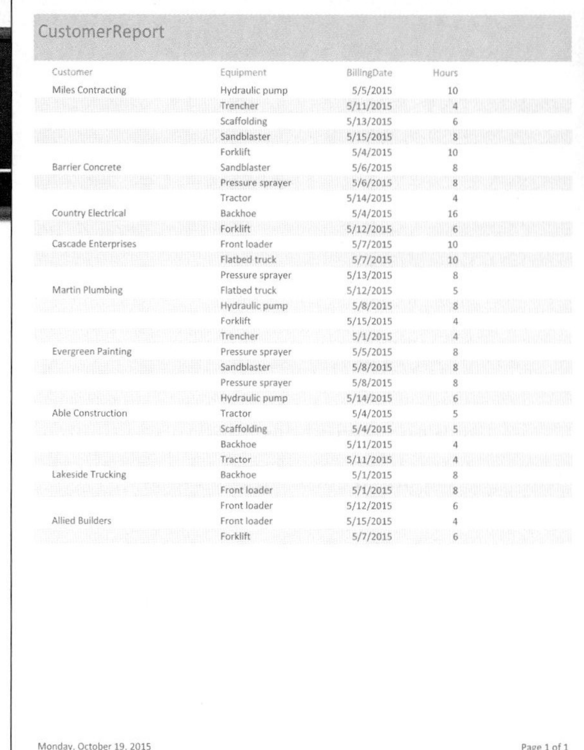

CustomerReport

Customer	Equipment	BillingDate	Hours
Miles Contracting	Hydraulic pump	5/5/2015	10
	Trencher	5/11/2015	4
	Scaffolding	5/13/2015	6
	Sandblaster	5/15/2015	8
	Forklift	5/4/2015	10
Barrier Concrete	Sandblaster	5/6/2015	8
	Pressure sprayer	5/6/2015	8
	Tractor	5/14/2015	4
Country Electrical	Backhoe	5/4/2015	16
	Forklift	5/12/2015	6
Cascade Enterprises	Front loader	5/7/2015	10
	Flatbed truck	5/7/2015	10
	Pressure sprayer	5/13/2015	8
Martin Plumbing	Flatbed truck	5/12/2015	5
	Hydraulic pump	5/8/2015	8
	Forklift	5/15/2015	4
	Trencher	5/1/2015	4
Evergreen Painting	Pressure sprayer	5/5/2015	8
	Sandblaster	5/8/2015	8
	Pressure sprayer	5/8/2015	8
	Hydraulic pump	5/14/2015	6
Able Construction	Tractor	5/4/2015	5
	Scaffolding	5/4/2015	5
	Backhoe	5/11/2015	4
	Tractor	5/11/2015	4
Lakeside Trucking	Backhoe	5/1/2015	8
	Front loader	5/1/2015	8
	Front loader	5/12/2015	6
Allied Builders	Front loader	5/15/2015	4
	Forklift	5/7/2015	6

Monday, October 19, 2015 Page 1 of 1

Project 1b, Hilltop Customer Report in Access

CustomerReport

Customer	Equipment	BillingDate	Hours
Miles Contracting	Hydraulic pump	5/5/2015	10
	Trencher	5/11/2015	4
	Scaffolding	5/13/2015	6
	Sandblaster	5/15/2015	8
	Forklift	5/4/2015	10
Barrier Concrete	Sandblaster	5/6/2015	8
	Pressure sprayer	5/6/2015	8
	Tractor	5/14/2015	4
Country Electrical	Backhoe	5/4/2015	16
	Forklift	5/12/2015	6
Cascade Enterprises	Front loader	5/7/2015	10
	Flatbed truck	5/7/2015	10
	Pressure sprayer	5/13/2015	8
Martin Plumbing	Flatbed truck	5/12/2015	5
	Hydraulic pump	5/8/2015	8
	Forklift	5/15/2015	4
	Trencher	5/1/2015	4
Evergreen Painting	Pressure sprayer	5/5/2015	8
	Sandblaster	5/8/2015	8
	Pressure sprayer	5/8/2015	8
	Hydraulic pump	5/14/2015	6
Able Construction	Tractor	5/4/2015	5
	Scaffolding	5/4/2015	5
	Backhoe	5/11/2015	4
	Tractor	5/11/2015	4
Lakeside Trucking	Backhoe	5/1/2015	8
	Front loader	5/1/2015	8
	Front loader	5/12/2015	6
Allied Builders	Front loader	5/15/2015	4
	Forklift	5/7/2015	6

Friday, October 19, 2012 Page 1 of 1

Project 1b, Hilltop Customer Report in Word

October 19, 2015

Miles Contracting
640 Smith Road
Aurora, CO 80041-6400

Ladies and Gentlemen:

Please join us June 1 for our annual equipment sales auction. Some of the choice items up for auction include three forklifts, two flatbed trucks, a front loader, and a bulldozer. We will also be auctioning painting equipment including pressure sprayers, ladders, and scaffolding.

The auction begins at 7:30 a.m. in the parking lot of our warehouse at 2605 Evans Avenue in Denver. For a listing of all equipment available for auction, stop by our store or call us at (303) 555-9066 and we will mail you the list.

Sincerely,

Lou Galloway
Manager

XX
HilltopLetter.docx

October 19, 2015

Barrier Concrete
220 Colorado Boulevard
Denver, CO 80125-2204

Ladies and Gentlemen:

Please join us June 1 for our annual equipment sales auction. Some of the choice items up for auction include three forklifts, two flatbed trucks, a front loader, and a bulldozer. We will also be auctioning painting equipment including pressure sprayers, ladders, and scaffolding.

The auction begins at 7:30 a.m. in the parking lot of our warehouse at 2605 Evans Avenue in Denver. For a listing of all equipment available for auction, stop by our store or call us at (303) 555-9066 and we will mail you the list.

Sincerely,

Lou Galloway
Manager

XX
HilltopLetter.docx

Project 1c, Hilltop Letters

October 19, 2015

Vernon Cook
1230 South Mesa
Phoenix, AZ 85018

Ladies and Gentlemen:

At the Grant Street West office of Copper State Insurance, we have hired two additional insurance representatives as well as one support staff member to ensure that we meet all your insurance needs. To accommodate the new staff, we have moved to a larger office just a few blocks away. Our new address is 3450 Grant Street West, Suite 110, Phoenix AZ 85003. Our telephone number, (602) 555-6300, has remained the same.

If you have any questions or concerns about your insurance policies or want to discuss adding or changing current coverage, please stop by or give us a call. We are committed to providing our clients with the most comprehensive automobile insurance coverage in the county.

Sincerely,

Lou Galloway
Manager

XX
AL1-C8-CSLtrs.docx

October 19, 2015

Helena Myerson
9032 45th Street East
Phoenix, AZ 85009

Ladies and Gentlemen:

At the Grant Street West office of Copper State Insurance, we have hired two additional insurance representatives as well as one support staff member to ensure that we meet all your insurance needs. To accommodate the new staff, we have moved to a larger office just a few blocks away. Our new address is 3450 Grant Street West, Suite 110, Phoenix AZ 85003. Our telephone number, (602) 555-6300, has remained the same.

If you have any questions or concerns about your insurance policies or want to discuss adding or changing current coverage, please stop by or give us a call. We are committed to providing our clients with the most comprehensive automobile insurance coverage in the county.

Sincerely,

Lou Galloway
Manager

XX
AL1-C8-CSLtrs.docx

Project 1d, Copper State Main Document

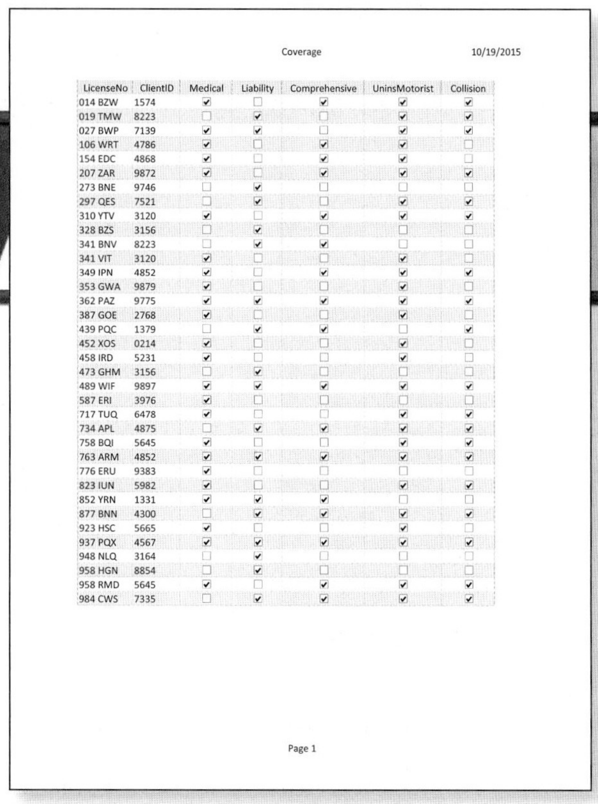

Coverage 10/19/2015

LicenseNo	ClientID	Medical	Liability	Comprehensive	UninsMotorist	Collision
014 BZW	1574	☑	☐	☑	☑	☑
019 TMW	8223	☐	☑	☐	☑	☑
027 BWP	7139	☑	☑	☐	☑	☑
106 WRT	4786	☑	☐	☑	☑	☐
154 EDC	4868	☑	☐	☑	☑	☐
207 ZAR	9872	☑	☐	☑	☑	☑
273 BNE	9746	☐	☑	☐	☐	☐
297 QES	7521	☐	☑	☐	☑	☑
310 YTV	3120	☑	☐	☑	☑	☑
328 BZS	3156	☐	☑	☐	☐	☐
341 BNV	8223	☐	☑	☑	☐	☐
341 VIT	3120	☑	☐	☐	☑	☐
349 IPN	4852	☑	☐	☑	☑	☑
353 GWA	9879	☑	☐	☐	☑	☐
362 PAZ	9775	☑	☑	☑	☑	☑
387 GOE	2768	☑	☐	☐	☑	☐
439 PQC	1379	☐	☑	☑	☐	☑
452 XOS	0214	☑	☐	☐	☑	☐
458 IRD	5231	☑	☐	☐	☑	☐
473 GHM	3156	☐	☑	☐	☐	☐
489 WIF	9897	☑	☑	☑	☑	☑
587 ERI	3976	☑	☐	☐	☐	☐
717 TUQ	6478	☑	☐	☐	☑	☑
734 APL	4875	☐	☑	☑	☑	☑
758 BQI	5645	☑	☐	☐	☑	☑
763 ARM	4852	☑	☑	☑	☑	☑
776 ERU	9383	☑	☐	☐	☐	☐
823 IUN	5982	☑	☐	☐	☑	☑
852 YRN	1331	☑	☑	☑	☐	☐
877 BNN	4300	☐	☑	☑	☑	☑
923 HSC	5665	☑	☐	☐	☑	☐
937 PQX	4567	☑	☑	☑	☑	☑
948 NLQ	3164	☐	☑	☐	☐	☐
958 HGN	8854	☐	☑	☐	☐	☐
958 RMD	5645	☑	☐	☑	☑	☑
984 CWS	7335	☐	☑	☑	☑	☑

Page 1

Project 1e, Copper State Coverage Table

Project 2 Import and Link Excel Worksheets with an Access Table

Project 2a

PolicyID	ClientID	Premium
110-C-39	0214	$1,450
115-C-41	3120	$935
120-B-33	3156	$424
122-E-30	1331	$745
127-E-67	3164	$893
129-D-55	3976	$770
131-C-90	4300	$1,255
135-E-31	4567	$1,510
136-E-77	4786	$635
139-B-59	4852	$338
141-E-84	4875	$951
143-D-20	1379	$920
145-D-12	5231	$1,175
147-C-10	5645	$1,005
150-C-36	5665	$805
152-B-01	5982	$411
155-E-88	6478	$988
168-B-65	7139	$1,050
170-C-20	7335	$875
173-D-77	7521	$556
180-E-05	8223	$721
185-E-19	2768	$734
188-D-63	8854	$1,384
192-C-29	1574	$1,390

Copper State Policies Table in Access

Project 2b

PolicyID	ClientID	Premium
110-C-39	0214	$ 1,450
122-E-30	1331	$ 850
143-D-20	1379	$ 920
192-C-29	1574	$ 1,390
185-E-19	2768	$ 734
115-C-41	3120	$ 935
120-B-33	3156	$ 424
127-E-67	3164	$ 893
129-D-55	3976	$ 770
131-C-90	4300	$ 1,255
135-E-31	4567	$ 1,510
136-E-77	4786	$ 635
139-B-59	4852	$ 338
141-E-84	4875	$ 951
145-D-12	5231	$ 1,175
147-C-10	5645	$ 1,005
150-C-36	5665	$ 805
152-B-01	5982	$ 411
155-E-88	6478	$ 988
168-B-65	7139	$ 1,050
170-C-20	7335	$ 875
173-D-77	7521	$ 556
180-E-05	8223	$ 721
188-D-63	8854	$ 1,384
190-C-28	3120	$ 685

Policies Table in Excel

Project 3 Collect Data in Word and Paste It into an Access Table

Project 3

CustomerID	Customer	StreetAddress	City	State	ZipCode
106	Miles Contracting	640 Smith Road	Aurora	CO	80041-6400
154	Barrier Concrete	220 Colorado Boulevard	Denver	CO	80125-2204
196	Country Electrical	12032 Sixth Avenue	Aurora	CO	80023-5473
209	Cascade Enterprises	24300 Quincy Avenue	Englewood	CO	80118-3800
267	Martin Plumbing	1010 Santa Fe Drive	Littleton	CO	80135-4886
275	Evergreen Painting	1045 Calfax Avenue	Denver	CO	80130-4337
305	Able Construction	8800 Evans Avenue	Denver	CO	80128-3488
310	Lakeside Trucking	566 Jewell Avenue	Denver	CO	80125-1298
316	Allied Builders	550 Alameda Avenue	Denver	CO	80135-7643
178	Stone Construction	9905 Broadway	Englewood	CO	80118-9008
225	Laughlin Products	997 Speer Boulevard	Denver	CO	80129-7446

Hilltop Customers Table

Model Answers

Project 1 Export Data to Excel and Export and Merge Data to Word

5 Parts

You will export a table and query to Excel and export a table and report to Word. You will also merge data in an Access table and query with a Word document.

Exporting Data

One of the advantages of using the Microsoft Office suite is the ability to exchange data between programs. Access, like other programs in the suite, offers a feature to export data from Access into Excel and/or Word. The Export group on the EXTERNAL DATA tab contains buttons for exporting a table, query, form, or report to other programs, such as Excel and Word.

Quick Steps

Export Data to Excel

1. Click desired table, query, or form.
2. Click EXTERNAL DATA tab.
3. Click Excel button in Export group.
4. Make desired changes at Export - Excel Spreadsheet dialog box.
5. Click OK.

Excel

Exporting Data to Excel

Use the Excel button in the Export group on the EXTERNAL DATA tab to export data in a table, query, or form to an Excel worksheet. Click the object containing the data you want to export to Excel, click the EXTERNAL DATA tab, and then click the Excel button in the Export group. The first Export - Excel Spreadsheet wizard dialog box displays, as shown in Figure 8.1.

Figure 8.1 Export - Excel Spreadsheet Wizard Dialog Box

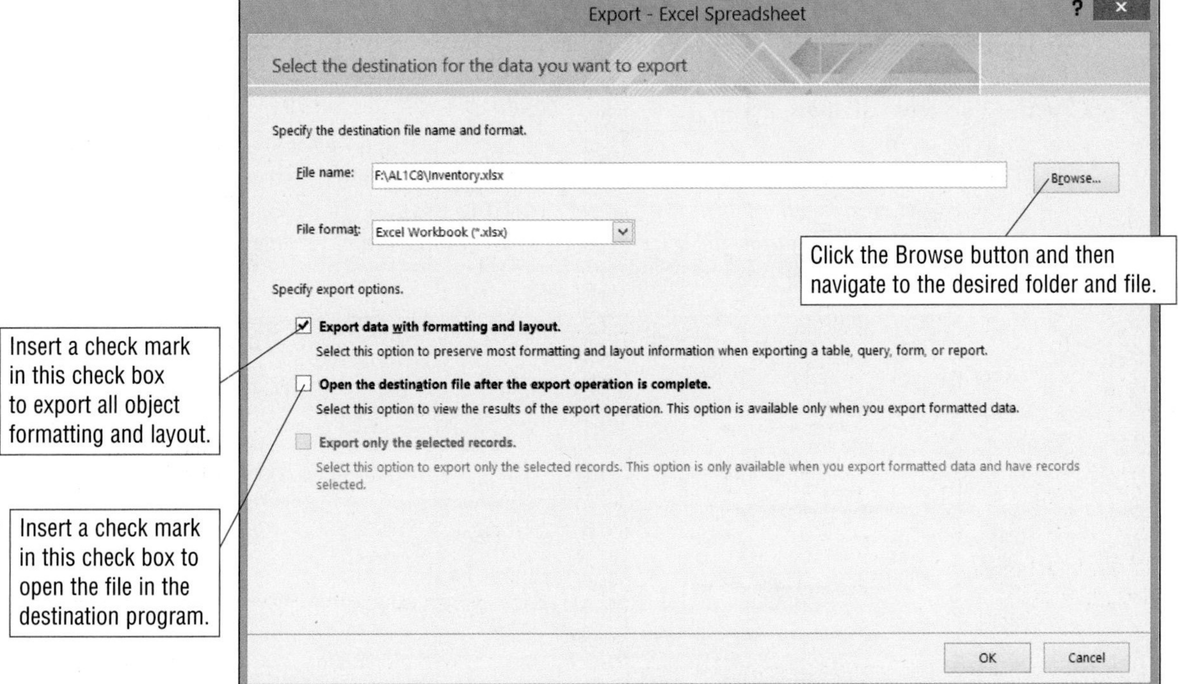

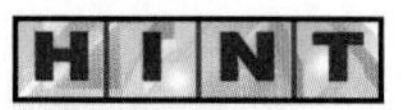

Data exported from Access to Excel is saved as an Excel workbook with the .xlsx file extension.

You can export only one database object at a time.

At the first wizard dialog box, Access uses the name of the object as the Excel workbook name. You can change this by selecting the current name and then typing a new name. You can also specify the file format with the *File format* option. Click the *Export data with formatting and layout* check box to insert a check mark. This exports all data formatting to the Excel workbook. If you want Excel to open with the exported data, click the *Open the destination file after the export operation is complete* option to insert a check mark. When you have made all desired changes, click the OK button. This opens Excel with the data in a workbook. Make any desired changes to the workbook and then save, print, and close the workbook. When you close Excel, Access displays with a second wizard dialog box, asking if you want to save the export steps. At this dialog box, insert a check mark in the *Save export steps* check box if you want to save the export steps or leave the check box blank and then click the Close button.

Project 1a Exporting a Table and Query to Excel — Part 1 of 5

1. Display the Open dialog box with the AL1C8 folder on your storage medium the active folder.
2. Open **AL1-C8-Hilltop.accdb** and enable the contents.
3. Save the Inventory table in the Tables group as an Excel workbook by completing the following steps:
   a. Click *Inventory* in the Tables group in the Navigation pane.
   b. Click the EXTERNAL DATA tab and then click the Excel button in the Export group.
   c. At the Export - Excel Spreadsheet wizard dialog box, click the Browse button.
   d. At the File Save dialog box, navigate to the AL1C8 folder on your storage medium and then click the Save button.
   e. Click the *Export data with formatting and layout* option to insert a check mark in the check box.
   f. Click the *Open the destination file after the export operation is complete* option to insert a check mark in the check box.

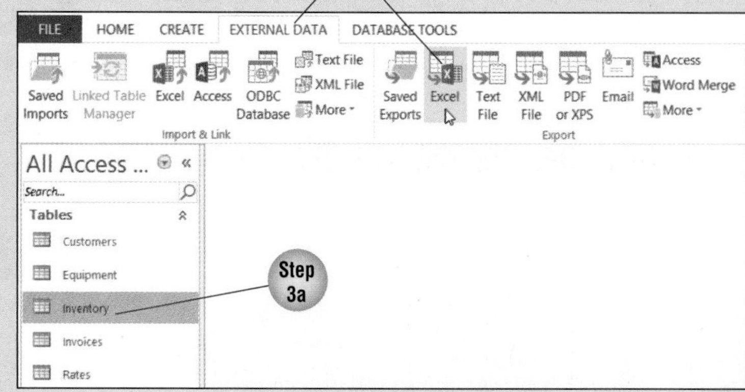

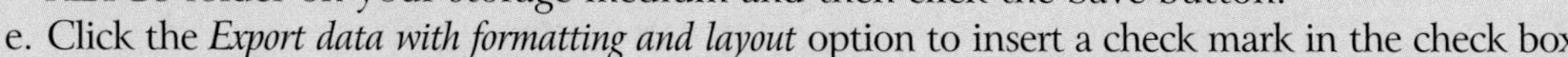

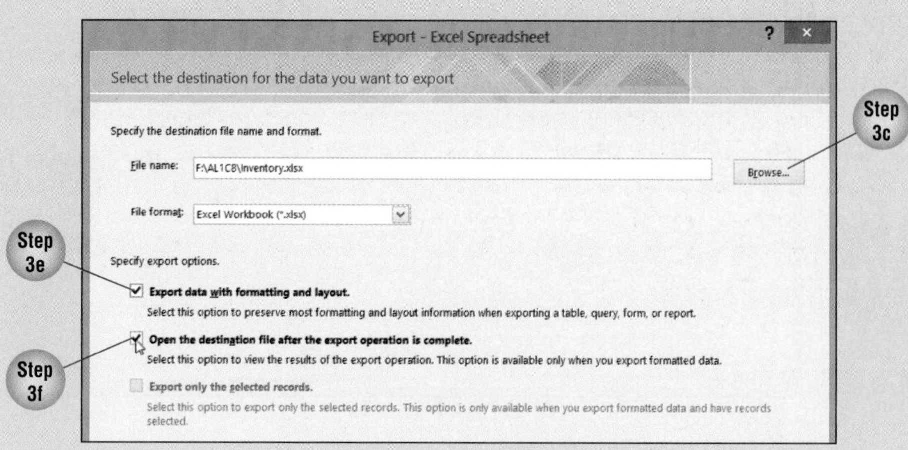

g. Click OK.
h. When the data displays on the screen in Excel as a worksheet, select cells A2 through A11 and then click the Center button in the Alignment group on the HOME tab.
i. Select cells D2 through F11 and then click the Center button.
j. Click the Save button on the Quick Access toolbar.
k. Print the worksheet by pressing Ctrl + P and then clicking the Print button at the Print backstage area.

Step 3h

	A	B	C	D	E	F
1	EquipmentID	PurchaseDate	PurchasePrice	AvailableHours	ServiceHours	RepairHours
2	10	01-Sep-10	$65,540.00	120	15	10
3	11	01-Feb-11	$105,500.00	125	20	15
4	12	01-Jun-11	$55,345.00	140	10	10
5	13	05-May-12	$86,750.00	120	20	20
6	14	15-Jul-12	$4,500.00	160	5	5
7	15	01-Oct-13	$95,900.00	125	25	20
8	16	01-Dec-13	$3,450.00	150	10	5
9	17	10-Apr-13	$5,600.00	160	5	10
10	18	15-Jun-14	$8,000.00	150	5	5
11	19	30-Sep-14	$42,675.00	120	20	25
12						
13						

l. Close the worksheet and then close Excel.

4. In Access, click the Close button to close the second wizard dialog box.
5. Design a query that extracts records from three tables with the following specifications:
   a. Add the Invoices, Customers, and Rates tables to the query window.
   b. Insert the *BillingDate* field from the *Invoices* field list box to the first *Field* row field.
   c. Insert the *Customer* field from the *Customers* field list box to the second *Field* row field.
   d. Insert the *Hours* field from the *Invoices* field list box to the third *Field* row field.
   e. Insert the *Rate* field from the *Rates* field list box to the fourth *Field* row field.
   f. Click in the fifth *Field* row field, type **Total: [Hours]*[Rate]**, and then press Enter.

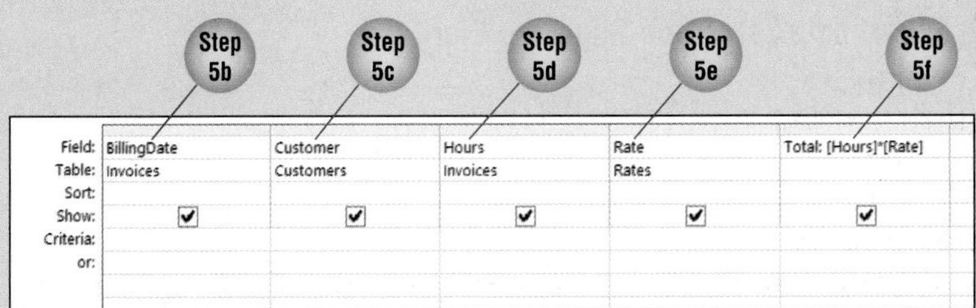

   g. Run the query.
   h. If necessary, automatically adjust the column width of the *Customer* field.
   i. Save the query and name it *CustomerInvoices*.
   j. Close the query.
6. Export the *CustomerInvoices* in the Queries group to Excel by completing the following steps:
   a. Click *CustomerInvoices* in the Queries group in the Navigation pane.
   b. Click the EXTERNAL DATA tab and then click the Excel button in the Export group.
   c. At the Export - Excel Spreadsheet wizard dialog box, click the *Export data with formatting and layout* option to insert a check mark in the check box.
   d. Click the *Open the destination file after the export operation is complete* option to insert a check mark in the check box.

e. Click OK.
f. When the data displays on the screen in Excel as a worksheet, select cells C2 through C31 and then click the Center button in the Alignment group on the HOME tab.
g. Click the Save button on the Quick Access toolbar.
h. Print the worksheet by pressing Ctrl + P and then clicking the Print button at the Print backstage area.
i. Close the worksheet and then close Excel.

7. In Access, click the Close button to close the second wizard dialog box.

Exporting Data to Word

Quick Steps

Export Data to Word
1. Click desired table, query, form, or report.
2. Click EXTERNAL DATA tab.
3. Click More button in Export group.
4. Click *Word*.
5. Make desired changes at Export - RTF File wizard dialog box.
6. Click OK.

More

Export data from Access to Word in a similar manner as exporting to Excel. To export data to Word, select the desired object in the Navigation pane, click the EXTERNAL DATA tab, click the More button in the Export group, and then click *Word* at the drop-down list. At the Export - RTF File wizard dialog box, make desired changes and then click OK. Word automatically opens and the data displays in a Word document that is saved automatically with the same name as the database object. The difference is that the file extension .rtf is added to the name. An RTF file is saved in rich-text format, which preserves formatting such as fonts and styles. You can export a document saved with the .rtf extension in Word and other Windows word processing or desktop publishing programs.

Project 1b **Exporting a Table and Report to Word** **Part 2 of 5**

1. With **AL1-C8-Hilltop.accdb** open, click *Invoices* in the Tables group in the Navigation pane.
2. Click the EXTERNAL DATA tab, click the More button in the Export group, and then click *Word* at the drop-down list.

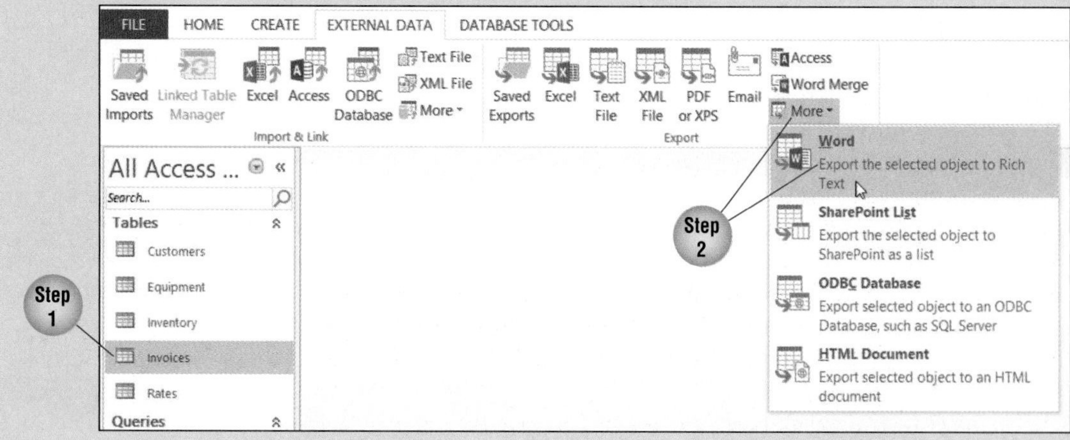

3. At the Export - RTF File wizard dialog box, click the Browse button.
4. At the File Save dialog box, make sure the AL1C8 folder on your storage medium is active and then click the Save button.
5. At the Export - RTF File wizard dialog box, click the *Open the destination file after the export operation is complete* check box to insert a check mark.

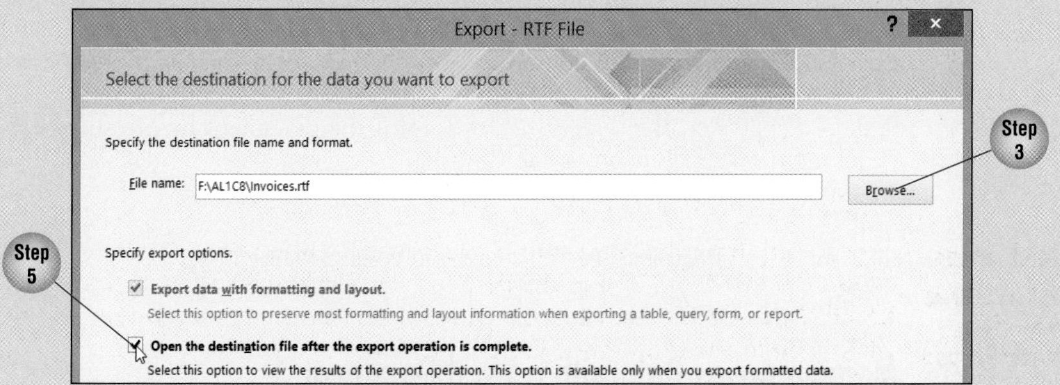

6. Click OK.
7. With the **Invoices.rtf** file open in Word, print the document by pressing Ctrl + P and then clicking the Print button at the Print backstage area.
8. Close the **Invoices.rtf** file and then close Word.
9. In Access, click the Close button to close the wizard dialog box.
10. Create a report with the Report Wizard by completing the following steps:
    a. Click the CREATE tab and then click the Report Wizard button in the Reports group.
    b. At the first Report Wizard dialog box, insert the following fields in the *Selected Fields* list box:
        From the Customers table:
            Customer
        From the Equipment table:
            Equipment
        From the Invoices table:
            BillingDate
            Hours
    c. After inserting the fields, click the Next button.
    d. At the second Report Wizard dialog box, make sure *by Customers* is selected in the list box in the upper left corner and then click the Next button.
    e. At the third Report Wizard dialog box, click the Next button.
    f. At the fourth Report Wizard dialog box, click the Next button.
    g. At the fifth Report Wizard dialog box, click *Block* in the *Layout* section and then click the Next button.
    h. At the sixth and final Report Wizard dialog box, select the current name in the *What title do you want for your report?* text box, type **CustomerReport**, and then click the Finish button.

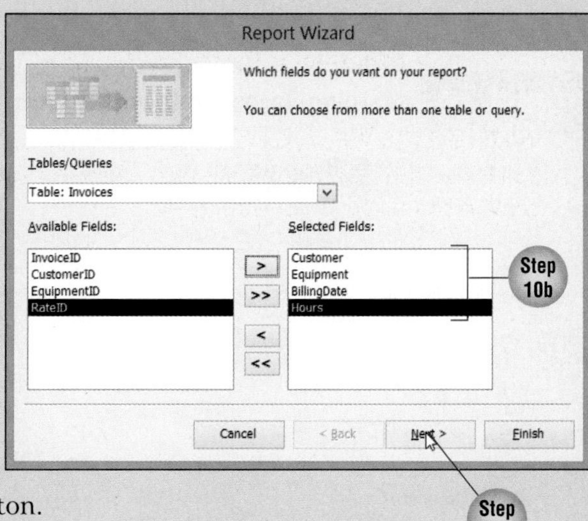

i. When the report displays in Print Preview, click the Print button at the left side of the PRINT PREVIEW tab and then click OK at the Print dialog box.
j. Save and then close the CustomerReport report.

11. Export the CustomerReport report to Word by completing the following steps:
    a. Click *CustomerReport* in the Reports group in the Navigation pane.
    b. Click the EXTERNAL DATA tab, click the More button in the Export group, and then click *Word* at the drop-down list.
    c. At the Export - RTF File wizard dialog box, click the *Open the destination file after export operation is complete* option to insert a check mark in the check box and then click OK.
    d. When the data displays on the screen in Word, print the document by pressing Ctrl + P and then clicking the Print button at the Print backstage area.
    e. Save and then close the CustomerReport document.
    f. Close Word.
12. In Access, click the Close button to close the second wizard dialog box.

Quick Steps

Merge Data with Word

1. Click desired table or query.
2. Click EXTERNAL DATA tab.
3. Click Word Merge button.
4. Make desired choices at each dialog box.

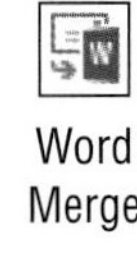

Word Merge

Merging Access Data with a Word Document

You can merge data from an Access table with a Word document. When merging data, the data in the Access table is considered the data source and the Word document is considered the main document. When the merge is completed, the merged documents display in Word.

To merge data, click the desired table in the Navigation pane, click the EXTERNAL DATA tab, and then click the Word Merge button. When merging Access data, you can either type the text in the main document or merge Access data with an existing Word document.

Project 1c Merging Access Data with a Word Document Part 3 of 5

1. With **AL1-C8-Hilltop.accdb** open, click *Customers* in the Tables group in the Navigation pane.
2. Click the EXTERNAL DATA tab.
3. Click the Word Merge button in the Export group.

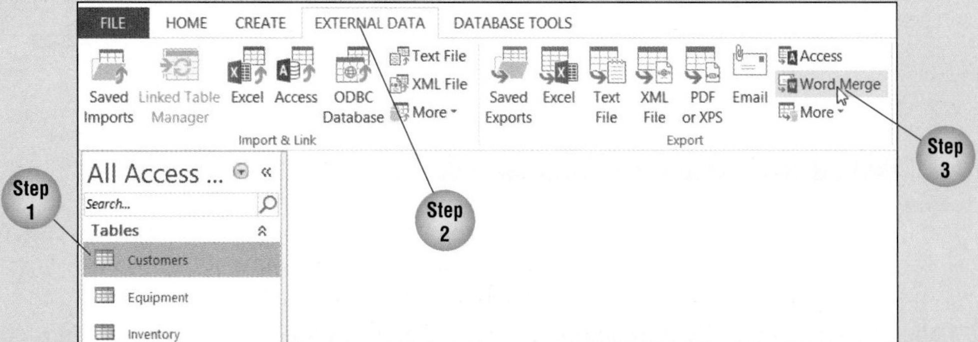

4. At the Microsoft Word Mail Merge Wizard dialog box, make sure *Link your data to an existing Microsoft Word document* is selected and then click OK.
5. At the Select Microsoft Word Document dialog box, make sure the AL1C8 folder on your storage medium is the active folder and then double-click the document named ***HilltopLetter.docx***.

6. Click the Word button on the Taskbar.
7. Click the Maximize button located at the right side of the HilltopLetter.docx Title bar and then close the Mail Merge task pane.
8. Press the down arrow key six times (not the Enter key) and then type the current date.
9. Press the down arrow key four times and then insert fields for merging from the Customers table by completing the following steps:
   a. Click the Insert Merge Field button arrow located in the Write & Insert Fields group and then click *Customer* in the drop-down list. (This inserts the *«Customer»* field in the document.)

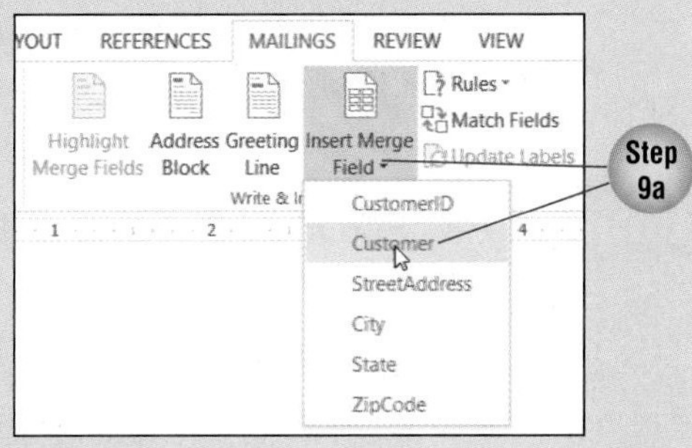

   b. Press Enter, click the Insert Merge Field button arrow, and then click *StreetAddress* in the drop-down list.
   c. Press Enter, click the Insert Merge Field button arrow, and then click *City* in the drop-down list.
   d. Type a comma (,) and then press the spacebar.
   e. Click the Insert Merge Field button arrow and then click *State* in the drop-down list.

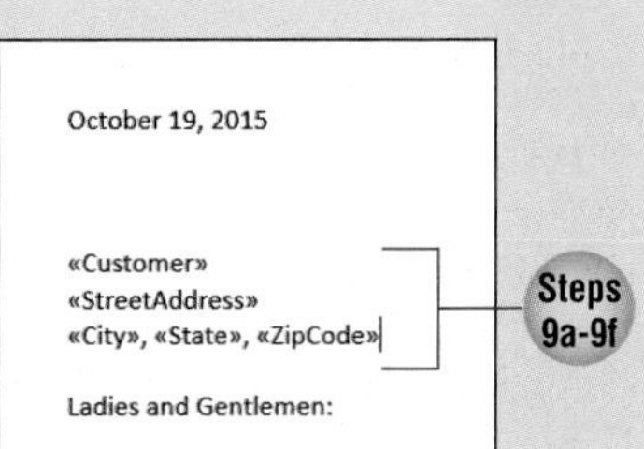

   f. Press the spacebar, click the Insert Merge Field button arrow, and then click *ZipCode* in the drop-down list.
   g. Replace the letters *XX* that display toward the bottom of the letter with your initials.
   h. Click the Finish & Merge button in the Finish group and then click *Edit Individual Documents* in the drop-down list.
   i. At the Merge to New Document dialog box, make sure *All* is selected and then click OK.
   j. When the merge is completed, save the new document and name it **AL1-C8-HilltopLtrs** in the AL1C8 folder on your storage medium.

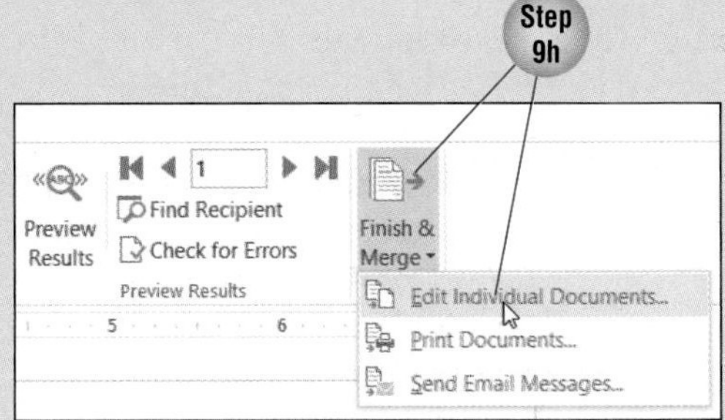

10. Print just the first two pages (two letters) of **AL1-C8-HilltopLtrs.docx**.
11. Close **AL1-C8-HilltopLtrs.docx** and then close **HilltopLetter.docx** without saving the changes.
12. Close Word.
13. Close **AL1-C8-Hilltop.accdb**.

Merging Query Data with a Word Document

You can perform a query in a database and then use the query to merge with a Word document. In Project 1c, you merged a table with an existing Word document. You can also merge a table or query and then type the Word document. You will create a query in Project 1d and then merge data in the query with a new document in Word.

In Project 1c, you inserted a number of merge fields for the inside address of a letter. You can also insert a field that will insert all of the fields required for the inside address of a letter with the Address Block button in the Write & Insert Fields group on the MAILINGS tab. When you click the Address Block button, the Insert Address Block dialog box displays with a preview of how the

Address Block

fields will be inserted in the document to create the inside address. The dialog box also contains buttons and options for customizing the fields. Click OK and the *«AddressBlock»* field is inserted in the document. The *«AddressBlock»* field is an example of a composite field, which groups a number of fields.

In Project 1c, you could not use the *«AddressBlock»* composite field because the *Customer* field was not recognized by Word as a field for the inside address. In Project 1d, you will create a query that contains the *FirstName* and *LastName* fields, which Word recognizes and uses for the *«AddressBlock»* composite field.

Project 1d Performing a Query and Then Merging with a Word Document — Part 4 of 5

1. Display the Open dialog box with the AL1C8 folder on your storage medium the active folder.
2. Open **AL1-C8-CopperState.accdb** and enable the contents.
3. Perform a query with the Query Wizard and modify the query by completing the following steps:
   a. Click the CREATE tab and then click the Query Wizard button in the Queries group.
   b. At the New Query dialog box, make sure Simple Query Wizard is selected and then click OK.
   c. At the first Simple Query Wizard dialog box, click the down-pointing arrow at the right of the *Tables/Queries* option box and then click *Table: Clients*.
   d. Click the All Fields button to insert all of the fields in the *Selected Fields* list box.
   e. Click the Next button.
   f. At the second Simple Query Wizard dialog box, make the following changes:
      1) Select the current name in the *What title do you want for your query?* text box and then type **ClientsPhoenixQuery**.
      2) Click the *Modify the query design* option.
      3) Click the Finish button.
   g. At the query window, click in the *Criteria* field in the *City* column, type **Phoenix**, and then press Enter.
   h. Click the Run button in the Results group. (Only clients living in Phoenix will display.)
   i. Save and then close the query.

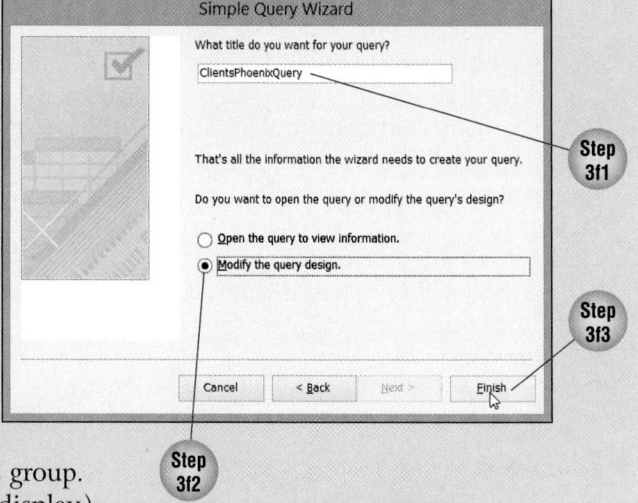

4. Click *ClientsPhoenixQuery* in the Queries group in the Navigation pane.
5. Click the EXTERNAL DATA tab and then click the Word Merge button in the Export group.
6. At the Microsoft Word Mail Merge Wizard dialog box, click the *Create a new document and then link the data to it* option and then click OK.

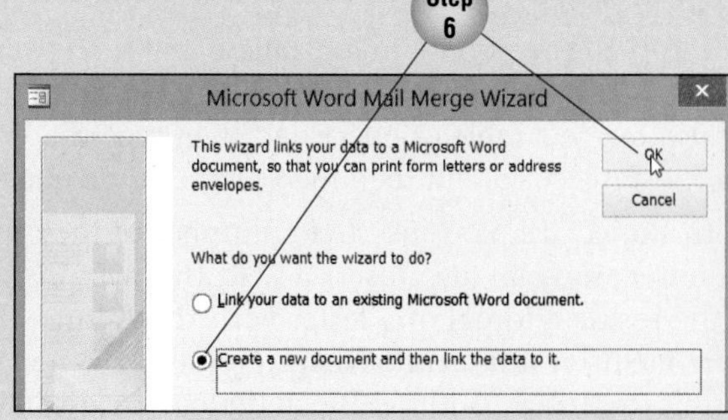

7. Click the Word button on the Taskbar.
8. Click the Maximize button located at the right side of the Document1 Title bar and then close the Mail Merge task pane.
9. Complete the following steps to type text and insert the *«AddressBlock»* composite field in the blank Word document:
   a. Click the HOME tab and then click the *No Spacing* style option in the Styles group.
   b. Press Enter six times.
   c. Type the current date.
   d. Press Enter four times.
   e. Click the MAILINGS tab.
   f. Insert the *«AddressBlock»* composite field by clicking the Address Block button in the Write & Insert Fields group on the MAILINGS tab and then clicking OK at the Insert Address Block dialog box. (This inserts the *«AddressBlock»* composite field in the document.)
   g. Press Enter twice and then type the salutation **Ladies and Gentlemen:**.
   h. Press Enter twice and then type the following paragraphs of text (press the Enter key twice after typing the first paragraph):

      At the Grant Street West office of Copper State Insurance, we have hired two additional insurance representatives as well as one support staff member to ensure that we meet all your insurance needs. To accommodate the new staff, we have moved to a larger office just a few blocks away. Our new address is 3450 Grant Street West, Suite 110, Phoenix AZ 85003. Our telephone number, (602) 555-6300, has remained the same.

      If you have any questions or concerns about your insurance policies or want to discuss adding or changing current coverage, please stop by or give us a call. We are committed to providing our clients with the most comprehensive automobile insurance coverage in the county.

   i. Press Enter twice and then type the following complimentary close at the left margin (press Enter four times after typing *Sincerely,*):

      Sincerely,

      Lou Galloway
      Manager

      XX (Type your initials instead of XX.)
      AL1-C8-CSLtrs.docx

   j. Click the Finish & Merge button in the Finish group on the MAILINGS tab and then click *Edit Individual Documents* in the drop-down menu.
   k. At the Merge to New Document dialog box, make sure *All* is selected, and then click OK.
   l. When the merge is complete, save the new document in the AL1C8 folder on your storage medium and name it **AL1-C8-CSLtrs**.
10. Print the first two pages (two letters) of **AL1-C8-CSLtrs.docx**.
11. Close **AL1-C8-CSLtrs.docx**.
12. Save the main document as **AL1-C8-CSMainDoc** in the AL1C8 folder on your storage medium and then close the document.
13. Close Word.

Exporting an Access Object to a PDF or XPS File

Quick Steps

Export an Access Object to a PDF File

1. Click object in the Navigation pane.
2. Click EXTERNAL DATA tab.
3. Click PDF or XPS button.
4. Navigate to desired folder.
5. Click Publish button.

PDF or XPS

With the PDF or XPS button in the Export group on the EXTERNAL DATA tab, you can export an Access object to a PDF or XPS file. As you learned in Chapter 7, the letters *PDF* stand for *portable document format*, which is a file format that captures all of the elements of a file as an electronic image. The letters *XPS* stand for *XML paper specification* and the letters *XML* stand for *extensible markup language*, which is a set of rules for encoding files electronically.

To export an Access object to PDF or XPS file format, click the desired object, click the EXTERNAL DATA tab, and then click the PDF or XPS button in the Export group. This displays the Publish as PDF or XPS dialog box with the *PDF (*.pdf)* option selected in the *Save as type* option box. If you want to save the Access object in XPS file format, click the *Save as type* option box and then click *XPS Document (*.xps)* at the drop-down list. At the Save As dialog box, type a name in the *File name* text box and then click the Publish button.

To open a PDF or XPS file in your web browser, open the browser, click *File* on the browser Menu bar, and then click *Open* at the drop-down list. At the Open dialog box, click the Browse button. At the browser window Open dialog box, change the *Files of type* to *All Files (*.*)*, navigate to the desired folder, and then double-click the file.

Project 1e **Exporting an Access Object to a PDF File** **Part 5 of 5**

1. With **AL1-C8-CopperState.accdb** open, export the Coverage table to PDF file format by completing the following steps:
   a. Click *Coverage* in the Tables group in the Navigation pane.
   b. Click the EXTERNAL DATA tab.
   c. Click the PDF or XPS button in the Export group.
   d. At the Publish as PDF or XPS dialog box, navigate to the AL1C8 folder on your storage medium, click the *Open file after publishing* check box to insert a check mark, and then click the Publish button.
   e. When the Coverage table data displays in Adobe Reader, scroll through the file and notice how it displays.
   f. Print the PDF file by clicking the Print button that displays at the left side of the toolbar and then clicking OK at the Print dialog box.
   g. Close Adobe Reader by positioning the mouse pointer at the top of the window (mouse turns into a hand), holding down the left mouse button, dragging down to the bottom of the screen, and then releasing the mouse button.
   h. At the Windows Start screen, click the Desktop icon.
2. In Access, click the Close button to close the wizard dialog box.

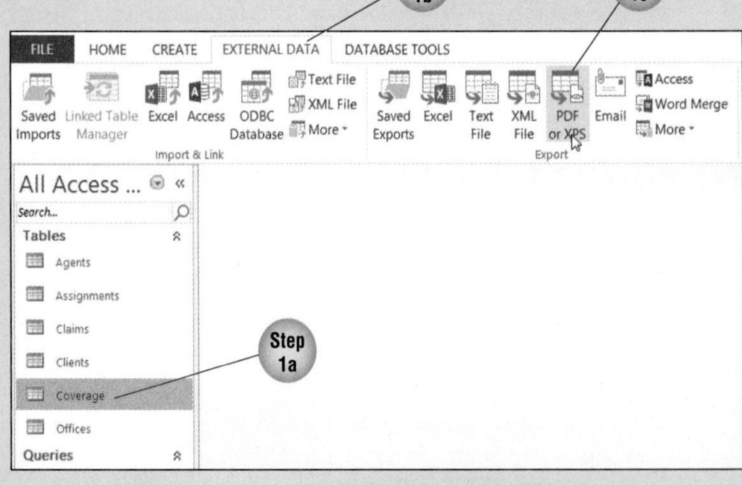

Project 2 Import and Link Excel Worksheets with an Access Table — 2 Parts

You will import an Excel worksheet into an Access table. You will also link an Excel worksheet to an Access table and then add a new record to the Access table.

Importing and Linking Data to New Tables

In this chapter, you have learned how to export Access data to Excel and Word. You can also import data from other programs into an Access table. For example, you can import data from an Excel worksheet and create a new table in a database using data from the worksheet. Data in the original program is not connected to the data imported into an Access table. If you make changes to the data in the original program, those changes are not reflected in the Access table. If you want the imported data connected to the original program, link the data.

Quick Steps

Import Data into a New Table

1. Click EXTERNAL DATA tab.
2. Click desired application in Import & Link group.
3. Click Browse button.
4. Double-click desired file name.
5. Make desired choices at each wizard dialog box.

Store data in Access and analyze it using Excel.

You can import and link data between Access databases.

Importing Data into a New Table

To import data, click the EXTERNAL DATA tab and then determine where you would like to retrieve data with options in the Import & Link group. At the Import dialog box that displays, click Browse and then double-click the desired file name. This activates the Import Wizard and displays the first wizard dialog box. The appearance of the dialog box varies depending on the file selected. Complete the steps of the Import Wizard, specifying information such as the range of data, whether the first row contains column headings, whether to store the data in a new table or existing table, the primary key, and the name of the table.

Project 2a Importing an Excel Worksheet into an Access Table — Part 1 of 2

1. With **AL1-C8-CopperState.accdb** open, import an Excel worksheet into a new table in the database by completing the following steps:
   a. Click the EXTERNAL DATA tab and then click the Excel button in the Import & Link group.
   b. At the Get External Data - Excel Spreadsheet dialog box, click the Browse button and then make the AL1C8 folder on your storage medium the active folder.
   c. Double-click ***AL1-C8-Policies.xlsx*** in the list box.
   d. Click OK at the Get External Data - Excel Spreadsheet dialog box.
   e. At the first Import Spreadsheet Wizard dialog box, make sure the *First Row Contains Column Headings* check box contains a check mark and then click the Next button.

f. At the second Import Spreadsheet Wizard dialog box, click the Next button.
g. At the third Import Spreadsheet Wizard dialog box, click the *Choose my own primary key* option (which inserts *PolicyID* in the option box located to the right of the option) and then click the Next button.

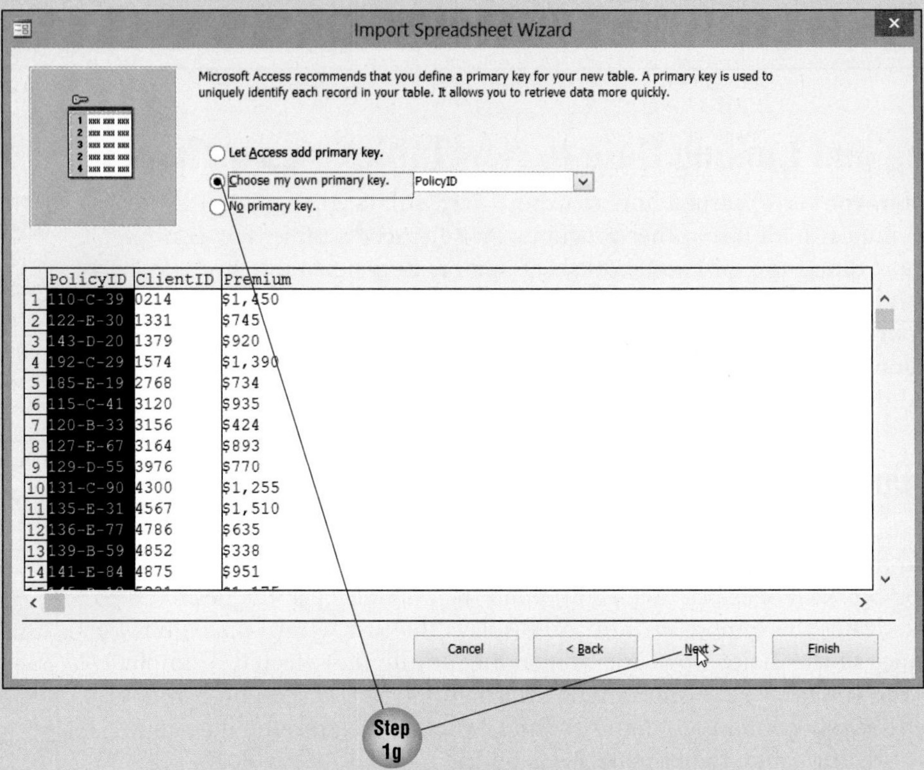

h. At the fourth Import Spreadsheet Wizard dialog box, type Policies in the *Import to Table* text box and then click the Finish button.

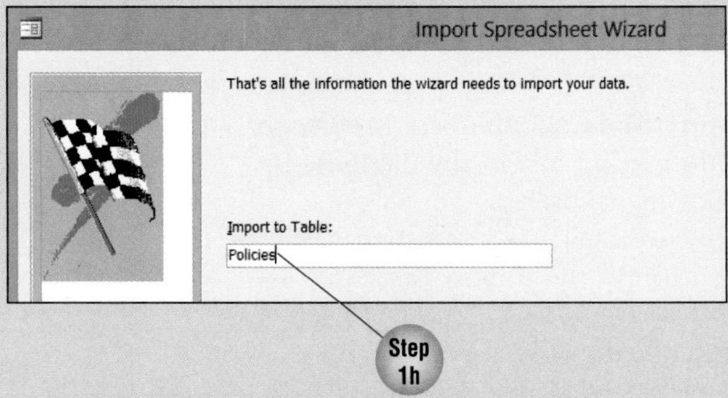

i. At the Get External Data - Excel Spreadsheet dialog box, click the Close button.
2. Open the new Policies table in Datasheet view.
3. Print and then close the Policies table.

Linking Data to an Excel Worksheet

Imported data is not connected to the source program. If you know that you will use your data only in Access, import it. However, if you want to update the data in a program other than Access, link the data. Changes made to linked data in the source program file are reflected in the destination program file. For example, you can link an Excel worksheet with an Access table and when you make changes in the Excel worksheet, the changes are reflected in the Access table.

Quick Steps

Link Data to an Excel Worksheet

1. Click EXTERNAL DATA tab.
2. Click Excel button in Import & Link group.
3. Click Browse button.
4. Double-click desired file name.
5. Click *Link to a data source by creating a linked table.*
6. Make desired choices at each wizard dialog box.

Excel

To link data to a new table, click the EXTERNAL DATA tab and then click the Excel button in the Import & Link group. At the Get External Data - Excel Spreadsheet dialog box, click the Browse button, double-click the desired file name, click the *Link to a data source by creating a linked table* option, and then click OK. This activates the Link Wizard and displays the first wizard dialog box. Complete the steps of the Link Wizard, specifying the same basic information as the Import Wizard.

Project 2b **Linking an Excel Worksheet to an Access Table** **Part 2 of 2**

1. With **AL1-C8-CopperState.accdb** open, click the EXTERNAL DATA tab and then click the Excel button in the Import & Link group.
2. At the Get External Data - Excel Spreadsheet dialog box, click the Browse button, make sure the AL1C8 folder on your storage medium is active, and then double-click ***AL1-C8-Policies.xlsx***.
3. At the Get External Data - Excel Spreadsheet dialog box, click the *Link to the data source by creating a linked table* option and then click OK.

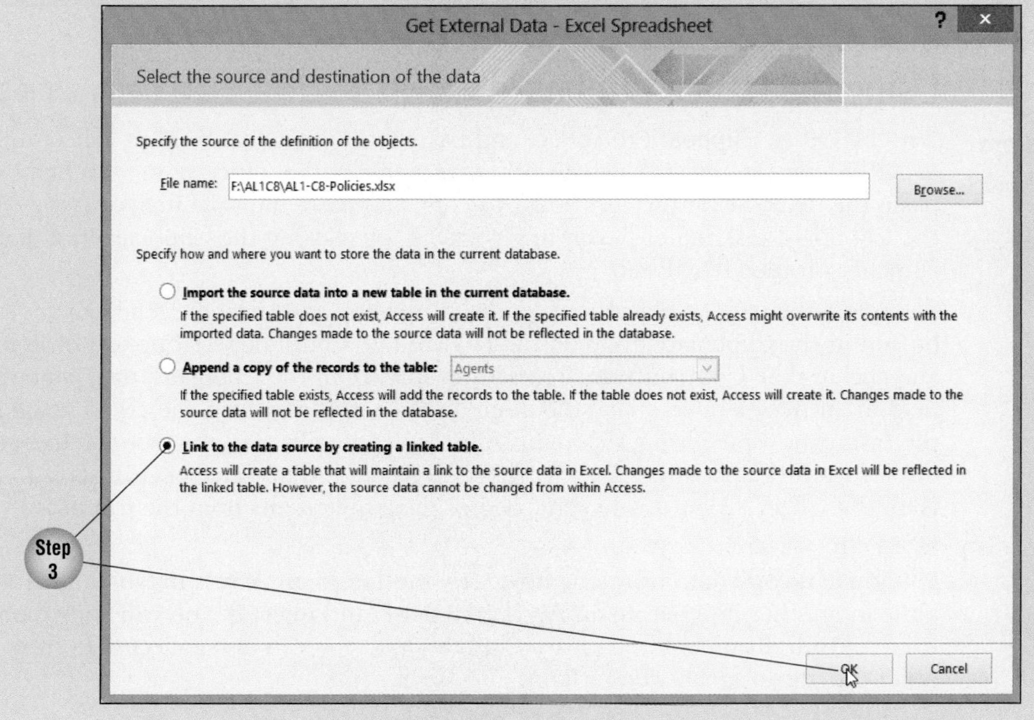

4. At the first Link Spreadsheet Wizard dialog box, make sure the *First Row Contains Column Headings* option contains a check mark and then click the Next button.
5. At the second Link Spreadsheet Wizard dialog box, type **LinkedPolicies** in the *Linked Table Name* text box and then click the Finish button.
6. At the message stating the linking is finished, click OK.
7. Open the new LinkedPolicies table in Datasheet view.
8. Close the LinkedPolicies table.
9. Open Excel, open the **AL1-C8-Policies.xlsx** workbook, and then make the following changes:
   a. Change the amount *$745* in cell C3 to *$850*.
   b. Add the following information in the specified cells:
      A26: **190-C-28**
      B26: **3120**
      C26: **685**

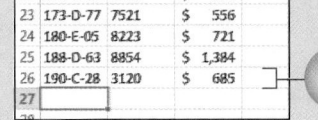

22	170-C-20	7335	$ 875
23	173-D-77	7521	$ 556
24	180-E-05	8223	$ 721
25	188-D-63	8854	$ 1,384
26	190-C-28	3120	$ 685
27			

Step 9b

10. Save, print, and then close **AL1-C8-Policies.xlsx**.
11. Close Excel.
12. With Access the active program and **AL1-C8-CopperState.accdb** open, open the LinkedPolicies table. Notice the changes you made in Excel are reflected in the table.
13. Close the LinkedPolicies table.
14. Close **AL1-C8-CopperState.accdb**.

Project 3 Collect Data in Word and Paste It into an Access Table 1 Part

You will open a Word document containing Hilltop customer names and addresses and then copy the data and paste it into an Access table.

Using the Office Clipboard

Quick Steps
Display the Clipboard Task Pane
Click Clipboard task pane launcher.

Use the Office Clipboard to collect and paste multiple items. You can collect up to 24 different items in Access or other programs in the Office suite and then paste the items in various locations. To copy and paste multiple items, display the Clipboard task pane, shown in Figure 8.2, by clicking the Clipboard task pane launcher on the HOME tab.

Select the data or object that you want to copy and then click the Copy button in the Clipboard group on the HOME tab. Continue selecting text or items and clicking the Copy button. To insert an item from the Clipboard task pane to a field in an Access table, make the desired field active and then click the button in the task pane representing the item. If the copied item is text, the first 50 characters display in the Clipboard task pane. After all desired items have been inserted, click the Clear All button to remove any remaining items from the Clipboard task pane.

You can copy data from one object to another in an Access database or from a file in another program to an Access database. In Project 3, you will copy data from a Word document and paste it into a table. You can also collect data from other programs, such as PowerPoint and Excel.

Figure 8.2 Office Clipboard Task Pane

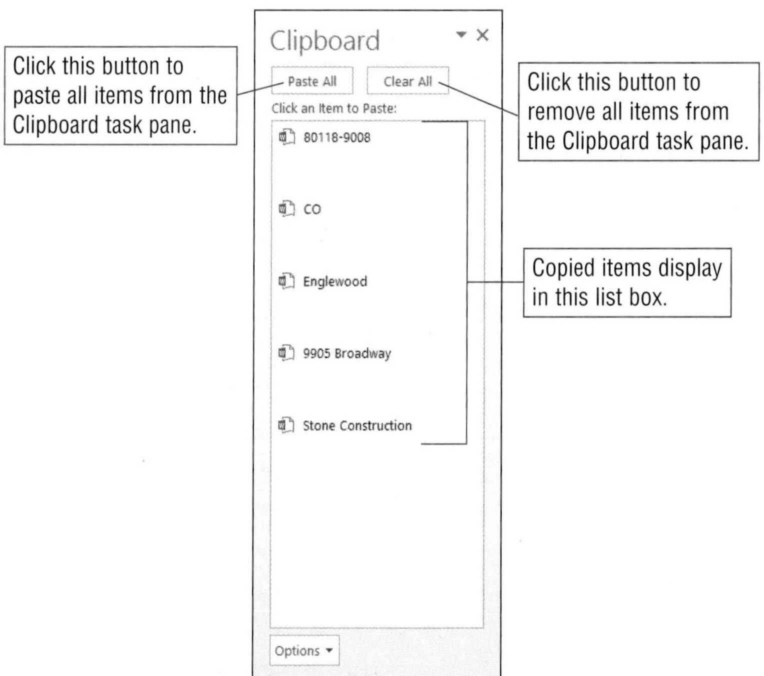

Project 3 Collecting Data in Word and Pasting It into an Access Table — Part 1 of 1

1. Open **AL1-C8-Hilltop.accdb**.
2. Open the Customers table.
3. Copy data from Word and paste it into the Customers table by completing the following steps:
   a. Open Word, make AL1C8 the active folder, and then open **HilltopCustomers.docx**.
   b. Make sure the HOME tab is active.
   c. Click the Clipboard task pane launcher to display the Clipboard task pane.
   d. Select the first company name, *Stone Construction*, and then click the Copy button in the Clipboard group.

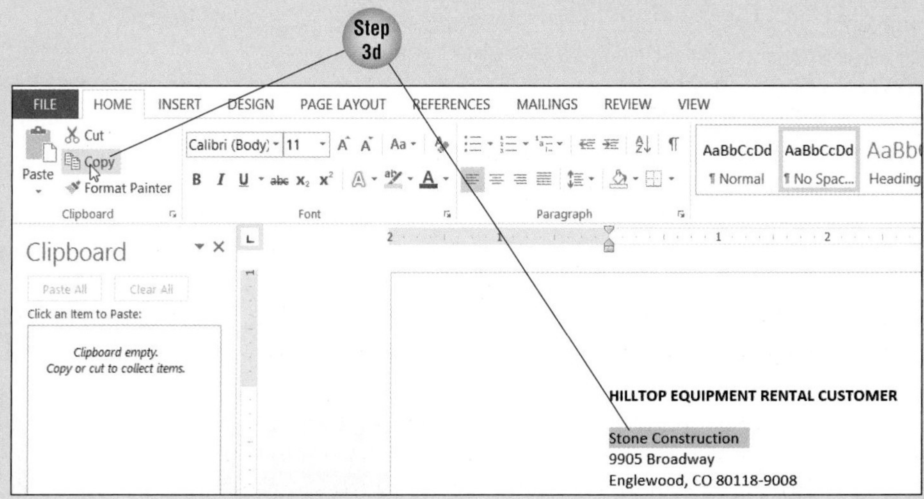

e. Select the street address, *9905 Broadway*, and then click the Copy button.
f. Select the city, *Englewood*, and then click the Copy button.
g. Select the state, *CO* (selecting only the two letters and not the space after the letters), and then click the Copy button.
h. Select the zip code, *80118-9008*, and then click the Copy button.
i. Click the button on the Taskbar representing Access. (Make sure the Customer table is open and displays in Datasheet view.)
j. Click in the first empty cell in the *CustomerID* field and then type 178.
k. Display the Clipboard task pane by clicking the HOME tab and then clicking the Clipboard task pane launcher.
l. Close the Navigation pane by clicking the Shutter Bar Open/Close Button.
m. Click in the first empty cell in the *Customer* field and then click *Stone Construction* in the Clipboard task pane.

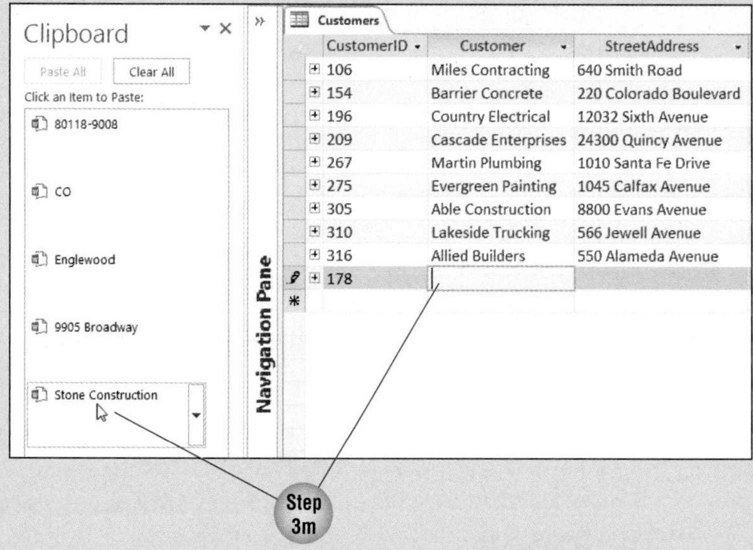

n. Click in the *StreetAddress* field and then click *9905 Broadway* in the Clipboard task pane.
o. Click in the *City* field and then click *Englewood* in the Clipboard task pane.
p. Click in the *State* field and then click *CO* in the Clipboard task pane.
q. Click in the *ZipCode* field, make sure the insertion point is positioned at the left side of the field, and then click *80118-9008* in the Clipboard task pane.
r. Click the Clear All button in the Clipboard task pane. (This removes all entries from the Clipboard.)

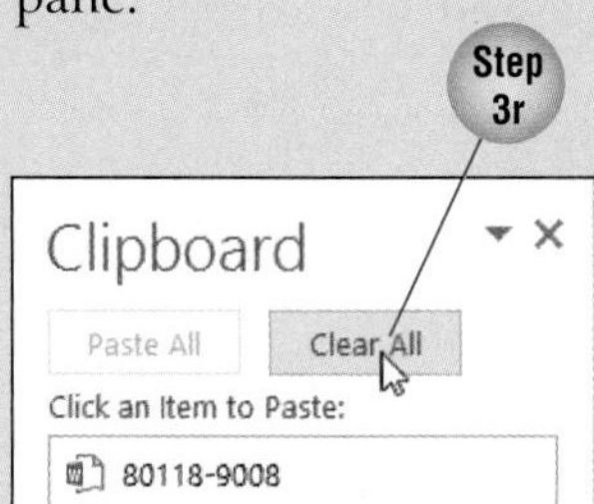

4. Complete steps similar to those in 3d through 3q to copy the information for Laughlin Products and paste it into the Customers table. (The customer ID number is 225.)
5. Click the Clear All button in the Clipboard task pane.
6. Close the Clipboard task pane by clicking the Close button (which contains an *X*) located in the upper right corner of the task pane.
7. Save, print, and then close the Customers table.
8. Open the Navigation pane by clicking the Shutter Bar Open/Close Button.
9. Make Word the active program, close **HilltopCustomers.docx** without saving changes, and then close Word.
10. Close **AL1-C8-Hilltop.accdb**.

Chapter Summary

- Use the Excel button in the Export group on the EXTERNAL DATA tab to export data in a table, query, or form to an Excel worksheet.
- Export data in a table, query, form, or report to a Word document by clicking the More button and then clicking *Word* at the drop-down list. Access exports the data to an RTF (rich-text format) file.
- Export an Access object to a PDF or XPS file with the PDF or XPS button in the Export group on the EXTERNAL DATA tab.
- You can merge Access data with a Word document. The Access data is the data source and the Word document is the main document. To merge data, click the desired table or query, click the EXTERNAL DATA tab, and then click the Word Merge button in the Export group.
- Use the Excel button in the Import group on the EXTERNAL DATA tab to import Excel data to an Access table.
- You can link imported data. Changes made to the data in the source program file are reflected in the destination source file.
- If you want to link imported data, click the *Link to the data source by creating a linked table* option at the Get External Data dialog box.
- Use the Clipboard task pane to collect up to 24 different items in Access or other programs and paste them in various locations.
- Display the Clipboard task pane by clicking the Clipboard task pane launcher on the HOME tab.

Commands Review

FEATURE	RIBBON TAB, GROUP	BUTTON
Clipboard task pane	HOME, Clipboard	
export object to Excel	EXTERNAL DATA, Export	
export object to PDF or XPS	EXTERNAL DATA, Export	
export object to Word	EXTERNAL DATA, Export	, *Word*
import Excel data	EXTERNAL DATA, Import & Link	
merge Access data with Word	EXTERNAL DATA, Export	

Concepts Check Test Your Knowledge 

Completion: In the space provided at the right, indicate the correct term, symbol, or command.

1. Click this tab to display the Export group. ______
2. Click this button in the Export group to display the Export - Excel Spreadsheet wizard dialog box. ______
3. At the first Export - Excel Spreadsheet wizard dialog box, click this option if you want Excel to open with the exported data. ______
4. To export Access data to Word, click this button in the Export group on the EXTERNAL DATA tab and then click *Word* at the drop-down list. ______
5. When you export Access data to Word, the document is saved in this file format. ______
6. When merging data, the data in the Access table is considered this. ______
7. To merge data, click this button in the Export group on the EXTERNAL DATA tab. ______
8. Import an Excel worksheet into an Access database with the Excel button in this group on the EXTERNAL DATA tab. ______
9. If you want imported data connected to the original program, do this to the data. ______
10. Use this task pane to collect and paste multiple items. ______

Skills Check Assess Your Performance

Assessment 1

EXPORT A FORM TO EXCEL AND A REPORT TO WORD

1. Open **AL1-C8-WarrenLegal.accdb** from the AL1C8 folder on your storage medium and enable the contents.
2. Create a form named *Billing* using the Form Wizard with the following fields:

   From the Billing table: *BillingID*
   ClientID
   BillingDate
   Hours

   From the Rates table: *Rate*
3. When the form displays, close it.
4. Export the Billing form to an Excel worksheet.
5. Make the following changes to the Excel Billing worksheet:
   a. Select columns A through E and then adjust the column widths.
   b. Select cells A2 through B42 and then click the Center button in the Alignment group on the HOME tab.
   c. Save the Billing worksheet.
   d. Print and then close the Billing worksheet.
   e. Close Excel.
6. In Access, close the Export Wizard.
7. Create a report named *ClientBilling* using the Report Wizard (at the fifth wizard dialog box, change the layout to *Block*) with the following fields:

   From the Clients table: *FirstName*
   LastName

   From the Billing table: *BillingDate*
   Hours

   From the Rates table: *Rate*
8. Close the report.
9. Create a Word document with the ClientBilling report and save it to the AL1C8 folder on your storage medium with the default name. In the Word document, make the following changes:
   a. Press Ctrl + A to select the entire document, change the font color to Black, and then deselect the text.
   b. Insert a space between *Client* and *Billing* in the title.
   c. Position the insertion point immediately right of the word *Billing*, press the spacebar, and then type **of Legal Services**.
10. Save and then print **ClientBilling.rtf**.
11. Close the document and then close Word.
12. In Access, close the wizard dialog box.

Assessment 2

MERGE TABLE AND QUERY DATA WITH A WORD DOCUMENT

1. With **AL1-C8-WarrenLegal.accdb** open, merge data in the Clients table to a new Word document using the Word Merge button.
2. Maximize the Word document, close the Mail Merge task pane, and then compose a letter with the following elements:
   a. Click the HOME tab and then click the *No Spacing* style option in the Styles group.
   b. Press Enter six times, type the current date, and then press Enter four times.
   c. Click the MAILINGS tab and then insert the «*AddressBlock*» composite field.
   d. Press Enter twice and then type the salutation **Ladies and Gentlemen:**.
   e. Press Enter twice and then type the following text (press Enter twice after typing the first paragraph of text):

      The last time you visited our offices, you may have noticed how crowded we were. To alleviate the overcrowding, we are leasing new offices in the Meridian Building and will be moving in at the beginning of next month.

      Stop by and see our new offices at our open house planned for the second Friday of next month. Drop by any time between 2:00 and 5:30 p.m. We look forward to seeing you.

   f. After typing the second paragraph, press Enter twice, type **Sincerely,**, and then press Enter four times. Type **Marjorie Shaw**, press the Enter key, and then type **Senior Partner**. Press Enter twice, type your initials, press Enter, and then type **AL1-C8-WLLtrs.docx**.
3. Merge to a new document and then save the document with the name **AL1-C8-WLLtrs**.
4. Print only the first two letters in the document and then close **AL1-C8-WLLtrs.docx**.
5. Save the main document and name it **AL1-C8-WLLtrMD1**. Close the document and then close Word.
6. With **AL1-C8-WarrenLegal.accdb** open, extract the records from the Clients table of those clients located in Kent and then name the query *ClientsKentQuery*. (Include all of the fields from the table in the query.)
7. Merge the ClientsKentQuery to a new Word document using the Word Merge button.
8. Maximize the Word document, close the Mail Merge task pane, and then compose a letter with the following elements:
   a. Click the HOME tab and then click the *No Spacing* style option in the Styles group.
   b. Press Enter six times, type the current date, and then press Enter four times.
   c. Click the MAILINGS tab and then insert the «*AddressBlock*» composite field.
   d. Insert a proper salutation (refer to step 2d).

e. Compose a letter to clients that includes the following information:

    The City of Kent Municipal Court has moved from 1024 Meeker Street to a new building located at 3201 James Avenue. All court hearings after the end of this month will be held at the new address. If you need directions to the new building, please call our office.

f. Include an appropriate complimentary close for the letter (refer to Step 2f). Use the name *Thomas Zeiger* and the title *Attorney* in the complimentary close and add your reference initials and the document name (**AL1-C8-WLKentLtrs.docx**).

9. Merge the letter to a new document and then save the document with the name **AL1-C8-WLKentLtrs**.
10. Print only the first two letters in the document and then close **AL1-C8-WLKentLtrs.docx**.
11. Save the main document and name it **AL1-C8-WLLtrMD2**, close the document, and then close Word.

Assessment 3

LINK AN EXCEL WORKBOOK

1. With **AL1-C8-WarrenLegal.accdb** open, link **AL1-C8-Cases.xlsx** into a new table named *Cases*.
2. Open the Cases table in Datasheet view.
3. Print and then close the Cases table.
4. Open Excel, open the **AL1-C8-Cases.xlsx** workbook and then add the following data in the specified cells:

    A8: 57-D
    B8: 130
    C8: 1,100

    A9: 42-A
    B9: 144
    C9: 3,250

    A10: 29-C
    B10: 125
    C10: 900

5. Apply the Accounting formatting with a dollar sign and no decimal places to cells C8, C9, and C10.
6. Save, print, and then close **AL1-C8-Cases.xlsx**.
7. Close Excel.
8. In Access, open the Cases table in Datasheet view. (Notice the changes you made in Excel are reflected in the table.)
9. Print and then close the Cases table.
10. Close **AL1-C8-WarrenLegal.accdb**.

Visual Benchmark Demonstrate Your Proficiency

CREATE A REPORT AND EXPORT THE REPORT TO WORD

1. Open **AL1-C8-Dearborn.accdb** and enable the contents.
2. Use the Report Wizard to create the report shown in Figure 8.3. (Use the Quotas table and Representatives table when creating the report and choose the *Block* layout at the fifth wizard dialog box.) Save the report and name it *RepQuotas* and then print the report.
3. Use the RepQuotas report and export it to Word (to your AL1C8 folder). Format the report in Word as shown in Figure 8.4. Print the Word document and then close Word.
4. In Access, close **AL1-C8-Dearborn.accdb**.

Figure 8.3 Visual Benchmark Report

RepQuotas

RepQuotas

Quota	RepName	Telephone
$100,000.00	Robin Rehberg	(317) 555-9812
	Andre Kulisek	(317) 555-2264
	Edward Harris	(317) 555-3894
	Cecilia Ortega	(317) 555-4810
$150,000.00	David DeBruler	(317) 555-8779
	Jaren Newman	(317) 555-6790
	Lee Hutchinson	(765) 555-4277
	Craig Johnson	(317) 555-4391
$200,000.00	Isabelle Marshall	(765) 555-8822
	Maureen Pascual	(317) 555-5513
	Linda Foster	(317) 555-2101
	Catherine Singleton	(317) 555-0172
$250,000.00	Kwan Im	(317) 555-8374
	William Ludlow	(317) 555-0991
	Lydia Alvarado	(765) 555-4996
$300,000.00	Gina Tapparo	(317) 555-0044

Figure 8.4 Visual Benchmark Word Document

Representatives Quotas

Quota	RepName	Telephone
$100,000.00	Robin Rehberg	(317) 555-9812
	Andre Kulisek	(317) 555-2264
	Edward Harris	(317) 555-3894
	Cecilia Ortega	(317) 555-4810
$150,000.00	David DeBruler	(317) 555-8779
	Jaren Newman	(317) 555-6790
	Lee Hutchinson	(765) 555-4277
	Craig Johnson	(317) 555-4391
$200,000.00	Isabelle Marshall	(765) 555-8822
	Maureen Pascual	(317) 555-5513
	Linda Foster	(317) 555-2101
	Catherine Singleton	(317) 555-0172
$250,000.00	Kwan Im	(317) 555-8374
	William Ludlow	(317) 555-0991
	Lydia Alvarado	(765) 555-4996
$300,000.00	Gina Tapparo	(317) 555-0044
	Alfred Silva	(317) 555-3211

Case Study Apply Your Skills

Part 1

As the office manager at Woodland Dermatology Center, you are responsible for managing the center database. In preparation for an upcoming meeting, open **AL1-C8-Woodland.accdb** and prepare the following with data in the database:

- Create a query that displays the patient identification number, first name, and last name; doctor last name; date of visit; and fee. Name the query *PatientBilling*.
- Export the PatientBilling query to an Excel worksheet. Apply formatting to enhance the appearance of the worksheet and then print the worksheet.
- Create mailing labels for the patients. ***Hint: Use the Labels button on the CREATE tab.***
- Export the patient labels to a Word (.rtf) document and then print the document.
- Import and link the **AL1-C8-Payroll.xlsx** Excel worksheet to a new table named *WeeklyPayroll*. Print the WeeklyPayroll table.

You have been given some updated information about the weekly payroll and need to make the following changes to the **AL1-C8-Payroll.xlsx** worksheet:

- Change the hours for Irene Vaughn to *30*
- Change the wage for Monica Saunders to *$10.50*
- Change the hours for Dale Jorgensen to *20*.

After making and saving the changes, open, print, and then close the WeeklyPayroll table.

Part 2

The center is expanding and will be offering cosmetic dermatology services at the beginning of next month to residents in the Altoona area. Design a query that extracts records of patients living in the city of Altoona and then merge the query with Word. At the Word document, write a letter describing the new services, which include microdermabrasion, chemical peels, laser resurfacing, sclerotherapy, and photorejuvenation, as well as an offer for a free facial and consultation. Insert the appropriate fields in the document and then complete the merge. Save the merged document and name it **AL1-C8-WLDLtr**. Print the first two letters of the document and then close the document. Close the main document without saving it and then close Word.

Part 3

The Woodland database contains critical information and you need to determine how often you should back up the database. (You learned how to back up a database in Chapter 7.) Use the Access Help files to learn more about the backup process and, more specifically, about guidelines for when to back up a database. Search the Access Help files using the phrase *backing up a database* and then read the hyperlinked article Protect your data with backup and restore processes. Since you are responsible for updating the clinic procedures manual, create a Word document that describes how often you think the Woodland database should be backed up and the rationale behind your backup plan. Include steps for creating a backup of the database. Save the completed document and name it **AL1-C8-CS-Manual**. Print and then close **AL1-C8-CS-Manual.docx**.

MICROSOFT® ACCESS® Performance Assessment

Note: Before beginning unit assessments, copy to your storage medium the AL1U2 subfolder from the AL1 folder on the CD that accompanies this textbook and then make AL1U2 the active folder.

Assessing Proficiency

In this unit, you have learned to create forms, reports, and mailing labels and filter data. You have also learned how to modify document properties, view object dependencies, and export, import, and link data between programs.

Assessment 1 Create Tables in a Clinic Database

1. Use Access to create a database for clients of a mental health clinic. Name the database **AL1-U2-LancasterClinic**. Create a table named *Clients* that includes the following fields. (You determine the field name, data type, field size, and description.)

   ClientNumber (primary key)
   ClientName
   StreetAddress
   City
   State
   ZipCode
   Telephone
   DateOfBirth
   DiagnosisID

2. After creating the table, switch to Datasheet view and then enter the following data in the appropriate fields:

   ClientNumber: 1831
   George Charoni
   3980 Broad Street
   Philadelphia, PA 19149
   (215) 555-3482
   DateOfBirth: 4/12/1961
   DiagnosisID: SC

   ClientNumber: 3219
   Marian Wilke
   12032 South 39th
   Jenkintown, PA 19209
   (215) 555-9083
   DateOfBirth: 10/23/1984
   DiagnosisID: OCD

ClientNumber: 2874
Arthur Shroeder
3618 Fourth Avenue
Philadelphia, PA 19176
(215) 555-8311
DateOfBirth: 3/23/1961
DiagnosisID: OCD

ClientNumber: 5831
Roshawn Collins
12110 52nd Court East
Cheltenham, PA 19210
(215) 555-4779
DateOfBirth: 11/3/1968
DiagnosisID: SC

ClientNumber: 4419
Lorena Hearron
3112 96th Street East
Philadelphia, PA 19132
(215) 555-3281
DateOfBirth: 7/2/1987
DiagnosisID: AD

ClientNumber: 1103
Raymond Mandato
631 Garden Boulevard
Jenkintown, PA 19209
(215) 555-0957
DateOfBirth: 9/20/1982
DiagnosisID: MDD

3. Automatically adjust the column widths.
4. Save, print, and then close the Clients table.
5. Create a table named *Diagnoses* that includes the following fields:

   DiagnosisID (primary key)
   Diagnosis

6. After creating the table, switch to Datasheet view and then enter the following data in the appropriate fields:

   DiagnosisID: AD
   Diagnosis: Adjustment Disorder

   DiagnosisID: MDD
   Diagnosis: Manic-Depressive Disorder

   DiagnosisID: OCD
   Diagnosis: Obsessive-Compulsive Disorder

   DiagnosisID: SC
   Diagnosis: Schizophrenia

7. Automatically adjust the column widths.
8. Save, print, and then close the Diagnoses table.
9. Create a table named *Fees* that includes the following fields. (You determine the field name, data type, field size, and description.)

   FeeCode (primary key)
   HourlyFee

10. After creating the table, switch to Datasheet view and then enter the following data in the appropriate fields:

FeeCode: A
HourlyFee: $75.00

FeeCode: B
HourlyFee: $80.00

FeeCode: C
HourlyFee: $85.00

FeeCode: D
HourlyFee: $90.00

FeeCode: E
HourlyFee: $95.00

FeeCode: F
HourlyFee: $100.00

FeeCode: G
HourlyFee: $105.00

FeeCode: H
HourlyFee: $110.00

11. Automatically adjust the column widths.
12. Save, print, and then close the Fees table.
13. Create a table named *Employees* that includes the following fields. (You determine the field name, data type, field size, and description.)

ProviderNumber (primary key)
ProviderName
Title
Extension

14. After creating the table, switch to Datasheet view and then enter the following data in the appropriate fields:

ProviderNumber: 29
ProviderName: James Schouten
Title: Psychologist
Extension: 399

ProviderNumber: 33
ProviderName: Janice Grisham
Title: Psychiatrist
Extension: 11

ProviderNumber: 15
ProviderName: Lynn Yee
Title: Child Psychologist
Extension: 102

ProviderNumber: 18
ProviderName: Craig Chilton
Title: Psychologist
Extension: 20

15. Automatically adjust the column widths.
16. Save, print, and then close the Employees table.
17. Create a table named *Billing* that includes the following fields. (You determine the field name, data type, field size, and description.)

BillingNumber (primary key; apply the AutoNumber data type)
ClientNumber
DateOfService (apply the Date/Time data type)
Insurer
ProviderNumber
Hours (Apply the Number data type, the *Field Size* option in the *Field Properties* section to *Double*, and the *Decimal Places* option in the *Field Properties* section in Design view to *1*. Two of the records will contain a number requiring this format.)
FeeCode

18. After creating the table, switch to Datasheet view and then enter the following data in the appropriate fields:

ClientNumber: 4419
DateOfService: 3/2/2015
Insurer: Health Plus
ProviderNumber: 15
Hours: 2
FeeCode: B

ClientNumber: 1831
DateOfService: 3/2/2015
Insurer: Self
ProviderNumber: 33
Hours: 1
FeeCode: H

ClientNumber: 3219
DateOfService: 3/3/2015
Insurer: Health Plus
ProviderNumber: 15
Hours: 1
FeeCode: D

ClientNumber: 5831
DateOfService: 3/3/2015
Insurer: Penn-State Health
ProviderNumber: 18
Hours: 2
FeeCode: C

ClientNumber: 4419
DateOfService: 3/4/2015
Insurer: Health Plus
ProviderNumber: 15
Hours: 1
FeeCode: A

ClientNumber: 1103
DateOfService: 3/4/2015
Insurer: Penn-State Health
ProviderNumber: 18
Hours: 0.5
FeeCode: A

ClientNumber: 1831
DateOfService: 3/5/2015
Insurer: Self
ProviderNumber: 33
Hours: 1
FeeCode: H

ClientNumber: 5831
DateOfService: 3/5/2015
Insurer: Penn-State Health
ProviderNumber: 18
Hours: 0.5
FeeCode: C

19. Automatically adjust the column widths.
20. Save, print in landscape orientation, and then close the Billing table.

Assessment 2 Relate Tables and Create Forms in a Clinic Database

1. With **AL1-U2-LancasterClinic.accdb** open, create the following one-to-many relationships and enforce referential integrity and cascade fields and records:
   a. *ClientNumber* in the Clients table is the "one" and *ClientNumber* in the Billing table is the "many."
   b. *DiagnosisID* in the Diagnoses table is the "one" and *DiagnosisID* in the Clients table is the "many."
   c. *ProviderNumber* in the Employees table is the "one" and *ProviderNumber* in the Billing table is the "many."
   d. *FeeCode* in the Fees table is the "one" and *FeeCode* in the Billing table is the "many."
2. Create a form with the data in the Clients table.

3. After creating the form, add the following record to the Clients form:

   ClientNumber: 1179
   Timothy Fierro
   1133 Tenth Southwest
   Philadelphia, PA 19178
   (215) 555-5594
   DateOfBirth: 12/7/1990
   DiagnosisID: AD

4. Save the form with the default name, print the form in landscape orientation, and then close the form.
5. Add the following records to the Billing table:

ClientNumber: 1179	*ClientNumber:* 1831
DateOfService: 3/6/2015	*DateOfService:* 3/6/2015
Insurer: Health Plus	*Insurer:* Self
ProviderNumber: 15	*ProviderNumber:* 33
Hours: 0.5	*Hours:* 1
FeeCode: C	FeeCode: H

6. Save and then print the Billing table in landscape orientation.
7. Close the Billing table.

Assessment 3 Create Forms Using the Form Wizard

1. With **AL1-U2-LancasterClinic.accdb** open, create a form with fields from related tables using the Form Wizard with the following specifications:
   a. At the first Form Wizard dialog box, insert the following fields in the *Selected Fields* list box:

      From the Clients table: *ClientNumber*
      DateOfBirth
      DiagnosisID
      From the Billing table: *Insurer*
      ProviderNumber

   b. Do not make any changes at the second Form Wizard dialog box.
   c. Do not make any changes at the third Form Wizard dialog box.
   d. At the fourth Form Wizard dialog box, type the name ProviderInformation in the *Form* text box.
2. When the first record displays, print the first record.
3. Close the form.

Assessment 4 Create Labels with the Label Wizard

1. With **AL1-U2-LancasterClinic.accdb** open, use the Label Wizard to create mailing labels with the client names and addresses and sort by zip code. Name the mailing label report **ClientMailingLabels**.
2. Print the mailing labels.
3. Close the mailing labels report.

Assessment 5 Filter Records in Tables

1. With **AL1-U2-LancasterClinic.accdb** open, open the Billing table and then filter the records to display the following records:
   a. Display only those records with the Health Plus insurer. Print the results in landscape orientation and then remove the filter.
   b. Display only those records with a client ID number of 4419. Print the results and then remove the filter.
2. Filter records by selection to display the following records:
   a. Display only those records with a fee code of C. Print the results and then remove the filter.
   b. Display only those records between the dates of 3/2/2015 and 3/4/2015. Print the results and then remove the filter.
3. Close the Billing table without saving the changes.
4. Open the Clients table and then use the *Filter By Form* option to display clients in Jenkintown or Cheltenham. Print the results and then remove the filter.
5. Close the Clients table without saving the changes.

Assessment 6 Export a Table to Excel

1. With **AL1-U2-LancasterClinic.accdb** open, export the Billing table to an Excel workbook to your AL1U2 folder.
2. Apply formatting to the cells in the Excel workbook to enhance the appearance of the data.
3. Change the page orientation to landscape.
4. Save, print, and then close the workbook.
5. Close Excel.

Assessment 7 Merge Records to Create Letters in Word

1. With **AL1-U2-LancasterClinic.accdb** open, merge data in the Clients table to a blank Word document. ***Hint: Use the Word Merge button in the Export group on the EXTERNAL DATA tab.*** You determine the fields to use in the inside address (you cannot use the *AddressBlock* field) and an appropriate salutation. Type March 12, 2015, as the date of the letter and type the following text in the body of the document:

   The building of a new wing for the Lancaster Clinic will begin April 1, 2015. We are excited about this new addition to our clinic. With the new facilities, we will be able to offer additional community and group services along with enhanced child-play therapy treatment.

   During the construction, the main entrance will be moved to the north end of the building. Please use this entrance until the construction of the wing is completed. We apologize in advance for any inconvenience this causes you.

   Include an appropriate complimentary close for the letter. Use the name and title *Marianne Lambert, Clinic Director* for the signature and add your reference initials and the document name (**AL1-U2-A7-LCLtrs.docx**).
2. Merge to a new document and then save the document with the name **AL1-U2-A7-LCLtrs**.

3. Print the first two letters of the document and then close **AL1-U2-A7-LCLtrs.docx**.
4. Save the main document as **AL1-U2-A7-ConstLtrMD** and then close the document.
5. Close Word.

Assessment 8 Import and Link Excel Data to an Access Table

1. With **AL1-U2-LancasterClinic.accdb** open, import and link **AL1-U2-StaffHours.xlsx** to a new table named *StaffHours*.
2. Open the StaffHours table in Datasheet view.
3. Print and then close the StaffHours table.
4. Open **AL1-U2-StaffHours.xlsx** in Excel.
5. Insert a formula in cell D2 that multiplies B2 with C2 and then copy the formula down to cells D3 through D7.
6. Save and then close **AL1-U2-StaffHours.xlsx**.
7. Close Excel.
8. In Access with **AL1-U2-LancasterClinic.accdb** open, open the StaffHours table.
9. Print and then close the StaffHours table.

Writing Activities

The following activities give you the opportunity to practice your writing skills while you demonstrate your understanding of some of the important Access features you have mastered in this unit. Use correct grammar, appropriate word choices, and clear sentence constructions.

Activity 1 Add a Table to the Clinic Database

The director at Lancaster Clinic has asked you to add information to **AL1-U2-LancasterClinic.accdb** on insurance companies contracted by the clinic. You need to create a table that will contain information on insurance companies. The director wants the table to include the insurance company name, address, city, state, and zip code, along with the telephone number and name of the representative. You determine the field names, data types, field sizes, and description for the table and then include the following information (in the appropriate fields):

Health Plus
4102 22nd Street
Philadelphia, PA 19166
(212) 555-0990
Representative: Byron Tolleson

Penn-State Health
5933 Lehigh Avenue
Philadelphia, PA 19148
(212) 555-3477
Representative: Tracey Pavone

Quality Medical
51 Cecil B. Moore Avenue
Philadelphia, PA 19168
(212) 555-4600
Representative: Lee Stafford

Delaware Health
4418 Front Street
Philadelphia, PA 19132
(212) 555-6770
Representative: Melanie Chon

Save the insurance company table, print it in landscape orientation, and then close the table. Open Word and then write a report to the clinic director detailing how you created the table. Include a title for the report, steps on how you created the table, and any other pertinent information. Save the completed report and name it **AL1-U2-Act1-LCRpt**. Print and then close **AL1-U2-Act1-LCRpt.docx**.

Activity 2 Merge Records to Create Letters to Insurance Companies

Merge data in the insurance company database to a blank Word document. You determine the fields to use in the inside address (you cannot use the Address Block button) and an appropriate salutation. Compose a letter to the insurance companies informing them that Lancaster Clinic is providing mental health counseling services to people who have health insurance through their employers. You are sending an informational brochure about Lancaster Clinic and are requesting information from the insurance companies on services and service limitations. Include an appropriate complimentary close for the letter. Use the name and title *Marianne Lambert, Clinic Director* for the signature and add your reference initials. When the merge is completed, name the document containing the merged letters **AL1-U2-Act2-LCIns**. Print the first two letters in the merged document and then close **AL1-U2-Act2-LCIns.docx**. Close the main document without saving it and then close Word. Close **AL1-U2-LancasterClinic.accdb**.

Internet Research

Health Information Search

In this activity, you will search the Internet for information on a health concern or disease that interests you. You will be looking for specific organizations, interest groups, or individuals who are somehow connected to the topic you have chosen. You may find information about an organization that raises money to support research, a support group that posts information or answers questions, or clinics or doctors that specialize in your topic. Try to find at least 10 different organizations, groups, or individuals that support the health concern you are researching.

Create a database in Access and then create a table that includes information from your research. Design the table so that you can store the name, address, phone number, and web address of each organization, group, or individual you find. Also identify the connection the organization, group, or individual has to your topic (supports research, interest group, treats patients, etc.). Create a report to summarize your findings. In Microsoft Word, create a letter that you can use to write for further information about the organization. Use the names and addresses in your database to merge with the letter. Select and then print the first two letters that result from the merge. Finally, write a paragraph describing information you learned about the health concern that you previously did not know.

Job Study

City Improvement Projects

In this activity, you will work with the city council in your area to keep the public informed of the progress being made on improvement projects throughout the city. These projects are paid for through tax dollars voted on by the public, and the city council feels that keeping area residents informed will lead to good voter turnout when it is time to make more improvements.

Your job is to create a database and table in the database that will store the following information for each project: a project ID number, a description of the project, the budgeted dollar amount to be spent, the amount of money spent so far, the amount of time allocated to the project, and the amount of time spent so far. Enter five city improvement projects into the table (using sample data created by you). Create a query based on the table that calculates the percentage of budgeted dollars spent so far and the percentage of budgeted time spent so far. Print the table and the query.

Index

A

Access
- exporting object to PDF or XPS file, 304
- merging data in Word document, 300–301
- opening, 5–6

Add a group button, 244
Add a sort button, 245
Add Existing Fields button, 207
adding, records to form, 189–190
Address Block button, 301
Advanced button, 272
aggregate function, designing queries with, 109–112
Align Left button, 148
Align Right button, 148
Alternate Row Color button, 148
And criteria, queries designed with, 96–100
Ascending button, 147, 189, 236
Attachment data type, 134
AutoNumber data type, 134
AutoNumber field, 23, 47
- changing, 29

B

Background button, 241
Background Color button, 148
Background Image button, 202
backing up database, 282–283
Backstage view, getting help in, 159–160
Back Up Database option, 282
Bold button, 148
Build button, 137
Builder button, 107

C

Calculated data type, 134
Caption text box, 27
Cascade Update Related Fields, 52, 60
Center button, 148
Clear All button, 308
Close button, 8
Close Print button, 18
closing
- database, 8–10
- objects, 8–10

collapse indicator, 65
Colors button, 193
columns. *See also* fields
- hiding, unhiding, freezing and unfreezing, 15–17
- width changes, 15–17

compacting, database, 276–278
Compact & Repair Database button, 276
conditional formatting, 203–207
Conditional Formatting button, 203–204
Control Margins button, 198
control objects
- arranging in form, 198–201
- defined, 192
- deleting, 193–194
- inserting, 194
- modifying
  - in forms, 193–194
  - in reports, 235–236
- moving form table, 197

Control Padding button, 198
Copy button, 308
Create button, 5
CREATE tab, 82, 186
criterion
- criteria examples, 85
- establishing query criteria, 84–85
- queries with *Or* and *And* criteria, 96–100

crosstab query, 112–115
Crosstab Query Wizard, 113
Currency data type, 24, 134
Current Record box, 11
customizing
- database properties, 278–280
- forms, 192–210
- reports
  - layout view, 240–244
  - in print preview, 236

D

data
- collecting data in Word and pasting in Access table, 309–310
- exporting
  - to Excel, 295–298
  - to Word, 298–300
- filtering
  - by Filter button, 265–266
  - by *Filter By Form* button, 272–273
  - in query and report, 268–270
  - records in table, form and report, 267–268
  - removing a filter, 266
  - by selection, 270–272
  - by shortcut menu, 271
  - on specific values, 268
- finding and replacing, 154–157
- formatting in table data, 148–149
- grouping and sorting in reports, 244–247
- importing into new table, 305–306
- inserting in form header, 193
- linking, to Excel worksheet, 307–308
- merging
  - Access data with Word document, 300–301
  - query data with Word document, 301–303
- reports, finding in, 237–240
- sorting in records, 147

database
- backing up, 282–283
- closing, 8–10
- compacting and repairing, 276–278
- creating new database, 5
- defined, 5
- design principles for, 22–23
- encrypting with password, 277
- naming, 5

opening, 6
pinning to Recent list, 7–8
relational, 22
saving, 6, 281–283
viewing and customizing database properties, 278–280
viewing object dependencies, 274–275
Database Password dialog box, 277
DATABASE TOOLS tab, 274
Datasheet view, 11
creating split forms and, 210–211
creating tables in, 23–32
assigning default value, 29
assigning field size, 29
changing AutoNumber field, 29
data types, 23–25
defining the table structure, 23
inserting field name, caption, description, 27–28
inserting Quick Start fields, 28–29
renaming field heading, 27
formatting data in table, 148–149
formatting table data in, 148–152
data types, 23–24, 134
Date and Time button, 193
Date Filters, 268
Date & Time data type, 24, 134
Decrypt Database button, 277
default value, assigning, 29, 136–137
Default Value button, 29
defining the table structure, 23
Delete button, 11, 189, 236
Delete Rows button, 143
deleting
control object, 193–194
fields, 13–15
in Design View, 142–147
forms, 187–188
query, 95
records, 11–13
in forms, 189–190
in related tables, 60–61
relationships, 56
report, 236
table, 17
Descending button, 147, 189, 236
Description text box, 27
Design view, 186
creating tables in, 132–136
assigning default value, 136–137
inserting, moving and deleting fields, 142–147
inserting Total row, 143
overview, 132–136
using Input Mask, 137–138
using Lookup Wizard, 141–142
validating field entries, 141
determining primary key, 47
displaying table in, 47
Properties table in, 132–133
Detail section, 187, 192, 234, 235
dialog box, getting help in, 159–160

E

editing, relationships, 56–59
Edition Relationships button, 56
Edit Relationships dialog box, 50–51
Enable Content button, 8
encrypting database with password, 277
Encrypt with Password button, 277
Enforce Referential Integrity, 50, 52, 60
Enter Fields Properties dialog box, 27
entity integrity, 47
Excel button, 295, 307
Excel worksheet
exporting data to, 295–298
Word document, 298–300
linking data to, 307–308
expand indicator, 64–65
exporting
Access object to PDF or XPS file, 304
data to Excel document, 295–298
data to Word document, 298–300
Expression Builder dialog box, 107
EXTERNAL DATA tab, 295, 298

F

Field List task pane, 207–208
field names, 10
inserting, 27–28
renaming, 27
fields
assigning default value, 29
assigning size, 29
calculated field, 107–108
creating, in Design view, 132–133
data types, 23–25
defined, 23
deleting, 13–15
in Design View, 142–147
filtering on specific field, 268–270
inserting, 13–15
in Design View, 142–147
in forms, 207–210
name, caption and description, 27–28
in query design grid, 83–84
Quick Start fields, 28–29
moving, 13–15
in Design View, 142–147
primary key field, 46–49
in query
arranging, 92
showing/hiding, 92
sorting, 92–94

validating entries, 141
file management system, 45
FILE tab, 7
filter
defined, 265
removing, 266
Filter button, 265–266
Filter by Form option, 272–273
filtering
by Filter button, 265–266
by *Filter By Form* button, 272–273
in query and report, 268–270
records in table, form and report, 267–268
by selection, 270–272
by shortcut menu, 271
on specific values, 268
find and replace, data, 154–157
Find and Replace dialog box, 154
Find button, 154, 237
Find dialog box, 237
find duplicate query, 115–118
Find Duplicates Query Wizard, 115
finding, data in report, 237–240
find unmatched query, 118–119
Find Unmatched Query Wizard, 118
First record button, 11, 187
flat file database, 45
folder, pinning to Recent list, 7–8
Font Color button, 148
Fonts button, 193
foreign key field, 46, 48
formatting
forms, 201–207
conditional, 203–207
report, 240–244
table data, 148–149
Form button, creating form with, 186–188
Form Header section, 193
FORM LAYOUT TOOLS ARRANGE tab, 198
FORM LAYOUT TOOLS DESIGN tab, 186, 192, 193
FORM LAYOUT TOOLS FORMAT tab, 201, 203
forms, 183–217
changing views, 186
creating
Form button, 186, 188
Form Wizard, 214–217
Multiple Items button, 213
with related tables, 190–192
Split Form button, 210–213
customizing, 192–210
adding existing fields, 207–210
applying themes, 193
arranging objects, 198–201
inserting control, 194
inserting data in form header, 193
modifying control object, 193–194
moving form table, 197
as database object, 8
defined, 186
deleting, 187–188
description of, 8
filtering records in, 267–268
formatting, 201–207
conditional formatting, 203–207
navigating in, 187
printing, 186–187
records
adding and deleting, 189–190
sorting, 189
form table, 187
Form view, 186
Form Wizard, creating forms using, 214–216
Form Wizard button, 214
freezing, columns, 15–17

G

Gridlines button, 148
Group, Sort, and Total pane, 244–245
grouping records
in reports, 244–247
using aggregate functions and, 111–112
Group & Sort button, 244

H

Header/Footer group, 193
Header section, 187, 192, 234, 235
Help button, 157
Help feature, 157–160
on button, 157–159
in dialog box or backstage area, 159–160
Hide All hyperlink, 157
hiding
columns, 15–17
fields in query, 92
HOME tab, 148
horizontal scroll bar, 10
Hyperlink data type, 134

I

ID field, 47
importing, data into new table, 305–306
Import Wizard, 305
Info backstage are, using options at, 276–280
Input Mask field property, 137–138
Input Mask Wizard, 137–140
Insert Above button, 198
Insert Below button, 198
inserting
control in form, 194
data in form header, 193
field name, caption and description, 27–28
fields, 13–15
in Design View, 142–147
records, 11–13
in related tables, 60–61

Insert Row button, 142
Insert Subdatasheet dialog box, 65
Italic button, 148

J

join, 50
join lines, 22, 51

K

keyboard shortcuts
- close object, 9
- closing database, 8
- navigate in form, 187
- Open backstage area, 6
- opening/closing Navigation pane, 9
- Zoom box, 88

L

label control object, 193, 194
Labels button, 252
Label Wizard dialog box, 252–254
Landscape button, 19
landscape orientation, 19
Last record button, 11, 187
Layout view, 186
- creating split forms and, 210–211

linking data, to Excel worksheet, 307–308
live preview feature, 193
Logo button, 193
Long Text data type, 134
Lookup Wizard, using, 141–142, 144–145
Lookup Wizard data type, 134
Lookup Wizard dialog box, 142

M

mailing labels, preparing, 252–255
margins, changing, 18
Margins button, 18
Merge button, 198
merging
- Access data with Word document, 300–301
- query data with Word document, 301–303

message bar, 7
modifying
- control objects in reports, 235–236
- queries, 95–96, 104–106
- record source in report, 234

More button, 15, 298
More Fields button, 24
More Forms button, 210
Move Down button, 198
Move Up button, 198
moving, fields, 13–15
- in Design View, 142–147

Multiple Item forms, 213

N

Name & Caption button, 27
Name text box, 27
navigating, in form, 187
Navigation pane, 7, 8
- controlling what displays in, 8–9
- opening/closing keyboard shortcut, 9

New button, 11
New Formatting Rule dialog box, 203–204
New (blank) record button, 11, 189
Next record button, 11, 187
Number data type, 24, 134
Number Filters, 268

O

Object button, 201
Object Dependencies task pane, 274–275
objects
- arranging in form, 198–201
- closing, 8–10
- exporting to PDF or XPS file, 304
- opening, 8–10
- saving in PDF or XPS file format, 281–282
- types of, 8
- viewing object dependencies, 274–275

object tab, 10
Office Clipboard, using, 308–310
OLE Object data type, 134
one-to-many relationships
- creating, 62–64
- relating tables in, 50–52

one-to-one relationships, creating, 61–64
opening
- database, 6
- objects, 8–10

Or criteria, queries designed with, 96–100
orientation
- landscape, 19
- portrait, 17, 19

P

page layout, changing, 19–21
Page Setup button, 19
Page Setup dialog box, 19
page size, changing, 18
password, encrypting database with, 277
paste data, 308–310
PDF file format
- exporting Access object to, 304
- saving object as, 281–282

pinning, database file or folder to, 7–8
portrait orientation, 17, 19
Previous record button, 11, 187
primary key, 22
- defining, 46–49

Primary Key button, 47
primary key field, defining, 46–49
primary table, 50
Print Backstage area, 17
Print button, 18

printing
forms, 186–187
relationships, 53
specific records, 147
tables, 17–21
changing page layout, 19–21
changing page size and margins, 18
previewing, 18
Print Preview, displaying and customizing report in, 236
Print Preview button, 18, 236
Properties dialog box, 278–279

Q

query
crosstab query, 112–115
as database object, 8
defined, 82
deleting, 95
description of, 8
designing, 82–100
with aggregate function, 107–112
arranging fields in, 92
establishing query criteria, 84–85
with *Or* and *And* criteria, 96–100
overview, 82–84
showing/hiding fields in, 92
sorting fields in, 92–94
exporting, to Excel, 296–298
filtering records in, 268–270
find duplicate query, 115–118
find unmatched query, 118–119
inserting calculated fields, 107–108
merging query data with Word document, 301–303
modifying, 95–96
performing
on related tables, 89–91
with Simple Query Wizard, 100–106
on tables, 85–88
renaming, 95
Query Design button, 82
Query Wizard button, 100
Quick Access toolbar, 6–7
Quick Print button, 17
Quick Start fields, 28–29

R

Recent list
opening database from, 6
pinning database file or folder to, 7–8
Record Navigation bar, 10, 187, 189
buttons on, 11
records
collapse indicator, 65
defined, 23
deleting, 11–13
in related tables, 60–61
displaying related records in subdatasheets, 64–67
expand indicator, 64–65
forms
adding and deleting, 189–190
sorting, 189
inserting, 11–13
in related tables, 60–61
modifying record source in report, 234
printing specific, 147
in reports
grouping and sorting, 244–247
sorting, 236
sorting data in, 147
record selector bar, 10
referential integrity
defined, 50
specifying, 52
related tables
creating, 45–61
defining primary key, 46–49
deleting records in, 60–61
deleting relationship, 56
determining relationships, 46
displaying related records in subdatasheets, 64–67
editing relationship, 56–59
inserting records in, 60–61
one-to-many relationships, 50–52, 62–64
one-to-one relationships, 61–64
printing relationships, 53
showing tables, 56
specifying referential integrity, 52
creating form with, 190–192
defined, 50
performing queries on, 89–91
relational database, 22
relational database management system, 45–46
Relationship Report button, 53
relationships
creating
one-to-many relationships, 50–52, 62–64
one-to-one, 61–64
between tables, 45–61
defined, 22
deleting, 56
determining, 46
editing, 56–59
printing, 53
Relationships button, 50
renaming, table, 17
repairing, database, 276–278
Replace button, 154
Report button, creating report with, 233–235
REPORT LAYOUT TOOLS ARRANGE tab, 240
REPORT LAYOUT TOOLS DESIGN tab, 233–234, 240
REPORT LAYOUT TOOLS FORMAT tab, 240
REPORT LAYOUT TOOLS PAGE SETUP tab, 241
reports, 229–252
creating
with fields from multiple tables, 251–252

with Report button, 233–235
with Report Wizard, 248–252
customizing, 240–244
as database object, 8
deleting, 236
description of, 8
displaying and customizing, in print preview, 236
filtering records in, 267–268, 268–270
finding data in, 237–240
formatting, 240–244
grouping and sorting records, 244–247
modifying control objects, 235–236
modifying record source, 234
purpose of, 233
sorting records, 236
Report Wizard, creating report with, 248–252
Report Wizard dialog box, 248–250
ribbon, 7
Run button, 83

S

Save As option, 281, 282
saving
database, 6, 281–283
object in PDF or XPS file format, 281–282
security message warning bar, 8
Select All button, 201
Select button, 194
Select Column button, 198
selection, filtering by, 270–272
Selection button, 270
Select Row button, 198
shortcut menu, filtering by, 271
Short Text button, 28
Short Text data type, 24, 134
Show All hyperlink, 157
showing, fields in query, 92
Show Table button, 56
Show Table dialog box, 56, 83
Shutter Bar Open/Close button, 9
Simple Query Wizard, performing queries with, 100–106
Simple Query Wizard dialog box, 100–101
Size button, 18
sorting
data in records, 147
fields in query, 92–94
records in forms, 189
records in reports, 236, 244–247
Spelling button, 152
spelling check feature, 152–153
Spelling dialog box, 152
split form, creating, 210–213
Split Horizontally button, 198
Split Vertically button, 198
Status bar, 7
subdatasheet
defined, 64
displaying related records in, 64–67
synchronous, 210

T

Table button, 23, 132
table move handle, 187, 197, 234, 235, 240
tables
collecting data in Word and pasting in, 309–310
columns
hiding, unhiding, freezing and unfreezing, 15–17
width changes, 15–17
creating in Datasheet view, 23–32
assigning default value, 29
assigning field size, 29
changing AutoNumber field, 29
data types, 23–25
defining the table structure, 23
inserting field name, caption, description, 27–28
inserting Quick Start fields, 28–29
renaming field heading, 27
creating in Design View, 132–147
assigning default value, 136–137
inserting, moving and deleting fields, 142–147
inserting Total row, 143
overview, 132–136
using Input Mask, 137–138
using Lookup Wizard, 141–142
validating field entries, 141
database design principles, 22–23
as database object, 8
defined, 23
deleting, 17
description of, 8
exporting, to Excel, 296–298
fields
deleting, 13–15
inserting, 13–15
moving, 13–15
filtering records in, 267–268
finding and replacing data in, 154–157
formatting data in, 148–152
importing data into new, 305–306
linking Excel worksheet to, 307–308
performing queries on, 85–88
primary table, 50
printing, 17–21
changing page layout, 19–21

changing page size and margins, 18
previewing, 18
records
deleting, 11–13
inserting, 11–13
related tables
creating, 45–61
creating form with, 190–192
defined, 50
renaming, 17
showing, 56
spell checking, 152–153
TABLE TOOLS DESIGN tab, 142
TABLE TOOLS FIELDS tab, 27, 28
tabs, 7
Text Box button, 194
text box control object, 193, 194
Text Filter option, 268
Text Formatting buttons, 148
Theme button, 193
themes, applying to forms, 193
Title bar, 7
Title button, 193
Toggle Filter button, 266
Total row, inserting, 143
Totals button, 109, 143, 240

U

Underline button, 148
unfreezing, columns, 15–17
unhiding, columns, 15–17

V

Validation Rule property box, 141
View button, 132, 186, 236
viewing, database properties, 278–280

W

wildcard character, 84
Word document
collecting data in, and pasting in Access table, 309–310
exporting data to, 298–300
merging Access data with, 300–301
merging query data with, 301–303
Word Merge button, 300
Work area, 7

X

XPS file format
exporting Access object to, 304
saving object as, 281–282

Y

Yes/No data type, 24, 134

Z

Zoom box, 88

MICROSOFT®

POWERPOINT®

Unit 1 ■ Creating and Formatting PowerPoint Presentations

Chapter 1 ■ Preparing a PowerPoint Presentation

Chapter 2 ■ Modifying a Presentation and Using Help

Chapter 3 ■ Formatting Slides

Chapter 4 ■ Inserting Elements in Slides

MICROSOFT® POWERPOINT®

Preparing a PowerPoint Presentation

PERFORMANCE OBJECTIVES

Upon successful completion of Chapter 1, you will be able to:

- **Open, save, run, print, close, and delete a presentation**
- **Pin a presentation to a recent list**
- **Plan a presentation**
- **Create a presentation using a theme template**
- **Insert slides, insert text in slides, and choose slide layouts**
- **Change presentation views**
- **Navigate and edit slides**
- **Preview and print a presentation**
- **Apply a design theme and variant to a presentation**
- **Prepare a presentation from a blank presentation**
- **Prepare a presentation in Outline view**
- **Add transitions, sounds, and timings to a presentation**

Tutorials

1.1 Opening, Running, and Closing a Presentation

1.2 Creating and Saving a Presentation

1.3 Navigating and Inserting Slides in a Presentation

1.4 Changing Views and Slide Layout

1.5 Previewing Slides and Printing a Presentation

1.6 Running a Presentation

1.7 Adding Transition and Sound

During a presentation, the person doing the presenting may use visual aids to strengthen the impact of the message as well as help organize the presented information. Visual aids may include transparencies, slides, photographs, or an on-screen presentation. With Microsoft's PowerPoint program, you can easily create visual aids for a presentation and then print copies of the aids as well as run the presentation. PowerPoint is a presentation graphics program that you can use to organize and present information. Model answers for this chapter's projects appear on the following page.

PC1

Note: Before beginning the projects, copy to your storage medium the PC1 subfolder from the PowerPoint folder on the CD that accompanies this textbook. Steps on how to copy a folder are presented on the inside of the back cover of this textbook. Do this every time you start a chapter's projects.

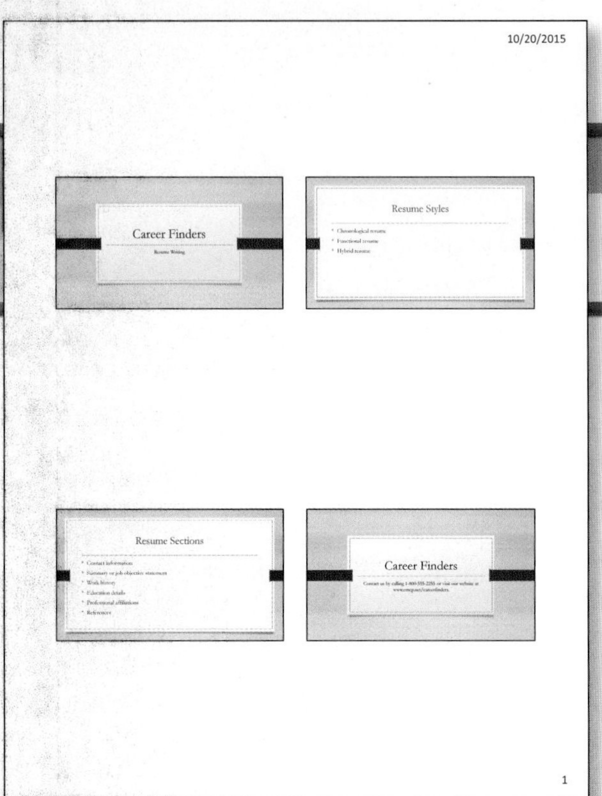

Project 2 Create an Internet Presentation Using a Theme Template
P-C1-P2-Resumes.pptx

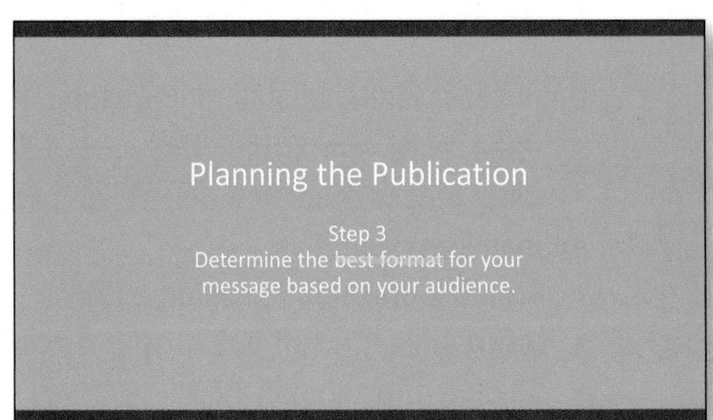

Project 3 Create a Planning Presentation from an Existing Presentation
P-C1-P3-PlanningPres-Ink.pptx

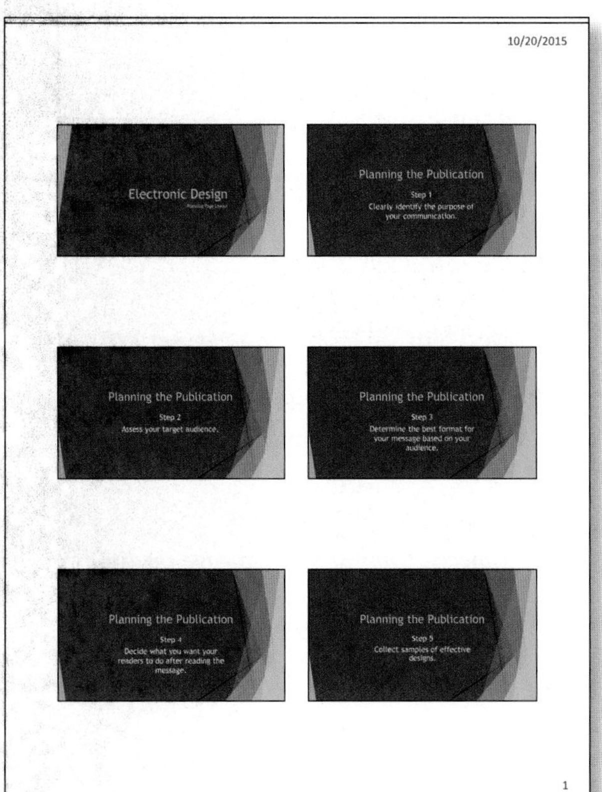

P-C1-P3-PlanningPres.pptx

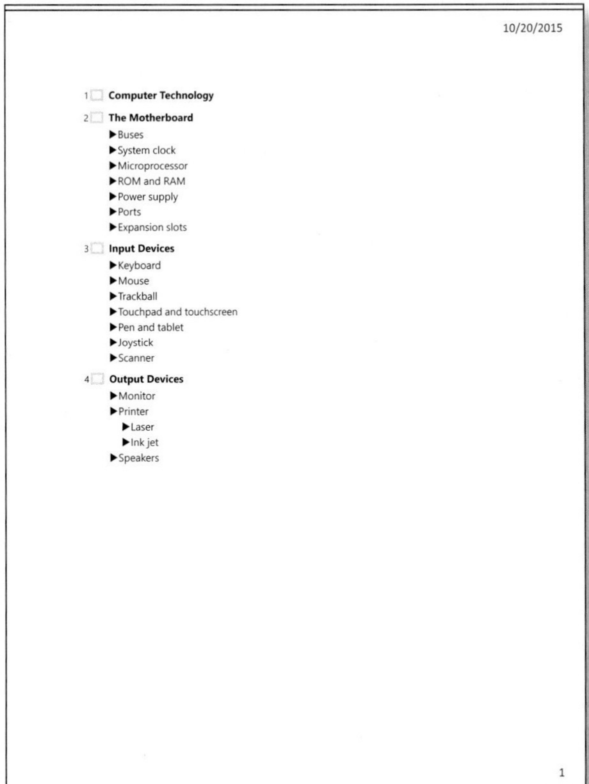
10/20/2015

1 **Computer Technology**

2 **The Motherboard**
- Buses
- System clock
- Microprocessor
- ROM and RAM
- Power supply
- Ports
- Expansion slots

3 **Input Devices**
- Keyboard
- Mouse
- Trackball
- Touchpad and touchscreen
- Pen and tablet
- Joystick
- Scanner

4 **Output Devices**
- Monitor
- Printer
  - Laser
  - Ink jet
- Speakers

1

Project 4 Create a Technology Presentation in Outline View
P-C1-P4-Computers.pptx

Model Answers

Project 1 Open and Run a Presentation — 1 Part

You will open a presentation, run the presentation, and then close the presentation.

Creating a PowerPoint Presentation

PowerPoint provides several methods for creating a presentation. You can create a presentation using a theme template or starting with a blank slide. The steps you follow to create a presentation will vary depending on the method you choose, but will often follow these basic steps:

1. Open PowerPoint.
2. Choose the desired theme template or start with a blank presentation.
3. Type the text for each slide, adding additional elements, such as graphic images, as needed.
4. If necessary, apply a design theme.
5. Save the presentation.
6. Print the presentation as slides, handouts, notes pages, or an outline.
7. Run the presentation.
8. Close the presentation.
9. Close PowerPoint.

After you choose the specific type of presentation you want to create, you are presented with the PowerPoint window in the Normal view. What displays in the window will vary depending on the type of presentation you are creating. However, the PowerPoint window contains some consistent elements, as shown in Figure 1.1 on the next page. The PowerPoint window contains many elements similar to those in other Microsoft Office programs such as Word and Excel. For example, the PowerPoint window, like the Word window, contains a FILE tab, Quick Access toolbar, tabs, ribbon, vertical and horizontal scroll bars, and Status bar. The PowerPoint window elements are described in Table 1.1 on the next page.

PowerPoint, like other Microsoft Office programs, provides enhanced ScreenTips for buttons and options. Hover the mouse pointer over a button or option and, after approximately one second, an enhanced ScreenTip will display near the button or option. The enhanced ScreenTip displays the name of the button or option, any shortcut command if one is available, and a description of the button or option.

Figure 1.1 PowerPoint Window

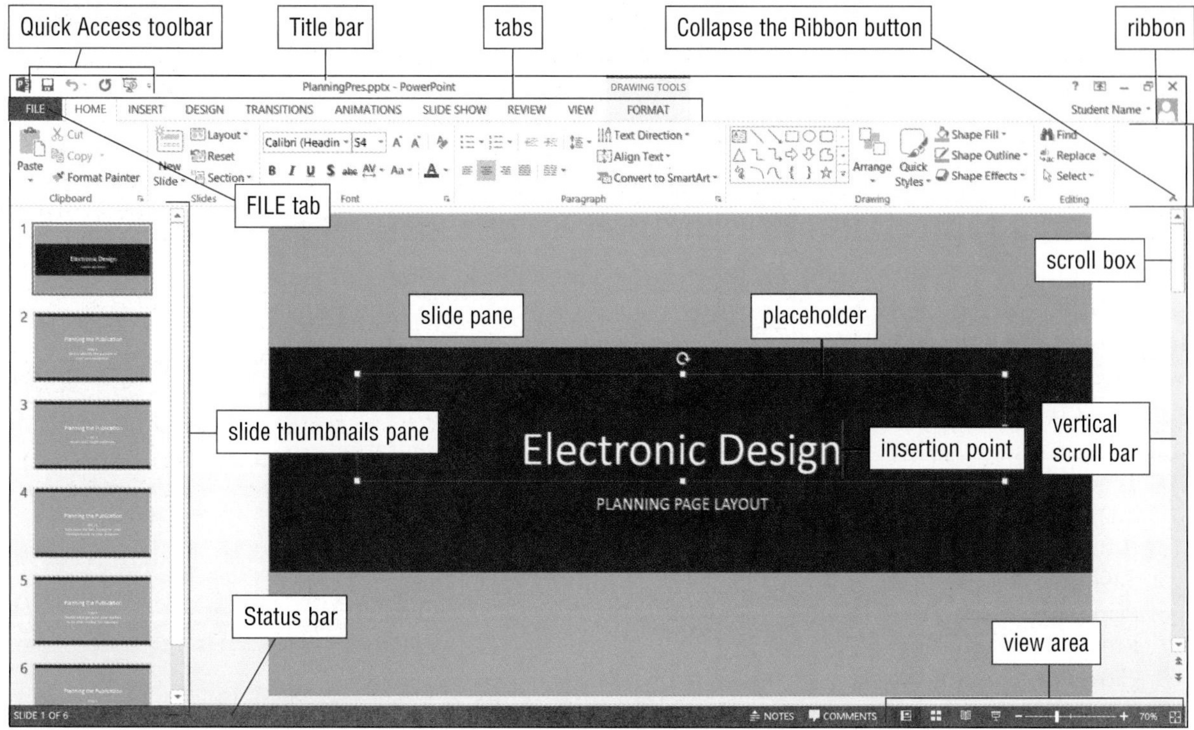

Table 1.1 PowerPoint Window Elements

Feature	*Description*
Collapse the Ribbon button	When clicked, removes the ribbon from the screen.
FILE tab	Click the FILE tab and the backstage area displays containing options for working with and managing presentations.
horizontal scroll bar	Shift text left or right in the slide pane.
I-beam pointer	Used to move the insertion point or to select text.
insertion point	Indicates the location of the next character entered at the keyboard.
placeholder	Location on a slide that holds text or objects.
Quick Access toolbar	Contains buttons for commonly used commands.
ribbon	Area containing the tabs and commands divided into groups.
slide pane	Displays the slide and slide contents.
slide thumbnails pane	The left side of the screen that displays slide thumbnails.
Status bar	Displays the slide number and number of slides, buttons for inserting notes and comments, view buttons, and the Zoom slider bar.
tabs	Contain commands and features organized into groups.
Title bar	Displays presentation name followed by the program name.
vertical scroll bar	Display specific slides using this scroll bar.
view area	Located toward the right side of the Status bar and contains buttons for changing the presentation view.

Opening a Presentation

When you create, save, and then close a presentation, you can open the presentation at the Open dialog box. To display this dialog box, click the FILE tab and then click the *Open* option. This displays the Open backstage area, as shown in Figure 1.2. You can also display the Open backstage area by clicking the Open Other Presentations hyperlink that displays in the lower left corner of the PowerPoint 2013 opening screen or with the keyboard shortcut Ctrl + O. Another method for displaying the Open backstage area is to insert an Open button on the Quick Access toolbar and then click the button.

At the Open backstage area, click the desired location, such as your OneDrive or the *Computer* option, and then click the Browse button. (If you are opening a presentation from your computer's hard drive or removable drive, you can double-click the *Computer* option.) When you click the Browse button (or double-click the *Computer* option), the Open dialog box displays. At this dialog box, open a presentation by double-clicking the presentation name in the Content pane. You can go directly to the Open dialog box without displaying the Open backstage area by pressing the keyboard shortcut Ctrl + F12.

At the Open backstage area with your OneDrive or the *Computer* option selected, the most recently accessed folder names display in the Recent Folders list. If you open PowerPoint and then access a presentation from a particular folder, that folder name will display above the Recent Folders list below the heading *Current Folder* at the Open backstage area with your OneDrive or the *Computer* option selected. Click the folder name in the Current Folder list or Recent Folders list if you want to open a presentation from the folder.

Quick Steps

Open a Presentation
1. Click FILE tab.
2. Click *Open* option.
3. Click desired location.
4. Click Browse button.
5. Navigate to desired folder or drive.
6. Double-click presentation.

Press Ctrl + F12 to display the Open dialog box without displaying the Open backstage area.

Figure 1.2 Open Backstage Area

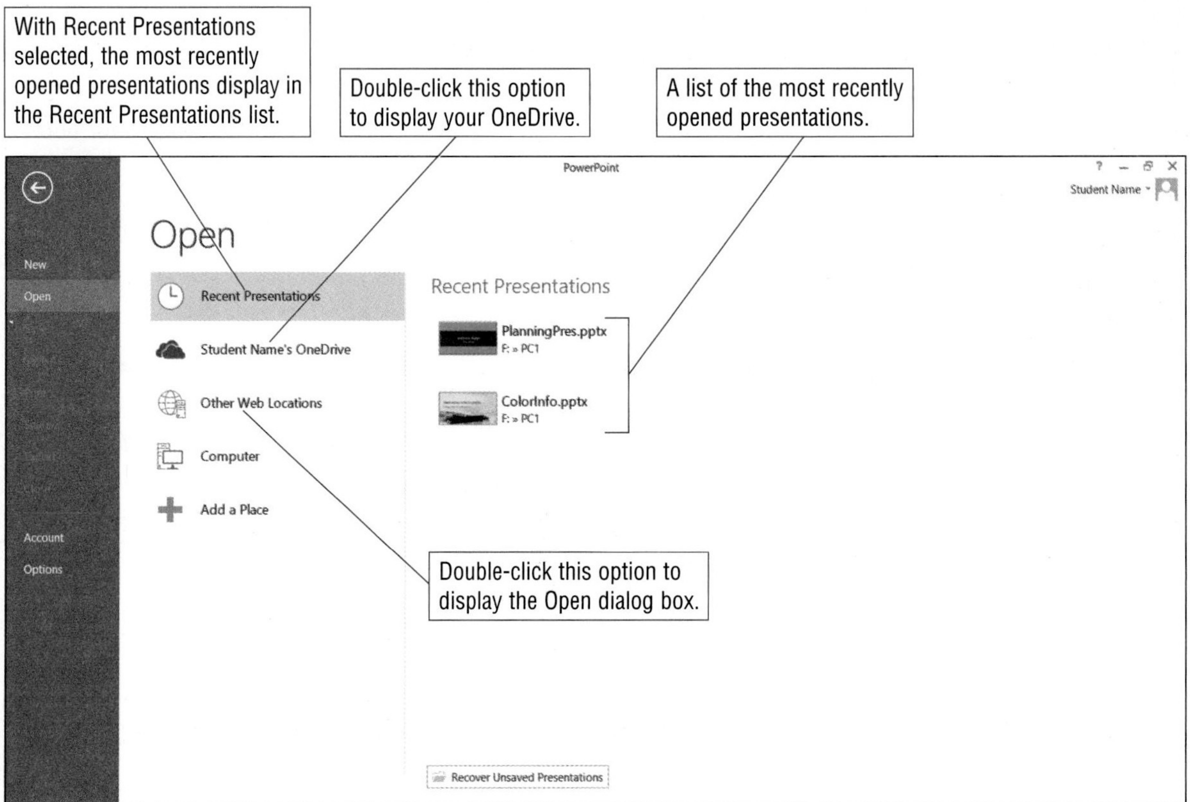

Opening a Presentation from the Recent Presentations List

At the Open backstage area with Recent Presentations selected, the Recent Presentations list displays up to 25 of the most recently opened presentations. The PowerPoint 2013 opening screen also contains a Recent list with the most recently opened presentations. To open a presentation from the Recent list, open PowerPoint to display the opening screen or display the Open backstage area with Recent Presentations selected and then click the desired presentation in the list.

Quick Steps

Pin a Presentation to a Recent List
1. Display PowerPoint 2013 opening screen or Open backstage area.
2. Hover mouse over presentation in list.
3. Click left-pointing stick pin.

Run a Presentation
1. Click Start From Beginning button on Quick Access toolbar.
2. Click left mouse button to advance slides.

OR
1. Click Slide Show button in view area on Status bar.
2. Click left mouse button to advance slides.

OR
1. Click SLIDE SHOW tab.
2. Click From Beginning button.
3. Click left mouse button to advance slides.

Close a Presentation
1. Click FILE tab.
2. Click *Close* option.

OR
Press Ctrl + F4.

Pinning a Presentation to a Recent List

If you want a presentation to remain in the Recent Presentations list at the Open backstage area or the Recent list at the PowerPoint 2013 opening screen, "pin" the presentation to the list. To pin a presentation, position the mouse pointer over the desired presentation name in the Recent Presentations list or Recent list and then click the left-pointing stick pin that displays at the right of the presentation name. This turns the stick pin into a down-pointing stick pin. The next time you open PowerPoint or display the Open backstage area, the presentation you "pinned" displays at the top of the list. To "unpin" a presentation, click the pin to change it from a down-pointing pin to a left-pointing pin. You can pin more than one presentation to the list.

When you click your OneDrive or the *Computer* option at the Open backstage area, the most recently accessed folders display in the Recent Folders list. You can pin a folder to the Recent Folders list in the same way you pin a presentation. If you access a particular folder on a regular basis, consider pinning it to the list.

Running a Presentation

Start from Beginning

When you open a presentation, the presentation displays in Normal view. In this view, you can edit and customize the presentation. To run the presentation, click the Start From Beginning button on the Quick Access toolbar, click the Slide Show button in the view area on the Status bar, or click the SLIDE SHOW tab and then click the From Beginning button in the Start Slide Show group. Navigate through slides in the presentation by clicking the left mouse button.

Closing a Presentation

To remove a presentation from the screen, close the presentation. Close a presentation by clicking the FILE tab and then clicking the *Close* option. You can also close a presentation with the keyboard shortcut Ctrl + F4. If you made any changes to the presentation, you will be asked if you want to save the presentation.

Project 1 Opening, Running, and Closing a Presentation

Part 1 of 1

1. Open PowerPoint by clicking the PowerPoint 2013 tile at the Windows Start screen. (Depending on your operating system, these steps may vary.)
2. At the PowerPoint 2013 opening screen, click the Open Other Presentations hyperlink that displays in the lower left corner of the screen.
3. At the Open backstage area, click the location where the PC1 folder containing your student data files is located. (For example, click your OneDrive or click the *Computer* option.)
4. Click the Browse button.
5. At the Open dialog box, navigate to the PC1 folder on your storage medium and then double-click ***ColorInfo.pptx***.

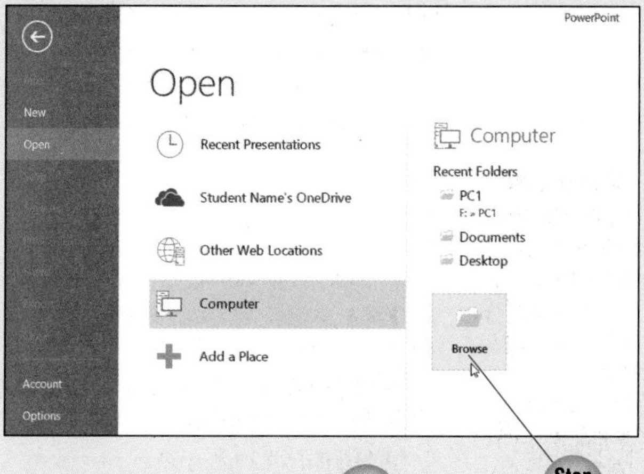

6. Run the presentation by completing the following steps:
   a. Click the Start From Beginning button on the Quick Access toolbar.
   b. Read the information in the first slide in the presentation and then click the left mouse button.
   c. Continue reading information in slides and clicking the left mouse button to advance slides.
   d. At the black screen with the message *End of slide show, click to exit.*, click the left mouse button. (This returns the presentation to Normal view.)

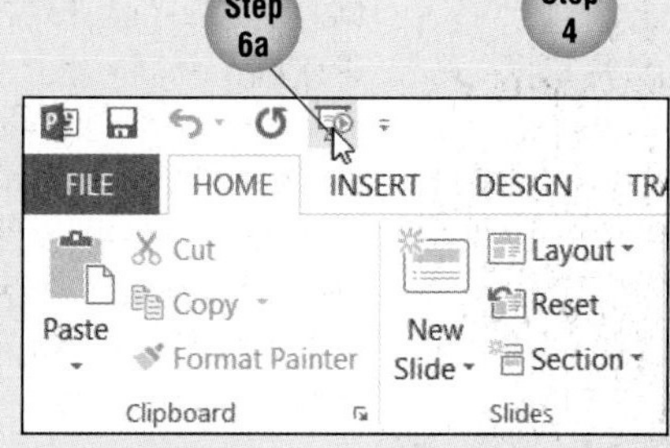

7. Close the presentation by clicking the FILE tab and then clicking the *Close* option.
8. Pin **ColorInfo.pptx** to the Recent Presentations list by completing the following steps:
   a. Click the FILE tab.
   b. At the Open backstage area with Recent Presentations selected, hover your mouse over the **ColorInfo.pptx** presentation name that displays at the top of the Recent Presentations list and then click the stick pin that displays to the right of the presentation name.
   c. Click the Back button to return to the blank presentation screen. (The Back button is located in the upper left corner of the backstage area and displays as a circle with a left-pointing arrow.)

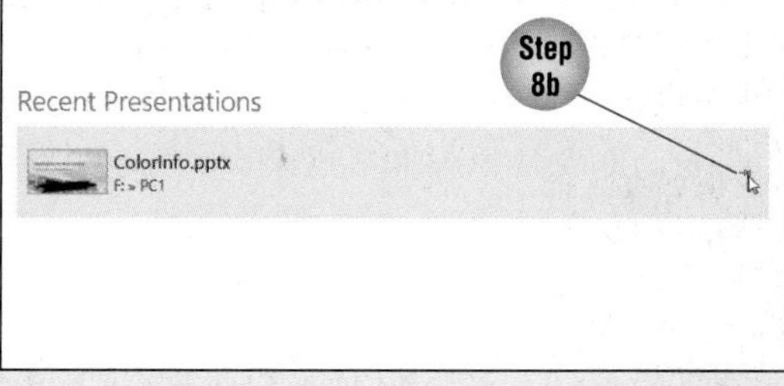

9. Close PowerPoint by clicking the Close button that displays in the upper right corner of the screen.
10. Open PowerPoint by clicking the PowerPoint 2013 tile at the Windows 8 Start screen. (These steps may vary; check with your instructor.)
11. At the PowerPoint 2013 opening screen, notice that **ColorInfo.pptx** is pinned to the Recent list. Open the presentation by clicking ***ColorInfo.pptx*** at the top of the list.
12. Close **ColorInfo.pptx**.
13. Unpin **ColorInfo.pptx** from the recent list by completing steps 8a through 8c.

Project 2 Create a Resume Style Presentation Using a Theme Template — 3 Parts

You will use a theme template to create a presentation, insert text in slides in the presentation, choose a slide layout, insert new slides, change views, navigate through the presentation, edit text in slides, and then print the presentation.

Planning a Presentation

When planning a presentation, first define the purpose of the presentation. Is the intent to inform? educate? sell? motivate? and/or entertain? In addition, consider the audience who will be listening to and watching the presentation. Determine the content of the presentation and the medium that will be used to convey the message. Will a computer monitor be used to display the presentation or will the presentation be projected onto a screen? Some basic guidelines to consider when preparing the content of a presentation include:

- **Determine the main purpose of the presentation.** Do not try to cover too many topics — this may strain the audience's attention or cause confusion. Identifying the main point of the presentation will help you stay focused and convey a clear message to the audience.
- **Determine the output.** Is the presentation going to be presented on a computer or will the slides be projected? To help determine which type of output to use, consider the availability of equipment, the size of the room where the presentation will be given, and the number of people who will be attending the presentation.
- **Show one idea per slide.** Each slide in a presentation should convey only one main idea. Too many thoughts or ideas on a slide may confuse the audience and cause you to stray from the purpose of the slide. Determine the specific message you want to convey to the audience and then outline the message to organize your ideas.
- **Maintain a consistent layout.** Using a consistent layout and color scheme for slides in a presentation will create continuity and cohesiveness. Do not get carried away by using too many colors, pictures, and/or other graphic elements.
- **Keep slides simple.** Keep slides uncluttered so that they are easy for the audience to read. Keep words and other items, such as bullets, to a minimum.
- **Determine the output needed.** Will you be providing audience members with handouts? If so, will these handouts consist of a printing of each slide? an outline of the presentation? a printing of each slide with space for taking notes?

Quick Steps

Create a Presentation Using a Design Theme Template

1. Click FILE tab.
2. Click *New* option.
3. Click desired theme template.
4. Click color variant.
5. Click Create button.

Creating a Presentation Using a Design Theme Template

PowerPoint provides built-in design theme templates you can use when creating slides for a presentation. These design theme templates include formatting such as color, background, fonts, and so on. Choose a design theme template at the New backstage area, as shown in Figure 1.3. Display the New backstage area by clicking the FILE tab and then clicking the *New* option. At this backstage area, click the desired design theme template or search for a template or theme at Office.com by typing a category in the search text box or clicking one of the categories listed

Figure 1.3 New Backstage Area

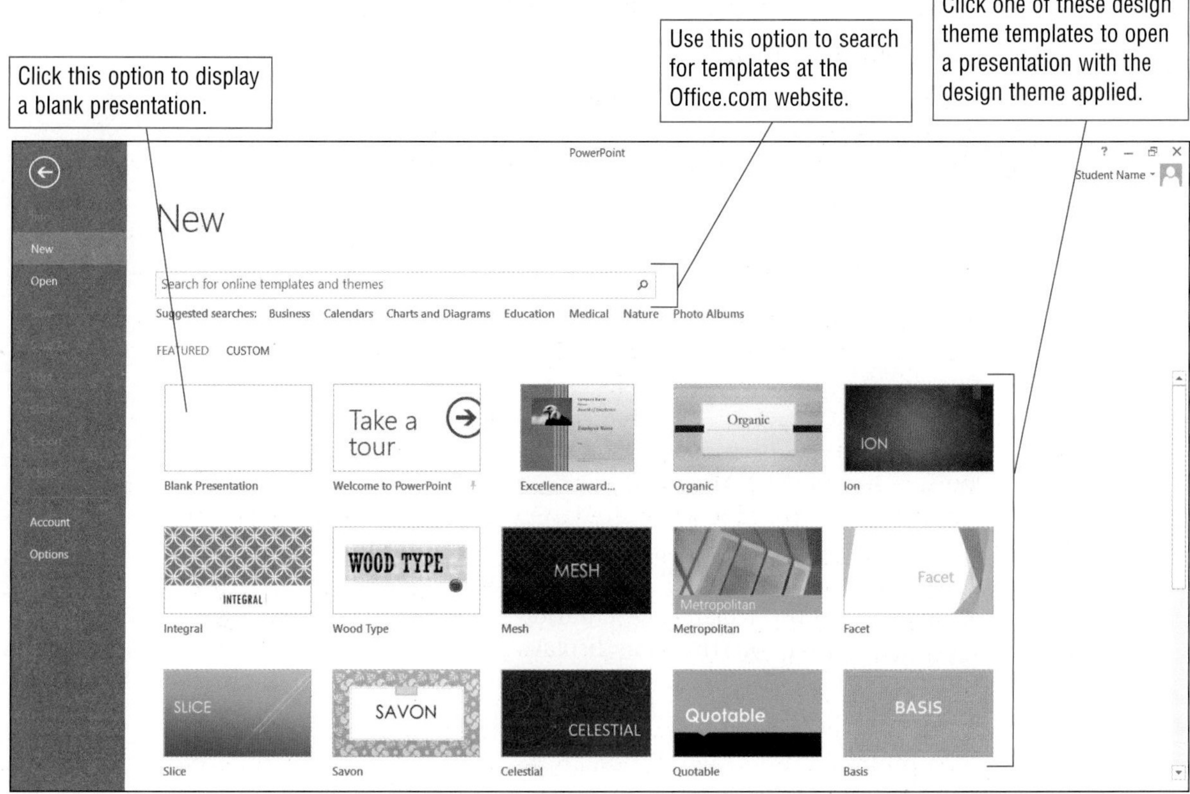

next to *Suggested searches* below the search text box. Microsoft provides a variety of predesigned templates in many different categories at Office.com.

When you click a design theme template at the New backstage area, a window opens containing a slide with the design theme applied as well as theme color variants. The color variants display at the right side of the window and provide color options for the theme. If you want to change the color of the theme, click the desired color variant and then click the Create button. This opens a presentation with the design theme and theme colors applied.

Creating Slides in a Presentation

When you choose a blank presentation template or design theme template at the New backstage area, a slide displays in the slide pane in Normal view. The slide displays with a default Title Slide layout. This layout contains placeholders for entering the slide title and subtitle. To insert text in a placeholder, click the placeholder text. This moves the insertion point inside the placeholder, removes the default placeholder text, and makes the placeholder active. An active placeholder displays surrounded by a dashed border with sizing handles and a white rotation handle, as shown in Figure 1.4.

With the insertion point positioned in a placeholder, type the desired text. Edit text in a placeholder in the same manner as you would edit text in a Word document. Press the Backspace key to delete the character immediately left of the insertion point and press the Delete key to delete the character immediately right of the insertion point. Use the arrow keys on the keyboard to move the insertion point in the desired direction.

Figure 1.4 Slide Placeholders

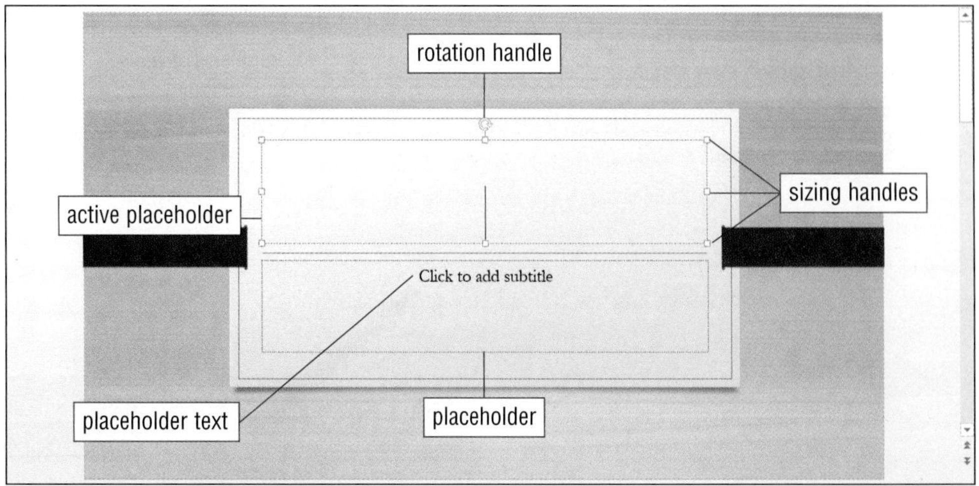

Quick Steps
Choose a Slide Layout
1. Click Layout button.
2. Click desired layout option in drop-down list.

Layout

Choosing a Slide Layout

When you choose a blank presentation template or design theme template to create a presentation, the slide displays in the Title Slide layout. You can change the slide layout with the Layout button in the Slides group on the HOME tab. Click the Layout button and a drop-down list of layouts displays. Click the desired layout at the drop-down list and the layout is applied to the current slide.

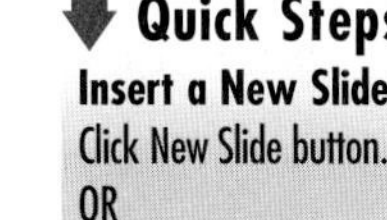

PowerPoint includes nine built-in standard layouts.

Quick Steps
Insert a New Slide
Click New Slide button.
OR
Press Ctrl + M.

New Slide

Inserting a New Slide

Create a new slide in a presentation by clicking the New Slide button in the Slides group on the HOME tab or by pressing Ctrl + M. By default, PowerPoint inserts a new slide with the Title and Content layout. Choose a different slide layout for a new slide by clicking the New Slide button arrow and then clicking the desired layout at the drop-down list. You can also change the slide layout by clicking the Layout button in the Slides group on the HOME tab and then clicking the desired layout at the drop-down list.

Quick Steps
Save a Presentation
1. Click Save button.
2. At Save As backstage area, click desired location.
3. Click Browse button.
4. At Save As dialog box, navigate to desired folder.
5. Type presentation name in *File name* text box.
6. Press Enter or click Save button.

Save

Saving a Presentation

After creating a presentation, save it by clicking the Save button on the Quick Access toolbar, by clicking the FILE tab and then clicking the *Save As* option, or with the keyboard shortcut Ctrl + S. This displays the Save As backstage area. At this backstage area, click the desired location where you want to save the presentation. For example, click your OneDrive or click the *Computer* option if you are saving to your computer's hard drive or removable drive. After specifying the location, click the Browse button and the Save As dialog box displays. If you are saving the presentation to your computer's hard drive or removable drive, you can double-click the *Computer* option at the Save As backstage area to display the Save As dialog box. At the Save As dialog box, type a name for the presentation in the *File name* text box and then press Enter or click the Save button. You can press the F12 function key to go directly to the Save As dialog box without displaying the Save As backstage area.

When you click your OneDrive or the *Computer* option at the Save As backstage area, the names of the most recently accessed folders display below the *Recent Folders* heading in the *Computer* section. Open a folder by clicking the folder name.

A presentation file name can contain up to 255 characters, including drive letter and any folder names, and can include spaces. You cannot give a presentation the same name in first uppercase and then lowercase letters. Also, some symbols cannot be used in a file name, including /, ?, \, “, >, :, <, ;, *, and |.

Press F12 to display the Save As dialog box without displaying the Save As backstage area.

Project 2a Creating a Presentation Using a Design Theme Template — Part 1 of 3

1. With PowerPoint open, click the FILE tab and then click the *New* option.
2. At the New backstage area, click the *Organic* design theme template.

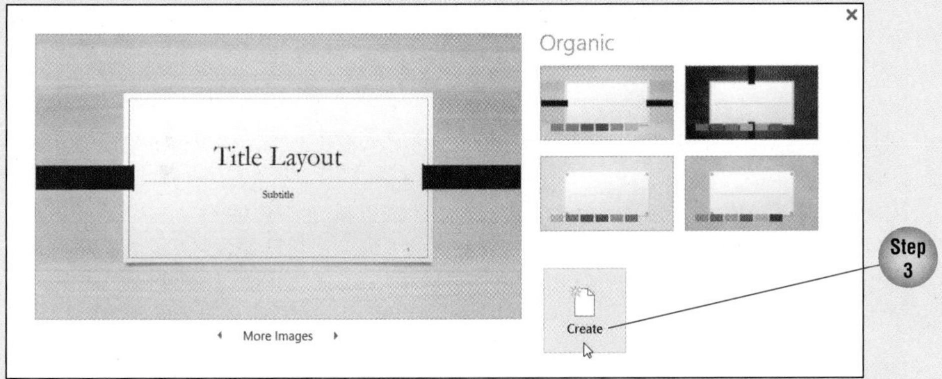

3. At the window that displays, click the Create button.
4. Click in the placeholder text *Click to add title* and then type **Career Finders.**
5. Click in the placeholder text *Click to add subtitle* and then type **Resume Writing**.
6. Click the New Slide button in the Slides group on the HOME tab. (This inserts a slide with the Title and Content layout.)

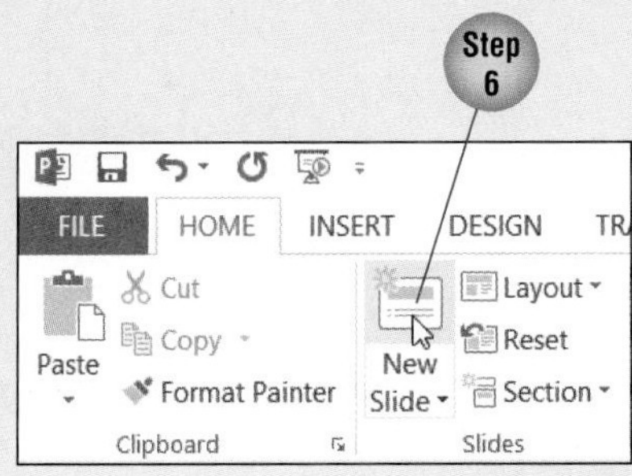

7. Click the placeholder text *Click to add title* and then type **Resume Styles.**
8. Click the placeholder text *Click to add text* and then type **Chronological resume.**
9. Press the Enter key (this moves the insertion point to the next line and inserts a bullet) and then type **Functional resume.**
10. Press the Enter key and then type **Hybrid resume.**

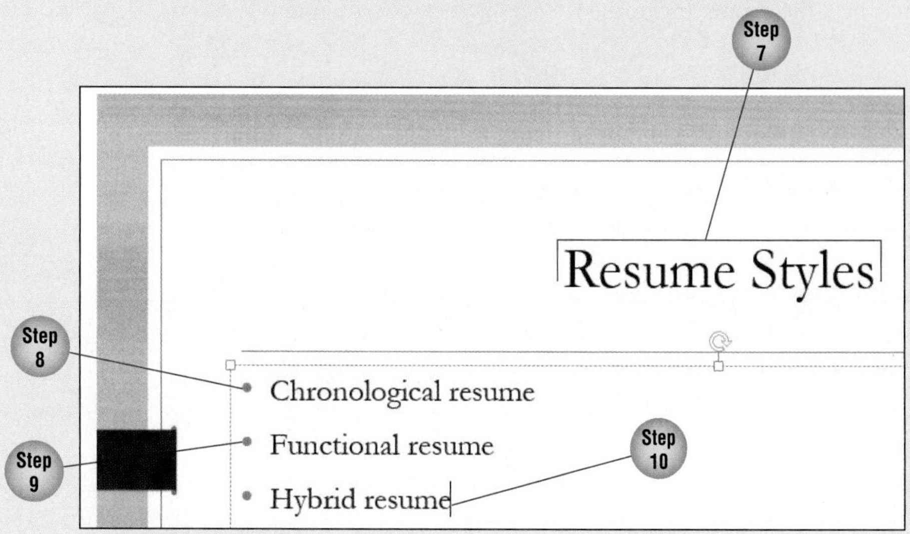

11. Click the New Slide button in the Slides group.
12. Click the placeholder text *Click to add title* and then type **Resume Sections.**
13. Click the placeholder text *Click to add text* and then type **Contact information.**
14. Press the Enter key and then type **Summary or job objective statement.**
15. Press the Enter key and then type **Work history.**
16. Press the Enter key and then type **Education details.**
17. Press the Enter key and then type **References.**

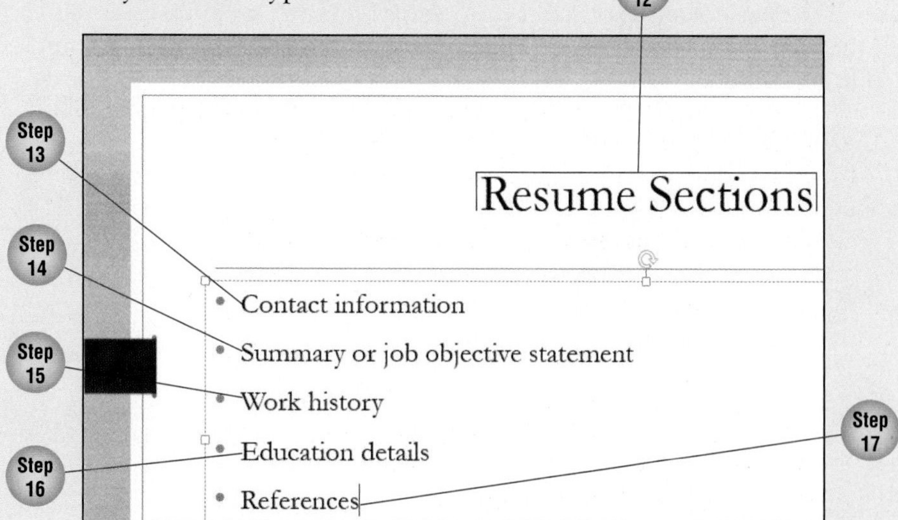

18. Click the New Slide button arrow and then click the *Title Slide* layout option.

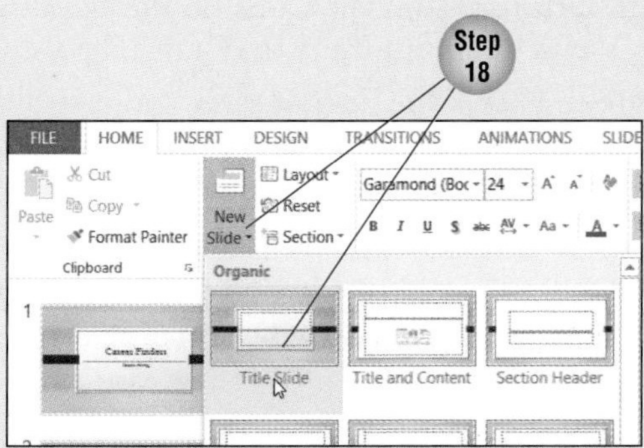

19. Click the placeholder text *Click to add title* and then type **Career Finders**.
20. Click the placeholder text *Click to add subtitle* and then type **Contact us by calling 1-800-555-2255**.

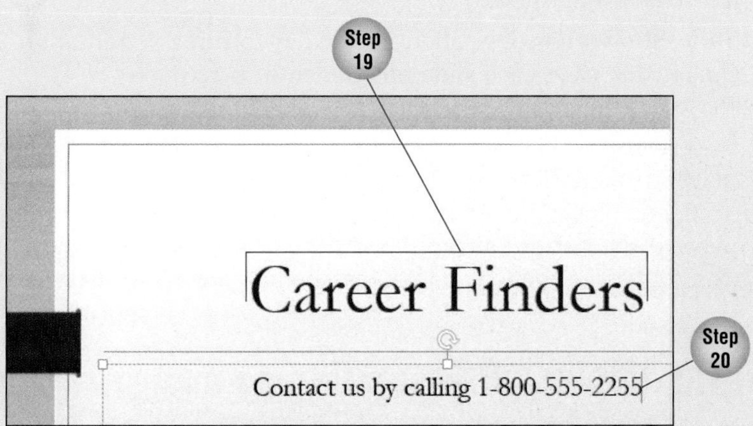

21. Click in the slide pane but outside the slide. (This deselects the placeholder.)
22. Save the presentation by completing the following steps:
    a. Click the Save button on the Quick Access toolbar.
    b. At the Save As backstage area, click the desired location, such as your OneDrive or *Computer* option, and then click the Browse button.
    c. At the Save As dialog box, navigate to the PC1 folder on your storage medium.
    d. Select the text in the *File name* text box and then type **P-C1-P2-Resumes** (*P* for PowerPoint, *C1* for Chapter 1, *P2* for Project 2, and *Resumes* because that is topic of the presentation).
    e. Press Enter or click the Save button.

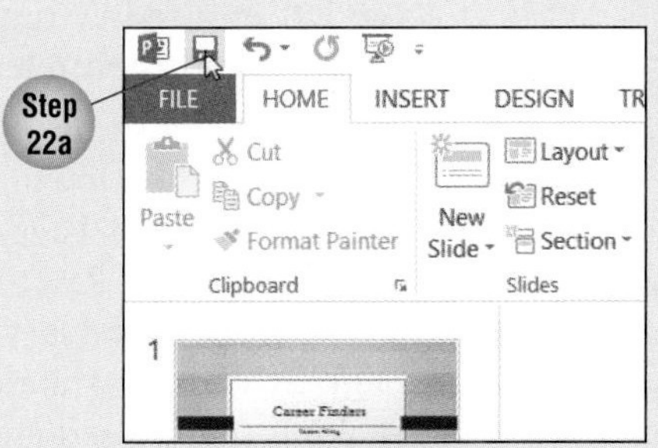

Changing Views

HINT

In Normal view, you can increase or decrease the size of the slide thumbnails pane.

VIEW tab	Status bar
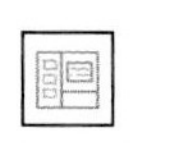 Normal	 Normal
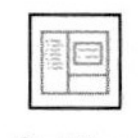 Outline View	 Slide Sorter
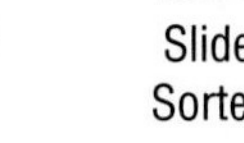  Slide Sorter	 Reading View
 Page Notes	 Slide Show
 Reading View	

PowerPoint provides a variety of viewing options for a presentation. Change the view with buttons in the view area on the Status bar or with options in the Presentation Views group on the VIEW tab. The viewing choices include:

- **Normal view.** This is the default view and displays two panes — the slide pane and the slide thumbnails pane. You can enter text in a slide in the slide pane and manage slides in the slide thumbnails pane.
- **Outline view.** In Outline view, the slide thumbnails pane changes to an outline pane where you can type text for slides.
- **Slide Sorter view.** Choosing Slide Sorter view displays all slides in the presentation as thumbnails. In this view, you can easily add, move, rearrange, and delete slides.
- **Notes Page view.** Change to Notes Page view and an individual slide displays on a page with any added notes displayed below the slide.
- **Reading view.** Use Reading view when you deliver your presentation to someone viewing the presentation on his or her own computer. This view allows you to play the slide show in the PowerPoint window without switching to a full-screen slide show.
- **Slide Show view.** Use Slide Show view to run a presentation. When you choose this view, each slide fills the entire screen.

The view area on the Status bar contains four buttons for changing the view — Normal, Slide Sorter, Reading View, and Slide Show. The active button displays with a dark orange background. The Status bar also contains a NOTES button and COMMENTS button. Click the NOTES button and a notes pane displays at the bottom of the slide in the slide pane. Click the COMMENTS button to display the Comments task pane, where you can type a comment.

Navigating in a Presentation

Previous Slide

Next Slide

In the Normal view, change slides by clicking the Previous Slide or Next Slide buttons located at the bottom of the vertical scroll bar. You can also change to a different slide using the mouse pointer on the vertical scroll bar. To do this, position the mouse pointer on the scroll box on the vertical scroll bar, hold down the left mouse button, drag up or down until a box displays with the desired slide number, and then release the button.

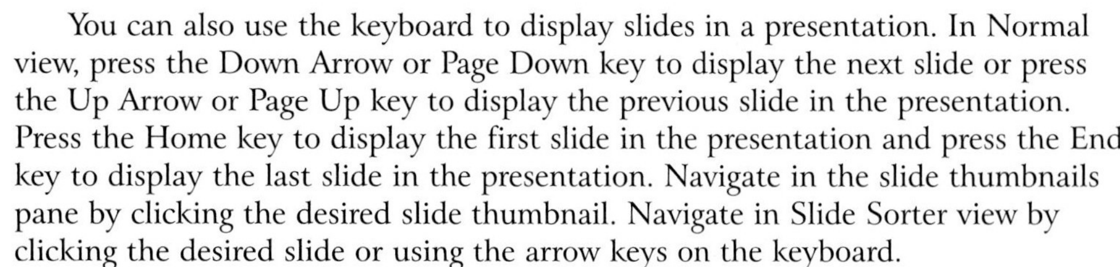

You can also use the keyboard to display slides in a presentation. In Normal view, press the Down Arrow or Page Down key to display the next slide or press the Up Arrow or Page Up key to display the previous slide in the presentation. Press the Home key to display the first slide in the presentation and press the End key to display the last slide in the presentation. Navigate in the slide thumbnails pane by clicking the desired slide thumbnail. Navigate in Slide Sorter view by clicking the desired slide or using the arrow keys on the keyboard.

Project 2b Navigating and Editing Slides in a Presentation Part 2 of 3

1. With **P-C1-P2-Resumes.pptx** open, navigate in the presentation by completing the following steps:
   a. Make sure no placeholders are selected.
   b. Press the Home key to display Slide 1 in the slide pane.
   c. Click the Next Slide button located toward the bottom of the vertical scroll bar.
   d. Press the End key to display the last slide in the slide pane.
   e. Click the Slide Sorter button in the view area on the Status bar.

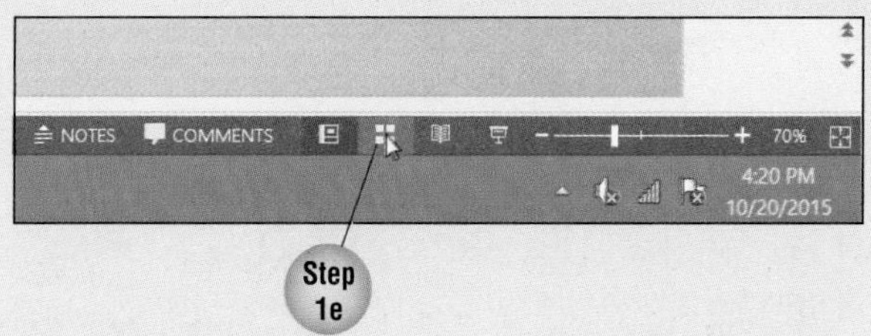

   f. Click Slide 1. (Notice that the active slide displays with an orange border.)
   g. Double-click Slide 3. (This closes Slide Sorter view and displays the presentation in Normal view with Slide 3 active.)
2. Insert text in slides by completing the following steps:
   a. Click any character in the bulleted text. (This positions the insertion point inside the placeholder.)
   b. Move the insertion point so it is positioned immediately right of *Education details*.
   c. Press the Enter key and then type **Professional affiliations**.

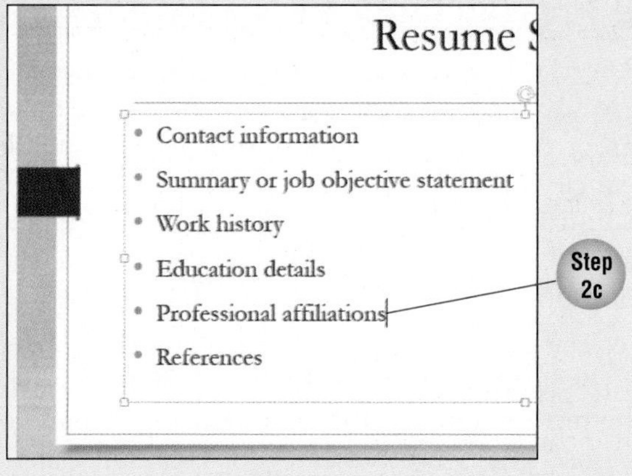

   d. Click Slide 4 in the slide thumbnails pane. (This displays Slide 4 in the slide pane.)
   e. Click in the text containing the telephone number, move the insertion point so it is positioned immediately right of the telephone number, press the spacebar, and then type **or visit our website at www.emcp.net/careerfinders.**

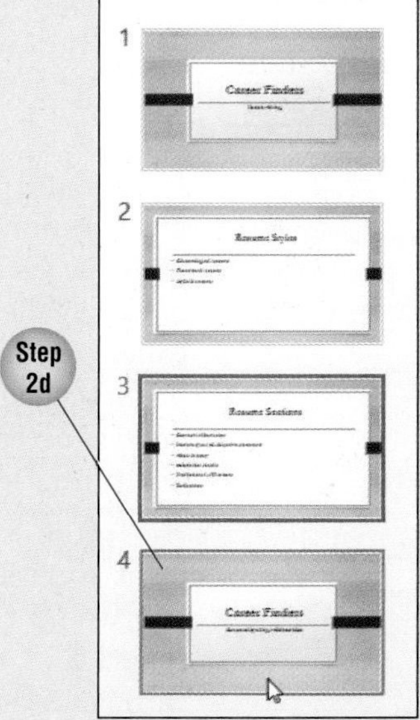

3. Type a note in the notes pane by completing the following steps:
   a. Click Slide 2 in the slide thumbnails pane.
   b. Click the NOTES button on the Status bar.
   c. Click the text *Click to add notes* that displays in the notes pane.

d. Type Distribute resume examples to the audience.

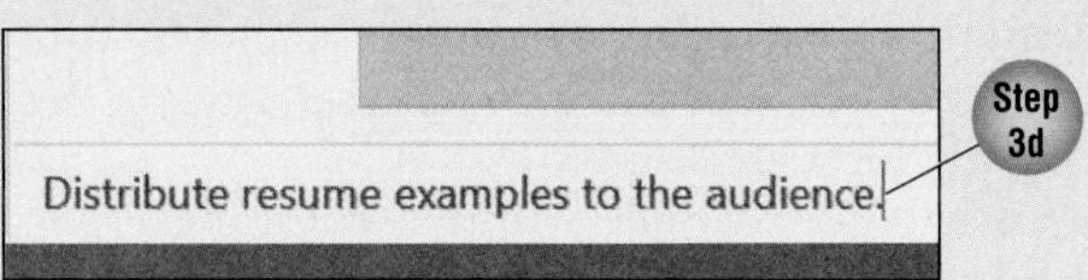

e. Display the slide in Notes Page view by clicking the VIEW tab and then clicking the Notes Page button in the Presentation Views group. (Notice the note you typed displays below the slide in this view.)

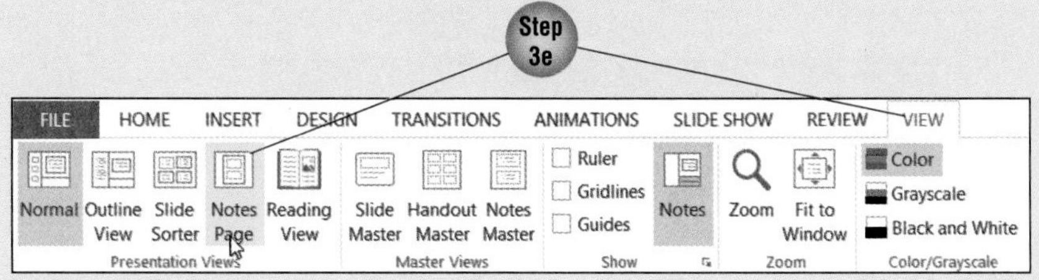

f. Return to Normal view by clicking the Normal button in the view area on the Status bar.
g. Click the NOTES button on the Status bar to close the notes pane.
h. Press the Home key to make Slide 1 the active slide.

4. Save the presentation by clicking the Save button on the Quick Access toolbar.

Printing and Previewing a Presentation

Quick Steps

Print a Presentation

1. Click FILE tab.
2. Click *Print* option.
3. Click Print button.

Printing a hard copy of your presentation and distributing it to your audience helps reinforce your message.

You can print a PowerPoint presentation in a variety of formats. You can print each slide on a separate piece of paper; print each slide at the top of the page, leaving the bottom of the page for notes; print a specific number of slides (up to nine slides) on a single piece of paper; or print the slide titles and topics in outline form. Use options in the Print backstage area, shown in Figure 1.5, to specify what you want printed. To display the Print backstage area, click the FILE tab and then click the *Print* option or use the keyboard shortcut Ctrl + P.

The left side of the Print backstage area displays three categories—*Print*, *Printer*, and *Settings*. Click the Print button in the *Print* category to send the presentation to the printer and specify the number of copies you want printed with the *Copies* option. The two other categories contain galleries. For example, use the gallery in the *Printer* category to specify the desired printer. Click the first gallery in the *Settings* category and options display for specifying what you want printed such as all of the presentation or specific slides in the presentation. The *Settings* category also contains a number of galleries that describe how the slides will print.

In the *Settings* category, you can print a range of slides using the hyphen and print specific slides using a comma. For example, to print Slides 2 through 6, you would type *2-6* in the *Slides* text box. To print Slides 1, 3, and 7, you would type *1,3,7*. You can combine a hyphen and comma. For example, to print Slides 1 through 5 and Slide 8, you would type *1-5,8* in the *Slides* text box.

Figure 1.5 Print Backstage Area

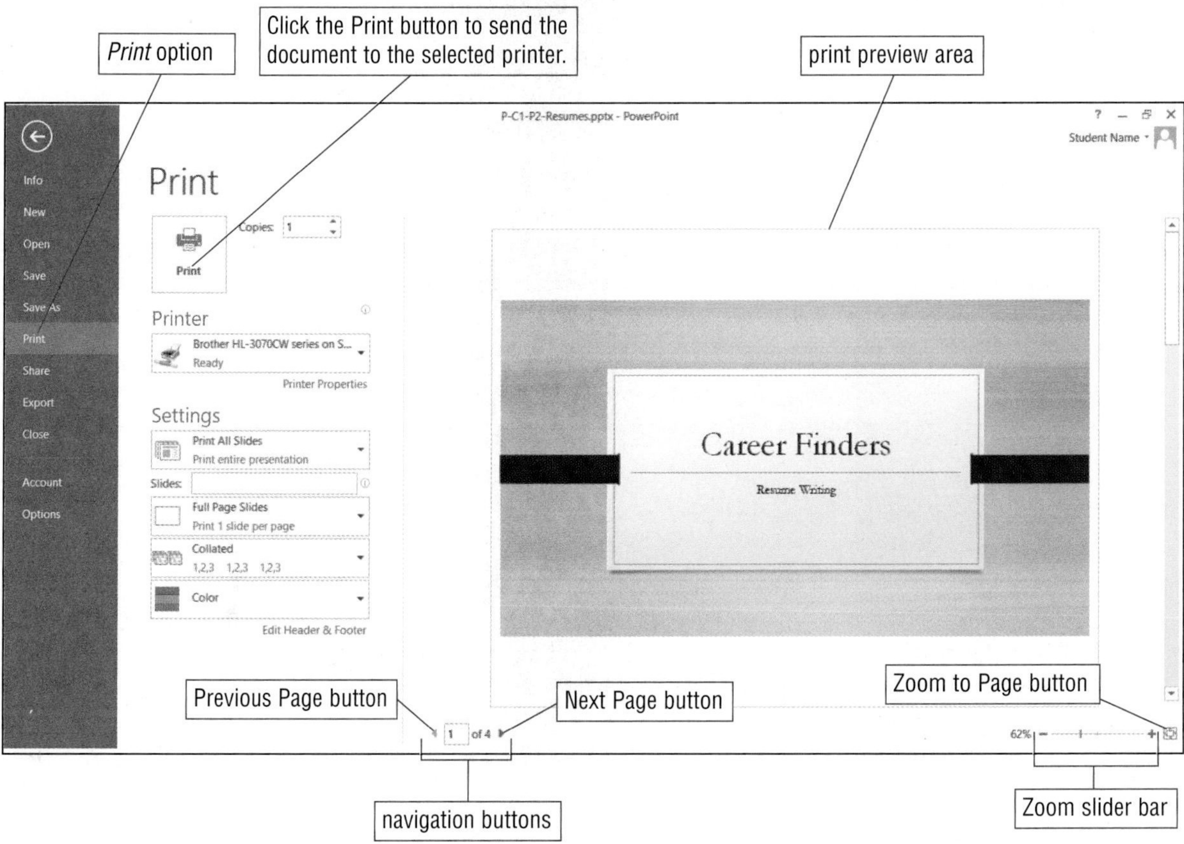

A preview of how a slide or slides will print displays at the right side of the Print backstage area. If you have a color printer selected, the slide or slides that display at the right side of the Print backstage area display in color, and if you have a black-and-white printer selected, the slide or slides will display in grayscale. Use the Next Page button (right-pointing arrow) located below and to the left of the page to view the next slide in the presentation, click the Previous Page button (left-pointing arrow) to display the previous slide in the presentation, use the Zoom slider bar to increase or decrease the size of the slide, and click the Zoom to Page button to fit the slide in the viewing area in the Print backstage area.

You can choose to print a presentation as individual slides, handouts, notes pages, or an outline. If you print a presentation as handouts or an outline, PowerPoint will automatically print the current date in the upper right corner of the page and the page number in the lower right corner. If you print the presentation as notes pages, PowerPoint will automatically print the page number in the lower right corner. PowerPoint does not insert the date or page number when you print individual slides.

Project 2c Printing a Presentation Part 3 of 3

1. With **P-C1-P2-Resumes.pptx** open, click the FILE tab and then click the *Print* option.
2. Click the Next Page button (located below and to the left of the slide in the viewing area) twice to display Slide 3 in the print preview area.

3. Click the Previous Page button twice to display Slide 1.
4. Change the zoom by completing the following steps:
   a. Position the mouse pointer on the Zoom slider bar button (located at the bottom right of the Print backstage area), drag the button to the right to increase the size of the slide in the print preview area of the Print backstage area, and then to the left to decrease the size of the slide.
   b. Click the percentage that displays at the left side of the Zoom slider bar. (This displays the Zoom dialog box.)
   c. Click the *50%* option in the Zoom dialog box and then click OK.
   d. Click the Zoom to Page button located to the right of the Zoom slider bar. (This increases the size of the slide to fill the print preview area.)

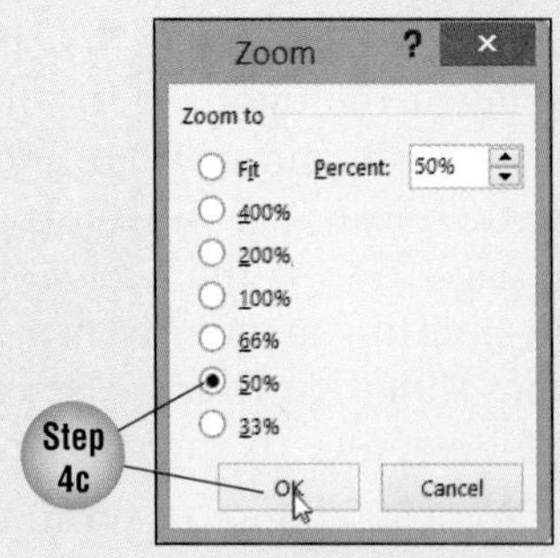

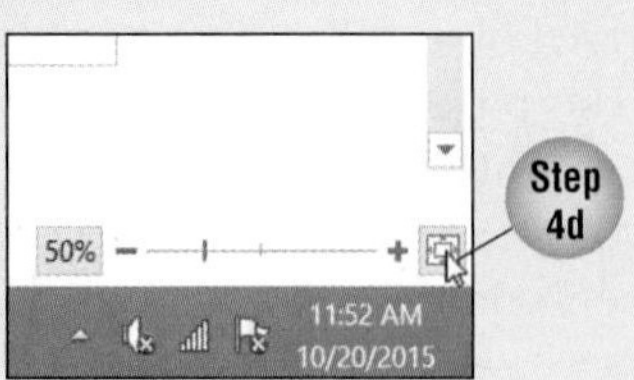

5. Print the presentation as a handout with four slides horizontally on the page by completing the following steps:
   a. At the Print backstage area, click the second gallery (displays with *Full Page Slides*) in the *Settings* category and then click *4 Slides Horizontal* in the *Handouts* section.

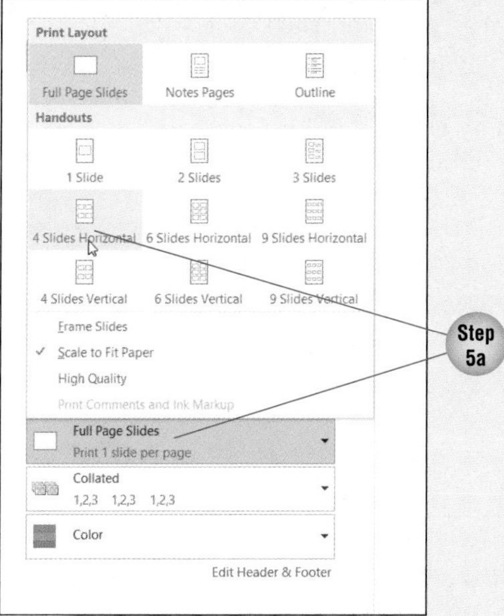

   b. Click the Print button.
6. Print Slide 2 as a notes page by completing the following steps:
   a. Click the FILE tab and then click the *Print* option.
   b. At the Print backstage area, click in the *Slides* text box located in the *Settings* category, and then type 2.
   c. Click the second gallery (displays with *4 Slides Horizontal*) in the *Settings* category and then click *Notes Pages* in the *Print Layout* section.
   d. Click the Print button.

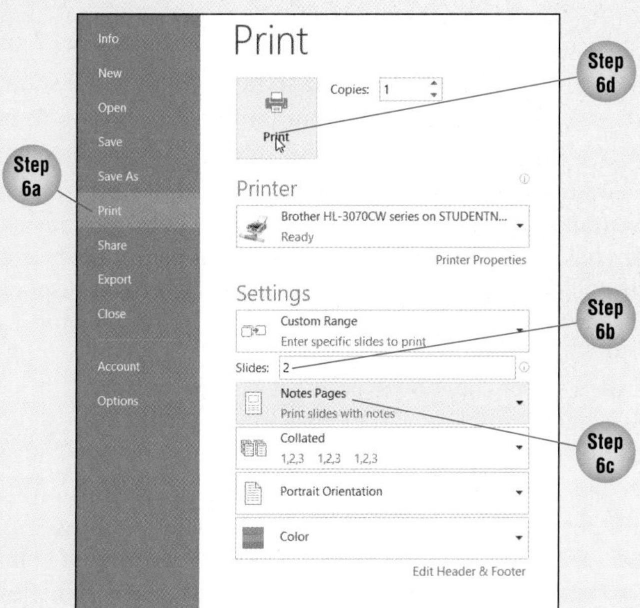

7. Print Slides 1, 2, and 4 by completing the following steps:
   a. Click the FILE tab and then click the *Print* option.
   b. At the Print backstage area, click in the *Slides* text box located in the *Settings* category and then type 1-2,4.
   c. Click the second gallery (displays with *Notes Pages*) in the *Settings* category and then click *Slides Horizontal* in the *Handouts* section.
   d. Click the Print button.
8. Close the presentation by clicking the FILE tab and then clicking the *Close* option.

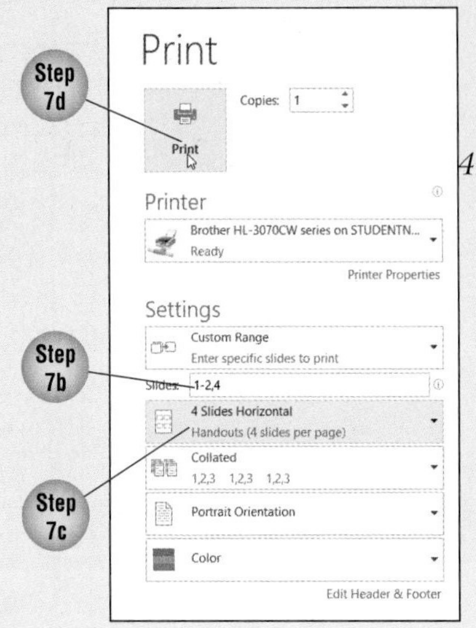

Project 3 Opening and Running a Presentation and Changing the Presentation Design Theme — 3 Parts

You will open a presentation, run the presentation using buttons on the Slide Show toolbar, apply a different design theme to the presentation, and then delete the presentation.

Running a Slide Show

From Beginning

From Current Slide

As you learned earlier in this chapter, you can run a presentation by clicking the Start From Beginning button on the Quick Access toolbar, clicking the Slide Show button in the view area on the Status bar, or by clicking the SLIDE SHOW tab and then clicking the From Beginning button in the Start Slide Show group. This group also contains a From Current Slide button. Use this button to begin running the slide show with the currently active slide rather than the first slide in the presentation.

PowerPoint offers a number of options for navigating through slides in a presentation. You can click the left mouse button to advance slides in a presentation, right-click in a slide and then choose options from a shortcut menu, or use buttons on the Slide Show toolbar. The Slide Show toolbar displays in the lower left corner of a slide when you are running the presentation. Figure 1.6 identifies the buttons on the Slide Show toolbar. To display the Slide Show toolbar, run the presentation and then hover the mouse pointer over the buttons. Click the Next button (displays with a right arrow) on the toolbar to display the next slide and click the Previous button (displays with a left arrow) to display the previous slide.

Click the Pen button (displays with a pen icon) on the Slide Show toolbar and a pop-up list displays with the following options: *Laser Pointer*, *Pen*, *Highlighter*, *Eraser*, and *Erase All Ink on Slide*, along with a row of color options. Click the *Laser Pointer* option and the pointer displays as a red, glowing circle you can use to point to specific locations on the slide. Use the *Pen* option to draw in the slide

Figure 1.6 Slide Show Toolbar

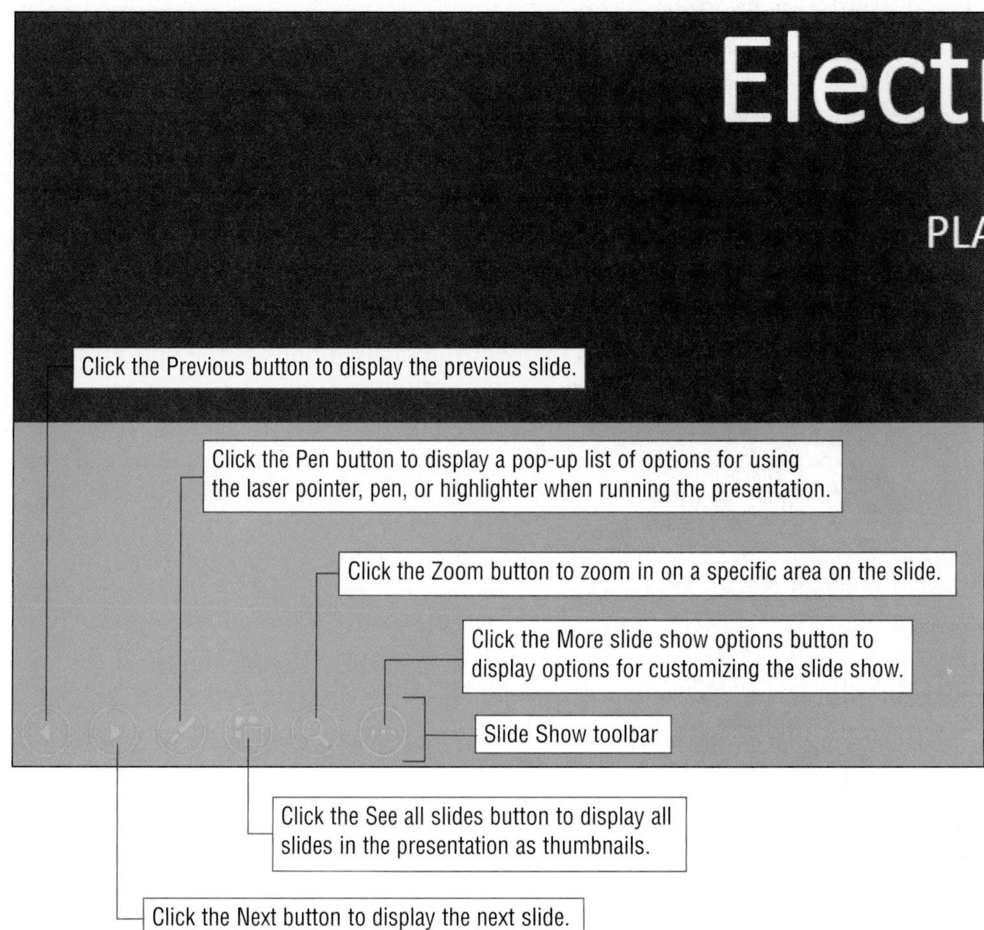
Elect
PL
Click the Previous button to display the previous slide.
Click the Pen button to display a pop-up list of options for using the laser pointer, pen, or highlighter when running the presentation.
Click the Zoom button to zoom in on a specific area on the slide.
Click the More slide show options button to display options for customizing the slide show.
Slide Show toolbar
Click the See all slides button to display all slides in the presentation as thumbnails.
Click the Next button to display the next slide.

and use the *Highlighter* option to highlight specific items in the slide. Select the *Pen* or *Highlighter* option and then drag with the mouse in the slide to draw or highlight items. If you draw or highlight in a slide, you can erase the drawing or highlighting by clicking the Pen button on the Slide Show toolbar, clicking the *Eraser* option, and then dragging with the mouse to erase the drawing or highlighting. If you want to erase all drawing or highlighting in the slide, click the Pen button and then click the *Erase All Ink on Slide* option.

Change the pen or highlighter color by clicking the Pen button and then clicking a color option in the color row. If you draw in a slide with the Pen or Highlighter, PowerPoint will ask you at the end of the slide show if you want to keep or discard the ink annotations. At this message, specify what you want to do with the ink annotations. Return the laser pointer, pen, or highlighter option back to the mouse pointer by pressing the Esc key on your keyboard.

Click the See all slides button on the Slide Show toolbar and all slides in the presentation display on the screen. Use this feature if you want to display all of the slides in the presentation and/or move to a different slide by clicking the desired slide.

Zoom in on a portion of a slide by clicking the Zoom button (contains an image of a magnifying glass) on the Slide Show toolbar. Clicking this button creates a magnification area and dims the remainder of the slide. Drag the

Quick Steps

Use the Pen or Highlighter During a Presentation

1. Run presentation.
2. Display desired slide.
3. Click Pen button on Slide Show toolbar.
4. Click pen or highlighter option.
5. Drag to draw line or highlight text.

HINT

If you use the pen or highlighter on a slide when running a presentation, choose an ink color that the audience can see easily.

magnification area with the mouse to specify what you want magnified and then click the left mouse button. Return to the normal zoom by pressing the Esc key or right-clicking in the slide.

Click the More slide show options button (the last button on the Slide Show toolbar; contains three dots) and a pop-up list displays with a variety of options. The pop-up list contains options for displaying a custom show or switching to Presenter view; changing the screen display, display settings, and arrow options; and pausing or ending the show. Click the *Help* option and the Slide Show Help dialog box displays, as shown in Figure 1.7. This dialog box contains various tabs that describe the keyboard options available when running a presentation.

In addition to the options on the Slide Show toolbar, right-click in a slide and a shortcut menu displays with many of the same options as the options that display when you click the More slide show options button.

When running a presentation, the mouse pointer is set, by default, to be hidden automatically after three seconds of inactivity. The mouse pointer will appear again when you move the mouse. You can change this default setting by clicking the More slide show options button on the Slide Show toolbar, pointing to *Arrow Options*, and then clicking *Visible* if you want the mouse pointer always visible or *Hidden* if you do not want the mouse to display at all as you run the presentation. The *Automatic* option is the default setting.

If you have selected the pen or highlighter and then want to return to the regular mouse pointer, press the Esc key or click the More slide show options button on the Slide Show toolbar, click *Arrow Options* at the pop-up list, and then click *Visible*.

Figure 1.7 Slide Show Help Dialog Box

Slide Show Help

General | Rehearse/Record | Media | Ink/Laser Pointer | Touch

General shortcuts

'N', left click, space, right or down arrow, enter, or page down	Advance to the next slide or animation
'P', backspace, left or up arrow, or page up	Return to the previous slide or animation
Right-click	Popup menu/Previous slide
'G', '-', or Ctrl+'-'	Zoom out of a slide; See all the slides
'+' or Ctrl+'+'	Zoom in a slide
Number followed by Enter	Go to that slide
Esc, or Ctrl+Break	End slide show
Ctrl+S	All Slides dialog
'B' or '.'	Blacks/Unblacks the screen
'W' or ','	Whites/Unwhites the screen
'S'	Stop/Restart automatic show
'H'	Go to next slide if hidden
Hold both the Right and Left Mouse buttons down for 2 seconds	Return to first slide
Ctrl+T	View task bar
Ctrl+H/U	Hide/Show arrow on mouse move

OK

Project 3a Opening and Running a Presentation — Part 1 of 3

1. Click the FILE tab and then click the *Open* option.
2. At the Open backstage area, click your OneDrive if you are opening presentations from your OneDrive or click the *Computer* option if you are opening presentations from the computer's hard drive or a USB flash drive.
3. Click the Browse button.
4. At the Open dialog box, navigate to the PC1 folder on your storage medium and then double-click ***PlanningPres.pptx***.
5. Save the presentation by completing the following steps:
   a. Click the FILE tab and then click the *Save As* option.
   b. At the Save As backstage area, click the *PC1* folder name that displays below the *Current Folder* heading in the *Computer* section of the backstage view. (If this folder name does not display, double-click your OneDrive or the *Computer* option.)
   c. At the Save As dialog box, make sure the PC1 folder on your storage medium is active and then type **P-C1-P3-PlanningPres** in the *File name* text box.
   d. Press Enter or click the Save button.
6. Run the presentation by completing the following steps:
   a. Click the Slide Show button in the view area on the Status bar.
   b. When Slide 1 fills the screen, move the mouse to display the Slide Show toolbar. (This toolbar displays in a dimmed manner in the lower left corner of the slide.)
   c. Click the Next button (contains a right arrow) to display the next slide.
   d. Continue clicking the Next button until a black screen displays.
   e. Click the left mouse button. (This displays the presentation in Normal view.)

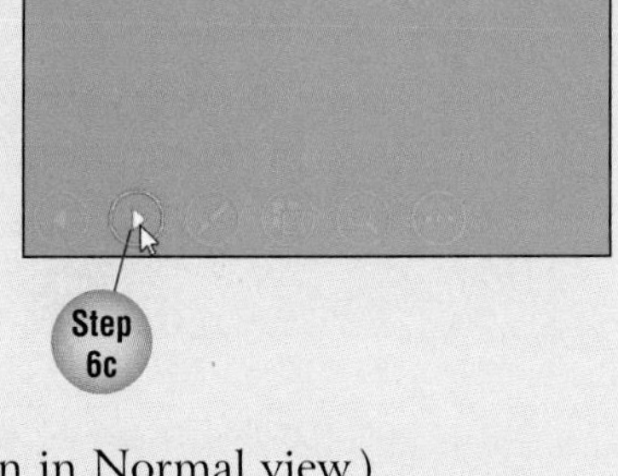

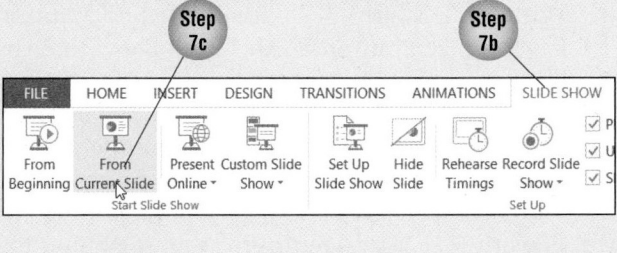

7. Run the presentation from the current slide by completing the following steps:
   a. Click Slide 4 in the slide thumbnails pane. (This makes Slide 4 active.)
   b. Click the SLIDE SHOW tab.
   c. Click the From Current Slide button in the Start Slide Show group.
8. With Slide 4 active, zoom in on the step text by completing these steps:
   a. Move the mouse to display the Slide Show toolbar.
   b. Click the Zoom button on the Slide Show toolbar.
   c. Using the mouse, drag the magnification area so it displays the step text and then click the left mouse button.
   d. Press the Esc key to return to the normal zoom.
9. Click the See all slides button on the Slide Show toolbar and then click the Slide 2 thumbnail.
10. With Slide 2 active, use the pen to draw in the slide by completing the following steps:
    a. Move the mouse to display the Slide Show toolbar.
    b. Click the Pen button on the Slide Show toolbar and then click *Pen* at the pop-up list. (This changes the mouse pointer to a small circle.)

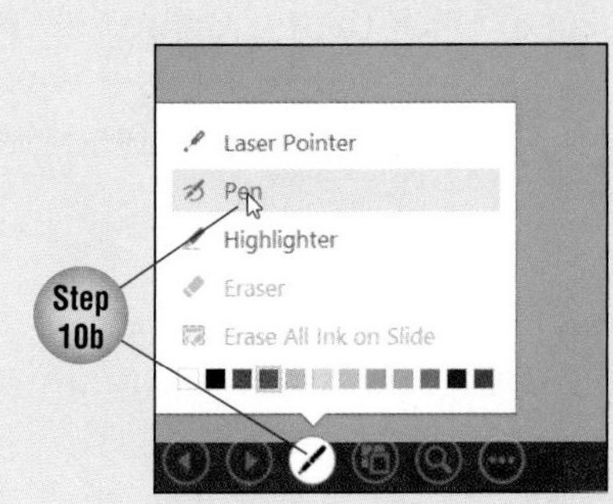

c. Using the mouse, draw a circle around the text *Step 1*.
d. Draw a line below the word *identify*.
e. Press the Esc key to return the mouse pointer to an arrow.

11. Erase the pen markings by clicking the Pen button on the Slide Show toolbar and then clicking *Erase All Ink on Slide* at the pop-up list.

12. Click the Next button to display Slide 3.
13. Click the Pen button and then click *Highlighter*.
14 Click the Pen button and then click the *Light Green* color (sixth option in the bottom row).
15. Drag through the text *Assess your target audience.*

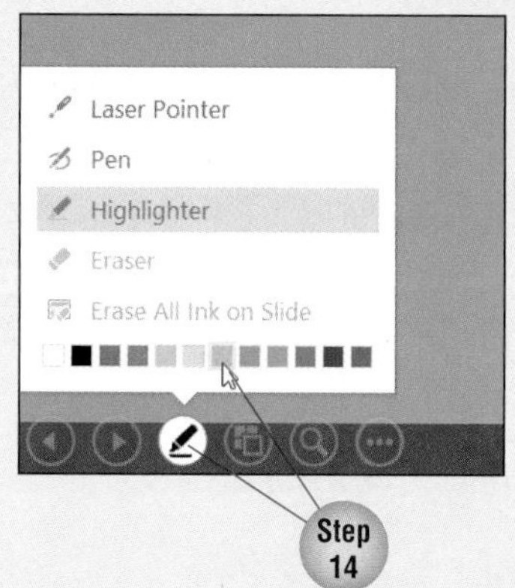

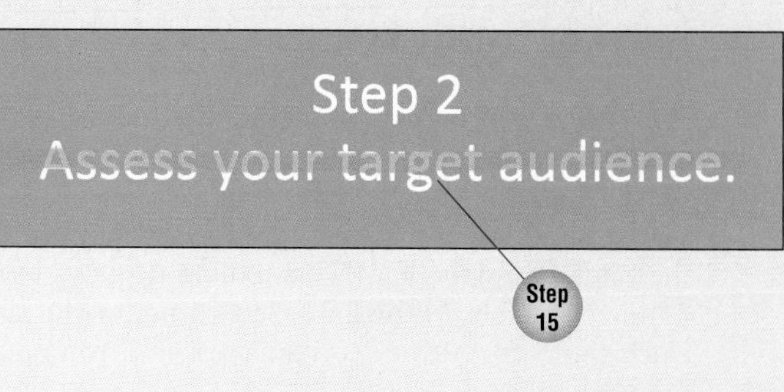

16. Press the Esc key to return the mouse pointer to an arrow.
17. Press the Esc key to end the slide show. Click the Discard button at the message asking if you want to keep or discard the ink annotations.
18. With Slide 3 active, click the Slide Show button on the Status bar to start the slide show.
19. Click the Pen button on the Slide Show toolbar and then click *Laser Pointer* at the pop-up list.
20. Use the laser pointer to point to various locations on the slide.
21. Press the Esc key to return to the mouse pointer to an arrow.
22. Click the Next button on the Slide Show toolbar. (This displays Slide 4.)
23. Turn on the highlighter and then drag through the words *best format* to highlight them.
24. Press the Esc key to return the mouse pointer to an arrow.
25. Continue clicking the left mouse button to move through the presentation.
26. At the black screen, click the left mouse button.
27. At the message asking if you want to keep your ink annotations, click the Keep button.
28. Save the presentation with a new name by completing the following steps:
    a. Click the FILE tab and then click the *Save As* option.
    b. Click the *PC1* folder name that displays below the *Current Folder* heading. (If the PC1 folder name does not display, double-click the *Computer* option.)
    c. At the Save As dialog box, make sure the PC1 folder on your storage medium is the active folder, type **P-C1-P3-PlanningPres-Ink** in the *File name* text box, and then press Enter.
29. Print Slide 4 as a handout.
30. Close **P-C1-P3-PlanningPres-Ink.pptx**.

Applying a Design Theme and Color Variant

As you have learned, PowerPoint provides a variety of built-in design theme templates you can use when creating slides for a presentation. Choose a design theme template at the New backstage area or with options in the Themes group on the DESIGN tab. Click the DESIGN tab and theme thumbnails display in the Themes group. Click one of these themes to apply it to the current presentation. Click the More button at the right side of the theme thumbnails to display any additional themes. You can also click the up-pointing or down-pointing arrows at the right side of the theme thumbnails to scroll through the list. Hover your mouse pointer over a theme and the active slide in the presentation displays with the theme formatting applied. This is an example of the ***live preview*** feature, which allows you to see how theme formatting will affect your presentation.

Each design theme contains color variations that display in the Variants group on the DESIGN tab. These are the same theme color variants that display when you apply a theme template at the New backstage area. Click a color variant thumbnail in the Variants group to apply the colors to the slides in the presentation.

Hover the mouse pointer over a theme thumbnail and a ScreenTip displays (after approximately a second) containing the theme name. Theme names in PowerPoint are similar to those in Word, Excel, Access, and Outlook and apply similar formatting. With the availability of the themes across these applications, you can "brand" your business documents, workbooks, and presentations with a consistent, uniform appearance.

Quick Steps

Apply a Design Theme
1. Click DESIGN tab.
2. Click desired theme in Themes group.

More

HINT

Design themes were designed by professional graphic artists who understand the use of color, space, and design.

Project 3b **Applying a Design Theme and Variant** **Part 2 of 3**

1. Open **P-C1-P3-PlanningPres.pptx**.
2. Make sure Slide 1 is active and that the presentation displays in Normal view.
3. Apply a different design theme to the presentation by completing the following steps:
   a. Click the DESIGN tab.
   b. Hover the mouse pointer over the *Ion* theme thumbnail in the Themes group and notice the theme formatting applied to the slide in the slide pane.
   c. Click the *Ion* theme.

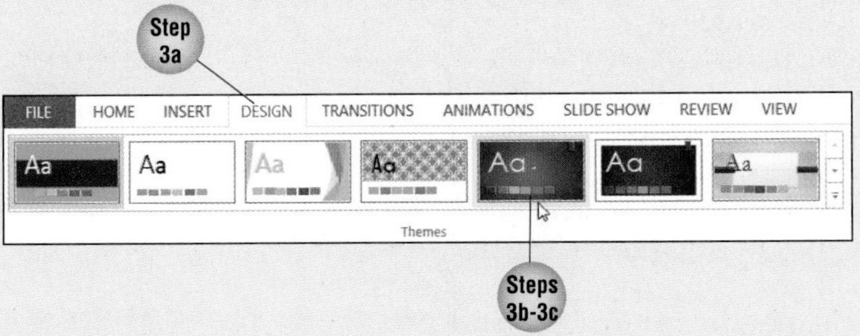

4. Run the presentation and notice the formatting applied by the theme.
5. With the presentation displayed in Normal view, apply a different design theme by clicking the *Facet* theme thumbnail in the Themes group on the DESIGN tab.

6. Apply a color variant by clicking the fourth thumbnail in the Variants group.

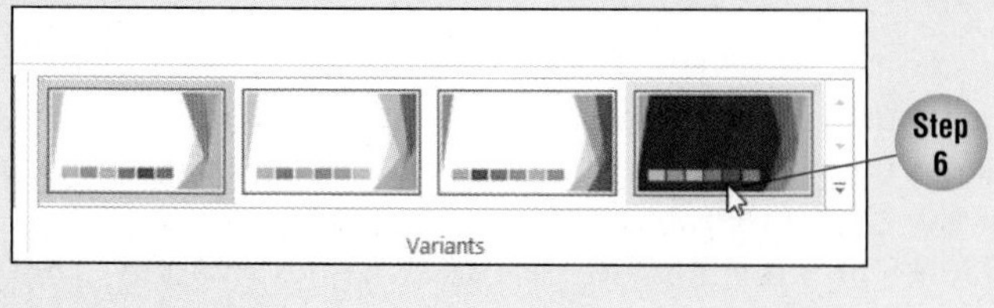

7. Run the presentation.
8. Print the presentation as a handout by completing the following steps:
   a. Click the FILE tab and then click the *Print* option.
   b. At the Print backstage area, click the second gallery (displays with *Full Page Slides*) in the *Settings* category and then click *6 Slides Horizontal* in the *Handouts* section.
   c. Click the Print button.
9. Save and then close **P-C1-P3-PlanningPres.pptx**.

Quick Steps

Delete a Presentation
1. Display Open dialog box.
2. Navigate to desired folder or drive.
3. Click the presentation.
4. Click Organize button, *Delete*.
5. Click Yes.

Deleting a Presentation

File management tasks in PowerPoint can be performed at the Open dialog box or Save As dialog box. To delete a PowerPoint presentation, display the Open dialog box, click the presentation you want deleted, click the Organize button on the toolbar, and then click *Delete* at the drop-down list. At the message asking if you are sure you want to delete the presentation, click the Yes button. The presentation file must be closed to be deleted.

Project 3c Deleting a PowerPoint Presentation

Part 3 of 3

1. Click the FILE tab and then, if necessary, click the *Open* option.
2. At the Open backstage area, click your OneDrive or the *Computer* option.
3. Click the *PC1* folder name that displays below the *Recent Folder* heading in the *Computer* section of the backstage area. (If this folder name does not display, double-click your OneDrive or the *Computer* option.)
4. At the Open dialog box, make sure the PC1 folder on your storage medium is the active folder and then click ***PlanningPres.pptx*** in the Content pane.
5. Click the Organize button on the toolbar and then click *Delete* at the drop-down list.
6. At the message asking if you are sure you want to delete the presentation, click Yes.

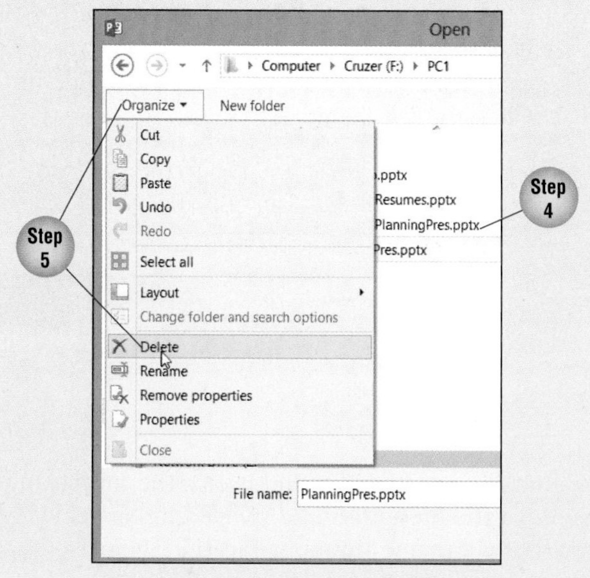

7. Click the Cancel button to close the Open dialog box.

Project 4 Create a Technology Presentation in the Outline Pane

3 Parts

You will create a computer technology presentation in the outline pane, add and remove transitions and sounds to the presentation, and set up the presentation to advance slides automatically after a specified amount of time.

Preparing a Presentation from a Blank Presentation

If you want to create a presentation without a design theme applied, open a blank presentation. Open a blank presentation at the PowerPoint opening screen or at the New backstage area by clicking the Blank Presentation template. You can also open a blank presentation with the keyboard shortcut Ctrl + N.

Quick Steps

Prepare a Presentation from a Blank Presentation

1. Click FILE tab.
2. Click *New* option.
3. Click *Blank Presentation.*

OR

Press Ctrl + N.

Preparing a Presentation in Outline View

You can create slides in a presentation by typing the slide text in the outline pane. Display this pane by clicking the VIEW tab and then clicking the Outline View button in the Presentation Views group. The outline pane replaces the slide thumbnails pane at the left side of the screen. A slide number displays in the pane followed by a small slide icon. When typing text in the outline pane, press the Tab key to move the insertion point to the next tab stop. This moves the insertion point and also changes the formatting. The formatting will vary depending on the theme you chose. Press Shift + Tab to move the insertion point to the previous tab stop. Moving the insertion point back to the left margin will create a new slide.

Project 4a Preparing a Presentation in Outline View

Part 1 of 3

1. At a blank screen, click the FILE tab and then click the *New* option.
2. At the New backstage area, click the *Blank Presentation* template.
3. At the blank presentation, click the VIEW tab and then click the Outline View button in the Presentation Views group.

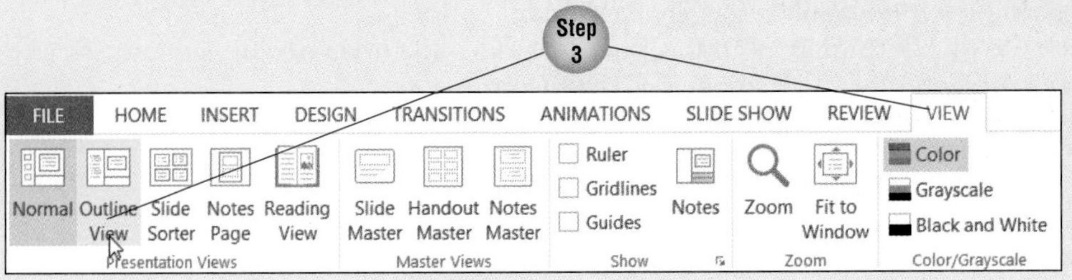

4. Click in the outline pane immediately right of the slide icon.
5. Type the first slide title shown in Figure 1.8 (*Computer Technology*), and then press Enter. (The text you type displays immediately right of the small orange slide icon that displays in the outline pane.)
6. Type the second slide title shown in Figure 1.8 (*The Motherboard*) and then press Enter.
7. Press the Tab key, type the text after the first bullet in Figure 1.8 (*Buses*), and then press Enter.
8. Continue typing the text as it displays in Figure 1.8. Press the Tab key to move the insertion point to the next tab stop or press Shift + Tab to move the insertion point back to a previous tab stop.

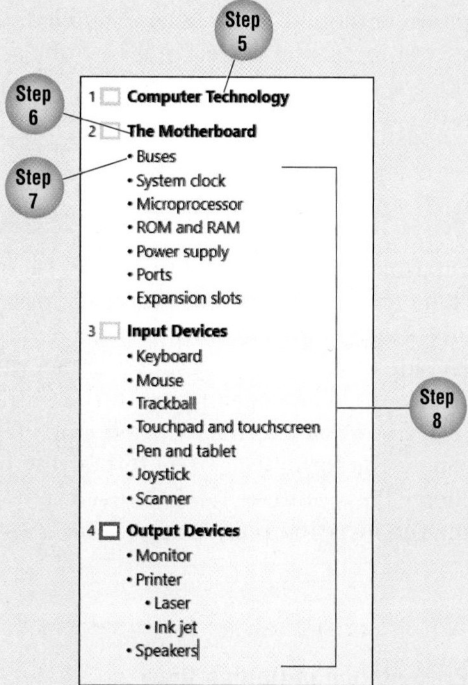

9. After typing all of the information as shown in Figure 1.8, click the Normal button in the Presentation Views group on the VIEW tab.
10. Click Slide 1 in the slide thumbnails pane. (This displays Slide 1 in the slide pane.)
11. Apply a design theme by completing the following steps:
    a. Click the DESIGN tab.
    b. Click the *Ion* thumbnail in the Themes group.
    c. Click the fourth thumbnail in the Variants group (the orange color variant).
12. Save the presentation and name it **P-C1-P4-Computers**.
13. Run the presentation.

Figure 1.8 Project 4a

1 Computer Technology
2 The Motherboard
- Buses
- System clock
- Microprocessor
- ROM and RAM
- Power supply
- Ports
- Expansion slots

3 Input Devices
- Keyboard
- Mouse
- Trackball
- Touchpad and touchscreen
- Pen and tablet
- Joystick
- Scanner

4 Output Devices
- Monitor
- Printer
  - Laser
  - Ink jet
- Speakers

Adding Transitions and Sound Effects

You can apply interesting transitions and sounds to a presentation. A ***transition*** is how one slide is removed from the screen during a presentation and the next slide is displayed. You can apply transitions such as cut, fade, push, wipe, split, reveal, and random bars. To add transitions and sounds, open a presentation, and then click the TRANSITIONS tab. This displays transition buttons and options, as shown in Figure 1.9.

Transitions and sounds apply by default to the active slide. If you want transitions and sound to affect all slides, click the Apply To All button in the Timing group. In Slide Sorter view, you can select all slides by pressing Ctrl + A (or by clicking the HOME tab, clicking the Select button, and then clicking *Select All* at the drop-down list) and then apply the desired transition and/or sound.

Apply To All

Figure 1.9 TRANSITIONS Tab

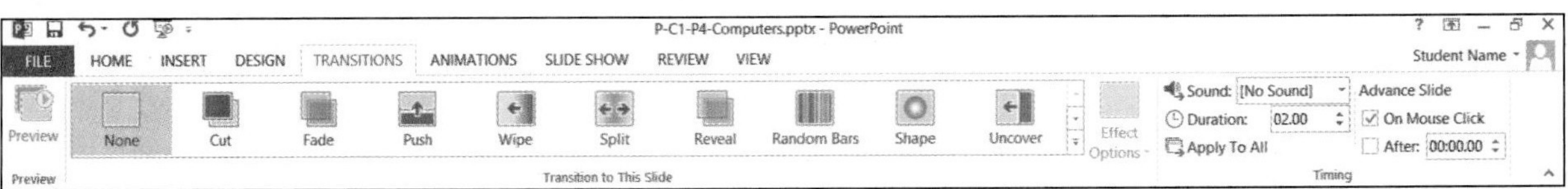

Adding Transitions

Quick Steps

Apply a Transition to Slides

1. Click TRANSITIONS tab.
2. Click desired transition in Transition to This Slide group.
3. Click Apply To All button.

Apply Sound to Slides

1. Click TRANSITIONS tab.
2. Click down-pointing arrow at right of *Sound* option.
3. Click desired sound.
4. Click Apply To All button.

Make a presentation more appealing by adding effects such as transitions and sounds.

To add a transition, click a transition thumbnail in the Transition to This Slide group on the TRANSITIONS tab. When you click a transition thumbnail, the transition displays in the slide in the slide pane. Use the down-pointing and up-pointing arrows at the right side of the transition thumbnails to display additional transitions. Click the More button that displays at the right side of the visible transition thumbnails and a drop-down gallery displays with additional transition options. Use the *Duration* measurement box to specify the duration of slide transitions when running the presentation. Click the up- or down-pointing arrows at the right side of the *Duration* measurement box to change the duration time. You can also select the current time in the measurement box and then type the desired time.

When you apply a transition to slides in a presentation, animation icons display below the slides in the slide thumbnails pane and in Slide Sorter view. Click an animation icon for a particular slide and the slide will display the transition effect.

Adding Sounds

You can also add sounds to your transitions. To add a sound, click the down-pointing arrow at the right side of the *Sound* option box and then click the desired sound at the drop-down list. Preview a transition and or sound applied to a slide by clicking the Preview button located at the left side of the TRANSITIONS tab.

Removing Transitions and Sounds

You can remove a transition and/or sound from specific slides or from all slides in a presentation. To remove a transition, click the *None* transition thumbnail in the Transition to This Slide group. To remove transitions from all slides, click the Apply To All button in the Timing group. To remove sound from a slide, click the down-pointing arrow at the right side of the *Sound* option and then click *[No Sound]* at the drop-down gallery. To remove sound from all slides, click the Apply To All button.

Project 4b **Adding Transitions and Sounds to a Presentation** **Part 2 of 3**

1. With **P-C1-P4-Computers.pptx** open, click the TRANSITIONS tab.
2. Apply transitions and sound to all slides in the presentation by completing the following steps:
   a. Click the More button at the right side of the transition thumbnails.
   b. Click the *Fall Over* option in the *Exciting* section.

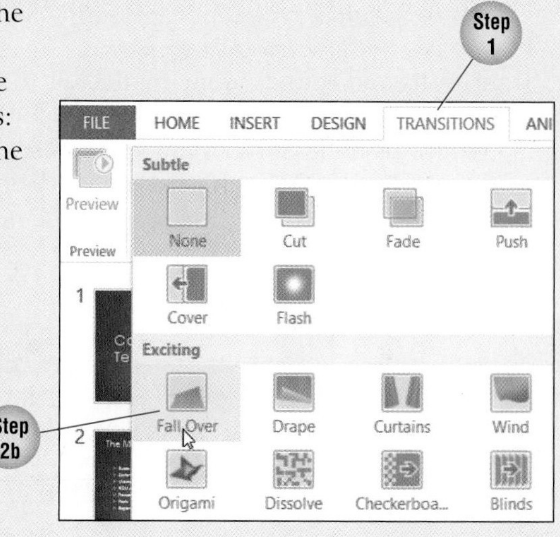

c. Click the Effect Options button in the Transition to This Slide group and then click *Right* at the drop-down list.
d. Click in the *Duration* measurement box in the Timing group, type 1, and then press Enter.
e. Click the down-pointing arrow at the right side of the *Sound* option box in the Timing group and then click *Chime* at the drop-down list.
f. Click the Apply To All button in the Timing group.

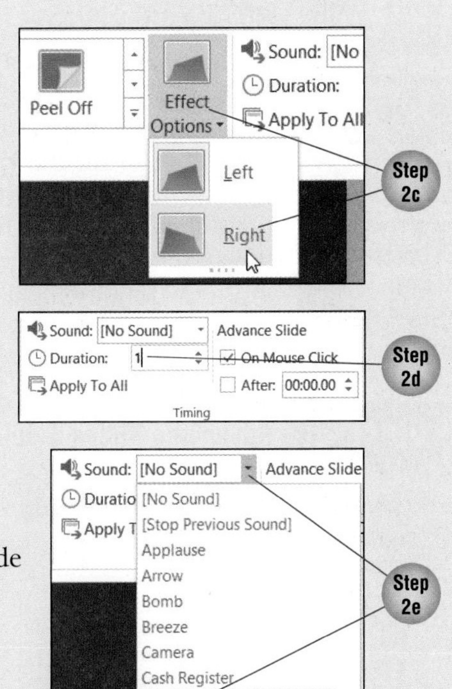

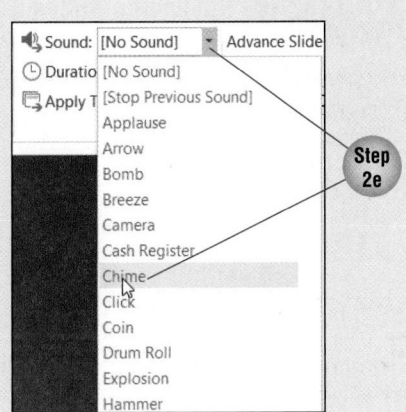

3. Run the presentation. (Notice the transitions and sound as you move from slide to slide.)
4. With the presentation in Normal view and the TRANSITIONS tab active, remove the transitions and sound by completing the following steps:
   a. Click the More button at the right side of the transition thumbnails in the Transition to This Slide group and then click the *None* thumbnail.
   b. Click the down-pointing arrow at the right side of the *Sound* option box and then click *[No Sound]* at the drop-down list.
   c. Click the Apply To All button.
5. Apply transitions and sounds to specific slides by completing the following steps:
   a. Make sure the presentation displays in Normal view.
   b. Click Slide 1 in the slide thumbnails pane.
   c. Hold down the Shift key and then click Slide 2. (Slides 1 and 2 will display with orange backgrounds.)
   d. Click the More button at the right side of the transition thumbnails and then click the *Ferris Wheel* option in the *Dynamic Content* section.
   e. Click the down-pointing arrow at the right side of the *Sound* option box and then click the *Breeze* option.
   f. Click Slide 3 in the slide pane.
   g. Hold down the Shift key and then click Slide 4.
   h. Click the More button at the right side of the transition thumbnails and then click the *Glitter* option in the *Exciting* section.
   i. Click the down-pointing arrow at the right side of the *Sound* option box and then click the *Wind* option.
6. Run the presentation from the beginning.
7. Remove the transitions and sounds from all slides. (Refer to Step 4.)
8. Save **P-C1-P4-Computers.pptx**.

Quick Steps

Advance Slides Automatically
1. Click TRANSITIONS tab.
2. Click *After* check box.
3. Insert desired number of seconds in measurement box.
4. Click *On Mouse Click* check box.
5. Click Apply To All button.

Advancing Slides Automatically

You can advance slides in a slide show after a specific number of seconds with options in the Timing group on the TRANSITIONS tab. To advance slides automatically, click in the *After* check box and then insert the desired number of seconds in the measurement box. You can select the current time in the measurement box and then type the desired time or click the up- or down-pointing arrows to increase or decrease the time. Click the *On Mouse Click* check box to remove the check mark. If you want the transition time to affect all slides in the presentation, click the Apply To All button. In Slide Sorter view, the transition time displays below each affected slide.

Project 4c **Advancing Slides Automatically** **Part 3 of 3**

1. With **P-C1-P4-Computers.pptx** open, make sure the TRANSITIONS tab is active.
2. Click in the *After* check box in the Timing group to insert a check mark.
3. Click the *On Mouse Click* check box to remove the check mark.
4. Click the up-pointing arrow at the right side of the *After* measurement box until *00:04.00* displays in the box.
5. Click the Apply To All button.
6. Run the presentation from the beginning. (Each slide will advance automatically after four seconds.)
7. At the black screen, click the left mouse button.

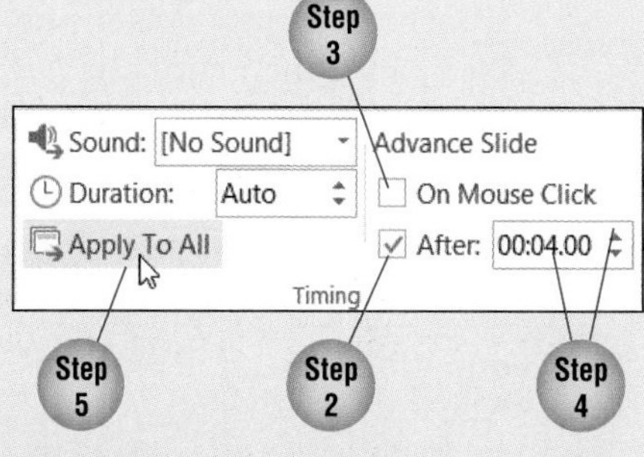

8. Print the presentation as an outline by completing the following steps:
   a. Click the FILE tab and then click the *Print* option.
   b. At the Print backstage area, click the second gallery (displays with *Full Page Slides*) in the *Settings* category and then click *Outline* in the *Print Layout* section.
   c. Click the Print button.
9. Save and then close **P-C1-P4-Computers.pptx**.

Chapter Summary

- PowerPoint is a presentation graphics program you can use to create slides for an on-screen presentation.
- Open a presentation at the Open dialog box. Display this dialog box by clicking the FILE tab and then clicking the *Open* option. At the Open backstage area, click your OneDrive or the *Computer* option and then click the Browse button.
- You can pin a presentation to and unpin a presentation from the Recent list at the PowerPoint 2013 opening screen and the Recent Presentations list at the Open backstage area.
- Start running a presentation by clicking the Start From Beginning button on the Quick Access toolbar, clicking the Slide Show button in the view area on the Status bar, or by clicking the VIEW tab and then clicking the From Beginning button.
- Close a presentation by clicking the FILE tab and then clicking the *Close* option or with the keyboard shortcut Ctrl + F4.

- Before creating a presentation in PowerPoint, plan the presentation by defining the purpose and determining the content and medium.
- Build-in presentation design theme templates are available at the New backstage area. Display this backstage area by clicking the FILE tab and then clicking the *New* option.
- To insert text in a slide, click the desired placeholder and then type the text.
- A slide layout provides placeholders for specific data in a slide. Choose a slide layout by clicking the Layout button in the Slides group on the HOME tab.
- Insert a new slide in a presentation with the Title and Content layout by clicking the New Slide button in the Slides group on the HOME tab. Insert a new slide with a specific layout by clicking the New Slide button arrow and then clicking the desired layout at the drop-down list.
- Save a presentation by clicking the Save button on the Quick Access toolbar or clicking the FILE tab and then clicking the *Save As* option. At the Save As backstage area, click your OneDrive or the *Computer* option and then click the Browse button. At the Save As dialog box, type a name for the presentation.
- View a presentation in one of the following six views: Normal view, which is the default and displays two panes — the slide thumbnails pane and the slide pane; Outline view, which displays the outline pane for typing text in slides; Slide Sorter view, which displays all slides in the presentation in slide thumbnails; Reading view, which delivers a presentation to someone viewing it on his or her own computer; Notes Page view, which displays an individual slide with any added notes displayed below the slide; and Slide Show view, which runs the presentation.
- Navigate to various slides in a presentation using the mouse and/or keyboard. You can use the Previous Slide and Next Slide buttons located at the bottom of the vertical scroll bar, the scroll box on the vertical scroll bar, arrow keys on the keyboard, or the Page Up and Page Down keys on the keyboard.
- Click the FILE tab and the backstage area displays options for working with and managing presentations.
- With options at the Print backstage area, you can print presentations with each slide on a separate piece of paper; each slide at the top of the page, leaving room for notes; all or a specific number of slides on a single piece of paper; or slide titles and topics in outline form.
- When running a presentation, the Slide Show toolbar displays in the lower left corner of the slide. This toolbar contains buttons and options for running a presentation. Use the buttons to navigate to slides, make ink notations on slides, display slide thumbnails, zoom in on a specific location in a slide, and display a Help menu.
- Apply a design theme to a presentation by clicking the DESIGN tab and then clicking the desired theme in the Themes group. Apply a color variation to a theme by clicking the desired thumbnail in the Variants group on the DESIGN tab.
- Delete a presentation at the Open dialog box by clicking the presentation file name, clicking the Organize button on the toolbar, and then clicking *Delete* at the drop-down list.
- Open a blank presentation by displaying the New backstage area and then clicking the *Blank Presentation* template or with the keyboard shortcut Ctrl + N.

- Type text in a slide in the slide pane or in the outline pane. Display the outline pane by clicking the VIEW tab and then clicking the Outline View button.
- Enhance a presentation by adding transitions (how one slide is removed from the screen and replaced with the next slide) and sound. Add transitions and sound to a presentation with options on the TRANSITIONS tab.
- Advance slides automatically in a slide show by removing the check mark from the *On Mouse Click* check box on the TRANSITIONS tab, inserting a check mark in the *After* check box, and then specifying the desired time in the time measurement box.
- Click the Apply To All button to apply transitions, sounds, and/or time settings to all slides in a presentation.

Commands Review

FEATURE	RIBBON TAB, GROUP/OPTION	BUTTON, OPTION	KEYBOARD SHORTCUT
close presentation	FILE, *Close*		Ctrl + F4
design theme	DESIGN, Themes		
New backstage area	FILE, *New*		
new slide	HOME, Slides		Ctrl + M
Normal view	VIEW, Presentation Views		
Notes Page view	VIEW, Presentation Views		
Open backstage area	FILE, *Open*		Ctrl + O
Outline view	VIEW, Presentation Views		
Print backstage area	FILE, *Print*		Ctrl + P
run presentation	SLIDE SHOW, Start Slide Show OR Quick Access Toolbar		F5
Save As backstage area	FILE, *Save* OR *Save As*		Ctrl + S
slide layout	HOME, Slides		
Slide Sorter view	VIEW, Presentation Views		
sound	TRANSITIONS, Timing		
transition	TRANSITIONS, Transition to This Slide		
transition duration	Transitions, Timing		

Concepts Check Test Your Knowledge

Completion: In the space provided at the right, indicate the correct term, command, or number.

1. Click this tab to display options for working with and managing presentations. ________________
2. This toolbar contains buttons for commonly used commands. ________________
3. This area contains the tabs and commands divided into groups. ________________
4. This is the keyboard shortcut to close a presentation. ________________
5. Display design theme templates in this backstage area. ________________
6. Insert a new slide by clicking the New Slide button in this group on the HOME tab. ________________
7. Change to this view to view all slides in the presentation as slide thumbnails. ________________
8. This is the default view and displays two panes. ________________
9. Click this button on the VIEW tab to display the outline pane. ________________
10. The Previous Slide and Next Slide buttons display in this location. ________________
11. To run a presentation beginning with Slide 1, click this button on the Quick Access toolbar. ________________
12. Apply a design theme to a presentation by clicking this tab and then clicking the desired theme in the Themes group. ________________
13. To add a transition, click a transition thumbnail in the Transition to This Slide group on this tab. ________________
14. When you apply a transition to slides in a presentation, these display below the slide numbers in the slide thumbnails pane. ________________
15. To advance slides automatically, remove the check mark from the *On Mouse Click* check box, insert a check mark in this check box, and then insert the desired number of seconds. ________________

Skills Check Assess Your Performance

Assessment 1

CREATE A PRESENTATION ON TYPES OF RESUMES

1. Create a presentation with the text shown in Figure 1.10 on the next page by completing the following steps:
   a. With PowerPoint open, click the FILE tab and then click the *New* option.
   b. At the New backstage area, click the *Wood Type* theme, click the variant in the top row in the second column, and then click the Create button.
   c. Create slides with the text shown in Figure 1.10. Use the Title Slide layout for slides 1 and 5 and use the Title and Content layout for slides 2, 3, and 4.
2. Save the completed presentation in the PC1 folder on your storage medium and name the presentation **P-C1-A1-ResumeTypes**.
3. Apply the Push transition (located in the *Subtle* section) with a From Left effect to all slides in the presentation.
4. Change the transition duration to 01.50 seconds.
5. Apply the Wind sound to all slides in the presentation.
6. Run the presentation.
7. Print the presentation as a handout with six slides printed horizontally per page.
8. Save and then close **P-C1-A1-ResumeTypes.pptx**.

Assessment 2

CREATE A PRESENTATION ON PREPARING A COMPANY NEWSLETTER

1. At the blank screen, click the FILE tab and then click the *New* option.
2. At the New backstage area, click the *Blank Presentation* template.
3. Create slides with the text shown in Figure 1.11 on page 40.
4. Apply the Basis design theme and the orange variant (third thumbnail in the Variants group).
5. Run the presentation.
6. Print the presentation as a handout with all six slides printed horizontally on the page.
7. Make the following changes to the presentation:
   a. Apply the Parallax design theme and the red variant (fourth thumbnail in the Variants group).
   b. Add the Switch transition (located in the *Exciting* section) with a Left effect to all slides.
   c. Add the Camera sound to all slides.
   d. Specify that all slides advance automatically after five seconds.
8. Run the presentation.
9. Save the presentation and name it **P-C1-A2-Newsletter**.
10. Close **P-C1-A2-Newsletter.pptx**.

Figure 1.10 Assessment 1

Slide 1	Title	=	Career Finders
	Subtitle	=	Types of Resumes
Slide 2	Title	=	Functional Resume
	Bullets	=	• Emphasizes skills and achievements • Used when you lack a formal education • Used when you have had many different jobs with no clear pattern or progression
Slide 3	Title	=	Chronological Resume
	Bullets	=	• List more recent training or jobs first and then proceed backwards • Components include: - personal contact information - employment history including employers, employment dates, positions held, and achievements - educational qualifications - professional development
Slide 4	Title	=	Hybrid Resume
	Bullets	=	• Combines best of chronological and functional resume • Contains fixed order of chronological resume • More emphasis on skills and achievements
Slide 5	Title	=	Career Finders
	Subtitle	=	Sign up today for Career Finder's resume writing workshop!

Visual Benchmark Demonstrate Your Proficiency

CREATE A PRESENTATION ON PREPARING A NEWSLETTER

1. Create the presentation shown in Figure 1.12 with the following specifications:
   a. Create the presentation with the Organic design theme template and apply the appropriate variant.
   b. Create the slides as shown in the figure (reading from left to right).
   c. Apply a transition, sound, and transition duration time of your choosing to each slide in the presentation.
2. Save the completed presentation and name it **P-C1-VB-Interview**.
3. Run the presentation.
4. Print the presentation as a handout with all six slides printed horizontally on the page.
5. Close the presentation.

Figure 1.11 Assessment 2

Slide 1	Title	=	PREPARING A COMPANY NEWSLETTER
	Subtitle	=	Planning and Designing the Layout
Slide 2	Title	=	Planning a Newsletter
	Bullets	=	• Use pictures of different people from your organization in each issue. • Distribute contributor sheets soliciting information from employees. • Keep the focus of the newsletter on issues of interest to employees.
Slide 3	Title	=	Planning a Newsletter
	Bullets	=	• Make sure the focus is on various levels of employment; do not focus on top management only. • Conduct regular surveys to see if your newsletter provides a needed source of information.
Slide 4	Title	=	Designing a Newsletter
	Bulllets	=	• Maintain consistent elements from issue to issue such as: - Column layout - Nameplate formatting and location - Formatting of headlines - Use of color
Slide 5	Title	=	Designing a Newsletter
	Bullets	=	• Consider the following elements when designing a newsletter: - Focus - Balance - White space - Directional flow
Slide 6	Title	=	Creating a Newsletter Layout
	Bullets	=	• Choose paper size • Choose paper weight • Determine margins • Specify column layout

Figure 1.12 Visual Benchmark

Company Research

- Gather company background information.
- Review the company's website.
- Ask the employer for company history.
- Search online for information on the company.

Practice

- Practice interviewing with a friend.
- Record interview responses and listen to determine how well you did.
- Prepare answers to commonly-asked interview questions.

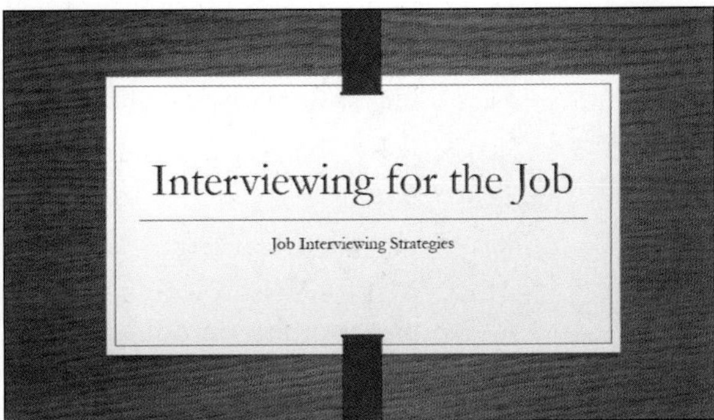

Prepare for the Interview

- Prepare a list of questions for the interviewer.
- Bring extra copies of your resume and list of references.
- Be on time for the interview.
- Know the interviewer's name and use it during the interview.

Maintain Composure

- Ask for clarification on questions.
- Take a moment or two to frame your responses.
- At the end of the interview:
  - Thank the interviewer.
  - Reiterate your interest in the position.
- Send a thank you note restating your interest in the position.

Case Study Apply Your Skills

Part 1

You work for Citizens for Consumer Safety, a nonprofit organization providing information on household safety. Your supervisor, Melinda Johansson, will be presenting information on smoke detectors at a community meeting and has asked you to prepare a PowerPoint presentation. Open the Word document named **PPSmokeDetectors.docx**. Read over the information and then use the information to prepare a presentation. Consider the information in the *Planning a Presentation* section of this chapter and then prepare at least five slides. Apply an appropriate design theme and add a transition and sound to all slides. Save the presentation and name it **P-C1-CS-PPSmokeDetectors**. Run the presentation and then print the presentation as a handout with all slides on one page.

Part 2

Ms. Johansson has looked at the printout of the presentation and has asked you to print the presentation with two slides per page and in grayscale. Use the Help feature to learn about printing in grayscale and then print the presentation in grayscale with two slides per page.

Part 3

Ms. Johansson would like to provide information to participants at the presentation on online companies that sell smoke detectors. Using the Internet, locate at least three online stores that sell smoke detectors. Insert a new slide in the **P-C1-CS-PPSmokeDetectors.pptx** presentation that includes the names of the stores, web addresses, and any additional information you feel is important. Save the presentation and then print the presentation in Outline view. Close the presentation.

MICROSOFT® POWERPOINT®

Modifying a Presentation and Using Help

PERFORMANCE OBJECTIVES

Upon successful completion of Chapter 2, you will be able to:

- **Check spelling**
- **Use the Thesaurus**
- **Insert and delete text in slides**
- **Find and replace text in slides**
- **Cut, copy, and paste text in slides**
- **Rearrange text in the slide thumbnails pane**
- **Size and rearrange placeholders**
- **Insert, delete, move, and copy slides**
- **Copy slides between presentations**
- **Duplicate slides**
- **Reuse slides**
- **Create and manage sections**
- **Customize the Quick Access toolbar**
- **Use the Help feature**

Tutorials

2.1 Using the Spelling and Thesaurus Features

2.2 Modifying Placeholders

2.3 Finding and Replacing Text

2.4 Cutting, Copying, Pasting, and Aligning Text

2.5 Rearranging, Deleting, and Hiding Slides

2.6 Duplicating and Reusing Slides

2.7 Creating Sections within a Presentation

2.8 Customizing the Quick Access Toolbar

2.9 Using Help in PowerPoint

When preparing a presentation, you may need to modify it by inserting and deleting text in slides or finding and replacing specific text. Improve the quality of your presentation by completing a spelling check to ensure that the words in your presentation are spelled correctly and use the Thesaurus to find synonyms and antonyms for words. Additional modifications you may need to make to a presentation include sizing and rearranging placeholders and rearranging, inserting, deleting, or copying slides. In this chapter, you will learn how to make these modifications to a presentation as well as how to preview a presentation and use the Help feature. Model answers for this chapter's projects appear on the following pages.

Note: Before beginning the projects, copy to your storage medium the PC2 subfolder from the PowerPoint folder on the CD that accompanies this textbook and then make PC2 the active folder.

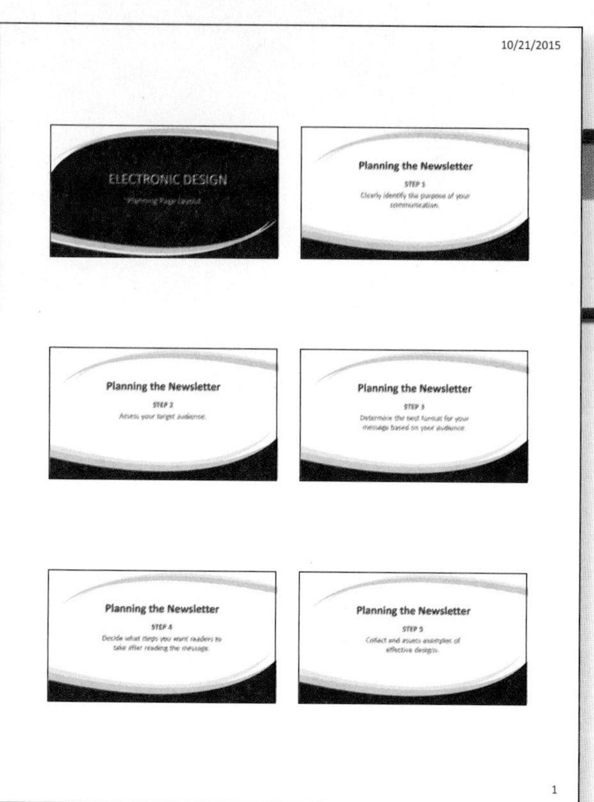

Project 1 Check Spelling and Manage Text in a Design Presentation P-C2-P1-ElectronicDesign.pptx

10/21/2015

Network System

TIME
- How quickly can information be delivered?
- What is the estimated training time for a new system?
- Will improved efficiency translate into lowered personnel costs?
- What is the time frame for implementing a new system?

EFFICIENCY
- How does the effectiveness of a new system compare with the current system?
- What is the time frame for implementing a new system?
- Will improved efficiency translate into lowered personnel costs?

BUDGET
- Can the system be purchased with funds from the existing budget?
- Will the system require ongoing funds?
- Who will manage the budget?
- What are the long-term ramifications on the budget?

1

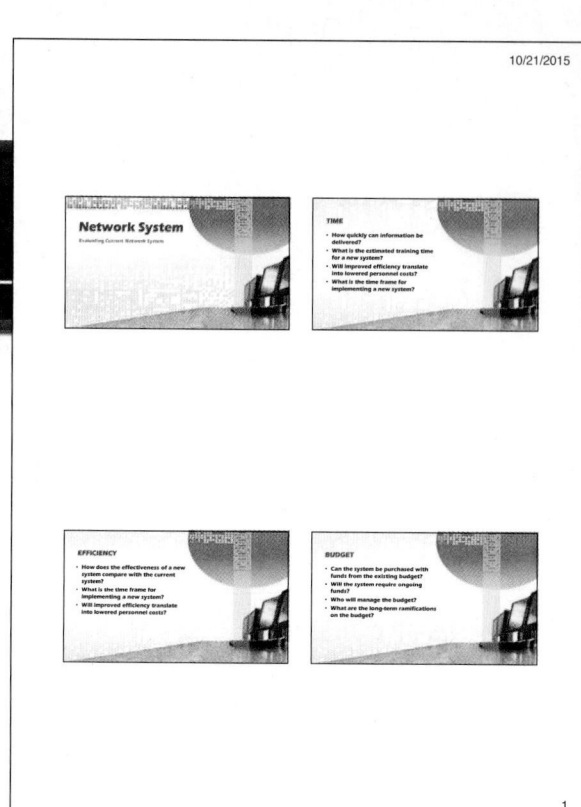

Project 2 Cut, Copy, Paste, Rearrange, and Manage Slides in a Network Presentation P-C2-P2-NetworkSystem.pptx

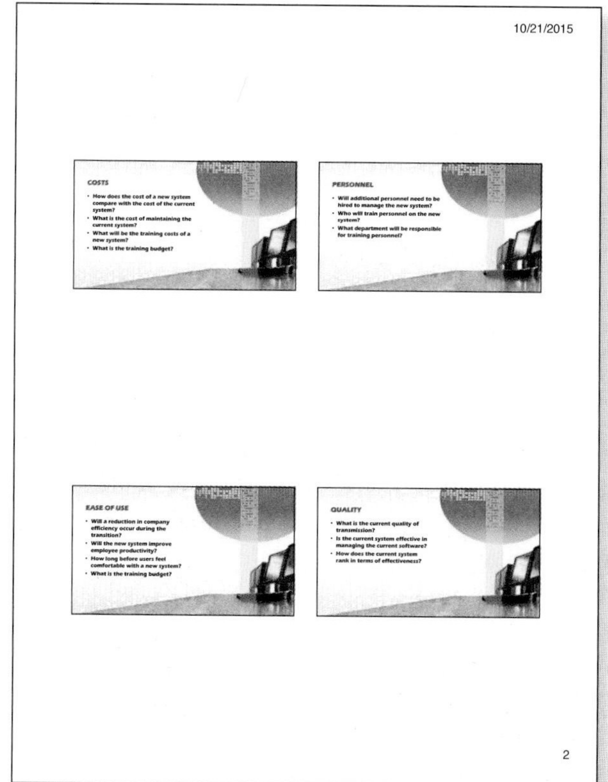

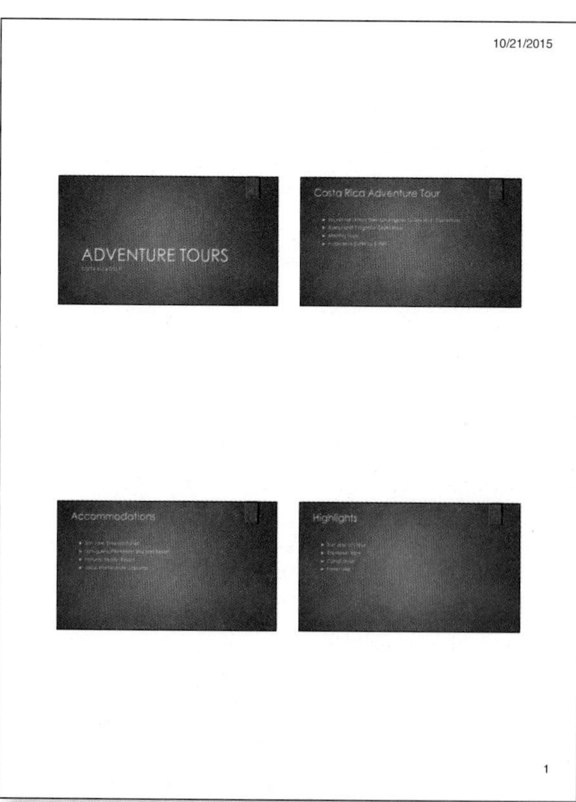

Project 3 Insert and Manage Slides in an Adventure Tours Presentation P-C2-P3-AdvTours.pptx

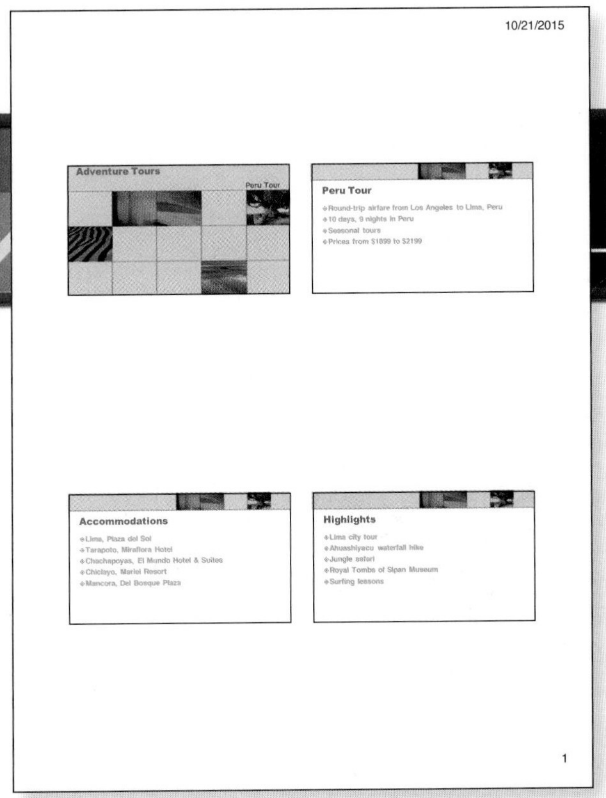

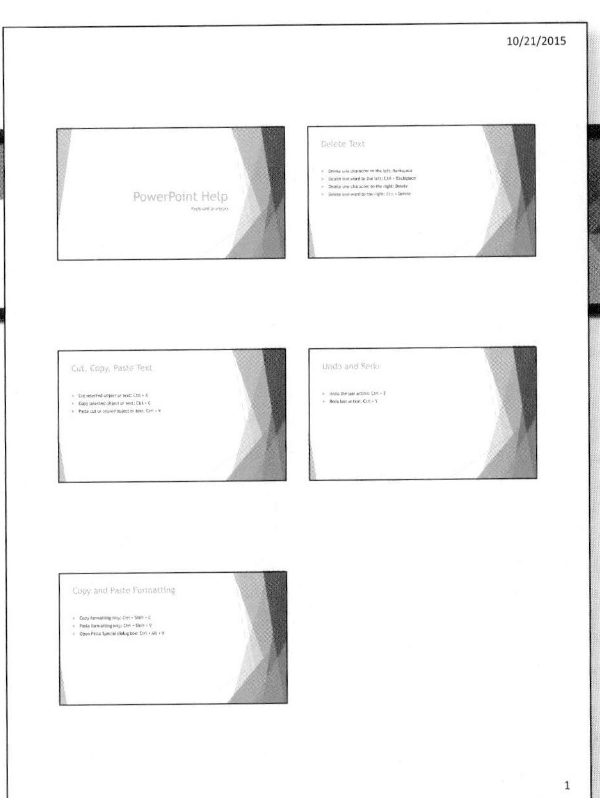

Project 4 Use PowerPoint Help Feature and Create a Presentation P-C2-P4-Shortcuts.pptx

Project 1 Check Spelling, Use the Thesaurus, and Manage Text in a Design Presentation — 3 Parts

You will open a presentation on steps for planning a design publication, complete a spelling check on the text in the presentation, use the Thesaurus to find synonyms, and find and replace specific text in slides.

Checking Spelling

When preparing a presentation, perform a spelling check on text in slides using PowerPoint's spelling checker feature. The spelling checker feature compares words in slides in a presentation with words in its dictionary. If a match is found, the word is passed over. If a match is not found, the Spelling task pane displays with replacement suggestions. At this task pane, you can choose to change the word or ignore the word and leave it as written. To perform a spelling check, click the REVIEW tab and then click the Spelling button in the Proofing group. You can also start the spelling checker by pressing the F7 function key on the keyboard.

When you begin checking spelling in the presentation in Project 1a, the spelling checker will stop at the misspelled word *Layuot* and display the Spelling task pane as shown in Figure 2.1. The options available in the Spelling task pane are described in Table 2.1 on the next page.

Quick Steps

Complete a Spelling Check
1. Click REVIEW tab.
2. Click Spelling button.
3. Change or ignore errors.
4. Click OK.

Spelling

Figure 2.1 Spelling Task Pane

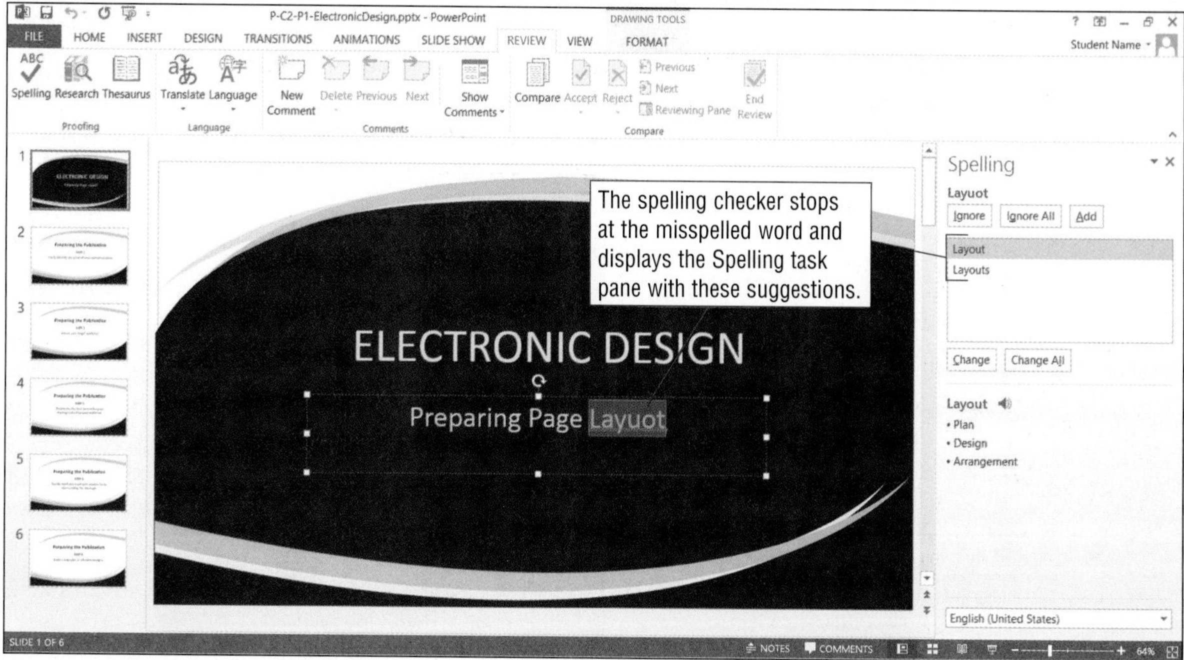

Table 2.1 Spelling Task Pane Options

Button	*Function*
Add	Adds selected word to the main spelling check dictionary.
Change	Replaces selected word in slide with selected word in the task pane list box.
Change All	Replaces selected word in slide with selected word in the task pane list box and all other occurrences of the word in all slides.
Delete	Deletes the currently selected word(s).
Ignore	Skips that occurrence of the word.
Ignore All	Skips that occurrence of the word and all other occurrences of the word in all slides.

Quick Steps

Using the Thesaurus
1. Click desired word.
2. Click REVIEW tab.
3. Click Thesaurus button.
4. Position mouse pointer on desired replacement word in Thesaurus task pane.
5. Click down-pointing arrow at right of word.
6. Click *Insert*.

Thesaurus

Using the Thesaurus

Use the Thesaurus to find synonyms, antonyms, and related words for a particular word. Synonyms are words that have the same or nearly the same meaning and antonyms are words with opposite meanings. To use the Thesaurus, click the word for which you want to display synonyms and antonyms, click the REVIEW tab, and then click the Thesaurus button in the Proofing group. This displays the Thesaurus task pane with information about the word where the insertion point is positioned. Hover the mouse over the desired synonym or antonym, click the down-pointing arrow that displays at the right of the word, and then click *Insert* at the drop-down list. You can also display and insert synonyms for words by right-clicking the word, pointing to *Synonyms*, and then clicking the desired word at the side menu.

Project 1a Checking the Spelling in a Presentation Part 1 of 3

1. Open **ElectronicDesign.pptx** and then save the presentation with Save As and name it **P-C2-P1-ElectronicDesign**.
2. With the presentation in Normal view, run a spelling check by completing the following steps:
   a. Click the REVIEW tab.
   b. Click the Spelling button in the Proofing group.
   c. The spelling checker selects the misspelled word *Layuot* and displays the Spelling task pane. The proper spelling (*Layout*) is selected in the Spelling task pane list box, so click the Change button (or the Change All button).
   d. The spelling checker selects the misspelled word *Clerly*. The correct spelling is selected in the Spelling task pane list box, so click the Change button (or the Change All button).

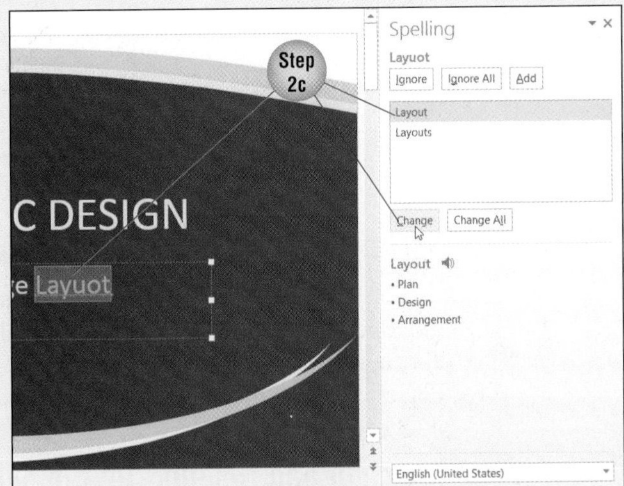

   e. When the spelling checker selects the misspelled word *massege*, click *message* in the Spelling task pane list box and then click the Change button (or the Change All button).

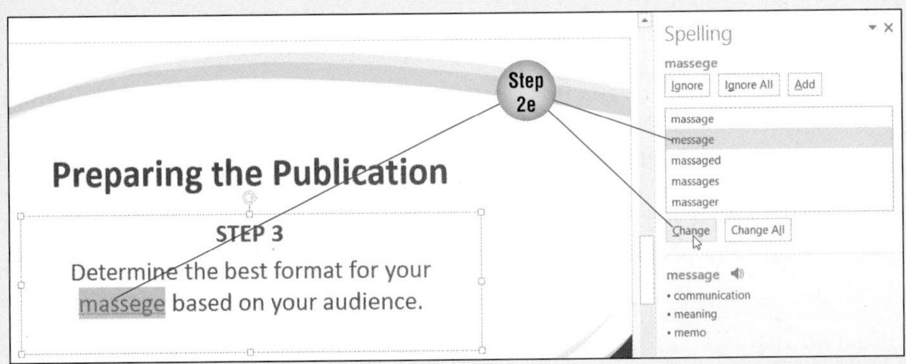

   f. The spelling checker selects the misspelled word *fo*. The correct spelling is selected in the Spelling task pane list box, so click the Change button (or the Change All button).
   g. At the message telling you that the spelling check is complete, click the OK button.
3. Make Slide 2 active and then use the Thesaurus to find a synonym for *point* by completing the following steps:
   a. Click in the word *point*.
   b. Click the REVIEW tab, if necessary, and then click the Thesaurus button.
   c. At the Thesaurus task pane, scroll down the task pane list box to display *purpose* (below *purpose (n.)*).
   d. Hover your mouse pointer over the word *purpose* in the task pane, click the down-pointing arrow, and then click *Insert* at the drop-down list.
   e. Close the Thesaurus task pane.

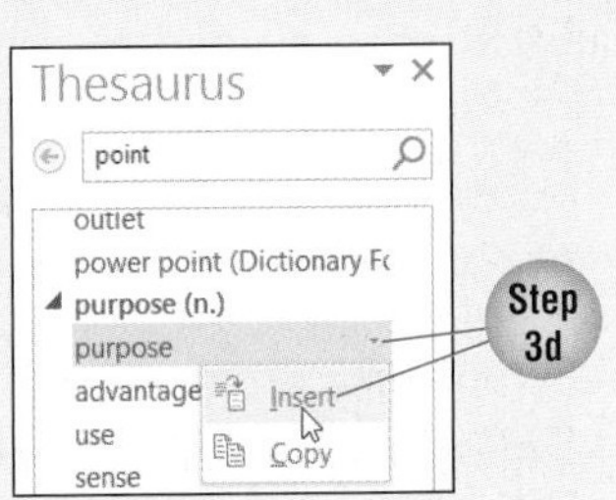

4. Make Slide 6 active and right-click the word *Gather*.
5. Point to *Synonyms* and then click *Collect* at the side menu.
6. Save **P-C2-P1-ElectronicDesign.pptx**.

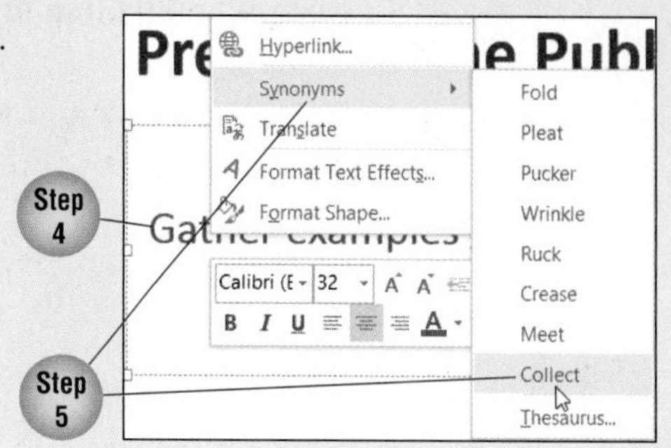

Managing Text in Slides

As you enter text in new slides or manage existing slides, you may need to edit, move, copy, or delete text. You may also want to find specific text in slides and replace it with other text. Text is generally inserted in a slide ***placeholder***. Placeholders can be moved, sized, and/or deleted.

Inserting and Deleting Text in Slides

To insert or delete text in an individual slide, open the presentation, edit the text as needed, and then save the presentation. If you want to delete more than one character, consider selecting the text first. This will help reduce the amount of times you have to press the Delete key or Backspace key. Several methods can be used for selecting text, as described in Table 2.2.

Text in a slide is positioned inside a placeholder. Slide layouts provide placeholders for text and generally display with a message suggesting the type of text to be entered in the slide. For example, the Title and Content slide layout contains a placeholder with the text *Click to add title* and another with the text *Click to add text*. Click in the placeholder text and the insertion point is positioned inside the placeholder, the default text is removed, and the placeholder is selected.

Table 2.2 Selecting Text

To select	*Perform this action*
text the mouse pointer passes through	Click and drag the mouse.
an entire word	Double-click the word.
an entire paragraph	Triple-click anywhere in the paragraph.
all text in a selected placeholder	Click Select button in Editing group on HOME tab and then click Select All, or press Ctrl + A.

Project 1b Inserting and Deleting Text in Slides Part 2 of 3

1. With **P-C2-P1-ElectronicDesign.pptx** open and the presentation in Normal view, click the Previous Slide button or the Next Slide button (located at the bottom of the vertical scroll bar) until Slide 5 displays.
2. Edit Slide 5 by completing the following steps:
   a. Position the I-beam pointer in the sentence below *STEP 4* and then click the left mouse button. (This selects the placeholder.)
   b. Edit the sentence so it reads *Decide what steps you want readers to take after reading the message.* (Use deleting and inserting commands to edit this sentence.)

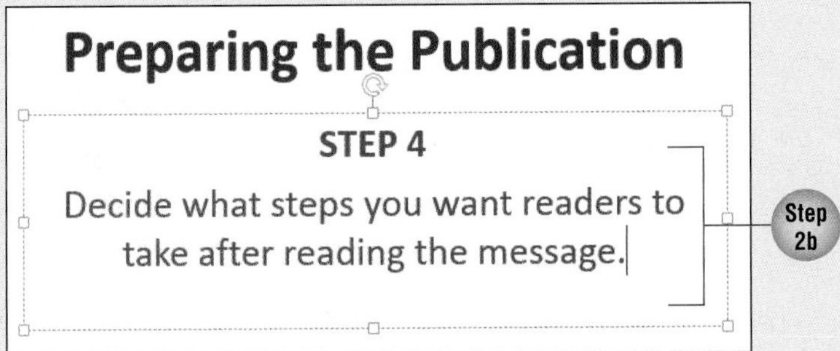

3. Click the Next Slide button to display Slide 6 and then edit Slide 6 in the outline pane by completing the following steps:
   a. Click the VIEW tab and then click the Outline View button in the Presentation Views group.
   b. In the outline pane, click in the sentence below *STEP 5* and then edit the sentence so it reads *Collect and assess examples of effective designs*.
   c. Click the Normal button in the Presentation Views group on the VIEW tab.
   d. Click the NOTES button on the Status bar to close the notes pane.
   e. Click the HOME tab.
4. Save **P-C2-P1-ElectronicDesign.pptx**.

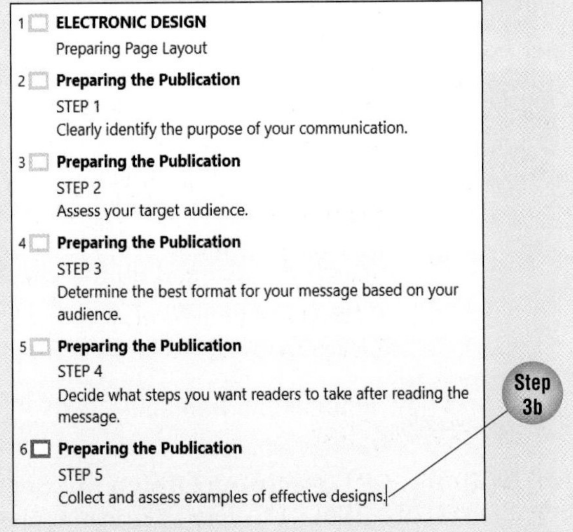

Finding and Replacing Text in Slides

Use the Find feature to look for specific text in slides in a presentation and use the Find and Replace feature to look for specific text in slides in a presentation and replace it with other text. Begin a search by clicking the Find button in the Editing group on the HOME tab. This displays the Find dialog box, as shown in Figure 2.2. In the *Find what* text box, type the text you want to find and then click the Find Next button. Continue clicking this button until a message displays telling you that the search is complete. At this message, click OK.

Use options at the Replace dialog box, shown in Figure 2.3, to search for text and replace it with other text. Display this dialog box by clicking the Replace button on the HOME tab. Type the text you want to find in the *Find what* text

Figure 2.2 Find Dialog Box

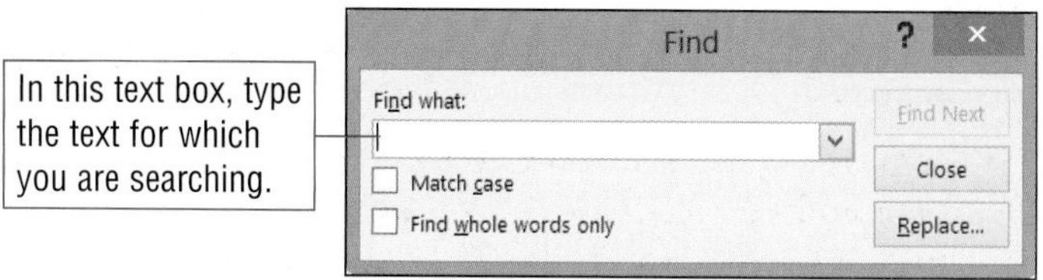

Figure 2.3 Replace Dialog Box

In this text box, type the text for which you are searching.

In this text box, type the replacement text.

Replace
Find what:
Replace with:
Match case
Find whole words only
Find Next
Close
Replace
Replace All

Quick Steps

Find Text
1. Click Find button.
2. Type text for which you are searching.
3. Click Find Next button.

Replace Text
1. Click Replace button.
2. Type text for which you are searching.
3. Press Tab key.
4. Type replacement text.
5. Click Replace All button.

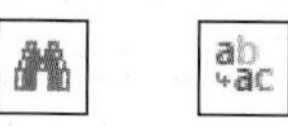

box, press the Tab key, and then type the replacement text in the *Replace with* text box. Click the Find Next button to find the next occurrence of the text and then click the Replace button to replace it with the new text, or click the Replace All button to replace all occurrences in the presentation.

Both the Find dialog box and the Replace dialog box contain two additional options. Insert a check mark in the *Match case* check box to specify that the text in the presentation should exactly match the case of the text in the *Find what* text box. For example, if you search for *Planning*, PowerPoint will stop at *Planning* but not *planning* or *PLANNING*. Insert a check mark in the *Find whole words only* check box to specify that the text is a whole word and not part of a word. For example, if you search for *plan* and do not check the *Find whole words only* option, PowerPoint will stop at ex*plan*ation, *plan*ned, *plan*ning, and so on.

Project 1c Finding and Replacing Text

Part 3 of 3

1. With **P-C2-P1-ElectronicDesign.pptx** open, make Slide 1 active.
2. Find all occurrences of *Preparing* in the presentation and replace them with *Planning* by completing the following steps:
   a. With Slide 1 active, click the Replace button in the Editing group on the HOME tab.
   b. At the Replace dialog box, type **Preparing** in the *Find what* text box.
   c. Press the Tab key.
   d. Type **Planning** in the *Replace with* text box.
   e. Click the Replace All button.
   f. At the message telling you that six replacements were made, click OK.
   g. Click the Close button to close the Replace dialog box.
3. Find all occurrences of *Publication* and replace them with *Newsletter* by completing steps similar to those in Step 2.

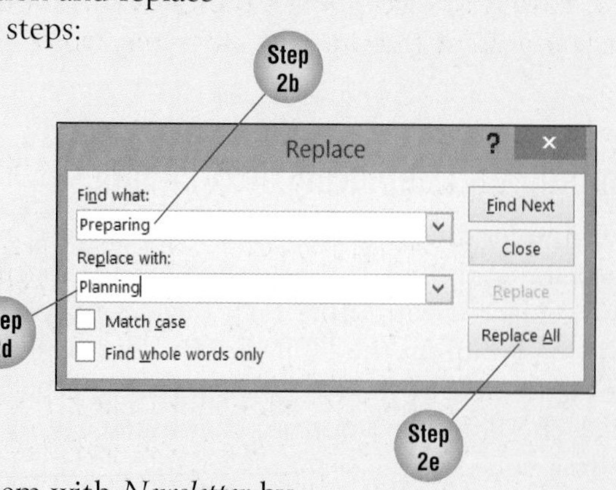

4. Save the presentation.
5. Apply a transition and sound of your choosing to all slides in the presentation.
6. Run the presentation.
7. Print Slide 1 by completing the following steps:
   a. Click the FILE tab and then click the *Print* option.
   b. At the Print backstage area, click in the *Slides* text box in the *Settings* category and then type 1.
   c. Click the Print button.
8. Print the presentation as a handout with six slides printed horizontally on the page. (Change the second gallery in the *Settings* category to *6 Slides Horizontal* and delete the *1* in the *Slides* text box.)
9. Save and then close **P-C2-P1-ElectronicDesign.pptx**.

Project 2 Cut, Copy, Paste, Rearrange, and Manage Slides in a Network Presentation

5 Parts

You will open a network evaluation presentation and then cut, copy, and paste text in slides; rearrange text in the slide thumbnails pane; size and rearrange placeholders in slides; and manage slides by inserting, deleting, moving, and copying them. You will also create sections within a presentation and copy slides between presentations.

Cutting, Copying, and Pasting Text in Slides

With buttons in the Clipboard group on the HOME tab and/or shortcut menu options, you can cut, copy, and paste text in slides. For example, to move text in a slide, click once in the placeholder containing the text to be moved, select the text, and then click the Cut button in the Clipboard group. Position the insertion point where you want to insert the text and then click the Paste button in the Clipboard group. To cut and paste with the shortcut menu, select the text you want to move, right-click the text, and then click *Cut* at the shortcut menu. Position the insertion point where you want to insert the text, right-click the location, and then click *Paste* at the shortcut menu. Complete similar steps to copy and paste text, except click the Copy button instead of the Cut button or click the *Copy* option at the shortcut menu instead of the *Cut* option.

Ctrl + X is the keyboard shortcut to cut selected text, Ctrl + C is the keyboard shortcut to copy selected text, and Ctrl + V is the keyboard shortcut to paste cut or copied text.

Cut

Copy

Paste

Project 2a Cutting, Copying, and Pasting Text in Slides

Part 1 of 5

1. Open **NetworkSystem.pptx**, located in the PC2 folder on your storage medium, and then save the presentation with Save As and name it **P-C2-P2-NetworkSystem**.
2. Insert a new slide by completing the following steps:
   a. Make Slide 4 active.
   b. Click the New Slide button in the Slides group on the HOME tab.
   c. Click in the *Click to add title* placeholder and then type TIME.
3. Cut text from Slide 3 and paste it into Slide 5 by completing the following steps:
   a. Make Slide 3 active.
   b. Click any character in the bulleted text in the slide pane.

c. Using the mouse, select the text following the bottom three bullets. (The bullets will not be selected.)
d. With the text selected, click the Cut button in the Clipboard group on the HOME tab.

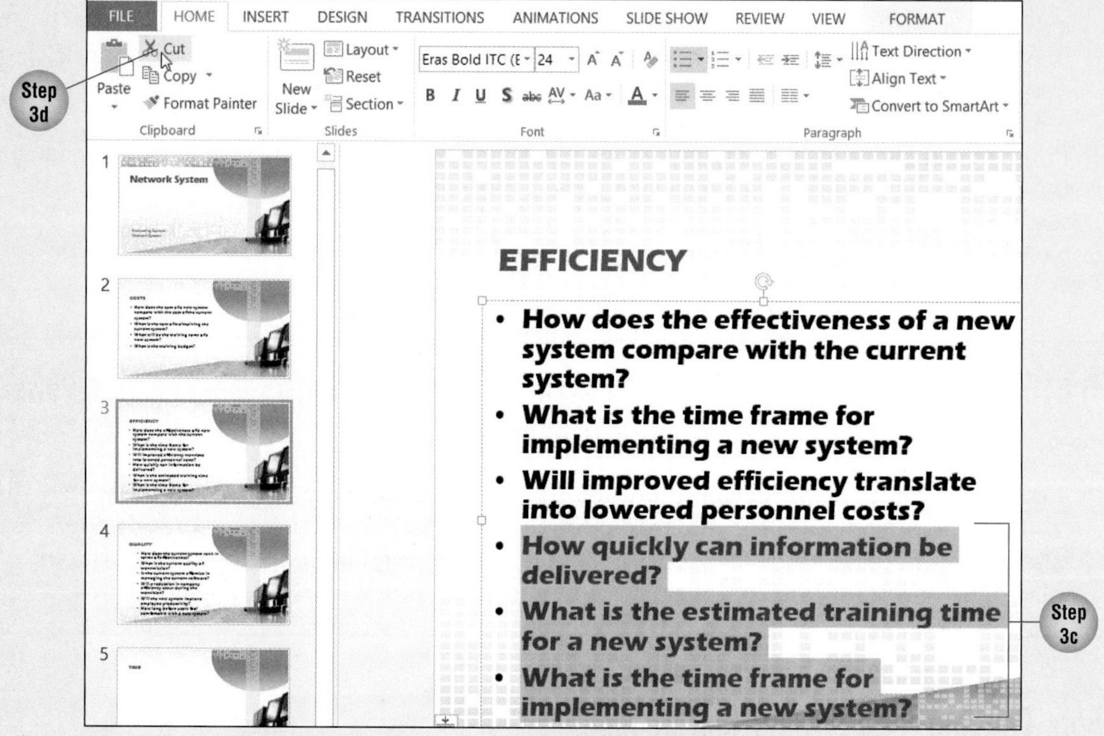

e. Make Slide 5 the active slide (contains the title *TIME*).
f. Click in the *Click to add text* placeholder.
g. Click the Paste button in the Clipboard group.
h. If the insertion point is positioned below the third bulleted item following a bullet, press the Backspace key twice. (This removes the bullet and deletes the blank line below the bullet.)

4. Insert a new slide by completing the following steps:
   a. With Slide 5 the active slide, click the New Slide button in the Slides group on the HOME tab.
   b. Click in the *Click to add title* placeholder and then type EASE OF USE.
5. Cut text from Slide 4 and paste it into Slide 6 by completing the following steps:
   a. Make Slide 4 active.
   b. Click any character in the bulleted text.
   c. Select the text following the bottom three bullets.
   d. Click the Cut button in the Clipboard group on the HOME tab.
   e. Make Slide 6 active (contains the title *EASE OF USE*).
   f. Click in the *Click to add text* placeholder.
   g. Click the Paste button in the Clipboard group.
   h. If the insertion point is positioned below the third bulleted item following a bullet, press the Backspace key twice.
6. Copy text from Slide 3 to Slide 5 by completing the following steps:
   a. Make Slide 3 active.
   b. Click any character in the bulleted text.

c. Position the mouse pointer on the last bullet until the pointer turns into a four-headed arrow and then click the left mouse button. (This selects the text following the bullet.)

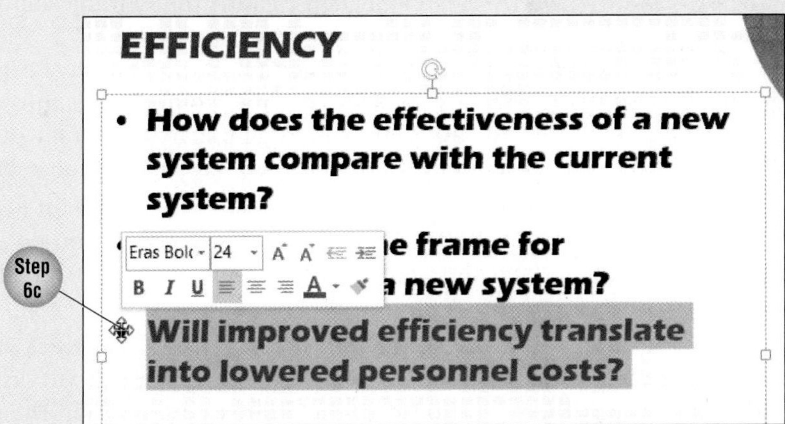

d. Click the Copy button in the Clipboard group.
e. Make Slide 5 active.
f. Click in the bulleted text and then move the insertion point so it is positioned immediately right of the question mark at the end of the second bulleted item.
g. Press the Enter key. (This moves the insertion point down to the next line and inserts another bullet.)
h. Click the Paste button in the Clipboard group.

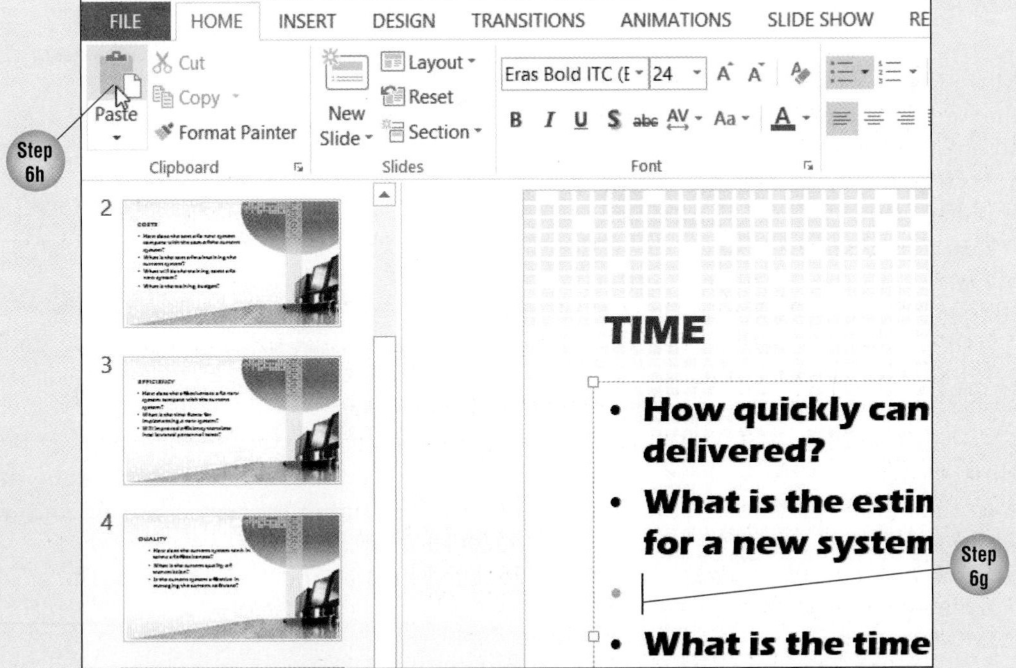

i. If a blank line is inserted between the third and fourth bullets, press the Backspace key twice.

7. Save **P-C2-P2-NetworkSystem.pptx**.

Rearranging Text in the Outline Pane

You can move and copy text in slides in the outline pane. Display the outline pane by clicking the VIEW tab and then clicking the Outline View button in the Presentation Views group or with the keyboard shortcut Ctrl + Shift + Tab. To move text in the outline pane, position the mouse pointer on the slide icon or bullet at the left side of the text until the arrow pointer turns into a four-headed arrow. Hold down the left mouse button, drag the arrow pointer (a thin horizontal line displays) to the desired location, and then release the mouse button.

If you position the arrow pointer on the slide icon and then hold down the left mouse button, all of the text in the slide is selected. If you position the arrow pointer on the bullet and then hold down the left mouse button, all text following that bullet is selected.

Dragging selected text with the mouse moves the selected text to a new location in the presentation. You can also copy selected text. To do this, click the slide icon or click the bullet to select the desired text. Position the arrow pointer in the selected text, hold down the Ctrl key, and then the left mouse button. Drag the arrow pointer (displays with a light gray box and a plus sign attached) to the desired location, release the mouse button, and then release the Ctrl key.

Project 2b **Rearranging Text in the Slide Thumbnails Pane** **Part 2 of 5**

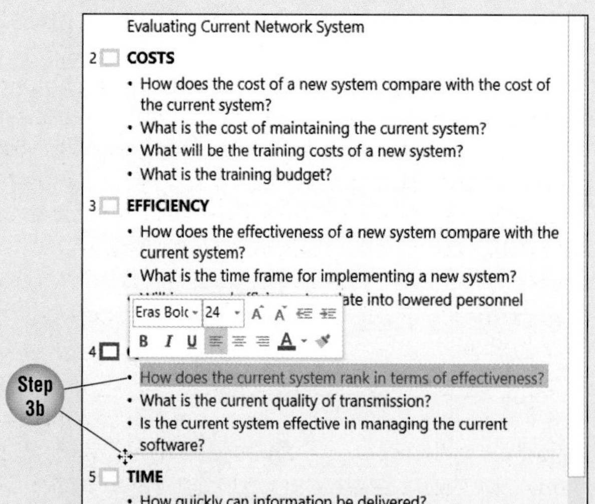

1. With **P-C2-P2-NetworkSystem.pptx** open, make Slide 1 active.
2. Press Ctrl + Shift + Tab to display the outline pane
3. Move the first bulleted item in Slide 4 in the outline pane to the end of the list by completing the following steps:
   a. Position the mouse pointer on the first bullet below *QUALITY* until it turns into a four-headed arrow.
   b. Hold down the left mouse button, drag the arrow pointer down until a thin horizontal line displays below the last bulleted item, and then release the mouse button.
4. Copy and paste text by completing the following steps:
   a. In the outline pane, move the insertion point to the end of the text in Slide 6 and then press the Enter key. (This inserts a new bullet in the slide.)
   b. Scroll up the outline pane until the last bulleted item in Slide 2 is visible in the outline pane as well as the last bullet in Slide 6.

c. Position the mouse pointer near the last bulleted item in Slide 2 until it turns into a four-headed arrow and then click the left mouse button. (This selects the text.)

d. Position the mouse pointer in the selected text, hold down the left mouse button, hold down the Ctrl key, and then drag down until the arrow pointer and light gray vertical line display on the blank line below the text in Slide 6.

e. Release the mouse button and then release the Ctrl key.

5. Press Ctrl + Shift + Tab to return to the slide thumbnails pane.
6. Click the NOTES button on the Status bar to close the notes pane.
7. Save **P-C2-P2-NetworkSystem.pptx**.

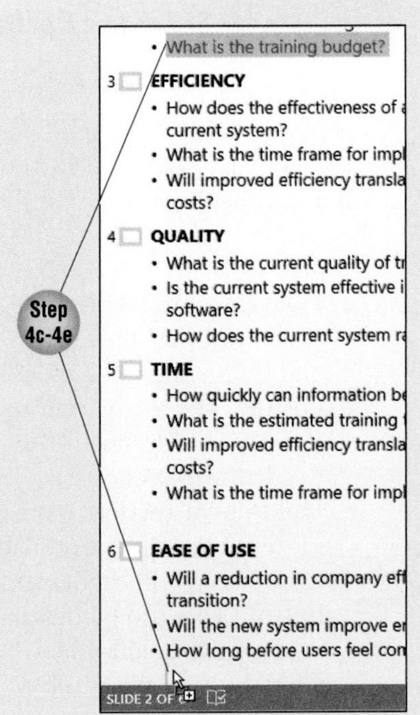

Sizing and Rearranging Placeholders in a Slide

When you click inside a placeholder, the placeholder is selected and white sizing handles and a white rotation handle display around the placeholder border. Use the sizing handles to increase or decrease the size of the placeholder by positioning the arrow pointer on a sizing handle until the pointer turns into a double-headed arrow and then dragging the placeholder border to the desired size. To move a placeholder, position the arrow pointer on the placeholder border until the arrow pointer displays with a four-headed arrow attached. Hold down the left mouse button, drag the placeholder to the desired position, and then release the mouse button.

Dragging a selected placeholder with the mouse moves the placeholder. If you want to copy a placeholder, hold down the Ctrl key while dragging the placeholder. When the placeholder is in the desired position, release the mouse button, and then release the Ctrl key. If you make a change to the size and/or location of a placeholder, click the Reset button in the Slides group on the HOME tab to return the formatting of the placeholder back to the default.

As you drag a placeholder on a slide, guidelines may display. Use these guidelines to help you position placeholders. For example, you can use a guideline to help you align a title placeholder with a subtitle placeholder.

Project 2c Sizing and Rearranging Placeholders

1. With **P-C2-P2-NetworkSystem.pptx** open, make Slide 1 active.
2. Size and move a placeholder by completing the following steps:
   a. Click any character in the subtitle *Evaluating Current Network System*.
   b. Position the arrow pointer on the sizing handle that displays in the middle of the right border until the pointer turns into a left-and-right-pointing arrow.
   c. Hold down the left mouse button, drag to the right until the subtitle text appears on one line, and then release the mouse button.

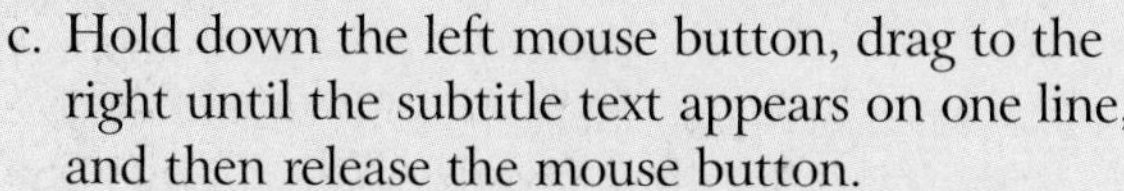

   d. Position the arrow pointer on the border of the placeholder until the pointer turns into a four-headed arrow.
   e. Hold down the left mouse button, drag the placeholder up so the placeholder is positioned as shown at the right, and then release the mouse button. Use the guideline that displays to the left of the title to left-align the subtitle placeholder with the title placeholder.

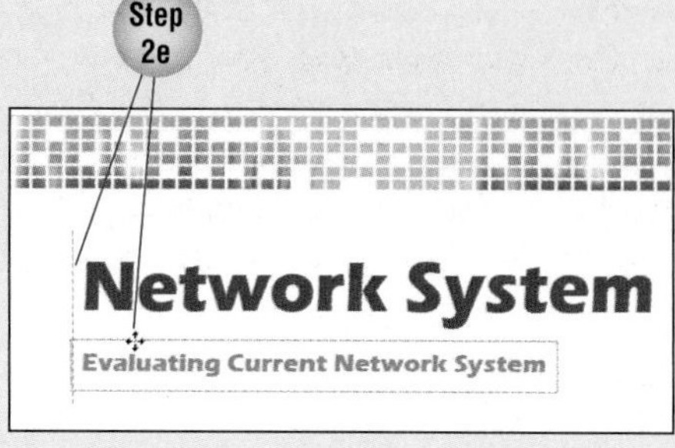

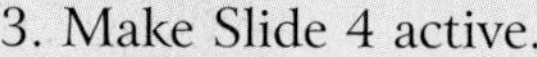

3. Make Slide 4 active.
4. Size and move a placeholder by completing the following steps:
   a. Click any character in the bulleted text.
   b. Position the arrow pointer on the sizing handle that displays in the middle of the right border until the pointer turns into a left-and-right-pointing arrow.
   c. Hold down the left mouse button and then drag to the left until the right border displays just to the right of the question mark in the second bulleted text.
   d. Drag the middle sizing handle on the bottom border up until the bottom border of the placeholder displays just below the last bulleted text.
   e. Position the arrow pointer on the border of the placeholder until the pointer turns into a four-headed arrow.
   f. Hold down the left mouse button and then drag the placeholder to the left until the vertical guideline displays left of the title (see image at the right) and then release the mouse button.
5. Save **P-C2-P2-NetworkSystem.pptx**.

Managing Slides

As you edit a presentation, you may need to reorganize slides, insert new slides, or delete existing slides. Manage slides in the slide thumbnails pane or in Slide Sorter view. Switch to Slide Sorter view by clicking the Slide Sorter button in the view area on the Status bar or by clicking the VIEW tab and then clicking the Slide Sorter button in the Presentation Views group.

Quick Steps

Insert Slide
Click New Slide button.
OR
Press Ctrl + M.
OR
1. Click Slide Sorter button in view area of Status bar.
2. Click slide that will immediately precede new slide.
3. Click New Slide button.

Delete Slide
1. Click slide thumbnail in slide thumbnails pane.
2. Press Delete key.
OR
1. Click Slide Sorter button in view area of Status bar.
2. Click desired slide thumbnail.
3. Press Delete key.

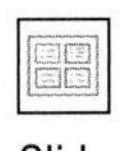
Slide Sorter

Inserting and Deleting Slides

As you learned in Chapter 1, clicking the New Slide button in the Slides group on the HOME tab inserts a new slide in the presentation immediately following the currently active slide. You can also insert a new slide in Slide Sorter view. To do this, click the slide that you want to immediately precede the new slide and then click the New Slide button in the Slides group. Delete a slide in Normal view by clicking the slide thumbnail in the slide thumbnails pane and then pressing the Delete key. You can also delete a slide by switching to Slide Sorter view, clicking the slide thumbnail, and then pressing the Delete key.

Moving Slides

Move slides in a presentation in Normal view or Slide Sorter view. In Normal view, click the desired slide in the slide thumbnails pane and then position the mouse pointer on the selected slide. Hold down the left mouse button, drag up or down until the slide thumbnail is in the desired location, and then release the mouse button. Complete similar steps to move a slide in Slide Sorter view. Click the desired slide, hold down the left mouse button, drag the slide to the desired location, and then release the mouse button.

Press Ctrl + X to cut the selected slide and then press Ctrl + V to insert the cut slide.

Copying a Slide

You may want some slides in a presentation to contain similar text, objects, and/or formatting. Rather than creating new slides in these presentations, consider copying an existing slide. To do this, display the presentation in Slide Sorter view, position the mouse on the desired slide, hold down the Ctrl key and then the left mouse button. Drag the copy of the slide thumbnail to the location where you want it inserted, release the mouse button, and then release the Ctrl key.

Press Ctrl + C to copy the selected slide and then press Ctrl + V to insert the copied slide.

You can also copy a slide in Normal view or Slide Sorter view with buttons in the Clipboard group on the HOME tab. To copy a slide, click the desired slide and then click the Copy button in the Clipboard group. Make active the slide that you want to precede the copied slide and then click the Paste button in the Clipboard group.

Project 2d Moving and Copying Slides Part 4 of 5

1. With **P-C2-P2-NetworkSystem.pptx** open in Normal view, move slides by completing the following steps:
   a. Click Slide 3 (*EFFICIENCY*) in the slide thumbnails pane.
   b. Position the mouse pointer on Slide 3, hold down the left mouse button, drag up until the slide thumbnail displays between Slides 1 and 2, and then release the mouse button.
   c. Click Slide 4 (*QUALITY*) in the slide thumbnails pane.
   d. Position the mouse pointer on Slide 4, hold down the left mouse button, drag down until the slide thumbnail displays below Slide 6, and then release the mouse button.
2. Move and copy slides in Slide Sorter view by completing the following steps:
   a. Click the Slide Sorter button in the view area on the Status bar.
   b. Click Slide 4 to make it the active slide. (The slide thumbnail displays with an orange border.)
   c. Position the mouse pointer on Slide 4, hold down the left mouse button, drag the slide thumbnail between Slides 1 and 2, and then release the mouse button.

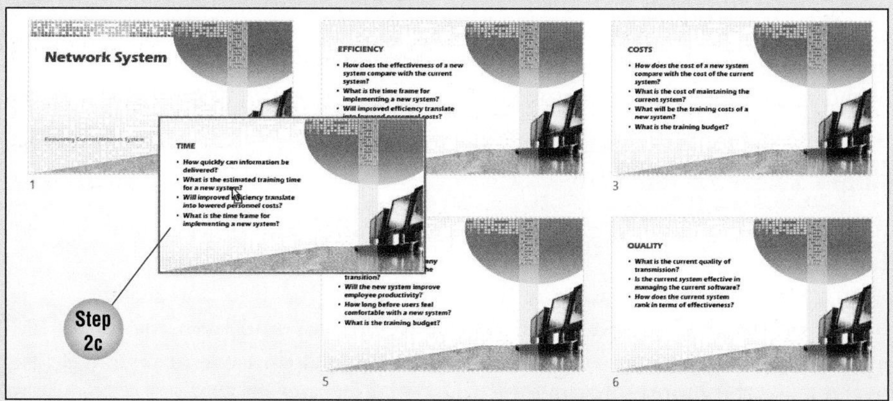

   d. Click Slide 1 to make it the active slide.
   e. Position the mouse pointer on Slide 1, hold down the left mouse button, and then hold down the Ctrl key.
   f. Drag the slide thumbnail down and to the right of Slide 6.
   g. Release the mouse button and then release the Ctrl key.

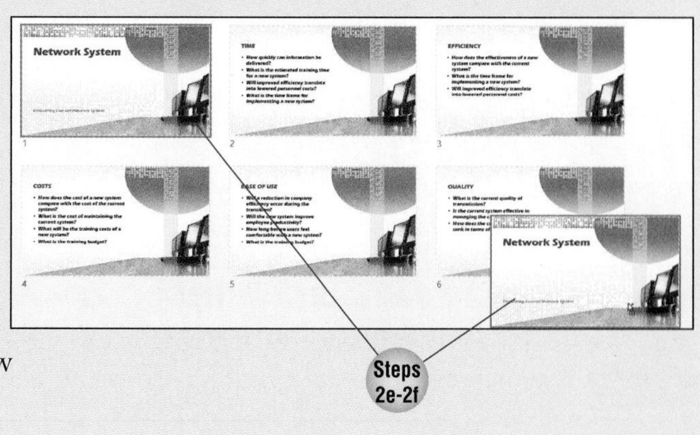

3. Click the Normal button in the view area on the Status bar.
4. Save **P-C2-P2-NetworkSystem.pptx**.

Copying a Slide between Presentations

You can copy slides between presentations as well as within them. To copy a slide, click the slide you want to copy (either in Slide Sorter view or in the slide thumbnails pane in Normal view) and then click the Copy button in the Clipboard group on the HOME tab. Open the presentation into which the slide is to be copied (in either Normal view or Slide Sorter view). Click in the location where you want to position the slide and then click the Paste button. The copied slide will take on the design theme of the presentation into which it is copied.

Project 2e Copying Slides between Presentations — Part 5 of 5

1. With **P-C2-P2-NetworkSystem.pptx** open, open the presentation named **EvalNetwork.pptx** located in the PC2 folder on your storage medium.
2. Copy Slide 2 to the **P-C2-P2-NetworkSystem.pptx** presentation by completing the following steps:
   a. Click Slide 2 in the slide thumbnails pane to make it the active slide.
   b. Click the Copy button in the Clipboard group on the HOME tab.
   c. Click the PowerPoint button on the Taskbar and then click the ***P-C2-P2-NetworkSystem.pptx*** thumbnail.
   d. Click Slide 4 (*COSTS*) in the slide thumbnails pane.
   e. Click the Paste button in the Clipboard group.
   f. Click the PowerPoint button on the Taskbar and then click the ***EvalNetwork.pptx*** thumbnail.
3. Copy Slide 3 to the **P-C2-P2-NetworkSystem.pptx** by completing the following steps:
   a. Click Slide 3 in the slide thumbnails pane.
   b. Position the mouse pointer on Slide 3 and then click the right mouse button. (This displays a shortcut menu.)
   c. Click *Copy* at the shortcut menu.
   d. Click the PowerPoint button on the Taskbar and then click the ***P-C2-P2-NetworkSystem.pptx*** thumbnail.
   e. Right-click Slide 3 in the slide thumbnails pane.
   f. Click the Use Destination Theme button that displays in the *Paste Options* section.

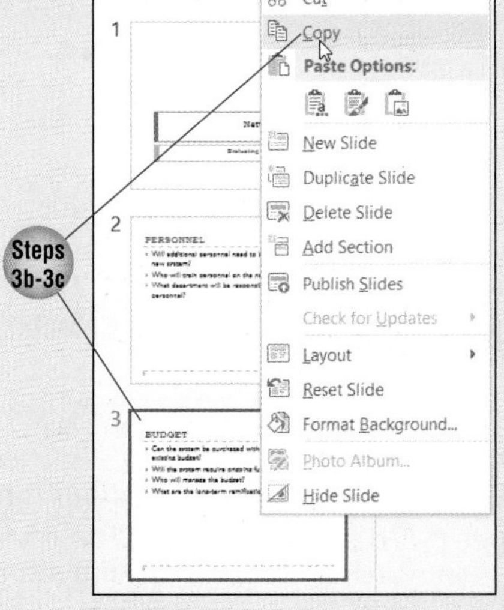

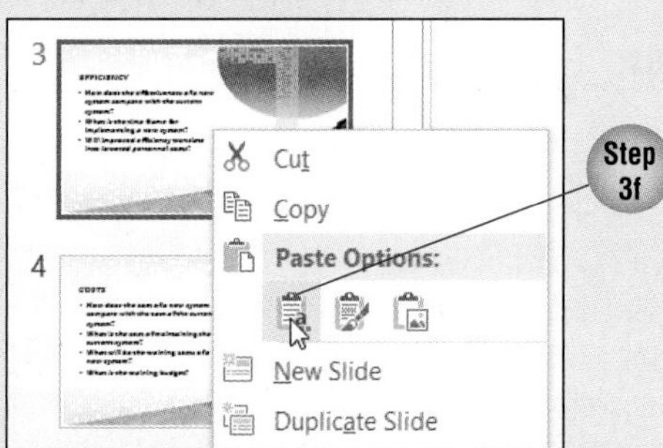

4. Click the PowerPoint button on the Taskbar and then click the **EvalNetwork.pptx** thumbnail.
5. Close the presentation.

6. With **P-C2-P2-NetworkSystem.pptx** open, delete Slide 9 by completing the following steps:
   a. If necessary, scroll down the slide thumbnails pane until Slide 9 is visible.
   b. Click Slide 9 to select it.
   c. Press the Delete key.
7. Save the presentation.
8. Print the presentation as a handout with four slides printed horizontally per page.
9. Close **P-C2-P2-NetworkSystem.pptx**.

Project  Insert and Manage Slides in an Adventure Tours Presentation — 4 Parts

You will open a presentation on Adventure Tours and then insert additional slides in the presentation by duplicating existing slides in the presentation and reusing slides from another presentation. You will also divide the presentation into sections and print a section.

Duplicating Slides

Quick Steps

Duplicate Slides
1. Select desired slides in slide thumbnails pane.
2. Click New Slide button arrow.
3. Click *Duplicate Selected Slides* at drop-down list.

In Project 2, you used the Copy and Paste buttons in the Clipboard group and options from a shortcut menu to copy slides in a presentation. You can also copy slides in a presentation using the *Duplicate Selected Slides* option from the New Slide button drop-down list or by clicking the Copy button arrow and then clicking *Duplicate* at the drop-down list. In addition to duplicating slides, you can use the *Duplicate* option from the Copy button drop-down list to duplicate a selected object in a slide, such as a placeholder.

You can duplicate a single slide or multiple selected slides. To select adjacent (sequential) slides, click the first slide you want to select in the slide thumbnails pane, hold down the Shift key, and then click the last slide you want to select. To select nonadjacent (nonsequential) slides, hold down the Ctrl key while clicking each desired slide.

Project 3a Duplicating Selected Slides — Part 1 of 4

1. Open **AdvTours.pptx** and then save the presentation with Save As and name it **P-C2-P3-AdvTours**.
2. Make sure the presentation displays in Normal view.
3. Select and then duplicate slides by completing the following steps:
   a. Click Slide 1 in the slide thumbnails pane.
   b. Hold down the Ctrl key.
   c. Click Slide 3, Slide 4, and Slide 5.
   d. Release the Ctrl key.

e. Click the New Slide button arrow in the Slides group on the HOME tab and then click *Duplicate Selected Slides* at the drop-down list.

4. With Slide 6 active in the slide pane, change *Fiji Tour* to *Costa Rica Tour*.
5. Make Slide 7 active, select *Fiji* and then type **Costa Rica**. Select and delete the existing bulleted text and then type the following bulleted text:
   - **Round-trip airfare from Los Angeles to San Jose, Costa Rica**
   - **8 days and 7 nights in Costa Rica**
   - **Monthly tours**
   - **Prices from $1099 to $1599**

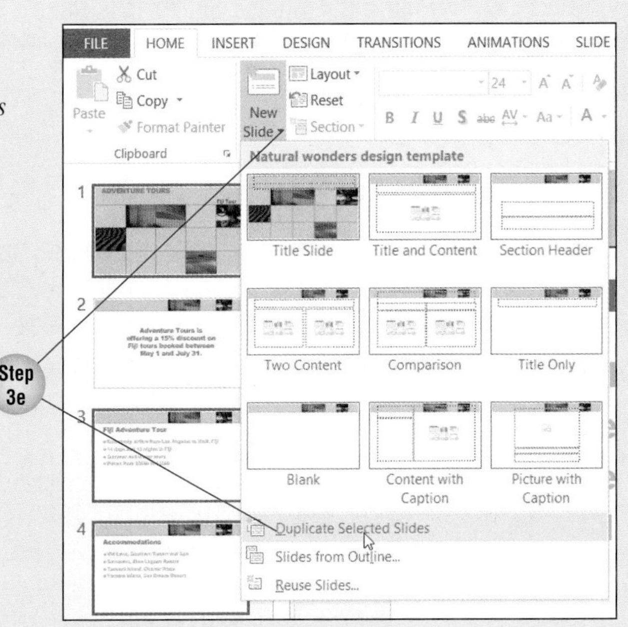

6. Make Slide 8 active, select and delete the existing bulleted text, and then type the following bulleted text:
   - **San Jose, Emerald Suites**
   - **Tortuguero, Plantation Spa and Resort**
   - **Fortuna, Pacific Resort**
   - **Jaco, Monteverde Cabanas**
7. Make Slide 9 active, select and delete the existing bulleted text, and then type the following bulleted text:
   - **San Jose city tour**
   - **Rainforest tram**
   - **Canal cruise**
   - **Forest hike**
8. Save **P-C2-P3-AdvTours.pptx**.

Reusing Slides

PowerPoint provides another method for copying slides from one presentation to another. Click the New Slide button arrow and then click the *Reuse Slides* option at the drop-down list to display the Reuse Slides task pane at the right side of the screen, as shown in Figure 2.4. At this task pane, click the Browse button and then click *Browse File* at the drop-down list and the Browse dialog box displays. At this dialog box, navigate to the desired folder and then double-click the desired presentation. This inserts the presentation slides in the Reuse Slides task pane. Click a slide in the Reuse Slides task pane to insert it in the currently open presentation.

Quick Steps

Reuse Slides
1. Click New Slide button arrow.
2. Click *Reuse Slides*.
3. Click Browse button.
4. Click *Browse File*.
5. Navigate to desired folder.
6. Double-click desired presentation.
7. Click desired slide in Reuse Slides task pane.

You can also share and reuse slides from a Slide Library on a server running Office SharePoint Server or Microsoft SharePoint Server. You can add slides to a Slide Library and insert slides from a Slide Library into a presentation. Before reusing slides from a Slide Library, the Slide Library must be created. Refer to the SharePoint help files to learn how to create a Slide Library. To reuse slides from a Slide Library in a presentation, click the Open a Slide Library hyperlink located

Figure 2.4 Reuse Slides Task Pane

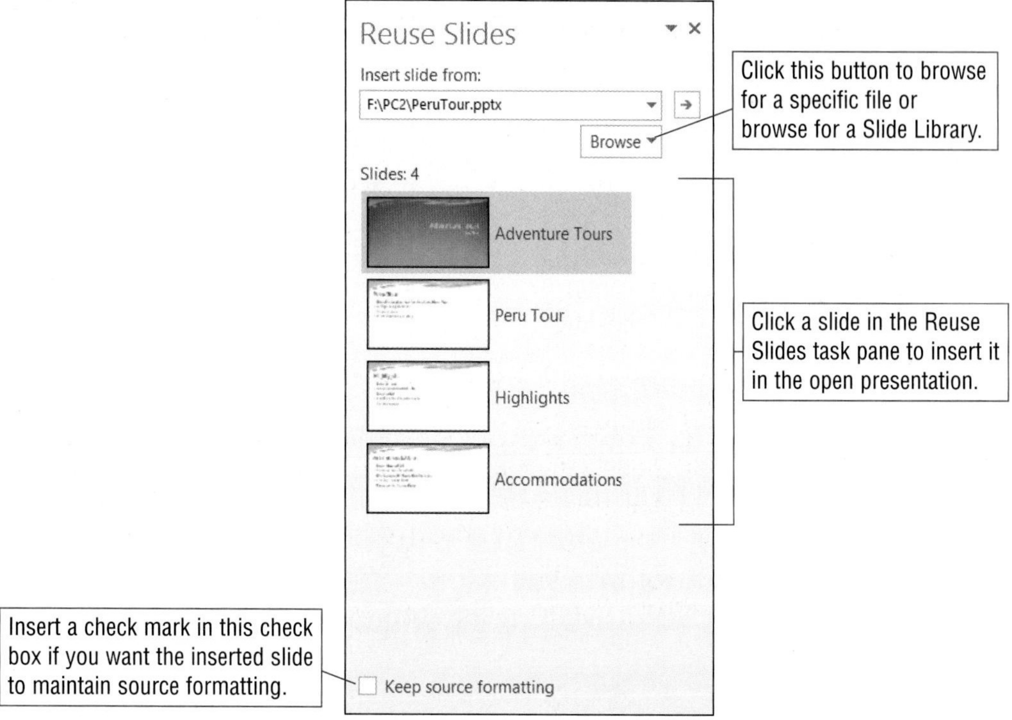
Reuse Slides
Insert slide from:
F:\PC2\PeruTour.pptx
Browse
Slides: 4
Adventure Tours
Peru Tour
Highlights
Accommodations
Keep source formatting
Click this button to browse for a specific file or browse for a Slide Library.
Click a slide in the Reuse Slides task pane to insert it in the open presentation.
Insert a check mark in this check box if you want the inserted slide to maintain source formatting.

in the Reuse Slides task pane. You can also click the Browse button in the Reuse Slides task pane and then click *Browse Slide Library* at the drop-down list. This displays the Select a Slide Library dialog box. At this dialog box, navigate to the location of the desired library and then double-click the library.

By default, the slides you insert from the Reuse Slides task pane into the currently open presentation take on the formatting of the current presentation. If you want the slides to retain their original formatting when inserted in the presentation, insert a check mark in the *Keep source formatting* check box located toward the bottom of the Reuse Slides task pane.

Project 3b Reusing Slides — Part 2 of 4

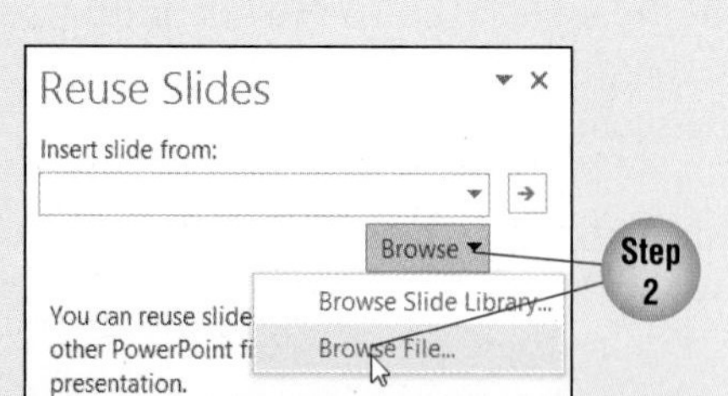
Reuse Slides
Insert slide from:
Browse
You can reuse slide
other PowerPoint fi
presentation.
Browse Slide Library...
Browse File...
Step 2

1. With **P-C2-P3-AdvTours.pptx** open, click the New Slide button arrow in the Slides group on the HOME tab and then click *Reuse Slides* at the drop-down list. (This displays the Reuse Slides task pane at the right side of the screen.)
2. Click the Browse button in the Reuse Slides task pane and then click *Browse File* at the drop-down list.
3. At the Browse dialog box, navigate to the PC2 folder on your storage medium and then double-click ***PeruTour.pptx***.
4. In the slide thumbnails pane, scroll down the slide thumbnails until Slide 9 displays and then click below Slide 9. (This inserts a thin, horizontal line below the Slide 9 thumbnail in the slide thumbnails pane.)

5. Click the first slide thumbnail (*Adventure Tours*) in the Reuse Slides task pane. (This inserts the slide in the open presentation immediately below Slide 9.)

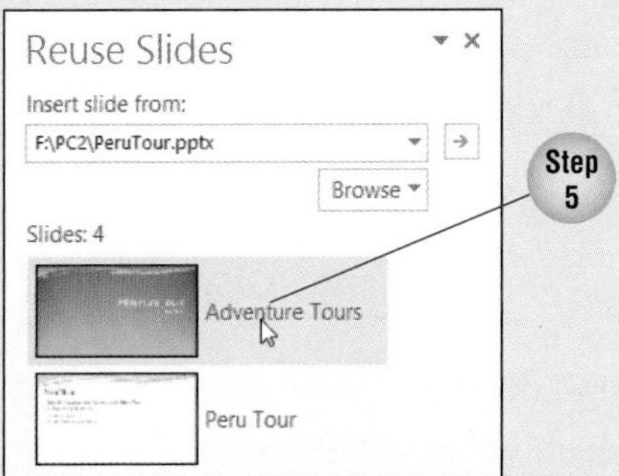

6. Click the second slide thumbnail (*Peru Tour*) in the Reuse Slides task pane.
7. Click the fourth slide thumbnail (*Accommodations*) in the Reuse Slides task pane.
8. Click the third slide thumbnail (*Highlights*) in the Reuse Slides task pane.
9. Close the Reuse Slides task pane by clicking the Close button (contains an *X*) located in the upper right corner of the task pane.
10. Save **P-C2-P3-AdvTours.pptx**.

Creating Sections within a Presentation

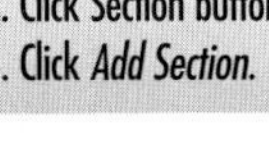

Quick Steps

Create Section

1. Select first slide for new section.
2. Click Section button.
3. Click *Add Section*.

Section

If you are working on a presentation with others in a group, or you are working in a presentation containing numerous slides, consider dividing related slides in the presentation into sections. Dividing a presentation into sections allows you to easily navigate and edit slides within a presentation. Create a section by selecting the first slide you want to place in the new section in the slide thumbnails pane, clicking the Section button in the Slides group on the HOME tab, and then clicking *Add Section* at the drop-down list. A section title bar displays in the slide thumbnails pane. By default, the section title is *Untitled Section*. Rename a section by clicking the Section button in the Slides group on the HOME tab and then clicking *Rename Section* at the drop-down list. You can also rename a section by right-clicking the section title bar in the slide thumbnails pane and then clicking *Rename Section* at the shortcut menu. Remove, move, collapse, and expand sections with options in the Section button drop-down list or by right-clicking the section title bar and then clicking the desired option. You can also apply different formatting to an individual section by clicking the section title bar to select the section and then applying the desired formatting.

When you create sections within a presentation, you have the ability to print only certain sections of the presentation. To print a section of a presentation, click the FILE tab, click the *Print* option, click the first gallery in the *Settings* category, click the desired section in the drop-down list, and then click the Print button.

Project 3c Creating and Printing Sections

1. With **P-C2-P3-AdvTours.pptx** open, create a section for slides about Fiji by completing the following steps:
   a. Click Slide 1 in the slide thumbnails pane.
   b. Click the Section button in the Slides group on the HOME tab and then click *Add Section* at the drop-down list.

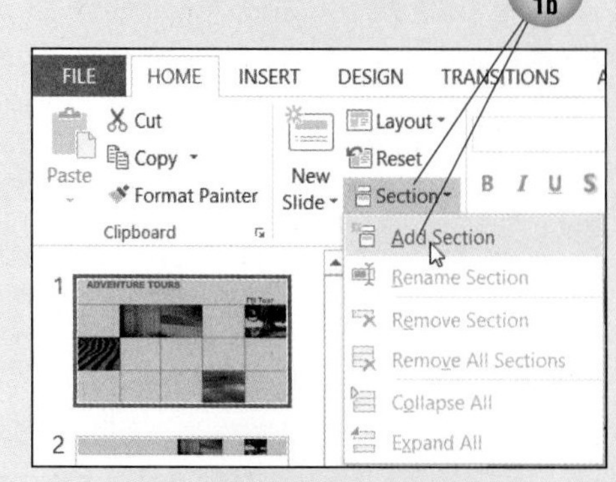

2. Rename the new section by completing the following steps:
   a. Click the Section button and then click *Rename Section* at the drop-down list.
   b. At the Rename Section dialog box, type **Fiji Tour** and then click the Rename button.

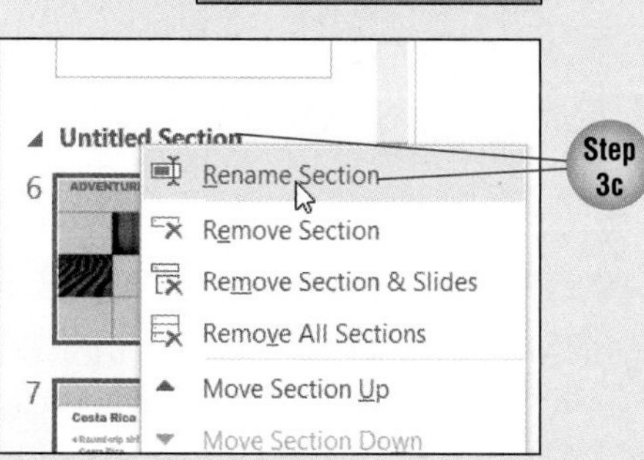

3. Create a section for slides about Costa Rica by completing the following steps:
   a. Click Slide 6 in the slide thumbnails pane.
   b. Click the Section button in the Slides group and then click *Add Section* at the drop-down list.
   c. Right-click in the section title bar (contains the text *Untitled Section*) and then click *Rename Section* at the shortcut menu.
   d. At the Rename Section dialog box, type **Costa Rica Tour** and then press Enter.
4. Complete steps similar to those in Step 3 to create a section beginning with Slide 10 and rename the section *Peru Tour*.

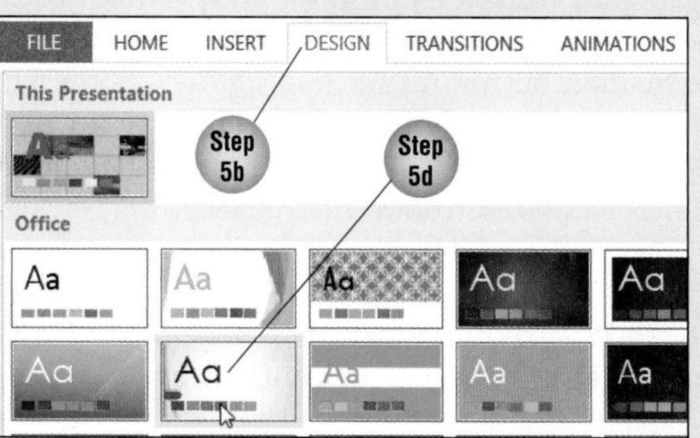

5. Change the design theme of a section by completing the following steps:
   a. Click the *Fiji Tour* section title bar located at the top of the slide thumbnails pane.
   b. Click the DESIGN tab.
   c. Click the More button located at the right of the themes thumbnails.
   d. Click *Wisp* at the drop-down gallery.
   e. Display Slide 2 in the Slides pane and move the placeholder down so the first line of text is aligned approximately with the orange shape at the left side of the slide.

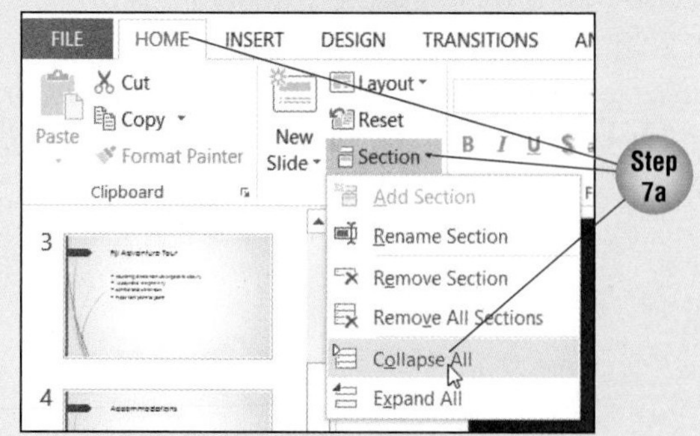

6. Complete steps similar to those in Steps 5a through 5d to apply the Ion design theme to the *Costa Rica Tour* section.
7. Display only slides in the *Costa Rica Tour* section by completing the following steps:
   a. Click the HOME tab, click the Section button in the Slides group, and then click *Collapse All* at the drop-down list.

b. Double-click the *Costa Rica Tour* section title bar in the slide thumbnails pane. (Notice that only Slides 6 through 9 display in the slide thumbnails pane and that the slides in the *Fiji Tour* and *Peru Tour* sections are hidden.)

8. Redisplay the *Fiji Tour* section slides by double-clicking the *Fiji Tour* section title bar in the slide thumbnails pane.
9. Display all sections by clicking the Section button in the Slides group and then clicking *Expand All* at the drop-down list.
10. Print only the *Costa Rica Tour* section by completing the following steps:
    a. Click the FILE tab and then click the *Print* option.
    b. At the Print backstage area, click the first gallery in the *Settings* category and then click *Costa Rica Tour* in the *Sections* section (located toward the bottom of the drop-down list).
    c. Click the second gallery (contains the text *Full Page Slides*) in the *Settings* category and then click *4 Slides Horizontal* in the *Handouts* section.
    d. Click the Print button.
11. Complete steps similar to those in Step 10 to print only the *Peru Tour* section.
12. Save **P-C2-P3-AdvTours.pptx**.

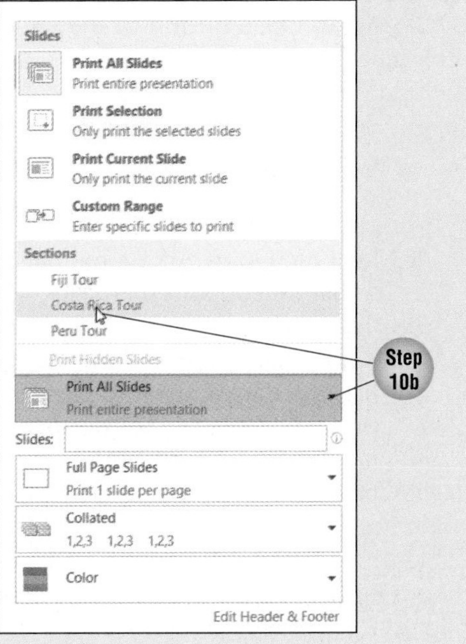

Customizing the Quick Access Toolbar

The Quick Access toolbar contains buttons for some of the most commonly performed tasks. By default, the toolbar contains the Save, Undo, Redo, and Start From Beginning buttons. You can easily add or delete buttons to and from the Quick Access toolbar. To add a button to or delete a button from the Quick Access toolbar, click the Customize Quick Access Toolbar button that displays at the right side of the toolbar. At the drop-down list that displays, insert a check mark next to those buttons you want to display on the toolbar and remove the check mark from those you do not want to appear.

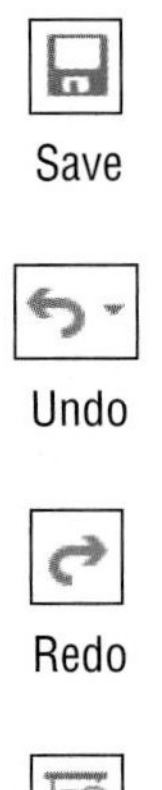

Click the *More Commands* option at the drop-down list and the PowerPoint Options dialog box displays with *Quick Access Toolbar* selected in the left panel. With options at this dialog box, you can choose to add a button from a list of PowerPoint commands. You can also click the Reset button at the dialog box to reset the Quick Access toolbar back to the default.

By default, the Quick Access toolbar displays above the ribbon tabs. You can display the Quick Access toolbar below the ribbon by clicking the Customize Quick Access Toolbar button that displays at the right side of the toolbar and then clicking the *Show Below the Ribbon* option at the drop-down list.

Project 3d Customizing the Quick Access Toolbar Part 4 of 4

1. With **P-C2-P3-AdvTours.pptx** open, add a New button to the Quick Access toolbar by clicking the Customize Quick Access Toolbar button that displays at the right side of the Quick Access toolbar and then clicking *New* at the drop-down list.
2. Add an Open button to the Quick Access toolbar by clicking the Customize Quick Access Toolbar button and then clicking *Open* at the drop-down list.
3. Add a Print Preview and Print button to the Quick Access toolbar by clicking the Customize Quick Access Toolbar button and then clicking *Print Preview and Print* at the drop-down list.

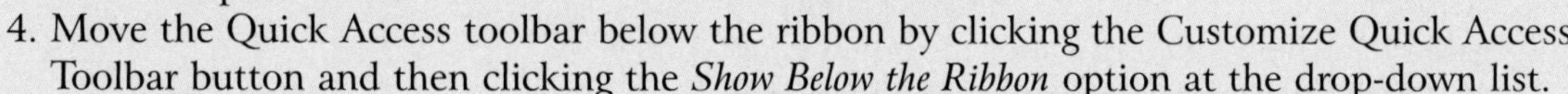

4. Move the Quick Access toolbar below the ribbon by clicking the Customize Quick Access Toolbar button and then clicking the *Show Below the Ribbon* option at the drop-down list.
5. Click the Print Preview and Print button on the Quick Access toolbar. (This displays the Print backstage area.)
6. Click the Back button to close the Print backstage area and return to the presentation.
7. Close **P-C2-P3-AdvTours.pptx.**
8. Click the New button to open a new blank presentation.
9. Click the Open button to display the Open backstage area.
10. Press the Esc key to return to the blank presentation and then close the presentation.
11. Move the Quick Access toolbar back to the original position by clicking the Customize Quick Access Toolbar button at the right side of the Quick Access toolbar and then clicking the *Show Above the Ribbon* option at the drop-down list.
12. Remove the New button by clicking the Customize Quick Access Toolbar button and then clicking *New* at the drop-down list.
13. Remove the Open button by right-clicking the button and then clicking *Remove from Quick Access Toolbar* at the drop-down list.
14. Remove the Print Preview and Print button from the Quick Access toolbar.

Project 4 Use PowerPoint Help Feature and Create a Presentation 1 Part

You will use the Help feature to learn more about PowerPoint features. You will also use the Help feature to find information on keyboard shortcuts and then use the information to create a presentation.

Using Help

Microsoft PowerPoint includes a Help feature that contains information about PowerPoint features and commands. This on-screen reference manual is similar to Windows Help and the Help features in Word, Excel, and Access.

Click the Microsoft PowerPoint Help button (the question mark) located in the upper right corner of the screen or press the keyboard shortcut F1 to display the PowerPoint Help window, shown in Figure 2.5. In this window, click in the search text box, type a topic, feature name, or question, and then press the Enter key. Topics related to the search text display in the PowerPoint Help window. Click a topic that interests you. If the topic window contains a Show All hyperlink in the upper right corner, click this hyperlink to expand the topic options to show additional related information. When you click the Show All hyperlink, it becomes the Hide All hyperlink.

Quick Steps

Use the Help Feature

1. Click Microsoft PowerPoint Help button.
2. Click in search text box.
3. Type topic or feature name.
4. Press Enter.
5. Click desired topic.

?

Help

Getting Help on a Button

When you position the mouse pointer on a button, a ScreenTip displays with information about the button. Some button ScreenTips display with a Help icon and the text *Tell me more*. Click this hyperlinked text or press F1 and the PowerPoint Help window opens with information about the button feature.

Getting Help in a Dialog Box or Backstage Area

Some dialog boxes and backstage areas contain a help button you can click to display the PowerPoint Help window with specific information about the dialog box or backstage area. After reading and/or printing the information, close a dialog box by clicking the Close button located in the upper right corner of the dialog box or close the backstage area by clicking the Back button or pressing the Esc key.

Figure 2.5 PowerPoint Help Window

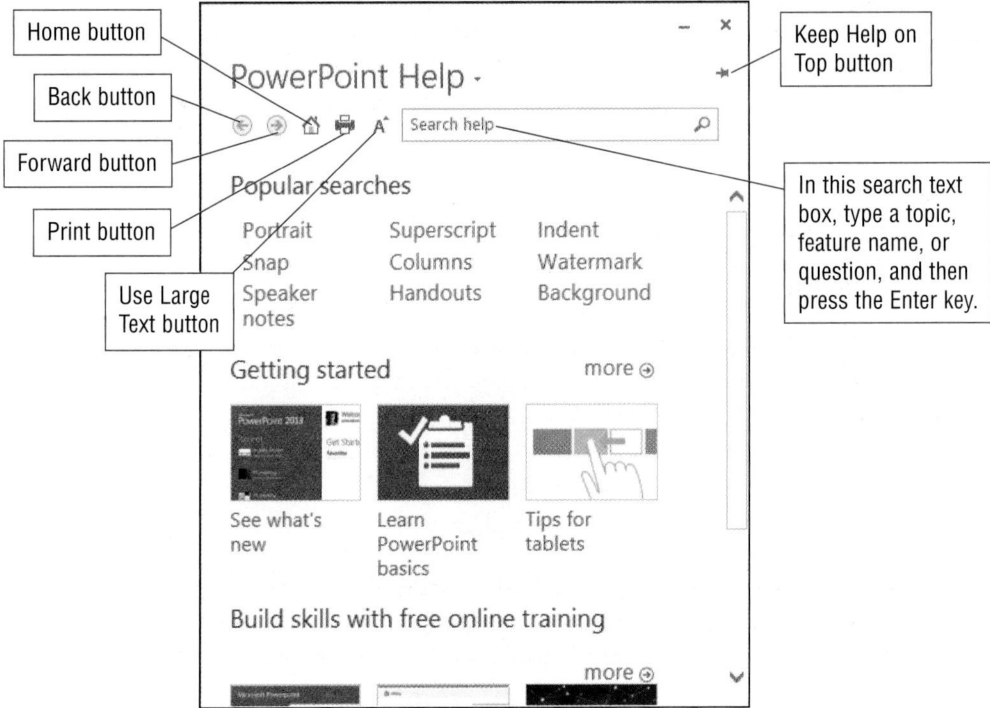

Project 4 Using the Help Feature and Creating a Presentation — Part 1 of 1

1. At the blank PowerPoint screen, press Ctrl + N to display a blank presentation. (Ctrl + N is the keyboard shortcut to open a blank presentation.)
2. Click the Microsoft PowerPoint Help button located in the upper right corner of the screen.

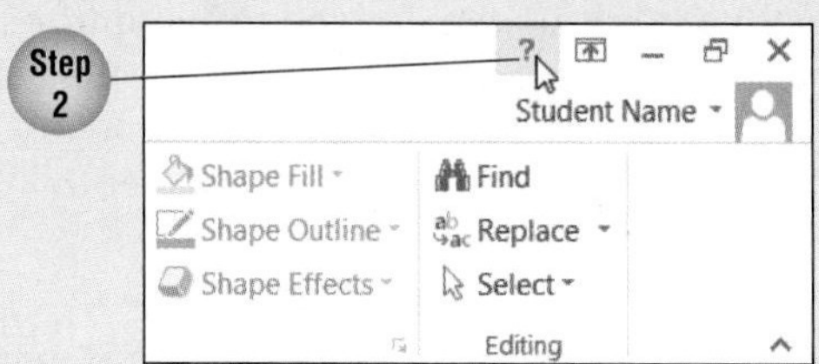

3. At the PowerPoint Help window, click in the search text box, type **create a presentation**, and then press the Enter key.
4. When the list of topics displays, click the Basic tasks for creating a PowerPoint 2013 presentation hyperlink. (If your PowerPoint Help window does not display this hyperlink, click a similar hyperlink.)
5. Read the information in the article. (If you want a hard copy of the information, you can click the Print button that displays to the left of the search text box in the PowerPoint Help window and then click the Print button at the Print dialog box.)
6. Close the PowerPoint Help window by clicking the Close button in the upper right corner of the window.

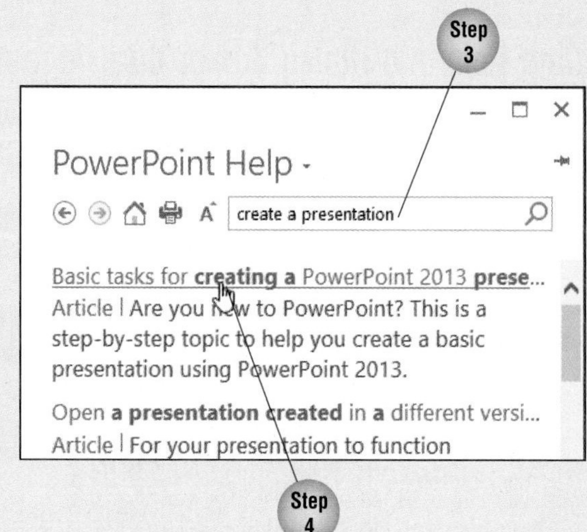

7. Hover the mouse over the New Slide button in the Slides group on the HOME tab and then click the *Tell me more* text that displays toward the bottom of the ScreenTip.
8. At the PowerPoint Help window, read the information on adding, rearranging, and deleting slides and then click the Close button in the upper right corner of the PowerPoint Help window.
9. Click the FILE tab and then click the *Open* option.
10. At the Open backstage area, click the Microsoft PowerPoint Help button that displays in the upper right corner of the backstage area.
11. Read the information that displays in the PowerPoint Help window.
12. Click in the search text box, type **keyboard shortcuts**, and then press the Enter key.
13. When the list of topics displays, click the Keyboard shortcuts for use while creating a presentation in PowerPoint 2013 hyperlink. (Not all of the hyperlink text will be visible.)
14. Scroll down the list of topics, display the *Common tasks in PowerPoint* section, and then click the Delete and copy text and objects hyperlink. (This displays a list of keyboard shortcuts for deleting and copying text and objects.)

15. Select the list of keyboard shortcuts for deleting and copying text and objects by positioning the mouse pointer at the left side of the heading *TO DO THIS*, holding down the left mouse button, dragging down to the lower right corner of the list of keyboard shortcuts, and then releasing the mouse button.
16. With the information selected, click the Print button that displays to the left of the search text box in the PowerPoint Help window.
17. At the Print dialog box, click the *Selection* option in the *Page Range* section and then click the Print button.
18. Close the PowerPoint Help window.
19. Press the Esc key to return to the blank presentation.
20. At the blank presentation, click the text *Click to add title* and then type **PowerPoint Help**.

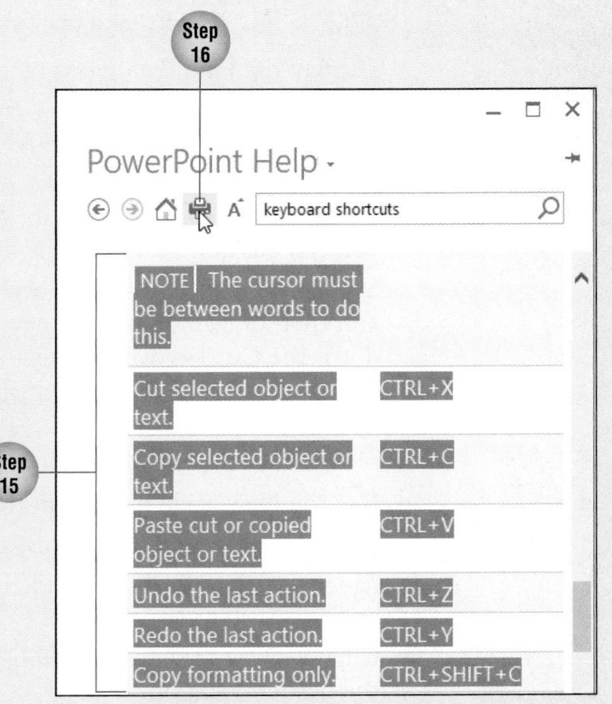

21. Click the text *Click to add subtitle* and then type **Keyboard Shortcuts**.
22. Using the information you printed, create slides with the following information:
    - Slide 2: Insert the text **Delete Text** as the title and then insert the four delete keyboard shortcuts as bulleted text. (For each keyboard shortcut, type the description followed by a colon and then the keyboard shortcut. For example, type **Delete one character to the left: Backspace** as the first bulleted item in the slide.)
    - Slide 3: Insert the text **Cut, Copy, Paste Text** as the title and then insert the three cut, copy, and paste keyboard shortcuts as bulleted text.
    - Slide 4: Insert the text **Undo and Redo** as the title and then insert the two undo and redo keyboard shortcuts as bulleted text.
    - Slide 5: Insert the text **Copy and Paste Formatting** as the title and then insert the three copy and paste formatting keyboard shortcuts as bulleted text.
23. Apply the Facet design theme with the blue variant to the presentation.
24. Apply a transition and sound of your choosing to all slides in the presentation.
25. Print the presentation as a handout with six slides printed horizontally per page.
26. Save and then close **P-C2-P4-Shortcuts.pptx**.

Chapter Summary

- Use the spelling checker feature to check the spelling of the text in a presentation. Begin a spelling check by clicking the REVIEW tab and then clicking the Spelling button in the Proofing group.
- Use the Thesaurus to find synonyms and antonyms for words in a presentation. Display synonyms at the Thesaurus task pane or by right-clicking a word and then pointing to *Synonyms* at the shortcut menu.

- Click in a placeholder to select the placeholder and position the insertion point inside the placeholder.
- Display the Find dialog box by clicking the Find button in the Editing group on the HOME tab.
- Display the Replace dialog box by clicking the Replace button in the Editing group on the HOME tab.
- With buttons in the Clipboard group or with options from a shortcut menu, you can cut and paste or copy and paste text in slides.
- You can use the mouse to move text in the slide thumbnails pane by selecting and then dragging text to a new location. To copy text to a new location, hold down the Ctrl key while dragging.
- Use the sizing handles that display around a selected placeholder to increase or decrease the size of the placeholder. Use the mouse to drag a selected placeholder to a new location in the slide.
- Use the New Slide button on the HOME tab to insert a slide in a presentation.
- Delete a selected slide by pressing the Delete key.
- Move or delete a selected slide in Normal view in the slide thumbnails pane or in Slide Sorter view.
- Copy a selected slide by holding down the Ctrl key while dragging the slide to the desired location.
- Use the Copy and Paste buttons in the Clipboard group on the HOME tab to copy a slide between presentations.
- Select adjacent slides in the slide thumbnails pane or in Slide Sorter view by clicking the first slide, holding down the Shift key, and then clicking the last slide. Select nonadjacent slides by holding down the Ctrl key while clicking each desired slide.
- Duplicate slides in a presentation by selecting the desired slides in the slide thumbnails pane, clicking the New Slide button arrow, and then clicking the *Duplicate Selected Slides* option or clicking the Copy button arrow and then clicking *Duplicate* at the drop-down list.
- Divide a presentation into sections to easily navigate and edit slides in a presentation.
- You can copy slides from a presentation into the open presentation with options at the Reuse Slides task pane. Display this task pane by clicking the New Slide button arrow and then clicking *Reuse Slides* at the drop-down list.
- Customize the Quick Access toolbar by clicking the Customize Quick Access Toolbar button that displays at the right side of the toolbar and then clicking the desired button or option at the drop-down list. You can add buttons to or remove buttons from the Quick Access toolbar and display the toolbar below the ribbon.
- Click the Microsoft PowerPoint Help button or press F1 to display the PowerPoint Help window.
- Some dialog boxes and backstage areas contain a help button you can click to display information specific to the dialog box or backstage area.

Commands Review

FEATURE	RIBBON TAB, GROUP	BUTTON, OPTION	KEYBOARD SHORTCUT
copy text or slide	HOME, Clipboard		Ctrl + C
create section	HOME, Slides		
cut text or slide	HOME, Clipboard		Ctrl + X
duplicate slide	HOME, Slides	, *Duplicate Selected Slides*	
Find dialog box	HOME, Editing		Ctrl + F
paste text or slide	HOME, Clipboard		Ctrl + V
PowerPoint Help window			F1
Replace dialog box	HOME, Editing		Ctrl + H
Reuse Slides task pane	HOME, Slides	, *Reuse Slides*	
spelling checker	REVIEW, Proofing		F7
Thesaurus task pane	REVIEW, Proofing		Shift + F7

Concepts Check

Test Your Knowledge

Completion: In the space provided at the right, indicate the correct term, symbol, or command.

1. The Spelling button is located in the Proofing group on this tab. ____________________
2. This is the keyboard shortcut to select all text in a placeholder. ____________________
3. The Find button is located in this group on the HOME tab. ____________________
4. To copy text to a new location in the slide thumbnails pane, hold down this key while dragging text. ____________________
5. The border of a selected placeholder displays these handles as well as a white rotation handle. ____________________
6. You can reorganize slides in a presentation in the slide thumbnails pane or in this view. ____________________
7. Copy selected slides in a presentation using this option from the New Slide button drop-down list. ____________________

8. To select adjacent slides, click the first slide, hold down this key, and then click the last slide. ____________

9. Click the New Slide button arrow and then click the *Reuse Slides* option at the drop-down list to display this. ____________

10. Divide a presentation into these to easily navigate and edit slides in a presentation. ____________

11. Display the Quick Access toolbar below the ribbon by clicking this button located at the right side of the toolbar and then clicking the *Show Below the Ribbon* option at the drop-down list. ____________

12. This is the keyboard shortcut to display the PowerPoint Help window. ____________

Skills Check Assess Your Performance

Assessment 1

CREATE AN ELECTRONIC DESIGN PRESENTATION

SNAP Grade It

1. Create the presentation shown in Figure 2.6 using the Wisp design theme and the second variant. (When typing bulleted text, press the Tab key to move the insertion point to the desired tab level.)
2. After creating the slides, complete a spelling check on the text in the slides.
3. Save the presentation into the PC2 folder on your storage medium and name the presentation **P-C2-A1-ElecDesign**.
4. Run the presentation.
5. Print the presentation as a handout with four slides printed horizontally per page.
6. Make the following changes to the presentation:
   a. Change to Slide Sorter view and then move Slide 3 between Slides 1 and 2.
   b. Move Slide 4 between Slides 2 and 3.
   c. Change to Normal view.
   d. Search for the word *document* and replace it with the word *brochure*. (After the replacements, make Slide 1 active and, if necessary, capitalize the "b" in *brochure*.)
   e. Add the Uncover transition and Hammer sound to each slide.
7. Save the presentation.
8. Display the Reuse Slides task pane, browse to the PC2 folder on your storage medium, and then double-click ***LayoutTips.pptx***.
9. Insert the *Layout Punctuation Tips* slide below Slide 4.
10. Insert the *Layout Tips* slide below Slide 5.
11. Close the Reuse Slides task pane.
12. Find all occurrences of *Layout* and replace with *Design*. (Insert a check mark in the *Match case* check box.)
13. Move Slide 5 between Slides 1 and 2.
14. Move Slide 6 between Slides 2 and 3.

Figure 2.6 Assessment 1

Slide I	Title	=	Electronic Design and Production
	Subtitle	=	Designing a Document
Slide 2	Title	=	Creating Balance
	Bullets	=	• Symmetrical balance: Balancing similar elements equally on a page (centered alignment) of the document • Asymmetrical balance: Balancing contrasting elements on a page of the document
Slide 3	Title	=	Creating Focus
	Bullets	=	• Creating focus with titles, headings, and subheads in a document • Creating focus with graphic elements in a document o Clip art o Watermarks o Illustrations o Photographs o Charts o Graphs
Slide 4	Title	=	Providing Proportion
	Bullets	=	• Evaluating proportions in a document • Sizing graphic elements in a document • Using white space in a document

15. Change to Normal view and then save the presentation.
16. Print the presentation as a handout with six slides printed horizontally per page.
17. Beginning with Slide 2, create a section named *Design Tips*.
18. Beginning with Slide 4, create a section named *Design Features*.
19. Print only the Design Features section as a handout with four slides printed horizontally per page.
20. Save and then close **P-C2-A1-ElecDesign.pptx**.

Assessment 2

CREATE A NETIQUETTE PRESENTATION

SNAP Grade It

1. Create a presentation with the text shown in Figure 2.7 on the next page. You determine the slide layout. Apply the Organic design theme (in the Themes group) and the fourth variant (in the Variants group).
2. If necessary, size and move placeholders so the text is positioned attractively on the slide.
3. Select Slides 4 through 6 and then duplicate the slides.

Figure 2.7 Assessment 2

Slide l	Title	=	CONNECTING ONLINE
	Subtitle	=	Internet Applications
Slide 2	Title	=	Internet Community
	Bullets	=	• Email • Internet voice services • Moderated environments • Netiquette
Slide 3	Title	=	Netiquette Rule
	Subtitle	=	Remember you are dealing with people.
Slide 4	Title	=	Netiquette Rule
	Subtitle	=	Adhere to the same standards of behavior online that you follow in real life.
Slide 5	Title	=	Netiquette Rule
	Subtitle	=	Respect the privacy of others.
Slide 6	Title	=	Netiquette Rule
	Subtitle	=	Share expert knowledge.

4. Type the following text in place of the existing text in the identified slides:
   a. Slide 7: Select the placeholder netiquette rule text and then type **Do not plagiarize.**
   b. Slide 8: Select the netiquette rule text in the placeholder and then type **Respect and accept people's differences.**
   c. Slide 9: Select the netiquette rule text in the placeholder and then type **Respect others' time.**
5. Complete a spelling check on text in the presentation.
6. Save the presentation and name it **P-C2-A2-InternetApps**.
7. Print the presentation as a handout with six slides printed horizontally per page.
8. Make the following edits to the presentation:
   a. Display the presentation in Slide Sorter view.
   b. Move Slide 3 between Slide 5 and Slide 6.
   c. Move Slide 7 between Slide 3 and Slide 4.
9. Add the Split transition, the Click sound, and change the duration to 01.00 second for all slides in the presentation.
10. Save the presentation.
11. Run the presentation.
12. Print the presentation as a handout with nine slides printed horizontally per page.
13. Close **P-C2-A2-InternetApps.pptx**.

Assessment 3

DOWNLOAD A DESIGN THEME

1. If your computer is connected to the Internet, Office.com provides a number of design themes you can download to your computer. Display the New backstage area, click in the search text box, type **Digital blue tunnel presentation**, and then press Enter.
2. Click the *Digital blue tunnel presentation (widescreen)* template (all of the template name may not be visible) and then click the Create button.
3. When the design theme is downloaded and a presentation is opened with the design theme applied, open **P-C2-A2-InternetApps.pptx**.
4. Select the nine slides in the **P-C2-A2-InternetApps.pptx** presentation and then click the Copy button.
5. Click the PowerPoint button on the Taskbar and then click the thumbnail representing the presentation with the downloaded design theme applied.
6. Click the Paste button to paste the nine slides in the current presentation.
7. Delete Slide 1 and then select and delete Slides 10 through 19.
8. Scroll through and look at each slide and, if necessary, make any changes required so the text is positioned attractively on each slide.
9. Save the presentation and name it **P-C2-A3-InternetApps**.
10. Run the presentation.
11. Print the presentation as a handout with nine slides printed horizontally per page.
12. Close **P-C2-A3-InternetApps.pptx** and then close **P-C2-A2-InternetApps.pptx**.

Visual Benchmark Demonstrate Your Proficiency

FORMATTING A PRESENTATION ON ONLINE LEARNING

1. Open **OnlineLearning.pptx** in the PC2 folder and then save the presentation with Save As and name it **P-C2-VB-OnlineLearning**.
2. Format the presentation so it appears as shown in Figure 2.8 on the next page with the following specifications:
   a. Apply the Parallax design theme and the fourth variant.
   b. Use the *Reuse Slides* option from the New Slide button drop-down list to insert the last two additional slides from the **Learning.pptx** presentation.
   c. Arrange the slides to match what you see in Figure 2.8. (Read the slides from left to right.)
   d. Size and/or move placeholders so text displays in each slide as shown in Figure 2.8.
3. Add a transition and sound of your choosing to each slide.
4. Run the presentation.
5. Print the presentation as a handout with six slides printed horizontally per page.
6. Save and then close **P-C2-VB-OnlineLearning.pptx**.

Figure 2.8 Visual Benchmark

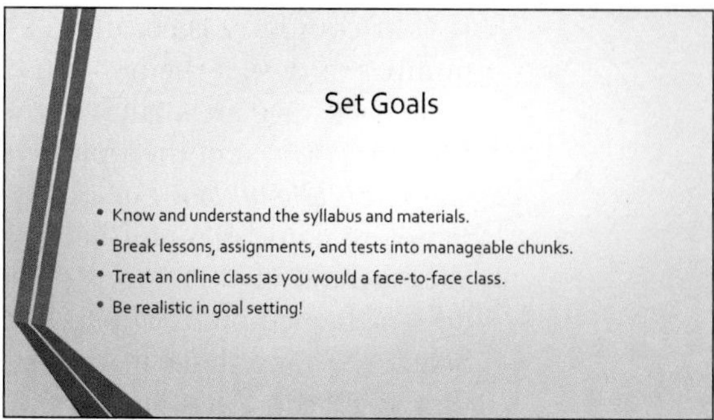

Establish Schedule

- Keep calendar of important deadlines.
- Determine what times during the week are best for you to complete lessons/assignments.
- Try to find a comfortable study place.
- Pace yourself!

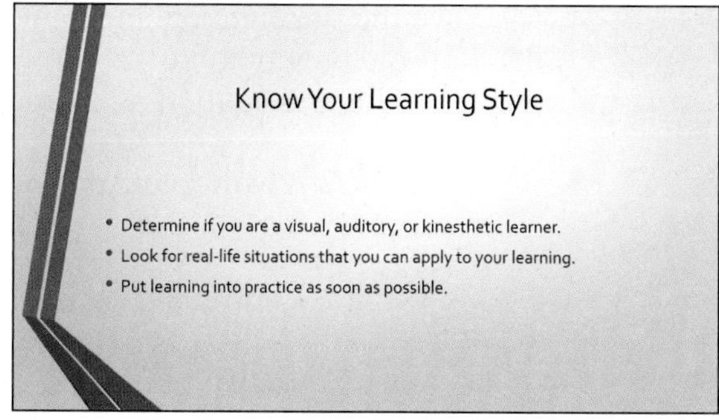

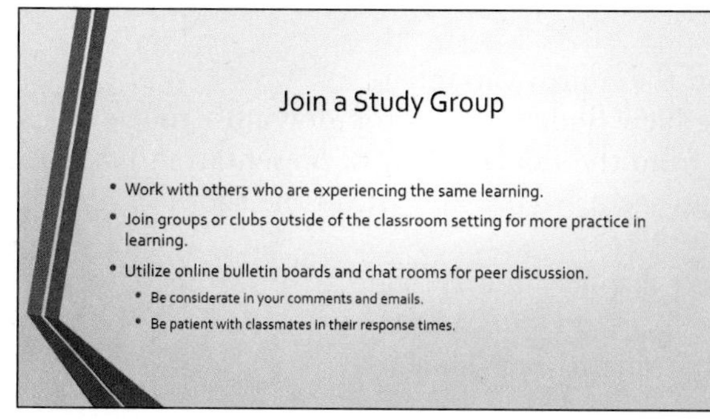

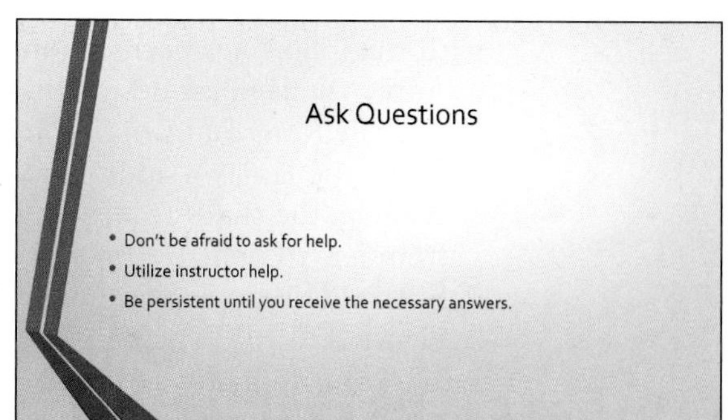

Case Study Apply Your Skills

Part 1

You are the office manager at the Career Finders agency. One of your responsibilities is to conduct workshops to prepare individuals for the job search process. A coworker has given you a presentation for the workshop but the presentation needs some editing and modifying. Open **JobAnalysis.pptx** and then save the presentation with Save As and name it **P-C2-CS-JobAnalysis**. Check each slide in the presentation and then make modifications to maintain consistency in the size and location of placeholders (consider using the Reset button to reset the formatting and size of the placeholders), maintain consistency in heading text, move text from an overcrowded slide to a new slide, complete a spelling check, apply a design theme, and make any other modifications to improve the presentation. Save **P-C2-CS-JobAnalysis.pptx**.

Part 2

After reviewing the presentation, you realize that you need to include slides on resumes. Open the **ResumePres.pptx** presentation and then copy Slides 2 and 3 into the **P-C2-CS-JobAnalysis.pptx** presentation (at the end of the presentation). You want to add additional information on resume writing tips and decide to use the Internet to find information. Search for tips on writing a resume and then create a slide (or two) with the information you find. Add a transition and sound to all slides in the presentation. Save **P-C2-CS-JobAnalysis.pptx**.

Part 3

You know that Microsoft Word offers a number of resume templates you can download from the Office.com website. You decide to include information in the presentation on how to find and download resumes. Open Microsoft Word and then click the *Blank document* template at the Word 2013 opening screen. At the blank document, click the FILE tab and then click the *New* option. At the New backstage area, click in the search text box, type **resume**, and then press Enter. Scroll through the list of resume templates that displays and then experiment with downloading a template. With the **P-C2-CS-JobAnalysis.pptx** presentation open, add an additional slide to the end of the presentation that provides steps on how to download a resume in Microsoft Word. Print the presentation as a handout with six slides printed horizontally per page. Save, run, and then close the presentation.

MICROSOFT® POWERPOINT®

CHAPTER 3

Formatting Slides

PERFORMANCE OBJECTIVES

Upon successful completion of Chapter 3, you will be able to:

- **Apply font and paragraph formatting to text in slides**
- **Apply formatting with the Mini toolbar and Format Painter**
- **Customize bullets and numbers**
- **Change page setup**
- **Customize slide backgrounds**
- **Create custom themes including custom theme colors and theme fonts**
- **Delete custom themes**

Tutorials

3.1 Applying Formatting Using the Font Group
3.2 Applying Formatting Using the Font Dialog Box
3.3 Formatting with Format Painter
3.4 Changing Paragraph Formatting
3.5 Customizing Bullets and Numbering
3.6 Customizing Placeholders
3.7 Changing Page Setup
3.8 Changing Slide Size, Design Themes, and Background Styles
3.9 Creating and Deleting Custom Themes

The Font and Paragraph groups on the HOME tab contain a number of buttons and options for formatting text in slides. PowerPoint also provides a Mini toolbar and the Format Painter feature to help you format text. You can modify the design theme colors and fonts provided by PowerPoint and create your own custom themes. You will learn to use these features in this chapter along with how to change page setup options. Model answers for this chapter's projects appear on the following pages.

Note: Before beginning the projects, copy to your storage medium the PC3 subfolder from the PowerPoint folder on the CD that accompanies this textbook and then make PC3 the active folder.

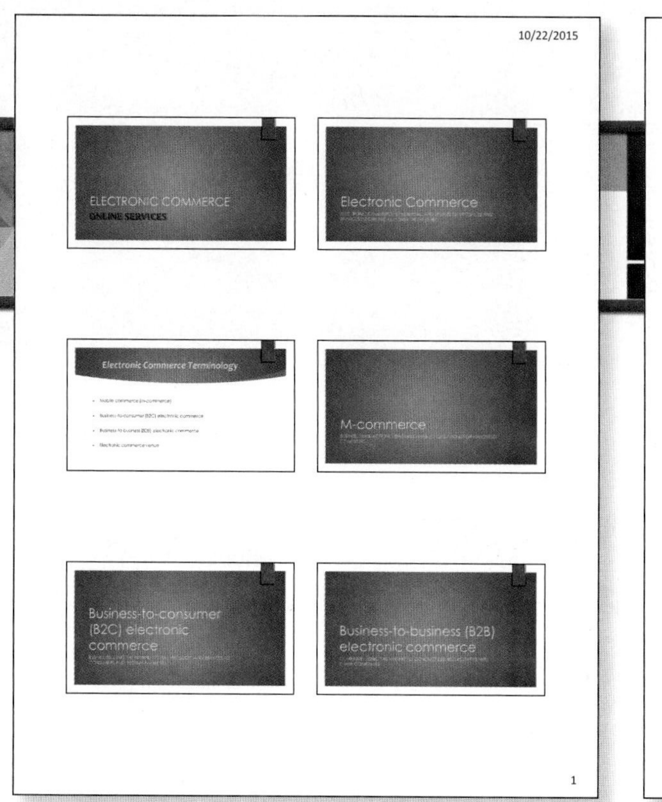

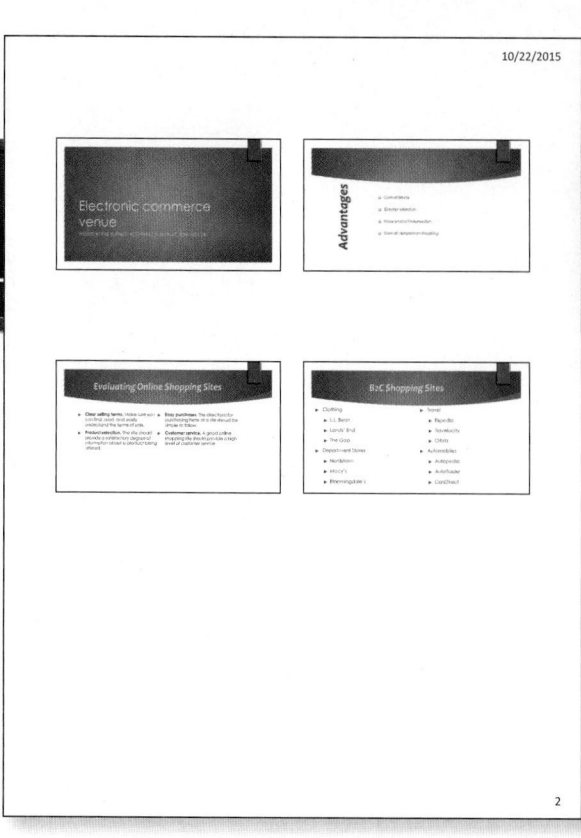

Project 1 Format an E-Commerce Presentation
P-C3-P1-E-Commerce.pptx

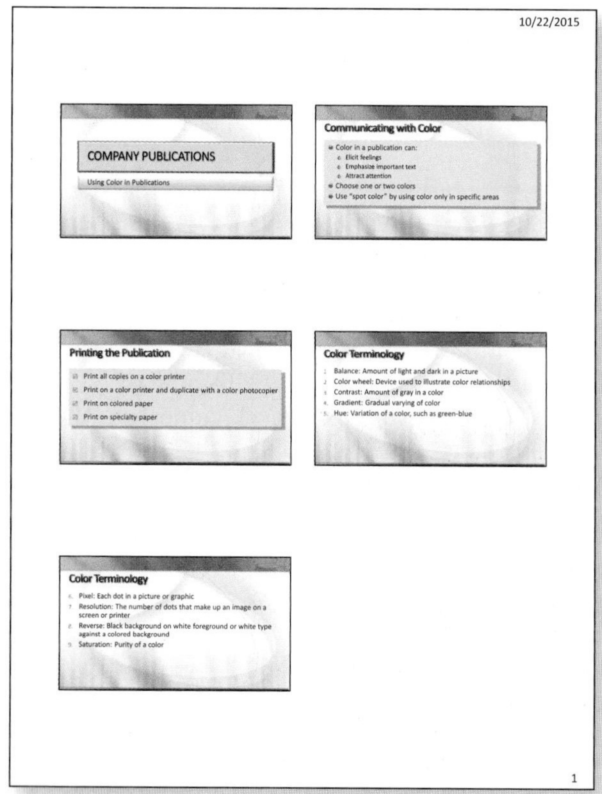

Project 2 Customize Bullets and Numbers in a Color Presentation
P-C3-P2-ColorPres.pptx

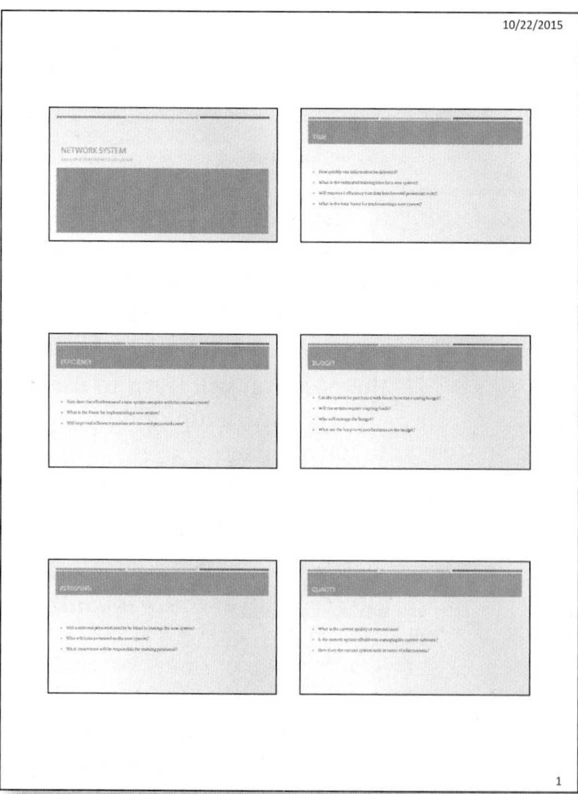

Project 3 Modify the Theme and Slide Background of a Network Presentation
P-C3-P3-NetworkPres.pptx

JOB SEARCH
Strategies for Success
Writing Your Resume
Resume Suggestions

Project 4 Create and Apply Custom Themes to Presentations
P-C3-P4-JobSearch.pptx

P-C3-P4-ResumePres.pptx

Project 1 Format an E-Commerce Presentation — 5 Parts

You will open an e-commerce presentation, apply font and paragraph formatting, apply formatting with Format Painter, apply column formatting to text in placeholders, and rotate and vertically align text in placeholders.

Formatting a Presentation

PowerPoint provides a variety of design themes you can apply to a presentation. These themes contain formatting such as font, color, and graphics. In some situations, the formatting provided by the theme is appropriate; in other situations, you may want to change or enhance the formatting of a slide in a presentation.

Applying Font Formatting

The Font group on the HOME tab contains a number of buttons for applying font formatting to text in a slide. Use these buttons to change the font, font size, and font color, as well as apply font effects. Table 3.1 describes the buttons in the Font group along with any keyboard shortcuts for applying font formatting.

Changing Fonts

Design themes apply a certain font (or fonts) to text in slides. You may want to change the font to change the mood of a presentation, enhance the visual appearance of slides, or increase the readability of the text. Change the font with the Font and Font Size buttons in the Font group on the HOME tab.

When you select text and then click the Font button arrow, a drop-down gallery displays with font options. Hover your mouse pointer over a font option and the selected text in the slide displays with the font applied. You can continue hovering your mouse pointer over different font options to see how the selected text displays in the specified font. The Font button drop-down gallery is an example of the ***live preview*** feature, which allows you to see how different formatting options look before you actually apply them. The live preview feature is also available when you click the Font Size button arrow.

Consider using a sans serif typeface for titles and headings and a serif typeface for body text.

Use options at the Font dialog box with the Character Spacing tab selected to increase or decrease spacing between characters and to apply kerning to text.

Fonts may be decorative or plain and generally fall into one of two categories: ***serif fonts*** or ***sans serif fonts***. A ***serif*** is a small line at the end of a character stroke. A serif font is easier to read and is generally used for large blocks of text. A sans serif font does not have serifs (*sans* is French for *without*). Sans serif fonts are generally used for titles and headings.

In addition to buttons in the Font group on the HOME tab, you can use options at the Font dialog box, shown in Figure 3.1, to apply character formatting to text. Display the Font dialog box by clicking the Font group dialog box launcher or with the keyboard shortcut Ctrl + Shift + F. (The dialog box launcher is the small button containing a diagonal arrow that displays in the lower right corner of the group.) Use options at the Font dialog box to choose a font, font style, and font size and to apply special effects to text in slides such as superscript, subscript, and double strikethrough.

Table 3.1 PowerPoint HOME Tab Font Group Buttons

Button	Name	Function	Keyboard Shortcut
B	Bold	Adds or removes bold formatting to or from selected text.	Ctrl + B
Aa	Change Case	Changes the case of selected text.	Shift + F3
AV	Character Spacing	Adjusts spacing between characters.	
	Clear All Formatting	Clears all character formatting from selected text.	Ctrl + Spacebar
A	Decrease Font Size	Decreases font size of selected text to next available smaller size.	Ctrl + Shift + <
Calibri (Body)	Font	Changes selected text to a different font.	
A	Font Color	Changes the font color for selected text.	
32	Font Size	Changes selected text to a different font size.	
A	Increase Font Size	Increases font size of selected text to next available larger size.	Ctrl + Shift + >
I	Italic	Adds or removes italic formatting to or from selected text.	Ctrl + I
abc	Strikethrough	Inserts or removes a line through the middle of selected text.	
S	Text Shadow	Adds or removes shadow formatting to or from selected text.	
U	Underline	Adds or removes underline formatting to or from selected text.	Ctrl + U

Figure 3.1 Font Dialog Box

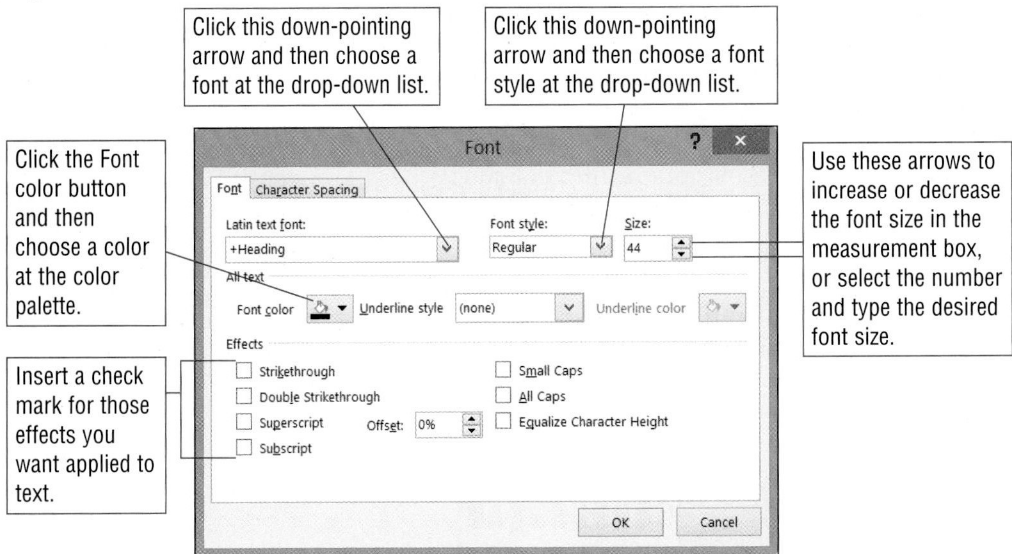

Formatting with the Mini Toolbar

When you select text, the Mini toolbar displays above the selected text. Click a button on the Mini toolbar to apply formatting to selected text. If you do not want the Mini toolbar to display when you select text, you can turn it off. To do this, click the FILE tab and then click *Options*. At the PowerPoint Options dialog box with the *General* option selected in the left panel, click the *Show Mini Toolbar on selection* check box to remove the check mark.

Project 1a **Applying Font Formatting to Text** **Part 1 of 5**

1. Open **E-Commerce.pptx** and then save the presentation with Save As and name it **P-C3-P1-E-Commerce**.
2. Apply the Ion Boardroom design theme with the green variant to the presentation by completing the following steps:
   a. Click the DESIGN tab.
   b. Click the More button located to the right of the theme thumbnails.
   c. Click the *Ion Boardroom* theme thumbnail.
   d. Click the green variant in the Variants group (second thumbnail).
3. Change the font formatting of the Slide 1 subtitle by completing the following steps:
   a. With Slide 1 active, click any character in the subtitle and then select *ONLINE SERVICES*.
   b. Click the HOME tab.
   c. Click the Font button arrow, scroll down the drop-down gallery, and then click *Cambria*.

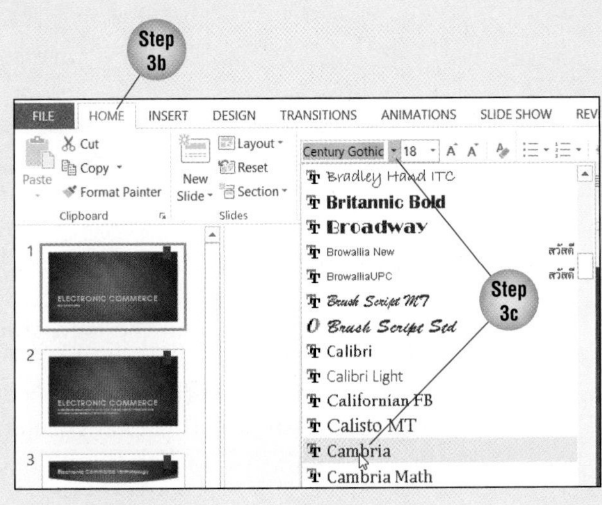

d. Click the Font Size button arrow and then click *40* at the drop-down gallery.
e. Click the Bold button in the Font group.
f. Click the Text Shadow button.
g. Click the Font Color button arrow and then click the *Dark Red, Accent 1, Darker 25%* option (fifth column, fifth row).

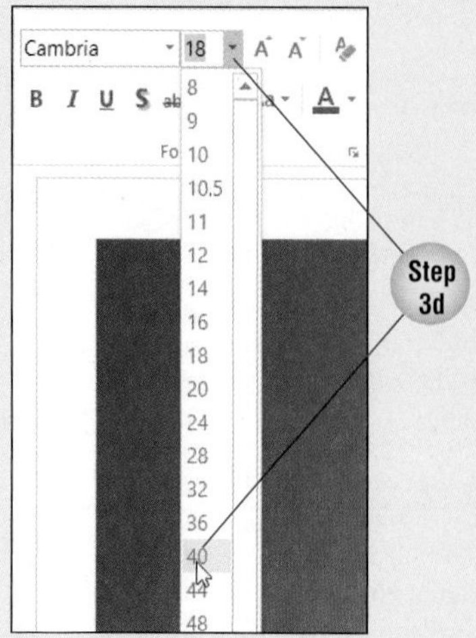

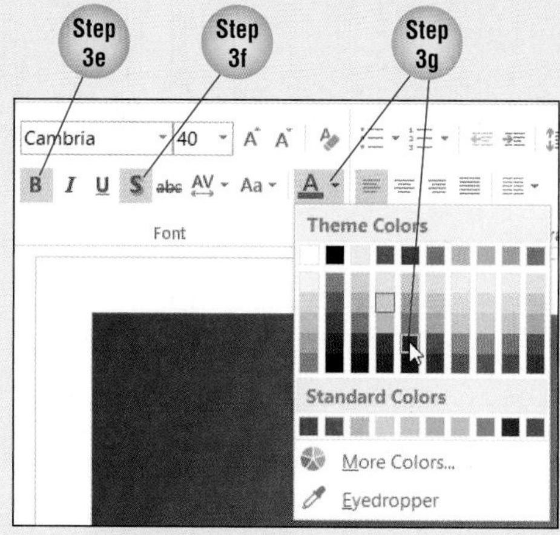

4. Change the size of the title text by completing the following steps:
   a. Click any character in the title *ELECTRONIC COMMERCE* and then click the placeholder border to change the border line to a solid line.
   b. Click once on the Decrease Font Size button in the Font group.
5. Change the case of the title text by completing the following steps:
   a. Make Slide 2 active.
   b. Click in the title *ELECTRONIC COMMERCE* and then click the placeholder border to change the border line to a solid line.
   c. Click the Change Case button in the Font group and then click *Capitalize Each Word* at the drop-down list.

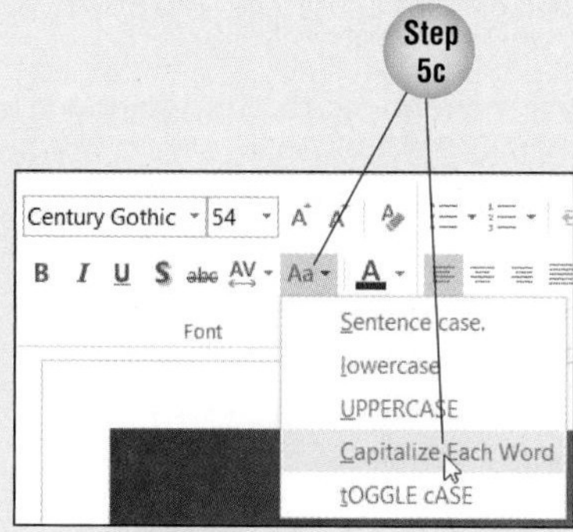

6. Apply and then clear formatting from the content text by completing the following steps:
   a. Make Slide 3 active.
   b. Click in the placeholder containing the bulleted text.
   c. Select *m-commerce* (located in parentheses).
   d. Click the Underline button in the Font group on the HOME tab.
   e. Click the Bold button in the Font group.
   f. After looking at the text with underlining and bold formatting applied, remove the formatting by clicking the Clear All Formatting button in the Font group.
   g. With the text still selected, click the Italic button in the Font group on the HOME tab.

7. Apply italic formatting with the Mini toolbar by completing the following steps:
   a. Select *B2C* in the second bulleted item and then click the Italic button on the Mini toolbar.
   b. Select *B2B* in the third bulleted item and then click the Italic button on the Mini toolbar.
8. Save **P-C3-P1-E-Commerce.pptx**.

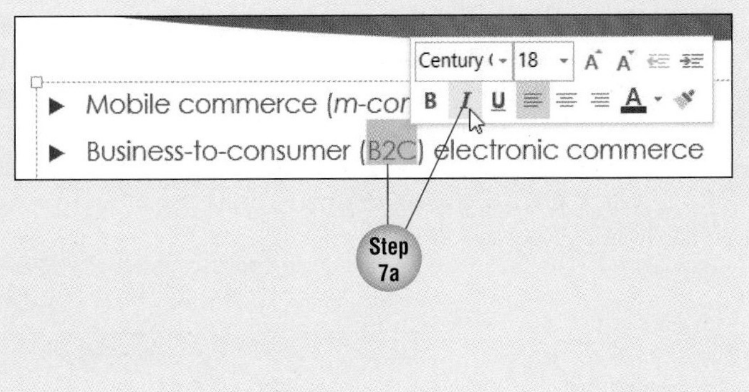

Formatting with Format Painter

If you apply character and/or paragraph formatting to text in a slide and want to apply the same formatting to additional text in that slide or other slides, use the Format Painter. With Format Painter, you can apply the same formatting in more than one location in a slide or slides. To use the Format Painter, apply the desired formatting to text, position the insertion point anywhere in the formatted text, and then double-click the Format Painter button in the Clipboard group on the HOME tab. Using the mouse, select the additional text to which you want to apply the formatting. After applying the formatting in the desired locations, click the Format Painter button to deactivate it. If you need to apply formatting in only one other location, click the Format Painter button once. The first time you select text, the formatting is applied and the Format Painter is deactivated.

Quick Steps

Format with Format Painter
1. Click text containing desired formatting.
2. Double-click Format Painter button.
3. Select or click on text.
4. Click Format Painter button.

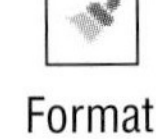

Format Painter

HINT

You can also turn off Format Painter by pressing the Esc key.

Project 1b **Applying Formatting with Format Painter** **Part 2 of 5**

1. With **P-C3-P1-E-Commerce.pptx** open, make sure Slide 3 is active.
2. Apply formatting to the title by completing the following steps:
   a. Click in the title text and then click the placeholder border to change the border line to a solid line.
   b. Click the Font group dialog box launcher on the HOME tab.

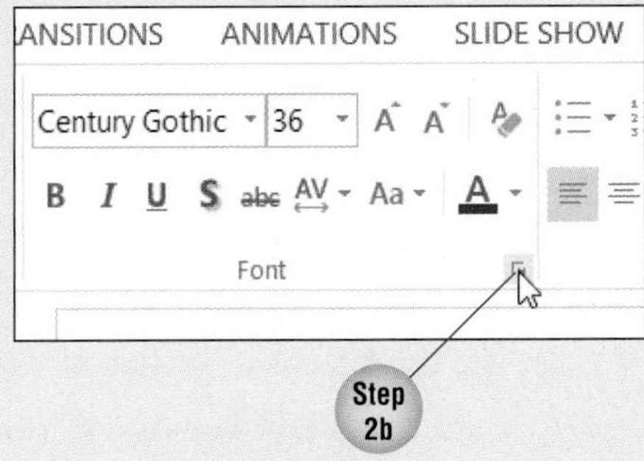

c. At the Font dialog box, click the down-pointing arrow at the right side of the *Latin text font* option box, scroll down the drop-down list, and then click *Candara*.
d. Click the down-pointing arrow at the right side of the *Font style* option box and then click *Bold Italic* at the drop-down list.
e. Select the current number in the *Size* measurement box and then type 40.
f. Click OK to close the dialog box.

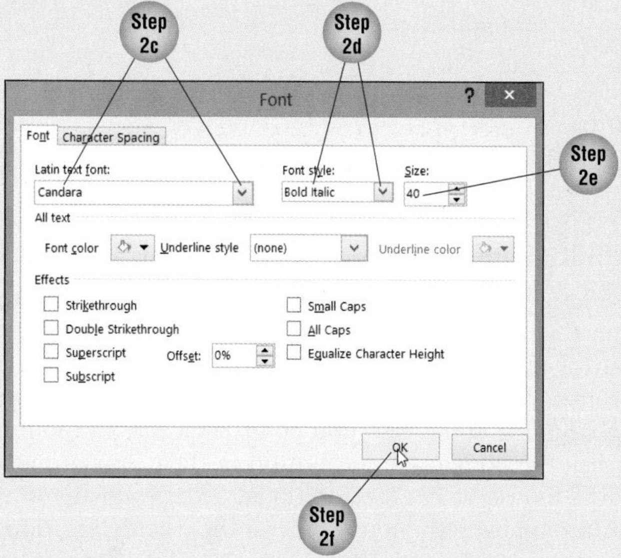

3. Click any character in the title.
4. Double-click the Format Painter button in the Clipboard group on the HOME tab.

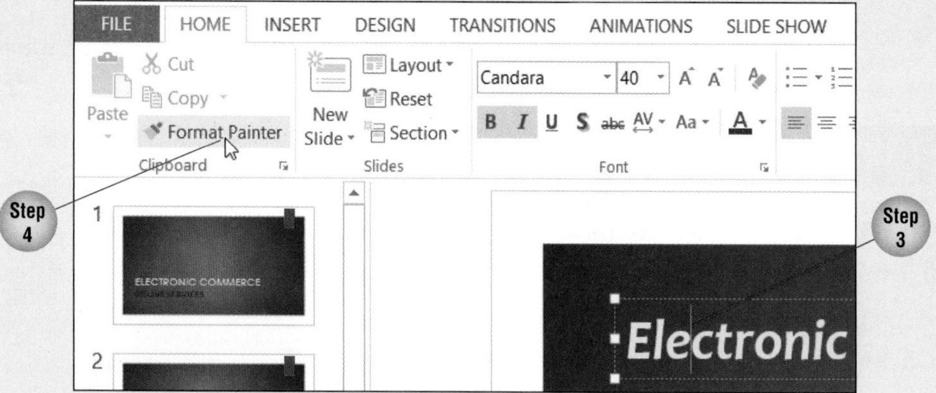

5. Make Slide 8 active.
6. Using the mouse, select the title *Advantages of Online Shopping*. (The mouse pointer displays as an I-beam with a paintbrush attached. Instead of selecting the whole title, you can also click each word in the title to apply the formatting. However, clicking individual words will not format the spaces between the words in multiple-word titles.)
7. Make Slide 9 active and then select the title (or click each word in the title).
8. Make Slide 10 active and then select the title (or click each word in the title).
9. Click the Format Painter button to deactivate it.
10. If necessary, deselect the text.
11. Save **P-C3-P1-E-Commerce.pptx**.

Formatting Paragraphs

The Paragraph group on the HOME tab contains a number of buttons for applying paragraph formatting to text in a slide, such as applying bullets and numbers, increasing and decreasing list levels, changing the horizontal and vertical alignment of text, changing line spacing, and rotating text in a placeholder. Table 3.2 describes the buttons in the Paragraph group along with any keyboard shortcuts.

Fitting Contents in a Placeholder

When text in a placeholder exceeds the size of the placeholder, you can use the AutoFit Options button to decrease the spacing between bulleted items or decrease the font size to ensure that all the text fits in the placeholder. The AutoFit Options button displays in the lower left corner of the placeholder when text no longer fits inside the placeholder. Click the AutoFit Options button to display a list of options such as *Autofit Text to Placeholder, Stop Fitting Text to This Placeholder, Split Between Two Slides, Continue on a New Slide, Change to Two Columns*, and *Control AutoCorrect Options*.

AutoFit Options

Table 3.2 Buttons in the Paragraph group on the HOME tab

Button	Name	Function	Keyboard Shortcut
	Bullets	Adds or removes bullets to or from selected text.	
	Numbering	Adds or removes numbers to or from selected text.	
	Decrease List Level	Moves text to the previous tab stop (level).	Shift + Tab
	Increase List Level	Moves text to the next tab stop (level).	Tab
	Line Spacing	Increases or reduces spacing between lines of text.	
	Align Left	Left-aligns text.	Ctrl + L
	Center	Center-aligns text.	Ctrl + E
	Align Right	Right-aligns text.	Ctrl + R
	Justify	Justifies text.	
	Add or Remove Columns	Splits text into two or more columns.	
	Text Direction	Rotates or stacks text.	
	Align Text	Changes the alignment of text within a text box.	
	Convert to SmartArt Graphic	Converts selected text to a SmartArt graphic.	

Project 1c Applying Paragraph Formatting to Text Part 3 of 5

1. With **P-C3-P1-E-Commerce.pptx** open, change bullets by completing the following steps:
   a. Make Slide 3 active.
   b. Click any character in the bulleted text.
   c. Select the bulleted text.
   d. Click the Bullets button arrow in the Paragraph group on the HOME tab and then click the *Filled Square Bullets* option at the drop-down gallery.

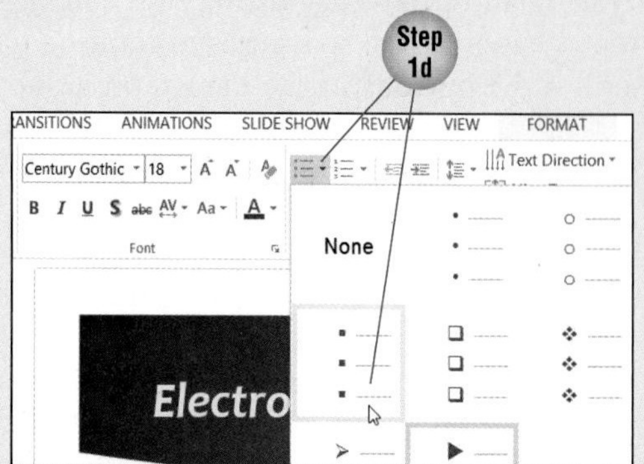

2. Change the bullets to letters by completing the following steps:
   a. Make Slide 8 active.
   b. Click any character in the bulleted text.
   c. Select the bulleted text.
   d. Click the Numbering button arrow in the Paragraph group on the HOME tab and then click the *A. B. C.* option at the drop-down gallery.

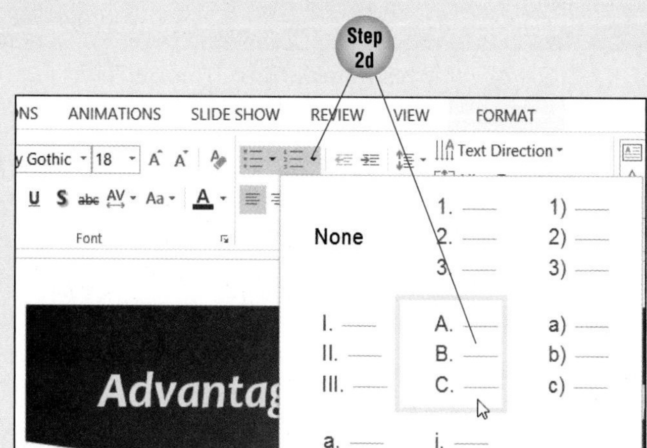

   e. After looking at the letters, change to numbers by clicking the Numbering button arrow and then clicking the *1. 2. 3.* option at the drop-down gallery.
3. Decrease and increase list levels by completing the following steps:
   a. With Slide 8 active and the numbered text selected, click the Increase List Level button in the Paragraph group on the HOME tab.
   b. With the text still selected, click the Font Color button arrow in the Font group on the HOME tab and then click *Teal, Accent 5, Darker 50%* at the drop-down gallery (ninth column, bottom row in the *Theme Colors* section).
   c. Make Slide 10 active.
   d. Click any character in the bulleted text.

e. Move the insertion point so it is positioned immediately left of the *N* in *Nordstrom*.
f. Click the Decrease List Level button in the Paragraph group on the HOME tab.
g. Move the insertion point so it is positioned immediately left of the *M* in *Macy's*.
h. Press Shift + Tab.
i. Move the insertion point so it is positioned immediately left of the first *L.* in *L.L. Bean*.
j. Click the Increase List Level button in the Paragraph group.
k. Move the insertion point so it is positioned immediately left of the *T* in *The Gap*.
l. Press the Tab key.
m. Complete similar steps to those in 3j or 3l to indent *Bloomingdale's, Expedia, Travelocity,* and *Orbitz* to the next level.

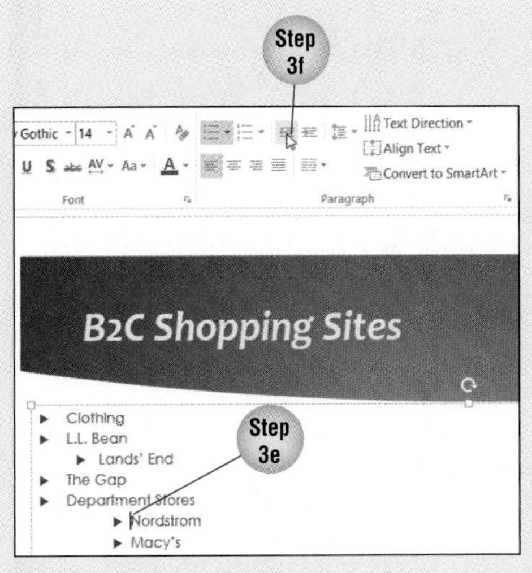

4. Increase the size of the text and make sure the content fits within the Slide 10 placeholder by completing the following steps:
   a. With Slide 10 active, select all the bulleted items and then change the font size to 16 points.
   b. Click anywhere in the bulleted text to deselect the text.
   c. Click the AutoFit Options button that displays in the lower left corner of the placeholder and then click *AutoFit Text to Placeholder* at the drop-down list. (This decreases the spacing between the bulleted items to ensure all items fit in the placeholder.)

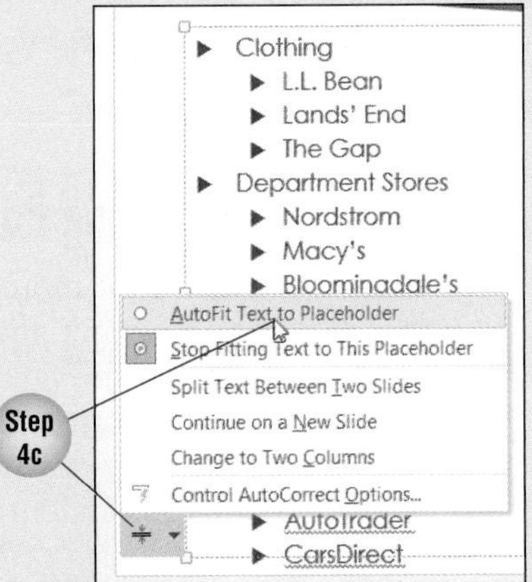

5. Change the line spacing of the text by completing the following steps:
   a. Make Slide 3 active.
   b. Click in the bulleted text and then select the bulleted text.
   c. Click the Line Spacing button in the Paragraph group on the HOME tab and then click *1.5* at the drop-down list.
   d. Make Slide 8 active.
   e. Click in the numbered text and then select the numbered text.
   f. Click the Line Spacing button and then click *2.0* at the drop-down list.

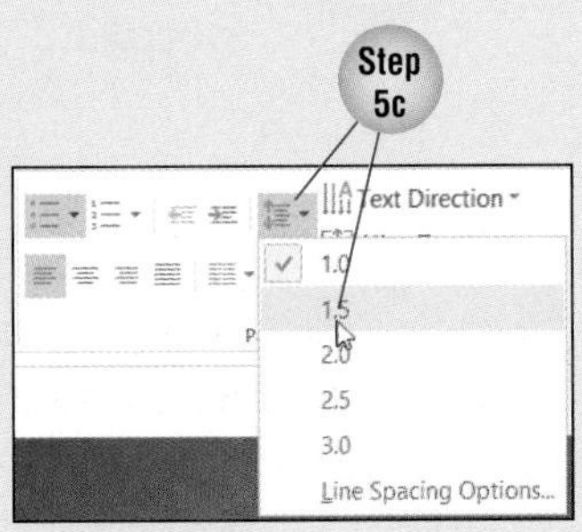

6. Change paragraph alignment by completing the following steps:
   a. Make Slide 3 active, click any character in the title, and then click the Center button in the Paragraph group.

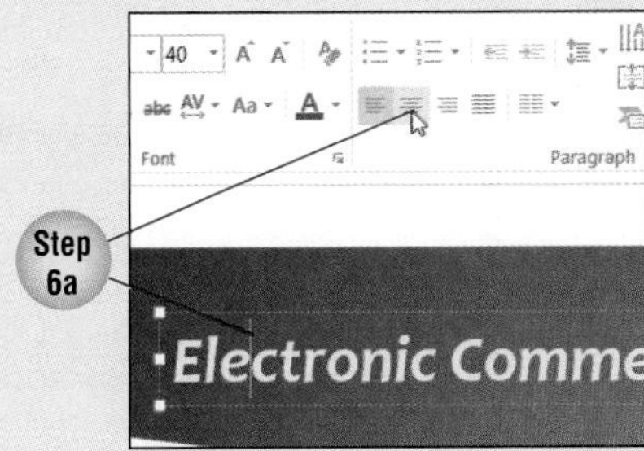

b. Make Slide 8 active, click any character in the title, and then click the Center button.
c. Make Slide 9 active, click any character in the title, and then click the Center button.
d. Make Slide 10 active, click any character in the title, and then click the Center button.

7. Split text into two columns by completing the following steps:
   a. Make Slide 9 active.
   b. Click in the bulleted text and then select the bulleted text.
   c. Click the Add or Remove Columns button in the Paragraph group and then click *Two Columns* at the drop-down list.
   d. Select the first sentence in the first bulleted paragraph (*Clear selling terms.*) and then click the Bold button.
   e. Select and then bold the first sentence in each of the remaining bulleted paragraphs in Slide 9.
   f. Drag the bottom border of the bulleted text placeholder up until two bulleted items display in each column.
8. Save **P-C3-P1-E-Commerce.pptx**.

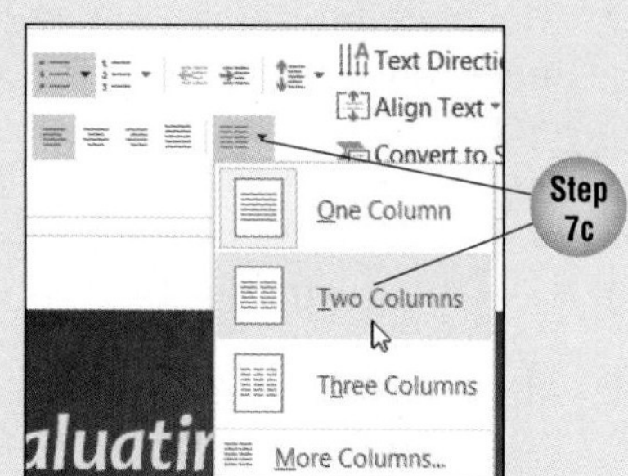

Customizing Paragraphs

Line Spacing

If you want more control over paragraph alignment, indenting, and spacing, click the Paragraph group dialog box launcher. This displays the Paragraph dialog box, as shown in Figure 3.2. You can also display this dialog box by clicking the Line Spacing button in the Paragraph group and then clicking *Line Spacing Options* at the drop-down list. Use options at this dialog box to specify text alignment, paragraph indentation, spacing before and after paragraphs, and line spacing.

Figure 3.2 Paragraph Dialog Box

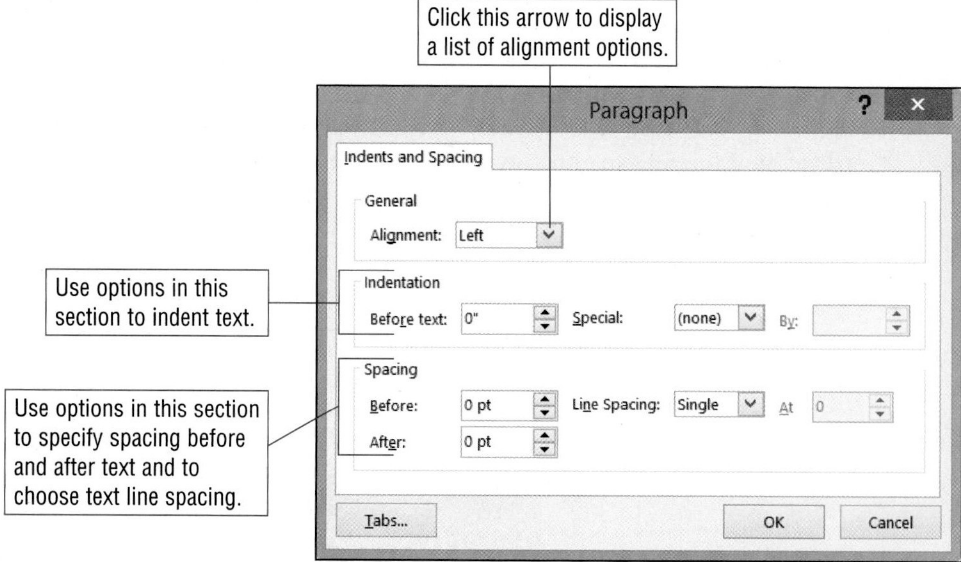

Customizing Columns

Click the Add or Remove Columns button in the Paragraph group to specify one, two, or three columns for your text. If you want to use more than three columns or if you want to control spacing between columns, click the *More Columns* option at the drop-down list. This displays the Columns dialog box, as shown in Figure 3.3. With options in this dialog box, you can specify the number of columns and the amount of spacing between them.

Add or Remove Columns

Format text into columns to make it attractive and easy to read.

Figure 3.3 Columns Dialog Box

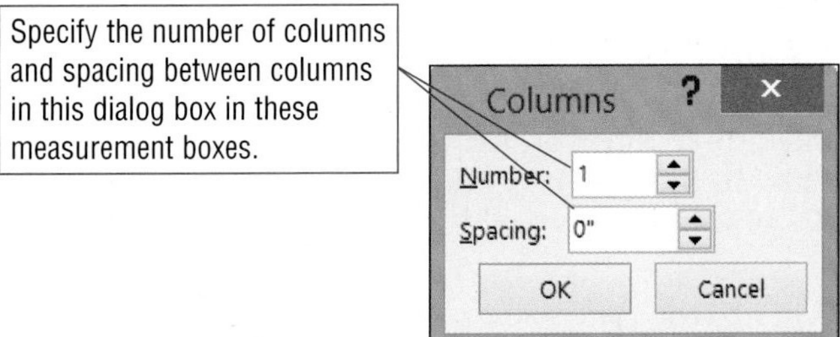

Project 1d **Customizing Paragraph and Column Formatting** **Part 4 of 5**

1. With **P-C3-P1-E-Commerce.pptx** open, change line and paragraph spacing by completing the following steps:
   a. Make Slide 3 active.
   b. Click in the bulleted text and then select the bulleted text.
   c. Click the Paragraph group dialog box launcher.
   d. At the Paragraph dialog box, click three times on the up-pointing arrow at the right side of the *Before text* measurement box in the *Indentation* section. (This inserts *0.6"* in the measurement box.)
   e. Click twice on the up-pointing arrow at the right side of the *After* measurement box in the *Spacing* section. (This inserts *12 pt* in the box.)
   f. Click the down-pointing arrow at the right side of the *Line Spacing* option box and then click *Multiple* at the drop-down list.
   g. Select the current measurement in the *At* measurement box and then type 1.8.
   h. Click OK.

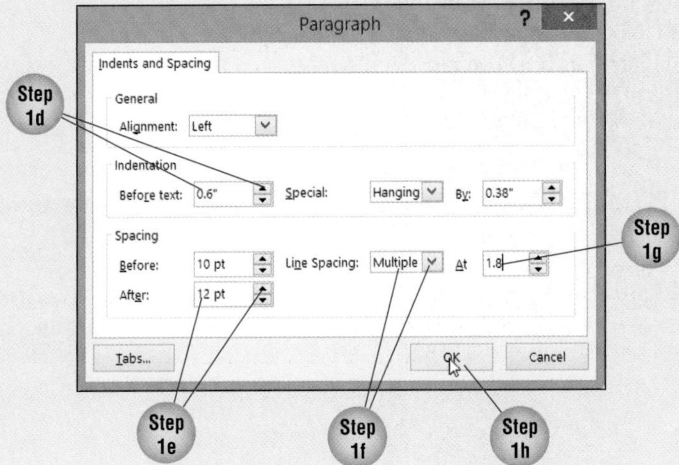

2. Format text in columns by completing the following steps:
   a. Make Slide 10 active.
   b. Click in the bulleted text and then select the text.
   c. Click the Add or Remove Columns button in the Paragraph group and then click *More Columns* at the drop-down list.
   d. At the Columns dialog box, click once on the up-pointing arrow at the right side of the *Number* measurement box. (This inserts a *2* in the measurement box.)
   e. Click the up-pointing arrow at the right side of the *Spacing* measurement box until *0.5"* displays in the measurement box.
   f. Click OK.
   g. With the text still selected, click the Paragraph group dialog box launcher.
   h. At the Paragraph dialog box, click three times on the up-pointing arrow at the right side of the *After* measurement box in the *Spacing* section. (This inserts *18 pt* in the measurement box.)
   i. Click OK.
3. With the bulleted text selected, change the font size to 20 points.
4. Save **P-C3-P1-E-Commerce.pptx**.

Rotating and Vertically Aligning Text

Text Direction

Align Text

If you click the Text Direction button in the Paragraph group on the HOME tab, a drop-down list displays with options for rotating and stacking text. Click the Align Text button in the Paragraph group and a drop-down list displays with options for changing the alignment to the top, middle, or bottom of the placeholder.

Project 1e Rotating and Vertically Aligning Text — Part 5 of 5

1. With **P-C3-P1-E-Commerce.pptx** open, change the vertical alignment of text by completing the following steps:
   a. Make Slide 3 active.
   b. Click any character in the bulleted text.
   c. Click the Align Text button in the Paragraph group on the HOME tab and then click *Middle* at the drop-down list.

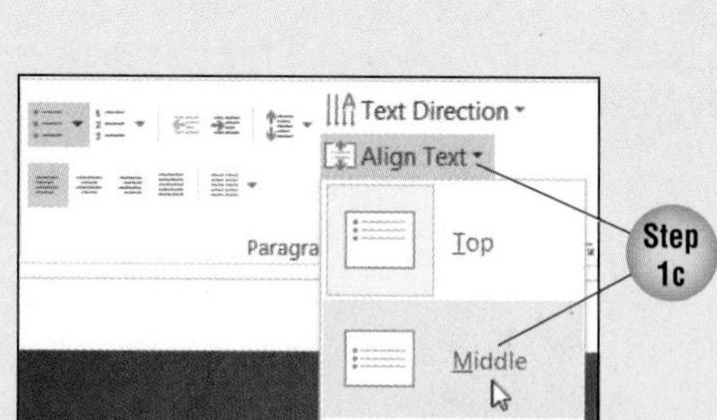

2. Make Slide 8 active and then modify the slide so it displays as shown in Figure 3.4 on page 94 by completing the following steps:
   a. Click in the numbered text and then select the numbered text.
   b. Click the Bullets button arrow and then click the *Hollow Square Bullets* option.
   c. Decrease the size of the bulleted text placeholder so the placeholder borders display just outside the text.

d. Drag the placeholder to the middle of the slide until the guideline (a vertical dashed line) displays and then release the mouse button. (Refer to Figure 3.4 for the postion of the placeholder.)
e. Click any character in the title *Advantages of Online Shopping*.
f. Delete the text *of Online Shopping*.
g. Select *Advantages* and then change the font size to 54 points.
h. Drag the right border of the placeholder to the left so it is positioned just outside the text.
i. Click the Text Direction button in the Paragraph group and then click *Rotate all text 270°*.
j. Using the sizing handles that display around the title placeholder, increase the height and decrease the width of the placeholder and then drag the placeholder so the title displays as shown in Figure 3.4. Use the horizontal guideline (a dashed line) to help you vertically center the placeholder on the slide.

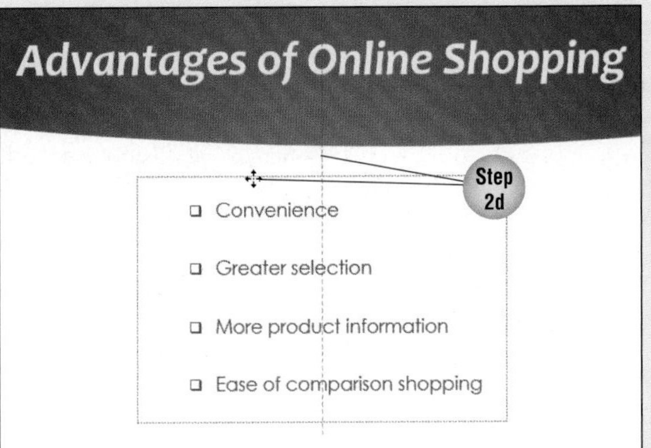

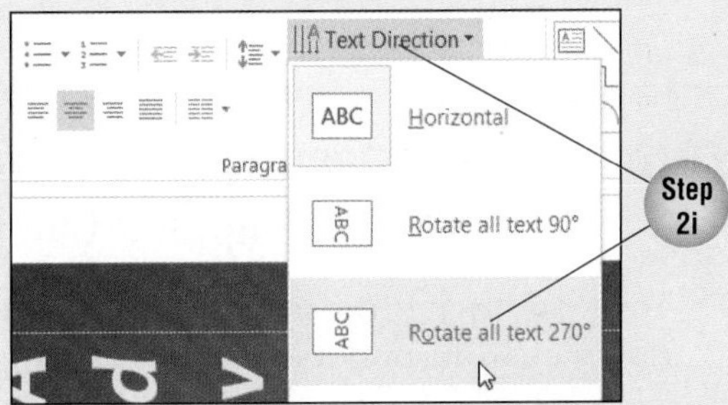

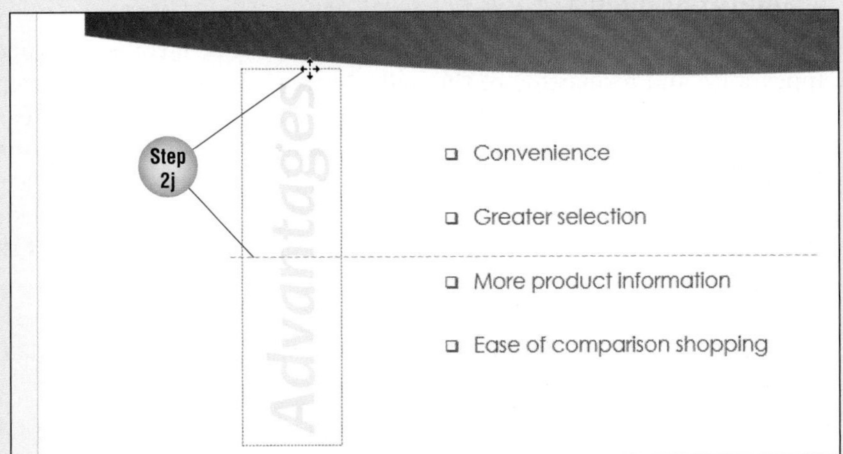

k. With the title placeholder selected, click the Font Color button arrow in the Font group and then click *Dark Red, Accent 1, Darker 25%* at the drop-down gallery (fifth column, fifth row in the *Theme Colors* section).

3. Apply a transition and sound to all slides in the presentation.
4. Print the presentation as a handout with six slides printed horizontally per page.
5. Save and then close **P-C3-P1-E-Commerce.pptx**.

Figure 3.4 Project 1e, Slide 8

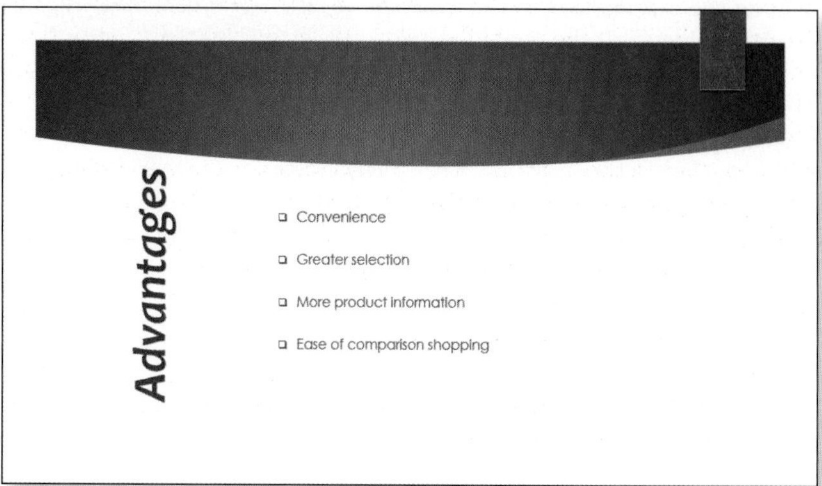

Project 2 Customize Bullets and Numbers and Change Page Setup in a Color Presentation — 4 Parts

You will open a presentation on using colors in publications and then create and apply custom bullets and numbering.

Quick Steps

Customize Bullets
1. Click in bulleted text.
2. Click Bullets button arrow.
3. Click *Bullets and Numbering* at drop-down gallery.
4. Make desired changes.
5. Click OK.

Bullets

Customizing Bullets

Each design theme contains a Title and Content slide layout with bullets. The appearance and formatting of the bullets vary with each design theme. You can choose to use the bullet style provided by the design theme, or you can create custom bullets. Customize bullets with options at the Bullets and Numbering dialog box with the Bulleted tab selected, as shown in Figure 3.5. Display this dialog box by clicking in a placeholder containing a bulleted list, clicking the Bullets button arrow in the Paragraph group on the HOME tab, and then clicking *Bullets and Numbering* at the drop-down gallery.

Figure 3.5 Bullets and Numbering Dialog Box with Bulleted Tab Selected

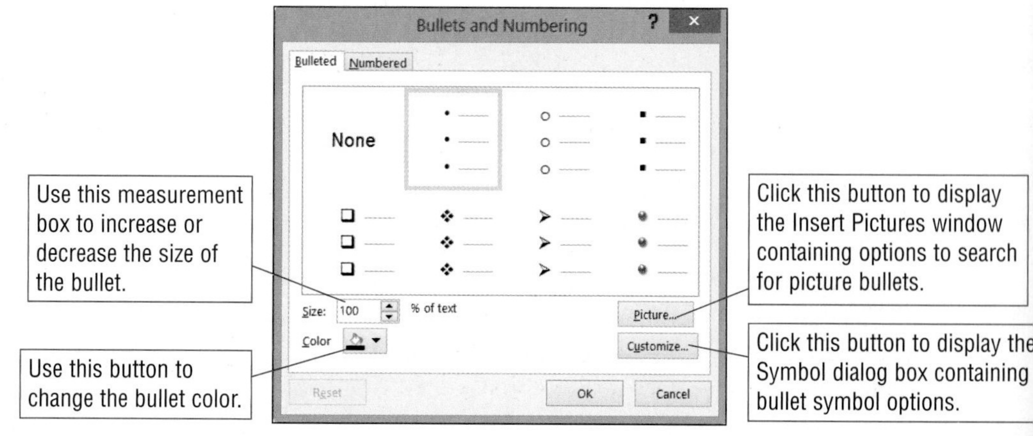

At the Bullets and Numbering dialog box, choose one of the predesigned bullets from the list box, change the size of the bullets (measured by percentage in relation to the size of the text), change the bullet color, and/or specify a picture or symbol to use as a bullet. Click the Picture button located toward the bottom of the dialog box and the Insert Pictures window displays. Click the Browse button to the right of the *From a file* option, navigate to the desired folder in the Insert Picture dialog box, and then double-click the desired picture. You can also search for images online in the Insert Pictures window. Click the Customize button located toward the bottom of the Bullets and Numbering dialog box and the Symbol dialog box displays. Choose a symbol bullet option at the Symbol dialog box and then click OK. Picture or symbol bullets are particularly effective for adding visual interest to a presentation.

HINT

Choose a custom bullet that matches the theme or mood of the presentation.

To insert a new, blank bullet point in a bulleted list, press Enter. If you want to move the insertion point down to the next line without inserting a new bullet, press Shift + Enter. This inserts a line break without inserting a bullet. A new bullet will be inserted the next time you press Enter.

Project 2a Customizing Bullets and Numbers

Part 1 of 4

1. Open **ColorPres.pptx** and then save the presentation with Save As and name it **P-C3-P2-ColorPres**.
2. Increase the list level of text and create custom bullets by completing the following steps:
   a. Make Slide 2 active.
   b. Select the second, third, and fourth bulleted paragraphs.
   c. Click the Increase List Level button in the Paragraph group on the HOME tab.
   d. With the three bulleted paragraphs still selected, click the Bullets button arrow and then click *Bullets and Numbering* at the drop-down list.
   e. At the Bullets and Numbering dialog box with the Bulleted tab selected, select the current number (*100*) in the *Size* measurement box and then type 75.
   f. Click the Picture button located toward the bottom right corner of the dialog box.
   g. At the Insert Pictures window, click in the search text box to the right of *Office.com Clip Art*, type **colorful bullet icon**, and then press Enter.
   h. When the search results display, double-click the colorful, round bullet, as shown at the right.

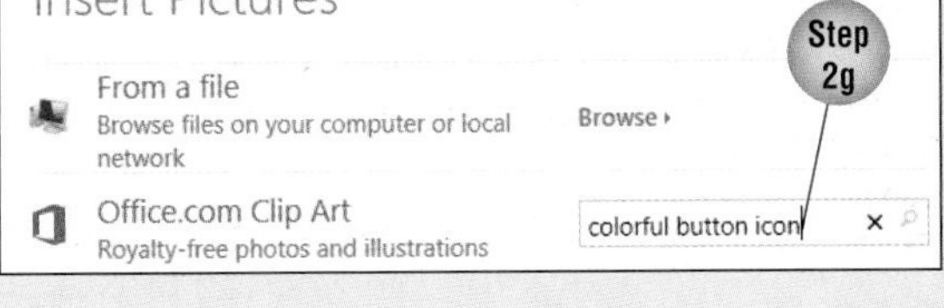

3. Insert symbol bullets by completing the following steps:
   a. Make Slide 3 active.
   b. Select all of the bulleted text.
   c. Click the Bullets button arrow and then click *Bullets and Numbering* at the drop-down list.
   d. At the Bullets and Numbering dialog box with the Bulleted tab selected, click the down-pointing arrow at the right side of the *Size* measurement box until *80* displays.
   e. Click the Customize button located toward the bottom right corner of the dialog box.

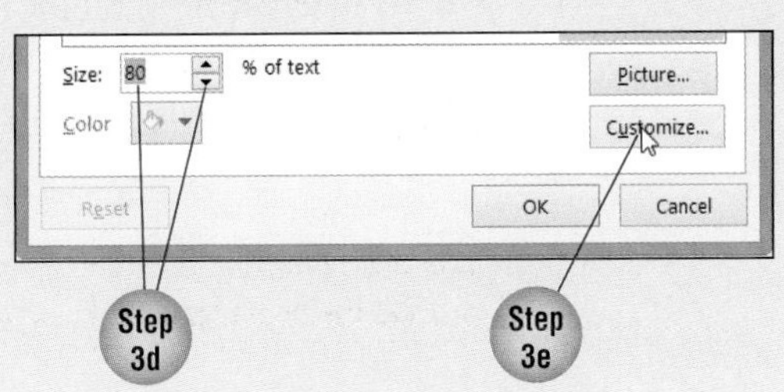

f. At the Symbol dialog box, click the down-pointing arrow at the right side of the *Font* option box, scroll down the drop-down list, and then click *Wingdings*. (This option is located toward the bottom of the list.)

g. Scroll to the bottom of the list box until the last row of symbols displays and then click the second symbol from the right in the bottom row (a check mark inside of a square).

h. Click OK.

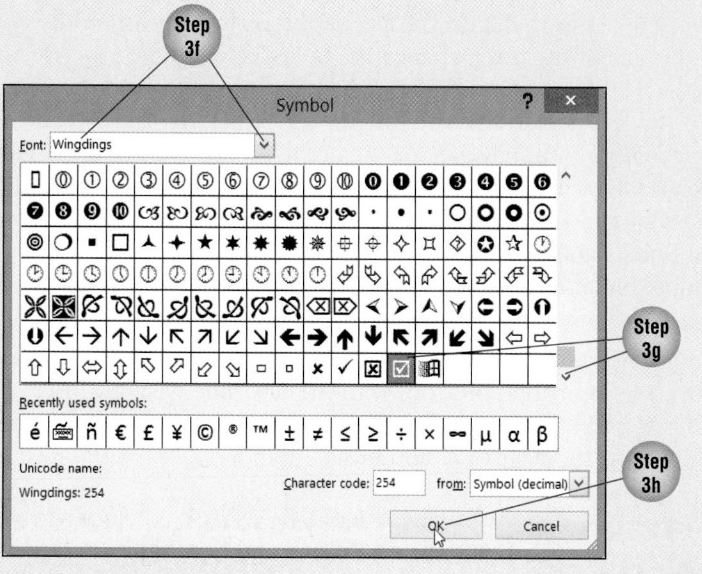

i. At the Bullets and Numbering dialog box, click the Color button and then click *Purple, Accent 6* (last column, first row in the *Theme Colors* section).

j. Click OK to close the Bullets and Numbering dialog box. (This applies the purple check mark symbol bullets to the selected text.)

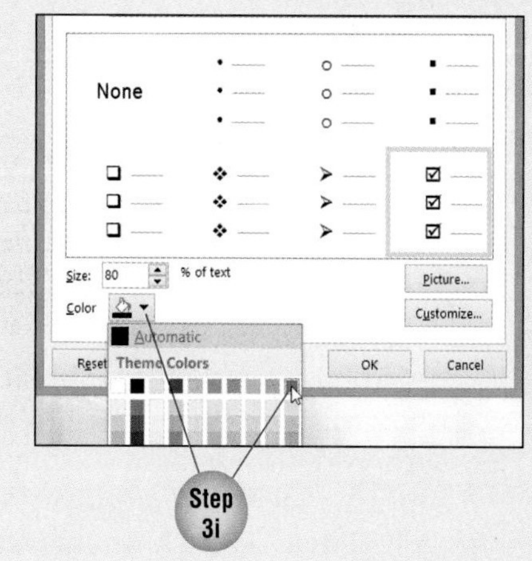

4. Increase the spacing between the bullets and the text by completing these steps:
   a. With the bulleted text selected, click the Paragraph group dialog box launcher.
   b. At the Paragraph dialog box, select the current measurement in the *By* measurement box (located in the *Indentation* section), type 0.6, and then press Enter.
5. Save **P-C3-P2-ColorPres.pptx**.

Customizing Numbering

Click the Numbering button arrow in the Paragraph group and several numbering options display in a drop-down gallery. Customize numbering with options at the Bullets and Numbering dialog box with the Numbered tab selected, as shown in Figure 3.6. Display this dialog box by clicking the Numbering button arrow and then clicking *Bullets and Numbering* at the drop-down gallery. Use options at this dialog box to change the size and color of numbers as well as the starting number.

To insert a new, blank numbered item in a numbered list, press Enter. If you want to move the insertion point down to the next line without inserting the next number, press Shift + Enter. The next number will be inserted the next time you press Enter.

Quick Steps

Customize Numbering
1. Click in numbered text.
2. Click Numbering button arrow.
3. Click *Bullets and Numbering* at drop-down gallery.
4. Make desired changes.
5. Click OK.

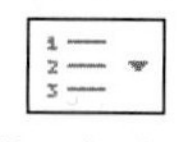

Numbering

Figure 3.6 Bullets and Numbering Dialog Box with Numbered Tab Selected

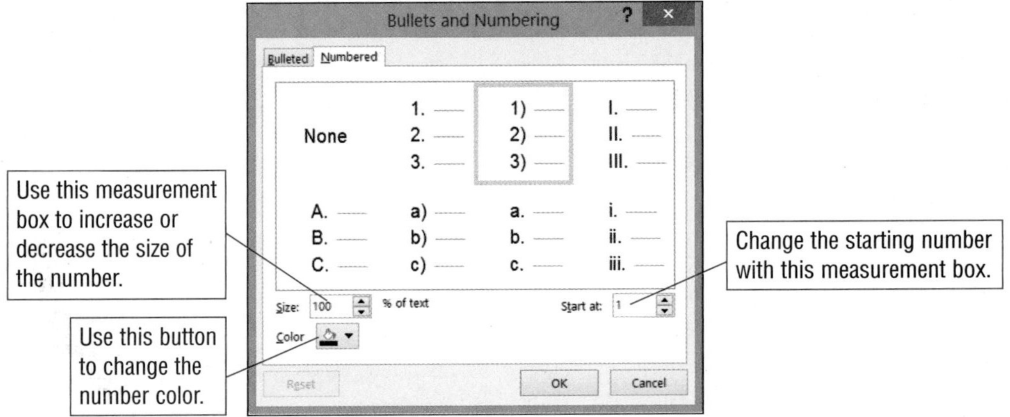

Project 2b Customizing Numbers

Part 2 of 4

1. With **P-C3-P2-ColorPres.pptx** open, make sure the presentation displays in Normal view.
2. Create and insert custom numbers by completing the following steps:
   a. Make Slide 4 active.
   b. Select the bulleted text in the slide.
   c. Click the Numbering button arrow in the Paragraph group on the HOME tab and then click the *Bullets and Numbering* option at the drop-down list.
   d. At the Bullets and Numbering dialog box with the Numbered tab selected, click the *1. 2. 3.* option (second option from the left in the top row).
   e. Select the number in the *Size* measurement box and then type 80.
   f. Click the Color button and then click *Purple, Accent 6* (last column, first row in the *Theme Colors* section).
   g. Click OK.

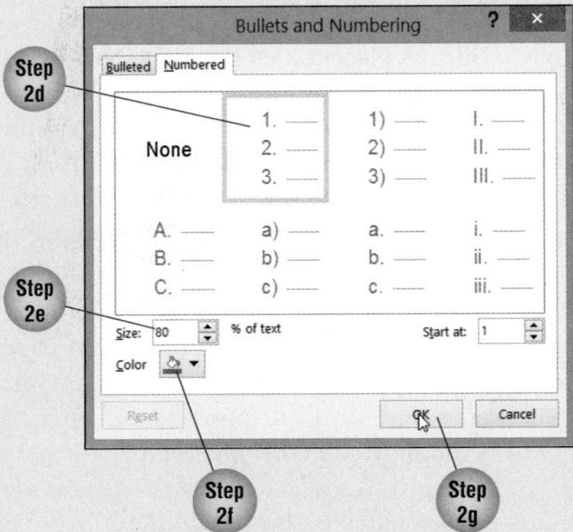

   h. Make Slide 5 active.
   i. Select the bulleted text in the slide.
   j. Click the Numbering button arrow and then click the *Bullets and Numbering* option at the drop-down list.

k. At the Bullets and Numbering dialog box with the Numbered tab selected, click the *1. 2. 3.* option (second option from the left in the top row).

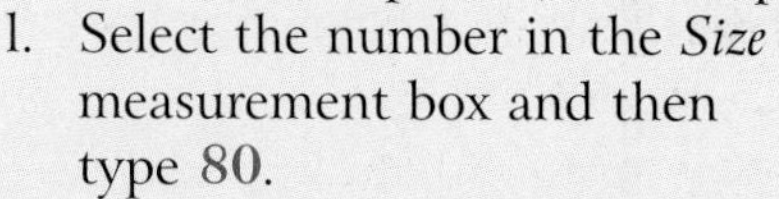

l. Select the number in the *Size* measurement box and then type 80.

m. Click the Color button and then click *Purple, Accent 6* (last column, first row in the *Theme Colors* section).

n. Click the up-pointing arrow at the right of the *Start at* measurement box until *6* displays.

o. Click OK.

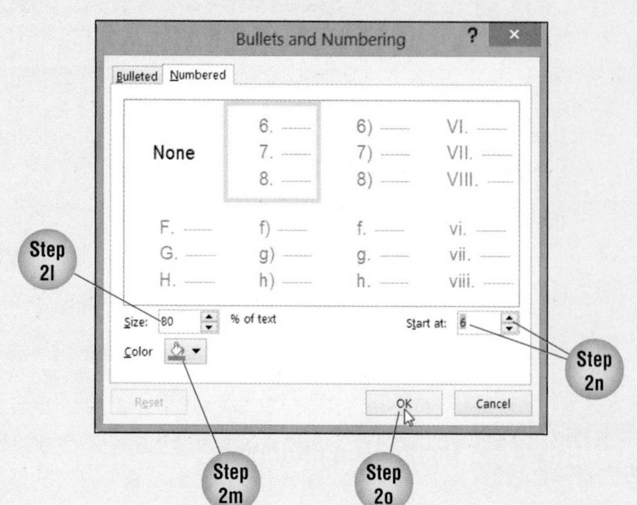

3. Add a transition and sound of your choosing to all slides in the presentation.
4. Run the presentation.
5. Save **P-C3-P2-ColorPres.pptx**.

Customizing Placeholders

You can also use options on the DRAWING TOOLS FORMAT tab to customize a placeholder.

Quick Styles

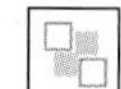
Arrange

Shape Fill

Shape Outline

Shape Effects

Quick Steps

Apply Color with the Eyedropper

1. Click desired object.
2. Click Shape Fill button.
3. Click *Eyedropper*.
4. Click desired color.

Customize a placeholder in a slide with buttons in the Drawing group on the HOME tab. Use options in the Drawing group to choose a shape, arrange the placeholder, apply a quick style, change the shape fill and outline colors, and apply a shape effect.

Click the Quick Styles button in the Drawing group and a drop-down gallery of styles displays. Choose a quick style from this gallery or click the *Other Theme Fills* option to display a side menu with additional fills. Arrange, align, and rotate a placeholder with options at the Arrange button drop-down list. Use the Shape Fill button to apply a fill to a placeholder. Click the Shape Fill button arrow and a drop-down gallery displays with options for applying a color, picture, gradient, or texture to the placeholder. Use the Shape Outline button to apply an outline to a placeholder and specify the outline color, weight, and style. With the Shape Effects button, you can choose from a variety of effects such as shadow, reflection, glow, and soft edges.

Both the Shape Fill and Shape Outline buttons in the Drawing group contain drop-down galleries with the *Eyedropper* option. Use the eyedropper to capture an exact color from one object and apply it to another object in the slide. To use the eyedropper to apply a fill color, click the object to which you want to apply fill color, click the Shape Fill button arrow, and then click *Eyedropper* at the drop-down gallery. The mouse pointer displays as an eyedropper. Position the tip of the eyedropper on the desired color and then click the mouse button. The color you click on is applied to the selected object. As you move the eyedropper, a live preview box displays above and to the right of the eyedropper. Use this live preview box to make sure you are pointing to the desired color. To pick a color outside the slide pane, hold down the Ctrl key, hold down the left mouse button, and then drag outside the slide pane. Position the tip of the eyedropper on the desired color and then release the mouse button and the Ctrl key. The *Eyedropper* option is also available with the Shape Fill, Shape Outline, and Font Color buttons on the HOME tab as well as with buttons on other tabs that apply color.

Customizing Placeholders at the Format Shape Task Pane

With options in the Format Shape task pane, apply shape options to a placeholder or apply text options to the text within a placeholder. The SHAPE OPTIONS tab of the Format Shape task pane displays three icons: Fill & Line, Effects, and Size & Properties, each with different options for formatting a placeholder. After clicking an icon, you may need to display (expand) the formatting options within the icons. For example, click *FILL* with the Fill & Line icon selected on the SHAPE OPTIONS tab to display options for applying a fill to a placeholder, as shown in Figure 3.7. The TEXT OPTIONS tab of the Format Shape task pane displays three icons: Text Fill & Outline, Text Effects, and Textbox, each with different options for formatting text within a placeholder. Display the Format Shape task pane by clicking the Drawing group task pane launcher on the HOME tab.

Align text in a placeholder with options at the Format Shape task pane with the Size & Properties icon selected. Scroll down the task pane list box to display the *TEXT BOX* section. With options in this section, you can align text in a placeholder as well as change text direction, autofit contents, and change internal margins.

When you apply formatting to a placeholder, you may need to move text within the placeholder. You can do this with the margin measurements in the Format Shape task pane. Display the margin measurements by clicking the Size & Properties icon and then scrolling down the task pane list box to the *TEXT BOX* section. Use the *Left margin*, *Right margin*, *Top margin*, and *Bottom margin* measurement boxes to specify internal margins for text inside a placeholder.

Figure 3.7 Format Shape Task Pane with SHAPE OPTIONS Tab Selected

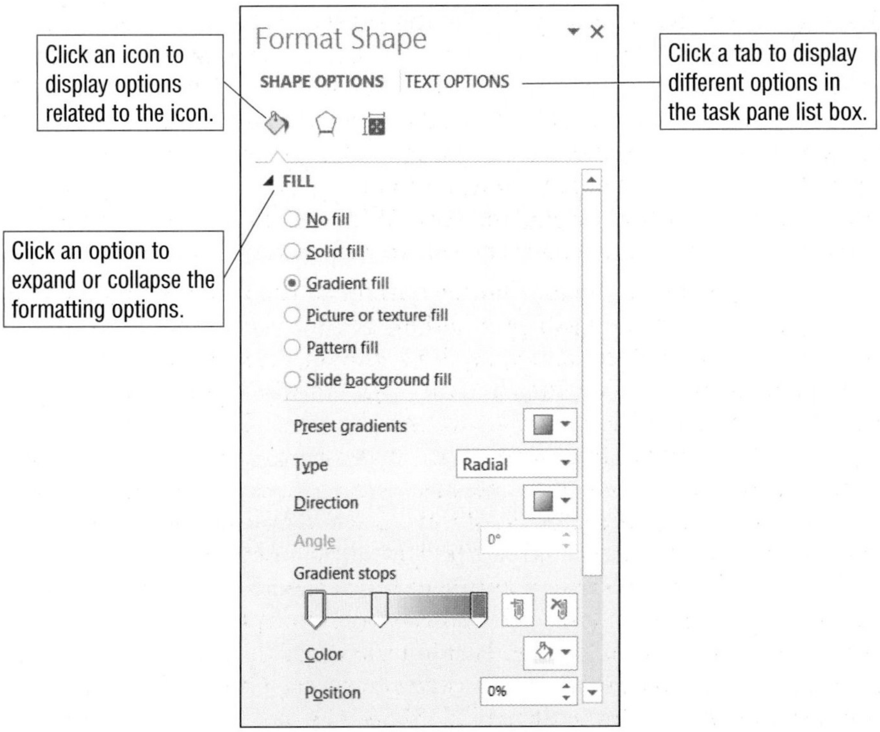

Click an icon to display options related to the icon.

Click an option to expand or collapse the formatting options.

Click a tab to display different options in the task pane list box.

Format Shape
SHAPE OPTIONS TEXT OPTIONS
FILL
No fill
Solid fill
Gradient fill
Picture or texture fill
Pattern fill
Slide background fill
Preset gradients
Type Radial
Direction
Angle 0°
Gradient stops
Color
Position 0%

Project 2c Customizing Placeholders Part 3 of 4

1. With **P-C3-P2-ColorPres.pptx** open, customize the title placeholder in Slide 1 by completing the following steps:
   a. If necessary, make Slide 1 active.
   b. Click in the title to select the placeholder.
   c. If necessary, click the HOME tab.
   d. Click the Quick Styles button in the Drawing group.
   e. Click the *Subtle Effect - Purple, Accent 6* option at the drop-down gallery (last column, fourth row).
   f. Click the Shape Outline button arrow in the Drawing group and then click *Purple, Accent 6, Darker 50%* (last column, last row in the *Theme Colors* section).
   g. Click the Shape Outline button arrow, point to *Weight*, and then click *3 pt* at the side menu.
   h. Click the Shape Effects button, point to *Bevel*, and then click *Cool Slant* at the side menu (fourth column, first row in the *Bevel* section).

Step 1d

Step 1e

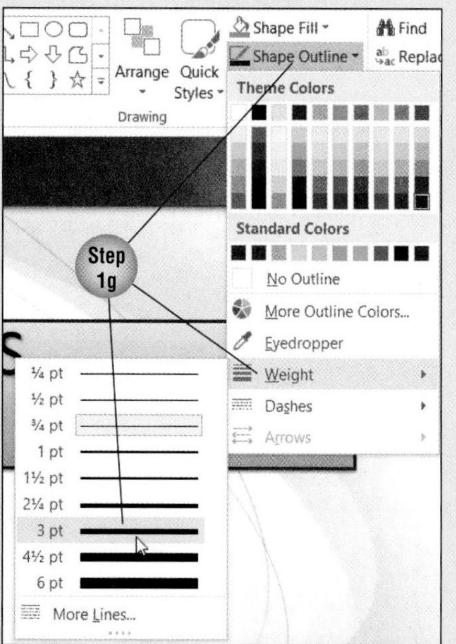

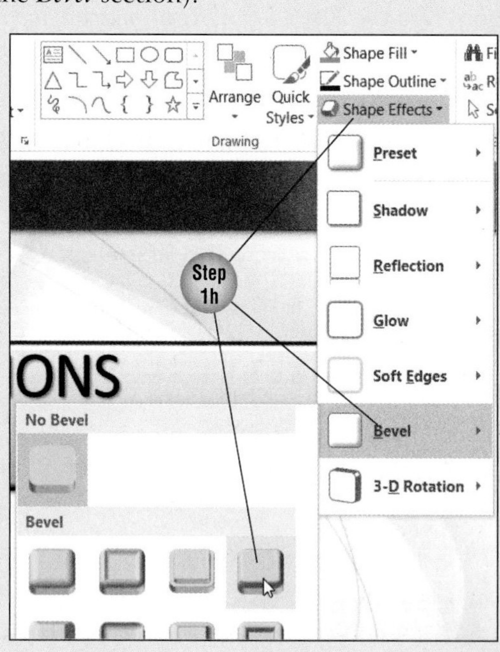

   i. Change the fill color by clicking the Quick Styles button in the Drawing group, pointing to *Other Theme Fills* at the bottom of the drop-down gallery, and then clicking *Style 6* at the side menu (second column, second row).

2. Change the alignment of the text within the placeholder by completing the following steps:
   a. With the title placeholder selected, click the Drawing group task pane launcher.
   b. At the Format Shape task pane with the SHAPE OPTIONS tab selected, click the Size & Properties icon.
   c. Click *TEXT BOX* to display the list of options.
   d. Click the down-pointing arrow at the right of the *Vertical alignment* option and then click *Middle* at the drop-down list.
   e. Click the up-pointing arrow at the right side of the *Left margin* measurement box until *0.5*" displays in the measurement box.
3. Close the Format Shape task pane by clicking the Close button in the upper right corner of the task pane.
4. Customize the subtitle placeholder by completing the following steps:
   a. Click in the subtitle text to select the placeholder.
   b. Click the Shape Fill button arrow in the Drawing group, point to *Texture*, and then click *Blue tissue paper* at the drop-down gallery (first column, fifth row).
   c. Click the Shape Effects button, point to *Bevel*, and then click *Cool Slant* at the side menu (fourth column, first row in the *Bevel* section).
5. You decide the texture fill does not match the theme of the presentation. Change the subtitle placeholder fill by completing the following steps:
   a. With the subtitle placeholder selected, click the Drawing group task pane launcher.
   b. Make sure the SHAPE OPTIONS tab is selected, click the Fill & Line icon, and then click *FILL* to display the list of options options.
   c. Click *Gradient fill.*
   d. Click the Preset gradients button and then click *Light Gradient, Accent 6* (sixth column, first row).
6. At the Format Shape task pane, click the Size & Properties icon, make sure the *TEXT BOX* options display, click the down-pointing arrow at the ride of the *Vertical alignment* option, and then click *Middle* at the drop-down list.

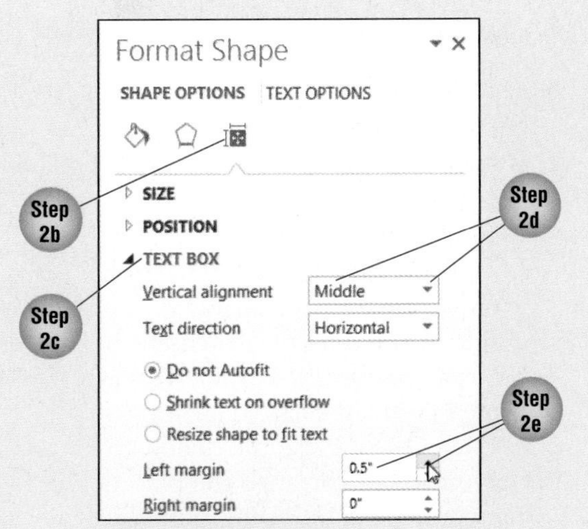

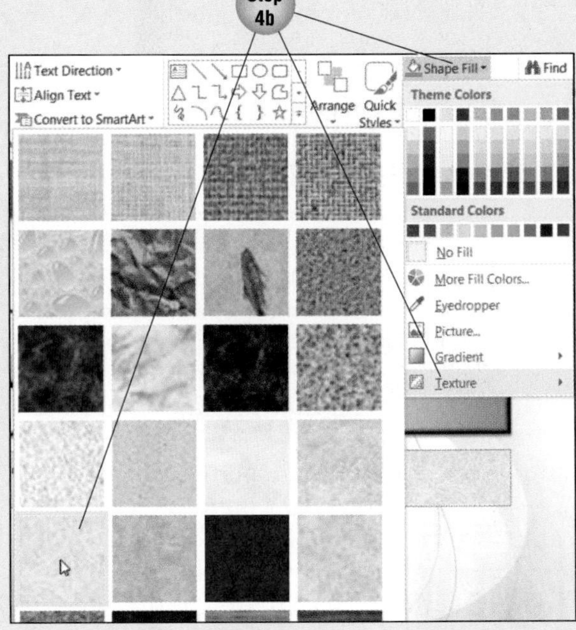

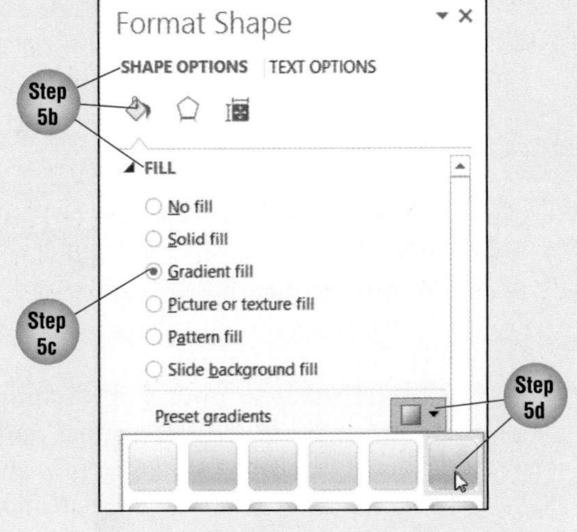

7. Click the up-pointing arrow at the right side of the *Left margin* measurement box until *0.5″* displays in the measurement box.
8. Make Slide 3 active and then change the spacing after paragraphs by completing the following steps:
   a. Select the bulleted text.
   b. Click the Paragraph group dialog box launcher.
   c. At the Paragraph dialog box, click twice on the up-pointing arrow at the right side of the *After* measurement box in the *Spacing* section to display *12 pt* in the measurement box.
   d. Click OK to close the dialog box.

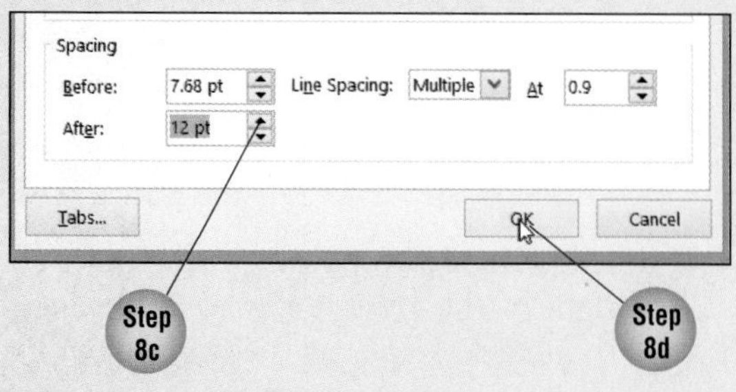

9. Customize and arrange the placeholder by completing the following steps:
   a. With the bulleted text placeholder selected and the Format Shape task pane open, click the Fill & Line icon, make sure the *FILL* options display, and then click *Solid fill*.
   b. Click the Color button and then click *Purple, Accent 6, Lighter 80%* (last column, second row in the *Theme Colors* section).
   c. Click the Effects icon and then click *SHADOW* to display the list of options.
   d. Click the Presets button and then click *Offset Diagonal Bottom Right* (first column, first row in *Outer* section).
   e. Click the Color button and then click *Purple, Accent 6, Darker 50%* (last column, bottom row in *Theme Colors* section).
   f. Click the up-pointing arrow at the right of the *Distance* measurement box until *15 pt* displays.
   g. Click the Size & Properties icon, make sure the *TEXT BOX* options display, and then change the left, top, and bottom measurements to 0.2 inches.
   h. Click the Arrange button in the Drawing group on the HOME tab, point to *Align* in the drop-down list, and then click *Distribute Vertically* in the side menu.

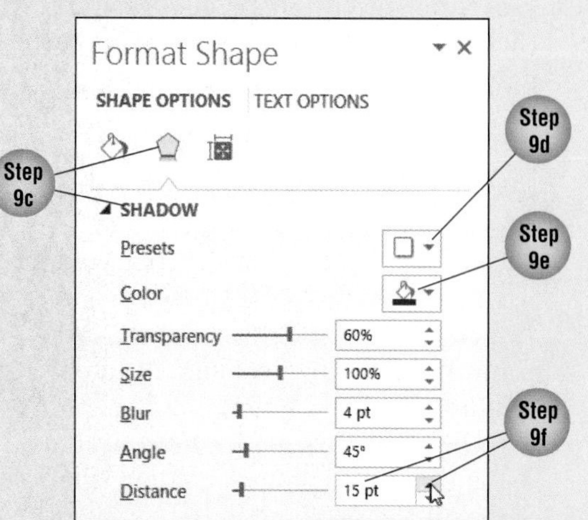

10. Make Slide 2 active, click in the bulleted text, and then customize and arrange the placeholder by completing the steps in Step 9.
11. Close the Format Shape task pane.
12. Make Slide 1 active and then use the eyedropper to apply fill color from the subtitle placeholder to the title placeholder by completing the following steps:
    a. Click the title placeholder.
    b. Click the Shape Fill button arrow in the Drawing group on the HOME tab.
    c. Click the *Eyedropper* option at the drop-down gallery.
    d. Position the tip of the eyedropper on the purple color below the word *Publications* in the subtitle placeholder and then click the left mouse button.

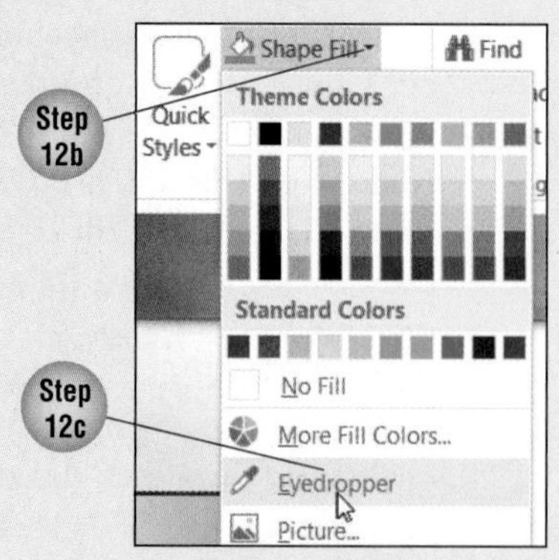

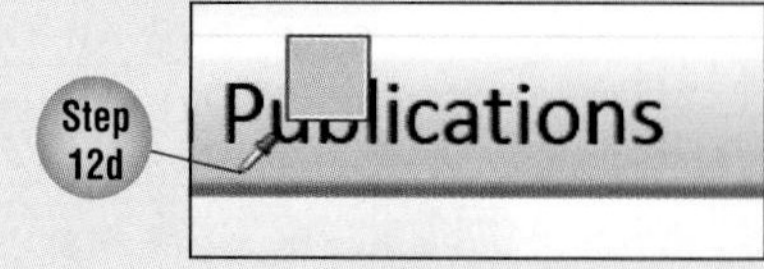

13. Run the presentation.
14. Print the presentation as a handout with six slides printed horizontally per page.
15. Save **P-C3-P2-ColorPres.pptx**.

Changing Page Setup

Control page setup and the orientation of slides with options in the Slide Size dialog box, as shown in Figure 3.8. Display the Slide Size dialog box by clicking the Slide Size button in the Customize group on the DESIGN tab and then clicking *Custom Slide Size* at the drop-down list. With options in the dialog box, change slide orientation, specify how you want the slides sized, change the slide size ratio, and change the starting slide number. By default, slides are sized for an on-screen show with a widescreen 16:9 ratio. If you change a widescreen size (16:9) presentation to a standard size (4:3) presentation, you will need to maximize the size of the content to fit in the new slide size or scale down the slide content to ensure that all content fits on the new slide. Click the down-pointing arrow at the right side of the *Slides sized for* option box and a drop-down list displays with options for changing the slide size ratio and choosing other paper sizes. You can also change the orientation of notes, handouts, and outline pages.

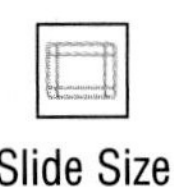
Slide Size

Figure 3.8 Slide Size Dialog Box

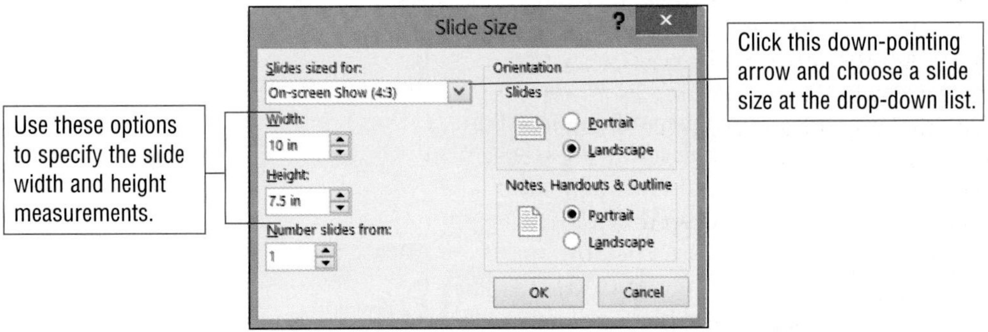

Project 2d **Changing Orientation and Page Setup** **Part 4 of 4**

1. With **P-C3-P2-ColorPres.pptx** open, change the slide size by completing the following steps:
   a. Click the DESIGN tab.
   b. Click the Slide Size button in the Customize group and then click *Standard (4:3)* at the drop-down list.
   c. At the Microsoft PowerPoint dialog box, click the Ensure Fit button.

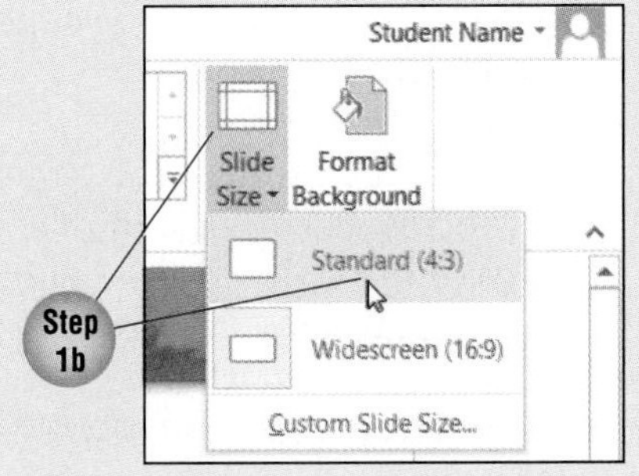

2. Run the presentation and notice how the slides appear in the standard size.
3. Change the slide orientation by completing the following steps:
   a. Click the Slide Size button in the Customize group and then click *Custom Slide Size* at the drop-down list.
   b. At the Slide Size dialog box, click the *Portrait* option in the *Slides* section, and then click OK.
   c. Click the Ensure Fit button at the Microsoft PowerPoint dialog box.
4. Run the presentation and notice how the slides appear in portrait orientation.
5. After running the presentation, change the page setup by completing the following steps:
   a. Click the Slide Size button and then click *Custom Slide Size* at the drop-down list.
   b. At the Slide Size dialog box, click the *Landscape* option in the Slides section.
   c. Click the down-pointing arrow at the right side of the *Slides sized for* option box and then click *On-screen Show (16:10)*. (Notice that the slide height changed from *10* to *6.25* in the *Height* measurement box.)
   d. Click OK.
   e. Click the Maximize button at the Microsoft PowerPoint dialog box.
6. Run the presentation.
7. Specify slide width and height and change slide numbering by completing the following steps:
   a. Click the Slide Size button and then click *Custom Slide Size* at the drop-down list.
   b. At the Slide Size dialog box, click the down-pointing arrow at the right side of the *Width* measurement box until *9 in* displays in the box.
   c. Click the down-pointing arrow at the right side of the *Height* measurement box until *6 in* displays in the box.
   d. Click the up-pointing arrow to the right of the *Number slides from* measurement box until *6* displays.
   e. Click OK.
   f. Click the Ensure Fit button at the Microsoft PowerPoint dialog box.
8. Notice the slide numbering in the slide thumbnails pane begins with Slide 6.
9. Run the presentation.
10. Save and then close **P-C3-P2-ColorPres.pptx**.

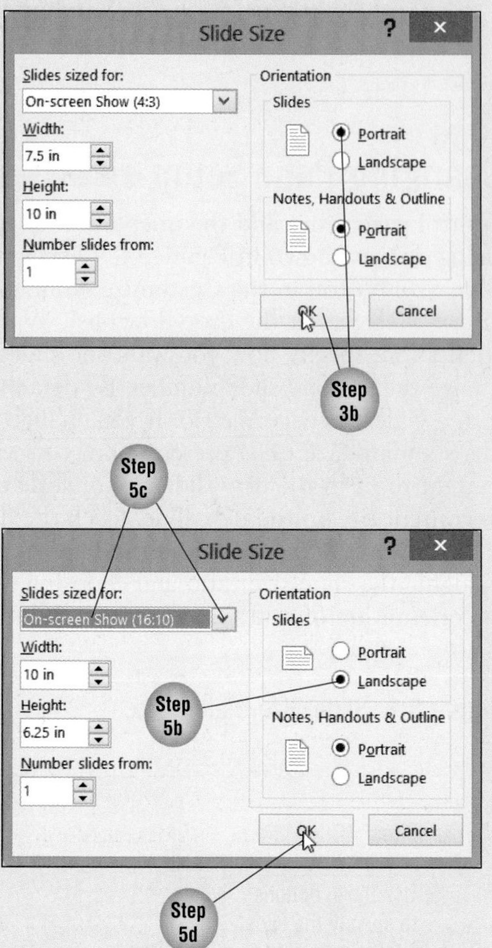

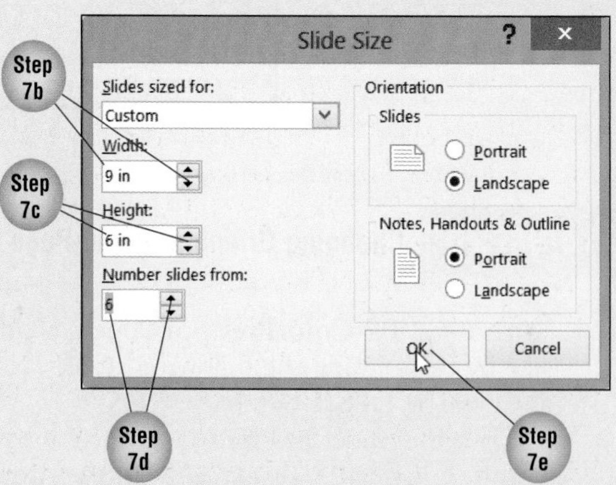

Project 3 Modify the Theme and Slide Background of a Network Presentation — 1 Part

You will open a network presentation, apply a design theme, and then change the theme colors and fonts. You will also apply and customize a background style.

Modifying Theme Colors and Fonts

A design theme is a set of formatting choices that includes a color theme (a set of colors), a font theme (heading and text fonts), and an effects theme (a set of lines and fill effects). Click the More button located to the right of the Variants group on the DESIGN tab to display options for changing design theme colors, fonts, and effects.

A theme contains specific color formatting you can change with color options. Display color options by clicking the More button at the right side of the Variants group. At the drop-down menu that displays, point to the *Colors* option and a drop-down gallery displays with named color schemes. Each theme applies specific fonts, which you can change with options from the Fonts option in the More drop-down list in the Variants group. Point to this option and a drop-down gallery displays with font choices. Each font group in the drop-down gallery contains two choices. The first choice in the group is the font that is applied to slide titles and the second choice is the font that is applied to slide subtitles and text. If you are formatting a presentation that contains graphic elements such as illustrations, pictures, clip art, or text boxes, you can specify theme effects at the Effects option drop-down gallery in the Variants group.

Themes are shared across Office programs such as PowerPoint, Word, and Excel.

Customizing Slide Backgrounds

Format a slide background with background styles or with options at the Format Background task pane. Display background styles by clicking the More button in the Variants group on the DESIGN tab and then pointing to the *Background Styles* option. Apply a background style by clicking an option at the side menu.

Quick Steps

Change a Slide Background

1. Click DESIGN tab.
2. Click Format Background button.
3. Make desired changes at Format Background task pane.

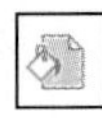

Format Background

Click the Format Background button in the Customize group on the DESIGN tab to display the Format Background task pane, as shown in Figure 3.9. With options in the Format Background task pane you can apply fill, effects, or a picture to a slide background. Apply the desired slide background to all slides in the presentation by clicking the Apply to All button located toward the bottom of the task pane. If you make changes to the slide background, you can reset the background to the default by clicking the Reset Background button located toward the bottom of the Format Background task pane.

Some of the design themes provided by PowerPoint contain a background graphic. You can remove this graphic from a slide by clicking the *Hide background graphics* check box in the *FILL* section of the Format Background task pane with the Fill icon selected and then clicking the Apply to All button.

Figure 3.9 Format Background Task Pane

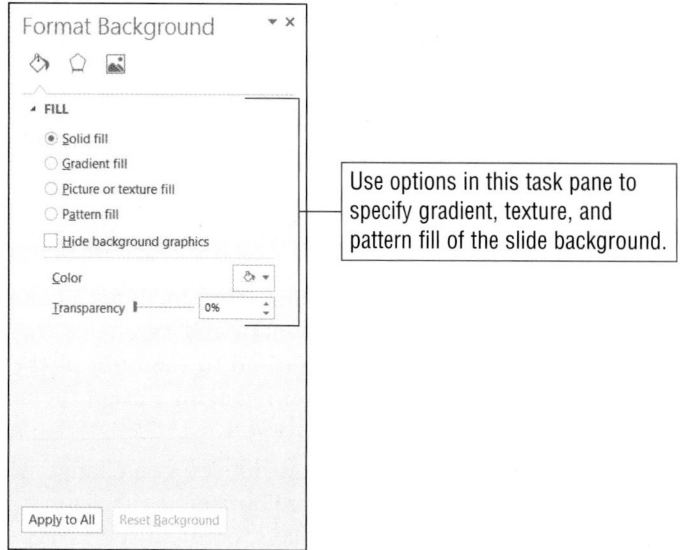

Project 3 Customizing Theme Colors, Theme Fonts, and Slide Background

Part 1 of 1

1. Open **NetworkPres.pptx** and then save the presentation with Save As and name it **P-C3-P3-NetworkPres.pptx**.
2. Apply a design theme by completing the following steps:
   a. Click the DESIGN tab.
   b. Click the More button at the right side of the design theme thumbnails and then click *Dividend* at the drop-down gallery.
3. Change the theme colors by clicking the More button located to the right of the Variants group thumbnails, pointing to *Colors*, scrolling down the color option list, and then clicking *Marquee* at the side menu.

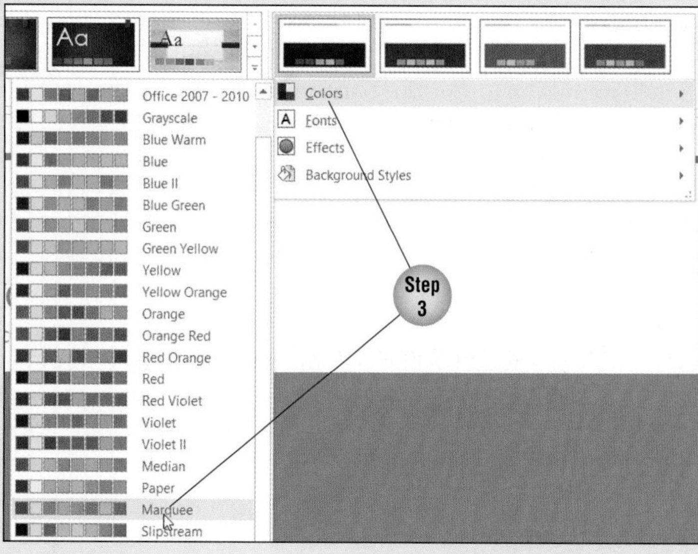

4. Change the theme fonts by clicking the More button in the Variants group, pointing to *Fonts*, scrolling down the font list, and then clicking *Calibri-Cambria* at the side menu.
5. Change the background style by clicking the More button in the Variants group, pointing to *Background Styles*, and then clicking *Style 5* at the side menu (first column, second row).

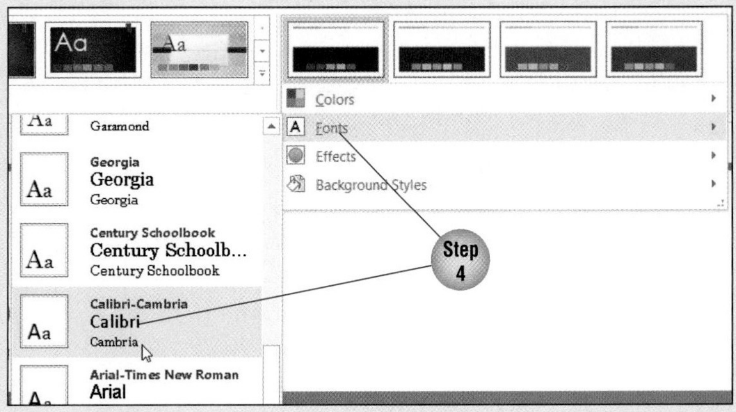

6. With Slide 1 active, run the presentation and notice the formatting applied by the design theme, theme colors, theme fonts, and background style.
7. Make sure Slide 1 is active and then apply and customize the background style of all slides by completing the following steps:
   a. Click the DESIGN tab.
   b. Click the Format Background button in the Customize group.
   c. At the Format Background task pane with the Fill icon selected and the *FILL* options displayed, click the *Picture or texture fill* option.
   d. Click the Texture button (located below the Online button) and then click the *Stationery* option (first column, bottom row).
   e. Click the up-pointing arrow at the right of the *Transparency* measurement box until *25%* displays.
   f. Click the Apply to All button located near the bottom of the task pane.
   g. Close the Format Background task pane.

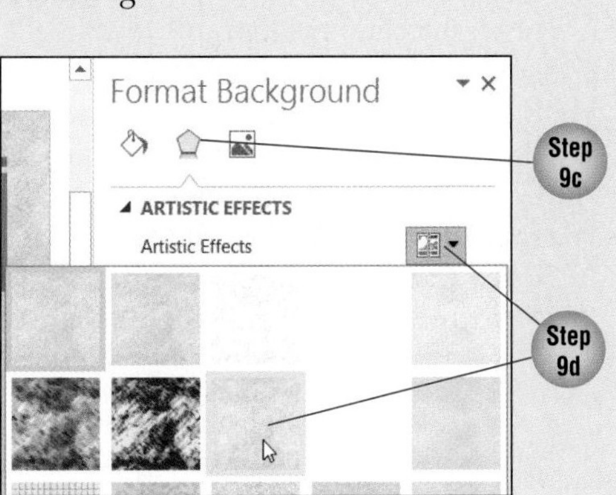

8. Run the presentation and notice the background formatting.
9. Apply an artistic effect to all slides in the presentation by completing the following steps:
   a. Make Slide 2 active.
   b. Click the Format Background button in the Customize group on the DESIGN tab.
   c. Click the Effects icon in the Format Background task pane.
   d. Click the Artistic Effects option button and then click the *Paint Brush* option (third column, second row).
   e. Click the Apply to All button located toward the bottom of the task pane.

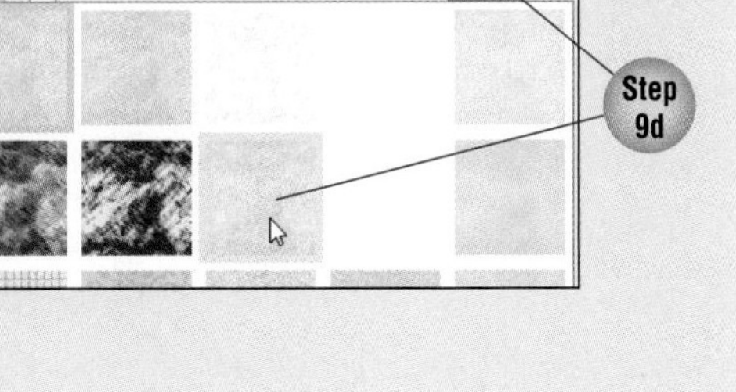

10. Run the presentation and notice the artistic effect applied to all slides in the presentation.

11. Change the background to a gradient fill rather than an artistic effect by completing the following steps:
    a. Click the Fill icon in the Format Background task pane.
    b. Click the *Gradient fill* option.
    c. Click the Preset gradients button and then click *Light Gradient - Accent 2* (second column, first row).
    d. Click the down-pointing arrow to the right of the *Type* option box and then click *Radial* at the drop-down list.
    e. Click the Direction button and then click the *From Bottom Left Corner* option (second option from the left).
    f. Select the *0%* in the *Position* measurement box, type 25, and then press Enter.
    g. Click the Apply to All button.

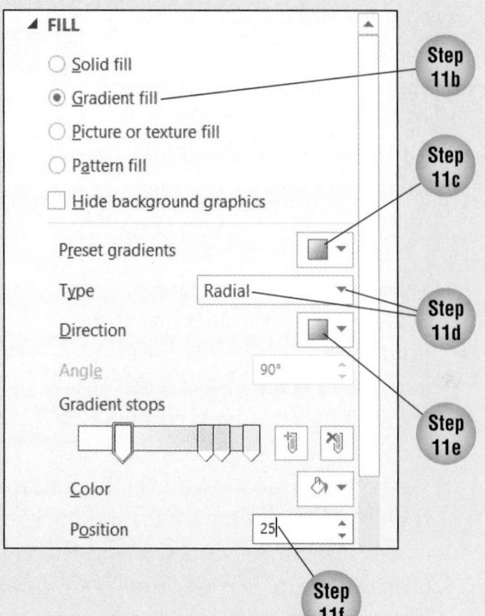

12. Look at the slides in the slide thumbnails pane and notice the gradient fill applied to all slides.
13. Apply a pattern fill to Slide 1 by completing the following steps:
    a. If necessary, click Slide 1 in the slide thumbnails pane.
    b. At the Format Background task pane, click the *Pattern fill* option.
    c. Click the *Divot* pattern fill in the *Pattern* section (first column, seventh row).
    d. Click the Background button and then click the *Green, Accent 2, Lighter 80%* option (sixth column, second row in the *Theme Colors* section).

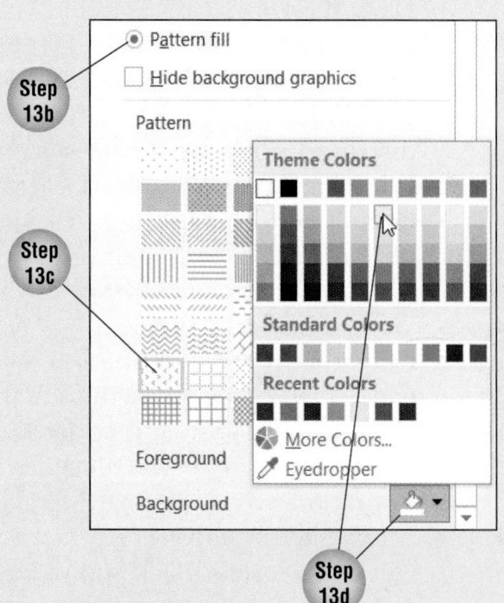

14. After viewing the pattern fill in the slide pane, reset the slide background of Slide 1 to the gradient fill background by clicking the Reset Background button located toward the bottom of the Format Background task pane.
15. Close the Format Background task pane.
16. Run the presentation and notice the background formatting.
17. Print the presentation as a handout with six slides printed horizontally per page.
18. Save and then close **P-C3-P3-NetworkPres.pptx**.

Project 4 Create and Apply Custom Themes to Presentations

4 Parts

You will create custom theme colors and custom theme fonts and then save the changes as a custom theme. You will then apply the custom theme to a job search presentation and a resume writing presentation.

Creating Custom Themes

If the default themes, theme colors, and theme fonts do not provide the formatting you desire for your presentation, you can create your own custom theme colors, custom theme fonts, and a custom theme. A theme you create will display in the *Custom* section of the Themes drop-down gallery. To create a custom theme, change the theme colors, theme fonts, and/or theme effects.

Click the More button in the Variants group on the DESIGN tab and the options at the drop-down list display a visual representation of the current theme. If you change the theme colors, the colors are reflected in the small color squares on the *Colors* option. If you change the theme fonts, the *A* on the *Fonts* option reflects the change.

Quick Steps

Create Custom Theme Colors

1. Click DESIGN tab.
2. Click More button in Variants group.
3. Point to *Colors*.
4. Click *Customize Colors*.
5. Change to desired background, accent, and hyperlink colors.
6. Type name for custom theme colors.
7. Click Save button.

Creating Custom Theme Colors

To create custom theme colors, click the DESIGN tab, click the More button located to the right of the Variants group, point to the *Colors* option at the drop-down list, and then click *Customize Colors* at the side menu. This displays the Create New Theme Colors dialog box, similar to the one shown in Figure 3.10. Theme colors contain four text and background colors, six accent colors, and two hyperlink colors, as shown in the *Themes color* section of the dialog box. Change a color in the option box by clicking the color button at the right side of the color option and then clicking the desired color at the color palette. If you make changes to colors at the Create New Theme Colors dialog box and then decide you do not

Figure 3.10 Create New Theme Colors Dialog Box

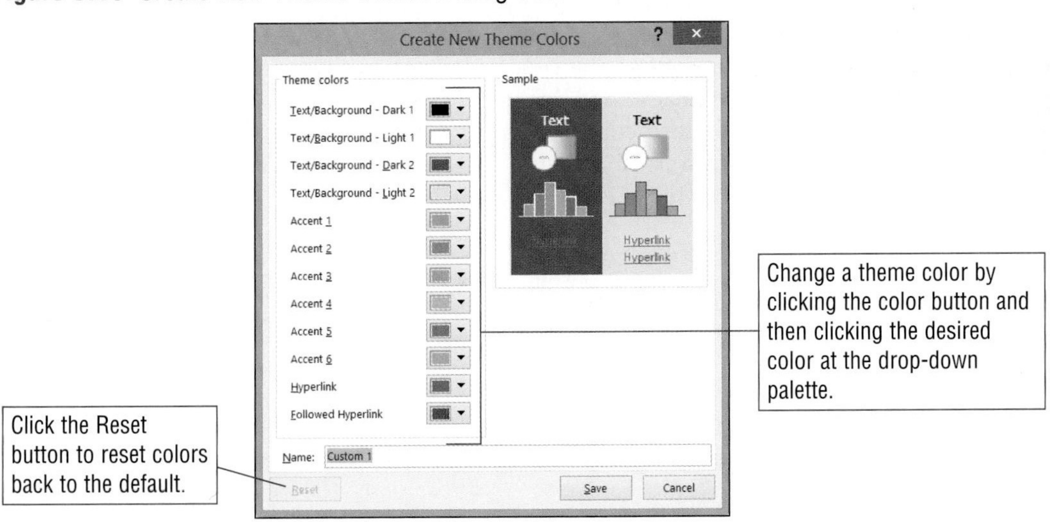

like the color changes, click the Reset button located in the lower left corner of the dialog box.

After you have made all desired changes to colors, click in the *Name* text box, type a name for the custom theme colors, and then click the Save button. This saves the custom theme colors and applies the color changes to the currently open presentation.

When you create custom theme colors, apply the theme to a presentation by clicking the More button in the Variants group on the DESIGN tab, pointing to the *Colors* option, and then clicking the custom theme colors that display toward the top of the drop-down gallery in the *Custom* section.

Project 4a Creating Custom Theme Colors

Part 1 of 4

Note: If you are running PowerPoint 2013 on a computer connected to a network in a public environment such as a school, you may need to complete all four parts of Project 4 during the same session. Network system software may delete your custom themes when you close PowerPoint. Check with your instructor.

1. At a blank presentation, click the DESIGN tab, click the More button at the right side of the theme thumbnails in the Themes group, and then click Wisp at the drop-down gallery.
2. Click the third thumbnail in the Variants group (light blue color).
3. Create custom theme colors by completing the following steps:
   a. Click the More button in the Variants group, point to the *Colors* option, and then click the *Customize Colors* option at the side menu.
   b. At the Create New Theme Colors dialog box, click the color button that displays at the right side of the *Text/Background - Dark 2* option and then click the *Dark Blue, Accent 3, Darker 25%* option (seventh column, fifth row in the Theme Colors section).
   c. Click the color button that displays at the right side of the *Text/Background - Light 2* option and then click the *Purple, Accent 4, Lighter 80%* option (eighth column, second row in the Theme Colors section).
   d. Click the color button that displays at the right side of the *Accent 1* option and then click the *Purple, Accent 4, Darker 50%* option (eighth column, last row in the Theme Colors section).
4. Save the custom colors by completing the following steps:
   a. Select the current text in the *Name* text box.
   b. Type your first and last names.
   c. Click the Save button.
5. Save the presentation and name it **P-C3-P4-CustomTheme**.

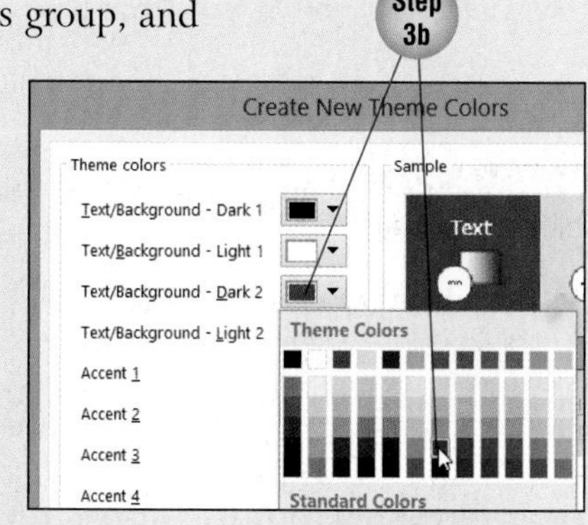

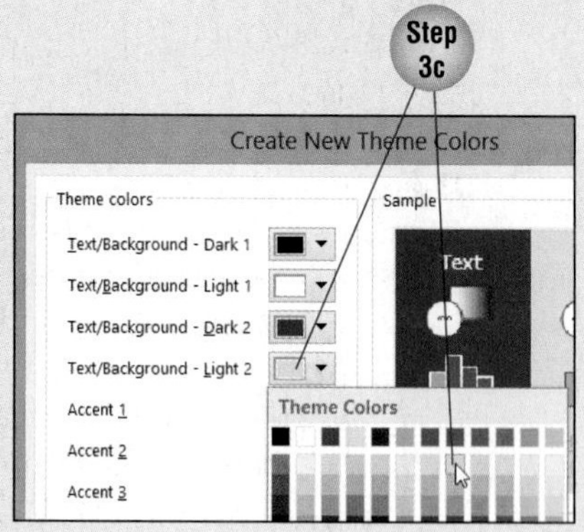

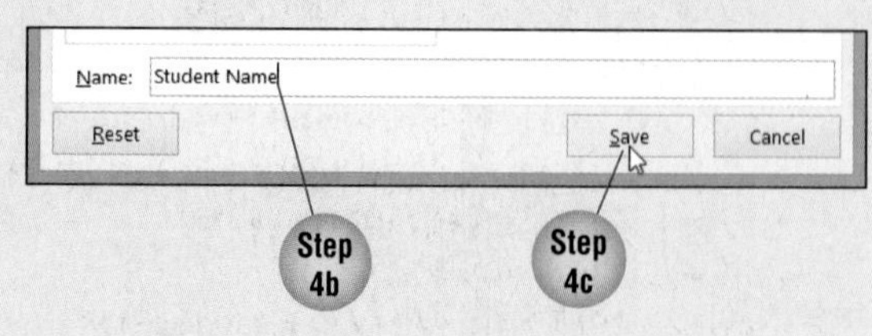

Creating Custom Theme Fonts

To create custom theme fonts, click the DESIGN tab, click the More button in the Variants group, point to the *Fonts* option, and then click *Customize Fonts* at the side menu. This displays the Create New Theme Fonts dialog box similar to the one shown in Figure 3.11. At this dialog box, choose a heading font and body font. Type the name of the custom theme fonts in the *Name* box and then click the Save button.

Quick Steps

Create Custom Fonts
1. Click DESIGN tab.
2. Click More button in Variants group.
3. Point to *Fonts*.
4. Click *Customize Fonts*.
5. Choose desired fonts.
6. Type name for custom theme fonts.
7. Click Save button.

Figure 3.11 Create New Theme Fonts Dialog Box

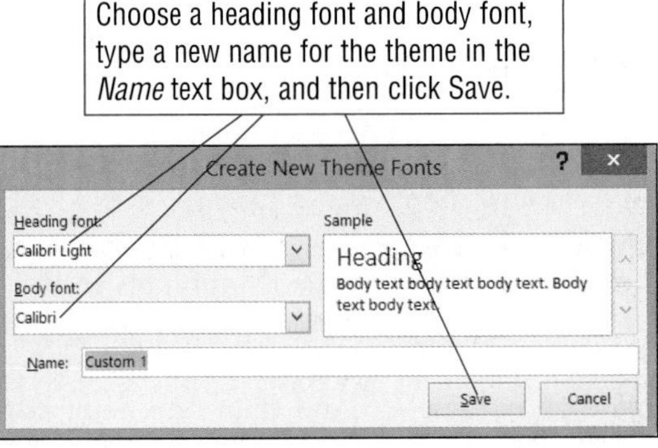

Project 4b **Creating Custom Theme Fonts** **Part 2 of 4**

1. With **P-C3-P4-CustomTheme.pptx** open, create custom theme fonts by completing the following steps:
   a. If necessary, click the DESIGN tab.
   b. Click the More button in the Variants group, point to the *Fonts* option, and then click the *Customize Fonts* option at the drop-down gallery.
   c. At the Create New Theme Fonts dialog box, click the down-pointing arrow at the right side of the *Heading font* option box, scroll up the drop-down list, and then click *Candara*.
   d. Click the down-pointing arrow at the right side of the *Body font* option box, scroll down the drop-down list, and then click *Constantia*.
2. Save the custom theme fonts by completing the following steps:
   a. Select the current text in the *Name* text box.
   b. Type your first and last names.
   c. Click the Save button.
3. Save **P-C3-P4-CustomTheme.pptx**.

Quick Steps

Save a Custom Theme
1. Click DESIGN tab.
2. Click More button in Themes group.
3. Click *Save Current Theme.*
4. Type name for custom theme.
5. Click Save button.

Saving a Custom Theme

When you have customized theme colors and fonts, you can save these as a custom theme. To do this, click the More button at the right side of the Themes group on the DESIGN tab and then click *Save Current Theme*. This displays the Save Current Theme dialog box with many of the same options as the Save As dialog box. Type a name for your custom theme in the *File name* text box and then click the Save button. To apply a custom theme, click the More button in the Themes group, and then click the desired theme in the *Custom* section of the drop-down gallery.

Project 4c Saving and Applying a Custom Theme — Part 3 of 4

1. With **P-C3-P4-CustomTheme.pptx** open, save the custom theme colors and fonts as a custom theme by completing the following steps:
   a. If necessary, click the DESIGN tab.
   b. Click the More button at the right side of the theme thumbnails in the Themes group.
   c. Click the *Save Current Theme* option that displays at the bottom of the drop-down gallery.
   d. At the Save Current Theme dialog box, type C3 and then type your last name in the *File name* text box.
   e. Click the Save button.

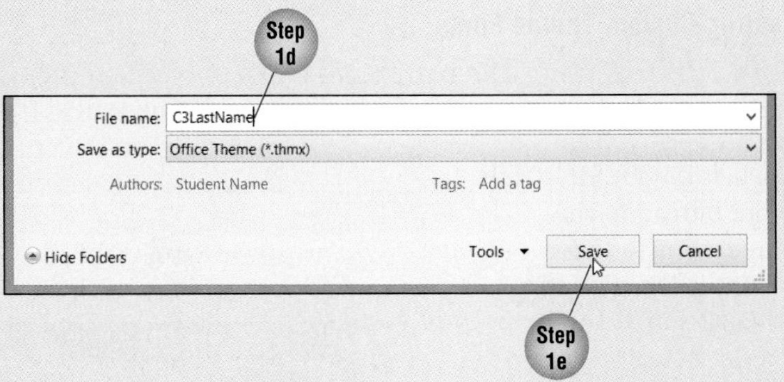

2. Close **P-C3-P4-CustomTheme.pptx**.
3. Open **JobSearch.pptx** and then save the presentation with Save As and name it **P-C3-P4-JobSearch**.
4. Apply your custom theme by completing the following steps:
   a. Click the DESIGN tab.
   b. Click the More button that displays at the right side of the theme thumbnails.
   c. Click the custom theme that begins with *C3* followed by your last name. (The theme will display in the *Custom* section of the drop-down gallery.)
5. Run the presentation and notice how the slides display with the custom theme applied.
6. Print Slide 1 of the presentation.
7. Save and then close **P-C3-P4-JobSearch.pptx**.

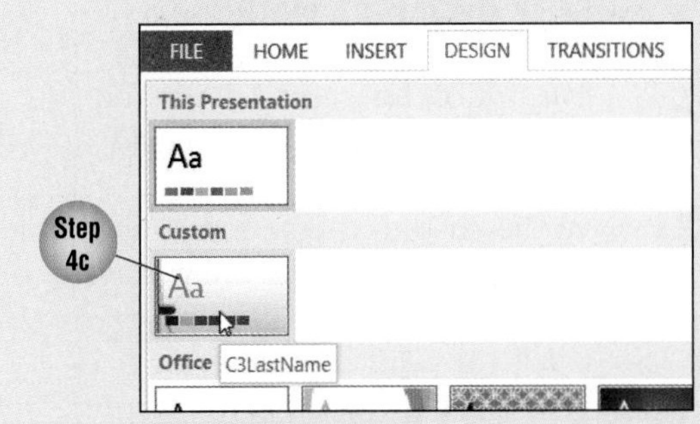

8. Open **ResumePres.pptx** and then save the presentation with Save As and name it **P-C3-P4-ResumePres**.
9. Apply your custom theme (the theme that displays beginning with *C3* followed by your last name).
10. Run the presentation.
11. Print Slide 1 of the presentation.
12. Save and then close **P-C3-P4-ResumePres.pptx**.

Editing Custom Themes

You can edit the custom theme colors and custom theme fonts. To edit the custom theme colors, click the More button in the Variants group on the DESIGN tab and then point to the *Colors* option. At the side menu of custom and built-in themes, right-click your custom theme and then click *Edit* at the shortcut menu. This displays the Edit Theme Colors dialog box that contains the same options as the Create New Theme Colors dialog box shown in Figure 3.10 on page 109. Make the desired changes to theme colors and then click the Save button.

To edit custom theme fonts, click the More button in the Variants group on the DESIGN tab, point to the *Fonts* option, right-click your custom theme fonts, and then click *Edit* at the shortcut menu. This displays the Edit Theme Fonts dialog box that contains the same options as the Create New Theme Fonts dialog box shown in Figure 3.11 on page 111. Make the desired changes and then click the Save button.

Deleting Custom Themes

You can delete custom theme colors from the *Colors* option side menu, delete custom theme fonts from the Fonts option side menu, and delete custom themes from the Themes drop-down gallery or the Save Current Theme dialog box. To delete custom theme colors, click the More button in the Variants group, point to the *Colors* option, right-click the theme you want to delete, and then click *Delete* at the shortcut menu. At the message asking if you want to delete the theme colors, click Yes. Complete similar steps to delete custom theme fonts.

Delete a custom theme by clicking the More button at the right side of the Themes group on the DESIGN tab, right-clicking the custom theme, and then clicking *Delete* at the shortcut menu. A custom theme can also be deleted at the Save Current Theme dialog box. To display this dialog box, click the More button at the right side of the Themes group on the DESIGN tab and then click *Save Current Theme* at the drop-down gallery. At the dialog box, click the custom theme file name, click the Organize button on the toolbar, and then click *Delete* at the drop-down list. At the message asking if you are sure you want to send the theme to the Recycle Bin, click Yes.

Quick Steps

Edit Custom Theme Colors
1. Click DESIGN tab.
2. Click More button in Variants group.
3. Point to *Colors* option.
4. Right-click desired custom theme.
5. Click *Edit*.
6. Make desired changes.
7. Click Save button.

Edit Custom Theme Fonts
1. Click DESIGN tab.
2. Click More button in Variants group.
3. Point to *Fonts* option.
4. Right-click desired custom theme.
5. Click *Edit*.
6. Make desired changes.
7. Click Save button.

Delete Custom Theme Colors
1. Click DESIGN tab.
2. Click More button in Variants group.
3. Point to *Colors* option.
4. Right-click desired custom theme.
5. Click *Delete*.
6. Click Yes.

Delete Custom Theme Fonts
1. Click DESIGN tab.
2. Click More button in Variants group.
3. Point to *Fonts* option.
4. Right-click desired custom theme.
5. Click *Delete*.
6. Click Yes.

Delete Custom Theme
1. Click DESIGN tab.
2. Click More button in Themes group.
3. Right-click desired custom theme.
4. Click *Delete*.
5. Click Yes.

Project 4d Deleting Custom Themes Part 4 of 4

1. At a blank presentation, delete the custom theme colors by completing the following steps:
   a. Click the DESIGN tab.
   b. Click the More button in the Variants group and then point to the *Colors* option.
   c. Right-click the custom theme colors named with your first and last names.
   d. Click *Delete* at the shortcut menu.
   e. At the message asking if you want to delete the theme colors, click Yes.

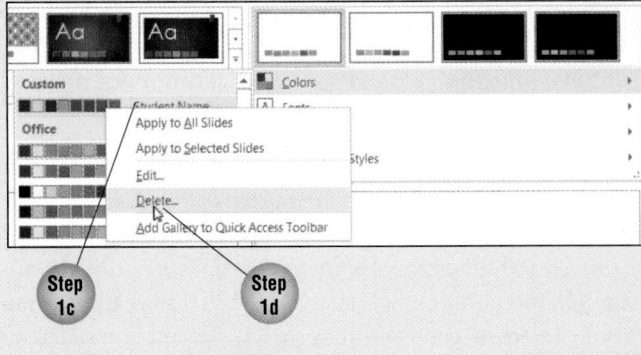

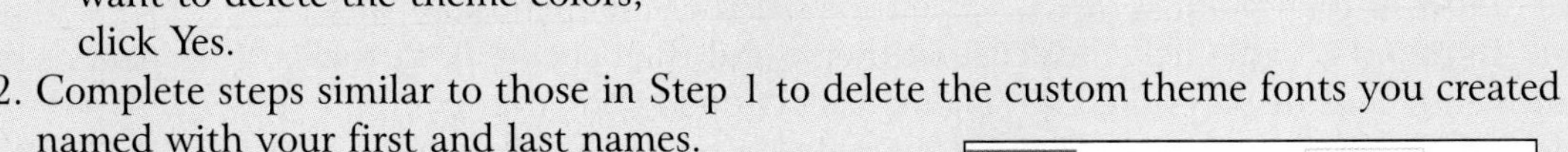

2. Complete steps similar to those in Step 1 to delete the custom theme fonts you created named with your first and last names.
3. Delete the custom theme by completing the following steps:
   a. Click the More button that displays at the right side of the theme thumbnails.
   b. Right-click the custom theme that begins with *C3* followed by your last name.
   c. Click *Delete* at the shortcut menu.
   d. At the message asking if you want to delete the theme, click Yes.
4. Close the presentation without saving it.

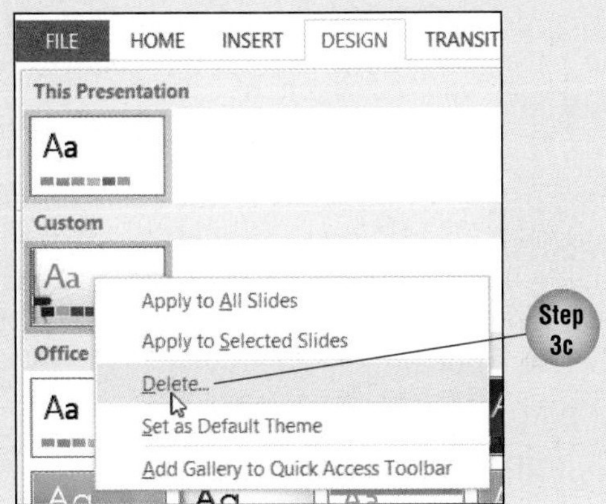

Chapter Summary

- The Font group on the HOME tab contains buttons for applying character formatting to text in slides.
- Design themes apply a font to text in slides. Change this default font with the Font and Font Size buttons in the Font group.
- Some buttons, such as the Font and Font Size buttons, contain the live preview feature, which allows you to see how the formatting affects your text without having to return to the presentation.
- You can also apply character formatting with options at the Font dialog box. Display this dialog box by clicking the Font group dialog box launcher.
- Select text in a slide and the Mini toolbar displays above the selected text. Apply formatting with buttons on this toolbar.

- Use the Format Painter feature to apply formatting to more than one location in a slide or slides.
- The Paragraph group on the HOME tab contains a number of buttons for applying paragraph formatting to text in slides.
- Customize paragraph formatting with options at the Paragraph dialog box with the Indents and Spacing tab selected. Display this dialog box by clicking the Paragraph group dialog box launcher or by clicking the Line Spacing button in the Paragraph group and then clicking *Line Spacing Options* at the drop-down list.
- Use the Add or Remove Columns button in the Paragraph group or options at the Columns dialog box to format selected text into columns. Display the Columns dialog box by clicking the Add or Remove Columns button and then clicking *More Columns* at the drop-down list.
- Use the Text Direction button or options at the Format Shape task pane to rotate or stack text in a slide. Display the Format Shape task pane by clicking the Drawing group task pane launcher on the HOME tab.
- Use the Align Text button or options at the Format Shape task pane to vertically align text in a slide.
- The SHAPE OPTIONS tab of the Format Shape task pane displays four icons: Fill & Line, Effects, Size & Properties, and Picture, each with different options for formatting a placeholder.
- Customize bullets with options at the Bullets and Numbering dialog box with the Bulleted tab selected. Display this dialog box by clicking the Bullets button arrow and then clicking *Bullets and Numbering* at the drop-down list.
- Customize numbering with options at the Bullets and Numbering dialog box with the Numbered tab selected. Display this dialog box by clicking the Numbering button arrow and then clicking *Bullets and Numbering* at the drop-down list.
- Click the Quick Styles button in the Drawing group on the HOME tab to apply formatting to a placeholder. The Drawing group also contains the Shape Fill, Shape Outline, and Shape Effects buttons for customizing a placeholder and the Arrange button for arranging slide elements.
- Click the Slide Size button and then click *Custom Slide Size* at the drop-down list to display the Slide Size dialog box. Use options in this dialog box to change the slide size and ratio, the start slide number, and the orientation of slides and notes, handouts, and outline pages.
- Use the Format Background task pane to customize the background of slides. Display the task pane by clicking the Format Background button in the Customize group on the DESIGN tab.
- Create custom theme colors with options at the Create New Theme Colors dialog box. Display this dialog box by clicking the More button in the Variants group on the DESIGN tab, pointing to the *Colors* option, and then clicking *Customize Colors* at the drop-down gallery.
- Create custom theme fonts with options at the Create New Theme Fonts dialog box. Display this dialog box by clicking the More button in the Variants group on the DESIGN tab, pointing to the *Fonts* option, and then clicking *Customize Fonts* at the drop-down gallery.

- Save a custom theme at the Save Current Theme dialog box. Display this dialog box by clicking the More button at the right side of the Themes group on the DESIGN tab and then clicking *Save Current Theme*.
- Edit custom theme colors with options at the Edit Theme Colors dialog box and edit custom theme fonts with options at the Edit Theme Fonts dialog box.
- Delete custom theme colors by clicking the More button in the Variants group, pointing to the *Colors* option, right-clicking the custom theme, and then clicking the *Delete* option.
- Delete custom theme fonts by clicking the More button in the Variants group, pointing to the *Fonts* option, right-clicking the custom theme, and then clicking the *Delete* option.
- Delete a custom theme by clicking the More button in the Themes group, right-clicking the custom theme, and then clicking *Delete* at the short cut menu. A custom theme also can be deleted at the Save Current Theme dialog box. Display this dialog box by clicking the Themes button and then clicking *Save Current Theme* at the drop-down gallery.

Commands Review

FEATURE	RIBBON TAB, GROUP	BUTTON, OPTION	KEYBOARD SHORTCUT
Bullets and Numbering dialog box with Bulleted tab selected	HOME, Paragraph	, *Bullets and Numbering*	
Bullets and Numbering dialog box with Numbered tab selected	HOME, Paragraph	, *Bullets and Numbering*	
Columns dialog box	HOME, Paragraph	, *More Columns*	
Create New Theme Colors dialog box	DESIGN, Variants	, *Colors, Customize Colors*	
Create New Theme Fonts dialog box	DESIGN, Variants	, *Fonts, Customize Fonts*	
Font dialog box	HOME, Font		Ctrl + Shift + F
Format Background task pane	DESIGN, Customize		
Format Painter	HOME, Clipboard		
Format Shape task pane	HOME, Drawing		
Paragraph dialog box	HOME, Paragraph		
Save Current Theme dialog box	DESIGN, Themes	, *Save Current Theme*	
slide size	DESIGN, Customize		

Concepts Check Test Your Knowledge 

Completion: In the space provided at the right, indicate the correct term, symbol, or command.

1. The Font button drop-down gallery is an example of this feature, which allows you to see how formatting will affect your text before you actually apply it. ____________
2. Click this button to clear character formatting from selected text. ____________
3. Click this to display the Font dialog box. ____________
4. Select text in a slide and this displays above the selected text. ____________
5. The Format Painter button is located in this group on the HOME tab. ____________
6. Press this key to move text to the next tab stop (level). ____________
7. Use options at this dialog box to change text alignment, indentation, and spacing. ____________
8. Click this button in the Paragraph group and a drop-down list displays with options for rotating and stacking text. ____________
9. Use the Align Text button or options at this task pane with the Size & Properties icon selected to vertically align text in a slide. ____________
10. Customize numbering with options at the Bullets and Numbering dialog box with this tab selected. ____________
11. The Quick Styles button is located in this group on the HOME tab. ____________
12. Click this button to apply an outline to a placeholder. ____________
13. Change slide orientation with options in this dialog box. ____________
14. Click this button in the Customize group on the DESIGN tab to display the Format Background task pane. ____________
15. Create custom theme colors with options at this dialog box. ____________
16. Save a custom theme at this dialog box. ____________

Skills Check Assess Your Performance

Assessment 1

CREATE, FORMAT, AND MODIFY A BENEFITS PRESENTATION

1. At a blank presentation, create the slides shown in Figure 3.12.
2. Apply the Facet design theme and then apply the blue variant.
3. Make Slide 1 active and then make the following changes:
   a. Select the title *BENEFITS PROGRAM*, change the font to Candara and the font size to 60 points, apply the Turquoise, Accent 1, Darker 50% font color, and apply italic formatting.
   b. Select the subtitle *Changes to Plans*, change the font to Candara and the font size to 32 points, apply the Turquoise, Accent 1 font color, and apply bold and shadow formatting.
   c. Click the title placeholder and then click the Center button in the Paragraph group.
   d. Center the subtitle in the placeholder.
4. Make Slide 2 active and then make the following changes:
   a. Select the title *INTRODUCTION*, change the font to Candara and the font size to 44 points, apply the Turquoise, Accent 1, Darker 50% font color, and apply shadow formatting.
   b. Using Format Painter, apply the title formatting to the titles in the remaining slides.
5. Center-align and middle-align the titles in Slides 2 through 5.
6. Make Slide 2 active, select the bulleted text, and then change the line spacing to double spacing (2.0).
7. Make Slide 3 active, select the bulleted text, and then change the line spacing to double spacing (2.0).
8. Make Slide 4 active, select the bulleted text, and then change the line spacing to 1.5.
9. Make Slide 5 active, select the bulleted text, and then change the spacing after paragraphs to *18 pt*. ***Hint: Do this at the Paragraph dialog box.***
10. Make Slide 2 active and then select the text in the content placeholder. Display the Bullets and Numbering dialog box with the Numbered tab selected, choose the *1. 2. 3.* option, change the size to 90%, apply the Turquoise, Accent 1, Darker 50% color, and then close the dialog box.
11. Make Slide 3 active and then select the text in the content placeholder. Display the Bullets and Numbering dialog box with the Numbered tab selected, choose the *1. 2. 3.* option, change the size to 90%, apply the Turquoise, Accent 1, Darker 50% color, change the starting number to 5, and then close the dialog box.
12. Make Slide 4 active, select the text in the content placeholder, and then change the bullets to *Hollow Square Bullets*.
13. Make Slide 5 active, select the text in the content placeholder, and then change the bullets to *Hollow Square Bullets*.
14. Save the presentation and name it **P-C3-A1-Benefits**.
15. Print the presentation as a handout with six slides printed horizontally per page.
16. Apply the Organic design theme.

Figure 3.12 Assessment 1

Slide 1	Title	=	BENEFITS PROGRAM
	Subtitle	=	Changes to Plans
Slide 2	Title	=	INTRODUCTION
	Content	=	• Changes made for 2015 • Description of eligibility • Instructions for enrolling new members • Overview of medical and dental coverage
Slide 3	Title	=	INTRODUCTION
	Content	=	• Expanded enrollment forms • Glossary defining terms • Telephone directory • Pamphlet with commonly asked questions
Slide 4	Title	=	WHAT'S NEW
	Content	=	• New medical plans o Plan 2015 o Premier Plan • Changes in monthly contributions • Paying with pretax dollars • Contributions toward spouse's coverage
Slide 5	Title	=	COST SHARING
	Content	=	• Increased deductible • New coinsurance amount • Higher coinsurance amount for retail prescription drugs • Co-payment for mail-order medicines • New stop loss limit

17. Apply a transition and sound of your choosing to each slide.
18. Run the presentation.
19. Print the presentation as a handout with six slides printed horizontally per page.
20. Save and then close **P-C3-A1-Benefits.pptx**.

Assessment 2 FORMAT AND MODIFY A PERENNIALS PRESENTATION

1. Open **PerennialsPres.pptx** and then save the presentation with Save As and name it **P-C3-A2-PerennialsPres**.
2. Make Slide 3 active, format the bulleted text into two columns, and change the line spacing to double spacing (2.0). Make sure each column contains four bulleted items. With the bulleted items selected, display the Paragraph dialog box, change the *By* option (in the *Indentation* section) to 0.4, and then close the dialog box.

3. Make Slide 2 active, click anywhere in the bulleted text, click the Drawing group task pane launcher and then make the following changes at the Format Shape task pane:
   a. With the Fill & Line icon selected, click *FILL* to expand the options, click the *Gradient fill* option, change *Type* to Rectangular, and then change *Color* to Green, Accent 1, Lighter 60% (fifth column, third row in the *Theme Colors* section).
   b. Click the Effects icon, click the SHADOW option, click the Presets button, and then click the *Offset Right* option (first column, second row).
   c. Click the Size & Properties icon and then click *TEXT BOX* to expand the options.
   d. Change the left margin measurement to 1 inch and the top margin to 0.4 inch.
   e. Close the task pane.
4. Make Slide 1 active, click the subtitle placeholder, and then apply the following shape and outline fill:
   a. Click the Shape Fill button arrow on the HOME tab and then click the *Eyedropper* option.
   b. Point the eyedropper to the light green border at the top of the slide and then click the left mouse button.
   c. Click the Shape Outline button arrow and then click the *Eyedropper* option.
   d. Position the tip of the eyedropper on a yellow colored flower in the Greenspace Architects logo and then click the left mouse button.
5. Make Slide 2 active, click the DESIGN tab, click the Format Background button, and then apply the following formatting:
   a. At the Format Background task pane with the Fill icon selected, click the *Solid fill* option.
   b. Click the Color button and then click the *Aqua, Accent 5, Lighter 80%* option (ninth column, second row in the *Theme Colors* section).
   c. Click the Apply to All button.
   d. Close the task pane.
6. Print the presentation with six slides printed horizontally per page.
7. Add a transition and sound of your choosing to all slides in the presentation.
8. Run the presentation.
9. Save and then close **P-C3-A2-PerennialsPres.pptx**.

Assessment 3

CREATE AND APPLY A CUSTOM THEME TO A TRAVEL PRESENTATION

1. At a blank presentation, apply the Parallax design theme.
2. Create custom theme colors named with your first and last names that changes the following colors:
   a. At the Create New Theme Colors dialog box, change the *Text/Background - Light 2* option to *Red, Accent 4, Lighter 80%* (eighth column, second row in the *Theme Colors* section).
   b. Change the *Accent 1* option to *Red, Accent 4, Darker 50%* (eighth column, bottom row in the *Theme Colors* section).
3. Create custom theme fonts named with your first and last names that applies the following fonts:
   a. At the Create New Theme Fonts dialog box, change the Heading font to *Copperplate Gothic Bold*.
   b. Change the Body font to *Rockwell*.

4. Save the current theme as a custom theme named with your first and last names. ***Hint: Do this at the Save Current Theme dialog box.***
5. Close the presentation without saving it.
6. Open **TravelEngland.pptx** and then save the presentation with Save As and name it **P-C3-A3-TravelEngland**.
7. Apply the custom theme named with your first and last names.
8. Improve the visual display of the bulleted text in Slides 2 and 3 by increasing the spacing between items and positioning the bulleted item placeholders attractively in the slides.
9. Make Slide 4 active, increase the spacing between bulleted items and then format the text into two columns. Make sure that each column contains three bulleted items. Consider decreasing the size of the placeholder.
10. Format the bulleted text in Slides 5 and 6 into two columns with four bulleted items in each column. Consider decreasing the size of the placeholder.
11. Print the presentation as a handout with six slides printed horizontally per page.
12. Add a transition and sound of your choosing to all slides in the presentation.
13. Run the presentation.
14. Save and then close **P-C3-A3-TravelEngland.pptx**.
15. Display a blank presentation and then delete the custom theme colors, custom theme fonts, and custom theme you created for this assessment.
16. Close the presentation without saving it.

Assessment 4

PREPARE A PRESENTATION ON ONLINE SHOPPING

1. Open Microsoft Word and then open the document **OnlineShopping.docx** that is located in the PC3 folder on your storage medium.
2. Print the document by clicking the FILE tab, clicking the *Print* option, and then clicking the Print button at the Print backstage area.
3. Close **OnlineShopping.docx** and then close Word.
4. At a blank PowerPoint presentation, use the information you printed to create a presentation on online shopping with the following specifications:
   a. Create a slide with the title of your presentation. Type your name as the subtitle.
   b. Create slides that summarize the information you printed. (You determine the number of slides in the presentation. Make sure the slides are not crowded with too much information.)
   c. Apply a design theme of your choosing.
   d. Apply a transition and sound of your choosing to all slides.
5. Save the presentation and name it **P-C3-A4-OnlineShopping**.
6. Run the presentation.
7. Print the presentation as a handout with six slides printed horizontally per page.
8. Close **P-C3-A4-OnlineShopping.pptx**.

Visual Benchmark Demonstrate Your Proficiency

FORMAT A PRESENTATION ON HOME SAFETY

1. Open **HomeSafety.pptx** and then save the presentation with Save As and name it **P-C3-VB-HomeSafety**.
2. Format the presentation so the slides appear as shown in Figure 3.13 with the following specifications.
   a. Apply the Facet design theme and the blue variant color.
   b. Delete and rearrange slides as shown in the figure.
   c. Apply the Parchment texture slide background and change the slide background transparency to 50% for all slides in the presentation. ***Hint: Apply these options using the Format Background task pane.***
   d. Change the font size of the title in Slide 1 to 60 points, apply bold formatting, apply the Blue, Accent 2, Darker 25% font color, and center-align the title.
   e. Change the font size of the subtitle in Slide 1 to 28 points, apply italics, change the font color to Turquoise, Accent 1, Darker 25%, and center-align the subtitle.
   f. Change the font size of the titles in Slides 2 through 6 to 48 points and the font color to Turquoise, Accent 1, Darker 50%.
   g. Change the line spacing, spacing after, column formatting, and bullet styles so your slides display in a manner similar to the slides in Figure 3.13.
   h. Select the bulleted text placeholder in Slide 6, display the Format Shape task pane, select the *Solid fill* option, and then change the color to Turquoise, Accent 1, Lighter 80%. Display the Format Shape task pane with the TEXT OPTIONS tab selected and the Textbox icon selected, then change the left margin to 1 inch and the top margin to 0.2 inch.
3. Print the presentation as a handout with six slides printed horizontally per page.
4. Save and then close the presentation.

Figure 3.13 Visual Benchmark

Safety at Home

Children and Babies

Stairs

- Fit stair gates at the bottom or top of stairs.
  - Bars of gates should be no more than 2.5 inches apart.
  - Never climb over gate because child may copy you.
- Regularly check that your banister is secured.
- Replace loose or damaged carpet or steps.

Kitchen

- Put safety locks on cabinets and drawers, especially those containing dangerous objects.
- Keep garbage containers in a cabinet with a child-restraint lock.
- Always be aware of what your child can reach and keep dangerous objects out of child's reach on work areas.
- Keep child away from oven doors as some get very hot while the oven is in use.

Bathroom

- Never leave a young child or baby alone in bathtub.
- Keep constant check on water temperature in bathtubs and showers.
- Keep toilet seat closed.
- Store bathroom chemicals in a cabinet with a safety lock.

Outdoor

- Keep baby and toddler away from poisonous plants.
- Keep sheds containing tools, equipment, and chemicals locked.
- Never leave child unattended when playing in or near water.
- Don't apply chemicals or mow the lawn when child will be playing in the yard.

Safety Supplies

- Plastic outlet covers
- Smoke detectors
- Safety gates
- Safety locks
- Water thermometer
- Nonslip mats
- Fireplace screen
- Bicycle helmets

Case Study Apply Your Skills

Part 1

You are the assistant to Gina Coletti, manager of La Dolce Vita, an Italian restaurant. She has been working on a new lunch menu and wants to present the new menu at the upcoming staff meeting. She has asked you to prepare a presentation she can use at the meeting. Open the Word document named **LunchMenu.docx** and then print the document. Close the document and then close Word. In PowerPoint, display the New backstage area, search for the *Fresh food presentation* design theme template at Office.com, and then download the template that contains the vegetables on the title slide. Create a presentation with the design theme template you downlaoded with the information you printed. Make any formatting changes to improve the visual appearance of the presentation. Save the presentation and name it **P-C3-CS-LunchMenu**.

Part 2

Ms. Coletti has looked over the presentation and has asked you to apply color and font formatting consistent with other restaurant publications. With **P-C3-CS-LunchMenu.pptx** open, create custom theme colors that change the *Text/Background - Light 1* color to *Gold, Accent 2, Lighter 80%* and the *Accent 3* color to *Blue*. Create custom theme fonts that apply Monotype Corsiva as the heading font and Garamond as the body font. Save the custom theme and name it *LaDolceVita* followed by your initials. Add a transition and sound to all slides in the presentation. Print the presentation as a handout with six slides printed horizontally per page. Save and then close **P-C3-CS-LunchMenu.pptx**.

Part 3

Ms. Coletti needs further information for the meeting. She wants you to use the Internet to search for two companies that print restaurant menus, two companies that design restaurant menus, and the names of two restaurant menu design software programs. Prepare a presentation with the information you find on the Internet using the design theme template you downloaded in part 1. Make any formatting changes to improve the visual appeal of each slide. Add a transition and sound to each slide in the presentation. Save the presentation and name it **P-C3-CS-RestMenus.pptx**. Print the presentation as a handout with six slides printed horizontally per page.

Part 4

When running **P-C3-CS-RestMenus.pptx**, Ms. Coletti would like to link to a couple of the sites you list in the presentation. Use PowerPoint's Help feature to learn how to insert a hyperlink in a slide to a web page or website. Create at least two hyperlinks between sites you list in the presentation and the web page or website. Print the slide(s) containing the hyperlinks. Save and then close **P-C3-CS-RestMenus.pptx**.

MICROSOFT® POWERPOINT®

CHAPTER 4

Inserting Elements in Slides

PERFORMANCE OBJECTIVES

Upon successful completion of Chapter 4, you will be able to:

- **Insert, format, select, and align a text box**
- **Set tabs in a text box**
- **Insert, format, and copy shapes**
- **Display rulers, gridlines, and guides**
- **Group and ungroup objects**
- **Insert, crop, size, move, and format a picture**
- **Insert a picture as a slide background**
- **Insert, size, scale, rotate, and position a clip art image**
- **Create and insert a screenshot**
- **Create and format WordArt text**
- **Insert objects such as a header, footer, date, slide number, and symbol**

Tutorials

4.1 Displaying Gridlines; Inserting a Text Box; Copying and Rotating Shapes
4.2 Formatting a Text Box
4.3 Drawing and Customizing Shapes
4.4 Grouping/Ungrouping Objects
4.5 Inserting and Formatting Images
4.6 Inserting and Formatting Clip Art Images
4.7 Creating and Inserting Screenshots
4.8 Inserting and Formatting WordArt
4.9 Inserting Headers and Footers

A presentation consisting only of text slides may have important information in it that will be overlooked by the audience because a slide contains too much text. Adding visual elements, where appropriate, can help deliver the message to your audience by adding interest and impact to the information. In this chapter, you will learn how to create visual elements on slides such as text boxes, shapes, pictures, clip art images, screenshots, and WordArt text. These elements will make the delivery of your presentation a dynamic experience for your audience. The model answer for this chapter's project appears on the following page.

Note: Before beginning the project, copy to your storage medium the PC4 subfolder from the PowerPoint folder on the CD that accompanies this textbook and then make PC4 the active folder.

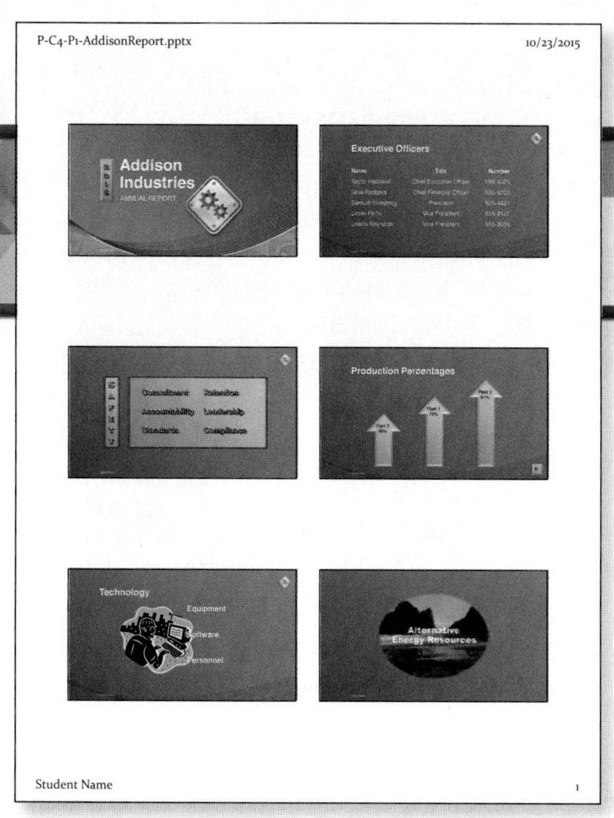

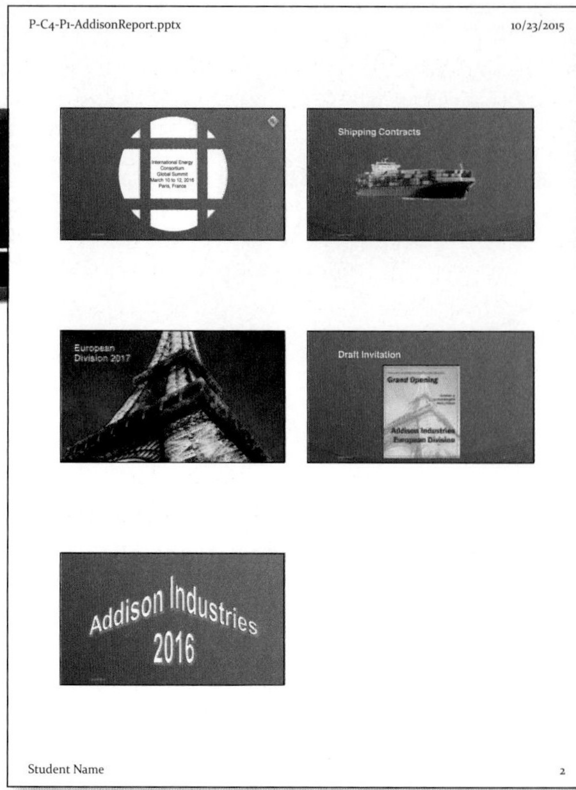

Model Answers

Project 1 Create a Company Presentation Containing Text Boxes, Shapes, and Images P-C4-P1-AddisonReport.pptx

Project 1 Create a Company Presentation Containing Text Boxes, Shapes, and Images — 14 Parts

You will create a company presentation that includes slides with text boxes, a slide with tabbed text in a text box, slides with shapes and text, slides with pictures, and slides with clip art images. You will also insert elements in slides such as slide numbers, headers, footers, the date, and symbols.

Inserting and Formatting Text Boxes

Quick Steps

Draw a Text Box
1. Click INSERT tab.
2. Click Text Box button.
3. Click or drag in slide to create box.

Text Box

Many slide layouts contain placeholders for entering text and other elements in a document. Along with placeholders, you can insert and format a text box. To insert a text box in a slide, click the INSERT tab, click the Text Box button in the Text group, and the mouse pointer displays as a thin, down-pointing arrow. Using the mouse, drag in the slide to create the text box. You can also click in the desired location and a small text box is inserted in the slide.

Formatting a Text Box

When you insert a text box in the document, the HOME tab displays. Use options in the Drawing group to format the text box by applying a Quick Style or adding a shape fill, outline, or effect. Format a text box in a manner similar to formatting a placeholder. You can also apply formatting to a text box with options on the DRAWING TOOLS FORMAT tab. Click this tab and the ribbon displays, as shown in Figure 4.1. The Shape Styles group contains the same options as the Drawing group on the HOME tab. With other options on the tab, apply WordArt formatting to text and arrange and size the text box.

Move a text box in the same way you move a placeholder. Click the text box to select it, position the mouse pointer on the text box border until the pointer displays with a four-headed arrow attached, and then drag the text box to the desired position. Change the size of a selected text box using the sizing handles that display around the box. You can also use the *Shape Height* and *Shape Width* measurement boxes in the Size group on the DRAWING TOOLS FORMAT tab to specify the text box height and width.

As you learned in Chapter 3, PowerPoint provides a task pane with a variety of options for formatting a placeholder. The same task pane is available with options for formatting and customizing a text box. Click the Shape Styles task pane launcher and the Format Shape task pane displays at the right side of the screen with options for formatting the text box fill, effects, and size; options for formatting a picture in the text box; and options for formatting text in a text box. Click the WordArt Styles task pane launcher and the Format Shape task pane displays text formatting options. Click the Size task pane launcher and the Format Shape task pane displays size and position options.

You can apply the same formatting to text in a text box that you apply to text in a placeholder. For example, use the buttons in the Paragraph group on the HOME tab to align text horizontally and vertically in a text box, change text direction, set text in columns, and set internal margins for the text in the text box.

HINT

Use a text box to place text anywhere in a slide. Text in inserted text boxes does not appear in the Outline view.

To select an object that is behind another object, select the top object and then press the Tab key to cycle through and select the other objects.

Selecting Multiple Objects

You can select multiple text boxes and other objects in a slide and then apply formatting or align and arrange the objects in the slide. To select all objects in a slide, click the Select button in the Editing group on the HOME tab and then click *Select All* at the drop-down list. Or, select all objects in a slide with the keyboard shortcut Ctrl + A. To select specific text boxes or objects in a slide, click the first object, hold down the Shift key, and then click each of the other desired objects.

Quick Steps

Select All Text Boxes

1. Click Select button.
2. Click *Select All*.

OR

Press Ctrl + A.

Select

Aligning Text Boxes

Use the Align button in the Arrange group on the DRAWING TOOLS FORMAT tab to align the edge of multiple objects in a slide. Click the Align button and a drop-down list of alignment options displays including options for aligning objects vertically and horizontally and distributing objects.

Align

Figure 4.1 DRAWING TOOLS FORMAT Tab

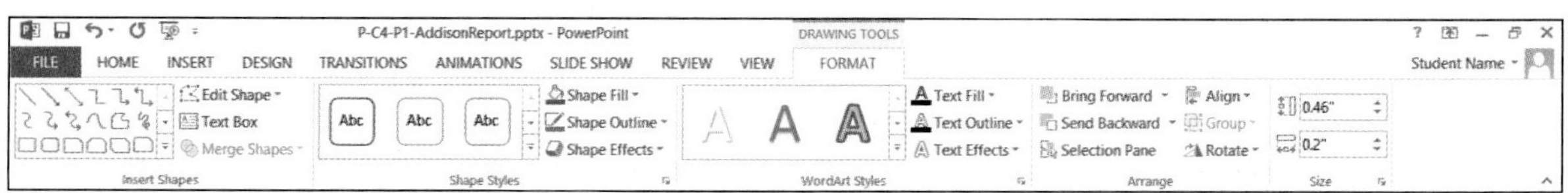

Project 1a Inserting and Formatting Text Boxes

1. Open **AddisonReport.pptx** and then save the presentation with Save As and name it **P-C4-P1-AddisonReport**.
2. Insert a new slide with the Blank layout by completing the following steps:
   a. Click the New Slide button arrow in the Slides group on the HOME tab.
   b. Click *Blank* at the drop-down list.
3. Insert and format the *Safety* text box shown in Figure 4.2 (on page 131) by completing the following steps:
   a. Click the INSERT tab.
   b. Click the Text Box button in the Text group.
   c. Click anywhere in the slide. (This inserts a small, selected text box in the slide.)
   d. Type **Safety**.
   e. Select the text and then change the font to Copperplate Gothic Bold and the font size to 36 points.
   f. Click the Text Direction button in the Paragraph group on the HOME tab and then click *Stacked* at the drop-down list.
   g. Click the DRAWING TOOLS FORMAT tab.
   h. Click the More button that displays at the right side of the style thumbnails in the Shape Styles group and then click the *Moderate Effect - Aqua, Accent 5* option (sixth column, fifth row).

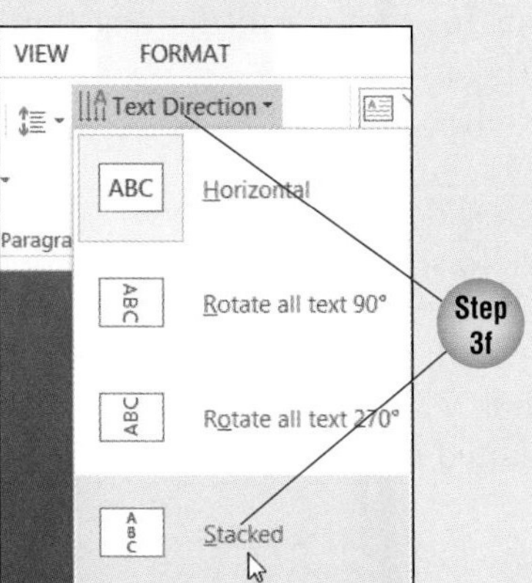

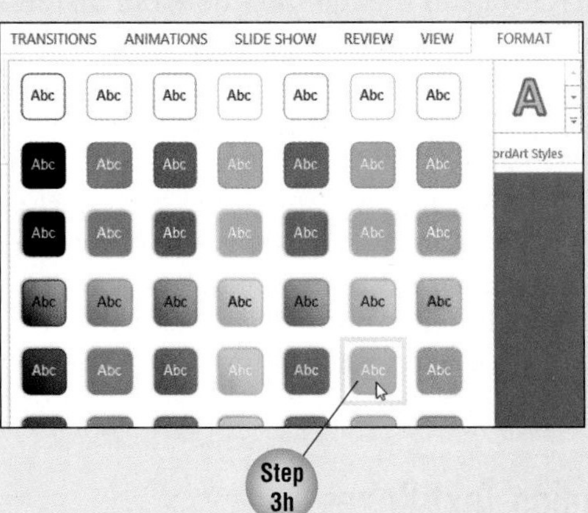

   i. Click the Shape Outline button arrow in the Shape Styles group and then click the *Blue* color (eighth option in the *Standard Colors* section).
   j. Click the Shape Outline button arrow, point to *Weight*, and then click the *1½ pt* option.
   k. Click the Shape Effects button, point to *Bevel*, and then click the *Circle* option (first option in the *Bevel* section).
   l. Click the More button at the right side of the WordArt style thumbnails in the WordArt Styles group and then click the *Fill - White, Text 1, Outline - Background 1, Hard Shadow - Background 1* option (first column, third row).
   m. Click in the *Shape Height* measurement box, type 4, and then press Enter.
   n. Drag the text box so it is positioned as shown in Figure 4.2 (located on page 131).

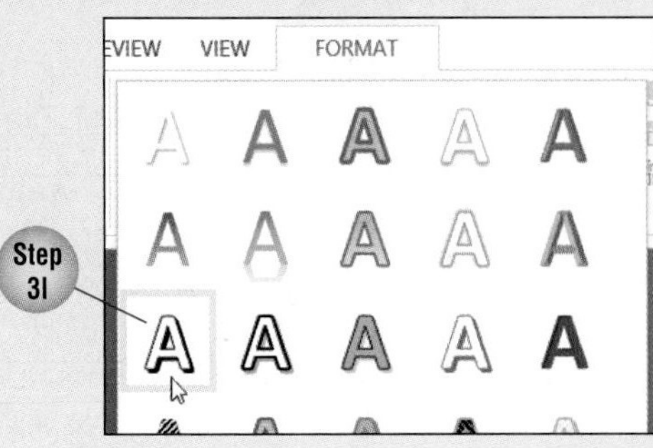

4. Insert and size the other text box shown in Figure 4.2 by completing the following steps:
   a. Click the INSERT tab.
   b. Click the Text Box button in the Text group.
   c. Drag in the slide to create a text box. (Drag to the approximate width of the text box in Figure 4.2.)
   d. Type the text shown in the text box in Figure 4.2 in a single column. Type the text in the first column and then type the text in the second column. (Your text will display as shown at the right in one column, in a smaller font, and with different line spacing than in Figure 4.2.)

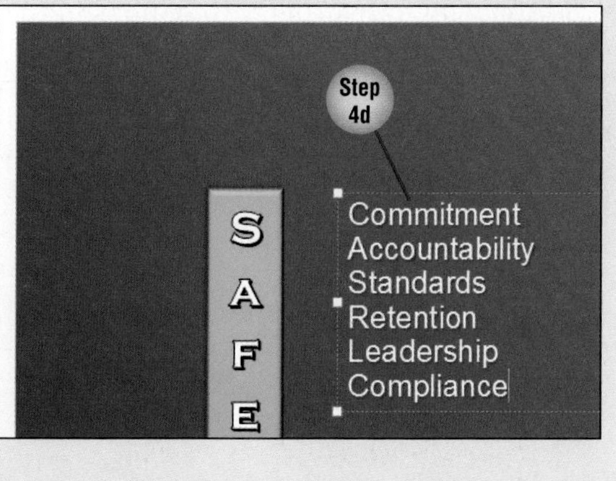

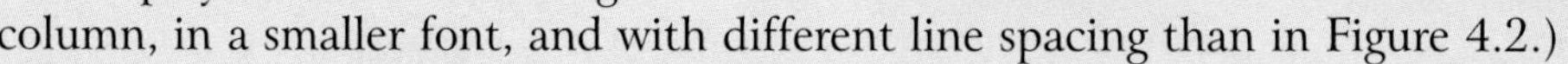

   e. Select the text and then change the font size to 32 points.
   f. Click the Line Spacing button in the Paragraph group and then click *2.0* at the drop-down list. (The text will flow off the slide.)
   g. Click the Add or Remove Columns button in the Paragraph group and then click *Two Columns* at the drop-down list. (The text in the slide will not display in two columns until you complete steps 7k and 7l.)
5. Click the DRAWING TOOLS FORMAT tab.
6. Apply a WordArt style by completing the following steps:
   a. Click the More button at the right side of the WordArt style thumbnails in the WordArt Styles group.
   b. Click the *Fill - White, Text 1, Outline - Background 1, Hard Shadow - Background 1* option (first column, third row).
7. Change the height, width, and internal margin measurements of the text box and turn off Autofit in the Format Shape task pane by completing the following steps:
   a. Click the Size group task pane launcher.
   b. At the Format Shape task pane, make sure the Size & Properties icon is selected.
   c. If necessary, click *TEXT BOX* in the task pane to display the text box options.
   d. If necessary, scroll down to the bottom of the task pane list box.
   e. Click the *Do not Autofit* option.
   f. Select the current measurement in the *Left margin* measurement box and then type 0.8.
   g. Select the current measurement in the *Right margin* measurement box and then type 0.
   h. Select the current measurement in the *Top margin* measurement box, type 0.2, and then press Enter.
   i. Scroll up to the top of the task pane list box.
   j. If necessary, click *SIZE* to display the size options.
   k. Select the current measurement in the *Height* measurement box and then type 4.
   l. Select the current measurement in the *Width* measurement box, type 8, and then press Enter.

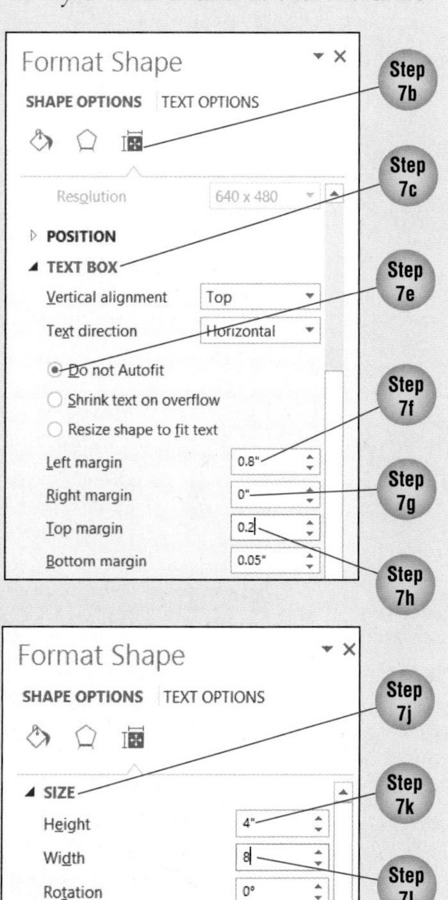

8. Apply fill formatting with options in the Format Shape task pane by completing the following steps:
   a. Click the Fill & Line icon in the task pane.
   b. Click *FILL* to display the fill options.
   c. Click the *Gradient fill* option. Notice the options available for customizing the gradient fill.
   d. Click the *Pattern fill* option and notice the pattern options that display.
   e. Click the *Picture or texture fill* option.
   f. Click the File button in the task pane.

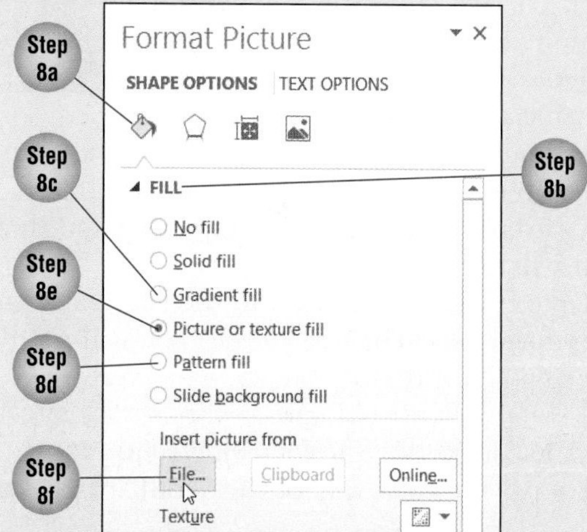

   g. At the Insert Picture dialog box, navigate to the PC4 folder on your storage medium and then double-click ***Ship.jpg***.
   h. Select *0%* in the *Transparency* measurement box, type **10**, and then press Enter.
   i. Close the task pane by clicking the Close button located in the upper right corner of the task pane.
9. Click in the slide outside the text box.
10. Arrange the text boxes by completing the following steps:
    a. Press Ctrl + A to select both text boxes.
    b. Click the DRAWING TOOLS FORMAT tab.
    c. Click the Align button in the Arrange group and then click *Align Bottom* at the drop-down list.

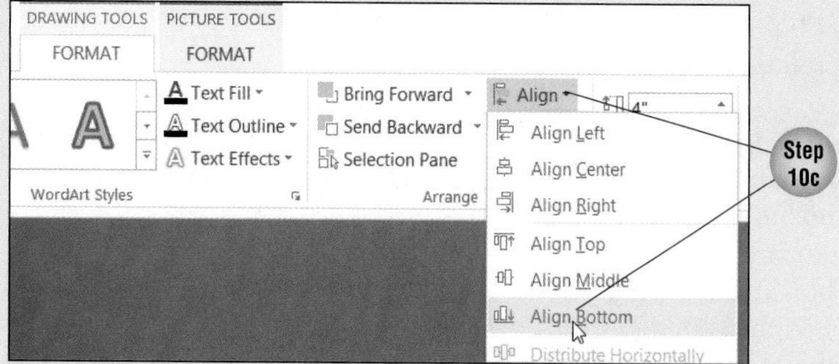

    d. Drag both boxes to the approximate location in the slide as shown in Figure 4.2.
11. Save **P-C4-P1-AddisonReport.pptx**.

12. Print only slide 2 by completing the following steps:
    a. Press Ctrl + P to display the Print backstage area.
    b. Click in the *Slides* text box in the *Settings* category and then type 2.
    c. Click the Print button.
13. Select the text box containing the image of the ship.
14. Make sure the DRAWING TOOLS FORMAT tab is active.
15. Click the More button that displays at the right side of the style thumbnails in the Shape Styles group and then click the *Moderate Effect - Aqua, Accent 5* option (sixth column, fifth row).
16. Click the Shape Outline button arrow in the Shape Styles group and then click the *Blue* color (eighth option in the *Standard Colors* section).
17. Click the Shape Outline button arrow, point to *Weight*, and then click the *1½ pt* option.
18. Click the Shape Effects button, point to *Bevel*, and then click the *Circle* option (first option in the *Bevel* section).
19. Save **P-C4-P1-AddisonReport.pptx**.

Figure 4.2 Project 1a, Slide 2

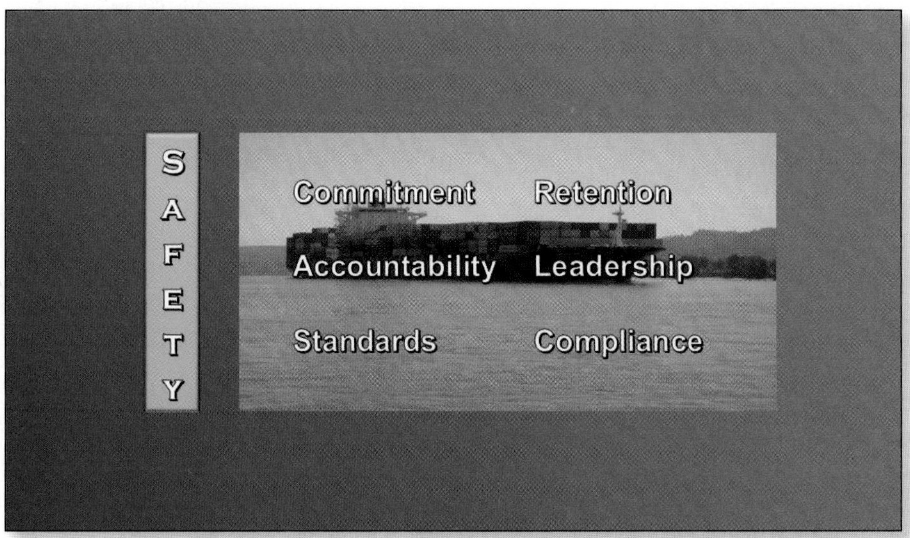

You can display the Format Shape task pane using a shortcut menu. To do this, position the mouse pointer on the border of the text box until the pointer displays with a four-headed arrow attached and then click the right mouse button. At the shortcut menu, click the *Size and Position* option to display the Format Shape task pane with the Size & Properties icon active. Click the *Format Shape* option at the shortcut menu and the Format Shape task pane displays with the Fill & Line icon active. If you apply formatting to a text box and then want that formatting to be the default for other text boxes in the current presentation, click the *Set as Default Text Box* option at the shortcut menu.

Project 1b Formatting a Text Box and Setting the Default Text Box Part 2 of 14

1. With **P-C4-P1-AddisonReport.pptx** open, make sure Slide 2 is the active slide and then complete the following steps:
   a. Click the INSERT tab, click the Text Box button, and then click in the lower right corner of the slide.
   b. Type **Default text box.** (In the next step you will change the default text box. You will use the text box you just inserted to return to the original text box.)
2. Set as default the text box containing the word *SAFETY* by completing the following steps:
   a. Position the mouse pointer on the border of the text box containing the word *SAFETY* until the pointer displays with a four-headed arrow attached and then click the right mouse button.
   b. Click the *Set as Default Text Box* option at the shortcut menu.
3. Make Slide 1 active.
4. Insert a text box by clicking the INSERT tab, clicking the Text Box button, and then clicking between the company name and the left side of the slide.
5. Type **2016** in the text box.
6. Change the *Autofit* option, wrap text in the text box, and size the text box by completing the following steps:
   a. Position the mouse pointer on the border of the text box until the pointer displays with a four-headed arrow attached and then click the right mouse button.
   b. Click the *Size and Position* option at the shortcut menu.
   c. At the Format Shape task pane with the Size & Properties icon selected, click *TEXT BOX* to display the options, scroll to the bottom of the task pane list box, and then click in the *Wrap text in shape* check box to insert a check mark.
   d. Click the *Shrink text on overflow* option.
   e. Scroll up to the top of the task pane.
   f. Select the current measurement in the *Height* measurement box in the *SIZE* section and then type **2.4**.
   g. Select the current measurement in the *Width* measurement box, type **0.8**, and then press Enter.

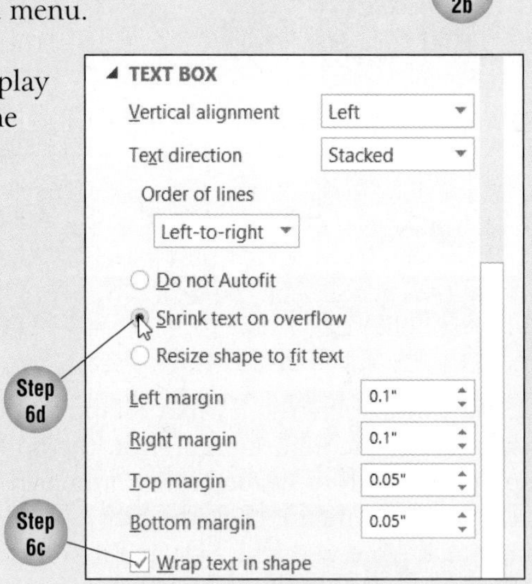

7. With the text box selected, change the shape of the text box by completing the following steps:
   a. Click the DRAWING TOOLS FORMAT tab to make the tab active.
   b. Click the Edit Shape button in the Insert Shapes group, point to *Change Shape*, and then click the *Bevel* option (last option, second row in the *Basic Shapes* section).
8. Precisely position the text box by completing the following steps:
   a. If necessary, scroll down the Format Shape task pane list box to the *POSITION* section and then click *POSITION* to display the options.
   b. Select the current measurement in the *Horizontal position* measurement box and then type 1.8.
   c. Select the current measurement in the *Vertical position* measurement box, type 2, and then press Enter.
9. Close the Format Shape task pane.
10. Return to the original text box by completing the following steps:
    a. Make Slide 2 active.
    b. Click in the text box containing the words *Default text box*.
    c. Position the mouse pointer on the border of the text box until the pointer displays with a four-headed arrow attached and then click the right mouse button.
    d. Click the *Set as Default Text Box* option at the shortcut menu.
    e. Press the Delete key to delete the text box.
11. Save **P-C4-P1-AddisonReport.pptx**.

Step 7b

Setting Tabs in a Text Box

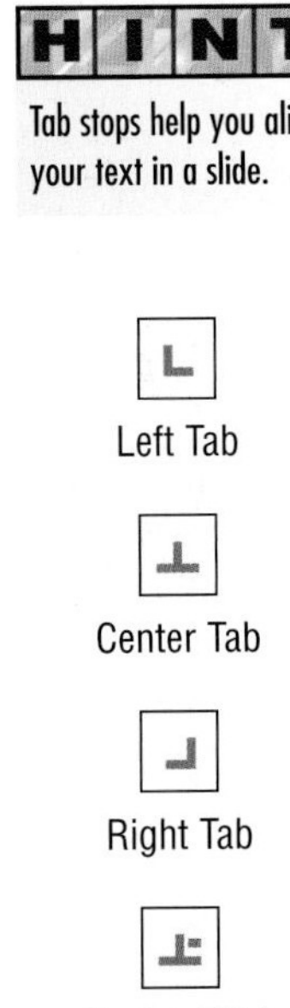

Inside a text box you may want to align text in columns using tabs. A text box, by default, contains left alignment tabs that display as gray marks along the bottom of the horizontal ruler. (If the ruler is not visible, display the horizontal ruler as well as the vertical ruler by clicking the VIEW tab and then clicking the *Ruler* check box in the Show group to insert a check mark.) These default left alignment tabs can be changed to center, right, or decimal. To change to a different tab alignment, click the Alignment button located at the left side of the horizontal ruler. Display the desired tab alignment symbol and then click at the desired position on the horizontal ruler. When you set a tab on the horizontal ruler, any default tabs to the left of the new tab are deleted. Move tabs on the horizontal ruler by using the mouse to drag the tab to the desired position. To delete a tab, use the mouse to drag the tab off of the ruler.

You can also set tabs with options at the Tabs dialog box. To display this dialog box, click the Paragraph group dialog box launcher. At the Paragraph dialog box, click the Tabs button that displays in the lower left corner. At the Tabs dialog box, type a tab position in the *Tab stop position* measurement box, choose a tab alignment with options in the *Alignment* section, and then click the Set button. Clear a specific tab by typing the tab stop position in the *Tab stop position* measurement box and then clicking the Clear button. Clear all tabs from the horizontal ruler by clicking the Clear All button. When all desired changes are made, click OK to close the Tabs dialog box and then click OK to close the Paragraph dialog box.

Project 1c Creating a Text Box and Setting Tabs Part 3 of 14

1. With **P-C4-P1-AddisonReport.pptx** open, make Slide 1 active and then click the HOME tab.
2. Click the New Slide button arrow and then click the *Title Only* layout.
3. Click in the placeholder text *Click to add title* and then type Executive Officers.
4. Draw a text box by completing the following steps:
   a. Click the INSERT tab.
   b. Click the Text Box button in the Text group.
   c. Draw a text box in the slide that is approximately 10 inches wide and 0.5 inch tall.
5. Change tabs in the text box by completing the following steps:
   a. Display the horizontal ruler by clicking the VIEW tab and then clicking the *Ruler* check box in the Show group to insert a check mark.
   b. With the insertion point inside the text box, check the Alignment button at the left side of the horizontal ruler and make sure the left tab symbol displays.
   c. Position the tip of the mouse pointer on the horizontal ruler below the 0.5-inch mark and then click the left mouse button.

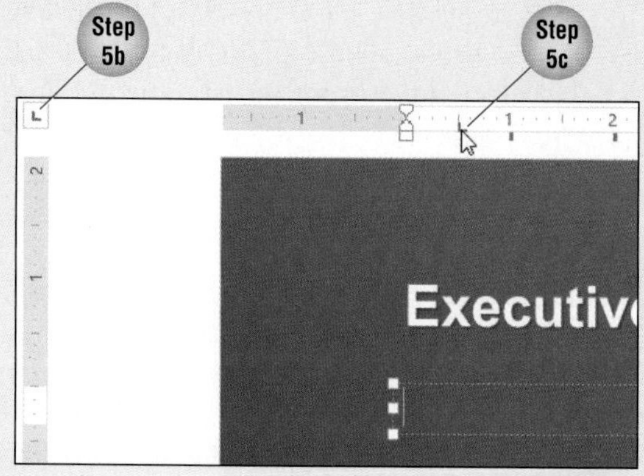

   d. Click once on the Alignment button to display the Center alignment symbol.
   e. Click immediately below the 5-inch mark on the horizontal ruler.
   f. Click once on the Alignment button to display the Right alignment symbol.

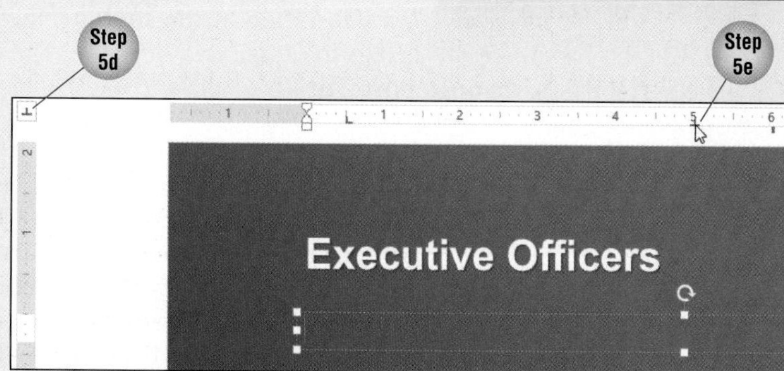

   g. Click on the horizontal ruler immediately below the 9.5-inch mark. (You may need to expand the size of the text box to set the tab at the 9.5-inch mark.)
6. Type the text in the text box as shown in the slide in Figure 4.3. Make sure you press the Tab key before typing text in the first column. (This moves the insertion point to the first tab, which is a left alignment tab.) Bold the three column headings—*Name*, *Title*, and *Number*.
7. When you are finished typing the text in the text box, press Ctrl + A to select all of the text in the text box.
8. Drag the left alignment marker on the horizontal ruler from the 0.5-inch mark to the 0.25-inch mark and then drag the center alignment marker on the horizontal ruler from the 5-inch mark on the ruler to the 5.5-inch mark.
9. With the text selected, click the Line Spacing button in the Paragraph group on the HOME tab and then click the *1.5* option.
10. Position the text box as shown in Figure 4.3.
11. Save **P-C4-P1-AddisonReport.pptx**.

Figure 4.3 Project 1c, Slide 2

Executive Officers

Name	Title	Number
Taylor Hallowell	Chief Executive Officer	555-4321
Gina Rodgers	Chief Financial Officer	555-4203
Samuel Weinberg	President	555-4421
Leslie Pena	Vice President	555-3122
Leticia Reynolds	Vice President	555-3004

Inserting, Formatting, and Copying Shapes

You can draw shapes in a slide with shapes in the Drawing group or with the Shapes button in the Illustrations group on the INSERT tab. Use the Shapes button drop-down list to draw shapes including lines, basic shapes, block arrows, flow chart symbols, callouts, stars, and banners. Click a shape and the mouse pointer displays as crosshairs (plus sign). Click in the slide to insert the shape or position the crosshairs in the slide and then drag to create the shape. Apply formatting to a shape in a manner similar to formatting a text box. Format a shape with buttons in the Drawing group on the HOME tab, with buttons on the DRAWING TOOLS FORMAT tab, options in the Format Shape task pane, or with options at the shortcut menu. When drawing an enclosed object, you can maintain the proportions of the shape by holding down the Shift key while dragging with the mouse to create the shape.

If you draw and format a shape and decide that you want to use the same formatting for other shapes in the presentation, save the shape as the default. To do this, right-click the border of the shape and then click *Set as Default Shape*.

To copy a shape, select the shape and then click the Copy button in the Clipboard group on the HOME tab. Position the insertion point at the location where you want the copied image and then click the Paste button. You can also copy a selected shape by holding down the Ctrl key while dragging the shape to the desired location.

Quick Steps

Insert a Shape

1. Click INSERT tab.
2. Click Shapes button.
3. Click desired shape at drop-down list.
4. Click or drag in slide to create shape.

Shapes

HINT

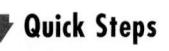

Many shapes have an adjustment handle you can use to change the most prominent feature of the shape.

Quick Steps

Copy a Shape

1. Select desired shape.
2. Click Copy button.
3. Position insertion point at desired location.
4. Click Paste button.

OR

1. Select desired shape.
2. Hold down Ctrl key.
3. Drag shape to desired location.

Displaying Rulers, Gridlines, and Guides

PowerPoint provides a number of features to help you position objects such as placeholders, text boxes, and shapes. You can display horizontal and vertical rulers, gridlines, and/or drawing guides and use Smart Guides as shown in Figure 4.4. Turn the horizontal and vertical rulers on and off with the *Ruler* check box in the Show group on the VIEW tab as you did in Project 1c. The Show group also contains a *Gridlines* check box. Insert a check mark in this check box and gridlines display in the active slide. Gridlines are intersecting lines that create a grid on the slide and are useful for aligning objects. You can also turn the display of gridlines on and off with the keyboard shortcut, Shift + F9.

Turn on drawing guides to help position objects on a slide. Drawing guides are horizontal and vertical dashed lines that display on the slide in the slide pane as shown in Figure 4.4. To turn on the drawing guides, display the Grid and Guides dialog box shown in Figure 4.5. Display this dialog box by clicking the Show group dialog box launcher on the VIEW tab. At the dialog box, insert a check mark in the *Display drawing guides on screen* check box. By default, the horizontal and vertical drawing guides intersect in the middle of the slide. You can move these guides by dragging the guide with the mouse. As you drag the guide, a measurement displays next to the mouse pointer. Drawing guides and gridlines display on the slide but do not print.

Figure 4.4 Rulers, Gridlines, Drawing Guides, and Smart Guides

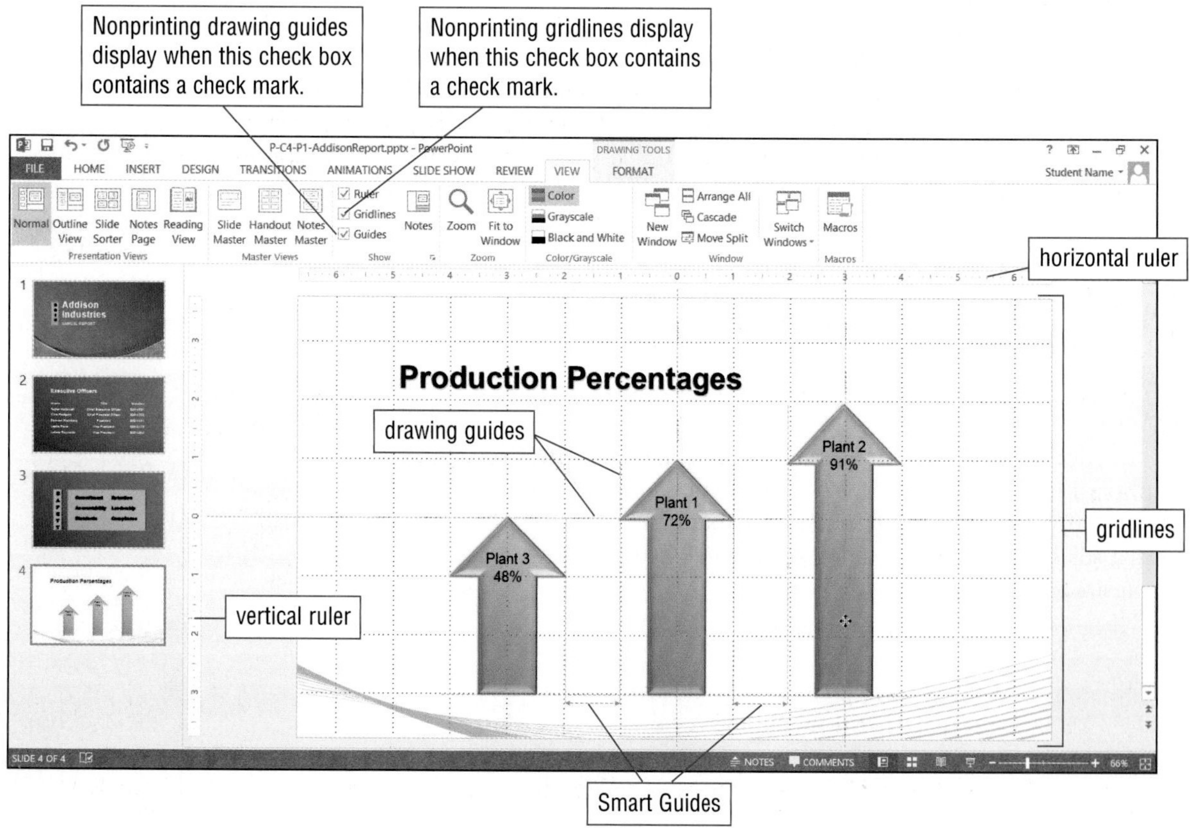

Figure 4.5 Grid and Guides Dialog Box

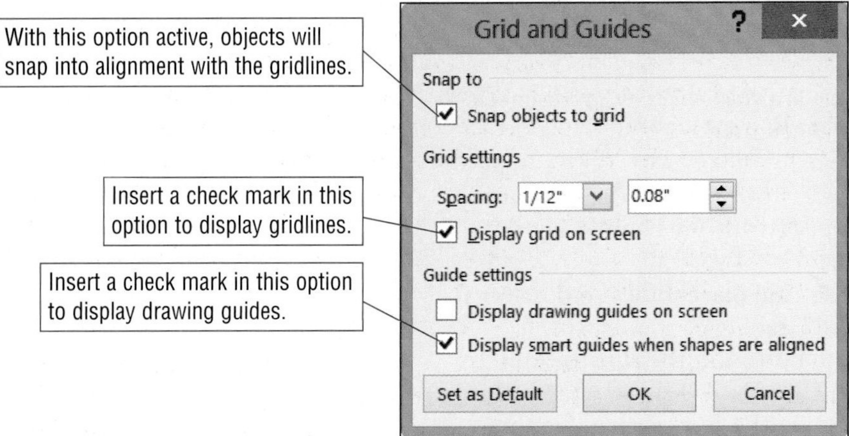

PowerPoint includes Smart Guides, which appear when you move objects that are close together on a slide. Use these guides to help you align and evenly space the objects on the slide. Turn on gridlines with the *Gridlines* check box on the VIEW tab or by inserting a check mark in the *Display grid on screen* check box at the Grid and Guides dialog box. The horizontal and vertical spacing between the gridlines is 0.08 inch by default. You can change this measurement with the *Spacing* option at the Grid and Guides dialog box.

As you drag or draw an object on the slide, it is pulled into alignment with the nearest intersection of gridlines. This is because the *Snap objects to grid* option at the Grid and Guides dialog box is active by default. If you want to position an object precisely, turn off this option by removing the check mark from the *Snap objects to grid* check box or by holding down the Alt key while dragging an object. Smart Guides display when shapes are aligned. If you do not want Smart Guides to display, click the *Display smart guides when shapes are aligned* check box in the Grid and Guides dialog box to remove the check mark.

Project 1d Drawing and Formatting Shapes — Part 4 of 14

1. With **P-C4-P1-AddisonReport.pptx** open, make Slide 3 active and then insert a new slide by clicking the New Slide button arrow in the Slides group on the HOME tab and then clicking the *White Background* layout at the drop-down list.
2. Turn on the display of gridlines by clicking the VIEW tab and then clicking *Gridlines* to insert a check mark in the check box.
3. Click in the title placeholder and then type **Production Percentages**.
4. Turn on the drawing guides and turn off the snap-to-grid feature by completing the following steps:
   a. Make sure the VIEW tab is active and then click the Show group dialog box launcher.

b. At the Grid and Guides dialog box, click the *Snap objects to grid* check box to remove the check mark.
c. Click the *Display drawing guides on screen* check box to insert a check mark.
d. Click OK.

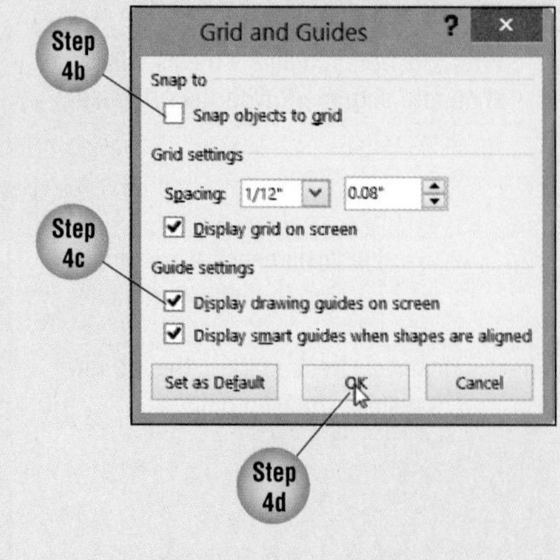

5. Insert the left-most arrow in the slide, as shown in Figure 4.6 (on page 140), by completing the following steps:
   a. Click outside the title placeholder to deselect it.
   b. Click the INSERT tab.
   c. Click the Shapes button in the Illustrations group and then click the *Up Arrow* shape (third column, first row in the *Block Arrows* section).
   d. Position the crosshairs at the intersection of the horizontal drawing guide and the third vertical gridline from the left.
   e. Hold down the left mouse button, drag down and to the right until the crosshairs are positioned on the intersection of the fifth vertical line from the left and the first horizontal line from the bottom, and then release the mouse button. (Your arrow should be the approximate size shown in Figure 4.6.)

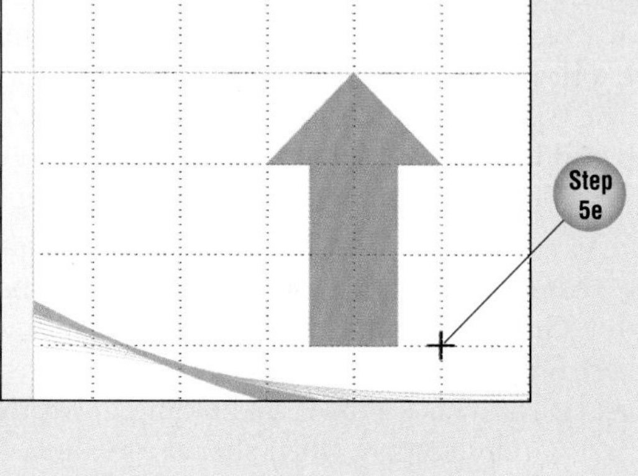

   f. With the arrow selected and the DRAWING TOOLS FORMAT tab active, click the Shape Fill button arrow in the Shape Styles group, and then click *Aqua, Accent 5* at the drop-down gallery (ninth column, first row in the *Theme Colors* section).
   g. Click the Shape Outline button arrow and then click *Dark Blue* at the drop-down gallery (ninth option in the *Standard Colors* section).
   h. Apply a shape style to the arrow by clicking the More button at the right side of the shape style thumbnails and then clicking the *Subtle Effect - Blue, Accent 1* option (second column, fourth row).
   i. Click the Shape Effects button in the Shape Styles group, point to *Bevel*, and then click the *Soft Round* option (second column, second row in the *Bevel* section).
6. Insert text in the arrow by completing the following steps:
   a. With the arrow selected, type Plant 3, press the Enter key, and then type 48%.
   b. Click the HOME tab, click the Align Text button in the Paragraph group, and then click the *Top* option at the drop-down list.

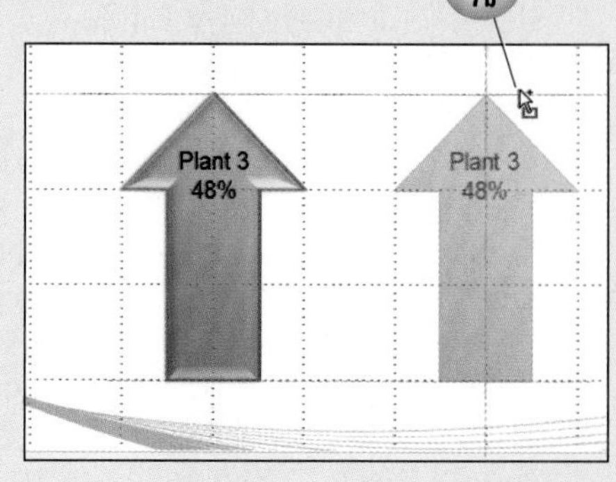

7. Copy the arrow by completing the following steps:
   a. Position the mouse pointer on the border of the selected arrow until the mouse pointer displays with a four-headed arrow attached.
   b. Hold down the Ctrl key and drag the arrow to the right so the tip of the arrow is positioned at the intersection of the horizontal and vertical drawing guides.

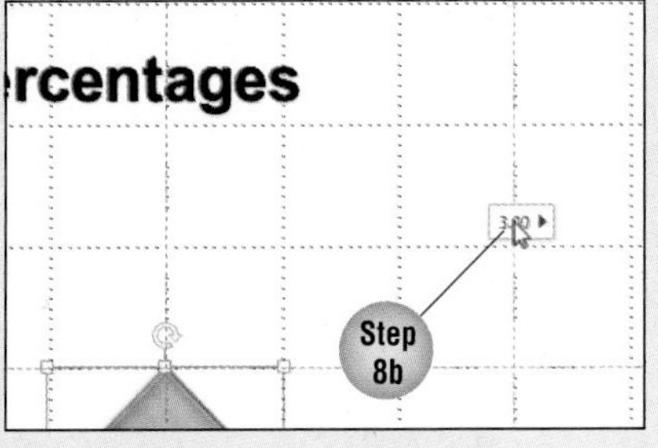

8. Move the vertical drawing guide and then copy the arrow by completing the following steps:
   a. Click outside the arrow to deselect the arrow.
   b. Position the mouse pointer on the vertical drawing guide, hold down the left mouse button, drag right until the mouse pointer displays with *3.00* and a right-pointing arrow in a box, and then release the mouse button.

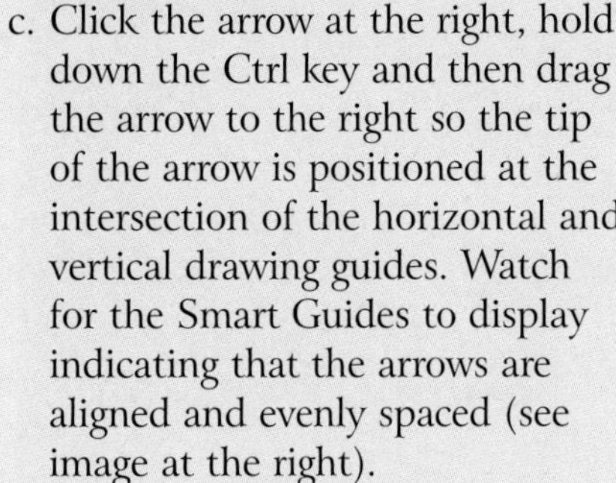

   c. Click the arrow at the right, hold down the Ctrl key and then drag the arrow to the right so the tip of the arrow is positioned at the intersection of the horizontal and vertical drawing guides. Watch for the Smart Guides to display indicating that the arrows are aligned and evenly spaced (see image at the right).

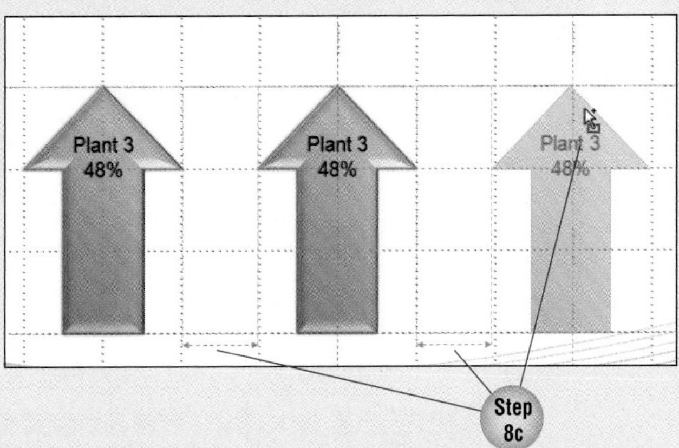

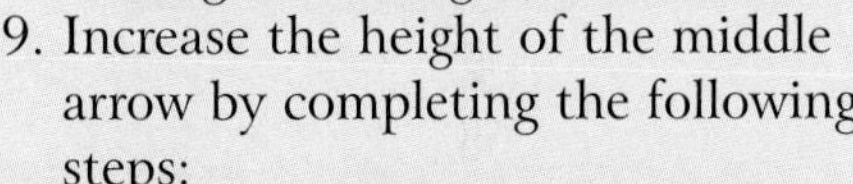

9. Increase the height of the middle arrow by completing the following steps:

   a. Click the middle arrow to select it.

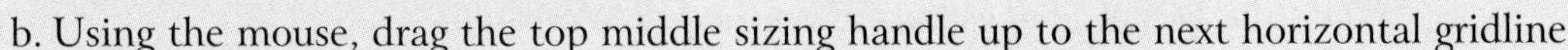

   b. Using the mouse, drag the top middle sizing handle up to the next horizontal gridline.

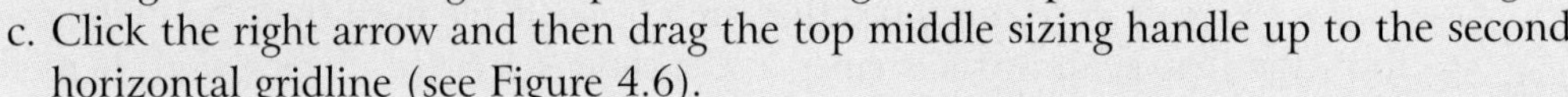

   c. Click the right arrow and then drag the top middle sizing handle up to the second horizontal gridline (see Figure 4.6).
   d. Change the text in the middle arrow to *Plant 1 72%* and change the text in the arrow at the right to *Plant 2 91%* (see Figure 4.6).
10. Turn on the snap-to-grid feature and turn off the gridlines and drawing guides by completing the following steps:
    a. Click the VIEW tab.
    b. Click the Show group dialog box launcher.
    c. At the Grid and Guides dialog box, click the *Snap objects to grid* check box to insert a check mark.
    d. Click the *Display grid on screen* option to remove the check mark.
    e. Click the *Display drawing guides on screen* check box to remove the check mark.
    f. Click OK.
11 Change the slide layout by clicking the HOME tab, clicking the Layout button in the Slides group, and then clicking the *Title Only* layout.
12. Set the formatting of the arrow shape as the default by completing the following steps:
    a. Click the first arrow shape.
    b. Position the mouse pointer on the arrow shape border until the pointer displays with a four-headed arrow attached and then click the right mouse button.
    c. Click the *Set as Default Shape* option at the shortcut menu.
13. Draw a shape by completing the following steps:
    a. Click the INSERT tab, click the Shapes button, and then click the Bevel shape (first option, third row in the *Basic Shapes* section).
    b. Click in the lower right corner of the slide.
    c. Change the height and width of the shape to 0.6 inch.
    d. Type **AI** in the shape.
    e. Position the shape in the slide as shown in Figure 4.6.
14. Save **P-C4-P1-AddisonReport.pptx**.

Figure 4.6 Project 1d, Slide 4

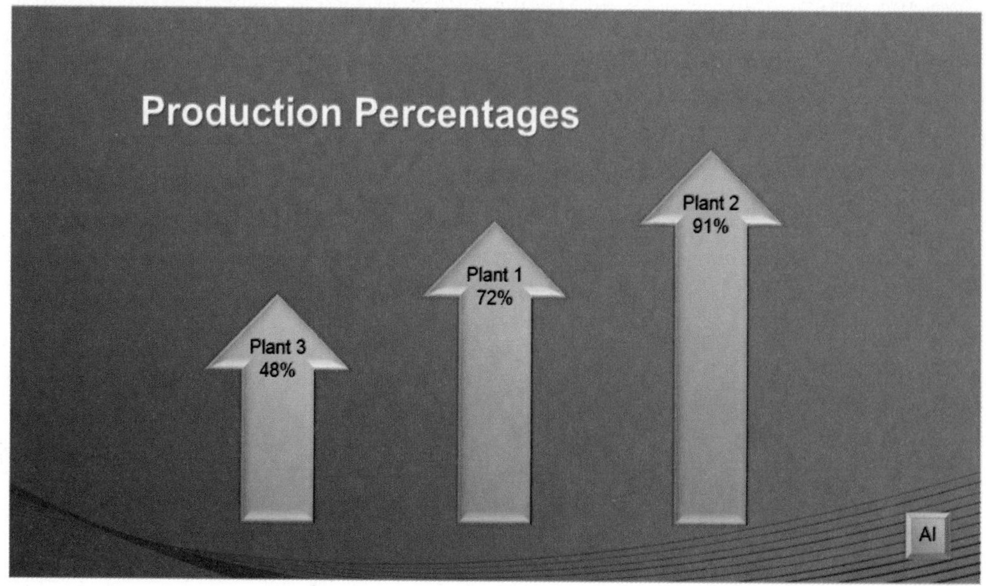

Merging Shapes

Merge Shapes

Use the Merge Shapes button on the DRAWING TOOLS FORMAT tab to merge shapes to create custom shapes that are not available with the default shapes. To merge shapes, draw the shapes in the slide, select the shapes, and then click the Merge Shapes button in the Insert Shapes group on the DRAWING TOOLS FORMAT tab. At the drop-down list that displays, choose one of the options. The options include *Union*, *Combine*, *Fragment*, *Intersect*, and *Subtract*. Each option merges the cells in a different manner.

Project 1e Merging Shapes — Part 5 of 14

1. With **P-C4-P1-AddisonReport.pptx** open, make Slide 4 active and then insert a slide from another presentation by completing the following steps:
   a. Make the HOME tab active.
   b. Click the New Slide button arrow and then click *Reuse Slides* at the drop-down list.
   c. At the Reuse Slides task pane, click the Browse button and then click *Browse File* at the drop-down list.
   d. At the Browse dialog box, navigate to the PC4 folder on your storage medium and then double-click ***IEC.pptx***.
   e. Click the second slide thumbnail in the Reuse Slides task pane.
   f. Close the Reuse Slides task pane by clicking the Close button in the upper right corner of the task pane.

2. The slide you inserted contains a circle shape and four rectangle shapes already drawn for you. Merge the shapes to create an image for the International Energy Consortium by completing the following steps:
   a. Click the slide in the slide pane and then press Ctrl + A to select all of the shapes in the slide.
   b. Click the DRAWING TOOLS FORMAT tab.
   c. Click the Merge Shapes button in the Insert Shapes group.
   d. Hover your mouse over each option in the drop-down list, notice how the option merges the shapes in the slide, and then click the *Subtract* option. (This merges the shapes into one shape.)

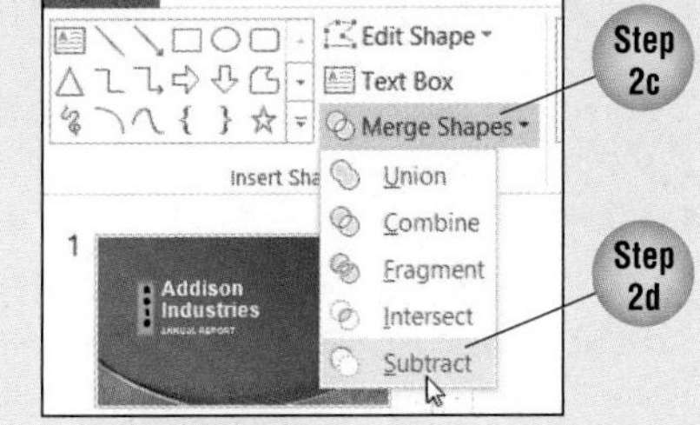

3. Apply formatting to the shape and type text in the shape by completing the following steps:
   a. Click the Shape Fill button arrow in the Shape Styles group and then click the *White, Text 1* option (second column, first row in the *Theme Colors* section).
   b. Click the Text Fill button arrow in the WordArt Styles group and then click the *Black, Background 1* option (first column, first row in the *Theme Colors* section).
   c. Type the following in the shape pressing the Enter key to end the lines as shown:

      International Energy
      Consortium
      Global Summit
      March 10 to 12, 2016
      Paris, France

   d. Select the text you just typed and then change the font size to 20 points.
4. Save **P-C4-P1-AddisonReport.pptx**.

Grouping/Ungrouping Objects

If you want to apply the same formatting or make the same adjustments to the size or rotation of objects, group the objects. If you group objects and then apply formatting such as a shape fill, effect, or shape style, the formatting is applied to each object within the group. With objects grouped, you can apply formatting more quickly to objects in the slide. To group objects, select the objects you want included in the group by clicking each object while holding down the Shift key or draw a border around the objects you want to include. With the objects selected, click the DRAWING TOOLS FORMAT tab, click the Group button in the Arrange group, and then click *Group* at the drop-down list.

An individual object within a group can be formatted. To do this, click any object in the group and the group border displays around the objects. Click the individual object and then apply the desired formatting. If you no longer want objects grouped, click the group to select it, click the DRAWING TOOLS FORMAT tab, click the Group button in the Arrange group, and then click *Ungroup* at the drop-down list.

Quick Steps

Group Objects
1. Select desired objects.
2. Click DRAWING TOOLS FORMAT tab.
3. Click Group button.
4. Click *Group* at drop-down list.

Group

Group objects so you can move, size, flip, or rotate objects at one time.

Project 1f Grouping and Formatting Objects

Part 6 of 14

1. With **P-C4-P1-AddisonReport.pptx** open, make Slide 3 active.
2. Group the objects and apply formatting by completing the following steps:
   a. Using the mouse, draw a border around the two text boxes in the slide to select them.
   b. Click the DRAWING TOOLS FORMAT tab.
   c. Click the Group button in the Arrange group and then click *Group* at the drop-down list.

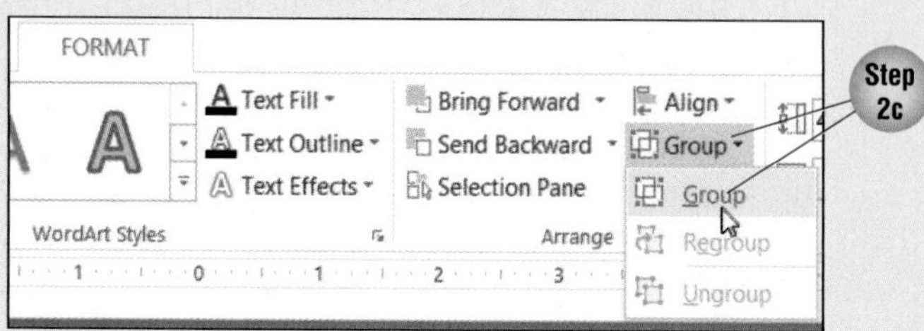

   d. Click the More button at the right side of the shape style thumbnails in the Shape Styles group and then click the *Subtle Effect - Blue, Accent 1* option at the drop-down gallery (second column, fourth row).
   e. Click the Shape Outline button arrow and then click the *Dark Blue* color (ninth color in the *Standard Colors* section.
   f. Click the Shape Outline button arrow, point to *Weight*, and then click *4½ pt*.
3. With the text boxes selected, ungroup the text boxes by clicking the Group button in the Arrange group and then clicking *Ungroup* at the drop-down list.
4. Click the text box containing the columns of text, click the More button at the right side of the WordArt style thumbnails, and then click the *Fill - White, Text 1, Outline - Background 1, Hard Shadow - Background 1* option (first column, third row).
5. Click Slide 1, click the text box containing *2016*, click the Quick Styles button in the Drawing group on the HOME tab, and then click the *Subtle Effect - Blue, Accent 1* option at the drop-down gallery (second column, fourth row).
6. Save **P-C4-P1-AddisonReport.pptx**.

Inserting an Image

Quick Steps

Insert a Picture
1. Click INSERT tab.
2. Click Pictures button.
3. Navigate to desired folder.
4. Double-click desired picture.

Pictures

Insert a picture from your camera by downloading the picture to your computer and then copying the picture into PowerPoint.

Insert an image such as a picture or clip art in a slide with buttons in the Images group on the INSERT tab. To insert a picture in a presentation, click the INSERT tab and then click the Pictures button in the Images group. At the Insert Picture dialog box, navigate to the folder containing the desired picture and then double-click the picture. Use buttons on the PICTURE TOOLS FORMAT tab to format and customize the picture.

Customizing and Formatting an Image

When you insert an image in a slide, the image is selected and the PICTURE TOOLS FORMAT tab is active as shown in Figure 4.7. Use buttons on this tab to apply formatting to the image. Use options in the Adjust group on the PICTURE TOOLS FORMAT tab to remove unwanted portions of the image, correct the brightness and contrast, change the image color, apply artistic effects, compress the size of the image file, change to a different image, and reset the image back to the original formatting.

Use buttons in the Picture Styles group to apply a predesigned style to the image, change the image border, or apply other effects to the image. With options in the Arrange group, you can position the image on the page, specify how text will wrap around it, align the image with other elements in the document, and rotate the image. Use options in the Size group to crop the image and change the size of the image.

Figure 4.7 PICTURE TOOLS FORMAT Tab

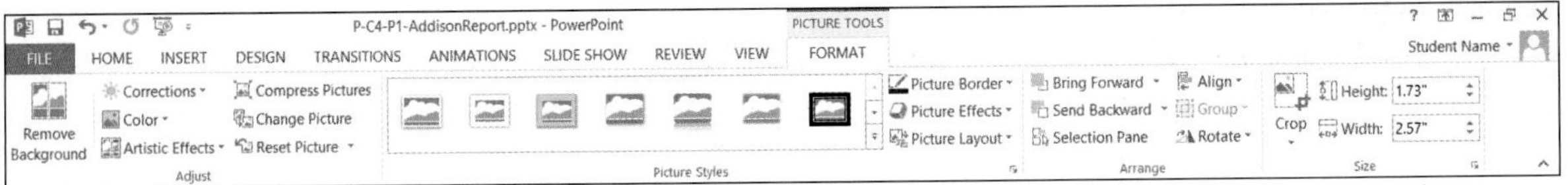

Sizing, Cropping, and Moving an Image

Change the size of an image with the *Shape Height* and *Shape Width* measurement boxes in the Size group on the PICTURE TOOLS FORMAT tab or with the sizing handles that display around the selected image. To change size with a sizing handle, position the mouse pointer on a sizing handle until the pointer turns into a double-headed arrow and then hold down the left mouse button. Drag the sizing handle in or out to decrease or increase the size of the image and then release the mouse button. Use the middle sizing handles at the left or right side of the image to make the image wider or thinner. Use the middle sizing handles at the top or bottom of the image to make the image taller or shorter. Use the sizing handles at the corners of the image to change both the width and height at the same time.

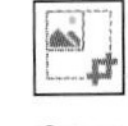
Crop

The Size group on the PICTURE TOOLS FORMAT tab contains a Crop button. Use this button to remove portions of an image. Click the Crop button and the mouse pointer displays with the crop tool attached, which is a black square with overlapping lines, and the image displays with cropping handles around the border. Drag a cropping handle to remove a portion of the image.

Move a selected image by dragging it to the desired location. Move the image by positioning the mouse pointer on the image border until the arrow pointer turns into a four-headed arrow. Hold down the left mouse button, drag the image to the desired position, and then release the mouse button. You can use the arrow keys on the keyboard to move the image in the desired direction. If you want to move the image in small increments (called ***nudging***), hold down the Ctrl key while pressing an arrow key.

Use the rotation handle to rotate an image by positioning the mouse pointer on the white, round rotation handle until the pointer displays as a circular arrow. Hold down the left mouse button, drag in the desired direction, and then release the mouse button.

Arranging Images

Bring Forward

Send Backward

Use the Bring Forward and Send Backward buttons in the Arrange group on the DRAWING TOOLS FORMAT tab or the PICTURE TOOLS FORMAT tab to layer one object on top of another. Click the Bring Forward button and the selected object is moved forward one layer. For example, if you have three objects layered on top of each other, selecting the object at the bottom of the layers and then clicking the Bring Forward button will move the object in front of the second object (but not the first object). If you want to move an object to the top layer, select the object, click the Bring Forward button arrow, and then click the *Bring to Front* option at the drop-down list. To move the selected object back one layer, click the Send Backward button. If you want to move the selected object behind all other objects, click the Send Backward button arrow and then click the *Send to Back* option at the drop-down list.

Project 1g Inserting and Formatting Pictures Part 7 of 14

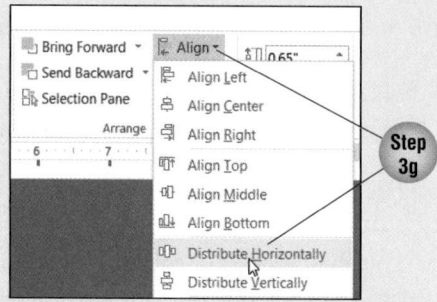

1. With **P-C4-P1-AddisonReport.pptx** open, make Slide 4 active and click the INSERT tab.
2. Insert a new slide by clicking the New Slide button arrow in the Slides group and then clicking *Blank* at the drop-down list.
3. Insert a text box by completing the following steps:
   a. Click the Text Box button in the Text group on the INSERT tab.
   b. Click in the middle of the slide.
   c. Change the font to Arial Black and the font size to 36 points.
   d. Click the Center button in the Paragraph group.
   e. Type Alternative, press the Enter key, and then type Energy Resources.
   f. With the text box selected, click the DRAWING TOOLS FORMAT tab.
   g. Click the Align button in the Arrange group and then click *Distribute Horizontally* at the drop-down list.
   h. Click the Align button and then click *Distribute Vertically* at the drop-down list.
4. Insert a picture by completing the following steps:
   a. Click the INSERT tab.
   b. Click the Pictures button in the Images group.
   c. At the Insert Picture dialog box, navigate to the PC4 folder on your storage medium and then double-click ***Mountain.jpg***.
5. You decide to insert a picture of the ocean rather than a mountain. Change the picture by completing the following steps:
   a. With the image of the mountain selected, click the Change Picture button in the Adjust group.
   b. At the Insert Pictures window that displays, click the Browse button located to the right of the *From a file* option.
   c. At the Insert Picture dialog box, make sure the PC4 folder on your storage medium is selected and then double-click ***Ocean.jpg***.
6. Crop the picture and then crop the picture to a shape by completing the following steps:
   a. With the picture selected, click the Crop button in the Size group on the PICTURE TOOLS FORMAT tab.
   b. Position the mouse pointer (displays with the crop tool attached) on the cropping handle in the middle of the right side of the picture.
   c. Hold down the left mouse button and then drag to the left approximately 0.25 inch. (Use the guideline that displays on the horizontal ruler to crop the picture 0.25 inch.)
   d. Click the Crop button to turn off cropping.

e. Click the Crop button arrow, point to the *Crop to Shape* option at the drop-down list, and then click the Oval shape (first option) in the *Basic Shapes* section of the side menu.
7. Click in the *Shape Height* measurement box in the Size group, type 5, and then press Enter.
8. Click the Send Backward button in the Arrange group. (This moves the picture behind the text in the text box.)
9. Align the picture by completing the following steps:
   a. Click the Align button in the Arrange group on the PICTURE TOOLS FORMAT tab and then click the *Distribute Horizontally* option.
   b. Click the Align button and then click the *Distribute Vertically* option.
10. Format the picture by completing the following steps:
    a. Click the Artistic Effects button in the Adjust group and then click the *Cutout* option (first column, bottom row).
    b. Click the Corrections button in the Adjust group and then click the *Soften: 25%* option (second option in the *Sharpen/Soften* section).

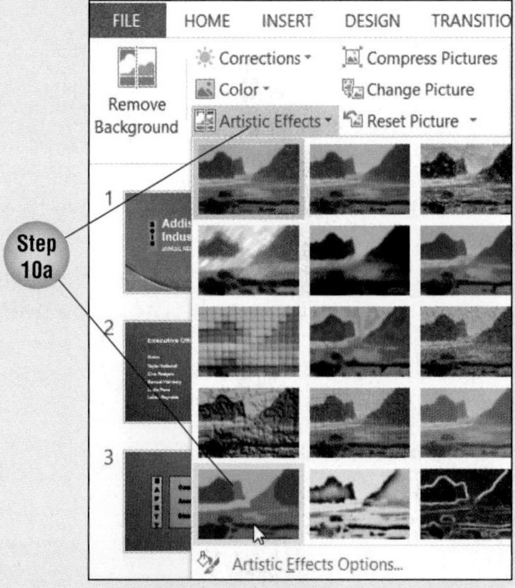

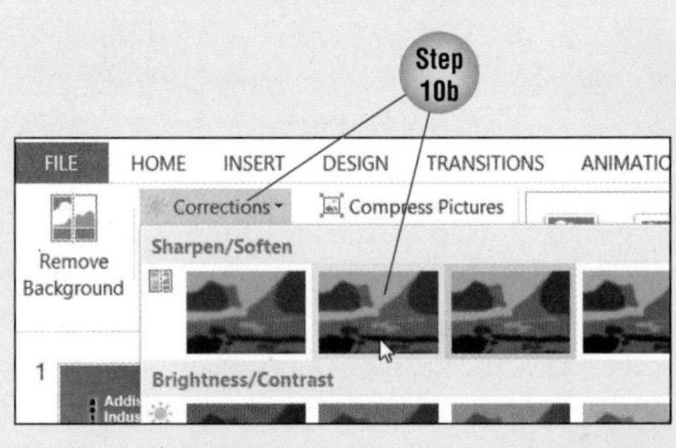

    c. Click the Picture Border button arrow in the Picture Styles group and then click the *Dark Blue* color (ninth option in the *Standard Colors* section).
11. After viewing the effects applied to the picture, reset the picture to the original effects by clicking the Reset Picture button arrow in the Adjust group and then clicking *Reset Picture* at the drop-down list.

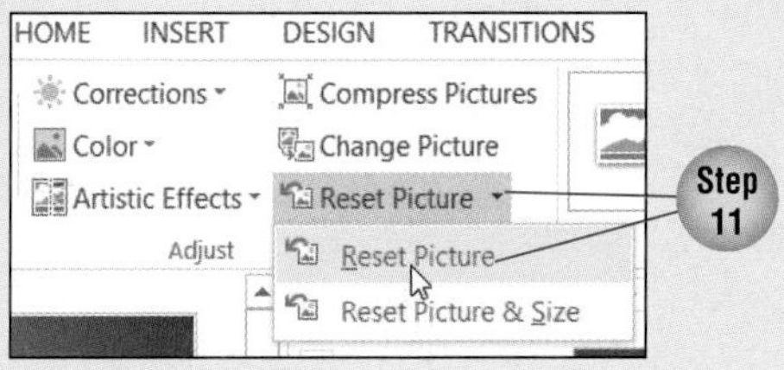

12. Format the picture by completing the following steps:
    a. Click the Corrections button in the Adjust group and then click the *Brightness: -20% Contrast: +40%* option (second column, bottom row in the *Brightness/Contrast* section).
    b. Click the Corrections button and then click the *Sharpen: 25%* option (fourth option in the *Sharpen/Soften* section).
    c. Click the More button that displays at the right side of the picture style thumbnails and then click the *Soft Edge Oval* option at the drop-down gallery (sixth column, third row).

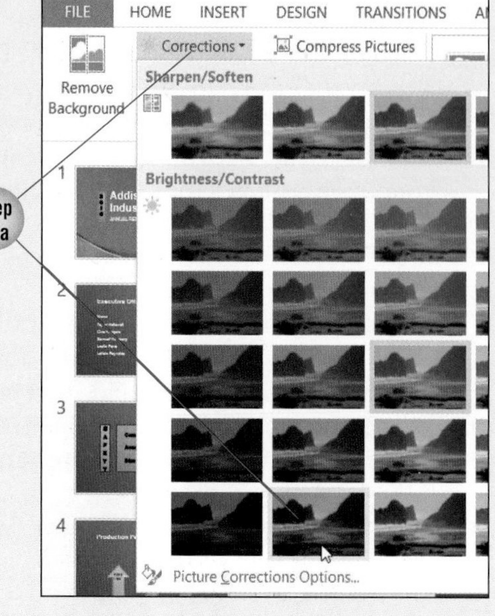

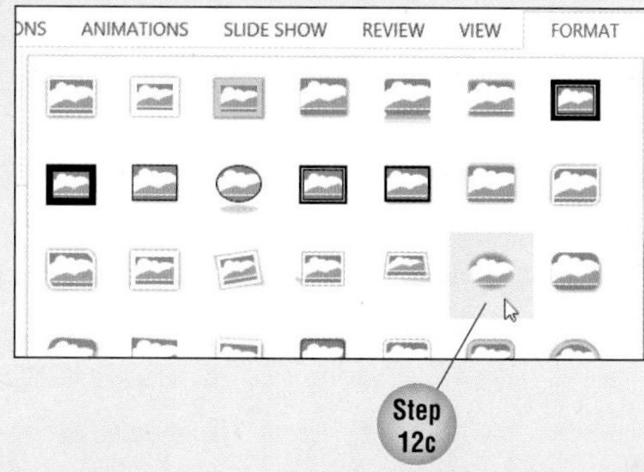

    d. Click the Compress Pictures button in the Adjust group. At the Compress Pictures dialog box, click OK.
13. Make Slide 6 active and then insert a new slide by clicking the HOME tab, clicking the New Slide button arrow in the Slides group, and then clicking *Title Only* at the drop-down list.
14. Click in the title placeholder and then type **Shipping Contracts**.
15. Insert a picture by completing the following steps:
    a. Click the INSERT tab and then click the Pictures button in the Images group.
    b. At the Insert Picture dialog box, make sure the PC4 folder on your storage medium is active and then double-click ***Ship.jpg***.
16. With the ship picture selected, remove some of the background by completing the following steps:
    a. Click the Remove Background button in the Adjust group on the PICTURE TOOLS FORMAT tab.
    b. Using the left middle sizing handle, drag the border to the left to include the back of the ship (see image at the right).
    c. Click the Mark Areas to Remove button in the Refine group on the BACKGROUND REMOVAL tab.
    d. Click anywhere in the water that displays below the ship. (This removes the water from the picture. If all of the water is not removed, you will need to click again in the remaining water.)

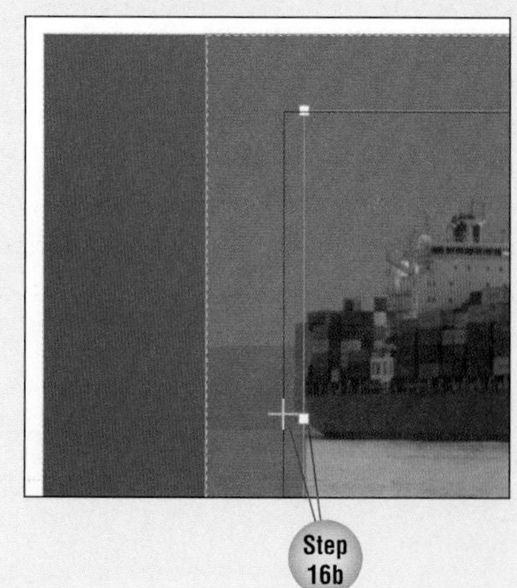

e. Using the right middle sizing handle, drag the border to the left so the border is near the front of the ship.
f. If part of the structure above the front of the ship has been removed, include it in the picture. To begin, click the Mark Areas to Keep button in the Refine group. (The mouse pointer displays as a pencil.)
g. Using the mouse, position the pencil at the top of the structure (as shown at the right), drag down to the top of the containers on the ship, and then release the mouse button.
h. Click the Keep Changes button in the Close group on the BACKGROUND REMOVAL tab.

Step 16g

17. Click the Corrections button in the Adjust group on the PICTURE TOOLS FORMAT tab and then click the *Brightness: +40% Contrast: +40%* option at the drop-down gallery (last column, bottom row in the *Brightness/Contrast* section).
18. Click the Corrections button in the Adjust group and then click the *Sharpen: 50%* option at the drop-down gallery (last option in the *Sharpen/Soften* section).
19. Drag the picture down to the middle of the slide.
20. Click outside the picture to deselect it.
21. Save **P-C4-P1-AddisonReport.pptx**.

Inserting a Picture as a Slide Background

A picture can be inserted as a slide background. To do this, click the DESIGN tab and then click the Format Background button in the Customize group. This displays the Format Background task pane with the Fill icon selected. Click the *Picture or texture fill* option in the FILL section of the task pane and then click the File button. At the Insert Picture dialog box, navigate to the desired folder and then double-click the picture. Click the Close button to close the Format Background task pane. If you want the picture background to display on all slides, click the Apply to All button at the Format Background task pane.

Use options in the Format Background task pane to apply formatting to the background picture. When you insert a picture in a slide, the Format Background task pane (with the Fill icon selected) includes options for hiding background graphics, applying a texture, changing the picture transparency, and offsetting the image on the slide either at the left, right, top, or bottom. Click the Effects icon and then click the Artistic Effects button and a drop-down palette of artistic options displays. Click the Picture icon and options display in the task pane for correcting the sharpness, softness, brightness, and contrast of the picture and for changing the picture color saturation and tone.

Quick Steps

Insert a Picture as a Slide Background
1. Click DESIGN tab.
2. Click Format Background button.
3. Click *Picture or texture fill* option.
4. Click File button.
5. Navigate to desired folder.
6. Double-click desired picture.
7. Click Close button.

Project 1h Inserting a Picture as a Slide Background

Part 8 of 14

1. With **P-C4-P1-AddisonReport.pptx** open, make sure both Slide 7 and the HOME tab are active.
2. Click the New Slide button arrow in the Slides group and then click the *Title Only* layout at the drop-down list.
3. Insert a picture background on Slide 8 by completing the following steps:
   a. Click the DESIGN tab.
   b. Click the Format Background button in the Customize group.
   c. At the Format Background task pane, click the *Picture or texture fill* option in the FILL section.
   d. Click the File button in the task pane that displays below the text *Insert picture from*.
   e. At the Insert Picture dialog box, navigate to the PC4 folder on your storage medium and then double-click ***EiffelTower.jpg***.
4. Apply formatting to the picture background by completing these steps:
   a. Click the *Hide background graphics* check box to insert a check mark.
   b. Select the current percentage in the *Transparency* measurement box, type 5, and then press Enter.
   c. Select the current number in the *Offset top* measurement box, type -50, and then press Enter. (Decreasing the negative number displays more of the top of the Eiffel Tower.)
   d. Click the Effects icon in the task pane and then, if necessary, click ARTISTIC EFFECTS to display the formatting options.
   e. Click the Artistic Effects button and then click the *Glow Diffused* option (fourth column, second row).

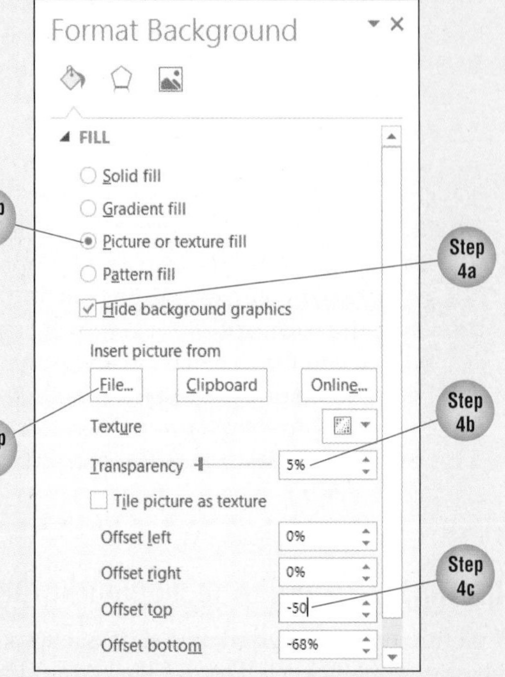

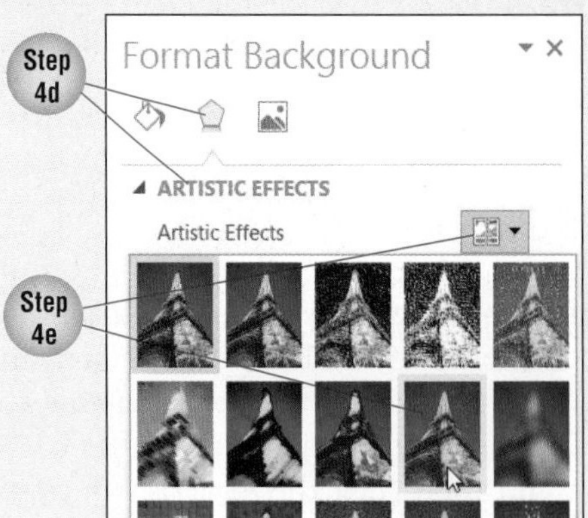

f. Click the Picture icon and, if necessary, expand the *PICTURE CORRECTIONS* section.
g. Select the current number in the *Contrast* text box, type 25, and then press Enter.
h. If necessary, expand the *PICTURE COLOR* section.
i. Select the current number in the *Saturation* measurement box, type 80, and then press Enter.

5. Remove the artistic effect by clicking the Effects icon, clicking the Artistic Effects button, and then clicking the *None* option (first option).
6. Close the Format Background task pane.
7. Click in the title placeholder, type **European**, press Enter, and then type **Division 2017**. Drag the placeholder so it is positioned attractively on the slide in the upper left corner.
8. Save **P-C4-P1-AddisonReport.pptx**.

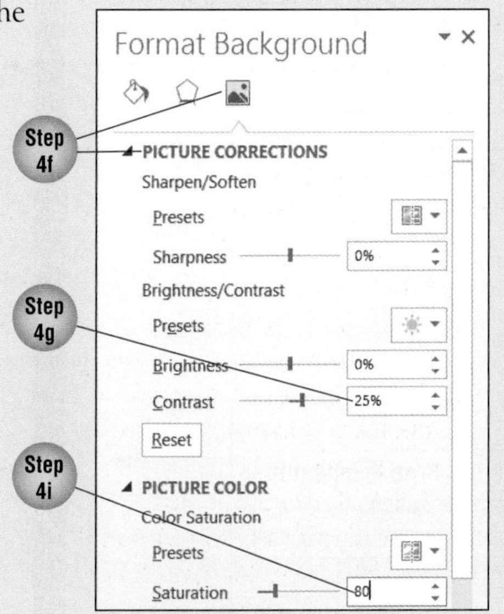

Inserting an Image from Office.com

Microsoft Office includes a gallery of media images you can insert in a slide, such as clip art images and photographs. To insert an image in a presentation, click the INSERT tab and then click the Online Pictures button in the Images group. This displays the Insert Pictures window, as shown in Figure 4.8 on the next page.

At the Insert Pictures window, click in the search text box to the right of Office.com Clip Art, type the search term or topic, and then press Enter. Images that match your search term or topic display in the window. To insert an image, click the desired image and then click the Insert button or double-click the image. This downloads the image from the Office.com website to your slide.

When you insert an image in a slide, the image is selected and the PICTURE TOOLS FORMAT tab is active. Use buttons on this tab to customize an image just as you customize a picture.

Quick Steps

Insert Images from Office.com

1. Click INSERT tab.
2. Click Online Pictures button.
3. Type search word or topic.
4. Press Enter.
5. Double-click desired image.

Online Pictures

For additional clip art images, consider buying a commercial package of images.

Figure 4.8 Insert Pictures Window

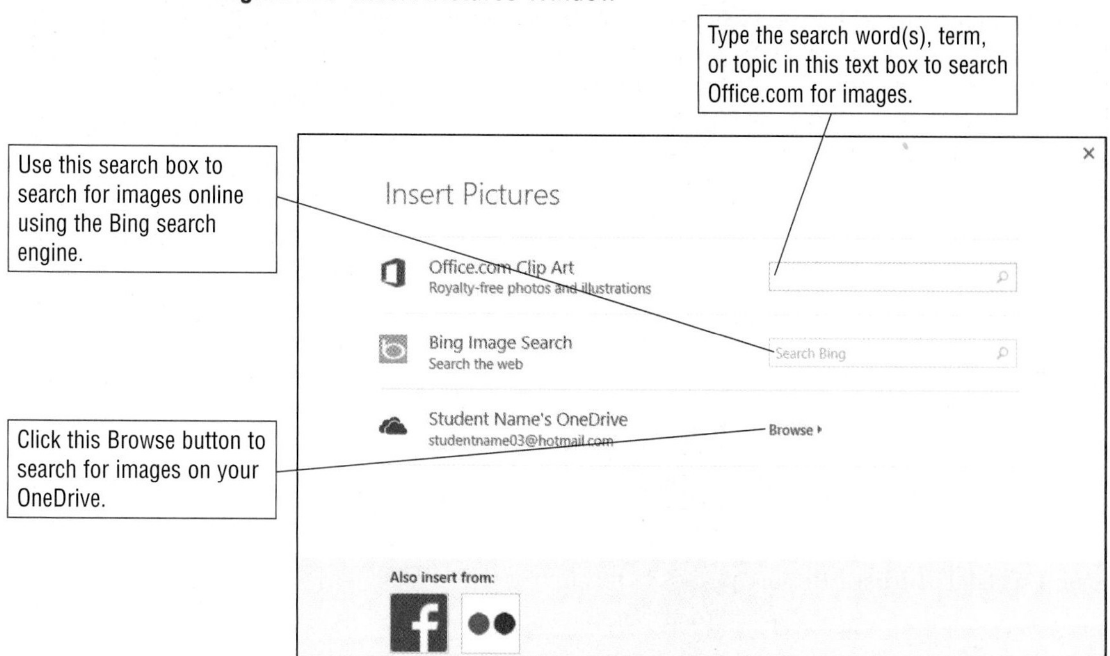
Type the search word(s), term, or topic in this text box to search Office.com for images.
Use this search box to search for images online using the Bing search engine.
Click this Browse button to search for images on your OneDrive.
Insert Pictures
Office.com Clip Art
Royalty-free photos and illustrations
Bing Image Search
Search the web
Search Bing
Student Name's OneDrive
studentname03@hotmail.com
Browse
Also insert from:

Sizing, Rotating, and Positioning Objects

Shape Height

Shape Width

PowerPoint provides a variety of methods for sizing and positioning an object such as a shape, text box, or image on a slide. As you learned earlier in this chapter, you can use the sizing handles that display around an object and use the *Shape Height* and *Shape Width* measurement boxes to increase or decrease the size of an object. You positioned shapes and text boxes by dragging the objects with the mouse. You also used options at the Format Shape task pane with the Size & Properties icon selected to size and position a shape and a text box. You can size and position an image in a similar manner using options at the Format Picture task pane with the Size & Properties icon selected. Display this task pane by selecting an image and then clicking the Size group task pane launcher location on the PICTURE TOOLS FORMAT tab.

Project 1i **Inserting and Formatting a Clip Art Image** **Part 9 of 14**

1. With **P-C4-P1-AddisonReport.pptx** open, make Slide 4 active.
2. Click the New Slide button arrow in the Slides group on the HOME tab and then click the *Two Content* layout at the drop-down list.
3. Click the placeholder text *Click to add title* and then type **Technology**.
4. Click the placeholder text *Click to add text* located at the right side of the slide.
5. Click the Bullets button in the Paragraph group to turn off bullets.
6. Change the font size to 32 points and turn on bold formatting.
7. Type **Equipment** and then press the Enter key twice.
8. Type **Software** and then press the Enter key twice.
9. Type **Personnel**.

10. Insert a clip art image by completing the following steps:
    a. Click the Online Pictures button that displays in the middle of the placeholder at the left side of the slide.
    b. At the Insert Pictures window, type **computer construction worker** in the search text box and then press Enter.

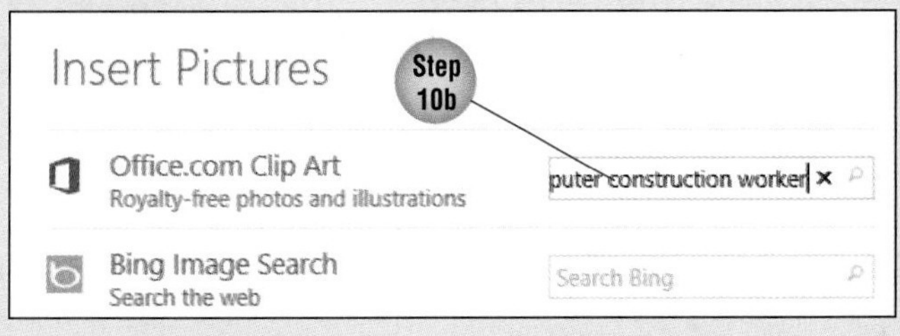

    c. Double-click the clip art image in the window as shown below and to the right.

11. Scale, rotate, and position the clip art image by completing the following steps:
    a. With the clip art image selected, click the Rotate button in the Arrange group on the PICTURE TOOLS FORMAT tab and then click *Flip Horizonal* at the drop-down list.
    b. Click the Size group task pane launcher.
    c. At the Format Picture task pane with the Size & Properties icon selected, if necessary, click *SIZE* to expand the options.
    d. Select the *0°* in the *Rotation* measurement box and then type 15.
    e. Select the current percentage in the *Scale Height* measurement box and then type 225.

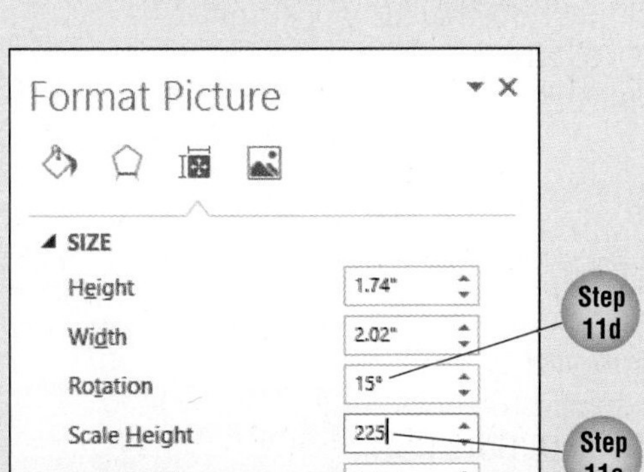

    f. Click *POSITION* to expand the options.
    g. Select the current measurement in the *Horizontal position* measurement box and then type 2.9. (The image will slightly overlap the text.).
    h. Select the current measurement in the *Vertical position* measurement box, type 2, and then press Enter.
    i. Close the Format Picture task pane.

POSITION
Horizontal position 2.9"
From Top Left Corner
Vertical position 2
From Top Left Corner
Step 11g
Step 11h

12. Save **P-C4-P1-AddisonReport.pptx**.

Copying Objects within and between Presentations

An object pasted to a different slide is positioned in the same location as the copied object.

Earlier in this chapter you learned how to copy shapes within a slide. You can also copy shapes as well as other objects to other slides within the same presentation or to slides in another presentation. To copy an object, select the object and then click the Copy button in the Clipboard group on the HOME tab. Make the desired slide active or open another presentation and display the desired slide and then click the Paste button in the Clipboard group. You can also copy an object by right-clicking the object and then clicking *Copy* at the shortcut menu. To paste the object, make the desired slide active, click the right mouse button, and then click *Paste* at the shortcut menu.

Project 1j **Copying an Object within and between Presentations** **Part 10 of 14**

1. With **P-C4-P1-AddisonReport.pptx** open, make Slide 1 active.
2. Open **Addison.pptx**.
3. Click the clip art image in Slide 1, click the Copy button in the Clipboard group, and then close **Addison.pptx**.
4. With **P-C4-P1-AddisonReport.pptx** open, click the Paste button. (This inserts the clip art image in Slide 1.)
5. With the clip art image selected, make Slide 2 active and then click the Paste button.
6. Decrease the size and position of the clip art by completing the following steps:
   a. Click the PICTURE TOOLS FORMAT tab.
   b. Click in the *Shape Height* measurement box, type **0.8**, and then press Enter.
   c. Drag the clip art image so that it is positioned in the upper right corner of the slide.

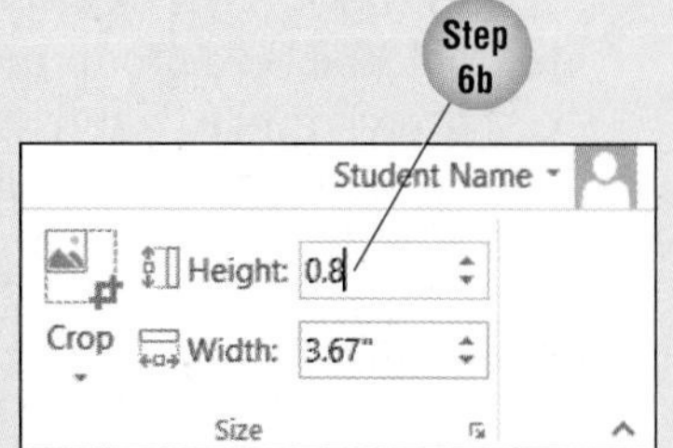

7. Copy the clip art image to other slides by completing the following steps:
   a. With the clip art image selected in Slide 2, click the HOME tab and then click the Copy button in the Clipboard group.
   b. Make Slide 3 active and then click the Paste button in the Clipboard group.
   c. Paste the clip art image to slides Slide 5 and 7.
8. Save **P-C4-P1-AddisonReport.pptx**.

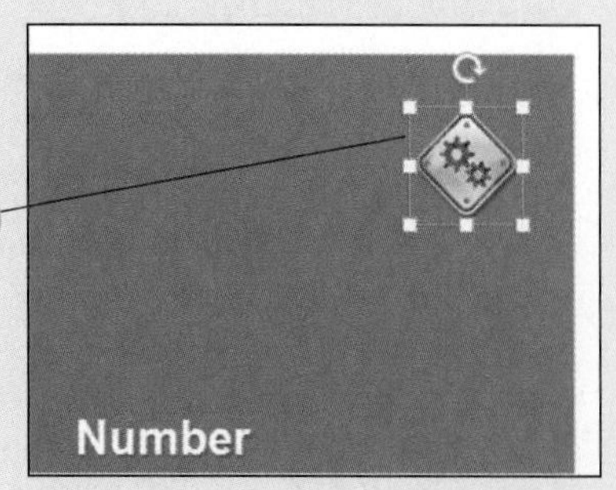

Creating Screenshots

Screenshot

The Images group on the INSERT tab contains a Screenshot button you can use to capture the contents or a portion of a screen as an image. This is useful for capturing information from a web page or from a file in another program. If you want to capture the entire screen, display the desired web page, or open the desired file from a program, make PowerPoint active, and then open a presentation. Click the INSERT tab, click the Screenshot button, and then click the desired screen thumbnail at the drop-down list. The currently active presentation does not display as a thumbnail at the drop-down list. Instead, any other file or program you have open displays. If you do not have another file or program open, the Windows desktop displays. When you click the desired thumbnail, the screenshot is inserted as an image in the active slide in the open presentation, the image is selected, and the PICTURE TOOLS FORMAT tab is active. Use buttons on this tab to customize the screenshot image.

In addition to making a screenshot of an entire screen, you can make a screenshot of a specific portion of the screen by clicking the *Screen Clipping* option at the Screenshot button drop-down list. When you click this option, the open web page, file, or Windows desktop displays in a dimmed manner and the mouse pointer displays as crosshairs. Using the mouse, draw a border around the specific area of the screen you want to capture. The specific area you identify is inserted in the active slide in the presentation as an image, the image is selected, and the PICTURE TOOLS FORMAT tab is active.

Quick Steps

Insert a Screenshot

1. Open presentation.
2. Open another file.
3. Display desired information.
4. Make presentation active.
5. Click INSERT tab.
6. Click Screenshot button.
7. Click desired window at drop-down list.

OR

6. Click Screenshot button, *Screen Clipping*.
7. Drag to specify capture area.

Project 1k **Inserting and Formatting a Screenshot** **Part 11 of 14**

1. With **P-C4-P1-AddisonReport.pptx** open, make sure that no other programs are open.
2. Make Slide 9 active and then insert a new slide by clicking the New Slide button arrow in the Slides group on the HOME tab and then clicking the *Title Only* layout.
3. Click in the title placeholder and then type **Draft Invitation**.
4. Open Word and then open the document named **AddIndInvite.docx** from the PC4 folder on your storage medium.
5. Click the PowerPoint button on the Taskbar.
6. Insert a screenshot of the draft invitation in the Word document by completing the following steps:
   a. Click the INSERT tab.
   b. Click the Screenshot button in the Images group and then click *Screen Clipping* at the drop-down list.
   c. When the **AddIndInvite.docx** document displays in a dimmed manner, position the mouse crosshairs in the upper left corner of the invitation, hold down the left mouse button, drag down to the lower right corner of the invitation, and then release the mouse button.

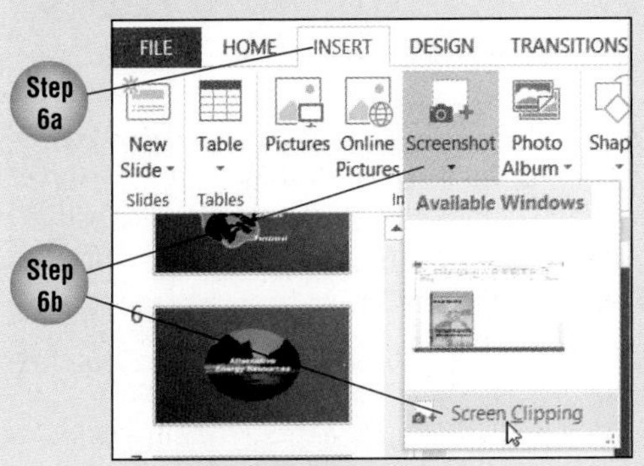

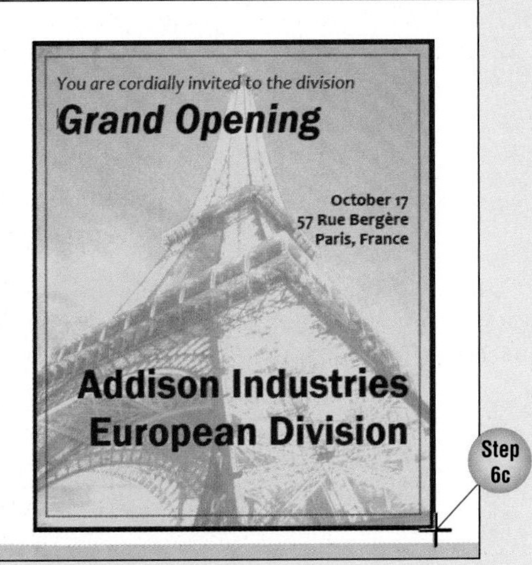

7. With the screenshot image inserted in the slide in the presentation, make the following changes:
   a. Click in the *Shape Width* measurement box in the Size group on the PICTURE TOOLS FORMAT tab, type 4.5, and then press Enter.
   b. Click the Corrections button in the Adjust group and then click the *Sharpen:25%* option (fourth option in the *Sharpen/Soften* section).
   c. Using the mouse, drag the screenshot image so it is centered on the slide.
8. Click outside the screenshot image to deselect it.
9. Save **P-C4-P1-AddisonReport.pptx**.
10. Click the Word button, close **AddIndInvite.docx**, and then close Word.

Creating and Formatting WordArt Text

Quick Steps

Create WordArt Text
1. Click INSERT tab.
2. Click WordArt button.
3. Click desired WordArt style.
4. Type WordArt text.

WordArt

Text Fill

Text Outline

Use the WordArt feature to insert preformatted, decorative text in a slide and to modify text to conform to a variety of shapes. Consider using WordArt to create a company logo, letterhead, flier title, or heading. Insert WordArt in a slide by clicking the INSERT tab and then clicking the WordArt button in the Text group. This displays the WordArt drop-down list as shown in Figure 4.10. Click the desired WordArt style at this drop-down list and a text box is inserted in the slide containing the text *Your Text Here*. Type the desired WordArt text and then use the options in the DRAWING TOOLS FORMAT tab to customize the WordArt text.

When you insert WordArt text in a document, the DRAWING TOOLS FORMAT tab is active. Use options and buttons on this tab to format the WordArt text. Use the WordArt styles to apply predesigned formatting to the WordArt text. Customize the text with the Text Fill, Text Outline, and Text Effects buttons in the WordArt Styles group. Use the Text Fill button to change the fill color, the Text Outline button to change the text outline color, and the Text Effects button to apply a variety of text effects and shapes.

Figure 4.10 WordArt Drop-down List

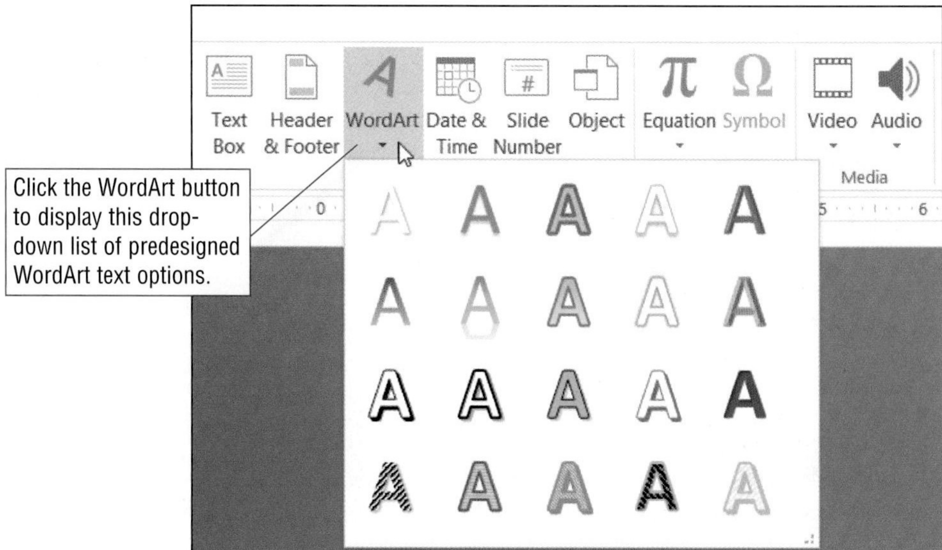

Click the Text Effects button and then point to *Transform* and a side menu displays with shaping and warping options as shown in Figure 4.11. Use these options to conform the WordArt text to a specific shape.

Text Effects

Use WordArt to create interesting text effects in slides.

Edit WordArt by double-clicking the WordArt text.

Figure 4.11 Text Effects *Transform* Side Menu

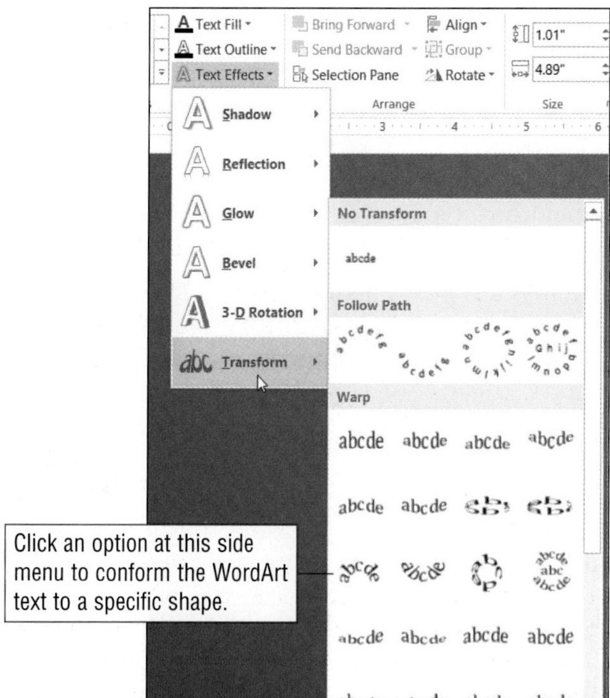

Click an option at this side menu to conform the WordArt text to a specific shape.

Project 1l Inserting and Formatting WordArt

Part 12 of 14

1. With **P-C4-P1-AddisonReport.pptx** open, make sure Slide 10 is active and the HOME tab is active.
2. Click the New Slide button arrow in the Slides group and then click the *Blank* layout.
3. Click the INSERT tab.
4. Click the WordArt button in the Text group and then click the *Fill - White, Text 1, Outline - Background 1, Hard Shadow - Accent 1* option (second column, third row).
5. Type **Addison Industries**, press the Enter key, and then type **2016**.
6. Click the WordArt text border to change the border from a dashed line to a solid line. (This selects the text box.)

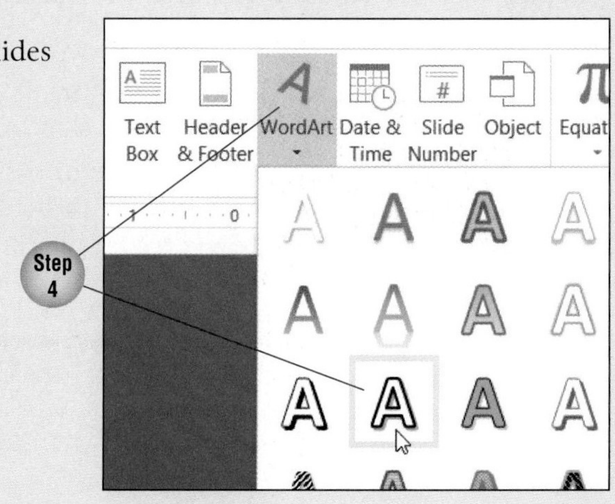

7. Click the Text Outline button arrow in the WordArt Styles group and then click the *Dark Blue* color (ninth option in the *Standard Colors* section).
8. Click the Text Effects button, point to *Glow*, and then click *Blue, 11 pt glow, Accent color 1* at the side menu (first column, third row in the *Glow Variations* section).
9. Click the Text Effects button, point to *Transform*, and then click the *Triangle Up* option (third column, first row in the *Warp* section).
10. Click in the *Shape Height* measurement box, type 5, and then press Enter.
11. Click in the *Shape Width* measurement box, type 10, and then press Enter.
12. Click the Align button in the Arrange group and then click *Distribute Horizontally*.
13. Click the Align button and then click *Distribute Vertically*.
14. Save **P-C4-P1-AddisonReport.pptx**.

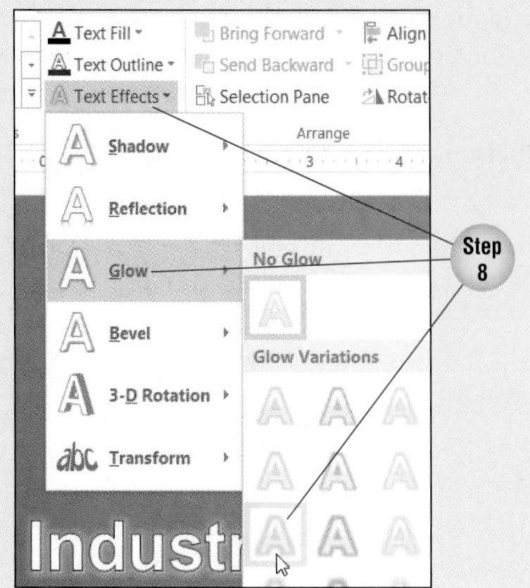

Inserting Symbols

Symbol

Insert symbols in a slide in a presentation with options at the Symbol dialog box. Display this dialog box by clicking the Symbol button in the Symbols group on the INSERT tab. At the Symbol dialog box, choose a symbol font with the *Font* option in the dialog box, click the desired symbol in the list box, click the Insert button, and then click the Close button. The symbol is inserted in the slide at the location of the insertion point.

Project 1m Inserting Symbols in a Presentation — Part 13 of 14

1. With **P-C4-P1-AddisonReport.pptx** open, insert a symbol by completing the following steps:
   a. Make Slide 2 active.
   b. Click in the text box containing the names, titles, and telephone numbers. (This selects the text box.)
   c. Delete the *n* in *Pena* (the last name of the fourth person).
   d. Click the INSERT tab and then click the Symbol button in the Symbols group.

e. At the Symbol dialog box, click the down-pointing arrow at the right side of the *Font* option box, scroll down the drop-down list to the *Century Gothic* option, and then click the option.
f. Scroll down the symbol list box and then click the ñ symbol (located in approximately the ninth, tenth, or eleventh row).
g. Click the Insert button and then click the Close button.

2. Save **P-C4-P1-AddisonReport.pptx**.

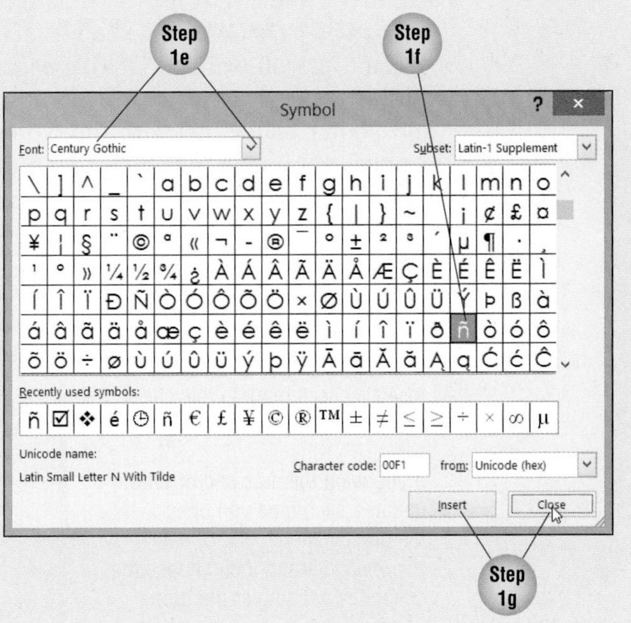

Inserting Headers and Footers

As you learned in Chapter 1, if you print a presentation as a handout or an outline, PowerPoint will automatically print the current date in the upper right corner of the page and the page number in the lower right corner. If you print the presentation as notes pages, PowerPoint will automatically print the page number when you print the individual slides. The date and page numbers are considered header and footer elements. You can modify existing header and footer elements or insert additional elements with options in the Header and Footer dialog box. Display the Header and Footer dialog box shown in Figure 4.12 by clicking the Header & Footer button in the Text group on the INSERT tab, clicking the Date & Time button in the Text group, or clicking the Slide Number button in the Text group. You can also display the Header and Footer dialog box by displaying the Print backstage area and then clicking the Edit Header & Footer hyperlink that displays below the galleries in the *Settings* category.

Header & Footer

Slide Number

The Header and Footer dialog box has two tabs, the Slide tab and the Notes and Handouts tab, and the options in the dialog box are similar with either tab selected. With options at the dialog box, you can insert the date and time, a header, a footer, and page numbers. If you insert the date and time in a presentation, you can choose the *Update automatically* option if you want the date and time updated each time the presentation is opened. Choose the date and time formatting by clicking the down-pointing arrow at the right side of the *Update automatically* option box and then choose the desired formatting at the drop-down list. If you choose the *Fixed* option, type the desired date and/or time in the *Fixed* text box. Type header text in the *Header* text box and type footer text in the *Footer* text box.

If you want to print the slide number on slides, insert a check mark in the *Slide number* check box in the Header and Footer dialog box with the Slide tab selected. If you want to include page numbers on handouts, notes pages, or outline pages, insert a check mark in the *Page number* check box in the Header and Footer dialog box with the Notes and Handouts tab selected. If you want all changes you make to the Header and Footer dialog box to apply to all slides or all handouts, notes pages, and outline pages, click the Apply to All button located in the lower right corner of the dialog box.

Figure 4.12 Header and Footer Dialog Box with the Notes and Handouts Tab Selected

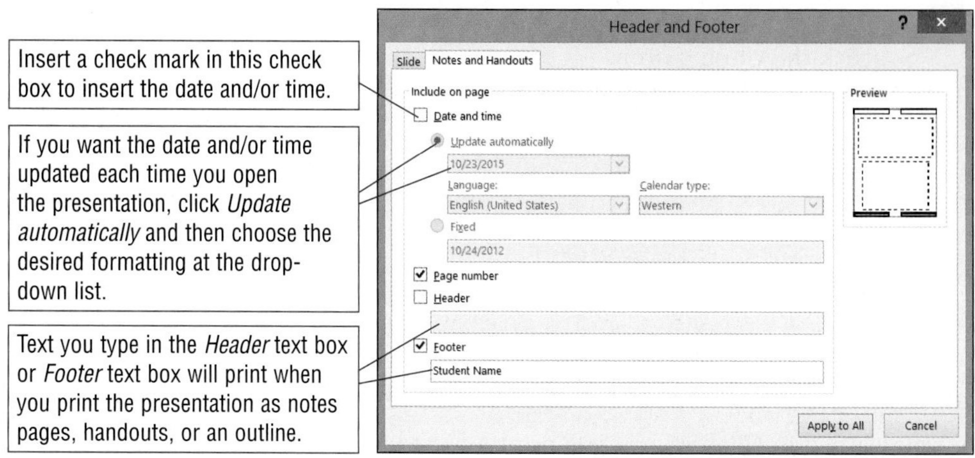

Project 1n **Inserting Headers and Footers** **Part 14 of 14**

1. With **P-C4-P1-AddisonReport.pptx** open, insert slide numbers on each slide in the presentation by completing the following steps:
   a. Make Slide 1 active.
   b. Click the INSERT tab.
   c. Click the Slide Number button in the Text group.
   d. At the Header and Footer dialog box with the Slide tab selected, click the *Slide number* check box to insert a check mark.
   e. Click the Apply to All button.
   f. Scroll through the slides and notice the slide number that displays in the lower right corner of each slide.

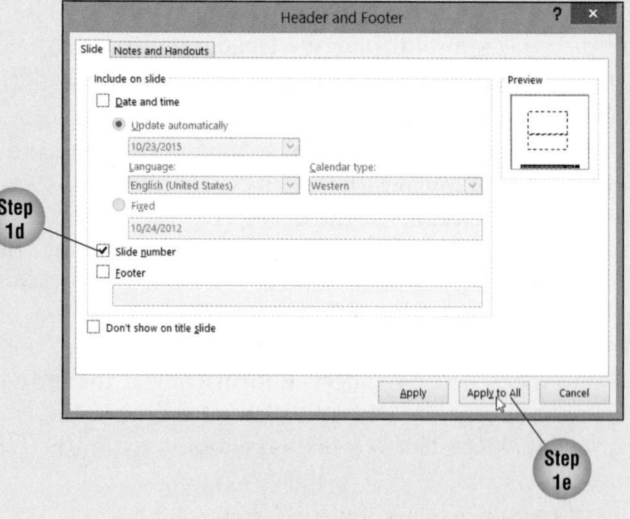

2. Insert your name as a footer that displays on each slide in the presentation by completing the following steps:
   a. Click the Header & Footer button in the Text group.

b. Click the *Footer* check box to insert a check mark, click in the *Footer* text box, and then type your first and last names.
c. Click the Apply to All button.
d. Run the presentation and notice that your name displays at the bottom left side of each slide.

3. You decide that you also want your name to print as a footer on handout pages. To do this, complete the following steps:
   a. Click the Header & Footer button in the Text group.
   b. At the Header and Footer dialog box, click the Notes and Handouts tab.
   c. Click the *Footer* check box to insert a check mark, click in the *Footer* text box, and then type your first and last names.
   d. Click the Apply to All button.
4. Insert the current date as a header that prints on handout pages by completing the following steps:
   a. Click the Date & Time button in the Text group.
   b. At the Header and Footer dialog box, click the Notes and Handouts tab.
   c. Click the *Date and time* check box to insert a check mark.
   d. Click the Apply to All button.
5. Insert the presentation name as a header that prints on handout pages by completing the following steps:
   a. Click the FILE tab and then click the *Print* option.
   b. At the Print backstage area, click the Edit Header & Footer hyperlink that displays below the galleries in the *Settings* category.
   c. At the Header and Footer dialog box, click the Notes and Handouts tab.
   d. Click the *Header* check box to insert a check mark, click in the *Header* text box, and then type **P-C4-P1-AddisonReport.pptx**.
   e. Click the Apply to All button.

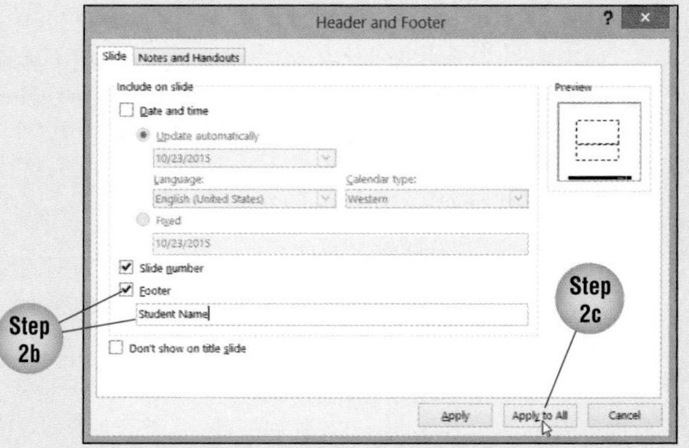

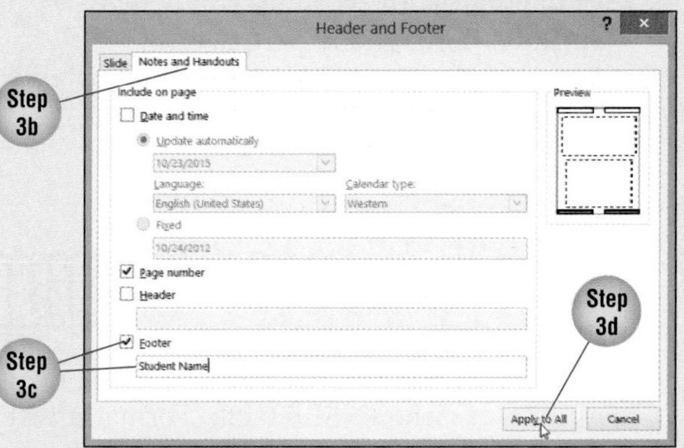

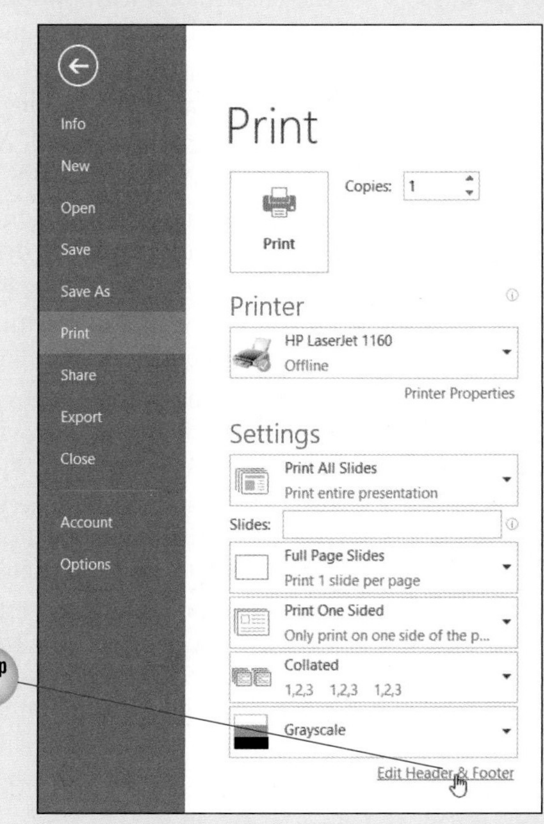

f. Click the second gallery in the *Settings* category and then click *6 Slides Horizontal* at the drop-down list. (If a number apears in the *Slides* text box, delete the number.)
g. Display the next handout page by clicking the Next Page button that displays toward the bottom of the Print backstage area.
h. Click the Previous page button to display the first handout page.
i. Click the Print button to print the presentation as a handout with six slides printed horizontally per page.

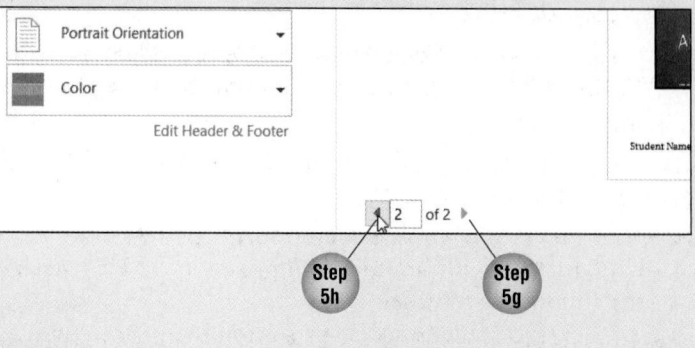

6. Save and then close **P-C4-P1-AddisonReport.pptx**.

Chapter Summary

- Insert a text box in a slide using the Text Box button in the Text group on the INSERT tab. Format a text box with options in the Drawing group on the HOME tab, with options on the DRAWING TOOLS FORMAT tab, with options at the shortcut menu, or with options at the Format Shape task pane.
- Select all objects in a slide by clicking the Select button in the Editing group on the HOME tab and then clicking *Select All* or with the keyboard shortcut, Ctrl + A.
- Align selected objects with options from the Align button in the Arrange group on the DRAWING TOOLS FORMAT tab.
- Set tabs in a text box by clicking the Alignment button at the left side of the horizontal ruler until the desired symbol displays and then clicking on a specific location on the ruler. You can set a left, center, right, or decimal tab.
- Insert a shape in a slide with shapes in the Drawing group on the HOME tab or the Shapes button in the Illustrations group on the INSERT tab.
- With options in the Shapes button drop-down list, you can draw a line, basic shapes, block arrows, flow chart symbols, callouts, stars, and banners.
- Copy a shape by selecting the shape, clicking the Copy button in the Clipboard group, positioning the insertion point in the desired position, and then clicking the Paste button in the Clipboard group. You can also copy a shape by holding down the Ctrl key and then dragging the shape to the desired location.
- Turn the horizontal and vertical rulers on and off with the *Ruler* check box in the Show group on the VIEW tab and turn gridlines on and off with the *Gridlines* check box. You can also turn gridlines as well as drawing guides and the snap-to-grid feature on and off with options at the Grid and Guides dialog box.

- You can group objects and then apply the same formatting to all objects in the group. To group objects, select the objects, click the Group button in the Arrange group on the DRAWING TOOLS FORMAT tab, and then click *Group* at the drop-down list.
- Size images with the *Shape Height* and *Shape Width* measurement boxes on the PICTURE TOOLS FORMAT tab or with the sizing handles that display around a selected image.
- Use the Crop button in the Size group on the PICTURE TOOLS FORMAT tab to remove portions of an image.
- Move an image by dragging it to the new location. Move an image in small increments, called *nudging*, by holding down the Ctrl key while pressing an arrow key on the keyboard.
- Specify how you want to layer objects with the Bring Forward and Send Backward buttons in the Adjust group on the DRAWING TOOLS FORMAT tab or the PICTURE TOOLS FORMAT tab.
- Insert a picture in a slide with the Pictures button in the Images group on the INSERT tab.
- Insert a picture as a slide background with options at the Format Background task pane. Display this task pane by clicking the Format Background button in the Customize group on the DESIGN tab.
- Insert an image from Office.com with options at the Online Pictures window. Display this window by clicking the Online Pictures button in the Images group on the INSERT tab or clicking the Online Pictures button in a layout content placeholder.
- Size objects with options at the Format Shape or Format Picture task pane with the Size & Properties icon selected.
- Use the Screenshot button in the Images group on the INSERT tab to capture the contents of a screen or capture a portion of a screen.
- Use the WordArt feature to distort or modify text to conform to a variety of shapes. Insert WordArt with the WordArt button in the Text group on the INSERT tab. Format WordArt with options on the DRAWING TOOLS FORMAT tab.
- Insert symbols in a slide with options at the Symbol dialog box. Display this dialog box by clicking the Symbol button in the Symbols group on the INSERT tab.
- Click the Header & Footer button, the Date & Time button, or the Slide Number button located in the Text group on the INSERT tab to display the Header and Footer dialog box. You can also display the dialog box by clicking the <u>Edit Header & Footer</u> hyperlink at the Print backstage area.

Commands Review

FEATURE	RIBBON TAB, GROUP	BUTTON, OPTION	KEYBOARD SHORTCUT
date and time	INSERT, Text		
Format Background task pane	DESIGN, Customize		
Format Picture task pane	PICTURE TOOLS FORMAT, Picture Styles OR Size		
Grid and Guides dialog box	VIEW, Show		
gridlines	VIEW, Show	*Gridlines*	Shift + F9
header and footer	INSERT, Text		
Insert Picture dialog box	INSERT, Images		
Insert Pictures window	INSERT, Images		
rulers	VIEW, Show	*Ruler*	
screenshot	INSERT, Images		
shape	INSERT, Illustrations OR HOME, Drawing		
slide number	INSERT, Text	#	
Symbol dialog box	INSERT, Symbols	Ω	
text box	INSERT, Text		
WordArt	INSERT, Text		

Concepts Check Test Your Knowledge 

Completion: In the space provided at the right, indicate the correct term, symbol, or command.

1. The Text Box button is located in the Text group on this tab. ____________________
2. Use the sizing handles or these measurement boxes to change the size of a text box. ____________________
3. This is the keyboard shortcut to select all objects in a slide. ____________________
4. A text box, by default, contains tabs with this alignment. ____________________
5. The Illustrations group on this tab contains a Shapes button. ____________________
6. When dragging a shape to change the size, hold down this key to maintain the proportions of the shape. ____________________
7. Copy a shape by holding down this key while dragging the shape to the desired location. ____________________
8. Turn drawing guides on and off with options in this dialog box. ____________________
9. The Group button is located in this group on the DRAWING TOOLS FORMAT tab. ____________________
10. Click the Online Pictures button and this window displays. ____________________
11. Use this button in the Size group on the PICTURE TOOLS FORMAT tab to remove any unnecessary parts of an image. ____________________
12. With the Bring Forward button and this button in the Arrange group on the DRAWING TOOLS FORMAT tab or the PICTURE TOOLS FORMAT tab you can layer one object on top of another. ____________________
13. To capture a portion of a screen, click the Screenshot button in the Images group on the INSERT tab and then click this option at the drop-down list. ____________________
14. Use this feature to distort or modify text to conform to a variety of shapes. ____________________
15. The Symbol button is located in the Symbols group on this tab. ____________________
16. Click this hyperlink at the Print backstage area to display the Header and Footer dialog box. ____________________

Skills Check Assess Your Performance

Assessment 1

FORMAT AND ADD ENHANCEMENTS TO A TRAVEL PRESENTATION

1. Open **TravelEngland.pptx** and then save the presentation with Save As and name it **P-C4-A1-TravelEngland**.
2. Make Slide 8 active and then insert the slide shown in Figure 4.13 with the following specifications:
   a. Insert a new slide with the Title Only layout.
   b. Type the title *Travel England* as shown in the slide.
   c. Draw a text box in the slide and then type the text shown in Figure 4.13. Select and then change the text font size to 40 points and apply the Tan, Background 2, Darker 75% font color.
   d. Apply the Tan, Background 2, Darker 10% shape fill to the text box.
   e. Apply the Dark Teal, 8 pt glow, Accent color 4 shape effect (from the *Glow* side menu).
   f. Display the Format Shape task pane with the Size & Properties icon selected, change the height to 2.8 inches and the width 9 inches (in the *SIZE* section). Change the left, right, top, and bottom margins to 0.4 inch (in the *TEXT BOX* section). Close the Format Shape task pane.
   g. Distribute the text box horizontally and vertically on the slide. (Do this with the Align button on the DRAWING TOOLS FORMAT tab.)
3. Make Slide 2 active, select the text in the text box and then set a left tab at the 0.5-inch mark on the horizontal ruler, a center tab at the 6-inch mark, and a right tab at the 9.5-inch mark. Bold the headings in the first row.
4. Make Slide 6 active, select the picture, and then make the following changes:
   a. Use the Corrections button on the PICTURE TOOLS FORMAT tab to sharpen the image 25%.
   b. Display the Format Picture task pane with the Size & Properties icon selected.
   c. Change the scale height to 150%, the horizontal position to 5.5 inches, the vertical position to 2.2 inches, and then close the task pane.
5. Make Slide 4 active and then insert the picture named ***Stonehenge.jpg*** located in the PC4 folder on your storage medium with the following specifications:
   a. Crop the picture so it displays as shown in Figure 4.14.
   b. Send the picture behind the text.
   c. Size and move the picture so it displays as shown in Figure 4.14.
   d. Size and move the bulleted text placeholder so it displays as shown in the figure.
6. Make Slide 7 active and then insert a clip art image as shown in Figure 4.15 with the following specification:
   a. At the Insert Pictures window, search for *green umbrella* and then download the umbrella image shown in Figure 4.15.
   b. Flip the umbrella horizontally. (Do this with the Rotate button.)
   c. Correct the image to *Brightness: -40% Contrast: +20%*.
   d. Change the height of the image to 4 inches.
   e. Change the horizontal position to 6.8 inches and the vertical position to 2 inches at the Format Picture task pane with the Size & Properties icon selected.
7. Make Slide 8 active, display the Format Background task pane (use the Format Background button on the DESIGN tab), and insert the picture shown in Figure 4.16 with the following specifications:

a. Insert the picture with the File button in the Format Background task pane with the Fill icon selected. The picture is named **BigBen.jpg** and is located in the PC4 folder on your storage medium.
b. Click the Fill icon in the Format Background task pane and then change the *Offset top* option to -30% and the *Offset bottom* option to -125%.
c. Display the Format Background task pane with the Picture icon selected.
d. Change the sharpness to 25% and the contrast to 30%.
e. Size and move the text in placeholders so the text is positioned as shown in Figure 4.16.

8. Make Slide 9 active and then insert a new slide with the Title Only layout. Insert the title and insert and format a shape as shown in Figure 4.17 with the following specifications:
   a. Type the title *Travel Discounts!* as shown in Figure 4.17.
   b. Draw the shape shown in the slide using the Horizontal Scroll shape.
   c. Change the height of the shape to 5 inches and the width to 10 inches.
   d. Apply the Subtle Effect - Dark Teal, Accent 4 shape style to the shape.
   e. Type the text in the shape as shown in the figure. Change the font size for the text to 36 points; apply the Tan, Background 2, Darker 75% font color, and then turn on bold formatting.
   f. Distribute the shape horizontally and vertically on the slide.
9. Apply the Peel Off transition to each slide.
10. Insert slide numbers on each slide.
11. Insert a footer for notes and handouts pages that prints your first and last names.
12. Run the presentation.
13. Print the presentation as a handout with six slides printed horizontally per page.
14. Save and then close **P-C4-A1-TravelEngland.pptx**.

Figure 4.13 Assessment 1, Step 2

Travel England
"With 6000 years of history, there is so much to see and enjoy that you will want to return time and again."

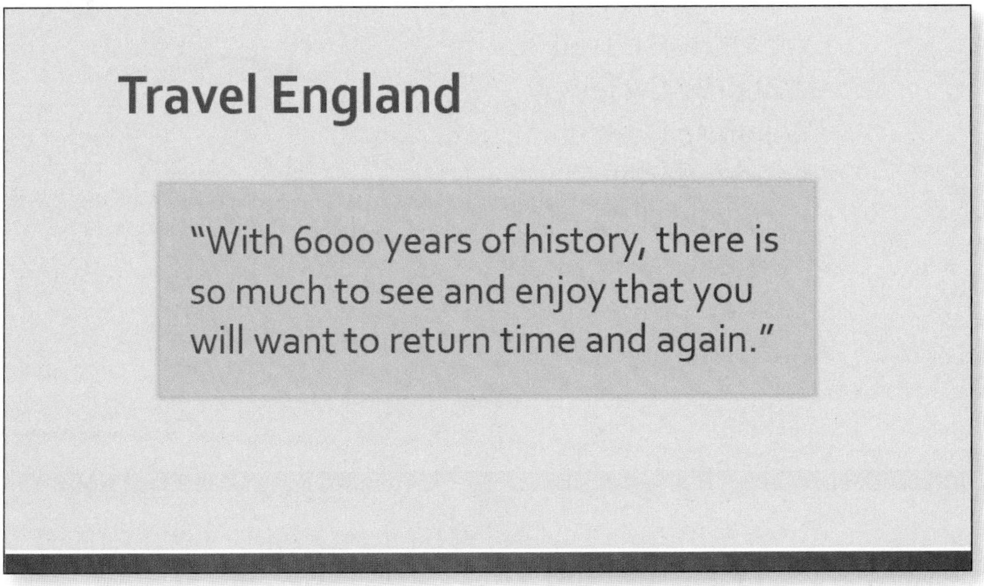

Figure 4.14 Assessment 1, Step 5

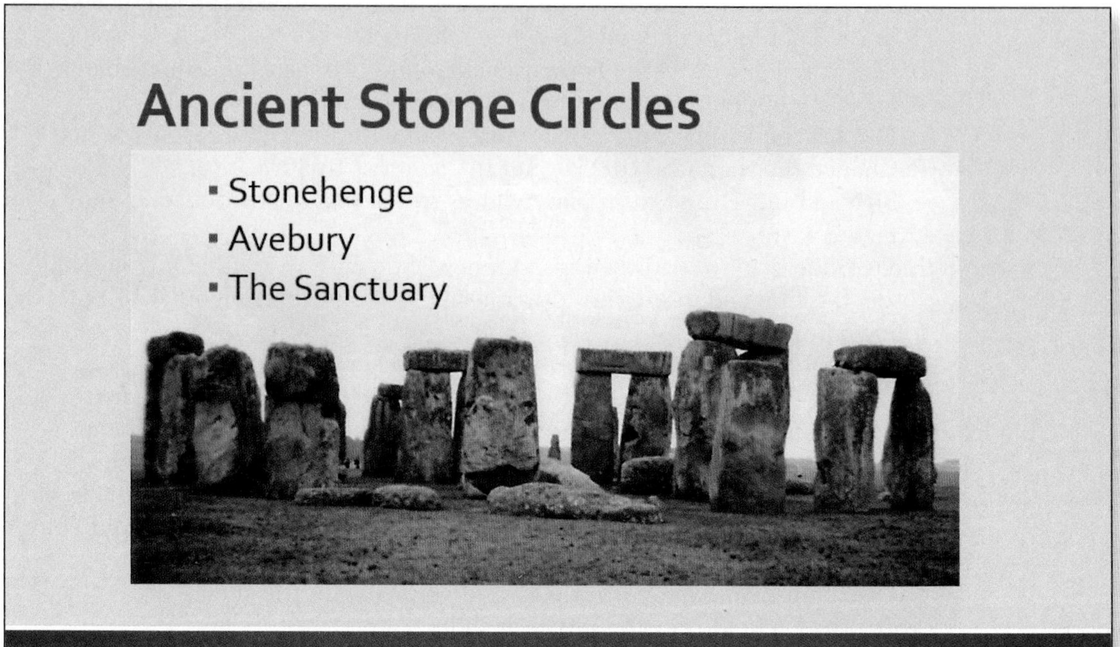

Figure 4.15 Assessment 1, Step 6

Outdoor Activities

- White Horse Trail
- Wiltshire Cycleway
- Wiltshire Downs
- Kennet Canal
- Cotswold Water Park
- Keynes Country Park
- Castle Combe Circuit
- Lydiard Country Park

Figure 4.16 Assessment 1, Step 7

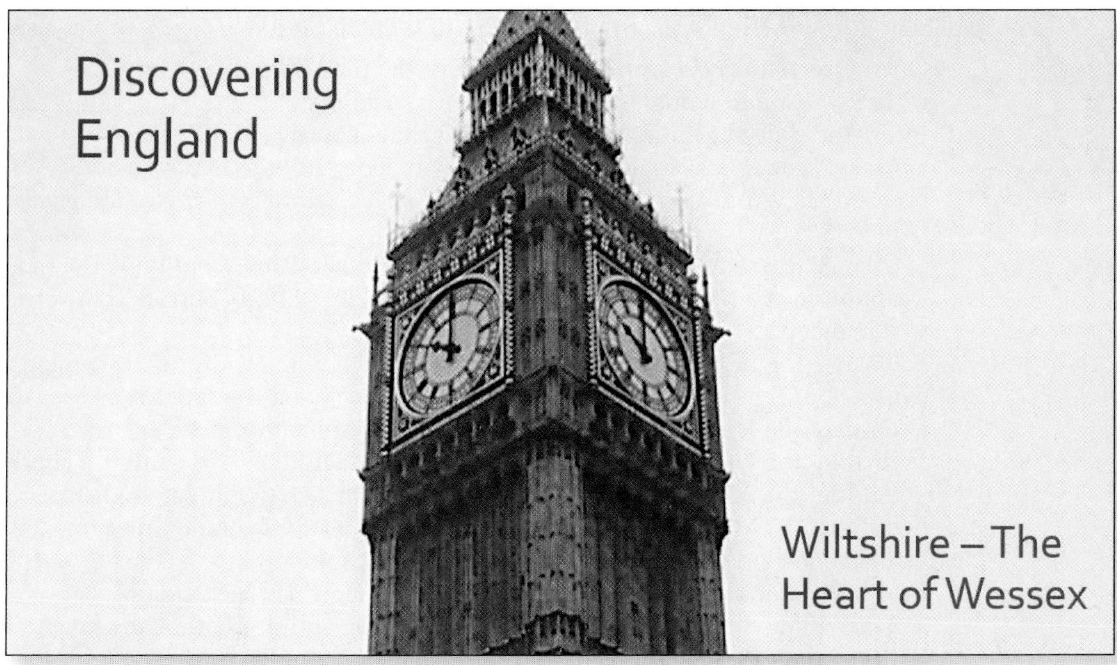

Figure 4.17 Assessment 1, Step 8

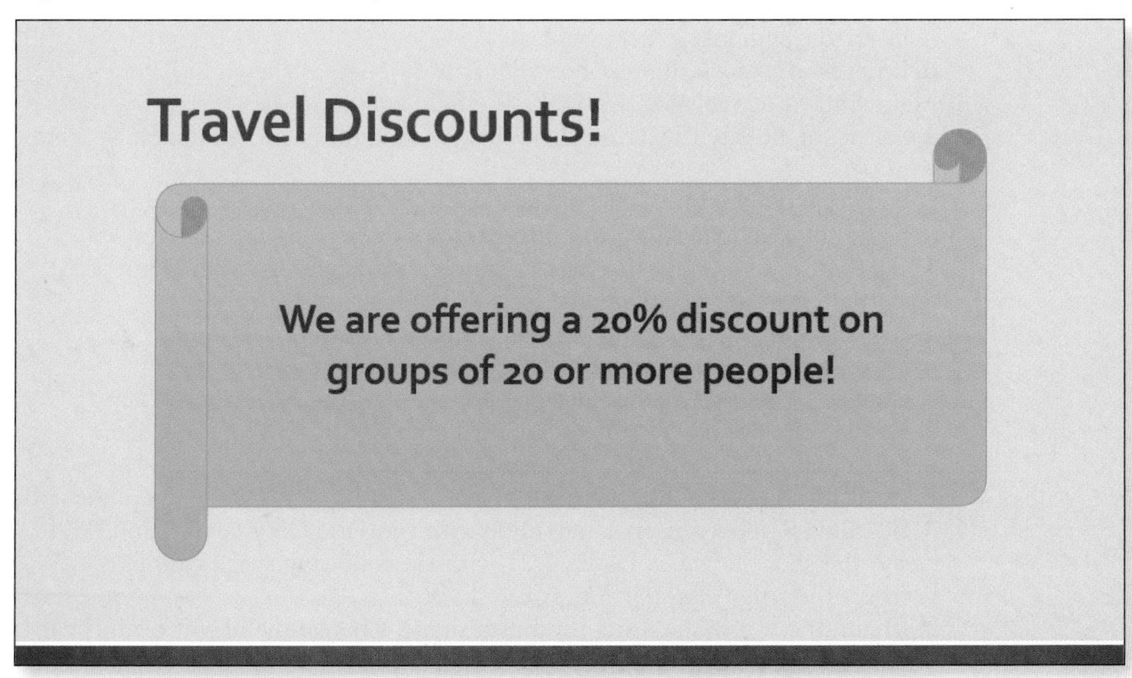

Assessment

2 FORMAT AND ADD ENHANCEMENTS TO A GARDENING PRESENTATION

1. Open **GreenspacePres.pptx** and then save the presentation with Save As and name it **P-C4-A2-GreenspacePres**.
2. Insert the slide shown in Figure 4.18 with the following specifications:
   a. Make Slide 2 active and then insert a new slide with the Blank layout.
   b. Insert the WordArt text using *Pattern Fill - Gold, Accent 3, Narrow Horizontal, Inner Shadow* (second column, bottom row).
   c. Change the shape of the WordArt to *Wave 1*. (The *Wave 1* option is the first option in the fifth row in *Warp* section of the Text Effects button Transform side menu.)
   d. Change the height of the WordArt to 4 inches and the width to 10 inches.
   e. Distribute the WordArt horizontally and vertically on the slide.
   f. Display the Format Background task pane. (Display this task pane by clicking the Format Background button on the DESIGN tab.) Insert a check mark in the *Hide background graphics* check box. Click the Preset gradients button, click the *Light Gradient - Accent 3* option (third column, first row), and then close the task pane.
3. Insert the slide shown in Figure 4.19 with the following specifications:
   a. Make Slide 8 active and then insert a new slide with the Title Only layout.
   b. Insert the title *English/French Translations* as shown in Figure 4.19.
   c. Insert a text box, change the font size to 28 points, set left tabs at the 1-inch and the 5.5-inch marks on the horizontal ruler, and then type the text shown in Figure 4.19 in columns. Bold the headings *English Name* and *French Name* and use the Symbol dialog box to insert the special symbols in the French names. Use the (normal text) font at the Symbol dialog box to insert the symbols.
   d. If necessary, move the text box so it is positioned as shown in Figure 4.19.
4. Make Slide 4 active and then make the following changes:
   a. Select the bulleted text and then change the line spacing to double spacing (2.0).
   b. With the bulleted text selected, set the bulleted text in two columns.
   c. Size the placeholder so four bulleted items display in each column.
5. Make Slide 5 active and then insert the clip art image shown in Figure 4.20 with the following specifications:
   a. Use the words *watering can gardening tools* to search for the image.
   b. Flip the image horizontally.
   c. Change the height of the image to 4 inches.
   d. Display the Format Picture task pane with the Size & Properties icon selected and then change the horizontal position to 6 inches and the vertical position to 2.2 inches.
6. Make Slide 9 active, insert a new slide with the Title Only layout, and then create the slide shown in Figure 4.21 with the following specifications:
   a. Insert the title *Gardening Magazines*.
   b. Create the top shape using the Bevel shape. Change the height of the shape to 1.1 inches and the width to 10 inches.
   c. Change the font size to 32 points and then type the text in the top shape. Insert the registered symbol at the Symbol dialog box with the (normal text) font selected.
   d. Select and then copy the shape two times. Use the guidelines and Smart Guides to help you align and position the shapes.

e. Change the text in the second and third shapes to match what you see in Figure 4.21.
f. Group the three shapes, apply the Dark Green, Text 2, Lighter 60% shape fill color, the Olive Green, Accent 1, Darker 50% shape outline, and the Dark Green, Text 2, Darker 25% text fill color.

7. With Slide 10 active, insert a new slide with the Title Only layout. Type **Gift Certificate** as the title and then insert a screenshot with the following specifications:
   a. Open Word and then open the document named **GAGiftCert.docx** from the PC4 folder on your storage medium.
   b. Click the PowerPoint button on the Taskbar and then use the *Screen Clipping* option from the Screenshot button drop-down list to capture only the gift certificate in the Word document.
   c. With the gift certificate screenshot inserted in the slide, change the height to 3.5 inches and distribute the certificate horizontally and vertically on the slide.
   d. Make Word active and then close Word.
8. Run the presentation.
9. Print the presentation as a handout with six slides printed horizontally per page.
10. Save **P-C4-A2-GreenspacePres.pptx**.

Figure 4.18 Assessment 2, Step 2

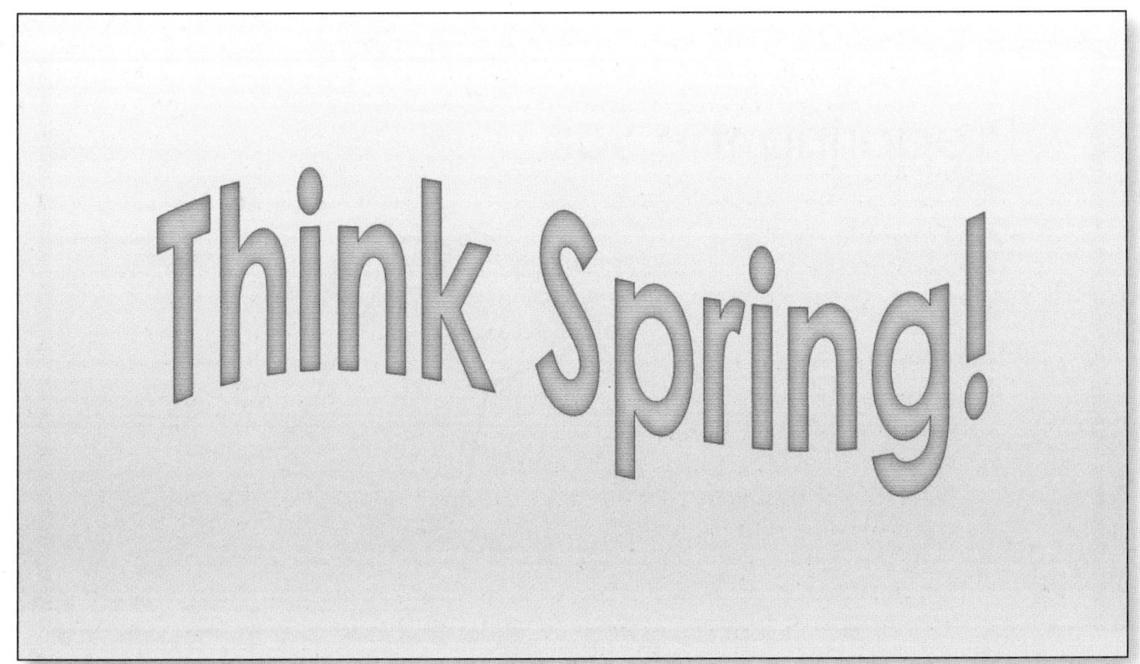

Figure 4.19 Assessment 2, Step 3

English/French Translations

English Name	French Name
Ash	Frêne èlevè
Chestnut	Chataignier
Cypress	Cyprès
Fir	Sapin
Oak	Chene

Figure 4.20 Assessment 2, Step 5

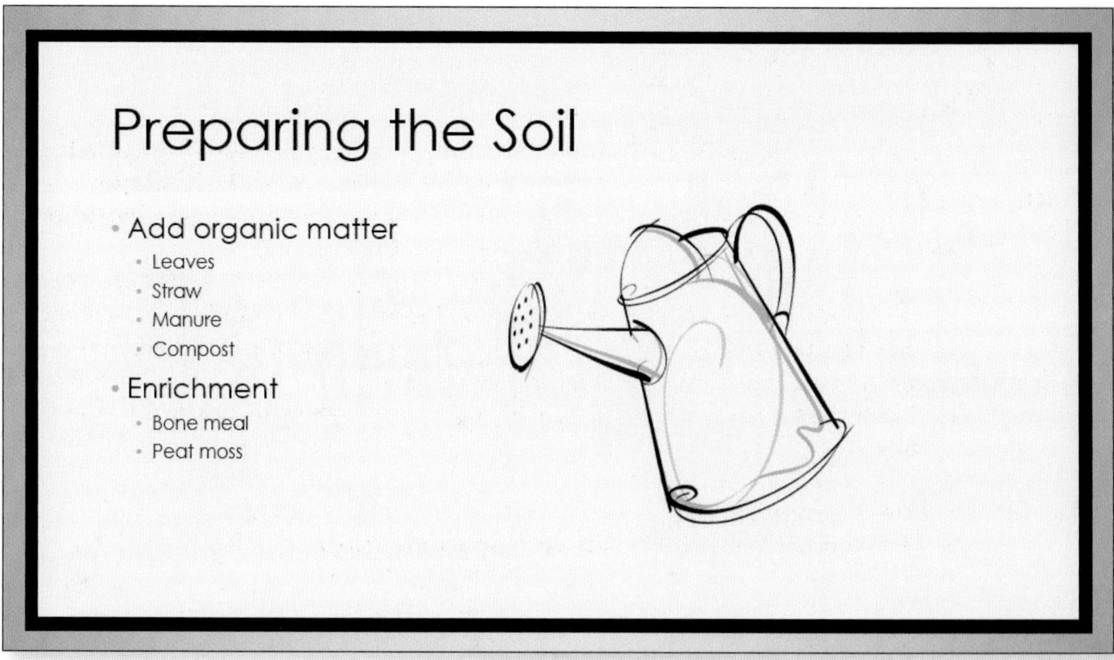

Preparing the Soil
Add organic matter
Leaves
Straw
Manure
Compost
Enrichment
Bone meal
Peat moss

Figure 4.21 Assessment 2, Step 6

Assessment 3

COPY A PICTURE FROM A WEBSITE TO A PRESENTATION

1. With **P-C4-A2-GreenspacePres.pptx** open, make Slide 6 active.
2. Use the Help feature to find information on copying a picture from a web page. (Begin by typing **insert a picture** in the PowerPoint Help window search text box, and then pressing Enter. Click the Insert a picture hyperlink and then click the Insert a picture from the web hyperlink.)
3. Using the information you learned about inserting a picture from a web page, use the *Bing Image Search* text box (at the Insert Pictures window) to search for a picture of flowers on the web and then insert the picture in Slide 6. Size and move the picture so it is positioned attractively in the slide. (Consider inserting at least one more picture of one of the flowers mentioned in the slide.)
4. Print only Slide 6.
5. Run the presentation.
6. Save and then close **P-C4-A2-GreenspacePres.pptx**.

Visual Benchmark Demonstrate Your Proficiency

CREATING A STUDY ABROAD PRESENTATION

1. At a blank presentation, create the presentation shown in Figure 4.22 with the following specifications:
   a. Apply the Quotable design theme and choose the purple variant.
   b. In Slide 1, increase the font size for the subtitle to 36 points.
   c. In Slide 2, insert the WordArt using the *Pattern Fill – Purple, Accent 1, 50%, Hard Shadow - Accent 1* option. Apply the *Deflate* transform text effect and size and position the WordArt on the slide as shown in Figure 4.22.
   d. Change the line spacing to double spacing (2.0) for the bulleted text in Slides 3 and 4 and change the line spacing to one-and-a-half spacing (1.5) for the bulleted text in Slide 5.
   e. Use the words *apartment building* to search for the clip art image in Slide 4. The original color of the clip art image is dark pink. Change the color to *Purple, Accent color 1 Light*. (If this clip art image is not available, choose a similar image.) Size and position the image as shown in Figure 4.22.
   f. Insert the picture **Colosseum.jpg** in Slide 5. (This image is located in the PC4 folder on your storage medium.) Size and position the image as shown in Figure 4.22.
   g. In Slide 6, use the Bevel shape in the *Basic Shapes* section of the Shapes button drop-down list to create the shape. Change the font size to 20 points for the text in the shapes.
   h. Make any other changes to placeholders and other objects so your slides display similar to what you see in Figure 4.22.
2. Apply a transition and sound of your choosing to all slides in the presentation.
3. Save the presentation and name it **P-C4-VB-RomeStudy**.
4. Print the presentation as a handout with six slides printed horizontally per page.
5. Close **P-C4-VB-RomeStudy.pptx**.

Figure 4.22 Visual Benchmark

continues

Figure 4.22 Visual Benchmark—*continued*

Courses

- Italian Language
- Renaissance and Baroque Art History
- Rome Through the Ages
- Roman Mythology
- Roman Archeology

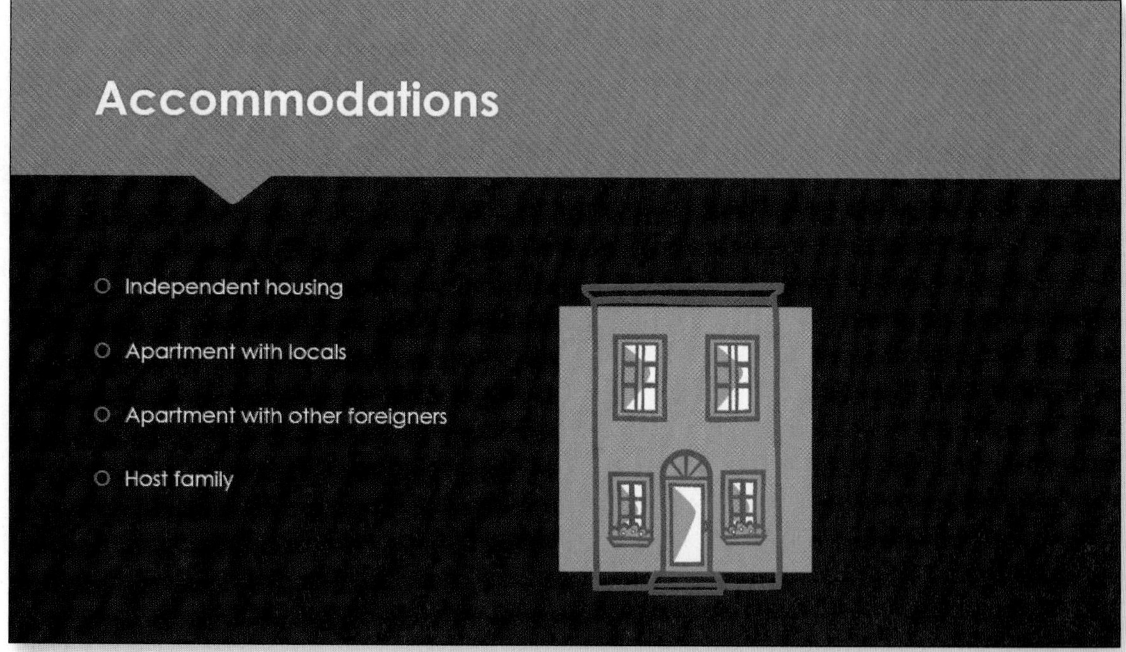

continues

Figure 4.22 Visual Benchmark—*continued*

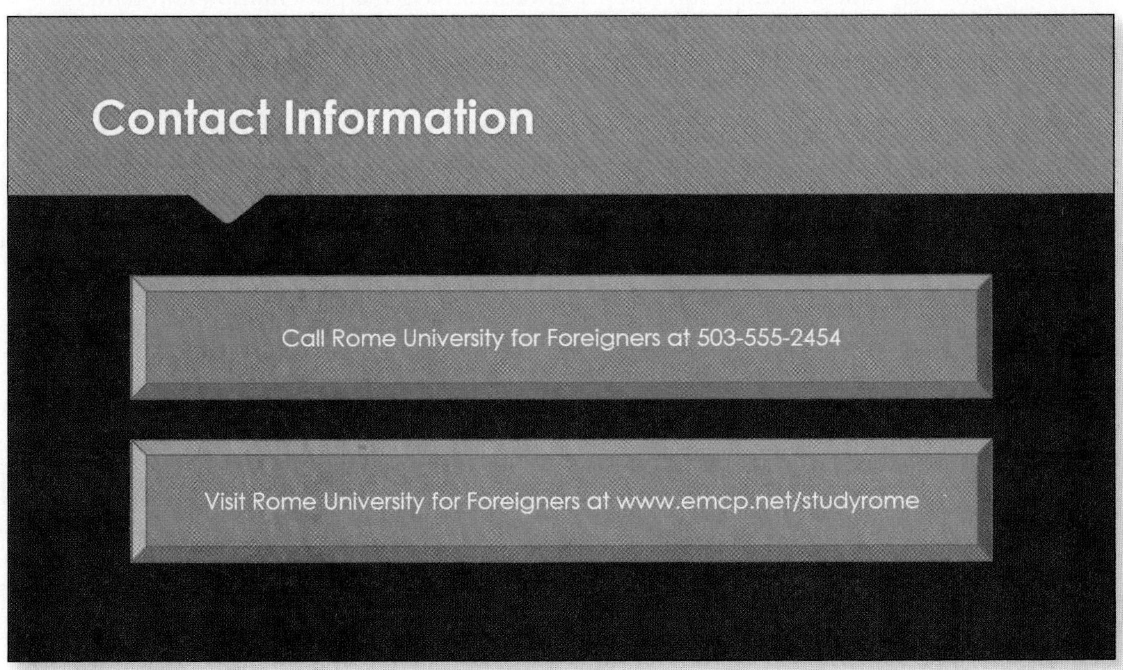

Case Study Apply Your Skills

Part 1

You work for Honoré Financial Services and the Office Manager, Jason Monroe, has asked you to prepare a presentation for a community workshop he will be conducting next week. Open the Word document named **HFS.docx** and then use the information in the document to create a presentation with the following specifications:

- Slide 1: Include the company name Honoré Financial Services (use the Symbol feature to create the é in Honoré) and the subtitle *Managing Your Money*.
- Slide 2: Insert the word *Budgeting* as WordArt.
- Slides 3, 4, and 5: Use the bulleted and numbered information to create these slides.
- Slide 6: Create a text box, set tabs, and then type the information in the *Managing Records* section that is set in columns.
- Slide 7: Create a shape and then insert the following slogan *"Retirement Planning Made Easy"*.
- Include at least one picture and one clip art in the presentation.

Apply a design theme of your choosing and add any additional features to improve the visual appearance of the presentation. Insert a transition and sound to each slide and then run the presentation. Save the presentation and name it **P-C4-CS-HFS.pptx**. Print the presentation as a handout with four slides printed horizontally per page.

Part 2

Mr. Monroe will be conducting a free workshop titled *Financial Planning for the College Student*. Create a slide in the **P-C4-CS-HFS.pptx** presentation (make it the last slide in the presentation) that includes a shape with text inside that includes information about the workshop. You determine the day, the time, and the location for the workshop. Print the slide.

Part 3

Mr. Monroe would like to post the information about the workshop in various locations in the community and wants to print a number of copies. You decide to copy the shape and then insert it in a blank Word document. In Word, change the orientation of the page to landscape, increase the size of the shape, and then drag the shape to the middle of the page. Save the Word document and name it **P-C4-CS-HFSWorkshop**. Print and then close **P-C4-CS-HFSWorkshop.docx**.

Part 4

Mr. Monroe has asked you to locate online finance and/or budgeting resources such as newsletters and magazines. He would like you to locate resources and then create a slide with hyperlinks to the resources. Locate at least two online resources and then insert this information with the hyperlinks in a new slide at the end of the **P-C4-CS-HFS.pptx** presentation. Print the slide and then save and close the presentation.

MICROSOFT® POWERPOINT® Performance Assessment

PU1

Note: Before beginning unit assessments, copy to your storage medium the PU1 folder from the PowerPoint folder on the CD that accompanies this textbook and then make PU1 the active folder.

Assessing Proficiency

In this unit, you have learned to create, print, save, close, open, view, run, edit, and format a PowerPoint presentation. You have also learned how to add transitions and sound to presentations; rearrange slides; customize presentations by changing the design theme; and add visual appeal to slides by inserting text boxes, shapes, pictures, clip art, screenshots, and symbols.

Assessment 1 Prepare, Format, and Enhance a Conference Presentation

1. Create a presentation with the text shown in Figure U1.1 using the Quotable design theme. Use the appropriate slide layout for each slide. After creating the slides, complete a spelling check on the text in the slides.
2. Add a transition and sound of your choosing to all slides.
3. Save the presentation and name it **P-U1-A1-CSConf**.
4. Run the presentation.
5. Make Slide 1 active and then find all occurrences of *Area* and replace them with *Market*.
6. Make the following changes to Slide 2:
   a. Replace the text *Net income* with *Net income per common share*.
   b. Delete the text *Return on average equity*.
7. Make the following changes to Slide 4:
   a. Delete *Shopping*.
   b. Type **Business finance** between *Personal finance* and *Email*.
8. Rearrange the slides in the presentation so they are in the following order (only the slide titles are shown below):
   Slide 1 = CORNERSTONE SYSTEMS
   Slide 2 = Corporate Vision
   Slide 3 = Future Goals
   Slide 4 = Industrial Market
   Slide 5 = Consumer Market
   Slide 6 = Financial Review
9. Increase the line spacing to 1.5 for the bulleted text in Slides 2, 3, 5, and 6.
10. Make Slide 4 active, increase the line spacing to 2.0 for the bulleted text, and then format the bulleted text into two columns with three entries in each column. (You may need to decrease the size of the placeholder.)
11. Save and then run the presentation.

12. Print the presentation as a handout with six slides printed horizontally per page.
13. Display the Reuse Slides task pane, browse to the PU1 folder on your storage medium, and then double-click ***CSMktRpt.pptx***.
14. Insert the *Department Reports* slide below Slide 4.
15. Insert the *Services* slide below Slide 2.
16. Close the Reuse Slides task pane.
17. Make Slide 8 active, select the bulleted text, and then create and apply a custom bullet using a dollar sign in a complementary color and set the size to 100%. (You can find a dollar sign in the normal text font in the Symbol dialog box.)
18. With Slide 8 active, insert a clip art image related to money or finances. Format, size, and then position the clip art attractively on the slide.
19. Move Slide 4 (*Future Goals*) to the end of the presentation.
20. Insert a new slide with the Title and Content layout at the end of the presentation with the following specifications:
    a. Insert *Future Goals* as the title.
    b. Type **International market** as the first bulleted item and then press Enter.
    c. Copy *Acquisitions*, *Production*, *Technology*, and *Marketing* from Slide 8 and paste them in the content area of the new slide below the first line of bulleted text. (When copied, the items should be preceded by a bullet. If a bullet displays on a blank line below the last text item, press the Backspace key twice.)
    d. Select the bulleted text and then change the line spacing to 1.5.
21. Make Slide 8 active, select the bulleted items, and then apply numbering.
22. Make Slide 9 active, select the bulleted items, apply numbering, and then change the beginning number to *6*.
23. With Slide 9 active, create a new slide with the Blank layout with the following specifications:
    a. Insert **Nightscape.jpg** as a background picture and hide the background graphics. ***Hint: Do this with the Format Background button on the DESIGN tab.***
    b. Create a text box toward the top of the slide, change the font color to White, Text 1, increase the font size to 36 points, and then change the alignment to center.
    c. Type **National Sales Meeting**, press Enter, type **New York City**, press Enter, and then type **March 4 to 6, 2015**.
    d. Move and/or size the text box so the text is positioned centered above the buildings in the picture.
24. With Slide 10 active, insert a new slide with the Title Only layout. Type **Doubletree Guest Suites** as the title and then insert a screenshot with the following specifications:
    a. Open Word and then open **HotelMap.docx** from the PU1 folder on your storage medium.
    b. Click the PowerPoint button on the Taskbar and then use the *Screen Clipping* option from the Screenshot button drop-down list to capture only the map in the Word document.
    c. With the map screenshot inserted in the slide, apply the Sharpen: 25% correction. Size and position the map attractively on the slide.
25. Insert slide numbers on each slide.
26. Insert a footer for notes and handouts pages that prints your first and last names.
27. Save and then run the presentation.

28. Print the presentation as a handout with six slides printed horizontally per page.
29. Close **P-U1-A1-CSConf.pptx**.

Figure U1.1 Assessment 1

Slide 1	Title	=	CORNERSTONE SYSTEMS
	Subtitle	=	Executive Conference
Slide 2	Title	=	Financial Review
	Bullets	=	• Net revenues • Operating income • Net income • Return on average equity • Return on average asset
Slide 3	Title	=	Corporate Vision
	Bullets	=	• Expansion • Increased productivity • Consumer satisfaction • Employee satisfaction • Area visibility
Slide 4	Title	=	Consumer Area
	Bullets	=	• Travel • Shopping • Entertainment • Personal finance • Email
Slide 5	Title	=	Industrial Area
	Bullets	=	• Finance • Education • Government • Production • Manufacturing • Utilities
Slide 6	Title	=	Future Goals
	Bullets	=	• Domestic market • Acquisitions • Production • Technology • Marketing

Assessment 2 Format and Enhance a Kraft Artworks Presentation

1. Open **KAPres.pptx** and then save the presentation with Save As and name it **P-U1-A2-KAPres**.
2. With Slide 1 active, insert the text *Kraft Artworks* as WordArt and apply the following formatting:
   a. Transform the shape of the WordArt.
   b. Change the size so the WordArt better fills the slide.
   c. Change the text fill to a purple color.
   d. Apply any other formatting to improve the visual appearance of the WordArt.
3. Duplicate Slides 2 and 3.
4. Change the goal number in Slide 4 from *1* to *3* and change the goal text to *Conduct six art workshops at the Community Center.*
5. Change the goal number in Slide 5 from *2* to *4* and change the goal text to *Provide recycled material to public schools for art classes.*
6. With Slide 5 active, insert a new slide with the Title Only layout with the following specifications:
   a. Insert the title *Clients* and then format, size, and position the title in the same manner as the title in Slide 5.
   b. Insert a text box, change the font to Comic Sans MS and the font size to 20 points, apply the Lavender, Accent 1, Darker 50% font color and then type the following text in columns (you determine the tab settings):

School	**Contact**	**Number**
Logan Elementary School	Maya Jones	555-0882
Cedar Elementary School	George Ferraro	555-3211
Sunrise Elementary School	Avery Burns	555-3444
Hillside Middle School	Joanna Myers	555-2211
Douglas Middle School	Ray Murphy	555-8100

   c. Select all of the text in the text box and then change the line spacing to 1.5.
7. With Slide 6 active, insert a new slide with the Blank layout, hide the background graphic, and then create the slide shown in Figure U1.2 with the following specifications:
   a. Use the Explosion 1 shape (in the *Stars and Banners* section) to create the first shape.
   b. Apply the Light Green shape fill color and apply the Lavender, 18 pt glow, Accent color 2 glow effect.
   c. With the shape selected, change the font to 40-point Comic Sans MS with bold formatting and in the Lavender, Accent 1, Darker 50% font color and then type the text shown in Figure U1.2.
   d. Copy the shape twice and position the shapes as shown in Figure U1.2.
   e. Type the appropriate text in each shape as shown in Figure U1.2.
8. With Slide 7 active, insert a new slide with the Blank layout, hide the background graphic, and then create the slide shown in Figure U1.3 with the following specifications:
   a. Set the text in the two text boxes at the left and right sides of the slide in 54-point Comic Sans MS with bold formatting and in the Lavender, Accent 1, Darker 50% font color. Rotate, size, and position the two text boxes as shown in Figure U1.3.
   b. Use the Explosion 1 shape to create the shape in the middle of the slide.
   c. Apply the Light Green shape fill color, the Lavender, 18 pt glow, Accent color 2 glow effect, the Perspective Diagonal Upper Left shadow effect, the Lavender, Accent 1, Darker 50% shape outline color, and the 2¼ points shape outline weight.

d. Insert the text in the shape and then change the font to 28-point Comic Sans MS, apply bold formatting, and then apply the Lavender, Accent 1, Darker 50% font color. Change the alignment to *Center* and change the vertical alignment to *Middle*.

9. Create a footer that prints your first and last names and the current date on handout pages.
10. Print the presentation as a handout with four slides printed horizontally per page.
11. Save and then close **P-U1-A2-KAPres.pptx**.

Figure U1.2 Assessment 2, Slide 7

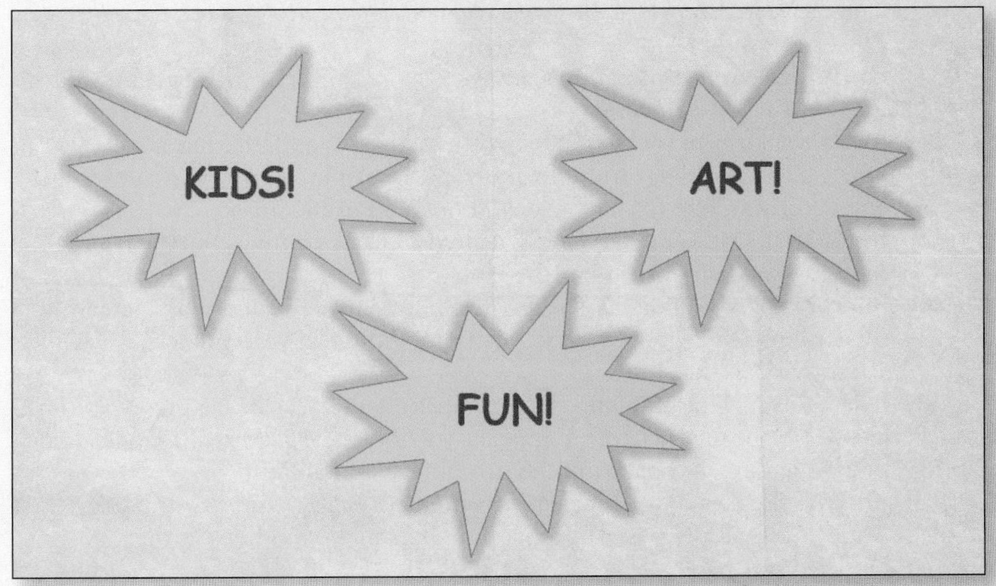

Figure U1.3 Assessment 2, Slide 8

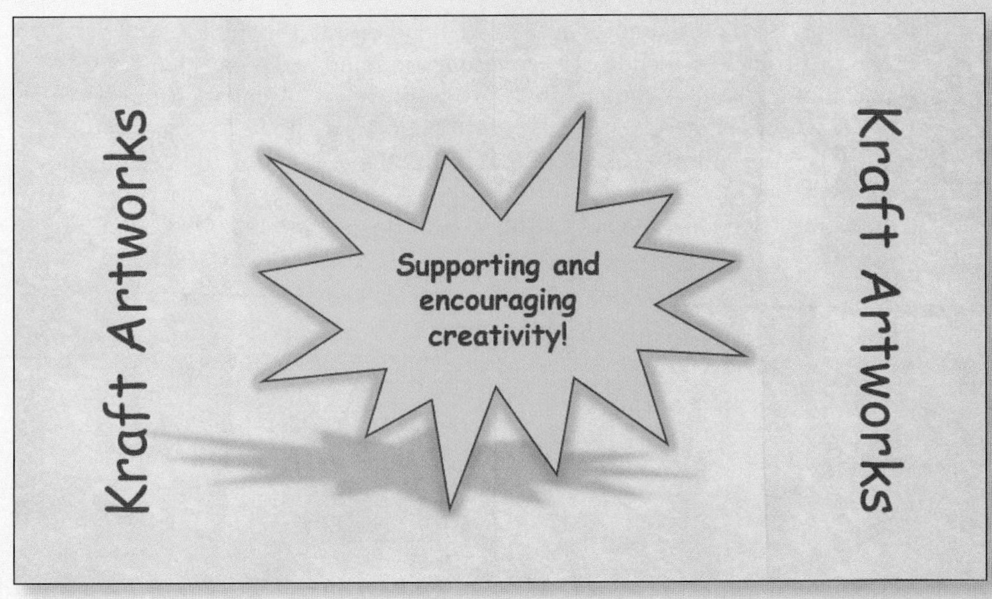

Assessment 3 Create and Apply a Custom Theme to a Job Search Presentation

1. At a blank presentation, apply the Dividend design theme and the green variant (third option in the Variants group).
2. Create custom theme colors named with your first and last names that change the following colors:
   a. Change the Accent 1 color to *Brown, Accent 6, Darker 50%.*
   b. Change the Accent 2 color to *Olive Green, Accent 2, Darker 25%.*
   c. Change the Accent 3 color to *Orange, Accent 5, Darker 25%.*
3. Create custom theme fonts named with your first and last names that changes the heading font to Constantia and the body font to Cambria.
4. Save the current theme as a custom theme named with your first and last names. ***Hint: Do this at the Save Current Theme dialog box.***
5. Close the presentation without saving it.
6. Open **JobSearch.pptx** and then save the presentation with Save As and name it **P-U1-A3-JobSearch**.
7. Apply the custom theme named with your first and last names.
8. Insert a clip art image in Slide 5 related to telephone, people, or Internet. You determine the format, size, and position of the image.
9. Insert a clip art image in Slide 6 related to clock or time. You determine the format, size, and position of the image.
10. Improve the visual display of text in Slides 2, 3, 7, 8, and 9 by increasing the spacing between items and positioning the text placeholders attractively in the slides.
11. Insert the current date and slide number on all slides in the presentation.
12. Create the header *Job Search Seminar*, the footer *Employment Strategies*, and insert the date and page number for notes and handouts.
13. Add the speaker note *Distribute list of Internet employment sites.* to Slide 5.
14. Apply a transition and sound of your choosing to all slides in the presentation.
15. Save and then run the presentation.
16. Print the presentation as a handout with six slides printed horizontally per page.
17. Print Slide 5 as a notes page.
18. Change the slide size to *Standard (4:3)* and ensure the fit.
19. Scroll through each slide of the presentation and make any changes to placeholders and/or clip art images to improve the visual appearance of the slides.
20. Print the presentation as a handout with nine slides printed horizontally per page.
21. Save and then close **P-U1-A3-JobSearch.pptx**.

Assessment 4 Format and Enhance a Medical Plans Presentation

1. Open **MedicalPlans.pptx** and then save the presentation with Save As and name it **P-U1-A4-MedicalPlans**.
2. Apply a design theme of your choosing.
3. Create a new slide with a Blank layout between Slides 1 and 2 that contains a shape with the text *Medical Plans 2015 to 2016* inside the shape. You determine the format, position, and size of the shape and the formatting of the text.
4. Change the bullets in Slides 3, 4, and 5 to custom bullets (you determine the picture or symbol).
5. Insert a clip art image related to medicine in Slide 4. You determine the color, size, and position of the image.
6. Make Slide 5 active, and then apply the following formatting:
   a. Move the insertion point to the beginning of *Eugene* and then press the Enter key two times.
   b. Select all of the bulleted text and then change the line spacing to 2.0.
   c. With the bulleted text selected, format the text into two columns. (Make sure each column contains four entries.)
   d. Size and/or move the placeholder so the bulleted text displays attractively in the slide.
7. Apply any additional formatting or elements to improve the visual appearance of the slides.
8. Add a transition and sound of your choosing to the presentation.
9. Run the presentation.
10. Print the presentation as a handout with six slides printed horizontally per page.
11. Save and then close **P-U1-A4-MedicalPlans.pptx**.

Writing Activities

The following activities provide you with the opportunity to practice your writing skills along with demonstrating an understanding of some of the important PowerPoint features you have mastered in this unit. Use correct spelling, grammar, and appropriate word choices.

Activity 1 Prepare and Format a Health Plan Presentation

Open Word and then open, print, and close **KLHPlan.docx**. Looking at the printout of this document, create a presentation in PowerPoint that presents the main points of the plan. (Use bullets in the presentation.) Add a transition and sound to the slides. Apply formatting and/or insert images to enhance the visual appearance of the presentation. Save the presentation and name it **P-U1-Act1-KLHPlan**. Run the presentation. Print the presentation as a handout with six slides printed horizontally per page. Save and then close **P-U1-Act1-KLHPlan.pptx**.

Activity 2 Prepare and Format a Presentation on Saving an Image as a JPG

At a blank presentation, use the Help feature to find information on inserting a picture or clip art image. ***Hint: Display the PowerPoint Help window, type*** *save image as a jpg*, ***press Enter, and then click the*** ***<u>Save a picture as a separate file</u>*** ***hyperlink that displays in the window.*** Print and read the information and then use the information to create a presentation that includes at least three slides (a title slide, a slide with the steps on saving an image in the JPG format, and a slide on the various file formats for saving an image). Format and add visual appeal to the presentation. With the presentation still open, open the **KLHPLogo.pptx** presentation. Group the image and the text and then save the grouped image as a JPG file named **KLHPLogo.jpg** in the PU1 folder on your storage medium. Close **KLHPLogo.pptx**. With your presentation open, insert the **KLHPLogo.jpg** file in the slide with the steps for saving in the JPG format. Size and position the logo attractively on the slide. Save the completed presentation and name it **P-U1-Act2-JPGPres**. Add a transition and sound of your choosing to each slide and then run the presentation. Print the presentation as a handout with four slides printed horizontally per page. Close **P-U1-Act2-JPGPres.pptx**.

Internet Research

Analyze a Magazine Website

Make sure you are connected to the Internet and then explore the *Time*® magazine website at www.time.com. Explore the site to discover the following information:

- The different sections of the magazine
- The type of information presented in each section
- Details on how to subscribe

Use the information you found on the *Time* magazine website to create a PowerPoint presentation that presents the information in a clear, concise, and logical manner. Add formatting and enhancements to the presentation to make it more interesting. When the presentation is completed, save it and name it **P-U1-TimeMag**. Run, print, and then close the presentation.

MICROSOFT® POWERPOINT®

Unit 2 ■ Customizing and Enhancing PowerPoint Presentations

Chapter 5 ■ Creating Tables, Charts, and SmartArt Graphics

Chapter 6 ■ Using Slide Masters and Action Buttons

Chapter 7 ■ Applying Custom Animation and Setting Up Shows

Chapter 8 ■ Integrating, Sharing, and Protecting Presentations

MICROSOFT®

POWERPOINT®

Creating Tables, Charts, and SmartArt Graphics

PERFORMANCE OBJECTIVES

Upon successful completion of Chapter 5, you will be able to:

- **Create and format a table**
- **Modify the design and layout of a table**
- **Insert an image in a table**
- **Create SmartArt graphics**
- **Modify the design and layout of SmartArt**
- **Convert text to a SmartArt graphic**
- **Create and format charts**
- **Modify the design and layout of charts**
- **Select and format chart elements**
- **Create, edit, and format a photo album**

Tutorials

5.1 Creating a Table in a Slide

5.2 Inserting and Formatting an Excel Spreadsheet

5.3 Inserting and Formatting SmartArt

5.4 Converting Text and WordArt to a SmartArt Graphic; Converting a SmartArt Graphic to Text or Shape

5.5 Creating and Formatting Charts

5.6 Creating a Photo Album

If you want to present numbers and lists in a slide, consider inserting the information in a table. Use the Tables feature to create data in columns and rows in a manner similar to a spreadsheet. Display data in a slide in a more visual way by creating a SmartArt graphic. The SmartArt feature provides a number of predesigned graphics such as diagrams and organizational charts. You can create a SmartArt graphic and then modify the design and layout of the graphic.

While a table does an adequate job of representing data, create a chart from data to provide a more visual representation of the data. A chart is sometimes referred to as a ***graph*** and is a picture of numeric data. If you have Microsoft Excel installed on your computer, you can create a chart in a PowerPoint slide. If you do not have Excel installed on your computer, PowerPoint uses the Microsoft Graph feature to create your chart. Projects and assessments in this chapter assume that you have Excel installed on your computer.

You can create a photo album presentation to attractively display personal or business photographs. Use the Photo Album feature to insert pictures and then format the appearance of the pictures in the presentation. Model answers for this chapter's projects appear on the following page.

Note: Before beginning the projects, copy to your storage medium the PC5 folder from the PowerPoint folder on the CD that accompanies this textbook and then make PC5 the active folder.

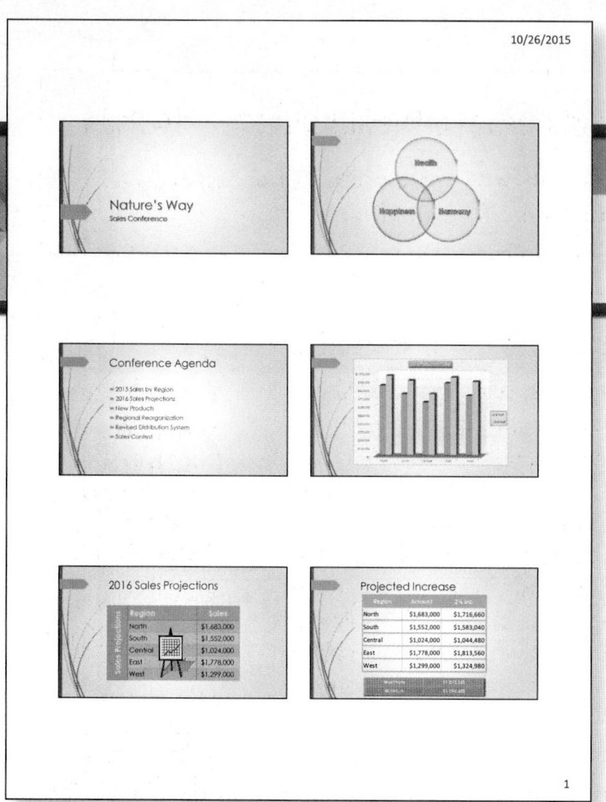

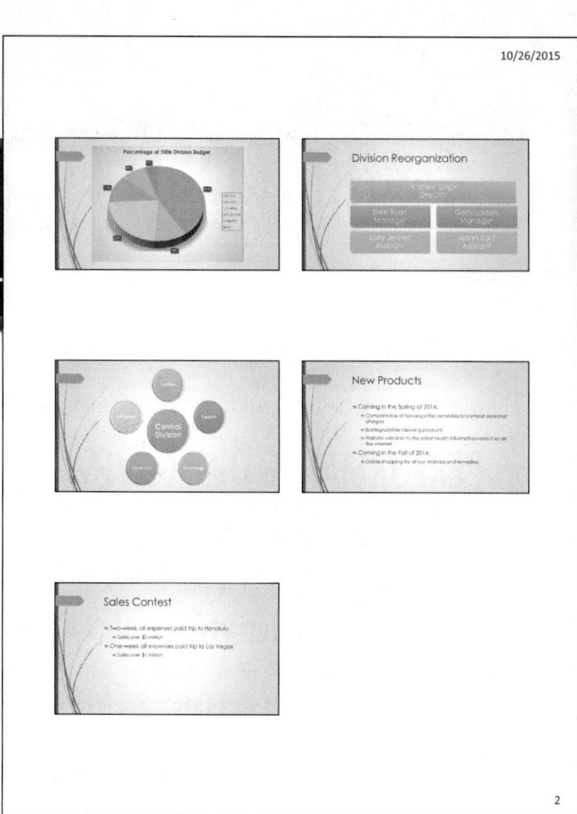

Project 1 Create a Company Sales Conference Presentation

P-C5-P1-Conference.pptx

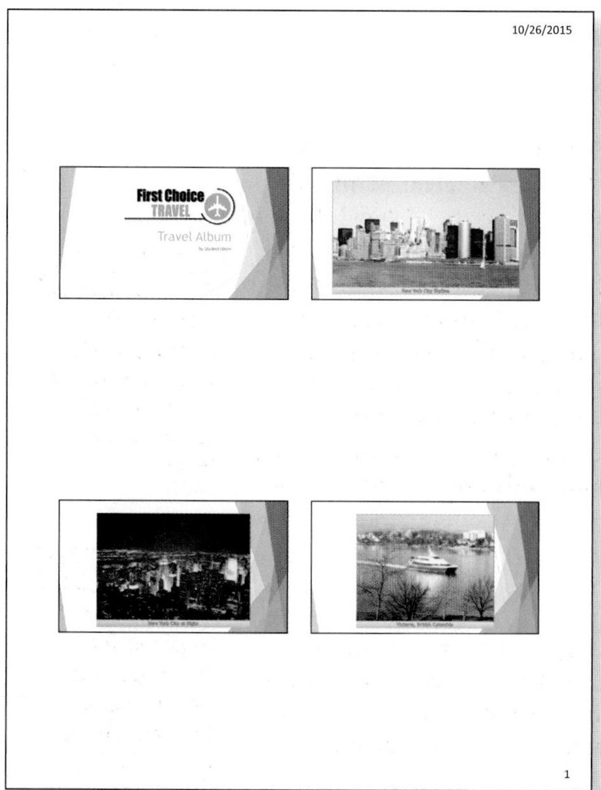

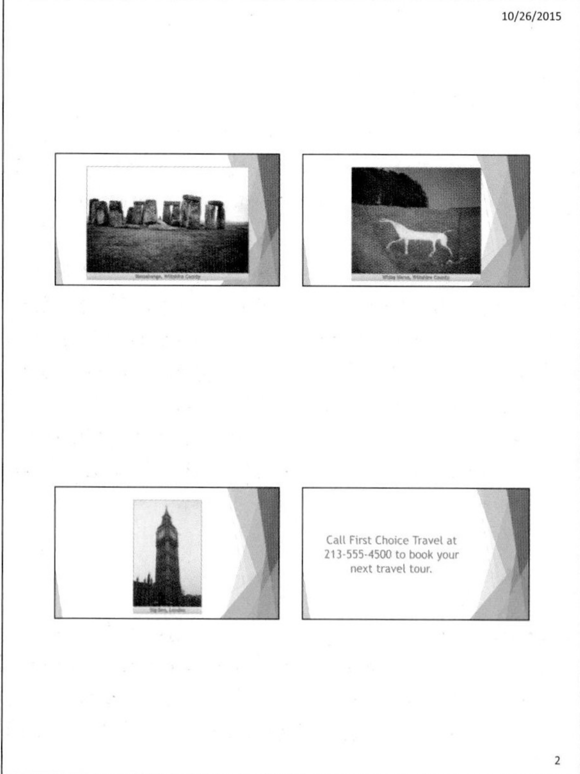

Project 2 Create and Format a Travel Photo Album

P-C5-P2-Album.pptx

Model Answers

Project 1 Create a Company Sales Conference Presentation 14 Parts

You will create a sales conference presentation for Nature's Way that includes a table, a column chart, a pie chart, and four SmartArt graphics.

Creating a Table

Use the Tables feature to create boxes of information called ***cells***. A cell is the intersection between a row and a column. A cell can contain text, characters, numbers, data, graphics, or formulas. If you want to arrange the content of a slide in columns and rows, insert a new slide with a slide layout that includes a content placeholder. Click the Insert Table button in the content placeholder and the Insert Table dialog box displays. At the Insert Table dialog box, type the number of columns, press the Tab key, type the number of rows, and then press Enter or click OK. You can also insert a table using the Table button in the Tables group on the INSERT tab. Click the Table button, drag the mouse down and to the right to select the desired number of columns and rows, and then click the left mouse button.

Quick Steps

Insert a Table

1. Click Insert Table button in content placeholder.
2. Type number of columns.
3. Press Tab.
4. Type number of rows.
5. Click OK.

OR

1. Click INSERT tab.
2. Click Table button.
3. Drag in grid to desired number of columns and rows.

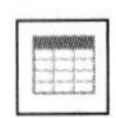

Table

When you create a table, the insertion point is located in the cell in the upper left corner of the table. Cells in a table contain a cell designation. Columns in a table are lettered from left to right, beginning with *A*. Rows in a table are numbered from top to bottom beginning with *1*. The cell in the upper left corner of the table is cell A1. The cell to the right of A1 is B1, the cell to the right of B1 is C1, and so on.

Entering Text in Cells

With the insertion point positioned in a cell, type or edit text. Move the insertion point to other cells by clicking in the desired cell. If you are using the keyboard, press the Tab key to move the insertion point to the next cell or press Shift + Tab to move the insertion point to the previous cell.

If the text you type does not fit on one line, it wraps to the next line within the same cell. If you press Enter in a cell, the insertion point is moved to the next line within the same cell. The cell vertically lengthens to accommodate the text, and all cells in that row also lengthen. Pressing the Tab key in a table causes the insertion point to move to the next cell. If you want to move the insertion point to a tab stop within a cell, press Ctrl + Tab. If the insertion point is located in the last cell of a table and you press the Tab key, PowerPoint adds another row to the table.

HINT

Add a row to the bottom of a table by positioning the insertion point in the last cell and then pressing the Tab key.

Selecting Cells

You can apply formatting to an entire table or to specific cells, rows, or columns in a table. To identify cells for formatting, select the specific cells using the mouse or the keyboard. Press the Tab key to select the next cell or press Shift + Tab to select the previous cell. Refer to Table 5.1 for additional methods for selecting in a table.

HINT

You can move text to a different cell by selecting the text and then dragging the selected text to a different cell.

Table 5.1 Selecting in a Table

To select this	*Do this*
A cell	Position the mouse pointer at left side of the cell until pointer turns into a small, black, diagonally pointing arrow and then click the left mouse button.
A column	Position the mouse pointer outside the table at the top of the column until the pointer turns into a small, black, down-pointing arrow and then click the left mouse button. Drag to select multiple columns.
A row	Position the mouse pointer outside the table at the left edge of the row until the pointer turns into a small, black, right-pointing arrow and then click the left mouse button. Drag to select multiple rows.
All cells in a table	Drag to select all cells or press Ctrl + A.
Text within a cell	Position the mouse pointer at the beginning of the text and then hold down the left mouse button as you drag the mouse across the text. (When a cell is selected, the cell background color changes to gray. When text within a cell is selected, only those lines containing text are highlighted in gray.)

Project 1a Creating a Table

Part 1 of 14

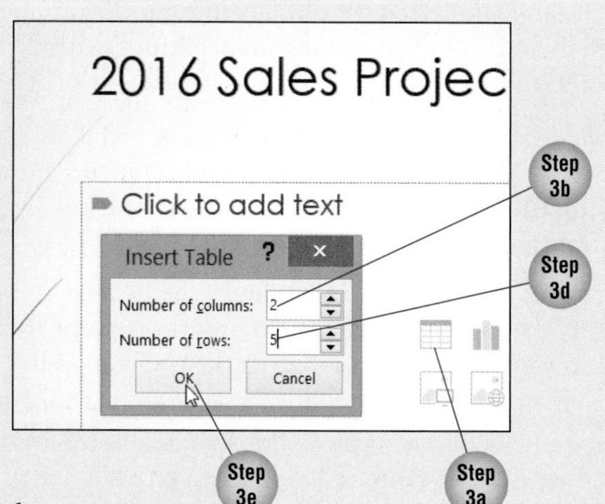

1. Open **Conference.pptx** and then save the presentation with Save As and name it **P-C5-P1-Conference**.
2. Make Slide 3 active.
3. Insert a table in the slide and enter text into the cells by completing the following steps:
   a. Click the Insert Table button located in the middle of the slide in the content placeholder.
   b. At the Insert Table dialog box, select the current number in the *Number of columns* measurement box and then type 2.
   c. Press the Tab key.
   d. Type 5 in the *Number of rows* measurement box.
   e. Click OK or press Enter.
   f. Type the text as displayed in the table below. Press the Tab key to move the insertion point to the next cell or press Shift + Tab to move the insertion point to the previous cell. Do not press Tab after typing the last cell entry.

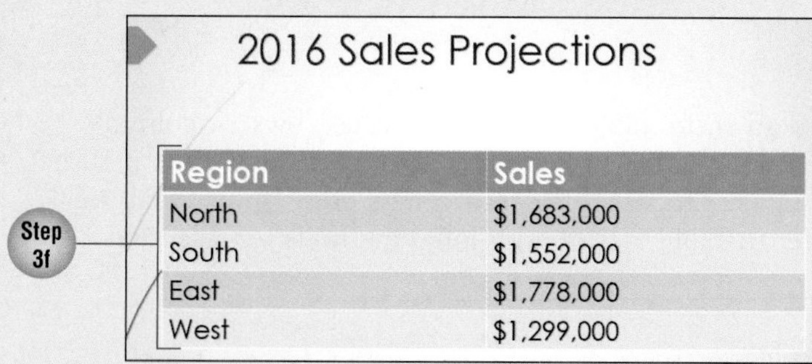

4. Apply formatting to text in specific cells by completing the following steps:
   a. With the insertion point positioned in the table, press Ctrl + A to select all of the text in the table.
   b. Click the HOME tab and then change the font size to 32 points.
   c. Set the text below the headings in a smaller point size by positioning the mouse pointer at the left edge of the second row (to the left of the cell containing *North*) until the pointer turns into a small, black, right-pointing arrow. Hold down the left mouse button, drag down so the remaining rows are selected, and then change the font size to 28 points.
   d. Click outside the table to deselect it.
5. Save **P-C5-P1-Conference.pptx**.

Changing Table Design

When you create a table, the TABLE TOOLS DESIGN tab displays. This tab contains a number of options for enhancing the appearance of the table, as shown in Figure 5.1. With options in the Table Styles group, apply a predesigned style that applies color and border lines to a table. Maintain further control over the predesigned style formatting applied to columns and rows with options in the Table Style Options group. For example, if you want your first column to be formatted differently than the other columns in the table, insert a check mark in the *First Column* check box. Apply additional design formatting to cells in a table with the Shading, Borders, and Effects buttons in the Table Styles group and the options in the WordArt Styles group. Draw a table or draw additional rows and/or columns in a table by clicking the Draw Table button in the Draw Borders group. Click this button and the mouse pointer turns into a pencil. Drag in the table to create the desired columns and rows. Click the Eraser button and the mouse pointer turns into an eraser. Drag through the column and/or row lines you want to erase in the table.

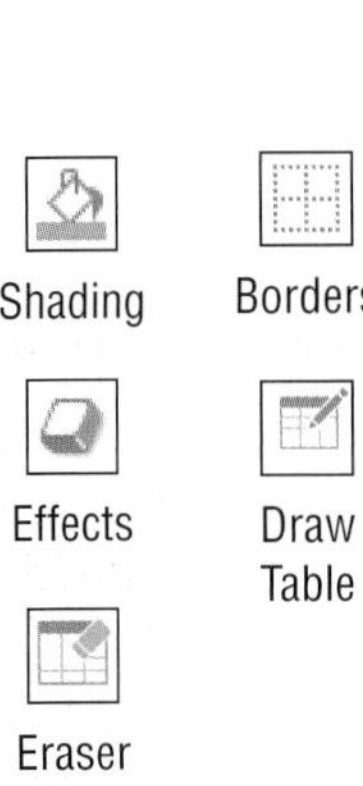

Figure 5.1 TABLE TOOLS DESIGN Tab

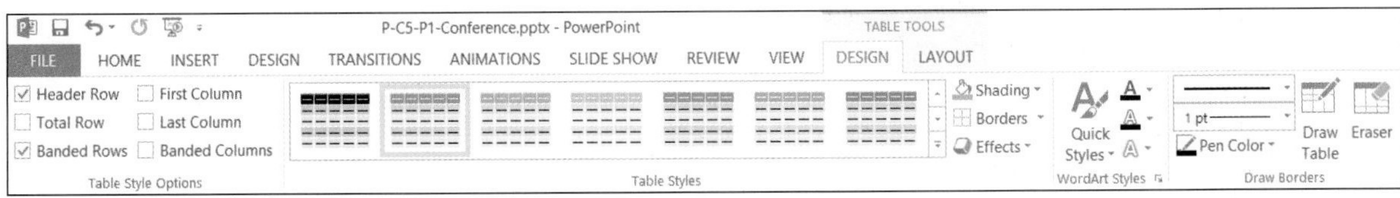

Project 1b Modifying the Table Design Part 2 of 14

1. With **P-C5-P1-Conference.pptx** open, make sure Slide 3 is active, click in a cell in the table, and then click the TABLE TOOLS DESIGN tab.
2. Click the *First Column* check box in the Table Style Options group to insert a check mark. (This applies bold formatting to the text in the first column and applies darker shading to the cell.)
3. Click the More button that displays at the right side of the table style thumbnails and then click the *Themed Style 1 - Accent 1* thumbnail (second column, first row in the *Best Match for Document* section).

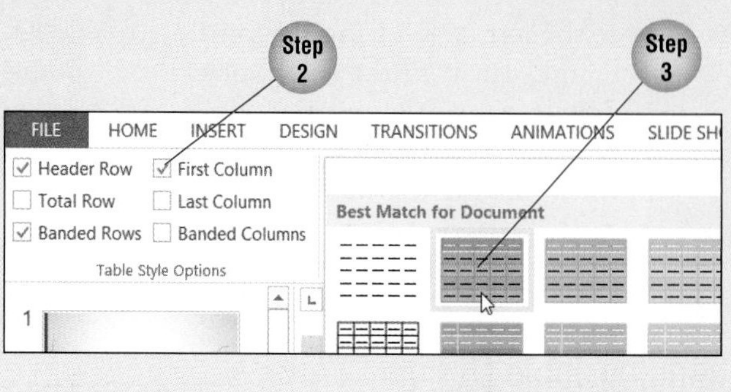

4. Select the first row of the table and then apply the following formatting:
   a. Click the Quick Styles button in the WordArt Styles group and then click the *Fill - White, Outline - Accent 2, Hard Shadow - Accent 2* option (fourth column, third row).
   b. Click the Text Fill button arrow in the WordArt Styles group and then click *Lime, Accent 3, Lighter 80%* (seventh column, second row in the *Theme Colors* section).
   c. Click the Text Outline button arrow in the WordArt Styles group and then click *Green, Accent 1, Lighter 80%* (fifth column, second row in the *Theme Colors* section).

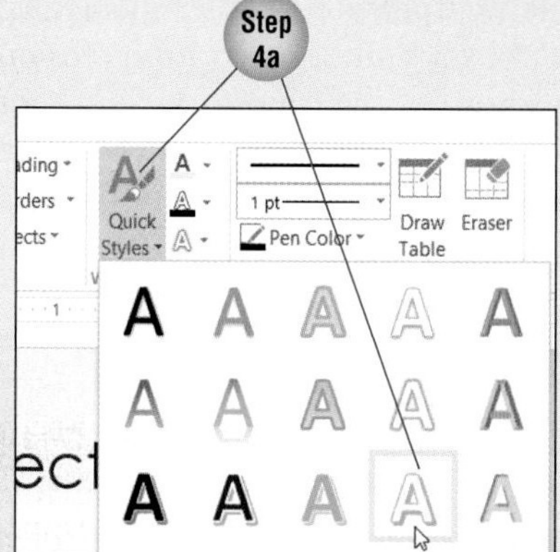

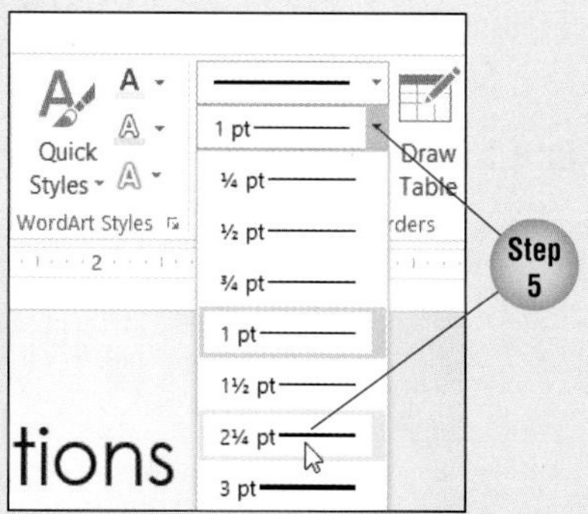

5. Click the Pen Weight button arrow in the Draw Borders group and then click *2¼ pt*. (This activates the Draw Table button.)
6. Click the Pen Color button in the Draw Borders group and then click *Green, Accent 1, Darker 25%* (fifth column, fifth row in the *Theme Colors* section).
7. Draw along the border that separates the two columns from the top of the first row to the bottom of the last row.
8. Draw along the border that separates the first row from the second row.
9. Click the Draw Table button to deactivate it.
10. Save **P-C5-P1-Conference.pptx**.

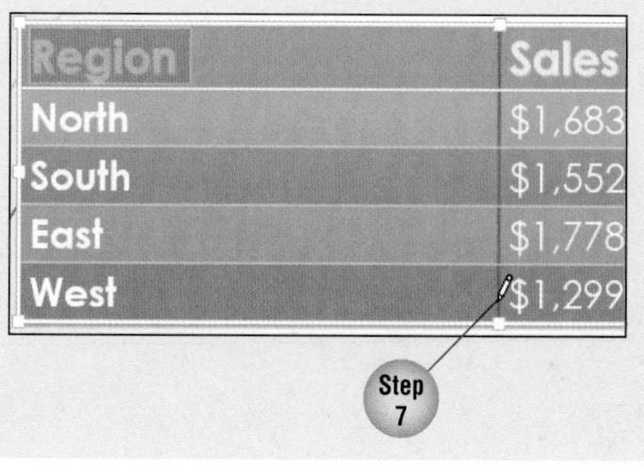

Changing Table Layout

To further customize a table, consider changing the table layout by inserting or deleting columns or rows and specifying cell alignments. Change the table layout with options on the TABLE TOOLS LAYOUT tab, shown in Figure 5.2. Use options and buttons on the tab to select specific cells, delete and insert rows and columns, merge and split cells, specify cell and table height and width, specify text alignment in cells, and arrange elements in a slide.

If you make a mistake while formatting a table, immediately click the Undo button on the Quick Access toolbar.

Figure 5.2 TABLE TOOLS LAYOUT Tab

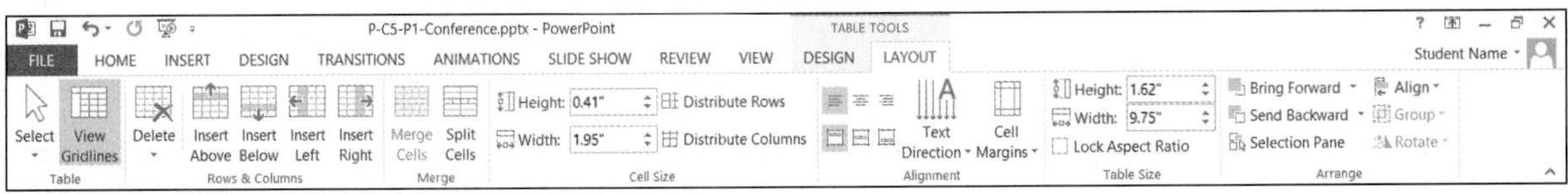

Project 1c **Modifying the Table Layout** **Part 3 of 14**

1. With **P-C5-P1-Conference.pptx** open, make sure Slide 3 is active.
2. Click in any cell in the table and then click the TABLE TOOLS LAYOUT tab.
3. Click in the cell containing the word *East*.
4. Click the Insert Above button in the Rows & Columns group.
5. Type **Central** in the new cell at the left, press the Tab key, and then type **$1,024,000** in the new cell at the right.
6. Click in the cell containing the word *Region*.
7. Click the Insert Left button in the Rows & Columns group.
8. Click the Merge Cells button in the Merge group.
9. Type **Sales Projections** in the new cell.
10. Click the Text Direction button in the Alignment group and then click *Rotate all text 270°* at the drop-down list.
11. Click the Center button in the Alignment group and then click the Center Vertically button in the Alignment group.
12. Click in the *Width* measurement box in the Cell Size group, type 1.2, and then press Enter.

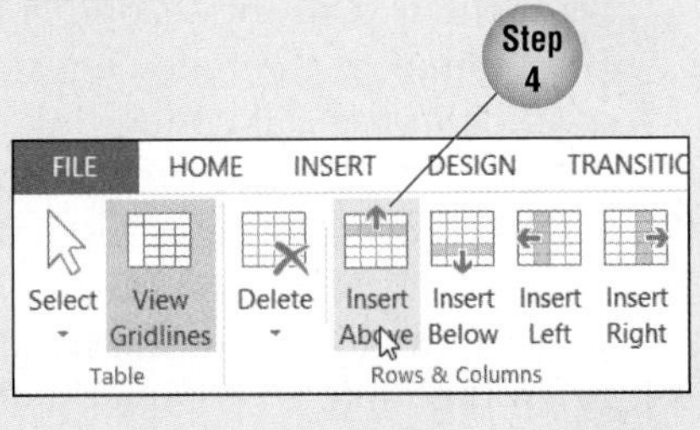

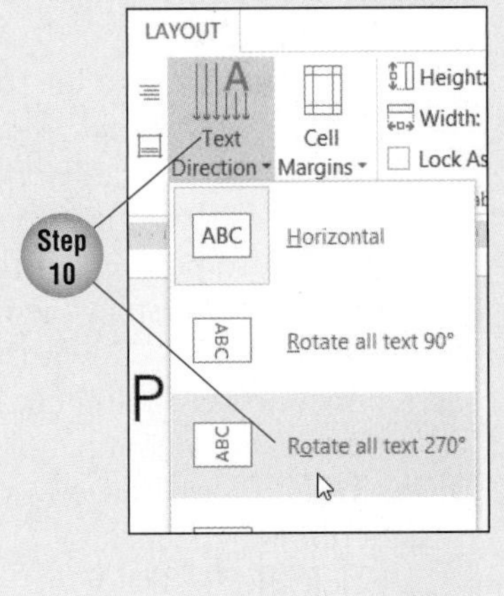

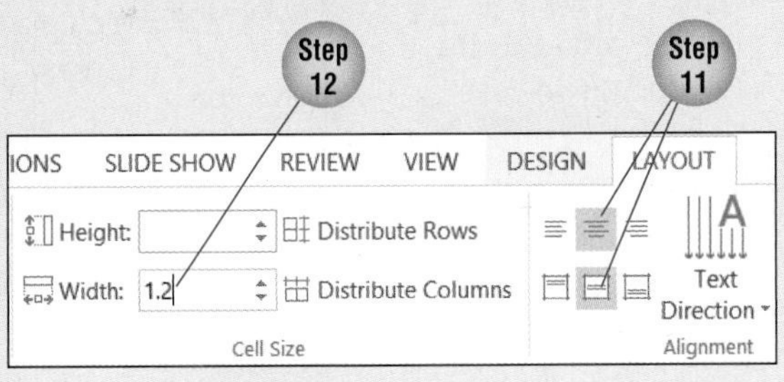

13. Click the TABLE TOOLS DESIGN tab.
14. Click the Borders button arrow in the Table Styles group and then click *Bottom Border* at the drop-down list.
15. Click in the cell containing the text *Sales* and then click the TABLE TOOLS LAYOUT tab.
16. Click in the *Height* measurement box in the Cell Size group and type 0.7.
17. Click in the *Width* measurement box in the Cell Size group, type 2.5, and then press Enter.
18. Click in the cell containing the text *Region*.
19. Click in the *Width* measurement box in the Cell Size group, type 4, and then press Enter.
20. Click in the *Height* measurement box in the Table Size group, type 4.2, and then press Enter.
21. Click the Select button in the Table group and then click *Select Table* at the drop-down list.
22. Click the Center button and then click the Center Vertically button in the Alignment group.
23. After looking at the text in cells, you decide that you want the text in the second column left-aligned. To do this, complete the following steps:
    a. Click in the cell containing the text *Region*.
    b. Click the Select button in the Table group and then click *Select Column* at the drop-down list.
    c. Click the Align Left button in the Alignment group.
    d. Click in any cell in the table.
24. Align the table by completing the following steps:
    a. Click the HOME tab.
    b. Click the Arrange button in the Drawing group, point to *Align*, and then click *Distribute Horizontally*.
    c. Click the Arrange button, point to *Align*, and then click *Distribute Vertically*.
    d. Looking at the table, you decide that it should be moved down in the slide. To do this, position the mouse pointer on the table border until the pointer displays with a four-headed arrow attached. Hold down the left mouse button, drag down approximately 0.5 inch, and then release the mouse button.
25. Insert a clip art image in the table by completing the following steps:
    a. Click the INSERT tab.
    b. Click the Online Pictures button in the Images group.

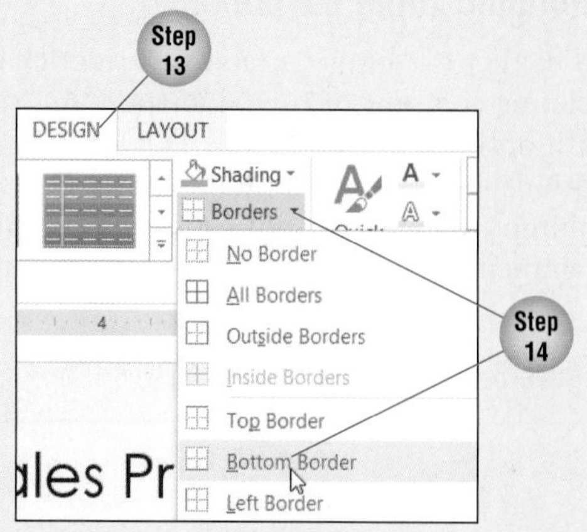

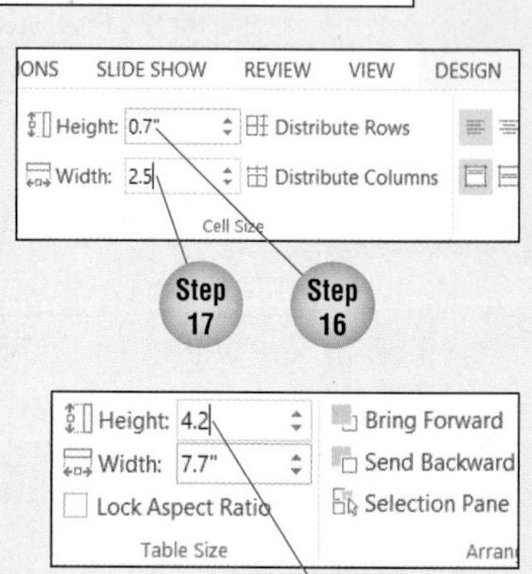

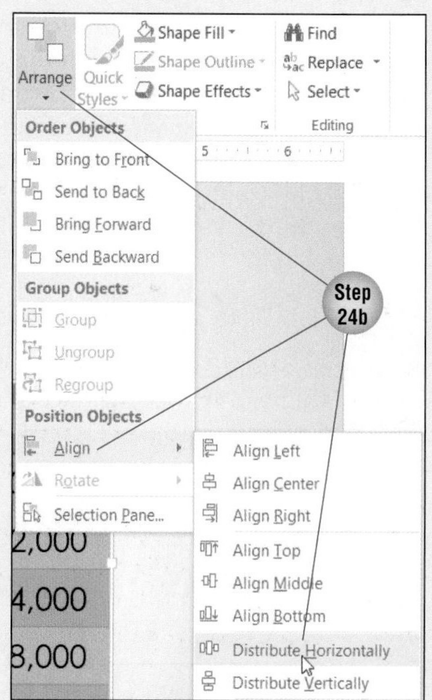

c. At the Insert Pictures window, type **flip chart sales** in the search text box and then press Enter.

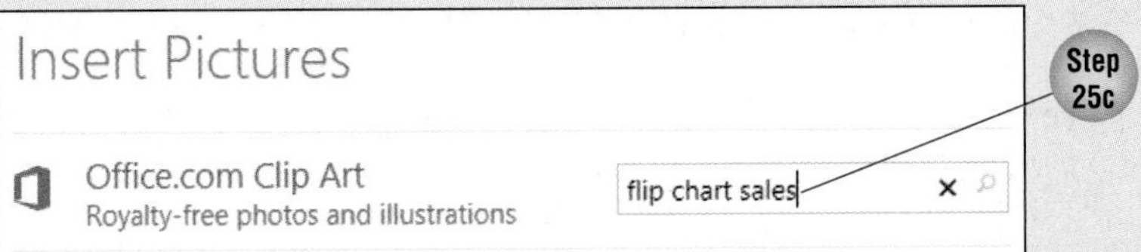

d. Double-click the image shown in Figure 5.3. (If this image is not available, choose a similar clip art image related to sales.)
e. With the image selected, click in the *Shape Height* measurement box in the Size group on the PICTURE TOOLS FORMAT tab, type 2.8, and then press Enter.
f. Drag the clip art image so it is positioned in the table as shown in Figure 5.3.
g. Click outside the clip art image to deselect it.

26. Save **P-C5-P1-Conference.pptx**.

Figure 5.3 Project 1c, Slide 3

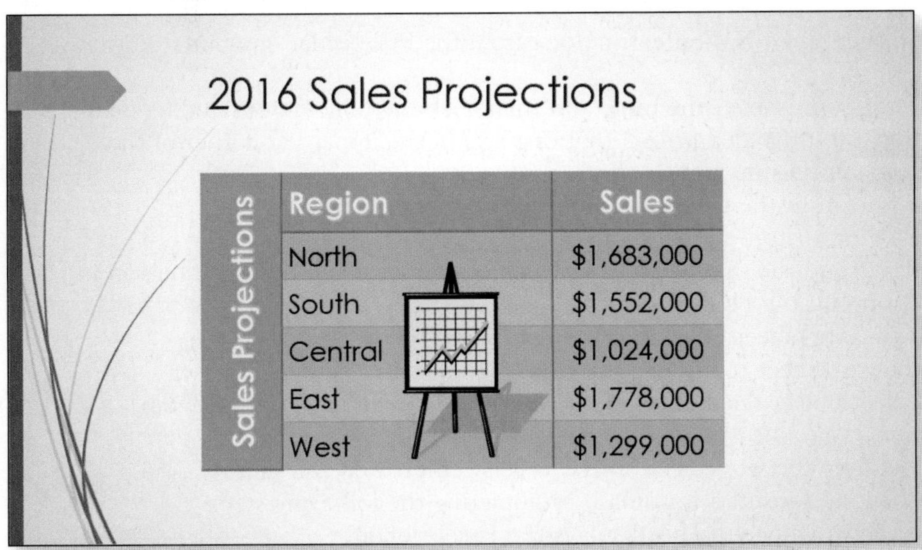

Inserting an Excel Spreadsheet

In addition to inserting a table in a slide, you can insert an Excel spreadsheet, which provides you with some Excel functions. To insert an Excel spreadsheet, click the INSERT tab, click the Table button in the Tables group, and then click the *Excel Spreadsheet* option at the drop-down list. This inserts a small worksheet in the slide with two columns and two rows visible. Increase the number of visible cells by dragging the sizing handles that display around the worksheet. Click outside the worksheet and the cells display as an object that you can format with options on the DRAWING TOOLS FORMAT tab. To format the worksheet with Excel options, double-click the worksheet and the ribbon displays with Excel tabs.

Project 1d Inserting and Formatting an Excel Spreadsheet in a Slide Part 4 of 14

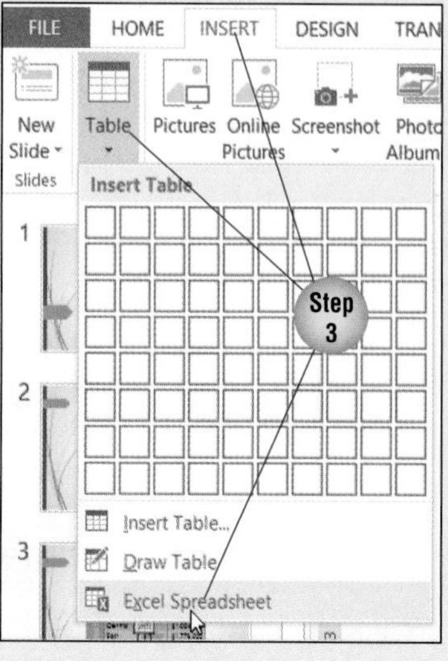

1. With **P-C5-P1-Conference.pptx** open, make sure Slide 3 is active and then insert a new slide with the Title Only layout.
2. Click the text *Click to add title* and then type **Projected Increase**.
3. Insert an Excel spreadsheet by clicking the INSERT tab, clicking the Table button in the Tables group, and then clicking *Excel Spreadsheet* at the drop-down list.
4. Increase the size of the worksheet by completing the following steps:
   a. Position the mouse pointer on the sizing handle (small black square) located in the lower right corner of the worksheet until the pointer displays as a black, diagonal, two-headed arrow.
   b. Hold down the left mouse button, drag down and to the right, and then release the mouse button. Continue dragging the sizing handles until columns A, B, and C and rows 1 through 6 are visible.
5. Copy a Word table into the Excel worksheet by completing the following steps:
   a. Open Word and then open **NWSalesInc.docx** from the PC5 folder on your storage medium.
   b. Hover your mouse pointer over the table and then click the table move handle (small square containing a four-headed arrow) that displays in the upper left corner of the table. (This selects all cells in the table.)
   c. Click the Copy button in the Clipboard group on the HOME tab.
   d. Click the PowerPoint button on the Taskbar.
   e. With Slide 4 active and the first cell in the worksheet active, click the Paste button in the Clipboard group on the HOME tab.
6. Size and position the worksheet object by completing the following steps:
   a. Click outside the worksheet to remove the Excel ribbon tabs.
   b. With the worksheet object selected, click the DRAWING TOOLS FORMAT tab.
   c. Click in the *Shape Width* measurement box, type 7, and then press Enter.
   d. Using the mouse, drag the worksheet object so it is centered on the slide.
7. Format the worksheet and insert a formula by completing the following steps:
   a. Double-click in the worksheet. (This displays the Excel ribbon tabs.)
   b. Click in cell C2, type the formula **=B2*1.02**, and then press Enter.

Step 7b

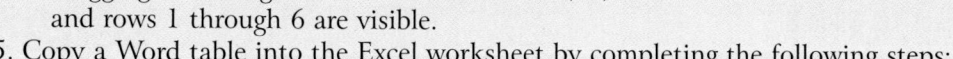

	B	C
Increase		
	Amount	2% Inc.
	$1,683,000	=B2*1.02

8. Copy the formula in C2 to cells C3 through C6 by completing the following steps:
   a. Position the mouse pointer (white plus symbol) in cell C2, hold down the left mouse button, drag down to cell C6, and then release the mouse button.
   b. Click the Fill button in the Editing group on the HOME tab and then click *Down* at the drop-down list.
   c. With cells C2 through C6 selected, click two times on the Decrease Decimal button in the Number group.
9. Click outside the worksheet to remove the Excel ribbon tabs.
10. Make the following changes to the table:
    a. Click the DRAWING TOOLS FORMAT tab.

b. Click the Align button and then click *Distribute Horizontally* at the drop-down list.
c. Click the Align button and then click *Distribute Vertically* at the drop-down list.

11. Click the Word button on the Taskbar and then close Word.
12. Save **P-C5-P1-Conference.pptx**.

Drawing a Table

You can draw a table in a slide using the *Draw Table* option at the Table button drop-down list. When you click the Table button and then click the *Draw Table* option, the mouse pointer displays as a pen. Drag in the slide to create the table. Use buttons on the TABLE TOOLS DESIGN tab and TABLE TOOLS FORMAT tab to format the table.

Project 1e Drawing a Table

Part 5 of 14

1. With **P-C5-P1-Conference.pptx** open, make sure Slide 4 is active.
2. Draw a table and then split the table into two columns and two rows by completing the following steps:
   a. Click the INSERT tab, click the Table button in the Tables group, and then click the *Draw Table* option at the drop-down list.
   b. Position the mouse pointer (displays as a pen) below the worksheet and then drag to create a table that is approximately 7 inches wide and 1 inch tall.
   c. Click the TABLE TOOLS LAYOUT tab and then click the Split Cells button in the Merge group.
   d. At the Split Cells dialog box, press the Tab key, type 2, and then click the OK button. (This splits the table into two columns and two rows.)
   e. Select the current measurement in the *Height* measurement box in the Table Size group and then type 1.
   f. Select the current measurement in the *Width* measurement box in the Table Size group, type 7, and then press Enter.

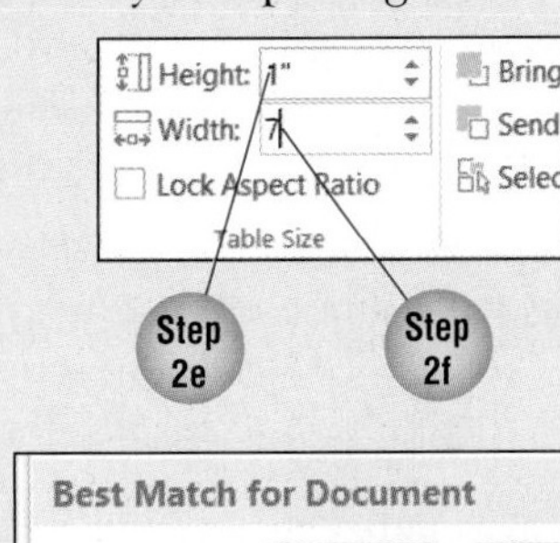

3. With the table selected, make the following formatting changes:
   a. Click the TABLE TOOLS DESIGN tab.
   b. Click the More button at the right side of the table style thumbnails and then click the *Themed Style 2 - Accent 1* thumbnail (second column, second row in the *Best Match for Document* section).
   c. Click the Effects button in the Table Styles group, point to *Cell Bevel*, and then click the *Relaxed Inset* option (second column, first row in the *Bevel* section).
   d. Click the HOME tab, click the Bold button, and then click the Center button.

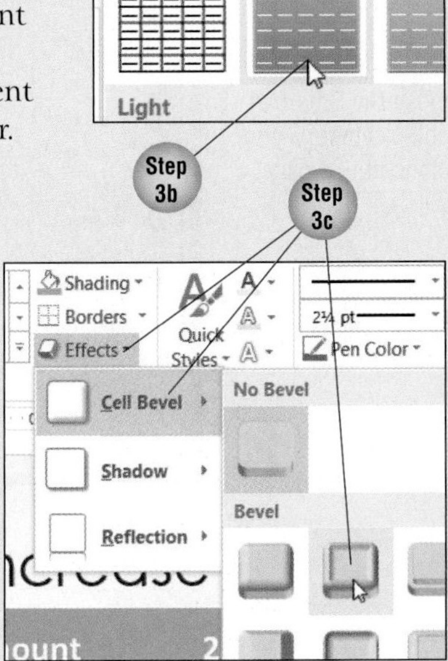

e. Click the Align Text button and then click *Middle* at the drop-down list.
f. Make sure the table is positioned evenly between the bottom of the top table and the bottom of the slide.
g. Click the Arrange button in the Drawing group, point to *Align*, and then click *Distribute Horizontally* at the side menu.

4. Type **Maximum** in the first cell in the table, press the Tab key, and then type **$1,813,360**.
5. Press the Tab key and then type **Minimum**.
6. Press the Tab key and then type **$1,044,480**.
7. Click outside the table to deselect it.
8. Save **P-C5-P1-Conference.pptx**.

Quick Steps

Insert a SmartArt Graphic
1. Click Insert a SmartArt Graphic button in content placeholder.
2. Double-click desired diagram.

OR
1. Click INSERT tab.
2. Click SmartArt button.
3. Double-click desired diagram.

SmartArt

Creating SmartArt

Use the SmartArt feature to insert graphics such as diagrams and organizational charts in a slide. SmartArt offers a variety of predesigned graphics that are available at the Choose a SmartArt Graphic dialog box, shown in Figure 5.4. Display the Choose a SmartArt Graphic dialog box by clicking the Insert a SmartArt Graphic button that displays in a content placeholder or by clicking the INSERT tab and then clicking the SmartArt button in the Illustrations group. At the dialog box, *All* is selected in the left panel and all available predesigned graphics display in the middle panel.

Figure 5.4 Choose a SmartArt Graphic Dialog Box

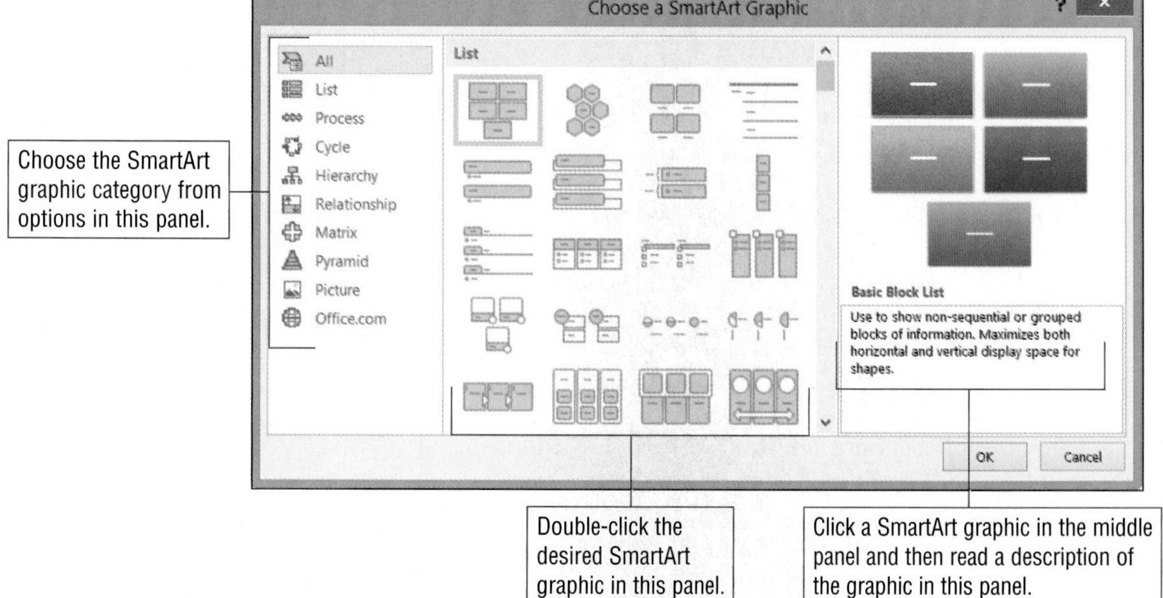
Choose a SmartArt Graphic
All
List
Process
Cycle
Hierarchy
Relationship
Matrix
Pyramid
Picture
Office.com
List
Basic Block List
Use to show non-sequential or grouped blocks of information. Maximizes both horizontal and vertical display space for shapes.
OK
Cancel
Choose the SmartArt graphic category from options in this panel.
Double-click the desired SmartArt graphic in this panel.
Click a SmartArt graphic in the middle panel and then read a description of the graphic in this panel.

Modifying SmartArt

Use SmartArt to communicate your message and ideas in a visual manner.

Limit the number of shapes and the amount of text to key points in a slide.

Predesigned graphics display in the middle panel of the Choose a SmartArt Graphic dialog box. Use the scroll bar at the right side of the middle panel to scroll down the list of graphic choices. Click a graphic in the middle panel and the name of the graphic displays in the right panel along with a description of the graphic type. SmartArt includes graphics for presenting a list of data; showing data processes, cycles, and relationships; and presenting data in a matrix or pyramid. Double-click a graphic in the middle panel of the dialog box and the graphic is inserted in the slide.

When you double-click a graphic at the dialog box, the graphic is inserted in the slide and a text pane may display at the left side of the graphic. You can type text in the text pane or directly in the graphic. Apply design formatting to a graphic with options on the SMARTART TOOLS DESIGN tab, shown in Figure 5.5. This tab is active when the graphic is inserted and selected in the slide. Use options and buttons on this tab to change the graphic layout, apply a style to the graphic, and reset the graphic back to the original formatting.

Figure 5.5 SMARTART TOOLS DESIGN Tab

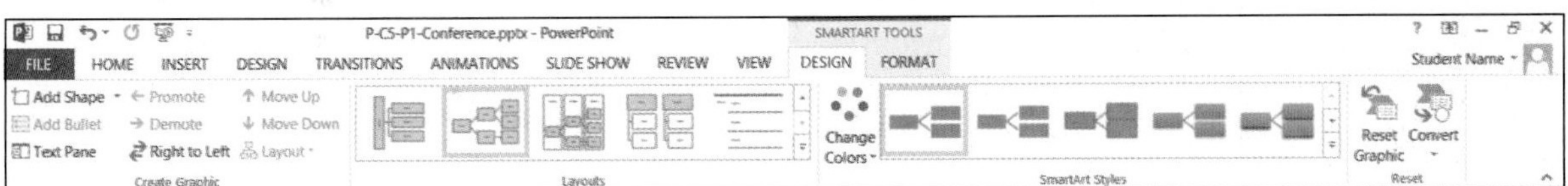

Project 1f Inserting and Modifying a SmartArt Graphic — Part 6 of 14

1. With **P-C5-P1-Conference.pptx** open, make sure Slide 4 is active and then insert a new slide with the Title and Content layout.
2. Click in the title placeholder and then type **Division Reorganization**.
3. Click the Insert a SmartArt Graphic button located in the middle of the slide in the content placeholder.
4. At the Choose a SmartArt Graphic dialog box, click *Hierarchy* in the left panel of the dialog box.
5. Double-click the *Horizontal Hierarchy* option.
6. If a *Type your text here* pane displays at the left side of the organizational chart, close the pane by clicking the Text Pane button in the Create Graphic group.

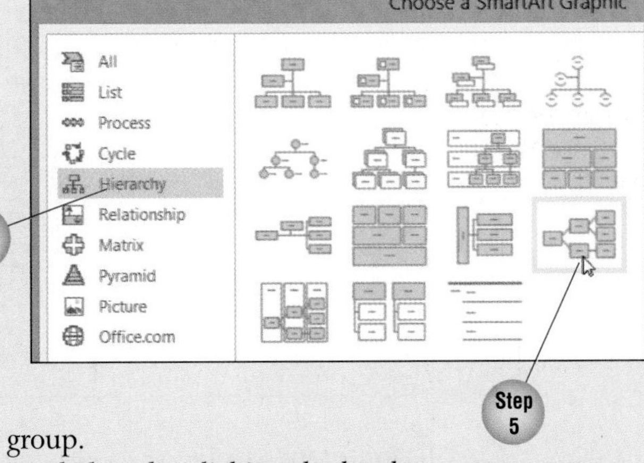

7. Delete one of the boxes in the organizational chart by clicking the border of the top box at the right side of the slide (the top box of the three stacked boxes) and then pressing the Delete key. (Make sure that the selection border that surrounds the box is a solid line and not a dashed line. If a dashed line displays, click the box border again. This should change it to a solid line.)

8. Click *[Text]* in the first box at the left, type **Andrew Singh**, press Shift + Enter, and then type **Director**. Click in each of the remaining boxes and type the text as shown below. (Press Shift + Enter after each name.)

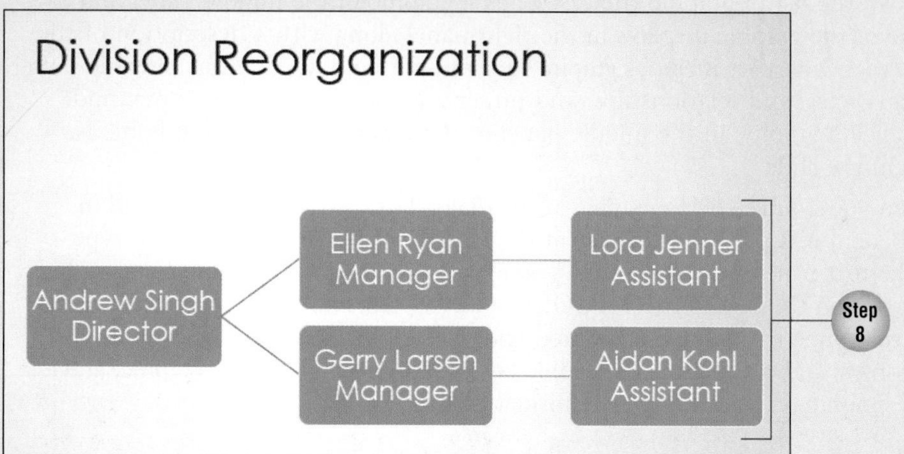

9. Click inside the SmartArt border but outside of any shape and then click the SMARTART TOOLS DESIGN tab.
10. Click the More button at the right side of the style thumbnails in the SmartArt Styles group and then click the *Polished* thumbnail (first column, first row in the *3-D* section).
11. Click the Change Colors button in the SmartArt Styles group and then click *Colorful Range - Accent Colors 3 to 4* (third option in the *Colorful* section).
12. Change the layout of the organizational chart by clicking the More button at the right side of the thumbnails in the Layouts group and then clicking *Table Hierarchy* at the drop-down list. Your slide should now look like the slide shown in Figure 5.6.

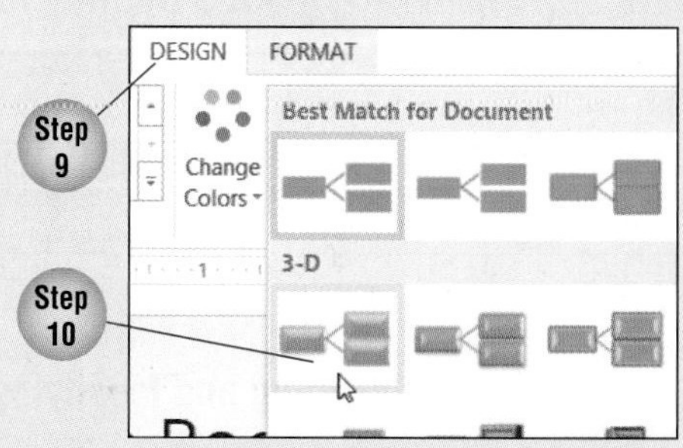

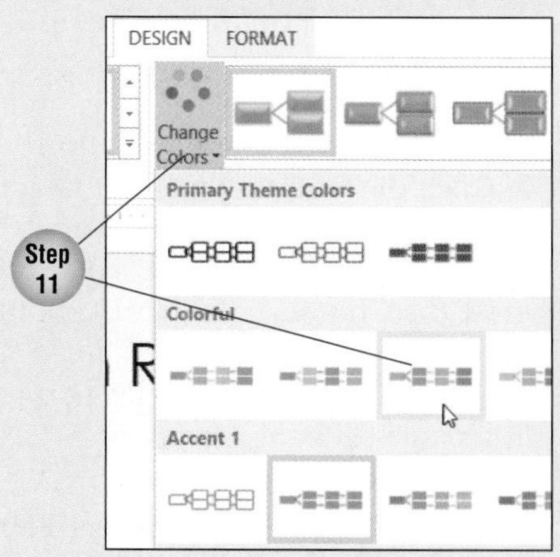

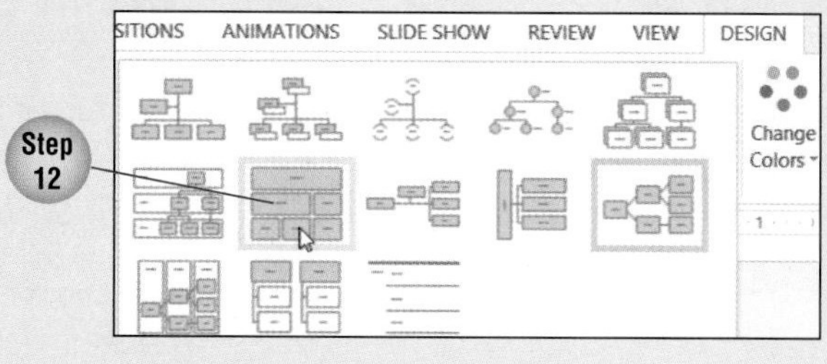

13. Save **P-C5-P1-Conference.pptx**.

Figure 5.6 Project 1f, Slide 5

Formatting SmartArt

Apply formatting to a SmartArt graphic with options on the SMARTART TOOLS FORMAT tab, shown in Figure 5.7. With options and buttons on this tab change the size and shape of objects in the graphic; apply shape styles and WordArt styles; change the shape fill, outline, and effects; and arrange and size the graphic. Move the graphic by positioning the arrow pointer on the graphic border until the pointer turns into a four-headed arrow, holding down the left mouse button, and then dragging the graphic to the desired location.

Nudge selected shape(s) with the up, down, left, or right arrow keys on the keyboard.

Figure 5.7 SMARTART TOOLS FORMAT Tab

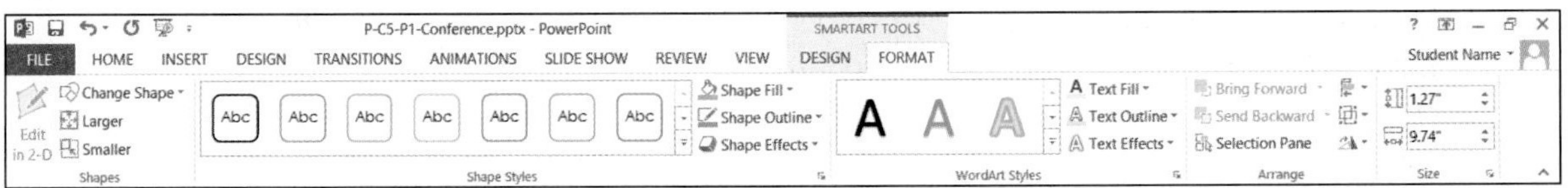

Project 1g **Inserting and Formatting a SmartArt Graphic** **Part 7 of 14**

1. With **P-C5-P1-Conference.pptx** open, make Slide 1 active and then insert a new slide with the Blank layout.
2. Click the INSERT tab and then click the SmartArt button in the Illustrations group.
3. At the Choose a SmartArt Graphic dialog box, click *Relationship* in the left panel of the dialog box.
4. Double-click the *Basic Venn* option shown at the right. (You will need to scroll down the list to display this diagram.)

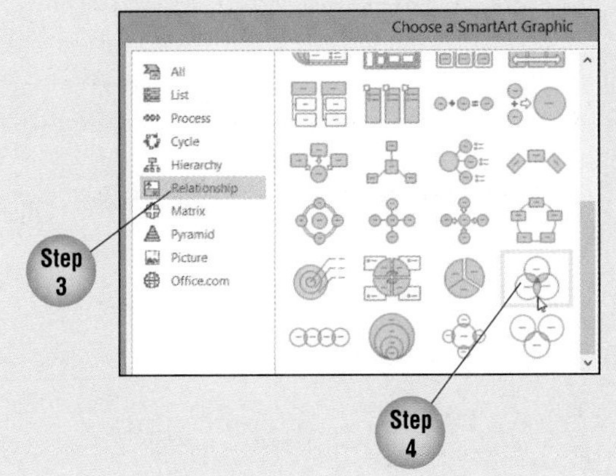

5. Click in the top shape and type **Health**.
6. Click in the shape at the left and type **Happiness**.
7. Click in the shape at the right and type **Harmony**.
8. Click inside the SmartArt border but outside of any shape.
9. Click the Change Colors button in the SmartArt Styles group and then click *Colorful Range - Accent Colors 3 to 4* (third option in the *Colorful* section).

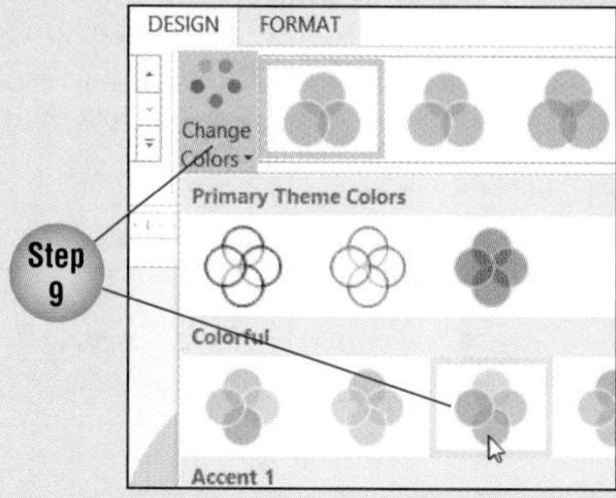

10. Click the More button at the right side of the thumbnails in the SmartArt Styles group and then click *Cartoon* at the drop-down gallery (third option in the *3-D* section).

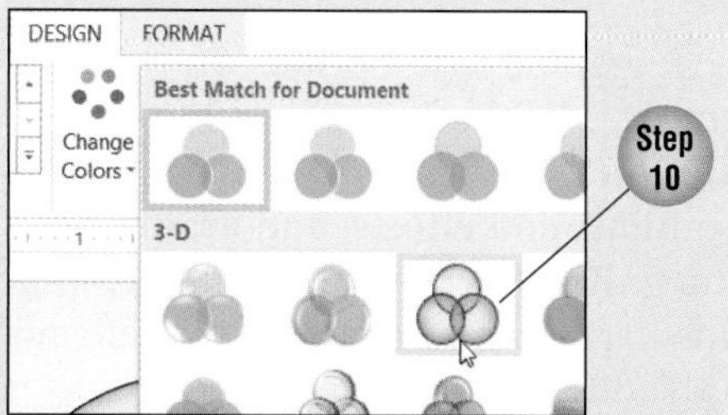

11. Click the SMARTART TOOLS FORMAT tab.
12. Click the More button at the right side of the WordArt Styles thumbnails and then click *Pattern Fill - Green, Accent 1, 50%, Hard Shadow - Accent 1* (third column, bottom row).
13. Click the Text Outline button arrow in the WordArt Styles group and then click *Green, Accent 1, Darker 50%* (fifth column, bottom row in the *Theme Colors* section).
14. Click in the *Shape Height* measurement box in the Size group and then type **6**.
15. Click in the *Shape Width* measurement box in the Size group, type **9**, and then press Enter.

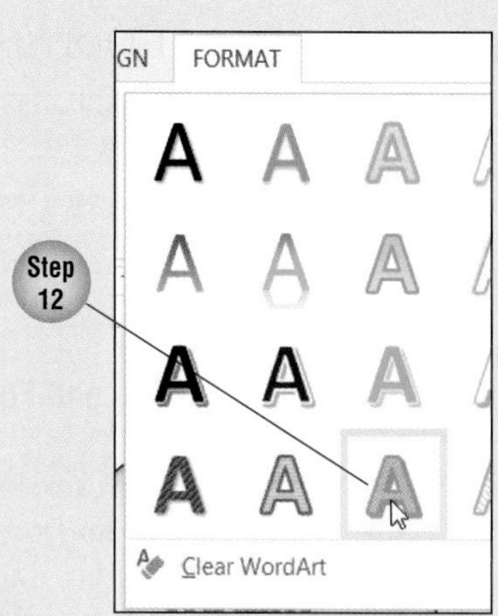

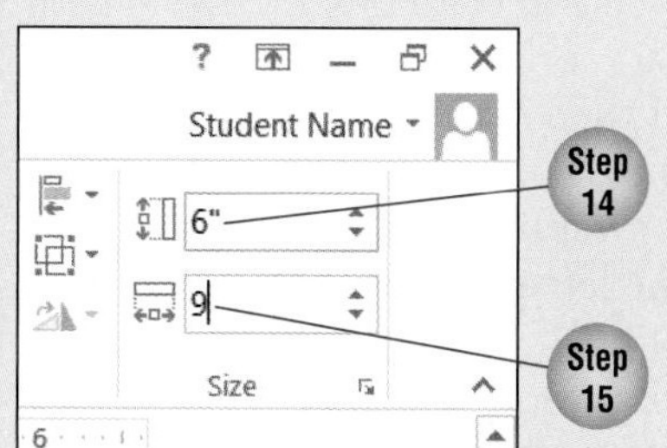

16. Save **P-C5-P1-Conference.pptx**.

Converting Text and WordArt to a SmartArt Graphic

To improve the visual display of text or WordArt and to create a professionally designed image, consider converting text or WordArt to a SmartArt graphic. To do this, select the placeholder containing the text or WordArt and then click the Convert to SmartArt Graphic button in the Paragraph group on the HOME tab. Click the desired SmartArt graphic at the drop-down gallery or click the *More SmartArt Graphics* option and then choose a SmartArt graphic at the Choose a SmartArt Graphic dialog box.

Convert to SmartArt Graphic

Inserting Text in the Text Pane

Enter text in a SmartArt shape by clicking in the shape and then typing the text or by typing text in the Text pane. Display the Text pane by clicking the Text Pane button in the Create Graphic group on the SMARTART TOOLS DESIGN tab.

Text Pane

Project 1h **Creating a SmartArt Graphic with Text and WordArt** **Part 8 of 14**

1. With **P-C5-P1-Conference.pptx** open, make Slide 7 active. (This slide contains WordArt text.)
2. Click on any character in the WordArt text.
3. If necessary, click the HOME tab.
4. Click the Convert to SmartArt Graphic button in the Paragraph group.
5. Click the *More SmartArt Graphics* option that displays at the bottom of the drop-down gallery.
6. At the Choose a SmartArt Graphic dialog box, click *Cycle* in the left panel and then double-click *Diverging Radial* in the middle panel.

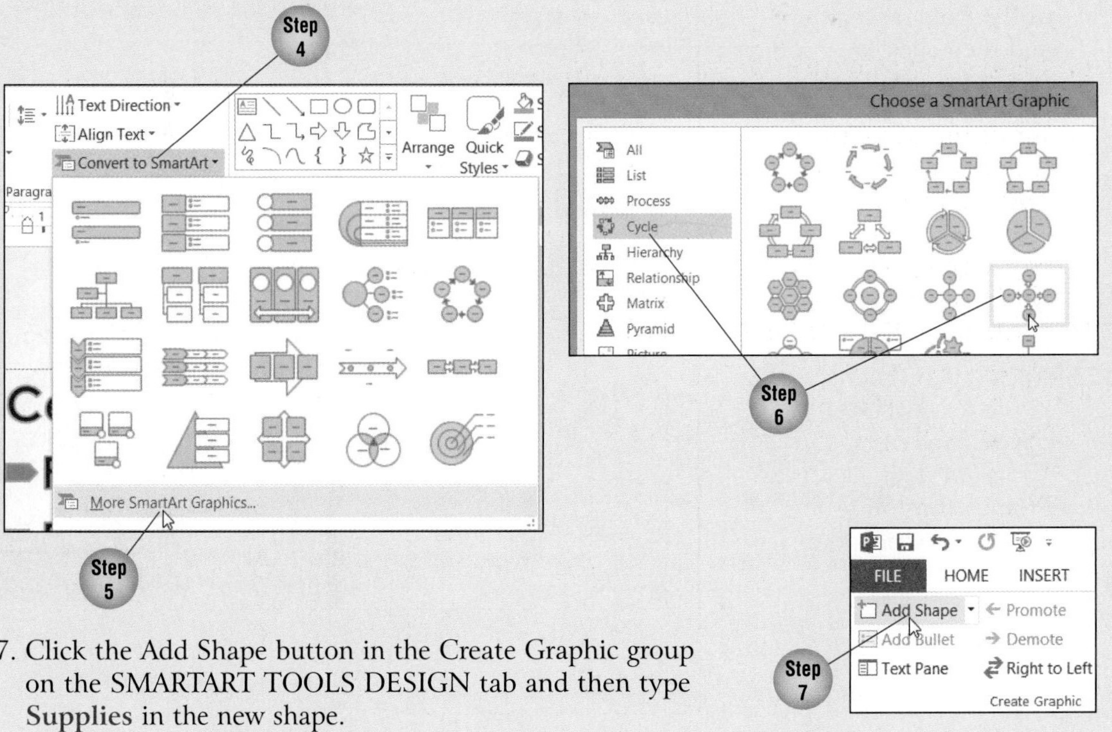

7. Click the Add Shape button in the Create Graphic group on the SMARTART TOOLS DESIGN tab and then type **Supplies** in the new shape.

8. Change the order of the text in the shapes at the left and right sides of the graphic by clicking the Right to Left button in the Create Graphic group.
9. Click the Change Colors button in the SmartArt Styles group and then click *Colorful - Accent Colors* (first option in the *Colorful* section).
10. Click the More button at the right of the style thumbnails in the SmartArt Styles group and then click *Inset* (second option in the *3-D* section).
11. Click the SMARTART TOOLS FORMAT tab.
12. Click the middle circle (contains the text *Central Division*).
13. Click three times on the Larger button in the Shapes group.
14. Click inside the SmartArt border but outside of any shape.
15. Click in the *Shape Height* measurement box in the Size group and then type 6.6.
16. Click in the *Shape Width* measurement box, type 8.2, and then press Enter.
17. Click the HOME tab.
18. With the SmartArt graphic selected, click the Arrange button in the Drawing group, point to *Align*, and then click *Distribute Horizontally*.
19. Click the Arrange button, point to *Align*, and then click *Distribute Vertically*.
20. Click the Bold button in the Font group.
21. Make Slide 9 active.
22. Click in any character in the bulleted text and, if necessary, click the HOME tab.
23. Click the Convert to SmartArt Graphic button in the Paragraph group and then click *Vertical Block List* at the drop-down list (second column, first row).
24. Click the shape containing the text *Sales over $2 million* and then click the Demote button in the Create Graphic group on the SMARTART TOOLS DESIGN tab.
25. Click on any character in the text *One-week all expenses paid trip to Las Vegas* and then click the Promote button in the Create Graphic group.

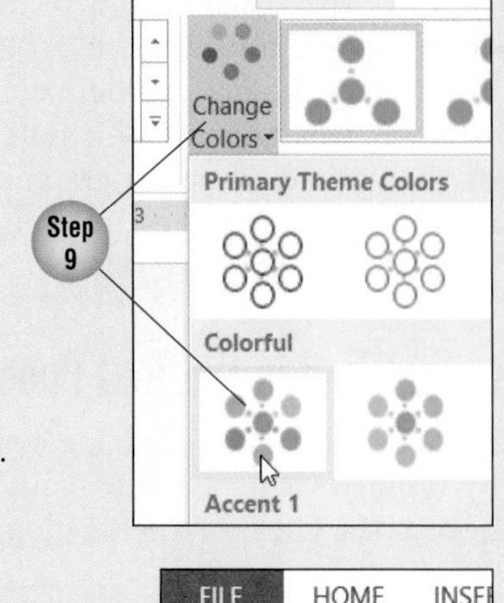

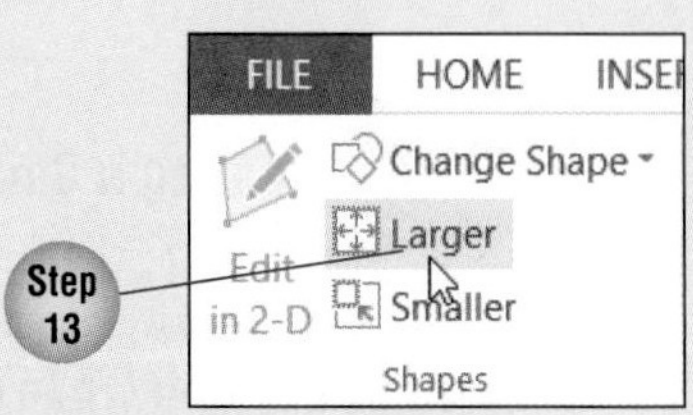

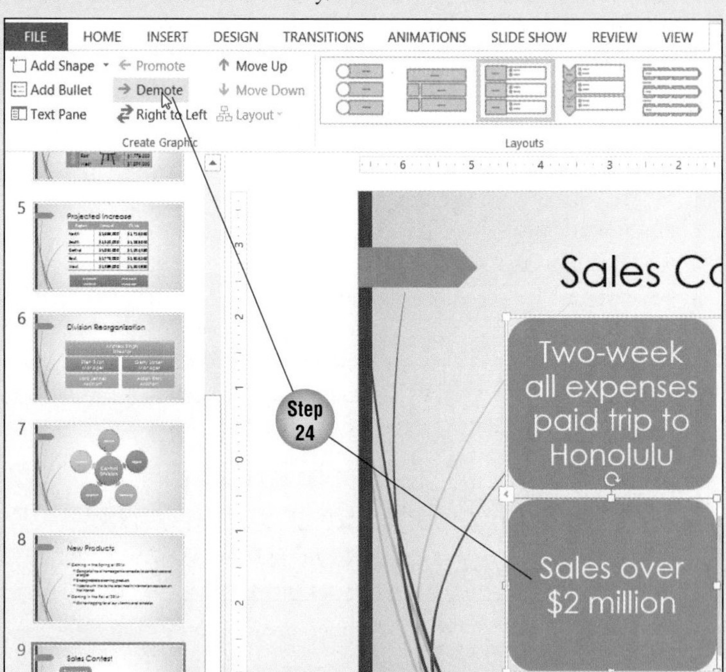

26. Click the Text Pane button in the Create Graphic group to display the *Type your text here* text pane.
27. Click immediately right of the *s* in *Vegas* in the text pane and then press the Enter key.
28. Press the Tab key and then type **Sales over $1 million**.
29. Close the text pane by clicking the Close button that displays in the upper right corner of the pane.
30. Click the More button that displays at the right side of the SmartArt Styles thumbnails and then click the *Inset* thumbnail (second column, first row in the *3-D* section).
31. Save **P-C5-P1-Conference.pptx**.
32. Print Slides 7 and 9.

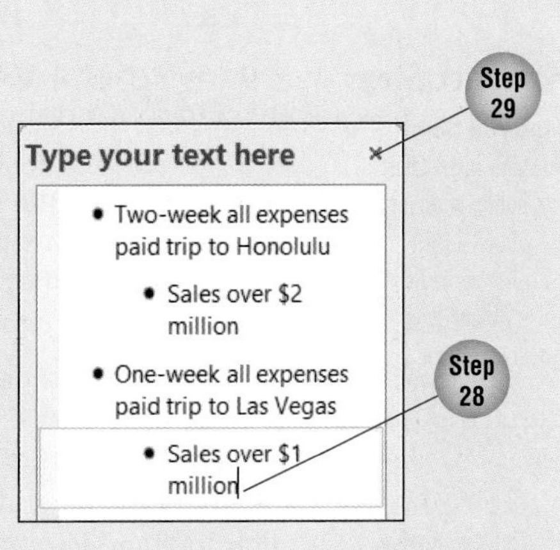

Converting a SmartArt Graphic to Text or Shapes

Reset Graphic

Convert

If you want to remove all formatting from a SmartArt graphic, click the Reset Graphic button in the Reset group on the SMARTART TOOLS DESIGN tab. With the Convert button, you can convert a SmartArt graphic to text or shapes. Click the Convert button and then click the *Convert to Text* option at the drop-down list to convert the SmartArt graphic to bulleted text. Click the *Convert to Shapes* option at the drop-down list to convert a SmartArt graphic to shapes. With the SmartArt graphic converted to shapes, you can move, resize, or delete a shape independently from the other shapes.

Project 1i **Converting SmartArt to Text and to Shapes** **Part 9 of 14**

1. With **P-C5-P1-Conference.pptx** open, make sure Slide 9 is active.
2. Click the SmartArt graphic to select it.
3. Click the SMARTART TOOLS DESIGN tab.
4. Click the Reset Graphic button in the Reset group.
5. With the SmartArt graphic still selected, click the Convert button in the Reset group and then click *Convert to Text* at the drop-down list.
6. Make Slide 7 active.
7. Click the SmartArt graphic to select it.
8. Click the SMARTART TOOLS DESIGN tab, click the Convert button in the Reset group, and then click *Convert to Shapes* at the drop-down list.
9. Select and then delete each of the arrows that points from the middle circle to each of the outer circles.
10. Save **P-C5-P1-Conference.pptx**.

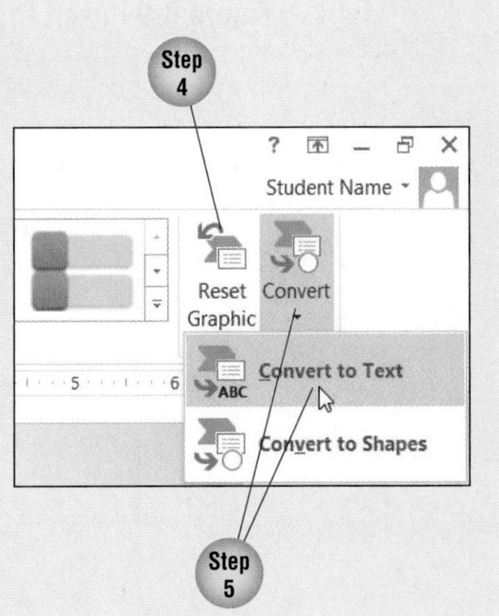

Creating a Chart

Quick Steps

Insert a Chart
1. Click Insert Chart button in content placeholder.
2. Click desired chart style and type.
3. Enter data in Excel worksheet.
4. Close Excel.

OR
1. Click INSERT tab.
2. Click Chart button.
3. Click desired chart type and style.
4. Enter data in Excel worksheet.
5. Close Excel.

Chart

You can create a variety of charts including bar and column charts, pie charts, area charts, and much more. To create a chart, click the Insert Chart button in a content placeholder or click the INSERT tab and then click the Chart button in the Illustrations group. This displays the Insert Chart dialog box, as shown in Figure 5.9. At this dialog box, choose the desired chart type in the list at the left side, click the chart style, and then click OK. Table 5.2 describes the ten basic chart types you can create in PowerPoint.

When you click OK at the Insert Chart dialog box, a sample chart is inserted in your slide and Excel opens with sample data, as shown in Figure 5.10. Type the desired data in the Excel worksheet cells over the existing data. As you type data, the chart in the slide reflects the typed data. To type data in the Excel worksheet, click in the desired cell, type the data, and then press the Tab key to make the next cell active, press Shift + Tab to make the previous cell active, or press Enter to make the cell below active.

The sample worksheet contains a data range of four columns and five rows and the cells in the data range display with a light fill color. Excel uses the data in the range to create the chart in the slide. You are not limited to four columns and five rows. Simply type data in cells outside the data range and Excel will expand the data range and incorporate the new data in the chart. This is because the table AutoExpansion feature is on by default. If you type data in a cell outside the data range, an AutoCorrect Options button displays in the lower right corner of the cell when you move away from the cell. Use this button if you want to turn off AutoExpansion. If you do not insert data in all four columns and five rows, decrease the size of the data range. To do this, position the mouse pointer on the small, square, blue icon that displays in the lower right corner of cell E5 until the pointer displays as a diagonally pointing two-headed arrow and then drag up to decrease the number of rows in the range and/or drag left to decrease the number of columns.

Figure 5.9 Insert Chart Dialog Box

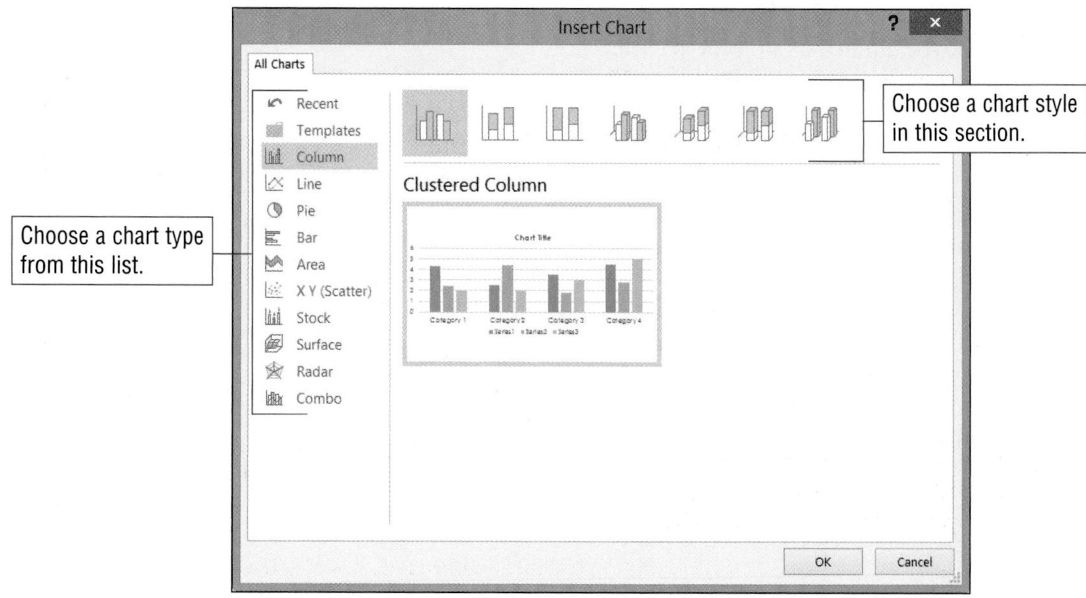

Once all data is entered in the worksheet, click the Close button that displays in the upper right corner of the screen. This closes the Excel window and displays the chart in the slide.

Table 5.2 Types of Charts

Type	*Description*
area	Emphasizes the magnitude of change, rather than time and the rate of change. It also shows the relationship of parts to a whole by displaying the sum of the plotted values.
bar	Shows individual figures at a specific time, or shows variations between components but not in relationship to the whole.
column	Compares separate (noncontinuous) items as they vary over time.
combo	Combines two or more chart types to make data easy to understand.
line	Shows trends and change over time at even intervals. It emphasizes the rate of change over time rather than the magnitude of change.
pie	Shows proportions and relationships of parts to the whole.
radar	Emphasizes differences and amounts of change over time and variations and trends. Each category has its own value axis radiating from the center point. Lines connect all values in the same series.
stock	Shows four values for a stock—open, high, low, and close.
surface	Shows trends in values across two dimensions in a continuous curve.
xy(scatter)	Either shows the relationships among numeric values in several data series or plots the interception points between *x* and *y* values. It shows uneven intervals of data and is commonly used in scientific data.

Figure 5.10 Sample Chart

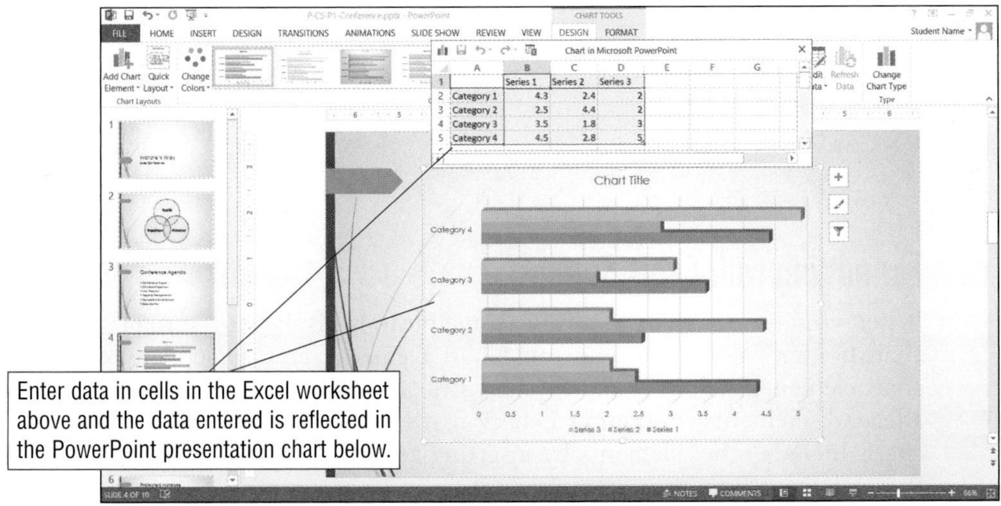

Project 1j Creating a Chart

Part 10 of 14

1. With **P-C5-P1-Conference.pptx** open, make Slide 3 active and then insert a new slide with the Blank layout.
2. Click the INSERT tab and then click the Chart button in the Illustrations group.
3. At the Insert Chart dialog box, click *Bar* in the left panel.
4. Double-click the *3-D Clustered Bar* option that displays at the top of the dialog box (fourth option).
5. In the Excel worksheet, position the mouse pointer in the bottom right corner of the cell D5 border until the mouse pointer displays as a diagonally pointing two-headed arrow. Hold down the left mouse button, drag to the left until the border displays at the right side of column C, and then release the mouse button.
6. Type the text in cells as shown below by completing the following steps:
   a. Click in cell B1 in the Excel worksheet, type **1st Half**, and then press the Tab key.
   b. With cell C1 active, type **2nd Half** and then press the Tab key.
   c. Click in cell A2, type **North**, and then press the Tab key.
   d. Type **$853,000** and then press the Tab key.
   e. Type **$970,000** and then press the Enter key.
   f. Continue typing the remaining data in cells as indicated at the right. (The data range will automatically expand to include row 6.)
7. Click the Close button that displays in the upper right corner of the Excel window.

Insert Chart

All Charts

Recent
Templates
Column
Line
Pie
Bar
Area

Clustered Bar

Step 3

Step 4

Chart in Microsoft PowerPo

	A	B	C	D
1		Series 1	Series 2	Series 3
2	Category 1	4.3	2.4	2
3	Category 2	2.5	4.4	2
4	Category 3	3.5	1.8	3
5	Category 4	4.5	2.8	5

Step 5

	A	B	C	D
1		1st Half	2nd Half	Series 3
2	North	$853,000	$970,000	2
3	South	$750,000	$910,000	2
4	Central	$720,000	$750,000	3
5	East	$880,000	$950,000	5
6	West	$830,000	$900,000	
7				

Step 6

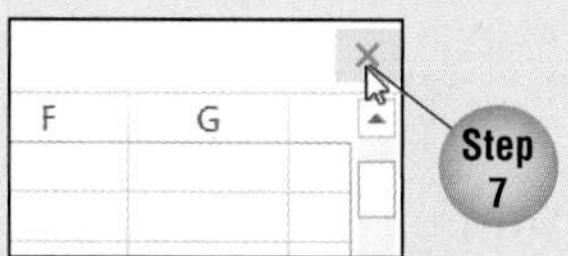

Step 7

8. Save **P-C5-P1-Conference.pptx**.

Formatting with Chart Buttons

Chart Elements

Chart Styles

When you insert a chart in a slide, three buttons display at the right side of the chart border. Click the top button, Chart Elements, and a side menu displays with chart elements such as axis title, chart title, data labels, data table, gridlines, and a legend. Elements containing a check mark in the check box are included in the chart. Include other elements by inserting a check mark in the check boxes for those elements you want in your chart.

You can apply a variety of chart styles to your chart. Click the Chart Styles button that displays at the right side of the chart and a side menu gallery of styles displays. Scroll down the gallery, hover your mouse over an option, and the style formatting is applied to your chart. In this way you can scroll down the gallery and preview the style before you apply it to your chart. In addition to applying a chart style, use the Chart Styles button side menu gallery to change the chart colors. Click the Chart Styles button and then click the COLOR tab that displays to the right of the STYLE tab. Click the desired color option at the color palette that displays. Hover your mouse over a color option to view how the color change affects the elements in your chart.

Chart Filters

Use the bottom button, Chart Filters, to isolate specific data in your chart. When you click the button, a side menu displays. Specify the series or categories you want to display in your chart. To do this, remove check marks from those elements that you do not want to appear in your chart. After removing the check marks, click the Apply button that displays toward the bottom of the side menu. Click the NAMES tab at the Chart Filters button side menu and options display for turning on/off the display of column and row names.

Project 1k Creating a Chart

Part 11 of 14

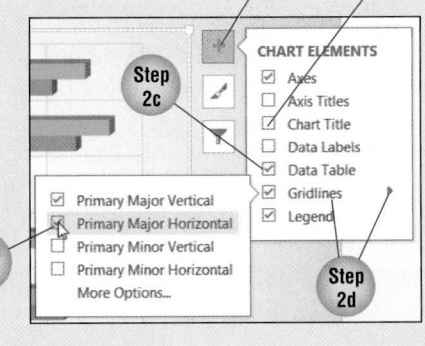

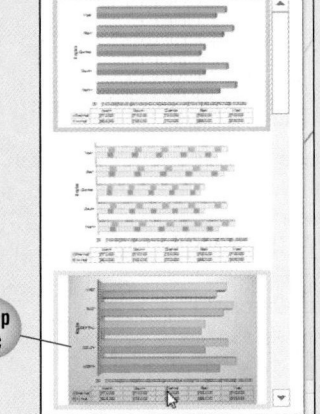

1. With **P-C5-P1-Conference.pptx** open, make sure Slide 4 is the active slide and that the chart in the slide is selected. (Make sure the chart is selected and not an element in the chart.)
2. Insert and remove chart elements by completing the following steps:
   a. Click the Chart Elements button that displays outside the upper right side of the chart.
   b. At the side menu that displays, click the *Chart Title* check box to remove the check mark.
   c. Click the *Data Table* check box to insert a check mark.
   d. Hover your mouse pointer over *Gridlines* in the Chart Elements button side menu and then click the right-pointing arrow that displays.
   e. At the other side menu that displays, click the *Primary Major Horizontal* check box to insert a check mark.
   f. Click the *Legend* check box to remove the check mark.
   g. Hover your mouse pointer over *Axis Titles* in the Chart Elements button side menu and then click the right-pointing arrow that displays.
   h. At the other side menu that displays, click the *Primary Vertical* check box to insert a check mark.
   i. With *Axis Title* selected in the rotated box at the left side of the chart, type **Region**.
3. Apply a different chart style by completing the following steps:
   a. Click the chart border to redisplay the chart buttons.
   b. Click the Chart Styles button that display to the right of the chart below the Chart Elements button.
   c. At the side menu gallery, click the *Style 3* option (third option in the gallery).

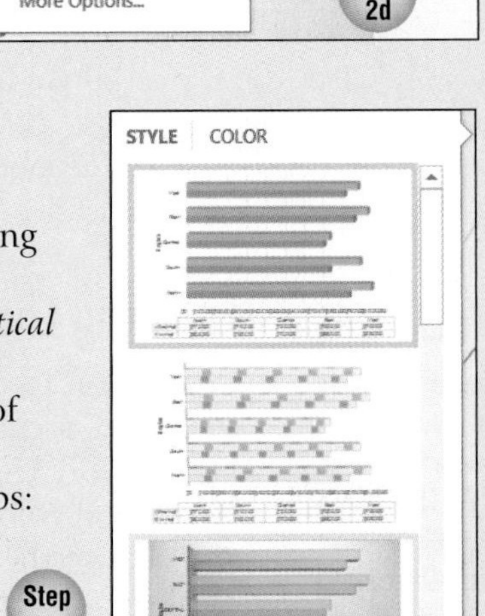

d. Click the COLOR tab at the top of the side menu and then click the *Color 2* option at the drop-down gallery (second row of color options in the *Colorful* section).
e. Click the Chart Styles button to remove the side menu.

4. Remove the horizontal axis title by completing these steps:
   a. Click the Chart Elements button.
   b. Hover your mouse pointer over Axes in the Chart Elements button side menu and then click the right-pointing arrow that displays.
   c. At the other side menu that displays, click the *Primary Horizontal* check box to remove the check mark.
   d. Click the Chart Elements button to remove the side menu.
5. Display only the North and South sales by completing the following steps:
   a. Click the Chart Filters button that displays below the Chart Styles button.
   b. Click the *Central* check box in the *CATEGORIES* section to remove the check mark.
   c. Click the *East* check box in the *CATEGORIES* section to remove the check mark.
   d. Click the *West* check box in the *CATEGORIES* section to remove the check mark.
   e. Click the Apply button that displays toward the bottom of the side menu.
   f. Click the Chart Filters button to remove the side menu.
   g. After viewing only the *North* and *South* sales, redisplay the other regions by clicking the Chart Filters button, clicking the *Central*, *East*, and *West* check boxes, and then clicking the Apply button.
   h. Click the Chart Filters button to remove the side menu.
6. Save **P-C5-P1-Conference.pptx**.

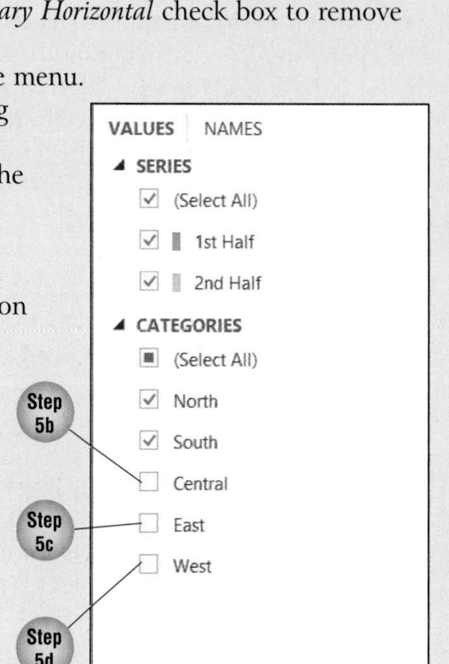

Quick Steps

Change the Chart Type and Style
1. Make the chart active.
2. Click CHART TOOLS DESIGN tab.
3. Click Change Chart Type button.
4. Click desired chart type.
5. Click desired chart style.
6. Click OK.

Change Chart Type

Changing Chart Design

In addition to the buttons that display outside the chart border, you can customize a chart with options on the CHART TOOLS DESIGN tab, shown in Figure 5.11. Use options on this tab to add a chart element, change the chart layout and colors, apply a chart style, select data and switch rows and columns, and change the chart type.

After you create a chart, you can change the chart type by clicking the Change Chart Type button in the Type group on the CHART TOOLS DESIGN tab. This displays the Change Chart Type dialog box. This dialog box contains the same options as the Insert Chart dialog box shown in Figure 5.9. At the Change Chart Type dialog box, click the desired chart type in the left panel and click the desired chart style in the right panel.

Figure 5.11 CHART TOOLS DESIGN Tab

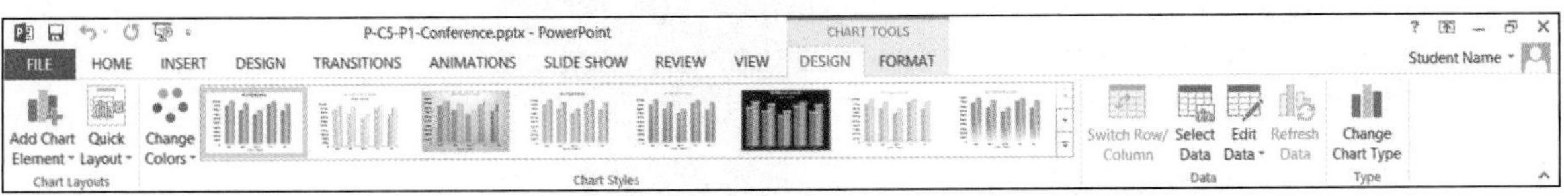

Select Data

Switch Row/Column

Edit Data

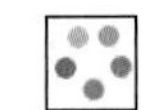
Change Colors

Quick Layout

Use options in the Data group on the CHART TOOLS DESIGN tab to change the grouping of the data in the chart, select specific data, edit data, and refresh the data. When you create a chart, the cells in the Excel worksheet are linked to the chart in the slide. Click the Select Data button in the Data group and Excel opens and the Select Data Source dialog box displays. At the Select Data Source dialog box, click the Switch Row/Column button to change the grouping of the selected data. Filter data at the dialog box by removing the check mark from those items in the dialog box that you do not want to appear in the chart. If you need to edit data in the chart, click the Edit Data button and the Excel worksheet opens. Make the desired changes to cells in the Excel worksheet and then click the Close button.

Apply predesigned chart styles with options in the Chart Styles group and use the Change Colors button to change the color of the selected element or chart. Click the Quick Layout button in the Chart Layouts group to display a drop-down gallery of layout options and add an element to the chart with the Add Chart Element button.

Project 1I Changing the Chart Design Part 12 of 14

1. With **P-C5-P1-Conference.pptx** open, make sure Slide 4 is active and the chart is selected. Click the CHART TOOLS DESIGN tab to make it active.
2. Looking at the chart, you decide that the bar chart was not the best choice for the data and decide to change to a column chart. Do this by completing the following steps:
   a. Click the Change Chart Type button in the Type group on the CHART TOOLS DESIGN tab.
   b. At the Change Chart Type dialog box, click the *Column* option in the left panel.
   c. Click the *3-D Clustered Column* option (fourth option at the top of the dialog box).
   d. Click OK to close the dialog box.
3. Change to a different layout by clicking the Quick Layout button in the Chart Layouts group and then clicking the *Layout 10* option (the last option).

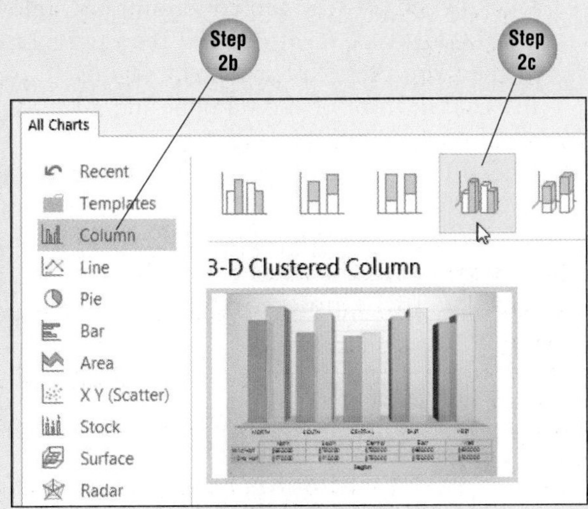

4. Click the Add Chart Element button in the Chart Layouts group, point to *Chart Title* at the drop-down list, and then click *Above Chart* at the side menu.
5. Type **2015 Regional Sales** as the chart title.
6. Click the chart border to deselect the chart title.
7. Click the *Style 1* thumbnail in the Chart Styles group (first thumbnail).
8. Select data and switch rows and columns by completing the following steps:
   a. Click the Select Data button in the Data group. (This opens Excel and displays the Select Data Source dialog box.)
   b. Click the Switch Row/Column button in the Select Data Source dialog box.

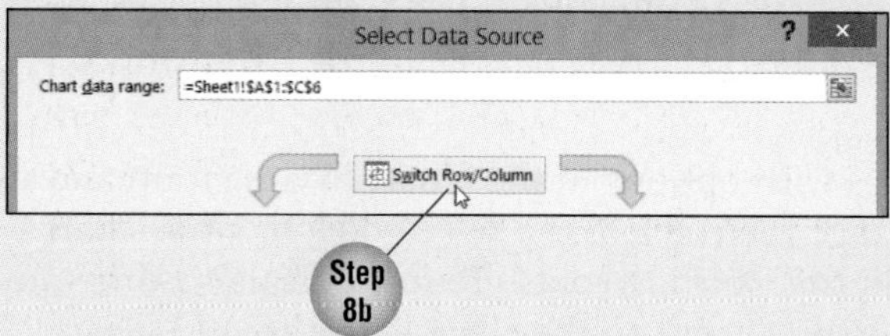

   c. Click OK. (This switches the grouping of the data from *Region* to *Half Yearly Sales*.)
9. After viewing the chart, switch the rows and columns back to the original groupings by dragging the Excel window so the Switch Row/Column button is visible in the Data group on the CHART TOOLS DESIGN tab, clicking in the chart, and then clicking the Switch Row/Column button.
10. Close the Excel window by clicking the Close button that displays in the upper right corner of the Excel window.
11. Click the Edit Data button in the Data group.
12. Click in cell B4 (the cell containing the amount *$720,000*), type **650000**, and then press Enter. (When you press Enter, a dollar sign is automatically inserted in front of the number and a thousand separator comma is inserted.)
13. Click in cell B6 (the cell containing the amount *$830,000*), type **730000**, and then press Enter.
14. Click the Close button that displays in the upper right corner of the Excel window.
15. Save **P-C5-P1-Conference.pptx**.

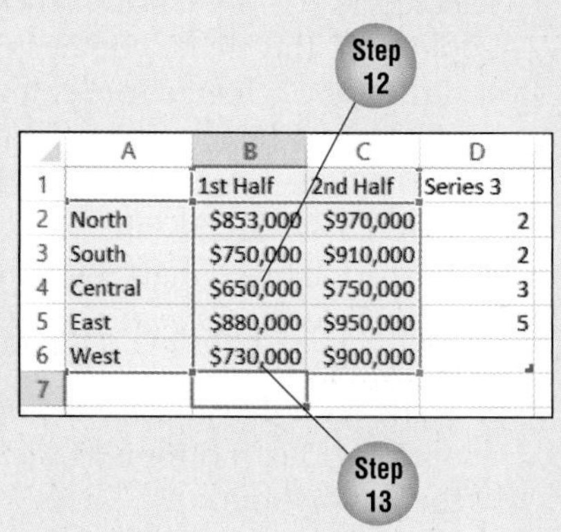

	A	B	C	D
1		1st Half	2nd Half	Series 3
2	North	$853,000	$970,000	2
3	South	$750,000	$910,000	2
4	Central	$650,000	$750,000	3
5	East	$880,000	$950,000	5
6	West	$730,000	$900,000	
7				

Formatting a Chart and Chart Elements

Apply formatting to a chart or chart elements with options in the Drawing group on the HOME tab. Apply a predesigned style to a chart or chart element with the Quick Styles button. Use other buttons in the group to add fill and outline color and apply effects.

In addition to the buttons in the Drawing group on the HOME tab, you can format and customize a chart and chart elements with options on the CHART TOOLS FORMAT tab, as shown in Figure 5.12. To format or modify a specific element in a chart, select the element. Do this by clicking the element or by clicking the Chart Elements button in the Current Selection group and then clicking the element at the drop-down list. With the element selected, apply the desired formatting. Click the Format Selection button in the Current Selection group and a task pane displays with options for formatting the selected element. Insert shapes with options in the Insert Shapes group. Click a shape or click the More button and then click a shape at the drop-down list and then drag in the chart to create the shape. Click the Change Shape button if you want to change the shape to a different shape.

Right-click text in a chart element to display the Mini toolbar.

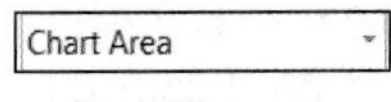

Chart Elements

Format Selection

Chart elements can be repositioned for easier viewing.

The Shape Styles group on the CHART TOOLS FORMAT tab contains predesigned styles you can apply to elements in the chart. Click the More button at the right side of the style thumbnails and a drop-down gallery displays of shape styles. Use the buttons that display at the right side of the Shape Styles group to apply fill, an outline, and an effect to a selected element. The WordArt Styles group contains predesigned styles you can apply to text in a chart. Use the buttons that display at the right side of the WordArt Styles group to apply fill color, an outline color, or an effect to text in a chart. Use options in the Arrange group to specify the layering, alignment, rotation, and size of a chart or chart element.

Additional formatting options are available at various task panes. Display a task pane by the clicking Format Selection button or by clicking a group task pane launcher. The Shape Styles, WordArt Styles, and Size groups on the CHART TOOLS FORMAT tab contain a task pane launcher. The task pane that opens at the right side of the screen depends on the chart or chart element selected.

Figure 5.12 CHART TOOLS FORMAT Tab

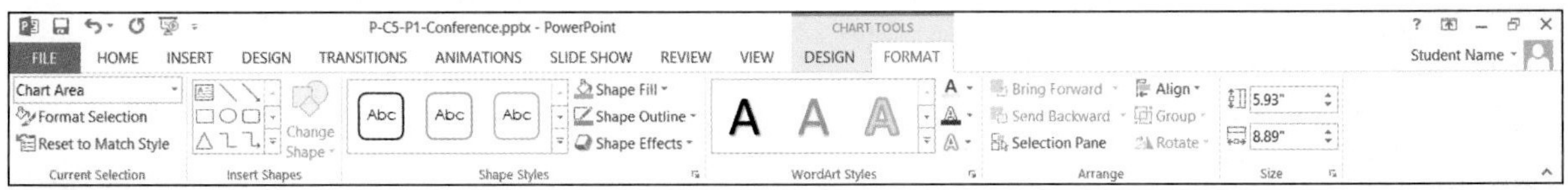

Project 1m Formatting a Chart and Chart Elements Part 13 of 14

1. With **P-C5-P1-Conference.pptx** open, make sure Slide 4 is active and the chart is selected.
2. Reposition and format the legend by completing the following steps:
   a. Click the Chart Elements button that displays at the right side of the chart.
   b. Hover your mouse pointer over *Legend*, click the right-pointing arrow at the right side of *Legend* in the side menu, and then click the *Right* option at the other side menu.
   c. Click the Chart Elements button again to remove the side menu.
   d. Click the legend to select it.
   e. If necessary, click the HOME tab.

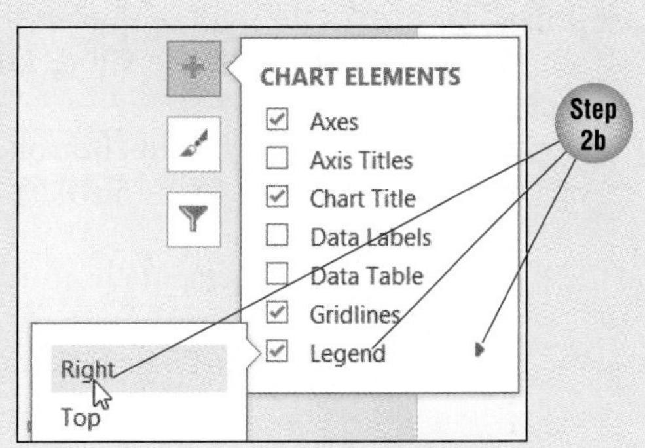

f. Click the Quick Styles button in the Drawing group and then click the *Subtle Effect - Lime, Accent 3* option (fourth column, fourth row).
g. Click the Shape Outline button arrow in the Drawing group and then click *Green, Accent 1, Darker 50%* (fifth column, bottom row in the *Theme Colors* section).
h. Increase the size of the legend by dragging down the bottom middle sizing handle about 0.25 inch.

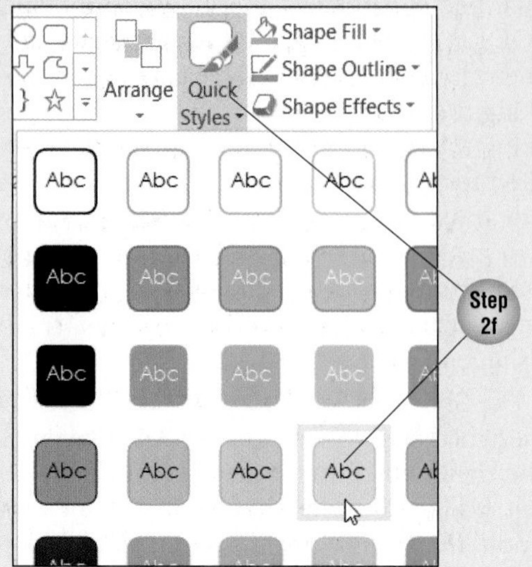

3. Format the title by completing the following steps:
   a. Click the CHART TOOLS FORMAT tab.
   b. Click the Chart Elements button arrow in the Current Selection group and then click *Chart Title* at the drop-down list.
   c. Click the More button at the right side of the style thumbnails in the Shape Styles group and then click *Intense Effect - Green, Accent 1* (second column, bottom row).
   d. Click the Shape Effects button, point to *Bevel*, and then click the *Cross* option (third column, first row in the *Bevel* section).

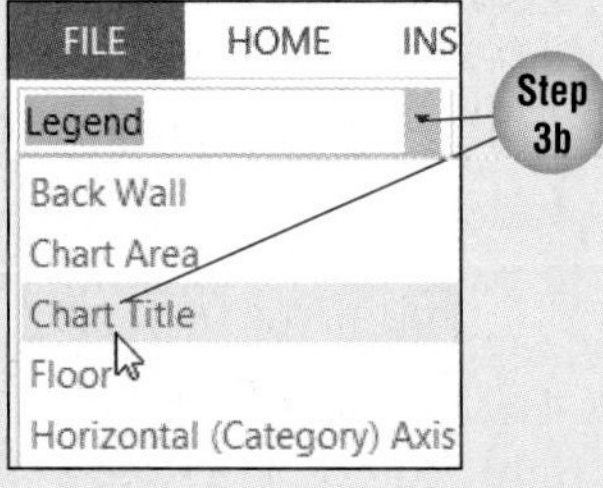

4. Customize the chart wall and floor by completing the following steps:
   a. Click the Chart Elements button arrow in the Current Selection group and then click *Back Wall* at the drop-down list.
   b. Click the Format Selection button in the Current Selection group. (This displays the Format Wall task pane.)

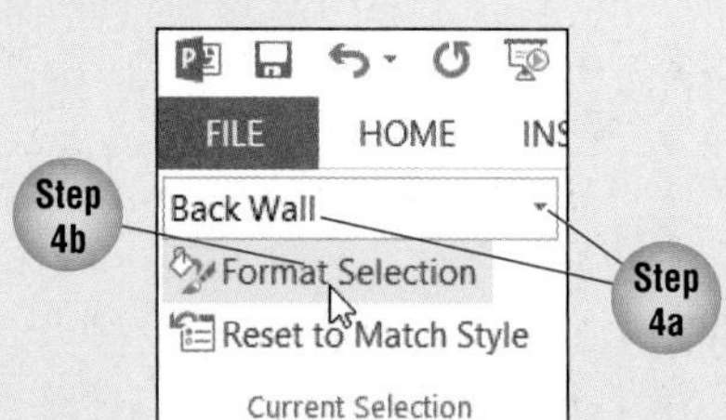

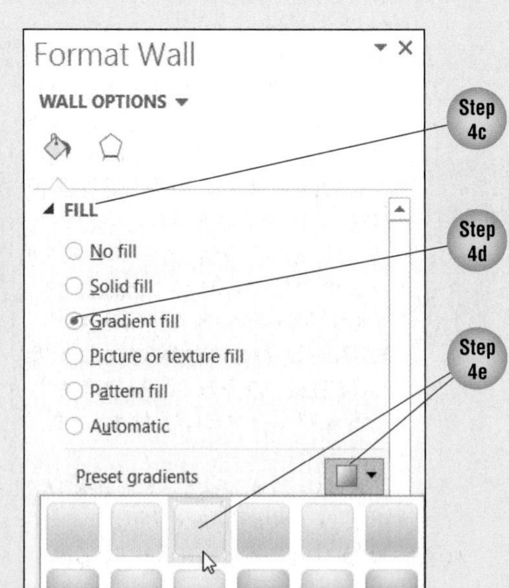

   c. Click *FILL* to display the options.
   d. Click the *Gradient fill* option in the Format Wall task pane with the Fill & Line icon selected.
   e. Click the Preset gradients button and then click the *Light Gradient - Accent 3* option (third column, first row).
   f. Click the Chart Elements button arrow and then click *Floor* at the drop-down list. (This displays the Format Floor task pane.)
   g. Click the *Solid fill* option.

5. Customize the 1st Half data series by completing the following steps:
   a. Click the Chart Elements button arrow and then click *Series "1st Half"* at the drop-down list.
   b. Click the Effects icon in the Format Data Series task pane.
   c. Click *3-D FORMAT* to display the options.
   d. Click the Material button in the task pane.
   e. At the gallery that displays, click the *Dark Edge* option (first option in the *Special Effect* section).
   f. Click the Bottom bevel button and then click the *Hard Edge* option (third column, third row in the *Bevel* section).

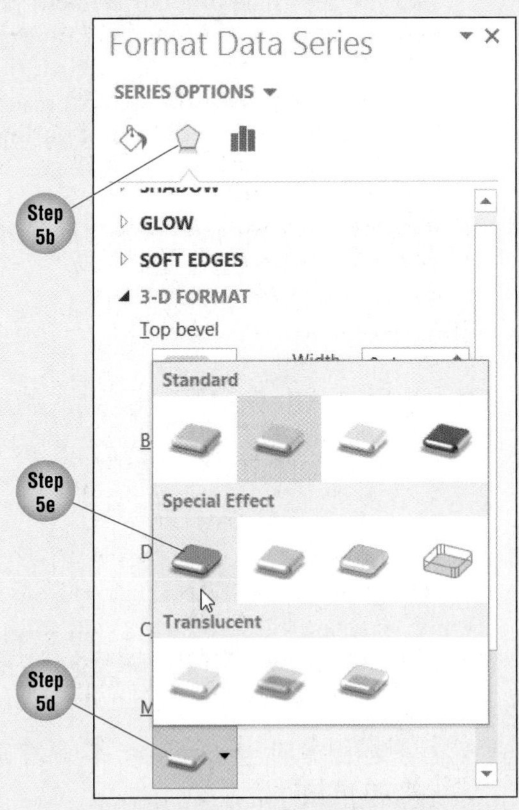

6. Complete steps similar to those in Step 5a through 5f to format the *Series "2nd Half"* chart element.
7. Customize the chart by completing the following steps:
   a. Click the Chart Elements button arrow and then click *Chart Area* at the drop-down list.
   b. Click the Fill & Line icon and make sure fill options display in the Format Chart Area task pane. (If necessary, click *FILL* to expand the options.)
   c. Click the *Picture or texture fill* option.
   d. Click the Texture button (displays below the Online button)
   e. Click the *Parchment* option (last column, third row).
   f. Scroll down the task pane to the *BORDER* section and, if necessary, click *BORDER* to expand the options.
   g. Click the *Solid line* option in the *BORDER* section.
   h. Click the Size & Properties icon.
   i. Click *SIZE* to display the options.
   j. Select the current measurement in the *Height* measurement box and then type 6.
   k. Select the current measurement in the *Width* measurement box, type 9, and then press Enter.
   l. Click *POSITION* to display the options.
   m. Select the current measurement in the *Horizontal position* measurement box and then type 2.5.
   n. Select the current measurement in the *Vertical position* measurement box, type 0.8, and then press Enter.
   o. Close the task pane by clicking the Close button in the upper right corner of the task pane.

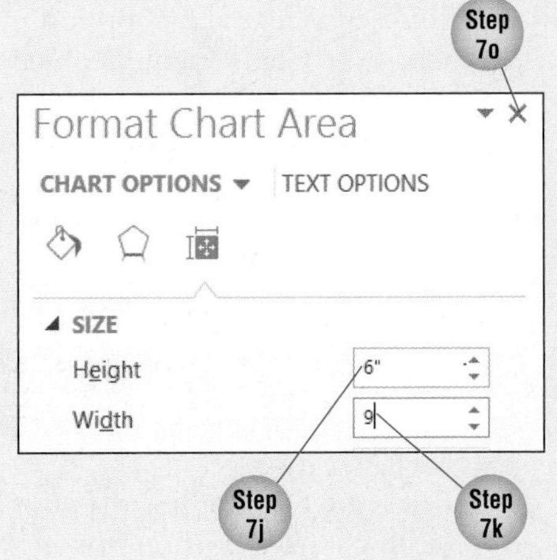

8. Save **P-C5-P1-Conference.pptx**.

Another method for formatting a chart or chart elements is to use options at the shortcut menu. Some of the options on the shortcut menu vary depending on the chart or chart element selected. Some common options include deleting the element, editing data, rotating the element, and adding data labels. To display the shortcut menu, right-click the element or the chart. In addition to the shortcut menu, the Mini toolbar also displays. The Mini toolbar contains options for applying fill color and outline color.

Project 1n Creating and Formatting a Pie Chart — Part 14 of 14

1. With **P-C5-P1-Conference.pptx** open, make Slide 6 active and then insert a new slide with the Blank layout.
2. Click the INSERT tab and then click the Chart button in the Illustrations group.
3. At the Insert Chart dialog box, click *Pie* in the left panel.
4. Double-click the *3-D Pie* option at the top of the dialog box (second option).
5. Type the text in cells in the Excel worksheet as shown at the right.

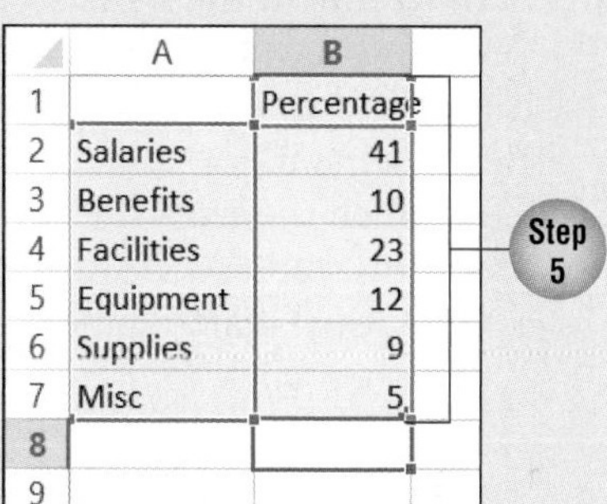

	A	B
1		Percentage
2	Salaries	41
3	Benefits	10
4	Facilities	23
5	Equipment	12
6	Supplies	9
7	Misc	5
8		
9		

6. When all data is entered, click the Close button that displays in the upper right corner of the Excel window.
7. Click the Chart Styles button that displays at the right side of the pie chart, click the *Style 3* chart style, and then click the Chart Styles button again to remove the side menu.
8. Move the data labels to the outside of the pie by completing the following steps:
   a. Click the Chart Elements button that displays at the right side of the chart.
   b. Hover your mouse pointer over the *Data Labels* option in the side menu and then click the right-pointing arrow that displays.
   c. Click the *Outside End* option.
   d. Click the Chart Elements button to remove the side menu.

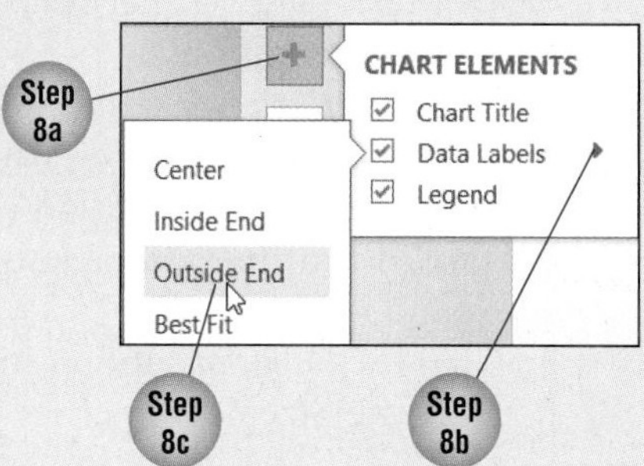

9. Apply formatting to the legend by completing the following steps:
   a. Hover your mouse just above the word *Salaries* in the legend until the mouse pointer displays with a four-headed arrow attached and then click the right mouse button.
   b. Click the Fill button on the Mini toolbar and then click *Tan, Background 2* (third column, first row in the *Theme Colors* section).
   c. Click the Outline button on the Mini toolbar and then click *Green, Accent 1, Darker 50%* (fifth column, bottom row in the *Theme Colors* section).
   d. Increase the size of the legend by dragging the bottom middle sizing handle down about 0.25 inch.

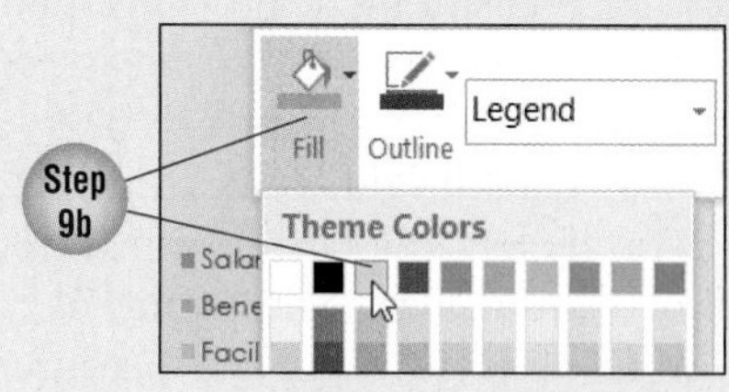

10. Edit the title by completing the following steps:
    a. Right-click the title *Percentage* and then click *Edit Text* in the shortcut menu.
    b. With the insertion point positioned in the title, press the End key to move the insertion point to the right of *Percentage*, press the spacebar, and then type **of 100k Division Budget**.
11. Click outside the title but inside the chart to select the chart.
12. Click the CHART TOOLS FORMAT tab.
13. Change the chart height to 6.5 inches and the chart width to 9 inches.
14. Click the Align button in the Arrange group and then click *Distribute Horizontally*.
15. Click the Align button in the Arrange group and then click *Distribute Vertically*.
16. Apply a transition and sound of your choosing to all slides in the presentation.
17. Save **P-C5-P1-Conference.pptx**.
18. Run the presentation.
19. Print the presentation as a handout with six slides printed horizontally per page.
20. Close **P-C5-P1-Conference.pptx**.

Step 10a

Perce

Delete

Reset to Match Style

Edit Text

Font...

Project 2 Create and Format a Travel Photo Album — 3 Parts

You will use the photo album feature to create a presentation containing travel photographs. You will also apply formatting and insert elements in the presentation.

Creating a Photo Album

With PowerPoint's photo album feature, you can create a presentation containing personal or business pictures. Customize and format the appearance of pictures by applying interesting layouts, frame shapes, and themes and insert elements such as captions and text boxes. To create a photo album, click the INSERT tab, click the Photo Album button arrow in the Images group, and then click *New Photo Album* at the drop-down list. This displays the Photo Album dialog box, as shown in Figure 5.14.

To insert pictures in the photo album, click the File/Disk button to display the Insert New Pictures dialog box. At this dialog box, navigate to the desired folder and then double-click the picture you want to insert in the album. This inserts the picture name in the *Pictures in album* list box in the dialog box and also displays the picture in the *Preview* section. As you insert pictures in the photo album, the picture names display in the *Pictures in album* list box in the order in which they will appear in the presentation. When you have inserted all of the desired pictures into the photo album, click the Create button. This creates the photo album as a presentation and displays the first slide. The photo album feature creates the first slide with the title *Photo Album* and the user's name.

Quick Steps

Create a Photo Album
1. Click INSERT tab.
2. Click Photo Album button arrow.
3. Click *New Photo Album.*
4. Click File/Disk button.
5. Double-click desired picture.
6. Repeat Steps 4 and 5 for all desired pictures.
7. Make desired changes at Photo Album dialog box.
8. Click Create button.

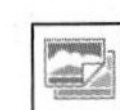

Photo Album

Figure 5.14 Photo Album Dialog Box

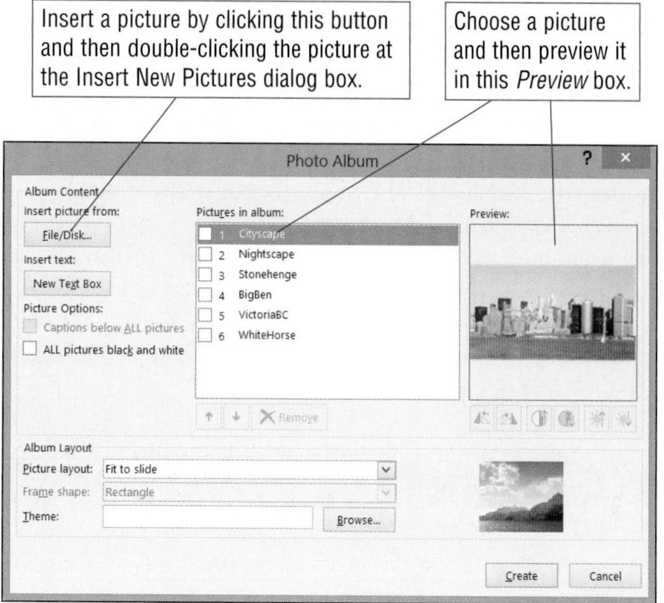

Project 2a Creating a Travel Photo Album

Part 1 of 3

1. At a blank screen, click the INSERT tab, click the Photo Album button arrow in the Images group, and then click *New Photo Album* at the drop-down list.
2. At the Photo Album dialog box, click the File/Disk button.
3. At the Insert New Pictures dialog box, navigate to the PC5 folder on your storage medium and then double-click ***Cityscape.jpg***.
4. At the Photo Album dialog box, click the File/Disk button, and then double-click ***Nightscape.jpg*** at the Insert New Pictures dialog box.
5. Insert the following additional pictures: ***Stonehenge.jpg***, ***WhiteHorse.jpg***, ***BigBen.jpg***, and ***VictoriaBC.jpg***.
6. Click the Create button. (This opens a presentation with each image in a separate slide. The first slide contains the default text *Photo Album* followed by your name (or the user name for the computer).
7. Save the presentation and name it **P-C5-P2-Album.pptx**.
8. Run the presentation.

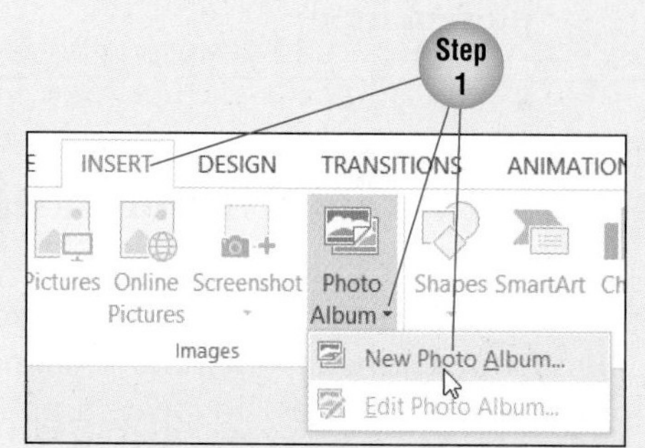

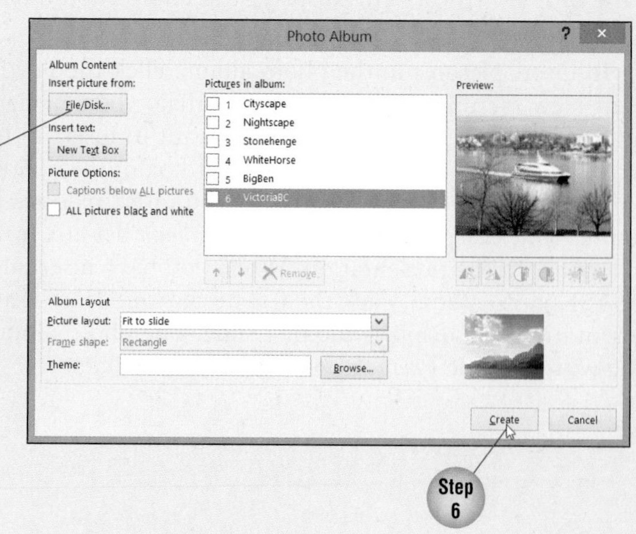

Editing and Formatting a Photo Album

If you want to make changes to a photo album presentation, open the presentation, click the INSERT tab, click the Photo Album button arrow in the Images group, and then click *Edit Photo Album* at the drop-down list. This displays the Edit Photo Album dialog box, which contains the same options as the Photo Album dialog box.

Rearrange the order of slides in a photo album presentation by clicking the desired slide in the *Pictures in album* list box and then clicking the button containing the up-pointing arrow to move the slide up in the order or clicking the button containing the down-pointing arrow to move the slide down in the order. Remove a slide by clicking the desired slide in the list box and then clicking the Remove button. Use buttons below the *Preview* box in the Edit Photo Album dialog box, to rotate the picture in the slide and increase or decrease the contrast or brightness of the picture.

The *Picture layout* option in the Album Layout group has a default setting of *Fit to slide*. At this setting the picture in each slide will fill most of the slide. You can change this setting by clicking the *Picture layout* option box arrow. With options at the drop-down list, specify whether you want one picture, two pictures, or four pictures inserted into the slide. You can also specify that you want the pictures inserted with titles.

If you change the *Picture layout* option to something other than the default of *Fit to slide*, the *Frame shape* option becomes available. Click the *Frame shape* option box arrow and a drop-down list displays with framing options. You can choose a rounded, simple, or double frame, or a soft or shadow effect frame.

Apply a theme to the photo album presentation by clicking the Browse button located at the right side of the *Theme* option box and then double-clicking the desired theme in the Choose Theme dialog box. This dialog box contains the predesigned themes provided by PowerPoint.

If you want to include captions with the pictures, change the *Picture layout* to one, two, or four slides and then click the *Captions below ALL pictures* check box located in the *Picture Options* section of the Edit Photo Album dialog box. PowerPoint will insert below each picture a caption containing the name of the picture. You can edit the caption in the slide in the presentation. If you want to display all of the pictures in your photo album in black and white, click the *ALL pictures black and white* check box in the *Picture Options* section of the dialog box.

Click the New Text Box button in the Edit Photo Album dialog box and a new slide containing a text box is inserted in the presentation. You can edit the information in the text box in the presentation. Once all changes have been made to the photo album, click the Update button located toward the bottom right side of the dialog box.

Quick Steps

Edit a Photo Album

1. Click INSERT tab.
2. Click Photo Album button arrow.
3. Click *Edit Photo Album*.
4. Make desired changes at Edit Photo Album dialog box.
5. Click Update button.

Project 2b **Editing and Formatting a Photo Album** **Part 2 of 3**

1. With **P-C5-P2-Album.pptx** open, make sure the INSERT tab is active, click the Photo Album button arrow in the Images group, and then click *Edit Photo Album* at the drop-down list.

2. At the Edit Photo Album dialog box, make the following changes:
   a. Click the *ALL pictures black and white* check box to insert a check mark.
   b. Click in the *VictoriaBC* check box in the *Pictures in album* list box and then click three times on the up-pointing arrow that displays below the list box. (This moves *VictoriaBC* so it is positioned between *Nightscape* and *Stonehenge*).

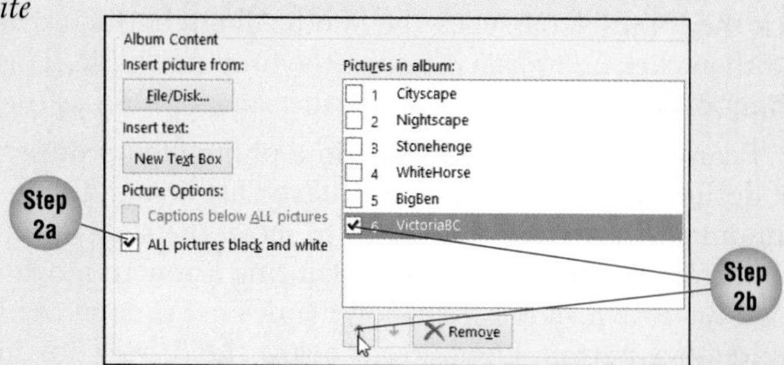

   c. Click once on the Rotate button located below the *Preview* box (the first button from the left below the picture). Click three more times on the Rotate button to return the image to the original orientation.
   d. Click the *VictoriaBC* check box in the *Pictures in album* list box to remove the check mark.
   e. Click the *Cityscape* check box in the *Pictures in album* list box and then click twice on the Increase Contrast button located under the *Preview* box.

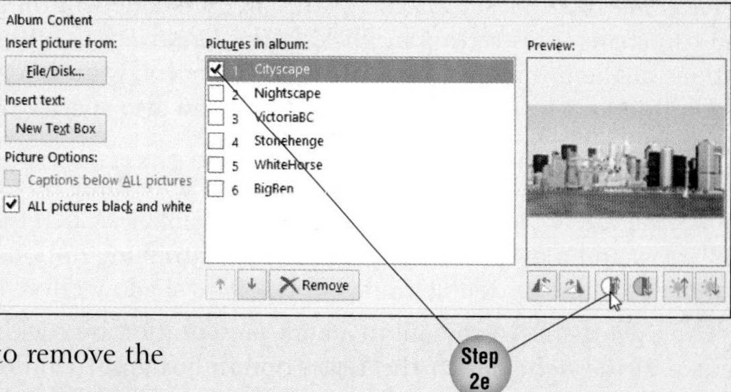

   f. Click the *Cityscape* check box to remove the check mark.
   g. Click the *Stonehenge* check box in the *Pictures in album* list box, click twice on the Increase Contrast button under the *Preview* box and then click twice on the Increase Brightness button (fifth button to the right of the Remove button).
   h. Click the *Picture layout* option box arrow and then click *1 picture* at the drop-down list.

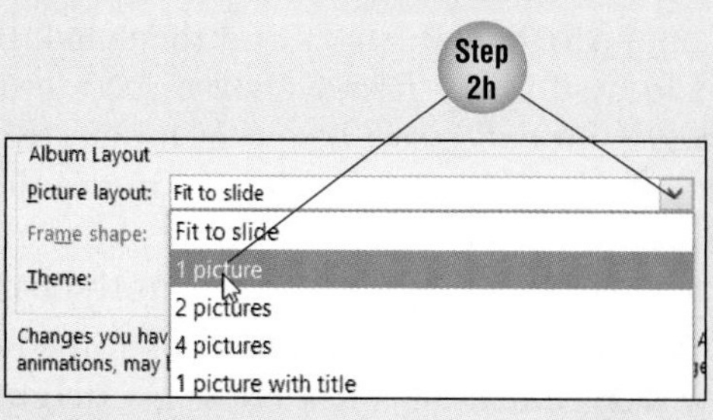

   i. Click the *Frame shape* option box arrow and then click *Center Shadow Rectangle* at the drop-down list.
   j. Click the Browse button located at the right side of the *Theme* option box. At the Choose Theme dialog box, double-click ***Facet.thmx***.
   k. Click the *Captions below ALL pictures* check box to insert a check mark.
   l. Click the *Stonehenge* check box in the *Pictures in album* list box to remove the check mark and then click the *BigBen* check box in the *Pictures in album* list box to insert a check mark.

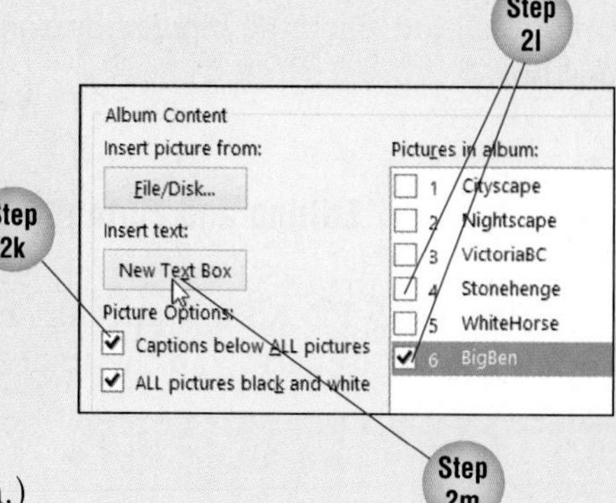

   m. Click the New Text Box button that displays at the left side of the list box. (This inserts a new slide containing a text box at the end of the presentation.)
   n. Click the Update button located in the lower right corner of the dialog box.

3. At the presentation, make the following formatting changes:
    a. Click the DESIGN tab.
    b. Click the blue variant in the Variants group (second variant).
4. With Slide 1 active, make the following changes:
    a. Select the text *Photo Album* and then type **Travel Album**.
    b. Select any text that displays after the word *by* and then type your first and last names.
    c. Click the INSERT tab and then click the Pictures button.
    d. At the Insert Picture dialog box, navigate to the PC5 folder on your storage medium and then double-click ***FCTLogo.jpg***.
    e. Click the Color button in the Adjust group on the PICTURE TOOLS FORMAT tab and then click *Set Transparent Color* at the drop-down list.
    f. Move the mouse pointer (pointer displays with a tool attached) to any white portion of the logo and then click the left mouse button. (This changes the white fill to transparent fill and allows the title to show through.)
    g. Change the height of the logo to 3.5 inches and then position the logo attractively in the slide.

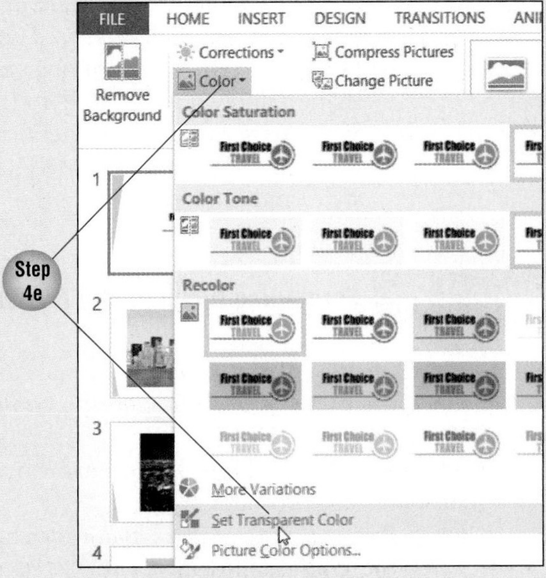

5. Make Slide 2 active and then edit the caption by completing the following steps:
    a. Click on any character in the caption *Cityscape*.
    b. Select *Cityscape* and then type **New York City Skyline**.

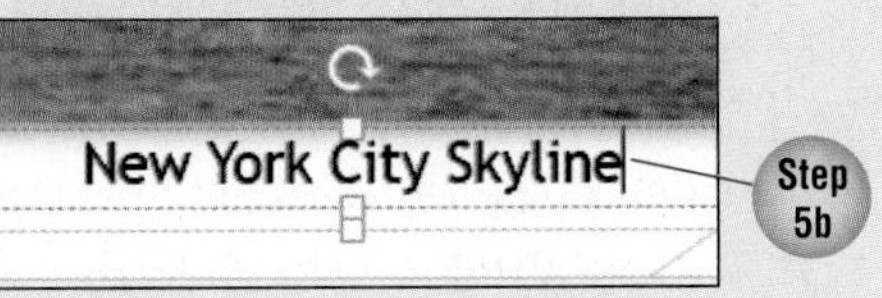

6. Complete steps similar to those in Step 5 to change the following captions:
    a. In Slide 3, change *Nightscape* to *New York City at Night*.
    b. In Slide 4, change *VictoriaBC* to *Victoria, British Columbia*.
    c. In Slide 5, change *Stonehenge* to *Stonehenge, Wiltshire County*.
    d. In Slide 6, change *WhiteHorse* to *White Horse, Wiltshire County*.
    e. In Slide 7, change *BigBen* to *Big Ben, London*.
7. Make Slide 8 active and then make the following changes:
    a. Select the text *Text Box* and then type **Call First Choice Travel at 213-555-4500 to book your next travel tour.**
    b. Select the text, change the font size to 48 points, apply the Blue font color, and center align the text.
    c. Change the width of the placeholder to 9 inches. (Do this with the *Shape Width* measurement box on the DRAWING TOOLS FORMAT tab.)
8. Apply a transition and sound of your choosing to all slides.
9. Run the presentation.
10. Save **P-C5-P2-Album.pptx**.

Formatting Pictures

If you format slides in the presentation instead of the Edit Photo Album dialog box, you may lose some of those changes if you subsequently display the Edit Photo Album dialog box, make changes, and then click the Update button. Consider making your initial editing and formatting changes at the Edit Photo Album dialog box and then make final editing and formatting changes in the presentation.

Since a picture in a slide in a photo album is an object, you can format it with options on the DRAWING TOOLS FORMAT tab and the PICTURE TOOLS FORMAT tab. With options on the DRAWING TOOLS FORMAT tab, insert shapes, apply a shape style to the picture and caption (if one is displayed), apply a WordArt style to caption text, and arrange and size the picture. Use options on the PICTURE TOOLS FORMAT tab to adjust the color of the picture, apply a picture style, and arrange and size the picture.

Project 2c Formatting Pictures in a Presentation — Part 3 of 3

1. With **P-C5-P2-Album.pptx** open, make Slide 2 active.
2. Change the pictures back to color by completing the following steps:
   a. Click the INSERT tab.
   b. Click the Photo Album button arrow in the Images group and then click *Edit Photo Album* at the drop-down list.
   c. Click the *ALL pictures black and white* check box to remove the check mark.
   d. Click the Update button.
3. Format the picture in Slide 2 by completing the following steps:
   a. Click the picture to select it.
   b. Click the DRAWING TOOLS FORMAT tab.
   c. Click the More button at the right side of the thumbnails in the Shape Styles group and then click *Subtle Effect - Turquoise, Accent 1* (second column, fourth row).

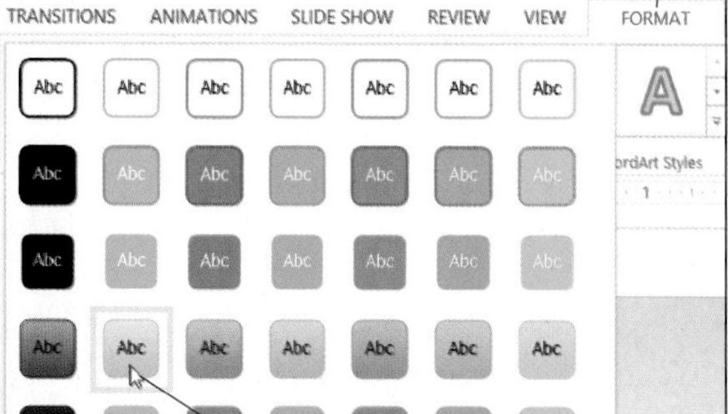

4. Apply the same style to the pictures in Slides 3 through 7 by making each slide active, clicking the picture, and then pressing F4. (Pressing F4 repeats the style formatting.)
5. Make Slide 2 active and then apply a WordArt style to the caption text by completing the following steps:
   a. With Slide 2 active, click the picture to select it.
   b. Click the DRAWING TOOLS FORMAT tab.
   c. Click the More button at the right side of the thumbnails in the WordArt Styles group and then click *Fill - Blue, Accent 2, Outline - Accent 2* (third column, first row).
6. Apply the same WordStyle style to the caption text in Slides 3 through 7 by making each slide active, clicking the picture, and then pressing F4.
7. Make Slide 8 active and then change the width of the placeholder to 9 inches.
8. Run the presentation.
9. Print the presentation as a handout with four slides horizontally per page.
10. Save and then close **P-C5-P2-Album.pptx**.

Chapter Summary

- With the Table button in the Tables group on the INSERT tab, you can create a table, insert an Excel spreadsheet, and draw a table in a slide.
- Change the table design with options and buttons on the TABLE TOOLS DESIGN tab. Change the table layout with options and buttons in the TABLE TOOLS LAYOUT tab.
- Use the SmartArt feature to insert predesigned graphics such as diagrams and organizational charts in a slide.
- Use options and buttons in the SMARTART TOOLS DESIGN tab to change the graphic layout, apply a style to the graphic, and reset the graphic back to the original formatting.
- Use options and buttons in the SMARTART TOOLS FORMAT tab to change the size and shapes of objects in the graphic; apply shape styles; change the shape fill, outline, and effects; and arrange and size the graphic.
- Insert text directly into a SmartArt graphic shape or at the Text pane. Display this pane by clicking the Text Pane button in the Create Graphic group on the SMARTART TOOLS DESIGN tab.
- You can convert text or WordArt to a SmartArt graphic and convert a SmartArt graphic to text or shapes.
- A chart is a visual presentation of data. You can create a variety of charts, as described in Table 5.2.
- To create a chart, display the Insert Chart dialog box by clicking the Insert Chart button in a content placeholder or clicking the Chart button in the Illustrations group on the INSERT tab.
- Enter chart data in an Excel worksheet. When entering data, press Tab to make the next cell active, press Shift + Tab to make the previous cell active, and press Enter to make the cell below active.
- Modify a chart design with options and buttons on the CHART TOOLS DESIGN tab.
- Cells in the Excel worksheet used to create a chart are linked to the chart in the slide. To edit chart data, click the Edit Data button on the CHART TOOLS DESIGN tab and then make changes to the text in the Excel worksheet.
- Customize the format of a chart and chart elements with options and buttons on the CHART TOOLS FORMAT tab. You can select the chart or a specific element, apply a style to a shape, apply a WordArt style to text, and arrange and size the chart.
- Use the Photo Album feature in the Images group on the INSERT tab to create a presentation containing pictures and then edit and format the pictures.
- At the Photo Album dialog box (or the Edit Photo Album dialog box), insert pictures and then use options to customize the photo album.
- Use options on the DRAWING TOOLS FORMAT tab and the PICTURE TOOLS FORMAT tab to format pictures in a photo album presentation.

Commands Review

FEATURE	RIBBON TAB, GROUP	BUTTON, OPTION	PLACEHOLDER BUTTON
Choose a SmartArt Graphic dialog box	INSERT, Illustrations		
convert bulleted text to SmartArt	HOME, Paragraph		
create photo album	INSERT, Images	, *New Photo Album*	
edit photo album	INSERT, Images	, *Edit Photo Album*	
Insert Chart dialog box	INSERT, Illustrations		
Insert Table dialog box	INSERT, Tables	, *Insert Table*	
Text pane	SMARTART TOOLS DESIGN, Create Graphic		

Concepts Check

Test Your Knowledge

Completion: In the space provided at the right, indicate the correct term, symbol, or command.

1. This term refers to the intersection between a row and a column. ______________
2. Display the Insert Table dialog box by clicking this button in a content placeholder. ______________
3. Press this key on the keyboard to move the insertion point to the next cell. ______________
4. Press these keys on the keyboard to select all cells in a table. ______________
5. The Table Styles group is located on this tab. ______________
6. Use options and buttons on this tab to delete and insert rows and columns and merge and split cells. ______________
7. Click this button in a content placeholder to display the Choose a SmartArt Graphic dialog box. ______________
8. When you insert a SmartArt graphic in a slide and the graphic is selected, this tab is active. ______________
9. Create a SmartArt graphic with bulleted text by clicking in the text placeholder, clicking this button, and then clicking the desired SmartArt graphic at the drop-down gallery. ______________

10. Click the Chart button in this group on the INSERT tab to display the Insert Chart dialog box. ____________________

11. Insert a chart in a slide and this tab is active. ____________________

12. To edit data in a chart, click the Edit Data button in this group on the CHART TOOLS DESIGN tab. ____________________

13. This group on the CHART TOOLS FORMAT tab contains predesigned styles you can apply to elements in a chart. ____________________

14. This group on the CHART TOOLS FORMAT tab contains predesigned styles you can apply to chart text. ____________________

15. To create a photo album, click the INSERT tab, click the Photo Album button arrow, and then click this at the drop-down list. ____________________

16. Click the down-pointing arrow at the right of this option in the Edit Photo Album dialog box to display a list of framing choices. ____________________

17. To insert captions below pictures in a photo album, insert a check mark in this check box in the Edit Photo Album dialog box. ____________________

Skills Check Assess Your Performance

Assessment 1

CREATE AND FORMAT TABLES AND SMARTART IN A RESTAURANT PRESENTATION

1. Open **Dockside.pptx** and then save the presentation with Save As and name it **P-C5-A1-Dockside**.
2. Make Slide 6 active and then create the table shown in the slide in Figure 5.15 on page 227 with the following specifications:
   a. Create a table with three columns and six rows.
   b. Type the text in cells as shown in Figure 5.15.
   c. Apply the Medium Style 1 - Accent 2 style to the table (third column, first row in the *Medium* section).
   d. Select all of the text in the table, center the text vertically, change the font size to 20 points, and change the font color to *Turquoise, Accent 2, Darker 50%* (sixth column, bottom row in the *Theme Colors* section).
   e. Change the height of the table to 3.7 inches and the width to 9 inches.
   f. Center the text in the first row.
   g. Center the data in the third column.
   h. Horizontally distribute the table.

3. Make Slide 4 active and then create the table shown in the slide in Figure 5.16 with the following specifications:
   a. Create a table with four columns and three rows.
   b. Select the entire table, change the vertical alignment to center, and then change the font size to 28 points.
   c. Merge the cells in the first column, change the text direction to *Rotate all text 270°*, change the alignment to center, change the font size to 40 points, and then type **Lunch**.
   d. Merge the cells in the third column, change the text direction to *Rotate all text 270°*, change the alignment to center, change the font size to 40 points, and then type **Dinner**.
   e. Type the remaining text in cells as shown in Figure 5.16.
   f. Change the height of the table to 3 inches.
   g. Change the width of the first and third columns to 1.2 inches.
   h. Change the width of the second and fourth columns to 2.5 inches.
   i. Insert a check mark in the *Banded Columns* check box in the Table Style Options group on the TABLE TOOLS DESIGN tab and remove the check marks from the other check boxes in the group.
   j. Apply the Light Style 3 - Accent 2 style to the table.
   k. Select all of the text in the table and then change the font color to *Light Turquoise, Background 2, Darker 75%*.
   l. Distribute the table horizontally on the slide.
4. Make Slide 5 active and then create the SmartArt organizational chart shown in the slide in Figure 5.17 with the following specifications:
   a. Choose the Half Circle Organization Chart graphic at the Choose a SmartArt Graphic dialog box.
   b. Select and then delete the second box (select the text box) so your chart appears with the same number of boxes and in the same order as the organizational chart in Figure 5.17.
   c. Type the text in the boxes as shown in Figure 5.17 (Press Enter after typing each name.).
   d. Change the color to *Colorful Range - Accent Colors 3 to 4*.
   e. Apply the Polished SmartArt style.
   f. Change the text fill color to *Dark Teal, Text 2, Darker 25%*.
   g. Change the height of the organizational chart to 6.5 inches and change the width to 10 inches.
   h. Distribute the SmartArt organizational chart horizontally on the slide.
5. Make Slide 1 active and then format the title and create the SmartArt graphic shown in the slide in Figure 5.18 with the following specifications:
   a. Create the SmartArt graphic with the Linear Venn option located in the Relationship group.
   b. Type the text in the shapes as shown in Figure 5.18.
   c. Change the colors to *Colorful - Accent Colors*.
   d. Apply the Cartoon SmartArt style.
   e. Change the height of the graphic to 3 inches and the width to 9 inches.
   f. Align the SmartArt at the bottom of the slide. (Use the Align button in the Arrange group on the SMARTART TOOLS FORMAT tab.)
6. Make Slide 2 active, select the bulleted text placeholder, and then convert the bulleted text to a Basic Matrix SmartArt graphic as shown in the slide in Figure 5.19 with the following specifications:
   a. Change the colors to *Colorful - Accent Colors*.
   b. Apply the Cartoon SmartArt style.
   c. Change the height of the graphic to 4.5 inches.

7. Apply a transition and sound of your choosing to all slides in the presentation.
8. Run the presentation.
9. Print the presentation as a handout with six slides horizontally per page.
10. Save and then close **P-C5-A1-Dockside.pptx**.

Figure 5.15 Assessment 1, Slide 6

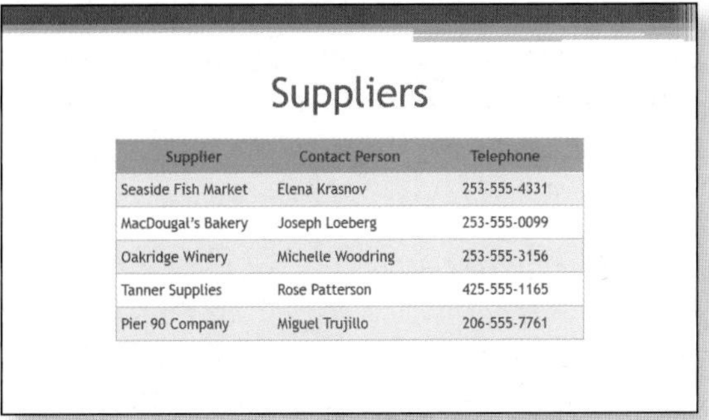

Supplier	Contact Person	Telephone
Seaside Fish Market	Elena Krasnov	253-555-4331
MacDougal's Bakery	Joseph Loeberg	253-555-0099
Oakridge Winery	Michelle Woodring	253-555-3156
Tanner Supplies	Rose Patterson	425-555-1165
Pier 90 Company	Miguel Trujillo	206-555-7761

Figure 5.16 Assessment 1, Slide 4

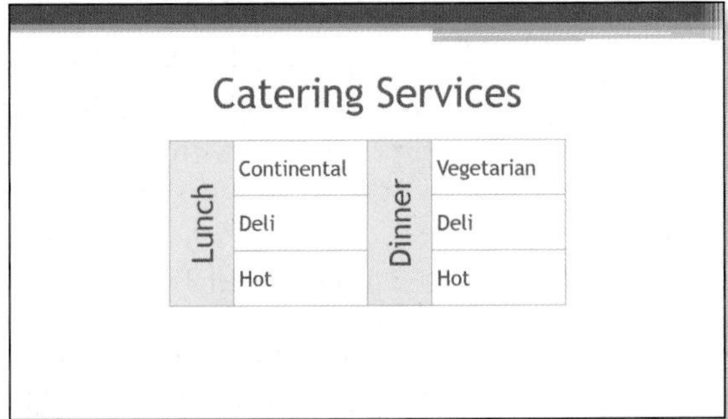

Figure 5.17 Assessment 1, Slide 5

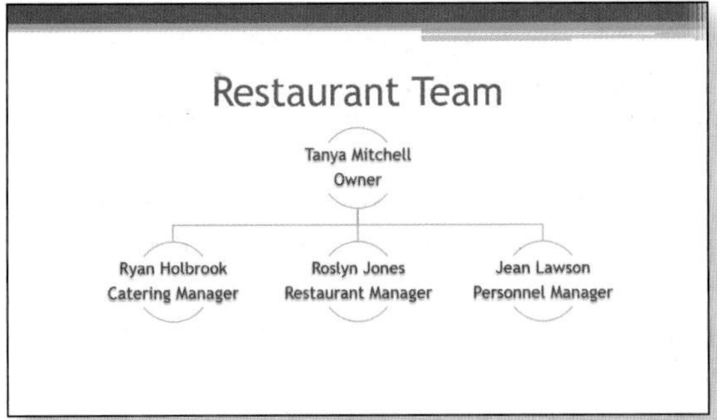

Figure 5.18 Assessment 1, Slide 1

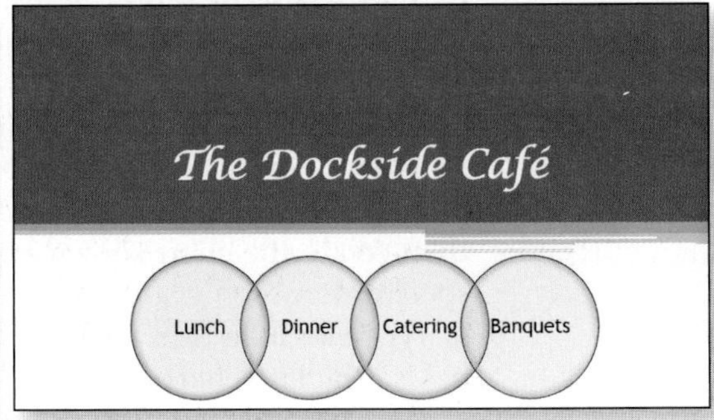

Figure 5.19 Assessment 1, Slide 2

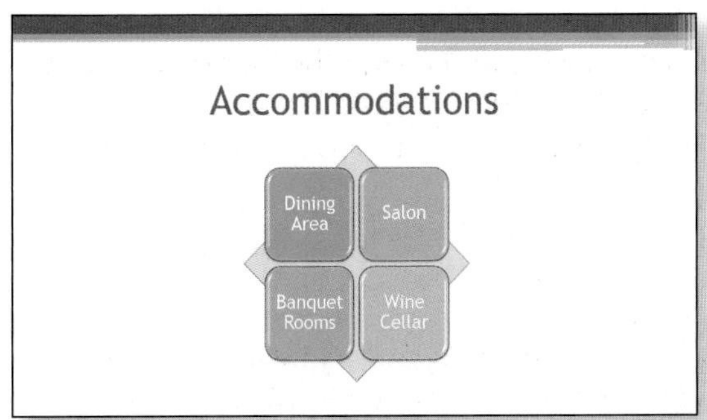

Assessment 2

CREATE AND FORMAT CHARTS IN A MARKETING PRESENTATION

1. Open **MarketingPres.pptx** and save the presentation with Save As and name it **P-C5-A2-MarketingPres**.
2. Make Slide 2 active, insert a new slide with the Title and Content layout, and then create the chart shown in the slide in Figure 5.20 with the following specifications:
   a. Type the slide title as shown in Figure 5.20 on the next page.
   b. Use the pie chart *3-D Pie* option to create the chart.
   c. Type the following information in the Excel worksheet:

	Percentage
Salaries	47%
Equipment	18%
Supplies	4%
Production	21%
Distribution	10%

   d. Apply the Layout 7 chart layout using the Quick Layout button.
   e. Apply the Style 5 chart style.
   f. Move the legend to the right.
   g. Select the legend and then change the font size to 24 points.
   h. Insert data labels on the inside end.
   i. Select the data labels and then change the font size to 20 points.
3. Print Slide 3.
4. After looking at the slide, you realize that two of the percentages are incorrect. Edit the Excel data and change *47%* to *42%* and change *10%* to *15%*.
5. With Slide 3 active, insert a new slide with the Title and Content layout and then create the chart shown in the slide in Figure 5.21 with the following specifications:
   a. Type the slide title as shown in Figure 5.21.
   b. Use the line chart *Line with Markers* option to create the chart.
   c. Type the following information in the Excel worksheet:

	Revenues	Expenses
1st Qtr	$789,560	$670,500
2nd Qtr	$990,450	$765,000
3rd Qtr	$750,340	$780,000
4th Qtr	$980,400	$875,200

   d. Apply the Style 4 chart style.
   e. Add primary major vertical gridlines.
   f. Add a data table with legend keys.
   g. Remove the title and remove the legend.
   h. Select the chart area and then change the font size to 18 points.
   i. With the chart area still selected, display the Format Chart Area task pane and then specify a gradient fill of *Light Gradient - Accent 2*.
   j. Select the Revenues series and then change the weight of the line to 4 ½ points. (Do this with the Shape Outline button in the Shape Styles group on the CHART TOOLS FORMAT tab.)
   k. Select the Expenses series and then change the weight of the line to 4 ½ points.
6. Apply a transition and sound of your choosing to each slide in the presentation.

Figure 5.20 Assessment 2, Slide 3

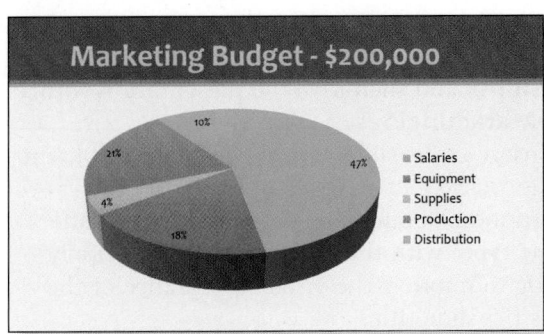

Figure 5.21 Assessment 2, Slide 4

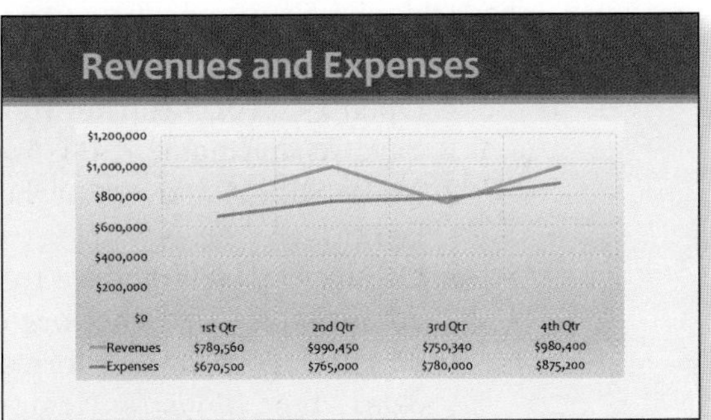

7. Run the presentation.
8. Print the presentation as a handout with six slides printed horizontally per page.
9. Save and then close **P-C5-A2-MarketingPres.pptx**.

Assessment 3

CREATE A SCENERY PHOTO ALBUM

SNAP Grade It

1. At a blank screen, create a new photo album.
2. At the Photo Album dialog box, insert the following images:

   AlderSprings.jpg
   CrookedRiver.jpg
   Mountain.jpg
   Ocean.jpg
   Olympics.jpg
   River.jpg
3. Change the *Picture layout* option to *1 picture with title*.
4. Change the *Frame shape* option to *Simple Frame, White*.
5. Apply the Integral theme.
6. Click the Create button.
7. At the presentation, click the DESIGN tab and then click the fourth variant.
8. Insert the following titles in the specified slides:
   Slide 2 *Alder Springs, Oregon*
   Slide 3 *Crooked River, Oregon*
   Slide 4 *Mt. Rainier, Washington*
   Slide 5 *Pacific Ocean, Washington*
   Slide 6 *Olympic Mountains, Washington*
   Slide 7 *Salmon River, Idaho*
9. Make Slide 1 active, select any name that follows *by*, and then type your first and last names.
10. Save the presentation and name it **P-C5-A3-PhotoAlbum**.
11. Print the presentation as a handout with four slides printed horizontally per page.
12. Close **P-C5-A3-PhotoAlbum.pptx**.

Assessment 4

CREATE A SALES AREA CHART

1. Open **P-C5-A2-MarketingPres.pptx** and then save the presentation with Save As and name it **P-C5-A4-MarketingPres**.
2. Make Slide 4 active and then insert a new slide with the Title and Content layout.
3. Use Excel's Help feature to learn more about chart types and then create an area chart (use the *Area* chart type) with the data shown below. Apply design, layout, and/or formatting to improve the visual appearance of the chart. Type **Sales by Region** as the slide title.

	Region 1	Region 2	Region 3
Sales 2012	$650,300	$478,100	$225,500
Sales 2013	$623,100	$533,600	$210,000
Sales 2014	$725,600	$478,400	$296,500

4. Print Slide 5.
5. Save and then close **P-C5-A4-MarketingPres.pptx**.

Visual Benchmark Demonstrate Your Proficiency

CREATE AND FORMAT A MEDICAL CENTER PRESENTATION

1. Open **RMCPres.pptx** and then save the presentation with Save As and name it **P-C5-VB-RMCPres**.
2. Create the presentation shown in Figure 5.22 with the following specifications:
   a. Create Slide 2 with the SmartArt Hierarchy relationship graphic and apply the Colorful Range - Accent Colors 2 to 3 colors to the graphic. (Press Enter after typing each title.)
   b. Create Slide 3 with the SmartArt Basic Radial relationship graphic and apply the Colorful - Accent Colors to the graphic.
   c. Create Slide 4 and insert the table as shown in Slide 5. Apply the Medium Style 2 - Accent 1 table style and apply other formatting so your table looks similar to the table in the figure.
   d. Use the information shown in the data table to create the 3-D Clustered Column chart as shown in Slide 5. Apply formatting so your chart looks similar to the chart in the figure. As the last formatting step, select the entire chart and change the font size to 16 points and apply the Black, Text 1 font color.
   e. Use the information shown in the legend and the data information at the outside end of each pie to create a 3-D pie chart as shown in Slide 6. Apply formatting so your pie chart looks similar to the chart in the figure. As the last formatting step, select the entire chart and change the font size to 16 points and apply the Black, Text 1 font color.
3. Apply a transition and sound of your choosing to all slides in the presentation.
4. Print the presentation as a handout with six slides printed horizontally per page.
5. Save and then close **P-C5-VB-RMCPres.pptx**.

Figure 5.22 Visual Benchmark

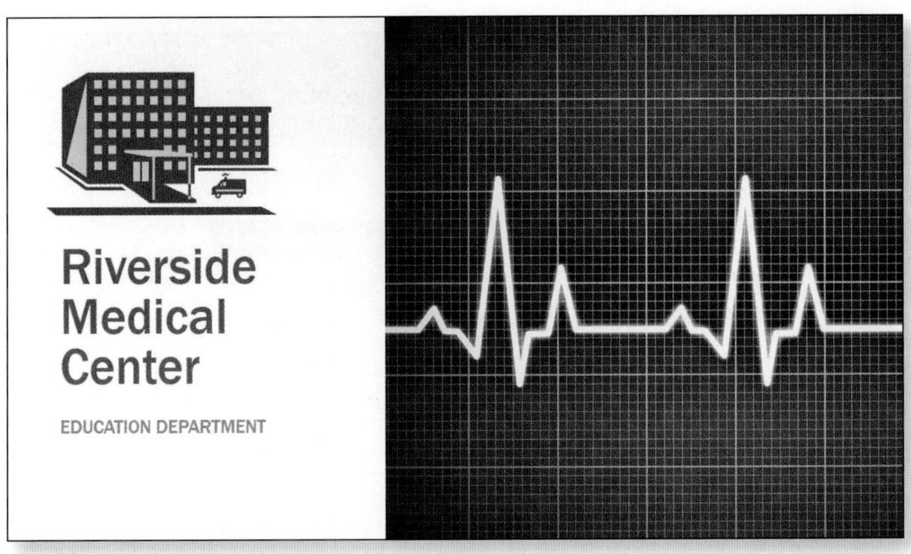

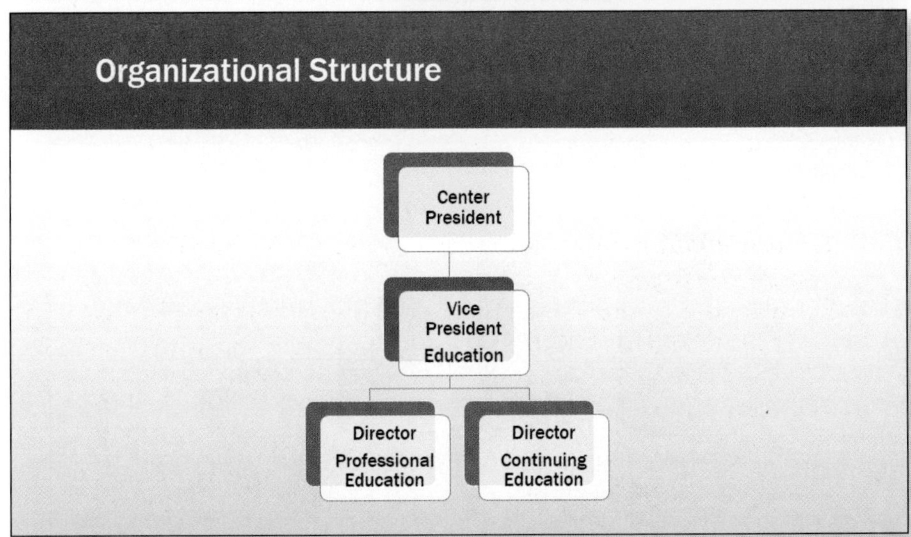

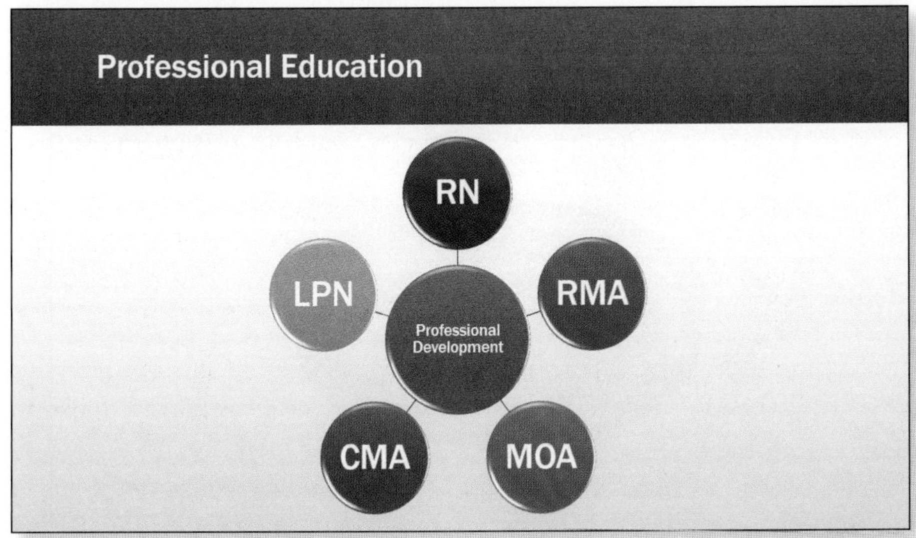

continues

Figure 5.22 Visual Benchmark—*continued*

Course Offerings

Course	Session 1	Session 2
AHA Basic Life Support	October 1	October 3
AHA First Aid	October 9	October 11
Basic Cardiac Care	October 15	October 17
Advanced Cardiac Life Support	October 30	November 1
Trauma Nursing Care	November 6	November 8
Emergency Pediatric Nursing Care	November 12	November 14

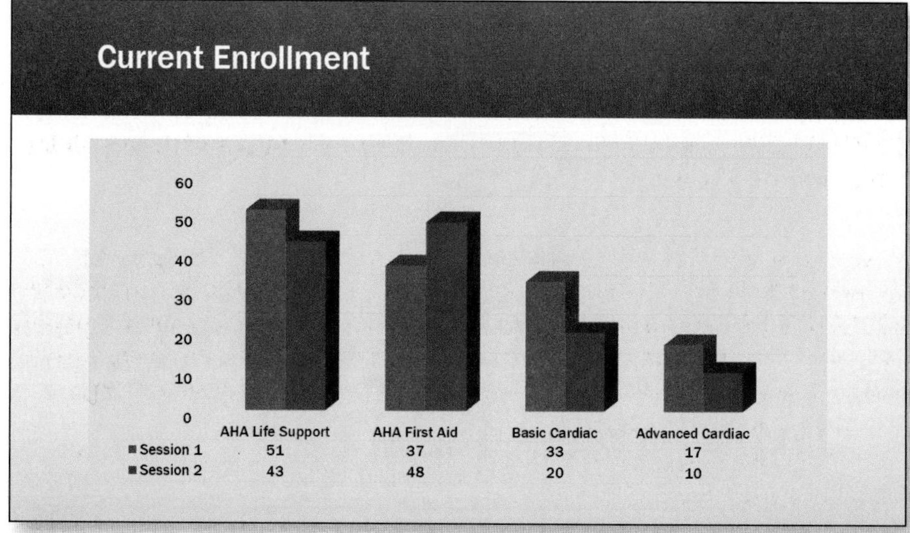

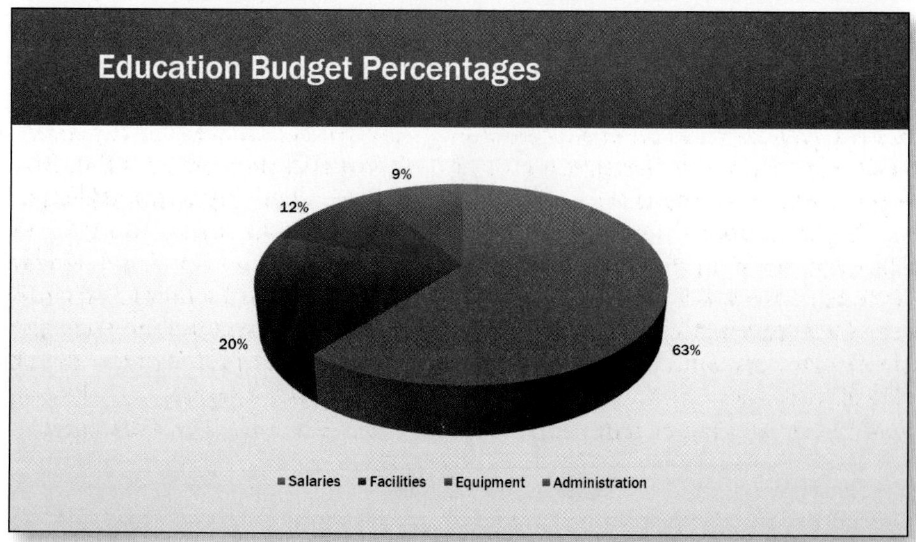

Case Study Apply Your Skills

Part 1

You are an administrator for Terra Energy Corporation and you are responsible for preparing a presentation for a quarterly meeting. Open the Word document named **TerraEnergy.docx** and then use the information to prepare a presentation with the following specifications:

- Create the first slide with the company name and the subtitle *Quarterly Meeting*.
- Create a slide that presents the Executive Team information in a table.
- Create a slide that presents the phases information in a table (the three columns of text in the *Research and Development* section). Insert a column at the left side of the table that includes the text *New Product* rotated.
- Create a slide that presents the development team information in a SmartArt organizational chart.
- Create a slide that presents the revenues information in a chart (you determine the type of chart).
- Create a slide that presents the United States sales information in a chart (you determine the type of chart).

Apply a design theme of your choosing and add any additional features to improve the visual appearance of the presentation. Insert a transition and sound to each slide and then run the presentation. Save the presentation and name it **P-C5-CS-TECPres.pptx**. Print the presentation as a handout with four slides printed horizontally per page.

Part 2

Last year, a production project was completed and you want to display a graphic that illustrates the primary focus of the project. Create a new slide in the **P-C5-CS-TECPres.pptx** presentation and insert a *Funnel* SmartArt graphic (in the *Relationship* group) with the following information in the shapes inside the funnel (turn on the Text pane to type the information in the shapes):

Updated Systems
Safety Programs
Market Expansion

Insert the information *Higher Profits* below the funnel. Apply formatting to the SmartArt graphic to improve the visual appeal. Print the slide and then save **P-C5-CS-TECPres.pptx**.

Part 3

You have created an Excel chart containing information on department costs. You decide to improve the appearance of the chart and then create a link from the presentation to the chart. Open Excel and then open **DepartmentCosts.xlsx**. Apply additional formatting to the pie chart to make it easy to read and understand the data. Save and then close the workbook and exit Excel. Create a new slide in the **P-C5-CS-TECPres.pptx** presentation that includes a hyperlink to the **DepartmentCosts.xlsx** workbook. Run the presentation and when the slide displays containing the hyperlinked text, click the hyperlink, view the chart in Excel, and then exit Excel. Print the presentation as a handout with four slides printed horizontally per page. Save and then close **P-C5-CS-TECPres.pptx**.

MICROSOFT® POWERPOINT®

CHAPTER 6

Using Slide Masters and Action Buttons

PERFORMANCE OBJECTIVES

Upon successful completion of Chapter 6, you will be able to:

- **Format slides in Slide Master view**
- **Apply themes and backgrounds in Slide Master view**
- **Delete placeholders and slide master layouts**
- **Insert elements in Slide Master view**
- **Create and rename a custom slide layout**
- **Insert a new slide master**
- **Save a presentation as a template**
- **Customize a handout in Handout Master view**
- **Customize notes pages in Notes Master view**
- **Change zoom, manage windows, and view presentations in color and grayscale**
- **Insert action buttons**
- **Insert hyperlinks**

Tutorials

6.1 Formatting with a Slide Master

6.2 Working in Slide Master View

6.3 Saving a Presentation as a Template

6.4 Customizing a Handout and Notes Master

6.5 Using VIEW Tab Options

6.6 Inserting Action Buttons and Hyperlinks

If you make design or formatting changes and you want the changes to affect all slides in the presentation, consider making the changes in a slide master in the Slide Master view. Along with the Slide Master view, you can make changes to all pages in a handout with options in the Handout Master view and all notes pages in the Notes Master view. Insert action buttons in a presentation to connect to slides within the same presentation, connect to another presentation, connect to a website, or connect to another program. You can also connect to a website by inserting a hyperlink to the site. Model answers for this chapter's projects appear on the following pages.

Note: Before beginning the projects, copy to your storage medium the PC6 folder from the PowerPoint folder on the CD that accompanies this textbook and then make PC6 the active folder.

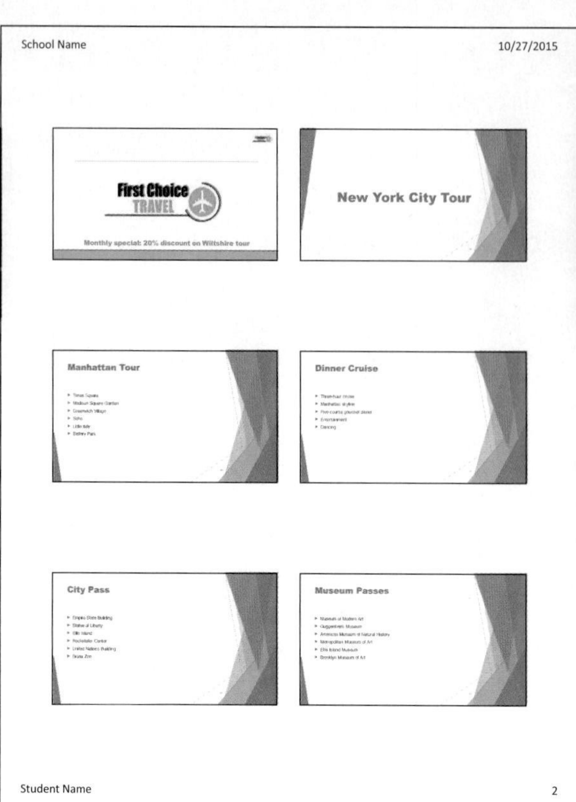

Project 1 Create a Travel Presentation and Apply Formatting in Slide Master View P-C6-P1-England.pptx

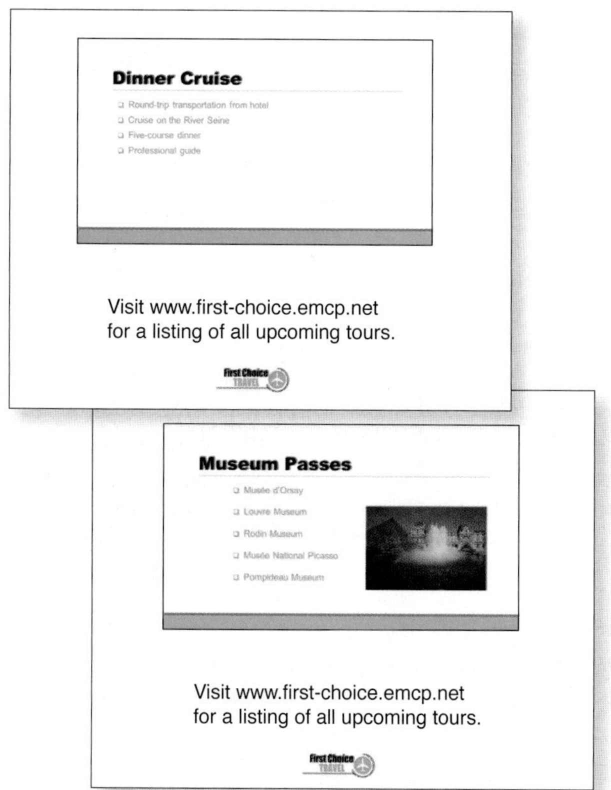

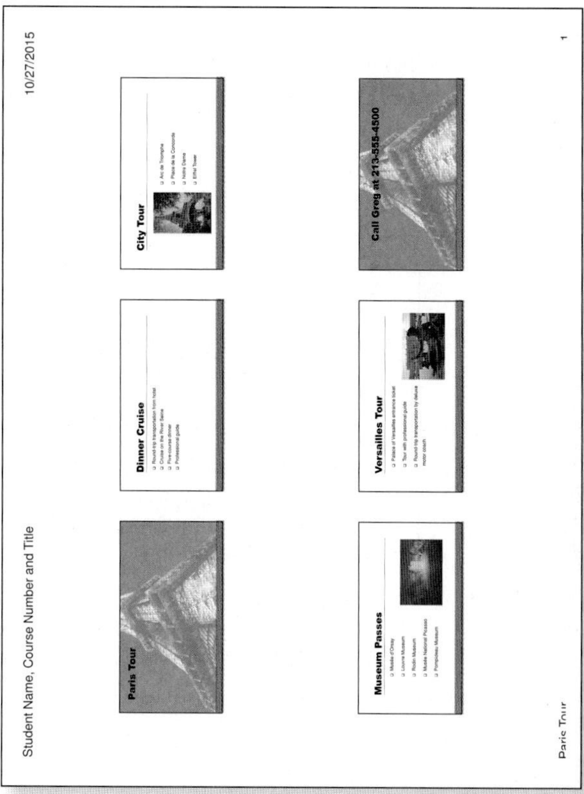

Project 2 Save a Template and Create a Travel Presentation with the Template P-C6-P2-ParisTour.pptx, Slides 2 and 4

P-C6-P2-ParisTour.pptx

Model Answers

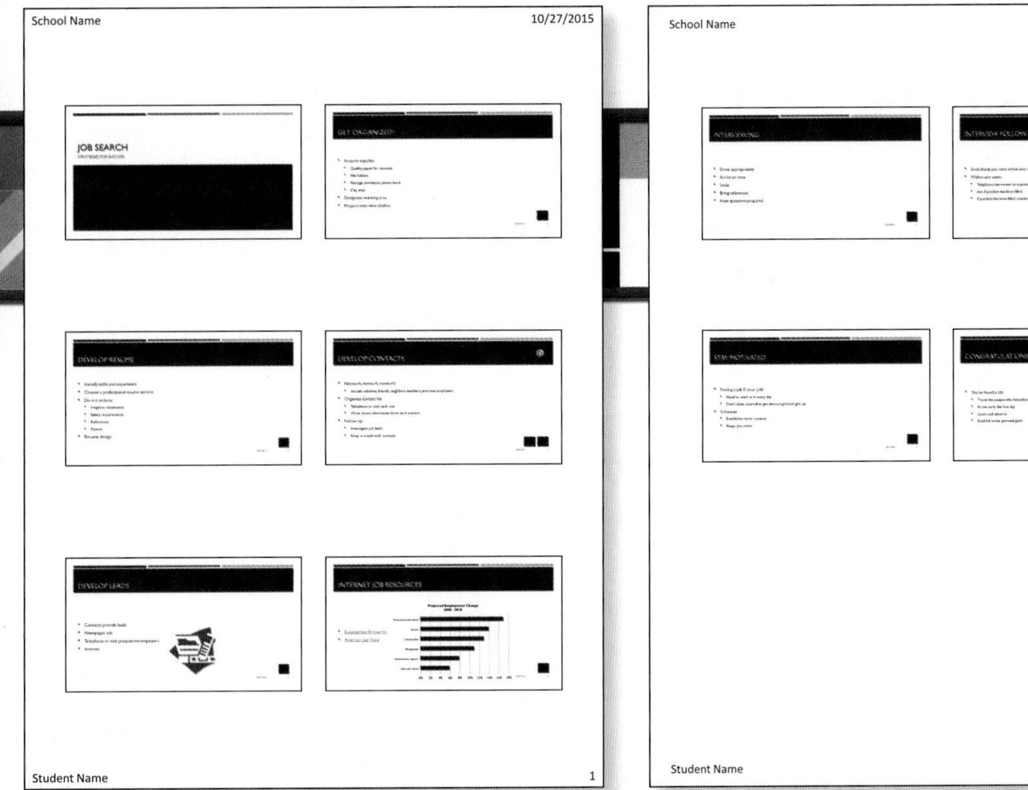

Project 3 Insert Action Buttons and Hyperlinks in a Job Search Presentation P-C6-P3-JobSearch.pptx

Project 1 Create a Travel Presentation and Apply Formatting in Slide Master View — 6 Parts

You will apply formatting to a blank presentation in Slide Master view, insert slides in the presentation, insert elements in Slide Master view, insert a custom slide layout, and insert a new slide master.

Customizing Slide Masters

If you make changes to a slide and want the changes to affect multiple slides in the presentation, make the change in a slide master. Customize a slide master by changing the theme, theme colors, or theme fonts; inserting or changing the location of placeholders; applying a background style; and changing the page setup and slide orientation. If you know how you want to customize your slides, apply the formatting in Slide Master view before you create each slide.

Quick Steps

Display the Slide Master View
1. Click VIEW tab.
2. Click Slide Master button.

Slide Master

If you edit the formatting of text in a slide in Normal view, that slide's link to the slide master is broken. Changes you make in Slide Master view will not affect the individually formatted slide. For this reason, make global formatting changes in Slide Master view before editing individual slides in a presentation.

To display Slide Master view, click the VIEW tab and then click the Slide Master button in the Master Views group. This activates the SLIDE MASTER tab, displays a blank slide master in the slide pane, and inserts slide master thumbnails

Figure 6.1 Slide Master View

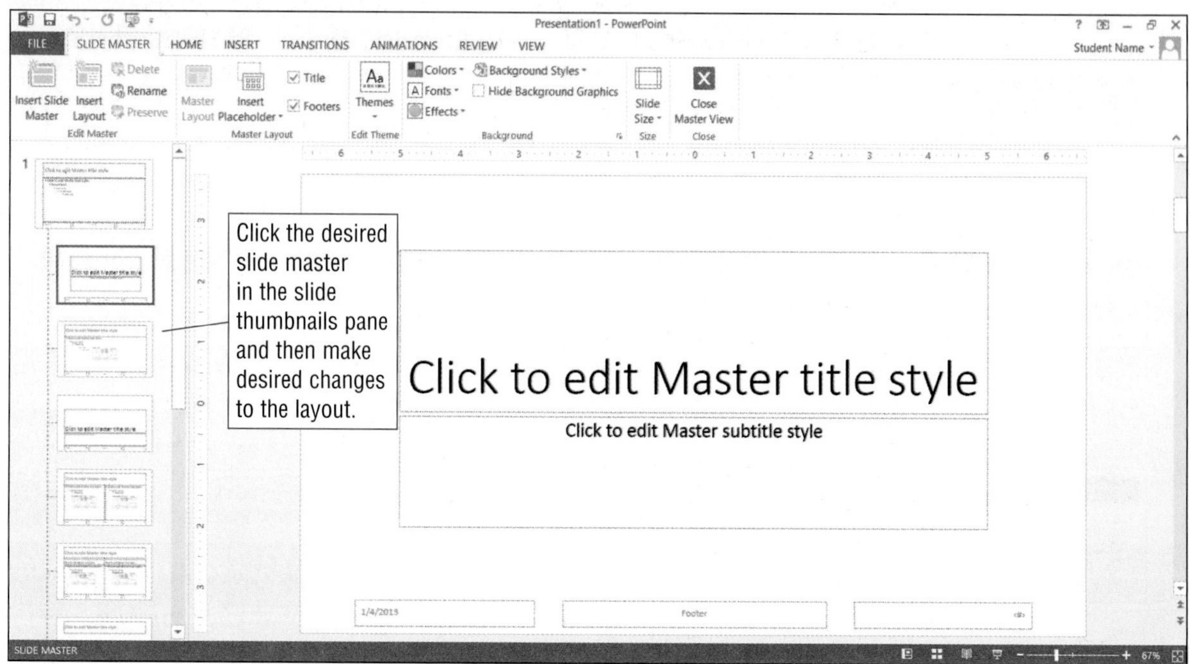

Create a consistent look for your slides by customizing them in Slide Master view.

Close Master View

Themes

in the slide thumbnails pane. The largest thumbnail in the pane is the slide master, and the other thumbnails represent associated layouts. Position the mouse pointer on a slide thumbnail and the name of the thumbnail displays in a ScreenTip by the thumbnail along with information on what slides in the presentation use the slide master. Figure 6.1 shows a blank presentation in Slide Master view. To specify the slide master or layout you want to customize, click the desired thumbnail in the slide thumbnails pane. With the slide master layout displayed in the slide pane, make the desired changes and then click the Close Master View button.

Applying Themes to Slide Masters

Apply themes, theme colors, theme fonts, and theme effects to a slide master with buttons in the Edit Theme group on the SLIDE MASTER tab. Click the Themes button and a drop-down gallery displays with available predesigned themes as well as any custom themes you have created. Click the desired theme and the theme formatting is applied to the slide master. Complete similar steps to apply theme colors, theme fonts, and theme effects.

Project 1a Formatting a Slide Master — Part 1 of 6

1. Open a blank presentation.
2. Click the VIEW tab and then click the Slide Master button in the Master Views group.

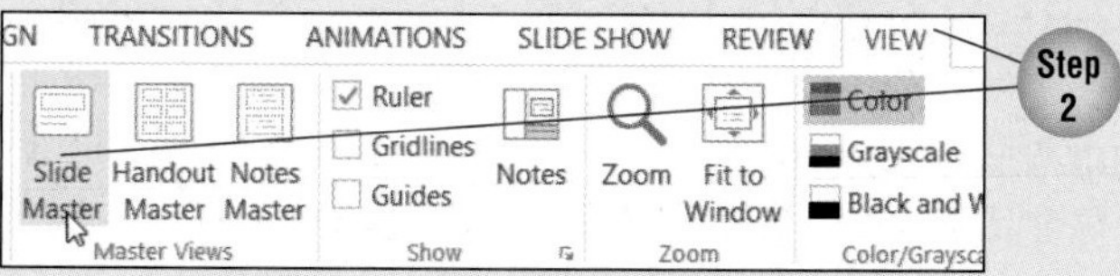

3. Scroll up the slide thumbnails pane and then click the top (and largest) slide master thumbnail in the slide thumbnails pane (Office Theme Slide Master). This displays the slide master layout in the slide pane.
4. Click the Themes button in the Edit Theme group on the SLIDE MASTER tab.
5. Click *Retrospect* at the drop-down gallery.
6. Click the Colors button in the Background group and then click *Blue* at the drop-down gallery.
7. Click the Fonts button in the Background group, scroll down the drop-down gallery, and then click the *Arial Black-Arial* option.

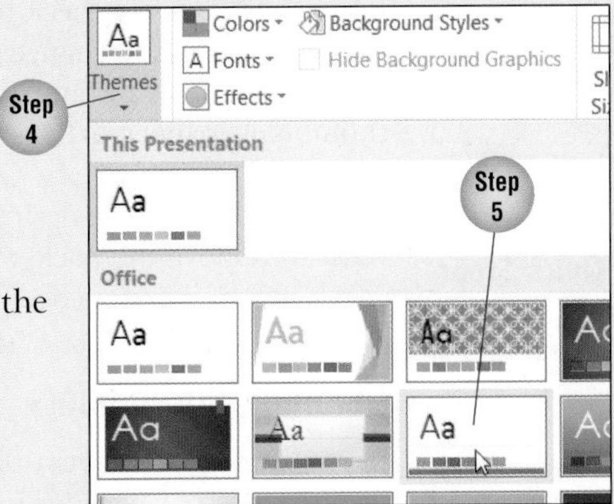

8. Change the font color for the title style by completing the following steps:
   a. Select the text *Click to edit Master title style* that displays in the slide master in the slide pane.
   b. Click the HOME tab.
   c. Click the Font Color button arrow in the Font group and then click *Black, Text 1* (second column first row in the *Theme Colors* section).

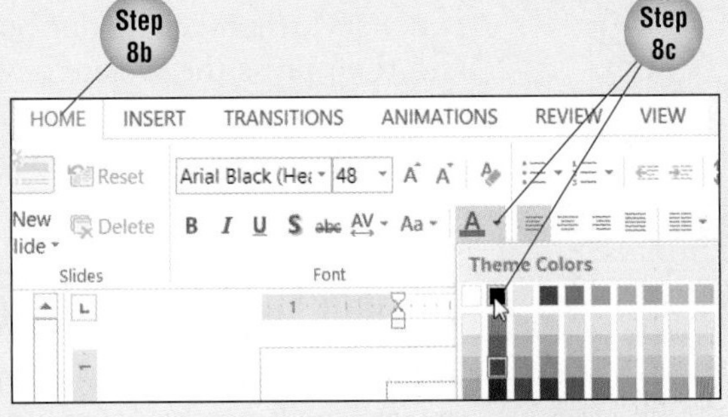

9. Change the font size and color and apply custom bullets by completing the following steps:
   a. Select the text *Click to edit Master text styles*.
   b. With the HOME tab selected, click the Font Size button arrow and then click *24* at the drop-down gallery.
   c. Click the Font Color button arrow and then click the *Light Blue, Background 2, Darker 50%* option (third column, fourth row in the *Theme Colors* section).
   d. Click the Bullets button arrow in the Paragraph group and then click *Bullets and Numbering* at the drop-down gallery.
   e. At the Bullets and Numbering dialog box, click the *Hollow Square Bullets* option.
   f. Click the Color button and then click the *Light Blue, Background 2, Darker 50%* option (third column, fourth row in the *Theme Colors* section).
   g. Select *100* in the Size measurement box and then type 80.
   h. Click OK to close the dialog box.
   i. Click the Paragraph group dialog box launcher.
   j. At the Paragraph dialog box, select the measurement in the *By* measurement box and then type 0.4.
   k. Click OK to close the dialog box.

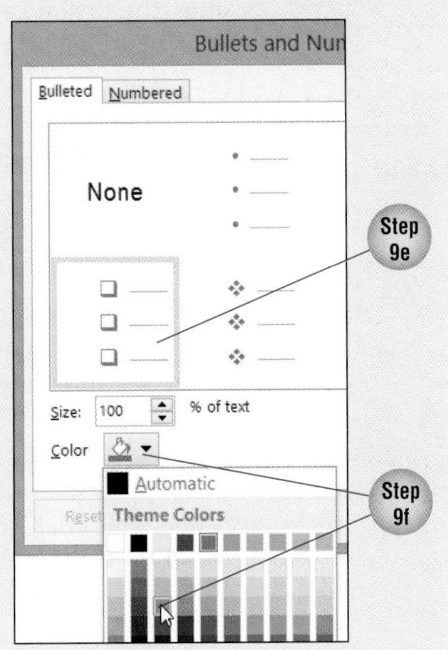

10. Click the SLIDE MASTER tab.
11. Click the Close Master View button.
12. Save the presentation and name it **P-C6-P1-TravelMaster.pptx**.

Applying and Formatting Backgrounds

In addition to the theme colors, fonts, and effects buttons the Background group on the SLIDE MASTER tab contains the Background Styles button and the *Hide Background Graphics* check box. If you want to change the background graphic for all slides, make the change at the slide master. To do this, display the presentation in Slide Master view and then click the desired slide master layout in the slide thumbnails pane. Click the Background Styles button and then click a background at the drop-down gallery. Or, click the *Format Background* option at the drop-down gallery and select the desired settings at the Format Background task pane. If you want to remove the background graphic for slides, click the *Hide Background Graphics* check box to insert a check mark.

Quick Steps

Delete a Slide Master Layout
1. Display presentation in Slide Master view.
2. Click desired slide layout thumbnail.
3. Click Delete button.

Delete

HINT

You can also delete a slide master layout by right-clicking the layout in the slide thumbnails pane and then clicking *Delete Layout* at the shortcut menu.

Deleting Placeholders

If you want to remove a placeholder for all slides in a presentation, consider deleting the placeholder in Slide Master view. To do this, display the presentation in Slide Master view, click the desired slide master layout in the slide thumbnails pane, click the placeholder border (make sure the border displays as a solid line), and then press the Delete key. You can also remove a title placeholder from a slide master by clicking the *Title* check box in the Master Layout group to remove the check mark. Remove footer placeholders by clicking the *Footer* check box to remove the check mark.

Deleting Slide Master Layouts

In Slide Master view, a slide master displays for each available layout. If you know that you will not be using a particular layout in the presentation, you can delete the slide master layout. To do this, display the presentation in Slide Master view, click the desired slide layout thumbnail in the slide thumbnails pane, and then click the Delete button in the Edit Master group.

Project 1b **Applying and Formatting Background Graphics** **Part 2 of 6**

1. With **P-C6-P1-TravelMaster.pptx** open, click the VIEW tab and then click the Slide Master button in the Master Views group.
2. Apply a picture to the background of the title slide layout (the picture will appear only on slides with this layout) by completing the following steps:
   a. Make sure the second slide layout thumbnail (Title Slide Layout) is selected in the slide thumbnails pane.
   b. Select the text *Click to edit Master title style*, click the HOME tab, change the font size to 48 points, apply the Black, Text 1 font color (second column, first row in the *Theme Colors* section), and click the Center button in the Paragraph group.
   c. Click the SLIDE MASTER tab and then make sure the *Hide Background Graphics* check box in the Background group contains a check mark.

d. Click the Background Styles button in the Background group and then click *Format Background* at the drop-down list.

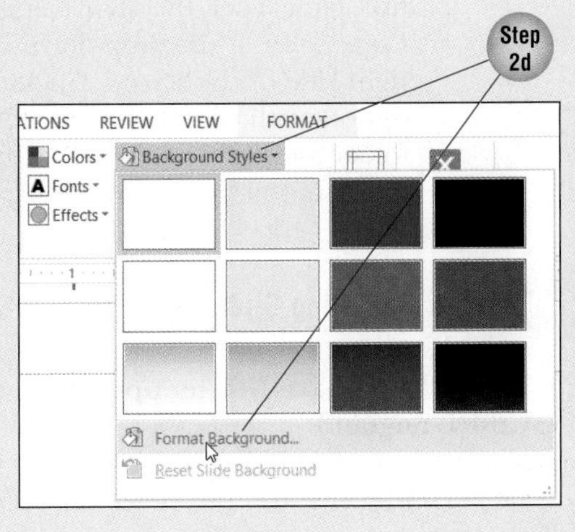

e. At the Format Background task pane, click the *Picture or texture fill* option.

f. Click the File button.

g. At the Insert Picture dialog box, navigate to the PC6 folder on your storage medium and then double-click ***Stonehenge.jpg***.

h. Close the Format Background task pane.

i. Drag the master title placeholder so it is positioned above the stones and centered horizontally. (Make sure the bottom border of the placeholder is positioned above the stones.)

j. Delete the master subtitle placeholder by clicking the placeholder border (make sure the border displays as a solid line) and then pressing the Delete key.

k. Click the thin horizontal line that displays below the stones and then press the Delete key.

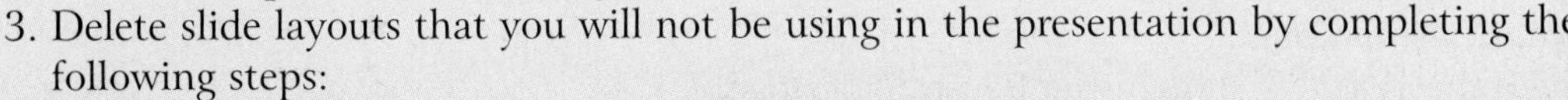

3. Delete slide layouts that you will not be using in the presentation by completing the following steps:
   a. Click the fourth slide layout thumbnail (Section Header Layout) in the slide thumbnails pane.
   b. Scroll down the pane until the last slide layout thumbnail is visible.
   c. Hold down the Shift key and then click the last slide layout thumbnail.
   d. Click the Delete button in the Edit Master group. (The slide thumbnails pane should now contain only one slide master and two associated layouts.)

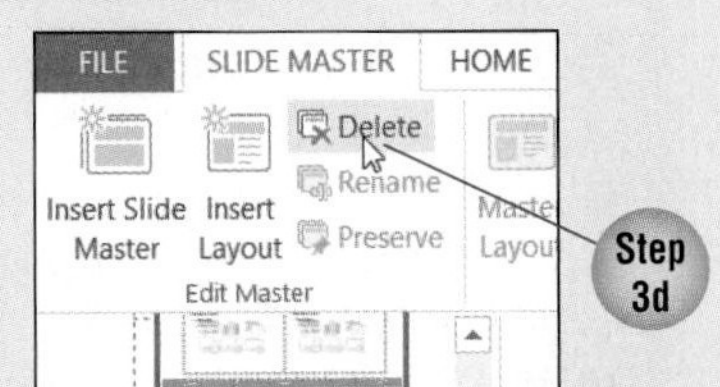

4. Click the Close Master View button.
5. Delete the slide that currently displays in the slide pane. (This displays a gray background with the text *Click to add first slide*. The presentation does not contain any slides, just formatting.)
6. Save **P-C6-P1-TravelMaster.pptx**.

Inserting Slides in a Customized Presentation

If you customize slides in a presentation in Slide Master view, you can use the presentation formatting in other presentations. To do this, either save the formatted presentation as a template or save the presentation in the normal manner, open the presentation, save it with a new name, and then type text in slides. You can also insert slides into the current presentation using the Reuse Slides task pane. (You learned about this task pane in Chapter 2.) To use this task pane, click the HOME tab, click the New Slide button arrow, and then click *Reuse Slides* at the drop-down list. This displays the Reuse Slides task pane at the right side of the screen. Click the Browse button and then click the *Browse File* option at the drop-down list. At the Browse dialog box, navigate to the desired folder and then double-click the desired presentation. Insert slides into the current presentation by clicking the desired slide in the task pane.

Project 1c Inserting Slides in a Presentation — Part 3 of 6

1. With **P-C6-P1-TravelMaster.pptx** open, save the presentation with Save As and name it **P-C6-P1-England**.
2. Make sure the HOME tab is active, click the New Slide button arrow, and then click *Title Slide* at the drop-down list.

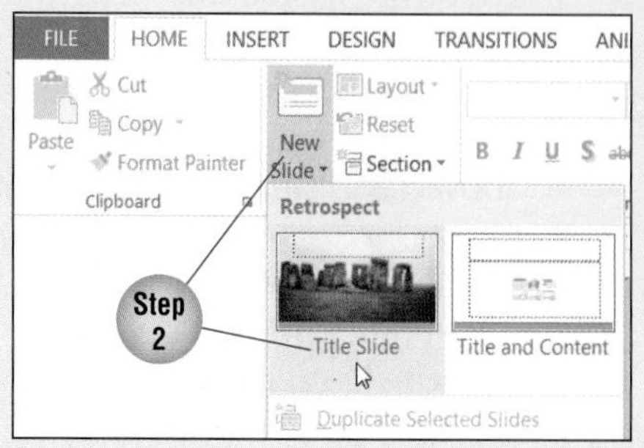

3. Click the *Click to add title* text in the current slide and then type **Wiltshire, England**.
4. Insert slides into the current presentation from an existing presentation by completing the following steps:
   a. Click the New Slide button arrow and then click *Reuse Slides* at the drop-down list.
   b. Click the Browse button in the Reuse Slides task pane and then click *Browse File* at the drop-down list.
   c. At the Browse dialog box, navigate to the PC6 folder on your storage medium and then double-click ***TravelEngland.pptx***.
   d. Click the *Wiltshire* slide in the Reuse Slides task pane. (This inserts the slide in the presentation and applies the custom formatting to the slide.)

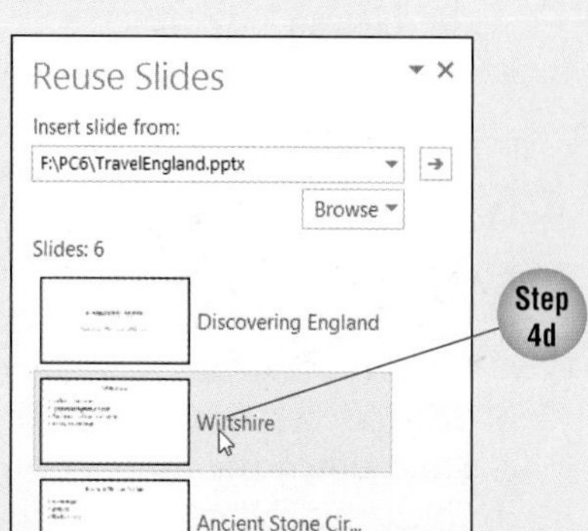

   e. Click the *Ancient Stone Circles* slide in the Reuse Slides task pane.
   f. Click the *Ancient Wiltshire* slide in the Reuse Slides task pane.
   g. Click the *White Horses* slide in the Reuse Slides task pane.
   h. Click the Close button located in the upper right corner of the Reuse Slides task pane to close the task pane.
5. With Slide 5 active, format the bulleted text into two columns by completing the following steps:
   a. Click any character in the bulleted text.
   b. Move the insertion point so it is positioned immediately following *Marlborough*.
   c. Press the Enter key (to insert a blank line) and then click the Bullets button in the Paragraph group on the HOME tab to remove the bullet.
   d. Press Ctrl + A to select all of the bulleted text.
   e. Click the Line Spacing button in the Paragraph group and then click *2.0* at the drop-down list.
   f. Click the Add or Remove Columns button in the Paragraph group and then click *Two Columns* at the drop-down list.
6. With Slide 5 active, insert a new slide by completing the following steps:
   a. Click the New Slide button arrow and then click *Title Slide* at the drop-down list.
   b. Click in the text *Click to add title* and then type **Call Lucy at 213-555-4500**.
7. Save **P-C6-P1-England.pptx**.

Inserting Elements in a Slide Master

As you learned in Chapter 4, you can insert a header, footer, or the date and time that will print on every slide in the presentation. You can also insert these elements in a slide master. For example, to insert a header or footer in a slide master, display the presentation in Slide Master view, click the INSERT tab, and then click the Header & Footer button in the Text group. At the Header and Footer dialog box with the Slide tab selected, make the desired changes, click the Notes and Handouts tab, make the desired changes, and then click the Apply to All button. You can also insert additional elements in Slide Master view, such as a picture, clip art image, shape, SmartArt graphic, or chart. Insert any of these elements in Slide Master view just as you would in Normal view.

Project 1d **Inserting Elements in Slide Master View** **Part 4 of 6**

1. With **P-C6-P1-England.pptx** open, insert a header, a footer, and the date and time by completing the following steps:
   a. Click the View tab.
   b. Click the Slide Master button in the Master Views group.
   c. Click the slide master thumbnail (the top slide thumbnail in the slide thumbnails pane).
   d. Click the INSERT tab.
   e. Click the Header & Footer button in the Text group.
   f. At the Header and Footer dialog box with the Slide tab selected, click the *Date and time* check box to insert a check mark.
   g. Make sure the *Update automatically* option is selected. (With this option selected, the date and/or time will automatically update each time you open the presentation.)
   h. Click the *Slide number* check box to insert a check mark.
   i. Click the *Footer* check box to insert a check mark, click in the *Footer* text box, and then type your first and last names.
   j. Click the Notes and Handouts tab.
   k. Click the *Date and time* check box to insert a check mark.
   l. Make sure the *Update automatically* option is selected.
   m. Click the *Header* check box to insert a check mark, click in the *Header* text box, and then type the name of your school.
   n. Click the *Footer* check box to insert a check mark, click in the *Footer* text box, and then type your first and last names.
   o. Click the Apply to All button.

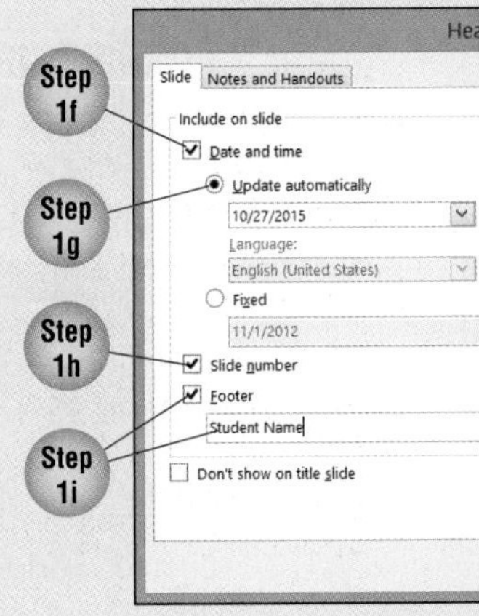

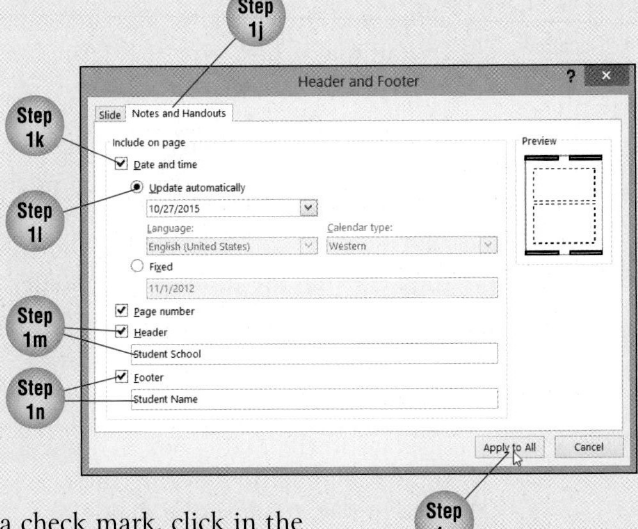

2. Insert the First Choice Travel logo in the upper right corner of the slide master by completing the following steps:
   a. Click the Pictures button in the Images group.
   b. At the Insert Picture dialog box, navigate to the PC6 folder on your storage medium and then double-click ***FCTLogo.jpg***.
   c. Click in the *Shape Height* measurement box in the Size group on the PICTURE TOOLS FORMAT tab, type **0.6**, and then press Enter.
   d. Drag the logo so it is positioned in the upper right corner of the slide as shown at the right.
   e. Click outside the logo to deselect it.
3. If necessary, click the SLIDE MASTER tab.
4. Click the Close Master View button.
5. Run the presentation and notice the logo and other elements in the slides.
6. Save **P-C6-P1-England.pptx**.

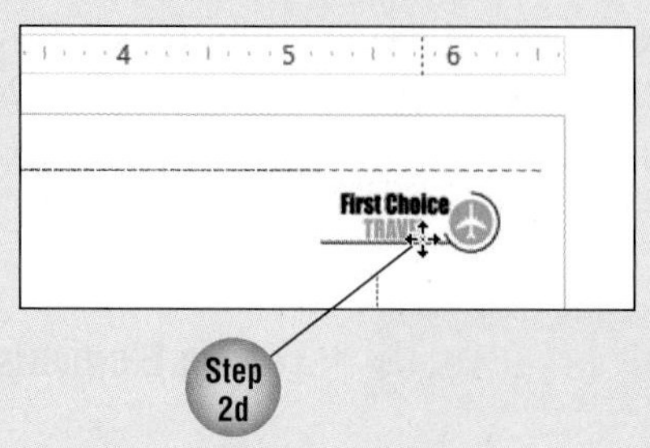

Creating and Renaming a Custom Slide Layout

Insert Layout

You can create your own custom slide layout in Slide Master view and then customize the layout by inserting or deleting elements and applying formatting to placeholders and text. To create a new slide layout, click the Insert Layout button in the Edit Master group on the SLIDE MASTER tab. This inserts in the slide pane a new slide containing a master title placeholder and footer placeholders. Customize the layout by inserting or deleting placeholders and applying formatting to placeholders.

Rename

PowerPoint automatically assigns the name *Custom Layout* to a slide layout you create. If you create another slide layout, PowerPoint will name it *1_Custom Layout*, and so on. Consider renaming your custom layout with a name that describes the layout. To rename a layout, make sure the desired slide layout is active and then click the Rename button in the Edit Master group. At the Rename Layout dialog box, type the desired name and then click the Rename button.

Inserting Placeholders

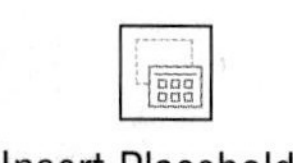
Insert Placeholder

Master Layout

You can insert placeholders in a predesigned slide layout or you can insert a custom slide layout and then insert placeholders. Insert a placeholder by clicking the Insert Placeholder button arrow in the Master Layout group and then clicking the desired placeholder option at the drop-down list. If you click the slide master, the Insert Placeholder button is dimmed. If you delete a placeholder from the slide master, you can reinsert the placeholder with options at the Master Layout dialog box. Display this dialog box by clicking the Master Layout button. Any placeholder that has been removed from the slide master displays in the dialog box as an active option with an empty check box. Reinsert the placeholder by clicking the check box to insert a check mark box and then clicking OK to close the dialog box.

Creating Custom Prompts

Some placeholders in a custom layout may contain generic text such as *Click to add Master title style* or *Click to edit Master text styles*. In Slide Master view, you can select this generic text and replace it with custom text. For example, you might want to insert text that describes what you want entered into the placeholder.

Project 1e Inserting a Layout and Placeholder Part 5 of 6

1. With **P-C6-P1-England.pptx** open, click the VIEW tab and then click the Slide Master button in the Master Views group.
2. Click the bottom slide layout thumbnail in the slide thumbnails pane.
3. Click the Insert Layout button in the Edit Master group. (This inserts in the slide pane a new slide with a master title placeholder, the logo, and the footer information.)
4. Remove the footer by clicking the *Footers* check box in the Master Layout group to remove the check mark.
5. Format and move the placeholder by completing the following steps:
   a. Select the text *Click to edit Master title style*.
   b. Click the HOME tab, change the font size to 28 points, apply the Light Blue, Background 2, Darker 50% font color (third column, fourth row in the *Theme Colors* section), and click the Center button in the Paragraph group.
   c. Move the placeholder so it is positioned along the bottom of the slide, just above the footer placeholder (as shown below).

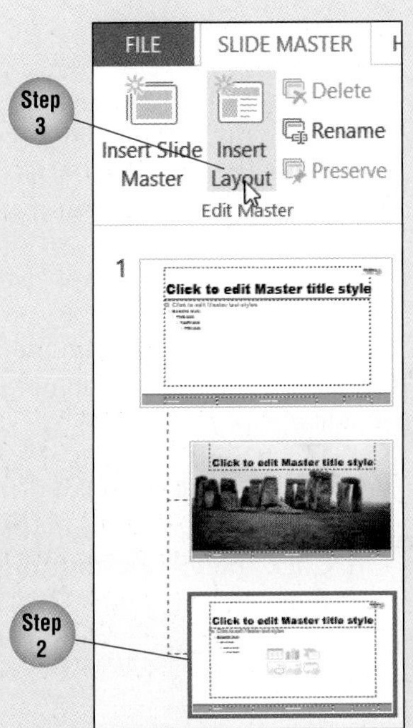

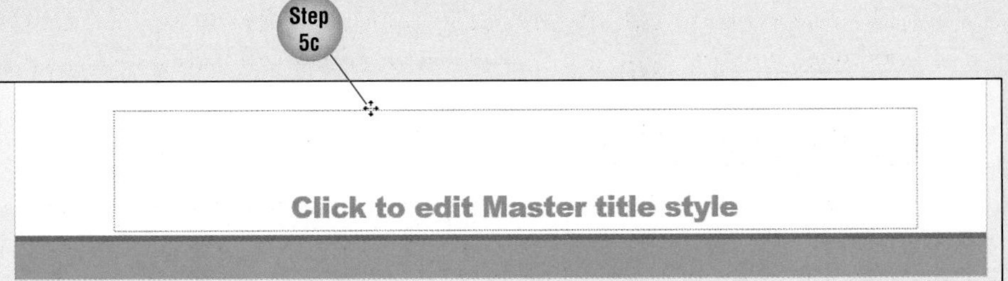

6. Click the SLIDE MASTER tab.
7. Insert a picture placeholder by completing the following steps:
   a. Click the Insert Placeholder button arrow.
   b. Click *Picture* at the drop-down list.
   c. Click in the slide to insert a placeholder.

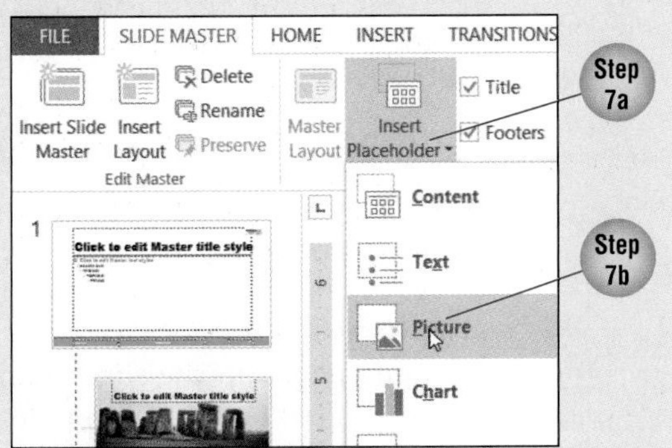

d. With the DRAWING TOOLS FORMAT tab active, click in the *Shape Height* measurement box and then type 3.5.
e. Click in the *Shape Width* measurement box, type 7.5, and then press Enter.
f. Drag the placeholder so it is positioned about 0.5 inch below the thin black line in the slide and centered horizontally. (The picture placeholder will overlap the title placeholder.)
g. Click anywhere in the word *Picture* in the placeholder. (This removes the word *Picture* and positions the insertion point in the placeholder.)
h. Type **Insert company logo** and then click outside of the placeholder.

8. Rename the custom slide layout by completing the following steps:
   a. Click the Rename button in the Edit Master group on the SLIDE MASTER tab.
   b. At the Rename Layout dialog box, select the text that displays in the *Layout name* text box and then type **Logo**.
   c. Click the Rename button.
9. Click the Close Master View button.
10. Insert a slide using the new slide layout by completing the following steps:
    a. Make Slide 6 active.
    b. Click the New Slide button arrow.
    c. Click *Logo* at the drop-down list.
    d. Click the Pictures button in the slide.

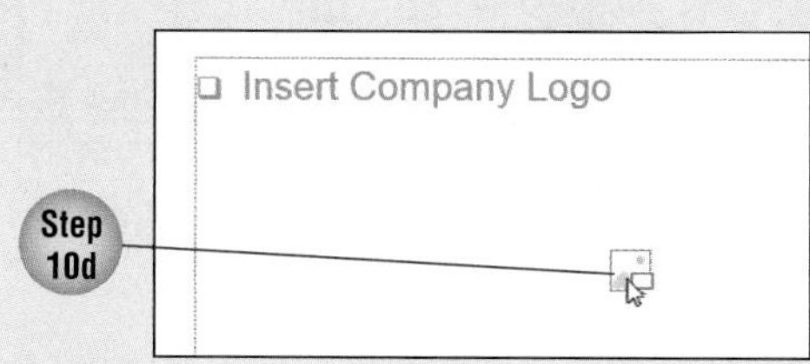

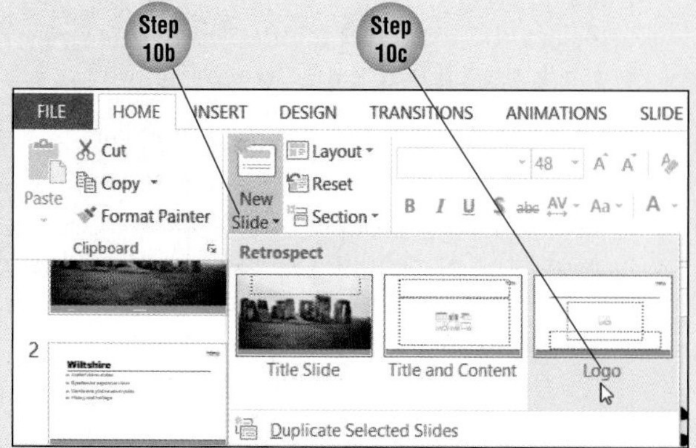

    e. At the Insert Picture dialog box, navigate to the PC6 folder on your storage medium and then double-click ***FCTLogo.jpg***.
    f. Click in the text *Click to add title* and then type **Monthly special: 20% discount on Wiltshire tour**.
11. Save **P-C6-P1-England.pptx**.

Inserting a New Slide Master

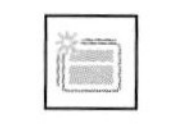
Insert Slide Master

A PowerPoint presentation can contain more than one slide master (and associated layouts). To insert a new slide master, display the presentation in Slide Master view and then click the Insert Slide Master button in the Edit Master group. This inserts a new slide master and all associated layouts below the existing slide master and layouts in the slide thumbnails pane. You can also insert a slide master and all associated layouts with a design theme applied. To do this, click below the existing slide master and associated layouts, click the Themes button in the Edit Theme group, and then click the desired theme at the drop-down gallery. A slide master containing the chosen design theme is inserted below the existing thumbnails.

Preserving Slide Masters

If you delete all of the slide layouts that follow a slide master, PowerPoint will automatically delete the slide master. You can protect a slide master from being deleted by preserving the master. To do this, click the desired slide master thumbnail and then click the Preserve button in the Edit Master group. If you insert a slide master using the Insert Slide Master button, the Preserve button is automatically active. When a slide master is preserved, a preservation icon displays below the slide number in the slide thumbnails pane.

Quick Steps

Preserve a Slide Master

1. Display presentation in Slide Master view.
2. Click desired slide master thumbnail.
3. Click Preserve button.

Preserve

Changing Page Setup

Click the Slide Size button in the Size group on the SLIDE MASTER tab and a drop-down list displays with options for choosing standard or widescreen size. In addition to these two options, the drop-down list also includes the *Custom Slide Size* option. Click this option and the Slide Size dialog box displays. This is the same dialog box you learned about in Chapter 3. The dialog box contains options for changing slide width, height, and numbering and applying slide orientation to slides, notes, handouts, and outline pages.

Project 1f Applying a Second Slide Master

Part 6 of 6

1. With **P-C6-P1-England.pptx** open, preserve the Retrospect slide master by completing the following steps:
   a. Click the VIEW tab and then click the Slide Master button in the Master Views group.
   b. Click the first slide master (Retrospect Slide Master) in the slide thumbnails pane.
   c. Click the Preserve button in the Edit Master group. (This inserts a preservation icon below the slide number in the slide thumbnails pane).
2. Insert a second slide master by completing the following steps:
   a. Click below the bottom slide layout in the slide thumbnails pane. (You want the second slide master and associated layouts to display below the original slide master and not take the place of the original.)
   b. Click the Themes button in the Edit Theme group and then click *Facet* at the drop-down gallery.
   c. Notice the slide master and associated layouts that display in the slide thumbnails pane below the original slide master and associated layouts and notice the preservation icon that displays below the second slide master.
   d. Click the new slide master (Facet Slide Master) in the slide thumbnails pane.

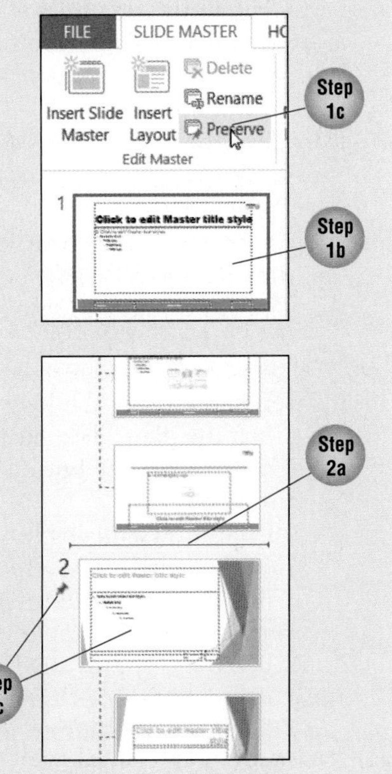

e. Click the Colors button in the Background group and then click *Blue* at the drop-down gallery.
f. Click the Fonts button and then click *Arial Black-Arial* at the drop-down gallery.
3. Click the first layout below the new slide master (Title Slide Layout) and then select and delete the master subtitle placeholder.
4. Click the third layout below the new slide master (Section Header Layout), scroll down to the bottom of the slide thumbnails pane, hold down the Shift key, click the bottom thumbnail, and then click the Delete button in the Edit Master group. (This deletes all but two of the layouts associated with the new slide master.)
5. Click the Close Master View button.
6. Insert a new slide by completing the following steps:
a. Make Slide 7 active.
b. Click the New Slide button arrow and then click *Title Slide* in the *Facet* section.

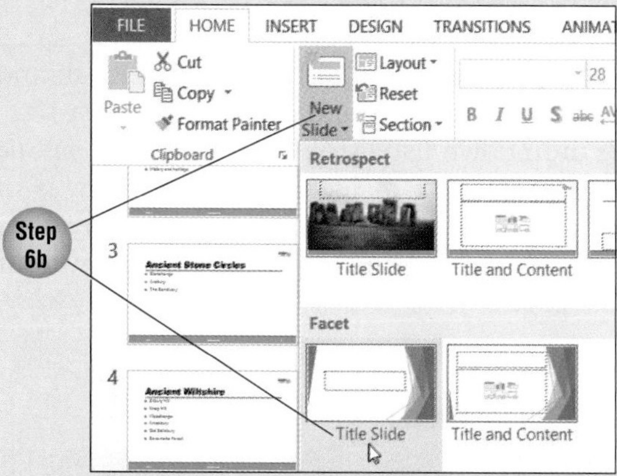

c. Click in the text *Click to add title* and then type **New York City Tour**.
7. Insert a new slide by completing the following steps:
a. With Slide 8 active, click the New Slide button. (This inserts a slide with the Facet Title and Content layout.)
b. Click the text *Click to add title* and then type **Manhattan Tour**.
c. Click the text *Click to add text* and then type the following bulleted text:
Times Square
Madison Square Garden
Greenwich Village
Soho
Little Italy
Battery Park
8. Insert slides using the Reuse Slides task pane by completing the following steps:
a. Click the New Slide button arrow and then click *Reuse Slides* at the drop-down list.
b. Click the Browse button in the Reuse Slides task pane and then click *Browse File* at the drop-down list.
c. At the Browse dialog box, navigate to the PC6 folder on your storage medium and then double-click ***FCTNewYork.pptx***.
d. Click the *Dinner Cruise* slide in the Reuse Slides task pane. (This inserts the slide in the presentation and applies the custom formatting to the slide.)
e. Click the *City Pass* slide in the Reuse Slides task pane.
f. Click the *Museum Passes* slide in the Reuse Slides task pane.
g. Click the Close button located in the upper right corner of the Reuse Slides task pane to close the task pane.

9. Assume that the presentation is going to be inserted into a larger presentation and that the starting slide will be Slide 12 (instead of Slide 1). Change the beginning slide number by completing the following steps:
   a. Click the VIEW tab and then click the Slide Master button.
   b. Click the top slide master in the slide thumbnails pane.
   c. Click the Slide Size button in the Size group and then click *Custom Slide Size* at the drop-down list.
   d. At the Slide Size dialog box, select the current number in the *Number slides from* measurement box and then type 12.
   e. Click OK to close the dialog box.

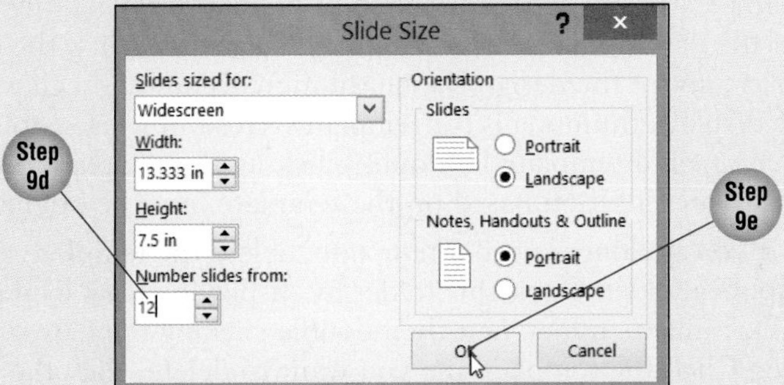

   f. Click the second slide master in the slide thumbnails pane (Facet Slide Master thumbnail).
   g. Click the INSERT tab and then click the Slide Number button in the Text group.
   h. At the Header and Footer dialog box, click the *Slide number* check box to insert a check mark and then click the Apply to All button.
   i. Click the SLIDE MASTER tab.
   j. Click the Close Master View button.
10. Make Slide 12 active (the first slide in the presentation) and then run the presentation.
11. Print the presentation as a handout with six slides horizontally per page.
12. Save and then close **P-C6-P1-England.pptx**.

Project 2 Save a Template and Create a Travel Presentation with the Template — 4 Parts

You will save a travel presentation as a template and then use the template to create and format a travel presentation. You will insert elements in the presentation in Handout Master view and Notes Master view, change the presentation zoom, and view the presentation in grayscale and black and white.

Saving a Presentation as a Template

Quick Steps

Save a Presentation as a Template

1. Display Save As dialog box.
2. Click *Save as type* option.
3. Click *PowerPoint Template (*.potx)*.
4. Type presentation name.
5. Click Save button.

Open a Presentation Based on a Template

1. Click FILE tab.
2. Click *New*.
3. Click *CUSTOM*.
4. Click *Custom Office Templates*.
5. Double-click template thumbnail.

If you create custom formatting to be used for future presentations, consider saving the presentation as a template. The advantage to saving your presentation as a template is that you cannot accidentally overwrite the presentation. Save a custom template in the Custom Office Templates folder in the Documents folder on the hard drive. Check to determine the default custom template folder location by displaying the PowerPoint Options dialog box with *Save* selected in the left panel. The *Default personal templates location* option should display the Custom Office Templates folder in the Documents folder as the default location. If this is not the default location, check with your instructor.

To save a presentation as a template, display the Save As dialog box, click the *Save as type* option button, and then click *PowerPoint Template (*.potx)* at the drop-down list. Type a name for the template in the *File name* text box and then click the Save button.

To create a presentation based on a template, click the FILE tab and then click the *New* option. At the New backstage area, click the *CUSTOM* option that displays above the design theme thumbnails and then click *Custom Office Templates*. This displays thumbnails for templates saved in the Custom Office Templates folder. Open a template by double-clicking the template thumbnail. PowerPoint opens a presentation based on the template, not the original template file.

If you no longer need a template, delete the template at the Custom Office Templates folder. Open this folder by displaying the Open dialog box, displaying the Documents folder, and then double-clicking the Custom Office Templates folder. Click the template file you want to delete, click the Organize button, and then click *Delete* at the drop-down list.

Project 2a Saving a Presentation as a Template — Part 1 of 4

Note: If you are using PowerPoint 2013 in a school setting on a network system, you may need to complete Project 2a and 2b in the same day. Check with your instructor for any specific instructions.

1. Open **P-C6-P1-TravelMaster.pptx**.
2. Press F12 to display the Save As dialog box.
3. At the Save As dialog box, type **XXXTravelTemplate** in the *File name* text box. (Type your initials in place of the *XXX*.)
4. Click the *Save as type* option button and then click *PowerPoint Template (*.potx)* at the drop-down list.
5. Click the Save button.
6. Close the **XXXTravelTemplate.potx** template.

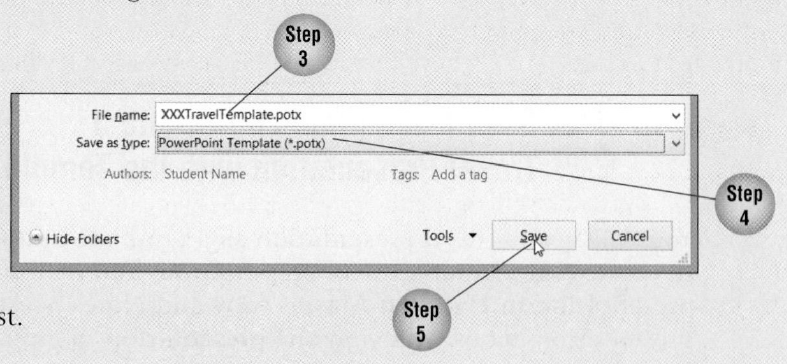

7. Open the template and save it as a presentation by completing the following steps:
   a. Click the FILE tab and then click the *New* option.
   b. At the New backstage area, click the *CUSTOM* option (located above the template thumbnails) and then click *Custom Office Templates*.

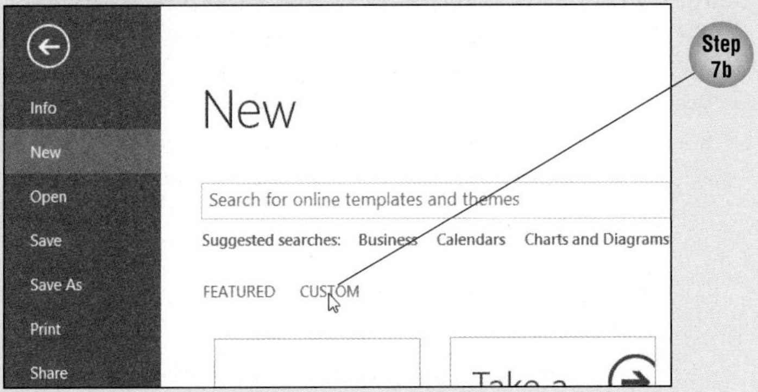

   c. Double-click the ***XXXTravelTemplate.potx*** template thumbnail.
8. Save the presentation with Save As and name it **P-C6-P2-ParisTour**.

Customizing the Handout Master

As you learned in Chapter 1, you can choose to print a presentation as individual slides, handouts, notes pages, or an outline. If you print a presentation as handouts or an outline, PowerPoint will automatically print the current date in the upper right corner of the page and the page number in the lower right corner. Customize a handout with options in the Handout Master view. Display a presentation in Handout Master view by clicking the VIEW tab and then clicking the Handout Master button in the Master Views group. Use options on the HANDOUT MASTER tab to move, resize, and format header and footer placeholders, change page orientation, add or remove placeholders, and specify the number of slides you want printed on each page.

Handout Master

With buttons in the Page Setup group, change the handout orientation, display the Slide Size dialog box with options for changing the size and orientation of the handout page, and specify the number of slides you want printed on the handout page. By default, a handout will contain a header, footer, date, and page number placeholder. Remove any of these placeholders by removing the check mark before the placeholder option in the Placeholders group.

The Edit Theme group contains buttons for changing the theme color, font, and effects. Click the Themes button and the options in the drop-down gallery are dimmed, indicating that the themes are not available for the handout. If you apply a background style to the handout master, you can change theme colors by clicking the Colors button and then clicking the desired color theme at the drop-down gallery. Apply theme fonts by clicking the Fonts button and then clicking the desired font theme at the drop-down gallery.

Apply a background style to the handout page by clicking the Background Styles button in the Background group and then clicking one of the predesigned styles. You can also click the *Format Background* option and then make changes at the Format Background task pane. Remove any background graphics by clicking the *Hide Background Graphics* check box to insert a check mark.

Background Styles

Project 2b Customizing the Handout Master Part 2 of 4

1. With **P-C6-P2-ParisTour.pptx** open, click the New Slide button arrow in the Slides group on the HOME tab and then click *Reuse Slides* at the drop-down list.
2. In the Reuse Slides task pane, click the Browse button and then click the *Browse File* option at the drop-down list.
3. Navigate to the PC6 folder on your storage medium and then double-click ***ParisTour.pptx***.
4. Insert the second, third, fourth, and fifth slides from the Reuse Slides task pane into the current presentation.
5. Close the Reuse Slides task pane.
6. Edit the Title Slide Layout in Slide Master view by completing the following steps:
   a. Click the VIEW tab and then click the Slide Master button.
   b. Click the second thumbnail in the slide thumbnails pane (Title Slide Layout).
   c. Click the Background Styles button in the Background group and then click *Format Background* at the drop-down list.
   d. At the Format Background task pane, click the File button (displays below the text *Insert picture from*).
   e. At the Insert Picture dialog box, navigate to the PC6 folder on your storage medium and then double-click ***EiffelTower.jpg***.

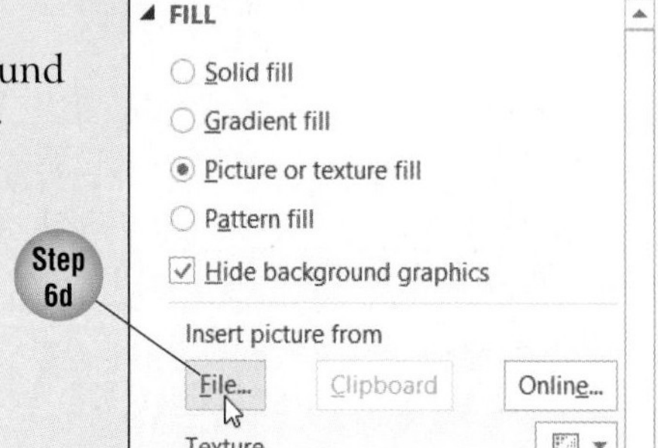

   f. Close the Format Background task pane.
   g. Select the text *Click to edit Master title style*, click the HOME tab, click the Font Color button arrow, and then click *Turquoise, Accent 2, Lighter 60%* (sixth column, third row in the *Theme Colors* section).
   h. Click the SLIDE MASTER tab.
   i. Click the Close Master View button.
   j. Make Slide 1 active, click in the text *Click to add title*, and then type **Paris Tour**.
   k. Size and move the text placeholder so *Paris Tour* displays in a blue area of the slide (not over the tower).
7. Make Slide 5 active and then create a new slide with the Title Slide layout. Type **Call Greg at 213-555-4500** in the title placeholder. (Leave the placeholder in the default location).
8. Save **P-C6-P2-ParisTour.pptx**.
9. Click the VIEW tab and then click the Handout Master button in the Master Views group.

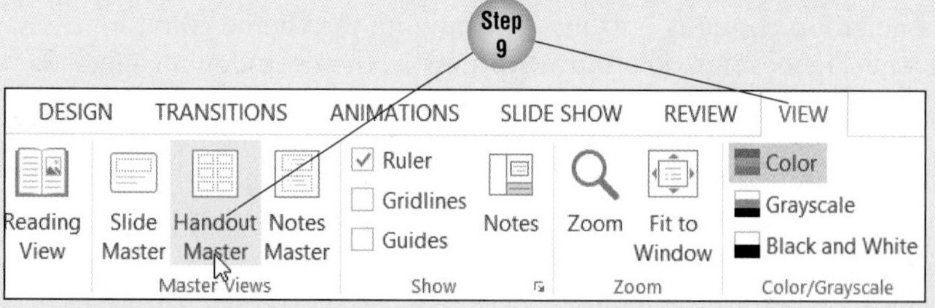

10. Click the Handout Orientation button in the Page Setup group and then click *Landscape* at the drop-down list.

11. Click in the Header placeholder on the page and then type your first and last names.
12. Click in the Footer placeholder and then type **Paris Tour**.
13. Click the Background Styles button and then click *Style 9* at the drop-down list (first column, third row).
14. Click the Colors button in the Background group and then click *Blue* at the drop-down list.
15. Click the Fonts button in the Background group, scroll down the drop-down gallery, and then click *Arial Black-Arial*.
16. Edit the header text by completing the following steps:
    a. Click in the header placeholder and then click any character in your name.
    b. Move the insertion point so it is positioned immediately right of the last character in your last name.
    c. Type a comma, press the spacebar, and then type your course number and title.
    d. Click in the handout page outside of any placeholder.
17. Click the Close Master View button.
18. Save **P-C6-P2-ParisTour.pptx**

Customizing the Notes Master

You can insert notes in a presentation and then print the presentation as notes pages, with the notes printed below the slides. If you want to insert or format text or other elements as notes on all slides in a presentation, consider making the changes in the Notes Master view. Display this view by clicking the VIEW tab and then clicking the Notes Master button in the Master Views group. This displays a notes page along with the NOTES MASTER tab. Many of the buttons and options on this tab are the same as those on the HANDOUT MASTER tab.

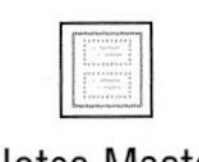

Notes Master

Project 2c Customizing the Notes Master — Part 3 of 4

1. With **P-C6-P2-ParisTour.pptx** open, click the VIEW tab and then click the Notes Master button in the Master Views group.
2. Click the *Body* check box in the Placeholders group to remove the check mark.
3. Click the Fonts button in the Background group, scroll down the drop-down gallery, and then click *Arial Black-Arial*.
4. Click the INSERT tab.
5. Click the Text Box button in the Text group.
6. Click in the notes page below the slide.

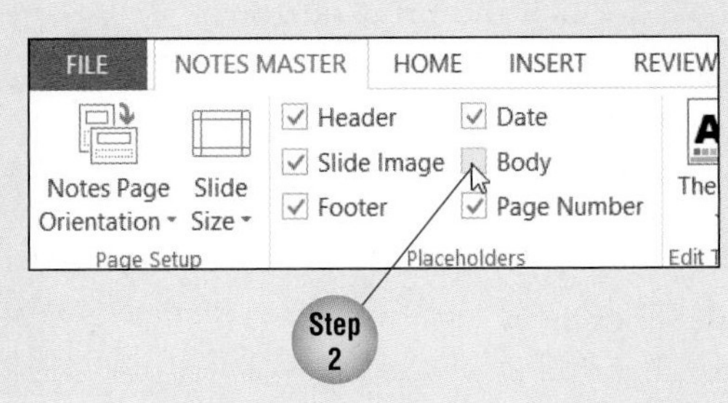

7. Type Visit www.first-choice.emcp.net for a listing of all upcoming tours.

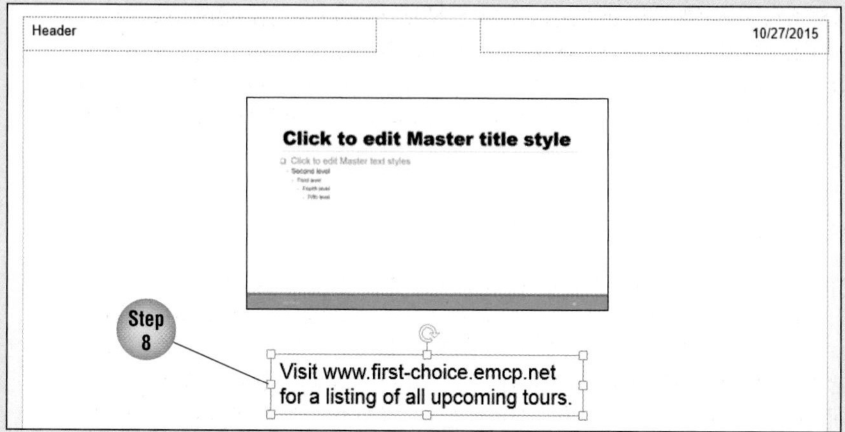

8. Size and position the text box below the slide as shown below.
9. Click the INSERT tab and then click the Pictures button in the Images group.
10. At the Insert Picture dialog box, navigate to the PC6 folder on your storage medium and then double-click ***FCTLogo.jpg***.
11. Change the height of the logo to 0.5 inch. (This changes the width to 1 inch.)
12. Drag the logo so it is positioned below the text.
13. Click the NOTES MASTER tab and then click the Close Master View button.
14. Print Slides 2 and 4 as notes pages by completing the following steps:
    a. Display the Print backstage area.
    b. Click the second gallery in the *Settings* category and then click *Notes Pages* in the *Print Layout* section.
    c. Click in the *Slides* text box located below the first gallery in the *Settings* category and then type 2,4.
    d. Click the Print button.
15. Save **P-C6-P2-ParisTour.pptx**.

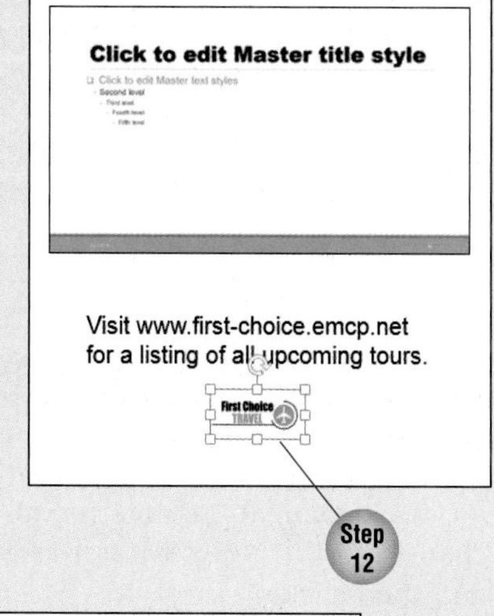

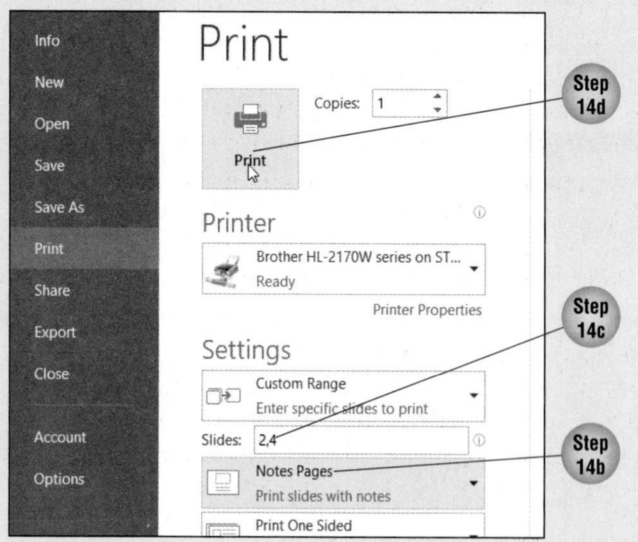

Using VIEW Tab Options

You have used buttons in the Presentation Views group and Master Views group on the VIEW tab to display your presentation in various views such as Normal, Slide Sorter, Slide Master, Handout Master, and Notes Master. In addition to viewing buttons, the VIEW tab includes options for showing or hiding the ruler and gridlines; displaying the Notes pane below the slide pane; zooming in or out in the slide; viewing the slide in color, grayscale, or black and white; and working with windows.

Changing the Zoom

Change the display size of the slide in the slide pane or the slides in the slide thumbnails pane with the Zoom button on the VIEW tab or with the Zoom slider bar located at the right side of the Status bar. Click the Zoom button on the VIEW tab and the Zoom dialog box displays. Use options in this dialog box to increase or decrease the display size of slides in the slide pane or slide thumbnails pane. To change the zoom with the Zoom slider bar, use the mouse to drag the slider bar button to the left to decrease the display size or to the right to increase the display size. Click the Zoom Out button (the minus symbol that displays at the left side of the Zoom slider bar) to decrease the display percentage or click the Zoom In button (the plus symbol that displays at the right side of the Zoom slider bar) to increase the display percentage. Click the percentage number that displays at the right side of the slider bar and the Zoom dialog box displays.

Zoom

Managing Windows

Use buttons in the Window group on the VIEW tab to work with presentation windows. Work in two locations in the same presentation by opening the presentation and then opening a new window with the same presentation. This is helpful if you want to view and edit slides in two different locations in the presentation. Open a new window by clicking the New Window button in the Window group.

New Window

Arrange All

Cascade

If you have more than one presentation open, you can arrange them so a portion of each presentation displays. Click the Arrange All button in the Window group and each open presentation displays as a tile on the screen. Click the Cascade button in the Window group and the open presentations are displayed in a layered manner, with the title bar of each presentation visible.

If you have more than one presentation open, you can switch presentations by clicking the Switch Windows button in the Window group. Click this button and a drop-down list with the names of the open presentations displays with a check mark in front of the active presentation. Make another presentation active by clicking the presentation name at the drop-down list.

Switch Windows

Increase or decrease the viewing area of each section of the presentation window with the Move Split button. Click this button and the mouse pointer displays as a four-headed arrow. Use the arrow keys on the keyboard to increase or decrease the viewing area of the slide pane and slide thumbnails pane. Click the left mouse button to deactivate the feature.

Move Split

Viewing in Color and Grayscale

Color

Grayscale

Black and White

By default, the slides in a presentation display in color. You can change the slides to grayscale or black and white with buttons in the Color/Grayscale group on the VIEW tab. Click the Grayscale button and the slides in the presentation display in grayscale and the GRAYSCALE tab becomes active. This tab contains a variety of options for changing the grayscale display, such as light grayscale, inverse grayscale, and gray or black with grayscale fill. Return to the color view by clicking the Back to Color View button on the GRAYSCALE tab. Click the Black and White button in the Color/Grayscale group and the slides in the presentation display in black and white and the BLACK AND WHITE tab becomes active. This tab contains many of the same options as the GRAYSCALE tab.

Project 2d **Viewing a Presentation** **Part 4 of 4**

1. With **P-C6-P2-ParisTour.pptx** open, make Slide 1 active and then click the slide in the slide pane.
2. Click the VIEW tab.
3. Increase and decrease the zoom by completing the following steps:
   a. Click the Zoom button in the Zoom group.
   b. At the Zoom dialog box, click the *33%* option and then click OK.
   c. Click the Zoom button, click the *100%* option in the Zoom dialog box, and then click OK.
   d. Click the Slide 2 thumbnail in the slide thumbnails pane.
   e. Click the Zoom button, click the *66%* option in the Zoom dialog box, and then click OK. (Because the slide was active in the slide thumbnails pane, the percentage display changed for the thumbnails in the pane.)
   f. Position the mouse pointer on the Zoom slider bar button (located at the right side of the Status bar), drag the button to the right to increase the size of the slide in the slide pane, and then drag the slider bar to the left to decrease the size of the slide.
   g. Click the percentage number that displays at the right side of the Zoom slider bar. This displays the Zoom dialog box.
   h. Click the *100%* option in the Zoom dialog box and then click OK.
   i. Click the Fit to Window button in the Zoom group on the VIEW tab.

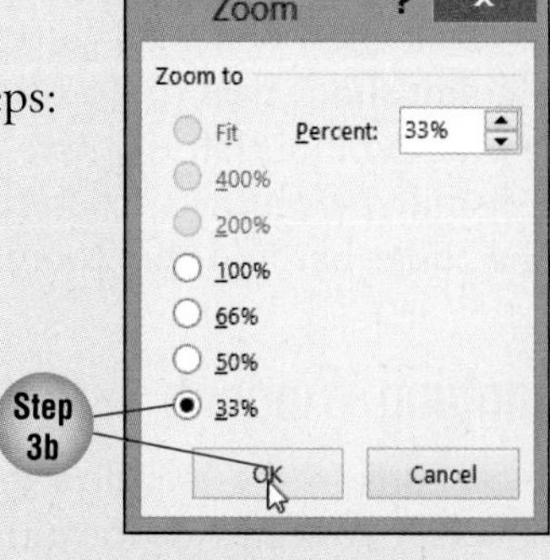

Step 3b

4. View the slides in grayscale by completing the following steps:
   a. Click the Grayscale button in the Color/Grayscale group on the VIEW tab.
   b. Click the slide in the slide pane.
   c. Click some of the buttons on the GRAYSCALE tab to display the slides in varying grayscale options.
   d. Click the Back To Color View button.

SLIDE SHOW REVIEW VIEW
Notes Zoom Fit to Window Color Grayscale Black and White
Zoom Color/Grayscale
Step 4a

5. View the slides in black and white by completing the following steps:
   a. Click the VIEW tab and then click the Black and White button in the Color/Grayscale group.
   b. Click some of the buttons in the BLACK AND WHITE tab to display the slides in varying black and white options.
   c. Click the Back To Color View button.

6. Open a new window and arrange the windows by completing the following steps:
   a. Click the VIEW tab and then click the New Window button in the Window group. (This opens the same presentation in another window. Notice that the name on the title bar displays followed by a colon and the number 2.)
   b. Click the VIEW tab and then click the Arrange All button to arrange the two presentation in two side-by-side windows.
   c. Click the Window button in the window at the left side of the screen and then click the Cascade button at the drop-down list. (This arranges the two presentations with the presentations overlapping with the title bar for each presentation visible.)
   d. Click the Switch Windows button and then click the *P-C6-P2-ParisTour.pptx:1* option at the drop-down list.
   e. Click the Close button that displays in the upper right corner of the currently active presentation.
   f. Click the Maximize button that displays in the upper right corner of the presentation window. (The Maximize button displays immediately left of the Close button.)

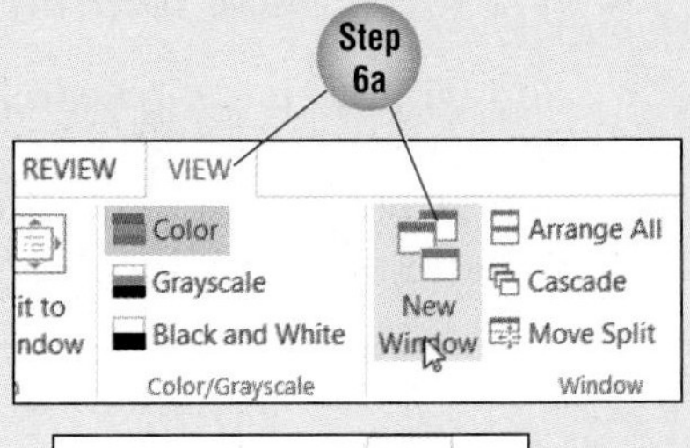

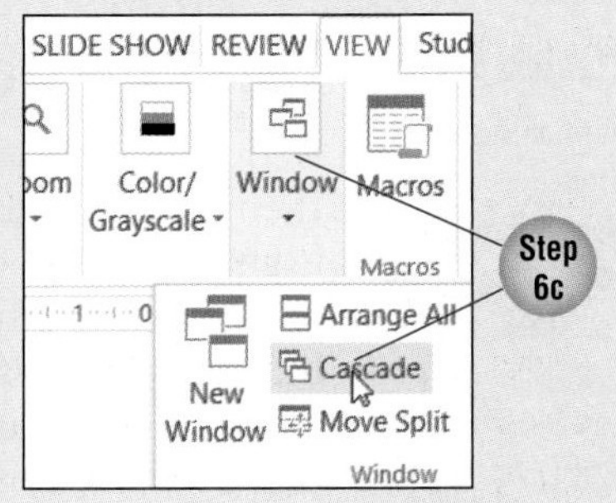

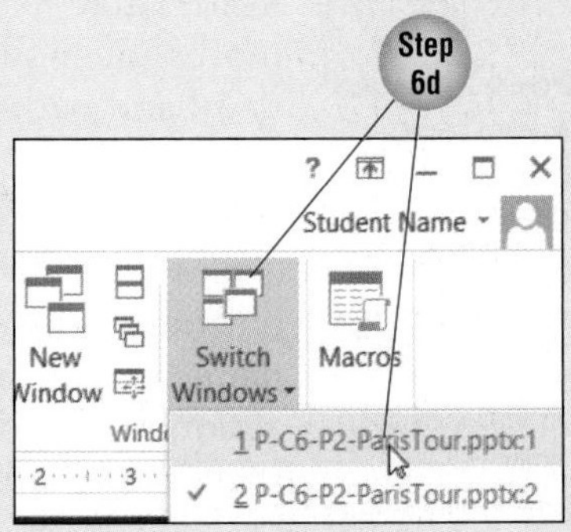

7. Use the Move Split button by completing these steps:
   a. Click the Move Split button in the Window group. (The mouse displays as a four-headed arrow.)
   b. Press the Right Arrow key on the keyboard several times and notice the slide thumbnails pane increasing in size.
   c. Press the Left Arrow key several times.
   d. Press the Up Arrow key several times and notice that the slide in the slide pane decreases in size and the notes pane displays.
   e. Press the Down Arrow key until the slide in the slide pane returns to the original size and the notes pane has closed.
8. With the VIEW tab active, click the Grayscale button in the Color/Grayscale group and then click the Light Grayscale button in the Change Selected Object group.
9. Print the presentation by completing the following steps:
   a. Display the Print backstage area.
   b. If any text displays in the *Slides* text box, select and then delete the text.
   c. If you are using a color printer, click the *Color* gallery that displays at the bottom of the *Settings* category and then click *Grayscale*. (Skip this step if you are using a black and white printer.)
   d. Click the second gallery in the *Settings* category and then click *6 Slides Horizontal* in the *Handouts* section.
   e. Click the Print button.
10. Click the Back To Color View button on the GRAYSCALE tab.
11. Make Slide 1 active and then run the presentation.
12. Save and then close **P-C6-P2-ParisTour.pptx**.

Project 3 Insert Action Buttons and Hyperlinks in a Job Search Presentation — 5 Parts

You will open a job search presentation and then insert action buttons that display the next slide, the first slide, a website, and another presentation. You will also create a hyperlink from text, a graphic image, and a chart in a slide to a website, a Word document, and another presentation.

Quick Steps

Create an Action Button
1. Make desired slide active.
2. Click INSERT tab.
3. Click Shapes button.
4. Click desired action button.
5. Click or drag in slide to create button.
6. Make desired changes at Action Settings dialog box.
7. Click OK.

Apply formatting to an action button with options on the DRAWING TOOLS FORMAT tab.

Inserting Action Buttons

Action buttons are drawn objects on a slide that have a routine attached to them which is activated when the viewer or the presenter clicks the button. For example, you could include an action button that displays the next slide in the presentation, a file in another program, or a specific web page. Creating an action button is a two-step process. You draw the button using an Action Button shape in the Shapes button drop-down list and then you define the action that will take place with options in the Action Settings dialog box. Customize an action button in the same manner as customizing a drawn object. When the viewer or presenter moves the mouse over an action button during a presentation, the pointer changes to a hand with a finger pointing upward to indicate clicking will result in an action.

To display the available action buttons, click the INSERT tab and then click the Shapes button in the Illustrations group. Action buttons display at the bottom of the drop-down list. Hover the mouse pointer over a button and the name and the action it performs display in a ScreenTip above the button. The action attached to an action button occurs when you run the presentation and then click the button.

Project 3a Inserting Action Buttons — Part 1 of 5

1. Open **JobSearch.pptx** and then save the presentation with the name **P-C6-P3-JobSearch**.
2. Make the following changes to the presentation:
   a. Apply the Dividend design theme.
   b. Click the INSERT tab and then click the Header & Footer button in the Text group.
   c. At the Header and Footer dialog box with the Slide tab selected, click the *Date and time* check box and make sure *Update automatically* is selected.
   d. Click the *Slide number* check box to insert a check mark.
   e. Click the Notes and Handouts tab.
   f. Click the *Date and time* check box and make sure *Update automatically* is selected.
   g. Click the *Header* check box to insert a check mark, click in the *Header* text box, and then type the name of your school.
   h. Click the *Footer* check box to insert a check mark, click in the *Footer* text box, and then type your first and last names.
   i. Click the Apply to All button.

3. Insert an action button in Slide 1 that will display the next slide by completing the following steps:
   a. Make sure Slide 1 is active.
   b. Click the INSERT tab and then click the Shapes button.
   c. Scroll down the drop-down list and then click the *Action Button: Forward or Next* button (second button in the *Action Buttons* group).
   d. Move the crosshair pointer to the lower right corner of the slide and then drag to create a button that is approximately 0.5 inch in height and width (see below).

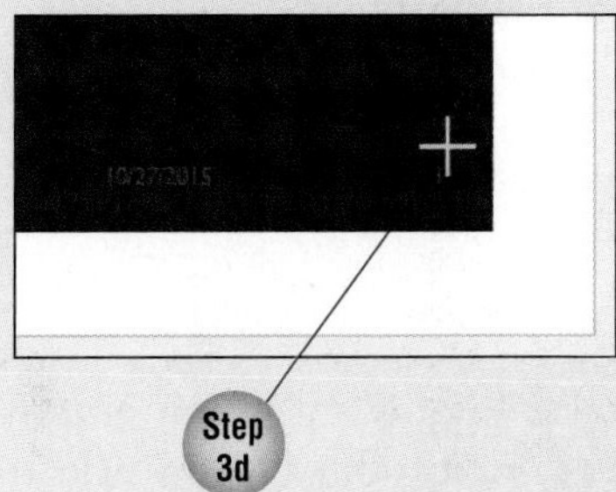

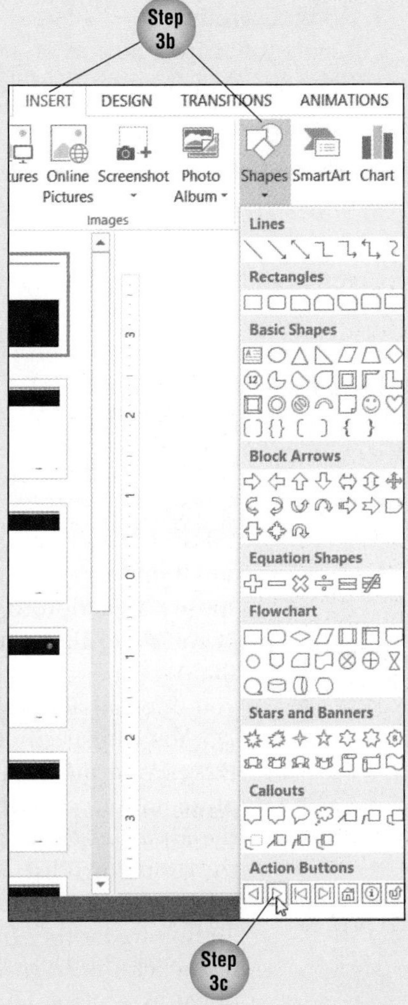

   e. At the Action Settings dialog box, click OK. (The default setting is *Hyperlink to Next Slide*.)
4. Insert an action button in Slide Master view that will display the next slide by completing the following steps:
   a. Display the presentation in Slide Master view.
   b. Click the top slide master thumbnail (*Dividend Slide Master*).
   c. Click the INSERT tab and then click the Shapes button.
   d. Scroll down the drop-down list and then click the *Action Button: Forward or Next* button (second button in the *Action Buttons* group).
   e. Move the crosshair pointer to the lower right corner of the slide master and then drag to create a button as shown at the right.
   f. At the Action Settings dialog box, click OK. (The default setting is *Hyperlink to Next Slide*.)
   g. Click the SLIDE MASTER tab and then click the Close Master View button.

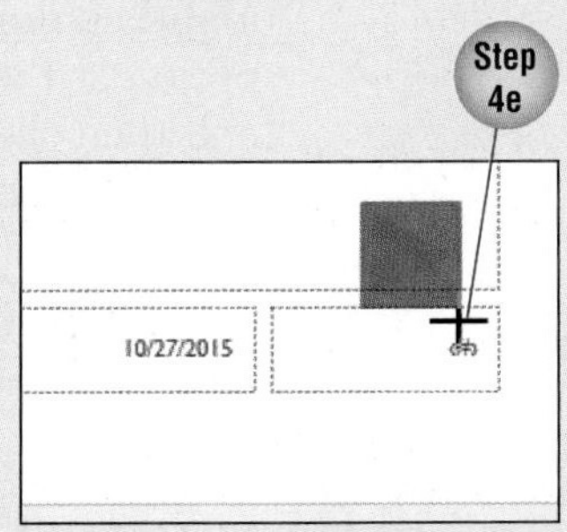

5. Make Slide 1 active and then run the presentation, clicking the action button to advance slides. When you click the action button on the last slide (Slide 9) nothing happens because it is the last slide. Press the Esc key to end the presentation.
6. Change the action button on Slide 9 by completing the following steps:
   a. Make Slide 9 active.
   b. Click the INSERT tab and then click the Shapes button.

c. Scroll down the drop-down list and then click the *Action Button: Home* button (fifth button in the *Action Buttons* group).
d. Drag to create a button on top of the previous action button. (Make sure it completely covers the previous action button.)
e. At the Action Settings dialog box with the *Hyperlink to: First Slide* option selected, click OK.
f. Deselect the button.

7. Display Slide 1 in the slide pane and then run the presentation. Navigate through the slide show by clicking the action button. When you click the action button on the last slide, the first slide displays. End the slide show by pressing the Esc key.
8. Save **P-C6-P3-JobSearch.pptx**.

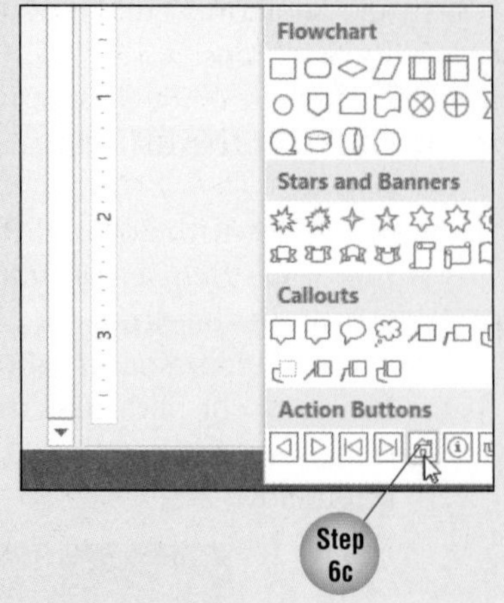

Applying an Action to an Object

Action

The Links group on the INSERT tab contains an Action button you can use to specify an action to a selected object. To use this button, select the desired object in the slide, click the INSERT tab, and then click the Action button. This displays the Action Settings dialog box, which is the same dialog box that displays when you draw an action button in a slide.

You can specify that an action button or a selected object link to another PowerPoint presentation, another file, or a website. To link to another PowerPoint presentation, click the *Hyperlink to* option at the Action Settings dialog box, click the *Hyperlink to* option box arrow, and then click *Other PowerPoint Presentation* at the drop-down list. At the Hyperlink to Other PowerPoint Presentation dialog box, navigate to the desired folder, and then double-click the PowerPoint presentation. To link to another file, click the *Hyperlink to* option at the Action Settings dialog box, click the *Hyperlink to* option box arrow, and then click *Other File* at the drop-down list. At the Hyperlink to Other File dialog box, navigate to the desired folder and then double-click the file name. To link to a website, click the *Hyperlink to* option at the Action Settings dialog box, click the *Hyperlink to* option box arrow, and then click *URL* at the drop-down list. At the Hyperlink To URL dialog box, type the web address in the *URL* text box, and then click OK. Click OK to close the Action Settings dialog box. Other actions you can link to using the *Hyperlink to* drop-down list include *Next Slide*, *Previous Slide*, *First Slide*, *Last Slide*, *Last Slide Viewed*, *End Show*, *Custom Show*, *Slide*, and *Other File*.

Project 3b **Linking to Another Presentation and a Website** **Part 2 of 5**

1. With **P-C6-P3-JobSearch.pptx** open, add an action button that will link to another presentation by completing the following steps:
   a. Make Slide 4 active.
   b. Click the INSERT tab and then click the Shapes button in the Illustrations group.
   c. Scroll down the drop-down list and then click *Action Button: Help* (second button shape from the right in the *Action Buttons* section).

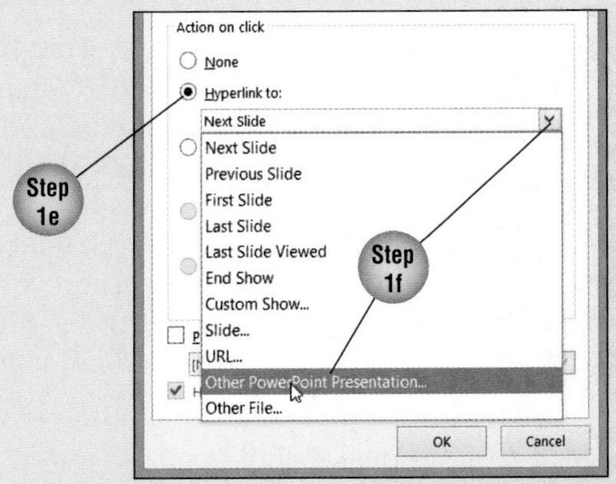

d. Draw the action button to the left of the existing button located in the lower right corner of the slide.
e. At the Action Settings dialog box, click the *Hyperlink to* option.
f. Click the *Hyperlink to* option box arrow and then click *Other PowerPoint Presentation* at the drop-down list.
g. At the Hyperlink to Other PowerPoint Presentation dialog box, navigate to the PC6 folder on your storage medium and then double-click ***Contacts.pptx***.
h. At the Hyperlink to Slide dialog box, click OK.
i. Click OK to close the Action Settings dialog box.

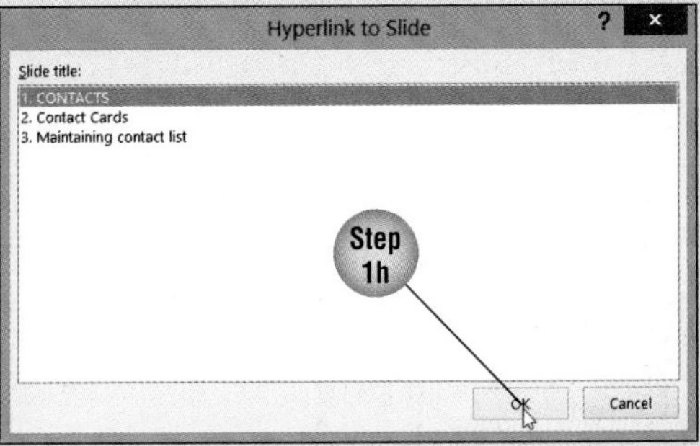

2. Apply an action to the clip art image in Slide 5 that links to a website by completing the following steps:
   a. Make Slide 5 active and then click the clip art image to select it.
   b. Click the INSERT tab and then click the Action button in the Links group.
   c. At the Action Settings dialog box, click the *Hyperlink to* option.
   d. Click the *Hyperlink to* option box arrow, and then click *URL* at the drop-down list.
   e. At the Hyperlink to URL dialog box, type **www.usajobs.gov** in the *URL* text box and then click OK.
   f. Click OK to close the Action Settings dialog box.
   g. Click outside the clip art image to deselect it.
3. Run the presentation by completing the following steps:
   a. Make sure you are connected to the Internet.
   b. Make Slide 1 active.
   c. Click the Slide Show button in the view area on the Status bar.
   d. Navigate through the slide show to Slide 4.
   e. Click the action button in Slide 4 containing the question mark. (This displays Slide 1 of **Contacts.pptx**.)
   f. Navigate through the three slides in **Contacts.pptx**. Continue clicking the mouse button until you return to Slide 4 of **P-C6-P3-JobSearch.pptx**.
   g. Display Slide 5 and then click the clip art image. (If you are connected to the Internet, the job site of the United States Federal Government displays.)
   h. Search for information on a specific job title that interests you and then click a few links at the website.
   i. When you have finished viewing the website, close your web browser.
   j. Continue viewing the remainder of the presentation by clicking the action button in the lower right corner of each slide.
   k. When Slide 1 displays, press the Esc key to end the presentation.
4. Save **P-C6-P3-JobSearch.pptx**.

Inserting Hyperlinks

Quick Steps

Insert a Hyperlink
1. Click INSERT tab.
2. Click Hyperlink button.
3. Make desired changes at Insert Hyperlink dialog box.
4. Click OK.

In Project 3b, you created hyperlinks with options at the Action Settings dialog box. You can also create hyperlinks with options at the Insert Hyperlink dialog box shown in Figure 6.2. To display this dialog box, select a key word, phrase, or object in a slide, click the INSERT tab, and then click the Hyperlink button in the Links group or press Ctrl + K, which is the keyboard shortcut to display the Insert Hyperlink dialog box. You can link to a website, another presentation, a place in the current presentation, a new presentation, or to an email address. To insert a hyperlink to a website or an existing presentation, click the Existing File or Web Page button in the *Link to* group at the Insert Hyperlink dialog box.

Figure 6.2 Insert Hyperlink Dialog Box

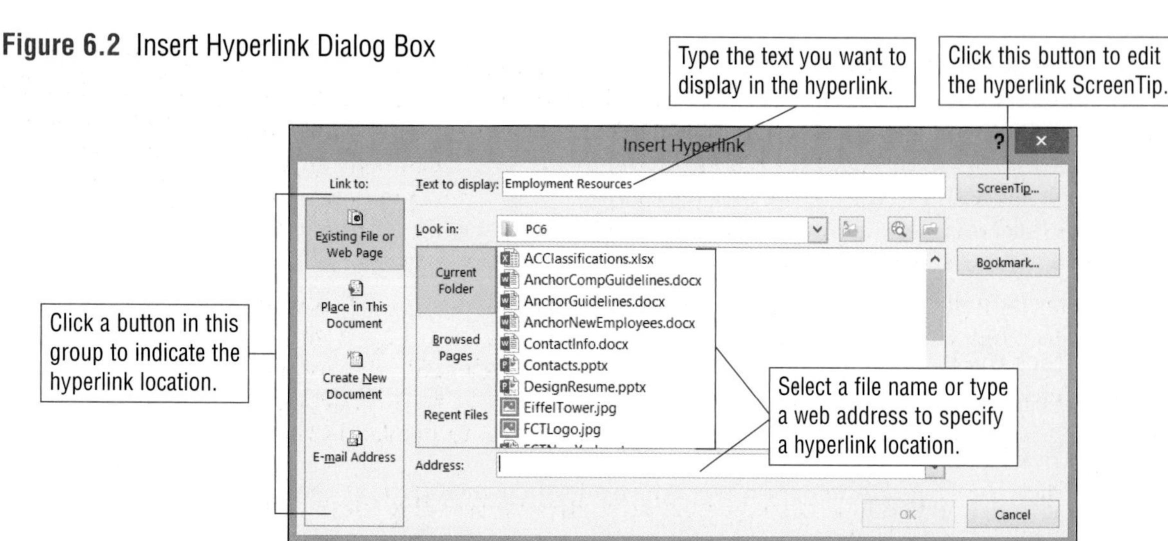

Project 3c **Inserting Hyperlinks to a Website** **Part 3 of 5**

1. With **P-C6-P3-JobSearch.pptx** open, insert a new slide by completing the following steps:
   a. Make Slide 5 active.
   b. Click the HOME tab.
   c. Create a new slide with the Title and Content layout.
   d. Click the text *Click to add title* and then type **Internet Job Resources**.
   e. Click the text *Click to add text,* type **Employment Resources**, press Enter, and then type **America's Job Bank**.
2. Add a hyperlink to the Employment Resources site by completing the following steps:
   a. Select *Employment Resources* in Slide 6.
   b. Click the INSERT tab and then click the Hyperlink button in the Links group.
   c. At the Insert Hyperlink dialog box, type **www.employment-resources.com** in the *Address* text box. (PowerPoint automatically inserts *http://* at the beginning of the address.)
   d. Click OK to close the Insert Hyperlink dialog box.

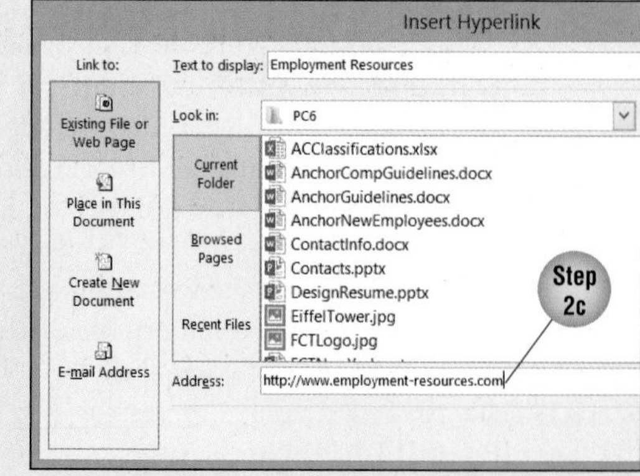

3. Add a hyperlink to the America's Job Bank website by completing the following steps:
   a. Select *America's Job Bank* in Slide 6.
   b. Click the Hyperlink button in the Links group.
   c. At the Insert Hyperlink dialog box, type www.ajb.dni.us in the *Address* text box.
   d. Click OK to close the Insert Hyperlink dialog box.
4. Save **P-C6-P3-JobSearch.pptx**.

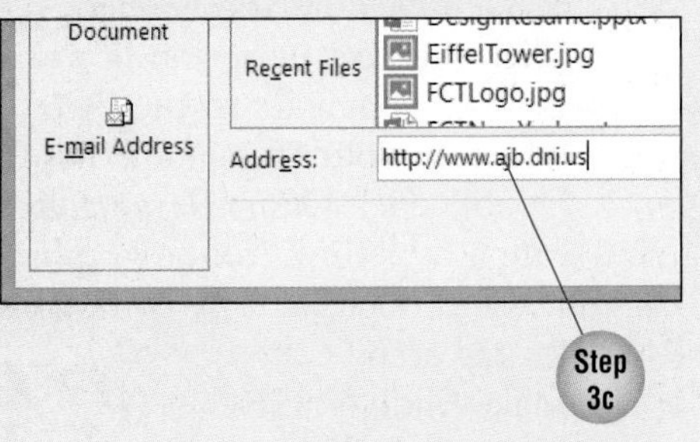

In addition to linking to a website, you can create a hyperlink to another location in the presentation with the Place in This Document button in the *Link to* group in the Insert Hyperlink dialog box. Click the slide you want to link to in the *Select a place in this document* list box. Use the Create New Document button in the Insert Hyperlink dialog box to create a hyperlink to a new presentation. When you click this button, you will be prompted to type a name for the new presentation and specify if you want to edit the new presentation now or later.

Hyperlinks are active when running the presentation, not when creating it.

You can use a graphic such as a clip art image, picture, chart, or text box, to hyperlink to a file or website. To hyperlink with a graphic, select the graphic, click the INSERT tab, and then click the Hyperlink button or right-click the graphic and then click *Hyperlink* at the shortcut menu. At the Insert Hyperlink dialog box, specify what you want to link to and the text you want to display in the hyperlink.

You can insert a hyperlink to an email address at the Insert Hyperlink dialog box. To do this, click the E-Mail Address button in the *Link to* group, type the desired address in the *E-mail address* text box, and type a subject for the email in the *Subject* text box. Click in the *Text to display* text box and then type the text you want to display in the document. To use this feature, the email address you use must be set up in Outlook.

Navigate to a hyperlink by clicking the hyperlink in the slide. Hover the mouse over the hyperlink and a ScreenTip displays with the hyperlink. If you want specific information to display in the ScreenTip, click the ScreenTip button in the Insert Hyperlink dialog box, type the desired text in the Set Hyperlink ScreenTip dialog box, and then click OK.

Project 3d Inserting Hyperlinks to a Website, to Another Presentation, and to a Word Document

Part 4 of 5

1. With **P-C6-P3-JobSearch.pptx** open, make Slide 3 active.
2. Create a link to another presentation by completing the following steps:
   a. Move the insertion point immediately right of the word *Picture*, press the Enter key, press Shift + Tab, and then type **Resume design**.
   b. Select *Resume design*.
   c. Make sure the INSERT tab is active and then click the Hyperlink button in the Links group.

d. At the Insert Hyperlink dialog box, make sure the Existing File or Web Page button is selected.
e. Click the *Look in* option box arrow and then navigate to the PC6 folder on your storage medium.
f. Double-click ***DesignResume.pptx***.

3. Create a hyperlink from a graphic to a Word document by completing the following steps:
a. Make Slide 4 active.
b. Right-click the small clip art image that displays in the upper right corner of the slide and then click *Hyperlink* at the shortcut menu.
c. At the Insert Hyperlink dialog box, make sure the Existing File or Web Page button is selected.
d. Click the *Look in* option box arrow and then navigate to the PC6 folder on your storage medium.
e. Double-click ***ContactInfo.docx***.

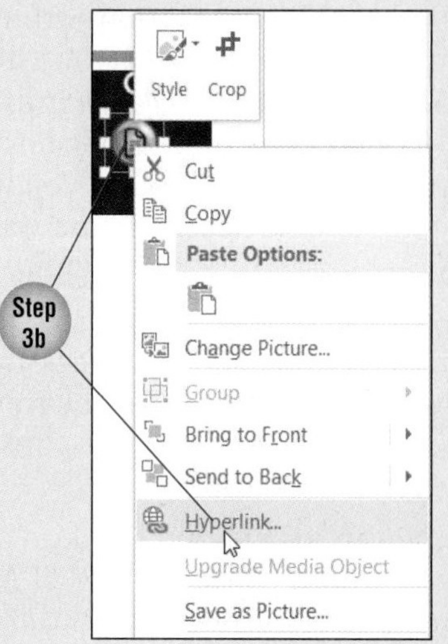

4. Make Slide 6 active and then insert a chart by completing the following steps:
a. Press Ctrl + F12 to display the Open dialog box.
b. Navigate to the PC6 folder on your storage medium and then double-click ***USBLSChart.pptx***.
c. Select the chart.
d. Click the Copy button.
e. Click the PowerPoint button on the Taskbar and then click the thumbnail representing **P-C6-P3-JobSearch.pptx**.
f. Click the Paste button.
g. With the chart selected, drag the chart down so it is positioned attractively on the slide.

5. Create a hyperlink from the chart to the United States Bureau of Labor Statistics website by completing the following steps:
a. With the chart selected, click the Hyperlink button in the Links group on the INSERT tab.
b. At the Insert Hyperlink dialog box, make sure the Existing File or Web Page button is selected and then type **www.bls.gov** in the *Address* text box.
c. Click OK to close the Insert Hyperlink dialog box.

6. Hover the mouse pointer on the PowerPoint button on the Taskbar, click the thumbnail representing **USBLSChart.pptx**, and then close the presentation.

7. Run the presentation by completing the following steps:
a. Make sure you are connected to the Internet.
b. Make Slide 1 active.
c. Click the Slide Show button in the view area on the Status bar.
d. Navigate through the slides to Slide 3 and then click the Resume design hyperlink in the slide.

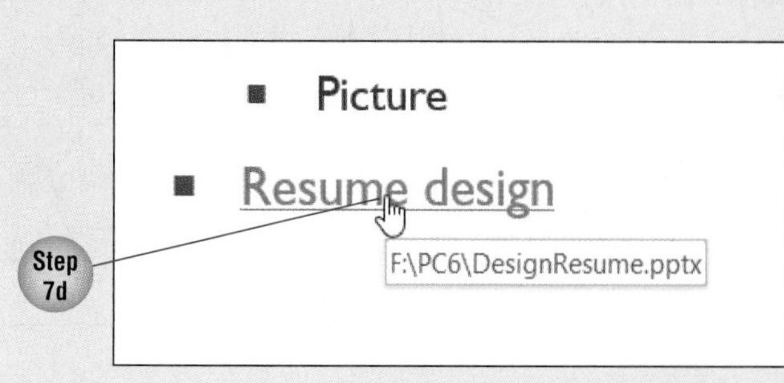

e. Run the **DesignResume.pptx** presentation that displays and then press the Esc key when the presentation has ended.
f. Click the mouse button to display Slide 4.
g. Display the Word document by clicking the small clip art image in the upper right corner of the slide.
h. Look at the information that displays in the Word document and then click the Close button located in the upper right corner of the Word window.
i. Continue running the presentation to Slide 6.
j. At Slide 6, click the Employment Resources hyperlink.
k. Scroll through the employment website and then close the web browser.
l. Click the America's Job Bank hyperlink.
m. Scroll through the America's Job Bank website and then close the web browser.
n. Click the chart.
o. Scroll through the Bureau of Labor Statistics website and then close the web browser.
p. Continue viewing the remainder of the presentation using the Action buttons. (When Slide 1 displays, press the Esc key to end the presentation.)

8. Save **P-C6-P3-JobSearch.pptx**.

You can modify or change hyperlink text or the hyperlink destination. To do this, right-click the hyperlink and then click *Edit Hyperlink* at the shortcut menu. At the Edit Hyperlink dialog box, make any desired changes and then close the dialog box. The Edit Hyperlink dialog box contains the same options as the Insert Hyperlink dialog box.

In addition to modifying the hyperlink, you can edit hyperlink text by making the desired editing changes. For example, you can apply a different font or font size, change the text color, and apply a text effect. Remove a hyperlink from a slide by right-clicking on the hyperlinked text and then clicking *Remove Hyperlink* at the shortcut menu.

Project 3e Modifying, Editing, and Removing a Hyperlink Part 5 of 5

1. With **P-C6-P3-JobSearch.pptx** open, make Slide 4 active and then modify the hyperlink in the clip art image by completing the following steps:
   a. Position the mouse pointer on the small clip art image in the upper right corner of the slide, click the right mouse button, and then click *Edit Hyperlink* at the shortcut menu.
   b. At the Edit Hyperlink dialog box, click the ScreenTip button located in the upper right corner of the dialog box.
   c. At the Set Hyperlink ScreenTip dialog box, type **Click this image to display information on typing contact information.**
   d. Click OK to close the Set Hyperlink ScreenTip dialog box.
   e. Click OK to close the Edit Hyperlink dialog box.

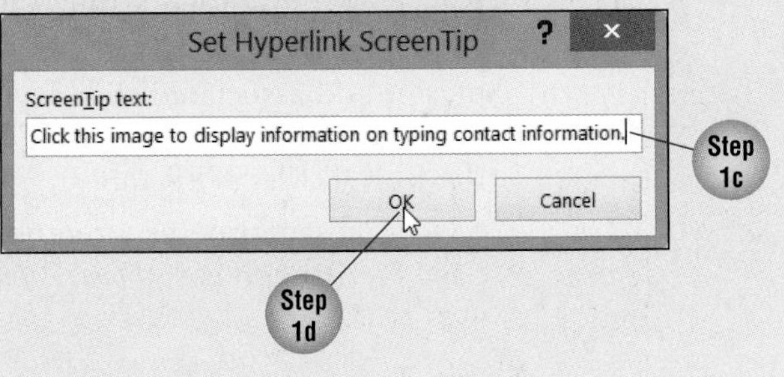

2. Make Slide 3 active and then remove the Resume design hyperlink by right-clicking the hyperlinked text (the text is dimmed and barely visible) and then clicking *Remove Hyperlink* at the shortcut menu.
3. Run the presentation and click the hyperlinks as they appear in slides.
4. Print the presentation as a handout with six slides horizontally per page.
5. Save and then close **P-C6-P3-JobSearch.pptx**.

Chapter Summary

- Display a presentation in Slide Master view by clicking the VIEW tab and then clicking the Slide Master button in the Master Views group. In Slide Master view, slide master thumbnails display in the slide thumbnails pane.
- Use buttons in the Background group on the SLIDE MASTER tab to change theme colors and fonts, apply a predesigned background style, display the Format Background task pane with options for applying background styles, and hide background graphics.
- Delete a placeholder by clicking in the placeholder, clicking the placeholder border, and then pressing the Delete key.
- Delete a slide master in Slide Master view by clicking the desired slide master thumbnail in the slide thumbnails pane and then clicking the Delete button in the Edit Master group.
- In Slide Master view, you can display the Header and Footer dialog box with the Slide tab selected and then insert the date and time, slide number, and/or a footer. At the Header and Footer dialog box with the Notes and Handouts tab selected, you can insert the date and time, a header, page numbers, and/or a footer.
- Create a custom slide layout by clicking the Insert Layout button in the Edit Master group on the SLIDE MASTER tab. Rename the custom slide layout with the Rename button in the Edit Master group.
- Insert placeholders in a slide layout or custom slide layout by clicking the Insert Placeholder button arrow in the Master Layout group and then clicking the desired placeholder at the drop-down list.
- In Slide Master view, create a custom prompt by selecting generic text in a placeholder and then typing the desired text.
- Click the Insert Slide Master button in Slide Master view to insert a new slide master and associated slide layouts. You can also insert a new slide master by applying a design theme using the Themes button in th Edit Theme group on the SLIDE MASTER tab.
- Save a presentation as a template by changing the *Save as type* option at the Save As dialog box to *PowerPoint Template (*.potx)*.

- Open a presentation based on a template by clicking the CUSTOM option at the New backstage area, clicking *Custom Office Templates*, and then double-clicking the desired template thumbnail.
- Customize a handout with options in the Handout Master view and customize notes pages with options in the Notes Master view.
- In addition to changing views, you can use buttons on the VIEW tab to show/hide the ruler and/or gridlines; change the zoom display; view slides in color, grayscale, or black and white; and work with multliple windows.
- Action buttons are drawn objects in a slide that have a routine attached, such as displaying the next slide, the first slide, a website, or another PowerPoint presentation.
- Create an action button by clicking the INSERT tab, clicking the Shapes button, clicking the desired button at the drop-down list, and then clicking or dragging in the slide to create the button.
- Apply an action to text or an object in a slide by selecting the text or object, clicking the INSERT tab, and then clicking the Action button.
- With options at the Insert Hyperlink dialog box, you can create a hyperlink to a web page, another presentation, a location within a presentation, a new presentation, or to an email. You can also create a hyperlink using a graphic.
- You can modify, edit, and remove hyperlinks.

Commands Review

FEATURE	RIBBON TAB, GROUP/OPTION	BUTTON	KEYBOARD SHORTCUT
action buttons	INSERT, Illustrations		
Action Settings dialog box	INSERT, Links		
Handout Master view	VIEW, Master Views		
Insert Hyperlink dialog box	INSERT, Links		Ctrl + K
New backstage area	FILE, *New*		
Notes Master view	VIEW, Master Views		
Slide Master view	VIEW, Master Views		

Concepts Check Test Your Knowledge 

Completion: In the space provided at the right, indicate the correct term, symbol, or command.

1. To display a presentation in Slide Master view, click this tab and then click the Slide Master button. ____________
2. Click this button to close Slide Master view. ____________
3. This group on the SLIDE MASTER tab contains buttons for applying theme colors and theme fonts. ____________
4. This dialog box with the Slide tab selected contains options for inserting the date and time, a slide number, and a footer. ____________
5. To create a new slide layout in Slide Master view, click this button in the Edit Master group. ____________
6. To save a presentation as a template, choose this option at the *Save as type* option drop-down list in the Save As dialog box. ____________
7. Change to this view to customize handouts. ____________
8. Change to this view to customize notes pages. ____________
9. The Zoom slider bar is located at the right side of this bar. ____________
10. Click this button to display a drop-down list that includes action buttons. ____________
11. Insert this action button in a slide to display the next slide in the presentation. ____________
12. Insert this action button in a slide to display the first slide in the presentation. ____________
13. This is the keyboard shortcut to display the Insert Hyperlink dialog box. ____________

Skills Check Assess Your Performance

Assessment 1

FORMAT A PRESENTATION IN SLIDE MASTER VIEW AND THEN SAVE THE PRESENTATION AS A TEMPLATE

Note: If you are using PowerPoint 2013 in a school setting on a network system, you may need to complete Assessments 1 and 2 in the same day. Check with your instructor for any specific instructions.

1. Open a blank presentation, click the VIEW tab, and then click the Slide Master button.
2. Click the top slide master thumbnail in the slide thumbnails pane.
3. Apply the Wood Type theme and apply the Yellow Orange theme colors.
4. Select the text *Click to edit Master text styles*, click the HOME tab and then change the font size to 24 points.
5. Select the text *Second level* in the slide master and then change the font size to 20 points.
6. Insert the **WELogo.jpg** image in the master slide, change the height of the logo to 0.5 inch, and then drag the logo to the upper right corner of the slide master.
7. Click the SLIDE MASTER tab.
8. Click the first slide layout below the slide master.
9. Click the *Footers* check box to remove the check mark in the Master Layout group to remove the footer and date placeholders.
10. Select and then delete the slide layouts from the third layout below the slide master (the *Section Header Layout*) to the last layout.
11. Preserve the slide master by clicking the top slide master in the slide thumbnails pane and then clicking the Preserve button in the Edit Master group.
12. Click the Close Master View button.
13. Save the presentation as a template and name the template **XXXPublicationTemplate** (use your initials in place of the *XXX*).
14. Close **XXXPublicationTemplate.potx**.

Assessment 2

USE A TEMPLATE TO CREATE A PUBLICATIONS PRESENTATION

1. Open a presentation based on the **XXXPublicationTemplate.potx** template presentation (where the XXX represents your initials). (To do this, display the New backstage area, click the CUSTOM option, click *Custom Office Templates*, and then double-click the ***XXXPublicationTemplate.potx*** template thumbnail.)
2. Save the presentation and name it **P-C6-A2-WEnterprises**.
3. Click the *CLICK TO ADD TITLE* text in the current slide and then type **Worldwide Enterprises**.
4. Click the *Click to add subtitle* text and then type **Company Publications**.
5. Display the Reuse Slides task pane, browse to the PC6 folder on your storage medium, and then double-click **Publications.pptx**.

6. Insert the second, third, fourth, and fifth slides from the Reuse Slides task pane into the current presentation and then close the task pane.
7. Insert a second slide master with the following specifications:
   a. Display the presentation in Slide Master view.
   b. Click in the slide thumbnails pane below the bottom slide layout.
   c. Apply the Frame theme.
   d. Click the Frame Slide Master thumbnail in the slide thumbnails pane and then apply the Yellow Orange theme colors.
   e. Apply the Style 9 background style.
8. Select and then delete slide layouts from the third layout (*Section Header Layout*) below the new slide master to the last layout.
9. Insert headers, footers, slide numbers, and dates with the following specifications:
   a. Click the INSERT tab, display the Header and Footer dialog box with the Slide tab selected, insert the date to update automatically, and insert slide numbers.
   b. Click the Notes and Handouts tab, insert the date to update automatically, insert a header that prints your first and last names, insert a footer that prints *Worldwide Enterprises*, and then click the Apply to All button.
10. Close Slide Master view.
11. Make Slide 5 active and then insert a new slide using the new Frame Title Slide layout and then type **Worldwide Enterprises** as the title and **Preparing the Company Newsletter** as the subtitle.
12. Insert the following text in slides using the Frame Title and Content layout:

    Slide 7 Preparing the Newsletter
    - Maintain consistent elements from issue to issue
    - Consider the following when designing the newsletter
      - Focus
      - Balance
      - White space
      - Directional flow

    Slide 8 Preparing the Newsletter
    - Choose paper size and weight
    - Determine margins
    - Specify column layout
    - Choose nameplate layout and format
    - Specify heading format
    - Determine newsletter colors
13. Insert a transition and sound of your choosing to all slides in the presentation.
14. Run the presentation.
15. Print the presentation as a handout with four slides printed horizontally per page.
16. Save and then close **P-C6-A2-WEnterprises.pptx**.

Assessment 3

INSERT ACTION BUTTONS IN A GARDENING PRESENTATION

1. Open **GAPres.pptx** and then save the presentation with the name **P-C6-A3-GAPres**.
2. Make Slide 1 active and then insert an action button in the lower right corner of the slide that displays the next slide.
3. Display the presentation in Slide Master view, click the top slide master in the slide thumbnails pane, create an action button in the lower right corner of the slide that displays the next slide, and then close Slide Master view.
4. Make Slide 8 active and then create an action button that displays the first slide in the presentation.
5. Make Slide 2 active, click the flowers clip art image, and then create a link to the presentation **MaintenancePres.pptx** (located in the PC6 folder on your storage medium). ***Hint: Use the Action button in the Links group on the INSERT tab.***
6. Display Slide 8 and then make the following changes:
   a. Delete the text *Better Homes and Gardens®* and then type **Organic Gardening®**.
   b. Select *Organic Gardening®* and then create a hyperlink with the text to the website www.organicgardening.com.
7. Make sure you are connected to the Internet and then run the presentation beginning with Slide 1. Navigate through the slide show by clicking the next action button and display the connected presentation by clicking the clip art image in Slide 2. At Slide 8, click the Organic Gardening® hyperlink. Scroll through the website and click a few different hyperlinks that interest you. After viewing a few web pages in the magazine, close your web browser. When you click the action button on the last slide, the first slide displays. End the slide show by pressing the Esc key.
8. Print the presentation as a handout with four slides printed horizontally per page.
9. Save and then close **P-C6-A3-GAPres.pptx**.

Assessment 4

CREATE AN ACTION BUTTONS PRESENTATION

1. In this chapter, you learned to insert a number of action buttons in a slide. Experiment with the other action buttons (click the INSERT tab, click the Shapes button, and then point to the buttons in the *Action Buttons* section) and then prepare a PowerPoint presentation with the following specifications:
   a. The first slide should contain the title of your presentation.
   b. Choose four action buttons and then create one slide for each of the action buttons that includes the specific name as well as an explanation of the button.
   c. Apply a design theme of your choosing to the presentation.
2. Save the presentation and name it **P-C6-A4-ActionButtons**.
3. Print the presentation as a handout with six slides printed horizontally per page.
4. Close **P-C6-A4-ActionButtons.pptx**.

Visual Benchmark Demonstrate Your Proficiency

CREATE AND FORMAT A COMPANY BRANCH OFFICE PRESENTATION

1. Create the presentation shown in Figure 6.3 with the following specifications:
   a. Apply the Parallax design theme, the gray/orange variant, the Arial Black-Arial theme fonts and the Style 1 background style.
   b. In Slide 1, delete the title placeholder and insert the text shown in the figure in the subtitle placeholder. Insert **WELogo.jpg** and then size and position the logo as shown in the figure. Insert the Forward or Next action button in the lower right corner of the slide as shown in the figure.
   c. Display the presentation in Slide Master view and then click the top slide master thumbnail. Insert **WELogo.jpg**, change the height of the logo to 0.5 inch, and then position the logo in the upper right corner of the slide as shown in Figure 6.3. Select the text *Click to edit Master title style*, click the HOME tab, and then change the font color to *Orange, Accent 1, Darker 25%*. Insert the Forward or Next action button in the lower right corner of the slide master as shown in the figure and then close the Slide Master view.
   d. In Slide 4, create the 3-D clustered column chart as shown in the figure using the following numbers:

	>$25,000	>$50,000	>$100,000
Under 25	184	167	0
25 to 44	1,228	524	660
45 to 64	519	1,689	1,402
Over 64	818	831	476

   e. In Slide 5 (the *Top Public Employers* slide), insert the Information action button that links to the website www.clearwater-fl.com/gov and then size and position the action button as shown in the figure.
   f. In Slide 6, insert the clip art image of a hospital (use the search words *hospital* and *ambulance*), correct the color of the clip art image to *Brightness: -20% Contrast: +20%*, and then size and position the clip art as shown in the figure. Insert a Home action button over the Forward or Next action button.
   g. Change the line spacing in Slides 5 and 6 so your slides display similar to the slides in Figure 6.3.
2. Apply a transition and sound of your choosing to all slides in the presentation.
3. Save the presentation and name it **P-C6-VB-WEClearwater**.
4. Run the presentation.
5. Print the presentation as a handout with six slides printed horizontally per page.
6. Close **P-C6-VB-WEClearwater.pptx**.

Figure 6.3 Visual Benchmark

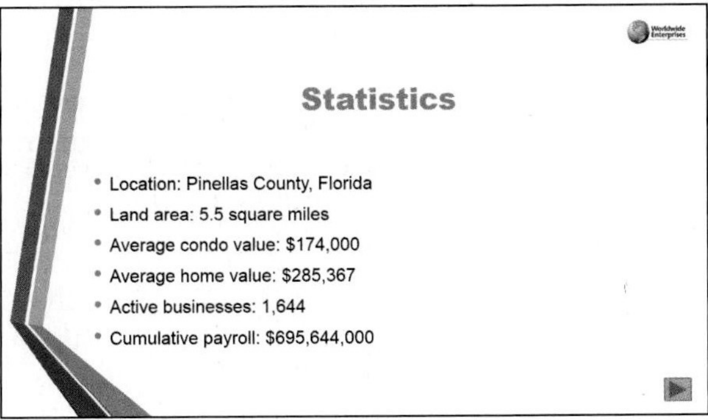

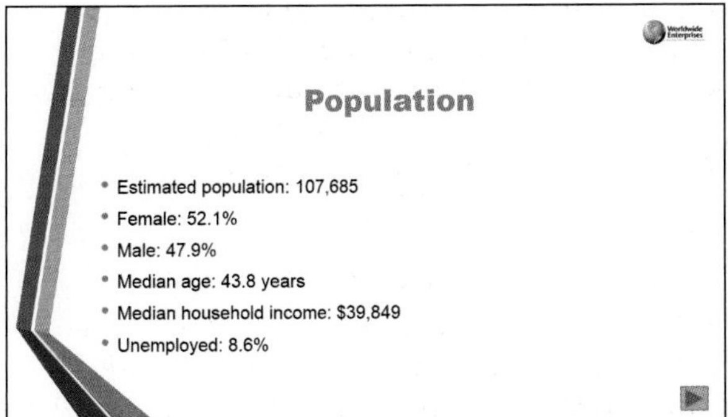

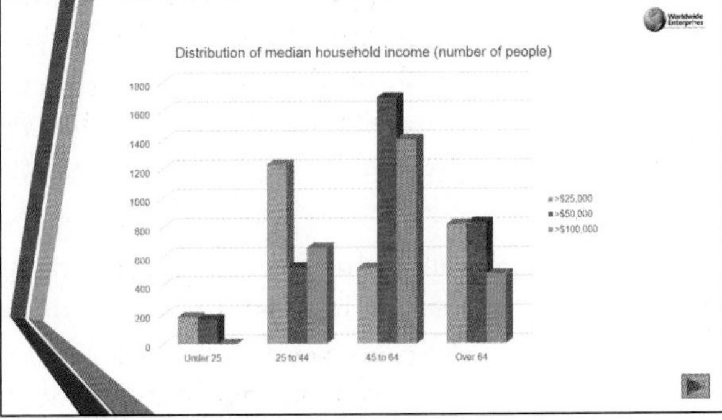

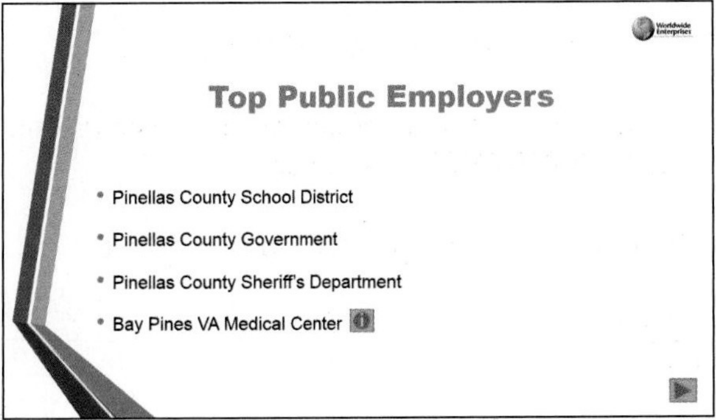

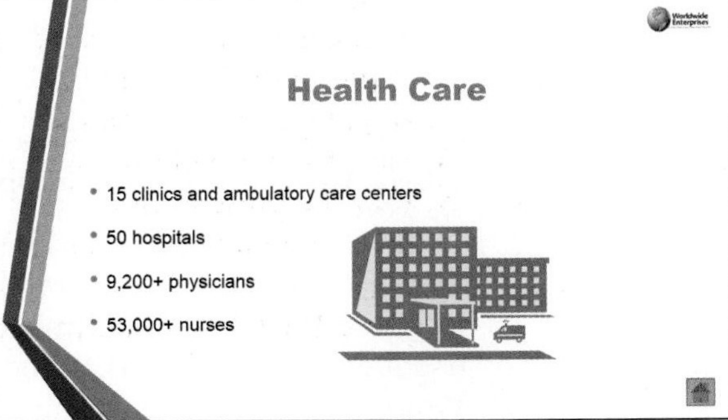

Case Study Apply Your Skills

Part 1

You are the training manager for Anchor Corporation and one of your job responsibilities is conducting new employee orientations. You decide that a PowerPoint presentation will help you deliver information to new employees during the orientation. You know that you will be creating other PowerPoint presentations so you decide to create a template. Create a presentation template with attractive formatting that includes a design theme, theme colors, and theme fonts. Include an anchor clip art image in all of the slides. Apply any other formatting or design elements to increase the appeal of the presentation. Save the presentation as a template with the name **XXXAnchorTemplate** (insert your initials in place of the XXX) and then close the template.

Part 2

You have a document with notes about information on types of employment appointments, employee performance, and compensation. Open the Word document named **AnchorNewEmployees.docx** and then use the information to prepare a presentation using the **XXXAnchorTemplate.potx** template. Save the completed presentation with the name **P-C6-CS-AnchorEmp** and make sure it has the file extension *.pptx*. Apply a transition and sound to all slides in the presentation, print the presentation as a handout, and then close the presentation.

Part 3

Open the Word document named **AnchorGuidelines.docx** and then use the information in the document to prepare a presentation using the **XXXAnchorTemplate.potx** template. Save the completed presentation with the name **P-C6-CS-AnchorGuidelines** and make sure it contains the file extension *.pptx*. Apply a transition and sound to all slides in the presentation, print the presentation as a handout, and then close the presentation.

Part 4

During the new employee presentation you want to refer to a chart of employee classifications, so you decide to create a link to an Excel spreadsheet. Open the **P-C6-CS-AnchorEmp.pptx** presentation and then create a new slide that contains a hyperlink to the Excel workbook named **ACClassifications.xlsx**. Run the presentation, link to the Excel chart, and then continue running the remaining slides in the presentation. Print only the new slide and then save and close **P-C6-CS-AnchorEmp.pptx**.

Part 5

The information you used to create the **P-C6-CS-AnchorGuidelines.pptx** presentation was taken from a document that is part of a new employee handbook. You decide that you want to create a link in your presentation to the Word document to show employees the additional information in the document. Create a new slide in the **P-C6-CS-AnchorGuidelines.pptx** presentation that includes an action button that links to the Word document named **AnchorCompGuidelines.docx**. Include other action buttons for navigating in the presentation. Run the presentation, link to the Word document, and then continue running the remaining slides in the presentation. Print only the new slide and then save and close **P-C6-CS-AnchorGuidelines.pptx**.

MICROSOFT® POWERPOINT®

CHAPTER 7

Applying Custom Animation and Setting Up Shows

PERFORMANCE OBJECTIVES

Upon successful completion of Chapter 7, you will be able to:

- **Apply animations**
- **Modify and remove animations**
- **Apply a build**
- **Animate shapes, images, SmartArt, and chart elements**
- **Draw motion paths**
- **Set up a slide show**
- **Set rehearse timings for slides**
- **Hide slides**
- **Create, run, edit, and print a custom show**
- **Insert and customize audio and video files**

Tutorials

7.1 Applying Animation to Objects and Text

7.2 Animating Shapes, Images, SmartArt, and Chart Elements

7.3 Setting Up a Slide Show

7.4 Applying Sound to Animations

7.5 Setting Timings for a Presentation

7.6 Creating and Running a Custom Show

7.7 Adding Audio and Video

7.8 Modifying Audio and Video Files

Animation, or movement, can add visual appeal and interest to your presentation when used appropriately. PowerPoint provides a number of animation effects you can apply to elements in a slide. In this chapter, you will learn how to apply animation effects as well as how to insert audio and video files to create dynamic presentations.

In some situations, you may want to prepare an automated presentation that runs on a continuous loop. You can customize a presentation to run continuously and set the time you want each slide to remain on the screen. You can also create a custom slide show to present only specific slides in a presentation. In this chapter, you will learn how to prepare automated presentations and how to create and edit custom slide shows. Model answers for this chapter's projects appear on the following pages.

Note: Before beginning the projects, copy to your storage medium the PC7 folder from the PowerPoint folder on the CD that accompanies this textbook and then make PC7 the active folder.

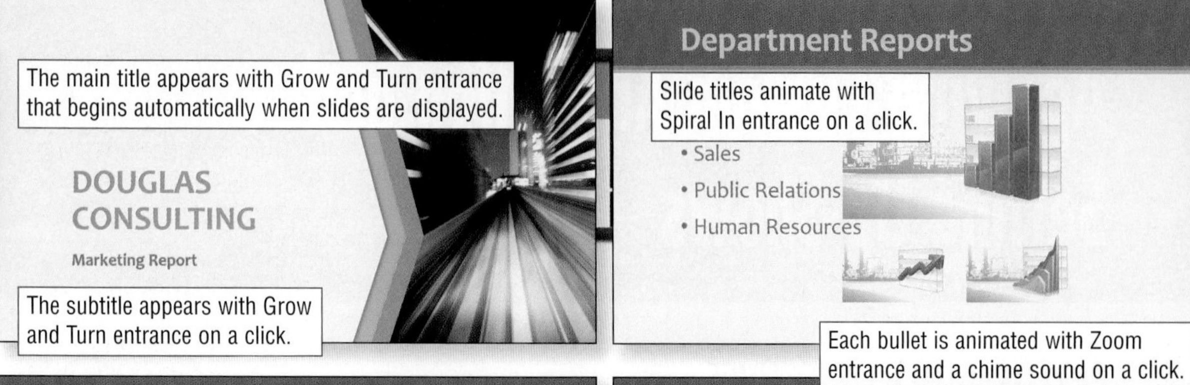
The main title appears with Grow and Turn entrance that begins automatically when slides are displayed.
DOUGLAS CONSULTING
Marketing Report
The subtitle appears with Grow and Turn entrance on a click.
Department Reports
Slide titles animate with Spiral In entrance on a click.
• Sales
• Public Relations
• Human Resources
Each bullet is animated with Zoom entrance and a chime sound on a click.

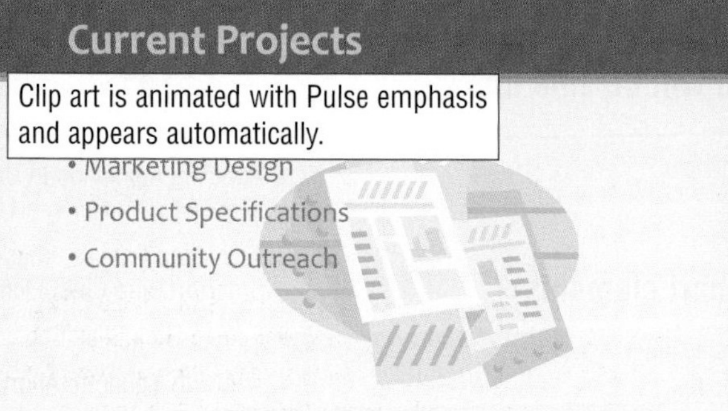
Current Projects
Clip art is animated with Pulse emphasis and appears automatically.
• Marketing Design
• Product Specifications
• Community Outreach

Services

• Project Management
• Research and Development
• Inventory Management
• Quality Control

Project 1 Apply Animation Effects to Elements in a Marketing Presentation

P-C7-P1-MarketingPres.pptx

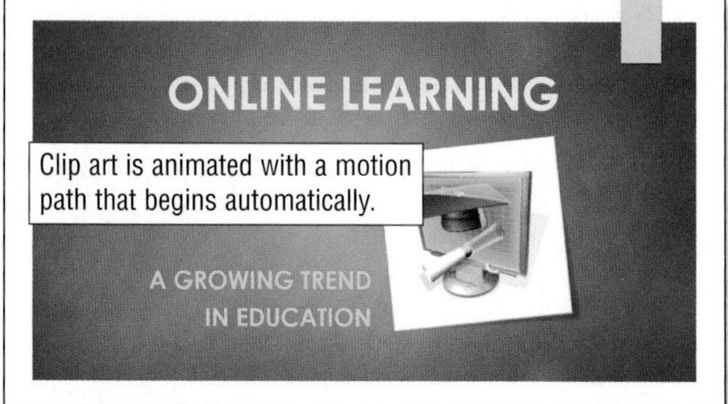
ONLINE LEARNING
Clip art is animated with a motion path that begins automatically.
A GROWING TREND IN EDUCATION

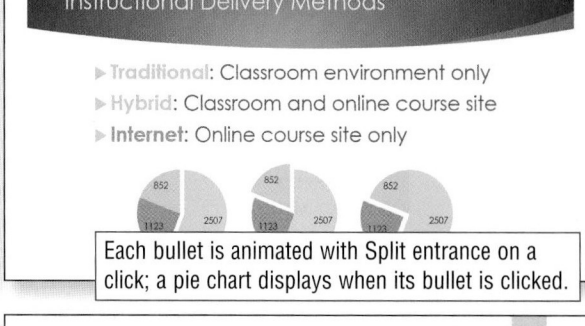

Instructional Delivery Methods

▸ Traditional: Classroom environment only
▸ Hybrid: Classroom and online course site
▸ Internet: Online course site only

852 1123 2507 | 852 1123 2507 | 852 1123 2507

Each bullet is animated with Split entrance on a click; a pie chart displays when its bullet is clicked.

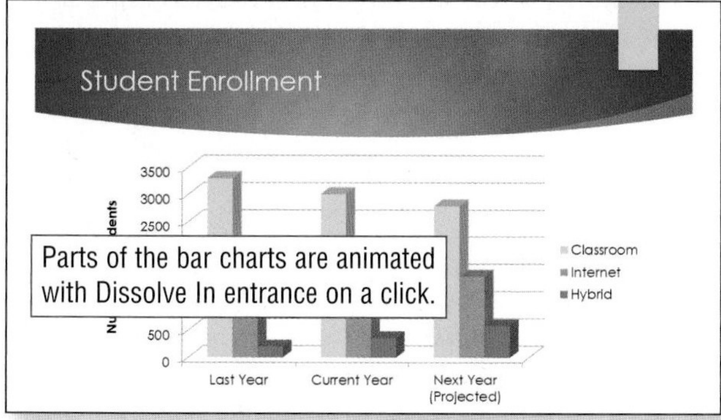
Student Enrollment
3500
3000
2500
500
0
Parts of the bar charts are animated with Dissolve In entrance on a click.
Classroom
Internet
Hybrid
Last Year
Current Year
Next Year (Projected)

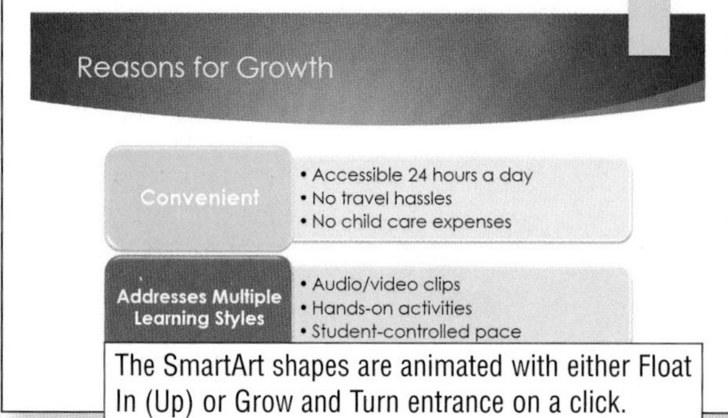
Reasons for Growth
Convenient
• Accessible 24 hours a day
• No travel hassles
• No child care expenses
Addresses Multiple Learning Styles
• Audio/video clips
• Hands-on activities
• Student-controlled pace
The SmartArt shapes are animated with either Float In (Up) or Grow and Turn entrance on a click.

Project 2 Apply Custom Animation Effects to Elements in Slides in an Online Learning Presentation, Slides 1–4

P-C7-P2-OLLearning.pptx

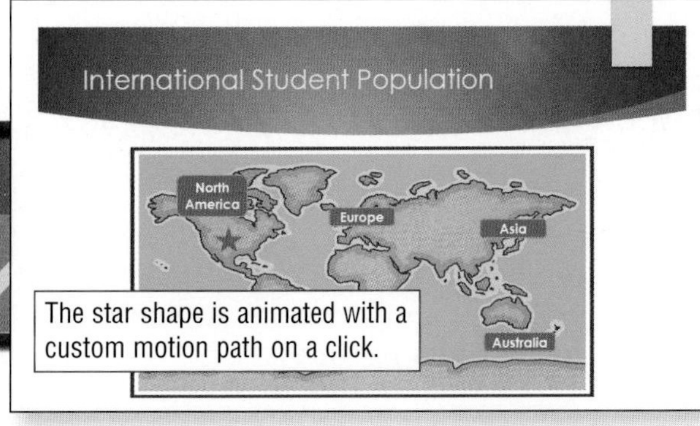

International Student Population

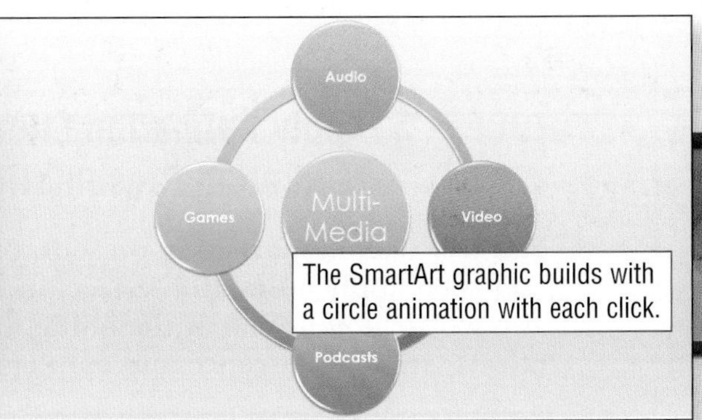

The SmartArt graphic builds with a circle animation with each click.

Each bullet is animated with Fly In entrance on a click and then dims.

- Electronic submission of assignments
- Evidence of online participation
- Peer evaluations
- Proctored exams

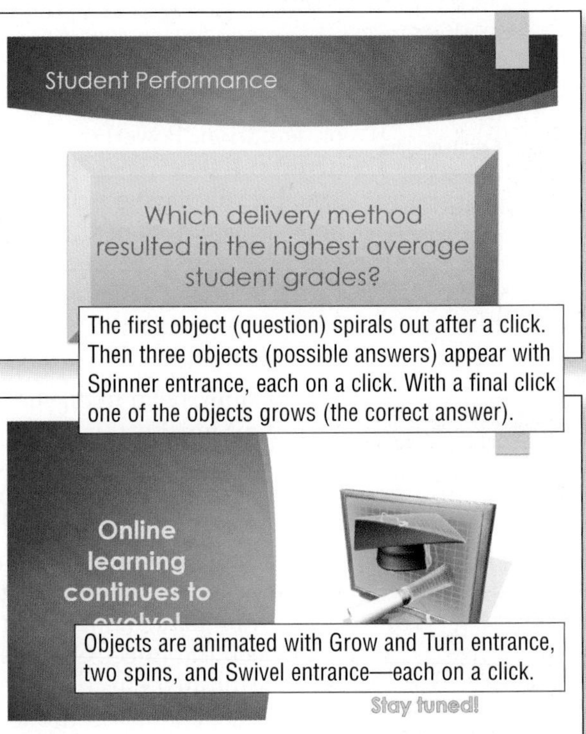

Student Performance
Which delivery method resulted in the highest average student grades?
The first object (question) spirals out after a click. Then three objects (possible answers) appear with Spinner entrance, each on a click. With a final click one of the objects grows (the correct answer).
Online learning continues to
Objects are animated with Grow and Turn entrance, two spins, and Swivel entrance—each on a click.
Stay tuned!

Project 2 Apply Custom Animation Effects to Elements in Slides in an Online Learning Presentation, Slides 5–9

P-C7-P2-OLLearning.pptx

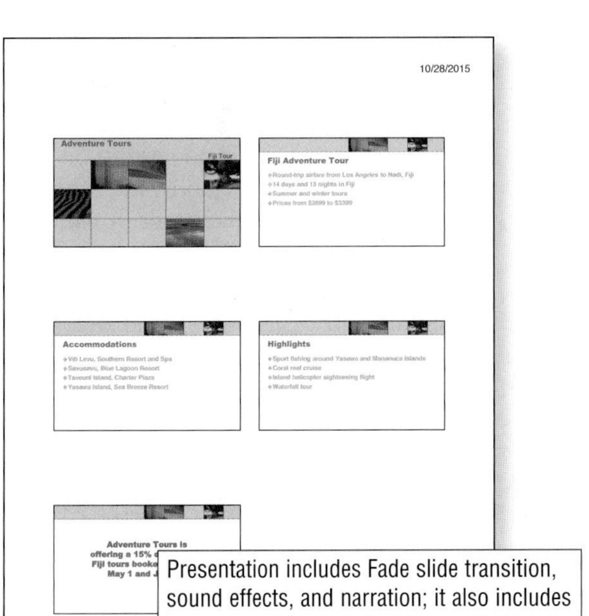

Presentation includes Fade slide transition, sound effects, and narration; it also includes two custom shows—Peru tour and Fiji tour.

Project 3 Prepare a Self-Running Adventure Presentation and Create Custom Shows

P-C7-P3-AdvTours-Custom.pptx

Video file inserted in slide that plays automatically. Video file deleted and then audio file inserted that plays throughout all slides as each slide advances automatically after five seconds.

Project 4 Insert Audio and Video Files in a Presentation

P-C7-P4-EcoTours.pptx

Project 1 Apply Animation Effects to Elements in a Marketing Presentation

6 Parts

You will open a marketing presentation, apply animation effects to the title slide, and then apply animation effects in Slide Master view to the remaining slides. You will remove some of the animation effects and then apply custom animation effects, such as entrance and emphasis effects, to elements in slides.

Applying and Removing Animations

Quick Steps

Apply an Animation
1. Click desired item.
2. Click ANIMATIONS tab.
3. Click More button in Animation group.
4. Click desired animation at drop-down gallery.

You can animate text, objects, graphics, SmartArt diagrams, charts, hyperlinks, and sound.

Effects Options

Preview

Animate items such as text or objects in a slide to add visual interest to a presentation. PowerPoint includes a number of animations you can apply to items in a slide. These animations can be modified to fit your specific needs. For example, displaying items one at a time helps your audience focus on each topic or point as you present it, so you may want items to appear individually or in groups. You can control the direction that an item enters from and the rate of speed at which it enters. Try not to overwhelm your audience with too much animation. In general, you want them to remember the content of your presentation rather than the visual effects.

To animate an item, click the desired item, click the ANIMATIONS tab, click the More button at the right side of the animations in the Animation group, and then click the desired animation at the drop-down gallery. Once you have applied an animation, you can specify the animation effects with options in the Effect Options button drop-down gallery. Some of the animation effect options may include the direction from which you want the item to appear, and whether you want items such as bulleted text or SmartArt to appear as one object, all at once, or by paragraph. To apply effects to an animation, apply an animation to an item, click the Effect Options button located in the Animation group, and then click the desired effect at the drop-down gallery. (The appearance of this button changes depending on the selected effect.) Use options in the Timing group on the ANIMATIONS tab to specify when the animation needs to start on a slide, the duration of the animation, the delay between animations, and the order in which animations should appear on the slide.

If you want to see the animation in your slide without running the presentation, click the Preview button on the ANIMATIONS tab. Click this button and the animation effect you applied to the active slide displays on the slide in the slide pane. When you apply animation effects to items in a slide, an animation icon displays below the slide number in the slide thumbnails pane.

If you add or change an animation, PowerPoint will automatically preview the animation in the slide. If you want to turn off this feature, click the Preview button arrow and then click *AutoPreview* at the drop-down list to remove the check mark.

Project 1a Applying Animations Part 1 of 6

1. Open **MarketingPres.pptx** and save the presentation with the name **P-C7-P1-MarketingPres**.
2. Make sure Slide 1 is active and then apply animations to the title and subtitle by completing the following steps:
   a. Click anywhere in the title *DOUGLAS CONSULTING*.
   b. Click the ANIMATIONS tab.
   c. Click the *Fade* animation in the Animation group.

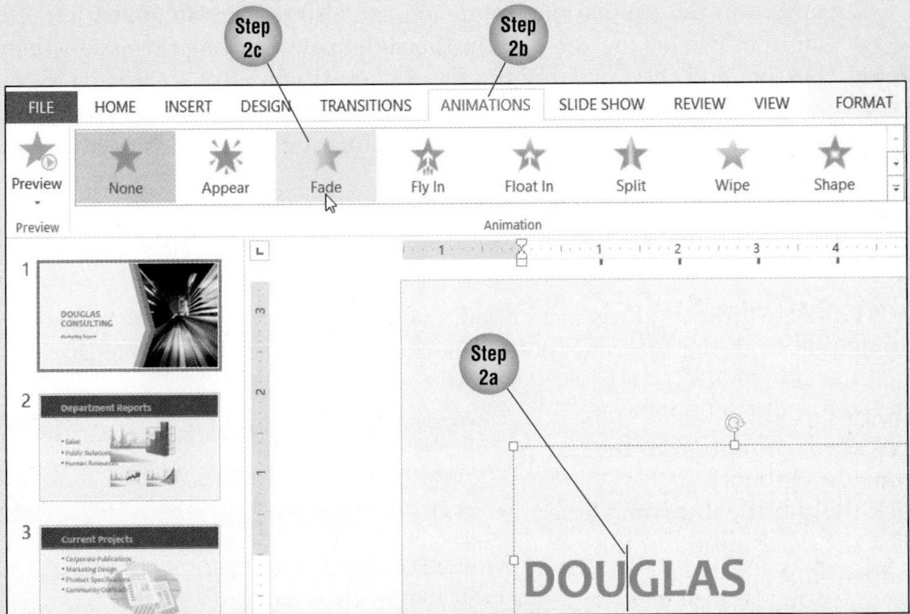

   d. Click anywhere in the subtitle *Marketing Report*.
   e. Click the *Fade* animation that displays in the Animation group.
   f. Click the Effect Options button in the Animation group and then click *All at Once* at the drop-down gallery.
   g. Click the Preview button on the ANIMATIONS tab to see the animation effects in the slide pane.

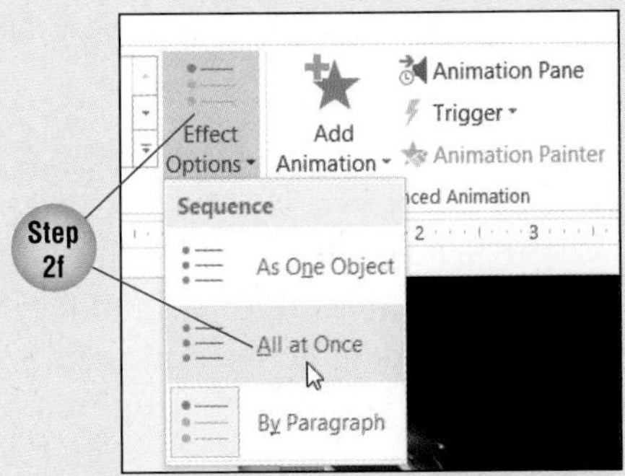

3. Apply animations to Slides 2 through 4 in Slide Master view by completing the following steps:
   a. Click the VIEW tab and then click the Slide Master button in the Master Views group.
   b. Click the third slide master layout in the slide thumbnails pane (Title and Content Layout).
   c. Click the text *Click to edit Master title style*.
   d. Click the ANIMATIONS tab and then click the *Fly In* animation that displays in the Animation group.
   e. Click the bulleted text *Click to edit Master text styles*.
   f. Click the *Fly In* animation that displays in the Animation group.
   g. Click the SLIDE MASTER tab and then click the Close Master View button.

4. Make Slide 1 active and then run the presentation. Click the mouse button to advance items in slides and to move to the next slide. Notice how the bulleted text in Slides 2 through 4 displays one item at a time.
5. Save **P-C7-P1-MarketingPres.pptx**.

Quick Steps

Remove an Animation
1. Click desired item.
2. Click ANIMATIONS tab.
3. Click *None* option.

If you want to remove an animation effect from an item, click the item in the slide in the slide pane, click the ANIMATIONS tab, and then click the *None* option in the Animation group. You can also remove an animation effect from an item by clicking the item in the slide pane, clicking the assigned animation button, and then pressing the Delete key. If you want to apply a different animation to an item, make sure to delete any existing animations first. If you do not delete the first animation, both animations will be assigned to the item.

Project 1b Removing Animations — Part 2 of 6

1. With **P-C7-P1-MarketingPres.pptx** open, make Slide 1 active and then remove the animation from the title and subtitle by completing the following steps:
   a. Click the title *DOUGLAS CONSULTING*.
   b. Click the ANIMATIONS tab.
   c. Click the *None* option in the Animation group.
   d. Click the subtitle *Marketing Report*.
   e. Click the *None* option in the Animation group.

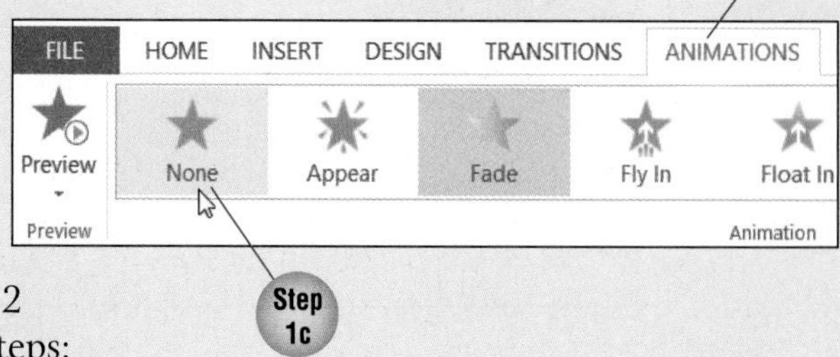

2. Remove the animation effects for Slides 2 through 4 by completing the following steps:
   a. Click the VIEW tab and then click the Slide Master button in the Master Views group.
   b. Click the third slide master layout in the slide thumbnails pane (Title and Content Layout).
   c. Click in the text *Click to edit Master title style*.
   d. Click the ANIMATIONS tab and then click the *None* option in the Animation group.
   e. Click in the text *Click to edit Master text styles*.
   f. Click the *None* option in the Animation group.
   g. Click the SLIDE MASTER tab and then click the Close Master View button.
3. Make Slide 1 active and then run the presentation.
4. Save **P-C7-P1-MarketingPres.pptx**.

Applying Animation Effects

The Add Animation button in the Advanced Animation group on the ANIMATIONS tab provides four types of animation effects that can be applied to an item. You can apply an effect as an item enters the slide, as an item exits the slide, as emphasis to an item, and as a motion path that will cause an item to move in a specific pattern on, or even off, the slide.

To apply an entrance effect to an item, click the Add Animation button in the Advanced Animation group and then click the desired animation effect in the *Entrance* section of the drop-down gallery. Customize the entrance effect by clicking the Effect Options button in the Animation group and then clicking the desired entrance effect. Additional entrance effects are available at the Add Entrance Effect dialog box. Display this dialog box by clicking the Add Animation button and then clicking *More Entrance Effects* at the drop-down gallery. Complete similar steps to apply an emphasis effect and an exit effect. Display additional emphasis effects by clicking the Add Animation button and then clicking *More Emphasis Effects*. Display additional exit effects by clicking the Add Animation button and then clicking *More Exit Effects*.

Quick Steps

Apply an Animation Effect
1. Click desired item.
2. Click ANIMATIONS tab.
3. Click Add Animation button.
4. Click desired animation effect at drop-down gallery.

Apply Effects with Animation Painter
1. Click item, then apply desired animation effect.
2. Click item with animation effect.
3. Double-click Animation Painter button.
4. Click each item to which you want animation effect applied.
5. Click Animation Painter button to deactivate it.

Add Animation

Animation Painter

Applying Animations with Animation Painter

If you apply an animation or animations to items in a slide and want to apply the same animation in more than one location in a slide or slides, use the Animation Painter. To use the Animation Painter, apply the desired animation to an item, position the insertion point anywhere in the animated item, and then double-click the Animation Painter button in the Advanced Animation group on the ANIMATIONS tab. Using the mouse, select or click on additional items to which you want the animation applied. After applying the animation in the desired locations, click the Animation Painter button to deactivate it. If you need to apply animation in only one other location, click the Animation Painter button once. The first time you click an item, the animation is applied and the Animation Painter is deactivated.

Project 1c **Applying Animation Effects** **Part 3 of 6**

1. With **P-C7-P1-MarktingPres.pptx** open, apply an animation effect to the title and subtitle in Slide 1 by completing the following steps:
   a. Make Slide 1 active.
   b. Click the title *DOUGLAS CONSULTING*.
   c. Click the ANIMATIONS tab.
   d. Click the Add Animation button in the Advanced Animation group and then click the *Wipe* animation in the *Entrance* section of the drop-down gallery.

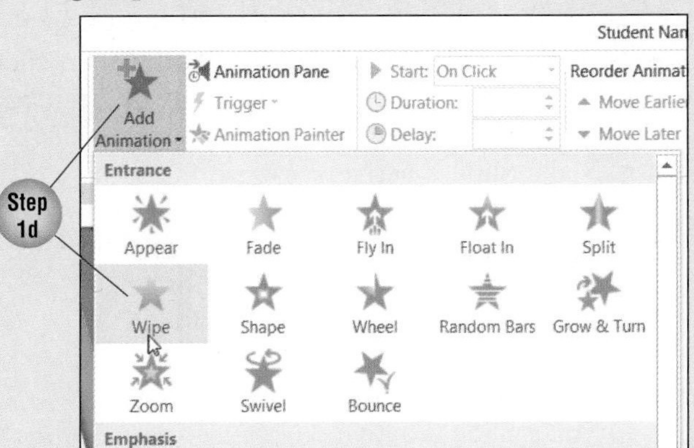

e. Click the Effect Options button in the Animation group and then click *From Top* at the drop-down gallery.
f. Click the subtitle *Marketing Report*.
g. Click the Add Animation button and then click the *Zoom* animation in the *Entrance* section.

2. Apply an animation effect to the titles in Slides 2 through 4 by completing the following steps:
   a. Click the VIEW tab and then click the Slide Master button in the Master Views group.
   b. Click the third slide master layout in the slide thumbnails pane (Title and Content Layout).
   c. Click in the text *Click to edit Master title style*.
   d. Click the ANIMATIONS tab, click the Add Animation button in the Advanced Animation group, and then click the *More Emphasis Effects* option at the drop-down gallery.
   e. At the Add Emphasis Effect dialog box, click the *Grow With Color* option in the *Moderate* section.
   f. Click OK to close the dialog box.

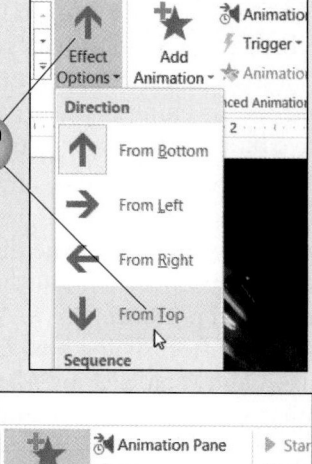

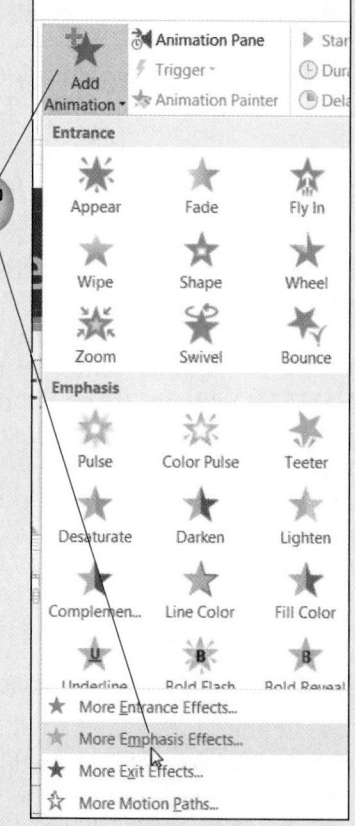

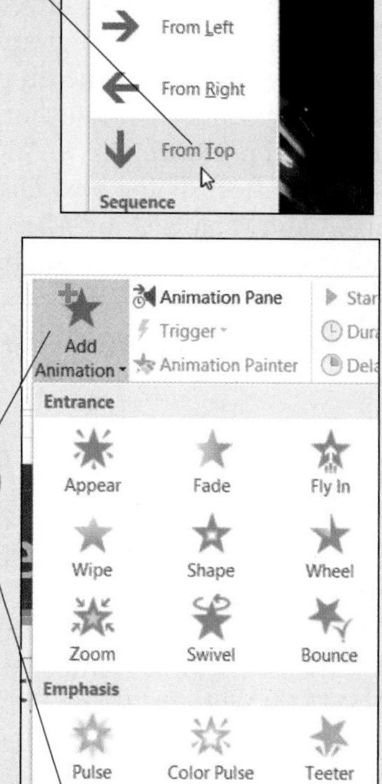

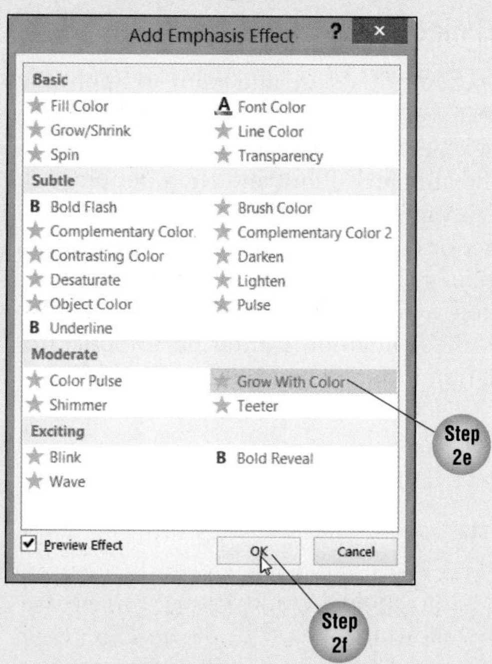

   g. Click the SLIDE MASTER tab and then click the Close Master View button.

3. Use the Animation Painter to apply an animation effect to the bulleted text in Slides 2 through 4 by completing the following steps:
   a. Make Slide 2 active.
   b. Click anywhere in the bulleted text to make the placeholder active.
   c. Click the ANIMATIONS tab, click the Add Animation button, and then click the *Split* animation in the *Entrance* section.
   d. Click anywhere in the bulleted text.
   e. Double-click the Animation Painter button in the Advanced Animation group.
   f. Make Slide 3 active.

g. Click anywhere in the bulleted text. (The mouse pointer displays as an arrow with a paintbrush attached. The animations are applied to all four bulleted items.)
h. Make Slide 4 active and then click anywhere in the bulleted text.
i. Click the Animation Painter button to deactivate it.
4. Click the Preview button to view the animation effects.
5. Run the presentation by clicking the Start From Beginning button on the Quick Access toolbar. Click the mouse button to advance slide elements and to move to the next slide.
6. Save **P-C7-P1-MarketingPres.pptx**.

Modifying Animation Effects

Start

When you apply an animation effect to an item, you can use options in the Timing group to modify the animation effect. Use the *Start* option box drop-down list to specify when you want the item inserted in the slide. Generally, items display in a slide when you click the mouse button. Click the *Start* option box arrow and then click *With Previous* or *With Next* at the drop-down list to make the item appear on the slide with the previous item or the next item.

Duration

Use the *Duration* measurement box to specify the length of an animation. For example, click the up-pointing arrow at the right of the *Duration* measurement box to increase the length of time the animation displays on the slide and click the down-pointing arrow to decrease the length of time the animation displays. You can also select the current time in the *Duration* measurement box and then type the desired time.

Delay

The *Delay* measurement box allows you to tell an animation to play a certain number of seconds after the previous animation plays. Click the up-pointing arrow to increase this amount of time and click the down-pointing arrow to decrease this amount of time. You can also select the current time in the *Delay* measurement box and then type the desired time.

Reordering Items

When you apply an animation effect to an item, an animation number displays next to the item in the slide pane. This number indicates the order in which the item will appear in the slide. When more than one item displays in the slide, you can change the order with options in the *Reorder Animation* section of the Timing group on the ANIMATIONS tab. Click the Move Earlier button to move an item before another item or click the Move Later button to move an item after another item.

Quick Steps
Reorder an Animation Item
1. Click item in slide.
2. Click Move Earlier button or Move Later button.

Move Earlier

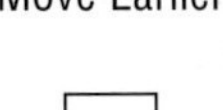
Move Later

Project 1d **Removing, Modifying, and Reordering Animation Effects** **Part 4 of 6**

1. With **P-C7-P1-MarketingPres.pptx** open, make Slide 1 active.
2. Modify the start setting for the animation effect you applied to the slide title by completing the following steps:
a. Click anywhere in the title to activate the placeholder.

b. Click the down-pointing arrow at the right of the *Start* option box in the Timing group on the ANIMATIONS tab.

c. Click *With Previous* at the drop-down list. (At this setting, the title animation effect will begin as soon as the slide displays, without you having to click the mouse button. Notice that the number *1* located to the left of the item in the slide changes to a zero.)

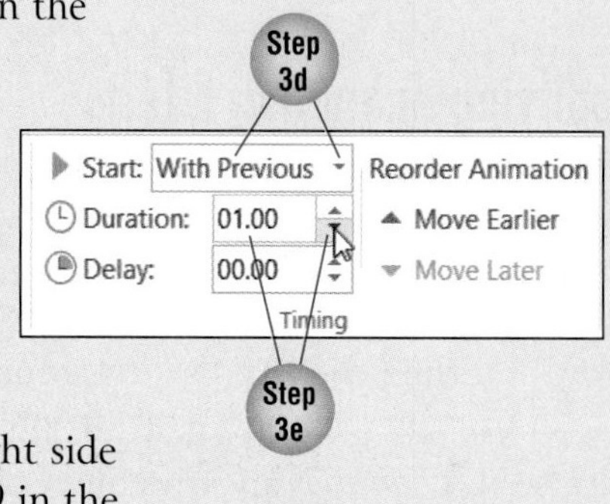

3. Change the animation effect applied to the subtitle and modify the new animation effect by completing the following steps:
   a. Click anywhere in the subtitle *Marketing Report* in the slide.
   b. Click the More button at the right of the thumbnails in the Animation group and then click the *None* option in the drop-down gallery.
   c. Click the Add Animation button in the Advanced Animation group and then click the *Grow/Shrink* animation in the *Emphasis* section.
   d. Click the down-pointing arrow at the right side of the *Start* option box and then click *With Previous* at the drop-down list.
   e. Click four times on the down-pointing arrow at the right side of the *Duration* measurement box. (This displays *01.00* in the measurement box.)

4. Remove animations from slide titles in Slide Master view by completing the following steps:
   a. Click the VIEW tab and then click the Slide Master button in the Master Views group.
   b. Click the third slide master layout in the slide thumbnails pane (Title and Content Layout).
   c. Click in the text *Click to edit Master title style*.
   d. Click the ANIMATIONS tab.
   e. Click the More button at the right of the thumbnails in the Animation group and then click the *None* option in the Animation group.
   f. Click the SLIDE MASTER tab and then click the Close Master View button.
5. Remove animations from the bulleted text in Slides 2 through 4 by completing the following steps:
   a. Make Slide 2 active.
   b. Click in the bulleted text.
   c. Click the ANIMATIONS tab and then click the *None* option in the Animation group.
   d. Make Slide 3 active, click in the bulleted text, and then click the *None* option in the Animation group.
   e. Make Slide 4 active, click in the bulleted text, and then click the *None* option in the Animation group.
6. Make Slide 2 active and then apply and customize animation effects by completing the following steps:
   a. Click the title *Department Reports*.
   b. Click the Add Animation button in the Advanced Animation group and then click the *More Entrance Effects* option at the drop-down gallery.
   c. At the Add Entrance Effect dialog box, scroll down the list box and then click *Spiral In* in the *Exciting* section.
   d. Click OK to close the dialog box.

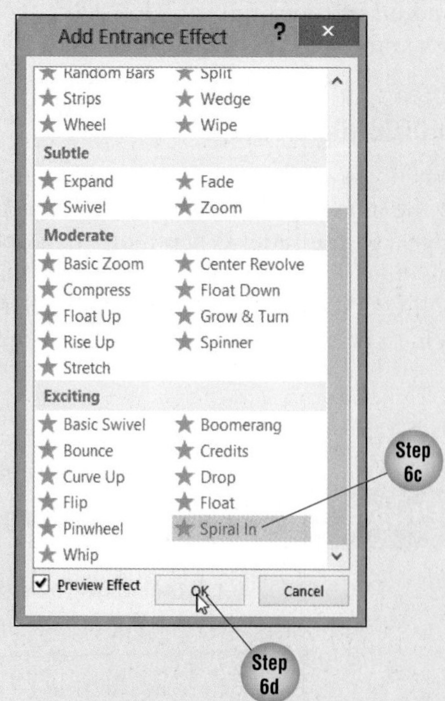

e. Click the bulleted text.
f. Click the Add Animation button and then click the *Zoom* animation in the *Entrance* section.
g. Click the clip art image.
h. Click the Add Animation button and then click the *Zoom* animation in the *Entrance* section.

7. Click the Preview button located at the left side of the ANIMATIONS tab to view the animation effects.
8. After viewing the animation effects, you decide that you want the clip art to animate before the bulleted text and you want the animation effects to begin with the previous animation (instead of with a mouse click). With Slide 2 active, complete the following steps:
   a. Click the clip art image. (The number 5 will display at the left of the clip art placeholder because the clip art is the fifth item to enter the slide.)
   b. Click the Move Earlier button in the *Reorder Animation* section of the Timing group. The number displayed to the left of the clip art image changes to 2 because you moved the clip art animation before the three bulleted items.)
   c. Click the down-pointing arrow at the right side of the *Start* option box in the Timing group and then click *With Previous* at the drop-down list.

   d. Click the title *Department Reports*.
   e. Click the down-pointing arrow at the right side of the *Start* option box in the Timing group and then click *With Previous* at the drop-down list.
9. Make Slide 3 active and then apply the same animation effects you applied in Slide 2. (Do this by completing steps similar to those in Steps 6a through 6h and Steps 8a through 8e.)
10. Make Slide 4 active and then apply the same animation effects you applied to Slide 2. (Do this by completing steps similar to those in Steps 6a through 6f and Steps 8d through 8e.)
11. Make Slide 1 active and then run the presentation.
12. Save **P-C7-P1-MarketingPres.pptx**.

Customizing Animation Effects at the Animation Pane

You can use the Animation Pane to customize and modify animation effects in a presentation. Display the Animation Pane, shown in Figure 7.1, by clicking the Animation Pane button in the Advanced Animation group on the ANIMATIONS tab. When you apply an animation to an item, the item name or description displays in the Animation Pane. Hover the mouse pointer over an item and a description of the animation effect applied to the item displays in a box below the item. If you click the down-pointing arrow at the right side of an item in the Animation Pane, a drop-down list displays with options for modifying or customizing the animation effect. For example, use options at the drop-down list to specify when you want the item to display on the slide, the delay and duration of the animation, and to remove an animation effect.

When you apply an effect to an item, the item name and/or description displays in the Animation Pane preceded by a number. This number indicates the order in which items will appear in the slide. When more than one item displays in the Animation Pane, you can change the order of an item by clicking the item and then clicking the Move Earlier button or the Move Later button located toward the top of the Animation Pane.

Quick Steps

Reorder Animation Items
1. Click item in Animation Pane.
2. Click Move Earlier button or Move Later button.

Remove an Animation Effect
1. Click item in Animation Pane.
2. Click down-pointing arrow.
3. Click *Remove*.

Animation Pane

Figure 7.1 Animation Pane

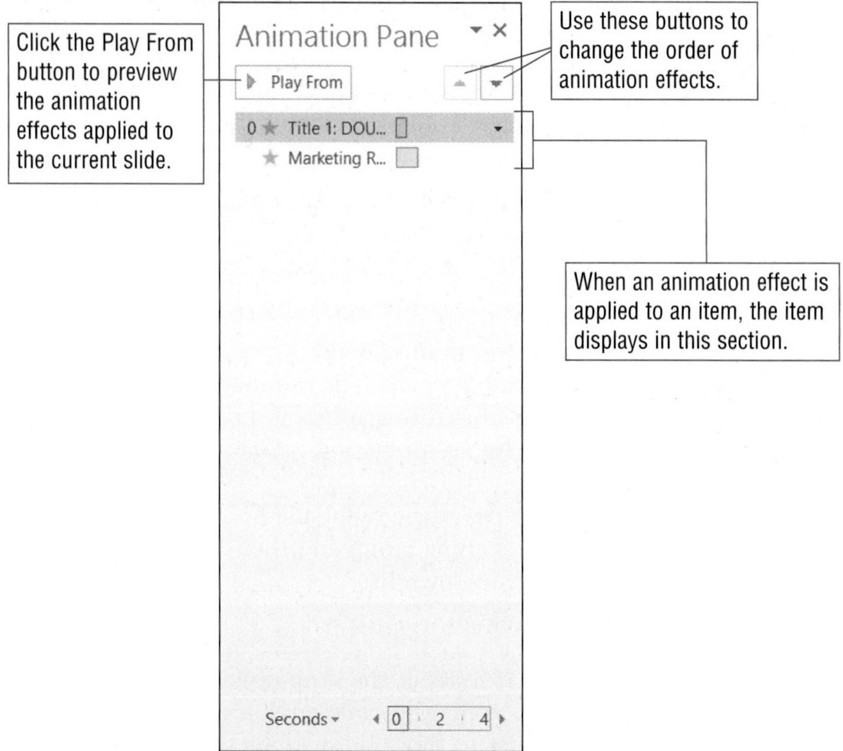
Click the Play From button to preview the animation effects applied to the current slide.
Animation Pane
Play From
Use these buttons to change the order of animation effects.
0 Title 1: DOU...
Marketing R...
When an animation effect is applied to an item, the item displays in this section.
Seconds
0 2 4

When you apply an animation effect or effects to a slide, you can play all the animations in the Animation Pane by clicking the Play All button at the top of the pane. (The name of the button varies depending on the contents of the Animation Pane and what is selected in the pane.) The animation effects display in the slide in the slide pane and a time indicator displays along the bottom of the Animation Pane with a vertical line indicating the progression of time (in seconds). You can also play only the selected animation effect in the Animation Pane by clicking the animation effect in the pane and then clicking the Play From button at the top of the pane.

Project 1e Removing, Modifying, and Reordering Animation Effects in the Animation Pane

Part 5 of 6

1. With **P-C7-P1-MarketingPres.pptx** open, make Slide 1 active.
2. Click in the title *DOUGLAS CONSULTING*, click the ANIMATIONS tab, and then click the *None* option in the Animation group.
3. With the title placeholder selected, click the Add Animation button in the Advanced Animation group and then click the *Grow & Turn* animation in the *Entrance* section.
4. Click twice on the down-pointing arrow at the right side of the *Duration* measurement box. (This displays *00.50* in the measurement box.)
5. Click in the subtitle *Marketing Report*, click the More button at the right of the animation thumbnails in the Animation group, and then click the *None* option.
6. With the subtitle placeholder selected, click the Add Animation button in the Advanced Animation group and then click the *Grow & Turn* animation in the *Entrance* section.
7. Click twice on the down-pointing arrow at the right side of the *Duration* measurement box. (This displays *00.50* in the measurement box.)

8. Modify the start setting for the slide title animation effect in the Animation Pane by completing the following steps:
   a. Click the Animation Pane button located in the Advanced Animation group on the ANIMATIONS tab. (This displays the Animation Pane at the right side of the screen.)
   b. Click the Title 1 item that displays in the Animation Pane.
   c. Click the down-pointing arrow at the right side of the item and then click *Start With Previous* at the drop-down list.

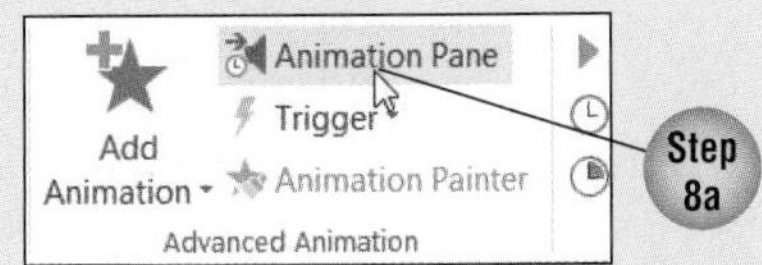

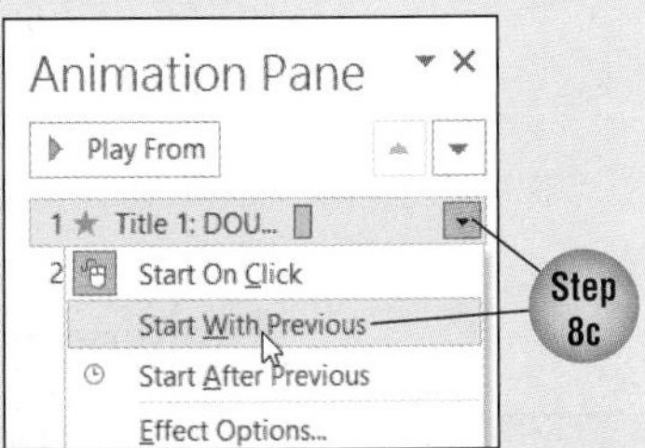

9. Remove animations from slides using the Animation Pane by completing the following steps:
   a. Make Slide 2 active.
   b. Click the Picture 3 item in the Animation Pane.
   c. Click the down-pointing arrow at the right side of the item and then click *Remove* at the drop-down list.
   d. Click the clip art image in the slide pane, click the Add Animation button in the Advanced Animation group, and then click the *Pulse* animation in the *Emphasis* section.

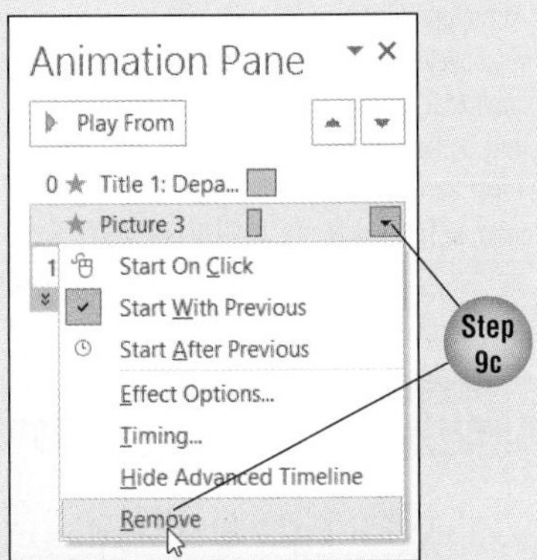

10. Make Slide 3 active and then complete steps similar to those in Steps 9b through 9d to remove the animation effect from the clip art image and add the *Pulse* emphasis effect.
11. With the Picture 3 image selected in the Animation Pane, click the Play From button located toward the top of the pane to view the animation effect applied to the clip art.
12. Play all animation effects applied to the slide by clicking anywhere in the blank area below the animation effects in the Animation Pane (this deselects the Picture 3 animation effect) and then click the Play All button (previously the Play From button) at the top of the pane.

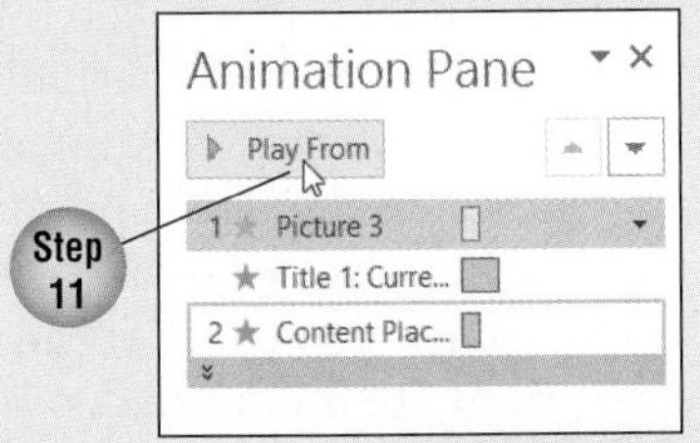

13. After viewing the animation effect, you decide that you want the clip art image to animate before the title and bulleted text and you want the animation effect to begin with the previous animation. With Slide 3 active, complete the following steps:
   a. Click the Picture 3 item in the Animation Pane.
   b. Click twice on the Move Earlier button located at the top of the Animation pane. (This moves the Picture 3 item above the Title 1 and the content placeholder items.)
   c. Click the down-pointing arrow at the right side of the Picture 3 item and then click *Start With Previous* at the drop-down list.

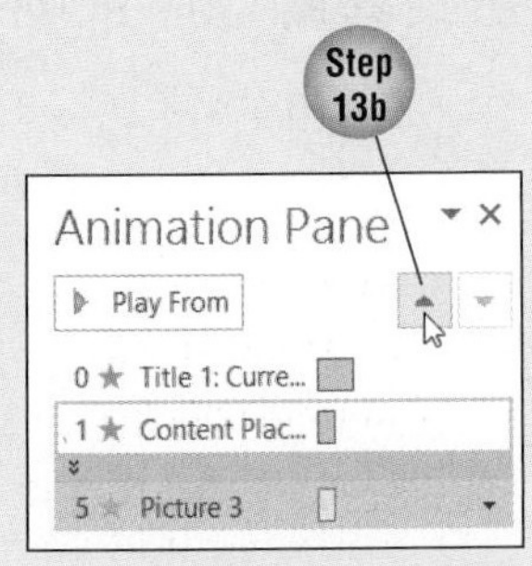

14. Reorder animation effects in Slide 2 to match the changes made to Slide 3.
15. Make Slide 1 active and then run the presentation.
16. Close the Animation Pane.
17. Save **P-C7-P1-MarketingPres.pptx**.

Applying Sound to Animations

Enhance an animation by applying a sound to the animation. To apply a sound, click the Animation Pane button to display the Animation Pane, click the desired animated item in the Animation Pane, click the down-pointing arrow at the right side of the item, and then click *Effect Options* at the drop-down list. At the effect options dialog box with the Effect tab selected, click the down-pointing arrow at the right side of the *Sound* option box and then click the desired sound at the drop-down list. The name of the dialog box will vary depending on the animation effect selected. You can also apply sound to an animation by clicking the desired animated item in the slide in the slide pane, clicking the Animation group dialog box launcher, and then choosing the desired sound effect at the dialog box that displays.

Applying a Build

You can group text (in a bulleted text placeholder) at the Effect Options dialog box by first, second, third, fourth, or fifth levels.

In Project 1a, you applied a build to bulleted text in a slide. A ***build*** displays important points on a slide one point at a time, keeping the audience's attention focused on the current point. You can further customize a build by causing a previous point to dim when the next point displays. To customize a build, click the Animation Pane button to display the Animation Pane, click the desired bulleted item in the Animation Pane, click the down-pointing arrow at the right side of the item, and then click *Effect Options* at the drop-down list. At the effect options dialog box with the Effect tab selected, choose a color option with the *After animation* option box.

Project 1f **Applying Sound and a Build to Animations** **Part 6 of 6**

1. With **P-C7-P1-MarketingPres.pptx** open, make Slide 2 active and then apply sound and a build to the bulleted text by completing the following steps:
   a. Click in the bulleted text.
   b. Open the Animation Pane by clicking the Animation Pane button in the Advanced Animation group on the ANIMATIONS tab.
   c. Click the down-pointing arrow at the right side of the Content Placeholder item in the Animation Pane and then click *Effect Options* at the drop-down list.
   d. At the Zoom dialog box, make sure the Effect tab is selected, click the down-pointing arrow at the right side of the *Sound* option box, scroll down the list box, and then click the *Chime* option.
   e. Click the down-pointing arrow at the right side of the *After animation* option box and then click the light gray color (last option).
   f. Click OK to close the dialog box.

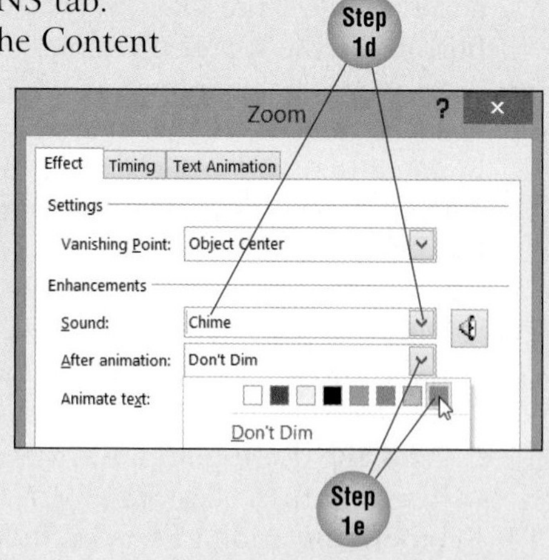

2. Click in the bulleted text in the slide.
3. Double-click the Animation Painter button.
4. Display Slide 3 and click anywhere in the bulleted text.
5. Display Slide 4 and click anywhere in the bulleted text.
6. Click the Animation Painter button to deactivate it.
7. Close the Animation Pane.
8. Make Slide 1 active and then run the presentation.
9. Save and then close **P-C7-P1-MarketingPres.pptx**.

Project 2 Apply Custom Animation Effects to Elements in Slides in an Online Learning Presentation — 6 Parts

You will open an online learning presentation and then apply animation effects to shapes, a clip art image, elements in SmartArt graphics, and elements in a chart. You will also draw a motion path in a slide.

Animating Shapes and Images

Animate individual shapes or images such as clip art images in a slide in the same way you animate a title or text content placeholder. You can select more than one shape and then apply the same animation effect to the shapes. To select more than one shape, click the first shape, hold down the Shift key, and then click any additional shapes.

Project 2a Animating Shapes and a Clip Art Image — Part 1 of 6

1. Open **OLLearning.pptx** and then save the presentation with Save As and name it **P-C7-P2-OLLearning**.
2. Make Slide 8 active (this slide contains one large object with three smaller objects hidden behind it) and then animate objects and apply exit effects by completing the following steps:
   a. Click the ANIMATIONS tab and then click the Animation Pane button in the Advanced Animation group.
   b. Click the large shape in the slide.
   c. Click the Add Animation button in the Advanced Animation group and then click the *More Exit Effects* option at the drop-down gallery.
   d. At the Add Exit Effect dialog box, click the *Spiral Out* option in the *Exciting* section. (You will need to scroll down the list to display this option.) Watch the animation effect in the slide and then click OK.
   e. Click the large object to select it and then drag it up the slide to display a portion of the three objects behind.
   f. Click the small object at the left, click the Add Animation button, and then click the *More Entrance Effects* option at the drop-down gallery.
   g. At the Add Entrance Effect dialog box, click *Spinner* in the *Moderate* section, and then click OK.
   h. Select the middle object, hold down the Shift key, and then click the object at the right. (This selects both objects.)
   i. Click the Add Animation button and then click the *More Entrance Effects* option at the drop-down gallery.

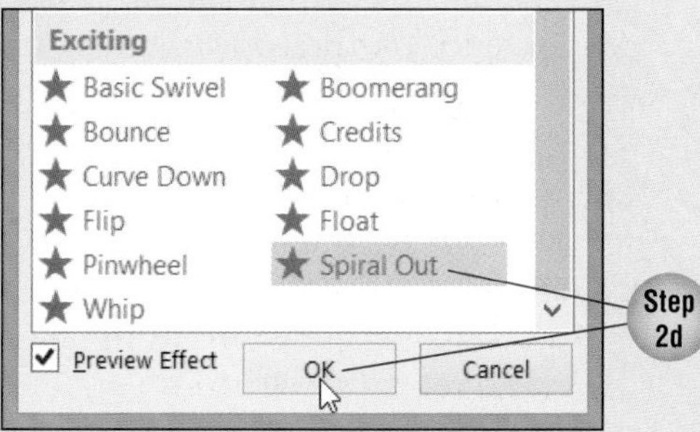

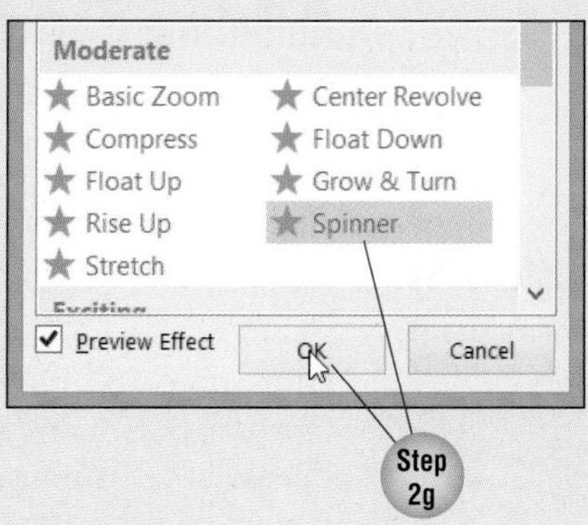

j. At the Add Entrance Effect dialog box, click *Spinner* in the *Moderate* section and then click OK. (Notice that the two objects are numbered *3* in the Animation Pane and are set to enter the slide at the same time. You will change this in the next step.)
k. Click the small object at the right, click the down-pointing arrow at the right of the *Start* option box in the Timing group, and then click *On Click* at the drop-down list.
l. Apply emphasis to the middle object by clicking the middle object, clicking the Add Animation button, and then clicking the *Grow/Shrink* option in the *Emphasis* section of the drop-down gallery.
m. Click the large object to select it and then reposition it over the three smaller objects.
n. Click the Preview button to play the animation effects in the slide.

3. Make Slide 9 active and apply and modify animation effects and change animation order by completing the following steps:
   a. Click in the text *Online learning continues to evolve!* (this selects the text box), click the Add Animation button, and then click *Grow & Turn* in the *Entrance* section.
   b. Click in the text *Stay tuned!* (this selects the text box), click the Add Animation button, and then click the *Swivel* option in the *Entrance* section.
   c. Click the clip art image to select it.
   d. Click the Add Animation button and then click the *Spin* animation in the *Emphasis* section.
   e. Click the Effect Options button in the Animation group and then click *Two Spins* at the drop-down gallery.
   f. Click the down-pointing arrow at the right side of the *Duration* measurement box until *01.00* displays.
   g. Click once on the Move Earlier button in the Timing group. This moves the clip art image item in the list box above the *Stay tuned!* text box item.
   h. Click the Preview button to play the animation effects in the slide.

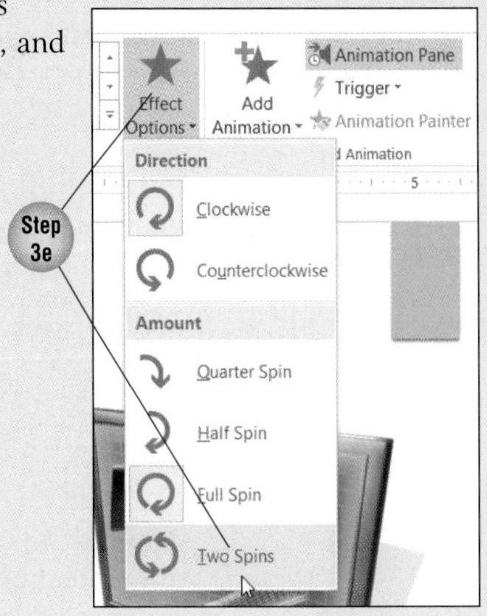

4. Save **P-C7-P2-OLLearning.pptx**.

Animating a SmartArt Graphic

You can apply animation effects to a SmartArt graphic and specify whether you want the entire SmartArt graphic to display at once or the individual elements in the SmartArt graphic to display one at a time. Specify a sequence for displaying elements in a SmartArt graphic with the Effect Options button in the Animation group.

Quick Steps

Animate a SmartArt Graphic
1. Click SmartArt graphic.
2. Apply animation effect.
3. Click Effect Options button.
4. Specify the desired sequence.

When you apply an animation effect to a SmartArt graphic, you can apply animations to individual elements in the graphic. To do this, click the Effect Options button and then click the *One by One* option at the drop-down list. Display the Animation Pane and then expand the list of SmartArt graphic objects by clicking the small double arrows that display in a gray shaded box below the item in the Animation Pane. Click the individual item in the Animation Pane to which you want to apply a different animation effect and then click the desired animation in the Animation group.

Project 2b Animating SmartArt

Part 2 of 6

1. With **P-C7-P2-OLLearning.pptx** open, make Slide 4 active and then animate objects in the SmartArt graphic by completing the following steps:
   a. Click the shape in the SmartArt graphic containing the word *Convenient*. (Make sure white sizing handles display around the shape.)
   b. Make sure the ANIMATIONS tab is selected and then click the *Float In* animation in the Animation group.
   c. Click the Effect Options button in the Animation group and then click *One by One* at the drop-down gallery. (This will allow you to apply different effects to the objects in the SmartArt graphic.)
   d. Make sure the Animation Pane displays. (If not, click the Animation Pane button in the Advanced Animation group.)
   e. Expand the list of SmartArt graphic objects in the Animation Pane by clicking the small double arrows that display in a gray shaded box below the content placeholder item. (This expands the list to display four items.)
   f. Click the second item in the Animation Pane (the item that begins with the number *2*).
   g. Click the More button at the right side of the animations in the Animation group and then click the *Grow & Turn* animation in the *Entrance* section.
   h. Click the fourth item in the Animation Pane (the item that begins with the number *4*).
   i. Click the More button at the right side of the animations in the Animation group and then click the *Grow & Turn* animation in the *Entrance* section.
2. Click the Preview button on the ANIMATIONS tab to view the animation effects applied to the SmartArt graphic objects.
3. Make Slide 6 active and then apply animation effects by completing the following steps:
   a. Click the shape in the SmartArt graphic containing the text *Multi-Media*. (Make sure white sizing handles display around the shape.)
   b. Click the Add Animation button and then click the *More Entrance Effects* option.
   c. At the Add Entrance Effect dialog box, click the *Circle* option in the *Basic* section.
   d. Click OK to close the dialog box.
   e. Click the Effect Options button in the Animation group and then click *Out* in the *Direction* section of the drop-down list.
   f. Click the Effect Options button and then click *One by One* in the *Sequence* section of the drop-down list.
   g. Click the down-pointing arrow at the right of the *Duration* measurement box until *00.50* displays.

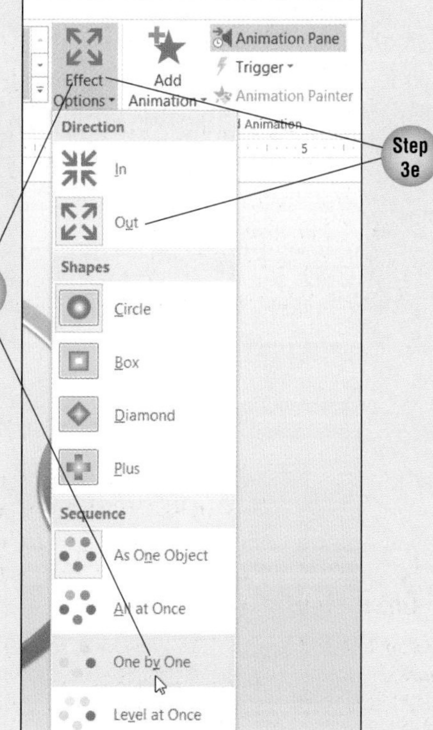

4. Click the Play Selected button located toward the top of the Animation Pane to view the animation effects applied to the SmartArt graphic objects.
5. Save **P-C7-P2-OLLearning.pptx**.

Animating a Chart

Like a SmartArt graphic, you can animate a chart or elements in a chart. Displaying data in a chart may have a more dramatic effect if the chart is animated. Bringing in one element at a time also allows you to discuss each piece of the data as it displays. Specify how you want the chart animated in the slide and how you want chart elements grouped. For example, group chart elements on one object or by series or category. Apply animation to elements in a chart in a manner similar to animating elements in a SmartArt graphic.

Project 2c **Animating Elements in a Chart** **Part 3 of 6**

1. With **P-C7-P2-OLLearning.pptx** open, make Slide 3 active and then animate chart elements by completing the following steps:
   a. Click in the chart placeholder to select the chart. (Make sure you do not have a chart element selected and that the ANIMATIONS tab is selected.)
   b. Click the Add Animation button and then click the *More Entrance Effects* option.
   c. At the Add Entrance Effect dialog box, click the *Dissolve In* option in the *Basic* section.
   d. Click OK to close the dialog box.
   e. Make sure the Animation Pane displays and then click the down-pointing arrow at the right side of the Content Placeholder item in the list box.
   f. At the drop-down list that displays, click *Effect Options*.
   g. At the Dissolve In dialog box, click the down-pointing arrow at the right side of the *Sound* option box, scroll down the drop-down list, and then click the *Click* option.
   h. Click the Timing tab.
   i. Click the down-pointing arrow at the right side of the *Duration* option box and then click *1 seconds (Fast)* at the drop-down list.
   j. Click the Chart Animation tab.
   k. Click the down-pointing arrow at the right side of the *Group chart* option box and then click *By Category* at the drop-down list.

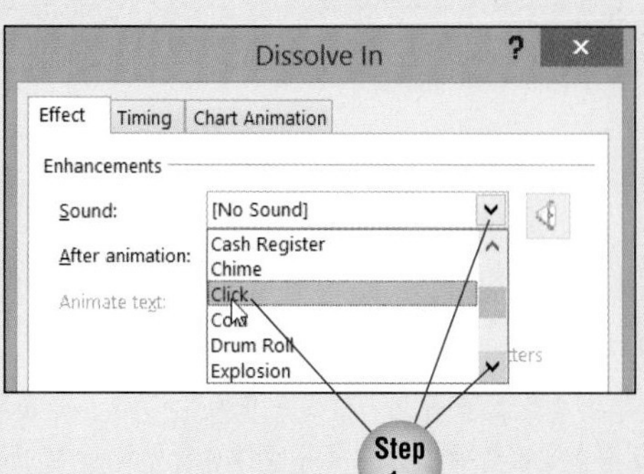

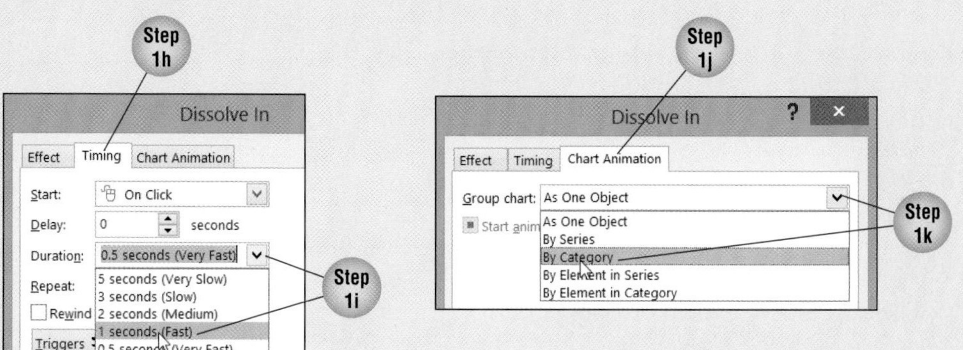

   l. Click OK to close the dialog box.

2. Make Slide 7 active and then apply a build animation effect to the bulleted text by completing the following steps:
   a. Click in the bulleted text.
   b. Click the *Fly In* animation in the Animation group on the ANIMATIONS tab.
   c. Click the Effect Options button and then click *From Right* at the drop-down gallery.
   d. Make sure the Animation Pane displays, click the down-pointing arrow at the right side of the Content Placeholder item in the pane, and then click *Effect Options* at the drop-down list.
   e. At the Fly In dialog box, make sure the Effect tab is selected, click the down-pointing arrow at the right side of the *After animation* option box, and then click the light green color (second from the right).
   f. Click OK to close the dialog box.
3. Save **P-C7-P2-OLLearning.pptx**.

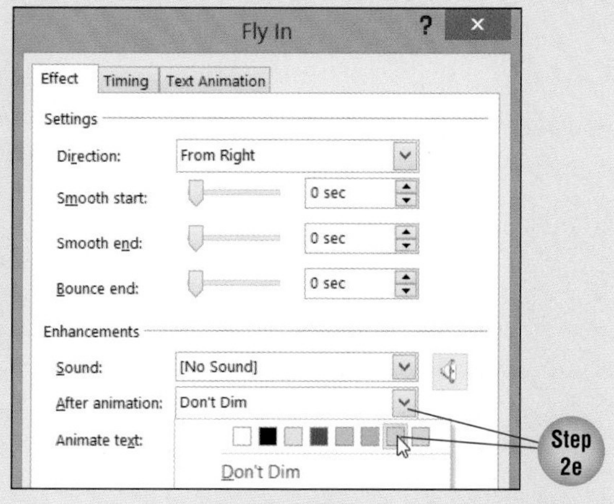

Creating a Motion Path

With options in the *Motion Paths* section of the Add Animation button drop-down gallery, you can specify a motion path. A ***motion path*** is a path you create for an object that specifies the movements of the object when you run the presentation. Click the Add Animation button in the Advanced Animation group, and a gallery of options for drawing a motion path in a specific direction can be found in the *Motion Paths* section. For example, if you want an item to move left in a line when running the presentation, click the Add Animation button in the Advanced Animation group and then click the *Lines* option in the *Motion Paths* section of the drop-down gallery. Click the Effect Options button in the Animation group and then click *Left* at the drop-down gallery. You can also apply a motion path by clicking the Add Animation button, clicking *More Motion Paths* at the drop-down gallery, and then clicking the desired motion path at the Add Motion Path dialog box.

To draw your own motion path, select the object in the slide you want to move in the slide, click the Add Animation button, and then click the *Custom Path* option in the *Motion Paths* section of the drop-down gallery. Using the mouse, drag in the slide to create the path. When the path is completed, double-click the mouse button.

Quick Steps

Insert a Motion Path
1. Click desired item in slide.
2. Click ANIMATIONS tab.
3. Click Add Animation button.
4. Click desired path in *Motion Paths* section.

Draw a Motion Path
1. Click desired item in slide.
2. Click ANIMATIONS tab.
3. Click Add Animation button.
4. Click *Custom Path* in *Motion Paths* section.
5. Drag in slide to create path.
6. Double-click mouse button.

Project 2d **Drawing a Motion Path** **Part 4 of 6**

1. With **P-C7-P2-OLLearning.pptx** open, make Slide 1 active and then apply a motion path to the clip art image by completing the following steps:
   a. Click the clip art image.
   b. Click the Add Animation button and then click the *More Motion Paths* option at the drop-down gallery.

c. At the Add Motion Path dialog box, scroll down the list box and then click the *Spiral Right* option in the *Lines Curves* section.
d. Click OK to close the dialog box.
e. Notice that a spiral line object displays in the slide and a dimmed copy of the clip art is selected. Hover the mouse pointer over the spiral line until the mouse pointer turns into a right-pointing arrow with a four-headed arrow attached and then drag the spiral line and dimmed copy of the clip art object so they are positioned over the original clip art (see the image above).

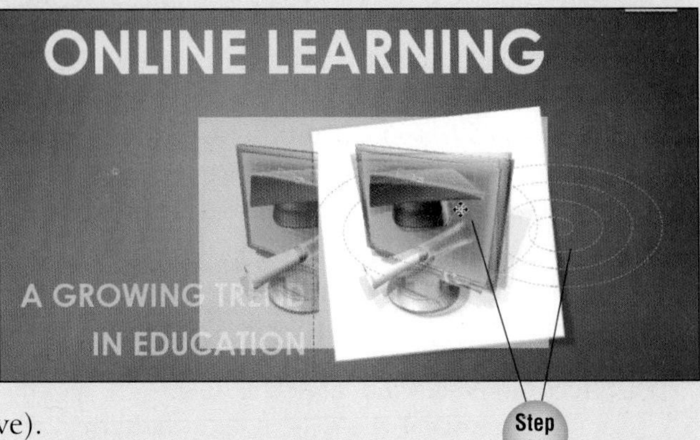

f. Click the down-pointing arrow at the right side of the *Start* option box in the Timing group and then click *With Previous* at the drop-down list.
g. Click the up-pointing arrow at the right side of the *Duration* measurement box in the Timing group until *03.00* displays in the measurement box.
h. Click the up-pointing arrow at the right side of the *Delay* measurement box in the Timing group until *01.00* displays in the measurement box.
i. Click outside the clip art to deselect it.

2. Make Slide 5 active and then animate the star on the map by completing the following steps:
   a. Click the star object in the slide (located below the heading *North America*).
   b. Click the Add Animation button, scroll down the drop-down gallery, and then click the *Custom Path* option in the *Motion Paths* section.
   c. Position the mouse pointer (displays as crosshairs) on the star, hold down the left mouse button, drag a path through each of the five locations on the map ending back in the original location, and then double-click the left mouse button.

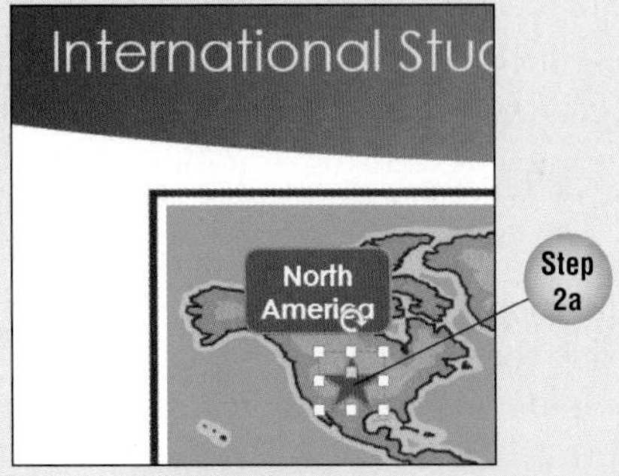

3. Run the presentation and click the mouse to advance slides and elements on slides as needed.
4. Save **P-C7-P2-OLLearning.pptx**.

Applying a Trigger

Use the Trigger button in the Advanced Animation group to make an animation effect occur by clicking an item on the slide during a slide show. A ***trigger*** creates a link between two items. For example, you can apply a trigger to a bulleted item that causes another item such as a picture or chart that provides additional information about the bulleted item to appear. When running the presentation, you hover the mouse over the item containing the trigger until the mouse pointer displays as a hand and then you click the mouse button. This displays the trigger item.

The advantage to applying a trigger to an item is that you can control whether or not the item displays when running the presentation. For example, suppose you created a presentation with product sales information and you wanted to provide additional specific sales data to one group but not another. When presenting to the group with whom you want to share the additional sales data, click the item to trigger the display of the data. When presenting to the other group, do not click the item and the sales data will remain hidden.

To insert a trigger, apply an animation effect to both items, display the Animation Pane, and then click the item to which you want to apply the trigger. Click the Trigger button in the Advanced Animation group, point to *On Click of*, and then click the item you want triggered at the side menu.

Quick Steps

Apply a Trigger

1. Click desired object in slide.
2. Click ANIMATIONS tab.
3. Click Trigger button, point to *On Click of*, and then click trigger object.

Trigger

Project 2e Inserting Triggers Part 5 of 6

1. With **P-C7-P2-OLLearning.pptx** open, make Slide 2 active.
2. Apply animation effects to the text and charts by completing the following steps:
   a. Click anywhere in the bulleted text.
   b. Click the ANIMATIONS tab.
   c. Click the *Split* animation in the Animation group.
   d. Select the pie chart at the left. (To do this, click in the chart and then click within the chart border but not on a specific item in the chart. Make sure the chart is selected and not an individual chart element.)
   e. Click the *Split* animation in the Animation group.
   f. Select the middle pie chart and then click the *Split* animation. (Make sure you select the chart and not a chart element.)
   g. Select the pie chart at the right and then click the *Split* animation. (Make sure you select the chart and not a chart element.)
3. Make sure the Animation Pane displays.
4. Apply a trigger to the first bulleted item that, when clicked, will display the chart at the left by completing the following steps:
   a. Click the *Chart 5* item in the Animation Pane.
   b. Click the Trigger button in the Advanced Animation group, point to *On Click of*, and then click *Content Placeholder 2* at the side menu.
   c. Click the *Chart 6* item in the Animation Pane, click the Trigger button, point to *On Click of*, and then click *Content Placeholder 2* at the side menu.
   d. Click the *Chart 7* item in the Animation Pane, click the Trigger button, point to *On Click of*, and then click *Content Placeholder 2* at the side menu.

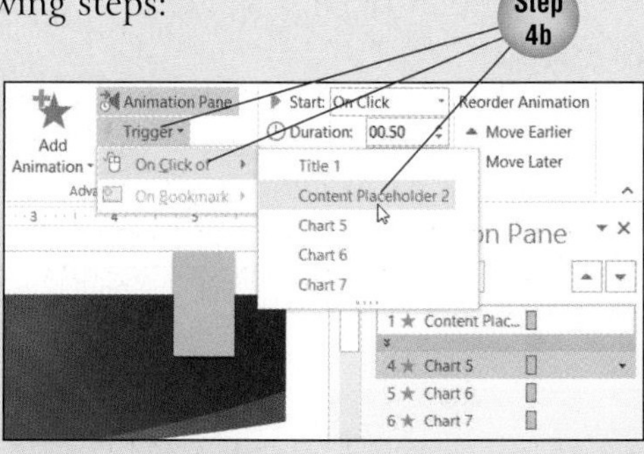

5. Close the Animation Pane.
6. Run the presentation by completing the following steps:
   a. Run the presentation from the beginning and when you get to Slide 2, click the mouse button until the first bulleted item displays (the item that begins with *Traditional*).

b. Hover your mouse over the bulleted text until the pointer turns into a hand and then click the left mouse button. (This displays the first chart.)
c. Position the mouse pointer anywhere in the white background of the slide and then click the left mouse button to display the second bulleted item (the item that begins with *Hybrid*).

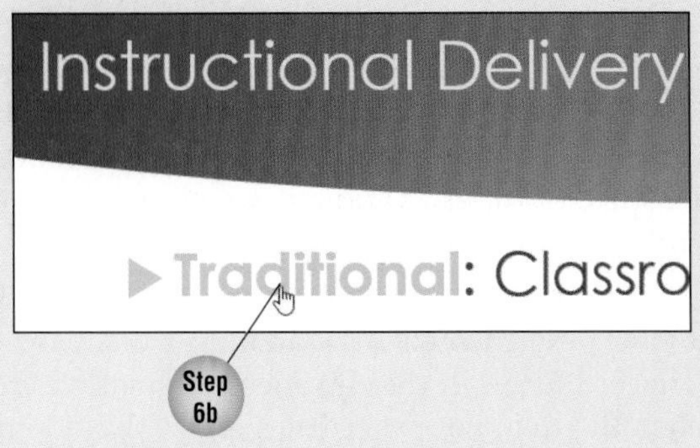

d. Hover your mouse over the text in the second bulleted item until the pointer turns into a hand and then click the left mouse button. (This displays the middle chart.)
e. Position the mouse pointer anywhere in the white background of the slide and then click the left mouse button to display the third bulleted item (the item that begins with *Internet*).
f. Hover your mouse over the text in the third bulleted item until the pointer turns into a hand and then click the left mouse button. (This displays the third chart.)
g. Continue running the remaining slides in the presentation.

7. Save **P-C7-P2-OLLearning.pptx**.
8. Print the presentation as a handout with all nine slides printed horizontally on the page.

Setting Up a Slide Show

Set Up Slide Show

Control how the presentation displays with options at the Set Up Show dialog box, shown in Figure 7.2. With options at this dialog box, set slide presentation options, specify how you want slides to advance, and set screen resolution. Display the Set Up Show dialog box by clicking the SLIDE SHOW tab and then clicking the Set Up Slide Show button in the Set Up group.

Figure 7.2 Set Up Show Dialog Box

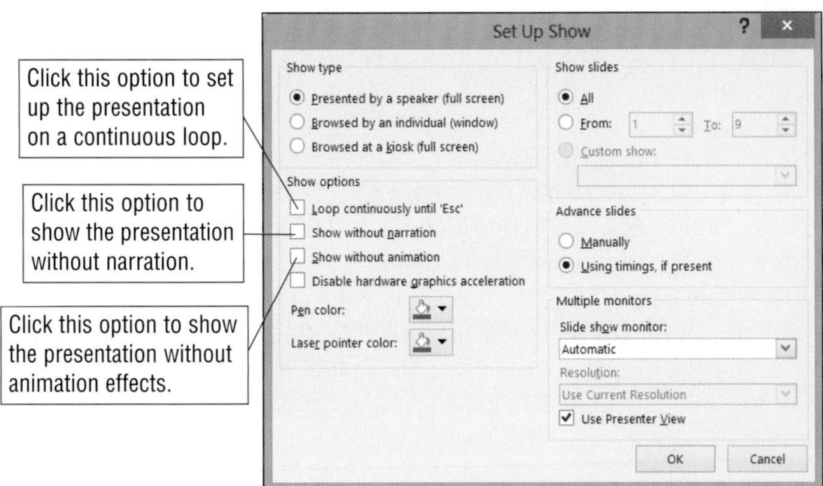

Running a Presentation without Animation

You can choose to run a presentation without the animations. To do this, display the Set Up Show dialog box, click the *Show without animation* check box to insert a check mark, and then click OK. Changes you make to the Set Up Show dialog box are saved with the presentation.

Quick Steps

Run a Presentation without Animation
1. Click SLIDE SHOW tab.
2. Click Set Up Slide Show button.
3. Click *Show without animation.*
4. Click OK.

Project 2f **Running a Presentation without Animation** **Part 6 of 6**

1. With **P-C7-P2-OLLearning.pptx** open, specify that you want to run the presentation without animation by completing the following steps:
   a. Click the SLIDE SHOW tab.
   b. Click the Set Up Slide Show button in the Set Up group.
   c. At the Set Up Show dialog box, click the *Show without animation* check box to insert a check mark.
   d. Click OK to close the dialog box.
2. Run the presentation and notice that the animation effects do not play.
3. Specify that you want the presentation to run with animations by completing the following steps:
   a. Click the Set Up Slide Show button on the SLIDE SHOW tab.
   b. At the Set Up Show dialog box, click the *Show without animation* check box to remove the check mark and then click OK.
4. Save and then close **P-C7-P2-OLLearning.pptx**.

Project 3 Prepare a Self-Running Adventure Presentation and Create Custom Shows — 6 Parts

You will open a travel tour presentation and then customize it to be an automated presentation set on a continuous loop. You will also hide slides and create and edit custom shows.

Setting Up a Presentation to Loop Continuously

In Chapter 1, you learned how to set automatic times for advancing slides. To advance a slide automatically, insert a check mark in the *After* check box in the Advance Slide section in the Timing group on the TRANSITIONS tab and then insert the desired number of seconds in the measurement box. If you want to be able to advance a slide before the specified amount of time has elapsed, leave the check mark in the *On Mouse Click* option. With this option active, you can let the slide advance after the specified number of seconds or you can click the left mouse button to advance the slide sooner. Remove the check mark from the *On Mouse Click* button if you do not want to advance slides with the mouse.

Quick Steps

Loop a Presentation Continuously
1. Click SLIDE SHOW tab.
2. Click Set Up Slide Show button.
3. Click *Loop continuously until 'Esc'.*
4. Click OK.

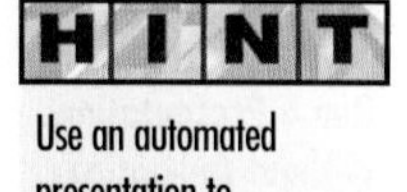

Use an automated presentation to communicate information without a presenter.

In some situations, such as at a trade show or convention, you may want to prepare an automated presentation. An automated presentation is set up on a continuous loop and does not require someone to advance the slides or restart the presentation. To design an automated presentation, display the Set Up Show dialog box and then insert a check mark in the *Loop continuously until 'Esc'* option. With this option active, the presentation will continue running until you press the Esc key.

Project 3a Preparing a Self-Running Presentation Part 1 of 6

1. Open **AdvTours.pptx** and then save the presentation with the name **P-C7-P3-AdvTours**.
2. Insert slides by completing the following steps:
   a. Click below the last slide thumbnail in the slide thumbnails pane.
   b. Make sure the HOME tab is selected, click the New Slide button arrow, and then click *Reuse Slides* at the drop-down list.
   c. At the Reuse Slides task pane, click the Browse button and then click *Browse File*.
   d. At the Browse dialog box, navigate to the PC7 folder on your storage medium and then double-click ***PeruTour.pptx***.
   e. Click each slide in the Reuse Slides task pane in the order in which they display, beginning with the top slide.
   f. Close the Reuse Slides task pane.
3. Add transition and sound effects and specify a time for automatically advancing slides by completing the following steps:
   a. Click the TRANSITIONS tab.
   b. Click in the *After* check box in the Timing group to insert a check mark.
   c. Click the up-pointing arrow at the right side of the *After* measurement box until *00:05.00* displays.
   d. Click the *On Mouse Click* check box to remove the check mark.
   e. Click the *Fade* slide transition in the Transition to This Slide group.
   f. Click the down-pointing arrow at the right side of the *Sound* option box in the Timing group and then click *Breeze* at the drop-down list.
   g. Click the Apply To All button.

Step 3d

Sound: [No Sound]
Duration: 02.00
Apply To All
Advance Slide
On Mouse Click
After: 00:05.00
Timing

Step 3b
Step 3c

Step 3f

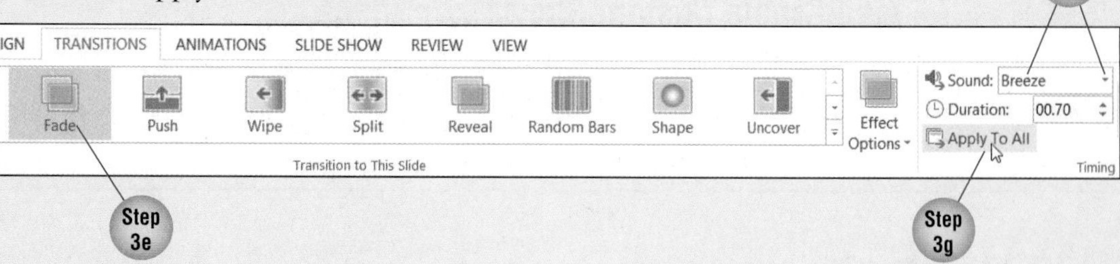

Step 3e
Step 3g

4. Set up the presentation to run continuously by completing the following steps:
   a. Click the SLIDE SHOW tab.
   b. Click the Set Up Slide Show button in the Set Up group.
   c. At the Set Up Show dialog box, click in the *Loop continuously until 'Esc'* check box to insert a check mark. (Make sure *All* is selected in the *Show slides* section and *Using timings, if present* is selected in the *Advance slides* section.)
   d. Click OK to close the dialog box.

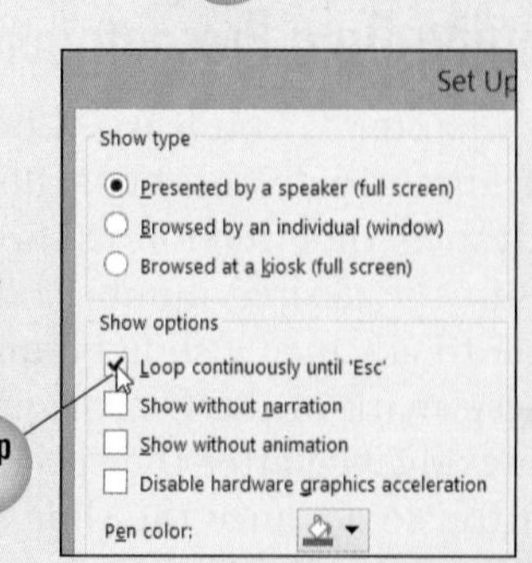

Step 4c

5. Click Slide 1 to select it and then run the presentation. (The slides will advance automatically after five seconds.)
6. After viewing the presentation, press the Esc key on the keyboard.
7. Save **P-C7-P3-AdvTours.pptx**.

Setting Automatic Times for Slides

Quick Steps

Set Automatic Times for Slides

1. Click SLIDE SHOW tab.
2. Click Rehearse Timings button.
3. Using Recording toolbar, specify time for each slide.
4. Click Yes.

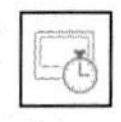

Rehearse Timings

Enter a specific recording time by selecting the time in the *Slide Time* text box, typing the desired time, and then pressing Enter.

Applying the same time to all slides is not very practical unless the same amount of text appears on every slide. In most cases, some slides should be left on the screen longer than others. Apply specific times to a slide with buttons on the Recording toolbar. Display this toolbar by clicking the SLIDE SHOW tab and then clicking the Rehearse Timings button in the Set Up group. This displays the first slide in the presentation in Slide Show view with the Recording toolbar located in the upper left corner of the slide. The buttons on the Recording toolbar are identified in Figure 7.3.

When the slide displays on the screen, the timer on the Recording toolbar begins. Click the Next button on the Recording toolbar when the slide has displayed for the appropriate amount of time. If you want to stop the timer, click the Pause button. Click the Resume Recording button to resume the timer. Use the Repeat button on the Recording toolbar if you get off track and want to reset the time for the current slide. Continue through the presentation until the slide show is complete. After the last slide, a message displays showing the total time for the presentation and asks if you want to record the new slide timings. At this message, click Yes to set the times for each slide recorded during the rehearsal. If you do not want to use the rehearsed timings when running a presentation, click the SLIDE SHOW tab and then click in the *Use Timings* check box to remove the check mark.

The times you apply to slides will display below each slide in the Slide Sorter view. The time that displays below the slide will generally be one second more than the time you applied to the slide. So, if you applied 5 seconds to Slide 1, *00.06* will display below the slide in Slide Sorter view.

If you need to edit the slide time for individual slides after you have recorded the times, you can do so with the *After* measurement box in the Advance Slide section in the Timing group on the TRANSITIONS tab. Make the slide active in the slide pane or click the slide in the Slide Sorter view and then click the up- or down-pointing arrows to change the slide duration to the desired time.

Figure 7.3 Recording Toolbar

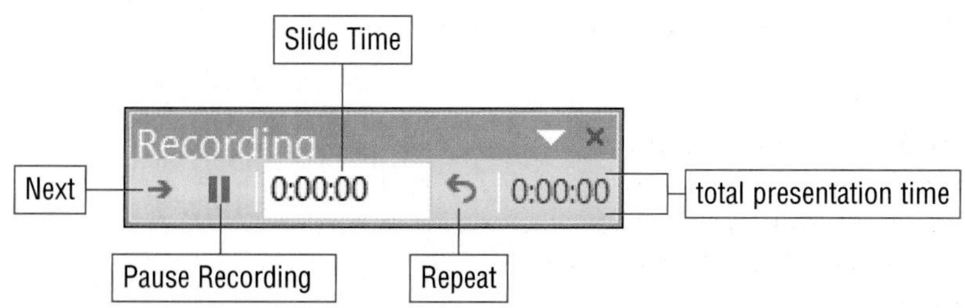

Project 3b Setting Rehearse Timings for Slides

Part 2 of 6

1. With **P-C7-P3-AdvTours.pptx** open, remove the automatic times for slides by completing the following steps:
   a. Click the SLIDE SHOW tab.
   b. Click the Set Up Slide Show button.
   c. At the Set Up Show dialog box, click the *Loop continuously until 'Esc'* check box to remove the check mark.
   d. Click OK to close the dialog box.
2. Set times for the slides to display during a slide show by completing the following steps:
   a. Make Slide 1 active.
   b. With the SLIDE SHOW tab active, click the Rehearse Timings button in the Set Up group.
   c. The first slide displays in Slide Show view and the Recording toolbar displays. Wait until the time displayed for the current slide reaches four seconds and then click Next. (If you miss the time, click the Repeat button to reset the clock back to zero for the current slide.)

Step 2c

Recording 0:00:04 0:00:04

   d. Set the times for remaining slides as follows:
      Slide 2 = 5 seconds
      Slide 3 = 6 seconds
      Slide 4 = 5 seconds
      Slide 5 = 6 seconds
      Slide 6 = 3 seconds
      Slide 7 = 6 seconds
      Slide 8 = 7 seconds
      Slide 9 = 7 seconds
   e. After the last slide displays, click Yes at the message asking if you want to record the new slide timings. (The slide times may display with one additional second for each.)
   f. If necessary, click the Normal button in the view area on the Status bar.
3. Click the Set Up Slide Show button to display the Set Up Show dialog box, click the *Loop continuously until 'Esc'* check box to insert a check mark, and then click OK to close the dialog box.
4. Run the presentation. (The slide show will start and run continuously.) Watch the presentation until it has started for the second time and then end the show by pressing the Esc key.
5. Save **P-C7-P3-AdvTours.pptx**.

Recording Narration

Quick Steps

Record a Narration
1. Click SLIDE SHOW tab.
2. Click Record Slide Show button.
3. Click Start Recording button.
4. Narrate slides.

You can record narration with your presentation that will play when the presentation is running. To record narration you must have a microphone connected to your computer. To begin the narration, click the Record Slide Show button in the Set Up group on the SLIDE SHOW tab. At the Record Slide Show dialog box, click the Start Recording button. Your presentation begins and the first slide fills the screen. Begin your narration, clicking the mouse to advance each slide. When you have narrated all of the slides in the presentation, your presentation may display in Slide Sorter view.

Clicking the Record Slide Show button arrow displays a drop-down list with three options. Click the *Start Recording from Beginning* option to begin recording your narration with the first slide in the presentation or click the *Start Recording from Current Slide* option if you want to begin recording your narration with the currently active slide. Position your mouse on the third option, *Clear*, and a side menu displays with options for clearing the timing on the current slide or all slides and clearing the narration from the current slide or all slides.

Record Slide Show

When you click the Record Slide Show button on the SLIDE SHOW tab, the Record Slide Show dialog box displays. This dialog box contains two options: *Slide and animation timings* and *Narrations and laser pointer*. You can choose to record just the slide timings, just the narration, or both at the same time. With the *Slide and animation timings* option active (containing a check mark), PowerPoint will keep track of the timing for each slide. When you run the presentation, the slides will remain on the screen the number of seconds recorded. If you want to narrate a presentation but do not want slides timed, remove the check mark from the *Slide and animation timings* check box. With the *Narrations and laser pointer* option active (containing a check mark), you can record your narration and record laser pointer gestures you make with the mouse. To make laser pointer gestures, hold down the Ctrl key, hold down the left mouse button, and then drag in the slide.

The narration in a presentation plays by default when you run the presentation. You can run the presentation without the narration by displaying the Set Up Show dialog box and then clicking the *Show without narration* check box in the *Show options* section to insert a check mark.

Project 3c Optional: Recording Narration

Part 3 of 6

This is an optional project. Before beginning the project, check with your instructor to determine if you have a microphone available for recording.

1. With **P-C7-P3-AdvTours.pptx** open, save the presentation and name it **P-C7-P3-AdvTours-NarrateSlide**.
2. Make Slide 9 active and then narrate the slide by completing the following steps:
   a. Click the SLIDE SHOW tab.
   b. Click the Record Slide Show button arrow in the Set Up group and then click *Start Recording from Current Slide* at the drop-down list.
   c. At the Record Slide Show dialog box, make sure both options contain a check mark and then click the Start Recording button.
   d. Speak into the microphone the following text: Call Adventure Tours today to receive an additional ten percent savings when you book a Fiji or Peru tour.
   e. Press the Esc key to end the narration.
3. Make Slide 1 active and then run the presentation. If your computer has speakers, you will hear your narration when Slide 9 displays. After viewing the presentation at least once, press the Esc key to end it.
4. Save and then close **P-C7-P3-AdvTours-NarrateSlide.pptx**.

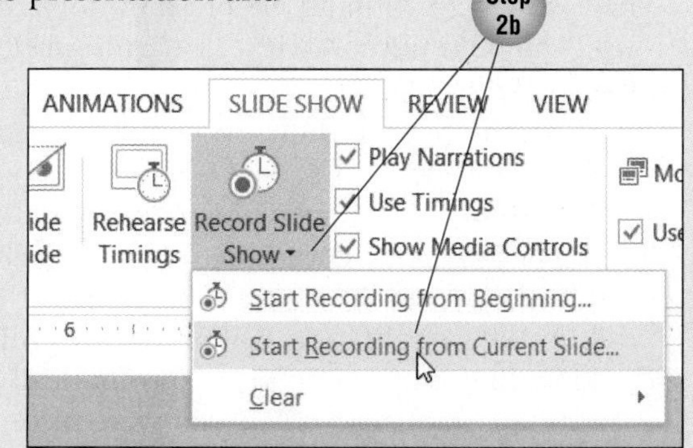

5. Open **P-C7-P3-AdvTours.pptx** and then save the presentation and name it **P-C7-P3-AdvTours-Narration**.
6. Remove the timings and the continuous loop option by completing the following steps:
   a. Click the SLIDE SHOW tab.
   b. Click the Record Slide Show button arrow, point to *Clear* at the drop-down list, and then click *Clear Timings on All Slides* at the side menu.
   c. Click the Set Up Slide Show button.
   d. At the Set Up Show dialog box, click the *Loop continuously until 'Esc'* check box to remove the check mark.
   e. Click OK to close the dialog box.

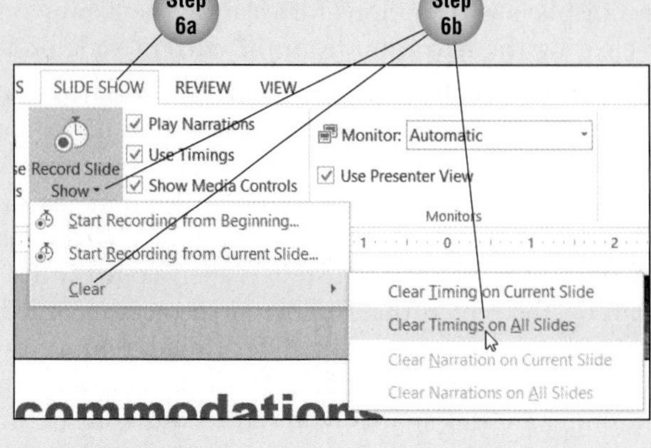

7. Make Slide 1 active and then record narration by completing the following steps:
   a. Click the Record Slide Show button in the Set Up group on the SLIDE SHOW tab.
   b. At the Record Slide Show dialog box, make sure both options contain a check mark and then click the Start Recording button.
   c. When the first slide displays, either read the information or provide your own narrative of the slide and then click the left mouse button. (You can also click the Next button on the Recording toolbar that displays in the upper left corner of the slide.)
   d. Continue narrating each slide (either using some of the information in the slides or creating your own narration). Try recording laser pointer gestures by holding down the Ctrl key, holding down the left mouse button, and then dragging in the slide.
   e. After you narrate the last slide (about accommodations for the Peru tour), the presentation may display in Slide Sorter view.
8. Make Slide 1 active and then run the presentation. If your computer has speakers, you will hear your narration as the presentation runs.
9. Run the presentation without narration by completing the following steps:
   a. Click the Set Up Slide Show button in the Set Up group on the SLIDE SHOW tab.
   b. At the Set Up Show dialog box, click the *Show without narration* check box to insert a check mark.
   c. Click OK.
   d. Run the presentation beginning with Slide 1. (The presentation will run automatically with the timing established when you were recording your narration but without the narration.)

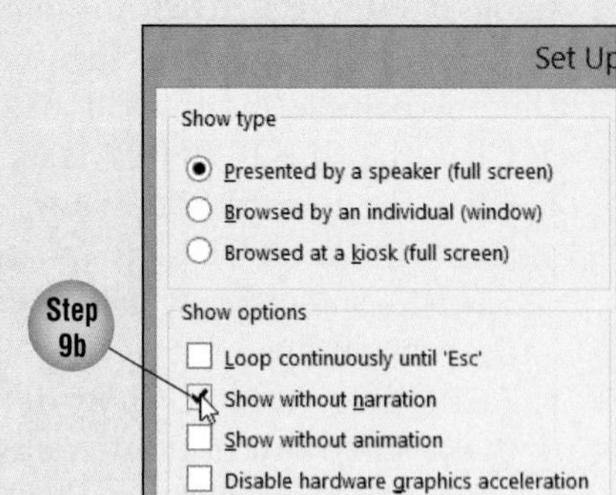

10. Save and then close **P-C7-P3-AdvTours-Narration.pptx**.

Quick Steps

Hide a Slide
1. Make slide active.
2. Click SLIDE SHOW tab.
3. Click Hide Slide button.

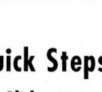

Hiding Slides

A presentation you create may be presented to a number of different groups or departments. In some situations you may want to hide specific slides in a presentation depending on the audience. To hide a slide in a presentation, make the desired slide active, click the SLIDE SHOW tab, and then click the Hide Slide button in the Set

Up group. When a slide is hidden, a slash displays over the slide number in the slide thumbnails pane. and the slide in the slide thumbnails pane displays in a dimmed manner. The slide is visible in the slide thumbnails pane in Normal view and also in the Slide Sorter view. To remove the hidden icon and redisplay the slide when running a presentation, click the slide miniature in the slide thumbnails pane, click the SLIDE SHOW tab, and then click the Hide Slide button.

Hide Slide

Managing Monitors

If you have two monitors connected to your computer or are running PowerPoint on a laptop with dual-display capabilities, you can determine on which monitor to run the presentation with the *Monitor* option in the Monitors group on the SLIDE SHOW tab. By default, PowerPoint automatically chooses a monitor to display the slide show. Change the desired monitor for viewing the presentation by clicking the *Monitor* option box arrow and then clicking the monitor at the drop-down list.

Using Presenter View

Insert a check mark in the *Use Presenter View* check box in the Monitors group on the SLIDE SHOW tab if you are running PowerPoint on a computer with two monitors or on a laptop with dual-display capabilities. With this option active, you display your presentation in full-screen view on one monitor and display your presentation in a special speaker view on the other, similar to what is shown in Figure 7.4. If you have two monitors or a laptop with dual-display capabilities, try exploring Presenter View on your own using the information in the figure.

Figure 7.4 Presenter View

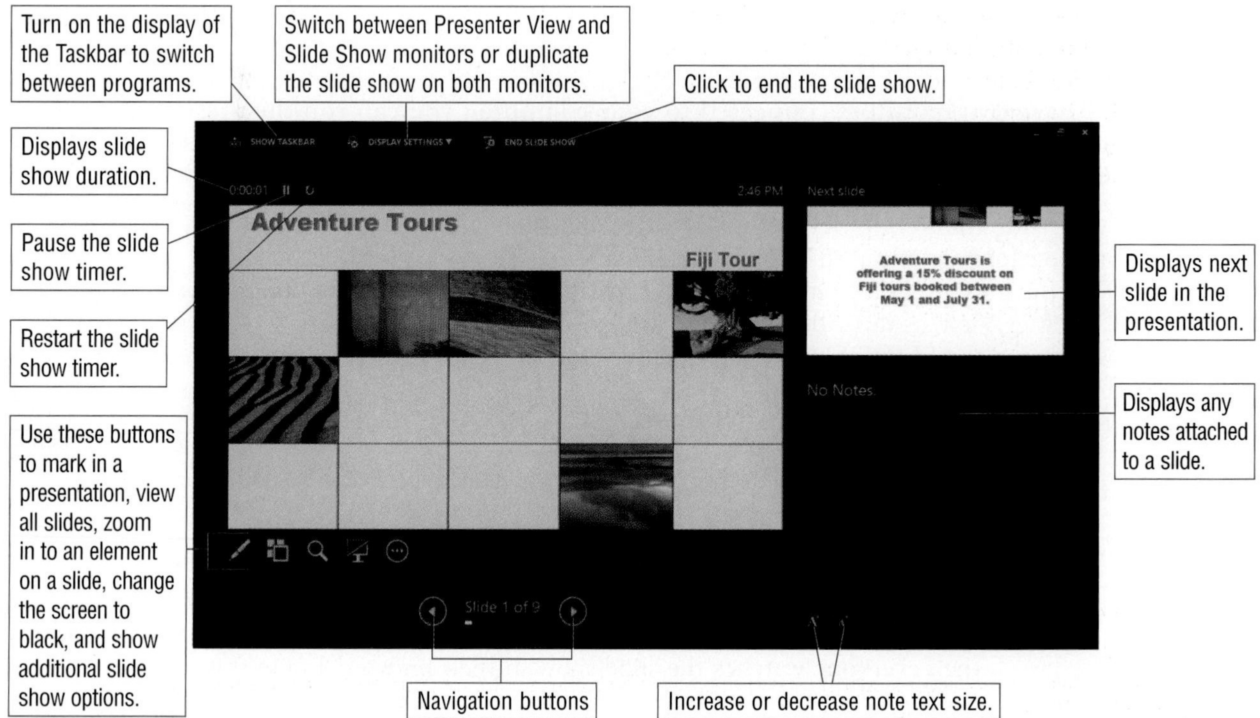
Turn on the display of the Taskbar to switch between programs.
Switch between Presenter View and Slide Show monitors or duplicate the slide show on both monitors.
Click to end the slide show.
Displays slide show duration.
Pause the slide show timer.
Restart the slide show timer.
Use these buttons to mark in a presentation, view all slides, zoom in to an element on a slide, change the screen to black, and show additional slide show options.
Adventure Tours
Fiji Tour
Adventure Tours is offering a 15% discount on Fiji tours booked between May 1 and July 31.
Displays next slide in the presentation.
Displays any notes attached to a slide.
Navigation buttons
Increase or decrease note text size.

Project 3d Hiding Slides and Using Presenter View Part 4 of 6

1. Open **P-C7-P3-AdvTours.pptx**.
2. Remove the continuous loop option and remove timings by completing the following steps:
   a. Click the SLIDE SHOW tab.
   b. Click the Set Up Slide Show button.
   c. At the Set Up Show dialog box, click the *Loop continuously until 'Esc'* check box to remove the check mark.
   d. Click OK to close the dialog box.
   e. Click the TRANSITIONS tab.
   f. Click the down-pointing arrow at the right side of the *After* measurement box until *00:00* displays in the box.
   g. Click the *After* check box to remove the check mark.
   h. Click the *On Mouse Click* option to insert a check mark.
   i. Click the Apply To All button.
3. Hide Slide 2 by completing the following steps:
   a. Click the Slide 2 thumbnail in the slide thumbnails pane.
   b. Click the SLIDE SHOW tab and then click the Hide Slide button in the Set Up group.
4. Run the presentation and notice that Slide 2 does not display (since it is hidden).
5. Unhide Slide 2 by clicking the Slide 2 thumbnail in the slide thumbnails pane and then clicking the Hide Slide button in the Set Up group on the SLIDE SHOW tab.

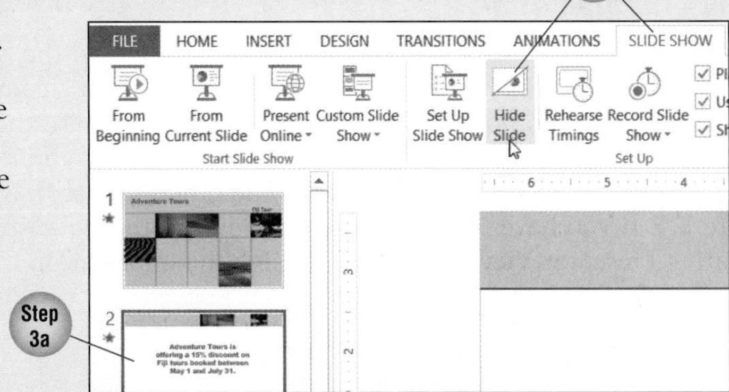

If you have two monitors connected to your computer, you can run the presentation in Presenter View. Complete these optional steps only if you have two monitors available with your computer.

6. Make sure the SLIDE SHOW tab is active and then click the *Use Presenter View* check box in the Monitors group to insert a check mark.
7. Run the presentation from Slide 1 and experiment with some of the options available in Presenter View, as described in Figure 7.4.
8. Make sure the SLIDE SHOW tab is active and then click the *Show Presenter View* check box to remove the check mark.
9. Save **P-C7-P3-AdvTours.pptx**.

Presenting a Presentation Online

With the Present Online feature, you can share a slide show with others over the Internet by sending a link to the people you want to view the presentation and then everyone watches the slide show in their browser. To use this feature, you need a network service to host the slide show. You can use the Office Presentation Service, which is available to anyone with a Windows Live ID, such as your

OneDrive, and Microsoft Office 2013. You can view an online presentation in Internet Explorer, Firefox, and Safari.

To present a presentation online, click the Present Online button in the Start Slide Show group on the SLIDE SHOW tab. At the Present Online window that displays, click the CONNECT button, and, if necessary, enter your Windows Live ID user name and password. When PowerPoint has connected to your account and prepared your presentation, the Present Online window will display with a unique link PowerPoint created for your presentation. Click the Copy Link hyperlink in the Present Online window to copy the unique link, and then paste the link into an email you are sending to the people who will be viewing your presentation. If you have an Outlook account, you can also click the Send in Email hyperlink to open Outlook and paste the link in a message window.

After everyone has opened the presentation link in a web browser, click the START PRESENTATION button in the Present Online window. People viewing your presentation do not need to have PowerPoint installed on their computers to view the presentation since the presentation will display through their web browsers. When the slide show has ended, click the End Online Presentation button on the PRESENT ONLINE tab. At the message that displays asking if you want to end the online presentation, click the End Online Presentation button. The PRESENT ONLINE tab provides options for running the slide show, managing monitors, sharing the presentation through OneNote, and displaying the unique link to send to more people. You can also access the Present Online window by clicking the FILE tab, clicking the *Share* option, clicking *Present Online*, and then clicking the Present Online button.

You can enable the viewers of your presentation to download the presentation and view the slides on their own without watching it live with you. To do this, click the *Enable remote viewers to download the presentation* check box at the Present Online window before your click the CONNECT button.

Quick Steps

Present Online
1. Click the SLIDE SHOW tab.
2. Click the Present Online button.
3. Click the CONNECT button.
4. If necessary, enter Windows Live ID user name and password.
5. Click Copy Link hyperlink.
6. Open email.
7. Paste link into email and send email.
8. Click START PRESENTATION button.

Present Online

Project 3e Optional: Presenting Online — Part 5 of 6

To complete this project, you will need a Windows Live ID account. Depending on your system configuration and what services are available, these steps will vary.

1. With **P-C7-P3-AdvTours.pttx** open, click the SLIDE SHOW tab and then click the Present Online button in the Start Slide Show group.
2. At the Present Online window that displays, click the CONNECT button.
3. Type your user name and password into the Windows Security dialog box.
4. At the Present Online window with the unique link selected, click the Copy Link hyperlink.
5. Send the link to colleagues by opening the desired email account, pasting the link into a new message window, and then sending the email to the viewers. Or, if you are using Microsoft Outlook, click the Send in Email hyperlink and Microsoft Outlook opens in a new message window with the link inserted in the message. In Outlook, send the link to people you want to view the presentation.
6. When everyone has received the link, click the START PRESENTATION button at the Present Online window.
7. Run the presentation.
8. When the slide show has ended, press the Esc key and then click the End Online Presentation button on the PRESENT ONLINE tab.
9. At the message that displays telling you that all remote viewers will be disconnected if you continue, click the End Online Presentation button.

Creating a Custom Show

A ***custom slide show*** is a presentation within a presentation. Creating a custom slide show might be useful in situations where you want to show only a select number of slides to a particular audience. To create a custom show, click the SLIDE SHOW tab, click the Custom Slide Show button in the Start Slide Show group, and then click *Custom Shows* at the drop-down list. At the Custom Shows dialog box, click the New button and the Define Custom Show dialog box displays, similar to what you see in Figure 7.5.

At the Define Custom Show dialog box, type a name for the custom presentation in the *Slide show name* text box. To insert a slide in the custom show, click the check box for the desired slide in the *Slides in presentation* list box to insert a check mark and then click the Add button. This inserts the slide in the *Slides in custom show* list box. Continue in this manner until all desired slides have been added to the custom show. You can also insert check marks in all the desired slide check boxes first and then click the Add button to add all the slides in the *Slides in custom show* list box at once. If you want to change the order of the slides in the *Slides in custom show* list box, click one of the arrow keys to move the selected slide up or down in the list box. When the desired slides have been inserted in the *Slides in custom show* list box and are arranged in the desired order, click OK. You can create more than one custom show in a presentation.

Quick Steps

Create a Custom Show
1. Click SLIDE SHOW tab.
2. Click Custom Slide Show button.
3. Click *Custom Shows*.
4. Click New button.
5. Make desired changes at Define Custom Show dialog box.
6. Click OK.

Run a Custom Show
1. Click SLIDE SHOW tab.
2. Click Custom Slide Show button.
3. Click desired custom show.

Edit a Custom Show
1. Click SLIDE SHOW tab.
2. Click Custom Slide Show button.
3. Click *Custom Shows*.
4. Click desired custom show.
5. Click Edit button.
6. Make desired changes at Define Custom Show dialog box.
7. Click OK.

Print a Custom Show
1. Display Print backstage area.
2. Click first gallery in *Settings* category.
3. Click desired custom show at drop-down list.
4. Click Print button.

Custom Slide Show

Create custom shows to customize a presentation for a variety of audiences.

Running a Custom Show

To run a custom show within a presentation, click the Custom Slide Show button on the SLIDE SHOW tab and then click the desired custom show at the drop-down list. You can also choose a custom show by displaying the Set Up Show dialog box and then clicking the *Custom show* option. If the presentation contains more than one custom show, click the down-pointing arrow at the right of the *Custom show* option box and then click the show name at the drop-down list.

Figure 7.5 Define Custom Show Dialog Box

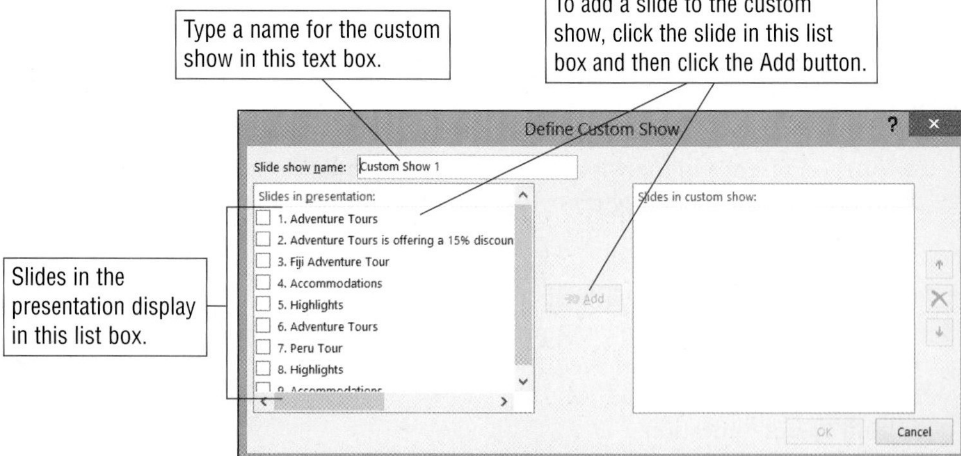

Editing a Custom Show

A custom show is saved with the presentation and can be edited. To edit a custom show, open the presentation, click the Custom Slide Show button on the SLIDE SHOW tab, and then click *Custom Shows* at the drop-down list. At the Custom Shows dialog box, click the custom show name you want to edit and then click the Edit button. At the Define Custom Show dialog box, make the desired changes to the custom show, such as adding or removing slides or changing the order of slides. When all changes have been made, click the OK button.

Printing a Custom Show

Print a custom show with options in the *Settings* category of the Print backstage area. To do this, click the FILE tab and then click the *Print* option to display the Print backstage area. Click the first gallery in the Settings category and then click the desired custom show in the *Custom Shows* section.

Project 3f **Creating, Editing, and Running Custom Shows** **Part 6 of 6**

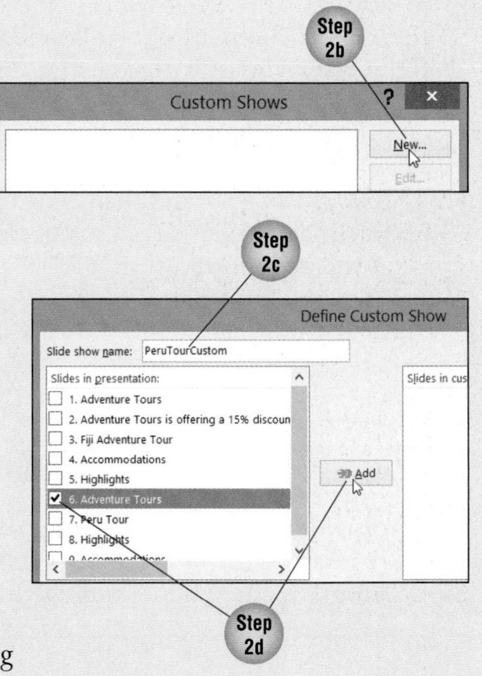

1. With **P-C7-P3-AdvTours.pptx** open, save the presentation and name it **P-C7-P3-AdvTours-Custom**.
2. Create two custom shows by completing the following steps:
   a. Click the SLIDE SHOW tab, click the Custom Slide Show button, and then click *Custom Shows* at the drop-down list.
   b. At the Custom Shows dialog box, click the New button.
   c. At the Define Custom Show dialog box, select the text in the *Slide show name* text box and then type **PeruTourCustom**.
   d. Click the Slide 6 check box in the *Slides in presentation* list box to insert a check mark and then click the Add button. (This adds the slide to the *Slides in custom show* list box.)
   e. Click the check boxes for Slides 7, 8, and 9 in the list box and then click the Add button.
   f. Click OK to close the Define Custom Show dialog box.
   g. At the Custom Shows dialog box, click the New button.
   h. At the Define Custom Show dialog box, select the text in the *Slide show name* text box and then type **FijiTourCustom**.
   i. Add Slides 1 through 5 to the *Slides in custom show* list box.
   j. Click OK to close the dialog box.
   k. Click the Close button to close the Custom Shows dialog box.
3. Run the *PeruTourCustom* custom show by completing the following steps:
   a. Click the Custom Slide Show button on the SLIDE SHOW tab and then click *PeruTourCustom* at the drop-down list.

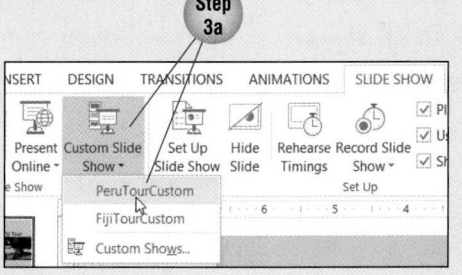

b. Click the left mouse button to advance slides.
c. Click the Custom Slide Show button, click *FijiTourCustom* at the drop-down list, and then view the presentation. (Click the left mouse button to advance the slides.)

4. Edit the FijiTourCustom custom slide show by completing the following steps:
   a. Click the Custom Slide Show button on the SLIDE SHOW tab and then click *Custom Shows* at the drop-down list.
   b. At the Custom Shows dialog box, click *FijiTourCustom* in the *Custom shows* list box and then click the Edit button. 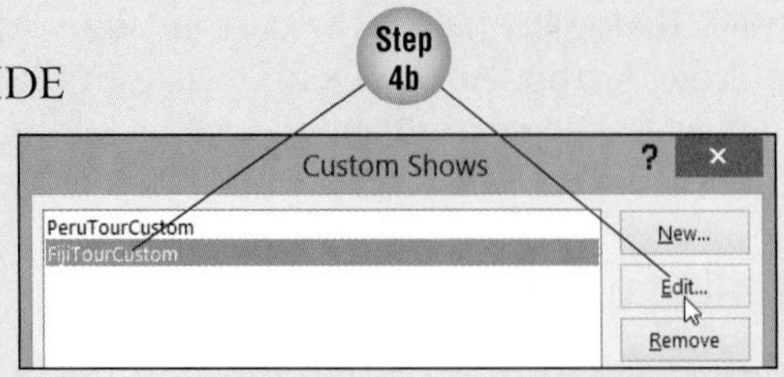
   c. At the Define Custom Show dialog box, click Slide 2 in the *Slides in custom show* list box and then click the Down button at the right side of the list box three times. (This moves the slide to the bottom of the list.)
   d. Click OK to close the dialog box.
   e. Click the Close button to close the Custom Shows dialog box. 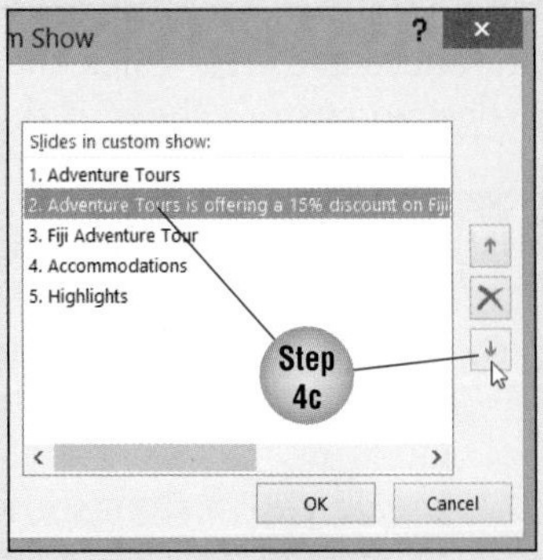
5. Run the FijiTourCustom custom show.
6. Print the FijiTourCustom custom show by completing the following steps:
   a. Click the FILE tab and then click the *Print* option.
   b. At the Print backstage area, click the first gallery in the *Settings* category and then click *FijiTourCustom* in the *Custom Shows* section.
   c. Click the second gallery in the *Settings* category and then click *6 Slides Horizontal* at the drop-down list.
   d. Click the Print button.
7. Save and then close **P-C7-P3-AdvTours-Custom.pptx**.

Project 4 Insert Audio and Video Files in a Presentation — 4 Parts

You will open a presentation and then insert an audio file, video file, and clip art image with motion. You will also customize the audio and video files to play automatically when running the presentation.

Inserting Audio and Video Files

Adding audio and/or video files to a presentation will turn a slide show into a true multimedia experience for your audience. Including a variety of elements in a presentation will stimulate interest in your presentation and keep the audience motivated.

Quick Steps

Insert an Audio File
1. Click INSERT tab.
2. Click Audio button.
3. Click *Audio on My PC*.
4. Double-click desired audio file.

Inserting an Audio File

To add an audio file to your presentation, click the INSERT tab, click the Audio button in the Media group, and then click *Audio on My PC* at the drop-down list. At the Insert Audio dialog box, navigate to the desired folder and then double-click the audio file.

You can search for and download audio files from Office.com. To do this, click the Audio button and then click *Online Audio* at the drop-down list. At the Insert Audio window, type a search word or topic and then press Enter. Double-click the desired audio to insert it in the slide. If you have an audio recording device attached to your computer, you can record audio for the presentation by clicking the Audio button and then clicking Record Audio at the drop-down list. At the Record Sound dialog box, name your audio, click the Record button, and then record your audio.

Audio

When you insert an audio file in a presentation, the AUDIO TOOLS FORMAT tab and the AUDIO TOOLS PLAYBACK tab display. Click the AUDIO TOOLS FORMAT tab and options similar to options on the PICTURE TOOLS FORMAT tab display. Click the AUDIO TOOLS PLAYBACK tab and options display for previewing the audio file, inserting a bookmark at a specific time in the audio file, specifying fade in and fade out times, and specifying how you want the audio file to play.

Project 4a **Inserting an Audio File** **Part 1 of 4**

1. Open **EcoTours.pptx** and then save the presentation with Save As and name it **P-C7-P4-EcoTours**.
2. Insert an audio file that plays music at the end of the presentation by completing the following steps:
   a. Make Slide 8 active and then click the INSERT tab.
   b. Click the Audio button in the Media group, and then click *Audio on My PC* at the drop-down list.
   c. At the Insert Audio dialog box, navigate to the PC7 folder on your storage medium and then double-click ***AudioFile-01.mid***.
   d. With the AUDIO TOOLS PLAYBACK tab active, click the down-pointing arrow at the right side of the *Start* option box in the Audio Options group and then click *Automatically* at the drop-down list.
   e. Click the *Loop until Stopped* check box in the Audio Options group to insert a check mark.
   f. Click the *Hide During Show* check box to insert a check mark.
3. Click the Start from Beginning button on the Quick Access toolbar to run the presentation starting with Slide 1. When the last slide displays, listen to the audio file and then press the Esc key to return to the Normal view.
4. Save **P-C7-P4-EcoTours.pptx**.

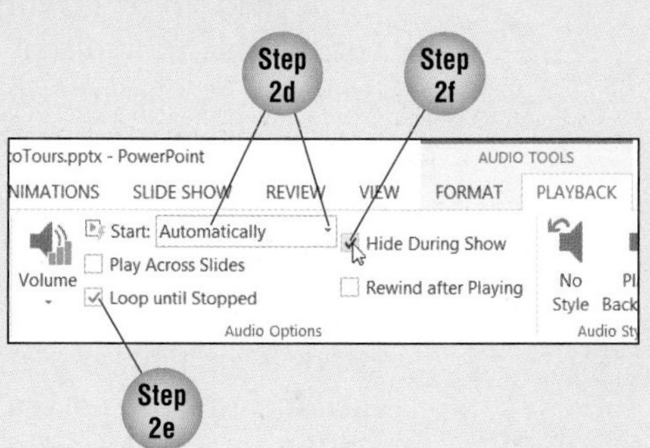

Inserting a Video File

Inserting a video file in a presentation is a similar process to inserting an audio file. Click the Video button in the Media group on the INSERT tab and then click *Video on My PC* at the drop-down list to display the Insert Video dialog box. At this dialog box, navigate to the folder containing the video file and then double-click the file.

Quick Steps

Insert a Video File
1. Click INSERT tab.
2. Click Video button.
3. Click *Video on My PC*.
4. Double-click desired video file.

Video

You can also click the Video button and then click *Online Video* to display the Insert Video window. At this window, search for videos online using the *Bing Video Search* option, search for a video in your OneDrive, or paste an embedded code into the *From a Video Embed Code* option to insert a video from a website. To embed code from a video you find online, locate and copy the embedded code of the desired video, paste the embedded code in the *From a Video Embed Code* section of the Insert Video window, and then click the Insert button. Another way to insert a video in a presentation is to click the Insert Video button in the content placeholder on a slide. This displays the Insert Video window with the additional option to browse for a file on your storage medium.

When you insert a video file in a presentation, the VIDEO TOOLS FORMAT tab and the VIDEO TOOLS PLAYBACK tab display. Click the VIDEO TOOLS FORMAT tab and options display for adjusting the video file color and frame, applying video styles, and arranging and sizing the video file. Click the VIDEO TOOLS PLAYBACK tab and options display that are similar to the options on the AUDIO TOOLS PLAYBACK tab. You can also apply formatting to a video with options in the Format Video task pane.

Optimizing and Compressing Audio and Video Files

If you insert a video in a presentation with an older file format, the Info backstage area may display an Optimize Compatibility button. Optimize compatibility of a video file to increase the likelihood that your video file will play on multiple devices.

Compress Media

If you insert an audio and/or video file in a presentation, consider compressing the file(s) to improve playback performance and save disk space. If a presentation contains audio and/or video files, the Info backstage area contains the Compress Media button. Click this button and a drop-down list displays with options for specifying the compressed quality of the video. Click the *Presentation Quality* option to save space and maintain the quality of the audio and/or video files. Click the *Internet Quality* option and the compressed video or audio files will be comparable to audio or video files streamed over the Internet. Choose the last option, *Low Quality*, to compress the audio or video files when space is limited such as when sending the presentation as an email attachment.

Showing and Hiding Media Controls

When a slide with an audio or video file displays during a slide show, media controls appear along the bottom of the audio icon or video window. Use these media controls to play the audio or video file, move to a specific location in the file, or change the audio level. The media controls display when you move the mouse pointer over the audio icon or video window. You can turn off the display of media controls by clicking the SLIDE SHOW tab and then clicking the *Show Media Controls* check box in the Set Up group to remove the check mark.

Project 4b **Inserting a Video File in a Presentation** **Part 2 of 4**

1. With **P-C7-P4-EcoTours.pptx** open, make Slide 8 active.
2. You will insert a video file in the slide that contains audio, so delete the audio file you inserted in Project 4a by clicking the audio file icon that displays in the middle of Slide 8 and then pressing the Delete key.

3. Insert a video file by completing the following steps:
   a. Click the INSERT tab
   b. Click the Video button in the Media group and then click *Video on My PC* at the drop-down list.
   c. At the Insert Video dialog box, navigate to the PC7 folder on your storage medium and then double-click the file named ***Wildlife.wmv***.
   d. Click the Play button in the Preview group (on the left side of the VIDEO TOOLS FORMAT tab) to preview the video file. (The video plays for approximately 30 seconds.)
4. Format the video by completing the following steps:
   a. Make sure the video image is selected on the slide and the VIDEO TOOLS FORMAT tab is selected.
   b. Click the *Beveled Frame, Gradient* thumbnail in the Video Styles group (fourth option).
   c. Click the Video Shape button in the Video Styles group and then click *Rounded Rectangle* at the drop-down gallery (second option in the *Rectangles* section).
   d. Click the Poster Frame button in the Adjust group and then click *Image from File* at the drop-down list.
   e. At the Insert Pictures window, click the Browse button to the right of the *From a file* option, navigate to the PC7 folder on your storage medium, and then double-click ***Olympics.jpg***.

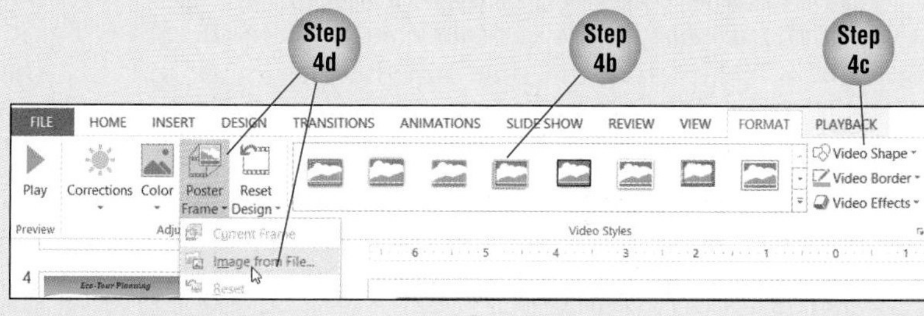

   f. Click the Corrections button in the Adjust group and then click *Brightness: 0% (Normal) Contrast: +20%* at the drop-down gallery (third column, fourth row).
   g. Click the Rotate button in the Arrange group and then click *Flip Horizontal* at the drop-down list.
   h. Click the Size group dialog box launcher to display the Format Video task pane.
   i. With the Size & Properties icon selected, make sure the *SIZE* options display.
   j. Select the current measurement in the *Height* measurement box and then type 4.9.
   k. Click *POSITION* to display the options.
   l. Select the current measurement in the *Horizontal position* measurement box and then type 2.3.
   m. Select the current measurement in the *Vertical position* measurement box and then type 1.8.
   n. Close the Format Video task pane.
   o. Click the VIDEO TOOLS PLAYBACK tab.
   p. Click the Volume button in the Video Options group and then click *Low* at the drop-down list.
   q. Click the *Loop until Stopped* check box in the Video Options group to insert a check mark.

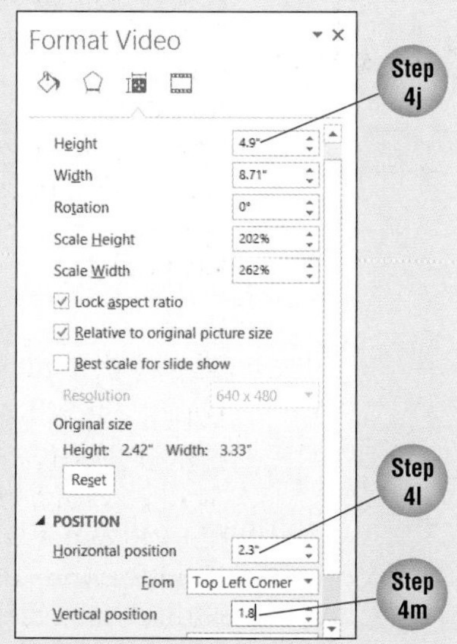

5. Make Slide 1 active and then run the presentation. When the slide containing the video file displays, move the mouse over the video file window and then click the play button located at the bottom left side of the window.

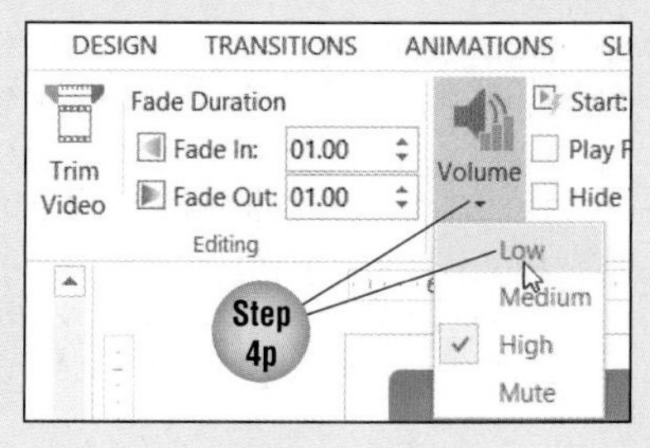

6. After viewing the video a couple of times, press the Esc key twice.
7. Specify that you want the video window to fill the slide, the video to automatically start when the slide displays, the video to play only once, and the display of media controls turned off by completing the following steps:
   a. Make sure Slide 8 is active, click the video file window, and then click the VIDEO TOOLS PLAYBACK tab.
   b. Click the *Play Full Screen* check box in the Video Options group to insert a check mark and click the *Loop until Stopped* check box to remove the check mark.
   c. Click the down-pointing arrow at the right side of the *Start* option box in the Video Options group and then click *Automatically* at the drop-down list.

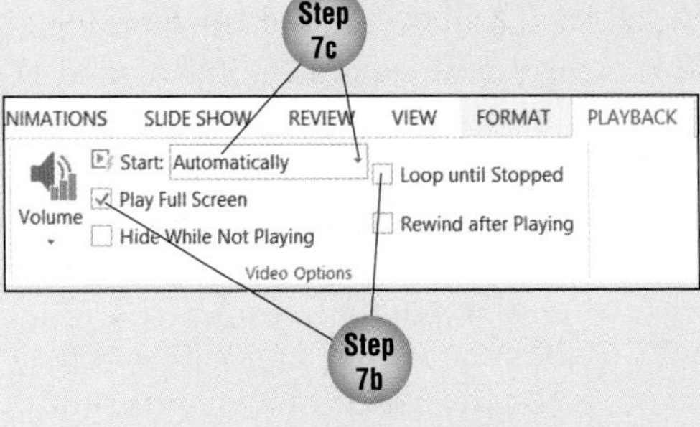

   d. Click the SLIDE SHOW tab.

   e. Click the *Show Media Controls* check box in the Set Up group to remove the check mark.
8. Make Slide 1 active and then run the presentation. When the slide displays containing the video, the video will automatically begin. When the video is finished playing, press the Esc key to return to Normal view.
9. Print Slide 8.
10. Compress the video file by completing the following steps:
    a. Make Slide 8 active and then click the video file window.
    b. Click the FILE tab.
    c. At the Info backstage area, click the Optimize Compatibility button.
    d. When the optimization is complete, click the Close button in the Optimize Media Compatibility dialog box.
    e. Click the Compress Media button and then click *Internet Quality* at the drop-down list.
    f. At the Compress Media dialog box, wait until the compression is complete (notice the progress bar along the bottom of the dialog box) and then notice the initial size of the video file and the number of megabytes saved by the compression.
    g. Click the Close button to close the dialog box and then click the Back button to return to the presentation.
11. Save **P-C7-P4-EcoTours.pptx**.

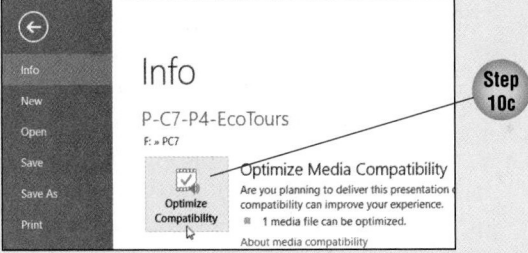

Complete these optional steps to insert a video from the Internet into a slide.

12. With Slide 8 active, insert a new slide with the Blank layout.
13. Click the INSERT tab, click the Video button in the Media group, and then click *Online Video* at the drop-down list.
14. Click in the *Bing Video Search* box, type Antarctica wildlife, and then press Enter.
15. At the search results window, double-click a video that interests you.
16. Size and position the video window in the slide to better fill the slide.
17. Make Slide 1 active and then run the presentation. When the slide with the video file you inserted displays, click the Play button in the video window. When the video is finished playing, press the Esc key to return to Normal view.
18. Save **P-C7-P4-EcoTours.pptx**.

Trimming a Video File

Use the Trim Video button on the VIDEO TOOLS PLAYBACK tab to trim the beginning and end of your video. This might be helpful in a situation where you want to remove a portion of the video that is not pertinent to the message in your presentation. You are limited to trimming a portion of the beginning of the video or the end.

To trim a video, insert the video file in the slide, click the VIDEO TOOLS PLAYBACK tab, and then click the Trim Video button in the Editing group. At the Trim Video dialog box, specify the time you want the video to start and/or the time you want the video to end. To trim the start of the video, you can insert a specific time in the *Start Time* text box or drag the green start point marker that displays on the slider bar below the video. You can zero in on a very specific starting point by clicking the Next Frame button or the Previous Frame button to move the display of the video a frame at a time. Complete similar steps to trim the ending of the video except use the red end point marker on the slider bar or insert the specific ending time in the *End Time* text box.

Quick Steps

Trim a Video File

1. Insert video file.
2. Click VIDEO TOOLS PLAYBACK tab.
3. Click Trim Video button.
4. Specify start time and/or end time.
5. Click OK.

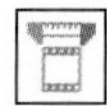

Trim Video

Project 4c **Trimming a Video** **Part 3 of 4**

1. With **P-C7-P4-EcoTour.pptx** open, make Slide 8 active.
2. Trim out the first part of the video that shows the running horses by completing the following steps:
   a. Click the video to select it and then click the VIDEO TOOLS PLAYBACK tab.
   b. Click the Trim Video button in the Editing group.
   c. At the Trim Video dialog box, position the mouse pointer on the green start point marker on the slider bar until the pointer displays as a double-headed arrow pointing left and right. Hold down the left mouse button, drag the start point marker to approximately the *00:04.0* time and then release the mouse button.
   d. Click the Next Frame button until the first image of the birds displays and the horses have completely disappeared off the screen. (Depending on where you dragged the start point marker, you may need to click the Previous Frame button.)
   e. Click the OK button.

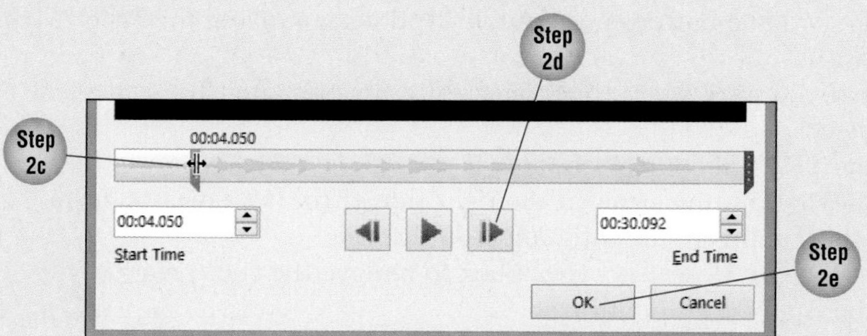

3. Click the up-pointing arrow at the right side of the *Fade In* measurement box in the Editing group until *01.00* displays and then click the up-pointing arrow at the right side of the *Fade Out* measurement box until *01.00* displays.
4. Run the presentation. Press the Esc key to return to Normal view.
5. Save **P-C7-P4-EcoTours.pptx**.

Playing an Audio File throughout a Presentation

In Project 4a, you inserted an audio file that played when a specific slide displayed. You can also insert an audio file in a presentation and have the audio play continually through all slides in the presentation. Generally you would add an audio file for the entire presentation when setting up an automated presentation. To specify that you want the audio file to play throughout the presentation, click the Play In Background button in the Audio Styles group on the AUDIO TOOLS PLAYBACK tab. When you click this button, the *Start* option box in the Audio Options group changes to *Automatically*, and check marks are inserted in the *Play Across Slides* check box, *Loop until Stopped* check box, and *Hide During Show* check box. To make the presentation automated, display the Set Up Show dialog box and then insert a check mark in the *Loop continuously until 'Esc'* check box.

Project 4d **Playing an Audio File throughout a Presentation** **Part 4 of 4**

1. With **P-C7-P4-EcoTours.pptx** open, make Slide 8 active and then make the following changes:
   a. Select and then delete the video file.
   b. Apply the Title Only slide layout.
   c. Type the title **Let the adventure begin!** and then change the font size to 54 points and the font color to Dark Blue.
   d. Distribute the title placeholder vertically on the slide.
2. Make Slide 1 active and then insert an audio file that plays throughout all files by completing the following steps:
   a. Click the INSERT tab, click the Audio button in the Media group, and then click *Audio on My PC* at the drop-down list.
   b. At the Insert Audio dialog box, navigate to the PC7 folder on your storage medium and then double-click ***AudioFile-02.mid***.
   c. With the AUDIO TOOLS PLAYBACK tab active, click the Play in Background button in the Audio Styles group. (Notice that when you click the Play in Background button, the *Start* option box in the Audio Options group changes to *Automatically*, and a check mark is inserted in the *Play Across Slides* check box, *Loop until Stopped* check box, and *Hide During Show* check box.)
   d. Click the Volume button in the Audio Options group and then click *Medium* at the drop-down list.
3. Specify that you want slides to automatically advance after five seconds by completing the following steps:
   a. Click the TRANSITIONS tab.
   b. Click the up-pointing arrow at the right side of the *After* measurement box in the Timing group until *00:05.00* displays.
   c. Click in the *On Mouse Click* check box to remove the check mark.
   d. Click the Apply To All button.

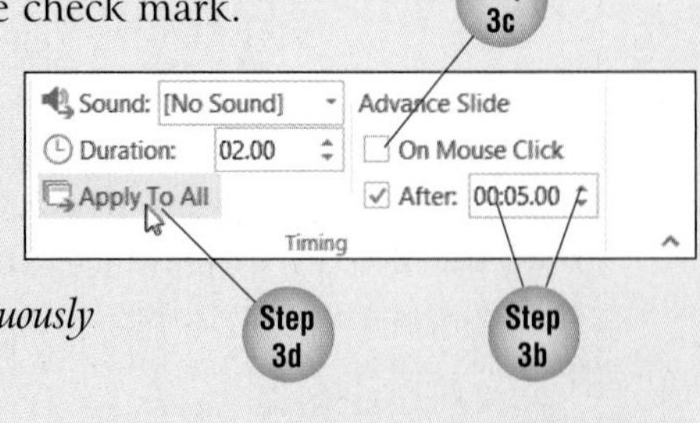

4. Set up the presentation to run continuously by completing the following steps:
   a. Click the SLIDE SHOW tab.
   b. Click the Set Up Slide Show button.
   c. At the Set Up Show dialog box, click in the *Loop continuously until 'Esc'* check box to insert a check mark.
   d. Click OK to close the dialog box.
5. Make Slide 1 active and then run the presentation. When the presentation begins for the second time, press the Esc key to return to Normal view.
6. Save and then close **P-C7-P4-EcoTours.pptx**.

Chapter Summary

- Apply animation to an item in a slide with options in the Animation group on the ANIMATIONS tab. Specify animation effects with options from the Effect Options button drop-down gallery.
- Click the Preview button on the ANIMATIONS tab to view the animation effects without running the presentation.
- Remove an animation effect from an item in a slide by clicking the *None* option in the Animation group on the ANIMATIONS tab.
- The Add Animation button in the Advanced Animation group on the ANIMATIONS tab provides four types of animation effects—entrance, exit, emphasis, and motion paths.
- Use the Animation Painter, located in the Advanced Animation group on the ANIMATIONS tab, to apply the same animation to items in more than one location in a slide or slides.
- Use options in the Timing group on the ANIMATIONS tab to determine when an animation starts on a slide, the duration of the animation, the delay between animations, and the order in which animations appear on the slide.
- Use the Animation Pane to customize and modify animation effects. Display the pane by clicking the Animation Pane button in the Advanced Animation group on the ANIMATIONS tab.
- Apply a sound to an animation with the *Sound* option box at the effect options dialog box with the Effect tab selected. The name of the dialog box varies depending on the animation effect selected.
- A build displays important points on a slide one point at a time. You can apply a build that dims the previous bulleted point with the *After animation* option box at the effect options dialog box with the Effect tab selected.
- Specify a path you want an item to follow when it displays on the slide with options in the *Motion Paths* section of the Add Animation button drop-down gallery. To draw a motion path, choose the *Custom path* option at the drop-down gallery.
- Use the Trigger button in the Advanced Animation group to specify that you want to make an animation effect occur during a slide show by clicking an item on the slide.
- Customize a slide show with options in the Set Up Show dialog box.
- To prepare an automated presentation, insert a check mark in the *Loop continuously until 'Esc'* check box at the Set Up Show dialog box.
- To apply specific times to slides, click the Rehearse Timings button in the Set Up group on the SLIDE SHOW tab. Use buttons on the Recording toolbar to set, pause, or repeat times.
- To record narration for a presentation, click the Record Slide Show button in the Set Up group on the SLIDE SHOW tab and then click the Start Recording button at the Record Slide Show dialog box.
- Hide or unhide a slide in a presentation by clicking the Hide Slide button in the Set Up group on the SLIDE SHOW tab.
- Specify on which monitor to run the presentation with the *Monitor* option in the Monitors group on the SLIDE SHOW tab.

- If you are running PowerPoint on a computer with two monitors or on a laptop with dual-display capabilities, you can display your presentation in full-screen view on one monitor and display your presentation in a special speaker view on the other monitor.
- Use the Present Online feature to share a slide show with others over the Internet. Send a link to the people you want to view the presentation and then everyone can watch the slide show in their browsers.
- Create a custom slide show, which is a presentation within a presentation, with options in the Define Custom Show dialog box.
- To run a custom slide show, click the Custom Slide Show button in the Start Slide Show group on the SLIDE SHOW tab and then click the desired custom show at the drop-down list.
- Print a custom show at the Print backstage area by clicking the first gallery in the *Settings* category and then clicking the desired custom show in the *Custom Shows* section.
- Insert an audio file in a slide by clicking the Audio button in the Media group on the INSERT tab, and then clicking *Audio on My PC*. Use options on the AUDIO TOOLS FORMAT tab and the AUDIO TOOLS PLAYBACK tab to format and customize the audio file.
- Insert a video file in a slide by clicking the Video button in the Media group on the INSERT tab and then clicking *Video on My PC*. Use options on the VIDEO TOOLS FORMAT tab and the VIDEO TOOLS PLAYBACK tab to format and customize the video file.
- When a slide show runs, media controls display along the bottom of an audio icon or video window in a slide when you move the mouse over the icon or window. Turn on or off the display of these media controls with the *Show Media Controls* check box in the Set Up group on the SLIDE SHOW tab.
- Compress audio and video files to improve playback performance and save disk space. Compress audio and video files by clicking the FILE tab to display the Info backstage area, clicking the Compress Media button, and then clicking the desired compression.
- Use the Trim Video button on the VIDEO TOOLS PLAYBACK tab to trim the beginning and end of your video.

Commands Review

FEATURE	RIBBON TAB, GROUP/OPTION	BUTTON, OPTION
add animations	ANIMATIONS, Advanced Animation	
Animation Painter	ANIMATIONS, Advanced Animation	
Animation Pane	ANIMATIONS, Advanced Animation	
animations	ANIMATIONS, Animation	
compress audio and video files	FILE, *Info*	

FEATURE	RIBBON TAB, GROUP/OPTION	BUTTON, OPTION
Define Custom Show dialog box	SLIDE SHOW, Start Slide Show	, *Custom Shows, New*
hide/unhide slide	SLIDE SHOW, Set Up	
insert audio file	INSERT, Media	
insert video file	INSERT, Media	
optimize video files	FILE, *Info*	
present online	SLIDE SHOW, Start Slide Show	
Recording toolbar	SLIDE SHOW, Set Up	
Set Up Show dialog box	SLIDE SHOW, Set Up	
Trim Video dialog box	VIDEO TOOLS PLAYBACK, Editing	

Concepts Check Test Your Knowledge

Completion: In the space provided at the right, indicate the correct term, symbol, or command.

1. Once you have applied an animation, specify the animation effects with options in this button drop-down gallery. ____________________
2. Remove an animation effect from an item in a slide by clicking this option in the Animation group on the ANIMATIONS tab. ____________________
3. The Add Animation button in the Advanced Animation group on the ANIMATIONS tab provides four types of animation effects you can apply to an item—entrance, exit, motion paths, and this. ____________________
4. Use this feature if you apply an animation or animations to items in a slide and want to apply the same animation in more than one location in a slide or slides. ____________________
5. The *Duration* measurement box is located in this group on the ANIMATIONS tab. ____________________
6. Display the Animation Pane by clicking the Animation Pane button in this group on the ANIMATIONS tab. ____________________
7. This term refers to displaying important points one at a time in a slide when running a presentation. ____________________

8. To draw your own motion path in a slide, click the Add Animation button on the ANIMATIONS tab and then click this option in the *Motion Paths* section of the drop-down gallery. ____________

9. The Hide Slide button is located on this tab. ____________

10. Specify the slides you want included in a custom show with options at this dialog box. ____________

11. The Audio and Video buttons are located in this group on the INSERT tab. ____________

12. The Volume button for an audio file is located in the Audio Options group on this tab. ____________

13. The Trim Video button is located on this tab. ____________

Skills Check Assess Your Performance

Assessment 1

APPLY ANIMATION EFFECTS TO A TRAVEL PRESENTATION

1. Open **FCTCruise.pptx** and then save the presentation with Save As and name it **P-C7-A1-FCTCruise**.
2. With Slide 1 active, click the company logo and then apply the Fade entrance animation. ***Hint: Click the ANIMATIONS tab***.
3. Click the subtitle *Vacation Cruise* and then apply the Fly In animation.
4. Display the presentation in Slide Master view, click the top slide master layout (Japanese Waves Slide Master) in the slide thumbnails pane, apply the Fade animation to the title style, and then close the Slide Master view.
5. Make Slide 2 active and then complete the following steps:
   a. Click in the bulleted text.
   b. Apply the Wipe entrance animation.
   c. Change the direction to *From Left*. ***Hint: Change the direction with the Effect Options button***.
   d. Click in the bulleted text.
   e. Double-click the Animation Painter button.
   f. Make Slide 3 active and then click in the bulleted text.
   g. Make Slide 4 active and then click in the bulleted text.
   h. Make Slide 5 active and then click in the bulleted text.
   i. Click the Animation Painter button to deactivate it.
6. Make Slide 3 active and then insert a trigger by completing the following steps:
   a. Click the banner that displays toward the bottom of the slide and then apply the Wipe entrance animation and change the direction to *From Left*.
   b. Display the Animation Pane.
   c. Click the *Horizontal Scroll* item in the Animation Pane.
   d. Click the Trigger button, point to *On Click of*, and then click *Content Placeholder 2* at the side menu.
   e. Close the Animation Pane.

7. Run the presentation from the beginning and, when the third bulleted item displays in Slide 3, click the bulleted item to trigger the display of the banner.
8. Save and then close **P-C7-A1-FCTCruise.pptx**.

Assessment 2

APPLY ANIMATION EFFECTS TO AN EMPLOYEE ORIENTATION PRESENTATION

1. Open **GEOrientation.pptx** and then save the presentation with Save As and name it **P-C7-A2-GEOrientation**.
2. Make Slide 2 active and then apply the following animations to the SmartArt graphic:
   a. Apply the Blinds entrance animation effect. ***Hint: You will need to click the More button at the right of the animations in the Animation group and then click*** **More Entrance Effects.**
   b. Change the SmartArt animation so the sequence is *One by One* and change the direction to *Vertical*. ***Hint: Do this with the Effect Options button.***
3. Make Slide 3 active and then apply the following animations to the organizational chart:
   a. Apply the Blinds entrance animation effect.
   b. Change the SmartArt animation so the sequence is *Level at Once*.
4. Make Slide 4 active and then apply the following animations to the bulleted text (click on any character in the bulleted text):
   a. Apply the Zoom entrance animation effect.
   b. Display the Animation Pane and then set the text to dim after animation to a dark blue color. ***Hint: Click the down-pointing arrow at the right side of the content placeholder in the Animation Pane and then click*** **Effect Options.**
5. Apply the following animations to the clip art image in Slide 4:
   a. Apply the Spin emphasis animation effect.
   b. Set the amount of spin for the clip art image to *Two Spins* and change the duration to *01.00*.
   c. Change the *Start* option to *With Previous*.
   d. Reorder the items in the Animation Pane so the clip art displays first when running the presentation.
6. Make Slide 5 active, select the SmartArt graphic, and then apply an entrance animation effect so the elements in the SmartArt graphic fade in one by one.
7. Make Slide 6 active and then apply the following animation effects to the images with the following specifications:
   a. Apply the Fly Out exit animation effect to the *Free Education* gift package, change the direction to *To Right*, and change the duration to *00.25*.
   b. Apply the Shape entrance animation effect to the diploma/books clip art image and change the duration to *01.00*.
   c. Move the *Free Education* gift package so the bulleted text underneath displays, apply the Grow & Turn entrance animation effect to the bulleted text, and then move the gift package back to the original location.
   d. Apply the Fly Out exit animation effect to the *Free Toys and Fitness* gift package, change the direction to *To Left*, and change the duration to *00.25*.
   e. Apply the Shape entrance animation effect to the notebook computer clip art image and change the duration to *01.00*.
   f. Move the *Free Toys and Fitness* gift package so the bulleted text underneath displays, apply the Grow & Turn entrance animation effect to the bulleted text, and then move the gift package back to the original location.

g. Close the Animation Pane.
8. Make Slide 1 active and then run the presentation.
9. Save **P-C7-A2-GEOrientation.pptx**.
10. Display the presentation in Slide Master view, click the top slide master layout in the slide thumbnails pane, apply an entrance animation effect of your choosing to the title, and then close Slide Master view.
11. Make Slide 1 active and then apply the following animation effects:
    a. Click the globe clip art image and then draw a motion path (using the *Custom Path* option) so the image will circle around the slide and return back to the original location.
    b. Apply the *Spiral In* entrance animation effect to the *New Employee Orientation* placeholder.
12. Run the presentation.
13. Print the presentation as a handout with nine slides printed horizontally per page.
14. Save and then close **P-C7-A2-GEOrientation.pptx**.

Assessment 3

APPLY ANIMATION EFFECTS, VIDEO, AND AUDIO TO A JOB SEARCH PRESENTATION

1. Open **JobSearch.pptx** and then save the presentation with Save As and name it **P-C7-A3-JobSearch**.
2. Apply the Wisp design theme and the blue-colored variant (third thumbnail) to the presentation.
3. Add appropriate clip art images to at least two slides.
4. Make Slide 10 active and then insert the video file named **Flight.mov** from the PC7 folder on your storage medium. Make the following changes to the video:
    a. Click the VIDEO TOOLS FORMAT tab and then change the height to 5 inches.
    b. Distribute the video horizontally on the slide.
    c. Click the VIDEO TOOLS PLAYBACK tab and then specify that you want the video to play automatically (do this with the *Start* option box), that you want the video to play full screen, and that you want the video to hide while not playing.
    d. Click the Trim Video button and then trim approximately the first nine seconds from the start of the video. Click OK to close the dialog box.
5. With Slide 10 active, insert the **AudioFile-03.mid** audio file in the slide (located in the PC7 folder on your storage medium) so it plays automatically, loops until stopped, and is hidden when running the presentation.
6. Compress the video file for Internet quality.
7. Run the presentation. After listening to the music for a period of time, end the presentation.
8. Print only Slide 10.
9. Create a custom show named *Interview* that contains Slides 1, 3, 6, 7, and 9.
10. Run the Interview custom show.
11. Print the Interview custom show as a handout with all slides printed horizontally on one page.
12. Edit the Interview custom show by removing Slide 2.
13. Print the Interview custom show again as a handout with all slides printed horizontally on one page.
14. Save and then close **P-C7-A3-JobSearch.pptx**.

Assessment 4

INSERT AN AUDIO FILE FROM OFFICE.COM

1. Open **JamaicaTour.pptx** and then save the presentation with Save As and name it **P-C7-A4-JamaicaTour**.
2. Click the INSERT tab, click the Audio button arrow, and then click *Online Audio*. (This displays the Insert Audio window.)
3. Type **Jamaica** in the Office.com Clip Art search box and then press Enter. Double-click *Jamaica Bounce (1* or *2)*. (If this audio file is not available, choose another audio file such as *Rainforest music*, *African song*, or a different audio file of your choosing.)
4. Set the audio file to start automatically, play across all slides, and hide when running the presentation.
5. Display the TRANSITIONS tab and specify that each slide should advance automatically after five seconds.
6. Set up the presentation to run on an endless loop. (Do this at the Set Up Show dialog box.)
7. Run the presentation.
8. Print the presentation as a handout with the six slides printed horizontally on the page.
9. Save and then close **P-C7-A4-JamaicaTour.pptx**.

Visual Benchmark Demonstrate Your Proficiency

CREATE AND FORMAT A MEDICAL CENTER PRESENTATION

1. Open **RMCPres.pptx** and then save the presentation with Save As and name it **P-C7-VB-RMCPres**.
2. Create the presentation shown in Figure 7.6 on pages 323–324 with the following specifications:
   a. Find the clip art image for Slide 2 (this is a caduceus symbol) by using the search words *caduceus healthcare*. Size and position the clip art as shown in the figure.
   b. Create the SmartArt in Slide 3 using the *Staggered Process* diagram (located in the *Process* section) and apply the *Colorful Range - Accent Colors 4 to 5* option to the diagram.
   c. Use the information shown in the legend and the data information shown above the bars to create a *Clustered Column* chart as shown in Slide 4. Increase the text size of all elements on the chart to 16 points.
   d. Use the Heart shape (located in the *Basic Shapes* section) to create the hearts in Slide 5. Apply the Subtle Effect - Red, Accent 1 shape style and change the shape outline weight to 4½ pt for all three shapes.
   e. Use the Frame shape (located in the *Basic Shapes* section) to create the shape in Slide 6.
3. Apply the following animation effects to items in slides:
   a. Display the presentation in Slide Master view, click the top slide master layout in the slide thumbnails pane (Medical Health 16x9 Slide Master), apply the Float In animation to the title style, and then close the Slide Master view.
   b. Make Slide 1 active and then apply an animation effect of your choosing to the subtitle.

c. Make Slide 2 active, apply an animation effect of your choosing to the clip art image, and then apply an animation effect to the bulleted text.
d. Make Slide 3 active, apply an animation effect of your choosing to the SmartArt, and then specify a sequence of *One by One*.
e. Make Slide 4 active, apply an animation effect of your choosing to the chart, and then specify a sequence of *By Category*.
f. Make Slide 5 active and then apply the *Shape* entrance animation effect to the heart at the left side of the slide. Using the Add Animation button, apply the *Pulse* emphasis animation effect. Click the same heart and then use the Animation Painter button to apply the entrance and emphasis animation effect to the middle heart and the heart at the right side of the slide.
g. Make Slide 6 active and then insert the **AudioFile-04.mid** audio file to play automatically, loop until stopped, and be hidden when running the presentation.

4. Run the presentation.
5. Print the presentation as a handout with six slides printed horizontally per page.
6. Save and then close **P-C7-VB-RMCPres.pptx**.

Case Study Apply Your Skills

Part 1

You are a trainer in the Training Department at Summit Services. You are responsible for coordinating and conducting software training in the company. Your company hires contract employees and some of those employees work at home and need to have a computer available. You will be conducting a short training for contract employees on how to purchase a personal computer. Open the Word document named **PCBuyGuide.docx** and then use the information in the document to prepare your presentation. Make sure you keep the slides uncluttered and easy to read. Consider inserting clip art or other images in some of the slides. Insert custom animation effects to each slide in the presentation. Run the presentation and then make any necessary changes to the animation effects. Save the presentation and name it **P-C7-CS-PCBuyGuide**. Print the presentation as a handout.

Part 2

Some training sessions on purchasing a personal computer are only scheduled for 20 minutes. For these training sessions, you want to cover only the information about selecting computer hardware components. With the **P-C7-CS-PCBuyGuide.pptx** presentation open, create a custom show (you determine the name) that contains only the slides pertaining to selecting hardware components. Run the custom show and then print the custom show. Save **P-C7-CS-PCBuyGuide.pptx**.

Part 3

You would like to insert an audio file that plays at the end of the presentation and decide to find free audio files on the Internet. Log on to the Internet and then use a search engine to search for “free audio files for PowerPoint” or “free audio clips for PowerPoint.” When you find a site, make sure that you can download and use the audio file without violating copyright laws. Download an audio file and then insert it in the last slide in your presentation. Set up the audio file to play after all of the elements display on the slide. Save and then close **P-C7-CS-PCBuyGuide.pptx**.

Figure 7.6 Visual Benchmark

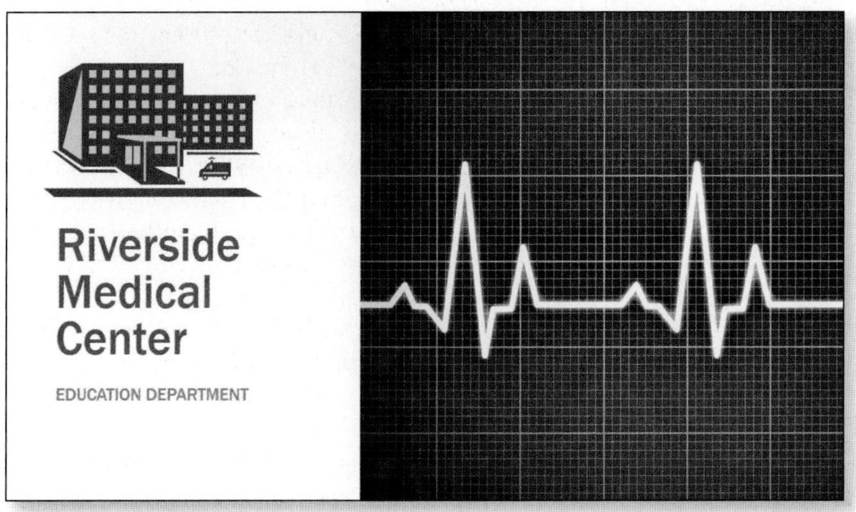

Education Development

- Current training courses
- Proposed training courses
- Course updates
- Staffing requirements
- Budgeting
- Future planning

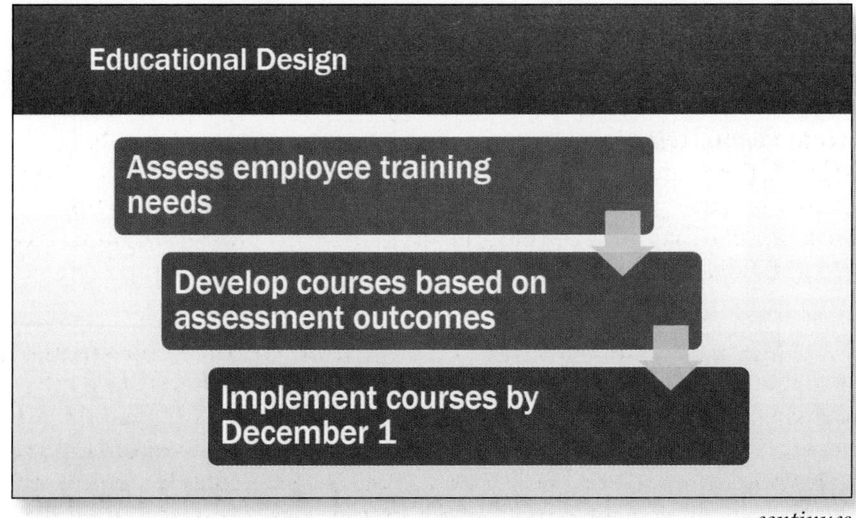

continues

Figure 7.6 Visual Benchmark—*continued*

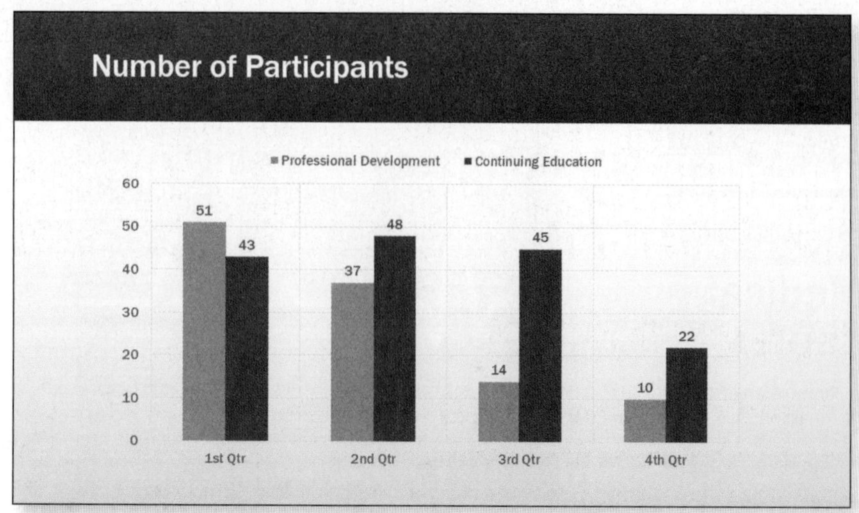

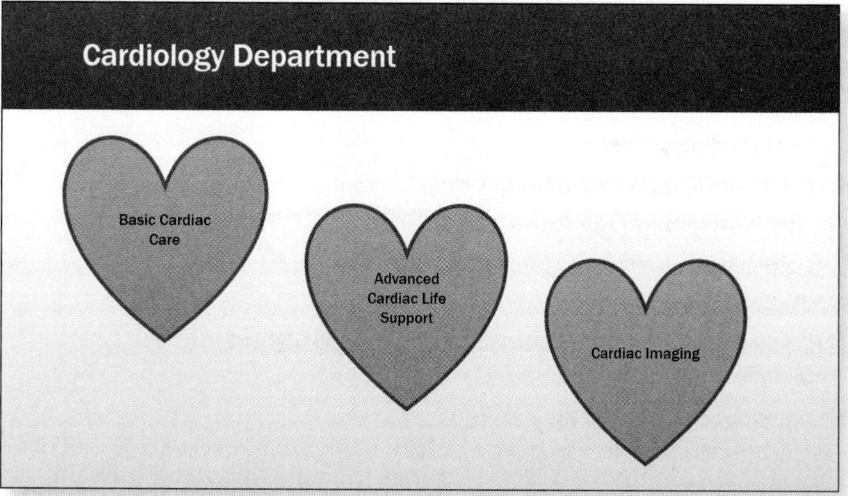

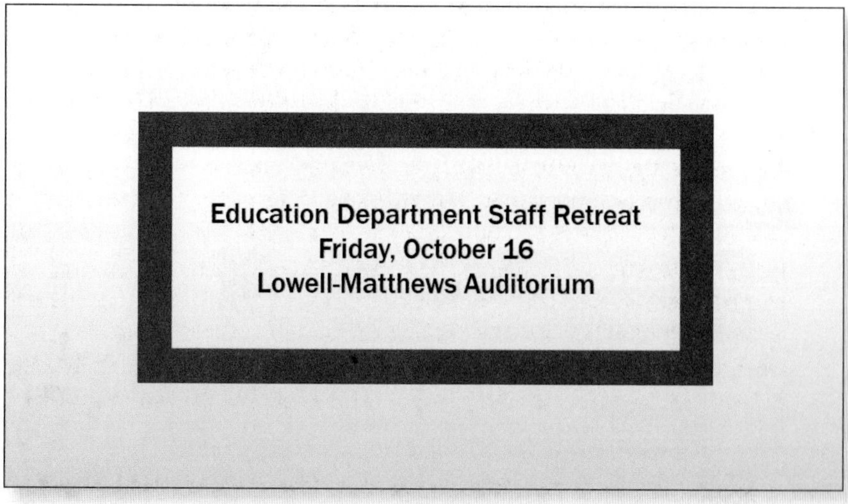

MICROSOFT® POWERPOINT®

CHAPTER 8

Integrating, Sharing, and Protecting Presentations

PERFORMANCE OBJECTIVES

Upon successful completion of Chapter 8, you will be able to:

- **Import a Word outline into a presentation**
- **Copy and paste data between programs and use the Clipboard**
- **Share presentations with others**
- **Export a presentation to Word**
- **Save a presentation in different file formats**
- **Embed and link objects**
- **Download templates**
- **Compare and combine presentations**
- **Insert, edit, and delete comments**
- **Manage presentation properties**
- **Protect a presentation**
- **Inspect a presentation and check for accessibility and compatibility issues**
- **Manage versions of presentations**
- **Customize PowerPoint options**

Tutorials

8.1 Integrating with Word and Excel

8.2 Exporting Presentations

8.3 Saving a Presentation in a Different Format

8.4 Embedding and Linking Objects

8.5 Downloading and Applying a Design Template

8.6 Comparing and Combining Presentations; Inserting and Deleting Comments

8.7 Managing Presentation Information and Properties

8.8 Customizing PowerPoint Options

Share data between programs in the Microsoft Office suite by importing and exporting data, copying and pasting data, copying and embedding data, or copying and linking data. The method you choose depends on how you use the data and whether the data is static or dynamic. Use options in the Share backstage area to share a presentation online or as an email attachment and use options at the Export backstage area to create a video or handout of a presentation and save a presentation in a variety of file formats. If you use PowerPoint in a collaborative environment, you may want to insert comments in a presentation and then share the presentation with others. Use options in the Info backstage area to manage presentation properties, password protect a presentation, insert a digital signature, inspect a presentation, and manage versions. In this chapter, you will learn how to complete these tasks as well as how to download design templates from Office.com. Model answers for this chapter's projects appear on the following pages.

Note: Before beginning the projects, copy to your storage medium the PC8 subfolder from the PowerPoint folder on the CD that accompanies this textbook and then make PC8 the active folder.

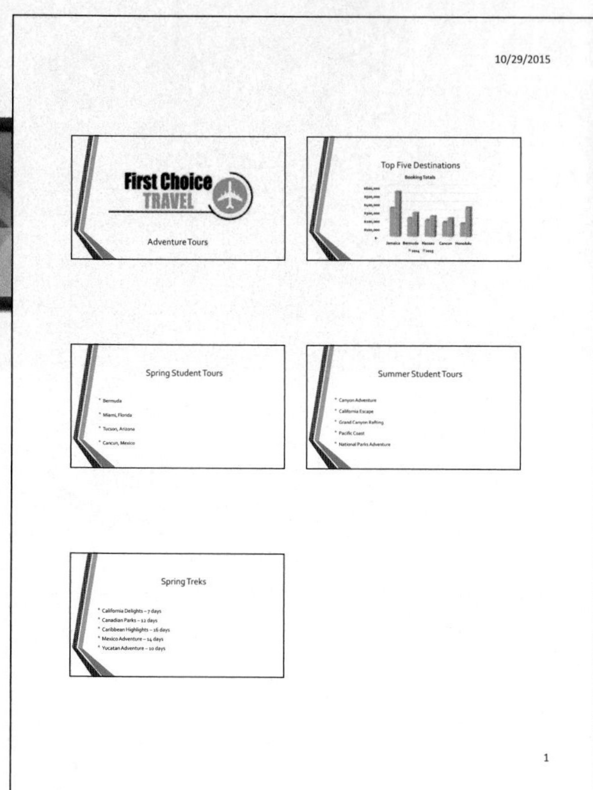

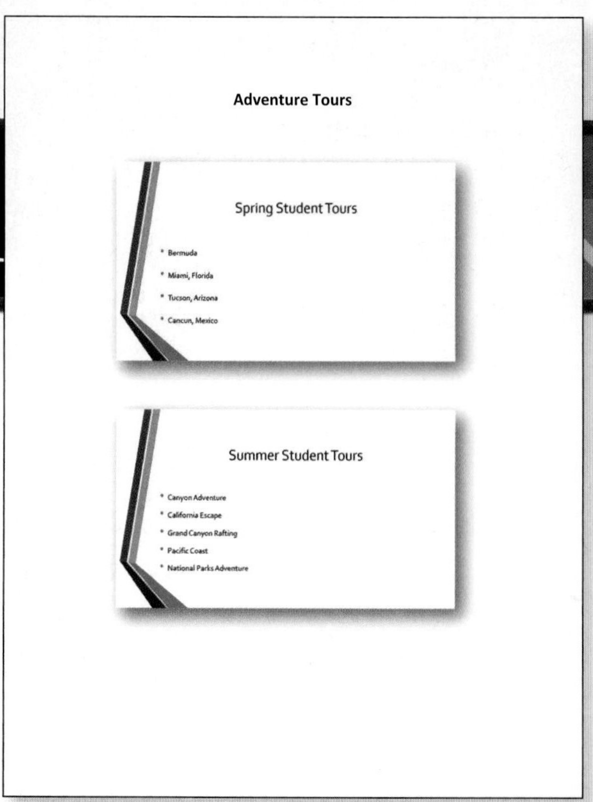

Project 1 Import a Word Outline, Save the Presentation in Different File Formats, and Copy and Paste Objects between Programs

P-C8-P1-ATTopFive.pptx

P-C8-P1-ATTours.docx

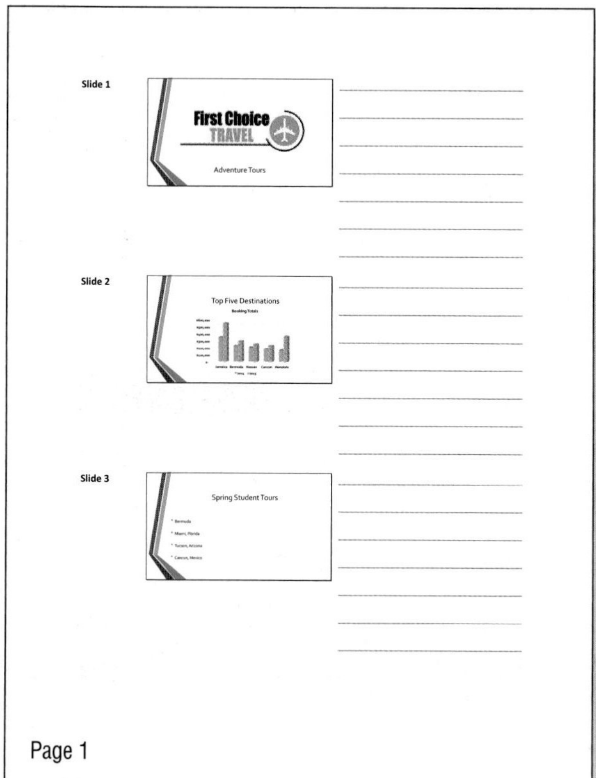

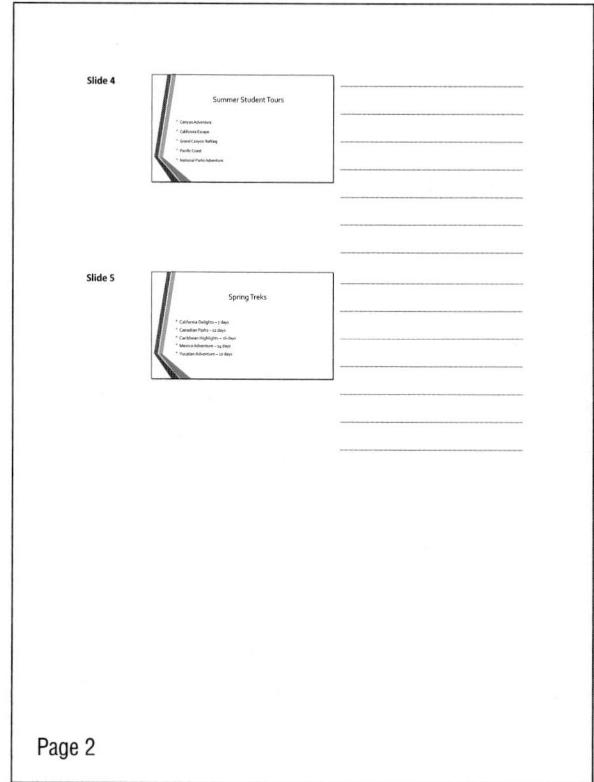

P-C8-P1-ATTopTours.docx

Model Answers

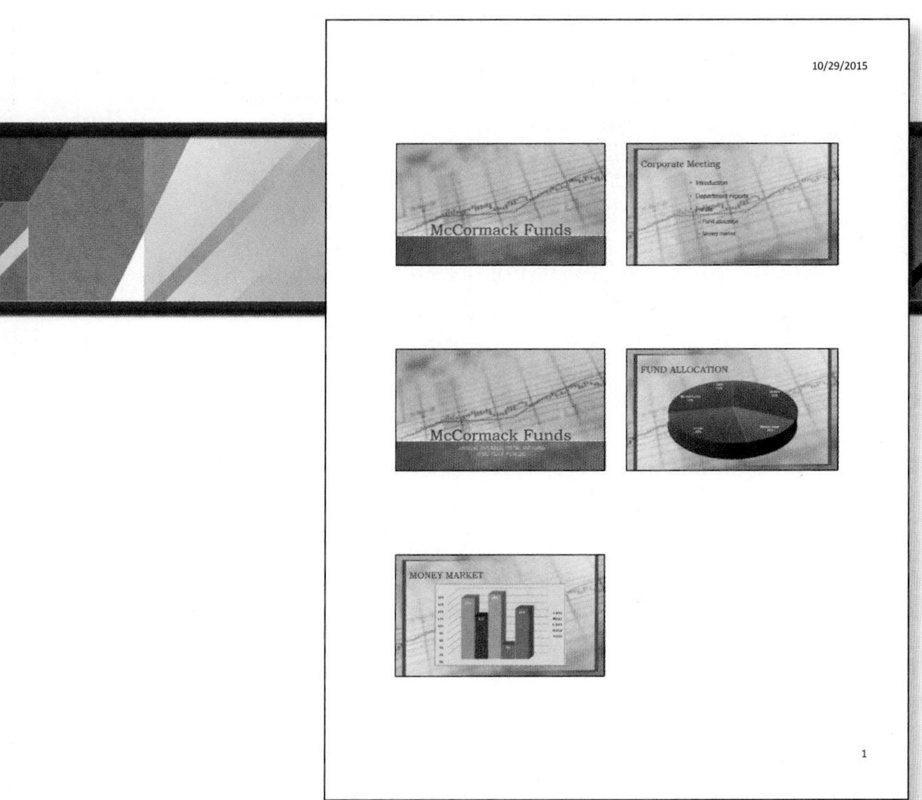

Project 2 Embed and Link Excel Charts to a Presentation

P-C8-P2-FundsPres.pptx

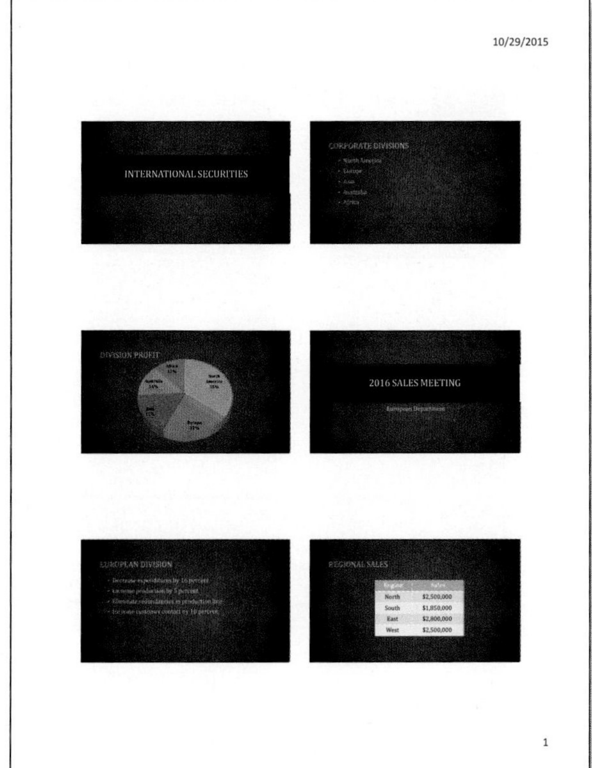

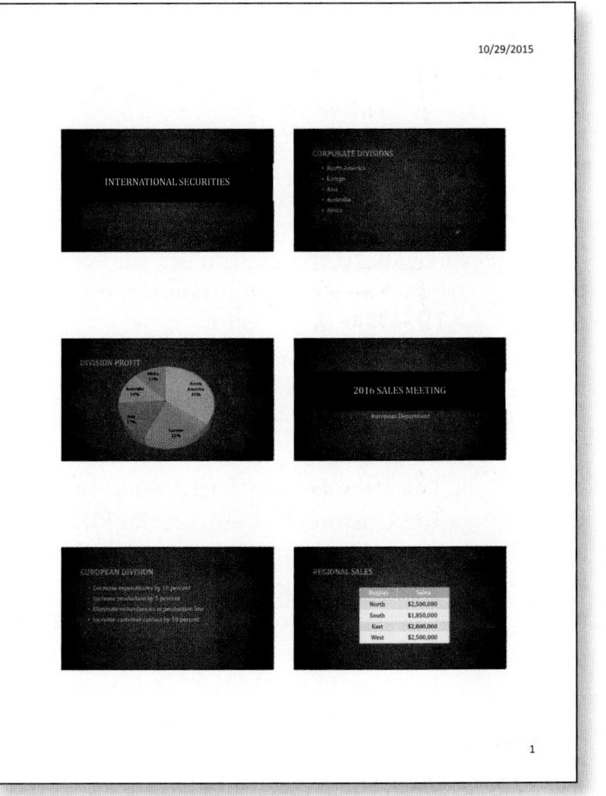

Project 3 Download and Apply a Design Template to a Presentation and Prepare a Presentation for Sharing

P-C8-P3-ISPres.pptx

Project  Import a Word Outline, Save the Presentation in Different File Formats, and Copy and Paste Objects between Programs

9 Parts

You will create a PowerPoint presentation using a Word document, save the presentation in different file formats, and then copy and paste an Excel chart and a Word table into slides in the presentation.

Importing a Word Outline

Quick Steps

Import a Word Outline
1. Open blank presentation.
2. Click New Slide button arrow.
3. Click *Slides from Outline.*
4. Double-click desired document.

You can import a Word document containing text formatted as an outline with heading styles into a PowerPoint presentation. Text formatted with a Heading 1 style becomes the title of a new slide. Text formatted with a Heading 2 style becomes first-level text, paragraphs formatted with a Heading 3 style become second-level text, and so on. To import a Word outline, open a blank presentation, click the New Slide button arrow in the Slides group on the HOME tab, and then click *Slides from Outline* at the drop-down list. At the Insert Outline dialog box, navigate to the folder containing the Word document and then double-click the document. If text in the Word document does not have heading styles applied, PowerPoint creates an outline based on each paragraph of text in the document.

Project 1a **Importing a Word Outline** **Part 1 of 9**

1. At a blank presentation, click the New Slide button arrow in the Slides group on the HOME tab and then click *Slides from Outline* at the drop-down list.
2. At the Insert Outline dialog box, navigate to the PC8 folder on your storage medium and then double-click ***ATTopFive.docx***.
3. Click the DESIGN tab and then apply the Parallax design theme.
4. Change the background by completing these steps:
   a. Click the Format Background button in the Customize group on the DESIGN tab.
   b. At the Format Background task pane, click the *Solid fill* option.
   c. Click the Color button and then click the *White, Background 1* option (first column, first row in the *Theme Colors* section).
   d. Click the Apply to All button.
   e. Close the task pane.
5. Delete Slide 1.

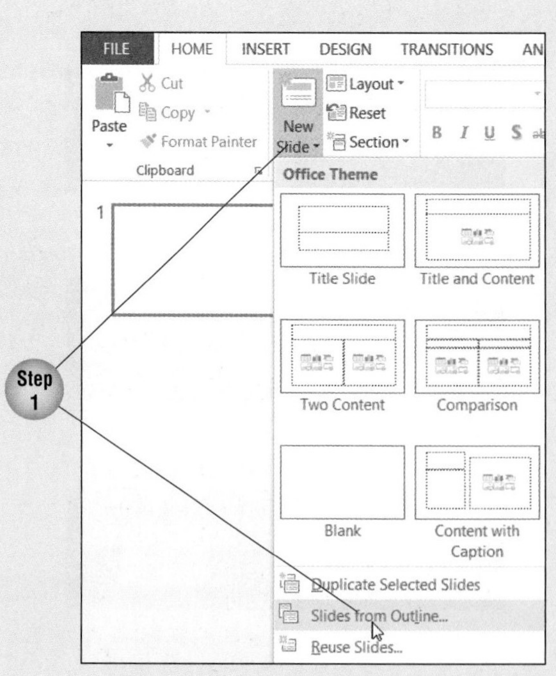

6. Format the new Slide 1 by completing the following steps:
   a. Change the slide layout by clicking the HOME tab, clicking the Layout button in the Slides group, and then clicking *Title Only* at the drop-down list.
   b. Drag the placeholder containing the text *Adventure Tours* toward the bottom of the slide and center it horizontally.
   c. Insert the **FCTLogo.jpg** located in the PC8 folder on your storage medium (do this with the Pictures button on the INSERT tab) and then increase the size of the logo so it fills a good portion of the white area of the slide.
7. Make Slide 2 active and then apply the Title Only layout.
8. Make Slide 3 active and then change the bulleted text line spacing to 2.0.
9. Make Slide 4 active and then change the bulleted text line spacing to 1.5.
10. Save the presentation and name it **P-C8-P1-ATTopFive**.

Copying and Pasting Data

Use the Copy and Paste buttons in the Clipboard group on the HOME tab to copy data such as text or an object from one program and then paste it into another program. For example, in Project 1b, you will copy an Excel chart and then paste it into a PowerPoint slide. You can move and size a copied object, such as a chart, like any other object.

Project 1b **Copying an Excel Chart to a PowerPoint Slide** **Part 2 of 9**

1. With **P-C8-P1-ATTopFive.pptx** open, make Slide 2 active.
2. Open Excel and then open **Top5Tours.xlsx**, located in the PC8 folder on your storage medium.
3. Click the chart to select it. (Make sure you select the chart and not just an element in the chart.)
4. Click the Copy button in the Clipboard group on the HOME tab.
5. Close **Top5Tours.xlsx** and then close Excel.
6. In PowerPoint, with Slide 2 active, click the Paste button in the Clipboard group on the HOME tab.
7. Move the chart so it is centered below the title *Top Five Destinations*.
8. Display Slide 1 in the slide pane and then run the presentation.
9. Print only Slide 2.
10. Save **P-C8-P1-ATTopFive.pptx**.

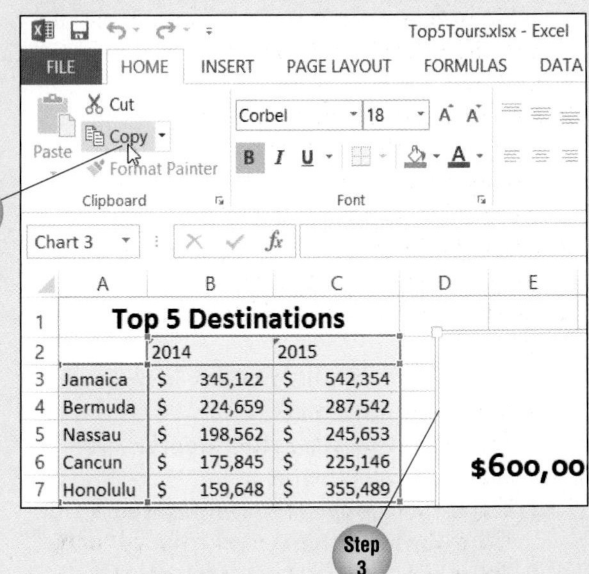

Click the Options button at the bottom of the Clipboard task pane to customize the display of the task pane.

Use the Clipboard task pane to collect and paste multiple items. You can collect up to 24 different items and then paste them in various locations. Turn on the display of the Clipboard task pane by clicking the Clipboard group task pane launcher. The Clipboard task pane displays at the left side of the screen.

Select data or an object you want to copy and then click the Copy button in the Clipboard group. Continue selecting text or items and clicking the Copy button. To insert an item, position the insertion point in the desired location and then click the button in the Clipboard task pane representing the item. If the copied item is text, the first 50 characters display. When all desired items are inserted, click the Clear All button to remove any remaining items from the Clipboard task pane. If you want to paste all items from the Clipboard task pane at once, click the Paste All button.

Project 1c Collecting and Pasting Text Between a Document and a Presentation — Part 3 of 9

1. With **P-C8-P1-ATTopFive.pptx** open, make Slide 4 active and then insert a new slide with the Title and Content layout.
2. Click the text *Click to add title* and then type **Spring Treks**.
3. Copy text from Word by completing the following steps:
   a. Open Word and then open **AdvTrek.docx**.
   b. Click the Clipboard group task pane launcher to display the Clipboard task pane.
   c. If any data displays in the Clipboard task pane, click the Clear All button located toward the top of the task pane.
   d. Select the text *Yucatan Adventure – 10 days* (including the paragraph mark following the text—consider turning on the display of nonprinting characters) and then click the Copy button in the Clipboard group.
   e. Select the text *Mexico Adventure – 14 days* and then click the Copy button.
   f. Select the text *Caribbean Highlights – 16 days* and then click the Copy button.
   g. Select the text *California Delights – 7 days* and then click the Copy button.
   h. Select the text *Canyon Adventure – 10 days* and then click the Copy button.
   i. Select the text *Canadian Parks – 12 days* and then click the Copy button.
   j. Select the text *Royal Canadian Adventure – 14 days* and then click the Copy button.
4. Click the PowerPoint button on the Taskbar and then paste items from the Clipboard task pane by completing the following steps:
   a. With Slide 5 active, click the text *Click to add text*.
   b. Click the Clipboard group task pane launcher to display the Clipboard task pane.
   c. Click the *California Delights* item in the Clipboard task pane.
   d. Click the *Canadian Parks* item in the Clipboard task pane.
   e. Click the *Caribbean Highlights* item in the Clipboard task pane.
   f. Click the *Mexico Adventure* item in the Clipboard task pane
   g. Click the *Yucatan Adventure* item in the Clipboard task pane. (Press the Backspace key twice to remove the bullet below *Yucatan Adventure* and the blank line.)

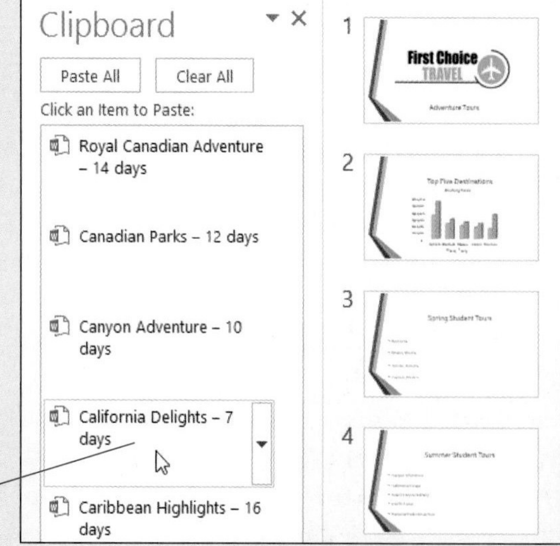

5. Clear the Clipboard task pane by clicking the Clear All button located in the upper right corner of the task pane.
6. Close the Clipboard task pane by clicking the Close button (contains an *X*) located in the upper right corner of the task pane.
7. Make Slide 1 the active slide and then run the presentation.
8. Print the presentation as a handout with all slides printed horizontally on one page. (Make sure the first gallery in the *Settings* category displays as *Print All Slides*.)
9. Save **P-C8-P1-ATTopFive.pptx**.
10. Make Word the active program, close the Clipboard task pane, close **AdvTrek.docx**, and then close Word.

Sharing Presentations

PowerPoint provides a number of options for sharing presentations between programs, sites on the Internet, other computers, and as attachments. Options for sending and sharing presentations are available at the Share backstage area. Display this view by clicking the FILE tab and then clicking the *Share* option.

With the *Invite People* option at the Share backstage area, you can invite people to view your presentation. To use this feature, your PowerPoint presentation must be saved to your OneDrive or a shared location such as a website or SharePoint library. (Microsoft SharePoint is a collection of products and software that includes a number of components. If your company or organization uses SharePoint, you can save a presentation in a library on your organization's SharePoint site so that you and your colleagues have a central location for accessing presentations.) If you have a PowerPoint presentation open from your OneDrive folder (or other shared location), the Share backstage area with the *Invite People* option selected will display, as shown in Figure 8.1. If you have a presentation open that is not saved to your OneDrive folder, the information at the right side of the backstage area will tell you to save your presentation. To do this, click the Save To Cloud button and, at the Save As backstage area, click your OneDrive and then click the Browse button. At the Save As dialog box, navigate to your OneDrive folder, and then click the Save button. In a few moments, the Share backstage area redisplays with the options shown in Figure 8.1.

When you click the *Invite People* option at the Share backstage area, options display for typing the names or email addresses of people you want to view and/or edit the presentation. Type more than one name or email address by separating the names or email addresses with a semicolon.

The option box to the right of the *Type names or e-mail addresses* text box contains the default setting *Can edit*. At this setting, the people you invite can edit the presentation. Change this option to *Can view* if you want the people you invite only to view the presentation. When all names or email addresses are entered, click the Share button. An email is sent to the email address(es) you typed and, in a few moments, the name or names display in the backstage area below the *Shared with* heading. Any time you open the presentation in the future and display the Share backstage area, the names you shared the presentation with will display below the *Shared with* heading. If you want to stop sharing the presentation with a person, right-click the person's name below the *Shared with* heading and then click *Remove User* at the shortcut menu.

Figure 8.1 Share Backstage Area with *Invite People* Option Selected

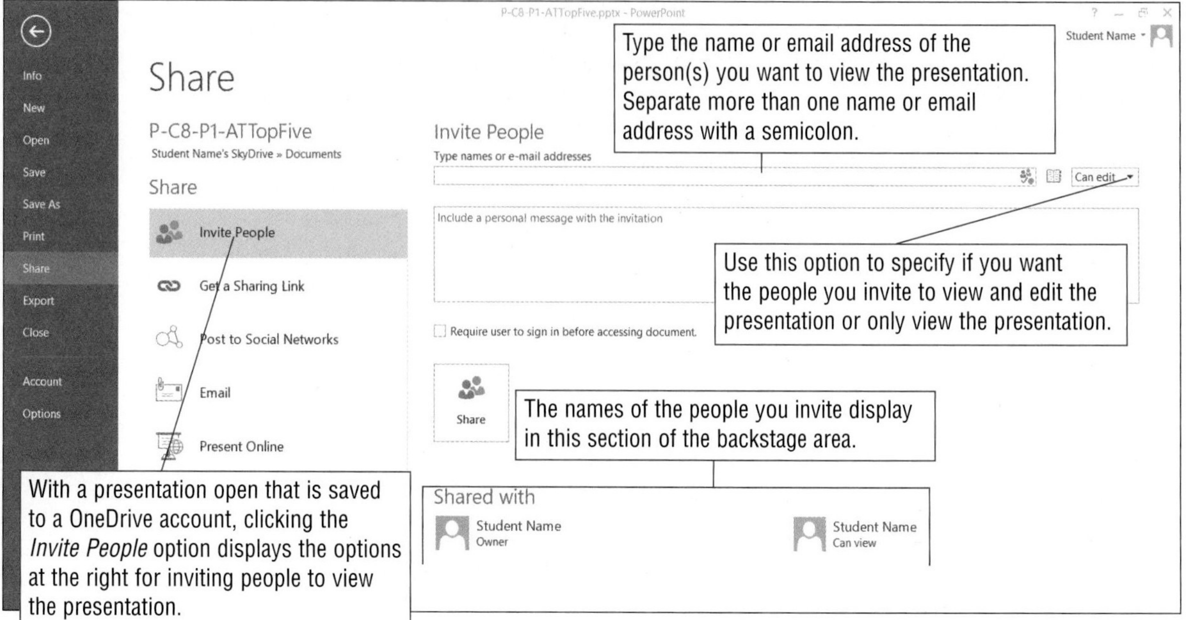

Project 1d Optional: Inviting People to View your Presentation — Part 4 of 9

Note: To complete this project, you need to have a OneDrive account.

1. With **P-C8-P1-ATTopFive.pptx** open, save the presentation to your OneDrive folder and name it **P-C8-P1-ATTopFive-Shared**.
2. With the **P-C8-P1-ATTopFive-Shared.pptx** presentation open, click the FILE tab and then click the *Share* option.
3. At the Share backstage area, click in the *Type names or e-mail addresses* text box.
4. Type the email address for your instructor and/or the email address of a classmate or friend.
5. Click the down-pointing arrow at the right side of the option box containing the text *Can edit* and then click *Can view* at the drop-down list.
6. Click the Share button.
7. After a few moments, notice the name(s) that display below the *Shared with* heading in the Share backstage area.
8. Check with your instructor, classmate, and/or friend to see if they were able to open the email containing the link to your PowerPoint presentation.
9. Remove the name (or one of the names) that displays below the *Shared with* heading by right-clicking the name and then clicking *Remove User* at the shortcut menu.
10. If you have the **P-C8-P1-ATTopFive.pptx** presentation saved on a removable device, close the **P-C8-P1-ATTopFive-Shared.pptx** presentation saved to your OneDrive and then reopen the **P-C8-P1-ATTopFive.pptx** presentation from your removable device.

Step 4 — Step 5 — Step 6

If you open a presentation saved to your)neDrive, the Share backstage area displays additional options including *Get a Sharing Link* and *Post to Social Networks*. Click *Get a Sharing Link* and options display for creating a link for viewing or for editing. Click the Create Link button that displays to the right of the *View Link* text box and a link displays for viewing the presentation. Click the Create Link button to the right of the *Edit Link* text box and a link displays in the text box for viewing and editing the presentation. If you want to paste a link for viewing your presentation without the ability to edit, select the link that displays in the *View Link* text box and then paste it in an email, instant message, social media site, and so on. If you want to paste a link for viewing and editing, click the Create Link button to the right of the *Edit Link* text box and then copy the link that displays.

Click the *Post to Social Networks* options to connect to and post your presentation to a social network such as Facebook or Twitter. Before being able to post, you must connect to the desired social network(s). If you are not connected, click the *Post to Social Networks* option and then click the Click here to connect social networks hyperlink.

Click the *Email* option at the Share backstage area and options display for sending a copy of the presentation as an attachment to an email, send a link to the presentation, attach a PDF or XPS copy of the open presentation to an email address, and send an email as an Internet fax.

To send the presentation as an attachment, you need to set up an Outlook email account. If you want to create an email that contains a link to the presentation, the presentation must be saved to your OneDrive or a shared location such as a website or SharePoint library.

Click the Send as PDF button and your presentation is converted to the PDF format and attached to the email. The letters PDF stand for *portable document format*, which is a file format developed by Adobe Systems that captures all of the elements of a presentation as an electronic image. Click the Send as XPS button and your presentation is converted to the XPS format and attached to the email. The XPS format is a Microsoft file format for publishing content in an easily viewable format. The letters XPS stand for *XML paper specification*, and the letters XML stand for *extensible markup language*, which is a set of rules for encoding presentations electronically. Information displays to the right of both buttons providing a brief description of the format.

Click the Send as Internet Fax button to fax the current presentation without using a fax machine. To use this button, you must be signed up with a fax service provider. If you have not previously signed up for a service, you will be prompted to do so.

Click the *Present Online* option at the Share backstage area, to present your presentation through the Office Presentation Service. You learned how to do this in Chapter 7.

Use the *Publish Slides* option at the Share backstage area to save slides in a shared location such as a slide library or a SharePoint site so that other people have access to the presentation and can review or make changes to it.

Project 1e Optional: Sending a Presentation as an Email Attachment Part 5 of 9

Note: Before completing this optional project, check with your instructor to determine if you have Outlook set up as your email provider.

1. With **P-C8-P1-ATTopFive.pptx** open, click the FILE tab and then click the *Share* option.
2. At the Share backstage area, click the *Email* option and then click the Send as Attachment button.
3. At the Outlook window, type your instructor's email address in the *To* text box.
4. Click the Send button.

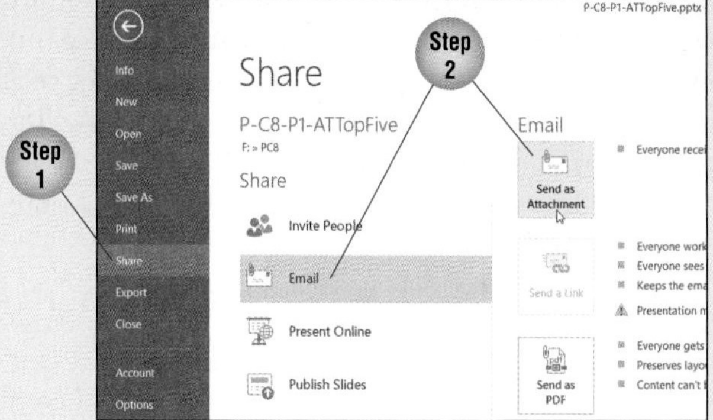

Exporting Presentations

The Export backstage area contains a number of options for saving and exporting a presentation. Options at the Export backstage area include saving a presentation in the PDF or XPS file format, creating a video of a presentation, packaging a presentation for a disc, creating handouts, and saving a presentation in a different file format.

Quick Steps
Save a Presentation in PDF/XPS Format
1. Open presentation.
2. Click FILE tab.
3. Click *Export* option.
4. Click *Create PDF/XPS Document* option.
5. Click Create PDF/XPS button.
6. At Publish as PDF or XPS dialog box, specify if you want to save in PDF or XPS format.
7. Click Publish button.

Saving a Presentation in the PDF or XPS Formats

As you learned earlier, the portable document format (PDF) captures all of the elements of a presentation as an electronic image and the XPS format is used for publishing content in an easily viewable format. To save a presentation in PDF or XPS format, click the FILE tab, click the *Export* option, make sure the *Create PDF/XPS Document* option is selected, and then click the Create PDF/XPS button. This displays the Publish as PDF or XPS dialog box with the *PDF (*.pdf)* option selected in the *Save as type* option box. If you want to save the presentation in XPS format, click the *Save as type* option box and then click *XPS Document (*.xps)* at the drop-down list. At the Save As dialog box, type a name in the *File name* text box and then click the Publish button.

You can open a PDF file in Adobe Reader, Internet Explorer, Microsoft Word, and Windows Reader. You can open an XPS file in Internet Explorer, Windows Reader, and XPS Viewer. One method for opening a PDF or XPS file is to open File Explorer, navigate to the folder containing the file, right-click on the file, and then point to *Open with*. This displays a side menu with the programs you can choose to open the file.

Quick Steps
Save a Presentation as a Video
1. Open presentation.
2. Click FILE tab.
3. Click *Export* option.
4. Click *Create a Video* option.
5. Click Create Video button.

Creating a Video of a Presentation

Create a video that incorporates all of a presentation's recorded timings and narrations and preserves animations and transitions using the *Create a Video* option. The information at the right side of the Export backstage area describes creating a video and provides a hyperlink to get help on burning a slide show video to a DVD or uploading it to the Web. Click the Get help burning your slide show video to DVD or uploading it to the Web hyperlink and information displays on burning your slide show video to disc and publishing your slide show video to YouTube.

Packaging a Presentation

Use the *Package Presentation for CD* option to copy a presentation and include all of the linked files, embedded items, and fonts. Click the *Package Presentation for CD* option and then click the Package for CD button and the Package for CD dialog box displays. At this dialog box, type a name for the CD and specify the files you want copied. You can copy the presentation to a CD or to a specific folder.

Quick Steps

Package a Presentation for CD
1. Open presentation.
2. Click FILE tab.
3. Click *Export* option.
4. Click *Package Presentation for CD* option.
5. Click Package for CD button.
6. Click Copy to CD button or Copy to Folder button.

Project 1f **Saving a Presentation in PDF and XPS Formats, as a Video, and Packaged for a CD** **Part 6 of 9**

1. With **P-C8-P1-ATTopFive.pptx** open, save the presentation in PDF format by completing the following steps:
   a. Click the FILE tab and then click the *Export* option.
   b. Make sure the *Create PDF/XPS Document* option is selected.
   c. Click the Create PDF/XPS button.
   d. At the Publish as PDF or XPS dialog box, make sure the *Save as type* option is set at *PDF (*.pdf)*, insert a check mark in the *Open file after publishing* check box and then click the Publish button. (In a few moments the presentation displays in PDF format in Adobe Reader.)
   e. Scroll through the presentation in Adobe Reader.
   f. Click the Close button located in the upper right corner of the window to close Adobe Reader.

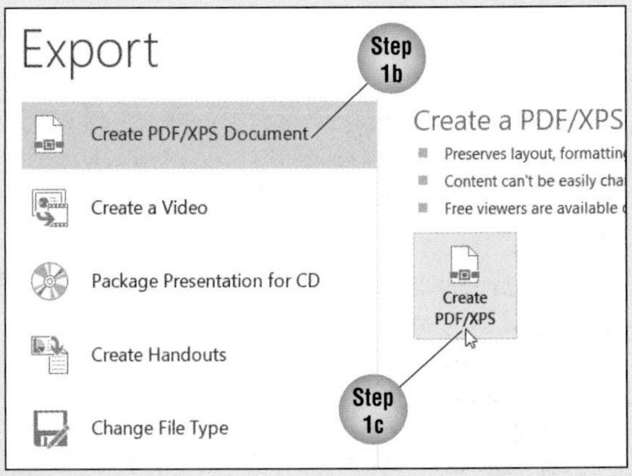

2. Save the presentation in XPS format by completing the following steps:
   a. Click the FILE tab and then click the *Export* option.
   b. With the *Create PDF/XPS Document* option selected, click the Create PDF/XPS button.
   c. At the Publish as PDF or XPS dialog box, click the *Save as type* option box and then click *XPS Document (*.xps)* at the drop-down list.
   d. Make sure the *Open file after publishing* check box contains a check mark and then click the Publish button. (In a few moments the presentation displays in the XPS Viewer.)
   e. Scroll through the presentation in the XPS Viewer.
   f. Close the XPS viewer by positioning the mouse pointer at the top of the screen (the pointer turns into a hand), dragging down to the bottom of the screen, and then releasing the mouse button.

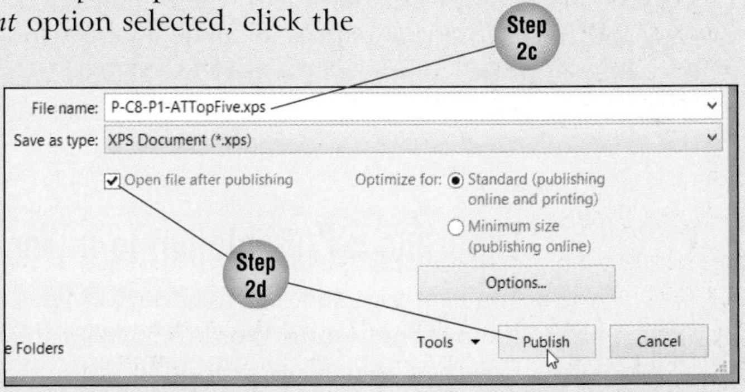

3. Save **P-C8-P1-ATTopFive.pptx** as a video by completing the following steps:
   a. Click the FILE tab and then click the *Export* option.
   b. Click the *Create a Video* option.
   c. Click the Create Video button.
   d. At the Save As dialog box, click the Save button. (Saving as a video takes a minute or so. The Status bar displays the saving progress.)
4. When the video has been saved, play the video by completing the following steps:
   a. Click the File Explorer button on the Taskbar.
   b. Navigate to the PC8 folder on your storage medium and then double-click ***P-C8-P1-ATTopFive.mp4***. (This opens the presentation video in a viewing window.)
   c. Watch the presentation video and, when it is finished, close the viewing window by using the mouse and dragging down from the top of the screen to the bottom.
   d. Close File Explorer.
5. With **P-C8-P1-ATTopFive.pptx** open, package the presentation by completing the following steps:
   a. Click the FILE tab and then click the *Export* option.
   b. Click the *Package Presentation for CD* option.
   c. Click the Package for CD button.
   d. At the Package for CD dialog box, select the text in the *Name the CD* text box and type ATTopFiveforCD.
   e. Click the Options button, at the Options dialog box make sure the Embedded TrueType fonts option includes a check mark, and then click OK.
   f. Click the Copy to Folder button.
   g. At the Copy to Folder dialog box, click the Browse button.
   h. Navigate to the PC8 folder on your storage medium.
   i. Click the Select button.
   j. At the Copy to Folder dialog box, click OK.
   k. At the message asking if you want to include linked files in the presentation, click the Yes button.
   l. When a window displays with the folder name and files, close the window by clicking the Close button in the upper right corner of the window.
   m. Close the Package for CD dialog box by clicking the Close button.

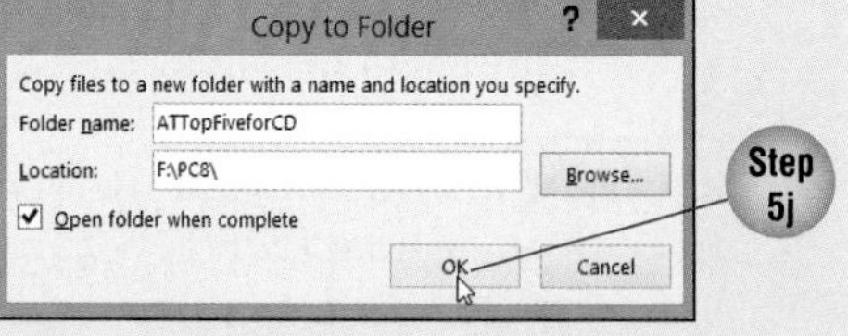

Exporting a Presentation to a Word Document

HINT Export a presentation to Word to gain greater control over formatting handouts.

You can print slides as handouts in PowerPoint; however, you may prefer to export the presentation to Word to have greater control over the formatting of the handouts. Use the *Create Handouts* option at the Export backstage area to export a PowerPoint presentation to a Word document. Open the presentation, click the FILE tab, click the *Export* option, click the *Create Handouts* option, and then click the Create Handouts button. This displays the Send to Microsoft Word dialog box, shown in Figure 8.3. At this dialog box, select the page layout you want to use in Word and then click OK.

The first four-page layout options will export slides as they appear in PowerPoint with lines to the right or below the slides. The last option will export the text only as an outline. If you select the *Paste link* option, the Word document will be automatically updated whenever changes are made to the PowerPoint presentation.

Figure 8.3 Send to Microsoft Word Dialog Box

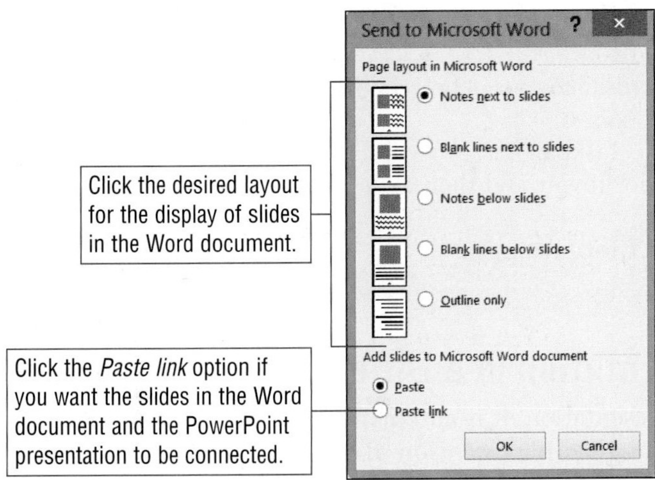

Exporting a Presentation to Word **Part 7 of 9**

1. Make sure **P-C8-P1-ATTopFive.pptx** is open, click the FILE tab, and then click the *Export* option.
2. At the Export backstage area, click the *Create Handouts* option.
3. Click the Create Handouts button.
4. At the Send to Microsoft Word dialog box, click the *Blank lines next to slides* option and then click OK.
5. Click the Word button on the Taskbar.
6. In Word, select the first column (the column that contains *Slide 1*, *Slide 2*, and so on) and then turn on bold formatting. (The presentation was inserted in a table in Word.)

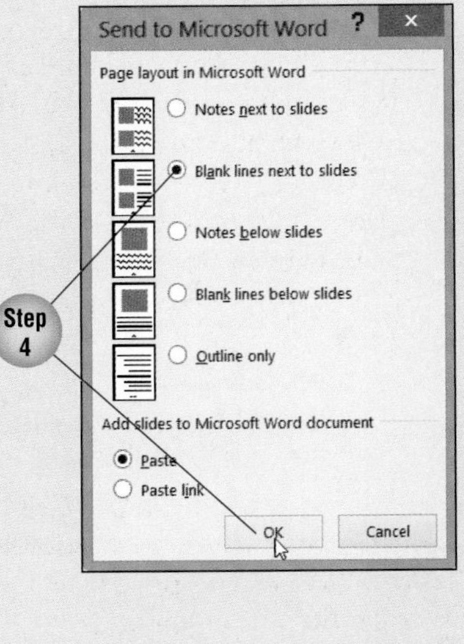

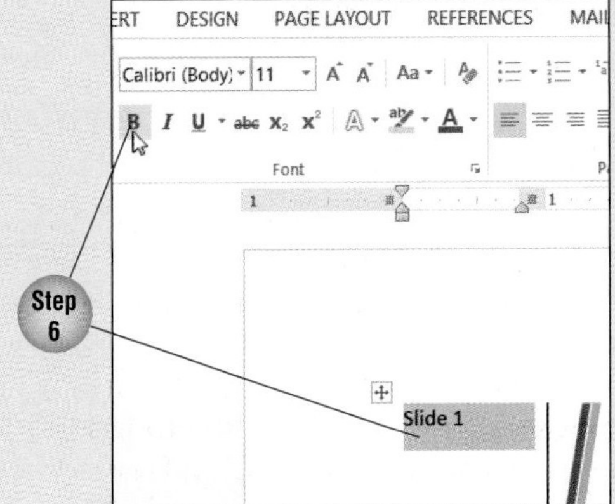

7. Select the third column (contains the lines) and then apply the Red font color.
8. Save the document and name it **P-C8-P1-ATTopTours**.
9. Print and then close **P-C8-P1-ATTopTours.docx**.
10. Close Word.
11. In PowerPoint, export **P-C8-P1-ATTopFive.pptx** as an outline by completing the following steps:
    a. Click the FILE tab and then click the *Export* option.
    b. At the Export backstage area, click the *Create Handouts* option.
    c. Click the Create Handouts button.
    d. At the Send to Microsoft Word dialog box, click the *Outline only* option and then click OK.
    e. Click the Word button on the Taskbar.
    f. In Word, scroll through the document and then close Word without saving the document.
12. In PowerPoint, save **P-C8-P1-ATTopFive.pptx**.

Saving a Presentation in a Different Format

When you save a presentation, it is automatically saved as a PowerPoint presentation with the .pptx file extension. If you need to share a presentation with someone who is using a different presentation program or a different version of PowerPoint, you may want to save the presentation in another format. At the Export backstage area, click the *Change File Type* option and the backstage area displays as shown in Figure 8.2.

Figure 8.2 Export Backstage Area with *Change File Type* Option Selected

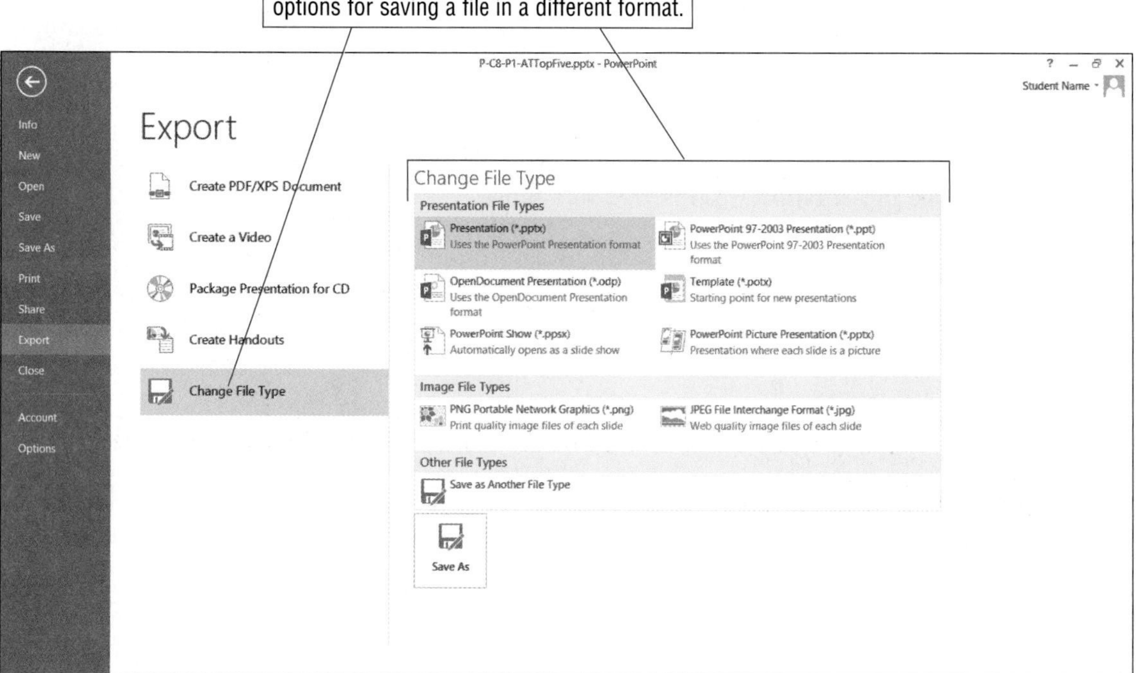

With options in the *Presentation File Types* section, you can choose to save a PowerPoint presentation with the default file format (.pptx) or to save a presentation in a previous version of PowerPoint. Use the *OpenDocument Presentation (*.odp)* option to save a presentation and make it available to open in other applications. The OpenDocument format enables files to be exchanged, retrieved, and edited with any OpenDocument-compliant software. Save a presentation as a template if you want to use the presentation as a basis for creating other presentations. (You learned how to do this at the Save As dialog box in Chapter 6.) If you save a presentation in the PowerPoint Show (*.ppsx) format, the presentation automatically starts when you open it. This might be useful, for example, in a situation where you email a presentation to a colleague or client and you want the presentation to automatically start when opened. When you save a presentation using the *PowerPoint Picture Presentation* option, the contents of the presentation are flattened to a single picture per slide. A presentation saved in this format can be opened and viewed but not edited.

Quick Steps

Save a Presentation in a Different Format

1. Click FILE tab.
2. Click *Export* option.
3. Click *Change File Type* option.
4. Click desired format.
5. Click Save As button.

Project 1h Saving a Presentation in Different Formats — Part 8 of 9

1. Make sure that **P-C8-P1-ATTopFive.pptx** is open.
2. Save the presentation as a PowerPoint Show by completing the following steps:
   a. Click the FILE tab and then click the *Export* option.
   b. At the Export backstage area, click the *Change File Type* option.
   c. Click the *PowerPoint Show (*.ppsx)* option in the *Presentation File Types* section and then click the Save As button.

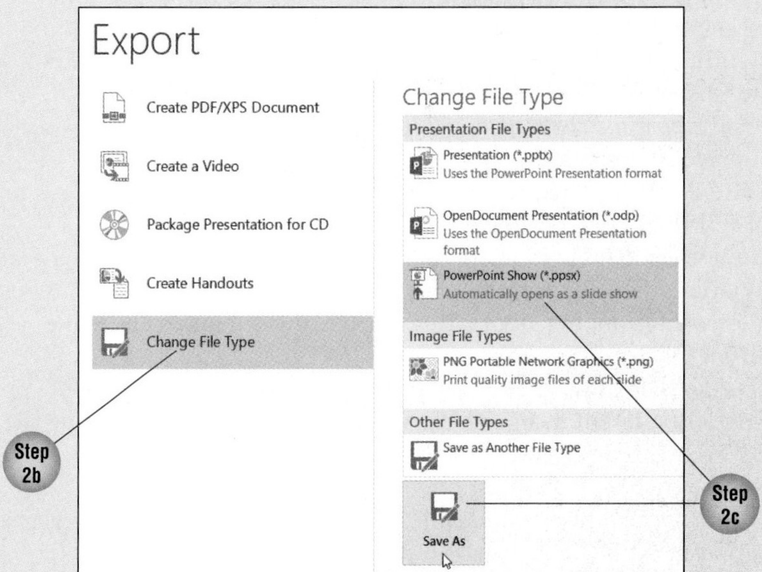

   d. At the Save As dialog box, click the Save button. (This saves the presentation with the file extension *.ppsx*.)
3. Close **P-C8-P1-ATTopFive.ppsx**.

4. Open the **P-C8-P1-ATTopFive.ppsx** file in File Explorer by completing the following steps:
   a. Click the File Explorer button (button containing yellow file folders) on the Taskbar.
   b. In File Explorer, double-click the drive representing your storage medium.
   c. Navigate to the PC8 folder on your storage medium and then double-click ***P-C8-P1-ATTopFive.ppsx***. (This starts the presentation in Slide Show view.)
   d. Run the presentation.
   e. When the presentation has ended, click the left mouse button.
   f. Close File Explorer by clicking the File Explorer button on the Taskbar and then clicking the Close button located in the upper right corner of the window.
5. Open **P-C8-P1-ATTopFive.pptx** (make sure you open the file with the .pptx file extension) and then save the presentation in a previous version of PowerPoint by completing the following steps:
   a. Click the FILE tab and then click the *Export* option.
   b. Click the *Change File Type* option.
   c. Click *PowerPoint 97-2003 Presentation (*.ppt)* in the *Presentation File Types* section and then click the Save As button.
   d. At the Save As dialog box, type **P-C8-P1-ATTopFive-2003format** in the *File name* text box and then click the Save button.
   e. At the Microsoft PowerPoint Compatibility Checker dialog box, click the Continue button.
   f. At the presentation, notice that the file name at the top of the screen displays followed by the words *[Compatibility Mode]*.
6. Close **P-C8-P1-ATTopFive-2003format.ppt**.
7. Open **P-C8-P1-ATTopFive.pptx** (make sure you open the file with the .pptx file extension) and then save the presentation in OpenDocument Presentation format by completing the following steps:
   a. Click the FILE tab and then click the *Export* option.
   b. Click the *Change File Type* option.
   c. Click *OpenDocument Presentation (*.odp)* in the *Presentation File Types* section and then click the Save As button.
   d. At the Save As dialog box, make sure *P-C8-P1-ATTopFive.odp* displays in the *File name* text box and then click the Save button.
   e. When a message displays stating that the presentation may contain features that are not compatible with the format, click the Yes button.
   f. Run the presentation and notice that formatting remained the same.
8. Close **P-C8-P1-ATTopFive.odp**.
9. Open **P-C8-P1-ATTopFive.pptx** (make sure you open the file with the .pptx file extension) and then save the presentation as a picture presentation by completing the following steps:
   a. Click the FILE tab and then click the *Export* option.
   b. Click the *Change File Type* option.
   c. Click *PowerPoint Picture Presentation (*.pptx)* in the *Presentation File Types* section and then click the Save As button.
   d. At the Save As dialog box, type **P-C8-P1-ATTopFive-Picture** in the *File name* text box and then click the Save button.
   e. At a message telling you that a copy of the presentation has been saved, click OK.
   f. Close **P-C8-P1-ATTopFive.pptx**.
   g. Open **P-C8-P1-ATTopFive-Picture.pptx**.
   h. Click Slide 1 in the slide pane and notice how the entire slide is selected rather than a specific element in the slide. In this format you cannot edit a slide.
10. Close **P-C8-P1-ATTopFive-Picture.pptx**.

Save slides in a presentation as graphic images in PNG or JPEG format with options in the *Image File Types* section of the Export backstage area. Save slides as PNG images if you want print quality, and save slides as JPEG images if you are going to post the slide images to the Internet. To save a slide or all slides as graphic images, click either the *PNG Portable Network Graphics (*.png)* option or the *JPEG File Interchange Format (*.jpg)* option in the *Image File Types* section and then click the Save As button. At the Save As dialog box, type a name for the slide or presentation and then click the Save button. At the message that displays, click the All Slides button if you want every slide in the presentation saved as a graphic image or click the Just This One button if you want only the current slide saved as a graphic image. If you click the All Slides button, a message displays telling you that all slides in the presentation were saved as separate files in a folder. The name of the folder is the name that you type in the *File name* text box in the Save As dialog box.

Project 1i Saving Slides as Graphic Images

Part 9 of 9

1. Open **P-C8-P1-ATTopFive.pptx**.
2. Click the FILE tab and then click the *Export* option.
3. At the Export backstage area, click the *Change File Type* option.
4. Click the *PNG Portable Network Graphics (*.png)* option in the *Image File Types* section and then click the Save As button.
5. At the Save As dialog box, make sure **P-C8-P1-ATTopFive.png** displays in the *File name* text box and then click the Save button.
6. At the message that displays, click the All Slides button.
7. At the message telling you that each slide has been saved as a separate file in the P-C8-P1-ATTopFive.png folder, click OK.
8. Open Word.
9. At a blank document, change the font size to 18 points, turn on bold formatting, change the alignment to center, and then type **Adventure Tours**.
10. Press the Enter key twice and then insert one of the slides saved in PNG format by completing the following steps:
    a. Click the INSERT tab and then click the Pictures button in the Illustrations group.
    b. At the Insert Picture dialog box, navigate to the P-C8-P1-ATTopFive folder in the PC8 folder on your storage medium and then double-click ***Slide3.PNG***.

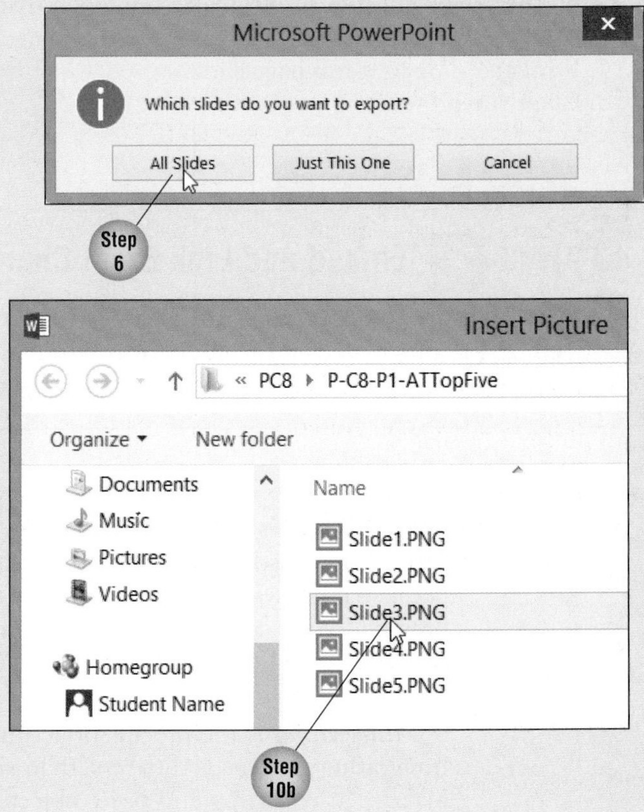

11. Format the image in the document by completing the following steps:
    a. Click in the *Shape Height* measurement box in the Size group on the PICTURE TOOLS FORMAT tab, type 2.8, and then press Enter.
    b. Click the *Drop Shadow Rectangle* option in the Picture Styles group (fourth thumbnail).
12. Press Ctrl + End to move the insertion point to the end of the document, press the Enter key, and then complete steps similar to those in Steps 10 and 11 to insert and format the image *Slide4.PNG* in the document.
13. Save the document and name it **P-C8-P1-ATTours**.
14. Print and then close **P-C8-P1-ATTours.docx**.
15. Close Word.
16. Capture an image of the Open dialog box and insert the image in a PowerPoint slide by completingthe following steps:
    a. Press Ctrl + N to display a new blank presentation.
    b. Click the Layout button in the Slides group on the HOME tab and then click *Blank* at the drop-down list.
    c. Press Ctrl + F12 to display the Open dialog box.
    d. At the Open dialog box, navigate to the PC8 folder on your storage medium.
    e. Click the option button that displays at the right side of the *File name* text box (option button that contains the text All PowerPoint Presentations) and then click *All Files (*.*)* at the drop-down list.
    f. Make sure all of your project files display. You may need to scroll down the list box to display the files.
    g. Hold down the Alt key and then press the Print Screen button on your keyboard. (This captures an image of the Open dialog box and not the entire screen.)
    h. Click the Cancel button to close the Open dialog box.
    i. Click the Paste button. (This inserts the image of the Open dialog box into the slide.)
17. Print the slide as a full page slide.
18. Close the presentation without saving it and then close **P-C8-P1-ATTopFive.pptx**.

Project 2 Embed and Link Excel Charts to a Presentation — 3 Parts

You will open a company funds presentation and then copy an Excel pie chart and embed it in a PowerPoint slide. You will also copy and link an Excel column chart to a slide and then update the chart in Excel.

Embedding and Linking Objects

One of the reasons the Microsoft Office suite is used extensively in business is because it allows data from one program to be seamlessly integrated into another program. For example, a chart depicting sales projections created in Excel can easily be added to a slide in a PowerPoint presentation to the company board of directors on the new budget forecast.

Integration is the process of adding content from other sources to a file. Integrating content is different than simply copying and pasting it. While it makes sense to copy and paste objects from one application to another when the content is not likely to change, if the content is dynamic, the copy and paste method becomes problematic and inefficient. To illustrate this point, assume one of the outcomes from the presentation to the board of directors is a revision to the sales projections, which means that the chart originally created in Excel has to be updated to reflect the new projections. If the first version of the chart was copied and pasted into PowerPoint, it would need to be deleted and then the revised chart in Excel would need to be copied and pasted into the slide again. Both Excel and PowerPoint would need to be opened and edited to reflect this change in projection. In this case, copying and pasting the chart would not be efficient.

To eliminate the inefficiency of the copy and paste method, you can integrate objects between programs. An ***object*** can be text in a presentation, data in a table, a chart, a picture, a slide, or any combination of data that you would like to share between programs. The program that was used to create the object is called the ***source*** and the program the object is linked or embedded to is called the ***destination***.

Embedding and linking are two methods you can use to integrate data in addition to the copy and paste method. When an object is embedded, the content in the object is stored in both the source and the destination programs. When you edit an embedded object in the destination program, the source program in which the program was created opens. If the content in the object is changed in the source program, the change is not reflected in the destination program and vice versa.

Linking inserts a code into the destination file connecting the destination to the name and location of the source object. The object itself is not stored within the destination file. When linking, if a change is made to the content in the source program, the destination program reflects the change automatically. Your decision to integrate data by embedding or linking will depend on whether the data is dynamic or static. If the data is dynamic, then linking the object is the most efficient method of integration.

Static data remains the same while dynamic data changes periodically or continually.

Embedding Objects

An object that is embedded is stored in both the source *and* the destination programs. The content of the object can be edited in *either* the source or the destination; however, a change made in one will not be reflected in the other. The difference between copying and pasting and copying and embedding is that embedded objects can be edited with the source program's editing tabs and options.

Quick Steps

Embed an Object

1. Open source program.
2. Select desired object.
3. Click Copy button.
4. Open destination program.
5. Click Paste button arrow.
6. Click *Paste Special*.
7. Click source of object.
8. Click OK.

Since embedded objects are edited within the source program, the source program must reside on the computer when the presentation is opened for editing. If you are preparing a presentation that will be edited on another computer, you may want to check before embedding any objects to verify that the other computer has the same programs.

To embed an object, open both programs and both files. In the source program, click the desired object and then click the Copy button in the Clipboard group on the HOME tab. Click the button on the Taskbar representing the destination program file and then position the insertion point at the location where you want the object embedded. Click the Paste button arrow in the Clipboard group and then click *Paste Special* at the drop-down list. At the Paste Special dialog box, click the source of the object in the *As* list box and then click OK.

Edit an embedded object by double-clicking the object. This displays the object with the source program tabs and options. Make any desired changes and then click outside the object to exit the source program tabs and options. You can apply animation effects to an embedded object with the same techniques you learned in Chapter 7.

Project 2a Embedding an Excel Chart in a Presentation Part 1 of 3

1. Open **FundsPres.pptx** and then save the presentation with Save As and name it **P-C8-P2-FundsPres**.
2. Open Excel and then open **Funds01.xlsx**, located in the PC8 folder on your storage medium.
3. Click the chart to select it. (Make sure the chart is selected and not an element in the chart.)
4. Click the Copy button in the Clipboard group on the HOME tab.
5. Click the PowerPoint button on the Taskbar.
6. Make Slide 4 active.
7. Click the Paste button arrow and then click *Paste Special* at the drop-down list.

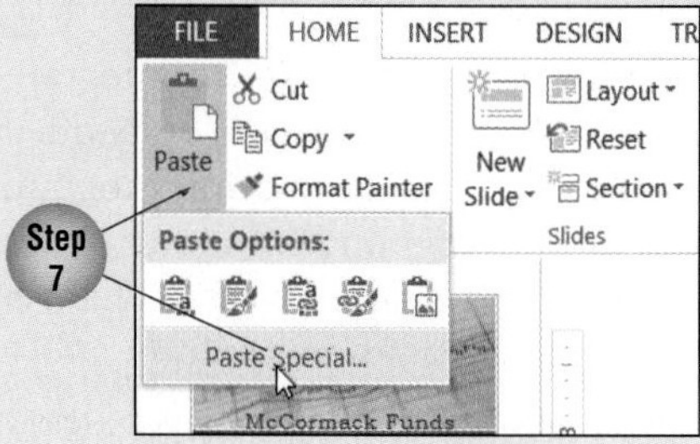

8. At the Paste Special dialog box, click *Microsoft Office Graphic Object* in the *As* list box and then click OK.

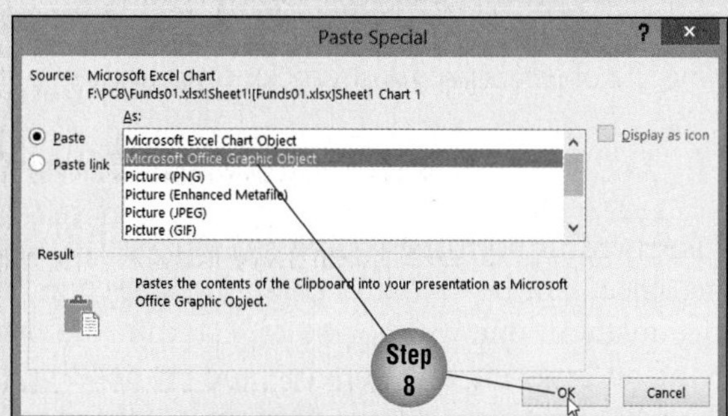

9. Click the CHART TOOLS FORMAT tab.
10. Change the height of the chart to 5.5 inches and change the width to 9 inches.
11. Center the pie chart in the slide below the title.
12. Save **P-C8-P2-FundsPres.pptx**.
13. Click the Excel button on the Taskbar, close the workbook, and then close Excel.

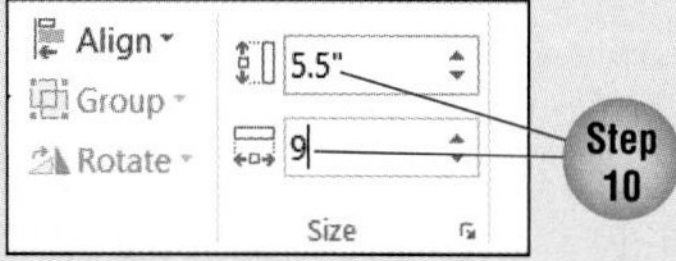

Linking Objects

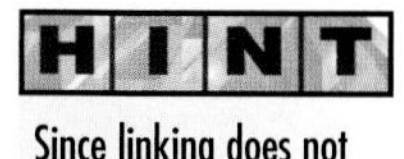

Since linking does not increase the size of the file in the destination program, consider linking objects if file size is a consideration.

If the content of the object that you will integrate between programs is likely to change, then link the object from the source program to the destination program. Linking the object establishes a direct connection between the source and destination programs. The object is stored in the source program only. The destination program will have a code inserted into it that indicates the name and location of the source of the object. Whenever the presentation containing the link is opened, a message displays saying that the presentation contains links and the user is prompted to update the links.

To link an object, open both programs and open both program files. In the source program file, click the desired object and then click the Copy button in the Clipboard group on the HOME tab. Click the button on the Taskbar representing the destination program file and then position the insertion point in the desired location. Click the Paste button arrow in the Clipboard group on the HOME tab and then click *Paste Special* at the drop-down list. At the Paste Special dialog box, click the source program for the object in the *As* list box, click the *Paste link* option located at the left side of the *As* list box, and then click OK.

Quick Steps

Link an Object

1. Open source program.
2. Select desired object.
3. Click Copy button.
4. Open destination program.
5. Click Paste button arrow.
6. Click *Paste Special*.
7. Click *Paste link* option.
8. Click OK.

Project 2b **Linking an Excel Chart to a Presentation** **Part 2 of 3**

1. With **P-C8-P2-FundsPres.pptx** open, open Excel and then open **Funds02.xlsx** located in the PC8 folder on your storage medium.
2. Save the workbook with Save As and name it **P-C8-P2-MMFunds**.
3. Copy and link the chart to a slide in the presentation by completing the following steps:
   a. Click the chart to select it.
   b. Click the Copy button in the Clipboard group on the HOME tab.
   c. Click the PowerPoint button on the Taskbar.
   d. Make Slide 5 active.
   e. Click the Paste button arrow and then click *Paste Special* at the drop-down list.
   f. At the Paste Special dialog box, click the *Paste link* option.
   g. Make sure *Microsoft Excel Chart Object* is selected in the *As* list box and then click OK.

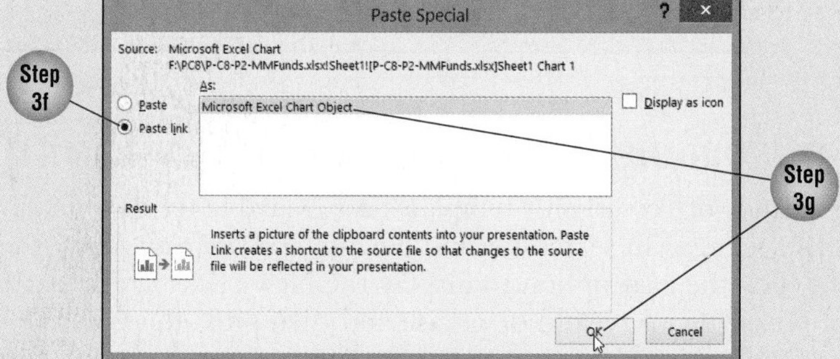

   h. Click the DRAWING TOOLS FORMAT tab, change the height of the chart to 5 inches, and then drag the chart so it is centered on the slide.
4. Click the Excel button on the Taskbar, close **P-C8-P2-MMFunds.xlsx**, and then close Excel.
5. Make Slide 1 active and then run the presentation.
6. Save and then close **P-C8-P2-FundsPres.pptx**.

Editing Linked Objects

Edit linked objects in the source program in which they were created. Open the document, workbook, or presentation containing the object; make the changes as required; and then save and close the file. If both the source and destination programs are open at the same time, the changed content is reflected immediately in both programs.

Project 2c Editing Linked Data

Part 3 of 3

1. Open Excel and then open **P-C8-P2-MMFunds.xlsx**.
2. Make the following changes to data in the following cells:
   a. Cell B2: Change *13%* to *17%*.
   b. Cell B3: Change *9%* to *12%*.
   c. Cell B6: Change *10%* to *14%*.
3. Click the Save button on the Quick Access toolbar to save the edited workbook.
4. Close **P-C8-P2-MMFunds.xlsx** and then close Excel.
5. In PowerPoint, open **P-C8-P2-FundsPres.pptx**.
6. At the message telling you that the presentation contains links, click the Update Links button.
7. Make Slide 5 active and then notice the changes in the chart data.
8. Print the presentation as a handout with six slides printed horizontally per page.
9. Save and then close **P-C8-P2-FundsPres.pptx**.

	A	B
1		Percentage
2	2011	17%
3	2012	12%
4	2013	18%
5	2014	4%
6	2015	14%

Step 2a
Step 2b
Step 2c

Project 3 Download and Apply a Design Template to a Presentation and Prepare a Presentation for Sharing

10 Parts

You will download a design template from Office.com and apply the template to a company presentation. You will insert, edit, and delete comments in the presentation; modify the presentation properties; inspect the presentation; and encrypt the presentation with a password.

Downloading Templates

Quick Steps

Download a Template

1. Click FILE tab.
2. Click *New* option.
3. Click in search text box.
4. Type key word or phrase.
5. Press Enter.
6. Double-click desired template.

Thousands of PowerPoint templates are available for downloading at the New backstage area. To search for and download a template, click the FILE tab and then click the *New* option to display the New backstage area. Click in the search text box, type a keyword or phrase and then press the Enter key or click the Start searching button that displays at the right side of the search text box. PowerPoint searches the Office.com templates gallery and displays templates that match your key word or phrase. To download a template, double-click the template or click once on the template to display a download window. At this window, you can read information about the template and view additional template images by clicking the right- or left-pointing arrows that display below the template image. If you want to download the template, click the Create button.

When you download a template, the template opens with most templates containing predesigned slides. Use these slides to help you create your presentation or delete the predesigned slides and create your own using the template layouts. If you download a template, make some changes to the presentation, and decide you want to use it for future presentations, save the presentation as a template to the Custom Office Templates folder (as you learned in Chapter 6).

If you want the downloaded template (not a customized version of the template) available for future presentations, pin the template to the New backstage area. To do this, display the New backstage area, hover your mouse over the template you want to pin and then click the stick pin that displays. Complete the same steps to unpin a template from the New backstage area.

If you saved a customized template to the Custom Office Templates folder, you can apply the template to an existing presentation. To do this, open the presentation, click the DESIGN tab, click the More button at the right side of the design thumbnails, and then click the *Browse for Themes* option at the drop-down list. At the Choose Theme or Themed Document dialog box, navigate to the Custom Office Templates folder in the Documents folder on the computer's hard drive and then double-click the desired template in the dialog box Content pane.

Project 3a Downloading and Applying a Design Template — Part 1 of 10

Note: Check with your instructor before downloading a design template. To download a template you must have access to the Internet and access to the hard drive. If you do not have access to the design template or cannot download it, open ISPres.pptx, save it with the name P-C8-P3-ISPres, apply a design theme of your choosing, and then continue with Step 16.

1. At a blank PowerPoint screen, click the FILE tab and then click the *New* option.
2. At the New backstage area, click one of the categories that displays below the search text box (such as *Business*, *Education*, and so on).
3. When templates display that match the category, scroll down the backstage list box and look at some of the templates.
4. Click the Home button that displays to the left of the search text box to return to the main New backstage area screen.
5. Click in the search text box, type **marketing plan**, and then press Enter.
6. Scroll down the backstage list box and view some of the templates.
7. Click in the search text box, type **red radial lines**, and then press Enter. (This displays the Red radial lines presentation (widescreen).)
8. Click the *Red radial lines presentation (widescreen)* template thumbnail.
9. At the template window, view some of the images for the template by clicking several times on the right-pointing arrow that displays below the template image.
10. Click the Create button. (This downloads the template and opens a presentation based on the template.)
11. Delete the sample slides in the presentation by completing the following steps:
    a. With the first slide selected in the slide thumbnails pane, scroll down the slide thumbnails pane to the last slide, hold down the Shift key, and then click the last slide. (This selects all of the slides in the presentation.)

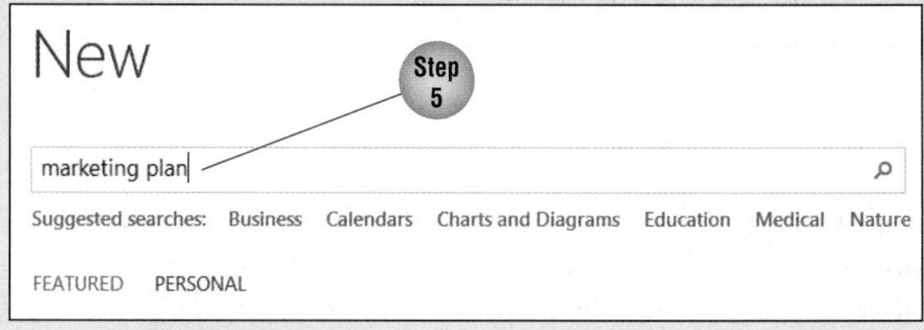

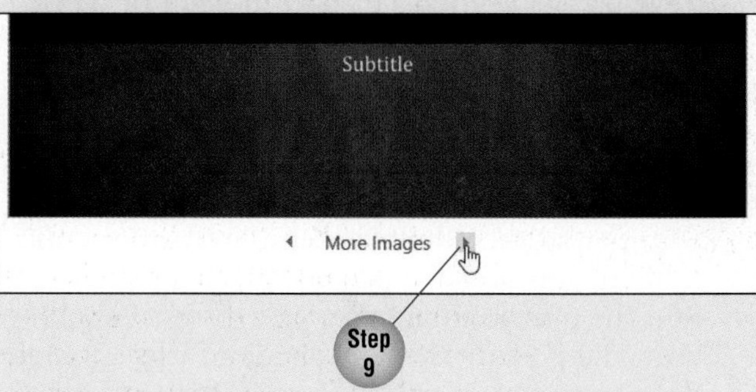

b. Press the Delete key. (When you press the Delete key, the slides are deleted and a gray screen displays with the text *Click to add first slide*.)

12. Save the presentation as a template to the Custom Office Templates folder by completing the following steps:
    a. Press the F12 function key to display the Save As dialog box.
    b. Click the *Save as type* option box and then click *PowerPoint Template (*.potx)* at the drop-down list. (Make sure the Custom Office Templates folder located in the Documents folder on the computer's hard drive is active.)
    c. Click in the *File name* text box, type **XXX-ISTemplate** (type your initials in place of the *XXX*) and then click the Save button.
    d. Close the **XXX-ISTemplate.potx** file.

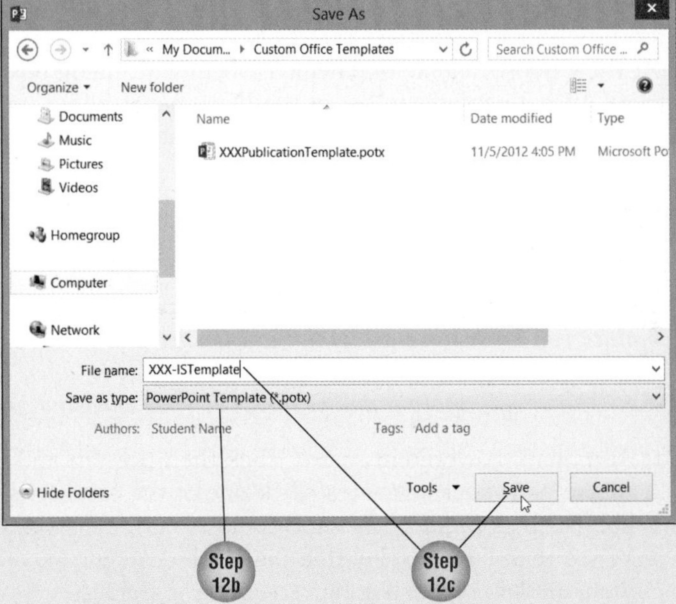

13. Open the **ISPres.pptx** presentation from the PC8 folder on your storage medium.
14. Save the presentation with Save As and name it **P-C8-P3-ISPres**.
15. Apply the **XXX-ISTemplate.potx** template to the presentation by completing the following steps:
    a. Click the DESIGN tab.
    b. Click the More button at the right side of the design thumbnails.
    c. Click the *Browse for Themes* option at the drop-down list.
    d. At the Choose Theme or Themed Document dialog box, double-click ***XXX-ISTemplate.potx*** (where your initials display in place of the *XXX*). (If the Custom Office Templates folder contents do not display in the Content pane of the Choose Theme or Themed Document dialog box, click the Documents folder located below the *Libraries* heading in the Navigation pane and then double-click the Custom Office Templates folder.)

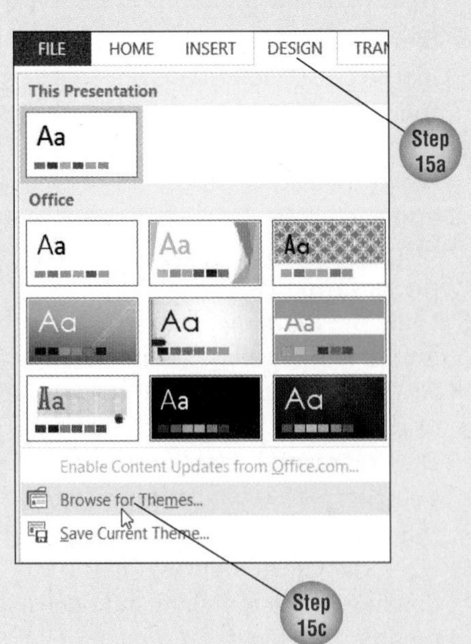

16. Run the presentation.
17. Print the presentation as a handout with all nine slides printed horizontally on the page.
18. Save **P-C8-P3-ISPres.pptx**.

Comparing and Combining Presentations

Use the Compare button in the Compare group on the REVIEW tab to compare two PowerPoint presentations to determine the differences between the presentations. You have the options of combining all of the changes, accepting only specific changes, and rejecting some or all of the changes. To compare and combine presentations, open the first presentation, click the REVIEW tab, and then click the Compare button in the Compare group. This displays the Choose File to Merge with Current Presentation dialog box. At this dialog box, navigate to the folder containing the presentation you want to compare with the current presentation, click the presentation name in the Content pane, and then click the Merge button. (You can also double-click the presentation name.)

When you click the Merge button (or double-click the presentation name), a Reviewing task pane with the heading *Revisions* displays at the right side of the screen containing changes to slides and changes to the presentation. In addition, a revision mark displays in a slide indicating a difference between slides in the two presentations. If a difference occurs to the entire presentation, such as a difference between design themes, a revision mark displays at the left side of the screen near the top of the slide thumbnails pane. Click a revision mark to expand it to display a revision check box followed by information about the change.

If you want to accept the change, click the revision check box and then click the Accept button in the Compare group. You can also accept a change by clicking the Accept button arrow. When you click the Accept button arrow, a drop-down list displays with options to accept the current change, accept all changes to the current slide, or accept all changes to the presentation. If you do not want to accept the change, click the Reject button in the Compare group. Click the Reject button arrow and options display for rejecting the current change, rejecting all changes to the current slide, or rejecting all changes to the presentation.

Use the Previous and Next buttons in the Compare group to navigate to changes in the presentation. Click the Reviewing Pane button to turn on or off the display of the Reviewing task pane. When you have finished comparing the presentations, click the End Review button and the review ends and the accept or reject decisions you made are applied.

Quick Steps

Comparing and Combining Presentations

1. Click REVIEW tab.
2. Click Compare button.
3. Navigate to folder containing presentation you want to compare with.
4. Click presentation.
5. Click Merge button.
6. Accept or reject changes.
7. Click End Review button.

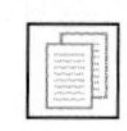

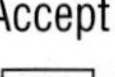

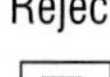

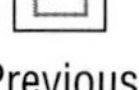

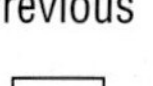

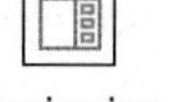

Project 3b Comparing and Combining Presentations — Part 2 of 10

1. With **P-C8-P3-ISPres.pptx** open, click the REVIEW tab and then click the Compare button in the Compare group.
2. At the Choose File to Merge with Current Presentation dialog box, navigate to the PC8 folder on your storage medium, click ***ISSalesMeeting.pptx*** in the Content pane, and then click the Merge button located toward the lower right corner of the dialog box.
3. Notice the Reviewing task pane (with the heading *Revisions*) that displays at the right side of the screen with the *DETAILS* option selected. This option contains a *Slide Changes* section and a *Presentation Changes* section. A message displays in the *Slide Changes* section indicating that the current slide (Slide 1) contains no changes. The *Presentation Changes* section indicates a change in the theme for Slides 1 through 9.

4. Click the revision check box that displays before the word *Theme* in the revision mark that displays near the top of the slide thumbnails pane. (When you insert a check mark in the check box, the design theme is removed from the presentation since the presentation to which you are comparing the current presentation does not include a design theme.)

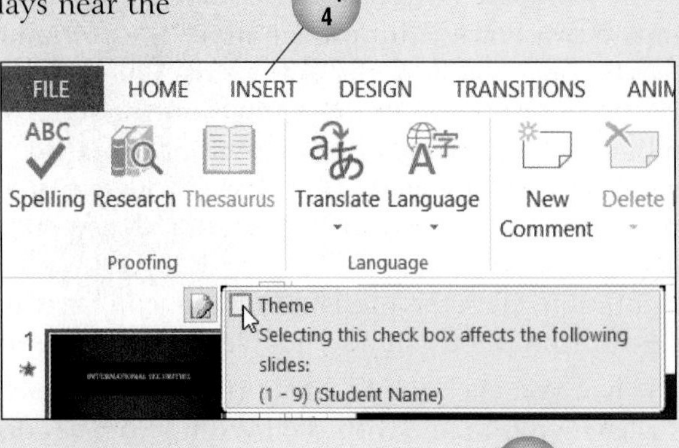

5. You decide that you want the design theme to remain, so click the Reject button in the Compare group. (You could also click again the revision check box before the word *Theme* in the revision mark.)

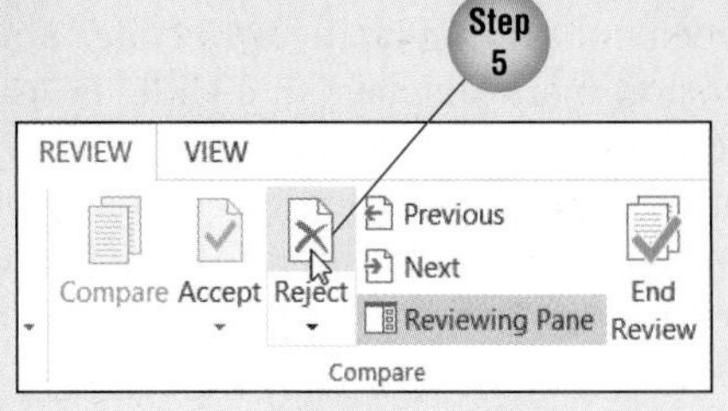

6. Click the Next button in the Compare group to display the next change.
7. Click the revision check box to the left of the text *All changes to Content Placeholder 2* located in the upper right corner of the slide in the slide pane.
8. Click the Reject button to reject this change.
9. Click the Next button.
10. Click the revision check box to the left of the text *Table contents* located at the right side of the table in the slide. Notice the change to the amount for the West region.
11. Click the revision check box again to remove the check mark and then click the Accept button in the Compare group to accept the change.
12. Click the Next button.
13. Click the revision check box to the left of the text *All changes to Content Placeholder 2* located in the upper right corner of the content placeholder in the slide, notice the changes made to the slide, and then click the check box to remove the check mark.
14. Accept all changes by clicking the Accept button arrow and then clicking *Accept All Changes to This Slide* at the drop-down list.

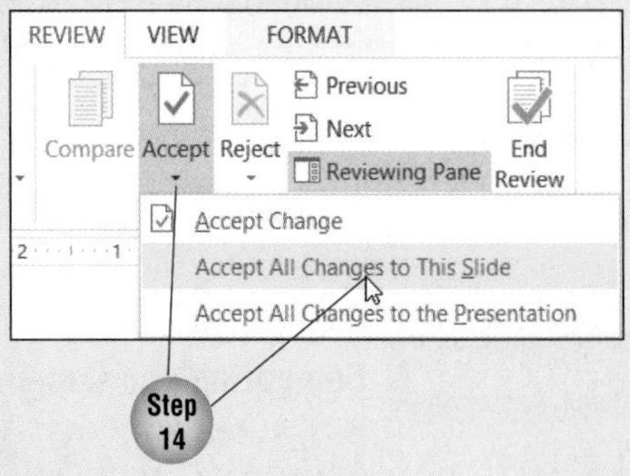

15. Click the Next button.
16. Click the Accept button to accept the changes to text in the content placeholder in Slide 9.
17. Click the Next button.
18. At the message that displays telling you that was the last change and asking if you want to continue reviewing from the beginning, click the Cancel button.
19. Click the End Review button in the Compare group.
20. At the message that displays asking if you are sure you want to end the review, click the Yes button.
21. Save **P-C8-P3-ISPres.pptx**.

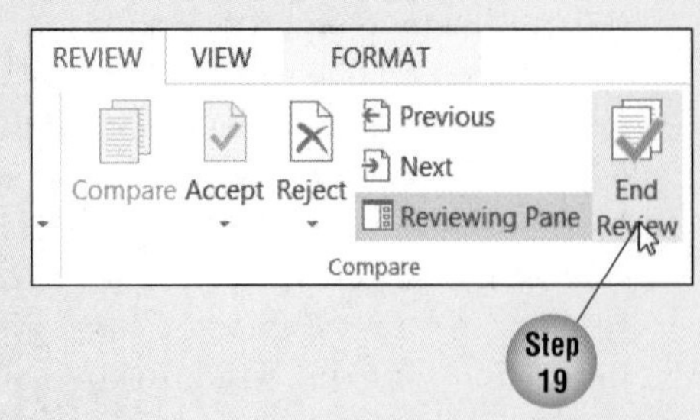

Managing Comments

If you are sending out a presentation for review and want to ask reviewers specific questions or provide information about slides in a presentation, insert a comment. To insert a comment, display the desired slide and then position the insertion point where you want the comment to appear or select an element in the slide. Click the REVIEW tab and then click the New Comment button in the Comments group. This displays an orange active icon at the location of the insertion point or next to the selected element and opens the Comments task pane with a text entry box in the pane. Type the desired comment in the text entry box and then click outside the text entry box, press the Tab key, or press the Enter key.

Quick Steps

Insert a Comment
1. Click REVIEW tab.
2. Click New Comment button.
3. Type comment text.

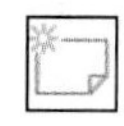

New Comment

To insert another comment in the presentation, position the insertion point or select the desired element in the slide and then click the New button in the Comments task pane or click the New Comment button in the Comments group and then type the comment in the text entry box. To view a comment in a presentation, click the comment icon and then read the information in the Comments task pane.

To move between comments in a presentation, click the Next button or Previous button located toward the upper right corner of the Comments task pane. You can also click the Previous button or Next button in the Comments group on the REVIEW tab.

Next

Previous

Other methods for displaying the Comments task pane include clicking the COMMENTS button on the Status bar or clicking the Show Comments button in the Comments group on the REVIEW tab. When the Comments task pane is open, the Show Comments button is active (displays with an orange background). Turn off the display of the Comments task pane by clicking the COMMENTS button on the Status bar, clicking the Show Comments button, or by clicking the Close button located in the upper right corner of the Comments task pane.

COMMENTS

Show Comments

To print comments, display the Print backstage area and then click the second gallery in the *Settings* category. (This is the gallery containing the text *Full Page Slides*.) At the drop-down list that displays, make sure the *Print Comments and Ink Markup* check box contains a check mark. Comments print on a separate page after the presentation is printed.

Project 3c **Inserting Comments** **Part 3 of 10**

1. With **P-C8-P3-ISPres.pptx** open, make Slide 2 active and then insert a comment by completing the following steps:
   a. Position the insertion point immediately to the right of the word *Australia*.
   b. Click the REVIEW tab.
   c. Click the New Comment button in the Comments group.
   d. Type the following in the text entry box in the Comments task pane: **Include information on New Zealand branch.**
2. Make Slide 3 active and then insert a comment by completing the following steps:
   a. Click in the chart to select it. (Make sure you select the chart and not a chart element.)

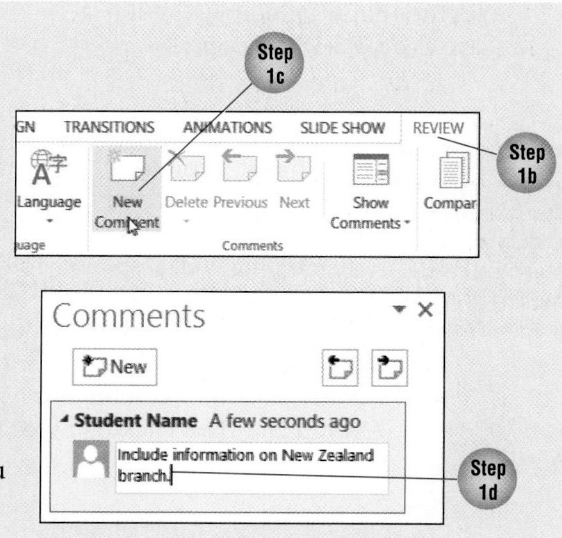

b. Click the New button in the Comments task pane.
c. Type the following in the text entry box: **Include a chart showing profit amounts.**

3. Make Slide 5 active, position the insertion point immediately to the right of the word *line* at the end of the third bulleted item, and then insert the comment **Provide detailed information on how this goal will be accomplished.**

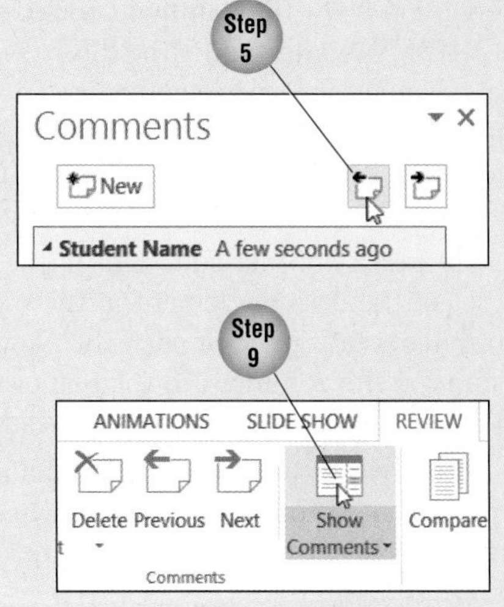

4. Make Slide 8 active, position the insertion point immediately to the right of the words *Hong Kong* in the second bulleted item, and then insert the comment **Who will be managing the Hong Kong office?**
5. Click the Previous button in the Comments task pane to display the comment box in Slide 5.
6. Click the Previous button in the Comments group on the REVIEW tab to display the comment box in Slide 3.
7. Click the Next button in the Comments task pane to display the comment in Slide 5.
8. Click the Next button in the Comments group on the REVIEW tab to display the comment in Slide 8.
9. Click the Show Comments button in the Comments group on the REVIEW tab to turn off the display of the Comments task pane.
10. Print the presentation and the comments by completing the following steps:
    a. Click the FILE tab and then click the *Print* option.
    b. At the Print backstage area, click the second gallery in the *Settings* category, make sure the *Print Comments and Ink Markup* option contains a check mark, and then click the *9 Slides Vertical* option.
    c. Click the Print button.
11. Make Slide 1 active and then run the presentation beginning with Slide 1.
12. Save **P-C8-P3-ISPres.pptx**.

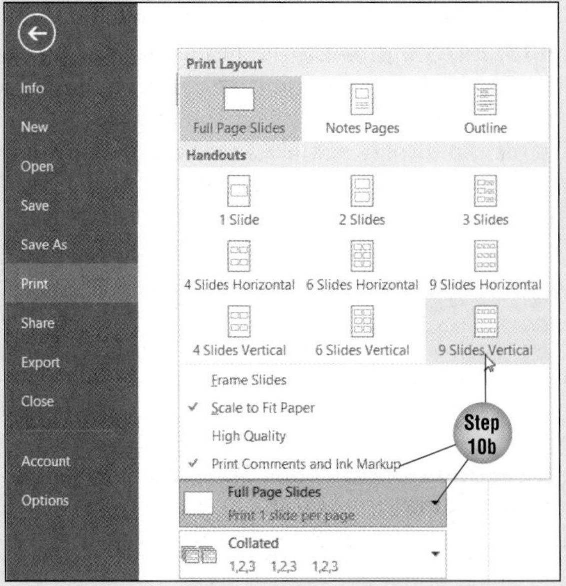

Move a comment in a slide by selecting the comment icon and then dragging it to the desired location.

Delete

To edit a comment, click the comment in the Comments task pane, click in the text entry box and then edit the comment. Reply to a comment by clicking the comment in the Comments task pane, clicking in the reply entry box and then typing your response. To delete a comment from a slide, click the comment icon and then click the Delete button in the Comments task pane or the Delete button in the Comments group on the REVIEW tab. You can also right-click the comment icon and then click *Delete Comment* at the shortcut menu. Delete all comments in a presentation by clicking the Delete button arrow in the Comments group and then clicking *Delete All Comments and Ink in This Presentation* at the drop-down list.

Project 3d Editing and Deleting Comments Part 4 of 10

1. With **P-C8-P3-ISPres.pptx** open, make Slide 8 active and then edit the comment by completing the following steps:
   a. Click the comment icon that displays to the right of *Hong Kong*. (This displays the Comments task pane.)
   b. Click in the text entry box in the Comments task pane.
   c. Delete the text in the comment box and then type **Check with Sandy Cates to determine who will be appointed branch manager.**
2. Delete the comment in Slide 3 by completing the following steps:
   a. Click twice on the Previous button located toward the upper right corner of the Comments task pane to display Slide 3 and the comment in the slide.
   b. Click the Delete button (contains an X) that displays in the upper right corner of the comment box.
3. Close the Comments task pane.
4. Print the presentation as a handout with all nine slides printed horizontally on the page and make sure the comments print.
5. Save **P-C8-P3-ISPres.pptx**.

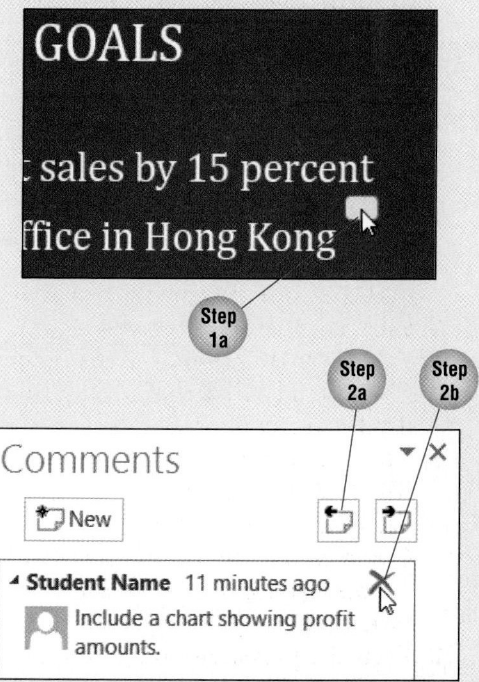

Managing Presentation Information

If you plan to distribute or share a presentation, you should check the presentation information and decide if you want to insert presentation properties in the presentation file, protect the presentation with a password, check the compatibility of the presentation, or access versions of the presentation. You can complete these tasks along with other tasks at the Info backstage area shown in Figure 8.4. Display this backstage area by clicking the FILE tab and then clicking the *Info* option.

Managing Presentation Properties

Each presentation you create has properties associated with it such as the type and location of the presentation and when the presentation was created, modified, and accessed. View and modify presentation properties at the Info backstage area and at the document panel.

Property information about a presentation displays at the right side of the Info backstage area. Add or update a presentation property by hovering your mouse over the information that displays at the right of the property (a rectangular box with a light orange border displays) and then typing the desired information. In the *Related Dates* section, dates display for when the

Figure 8.4 Info Backstage Area

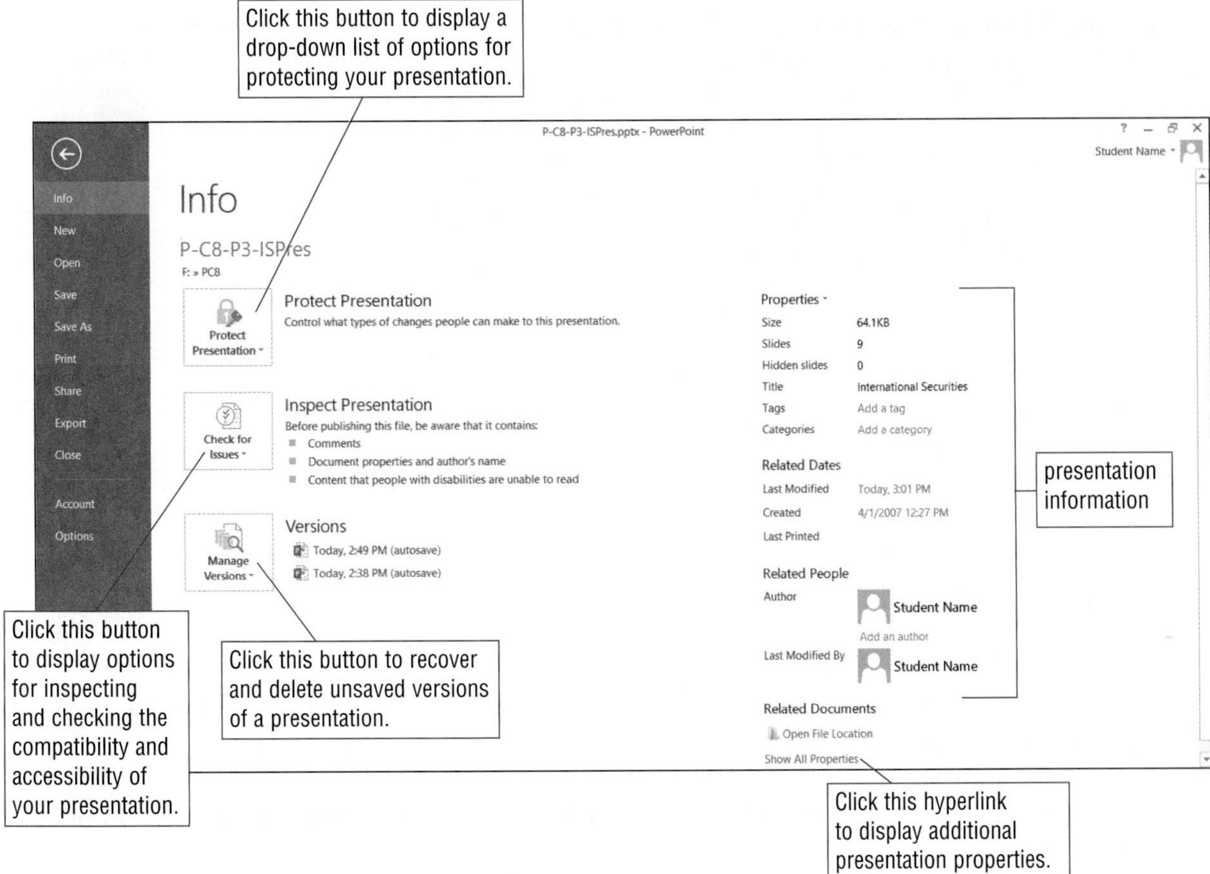

presentation was created and when it was last modified and printed. The *Related People* section displays the name of the author of the presentation and also contains options for adding additional author names. Click the folder below the *Related Documents* section to display the folder contents where the current presentation is located.

Display additional presentation properties by clicking the Show All Properties hyperlink. You can also manage presentation properties at the document panel shown in Figure 8.5. Display this panel by clicking the Properties button that displays at the top of the property information and then clicking *Show Document Panel* at the drop-down list. Inserting text in some of the text boxes can help you organize and identify your presentations.

Figure 8.5 Document Panel

Document Properties ▾ Location: F:\PC8\P-C8-P3-ISPres.pptx * Required field ✕

Author: Student Name | Title: International Securities | Subject: | Keywords: | Category: | Status:

Comments:

Project 3e Inserting Presentation Properties Part 5 of 10

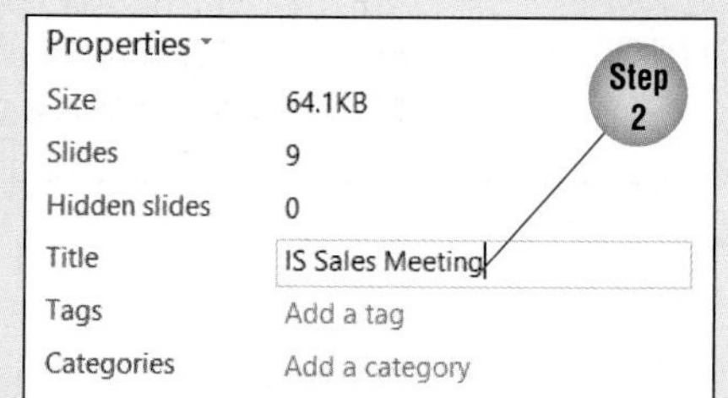

1. With **P-C8-P3-ISPres.pptx** open, click the FILE tab. (This displays the Info backstage area.)
2. At the Info backstage area, hover your mouse over the text *International Securities* that displays at the right of the *Title* property, click the left mouse button (this selects the text), and then type **IS Sales Meeting**.
3. Display the document panel by clicking the Properties button that displays at the top of the property information and then click *Show Document Panel* at the drop-down list.

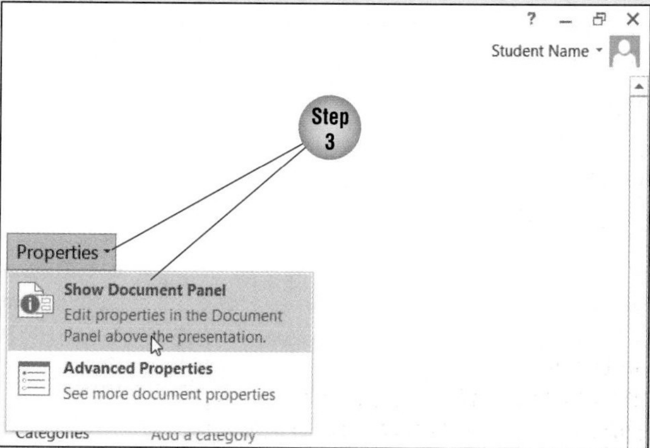

4. At the document panel, press the Tab key twice (this makes the *Subject* text box active) and then type **IS Corporate Sales Meeting**.
5. Press the Tab key and then type **International Securities, sales, divisions** in the *Keywords* text box.
6. Press the Tab key and then type **sales meeting** in the *Category* text box.
7. Press the Tab key twice and then type the following in the *Comments* text box: **This is a presentation prepared for the corporate sales meeting.**
8. Close the document panel by clicking the Close button located in the upper right corner of the panel.

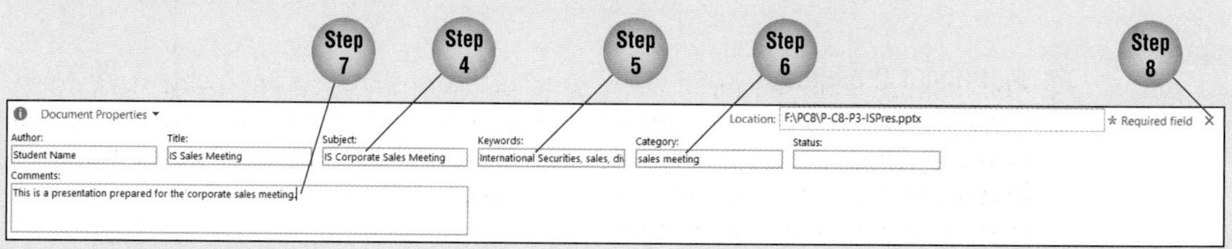

9. Save **P-C8-P3-ISPres.pptx**.

Protecting a Presentation

Click the Protect Presentation button in the middle panel at the Info backstage area and a drop-down list displays with the following options: *Mark as Final*, *Encrypt with Password*, *Restrict Access*, and *Add a Digital Signature*. Click the *Mark as Final* option to save the presentation as a read-only presentation. When you click this option, a message displays telling you that the presentation will be marked and then saved. At this message, click OK. This displays another message telling you that the presentation has been marked as final to indicate that editing is complete and

Quick Steps

Mark a Presentation as Final

1. Click FILE tab.
2. Click Protect Presentation button.
3. Click *Mark as Final*.

Protect Presentation

that it is the final version of the presentation. The message further indicates that when a presentation is marked as final, the status property is set to "Final"; typing, editing commands, and proofing marks are turned off; and that the presentation can be identified by the Mark As Final icon, which displays toward the left side of the Status bar. At this message, click OK. After a presentation is marked as final, a message displays above the ruler indicating that the author has marked the presentation as final and includes an Edit Anyway button. Click this button to edit the presentation. When a presentation is marked as final an additional message displays to the right of the Protect Presentation button in the Info backstage area stating "This presentation has been marked as final to discourage editing."

Encrypting a Presentation

Quick Steps

Encrypt a Presentation

1. Click FILE tab.
2. Click Protect Presentation button.
3. Click *Encrypt with Password.*
4. Type password, press Enter.
5. Type password again, press Enter.

Protect a presentation with a password by clicking the Protect Presentation button at the Info backstage area and then clicking the *Encrypt with Password* option at the drop-down list. At the Encrypt Document dialog box that displays, type your password in the text box (the text will display as round bullets) and then press the Enter key or click OK. At the Confirm Password dialog box, type your password again (the text will display as round bullets) and then press the Enter key or click OK. When you apply a password, the message *A password is required to open this document* displays to the right of the Protect Presentation button.

If you encrypt a presentation with a password, make sure you keep a copy of the password in a safe place because Microsoft cannot retrieve lost or forgotten passwords. If you do not remember your password you will not be able to open the presentation. You can change a password by removing the original password and then creating a new one. To remove a password, open the password-protected presentation, display the Encrypt Document dialog box, and then remove the password (round bullets) in the *Password* text box.

Project 3f **Marking a Presentation as Final** **Part 6 of 10**

1. With **P-C8-P3-ISPres.pptx** open, click the FILE tab.
2. At the Info backstage area, click the Protect Presentation button and then click *Mark as Final* at the drop-down list.
3. At the message telling you the presentation will be marked as final and saved, click OK.
4. At the next message that displays, click OK. (Notice the message that displays to the right of the Protect Presentation button.)
5. At the presentation, notice the message bar that displays above the ruler.
6. Close the presentation.

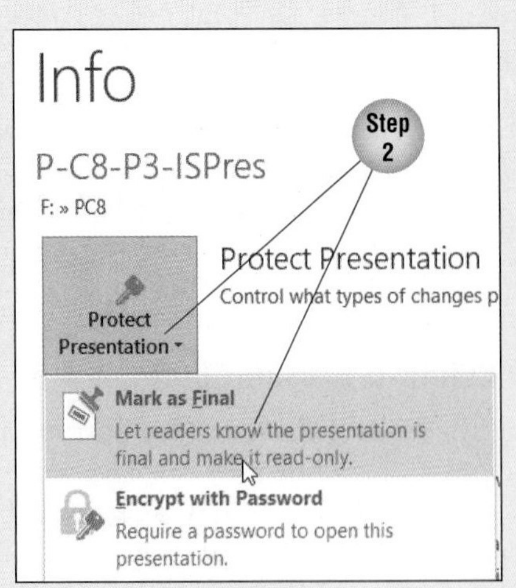

7. Open **P-C8-P3-ISPres.pptx**, click the Edit Anyway button on the yellow message bar, and then save the presentation.

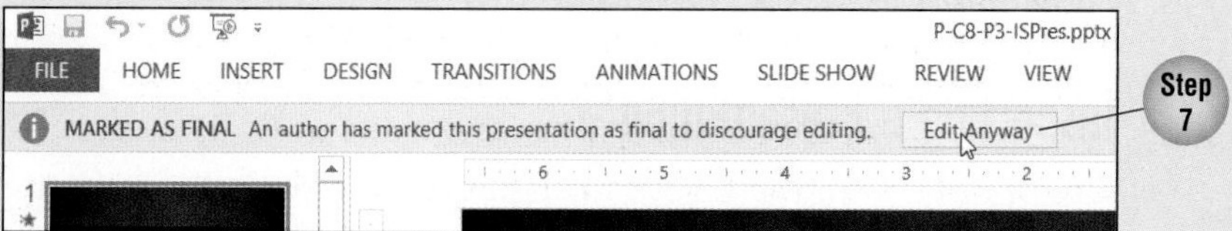

8. Encrypt the presentation with a password by completing the following steps:
   a. Click the FILE tab, click the Protect Presentation button at the Info backstage area, and then click *Encrypt with Password* at the drop-down list.
   b. At the Encrypt Document dialog box, type your initials in uppercase letters. (Your text will display as round bullets.)
   c. Press the Enter key.
   d. At the Confirm Password dialog box, type your initials again in uppercase letters (your text will display as bullets) and then press the Enter key.

Step 8b

Encrypt Document

Encrypt the contents of this file

Password:

Caution: If you lose or forget the password, it cannot be recovered. It is advisable to keep a list of passwords and their corresponding document names in a safe place. (Remember that passwords are case-sensitive.)

OK Cancel

9. Click the Back button to return to the presentation.
10. Save and then close **P-C8-P3-ISPres.pptx**.
11. Open **P-C8-P3-ISPres.pptx**. At the Password dialog box, type your initials in uppercase letters and then press the Enter key.
12. Change the password by completing the following steps:
    a. Click the FILE tab.
    b. At the Info backstage area, click the Protect Presentation button and then click *Encrypt with Password* at the drop-down list.
    c. At the Encrypt Document dialog box, delete the round bullets in the *Password* text box, type your first name in lowercase letters, and then press Enter.
    d. At the Confirm Password dialog box, type your first name again in lowercase letters and then press the Enter key.
    e. Press the Esc key to return to the document.
13. Save and then close **P-C8-P3-ISPres.pptx**.
14. Open **P-C8-P3-ISPres.pptx**. At the Password dialog box, type your first name in lowercase letters and then press Enter.
15. Remove the password protection by completing the following steps:
    a. Click the FILE tab.
    b. At the Info backstage area, click the Protect Presentation button and then click *Encrypt with Password* at the drop-down list.
    c. At the Encrypt Document dialog box, delete the round bullets in the *Password* text box and then press the Enter key.
    d. Press the Esc key to return to the presentation.
16. Save **P-C8-P3-ISPres.pptx**.

Adding a Digital Signature

Add a ***digital signature***, which is an electronic stamp that vouches for a presentation's authenticity, to a presentation to authenticate it and indicate that you agree with its contents. When you add a digital signature, the presentation is locked so that it cannot be edited or changed unless you remove the digital signature. Before adding

Quick Steps

Add a Digital Signature
1. Click FILE tab.
2. Click Protect Presentation button.
3. Click *Add a Digital Signature*.
4. Make desired changes at Sign dialog box.
5. Click OK.

Inspect a Presentation
1. Click FILE tab.
2. Click Check for Issues button.
3. Click *Inspect Document*.
4. Remove check marks from items you do not want to inspect.
5. Click Inspect button.
6. Click Close button.

Check for Issues

a digital signature, you must obtain one from a commercial certification authority. Once you have obtained a commercial digital signature, add it to a presentation by clicking the Protect Presentation button at the Info backstage area and then clicking *Digital Signature* at the drop-down list.

Inspecting a Presentation

Use options from the Check for Issues button drop-down list at the Info backstage area to inspect a presentation for personal and hidden data and to check a presentation for compatibility and accessibility issues. When you click the Check for Issues button, a drop-down list displays with the options *Inspect Document*, *Check Accessibility*, and *Check Compatibility*.

PowerPoint includes a document inspector feature you can use to inspect your presentation for personal data, hidden data, and metadata. Metadata is data that describes other data, such as presentation properties. You may want to remove some personal or hidden data before you share a presentation with other people. To check your presentation for personal or hidden data, click the FILE tab, click the Check for Issues button at the Info backstage area, and then click the *Inspect Document* option at the drop-down list. This displays the Document Inspector dialog box.

By default, the document inspector checks all of the items listed in the dialog box. If you do not want the inspector to check a specific item in your presentation, remove the check mark preceding the item. For example, if you know your presentation contains comments and/or ink annotations, click the *Comments and Annotations* check box to remove the check mark. Click the Inspect button located toward the bottom of the dialog box, and the document inspector scans the presentation to identify information.

When the inspection is complete, the results display in the dialog box. A check mark before an option indicates that the inspector did not find the specific items. If an exclamation point is inserted before an option, the inspector found items and displays a list of the items. If you want to remove the found items, click the Remove All button that displays at the right of the desired option. Click the Reinspect button to ensure that the specific items were removed and then click the Close button.

Project 3g **Inspecting a Presentation** **Part 7 of 10**

1. With **P-C8-P3-ISPres.pptx** open, click the FILE tab.
2. At the Info backstage area, click the Check for Issues button and then click *Inspect Document* at the drop-down list.

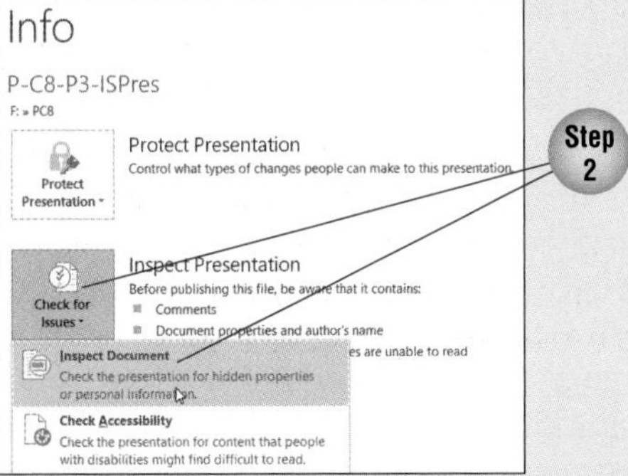

3. At the Document Inspector dialog box, you decide that you do not want to check the presentation for XML data, so click the *Custom XML Data* check box to remove the check mark.

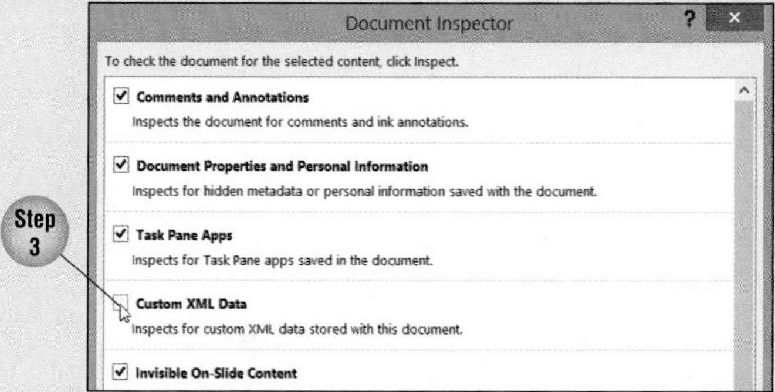

4. Click the Inspect button.
5. Read through the inspection results and then remove all comments by clicking the Remove All button that displays at the right side of the *Comments and Annotations* section.

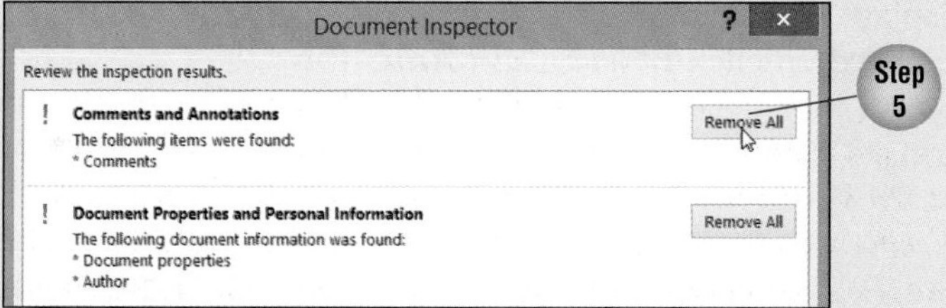

6. Click the Close button to close the Document Inspector dialog box.
7. Click the Back button to return to the presentation.
8. Save **P-C8-P3-ISPres.pptx**.

Checking the Accessibility of a Presentation

PowerPoint includes the accessibility checker feature, which checks a presentation for content that a person with disabilities, such as a visual impairment, might find difficult to read. Check the accessibility of a presentation by clicking the Check for Issues button at the Info backstage area and then clicking *Check Accessibility*. The accessibility checker examines the presentation for the most common accessibility problems in PowerPoint presentations and groups them into three categories: errors—content that is unreadable to a person who is blind; warnings—content that is difficult to read; and tips—content that may or may not be difficult to read. The accessibility checker examines the presentation, closes the Info backstage area, and displays the Accessibility Checker task pane.

Quick Steps

Check Accessibility
1. Click FILE tab.
2. Click Check for Issues button.
3. Click *Check Accessibility*.

At the Accessibility Checker task pane, unreadable errors are grouped in the *ERRORS* section, content that is difficult to read is grouped in the *WARNINGS* section, and content that may or may not be difficult to read is grouped in the *TIPS* section. Select an issue in one of the sections and an explanation of how to fix the issue and why displays at the bottom of the task pane.

Project 3h Completing an Accessibility Check

Part 8 of 10

1. With **P-C8-P3-ISPres.pptx** open, click the FILE tab.
2. At the Info backstage area, click the Check for Issues button and then click *Check Accessibility* at the drop-down list.
3. Notice the Accessibility Checker task pane that displays at the right side of the screen. The task pane displays an *ERRORS* section. Click *Content Placeholder 7 (Slide 3)* in the *ERRORS* section and then read the information that displays toward the bottom of the task pane describing why you should fix the error and how to fix it.

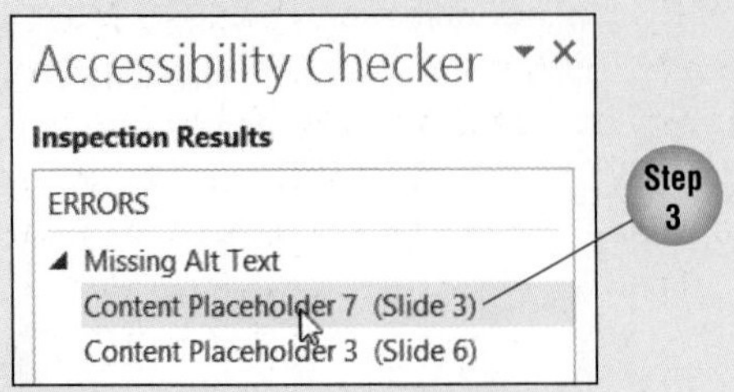

4. Add alternative text (which is a text-based representation of the chart) to the chart by completing the following steps:
   a. Make Slide 3 active, click the pie chart, right-click the chart border (mouse pointer displays with a four-headed arrow attached), and then click *Format Chart Area* at the shortcut menu.

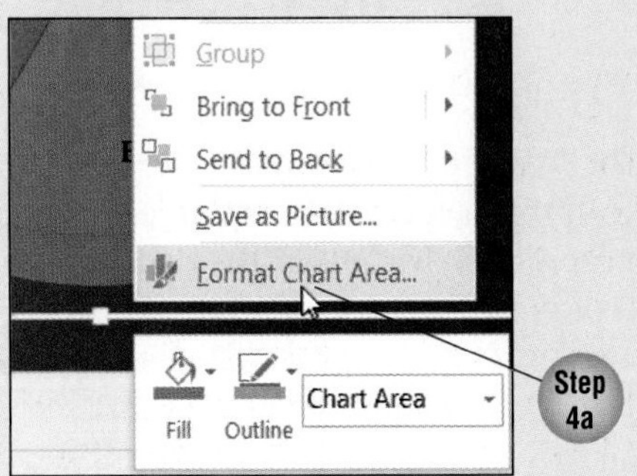

   b. At the Format Chart Area task pane, click the Size & Properties icon.
   c. Click *ALT TEXT* to display the options.
   d. Click in the *Title* text box and then type **Division Profit Chart**.
   e. Click in the *Description* text box and then type **Profits: North America, 35%; Europe, 22%; Asia, 17%; Australia, 14%; and Africa, 12%.**
   f. Close the Format Chart Area task pane.

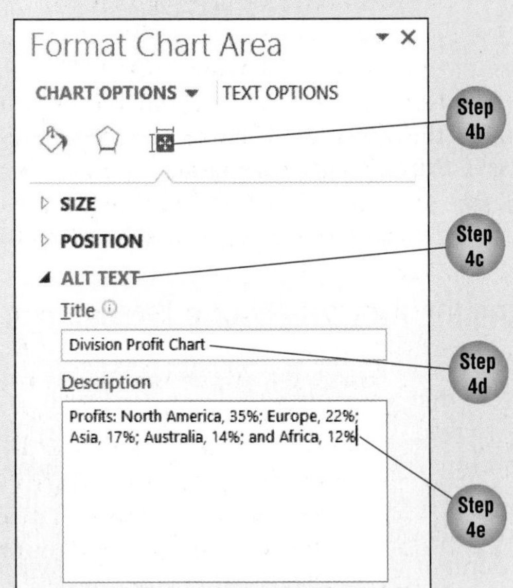

5. Click the remaining item in the Accessibility Checker task pane and then read the information that displays toward the bottom of the task pane.
6. Close the Accessibility Checker task pane by clicking the Close button located in the upper right corner of the task pane.
7. Save **P-C8-P3-ISPres.pptx**.

Checking the Compatibility of a Presentation

Use one of the Check for Issues button drop-down options, *Check Compatibility*, to check your presentation and identify elements that are either not supported or will act differently in previous versions of PowerPoint from PowerPoint 97 through PowerPoint 2003. To run the compatibility checker, open the desired presentation, click the Check for Issues button at the Info backstage area, and then click *Check Compatibility* at the drop-down list. This displays the Microsoft PowerPoint Compatibility Checker dialog box that displays a summary of the elements in the presentation that are not compatible with previous versions of PowerPoint and indicates what will happen when the presentation is saved and then opened in a previous version.

Quick Steps

Check Compatibility
1. Click FILE tab.
2. Click Check for Issues button.
3. Click *Check Compatibility*.
4. Click OK.

Managing Versions

As you work in a presentation, PowerPoint automatically saves your presentation every 10 minutes. This automatic backup feature can be very helpful if you accidentally close your presentation without saving it, or if the power to your computer is disrupted. The automatically saved versions of a presentation are listed to the right of the Manage Versions button in the Info backstage area. Each autosaved presentation displays with *Today*, followed by the time and *(autosave)*. When you save and then close your presentation, the autosaved backup presentations are deleted.

Manage Versions

To open an autosaved backup presentation, click the FILE tab to display the Info backstage area and then click the backup presentation you want to open at the right of the Manage Versions button. The presentation opens as a read-only presentation, and a yellow message bar displays with a Compare button and a Restore button. Click the Compare button and the autosave presentation is compared to the original presentation. You can then decide which changes you want to accept or reject. Click the Restore button and a message displays indicating that you are about to overwrite the last saved version with the selected version. At this message, click OK.

Quick Steps

Open an Autosaved Backup Presentation
1. Click FILE tab.
2. Click presentation name at right of Manage Versions button.

When you save a presentation, the autosaved backup presentations are deleted. However, if you close a presentation after 10 minutes without saving it or if the power is disrupted, PowerPoint keeps the backup file in the *UnsavedFiles* folder on the hard drive. You can access this folder by clicking the Manage Versions button in the Info backstage area and then clicking *Recover Unsaved Presentations*. At the Open dialog box that displays, double-click the desired backup file you want to open. You can also display the *UnsavedFiles* folder by clicking the FILE tab, clicking the *Open* option, and then clicking the Recover Unsaved Presentations button that displays at the bottom of the Recent Presentations list.

Project 3i Checking the Compatibility of Elements in a Presentation and Managing Versions

Part 9 of 10

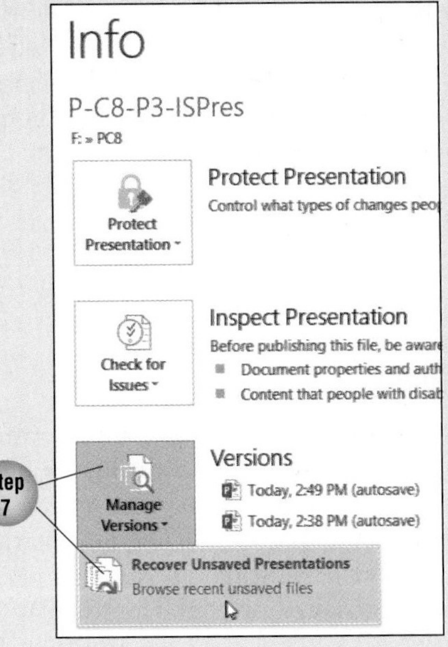

1. With **P-C8-P3-ISPres.pptx** open, click the FILE tab.
2. Click the Check for Issues button and then click *Check Compatibility* at the drop-down list.
3. At the Microsoft PowerPoint Compatibility Checker dialog box, read the information that displays in the *Summary* list box.
4. Click OK to close the dialog box.
5. Click the FILE tab and then check to see if any versions of your presentation display to the right of the Manage Versions button. If so, click the version (or the first version, if more than one displays). This opens the autosave presentation as read-only.
6. Close the read-only presentation.
7. Click the FILE tab, click the Manage Versions button, and then click *Recover Unsaved Presentations* at the drop-down list.
8. At the Open dialog box, check to see if recovered presentation file names display along with the date and time and then click the Cancel button to close the Open dialog box.
9. Save the presentation.

Customizing PowerPoint Options

Customize PowerPoint with options at the PowerPoint Options dialog box, shown in Figure 8.6. Display this dialog box by clicking the FILE tab and then clicking *Options*. The panel at the left side of the dialog box contains a number of options you can select to customize specific features in PowerPoint. For example, click the *General* option in the left panel and options display for turning on or off the display of the Mini toolbar when text is selected, enabling or disabling live preview, and changing the user name and password.

Click the *Save* option at the PowerPoint Options dialog box and the dialog box displays with options for customizing how presentations are saved. You can change the format in which files are saved from the default of *PowerPoint Presentation* to a macro-enabled PowerPoint presentation, a 97-2003 presentation, a strict open XML presentation, or an OpenDocument presentation. With other options you can specify, by minutes, how often you want PowerPoint to automatically save a presentation, specify whether or not you want to save an autosaved version of a presentation if you close a presentation without first saving it, and specify a default location for saving presentations.

Click the *Proofing* option at the PowerPoint Options dialog box and the dialog box displays with options for customizing the spell checker, such as specifying what you want and do not want to be checked during a spelling check and creating a custom spell check dictionary. Click the AutoCorrect Options button and the AutoCorrect dialog box displays with options for changing how PowerPoint corrects and formats text as you type.

Figure 8.6 PowerPoint Options Dialog Box

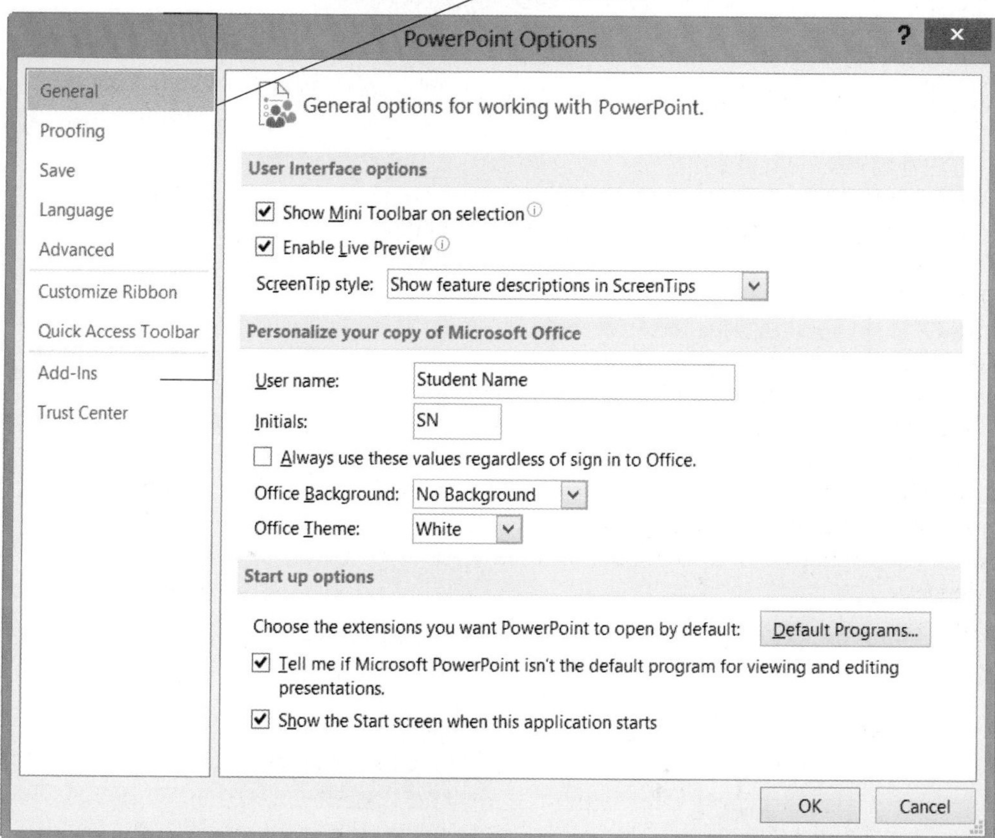

Project 3j Customizing PowerPoint Options

Part 10 of 10

1. With **P-C8-P3-ISPres.pptx** open, insert new slides in the presentation by completing the following steps:
   a. Click below the bottom slide in the slide thumbnails pane.
   b. Click the New Slide button arrow and then click *Reuse Slides* at the drop-down list.
   c. At the Reuse Slides task pane, click the Browse button and then click *Browse File* at the drop-down list.
   d. At the Browse dialog box, navigate to the PC8 folder on your storage medium and then double-click ***ISPresAfrica.pptx***.
   e. Click each of the three slides in the Reuse Slides task pane to insert the slides into the current presentation.
   f. Close the Reuse Slides task pane.
2. Make Slide 1 active.

3. Change PowerPoint options by completing the following steps:
   a. Click the FILE tab and then click *Options*.
   b. At the PowerPoint Options dialog box, click the *Save* option in the left panel.
   c. Click the down-pointing arrow at the right side of the measurement box containing *10* that is located to the right of the *Save AutoRecover information every* text until *1* displays in the measurement box.
   d. Specify that you want presentations saved in the 97-2003 format by clicking the down-pointing arrow at the right side of the *Save files in this format* option box and then clicking *PowerPoint Presentation 97-2003* at the drop-down list.

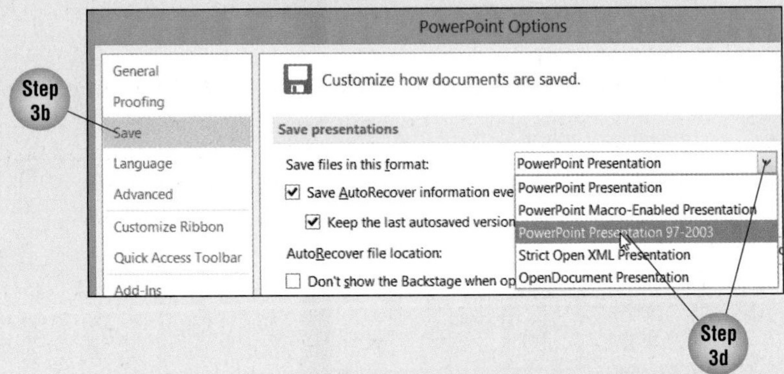

   e. Click the *Proofing* option in the left panel of the PowerPoint Options dialog box.
   f. Click the *Ignore words in UPPERCASE* check box to remove the check mark.
   g. Click the *Ignore words that contain numbers* check box to remove the check mark.

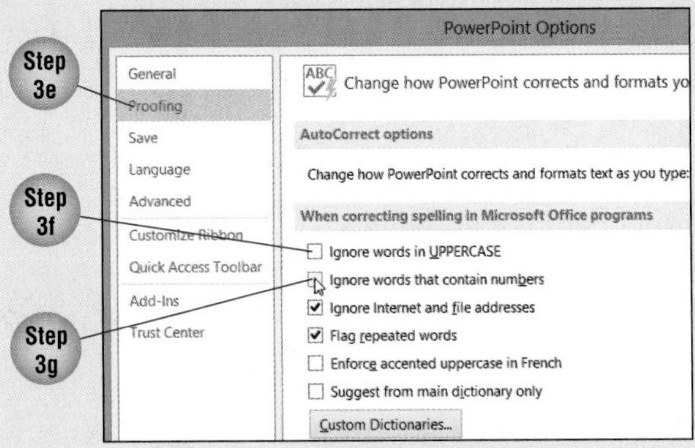

   h. Click OK to close the PowerPoint Options dialog box.

4. Complete a spelling check of the presentation and make changes as needed.
5. Move down the content placeholders on Slides 11 and 12 so they do not overlap the titles.
6. Save the presentation, print six slides horizontally per page, and then close the presentation.
7. Press Ctrl + N to open a new blank presentation.
8. Press F12 to display the Save As dialog box.
9. At the Save As dialog box, notice that the *Save as type* option is set at *PowerPoint 97-2003 Presentation (*.ppt)* because you changed the default format at the PowerPoint Options dialog box.
10. Click Cancel to close the dialog box.
11. Display the PowerPoint Options dialog box and then make the following changes:
    a. Click the *Save* option in the left panel.
    b. Change the number in the measurement box that is located to the right of the *Save AutoRecover information every* text to *10*.
    c. Click the down-pointing arrow at the right side of the *Save files in this format* option box and then click *PowerPoint Presentation* at the drop-down list.
    d. Click the *Proofing* option in the left panel of the PowerPoint Options dialog box.
    e. Click the *Ignore words in UPPERCASE* check box to insert a check mark.
    f. Click the *Ignore words that contain numbers* check box to insert a check mark.
    g. Click OK to close the PowerPoint Options dialog box.
    h. At the message that displays telling you that you are changing the default file format to Office Open XML and asking if you want to change this setting for all Microsoft Office applications, click the No button.
12. Close the blank presentation.

Chapter Summary

- Create a PowerPoint presentation by importing a Word document containing text with heading styles applied using the *Slides from Outline* option at the New Slides drop-down list.
- Use the Copy and Paste buttons in the Clipboard group to copy data from one program to another.
- Use the Clipboard task pane to collect and paste up to 24 items and paste the items into a presentation or other program files.
- With options at the Share backstage area, you can invite people to view and/or edit a presentation, send a presentation as an email attachment or in PDF or XPS format and as a fax, present a presentation online, and publish slides to a shared location.
- At the Export backstage area, create a PDF or XPS file with a presentation, create a video, package the presentation in a folder or on a CD, and create handouts.
- Click the *Change File Type* option at the Export backstage area and options display for saving a presentation in a different file format such as a previous version of PowerPoint, a PowerPoint show, an OpenDocument presentation, and as graphic images.
- An object created in one program in the Microsoft Office suite can be copied, linked, or embedded in another program in the suite. The program containing the original object is called the source program and the program the object is pasted to is called the destination program.
- An embedded object is stored in both the source and the destination programs. A linked object is stored in the source program only. Link an object if you want the contents in the destination program to reflect any changes made to the object stored in the source program.
- Download templates from the Office.com templates gallery at the New backstage area.
- If you download a template and then customize it, consider saving the template to the Custom Office Templates folder in the Documents folder on the computer's hard drive.
- Use the Compare button in the Compare group on the REVIEW tab to compare two presentations to determine the differences between the presentations. Use options in the Compare group to accept or reject differences and display the next or previous change.
- Insert, edit, and delete comments with buttons in the Comments group on the REVIEW tab.
- View and modify presentation properties at the Info backstage area and at the document panel. Display this panel by clicking the Properties button at the Info backstage area and then clicking *Show Document Panel* at the drop-down list.
- Use options from the Protect Presentation button drop-down list at the Info backstage area to mark a presentation as final, encrypt the presentation with a password, restrict access to the presentation, and add a digital signature.

- With options from the Check for Issues button drop-down list at the Info backstage area, you can inspect a document for personal and hidden data, check a presentation for content that a person with disabilities, such as a visual impairment, might find difficult to read, and check the compatibility of the presentation with previous versions of PowerPoint.
- PowerPoint automatically saves a presentation every 10 minutes. When you save a presentation, the autosave backup presentation(s) are deleted. Use the Manage Versions button at the Info backstage area to open an autosave backup presentation.
- Customize PowerPoint with options at the PowerPoint Options dialog box. Display this dialog box by clicking the FILE tab and then clicking *Options*.

Commands Review

FEATURE	RIBBON TAB, GROUP/OPTION	BUTTON, OPTION
Accessibility Checker task pane	FILE, *Info*	, *Check Accessibility*
Clipboard task pane	HOME, Clipboard	
compare presentations	REVIEW, Compare	
Document Inspector dialog box	FILE, *Info*	, *Inspect Document*
Encrypt Document dialog box	FILE, *Info*	, *Encrypt with Password*
Export backstage area	FILE, *Export*	
Insert Outline dialog box	HOME, Slides	, *Slides from Outline*
Microsoft PowerPoint Compatibility Checker dialog box	FILE, *Info*	, *Check Compatibility*
Package for CD dialog box	FILE, *Export*	
Paste Special dialog box	HOME, Clipboard	, *Paste Special*
Publish as PDF or XPS dialog box	FILE, *Export*	
Send to Microsoft Word dialog box	FILE, *Export*	
Share backstage area	FILE, *Share*	

Concepts Check Test Your Knowledge 

Completion: In the space provided at the right, indicate the correct term, symbol, or command.

1. Display the Insert Outline dialog box by clicking the New Slide button arrow and then clicking this option. ____________
2. Use this task pane to collect and paste multiple items. ____________
3. The *Invite People* option is available at this backstage area. ____________
4. If you save the presentation in PDF format, the presentation opens in this. ____________
5. With this option at the Export backstage area, you can export a PowerPoint presentation to a Word document. ____________
6. A presentation you save as a PowerPoint show will display with this file extension. ____________
7. With options in the *Image File Types* section of the Export backstage area with the *Change File Type* option selected, you can save slides in a presentation as graphic images as JPEG files or this type of file. ____________
8. Do this to an object if you want the contents in the destination program to reflect any changes made to the object stored in the source program. ____________
9. Download a template at this backstage area. ____________
10. Click the Merge button at the Choose File to Merge with Current Presentation dialog box when comparing presentations and this task pane displays. ____________
11. The New Comment button is located in the Comments group on this tab. ____________
12. Display additional presentation properties at the Info backstage area by clicking this hyperlink. ____________
13. Display the Encrypt Document dialog box by clicking the FILE tab, clicking the Protect Presentation button at the Info backstage area, and then clicking this option at the drop-down list. ____________
14. Use this feature to inspect your presentation for personal data, hidden data, and metadata. ____________

15. Use this feature to check a presentation for content that a person with a visual impairment might find difficult to read. ________________

16. Use this button at the Info backstage area to open an autosaved backup presentation. ________________

17. Customize PowerPoint with options at this dialog box. ________________

Skills Check Assess Your Performance

Assessment 1

COPY WORD AND EXCEL DATA INTO A SALES CONFERENCE PRESENTATION

1. Open **NWPres.pptx** and then save the presentation with Save As and name it **P-C8-A1-NWPres**.
2. Make Slide 2 active and then complete the following steps:
   a. Open Excel and then open the workbook named **SalesProj.xlsx** (located in the PC8 folder on your storage medium).
   b. Copy the chart and paste it into Slide 2.
   c. Resize the chart so it fills most of the slide below the title.
   d. Close the workbook and then close Excel.
3. Make Slide 4 active and then complete the following steps:
   a. Draw a text box in the slide.
   b. Open Word and then open the document named **HerbRemedies.docx**.
   c. Copy the first three terms and the paragraph below each term in the document to the text box in Slide 4.
   d. Move and/or resize the placeholder so it fills most of the slide below the title.
4. Make Slide 5 active and then complete the following steps:
   a. Draw a text box in the slide.
   b. Make active the **HerbRemedies.docx** Word document.
   c. Copy the last two terms and the paragraph below each term in the document and paste them into Slide 5 in the text box.
   d. Move and/or size the text box so it fills most of the slide below the title.
5. Make Word active, close **HerbRemedies.docx**, and then close Word.
6. With PowerPoint active, apply animation effects to each item on each slide.
7. Run the presentation.
8. Save **P-C8-A1-NWPres.pptx**.
9. Print the presentation as a handout with six slides printed horizontally per page.
10. Export the presentation to a Word document that prints blank lines next to slides.
11. Save the Word document and name it **P-C8-A1-NWPresHandout**.
12. Print and then close **P-C8-A1-NWPresHandout.docx** and then close Word.
13. In PowerPoint, close **P-C8-A1-NWPres.pptx**.

Assessment 2

COPY AND LINK WORD AND EXCEL DATA INTO A COMMUNICATIONS PRESENTATION

1. Open **CommPres.pptx** and then save the presentation with Save As and name it **P-C8-A2-CommPres**.
2. Open Word and then open the document named **VerbalSkills.docx** (located in the PC8 folder on your storage medium).
3. Copy the table and embed it (use the Paste Special dialog box and click Microsoft Word Document Object in the *As* list box) into Slide 5.
4. Resize the table so it better fills the slide.
5. Make Word active, close the **VerbalSkills.docx** document, and then close Word.
6. Open Excel and then open the workbook named **NVCues.xlsx** (located in the PC8 folder on your storage medium).
7. Copy the chart and link it to Slide 6. Resize the chart so it fills a majority of the slide below the title.
8. Save and then close **P-C8-A2-CommPres.pptx**.
9. Make the following changes to the chart in **NVCues.xlsx**:
   a. Change the amount in B2 from *35%* to *38%*.
   b. Change the amount in B3 from *25%* to *22%*.
10. Save and then close **NVCues.xlsx** and then close Excel.
11. In PowerPoint, open **P-C8-A2-CommPres.pptx**. (At the message that displays when you open the presentation, click the Update Links button.)
12. Make Slide 2 active and then insert the following comment after the second bulleted item: **Ask Lauren to provide a specific communication example.**
13. Make Slide 4 active and then insert the following comment after the third bulleted item: **Insert a link here to the writing presentation prepared by Sylvia.**
14. Make Slide 8 active and then insert the following comment after the third bulleted item: **Distribute evaluation forms to audience.**
15. Run the presentation.
16. Save the presentation and then print the presentation as a handout with four slides printed horizontally per page and make sure the comments print.
17. Run the Document Inspector and remove comments.
18. Run the accessibility checker and then create the following alt text (right-click chart, click *Format Object*, click the Size & Properties icon at the Format Object task pane, click *ALT TEXT*) for the chart in Slide 6 with the title *Top Five Nonverbal Cues* and the description *Eye contact, 38%; Smiling, 22%; Posture, 15%; Position, 15%; Gestures, 10%.*
19. Close the Format Object task pane and the Accessibility Checker task pane.
20. Save and then close **P-C8-A2-CommPres.pptx**.

Assessment

3 SAVE A SALES CONFERENCE PRESENTATION IN VARIOUS FORMATS

1. Open **P-C8-A1-NWPres.pptx** and then save the presentation in the PowerPoint 97-2003 Presentation (*.ppt) file format and name the presentation **P-C8-A3-NWPres-2003format**. (At the compatibility checker dialog box, click Continue.)
2. Close **P-C8-A3-NWPres-2003format.ppt**.
3. Open **P-C8-A1-NWPres.pptx** and then save each slide in the presentation as a JPEG image file.
4. Close **P-C8-A1-NWPres.pptx** without saving the changes.
5. Open Word and at a blank document, complete the following steps:
   a. Change the font to Century Gothic, change the font size to 24 points, change the alignment to center, and then type Nature's Way.
   b. Press the Enter key and then insert the **Slide4.JPG** slide. (Use the Pictures button on the INSERT tab to insert this slide. The slide is located in the **P-C8-A1-NWPres** folder in the PC8 folder on your storage medium.)
   c. Change the height of the slide to 2.8 inches.
   d. Press Ctrl + End, press the Enter key, and then insert the **Slide5.JPG** slide.
   e. Change the height of the slide to 2.8 inches.
   f. Save the Word document and name it **P-C8-A3-Herbs**.
   g. Print and then close **P-C8-A3-Herbs.docx** and then close Word.
6. Open **P-C8-A1-NWPres.pptx** and then save the presentation in PDF file format. When the presentation displays in Adobe Reader, scroll through the presentation and then close Adobe Reader.
7. In PowerPoint, close **P-C8-A1-NWPres.pptx**.
8. Capture an image of the Open dialog box and insert the image in a PowerPoint slide by completing the following steps:
   a. Press Ctrl + N to display a new blank presentation.
   b. Click the Layout button in the Slides group on the HOME tab and then click the *Blank* layout at the drop-down list.
   c. Press Ctrl + F12 to display the Open dialog box.
   d. At the Open dialog box, make sure the PC8 folder on your storage medium is the active folder.
   e. Click the option box that displays to the right of the *File name* text box (option box that contains the text *All PowerPoint Presentations*) and then click *All Files (*.*)* at the drop-down list.
   f. Click the Change your view button arrow that displays below the search text box in the Open dialog box, and then click *List* at the drop-down list.
   g. Make sure that all of your project and assessment files display. You may need to resize the dialog box to display the files.
   h. Hold down the Alt key and then press the Print Screen button on your keyboard. (This captures an image of the Open dialog box.)
   i. Click the Cancel button to close the Open dialog box.
   j. Click the Paste button. (This inserts the image of the Open dialog box into the slide.)
9. Print the slide as a full page slide.
10. Close the presentation without saving it.

Assessment 4

DOWNLOAD AND FILL IN AN AWARD CERTIFICATE

1. Create the certificate shown in Figure 8.7 with the following specifications:
   a. In PowerPoint, display the New backstage area, click in the search text box, type **award certificate**, and then press Enter. Download the *Excellence award (with eagle)* template.
   b. Type the company name as shown in Figure 8.7, type your name in place of *Student Name*, type the current date in place of *Date*, and type the name and title of the president/CEO as shown in the figure.
2. Save the certificate and name it **P-C8-A4-Certificate**.
3. Print and then close **P-C8-A4-Certificate.pptx**.

Figure 8.7 Assessment 4

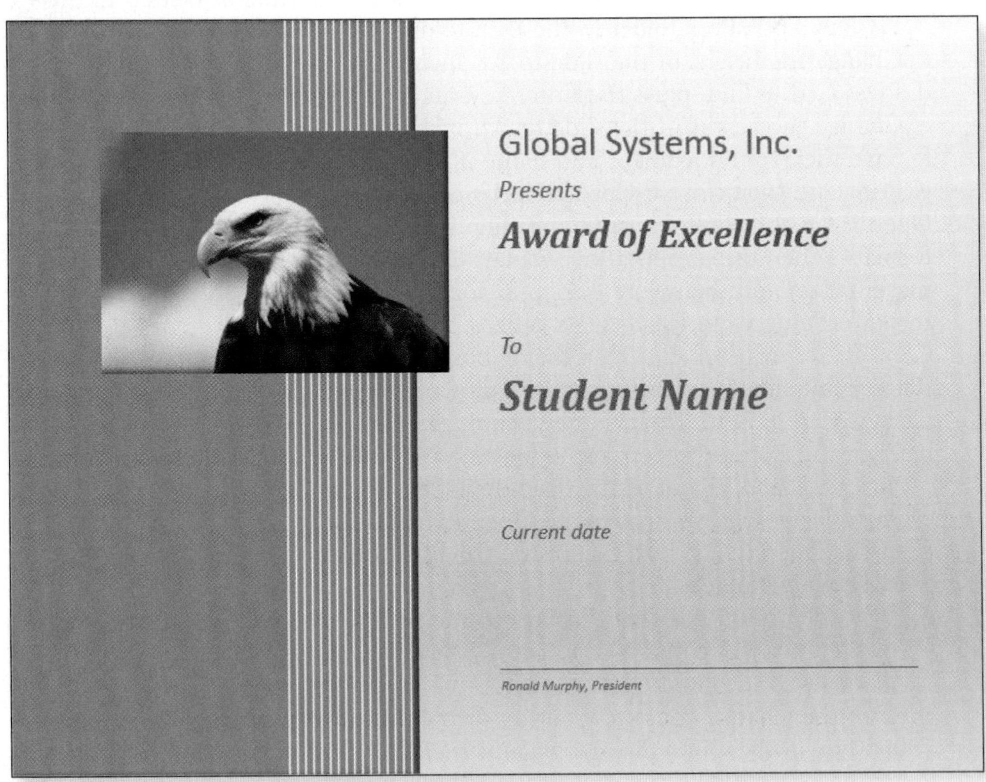

Visual Benchmark Demonstrate Your Proficiency

1 CREATE JPEG IMAGE FILES AND CREATE A WORD DOCUMENT

1. Open **FCTTours.pptx**, save all of the slides in the presentation in the JPEG graphic format, and then close **FCTTours.pptx** without saving the changes.
2. Open Word and, at a blank document, create the document shown in Figure 8.8 on the next page with the following specifications:
   a. Set the two lines of text in 24-point Calibri bold.
   b. Insert each slide and change the height of each slide to 2.5 inches, change the text wrapping to *Tight*, and size and position the slides as shown in Figure 8.8.
3. Save the completed Word document and name it **P-C8-VB1-FCTCovers**.
4. Print and then close **P-C8-VB1-FCTCovers.docx** and then close Word.

2 CREATE A TRAVEL COMPANY PRESENTATION

1. Create the presentation shown in Figure 8.9 on pages 375–376 with the following specifications:
   a. In PowerPoint, download the template named *Photo journal design template*.
   b. Delete all of the slides in the downloaded presentation.
   c. Use the **FCTQtrlyMtg.docx** Word outline document to create the slides in the presentation. ***Hint: Use the* Slides from Outline *option at the New Slide button drop-down list.***
   d. Insert a new slide at the beginning of the presentation using the Blank layout and then insert the **FCTLogo.jpg** image. (See the first slide in Figure 8.9.) Make the white background of the logo transparent. (Do this with the *Set Transparent Color* option from the Color button drop-down gallery on the PICTURE TOOLS FORMAT tab.) Size and position the logo as shown in Figure 8.9.
   e. Make Slide 5 active, apply the Title Only layout, and then copy and link the Excel chart in **Bookings.xlsx** to the slide. Size and position the chart as shown in Figure 8.9. (Close Excel after inserting the chart.)
2. Save the presentation and name it **P-C8-VB2-FCTQtrlyMtgPres**.
3. Print the presentation as a handout with six slides printed horizontally per page.
4. Close **P-C8-VB2-FCTQtrlyMtgPres.pptx**.
5. Open Excel, open **Bookings.xlsx**, and then make the following changes to the data in the specified cells:
   C2: Change *45* to *52*
   C3: Change *36* to *41*
   C4: Change *24* to *33*
   C5: Change *19* to *25*
6. After making the changes, save and then close **Bookings.xlsx** and then close Excel.
7. Open **P-C8-VB2-FCTQtrlyMtgPres.pptx** and update the links.
8. Print the presentation as a handout with six slides printed horizontally per page.
9. Save and then close **P-C8-VB2-FCTQtrlyMtgPres.pptx**.

Figure 8.8 Visual Benchmark 1

First Choice Travel
Proposed Tour Package Covers

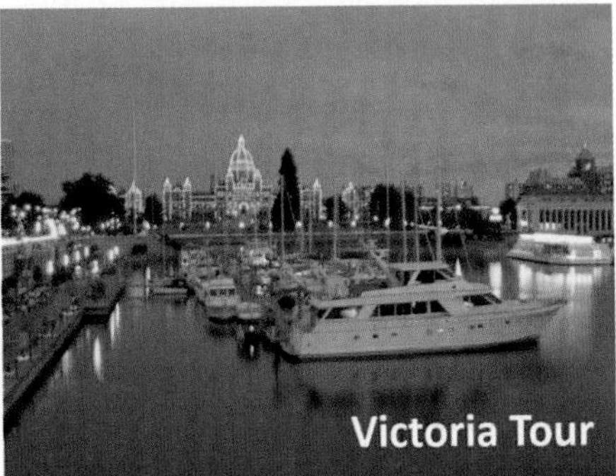

Figure 8.9 Visual Benchmark 2

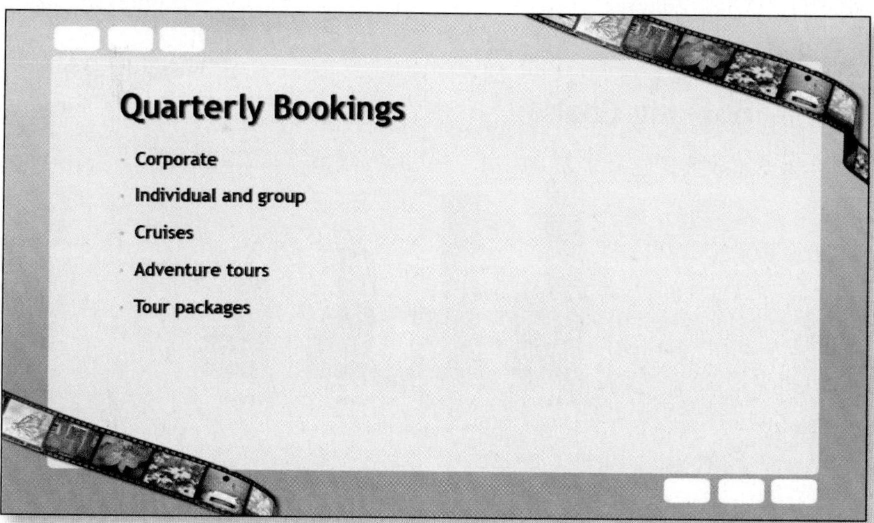

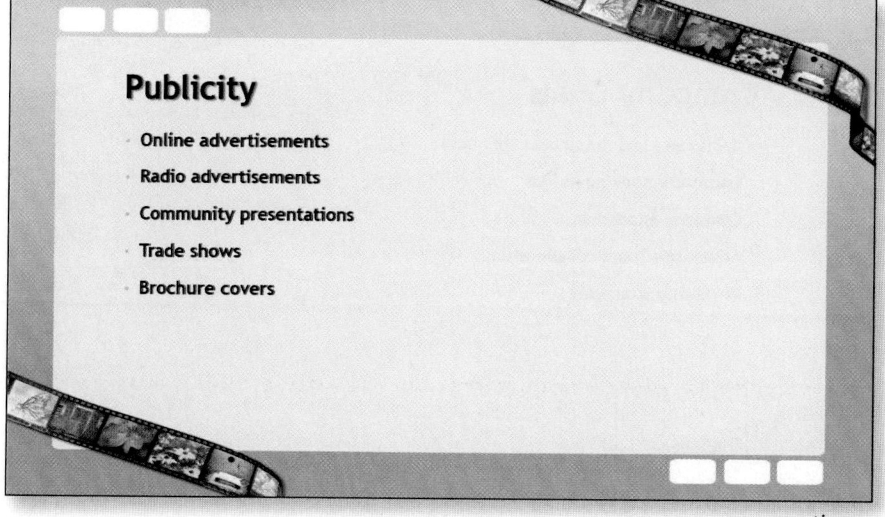

continues

Figure 8.9 Visual Benchmark 2—*continued*

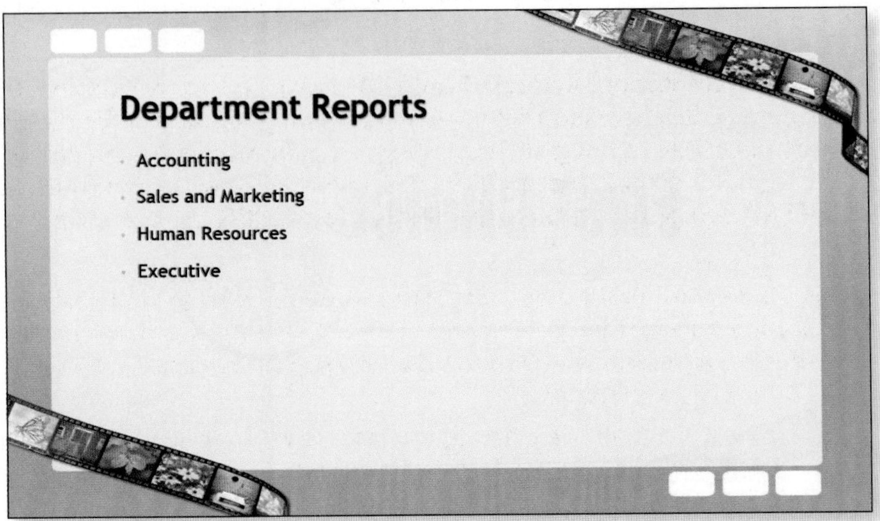

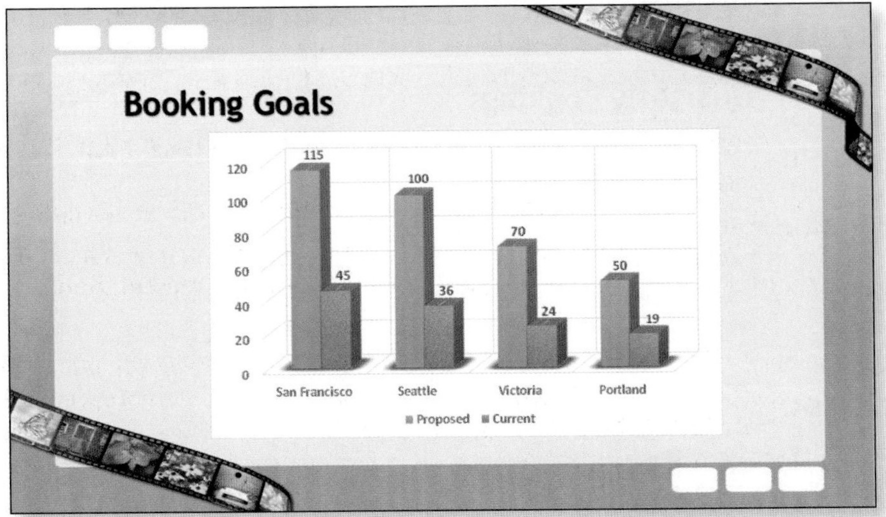

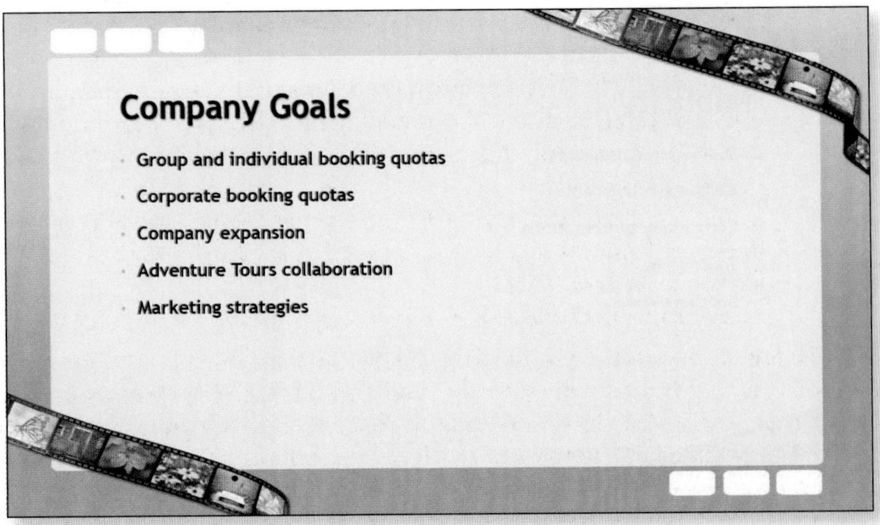

Case Study Apply Your Skills

Part 1

You work for Rocky Mountain Family Medicine and are responsible for preparing education and training materials and publications for the center. You want to be able to insert the center logo in publications so you decide to save the logo as a graphic image. To do this, open the presentation (one slide) named **RMFMLogo.pptx** and then save the slide as a JPEG graphic image.

Part 2

You are responsible for presenting information on childhood diseases at an education class at a local community center. Open the Word document named **ChildDiseases.docx** and then use the information to create a presentation with the following specifications:

- Open the **RMFMDesign.pptx** presentation and then save the presentation with the name **P-C8-CS-RMFMDiseases**.
- Use the Title Only layout for the first slide, type an appropriate title for the presentation, and then insert the **RMFMLogo.jpg** graphic image in the first slide. Set transparent color to the background of the logo image. (Do this with the *Set Transparent Color* option in the Color button drop-down list on the PICTURE TOOLS FORMAT tab.) Size and position the logo attractively on the slide.
- Create additional slides with the information in the **ChildDiseases.docx** Word document.
- Apply any additional enhancements to improve the presentation.

Save and then run the presentation. Print the presentation as a handout with six slides printed horizontally per page and then close the presentation.

Part 3

You need to prepare a presentation for an upcoming education and training meeting. Open **RMFMDesign.pptx** and then save the presentation and name it **P-C8-CS-RMFMClasses**. Import the Word outline document named **RMFMOutline.docx** and then make the following changes:

- Create the first slide with the Title Only layout, insert the **RMFMLogo.jpg** graphic image, and then format, size, and position the logo in the same manner as the first slide in **P-C8-CS-RMFMDiseases.pptx**. Insert the title *Education and Training* in the title placeholder.
- Apply the Title Only layout to the *Community Contacts* slide and then copy the table from the Word document **RMFMContacts.docx** and paste it into the *Community Contacts* slide. Increase the size of the table so it better fills the slide.
- Apply the Title Only layout to the *Current Enrollment* slide and then copy the chart from the Excel workbook **RMFMEnroll.xlsx** and link it to the *Current Enrollment* slide.
- Apply any additional enhancements to improve the presentation.

Save and then run the presentation. Print the presentation as a handout with six slides printed horizontally per page and then close the presentation. You check the enrollments for classes and realize that more people have enrolled, so you need to update the numbers in the Excel workbook. Open **RMFMEnroll.xlsx** and then change *46* to *52*, *38* to *40*, and *24* to *27*. Save and then close the workbook. Open **P-C8-CS-RMFMClasses.pptx** and then update the links. Print only the *Current Enrollment* slide and then close the presentation.

Part 4

You decide that you want to include information on measles in the **P-C8-CS-RMFMDiseases.pptx** presentation on measles. Using the Internet, search for information such as symptoms, complications, transmission, and prevention. Include this information in new slides in the **P-C8-CS-RMFMDiseases.pptx** presentation. Run the presentation and then print only the new slides. Save and then close the presentation.

MICROSOFT® POWERPOINT® Performance Assessment

Note: Before beginning unit assessments, copy to your storage medium the PU2 folder from the PowerPoint folder on the CD that accompanies this textbook and then make PU2 the active folder.

Assessing Proficiency

In this unit you have learned to add visual elements to presentations such as tables, charts, and SmartArt graphics; create a photo album; apply formatting in Slide Master view; insert action buttons; apply custom animation effects; and set up slide shows. You also learned how to copy, embed, and link data between programs; how to insert comments; and how to protect and prepare a presentation.

Assessment 1 Save and Insert a Slide in JPEG Format, Format a Slide Master, Create a Table and SmartArt Graphics, and Insert Comments

1. Open **GreenDesignLogo.pptx**, save the only slide in the presentation as a JPEG graphic image, and then close **GreenDesignLogo.pptx**.
2. Open **GreenDesignPres.pptx** and then save the presentation with the name **P-U2-A1-GreenDesignPres**.
3. Display the presentation in Slide Master view and then make the following changes:
   a. Click the top slide master thumbnail.
   b. Select the text *Click to edit Master text styles* (in the bulleted section), change the font color to Tan, Background 2, Darker 75% (third column, fifth row), and change the font size to 28 points.
   c. Select the text *Second level*, apply the Green, Accent 1 font color (fifth column, first row), and then change the font size to 24 points.
   d. Close Slide Master view.
4. Make Slide 1 active and then make the following changes:
   a. Insert the **GreenDesignLogo.jpg** graphic image.
   b. Set transparent color for the logo background (the white background). (Do this with the *Set Transparent Color* option at the Color button drop-down gallery on the PICTURE TOOLS FORMAT tab.)
   c. Reduce the size of the logo and position it in the white space in the upper right corner of the slide above the water image.
5. Make Slide 6 active and then insert the following data in a table. You determine the formatting and positioning of the table and its data (next page):

Project	Contact	Completion Date
Moyer-Sylvan Complex	Barry MacDonald	07/31/2016
Waterfront Headquarters	Jasmine Jefferson	02/15/2017
Linden Square	Marion Van Horn	09/30/2017
Village Green	Parker Alderton	12/31/2017
Cedar Place Market	Gerry Halderman	03/31/2018

6. Make Slide 7 active and then insert the data from Figure U2.1 in a SmartArt organizational chart. You determine the organization and formatting of the chart.
7. Make Slide 5 active and then create a bar chart with the following data. Delete the chart title and chart legend. You determine the formatting and layout of the chart.

	Revenues
1st Qtr	$25,250,000
2nd Qtr	$34,000,000
3rd Qtr	$22,750,000
4th Qtr	$20,500,000

8. Make Slide 8 active and then insert a SmartArt graphic with the *Repeating Bending Process* graphic (found in the *Process* group) with the following information (insert the information in the slides from left to right). You determine the design and formatting of the SmartArt graphic.
   Mission Analysis
   Requirements Analysis
   Function Allocation
   Design
   Verification
9. Check each slide and make any changes that improve the visual appearance of the slide.
10. Make Slide 1 active and then run the presentation.
11. Make Slide 3 active, click in the slide title placeholder, and then position the insertion point immediately right of the slide title. Display the Comments pane and then insert the comment **Check with Marilyn about adding River View Mall to this list.**
12. Make Slide 4 active, click immediately right of the word *Australia* in the bulleted text, and then insert the comment **What happened to the plans to open an office in Sydney?**
13. Print the presentation as a handout with four slides printed horizontally per page and make sure the comments print.
14. Save and then close **P-U2-A1-GreenDesignPres.pptx**.

Figure U2.1 Assessment 1

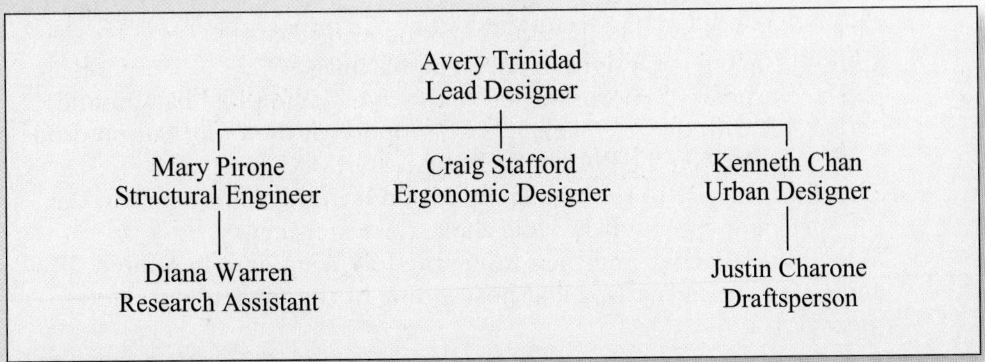

Assessment 2 Copy and Paste Data between Programs and Insert Action Buttons in a Travel Presentation

1. Open **NortonTravelPres.pptx** and then save the presentation with the name **P-U2-A2-NortonTravelPres**.
2. Make Slide 4 active and then create a new Slide 5 (with the Title Only layout) with the following specifications:
   a. Insert the title *Extreme Adventures* in the slide.
   b. Open Word and then open **NTExtremeAdventures.docx**.
   c. Display the Clipboard task pane. (Make sure the task pane is empty. If not, click the Clear All button.)
   d. Select and then copy *Small Groups*, the paragraph below it, and the blank line below the paragraph.
   e. Select and then copy *Comprehensive Itineraries*, the paragraph below it, and the blank line below the paragraph.
   f. Select and then copy *Custom Groups*, the paragraph below it, and the blank line below the paragraph.
   g. Select and then copy *Accommodations*, the paragraph below it, and the blank line below the paragraph.
   h. Display the **P-U2-A2-NortonTravelPres.pptx** presentation.
   i. Draw a text box below the title that is approximately 10 inches wide.
   j. Turn on the display of the Clipboard task pane.
   k. Paste the *Comprehensive Itineraries* item in the text box in the slide.
   l. Paste the *Small Groups* item in the text box.
   m. Paste the *Accommodations* item in the text box.
   n. Clear and then close the Clipboard.
   o. Make the **NTExtremeAdventures.docx** document active, close the Clipboard task pane, close the document, and then close Word.
3. Make Slide 1 active and then insert an action button with the following specifications:
   a. Use the *Action Button: Forward or Next* option to draw the button.
   b. Draw the button in the lower right corner of the slide and make it approximately one-half inch in size.
   c. Apply the Subtle Effect - Aqua, Accent 2 shape style.
4. Display the presentation in Slide Master view and then make the following changes:
   a. Click the top slide master thumbnail.
   b. Insert an action button in the lower right corner of the slide with the same specifications as those in Step 3.
   c. Close Slide Master view.
5. Run the presentation. (Use the action buttons to advance slides. At the last slide, press the Esc key.)
6. Create a footer that prints your first and last names at the bottom of each slide, create a footer for handouts that prints the presentation title *2016 Adventure Packages*, and insert the date in the upper right corner.
7. Print the presentation as a handout with six slides printed horizontally per page.
8. Save and then close **P-U2-A2-NortonTravelPres.pptx**.

Assessment 3 Save a Template Presentation and Copy, Embed, and Link Objects between Programs

1. Open **GSTemplate.pptx**.
2. Display the presentation in Slide Master view, insert **GSLogo.jpg** in the top slide master thumbnail (use the Picture button on the INSERT tab to insert the logo), change the height of the logo to one inch, and drag the logo to the lower right corner of the slide master, and then close Slide Master view.
3. Save the presentation as a template (to the Custom Office Templates folder) and name the presentation **XXXGSTemplate** (use your initials in place of the *XXX*).
4. Close **XXXGSTemplate.potx**.
5. Open **XXXGSTemplate.potx**. (To do this, display the New backstage area, click the CUSTOM option, and then double-click the ***XXXGSTemplate.potx*** thumbnail.)
6. Save the presentation and name it **P-U2-A3-GSMtg**.
7. Format the first slide with the following specifications:
   a. Change to the Blank layout.
   b. Use WordArt to create the text *Global Systems*. (You determine the shape and formatting of the WordArt text.)
8. Create the second slide with the following specifications:
   a. Choose the Title Slide layout.
   b. Type **2016 Sales Meeting** as the title.
   c. Type **European Division** as the subtitle.
9. Create the third slide with the following specifications:
   a. Choose the Title Only layout.
   b. Type **Regional Sales** as the title.
   c. Open Excel and then open **GSWorkbook01.xlsx**.
   d. Select cells A1 through D5 (the cells containing data) and then copy and embed the cells in Slide 3 as a Microsoft Excel Worksheet Object.
   e. Increase the size of the cells so they better fill the slide.
10. Create the fourth slide with the following specifications:
    a. Choose the Title and Content layout.
    b. Type **Company Goals** as the title.
    c. Type the following as the bulleted items:
       - **Increase product sales by 15 percent**
       - **Open a branch office in Spain**
       - **Hire one manager and two additional account managers**
       - **Decrease production costs by 6 percent**
11. Create the fifth slide with the following specifications:
    a. Choose the Title and Content layout.
    b. Type **Hiring Timeline** as the title.
    c. Create a table with two columns and five rows and then type the following text in the cells in the table. (You determine the formatting of the cells.)

Task	Date
Advertise positions	03/01/2016 to 04/30/2016
Review resumes	05/15/2016 to 06/01/2016
Conduct interviews	06/15/2016 to 07/15/2016
Hire personnel	08/01/2016

12. Create the sixth slide with the following specifications:
    a. Choose the Title Only layout.
    b. Type **Production Expenses** as the title.
    c. Make Excel the active program and then close **GSWorkbook01.xlsx**.
    d. Open **GSWorkbook02.xlsx**.
    e. Save the workbook with Save As and name it **GSExpensesWorkbook**.
    f. Copy and then link the pie chart in **GSExpensesWorkbook.xlsx** to Slide 6. Size and center the pie chart on the slide.
    g. Make Excel active, close **GSExpensesWorkbook.xlsx**, and then close Excel.
13. Run the presentation.
14. Create a footer for handouts that prints the presentation title *2016 Sales Meeting* and insert the date in the upper right corner.
15. Print the presentation as a handout with six slides printed horizontally per page.
16. Save and then close **P-U2-A3-GSMtg.pptx**.
17. Open Excel and then open **GSExpensesWorkbook.xlsx**.
18. Make the following changes:
    a. B2: Change *38% to 41%*
    b. B3: Change *35% to 32%*
    c. B4: Change *18%* to *21%*
    d. B5: Change *9%* to *6%*
19. Save, print, and close **GSExpensesWorkbook.xlsx** and then close Excel.
20. With PowerPoint the active program, open **P-U2-A3-GSMtg.pptx**. (At the message that displays, click the Update Links button.)
21. Display Slide 3, double-click the cells, and then make the following changes to the data in the embedded cells:
    a. C2: Change *2678450* to *2857300*
    b. C3: Change *1753405* to *1598970*
    c. C4: Change *1452540* to *1635400*
22. Run the presentation.
23. Print the presentation as a handout with six slides printed horizontally per page.
24. Save **P-U2-A3-GSMtg.pptx**.
25. Apply a transition and sound of your choosing to all slides in the presentation.
26. Use the Rehearse Timings feature to set the following times for the slides to display during a slide show (your actual time will display with an extra second for each slide):
    Slide 1 = 3 seconds
    Slide 2 = 3 seconds
    Slide 3 = 6 seconds
    Slide 4 = 5 seconds
    Slide 5 = 6 seconds
    Slide 6 = 5 seconds
27. Set up the slide show to run continuously.
28. Run the presentation beginning with Slide 1. Watch the slide show until the presentation has started for the second time and then end the show.
29. Save and then close the presentation.

Assessment 4 Apply Custom Animation Effects to a Travel Presentation

1. Open **NTAustralia.pptx** and then save the presentation with the name **P-U2-A4-NTAustralia**.
2. With Slide 1 active, apply a Fly In entrance animation effect to the subtitle *Australia Tour* that has the title fly in from the bottom.
3. Display the presentation in Slide Master view and then make the following changes:
   a. Click the third slide master thumbnail.
   b. Apply a Fly In entrance animation effect to the title that has the title fly in from the top.
   c. Apply a Fly In entrance animation effect to the bulleted text that has the text fly in from the left and then dims to a color of your choosing when the next bullet displays.
   d. Close Slide Master view.
4. Make Slide 5 active, select the sun shape that displays above *Sydney*, and then draw a freeform motion path from Sydney to Melbourne, Tasmania, Adelaide, Perth, Derby, Darwin, Cairns, and then back to Sydney. Change the duration to *04.00*.
5. Make Slide 6 active and then make the following changes:
   a. Click the bottom shape to select it. (You may want to move the top two shapes out of the way.)
   b. Apply the Grow & Turn entrance effect.
   c. Click the Add Animation button and then click the *Shrink & Turn* exit effect.
   d. Click the middle shape to select it and then apply the Grow & Turn entrance effect.
   e. Click the Add Animation button and then click the *Shrink & Turn* exit effect.
   f. Click the top shape to select it and then apply the Grow & Turn entrance effect.
   g. Position the shapes so they are stacked on top of each other so you do not see a portion of the shapes behind.
6. Save **P-U2-A4-NTAustralia.pptx**.
7. Make Slide 1 active, run the presentation, and then make sure the animation effects play correctly.
8. Print the presentation as a handout with all slides printed horizontally on one page.
9. Close **P-U2-A4-NTAustralia.pptx**.

Assessment 5 Inspect a Presentation and Save a Presentation in Different Formats

1. Open **P-U2-A1-GreenDesignPres.pptx** and then save the presentation with the name **P-U2-A5-GreenDesignPres**.
2. Inspect the presentation using the Document Inspector dialog box and remove comments from the presentation.
3. Run the compatibility checker. (Click OK at the Microsoft Compatibility Checker dialog box.)
4. Save the presentation in *PowerPoint 97-2003* format and name it **P-U2-A5-GreenDesignPres-2003format**. (Click the Continue button at the compatibility checker message.)
5. Close **P-U2-A5-GreenDesignPres-2003format.ppt**.

6. Open **P-U2-A5-GreenDesignPres.pptx** and then save the presentation as a PDF document.
7. View the presentation in Adobe Reader.
8. After viewing all of the slides, close Adobe Reader.
9. Close **P-U2-A5-GreenDesignPres.pptx** without saving the changes.
10. Capture an image of the Open dialog box and insert the image in a PowerPoint slide by completing the following steps:
    a. Press Ctrl + N to display a new blank presentation.
    b. Click the Layout button in the Slides group on the HOME tab and then click the *Blank* layout at the drop-down list.
    c. Press Ctrl + F12 to display the Open dialog box.
    d. At the Open dialog box, click the option button that displays to the right of the *File name* text box (option button that contains the text *All PowerPoint Presentations*) and then click *All Files (*.*)* at the drop-down list.
    e. Scroll down the Open dialog box list box to display your assessment files.
    f. Hold down the Alt key and then press the Print Screen button on your keyboard. (This captures an image of your Open dialog box.)
    g. Click the Cancel button to close the Open dialog box.
    h. Click the Paste button. (This inserts the image of your Open dialog box into the slide.)
11. Print the slide as a full page slide.
12. Close the presentation without saving it.

Writing Activities

The following activities give you the opportunity to practice your writing skills along with demonstrating an understanding of some of the important PowerPoint features you have mastered in this unit. Use correct grammar, appropriate word choices, and clear sentence structure.

Activity 1 Prepare and Format a Travel Presentation

You work for Norton Travel and you are responsible for preparing a presentation on travel vacations. Open the Word document named **NTVacations.docx** and then print the document. Close the document and then close Word. Using the information in the document, prepare a PowerPoint presentation with the following specifications:

1. Create a presentation that presents the main points of the document.
2. Rehearse and set times for the slides to display during a slide show. You determine the number of seconds for each slide.
3. Insert a song into the first slide from the Insert Audio window (type **summer** in the search text box).
4. Set up the presentation to run continuously and the audio to play automatically across all slides and continuously as long as the presentation is running.
5. Run the presentation. (The slide show will start and run continuously.) Watch the presentation until it has started for the second time and then end the show by pressing the Esc key.
6. Save the presentation and name it **P-U2-Act1-NTVacations**.
7. Print the presentation as a handout with six slides printed horizontally per page.
8. Close **P-U2-Act1-NTVacations.pptx**.

Activity 2 Prepare and Format a Presentation on Media Files

Using PowerPoint's Help feature, learn more about audio and video file formats compatible with PowerPoint 2013. (Use the search terms *video and audio file formats*.) Using the information you find in the Help files, create a presentation with *at least* the following specifications:

- A slide containing the title of the presentation and your name
- Two slides that each contain information on compatible audio file formats, including the file extensions
- Two slides that each contain information on compatible video file formats, including the file extensions
- Optional: If you are connected to the Internet, search for websites where you can download free audio clips and then include this information in a slide with a hyperlink to the site.

Save the completed presentation and name it **P-U2-Act2-AudioVideo**. Run the presentation and then print the presentation as a handout with six slides printed horizontally per page. Close **P-U2-Act2-AudioVideo.pptx**.

Internet Research

Presenting Office 2013

Make sure you are connected to the Internet and then explore the Microsoft website at www.microsoft.com. Browse the various categories and links on the website to familiarize yourself with how information is organized.

Create a PowerPoint presentation to deliver to someone who has just purchased Office 2013 and wants to know how to find more information about the software on the Microsoft website. Include tips on where to find product release information and technical support, as well as hyperlinks to other important pages. Add formatting and enhancements to make the presentation as dynamic as possible. Save the presentation and name it **P-U2-Int-Office2013**. Run the presentation and then print the presentation as a handout with four slides printed per page. Close **P-U2-Int-Office2013.pptx**.

Job Study

Creating a Skills Presentation

You are preparing a presentation to give at your local job fair. Open the Word document **JobDescriptions.docx**, print the document, and then close the document and close Word. Use the information in the document to prepare slides that describe each job (do not include the starting salary). Using the Internet, locate information on two other jobs that interest you and then create a slide about the responsibilities of each job. Determine the starting salary for the two jobs and then use that information along with the starting salary information for the jobs in the Word document to create a chart that displays the salary amounts. Locate at least two online job search websites and then include their names in your presentation along with hyperlinks to the sites. Save the presentation and name it **P-U2-JobStudy**. Run the presentation and then print the presentation as a handout with six slides printed horizontally per page. Close **P-U2-JobStudy.pptx**.

Index

A

accessibility check, 359–360
action buttons
applying action to object, 260–261
creating, 258–260
Action Settings dialog box, creating hyperlink, 260–261
Add Animation button, 281
adding
new slide, 12
sound effects, 31–32
transitions, 31–32
Align button, 127
alignment, of text boxes, 127
Align Text button, 92
animation
applying
with Animation Painter, 281
with ANIMATIONS tab, 278–280
build, 288
sound to, 288
chart, 292–293
creating motion path, 293–294
customizing, 285–287
images, 289–290
inserting trigger, 294–296
removing, 280
running presentation without, 297
shapes, 289–290
SmartArt graphic, 290–291
animation effects
applying, 281–283
modifying, 283, 286–287
removing, 286–287
reordering items, 283–285, 286–287
Animation Painter, 281
Animation Pane, 285–287
ANIMATIONS tab, 278
Apply To All button, 31
area chart, 207
Arrange All button, 255
Arrange button, 98
Audio button, 309
audio file
inserting, 308–309
optimizing and compressing, 310
playing throughout presentation, 314
showing and hiding media controls, 310
AutoExpansion feature, 206
AutoFit Options, 87
automatic backup, 361–362

B

background
applying and formatting for Slide Master, 240–241
inserting picture as, 147–149
background, customizing, 105–108
Background Styles button, 240, 251
Background Styles option, 105
bar chart, 207
Blank Presentation template, 29
Borders button, 191
Bring Forward button, 143
bubble chart, 207
build animation, applying, 288
bullets, customizing, 94–96
Bullets and Numbering dialog box, 94, 95, 96, 97

C

Cascade button, 255
CD, packaging a presentation for, 335
cells
cell designation, 189
defined, 189
entering text in, 189
selecting, 189–190
Center Tab button, 133
Change Chart Type dialog box, 210–212
Change Colors button, 211
Change File Type option, 338–342
chart, 206–217
animating, 292–293
creating, 206–208
customizing design of, 210–212
formatting, 212–216
with chart buttons, 208–210
with CHART TOOLS FORMAT tab, 213–215
with Drawing group, 212
shortcut menu, 216
pie chart, 216–217
sample chart, 206, 207
types of, 207
Chart Elements button, 208, 213
Chart Filters button, 209
Chart Styles button, 208–209
CHART TOOLS DESIGN tab, 210–212
CHART TOOLS FORMAT tab, 213
clip art, animating, 289–290
Clipboard task pane, 329–330
closing, presentation, 8–9
Collapse the Ribbon button, 6
color
changing theme color, 105
color variant in design theme template, 27
creating custom theme color, 109–110
Eyedropper option, 98
viewing presentation in, 256
column chart, 207
columns
customizing, 91–92
number of, in table, 189
selecting, in table, 190
setting tabs in text box, 133–134
Columns dialog box, 91
comments
editing and deleting, 352–353
inserting, 351–352
COMMENTS button, 16
Compare button, 349
compatibility check, 361
Compress Media button, 310
Convert button, 205
copying
objects within and between presentations, 152
shapes, 135
slides, 57–58
between presentations, 59–60
text between document and presentation, 329–331
text in slides, 51–53
Create Handouts option, 336–337
Create New Theme Colors dialog box, 109
Create New Theme Fonts dialog box, 111
Crop button, 143
cropping images, 143
customizing
animation effects, 285–287
bullets, 94–96
chart design, 210–212
columns, 91–92
Handout Master, 251–253
images, 142

Notes Master, 253–254
numbering, 96–98
paragraphs, 90
placeholders, 98–102
PowerPoint Options, 362–365
prompts, 245
Quick Access Toolbar, 65–66
slide show, 306–308
themes, 109–114
custom themes
deleting, 113–114
editing, 113
saving, 112–113
theme colors, 109–110
theme fonts, 111

D

date, inserting into Slide Master, 243–244
Decimal Tab button, 133
Delay measurement box, 283
deleting
comments, 352–353
custom theme, 113–114
presentation, 28
slides, 57
DESIGN tab, 27, 109
design theme templates
applying, 27
changing color, 105
changing fonts, 105
color variant, 27
creating presentation using, 10–11, 13–15
downloading, 346–348
live preview of, 27
names of, 27
destination, 343
dialog box launder, 82
digital signature, adding, 357–358
document panel, 354–355
doughnut chart, 207
drawing, table, 197–198
Drawing group, 98, 212
drawing guides, turn on/off, 136
DRAWING TOOLS FORMAT tab, 127, 135
Draw Table button, 191
duplicating slides, 60–61
Duration measurement box, 32, 283
DVD, burning video to, 334

E

Edit Data button, 211
editing
comments, 352–353
custom slide show, 307
custom theme, 113
hyperlinks, 265
linked objects, 345–346
photo album, 219–221
Effect Options button, 278
Effects button, 191
email address, insert hyperlink to, 263
email attachment, sending presentation as, 333, 334
embedding objects, 343–344
encrypt presentation, 356
Erase All Ink on Slide option, 23
Eraser button, 191
Eraser option, 23
Excel spreadsheet, inserting and formatting in slide, 195–197
exporting, presentations, 334–338
Eyedropper option, 98

F

FILE tab, 6
Find dialog box, 49–50
Font dialog box, 82–83
Font group buttons, 81–82
fonts
changing, 81–83
changing font theme, 105
creating custom theme fonts, 111
formatting, 81–84
dialog box, 82–83
Font group buttons, 81–82
with Mini toolbar, 83
live preview, 81
serif and sans serif, 82
footers, inserting, 157–160
into Slide Master, 243–244
Format Background button, 147
Format Background task pane, 105–106, 147, 148
Format Painter, 85–86
Format Selection button, 213
Format Shape task pane, 99, 127, 131
formatting
bullets and numbering, 94–98
chart, 208–210, 212–216
columns, 91–92
custom themes, 109–114
fonts, 81–84
Format Painter, 85–86
grouping/ungrouping objects, 141–142
images, 142
merging shapes, 140–141
page setup changes, 103–104
paragraphs, 87–90
photo album, 219–221
pictures, 222
placeholders, 87, 98–102
presentations, 81–102
rotating and vertically aligning text, 92–93
screenshots, 152–154
shapes, 135
Slide Master, 238–239
SmartArt, 201–202
text box, 126–134
WordArt text, 154–156
From Beginning button, 22
From Current Slide button, 22

G

graph, 187
graphic, hyperlink with, 263
GRAYSCALE tab, 256
Grid and Guides dialog box, 136–137
gridlines, turn on/off, 136–137
Group button, 140
grouping objects, 140–141

H

Handout Master, 235
customizing, 251–253
Handout Master button, 251
HANDOUT MASTER tab, 251
handouts
exporting presentation to Word to create, 336–338
printing presentation as, 19
Header and Footer dialog box, 157–158, 243
headers, inserting, 157–160
into Slide Master, 243–244
Help feature
dialog box and backstage area, 67
Help button, 67
running slide show, 24
ScreenTip, 67
Hide Background Graphics check box, 240
Hide Slide button, 302–303
Highlighter option, 23
HOME tab, 81, 82
horizontal ruler, turning on/off, 136
hyperlink

Action Settings dialog box, 260–261
to email address, 263
with graphic, 263
inserting, 262–265
linking to another presentation and website, 260–261
modifying, editing and removing, 265
ScreenTip, 263

I

images
animating, 289–290
arranging, 143
cropping, 143
customizing and formatting, 142
inserting, 142–147
from Office.com, 149–150
as slide background, 147–149
moving, 143
nudging, 143
sizing, 143
Info backstage area, 353–355
Insert Chart dialog box, 206
Insert Hyperlink dialog box, 262–263
inserting
action buttons, 258–260
audio file, 308–309
comments, 351–352
elements in Slide Master, 243–244
elements in slides
copying within and between presentations, 152
Excel spreadsheet, 195–197
headers and footers, 157–160
image from Office.com, 149–150
images, 142–147
merges shapes, 140–141
picture as slide background, 147–149
screenshots, 152–154
shapes, 135
sizing, rotating and positioning objects, 150–151
symbols, 156–157
text boxes, 126–134
WordArt text, 154–156
hyperlinks, 262–265
new slide, 12
new Slide Master, 246–247
placeholders in Slide Master, 244–246
presentation properties, 355
slides, 57
in customized presentations, 241–242
SmartArt graphic, 198
insertion point, 6
Insert Layout button, 244
Insert Picture dialog box, 95
Insert Placeholder button, 244
Insert Slide Master button, 246
INSERT tab, 142
Insert Table button, 189
inspect presentation, 358–359
integration, 342–343
Invite People option, 331

J

JPEG images, saving slides as, 341–342

K

keyboard shortcuts
cutting, copying and pasting, 51
Font dialog box, 82
to navigate slides, 16
Open backstage area, 7
Print backstage area, 18
Save As dialog box, 12

L

Laser Pointer option, 22
Layout button, 12
Left Tab button, 133
line chart, 207
Line Spacing Options, 90
linking objects, 344–345
editing, 345–346
live preview
design theme templates, 27
Eyedropper option, 98
fonts, 81

M

Manage Versions button, 361
Mark as Final, 355–357
Master Layout button, 244
media controls, showing and hiding, 310
Merge button, 349
Merge Shapes button, 140–141
Mini toolbar, formatting text with, 83
Monitor option, 303
More button, 109
More slide show options button, 23, 24
motion path, drawing, 293–294
mouse pointer, hiding/displaying, 24
Move Earlier button, 283, 285
Move Later button, 283, 285
Move Split button, 255
moving
images, 143
slides, 57–58

N

New backstage area, 10–11
New Comment button, 351
New Slide button, 57
New Window button, 255
Next button, 22, 23
Next Slide button, 16
Normal view, 16
NOTES button, 16
Notes Master, 235
customizing, 253–254
NOTES MASTER tab, 253
Notes Page view, 16
nudging, 143
numbering, customizing, 96–98

O

objects
applying action to, 260–261
copying within and between presentations, 152
defined, 343
embedding, to presentations, 342–344
grouping and ungrouping, 141–142
linking, to presentations, 344–346
sizing, rotating and positioning, 150–151
Office.com, inserting image from, 149–150
Online Pictures button, 149
On Mouse Click option, 297
Open backstage area, 7
Open button, 7
opening presentation
blank presentation, 29
from Open dialog box, 7
from Recent Presentations, 8
Optimize Compatibility button, 310

outline
importing Word outline, 328–329
printing presentation as, 19
outline pane, rearranging text in, 54–55
Outline View, 16, 29

P

page setup, changing in Slide Master, 247
Paragraph dialog box, 90
Paragraph group, 87
paragraphs
customizing, 90
formatting with Paragraph group, 87–90
pasting
text between document and presentation, 329–331
text in slides, 51–53
PDF, saving presentation in, 333, 334
Pen button, 22–23
Pen option, 22–23
photo album, 217–222
creating, 217–218
editing and formatting, 219–221
Photo Album dialog box, 217–218
pictures. See also images
creating photo album, 217–222
formatting, 222
inserting as bullet, 95
inserting as slide background, 147–149
PICTURE TOOLS FORMAT tab, 142–143
pie chart, 207
creating and formatting, 216–217
pin presentation, 8
placeholders, 6
AutoFit Options, 87
customizing, 98–102
with Drawing group, 98
Format Shape task pane, 99
deleting, in Slide Master, 240
elements of, 12
fitting contents in placeholder, 87
inserting in Slide Master, 244–246
inserting text in, 11, 48–49
sizing and rearranging, 55–56
planning, presentation, 10
PNG images, saving slides as, 341–342
positioning, objects, 150–151
PowerPoint Options dialog box, 362–365
PowerPoint window elements, 5–6
presentations
accessibility check, 359–360
closing, 8–9
comparing and combining, 349–350
compatibility check, 361
copying slides between, 59–60
creating
basic steps of, 5
from blank presentation, 29
with design theme templates, 10–11, 13–15
from Outline View, 29–30
slides in, 11–12
creating sections within, 63–65
custom slide show, 306–308
deleting, 28
embedding objects to, 342–344
encrypting, 356
exporting, 334–338
file name requirements, 13
formatting, 81–102
hiding slides, 302–303
inserting hyperlinks to another presentation, 263–265
inspecting, 358–359
linking
another presentation to website, 260–261
objects to, 344–346
managing monitors, 303
managing properties of, 353–355
navigating, 16–18
opening, 7–8
pinning to Recent Presentation list, 8
planning, 10
playing audio file throughout, 314
Presenter View, 303–304
Present Online feature, 304–305
printing, 18–22
protecting, 355–357
recording narration, 300–302
running, 8–9, 22–26
loop continuously, 297–299
setting automatic times for slides, 299
setting rehearse timings for, 300
without animation, 297
saving, 12–13
in different format, 338–342
as template, 250–251
sharing, 331–334
sound effects, 31–32
transitions, 31–32
viewing, 256
viewing options for, 16
Presenter View, 303–304
Present Online feature, 304–305
Preserve button, 247
Preview button, 280
Previous Slide button, 16
Print backstage area, 18–19
printing
custom slide show, 307
presentation, 18–22
slides, 18
print preview area, 19
prompts, creating custom, 245
Protect Presentation button, 355–356

Q

Quick Access toolbar, 6
customizing, 65–66
Quick Layout button, 211
Quick Styles button, 98

R

radar chart, 207
Reading view, 16
Recent Presentations list
opening presentation from, 8
pinning presentation to, 8
Recording toolbar, 299
Record Slide Show button, 300–301
Rename button, 244
Replace dialog box, 49–50
Reset Graphic button, 205
Reuse Slide task pane, 61–62, 242
reusing slides, 61–63
REVIEW tab, 349
ribbon, 6
Right Tab button, 133
rotating, objects, 150–151
rows
number of, in table, 189
selecting, in table, 190
ruler, turning on/off, 136
running

presentation, 8–9
slide show, 22–26

S

sans serif fonts, 82
Save As dialog box, 12
saving
autosaved presentations, 361–362
custom theme, 112–113
presentations, 12–13
in different format, 338–342
as template, 250–251
slides as graphic images, 341–342
scatter chart, 207
Screen Clipping option, 153
Screenshot button, 152
screenshots, creating, 152–154
ScreenTip, 67
with hyperlink, 263
scroll box, 6
sections, creating within presentations, 63–65
See all slides button, 23
Select Data button, 211
Send Backward button, 143
serif fonts, 82
serifs, 82
Set Up Slide Show dialog box, 296
Shading button, 191
Shape Effects button, 98
Shape Fill button, 98
SHAPE OPTIONS tab, 99
Shape Outline button, 98
shapes
animating, 289–290
converting SmartArt graphic to, 205
copying, 135
drawing and formatting, 135, 137–139
inserting, 135
merging, 140–141
set as default, 135
Shapes button, 135
Shape Styles task pane, 127
Share backstage area, 331–334
sizing
images, 143
objects, 150–151
Slide Library, 61–62
Slide Master, 235, 237–249
applying
backgrounds, 240–241
themes to, 238–239
changing page setup, 247
creating
custom prompts, 245
custom slide layout, 244
deleting
layout, 240
placeholders, 240
formatting, 238–239
inserting
header, footer, time, date in, 243–244
new Slide Master, 246–247
placeholders, 244–246
slides in customized presentation, 241–242
overview of, 237–238
preserving, 247
SLIDE MASTER tab, 237–238, 244
Slide Master view, 237–238
slide pane, 6
advancing automatically, 34
finding and replacing text in, 49–51
slides
background, customizing, 105–108
choosing slide layout, 12
copying, 57–58
between presentations, 59–60
creating, 11–12
cutting, copying, pasting text in, 51–53
deleting, 57
deleting text in, 48–49
duplicating, 60–61
hiding, 302–303
inserting
in customized presentation, 241–242
new, 12, 57
text in, 48–49
moving, 57–58
navigating, 16
automatically, 34
orientation, changing, 103–104
printing, 18
reusing, 61–63
saving, as graphic images, 341–342
size, changing, 103–104
sizing and rearranging placeholders in, 55–56
slide show
custom slide show, 306–308
hiding slides, 302–303
Presenter View, 303–304
Present Online feature, 304–305
recording narration, 300–302
running, 22–26
loop continuously, 297–299
setting automatic times for slides, 299
setting rehearse timings for, 300
without animation, 297
Set Up Show dialog box, 296
Slide Show button, 22
Slide Show Help dialog box, 24
SLIDE SHOW tab, 8, 22, 296
Slide Show toolbar, 22–23
Slide Show view, 16
Slide Size dialog box, 103–104
Slide Sorter view, 16
copying slides in, 57
inserting new slide, 57
moving slides in, 57–58
slide thumbnails pane, 6
navigate slides with, 16
SmartArt, 198–205
animating, 290–291
converting text and WordArt to, 203–205
converting to text or shapes, 205
formatting, 201–202
inserting graphic, 198
inserting text in Text pane, 203
modifying, 199–200
SmartArt Graphic dialog box, 198
SMARTART TOOLS DESIGN tab, 199
SMARTART TOOLS FORMAT tab, 201
Smart Guides, turn on/off, 136–137
sound
adding/removing, 32
applying to animation, 288
Sound option box, 288
source, 343
spelling, checking, 45–46
Spelling task pane, 45–46
Start From Beginning button, 8, 22
Start option box, 283
Status bar, 6
stock chart, 207
surface chart, 207
Switch Row/Column button, 211
Switch Windows button, 255
symbol, inserting as bullet, 95

Symbol button, 156
Symbol dialog box, 95, 96
symbols, inserting, 156–157

T

table, 189–198
AutoExpansion feature, 206
changing design of, 191–192
changing layout of, 193–195
creating, 189–191
drawing, 197–198
entering text in cells, 189
inserting Excel spreadsheet, 195–197
selecting cells, 189–190
Table button, 189
TABLE TOOLS DESIGN tab, 191–192, 197
TABLE TOOLS LAYOUT tab, 193–195, 197
tabs, 6
setting, in text box, 133–134
Tabs dialog box, 133
template
downloading, 346–348
saving presentation as, 250–251
text
checking spelling, 45–46
converting SmartArt graphic to, 205
converting to SmartArt, 203–205
cutting, copying and pasting in slides, 51–53
deleting in slide, 48–49
entering in cells, 189
finding and replacing, in slides, 49–51
fitting text in placeholder, 87
formatting
with Format Painter, 85–86
with Mini toolbar, 83
inserting
in placeholder, 11
in slide, 48–49
pasting text between document and presentation, 329–331
rearranging in outline pane, 54–55
rotating, 92–93
thesaurus, 46
vertically aligning, 92–93
WordArt text, 154–156
text box
aligning, 127
change size of, 127
formatting, 126–127
inserting, 126–131
moving, 127
selecting multiple objects, 127
set default, 131–133
setting tabs in, 133–134
Text Direction button, 92
Text Effects button, 155
Text Fill button, 154
TEXT OPTIONS tab, 99
Text Outline button, 154
Text pane, inserting text in, 203
themes
applying to Slide Master, 238–239
custom
deleting, 113–114
editing, 113
saving, 112–113
theme colors, 109–110
theme fonts, 111
design theme templates, 10–11, 13–15, 27
Thesaurus, 46
time, inserting, into Slide Master, 243–244
Title bar, 6
Title Slide layout, 11, 12
transitions
adding, 32
defined, 31
removing, 32
TRANSITIONS tab, 31–32, 297
trigger, applying for animation, 294–296

U

ungrouping objects, 140–141
unpin presentation, 8

V

vertical ruler, turning on/off, 136
vertical scroll bar, 6
navigate slides, 16
video, saving presentation as, 334–336
Video button, 310
video file
inserting, 309–310
optimizing and compressing, 310
showing and hiding media controls, 310
trimming, 313
view area, 6
views, changing, 16
VIEW tab, 16, 29
changing zoom, 255
managing windows, 255
viewing color and grayscale, 256
viewing presentation, 256

W

website
inserting hyperlinks, 262–265
linking, to another presentation, 260–261
WordArt, converting to SmartArt, 203–205
WordArt button, 154
Word document
exporting presentation to, 336–338
inserting hyperlinks, 263–265
Word outline, importing, 328–329

X

XPS format, 334
xy (scatter) chart, 207

Z

zoom, changing, 255
Zoom button, 23–24, 255
Zoom slider button, 255

Office 2013 Integrated Project

Now that you have completed the chapters in this textbook, you have learned to create documents in Word, build worksheets in Excel, organize data in Access, and design presentations in PowerPoint. To learn the various programs in the Microsoft Office 2013 suite, you have completed a variety of projects, assessments, and activities. This integrated project is a final assignment that allows you to apply the knowledge you have gained about the programs in the Office suite to produce a variety of documents and files.

Situation

You are the vice president of Classique Coffees, a gourmet coffee company. Your company operates two retail stores that sell gourmet coffee and related products to the public. One retail store is located in Seattle, Washington; the other in is located in Tacoma, Washington. The company is three years old and has seen approximately 10- to 20-percent growth in profit each year. Your duties as the vice president of the company include researching the coffee market; studying coffee buying trends; designing and implementing new projects; and supervising the marketing, sales, and personnel managers.

Activity 1 Write Persuasively

Using Word, compose a memo to the president of Classique Coffees, Leslie Steiner, detailing your research and recommendations:

- Research has shown 10-percent growth in the protein smoothie market.
- The target population for protein smoothies is people from ages 18 to 35.
- Market analysis indicates that only three local retail companies sell protein smoothies in the greater Seattle-Tacoma area.
- The recommendation is that Classique Coffees develop a suite of protein smoothies for market consumption by early next year. (Be as persuasive as possible.)

Save the completed memo and name it **ProjectAct01**. Print and then close **ProjectAct01.docx**.

Activity 2 Design a Letterhead

You are not satisfied with the current letterhead used by your company. Use Word to design a new letterhead for Classique Coffees according to the following specifications:

- Use a clip art image in the letterhead.
- Include the company name—Classique Coffees.
- Include the company address—355 Pioneer Square, Seattle, WA 98211.
- Include the company telephone number—(206) 555-6690.
- Include the company web address—www.ccoffees.emcp.net.
- Create a slogan that will help your business contacts remember your company.
- Add any other information or elements that you feel are appropriate.

When the letterhead is completed, save the Word document and name it **ProjectAct02**. Print and then close **ProjectAct02.docx**.

Activity 3 Prepare a Notice

Using Word, prepare a notice about an upcoming marketing seminar. Include the following information in the notice:

- Name of the seminar—Marketing to the Coffee Gourmet
- Location of the seminar—Conference room at the corporate office, 355 Pioneer Square, Seattle, WA 98211
- Date and time of seminar—Friday, October 16, 2015, 9:00 a.m. to 2:30 p.m.
- Topics that will be covered at the seminar:
    - Identifying coffee drinking trends
    - Assessing the current gourmet coffee market
    - Developing new products
    - Analyzing the typical Classique Coffees customer
    - Marketing a new product line
- Consider including a clip art image in the notice. (You determine an appropriate clip art image.)

When the notice is completed, save it and name it **ProjectAct03**. Print and then close **ProjectAct03.docx**.

Activity 4 Create an Organizational Chart

In preparation for an upcoming meeting, you need to prepare an organizational chart of the leadership team at Classique Coffees. Using Word, create an organizational chart using a SmartArt graphic that includes the following:

President
Vice President

Marketing Manager	Sales Manager	Personnel Manager
Marketing Assistants	Sales Associates	Assistant Manager

Apply formatting to improve the appearance of the chart. Save the Word document and name it **ProjectAct04**. Print and then close **ProjectAct04.docx**.

Activity 5 Create a SmartArt Graphic

In addition to the organizational chart, you also want to create a SmartArt graphic that illustrates the steps in a marketing plan. Those steps are:

- Planning
- Development
- Marketing
- Distribution

Apply formatting to improve the appearance of the graphic. Save the Word document and name it **ProjectAct05**. Print and then close **ProjectAct05.docx**.

Activity 6 Build a Budget Worksheet

Using Excel, prepare a worksheet containing the following information:

Annual Budget: $1,450,000

Department	**Percent of Budget**	**Total**
Administration	10%	
Purchasing	24%	
Sales	21%	
Marketing	23%	
Personnel	12%	
Training	10%	

Insert formulas to calculate the total amount for each department based on the specified percentage of the annual budget. When the worksheet is completed, save it, name it **ProjectAct06**, and then print **ProjectAct06.xlsx**.

Determine the impact of a 10-percent increase in the annual budget on the total amount for each department. With the amounts displayed for a 10-percent increase, save, print, and then close **ProjectAct06.xlsx**.

Activity 7 Determine Sales Quota Increases

The Marketing Department for Classique Coffees employs seven people who market the company products to customers. These employees are to meet a quota for yearly sales. You have determined that the quotas need to be raised for the upcoming year. You are not sure whether the quotas should be increased by 5 percent or 10 percent. Using Excel, prepare a worksheet with the following information:

CLASSIQUE COFFEES
Sales Quotas

Employee	Current Quota	Projected Quota
Berenstein	$125,000	
Evans	$100,000	
Grayson	$110,000	
Lueke	$135,000	
Nasson	$125,000	
Phillips	$150,000	
Samuels	$175,000	

Insert a formula to determine the projected quotas at 5 percent more than the current quotas. Save the worksheet, name it **ProjectAct07A**, and then print **ProjectAct07A.xlsx**. Insert formulas to determine the projected quotas at 10 percent more than the current quotas. Save the worksheet and name it **ProjectAct07B**. Print and then close **ProjectAct07B.xlsx**.

Activity 8 Build a Sales Worksheet and Create a Chart

Using Excel, prepare a worksheet containing the following information:

Type of Coffee	Percent of Sales
Regular blend	22%
Espresso blend	12%
Regular blend decaf	17%
Espresso blend decaf	10%
Flavored blend	25%
Flavored blend decaf	14%

Save the completed worksheet, name it **ProjectAct08**, and then print **ProjectAct08.xlsx**. With the worksheet still displayed, use the data in the worksheet to create a pie chart in a new sheet. Title the pie chart *Year 2015 Percentage of Sales*. When the chart is completed, save the workbook (now two sheets) with the same name (**ProjectAct08.xlsx**). Print only the sheet containing the pie chart and then close **ProjectAct08.xlsx**.

Activity 9 Build a Projected Sales Worksheet and Create a Chart

Using Excel, prepare a worksheet containing the following information:

Type of Coffee	Percent of Sales
Regular blend	21%
Espresso blend	10%
Regular blend decaf	16%
Espresso blend decaf	8%
Flavored blend	24%
Flavored blend decaf	16%
Protein smoothie	5%

Use the data in the worksheet to create a pie chart in a new sheet. Title the pie chart *Year 2016 Projected Percentage of Sales*. When the chart is completed, save the workbook and name it **ProjectAct09**. Print and then close **ProjectAct09.xlsx**.

Analyze the sales data by comparing and contrasting the pie charts in **ProjectAct08.xlsx** and **ProjectAct09.xlsx**. What areas in the projected sales percentages have changed? What do these changes indicate? Assume that the projected 2016 annual income for Classique Coffees is $2,200,000. What amount of that income will come from protein smoothies? Does this amount warrant marketing this new product? Use Word to prepare a memo to Leslie Steiner that includes your analysis. Add any other interpretations based on your analysis of the pie charts. Save the memo and name it **WordProject09**. Print and then close **WordProject09.docx**.

Activity 10 Design and Create a Presentation

Using PowerPoint, prepare a marketing presentation. Include the following information in the presentation:

- Classique Coffees 2016 Marketing Plan (Use this as the title.)
- Company reorganization (Insert the organizational chart you created in Activity 4.)
- 2015 sales percentages (Insert the pie chart from **ProjectAct08.xlsx**.)
- 2016 projected sales percentages (Insert the pie chart from **ProjectAct09.xlsx**.)
- Protein smoothie marketing strategy
    - Target customer
    - Analysis of competition
    - Wholesale resources
    - Pricing
    - Volume
- Product placement
    - Stocking strategies
    - Shelf allocation
    - Stock rotation schedule
    - Seasonal display

When preparing the slide presentation, you determine the presentation design theme and the layouts. Include any clip art images that might be appropriate and apply an animation scheme to all slides. When the presentation is completed, save it and name it **ProjectAct10**. Run the presentation and then print the presentation with six slides printed horizontally per page.

Activity 11 Create a Database File and Organize Data

Use Access to create a database for Classique Coffees that contains information on suppliers and products. Include the following fields in the Suppliers table and the Products table:

Suppliers table:

SupplierNo
SupplierName
Address
City
State
ZipCode
Email

Products table:

ProductNo
Product
SupplierNo

Type the following data in the Suppliers table:

SupplierNo	=	24	*SupplierNo*	=	62
SupplierName	=	Gourmet Blends	*SupplierName*	=	Sure Shot Supplies
Address	=	109 South Madison	*Address*	=	291 Pacific Avenue
City	=	Seattle	*City*	=	Tacoma
State	=	WA	*State*	=	WA
ZipCode	=	98032	*ZipCode*	=	98418
Email	=	gblends@emcp.net	*Email*	=	sssupplies@emcp.net

SupplierNo	=	36	*SupplierNo*	=	41
SupplierName	=	Jannsen Company	*SupplierName*	=	Bertolinos
Address	=	4122 South Sprague	*Address*	=	11711 Meridian East
City	=	Tacoma	*City*	=	Seattle
State	=	WA	*State*	=	WA
ZipCode	=	98402	*ZipCode*	=	98109
Email	=	jannsen@emcp.net	*Email*	=	bertolino@emcp.net

Type the following data in the Products table:

ProductNo	=	12A-0	*ProductNo*	=	59R-1
Product	=	Premium blend	*Product*	=	Vanilla syrup
SupplierNo	=	24	*SupplierNo*	=	62
ProductNo	=	12A-1	*ProductNo*	=	59R-2
Product	=	Cappuccino blend	*Product*	=	Raspberry syrup
SupplierNo	=	24	*SupplierNo*	=	62
ProductNo	=	12A-2	*ProductNo*	=	59R-3
Product	=	Hazelnut blend	*Product*	=	Chocolate syrup
SupplierNo	=	24	*SupplierNo*	=	62
ProductNo	=	21B-2	*ProductNo*	=	89T-3
Product	=	12-oz cup	*Product*	=	Napkins, 500 ct
SupplierNo	=	36	*SupplierNo*	=	41
ProductNo	=	21B-3	*ProductNo*	=	89T-4
Product	=	16-oz cup	*Product*	=	6-inch stir stick
SupplierNo	=	36	*SupplierNo*	=	41

Print both the Suppliers table and the Products table in landscape orientation. Prepare a report with the following information: supplier name, supplier number, supplier email, and product.

Merge the records of the suppliers located in Tacoma to a blank Word document. Compose a business letter that you will send to the contacts in Tacoma. You determine the inside address and an appropriate salutation. Include the following information in the letter:

- Explain that Classique Coffees is interested in selling protein smoothies in the greater Seattle-Tacoma area.
- Ask if the company offers any protein smoothie products.
- If the company does not currently offer any protein smoothie products, will these products be available in the future?
- Ask the company to send any materials on current products and specifically on protein smoothies.
- Ask someone at the company to contact you at the Classique Coffees address, by telephone at (206) 555-6690, or by email at ccoffees@emcp.net.
- Include any other information you think appropriate to the topic.

Merge to a new document and then save the document with the name **ProjectAct11**. Print and then close **ProjectAct11.docx**. Save the main document as **SmoothieLtrMD** and then close **SmoothieLtrMD.docx**.

Activity 12 Assess Your Work

Review the documents you developed and create a Word document assessing your work. To help you develop an objective perspective of your work, openly solicit constructive criticism from your teacher, peers, and contacts outside of school. Your self-assessment document should specify the weaknesses and strengths of each piece and your specific recommendations for revision and improvement.

MON COMMANDS FOR MICROSOFT 2013 OFFICE SUITE

WORD, EXCEL, POWERPOINT

Feature	Ribbon Tab, Group/Option	Button	Keyboard Shortcut
bold text	HOME, Font	B	Ctrl + B
Clipboard task pane	HOME, Clipboard		
close	FILE, *Close*		Ctrl + F4
close program		×	Alt + F4
copy	HOME, Clipboard		Ctrl + C
cut	HOME, Clipboard		Ctrl + X
Find	HOME, Editing		Ctrl + F
font	HOME, Font	Calibri (Body)	
font color	HOME, Font	A	
font size	HOME, Font	11	Ctrl + Shift + P
Format Painter	HOME, Clipboard		Ctrl + Shift + C
Help		?	F1
Insert Hyperlink dialog box	INSERT, Links		Ctrl + K
italicize text	HOME, Font	*I*	Ctrl + I
New backstage area	FILE, *New*		
Open backstage area	FILE, *Open*		Ctrl + O
paste	HOME, Clipboard		Ctrl + V
Print backstage area	FILE, *Print*		Ctrl + P
Save As backstage area	FILE, *Save* OR *Save As*		Ctrl + S
Save As dialog box			F12
shapes	INSERT, Illustrations		
SmartArt	INSERT, Illustrations		
table	INSERT, Tables		
text box	INSERT, Text		
underline text	HOME, Font	U	Ctrl + U
WordArt	INSERT, Text		

WORD

Feature	Ribbon Tab, Group/Option	Button	Keyboard Shortcut
align left, center, or right	HOME, Paragraph		Ctrl + L, E, or R
bullets	HOME, Paragraph		
columns	PAGE LAYOUT, Page Setup		
Envelopes and Labels dialog box	MAILINGS, Create		
header or footer	INSERT, Header & Footer		
line spacing, single or double	HOME, Paragraph		Ctrl + 1 or 2
Navigation pane	VIEW, Show		Ctrl + F
numbering	HOME, Paragraph		
online pictures	INSERT, Illustrations		
page break	INSERT, Pages		Ctrl + Enter
page number	INSERT, Header & Footer		
Page Setup dialog box	PAGE LAYOUT, Page Setup		
pictures	INSERT, Illustrations		
section break	PAGE LAYOUT, Page Setup		
Spelling & Grammar	REVIEW, Proofing		F7
themes	DESIGN, Document Formatting		
POWERPOINT			
add animation	ANIMATIONS, Advanced Animation		
audio file	INSERT, Media		
Font size, increase or decrease	HOME, Font		Ctrl + Shift + > Ctrl + Shift + <
layout	HOME, Slides		
list level, increase or decrease	HOME, Paragraph		Tab or Shift + Tab
new slide	HOME, Slides		Ctrl + M
screenshot	INSERT, Images		
Slide Sorter view	VIEW, Presentation Views		
video file	INSERT, Media		F7

EXCEL

Feature	Ribbon Tab, Group/Option	Button	Keyboard Shortcut
Accounting format	HOME, Number	$	
align left, center, or right	HOME, Alignment		
borders	HOME, Font		Ctrl + Shift + &
cell formulas	FORMULAS, Formula Auditing		Ctrl + `
change margins	PAGE LAYOUT, Page Setup OR FILE, *Print*		
column width or row height	HOME, Cells		
Comma format	HOME, Number	,	
create column, line, or pie chart	INSERT, Charts		F11
decimal, increase or decrease	HOME, Number		
delete cell, column, row, or worksheet	HOME, Cells		
fill color	HOME, Font		
format, move, copy, or rename worksheet	HOME, Cells		
indent, increase or decrease	HOME, Alignment		
insert cell, column, row, or worksheet	HOME, Cells		
insert comment	REVIEW, Comments		Shift + F2
insert function	FORMULAS, Function Library	*fx*	
merge and center	HOME, Alignment		
scale page width and/or height	PAGE LAYOUT, Scale to Fit OR FILE, Print		
sort	HOME, Editing		
Spelling or Thesaurus	REVIEW, Proofing		F7; Shift + F7
SUM function	HOME, Editing	Σ	Alt + =
theme	PAGE LAYOUT, Themes		
wrap text	HOME, Alignment		

ACCESS

Feature	Ribbon Tab, Group/Option	Button	Keyboard Shortcut
add fields to a form	FORM LAYOUT TOOLS DESIGN, Controls		
add or delete records	HOME, Records		Ctrl + +; Delete
change margins	PRINT PREVIEW, Page Size OR Page Layout		
column width	HOME, Records		
conditional formatting in form or report	FORM LAYOUT TOOLS FORMAT, Control Formatting OR REPORT LAYOUT TOOLS FORMAT, Control Formatting		
create table or create table in Design view	CREATE, Tables		
filter	HOME, Sort & Filter		
Find	HOME, Find		Ctrl + F
Form tool	CREATE, Forms		
Group, Sort, and Total pane	REPORT LAYOUT TOOLS DESIGN, Grouping & Totals		
insert or delete fields	TABLE TOOLS DESIGN, Tools		Delete
Labels Wizard	CREATE, Reports		
landscape orientation	PRINT PREVIEW, Page Layout		
primary key	TABLE TOOLS DESIGN, Tools		
Print Preview	FILE, *Print*		Ctrl + P
property sheet in query	QUERY TOOLS DESIGN, Show/Hide		Alt + Enter
Query Wizard or Query Design	CREATE, Queries		
relationships	DATABASE TOOLS, Relationships		
Report tool	CREATE, Reports		
run a query	QUERY TOOLS DESIGN, Results	!	
sort ascending or descending order	HOME, Sort & Filter		
Total row	HOME, Records	Σ	